ATHLET S
20

THE INTER NAL
TRACK AND FIELD ANNUAL

ASSOCIATION OF
TRACK & FIELD STATISTICIANS
EDITED BY PETER MATTHEWS

SPORTSBOOKS

Published by SportsBooks Ltd

SportsBooks Limited
PO Box 422
Worcester
WR1 1ZT
United Kingdom

Tel:	08700 713 965
Fax:	08700 750 888
e-mail	randall@sportsbooks.ltd.uk
Website	www.sportsbooks.ltd.uk

This publication incorporates the ATFS Annual.

Photographs supplied by Mark Shearman, 22 Grovelands Road, Purley, Surrey, CR8 4LA.
Tel: 0208-660-0156 Fax: 0208-660-3437

British Library Cataloguing in Publication Data

Athletics: the international track and
field annual – 2001
1. Athletics. Track & Field events –
Serials
1. International athletics annual (London)
796.4'2'05

ISBN 1 899807 11 X

Printed by Midas (UK) Ltd.

CONTENTS

INTRODUCTION

THE WORLD of athletics has changed enormously in the 50 years since the first ATFS Annual was published. With the wealth of statistics included in this series of Annuals we can, of course, measure the change in performance standards – and these have been dramatic. Only seven men's marks made in any event in 1950 would have qualified for the lists in 2000, even though we now list up to 200 deep per event! Women's lists were not given in 1950 but no women's mark made then meets our 2000 standards.

One must appreciate that conditions have changed very considerably – facilities, such as track surfaces, equipment, including footwear, and preparation of athletes have advanced apace. Many of the great athletes of 1950 were of similar calibre to the stars of today. At 10,000m the great Emil Zátopek set a world record at 29:02.6 and the second best man ran 30:07.0. This was a staggering margin of superiority and the fact that in the year 2000 I have recorded 245 men around the world who bettered 28:45.0 should not detract from Zátopek's feat.

Zátopek's death in 2000 was one of the saddest features of the year. We have a special feature on this wonderful man in this Annual. He also leads the cast in a new feature that we have introduced– the start of a Hall of Fame, to which we will be adding five athletes each year.

Athletics has changed a great deal as it has evolved over the past half century from an amateur sport to a professional one at the elite level. Some people feel that much has been lost in this process, but surely much more has been gained. The sport is now truly worldwide and participation of all peoples has increased enormously. Also, monetary rewards mean that talented athletes can stay in competition for much longer than was previously the case. Women's events now embrace distance running and the three 'new' field events – triple jump, hammer and pole vault – are all hugely popular. Not so, as yet, the steeplechase.

As the world emerged from the deprivations of World War II and as participation grew there was a proliferation of record breaking from the mid-1950s through the 1960s and 1970s. This has now slowed considerably so that in 2000 there was no world record at any standard men's event – the first time that this had happened since 1907 – and none at any women's event, apart from the 'new' ones referred to above.

This slow-down must be recognised by meeting promoters who should concentrate on head-to-head competition rather than trying to make almost every distance race at top events into record attempts. The near-inevitable 'failure' of such attempts produces negative comments in the media.

I am also much concerned at the misguided 'attacks' on the traditional patterns of field events. Every athletics fan that I have spoken to deplores the suggestion from the IAAF that the number of attempts should be reduced from six to four and, even more so, that vertical jump attempts should be reduced from three to two. We must all put pressure on our national federations to reject these misguided proposals.

The stated intention of such ideas is to shorten meetings – providing spectaculars of greater interest to television. But, as I have said before, any sport must avoid compromising its fundamental standards and ideals to chase presumed TV interest. In this case such changes in regulations would reduce the competitions in every way and deprive the spectators of much enjoyment. And the changes would make not a jot of difference to TV coverage as, all too often, they would still fail to cover field events properly. Administrators – please note that spectators enjoy the field events, where they can follow their favourites over a series of attempts, much more than they do interminable series of sprints heats.

So while change that enables the sport to progress is welcome and essential, change for change sake or to pander unsuccessfully to TV is to be resisted – please!

The plethora of competition in our sport flows on– and I hope that this Annual provides much assistance to those who will follow the major events this year. Already we have had the 2001 Worlds Indoor and Cross-Country Championships and details of these will be found at the end of this book.

Bon chance for the year ahead.

Peter Matthews

30 March 2001

Please send me information, results, corrections etc. to 10 Madgeways Close, Great Amwell, Ware, Herts SG12 9RU, England. **Fax** 44 1920-877392, **Email** peter@matthews.in2home.co.uk

These will be invaluable not only for next year's Annual – ATHLETICS 2002 – but also for publication during the year in *Athletics International*, the newsletter in which Mel Watman and I aim to publish all performances qualifying for detailed world lists (see details on page 124).

Information or requests re sales, distribution, publication etc. to our publisher, Randall Northam, SportsBooks Ltd, PO Box 422, Worcester, WR1 1HX. Fax 08700 750888.

Email: randall@sportsbooks.ltd.uk

ABBREVIATIONS

Meeting Abbreviations

The following abbreviations have been used for meetings with, in parentheses, the first year that they were held.

AAA (GBR) Amateur Athletic Association Championships (1880)
AAU (USA) Amateur Athletic Union Championships (1888) (now TAC)
AfCh African Championships (1979)
AfG African Games (1965)
Af-J African Junior Championships
AmCp America's Cup (World Cup Trial)
APM Adriaan Paulen Memorial, Hengelo
AsiC Asian Championships (1973)
AsiG Asian Games (1951)
Asi-J Asian Junior Championships
ASV Weltklasse in Köln, ASV club meeting (1934)
Athl Athletissima, Lausanne (1976)
Balk Balkan Games (1929), C - Championships
Barr (Cuba) Barrientos Memorial (1950)
BGP Budapest Grand Prix (1978)
Bisl Bislett Games, Oslo (1965)
Bol Bolivar Games (1938)
BrGP British Grand Prix
CAC Central American and Caribbean Championships (1967)
CAG Central American and Caribbean Games (1926)
CalR California Relays (1942)
C.Asian Central Asian Championships
CAU Inter-counties, GBR (1934)
CISM International Military Championships (1946)
CG Commonwealth Games (1930)
DNG DN Galan, Stockholm (1966)
Drake Drake Relays (1910)
Drz Druzhba/Friendship Games
EAsG East Asian Games
EC European Championships (1934)
ECCp European Clubs Cup (1975)
EChall European Challenge (10,000m) (1997)
ECp European Cup - track & field (1965), multi-events (1973)
EI European Indoor Championships (1970, Games 1966-9)
EJ European Junior Championships (1970)
EU23 European Under-23 Championships (1997) & European U-23 Cup (1992-4)
FlaR Florida Relays (1939)
FOT (USA) Final Olympic Trials (1920)
Franc Francophone Games
Gaz Gaz de France meeting, Paris, Lille or Villeneuve d'Ascq (was BNP) (1968)
GGala Golden Gala, Roma (from 1980), Verona (1988), Pescara (1989), Bologna (1990)
GNR Great North Run – Newcastle to South Shields, GBR (1981)
GO Golden Oval, Dresden
GP Grand Prix
GPF IAAF Grand Prix Final (1985)
GS Golden Spike, Ostrava (1969)
Gugl Zipfer Gugl Grand Prix, Linz (1988)
GWG Goodwill Games (1986)
Herc Herculis, Monte Carlo, Monaco (1987)
IAAF International Amateur Athletic Federation
IAAFg IAAF Golden events (1978)
IAC IAC meeting (1968), formerly Coca-Cola meeting
IAU International Association of Ultrarunners
IbAm Ibero-American Championships (1983)
ISTAF Internationales Stadionfest, Berlin (1921)
Izv (URS) Izvestia Cup
Jen Bruce Jenner Classic, San Jose (1979)
Jerome Harry Jerome Track Classic (1984)
JUCO Junior Colleges Championships, USA
KansR Kansas Relays, Lawrence (1923)
King Martin Luther King Games (1969)
Kuso Janusz Kusocinski Memorial (1954)
Kuts Vladimir Kuts Memorial
LAT Los Angeles Times indoors (1960, from 1968 at Inglewood)
LHum L'Humanité, St-Denis (1984)
Macc Maccabiah Games, Israel
MAI Malmö Al Galan, Sweden (formerly Idag) (1958)
Mal Malinowski Memorial, Poland
McV McVitie's Challenge, Crystal Palace, London (1985-9), Sheffield (1990-1)
Mast Masters pole vault, Grenoble (1987)
McD McDonald's Games, Sheffield or London (1992)
MedG Mediterranean Games (1951)
Mill Millrose Games, New York indoors (1908)
ModR Modesto Relays
MSR Mt. San Antonio College Relays (1959)
NA Night of Athletics, Heusden (2000) formerly Hechtel
NC National Championships
NC-w National Winter Championships
NCAA National Collegiate Athletic Association Championships (1921)
NCp National Cup
NG National Games
Nik Nikaïa, Nice (1976)
NM Narodna Mladezhe, Sofia (1955)
N.Sch National Schools
Nurmi Paavo Nurmi Games (1957)
NYG New York Games (1989)
OD Olympischer Tag (Olympic Day)
OG Olympic Games (1896)
OT Olympic Trials
Owens Jesse Owens Memorial (1981)
PAm Pan American Games (1951)
PArab Pan Arab Championships (G- Games)
PennR Pennsylvania Relays (1895)
Pepsi Pepsi Cola Invitational
PG Peugeot (Talbot) Games (1980), Royal Mail Parcels Games 1989-90, Parcelforce Games 1991
Prav (URS) Pravda Cup
PTS Pravda Televízia Slovnaft, Bratislava (1957) (now GPB)
Pre Steve Prefontaine Memorial (1976)

RdVin	Route du Vin Half Marathon, Luxembourg
RomIC	Romanian International Championships (1948)
Ros	Evzen Rosicky Memorial, Praha (1947)
R-W	Rot-Weiss meeting, Koblenz
SACh	South American Championships (1919)
SEAG	South East Asia Games
SEC	Southeast Conference Championships
SGP	Softeland Grand Prix (walking)
Slovn	Slovnaft, Bratislava (formerly PTS) (1990)
Spark	Sparkassen Cup, Stuttgart (indoor) (1987)
Spart	(URS) Spartakiad (1956)
Stra	Stramilano Half marathon, Milan
S&W	S & W Invitational, Modesto (previously CalR)
TAC	(USA) The Athletics Congress Championships (1980-91)
TexR	Texas Relays (1925)
Toto	Toto International Super Meet, Tokyo
TSB	TSB International, Crystal Palace, London (Formerly PG)
USOF	US Olympic Festival
VD	Ivo Van Damme Memorial, Brussels (1977)
Veniz	Venizelia, Haniá, Crete
WAAA	(GBR) Women's Amateur Athletic Association Championships (1922-91)
WAC	Western Athletic Conference Championships
WAfC	West African Championships
WCh	World Championships (1983)
WCp	World Cup - track & field (1977), marathon (1985)
	Walking – Lugano Trophy – men (1961), Eschborn Cup – women (1979)
WCT	World Championships Trial
WG	World Games, Helsinki (1961)
WI	World Indoor Championships (1987), World Indoor Games (1985)
WJ	World Junior Championships (1986)
WK	Weltklasse, Zürich (1962)
WmilG	World Military Games
WUG	World University Games (1923)
WY	World Youth Championships (1999)
Zat	Emil Zátopek Classic, Melbourne
Znam	Znamenskiy Brothers Memorial (1958)

-j, -y, -23 Junior, Youth or under-23
Dual and triangular matches are indicated by "v" (versus) followed by the name(s) of the opposition. Quadrangular and larger inter-nation matches are denoted by the number of nations and -N; viz 8-N designates an 8-nation meeting.

Events

CC	cross-country
Dec	decathlon
DT	discus
h	hurdles
Hep	heptathlon
HJ	high jump
HMar	half marathon
HT	hammer
JT	javelin
LJ	long jump
Mar	marathon
Pen	pentathlon
PV	pole vault
R	relay
SP	shot
St	steeplechase
TJ	triple jump
W	walk
Wt	weight

Miscellaneous abbreviations

+	Intermediate time in longer race
=	Tie (ex-aequo)
A	Made at an altitude of 1000m or higher
b	date of birth
D	Made in decathlon competition
dnf	did not finish
dnq	did not qualify
dns	did not start
exh	exhibition
h	heat
H	Made in heptathlon competition
hr	hour
i	indoors
kg	kilograms
km	kilometres
m	metres
M	mile
m/s	metres per second
mx	Made in mixed men's and women's race
O	Made in octathlon
P	Made in pentathlon
pb	personal best
Q	Made in qualifying round
qf	quarter final (or q in lists)
r	Race number in a series of races
sf	semi final (or s in lists)
w	wind assisted
WR	world record or best
WIR	world indoor record
y	yards
*	Converted time from yards to metres: For 200m: 220 yards less 0.11 second For 400m: 440 yards less 0.26 second For 110mh: 120yh plus 0.03 second

Countries

(IAAF membership reached 210 in 1999)
After the 2000 Olympic Games, the IAAF determined to align their abbreviations with those of the IOC, so we have switched also. Former IAAF abbreviations are shown in brackets in this list.

AFG	Afghanistan
AHO	Netherlands Antilles
AIA	Anguilla (ANG)
ALB	Albania
ALG	Algeria
AND	Andorra
ANG	Angola (ANO)
ANT	Antigua & Barbuda
ARG	Argentina
ARM	Armenia
ARU	Aruba
ASA	American Samoa (AMS)
AUS	Australia
AUT	Austria
AZE	Azerbaijan
BAH	Bahamas
BAN	Bangladesh
BAR	Barbados
BDI	Burundi (BUR)
BEL	Belgium
BEN	Benin
BER	Bermuda

BHU Bhutan
BIH Bosnia Herzegovina (BSH)
BIZ Belize
BLR Belarus
BOL Bolivia
BOT Botswana
BRA Brazil
BRK Burkina Faso
BRN Bahrain (BHR)
BRU Brunei
BUL Bulgaria
BUR Burkina Faso (BKF)
CAF Central African Republic
CAM Cambodia
CAN Canada
CAY Cayman Islands
CGO Congo
CHA Chad
CHI Chile
CHN People's Republic of China
CIV Côte d'Ivoire (Ivory Coast)
CMR Cameroon
COD Democratic Republic of Congo (ex ZAI Zaïre)
COK Cook Islands (CKI)
COL Colombia
COM Comoros
CPD Cape Verde Islands (CVD)
CRC Costa Rica
CRO Croatia
CUB Cuba
CYP Cyprus
CZE Czech Republic
DEN Denmark
DJI Djibouti
DMA Dominica (DMN)
DOM Dominican Republic
ECU Ecuador
EGY Egypt
ENG England
ERI Eritrea
ESA El Salvador
ESP Spain
EST Estonia
ETH Ethiopia
FIJ Fiji
FIN Finland
FRA France
FRG Federal Republic of Germany (1948-90)
FSM Micronesia
GAB Gabon
GAM The Gambia
GBR United Kingdom of Great Britain & Northern Ireland
GBS Guinea-Bissau
GDR German Democratic Republic (1948-90)
GEO Georgia
GEQ Equatorial Guinea
GER Germany (pre 1948 and from 1991)
GHA Ghana
GIB Gibraltar
GRE Greece
GRN Grenada
GUA Guatemala
GUI Guinea
GUM Guam
GUY Guyana
HAI Haiti
HKG Hong Kong, China
HON Honduras
HUN Hungary
INA Indonesia
IND India
IRI Iran (IRN)
IRL Ireland
IRQ Iraq
ISL Iceland
ISR Israel
ISV US Virgin Islands
ITA Italy
IVB British Virgin Islands (BVI)
JAM Jamaica
JOR Jordan
JPN Japan
KAZ Kazakhstan (KZK)
KEN Kenya
KGZ Kirgizstan
KIR Kiribati
KOR Korea
KSA Saudi Arabia (from SAU)
KUW Kuwait
LAO Laos
LAT Latvia
LBA Libya
LBR Liberia
LCA St Lucia (STL)
LES Lesotho
LIB Lebanon
LIE Liechtenstein
LTU Lithuania (LIT)
LUX Luxembourg
MAC Macao
MAD Madagascar
MAR Morocco
MAS Malaysia
MAW Malawi
MDV Maldives (MLD)
MEX Mexico
MGL Mongolia
MKD Former Yugoslav Republic of Macedonia
MLI Mali
MLT Malta
MNT Montserrat
MOL Moldova
MON Monaco
MOZ Mozambique
MRI Mauritius
MSH Marshall Islands
MTN Mauritania
MYA Myanmar (formerly BIR Burma)
NAM Namibia
NCA Nicaragua
NED Netherlands (changed from HOL)
NEP Nepal
NFI Norfolk Islands
NGR Nigeria
NGU Papua New Guinea (PNG)
NI Northern Ireland
NIG Niger
NMA Northern Marianas Isl.
NOR Norway
NRU Nauru (NAU)
NZL New Zealand
OMN Oman
PAK Pakistan
PAN Panama
PAR Paraguay
PER Peru
PHI Philippines
PLE Palestine (PAL)
PLW Palau
PNG Papua New Guinea
POL Poland
POR Portugal
PRK North Korea (DPR Korea)
PUR Puerto Rico
QAT Qatar
ROM Romania
RSA South Africa
RUS Russia
RWA Rwanda
SAM Western Samoa
SCO Scotland
SEN Sénégal
SEY Seychelles
SIN Singapore
SKN St Kitts & Nevis (STK)
SLE Sierra Leone
SLO Slovenia
SMR San Marino
SOL Solomon Islands
SOM Somalia
SRI Sri Lanka
STP São Tomé Principé
SUD Sudan
SUI Switzerland
SUR Surinam
SVK Slovakia
SWE Sweden
SWZ Swaziland
SYR Syria
TAH Tahiti
TAN Tanzania
TCH Czechoslovakia (to 1991)
TGA Tonga (TON)
THA Thailand
TJK Tadjikistan
TKM Turkmenistan
TKS Turks & Caicos Islands
TOG Togo
TPE Taiwan (Chinese Taipeh)
TRI Trinidad & Tobago
TUN Tunisia
TUR Turkey
UAE United Arab Emirates
UGA Uganda
UKR Ukraine
URS Soviet Union (to 1991)
URU Uruguay
USA United States
UZB Uzbekistan
VAN Vanuatu
VEN Venezuela
VIE Vietnam
VIN St Vincent & the Grenadines (STV)
WAL Wales
YEM Republic of Yemen
YUG Yugoslavia
ZAM Zambia
ZIM Zimbabwe

ACKNOWLEDGEMENTS

I AM once again most grateful to everybody who has helped to make this the supreme collection of information on our sport. Athletics statisticians strive for comprehensiveness and accuracy, and in a sport which has a limitless range of competitions it is not possible to get absolutely everything together. Nonetheless, we can take great pride in this and other ATFS publications, which benefit from the energies of many dedicated enthusiasts.

My thanks therefore to Richard Hymans and Mirko Jalava, whose lists formed the basis from which I started my work on the world lists; and to Jirí Havlín. Also to Marco Buccellato, Silvio Garavaglia, Winfried Kramer and Carlos Fernández who checked many of our lists so very thoroughly.

Then the area specialists, whose work is so vital include: *Africa*: Yves Pinaud, *Asia*: Heinrich Hubbeling, *Central and South America*: Eduardo Biscayart and Luis Vinker, *Europe*: Nejat Kök.

Further information on specific areas was provided by:

Records Martin Rix and Bob Sparks, *Juniors* Milan Skocovsky, *Marathon* Dr. David E Martin, *Ultrarunning* Andy Milroy, *Indoor marks* Ed Gordon, *Walks and Relays* Emmerich Götze, *Men's middle and long distance events* Ian Smith, *Multi events*: Hans van Kuijen, Enrique Tré, Enn Endjärv and Vaclav Klvana, *Heptathlon* Milan Urban.

The following specialists supplied information for their respective areas and countries and in many cases provided details beyond their boundaries:

Albania: Luigi Mengoni; *Australia*: Paul Jenes; *Austria*: Dr Karl Graf; *Belgium*: André de Hooghe and Alain Monet; *Bulgaria*: Grigor Khristov and Alexander Vangelov; *Caribbean*: Bernard Linley; *Canada*: Cecil Smith; *China*: Mirko Jalava; *Cuba*: Roberto Ávila and Néstor Calixto; *Czech Republic*: Milan Skocovsky and Jirí Havlín; *Denmark*: Erik Laursen; *Estonia*: Erlend Teemägi; *Finland*: Juhani Jalava, Mirko Jalava and Matti Hannus; *France*: Jean Gilbert, Alain Bouillé and Yves Pinaud; *Germany*: Klaus Amrhein and Eberhard Vollmer; *Greece*: Thomas Konstas and Nikos Kriezis; *Hungary*: György Csiki; *Iceland*: Fridrik Oskarsson; *India*: Ranjit Bhatia; *Ireland*: Liam Hennessy and Sean Naughton; *Israel*: David Eiger; *Italy*: Raul Leoni; *Jamaica:* Richard Ashenheim; *Japan*: Yoshimasa Noguchi, Tatsuya Yamada, Isao Sugawara and Ken Nakamura; *Kenya*: Phil Minshull; *Latvia*: Andris Stagis; *Lithuania*: Stepas Misunas; *Luxembourg*: Georges Klepper; *Netherlands*: Louis Weisscher and Wilmar Kortleever; *New Zealand*: Barry and Tony Hunt; *Norway*: Tore Johansen and Børre Lilloe; *Poland*: Zbigniew Jonik, Janusz Rozum and Tadeusz Wolejko; *Portugal*: Manuel Arons Carvalho; *Puerto Rico*: Dr Pedro Anibal Diaz; *Romania*: Alexandru Boriga; *Russia*: Sergey Tikhonov; San Marino: Dr Giorgio Rizzoli; *Slovakia*: Gabriel Bogdányi and Alfons Juck; *Slovenia*: Zdravko Peternelj; *South Africa*: Gert le Roux, Hans Prinsloo and Riël Haumann; *Spain*: José Luis Hernández, Carles Baronet and the AEEA team; *Sweden*: A.Lennart Julin, Owe Fröberg and Birger Fält; *Switzerland*: Alberto Bordoli and Antonin Hejda; *Syria and Arab world*: Fouad Habbash; *Turkey* Nejat Kök; Ukraine: Leonid Epshteyn; *UK*: Peter Matthews, Ian Hodge and NUTS members; *USA*: Hal Bateman, Scott Davis, Jack Shepard and Track Newsletter; *Yugoslavia*: Ozren Karamata. Also various national federation lists and to those who post results or ranking lists to various web sites.

Also to: Mark Butler, Ottavio Castellini, Eric Cowe, Arild Gjerde, Stan Greenberg, Garry Hill, Pino Mappa, Rooney Magnusson and Lionel Peters. And, as ever, for computer expertise and advice: Rob Whittingham.

My apologies to anybody whose name I may have missed or who have corresponded with other key ATFS personnel.

Keep the results flowing

DURING the year Mel Watman and I publish all marks that we know about to ATFS standards in Athletics International , of which there are 30 issues per year. This serves as a base from which the lists in this book can be compiled, together with the major magazines that are published around the world, such as *Track & Field News* (USA) with its results spin-off *Track Newsletter*, and *Leichtathletik* (Germany). Then there are the newsletters with particular spheres of interest such as Yves Pinaud's *Lettre de l'Athlétisme, Atletismo en España* by Francisco J Ascorbe and José Luis Hernández, Luis Vinker's South America Bulletin, and the Finnish newsletter *Tulossivut*.

Many of the national contributors to Athletics International are included in the list above. In order to ensure that the record of 2001 is as complete as possible I urge results contribution worldwide to AI, and then in turn our lists in Athletics 2002 will be as comprehensive as we can make them.

ATFS MEMBERS

Executive Committee
President
Paul Jenes AUS
Secretary General
Scott Davis USA
Treasurer
Rob Whittingham GBR
Past Presidents
Rooney Magnusson SWE
Dr Don Potts USA
Dr Roberto Quercetani ITA
Bob Sparks GBR
Committee
Jír]í Havlín CZE
A.Lennart Julin SWE
Nejat Kök TUR
Gert le Roux RSA
Bernard Linley TRI
Peter J Matthews GBR
Yves Pinaud FRA
Tatsumi Senda JPN
Luis R Vinker ARG

Members

Argentina
Rubén Aguilera
Eduardo Biscayart
Edgardo Fontana
Luis R.Vinker

Australia
Ron Casey
Paul Jenes
Stephen Lock
Fletcher McEwen
Roy McFadden
Michael J McLaughlin
Luciano Paolini
David Tarbotton

Austria
Karl Graf
Dr Georg Werthner

Belgium
André de Hooghe
Alain Monet

Bermuda
Robert Oliver

Brazil
José C Gonçalves
Ulf Lagerstrom

British Virgin Islands
Reynold O'Neal

Bulgaria
Georgi Kaburov
Grigor Khristov
Aleksander Vangelov

Canada
Gerard Dumas
Paul F Houde
Bill McNulty
Jonas Mureika
Ted Radcliffe
Cecil Smith

China
Gao Dianmin

Croatia
Mladen Delic

Cuba
Roberto Avila
Basilio Fuentes
Severo Nieto

Czech Republic
Milos Alter
Vladimír Braun
Svatopluk Dubsky
Ludek Follprecht
Pavel Formánek
Jírí Havlín
Jírí Hetfleis
Stanislav Hrncír
Dr Vladimír Jorda
Václav Klvana
Otto Kudelka
Frantis]ek Macák
Miroslav Maly
Karel Mísek
Miroslav Ondruska
Josef Potucek
Stanislav Sanda
Milan Skoc]ovsky
Dr Lubomír Slavíc]ek
Stepan Skorpil
Vladimír Tkacov
Milan Urban
Vladimír Visek
Jir]í Vycichlo

Denmark
Erik Laursen

Estonia
Leo Heinla
Jaan Otsason
Eugen Piisang
Ants Teder
Erlend Teemägi

Finland
Matti Hannus
Juhani Jalava
Mirko Jalava
Erkki Kiilunen
Asko Koski
Esa Laitinen
Matti Pesola
Esko Saarinen
Arvo Siltanen
Björn-Johan Weckman (HM)

France
Jean-Louis Absin de Cassière
André Alberty
Patrice Bertignon
Alain Bouillé
Jacques Carmelli
Vincenzo Guglielmelli
André Halphen
Guy Kerfant
Gérard Leconte
Robert Parienté (HM)
Jean-Claude Patinaud
Yves Pinaud
Daniel Urien

Georgia
Yevgeniy Gagua

Germany
Walter Abmayr
Klaus Amrhein
Dr Hans-Peter Car.
Werner Gessner
Heiner Göttke
Emmerich Götze

Hubert Hamacher
Max Heilrath
Raymund Herdt
Manfred Holzhausen
Heinrich Hubbeling
Heinz Klatt
Winfried Kramer
Rolf von der Laage
Dr Karl Lennartz
Jürgen Martin
Ekkehard zur Megede (HM)
Axel Schäfer
Fritz Steinmetz (HM)
Otto Verhoeven

Greece
Angelos Kokkonis
Thomas Konstas
Nikos Kriezis
Karolos Sargologos
Leandros J Slavis
Mihalis Syngros
Haralambos Zannias

Hungary
György Csiki
Endre Kahlich
György Lévai
Gabriel Szabó

India
Ranjit Bhatia
Rameshchandra G Kharkar
R Murali Krishnan

Iran
Fred Sahebjam

Ireland
Fionnbar Callanan
Brian Cullen
Liam Hennessy
Pierce O'Callaghan
Tony O'Donoghue

Israel
David Eiger
Moshe Genuth
Prof. Uri Goldbourt

Italy
Giancarlo Brunetti
Marco Buccellato
Roberto Camano
Prof. Paulo De Bartolomeis
Gianfranco Fioretti
Gianni Galeotti
Silvio Garavaglia
Michelangelo Granata
Raul Leoni
Fabio Majocchi
Giorgio Malisani
Gabriele Manfredini
Giuseppe Mappa
Michele Marescalchi
Salvatore Massara
Luigi Mengoni (HM)
Gianni Menicatti
Pietro Nava
Gustavo Pallica
Matteo Piombo
Dr Roberto Quercetani (HM)
Enzo Rivis
Dr Giorgio Rizzoli
Mauro Rossi
Pier Paulo Temeroli

Jamaica
Richard G Ashenheim

Japan
Atsushi Hoshino
Naoshi Ito
Wakaki Maeda
Yoshimasa Noguchi
Tatsumi Senda
Isao Sugawara
Seiichi Tanabe

Latvia
Andris Stagis

Malaysia
Balwant Singh Kler

Netherlands
Anton de Groot
Hans van Kuijen
Frieda Michiels

New Zealand
Barry Hunt
Tony Hunt

Nigeria
Samuel Fatula

Norway
Arild Gjerde
Hans T Halvorsen
Tore Johansen
Børre Lilloe
Jan Jørgen Moe
Einar Otto Øren
Ole Petter Sandvig
Bernt A Solaas

Papua New Guinea
Bob Snow

Poland
Marek Drzewowski
Wojciech Gaczkowski
Zygmunt Gluszek
Daniel Grinberg
Zbigniew Jonik
Henryk Kurzynski
Zbigniew Lojewski
Leszek Luftman
Adam Parczewski
Henryk Paskal
Maciej Petruczenko
Stefan J K Pietkiewicz
Józef Pliszkiewicz
Janusz Rozum
Maciej Rychwalski
Leslaw Skinder
Tadeusz Smolarski
Wlodzimierz Szymanski
Janusz Wasko
Edward Wiecek
Tadeusz Wolejko

Portugal
M Arons Carvalho
Vitor Gomes da Silva
Luis Leite

Puerto Rico
Pedro Anibal Díaz

Romania
Alexandru Boriga
Adrian Ionescu
Nicolae Marasescu

Russia
Vladimir Andreyev
Nikolay Ivanov
Rostislav V Orlov
Vladimir A Otkalenko (HM)
Vladimir Spychkov
Sergey Tikhonov

Singapore
T C Ong

Slovakia
Gabriel Bogdanyi
Alfons Juck
Ladislav Krnác
Marián Malek

Slovenia
Zdravko Peternelj
Marko Racic

South Africa
Naomi Beinart
Riël Haumann
DeVilliers Lamprecht
Gert J J le Roux
Hans Prinsloo
Johann Russouw
Johan van Wyk
Frik Vermaak

Spain
Andres de Acuña
Ignacio de Alava
Francisco Ascorbe
Carles Baronet
Felix Capilla
José Javier Etayo
Carlos Fernández
José María García
José Luis Hernández
Ignacio Mansilla
Ignacio Romo
Alberto Sánchez
Enrique Tré
Gabriel Velasco
Manuel Villuendas

Sweden
Mats Åkerlind
Mats Åkesson
Owe Fröberg
Jöran Hedberg
Bengt Holmberg
A.Lennart Julin
Ove Karlsson
Peter Larsson
Rooney Magnusson (HM)
Anders Melkersson
Stig L Nilsson (HM)
Ture Widlund

Switzerland
Alberto Bordoli
Antonin Hejda

Syria
Fouad Habbash

Trinidad & Tobago
Bernard A Linley

Turkey
Turhan Göker
Nejat Kök
Cüneyt E Koryürek
I Süreyya Yigit

Ukraine
Leonid Epshteyn

UK
Ian Buchanan
Mark Butler
Eric L Cowe
Leslie J Crouch
Dr David P Dallman
Stan Greenberg
Roger W H Gynn
Ian M M Hodge
Andrew Huxtable (HM)
Richard Hymans
Tony Isaacs
Alan Lindop
Peter H Lovesey
Tim Lynch-Staunton
Norris D McWhirter (HM)
Peter V Martin
Peter J Matthews
Stuart Mazdon
Lionel Peters
Martin Rix
Michael Sheridan
Ian R Smith
Bob Sparks
Ian Tempest
M David Terry
Chris Turner
Mel Watman
Rob Whittingham

USA
Jon W Alquist
David A Batchelor
Hal Bateman
John Blackburn
Norman Brand
Jed Brickner
Dave Carey
Tom Casacky
Roger Cass
Pete Cava
Gene Cherry
Al Crepinsek
Scott S Davis
David Donley
James O Dunaway
Tom Feuer
Edward C Gordon
George Grenier
Robert Hersh
Jeff Hollobaugh
Basil Honikman
Mike Hubbard
David Johnson
Michael Kennedy
Dr Clifford E Larrabee
Charles Letcher
Frank Litsky
Roar Lund
Dr Bill Mallon
Dr David E Martin
Alan Mazursky
K Ken Nakamura
Cordner B Nelson (HM)
Rich Perelman
Jack Pfeifer
Martin A Post
Dr Donald H Potts (HM)
Shawn Price
Stan Saplin
Kevin Saylors
Alan Sigmon
James I Spier
Carol R Swenson
Michael Takaha
Frank Zarnowski

Yugoslavia
Olga Acic;
Ljubisa Gajic;
Ozren Karamata

For details of ATFS Membership, which is open to keen statisticians, apply to the secretary:
Scott Davis, 4432 Snowbird Circle, Cerritos, California 90703, USA.
EMail address
ssd@aol.com

In Memoriam - died in 2000
Josep Corominas ESP
Nic Lemmens NED
Ingmund Ofstad SWE
Dr István Zahumenszky HUN

In Memoriam - died in 2001
Dr Alphonse Juilland USA
Louis Weisscher NED

METRIC – IMPERIAL CONVERSION TABLES

THROUGHOUT THIS book measurements are given in the metric system. For those readers who are more familiar with imperial units we give a basic conversion table which specifically covers those distances achieved by top class athletes in the field events.

1.70m	5ft 7in	17.50m	57ft 5in	5.80	18ft 0 ¾in	68.00	223ft 1in
1.75	5ft 8¾in	18.00	59ft 0%in	6.00	19ft 8 ¼in	70.00	229ft 8in
1.80	5ft 10 ¾in	18.50	60ft 8 ½in	6.25	20ft 6 ¼in	72.00	236ft 3in
1.85	6ft 0 ¾in	19.00	62ft 4in	6.50	21ft 4in	74.00	242ft 9in
1.90	6ft 2 ¾in	19.50	63ft 11 ¾in	6.75	22ft 1 ¾in	76.00	249ft 4in
1.95	6ft 4 ¾in	20.00	65ft 7 ½in	7.00	22ft 11 ¾in	78.00	255ft 11in
2.00	6ft 6 ¾in	20.50	67ft 3 1/4in	7.25	23ft 9 ½in	80.00	262ft 5in
2.05	6ft 8 ¾in	21.00	68ft 10 ¾in	7.50	24ft 7 ¼in	82.00	269ft 0in
2.10	6ft 10 ¾in	21.50	70ft 6 ½in	7.75	25ft 5 ¼in	84.00	275ft 7in
2.15	7ft 0 ½in	22.00	72ft 2 ¼in	8.00	26ft 3in	86.00	282ft 2in
2.20	7ft 2 ½in	22.50	73ft 10in	8.25	27ft 0 ¾in	88.00	288ft 8in
2.25	7ft 4 ½in	23.00	75ft 5 ½in	8.50	27ft 10 ¾in	90.00	295ft 3in
2.30	7ft 6 ½in	50.00	164ft 0in	8.75	28ft 8 ½in	92.00	301ft 10in
2.35	7ft 8 ½in	52.00	170ft 7in	9.00	29ft 6 ½in	94.00	308ft 5in
2.40	7ft 10 ½in	54.00	177ft 2in	15.00	49ft 2 ½in	96.00	314ft 11in
4.60	15ft 1in	56.00	183ft 9in	15.50	50ft 10 ¼in	98.00	321ft 6in
4.80	15ft 9in	58.00	190ft 3in	16.00	52ft 6in	100.00	328ft 1in
5.00	16ft 4 ¾in	60.00	196ft 10in	16.50	54ft 1 ¾in	102.00	334ft 8in
5.20	17ft 0 ¾in	62.00	203ft 5in	17.00	55ft 9 ¼in	104.00	341ft 2in
5.40	17ft 8 ¾in	64.00	210ft 0in				
5.60	18ft 4 ¾in	66.00	216ft 6in				

Yards	*Metres*
50	45.72
54.68	50
60	54.86
65.62	60
100	91.44
109.36	100
218.72	200
220	201.17
437.44	400
440	402.34
874.89	800
880	804.67
1000	914.40
1093.61	1000

Miles	*Yards*	*Metres*
1m		1609.34
1m	427.23	2000
1m	1520.84	3000
2m		3218.69
3m		4828.03
3m	188.07	5000
6m		9656.06
6m	376.13	10000
10m		16093.44
12m	752.27	20000
18m	1128.40	30000
26m	385	42194.99(mar)
31m	120.66	50,000

IN THE biographies section, athletes' weights are given in kilograms, the following guide will help those who are more familiar with weights in pounds:

kg	*lbs*
50	110
60	132
70	154
80	176
90	198
100	220
110	243
120	265
130	287
140	309

DIARY OF 2000

by Peter Matthews

A chronological survey of highlights in major events in the world of track and field athletics during the year.

January

1 **Rome**, Italy. The Rome Millennium Marathon was won by Josephat Kiprono in 2:08:27 and the women's winner was the indefatigable Tegla Loroupe in 2:32:04 – on a route which began in St. Peter's Square, where runners were blessed by the Pope, and which took in many historic sites in the Eternal City.

8 **Lawrence**, Kansas, USA. The first world best of the year came in the women's weight indoors, as Dawn Ellerbe added 2cm to her previous mark with 23.06. She was to add a further three improvements to 23.60 during the season.

9 **Amorebieta**, Spain. Sergey Lebed showed his continuing progress with a rare European men's win over a top-class field in a major cross-country race. Gete Wami was the women's winner.

10 **Tokyo**, Japan. Ken-ichi Takahashi set a Asian half marathon record of 60:30 to win on a course that is now out-and-back. He won by over a minute from Gert Thys 61:56 and Elana Meyer was the women's winner in 67:33 from Esther Wanjiru 67:41.

16 **Seville (Santiponce)**, Spain. Charles Kamathi beat fellow-Kenyans Paul Tergat and Patrick Ivuti in the men's race and after Paula Radcliffe had tried to get away from the women's field, she was out-sprinted by Gete Wami and Jackline Maranga in this IAAF World Cross Challenge series event.

21-22 **Reno**, USA. Jeff Hartwig's 5.90 was the top mark at the annual US Pole vault Summit at which there were 35 competitions involving about 1000 vaulters.

22 **Durham**, GBR. Sergey Lebed had another fine win over top African opposition and Gete Wami won again – from Jackline Maranga, Susan Chepkemei and Paula Radcliffe.

28 **Pocatello**, USA. Having missed her opening height a week earlier at the Pole vault Summit, Stacy Dragila here set a US Indoor record of 4.51.

29-30 **AAA Indoor Championships**, Birmingham, GBR. Jason Gardener starred as his 6.53 for 60m took 0.02 off Linford Christie's Championship record. Judy Oakes took a record 18th national indoor title at the shot.

29-30 **Tallinn**, Estonia. Roman Sebrle was a clear winner of the Erki Nool heptathlon with 6358; Erki himself was third at 6137.

30 **Dortmund**, Germany. Yuriy Borzakovskiy burst through from fourth to first approaching 700m and won the 800m in a hugely impressive world junior record 1:44.35.

30 **Osaka**, Japan. Lidia Simon of Romania won her third consecutive Osaka Women's Marathon. She won the 1998 race in 2:28:31, set what was then a world best in a women only race on an out and back course with 2:23:24 in 1999, and this time ran 2:22:54 (70:48 and 72:06) for a course record, Harumi Hiroyama was runner-up in 2:22:56 and these two moved to eighth and ninth on the world all-time list. Esther Wanjiru was third in 2:23:31.

February

2 **Erfurt**, Germany. Tony Dees is aged 36, but won the 60m hurdles in a personal best time of 7.42 from Anier Hernández, CAC record of 7.45.

2 **Valencia**, Spain. Sergey Bubka, now 36 and out of competition through a foot injury for 17 months, made a splendid comeback to win the vault at 5.60.

4 **Millrose Games**, New York, USA. Maurice Greene, with a meet record 6.45 for 60m, Regina Jacobs, 1 mile 4:24.04 and Dawn Ellerbe, world best 23.11 for women's weight, produced the headlines. This was the 93rd edition of this famous meeting , with a new sponsor, the US Air Force, and a new Mondo track (still a tight 11 laps to the mile).

4-6 **Russian Championships**, Volgograd. Yelena Isinbayeva won the women's pole vault with a world junior record 4.45.

5 **Perth**, Australia. Emma George showed a welcome return to form with 4.50 in the pole vault, before narrowly missing a world record 4.61.

6 **Boston (Roxbury)**, USA. The world indoor record for 4 x 800m (7:17.8 USSR 1971)

was beaten by all three teams as a new mark was set by the US squad of Joey Woody 1:49.34, Karl Paranya 1:48.31, Rich Kenah 1:48.48 and David Krummenacker 1:47.81 for &:13.94. Khadevis Robinson ran 1:46.19 for the last leg to bring Santa Monica into 3rd at 7:16.59 as Reebok Enclave ran 7:14.78.
6 **Stuttgart**, Germany. Wilson Kipketer produced the first major record of the new century when he shaved 0.01 sec. from Noureddine Morceli's 1992 world indoor 1000m record 2:15.25 in the Sparkassen Cup meeting. Kennedy Kimwetich pushed him hard and was rewarded with a Commonwealth record 2:15.50. Kipketer led at 800m in 1:47.91. Gabriela Szabo had to struggle to win the mile in 4:23.90 from Lidia Chojecka 4:24.44, and Jason Gardener continued an impressive season with a 60m win in 6.49.
7 **Tampere**, Finland. Mika Halvari threw a staggering 22.09 in the first round of the shot, followed by five fouls, to become the fourth longest thrower on the world all-time indoor list. He had been suffering from Achilles tendon problems since early in 1996 and his previous Finnish indoor record was 20.83 in 1995.
8 **Pireás**, Greece. Anier García regained the CAC 60m hurdles record with 7.37 at the Nebiolo Memorial meeting.
11 **Gent**, Belgium. Highlight of the first of the four Ricoh Tour meetings was the win at 800m of Stephanie Graf over Maria Mutola, 1:59.13 to 1:59.23. Philomenah Mensah set a world leading time of 7.02 for 60m, to equal her Canadian record.
13 **Liévin**, France. Round Two of the Ricoh Tour and, as usual, there were fast 200m times from lane 6: Nanceen Perry 22.51 and Marcin Urbas 20.60 posting world-leading times. Michelle Freeman ran the year's fastest times for 60m hurdles: first 7.81 in her heat and then 7.78 in the final, and Hailu Mekonnen ran the season's fastest mile, 3:54.78.
13 **Sydney**, Australia. Sonia O'Sullivan, who had given birth to daughter Ciara in June 1999, had a fine win at 5000m in 15:10.24 (she had won at 1500m in 4:22.1 in her first race back two days earlier).
13 **Tokyo**, Japan. marathon. Japhet Kosgei made his record four wins in four marathons as he won in 2:07:15 from Lee Bong-ju, who set a Korean record 2:07:20.
15 **Pátra**, Greece. Kajsa Bergqvist joined the 2m club, her 2.00 was the world's best of the 2000 indoor season.
16 **Madrid**, Spain. Jason Gardener tied the European 50m record of 5.61 en route to his win at 60m in 6.48 from Freddy Mayola's CAC record 6.49.
17 **Stockholm**, Sweden. This Ricoh Tour meeting lacked a little of the quality of the other three in the series but Stephanie Graf made further progress at 800m, with a win over Natalya Tsyganova, 1:58.43 to 1:58.96.
18 **Chemnitz**, Germany. Tim Lobinger's 5.95 was the world's best pole vault mark of the indoor season and the amazing Tony Dees improved again, to win the 60m hurdles in 7.37, well clear of Colin Jackson, 7.59 on his seasonal debut.
18 **Spala**, Poland. Artur Partyka won the pole vault at 2.27, well clear of Vyacheslav Voronin, who had earlier wins at Balingen with 2.34 and Arnstadt 2.35.
19 **Pocatello**, USA. Stacy Dragila set world indoor vault records at 4.57 and 4.61 before setting the bar at an unprecedented 4.90 (for practice!). Also, Jearl Miles-Clark ran a world best for 500m, 1:00.61, at this high (1361m) altitude venue.
19-20 **Russian Winter Walk Championships**, Adler. As usual there was a mass of fast times, headed by senior winners: 20km Roman Rasskazov 1:18:07, 35km Yevgeniy Shmalyuk 2:27:02, women 20km Irina Stankina 1:28:08.
20 **Birmingham**, GBR (Ricoh Tour Final). Bonus cheques of $50,000 were collected by two world-record setters. First Hailu Mekonnen shattered the 2 mile mark (8:13.2 Emile Puttemans back in 1973) with 8:09.66 and then Wilson Kipketer took his 1000m record despite over-fast early pacemaking (24.62, 50.48 and 1:17.29). He had been some five metres behind and held on to take 0.29 off his 14-day-old mark; his 200m splits were 25.3, 50.9, 1:17.8, 1:46.3, 2:14.96. Million Wolde. At the end of the meeting Gabriela Szabo had a brave go at the women's 3000m mark, but, out on her own after seven laps, she just missed at 8:35.42. Stephanie Graf lowered her Austrian record to 1:57.80 as she ran the fastest 800m of the indoor season.
24-27 **Australian Championships**, Sydney. Cathy Freeman won the 400m in 50.00 and came back the next day to win the 200m in 22.78. Another to return to form was Sonia O'Sullivan, with 31:43.07 for 10,000m. *See Kenya section for winners.*
25-27 European Indoor Championships, Gent, Belgium. Tomás Dvorák added six points to the European heptathlon record with 6424 and Jason Gardener tied the Championship record of 6.49 for 60m, but the star, despite his slow winning time of 1:47.92 was the awe-inspiring Russian, Yuriy Borzakovskiy, who was a class-apart in the 800m, easing clear of the field and running the last 200m in 25.2.

Gabriela Szabo (at 3000m) was the only athlete to retain a title from 1998. Kajsa Bergqvist tied her Swedish record of 2.00 to win the high jump. *For leading results see Athletics2000 p.591.*

March

2 **Melbourne**, Australia. The first IAAF Grand Prix II meeting of the year held on a hot day (37°C) included notable wins for Kenyans David Lelei, a pb 1:43.97 for 800m, William Chirchir. 3:32.55 well clear of Noah Ngeny 3:33.45 at 1500m, and John Kosgei, 8:19.47 steeplechase. Cathy Freeman won the 400m in 50.31.

3-4 **US Indoor Championships**, Atlanta. Stacy Dragila set her third world indoor vault record of the year with a first-time clearance at 4.62 and Matt Hemingway sealed a great return after 2 1/2 years out of the sport by winning the high jump at 2.38. Lance Deal won a 12th title at 35lb weight, the most wins at any event, and Dawn Ellerbe improved her women's world record with the 20lb weight to 23.60. Thus field eventers were the stars but were all relegated to before the televised Saturday afternoon session which had track events only, and must have been very boring for spectators, but Jon Drummond won the 60m in 6.46 and Regina Jacobs set a meeting record for 1 mile at 4:25.92.

5 **CGU International**, Glasgow, GBR. Vyacheslav Voronin soared over 2.37 in the high jump to lead the Russian team to a clear victory over the All-Stars, Britain, France and Canada.

6 **Lake Biwa**, Japan. Martín Fiz achieved his 8th win in 16 marathons with 2:08:14.

10-11 **NCAA Indoor Championships**, Fayetteville, Arkansas. Arkansas (men, for the 16th time in 17 years) and UCLA (women, first ever indoors) were the team winners. Stanford, 2nd in the men's match, were helped by a distance medley world best of 9:28.83 (Gabe Jennings 1200m 2:52.1, Evan Kelty 400m 48.3, Michael Stember 800m 1:48.4, Jonathon Riley 1600m 4:00.0), but Melvin Lister scored a crucial LT/TJ double for Arkansas with 8.14 and 16.65. Shaun Crawford ran a Collegiate 200m record 20.33 in the heats and broke the US record with 20.26 in the final, but that mark was also run by 2nd placer John Capel. For UCLA Tracy O'Hara set three Collegiate vault records: 4.28, 4.35 and 4.42. Terrence Trammell won both 60m (6.54) and 60mh (7.55); he was the one champion to have also won at the previous weekend's Nationals.

12 **Nagoya**, Japan. Naoko Takahashi showed that she had returned to full fitness with a brilliant win in 2:22:19, after 1:12:40 at halfway; this was her first marathon since her amazing 2:21:47 in tropical conditions at the 1998 Asian Games.

18 **Pietersburg**, South Africa. He was helped by high altitude, but 19.71 was still a remarkable 200m time for a season's debut by Michael Johnson. Jane Pittman set a world junior record 55.20 for 400m hurdles and in the men's event Llewellyn Herbert ran a world-leading 48.50.

18-19 **World Cross-Country Championships, Vilamoura, Portugal.** Kenyan supremacy was maintained with team wins in all three men's races (and the junior women's) but in the men's 12km they had to settle for places 3-4-5-7 behind Mohammed Mourhit and Assefa Mezegebu, so Paul Tergat, 3rd, was unable to complete a sixth consecutive win. He said later that he had been up until 4 am on the eve of the race in a row between team members and Kenyan officials. Derartu Tulu made a wondrous comeback to win the women's title that she had won twice before with defending champion Gete Wami 2nd in the 8km race in which they helped Ethiopia to a narrow win over Kenya, and the women's short-course race featured a tremendous finish, in which Kutre Dulecha produced an unanswerable sprint to take the title after seeming a beaten 4th just 20m from the line; good packing earned Portugal that team title. Paul Tergat and Lydia Cheromei (4th 8km) took the IAAF World Cross Challenge awards. *For details see Athletics 2000 p.592.*

24 **Pretoria**, South Africa. Engen Grand Prix. Taking advantage of 1400m high altitude, Michael Johnson smashed the best time ever recorded for 300m, his 30.85 being a huge improvement on the previous best of 31.48. He went through 100m in 10.68 and 200m in 20.11, the times confirming that he really blasted the bend and that he decelerated considerably in the closing stages. Jan Zelezny confirmed his recovery from his shoulder operation with his first 90m plus throw (90.59) since 1997.

26 **Carlsbad**, USA. Sammy Kipketer ran a world road best for 5km of 13:00.

26 **Lisbon**, Portugal. Paul Tergat, frustrated by the late night row which had cost him sleep before the World CC race, improved his 1996 world best for the half marathon by 11 seconds to 59:06 to earn a bonus of $100,000. It should be noted, however, that this course drops 40m in the opening 5km. Behind him Hendrick Ramaala (59:20), Patrick Ivuti (59:31) and Faustin Baha (59:38) moved to places 2-4 on the world all-time list, while William Kiplagat (59:51) also broke the hour. Never before have more than two men dipped under the

hour. The leaders reached 10k in 27:34 and 15k in 42:03 and Tergat was alone at 20k in 55:57. Tegla Loroupe was the women's winner in 67:24, 40 secs ahead of Derartu Tulu.

31 **Cape Town**, South Africa. Engen Grand Prix Final. Michael Johnson ended his three-meeting tour of South Africa with the fastest ever time clocked over 400m on the African continent, 43.9 in his first race of 2000 at this distance.

April

1 **European Challenge 10,000m**, Lisbon, Portugal. Rain and wind held back times with the men's race won by Enrique Molina in 27:59.80, but there was an outstanding breakthrough in the women's race, won by Jelena Prokopcuka in a Latvian record 31:27.86; her previous best was 33:29.04 (1998) and she won by over 15 seconds. *See Championships section for medallists.*

9 **Paris Marathon**, France. Marlene Renders won the women's race in a Belgian record 2:23:43.

14-16 **Mt SAC Relays**, Walnut, California, USA. For the third year in a row, Marion Jones came West to run the 400m and this time there was an explosive result as she ran 49.59 for the world's fastest time since 1998 in her first competition since her injury at the 1999 World Championships. Husband C J Hunter produced a mighty shot effort of 21.74 in his first meet of 2000, and the 1992 Olympic champion, Mike Marsh, had his seventh Mt SAC win with a surprise 9.90w for 100m.

16 **London Marathon**. António Pinto sped to a European record 2:06:36, fifth best of all-time, 1:19 inside his course record set in 1997. For this he won $130,000 in addition to his appearance fee. After halfway in 63:52, Pinto broke clear before 30k (1:30:36), putting in an astonishing 4:32 for the 20th mile of the race. The 1999 winner, Abdelkader El Mouaziz, was 2nd in a pb 2:07:33 and Khalid Khannouchi 3rd in 2:08:36. Tegla Loroupe (2:24:33), Lidia Simon (2:24:46) and Joyce Chepchumba (2:24:56) were the women's 1-2-3, with a record nine runners under 2:27. A new record was set for the number of finishers at 31,648.

16 **Rotterdam Marathon**, Netherlands. Kenneth Cheruiyot won in 2:08:22, leading four others under 2:09.

17 **Boston Marathon**, USA. A Kenyan man won in Boston for the tenth successive year – this time Elijah Lagat 2:09:47, outkicking Gezahegne Abera and Moses Tanui in a furious sprint finish. Another Kenyan, Catherine Ndereba, was women's winner in 2:26:11, with Irina Bogacheva also passing 1997-9 winner Fatuma Roba to snatch second place on the line.

27-29 **106th Penn Relays**, Philadelphia, USA. One of the oldest world records in the book fell, and decisively, when a US team of LaTasha Jenkins, LaTasha Collander-Richardson, Nanceen Perry and Marion Jones (20.8) ran 1 :27.46 for 4x200m. The previous best was 1:28.15 by the GDR back in 1980. Maurice Greene anchored US teams to top marks at 4x100m (38.22) and 4x200m (1:19.92) and Tyree Washington and Michael Johnson each contributed 43.7 legs to the US team's 2:56.60 at 4x400m. There was a record three-day total attendance of 102,193.

May

7 **European Clubs 15km Championships for Women**, Moscow, Russia. Manuela Machado POR won in 49:35, but was followed by four members of SC Luch, Russia, who took the team title.

11-14 **SEC Conference**, Baton Rouge, USA. Melvin Lister long jumped a world-leading 8.49.

13 59th **Modesto Relays**, USA. Stacy Dragila tied the world pole vault record with a second-time clearance of 4.60. Jeff Hartwig won the men's event with 5.92.

13 **Osaka** GP, Japan. Seasonal debuts for Maurice Greene and Marion Jones at 100m resulted in clear wins in 9.91 and 10.84 respectively. C J Hunter won the shot with 21.33.

14 **Rio de Janeiro**, Brazil. Standards were generally modest at this IAAF GP I meeting, but Fiona May long jumped 7.09 (just 2cm behind her legal best) to Maurren Maggi's 6.93, easily the longest ever by a South American at or near sea level.

19-21 **Russian Walks Championships**, Moscow. Held in ideal weather conditions over a 2.5km lap on the bank of the Moscow river. On the first day five women were under the world best of 1:27:30 in the 20km, headed by Tatyana Gudkova in 1:25:18, and Roman Rasskazov equalled the men's world best for 20k on the road with 1:17:46. Two days later Valeriy Spitsyn took 15 seconds off the world 50km best with 3:37:26. Viktor Burayev (born 1982) set a world junior and Russian senior record of 38:46.4 for 10,000m on the track, while in the women's event Lyudmila Yefimkina clocked 43:35.2 for a European junior record.

20-21 **Ibero-American Championships**, Rio de Janeiro, Brazil. The host nation was by far the most successful with 45 medals (18 gold, 16 sil-

ver, 11 bronze) to 21 by the next best, Spain. *See Championships section for details.*
27 **Halle**, Germany. Yipsi Moreno won the hammer with a new CAC record 69.09 and there were wins at this annual throws international by top German throwers: Lars Riedel DT 66.89, Karsten Kobs 79.13, Astrid Kumbernuss SP 19.93, Franka Dietzsch DT 67.13, Steffi Nerius JT 65.47.
27 **Phoenix**, USA. Stacy Dragila added two centimetres to the women's world record for the pole vault with a first-time clearance (and ninth vault of the day) at 4.62. She then had three tries at 4.70.
27-28 European Champion Clubs Cup, Vila Real San António, Portugal. *See Championships section for details***.**
28 **Hengelo**, Netherlands. After Igor Astapkovich had won the hammer with 80.90 the meeting was abandoned due to a huge storm – an unprecedented occurrence for a major meeting in the all-weather track era.
28 **Saransk**, Russia. Roman Rasskazov set an amazing road best for 10km with 37:11 and Olga Polyakova's 20:05 for 5km was also a world women's best.
31-Jun 3 **NCAA Championships**, Durham, NC, USA. The eight-year win streak by Arkansas was ended when Stanford beat them 72 to 59 in the men's competition, and the women's winners were Louisiana State narrowly from USC 58-54. The sprinting was spectacular as Shaun Crawford 20.09 and Coby Miller 20.12 went 1-2 at 200m, and Bernard Williams won the 100m in 10.03 from Miller 10.14, after they had run 9.99 and 9.98 respectively in the semis. LSU owed much to Peta-Gaye Dowdie, 1st at 200m and 2nd at 100m and anchor leg on 2nd placed 4x100m team with a 51.5 400m leg for 7th place. With a 61.20 discus victory Seilala Sua became only the second woman ever to win four successive titles at the same event (after Suzy Hamilton 1500m 1987-90) and she also retained the shot title with 17.36. Her 107 points at shot, discus and weight indoors (38) and out (69) is a new NCAA record for any athlete. *See USA section for winners.*

June

2-4 **Russia Cup, Tula**. Olga Kuzenkova improved her national hammer record to 75.16 and 75.68.
3 **Jena**, Germany. Iván Pedroso won the long jump with the best jump of the year, 8.65, while his compatriot Lisette Cuza's 6.99 was the second best at the time.
3-4 **Götzis,** Austria. Tomás Dvorák and Eunice Barber amassed the second highest scores of their careers. Dvorák was on course for the first 9000 total in history with the current decathlon tables, but finished with 8900, 94 points below his world record. For the first time ever three men exceeded 8700 – 2nd Roman Sebrle 8757 and 3rd Erki Nool 8742 and a record eight men went over 8400. Barber expressed satisfaction with her 6842 to win the women's heptathlon, just 19 points shy of her inspired performance in Seville. Natalya Roshchupkina was 2nd with 6513 and Sabine Braun 3rd 6464.
4 **Kalamata,** Greece. Bulgarians set two world-leading marks: Tereza Marinova TJ 14.90 and Venelina Veneva, HJ 2.01.
5 **Prague,** Czech Republic. Jan Zelezny starred at the Josef Odlozil Memorial Meeting with 90.56, his second 90m+ javelin win of the year, and Zuzana Hlavonová set a Czech high jump record of 2.00m.
7 **Milano**, Italy. Haile Gebrselassie started his season with a 5000m win in 13:01.6 and Fabrizio Donato produced an extraordinary improvement at triple jump from 16.73 and 17.11w to 17.60 for the Italian record after Paolo Camossi had earlier broken that with 17.45. Chris Rawlinson upset Fabrizio Mori at 400mh 48.22 to 48.41.
7-8 **Jinzhou,** China. The last of the Chinese Grand Prix series also served as Olympic Trials. Two of the women's distance stars of 1997 showed top form, Lan Lixin winning at 1500m in 4:03.95 and Dong Yanmei at 15:03.99 for 5000m.
9 **Seville**, Spain (GP II). Michael Johnson ran a impressive 19.91 for 200m and Hicham El Guerrouj started his season with a 1500m win in 3:33.48.
10 **Réthimno**, Greece. The two top javelin throwers of the year to date met – and Jan Zelezny beat Kostas Gatsioúdis 88.84 to 84.60. The first women's 15m triple jumps of the season came from Tereza Marinova 15.07w and Tatyana Lebedeva 15.00w.
11 **Santa Barbara**, USA. Stacy Dragila won $50,000 by clearing 4.70 in the pole vault. Due to the elevated wooden runway built on the sand of Leadbetter Beach this could not be ratified as a world record, but the Beach Vault was a USATF-certified competition, with regulation officials and rules, and thus considered statistically valid.
12 **Copenhagen** to **Malmö**. Over 80,000 runners started the half marathon to celebrate the new bridge (7845m) between Denmark and Sweden; a record for the distance. Tesfaye Tolla won in an Ethiopian record 59:51 and first woman was Restituta Joseph 67:59.

14 **Jonesboro**, USA. Jeff Hartwig set an American record and world best for the year with a 6.03 vault before three failures at 6.10.
15 **Helsinki**, Finland. Maurice Greene suffered a shock defeat at 100m, 10.08 to Brian Lewis 10.06 at this GP II meeting. Wilson Kipketer ran an impressive 1:44.27 in his first race of the year at 800m, but did not compete again for over two months. Svetlana Feofanova's 4.50 vault was a Russian record.
17 **Raleigh**, NC, USA. Top mark of the Pontiac Grand Prix came in the shot, won by C J Hunter at 21.86 from Adam Nelson 21.40. Chandra Sturrup won the 100m in 11.09 and then made a rare appearance in the long jump, rewarded with a pb 6.70 and a win over Marion Jones (6.55).
17 **Villeneuve d'Ascq**, France. Top marks in this IAAF Permit meeting included an easy 10.08 100 win for Bruny Surin, 27:19.70 10,000 by Assefa Mezegebu with three other Africans inside 27:24, and leaps of 8.41 by James Beckford and 2.02 by Monica Dinescu.
17-18 **European Cup of Race Walking**, Eisenhüttenstadt, Germany. Robert Korzeniowksi won the men's 20km in a Polish record 1:18:29 with further national records from 2-3-4 and Jesús Angel García won the 50km in 3:42:51. The women's 20km was of an exceptional standard as Olympiada Ivanova 1:26:48 led seven women under 1:30 and 30 under 1:35. *See Championships section for details.*
17-18 **Znamenskiy Memorial, Moscow**, Russia. Perhaps the best of a solid set of results came from Irina Mistyukevich, 800m 1:57.49, Olga Kuzenkova, hammer 71.81, and Svetlana Krivelyova, SP 20.15.
20 **Vantaa**, Finland. Aki Parviainen went to the top of the world javelin rankings as his 90.80 was well ahead of Kostas Gatsioúdis 87.93.
22 **Bratislava**, Slovakia. This GP II meeting was held in very hot weather in complete contrast to 1999. The junior John Cheruiyot Korir won the 5000m in 13:11.04. Unfortunately the meeting was marred by the ill-considered EAA experiment to allow the throwers only four goes each and the vertical jumpers only two attempts at each height.
23 **Saint-Denis**, France. The distance races provided the top results from the first Golden League meeting of the year. This Meeting Gaz de France Paris Saint-Denis brought together, at the Stade de France, the Paris GP meeting, held from 1995 at the Stade de Charléty, and the Saint-Denis meeting, first held in 1984 and which moved to this superb new stadium in 1999. Then there were 57,524 spectators, but this time, despite the Golden League status, there were about 30,000 present. The four fastest times of the year were in the men's and the women's 3000m – winners were Ali Saïdi-Sief 7:27.67 and Lidia Chojecka who set a Polish record of 8:33.35. Ali Ezzine's Moroccan record 8:03.57 headed a field containing ten Kenyans and it was the best ever by a non-Kenyan.
23-24 **Vienna**, Austria. 1011 competitors, spilt into 52 groups, scored points in the world's biggest decathlon competition, organised by Georg Werthner. The highest score came from Eugenio Balanque 7958.
24 **Kuortane**, Finland. The javelin throws of Kostas Gatsioúdis 91.69 and Aki Parviainen 90.97 were to remain the top throws of 2000. Jan Zelezny was third at 87.80.
24 **Prefontaine Classic**, Eugene, USA. Michael Johnson, in just his second 400m race of the year, ran a stunning 43.92 and other US superstars in top form were Marion Jones, who won the 100m in 10.93w, Gail Devers, 100mh 12.64, and Maurice Greene, 19.93w for 200m. Top race was undoubtedly the women's 1500m, where Gabriela Szabo had to dig deep to beat Suzy Favor Hamilton by just 0.06 in 4:00.73.
25 **Lake Saroma**, Japan. Tomoe Abe set an astonishing world best for 100km with 6:33:11, 27:37 inside the previous best ever time by a woman. She went through 50k in 3:15:09 and was only slowed by slight head winds over the final 10k. Only one man, Yasumi Mukami 6:27:13, beat her.
25 **Nürnberg**, Germany. Haile Gebrselassie maintained his winning run with 5000m in 13:01.07. Seventh in this race at 13:18.78 was Dieter Baumann, whose drugs ban had been lifted just two days earlier by the German Federation's legal panel.
27 **Luzern**, Switzerland. Donovan Bailey won the 100m in 9.98, but observers were clear that he got away to a blatant false start, and therefore this time is shown in world lists as a footnote.
28 **Athens**, Greece. The pole vault, won by Svetlana Feofanova in a Russian record 4.50, set records for three women over 4.50 (also Daniela Bártová and Yelena Belyakova) and eleven over 4.30. Dong Yanmei, in a rare appearance by a top Chinese runner at a GP meeting, won the 3000m in 8:33.07.
30 **Golden Gala**, Rome, Italy. Trine Hattestad's world record 68.22 javelin throw was one of six world leading marks at this, the second Golden League meeting of 2000. In only his second ever 5000m race, Ali Saïdi-Sief

reduced Noureddine Morceli's Algerian record for 5000m from 13:03.85 to 12:50.86. He ran away from the field after 4000m and six Kenyans and two Ethiopians followed him before Marius Bakken's Norwegian record 13:11.30 in tenth place. In ideal conditions, Maurice Greene won 100m in 9.97 and 200m in 20.02 and Gail Devers ran brilliantly to take the 100m hurdles in 12.47 in just her third race of the year, and Nezha Bidouane the 400mh in 53.53 on her seasonal debut.

July

1 **IMSS Grand Prix**, Mexico City. Ana Guevara took advantage of the high altitude to run a Mexican record 49.70 for 400m.

1 **Stanford** (Palo Alto), USA. The third of UST&F's Golden Spike Tour meetings. Stacy Dragila and Kellie Suttle vaulted 4.53 before failing at the world record height of 4.63. Adam Nelson added 30cm to his shot best with 21.70.

1-2 **European Cup for Combined Events**. France (decathlon) and Russia (heptathlon) were Super League winners. *See Championships section for details.*

1-2 **Balkan Games**, Kavalá, Greece. *See Championships section for winners.*

2 **GBR v USA**, Glasgow, UK. The US had a narrow 177.5 to 170.5 victory, with the biggest shock on a windy day being Maurice Greene's fifth place in 10.54 in the 100m won by Jason Gardener 10.40/-3.8m/s.

3 **Zagreb**, Croatia. Allen Johnson starred at this GP II meeting with 110mh victory in 13.10, but Gail Devers lost to Delloreen Ennis-London, 12.80 to 12.78.

5 **Athletissima, Lausanne**, Switzerland. Ato Boldon sped to a splendid double in 9.95 and 19.97 from Francis Obikwelu 9.97 and 20.01 and André Bucher delighted the Swiss with an 800m win in 1:43.12 from Djabir Saïd-Guerni 1:43.32. Anier García just held off Allen Johnson, 13.06 to 13.07 for 110mh. There were world-leading women's marks from Cathy Freeman 400m 49.56, and Debbie Ferguson, 200m 22.43 with Marie-José Pérec second in 22.71.

6-17 **European Veterans Championships**, Jyväskylä, Finland. There was an entry of 2887 athletes from 49 of the 49 European nations. Notable performances included the fourth consecutive 100m/200m/400m treble at these biennial championships by Stephen Peters GBR (now M45).

8 **Dortmund**, Germany. Virgilijus Alekna maintained his supremacy in world discus throwing, beating Lars Riedel for the fourth time in four meetings this year, 68.48 to 67.13.

8 **Nikaïa**, Nice, France. Greatest interest was in Marie-José Pérec, who in her first 400m since 1996 was third to Katharine Merry 50.05 and Lorraine Graham 50.10 at 400m in 50.32. Brahim Boulami won the steeplechase in a Moroccan record 8:03.30, thus supplanting Ali Ezzine, who was second in 8:04.06, as the fastest ever non-Kenyan. Paula Ivan's 4:06.70 in sixth place in the women's 1500m was her fastest time since 1989 when she set a world mile record in Nice.

8-9 **European Cup, First and Second Leagues**. Promotion to the Super League was won by Poland and Spain (men) and Belarus and Czech Republic (women). *See Championships section for details.*

10-14 **African Championships**, Alger, Algeria. There were some interesting performances but the very weak participation by such nations as Kenya (many of their athletes had visa problems), Ethiopia, Nigeria, Morocco and South Africa meant that these were hardly worthy of the status of Continental Championships. The best marks came in the jumps: Abderrahmane Hammad high jumped 2.34 for a new African record and Younès Moudrik long jumped a legal 8.34. Abdul Aziz Zakari sprinted to treble success. *See Championships section for medallists.*

11-12 **Moscow Championships**, Russia. Irina Privalova made a startling debut at 400m hurdles, winning in 54.49.

14-23 **US Championships and Olympic Trials**, Sacramento. The total attendance at Sacramento State's Hornet Stadium for the eight days of the Trials was a record 187,104. Stacy Dragila added a centimetre to her pole vault world record with 4.63 and there were American records from Gail Devers, 12.33 for 100mh, and Regina Jacobs, 14:45.35. Jacobs also won the 1500m, but Marion Jones did even better, with triple success, 100m 10.88, 200m 21.94 and long jump 7.02 (after two fouls). As ever there were shocks, none bigger than Jeff Hartwig, the world leader in the pole vault, who failed to clear his opening height of 5.55 in qualifying, except for the fact that both Michael Johnson and Maurice Greene pulled up with injury in the final of the 200m. Both had, however, sealed their Olympic places – Greene winning the 100m in 10.10 and Johnson the 400m in 43.68, a world-leading mark that left second-placer Alvin Harrison well behind at 44.63. Other marks to top the 2000 world rankings came from Allen Johnson, a record eighth sub-13 time 12.97 at 110mh, Angelo Taylor 400mh 47.62, Adam Nelson SP 22.12 and Sandra

Glover, 400mh 53.33. The Clark family took all three places in the women's 800m, Hazel winning in 1:58.97 from sister-in-law Jearl and sister Joetta, *See USA section for winners.*

15-16 **European Cup Super League**, Gateshead, UK. The British men's team rose to the occasion to repeat the success they had in 1989, when this event was previously staged at Gateshead. Larry Achike stood in for Jonathan Edwards and won the triple jump with 17.31w and Darren Campbell, a last-minute substitute for Jason Gardener, won the 100m in 10.09w. Russia retained the women's cup and there was a great battle in the women's hammer where Mihaela Melinte beat Olga Kuzenkova on second best as both threw 70.20. There were new Cup records from Sergey Makarov, 89.92 javelin, and Tatyana Lebedeva, 14.98 triple jump. Campbell and Ekateríni Thánou (10.84w 100m) were named as athletes of the meeting by the EAA, *See Championships section for details.*

16 **Lapinlahti**, Finland. Aki Parviainen, 90.34, was again over 90m in the javelin.

20-22 **Jamaican Championships**, Kingston. Delloreen Ennis-London won the 100m hurdles in 12.52 from Michelle Freeman 12.57, thus tying the latter's CAC record. Merlene Ottey was only fourth in the 100m won by Peta-Gaye Dowdie 11.19, but was selected to her sixth Olympic team. *See Jamaica section for winners.*

20-22 **Kenyan Championships**, Nairobi. John Korir, still a junior, ran the fastest ever 10,000m at high altitude, 27:48.42 (previously 27:53.0 Josphat Machuka in 1995). A straight 1-2-3 Olympic selection system provided some shocks, with fourth placers such as Sammy Kipketer (5000m) and William Chirchir (1500m) amongst top names to miss-out on initial selection. Reuben Koskei outsprinted Bernard Barmasai to win the steeplechase in 8:17.6 and Julius Gitahi was an impressive winner of the 5000m in 13:24.4 with a fast last lap as Richard Limo challenged him in the last 200m.*See Kenya section for winners.*

21-22 **Bahamas Championships**, Nassau. Chandra Sturrup won the 100m in 10.86 from pbs by Debbie Ferguson 10.96 and Pauline Davis 10.97 with Sevatheda Fynes 4th in 11.04 – confirming this squad's hopes for Olympic relay success. Ferguson won the 200m in 22.46 from Davis 22.48 and Sturrup 22.57. *See Bahamas section for winners.*

25 **Barcelona**, Spain. Inessa Kravets long jumped 7.10w/+2.1, but was later found to have tested positive for drugs at this meeting.

28 **Bislett Games**, Oslo, Norway. Trine Hattestad added to the world record (68.22) that she had set in the Golden League meeting in Rome, with a last round 69.48 on home ground. Suzy Favor-Hamilton missed Mary Decker's 17 year-old US record by a mere 0.28 secs in winning the 1500m in 3:57.40 from Lidia Chojecka, Polish record 3:59.22, Violeta Szekely 3:59.34 and Kutre Dulecha 4:00.60. Hicham El Guerrouj won the mile in 3:46.24 from William Chirchir 3:47.94. Still a junior, Sammy Kipketer ran 12:55.03 to lead a record eight men under 13 minutes and 12 under 13:06 in the 5000m.

29-30 **German Championships**, Braunschweig. The overall standard was somewhat disappointing, with adverse winds holding back times, but the world class throwers came through well. Karsten Kobs produced his first 80m hammer throw of the year and Oliver-Sven Buder, in taking his seventh successive shot title, also produced a season's best 20.41. Lars Riedel won his eighth discus title with 65.67. Tanja Damaske was just 18cm short of her German record in the javelin at 66.73 and Franka Dietzsch won her fourth successive discus title with 65.25. *See Germany section for winners*

29-30 **Talence**, France. Denise Lewis returned from injury to add 95 points to her British and Commonwealth record with a 6831 heptathlon, setting new personal bests at 100mH (13.13), 200m (24.01w), LJ (6.69), new JT (49.42) and 800m (2:12.20, by 4.5 secs!). A great battle in the decathlon was won by Tomás Dvorák 8733 from Erki Nool 8706.

29 - Aug 1 **Russian Championships**, Tula. Natalya Tsyganova ran a world-leading 1:56.60 for 800m to beat Olga Raspopova 1:56.85, and other top women's marks included Yelena Prokhorova, 6765 heptathlon, Natalya Sadova, 67.33 discus, Tatyana Lebedeva 14.82 triple jump and 54.21 by Irina Privalova at her new event, the 400mh. Vasiliy Sidorenko won the hammer with 81.75. *See Russia section for winners.*

August

1 **DN Galan**, Stockholm, Sweden. Marion Jones moved into top gear, winning the 100m in 10.68w/+2.2, with Zhanna Pintusevich far back second in 10.98, and Trine Hattestad maintained her form with 67.92 in the javelin. Japheth Kimutai's 2:14.28 was to remain the year's fastest for 1000m. Olga Yegorova won the 5000m in 14:42.91 from Gete Wami 14:44.34 and Derartu Tulu 14:44.57. Eight women ran under 14:50 and 13 under 15 min, with the best ever times for places 7-18, all under 15:20. Five women vaulters over 4.40 tied the record, and Anzhela Balakhonova beat Stacy Dragila, 4.50 to 4.45.

3-4 **Lithuanian Championships**, Kaunas.

In the first round Virgilijus Alekna threw 70.22. Then he added over two metres to that, and his 72.35 has only been bettered by one throw in history – Jürgen Schult's amazing 74.08 at Neubrandenburg in 1986. But Alekna was not finished, for after 69.26 in the third round he whirled out the discus to 73.88. *See Lithuania section for winners.*

3-5 **North American and CAC U25 Championships**, Monterrey, Mexico. Although not contested by many of the best athletes who were eligible, this new event provided extra competition for those on the edge of international class.

4-6 **Polish Championships**, Kraków. Szymon Ziolkówski was over 80m for the first time in the hammer with a national record 80.39. Artur Partyka won his 12th successive high jump title at 2.22. *See Poland section for winners.*

5 **British Grand Prix**, London (CP), UK. On his final attempt Vyacheslav Voronin cleared 2.40 in the high jump, the best jump in the world since 1995. Three other world-leading marks for the year were: Hicham El Guerrouj 1 mile in 3:45.96, Marion Jones 10.78 for 100m, and Ayelech Worku 14:41.23 for 5000m, a mark that was bettered a few hours later by Gete Wami. UK all-comers records fell to El Guerrouj (3:30.2 at 1500m en route as well as the mile time), Haile Gebrselassie (13:06.23 5000), Jones and Worku, while perhaps the most remarkable mark came in an invitation 100 where Mark Lewis-Francis, whose previous best was 10.25, ran 10.10 to break the world age-17 best. Gabriela Szabo was outpaced in the closing stages of the 1500, her first defeat since 7 Feb 1999 (indoors by Kutre Dulecha at 1500m), by Violeta Szekely.

5 **Heusden, Belgium**. Gete Wami sped to 14:30.88 for 5000m, a time bettered only by two Chinese women and there was also a world-leading mark for the year from her fellow-Ethiopian, Berhane Adere, 30:51.30 for 10,000m with Leah Malot and Merima Hashim also under 31 minutes and national records from Marlene Renders and Maura Viceconte at just outside this time. This was a new venue for the 'Night of Athletics' annual meeting formerly held at Hechtel.

6-7 **Romanian Championships**, Bucharest. Cristina Iloc-Casandra set a women's world best for 3000m steeplechase with 9:43.64. *See Romania section for winners.*

7 **Malmö**, Sweden. Kajsa Bergqvist high jumped 2.00 for the first time outdoors. Adam Nelson maintained his fine form in the shot with 21.53.

8 **Linz**, Austria. Highlight of this GP II meeting was a European record 4.56 by Anzhela Balakhonova in the women's pole vault. She was close to 4.64 on her final attempt at a new world record.

11 **Weltklasse, Zürich**, Switzerland. Virgilijus Alekna won the discus with 71.12 and had all six throws ahead of the best of the rest; he was over 70m an unprecedented four times – brilliant in the confines of a stadium without beneficial wind conditions. Maurice Greene ran 9.94 for 100m into a head wind of 1.0 m/s, but Marion Jones, after a poor pick-up, only just beat Inger Miller, 10.95 to 10.96. Jones, however, won the long jump at 6.93 from Iva Prandzheva, pb 6.92, and Heike Drechsler 6.91. Noah Ngeny 3:28.12 and Bernard Lagat 3:28.51 were both inside the Kenyan record for 1500m, yet could make no impression on Hicham El Guerrouj, who sped to a 54.97 last lap for 3:27.21, the third best 1500m time ever. Maria Mutola, 1:56.90, had a record eighth successive Weltklassse win at 800m and Gail Devers ran her third fastest ever time for 100mh (12.39). Gabriela Szabo ran the year's fastest time for 3000m, 8:26.35, from Sonia O'Sullivan 8:27.58 and there were three national records in the next four places. André Bucher produced a crowd-pleasing performance to win the 800m in 1:43.72. Andreas Brügger retired after directing 28 editions of this marvellous meeting.

11-13 **Olympic Trials and AAA Championships**, Birmingham. Colin Jackson won his tenth AAA title at 110mh and Robert Weir his eighth at discus, but these totals were far behind that of Judy Oakes who took her 17th and last shot title. Dwain Chambers returned to form to take the 100m in 10.11 from Darren Campbell 10.12. *See UK section for winners.*

12 **Gijón**, Spain, José Rios impressed to take the Spanish 10,000 title in 27:22.20 and guest Derartu Tulu won the women's race in 30:56.4.

13 **La Chaux de Fonds**. Mary Onyali took advantage of the 997m altitude to return to top form with a 100m/200m double in 10.99 and 22.49.

13 **Rüdlingen**, Switzerland. Although well behind Mihaela Melinte's 74.80, Kamila Skolimowska set a world junior hammer record with 70.62. Vasiliy Sidorenko won the men's event with 81.57.

17-19 **Australian Olympic Trials**, Sydney. Emma George returned to form to win the pole vault at 4.40, but both women javelin throwers, Louise Currey (1st with 63.59) and Joanna Stone aggravated injuries.

18 **Herculis Zepter GP**, Monaco. Ali

Saïdi-Sief again showed magnificent form with 7:25.02 for 3000m which took him to third on the world all-time list; he ran his last 800m in around 1:55. Three women bettered 4 minutes in the 1500m won by Violeta Szekely, who, at the age of 35, ran a personal best time of 3:58.29. Her 37 year-old compatriot, Paula Ivan, who was retired in 1993-8, was fifth in 4:04.66. Bernard Barmasai in 8:02.76 and Brahim Boulami (again setting the best ever by a non-Kenyan) 8:02.90 ran the two fastest times of the year in the steeplechase, while Raymond Yator broke the world junior record by four seconds with 8:03.74 and there were the fastest ever times for 7th, 8th and 9th (8:11.29). Irina Privalova, in only her third race at 400mh, set off hard and maintained outstanding form over the hurdles for the first 300m to finish in 54.06. Inger Miller, without Marion Jones, showed, as in Zürich, that she was rounding into impressive form, with a superb 100m win in 10.91. Tatyana Shikolenko smashed the Russian javelin record with 67.20 in ending Trine Hattestad's run of eight victories.

18 **Stayki**, Belarus. Igor Astapkovich's 82.58 was the world's longest hammer throw of 2000.

18-20 **Swedish Championships**, Uppsala. Kajsa Bergqvist improved her national high jump record to 2.01. *See Sweden section for winners.*

20 **Leverkusen**, Germany. Jonathan Edwards sprang to a world-leading 17.62 in the triple jump and Colin Jackson won the 100mh in 13.10 from Dominique Arnold 13.11.

23 **Cottbus**, Germany. Frantz Kruger set an African and Commonwealth discus record of 68.13.

25 **Van Damme Memorial, Brussels**, Belgium. The largest crowd of the GP season (c. 40,000) was treated to a very high quality meeting, with especially notable distance running. A great men's 5000m completed the programme, and in this Brahim Lahlafi sped home in a Moroccan record 12:49.28 from ex-Moroccan Mohammed Mourhit, whose 12:49.71gave him the Belgian and European records. Marion Jones won the 100m into a headwind of 1.3 m/s and Maurice Greene impressed to win the men's race in 9.88w/2.1. Gail Devers completed her five Golden League wins to book a share of the jackpot with the 100mh in 12.53. Paul Tergat set his sights on the world's fastest 10,000m of 2000 in an attempt to persuade the Kenyan selectors to switch him to this event from the 5000m that he had run at the Kenyan Trials. He succeeded with a win in 27:03.87, although at halfway in 13:18.98 he was headed for a much faster time. Felix Limo surprised everybody to come through the field for second in 27:04.54 with Patrick Ivuti, who had been Tergat's main rival for most of the race, third in 27:09.79. Wilson Kipketer was third to Djabir Saïd-Guerni (1:43.25) and André Bucher (1:43.31) in the 800m, but his 1:43.55 was excellent in his first race since 15 June. Michael Johnson's 400m win in 44.07 was his first race since the US Trials.

26-27 **Kuts Memorial**, Moscow. Larisa Peleshenko had all five valid puts in excess of the previous world best shot mark of 2000, topped by a fifth-round 21.46. Irina Privalova won at both 400m (51.63) and 400mh (54.52).

28 **Gateshead**, UK. On a cool, wet day Dwain Chambers (10.11) score a notable win over Bernard Williams (10.17) and Maurice Greene (10.24) in the 100m, but Greene did not seem unduly concerned and had earlier helped a US team to run the year's fastest 4x100m of 37.95. Ali Saïdi-Sief ran just his second 1500m of the year, and finished well ahead of Paul Bitok (3:36.17) as his 3:30.82 took 4.28 off Steve Cram's stadium record. Sonia O'Sullivan won the 3000m in 8:33.00 from Libbie Hickman, who at the age of 35 improved her best from 8:43.32 to 8:35.02.

28 **Nitra**, Slovakia. The 25th edition of this meeting featured a 74.32 hammer throw by Mihaela Melinte.

28-31 **Asian Championships**, Jakarta, Indonesia. Ibrahim Ismail won his sixth Asian 400m title (also 1989, 1991, 1993-5) in a Qatar record 44.66 and Mohammed Suleiman took his sixth at 1500m (also 1990-1, 1994-5, 1998). Hussein Al-Sabee won the long jump with 8.33 and Damayanthi Dharsha set championship records to win both 200m and 400m in 22.84/51.05. *See Championships section for details.*

30 **Reims**, France. Cristina Iloc-Casandra improved her women's world best for 3000m steeplechase to 9:40.20.

30 **Rovereto**, Italy. Despite heavy rain throughout the meeting, Andrea Longo ran a European best 1:14.41 for 600m.

30 **Thessaloniki**, Greece. The ever-astonishing Merlene Ottey improved the women's over-40 record to 10.99 despite a headwind of 1.2 m/s.

September

1 **ISTAF, Berlin**, Germany. Maurice Greene won the 100m in a world-leading 9.86 despite a headwind of 0.2 m/s and returned to anchor the US/HIS team to 37.65, the sixth fastest ever time for 4x100m. He was one of five athletes to complete the five wins in the Golden

league events that qualified for a share of the jackpot, being joined here by Hicham El Guerrouj (1500m in 3:30.90) and two women who came from behind to win their events in impressive style – Tatyana Kotova (LJ 6.96 by just 1cm from Heike Drechsler) and Trine Hattestad (JT 68.31 after Osleidys Menéndez had a set a CAC record of 67.81. Virgilijus Alekna came to Berlin with a 6-0 record against Lars Riedel in 2000, but here Riedel produced a season's best 69.72 to top Alekna's 69.70 in the discus. Leah Malot, not selected for the Olympics, had an upset victory in the women's 5000m with a Commonwealth record 14:39.83 to Gabriela Szabo's 14:40.61. Notable sprint finishes to victory came from Violeta Szekely, 1500m 4:02.80, and Ali Saïdi-Sief, 3000m 7:30.76. *See Championships section for all Golden League event winners.*

2-3 **Sweden v Finland**, Helsinki. Sweden were men's winners 216-194 and Finland women's winners 219-191 in the annual match. Stefan Holm high jumped 2.34.

3 **Rieti**, Italy. GP II meeting. Andrea Longo's 1:43.74 was later accepted as an Italian record to equal the 1:43.7 that Marcelo Fiasconaro had run back in 1973. Noah Ngeny, a year after his 1000m world record here, won the 1500m in 3:30.42.

8 **Brisbane**, Australia. Alvin Harrison set an Australian all-comers record for 400m in 44.18, for second to Michael Johnson on the 2000 world list.

9 **IAU World 100km Challenge**. Winschoten, Netherlands. Pascal Fétizon won in a national record time of 6:23:15 and led France to the team title. Edit Bercés was the women's winner in 7:25:21 with Germany as team winners. *See Championships section for medallists.*

9 **Yokohama**, Japan. Tatyana Lebedeva set a Russian triple jump record with 15.32 for second on the world all-time list and had a record four jumps in a series over 15m. Koji Murofushi thrilled the local crowd with his Japanese hammer record 81.08. Obadele Thompson set a Barbadian record of 19.97 for 200m and Susanthika Jayasinghe showed her readiness for the Olympics with Sri Lankan sprint records of 11.04 and 22.32, but Allen Johnson pulled up with a hamstring injury in the 110m hurdles.

9-10 **Lage, Germany**. Marie Collonvillé improved the world best for the women's decathlon from 7615 to 7731.

9-10 **World Mountain Running Trophy**, Bergen, Norway. *See Championships section for medallists*

22-Oct 1 **Olympic Games**, Sydney, Australia. The Games of the 27th Olympiad provided a joyous feast of sport, enthusiastically presented and supported. *See Olympic Games section for details.*

10 **Gold Coast (Runaway Bay)**, Australia. 40 year-old Merlene Ottey ran 100m in 10.91w (+2.4) and Peter Burge long jumped 8.48w (+3.4).

10 **Berlin Marathon**, Germany. Having originally been the designated pacemaker, Simon Biwott won in 2:07:42 from Antonio Peña 2:07:47. Kazumi Matsuo overtook France Fiacconi 4km from the finish to win in 2:26:15 to Fiacconi 2:26:42.

October

5 **IAAF Grand Prix Final**, Doha, Qatar. While there were a lot of tired athletes so soon after the Olympic Games held at the end of the season, the $3.4 million prize money ensured that not too many men and women passed the chance of sealing their season here. Angelo Taylor, who just beat Hadi Al-Somaily 48.14 to 48.18 won the overall Grand Prix for men ($200,000), and Trine Hattestad, having set two world records earlier in the year won the women's award, even though she was beaten in the javelin by Sonia Bisset. Maurice Greene and Hicham El-Guerrouj did not compete and thus passed their share of the Golden League jackpot to the other three winners. One of those was Gail Devers, who after pulling up in Sydney, was not expected to be fit; but she managed to win the 100m hurdles in 12.85 while Olga Shishigina came to a halt after just one hurdle. Top competition came in the men's shot with three Americans over 21.50: Andy Bloom 21.82, a pb by 21 cm in the final round, Adam Nelson 21.66 and John Godina 21.51. *See Championships section for details.*

15 **Pettinengo,** Italy. Paul Kosgei set a world road best for 10km with 27:03.

17-22 **World Junior Championships,** Santiago de Chile. Hamdam Al-Bishi won the men's 400m by the huge margin of 1.07 sec in 44.66, a time bettered by just one junior in history, Steve Lewis. Almost as impressive was Mark Lewis-Francis, who equalled the championships record of 10.12 in the 100m, looking a class apart from the rest. He later came from behind to take the British 4x100m team to gold in a European junior record time of 39.05. Two women scored impressive doubles, Veronica Campbell 100m/200m and Jan Pittman 400m/400mh, but the Olympic gold medallist from the women's hammer, Kamila Skolimowska, failed to even qualify for the final here with just 51.84 and two no-throws. Kenyan men won all the titles from 800m to 10,000m, the latter by the youngest winner, Robert Kipchumba at 16-235, with Raymond Yator winning the steeplechase by 15.61 secs in 8:16.34. Anastasiya Ilyina produced the outstanding women's mark, 14.52 in the qualifying round of the triple jump before taking gold with 14.24. *See Championships section for medallists.*

21-22 **European 24 Hours Challenge**, Uden, Netherlands. *See Championships section for medallists.*

22 **Chicago Marathon,** USA. Running his first marathon since becoming an American citizen in May, Khalid Khannouchi maintained his astonishing sequence in the Chicago event by winning in the US record time of 2:07:01. The former Moroccan had won in the Windy City in 1997 in what was a world's fastest debut time of 2:07:10, placed second in 1998 in 2:07:19 despite a stress fracture in his heel and triumphed in 1999 in a world record 2:05:42. Josephat Kiprono and Moses Tanui followed Khannouchi under 2:08, Peter Githuka finished only 2 sec outside that time for a three minute improvement and Fred Kiprop finished as fourth Kenyan home in 2:08:23, a world's best for fifth place. Kenyans shone also in the women's race as Catherine Ndereba ran negative splits (71:04 at halfway) to post a world year best of 2:21:33 with Lornah Kiplagat (leading at halfway in 70:58) second in 2:22:36. Both winners collected $105.000 in prize money and time bonuses. There were 27,956 finishers, a total beaten only at Boston in its centennial edition), London and New York.

22 **Great North Run,** Newcastle to South Shields, GBR. 18 year-old Faustin Baha, in his seventh half marathon of the year, was the winner in 61:57, but the headlines were taken by women's winner Paula Radcliffe, who, in her second try at the distance, ran a European record time of 67:07, winning by exactly three minutes from Tegla Loroupe. She was thus far in excess of her target of beating Grete Waitz's course record of 68:19 (1988). The total of 36,546 finishers made this, once again, Britain's largest ever race.

29 **Scanzorosciate,** Italy. Viktor Ginko smashed the world best for 100k walk at with 8:43:30 (previously 8:54:35 by Aleksey Rodionov at the same venue in 1998).

November

5 **New York Marathon**, USA. Abdelkader El Mouaziz had close to half a mile to spare over his nearest rivals when winning in 2:10:09. The relatively modest time was due to an over-fast first half (63:07) in cool, windy conditions. Lyudmila Petrova, the first Russian to succeed in this race, won $90,000, $15,000 more than El Mouaziz, on account of her superior time of 2:25:45 – a huge improvement over her previous best of 2:29:13 despite the conditions.

12 **World Half Marathon Championships,** Veracruz, Mexico. Paul Tergat maintained his six-year unbeaten run at the distance by retaining his title. His time of 63:47 was by over two minutes the slowest of his career (13 half marathons from 1992), but the race was run in high temperature and humidity and although his margin was just one second over Faustin Baha, he looked very relaxed. With Tergat followed by Kenyan team mates finishing 4-5-6, they took the team title easily (for the sixth time). Three weeks after her European record, Paula Radcliffe won the women's title by 33 seconds from Joyce Chepchumba. Third-placed Lidia Simon took her fourth medal, and led Romania to their sixth women's team title in the nine editions of this event. *See Championships section for details.*

19 **Tokyo**, Japan. Joyce Chepchumba became the first African winner of the annual international marathon. She won in 2:24:02 from Reiko Tosa 2:24:47 and Derartu Tulu 2:26:38.

23 **Chiba**, Japan. the international Ekiden relay was won by the Japanese men for the third successive year (1:59:47) and women for the ninth successive year (2:15:30).

December

3 **Fukuoka**, Japan. In his first marathon since 6th place in the 1999 World Championships and third of his career, Atsushi Fujita set an Asian record of 2:06:51, the world's second fastest of 2000. He won very easily as Lee Bong-ju was second in 2:09:04. Gezahegne Abera was with Fujita until 35k, but then fell back to fifth in 2:09:45 as Fujita covered the 5k from 35k to 40k in 14:11.

10 **European Cross-country Championships**, Malmö, Sweden. Paulo Guerra won his fourth men's title and Katalin Szentgyörgy returned from the injury that had caused her to miss the 2000 track season to win the women's race. Team titles went to France (senior men), Portugal (senior women and junior men) and Britain (junior women). *See Cross-country section for details.*

IAAF Council Decisions

● The IAAF Council has decided that in order to qualify for world best performances the women's race must start 15 minutes before the men's in mixed marathons.

● Starting from 2001, prize money will be awarded to leading teams at the IAAF World Cross Country Champs, World Race Walking Cup and World Cup.

● The IAAF Council agreed on a number of proposals from the newly constituted IAAF Competitions Commission to make the number of IAAF Events in odd and even years more evenly balanced. To this end, it was agreed that the IAAF World Indoor Championships would be moved to an even year schedule from 2004. To make this transition as smooth as possible, and so as not to prejudice the organisation of the European Indoor Championships unduly, it was agreed that the World Indoor Championships would be held on successive years - 2003 and 2004. The following schedule will apply: 2001, 2003, 2004, 2006 World Indoor Championships; 2002, 2005 European Indoor Championships

● Council also agreed, in principle, to move the IAAF World Race Walking Cup to even years, and be held at a different time of year - autumn instead of spring.

● For indoor athletics, in future, lanes 1 and 2 would not be used for 200 metres races, to make the event fairer for all competitors.

Change of Citizenship 2000

Name	*From*	*To*
Men		
Youcef Abdirahman	ALG	AUS Jul 2000
Abdihakem Abdirahman	SOM	USA
Charles Allen	CAN	GUY
Sisay Bezabeh	ETH	AUS
Jean Destine	HAI	USA
Eddie Hellebuyck	BEL	USA
Boris Kaveshnikov	KGZ	RUS Feb 2000
Khalid Khannouchi	MAR	USA 2 May 2000
Hassan Lahssini	MAR	FRA 22 Mar 2001
James McIlroy	IRL	GBR
Anton Savkin	UZB	RUS
Ismail Sghir	MAR	FRA 24 Sep 2002
Vitaliy Sidorov	UKR	RUS
Ibrahima Wade	SEN	FRA 29 Aug 2000
Women		
Norfalia Carabali	COL	ESP 26 Jun 2000
Chen Yueling	CHN	USA April 2000
Florence Ekpo-Umoh	NGR	GER
Melissa Feinstein	USA	CAN
Natasha Alleyne-Gibson	TRI	USA
Nicole Haynes	USA	CAN
Irie Hill	GER	GBR
Adrienne McIvor	AUS	IRL
Alice Matejková	CZE	ESP
Nadia Prasad	FRA	USA
Sarah Reilly (Oxley)	GBR	IRL
Simona Staicu	ROM	HUN

IAAF Council Decisions – Nov. 2000

IT WAS agreed that a new structure of IAAF Competition Awards, designed to reward greater numbers of athletes, would be introduced for the period 2001-03.

● Awards for the top eight at the outdoor World Championships: individual events – $60,000, $30,000, $20,000, $15,000, $10,000, $6000, $5000, $4000; relays – $80,000, $40,000, $20,000, $16,000, $12,000, $8000, $6000, $4000. Top six in the Indoor World Championships: individual events – $40,000, $20,000, $10,000, $8000, $6000, $4000; relays – $40,000, $20,000, $10,000, $8000, $6000, $4000.

● Awards for all eight competitors in the World Cup including relays (individual from $30,000 to $1000, relay from $30,000 to $3000), World Cross Country team awards (individual from $30,000 to $3000 for sixth place and team from: $20,000 to $4000 for sixth place), World Half Marathon (individual from $30,000 to $3000 for sixth place and team from $15,000 to $3000 for sixth place) and World Race Walking Cup (individual from $30,000 to $3000 for sixth place and teams from $15,000 to $3000 for sixth place).

● Team awards in the World Marathon Cup (held in conjunction with the outdoor World Championships), from $20,000 for first to $6000 for sixth place.

● In the year 2000, $9,223,000 in competition awards from IAAF World Athletic Series and Golden League events was paid to 515 athletes (306 men and 209 women).

● Council also proposed that some recommendations of the Race Walking Working Group should be discussed by the Walking Committee with the aim of full implementation in time for the 2001 World Championships. The aim was to improve the credibility of race walking following some controversial incidents at the Olympic Games and recent World Junior Championships. In particular, the role of the Chief Judge is to be simplified, communications between judges will be improved, and the Chief Judge will now be present in the stadium at the end of the race and have the authority to disqualify an athlete who flagrantly breaches the rules.

The IAAF Walking Committee would also study the feasibility of using a new invention by Dr Dennis Furlong called the "intelligent shoe", which aims to make the judging of walking less subjective. This shoe is claimed to permit the instant detection of loss of contact with the ground by a walker. The system apparently provides first an audible beep, and after a pre-programmed number of faults, a visible red signal.

● Council also agreed to introduce entry standards for team members at the World Cross Country Champs, World Half Marathon Champs and the Race Walking World Cup. This will commence at the World Half Marathon Champs in Bristol in Autumn 2001.

ATHLETES OF 2000

By Peter Matthews

MARION JONES was an obvious choice for woman athlete of the year – unbeaten at 100m and 200m and taking the Olympic titles by huge margin. However, the choice of male athlete of the year was very difficult in 2000. We can look for Olympic success, for world records, for a series of top-class performances. One can look for perfection, because if an athlete is to be a prime contender for the accolade as THE athlete of the year, then one looks at athletes who stand out as supreme amongst their peers – and best of all, those who went through the year undefeated.

Marion Jones on the track in 2000

Date	*Meeting*	*Venue*	*Distance*	*Place*	*Time*
Apr 16	MSR	Walnut	400m	1	49.59
May 13	GP	Osaka	100m	1	10.84
Jun 24	GP	Eugene	100m	1	10.93w
Jun 30	GGala	Rome	100m	1	10.91
Jul 15	US Ch	Sacramento	100m	1	10.88
	(1h1 10.92 on Jul 14, 1s1 10.93 on Jul 15)				
Jul 23	US Ch	Sacramento	200m	1	21.94
	(1h1 22.62 on Jul 22, 1s1 22.08w on Jul 23)				
Aug 1	DNG	Stockholm	100m	1	10.68w
Aug 5	BrGP	London (CP)	100m	1	10.78
Aug 11	WK	Zürich	100m	1	10.95
Aug 25	VD	Brussels	100m	1	10.83
Sep 1	ISTAF	Berlin	100m	1	10.78
Sep 23	OG	Sydney	100m	1	10.75
	(1h6 11.20 & 1q2 10.83 on Sep 22, 1s2 11.01 on Sep 23				
Sep 28	OG	Sydney	200m	1	21.84
	(1h1 22.75 & 2q2 22.50 on Sep 27, 1s1 22.40 on Sep 28)				
Oct 5	GPF	Doha	100m	1	11.00

In 2000 the situation is complicated as most of the top men suffered a few defeats. Maurice Greene for instance lost four times at 100m, although he won when it really mattered. Michael Johnson was perfect at 400m, but not at 200m, as he failed to finish through injury in the final of the US Olympic Trials 200m, and he did not compete much. Virgilijus Alekna produced the second and third longest discus throws in history but lost five times. Jan Zelezny produced one of the greatest ever competitive efforts to take the Olympic javelin title, but he did not have a perfect season, losing one of his seven javelin competitions and Jonathan Edwards lost twice at the triple jump.

Naoko Takahashi in 2000

Date	*Meeting*	*Venue*	*Distance*	*Place*	*Time*
Jan 23		Chiba	HMar	1	68:55
Mar 12		Nagoya	Mar	1	2:22:19
Jul 2		Sapporo	HMar	1	69:10
Sep 24	OG	Sydney	Mar	1	2:23:14

Haile Gebrselassie in 2000

Date	*Meeting*	*Venue*	*Distance*	*Place*	*Time*
Jun 7	Milan		5000m	1	13:01.6
Jun 25	Nuremberg		5000m	1	13:01.07
Aug 5	BrGP	London (CP)	5000m	1	13:06.23
Aug 11	WK	Zürich	5000m	1	12:57.95
Sep 25	OG	Sydney	10000m	1	27:18.20
			(1h1 27:50.01 on Sep 22)		

In fact just two main contenders for athlete of the year honours, both Olympic champions, went undefeated at any event.

The wonderful Haile Gebrselassie won all his races, but competed infrequently through injury and was way off his best – but still good enough to take Olympic gold in one of the greatest races of all-time.

Naoko Takahashi became a super-star in Japan through Olympic marathon success and won all her preceding races.

The seasons of these two athletes were, however, too restricted to earn absolute top rankings against all comers at all events.

Female Athlete of the Year

Robert Korzeniowski in 2000					
Date	Meeting	Venue	Distance	Place	Time
Feb 13	POL Ch	Spala (ind)	5000m	1	19:00.53
Feb 19	FRA Ch	Liévin (ind)	5000m	1	18:53.71
Mar 5		Ponte de Sôr	50km	1	3:41:50
May 7		Villeneuve d'Ascq	5000m	1	19:16.30
May 21		Belfort	5000m	1	18:58.29
Jun 3		Kraków	10km	3	38:48
	(1. Ilya Markov 38:42, 2. Vladimir Andreyev 38:47)				
Jun 10		Spala	5000m	1	18:48.92
Jun 17	Eur Cup	Eisenhüttenstadt	20km	1	1:18:29
Jun 24		Warsaw	5000m	1	19:02.88
Jul 9		Hildesheim	20km	1	1:18:22
Aug 5	POL Ch	Kraków	20km	1	1:20:52
Sep 22	OG	Sydney	20km	1	1:18:59
Sep 29	OG	Sydney	50km	1	3:42:22

As mentioned above, the incomparable Marion Jones, must be the woman athlete of the year. She won only three of her eight long jump competitions, but was unbeaten on the track:

Other women competing at world-class level who were unbeaten at their main event were:

Cathy Freeman 10/10 at 400m, but losses at 200m; Irina Privalova 5/5 at 400mh and 1/1 at 400m, but losses at 100m and 100mh; Catherine Ndereba 2/2 at both half marathon and marathon, but lost three of ten other road races; Derartu Tulu 3/3 at 10000m; Lornah Kiplagat 3/3 at half marathon; Paula Radcliffe 2/2 at half marathon; Denise Lewis 2/2 at heptathlon; Maria Mutola was unbeaten in five outdoor races at 800m, but lost one of two indoor races at this distance.

There were world records in standard events only at the 'new' events of triple jump and new specifiaction javelin, two apiece for Stacy Dragila and Trine Hattestad and both became Olympic champions after fine seasons, Hattestad losing only three of 16 competitions and Dragila six of 24.

My top ten selection of the top 10 athletes of 2000 together with the list compiled by international experts polled by *Track & Field News* and those of *Athletics International* readers (who only voted for 1-2-3) is as follows:

Women	PJM	T&FN	AI
Marion Jones	1	1	1
Derartu Tulu	2	6	8
Trine Hattestad	3	4	3
Naoko Takahashi	4	5	9
Cathy Freeman	5	3	2
Stacy Dragila	6	2	5
Maria Mutola	7	9	–
Irina Privalova	8	8	6=
Tereza Marinova	9	(12)	–
Heike Drechsler	10	(13)	4
The IAAF 12 included all the above and			
Gabriela Szabo	–	7	6=
Denise Lewis		(11)	10
T&FN also had			
Gail Devers	–	10	

Note (re Tulu) that I include cross-country whereas T&FN does not.

Male Athlete of the Year

There are many in the athletics community who will not contemplate voting for a walker. Unfair perhaps, although perhaps they have some reason on their side, in that it could be argued that walking is a less competitive activity (in terms of numbers throughout the world) than say sprinting and distance running. Nonetheless, one man stands out for his overall competitive record throughout the year, and indeed he is my selection as athlete of the year. This is the double Olympic champion Robert Korzeniowski, who lost just once – under distance at 10 kilometres in a race that he organised himself.
Other men unbeaten at their main event were:

Michael Johnson 7/7 at 400m and 1/1 at 300m, but one loss in three competitions at 200m; Paul Tergat 2/2 at half marathon; Simon Biwott 2/2 at marathon.

It was noticeable that for the first time since 1907 there was no world record in men's athletics outdoors. But we should not be obsessed by records and in many events, despite the continuing decline in endurance events in the developed world, standards in depth set new records.

Here are my selections of the top 10 athletes of 2000 together with those of the international experts polled by *Track & Field News* and those of *Athletics International* readers (who only voted for 1-2-3).

Men	PJM	T&FN	AI
Robert Korzeniowski	1	4	3=
Jan Zelezny	2	5	1
Maurice Greene	3	3	6
Michael Johnson	4	2	2
Virgilijus Alekna	5	1	5
Haile Gebrselassie	6	6	3=
Jonathan Edwards	7	7	7
Paul Tergat	8		8=
Anier García	9	10	–

Noah Ngeny	10	(12)	8=
Angelo Taylor	–	(11)	10
Iván Pedroso	–	8	–
Hicham El Guerrouj	–	9	

100 Metres

MAURICE GREENE remained undoubtedly the "world's fastest man". His season was not perfect, as he lost four times, but he won when it really mattered and he ran the five fastest times of the year. His winning time at the Olympics of 9.87, was worth much faster in warmer weather and considering that there was a head wind (-0.3 m/s) and that it could also have been 0.05 faster if the starter had been nearer to the athletes, it might be intrinsically the best 100m ever run.

After a 9.91 win at Osaka, Greene lost in Helsinki with 10.08 to Brian Lewis 10.06, and was 4th in Athens in 10.16 behind Greg Saddler 10.08, Ato Boldon 10.11 and Tim Montgomery 10.15. Then he had two poor runs in bad weather in Britain – 5th in Glasgow in 10.54 and 3rd in Gateshead in 10.24 – but otherwise he was supreme and ran the world's fastest of the year, 9.86, in his final pre-Olympic meeting in Berlin with Jon Drummond second in 9.96. Boldon also broke 10 seconds in Sydney and had run 9.95 when he beat Francis Obikwelu 9.97 in Lausanne.

The other 'legal' sub-ten times came in Zürich: Greene 9.94 and Obadele Thompson 9.97 (Boldon 3rd 10.00), and from Coby Miller 9.98 and Bernard Williams 9.99 in their semi at the NCAAs before Williams reversed the order in the final 10.03 to 10.14. Thompson took Olympic bronze and although 1-3 down to Obikwelu, also had 3-1 win-loss advantages over two top Americans Brian Lewis and Tim Montgomery, who were 4th and 5th in Zürich. Those two missed the Olympics by placing 4th and 6th in the US Champs (Drummond 3rd, Kenny Brokenburr 5th, Williams 7th) but had solid seasons in Europe and had a case for a higher ranking than the two British Olympic finalists.

Lewis had positive win-loss records against Obikwelu 2-1, Drummond 4-2, Dwain Chambers 4-0 and Darren Campbell 4-3 and Montgomery, 4-4 v Lewis, was 2-1 v Chambers and Obikwelu. Drummond beat Montgomery 3-1. Chambers recovered from a poor start to the year to beat European Cup winner Campbell at the AAAs and at the Olympics, where they were 4th and 6th with Drummond 5th. Campbell ended a breakthrough year with a win at the Grand Prix Final, where Montgomery, Saddler, Miller and Lewis followed him. Determination of the rankings positions from 4th onwards was very tricky. Miller beat Williams 3-2, but the later did better in the Championships races (Miller 5th US Champs semi) and had positive win-loss records against Obikwelu, Drummond and Campbell. However, Brokenburr was 2-2 v Miller and beat Williams 4-0, although he had a slightly slower set of times. Also just missing a top ten ranking was the African champion Abdul Aziz Zakari, who did not finish in the Olympic final.

1. Greene, 2. Boldon, 3. Thompson,
4. Obikwelu, 5. Lewis, 6. Drummond,
7. Chambers, 8. Campbell, 9. Montgomery,
10. Brokenburr

200 Metres

KONSTADÍNOS KEDÉRIS was the most surprising Olympic champion, but ran well there with a Greek record 20.14 in his quarter-final, 20.20 in the semi and another record of 20.09 in the final. He had four races at 200m prior to Sydney, the first of three wins in Greece had been a Greek record of 20.25, but he was only third at the European Cup behind Christian Malcolm and Alessandro Cavallaro. Many of the world's top sprinters concentrated on the blue riband event of the 100m, and had rather thin seasons at 200m.

Ato Boldon, Obadele Thompson and Francis Obikwelu were perhaps the favourites in Sydney and the first two came in 3rd and 4th, but Obikwelu disappointed by coming only 7th in his semi through injury. Passing them all was Darren Campbell, who beat Malcolm to take the AAA title in 20.49, just 0.01 off his pb, but then excelled in Sydney with 20.13, 20.23 and 20.14. He had won the World Junior silver behind Boldon back in 1992, but since then had concentrated on 100m. Boldon beat both Thompson and Obikwelu 3-0 and had a good claim to top ranking with big race wins at Lausanne, Oslo and Brussels.

Both Boldon (at Lausanne) and Thompson (at Yokohama) had season's bests of 19.97, but the dilemma for ranking is how to treat the two men who sensationally pulled out with injuries in the US Trials final – both having won their only other two competitions at this distance: Michael Johnson ran 19.71 at altitude in Pietersburg and 19.91 in Seville with another sub-20, 19.91 in the US semi, and Maurice Greene ran 19.93w in Eugene and 20.02 in Rome. There is no really satisfactory answer, but I have rated both highly, principally because the form of other men was not in such sub-20 league. John Capel came through to win the US title in 19.85 followed under 20 secs by Floyd Heard and Coby Miller and with Bernard Williams just outside. Capel looked the likely Olympic champion when he won his semi in Sydney in 20.10, but settled back in his blocks at the start of the final and was virtually left, to come home last in 20.49. His ranking was also affected by poor runs in his two European races: 8th in Brussels in 20.72 and 3rd in Gateshead in 20.59, so that he lost 3-0 to Malcolm. Claudinei da Silva and Miller were 6th and 7th at the Olympics; Obikwelu, who beat da Silva 3-2, was behind both in his Olympic semi.

1. Boldon, 2. Johnson, 3. Kedéris,
4. Thompson, 5. Greene, 6. Campbell,
7. Malcolm, 8. Capel, 9. da Silva, 10. Miller

400 Metres

MICHAEL JOHNSON maintained his decade-long run as the world's top 400m runner – and indeed incontestably the greatest ever. He won all his seven 400m competitions and became the first man ever to retain an Olympic title. He now has a total from 200m, 400m and relay of 14 global gold medals (and no other colour). Alvin Harrison ranked second on the world list with his pre-Olympic 44.18 and was a clear silver medallist, but Johnson bettered that time five times, headed by the 43.68 with which he had won the US title from Harrison, Antonio Pettigrew, Jerome Young and Calvin Harrison. The rest of the world was a long way behind Johnson, but Greg Haughton, although his best was modest at 44.70, beat Harrison in Zürich and beat Sanderlei Parrela for the Olympic bronze by over three metres.

However, Parrela beat Haughton on the other three occasions they met; this included 2nd to 5th at the Grand Prix Final where the winner was Mark Richardson. The British runner had tested marginally positive for Nandrolene the previous winter and had been fiercely protesting his innocence but, having returned to fine form in the month leading up to Sydney, withdrew from the Games to delay his IAAF hearing and further assemble the evidence of Nandrolene being possibly produced in small quantities from legal products. His season's record of two wins, four seconds and a third in major races ensures him of a high ranking. Richardson had two wins over Pettigrew, who was third in the GP final and who was 7th, behind Robert Mackowiak and Hendrik Mokganyetsi in the Olympic final, but with a superior overall record to those men.

Parrela's fate was different to Richardson; it was reported that he had tested positive at Rio on 14 May, and he stopped competing from the end of June, but, with sampling variances, he was let off by his national federation and unexpectedly returned to run at the Olympics. Angelo Taylor, Olympic champion at 400m hurdles, ran the flat 400m four times, and won three times, losing only to Pettigrew but with a win over Richardson, Danny McCray, Arvad Moncur and Young in Gateshead. Tyree Washington beat Mokganyetsi twice in European races in June and was second in Eugene between Johnson and Parrela, but then managed only 46.02 and did not advance from the heats of the US Championships and did not run again. Alejandro Cárdenas exited the Olympics at the quarter-final stage, but beat Young 4-0 and Mokganyetsi 2-1.

Most sub-45 second times: A Harrison 10, Johnson 8, Haughton 6, Mokganyetsi, Parrela & Pettigrew 4; Cárdenas, Ja'Warren Hooker, Ibrahim Ismail, Moncur & Washington 3. Mackowiak's best was only 45.01.

1. Johnson, 2. A Harrison, 3. Parrela,
4. Haughton, 5. Richardson, 6. Pettigrew,
7. Taylor, 8. Cárdenas, 9. Washington,
10. Mokganyetsi

800 Metres

NILS SCHUMANN added to his superb championships record with the Olympic gold. He had a season's best of 1:44.87 prior to the Games, with 3 wins in 6 races, but then ran 1:44.22 in his semi in Sydney. The problem was that the Olympic final was a thoroughly unsatisfactory race with the other seven finalists all running bad races. Perhaps they (and the same can be said for the men in the 5000m and perhaps 1500m) have got so used to paced races on the Grand Prix circuit that they cannot cope properly when they have to make the decisions.

The Golden League season was headed by two men who met lots of problems in that Olympic final to end 3rd and 5th – Djabir Saïd-Guerni and André Bucher, the former having a 4-2 advantage overall and with four and three times respectively under 1:44. Wilson Kipketer won in Helsinki in June and then returned with two good runs before taking the Olympic silver: he was third behind Saïd-Guerni and Bucher in Brussels and second to Bucher in Gateshead. Hezekiel Sepeng (4 OG) went 5-4-3-4 at the Golden League meetings of Oslo, Zürich, Monaco and Brussels and Japheth Kimutai was second in the first three of those, but had lost to Patrick Konchellah at the Kenyan Championships and went out in his Olympic semi-final.

The brilliant young Russian, Yuriy Borzakovskiy, had moved to second on the world indoor all-time list with 1:44.35 and added European Junior records at 1:44.63 for 4th in Lausanne and 1:44.33 in his Olympic semi-final before 6th in the final. He also had a 2-1 record v Kimutai, but continued to both exasperate and amaze by his tactic of hanging far back off the pace before trying to charge through the field.

Andrea Longo was only fourth in the European Cup (won by Mehdi Baala from Schumann) but won in Rieti in 1:43.97 and came in sixth in the Olympic final only to be disqualified for pushing Bucher off the track. Several Kenyans come into contention for rankings spots. William Chirchir was the fastest with 1:43.84 for 3rd in Lausanne, but was 9th in Rome and 8th in Zürich a place behind William Yiampoy, who ran five 1:44 times. Better than either, however, were Noah Ngeny, 2-0 v Yiampoy and winner in Oslo ahead of Kimutai, Vebjørn Rodal, Konchellah and Sepeng, and Konchellah, who beat Yiampoy 5-0 but who had to withdraw from the Olympics through illness. However, Jean-Patrick Ndumimana though losing to Konchellah, beat Ngeny 1-0 and Yiampoy 3-1 and had better times.

Most times sub-1:45: Bucher 8, Saïd-Guerni 7, Sepeng, Kimutai & Yiampoy 5; Kipketer & Nduwimana 4, William Bungei, William Chirchir, David Kiptoo 3; Borzakhovskiy 2+1i

1. Saïd-Guerni, 2. Bucher, 3. Schumann,
4. Kipketer, 5. Kimutai, 6. Sepeng,
7. Borzakovskiy, 8. Longo, 9. Nduwimana,
10. Ngeny

1500 Metres

HICHAM EL GUERROUJ stretched his unbeaten record at 1500m and 1 mile to 25 finals from the end of 1997 with seven wins in the major European races. And yet he had seemed to experts to be vulnerable, so that it was less of a surprise than it might have been that he lost to Noah Ngeny at the Olympics. After a very uneven pace over the first two laps he was out in the front and unable to resist the kick of the hugely talented Ngeny, who had followed him home in the world record runs at 1500m and 1 mile in Rome in 1998 and 1999.

Ngeny won with 3:32.07 to 3:32.32, yet who should be ranked first for the year? El G had beaten Ngeny at London 3:45.96 to 3:47.67 over 1 mile and 3:27.21 to 3:28.12 at Zürich, and Ngeny had a third loss in his nine competitions at this event, as he had been beaten by William Chirchir at Melbourne in March. Ngeny went on to win the GP Final from Bernard Lagat, who had taken the Olympic bronze. Chirchir went out in his Olympic heat after running into trouble, but had been second in the Brussels mile behind El Guerrouj with Lagat fourth on the only time that they had met. Benjamin Kipkurui was third in that race, but had been beaten 3-0 by Chirchir and also by the under-rated Kevin Sullivan, who was 5th in Sydney and 3rd in the GP final.

Also rating highly was Mehdi Baala, who won the 800m/1500m double for France in the European Cup and who went on the 4th in Sydney, although he was only sixth in Zürich when he ran his fastest time of 3:32.05. In that race, contested by most of the top men: El Guerrouj, Ngeny and Lagat had been 1-2-3, followed by the men who went on to be 7th and 8th at the Olympics, Andrés Díaz and Driss Maazouzi. The fourth fastest man of the year was Ali Saïdi-Sief, and one can only speculate what might have been had he chosen this distance at the Olympics; but as it was he ran only two 1500m races: winning at Algiers in 3:32.99 and at Gateshead in 3:30.82 and did not meet the top men.

Most times sub-3:34 or 3:51M: El Guerrouj 8, Ngeny 7, Lagat & Chirchir 6, Sullivan 4, Díaz, Kipkurui, Benson Koech, Maazouzi & Vyacheslav Shabunin 3

1. El Guerrouj, 2. Ngeny, 3. Lagat,
4. W Chirchir, 5. Baala, 6. Sullivan, 7. Díaz,
8. Maazouzi, 9. Kipkurui, 10. Saïdi-Sief

3000 Metres/2 Miles

INDOORS THE fastest times of the year came at Stuttgart when Million Wolde beat Ali Saïdi-Sief and Moses Kiptanui. Two weeks later Hailu Mekonnen broke the world best for 2 miles at Birmingham, running 8:09.66 to finish well clear of Wolde's 8:17.68. Saïdi-Sief had a good win at Stockholm over Kiptanui and was hugely impressive outdoors with three Golden League wins at this event: 7:27.67 in Paris, an Algerian record 7:25.02 in Monaco and 7:30.79 in Berlin. But after taking the Olympic silver medal at 5000m, he again had to settle for second in a slow race, this time in the GP Final 3000m behind Luke Kipkosgei, who had been nearly ten seconds behind him when 6th in Monaco and six seconds behind when fourth in Berlin.

Although only fifth in the GP Final, Daniel Komen had a solid season with two wins in seven races at 3000m, including second in Paris and thirds in Monaco and Berlin. Mohammed Mourhit set a European record 7:26.62 when second in Berlin, but was only third in his European Cup race at this distance and dropped out in Berlin. Noah Ngeny won his only (and debut) race at 3000m in Seville from Brahim Lahlafi and the latter went on to 5th, 4th, 2nd and 6th at Paris, Monaco, Berlin and GP Final. Wolde was third in Paris in his only outdoor 3000m.

1. Saïdi-Sief, 2. Komen, 3. Lahlafi,
4. Kipkosgei, 5. Mourhit

5000 Metres

IT IS a confusing picture at 5000m! Only four of the top 20 fastest men of the year (and 8 of the top 30) ran this event at the Olympic Games, and the race in Sydney was a most unsatisfactory one. This was not just that it was slow, but that some of the top protagonists, notable Ali Saïdi-Sief, did not seem to have much idea of how they wanted to run the race.

All credit, however, to Million Wolde who sped to gold with a 53.83 last lap from Saïdi-Sief and Brahim Lahlafi. Yet Wolde's fastest time of the year was 13:02.96 and that rates him 19th on the world list! That came with 4th in Lausanne and his other 5000 races were: 6th Rome 13:03.08, 6th London 13:10.99 and 13th Zürich 13:12.26 – a very respectable set of performances but not worth a top ten rating other than for his Olympic triumph. One man stands out from much conflicting evidence on an analysis of the year's form – Haile Gebrselassie – for while he ran the 10k in Sydney, he won all his four 5000m races in 2000: Milan, Nuremberg, London and Zürich, where he ran his best time of the year 12:57.95 ahead of a top-class field. Even so, that ranked Geb only ninth on the year list, which was headed by two men who broke 12:50 in Brussels, Lahlafi and Mohammed Mourhit. In that race Daniel Komen was 3rd and Luke Kipkosgei 4th, but, slightly spoiling his record, 9th was Sammy Kipketer. However, this was Kipketer's eighth top 5000m race in less than three months, and he had broken 13 minutes three times: when second to Saïdi-Sief in Rome, first in Oslo and third in Zürich.

After his brilliant 3000m in Paris, I made Saïdi-Sief Olympic favourite for the 5000m even before he started to run the distance (we later found that he had run 13:39.5 in 1999), and he showed his potential with 12:50.86 in Rome, but, after winning the African title, the Olympics was only his fourth meeting at this event. Paul Tergat broke 13 minutes when third in Rome and second in Zürich and the best depth of times came at Oslo, where eight men broke 13 minutes: Kipketer, Mark Bett, Benjamin Limo, Lahlafi, Kipkosgei, Mourhit, Ismail Sghir and Albert Chepkirui, with Salah Hissou just 0.06 outside. Hissou, also 5th London and Zürich and 6th Brussels, beat Wolde 3-0! Julius Gitahi won the Kenyan title in 13:24.4 from Richard Limo (10 OG), Tergat, Kipketer, Benjamin Limo and Chepkirui , but was 9th in Sydney and had a best of 13:23.12. Richard Limo beat his namesake Benjamin 4-0. Komen was ahead of Hissou in Brussels and won in Rieti, but went out in the Kenyan Champs heats. The Olympic 4th placer was Fita Bayissa, whose other races were 7th Rome, 12th London and 18th Zürich, and fifth was David Chelule, switched to this event from his preferred 10000m, who had been 15th Oslo and 8th Brussels.

1. Gebrselassie, 2. Saïdi-Sief, 3. S Kipketer,
4. Lahlafi, 5. Tergat, 6. Mourhit, 7. R Limo,
8. B Limo, 9. Hissou, 10. Wolde

10,000 Metres

THE OLYMPIC 10,000m was one of the greatest races ever seen, a fascinating tactical battle between three Kenyans and two Ethiopians, culminating in an all-out sprint for the line in which Haile Gebrselassie, not yet back to his superb best after an Achilles injury, somehow imposed his will and overcame Paul Tergat, who once again had to settle for silver behind the world's greatest ever distance runner (as I now see him over the claims of the likes of 'gods' Nurmi and Zátopek). Assefa Mezegebu, Patrick Ivuti and John Korir rank in their Olympic order.

Korir had won in Prague and at the Kenyan Championships, at which Tergat declined running the 10,000m and earned his place on the Kenyan team at 5000m. He later set out to run the year's fastest time at Brussels and having done so persuaded his nations selectors to re-arrange their team and allow him into the 10,000m. They did so by moving 10k second placer David Chelule (who had no other races at this distance in 2000) to the 5000m.

The third placer, Ivuti, had shown his sharpness by placing third at Brussels, passed on the last lap for second by Felix Limo, who was thought at the time to have been lapped. Ivuti had also been third at the African Championships and was under 27:30 at Brussels, Sydney and at Barakaldo, where he beat José Rios, who later ran the fastest time of the year by a European, 27:22.20 to win the Spanish title but who was only 18th in Sydney. Mezegebu had a significant win at Lille, beating Girma Tolla (OG 11th), Evans Rutto and Simon Maina, as all these four were under 27:24. Saïd Bérioui was sixth both in Lille and Sydney in nearly identical times, but Olympic 7th placer Toshinari Takaoka was over a minute back in 14th in Lille. Maina also had two fast wins in Japan and was fifth in Brussels, a place behind William Kalya, and two ahead of Rutto.

1. Gebrselassie, 2. Tergat, 3. Mezegebu,
4. Ivuti, 5. Korir, 6. F Limo, 7. G Tolla, 8. Maina,
9. Rutto, 10. Bérioui

Half Marathon

PAUL TERGAT, unbeaten at the half marathon since 1994, ran the fastest ever time for the distance at Lisbon in March. His time of 59:06 will not, however be recognised as a world best under the strictest rules as the first 5km is downhill by 40m from the bridge starting point to sea level. Then, in October, he won the World Championship in hot and very humid conditions in Brazil in 63:47.

The first seven in the World title race all came from East Africa, as Tergat was followed by Faustin Baha, Tesfaye Jifar, Joseph Kimani, David Rutto, John Gwako and Zebedayo Bayo. In Lisbon five men had broken the hour in ideal conditions: Tergat, Hendrik Ramaala, Patrick Ivuti, Baha and William Kiplagat. The other sub-60 came with a strong following wind on the bridge run from Copenhagen to Malmö, with Tesfaye Tolla running 59:51 from Philip Rugut 60:00 and Baha 60:05. Baha was a prolific racer at this distance as he ran eight half marathons, with wins at Nice, Göteborg and in the Great North Run. Ivuti added a win over Mohammed Mourhit and Joseph Waweru in the Stramilano (60:49), but Ramaala was third in Durban behind Lahoussine Mrikik (who was also second at Paris and Ivry) and Shadrack Hoff and then a poor tenth in the Portuguese Championships race. Jifar and Kimani had no other half marathons to back up their World placings, but Rutto won in Gargnano (60:44), Gwako was first in Rio and second in Zaandam, and Bayo won in Paris (60:50) and Den Haag (61:07). Kiplagat was second in Lille and third Zaandam (winner Christopher Cheboiboch 60:49). Khalid Khannouchi, sixth in Lisbon in 60:28, also won in Philadelphia (61:17).

1. Tergat, 2. Baha, 3. Ivuti, 4, Ramaala,
5, Rutto, 6. Gwako, 7. Bayo, 8, Mrikik,
9, Kiplagat, 10. Khannouchi

Marathon

THE FASTEST marathon time of 2000 was run by António Pinto, 2:06:36 in London. This took 36 seconds off Carlos Lopes's 15 year-old European record and was a remarkable run, not least because the London course is not as easy as those of, for instance, Rotterdam, Berlin and Chicago. This was Pinto's third win in London (with a second and two thirds). Pinto was thus a favourite for the Olympic title, but in warmer weather and on a tough course in Sydney, he could manage only 11th place in 2:15:11.

The Olympic champion was Gezahegne Abera in 2:10:11 after a fascinating race with Eric Wainaina, Tesfaye Tolla and Jon Brown. Abera had previously been second to Elijah Lagat (dnf OG) in Boston in 2:09:47. Wainaina had won at Nagano in 2:10:17 and Tolla only 15th in Rotterdam in 2:11:42. It is always difficult to compare course and conditions but at a guess the Olympic times might be worth about three minutes quicker in perfect conditions. At the end of the year the Fukuoka marathon was won in 2:06:51 by Atsushi Fujita (who had no other marathons in 2000) by a margin of 2:13 from Lee Bong-ju (24th OG), with Abera fifth in 2:09:45.

The fastest marathoner of all-time Khalid Khannouchi just beat the deadline to become a US citizen but had to withdraw from the US Olympic Trials through injury. Instead he came third in London, and showed a return to full fitness by winning for the third time in Chicago in 2:07:01, the third fastest of the year. The next best was 2:07:15 by Japhet Kosgei, the Tokyo winner, who did not finish in London and later was over two minutes behind Abdelkader El Mouaziz for second in New York. The latter's performance was especially noteworthy in adverse conditions and he had also been second in London in 2:07:33, if a little off the pace with 7th at the Olympics. Josephat Kiprono won the Millennium Marathon on 1 January in Rome and went on to second in Prague (to Simon Chemoiywo) and Chicago. Moses Tanui was third in both Boston and Chicago and Simon Biwott won in Berlin and in Milan. Joining Khannouchi and Kiprono with two marathons under 2:09 were Fr.Javier Cortes, 2nd in Rotterdam and 1st in Amsterdam, and Antonio Peña, 5th in Rotterdam and 2nd in Berlin. Giacomo Leone, 5th OG was also 2nd in Rome, and Martín Fiz, 6th OG, also won the Lake Biwa race. With athletes choosing different races, any attempt at marathon ranking, where I prefer at least two good races if possible, is doomed to endless dispute!

1. Khannouchi, 2. Abera, 3. El Mouaziz,
4. Wainaina, 5. J Kiprono, 6. Pinto,
7. J Kosgei, 8. Biwott, 9. M Tanui, 10. Fujita

3000 Metres Steeple

KENYANS WERE slightly less dominant than usual this year, as my top ten only has five of them, with two Moroccans, two Spaniards and an Austrian included. Nonetheless it was a Kenyan 1-2-4 at the Olympics. Reuben Kosgei, the World Junior champion of 1998 improved from 8:12.33 in 1999 to 8:03.93 this year and won the Kenyan title before taking Olympic gold. He had a 3-1 advantage over the Olympic silver medallist Wilson Boit Kipketer and 5-0 over Bernard Barmasai. Boit Kipketer was only the seventh fastest of the year and only had two sub-8:10 times, while Barmasai beat him 3-2 and had the year's fastest time of 8:02.76.

Nonetheless, a good win in Zürich with Reuben Kosgei, Barmasai, Raymond Yator, Eliseo Martín, Brahim Boulami and Kipkirui Misoi following, helps Boit K to second ranking. The Moroccans Ali Ezzine (in Paris, where he beat Reuben K and Barmasai) and Brahim Boulami (in Nice where he beat Ezzine, and then when second to Barmasai in Monaco) both became the fastest ever non-Kenyans at the event, so that at the end of the year they ranked fourth and sixth on the world all-time list which a year earlier had Kenyans in the first 12 places before Ezzine at 13.

Boulami fell back a little to 7th in Sydney, where the two Spanish Martíns, Luis 5th and Eliseo 6th were ahead of him. Almost inseparable were the Kenyans Raymond Yator and Kipkurui Misoi, 3-3 on win loss. Yator's 8:03.73 for third in Monaco was, however, much quicker than Misoi's best of 8:07.21 run when second to Boulami in Rome. Yator won the World Junior title by a huge margin. The sixth best Kenyan was Abraham Cherono, who beat Jonathan Kandie 4-1 and also had a 2-1 advantage over another man with a faster season's best, Laïd

Bessou (11 OG). But Günther Weidlinger beat Cherono in Linz before taking eighth place in the Olympic final and is preferred for the final ranking place.

1. R Kosgei, 2. Boit Kipketer, 3. Ezzine,
4. Barmasai, 5. Boulami, 6. Yator, 7. Misoi,
8. L Martín, 9. E Martín, 10. Weidlinger

110 Metres Hurdles

IT SEEMED to be a case of the old order changing as Anier García and Terrence Trammell, aged 24 and 21 respectively, took Olympic gold and silver and Mark Crear, Allen Johnson, Colin Jackson and Florian Schwarthoff, aged 31, 29, 33 and 32 respectively followed 3rd to 6th. García had a clear claim to top ranking and he beat Allen Johnson 4-2 as both men had 13 wins from 18 races. Johnson was 3-1 up on Crear and 5-1 on Trammell and had looked to be the favourite for Sydney until he had pulled up favouring an injury in his last pre-Olympic race in Yokohama. He had beaten García 13.17 to 13.36 in Zürich. Trammell was 1-1 with Jackson and 3-3 v Crear, who had disappointed in his big races in Europe: 7th Linz, 8th Zürich, 4th Brussels.

Another American Dominique Arnold missed a chance of going to the Olympics when he fell in the final of the US Trials, but had an excellent season in Europe and beat Crear 3-1. Jackson, however, is ahead of Arnold with 3-1 advantage. There is a big gap after the top six, and the remaining spots are close. The Germans Schwarthoff and Balzer were 3-3, but while Balzer beat Robin Korving (who missed the Olympics through injury) 3-0, Schwarthoff was 0-2 down to Korving! Dudley Dorival and Robert Kronberg made the Olympic final, but did not have records as good as the semi-finalists, Yoel Hernández, Stanislavs Olijars and Balzer. Olijars beat Balzer 3-1 and Hernández 4-2. Hernández beat Balzer 2-1.

Most times under 13.30: Johnson 12+2w, Garcia 10+4w, Jackson 7, Crear 5+2w, Trammell & Arnold 5, Balzer & Olijars 4, Hernández 2+1w

1. García, 2. Johnson, 3. Trammell,
4. Jackson, 5. Arnold, 6. Crear,
7. Schwarthoff, 8. Olijars, 9. Hernández,
9. 10. Balzer

400 Metres Hurdles

ANGELO TAYLOR came from the inside lane to take the Olympic final in the fastest time of the year, but he only just beat the hugely talented Hadi Soua'an Al-Somaily, who set Saudi records in Sydney of 48.14 and then the startling 47.53. Llewellyn Herbert improved his South Africa record to 47.81 in taking the bronze medal and was 3-3 against Taylor and 4-2 v Al-Somaily overall. James Carter had surprised by improving his personal best from 49.03 to 48.45 to take third place at the US Trials and without any further runs after that until the Olympics made further progress to 48.04 in fourth place after an easy 48.48 in his semi-final.

Nonetheless, Eric Thomas (US Trials 2nd), despite being only fifth in his Olympic semi, rates ahead after a long hard season in which he beat Al-Somaily 4-2, Samuel Matete 6-4 and Eronilde de Araújo 7-2. Araújo was 5th in Sydney and kept Matete out of a place in the Olympic final, but these two were 5-5 overall. Pawel Januszewski was 6th in Sydney and 5th at the GP Final (behind Taylor, Al-Somailly, Matete and Herbert with Chris Rawlinson, Araújo and Thomas finishing tired men behind them) and he beat Rawlinson, who faded after an excellent start to the year 2-1. Rawlinson beat Ruslan Mashchenko and Fabrizio Mori (OG 7th) in the European Cup. Joey Woody was 4th in the US Trials, but was beaten 2-0 by Mori, and he and Felix Sanchez just miss a ranking.

Most times under 49.00: Matete 13, Herbert 12, Taylor & Thomas 11, Araújo 9, Al-Somailly 8, Januszewski, Rawlinson & Joey Woody 7, Carter, Mori & Felix Sanchez 4, Thomas Goller 3

1. Taylor, 2. Herbert, 3. Al-Somaily,
4. Thomas, 5. Carter, 6. Araújo, 7. Matete,
8. Januszewski, 9. Rawlinson, 10. Mori

High Jump

ALTHOUGH HE had an off-day at the Olympcs, 10th at 2.29, Vyacheslav Voronin was surely the top high jumper of 2000. His 2.40 at the British GP was by 4cm the best jump of the year outdoors and he had 7 wins in 11 outdoor competions and 8 in 11 indoors; he came back from his Sydney disappointment to win at the GP Final. He beat the Olympic champion Sergey Klyugin 5-3 outdoors and 3-1 indoors. Klyugin had pretty much wrapped up the gold medal in Sydney by clearing 2.35 first time before the rains came, but the places of the six men who cleared 2.32 could well have been affected.

The order was 2. Javier Sotomayor, 3, Abderrahmane Hammad, 4. Stefan Holm, 5. Konstantin Matusevich, 6= Steffan Strand and Mark Boswell. Of those, Boswell had looked the most likely to go higher and he may deserve a higher ranking, although after the top two there is little between the rest of the men. Boswell won NCAA titles indoors and out, was 2-2 against Hammad but 1-3 down to Holm, and had marks of 2.35, 2.33, 2.32 (3), 2.31 (2) and 2.30 (2) outdoors and 2.33 and 2.32 indoors, a much better collection than all but Voronin.

Even Klyugin's was not as good, but he beat Boswell 5-2. Sotomayor came back from his cocaine suspension to take Olympic silver but did not have the depth of marks of the others, with 2.32, 2.30 and two 2.28s. The Swedes Holm and Strand were as ever closely matched, the score being Holm ahead 6-4 outdoors, but Strand winning 3-1 indoors. Matusevich beat Strand 5-2. Kwaku Boateng slipped to 12th at the Olympics and 5th at the GP Final, but had positive win-loss records outdoors against Holm 4-1, Matusevuch 4-2, Kreissig 3-1, Strand 7-4 and Nathan Leeper (11 OG, 2 GPF). Kreissig was 3-1 v Strand (but 0-2 and 1 tie indoors) and 3-0 (& 3-1 in) v US champion Charles Austin. Although the Americans Austin and Leeper had better marks, Strand was 4-3 and 5-3 up on them respectively outdoors and a further 4-0 against Austin indoors. The three medallists at the European Indoors all cleared 2.34: 1. Voronin, 2. Martin Buss, who did not compete outdoors, and 3. Dragutin Topic, with Holm fourth at 2.32.

Most competitions over 2.30m (outdoors/ in): Voronin 8/10, Boswell 9/3, Matusevich 8/-, Topic 5/4, Boateng 5/-, Holm 4/3, Klyugin & Kreissig 4/1, Hammad & Leeper 4/-, Hemingway 2/3, Strand 2/1, Martin Buss 0/5, Artur Partyka 0/3

1. Voronin, 2. Klyugin, 3. Hammad,
4. Boswell, 5. Sotomayor, 6. Boateng (7),
7. Holm (6), 8. Matusevich, 9. Kreissig (-), 10. Strand (-) (inc. indoors: 9. Buss, 10. Topic)

Pole Vault

PUNDITS RECKONED that the Olympic pole vault was open to all sorts of possibilities. Nick Hysong was not especially favoured, but he won in Sydney as four men cleared 5.90, and when one examines the overall season's records of the top men, then Hysong's excellent year is confirmed for he beat his compatriot, Lawrence Johnson, who completed the first US PV 1-2 for 40 years, 8-2 outdoors (although Johnson had won 3-0 indoors). Hysong also beat Maksim Tarasov 5-3 and was 6-6 (and 0-4 indoors) against Jeff Hartwig, who had problems with his eyes at the US Trials and failed to clear a height in the qualifying competition.

It was Hartwig, however, who was the one man to clear 6 metres in 2000, improving his US record to 6.03 at Jonesboro in June; he also cleared 6.00 in an exhibition at Köln. The next best vaulters cleared 5.95: Tim Lobinger indoors and Michael Stolle outdoors. Johnson won US titles indoors and out and was 4-4 outdoors (1-2 in) against Hartwig.

Tarasov has been the world's best vaulter in the post-Bubka era and his Olympic bronze was quite a triumph considering that he was vaulting with a broken jaw, just one of a series of injuries that he suffered in 2000. Tarasov's claim to a high ranking is confirmed by his win-loss advantage of 5-2 over Johnson and 5-3 over Hartwig. Lobinger was, as usual, a prolific competitor, with 11 indoor and 33 outdoor competitions. He was last in the Olympic final at 5.50, but returned to win the GP Final and proved to be the best of the Germans as outdoors he beat Stolle (OG 4th at 5.90) 14-5 and both Johnson and Danny Ecker 6-4, Ecker in turn was 6-3 v Stolle (0-1 indoors) and also beat Okkert Brits 9-8 outdoors and 6-1 indoors. Stolle beat Brits 3-0 indoors, but was 5-7 down outdoors. The 'new' Australians Dmitriy Markov and Viktor Chistiakov tied for fifth at the Olympics at 5.80, a height also cleared by the 7th and 8th placers, Brits and Ecker. Chistiakov's next best was 5.70, and Markov was beaten 6-3 by Brits and 4-3 by Stolle. The European Indoor champion Aleksandr Averbukh beat Russian champion Pavel Gerasimov 2-1, but was beaten 3-0 with one tie (10= OG) by European Cup winner, Yevgeniy Smiryagin, who takes the final ranking.

Most competitions over 5.80m (outdoors/ in, exhibitions = ex): Lobinger 10/3, Hartwig 6+1ex/3, Tarasov 6/2, Hysong 6/1, Brits 5+2ex, Markov 5/-, Ecker & Gerasimov 4/-, Stolle 3/3, Johnson 3/2, Averbukh 2/1

1. Hysong, 2. Tarasov, 3. Johnson,
4. Hartwig, 5. Lobinger, 6. Brits, 7. Ecker,
8. Stolle, 9. Markov, 10. Smiryagin

Long Jump

AFTER SEVEN world titles (four indoors and three out) it was right and proper that Iván Pedroso should win the Olympic gold medal, particularly as he could only manage 12th in 1996 after his hamstring surgery. In 2000 he won 3/4 indoors (beaten by James Beckford at Birmingham) and 13/15 outdoors. Kareem Streete-Thomspon beat him at Linz and he was only fourth at Salamanca. He was given a great battle in Sydney by the exciting Jai Taurima and indeed Pedroso had come from behind to win the gold medal with his last jump.

Prior to the Olympics, Taurima had been below his best and indeed had been beaten 6-1 by Peter Burge, with season's bests of 8.13/8.24w. However, when it mattered, in the Olympic final, he produced successive jumps of 8.34, 8.40 and an Australian record 8.49. Roman Shchurenko and Aleksey Lukashevich had solid seasons, capped by Olympic 3-4, but Beckford had much better marks and performances prior to his disappointing 7.98 in failing to make the Olympic final and Burge won 11/14 prior to his 6th place in Sydney.

Kofi Amoah Prah excelled with 2nd to Vitaliy Shkurlatov (whose season ended at the beginning of August) at the European Cup and 5th at the Olympics, but did not have the depth of marks as such men as Luis Meliz (7 OG) or the top Americans. Dwight Phillips was the best of these in Sydney (8th) but had been beaten by Melvin Lister at the US Championships and Lister had jumped 8.49, equal second on the world list, earlier. But Lister and Savante Stringfellow, who won NCAA titles indoors and outdoors respectively, were only 25th and 22nd in the Olympic qualifying round, where Streete-Thompson missed the final by one place. Phillips was 4-1 v Lister, and Stringellow 5-3 v Lister and 3-3 v Phillips. Petar Dachev won the Euopean Indoor title, with Shkurlatov third, and was 11th in Sydney.

Most competitions over 8.20m (outdoors/in): Pedroso 9/3, Beckford 9, Streete-Thompson 5, Stringfellow 3+2w, Lukashevich 3/1, Lister & Shchurenko 3, Shkurlatov 2/2, Meliz 2/1, Burge 2+2w, Petar Dachev 1/2, Bogdan Tarus -/3.

1. Pedroso, 2. Beckford, 3. Taurima,
4. Shchurenko,5. Lukashevich, 6. Burge,
7. Meliz, 8. Streete-Thompson, 9. Stringfellow (-), 10. Prah (-). (inc. indoors 9. Shkurlatov, 10. Dachev).

Triple Jump

JONATHAN EDWARDS sealed his reputation as the star triple jumper of the modern era, as he added Olympic gold to the silver he had won in 1996 and his World and Eyropean titles and three world records. He seemed to have come to terms with the fact that he was no longer able to challenge his sensational form of 1995 when he jumped 18.29 and 18.43w, and that 17.71 was enough to lead the world. He won 10 of his 12 competitions in 2000, his only losses being when he was 4th in Rome behind Rostislav Dimitrov, Yoelbi Quesada and Charles Friedek in Rome and when he did three no-jumps in Berlin.

I have ranked the Olympic 2-3-4-5 in that order, but the fifth placer Larry Achike had the best set of marks throughout the year. He stood in for Edwards to win at the European Cup for Britain, but he was beaten 2-1 by Quesada. The silver medallist Yoel García was 4-2 v Quesada and the bronze medallist Denis Kapustin only had four competitions during the year. Friedek and Dimitrov, the European Indoor gold and silver medallists, disappointed with no mark and 9th respectively in the Olympic final, but deserved higher rankings, with Dimitrov 4-2 v Friedek (and 2-1 indoors) and 2-1 v Quesada.

Achike beat Friedek 4-1 and was 3-3 v Dimitrov. Phillips Idowu, an exciting talent, beat Achike to take the AAA title and was 6th in Sydney for an unprecedented three British jumpers in the top six. The Italians Fabrizio Donato and Paolo Camossi complete the top ten rankings, but their best marks of 17.60 and 17.45 were far head of their next bests. Donato was second to Achike in the European Cup and beat Camossi 2-1 outdoors, although he failed to make the Olympic final where Camossi was eighth. Camossi was third and Donato sixth at the European Indoors. Robert Howard was US champion and 7th in Sydney, but very moderate otherwise.

Most competitions over 17m (outdoors/in): Edwards 11, Friedek 6+1w/1, Dimitrov 5+1w/1, Achike & García 4+1w, Idowu & Kapustin 3, Czingler 2/2, Quesada 2+1w/1, Camossi 2/1, Donato 1+2w

1. Edwards, 2. García, 3. Kapustin,
4. Quesada, 5. Achike, 6. Dimitrov,
7. Friedek, 8. Idowu, 9. Donato (10),
10. Camossi (9)

Shot

THERE WAS an upset at the Olympics as Arsi Harju surprised his rivals with 21.39 in the qualifying round (an improvement of 35cm on his pb) and then 21.29 in the final, although Adam Nelson 21.21 and John Godina 21.20 were close behind. Harju had struggled in the first part of the year, and did not pass 20m until August; and even then his 20.01 at Turku made him only the fourth best Finn, as he had been at Helsinki and Tampere.

But he came through with important wins in the Finnish Championships (20.84) and in the match against Sweden (20.50). His compatriot Mika Halvari led the world rankings indoors with a mighty 22.09, but fouled out at the European Indoors; however he beat Harsu 2-0 indoors and 4-0 outdoors before injury ended his season. The top throw of the year came at the US Trials where Nelson won a superb competition with 22.12 as he was followed by C J Hunter 21.87, Adam Bloom 21.61, Godina 21.09 and Kevin Toth 19.58, with the top three all recording their best marks in the final round. It then looked as though Godina would miss the Olympics, but despite only one shot competition from then until Sydney he came in for Hunter and took the bronze. It is Nelson, though, who ranks first. He matched his preseason best of 20.64 in his fourth competition of 2000 and then exceeded it in all but two of the rest of his competitions, winning in all 10 of 16.

At the Grand Prix Final three Americans beat 21.50: Bloom (4 OG) a pb 21.82, Nelson 21.66 and Godina 21.51, and they were followed by Yuriy Belonog (5 OG), Oliver-Sven Buder (8 OG), Miroslav Menc (10 OG) and Burger Lambrechts (14 OG). Bloom beat Godina 3-2 during the year and Godina also had a 3-2 advantage over the consistent Belonog and 2-1 over Harju. Menc beat Buder 8-2. In Sydney, Manuel Martínez was sixth at 20.55, but did not otherwise beat 20m outdoors, and Janus Robberts was fourth, but his four competitions over 20m was much less than other rivals.

Aleksandr Bagach lost the European Indoor title due to a positive drugs test and the medallists then became 1. Timo Aaltonen, 2. Martínez, 3. Menc. Then, on the eve of the Olympics, from which he had withdrawn through injury, it was reported than Hunter had failed a drugs test at

Oslo and possibly several other occasions, so he and Bagach are not ranked.

Most competitions over 21m/20m (indoors and out): Nelson 10/18, Belonog 6/15, Godina 5/11, Toth 4/9, Halvari 4/8, Harju 2/9, Menc 0/18, Aaltonen 0/17, Buder 0/14, Lambrechts 0/12, Gheorghe Guset 0/9, Paulo Dal Soglio 0/6 (Hunter 9/13, Bagach 2/6). Menc beat Buder 8-2 and Martínez 5-1 outdoors, and Aaltonen (12 OG) was 2-0 up on Lambrechts.

1. Nelson, 2. Bloom, 3. Godina, 4. Belonog, 5. Harju (6), 6. Toth (7), 7. Halvari (5), 8. Menc, 9. Buder, 10. Aaltonen. In brackets are changes including indoor form.

Discus

VIRGILIJUS ALEKNA had a marvellous season, in which he produced the second and third longest throws in history (73.88 and 72.35) at the Lithuanian Championships, was over 70m four times in windless conditions in Zürich, and ended with Olympic gold. He had 17 wins during the year; losing four times in February-March in South Africa, but otherwise just once to Lars Riedel.

That win, in the final Golden League meeting, gave hope to Riedel after seven losses to Alekna, but he had to settle for silver 80cm behind the Lithunaian in Sydney. Frantz Kruger took the bronze after upping his RSA record three times and going 3-3 with Riedel. The rest of the Olympic final placings pretty much determine the rankings, although Jürgen Schult, 8th in Sydney, moves up two places on his consistent overall record and so too does Aleksandr Tammert (9 OG) who beat Jason Tunks (6 OG) 5-3.

Vasiliy Kaptyukh had only six competitions that I know of, but beat his Belarus colleague Vladimir Dubrovshchik 3-2. US champion Adam Setliff did not contest the Golden League meetings but beat Schult 2-0 and Tunks 3-0. The final two spots in the Olympic final were taken by Dmitriy Shevchenko, who had two wins in Russia over 66m but who only competed four times, and the disappointing world champion Anthony Washington. Probably more worthy of a ranking were the Hungarians who did not qualify for the Olympic final, with Róbert Fazekas beating Zoltán Kövágó 6-1 overall and Kövágó 4-2 up on Gábor Máté. Also close is Olympic 10th placer, Michael Möllenbeck, 1-1 v Fazekas.

Most competitions over 65m: Alekna 19, Riedel 12, Kruger 11, Fazekas 7, Tammert & Washington 5, Dubrovshchik, Kaptyukh & Setliff 4; John Godina, Schult, Shevchenko & Tunks 3

1. Alekna, 2. Riedel, 3. Kruger, 4. Kaptyukh, 5. Setliff, 6. Dubrovshchik, 7. Schult, 8. Tammert, 9. Tunks, 10. Fazekas

Hammer

IN ANTICIPATION, the hammer looked to be one of the most open events at the Olympics, with a dozen or so possible winners. At the Games a large number of the big names did not qualify for the final, including the champions of the USA, Russia and Finland: Lance Deal, Vasiliy Sidorenko and Olli-Pekka Karjalainen, the European Cup 1-2 Christophe Epalle and Vladislav Piskunov, and the last three world champions. Andrey Abduvaliyev, Karsten Kobs and Heinz Weis.

Szymon Ziolkówski proved to be the one man to overcome the difficulty of a wet and slippery circle and exceed 80m in the final; and he had a good season overall with 12 wins in 15 competitions. Nicola Vizzoni took silver and won all his other six competitions (all in Italy), but did not exceed 80m, so it is difficult to rank him highly. Bronze medallist Igor Astapkovich did enough to justify this position, but ranks behind the Olympic seventh placer, Tibor Gécsek, who had the best overall record. He did not meet Ziolkówski elsewhere but had win-loss advantages over other strong contenders such as 4-1 v Astapkovich, 7-2 v Andrey Skvaruk (10 OG) and 5-2 v Koji Murofushi (9 OG). After Sydney it was notable that all but one (Vladimir Maska) of the eight competitors in the Grand Prix Final threw further in Doha than they had in Sydney.

Skvaruk revelled in the excellent conditions to win the $50,000 prize with a throw of 81.43 and Murofushi, who was 9th in Sydney (a place lower than his father had achieved at the 1972 Olympics) was also over 80m and beat Skvaruk 4-3 overall. Kobs, Zsolt Németh and Weis returned from 31st, 25th and 26th in the Olympic qualifying to place 3-4-5 in the GP Final ahead of Gécsek. Sidorenko backed up his 81.75 at the Russian Champs with a win at Rüdlingen over Ilya Konovalov, Weis, Ziolkówksi and Kobs. Epalle was undefeated prior to his 23rd place in Sydney. Olli-Pekka Karjalainen looked good until managing only 69.64 in Olympic qualifying, and Alexandros Padadimitríou, OG 12th, is another close to ranking in a confused situation.

Most competitions over 79m: Ziolkówski 11, Gécsek 8, Astapkovich 7, Kobs 6, Epalle, Karjalainen. Murofushi & Skvaruk 5, Piskunov, Sidorenko, Vizzoni & Weis 4; the Olympic 4th placer Ivan Tikhon had two, and 5th and 6th placers Konovalov and Loris Paoluzzi had only one each

1. Ziolkówski, 2. Gécsek, 3. I Astapkovich, 4. Murofushi, 5. Skvaruk, 6. Sidorenko, 7. Epalle, 8. Vizzoni, 9. Tikhon, 10. Konovalov

Javelin

JAN ZELEZNY added to his reputation as the greatest ever javelin thrower by winning his third successive Olympic gold (and a silver before that as well) – an astonishing record, especially considering that his career seemed to have been ended by chronic injury just two years earlier. He lost just one of his seven competitions, third at 87.80 behind Kostas Gatsioudis (Greek record 91.69) and Aki Parviainen (90.97), and four times went over 90m. Steve Backley competed even less – just five times, with three wins and two seconds (85.84 in London behind Parviainen's 87.81 and at the Olympics).

Parviainen had a much better depth of marks and had a record of eight wins, three second places and 5th in Sydney, which meant that the certainty of second ranking was in doubt. He was 1-1 with Backley and 2-1 over the Olympic bronze medallist Sergey Makarov. Gatsioúdis also has strong claims for a high ranking with a 3-2 advantage over Parviainen, but 2-2 v Makarov and slipping to 6th in Sydney. Raymond Hecht came to Sydney with a season's best of 83.84, but after 84.00 in qualifying was a fine fourth at 87.76, However, he was beaten 7-2 by Boris Henry who was 7th in Sydney. Emeterio González, 8th in Sydney, had a 4-1 win-loss advantage over Henry. The top eight were clear, but after them Pål Fagernes led the Olympic qualifying with 86.74 and was ninth in the final, but had only one other competition (84.88). The Finns Harri Haatainen and Harri Hakkarainen were 4-4, but Dariusz Trafas, 10th in Sydney, and Eriks Rags are close.

Two or more competitions over 85m: Gatsioúdis 14, Parviainen 12, Makarov 9, Zelezny 8, Backley & González 3, Hakkarainen & Henry 2

1. Zelezny, 2. Parviainen, 3. Backley,
4. Makarov, 5. Gatsioúdis, 6. González,
7. Henry, 8. Hecht, 9. Hakkarainen,
10. Haatainen

Decathlon

THE OLYMPIC order determines my rankings – with just one major exception. Tomás Dvorák was below par in Sydney for sixth place at 8385 points as he was held back by injury. But he produced easily the highest score of the year, 8900 to win at Götzis (2. Roman Sebrle, 3. Erki Nool, 4. Aleksandr Yurkov, 5. Attila Zsivóczky, 6. Frank Busemann, 7. Mike Maczey, 8. Stefan Schmid) and also won at Talence with 8733 (2. Nool, 3. Zsivóczky, 4. Sebrle), and this record is worthy of top ranking.

Nool, over 8700 in both those major events, won in Sydney with 8641. He would have been very unlucky, but he undoubtedly should have been disqualified at the Olympics for three no throws in the discus, as originally ruled by the judges. Chris Huffins did not finish the 1500m at Götzis and was beaten by Tom Pappas for the US title, but showed his competitive strength when he had to run hard in his worst event, the 1500m, in Sydney – and did so in taking 12.5 seconds off his pb to ensure that he took the bronze medal ahead of Dean Macey, who amazingly came into the Olympics with no decathlons and just one day of individual competition behind him in 2000.

1. Dvorák, 2. Nool, 3. Sebrle, 4. Huffins,
5. Macey, 6. Pappas, 7. Busemann,
8. Zsivóczky, 9. Schmid, 10. Yurkov

20 Kilometres Walk

ROBERT KORZENIOWSKI had a perfect season, winning all his four 20km races. He set Polish records in the first two, in the European Cup and at Hildesheim, and then won the Polish and Olympic titles. I have only changed the Olympic finishing order in two respects to get the world rankings. I swapped the Olympic 4th and 5th placers, Jefferson Pérez and Andreas Erm, as Erm won at Naumburg, where Pérez did not finish, and was also second in the European Cup, while Pérez, although a winner at Fana and Turku, was only 4th in the Pan-American Cup. I then brought into the rankings the winner of that race, Bernardo Segura, He, of course, had celebrated winning Olympic gold only to learn of his disqualification some 15 minutes after he had crossed the line ahead of Korzeniowski. The fasstest time of the year (and indeed a world best) was posted by Roman Rasskazov in the Russian Championships, but some have felt that course to be short. Razzkazov also won the Russian winter title in the next best time of the year, but was sixth in Sydney.

1. Korzeniowski, 2. Hernández, 3. Andreyev,
4. Erm, 5. J Pérez, 6. Rasskazov,
7. Fernández, 8. Deakes, 9. Segura,
10. Gandellini

50 Kilometres Walk

AS AT 20km the Olympic order needs few adjustments for the world rankings. Robert Korzeniowski also won in Portugal before retaining his Olympic title and completing the unique 20km/50km double. Valeriy Spitsyn set a world best time of 3:37:26 to win the Russian title from Vladimir Potomin and Nikolay Matyukhin, but he did not finish in Sydney and Potemin was 26th whereas Matyukhin was fifth. Miguel Rodríguez moves up a place from his Olympic position as he also beat Joel Sánchez (OG 3) to win the Pan-Am Cup, and Valentí Massana is down a place as his other 50k race was a dnf in the Spanish Champs. Jesús Angel García was 12th at the Olympics but won two other important races, the Spanish Champs and European Cup. Nathan Deakes completed a notable Olympic double, with 8th at 20km and 6th at 50km.

1. Korzeniowski, 2. Fadejevs, 3. J Sánchez,
4. Matyukhin, 5. Massana, 6. Rodríguez,
7. J A García, 8. Deakes, 9. Magdziarczyk,
10. Spitsyn

WOMEN ATHLETES OF 2000

100 Metres

MARION JONES maintained her dominance of women's sprinting. This year at 100m she won all her 11 competitions and had a huge victory margin of 0.37 secs over the runner-up, Ekateríni Thánou, at the Olympic Games. Jones ran the six fastest times of the year and eight of the top ten. Inger Miller was the only athlete to get close to her as, after finishing 0.17 back at the US Trials, she ran 10.96 in Zürich behind Jones's 10.95.

Miller then ran a season's best 10.91 to win in Monaco, but was then fifth in Brussels and missed the Olympics through injury. Thánou lost only that Olympic final, and Tayna Lawrence was the surprise bronze medallist, just ahead of Merlene Ottey and Zhanna Pintusevich.

Although Lawrence had a season's best of only 11.07, she beat Ottey 3-0 and Ottey, in turn, was 2-0 up on Pintusevich, who beat the Olympic 6th placer, Chandra Sturrup 7-1. Sturrup was the year's second fastest women with the 10.86 that she ran to win the Bahamas title, but the three Bahamanian's were otherwise very close on times, their rankings determined by win-loss: Sturrup 6-5 v Sevatheda Fynes (OG 7th) and 4-3 v Debbie Ferguson (OG 8th), Fynes 8-4 v Ferguson and 8-3 against the US no. 3 Chryste Gaines. Gaines, who missed the Olympic final by one place ranks 10th as she beat Ferguson 6-3 (and indeed Sturrup 3-2). Christine Arron was second to Thánou in the European Cup, but lost form through illness to run only 7th in her Olympic semi; she was, however, 3-2 v Sturrup, 4-2 v Fynes and 4-1 v Gaines.

Most times under 11.10: Jones 13+2w, Fynes & Miller 7+1w, Torri Edwards 5+3w, Ottey, Pintusevich, Sturrup & Thánou 5+1w, Ferguson & Gaines 4+1w, Arron 3+2w

1. Jones, 2. Thánou, 3. Miller, 4. Lawrence, 5. Ottey, 6. Pintusevich, 7. Sturrup, 8. Arron, 9. Fynes, 10. Gaines

200 Metres

MARION JONES ran the 200m just in the Championships; she won the US title in 21.94 (from Inger Miller 22.09) and the Olympic title in 21.84 (from Pauline Davis-Thompson 22.22). Debbie Ferguson was 5th in Sydney, with Susanthika Jayasinghe and Bev McDonald also ahead of her, but she beat Davis-Thompson 3-1, having won all her six competitions prior to the Olympics. Melinda Gainsford-Taylor beat her Australian rival Cathy Freeman 4-1 and they finished 6th and 7th at the Olympics, with Zhanna Pintusevich 8th. A problem at this event was the dearth of competition as the 200m was not a Grand Prix event.

The US Trials 2-3, Miller and Nanceen Perry did enough to attain top ten rankings, but others with fast times, such as LaTasha Colander-Richardson and Mary Onyali at 22.49 produced too little and perhaps better claimants to a rankings place were the African champion Myriam Mani and NCAA champion Peta-Gaye Dowdie.

Most times under 22.70: Gainsford 8+1w, Ferguson & McDonald 7, Jones 5+1w, Davis & Jayasinghe 5, Perry 4+1w (and 2 indoor), Mani 4, Miller 3+1w, Freeman 3

1. Jones, 2. Ferguson, 3. Davis-Thompson, 4. Jayasinghe, 5. McDonald, 6. Gainsford-Taylor, 7. Freeman, 8. Miller, 9. Perry, 10. Pintusevich

400 Metres

THE BURDEN of expectation on Cathy Freeman at the Olympic Games was huge, but she delivered in great style for her 41st win in 42 finals since the 1996 Olympics. Her 49.11 was the fastest time of the year and those who followed in 2nd, 3rd and 4th places all set personal bests: Lorraine Graham 49.58, Katharine Merry 49.72 and Donna Fraser 49.79. Two other women get into the world's top six: Marion Jones who ran 49.59 in her one 400m race of the year at Walnut and Anna Guevara, who ran 49.70 at Mexico City before taking fifth in Sydney in 49.96.

Heide Seyerling, Falilat Ogunkoya and Olga Kotlyarova completed the Olympic final, and there is little reason to go beyond these eight for the top rankings, with some adjustments for their overall records. LaTasha Colander-Richardson won the US title in 49.87, but her next fastest was 50.50 and she did not advance from the quarter-finals in Sydney. Next best on times was Michelle Collins, but she was limited by a right hip stress fracture and ran only 53.66 in her heat at the Olympics.

Most times under 51.0: Freeman, Graham, Guevara & Ogunkoya 11, Merry 9, Collins 7, Svetlana Goncharova & Kotlyarova 6, Colander-Richardson & Seyerling 5, Fraser, Svetlana Pospelova, Sandie Richards & Olesya Zykina 4

1. Freeman, 2. L Graham, 3. Merry, 4. Guevara, 5. Ogunkoya, 6. Fraser, 7. Seyerling, 8. Kotlyarova, 9. Colander-Richardson, 10. Collins

800 Metres

MARIA MUTOLA won the Olympic title at her fourth attempt and takes top ranking at this event for the sixth time. She raced sparingly, twice indoors, a loss to Stephanie Graf at Gent and a win at Stuttgart, and then wins in all her seven races at five meeting outdoors. Three of the four fastest times of the year were set in Sydney by the medallists, Mutola, Graf and Kelly Holmes. The second and fifth fastest times came at the Russian Championships from Natalya Tsyganova and Olga Raspopova, and amazingly both these women failed to advance from third places in their heats at the Olympics. Poor preparation was blamed for their team's performances, but they, and the Russian third-placer Irina Mistyukevich, who went out in the Olympic semis, had good depth of performances. Mistyukevich won the European Cup and the others ran well in the top international races.

At Zürich five women beat 1:58, in order: Mutola, Graf, Ludmila Formanová, Tsyganova and Raspopova with Claudia Gesell sixth, and at Stockholm six were under 1:58.1: Mutola, Graf, Raspopova, Formanová, Mistyukevich and Tsyganova. Formanová fell foul of an injured leg at Sydney, but had a good overall record and beat Tsyganova 2-0. Tsyganova was 4-1 and Mistyukevich 3-2 against Raspopova. Holmes returned from injury to win the AAA title in 2:02.08 and then had three races just outside 2 minutes. So her Olympic form of 1:58.45 semi and 1;56.80 for bronze was just wonderful. Brigita Langerholc and Helena Fuchsová ran personal bests for 4th and 5th at Sydney, but 8th placed Hasna Benhassi had much better pre-Ollympic form with seven wins in nine races, including the African title.

1. Mutola, 2. Graf, 3. Formanová,
4. Tsyganova, 5. Mistyukevich,
6. Raspopova, 7. Holmes, 8. Benhassi,
9. Langerholc, 10. Fuchsová

1500 Metres

THE OLYMPIC final was such a curious race that the rankings are harder than they might have been. Nouria Mérah-Benida ran well to take the title, but her overall record at the event was three wins from nine competitions. After the Games she was third in a slow Grand Prix Final behind Violeta Szekely and Kutre Dulecha, and those two, 2nd and 4th at the Olympics, had records of four wins from ten and three wins from eight.

The Olympic silver medallist was Gabriela Szabo who came from some 30m down after she had tripped over the falling Hayley Tullett, but she had only two other 1500m competitions – first a fine win in a great race against Suzy Favor Hamilton in Eugene and then second to Szekely at the British GP. Favor Hamilton looked set for a medal but then collapsed in the finishing straight in Sydney; she had run the year's fastest time of 3:57.40 to win at Oslo from Lidia Chojecka (OG 4th), Szekely, Dulecha, Svetlana Masterkova (dnf OG heat) and Carla Sacramento (OG 10th). Szekely, with positive win-loss records of 4-3 v Dulecha, 4-2 v Mérah-Benida and 2-0 v Szabo just takes the top ranking. Dulecha was 5-1 v Mérah-Benida to ensure second place.

Regina Jacobs won the US title in 4:01.01 but had only one other outdoor race at this event; she did, however, have three good 1 mile wins indoors. The other significant indoor race was the mile at Stuttgart won by Szabo from Chojecka, Olga Yegorova, Dulecha, Tullett and Mérah-Benida.

Most times under 4:05: Dulecha and Szekely 6, Chojecka and Natalya Gorelova 5, Mérah-Benida, Olga Komyagina, Olga Kuznetsova, Olga Nelyubova and Sacramento 4, Favor Hamilton and Yuliya Kosenkova 3

1. Szekely, 2. Dulecha, 3. Mérah-Benida,
4. Szabo, 5. Chojecka, 6. Favor-Hamilton,
7. Sacramento, 8. Masterkova, 9. Tullett,
10. Gorelova (-). With indoors: 10. Jacobs.

3000 Metres

THE TOP six places in the world rankings all came at Zürich, where Gabriela Szabo won in 8:26.35 from Sonia O'Sullivan, Marta Domínguez, Paula Radcliffe, Lydia Cheromei and Irina Mikitenko. Seventh was Tegla Loroupe who ran a little quicker, 8:30.95 for seventh on the world lists, when second to Cheromei at Monaco. Szabo won at the European Cup in her only other outdoor 3000m race after indoors wins at Birmingham and at the European Indoors. O'Sullivan had seven races, winning three, including the Grand Prix final. Although her best time of 8:36.92 was only 15th on the world list, Gete Wami ranks highly as she had two other sub-8:40 races and won two of three. Her one loss was to Tatyana Tomashova at Nice, ahead of Loroupe and O'Sullivan. Lidia Chojecka, ninth best by time, won twice outdoors, beating Dong Yanmei, O'Sullivan and Cheromei in Paris, and had also taken the European Indoor silver with Domínguez taking the bronze.

1. Szabo, 2. O'Sullivan, 3. Chojecka,
4. Wami, 5. Domínguez

5000 Metres

TOP FOUR in the rankings were the Olympic top four, but I have made one change in the order, with Gete Wami (3rd) swapping places with Sonia O'Sullivan (2nd) as Wami ran much the year's fastest time, 14:30.88 in Heusden and was also second in Stockholm in 14:45.50

whereas O'Sullivan did not beat 15:10 in her three other 5000m races and was only ninth at the British GP. Gabriela Szabo is top for the fourth successive year, but after her heroics of 1999, raced sparingly in 2000 and had only one 5000m race before Sydney. That was at Berlin where she was second to Leah Malot, who ran the year's second fastest time of 14:39.83. Malot, however, had lost her chance of Olympic glory by not running the event at the Kenyan Trials (she was 5th at 10,000m), and although she also won at Lille and Yokohama, she was only 12th at Stockholm.

This race and the Olympic final produced the greatest depth of times with 13 and 12 women under 15 minutes respectively. The Stockholm winner was Olga Yegorova, who was also 2nd in the Russian Championships and 8th in Sydney. Derartu Tulu was third at Stockholm in her only 5000m of the year and Ayelech Worku fourth as she was in Sydney. Worku won the British GP from Paula Radcliffe (also AAA champion), Tegla Loroupe (also 3rd Berlin and 7th Stockholm), Lydia Cheromei (6th OG , 8th Stockholm) and Irina Mikitenko (5th OG, 2nd Lille). Worknesh Kidane just misses a ranking with 3rd Lille, 8th British GP and 7th OG.

1. Szabo, 2. O'Sullivan, 3. Wami, 4. Worku, 5. Malot, 6. Radcliffe, 7. Mikitenko, 8. Yegorova, 9. Loroupe, 10. Cheromei

10,000 Metres

PAULA RADCLIFFE, just as she had done in Seville 1999, made the Olympic final a great race. Her tactics of running fast from the gun failed to get her a medal but once again earned her huge admiration. The kickers passed her at the end and the smooth styles of Derartu Tulu and Gete Wami earned Ethiopia gold and silver. Tulu regained the title she had won at Barcelona in 1992 and this time she smashed the Olympic and African records; her 30:17.49 being a huge improvement on her previous best of 30:56.4. Wami's 30:22.48 was the fifth fastest ever and Fernanda Ribeiro's 30:22.88 the sixth.

Radcliffe took 0.15 off her Commonwealth record for eighth on the all-time list and of the top twelve, eight set personal bests and five national records. Tegla Loroupe was fifth, just outside her 1999 best, but the sixth placer Sonia O'Sullivan took 36 seconds off her previous best. There were four sub-31 times outside the Sydney final in 2000, three of them at Heusden, where Berhane Adere (OG 12th) won in 30:51.30 from Leah Malot and Merima Hashim, and also from Tulu in Gijón, 30:56.4.

Tulu had three wins in three 10,000m races as she also won at Brunswick in 31:08.27 from Yuko Kawakami (OG 10th) who had two wins at 10,000m, as did Loroupe and the Olympic eighth placer Elana Meyer. Li Ji (7th OG) won her other three 10,000m races. The Olympics was the only 10,000m competition of the year for Wami and Radcliffe, while Ribeiro's other race was a win at Barakaldo. Lidiya Grigoryeva, 9th in Sydney after 2nd in the Russian Champs, just misses a ranking.

1. Tulu, 2. Wami, 3. Ribeiro, 4. Radcliffe, 5. Loroupe, 6. O'Sullivan, 7. Li Ji, 8. Meyer, 9. Kawakami, 10. Adere

Half Marathon

PAULA RADCLIFFE had made her half marathon debut with third place in the 1999 Great North Run. This year she ran away with that race and set a European best of 67:07. Two weeks later she ran exactly two minutes slower to win the World title in the heat and humidity of Veracruz. Lornah Kiplagat ran the year's fastest time of 66:56 to win at Den Haag and won her other two half marathons: Ein Gedi 71:21 and Zaandam 67:37. Third fastest was Tegla Loroupe with her Lisbon win in 67:24, but she was three minutes behind Radcliffe in the Great North Run.

The next three fastest times came in Tokyo in January, when Elana Meyer won in 67:33 from Esther Wanjiru and Kerryn McCann. Significantly Lidia Simon was fourth in that race; she went on to third in the Worlds. Meyer and Wanjiru were again 1-2 at Sendai, but Meyer was beaten by Naoko Takahashi at Sapporo. Takahashi won both her half marathons (also Chiba) as did Catherine Ndereba (Como and Philadelphia). Derartu Tulu was second to Loroupe in Lisbon in March and in the same city, but a different course, won in October from Susan Chepkemei (4th Zaandam and 2nd Worlds) and Joyce Chepchumba, who had three wins: Berlin, Glasgow and Altötting as well as second to Restituta Joseph in the Copenhagen-Malmö bridge race. Joseph also won in Nice and was fifth in Lisbon.

1. Radcliffe, 2. Kiplagat, 3. Takahashi, 4. Meyer, 5. Loroupe, 6. Tulu, 7. Chepkemei, 8. Wanjiru, 9. Simon, 10, Joseph

Marathon

THE TWO fastest women marathoners of the year both won their two marathons of the year, but while Catherine Ndereba was faster (2:21:33 in Chicago, as well as 2:26:11 in Boston), Naoko Takahashi takes top ranking. She won in Nagoya in 2:22:19 and then ran wonderfully well to win the Olympic title on a tougher course in Sydney in 2:23:14. Lidia Simon took the Olympic silver medal and Joyce Chepchumba the bronze and both ran sub-2:25 in all their three marathons. Simon beat a classy field in Osaka (2:22:54), followed by Harumi Hiroyama (who had no other marathons), Esther Wanjiru (4 OG), Elefenesh Alemu (6 OG and 1st

Nagano), all under 2:25. Then Simon ran in another top-class race in London, where the order was 1. Tegla Loroupe 2:24:33 (13 OG when ill, 1st Rome, 6th New York), 2. Simon, 3. Chepchumba, 4. Adriana Fernández (16 OG, 13 New York). In October Chepchumba ran the fastest of her three 2:24 times – 2:24:02 to win in Tokyo from Reiko Tosa, whose 2:24:47 almost matched her 2:24:36 for second at Nagoya, and Derartu Tulu, who was also sixth in London.

1. Takahashi, 2. Ndereba, 3. Simon,
4. Chepchumba, 5. Wanjiru, 6. Kiplagat,
7. Alemu, 8. Tosa, 9. Loroupe, 10. Tulu

100 Metres Hurdles

GAIL DEVERS was unquestionably the top sprint hurdler of the year, with 9 wins in 11 events, but she was forced out of her semi in the Olympics with a hurt left hamstring. She ran the four fastest times of the year and a further four of the top 12. Surprisingly she was able to run again at the Grand Prix final after the Olympics, and won there – just as well too, as she protected her share of the Golden League jackpot as well as winning $50,000 for her event win plus a tie for second in the overall Grand Prix. Delloreen Ennis-London, at Zagreb, handed Devers her only other loss during the year.

Olga Shishigina, Glory Alozie and Melissa Morrison took the Olympic medals, but Alozie had faster times and beat Shishigina 4-3. Shishigina beat Morrison 4-2, although she did not finish at the GP final. Ennis-London was 4th in Sydney and 4th at the Olympics and was also 5-4 with Morrison, so these two are very close. There is quite a gap after them, with Michelle Freeman favoured for sixth ranking. She was 8-1 down to Ennis-London, but 2-1 against Anjanette Kirkland, who fell in her semi at the US Trials. There was little between those ranked in the final places. Aliuska López and Nicole Ramalalanirina were 5th and 6th ahead of unranked Linda Ferga and Bridgette Foster in Sydney. But Sharon Couch-Jewell (6th OG semi) was 3-1 v López. Ramalalanirina was 2-1 against both Couch and Ferga.

Most times under 12.80: Devers 11 (+1w), Alozie, Ennis-London, Morrison and Shishigina 8; Freeman 5, Couch, Foster, Kirkland and Ramalalanirina 3.

1. Devers, 2. Alozie, 3. Shishigina,
4. Morrison, 5. Ennis-London, 6. Freeman,
7. Kirkland, 8. Couch-Jewell, 9. López,
10. Ramalalanirina

400 Metres Hurdles

IRINA PRIVALOVA ran 60m hurdles indoors twice in January, but few could then have anticipated her later progress over hurdles. She made her debut at 400mh at Moscow on 12 July with a splendid 54.49, and improved to 54.21 at the Russian Championships, 54.06 in Monaco (where she looked superb over the first 300m before easing) and then 54.02 in the semi and 53.02 to take Olympic gold – eight wins in eight races including heats. Deon Hemmings and Nezha Bidouane followed to take Olympic silver and bronze and they were 2-2 and 4-0 respectively against the prolific Sandra Glover.

Glover ran the year's second fastest time to take the US title and won 12 of her 18 competitions, but faded a little at the end and went out in the semis in Sydney. Nonetheless she ranks higher than the Olympic 4-5, Daimí Pernía and Tatyana Tereshchuk.

Pernía had only six competitions but beat Tereshchuk 2-0. Ionela Tîrlea, who had raced so well in 1999 before injury, did not return until the Olympics, where she excelled for sixth in the final. But she is ranked behind Gudrun Arnardótttir (7 OG), and semi-finalists Ulrike Urbansky and Andrea Blackett, who all had full seasons. Blackett beat the Olympic 8th placer, NCAA champion Natasha Danvers, 2-0.

Most times under 55.0: Glover 12, Hemmings 10, Tereshchuk 8, Privalova 7, Blackett 5, Bidouane and Pernía 4, Urbansky 3.

1. Privalova, 2. Hemmings, 3. Bidouane,
4. Glover, 5. Pernía, 6. Tereshchuk,
7. Arnardóttir, 8. Urbansky, 9. Blackett,
10. Tîrlea

High Jump

SEVEN WOMEN cleared the benchmark height of 2 metres in 2000 – and two of them did so at the Olympic Games, where Yelena Yelesina took the gold on count-back from Hestrie Cloete. Another of the seven, Kajsa Bergqvist shared the bronze at 1.99 before coming closer than the others to clearing 2.03. Bergqvist had twice jumped 2.00 indoors, and outdoors set Swedish records in August at 2.00 and 2.01; she had nine wins in 13 outdoor competitions (and 6 in 8 indoors), Cloete had 9 wins from 14 and Yelesina 5 from 12.

Although losing all her mid-season events in Europe, Yelesina beat Cloete 2-1 and Cloete beat Bergqvist 2-1 with Bergqvist only meeting Yelesina in Sydney. The big surprise in Sydney was that Oana Pantelimon took her pb up from 1.94 to 1.96 and then to 1.99 to tie for third place. In limited competition, she had won 4/5 outdoors pre-Sydney, the one loss being at 1.90 at the Romanian Championships behind Monica Dinescu's 1.95.

Dinescu had the year's best jump of 2.02 at Paris in June and won at the European Cup, but was outjumped 1.96 to 1.93 in Sydney by the 5-6-7 placers: Inga Babakova, Svetlana Zalevskaya and Viktoriya Palamar. Babakova (twice), Venelina Veneva (twice) and Zuzana Hlavonová were the other 2m jumpers. Babakova beat Dinescu 5-3 and Veneva 4-1 outdoors but the later two were as equal as they could be – for they shared ninth place in Sydney and otherwise were 2-2 outdoors (although Veneva won their one indoor clash). Zalevskaya beat Hlavonová 3-1 and the latter beat Olympic 8th placer Amewu Mensah 2-1. Indoors, Bergqvist took the European title from Hlavonová, Olga Kaliturina, Veneva and Palamar.

Most competitions over 1.95m (outdoors/in): Bergqvist 8/4, Dinescu 8, Veneva 4/3, Babakova 6, Hlavonová 5/1, Cloete & Palamar 5, Yelesina 3

1. Yelesina (2), 2. Cloete (3), 3. Bergqvist (1), 4. Babakova, 5. Dinescu (6), 6. Veneva (5), 7. Pantelimon, 8. Zalevskaya, 9. Palamar (10), 10. Hlavonová (9). In brackets are changes including indoor form.

Pole Vault

STACY DRAGILA is clearly the queen of women's pole vaulting. She set world records indoors at 4.57, 4.61 and 4.62 and outdoors at 4.60, 4.62 and 4.63 – and she went over 4.70 in the beach vault at Santa Barbara, which, although not allowed for record purposes, was held under regular conditions. She sealed a great season of five wins in six indoor competitions and 13 in 18 outdoors with Olympic victory at 4.60.

Behind her, however, the situation was extremely confused. Take the two Australians for instance: Tatiana Grigorieva came to the Olympics with a season's best of just 4.30, but in Sydney cleared that in qualifying and then 4.35, 4.40, 4.45, 4.50 and 4.55 for the silver medal. Emma George on the other hand was 15= in the Olympic qualifying at 4.25 – but she beat Grigorieva 8-2 and had 11 competitions (second only to Dragila) over 4.40.

Clearing 4.50 in Sydney for 3rd and 4th were Vala Flosadóttir and Daniela Bártová, but the former had a next best of 4.30 (4.40 indoors). Bártová had more consistent form although she had no-heighted at the European Indoors won by Pavla Hamácková from Yelena Belyakova and Christine Adams (tied for silver) and Flosadóttir 4th.

Anzhela Balakhonova improved her European record to 4.56 and although she no-heighted in the Olympic final, might just justify second ranking, beating Bártová 3-2 (and 3-0 indoors). However, she was beaten 3-1 by Nicole Humbert (5 OG 4.45). Humbert in turn was 5-4 up on Yvonne Buschbaum (6 OG 4.40) outdoors (but 1-2 down indoors) and 3-1 against George.

Two Russians come into the picture despite not clearing a height in the Olympic qualifying, as both had season's bests of 4.50: Svetlana Feofanova ahead of Yelena Belyakova 7-2 on win-loss (0-1 indoors). Outdoors Feofanova was 2-2 v Bártová, 2-1 v Humbert and 3-1 v Buschbaum and Belyakova beat George 3-2. Of the US 2-3, Kellie Suttle beat Mel Mueller 4-2 outdoors (but 1-2 indoors), but was 1-2 down to George.

Most competitions over 4.40m (outdoors/in, exhibitions = ex): Dragila 13/4, George 11, Balakhonova 8/3, Feofanova 8/1, Humbert 8+1ex, Suttle 7/1, Bártová 6+1ex/3, Buschbaum 4/2, Belyakova 4/1, Mueller 3/2, Mary Sauer 3, Elmarie Gerryts 2.2, Tracy O'Hara 2/1, Hamácková 1/2, Flosadóttir & Yelena Isinbayeva 1/1

1. Dragila, 2. Balakhonova, 3. Bártová, 4. Feofanova, 5. Humbert (7), 6. Grigorieva (8), 7. Buschbaum (9), 8. Belyakova (5), 9. George (10), 10. Suttle (-). - Flosadóttir (6). In brackets are changes including indoor form

Long Jump

THIS IS another event in which the number one is not clear cut, but the marvellous Heike Drechsler, 17 years after taking her first world title, ended the year with wins at both the Olympic Games and Grand Prix Final and ranks first despite only winning five of her 13 outdoor competitions (and 4 of 9 indoors). Tatyana Kotova shared the Golden League jackpot by winning at Paris, Rome, Oslo, Brussels and Berlin.

This was especially notable as she returned from a serious car accident to win the last two, although the effects of that crash held her back to 4th in the Olympics and 5th at the GP Final. Fiona May and Marion Jones won the other two Olympic medals, but were beaten 4-2 and 2-1 respectively by Kotova. May was also beaten (3rd to 4th) at the GP Final by Niurka Montalvo, who was not cleared by Cuba to compete for her new country, Spain, in Sydney.

Dawn Burrell and Erica Johansson were 4-4, but Burrell was ahead at the Olympics (11th to 17th) and GP Final (2nd to 6th). Both had win loss advantage over Inessa Kravets, who joined May, Kotova and Jones with 'legal' 7m jumps.

Olga Rublyova was 6th at the Olympics and won at the European Cup, but was 10th in Paris in her only Golden League competition. Lyudmila Galkina was ninth in Sydney and beat Rublyova 2-1. The European Indoor 1-2-3-4 was: Johansson, Drechsler, Iva Prandzheva (later suspended for drugs) and Rublyova.

Most competitions over 6.80m (outdoors/in): May 11, Kotova 9/1, Drechsler 7+1w/2, Burrell 6, Johansson & Montalvo 4+1w/2, Jones 4, Guan Yingnan 3+1w, Kravets 3, Rublyova 2+1w/1; (dq, Prandzheva 5/2)

1. Drechsler, 2. Kotova, 3. May, 4. Jones, 5. Burrell, 6. E Johansson, 7. Montalvo, 8. Rublyova, 9. Galkina, 10. Guan Yingnan

Triple Jump

THE OLYMPIC medallists were a class apart from the rest as world standards were well down this year (10th best at 14.52 compared to 14.70 in 1999). The Olympic medals went to Tereza Marinova 5,20, Tatyana Lebedeva 15.00 and Yelena Govorova 14.96, with Yamilé Aldama fourth with 14.30. Of course some of the others might have jumped further but for the heavy rain which fell in Sydney after the first round. Lebedeva had come to Sydney as clear favourite after winning 6/6 indoors and 7/8 outdoors and with Russian records at 15.15 and 15.32 in Yokohama just two weeks earlier. But Marinova had beaten her 15.07w to 15.00w at Réthimno in May.

Marinova's overall record was seven wins from nine events. Govorova had nine competitions better than Aldama's best of the year, but the latter did enough to rank fourth. The Olympic 5-6-7-8, Baya Rahouli, Cristina Nicolau, Olga Vasdeki and Oksana Rogova had outdoor season's bests of only 14.30, 14.19, 14.26 and 14.27 respectively, although if we add indoor form, then Nicolau comes into the picture with 14.94, 14.63 for European Indoor bronze behind Lebedeva, and 14.53. Anja Valant, Olympic 9th, exceeded 14.60 twice and Natalya Safronova, dnq 15th in Sydney, had a best of 14.65 heading six competitions over 14.20. Rogova was 2nd in the Russian Champs ahead of Inna Lasovskaya and Olga Yershova with Anna Biryukova 6th, and the last two have a reasonable set of marks. Not ranked is Iva Prandzheva who got a drugs ban and whose performances, headed by 15.04, would otherwise have ranked her third.

1. Marinova, 2. Lebedeva, 3. Govorova, 4. Aldama, 5. Valant (6), 6. Safronova (7), 7. Rahouli (8), 8. Rogova (9), 9. Yershova (10), 10. Biryukova (-). - Nicolau (5). In brackets are changes including indoor form.

Shot

YANINA KOROLCHIK has become a formidable big meeting competitor. In 1998 she took the European bronze medal with 19.23, a 33cm improvement to her pb; in 1999 she was 4th in the Worlds, and in Sydney 2000 she improved her best from 20.31 to 20.56 to take the gold medal. However, each of the Olympic 2-3-4. Larisa Peleshenko, Astrid Kumbernuss and Svetlana Krivelyova could also be considered for top ranking. Easily the best mark of 2000 was Larisa Peleshenko's 21.46 at the Kuts Memorial in August, but Krivelyova won her three outdoor competitions, including the Russian Championships, prior to the Olympics and beat Peleshenko each time.

The Russians did not meet Korolchik, but Kumbernuss beat Korolchik 2-1 overall. Each had three outdoor competitions over 20m and perhaps the Olympic order must decide the rankings. If we add indoor form, however, the case for Peleshenko becomes clear, for she won 4/4 and was over 20m three times. She beat Krivelyova twice including at the European Indoors, where the order was 1. Peleshenko, 2. Nadine Kleinert-Schmitt, 3. Kumbernuss, 4. Krivelyova. Korolchik had just two indoor competitions and was sixth in each at below 18m. Kleinert-Schmitt slipped a little at the Olympics to 8th, but beat the Olympic 6th placer, Yumileidi Cumbá 5-2 outdoors (5-3 inc. indoor).

Krystyna Zabawska, 5th at the Olympics and at the European Indoors, had poorer marks outdoors, but was over 19m three times indoors where she beat Cumbá 2-0. Kumbernuss v Kleinert-Schmitt was 9-3 outdoors and 3-3 indoors. Kalliopi Ouzoúni set a Greek record of 18.63 to take 7th in Sydney, but Olga Ryabinkina and Lyudmila Sechko, 3rd and 4th at the Russian Championships, were twice over 19m and the Chinese Cheng Xiaoyan (11 OG) and Yu Xin (24 OG) also had better marks. Nadezhda Ostapchuk took the Belarus title at 18.81 and was over 19m indoors but did not compete at the Olympics.

Most competitions over 20m/19m (indoors and out): Peleshenko 6/11, Krivelyova 4/7, Kumbernuss 3/18, Korolchik 3/4, Kleinert-Schmitt 0/16, Zabawska 0/4, Cumbá 0/3

1. Korolchik (3), 2. Peleshenko (1), 3. Kumbernuss (2), 4. Krivelyova, 5. Kleinert-Schmitt, 6. Cumbá (7), 7. Zabawska (6), 8. Ryabinkina (10), 9. Sechko (-), 10. Cheng (-), - Ostapchuk (8), Ouzoúni (9). In brackets are changes including indoor form.

Discus

ELLINA ZVEREVA became, at 39, the oldest ever Olympic women's champion at athletics. During 2000 she beat the silver medallist Anastasiá Kelesídou 3-1, the bronze medallist Irina Yatchenko 3-0 and the 4th placer Natalya Sadova 2-0. But the Olympic 6th placer was Franka Dietzsch who otherwise had the best season, beating Zvereva 4-1 and Kelesídou 2-1, although 1-2 to Sadova. Dietzsch had 15 wins in 18 competitions, including coming back from Sydney to win the GP Final from Zvereva, Beatrice Faumuiná (12 OG), Nicoleta Grasu (19 OG) and Lisa-Marie Vizaniari (8 OG).

Grasu failed to make the Olympic final, but otherwise had a solid season, including a win in the European Cup over Ilke Wyludda (7 OG) and Kelesídou, and she was 3-1 up on the Olympic 5th place Stiliani Tsikoúna and 1-2 down to Yatchenko. Grasu's 68.70 in February topped the world lists from Zvereva's Olympic winning distance of 68.40 and Dietzsch 68.06.

Contenders for the final place in the top ten rankings include Seilala Sua, Faumuiná, Yelena Antonova and Suzy Powell, who were 10th, 12th, 13th and 15th respectively at the Olympics. They come some way after the top nine, as indicated by Vizaniari's 8-1 advantage over Faumuiná.

Most competitions over 64m: Dietzsch 13, Grasu 11, Zvereva 8, Sadova 7, Yatchenko 6, Vizaniari 5, Antonova, Kelesídou, Powell, Tsikoúna & Wyludda 4, Faumuiná 3

1. Zvereva, 2. Dietzsch, 3. Sadova,
4. Kelesídou, 5. Yatchenko, 6. Grasu,
7. Tsikoúna, 8. Wyludda, 9. Vizaniari, 10. Sua

Hammer

IT WAS anticipated that there would be a great struggle for gold between Mihaela Melinte and Olga Kuzenkova. Melinte's three-year run of 42 successive wins had been ended when Kuzenkova beat her twice in June before Melinte came back to beat her great rival in the European Cup on second best throw as both recorded 70.20. Kuzenkova had improved her national record to 75.68 at the Russian Cup and Melinte produced a season's best of 74.80 to win at Rüdlingen. Melinte had 11 and Kuzenkova 6 marks better than the world's third best, a French record 71.18 by Manuela Montebrun.

But just as the Olympic qualifying round was due to start came news of Melinte's drugs disqualification from a positive test back on June 7. As expected Kuzenkova led the qualifying in Sydney with 70.60, but could only manage 69.77 for the silver in the final, where the 17 year-old Kamila Skolimowska set her third world junior record of the year with 71.16 (previously 69.13 and 70.62). Skolimowska followed that with the anti-climax of not even qualifying for the World Juniors final, her 51.84 following two no throws. However, she won 10/13 overall. Kirsten Münchow and Yipsi Moreno were 3-4 at the Olympics and had the depth of performances to support those positions in the rankings, but Debbie Sosimenko is ranked lower than her splendid Olympic fifth place, as she had had a modest season until then, and Amy Palmer also is a little lower than her 8th place in Sydney. Series of marks and win-loss records determined 5-10 rankings, but there was little between these women.

The annual get-together at Rüdlingen weighed heavily as most of the world's best were there: 1. Melinte, 2. Skolimowska, 3. Dawn Ellerbe (7 OG), 4. Lisa Misipeka (14 OG), 5. Münchow, 6. Katalin Divós (13 OG), and some win-loss records included: Lyudmila Gubkina (6 OG) beat Lorraine Shaw (9 OG) 2-0 and was 1-1 with Divos, Shaw beat Sosimenko 3-1 and was 3-3 with Divós, Divós beat Misipeka 3-2 and was 2-1 with Sosimenko. Montebrun was a good 4th at the European Cup (Münchow 3rd, Shaw 5th) but managed to throw only 57.77 in the Olympic qualifying.

Most competitions over 68m: Kuzenkova 13, Ellerbe 6, Münchow & Skolimowska 5, Moreno 4, Divós & Montebrun 3; (Melinte 14)

1. Kuzenkova, 2. Skolimowska,
3. Münchow, 4. Moreno, 5. Ellerbe,
6. Gubkina, 7. Divós, 8. Shaw,
9. Sosimenko, 10. Palmer

Javelin

TRINE HATTESTAD announced her retirement after a great year in which she set world records in the Golden League meetings in Rome and Oslo, won the overall IAAF GP prize and at her fifth Olympic Games took the gold medal in Sydney. Overall she won 13 of 16 competitions, her losses being 5th in Paris (1. Tatyana Shikolenko, 2. Osleidys Menéndez, 3. Tanja Damaske, 4. Yekaterina Ivakina), 2nd in Monaco to Shikolenko and 2nd at the GP Final to Sonia Bisset. Mirela Tzelíli was second in Sydney where she twice set a Greek record of 67.51, but had only won two of her four other competitions, and threw only 57.84 for 3rd at the European Cup. Much stronger seasons were compiled by Menéndez (3 OG and 3 GPF) and Shikolenko (7 OG and 4 GPF), with Menéndez 7-3 ahead on win-loss. Tanja Damaske had to withdraw from the Olympics through injury but beat Steffi Nerius (4 OG) 6-0 and Bisset (5 OG) 3-0; she was 2-3 down to Shikolenko. Bisset's GP win and 6-3 win-loss advantage moves her ahead of Nerius. Xiomara Rivero was 6th at the Olympics with her best mark of the year, 62.92, but that was bettered often by several others, including Nikola Tomecková and Mikaela Ingberg who were 8-9 at the Olympics and 6-7 at the GP Final, and also Yekaterina Ivakina, although she was only 24th in the Olympic qualifying.

1. Hattestad, 2. Menéndez, 3. Shikolenko,
4. Damaske, 5. Tzelíli, 6. Bisset, 7. Nerius,
8. Tomecková, 9. Ingberg, 10. Ivakina

Heptathlon

DESPITE INJURY, Denise Lewis held on to take the Olympic title with 6584 points and this, together with her win in Talence at 6831, ensures her of top ranking. The silver medallist Yelena Prokhorova had won her two previous heptathlons, the Russian Cup 6520 and Russian Championships 6765. Eunice Barber was unable to finish in Sydney after being held back by injury since her win at Götzis when she recorded the year's top score of 6842. Natalya Roshchupkina was a long way behind her then with second in 6513 and slipped a little to 6th at the Olympics but also won the European Cup and was second at the Russian Champs. Further

Götzis positions were: 3. Sabine Braun (5 OG), 4. Shelia Burrell (26 OG with no height in the high jump), 5. Karin Ertl (7 OG), 6. Kathleen Gutjahr, 7. Astrid Retzke and other top names further back: 9, Natalya Sazanovich, 10. Tiia Hautala, 12. DeDee Nathan. Sazanovich then won the European Cup First League and was third in the Olympics, where Hautala and Nathan came 8th and 9th. Ursula Wlodarczyk again had a busy year with six heptathlons; she was second to Lewis in Talence and came 4th in Sydney. Retzke did not finish in Sydney, but her win over Braun, Ertl and Wlodarczyk in the German Trials meeting helps her ranking.

1. Lewis, 2. Prokhorova, 3. Barber, 4. Roshchupkina, 5. Sazanovich, 6. Wlodarczyk, 7. Braun, 8. Burrell, 9. Ertl, 10. Retzke

20 Kilometres Walk

AS EVER a ranking in this event is extremely difficult. My top two both won all their three competitions at this distance, but surprisingly, both being Chinese, did not meet. Wang Liping won the two top Chinese races before taking Olympic gold while Liu Hongyu won three major races in Europe but did not compete in Sydney. The last of those wins was at Naumburg where she was followed by Kerry Saxby-Junna (later 7 OG) and Jane Saville, who had the misfortune to be disqualified when leading the Olympic race just as she was about to enter the stadium in triumph. Also at Naumburg Guadeloupe Sánchez (5 OG) was 5th and Kjersti Plätzer, the Olympic silver medallist, 10th. Other significant races were: the Australian Championships – where the visiting Italians Erica Alfridi (4 OG) and Elisabetta Perrone (dq OG) beat the locals Saville and Saxby-Junna; Leamington – Liu won from Wang Yan, Perrone and Maria Vasco (Olympic bronze medallist); the European Cup – Olimpiada Ivanova won from Perrone, Plätzer, Alfridi, Annarita Sidoti and Norica Cîmpean (6 OG); and Turku –1-2-3 Plätzer, Sánchez and Saville. The five fastest times of the year came at the Russian Championships, won by Tatyana Gudkova in 1:25:18 from Olga Polyakova, Irina Stankina, Tamara Kovalenko, Ivanova and Nadezhda Ryashkina. Gudkova was 8th and Polyakova and Stankina non-finishers at the Olympics, but Stankina had earlier won the Russian winter title from Ryashkina and Ivanova with Gudkova 5th. Saville also beat Sánchez (the Pan-Am Cup winner) at Copenhagen.

1. Wang Liping, 2. Liu Hongyu, 3. Plätzer, 4. Stankina, 5. Ivanova, 6. Alfridi, 7. Perrone, 8. Vasco, 9. G Sánchez, 10. J Saville

IAAF WORLD RANKINGS

IN JUNE 2000, the IAAF experimentally introduced a ranking system for our sport. The IAAF Rankings were presented at a press conference in Paris on the eve of the Paris-St. Denis Golden League Meeting, and have since been published on the IAAF web site (www.iaaf.org) on a weekly basis. Marion Jones and Hicham El Guerrouj headed the first IAAF World Rankings issued on June 27. The IAAF hoped that its World Rankings would be a new way of promoting athletics and its champions among the media and the public at large.

The IAAF World Rankings are formulated on the basis of the best five performances achieved during the period of 1 year prior to the date of the Rankings. The points accumulated are then corrected using a formula that takes into account the race conditions: electric or manual timing, wind readings (positive or negative), the category of the competition, placing and type of event (e.g. 100m or 60m indoor, 1500 or mile, 3000m/2000m steeplechase etc.).

The Ranking score is the average Performance score or points achieved by the athlete. The Performance score is made up of a Result score (calculated using the IAAF scoring tables and may be altered by hand timing or wind readings, with a bonus for a world record) and a Placing Score (determined from finals of major competitions, weighted according to importance).

The results are interesting and the IAAF must be commended for their initiative in trying to achieve a higher profile for the sport. Certainly the rankings show the prominence of leading athletes, but there are many flaws in the system and indeed experts doubt that any such system can properly determine athletes' merit even after modifications that the IAAF may make in the methodology.

Unlike sports such as motor racing or golf where the world top contestants compete regularly against one another throughout the year, athletes will have very different competitive programmes, and the quantity of competitions will vary according to individual preferences and according to the type of event at which an athlete competes.

The IAAF choice of five qualifying performances virtually rules out marathon runners, decathletes and heptathletes, and many great athletes therefore do not appear in these rankings. To make greater sense the system will need to be adapted to vary the number of qualifying performances for differing disciplines. But then is it really possible to devise scoring tables which can judge the merits of performances in different events – a 400m to a javelin to a 50km walk etc.? The IAAF scoring tables are based on world records and performances in depth, but if substantially more people compete at some events than others, then surely it must be 'easier' to rate highly in less popular ones.

Those of us who attempt merit rankings assess much weight to win-loss records between major athletes and this approach is not used in the IAAF rankings, where an athlete will do best if they compete often – not only in major championships but also the Golden League and other Grand Prix meetings. But that gives an in-built advantage to those who do that, which may well exclude those from major European countries because of the anomaly whereby that although the large majority of Grand Prix events are in Europe, those who compete most often in these come from nations outside the region. Athletes from, say, Germany, France and Italy have a large number of competitive domestic meetings and may naturally prefer and indeed be encouraged to compete at these rather than travel from GP to GP, in contrast to Americans, who without an extensive season at home during the summer, will travel throughout Europe.

Also points are given for success at continental and national championships, but the merits of achievements in such events will vary substantially. For example to come 1-2-3 in the Finnish javelin championship is of much greater significance than to do so at 400m, whereas almost the reverse would be true for the USA.

PJM.

IAAF World Rankings as at the end of 2000

Men's Overall Ranking

1.	Maurice Greene USA	1469.08	100m
2.	Hicham El Guerrouj MAR	1447.60	1500m
3.	Michael Johnson USA	1445.80	400m
4.	Noah Ngeny KEN	1432.72	MD
5.	Angelo Taylor USA	1420.60	400mh
6.	Virgilijus Alekna LTU	1415.80	DT
7.	Ali Saidi-Sief ALG	1415.40	5000m ()
8.	Ato Boldon TRI	1411.60	Sprints
9.	Anier Garcia CUB	1409.88	110mh
10.	Paul Tergat KEN	1409.05	LD
11.	Haile Gebrselassie ETH	1401.18	LA
12.	Adam Nelson USA	1398.60	SP
13.	Wilson Kipketer DEN	1398.16	800m
14.	Obadele Thompson BAR	1397.06	Sprints
15.	Allen Johnson USA	1395.00	110mh
16.	Llewellyn Herbert RSA	1393.20	400mh
17.	Bernard Barmasai KEN	1391.70	3000mst
18.	Mohammed Mourhit BEL	1387.80	5000m
19.	Iván Pedroso CUB	1383.60	LJ
20.	Brahim Lahlafi MAR	1381.94	5000m
21.	Bernard Lagat KEN	1381.00	1500m
22.	Maxim Tarasov RUS	1379.79	PV
23.	Sammy Kipketer KEN	1379.00	5000m (
24.	Jonathan Edwards GBR	1378.74	TJ
25.	Ali Ezzine MAR	1377.36	3000mst
26.	Jan Zelezny CZE	1376.52	JT
27.	Djabir Said-Guerni ALG	1374.60	800m
28.	Hadi Soua'an Al Somaliy KSA	1373.80	400mh
29.	Wilson Boit Kipketer KEN	1373.76	3000mst
30.	Reuben Kosgei KEN	1373.00	3000mst
31.	Brahim Boulami MAR	1371.60	3000mst
32.	William Chirchir KEN	1370.60	1500m
33.	Daniel Komen KEN	1365.46	5000m
34.	Vyacheslav Voronin RUS	1364.80	HJ
35.	André Bucher SUI	1360.60	800m
36.	Nick Hysong USA	1359.68	PV
37.	Darren Campbell GBR	1357.80	Sprints
38.	Benjamin Limo KEN	1357.72	5000m
39.	Terrance Trammell USA	1357.20	110mh
40.	John Godina USA	1356.39	SP
41.	Francis Obikwelu NGR	1355.01	Sprints
42.	Eric Thomas USA	1354.40	400mh
43.	Million Wolde ETH	1353.80	5000m
44.	Lars Riedel GER	1353.79	DT
45.	C.J. Hunter USA	1353.40	SP
46.	Japheth Kimutai KEN	1350.07	MD
47.	Daniel Ecker GER	1349.48	PV
48.	Patrick Ivuti KEN	1347.20	LD
49.	Kipkurui Misoi KEN	1346.52	3000mst
50.	Hezekiel Sepeng RSA	1344.64	800m
51.	Assefa Mezegebu ETH	1344.25	LD
52.	Mark Crear USA	1343.01	110mh
53.	Andrés Manuel Diaz ESP	1342.16	1500m
54.	Eronildo De Araujo BRA	1341.68	400mh
55.	Yuriy Bilonog UKR	1340.40	SP
56.	Frantz Kruger RSA	1338.76	DT
57.	Jon Drummond USA	1338.68	100m
58.	Dominique Arnold USA	1338.60	110mh
59.	Sanderlei Parrela BRA	1338.12	400m
60.	Claudinei Da Silva BRA	1337.56	200m
61.	Michael Stolle GER	1336.72	PV
62.	Colin Jackson GBR	1335.24	110mh
63.	Samuel Matete ZAM	1335.01	400mh
64.	Luke Kipkosgei KEN	1334.98	5000m
65.	Brian Lewis USA	1334.20	100m
66.	Sergey Klyugin RUS	1333.40	HJ
67.	Dmitriy Markov AUS	1333.35	PV
68.	Kevin Sullivan CAN	1332.60	1500m
69.	Andy Bloom USA	1331.04	SP
70.	Florian Schwarthoff GER	1330.16	110mh
71.	Jeff Hartwig USA	1330.12	PV
72.	Sergey Makarov RUS	1329.52	JT
73.	Kostas Gatsioudis GRE	1328.96	JT
74.	Greg Haughton JAM	1327.60	400m
75.	Salah Hissou MAR	1326.24	5000m

76.	Mehdi Baala FRA	1325.00	1500m
77.	Stanislavs Olijars LAT	1324.40	110mh
78.	Coby Miller USA	1323.60	Sprints
79.	Tim Lobinger GER	1323.50	PV
80.	Driss Maazouzi FRA	1323.30	1500m
81.	Lawrence Johnson USA	1321.44	PV
82.	Abdul Aziz Zakari GHA	1321.20	Sprints
83.	Pawel Januszewski POL	1321.09	400mh
84.	Mark Richardson GBR	1320.07	400m
85.	Abderrahmane Hamad ALG	1319.60	HJ
86.	Raymond Yator KEN	1319.20	3000mst
87.	Robin Korving NED	1318.56	110mh
88.	Nils Schumann GER	1317.91	800m
89.	Koji Murofushi JPN	1317.80	HT
90.	Benjamin Kipkurui KEN	1317.60	1500m
91.	Aki Parviainen FIN	1317.36	JT
92.	Tim Montgomery USA	1317.18	100m
93.	Dwain Chambers GBR	1316.14	100m
94.	John Kibowen KEN	1316.00	1500m
95.	Bruny Surin CAN	1315.84	100m
96.	Charles Michel Friedek GER	1315.82	TJ
97.	Antonio Pettigrew USA	1315.46	400m
98.	Mark Boswell CAN	1315.44	HJ
99.	Yuriy Borzakovskiy RUS	1315.00	800m
100.	Alvin Harrison USA	1314.40	400m

Women's Overall Ranking

Pl.	Athlete Nat	Score	Events
1.	Marion Jones USA	1463.04	Sprints,LJ
2.	Trine Hattestad NOR	1454.00	JT
3.	Gabriela Szabo ROM	1421.88	MD
4.	Gete Wami ETH	1406.12	LD
5.	Maria Lurdes Mutola MOZ	1404.52	800m
6.	Cathy Freeman AUS	1403.55	400m
7.	Gail Devers USA	1398.96	100mh
8.	Glory Alozie NGR	1389.90	100mh
9.	Olga Shishigina KAZ	1386.24	100mh
10.	Sonia O'Sullivan IRL	1384.80	LD
11.	Violetta Szekely ROM	1381.52	1500m
12.	Heike Drechsler GER	1371.80	LJ
13.	Deon Hemmings JAM	1370.92	400mh
14.	Kutre Dulecha ETH	1370.00	1500m
15.	Tatyana Kotova RUS	1369.00	LJ
16.	Lorraine Graham JAM	1368.60	400m
17.	Katerina Thanou GRE	1364.66	100m
18.	Paula Radcliffe GBR	1364.48	LD
19.	Stephanie Graf AUT	1362.04	800m
20.	Osleidys Menendez CUB	1361.20	JT
20.	Lidia Chojecka POL	1361.20	1500m
22.	Tatyana Lebedeva RUS	1358.56	TJ
23.	Tegla Loroupe KEN	1357.92	LD
24.	Melissa Morrison USA	1355.68	100mh
25.	Derartu Tulu ETH	1355.60	LD
26.	Fiona May ITA	1355.37	LJ
27.	Nouria Mérah-Benida ALG	1353.60	MD
28.	Stacy Dragila USA	1352.92	PV
29.	Inger Miller USA	1352.64	100m
30.	Lydia Cheromei KEN	1350.20	5000m
31.	Zhanna Pintusevich UKR	1349.67	Sprints
32.	Failat Ogunkoya NGR	1347.85	400m
33.	Nezha Bidouane MAR	1341.55	400mh
34.	Tetyana Tereshchuk UKR	1340.18	400mh
35.	Ayelech Worku ETH	1338.00	5000m
35.	Sevatheda Fynes BAH	1338.00	100m
37.	Ana Guevarra MEX	1337.28	400m
38.	Deloreen Ennis-London JAM	1336.80	100mh
39.	Debbie Ferguson BAH	1334.80	Sprints
40.	Inga Babakova UKR	1332.60	HJ
41.	Katharine Merry GBR	1331.96	400m
42.	Kajsa Bergqvist SWE	1328.64	HJ
43.	Sandra Glover USA	1327.32	400mh
44.	Tereza Marinova BUL	1326.38	TJ
45.	Irina Privalova RUS	1325.61	400mh
46.	Carla Sacramento POR	1325.56	1500m
47.	Daimi Pernia CUB	1325.32	400m,400mh
48.	Pauline Davis-Thompson BAH	1321.20	Sprints
49.	Michelle Freeman JAM	1320.00	100mh
50.	Tatyana Shikolenko RUS	1319.80	JT
51.	Ludmila Formanová CZE	1319.52	800m
52.	Irina Mikitenko GER	1319.16	5000m
53.	Chandra Sturrup BAH	1317.80	100m
54.	Olga Yegorova RUS	1317.00	5000m
55.	Hestrie Cloete RSA	1316.92	HJ
56.	Christine Arron FRA	1316.42	100m
57.	Fernanda Ribeiro POR	1315.91	LD
58.	Hasna Benhassi MAR	1314.15	800m
59.	Chryste Gaines USA	1314.00	100m
60.	Erica Johansson SWE	1309.20	LJ
61.	Olena Govorova UKR	1307.88	TJ
62.	Natalya Tsyganova RUS	1307.20	800m
63.	Merlene Ottey JAM	1305.71	100m
64.	Leah Malot KEN	1304.72	LD
65.	Franka Dietzsch GER	1303.74	DT
66.	Linda Ferga FRA	1303.60	100mh
67.	Anjanette Kirkland USA	1303.40	100mh
67.	Susanthika Jayasinghe SRI	1303.40	200m
69.	Dawn Burrell USA	1303.15	LJ
70.	Larisa Peleshenko RUS	1302.00	SP
71.	Beverly Mcdonald JAM	1301.36	Sprints
72.	Yelena Yelesina RUS	1301.32	HJ
73.	Ellina Zvereva BLR	1301.00	DT
74.	Tanya Lawrence JAM	1300.60	100m
75.	Monica Dinescu ROM	1299.25	HJ
76.	Andrea Blackett BAR	1298.50	400mh
77.	Regina Jacobs USA	1295.86	MD
78.	Léonie Myriam Mani CMR	1295.60	Sprints
79.	Gudrún Arnardóttir ISL	1295.24	400mh
80.	Anzhela Balakhonova UKR	1291.90	PV
81.	Tanja Damaske GER	1289.74	JT
82.	Sonia Bisset CUB	1289.40	JT
83.	Sharon Couch-Jewell USA	1289.00	100mh
84.	Jearl Miles-Clark USA	1287.86	MD
85.	Suzy Hamilton USA	1287.80	MD
86.	Helena Fuchsová CZE	1287.60	MD
87.	Olga Kotlyarova RUS	1287.40	400m
88.	Donna Fraser GBR	1287.20	400m
89.	Torri Edwards USA	1284.80	100m
90.	Tatyana Tomashova RUS	1283.80	5000m
91.	Latasha Colander-Richardson USA	1283.60	400m
92.	Daniela Bártová CZE	1282.22	PV
93.	Michelle Collins USA	1282.20	400m
94.	Niurka Montalvo ESP	1282.08	LJ
95.	Olga Kuzenkova RUS	1281.93	HT
96.	Kelly Holmes GBR	1281.36	MD
97.	Olga Kuznetsova RUS	1281.00	1500m
98.	Nanceen Perry USA	1280.40	Sprints
99.	Svetlana Feofanova RUS	1279.60	PV
100.	Olga Nelyubova RUS	1278.82	1500m

Jan Zelezny – Proud father, fisher, but mainly great javelin thrower

Alfons Juck pays tribute

WHEN YOU meet him, he doesn´t look like a javelin thrower. But he is, and one of the best if not the best ever. He won the Olympics three times in a row, and one silver before legislators changed the javelin, but nothing stopped him and he came near the danger line – at 100 metres. He is a proud father and husband who besides family and javelin loves fishing; a normal young man who never will behave as a superstar. But for sure, he is.

Every year he gets more and more recognition. Recently he became an IOC Member and he is well able to spread his opinions. For example about the bid of Beijing for Olympic Games 2008. "I think that in China democracy is not working. From a technical point view, there is no danger about this bid," he was quoted by international agencies. He is still not thinking about retirement and wants to compete this year. His main problem is not motivation, but his body and health situation. "I do not want to announce something and then change. I´m not the type of person to clarify the retirement situation. There is a slight risk, I admit," he said recently. And he speaks openly about Athens 2004. "I think I still can throw farther then ever, I just need to be totally healthy and everything should work on that day more than 100 per cent."

One thing he does not like are official celebrations, where he is observed by many but not in the stadium. As in November in Monte Carlo, where he was presented with the award for the Best Male World Athlete of 2000. Black tie is something unusal, as is to speak in English. Not that he cannot speak English (every year he getsbetter); he just a kind of person who doesn´t like big speeches in front of big audiences. He likes to speak with his throws. In 2000 he did not compete very often. But he was able to win in Oslo even with rib problems and came from behind to win. It was the same again in Sydney, when his main rival and close friend Steve Backley was also surprised. Jan is now a complete competitor, he can throw far, he can get better during the competition.

In January in London he met boxing legend Muhammad Ali and for him that was a dream come true. He is a superstar who admits to having heroes. After that he went as usual to South Africa and was there until April for his usual time spent in hot weather. "I was very tired from all the official appointments. South Africa is something special, I like a quiet atmosphere, enough sleep, training, and also that is an important time for fishing," said Zelezny. In 2001 he will be a member of a Finnish club and have a main sponsor from Finland, the country with the biggest love and tradition for javelin in the world. *Track and Field News* voters had him only in fifth place in 2000 and the World Sports Awards celebration in London gave the best athlete honour to Michael Johnson. Never mind, for many he was the athlete of 2000. Not least because he is normal and speaks with everybody without any pressure from being a superstar. That´s why he is a big hero in his country and his first words after winning in Sydney were about his family and two children. "It is very important, I will be remembered for my javelin results. But even more important for me is, that my children will have in their minds the feeling that I´m a good father. That is really important."

Jan Zelezny's Career

by Peter Matthews

Born 16 June 1966 Mladá Boleslav.

Annual bests: 1979- 44.44 (800g), 1980- 48.90 (600g), 1981- 64.42 (600g), 1982- 57.22 (800g)

1983-85 with old javelin

Year	*Best*	*Comps*	*Wins*	*Championships*
1983	74.34	5	2	6 EJ, 1 CS-J
1984	80.32 (126)	13	8	1 CS-J, 1 CS-Y
1985	84.68 (51)	12	3	4 EJ

Career from 1986 with new javelin

Year	*Best*	*Comps*	*Wins*	*Championships*	*Competitions over*		
					90m	*85m*	*80m*
1986	82.48 (6)	14	8	dnq 16 EC, 1 CS	-	-	4
1987	87.66 (1)	14	7	3 WCh, 3 ECp	-	2	11
1988	86.88 (1)	10	8	2 OG	-	4	9
1989	84.74 (6)	13	5	2 ECp	-	-	8
1990	89.66 (2)	12	5	dnq 13 EC, 1 CS	-	4	9
1991	90.72 (5)	12	10	dnq 18 WCh, 1 ECp, 1 GPF	2	9	11
1992	94.74R (1)	12	11	1 OG, 1 WCp	3	8	11
1993	95.66 (1)	14	13	1 WCh, 1 ECp, 1 GPF	5	12	15
1994	91.82 (1)	20	17	3 EC, 1 CZE	4	12	19
1995	92.28 (2)	17	13	1 WCh, 1 GPF	7	15	17
1996	98.48 (1)	15	14	1 OG, 1 CZE	6	16	16
1997	94.02 (1)	18	11	9 WCh, 1 GPF	3	13	19
1998	did not compete						
1999	89.06 (4)	10	3	3 WCh, 2 GPF	-	5	11
2000	90.59A (3)	7	6	1 OG	4	8	8

Position in world list shown in brackets after year's best.
Note that competions over 80m etc. include qualifying competitions (not included in annual totals).
I am indebted to the detailed career record that Richard Hyman has compiled for Zelezny. This also shows the average of his best throws:
10- 94.60, 20- 93.23, 30- 92.57, 50- 91.77, 100- 90.56, 200- 89.00, 300- 87.72, 400- 86.40, 500- 84.75.

Lifetime win-loss against major competition

Steve Backley	30-16	Tapio Korjus	4-2	Vladimir Sasimovich	33-1
Patrik Bodén	25-4	Gavin Lovegrove	28-1	Klaus Tafelmeier	11-5
Kostas Gatsioúdis	6-6	Sergey Makarov	16-7	Einar Vihljalmsson	14-7
Harri Hakarainen	16-1	Andrey Moruyev	21-2	Gerald Weiss	5-2
Raymond Hecht	34-9	Aki Parviainen	12-6	Dag Wennlund	31-2
Boris Henry	22-8	Tom Petranoff	14-3	Viktor Yevsyukov	7-6
Mick Hill	46-7	Tom Pukstys	30-1		
Kimmo Kinnunen	22-3	Seppo Räty	20-7		

Steve Backley (b. 12 Feb 1969) has been his greatest rival. Here is a record of all their clashes:

Date	*Venue*	*Zelezny*	*Backley*
3 Jul 89	Stockholm	3- 81.18	2- 81.20
5 Aug 89	Gateshead ECp	2- 79.44	1- 82.92
8 Aug 89	Budapest	5- 80.96	1- 85.86
16 Aug 89	Zürich	7- 77.22	1- 84.90
18 Aug 89	Berlin	7- 77.14	1- 83.58
14 Jul 90	Oslo	1- 89.66	2- 87.94
20 Jul 90	London (CP)	2- 85.84	1- 90.98
15 Aug 90	Zürich	4- 79.08	1- 85.04
27 Aug 90	Split – EC	13- 77.64	q- 82.24
12 Jul 91	London (CP)	1- 89.86	2- 88.04
7 Aug 91	Zürich	1- 88.78	2- 87.16
25 Aug 91	Tokyo – WCh	18- 76.26	q-78.24
15 Sep 91	Sheffield	2- 89.58	1- 91.36
4 Jul 92	Oslo	1- 94.74	2- 85.06
8 Aug 92	Barcelona	1- 89.66	3- 83.32
23 Jul 93	London (CP)	1- 86.78	2- 85.10
16 Aug 93	Stuttgart –WCh	1- 85.98	4- 81.80
29 Jun 94	Helsinki	1- 88.04	2- 84.66
1 Jul 94	Gateshead	1- 91.68	9- 76.14
8 Aug 94	Helsinki –EC	3- 82.58	1- 85.20
17 Aug 94	Zürich	1- 81.20	2- 81.16
30 Aug 94	Berlin	3- 83.16	5- 82.28
4 Sep 94	Sheffield	1- 91.82	3- 84.78
15 Sep 94	Tokyo	1- 86.34	4- 79.94
7 Jul 95	London (CP)	2- 88.16	1- 88.54
21 Jul 95	Oslo	2- 89.30	3- 86.46
13 Aug 95	Göteborg –WCh	1- 89.58	2- 86.30
16 Aug 95	Zürich	2- 86.98	3- 85.90
25 Aug 95	Bruxelles	1- 90.50	3- 84.78
27 Aug 95	London (CP)	1- 92.12	6- 81.90
9 Sep 95	Monaco – GPF	1- 92.28	3- 83.84
3 Aug 96	Atlanta – OG	1- 88.16	2- 87.44
16 Sep 96	Tokyo	1- 89.32	3- 84.46
8 Jun 97	Moskva	1- 86.92	2- 83.90
18 Jun 97	Helsinki	4- 83.30	1- 87.96
4 Jul 97	Oslo	4- 85.22	5- 84.32
5 Aug 97	Athína – WCh	9- 82.04	2- 86.80
13 Aug 97	Zürich	4- 85.22	5- 84.32
16 Aug 97	Monaco	5- 84.94	7- 84.48
22 Aug 97	Bruxelles	4- 83.46	1- 85.30
13 Sep 97	Fukuoka – GPF	1- 89.58	7- 81.58
1 Jun 99	Tartu	2- 84.77	3- 83.66
4 Aug 99	Monaco	6- 83.48	4- 83.51
7 Aug 99	London (CP)	2- 84.43	3- 84.24
29 Aug 99	Sevilla – WCh	3- 87.67	8- 83.84
23 Sep 00	Sydney –OG	1- 90.17	2- 89.85

CROSS-COUNTRY - NATIONAL CHAMPIONS 2000

	MEN (longer distance)	WOMEN (longer distance)
Argentina	Oscar Amaya	Verónica Páez
Australia	Lee Troop	Kerryn McCann
Austria	Micheal Buchleitner	Sandra Baumann
Belgium	Jerry Van den Eede	Anja Smolders
Brazil	Marilson dos Santos	Adriana de Souza
Bulgaria	Dimitar Dimitrov	Rumyana Panovska
Canada	Mark Bomba	Courtney Babcock
Denmark	Dennis Jensen	Tina H Jensen
England	Glynn Tromans	Tara Krzywicki
Estonia	Heiki Sarapuu	Maile Mangusson
Finland	Jussi Utriainen	Annemari Sandell
France	Abdellah Béhar	Rakiya Quétier-Maraoui
Germany (Dec)	Sebastian Hallmann	Irina Mikitenko
Greece	Panayiótis Haramis	María Protópappa
Hungary	Zsolt Benedek	Simona Staicu
Ireland	Seamus Power	Anne Keenan-Buckley
Israel	Asaf Bimro	Nili Avramski
Italy	Rachid Berradi	Agata Balsamo
Kenya	Paul Tergat	Lydia Cheromei
Latvia	Aleksandrs Proscenko	Inna Poluskina
Luxembourg	Josy Bourggraff	Pascale Schmoetten
Northern Ireland	John Ferrin	Catriona McGranaghan
Norway	Karl Johan Rasmussen	Bente Landøy
Poland	Leszek Beblo	Justyna Bak
Portugal	Eduardo Henriques	Carla Sacramento
Romania	Adrian Maghiar	Mihaela Botezan
Scotland	Robert Quinn	Hayley Haining
Slovenia	Romeo Zivko	Sonja Roman
South Africa (Trial)	George Mofokeng	Theresa du Toit
Spain	Enrique Molina	María Abel
Sweden	Alfred Shemweta	Marie Söderström-Lundberg
Switzerland	Mehdi Khelifi TUN	Anita Weyermann
UK	Keith Cullen	Tara Krzywicki
USA	Adam Goucher	Deena Drossin
Wales	Nick Comerford	Catherine Dudgale
Yugoslavia	Dragoslav Prpa	Olivera Jevtic
Pan-Arab	Mohamed Yaacoub SUD (won 12k and 4k)	
European Clubs	Eduardo Henriques POR	Marina Bastos POR
Teams	Maratona de Maia POR	Maratona de Maia POR
S.American & CAC	Daniel Ferreira BRA	Bertha Sánchez COL
World Military	Mustapha Bamouh MAR	Zhor El-Kamch MAR
Teams	Morocco	Italy
World Universities	Günther Weidlinger AUT	Analia Rosa POR
Teams	Morocco	South Africa

	Men (short distance)	Women (short distance)
Argentina	José Mansilla	Claudia Camargo
Austria	Günther Weidlinger	–
Belgium	Patrick Grammens	Véronique Collard
Brazil	Emerson Iser Bem	Fatima da Silva
Bulgaria	Stanislav Lambev	Rumyana Panovska
Denmark	Dennis Jensen	Jytte Pedersen
Finland	Marko Kotila	
France	Driss Maazouzi	Yamna Belkacem

Germany (Dec)	Jan Fitschen	Irina Mikitenko
Hungary	Norbert Kömüves	–
Israel	Haiel Satain	–
Italy	Luciano Di Pardo	Giovanna Arici
Kenya	John Kibowen	Margaret Ngotho
New Zealand	Alan Bunce	Sonia Barry
Poland	Dariusz Kruczkowski	
Portugal	Rui Silva	Anália Rosa
Romania	Andreescu	Elena Fidatov
South Africa (Tr)	Whaddon Niewoudt	Runel Thomas
Switzerland	Yarba Lakhal MAR	Anita Weyermann
UK	Rob Whalley	Hayley Tullett
USA	Adam Goucher	Deena Drossin
Nordic (10 Nov)	Denis Jensen DEN	Gunhild Haugen NOR
S.American & CAC	Daniel Ferreira BRA	Fatima da Silva BRA
World Military	Driss El-Himer FRA	

European Cross-Country Championships 2000

At Malmö, Sweden 10 December

Senior Men (9705m)

1. Paulo Guerra POR 29.29
2. Sergey Lebed UKR 29:39
3. Driss El Himer FRA 29:45
4. Lyes Ramoul FRA 29:47
5. Mustapha El Ahmadi FRA 29:47
6. Carlos Adan ESP 29:48
7. Kamiel Maase NED 29:49
8. Tom Van Hooste BEL 29:51
9. José M. Martínez ESP 29:52
10. Peter Matthews IRL 29:53
11. Yann Millon FRA 29:54
12. Jose Ramos POR 29:55
13. Alberto Maravilha POR 29:56
14. Seamus Power IRL 29:58
15. Claes Nyberg SWE 30:01

83 finished

Teams: 1. FRA 23, 2. ESP 51, 3. IRL 72, 4. POR 74, 5. BEL 98, 6. GBR 103, 7. ITA 144, 8. RUS 156, 9. UKR 166, 10. GER 168, 11, DEN 189, 12. SWE 189, 13, POL 257, 14. TUR 281.

Senior Women (4945m)

1. Katalin Szentgyörgyi HUN 16.34
2. Analidia Torre POR 16.35
3. Olivera Jevtic YUG 16.39
4. Zahia Dahmani FRA 16:49
5. Kathy Butler GBR 16:51
6. Monica Rosa POR 16:55
7. Anja Smolders BEL 16:55
8. Liz Yelling GBR 16:55
9. Anne Keenan-Buckley IRL 16:56
10. Analia Rosa POR 16:57
11. Gunhild Halle-Haugen NOR 16:57
12. Jacqueline Martin ESP 17:00
13. Michaela Möller GER 17:02
14. Rakiya Quetier-Maraoui FRA 17:02
15. Rosemary Ryan IRL 17:03

67 finished.

Teams: 1. POR 18, 2. GBR 33, 3. GER 54, 4. BEL 55, 5. ROM 60, 6. IRL 60, 7. FRA 60, 8. ESP 73, 9. ITA 106, 10. SWE 140, 11. POL 147.

Junior Men (6135m)

1. Wolfram Müller GER 18:58
2. Chris Thompson GBR 19:00
3. Martin Pröll AUT 19:05
4. Rui Pedro Silva POR 19:10
5. Mickael André FRA 19:11
6. Bruno Silva POR 19:11
7. Mohamed Farah GBR 19:12
8. Aleksandr Sekletov RUS 19:16
9. Henrik Ahnström SWE 19:17
10. Benoit Charpantier FRA 19:26

93 finished.

Teams:

1. POL 21, 2. GBR 25, 3. FRA 30, 4. ESP 48, 5. GER 62. 6. ITA 74, 7, SWE 85, 8. RUS 86, 9. NED 121, 10. BLR 126, 11. BEL 129, 12. UKR 142, 13. TUR 143, 14. AUT 144, 15. IRL 178, 16. SUI 194, 17. CZE 213, 18. HUN 214, 19. SLO 247.

Junior Women (3755m)

1. Jessica Augusto POR 12:55
2. Nicola Spirig SUI 12:56
3. Elvan Can TUR 12:56
4. Tatyana Chulakh RUS 12:56
5. Juliet Potter GBR 13:02
6. Olga Krivyak UKR 13:14
7. Jane Potter GBR 13:14
8. Olesya Dubovik UKR 13:15
9. Collette Fagan GBR 13:15
10. Türkan Erismis TUR 13:17

85 finished.

Teams: 1. GBR 21, 2. TUR 40, 3. SWE 49, 4. POR 55, 5. FIN 60, 6. UKR 69, 7. RUS 71, 8. ROM 83, 9. ESP 84, 10. BEL 102, 11. FRA 108, 12. BLR 115, 13. HUN 124, 14. SUI 126, 15. GER 140, 16. ITA 148, 17. YUG 161, 18. IRL 200, 19. NED 204, 20. CZE 224.

IAAF Cross-country Challenge 1999/2000

See *Athletics 2000* page 592 for the results of the 1999/2000 IAAF Cross Challenge series, which has not been contained in 2000/01.

First three in major international races 2000/01 season

	1st	*2nd*	*3rd*
Llodio 26/11	Abraham Chebii KEN	Hailu Mekonnen ETH	Patrick Ivuti KEN
Figaro, Paris 10/12	Evans Rutto KEN	Hosea Kogo KEN	Reuben Cheruiyot KEN
Brussels 17/12 *	Paulo Guerra POR	Patrick Ivuti KEN	Mustapha Al Ahmadi FRA
Consett 30/12 *	Paul Kosgei KEN	Paulo Guerra	Kamel Maase NED
Amorebieta 7/1 #	Paul Kosgei	Charles Kamathi KEN	Salim Kipsang KEN
Sevilla 14/1 *	Charles Kamathi	Sergey Lebed UKR	Paula Guerra
Belfast 20/1 #	Daniel Gachara KEN	Joseph Giri KEN	Luka Keitany KEN
Elgoibar 21/1	Abraham Chebii	Paul Tergat KEN	Albert Chepkurui KEN
Tourcoing 28/1 *	Driss El Himer FRA	Mohammed Mourhit BEL	Julius Kiptoo KEN
San Sebastián 28/1	Abraham Chebii	Evans Rutto	Bernard Barmasai KEN
Vilamoura 4/2 *	Patrick Ivuti	Bernard Barmasai	Sergey Lebed
Diekirch 18/2 #	Abderrahim Goumri MAR	Lyes Ramoul FRA	Luciano Di Pardo ITA
Chiba 18/2 #	Samuel Kabiru KEN	Satoshi Irifune JPN	Mobuya Matsunaga JPN
San Vittore Olona 4/3 *	Charles Kamathi	Sergey Lebed	Mohammed Mourhit
WOMEN			
Llodio 26/11	Merima Denboba ETH	Ayelech Worku ETH	Hawa Hussein ETH
Figaro, Paris 10/12	Irene Limika KEN	Chantal Dällenbach FRA	Nancy Omwenga KEN
Brussels 17/12 *	Susan Chepkemei KEN	Lydia Cheromei KEN	Paula Radcliffe GBR
Consett 30/12 *	Paula Radcliffe	Derartu Tulu ETH	Kathy Butler GBR
Amorebieta 7/1 #	Naomi Mugo KEN	Ejagayou Diababa ETH	Eyerusalm Kuma ETH
Sevilla 14/1 *	Paula Radcliffe	Olivera Jevtic YUG	Anja Smolders BEL
Belfast 20/1 #	Paula Radcliffe	Tara Krzywicki GBR	Helen Pattinson GBR
Elgoibar 21/1	Leah Malot KEN	Merima Denboba	Carla Sacramento POR
Tourcoing 28/1 *	Paula Radcliffe	Leah Malot	Anja Smolders
San Sebastián 28/1	Lydia Cheromei	Ruth Kutol KEN	Hareg Sidelil ETH
Vilamoura 4/2 *	Lydia Cheromei	Elena Fidatov ROM	Svetlana Baygulova RUS
Diekirch 18/2 #	Anja Smolders	Natalie Harvey AUS	Sabine Fischer SUI
Chiba 18/2 #	Iulia Olteanu ROM	Yoshiko Fujinaga JPN	Chiemi Takahashi JPN
San Vittore Olona 4/3 *	Olivera Jevtic	Kathy Butler	Agata Balsamo ITA*

European CrossCup series, # other IAAF Permit races

See page 592 for results of the 2001 World Cross-Country Championships.

16 Marathons Inside 2:20 in One Year

The Italian runner, **Giorgio Calcaterra** ran 16 marathon races during 1999 (with a best of 2:17:48 at Pompeii on Nov 21) ending with 2:24:05 for 3rd at Assisi on Dec 31. In 2000 he ran much faster and broke the previous record of thirteen sub-2:20 marathons in a year, set by El-Hadi Moumou in 1994. Note the nine in succession in ten weeks in October-December. Giorgio's races:

Jan 1	Roma (day after 2:24:05!)	36th 2:29:00
Feb 13	Busseto	1st 2:15:03
Mar 5	Piacenza	1st 2:15:51
Mar 12	Vigarano Mainarda	2nd 2:13:15
Apr 2	Egna	5th 2:16:24
Apr 30	Madrid	4th 2:20:05
May 7	Trieste	3rd 2:16:33
Jun 3	Stockholm	2nd 2:18:54
Sep 10	Grottazzolina	1st 2:17:50
Sep 23	Borgo S.Lorenzo	1st 2:24:13
Oct 8	Cesano Boscone	5th 2:14:24
Oct 15	München	9th 2:19:39
Oct 22	Venezia	11th 2:17:55
Oct 29	Calderara di Reno	1st 2:19:07
Nov 12	Livorno	2nd 2:16:16
Nov 19	Pompeii	2nd 2:17:43
Nov 26	Firenze	6th 2:18:34
Dec 3	Milano	11th 2:19:46
Dec 10	Latina	3rd 2:18:54
Dec 31	Assisi	7th 2:27:41

WORLD MARATHON REVIEW 2000

By David E Martin

AN OLYMPIC year is especially intriguing for the marathon as national governing bodies attempt various strategies for selecting their best athletes, sometimes with disastrous results. The Sydney Games began during the Australian winter, ending in its springtime, which meant that they were summer/autumn Games in the Northern Hemisphere. The women raced on September 24, the men one week later, on October 1, as the final competitive event. Most athletes were thus selected for the Games on the basis of performances achieved from the latter half of 1999 through the first half of 2000. For those nations having top-level marathoners, time standards of sub-2:14:00 for men and sub-2:33:00 for women were intended to help reduce the size of the fields. The women's standard was relatively more difficult than the men's. As an example, during calendar year 2000, 35 nations had men under 2:14:00 (291 performances) compared to 23 with women under 2:33:00 (171 total performances). A more appropriate women's standard would have been sub-2:36:00 – 34 nations met that during 2000 (275 total performances).

It had been the plan of IAAF President Primo Nebiolo to bring worldwide attention to the sport of athletics by staging a Millennium Marathon on New Year's Day. His death 54 days earlier thus resulted in the event becoming a living memorial for his contributions to the sport, with a superb elite field leading more than 5000 through the streets of Rome. Kenyans won both the men's (Josephat Kiprono) and women's (Tegla Loroupe) divisions. Although the Italians had pre-selected their men's Olympic marathon team (Vicenzo Modica, Danilo Goffi, and Stefano Baldini), a fine runner-up performance in Rome by Giacomo Leone prompted his eventual substitution for Goffi. It was a wise decision, for Leone placed fifth at Sydney – Modica and Baldini did not finish.

Two early Japanese women's marathons – Osaka in late January and Nagoya in early March – provided competition of the highest quality for athletes of several nations. Ari Ichihashi and Eri Yamaguchi had been preselected for the Japanese Olympic team based upon their 1999 Sevilla runner-up and Tokyo winning efforts, respectively, and thus one spot remained. At Osaka, 10,000 m track star Hiromi Hiroyama challenged Romania's two-time Osaka winner Lidia Simon. It was a third victory by Simon in a quick 2:22:54 – with Hiroyama only two seconds behind in a made-for-TV thriller seeing the two duel side-by-side over the final track lap. Kenya's Esther Wanjiru and Ethiopia's Elfenesh Alemu were third and fourth. All four eventually got to Sydney, but not all in the marathon. At Nagoya the incomparable Naoko Takahashi – running her first marathon since her Asian Championships gold medal in hot, humid Bangkok in 1998, overpowered a quality Japanese women's field. Her 2:22:19 was not only faster than Hiroyama at Osaka but also a victory by more than two minutes. Takahashi thus earned the third Japanese Olympic marathon spot, with Hiroyama relegated to the 10,000 m team. Takahashi's magnificent gold medal performance at Sydney ensured her distinction as the year's top woman marathoner. Osaka finishers Wanjiru and Alemu placed 4th and 6th at Sydney. Yamaguchi's 7th and Ichihashi's 15th place gave Japan the runner-up informal Olympic marathon team ranking behind Kenya's winning combination of 3rd (Chepchumba), 4th (Wanjiru), and 13th (Loroupe).

The Japanese men's team was similarly selected by a committee, based upon performances at key competitions. At Tokyo in February, national record-holder Takayuki Inubushi placed 4th as the first Japanese (behind winner Japhet Kosgei, runner-up Lee Bong-ju with a Korean NR, and Portugal's Alberto Juzdado). Only Lee and Juzdado of this quartet earned Sydney team spots, Lee placing 24th and Juzdado 42nd. Then, at the Lake Biwa marathon in Otsu, Shinji Kawashima was runner-up to Spain's defending champion Martín Fiz, and both were named to their respective Olympic teams. Fiz performed well at Sydney, placing 6th, whereas Kawashima headed a disastrous Japanese team showing, finishing only 21st as their top performer.

There was frustration at the South African championships in Cape Town, where it was announced pre-race that the men had to better 2:11:00 – three minutes faster than the IAAF standard – to achieve Olympic selection. Despite cool conditions and a flat course, the top three all broke 2:12 but not 2:11. Atlanta Olympic gold medallist Josiah Thugwane was not one of them. Subsequent reconsideration by the federation selected a team consisting of Johannes Maremane (who placed 43rd at Sydney), and two quality London marathon performers (Hendrick Ramaala, 5th, and Thugwane, 8th). At Sydney, Ramaala placed 12th and Thugwane 20th, making South Africa the informal runner-up team behind Ethiopia's 1st, 3rd, and 22nd.

Such selection frustration, however, paled in comparison to the situation confronting the USA. The IAAF A-level marathon time standards were not announced until mid-1999. By then, the venues for the USA's plan to choose its teams using its well-known 'first-past-the-post' system were already selected – they involved challenging courses not conducive to fast times. Event sponsors, who had made huge financial contributions, insisted that the winner of each race be selected to the team, even if the winning time was below the A standard and thus limiting the 'team' to that single athlete. Unfortunately, at both venues – Columbia, South Carolina for the women in February and Pittsburgh, Pennsylvania for the men in May – freakish weather brought hot days for both events. Had an athlete with a previous A standard time won each race, other A standard athletes behind them could also have been selected. But the two winners – Christine Clark for the women and Rodney De Haven for the men, did not have such times, and thus these two comprised the USA marathon team. To her credit, Clark (a 37-year-old Alaskan pathologist and mother of two) performed well, achieving a personal best by 7:07to win the trials, and lowering that by another 1:54 to place 19th at Sydney.

The fields assembled at London in mid-April to celebrate the event's 20th anniversary were absolutely top-class, and after days of a cold chilly wind with rain, a sunny cool day provided superb racing conditions. The event became the year's largest marathon (24,694 men and 6964 women finishers). Portugal's two-time past winner António Pinto this time did not allow Morocco's Abdelkader El Mouaziz to develop a lead with the pacemakers, which relegated Pinto to the runner-up position in 1999. Pinto dominated with a 57-second victory – his 2:06:36 was a European record and became the year's fastest time. Both athletes experienced Olympic frustration, failing to keep pace with the eventual medallists when the pack broke up (El Mouaziz placed 7th and Pinto 11th). Fine performances at London by such athletes as Ramaala (5th), Baldini (6th), and Thugwane (8th) mentioned earlier made this a major men's Sydney selection event.

For the women at London, Tegla Loroupe was bothered by a sore hip and thus initially fell behind the assigned pacemakers until getting thoroughly warmed up. Rivals Lidia Simon and Joyce Chepchumba did the same, but the three eventually found themselves in front, and finished in that order, all earning berths on their respective Olympic teams. Had Loroupe won at Sydney, she would have joined only Kitei Son and Abebe Bikila as world-record-holders who also won gold, but stomach problems relegated her to 13th, with Simon and Chepchumba taking the Olympic silver and bronze medals.

The following day in Boston, the men's race was billed as the Kenyan Olympic trials, and indeed, only Ethiopia's Gezahegne Abera's placing second behind winner Elijah Lagat interrupted the parade of top Kenyan stars. It was the closest men's race in Boston history, with Lagat and Abera achieving the same time (2:09:47), and Moses Tanui being only a second behind. The Kenyan selectors initially chose Lagat (1st), Tanui (3rd) and Rome winner Japhet Kosgei for their Olympic team. However, following the Kenyan track championships in July, the selection committee changed its mind, replacing them with Atlanta bronze medallist Eric Wainaina, Kennedy Cheruiyot (Rotterdam winner), and Ondoro Osoro (4th at Boston). The day following this announcement, Osoro fell victim to a carjacking and was shot in the neck; Lagat was then reinstated. Wainaina's selection was fortuitous, for in Sydney he split the Ethiopian contingent of Abera and Tesfaye Tolla to take the silver medal. Neither Lagat or Cheruiyot finished the Olympic race.

At Boston the women's race was also the closest in race history, with Catherine Ndereba expecting to join Loroupe and Chepchumba onto the Kenyan Olympic team. Ndereba's 2:26:11 was 16 seconds faster than the identical 2:26:27 achieved by 2nd and 3rd Irina Bogacheva and Atlanta gold medallist Fatuma Roba. But the Kenyan selectors opted to give the third Olympic team spot to Esther Wanjiru for her faster Osaka time. Roba placed 9th at Sydney while Ndereba stayed home, her hunger for competition making her a strong contender at Chicago in October.

At Sydney, although the same marathon course was used for the men's and women's races, the two events were really quite different. The women started at 9 a.m. under calm conditions (clear, 14°C, 91% humidity), and the men started at 4 p.m. (clear, 23°C, 45% humidity) with strong headwinds gusting to >30km/hr over the final 14km of rolling pavement. The point-to-point course showcased the two major city bridges and the central business district. It was net downhill, starting at 80m elevation and ending at 12m.

In both Olympic races, an inappropriately quick-starting athlete kept those on the lead press truck from observing the inner dynamics of the front pack during the initial dozen kilometers. The early women's leader was Belgium's Marleen Renders, a top-class athlete who should have known better (and who later dropped out). For the men it was Botswanian Tiyapo Maso (PB of 2:17:04) who slowed from world record pace (29:58 for 10km!) to place

77th out of 81 finishers. Both races had the usual large assortment of national representation: 53 athletes from 36 countries among the women, 100 athletes from 67 countries among the men. For the first time in Olympic history, all three men medallists represented Africa. In the women's race, Takahashi became a national heroine. Her victory came in an Olympic record and she became history's first Japanese-born Olympic marathon winner for either sex (1936 gold medallist Kitei Son was born in Korea). Of the 45 women finishers, a record 13 of them finished under the 2:30:00 mark.

Despite the proximity of the Games to the autumn marathon season in the Northern Hemisphere, both fast times and deep fields continued at the major city marathons. The Berlin event was staged on September 10th, one week prior to the Olympic opening ceremonies. One of its male pacemakers, Simon Biwott, continued onward after 28km, when his 'official' duties ended, and won with a 5-second victory over Antonio Peña. An unprecedented 27,017 runners finished the race. At Beijing on October 15th, it was the women who made special headlines as 20-year-old Wei Yanan debuted and won in 2:26:34. Not far behind was 15-year-old Shi Hongjuan in 12th (2:45:11), a world best for her age. As well, 16-year-old Li Zhuhong's 2:15:07 for 10th in the men's race also set a world age-best mark.

The Chicago marathon on October 22nd continued its recent spectacular success story under the guidance of race director Carey Pinkowski. Its 27,956 finishers was an event record. Eight American men broke 2:20:00, five achieving personal bests, signaling perhaps a turn-around in that nation's recent performance doldrums. Khalid Khannouchi's 28-second 2:07:01 victory over Rome winner Josephat Kiprono gave him a unique set of double credentials. First, his five-race career average of 2:07:10, including four runs at Chicago (averaging 2:06:48) is unsurpassed. Second, having acquired United States citizenship last May 4th, this newest performance makes him the current national marathon record-holder for both Morocco and the USA, and as well, he now holds simultaneously the African and North American continental marathon records. So fast were the men finishers, commanded by the Kenyan juggernaut of Kiprono, Moses Tanui, Peter Githuka, and Fred Kiprop – all behind Khannouchi – that Kiprop's 2:08:23 was a world best-for-5th-place. The women were nearly as superlative, with Kenyans again up front. Boston winner Ndereba took control from Lornah Kiplagat at 23 miles, developing a huge 63-second lead with negative splits (71:04 + 70:29) on this flat course to become the fourth fastest woman ever (2:21:33), behind only Loroupe, Kristiansen, and Benoit-Samuelson.

Two weeks later, at New York's 25th anniversary of its marathon run through its five boroughs, both the men's and women's fields included a mix of athletes who either were unhappy with their Olympic performance or who were denied a team spot. Moroccan Abdelkader El Mouaziz wanted redemption and got it; never had someone vaulted into the lead here so early (23 seconds in front of Josiah Thugwane at half-way) and maintained it; he won (2:10:09) by 2:21 over Tokyo winner Japhet Kosgei on a cool, windy, gray day. Not only was this the first Moroccan victory at New York but on the women's side it was also an inaugural victory for Russia as Lyudmila Petrova (4th here in 1998) took 3:38 off her personal best to defeat a superb field that included former winners Franca Fiacconi (2nd), Tegla Loroupe (6th), and Adriana Fernández (13th). The 21,041 men and 8,332 women finishers made it the year's second largest marathon, behind London.

Japanese marathons also provided some surprises. Tokyo's all-women's marathon on November 19th produced the first African winner (2:24:02) in its 22-year history as Sydney bronze medallist Joyce Chepchumba broke a five-year Japanese winning streak by defeating Reiko Tosa and Sydney 10,000 m gold medallist Derartu Tulu. Chepchumba's 2:24:02 at Tokyo, 2:24:45 at Sydney, and 2:24:56 at London made her the most consistent top-level woman marathoner, ahead of Lidia Simon's 2:22:54 at Osaka, 2:23:22 at Sydney, and 2:24:46 at London. These two women led an unprecedented increase in quality marathon racing during 2000 with 94 performances under 2:30:00 (81 in 1999) and 230 under 2:35:00 (202 in 1999).

Two weeks after the women's race, Japan's Atsushi Fujita ended a nine-year foreign domination of the 54-year-old Fukuoka men's marathon with his national (and Asian) record 2:06:51, beating Atlanta silver medallist Lee Bong-ju (runner-up, three seconds behind) and Sydney gold medallist Gezahegne Abera. Only Pinto at London ran faster during 2000. Both Tosa and Fujita were declared as members of Japan's team bound for the 2001 IAAF World Athletics Championships at Edmonton.

Once again the Honolulu marathon accurately mirrored the year's trends, from several points of view. First, marathon participation continues to increase worldwide, and Honolulu's 22,699 finishers (59% Japanese!) was an increase over 1999. Second, for the men, Jimmy Muindi led an army of Kenyans to the finish line, taking four of the five spots. [The world dominance by Kenyan men is seen in the accompanying summary of 172 major races – 65 victories (37.8%). The year's total of 298 sub-2:20:00 performances by 174 Kenyan athletes is matched only by the 268 such performances by 190 USA men way back in 1983!]. Third, the enormous improvement by women at the top-level worldwide also occurred at Honolulu as three athletes bettered the event's previous fastest time despite warm, humid weather. Fourth, the world dominance by Russian women marathoners (note the 28 Russian victories {16.4%} in the accompanying list of 170 world marathons) is seen at Honolulu with their capturing three of the four top spots. Lyubov Morgunova's victory (2:28:33) was a welcome consolation for her poor (23rd) Olympic performance, bringing her $35,000 with record-breaking bonuses.

Honolulu runner-up Svetlana Zakharova and third-placed Franca Fiacconi were running their fourth and fifth marathons in 2000, respectively. More than two dozen elite-level women athletes managed four or more such finishes, a pattern seen rarely among top-level men, who seldom run more than three. One notable exception, however, occurred during 2000 when a 28-year-old Roman cab driver named Giorgio Calcaterra ran 21 (averaging 2:19:02), 16 of which ranged between 2:13:15 and 2:19:46 (averaging 2:17:15). This surpasses the previous 'record' of 13 sub-2:20:00 performances set by Moroccan El-Hadi Moumou in 1994.

Leading International marathons 2000

1 Jan	Roma	Josephat Kiprono KEN	2:08:27	Tegla Loroupe KEN	2:32:04
6 Jan	Tiberias	Asaf Bimro ISR	2:19:45	Nili Avramski ISR	2:42:06
14 Jan	Dubai	Wilson Kibet KEN	2:12:21	Ramilya Burangulova RUS	2:40:22
16 Jan	Carlsbad	Andrey Gordeyev BLR	2:18:21	Galina Karnatsevich BLR	2:44:04
16 Jan	Hamilton BER	Boubker El Affaoui MAR	2:23:15	Lyudmila Korchagina RUS	2:52:51
16 Jan	Houston	Stephen Ndungu KEN	2:11:28	Tatyana Pozdnyakova UKR	2:32:25
30 Jan	Osaka	Women only		Lidia Simon ROM	2:22:54
30 Jan	Port of Spain	Pamenos Ballentyne STV	2:19:20	Salina Chirchir KEN	2:51:41
5 Feb	Apeldoorn	Dmitriy Ryushkin RUS	2:20:31	Yelena Plastinina RUS	2:44:27
6 Feb	Caracas	Alejandro Semprún VEN	2:12:58	Rosa Rodríguez VEN	2:53:23
6 Feb	Las Vegas	Robert Reeder USA	2:17:15	Joanna Gront POL	2:36:01
6 Feb	Oita	Kazutaka Enoki JPN	2:10:44	Men only	
6 Feb	Valencia	Thomas Magut KEN	2:15:05	Maria Luisa Muñoz ESP	2:32:34
13 Feb	Busseto	Giorgio Calcaterra ITA	2:15:03	Deborah Bruni ITA	2:48:14
13 Feb	Guadalajara	Jose Ledezma MEX	2:19:11	Emma Cabrera MEX	2:41:49
13 Feb	Tokyo	Japhet Kosgei KEN	2:07:15	Men only	
20 Feb	Austin	Janko Bensa YUG	2:14:12	Tatyana Titova RUS	2:34:03
20 Feb	Hong Kong	Henry Kosgei Cherono KEN	2:21:09	Irina Safarova RUS	2:46:59
20 Feb	Senshu	Kazunari Kamagome JPN	2:15:24	Tomoe Abe JPN	2:29:09
26 Feb	Columbia	Women only (OT)		Christine Clark USA	2:33:31
27 Feb	Nobeoka	Yukiyasu Ogura JPN	2:14:45	Men only	
27 Feb	Sevilla	Aleksandr Krestianinov RUS	2:16:52	Irina Suvorova RUS	2:33:48
5 Mar	Los Angeles	Benson Mbithi KEN	2:11:55	Jane Salumäe EST	2:33:34
5 Mar	Otsu	Martín Fiz ESP	2:08:14	Men only	
5 Mar	Piacenza	Giorgio Calcaterra ITA	2:15:51	Irene Kipkorir KEN	2:43:43
5 Mar	Pinelands	Johannes Maremane RSA	2:11:15	Gwen van Lingen RSA	2:39:08
5 Mar	Torreon	Benjamin Paredes MEX	2:11:24	Lucia Rendón MEX	2:37:25
12 Mar	Ferrara	Ezekiel Kibiwott KEN	2:13:08	Giustina Menna ITA	2:43:05
12 Mar	Nagoya	Women only		Naoko Takahashi JPN	2:22:19
18 Mar	Virginia Beach	Jerry Lawson USA	2:19:33	Roxi Erickson USA	2:51:24
19 Mar	Barcelona	William Musyoki KEN	2:12:18	Griselda González ESP	2:31:12
19 Mar	Seoul	Chung Nam-kyun KOR	2:11:29	Park Ko-eun KOR	2:33:06
26 Mar	Como	Emanuele Zenucchi ITA	2:15:25	Tatyana Maslova RUS	2:39:45
26 Mar	Torino	Simretu Alemayehu ETH	2:08:33	Florence Barsosio KEN	2:27:58
2 Apr	Egna	David Kirui KEN	2:12:25	Karina Szymanska POL	2:36:44
2 Apr	Jinan NC	Zhu Ronghua CHN	2:15:26	Ren Xiujuan CHN	2:25:32
2 Apr	Napoli	Andrew Eyapan KEN	2:11:09	Lucilla Andreucci ITA	2:36:24
9 Apr	Kunsan	Hyung Jae-young KOR	2:11:39	Oh Mi-ja KOR	2:29:44
9 Apr	Nagano	Eric Wainaina KEN	2:10:17	Elfenesh Alemu ETH	2:24:55
9 Apr	Nantes	Pascal Fétizon FRA	2:15:44	Valentina Lunegova RUS	2:41:04
9 Apr	Paris	Mohamed Ouaadi FRA	2:08:49	Marleen Renders BEL	2:23:43
9 Apr	Pyongyang	Nelson Ndereva KEN	2:11:05	Hong Myong-hui PRK	2:31:28
16 Apr	Albi	Joseph Mutinda KEN	2:16:23	Marina Pilyavina RUS	2:39:55
16 Apr	Debno	Piotr Poblocki POL	2:15:28	Alena Peterková CZE	2:34:22

16 Apr	Hamburg	Piotr Gladki POL	2:11:06	Manuela Zipse GER	2:31:37
16 Apr	London	António Pinto POR	2:06:36	Tegla Loroupe KEN	2:24:33
16 Apr	Rotterdam	Kenneth Cheruiyot KEN	2:08:22	Ana Isabel Alonso ESP	2:30:21
16 Apr	Santiago	Ivan Condori BOL	2:20:35	Erika Olivera CHI	2:36:34
17 Apr	Boston	Gezahegne Abera ETH	2:09:47	Catherine Ndereba KEN	2:26:11
22 Apr	Beograd	Thabiso Moqhali LES	2:15:08	Cristina Pomacu ROM	2:36:54
23 Apr	Santa Rosa	Oscar Cortínez ARG	2:13:42	Claudia Camargo ARG	2:46:17
24 Apr	de Meern	Andrey Romashchenko RUS	2:18:43	Tatyana Perepelkina RUS	2:42:56
25 Apr	Pisa	Philemon Kipkering KEN	2:20:37	Monica Bondioli ITA	2:49:35
29 Apr	Bratislava	Mikola Antonenko UKR	2:18:23	Anna Balosaková SVK	2:52:55
29 Apr	Nashville dh	Lukas Kibet KEN	2:12:55	Lucia Subano KEN	2:37:02
29 Apr	Rotorua	Philip Costley NZL	2:23:08	Megan Edhouse NZL	2:45:47
30 Apr	Cleveland	Pavel Kokin RUS	2:10:29	Wioletta Kryza POL	2:34:27
30 Apr	Duisburg	Matthias Korner GER	2:20:04	Ines Cronjager GER	2:40:59
30 Apr	Kuala Lumpur	John Kemboi KEN	2:30:58	Yuan Yufang MAS	2:49:28
30 Apr	Madrid	John Milka KEN	2:16:05	Marina Pilyavina RUS	2:39:33
30 Apr	Padova	Migidio Bourifa ITA	2:13:55	Franca Fiacconi ITA	2:30:20
30 Apr	Sydney	Rod de Highden AUS	2:16:36	Susan Hobson AUS	2:35:20
30 Apr	Wroclaw	Marek Dryja POL	2:21:23	Yelena Vinitskaya BLR	2:46:26
7 May	La Habana	Iram Trutié CUB	2:14:54	Maribel Durruty CUB	2:47:16
7 May	Pittsburgh	Rodney De Haven USA	2:15:30	Tammy Slusser USA	2:53:30
7 May	Porto Alegre	William Musyoki BRA	2:13:49	Marcia Narloch BRA	2:34:18
7 May	Trieste	Michael Kite KEN	2:13:22	Irina Sklyarenko RUS	2:44:33
7 May	Vancouver	Ulrich Steidl GER	2:18:53	Krystyna Pieczulis POL	2:45:32
7 May	Warszawa	Miroslaw Plawgo POL	2:15:57	Ewa Fliegert POL	2:51:02
14 May	Hannover	Waldemar Glinka POL	2:12:55	Birgit Behrend GER	2:54:39
14 May	Ottawa	Bruce Deacon CAN	2:17:13	Véronique Vandersmissen CAN	2:36:46
20 May	Radenci	Mikhail Romanov RUS	2:16:20	Gigliola Borghini ITA	2:38:33
21 May	København	Samuel Kiplimo KEN	2:21:30	Michaela McCallum GBR	2:42:25
21 May	Moskva	Aleksey Korobov RUS	2:14:50	Irina Safarova RUS	2:34:45
21 May	Praha	Simon Chemoiywo KEN	2:10:35	Alina Ivanova RUS	2:27:42
21 May	Wien	Wilson Cheruiyot KEN	2:08:48	Maura Viceconte ITA	2:23:47
28 May	Bergamo	Philip Malakwen KEN	2:15:04	Blanca James Nyambo KEN	2:54:13
28 May	Laredo	Mohamed Aoulhab MAR	2:19:15	Remedios Alonso ESP	3:04:10
3 Jun	Stockholm	Alfred Shemweta TAN	2:18:49	Marie Söderström SWE	2:37:57
4 Jun	Bilbão	Daniel Komen Kipcheru KEN	2:16:30	Chiara Barale ITA	2:57:50
4 Jun	Regensburg	Samson Loywapet KEN	2:15:38	Monika Hirt GER	3:00:25
4 Jun	San Diego	Belaye Wolashe ETH	2:12:45	Margaret Okayo KEN	2:27:05
10 Jun	Spitzbergen	Nils Haugen NOR	3:07:52	Jenni de Groot NED	3:54:11
11 Jun	Katharagama	Ajith Bandara SRI	2:25:09	N.A. Chandrawathi SRI	3:00:45
11 Jun	Leiden	Abraham Limo KEN	2:18:28	Karina Szymanska POL	2:41:33
11 Jun	São Paolo	David Ngetich KEN	2:15:21	Marcia Narloch BRA	2:40:15
17 Jun	Bordeaux	John Kemboi KEN	2:22:08	Natalya Sharanova RUS	2:56:02
17 Jun	Duluth	Pavel Andreyev RUS	2:14:31	Svetlana Shepeleva MOL	2:33:53
18 Jun	Caen	David Kiptoo Kirui KEN	2:17:12	Lyudmila Smirnova RUS	2:44:19
18 Jun	Lebork	Yuriy Hichun UKR	2:20:37	Galina Karnatsevich BLR	2:44:27
25 Jun	Mont St.Michel	Julius Sugut KEN	2:14:22	Judit Nagy HUN	2:38:07
25 Jun	Gold Coast	Joseph Kahugu KEN	2:16:38	Samantha Hughes AUS	2:44:04
26 Jun	Green Bay	Vladimir Epanov RUS	2:21:10	Lucia Subano KEN	2:42:07
2 Jul	Rio de Janeiro	Reginaldo dos Santos BRA	2:18:01	Rizoneide Wanderlei BRA	2:43:53
9 Jul	Brugge	Filip Vanhaecke BEL	2:18:54	Grace Chebet KEN	2:37:04
9 Jul	Turku	Joseph Mutinda KEN	2:23:46	Tatyana Maslova RUS	2:45:55
23 Jul	Toral de los Vados	José Ramon Rey ESP	2:14:56	Alzira Lario POR	3:03:24
30 Jul	Blumenau	Diamantino dos Santos BRA	2:16:07	Josefa Madalena da Silva BRA	2:42:48
5 Aug	Omsk	Mikhail Khobotov RUS	2:18:05	Irina Timofeyeva RUS	2:34:07
13 Aug	Arusha	John Nada Saya TAN	2:17:03	Banuela Mrashani TAN	2:47:22
15 Aug	Gdynia	Benjamin Mutua Matolo KEN	2:19:28	Natalya Galushko BLR	2:50:50
19 Aug	Helsinki	Nikolaos Pollias GRE	2:18:46	Tatyana Zolotareva RUS	2:44:31
20 Aug	Edmonton	Chris Glowach CAN	2:32:24	Meghan Behrens USA	3:03:14
20 Aug	Glasgow	Wilson Cheruiyot KEN	2:22:45	Alevtina Naumova RUS	2:48:50
27 Aug	Ciudad de México	Enrique Montiel MEX	2:16:10	Patricia Jardón MEX	2:41:50

27 Aug	Sapporo	Dionicio Cerón MEX	2:17:14	Mayumi Ichikawa JPN	2:32:30
2 Sep	Klagenfurt	Pavel Kryska CZE	2:23:16	Ida Kovács HUN	2:46:11
3 Sep	Cape Town	Sicelo Baba RSA	2:24:29	Kathleen Shuttleworth RSA	2:49:59
10 Sep	Berlin	Simon Biwott KEN	2:07:42	Kazumi Matsuo JPN	2:26:15
10 Sep	Chantilly	Azzeddine Sakhri ALG	2:17:27	Olga Michurina RUS	2:45:42
10 Sep	Grottazzolina	Giorgio Calcaterra ITA	2:17:50	Margherita Grosso ITA	2:45:04
10 Sep	Moskva	Anatoliy Archakov RUS	2:16:57	Viktoriya Klimina RUS	2:39:02
17 Sep	Karlsruhe	Aleksandr Kuzin RUS	2:15:39	Krystyna Pieczulis POL	2:47:42
17 Sep	Otterndorf	Simon Mbethuka KEN	2:14:16	Wioletta Uryga POL	2:47:32
17 Sep	Wachau	James Tanui KEN	2:14:32	Karina Szymanska POL	2:38:47
1 Oct	Budapest	Nikolai Rudik UKR	2:19:32	Erika Csomor HUN	2:41:59
1 Oct	Köln	Benson Lokorwa KEN	2:15:51	Malgorzata Sobanska POL	2:28:42
1 Oct	Kosice	Ernest Kipyego KEN	2:14:35	Ivana Martincová CZE	2:46:17
1 Oct	Lyon	David Kiptoo Kirui KEN	2:11:43	Zhanna Malkova RUS	2:36:13
8 Oct	Cesano Boscone	Yuriy Chizhov RUS	2:11:46	Tiziana Alagia ITA	2:33:19
8 Oct	Eindhoven	Wilson Cheruiyot KEN	2:09:55	Wilma van Onna NED	2:39:35
8 Oct	Le Havre	Viktor Rozgovoy RUS	2:19:28	Olga Michurina RUS	2:45:35
8 Oct	St. Paul	Sergey Fedetov RUS	2:12:40	Zinaida Semyonova RUS	2:29:37
14 Oct	Hartford	John Mwai KEN	2:17:00	Yelena Plastinina RUS	2:44:22
15 Oct	Amsterdam	Francisco J Cortes ESP	2:08:57	Abeba Tola ETH	2:29:54
15 Oct	Beijing	Nelson Ndereva KEN	2:13:52	Wei Yanan CHN	2:26:34
15 Oct	Carpi	Gideon Chirchir KEN	2:12:51	Jackline Jerotich KEN	2:28:32
15 Oct	Istanbul	Josephat Kipchoge Rop KEN	2:17:03	Adriana Chirita ROM	2:37:39
15 Oct	München	Michael Kite KEN	2:09:46	Elzbieta Jarosz POL	2:37:34
15 Oct	Odense	Daniel Cheribo KEN	2:14:17	Gitte Karlshøj DEN	2:35:39
15 Oct	Poznan	Andrzej Krzyscin POL	2:17:23	Dorota Gruca POL	2:37:22
15 Oct	Toronto	El Mostafa Damaoui MAR	2:15:18	Jennifer Cooper CAN	2:59:05
22 Oct	Chicago	Khalid Khannouchi USA	2:07:01	Catherine Ndereba KEN	2:21:33
22 Oct	Chunchon	Kim Ye-kyong KOR	2:13:57	Yun Sun-sook KOR	2:37:02
22 Oct	Echternach	Mikhail Khobotov RUS	2:20:02	Wioletta Kryza POL	2:38:27
22 Oct	Lausanne	Tesfaye Eticha ETH	2:16:25	Irina Kazakova FRA	2:38:42
22 Oct	Ljubljana	Patrick Chumba KEN	2:13:35	Maria Luisa Costetti ITA	3:08:38
22 Oct	Niagara Falls	Joseph Maina KEN	2:21:46	Danuta Bartoszek CAN	2:38:30
22 Oct	Reims NC	Benoit Zwierzchlewski FRA	2:10:47	Chantal Dällenbach FRA	2:33:34
22 Oct	Venezia	John Bungei KEN	2:09:50	Ruth Kutol KEN	2:28:16
29 Oct	Calderara di Reno	Giorgio Calcaterra ITA	2:19:07	Sara Ferroglia ITA	2:51:35
29 Oct	Columbus	Elly Rono KEN	2:15:27	Marzena Helbik POL	2:36:28
29 Oct	Dalian	Zhong Weifu CHN	2:18:52	Sun Jingchu CHN	2:40:54
29 Oct	Frankfurt	Henry Kosgei Cherono KEN	2:10:40	Esther Barmasai KEN	2:31:04
29 Oct	San Jose	Simon Sawe KEN	2:20:54	Sandy Jacobson CAN	2:39:42
30 Oct	Dublin	Simon Pride GBR	2:18:59	Sonia O'Sullivan IRL	2:35:42
5 Nov	New York	Abdelkader El Mouaziz MAR	2:10:09	Lyudmila Petrova RUS	2:25:45
5 Nov	Soweto @	Honest Mutsakani ZIM	2:18:28	Sarah Mahlangu RSA	2:56:47
12 Nov	Livorno	Fabio Rinaldi ITA	2:13.58	Galina Zhulyayeva UKR	2:38:54
12 Nov	Long Beach	James Bungei KEN	2:16:49	Irina Safarova RUS	2:37:40
12 Nov	Providence (46m dh)	Igor Osmak UKR	2:14:24	Olga Kovpotina RUS	2:37:53
12 Nov	Shanghai	Lu Zhenghua CHN	2:18:17	Zhong Guoshang CHN	2:46:49
19 Nov	Philadelphia	Brian Clas USA	2:18:03	Elvira Kolpakova RUS	2:41:56
19 Nov	Pompeii	David Ndegwa KEN	2:17:11	Jean D'Argenio ITA	2:44:34
19 Nov	Tokyo	Women only		Joyce Chepchumba KEN	2:24:02
26 Nov	Bangkok	Vladimir Kotov BLR	2:31:11	Sunisa Sailomyen THA	2:54:01
26 Nov	Firenze	Angelo Carosi ITA	2:14:11	Tiziana Alagia ITA	2:32:18
26 Nov	La Rochelle	John Ngeny KEN	2:18:35	Valentina Lunegova RUS	2:40:03
26 Nov	Lisboa	William Musyoki KEN	2:16:10	Fatima Silva POR	2:34:40
26 Nov	San Sebastián	Turbo Tumo ETH	2:12:18	Gadissie Edato ETH	2:38:08
3 Dec	Bridgetown	Benedict Ballantyne STV	2:27:40	Kimberly Goff USA	3:10:43
3 Dec	Fukuoka	Atsushi Fujita JPN	2:06:51	Men only	
3 Dec	Macau	Willie Mtolo KEN	2:19:25	Lu Jingbo CHN	2:47:15
3 Dec	Mazatlan	Kipkemboi Cheruiyot KEN	2:15:40	Martha Tenorio ECU	2:34:00
3 Dec	Milano	Simon Biwott KEN	2:09:00	Lucilla Andreucci ITA	2:29:43
3 Dec	Palermo	Joseph Ngolepus KEN	2:13:48	Irene Kipkorir KEN	2:50:31

3 Dec	Sacramento	Elly Rono KEN	2:15:38	Kristin Schwartz USA	2:38:16
3 Dec	Singapore	Nixon Nkodima RSA	2:27:07	Ruwiyati INA	2:53:11
3 Dec	Tucson	Bassirima Sori CIV	2:18:32	Jane Johnson USA	2:56:12
9 Dec	Huntsville	Andrey Shalagin RUS	2:21:38	Michelle Lafleur USA	2:44:52
10 Dec	Calvia	Jan Blaha CZE	2:21:24	Janina Malska POL	2:49:30
10 Dec	Honolulu	Mwangangi Muindi KEN	2:15:19	Lyubov Morgunova RUS	2:28:33
10 Dec	Latina	Josephat Kipchoge Rop KEN	2:17:36	Giustina Menna ITA	2:40:31
10 Dec	Reggio Emilia	Emanuele Zenucchi ITA	2:15:51	Ida Koáacs HUN	2:41:45
17 Dec	Hofu	Waldemar Glinka POL	2:11:40	Men only	
31 Dec	Assisi	Graziano Calvaresi ITA	2:22:00	Sara Ferrari ITA	2:48:42

See also Championships section

@=altitude > 1000

WORLD ROAD RACE REVIEW 2000

By David E Martin

THE ACCOMPANYING global summary of top-level road races summarizes briefly what is arguably the most free-wheeling element of the sport of athletics. These events often are not contested over standard distances familiar to track enthusiasts – they may extend from one city to another, or consist of several loops along village streets. Road courses have variable terrain, and may be net downhill or uphill. Many are held at higher altitudes. Whereas several nations (notably France, Great Britain, Japan, South Africa, and the United States) are leaders in implementing both technology and record-keeping to ensure that course lengths and athlete performances are accurately ascertained, such activities are not uniform, and vary considerably in other countries. Thus, not all road races can be expected to actually extend over the stated distance. Appreciating the pace maintained by the top athletes therefore becomes less consequential than who wins or whether the course record is bettered (see asterisk on the lists). Both prize money and appearance money are available, distributed in varying amounts depending upon budget and desire of the event to attract stars.

The summary of winners clearly indicates the global nature of road racing with winners coming form over 30 nations. Most impressive is the enormous Kenyan excellence – 147 victories by Kenyan men (59% of the total!) are listed here, 98 by the women (37.7%). This dominance is especially noteworthy in view of the barely half dozen venues listed here for the entire African continent. These athletes thus travel great distances to compete. Behind these winners is a much larger reservoir of talented countrymen who cause utter Kenyan domination at many races. Nine of the top ten at the Utica (New York) Boilermaker 15km were Kenyans, for example, along with 12 of the top 13 at the Falmouth (Massachusetts) Road Race (7.1 miles) and all of the top 13 at the Crim 10 miler at Flint, Michigan. Whatever the continent, time of year, or race distance, well-organized agents mobilize Kenyan talent around the world to race for money. After taking a variable percentage of prize-money winnings as payment for services, it is the agents who ultimately profit most, as the runners come and go, most managing a competitive lifetime of but a year or two, succumbing to the stress of global travel, high-volume training, and enormously intense competition.

Road races fit in varying ways into athletes' yearly schedules. Some focus primarily on road races, appearing only occasionally on the track or at cross country competitions. In this regard, among the men such athletes as Reuben Kiprop Cheruiyot deserve special mention (eight victories, two runner-ups, and three 3rd-placings over a range from 8km through the half marathon). Another is Ethiopia's Alene Amere, who won the Professional Road Racing Organization (PRRO) World Championships – ahead of 13 of Kenya's best! Staged this year at Atlanta's 10km Peachtree Road Race on July 4, the PRRO championships brings together the top placers from a series of six other major North American road races held during the 12 months preceding (Utica Boilermaker 15km, Davenport Bix 7M, and Tulsa Run 15km during 1999; Washington Cherry Blossom 10M, Washington Sallie Mae 10km, and Spokane Bloomsday 12km during 2000). Among the women, a strong candidate for road-racer of the year would have to be Catherine Ndereba, who achieved 10 victories and three runner-ups from 5 miles through the half marathon in addition to marathon victories at Boston and Chicago. Her countrywoman Lornah Kiplagat, however, challenged her by winning the PRRO Championships and six other road races, with three runner-up placings as well.

Athletes considering themselves as

marathon specialists often identify specific road races – especially at the half-marathon distance – to assess their fitness for an upcoming marathon. Khalid Khannouchi, for example, used the September 17th Philadelphia Distance Run (winning in 61:17) as an indicator of readiness for the Chicago marathon on October 24th, which he won. And Naoko Takahashi used the Sapporo half marathon on July 2nd (winning in 62:16) to test her fitness for the Sydney Olympic marathon on September 24th, which she also won.

A relatively small minority of distance runners perform superbly on road, track, and turf, possessing a remarkable ability to craft carefully their training, racing, and recovery to ensure consistent quality on all venues through the year. Last year we summarized the remarkable saga of Tegla Loroupe in this regard, and in 2000 she performed nearly as well. Two other outstanding examples in 2000 were Great Britain's Paula Radcliffe and Kenya's Paul Tergat.

At the World Cross Country Champ-ionships Radcliffe ran both the 4 and 8km races, finishing 4th and 5th, respectively – the only non-African among the top five. On the track at the Sydney Games, she found the same athletes around her. Just as it was Derartu Tulu and Gete Wami going one-two in the 8km turf race, so it was Tulu and Wami at the Sydney Games, with Paula again a fine 4th. She then switched focus to road racing, hoping for a good performance at the IAAF World Half Marathon Champ-ionships on November 12th in hot, humid Veracruz. Running a European best for the distance at the Great North Run in South Shields three weeks prior, she captured the world title with a striking 33-second victory in 69:09 – even beating the best time of her male teammates!

Similarly for the men, if the half marathon and cross country were Olympic events, Paul Tergat would likely be a multiple medallist. The five-time (successively!) World Cross Country champion finally faltered (by only two seconds!) this year at Vilamoura, but scored a 59:06 victory in the downhill Lisbon half marathon one week later – his 7th victory over the distance in as many races, dating back to 1994! He too had an excellent Olympic track performance, being edged at the tape by only 0.09 second by Haile Gebrselassie in the epic thriller over 10,000 m. Racing sparingly thereafter, he was determined to achieve victory at Veracruz, and his sprint finish victory (by one second) over Faustin Baha made him the first to win the IAAF half marathon title twice (the other being at Palermo in 1999).

Road racing as a sport remains as healthy among the masses as does marathon running, with more than a dozen events exceeding 40,000 participants. A 'world record' of sorts occurred on June 12th when more than 80,000 ran the half marathon distance from København to Malmö through a 4km tunnel and over a 7.8km bridge connecting Denmark with Sweden. The event commemorated the opening of this important road link, but was a challenge for organizers, as they had to transport the finishers back to København! Although runners had to cope with a 70m climb up the bridge, they encountered a 6 m/km assisting tailwind. Such are the challenges that make road racing a unique aspect of our sport.

Leading International Road Races 2000

2 Jan	Ratingen 10km	Assefa Mezgebu ETH 28:30	Leah Malot KEN 33:22
5 Jan	Punta del Este 10km	Paul Tergat KEN 28:04	Jane Omoro KEN 33:21
6 Jan	Miyazaki HMar	Women only	Hiromi Ominami JPN 69:40
6 Jan	San Sebastián 9.2/5km	James Kosgei KEN 27:48	Tereza Yohannes ETH 17:23
7 Jan	Montevideo 10km	Hendrick Ramaala RSA 27:57	Jane Omoro KEN 32:37
9 Jan	Egmond aan Zee HMar	Wilson Kigen KEN 62:41	Tegla Loroupe KEN 72:14
10 Jan	Tokyo HMar	Ken-ichi Takahashi JPN 60:30	Elana Meyer RSA 67:33
15 Jan	Hamilton BFR 10km	Sammy N'geno KEN 30:14	Courtney Babcock CAN 34:44
16 Jan	Oakland HMar	Philip Kemei KEN 62:52*	Karolina Szabó HUN 74.15*
16 Jan	San Diego HMar	Janko Bensa KEN 62:38	Deena Drossin USA 73:16
23 Jan	Chiba HMar	Women only	Naoko Takahashi JPN 68:55
23 Jan	Granollers HMar	Philip Kirui KEN 61:07	Esther Kiplagat KEN 71:57
25 Jan	São Paolo 10km	Emerson Iser Bem BRA 29:21	Lidia Karwowski BRA 34:42
28 Jan	Nairobi 30km @	Peter Ndirangu KEN 1:34:11	Men only
30 Jan	Naples HMar	Rod DeHaven USA 63:12	Tatyana Pozdnyakova UKR 72:40
30 Jan	Redondo Beach 10km	Philip Kimei KEN 29:42	Kim Fitchen USA 33:02
5 Feb	Ein Gedi HMar	John Kipsang KEN 65:46	Lornah Kiplagat KEN 71:21*
6 Feb	Austin HMar	William Cheseret KEN 62:26	Tatyana Pozdnyakova UKR 73:39
6 Feb	Barcelona HMar	Abel Antón ESP 63:11*	Eva Sanz ESP 73:47
6 Feb	Coamo HMar	Khalid Khannouchi MAR 65:02	Margaret Okayo KEN 76:52
6 Feb	Las Vegas HMar	Tom Lentz USA 63:38	Melody Fairchild USA 71:38
6 Feb	Marugame HMar	Kazuhito Yokota JPN 62:59	Rie Ueno JPN 69:57

13 Feb	Karatsu 10M/10km	Ken-ichi Takahashi JPN 45:48	Emiko Kojima JPN 32:44
13 Feb	Vancouver HMar	Norman Tinkham CAN 67:49	Lisa Harvey CAN 75:42
20 Feb	Cape Town HMar	Owen MacHelm RSA 73:20	Elana Meyer RSA 81:37
20 Feb	Ferrara HMar	Eliud Lagat KEN 61:43*	Silvana Trampuz AUS 76:00
20 Feb	Kumamoto 30km	Ken-ichi Takahashi JPN 1:29:55	Men only
20 Feb	Ome 30km	Takayuki Matsumiya JPN 1:31:18	Tomoko Kai JPN 1:47:43
20 Feb	Schoorl HMar	Greg van Hest NED 62:20*	Wilma van Onna NED 75:14
27 Feb	Inuyama HMar	Naruhito Terao JPN 63:14	Fumi Murata JPN 71:12
27 Feb	Osaka HMar	Yoshiteru Morishita JPN 63:33	Masami Deto JPN 72:23
27 Feb	San Juan 10km	Khalid Khannouchi MAR 28:35	Tegla Loroupe KEN 31:30
4 Mar	Jacksonville 15km NC	Daniel Browne USA 44:26	Deena Drossin USA 49:40
11 Mar	Frankfurt HMar	Julius Maritim KEN 62:19	Pamela Chepchumba KEN 71:07
12 Mar	Alphen aan den Rijn 20km	Hendrick Ramaala RSA 57:58	Joyce Chepchumba KEN 65:16
12 Mar	Kyoto HMar	Ondoro Osoro KEN 61:50	Fatuma Roba ETH 70:16
12 Mar	Leverkusen 10km	Women only	Sonja Oberem GER 32:29
12 Mar	Paris HMar	Zebedayo Bayo TAN 60:50	Anne Njeri KEN 70:40
12 Mar	Reading HMar	Samuel Bitok KEN 62:56	Berhane Dagne ETH 74:23
12 Mar	Sendai HMar	James Wainaina KEN 62:28	Elana Meyer RSA 69:04
12 Mar	San Jose 10km	Simon Sawe KEN 30:04	Colleen de Reuck RSA 32:50*
12 Mar	São Paolo 9.5km	Daniel Lopes Ferreira BRA 28:07	Fabiana da Silva BRA 32:55
12 Mar	Yamaguchi HMar	Susumu Ichinose JPN 61:30*	Yukiko Okamoto JPN 69:12*
18 Mar	Virginia Beach 8km	Reuben Kiprop Cheruiyot KEN 22:21	Cathy Vasto USA 27:16
19 Mar	Brasilia 10km	Marilson dos Santos BRA 29:03	Viviany Anderson BRA 34:21
19 Mar	Hastings HMar	Simon Kasimili KEN 63:45	Esther Kiplagat KEN 72:19
19 Mar	Ostia HMar	Francesco Ingargiola ITA 61:19	Maura Viceconte ITA 71:07
20 Mar	Matsue HMar	Women only	Yoko Shibui JPN 69:31
25 Mar	Den Haag HMar	Zebedayo Bayo TAN 61:07	Lornah Kiplagat KEN 66:56
25 Mar	Freiburg HMar NC	Carsten Eich GER 62:47	Katrin Dörre-Heinig GER 71:44
25 Mar	Mobile 10km	Dominic Kirui KEN 27:49	Jane Omoro KEN 32:39
25 Mar	Praha HMar	Isaac Kiprono KEN 63:28	Jana Klimesová CZE 74:17
26 Mar	Azpeitia HMar	Simon Kasimili KEN 62:42	Rocio Rios ESP 72:28
26 Mar	Berlin HMar	Joseph Mereng KEN 61:52	Joyce Chepchumba KEN 68:22
26 Mar	Carlsbad 5km	Sammy Kipketer KEN 13:00WB	Deena Drossin USA 15:08
26 Mar	Como HMar	Philip Kipketer KEN 62:05	Catherine Ndereba KEN 69:02
26 Mar	Hamilton CAN 30km	Joseph Ndiritu KEN 1:32:54*	Véronique Vandersmissen CAN 1:52:34
26 Mar	Lisboa HMar#	Paul Tergat KEN 59:06	Tegla Loroupe KEN 67:24
26 Mar	Zapopan HMar	Samson Limareng KEN 63:56*	Pamela Chepchumba KEN 73:25*
1 Apr	Charleston 10km	James Kosgei KEN 27:40*	Catherine Ndereba KEN 31:42
2 Apr	Vitry sur Seine HMar	John Nada Saya TAN 61:19	Irene Kwambai KEN 71:41
7 Apr	Zaragoza 8km	Isaac Viciosa ESP 24:15	Bertha Sánchez COL 25:51
8 Apr	Toronto 8km	James Kosgei KEN 23:17	Sally Barsosio KEN 27:06
8 Apr	Washington 10M	Reuben Kiprop Cheruiyot KEN 46:07	Teresa Wanjiku KEN 55:53
9 Apr	Brunssum 10km	Paul Kosgei KEN 27:38	Susan Chepkemei KEN 32:25
9 Apr	Korschenbroich 10/5km	Tendai Chimusasa ZIM 28:38*	Luminita Zaituc ROM 15:51*
9 Apr	Madrid 20km	Mohamed Zouak MAR 60:52	Margaret Ngadi TAN 72:27
15 Apr	Milano HMar	Patrick Ivuti KEN 60:49	Men only
15 Apr	Turku HMar	Jussi Utarainen FIN 65:47	Marianne Lundberg SWE 79:26
16 Apr	Iurreta 8.6km	Enrique Molina ESP 23:38	Amaia Piedra ESP 14:23
16 Apr	Nice HMar	Faustin Baha TAN 61:27	Restituta Joseph TAN 68:47*
16 Apr	Nyiregyháza HMar	Samuel Maritim KEN 63:25	Erika Csomor HUN 72:06
16 Apr	São Paolo HMar	Emerson Iser Bem BRA 64:08	Marlene Fortunato BRA 75:30
16 Apr	Vancouver 10km	James Kosgei KEN 27:36	Sally Barsosio KEN 32:24
22 Apr	New Orleans 10km	James Kosgei KEN 27:38	Colleen de Reuck RSA 31:58
22 Apr	Paderborn 10km	Benjamin Itok KEN 28:39	Restituta Joseph TAN 32:17
22 Apr	Balmoral 5M	Fita Bayissa ETH 22:29	Sonia O'Sullivan IRL 24:50
23 Apr	Nizhniy Novgorod HMar	Women only	Irina Timofeyeva RUS 71:09
30 Apr	Berlin 25km	Róbert Stefko SVK 1:15:31	Madina Biktagirova BLR 1:26:01
30 Apr	Cleveland 10km	Reuben Kiprop Cheruiyot KEN 28:09	Jane Ngotho KEN 32:17
30 Apr	Merano HMar	Michael Kite KEN 61:42	Margarete Atodonyang KEN 72:56
30 Apr	St. Denis 15km	Andrew Sambu TAN 43:49	Leah Malot KEN 49:03
30 Apr	Trutnov HMar	Miroslav Vitek CZE 67:04	Alena Peterková CZE 73:30
30 Apr	Washington 10km	Kibet Cherop KEN 29:18	Grace Momanyl KEN 34:03

1 May	Wellington RSA HMar	Owen MacHelm RSA 65:18	Theresa du Toit RSA 76:49
6 May	Indianapolis HMar	Philip Kemei KEN 64:19	Lidiya Grigoryeva RUS 72:23
6 May	Luzern 8.5/4.25km	Tendai Chimusasa ZIM 24:46	Tegla Loroupe KEN 13:13
7 May	Almeria HMar	Abdelkarim Kabouri MAR 65:37	Teresa Pulido ESP 75:54
7 May	Moskva Eur Clubs 15km	Women only	Maria Machado POR 49:35
7 May	Setúbal HMar	Anthony Korir KEN 62:04	Helena Sampaio POR 72:21
7 May	Spokane 12km	Reuben Kiprop Cheruiyot KEN 34:10	Jane Omoro KEN 40:08
7 May	Toronto 10km	Paul Mbugua KEN 29:17	Lucia Subano KEN 33:33
12 May	Aschaffenburg 7.9km	Thomas Omwenga KEN 22:06*	Petra Wassiluk GER 25:29
13 May	Bern 10M	Elijah Korir KEN 47:19	Leah Malot KEN 54:14
13 May	Evansville HMar	Reuben Kiprop Cheruiyot KEN 34:57	Jane Ngotho KEN 40:13
13 May	Göteborg HMar	Faustin Baha TAN 62:42	Stine Larsen NOR 69:28*
13 May	Grand Rapids 20km	Joseph Kariuki KEN 1:16:26	Svetlana Zakharova RUS 1:27:35
14 May	Glasgow 10km	Women only	Lornah Kiplagat KEN 31:46*
14 May	Kassel 10/5km	Thomas Omwenga KEN 28:42	Irina Mikitenko GER 15:17
14 May	Pietramurata HMar	Jackson Koech KEN 62:46	Margarete Atodonyang KEN 71:28
20 May	Flemington 9.9km	Steve Moneghetti AUS 28:15	Anne Cross AUS 32:02
21 May	Barcelona 11km	Driss Lakhouaja MAR 32:42	Eva Sanz ESP 38:22
21 May	Coban HMar	Ben Kimondiu KEN 65:46	Lucia Subano KEN 76:57
21 May	Milano 10km	Women only	Sonia O'Sullivan IRL 30:59*
21 May	San Francisco 12km	Reuben Kiprop Cheruiyot KEN 34:54	Colleen de Reuck RSA 38:42
21 May	Sydney HMar	Joseph Waweru KEN 64:05	Heather Turland AUS 77:28
21 May	Utrecht HMar	Mohammed Baket PAL 65:04	Marina Pilyavina RUS 79:02
27 May	Wheeling 20km	Abel Ondeyo KEN 62:43	Elfenesh Alemu ETH 71:38
28 May	Arusha HMar @	Zebedayo Bayo TAN 64:06	Men only
28 May	Paris 10km	Eljah Korir KEN 29:38	Isabella Ochichi KEN 33:40
29 May	Boulder 10km @	Joseph Kimani KEN 28:55	Derartu Tulu ETH 33:09
3 Jun	Albany 5km NC	Women only	Elizabeth Hickman USA 15:35
3 Jun	Comacchio 10/6km	David Ngeny Cheruiyot KEN 28:50	Maria Guida ITA 19:39
3 Jun	Logrono HMar	Antonio Peña ESP 63:45	Tereza Johannes TAN 77:07
4 Jun	Kansas City MO HMar	Eric Biyasse RSA 67:07	Lucia Subano KEN 82:08
4 Jun	Tilburg 10 M/10km	Eliud Kurgat KEN 46:53	Lornah Kiplagat KEN 31:14
10 Jun	Groesbeek 10km	Ambesse Tolossa ETH 27:56	Janet Rotich KEN 32:42
10 Jun	Green Bay 10km	Joseph Kimani KEN 28:23	Elana Meyer RSA 32:33
10 Jun	Maasdijk 15km	Hilaire N'tirampeba BDI 43:55	Lyudmila Afonyushkina RUS 54:25
10 Jun	New York 10km	Women only	Tegla Loroupe KEN 31:37
10 Jun	Peoria 4M	Jon Brown GBR 18:16	Colleen de Reuck RSA 20:05
11 Jun	Castellarano 10km	Roberto Barbi ITA 29:06	Deborah Mencich KEN 33:19
12 Jun	Malmö HMar	Tesfaye Tolla ETH 59:51	Restituta Joseph TAN 67:59
17 Jun	Borgholzhausen 10M	Thomas Omwenga KEN 47:19	Helen Chepngeno KEN 55:56
17 Jun	Dallas 5km	Janko Bensa YUG 13:52*	Colleen de Reuck RSA 15:43*
18 Jun	Albacete HMar	James Moiben KEN 64:32	Faustina Maria Ramos ESP 76:51
18 Jun	Bern 5km	Women only	Lydia Cheromei KEN 15:18
18 Jun	Phalempin HMar NC	Mohamed Serbouti FRA 63:21	Chantal Dällenbach FRA 73:08
21 Jun	Darmstadt 7.6/4.9km	Thomas Omwenga KEN 21:07	Lornah Kiplagat KEN 15:12
24 Jun	Lelystad 10M	Greg van Hest NED 46:45	Denisa Costescu ROM 55:32
24 Jun	Ludwigshafen 9.2km	Laban Chege KEN 27:18	Joyce Chepchumba KEN 31:12
24 Jun	Neuss 8.2km	Tendai Chimusasa ZIM 23:34	Petra Drajzlajtlová CZE 26:37
25 Jun	Durban 10km	Women only	Colleen de Reuck RSA 31:38*
25 Jun	Fairfield HMar	Ben Kimondiu KEN 64:12	Mary Lynn Currier USA 77:34
25 Jun	Gold Coast HMar	Cosmas Ndeti KEN 63:30	Takako Kotorida JPN 71:16
25 Jun	Vancouver HMar	Julius Gwako KEN 64:46	Véronique Vandersmissen CAN 75:23
2 Jul	Sapporo HMar	Laban Kagika KEN 62:16	Naoko Takahashi JPN 69:10
4 Jul	Atlanta 10km	Alene Emere ETH 28:04	Lornah Kiplagat KEN 30:52
8 Jul	Recanati 10km	Titus Munji KEN 28:21	Men only
9 Jul	Utica 15km	Reuben Kiprop Cheruiyot KEN 43:07	Catherine Ndereba KEN 48:47*
10 Jul	Tessenderlo 10km	Greg van Hest NED 28:32	Marleen Renders BEL 32:18
14 Jul	Borgholm 8.5km	Meshack Sang KEN 25:53	Zakia Mrisho TAN 30:17
14 Jul	Chicago 5km	Joseph Kimani KEN 13:42	Colleen de Reuck RSA 15:48*
15 Jul	Buffalo 4M	Ronald Mogaka KEN 17:58*	Lucia Subano KEN 21:45
15 Jul	Kingsport 8km	Reuben Kiprop Cheruiyot KEN 22:25	Naomi Wangui KEN 26:22
15 Jul	London 3M	Women only	Tegla Loroupe KEN 15:08*

16 Jul	Sydney City to Surf 14km	Laban Chege KEN 40:25	Susan Hobson AUS 48:24
17 Jul	Forssa HMar	Dmitriy Kapitonov RUS 63:36*	Maria Lundberg SWE 77:21
19 Jul	Voorthuizen 10km	Thomas Omwenga KEN 28:42	Nadezhda Wijenberg NED 33:28
22 Jul	Kaapstad 10km	Makhosonke Fika RSA 30:01	Theresa du Toit RSA 34:06
22 Jul	Davenport 7M	Mark Yatich KEN 32:31	Colleen de Reuck RSA 36:42
22 Jul	Davos 8.05/5.4km @	Mark Bett KEN 23:04	Joyce Chepchumba KEN 17:23
23 Jul	Capitola 6M	John Gwako KEN 27:55	Kelly Cordell USA 32:41
23 Jul	Mende HMar	Robert Cheruiyot KEN 62:57	Alena Peterková CZE 85:28
24 Jul	Salt Lake City 10km# @	Simon Sawe KEN 28:45	Katrina Price USA 33:06
29 Jul	Clarksburg 10km	Reuben Kiprop Cheruiyot KEN 28:57	Naomi Wangui KEN 33:36
29 Jul	New Milford 8M	Daniel Kirwa Too KEN 38:13	Christine Junkermann USA 46:07
29 Jul	Phalaborwa HMar	Gert Thys RSA 63:06	Irina Safarova RUS 75:10
30 Jul	Zelenograd HMar	Aleksey Korobov RUS 64:30	Lydia Vasilevskaya RUS 70:23
3 Aug	Hartford 5km	Titus Munji KEN 14:02	Naomi Wangui KEN 16:11
4 Aug	Pombal HMar	Benson Ogato KEN 65:31	Helena Sampaio POR 71:45
5 Aug	Berlin 10km	Carsten Eich GER 29:10	Claudia Dreher GER 32:39
5 Aug	Cape Elizabeth 10km	Joseph Kimani KEN 28:07	Catherine Ndereba KEN 32:19
6 Aug	Bogotá HMar @	Armando Quintanilla MEX 64:20	Martha Tenorio ECU 72:07
6 Aug	Durban HMar	Lahoussine Mrikik MAR 61:09	Milka Chepkieny KEN 74:34
12 Aug	Almaty HMar @	Women only	Garifa Kuku KZK 71:44
12 Aug	Red Bank 5M	Titus Munji KEN 23:05	Catherine Ndereba KEN 26:27
12 Aug	Stockholm 10km	Karl Johan Rasmussen SWE 29:58	Zakia Mrisho TAN 34:32
13 Aug	San Diego HMar	Peter Githuka KEN 62:24	Cristina Pomacu ROM 70:44
15 Aug	Falmouth 7.1M	Mark Yatich KEN 31:43	Lornah Kiplagat KEN 35:02*
19 Aug	Arco 10km	Paul Kosgei ITA 28:16	Men only
19 Aug	Le Touquet 20km	Patrick Tambwen KEN 62:33	Svetlana Demidenko RUS 72:39
19 Aug	Parkersburg HMar	Rod De Haven USA 63:06 (NC)	Libbie Hickman USA 71:01*
19 Aug	Schortens 10M	Julius Maritim KEN 46:45	Milkah Chepkieny KEN 53:07*
19 Aug	Siete Aguas 15.2km	Enock Keter KEN 46:53	María Abel ESP 55:23
20 Aug	Glasgow HMar	António Pinto POR 62:04	Joyce Chepchumba KEN 68:52*
20 Aug	Nottingham 10M	Timothy Cherigat KEN 46:28	Andrea Green GBR 55:57
21 Aug	Rio de Janeiro HMar	John Gwako KEN 61:48*	Margaret Okayo KEN 71:22*
26 Aug	Flint 10M	Mark Yatich KEN 47:36	Catherine Ndereba KEN 53:01
27 Aug	Noosa HMar NC	Scott Westcott AUS 63:03*	Nicky Carroll AUS 72:39*
27 Aug	Pila HMar	Jan Bialk POL 63:38	Dorota Gruca POL 73:03
27 Aug	Zamora HMar	Antonio Peña ESP 63:14	Helena Sampaio POR 70:15
27 Aug	Stockholm 10km	Women only	Marie Lundberg SWE 33:29
27 Aug	Vitoria 10M	Joseph Waweru KEN 47:24	Marcia Narloch BRA 55:52
2 Sep	Charleston 15M	Gideon Mutisya KEN 1:15:29	Svetlana Zakharova RUS 1:27:17*
2 Sep	Lille HMar	Abdellah Béhar FRA 61:30	Nuta Olaru ROM 71:08
3 Sep	Altötting HMar	Christopher Kandie KEN 63:47	Joyce Chepchumba KEN 69:13
3 Sep	Düsseldorf 10km	Tendai Chimusasa ZIM 28:38	Christine Chepkonga KEN 32:36
3 Sep	Heerlen 10M	Wilson Kibet KEN 46:52*	Nadezhda Wijenberg NED 54:11
3 Sep	Ortonovo HMar	Roberto Barbi ITA 62:48	Men only
3 Sep	Ravanusa 10km	Vincenzo Modica ITA 28:11	Men only
3 Sep	Tallinn HMar	Pavel Loskutov EST 63:23	Zivile Balciunaite LIT 75:24
4 Sep	Atlanta 10km	Charles Kamathi KEN 29:05	Catherine Ndereba KEN 34:21
4 Sep	New Haven 20km	William Kiptum KEN 59:43	Lyudmila Petrova RUS 68:38
4 Sep	Park Forest 10M	David Njuguna KEN 47:30	Naomi Wangui KEN 54:36
10 Sep	Bradford 10km	Julius Kimtai KEN 29:06	Esther Kiplagat KEN 33:01
10 Sep	Buenos Aires HMar	Patrik Boiyo KEN 64:57	Cleuza Irineu BRA 77:14
10 Sep	Medellin HMar @	Silvio Guerra ECU 63:13	Ramilya Burangulova RUS 74:15
10 Sep	Parma HMar	Martin Sulle KEN 61:54	Rosalba Console ITA 72:36
17 Sep	Koblenz 23.8km	Isaac Chemobwo KEN 1:15:36	Jana Klimecová CZE 1:28:57
17 Sep	Philadelphia HMar	Khalid Khannouchi USA 61:17	Catherine Ndereba KEN 70:01
17 Sep	Providence 5km	Evans Ruto KEN 13:34	Jane Ngotho KEN 15:50
17 Oct	Torino HMar	Barnabas Rutto KEN 62:41	Hellen Kimutai KEN 69:59
17 Sep	Uster HMar	Sammy Kipruto KEN 63:55	Milkah Chepkieny KEN 72:25
17 Sep	Zaandam HMar	Christopher Cheboiboch KEN 60:49	Lornah Kiplagat KEN 67:37
18 Sep	Guatemala 10km @	Ben Kimondiu KEN 29:25	Jackline Tororo KEN 35:47
23 Sep	Lynchburg 10M	Peter Githuka KEN 47:33	Catherine Ndereba KEN 55:03*
24 Sep	Den Bosch 10km	John Kipchumba KEN 28:43	Christine Chepkonga KEN 32:52

24 Sep	Gargnano HMar	David Rutto KEN 60:44	Galina Zhulyayeva UKR 72:42
24 Sep	Gravellona HMar	Salaho Ngadi TAN 61:53	Margherita Grosso ITA 75:37
24 Sep	Haarlem HMar	Jackson Koech KEN 62:07	Wilma van Onna NED 71:12*
24 Sep	Montbeliard HMar	Robert Cheruiyot KEN 63:13	Mami Kusunoki JPN 72:23
24 Sep	Pittsburgh 10km #	Alene Amere ETH 27:49	Jane Ngotho KEN 32:06
24 Sep	St. Denis HMar	Eduardo Henriques POR 62:20	Klara Kashapova RUS 75:28
24 Sep	Swansea 10km	Laban Kipkemboi KEN 28:17	Grace Misati KEN 33:32
24 Sep	Toronto HMar	Joseph Kamau KEN 64:03	Lucia Subano KEN 73:05
1 Oct	Attleboro 5M	Alene Amere ETH 22:36	Jane Ngotho KEN 25:51
1 Oct	Breda HMar	Jackson Koech KEN 62:11	Simona Staicu ROM 72:50
1 Oct	Fribourg 17.2km	Sammy Kipruto KEN 54:18	Svetlana Nechayeva RUS 64:16
1 Oct	Udine HMar	Japhet Kosgei KEN 60:22	Margaret Okayo KEN 69:03
1 Oct	Versailles 16.3km	Francis Komu KEN 48:45	Isabella Ochichi KEN 54:35
7 Oct	Durham 10km	Julius Kimtai KEN 28:45*	Birhan Dagne ETH 34:08
7 Oct	Port Elizabeth 10km	Shadrack Hoff RSA 28:12	Elana Meyer RSA 32:36
8 Oct	Boston 10km	Women only	Catherine Ndereba KEN 32:46
8 Oct	Groningen 6.7km	Barnard Barmasai KEN 18:25	Lydia Cheromei KEN 20:07*
8 Oct	Youngstown 10km	Thomas Omwenga KEN 28:33	Lucia Subano KEN 33:07
15 Oct	Burnie 10km	Shaun Creighton AUS 29:25	Susan Michelsson AUS 34:13
15 Oct	Chula Vista 10km	Joseph Waweru KEN 28:33	Jane Ngotho KEN 33:01
15 Oct	Guadalajara HMar @	Dominic Ayabuto KEN 63:31	Pamela Chepchumba KEN 73:32
15 Oct	Istanbul 15km	Abdulkadir Türk TUR 45:23	Ebru Kavaklioglu TUR 52:25
15 Oct	Loughrea 5M	John Mayock GBR 23:53	Paula Radcliffe GBR 25:04
15 Oct	Pettinengo 9.8/4km	Paul Kosgei KEN 27:03	Lydia Cheromei KEN 12:36
15 Oct	Remich HMar	Joseph Mereng KEN 62:24	Ikumi Nagayama JPN 70:25
15 Oct	Washington 10M	Sammy Ngatia KEN 48:50	Naoko Ishibe JPN 56:40
20 Oct	Paris 20km	Francis Komu KEN 59:35	Hellen Kimutai KEN 65:28
22 Oct	Lisboa HMar	David Makori KEN 61:40	Derartu Tulu ETH 69:09
22 Oct	Pietramarazzi HMar	Godfrey Nyombi UGA 63:43	Galina Zhulyayeva UKR 74:32
22 Oct	South Shields HMar	Faustin Baha TAN 61:57	Paula Radcliffe GBR 67:07*
22 Oct	Stroud HMar	Laban Kipkemboi KEN 61:50	Liz Yelling GBR 72:31
28 Oct	Ocean City 10M	Paul Mwangi KEN 48:16	Olga Kovpotina RUS 56:11
28 Oct	Tulsa 15km	Simon Rono KEN 43:42	Irina Suvorova RUS 50:22
29 Oct	Cassis 20.3km	David Makori KEN 60:49	Susan Chepkemei KEN 68:30
4 Nov	Heerenburg 15km	Kenisisa Bekele ETH 43:09*	Irma Heeren NED 46:10
4 Nov	Mobile 10km	Scott Strand USA 29:01	Elva Dryer USA 32:53
5 Nov	São Paolo 10km	Elenilson da Silva BRA 29:25	Cleuza Irineu BRA 34:01
5 Nov	Verl HMar	Francis Naali TAN 63:19	Restituta Joseph TAN 72:18
12 Nov	Phoenix 10km	Aurelio Miti ANO 28:58	Gladys Asiba KEN 33:33
19 Nov	Barcelona 9533m/6450m	Driss Lakhouaja MAR 27:59	Fernanda Ribeiro POR 20:50
19 Nov	Belo Horizonte 17.85km	David Cheruiyot KEN 53:13	Cleuza Irineu BRA 61:48
19 Nov	Civitavecchia HMar	Godfrey Nyombi UGA 62:56	Anne Kosgei KEN 77:27
19 Nov	Nijmegen 15km	Felix Limo KEN 42:53	Birhane Adere ETH 48:06*
23 Nov	Manchester CT 4.748M	Mark Carroll IRL 21:19	Amy Rudolph USA 24:26
25 Nov	Basel 10/7.8km	Mike Tanui KEN 28:46	Leah Malot KEN 25:17
26 Nov	Bilbão 14.7km	George Okworo KEN 42:07	Tereza Yohannes ETH 50:05
26 Nov	Chihuahua HMar	Lazarus Nyakeraka KEN 62:34	Pamela Chepchumba KEN 74:17
26 Nov	Monte Carlo 10km	Philip Tanui KEN 28:35	Jackline Jerotich KEN 34:04
26 Nov	Portsmouth 10M	Gert Thys RSA 48:26	Restituta Joseph TAN 55:10
26 Nov	São Paolo 10km	David Cheruiyot KEN 28:46	Leah Kiprono KEN 33:35
3 Dec	Mazatlan HMar	Francisco Ledezma MEX 65:49	Colleen de Reuck RSA 76:48
3 Dec	Okayama HMar	Women only	Mizuki Noguchi JPN 69:44
3 Dec	Tequila HMar	Lazarus Nyakeraka KEN 63:30	Gladys Asiba KEN 76:02
10 Dec	Phoenix 10km	Women only	Milena Glusac USA 33:40
16 Dec	Dronten HMar	Keter Enock Kiptoo KEN 62:14	Irma Heeren NED 73:40
17 Dec	Kobe 20km	Women only	Esther Wanjiru KEN 64:01WB
31 Dec	Bolzano 10.1km/5.07k	John Cheruiyot Korir KEN 28:27	Merima Denboba ETH 16:08
31 Dec	Madrid c.10km	Isaac Viciosa ESP 28:45	Patricia Arriba ESP 32:22
31 Dec	Sâo Paulo 15km	Paul Tergat KEN 43:57	Lydia Cheromei KEN 50:33
31 Dec	Trier 8/5km	Enock Keter Kiptoo KEN 22:47	Lornah Kiplagat KEN 15:15*

@=altitude > 1000m, *=course record, WB=world best, #=> 3m/km downhill

See also Championships section for road races within major championships.

ULTRA SUMMARY 2000

by Andy Milroy

THE PREVIOUSLY dominant Ultrarunning nations beginning to face serious challenges to their superiority in 2000. The strength of Russian ultrarunning was still there in depth but at the highest level it was no longer the force it once was. South Africa, once the power house of the sport, is now being squeezed from its last bastion, the Comrades.

The threat to the Russian dominance came from Japanese runners, who had a breakthrough year, from Western Europeans, continuing the revival of the last two years, Eastern Europe where outstanding runners continued to make a major impact, and from new blood coming into the United States national team. The growth of Ultrarunning continued, particularly in the Far East, where Korea and Nepal joined the other newly emergent ultra nations of the area.

Western Europeans were again to the fore in the World 100km Challenge. Britons Carolyn Hunter-Rowe and Simon Pride had won in '98 and '99 and a newcomer to the sport, Frenchman Pascal Fétizon, was the winner at Winschoten in 2000. Russians Dmitriy Radyuchenko and Oleg Kharitonov were second and third, all running under 6:30, but France took the team title, with the US second. Edit Bérces HUN won the women's race in 7:25:21, from Elvira Kolpakova RUS and Constanze Wagner GER. The German women, always strong, took the team title, from France.

Ranking the top men this year is not easy, but Takahiro Sunada of Japan takes the No.1 spot for producing the best time in the world for 2000 against strong international competition, when he decided to contest the open race held in association with the European Championships at Belvès in France in April. On an undulating course he ran away from a field that included the leading Russians, in 6:17:17. Fétizon is ranked second for his win in the World Challenge in the third best time of the year. The next three runners, the Russians Radyuchenko, Grigoriy Murzin and Farit Ganiyev (European champion and winner at Torhout) are difficult to rank as there is no strong win/loss record to go on. Radyuchenko's second in the World Challenge was his one good run of the year and he was beaten decisively by Murzin when the latter, a former winner of the World Challenge, ran the second fastest time of the year, 6:23:14 in Spain. Ganiyev had the most consistent record of the three, finishing first or second in three of his four 100km races, but only finished fifth in the World Challenge. Radichenko just shades Ganiyev with Murzin fifth. The only other man to better 6:30 was Yasufumi Makimi who ran 6:27:13 at Yufutsu in Japan.

Edit Bérces won every 100km she ran, taking the World and European titles, as well as winning at Torhout and Boston. However she was relegated in to second place on the world list for the year by a performance which caused considerable ripples way beyond the world of Ultrarunning. Tomoe Abe, a former Japanese national record holder for the marathon in 2:26:09, was entered in the Lake Saroma 100km as a training run as part of her preparation for the marathon. Her 100km finishing time was greeted with incredulity when first relayed across the globe. She ran 6:33:11 – over an hour faster than the second placed woman in the World Challenge. The Yufutsu course at Lake Saroma is point to point and there is some evidence that her mark had some limited wind assistance, but this scarcely detracts from Abe's astounding performance. In second place Makiko Hotta ran 7:30:26 but other marks set in the race were not that exceptional.

Abe is clearly No.1 despite the absence of serious international competition at Yufutsu. Her margin of superiority over the rest of the world makes such considerations academic. In second is Bérces, who would have been a clear No.1 in virtually any other year. Kolpakova is third, with Wagner, and Maggliolini taking fourth and fifth places.

At 24 Hours the competition was close, and perhaps because he is growing older, perhaps because he no longer wishes to push himself to the limit, Yiannis Kouros' margin of superiority over the rest of the pack is slowly being eroded. He ran 265km on the track in Verona against limited opposition, which left him just ahead of the next best marks of the year set by Russian Anatoliy Kruglikov at 261km, and by Alain Prual's 260km in the French championships.

The major championship of the year, the European Challenge, was won by the Slovakian, Lubomir Hrmo, with 259km from Andrey

Kazantsev of Russia 257km and Prual's 255km. Kazantsev also won the Russian track championships in 256km. Jean-Pierre Guyomarc'h of France showed great consistency with fourth in the European event, with 254km, just short of his distance in the French championships. My ranking for the event is Kouros first, with Hrmo second, Kazantsev third, and Prual fourth. Kruglikov just shades Guyomarc'h for fifth.

Japan now has several 100km events with over a thousand runners, with over 10,000 ultrarunners competing each year. They have yet, however to take the 24 Hour event seriously, but Kenji Okiyama ran 252.748km on the road in Tokyo, the greatest distance yet achieved in Japan. (Seigi Arita has, of course, run further in France).

The leading woman performer at 24 hours was the consistent Irina Reutovich of Russia who produced three of the four top marks of the year, topped by 230km at the Russian track championships. She then took the European Challenge with 225km and ran 221km as a split in the longer 48 hour event.

The rankings for women match the order of the top five in the European. Joëlle Semur FRA, was second with 219km, Rimma Paltseva RUS third with 216km, Helga Backhaus GER fourth with 215km and Colette Musy fifth with 209km. Paltseva had earlier run the second best distance in the world for the year with 225km on the road in St Petersburg.

There were major races in four continents at 48 hours. Two men went over 400km: Yiannis Kouros, as a split in a 6 day race in Australia, and Jaroslav Kocourek, when he took an international championship event in the Czech Republic dominated by Czechs. Kouros also ran over 400km at Surgères, the most closely contested event of the year with Seigi Arita of Japan running 378km and Roy Pirrung 372km. There were also notable events in Phoenix, Arizona USA and São Paulo in Brazil, both races won by Luciano dos Santos of Brazil.

The top female 48 hour performer was Irina Reutovich, whose 368km (from Helga Backhaus 333km) in the indoor international race at Brno was the second best mark of all-time. She subsequently won at Köln with 337km. The other top performer was Susan Olsen of the United States who won at Surgères with 332km.

An unusual 72 hour race held at Devanter, Netherlands was won by Hans Peter Heise of Germany with 500.461km, with Dutch woman Ria Buiten the first woman with 449.117km

The top 6 Day mark of the year came in the New York road race where David Luljak ran 807km from Rimas Jakelaitis of Lithuania 804, and the top women's mark by the Anglo-Australian Catherine Dipali Cunningham 733.8km. Yiannis Kouros ran 801km at Colac in Australia.

The best 1000 mile mark of the year came in New York when Lithuanian Rimas Jakelaitis ran a pending world road best of 11d 23:07:21. The 1000 mile track championships at Nanango in Queensland had a small field and was won by Petras Silkinas of Lithuania with 13d 05:36:20 with Martina Hausmann of Germany recording 14d 22:22:42. However for some such a race is just not long enough and Pekka Aalto of Finland won the world's longest certified footrace, the Sri Chinmoy 3100-Miler. He completed 5000km in 47d 16:05:13

The 50th London to Brighton had one of the strongest fields for some years. The course record holder Sarel Akermann RSA produced a fine 5:56:50 to win, with four time winner Stephen Moore GBR a distant second in 6:24:17 and Danny de Chaumont RSA third in 6:33:26. The women's race was won by Danielle Sanderson GBR 7:07:12 from Karen Bradford RSA 7:16:24 and Hilary Walker GBR 8:17:23.

There was further erosion of South African superiority in the 75th Comrades race from Durban to Pietermaritzburg as for the first time ever there was no South African in the top three in the men's event, and their first woman was only third. The level of prize money assured a very competitive race with a strong international field. Russian born Vladimir Kotov, twenty years after he narrowly missed a medal in the Moscow Olympic marathon in 2:10:58, came through strongly at the end of the 90km race to break the course record by nearly a minute. His 5:25:33 put him well clear of two more Russians, Aleksey Volgin 5:27:07 and Dmitriy Grishin 5:32:47.

The women's race was dominated by German Maria Bak, back after a two year suspension for doping. Her time of 6:15:35 was close to the course record and put her well clear of her fellow country woman, the 1999 winner Birgit Lennartz 6:33:54. Third was Grace de Oliveira RSA in 6:38:44. The race was the biggest ultrarunning event ever with 23,961 registered and 20,046 finishers within the 12 hour deadline.

There was a Japanese double in the Spartathlon in Greece. Masayuki Otaki took an early lead to win in 24:01:10, almost an hour ahead of the 1999 winner Jens Lukas GER 24:59:54 with Cees Verhagen NED third in 25:35:60. First woman was Hiroko Okiyama in 29:16:37, with the former US runner Mary Larsson second in 30:56:16 and Helga Backhaus third in 31:35:24. 88 runners from 14 countries finished within the 36-hour time limit.

OBITUARY 2000

See also Athletics 2000 *for* Auden BOYSEN, Henry ERIKSSON, Mae FAGGS, Masao HARADA, John LJUNGGREN, Edith PEACOCK, Raphaël PUJAZON and Masami YOSHIDA.

Hyginus ANUGO (Nigeria) (b. 29 Nov 1977) was knocked down and killed by a car while crossing the road to catch a bus in Sydney on 7 September. The fiancée of Glory Alozie, he had a 400m best of 45.89 (1999).

Serge AVEDISSIAN (France) (25 Mar 1964 Yerevan, USSR) was killed during a training session at Colombes in April when he was hit on the head by a flying 10kg hammer while he was recovering his discus). French discus champion in 1987, pb 59.96 (1987).

George BAILEY (UK) (b. 29 April 1906). He was the inaugural Empire Games champion at the steeplechase (9:52.0 for less than 2 miles) in 1930 and at the 2 miles steeplechase won the AAA title at that event in 1930 and 1935 and had a best of 10:14.8 in 1932 and 1935. He set a UK 3000m steeplechase record with 9:16.0 in the heats of the 1932 Olympics in Los Angeles, and crossed the line at that distance in the final in second place only to fade to 5th as the athletes had, wrongly, to run an extra lap. He also won the 1933 AAA 10 miles in 50:51.0; that would have been a UK record, but the track was found to be 4 ft 4 ins short per lap (also 30:08.4 at 6 miles in this race). He represented England in the International Cross-country Championships five times between 1930 and 1937, with a best of 5th in 1932 and 1933. Other bests: 2M 9:27.8 (1932), 5000m 15:36.8 (1933), Mar 2:40:14 (1936).

GÖSTA BJÖRKMAN (Sweden) (b. 17 Mar 1924) on 14 March. Probably one of the oldest national champions of all time. In 1987, at age 63, he placed 4th in the Swedish 50 km walking championship and belonged to the winning team of Mälarhöjdens IK in the 3-men team scoring.

Dieter BOGATZKI (Germany) (b. 25 Jan 1942 Konitz) in December. His two finest achievements were placing 7th in the 1964 Olympic 800m, the first European finisher, and contributing to a world 4x800m relay record of 7:08.6 in 1966 along with German team-mates Manfred Kinder, Walter Adams and Franz-Josef Kemper. Eight internationals 1964-6. Pbs: 400m 48.3 (1963), 800m 1:46.5 (1966), 1000m 2:21.1 (1965), 1500m 3:49.6 (1966).

Kurt BONAH (Germany) (b. 18 Sep 1928 Detmold) on 12 July in Koblenz. German champion at 400mh 1954 and 1956. 22 internationals 1951-6 including 1954 European Championships. Pbs: 400m 47.9 (1955), 800m 1:52.0 (1951), 400mh 51.5 (German record, 1954).

Rod BONELLA (Australia) following a long fight with cancer, aged 63. He was the 1962 Commonwealth Games marathon bronze medallist (behind Brian Kilby and Dave Power) in 2:24:07.

Eric BORCHMEYER (Germany) (b 23 Jan 1905 Münster) on 17 August in Bielefeld. At the Olympics he was a silver medallist in 1932 and bronze in 1936 at 4x100m, semi-finalist at 200m in 1932 and 5th at 100m in 1936. At the 1934 Europeans he was 2nd at 100m and was a member of the winning German 4x100m team. In 1933 he unofficially equalled the world 100m record of 10.3, and did so again on two occasions in 1934. He ran on the German 4x100m teams that set a world record in 1932 and a European record 40.1 in 1939 and also set a German record for 200m (turn) with 21.4 in 1929. German champion 100m 1933-5 and 1937; 200m 1933; 19 internationals 1930-8.

Annual progression at 100m, 200m (° half turn): 1927- 22.3, 1928- 10.7, 22.0; 1929- 10.6/10.4dh, 21.4°; 1930- 10.6, 21.5; 1931- 10.6, 21.6°; 1932- 10.5, 21.7; 1933- 10.3, 21.4°/21.5; 1934- 10.3, 21.5; 1935- 10.5/10.4w, 21.4; 1936- 10.5/10.3dh, 21.7; 1937- 10.5, 21.8; 1938- 10.6, 21.9; 1939- 10.5, 22.5; 1940- 10.8. Other pbs: 60m 6.7i (1936), 300m 34.3 (1931), 400m 49.1 (1935), LJ 7.19 (1930), 7.24w (1929); TJ 14.90 (1936).

LEIF CHRISTERSSON (Sweden) (b. 22 Jan 1932 Eksjö) on 14 December. He was a member of the Swedish 4x100 m team which placed a surprising 3rd in the 1950 European championships. Still a junior he was Swedish champion in 1950 (100 m) and 1951 (200 m). He participated in eight international matches 1950-6. In 1959 he ran in the Bromma IF team, which won the Swedish 4x400 m championship. Pbs: 100m 10.6 (1956), 200m 21.7 (1958), 400m 48.9 (1958).

Josep COROMINAS (Spain) (b. 22 Nov 1912) on 27 October in L'Hospitalet de Llobregat. A statistician since 1930, he was a long-time ATFS and AEEA member and a respected sports journalist. He was President of the Catalonian Athletics Federation and Vice-President of the Spanish Federation (RFEA).

Dr **Max DANZ** (Germany) (b. 6 Sep 1908 Kassel) on 20 June. He was 2nd in the German 800m in 1931 and 1932 and ran at the 1932 Olympics. At the World University Games he was 3rd in 1930 and 2nd in 1933 at 800m and won a gold and two silver medals at relays. Pbs: 400m 48.8 (1929), 800m 1:52.6 (1934). He was for many years one of the world's leading officials. He was President of the DLV 1949-70, a member of the European Committee of the IAAF 1952-76, a founder EAA Council Member 1970, IAAF Council Member 1956-81 and IAAF Honorary Life Vice President from 1981.

Peter DENTON (Australia) (b. 10 Jun 1926) on 3 December in Sydney. The Commonwealth Games bronze medallist at pole vault in 1950 and 8th in 1954, he also competed at the 1956 Olympic Games. Australian champion 1949-50 and 1952-3. pb 4.04 (1954).

Helen FILKEY (later Warren, then De Vrye) USA) (b. 18 Mar 1908) on 24 November. She was AAU champion at 60yh 1925-8 and 80mh 1929, adding two further titles in 1925 (100y and LJ) when she was aged 17. Her 16 US outdoor records included two at 100y 11.6 (1923) and 11.4 (1925), three at 60 yards hurdles to 8.0 in 1928, four at 80mh to 12.3 in 1931 and three at long jump to 5.19 in 1925.

David GUINEY (Ireland) (b. 31 Jan 1921) on 14 October in Dublin. He won the AAA shot title in 1947 and 1948 and represented Ireland in the London Olympic Games in 1948. He broke the Irish record several times, with a best of 15.19 in 1953, and was ranked number one in Ireland each year from 1943 to 1956. He became a leading sports journalist and wrote many books on sport, including athletics and the Olympics.

Hideo HAMAMURA (Japan) (b. Jul 1928) of cancer on 7 May in Hofu, Yamaguchi prefecture. He won the 1953 Asahi Marathon (held in Nagoya that year) in 2:27:26, and the 1955 Boston marathon in 2:18:22 (the course was short). He was 16th in the 1956 Olympic Games marathon and 5th in the 1958 Asian Games, and later took up coaching

Takahiro HATTORI (Japan) (b. 27 Nov 1971) in a car accident on 29 June. He was 40th at marathon in the 1997 World Championships after running a pb 2:10:21 for 2nd in the Tokyo marathon.

Leonard HILTON (USA) (b. 28 Sep 1947) on 3 July in Houston of pancreatic cancer. He ran in the 1972 Olympic 5000m after 3rd in the US Trials in a pb 13:40.2 and won the US 1 mile 1973 and 1500m 1975 and the indoor 3 miles in 1972. He was the first Texas-born athlete to break four minutes for the mile. Other pbs: 800m 1:48.7 (1973), 1500m 3:36.4 (1974), 1M 3:55.9 (1973), 2M 8:35.6 (1972), 3M 13:04.4 (1972), 6M 28:30.4 (1972).

Teruo ITOKAWA (Japan) (b. 20 Oct 1940) on 4 October in Tokyo. Asian Games champion in 1962 and Japanese champion 1961 and 1962 at the shot, at which he set five Japanese records from 15.54 in 1962 to 16.23 in 1964.

Helmut JANZ (Germany) (b. 11 Apr 1934 Gladbeck) on 19 November. He placed fourth (behind three Americans) in the 1960 Olympic 400 hurdles in 49.9 (50.04) to become the first European to break 50 sec (on hand timing). This was his fifth German record (from 51 5 in 1957). He was European bronze medallist in 1962. He made 53 international appearances for FR Germany 1955-64 and was German champion at 400mh 1957-63.

Annual progression at 400mh (position on world list): 1954- 55.4, 1955- 53.2 (39=), 1956- 51.8 (16=), 1957- 51.5 (8=), 1958- 50.9 (6), 1959- 51.0 (5). 1960- 49.9 (6=), 1961- 50.2 (4), 1962- 50.4 (6), 1963- 49.9 (2), 1964- 51.1 (28=), 1965- 53.5, 1966- 54.1. Other pbs: 400m 47.8 (1960), 800m 1:51.9 (1961), 1000m 2:26.0 (1957).

Aleksandr KLIMENKO (Ukraine) (b 27 Mar 70) died on 7 March in Kiev three weeks before his 30th birthday, allegedly murdered. At the shot he won the World Junior title in 1988, European Juniors 1989, World University Games 1991 and 1993 and Europeans 1994. He was 2nd at the 1992 European Indoors and 1994 World Cup, 3rd at the 1991 World Championships and 8th at the 1992 Olympics. He set his personal best of 20.84 to win the Ukrainian title in 1992.

Henry LASKAU (USA) (b. 12 Sep 1916 Berlin) on 7 May. He was a 1500m runner in Germany before, as a Jew, fleeing the country in 1938. He moved to the United States and served in the US Army during World War II before starting his competitive walking career in 1946. His total of 42 national titles (1947-57) is one of the highest on record. He competed in the 1948, 1952 and 1956 Olympic Games, placing 12th at 20k in 1956. He was 1951 Pan American Games 10km champion and also was a four-time winner at the Maccabiah Games in Israel. During an 11-year career, he set five national records, and during nine years of that period he was unbeaten by any American. He remained active as an official in the sport. Pbs: 10,000mW 46:45.0 (1951), 20kmW 1:37:04 (1952), 1:32:01 short? (1956).

Nic LEMMENS (Netherlands) (b. 11 July 1916 Maastricht) on 10 May at Waalre. A high jumper and long jumper as a young man, he was a member of the council of the KNAU 1948-67, particularly active as a cross-country promoter and international team manager. For 35 years he was the editor of the Dutch athletic magazine *de Atletiekwereld* and he was an ATFS member from 1969.

Håkan LIDMAN (Sweden) (b.31 Jan 1915 Göteborg) on 6 June. His first effort at 110m low hurdles was 16.8 and a week later, in September 1933, he won the Swedish schools title in 16.1. On 11 May 1934 he at once improved to 15.3 and ten days later at the British Games against top class hurdlers confirmed that he was already established at international level. From that year he dominated his event for several years winning the Swedish 110mh title 14 times (1934-45 and 1947-8) as well as winning his event in his 21 appearances in Sweden's 22 international matches 1935-48 (after 2 in 1934). In 1946 he stayed away from the Swedish championships and an international match, protesting against the way in which the amateur issue had been handled. However he won the 1946 European title (after 2nd in 1938). In the Olympic Games he was 4th in 1936 and 6th in 1948. His 1940 European record of 14.0 was not beaten until 1956. He won Swedish Championships medals also in other events: as a member of Örgryte IS he won at 4x100m in 1941 and won another 5 medals in 4x100 m and 4x400 m and three medals at Standing HJ. In 1943 he placed 2nd in the 200 m behind Lennart Strandberg.

Annual progression: 1933- 16.8; 1934- 14.9; 1935- 14.6; 1936- 14.3; 1937- 14.5; 1938- 14.3; 1939- 14.2; 1940- 14.0; 1941- 14.2; 1942- 14.2; 1943- 14.3; 1944- 14.5; 1945- 14.3; 1946- 14.5; 1947- 14.0; 1948- 14.4; 1949- 15.4; 1954- 15.3. Other pbs: 100m 10.9 (1943), 200m 22.2 (1943), 200mh 24.0 (1943, Swedish record), 400mh 58.2 (1937), Standing HJ 1.55 (1938).

Jacobus F **'Poena' MALAN** (South Africa) (b. 28 Jul 1935) died after suffering a heart attack at his home in Dana Bay, in the Southern Cape on 2 July. Between 1958 and 1962 he won four SA titles at 120yh, 220yh in 1958 and decathlon in 1957. He equalled the national record of 14.1 for 120yh at the Commonwealth Games trials in Durban in 1958, but fell in his semi-final at the Games in Cardiff. In 1961 he set a SA record at 110mh with 14.2. His first wife, Gale won three SA titles in 1962 (100y, 220y and 80mh). In later years he suffered many setbacks with his health and had both his legs amputated. Other pbs: 220yh half turn 23.4 (1959), 440yh 53.0A (1958), LJ 7.21A (1959).

Norma MARSH (b. 11 Dec 1909, née Wilson) on 11 July. New Zealand's first Olympic track and field athlete (100m semis at Amsterdam 1928). In the late 1920s and early 1930s she was reputed to have equalled or broke the official world records for 100y with times of 11.2w, 11.2 (track 7 inches short), 11.2 (valid, but NZ not affiliated with the FSFI), 11.2 and 11.0 (both downhill). She was NZ champion in 1928 and 1933. She was formerly married to the boxer Ted Morgan, welterweight gold medallist at Amsterdam.

Prof Dr **Eberhard MUNZERT** (Germany) (b. 23 Mar 1932 Hannover) on 9 April. President of the German Athletics Federation (DLV) 1985-8 and member European AA Council 1987-8.

Seikan OKI (Japan) (b. 14 Jan 1907) on 19 October in Saitama prefecture. He was a member of Japanese 4x400m team that finished fifth (3:14.6) in the 1932 Olympic Games in Los Angeles, where he was also a quarter-finalist at 400m.

Julius ONDIEKI (Kenya) (b. 10 Jul 69) in December of liver disease. He was a member of Kenya's winning team in the 1995 World Cross Country Championships, finishing 15th, and had pbs: 5000m 13:19.73 (1995), 10,000 27:45.47 (1996), Mar 2:13:16 (1998).

Karl-Heinz PAPE (Germany) (b. 23 Apr 1939) on 16 February. German champion at 20km walk in 1962 and 1966-7 and at 50km in 1965. In the European Championships he was 14th in 1962 and 11th in 1966 at 20km. FRG records: 5000m 22:04.6 (1960), 10000m 45:18.6 (1966), 20km 1:30:46 (1965) and 1:29:18.0 (1967). pb 50km 4:27:12.8 (1965).

Sam PERRY (USA) at Southport, Connecticut on 18 July aged 55. In 1965 he twice equalled Bob Hayes' world indoor 60 yards record of 5.9. He was AAU indoor champion at 60y in 1963 and 1965. Outdoors he had a 100y best of 9.4 in 1963.

William Franklin **'Bill" PORTER** (USA) (b. 24 Mar 1926 Jackson, Michigan) on 10 March at Irvine, California. Following graduation from the Hill School in Pottstown, Pa., Porter was at Western Michigan University 1944-5 and then transferred to Northwestern, where he graduated in 1947 with a degree in business administration. Having fared best at 220yh in 1945-6, in 1947 he was second to Harrison Dillard in the NCAAs, held at altitude in Salt Lake City, at 120yh (improving his pb from 14.1 to 14.0 in a heat) and at 220y hurdles (straight track) when he tied the former world record of 22.5 in placing second to Dillard's 22.3. He had earlier beaten Dillard in Los Angeles at this event, 22.7 to 22.8. Dillard, who had set a world 120y record of 13.6 in April 1948 and had chalked up 82 consecutive victories, was considered a certainty to lift the Olympic title in London... but he slammed into several hurdles at the US Olympic Trials, failed to finish and had to content himself with selection for his second-string event, the 100m (which he went on to win!). Porter, who had been second in 13.8w to Clyde Scott's 13.7w at the NCAAs, won at the US Trials in 13.9 and duplicated that time at Wembley for an Olympic record in leading an American clean sweep of the medals. He was employed for many years by American Hospital Supply in Kenilworth, Illinois, ending as Executive Vice President.

Progression at 110mh/120yh (position on world list): 1944- 14.9y (13=), 1947- 14.0yA (2=), 1948- 13.8w/13.9 (3).

John Wilson **'Paddy' PROCTOR** (GBR) (b. 3 Sep 1923 Ballyclare) on 26 October. In 1950 he was fifth in the European 50km walk after setting a pb 4:43:04 to win the RWA title in Sheffield, where he was a member of the local club. He also won the RWA 20 miles in 1952.

Mona-Lisa PURSIAINEN (Finland) (née Strandvall, b. 21 Jun 1951), on 7 August after fighting breast cancer for many years. Finland´s greatest woman sprinter, she won 41 Finnish Championships medals, including 14 golds individually (nine at 100m 1967-70 and 1973-7, four at 200m 1967-70, one at 400m 1970) and 12 in relays for Gamlakarleby IF teams. Against Sweden, she had 44 races 1966-78, including 100m every year. A sports teacher and later mother of three children, she ran Finnish records 22 times from 1966, improving at 100m from 12.0 in 1966 to 11.19, at 200m from 24.6 in 1968 to 22.39 at the Moscow Universiade – just 0.01 from Renate Stecher´s world record, still intact as a national record 27 years later – and three at 400m 52.53 in 1972 to 51.27, all the bests in her big year of 1973, when she was elected Sportsman of the Year in Finland (the first woman to have this honour).

Besides her 100 and 200m Universiade victories in 1973, Pursiainen took 200m bronze and 4x400m silver (running her leg in 49.5) at the 1974 European Championships in Rome. She also competed in the 1969, 1971 and 1978 Europeans and 1972 and 1976 Olympic Games. Her husband Pauli Pursiainen was the Finnish 110H champion in 1972-3. Her uncle Börje Strandvall just missed the 400m Olympic final in 1932, and 1946 European 400m hurdles champion Bertel Storskrubb was also a relative.

Michael Arthur **'Mike' RAWSON** (GBR) (b. 26 May 1934 Hall Green, Birmingham) on 26 October in Birmingham. His greatest success came at the 1958 European Championships when he took the gold medal at 800m in 1:47.8; but not before a traumatic time as he was at first disqualified for leaving the track; he had been swept off in the stampede for the first bend in a rough race (before the runners in 800m races ran the first 110m in lanes). He had recovered from that to run with great judgement and sped from 4th to 1st in the final 20m of the race. The Jury of Appeal named him as champion after an agonizing two hours. Earlier that year he had taken the bronze medal at 880y at the Empire Games and he went on to run a personal best for 800m of 1:47.0 just behind Brian Hewson (who had won the European 1500m) for Britain against France. A member of Birchfield Harriers, he was a semi-finalist at the 1956 Olympics and AAA champion at 880y in 1956 before 2nd each year 1957-9. He won seven times in 14 international appearances for Britain at 800m 1956-9 and then had a 15th international at 400m indoors in 1965 after winning the AAA indoor 440y title. He set a British indoor record for 880y with 1:54.5 in New York in 1959. He became a respected coach and broadcaster.

Annual progression at 800m (* 880y time les 0.7 secs): 1949- 2:27.3*, 1950- 2:20.5*, 1951- 2:13.3*, 1952- 2:06.5*, 1953- 2:02.3*, 1954- 1:56.0*, 1955- 1:53.5*, 1956- 1:49.7, 1957- 1:47.5, 1958- 1:47.0, 1959- 1:48.6*, 1960- 1:50.3*, 1961- 1:50.7, 1962- 1:53.3*, 1964- 1:50.4*, 1965- 1:51.2*. Other pbs: 440y 47.6 (1957), 600y 1:11.6i (1959), 1000m 2:23.2 (1957).

RHADI ben Abdesselem (Morocco) (b. 28 Feb 1929 Ksar-es-Sauk) at Fez on 4 October. The International cross country champion in 1960, later that year he was second 25 sec behind Abebe Bikila in the Rome Olympics marathon in 2:15:42, his only race at the distance. This was two days after placing 14th in the 10,000m. He had three other top 20 placings in the International CC: 1958- 15, 1959- 8, 1962- 10. On the track he had bests (all in 1960) of: 10,000m 29:20.8, 10M 48:17.4, 1 Hour 19,907m.

Edith Frances **'Edie' ROBINSON/PAYNE** (Australia) (b. 26 Sep 1906) on 7 October in Sydney just weeks after she cut the ribbon to open the Olympic Village as Australia's oldest Olympian. Edie Robinson competed in the 100m (semis) and 800m (dnf ht) at the Amsterdam Games of 1928, the first Olympics with women's athletics events. She attended the Opening Ceremony in Sydney with her granddaughter Kylie Sutton, who said: "She was sick early this year, but I think she was keeping herself going just for the Olympics. She was very emotional." She was national champion at 100y in 1935 and 220y in 1935-6 and set AUS records for 220y: 26.2 (twice) in 1929 to 25.6 in 1932. Other pbs: 100y 11.0 (1934), 440y 61.0 (1933).

Mabel ROBINSON (Australia) (b. 23 Jan 1909, née Moad) on 18 January in Melbourne. President of the Australian Women's AAU from 1962 to 1978 when this union amalgamated with the men's. She was then Vice-President of Athletics Australia 1978-83. She was the Australian 880y walk champion in 1933 and second in the next three championships; she was an official from 1931 to 1997.

Matthew **Mack ROBINSON** (USA) (b. 18 Jul 1914 Cairo, Georgia) on 12 March in Pasadena, California. At the 1936 Olympics in Berlin, Robinson won the 200m silver medal in 21.1, four metres behind Jesse Owens. After the Games he went to the University of Oregon and had career bests of 100m 10.4 (1936), 200m 20.8 (1936) and long jump 7.76 (1937). In 1938 he won the NCAA 220y and AAU 200m titles. In 1947 his younger brother Jackie Robinson became the first African American major league baseball player of the 20th century.

Mack wasn't considered an athletic prospect when he attended John Muir Technical High School in Pasadena. Doctors had warned that athletics participation could be fatal due to a heart condition. Undaunted, he developed into a star sprinter and long jumper and after he set several junior college records local businessmen paid Robinson's way to the 1936 US Olympic Trials in New York, where, in the 200m final, he took the lead with 75m to go and held it until Owens flew past him 40m from the finish. Owens finished first in American record time of 21.0, with Robinson second in 21.3.

Ernst SCHMIDT (Germany) (b. 1 Feb 1920 Garsebach) on 15 September in Oranienburg. He was German champion in 1942 at pentathlon and decathlon – with a world's best score for the year of 7280 points (6802 on current tables). He won 11 GDR titles: 6 at shot, 4 at discus, 1 at decathlon between 1949 and 1954 and set 22 GDR records, 12 at shot from 13.35 in 1949 to 15.85 in 1952, 8 at discus from 39.20 in 1949 to 46.24 in 1954, and 2 at decathlon. 6320 in 1950 and 6484 in 1951. Other pbs: 100m 11.2 (1941), 400m 49.8 (1942), 110mh 15.8 (1942), HJ 1.81 (1942), PV 3.50 (1942), LJ 7.25 (1942), HT 46.51 (1953), JT 57.78 (1952). He became a coach and was the father of Wolfgang Schmidt, who set a world discus record of 71.16 in 1978.

Satoru SHIMIZU (Japan) (b. 13 Aug 1963) on 14 October due to sudden heart failure in Hofu, Yamaguchi prefecture. He was second in the 1990 Asian Games in Beijing and set a personal best of 2:12:26 when he won the 1989 Beppu-Oita Mainichi marathon. He was also sixth in the 1990 Tokyo Marathon in 2:12:49.

Barbara SOBOTTA (Poland) (b. 4 Dec 1936 Poznan, née Lerczak, then Janiszewska) on 20 November in Kraków. She first competed at the European Championships in 1954, fourth at 200m, then in Stockholm in 1958 she won the gold medal for 200m and bronze for 4x100m, and in 1962 she took bronze medals at 200m and 4x100m. She took part in three Olympic Games, with a relay bronze in 1960 and at 200m fifth in 1960 and sixth in 1964. Running for AZS Poznan and later AZS Kraków, she won 14 Polish titles: 100m (4) 1953-4, 1957-8, 200m (10) 1953-5 and 1957-63; she also set Polish records for 100m 11.4 (1963) and 200m 23.6 (1964). Besides her athletic talent she was also known for her beauty. She married three times, to Zbigniew Janiszewski (PV), Piotr Sobotta (HJ) and Jan Nowicki (famous Polish actor). In the last years of her life she ran a cafe at one of the famous theatres in Kraków.

Annual progression at 100m, 200m (position on world list, all=): 1952- 12.4, 26.6; 1953- 12.5, 25.4; 1954- 12.1 (33), 24.4 (8); 1955- 12.1 (54), 24.6 (18); 1956- 11.8 (29), 23.8 (6); 1957- 12.0 (44), 24.1 (9); 1958- 11.6 (5), 23.9 (8); 1959- 11.9 (48), 24.2 (16); 1960- 11.7 (22), 23.6 (4); 1961- 11.8 (28), 24.1 (10); 1962- 11.6 (7), 23.8 (7); 1963- 11.4 (2), 24.2 (30); 1964- 11.6/11.84 (20), 23.6/23.97 (10). Pb 80mh 11.0 (1960).

Endre SZABÓ (Hungary) (b. 25 Apr 1913 Nagykörös) on 20 March in Stockholm, where he had been living since several decades. He was Hungarian 110m hurdles champion in 1938 and 1939, pb 14.8w/14.9 (both in 1941).

Miklós SZABÓ (Hungary) (b. 6 Dec 1908 Budapest) in Budapest on 3 December. He won the 1934 European 800m title ahead of Mario Lanzi and was second in the 1500m to Luigi Beccali. He placed 7th in the 1936 Olympic 1500m (and semi-finalist at 800m) and set world records at 2000m (5:20.4 in 1936) and 2 miles (8:56.0 in 1937), and a European 1500m record of 3:48.6 in 1937. He set a total of 23 Hungarian records and won 16 national titles: 800m 1933-7, 1500m 1929-30, 1932-7; 5000m 1943, 3000mSt 1944, CC 1934. Other pbs: 800m 1:52.0 (1934), 1000m 2:25.8 (1936), 1M 4:16.2 (1937), 3000m 8:17.8 (1937), 5000m 14:33.8 (1937), 10,000m 30:47.2 (1940), 3000mSt 9:39.6 (1941). He coached in Sweden between 1947 and 1980.

Annual progression at 800m, 1500m, 5000m (position on world list); 1927- 1:59.2, 4:11.6; 1928- 1:58.4, 1929- 4:00.4 (14), 1930- 3:59.8 (13), 1931- 1:58.2, 4:03.6 (48=), 16:15.0; 1932- 1:56.0, 3:59.2 (24=), 15:15.0 (38); 1933- 1:54.4 (29=), 3:52.6 (4); 1934- 1:52.0 (6), 3:55.1 (11); 1935- 1:54.8 (61=), 3:59.2 (46); 1936- 1:53.9 (36=), 3:53.0 (9=), 14:39.4 (10); 1937- 1:53.2 (34=), 3:48.6 (1), 14:33.8 (7); 1938- 3:53.4 (15=), 14:35.6 (6); 1939- 3:53.6

(17), 14:52.4 (38); 1940- 1:53.8 (37=), 3:52.8 (9=), 14:48.6 (26); 1941- 1:56.0, 3:52.6 (9=), 14:55.0 (38); 1942- 3:56.6 (48=), 14:48.2 (22=); 1943- 3:56.8 (34), 14:40.2 (9).

Per-Owe TROLLSÅS (Sweden) (b. 18 Jan 1933 Nässkott) on 5 November. Silver medallist in the 1958 European Championships at 400m hurdles after running his best ever time of 51.0 in the semi-finals. He was Swedish 100 m champion in 1952 and 1953 and participated in 6 international matches. He came back for another 20 international matches from 1956 to 1961 and soon concentrated on the 400m hurdles, at which he was Swedish champion 1957-60 and also competed at the 1960 Olympic Games. In 1958 he was Swedish 4x400 m champion with Bromma IF. Pbs: 100m 10.6 (1956)/10.3w (1957), 200m 21.6 (1958), 400 m 47.8 (1958), 800 m 1:55.0 (1958), 110mh 15.3 (1957), 200mh 23.7 (1961, Swedish record), 400mh 51.0 (1958), LJ 7.03w (1957).

Camille VIALE (France) (b. 28 Apr 1947) of cancer at Saint-Etienne on 15 April. He was French national coach for road running and a former national middle distance coach. He was an international in 1966-7. Pbs: 1000m 2:22.0 (1973), 1500m 3:43.9 (1972).

Petar VUKOVIC (Yugoslavia) (b. 12 Jun 1922) on 9 March in Belgrade. 12th at the European Championships in 1946, he was the Yugoslav high jump champion in 1945 and 1947, and set national records at 1.88 (1946) and 1.89 (1947).

Perrin WALKER (USA) (b. 27 Sep 1912) at Lawrenceville, Georgia on 17 July. AAU champion at 100m in 1937 and twice placed at 200m – 2nd 1938, 3rd 1939. He tied the world indoor 60y record at 6.1 in 1938. Pbs: 100y 9.6 (1936), 100m 10.4 (1937), 200m half turn 20.9 (1938), 220y straight 20.8 (1936)

Jack WEIERSHAUSER (USA) (b. 21.12.1915) in San Diego on 19 May. He anchored Stanford University's world record breaking 4x200m/4x220y relay team (1:25.0 in 1937) and was American AAU 220 yards champion and 2nd in the NCAA 220y in 1937. That year he was second on the world list at 200m with 20.9 and he ran 20.7 for 220y on a straight track and an estimated 47.9 for 440y. He had been 4th in the 1936 NCAA 400m. He later became head coach at Washington State University and Stanford.

Mildred WILEY (USA) (b. 3 Dec 1901 Taunton, Mass) in Bourne, Massachusetts on 7 February at the age of 98. She won the bronze medal in the 1928 Olympic high jump with a pb 1.56, when she tied for second behind the world record 1.59 of Canada's Ethel Catherwood but lost a jump-off against Carolina Gisolf of the Netherlands. Standing 1.81m, she was AAU champion indoors in 1927-8 and outdoors in 1928.

Harry WILLIAMSON (USA) (b. 11 July 1913) on 8 April in Charlotte, North Carolina. 4th in 1934 and 2nd in 1935 in the NCAA 1 mile while at the University of North Carolina, he went on take 3rd place in the US Olympic Trials in 1936, finishing with a great rush, and then to place 6th in the Olympic 800m. In his last race he ran the third leg for the USA against the British Empire on the 4x880y team that set a world record of 7:35.8 at the White City Stadium, London. Pbs: 800m 1:51.2 (1936), 1M 4:15.3 (1934).

Vern WOLFE (USA) on 25 October in Fallbrook, California at the age of 78. He guided the University of Southern California to seven men's NCAA championships (outdoors 1963, 1965, 1967-8, 1976; indoors 1967. 1972) during his 22 years as coach 1963-84. He coached six Olympic champions: Dallas Long, Rex Cawley, Mike Larrabee, Bob Seagren, Randy Williams and Don Quarrie.

Rie YAMAUCHI (Japan) (b. 15 Feb 1922) on 8 October in Kyoto. Set six Japanese records at high jump from 1.55 in 1936 to 1.63 in 1946 (record stood until 1959) and two records at long jump in 1947: 6.01 (beating Kinue Hitomi's 5.98, a world record in 1928) and 6.07 (stood until 1961). She won five Japanese titles at both HJ (1939-40, 1942, 1946 and 1951) and LJ (1939, 1942, 1946-8) as well as 200m 1942, shot 1946 and pentathlon 1947.

Emil ZATOPEK (Czech Republic) (b. 19 Sep 1922 Koprivnice, Moravia) on 21 November in Prague.

Zátopek was a running genius, whose dedicated hard work brought him unprecedented success. His seemingly agonised, head-rolling gait belied his control and indeed his charming personality. In 1948 he won the Olympic gold medal at 10,000m and silver at 5000m, when he left his sprint finish far too late, and in 1952 he completed a unique triple with wins at both these events and the marathon in his first attempt at the distance. In his last Olympic appearance he was 6th in the 1956 marathon.

His first Czech records were set in 1944 and he was national champion eight times at 5000m and twice at 10,000m. He won his first 38 races at 10,000m from 1948 to 1954, including the European titles of 1950 and 1954, and in his whole career won 261 of 334 races at all distances. At 5000m he was 5th in the Europeans of 1946, 1st in 1950 and 3rd in 1954. At his peak supremacy, the three years 1949-51, he won all 69 races at various distances and was far superior to anyone else in the world. In all he set 18 world records: five at 10,000 from 29:28.2 in 1949 to 28:54.2 in 1954, the latter just one day after he had run a world record 13:57.2 for 5000m; two each at 6 miles, 20km, 1 hour, 15 miles, and 25km; and one each at 10 miles and 30km. At Stara Boleslav in 1951 he became the first to run more than 20km in an hour, 59:51.6 at 20km and 20,052m in all, passing 10 miles in a record 48:12.0.

Zátopek was a national hero, but his support for the 'Prague Spring' cost him his Communist Party membership and his rank as a colonel in the army. He was sent to work in a uranium mine for six years, but after this hardship he returned to public life, his indomitable spirit triumphing as always. The government employed him to work for the Ministry of Sport in 1982 and eventually the new freedom in his country meant that once again he could accept invitations to travel around the world. He was a wonderfully warm-hearted man – a hero to generations of runners.

Died in early 2001

Colin ANDREWS (GBR) (b. 1 Sep 1931 Cleckheaton) in Clevedon on 27 January. AAA decathlon champion 1958-60, in the last of these he set a British record of 6176 (1950 tables), equating to 6481 on the 1985 tables. Five internationals for Britain 1959-62.

Igor CAGIGAS (Spain) (b. 1 Feb 1977) in a car accident on 30 January, just two days after winning an outdoor shot competition in Bilbao. In 2000 he became Spain's seventh longest shot putter of all time with 18.28.

József CSERMÁK (Hungary) (b. 14 Feb 1932 Szenc) on 12 January in Tapolca. He became the world's first 60m hammer thrower with a third round 60.34 to win the Olympic gold medal in Helsinki in 1952; only 20 at the time, he remains the youngest ever Olympic male champion in this event. Csermák succeeded as champion and record holder his own coach, Imre Németh, and he in turn helped maintain Hungary's tradition by helping to coach Attila Zsivótzky to the title in 1968.

Csermák went on to place third in the 1954 European Championships, fifth in the 1956 Olympics (with a longer throw than his world record of four years before) and eighth in the 1958 European Champs. He raised the Hungarian record seven times, his personal best being 64.23 in 1960, by when world standards had risen considerably, and was Hungarian champion in 1953-4, 1956-7.

Annual progression at HT (position on world list): 1950- 46.48, 1951- 55.85 (9), 1952- 60.34 (4), 1953- 60.22 (4), 1954- 61.39 (4), 1955- 61.48 (4=), 1956- 62.59 (11), 1957- 62.00 (18), 1958- 61.95 (29), 1959- 63.03 (21), 1960- 64.23 (23), 1961- 63.04 (29), 1962- 63.15 (37).

Adhemar Ferreira da SILVA (Brazil) (b. 29 Sep 1927) in São Paulo on 12 January of a cardiac arrest after being admitted to hospital with pneumonia. Having opened his Olympic career with 11th place in 1948 he won Olympic gold at the triple jump in 1952 and 1956 and bowed out at the 1960 Games but, reportedly suffering from tuberculosis, he could place only 14th.

His started modestly enough with a leap of 13.05 in March 1947 but his German-born coach, Dietrich Gerner immediately predicted that the 19 year-old would one day break the world record of 16m. He set the first of seven South American records at 15.51 in 1949 and in 1950 in São Paulo, he equalled Naoto Tajima's world record, which had stood since the 1936 Olympics, In 1951 he claimed sole possession of that record with 16.01 in Rio. In Helsinki in 1952 he became Brazil's first ever Olympic champion and South America's first field event gold medallist; he raised the world record to 16.12 in the second round and then to 16.22 in the fifth. Two other jumps (16.09 in round 4 and 16.05 in round 6) were also beyond the listed world record and he took a well-merited lap of honour, a rarity in those less demonstrative days. A natural talent who trained just three or four times a week and who triple jumped only in competition, he went undefeated in 60 contests 1950-6. At the 1955 Pan American Games (a title he won also in 1951 and 1959), at high altitude in Mexico City, he regained the world record he had lost to the USSR's Leonid Shcherbakov (16.23 in 1953) with a resounding 16.56, that 33cm margin being the biggest ever improvement. He claimed the jump was actually worth around 17m as he took off some 30cm behind the board. He was South American champion in 1952, 1954 and 1958 (3rd 1949).

The son of a railway worker and a cook, growing up in a poor section of São Paulo, da Silva was not just a phenomenal athlete. He could speak six languages, took degrees in fine arts, physical education and law, and served as Brazil's cultural attaché to Nigeria during the sixties. In his time a poet, singer, dancer and sculptor, he portrayed Death in Marcel Camus' Academy Award winning film Orfeu Negro (Black Orpheus) in 1958.

Annual progression at TJ (position on world list): 1947- 14.64 (16), 1948- 15.00 (10), 1949- 15.51 (1), 1950- 16.00 (1), 1951- 16.01 (1), 1952- 16.22 (1), 1953- 15.92 (2), 1954- 16.22 (1), 1955- 16.56A (1), 1956- 16.35 (3), 1957- 15.92 (9), 1958- 16.25 (4), 1959- 15.95 (15), 1960- 16.06 (14). Other pbs: 220ySt 21.0w (1958), LJ 7.33 (1954).

Martin **'Marty' GLICKMAN** (USA) (b. 14 Aug 1917 New York City) on 3 January. He was fifth at 100m in the 1936 US Olympic Trials (although a film of the race shows that he was really fourth) and a reserve for the Berlin Olympics. There he was originally announced as competing in the 4x100m but was omitted at the last minute. It was oft alleged that he and Sam Stoller were left out because they were Jewish but actually the US decided to go for a full strength team and added Jesse Owens and Ralph Metcalfe. Owens was on record as wanting Glickman and Stoller in the team ("I've already won my three gold medals; let them run, they deserve it"), but was ordered by assistant head coach Dean Cromwell to do as he was told. After the Games, Glickman ran on the US team that won at 4x100 yards (in a 'world best' 37.4) against the British Empire at the White City, London. A graduate of Syracuse University, New York, he became a notable TV and radio sports commentator in the New York area, particularly on American football and basketball and received numerous awards.

Annual progression at 100y, 100m: 1935- 9.7y, 1936- 10.6, 1937- 9.7y, 1938- 9.5y. pb 220y St 21.4 (1937).

Bret HYDE (USA) (b. 3 Jul 1959) on 14 January of Lou Gehrig's Disease. He was 2nd in the AAU 3000m steeplechase in 1984 and ran a pb 8:25.39 in the semi-finals of the Olympic Trials that year before placing 8th in the final after leading for much of the way into the last lap.

Sam JEFFERSON (USA) (b. 19 Apr 1971) in his hometown of Waco, Texas, on 20 January after a long illness, aged just 29. He was the 1994 NCAA 100m champion and won gold (4x100m) and silver (100m) at the 1993 World University Games. He also ran on the third-placed US 4x400m team at the 1994 World Cup. Pbs: 100m 10.12 (1994), 9.9/10.01w (1995); 200m 20.32 (1993).

Sándor NOSZÁLY (Hungary) (b. 8 Mar 1940 Nagykálló) on 27 January. Four times Hungarian high jump champion between 1960 and 1968, his final Hungarian record being 2.10 in 1967. He placed 13th in the 1960 Olympics and 9th in the 1962 European Champs. He worked as a coach from 1973.

Keith PARDON (Australia) (b. 16 Mar 1912) on 15 February in Sydney. The Commonwealth Games silver medallist at hammer in 1938 and 1950 and 5th and 4th respectively at the discus and Australian champion at hammer 1937, 1950-3 and 1955, and discus 1937, 1947, 1951-3. Pbs: DT 44.32 (1953), HT 49.52 (1952).

Papa Gallo THIAM (Senegal) (b. 24 Jan 1930) on 14 January in Paris. As Senegal was not then independent, he competed for France in 24 internationals 1948-56 at high jump and set French records at 1.97 and 1.99 in 1949 and 2.03 in 1950, 8cm below the existing world record, using the Western roll technique. He was French champion in 1950 and 1954-5. He later became president of the Senegalese Athletics federation and was treasurer of the African Athletic Confederation.

Died in 1999

Wilhelmina **'Mien' DUCHATEAU** (Netherlands) (b. 9 Nov 1904) on 28 April 1999. She competed at 800m in the 1928 Olympic Games.

Hildegard KLUSENWERTH (Germany) (b. 15 Jul 1910 Charlottenburg) on 2 December 1999. Although already married (Le Viseur) she competed under her maiden name at 80m hurdles in the 1936 Olympic Games. In German Championships she was 2nd at 80mh 1933, 3rd at 80mh 1934 and 1936 and HJ 1933. Pbs: 80mh 12.0, HJ 1.55, DT 37.65 (all 1934), LJ 5.44 (1931).

Ida KÜHNEL (was Adler, later Pleschak) (Germany) (b. 22 Apr 1920) on 20 July. 5th at 100m and gold medal at 4x100m at 1938 European Championships. German champion at 100m 1939 and 1941, 2nd 1940. Pbs: 100m 11.9 (ranked her first equal in the world in 1939), 200m 24.7 (1938), LJ 5.55 (1941).

Stig LINDBÄCK (Sweden) (b.2 Oct 1937 Luleå) on 14 March. With his pbs of 1:48.6 and 3:41.8 (both in 1964) he was then 3rd on the Swedish all-time lists for 800m and 1500m. He participated in the 1964 Olympic Games, represented Sweden in 10 international matches and was Swedish 800m champion in 1962.

Rui da SILVA (Brazil) (b. 15 Sep 51) was shot in a "favela" on 5 May 1999 while on police duty in Rio de Janeiro. He was 5th in the 1976 Olympic 200m in 20.84, having set a pb of 20.76 in the quarter-finals. He won nine gold medals at the South American Championships: 100m, 200m and 4x100m 1974-5 and 1977. At the Pan Am Games at 100m, he was 7th in 1975 and 5th in 1979 and at 4x100m helped Brazil to 4th in 1975 (39.18 South American Record) and 3rd in 1979. 100m pb 10.36A (1975).

James **'Jim' SMITH** (USA) (b. 17 Sep 1913) on 23 October. While at the University of Indiana he was 4th in the NCAA 5000m in 1936, improving to 2nd at 1 mile in 1937 before 4th at 1 mile in 1938. In the AAUs he was 2nd at 1500m in 1937 and 3rd at 5000m in 1936. His 1 mile pb of 4:11.0 ranked him 7th in the world in 1937. Pbs 1500m 3:54.0 (1937), 2M 9:04.0i (1937), 5000m 14:47.8i (1937).

EMIL ZATOPEK – SIMPLY THE GREATEST

Mel Watman paid tribute to one of his supreme heroes in ATHLETICS INTERNATIONAL

Track and field fans love to compare the merits of past champions with those of the current era to determine who is the greatest athlete of all time. It's a futile, subjective but enjoyable exercise, but I will guarantee that every knowledgeable enthusiast who has more than a stopwatch for a heart will have the name of Emil Zátopek at or near the top of their list. One could argue that Haile Gebrselassie has by now overtaken Zátopek and Paavo Nurmi as the most consistently successful long distance track runner the world has ever seen, or that Carl Lewis' achievements outshine those of every other athlete. But there should be more to this than mere facts and figures. Zátopek was an exceptional athlete, agreed, but transcending that was his humanity.

He was the personification of all that is worthy in sport, and in life. He was ambitious and successful but never lost his humility or sense of wonder. He had the capacity to enjoy himself and enrich the lives of others but also a stoicism born of early hardship which carried him through the bad times when he found himself on the wrong side of the political fence. His courage, on and off the track, was remarkable.

As a runner Zátopek broke through the barriers of what was deemed humanly possible by dint of training much harder than anyone before him and by pushing himself closer to the limits than his rivals; he was an uncompromising opponent who could destroy the field from the front as in most of his 10,000m races or by summoning a fearsome kick as in the classic 1952 Olympic 5000m. He won every honour during a long career and yet remained an intensely modest man, always somewhat bemused that long after his retirement he would still be recognised and honoured wherever he travelled.

His tortured expression and torso-rolling action, each stride looking as though it would be his last before collapsing, endeared him to fans the world over. Even his closest rivals, like Alain Mimoun and Gordon Pirie, had enormous affection as well as respect for the man dubbed "The Human Locomotive" and "The Bouncing Czech". His open, friendly personality won over everybody; he was always happy to share his training "secrets" and even in Olympic heats he would encourage or joke with his fellow competitors in a bewildering variety of languages. Such was his aura that even hard-bitten journalists would queue patiently to secure his autograph. Many an outstanding athlete is admired, hero worshipped even ... Emil Zátopek was universally loved.

It was 36 years ago, in the first edition of my *Encyclopaedia of Athletics* that I wrote: "In the eyes of many athletics experts, Emil Zátopek's triple triumph at the 1952 Olympics represents the sport's supreme achievement. Even to attempt the 5000m, 10,000m and marathon against the cream of the world's athletes is startling; to win all three – each in Olympic record time – is well nigh incredible." Nothing has changed since then to revise that opinion.

Another of Zátopek's legendary feats, which surely will never be matched, is his win-streak at 10,000m. Haile Gebrselassie, a worthy successor both on the track and by virtue of his winning personality, has not lost a race at that distance for seven years, a stunning achievement. But his sequence covers 11 races, whereas Zátopek won a phenomenal 38 consecutive 10,000's between May 1948 and July 1954! He then lost one close race (to Jozef Kovács) before winning another nine on the trot for 47 victories out of 48.

On a personal note, although I was too young to see Zátopek at his zenith in the Helsinki Olympics I was privileged to watch my hero in a few races towards the end of his career. It was largely due to the enticing prospect of viewing him in action at the 1955 World Youth Festival in Warsaw that, at 17, I made my first trip abroad and had my first by-lined report published in *Athletics Weekly*, an event that was to determine the direction of my journalistic career.

For perhaps the best example of Zátopek's character and generosity we turn to another legendary distance runner, Ron Clarke, a man who set a stack of world records but never managed to win a major title. Writing in *Athletics Weekly* in 1987, the Australian recalled the end of his first visit to Zátopek nearly 20 years earlier. "As he marched me through customs and onto the plane on my way out of Prague, he shook hands and, in so doing, secretly transferred a small package into my grip. I thought I was smuggling some message to the outside world for him so did not dare open the little parcel until the plane was well outside Czechoslovakian territory.

"When I opened it up it was his 1952 Olympic 10,000m gold medal. I thought back to the words he said as he passed it across to me, which at the time I did not understand: "Because you deserved it", he said. I wish I had. I do know no-one cherishes any gift more than I do, my only Olympic gold medal and not because of what it is ... but because of the man whose spirit it represents."

Emil Zátopek – Annual Progression

With position on world lists and wins/races for 5000m and 10,000m

Year	1500m	3000m	5000m	5000m races	10,000m	10,000m races
1941	4:20.3					
1942	4:13.9	9:12.2	16:25.0	1/1		(2:02.8 - 800m)
1943	4:01.6	8;56.0	15:26.6	1/1		(1:58.7)
1944	3:59.5	8:34.0	14:54.9 (29)	1/2		(1:59.8)
1945	4:01.4	8:33.4	14:50.8 (23)	2/2		
1946	3:57.6	8:21.0 (10=)	14:25.8 (5)	5/6		
1947	3:52.8 (21=)	8:08.8 (1)	14:08.2 (1)	12/12		
1948		8:07.8 (1)	14:10.0 (1)	9/11 + 1ht	29:37.0 (1)	5/5
1949	3:57.0	8:19.2 (6)	14:10.2 (1)	12/12	29:21.2 (1)	11/11
1950		8:16.09)	14:03.0 (1)	19/19 + 1ht	29:02.6 (1)	7/7
1951	Marathon	8:17.6 (7)	14:11.6 (2)	12/12	29:21.8 (1)	3/3 and 2/2 at 20km
1952	2:23:02.2 (1)	8:32.4	14:06.4 (1)	13/14 + 1ht	29:17.0 (1)	6/6 and 1/1 at 30km
1953		8:13.8 (10)	14:03.0 (5)	9/9	29:01.6 (1)	4/4
1954		8;19.0 (25)	13:57.0 (3)	9/11 + 1ht	28:54.2 (1)	6/7
1955		8:26.8	14:04.0 (11=)	5/11	29:25.6 (8)	5/7 and 1/1 at 25km
1956	2:29:34		14:14.8 (49=)	2/3	29:33.4 (17)	1/1
1957			14:06.4 (24)	5/9	29:25.8 (11)	5/10
1958			15:13.0		31:13.0	

Other bests: 2000m 5:20.5 (1947), 3M 13:31.2 (1954), 6M 27:59.2 (1954)

Championships

Won Czechoslovak 5000m 1945-8, 1950, 1952-4; 10,000m 1952-3, cross-country 1948-9, 1952, 1954-5

World Records

5000m	13:57.2	Colombes	30 May 1954
6M	28:08.4	Stara Boleslav	1 Nov 1953
	27:59.2	Bruxelles	1 Jun 1954
10,000m	29:28.2	Ostrava	11 Jun 1949
	29:21.2	Ostrava	22 Oct 1949
	29:02.6	Turku	4 Aug 1950
	29:01.6	Stara Boleslav	1 Nov 1953
	28:54.2	Bruxelles	1 Jun 1954
10M	48:12.0	Stara Boleslav	29 Sep 1951
20,000m	1:01:15.8	Praha	15 Sep 1951
	59:51.8	Stara Boleslav	29 Sep 1951
1 Hour	19,558m	Praha	15 Sep 1951
	20,052m	Stara Boleslav	29 Sep 1951
15M	1:16:26.4	Stara Boleslav	26 Oct 1952
	1:14:01.0	Celakovice	29 Oct 1955
25,000m	1:19:11.8	Stara Boleslav	26 Oct 1952
	1:16:36.4	Celakovice	29 Oct 1955
30,000m	1:35:23.8	Stara Boleslav	26 Oct 1952

Career Summary and national records

2000m: 4 CS records from 5:33.4 (1944) to 5:20.6 (1947)
3000m: 9 CS records from 8:34.8 (1944) to 8:07.8 (1948). From his first record in September 1944 to October 1957, he won 40 of his 46 races at 3000m.
5000m: Won 117 of his 135 finals 1942-57. 10 CS records from 14:55.0 (1944) to 13:57.0 (1954).
10,000m: Won 53 of his 61 races. 7 CS records from 30:28.4 (1948 on his debut at 10,000m) to 28:54.2 (1954).
Longer distances: National records as per world records above, plus one more at 10 miles – 49:32.6 (1951).
4x1500m relay: 6 CS records from 17:01.6 (1942) to 15:45.4 (1951).

DRUGS BANS

THE IAAF has a longstanding history in the fight against doping and continues to take a lead in the world of sport, conducting far more tests than any other international federation.

The following cases were reported of athletes failing drug tests in 2000

Suspension: Life - life ban, 4y/2y = 4/2 years, 3m = 3 months, W = warning and disqualification, P = pending hearing

Leading athletes

Men *Name*	*Date*	
Aleksandr Bagach UKR	12 Feb	Life
Vadim Devyatovskiy BLR	18 Sep	2y
Gabor Dobos HUN	19 Feb	2y
Daniel Effiong NGR	14 May	P
Mark Findlay GBR	27 Jul	2y
Floyd Heard USA	25 Jun	W
Claus Hirsbro DEN	12 Aug	Life
Samir Haouam ALG	10 Jul	W
C J Hunter USA	27 Jul	P
Simon Kemboi KEN	21 Aug	2y
Liu Yunfeng CHN	13 Jul	P
João Pires POR	7 May	W
Josephus Thomas SLE	2 Mar	P
Roland Varga HUN	5 Aug	W
Zhou Wei CHN	7 Jun	2y
Women		
Martha Adusei CAN	25 Feb	W
Yelena Andreyeva RUS	30 Jan	2y
Claudia Iovan ROM	20 May	2y
Yumiko Ito JPN	28 Oct	W
Inessa Kravets ROM	24 Jul	2y
Robin Lyons CAN	13 Aug	4y
Rodica Mateescu ROM	May	Life
Mihaela Melinte ROM	7 Jun	P
Svetlana Pospelova RUS	25 Sep	2y
Iva Prandzheva BUL	5 Aug	P
Judit Szekeres HUN	12Jan	2y
Elena Teloni CYP	6 May	W
Tressa Thompson USA	25 Jun	2y
Yin Yili CHN	12 Jul	2y

Others: **2y**: Adnir Bregu ALB (12 Feb), Tania Ciuciula ITA (20 Feb), Angel Lopez Navarro ESP (5 Mar), Csaba Németh HUN (30 Apr), Alexandra Tziouti GRE (10 Jul), Frantisek Drab CZE (13 Jul), Dmitriy Barannik RUS (27 Aug), Galina Kovalenko RUS (15 Sep); **3m**: Davide Comunello ITA (13 Feb), Daniel Garzon ESP (5 Apr), Fernando Cipollini ITA (3 Jun), Al Hough CAN (22 Jul); **Warning**: Lucy Carr FRA (24 Jan), Wynand Harmse RSA (18 Feb), Stiaan du Plessis RSA (18 Mar), Moktar Ajajy FRA (1 May), Solomon Khambule RSA (3 Jun), Tatiana Orcy BRA (12 Jun), Lauren Reimer USA (24 Jun), Samir Haouam ALG (10 Jul), Hussein S Mohamed EGY (12 Jul), Fabrizio Romero BRA (6 Aug), Eric Labiau FRA (2 Sep); **Pending**: Dupe Osime NGR (14 Aug)

Add to list of athletes failing drug tests in 1999

Men		
Innocent Asonze NGR	24 Jun	2y
Giuliano Battocletti ITA	12 Jun	16m
Dieter Baumann GER	19 Oct	2y
Linford Christie GBR	13 Feb	2y
Mike Edwards GBR	3 Mar	P
Davidson Ezinwa NGR	22 Aug	2y
Paul Henderson AUS	23 Mar	2y
Luis Jesús POR	31 Jan	2y
Ben Johnson CAN	7 Oct	Life
Carl Myerscough GBR	28 May (to 12 Feb 2002)	2y
Sergey Nikolayev RUS	1 Aug	2y
Mark Richardson GBR	27 Oct	P
Leonard Scott USA	19 Jun	W
Wu Ji CHN	17 Oct	2y
Women		
Delillah Asiago KEN	31 Dec	2y
Cynthia Rhodes USA	27 Feb	P
Deng Xiaochen CHN	8 Jul	2y
Sonata Milusauskaité LIT	31 Oct	W
Kristina Saltanovic LIT	31 Oct	W

Others: **4y**: Jean Fletcher CAN (13 Feb); **2y**: Kathleen Jager USA (1 Aug), Michael Tietz GBR 1 Aug, Ashoka Jayasundra SRI (29 Sep), Gerard Duffy AUS (8 Oct), Robert Koss AUT (4 Nov); 16m: Ilaria Sighele (27 Jun); **Warning**: Basil Bizuneh USA (14 Feb), Dionte Campbell USA (20 Jun), Scott Wiegand (20 Jun), Oksana Titenko (3 Jul), Louis Chisari USA (6 Aug), Roberto Defendenti ITA (31 Oct).

1998		
Bryan Bronson USA	14 Jul	2y
Gary Cadogan GBR	28 Nov	2y
Jan Christian Torvestad NOR	16 Sep	18m
Doug Walker GBR	1 Dec	2y
José Carlos Hernandez ESP	6 Dec	3m
1997		
Kory Tarpenning USA	14 Jul	2y

It was announced on 3 Jul 2000 that the IAAF Arbitration Panel decided that there were not the grounds to maintain the suspension of Merlene Ottey from competition and accordingly the suspension, applied in conformity with Rule 59.2, ended with immediate effect. The Jamaican athlete was the subject of an adverse finding on 5 July 1999 in Lucerne, Switzerland. The Arbitration Panel considered that the testing laboratory had not taken into sufficient account factors regarding the specific gravity of the sample, which as a result did not exceed the IOC recommended reporting threshold.

OLYMPIC GAMES 2000

SYDNEY 2000 – the Games of the 27th Olympiad – provided wonderful sport in a superb setting. The joyous enthusiasm of the people of Sydney and world's top sporting nation, Australia, helped to make this a Games that will be well-nigh impossible to better in future.

In athletics, for the first time since 1948, there were no world records set, but despite that and the fact that winning marks were inferior to those set in the unfairly maligned Atlanta Games in 26 of the 43 events common to both occasions (plus two the same), the Sydney Olympics proved wildly successful. Unprecedented crowds, with attendances of between 85,806 and 97,432 for each of the morning sessions and from 99,428 to 112,524 for the evening sessions, totalling 1,597,104 in all (over 300,000 more than in Atlanta), provided a fantastic atmosphere and the athletes responded accordingly.

Much superb competition reached its apogee on the fourth day – one of the greatest in the history of our sport. The highlight for the crowd was undoubtedly Cathy Freeman's victory at 400m run in a massive roar of popular support and illuminated by the flashing of thousands of cameras as she strode around the track. But there was much else besides, with victories for all-time greats such as Michael Johnson, Jonathan Edwards, Maria Mutola and Gabriela Szabo, the closest approach to a world record at the Games from pole vault attempts by Stacy Dragila and Tatiana Grigorieva, and above all one of the greatest races we have ever seen, the men's 10,000 which culminated in an epic sprint to the finish in which the sheer mental strength of Haile Gebrselassie, below par all year, overcame the challenge from Paul Tergat.

Many seasoned veterans came through to fresh triumph. Jan Zelezny responded to a new Olympic record by Steve Backley to take his third Olympic gold medal in the javelin, Heike Drechsler regained her long jump title at the age of 35, Irina Privalova won the 400m hurdles in her first year at a new event and Ellina Zvereva became, at 39, the oldest ever women's champion. At the other end of the scale Kamila Skolimowska set a world junior record to take the women's hammer at the age of 17.

The Americans, led by Marion Jones' three gold and two bronze medals, were easily the strongest nation, although their 10 golds, including the inaugural women's pole vault, compared to 13 in 1988, 12 in 1992 and 13 in 1996. They also had many disappointing results from their athletes below the super-star level so that they were well down on the points table for top eight placings. In all 44 nations won medals (compared to 42 in Atlanta), 21 of whom won just one.

There was a general reduction in performance levels which meant that there were far fewer national records than usual and there maybe three main reasons for this:

1. The climate. While conditions in Sydney were generally good, and indeed better than anticipated, the temperatures were considerably less than at other recent Olympics and World Championships, and thus times at non-distance events were slower. Also swirling winds at some times were a factor.

2. The time of year. Some athletes showed the effects of competing at the end of their season.

3. The increased drug testing regime.

In brackets after the headings for each event are the dates of the final, followed for sprints by the wind speed.

1264 men and 883 women from a total of 194 nations (including East Timor) took part.

* *Olympic records*

Sydney, Australia, September 22 – October 1

100 Metres (23, -0.3)

Greene was back to top form when it mattered and became the first American 100 champion since Carl Lewis in 1988, and his winning margin of 0.12 over training companion Boldon was the widest since Lewis in 1984. Greene's 9.87 into a slight wind was the second fastest ever Olympic time and in the cool conditions a strong contender for the greatest ever 100m performance. Chambers looked set for bronze until he dipped too early and was edged by Thompson, winning a first ever Olympic medal for Barbados. On reaction times Boldon was fastest away at 0.136 from Drummond 0.147, with Greene at a slow 0.197 and Thompson worst at 0.216. Defending champion Donovan Bailey suffered one injury too many and trailed home last in his quarter-final; other casualties included Bruny Surin (hamstring problems) in the semis after only just making it from round 1 as a fastest loser and Zakari (pulled hamstring) in the final. Boldon (10.04/1.9) was fastest in round one and Thompson matched that in the quarter-finals (+0.8). Chambers won the first semi in 10.14 before Greene took the second in 10.06 from Drummond 10.10.

1. Maurice Greene USA	9.87
2. Ato Boldon TRI	9.99
3. Obadele Thompson BAR	10.04
4. Dwain Chambers GBR	10.08
5. Jon Drummond USA	10.09
6. Darren Campbell GBR	10.13
7. Kim Collins SKN	10.17
dnf Abdul Aziz Zakari GHA	–

200 Metres (28, -0.6)

THE ABSENCE of Johnson and Greene made the event wide open, but the gold medal for Kedéris was the least expected of the Games. Prior to 2000 the Greek had a best of 20.50 and was better known as a 45.60 400 runner, although he had improved to 20.25 in June. Silver for Campbell was also a huge surprise for the European 100 champion came to Sydney with a 200 best of 20.48. These two produced startling results in the first quarter-final as Campbell ran 20.13 and Kedéris 20.14 with Boldon third in 20.28. There were also fast times in q2: Thompson 20.16, q3: Capel 20.13, Malcolm 20.19 and q4: Floyd Heard 20.24. Only two of these men ran faster in the semis, where US champion Capel clocked 20.10 in the first race, looking round, from Malcolm 20.19 and Boldon 20.20. Kedéris won the second semi from 20.20 to 20.23.

Capel had looked the potential champion but finished last in the final after being left at the start. He moved early and then rocked back onto his blocks as the gun went for a 0.348 reaction time (compared to 0.163 for Kedéris and Boldon and 0.174 for Campbell) – poor starting. Campbell led into the straight from Boldon and Thompson but Kedéris (27) came past to become the first Greek man to win an Olympic running title since 1896. It was the first time the USA has been out of the medals (excluding 1980 of course) since 1928!

1. Konstadínos Kedéris GRE	20.09
2. Darren Campbell GBR	20.14
3. Ato Boldon TRI	20.20
4. Obadele Thompson BAR	20.20
5. Christian Malcolm GBR	20.23
6. Claudinei da Silva BRA	20.28
7. Coby Miller USA	20.35
8. John Capel USA	20.49

400 Metres (25)

JOHNSON BECAME the first man to win a second Olympic 400 title. Haughton, in lane 8, went off fast through 100 in 10.9 and 200m in 21.2 from Johnson (lane 6) 11.4 and 21.6. Johnson caught him at 300 (both men timed at 32.1) and the great man drew away while Harrison (11.5, 21.8 and 32.6) overtook the Jamaican for a US 1-2. Johnson's 43.84 has been bettered by only three other men yet it ranks merely 13th on his own all-time list!

At 33, Johnson is the oldest man to win any Olympic title under 5000m. Parrela, who took fourth place, was a surprise entrant as he had tested positive for Nandrolene on May 14, but apparently he was let off by the Brazilian Federation citing "no evidence". In contrast Mark Richardson withdrew from the British team on the eve of the Games so as to have more time to prepare his case against just such a ban. There were only five sub-45 sec times in the preliminary rounds: Harrison in round 1 (44.96) and round 2 (44.25, finishing with a smile on his face) and again when Johnson (who had won his heat and quarter in 45.25 and 45.31) let him win their semi in 44.53 to 44.65 with Haughton third in 44.93. Avard Moncur BAH was fifth in this race in 45.18 and thus unlucky as the second semi was won in 45.24 by Pettigrew. Hamdam Al-Bishi KSA set an Asian junior record of 45.22 in the first round.

1. Michael Johnson USA	43.84
2. Alvin Harrison USA	44.40
3. Greg Haughton JAM	44.70
4. Sanderlei Parrela BRA	45.01
5. Robert Mackowiak POL	45.14
6. Hendrik Mokganyetsi RSA	45.26
7. Antonio Pettigrew USA	45.42
8. Danny McFarlane JAM	45.55

800 Metres (27)

AFTER EIGHT men broke 1:45 in the semis off first laps of 49.5-50.6, the final proved a disappointingly slow race. The first lap, with Bucher and Longo leading, took 53.43 as they dawdled through the second 200m in 28.4, with Borzakovskiy way behind even at that pedestrian pace. At 600 Longo pushed Bucher momentarily off the track, an action which led to his disqualification after finishing sixth. Entering the final straight it was Longo from Bucher and Schumann and it was the 22 year-old German, who had set a pb of 1:44.22 winning his semi, who timed his effort best and was indeed the only finalist who ran a sensible race. With less than a stride separating the first four he held on for Germany's first ever Olympic win in the men's 800.

Kipketer and (especially) Saïd-Guerni left themselves too much to do, finishing out in lanes 4 and 5 respectively! Kipketer revealed he was spiked at the moment he intended making a break but was pleased with the silver. Defending champion Rodal went out in the semis, where the winners of the three races were Schumann 1:44.22, Saïd-Guerni 1:44.19 and Kipketer 1:44.22. Borzakovskiy (1:45.39) had been the fastest in the heats and reduced his European junior record to 1:44.33 for second in s2 (he ran 400s splits of 51.6 and 52.7 as Japheth Kimutai went through 400 in 49.50 and faded to miss a place in the final with 1:45.64).

1. Nils Schumann GER	1:45.08
2. Wilson Kipketer DEN	1:45.14
3. Djabir Saïd-Guerni ALG	1:45.16
4. Hezekiel Sepeng RSA	1:45.29
5. André Bucher SUI	1:45.40
6. Yuriy Borzakovskiy RUS	1:45.83
7. Glody Dube BOT	1:46.24
dq. Andrea Longo ITA	(1:45.66)

1500 Metres (29)

EL GUERROUJ had not looked quite at his best all summer but was unbeaten at 1500 since falling in Atlanta four years ago and was desperate to overcome that loss. His team-mate Baba hared round the first lap in 54.14 with El G in close attendance, but took 60.63 for lap two (1:54.77) and El G then took charge. He stepped up the pace with a 56.90 (2:51.67) yet, ominously, Ngeny, Lagat and Baala remained in contact. Although Baala (who was to prove the most successful French athlete of the Games with 4th place!) dropped back during the 54.27 last lap, the Kenyan pair stayed close and for the first time serious doubts were raised over whether the Moroccan could find another gear to dispose of his pursuers.

With some 30m remaining, Ngeny moved ahead to claim a famous victory in 3:32.07, breaking Seb Coe's 1984 Olympic record, while El G only just salvaged second ahead of Lagat. Despite his world 1000 record and other brilliant achievements, Ngeny's triumph still came as a shock. Ngeny (21), who said he was not at all surprised by his success, had more joy awaiting him; next day his wife gave birth to a daughter, whom he has confusingly but understandably named Sydney! El Guerrouj was in tears after the race ("it just wasn't my day and Noah ran a very good race"). Defending champion Noureddine Morceli, who had not raced all year, jogged in last in his semi following a collision in the finishing straight.

1. Noah Ngeny KEN	3:32.07*
2. Hicham El Guerrouj MAR	3:32.32
3. Bernard Lagat KEN	3:32.44
4. Mehdi Baala FRA	3:34.14
5. Kevin Sullivan CAN	3:35.50
6. Daniel Zegeye ETH	3:36.78
7, Andrés Díaz ESP	3:37.27
8. Juan Carlos Higuero ESP	3:38.91
9. John Mayock GBR	3:39.41
10. Jason Pyrah USA	3:39.84
11. Driss Maazouzi FRA	3:45.46
12. Youssef Baba MAR	3:56.08

5000 Metres (30)

HAVING DECIDED to tackle the 5000 rather than the 1500, Saïdi-Sief was the favourite to win despite having seriously run the distance only twice before. But he was found wanting in the finishing straight, enabling Wolde to sprint past and become at 21 the youngest winner of this event for 80 years. In the slowest Olympic final since 1968, Arndt led at 1k in 2:45.36 (after being 25m clear at 800m), Alemu at 2k in 5:39.54 (2:54.18), Lahlafi at 3k in 8:21.79 (2:42.25) and 4k in 11:09.84 (2:48.05), at which point the entire field was still bunched.

Saïdi-Sief, who had been prominent throughout but who did not seem to know what to do at such a slow pace, constantly looking around, threw in a 60.36 lap to the bell, where he was 3m up on Wolde with Lahlafi (world leader at 12:49.28) third, but had no answer to the Ethiopian's 53.83 last lap (26.3/27.5). The final kilometre took just 2:25.64. For the first time in this event all of the top six placings were occupied by Africans. All but one of the 15 finalists bettered 13:30 in the heats, headed by Lahlafi 13:22.70. The 1996 champion Vénuste Niyongabo BDI, still struggling to recapture form after injury, finished 15th in his heat.

1. Million Wolde ETH	13:35.49
2. Ali Saïdi-Sief ALG	13:36.20
3. Brahim Lahlafi MAR	13:36.47
4. Fita Bayissa ETH	13:37.03
5. David Chelule KEN	13:37.13
6. Dagne Alemu ETH	13:37.17
7. Sergey Lebed UKR	13:37.80
8. Jirka Arndt GER	13:38.57
9. Julius Gitahi KEN	13:39.11
10. Richard Limo KEN	13:39.43
11. Réda Benzine ALG	13:40.95
12. Mizan Mehari AUS	13:42.03
13. Adam Goucher USA	13:43.20
14. Mohamed Suleiman QAT	13:45.10
15. Toshinari Takaoka JPN	13:46.90

10,000 Metres (25)

WINNING BY a smaller margin than Greene in the 100, Gebrselassie (27) joined the Olympic greats by becoming the fourth man – after Nurmi, Zátopek and Viren – to capture a second Olympic 10,000 title. Poor Tergat, so often his runner-up on the track, could have been excused for believing he had pulled it off at last when he spurted ahead 250m from home and unleashed a prodigious kick. It didn't seem possible that Gebrselassie, at one time a doubtful starter due to an Achilles tendon injury, could close the gap... but he did and, in the last ten metres, summoned up one last superhuman effort to edge past and maintain a seven-year unbeaten record at the distance. It was the closest ever finish to an Olympic distance race at 9/100ths. The last lap took 56.56 with the last 200 in 26.0 by Geb, the second 5000 covered in 13:32.32 and the last 3000 in 7:53.37.

East Africans occupied the top five places, Mezegebu taking bronze ahead of Ivuti and Korir (18) whose 27:24.75 ranks him 3rd on the world junior all-time list. The first European home was Britain's Keska (8th) who set pbs in heat (by 12 secs with 27:48.29) and final. The kilometre splits of what was a fascinating race throughout were 2:39.52, 2:43.79, 2:44.72 (all by Nizigama), 2:47.44 (Ivuti), 2:50.41 (Nizigama 13:45.88, Geb 2nd 13:46.1), 2:45.31 (Ivuti), 2:53.44 (Nizigama), 2:39.83, 2:39.63 (both by Korir) and 2:34.11. Korir led the major surge with six laps to go and Mourhit most surprisingly dropped back and then out after another lap leaving six men in the leading group. Korir still led with 600 to go before Tergat began his bid for victory. 16 men broke 28 minutes in the heats won by Gebrselassie 27:50.01 and Tolla 27:44.01.

1. Haile Gebrselassie ETH	27:18.20
2. Paul Tergat KEN	27:18.29
3. Assefa Mezegebu ETH	27:19.75
4. Patrick Ivuti KEN	27:20.44
5. John Korir KEN	27:24.75
6. Saïd Bérioui MAR	27:37.83
7. Toshinari Takaoka JPN	27:40.44
8. Karl Keska GBR	27:44.09
9. Aloÿs Nizigama BDI	27:44.56
10. Abdi Abdirahman USA	27:46.17
11. Girma Tolla ETH	27:49.75
12. Mebrahtom Keflezighi USA	27:53.63
13. David Galván MEX	27:54.56
14. José Ramos POR	28:07.43
15. Katsuhiko Hanada JPN	28:08.11
16. Samir Moussaoui ALG	28:17.25
17. Rachid Berradi ITA	28:45.96
18. José Rios ESP	28:50.31
dnf. Mohammed Mourhit BEL	–
dnf. Enrique Molina ESP	–

Marathon (Oct 1)

FOR THE first time in Olympic marathon history all three medals went to Africans, with fourth place unexpectedly going to Britain's Jon Brown. Josiah Thugwane and Lee Bong-ju, who fought out the closest ever Olympic marathon finish in Atlanta, finished well down this time (20th & 24th) but 1996 bronze medallist Wainaina, who was not one of Kenya's original selections for Sydney, was again heavily involved. The race began in warm, windy conditions at 4pm. Tiyapo Maso BOT sped through 10k in 29:58 (84 sec ahead of the main pack) and halfway 35 sec clear in 1:04:27. He was caught soon after 25k and went on to finish 77th nearly half an hour behind the winner. At 30k (1:32:48) and 35k (1:48:11) the leaders were Abera, Tolla and Wainaina with Brown 1 sec behind.

The Briton had to let them go soon afterwards when he suffered stitch and Tolla dropped back during the 39th kilometre, after beckoning to Abera to go on to challenge the Japanese-based Wainaina who had been pressing on hardest. The 22 year-old Ethiopian, whose last two marathons resulted in a 1 sec win in Fukuoka (2:07:54) and 2nd place in Boston in the same time (2:09:47) as the winner, pulled clear of Wainaina at 39k, passed 40k in 2:03:30 and had 20 sec to spare at the end in 2:10:11, a formidable time in the conditions on a hilly course and all the more remarkable as he fell after 17k, hurting his knee and losing about 20m in the process. Double world champion Abel Antón ESP was 53rd in 2:24:04. There were 81 finishers from 100 starters.

1. Gezahegne Abera ETH	2:10:11
2. Eric Wainaina KEN	2:10:31
3. Tesfaye Tolla ETH	2:11:10
4. Jon Brown GBR	2:11:17
5. Giacomo Leone ITA	2:12:14
6. Martín Fiz ESP	2:13:06
7. Abdelkader El Mouaziz MAR	2:13:49
8. Mohamed Ouaadi FRA	2:14:04
9. Tendai Chimusasa ZIM	2:14:19
10. Steve Moneghetti AUS	2:14:50
11. António Pinto POR	2:15:17
12. Hendrick Ramaala RSA	2:16;19
13. Kamiel Maase NED	2:16:24
14. Silvio Guerra ECU	2:16:27
15. Mathias Ntawulikura RWA	2:16:39
16. Thabiso Moqhali LES	2:16:43
17. João N'Tyamba ANO	2:16:43
18. Domingos Castro POR	2:16:52
19. Keith Cullen GBR	2:16:59
20. Josiah Thugwane RSA	2:16:59

3000 Metres Steeplechase (29)

THIS ALWAYS shaped up as a Kenyan/Moroccan affair and so it proved, although Boulami – the fastest non-Kenyan ever with 8:02.90 this year – placed no higher than 7th due to some fine running by the two Martíns from Spain. European champion Kallabis fell at the very first hurdle (he did an immaculate forward roll and immediately rejoined the field, but fell back later) as the race got away to a very slow start. Luis Martín led at 1k in 2:55.85 with Kosgei just ahead of the leading pack of 11 men at 2k in 5:43.91.

Kosgei (21), the 1998 world junior champion with a best of 8:03.92, held off all challenges during a 61.38 last lap, the most serious coming from 1997 world champion Boit Kipketer who drew level on the run in before a clash of arms caused him to falter, while Ezzine edged world record holder Barmasai for bronze. The final kilometre in this the slowest final since 1972 was covered in 2:37.52. Kenya has now won this title at every Games they have contested since 1968 and this was their fourth successive 1-2. All the finalists had run between 8:21.14 (Bessou) and 8:25.70 in the heats.

1. Reuben Kosgei KEN	8:21.43
2. Wilson Boit Kipketer KEN	8:21.77
3. Ali Ezzine MAR	8:22.15
4. Bernard Barmasai KEN	8:22.23
5. Luis M Martín ESP	8:22.75
6. Eliseo Martín ESP	8:23.00
7. Brahim Boulami MAR	8:24.32
8. Günther Weidlinger AUT	8:26.70
9. Jim Svenøy NOR	8:27.20
10. Khamis S Abdullah QAT	8:30.89
11. Laïd Bessou ALG	8:33.07
12. Simon Vroemen NED	8:37.87
13. Manuel Silva POR	8:38.63
14. Gaël Pencréach FRA	8:41.19
15. Damian Kallabis GER	9:09.78

110 Metres Hurdles (25, +0.6)

The youngsters beat the old guard, as García ran out a splendid, clear-cut winner in a Cuban and Central American record of 13.00, followed by the American pair of 10.04 100m man Trammell (in a pb 13.16) and Crear. The defending champion Johnson hit all ten barriers and world champion Jackson came fifth after hitting the second hurdle hard and is now reconciled to the fact that he will never be Olympic champion, having been 2nd in 1988, 7th in 1992 when as strong favourite he was hampered by an injury and 4th in 1996. Jackson and Crear were responsible for false starts, but while Jackson's reaction time was not quite as fast as usual, at 0.139 it was still easily the best, next Dorival 0.161 and García 0.172. Dorival was fastest in the first round in a Haitian record 13.33 and Jackson headed the quarter-finalists with 13.27. García won the first semi in 13.16 from Crear 13.23 and Trammell the second in 13.32.

1. Anier García CUB	13.00
2. Terrence Trammell USA	13.16
3. Mark Crear USA	13.22
4. Allen Johnson USA	13.23
5. Colin Jackson GBR	13.28
6. Florian Schwarthoff GER	13.42
7. Dudley Dorival HAI	13.49
8. Robert Kronberg SWE	13.61

400 Metres Hurdles (27)

TAYLOR, the 21-year-old US champion had plenty of motivation after failing dismally in last year's World Champs and seized the opportunity to prove he is currently the world's no 1. He lowered his personal best and world's leading mark for the year to 47.50– and, like Morgan Taylor in 1924 and John Akii-Bua in 1972, he did it from the inside lane, the penalty for finishing second to Herbert in his semi with only the seventh quickest time of the round (48.49). Fastest was Al-Somaily, whose 48.14 was an Asian record and he became the first Saudi Arabian ever to make an Olympic athletics final. There he went much faster still, leading in to the final straight and clocking 47.53 for a very close second ahead of fast finishing Herbert whose 47.81 was a South African record.

Carter took 0.42 off his pb with his fourth place time of 48.04, but had attracted one of the very few adverse reactions from the crowd after his taunting gesture to those behind him when he won his semi in 48.48. Some of the heats were affected by very strong winds, but Samuel Matete ZAM had decent conditions when he won h7 in 48.98, the fastest of the round. Matete, the Atlanta silver medallist, matched that time in his semi, but it was not enough to advance to the final.

1. Angelo Taylor USA	47.50
2. Hadi Al-Somaily KSA	47.53
3. Llewellyn Herbert RSA	47.81
4. James Carter USA	48.04
5. Eronilde de Araújo BRA	48.34
6. Pawel Januszewski POL	48.44
7. Fabrizio Mori ITA	48.78
8. Gennadiy Gorbenko UKR	49.01

High Jump (24)

A CLEAR favourite, world-leader at 2.40, was world champion Voronin, but he cleared 2.29 only on his final attempt before going out at 2.32. It was his less celebrated training companion Klyugin who triumphed. It was Klyugin's good fortune that his initial clearance at 2.35 (at a time when he had been in fourth place behind Sotomayor, Hammad and Holm) came before the heavy rain which ruined the rest of the contest and none of the other six men left in came close to succeeding, but as they would have had to jump 2.38 to beat Klyugin it is unlikely that the gold medal was affected. The controversially reinstated Sotomayor took silver to add to his 1992 gold and Hammad became the first African male athlete to win an Olympic field event medal. 2.27 proved to be enough to make the final and the stipulated qualifying height of 2.30 was not even attempted. Defending champion Austin (20th 2.20) was one of the casualties and for the first time ever the US failed to place in the top four.

1. Sergey Klyugin RUS	2.35
2. Javier Sotomayor CUB	2.32
3. Abderahmane Hammad ALG	2.32
4. Stefan Holm SWE	2.32
5. Konstantin Matusevich ISR	2.32
6= Staffan Strand SWE	2.32
6= Mark Boswell CAN	2.32
8. Wolfgang Kreissig GER	2.29
9. Sergey Dymchenko UKR	2.29
10. Vyacheslav Voronin RUS	2.29
11. Nathan Leeper USA	2.25
12. Kwaku Boateng CAN	2.25
13. Kenny Evans USA	2.20

Pole Vault (29)

An era came to an end when the greatest ever pole vaulter, Sergey Bubka, bade farewell. He departed not in a blaze of glory but with a typically audacious gesture; although injury has restricted him to a best of only 5.55 this summer he did not enter the qualifying competition until 5.70 … and failed to clear. Out too went defending champion Jean Galfione (16= 5.55). The final was full of surprises, one of which was the fact that only two Europeans – 1992 champion Tarasov and Stolle – made the top seven. Eight men were still in as the bar was raised to 5.90 and four cleared: Hysong added 5cm to his pb at his first attempt (even if the bar did bounce), Johnson with his second, Tarasov and Stolle with their third, and as all four (along with Markov who carried forward one final try) failed at 5.96 the result was the USA's first victory for 32 years. The Americans had won all of the first 15 quadrennial Olympic titles but since Seagren's 1968 success had played second fiddle to the Europeans. Now they had their first 1-2 since 1960, despite the fact that the world leader at 6.03, Hartwig, the US Trials. Eight men over 5.80 was a record for any PV competition.

1. Nick Hysong USA	5.90
2. Lawrence Johnson USA	5.90
3. Maksim Tarasov RUS	5.90
4. Michael Stolle GER	5.90
5= Dmitriy Markov AUS	5.80
5= Viktor Chistyakov AUS	5.80
7. Okkert Brits RSA	5.80
8. Danny Ecker GER	5.80
9. Montxu Miranda ESP	5.70
10= Yevgeniy Smiryagin RUS	5.50
10= Aleksandr Averbukh ISR	5.50
10= Giuseppe Gibilisco ITA	5.50
13. Tim Lobinger GER	5.50

Long Jump (28)

FOR THE first time since 1980, the Olympic long jump champion would be someone other than Carl Lewis. The universal favourite was Pedroso, with three outdoor and four indoor world titles, but he had to dig deep before the gold medal became a reality. In the qualifying contest he faced possible elimination after jumping only 7.70 and 7.99, only to pull out an 8.32 to head the field. His compatriot Meliz 8.21 was the only other man to make the stipulated 8.15. Among those narrowly eliminated were Streete-Thompson CAY (13th 7.99) and Beckford JAM (14th 7.98), while the US pair of Stringfellow and Lister came nowhere near. The final became a riveting duel between Pedroso and the flamboyant Australian, Taurima. The latter took the lead with his second jump of 8.18, only to be overtaken in that round by Pedroso's 8.34. In round 3 Taurima himself leapt 8.34 to take the lead on countback, but Pedroso struck back with a fourth round 8.41. Jumping next, Taurima fell 1cm short with a new Oceania record of 8.40, but in the fifth round, in which Pedroso fouled, Taurima drew a huge roar from the 110,000 crowd as he landed at 8.49.

Even Pedroso can't jump that far to order but, amid unbearable tension, he produced an 8.55. Taurima finished with 8.28 and the 27 year-old Cuban had won an Olympic crown to add to his seven world outdoor and indoor titles. Shchurenko moved from 6th to 3rd with his final effort of 8.31 while the only American finalist, Phillips, placed 8th for an all-time worst US showing.

1. Iván Pedroso CUB	8.55/0.4
2. Jai Taurima AUS	8.49/0.6
3. Roman Shchurenko UKR	8.31/0.3
4. Aleksey Lukashevich UKR	8.26/-0.2
5. Kofi Amoah Prah GER	8.19/-0.6
6. Peter Burge AUS	8.15/0.7
7. Luis Felipe Meliz CUB	8.08/0.1
8. Dwight Phillips USA	8.06/-0.1
9. Bogdan Tarus ROM	8.00/-0.8
10. Carlos Calado POR	7.94/0.3
11. Petar Dachev BUL	7.80/0.2
12. Vladimir Malyavin RUS	7.67/-0.6

Triple Jump (Q 16.95 23rd, F 25th)

FOUR YEARS after he was expected to become Olympic champion, the world record holder finally fulfilled his destiny. Now 34 (thus becoming easily the oldest ever winner of this event), Edwards has remained the world's no 1 for most of the time since Atlanta and, with the virtual retirement of Kenny Harrison, no truly outstanding challenger has emerged. The best has been Friedek, the 1999 world champion, but he was a questionable starter in Sydney following injury and although he made the final he failed to register a distance. Edwards' compatriot Achike, the Commonwealth champion, started the final on a high note. The leading qualifier of eight men over 17m with a pb of 17.30, he opened with 17.29 – a distance which would keep him in a medal position until close to the end.

Edwards went ahead with his second jump of 17.37, minutes later Kapustin responded with 17.46, but in round 3 Edwards leapt to 17.71, the world's longest of the year and the winning distance although some way short of his unavailing 17.88 behind Harrison in Atlanta. That's how it stayed until in the final round Quesada knocked Achike out of the medals with 17.37, only to be deposed himself by team-mate García's last gasp silver medal winning 17.47. With three in the top six this was Britain's best ever performance in an Olympic field event.

1. Jonathan Edwards GBR	17.71/0.2
2. Yoel García CUB	17.47/0.1
3. Denis Kapustin RUS	17.46/0.3
4. Yoelbi Quesada CUB	17.37/0.3
5. Larry Achike GBR	17.29/0.5
6. Phillips Idowu GBR	17.08/0.0
7. Robert Howard USA	17.05/0.5
8. Paolo Camossi ITA	16.96/0.3
9. Rostislav Dimitrov BUL	16.95/0.4
10. Andrew Murphy AUS	16.80/0.4
11. Walter Davis USA	16.61/-0.1
nm. Charles Friedek GER	–

Shot (22)

THE SURPRISE leader in the qualifying round was Harju, who improved his best from 21.04 to 21.39 (after an opening 19.40), and he consolidated that form in the final. He opened with 21.20, a distance matched in the second round by Nelson, but with his second put the Finn, looking like a gigantic pirate, reached what proved to be the winning distance of 21.29. Nelson improved slightly to 21.21 in round 3, while 1995 & 1997 world champion Godina went close with a fifth round 21.20, moving from fifth to third.

With just 9cm covering the medallists it was one of the closest ever Olympic contests. Harju (26), who fouled out in last year's World Champs final, became the first Finnish winner of the event since Pörhöla 80 years ago. All three medallists used the rotational technique. Godina only made the US team when C J Hunter withdrew (at first claiming injury, but with news of his positive drugs tests arriving in Sydney just as the Games began). Brad Snyder CAN missed the final by a place, his 19.77 was the best ever non-qualifying mark.

1. Arsi Harju FIN	21.29
2. Adam Nelson USA	21.21
3. John Godina USA	21.20
4. Andy Bloom USA	20.87
5. Yuriy Belonog UKR	20.84
6. Manuel Martínez ESP	20.55
7. Janus Robberts RSA	20.32
8. Oliver-Sven Buder GER	20.18
9. Andrey Mikhnevich BLR	19.48
10. Miroslav Menc CZE	19.39
11. Milan Haborák SVK	19.06
12. Timo Aaltonen FIN	18.64

Discus (25)

ALEKNA OPENED with a dreadful 58.55 before getting down to business. In the second round he threw 67.54 to take second place behind Kruger's 67.89 opener and a momentous third round saw, in sequence, defending champion Riedel take the lead with 68.50, Kruger improve to 68.19 and Alekna move ahead with 68.73. Although the other two were over 68m again in the next round their challenge ultimately petered out, particularly when Alekna progressed to 69.30 in round 5. The three medallists, all of superb athletic physique, are respectively 2.00, 1.99 and 2.03 tall! In a high level contest Kaptyukh threw a pb of 67.59 in fourth place.

World record holder Schult, the only man ever to have thrown beyond Alekna's best of 73.88, placed 8th at the age of 40; this was his fourth Olympic top eight placing (after 1st, 2nd and 6th 1988-92-96), and he has also always placed in the top six at seven World Championships and four Europeans in his great career. The 1999 world champion, Washington, however, came last. Riedel 68.15, Kruger 67.54 and Alekna 67.10 had produced the best qualifying marks.

1. Virgilijus Alekna LTU	69.30
2. Lars Riedel GER	68.50
3. Frantz Kruger RSA	68.19
4. Vasiliy Kaptyukh BLR	67.59
5. Adam Setliff USA	66.02
6. Jason Tunks CAN	65.80
7. Vladimir Dubrovshchik BLR	65.13
8. Jürgen Schult GER	64.41
9. Aleksander Tammert EST	63.25
10. Michael Möllenbeck GER	63.14
11. Dmitriy Shevchenko RUS	62.65
12. Anthony Washington USA	59.87

Hammer (24)

THE QUALIFYING round produced carnage among the world's elite throwers. A throw of 77.50 provided automatic entry to the final, but a metre less sufficed for a place among the 12 to advance. Nonetheless among those who bade farewell were world champion Karsten Kobs (31st 72.29), Atlanta silver medallist Lance Deal (16th 75.61), 1992 champion Andrey Abduvaliyev (15th 75.64), 1997 world champion Heinz Weis (26th 73.51) and 80m+ throwers in 2000: Gilles Dupray (19th 75.05), Christophe Epalle (23rd 74.22), Vladislav Piskunov(14th 78.08) and Vasiliy Sidorenko (21st 74.72).

The leading qualifier was Astapkovich at 79.81 and he started as the sentimental favourite;

four times a silver medallist in Olympics and World Champs and the world leader at 82.58. But although he did make the podium again it was only as bronze medallist. The 1994 world junior champion Ziólkowski took the lead with a second round 79.87 and improved to 80.02 with his fourth effort. That was commendable throwing considering the event started in rain, the circle remained wet and slippery, and the Pole had brought only one pair of shoes, designed for dry conditions. Meanwhile, in round 3 the left handed Vizzoni produced a pb silver medal winning 79.64, and Astapkovich nudged his compatriot Tikhon (79.17 in round 3) out of the bronze when he threw the same distance in round 5 but finished ahead on the basis of a superior second best.

1. Szymon Ziólkowski POL	80.02
2. Nicola Vizzoni ITA	79.64
3. Igor Astapkovich BLR	79.17
4. Ivan Tikhon BLR	79.17
5. Ilya Konovalov RUS	78.56
6. Loris Paoluzzi ITA	78.18
7. Tibor Gécsek HUN	77.70
8. Vladimir Maska CZE	77.32
9. Koji Murofushi JPN	76.60
10. Andrey Skvaruk UKR	75.50
11. David Chaussinand FRA	75.26
12. Aléxandros Papadimitríou GRE	73.30

Javelin (23)

BIDDING FOR a record breaking third Olympic javelin title, despite a rib injury sustained in training the previous month, Zelezny opened with a daunting 89.41 (improving the Olympic record 89.39 that he had set in qualifying), followed in quick succession by 88.67 from Makarov and 87.76 by Hecht. It was shaping up as a titanic contest (there were a record seven men over 85m and best ever marks for places 3, 5-10), and early in round 2 Backley threw an Olympic record (with current model) of 89.85.

But Zelezny, irritated at having to hold fire while the women's 100m victory ceremony was being staged, ploughed all his frustration as well as strength and skill into his third round effort. It landed at 90.17 and Backley knew he was destined once again to finish second best to the man who must be acknowledged as the greatest ever javelin thrower. As well as his three Olympic golds, in 1988 the Czech finished second, pipped in the final round. At 34 he became the oldest ever Olympic javelin winner. Backley became the first Briton in any event to win an Olympic medal in three Games. Makarov's opener held up for bronze, his father having won silver in 1980. Nick Nieland's 82.12 was the best ever non-qualifying mark as he was just 12cm short of his compatriot Hill, who made his 16th major championship final.

1. Jan Zelezny CZE	90.17*
2. Steve Backley GBR	89.85
3. Sergey Makarov RUS	88.67
4. Raymond Hecht GER	87.76
5. Aki Parviainen FIN	86.62
6. Konstadínos Gatsioúdis GRE	86.53
7. Boris Henry GER	85.78
8. Emeterio González CUB	83.33
9. Pål Arne Fagernes NOR	83.04
10. Dariusz Trafas POL	82.30
11. Mick Hill GBR	81.00
12. Breaux Greer USA	79.91

Decathlon (27-28)

ERKI NOOL became Estonia's first-ever Olympic athletics champion, winning a closely contested event, but was exceptionally lucky, because most would say that he had no valid throws in the discus. Following two fouls he faced oblivion when his third attempt was measured but was declared a foul. A protest succeeded as the referee overruled the judges, but experts who viewed the video were in no doubt that Nool foot faulted and it was amazing that the Jury of Appeal upheld the referee's decision when they examined the video evidence. Huffins set the pace right through to the last event and although this remains his weakest discipline the American smashed his 1500 best by 12.5 sec with 4:38.71 to hang on for the bronze behind Nool and Sebrle, leaving Macey – despite a pb – to end up fourth. Dvorák started the contest with abdominal and knee injuries and was unable to do himself justice, but came a brave sixth.

Huffins led after day 1 with 4554 but only by 8pts from Macey who in his first decathlon since Seville (where he also scored 4546) posted pbs at LJ 7.77 and 400 with a magnificent 46.41. Next came Nool 4505 (pb 15.11 shot), Pappas 4476 (with a brilliant 2.21 HJ) and Sebrle 4460. Had the wind not changed in the 100 from +0.4 for Huffins to -1.1 for Macey, the Briton would surely have led at halfway. Huffins widened his advantage after the hurdles, run in heavy rain, and discus. Although Huffins vaulted only 4.70 he was still well clear after 8 events with 7220. Nool, who has a best of 5.60, went no higher than 5.00 but even so moved to 2nd with 7067 just ahead of Sebrle 7054 and Macey 7035, who raised his best to 4.80, but who was handicapped in the throws following a right elbow operation. Nool's vastly superior javelin throwing (65.82 to 56.62) whittled the American's lead down to just 14pts (7907-7893) after nine events with Sebrle on 7853 and Macey on 7779. Projections for the 1500 indicated Nool would win overall, which he did with 8641 by 35pts from Sebrle, but although Macey set another pb (4:23.45) he was foiled by Huffins' determined run.

1. Erki Nool EST	8641
2. Roman Sebrle CZE	8606
3. Chris Huffins USA	8595
4. Dean Macey GBR	8567
5. Tom Pappas USA	8425
6. Tomás Dvorák CZE	8385
7. Frank Busemann GER	8351
8. Attila Zsivóczky HUN	8277
9. Stefan Schmid GER	8206
10. Henrik Dagård SWE	8178
11. Zsolt Kürtösi HUN	8149
12. Mário Anibal POR	8136
13. Lev Lobodin RUS	8071
14. Jirí Ryba CZE	8056
15. Raúl Duany CUB	8054
16. Aleksandr Yurkov UKR	7993
17. Indrek Kaseorg EST	7932
18. Klaus Ambrosch AUT	7917
19. Laurent Hernu FRA	7909
20. Wilfrid Boulineau FRA	7821

20 Kilometres Walk (22)

KORZENIOWSKI WOULD make further history in the 50k seven days later but by winning the 20k he became the first to win Olympic road walking titles at both 20k and 50k, the previous closest being Raul González, winner of the 50k and 2nd at 20k in 1984. Not that Korzeniowski, the 50k champion in Atlanta, knew that he had won when he crossed the line for he assumed he had finished a close second to Bernardo Segura.

Only 15 minutes later, after a lap of honour and while he was speaking on the phone to his nation's President, was it revealed that the Mexican had been disqualified, leaving the Pole the winner. Korzeniowski, who has his own bitter memories of being pulled out late in an Olympic race (he was second in the Barcelona 50k when disqualified just before the finish), reeled off 2k splits of 8:00, 7:57, 8:00, 7:58, 8:00, 7:58, 7:51, 7:44, 7:39 and 7:52; halves of 39:55 and 39:04. Hernández (21) finished just 4 sec behind in a pb of 1:19:03 while Andreyev took bronze well clear of defending champion Pérez. All three medallists were well ahead of the old Olympic record of 1:19:57 by Jozef Pribilinec in 1988. Just two of the 47 starters were disqualified and 44 men finished.

1. Robert Korzeniowski POL	1:18:59*
2. Noe Hernández MEX	1:19:03
3. Vladimir Andreyev RUS	1:19:27
4. Jefferson Pérez ECU	1:20:18
5. Andreas Erm GER	1:20:25
6. Roman Rasskazov RUS	1:20:57
7. Francisco Fernández ESP	1:21:01
8. Nathan Deakes AUS	1:21:03
9. Alessandro Gandellini ITA	1:21:14
10. Nick A'Hern AUS	1:21:34
11. Michele Didoni ITA	1:21:43
12. Daniel García MEX	1:22:05
13. Yu Guohui CHN	1:22:32
14. Aigars Fadejevs LAT	1:22:43
15. Ilya Markov RUS	1:23:03
16. Giovanni De Benedictis ITA	1:23:14
17. Andrey Makarov BLR	1:23:33
18. Costica Balan ROM	1:23:42
19. Jirí Malysa CZE	1:24:08
20. David Márquez ESP	1:24:36

50 Kilometres Walk (29)

HAVING WON the 20k, which he had regarded in the nature of a warm up for his best distance, Korzeniowski made history as he became the first road walker to win a third Olympic gold. Competing in hot, humid conditions he covered the first 20k in 1:30:00, the next in a murderous 1:26:28, eventually winning by over a minute in 3:42:22. His 10k splits were 45:53 (García led in 45:52), 44:07, 43:30, 42:58 and 45:54. Joel Sánchez was his closest rival but a warning prompted the Mexican to throttle back after being just a second down at 35k and 40k, and Korzeniowski, who received one caution during the race, pulled away at 43k. Fadejevs finished strongly to overtake Sánchez for second after being 55 secs behind the Mexican at 40k and 19 secs down at 45k. A great reception was accorded Chris Maddocks (43), the first British male athlete to compete in five Olympics and the oldest athletics competitor at the Games. In pain with a hamstring injury from the outset he finished in 4:52:12, an hour outside his best, the 39th and last finisher from 56 starters.

1. Robert Korzeniowski POL	3:42:22
2. Aigars Fadejevs LAT	3:43:40
3. Joel Sánchez MEX	3:44:36
4. Valentí Massana ESP	3:46:01
5. Nikolay Matyukhin RUS	3:46:37
6. Nathan Deakes AUS	3:47:29
7. Miguel A Rodríguez MEX	3:48:12
8. Roman Magdziarczyk POL	3:48:17
9. Modris Liepins LAT	3:48:36
10. Yang Yongjian CHN	3:48:42
11. Aleksandar Rakovic YUG	3:49:16
12. Jesús Angel García ESP	3:49:31
13. Wang Yinhang CHN	3:50:19
14. Denis Langlois FRA	3:52:56
15. Sergey Korepanov KAZ	3:53:30
16. Milos Holusa CZE	3:53:48
17. Peter Tichy SVK	3:54:47
18. Craig Barrett NZL	3:55:53
19. Mike Trautmann GER	3:56:19
20. Stefan Malik SVK	3:56:44

4 x 100 Metres Relay (30)

BRITAIN HAD high hopes of taking the silver medals as in the 1999 World Champs, perhaps even defeating the Americans, but the team didn't even survive the first round. Appalling baton passing by an experienced but poorly selected team led to last place (40.36) and subsequent disqualification (for both first and third changes) whereas the US was fastest in the heats (38.15) and semis (37.82) before taking the final by 3m in 37.61, sixth fastest ever behind five other US combinations. Chasing Maurice Greene on the anchor, Brazil's Claudinei da Silva overtook Cuba's Mayola for silver in the South American record time of 37.90. Japan tied the Asian record of 38.31 in their semi. In addition to Jon Drummond, Bernard Williams, Brian Lewis and Greene, Kenny Brokenburr and Tim Montgomery receive gold medals as they ran in the heats.

1. USA	37.61	Drummond, Williams, Lewis, Greene (also gold: Brokenburr, Montgomery)
2. BRA	37.90	V Lima, Ribeiro, A da Silva, C da Silva (also silver: C Sousa)
3. CUB	38.04	Cesar, Pérez-Rionda, I García, Mayola
4. JAM	38.20	
5. FRA	38.49	
6. JPN	38.66	
7. ITA	38.67	
8. POL	38.96	

4 x 400 Metres Relay (30)

WITH FOUR runners whose best times add up to 2:56.12 from standing starts there was a chance that the US team might threaten the world record of 2:54.20. Had Michael Johnson on the anchor run full out they would have been quite close. Alvin Harrison established a substantial lead on the first leg with a time of 44.5, Antonio Pettigrew followed with a 44.1 and Calvin Harrison (who had clocked a 43.56 split in the semis) covered his lap in 43.55. Needing a somewhat unlikely 42.07 for the record, Johnson contented himself with an unstraining 44.22 for a time of 2:56.35, the no 7 mark of all-time. In his final Olympic appearance Johnson thus brought his total of gold medals to five. Jerome Young and Angelo Taylor also won golds for their contribution in the heats and semis, the 400 hurdles champion being timed at 44.2 in his semi. The Bahamas were second for much of the final but were squeezed out of the medals on the last leg with Nigeria setting an African record of 2:58.68 just ahead of Jamaica.

1. USA	2:56.35	A Harrison, Pettigrew, C Harrison, Johnson
2. NGR	2:58.68	Chukwu, Monye, Bada, Udo-Obong (also silver: Awazie, Gadzama)
3. JAM	2:58.78	Blackwood, Haughton, C Williams, McFarlane (also bronze: McDonald, Ayre)
4. BAH	2:59.23	
5. FRA	3:01.02	
6. GBR	3:01.22	
7. POL	3:03.22	
8. AUS	3:03.91	

WOMEN'S EVENTS

100 Metres (23, -0.4)

JONES BEGAN her much publicised quest for five golds with a breathtaking display, winning her first Olympic title by nearly four metres. Even Flo-Jo in Seoul won by "only" 3m. It was the widest ever margin of victory at 100m for men or women; Marjorie Jackson, one of the Australian legends who played such a moving part in the Sydney opening ceremony, won by 0.38 in 1952 (11.67) but at today's higher speeds Jones' margin of 0.37 represents more track space. Her 10.75, into a slight wind, was the year's fastest. She ran her lap of honour holding the flag of Belize (her mother's home country) as well as the Stars and Stripes.

Lawrence, who edged out her much more celebrated fellow Jamaican, Ottey (40) for the bronze by 1/100th, was fastest away at 0.163 followed by Ottey 0.179 and Jones 0.189. Thánou, penalised for a false start, showed 0.206 but came through for silver. European record holder Arron, one of several French athletes suffering from a throat infection, failed to reach the final as did Chrstye Gaines USA, who ran fastest at 11.06 in the first round, but 11.23 for 5th in her semi. Jones 10.83 and Thánou 10.99 had a +1.0 wind in the first quarter-final and Jones was fastest, at 11.1 in the semis.

1. Marion Jones USA	10.75
2. Ekateríni Thánou GRE	11.12
3. Tanya Lawrence JAM	11.18
4. Merlene Ottey JAM	11.19
5. Zhanna Pintusevich UKR	11.20
6. Chandra Sturrup BAH	11.21
7. Sevatheda Fynes BAH	11.22
8. Debbie Ferguson BAH	11.29

200 Metres (28, +0.7)

REMAINING remarkably focussed and upbeat, at least in public, while the furore over her husband C J Hunter's drugs positives raged all week, Jones posted another world leading mark for the year of 21.84 for gold no 2, her winning margin being a good four metres and she gave the impression that there was something in reserve as she became the seventh woman, but first since Flo-Jo 1988, to complete the Olympic

100/200 double. Her only previous 200m competition of 2000 had been her win at the US Trials.

Finishing an ecstatic second was Davis-Thompson, competing in her fifth Olympics and winning her first medal after being a 100/200 semi-finalist in 1984, 1988 and 1992 and placing 4th over 400 in Atlanta. She ran a pb to edge Jayasinghe, who set a Sri Lankan record, by 1/100th, while two Aussies in the final ensured plenty of crowd support. McDonald was fastest (22.50 and 22.44) in the first two rounds where Jones ran 22.75 and 22.50 before taking the first semi in 22.40. Davis-Thompson won the second semi in 22.38 from Jayasinghe 22.45.

1. Marion Jones USA 21.84
2. Pauline Davis-Thompson BAH 22.27
3. Susanthika Jayasinghe SRI 22.28
4. Bev McDonald JAM 22.35
5. Debbie Ferguson BAH 22.37
6. Melinda Gainsford-Taylor AUS 22.42
7. Cathy Freeman AUS 22.53
8. Zhanna Pintusevich UKR 22.66

400 Metres (25)

CATHY FREEMAN triumphed in a race in which four of the five women that followed her set pbs. The dramatic departure from Sydney of reigning champion Marie-José Pérec, initially claiming she had feared for her safety but later admitting she had run away from the prospect of taking on Cathy Freeman, robbed the Games of what might have been one of the great Olympic duels ... but the vast majority of the 112,000 fans who packed the stadium for the final could not have cared less. It was unthinkable that Freeman (27), an icon of modern Australia who has become a symbol of reconciliation between the white community and the indigenous population, could lose this race and – despite the unbearable pressure of all the public expectation – she was fastest in the quarter-finals 50.31 and semis 50.01 and rose to the occasion in the final despite having to work hard to overcome her rivals. Graham (lane 4), entered the finishing straight narrowly ahead of Freeman (6) and Merry (3), and although the local heroine powered past for victory in 49.11, the world's fastest for four years, the Jamaican finished second 4m back in her first sub-50 run of the year.

Merry and fast finishing Fraser (lane 2) became (after Kathy Cook in 1984) the second and third Britons ever to crack 50, Fraser improving at the Games from 50.85 to 50.77 in round 2, 50.21 in her semi and 49.79 in the final. For the first time since 1964 no American made the final; they didn't even have a semi-finalist ... and yet the US would go on to win the 4x400! 300m splits Freeman 12.30, 24.08, 36.14; Graham 12.14, 23.70, 36.00; Merry 12.32, 23.80, 36.08.

1. Cathy Freeman AUS 49.11
2. Lorraine Graham JAM 49.58
3. Katharine Merry GBR 49.72
4. Donna Fraser GBR 49.79
5. Ana Guevara MEX 49.96
6. Heide Seyerling RSA 50.05
7. Falilat Ogunkoya NGR 50.12
8. Olga Kotlyarova RUS 51.04

800 Metres (25)

MUTOLA, still only 27 yet contesting her fourth Olympics, became the first athlete from Mozambique to win an Olympic title, the time of 1:56.15 being the world's best of 2000, while Graf set an Austrian record to take silver. Fuchsová set a tremendous pace, reaching 400 in 55.04 some 5m ahead of Langerholc with the main contenders well back. Holmes had been so short of training after her latest round of injuries that making the British Olympic team had seemed a forlorn hope, but she improved her season's best of 2:00.35 to 1:58.45 in her semi. Now she took the field by surprise with an early strike at 600m and led until 50m out, finishing in a remarkable 1:56.80, second only to her 1995 UK record of 1:56.21. She could not have been more delighted with her bronze.

There were shocks galore in the heats with world champion Ludmila Formanová CZE dropping out injured, the two Russians who headed the world list, Natalya Tsyganova and Olga Raspopova, eliminated (apparently the Russian team had prepared badly for the Games, spending the week immediately prior to the start of the athletics at a training camp in Japan where it rained most of the time). Then Jearl Miles-Clark USA went out in the semis with 1:59.44 in a race won by Mutola at 1:58.86. Graf had been fastest in round one at 1:58.39 and went faster in the second semi with 1:57.56.

1. Maria Mutola MOZ 1:56.15
2. Stephanie Graf AUT 1:56.64
3. Kelly Holmes GBR 1:56.80
4. Brigita Langerholc SLO 1:58.51
5. Helena Fuchsová CZE 1:58.56
6. Zulia Calatayud CUB 1:58.66
7. Hazel Clark USA 1:58.75
8. Hasna Benhassi MAR 1:59.27

1500 Metres (30)

FOR ALL but the winner this event proved to be full of anguish. Regina Jacobs never even got to the Games due to a viral infection, defending champion Svetlana Masterkova, who had raced only twice in 2000, hobbled off the track in her heat, while the final – described by Holmes as "the dirtiest 1500 I've ever been in" – was marred when Tullett fell at 800, Szabo (then in last place) having to hurdle her and losing valuable ground. The race started slowly with Runyan, the first near-blind athlete to reach an Olympic final, passing 400 in 70.56, but then Favor Hamilton, the world's fastest of 2000 at 3:57.40, pushed on and was ahead at 800 in 2:15.93 (65.37). Sacramento took over at the bell and led at 1200 (61.92 lap for 3:17.85).

Favor Hamilton then went ahead with just over 200 to go only for Mérah-Benida to dash in front early in the finishing straight and open up a significant lead. The American, trying to respond but suffering from severe dehydration (or as she said later, the effects of anti-inflammatory pills), hit the kerb and later her legs buckled while she was in 6th place, causing her to fall. The challenge to Mérah-Benida came first from Szekely and Dulecha, and then from a great burst of speed from Szabo (who was some 30m down at one point and 6th with 40m to go, finishing out in lane 4), but the Algerian scraped home with the last lap taking 63.0. Favor-Hamilton walked across the line. The semis had been won in 4:05.24 Mérah-Benida and 4:06.60 Szekely after Favor Hamilton had led the first round at 4:08.08.

1. Nouria Mérah-Benida ALG	4:05.10
2. Violeta Szekely ROM	4:05.15
3. Gabriela Szabo ROM	4:05.27
4. Kutre Dulecha ETH	4:05.33
5. Lidia Chojecka POL	4:06.42
6. Anna Jakubczak POL	4:06.49
7. Kelly Holmes GBR	4:08.02
8. Marla Runyan USA	4:08.30
9. Sabine Fischer SUI	4:08.84
10. Carla Sacramento POR	4:11.15
11. Hayley Tullett GBR	4:22.29
12. Suzy Favor Hamilton USA	4:23.05

5000 Metres (25)

THE GREAT Szabo kick had reaped a golden reward in the 5000 five days before the 1500 final. She held the early lead for no other reason than to slow the pace and succeeded as the first kilometre took 3:03.84. Wami made it more respectable with a second kilometre of 2:53.49 (5:57.33), during which O'Sullivan fell 20m behind, but a 3:01.00 (8:58.33) enabled her to catch up. At around 3700m Wami signalled for her colleague Kidane to move ahead and at 4k (11:53.60; 2:55.27 km) it was an Ethiopian 1-2-3 (Kidane, Worku, Wami) ahead of Szabo and O'Sullivan. Szabo showed ahead a lap later and after resisting a challenge from Mikitenko along the final back straight she held off O'Sullivan in a fantastic sprint for the line. With a last lap of 60.01 (31.4/28.6) and final kilometre of 2:47.19, Szabo (24) smashed the Olympic record with O'Sullivan setting a national record (for the first time in five years) while becoming Ireland's first ever female Olympic medallist. Wami and Worku battled for bronze, Ethiopia's first medal by a woman at a distance below 10,000. O'Sullivan 15:07.91 and Szabo 15:08.36 won their heats while Susanne Pumper AUT ran 15:16.66 for firth in her heat, the fastest ever non-qualifying mark.

1. Gabriela Szabo ROM	14:40.79*
2. Sonia O'Sullivan IRL	14:41.02
3. Gete Wami ETH	14:42.23
4. Ayelech Worku ETH	14:42.67
5. Irina Mikitenko GER	14:43.59
6. Lydia Cheromei KEN	14:47.35
7. Werknesh Kidane ETH	14:47.40
8. Olga Yegorova RUS	14:50.31
9. Jelena Prokopcuka LAT	14:55.46
10. Daniela Yordanova BUL	14:56.95
11. Rose Cheruiyot KEN	14:58.07
12. Jo Pavey GBR	14:58.27
13. Tatyana Tomashova RUS	15:01.28
14. Vivian Cheruiyot KEN	15:33.66
dnf Olivera Jevtic YUG	–

10,000 Metres (30)

LONG AFTER many a medallist from Sydney is forgotten, the vision of Radcliffe's brave front running will remain. Lacking the finishing powers of her main rivals her tactic is to make the pace so fast that the opposition fall back exhausted before the last lap is reached. In Seville 1999 she burned off everyone except Wami, clocking a Commonwealth record of 30:27.13. This time she ran even faster with 30:26.97, a time only four women had ever bettered prior to Sydney ... and yet came fourth.

By 3000 (9:01.99) even O'Sullivan – destined to break the Irish record and take 36 secs off her pb – had been dropped, but four formidable runners in Wami, 1992 champion Tulu, defending champion Ribeiro and Loroupe (seemingly unscathed after her distressing marathon experience) clung to the tall tortured-looking Briton through halfway in a searing 15:05.70 and on to 7k in 21:17.05. Just before 7800m the Ethiopians went ahead in order to slow it down (8k Wami 21:17.05), But before long Radcliffe was in charge again to 9k in 27:29.34. Loroupe was dropped on the penultimate lap and the heroic Radcliffe went from first to fourth as her three remaining opponents accelerated approaching the bell. Tulu (28) produced a stunning 60.26 finale, while Wami narrowly prevailed over Ribeiro.

Tulu's Olympic and African record shattered her previous best of 30:56.4. Kilometre splits – 3:01.66, 3:00.35, 2:59.98, 3:01.02, 3:02.69, 3:05.69, 3:05.66, 3:04.22, 3:08.07, 2:48.15. The first four went to 4-5-6-7 on the world all-time list, eight of the top 12 set personal bests with five national records and there were best ever marks for places 3-7 and 10-18. Tulu was fastest in the heats at 32:06.19.

1. Derartu Tulu ETH	30:17.49*

2. Gete Wami ETH	30:22.48
3. Fernanda Ribeiro POR	30:22.88
4. Paula Radcliffe GBR	30:26.97
5. Tegla Loroupe KEN	30:37.26
6. Sonia O'Sullivan IRL	30:53.37
7. Li Ji CHN	31:06.94
8. Elana Meyer RSA	31:14.70
9. Lydia Grigoryeva RUS	31:21.27
10. Yuko Kawakami JPN	31:27.44
11. Olivera Jevtic YUG	31:29.65
12. Berhane Adere ETH	31:40.52
13. Lyudmila Biktasheva RUS	31:47.10
14. Alice Timbilili KEN	31:50.22
15. Chiemi Takahashi JPN	31:52.59
16. Libbie Hickman USA	31:56.94
17. Sally Barsosio KEN	31:57.41
18. Asmae Laghzaoui MAR	31:59.21
19. Jelena Prokopcuka LAT	32:17.72
20. Harumi Hiroyama JPN	32:24.17

Marathon (24)

TAKAHASHI became the first Japanese-born winner of an Olympic marathon title – a feat that will practically deify her in a marathon-crazy country. The temperature for the race was reasonable but the high humidity and the severity of the course did not make for fast times, and yet the first three broke Joan Benoit's Olympic record of 2:24:52. Despite her experience Marleen Renders blazed away from the start and was 100m clear by 5k in 16:42. After passing 10k in 34:08 she was caught in the 12th kilometre and subsequently dropped out.

Now Loroupe was in trouble; she had been ill (food poisoning) before the race, and was only 23rd at 20k before improving to 13th at the finish in 2:29:45, and was put on a drip after the race. Takahashi, with her minimal arm action, led at halfway in 71:45 with only Ichihashi and Simon for company. At 25k Fernández was an isolated 4th but she was to drop away to 16th. Ichihashi also began to lose ground and at 30k was 47 sec behind Simon and Takahashi (1:41:39). By 35k Chepchumba was a clear third and at 40k Takahashi (2:15:19) held a 28 sec lead over Simon, although the Romanian narrowed that to 8 sec by the finish. The leader's 5k splits were 16:42, 17:26, 17:11, 16:51, 16:38, 16:51, 16:47, 16:53 plus 7:55. Defending champion Roba placed 9th and 14 women under 2:30 was a record for any marathon (previous best 12 London 2000) as was 26 under 2:35. Manuela Machado POR after ten top ten places in major championship marathons was 21st in 2:32:29 and there were 45 finishers from 53 starters.

1. Naoko Takahashi JPN	2:23:14*
2. Lidia Simon ROM	2:23:22
3. Joyce Chepchumba KEN	2:24:45
4. Esther Wanjiru KEN	2:26:17
5. Madina Biktagirova RUS	2:26:33
6. Elfenesh Alemu ETH	2:26:54
7. Eri Yamaguchi JPN	2:27:03
8. Ham Bong-sil PRK	2:27:07
9. Fatuma Roba ETH	2:27:38
10. Ren Xiujuan CHN	2:27:55
11. Kerryn McCann AUS	2:28:37
12. Maura Viceconte ITA	2:29:26
13. Tegla Loroupe KEN	2:29:45
14. Irina Bogachova KGZ	2:29:55
15. Ari Ichihashi JPN	2:30:34
16. Adriana Fernández MEX	2:30:51
17. Judit Földing-Nagy HUN	2:30:54
18. Ornella Ferrara ITA	2:31:32
19. Christine Clark USA	2:31:35
20. Jong Yong-ok PRK	2:31:40

100 Metres Hurdles (27, 0.0)

DEVERS was a very hot favourite; she had run 12.33, 12.39 and 12.47 while no one else had clocked faster than 12.52 in 2000 and she was really hungry for the title which had so tantalisingly eluded her in 1992. Despite two 100m titles and a relay gold she had never collected any Olympic medal as a hurdler. That looked about to change after running a 12.62 heat – the fastest time of the entire competition – but after 12.77 in her quarter-final she pulled up beyond the fourth hurdle in her semi, citing a hamstring problem despite walking off seemingly untroubled, although she was already behind in the race.

Another major casualty was Michelle Freeman JAM (7th qf 13.52). Asian record holder Shishigina, making her Olympic debut at 31 (she was serving a drugs ban at the time of the 1996 Games), grabbed the opportunity. Off to a sluggish start (reaction time 0.237, Ennis-London best at 0.156) she ran a brilliant second half to pip Alozie and give Kazakhstan its first ever Olympic athletics medal of any colour. Alozie dedicated her medal to the memory of her fiancé Hyginus Anugo, killed three weeks earlier in a Sydney traffic incident. Shishigina had run the fastest quarter-final in 12.66/1.5 and Alozie was quickest in the semis at 12.68/-0.4.

1. Olga Shishigina KAZ	12.65
2. Glory Alozie NGR	12.68
3. Melissa Morrison USA	12.76
4. Delloreen Ennis-London JAM	12.80
5. Aliuska López CUB	12.83
6. Nicole Ramalalanirina FRA	12.91
7. Linda Ferga FRA	13.11
8. Brigitte Foster JAM	13.49

400 Metres Hurdles (27)

PRIVALOVA, a world record holder for the indoor 60m, made history by winning at 400m hurdles in her first year at the event. Having made a sensational debut in Moscow on July 12 with 54.49 she had improved to 54.06 pre Sydney.

where she ran with the assurance of a veteran. She lowered her best to 54.02 when winning her semi and, in the fifth 400H final of her life, went a full second faster in the final. Hurdling confidently off either leg (although jumping higher than necessary), and with the luxury of the flat speed which enabled her to run a 48.47 relay leg in 1993, she finished 4m ahead of defending champion Hemmings, with former world champion Bidouane and current world champion Pernía a further one and two metres behind.

Her 53.02, fastest in the world this year, makes her no 9 of all time. At 31 she is the oldest, male or female, to win an Olympic 400mh title. After her heat (55.89) she said "I like this event. It's easier – you jump, then rest". Tîrlea remarkably made the final despite no previous 2000 form, but the three US women all disappointed: Kim Batten (6th sf 55.73) failed to make the final for the first time in her six global championships, and another Atlanta medallist Tanya Buford-Bailey ran only 57.02 for 4th in her heat; then the 2000 US champion Sandra Glover was 6th in her semi at 54.98. Pernía 55.38 was fastest in the heats and Hemmings 54.00 in the semis.

1. Irina Privalova RUS	53.02
2. Deon Hemmings JAM	53.45
3. Nezha Bidouane MAR	53.57
4. Daimí Pernía CUB	53.68
5. Tatyana Tereshchuk UKR	53.98
6. Ionela Tîrlea ROM	54.35
7. Gudrun Arnardóttir ISL	54.63
8. Natasha Danvers GBR	55.00

High Jump (30)

A RECORD seven women cleared 1.96 and the medals were determined from 1.99. First Cloete (who had incurred one costly failure at 1.96) and then Yelesina made it first time, followed at the second attempt by Bergqvist and the astonishing Pantelimon who had equalled her pb of 1.94 to qualify for the final and had raised it first to 1.96 and now 1.99 for a share of the bronze medal. After seeing Cloete and Yelesina clear 2.01 second time round, Bergqvist saved up her final two attempts at the next bar setting of 2.03... and came closer than anyone else to succeeding. Yelesina, the first Russian woman to have won the title, had been living in Australia all year. All finalists cleared 1.94 in qualifying.

1. Yelena Yelesina RUS	2.01
2. Hestrie Cloete RSA	2.01
3= Kajsa Bergqvist SWE	1.99
3= Oana Pantelimon ROM	1.99
5. Inga Babakova UKR	1.96
6. Svetlana Zalevskaya KAZ	1.96
7. Viktoriya Palamar UKR	1.96
8. Amewu Mensah GER	1.93
9= Venelina Veneva BUL	1.93
9= Monica Dinescu ROM	1.93
11= Yoko Ota JPN	1.90
11= Zuzana Hlavonová CZE	1.90
13. Eleonora Milusheva BUL	1.90

Pole Vault (25)

DRAGILA has now won all three inaugural global titles: World Indoors in 1997, World in 1999 and Olympics in 2000. All three Russians no-heighted in the qualifying competition, from which 13 women advanced to the final by clearing 4.30, and European champion Balakhonova did the same in the final. It was left to a former Russian turned Australian, Grigorieva, to test Dragila and thrill the home fans. However, the leader for a long time was Flosadóttir, who had a clean sheet up to and including 4.50. Bártová, with third clearances at 4.35 and 4.45, also made 4.50 first time, whereas Grigorieva needed two tries and Dragila her full quota.

Flosadóttir, who became the first Icelandic woman to win an Olympic medal, and Bártová didn't get any higher but Grigorieva leapt into the lead by clearing a personal best 4.55 first time and Dragila followed at the second. At 4.60, Dragila finally got her act together ("my earlier attempts were a little rushed"), flying clear at the first attempt while still chewing gum. Grigorieva failed and carried her two remaining attempts to a world record 4.65 but neither she nor Dragila succeeded. Four women over 4.50 was a record and seven over 4.40 tied the record from Seville 1999. Former world record holder Emma George was 15= at 4.25.

1. Stacy Dragila USA	4.60*
2. Tatiana Grigorieva AUS	4.55
3. Vala Flosadóttir ISL	4.50
4. Daniela Bártová CZE	4.50
5. Nicole Humbert GER	4.45
6. Yvonne Buschbaum GER	4.40
7. Monika Pyrek POL	4.40
8. Marie Rasmussen DEN	4.35
9. Doris Auer AUT	4.25
10. Gao Shuying CHN	4.15
11. Kellie Suttle USA	4.00
nh Elmarie Gerryts RSA	–
nh Anzhela Balakhonova UKR	–

Long Jump (29)

JONES' bid for five golds came to an end in her third event. She had her chances, with at least three of her four fouls being a potential winning jump, but her best valid mark of 6.92 gave her third place. "I don't regret it at all," she said. "I had a shot at it and it didn't pan out." May jumped the same distance but took her second Olympic silver by virtue of a superior second best: 6.82 to 6.68.

The gold went to an athlete who has enjoyed an even more remarkable and diverse career than Jones. Even before Sydney, Drechsler had done it all but in Sydney she was in exuberant form. Heading the qualifiers at 6.84 from May 6.81 and Jones 6.78, she jumped 6.99 at the start of round 3 – adding 4cm to her world veterans record and making her at 35 by far the oldest winner of this Olympic gold. The 17-year span separating her first and latest global titles is the widest in the history of athletics, surpassing Bubka's 14 years and Lewis's 13 years.

1. Heike Drechsler GER	6.99/1.9
2. Fiona May ITA	6.92/1.1
3. Marion Jones USA	6.92/1.0
4. Tatyana Kotova RUS	6.83/1.4
5. Olga Rublyova RUS	6.79/-0.9
6. Susen Tiedtke GER	6.74/0.1
7. Jackie Edwards BAH	6.59/0.9
8. Tünde Vaszi HUN	6.59/0.4
9. Lyudmila Galkina RUS	6.56w/2.9
10. Elva Goulbourne JAM	6.43/0.9
11. Dawn Burrell USA	6.38/0.1
12. Yelena Shekhovtsova UKR	6.37/0.8

Triple Jump (24)

Marinova, who set a world junior record of 14.62 to win at the 1996 World Junior Championships in Sydney, became the only champion from then to win again four years on. The favourite Lebedeva led the qualifying with 14.91 from Govorova 14.76 and Marinova 14.73. Marinova then set a national record of 15.20, the equal fourth longest of all time, in the first round of the final and this came before the heavy rain which affected the rest of the competition. Only two of her rivals managed anything in excess of 14.30 and Marinova herself had five no jumps. However, Govorova responded later in round 1 with a pb of 14.96, which held up for second place until the pre-event favourite Lebedeva jumped superbly in the conditions for 14.91, 1500 and 14.90 in the last three rounds.

1. Tereza Marinova BUL	15.20/-0.3
2. Tatyana Lebedeva RUS	15.00/1.3
3. Yelena Govorova UKR	14.96/0.7
4. Yamilé Aldama CUB	14.30/-0.9
5. Baya Rahouli ALG	14.17/-0.3
6. Cristina Nicolau ROM	14.17/0.6
7. Olga Vasdéki GRE	14.15/0.4
8. Oksana Rogova RUS	13.97/-1.5
9. Anja Valant SLO	13.59/-0.7
10. Françoise Mbango CMR	13.53/-2.1
11. Ashia Hansen GBR	13.44/0.4
nm Sárka Kaspárková CZE	-

Shot (28)

THE FIRST round determined the medal winners. Korolchik led with 19.43 to 19.38 by defending champion Kumbernuss and 19.16 by Peleshenko, who then moved ahead with a second round 19.92 and kept up the pressure with 19.79 in the third. The 1992 champion Krivelyova pressurised Kumbernuss for the bronze with 19.37 in the fifth round but Peleshenko's hold on the event looked secure as Korolchik had nothing better than 19.11 to show between rounds 2 and 5. In the final round Krivelyova reached 19.36 followed by 19.62 from Kumbernuss to lift her into second place before Korolchik sent the shot a lifetime best of 20.56. A thunderstruck Peleshenko had her chance to counterpunch but her effort went only 19.60. Judy Oakes GBR bade farewell at the age of 42, missing a place in the final by just 4cm with 17.81 as Korolchik 19.36, Ryabinkina 19.20 and Peleshenko led the qualifiers.

1. Yanina Korolchik BLR	20.56
2. Larisa Peleshenko RUS	19.92
3. Astrid Kumbernuss GER	19.62
4. Svetlana Krivelyova RUS	19.37
5. Krystyna Zabawska POL	19.18
6. Yumileidi Cumbá CUB	18.70
7. Kalliópi Ouzoúni GRE	18.63
8. Nadine Kleinert-Schmitt GER	18.49
9. Lieja Koeman NED	17.96
10. Olga Ryabinkina RUS	17.85
11. Cheng Xiaoyan CHN	17.85
12. Valentina Fedyushina AUT	17.14

Discus (27)

WITH world leader Grasu failing to qualify after two fouls and the no. 2 Dietzsch scraping through as the 12th and last qualifier at 60.74 there were shocks even before the final, to which Machado was added after a dispute about her qualifying throw. In the event Zvereva (who had led the qualifying with 64.81 from Sadova 64.62) was in unbeatable form, all four of her valid throws exceeding anything thrown by the opposition. She opened with 67.00, followed by 65.71 from Kelesídou which remained the silver medal throw throughout and 65.00 by Sadova. Zvereva improved to 68.40 in the third round, while her team-mate Yatchenko crept past Sadova to snatch bronze with 65.20 in round 5. Yatchenko's husband, Igor Astapkovich, had won a bronze in the hammer three days earlier. Defending champion Wyludda placed seventh, one position behind world champion Dietzsch. Zvereva, at 39 years 315 days, thus became the oldest ever woman to lift an Olympic title, the previous record being held by fellow discus thrower Lia Manoliu, who was 36 when she won in 1968.

1. Ellina Zvereva BLR	68.40
2. Anastasía Kelesídou GRE	65.71
3. Irina Yatchenko BLR	65.20
4. Natalya Sadova RUS	65.00
5. Stilianí Tsikoúna GRE	64.08
6. Franka Dietzsch GER	63.18
7. Ilke Wyludda GER	63.16
8. Lisa-Marie Vizaniari AUS	62.57
9. Ekateríni Vóggoli GRE	61.57

10.	Seilala Sua USA	59.85
11.	Teresa Machado POR	59.50
12.	Beatrice Faumuiná NZL	58.69
13.	Yu Xin CHN	58.34

Hammer (29)

MELINTE, the world record holder and co-favourite with Kuzenkova for this inaugural title, was led away from the arena just prior to her pool of the hammer qualifying starting, having just been informed that she had failed a drugs test – testing positive for Nandrolone in Milan on June 7. Although news of her suspension had been transmitted by the IAAF to the Romanian Federation two days previously, the athlete herself had not been told. An appeal next day by the Romanians for her to be added to the final was rejected by the Court of Arbitration for Sport in Sydney.

The qualifying contest also saw the end of Manuela Montebrun FRA, no. 3 on the world list this year with 71.18 but able to throw only a mere 57.77. That left Kuzenkova, world leader at 75.68, seemingly in a class of her own and her 70.60 was far ahead of the next best qualifier, Münchow 67.60. Sosimenko got the final off to a rousing start with a Commonwealth and Oceania record of 67.95, remaining in the lead until Skolimowska let loose in the third round with a stunning world junior record of 71.16. Kuzenkova's response was 69.64, but after a slight improvement to 69.77 in round 4 she fouled her remaining two efforts and Skolimowska had a fifth round throw of 69.91. Münchow, with a German record, and Moreno demoted Sosimenko in round 5. Skolimowska became, at 17 years 331 days, the youngest Olympic athletics champion since Ulrike Meyfarth won the 1972 high jump title at 16 and the youngest thrower to win since Mihaela Penes, javelin 1964.

1.	Kamila Skolimowska POL	71.16*
2.	Olga Kuzenkova RUS	69.77
3.	Kirsten Münchow GER	69.28
4.	Yipsi Moreno CUB	68.33
5.	Debbie Sosimenko AUS	67.95
6.	Lyudmila Gubkina BLR	67.08
7.	Dawn Ellerbe USA	66.80
8.	Amy Palmer USA	66.15
9.	Lorraine Shaw GBR	64.27
10.	Svetlana Sudak BLR	64.21
11.	Ivana Brkljacic CRO	63.20
12.	Sini Pöyry FIN	62.49

Javelin (30)

WORLD JUNIOR champion Menéndez, who led the way in the qualifying round with 67.34 from Nerius 65.76 and Hattestad 65.44, opened with 66.03 but her lead lasted only a minute or two as Hattestad's response was a mighty 68.91, which will count as an Olympic record with the new implement and is a distance which only the 34 year-old Norwegian herself has surpassed with that model. Although the Cuban improved a little to 66.18 with her final throw the main challenge came from the Albanian-born world champion Tzelili, who threw a Greek record of 67.51 in round 3 and matched that with her last throw.

Cubans took three of the top six places, but Shikolenko, world silver medallist last year, was below form in seventh place. The Australian pair of Stone and Currey, struggling with injuries, failed to make the final. Hattestad, competing in her fifth Olympics (5th 1984, dnq 1988, 5th 1992, 3rd 1996), became the first Norwegian woman ever to win an Olympic athletics title.

1.	Trine Hattestad NOR	68.91*
2.	Miréla Tzelíli GRE	67.51
3.	Osleidys Menéndez CUB	66.18
4.	Steffi Nerius GER	64.84
5.	Sonia Bisset CUB	63.26
6.	Xiomara Rivero CUB	62.92
7.	Tatyana Shikolenko RUS	62.91
8.	Nikola Tomecková CZE	62.10
9.	Mikaela Ingberg FIN	58.56
10.	Wei Jianhua CHN	58.33
11.	Li Lei CHN	56.83
12.	Claudia Coslovich ITA	56.74

Heptathlon (23-24)

LEWIS held on for gold, despite a foot injury sustained in the long jump that got progressively worse and meant that she nearly didn't make it to the javelin or the 1500m. The defending champion Shouaa pulled up almost immediately in the first event of 100m hurdles, but world champion Barber looked to be in fine shape as she flew to a 12.97 win from Lewis 13.23. Barber kept up the pressure with the equal highest jump of 1.84 but Lewis managed only 1.75 and dropped to 8th place after 2 events, 152pts behind Barber. Lewis made up with fine shot putting (15.55 to Barber's 11.27) and the positions were transformed with Atlanta silver medallist Sazanovich taking the lead by 30pts from Lewis.

For Barber, down to 8th, it was the beginning of the end; she was nearly a second behind her best at 200 and the next day took only one jump, a mediocre 5.93, before retiring injured. Sazanovich led overnight with 3903 from Roshchupkina 3872, Lewis 3852 and Wlodarczyk 3805. Lewis stayed in the hunt with a 6.48 LJ which was bettered only by Prokhorova and Sazanovich, but Roshchupkina mustered only 5.47 after two fouls and dropped to 8th. Lewis then threw the javelin 50.19 to take the lead with 5717 ahead of Sazanovich 5654 and Prokhorova 5571. Prokhorova (2:04.27 in July) went for it with a first lap of 62.38 in the 800m but could not sustain the pace and finished in 2:10.32, good enough to take the silver but Lewis, her legs heavily bandaged, did enough with 2:16.83 to win by 53 points.

1.	Denise Lewis GBR	6584
2.	Yelena Prokhorova RUS	6531
3.	Natalya Sazanovich BLR	6527
4.	Urszula Wlodarczyk POL	6470
5.	Sabine Braun GER	6355
6.	Natalya Roshchupkina RUS	6237
7.	Karin Ertl GER	6209
8.	Tiia Hautala FIN	6173
9.	DeDee Nathan USA	6150
10.	Jane Jamieson AUS	6104
11.	Magalys García CUB	6054
12.	Austra Skujyté LTU	6034
13.	Susanna Rajamäki FIN	6021
14.	Gertrud Bacher ITA	5989
15.	Diana Koritskaya RUS	5975
16.	Svetlana Kazanina KAZ	5898
17.	Yasmina Azzizi ALG	5896
18.	Viorica Tigau ROM	5893
19.	Nathalie Teppe FRA	5851
20.	Larisa Netseporuk UKR	5762

20 Kilometres Walk (28th)

THREE WOMEN were disqualified while in the lead before Wang Liping, fifth 12 seconds off the lead at 16km, eventually won by 28 secs from Plätzer, with Vasco a further 50 seconds behind in third place. The world champion Liu Hongyu, who had led at halfway in 44:54, was pulled out in the 17th kilometre and Atlanta 10k silver medallist Perrone in the 18th. The latter disgraced herself by openly jogging up the road to catch up Saville, who had passed by in the meantime. Then there was the utter disbelieving despair when, just as she was about to enter the stadium with a clear lead, to win gold for Australia, Saville, too, was shown the red card. Wang had received one warning, for a bent knee, while the other medallists had a clean sheet. Intermediate times: 4k/8k: Tsybulskaya BLR 18:33/35:55; 12k: Saville 53:40; 16k: Liu Hongyu 1:11:07. The 4k splits were 18:33, 17:22, 17:45, 17:27 and 17:58. 45 of the 57 starters finished.

1.	Wang Liping CHN	1:29:05*
2.	Kjersti Plätzer NOR	1:29:33
3.	María Vasco ESP	1:30:23
4.	Erica Alfridi ITA	1:31:25
5.	Guadalupe Sánchez MEX	1:31:33
6.	Norica Cîmpean ROM	1:31:50
7.	Kerry Saxby-Junna AUS	1:32:02
8.	Tatyana Gudkova RUS	1:32:35
9.	Natalya Misyulya BLR	1:33:08
10.	Gillian O'Sullivan IRL	1:33:10
11.	Athiná Papayiánni GRE	1:33:14
12.	Valentina Savchuk UKR	1:33:22
13.	Ana Maria Groza ROM	1:33:38
14.	Susana Feitor POR	1:33:53
15.	Yuan Yufang MAS	1:34:19
16.	Kristina Saltanovic LTU	1:34:24
17.	Michelle Rohl USA	1:34:26
18.	Mária Urbanik HUN	1:34:45
19.	Beate Gummelt GER	1:34:59
20.	Encarna Granados ESP	1:35:06

4 x 100 Metres Relay (30)

IT WAS just as well that Jones' five golds dream had already been shattered, for the US team – without Miller or Devers – was no match for the Caribbean islands and failed to take gold at this event for the first time since 1980. Jones pulled well clear of Arron (France) on the anchor, but that was for the bronze. Up front the slick-passing Bahamas, fielding the same personnel and running order as when they won last year's world title in 41.92 (and three of the Atlanta silver medal team), this time whizzed the stick around in 41.95 – a gold medal for a nation of 275,000, and for Pauline Davis-Thompson in her fifth Olympics. Jamaica took second place, anchored by Ottey who at 40 became the oldest women's medallist in Olympic history. She also became the most prolific female medallist ever with a total of eight spread over an astonishing 20-year period… three silvers and five bronzes. Jamaica were fastest in the heats 42.46 and semis 42.15.

1. BAH	41.95	
	Fynes, Sturrup, Davis-Thompson, Ferguson	
	(also gold: Clarke-Lewis)	
2. JAM	42.12	
	Lawrence, V Campbell, McDonald, Ottey	
	(also silver: Frazer)	
3. USA	42.20	
	Gaines, Edwards, Perry, Jones	
	(also bronze: P Richardson)	
4. FRA	42.42	
5. RUS	43.02	
6. GER	43.11	
7. NGR	44.05	
8. CHN	44.87	

4 x 400 Metres Relay (30)

JONES completed her marathon stint in style, bringing her tally to three golds and two bronzes. That total of five medals is the most ever amassed by a woman at one Games. After legs of 51.1 by Miles-Clark and 51.4 by Hennagan she took over for the third leg about level with Jamaica's Hemmings but handed over some 15m clear after completing her lap in 49.40. That gave Colander-Richardson a good safety margin as Graham (49.6), Privalova (49.6), Ogunkoya (49.7) and Freeman (49.4) set off in pursuit, and she won by five metres with a 50.68 leg. There were swift legs also for the British team by Fraser (50.2) and Merry (49.6). Australia set Oceania records of 3:24.05 (without Freeman) and 3:23.81. Nigeria were the fastest in the heats with 3:22.99

with the US team winning their race in 3:23.95.

1. USA 3:22.62
   Miles-Clark, Hennagan, Jones, Colander-Richardson
   (also gold: Anderson)
2. JAM 3:23.25
   Richards, Scott, Hemmings, Graham
   (also silver: Howell, Burgher)
3. RUS 3:23.46
   Sotnikova, Goncharenko, Kotlyarova, Privalova
   (also bronze: Zykina, Nazarova)
4. NGR 3:23.80
5. AUS 3:23.81
6. GBR 3:25.67
7. CZE 3:29.17
8. CUB 3:29.47

Crowd Numbers

Date	Morning	Evening
Sep 22	97,432	102,485
Sep 23	92.655	104,228
Sep 24	85,806	101,772
Sep 25	92,154	112,524
Sep 27	96,127	102,844
Sep 28	89,254	106,106
Sep 29	94,127	99,428
Sep 30		105,448
Oct 1		114,714

Note: Oct 1 was the closing ceremony – but also the finish of the Marathon.

Points Table for Places

Scoring 8 for 1st to 1 for 8th.

Nation	1	2	3	4	5	6	7	8	Total
USA	10	4	6	3	3	-	5	4	185
RUS	3	4	5	3	5	3	1	4	132
GER	2	1	2	3	5	5	4	7	100
GBR	2	2	2	5	3	4	1	2	95
ETH	4	1	3	3	-	3	1	-	83
CUB	2	2	2	4	2	3	1	2	83
KEN	2	3	2	3	3	1	-	-	79
JAM	-	4	3	4	-	-	-	2	68
POL	4	-	-	1	3	2	2	2	61
AUS	1	2	-	-	4	3	2	3	53
BLR	2	-	3	2	-	1	1	-	49
ROM	1	2	2	-	-	3	-	-	42.5
GRE	1	3	-	-	1	1	2	-	40
UKR	-	-	2	1	4	-	2	2	39
RSA	-	1	2	1	-	2	2	1	35
MAR	-	1	3	-	-	1	2	1	33
BAH	1	1	-	1	1	1	2	1	32
ALG	1	1	2	-	1	-	-	-	31
CZE	1	1	-	1	1	1	1	2	31
ITA	-	2	-	1	1	1	2	1	31
ESP	-	-	1	1	2	3	2	1	29
FRA	-	-	-	2	2	1	1	1	24
NGR	-	2	-	1	-	-	2	-	23
MEX	-	1	1	-	2	-	1	-	23
BRA	-	1	-	1	1	1	-	-	19
NOR	1	1	-	-	-	-	-	-	15
JPN	1	-	-	-	-	1	2	-	15
SWE	-	-	1	1	-	1	-	1	14
FIN	1	-	-	-	1	-	-	1	13
TRI	-	1	1	-	-	-	-	-	13
KAZ	1	-	-	-	-	1	-	-	11
CHN	1	-	-	-	-	-	1	1	11
BAR	-	-	1	1	-	-	-	-	11
IRL	-	1	-	-	-	1	-	-	10
CAN	-	-	-	-	1	2	-	-	9.5

Note: Points scores take account of ties.
In all 56 nations placed athletes in the top eight.

2000 CHAMPIONSHIPS

IAAF World Half Marathon Championships

At Veracruz, Mexico, November 12

Men

1. Paul Tergat KEN 63:47
2. Faustin Baha TAN 63:48
3. Tesfaye Jifar ETH 63:50
4. Joseph Kimani KEN 63:52
5. David Ruto KEN 63:59
6. John Gwako KEN 64:16
7. Zebedayo Bayo TAN 64:25
8. Oscar Fernández ESP 64:25
9. Marco Mazza ITA 64:26
10. Noureddine Betim ALG 64:40
11. Toshiyuki Hayata JPN 64:55
12. Ibrahim Seid ETH 65:19
13. Faustino Reynoso MEX 65:34
14. Gemechu Kebede ETH 65:36
15. Koen Allaert BEL 65:41
16. Mohammed Awdl ETH 65:51
17. Clint Verran USA 65:56
18. Satoshi Irifune JPN 66:08
19. George Mofokeng RSA 66:12
20. Bethuel Netshifhefhe RSA 66:18

119 starters. 100 finishers.

Teams: 1. KEN 3:11:38, 2. ETH 3:14:45, 3. BEL 3:18:35, 4. JPN 3:18:44, 5. ITA 3:19:21, 6. ESP 3:20:12, 7. RSA 3:20:28, 8. MEX 3:21:12, 9. MAR 3:21:25, 10. ALG 3:21:43, 11. AUS 2:23:54, 12. COL 3:24:09, 13. USA 3:25:36, 14. FRA 3:25:42, 15. BRA 3:31:53, 16. BLR 3:33:30, 17. GBR 3:35:43, 18. LES 3:38:22, 19. CRO 3:41:43, 20. ARU 3:58:06, 21. TJK 4:13:04.

Women

1. Paula Radcliffe GBR 69:07
2. Susan Chepkemei KEN 69:40
3. Lidia Simon ROM 70:24
4. Mizuki Noguchi JPN 71:11
5. Pamela Chepchumba KEN 71:33
6. Mihaela Botezan ROM 71:52
7. Cristiana Pomacu ROM 72:06
8. Yukiko Okamoto JPN 72:20
9. Yasuko Hashimoto JPN 72:54
10. Milena Glusac USA 73:53
11. Lidiya Grigoryeva RUS 74:26
12. Stine Larsen NOR 74:39
13. Galina Aleksandrova RUS 75:02
14. Selma dos Reis BRA 75:16
15. Wilma van Onna NED 75:17
16. Fumi Murata JPN 75:52
17. Aster Bacha ETH 75:52
18. María Luisa Muñoz ESP 75:54
19. Sarah Young-Wilkinson GBR 75:55
20. Abeba Tolla ETH 75:59

61 starters. 54 finishers

Teams: 1. ROM 3:34:22, 2. JPN 3:36:25, 3. RUS 3:45:41, 4. ETH 3:48;20, 5. USA 3:49:03, 6. GBR 3:49:55, 7. RSA 3:55:26, 8. MEX 3:56:55, 9. GUA 4:33:36, 10. CRO 4:41:29.

IAAF World Junior Championships 2000

THE EIGHTH edition of this biennial meeting was held at Santiago de Chile on 17-22 October. in excellent conditions, although it was hot for the distance races at between 28°C and 31°C each afternoon. Two sprinters were the stars – Hamdan Al-Bishi and Mark Lewis-Francis. Al-Bishi, who had run his second Asian junior record with 45.22 at the Olympic Games made another huge leap forward, as he won the title by the huge margin of 1.07 sec, his 44.66 improving the Championships record by 0.61 sec.

A championships record (Christian Malcolm's 10.12 from 1998) was equalled by Mark Lewis-Francis, who later overtook France's Leslie Djhone on the final leg of the sprint relay to bring Britain home in another Championships best for his second gold medal. The British team set a European Junior record time of 39.05 and all remain juniors for 2001.

Two juniors came into the Championships with Sydney Olympic medals. One – the gold medallist from the women's hammer, Kamila Skolimowska – had a disaster here as she failed even to make the final (after two no throws she managed only 51.84, almost as bad as when she had three no throws at the previous Championships in 1998!), but the other, sprint relay silver medallist Veronica Campbell, excelled to take the sprint double, both in Championship record times. Campbell, like Lewis-Francis still with a year to go in junior ranks, had a winning margin at 100m of 0.27 compared to 0.26 by Lewis-Francis and she was just as outstanding at 200m, where she won in a Jamaican junior record time of 22.87 to 23.20 by Sina Schielke. This was the first women's 100m/200m double at the World Juniors and there was another unique double from Jana Pittman, who won both 400m and 400m hurdles.

Kenyans took all the men's running titles from 800m to 10,000m and outstanding were Raymond Yator, who improved the Championships record for the steeplechase by over seven seconds, and Cornelius Chirchir, younger brother of William, who controlled the 1500m by leading from the start and running the first 400m in 57.99 and the last in 56.07. The four women's distance events from 800m upwards were shared between Kenya and Ethiopia, with 16 year-old Georgie Clarke of Australia having to settle for a silver and a bronze.

The outstanding women's mark came in the qualifying round of the triple jump, when Anastasiya Ilyina improved her best from 13.90 to 14.52 for the third best junior mark of all-time. She just held off teammate Anna Pyatkh, 14.24 to 14.18, to win the gold medal. The best throwing performances came from new Championships bests by Rutger Smith in the men's shot (in which four men beat 19m after only one in the entire history of these championships before) and Ivana Brkljajcic in the women's hammer.

Five women's titles went to athletes born in 1983, who will be eligible to defend their titles in two years time, including the hugely promising Carolina Klüft who added 242 points to her Swedish junior heptathlon record. The youngest winner of all, however, was the Kenyan Robert Kipchumba, born in 1984, who won the men's 10,000m at 16 years 235 days.

The Nigerian team were unable to compete due to visa problems and a major talking point was the very poor performance by the US team, who amazingly took just one medal – bronze in the men's pole vault – to come in 30th equal on the medal table. They also only had a further five top eight placings. Their lack of competition for juniors during the summer and the unwillingness to compete of some of those who had qualified at their Junior Championships cost them dearly.

Men

100 Metres (18) (+0.1)

1	Mark Lewis-Francis GBR	10.12*
2	Salem Mohamed Al-Yami KSA	10.38
3	Marc Burns TRI	10.40
4	Darrel Brown TRI	10.40
5	Michael Frater JAM	10.46
6	Ricardo Alves POR	10.52
7	Saad Faraj Al-Shahwani QAT	10.54
8	Edson Ollarves VEN	10.64

200 Metres (21) (+1.3)

1	Paul Gorries RSA	20.64
2	Marek Jedrusinski POL	20.87
3	Tim Benjamin GBR	20.94
4	Omar Brown II JAM	21.04
5	Yusuke Omae JPN	21.05
6	Marvin Anderson JAM	21.06
7	Dwayne Grant GBR	21.33
8	Johan Engberg SWE	21.38

400 Metres (20)

1	Hamdan Al-Bishi KSA	44.66*
2	Brandon Simpson JAM	45.73
3	Shinji Ishikawa JPN	45.77
4	Damion Barry TRI	45.86
5	William Hernández VEN	45.94
6	Richard Sharp RSA	45.97
7	Jonathan Palma VEN	46.36
8	Rafal Wieruszewski POL	46.37

800 Metres (20)

1	Nicholas Wachira KEN	1:47.16
2	Florent Lacasse FRA	1:47.61
3	António Reina ESP	1:47.90
4	Salem Al-Badri QAT	1:48.51
5	Arnoud Okken NED	1:49.10
6	Abdelkebir Louraïbi MAR	1:49.88
7	Jason Stewart II NZL	1:50.34
8	Aldwyn Sappleton JAM	1:50.63

1500 Metres (22)

1	Cornelius Chirchir KEN	3:38.80
2	Wolfram Müller GER	3:39.37
3	Philemon Kibet KEN	3:40.77
4	Jamal Noor QAT	3:42.27
5	Johan Cronje RSA	3:42.52
6	Ridouane Harroufi MAR	3:43.34
7	Abu Bakr Kamal QAT	3:44.12
8	Tarek Boukensa ALG	3:44.46

5000 Metres (21)

1	Gordon Mugi KEN	13:44.93
2	Kenenisa Bekele ETH	13:45.43
3	Cyrus Kataron KEN	13:46.12
4	Obed Mutanya ZAM	13:46.33
5	Biruk Deberework ETH	13:54.17
6	Khoudir Aggoune ALG	14:01.16
7	Cuthbert Nyasango ZIM	14:02.02
8	Aïssa Dghougi MAR	14:07.30

10,000 Metres (17)

1	Robert Kipchumba KEN	28:54.37
2	Duncan Lebo KEN	28:58.39
3	Abraha Hadush ETH	29:44.65
4	Kebede Tekeste ETH	29:44.69
5	Jeffrey Gwebu RSA	30:01.62
6	Jean Baptiste Simukeka RWA	30:08.87
7	Zhang Yunshan CHN	30:24.02
8	Vasiliy Matviychuk UKR	30:41.23

3000 Metres Steeplechase (21)

1	Raymond Yator KEN	8:16.34*
2	David Chemweno KEN	8:31.95
3	Abdellatif Chemlal MAR	8:43.57
4	Adelino Monteiro POR	8:45.34
5	Martin Pröll AUT	8:46.80
6	Itai Maghidi ISR	8:51.26
7	Jukka Keskisalo FIN	8:53.18

8 Rami Al-Faar KSA 8:53.48

110 Metres Hurdles (20) (-0.1)
1 Yunier Hernández CUB 13.60
2 Thomas Blaschek GER 13.80
3 Ladji Doucouré FRA 13.84
4 Liu Xiang CHN 13.87
5 Philip Nossmy SWE 13.92
6 Nassim Meziane QAT 14.14
7 Robert Newton GBR 14.22
8 Chris Baillie GBR 14.28

400 Metres Hurdles (21)
1 Marek Plawgo POL 49.23
2 Ter de Villiers RSA 50.52
3 Okkert Cilliers RSA 50.58
4 Christian Duma GER 50.60
5 Yevgeniy Meleshenko KAZ 51.05
6 Mikael Jakobsson SWE 51.48
7 Loic Clement FRA 52.26
8 Sean Avery AUS 54.95

High Jump (19)
1 Jacques Freitag RSA 2.24
2 Germaine Mason JAM 2.24
3 Tomasz Smialek POL 2.21
4 Jessé de Lima BRA 2.18
5 Matt Vincent USA 2.18
6 Andrey Chubsa BLR 2.15
7= Mickael Hanany FRA 2.10
7= Alfred Neale USA 2.10
7= Yohaav Shuster ISR 2.10

Pole Vault (22)
1 Aleksey Khanafin RUS 5.30
2 Aleksandr Korchmyd UKR 5.30
3 Rocky Danners USA 5.20
4 Steve Hooker AUS 5.20
5 Toshio Imura JPN 5.20
6 Vasiliy Petrov II RUS 5.20
7 Shunsuke Shimo JPN 5.20
8= Kewin Rans BEL 5.00
8= Alhahi Jeng SWE 5.00

Long Jump (22)
1 Cai Peng CHN 7.88/-0.5
2 Vladimir Zyuskov UKR 7.84/-0.6
3 Yoelmis Pacheco CUB 7.71/0.5
4 Victor Castillo VEN 7.66/0.6
5 Tim Parravicini AUS 7.65/-2.5
6 Imre Lórincz HUN 7.65/0.1
7 Daniel Kaczmarczyk POL 7.57/0.7
8 Luka Aracic CRO 7.50/-1.4

Triple Jump (20)
1 Marian Oprea ROM 16.41/1.9
2 Yoandri Betanzos CUB 16.34/0.5
3 Mohammed Hamdi Awadh QAT 16.29/-0.5
4 Gu Junjie CHN 16.26/0.7
5 Leevan Sands BAH 16.22/-1.3
6 Arvidas Nazarovas LTU 16.13/0.4
7 Marcelo da Costa BRA 16.10/-0.3
8 Ibrahim Mahmedin QAT 16.05/-0.4

Shot (19)
1 Rutger Smith NED 19.48*
2 Ivan Yushkov RUS 19.06
3 Tomasz Chrzanowski POL 19.00
4 Pavel Lyzhin BLR 19.00
5 Jeff Chakouian USA 18.89
6 Yuriy Belov BLR 18.83
7 Pavel Sofin RUS 18.26
8 Jaroslaw Cichocki II POL 18.26

Discus (21)
1 Hannes Hopley RSA 59.51
2 Niklas Arrhenius SWE 59.19
3 Rutger Smith NED 58.70
4 Michal Hodun POL 58.62
5 Rasheed Al-Dosari QAT 58.29
6 Loy Martínez CUB 56.94
7 Pavel Lyzhin BLR 56.24
8 Krishnakumar Sharma IND 52.01

Hammer (18)
1 Esref Apak TUR 69.97
2 Dylan Armstrong CAN 67.50
3 Aaron Fish AUS 67.44
4 Aleksey Yeliseyev RUS 65.82
5 Dilchod Nazarov TJK 63.43
6 Alessandro Beschi ITA 61.58
7 Jari Polvi FIN 60.15
8 Lucas Andino ARG 58.69

Javelin (22)
1 Hardus Pienaar RSA 78.11
2 Andreas Thorkildsen NOR 76.34
3 Park Jae-myong KOR 72.36
4 Janis Liepa LAT 71.93
5 Song Dong-hyun KOR 71.20
6 Aleksandr Ivanov II RUS 71.02
7 Chen Te-Chun TPE 68.39
8 Vadims Vasilevskis LAT 68.14

Decathlon (18/19)
1 Dennis Leyckes GER 7897
2 David Gómez ESP 7772
3 André Niklaus GER 7712
4 Dmitriy Karpov KAZ 7366
5 Indrek Turi EST 7222
6 Pavel Havlícek CZE 7131
7 Pavel Dubitskiy KAZ 6998
8 Mikk Joorits EST 6979

10,000 Metres Walk (19)
1 Cristian Berdeja MEX 40:56.47
2 Yevgeniy Demkov RUS 40:56.53
3 Viktor Burayev RUS 40:56.97
4 Takeaki Agatsuma JPN 42:39.08
5 Pei Chuang CHN 42:41.01
6 Patrick Ennemoser ITA 42:50.73
7 José Alessandro Bagio BRA 43:18.95
8 Aleksandr Kuzmin BLR 43:20.96

4 x 100 Metres (22)
1 GBR 39.05*
Tyrone Edgar, Dwayne Grant, Tim Benjamin, Mark Lewis-Francis
2 FRA 39.33
Ronald Pognon, Fabrice Calligny, Ladji Doucouré, Leslie Djhone

3	JPN	39.47
		Takashi Mogi, Kazuya Kitamura, Yusuke Omae, Hisashi Miyazaki
4	TRI	40.03
5	JAM	40.07
6	GER	40.42
7	HUN	40.57
–	POL	DNF

4 x 400 Metres (22)

1	JAM	3:06.06
		Sekou Clarke, Aldwyn Sappleton, Pete Coley, Brandon Simpson
2	GER	3:06.79
		Sebastian Gatzka, Christina Duma, Steffen Hönig, Bastian Swillims
3	POL	3:07.05
		Rafal Wieruszewski, Karol Terejils, Adrian Galaszewski, Marek Plawgo
4	RSA	3:07.66
5	ESP	3:09.22
6	VEN	3:09.71
7	CHI	3:12.25
8	AUS	3:14.44

Women

100 Metres (18) (+2.0)

1	Veronica Campbell JAM	11.12*
2	Katchi Habel GER	11.39
3	Fana Ashby TRI	11.47
4	Vida Anim GHA	11.58
5	Nadine Palmer JAM	11.59
6	Christa Kaufmann GER	11.66
7	Emily Maher IRL	11.73
8	Tathiana Regina Ignacio BRA	11.84

200 Metres (21) (+0.7)

1	Veronica Campbell JAM	22.87*
2	Sina Schielke GER	23.20
3	Vida Anim GHA	23.81
4	Malgorzata Flejszar POL	23.94
5	Vernicha James GBR	23.96
6	Emily Maher IRL	24.00
7	Melanie Kleeberg AUS	24.39
8	Kim Wall GBR	24.46

400 Metres (20)

1	Jana Pittman AUS	52.45
2	Aneta Lemiesz POL	52.78
3	Norma González COL	53.30
4	Maria Rus ROM	53.46
5	Natalya Ivanova RUS	53.58
6	Natalya Pigida UKR	53.69
7	Karen Gayle JAM	53.95
8	Martina McCarthy IRL	54.32

800 Metres (20)

1	Chebet Langat KEN	2:01.51
2	Georgie Clarke AUS	2:02.28
3	Lucia Klocová SVK	2:04.00
4	Alina Rîpanu ROM	2:04.60
5	Esther Desviat ESP	2:06.55
6	Tatyana Petlyuk UKR	2:07.26
7	Jeruto Kiptum KEN	2:08.97
–	Kerstin Werner GER	DNS

1500 Metres (21)

1	Abebech Negussie ETH	4:19.93
2	Rose Koskei KEN	4:20.16
3	Georgie Clarke AUS	4:20.21
4	Zanelle Grobler RSA	4:21.41
5	Rasa Drazdauskaite LTU	4:21.58
6	Chen Fang CHN	4:22.81
7	Florence Kyalo KEN	4:22.95
8	Melissa Rollison AUS	4:25.17

3000 Metres (22)

1	Beatrice Chepchumba KEN	9:08.80
2	Jane Chepkoech KEN	9:10.05
3	Etalemahu Kidane ETH	9:11.55
4	Chen Fang CHN	9:12.53
5	Mestawat Tufa ETH	9:16.73
6	Hewan Can TUR	9:28.20
7	Carol Henry CAN	9:31.88
8	Jessica Augusto POR	9:33.37

5000 Metres (17)

1	Dorcus Inzikuru UGA	16:21.32
2	Meseret Defaru ETH	16:23.69
3	Sharon Cherop KEN	16:23.73
4	Kayoko Fukushi JPN	16:25.01
5	Fridah Domongole KEN	16:28.35
6	Hewan Can TUR	16:33.77
7	Eyerusalem Kuma ETH	16:40.07
8	Wang Xiaoming CHN	16:46.75

100 Metres Hurdles (19) (-1.7)

1	Susanna Kallur SWE	13.02
2	Fanny Gérance FRA	13.21
3	Adrianna Lamalle FRA	13.27
4	Toni Ann Doyley JAM	13.29
5	Jacqui Munro AUS	13.30
6	Jenny Kallur SWE	13.30
7	Anay Tejeda CUB	13.38
8	Maíla Paula Machado BRA	13.50

400 Metres Hurdles (21)

1	Jana Pittman AUS	56.27
2	Marjorlein de Jong NED	56.50
3	Melanie Walker JAM	56.96
4	Lantosoa Razafinjanahary MAD	58.14
5	Irena Zauna LAT	58.93
6	Zofia Malachowska POL	59.03
7	Perla dos Santos BRA	59.36
8	Karolina Tlustochowska POL	59.49

High Jump (20)

1	Blanka Vlasic CRO	1.91
2	Marina Kuptsova RUS	1.88
3	Marisa Gertenbach RSA	1.88
4	Anna Chicherova RUS	1.85

5	Melanie Skotnik GER	1.85
6	Katja Schötz GER	1.85
7	Petrina Price AUS	1.80
8	Nicolize Steyn RSA	1.80

Pole Vault (18)

1	Yelena Isinbayeva RUS	4.20*
2	Annika Becker GER	4.10
3=	Vanessa Boslak FRA	4.10
3=	Fanni Juhász HUN	4.10
5	Martina Strutz GER	4.00
6=	Michaela Boulová CZE	3.70
6=	Bridgid Isworth AUS	3.70
6=	Lucie Palasová CZE	3.70

Long Jump (18)

1	Concepción Montaner ESP	6.47/0.6
2	Zhou Yangxia CHN	6.45w/2.9
3	Kumiko Ikeda JPN	6.43/0.8
4	Dana Veldaková SVK	6.35/0.7
5	Yevgeniya Stavchanska UKR	6.23/-1.0
6	Irina Simagina RUS	6.21/0.2
7	Maria Chiara Baccini ITA	6.20/-0.1
8	Nolle Graham JAM	6.16/0.5

Triple Jump (21)

1	Anastasiya Ilyina RUS (14.52/0.6* in qualifying)	14.24/-0.3
2	Anna Pyatykh RUS	14.18/1.2
3	Dana Veldaková SVK	13.92/1.4
4	Mabel Gay CUB	13.74w/3.2
5	Zhou Yangxia CHN	13.72/1.2
6	Song Ying CHN	13.46/1.1
7	Shelly-Ann Gallimore JAM	13.25w/2.3
8	Aurélie Talbot FRA	13.16/0.8

Shot (17)

1	Kathleen Kluge GER	17.37
2	Li Meiju CHN	16.57
3	Natalya Kharaneko BLR	16.40
4	Laura Gerraughty USA	15.71
5	Anna Tolokina RUS	15.42
6	Lucia Korceková SVK	15.30
7	Claudia Villeneuve FRA	15.09
8	Kamila Hlavacová CZE	14.98

Discus (19)

1	Seena Antil IND	55.27
2	Xu Shaoyang CHN	54.41
3	Jana Tucholke GER	53.97
4	Volha Hancharenka BLR	53.64
5	Julia Bremser GER	53.06
6	Vera Begic CRO	52.28
7	Natalya Fokina UKR	51.44
8	Claire Smithson GBR	50.18

Hammer (18)

1	Ivana Brkljajcic CRO	62.22*
2	Virginia Balut ROM	60.23
3	Yunaika Crawford CUB	59.98
4	Merja Korpela FIN	59.59
5	Martina Danisová SVK	57.75
6	Natalya Kravchenko UKR	56.51
7	Yuliya Denisova RUS	55.56
8	Debby van der Schilt NED	55.15

Javelin (20)

1	Jarmila Klimesová CZE	54.82
2	Inga Kozarenoka LAT	54.64
3	Galina Kakhava BLR	54.26
4	Magdalena Czenska POL	53.59
5	Yi Chunmei CHN	53.12
6	Goldie Sayers GBR	51.52
7	Hidemi Ueki JPN	50.88
8	Christina Obergföll GER	50.23

Heptathlon (19/20)

1	Carolina Klüft SWE	6056
2	Lidiya Bashlykova RUS	5898
3	Sanna Saarman FIN	5707
4	Barbora Spotáková CZE	5689
5	Jessica Zelinka CAN	5688
6	Olga Karas RUS	5584
7	Yvonne Wisse NED	5371
8	Lucia Tomaseková SVK	5353

10,000 Metres Walk (20)

1	Lyudmila Yefimkina RUS	44:07.74
2	Tatyana Kozlova RUS	44:24.43
3	Sabine Zimmer GER	46:49.97
4	Athanasía Tsoumeléka GRE	47:10.96
5	Vera Santos POR	47:11.18
6	Beatriz Pascual ESP	47:14.79
7	Melissa Rodriguez FRA	47:57.88
8	Zuzana Malíková SVK	48:00.84

4 x 100 Metres (22)

1	GER	43.91 Christa Kaufmann, Sina Schielke, Kerstin Grötzinger, Katchi Habel
2	JAM	44.05 Veronica Camell, Nadine Palmer, Kerron Stewart, Nolle Graham
3	SWE	44.78 Emma Rienas, Jenny Kallur, Susanna Kallur, Linda Fernström
4	ITA	44.80
5	AUS	45.04
6	POL	45.23
7	USA	45.43
–	FRA	DQ

4 x 400 Metres (22)

1	GBR	3:33.82 Kim Wall, Jennifer Meadows, Helen Thieme, Lisa Miller
2	JAM	3:33.99 Sheryl Morgan, Kareen Gayle, Aneisha McLaughlin, Melanie Walker
3	ROM	3:34.39 Diana Marchis, Liliana Barbulescu, Maria Rus, Alina Ripanu
4	POL	3:36.11
5	GER	3:36.70
6	UKR	3:37.83
7	AUS	3:38.66
8	NZL	3:49.87

World Juniors Points Table

8 points for 1s to 1 point for 8th

Nation	1	2	3	4	5	6	7	8	Total
GER	3	6	3	1	4	3	-	1	115
RUS	4	6	1	2	2	4	2	-	114
KEN	7	4	3	-	1	-	2	-	110
JAM	3	4	1	2	3	1	2	2	89
RSA	4	1	2	2	2	1	-	1	73
POL	1	2	3	4	-	2	1	1	71
CHN	1	3	-	3	3	2	1	1	65
AUS	2	1	2	1	3	1	3	3	64
ETH	1	2	2	1	2	-	1	-	49
FRA	-	3	3	-	-	-	4	1	48
GBR	3	-	1	-	1	1	2	3	44
SWE	2	1	1	-	1	2	-	2	41
JPN	-	-	3	2	2	-	2	-	40
CUB	1	1	2	1	-	1	1	-	37
UKR	-	2	-	-	1	4	1	1	33
ESP	1	1	1	-	2	1	-	-	32
ROM	1	1	1	2	-	-	-	-	31
BLR	-	-	2	2	-	2	1	1	31
NED	1	1	1	-	1	-	1	1	28
QAT	-	-	1	2	1	1	2	1	28
TRI	-	-	2	3	-	-	-	-	27
SVK	-	-	2	1	1	1	-	2	26
CZE	1	-	-	1	-	3	-	1	23
USA	-	-	1	1	2	-	2	-	23
CRO	2	-	-	-	-	1	-	1	20
KSA	1	1	-	-	-	-	-	1	16

Other nations to win medals (39 in all): 1 gold: IND, MEX, TUR, UGA; 1 silver: CAN, LAT, NOR; 1 bronze: COL, FIN, GHA, HUN, KOR, MAR

IAAF Combined Events Challenge 2000

Men Decathlon

1	Erki Nool	EST	26089	8742 Götzis	8706 Talence	8641 OG
2	Tomás Dvorák	CZE	26018	8900 Götzis	8733 Talence	8385 OG
3	Roman Sebrle	CZE	25591	8757 Götzis	8228 Talence	8606 OG
4	Stefan Schmid	GER	25136	8445 Götzis	8485 Ratingen	8206 OG
5	Attila Zsivóczky	HUN	25124	8554 Götzis	8293 Talence	8277 OG
6	Aleksandr Yurkov	UKR	24685	8574 Götzis	8118 Eur Cup	7993 OG
7	Chris Huffins	USA	24584	7704 Götzis	8285 US Ch	8595 OG
8	Zsolt Kürtösi	HUN	24156	8106 Götzis	7901 Eur Cup	8149 OG
9	Laurent Hernu	FRA	24030	7943 Eur Cup	8178 Talence	7909 OG
10	Klaus Ambrosch	AUT	23922	7892 AUT Ch	8113 Götzis	7917 OG

Women Heptathlon

1	Sabine Braun	GER	19151	6464 Götzis	6332 Ratingen	6355 OG
2	Natalja Roschchupkina	RUS	19127	6513 Götzis	6377 Eur Cup	6237 OG
3=	Natalya Sazanovich	BLR	19047	6232 Götzis	6288 Eur Cup 1	6527 OG
3=	Urszula Wlodarczyk	POL	19047	6351 Talence	6226 Ratingen	6470 OG
5	Karin Ertl	GER	18881	6396 Götzis	6276 Ratingen	6209 OG
6	DeDee Nathan	USA	18592	6099 Götzis	6343 US Ch	6150 OG
7	Tiia Hautala	FIN	18485	6219 Götzis	6093 Ratingen	6173 OG
8	Svetlana Kazanina	KAZ	18346	6111 Desenzano	6161 Götzis	6074 Asian Ch
9	Shelia Burrell	USA	18106	6422 Götzis	6339 US Ch	5345 OG
10	Nathalie Teppe	FRA	18087	6214 Talence	6022 Eur Cup	5851 OG

2000 African Championships

The 12th edition was held at Alger, Algeria, 10-14 July

Men

100m (-0.9)
1. Abdul Aziz Zakari GHA 10.13
2. Stéphane Buckland MRI 10.20
3. Kenneth Andam GHA 10.33

200m (0.2)
1. Abdul Aziz Zakari GHA 20.23
2. Joseph Batangdon CMR 20.31
3. Oumar Loum SEN 20.76

400m
1. Éric Milazar MRI 45.62
2. Malik Louahla ALG 45.78
3. Sofiene Labidi TUN 45.81

800m
1. Djabir Saïd-Guerni 1:45.88
2. Mbulaeni Mulaudzi RSA 1:46.28
3. Mohcine Chehibi MAR 1:46.47

1500m
1. Youssef Baba MAR 3:42.07
2. Adil El Kaouch MAR 3:42.53
3. Mohamed Khaldi ALG 3:42.77

5000m
1. Ali Saïdi-Sief 13:26.86
2. Saïd Bérioui MAR 13:31.75
3. Mohamed El Wardi MAR 13:30.01

10,000m
1. Abreta Hadish ETH 28:40.51
2. Birhanu Dejene ETH 28:41.11
3. Kamel Kohil 28:48.98

3000mSt
1. Lotfi Turki TUN 8:33.29
2. Laïd Bessou 8:35.89
3. David Chepkisa KEN 8:39.00

110mh (-0.3)
1. Berlioz Randriahihaja MAD 13.99
2. Doudou Sow SEN 14.38
3. Taoufik Dahmane ALG 15.10

400mh
1. Sylvester Omodiale NGR 49.81
2. Jean Dième SEN 50.29
3. Yvon Rakotoarimaindry MAD 50.39

HJ
1. Abderahmane Hammad 2.34*
2. Malcolm Hendriks RSA 2.20
3. Eugène Ernesta SEY 2.20

PV
1. Rafik Mefti ALG 5.00
2. Karm Sène SEN 4.80
3. Mohamed Benyahia ALG 4.65

LJ
1. Younès Moudrik MAR 8.34*/1.4
2. Hatem Mersal EGY 7.90/-0.7
3. Mehdi Ghazouani MAR 7.88/-0.1

TJ
1. Andrew Owusu GHA 16.69/-0.1
2. Samuel Okantey GHA 16.69/0.7
3. Olivier Sanou BKF 16.31/-0.7

SP
1. Chima Ugwu NGR 19.02
2. John Sullivan RSA 17.46
3. Hicham Aïtaha MAR 16.91

DT
1. Frits Potgieter RSA 60.35
2. Mickaël Conjungo CAF 59.58
3. Chima Ugwu NGR 57.91

HT
1. Samir Haouam 69.38
2. Mohamed K Horchani TUN 63.68
3. Yamine Hussein EGY 63.71

JT
1. Maher Ridane TUN 72.51
2. Khaled Essayed Yassine EGY 72.01
3. Walid Mohamed EGY 71.67

Dec
1. Rédouane Youcef ALG 7129
2. Maba Ndiaye SEN 6981
3. Adil Chakri MAR 6715

4x100m
1. GHA 39.90
(Duah, K.Andam, Mfum, Zakari)
2. MRI 40.07 3. GAB 40.53

4x400m
1. ALG 3:05.45
(M.Louahla, S.Louahla, Hecini, Saïd-Guerni)
2. BOT 3:06.07 3. SEN 3:06.53

20km W
1. Hatem Ghoula ALG 1:25:38*
2. Moussa Aouanouk ALG 1:25.42
3. Merzak Abbès ALG 1:32:37

Women

100m (-0.6)
1. Myriam Mani CMR 11.46
2. Aïda Diop SEN 11.46
3. Monica Twum GHA 11.47

200m (0.4)
1. Myriam Mani CMR 22.54
2. Aïda Diop SEN 23.01
3. Fatima Yusuf NGR 23.27

400m
1. Claudine Komgang CMR 51.35
2. Mireille Nguimgo CMR 51.81
3. Nadjina Kaltouma CHA 52.27

800m
1. Hasna Benhassi MAR 1:59.01
2. Nouria Mérah-Benida ALG 1:59.73
3. Gladys Wamuyu KEN 2:00.32

1500m
1. Nouria Mérah-Benida ALG 4:16.14
2. Gladys Wamuyu KEN 4:16.56
3. Birhane Hirpessa ETH 4:16.87

5000m
1. Asmae Laghzaoui MAR 15:43.46*
2. Meseret Defar ETH 15:49.86
3. Merima Denboba ETH 15:53.68

10,000m
1. Souad Aït Salem ALG 34:02.28
2. Genet Teka ETH 34:05.18
3. Bouchra Chaabi MAR 34:08.79

100mh (0.1)
1. Glory Alozie NGR 13.09
2. Rosa Rakotozafy MAD 13.21
3. Maria-Joëlle Conjungo CAF 13.77

400mh
1. M Tacko Diouf SEN 57.48
2. Gnima Touré SEN 58.96
3. Djami Nabila TUN 62.45

HJ
1. Hind Bounouar MAR 1.75
2. Amina Lemhjerbi ALG 1.70
3. Hamida Benhocine ALG 1.70

PV
1. Syrin Balti TUN 3.85*
2. Annelle van Wyk RSA 3.80
3. Rasha Abdel Khalek EGY 3.10

LJ
1. Kène Ndoye SEN 6.39/1.2
2. Elisa Cossa MOZ 6.20/0.0
3. Béryl Laramé SEY 6.18/-0.1

TJ
1. Baya Rahouli 14.23*/-1.1
2. Françoise Mbango CMR 13.87/0.4
3. Kène Ndoye SEN 13.81/0.3

SP
1. Hanaa Salah El Melegi EGY 16.01
2. Amel Ben Khaled TUN 15.39
3. Wafa Baghdadi EGY 14.97

DT
1. Monia Kari TUN 58.46*
2. Ndoumbé Gaye SEN 50.81
3. Felicia Nkiru Ojiego NGR 49.65

HT
1. Caroline Fournier MRI 59.60*
2. Marwa Ahmed Hussein EGY 57.15
3. Nawal Iallouléne ALG 49.72

JT
1. Aïda Sellam TUN 53.35*

	2. Lindy Leveaux SEY 50.88
	3. Hanaa Salah El Melegi EGY 42.31
Hep	1. Yasmina Azzizi-Kettab ALG 5837
	2. Maralize Fouché RSA 5726
	3. Patience Itanyi NGR 5611
4x100m	1. GHA 43.99 (Amoako, Twum, Bawuah, Anim)
	2. SEN 44.62 3. CMR 46.97
4x400m	1. CMR 3:32.89 (Nguimgo, Béwouda, Komgang, Mani)
	2. MAR 3:42.91 3. ALG 3:51.01
10kmW	1. Bahia Boussad ALG 49:33*
	2. Najoua Ibrahim Ali EGY 50:15
	3. Dounia Kara ALG 50:55

Asian Championships 2000

The 13th edition was held at Jakarta, Indonesia, 28-31 August

Men

100m (0.2)	1. Jamal Al-Safar KSA 10.32
	2. Anil Kumar IND 10.35
	3. Yin Hanzhao CHN 10.36
200m (0.4)	1. Masahiko Fukunaga JPN 20.78
	2. Sittichai Suwontrateep THA 20.79
	3. Mohammed Al-Hooti OMN 20.81
400m	1. Ibrahim Ismail QAT 44.66
	2. Hamdan Al-Bishi KSA 45.32
	3. Xu Zizhou CHN 45.55
800m	1. Mehdi Jelodarzadeh IRN 1:49.80
	2. Kim Soon-hyung KOR 1:50.06
	3. Lee Jae-hoon KOR 1:50.35
1500m	1. Mohamed Suleiman QAT 3:52.47
	2. Abubaker Ali Kamal 3:52.64
	3. Sun Wenli CHN 3:52.94
5000m	1. Ahmed Ibrahim QAT 13:53.10
	2. Gong Ke CHN 14:04.61
	3. Mohamed Suleiman QAT 14:10.79
10,000m	1. Ahmed Ibrahim QAT 29:53.00
	2. Gulab Chand IND 30:03.75
	3. Gong Ke CHN 30:05.11
3000mSt	1. Khamis S Abdullah QAT 8:47.33
	2. Hassan Al-Asmari KSA 8:52.25
110mh (0.7)	1. Mubarak Ata Mubarak KSA 14.02
	2. Shen Zhensheng CHN 14.13
	3. Park Tae-kyung KOR 14.16
400mh	1. Hadi Soua´an Al-Somaily KSA 49.13
	2. Harijan Ratnayaka SRI 49.44
	3. Zahiruddin Al-Najem SYR 49.67
HJ	1. Yuriy Pakhlyayev KAZ 2.23
	2. Wang Zhouzhou CHN 2.23
	3. Yoshiteru Kaihoko JPN 2.19
PV	1. Zhang Hongwei CHN 5.40
	2. Satoru Yasuda JPN 5.20
	3. Liu Yen-Sung TPE 5.10
LJ	1. Hussein Al-Sabee KSA 8.33*/0.8
	2. Sanjay Kumar Rai IND 8.03/0.4
	3. Abdulrahman Al-Nubi QAT 8.01/-0.4
TJ	1. Nattapol Namkunha THA 16.53/0.4
	2. Maksim Smetarin KGZ 16.33/0.2
	3. Salem Mouled Al-Ahmadi KSA 16.24/-1.1
SP	1. Shakti Singh IND 19.77*
	2. Bilal Saad Mubarak QAT 19.23
	3. Wen Jili CHN 18.18
DT	1. Anil Kumar IND 58.47
	2. Abbas Samini IRN 58.27
	3. Hridayanand Singh IND 56.96
HT	1. Wataru Ebihara JPN 69.50
	2. Yo Kuigang CHN 69.48
	3. Nasser Al-Jarallah KUW 66.98
JT	1. Jagdish Singh Bishnoi IND 76.81
	2. Chu Ki-young KOR 75.27
	3. Sun Shipeng CHN 74.34
Dec	1. Hitoshi Maruono JPN 7321
	2. Kim Kun-woo KOR 7031
	3. Kim Sang-ryong PRK 6970
20kW	1. Wu Ping CHN 1:28:04
	2. Hironori Kawai JPN 1:29:13
	3. Lee Dae-ro KOR 1:30:36
4x100m	1. THA 38.80* (Natenee, Sophanich, Janthana, Suwonprateep)
	2. JPN 39.18 (Fukunaga, Nakagawa, Takahashi, Yasui)
	3. KSA 39.60 (Al-Yami, Ata Mubarak, Al-Yami, Al-Saffar)
4x400m	1. SRI 3:02.71 (Perera, Ratnakumara, Wimalawansa, Kumara)
	2. IND 3:02.78 (Ramachandran, Manoj Lal, Thottan, Paramjit Singh)
	3. KSA 3:05.00 (Hamdan Al-Bishi, M Al-Bishi, Hamed Al-Bishi, Al-Somaily)

Women

100m (+1.0)	1. Lyubov Perepelova UZB 11.31
	2. Saraswati Dey IND 11.40
	3. Rachita Mistry IND 11.46
200m (+0.7)	1. Damayanthi Dharsha SRI 22.84*
	2. Lyubov Perepelova UZB 23.30
	3. Vinita Tripathy IND 23.39
400m	1. Damayanthi Dharsha SRI 51.05*
	2. K M Beenamol IND 51.41
	3. Chan Yuxiang CHN 52.81
800m	1. Lin Na CHN 2:03.46
	2. Wang Yuanping CHN 2:04.11
	3. Rosa Kutty IND 2:04.97
1500m	1. Wu Qingdong CHN 4:17.82
	2. Zhang Ling CHN 4:18.31
	3. Ok Tok-sun PRK 4:20.04
5000m	1. Wu Qingdong 15:58.83
	2. Naomi Sakashita JPN 16:01.53
	3. Supriati Sutono INA 16:03.85
10,000m	1. Supriati Sutono INA 33:47.24
	2. Aruna Devi IND 34:31.15
	3. Hong Myung-hui PRK 35:27.50
100mh (+0.8)	1. Su Yiping CHN 12.99
	2. Trecia Roberts THA 13.01
	3. Anuradha Biswal IND 13.40
400mh	1. Song Yinlan CHN 57.73
	2. Yasuko Igari JON 58.90
	3. Norasheela Mohd Khalid MAS 59.62

HJ	1. Bobby Aloysius IND 1.83
	2. Marina Korzhova KAZ 1.83
	3. Tatyana Efimenko KGZ 1.80
PV	1. Takayo Kondo JPN 4.00*
	2. Chang Hsin TAI 3.90
	3. Masumi Ono JPN 3.80
LJ	1. Yelena Bobrovskaya KGZ 6.66/0.2
	2. Liang Shuyan CHN 6.64/0.5
	3. Maho Hanaoka JPN 6.61/0.5
TJ	1. Yelena Parfyonova KAZ 14.08/0.7
	2. Miao Chunqing CHN 14.01/1.9
	3. Maho Hanaoka JPN 13.67/1.9
SP	1. Nada Kawar JOR 17.46
	2. Chinatsu Mori JPN 16.38
	3. Cho Jin-sook KOR 15.38
DT	1. Neelam Jaswant Singh IND 60.75
	2. Cao Qi CHN 58.71
	3. Li Yanfeng CHN 57.52
HT	1. Li Xiaoxue CHN 59.02
	2. Yuka Murofushi JPN 58.64
	3. Masami Aya JPN 55.97
JT	1. Lee Young-sun KOR 55.78*
	2. Gurmeet Kaur IND 55.65
	3. Zhang Li CHN 55.07
Hep	1. Svetlana Kazanina KAZ 6074
	2. G Pramila Ganapathy IND 6016
	3. Irina Naumenko KAZ 5937
10kW	1. Li Hong CHN 44:59.90*
	2. Sun Chunfang CHN 45:42.68
	3. Yuan Yufang MAS 46:12.66
4x100m	1. SRI 44.23
	(Samandeepika, Herath, De Zoysa, Dharsha)
	2. IND 44.48
	(Biswal, Tripathi, Dey, Mistry)
	3. CHN 44.80
	(Su Y, Chen Y, Yan J, Chen Y)
4x400m	1. IND 3:31.54*
	(P Kaur, Philips, Kutty, K Beenamol)
	2. JPN 3:37.15
	(Sugimori, Kakinuma, Nobuoka, Yoshida)
	3. KOR 3:48.29
	(Kim S-y, Jeon M-y, Kim S-k, Kim D-h)

Medal table of leading nations

	G	S	B	Total
CHN	9	10	10	29
IND	6	10	5	21
QAT	5	2	2	9
JPN	4	8	5	17
KSA	4	2	3	9
SRI	4	1	0	5
KAZ	3	1	1	5
THA	2	2	0	4
KOR	1	3	5	9

A total of 20 nations won medals. A men's record of five individual event gold medals was set by Ibrahim Ismail QAT (400m 1987-91-93-95-00) and Mohammed Suleiman QAT (1500m 1991-95-98-00, 5000m 1991).

CAC Junior Championships 2000

Jul 14-16, San Juan, Puerto Rico.

Men: 100m: Marvin Anderson JAM 10.56, **200m**: Omar Brown JAM 21.10, **400m**: Brandon Simpson JAM 46.49, **800m**: Alwyn Sappleton JAM 1:51.84, **1500m**: Heleodoro Navarro MEX 3:57.73, **5000m**: Antonio Cortez MEX 15:07.72, **10000m**: Sergio de León GUA 32:16.20, **3000mSt**: Erick Bonilla ESA 9:29.08, **110mh**: Dwayne Robinson JAM 14.21w, **400mh**: Jorge Chaverra COL 52.98, **HJ**: Germaine Mason JAM 2.15, **PV**: Kenith Goodridge TRI 3.95, **LJ**: Cleavon Dillon TRI 8.09w, **TJ**: Leevans Sands BAH 15.95w, **SP**: Manuel Repollet PUR 16.18, **DT**: Dwayne Henclewood JAM 51.10, **HT** Omar Ortiz PUR 45.95, **JT**: Edwin Cuesta VEN 69.91*, **Dec**: Rubén Arcia VEN 6387, **4x100m**: JAM (Anderson, Brown, Frater, Mullings) 40.39, **4x400m**: JAM (Coley, Sappleton, Clarke, Simpson) 3:08.42, **10000m** W: David Berdeja MEX 41:29.66*. **Women**: **100m**: Veronica Campbell JAM 11.18*, **200m**: Farna Ashby TRI 23.67w, **400m**: Hazel Ann Regis GRN 53.32, **800m**: Karen Gayle JAM 2:06.37*, **1500m/5000m**: Valentina Medina VEN 4:35.68/17:50.72, **3000m**: Meleshia Spencer JAM 10:15.96, **100mh**: Toni Ann Doyle JAM 13.30w, **400mh**: Melanie Walker JAM 59.65, **HJ**: Sheree Francis JAM 1.86*, **PV**: Yoisemil Fuentes VEN 3.25, **LJ**: Nolle Graham JAM 6.47, **TJ**: Shelly Ann Gallimore JAM 13.15w, **SP**: Yanira Hurtado VEN 14.18, **DT**: Chafree Baun BAH 44.05, **HT**: Dubraska Rodríguez VEN 47.46, **JT**: Ana Gutiérrez MEX 46.28, **Hep**: Keitha Moseley BAR 4723, **4x100m**: JAM (Lloyd, Palmer, Campbell, Graham) 44.26*, **4x400m**: JAM (Simpson, Morgan, Walker, Williams) 3:36.14, **5000mW**: Natalia García MEX 25:06.34.

European Cup 2000

Super-League at Gateshead, GBR 15-16 July

Men: 1. GBR 101.5, 2. GER 101, 3. FRA 97, 4. ITA 96.5, 5. RUS 88.5, 6. GRE 88.5, 7. SWE 75, 8. HUN 62.

100m	1. Darren Campbell GBR 10.09w
(2.3)	2. Roland Németh HUN 10.19
	3. Andrea Colombo ITA 10.23
200m	1. Christian Malcolm GBR 20.45
(0.0)	2. Alessandro Cavallaro ITA 20.48
	3. Konstadínos Kéderis GRE 20.48
400m	1. Jamie Baulch GBR 46.64
	2. Alessandro Attene ITA 46.71
	3. Jimisola Laursen SWE 46.93
800m	1. Mahdi Baala FRA 1:47.90
	2. Nils Schumann GER 1:47.94
	3. Balázs Korányi HUN 1:48.52
1500m	1. Mahdi Baala FRA 3:41.75
	2. JohnMayock GBR 3:42.32
	3. Vyacheslav Shabunin RUS 3:42.44

3000m 1. Driss Maazouzi FRA 7:58.7
2. Vyacheslav Shabunin RUS 7:59.0
3. Anthony Whiteman GBR 8:01.0
5000m 1. Mustapha Essaïd FRA 13:47.44
2. Dmitriy Maksimov RUS 13:48.43
3. Sebastian Hallmann GER 13:49.95
3000mSt 1. Bouabdallah Tahri FRA 8:27.28
2. Damian Kallabis GER 8:29.16
3. Giuseppe Maffei ITA 8:34.47
110mh (1.4) 1. Falk Balzer GER 13.52
2. Emiliano Pizzoli ITA 13.54
3. Robert Kronberg SWE 13.67
400mh 1. Chris Rawlinson GBR 48.84
2. Ruslan Mashchenko RUS 49.19
3. Fabrizio Mori ITA 49.98
HJ 1. Stefan Holm SWE 2.28
2. Wolfgang Kreissig GER 2.25
3= Sergey Klyugin RUS 2.20
3= Lábros Papakóstas GRE 2.20
PV 1. Yevgeniy Smiryagin RUS 5.85
2. Tim Lobinger GER 5.75
3. Patrik Kristiansson SWE 5.70
LJ 1. Vitaliy Shkurlatov RUS 8.22/1.8
2. Kofi Amoah Prah GER 8.15w/2.1
3. Peter Häggström SWE 8.08w/3.3
TJ 1. Larry Achike GBR 17.31w/4.4
2. Fabrizio Donato ITA 17.17w/2.8
3. Stamatis Lenis GRE 17.01/1.5
SP 1. Paolo Dal Soglio ITA 19.99
2. Michael Mertens GER 19.71
3. Jimmy Nordin SWE 19.46
DT 1. Lars Riedel GER 63.30
2. Róbert Fazekas HUN 62.15
3. Vitaliy Sidorov RUS 60.91
HT 1. Christophe Epalle FRA 78.51
2. Alexandros Papadimitríou GRE 77.64
3. Karsten Kobs GER 77.55
JT 1. Sergey Makarov RUS 89.92*
2. Kostas Gatsioúdis GRE 84.56
3. Boris Henry GER 82.83
4x100m 1. GBR 38.41
(Malcolm, Campbell, Devonish, Chambers)
2. GRE 38.07 3. ITA 39.17
4x400m 1. FRA 3:04.50
(Wavelet, Foucan, Demonière, Raquil)
2. GBR 3:05.24 3. HUN 3:05.88

Women: 1. RUS 124, 2. GER 111, 3. FRA 87, 4. ITA 79, 5. GBR 78, 6. ROM 72, 7. UKR 71, 8. GRE 56.

100m (2.9) 1. Ekateríni Thánou GRE 10.84w
2. Christine Arron FRA 11.02
3. Manuela Levorato ITA 11.13
200m (-0.3) 1. Muriel Hurtis FRA 22.70
2. Natalya Voronova RUS 22.81
3. Andrea Philipp GER 22.88
400m 1. Svetlana Pospelova RUS 50.63
2. Donna Fraser GBR 51.78
3. Uta Rohländer GER 52.17
800m 1. Irina Mistyukevich RUS 2:02.52
2. Linda Kisabaka GER 2:03.88
3. Patricia Djaté FRA 2:04.44
1500m 1. Helen Pattinson GBR 4:12.05
2. Yelena Zadorozhnaya RUS 4:12.20
3. Kristina da Fonseca-Wollheim GER 4:13.11
3000m 1. Gabriela Szabo ROM 8:43.33
2. Galina Bogomolova RUS 8:43.45
3. Hayley Tullett GBR 8:45.39
5000m 1. Tatyana Tomashova RUS 14:53.00
2. Irina Mikitenko GER 14:54.30
3. Yamna Belkacem FRA 14:57.05
100mh (0.2) 1. Linda Ferga FRA 12.93
2. Maya Shemchishina UKR 12.95
3. Yuliya Graudyn RUS 13.08
400mh 1. Tatyana Tereshchuk UKR 54.68
2. Ulrike Urbansky GER 56.10
3. Monika Niederstatter ITA 56.33
HJ 1. Monica Dinescu ROM 1.93
2. Yuliya Lyakhova RUS 1.91
3. Joanne Jennings-Steele GBR 1.86
PV 1. Svetlana Feofanova RUS 4.35*
2. Yvonne Buschbaum GER 4.30
3. Francesca Dolcini ITA 4.20
LJ 1. Olga Rublyova RUS 6.87/1.2
2. Yelena Shekhovtsova UKR 6.79/1.0
3. Fiona May ITA 6.74w/2.8
TJ 1. Tatyana Lebedeva RUS 14.98*/0.9
2. Yelena Govorova UKR 14.31/0.2
3. Barbara Lah ITA 13.86/0.8
SP 1. Astrid Kumbernuss GER 18.94
2. Kalliopi Ouzoúni GRE 18.16
3. Judy Oakes GBR 18.08
DT 1. Nicoleta Grasu ROM 63.35
2. Ilke Wyludda GER 62.45
3. Anastasia Kelesídou GRE 62.30
HT 1. Olga Kuzenkova RUS 70.20
2. Kirsten Münchow GER 68.31
3. Manuela Montebrun FRA 67.73
dq (1). Mihaela Melinte ROM 70.20
JT 1. Ana Mirela Termure ROM 63.23
2. Tatyana Shikolenko RUS 60.41
3. Mirela Tzelíli GRE 57.84
4x100m 1. FRA 42.97
(Benth, Hurtis, Dia, Arron)
2. RUS 43.38 3. GER 43.51
4x400m 1. RUS 3:25.50
(Zykina, Rosikhina, Kulikova, Sotnikova)
2. GER 3:27.70 3. GBR 3:28.12

First League Group A *at Nadderud, NOR 8-9 July*

Men: 1. ESP 116, 2. FIN 101, 3. NOR 98, 4. CZE 93, 5. POR 87, 6. SUI 85, 7. BEL 82, 8. DEN 54.
Winners. 100m: Geir Moen NOR 10.37w, **200m**: Patrick Stevens BEL 20.49w, **400m**: David Canal ESP 45.97, **800m**: André Bucher 1:44.80, **1500m**: José A Redolat ESP 3:47.81, **3000m**: Andrés Díaz 8:01.65, **5000m**: Alberto García ESP 13:36.17, **3000mSt**: José Luis Blanco ESP 8:36.42, **110mh**: Antti Haapakoski FIN 13.69, **400mh**: Jirí Muzík CZE 49.83, **HJ**: Arturo Ortiz ESP 2.24, **PV**: Vesa Rantanen FIN 5.60, **LJ**: Carlos Calado POR 7.97w, **TJ**: Johan Meriluoto FIN 16.76w, **SP**: Timo Aaltonen FIN 20.37, **DT**: Timo Tompuri FIN 59.27, **HT**: Olli-Pekka Karjalainen FIN 80.24, **JT**: Aki Parviainen FIN 89.88, **4x100m**: NOR 39.57, **4x400m**: CZE 3:05.90.

Women: 1. CZE 108, 2. SWE 106, 3. ESP 96, 4. FIN 89, 5. HUN 83, 6. POR 72, 7. NOR 71, 8. SUI 59. Winners: **100m**: Heidi Hannula FIN 11.74, **200m**: Mireille Donders SUI 23.22w, **400m**: Helena Fuchsová CZE 52.32, **800m**: Ludmila Formanová CZE 1:59.66, **1500m**: Carla Sacramento POR 4:06.46, **3000m**: Nuria Domínguez ESP 8:57.42, **5000m**: Gunhild Haugen NOR 15:39.68, **100mh**: Susanna Kallur SWE 13.10, **400mh**: Frida Svensson SWE 56.94, **HJ**: Zuzana Hlavanová CZE 1.95, **PV**: Daniela Bártová CZE 4.20, **LJ**: Erica Johansson SWE 7.01w, **TJ**: Camilla Johansson SWE 13.96, **SP**: Martina de la Puente ESP 17.60, **DT**: Anna Söderberg SWE 60.04, **HT**: Katalin Divós HUN 64.51, **JT**: Trine Hattestad NOR 66.96, **4x100m**: NOR 39.57, **4x400m**: CZE 3:05.90.

First League Group B at Bydgoszcz, POL 8-9 July

Men: 1. POL 134, 2. UKR 111, 3. NED 108, 4. BUL 86, 5. SLO 78.5, 6. ROM 77.5, 7. AUT 63, 8. CRO 59. **Winners 100m**: Konstantin Rurak UKR 10.25, **200m**: Patrick van Balkom NED 20.82, **400m**: Ilya Dzhivondov BUL 46.22, **800m**: Bram Som NED 1:50.84, **1500m**: Marko Koers NED 3:41.81, **3000m**: Simon Vroemen NED 8:20.79, **5000m**: Kamiel Maase NED 13:48.41, **3000mSt**: Florin Ionescu ROM 8:28.40, **110mh**: Robin Korving NED 13.49, **400mh**: Pawel Januszewski POL 49.69, **HJ**: Ruslan Glivinskiy UKR 2.22, **PV**: Ilian Efremov BUL 5.70, **LJ**: Petar Dachev BUL 8.00, **TJ**: Rostislav Dimitrov BUL 17.12, **SP**: Leszek Sliwa 19.62, **DT**: Olgierd Stanski 64.20, **HT**: Szymon Ziolkówski POL 79.66, **JT**: Gregor Högler AUT 79.72, **4x100m/4x400m**: POL 39.50/3:02.41.

Women: 1. BLR 118, 2. BUL 116, 3. POL 106, 4. SLO 94, 5. NED 71, 6. AUT 69, 7. IRL 63, 8. CRO 44. **Winners 100m/200m**: Alenka Bikar SLO 11.38/23.29, **400m**: Daniela Georgieva BUL 51.88, **800m**: Jolanda Ceplak SLO 2:03.00, **1500m/3000m**: Lidia Chojecka POL 4:02.69/ 8:44.32, **5000m**: Ann Keenan-Buckley IRL 15:58.44, **100mh**: Svetla Dimitrova BUL 12.96, **400mh**: Susan Smith IRL 56.16, **HJ**: Venelina Veneva BUL 1.97, **PV**: Monika Pyrek POL 4.30, **LJ/TJ**: Iva Prandzheva BUL 6.83/14.64, **SP**: Nadezhda Ostapchuk BLR 18.82, **DT**: Ellina Zvereva BLR 64.94, **HT**: Olga Tsander BLR 64.42, **JT**: Genowefa Patla POL 60.88, **4x100m/4x400m**: BLR 44.19/3:28.36.

Second League Group A at Kaunas, LTU 8-9 July

Men: 1. BLR 132, 2. IRL 125, 3. LTU 108, 4. EST 100, 5. LAT 94, 6. MDA 74, 7. LUX 43, 8. ARM 37
Women: 1. LTU 129, 2. BEL 115, 3. DEN 106, 4. EST 100, 5. LAT 94, 6. MDA 64, 7. LUX 41, 8. ARM 28

Second League Group B at Banská Bystrica, SVK 8-9 July

Men: 1. SVK 140, 2. YUG 136, 3. TUR 132, 4. CYP 127, 5. ISR 116.5, 6. ISL 70, 7. Small States 69, 8. BSH 53, 9. GEO 50.5
Women: 1. TUR 149.5, 2. YUG 136, 3. SVK 120, 4. ISR 116, 5. ISL 95, 6. CYP 83, 7. ALB 64.5, 8. GEO 42, 9. Small States 37

2001 Matches on 23-24 June

SPAR Super-League at Bremen, GER
Men: ESP, FRA, GBR, GER, GRE, ITA, RUS
Women: BLR, CZE, FRA, GBR, GER, ITA, ROM, RUS

First League Group A at Vaasa, FIN
Men: BLR, CZE, FIN, IRL, NOR, POR, SUI, SWE
Women: BEL, ESP, FIN, GRE, LTU, POL, POR, SWE

First League Group B at Budapest, HUN
Men: BUL, HUN, NED, ROM, SLO, SKV, UKR, YUG
Women: AUT, BUL, HUN, NED, SLO, TUR, UKR, YUG

Second League Group A at Riga, LAT
Men: ARM, DEN, EST, GEO, LAT, LTU, LUX, MDA, TUR
Women: ARM, DEN, EST, GEO, IRL, LAT, LUX, MDA, NOR

Second League Group B at Nicosia, CYP
Men: AUT, BEL, BIH, CRO, CYP, ISL, ISR, Small states
Women: ALB, CRO, CYP, ISL, ISR, SUI, SVK, Small states

European Cup for Combined Events 2000

Super League at Oulu, FIN 1-2 July

Men Dec: 1. FRA 23,496, 2. UKR 23,165, 3. RUS 23,144, 4. GER 23,006, 5. FIN 22,616, 6. HUN 22,523, 7. CZE 22,350, 8. ESP 22,229. **Ind:** 1. Aleksandr Yurkov UKR 8118, 2. Laurent Hernu FRA 7943, 3. Zsolt Kürtösi HUN 7901
Women Hep: 1. RUS 18,637, 2. POL 17,759, 3. FRA 17,710, 4. FIN 17,621, 5. GER 17,304, 6. CZE 17,197, 7. UKR 16.750, 8. NED 16,347. **Ind:** 1. Natalya Roshchupkina RUS 6377, 2. Tatyana Gordeyeva RUS 6154, 3. Yelena Chernyavskaya RUS 6106

First League at Schwyz-lbach, SUI 1-2 July

Men Dec: 1. SUI 23,419, 2. GRE 23,093, 3. EST 22,917, 4. NED 22,587, 5. ITA 22,007, 6. SWE 21,926, 7. POL 21,748, 8. NOR 21,538. **Ind:** 1. Pródromos Korkízoglou GRE 8069, 2. Philipp Huber SUI 8062, 3. Indrek Kaseorg EST 8024
Women Hep: 1. BLR 18,248, 2. ITA 17,324, 3. HUN 17,225, 4. GBR 16,553, 5. SUI 16,059, 6. SWE 15.914, 7. ESP 15,856, 8. EST 15,309. **Ind:** 1. Natalya Sazanovich BLR 6288, 2. Rita Ináncsi HUN 6177, 3. Tatyana Alisevich BLR 6146

Second League at Esbjerg, DEN 1-2 July.
Men Dec: 1. AUT 22,366, 2. LAT 21,573, 3. BLR 21,019, 4. GBR 20,793, 5. LTU 19,838, 6. DEN 19,779, incomplete POR. **Ind:** Rojs Piziks LAT 7746
Women Hep: 1. LTU 16,221, 2. GRE 15,806, 3. SLO 15,670, 4. NOR 15,629, 5. BEL 14,586, 6. DEN 14,534, 7. LAT 13,433. **Ind:** Austra Skujytė LTU 6104

2001 Matches

Super League at Arles, FRA 30 Jun - 1 Jul
Men: FIN, FRA, GER, GRE, HUN, RUS, SUI, UKR
Women: BLR, CZE, FIN, FRA, GER, ITA, POL, RUS

First League at Ried, AUT 30 Jun - 1 Jul
Men: AUT, CZE, ESP, EST, ITA, LAT, NED, SWE
Women: GBR, GRE, HUN, LTU, NED, SUI, SWE, UKR

Second League at Kaunas, LTU 30 Jun - 1 Jul
Men: BLR, DEN, GBR, ISL, LTU, NOR, POL, POR, SVK, SLO
Women: AUT, DEN, ESP, EST, ISL, LAT, NOR, POR, SLO

European Cup of Race Walking 2000

At Eusenhüttenstadt, Germany 17-18 June.
There were 216 participants in the five races of the third edition of this biennial competition.
Men 20km: 1. Robert Korzeniowski POL 1:18:29, 2. Andreas Erm GER 1:18:42, 3. Francisco Fernández ESP 1:18:56, 4. Jirí Malysa CZE 1:19:18 rec, 5. Dmitriy Yesipchuk RUS 1:19:56, 6. Aigars Fadejevs LAT 1:20:18, 7. Tomasz Lipiec POL 1:20:48, 8. Artur Meleshkevich BLR 1:20:53, 9. Valentin Kononen FIN 1:21:09, 10. Anthony Gillet FRA 1:21:28; 60 of 65 finished; **Teams:** 1. ESP 32, 2. POL 35, 3. GER 43. 4. ITA 44, 5. RUS 66, 6. SVK 72, 7. LAT 85, 8. FRA 91, 9. UKR 97, 10. GRE 90, 11. FIN 117, 12. YUG 140, 13. LTU 140, 14. SUI 177.
Men 50km: 1. Jesús Angel García ESP 3:42:51, 2. Yevgeniy Shmalyuk RUS 3:44:33, 3. Denis Langlois FRA 3:47:38, 4. René Piller FRA 3:47:49, 5. Sylvain Caudron FRA 3:48:09, 6. Mario Avellaneda ESP 3:49:50, 7. Denis Trautmann GER 3:50:28, 8. Santiago Pérez ESP 3:51:24, 9. Francesco Galdenzi ITA 3:53:01, 10. Trond Nymark NOR 3:53:24; 49 of 67 finished; **Teams:** 1. FRA 12, 2. ESP 15, 3. GER 30, 4. ITA 62, 5. RUS 72, 6. SVK 74, 7. POR 78, 8. UKR 85, 9. BLR 88, 10. LAT 104, 11. HUN 111, 12. GBR 116, 13. SUI 122.
Junior Men 10km: 1. Aleksandr Kuzmin BLR 41:16, 2. Jan Albrecht GER 41:17, 3. Andre Katzinski GER 41:59; 40 of 41 finished; **Teams:** 1. GER 5, 2. BLR 5, 3. ITA 15, 4. POL 16, 5. RUS 22, 6. SVK 30, 7. GRE 37, 8. ROM 42, 9. ESP 49, 10. SWE 54.
Women 20 km: 1. Olympiada Ivanova RUS 1:26:48, 2. Elisabetta Perrone ITA 1:27:42, 3. Kjersti Plätzer NOR 1:27:53, 4. Erica Alfridi ITA 1:28:06, 5. Annarita Sidoti ITA 1:28:38, 6. Norica Cîmpean ROM 1:28:59, 7. Valintina Savchuk UKR 1:29:16, 8. Valentina Tsybulskaya BLR 1:30:19, 9. Cristiana Pellino ITA 1:30:42, 10. Ana Maria Groza ROM 1:31:08; 53 of 65 finished; **Teams:** 1. ITA 11, 2. ROM 29, 3. UKR 38, 4. BLR 55, 5. RUS 58, 6. ESP 77, 7. GER 86, 8. LTU 92, 9. GRE 96, 10. SVK 114, 11. GBR 119, 12. POR 128.
Junior Women 10km: 1. Tatyana Kozlova RUS 45:28, 2. Marina Tikhonova BLR 45:35, 3. Alena Zenkova RUS 45:35; 36 of 38 finished; **Teams:** 1. RUS 4, 2. BLR 11, 3. GER 18, 4. POR 21, 5. GRE 25, 6. ESP 31.

European 10,000m Challenge 2000

April 1, Lisbon, Portugal.
Men: 1. Enrique Molina ESP 27:59.80, 2. Karl Keska GBR 28:00.56, 3. Alberto García ESP 28:01.11; Team: 1. ESP, 2. POR, 3. GBR, Women: 1. Jelena Prokopcuka LAT 31:27.86, 2. Fatima Yvelain FRA 31:43.29, 3. Gunhild Haugen NOR 31:47.89; **Teams:** 1. POR, 2. NOR, 3. ESP.

European Champion Clubs Cup 2000

Div 1 Men: *At Vila Real San António, POR May 27-28.*
1. Sporting POR 105.5, 2. Luch RUS 105, 3. Dukla Praha CZE 95, 4. Fiamme Galle ITA 85, 5. Partizan YUG 74, 6. Panellinios GRE 60.5, 7. Airtel ESP 55, dns. Celje SLO. **New Series record**: JT 87.29 Kostas Gatsioúdis (Panellínos, GRE).
Div 2 Men. *At Liège, BEL May 27-28.*
1. Belgrave H GBR 102, 2. CA Montreuil FRA 93, 3. Maccabi Tel-Aviv ISR 75, 4. UK Slavija SVK 55, 5. Amsterdam NED 55, 6. Olympia CYP 32.
Div 3 Men: *At Liège, BEL May 27-28.*
1. Sparta Copenhagen DEN 87, 2. Zrinevac CRO 85, 3. RFC Liège BEL 63, 4. Dublin City Harriers IRL 53, 5. SV Schwechat AUT 43, 6. CA Spora LUX 36
Div 1 Women: 1. Luch RUS 131, 2. Snam ITA 102, 3. Valencia Terra i Mar ESP 102, 4. Panellínos GRE 78, 5. Sporting POR 73, 6. PSK Praha CZE 69, 7. Fenerbahce TUR 62, 8. Montreuil FRA 49. **New series records: 400mh**: Natalya Torshina KAZ (SC Luch. RUS) 54.50, **JT** (new): Yekaterina Ivakina (Luch) 61.56
Div 2 Women: *At Dudelange, LUX May 27.*
1. AK Partizan. Beograd YUG 107, 2. Shaftesbury Barnet GBR 90, 3. SUK Bratislava SVK 83, 4. ZAK-Mass SLO 71, 5. Sparta DEN 67, 6. Amsterdam NED 63, 7. LUX 38.
Div 3 Women: *At Dudelange. LUX May 27.*

1. Maccabi ISR 108, 2. Ess-Halle BEL 90, 3. Haak-Mlad CRO 85, 4. Hässelby SWE 84, 5. TV Unterstrass SUI 59, 6. Salzburg AUT 59, 7. Dudelange LUX 33.

8th Gulf Championships

April 18-20, Kuwait.

Men: 100m: Jamal Al-Saffar KSA 10.56, **200m**: Mohamed Al-Houti OMN 20.97, **400m**: Ibrahim Ismail QAT 45.61, **800m**: Mohamed Al-Azimi KUW 1:53.46, **1500m**: Othman Mohamed Othman KSA 3:46.90, **5000m/3000mSt**: Khamis S Abdullah QAT 15:03.59/8:29.6, **10,000m**: Ahmed Ibrahim Warsama QAT 30:47.59, HMar: Ahmed Saleh QAT 71:38, **110mh**: Mubarak Ata Mubarak KSA 14.26, **400mh**: Bader Abdulrahman Aman KUW 51.47, **HJ**: Omar Moussa Masrahi KSA 2.09, **PV**: Abdullah Saoud Ghanem QAT 4.90, **LJ**: Hussein Taher Al-Sabee KSA 8.15, **TJ**: Salem Mouled Al-Ahmadi KSA 16.50, **SP**: Bilal Saad Mubarak QAT 19.19, **DT**: Rasheed S. Al-Dosari QAT 60.16, **HT**: Nasser Abd. Al-Jarallah KUW 68.49, **JT**: Ahmad Abou Jalala QAT 70.20, **Dec**: Ahmad Hassan Moussa QAT 7222, 10kmW: Waleed Ahmed Al-Sabee QAT 52:18.0, **4x100m**: KSA 39.90, **4x400m**: KUW 3:06.34.

9th Ibero-American Championships 2000

May 20-21, Rio de Janeiro, Brazil.

Men: 100m: Vicente de Lima BRA 10.28, **200m:** Claudinei da Silva BRA 20.23, **400m:** Sanderlei Parrela BRA 44.80, **800m/1500m:** Hudson de Souza BRA 1:47.18/3:42.21, **5000m:** José Ramos POR 13:43.86, **10,000m:** Elenilson da Silva BRA 28:57.98, **3000mSt:** José Blanco ESP 8:28.44, **110mh:** Márcio Souza BRA 13.76, **400mh:** Eronildo de Araújo BRA 49.35, **HJ:** Gilmar Mayo COL 2.24, **PV:** Nuno Fernandes POR 5.20, **LJ:** Nelson Ferreira Jr BRA 7.90, **TJ:** Michael Calvo CUB 17.05*/1.6, **SP:** Manuel Martínez ESP 19.70, **DT:** Frank Casañas CUB 59.87, **HT:** Juan Cerra ARG 74.32, **JT:** Emeterio González CUB 80.02*, **Dec:** Édson Bindilatti BRA 7538, **4x100m:** BRA (de Lima, Ribeiro, A da Silva, Cl da Silva) 38.24*, **4x400m:** BRA (A de Oliveira, Parrela, Eloy, V da Silva) 3:03.33, **20,000mW:** Noé Hernández MEX 1:24:50.46, **Women: 100m:** Liliana Allen MEX 11.57, **200m:** Felipa Palacios COL 23.18, **400m:** Norma González COL 53.00, **800m:** Luciana Mendes 2:01.77, **1500m:** Nuria Fernández ESP 4:18.03, **5000m:** Fernanda Ribeiro POR 15:29.47*, **10,000m:** Erika Olivera CHI 33:39.16, **3000mSt:** Soraya Telles-Teixiera BRA 10:49.52*, **100mh:** Yahumara Neyra CUB 13.17, **400mh:** Ana Paula Pereira BRA 57.59, **HJ:** Solange Witteveen ARG 1.87, **PV:** Alejandra García ARG 4.30*, **LJ:** Maurren Maggi BRA 6.70, **TJ:** Carlota Castrejana ESP 13.61, **SP:** Martina de la Puente ESP 17.44, **DT:** Katiuscia de Jesus BRA 51.41, **HT:** Dolores Pedrares ESP 61.39*, **JT:** Xiomara Rivero CUB 60.43, **Hep:** Mônica Marques BRA 5480, **4x100m:** COL (Brock, Palacios, González, Oliveros) 44.81, **4x400m:** COL (Brock, Palacios, González, Lucumi) 3:34.51, **10,000W:** Rosario Sánchez MEX 45:38.90*.

Medal winning nations: BRA 18G, 16S, 11B – 45 medals; ESP 6-5-10, CUB 5-2-1, COL 5-0-1, MEX 3-5-2, ARG 3-3-5, POR 3-3-3, CHI 1-3-4, VEN 0-3-1, PUR 0-1-3, BOL 0-1-1, 1 each for PAR, STP, ECU, URU.

Oceania Championships 2000

August 24-26, Adelaide, Australia

Men: 100m/200m: Peter Pulu PNG 10.46w/ 21.39w, **400m:** Jeffery Bai PNG 48.50, **800m:** Isireli Naikelekelevesi FIJ 1:51.49, **1500m:** Michael Bond AUS 4:03.11, **5000m/10,000m:** Brent Butler GUM 15:36.83/32:36.39, **HMar:** David Kanie PNG 1:12:43, **3000mSt:** Primo Higa SOL 9:58.06, **110mh:** Joseph Rodan FIJ 14.91, **400mh:** Ivan Wakit PNG 52.40, **HJ:** Glen Paterson NZL 2.00, **PV:** Eric Reuillard NC 4.80, **LJ:** David Lane NZL 7.10, **TJ:** Fagamanu Sofai SAM 14.92, **SP/DT:** Hohepa Poihipi NZL 14.03/47.85, **HT:** Brentt Jones NFI 55.01, **JT:** James Goulding FIJ 68.37, **4x100m/4x400m:** PNG 41.96/3:18.56. **Women: 100m:** Litiana Miller FIJ 12.03, **200m:** Nicola Morris NZL 25.14, **400m/400mh:** Mary-Estelle Kapalu VAN 55.37/60.62, **800m:** Rochelle Heron NZL 2:14.26, **1500m:** Salome Tabuatalei FIJ 5:15.11, **5000m:** Vasa Tulahe TON 19:58.34, **2000mSt:** Jacqui Falconer NZL 7:10.86, **100mh:** Laurence Upigit NC 14.86, **HJ/TJ:** Tatum Rickard NZL 1.68/11.87, **PV:** Nikki Beckett 3.20, **LJ:** Siulolo Liku TON 6.15, **SP/JT:** Anna Pou'hila TON 14.36/42.32, **DT:** Melehifo Uhi TON 47.04, **HT:** Sharyn Tennant AUS 47.42, **4x100m/4x400m:** NZL 48.36/3:54.19.

Pan-American Walks Cup

April 8-9, Poza Rica, Mexico

Men: 20km: 1. Bernardo Segura MEX 1:22:47, 2. Noe Hernández MEX 1:22:47, 3. Jefferson Pérez ECU 1:24:36, **50km**: 1. Miguel A. Rodriguez MEX 3:43:52, 2. Joel Sánchez MEX 3:47:55, 3. Carlos Mercenario MEX 3:50:28. **Women 20km:** 1. Guadalupe Sánchez MEX 1:34:39, 2 .Graciela Mendoza MEX 1:35:28; 3. Oslaidys Cruz CUB 1:36:01. **Overall teams:** 1. MEX, 2. USA, 3. CAN

South American Walks

March 18-19, Lima, Peru

Men: 20km: Jefferson Pérez ECU 1:30:50, **35km:** Luis Villagra CHI 3:07:43. **Women 20km:** Geovanna Irusta BOL 1:46:46.

South American Junior Championships 2000

July 14-16, San Juan, Puerto Rico.

Men: 100m: Bruno Campos BRA 10.74, **200m**: Pablo del Valle ARG 21.36w, **400m**: William Hernández VEN 46.43*, **800m**: Simoncito Silvera VEN 1:50.18, **1500m**: Sebastián Gesualdo ARG 3:54.43, **5000m**: César Pelaluisa ECU 15:01.38, **10000m**: Jonathan Monje CHI 30:36.01, **3000mSt**: Fernando Fernandes BRA 8:59.12, **110mh**: Matheus Inocêncio BRA 14.53, **400mh**: Jorge Chaverra COL 52.23, **HJ**: Jessé de Lima BRA 2.09, **PV**: José Francisco Nava CHI 5.10*, **LJ**: Víctor Castillo VEN 7.70, **TJ**: Marcelo da Costa BRA 16.22w, **SP**: Mateus Monari BRA 16.36, **DT**: Héctor Hurtado VEN 49.37, **HT**: Lucas Andino ARG 60.41, **JT**: Pablo Alfano ARG 68.90, **Dec**: Iván da Silva BRA 6874, **4x100m**: BRA 41.08, **4x400m**: VEN 3:16.77, **10,000mW**: Cristián Muñoz CHI 42:32.85. **Women**: **100m**: Thatiana Ignâcio BRA 11.89, **200m**: Norma González COL 24.23w, **400m**: Amanda Dias BRA 55.05, **800m**: Yenny Mejías VEN 2:08.47, **1500m**: Ana Cláudio Coimbra BRA 4:41.19, **3000m/5000m**: Lucélia Peres BRA 9:31.10/17:23.18, **100mh**: Maíla Paula Machado BRA 14.00, **400mh**: Sira Córdoba COL nt, **HJ**: Jorgelina Rodríguez ARG 1.82, **PV**: Fabiana Murer BRA 3.75*, **LJ**: Laurice Félix BRA 6.03w, **TJ**: Keila de Costa BRA 13.65w, **SP/DT**: Fernanda Resende BRA 15.02/46.64, **HT**: Jennifer Dahlgren ARG 54.95*, **JT**: Jurema César BRA 48.52*, Hep: Valeria Steffens CHI 5064, **4x100m**: VEN 46.87, **4x400m**: BRA 3:42.99, **10000mW**: Ariana Quino BOL 51:32.57.

IAU World 100km Challenge 2000

Sep 9, Winschoten, Netherlands

Men

1. Pascal Fétizon FRA 6:23:15
2. Dmitriy Radyuchenko RUS 6:29:13
3. Oleg Kharitonov RUS 6:29:29
4. Dan Held USA 6:33:12
5. Farid Ganiyev RUS 6:38:57
6. Thierry Guichard FRA 6:41:35

Teams: 1. FRA 19:46:25, 2. USA 20:45:42, 3. RSA 21:01:32

Women

1. Edit Bérces HUN 7:25:21
2. Elvira Kolpakova RUS 7:35:01
3. Constanze Wagner GER 7:39:35
4. Magali Maggiolini FRA 7:46:05
5. S ylvie Beaulieu FRA 7:52:50
6. Elke Hiebl GER 7:54:32

Teams: 1. GER 23:39:28, 2. FRA 24:06:31, 3. USA 25:03:01

IAU 100km European Championships

April 30, Belvès, France.

Men: 1. Farid Ganiyev RUS 6:33:26, 2. Piotr Sekowski POL 6:44:28, 3. Oleg Kharitonov RUS 6:47:00; Team: 1. RUS, 2. FRA, 3. BEL. **Women:** 1. Edit Berces HUN 7:53:12, 2. Karine Herry FRA 8:06:46, 3. Alzira Lario POR 8:16:53; Team: 1. FRA, 2. ITA.

IAU 24 Hours European Challenge

Oct 21-22, Uden, Netherlands

Men: 1. Lubomir Hrmo SVK 259.273k, 2. Andrey Kazantsev RUS 257.760, 3. Alain Prual FRA 255.501; **Teams:** 1. FRA 752.642k, 2. RUS 731.88k, 3. GBR 667.688k. **Women:** 1. Irina Reutovich RUS 225.418k, 2. Joëlle Semur FRA 219.260, 3. Rimma Paltseva RUS 216.299; **Teams:** 1. RUS 647.492k, 2. GER 608.129k, 3. FRA 608,040k.

European Mountain Racing Trophy 2000

July 2, Miedzygorze, Poland

Men: 11.692km, 818m uphill: 1. Massimo Galliano ITA 50:22, 2. Richard Findlow ENG 50:56, 3. Antonio Molinari ITA 51:03; **Teams:** 1. ITA, 2. GER, 3. FRA; **Women:** 7.068km, 488m uphill: 1. Izabella Zatorska POL 33:38, 2. Birgit Sonntag GER 33:53, 3. Rosita Rota Gelpi ITA 34:17; **Teams:** 1. ITA, 2. SCO, 3. FRA.

World Mountain Racing Trophy 2000

Sep 9-10, Bergen, Norway

Men: 11.6km. 1204m uphill: 1. Jonathan Wyatt NZL 47:29, 2. Hans Kogler AUT 49:48, 3. Alexis Gex-Fabry SUI 50:16; **Teams:** 1. ITA, 2. AUT, 3. NZL; **Junior men** 8.9k (1074m): Nebai Habteghergish ERI 44:08, **Team:** ITA. **Women:** 8.9k (1074m): 1. Angela Mudge GBR/SCO 49:24, 2. Birgit Sonntag GER 49:43, 3. Izabela Zatorska POL 50:11; **Team:** NZL; **Junior women** 4.5k (604m): Elise Marcot FRA 29:05, team: ITA.

Mountain Racing Grand Prix 2000

Winners: Men: Antonio Molinari ITA, **Women:** Angela Mudge GBR.

** = Championships record throughout this section*

IAAF GRAND PRIX

INTRODUCED IN 1985, the Grand Prix links the world's leading invitational meetings, so that athletes earn points over the season, with a final contested by the leaders in the points tables. Half the standard events are held each year. There is an Individual Event Grand Prix for each event and an Overall Grand Prix for men and women. There is now a three-tier Grand Prix structure. From 1998 the top GP meetings constitute the IAAF Golden League, and below them are Grand Prix and Grand Prix II meetings.

Qualified athletes for the Grand Prix are those who, in the current or preceding year have achieved a performance equal to or better than the 50th best in the world in the past year.

Scoring

- Golden League meetings: 12 points for 1st, then 10-9-8-7-6-5-4 for 2nd to 8th
- GP I meetings: 8 points for 1st, then 7-6-5-4-3-2-1 for 2nd to 8th
- GP II meetings: 5 points for 1st, then 4-3-2-1 for 2nd to 5th
- Long throws events in GP II events score as GP I.
- Additional points are awarded in GP events prior to the GP Final: 6 for breaking a world record, 3 for equalling a world record.
- Athletes qualify for the Grand Prix Final on their total points over the season from a maximum of eight meetings for each designated event.
- IAAF GP Final: 24 points for 1st, then 21-18-15-12-9-6-3 for 2nd to 8th

Award structure

Men's and women's overall Grand Prix awards (all events): first $200,000, second $100,000, third $50,000, fourth $20,000, fifth $15,000, sixth $13,000, seventh $12,000, eight $10,000.
World record (broken not equalled) $100,000

Prize Money Structure

The standard prize money structure for GP meetings was as follows – 1st column for IAAF Golden League events (in Euros), 2nd column for other events at GL meetings (in Euros), 3rd column for individual events at the IAAF Grand Prix Final.

Place	GL	Other	GP Final
1st	EU15,000	EU7500	$50,000
2nd	10,000	5000	30,000
3rd	6000	3000	20,000
4th	4000	2000	10,000
5th	3000	1500	8000
6th	2000	1000	7000
7th	1500	750	6000
8th	1000	500	5000

In addition a Golden League Jackpot of 50 kilograms of gold was divided equally among all athletes who won the same discipline at each GL meeting and the Final.

A bonus of 50,000 Euros was available for a world record set in any of the designated Golden League disciplines in a GL meeting. For the women's javelin, where the record with the new implement was established from 1 January 2000, the same rule applies as in the IAAF World Championships – the record bonus would be reduced by 50% in the first year and by 25% in the second year following the adoption of the new standard.

IAAF Golden League

The Golden League was initiated in 1998, bringing together the six leading Grand Prix meetings – Oslo, Zürich, Brussels, Berlin, Monte Carlo and Rome. In 1999 a seventh, Paris, was added. In 1998 and 1999 a jackpot of $1 million was divided amongst any athletes winning all of his or her Golden League events (provided that they also competed at the Grand Prix Final). A special bonus of $50,000 was paid to anyone breaking a world record in one of the Golden League events.

The IAAF Council decided that, in the interest of the athletes during an Olympic year, the Golden League Jackpot would be made easier to win in 2000. The IAAF Golden League Jackpot (50kg of gold bars) was to be shared among those competitors who win five Golden League events in total, as against the seven victories which were required in 1999. All Golden League meetings would therefore contain all the Golden League events, so that competitors had a choice of which meetings in which to participate. Jackpot contenders had to also compete (but not necessarily win) in the IAAF Grand Prix Final in Doha shortly after the Olympics.

Golden League Jackpot winners:

1998: Marion Jones (women's 100m), Hicham El Guerrouj (1500m), Haile Gebrselassie (3000m/5000m).
1999: Gabriela Szabo (women's 3000m/5000m), Wilson Kipketer (800m).
2000: Gail Devers (women's 100mh), Trine Hattestad (W JT), Tatyana Kotova (W LJ). Maurice Greene (100m) and Hicham El

Winners of IAAF Golden League Events 2000

Event	*Paris 23/6*	*Rome 30/6*	*Oslo 28/7*	*Zürich 11/8*	*Monaco 18/8*	*Brussels 25/8*	*Berlin 1/9*
Men							
100m	B Lewis	M Greene	A Boldon	M Greene	M Greene	M Greene	M Greene
1500m	H El Guerrouj	N Ngeny	H El Guerrouj	H El Guerrouj	W Chirchir	H El Guerrouj	H El Guerrouj
3/5000m	A Saïdi-Sief	A Saïdi-Sief	S Kipketer	H Gebrselassie	A Saïdi-Sief	B Lahlafi	A Saïdi-Sief
400mh	L Herbert	E Thomas	E Thomas	A Taylor	L Herbert	L Herbert	A Taylor
HJ	S Klyugin	V Voronin	V Voronin	C Austin	J Sotomayor	C Austin	M Boswell
PV	M Tarasov	M Tarasov	J Galfione	D Ecker	M Stolle	D Ecker	J Hartwig
SP	J Godina	C J Hunter	A Nelson	A Nelson	Y Belonog	A Nelson	A Nelson
Women							
100m	Z Pintusevich	M Jones	Z Pintusevich	M Jones	I Miller	M Jones	M Jones
1500m	K Dulecha	K Dulecha	S F Hamilton	L Chojecka	V Szekely	C Sacramento	V Szekely
LJ	T Kotova	T Kotova	T Kotova	M Jones	E Johansson	T Kotova	T Kotova
JT	T Shikolenko	T Hattestad	T Hattestad	T Hattestad	T Shikolenko	T Hattestad	T Hattestad

Guerrouj (1500m/1M) lost their share as they did not compete in the GP Final.

THE SEVEN Golden League meets will have a new format in 2001 in a move that organizers hope will draw larger crowds and TV audiences. The 14 events in each meet will be divided into premium events and classic events. The winners of premium events will collect $13,350, with $6,675 going to classic event winners. There will be no change, however, in the Golden League jackpot payout. Any athlete winning five of the seven meets - in a premium or classic event - will collect the end-of-season 50kgs of gold.

The men's premium events will be: 100, 800, 1500 or mile, and 3000 or 5000. For women they will be: 100, 800 and 3000 or 5000.

The classic events for men will be: 110 hurdles, 3000 steeplechase, javelin and long jump. For women: 1500 or mile, 400 hurdles and high jump.

The IAAF decided in December 2000 to maintain its current seven-meet format and venues through to 2002. The only change in 2002 will be moving the Oslo, Norway, meet from July 19 to June 27to start the series.

Grand Prix meetings 2000
Golden League

Jun 23 Gaz de France, Saint-Denis, FRA
Jun 30 Golden Gala, Rome, ITA
Jul 28 Mobil Bislett Games, Oslo, NOR
Aug 11 Weltklasse, Zürich, SUI
Aug 18 Herculis Zepter, Monaco, MON
Aug 25 Memorial Ivo van Damme, Brussels, BEL
Sep 1 ISTAF, Berlin, GER
Oct 5 **Grand Prix Final**: Doha, QAT

Grand Prix I meetings

May 13 Japan Grand Prix, Osaka, JPN
May 14 Grand Prix Brasil de Atletismo, Rio de Janeiro, BRA
Jun 17 Raleigh International, Raleigh, NC, USA
Jun 24 Prefontaine Classic, Eugene, Oregon, USA
Jun 28 Athens GP, GRE
Jul 5 Athletissima, Lausanne, SUI
Jul 8 Nikaïa, Nice, FRA
Aug 1 DN Galan, Stockholm, SWE
Aug 5 British Grand Prix, London (CP), GBR

Grand Prix II meetings - staging up to six Grand Prix events with points 5-4-3-2-1 adding to the main GP points:

Mar 2 Melbourne Track Classic, AUS
Mar 24 Engen Grand Prix, Pretoria, RSA
Jun 23 Gran Premio Diputacion, Sevilla, ESP
May 28 Adriaan Paulen Memorial, Hengelo, NED
Jun 15 Ericsson GP, Helsinki , FIN
Jun 22 Cena Slovenska, Bratislava, SVK
Aug 8 Gugl Grand Prix, Linz, AUT
Aug 28 Gateshead
Sep 3 Rieti

IAAF Permit meetings 2000:

Sydney 13/2, Cape Town (Engen GP Final) 31/3, Fort-de-France 29/4, Milano 7/6, Torino 10/6, Villeneuve d'Ascq (Lille) 17/6, Moskva (Znamenskiy Memorial) 17-18/6, Nürnberg 25/6, Portland 25/6, Zagreb 3/7, Budapest 22/7, Barcelona 25/7, Thessaloniki 30/8, Yokohama 9/9

IAAF GRAND PRIX FINAL 2000

At Doha, Qatar on 5 October
Results with scores (and positions in brackets) prior to the final, and leading scorers who did not compete in Doha. As the GP final was held at the end of the year, after the Olympic Games, more athletes than usual passed the chance of earning good money at this event.

Men

100 Metres (-0.5)
1. Darren Campbell GBR 10.25 42 (6)
2. Tim Montgomery USA 10.27 49 (4)
3. Gerg Saddler USA 10.41 34 (8)
4. Coby Miller USA 10.52 26 (9)
5. Brian Lewis USA 10.52 60.5 (3)
6. David Patros FRA 10.53 –

Other GP leaders prior to final:
Maurice Greene USA 77. Ato Boldon TRI 71.5, Obadele Thompson BAR 45, Francis Obikwelu NGR 35, Bruny Surin CAN 24

400 Metres
1. Mark Richardson GBR 45.20 30 (8)
2. Sanderlei Parrela BRA 45.25 27 (9)
3. Antonio Pettigrew USA 45.37 31 (6=)
4. Jerome Young USA 45.38 31 (6=)
5. Greg Haughton JAM 45.85 35 (2=)
6. Danny McCray USA 46.82 34 (4)

Other GP leaders prior to final:
Alejandro Cárdenas MEX 49, Hendrik Mokganyetsi RSA 35, Michael Johnson USA 32

1500 Metres
1. Noah Ngeny KEN 3:36.62 42 (5)
2. Bernard Lagat KEN 3:36.88 50 (3)
3. Kevin Sullivan CAN 3:37.16 36 (7)
4. Benjamin Kipkurui KEN 3:37.38 41 (6)
5. Vyacheslav Shabunin RUS 3:38.42 44 (4)
6. Driss Maazouzi FRA 3:41.16 35 (8)
7. Laban Rotich KEN 3:43.02 24 (11=)
8. John Mayock GBR 3:43.70 24 (11=)

Other GP leaders prior to final:
Hicham El Guerrouj MAR 73. William Chirchir KEN 58, John Kibowen KEN 27.5, Andrés Díaz ESP 26

3000 Metres
1. Luke Kipkosgei KEN 7:46.21 48 (3=)
2. Ali Saïdi-Sief ALG 7:47.16 48 (3=)
3. Sammy Kipketer KEN 7:47.31 54 (1)
4. Ismaïl Sghir FRA 7:47.49 21 (12)
5. Daniel Komen KEN 7:47.79 48 (3=)
6. Brahim Lahlafi MAR 7:47.83 51 (2)
7. James Koskei KEN 7:58.10 17 (14)
8. Aloÿs Nizigama BDI 7:59.98 –

Other GP leaders prior to final:
Benjamin Limo KEN 41, Mohammed Mourhit BEL 34, Paul Tergat KEN 25, Salah Hissou MAR 24, Million Wolde ETH 23, Richard Limo KEN 22, Haile Gebrselassie ETH 20

400 Metres Hurdles
1. Angelo Taylor USA 48.14 70 (2)
2. Hadi Soua'an Al-Somaily KSA 48.18 48 (6)
3. Samuel Matete ZAM 48.71 57 (4)
4. Llewellyn Herbert RSA 49.05 59 (3)
5. Pawel Januszewski POL 49.88 38 (8)
6. Chris Rawlinson GBR 50.53 42 (7)
7. Eronilde de Araújo BRA 51.32 50 (5)
8. Eric Thomas USA 55.91 74 (1)

Other GP leaders prior to final:
Jirí Muzík CZE 31, Felix Sanchez DOM 27, Joey Woody USA 22

High Jump
1. Vyacheslav Voronin RUS 2.32 50 (3)
2. Nathan Leeper USA 2.30 41.5 (6)
3. Dragutin Topic YUG 2.25 38 (7)
4. Staffan Strand SWE 2.25 49.5 (4)
5. Sergey Klyugin RUS 2.20 53 (2)
6. Kwaku Boateng CAN 2.15 60 (1)
7. Charles Austin USA 2.15 46 (5)

Other GP leaders prior to final:
Konstantin Matusevich ISR 37.5, Abderrahmane Hammad ALG 37, Mark Boswell CAN 27.5, Stefan Holm SWE 22.5, Matt Hemingway USA 22

Pole Vault
1. Tim Lobinger GER 5.70 53.5 (4)
2. Nick Hysong USA 5.60 65.5 (2)
3. Okkert Brits RSA 5.60 56 (3)
4. Jeff Hartwig USA 5.40 47.5 (5)
5. Michael Stolle GER 5.40 36.5 (8)
nh. Dmitriy Markov AUS 35.5 (9)
nh. Maksim Tarasov RUS 71 (1)

Other GP leaders prior to final:
Lawrence Johnson USA 43, Aleksandr Averbukh ISR 41.5, Danny Ecker GER 34

Triple Jump
1. Jonathan Edwards GBR 17.12/0.9 33 (3)
2. Rostislav Dimitrov BUL 17.1/0.4 31 (4)
3. Larry Achike GBR 16.49/0.2 34 (2)
4. Kjetil Hanstveit NOR 16.24/1.1 28 (5)
5. LaMark Carter USA 15.80/0.3 13 (9)
6. Charles Friedek GER 15.79/0.4 41 (1)

Other GP leaders prior to final:
Yoelbi Quesada CUB 20, Rogel Nachum ISR 19, Fabrizio Donato ITA 16

Shot

1. Andy Bloom USA 21.82	39 (7=)
2. Adam Nelson USA 21.66	72 (2)
3. John Godina USA 21.51	39 (7=)
4. Yuriy Belonog UKR 20.76	79 (1)
5. Oliver-Sven Buder GER 19.77	50 (6)
6. Miroslav Menc CZE 19.66	60 (4)
7. Burger Lambrechts RSA 19.46	51 (5)
8. Mikulas Konopka SVK 18.98	39 (9)

Other GP leaders prior to final:
C J Hunter USA 64, Mika Halvari FIN 29, Gheorghe Guset ROM 24

Hammer

1. Andrey Skvaruk UKR 81.43	24 (4=)
2. Koji Murofushi JPN 80.32	29 (3)
3. Karsten Kobs GER 79.22	20 (8)
4. Zsolt Németh HUN 78.67	30 (2)
5. Heinz Weis GER 77.97	23 (6)
6. Tibor Gécsek HUN 77.82	45 (1)
7. Lance Deal USA 77.47	24 (4=)
8. Vladimir Maska CZE 76.91	15 (13)

Other GP leaders prior to final:
Olli-Pekka Karkalainen FIN 22, Hristos Polyhroníou GRE 19, Igor Astapkovich BLR 17

Overall Final Standings

1. Angelo Taylor 101	77 (2=)
2. Yuriy Belonog 94	79 (1)
3. Adam Nelson 93	72 (6)
4. Nick Hysong 86.5	65.5 (9)
5. Bernard Lagat 78	57 (16)
6. Tim Lobinger 77.5	53.5 (20)
7= Maurice Greene USA 77	77 (2=)
7= Eric Thomas 77	74 (4)
9= Luke Kipksogei KEN 75	51 (23=)
9= Samuel Matete ZIM 75	57 (16=)

Other GP leaders prior to final:

15. Hicham El Guerrouj MAR 73	73 (5)
18. Ato Boldon TRI 71.5	71.5 (7)
19. Maksim Tarasov RUS 71	71 (8)
28. C J Hunter USA 64	64 (10)

Women

100 Metres (+1.6)

1. Marion Jones USA 11.00	80 (1)
2. Chryste Gaines USA 11.09	57 (3)
3. Sevatheda Fynes BAH 11.10	58.5 (2)
4. Zhanna Pintusevich UKR 11.16	55.5 (4)
5. Debbie Ferguson BAH 11.22	52 (6)
6. Chandra Sturrup BAH 11.40	52.5 (5)
7. Torri Edwards USA 11.54	44 (8)
8. Myriam Mani CMR 12.15	27.5 (10)

Other GP leaders prior to final:
Inger Miller USA 47.5, Christine Arron FRA 38, Nanceen Perry USA 23

400 Metres

1. Lorraine Graham JAM 50.21	49 (2)
2. Falilat Ogunkoya NGR 50.61	42 (3)
3. Charity Opara NGR 50.85	18 (10)
4. Sandie Richards JAM 50.92	27 (5)
5. Ana Guevara MEX 51.22	30 (4)
6. Bisi Afolabi NGR 52.28	16 (12=)

Other GP leaders prior to final:
Cathy Freeman AUS 57, LaTasha Colander-Richardson USA 23, Michelle Collins and Katharine Merry GBR 21, Monique Hennagan USA 20

1500 Metres

1. Violeta Szekely ROM 4:15.63	70 (1)
2. Kutre Dulecha ETH 4:15.75	60 (2)
3. Nouriah Mérah-Benida ALG 4:15.85	41 (4=)
4. Lidia Chojecka POL 4:18.26	41 (4=)
5. Carla Sacramento POR 4:19.35	40 (6)
6. Olga Nelyubova RUS 4:19.95	45 (3)
7. Yuliya Kosenkova RUS 4:21.15	30 (7)
8. Olga Kuznetsova RUS 4:21.75	27 (8)
9. Paula Ivan ROM 4:24.10	18 (13)
10. Naomi Mugo KEN 4:25.97	26 (9)

Other GP leaders prior to final:
Hareg Sidelil ETH 20, Suzy Favor Hamilton USA and Hayley Tullett GBR 19

3000 Metres

1. Sonia O'Sullivan IRL 8:52.01	29 (3)
2. Leah Malot KEN 8:52.73	27 (4)
3. Sally Barsosio KEN 8:52.99	11 (15=)
4. Lydia Cheromei KEN 8:54.85	40 (1)
5. Tegla Loroupe KEN 8:55.99	38 (2)
6. Asmae Leghzaoui MAR 9:02.13	22 (5=)
7. Yemenashu Taye ETH 9:18.86	19 (7)
8. Roberta Brunet ITA 9:19.50	–

Other GP leaders prior to final:
Gabriela Szabo 22, Dong Yanmei CHN and Paula Radccliffe GBR 18

100 Metres Hurdles (+1.2)

1. Gail Devers USA 12.85	80 (1)
2. Glory Alozie NGR 12.94	70 (2)
3. Delloreen Ennis-London JAM 12.96	63 (3)
4. Melissa Morrison USA 13.00	56 (5)
5. Sharon Couch-Jewell USA 13.06	38 (7=)
6. Michelle Freeman JAM 13.11	58 (4)
7. Dawn Burrell USA 13.23	–
dnf. Olga Shishigina KZK	55 (6)

Other GP leaders prior to final:
Anjanette Kirkland USA 38, Yelena Krasovskaya UKR 29, Katie Anderson USA 24

Long Jump

1. Heike Drechsler GER 7.07w/2.4	49 (5)
2. Dawn Burrell USA 6.99w/2.5	54 (4)
3. Niurka Montalvo ESP 6.87/0.6	47 (7=)
4. Fiona May ITA 6.72/1.7	68 (1)
5. Tatyana Kotova RUS 6.70/1.3	63 (2)
6. Erica Johansson SWE 6.69/0.3	62 (3)

Other GP leaders prior to final:
Marion Jones USA 48, Iva Prandzheva BUL 47, Maureen Maggi BRA 23, Guan Yingnan CHN 21

Discus

1. Franka Dietzsch GER 65.41	32 (1)
2. Ellina Zvereva BLR 63.96	27 (4)
3. Beatrice Faumuiná NZL 63.03	25 (6)
4. Nicoleta Grasu ROM 62.39	28 (3)
5. Lisa-Marie Vizaniari AUS 62.32	31 (2)
6. Alison Lever AUS 59.92	26 (5)
7. Suzy Powell USA 59.70	16 (8)
8. Anja Möllenbeck GER 57.55	21 (7)

Javelin

1. Sonia Bisset CUB 65.87	36 (6)
2. Trine Hattestad NOR 65.86	89 (1)
3. Osleidys Menéndez CUB 65.79	72 (3)
4. Tatyana Shikolenko RUS 63.06	73 (2)
5. Steffi Nerius GER 62.84	26 (9)
6. Nikola Tomecková CZE 62.59	34 (7)
7. Mihaela Ingberg FIN 62.57	29 (8)
8. Yekaterina Ivakina RUS 59.23	37 (5)

Other GP leaders prior to final:
Tanja Damaske GER 43

Overall Final Standings

1. Trine Hattestad 110	89 (1)
2= Gail Devers 104	80 (2=)
2= Marion Jones 104	80 (2=)
4. Violeta Szekely 94	70 (6=)
5. Glory Alozie 91	70 (6=)
6. Osleidys Menéndez 90	72 (5)
7. Tatyana Shikolenko 88	73 (4)
8. Fiona May 83	68 (8)
9= Kutre Dulecha 81	60 (12)
9= Delloreen Ennis-London 81	63 (9=)
Other GP leader prior to final:	
13= Tatyana Kotova 75	63 (9=)

Grand Prix Final Records

Men

100m	9.91	Dennis Mitchell USA 1996
200m	19.81	Frank Fredericks NAM 1997
400m	44.53	Michael Johnson USA 1996
800m	1:42.98	Wilson Kipketer DEN 1997
1500m	3:28.37	Noureddine Morceli ALG 1995
1 Mile	3:50.28	Steve Scott USA 1986
3000m	7:35.90	Haile Gebrselassie ETH 1995
5000m	12:52.38	Daniel Komen KEN 1996
10,000m	27:33.14	Francesco Panetta ITA 1988
3000mSt	8:02.45	Moses Kiptanui KEN 1995
110mh	13.03	Mark Crear USA 1997
400mh	47.89	Andre Phillips USA 1988
HJ	2.34	Igor Paklin URS 1986
	2.34	Sergey Malchenko RUS 1990
PV	6.05	Sergey Bubka UKR 1993 & 1997
LJ	8.54	Larry Myricks USA 1989
	8.54	Mike Powell USA 1993
TJ	17.68	Mike Conley USA 1994
SP	21.82	Andy Bloom USA 2000
DT	68.61	Lars Reidel GER 1999
HT	84.88	Sergey Litvinov RUS 1986
JT	92.28	Jan Zelezny CZE 1995

Women

100m	10.74	Merlene Ottey JAM 1996
200m	21.88	Merlene Ottey JAM 1990
	21.84w	Marion Jones USA 1997
400m	49.17	Marita Koch GDR 1986
800m	1:55.72	Maria Mutola MOZ 1995
1500m	4:00.24	Paula Ivan ROM 1988
1 Mile	4:17.00	Natalya Artyomova RUS 1991
3000m	8:25.83	Mary Slaney USA 1985
5000m	14:54.54	Roberta Brunet ITA 1996
100mh	12.47	Yordanka Donkova BUL 1986
	12.40w	Michelle Freeman JAM 1997
400mh	53.41	Deon Hemmings JAM 1999
HJ	2.03	Inga Babakova UKR 1995
LJ	7.21	Jackie Joyner-Kersee USA 1994
TJ	15.15	Ashia Hansen GBR 1997
SP	20.95	Astrid Kumbernuss GER 1997
DT	68.90	Tsvetanka Khristova BUL 1986
JT	70.64	Petra Felke GDR 1986
4x400m	3:18.58	USSR 1985

IAAF/MOBIL Overall Grand Prix winners

Year	*Men*	*Women*
1985	Doug Padilla USA	Mary Slaney USA
1986	Saïd Aouita MAR	Yordanka Donkova BUL
1987	Tonie Campbell USA	Merlene Ottey JAM
1988	Saïd Aouita MAR	Paula Ivan ROM
1989	Saïd Aouita MAR	Paula Ivan ROM
1990	Leroy Burrell USA	Merlene Ottey JAM
1991	Sergey Bubka URS	Heike Henkel GER
1992	Kevin Young USA	Heike Drechsler GER
1993	Sergey Bubka UKR	Sandra Farmer-Patrick USA
1994	Noureddine Morceli ALG	Jackie Joyner-Kersee USA
1995	Moses Kiptanui KEN	Maria Mutola MOZ
1996	Daniel Komen KEN	Ludmila Engquist SWE
1997	Wilson Kipketer DEN	Astrid Kumbernuss GER
1998	Hicham El Guerrouj MAR	Marion Jones USA
1999	Bernard Barmasai KEN	Gabriela Szabo ROM
2000	Angelo Taylor USA	Trine Hattestad NOR

WORLD CHAMPIONSHIPS

THE 8th IAAF World Championships in Athletics will be staged in Edmonton, Alberta, Canada from 3 to 12 August 2001. The Commonwealth Stadium, which was built for the 1978 Commonwealth Games, will be the venue for the track and field events. It has a capacity of 60,217 spectators and is situated at an altitude of 652m.

Previous Championships

Athletics events at the Olympic Games have had world championship status, but the first championships for athletics alone were staged in 1983. It should, however, be noted that separate World Championships were held for men's 50 kilometres walk in 1976 and for women's 3000m and 400m hurdles in 1980, as those events were not on the Olympic programme in those years.

Year	*Venue*	*Athletes*	*Nations*
1983	Helsinki, FIN	1572	153
1987	Rome, ITA	1741	157
1991	Tokyo, JPN	1551	164
1993	Stuttgart, GER	1624	187
1995	Göteborg, SWE	1804	191
1997	Athens, GRE	1882	198
1999	Sevilla, ESP	1821	201

World Championship Records

Men

100m	9.80	Maurice Greene USA	1999
	9.80w	Carl Lewis USA (qf)	1991
200m	19.79	Michael Johnson USA	1995
400m	43.18	Michael Johnson USA	1999
800m	1:43.06	Billy Konchellah KEN	1987
1500m	3:27.65	Hicham El Guerrouj MAR	1999
5000m	12:58.13	Salah Hissou MAR	1999
10,000m	27:12.95	Haile Gebrselassie ETH	1995
Mar	2:10:03	Rob de Castella AUS	1983
3000mSt	8:04.16	Moses Kiptanui KEN	1995
110mh	12.91	Colin Jackson GBR	1993
400mh	47.18	Kevin Young USA	1993
HJ	2.40	Javier Sotomayor CUB	1993
PV	6.02	Maksim Tarasov RUS	1999
LJ	8.95	Mike Powell USA	1991
TJ	18.29	Jonathan Edwards GBR	1995
SP	22.23	Werner Günthör SUI	1987
DT	69.08	Anthony Washington USA	1999
HT	83.06	Sergey Litvinov URS	1987
JT	90.12	Jan Zelezny CZE	1995
Dec	8837	Tomás Dvorák CZE	1997
4x100mR	37.40	USA	1993
4x400mR	2:54.29	USA	1993
20 kmW	1:19:37	Maurizio Damilano ITA	1991
50 kmW	3:40:53	Hartwig Gauder GDR	1987

Women

100m	10.70	Marion Jones USA	1999
200m	21.74	Silke Gladisch GDR	1987
400m	47.99	Jarmila Kratochvílová TCH	1983
800m	1:54.68	Jarmila Kratochvílová TCH	1983
1500m	3:58.56	Tatyana Samolenko URS	1987
3000m	8:28.71	Qu Yunxia CHN	1993
5000m	14:41.82	Gabriela Szabo ROM	1999
10,000m	30:24.56	Gete Wami ETH	1999
Mar	2:25:17	Rosa Mota POR	1987
100mh	12.34	Ginka Zagorcheva BUL	1987
400mh	52.61	Kim Batten USA	1995
HJ	2.09	Stefka Kostadinova BUL	1987
PV	4.60	Stacy Dragila USA	1999
LJ	7.36	Jackie Joyner-Kersee USA	1987
TJ	15.50	Inessa Kravets UKR	1995
SP	21.24	Natalya Lisovskaya URS	1987
DT	71.62	Martina Hellmann GDR	1987
HT	75.20	Mihaela Melinte ROM	1999
JT (old spec)	76.64	Fatima Whitbread GBR	1987
(new)	67.09	Mirela Tzelíli GRE	1999
Hep	7128	Jackie Joyner-Kersee USA	1987
4x100mR	41.47	USA	1997
4x400mR	3:16.71	USA	1993
10kmW	42:13	Irina Stankina RUS	1995
20kmW	1:30:50	Liu Hongyu CHN	1999

Winners of the most medals

14 Merlene Ottey JAM gold 4x100m 1991, 200m 1993 & 1995; silver 200m 1983, 100m 1993 & 1995, 4x100m 1995; bronze 4x100m 1983, 100m & 200m 1987 & 1991, 4x100m 1993, 200m 1997

10 Carl Lewis USA gold 100m, LJ & 4x100m 1983; 100m, LJ & 4x100m 1987, 100m & 4x100m 1991; silver LJ 1991; bronze 200m 1993

9 Michael Johnson USA gold 200m 1991 & 1995, 400m 1993, 1995, 1997 & 1999, 4x400m 1993, 1995 & 1999

8 Gwen Torrence USA gold 4x400m 1993, 100m & 4x100m 1995; silver 100m 1991, 200m 1991 & 1993, 4x100m 1993; bronze 100m 1993

8 Jearl Miles(-Clark) USA gold 400m 1993, 4x400m 1993 & 1995; silver 4x400m 1991, 1997, 1999; bronze 400m 1995 & 1997

7 Gail Devers USA gold 100m 1993, 100mh 1993, 1995 & 1999, 4x100m 1997; silver 100mh 1991, 4x100m 1993

6 Heike Daute/Drechsler GDR/GER gold LJ 1983 & 1993; silver 100m 1987, LJ 1991; bronze LJ 1987, 4x100m 1991

6 Irina Privalova USSR/RUS gold 4x100m 1993, silver 4x100m 1991 & 1993, 200m 1995; bronze 200m 1993, 100m 1995

6 Sergey Bubka PV 1983, 1987, 1991, 1993, 1995, 1997

6 Butch Reynolds USA gold 4x400m 1987, 1993 & 1995; silver 400m 1993 & 1995; bronze 400m 1987

Winners of the most gold medals

9 Michael Johnson *as above*
8 Carl Lewis *as above*
6 Sergey Bubka PV 1983, 1987, 1991, 1993, 1995, 1997
5 Gail Devers *as above*

Oldest world champions

Men
36yr 300d Abel Antón Mar 1999
36yr 75d Yuriy Sedykh HT 1991
Women
31yr 30 d Helena Fibingerová SP 1983

Oldest medallists

M: 40yr 71d John Powell USA 2nd DT 1987
W: 37yr 34d Maricica Puica ROM 2nd 3000m 1987

Youngest gold medallists

17yr 88d Nikole Mitchell JAM 4x100m 1991
18yr 135d Irina Stankina RUS 10kmW 1995
18yr 177d Ismael Kirui KEN 10000m 1993 (youngest man)
18yr 241d Heike Daute GDR LJ 1983

Youngest medallists

M: 18yr 5d Kunle Adejuyigbe NGR 4x400m 1995
W: 15yr 153d Sally Barsosio KEN 10,000m 1993

Timetable and Qualifying Standards

The Opening Ceremony starts at 6pm on Friday, 3 August and the men's marathon starts at the Stadium at 6.45 and follows a course through Edmonton to end back at the Stadium so that its conclusion is part of this ceremony.
As in Seville 1999, there will be four days with separate morning and afternoon/evening sessions and then five further days of competition. Start times for these sessiona are as follows:
4 Aug: 0830/1430, 5 Aug: 0830/1430, 6 Aug: 0900/1300, 7 Aug: 0900/1750, 8 Aug: 1800, 9 Aug: 1800, 10 Aug: 1910, 11 Aug: 1430, 12 Aug: 1430 (with women's marathon 0800).

Dates of successive rounds (all in August)

Event	*Days*	*Qual. standards A/B*
Men		
100m	4-4-5-5	10.26/10.38
200m	7-7-8-9	20.72/20.84
400m	4-5-6	45.72/46.10
800m	4-5-7	1:46.00/1:47.00
1500m	9-10-12	3:36.20/3:38.40
5000m	6-10	13:25.00/13:32.00
10,000m	5-8	28:00.00/28:23.00
Mar	3	no standard
3000mSt	6-8	8:25.00/8:29.00
110mh	6-7-8-9	13.70/13.85
400mh	7-8-10	49.70/50.00
HJ	5-8	2.31/2.26
PV	7-9	5.75/5.60
LJ	9-11	8.20/8.00
TJ	4-6	16.95/16.70
SP	4-4	19.95/19.40
DT	6-8	65.00/62.40
HT	4-5	77.65/76.30
JT	10-12	82.50/80.50
Dec	6/7	8070/7990
4x100mR	11-12-12	no standard
4x400mR	11-12	no standard
20kmW	4	1:23:00/1:25:30
50kmW	11	4:00:00/4:04:00
Women		
100m	5-5-6-6	11.36/11.47
200m	8-8-9-10	23.06/23.35
400m	5-6-7	52.00/52.70
800m	9-10-12	2:00.00/2:02.00
1500m	4-5-7	4:07.00/4:09.20
5000m	9-11	15:22.00/15:49.00
10000m	4-7	32:00.00/33:00.00
Mar	12	no standard
100mh	7-8-9	13.05/13.32
400mh	5-6-8	55.67/56.80
HJ	10-12	1.95/1.92
PV	4-6	4.40/4.20
LJ	5-7	6.75/6.65
TJ	8-10	14.15/14.00
SP	5-5	18.35/17.50
DT	9-11	62.80/60.25
HT	6-7	65.00/62.00
JT	4-6	60.30/59.00
Hep	4/5	6120/5820
4x100m	11-11-12	no standard
4x400m	11-12	no standard
20kmW	9	1:36:00/1:40:00

Amputees: men 200m and women 100m on 5th
Blind: men 100m and women 200m on 6th
Wheelchair: men 1500m and women 800m on 10th

Notes

QUALIFYING STANDARDS must be achived in the period 1 January 2000 to 23 July 2001. Indoor performances will be accepted, but not races in mixed events between male and female participants or hand times for 100m-400m events.

Each member nation may enter one athlete per event provided that they have achieved the B entry standard in that event. Two, three or four (three to compete) athletes can be entered provided that they have all achieved the A standard.

Member federations that have no athlete (either male or female) achieving the entry standards can enter one athlete in any of the Championship events with the exception of the combined events and the field events.

MAJOR INTERNATIONAL EVENTS 2001-2006

2001

European 10,000m Challenge – Barakaldo, Spain (7 Apr)
IAU European 100km Challenge – Belvès, France (30 Apr)
European Cup of Race Walking – Dudince, Slovakia (19 May)
East Asian Games, Osaka, Japan (23-26 May)
Games of the Small States of Europe, San Marino (30 May-1 June)
European Cup – First and Second Leagues (22-24 June)
European Cup – Super League – Bremen, Germany (23-24 June)
African Junior Championships, Mauritius
Asian Junior Championships – Brunei Darussalam
European Cup for Combined Events (30 June-1 July)
WAVA World Veterans Championships – Brisbane, Australia (4-14 July)
IAAF World Youth Championships – Debrecen, Hungary (12-15 July)
European Under 23 Championships – Amsterdam, Netherlands (12-15 July)
Maccabiah Games, Tel Aviv, Israel (16-17 July)
European Junior Championships – Grosseto, Italy (19-22 July)
Francophone Games – Ottawa-Hull, Canada (19-24 July)
European Youth Olympic Days – Murcia, Spain (23-26 July)
IAAF World Championships – Edmonton, Canada (3-12 Aug)
IAU World 100km Challenge – Cléder, France (26 Aug)
World University Games – Beijing, China (27 Aug - 1 Sep)
Goodwill Games, Brisbane, Australia (4-7 Sep)
Mediterranean Games – Tunis, Tunisia (3-6 Sep)
WMRA World Mountain Racing Trophy – Arta Terne, Italy (9 Sep?)
IAAF World Half Marathon Championships – Bristol, GBR (7 Oct)
IAU 24 Hours European Challenge – Uden, Netherlands (21 Oct)
1st Afro-Asian Games – New Delhi, India (3-11 Nov)
European Cross-country Championships – Thun, Switzerland (9 Dec)

2002

European Indoor Championships – Vienna, Austria (1-3 March)
IAAF World Cross-country Championships – Dublin, Ireland
IAAF World Half Marathon Championships – Kortrijk, BEL (5 or 12 May)
European Cup – Super League – Annecy, France (21-22 Jun)
IAAF World Junior Championships – Kingston, Jamaica (16-21 July)
Commonwealth Games – Manchester, GBR (26-30 July)
European Championships – Munich, Germany (6-11 Aug)
Asian Championships – Kandy, Sri Lanka
IAAF Grand Prix Final – Paris (Charléty), France (14 or 15 Sep)
IAAF World Cup – (20-22 Sep)
Asian Games – Pusan, Korea (29 Sep - 14 Oct)
IAAF World Race Walking Cup – Torino, Italy (12-13 Oct)
African Championships. Tunisia
IAAF World Road Relay Championships
IAU 100km World Challenge – Torhout, Belgium
European Cross-country Championships – Pula, Croatia

2003

IAAF World Indoor Championships – Birmingham, GBR
IAAF World Cross-country Championships – Lausanne, Switzerland
IAAF World Race Walking Cup – Naumburg, Germany (3-4 May)
European Cup of Race Walking – (18 May)
European Cup – Super League – Firenze, Italy (21-22 Jun)
Pan-American Games – Santo Domingo, Dominican Republic
IAAF World Youth Championships – Sherbrooke, Canada
IAAF World Championships – Paris, France (15-24 Aug)
WAVA World Veterans Championships – Kuala Lumpur, Malaysia
All-Africa Games, Abuja, Nigeria
IAAF World Half Marathon Championships – Vilamoura, Portugal
European Cross-country Championships – Edinburgh, GBR (14 Dec)

2004

IAAF World Indoor Championships – Budapest, Hungary (Mar)
IAAF World Cross-country Championships – Brussels, Belgium

Olympic Games – Athens, Greece (13-29 Aug)
European Cross-country Championships – Heringsdorf, Germany (12 Dec)

2005

European Indoor Championships
IAAF World Cross-country Championships – Le Mans, France
IAAF World Championships – London, GBR

2006

IAAF World Indoor Championships
Commonwealth Games – Melbourne, Australia (15-26 Mar)
Asian Games – Doha, Qatar

IAAF Grand Prix 2001 Dates

March

1	Grand Prix II, Melbourne AUS
23	Grand Prix II, Pretoria RSA
9-11	World Indoor Champs, Lisbon POR
24-25	World Cross Country Champs, Ostend BEL

May

6	Grand Prix, Rio de Janeiro BRA
12	Grand Prix, Osaka JPN
27	Grand Prix, Eugene USA

June

2	Grand Prix II, USA (tbd)
4	Grand Prix II, Hengelo NED
8	Grand Prix II, Seville ESP
9	Grand Prix, Palo Alto USA
11	Grand Prix, Athens GRE
12	Grand Prix II, Bratislava SVK
14	Grand Prix II, Helsinki FIN
29	Golden League, Rome ITA

July

2	Grand Prix II, Zagreb CRO
4	Grand Prix, Lausanne SUI
6	Golden League, Paris FRA
9	Grand Prix, Nice FRA
12-15	World Youth Champs, Debrecen HUN
13	Golden League, Oslo NOR
17	Grand Prix, Stockholm SWE
20	Golden League, Monte Carlo MON
22	Grand Prix, London (Crystal Palace) GBR

August

3-12	World Championships, Edmonton CAN
17	Golden League, Zürich SUI
20	Grand Prix II, Linz AUT
24	Golden League, Brussels BEL
27	Grand Prix II, Gateshead GBR
31	Golden League, Berlin GER

September

2	Grand Prix II, Rieti ITA
9	Grand Prix Final, Melbourne

October

7	World Half Marathon Champs, Bristol GBR

Date to be determined: Grand Prix meeting in Doha QAT.

Internet – Web sites

Sites of international and national federations:
(all start – http://)

IAAF	www.iaaf.org	
European AA	www.eaa-athletics.ch	
Australia	www.athletics.org.au	
Austria	www.oelv.at	
Belgium	www.val.be	
Brazil	www.cbat.org.br	
Britain	www.ukathletics.org	
Bulgaria	www.athletics.netbg.com	
Canada	www.athleticscanada.com	
Croatia	pubwww.srce.hr/has/	
Czech Republic	www.atletika.cz	
Denmark	www.dansk-atletik.dk/	
Finland	www.sul.fi	
France	www.athle.org	
Germany	www.dlv-sport.de	
Hungary	www.masz.hu	
Iceland	www.toto.is/sersamb/fri/	
Ireland	www.athleticsireland.ie	
Italy	www.fidal.it	
Japan	www.rikuren.or.jp	inJapanese
Korea	www.kaaf.or.kr	in Korean
Latvia	www.lat-athletics.lv	
Lithuania	www.laf.lt	
Luxembourg	www.fla.lu	
Monaco	www.fma.mc	
Netherlands	www.knau.nl	
New Zealand	www.athletics.org.nz	
Norway	www.friidrett.no	
Poland	www.pzla.pl	
Portugal	www.fpatletismo.pt	
Scotland	www.saf.or.uk	
Singapore	home1.pacific.net.sg/~saaa	
Slovakia	www.saz.sk	
Slovenia	www.slo-sport.org/azs	
Spain	www.sportec.com/rfea	
Sweden	www.friidrott.se	
Switzerland	www.swiss-athletics.ch	
Turkey	www.taag.org	
UK	www.ukathletics.org	
USA	www.usatf.org	
Yugoslavia	asj.org.yu	

NOTES FROM THE EDITOR

Controversial IAAF Proposals

IN MY INTRODUCTION I referred to the horror expressed by athletics enthusiasts at the IAAF proposals to shorten field event competitions. This was the information that came from them on this subject (with further points):

A number of important technical rule change proposals will be presented to the IAAF Congress in August for consideration. One is that an athlete in events under 400m shall be disqualified for making one false start, rather than two. It is also proposed that in vertical jumps, athletes shall exit a competition after two consecutive failures at a height rather than three; that the horizontal jumps and throws be limited to four rounds; that in the pole vault the pegs be reduced from 75mm to 55mm; and that the take-over zone in relays should be, in total, 30 rather than 20m long. The IAAF Council, meeting in Lisbon, agreed that some of these rule changes would be tested at IAAF Grand Prix II events prior to the Edmonton Congress.

Writing for the IAAF's website (www.iaaf.org), Sean Wallace-Jones explained that the intention of the no false starts proposal "is to discourage athletes from anticipating the gun or even play the tactic of false starting to put other competitors off their game. Reducing the number of false starts will also make for a better 'show' for competitors and avoid delays in the overall competition programme." The proposed field event changes, he states, are designed to speed up the competition and make it more 'spectator friendly'. That, of course, is exactly what the reduction of the competition would not do!

Council agreed that the decathlon would be introduced as a new event for women, although the heptathlon would be retained as the official championship event, and also decided to maintain the 200m at the World Indoor Championships.

Drugs

The whole issue of drugs in sport continues to be unsatisfactory, not least the problems of varying legal considerations around the world. The IAAF determine that any substance found in an athlete's body is the responsibility of that athlete. Of particular concern have been reports of the detection of the steroid nandrolene in several athletes – amongst them those with a very high reputation. There has been much speculation as to how nandrolene could have been found, and suspicion has fallen on food supplements admittedly taken by such athletes, but on the understanding that the supplements were legal and did not contain illegal performance-enhancing drugs. While there seems to be no confirmation of any such link with the supplements in question, the question of contamination remains.

Even before the disclosure in February 2000 that Mark Richardson had failed a drugs test, seemingly with low levels of the banned substance, a UK Athletics panel had cleared Doug Walker and Gary Cadogan, finding that it could not be proven beyond reasonable doubt that the substance present in the sample was derived from a prohibited substance.

The ability of governing bodies to control the drugs menace is under severe threat, with national federations, especially in the USA, Britain and other major nations, increasingly wary of legal problems and costs in enforcing drugs bans. At the time of going to press there were reports of years of dissatisfaction by the IAAF with the way that USA Track and Field have dealt with their doping cases and rumours of many unreported cases.

The IAAF are to be commended for their determination to deal with the drugs problem, but they are under constant attack from some critics and one can but speculate that they might get a better press if, on the nandrolene matter, the permitted levels were raised slightly while the scientific issues were investigated in depth. That would eliminate the bans on several athletes who may well have succumbed inadvertently from doubtful food supplements but ensure that anyone with substantial levels received bans without being included in the same 'benefit of doubt' category.

March IAAF Council Decisions

In March the IAAF Council, following the recommendations of the Anti-Doping Commission, decided to refer the case of Mihaela Melinte to Arbitration. Council was notified about the decision of Mark Richardson to withdraw from the Arbitration process and accept the application of IAAF rules, and considered, but did not accept, a request for early reinstatement for Richardson presented by UK Athletics. Nevertheless it welcomed a proposal from UK Athletics for Richardson to carry out a series of educational activities, warning young athletes about the dangers of contaminated food supplements, and agreed that it would reconsider the reinstatement request at a later date.
Council also expressed its dissatisfaction with earlier public announcements made by UK Athletics related to nandrolone analysis.

ATHLETICS REFERENCE BOOKS 2000/2001

Reviewed by Peter Matthews

Athletics: A History of Modern Track & Field Athletics (1860-2000) (English language edition), published by SEP Editrice, Milan. Roberto Quercetani, the world's most illustrious track and field statistician and historian, has updated his major work of ten years ago to present a brilliantly crafted history of the sport from 1860 to the present day. Facts and figures abound, of course, but there is also a wealth of anecdotal material and illuminating asides. He concentrates on one era at a time (1860-1900, 1901-20, 1921-40, 1941-60, 1961-80, 1981-99 for men, 1900-40, 1941-70, 1971-99 for women) and present the highlights of each event during that period. The evolution of performance is illustrated by the top ten all-time lists as at the end of each of those eras, and a marvellous collection of over 300 colour and black & white photos enhance the 450 pages. Highly recommended. £30 sterling plus £5 airmail postage & packaging for customers in Europe, £14 for USA and £15 for the rest of the world from Athletics International, 13 Garden Court, Marsh Lane, Stanmore, Middlesex HA7 4TE, England. The orders will be forwarded to the Italian publishers, who will despatch the books. Payment in cash or by cheque (drawn on a British bank) made payable to Athletics International. Or $45 plus $20 p&p for USA, $25 elsewhere – cash only.

ATFS Golden Jubilee Book. A5 180 pp. Roberto Quercetani, the first president of the ATFS, and Bob Phillips, a former ATFS secretary general, produced this fascinating book of immense appeal to all dedicated track nuts with contributions from 41 members to mark the golden jubilee of this organisation, which now has members in 57 countries. It is illustrated by many rare photos. Roberto describes how the Association was formed, Bob reflects on the athletics scene of 50 years ago, Norris McWhirter writes about Harold Abrahams, Peter Lovesey delves into the ancient history of athletics statistics, Peter Matthews explains how the ATFS Annual is prepared, Lennart Julin reveals the eye-opening facts behind many official results, Ladislav Krnác reminisces with the legendary Emil Zátopek ... and so much more. The book was named by *The Times* as one of their "sports books for 2000". Price £13 or US $20 to the ATFS from Les Crouch, 'Gentle Murmurs', Off Clos Llanfair, Wenvoe, Cardiff CF5 6EU, UK.

Honour of Empire, Glory of Sport --The History of Athletics at the Commonwealth Games, by Bob Phillips with a Foreword by David Moorcroft. Hardback, 320 pages, 40 photographs (b&w and colour). This is a very readable history of athletics at the Empire and Commonwealth Games, the first comprehensive review of this meeting ever to have been published. Full details are given of all finals (Note that the author is publishing complete details (including heats and qualifying rounds) in issues of Track Stats). £20 post free (UK only) from The Parrs Wood Press, FREEPOST, Manchester M15 9PW. For overseas orders visit website: www.parrswoodpress.com.

Who's Who of UK & GB International Athletics 1896-1939. A5 168pp. Ian Buchanan has produced a most important book in which there are profiles of every male athlete (484 in all) who competed for Britain up to World War II in the 38 international meetings from the first Olympic Games of 1896 to those of 1936, the international matches, which started in 1921 (against France) and the 1938 European Championships. The comprehensive statistics include full dates and places of birth and death and full details of each international appearance, with dates and performances achieved, and personal bests at all events and there are fascinating career profiles. Price including postage £10 UK, £13 rest of Europe, £15 outside Europe; from Rob Whittingham at Umbra Software Ltd, Unit 1, Bredbury Business Park, Bredbury Park Way, Stockport, SK6 2SN, England.

The Olympic Marathon by David E Martin & Roger W.H.Gynn; published by Human Kinetics, PO Box 5076, Champaign, IL 61825-5076, USA. 528 pages. Price $27.95 (£20.95). From the publishers (www.humankinetics.com) or in Britain from Human Kinetics, Units C2-C3 Wira Business Park, West Park Ring Road, Leeds LS16 6EB. (custserv@hkeurope.com). The co-authors of the definite book on the marathon, "The Marathon Footrace", Dr David E Martin and Roger Gynn have again combined to produce a book to treasure. Their research has been characteristically meticulous and the resulting text is both enthralling and informative, covering their subject from all angles from the first Olympic marathon when Spiridon Louis became a Greek national hero until 1996 when there was the closest race in Olympic history. Adding to the attractions are the many rare photos, maps of each course, complete results of each men's and women's race complete with athletes' date of birth, biographical notes on each medallist, and career records of the winners.

History of Olympic Track & Field Athletics by Mel Watman. 184 pages. £10 (£11 Europe, £13 elsewhere, or $15, 17, 20). This revised and updated version of his Olympic Track & Field Athletics Guide (1996); contains in-depth reports, trivia and results (up to top 8) of each Games from 1896 to 1996 plus features on Olympic greats. Orders to Athletics International, 13 Garden Court, Marsh Lane, Stanmore, Middlesex HA7 4TE, England; payment by cheque (pounds sterling only, drawn on a British bank and payable to Mel Watman) or cash.

Who's Who in Olympic Track and Field 2000 by Mel Watman. 152 pages. Published by Athletics International in conjunction with Shooting Star Media Inc. Details are given of nearly 2500 top athletes of today. Price £10 or $15 as above.

Weltrekorde und Weltrekordler 100m, 200m/220y. A4 180 pages. Manfred Holzhausen has produced a splendidly detailed survey (in German) of world records and world record holders at the men's sprints in the IAAF-era (i.e. from 1912). There are profiles (and illustrations) of all world-record-holders, with detailed surveys of their careers and a table of yearly world bests for each year 1900-2000. Price DM 25 (Europe) cash or IMO to Manfred Holzhausen, Dresdener Str. 4, 41516 Grevenbroich, Germany, Tel: +49 21823049, FAX: +49 2182811849.(*m.holzhausen @planet-interkom.de*).

Temps Automatiques 1932-1999, 100 Metres, 200 Metres, 400 Metres. A5 46-60pp by Jean-Claude Patinaud, Allée des Lauriers, 87130 Châteauneuf-la-Forêt, France. The author has updated his very deep world all-time automatic timing lists for the men's sprints in these three booklets with all performers to, respectively, 10.50, 21.00 and 46.50. Price inc. postage: £7 for one booklet, £12 for two or £15 for all three, or equivalents in main currencies, payable in banknotes.

Listas Mundiais de Sempre (World All-Time Lists) 220 pp A4. 300 deep for men and 200 deep for women. Luís Leite has updated and extended his lists to the end of 2000. One pre-war athlete still makes the list: Jesse Owens with his 8.13 long jump, ranked 249th equal. Available from Luis at: Av. Alm. Gago Coutinho 154, 1700-033 Lisboa, Portugal for $15 US within Europe, $20 US elsewhere.

Maailman paras maaottelu (The best dual match in the world) – the 75-year Jubilee book on the history of the Finland-Sweden match by Matti Hannus & Esa Laitinen, published by the Finnish Federation. A5 256 pages of stories (in Finnish), photos and full results of all matches 1925-99. £16 or US $23 in cash (including postage) from Esa Laitinen at Haapalammentie 20 A 3, 40800 Vaajakoski, Finland.

British Athletics 1950 by Michael Sheridan. A4 126 pages. The author has done a magnificent job is assembling the results and ranking lists for British Athletics in this one year, 50 years ago, the first of what I hope will be a distinguished series of year books for the period. Dorothy and John Parlett contribute a Foreword and are amongst the 51 athletes that are profiled. There are results of the Empire Games and European Championships and all the major British events in 1950 (first six at the AAAs, first three at Scottish, Welsh and area championships, inter-counties etc.). The detailed ranking lists, generally at least 20 deep for each event with performances as well to this level are accompanied by a detailed index of all performers. The author sets the scene in his extensive introduction and his review of what was happening in the world in 1950. Available at £10 in the UK and £12 elsewhere from the author at 27 Yew Tree Park, Congresbury, Somerset BS49 5ER, UK.

All-Time Lists for the Czech Republic at 31.12.1999 compiled by Ludek Follprecht. A4 144 pages. Lists are generally 100 deep for all men's and women's events, with shorter lists for non-standard events. Price 30 DM or equivalent in other major currencies post paid from Jirí Havlín, Pod Skalkou 2737, 150 00 Praha 5, Czech Republic.

German University Championships In Athletics 1898-2000 by Klaus Amrhein. A5 c.400p. Detailed results of all events for university championships: GER champions 1898-1941 and 1st 8 from 1949 (FRG) and 1962-90 (GDR) and a survey of all German students who are placed 1-8 in World Student CC & Universiade 1923-1999. Orders to: Allgemeiner Hochschulsportverband ADH, Max-Planck-Str. 2, 64807 Dieburg, Fax: 06071-207578, e-mail: adh@adh.de. 50 DM in cash banknotes or remittance in advance to: Sparkasse Dieburg, bank-no. 133101774 - bankcode 50852651.

Polish Lists 1920-39 by Henryk Kurzynski, Stefan Pietkiewicz (Pietkiewicz@delta.sggw.waw.pl) and Marian Rynkowski. A4 landscape 214pp. Introductions etc. in Polish, this book gives Polish top tens as at 1919, then detailed lists for each year 1920-39 followed by all-time lists, 100 deep per event, as at 1.1.1940 for both Poland and for Europe. There is also an addendum with leading Polish marks in the period 1940-4. All lists for men only.

Zlatna Knjiga Jugoslovenske Atletike – The Golden Book of Yugoslav Athletics by Ljubisa Gajic. 234x160mm 194p. This is a splendidly comprehensive compilation of all Yugoslav performances in international competition, at all levels and age groups from Balkan Games to all European Championships and Olympic Games. There is a directory of all internationals and statistical profiles by Ozren Karamata of 31 top Yugoslav athletes. Price 30 DM, cash only, from Ljubisa Gajic, Vukasina Stefanovica 9, YU – 35000 Jagodina, Yugoslavia.

World Junior Lists. Milan Skocovsky, with the help of Raul Leoni, is producing updated editions of his well-known Svetove juniorske tabulky produced in START 1973 to 1989. Two years will be included in each booklet, starting with 1974 and 1975 world junior lists. "1976 and 1977" will be available soon. Each booklet is 25,000 Italian lira by international money order (no cheques, please) to: Raul Leoni, Via Paolo Maria Martinez, 11 – 00151 Roma, Italy. The booklets will also be available directly from Milan, but we do not yet have the price in Czech crowns.

ANNUALS

For most Annuals below referring to 1999, there will be new issues covering 2000.

Combined Events Annual 2000 by Hans van Kuijen. A5, over 200p. The 8th edition of this attractively produced annual includes top 200 men's and women's lists for 2000, including all decathlons over 7500 points and heptathlons over 5600, and all-time world lists for decathlon, heptathlon and indoor multis. There are also results of major events, profiles and complete career details for 100 of the world's top multi-eventers, records etc. NLG 55 (international money order or Eurocheque) or for cash: £15 sterling, DM 50, FF 160 or US $25 (cash) in Europe; NLG 60 or US $30 (cash) elsewhere from Hans van Kuijen, de Bergen 66, 5706 RZ Helmond, Netherlands. email: hvankuijen@wxs.nl

TAFWA All-Time Indoor List 2001 by Ed Gordon. A5 200pp $15. The excellent annual compilation contains deep world all-time indoor lists of performers and performances for all events, men and women. The author prepared a 12-page supplement with lists for 'discontinued' events at Imperial distances such as 50y, 1000y and 2 miles.

World Junior Athletics Annual 1999/2000. A5 84pp. By Lionel Peters. Includes deep world junior lists for 1999, world all-time top tens, various record tables including world age bests, and results of last year's major events. Available from 40 Berkeley Road, London NW9 9DG, England, price £10 (Europe) or £12 (outside Europe) in currency or by cheque drawn on a British bank and made payable to World Junior Athletics News.

L'Athlétisme Africain/African Athletics 2000. A5, 152p. The 19th edition of this invaluable definitive work by Yves Pinaud. 100 deep men's and women's lists for Africa for 1999, with all-time lists, national championships and major meetings results. FF 130 (or US $20, 35 DM) from Polymédias, 103 rue de Paris, 94220 Charenton le Pont, France. (Previous annuals 1979-99 available at various prices from Polymédias). Also available at £11 from Tony Isaacs, 11 Manton Close, Trowbridge, Wiltshire BA14 0RZ, England.

Asian Athletics 1999 rankings. A5 88 pages. DM 30/US $15 in Europe, DM 40/US $20 outside Europe in cash or Eurocheque (in DM only) or by International Money Order from the author, Heinrich Hubbeling, Haydnstrasse 8, 48691 Vreden, Germany (or for £10 from Tony Isaacs, as above). Top 30s for 1999 for athletes from Asian nations, together with continuation lists for countries other than China and Japan and all new national records set during the year. Also included are Asian records. Some earlier years also available.

Athletics Australia 1999 Handbook of Records and Results A5 234p. 49th year of issue. The handbook, as usual, covers the Australian season to the end of March 2000, with comprehensive records, results and 30-deep all-time lists, but the basis of the ranking lists compiled by Paul Jenes has been changed to a calendar year basis, here for 1999. Price $13 from the publishers Athletics Australia.

Paul produces a round up of **Australian results**, issued regularly throughout the year, 60-70 pages in all. $30 from Paul Jenes, 23-25 Grandview Road, Warrandyte, Victoria, Australia 3113.

Jaarboek 2000 (Belgian Athletics Annual). 368 A4 pages include deep 2000 lists for all age groups plus all-time lists, championship results etc. in a massive volume. Price 600 Belgian francs plus postage from Michel Jordens, Koning Boudewijnstadion 119C, 1020 Brussel, Belgium.

British Athletics 2001. The NUTS Annual, edited by Rob Whittingham and Peter Matthews. 464 pages including 32 of colour photographs. Contents include deep UK ranking lists for all age groups in 2000, top 12 merit rankings, all-time lists, results etc. £15 UK, £17 rest of Europe, £18 outside Europe; from Umbra Software Ltd, Unit 1, Bredbury Business Park, Bredbury Park Way, Stockport, SK6 2SN, England.

Caribbean Athletics Annual 1999 A5, 136pp. £10 or US $16 ($20 outside Europe) by Bernard Linley. Results are given of major meetings and championships in the Caribbean in 1999, with 20-deep CAC lists for 1999 and c.40-deep all-time lists. Continuing the series policy, this year's major feature is the compilation of all medallists at the CAC Junior Championships 1974-98; and there are also 30 deep Trinidad and Tobago all-time lists. Price £10 from Tony Isaacs, 11 Menton Close, Trowbridge, Wiltshire BA14 0RZ, England.

Atletické Vykony 1999. A5 248pp. Deep ranking lists for all age groups in 1999 for the Czech Republic with results of championships etc. Published by Ceská Atletiky svaz, Mezi stadiony - PS 40, 160 17 Praha 6, Czech Republic.

Laursens's lille lommebog 2000. A6. 90pp, includes Danish ranking lists for 2000, and all-time indoor list for all events, with men's 1500m lists 1940-9. This book and others on Danish statistics from Erik Laursen, Sandbakken 95, 8270 Høbjerg, Denmark. Tel/fax 86 27 96 34 (Giro 1 46 5333).

Eesti Kergejõustiku Aastraamat 2001. 264pp. Edited by Ants Teder and Erlend Teemägi. Estonian ranking lists for 2000, with colour photographs, results and records are contained in this handbook from the national federation: Eesti Kergejõustikuliit, Regati pst. 1, 11911 Tallinn, Estonia.

European Athletics Yearbook 99-00. A5 710pp. The official yearbook of the European Athletic Association is a most attractive work, which has grown this year by 120 pages, published by Justus von Liebig Verlag, Alsfeder Straße 27, 64289 Darmstadt, Germany. Price DM30 in Europe (DM 35 overseas) payable to Druckerei Reinheimer, Darmstadt. Contents include deep European lists for 1999 (seniors, under-23 and juniors) and all-time compiled by Nejat Kök, results of major 1999 European events, records and useful addresses.

Yleisurheilu 2000. A5 636p. As usual the Finnish annual was the first to be produced and I received my copy, covering 2000, in December. There are very deep Finnish lists for all age groups – down to 9! – with results of championships and international matches. It also contains indoor and outdoor world lists for 2000 with information received by Mirko Jalava as at mid-November. 20 euro or equivalent from Tilastopaja Oy, Raskinpolku 9 E 88, 20360 Turku, Finland. Can be ordered by email from juhani@tilastopaja.fi – there is also a credit card facility.

Athlerama 2000. The French Annual, edited by Jean Gilbert. A5, 588pp. This splendid yearbook, again increased in size, is packed with information on French athletics – deep year lists for 2000, profiles, results, all-time lists. Special features include profiles of their 'athletes of the century' – Carl Lewis (world) and Alain Mimoun (France), with an event-by-event survey of top French athletes of the 20th century. 150 FF including postage from the FFA, 33 avenue Pierre de Coubertin, 75640 Paris CEDEX 13, France.

Deutsche Bestenliste 1999 A5 200 pp. 30 DM or US $20. Edited by Klaus Amrhein for the Deutschen Gesellschaft für Leichtathletik-Dokumentation (DGLD). Deep performance and performer year lists for Germany for 1999. See DGLD details at the end of this review.

DLV-Jahrbuch 2000/2001. A5 384pp. The official yearbook of the German Federation. Articles and review, with detailed results of 2000 meetings, records and top ten lists as well as illustrations, some in colour. 35 DM. plus postage (DM 5.50 or DM 18 outside Germany), from Leichtathletik Fördergesellschaft mbH, Postfach 11 04 63, 64219 Darmstadt, Germany.

DLV-Bestenliste 2000. A5 432pp. The DLV's ranking lists for 2000 for all events compiled by Eberhard Vollmer, generally 50-deep for seniors and Jugend-A, 30-deep for other age groups. DM 25 from Leichtathletik Fördergesellschaft mbH, Postfach 10 04 63, 64204 Darmstadt, Germany.

Israeli Amateur Athletic Association 2000 Annual compiled by David and Arik Cooks. 40pp 235 x 168mm. $5 US or equivalent from David Eiger, 10 Ezra Hozsofer Str, Herzliya 46 371, Israel. Records, championship results, 2000 top ten and all-time lists, and expanded this year to include profiles of leading Israeli athletes.

Japan Athletics Annual 2000. A5 256pp. Compiled for the Japan AAF. Up to 100 deep lists for seniors with further marks for juniors for 1999, all-time top 50s for seniors and juniors and all-comers top 10s, and championship results. Also articles on top athletes in English. Available from Yoshimasa Noguchi, Track & Field Magazine, BBM Co. Ltd., 3-10-10 Misaki-cho, Chiyoda-ku, Tokyo 101-8381, Japan.

Latvijas Vieglatletikas Gadagramata 2000. A5 374 pp. Most comprehensive coverage of Latvian athletics, including 1999 and all-time lists, results and biographies, compiled by Andris Stagis with Irma Jaunzeme. From the Latvian Athletic Association, 1 Augsiela, Riga LV-1009, Latvia.

Pacific Statistics. Booklet **No. 19** in this series contained Pacific Islands results, including the South Pacific Games and Oceania Youth Championships, and top 20 rankings for 1999. **No.20** was a 72-page edition covering Top-50 All-Time best performances (men and women) updated to 31.12.99. Both from the compiler: Tony Isaacs, 11 Manton Close, Trowbridge, Wilts BA14 0RZ, UK, price £5 in Europe, £6 elsewhere. Payment in £ sterling.

Scottish Athletics Yearbook 2000. A5 264p. Edited by Arnold Black for the SATS, this is a very comprehensive review of Scottish athletics in 1999. There are deep Scottish lists for all age groups, records and championship results; also lists of Scottish champions and articles. As ever, remarkable value at £6 including postage in the UK, £7 elsewhere, cheques payable to S.A.T.S. From Arnold Black, 19 Millbrae Crescent, Langside, Glasgow G42 9UW.

2000 SA Athletics Annual. A5 320p. This publication of the South African Athletics Statisticians (SAAS) is edited by Hans Prinsloo. Rand 40 by surface mail or R80 airmail from SA Athletics Annual, PO Box 35209, Menlo Park, 0102 South Africa. Detailed 1999 and all-time lists for South Africa, records, championship results and profiles of leading athletes. Voted as South Africa athletes of the century were were Gert Potgieter and Zola Budd-Pieterse.

El Atletismo Sudamericano 2000. A5, 130pp. By Luis Vinker and Edgardo Fontana for Confederación Sudamericana de Atletismo. South American ranking lists for 1999 with records, results and articles.

Spanish Athletics Annual 2000. A5, 638pp. This hugely comprehensive Annual includes deep Spanish year lists for all age groups, all-time lists and biographies with index of best Spanish athletes, as well as detailed results from the Spanish season in 2000. 3125 ptas including postage from Federación Española de Atletismo, Avda, Valladolid 81 – 1°, 28.008 Madrid, Spain.

Ránking de España en Pista Cubierta 1999/2000. A5 272pp. The first half of this book contains detailed records and results with ranking lists for the Spanish indoor season of early 2000. There follow Spanish indoor all-time lists and progressive indoor records and summaries of Spanish Championships and international results, and finally full results of the 2000 European Indoor Championships and World top 20 lists for 2000.

Sverige Bästa 1999. A5 240p. Editor A Lennart Julin maintains his impeccable presentation of detailed Swedish lists for the Svenska Friidrottsförbundet, Box 11, 171 18 Solna, Sweden.

Friidrott 1999. The seventh edition of the annual by Göran Lenz covering world and Scandinavian athletics. There are event-by-event narrative reviews, full results of World Championships, world outdoor top 50 year and all-time lists, top 25 Scandinavian year and all-time lists plus indoor top tens. 336 pages. $49 Europe, $52 rest of the world.

Swedish women's all-time lists will be published in June/July. Up to top-250 in each event both indoor and outdoor. Age lists up to top-25 for 13 – 22 years athletes. 320 pages. $37 Europe, $39 rest of the world.

Orders for both to Gordons Förlag, Bärnstensvägen 2, 226 51 Lund, Sweden tel & fax 46- 46 – 24 88 99, e-mail: goran.lenz@swipnet.se

Schweizer Leichtathletik-Jahrbuch 2000. A5 320p. Published by the Swiss Federation (SLV/FSA), this is a most comprehensive compilation of Swiss records, results and year lists (with all-time top tens as well). From the Schweizerischer Leichtathletik Verband (SLV), Postfach 8222, CH 3001, Bern.

2000 USA Track & Field Media Guide & Annual (general editors: Jill M Geer & Scott S Davis). A5 624pp. The 22nd edition of the FAST Annual, which has now been combined with the USATF Media Guide (first 176 pages of this edition). Packed with US statistics and extensive index material including annual progressions etc for all top American athletes. Compared to all other national annuals, however, the year lists section is remarkably small at just 42 pages and the senior lists lack full details. The editor pleads lack of space, but many would consider year lists to be more important than 132 pages of all-time lists. There is also duplication between the USATF and FAST athlete profiles. Price $20 in the USA, $27.50 to Europe, $30 elsewhere from Scott Davis, 4432 Snowbird Circle, Cerritos, CA 90703, USA), or £20 (inc. post & packing) from Richard Hymans, 235 Lonsdale Road, Barnes, London SW13 9QN.

Statistical bulletins

The **DGLD – German** statistical group, the Deutschen Gesellschaft für Leichtathletik-Dokumentation, was founded in 1990. Its members produce annual national ranking lists (see **Deutsche Bestenliste**) for Germany and most impressive quarterly bulletins of up to 268 pages, packed with historical articles and statistical compilations. A major feature in each issue is detailed statistical profiles of athletes born in that quarter 70 years ago, 75, 80, 85, 90 etc. In 2000 bulletins no. 27-29 were published (each DM 30 or US $20). Membership, with free Deutsche Bestenliste costs DM 90 (US $55) per year. Details from Hans Waynberg, Grefrather Weg 100, 41464 Neuss/Rh, Germany.

TRACK STATS. The NUTS quarterly bulletin, edited by Bob Phillips, includes a wealth of fascinating statistics and articles. A5 size, generally about 80 pages. Annual subscription (4 issues) is £17 (UK), £21 (rest of Europe) or £26 (elsewhere); contact Liz Sissons, 9 Fairoak Lane, Chessington, Surrey KT9 2NS.

The **April 2000** issue included a deep (242 marks) world all-time list for the one hour run, features on Fernando Mamede, Bill Land, Otis & Glenn Davis, Jack (Eddie) Webster and Raphaël Pujazon,and the career record of Joetta Clark from 1978 (344 800m or 880y races!).

July had a profile of Dorothy Tyler, Jackie Joyner-Kersee's career record 1980-97 and an article on early Trinidadian sprint stars by Ulf Lagerström.

September 2000 included a detailed explanation of the IAAF World Rankings system; an interview with former British miling star Bill Nankeville; a profile of Mike Agostini and a detailed listing of McDonald Bailey's races.

November 2000 included a fascinating interview with 93 year-old marathon legend Jack Holden, the story of the first notable Soviet distance runners, the Znamenskiy brothers, a profile of world record breaking hurdler Gert Potgieter and full results of the 1934 British Empire Games.

March 2001 included detailed profiles of Richard Webster and Micheline Ostermeyer, features on Swedish sprinters and Small Heath Harriers and a report by Bob Phillips on a nostalgic visit to Eskilstuna amidst much else – including full results of the 1938 British Empire Games.

High Jump – a Statistical Survey of British Jumping by Ian Tempest. A5, 88pp. This booklet is packed with information on British high jumping. There are progressive UK records, senior and U20, indoors and out, age bests and deep UK performer and performance all-time lists, followed by a brief history of UK high jumping with best performances for each decade from the 1850s. The results include all British international results, national and area champions, and there are biographies of 107 men and 67 women. Further statistics include career progressions for top jumpers and a review of progress over the years to 2000. Price including postage: £5 in UK (£5.50 outside Europe) in sterling cheques payable to NUTS or cash in sterling or equivalent in DM or US $, from Dave Terry, 34 Windmill Hill, Ruislip, Middlesex HA4 8PX, UK. (Email mdterry@dial.pipex.com).

Previous editions in this series **400 metres (men)** and **Javelin (men and women)** are also available from Dave Terry. Events due for publication in 2001 are **1500 metres (Men)** by Peter Matthews and **Triple Jump (Men and Women)** by Ian Tempest.

The **Spanish group**, the **AEEA** continues to flourish, with four A5 bulletins each year packed with statistical items.

AEEA bulletin 55 March 2000 (120 pp) included: The contents of the newsletter *Atletismo en España* for the whole of 1999 and thus detailed meeting results – also Spanish veterans lists and a review of Internet usage.

No. 56 Jun 2000 (134pp) included a survey of Spaniards included in World and European rankings in 1992-9 and in 1921-49, full details for the top ten Spaniards at each event ranked by the average of their top ten marks and Spanish indoor all-time lists.

No. 57 October 2000 (314pp) included world best performances for each event in 1999 (200 deep). Price: 2500 pesetas or £20, $25, 122FF or 38 DM payable in cash or eurocheque from: José Luis Hernández, Carril, 21 – 28.530 Morata de Tajuña. Madrid.

No. 58 December 2000 (232pp). The first 84 pages included World Indoor Lists for 1999/2000, generally 50 deep performances and performers, with detailed results with national rankings for the Spanish indoor season. The rest of the book is a Spanish Annual for the season 1950 with detailed ranking lists for that year and provincial records at that time. Price: 2000 pesetas or £12, $20 payable in cash or eurocheque from José Luis Hernández.

La Lettre de l'Athlétisme: For French results and much else of interest to any statistician; edited by Yves Pinaud. Annual subscription (12 issues) 270 French Francs; payment by cheque drawn on a French bank or by international money order. La Lettre de l'Athlétisme, Polymédias, 103 Rue de Paris, 94220 Charenton-le-Pont, France.

Polymédias stock a wide range of statistical books for athletics and other sports.

IAAF Handbooks
These and a long list of other productions from the IAAF, 17 rue Princesse Florestine, BP 359, MC 98007, Monaco. All prices (by Visa, Master Card or Eurocard) include postage by airmail.

IAAF Magazine/Newsletter. The quarterly magazine is a top-quality colour production (A4, 96-148 pages) with reports and results of major competitions and articles by leading authorities. The regular newsletters are generally 16 pages. $75 subscription for text in English and French.

IAAF Handbook 2000-2001. 169 x114mm. 212pp. Rules and regulations section re-designed In English, French or Spanish. Each $10.

IAAF Directory and Calendar 2000. A5, 216 pages. Contact details for officials, organisations and national federations, with calendar and lists of champions. $16.

Previous editions of the International Athletics Annual.
Early editions of the International Athletics Annual (from 1951) are rare and in much demand. Back issues 1984-94 may be obtained from Old Bakehouse Publications, Church Street, Abertillery, Gwent NP3 1EA, Wales. Issues for 1992 and from 1995 to date are obtainable from SportsBooks, PO Box 422, Worcester WR1 1ZT, England.

Volume 5 of the **ATFS Historical series**, covering the years 1911 to 1920, is in preparation, but not ready yet as the research is very difficult and more people are needed able to help with this invaluable project.

Note that previous books in this series are available – each 40 Swiss Francs in Europe (plus 10 Francs for postage), 55 Swiss Francs outside Europe (or 60 SF for airmail). From Rob Whittingham, Umbra Software Ltd, Unit 1, Bredbury Business Park, Bredbury Park Way, Stockport, SK6 2SN, England.
Volume 1 – 1929-36, Volume 2 – 1937-44, Volume 3 – 1945-50, Volume 4 – 1921-28.

Books for review would be welcomed by the editor: Peter Matthews, 10 Madgeways Close, Great Amwell, Ware, Herts SG12 9RU, England.

HALL OF FAME

WE INTRODUCE a new feature this year – the International Track & Field Annual Hall of Fame. Every year we will select five athletes – to be a mix of former greats and athletes with notable achievements during the past year to add to career brilliance over at least ten years. This year's initial selection is:

Sergey Bubka, Heike Drechsler, Michael Johnson, Emil Zátopek and Jan Zelezny

The marvellous **Emil Zátopek** is profiled in the Obituary section in this Annual. He was the world's top athlete of the late 1940s and early 1950s when the ATFS Annual was first published. If one looks at the world lists in our first annual it can be seen that Zátopek headed the world list for 10,000m with his world record of 29:02.6 at Turku on 4 August 1950.

Now that time would not even get close to the world top 200 as recorded in this annual for the year 2000. Such is the rate of progress in distance running, yet one can but judge people for the standards of their own generation, and it is staggering to see that the second best 10,000m time in 1950 was Ivan Semyonov's 30:07.0. In other words Zátopek was just about a lap superior to the best of the rest of the world at this distance! He also headed the 5000m list by 16.8 seconds.

Sergey Bubka was a master of his craft, combining great speed and strength with brilliant gymnastic ability. He was one of the few athletes in the history of sport to compete regularly over many years at a different level from all rivals. The surprise world champion in 1983, Bubka went on to dominate the world of pole vaulting, and was not beaten in a championship from then until his sixth place in the Europeans after injury earlier in 1990.

He set 17 world pole vault records, the most at any event, from 5.85m in 1984 to 6.14m in 1994, including the world's first six-metre jump at Paris in 1985. He also set 18 world indoor records from 5.81 in 1984 to 6.15 in 1993. On 15 Mar 1991 he became the first vaulter to clear 20 feet when he set his 13th world indoor record at 6.10m.

His championship gold medals include: Olympics 1988; Worlds 1983, 1987, 1991, 1993, 1995 and 1997; World Indoors 1985, 1987, 1991 and 1995; Europeans 1990; European Indoors 1985; World and European Cup 1985. He jumped 6 metres or higher in 44 competitions from 1985 to 1997.

Heike Drechsler has had a wonderful career over the past twenty years and we recognise her sustained brilliance after a year in which she regained the Olympic title she had previously won in 1992. She thus showed that she still competes at the top of her sport even though she now operates somewhat below her peak of 7.48m for long jump in 1988 and 1992 as well as her 7.63w (+2.1 m/s) at the high altitude of Sestriere in 1992 – the first 25 ft long jump by a woman.

See the Biographies section for details of her career.

Michael Johnson has announced his retirement from major championships, although he will run for at least one more year. Athletics enthusiasts had never been able to agree on who could be classified as the greatest male athlete of all-time at 400m – Lee Evans, Herb McKenley, Alberto Juantorena, Tommie Smith, Butch Reynolds....? But now there is no question – it is the man from Dallas, Texas.

From Olympic Games Johnson has five gold medals and is the only man to retain a 400m title, and at World Championships has a record nine gold medals including three at 200m and four at 400m. In Seville 1999 he found the combination of full fitness and ideal conditions to, at last, take the world record for 400m and his 43.18 will take some beating. Even more, so will the fantastic 19.32 for 200m with which he won the 1996 Olympic title in Atlanta.

See the Biographies section for details of his career.

Jan Zelezny, or cover athlete, is the subject of a detailed profile elsewhere in this Annual. His third Olympic gold medal at the javelin came after many had assumed that severe injury had terminated his career.

In an event which puts a terrific strain on its practitioners and which has often seen unpredictable results, Zelezny has compiled a record that puts into unquestionably on a Hall of Fame pedestal.

See the Biographies section for further details of his career and the review on pages 49 and 50.

Sergey Bubka: the greatest pole vaulter of them all retired last year. The first man to clear six metres and 20 feet, Bubka won six world titles in a row and one Olympic gold as well as setting 17 world records outdoors and 18 indoors.

A world title in 1983, an Olympic gold 18 years later. In between world records at long jump and 200 metres. Truly Heike Drechsler is one of the all-time greats, the first woman to clear 25 feet in the long jump

Michael Johnson finally settled the argument as to who is the best one lap runner of all-time when in Sydney he became the first man to successfully defend the Olympic 400 metres title. He has now retired from international championships.

Emil Zátopek, who died last year, entered athletic immortality when he won the 5000m, 10,000m and marathon at the 1952 Helsinki Olympics.

Jan Zelezny came back from career threatening injury to win his third Olympic title in Sydney, something no other javelin thrower has managed.

Two Olympic walking titles in one Games made Robert Korzeniowski the male athlete of the year. Hamdan Al-Bishi is the male junior athlete of the year after winning the world junior 400m title in a championship record.

Marion Jones was unquestionably the female athlete of the year, while Kamila Skolimowska (inset) takes the junior award after winning the Olympic hammer title.

Paul Tergat was male road runner of the year after winning the world half marathon title again while Naoko Takahashi, the first Japanese woman to win an Olympic marathon gold, is the women's road runner of 2000.

NATIONAL CHAMPIONS 2000 and BIOGRAPHIES OF LEADING ATHLETES

By Peter Matthews

THIS SECTION incorporates biographies of 726 of the world's top athletes, 405 men and 321 women, listed by nation. There are also national champions at standard events in 2000 for the leading countries prominent in athletics; I have added a few new nations this year.

Those profiled have, as usual, changed quite considerably from the previous year, not only that all entries have been updated, but also that many newcomers have been included to replace those who have retired or faded a little from the spotlight. The choice of who to include is always invidious, but I have concentrated on those who are currently in the world's top 10-15 per event, those who have the best championship records and some up-and-coming athletes who I consider may make notable impact during the coming year.

Since this section was introduced in the 1985 Annual, biographies have been given for a total of 2696 athletes (1584 men and 1112 women).

This year there are 118 newcomers (64 men, 54 women), with 24 (12 men, 12 women) reinstated from previous Annuals. Every year I review the list of athletes who have been featured in all editions of this Annual. Now there have been 17 Annuals from 1985 to 2001, and the number of athlestes is down to four (two men and two women):
Men – Jürgen Schult and Javier Sotomayor
Women – Heike Drechsler and Merlene Ottey.
Ottey would, of course, have been included every year from 1980.

As ever, no doubt some of those dropped from this compilation will also again make their presence felt; the keen reader can look up their credentials in previous Annuals, and, of course, basic details may be in the athletes' index at the end of this book. Athletes included in these biographies are identified in the index by * for those in this Annual and by ^ for these included in previous Annuals,

The biographical information includes:

a) Name; date and place of birth; height (in metres); weight (in kilograms).
b) Previous name(s) for married women; club or university; occupation.
c) Major championships record – all placings in such events as the Olympic Games, World Championships, European Championships, Commonwealth Games, World Cup and European Cup Super League; leading placings in finals of the World Indoor Championships, European or World Junior Championships, and other Continental Championships; and first three to six in European Indoors or World University Games. IAAF Grand Prix first three at each event or overall.
d) National titles won or successes in other major events.
e) Records set: world, continental and national; indoor world records/bests (WIR/WIB).
f) Progression of best marks over the years at major event(s).
g) Personal best performances at other events.
h) Other comments.

See Introduction to this Annual for lists of abbreviations used for events and championships. Note that for comparison purposes decathlons and heptathlons made before the introduction of the current tables have been rescored using the 1984 IAAF Tables, except those marked *, for which event breakdowns were unavailable. Women's pentathlons (p) have not been rescored.

Information given is as known at 27 March 2001 (to include performances at World Indoor Championships as well as Australian and South African Championships outdoors and the World Cross-country Championships).

I am most grateful to various ATFS members who have helped check these details. Additional information or corrections would be welcomed for next year's Annual.

ALBANIA

Governing body: Federata Shqiptare e Atletikes, Rruga Dervish Hima nr 31, Tirana.

National Championships first held in 1945 (women 1946). **2000 Champions**: **Men:** 100m: Arben Maka 10.3, 200m: Fation Serhanti 23.0, 400m: Fetjon Thana 51.6, 800m: Ervis Peza 2:00.2, 1500m/3000mSt: Gerard Qirici 4:11.0/9:38.7, 5000m: Genci Lugja 15:57.6, 10000m: Vullnet Manushi 34:00.3, 110mh: Elton Duka 15.6, 400mh: Ardian Zhuri 56.0, HJ: Elton Kodra 1.80, PV: NeritanTançica 4.50, LJ: Bendis Spaho 6.81, TJ: Edvin Grucka 13.71, SP/DT: Dhimitraq Cepa 14.60/45.33, HT: Alban Shehri 57.12, JT: Vladimir Sokoli 66.34. **Women**: 100m: Monika Bakllava 12.1, 200m/400m: Klodiana Shala 25.4/57.3, 800m: Sonila Çekini 2:21.7, 1500m: Eriola Xeka 4:50.0, 5000m/10000m: Miranda Gresa 18:09.2/38:39.7, 100mh/LJ: Suela Zoga 14.0/5.77, 400mh: Donika Smaçi 62.2, HJ/Hep: Laura Derhemi 1.65/5290, SP: Valbona Laukaj 14.84, HT: Emiliana Ciko 55.74, JT: Zhuje Bajka 46.18.

ALGERIA

Governing body: Fédération Algerienne d'Athlétisme, BP n°61, Dely-Ibrahim, Alger. Founded 1963.

Abderrahmane HAMMAD b. 27 May 1977 1.89m 70kg.
At HJ: OG: '00- 3; WCh: '99- 10=; WJ: '96- dnq 22=; AfG: '99- 2; AfCh: '98- 1, '00- 1, Af-J: '95- 1.
Three African high jump records 1999-2000.
Progression at HJ: 1993- 2.00, 1994- 2.10, 1995- 2.12, 1996- 2.16, 1997- 2.24, 1998- 2.21, 1999- 2.32, 2000- 2.34.

Noureddine MORCELI b. 28 Feb 1970 Ténès 1.72m 62kg.
At 1500m: OG: '92- 7, '96- 1, '00- sf; WCh: '91- 1, '93- 1, '95- 1, '97- 4; WJ: '88- 2; WI: '91- 1; WCp: '94- 1; AfCh: '89- 4. Algerian champion 1989, GWG 1M 1994. Won GP 1500m/1M 1990 (2nd overall), 1991, 1993, 1994 (1st overall); 2nd 1500m 1996. 9th World Jnr CC 1988.
World records 1500m 1992 & 1995, mile 1993, 2000m 1995, 3000m 1994. WIR 1500m 3:34.16 '91. ALG records 1990-5: 1500m (7), 1M (5), 2000m, 3000m & 5000m (2), 800m & 1000m (1). African indoor 1M records 3:53.50 and 3:50.81 '91.
Progression at 1500m, 1M, 5000m: 1986- 3:50.7, 1987- 3:53.1, 1988- 3:40.41, 1989- 3:37.87, 3:59.79, 13:56.3; 1990- 3:32.60, 3:53.06, 13:25.20; 1991- 3:31.00, 3:49.12; 1992- 3:28.86, 3:49.79, 1993- 3:29.20, 3:44.39; 1994- 3:30.61, 3:48.67, 13:03.85; 1995- 3:27.37, 3:45.19; 1996- 3:29.50, 3:48.95; 1997- 3:30.23, 3:48.64; 1998- 3:33.58, 3:50.68; 1999- 3:30.91, 2000- 3:38.41. pbs: 800m 1:44.79 '91, 1000m 2:13.73 '93, 2000m 4:47.88 '95, 3000m 7:25.11 '94.
The king of 1500m/1M when unbeaten in 45 finals at 1500m/1M from 1992 until 2nd to Hicham El Guerrouj at 1996 Grand Prix Final. Also unbeaten in 15 1500m/1M races in 1991, but lost four in 1992 including a poor run at the Olympics prior to getting the world record. Studied at Riverside CC, USA 1989-90. Coached by elder brother Abderahmane (1500m: 3 WUG, 4 WCp and pb 3:36.26 in 1977). His younger brother Ali (b. 1973) has often acted as his pacemaker.

Djabir SAÏD-GUERNI b. 29 Mar 1977 Algers 1.87m 70kg. Army sergeant.
At 800m: OG: '00- 3; WCh: '99- 3; WJ: '94- h; AfCh: '00- 1/1R; WUG: '99- 4.
Two Algerian 800m records 1999.
Progression at 800m: 1997- 1:46.84, 1998- 1:45.72, 1999- 1:43.09, 2000- 1:43.25. pbs: 400m 46.15 '00; 1000m 2:14.52 '99.
Made huge breakthrough at 1999 World Champs, when he reduced his pb of 1:45.99 to 1:45.65, 1:45.17 and 1:44.18 in successive rounds, taking the bronze medal with the later. In his next race he was 3rd in Brussels in 1:43.09. His older brother Chakib ran on the team that was 2nd at 4x100m in the 1994 African Junior Champs.

Ali SAÏDI SIEF b. 15 Mar 1978 Constantine 1.80m 68kg.
At 1500m: WCh: '97- h, '99- sf; WJ: '96- 7; AfCh: '98- 3. At 3000m: WI: '99- 9; 2nd GP 2000. At 5000m: OG: '00- 2; AfCh: '00- 1. World CC: '97- 17J, '00- 16 (4k).
Algerian records 3000m and 5000m 2000.
Progression at 1500m, 5000m: 1996- 3:41.6, 1997- 3:37.47, 1998- 3:35.87, 1999- 3:30.91, 13:39.5; 2000- 3:30.82, 12:50.86. pbs: 1M 3:51.90 '99, 2000m 4:56.43 '99, 3000m 7:25.02 '00.

Women

Nouria MÉRAH-BENIDA b. 19 Oct 1970 1.62m 52kg. née Mérah.
At (800m)/1500m: OG: '00- 1; WCh: '97- sf/h, '99- h; AfG: '95- 6, '99- 2/2; AfCh: '98- 4/4; '00- 2/1. 3rd GP 1500m 2000.
Progression at 800m, 1500m: 1994- 2:09.14, 1995- 2:02.8, 1996- 2:01.43, 4:10.67; 1997- 2:00.46, 4:07.69; 1998- 2:00.77, 4:14.22; 1999- 1:59.49, 4:05.44; 2000- 1:59.68, 3:59.12. pbs: 100m 11.7 '94, 200m 23.8 '94, 400m 54.1 '95, 1000m 2:34.60 '99, 1M 4:28.90i '00, 2000m 5:46.67i '00, 3000m 9:01.20 '00.

Baya RAHOULI b. 27 Jul 1979 1.76m 58kg.
At TJ(/LJ): OG: '00- 5; WCh: '99- 10; WJ: '96- 10, '98- 1; WCp: '98- 6; AfG:'95- 4, '99- 2/6; AfCh: '98- 1/3, '00- 1; Af-J: '95- 1/2, '97- 1/2 (1 100mh); WUG: '99- 4.
Six African triple jump records 1998-9. ALG LJ records 19989.
Progression at TJ: 1993- 11.76, 1994- 12.05, 1995- 13.09, 1996- 13.48, 1997- 13.55, 1998- 14.04, 1999- 14.64A/14.30, 2000- 14.30/14.42w. pbs: 100m 11.1/11.62/11.51w '99, 100mh 13.50 '98, LJ 6.70 '99.
Brother Hamimed Rahouli set African 50km walk record of 4:19:15 in 1987.

AMERICAN SAMOA

Governing body: American Samoa Track & Field Association, PO box 855, Pago Pago, American Samoa 96799. Founded 1976.

Lisa MISIPEKA b. 3 Jan 1975 1.70m 84kg. Was at University of South Carolina.
At HT: OG: '00- dnq 14; WCh: '99- 3; won NCAA 1998 At SP: OG: '96- dnq 25; WCh: '95- dnq 22. Samoan records at SP, DT, HT.
Progression at HT: 1994- 48.70, 1995- 53.20, 1996- 60.94dq/54.86, 1997- 63.24, 1998- 65.00, 1999- 67.00, 2000- 67.55. pbs: SP 16.67 '95, DT 51.76 '97.
At Seville 1999, won the first ever international medal for American Samoa. Three months drugs ban 1996.

ARGENTINA

Governing body: Confederación Argentina de Atletismo, 21 de Noviembre No. 207. 3260 Concepción del Uruguay, Entre Ríos.
National Championships first held in 1920 (men), 1939 (women). **2000 Champions: Men**: 100m: Gabriel Simón 10.47, 200m: Nicolás Arias Duval 22.15, 400m/800m: Gustavo Aguirre 46.65/1:51.80, 1500m/5000m: Javier Carriqueo 3:46.48/14:22.11, 10000m: José Mansilla 29:58.81, HMar: Oscar Cortínez 65:29, Mar: Juan Castro 2:20:35, 3000mSt: Mariano Tarilo 9:05.81, 110mh: Oscar Ratto 14.68, 400mh: Gabriel Heredia 52.51, HJ: Erasmo Jara 2.15, PV: Javier Benítez 5.15, LJ: Leandro Simes 7.36w, TJ: Mariano Sala 14.85, SP: Adrián Marzo 15.81, DT: Marcelo Pugliese 57.06, HT: Juan Cerra 71.75, JT: Pablo Pietrobelli 63.35, Dec: Enrique Aguirre 7042, 20kmW: Jorge Lorefice 1:34:26.6. **Women**: 100m/200m: Vanesa Wohlgemuth 11.80/25.08, 400m: Andrea Rosotti 55.72, 800m/1500m: María Peralta 2:13.23/4:36.05, 5000m: Nadia Rodríguez 17:55.33, 10000m: Claudia Camargo 36:17.51, HMar: Elisa Cobanea 75:45, Mar: Claudia Camargo 2:51:52, 100mh/400mh: Verónica Depaoli 14.19/62.17, HJ: Ana Berg 1.55, PV: Alejandra García 4.10, LJ/TJ: Andrea Ávila 6.27w/13.24, SP: Simone Gonçalves BRA 13.83, DT: María Eugenia Giggi 45.95, HT: Karina Moya 57.98, JT: Romina Maggi 45.95, Hep: Ana Berg 3775, 20kmW: Ofelia Puyol 1:53:42.7.

Alejandra GARCÍA b. 13 Jun 1973 Buenos Aires 1.74m 60kg.
At PV: OG: '00- dnq 18=; WCh: '99- 11; PAm, '99- 1; SACh: '95- 1, '97- 2, '99- 1. Won Ib Am 2000, ARG 100mh 1995-6, HJ 1992, 1996, PV 1995-2000. LJ 1995-6, Hep 1990.
23 South American pole vault records from 3.10m in 1995 to 2000.
Progression at PV: 1994- 3.00, 1995- 3.60, 1996- 3.82, 1997- 4.00, 1998- 4.16, 1999- 4.41, 2000- 4.42. pbs: 100m 12.28 '00, 11.9 '96; 100mh 13.84 '96, 13.6 '95, 13.4w '98; HJ 1.87 '96, LJ 6.19 '95, TJ 12.53 '95, Hep 5139 '95.
Started in HJ and Heptathlon (2nd at both at 1990 South American Juniors), and switched to PV for good in 1995. Won the inaugural edition of the event at the South American Champs that year. Has a son (Tomás) born in 1991.

AUSTRALIA

Governing body: Athletics Australia, Suite 22, Fawkner Tower, 431 St.Kilda Rd, Melbourne, Victoria 3004. Founded 1897.
National Championships first held in 1893 (men) (Australasian until 1927), 1930 (women).
2000 Champions: **Men**: 100m: Matt Shirvington 10.26, 200m: Darryl Wohlsen 20.64, 400m: Patrick Dwyer 45.21, 800m: Kris McCarthy 1:45.91, 1500m: Nick Howarth 3:40.19, 5000m: Michael Power 13:28.11, 10000m (Dec): Sisay Bezebeh 28:40.09, HMar: Scott Westcott 63:03, Mar: Rod De Highden 2:16:36, 3000mSt: Chris Unthank 8:36.35, 110mh: Tim Ewen 13.87, 400mh: Rohan Robinson 50.21, HJ: Nick Moroney 2.22, PV: Paul Burgess 5.50, LJ: Peter Burge 8.28, TJ: Andrew Murphy 16.56, SP: Justin Anlezark 19.24, DT: Chris Gaviglio 55.52, HT: Stuart Rendell 74.71, JT: Andrew Currey 81.81, Dec: Jagan Hames 7720, 20kmW: Nathan Deakes 1:21:47. **Women**: 100m: Melinda Gainsford-Taylor 11.53, 200m/400m: Cathy Freeman 22.75/50.00, 800m: Tamsyn Lewis 1:59.29, 1500m: Georgie Clarke 4:10.59, 5000m: Anne Cross 15:36.15, 10000m: Clair Fearnley 31:55.65, (Dec) Liz Miller 33:26.80, HMar: Nicole Carroll 72:39, Mar: Susan Hobson 2:35:20, 3000mSt: Melissa Rollison 10:10.73, 100mh: Sally Bult 13.50, 400mh: Lauren Poetschka 56.03, HJ: Alison Inverarity 1.85, PV: Emma George 4.40, LJ: Kylie Reed 6.57, TJ: Nicole Mladenis 13.59, SP: Helen Toussis 15.55, DT: Alison Lever 63.73, HT: Bronwyn Eagles 62.77, JT: Stephanie Hancock 49.58, Hep: Sherryl Morrow 5817, 10kmW: Lisa Paolini 47:42, 20kmW: Jane Saville 1:30:58.

Peter BURGE b. 3 Jul 1974 Townsville, Queensland 1.86m 75kg. Reebok. Fitness instructor.
At LJ: OG: '00- 6; CG: '98- 1; WI: '01- 4. At TJ: WJ: '92- 5. Won AUS TJ 1993, 2001; LJ 2000.
Progression at LJ: 1991- 7.17, 1992- 7.06, 1993- 7.58, 1994- 7.18/7.50w, 1995- 7.41, 1996- 7.37, 1997- 7.53/7.70w, 1998- 8.22, 1999- 7.87, 2000- 8.30/8.48w. pbs: 100m 10.46 '00, 10.3 '98; 200m 21.00w '98, TJ 16.19 '92.

Viktor CHISTIAKOV b. 9 Feb 1975 Moskva, Russia 2.02m 92kg. SASI.
At PV: OG: '96- dnq 17, '00- 5=; EI: '96- 3; WJ: '94- 1; EJ: '93- 3. AUS champion 1999.
Progression at PV: 1988- 3.00, 1989- 3.70, 1990- 4.30, 1991- 4.60, 1992- 5.10, 1993- 5.35, 1994- 5.70, 1995- 5.85, 1996- 5.81i/5.80, 1997- 5.80, 1998- 5.72, 1999- 5.90/5.95exh, 2000- 5.80.
Ex Russian, AUS from 1999, married to pole

vaulter Tatiana Grigorieva (qv). His mother Natalya Burda/Pechenkina/Chistyakova was 3rd in the 1968 Olympic 400m in her pb 52.25 and in the 1971 European 4x400m. His sister Nadezhda was world's 3rd best junior at 100mh (13.22) 1988.

Nathan DEAKES b. 17 Aug 1977 Geelong 1.83m 66kg. Bellarine. Sports administrator.
At 20kmW(/50kmW): OG: '00- 8/6; WCh: '99- 7; CG: '98- 3. At 10000mW: WJ: '96- 3. Won AUS 20kmW 2000-01, 50kmW 1999 (t).
Progression at 20kmW, 50kmW: 1997- 1:23:58, 1998- 1:23:25, 1999- 1:20:15, 3:52:53; 2000- 1:21:03, 3:47:29. pbs: 3000mW 11:17.0 '98, 5000mW 19:27.4 '97, 10000m 38:53.82 '01, 30kmW 2:11:10 '98.

Dmitriy MARKOV b. 14 Mar 1975 Vitebsk, BLR 1.82m 85kg. SASI.
At PV: OG: '96- 6, '00- 5=; WCh: '97- nh, '99- 2; EI: '96- 1; WJ: '94- 2; EJ: '93- 6. 3rd GP 1999. AUS champion 1998, 2001.
Three Belarus pole vault records 1996-7, two Australian 1999.
Progression at PV: 1991- 4.80, 1992- 5.10, 1993- 5.42, 1994- 5.50, 1995- 5.65, 1996- 5.86, 1997- 5.95, 1998- 6.00, 1999- 5.95, 2000- 5.85.
Became an Australian citizen in May 1999, a month after his wife Valentina, who was granted citizenship as a result of spending two consecutive years in Australia after becoming a permanent resident in April 1997.

Andrew MURPHY b. 18 Dec 1969 Melbourne 1.85m 82kg. Pacific AC. Marketing executive.
At TJ: OG: '96- dnq 34, '00- 10; WCh: '95- dnq 22, '99- 4; CG: '90- 6, '94- 10; WJ: '88- 10; WI: '97-5, '01- 3; WCp: '92- 7, '94- 8, '98- 6. Won AUS TJ 1990, 1994-2001.
Progression at TJ: 1986- 14.96/15.56w, 1987- 15.60, 1988- 15.84/16.33w, 1989- 17.18, 1990- 16.57, 1991- 16.64, 1992- 16.30, 1993- 16.29, 1994- 16.76, 1995- 16.79, 1996- 17.07/17.28w, 1997- 17.18, 1998- 16.89A/16.59, 1999- 17.32, 2000- 17.12, 2001- 17.20i/17.28w. pbs: 100m 10.46/10.35w '96, LJ 7.88 '91.
Set an Australian junior record in 1989 with 17.18, but did not better that with legal wind until the 1999 World Championships in Seville, when he excelled with 17.32 for 4th.

Matthew SHIRVINGTON b. 25 Oct 1978 Sydney 1.83m 79kg. Asics West. Student.
At 100m/200m/4x100mR: OG: '00- sf/qf; WCh: '99- sf/qf; CG: '98- 4/6/3R; WCp: '98 -5. At 60m: WI: '99- 4, '01- 5. Won AUS 100m 1998-2001, 200m 1999. Two Australian 100m records 1998.
Progression at 100m, 200m: 1995- 11.01, 1996- 10.60, 21.31; 1997- 10.29, 20.89; 1998- 10.03, 20.45; 1999- 10.07, 20.67; 2000- 10.11, 20.62A. pbs: 60m: 6.52i '99, 300m 33.4 '98.

Jai TAURIMA b. 26 Jun 1972 Southport, Queensland 1.88m 80kg. AIS.
At LJ: OG: '00- 2; WCh: '99- 4; CG: '94- 6, '98- 2; WCp: '98 -2. AUS champion 1994, 1996.
Three Oceania long jump records 1998-2000.
Progression at LJ: 1990- 7.17, 1991- 7.65, 1992- 7.88, 1993- 7.84, 1994- 7.98/8.10Aw, 1995- 7.89, 1996- 8.05, 1997- 7.88/8.00w, 1998- 8.32A/8.22/8.26w, 1999- 8.35, 2000- 8.49. pb 110mh 13.95 '92.

Women

Louise CURREY b. 24 Jan 1969 Port Kembla, NSW 1.75m 68kg. née McPaul, married to Andrew Currey (AUS javelin record 85.75 '98). Illawarra Blue Stars. Police officer.
At JT: OG: '92- 11, '96- 2, '00- dnq 31; WCh: '91- 6, '95- dnq 13, '99- 5; CG: '94- 1, '98- 1; WJ: '86- (13 Hep), 88- dnq 15; WCp: '94- 4; WUG: '91- 4. AUS champion 1990-1, 1993, 1995, 1998.
Commonwealth and Oceania best new javelin 1999 & 2000.
Progression at JT: 1984- 38.36, 1985- 38.50, 1986- 47.94, 1987- 51.30, 1988- 52.34, 1989- 50.50, 1990- 57.06, 1991- 63.34, 1992- 62.62, 1993- 60.86, 1994- 65.32, 1995- 65.80, 1996- 65.54, 1997- 62.92, 1998- 66.96; new 1999- 66.03, 2000- 66.80. pbs: 100mh 14.95 '93, HJ 1.80 '92, LJ 5.85 '93, TJ 11.98 '96, SP 13.12 '92, HT 45.82 '96, Hep 5709 '93.

Cathy FREEMAN b. 16 Feb 1973 Mackay, Qld 1.63m 52kg. Ringwood. Married Alexander Bodecker (USA) in September 1999.
At 400m/4x100mR (200m): OG: '92- qf, '96- 2 (sf), '00- 7 (1); WCh: '93- (sf); '95- 4 (sf, 3 4x400R), '97- 1, '99- 1; CG: '90- 1R, '94- 1/2R (1); WJ: '90- (5, sf 100m), '92- (2); WI: '99- 2 4x400mR; WCp: '94- 3R (3). Won GP 400m 1996, 2nd 1994. Won AUS 100m 1994, 1996; 200m 1990-1, 1994, 1996, 2000; 400m 1995, 1997-2000; AAA 200m 1993, 400m 1992.
AUS records: 200m (2), 400m (5) 1994-6.
Progression at 200m, 400m: 1988- 24.50, 55.53; 1989- 23.86, 1990- 23.36, 1991- 23.50, 54.24; 1992- 23.09, 51.14; 1993- 22.37, 51.34; 1994- 22.25, 50.04; 1995- 22.50, 50.21; 1996- 22.55/22.53w, 48.63; 1997- 22.68/22.50w, 49.39; 1998- 22.55, 50.02; 1999- 22.81, 49.67; 2000- 22.53, 49.11. pbs: 100y 10.62 '93, 100m 11.24/11.15w '94, 300m 35.97 '99.
Lit the flame at the Opening Ceremony for the 2000 Olympic Games in Sydney before going on to gold at 400m. First Aboriginal to represent AUS at Olympics and first world champion. At the 1994 Commonwealth Games she won both 200m and 400m, took silver at 4 x 100m, and crossed the line first in the 4x400, only to be disqualified for baulking Yusuf NGR on the final turn. Set four AUS 400m records in 1996, improving by 0.96 to take the Olympic silver medal. Unbeaten for 22 finals at 400m from 1996 to Oslo 1998, when season cut short by injury (bruised foot), then unbeaten again in 11 finals in 1999 and in 10 in 2000.

Melinda GAINSFORD-TAYLOR b. 1 Oct 1971 Narromine, NSW 1.72m 67kg. née Gainsford. Cumberland Ryde Hornsby.

At (100m/)200m/4x100mR (100m): OG: '92- qf/sf, '96- sf, '00- sf/6; WCh: '93- (sf), '95- sf/sf (3 4x400R), '97- sf/7; CG: '94- 4/3/2R, '98- 4; WI: '93- 2, '95- 1; WJ: '90- sf/sf; WCp '92- 4/4, '94- (4)/3R. 3rd GP 200m 1997. Won AUS 100m and 200m 1992-3, 1995, 1997-8; 100m 2000; AAA 100m & 200m 1992.
Australian records 100m 1994, 200m 1994 & 1997.
Progression at 100m, 200m: 1988- 12.14, 1989- 11.89/11.59w, 24.02/23.89w; 1990- 11.77/11.72w, 23.89/23.50dq; 1991- 11.61, 23.62; 1992- 11.38, 22.68/22.26w; 1993- 11.22/11.15w, 22.49, 1994- 11.12A, 22.32; 1995- 11.15, 22.33; 1996- 11.29, 22.70; 1997- 11.16, 22.23; 1998- 11.21/11.03w, 22.49; 1999- 11.68/11.4, 22.80; 2000- 11.24/11.02Aw, 22.42/ 22.18Aw. pbs: 100y 10.4 '94, 300m 36.9 '96, 400m 51.73 '00.

Emma GEORGE b. 1 Nov 1974 Beechworth, Victoria 1.72m 60kg. WA. Studied arts and commerce at Deakin University, Melbourne.
At PV: OG: '00- dnq 15=; WCh: '99- 14=; CG: '98- 1; WI: '97- 2, '99- 6; WUG: '97- 1. Won AUS 1997-8, 2000.
12 world and 18 Australian PV records 1995-9, including first 15ft vault by a woman (4.57 '98). Two world indoor records 1996 (4.30 and 4.40).
Progression at PV: 1994- 3.05, 1995- 4.28, 1996- 4.45, 1997- 4.55, 1998- 4.59, 1999- 4.60, 2000- 4.50. pbs: 100m 12.0, HJ 1.60, LJ 5.66w '91, TJ 11.15.
As a schoolgirl she was a trapeze artist in the Flying Fruit Flies Circus for four years. Just a year and two weeks after clearing 2.55m in her first pole vault competition (12 Nov 1994) she became the fourth Australian to set a world record in a field event with 4.25m. Below her best in the summer of 2000, and at the end of the year had surgery on her feet for three stress fractures.

Tatyana GRIGORIEVA b. 8 Oct 1975 St Petersburg 1.72m 60kg. SASI.
At PV: OG: '00- 2; WCh: '99- 3; WI: '99- 9=. Won AUS 1999.
Progression at PV: 1997- 3.90, 1998- 4.35, 1999- 4.50/4.55ex, 2000- 4.55. pb 400mh 58.54 '96.
She moved with her husband Viktor Chistyakov to Australia, where they are coached by Aleksandr Parnov.

Lauren HEWITT b. 25 Nov 1978 Warracknabeal, Victoria 1.70m 60kg. Ringwood. Student.
At 200m/4x100m (100m): OG: '96- 7R, '00- sf; WCh: '97- qf (qf), '99- 7; CG: '98- 3/1R (4); WJ: '96- 2 (8); WCp: '98- 6R (7). Won AUS 100m & 200m 1999, 2001.
Progression at 200m: 1993- 23.99, 1994- 23.91, 1995- 23.83, 1996- 23.24/23.2w, 1997- 23.09/ 22.66w, 1998- 22.62, 1999- 22.53, 2000- 22.52. pbs: 100m 11.28 '99, 11.18w '00.

Jana PITTMAN b. 9 Nov 1982 Sydney 1.79m 67kg. Baulkham Hills. Student.
At 400mh(/400m): OG: '00- h; WJ: '00- 1/1; WY: '99- 1/7. AUS champion 2001.
Equalled world junior record 400mh 2000.
Progression at 400mh: 1998- 59.75, 1999- 56.23, 2000- 55.20A. pbs: 200m 23.60 '99, 400m 51.76A '00, 51.80 '99; 100mh 13.92 '00.

Jane SAVILLE b. 5 Nov 1974 Sydney 1.64m 52kg. Randwick Botany H. Customer Service Officer.
At 20kmW: OG: '00- dq: WCh: '99- 7. At 10kmW: OG: '96- 26; WCh: '97- h; CG: '94- 8, '98- 1. At 5000mW: WJ: '92- 2. Won AUS 5000mW 1997, 10kmW 1991-2, 1997-8, 20kmW 2000.
Commonwealth 20km walk record 2000.
Progression at 10kmW, 20kmW: 1990- 52:24, 1991- 47:10, 1992- 46:02, 1993- 47:29.1, 1994- 46:04, 1995- 45:10, 1996- 45:22, 1997- 42:59, 1998- 43:38, 1:37:53; 1999- 42:15, 1:31:58; 2000- 44:06, 1:28:56. pbs: 3000mW 12:27.74 '93, 5000mW 21:32.26 '97.
Disqualified when leading just outside stadium at Sydney Olympics. Her sister Natalie (b. 7 Sep 1978) has represneted AUS at WJ and WCp, pbs: 10kmW 45:10 '97, 20kmW 1:36:32 '99.

Kerry SAXBY-JUNNA b. 2 Jun 1961 Ballina, NSW 1.65m 59kg. née Saxby. Ballina. Tour guide, Australian Institute of Sport.
At 10kmW: OG: '92- 15, '96- 12; WCh: '87- 2, '91- 5, '93- dnf, '95- 9, '99- 3; CG: '90- 1, '94- 1, '98- 2; WCp: '85- 10, '87- 4, '89- 2, '91- 5, '93- 5, '95- 5. Won GWG 1986. At 20kmW: OG: '00- 7; WCh: '99- 3; WCp: '99- 21. At 3000mW: WI: '89- 1, '91- 2, '93- 2. Record 26 AUS titles: 5000mW 1986-96, 1998; 10kmW 1986-90, 1999; 3000mW 1987, 20kmW 1984-9, 2001.
World walking bests 1985-96: road: 5km (4) to 20:34 '87, 10km (2) 1987-8, 15km 1:09:33 '85, 20km (3) 1985-8; track: 1500m (2) 5:50.51 '91; 3000m (5) 11:51.26 '91; 5000m (6) 20:13.26 '96 (and 20:03.0u); 10,000m (3) 42:14.2 '88 (mx) '89 & 42:25.2 '90. WIB 3000mW 12:01.65 '89. Four Commonwealth 10000mW track records.
Progression at 10kmW, 20kmW: 1983- 50:52, 1984- 48:22, 1985- 46:13, 1:33:30, 1986- 44:53, 1987- 42:52, 1:32:51; 1988- 41:30/42:14.2t, 1:29:40; 1989- 42:46.45t, 1:32:44; 1990- 41:57.22t, 1991- 42:30/43:53.41t, 1992- 42:23.9t, 1993- 42:22.6t, 1994- 43:09, 1995- 42:18/42:27.5t, 1996- 41:47, 1998- 42:52, 1:33:14; 1999- 43:09, 1:31:18; 2000- 44:59, 1:29:36.
Baby born 1997. Her sister Sharon won the AUS schools under-17 800m in 2:10.1 in 1978.

Debbie SOSIMENKO b. 5 Apr 1974 Sydney 1.70m 90kg. Bankstown Sports. Teacher.
At HT: OG: '00- 5; WCh: '99- 5; CG: '98- 1; WUG: '97- 3. AUS champion 1993-5, 1998-9.
14 Commonwealth, 15 AUS hammer records 1993-2000. World junior hammer record 1993.
Progression at HT: 1989- 32.30, 1990- 44.30, 1991- 47.14, 1992- 51.48, 1993- 58.90, 1994- 62.38, 1995- 65.24, 1996- 62.86, 1997- 66.60, 1998- 67.16, 1999- 66.78/67.40dh, 2000- 67.95. pb DT 45.00 '91.

Joanna STONE b. 4 Oct 1972 London, England 1.72m 63kg. Mayne Harriers. Police officer.

At JT: OG: '96- dnq 16, '00- dnq 17; WCh: '95- 5, '97- 2; CG: '94- 4; WCp: '98- 1. AUS champion 1994, 1996-7.
Progression at JT: 1988- 44.98, 1989- 46.70, 1990- 47.54, 1991- 49.34, 1992- 54.02, 1993- 57.92, 1994- 62.40, 1995- 66.28, 1996- 65.84, 1997- 68.64, 1998- 69.85; new: 2000- 64.62.
Injured her right (throwing) elbow when setting an Australian javelin record of 69.85 for victory in the 1998 World Cup, causing her to miss the Commonwealth Games, and in March 1999 she underwent surgery.

Lisa-Marie VIZANIARI b. 14 Dec 1971 Lake Cargellico, NSW 1.73m 100kg. Griffith University.
At DT (SP): OG: '96- 8, '00- 8; WCh: '95- dnq 14, '97- 12, '99- dnq 14; WJ: '90- 2; CG: '90- 1, '94- 6 (3), '98- 2; WCp: '89- 6. Won AUS DT 1996-9, AAA DT 1995.
Progression at DT: 1987- 48.56, 1988- 53.50, 1989- 57.92, 1990- 60.44, 1991- 53.30, 1992- 55.16, 1993- 50.72, 1994- 55.58, 1995- 63.90, 1996- 64.90, 1997- 65.86, 1998- 64.11, 1999- 62.37, 2000- 65.35. pb SP 16.61 '94.
Knee reconstruction following a long jump accident in 1990. Kick boxing enthusiast.

AUSTRIA

Governing body: Österreichischer Leichtathletik Verband, 1040 Vienna, Prinz Eugenstrasse 12. Founded 1900.
National Championships first held in 1911 (men), 1918 (women). **2000 Champions**: **Men**: 100m/200m: Martin Lachkovics 10.26/20.61, 400: Andreas Rechbauer 46.30, 800m: Mario Handle 1:53.41, 1500m: Günther Weidlinger 3:44.87, 5000m/10000m: Bernhard Richter 14:28.35/ 29:39.30, HMar: Roman Weger 66:52, Mar: Max Wenisch 2:17:45, 3000mSt: Georg Mlynek 9:14.30, 110mh: Elmar Lichtenegger 13.55, 400mh: Karl Lang 51.69, HJ: Pavel Vanicek 2.09, PV: Martin Tischler 5.00, LJ: Daniel Hagspiel 7.57, TJ: Boris Bjanov 15.80, SP/DT: Erwin Pirklbauer 17.69/ 55.88, HT: Walter Edletisch 64.80, JT: Gregor Högler 77.86, Dec: Thomas Lorber 7364, 20kmW/ 50kmW: Stephan Wögerbauer 1:37:33/4:56:32. **Women**: 100m/200m: Karin Mayr 11.41/23.57, 400m: Stephanie Graf 53.40, 800m: Brigitte Mühlbacher 2:05.08, 1500m/10000m: Susanne Pumper 4:15.13/33:08.69, 5000m: Sandra Baumann 16:51.60, HMar/Mar: Dagmar Rabensteiner 76:29/2:39:08, 100mh: Elke Wölfling 13.55, 400mh: Pamela Märzendorfer 60.67, HJ: Linda Horvath 1.93, PV: Doris Auer 4.20, LJ: Manuela Witting 5.98, TJ: Olivia Wöckinger 12.69, SP: Valentina Fedyushina 17.27, DT/HT: Claudia Stern 48.00/ 53.26, JT: Monika Brodschneider 44.34, Hep: Marion Obermayr 5060, 10kmW: Viera Toporek 55:04.

Günther WEIDLINGER b. 5 Apr 1978 Braunau 1.69m 54kg. SU Igla Harmonie Natternbach.
At 3000mSt: OG: '00- 8; WCh: '99- 9; EC: '98- h; WJ: '96- 6; EU23: '99- 1; EJ: '95- 8, '97- 1. Eur CC: '97- 2J, '98- 4. Won World Univs CC 2000. Won AUT 1500m 1999-2000, 3000mSt 1998-9.
Three Austrian 3000mSt records 1999.
Progression at 3000mSt, 1995- 9:02.15, 1996- 8:38.97, 1997- 8:31.43, 1998- 8:23.13, 1999- 8:10.83, 2000- 8:11.51. pbs: 1500m 3:34.69 '00, 3000m 7:47.79i '00, 5000m 14:32.58 '97, 10000m 29:23.28 '97.

Women

Doris AUER b. 10 May 1971 Wien 1.68m 55kg. LCC Wien. Teacher.
At PV: OG: '00- 9; EC: '98- dnq 17=; WUG: '97- 3. Austrian champion 1996-7, 1999-2000.
18 Austrian pole vault records 1996-2000.
Progression at PV: 1996- 3.60, 1997- 4.10, 1998- 4.12, 1999- 4.33, 2000- 4.40, 2001- 4.32i.

Stephanie GRAF b. 26 Apr 1973 Klagenfurt 1.70m 60kg. Klagenfurter LC.
At 800m: OG: '00- 2; WCh: '97- h, '99- 7; EC: '98- 3; WI: '99- 6, '01- 2; EI: '00- 1. Won AUT 400m 1997-2000, 800m 1994-7, 1500m 1993-4.
Five Austrian 800m records 1998-2000.
Progression at 800m: 1989- 2:12.72, 1990- 2:10.72, 1991- 2:12.80, 1992- 2:09.20, 1993- 2:06.22, 1994- 2:05.36, 1995- 2:05.06, 1996- 2:01.54, 1997- 2:00.27, 1998- 1:57.97, 1999- 1:57.07, 2000- 1:56.64, 2001- 1:57.53i. pbs: 200m 25.42 '96, 400m 52.69 '99, 1000m 2:34.47 '98, 1500m 4:13.58 '96.
Her mother Rita Graf (née Merva) was Austrian 800m champion in 1974, pb 2:09.4 '71.

AZERBAIJAN

Governing body: Azerbaijan Amateur Athletic Federation, Xan Xoyski pros. 98a, Baku 370072. Founded 1923.
National Championships first held 1922.
National Champions 2000: Men: 100m: Teymur Gasumov 10.46, 200m: Arif Ahundov 21.40, 400m: Valentin Bulichov 47.63: 800m: Sergey Anohin 1.52.70, 1500m: Faig Bagirov 3:54.20, LJ: Ziya Jabbarov 7.03, TJ: Sergei Bochkov 16.27. **Women**: 100m/200m/400m: Olesya Kulichkina 12.41/25.40/58.10: 800m: Adelya Aliyeva 2:14.50, 1500m: Nailya Novruzova 4:50.25, LJ/TJ: Juliya Kolesnikova 5.33/12.58, 20kmW Aida Isayeva 1:42:98.

BAHAMAS

Governing body: Bahamas Amateur Athletic Association, P.O Box SS 5517, Nassau. F'd 1952.
National Champions 2000: **Men**: 100m: Renward Wells 10.31, 200m: Dominic Demeritte 20.53, 400m: Avard Moncur 44.93, 800m: Gregory Chipman 1:55.13, 1500m: Devon Armbrister 4:07.54, 5000m: Delroy Boothe 16:09.45, 400mh/ HJ: James Role 51.74/2.16, LJ: Chris Wright 7.92w, TJ: Alan Mortimer 16.51, SP: Leslie White

13.17, DT: Arthur Thompson 35.42, JT: Henry Butler 51.60. **Women**: 100m: Chandra Sturrup 10.86, 200m: Debbie Ferguson 22.46, 400m: Christine Amertil 52.00, 800m: Vhelma Colebrooke 2:21.48, 1500m: Santisha Martin 5:09.23, LJ: Jackie Edwards 6.51, TJ: Althea Williams 13.42, SP: Doris Thompson 14.20, DT: Chafree Bain 49.66, JT: Lavern Eve 61.30.

Women

Pauline DAVIS-THOMPSON b. 9 Jul 1966 1.68m 57kg. Née Davis. University of Alabama, USA.
At 400m: OG: '96- 4; WCh: '95- 2, '97- 7 (qf 200). At 100m/200m/4x100mR: OG: '84, '88 & '92- sf/sf, 00- -/2/1R; WCh: '83- qf/qf, '87- qf/sf, '91- sf/7, '93- sf/sf, '99- 1R; CG: '90- 3/3, '94- -/5 (11 LJ); PAm: '87- 3/3, '99- -/4; WCp: '89- 4R/1 4x400mR; CAG: '86- 1/1/2R. At 60m: WI: '91- 5; 200m: WI: '95- 2, '99- 3. Won CAC 100m and NCAA 400m 1989. 2nd GP 400m 1990, 3rd 100m 1989, 400m 1996.
National records 100m, 200m, 400m.
Progression at 100m, 200m, 400m: 1983- 11.56/11.3, 23.57, 1984- 11.51/11.1, 22.97, 1985- 11.47, 23.37/23.22w, 1986- 11.27/11.11w, 22.83, 1987- 11.19/11.16w, 22.49/22.1w; 1988- 11.17/11.12w, 22.67, 51.11; 1989- 11.14/10.9, 22.50, 50.18A; 1990- 11.16, 22.55, 50.05; 1991- 11.18/11.08w, 22.73; 1992- 11.31/11.30w, 22.44, 51.30; 1993- 11.16, 22.89, 52.85; 1994- 11.37/11.28w, 22.52, 50.46; 1995- 22.68i/22.80/22.70w, 49.96; 1996- 11.33, 22.78, 49.28; 1997- 11.41, 23.00, 50.53; 1998- 11.07, 22.78, 50.78; 1999- 11.39/11.16w, 22.64; 2000- 10.97, 22.27. pbs: 55m 6.70i '88, 60m 7.16i '91, 300m 36.50 '93.
Th only woman to have competed at all seven World Championships 1983-99; she won her first Olympic medals (silver 200m and gold relay) at her fifth Games in 2000.

Debbie FERGUSON b. 16 Jan 1976 1.70m 57kg. Student at University of Georgia.
At 100m/4x100mR (/200m): OG: '96- sf/res (2)R, '00- 8/5/1RE; WCh: '95- 4R (h), '97- sf, '99- sf/5/1R; CG: 94 (sf); WJ: '92- qf/sf, '94- 5/4, PAm: '99- (1); won CAC 100m 1997, 200m 1995, NCAA 100m & 200m 1998, PAm-J 100m & 200m 1995, CAC-J 100m 1994.
Bahamas 200m record 1999
Progression at 100m, 200m: 1991- 11.75, 24.26; 1992- 11.79, 23.97w; 1993- 23.82/23.32w, 1994- 11.48/11.1, 23.32/23.1; 1995- 11.19/10.9w, 22.86/22.7; 1996- 11.26/11.07Aw, 22.92; 1997- 11.20, 1998- 10.97/10.94w, 22.53; 1999- 10.98/10.91w, 22.19; 2000- 10.96, 22.37. pbs: 55m 6.71i '99, 60m 7.24i '99, 400m 54.68 '92.

Savatheda FYNES b. 17 Oct 1974 Abaco 1.65m 58kg. Was at Michigan State University, USA.
At 100m/4x100mR: OG: '96- 2R (qf), '00- 7/1R; WCh: '95- qf (h), '97- 3, '99- sf/1R; PAm-J: '91- 3, '93- 2 (2, 3 4x400); won NCAA 100m 1997, 200m 1995, 1997. Won GP 200m 1999, 100m: 2nd 1998, 3rd 2000. At 60m: WI: '99- 5, '01- 4.
Bahamas 100m record 1999.
Progression at 100m, 200m: 1991- 11.58, 24.49; 1992- 11.52w, 23.49w; 1993- 11.55, 23.43A; 1994- 11.42/11.2w, 23.38/23.10w; 1995- 11.12/10.7w, 22.63; 1996- 11.24, 23.01; 1997- 11.03/11.00w, 22.60/22.51w; 1998- 11.02, 1999- 10.91, 22.32; 2000- 11.03, 22.87. pbs: 50m 6.05i '00, 55m 6.65i '97, 60m 7.01i '99, 400m 53.40 '95.

Chandra STURRUP b. 12 Sep 1971 1.63m 55kg. Was at Norfolk State University, USA.
At 100m/200m/4x100mR: OG: '96- 4/6/2R, '00- 6/qf/1R; WCh: '99- 7/sf/1R; CG: '98- 1/-; PAm: '99- 1 (100); CAG: '93- 3/5, '98- 1; WJ: '88- sf/sf, '90- sf/6; WCp: '98- 2/2R. At 60m: WI: '97- 2, '01- 1.
Bahamas records 100m (3) 1996-2000, 200m 1996.
Progression at 100m, 200m: 1987- 11.75, 1988- 11.93/11.70w, 23.96w; 1989- ?, 1990- 11.62, 23.77; 1992- 11.54, 23.55; 1993- 11.20, 22.85; 1994- 11.75, 1995- 11.39/11.35w/11.1w, 23.31/23.14w; 1996- 11.00, 22.33; 1997- 11.26, 22.77; 1998- 10.95, 23.52/22.64w; 1999- 10.96/10.94w, 22.75; 2000- 10.86, 22.57. pbs: 50m 6.11+ '99, 55m 6.73i '96, 60m 7.05i '01, 400m 54.77 '00, LJ 6.70 '00, 6.80w '95.

BARBADOS

Governing body: Amateur Athletic Association of Barbados, P.O.Box 46, Bridgetown. F'd 1947.
National Champions 2000: **Men**: 100m: Obadele Thompson 10.24, 200m: Keita Cline BVI 20.97, 400m: Fabian Rollins 46.40, 800m: Milton Browne 1:48.36, 110mh: Gabriel Burnett 13.62, 400mh: Steve Augustin BVI 51.01, LJ: Kevin Bartlett 7.67, TJ: Gregory Hughes 16.00, SP: Dave Stoute TRI, DT: Ivorn McKnee 46.38. **Women**: 100m: Sarah Wilhelmy GBR 11.53, 200m/400m: Tanya Oxley 23.33/52.26, 800m: Sheena Gooding 2:07.25, 1500m: Janil Williams ANT, 400mh: Stacia Small 61.90, HJ: Desiree Crichlow 1.70, DT: Shernelle Nicholls 43.18, JT: Dawn Barrow 40.20.

Obadele THOMPSON b. 30 Mar 1976 St Michael 1.75m 67kg. Studied business at University of Texas, El Paso, USA.
At 100m (/200m): OG: '96- sf /4, '00- 3/4; WCh: '95- qf/sf, '97- sf/6, '99- 4/4; CG: '94- sf, '98- 3; CAG: '98- 1; WJ: '94- 4/sf; WI: '99- (2); WUG: '95- 2; WCp: '98- 1. 2nd GP 100m 1998, 200m 1997. Won CAC 100m 1993, 1995, 1999; 200m 1995; NCAA 100m & 200m 1997, CAC-J 100m & 200m 1994.
World junior 100m record 1994. BAR records: 100m (6) 1994-8, 200m (4) 1996-7. World indoor best 55m 1997.
Progression at 100m, 200m: 1991- 10.81/10.5w, 22.26; 1992- 10.59w, 21.61; 1993- 10.71/10.30w, 21.18; 1994- 10.08A/10.0, 20.71; 1995- 10.18, 20.49A/20.57; 1996- 10.07A/9.69wA, 20.14; 1997- 10.09, 20.03; 1998- 9.87A/10.00, 20.38/20.17w; 1999- 9.96, 20.09; 2000- 9.97, 19.97. pbs:

50m 5.63+ '99, 55m 5.99Ai '97, 60m 6.50+ '99, 400m 45.38A '96.
Ran the fastest ever 100m at high altitude in El Paso 1996. His father won the British Universities 100y in 1966, while at the University of London.

Women

Andrea BLACKETT b. 24 Jan 1976 London, GBR 1.60m 51kg. Student at Rice University, USA.
At 400mh/4x400mR: OG: '00- sf; WCh: '97- 8, '99- 4; CG: '98- 1; PAm: '99- 2/3R; CAG: '98- 2/3R; WJ: '94- h; WCp: '98- 2R; 2nd GP 1999; won CAC 1997 (3rd 100mh), 1999; 2nd 1998. Barbadian 400mh records 1994-8, 100mh 1997-8.
Progression at 400mh: 1994- 58.75, 1995- 58.59, 1996- 57.35A, 1997- 54.74, 1998- 53.74, 1999- 53.36, 2000- 54.41. pbs: 55mh 7.65i '97, 200m 23.73 '00, 800m 2:10.47 '99, 100mh 13.2, 13.42, 13.41w '98.

BELARUS

Governing body: Track & Field Athletics Federation of the Republic of Belarus, 2a Surganov Street, Minsk 220012. Founded 1991.
National Champions 2000: *Partial*. **Men**: 100m: Yuriy Rydevskiy 10.52, 400m: Sergey Kozlov 46.63, 800m: Pavel Pelepyagin 1:45.8, 1500m/5000m: Azat Rakipov 3:44.0/14:02.7, HJ: Oleg Prokopov 2.20, LJ: Andrey Shablovskiy 7.24, TJ: Dmitriy Vasilyev 16.53, SP: Andrey Mikhnevich 20.12, DT: Leonid Cherevko 63.80, HT: Vadim Devyatovskiy 81.36, JT: Vladimir Sasimovich 84.42, 20000mW: Vitaliy Gordey 1:24:59.9. **Women**: 100m: Tatyana Barashko 11.36, 400m: Natalya Sologub 51.70, 800m/1500m: Tatyana Buloychik 2:01.8/4:14.1, 10000m: Oksana Vasylevska 34:31.5, 100mh: Tayisiya Dobrovitskaya 13.93, 400mh: Tatyana Kurochkina 57.09, HJ: Tatyana Shevchik 1.86, LJ/TJ: Natalya Safronova 6.60/14.26, SP: Nadezhda Ostapchuk 18.81, DT: Lyudmila Starovoytova 62.42, HT: Lyudmila Gubkina 67.73, 10000mW: Margarita Turova 45:34.5.

Igor ASTAPKOVICH b. 4 Jan 1963 Minsk 1.91m 118kg. Minsk. Sports instructor.
At HT: OG: '92- 2, '96- 7, '00- 3; WCh: '91- 2, '93- 2, '95- 2, '97- 5, '99- 9; EC: '90- 1, '94- 2, '98- 7; WUG: '87- 1, '89- 1; ECp: '89- 2, '91- 1. Won GWG 1990. USSR champion 1989-90, CIS 1992, BLR 2000. Won GP 1992, 2nd 1988, 1994, 1996.
BLR hammer record 1992.
Progression at HT: 1981- 66.56, 1982- 68.08, 1983- 75.02, 1984- 79.98, 1985- 80.16, 1986- 80.68, 1987- 82.96, 1988- 83.44, 1989- 82.52, 1990- 84.14, 1991- 84.26, 1992- 84.62, 1993- 82.28, 1994- 83.14, 1995- 82.60, 1996- 81.76, 1997- 82.44, 1998- 83.62, 1999- 80.12, 2000- 82.58.
He has won five major silver medals and was world number one in 1990. Married to Irina Yatchenko (qv). Brother Konstantin (b. 23 Oct 1970) has a best of 79.08 '99 and was BLR champion 1995 and 1998-9.

Vladimir DUBROVSHCHIK b. 7 Jan 1972 Grodno 1.91m 115kg. Grodno. PE student.
At DT: OG: '96- 2, '00- 7; WCh: '95- 2, '97- 4, '99- 7; EC: '94- 1, '98- 6; EJ: '91- 1; WUG: '97- 1; WCp: '94- 1. BLR champion 1993-6, 1999. 3rd GP 1995.
Progression at DT: 1989- 53.04, 1990- 56.76, 1991- 61.40, 1992- 61.80, 1993- 63.26, 1994- 65.80, 1995- 66.60, 1996- 67.90, 1997- 66.40, 1998- 65.78, 1999- 67.80, 2000- 69.28. pb SP 17.47i '99, 16.57 '94.
Won the first European gold medal for Belarus.

Viktor GINKO b. 7 Dec 1965 Sharkovshchina 1.86m 77kg. Sports instructor.
At 50kmW: OG: '96- 5, '00- dq; WCh: '93- 11, '95- dq, '97/9- dnf; WCp: '95- 6, '97- 12, '99- 7; EC: '94 & '98- dq; ECp: '98- 8. BLR champion 50kmW 1993, 20kmW 1995-6.
Progression at 50kmW: 1988- 4:09:16, 1990- 3:50:45, 1991- 3:51:35, 1992- 3:48:42/3:40:46sh, 1993- 3:53:41, 1994- 3:45:34, 1995- 3:42:20, 1996- 3:42:52, 1997- 3:44:45, 1998- 3:48:27, 1999- 3:43:15, 2000- 3:47:53. pb 20kmW 1:20:03sh '93, 1:20:31 '98; 30kmW 2:05:36 '93, 35kmW 2:31:58 '93, 100kmW 8:43:30 '00 (world best).

Aleksandr GLAVATSKIY b. 2 May 1970 Soligarsk 1.85m 72kg.
At LJ (TJ): OG: '96- 7; WCh: '93- 7, '95- dnq 22, '97- 6; EC: '94- 10, '98- dnq 13 (4); WI: '97- 9, '01- 8; WUG: '95- 5. Won BLR LJ & TJ 1998.
Progression at LJ, TJ: 1988- 7.57, 1989- 7.55, 1990- 8.10, 1991- 7.97, 1992- 7.88/7.97w, 16.28i; 1993- 8.05, 1994- 8.21, 17.12i/16.94; 1995- 8.22, 1996- 8.33A/8.30, 1997- 8.20/8.29w, 16.46; 1998- 8.26, 17.53; 2000- 16.68, 2001- 17.06i.

Vasiliy KAPTYUKH b. 27 Jun 1967 Molodechno 1.97m 120kg. Minsk TR. Sports instructor.
At DT: OG: '96- 3, '00- 4; WCh: '91- dns, '93- 7, '95- 3, '97- 11; EC: '90- 4; WJ: '86- 3; EJ: '85- 3. Won ECp B3 1993.
Progression at DT: 1985- 57.18, 1986- 60.24, 1988- 61.60, 1989- 62.92, 1990- 63.72, 1991- 62.88, 1992- 63.34, 1993- 66.18, 1994- 58.86, 1995- 66.30, 1996- 66.92, 1997- 65.52, 2000- 67.59.
Father Boris (1950s) and aunt Vera Kaptyukh (1960s, Pen) were prominent athletes.

Ivan TIKHON b. 24 Jul 1976 Slonim 1.88m 105kg.
At HT: OG: '00- 4; WCh: 97- nt (12); EC: '98- dnq 30; EU23: 97- 1; EJ: '95- 9.
Progression at HT: 1994- 62.66, 1995- 66.84, 1996- 75.32, 1997- 77.46, 1998- 78.03, 1999- 70.37, 2000- 79.85.

Women

Lyudmila GUBKINA b. 28 May 1972 Novopolotsk 1.70m 72kg. Novopolotsk TU.
At HT: OG: '00- 6; WCh: '99- 6; EC: '98- 6; WUG: '97- 4, '99- 2; ECp: '97- 3. Won BLR 1996, 2000.
Three BLR hammer records 1997-9.
Progression at HT: 1992- 55.90, 1993- 59.62, 1994- 57.58, 1995- 60.78, 1996- 65.02, 1997- 68.24, 1998- 67.83, 1999- 68.27, 2000- 69.92.

Yanina KOROLCHIK b. 26 Dec 1976 1.86m 87kg.
At SP: OG: '00- 1; WCh: '97- dnq 18; 99- 4; EC: '98- 3; EU23: '97- 3 (3 DT); EJ: '95- 2. BLR champion 2000.
Progression at SP: 1994- 16.00, 1995- 17.07, 1996- 17.48, 1997- 18.67, 1998- 19.23, 1999- 19.58, 2000- 20.56. pb DT 59.90 '97.

Nadezhda OSTAPCHUK b. 12 Oct 1980 1.80m 78kg.
At SP: WCh: '99- dnq 17; WJ: '98- 1; EJ: '99- 1; WI: '01- 2, EI: '00- 6. BLR champion 1999-2000.
Progression at SP: 1997- 14.23, 1998- 18.23, 1999- 18.73, 2000- 19.13i/18.83, 2001- 19.24i.

Natalya SAZANOVICH b. 15 Aug 1973 Baranovich 1.79m 65kg. Gomel. Sports instructor.
At Hep: OG: '96- 2, '00- 3; WCh: '97- 5; EC: '98- 3; ECp: '95- 7, '96- 1, '00- 1B; WJ: '92- 1; EJ: '91- 1; At Pen: WI: '01- 1. Won BLR LJ 1996.
Progression at Hep: 1989- 5431, 1990- 5725, 1991- 5896, 1992- 6036, 1995- 6020, 1996- 6563, 1997- 6442, 1998- 6410, 2000- 6527. pbs: 200m 23.62 '96, 800m 2:16.41 '00, 60mh 8.24i '96, 100mh 13.30 '96, HJ 1.84 '95, LJ 6.86 '96, SP 16.31i '01, 15.64 '96; JT 46.20 '96, 43.97N '00; Pen 4850i '96.

Svetlana SUDAK b. 20 Mar 1971 Grodno 1.74m 90kg. Grodno TU.
At HT: OG: '00- 10; WCh: '99- 9; EC: '98- 9; WUG: '97- 5. BLR champion 1992-5, 1998-9.
World hammer record 1994.
Progression at HT: 1991- 55.22, 1992- 62.70, 1993- 63.70, 1994- 67.34, 1995- 64.96, 1996- 66.14, 1997- 67.58, 1998- 64.23, 1999- 68.21, 2000- 67.15.
Changed from BLR to RUS in 1999.

Irina YATCHENKO b. 31 Oct 1965 Gomel 1.85m 94kg. Grodno. Sports instructor.
At DT: OG: '92- 7, '96- 12, '00- 3; WCh: '91- 7, '95- 9, '97- 5, '99- 9; EC: '90- 5, '98- 8; ECp: '95- 3, '96- 3. 2nd GP 1992. BLR champion 1997.
Progression at DT: 1982- 50.72, 1983- 57.04, 1984- 59.54, 1985- 60.56, 1986- 57.58, 1987- 63.00, 1988- 67.44, 1989- 62.38, 1990- 68.60, 1991- 64.92, 1992- 68.94, 1993- 58.74, 1995- 66.14, 1996- 65.80, 1997- 68.32, 1998- 64.00, 1999- 66.18, 2000- 66.51.
Married to Igor Astapkovich (qv).

Ellina ZVEREVA b. 16 Nov 1960 Dolgoprudny 1.85m 100kg. formerly Kisheyeva. Minsk Dyn. Sports instructor.
At DT: OG: '88- 5, '96- 3, '00- 1; WCh: '91- 9, '95- 1, '97- 2, '99- 10; EC: '90- 6, '94- 2, '98- 4; WCp: '94- 2; ECp: '93- 1B, '94- 3. 2nd GP 1996, 2000; 3rd 1994.
USSR champion 1986, BLR 1993, 2000.
BLR discus record 1988.
Progression at DT: 1979- 44.06, 1980- 51.38, 1981- 59.88, 1982- 62.52, 1983- 65.18, 1984- 68.56, 1985- 66.64, 1986- 68.96, 1987- 60.84, 1988- 71.58, 1990- 66.20, 1991- 63.80, 1992- 66.26/68.82dq, 1993- 66.32, 1994- 67.44, 1995- 68.84, 1996- 68.60, 1997- 65.94, 1998- 67.46, 1999- 67.60, 2000- 68.40.
Drugs ban reported after positive steroids test when first at CIS Trials 1992, but back in 1993. At 39y 315d she became the oldest ever women's champion at athletics in 2000.

BELGIUM

Governing bodies: Ligue Royale Belge d'Athlétisme, Stade Roi Baudouin, avenue du Marathon 199B, 1020 Bruxelles (KBAB). Vlaamse Atletiekliga (VAL); Ligue Belge Francophone d'Athlétisme (LBFA). Original governing body founded 1889.

National Championships first held in 1889 (women 1921). **2000 Champions**: **Men**: 100m/200m: Patrick Stevens 10.31/20.59, 400m: Kjell Provost 46.08, 800m: Nathan Kahan 1:49.60, 1500m: Luc Bernaert 3:48.15, 5000m/10000m: Koen Allaert 13:52.43/28:32.22, Mar: Peter De Vocht 2:23:11, 3000mSt: Hilaire Ntirampeba BUR 8:45.89, 110mh: Hubert Grossard 13.92, 400mh: Jean-Paul Bruwier 50.72, HJ: Patrick De Paepe 2.05, PV: Thibault Duval 5.50, LJ: David Branle 7.45, TJ: Djeke Mambo 15.60, SP: Filip Eeckhout 15.73, DT: Jo Van Daele 58.78, HT: Walter De Wyngaert 64.83, JT: Marc Van Mensel 70.25, 20000mW: Dirk Bogaert 1:58:39t. **Women**: 100m: Kim Gevaert 11.61, 200m: Katleen De Caluwe 24.00, 400m: Sandra Stals 53.53, 800m: Ludivine Michel 2:04.80, 1500m: Veerle Dejaeghere 4:16.01, 5000m: Anja Smolders 15:45.68, 10000m: Marleen Renders 32:01.79, Mar: Katja Merlin 2:45:17; 100mh: Nadine Grouwels 13.56, 400mh: Ann Mercken 57.06, HJ/Hep: Tia Hellebaut 1.85/5646, PV: Liesbet Van Roie 3.75, LJ: Sandrine Hennart 6.16, TJ: Sandra Swennen 13.16, SP/DT: Veerle Blondeel 15.46/51.35, HT: Hannelore Poissonnier 49.47, JT: Cindy Stas 51.71, 5000mW: L Desmet 30:41.

Mohammed MOURHIT b. 10 Oct 1970 Morocco 1.64m 55kg.
At 5000m: WCh: '99- 3. At 10000m: OG: '00- dnf; WCh: '97- dns. At 3000m: WI: '01- 2; EI: '00- 4. World CC: '97-8-9-00-01: 5/8/7/1/1; HMar: '97- 5; Eur CC: '98- 2. 3rd GP 3000m 1999. Won MAR 1500m 1992, 1995; 5000m 1993; BEL 1500m 1999, CC 1997-9.
Records: European 10000m 1999, 3000m & 5000m 2000; Belgian 3000m (2), 5000m (5), 10,000m (2), HMar 1997-9.
Progression at 5000m, 10000m: 1988- 13:57.91, 29:17.3; 1989- 14:05.59, 29:37.55; 1990- 14:08.52, 1991- 13:29.20, 1993- 13:47.7, 1996- 13:46.94, 1997- 13:05.49, 27:17.09; 1998- 13:06.20, 1999- 12:58.45, 26:52.30; 2000- 12:49.71, 27:45.75. pbs: 800m 1:48.23 '93, 1500m 3:36.14 '00, 1M 3:56.41 '91, 2000m 4:58.8 '00, 3000m 7:26.62 '00, 2M 8:14.88 '97, HMar 60:18 '97.
Ex-Moroccan with Belgian wife. BEL citizenship confirmed July 1997. His younger brother **Hassan** (b. 2 Jan 1982) ran 2M indoors in 8:31.77 and won a major Belgian CC race in February 2001.

Women

Marleen RENDERS b. 24 Dec 1968 1.66m 42kg.
At Mar: OG: '96- 25, '00- dnf; EC: '98- 5. At 10000m: WCh: '87- 12, '95- 17, '97- dnf, '99- 9; EC: '94- 10; WJ: '86- 3. World HMar: '94- 7, '95- 13. Won BEL 3000m 1987, 5000m 1995-6, 10000m 1988, 1994, 1998-2000; HMar 1994-5, 1998.
World junior 10000m record 1987. Belgian records: 10000m 2000, marathon (4) 1997-2000.
Progression at 10000m, Mar: 1986- 33:41.13, 1987- 32:12.51, 1988- 32:11.49, 1991- 32:04.2mx, 1994- 32:11.18, 1995- 32:33.38, 2:28:57; 1996- 32:02.55, 2:27:42; 1997- 31:57.87, 2:25:56; 1998- 32:01.80, 2:25:22; 1999- 31:51.21, 2:23:58; 2000- 31:03.60, 2:23:43. pbs: 1500m 4:18.07 '87, 3000m 9:03.64 '97, 5000m 15:19.20 '89, HMar 69:29 '94.
Won Antwerp marathon 1995, Paris 2000; 2nd Rotterdam. Berlin: 3rd 1997, 1st 1998, 2nd 1999.

BERMUDA

Governing body: Bermuda T & F Association, P.O.Box DV 397, Devonshire. Founded 1946.

Brian WELLMAN b. 8 Sep 1967 1.75m 72kg. University of Arkansas, USA.
At TJ: OG: '88- dnq, '92- 5, '96- 6, '00- dnq 20; WCh: '91- 6, '93- 8, '95- 2, '97- 5, '99- dnq 24; WJ: '86- 8; WI: '93- 3, '95- 1; CG: '90- 11, '94- 3; PAm: '91- 5, '99- 4; WUG: '91- 1. 2nd PAm Jnr 1986; Won NCAA 1991, CAC 1999. 3rd GP 1992.
Bermuda TJ records 1986-95, Commonwealth 1995.
Progression at TJ: 1986- 16.18, 1988- 16.38, 1989- 16.44w, 1990- 16.23, 1991- 17.07/17.41w, 1992- 17.24/17.30w, 1993- 17.27i/17.14, 1994- 17.41A, 1995- 17.72i/17.62A/17.75w, 1996- 17.51A/17.15/ 17.56Aw, 1997- 17.22, 1998- 16.98A/16.97/17.15Aw, 1999- 17.18, 2000- 17.05Ai/16.50/ 17.09Aw. pb LJ 7.61 '94.
Advanced to third in 1993 World Indoors after drugs disqualification of Nikolay Raev.

BRAZIL

Governing body: Confederação Brasileira de Atletismo (CBAT), Avenida Sete de Setembro 874, 4to. andar, Manaus, Amazonas 69005-140. Founded 1914 (Confederação 1977).
2000 National Champions: Men: 100m: Vicente de Lima 10.35, 200m: Claudinei da Silva 20.53, 400m: Valdinei da Silva 46.02, 800m: Osmar dos Santos 1:45.87, 1500m: Hudson de Souza 3:40.88, 5000m/10000m: Valdenor dos Santos 13:48.76/29:02.26, 3000mSt: Wander Moura 8:42.81, 110mh: Márcio de Souza 13.79, 400mh: Eronilde de Araújo 49.05, HJ: Vagner Príncipe 2.14, PV: Gustavo Rehder 5.00, LJ: Nelson Ferreira Jr 8.18, TJ: Sérgio dos Santos 16.68, SP: Édson Miguel 17.80, DT: João dos Santos 57.71, HT: Mário Leme 61.12, JT: Luiz F da Silva 79.50, Dec: Édson Bindilatti 7479, 20kmW: Sérgio Galdino 1:26:47. **Women:** 100m/200m: Lucimar de Moura 11.37/23.35, 400m: Luciana Mendes 53.53/2:02.81, 1500m/5000m: Fabiana C da Silva 4:14.86/16:07.72, 10000m: Marcía Narloch 34:23.87, 3000mSt: Michele Costa 10:26.00, 100mh/LJ: Maurren Maggi 13.27/6.72w, 400mh: Ana Paula Pereira 57.51, HJ: Thaís de Andrade 1.82, PV: Karen da Silva 3.80, TJ: Luciana dos Santos 13.68, SP/DT: Elisângela Adriano 17.21/58.63, HT: Josiane Soares 59.46, JT: Sueli dos Santos 51.63, Hep: Euzinete Reis 5558, 20000mW: Gianetti Bonfim 1:46:21.6.

Eronilde Nunes **de ARAÚJO** b. 31 Dec 1970 Bom Jesus da Lapa, Bahia 1.82m 78kg. Funilense.
At 400mh/4x400mR: OG: '92- sf, '96- 8, '00- 5; WCh: '95- 8, '99- 4; PAm: '91- 1, '95- 1, '99- 1/2R; WCp: '94- 3. Won SACh 1991, 1993, 1995, 1997, 1999; SA-J 1989, IbAm 1992, 1998, 2000; BRA 1991-2000.
Four S American 400mh records 1994-5.
Progression at 400mh: 1989- 50.15, 1990- 49.82, 1991- 49.28, 1992- 49.10, 1993- 49.15, 1994- 48.88, 1995- 48.04, 1996- 48.45, 1997- 48.95, 1998- 48.75, 1999- 48.13, 2000- 48.25. pbs: 400m 45.75 '97, 110mh 14.37 '90.

Sanderlei Claro **PARRELA** b. 7 Oct 1974 Santos, São Paulo 1.94m 77kg. Flamengo.
At 400m/4x400mR: OG: '96- qf, '00- 4; WCh: '95- h, '97- sf, '99- 2; PAm: '99- 4/2R; SACh: '95- 1/1R, '97- 1/1R. Won SA-J 1991, 1993; Ib-Am 1996, 2000; BRA 1996-7, 1999. 2nd GP 2000.
Six Brazilian and S.American 400m records 1997-9
Progression at 400m: 1990- 50.3, 1991- 47.74, 1992- 46.98, 1993- 47.86, 1994- 46.84/46.7, 1995- 45.74, 1996- 45.17, 1997- 44.96, 1998- 45.27, 1999- 44.29, 2000- 44.65. pbs: 100m 10.61 '00, 200m 20.60A '00, 20.83 '97; 300m 32.10+ '99, 800m 1:46.34 '98.
Failed a drugs test on 14 May 2000, but there were apparently discrepancies between his A and B samples and he was reinstated by his national federation in time to compete at Olympic Games.

Claudinei Quirino **da SILVA** b. 19 Nov 1970 Lençóis Paulista, São Paulo 1.86m 86kg. Funilense.
At 200m (100m/4x100mR): OG: '96- qf, '00- 6/2R; WCh: '95- 5, '97- 3, '99- 2/4R; PAm: 99- 1 (3, 1R/2R); SACh: '95- 2, '97- 1/1R. Won GP 200m 1999, Ib-Am 200m 2000, BRA 100m 1998-9, 200m 1996, 1998-2000.
South American 200m record 1999.
Progression at 100m, 200m: 1992- 10.59, 1993- 10.60, 1994- 10.41/10.26dt, 21.19/20.6; 1995- 10.41/10.27w/10.1w, 20.28; 1996- 10.28/10.08dt/ 10.2/10.0w, 20.51/20.0w; 1997- 10.28, 20.27/ 20.26w; 1998- 10.21, 20.46/20.28w; 1999- 10.12, 19.89; 2000- 10.16, 20.23. pb 400m 46.14 '01.
Ran 44.6 leg on Pan-Am 4x400m relay. Ran successive pbs of 20.22, 20.13 and 20.00 at 1999 Worlds, and then South American record 19.89 to beat Maurice Greene for GP title.

Women

Maurren Higa **MAGGI** b. 25 Jun 1976 São Carlos, São Paulo 1.73m 62kg. Funilense.
At LJ (/100mh): OG: '00- dnq 25; WCh: '99- 8/qf; PAm: '99- 1/2; SACh: '97- 2/1, 99- 1/1; WUG: '99- 3. Won IbAm LJ 2000, SA-J 100mh 1994, BRA 100mh 1997-2000, LJ 1999-2000.
Three Brazilian and one S.American long jump records 1999, 6 BRA & 3 SA 100mh records 1999.
Progression at 100mh, LJ: 1994- 14.13. 5.86; 1995- 14.46/14.3w, 5.75/6.02w; 1996- 13.99, 6.47; 1997- 13.67/13.53w, 6.54; 1998- 13.60, 6.42; 1999- 12.86, 7.26A/6.79/6.81w, 2000- 6.93. pb 60mh 8.12i '00 (S.Am rec).
Formerly a gymnast, made huge breakthrough in 1999 with her 7.26 LJ at the high altitude of Bogotá from a previous best of 6.79.

BULGARIA

Governing body: Bulgarian Athletics Federation, 75 bl. Vassil Levski, Sofia 1000. F'd 1924.
National Championships first held in 1926 (men), 1938 (women). **2000 Champions**: **Men**: 100m: Ruslan Rusidze GEO 10.51, 200m: Milen Petrov 22.01, 400m: Ilia Dzhivondov 46.95, 800m: Khristo Moisev 1:54.49, 1500m: Stanislav Lambev 4:00.60, 5000m/10000m/Mar: Petko Stefanov 14:42.6/30:51.4/2:22:48, HMar: Khristo Stefanov 66:10, 3000mSt: Georgi Georgiev 9:29.5, 110mh: Nikolay Koikov 14.58, 400mh: Plamen Nyagin 52.79, HJ: Angel Kararadev 2.15, PV: Ilian Efremov 5.60, LJ: Petar Dachev 8.18, TJ: Ivailo Rusenov 16.78, SP: Galin Kostadinov 16.42, DT: Encho Shterev 50.63, HT: Andrian Andreev 64.95, JT: Angel Mandzhukov 65.75, Dec: Marin Karailev 6042, 10000mW: Todor Ivanov 50:58.7, 20kmW: Tenyo Georgiev 1:45:15. **Women**: 100m/200m: Monika Gachevska 11.3/23.79, 400m: Daniela Georgieva 52.63, 800m/1500m: Yoana Parusheva 2:10.13/4:33.26, 5000m/10000m/HMar: Milka Mikhailova 16:25.53/34:04.6/74:02, Mar: Rumyana Panovska 2:51:45, 100mh: Gegana Stoyanova 13.69, 400mh: Desislava Stoyanova 61.79, HJ: Eleonora Milusheva 1.85, PV: TaniaKoleva 4.10, LJ: Maria Dimitrova 6.06, TJ: Iva Prandzheva 15.04, SP/HT: Anelia Yordanova 15.64/62.10, DT: Venera Getova 46.53, JT: Rumyana Karapetrova 43.11, 5000mW/20kmW: Nevena Mineva-Dimitrova 21:49.5/1:35:45.

Rostislav DIMITROV b. 26 Dec 1974 Ruse 1.82m 80kg. Chendini.
At TJ: OG: '00- 9; WCh: '97- dnq 18, '99- 2; EC: '98- 3; EJ: '93- 2; WI: '99- dq (2), '01- 5; EI: '00- 2. 2nd GP 2000. Won Balkan 1997, 1999.
Progression at TJ: 1990- 14.70, 1991- 15.49, 1992- 15.98, 1993- 16.35, 1994- 16.11, 1995- 16.18, 1996- 16.48, 1997- 16.88, 1998- 17.07/17.26w, 1999- 17.49, 2000- 17.30. pb LJ 7.48 '97.
Positive test for ephedrine cost him the silver medal from the 1999 World Indoor Champs.

Women

Svetla DIMITROVA b. 27 Jan 1970 Burgas 1.70m 65kg. Married name Pishtikova. Spirala.
At 100mh: OG: '96- sf, '00- sf; WCh: '97- 2, '99- 5; EC: '94- 1/3R, '98- 1; WCp: '94- 2. At Hep: OG: '88- 12, '92- 5; WCh: '93- 4; WJ: '86- 1, '88- 1; ECp: '89- 3dq. Won GP 100mh and 2nd overall 1994. Won BUL Hep 1989, 100mh 1992-3, 1998.
Progression at 100mh, Hep: 1986- 6041; 1988- 12.9w, 6343; 1989- 6534 dq/6428; 1992- 13.22, 6658; 1993- 12.71, 6594; 1994- 12.53/12.50w, 1996- 12.57, 1997- 12.58/12.4, 1998- 12.56, 1999- 12.72/12.64w, 2000- 12.78. pbs: 200m 23.06w '92, 23.10 '93; 800m 2:07.90 '92, 60mh 7.94i '00, HJ 1.88 '86, LJ 6.64 '92, SP 15.50 '93, JT 48.18 '93.
Suspended for a positive drugs test when third in the 1989 European Cup heptathlon in what would have been a world junior record. Won Götzis heptathlon 1993, but has since concentrated on hurdling. She was clearly the world's best in 1994. In November 1994 she left her husband and coach Ilian Pishtikov to seek Austrian citizenship, but returned in 1995. Her son Kristian was born on 30 Dec 1995.

Khristina KALCHEVA b. 29 May 1977 Aleksin, Russia 1.78m 57kg. Lokomotiv Plovdiv.
At HJ: OG: '00- dnq; EC: '98- dnq 17; WI: '99- 1. Bulgarian champion 1998.
Progression at HJ: 1995- 1.65, 1996- 1.76, 1997- 1.91, 1998- 1.99, 1999- 1.99i/1.90, 2000- 1.98.
Russian mother and Bulgarian father.

Tereza MARINOVA b. 5 Sep 1977 Pleven 1.73m 56kg. Chendini.
At TJ: OG: '00- 1; WCh: '97- 6; EC: '98- 3; WJ: '94- dnq 15, '96- 1; EJ: '95- 1; WI: '97- 8, '99- 4, '01- 1. Balkan champion 1996, 2000; BUL 1998.
Two world junior triple jump records (one unofficial) 1996. Bulgarian TJ record 2000.
Progression at TJ: 1993- 12.18, 1994- 13.23/13.51w, 1995- 13.90, 1996- 14.62, 1997- 14.34/14.53w, 1998- 14.67, 1999- 14.76i/14.64, 2000- 15.20, 2001- 14.91i. pb LJ 6.46 '00.
Smashed personal bests when winning European (1995) and World (1996) Junior gold medals and again to win 2000 Olympic title. Her father Moncho Marinov set a Bulgarian 800m record of 1:47.7 in 1974 and brother Tsvetomir (b. 10 Jul 1976) was 3rd in the 1995 European Junior 400m.

Petya PENDAREVA b. 20 Jan 1971 Kazanluk 1.63m 56kg. Athletik (Kazanlak). Sports instructor.
At 100m(/200m): OG: '96- h, '00- qf; WCh: '91- hR, '93/5/7/9- qf/sf/sf; EC: '94- 6, 98- 6; WJ: '90- sf. At 60m: WI: '99- 7, '01- 6; EI: '94- 4/6, '98- 6, '00- 2. Won BUL 100m 1993, 1997; 200m 1993.
Progression at 100m: 1990- 11.80, 1991- 11.67, 1992- 11.33, 1993- 11.14, 1994- 11.23/11.18w, 1995- 11.39/11.23w/11.0, 1996- 11.41, 1997- 11.22, 1998- 11.12, 1999- 11.16/11.04w, 2000- 11.23. pbs: 50m 6.14i '99, 60m 7.04i '01, 200m 22.78 '93.

Venelina VENEVA b. 13 Jun 1974 Ruse 1.79m 61kg. 'Champion' Sofia.
At HJ: OG: '96- dnq 29=, '00- 9=; WCh: '91- dnq, '95- dnq 14, '99- dnq 14=; EC: '98- 5; EJ: '91- 2; WI: '01- 3; EI: '00- 4. BUL champion 1995.
Progression at HJ: 1988- 1.80, 1989- 1.86, 1990- 1.93i/1.90, 1991- 1.91, 1992- 1.91, 1993- 1.89i/1.85, 1994- 1.90, 1995- 1.94, 1996- 1.94i/1.88, 1998- 2.03, 1999- 1.90, 2000- 2.01. pb TJ 12.51 '95.
Daughter Neapola born in 1997. World age-15 best of 1.93i in 1990.

CAMEROON

Governing body: Fédération Camerounaise d'Athlétisme, BP 353, Yaoundé. Founded 1957.

Léonie **Myriam MANI** b. 21 May 1977 1.64m 60kg.
At 100m(/200m): OG: '96- h, '00- sf/sf; WCh: '97- h, '99 – h/qf; CG: '98- 8, AfG: '95- (7), '99- 2/2; AfCh: '96- 3/3, '00-1/1.
CMR records 100m, 200m from 1998.
Progression at 100m, 200m: 1991- 24.2; 1992- 12.0, 24.5; 1993- 24.0, 1994- 23.6, 1995- 24.40A, 1996- 11.71/11.4, 23.33; 1997- 11.62/11.54w, 23.68; 1998- 11.35/11.1w, 23.01; 1999- 11.24A/11.22w, 22.66A; 2000- 11.01, 22.41. pbs: 60m 7.18i '00, 400m 53.0 '98.

CANADA

Governing body: Athletics Canada, Suite 606, 1185 Eglinton Avenue East, Toronto, Ontario, L3X 1T6. Formed as Canadian AAU in 1884.
National Championships first held in 1884 (men), 1925 (women). **2000 champions: Men**: 100m: Bruny Surin 10.05w, 200m: Pierre Browne 20.58w, 400m: Shane Niemi 45.79, 800m: Zach Whitmarsh 1:52.23, 1500m: Kevin Sullivan 3:46.59, 5000m: Sean Kaley 13:25.16, 3000mSt: Joel Bourgeois 8:38.53, Mar: Bruce Deacon 2:17:13, 110mh: Andrew Woodley 13.67w, 400mh: Nick Stewart 50.32, HJ: Mark Boswell 2.31, PV: Jason Pearce 5.10, LJ: Ian Lowe 7.70, TJ: Oral O'Gilvie 16.06, SP: Jason Gervais 19.03, DT: Jason Tunks 63.06, HT: Dylan Armstrong 66.67, JT: Scott Russell 75.92, Dec: Mike Nolan 7555, 20kmW: Arturo Huerta 1:21:24. **Women**: 100m: Esi Benyarku 11.30, 200m/400m: Ladonna Antoine 22.82w/51.63, 800m: Diane Cummins 2:03.80, 1500m: Leah Pells 4:13.27, 5000m: Tina Connelly 15:33.59, Mar: Véronique Vandemissen 2:36:46, 3000mSt: Kristin Brennand 11:08.41, 100mh: Perdita Felicien 13.15w, 400mh: Karlene Haughton 57.20, HJ: Wanita May 1.85, PV: Ardin Harrison 3.85, LJ: Alice Falaiye 6.39, TJ: Althea Williams 13.25w, SP: Georgette Reed 15.97, DT: Tina McDonald 51.48, HT: Robin Lyons 62.70, JT: Dominique Bilodeau 50.52, Hep: Nicole Haynes 5838, 20kmW: Janice McCaffrey 1:34:50.

Donovan BAILEY b. 16 Dec 1967 Manchester, JAM 1.82m 82kg. Phoenix TC. Consultant.
At 100m/4x100m: OG: '96- 1/1R, '00- qf; WCh: '95- 1/1R, '97- 2/1R, '99- hR; CG: '94- 1R; PAm: '91- 8/2R, '99- 2R. 2nd GP 1996. At 200m: WI: '95- 4. Won CAN 100m 1995-7.
World 100m record 1996, world indoor 50m record 1996. Two Canadian 100m records 1995-6.
Progression at 100m: 1984- 11.0, 1985- 11.37, 1991- 10.42, 1992- 10.42/10.15Aw, 1993- 10.36A, 1994- 10.03, 1995- 9.91, 1996- 9.84, 1997- 9.91, 1998- 9.93, 1999- 10.30/10.19w, 2000- 10.06/9.98r/ 10.00w. pbs: 50m 5.56Ai '96, 5.58+ '97; 60m 6.43+ '97, 150m 14.99i/15.01 '97, 200m 20.42 '98, 20.14w '97.
Emigrated to Canada in 1981. Did not break 11 secs until age 23 but went on to win World and Olympic golds at 100m. A ruptured Achilles cut short his 1998 season, but he returned in 1999.

Kwaku BOATENG b. 30 Jun 1974 Toronto 1.83m 80kg. St Laurent Select. Studying psychology at Concordia University.
At HJ: OG: '00- 12; WCh: '99- 6=; CG: '94- dnq; PAm: '99- 1=. Canadian champion 1997-9.
Progression at HJ: 1993- 2.13, 1994- 2.15, 1996- 2.24, 1997- 2.27i, 1998- 2.20, 1999- 2.29, 2000- 2.34.
Competed for Ghana at 1994 CG.

Mark BOSWELL b. 28 Jul 1977 Mandeville, Jamaica 1.89m 77kg. Lightning T&F. Student at University of Texas.
At HJ: OG: '00- 6=; WCh: '99- 2; WJ: '96: 1; PAm: '99- 1=; WUG '99- 2; Won NCAA 1999-2000, Canadian 1997, 2000.
Four Canadian high jump records 1999-2000.
Progression at HJ: 1994- 2.10, 1995- 2.00, 1996- 2.24, 1997- 2.28, 1998- 2.29, 1999- 2.35, 2000- 2.35
Moved to Canada in 1988.

Brad SNYDER b. 8 Jan 1976 Windsor, Ontario 1.96m 128kg. Windsor Legion. Was at University of South Carolina, USA.
At SP: OG: '96- dnq 30, '00- dnq 13; WCh: '97- dnq 21; WJ: '94- dnq 14; PAm: '99- 3; WUG: '99- 4. Won Pan-Am J 1995, NCAA 1998, Canadian 1996, 1998-9.
Progression at SP: 1994- 16.73, 1995- 17.34, 1996- 19.70, 1997- 19.68i/19.51, 1998- 20.40, 1999- 20.51, 2000- 20.24, 2001- 20.29i. pb DT 58.65 '99.

Kevin SULLIVAN b. 20 Mar 1974 Brantford, Ontario 1.80m 68kg. Windsor. Civil engineering graduate of University of Michigan, USA.
At 1500m: OG: '00- 5; WCh: '95- 5, '97- sf, '99- h; WJ: '92- 3; CG: '94- 2; 3rd GP 2000. At 800m: WJ: '90- h. World CC: '93- 13J. Won CAN 1500m 1992-5, 2000; PAmJ 800m 1993, NCAA 1500m 1995.
Canadian records 1M 1995 and 2000, 1500m 1997 and 2000.
Progression at 1500m: 1991- 3:46.52, 1992- 3:39.11, 1993- 3:39.43, 1994- 3:36.78, 1995- 3:35.77, 1996- 3:42.2, 1997- 3:35.19, 1998- 3:34.80, 1999- 3:34.61, 2000- 3:31.71. pbs: 800m 1:47.06 '95, 1000m 2:17.59 '00, 1M 3:50.26 '00, 3000m 7:51.65i '98, 2M 8:23.67i '01.
Married Karen Harvey on 8 Aug 1998.

Bruny SURIN b. 12 Jul 1967 Cap-Haïtien, Haiti 1.80m 81kg. Vidéotron, Montreal.
At 100m/4x100m: OG: '92- 4, '96- sf/1R, '00- sf; WCh: '91- 8, '93- 5/3R, '95- 2/1R, '97- 7/1R, '99- 2; CG: '90- 3 (7 LJ), '94- sf/1R. At LJ: OG: '88- dnq 15; PAm: '87- dnq 15. At TJ: WJ: '86- 11. At 60m: WI: '91- 8, '93- 1, '95- 1, '97- 5, '99- 8. Won Canadian 100m 1989-92, 1998-2000.
Six Canadian 100m records 1989-99. Commonwealth 100m record 1999.
Progression at 100m, LJ: 1986- 10.95, 7.66, 1987- 10.62, 8.03; 1988- 10.71, 8.02/8.19w; 1989- 10.14/10.1, 8.00; 1990- 10.24/10.12w, 7.85w; 1991- 10.07/10.01w, 1992- 10.05/9.9, 1993- 10.02, 1994- 10.08, 1995- 9.97/9.92w, 1996- 10.03, 1997- 10.06, 1998- 9.89, 1999- 9.84, 2000- 10.08/10.05w. pbs: 50m 5.53+ '99, 55m 6.15i '96, 60m 6.38+ '99, 200m 20.21 '99, TJ 15.96 '86.
Moved to Canada in 1975. Set four Canadian records 1989-92 and reached peak form in 1999, when in a record fifth successive World 100m final, he took the silver medal, equalling Donovan Bailey's Canadian (and former world) record of 9.84.

Jason TUNKS b. 7 May 1975 London, Ontario 1.97m 120kg. London Western. Was at Southern Methodist University, USA.
At DT (SP): OG: '96- dnq 33, '00- 6; WCh: '97- 9, '99- dnq 20; WJ: '94- 8 (10); CG: '98- 3; PAm: '99- 3 (5). Won NCAA 1997; Canadian SP 1997, DT 1995, 1997-2000.
Two Canadian (one Commonwealth) discus records 1998.
Progression at DT: 1992- 48.38, 1993- 51.52, 1994- 58.76, 1995- 58.66, 1996- 63.86, 1997- 65.20, 1998- 67.88, 1999- 65.54, 2000- 66.28. pb SP 19.06 '97.
Married to **Teri** (née Steer) (USA) pb SP 19.04i/18.80 '99, 3 WI '99, 3 PAm 99, 9 WCh 99, pb DT 56.60 '98.

Women

Keturah '**Katie**' **ANDERSON** b. 9 Jan 1968 Kingston, Jamaica 1.62m 63kg. Phoenix AA. Was at University of Alabama, USA.
At 100mh: OG: '92/96/00- qf; WCh: '93- sf, '97- 6, '99- qf; CG: '98- 3; Canadian champion 1998-9. At 60mh: WI: '97- 6, '99- 3. At 100m: OG: '88- sfR, WCh: '87- 6R; WJ: '86- 7 (sf 200m); WUG: '93- 3R; won PAm Jnr 1984 (3rd 1986).
Six Canadian 100mh records 1996-9.
Progression at 100mh: 1991- 13.68, 1992- 13.09, 1993- 13.23, 1994- 13.38, 1995- 13.49, 1996- 12.86, 1997- 12.80, 1998- 12.66, 1999- 12.61, 2000- 12.82. pbs: 100m 11.42 '88, 11.41w '92; 200m 23.81/23.69w '87, 50mh 6.78i '99, 55mh 7.48 '96, 60mh 7.90i '99.
Moved to Canada in 1975. Switched from sprinting to hurdling in 1992.

CAYMAN ISLANDS

Governing Body: Cayman Islands Amateur Athletic Association, PO Box 527, George Town, Grand Cayman. Founded 1980.

Kareem **STREETE-THOMPSON** b. 30 Mar 1973 Ithaca, New York 1.83m 84kg. Nike. Degree in political science from Rice University.
At LJ (100m): OG: '92- dnq (h), '00- dnq 13; WCh: '91- dnq, '95- 14, '99- dnq 24 (8); WI: '01- 2; CG: '90- 11 (qf); WJ: '88- dnq; '90- 3; PAm: '99- 2; WUG: '93- 1. Won CAC Jnr 1990 and 1992, NCAA 1995. 2nd GP 1995.
Cayman Islands records 100m 1999, LJ 1999-2000.
Progression at 100m, LJ: 1988- 6.84, 1989- 10.88, 7.83; 1990- 7.95, 1991- 10.59/10.50w, 8.09/8.40w; 1992- 10.57, 8.12/8.39w; 1993- 10.30/10.19Aw, 8.36A; 1994- 10.21A/10.29, 8.63/8.64w; 1995- 10.16, 8.56; 1996- 10.23, 8.34; 1997- 9.96, 8.08A/8.30Aw; 1998- 10.07, 8.17; 1999- 10.14, 8.15/8.22Aw; 2000- 10.22Aw, 8.31. pbs: 50m 5.76i '97, 55m 6.16i '94, 60m 6.53i '98, 200m 20.3 '97, 21.34 '93.
Until 1992 he represented the Cayman Islands, where he lived for the first 18 years of his life, apart from his first month as he was born in the USA of Jamaican parents while his mother was visiting friends. He became a US citizen in 1994, but in 1999 reverted to the Cayman Islands.

CHILE

Governing body: Federación Atlética de Chile, Calle Santo Toribio No 660, Ñuñoa, Santiago de Chile. Founded 1917.
2000 National Champions: **Men**: 100m: Rodrigo Roach 10.62, 200m: Javier Díaz 22.22, 400m: Juan Zapata 48.55, 800m: Ronny Bravo 1:51.29, 1500m: Ronny Bravo 3:55.47, 5000m: Patricio Contreras 14:53.36, 10000m: Wilson Wall 30:17.63, 3000mSt: Raúl Mora 8:55.38, 110mh: Francisco Schilling 14.85, 400mh: Carlos Zbinden 50.34, HJ: Felipe Apablaza 2.05, PV: José Francisco Nava 4.90, LJ: Claudio Bossay 7.36, TJ: Octavio Silva 14.05, SP/DT: Marco Antonio Verni 17.47/50.41, HT: José Manuel Llano 64.68, JT: Diego Moraga 72.42, Dec: Cristián Lyon 6174, 20kmW: Luis Villagra 1:35:20. **Women**. 100m/200m: Lisette Rondón 11,76/24.18, 400m: Roxana González 56.96, 800m: Magdalena Sánchez 2:18.87, 1500m: Anahí Soto 4:36.36, 5000m: Luz Silva 18:23.30, 10000m: Erika Olivera 34:24.49, 100mh: Annete Stotz 15.06, 400mh: Magdalena Sánchez 61.97, HJ: Ana María Urrutia 1.70, PV: Carolina González 3.30, LJ/TJ: Karen Faúndez 5.44/11.68, SP: Marisol Bengoa 12.86, DT: Bárbara Lewin 43.22, HT: Odette Palma 46.79, JT: Paula Palma 43.10, Hep: Valeria Steffens 4809, 10000mW: Mabel Vásquez 59:49.34.

CHINA

Governing body: Athletic Association of the People's Republic of China, 9 Tiyuguan Road, Beijing 100763.
National Championships first held in 1910 (men), 1959 (women). **2000 Champions**. **Men**:

100m: Chen Haijian 10.30, 200m/400m: Xu Zizhou 20.65/46.56, 800m: Li Guangming 1:50.65, 1500m: Dou Zhaobo 3:48.23, 5000m/10000m: Xia Fengyuan 13:51.12/29:17.03, Mar: Hu Gangjun 2:14:01, 3000mSt: Sun Wenli 8:43.29, 110mh: Zhang Feng 14.06, 400mh: Meng Yan 50.53, HJ: Zhou Zhongge 2.18, PV: Zhang Hongwei 5.45, LJ: Wang Cheng 7.96, TJ: Lao Jianfeng 16.26, SP: Liu Hao 18.62, DT: Li Shaojie 59.25, HT: Ye Kuigang 73.67, JT: Zhang Lianbiao 77.14, Dec: Du Xiaopeng 7732, 20kmW: Yu Guohui 1:23:17 & Li Zewen 1:23:04, 50kmW: Zhang Huiqiang 3:54:40 & Wang Yinhang 3:53:10. **Women**: 100m/200m: Li Xuemei 11.39/23.38, 400m: Bu Fanfang 51.95, 800m: Wang Yuanping 2:07.23, 1500m: Wu Qingdong 4:14.40, 5000m: Dong Yanmei 15:32.31, 10000m: Li Ji 33:28.77, Mar: Wei Yanan 2:26:34, 100mh: Su Yiping 13.18, 400mh: Li Yulian 55.83, HJ: Zhang Liwen 1.84, PV: Gao Shuying 4.20, LJ: Guan Yingnan 6.66, TJ: Ren Ruiping 14.04, SP: Song Feina 18.68, DT: Xiao Yanling 60.81, HT: Liu Yinghui 65.06, JT: Liang Lili 59.33, Hep: Liu Xing 5835, 10000mtW: Gao Hongmiao 44:36.0, 20kmW: Wang Liping 1:34:01 & 1:28:33.

LI Zewen b. 5 Dec 1973 Qujing, Yunnan Prov. 1.72m 55kg. Sports psychology student.
At 20kmW: OG: '96- 28, WCh: '95- 5, '97- 5, '99- 4; WCp: '95- 1, '97- 4, '99- 18; AsiG: '98- 3; AsiC: '98- 1. Won CHN National Games 1997.
Progression at 20kmW: 1992- 1:23:36.9, 1993- 1:22:30, 1995- 1:19:44, 1996- 1:19:41, 1997- 1:18:32, 1998- 1:22:53, 1999- 1:24:03, 2000- 1:21:12.

YU Guohui b. 30 Apr 1977 Qingdao, Shandong 1.82m 70kg. PE student in Shandong.
At 20kmW: OG: '96- 21, '00- 13; WCh: '97- 4, '99- 14; WCp: '97- 40, '99- 2; AsiG: '98- 1. Chinese champion 1997-8.
World junior 20km walk best 1996.
Progression at 20kmW: 1995- 1:23:06, 1996- 1:19:38, 1997- 1:22:08, 1998- 1:20:25, 1999- 1:20:21, 2000- 1:22:32. pb 50kmW 3:55:20 '00.

Women

CHENG Xiaoyan b. 30 Dec 1975 Shandong Prov. 1.74m 100kg.
At SP: OG: '00- 11; WCh: '99- 5; WI: '01- 7; WJ: '94- 1; WUG: '95- 2; AsiG: '98- 2; Won CHN 1999.
Progression at SP: 1993- 18.00, 1994- 20.02, 1995- 18.29, 1996- 18.40, 1997- 18.28, 1998- 18.55, 1999- 18.91, 2000- 19.31.

DONG Yanmei b. 16 Feb 1977 Xuengdong, Liaoning Prov. 1.66m 51kg
At 3000m: WI: '01- 5, Won CHN National Games 10000m 1997. World record 5000m 1997.
Progression at 1500m, 5000m, 10000m, Mar: 1993- 17:23.0, 1994- 16:09.37, 1995- 15:11.80, 32:04.42, 2:38:57; 1996- 4:18.41, 15:58.55, 33:24.19, 2:34:52; 1997- 3:55.07, 14:29.82, 30:38.09, 2:28:09; 1998- 32:59.85, 2000- 15:03.99, 32:23.21. pb 3000m 8:33.07 '00, 8:41.34i '01.

GAO Hongmiao b. 17 Mar 1974 Liaoning 1.62m 51kg. Computing student.
At 20kmW: WCh: '99- 15; WCp: '99- 7. At 10kmW: OG: '96- dq; WCh: '95- dq; WCp: '95- 1; AsiG: '94- 1; AsiC: '93- 1. At 5000mW: WJ: '92- 1. Won CHN 10kmW 1994, 1996.
World junior 10,000m walk records track 1992, road 1993. Asian 10 km walk record 1994.
Progression at 10kmW, 20kmW: 1991- 42:56.09, 1992- 42:49.7, 1993- 41:57, 1994- 41:38, 1995- 42:19, 1996- 42:16, 1999- 43:37, 1:30:03; 2000- 44:36.0t, 1:33:01. pb 5000mW 21:20.03 '92.
Disqualified outside the stadium when leading World 10km 1995. Date of birth originally shown as 8 Jul 1974, then as 1972. However, the Chinese federation confirmed in 1995 that her date of birth was as above.

GUAN Yingnan b. 25 Apr 1977 Liaoning Prov. 1.77m 58kg.
At LJ: OG: '00- dnq 19; WCh: '99- dnq 17; WJ: '96- 1; AsiG: '98- 1; AsiC: '98- 1; WI: '99- 6, '01- 7; WCp: '98- 3. Won Asi-J 1996, CHN 1998-2000.
Progression at LJ: 1995- 6.48, 1996- 6.68, 1997- 6.86, 1998- 6.91, 1999- 6.80, 2000- 6.95.

LAN Lixin b. 14 Feb 1979 Liaoning Prov. 1.66m 50kg.
At 1500m (3000m): WJ: '98- 1 (4). Won Asian Junior 3000m 1997.
World Junior 1500m record 1997.
Progression at 1500m, 5000m, 10000m: 1997- 3:53.97, 14:45.33, 30:39.41; 1998- 4:10.05, 15:56.84; 1999- 4:11.62, 15:29.25, 33:26.51; 2000- 4:03.95, 15:31.05. pb 3000m 8:39.67 '00.

LIU Hongyu b. 11 Jan 1975 Liaoning Prov. 1.64m 51kg.
At 20kmW: WCh: '99- 1; WCp: '99- 1. At 10kmW: WCh: '95- 8, '97- 4; WCp: '93- 18, '95- 3, '97- 12; AsiG: '98- 1. At 5000mW: WJ: '94- 8.
World best 20km walk 1995.
Progression at 10kmW, 20kmW: 1993- 43:49.5, 1994- 42:47, 1995- 42:38.24t, 1:27:30; 1996- 42:55, 1997- 42:57, 1:33:31; 1998- 43:57.28t, 1999- 41:45, 1:27:32; 2000- 44:08, 1:27:55. pbs: 5kmW: 21:15 '95.

REN Ruiping b. 1 Feb 1976 Shandong province 1.76m 64kg.
At TJ: OG: '96- 7, '00- dnq 26; WCh: '95- 6, '97- dnq 16, '99- dnq 16; WJ: '94- 2; WI: '95- 3; AsiG: '98- 1; AsiC: '93- 1, '95- 1, '98- 1; WCp: '94- 3, '98- 4. Won CHN TJ 1994-7, 1999; E.Asian 1997.
Three World junior triple jump records 1993-4, two Asian records 1996-7.
Progression at TJ: 1991- 13.10, 1993- 14.29, 1994- 14.36, 1995- 14.07i/14.25/14.00Aw, 1996- 14.56, 1997- 14.66, 1998- 14.50, 1999- 14.64/14.68w, 2000- 14.47. pb LJ 6.67 '00.

REN Xiujuan b. 14 Sep 1974 Dalian, Liaoning Prov. 1.60m 56kg. Business management student.
At Mar: OG: '96- 9, '00- 10. At 10000m: WCh: '97- 5. Won World HMar 1996. Won Chinese Mar 1996, 2000.

Progression at 10000m, Mar: 1994- 2:35:59, 1995- 32:34.64, 2:30:00; 1996- 31:13.21, 2:27:13; 1997- 31:50.63, 2:28:52; 1999- 32:47.66, 2:33:58; 2000- 2:25:32. pbs: 5000m 15:39.68 '96, HMar 70:39 '96, 5000W 21:39.6 '89.
Won Beijing marathon 1995 and 1996.

WANG Liping b. 8 Jul 1976 Liaoning Prov. 1.65m 48kg.
At 20kmW: OG: '00- 1. CHN champion 2000. At 10kmW: WCp: '97- 10.
Progression at 10kmW, 20kmW: 1994- 1:35:09, 1995- 46:19.83t, 1:29:26; 1997- 42:53, 1:36:22; 1998- 45:12, 2000- 44:55, 1:28:33.

WANG Yan b. 3 May 1971 Liaoning 1.68m 50kg. Student.
At 20kmW: WCh: '99- 2; WCp: '99- 5. At 10kmW: OG: '96- 3; WCh: '93- dq, '97- 12; AsiC: '98- 5; WCp: '93- 1, '95- 14. Chinese champion 1993, 1998.
World walk records in 1986: 3000m: 12:39.1, 5000m: 21:33.8, with the latter at 14 years 310 days the youngest ever to set a world record. World junior 10kmW record 1986, Asian 10km walks records 1993 and 1999.
Progression at 10kmW: 1984- 49:01, 1985- 46:09, 1986- 44:59.3t, 1987- 45:22.24t, 1992- 42:50, 1993- 42:26, 1995- 44:25, 1:28:54; 1996- 42:19, 1997- 42:42, 1998- 45:03, 1999- 41:16, 1:29:15; 2000- 43:11, 1:28:27. pbs: 5kmW 21:10 '97.

COLOMBIA

Governing body: Federación Colombiana de Atletismo, Calle 28 No. 25-18, Apartado Aéreo 6024, Santafé de Bogotá. Founded 1937.
National Games 2000: Men: 100m/200m: John Córdoba 10.2/20.91, 400m: Milcíades Cantillo 48.17, 800m: John Chávez 1:52.41, 1500m: Alonso Pérez 3:53.49, 5000m: Diego Colorado 14:32.18, 10000m Herder Vásquez 31:04.50, Mar: Hugo Jiménez 2:24:50, 3000mSt: Diego Grisales 9:40.0, 110mh: Paulo Villar 14.06, 400mh: Alexander Mena 52.01, HJ: Gilmar Mayo 2.18, PV: Oscar Sánchez 4.20, LJ: Alvin Rentería 7.37, TJ: Leigner Aragón 16.15, SP/DT: Orlando Ibarra 16.90/49.39, HT: Fabián Vera 55.45, JT: Noraldo Palacios 74.63, Dec: Jackson Angulo 6247, 20000mW: John Jairo García 1:31:40.0, 50kmW: Joaquín Córdoba 4:40:31. **Women:** 100m: Digna Luz Murillo 11.87, 200m: Felipa Palacios 23.19, 400m: Norma González 52.73, 800m: Janeth Lucumí 2:11.10, 1500m: Sandra Villa 4:44.99, 5000m/10000m: Stella Castro 17:15.19/36:14.95, Mar: Sandra León 3:03:00, 100mh/400mh: Princesa Oliveros 13.76/58.27, HJ: Lía Torres 1.66, PV: Milena Agudelo 3.50, LJ: Helena Guerrero 6.21, TJ: Clara Inés Córdoba 12.62, SP/DT: Luz Dary Castro 16.21/51.00, HT: María Eugenia Villamizar 57.06, JT: Zuleima Araméndiz 59.33, Hep: Zorobabelia Córdoba 5259, 20000mW: Cristina Bohorquez 1:48:41.0.

CROATIA

Governing body: Hrvatski Atletski Savez, Tg Sportova 11, 10000 Zagreb. Founded 1912.

Ivana BRKLJACIC b. 25 Jan 1983 Vinningen-Schweningen, Germany 1.70m 65kg. Mladost Zagreb.
At HT: OG: '00- 11; WJ: '98- dnq 15, '00- 1; WY: '99- 3; EJ: '99- 5.
Croatian hammer record from 1998.
Progression at HT: 1998- 56.84, 1999- 58.51, 2000- 68.18.

CUBA

Governing body: Federación Cubana de Atletismo, 13 y C Vedado 601, Zone Postal 4, La Habana 10400. Founded 1922.
National Champions 2000. Men: 100m: Freddy Mayola 10.14, 200m: Ivan García 20.80, 400m: Norberto Téllez 46.50, 800m: Omar Torres 1:51.18, 1500m: Ereisis Torres 3:49.97, 5000m: Henry Jaen 14:14.50, 10000m: Aguelmis Rojas 30:27.96, 3000mSt: Yunier González 8:58.80, 110mh: Anier García 13.18, 400mh: Jorge Moreno 50.85, HJ: Lazaro Suárez 2.15, PV: Amaury Fernández 5.10, LJ: Iván Pedroso 8.20, TJ: Michael Calvo 17.14, SP: Alexis Paumier 19.53, DT: Alexis Elizalde 61.98, HT: Yosmel Monte 71.20, JT: Emeterio González 82.77, Dec: Raúl Duany 8252, 20kmW: Francisco Gutierrez 1:28:23. **Women**: 100m: Ana López 11.58, 200m: Roxana Díaz 23.57, 400m: Julia Duporty 52.41, 800m: Zulia Calatayud 2:02.92, 1500m: Yoenny Mayacen 4:31.37, 5000m/10000m: Mariela González 16:20.22/34:59.87, 100mh: Aliuska López 13.12; 400mh: Yaznai Lescay 58.62, HJ: Ioamnet Quintero 1.90, PV: Katiuska Pérez 3.80, LJ: Lissette Cuza 6.72, TJ: Yamilé Aldama 14.07, SP: Yumileidi Cumbá 19.10, DT: Yania Ferrales 56.06, HT: Yipsi Moreno 65.35, JT: Osleidys Menéndez 64.76, Hep: Magalys García 5977, 20kmW: Yarelis Sánchez 1:49:40.

Alexis ELIZALDE b. 19 Sep 1967 Ciudad Habana 1.92m 118kg.
At DT: OG: '96- 9, '00- dnq 20; WCh: '93- dnq 14, '95- 7, '97- dnq 13; PAm: '95- 2, '99- 2; CAG: '93- 1, '98- 1; WCp: '94- 2, '98- 6; WUG: '91- 3, '93- 1. Won CAC 1997; IbAm 1998, Cuban 1996-2000.
Progression at DT: 1985- 47.40, 1986- 50.88, 1987- 52.54, 1988- 53.04, 1989- 57.76, 1990- 59.62, 1991- 62.52, 1992- 60.92, 1993- 64.12, 1994- 62.74, 1995- 63.28, 1996- 64.00, 1997- 65.76, 1998- 65.00, 1999- 64.26, 2000- 64.13. pb SP 16.10 '88.

Anier Octavio **GARCÍA** b. 9 Mar 1976 Santiago de Cuba 1.90m 88kg.
At 110mh: OG: '96- qf, '00- 1; WCh: '97- sf, '99- 2; WJ: '94- 5; PAm: '99- 1; CAG: '98- 1; WCp: '98- 3. Won PAm-J 1995, IbAm 1996, Cuban 1997-2000.
At 60mh: WI: '97- 1, '99- 6, '01- 2.
Five CAC & Cuban 110mh records 1997-2000.

CAC indoor records at 50mh & 60mh 2000.
Progression at 110mh: 1993- 14.61, 1994- 13.91, 1995- 13.63/13.6, 1996- 13.39A/13.43, 1997- 13.11, 1998- 13.14A/13.24, 1999- 13.07, 2000- 13.00. pb 50mh 6.36i '00, 60mh 7.37i '00.
Ricoh Tour 60h winner 2000. Withdrew from 1997 World 110mh semis due to a leg injury.

Yoel GARCÍA b. 25 Nov 1973 Nueva Gerona, Isla de la Juventud 1.82m 83kg. Adidas.
At TJ: OG: '96- dnq 20, '00- 2; WCh: '95- 5, '97- dnq 15, '99- dnq 21; WI: '97- 1; PAm: '95- 3. Cuban champion 1999.
Progression at TJ: 1990- 14.98, 1991- 15.36, 1993- 16.39, 1994- 16.62, 1995- 17.47, 1996- 17.36, 1997- 17.62i/17.37, 1998- 17.04, 1999- 17.07, 2000- 17.47. pb LJ 7.58 '95.

Emeterio GONZÁLEZ b. 11 Apr 1973 San Juan y Martínez, Pinar del Río 1.84m 94kg.
At JT: OG: '96- dnq 18, '00- 8; WCh: '95- dnq 17, '97- 7, '99- 7; WJ: '92- 6; : '94- 7; PAm: '95- 1, '99- 1; CAG: '93- 3, '98- 1; WUG: '97- 2, '99- 4; WCp: '98- 5. Won CUB 1996-2000, CAC 1997, Ib-Am 2000. Nine CAC & Cuban javelin records 1995-2000.
Progression at JT: 1989- 60.36, 1990- 67.40, 1991- 65.78, 1992- 73.56, 1993- 74.14, 1994- 78.18, 1995- 82.64, 1996- 82.10, 1997- 83.56, 1998- 84.20, 1999- 84.32, 2000- 87.12.

Yoel HERNÁNDEZ b. 12 Dec 1977 Manacas, Villa Clara 1.84m 77kg
At 110mh: OG: '00- sf; WCh: '99- 6; WJ: '94- sf, '96- 1; PAm: '99- 2. At 60mh: WI: '01- 5.
Progression at 110mh: 1994- 14.20, 1995- 13.81, 1996- 13.81/13.72w, 1997- 13.70, 1998- 13.45, 1999- 13.24, 2000- 13.24/13.20w. pbs: 100m 10.69 '99, 200m 21.18 '99, 50mh 6.42i '00, 60mh 7.40i '00.

Freddy Santiago **MAYOLA** b. 1 Nov 1977 Ciudad Habana 1.76m 74kg.
At 100m: OG: '00- qf/3R; WCh: '99- sf; PAm: '99- 2; CAG: '98- 4. Cuban champion 1998-2000. At 60m: WI: '01- 4.
Progression at 100m: 1996- 10.66, 1997- 10.35, 1998- 10.19, 1999- 10.10, 2000- 10.14/10.10w/10.00rw. pbs: 60m 6.49i '00, 200m 21.32 '98.
Ex weightlifter; indoors in 2000 he set four Cuban records at 60m when 6.52 to 6.49.

Luis Felipe **MELIZ** b. 11 Aug 1979 Villa Clara 1.77m 76kg
At LJ: OG: '00- 7; WCh: '99- dnq 18; WI: '01- 9; WJ: '98 - 3; PAm: '99- 3; WUG: '99- 2.
Progression at LJ: 1997- 7.65, 1998- 8.05, 1999- 8.14/8.23 irreg, 2000- 8.43.

Iván Lázaro **PEDROSO** b. 17 Dec 1972 Ciudad Habana 1.72m 70kg. Adidas.
At LJ: OG: '92- 4, '96- 12, '00- 1; WCh: '93- nj, '95- 1, '97- 1, '99- 1; WI: '93/95/97/99/00- 1; WJ: '90- 4; WUG: '97- 1; PAm: '91- 3, '95- 1, '99- 1; CAG: '98- 1; WCp: '92- 1, '98- 1. Won GP 1995, 1997, 1999; GWG 1998, PAm J 1991, IbAm 1992, CAC 1997, Cuban 1992-3, 1995, 1997-8, 2000.
Three CAC & Cuban long jump records 1992-5.
Progression at LJ: 1988- 7.43, 1989- 7.43, 1990- 8.06, 1991- 8.22, 1992- 8.53/8.79w, 1993- 8.49, 1994- 8.26i/8.16, 1995- 8.71/8.96Aw, 1996- 8.46i/8.32, 1997- 8.63, 1998- 8.54, 1999- 8.62i/8.60, 2000- 8.65. pb TJ 16.05 '91.
Won fourth successive World Indoor title in 1999. Clearly the world top long jumper in 1995, when he had a narrow foul at 9.03 at the Pan-American Games and jumped 8.96 at Sestriere. This was shown to have a wind of just 1.2 m/s, but allegations were made of interference by an official standing in front of the gauge and the mark was not recognised. Unbeaten in 26 LJ competitions 1995 to Jan 1996. Hamstring surgery in 1996 meant that he was not fully fit at the Olympics, but he was back at the top in 1997, and has won 69/77 competitions in 1997-2000. Cousin of Aliuska López (Pedroso) (qv).

Yoelbi Luis **QUESADA** b. 4 Aug 1973 Trinidad, Sancti Spíritus 1.81m 71kg. Adidas.
At TJ: OG: '92- 6, '96- 3, '00- 4; WCh: '91- 7, '93- 12, '95- 4, '97- 1, '99- 10; WI: '93- 5, '95- 2, '99- 4; WJ: '90- 2, '92- 1; WUG: '97- 1, '99- 1; WCp: '94- 1, '98- 3; PAm: '91- 1, '95- 1, '99- 1; CAG: '93- 1, '98- 1. Won CAC-J 1990, PAmJ 1991, IbAm 1992, Cuban 1991-5, 1997-8. 2nd GP 1996.
Cuban triple jump record 1997.
Progression at TJ: 1989- 16.11, 1990- 16.68, 1991- 17.13, 1992- 17.23, 1993- 17.68, 1994- 17.61, 1995- 17.67/17.97w, 1996- 17.75, 1997- 17.85, 1998- 17.43i/17.27, 1999- 17.40, 2000- 17.37. pb LJ 7.88 '94. Set world age bests for each age from 15 to 19 in 1989-93.

Javier SOTOMAYOR b. 13 Oct 1967 Limonar, Matanzas 1.93m 80kg. PE teacher, graduate of Habana Institute of PE. Adidas.
At HJ: OG: '92- 1, '96- 11=, '00- 2; WCh: '87- 9, '91- 2, '93- 1, '95- 2, '97- 1; PAm: '87- 1, '91- 1, '95- 1, '99- dq (1); CAG: '90- 1, '93- 1, '98- 1; WJ: '86- 1; WCp: '85- 3, '89- 3, '92- 2, '94- 1, '98- 2; WUG: '89- 1; WI: '85- 2, '87- 4, '89- 1, '91- 3=, '93- 1, '95- 1, '99- 1, '01- 5=. Won CUB 1984, 1986-9, 1991-5, 1998-9; GWG 1998, CAC 1985, 1989; PAm-J 1986; IbAm 1986, 1988, 1992, 1996; GWG 1994. Won GP 1988, 1994, 1998.
World high jump records 1988, 1989 (first 8ft jump), 1993. WIR 2.43m 1989. World junior record 1986, nine CAC & Cuban records 1984-93.
Progression at HJ: 1980- 1.65, 1981- 1.84, 1982- 2.00, 1983- 2.17, 1984- 2.33, 1985- 2.34, 1986- 2.36, 1987- 2.37, 1988- 2.43, 1989- 2.44, 1990- 2.36, 1991- 2.40, 1992- 2.36, 1993- 2.45, 1994- 2.42, 1995- 2.40, 1996- 2.38i/2.33, 1997- 2.37, 1998- 2.37, 1999- 2.36i/2.34, 2000- 2.32.
World number number one 1988-9, 1992-5, 1997-8. Master technician, with very fast, head-on approach. Set world age bests each year from 15 to 19 in 1983-7. Disqualified following positive test for cocaine at 1999 Pan-Americans; his federation exonerated him, and the IAAF

allowed him to compete again from August 2000. Has cleared 2.30m or better in 230 meetings (89 at 2.35 or more and 21 at 2.40 or more) 1984-2000. Married Maria del Carmen García (HJ 1.90 '90) in Sept. 1989.

Norberto TÉLLEZ b. 22 Jan 1972 Rodas, Cienfuegos 1.86m 78kg. Adidas.
At 800m: OG: '96- 4; WCh: '97- 2, '99- 4; WJ: '90- 3; PAm: '99- 2; CAG: '98- 1/1R; WUG: '97- 1, '99- 1; WCp: '98- 3. At 400m/4x400mR: OG: '92- 2R; WCh: '93- sf, '95- sf; PAm: '95- 1/1R; CAG: '93- 1/1R. Won Cuban 400m 1994-7, 1999-2000; 800m 1995, 1997-8; CAC 800m 1997.
Cuban 800m record 1996.
Progression at 400m, 800m: 1989- 48.98, 1:50.83; 1990- 46.83, 1:47.33; 1991- 46.69, 1:51.76; 1992- 45.70, 1993- 45.51, 1994- 45.27, 1995- 45.38, 1:47.85; 1996- 45.48, 1:42.85; 1997- 45.66, 1:44.00; 1998- 45.71, 1:44.51; 1999- 46.52, 1:44.05; 2000- 45.72, 1:45.39. pb 200m 21.10 '94.
Ran first sub-1:44 time with 1:43.79 in 1996 Olympic semi, improving to 1:42.85 in the final, to beat the national record set by Alberto Juantorena at 1:43.44 in 1977. Former baseball player, centerfield position.

Women

Yamilé ALDAMA b. 14 Aug 1972 Ciudad Habana 1.73m 62kg.
At TJ: OG: '00- 4; WCh: '97- dnq 13, '99- 2; PAm: '99- 1; CAG: '98- 1; WI: '97- 6, '99- 7; WCp: '98- 3. Won IbAm 1996, 1998. Won CUB 1997-2000.
Two CAC triple jump records 1999.
Progression at TJ: 1994- 13.92, 1995- 13.84, 1996- 14.43, 1997- 14.46, 1998- 14.55, 1999- 14.77, 2000- 14.47. pbs: 100mh 14.97/14.8 '92, HJ 1.88 '92, LJ 6.13 '95, Hep 5246 '93.

Sonia BISSET b. 1 Apr 1971 Palma Soriano, Santiago de Cuba 1.71m 69kg.
At JT: OG: '00- 5; WCh: '97- 6, '99- 6; CAG: '98- 1; WUG: '97- 2; WCp: '98- 2. CAC champion 1995, IbAm 1996, Cuban 1998, GP 2000.
Progression at JT: 1987- 50.40, 1988- 58.28, 1989- 55.94, 1990- 55.20, 1991- 57.64, 1992- 58.38, 1993- 59.52, 1994- 61.42, 1995- 62.52, 1996- 64.54, 1997- 68.24, 1998- 67.59; new: 1999- 63.52, 2000- 65.87.

Zulia Inés **CALATAYUD** b. 9 Nov 1979 Ciudad Habana 1.69m 59kg.
At 800m: OG:'00- 6; WCh: '99- h; PAm:'99- 2. At 400m: WJ: '98- sf. Won Cuban 400m 1999, 800m 1999-2000.
Progression at 800m: 1995- 2:18.9, 1996- 2:13.80, 1997- 2:12.7, 1999- 2:00.67, 2000- 1:58.66. pbs: 200m 24.33/24.2 '98, 400m 51.69 '00.

Yumileidi CUMBÁ b. 11 Feb 1975 Guantánamo 1.85m 85kg. PE student.
At SP: OG: '96- dnq 13, '00- 6; WCh: '99- 6; PAm: '95- 3, '99- 2; CAG: '93- 2, '98- 1; WJ: '92- 4, '94- 2; WI: '99- 6, '01- 5; WUG: '99- 1; WCp: '98- 4. Cuban champion 1994-5, 1998, 2000.
Progression at SP: 1990- 14.53, 1991- 15.84, 1992- 17.44, 1993- 17.70, 1994- 18.78, 1995- 19.11, 1996- 18.57, 1998- 19.20, 1999- 19.29, 2000- 19.48. pb DT 42.84 '93.

Aliuska Yanira **LÓPEZ** Pedroso b. 29 Aug 1969 Ciudad Habana1.69m 53kg. Adidas.
At 100mh: OG: '92- 6, '96- sf, '00- 5; WCh: '87- sf, '91- 7/6R, '93- 4/6R, '95- sf, '97- h, '99- sf; PAm: '87- 3/2R, '91- 1, '95- 1/2R, '99- 1; CAG: '90 & '93- 1/1R; WJ: '86- 2, '88- 1/2R; WUG: '87- 2, '89- 4; WCp: '92- 1, '94- 1. 3rd GP 1994. At 60mh: WI: '91- 3, '93- 5, '95- 1. Won CUB 100mh 1986-9, 1993-7, 1999-2000; CAC 1997, IbAm 1992.
Two world junior 100mh records 1987; seven Cuban records 1986-96.
Progression at 100mh: 1983- 15.5, 1984- 14.4, 1985- 13.97/13.5, 1986- 13.14, 1987- 12.84, 1988- 12.96, 1989- 12.87, 1990- 12.73, 1991- 12.91, 1992- 12.87, 1993- 12.73, 1994- 12.74, 1995- 12.89/12.68w, 1996- 12.67, 1997- 13.07, 1998- 13.26, 1999- 12.76, 2000- 12.82. pbs: 100m 11.53 '87, 200m 24.22 '87, 60mh 7.91i '95, 400mh 64.32 '86.
World age records each age 16-19. Cousin of Iván Pedroso (qv).

Osleidys MENÉNDEZ b. 14 Nov 1979 Martí, Matanzas 1.78m 80kg.
At JT: OG: '00- 3; WCh: '97- 7, '99- 4; WJ: '96- 1, '98- 1; PAm: '99- 1; CAG: '98- 2. Won PAm-J 1995, 1997; Cuban 1997, 1999-2000; CAC 1997. 3rd GP 2000.
Six CAC bests and one world best (66.45 '99) new javelin 1999-2000.
Progression at JT: 1994- 53.98, 1995- 54.30, 1996- 62.54, 1997- 66.92, 1998- 68.17, 1999- 67.59; new 1999- 66.49, 2000- 67.83.

Yipsi MORENO b. 19 Nov 1980 Camagüey 1.68m 70kg.
At HT: OG: '00- 4; WCh: '99- 18; WJ: '98- 4; PAm: '99- 2. Won PAm-J 1997, Cuban 2000.
World junior hammer record 1999, ten CAC records 1999-2000.
Progression at HT: 1996- 53.94, 1997- 61.96, 1998- 61.00, 1999- 66.34, 2000- 69.36.

Daimí PERNÍA b. 27 Dec 1976 La Palma, Pinar del Rio 1.73m 59kg. PE student.
At 400mh/4x400mR: OG: '00- 4; WCh: '99- 1; PAm: '99- 1/1R; WUG: '97- 3/2R, '99- 1. Won Cuban 400mh 1997 & 1999.
Seven Cuban 400mh records 1997-9.
Progression at 400mh: 1996- 59.2, 1997- 55.51, 1998- 57.40, 1999- 52.89, 2000- 53.68. pbs: 200m 23.43 '99, 400m 51.13 '00.
Formerly a basketball player.

Xiomara RIVERO b. 24 Dec 1968 Guane, Pinar del Río 1.77m 74kg. Adidas.
At JT: OG: '96- 5, '00- 6; WCh: '95- dnq 16, '99- dnq 19; PAm: '95- 1, '99- 2; WJ: '86- 1; CAG: '93- 2. Cuban champion 1994, Ib-Am 2000.

Progression at JT: 1983- 38.90, 1984- 48.36, 1985- 56.26, 1986- 64.56, 1987- 57.36, 1990- 55.56, 1991- 55.52, 1992- 60.10, 1993- 59.60, 1994- 62.44, 1995- 67.06, 1996- 66.14, 1997- 61.26, 1998- 65.07, 1999- 64.00; new: 1999- 62.46, 2000- 62.92, 2001- 65.29. Having been world junior champion in 1986 at the age of 17, she did not improve until 1995.

CYPRUS

Governing body: Amateur Athletic Association of Cyprus, 20 Ionos St, 4th Floor, Flat 40, Engomi, Nicosia. Founded 1983.

2000 Champions: **Men**: 100m: Anninos Marcoullides 10.37, 200m: Prodromos Katsantonis 20.84w, 400m: Antonis Agiomamites 48.36, 800m: Constantinos Hadjimarcou 1:51.19, 1500m: Yiannakis Cleanthous 4:02.63, 5000m: Christos Papapetrou 14:48.87, 10000m: Costas Constantinou 33:10.89,: Stathis Stasi 8:43.76, 110mh: Stefanos Ioannou 14.28w, 400mh: Costas Pochanis 51.56, HJ: Yiannos Constantinou 2.10, PV: Andreas Ioannou 4.80, LJ: Renos Kolokotronis 7.71w, TJ: Stelios Petrou 15.11, SP: Georgios Aresti 16.05, DT: Petros Mitsides 54.12, HT: Yiannos Apostolides 59.20, JT: Pieros Tsisios 65.24. **Women**: 100m: Marina Andreou 12.19w, 200m: Vaso Papaioannou 25.07, 400m: Daniella Ekpe 59.57, 800m: Louiza Nicolaou 2:18.41, 1500m: Photoula Fteroudi 4:51.81, 5000m: Christina Fysouni 18:56.03, 100mh: Morfo Baourda 15.08, 400mh: Maria Tsangaridou 63.14, HJ: Agni Charalambous 1.89, PV: Anna Fitidou 3.40, LJ: Irini Charalambous 6.21, TJ: Ioanna Lazarou 12.42, SP: Olympia Menelaou 14.57, DT: Kyriaki Pilia 44.64, HT/JT: Elena Teloni 52.17/43.87.

CZECH REPUBLIC

Governing body: Cesky atleticky svaz, Atletická 100/2, 16017 Praha 6, PO Box 40. AAU of Bohemia founded in 1897.

National Championships first held in 1907 (Bohemia), 1919 (Czechoslovakia), now CZE.

2000 Champions: **Men**: 100m: Martin Duda 10.63, 200m: Vít Havlícek 21.69, 400m: Karel Bláha 45.82, 800m: Roman Oravec 1:50.19, 1500m: Michal Sneberger 3:50.43, 5000m/3000mSt: Michael Nejedly 14:12.67/8:50.19, 10000m: Pavel Faschingbauer 29:29.18, HMar: Miroslav Vítek 67:04, Mar: Jan Bláha 2:18:43, 110mh: Tomás Dvorák 13.85, 400mh: Josef Rous 50.64, HJ: Tomás Janku 2.24, PV: Stepán Janácek 5.50, LJ: Milan Kovár 7.92, TJ: Jirí Kuntos 16.49, SP: Miroslav Menc 20.34, DT: Libor Kacek 55.99, HT: Vladimír Maska 80.98, JT: Miroslav Guzdek 78.76, Dec: Ales Pastrnák 7801, 20kmW: Jirí Malysa 1:25:25, 50kmW: Milos Holusa 4:06:49. **Women**: 100m: Lenka Ficková 11.78, 200m: Helena Fuchsová 23.96, 400m: Jitka Burianová 50.97, 800m: Ludmila Formanová 1:59.55, 1500m: Renata Hoppová 4:14.37, 5000m/10000m/HMar/Mar: Alena Peterková 16:00.78/32:27.68/73:30/2:31:08, 100mh: Michaela Hejová 13.57, 400mh: Dagmar Votocková 58.83, HJ: Zuzana Hlavonová 1.95, PV: Daniela Bártová 4.20, LJ/Hep: Sárka Beranková 6.37.6079, TJ: Sárka Kaspárková 13.73, SP: Zdenka Silhavá 16.43, DT: Vladimíra Racková 60.51, HT: Lucie Vrbenská 60.49, JT: Nikola Tomecková 63.22, 10kmW: Lucie Nedomová 49:39.

Tomás DVORÁK b. 11 May 1972 Gottwaldov (now Zlín) 1.86m 88kg. Dukla Praha. Soldier.
At Dec: OG: '96- 3 (h 110mh), '00- 6; WCh: '93- 10, '95- 5, '97- 1, '99- 1; EC: '94- 7, '98- 5; ECp: '94- 3, '95- 1, '99- 1; WJ: '90- 17; EJ: '91- 2. At Hep: WI: '95- 2, '99- 4; EI: '94- 4, '96- 2, '98- 4, '00- 1. Won Czech 110mh 1994-6, 1998-2000.
World decathlon record 1999, three Czech 1996-9. European indoor heptathlon record 2000.
Progression at Dec: 1989- 6911, 1990- 7251w/7138, 1991- 7748, 1992- 7392, 1993- 8054, 1994- 8313, 1995- 8347, 1996- 8664, 1997- 8837, 1998- 8592, 1999- 8994, 2000- 8900. pbs: 60m 6.90i '97. 100m 10.54 '99, 200m 21.39 '98, 400m 47.56 '97, 1500m 4:29.69 '94, 50mh 6.59i '96, 60mh 7.78i '97, 110mh 13.61/13.6 '97, HJ 2.09 '00, PV 5.00 '97, LJ 8.03 '00, SP 16.88 '00, DT 50.28 '00, JT 72.32 '99, Hep 6309i '99.
Set four pbs en route to Olympic bronze in 1996 and six pbs when he won World gold in 1997. In 1999 he added 103 points to Dan O'Briens' world record, missing 9000 by just six points and setting five pbs in this supreme effort. Won all four decathlons in 1999 and the IAAF Combined Events Challenge; on each occasion he scored more than the best by the second-best in the world in 1999; his win at Götzis came after 2nd there each year 1996-8. Won at Götzis and Talence 2000 before injury held him back to sixth in Sydney. Married Gabriela Vánová (pb LJ 6.28/6.30w '93, daughter of his coach).

Miroslav MENC b. 16 Mar 1971 Varnsdorf 1.97m 145kg. :IAZ Jablonec. Sports instructor.
At SP (DT): OG: '96- dnq 21, '00- 10; WCh: '95- dnq 27, '97- dnq 17; EC: '98- 6; WJ: 90- dnq (7); EJ: '89- 9 (6); WI: '97- 9, '01- 6; EI: 00- 4. Czech champion 1993-7, 2000.
Progression at SP: 1988- 15.08, 1989- 16.85, 1990- 17.47i/17.32, 1991- 17.80, 1992- 18.04, 1993- 18.63, 1994- 18.60, 1995- 19.32, 1996- 19.88, 1997- 20.15, 1998- 20.58i, 1999- (21.19ex), 2000- 20.64, 2001- 20.68i. pb DT 56.78 '97.
Two year drugs ban from 21 Feb 1998.

Roman SEBRLE b. 26 Nov 1974 Lanskroun 1.86m 88kg. Dukla Praha. Soldier.
At Dec: OG: '00- 2; WCh: '97- 9, '99- dnf; EC: '98- 6; WUG: '97- 1; ECp: '97-8-9: 1/2/2. At Hep: WI: '99- 3, '01- 1; EI: '00- 2. At 110mh: ECp: '99- 6. Won Czech Dec 1996, LJ 1998.
Progession at Dec: 1992- 6541, 1993- 7066, 1994- 7153, 1995- 7642, 1996- 8210, 1997- 8380, 1998-

8589, 1999- 8527, 2000- 8757. pbs: 60m 6.91i '99, 100m 10.64 '00, 200m 21.83 '00, 400m 47.76 '99, 1000m 2:27.86i '01, 1500m 4:28.79 '00, 60mh 7.86i '01, 110mh 13.79 '99, HJ 2.15 '00, PV 5.00 '99, LJ 8.03 '98, SP 15.76i '01, 15.43 '98; DT 47.41 '00, JT 68.62 '97, Hep 6420i '01.
Married Eva Kasalová (b. 4 Dec 1976, pb 800m 2:02.79 '98), on 14 Oct 2000.

Jan ZELEZNY b. 16 Jun 1966 Mladá Boleslav 1.86m 88kg. AC Start Karlovy Vary.
At JT: OG: '88- 2, '92- 1, '96- 1, '00- 1; WCh: '87- 3, '91- dnq 18, '93- 1, '95- 1, '97- 9, '99- 3; EC: '86- dnq 18, '90- dnq 13, '94- 3; EJ: '83- 6, '85- 4; WCp: '92- 1; ECp: '87-89-91-3: 3/2/1/1. Won GP JT 1991, 1993, 1995, 1997 (2nd overall first 3 years), 2nd 1999. Won CS 1986, 1990, CZE 1994, 1996.
Five world javelin records 1987-96, eight CS records 1986-93, five CZE records 1992-6.
Progression at JT: 1979- 44.44, 1982- 57.22, 1983- 74.34, 1984- 80.32, 1985- 84.68, new: 1986- 82.48, 1987- 87.66, 1988- 86.88, 1989- 84.74, 1990- 89.66, 1991- 90.72, 1992- 94.74, 1993- 95.66, 1994- 91.82, 1995- 92.28, 1996- 98.48, 1997- 94.02, 1999- 89.06, 2000- 90.59A.
His third successive Olympic gold in 2000 surely sealed Zelezny's place as the greatest ever javelin thrower. He won 98 of 125 competitions 1991-2000. In his career with the new javelin 1986-2000 his competition bests average 85.29, with 131 throws in all over 88m. His 100 best throws average 90.56m, 200 best 89.00 and 300 best 87.72. His 94.74 throw in 1992 was made with a new 'Németh' javelin, later ruled illegal by the IAAF. In 1993 he added 4.08m to Backley's world record with 95.44 at Pietersburg, South Africa in April, and threw 95.56 at Sheffield in August. Entered hospital at the end of the 1989 season due to a fractured vertebra, but recovered to regain the world record in 1990. In 1991 he was most unlucky not to qualify for the World final, when he fell, perhaps over the line, on a long throw; otherwise lost only once, to Steve Backley. Serious injury cost him the 1998 season amid fears that he might never compete again. but he was back in full training by the end of the year. In December 1999 he was amongst the first group of ten active participants to be elected a member of the IOC, having already been a member of its athletes' commission. His father, Jaroslav, threw the javelin 68.46m in 1969 and his mother Jana threw the javelin 43.23 in 1959.

Women

Daniela BÁRTOVÁ b. 6 May 1974 Ostrava 1.64m 63kg. Dukla Praha. PE student at Charles University.
At PV: OG: '00- 4; WCh: '99- 6=; EC: '98- dnq 19=; WI: '97- 5; EI: '96- 6, '98- 2; ECp: '98- 1. Czech champion 1993-8, 2000.
Ten world pole vault records 1995-6, 19 European records 1995-8. Five world indoor records 1996-8, 12 European indoor records to 4.48i 1996-8.
Progression at PV: 1992- 2.80, 1993- 3.50i/3.40/ 3.57exh, 1994- 3.75i/3.70, 1995- 4.22, 1996- 4.27, 1997- 4.33/4.40sq, 1998- 4.51, 1999- 4.40, 2000- 4.50. pbs: 100m 12.33 '99, 200m 25.46 '99.
Represented Czechoslovakia at gymnastics at the 1992 Olympics, and started running and pole vaulting after that. Her brother Radim Bárta has 800m best of 1:50.98 '98.

Ludmila FORMANOVÁ b. 2 Jan 1974 Cáslav 1.68m 60kg. AC Cáslav.
At 800m/4x400mR (400m): OG: '96- sf, '00- h; WCh: '93- 7R, '95- h (h), '97- 5/5R, '99- 1/4R; EC: '94- h, '98- sf/5R; WI: '95- sf/2R, '97- sf/4R, '99- 1; WJ: '92- h; EJ: '91- (6)/4R, '93- 1; WI: '99- 1; EI: '96- 4, '98- 1; ECp: '98- 3/2R. 2nd GP 1999. Won Czech 800m 1994-5, 1997, 1999-2000.
Progression at 800m: 1990- 2:15.5, 1991- 2:11.85, 1992- 2:05.29, 1993- 2:03.78, 1994- 2:02.54, 1995- 2:01.09, 1996- 1:59.28, 1997- 1:58.54, 1998- 1:59.44, 1999- 1:56.56, 2000- 1:57.53. pbs: 200m 24.30 '95, 400m 51.84 '95, 600m 1:26.0i '99, 1000m 2:35.06 '99.
Ran second fastest of all-time to win 1999 World Indoors – and later completed double with outdoor title. Out of action following an ankle operation on an injury which caused her to drop out of her heat at the Sydney Olympics. Coached by Jarmila Kratochvílová.

Helena FUCHSOVÁ b. 3 Jun 1965 Tábor 1.70m 68kg. née Dziurová. PSK Olymp Praha.
At 400m: OG: '96- qf; WCh: '93- 7R, '95- h, '97- 6, '99- sf/4R; EC: '98- 2; WI: '95- 2R, '97- 3; EI: '98- 3, '00- 3; WCp: '98- 4; ECp: '98- 1/2R. At 800m: OG: '00- 5; WI: '01- 3; ECp: '99- 2. Won Czech 200m 2000, 400m 1992, 1996-7, 1999; 800m 1992.
Progression at 400m, 800m: 1980- 61.0, 1981- 59.0, 1982- 58.00, 1985- 55.83, 1986- 54.79, 1987- 53.59, 2:06.14; 1988- 53.15, 2:06.6; 1989- 54.19, 2:04.81i; 1990- 54.35, 2:04.08; 1991- 54.58, 2:03.92i; 1992- 52.91, 2:03.50; 1993- 53.67, 2:09.75; 1994- 53.54, 2:08.19; 1995- 51.96, 2:04.53; 1996- 51.70, 2:08.34, 1997- 50.36, 1998- 50.21, 2:02.19i; 1999- 50.84, 1:58.81; 2000- 50.71, 1:58.56; 2001- 1:58.37i. pbs: 100m 11.97 '96, 200m 23.29 '97, 300m 36.44 '99, 1500m 4:34.05 '91, 400mh 62.0 '94.

Pavla HAMÁCKOVÁ b. 20 May 1978 Chomutov 1.70m 68kg. Dukla Praha.
At PV: OG: '00- dnq 22=; WCh: '99- 6=; EC: '98- 12=; EJ: '97- 5; EU23: '99- 7; WUG: '99- 1; WI: '99- 7, '01- 1; EI: '00- 1; ECp: '99- 3; Won CZE 1999.
Progression at PV: 1993- 2.40i, 1994- 3.20, 1995- 3.21i/3.28i exh, 1997- 3.95, 1998- 4.15, 1999- 4.40, 2000- 4.45, 2001- 4.56i.

Zuzana HLAVONOVÁ b. 16 Apr 1973 Sala, SVK 1.78m 60kg. née Kovácíková. USK Mogul NOCC Praha.
At HJ: OG: '96- 12, '00- 11=; WCh: '95- dnq 24=, '97- dnq 21, '99- 4=; EC: '94- 11, '98- 11; WJ: '92-

12; EJ: '91- 11; EU23: '94- 7=; WI: '99- 2; EI: '00- 2; ECp: '98- 1, '99- 3. 2= GP 1999; Czech champion 1994-7, 1999-2000.
Four Czech high jump records 1997-2000.
Progression at HJ: 1986- 1.57, 1987- 1.63, 1988- 1.71, 1989- 1.73, 1990- 1.77, 1991- 1.83, 1992- 1.88, 1993- 1.89, 1994- 1.94, 1995- 1.92, 1996- 1.94, 1997- 1.96, 1998- 1.98, 1999- 1.99, 2000- 2.00.
Expecting a baby and will miss the 2001 season.

Sárka KASPÁRKOVÁ b. 20 May 1971 Karviná 1.87m 68kg. USK NOCC Mogul Praha. Was at Masaryks University. Sports instructor.
At TJ: OG: '96- 3, '00- nj (12); WCh: '93- 7, '95- dnq 13, '97- 1, '99- 6; EC: '94- 6, '98- 2; WI: '93- 7, '95- 4, '97- 3, '99- 3; EI: '92- 4, '94- 4, '96- 2, '98- 2; WUG: '93- 2, '95- 1; ECp: '98- 2; 2nd GP 1997. At HJ: OG: '92- dnq; WJ: '88- 6; EJ: '89- 3. Won CS HJ 1988, CZE TJ 1993-4, 1996-8, 2000; Eur U23Cp TJ 1992, ECp I TJ 1994-5.
Ten Czech triple jump records 1992-7.
Progression at HJ, TJ: 1983- 1.42, 1984- 1.59, 1985- 1.71, 1986- 1.77, 1987- 1.80, 1988- 1.89, 1989- 1.91, 1990- 1.81, 1991- 1.78, 1992- 1.92, 14.00; 1993- 1.95i/1.84, 14.16; 1994- 1.82, 14.46i/14.14/14.20w; 1995- 1.82, 14.38; 1996- 1.80i/1.79, 14.98; 1997- 15.20, 1998- 1.81, 14.98; 1999- 14.87i/14.54, 2000- 14.34. pbs: 100mh 14.72 '94, LJ 6.56 '98.
Expecting a baby in 2001.

Nikola TOMECKOVÁ b. 25 Jun 1974 Gottwaldov (now Zlín) 1.80m 75kg. PSK Olympia Praha. Sports instructor.
At JT: OG: '96- dnq 25, '00- 8; WCh: '93- dnq 22, '95- dnq 17, '97- dnq 26, '99- dnq 21; EC: '98- dnq 13; WJ: '92- 11; EJ: '91- 2, '93- 5; ECp: '98- 2, '99- 5. Czech champion 1993-2000.
Seven Czech new javelin records 1999-2000.
Progression at JT: 1987- 32.22, 1988- 39.80, 1989- 42.24, 1990- 49.22, 1991- 55.80, 1992- 59.78, 1993- 57.48, 1994- 56.68, 1995- 63.80, 1996- 64.50, 1997- 62.96, 1998- 64.18; new: 1999- 60.92A, 2000- 64.19.

DENMARK

Governing body: Dansk Athletik Forbund, Idraettens Hus, Brøndby Stadion 20, DK-2605 Brøndby.
National Championships first held in 1894. **2000 Champions**: **Men**: 100m: Cristian Trajkovski 10.77, 200m/400m: Christian Birk 21.37/47.03, 800m/1500m: Paw Nielsen 1:50.85/3:43.42, 5000m: Dennis Jensen 13:57.15, 10000m: Klaus Hansen 29:20.30, HMar: Christian Madsen 67:20, Mar: Torben Juul Nielsen 2:27:46, 3000mSt: Jakob D Jensen 8:58.79, 110mh: Anders Sækmose 14.42, 400mh: Henrik Vincentsen 52.82, HJ: Christoffer Holst 2.06, PV: Martin Voss 5.40, LJ: Jesper Aabo 7.47, TJ: Jesper Riege 15.99, SP/DT: Joachim B Olsen 20.88/58.51, HT: Jan Bielecki 73.88, JT: Richard A Knudsen 72.68, Dec: Piotr Buciarski 7208, 20kmW/50kmW: Jacob Sørensen 1:35:37.4/4:20.13. **Women**: 100m/200m/400m/ Hep: Christina Schnohr 11.77/24.24/54.59/5321, 800m/1500m: Heidi Jensen 2:03.18/4:19.00, 5000m/HMar: Annemette Jensen 16:38.85/76:54, 10000m: Ann Thomsen 38:03.96, Mar: Anne Marie Simonsen 3:03:08, 100mh: Joanna B Zeberg-Jensen 14.26, 400mh: Rikke Sørensen 63.50, HJ: Kathrine Nielsen 1.73, PV: Anita Tørring 3.80, LJ/TJ: Renata Nielsen 5.87/12.29, SP: Henrietta Lykke 12.68, DT: Marianne Simonsen 46.21, HT: Vanessa S Mortensen 50.49, JT: Christina Scherwin 55.58.

Wilson KIPKETER b. 12 Dec 1970 Kenya 1.72m 62kg. Sparta. Student of electronic engineering.
At 800m: OG: '00- 2; WCh: '95- 1, '97- 1, '99- 1; EC: '98- 8; WI: '97- 1, '99- 2; WJ: '88- dq, '90- 4. Won GP 1997 (and overall), 1999 (3rd overall), 2nd 1995. Danish champion 1993-4.
Three world 800m records 1997. WIR: 800m (2) 1997, 1000m (2) 2000 (2:15.25 & 2:14.96). 12 Danish 800m records 1995-7.
Progression at 800m: 1985- 1:49.6, 1986- 1:50.3, 1987- c.1:52, 1988- 1:47.0, 1989- 1:47.2, 1990- 1:45.7, 1991- 1:46.19, 1992- 1:45.62, 1993- 1:45.46, 1994- 1:43.29, 1995- 1:42.87, 1996- 1:41.83, 1997- 1:41.11, 1998- 1:43.18, 1999- 1:42.27, 2000- 1:43.35. pbs: 400m 46.85 '94, 1000m 2:14.96i '00, 2:16.29 '95; 1500m 3:42.80 '93, 1M 3:59.57 '93.
Went to live in Denmark in 1990. Competed for Kenya in World Juniors with year of birth 1972, but back in 1985 he was shown as second fastest African junior at 1:49.6 with year of birth 1968! Came to prominence as world no.1 at 800m in 1994. Allowed by the IAAF to compete for Denmark when not yet a citizen in 1995, when he was seemingly a class apart from the rest of the world at 800m. In 1996 his Olympic entry was blocked by the Kenyan Federation, but he was again the world no. 1, running five successive 1:42 times, followed by a 1:43.43 and then just missing the world record with 1:41.83. Took the world indoor record from 1:44.84 to 1:43.96 in his heat and 1:42.67 in the final of the 1997 World Indoors. In 1997 he tied Seb Coe's WR for 800m at 1:41.73 in Stockholm and after retaining his world title, improved the record to 1:41.24 in Zürich and 1:41.11 in Köln. Unbeaten in 27 800m races in 1996 and 1997. 1998 season restricted due to malaria in January and later pneumonia, but in 1999 won third world title and a half share of the $1m Golden League jackpot.

DOMINICAN REPUBLIC

Felix SANCHEZ b. 30 Aug 1977 New York, USA 1.78m 73kg. University of Southern California.
At 400mh: OG: '00- sf; WCh: '99- ht; PAm: '99- 4. NCAA champion 2000.
Six DOM 400mh records 1997-2000.
Progression at 400mh: 1995- 51.33, 1996- 51.19, 1997- 50.11, 1999- 48.60, 2000- 48.33.

Born in New York and raised in California, he first competed for the Dominican Republic, where his parents were born, in 1999.

ECUADOR

Governing body: Federación Ecuatoriana de Atletismo, PO Box 3303, Guayaquil. F'd 1925.

Jefferson PÉREZ b. 1 Jul 1974 Cuenca 1.74m 59kg. Studied business management at University of Azuay.
At 20kmW: OG: '92- dnf, '96- 1, '00- 4; WCh: '95- 32, '97- 14, '99- 2; WCp: '97- 1; PAm: '95- 1; SAmCh: '93- 1. Won SAm Cup 1994-5, 1997-8. At 10kmW: WJ: '90- 3, '92- 1; won SAm-J 1989-93, PAm-J 1993. At 50km: WCp: '99- dnf.
South American 20km walk record 1997, 8 Ecuador records 1992-7.
Progression at 20kmW: 1992- 1:25:50.5, 1993- 1:24:03, 1994- 1:23:27, 1995- 1:22:53, 1996- 1:20:07/ 1:20:55.4t, 1997- 1:18:24, 1998- 1:19:19, 1999- 1:20:46, 2000- 1:20:18. pbs: 5000mW 19:49.54i '90, 10,000mW 39:50.73 '93.
In 1996 he became the youngest ever Olympic walking champion and Ecuador's first Olympic medallist at any sport. He then walked 459km from Quito, along the Pan-American Freeway at an altitude of between 2500 and 4800m, to his home-town of Cuenca, as a religious promise. The Ecuador postal authorities issued a stamp with his picture.

ESTONIA

Governing body: Eesti Kergejôustikuliit, Regati pst. 1, Tallinn EE0 103. Founded 1920.
National Championships first held in 1917. **2000 Champions**: **Men**: 100m/200m: Maidu Laht 10.78/21.80, 400m: Urmet Uusorg 48.02, 800m: Igor Holdai 1:55.59, 1500m/5000m: Margus Pirksaar 3:53.99/14:48.38, 10000m: Toomas Tarm 31:21.22, HMar: Pavel Loskutov 63:23, Mar: Einar Kaigas 2:43:57, 3000mSt: Kaupo Tiislär 9:02.37, 110mh: Tarmo Jallai 14.39, 400mh: Kristjan Suur 52.57, HJ: Marko Aleksejev 2.15, PV: Aivo Normak 4.80, LJ: Miik Joorits 7.18, TJ: Ilja Tumorin 16.04, SP: Margus Tammaru 18.62, DT: Aleksander Tammert 61.85, JT: Andrus Värnik 77.80, Dec: Aivo Normak 7461, 20000mW: Margus Luik 1:47:29.9, 50kmW: Lauri Lelumees 4:56:23. **Women**: 100m: Marianna Voronina 11.9, 200m/Hep: Rutti Luksepp 24.77/??, 400m: Maria Sahharova 56.77, 800m/1500m: Maile Mangusson 2:09.38/4:36.70, 5000m/HMar: Külli Kaljus 17:01.76/77:21, Mar: Kaja Mulla 3:05:36, 100mh: Jaanika Meriküll 14.10, 400mh: Milena Alver 60.86, HJ: Kärt Siilats 1.85, PV: Merle Kivimets 3.80, LJ: Riina Vals 6.03, TJ: Diana Nikitina 12.54, SP/DT: Eha Rünne 15.03/ 56.17, HT: Kadri-Liis Vähi 49.30, JT: Moonika Aava 53.70, 10000mW/20kmW: Kaity-Marin Tiitmaa 58:26.5/2:00:51.

Erki NOOL b. 25 Jun 1970 Vôru 1.84m 84kg. Tallinna West-Sport.
At Dec: OG: '92- dnf, '96- 6, '00- 1; WCh: '95- 4, '97- 6, '99- 14; EC: '94- 10, '98- 1; ECp: '94-6-7-8: 1C/1B/2/1. At Hep: WI: '95/7/9/01- 7/2/2/5; EI: '94- 5, '96- 1, '00- 3. Won EST 100m 1999, PV 1989, 1994, 1996-7; 110mh 1998-9, Dec 1990, 1992.
Estonian records: 200m and LJ 1995, Decathlon 1995, 1998 and 2000.
Progression at Dec: 1988- 6662, 1989- 7351, 1990- 7771, 1992- 8001, 1993- 7425, 1994- 8093, 1995 - 8575, 1996- 8543, 1997- 8534, 1998- 8672, 1999- 8664, 2000- 8742. pbs: 60m 6.72i '96, 100m 10.43 '95, 10.34w '97; 200m 21.03A '95, 400m 46.53 '97, 1500m 4:29.48 '00, 60mh 8.02i '01, 110mh 14.37 '00, HJ 2.05i '91, 2.03 '98; PV 5.60 '98, LJ 8.10 '95, 8.22w '96; SP 15.11 '00, DT 44.47 '99, JT 71.91 '98, Hep 6374i '99.
Won Götzis decathlon 1995 and 1998, IAAF Combined Events Challenge 1998 and 2000. Failed opening height (5.10) in 1999 World Champs; with 5.30 or higher he would have come 2nd. Became Estonia's first-ever Olympic athletics champion at Sydney, although very fortunate to avoid three no throws in the discus.

Aleksander TAMMERT b. 2 Feb 1973 Tartu 1.96m 117kg. Was at Southern Methodist University, USA.
At DT: OG: '96- dnq 25, '00- 9; WCh: '95- dnq 23, '97- 12, '99- 10; EC: '98- dnq 20; WUG: '97- 5, '99- 4.
Three Estonian discus records 1998-2000.
Progression at DT: 1990- 42.06, 1991- 48.24, 1992- 51.12, 1993- 54.54, 1994- 55.50, 1995- 60.24, 1996- 64.80, 1997- 64.78, 1998- 65.35, 1999- 66.95, 2000- 67.41. pb SP 18.06i '00, 18.05 '99.
Father (also Aleksander) was 1966 European Junior shot champion, pb 19.41 '76.

ETHIOPIA

Governing body: Ethiopian Athletic Federation, Addis Ababa Stadium, PO Box 3241, Addis Ababa. Founded 1961.

Gezahegne ABERA b. 23 Apr 1978 1.68m 57kg.
At Mar: WCh: '99- 11; OG: '00- 1. World 4k CC: '00- 14.
Progression at Mar: 1999- 2:07:54, 2000- 2:09:47. pbs: HMar 60:30 '00.
Won Fukuoka 1999 (his third marathon starting with 4th at LA 1999 in 2:13:59). and in 2000 was 2nd in Boston before taking Olympic gold.

Dagne ALEMU b. 15 Oct 1980 1.71m 58kg.
At 5000m: OG: '00- 6; AfG: '99- 4.
Progression at 5000m: 1997- 14:04.42, 1998- 13:21.60, 1999- 13:18.39, 2000- 13:07.73. pbs: 3000m 7:47.52 '00.

Fita BAYISSA b. 15 Dec 1972 Ambo 1.73m 52kg. Policeman.
At 5000m (10000m): OG: '92- 3 (9), '96- 10, '00- 4; WCh: '91- 2, '93- 3 (dnf), '95- 8, '97- 10, '99- 6;

WJ: '90- 1; AfG: '91- 1, '93- (2), '99- 2; AfCh: '98- 4 (3000m 3); WCp: '92- 1. At 3000m: WI: '97- 7. World CC: '90- 3J, '91- 3J, '92- 3, '93- 16; Rd Rly team: '94- 2, '98- 2.
World junior 5000m record 1991.
Progression at 5000m, 10000m: 1990- 13:42.59, 1991- 13:16.64, 1992- 13:13.03, 27:14.26; 1993- 13:05.40, 27:26.90; 1994- 13:07.70, 27:51.56; 1995- 13:18.53, 27:45.99; 1996- 13:07.44, 1997- 13:07.20, 1998- 13:16.37, 1999- 13:13.86, 2000- 13:08.15. pbs: 1500m 3:39.00 '98, 2000m 5:03.2 '96, 3000m 7:35.32 '96, 2M 8:16.84 '97.
Won IAAF World Cross Challenge 1991/2. Won at Oslo in 10,000m début in 27:14.26 in 1992.

Haile GEBRSELASSIE b. 18 Apr 1973 Arssi 1.64m 53kg.
At 10000m (5000m): OG: '96- 1, '00- 1; WCh: '93- 1 (2), '95- 1, '97- 1, '99- 1; WJ: '92- 1 (1); AfG: '93- 3 (2). At 3000m: WI: '97- 1, '99- 1 (1 1500m). Won GP 3000m 1995, 1998. World CC: '91- 8J, '92- 2J, '93- 7, '94- 3, '95- 4, '96- 5; Rd Rly team: '94- 2.
World records 5000m (4) 1994-8, 10000m (3) 1995-8. World best 2M 1995 (8:07.46) & 1997. World indoor records 2000m 1998, 3000m (7:30.72 '96, 7:26.14 '98), 5000m (13:10.98 '96, 12:59.04 '97, 12:50.38 '99). ETH records 1993-8: 1500m (2), 3000m (6), 5000m (5), 10000m (3).
Progression at 5000m, 10000m: 1992- 13:36.06, 28:03.99; 1993- 13:03.17, 27:30.17; 1994- 12:56.96, 27:15.00; 1995- 12:44.39, 26:43.53; 1996- 12:52.70, 27:07.34; 1997- 12:41.86, 26:31.32; 1998- 12:39.36, 26:22.75; 1999- 12:49.64, 27:57.27; 2000- 12:57.95, 27:18.20. pbs: 800m 1:49.35i '97, 1000m 2:20.3+i '98, 1500m 3:31.76i '98, 3:33.73 '99; 1M 3:52.39 '99, 2000m 4:52.86i '98, 4:56.1 '97; 3000m 7:25.09 '98, 2M 8:01.08 '97, Mar c.2:48 '88.
A beautifully smooth runner, whose right to be named as the greatest ever grows steadily. After finishing a place behind Ismael Kirui at two successive World Junior CC championships, he outkicked his rival for a brilliant double at the 1992 World Juniors. He set the first of his 15 world records in Hengelo in 1994 at 5000m and in 1995 he took 8.7 secs off the 10,000m WR and regained the 5000m record by taking 10.91 secs off Kiptanui's mark. Between these feats he won the World 10,000m, running the last 200m in 25.1!. He ran the second 5000m in c.13:11.6 to win the 1996 Olympic 10,000m and in 1997 took 6.76 secs off the world 10,000m record in Oslo. In 1998 he regained both the 5000m and 10000m world records. Has 12 wins in 13 competitions at 10,000m (his only loss 3rd in the 1993 African Champs), with 21 wins at 3000m/2M from 2nd to Noureddine Morceli at Monaco in 1994 to 2000, and 16 wins at 5000m from 2nd to Daniel Komen in Zürich 1996 to 2000. In 1997 and 1998 he lost just indoors once at 1500m in 1997 and once each at 800m in 1997 and 1998. In 1999 he won all 15 finals from 1500m to 10,000m and he was unbeaten in five races in 2000.

Lives during the summer in the Netherlands. His brother Tekeye was 13th in the 1991 London Marathon (World Cup) in 2:12:05, with pb 2:11:45 '94.

Habte JIFAR b. 29 Jan 1976 1.75m 63kg.
At 10000m (5000m): WCh: '97- 7, '99- 6; WJ: '94- 4 (2); AfG: '95- 2 (2), '99- 3; Af-J: '94- 1 (2). World CC: '93- 6J, '96-7-8-9: 17/11/13/9. Won ETH 5000m 1994, 10000m 1995, CC 1996.
Progression at 5000m, 10000m: 1994- 13:43.92, 29:04.57; 1995- 13:45.11A, 28:26.3A; 1996- 13:25.30, 1997- 13:12.88, 27:30.26; 1998- 13:10.74, 27:29.97; 1999- 13:21.01, 27:06.45. pb 3000m 7:54.54 '99.

Tesfaye JIFAR b. 23 Apr 1976.
World HMar: '99- 3, '00- 3.
Progression at Mar: 1998- 2:22:13, 1999- 2:06:49, 2000- 2:15:59. pbs: HMar 61:51 '99.
At Amsterdam in 1999 he took a second off Belayneh Dinsamo's Ethiopian marathon record, placing 2nd in 2:06:49, the fifth fastest of all-time. Missed 2000 Olympics through illness, from which he returned for 15th in Chicago Marathon and then third in the World Half marathon.

Hailu MEKONNEN b. 4 Apr 1980 1.72m 61kg.
At 5000m: WCh: '99- 7; WJ: '98- 6; AfCh: '98- 2 (4 3000m). At 1500m: OG: '00- sf; WI: '01- 7; AfG: '99- 1. World CC J & 4k: '97- 12J, '98-3J, '99- 1J/3, '00-01- 6/10. WIR 2 miles 2000. World junior record 3000m 1999. ETH 1500m record 2000.
Progression at 1500m, 5000m: 1998- 13:36.61, 1999- 3:35.63, 13:10.98; 2000- 3:33.14. pbs: 1M 3:53.40 '00, 2000m 5:02.06 '98, 3000m 7:33.00 '99, 2M 8:09.66i '00.
Placed third in the 4km race at the 1999 World CC Championships and returned the next day to win the junior race. Was unbeaten indoors in 2000 at distances from 1500m to 2 miles.

Assefa MEZEGEBU b. 19 Jun 1978 1.75m 55kg.
At 10000m (5000m): OG: '96- (sf), '00- 3; WCh: '95/7/9- 14/5/3; WJ: '96- 1 (1); AfG: '95- 8, '99- 1 (5). World CC: '95-6-7-8-9-00: 1J/2J/13/3/ 11/2.
Progression at 5000m, 10000m: 1995- 13:33.82, 27:56.06, 1996- 13:17.68, 28:27.78; 1997- 13:05.48, 27:25.01; 1998- 12:53.84, 1999- 13:13.77, 27:18.28; 2000- 13:06.13, 27:19.75. pbs: 1500m 3:35.58i '00, 1M 3:54.78i '00, 3000m 7:28.45 '98, 2M 8:09.96i '00.
Began running in 1994, and in 1995 won the World Junior CC at the age of 16. His brother **Ayele** (b. 6 Jan 1973) was 2nd at the 1992 World Junior 3000mSt and in the 1998 World Road relay team; pbs: 5000m 13:21.21 '94, 10000m 28:22.06 '97, 3000mSt 8:32.43 '92.

Girma TOLLA b. 13 Oct 1975 1.74m 57kg.
At 10000m: OG: '00- 11; WCh: '99- 4; AfG: '99- 6. World CC: '99- 17.
Progression at 5000m, 10000m: 1997- 28:55.67, 1998- 13:15.72, 27:32.02; 1999- 27:13.48, 2000- 13:21.04, 27:20.03. pbs: 2000m 5:02.01 '98, 3000m 7:38.68i '00, 7:42.98 '99.

Tesfaye TOLLA b. 19 Oct 1974 1.67m 60kg.
At Mar: OG: '00- 3; WCh: '99- 4. World HMar: '99- 8. Ethiopian Half marathon record 2000.
Progression at Mar: 1997- 28:55.67, 1998- 13:15.72, 27:32.02; 1999- 2:06:57, 2000- 2:11:10. pbs: 10000m 28:12.32 '99; road: 10M: 46:01 '99, HMar 59:51 '00.

Million WOLDE b. 17 Mar 1979 1.75m 59kg
At 5000m: OG: '00- 1; WCh: '99- 8; WJ: '98- 1. At 3000m: WI: '99- 3, '01- 5. At 3000mSt: WJ: '96- 6. World CC: '96-7-8: 8J/2J/1J, 4k: '99-00: 4/15; 2nd Rd Rly team '98.
Progression at 5000m: 1996- 13:28.86, 1997- 13:32.02, 1998- 12:59.39, 1999- 13:19.41, 2000- 13:02.94. pbs: 1500m 3:39.15 '98, 1M 3:58.21 '99, 2000m 5:01.6+ '00, 3000m 7:32.36 '00, 2M 8:12.10 '01, 8:24.53 '99; 3000mSt 8:29.21 '97.

Women

Birhane ADERE b. 21 Jul 1973 1.70m 48kg.
At 10000m: OG: '96- 18, '00- 12; WCh: '95- h, '97- 4, '99- 7; AfCh: '93- 1 (5 3000m). At 5000m: AfCh: '98- 1; WCp: '98- 3. World CC: '96-7-00: 10/14/14. Won Rd Rly team '96, Ethiopian 3000m & 10000m 1993.
Ethiopian 3000m record 1997.
Progression at 5000m, 10000m: 1992- 34:13.3, 1993- 32:48.52, 1995- 15:44.46, 32:02.94; 1996- 14:59.17, 32:21.09; 1997- 15:08.22, 31:48.95; 1998- 15:22.34, 32:06.42; 1999- 14:54.88, 31:32.51; 2000- 14:52.61, 30:51.30. pbs: 3000m 8:40.14 '97; road: 10M 53:16 '98, HMar 69:28 '00.

Elfenesh ALEMU b. 10 Jun 1975 1.71m 57kg.
At Mar: OG: '00- 6; WCh: '99- 5; WCp: '95- 18; AfG: '95- 3.
Progression at Mar: 1993- 2:57:32A, 1994- 3:08:05, 1995- 2:40:04, 1996- 2:36:29, 1997- 2:37:37, 1998- 2:30:19; 1999- 2:28:52, 2000- 2:24:47. pb HMar 69:46 '00.
2nd in Nagoya marathon 1998. Broke 2:25 twice in 2000: 4th Osaka and 1st Nagano before 2:26:45 at Olympics.

Merima DENBOBA b. 21 Aug 1974 1.68m 48kg.
At 5000m: OG: '96- h; WCh: '97- 10; AfG: '95- 5, '99- 4; AfCh: '98- 3, '00- 3. At 10000m: WJ: '92- 5. World CC: '91-2-3-4-5: 18/20/19/4/7, '97-8-9-00-01: 6/4/2/8/8 & 4 4k; Rd Rly team: '98- 1. Won ETH 10000m 1995, CC 1995, 1998 and 1997/8 World CC challenge.
Progression at 5000m, 10000m: 1992- 33:57.21, 1993- 35:15.5A, 1994- 15:47.86, 32:16.50; 1995- 15:47.12, 34:20.6A; 1996- 15:19.86, 1997- 15:11.71, 32:10.36; 1998- 15:30.06, 32:04.89; 1999- 15:08.52, 31:32.63; 2000- 15:15.17, 31:43.28. pbs: 1500m 4:14.60 '94, 3000m 8:44.21 '99.

Kutre DULECHA b. 22 Aug 1978 1.68m 48kg.
At 1500m (800m): OG: '96- sf (h), '00- 4; WCh: '97- 9, '99- 3; WI: '97- 9, '99- 8; WJ: '94- 5 (3), '96- 1; AfG: '95- 1 (3); Af-J: '94- 2 (2); 2nd GP 1998, 2000. World CC: '96- 1J, 4k: '98-9-00: 3/12/1.
Ethiopian records: 1500m (5) 1997-8, 800m 1999. World junior record indoor 1500m 1997.
Progression at 1500m: 1994- 4:15.59, 1995- 4:08.70, 1996- 4:07.69, 1997- 4:05.67, 1998- 3:58.38, 1999- 4:00.96, 2000- 3:59.02. pbs: 800m 1:59.17i/1:59.37 '99, 1000m 2:37.82 '99, 1M 4:23.33i '01, 4:39.04 '97.

Merima HASHIM b. 1981 1.62m 42kg.
At 10000m: WCh: '99- 6; AfG: '99- 2. Won Afr-J 1997. World CC: '97-8-00- 23J/8J/5J.
Progression at 10000m: 1997- 34:48.68, 1998- 35:40.1A, 1999- 31:32.06, 2000- 30:59.92. pbs: 3000m 9:07.71 '99, 5000m 15:14.42 '00.

Worknesh KIDANE b. 21 Nov 1981 1.58m 41kg.
At 5000m: OG: '00- 7; WJ: '98- 6; AfG: '99- 4. World CC: '97-8-9-00: 13J/3J/1J/9J; '01- 5 4k. At 3000m: WI: '01- 9.
Progression at 5000m: 1998- 15:50.10, 1999- 15:24.56, 2000- 14:47.40. pb 3000m 8:44.14 '00.

Fatuma ROBA b. 18 Dec 1973 1.60m 49kg.
At Mar: OG: '96- 1, '00- 9; WCh: '95- 19, '97- dnf, '99- 4. At 10000m: AfCh: '90- 4 (4 3000m), '93- 3. World CC: '91- 12; HMar: '92- 6, '94- 11.
Progression at Mar: 1993- 2:44:20A, 1994- 2:35:25, 1995- 2:39:27sh, 1996- 2:26:05, 1997- 2:26:23, 1998- 2:23:21, 1999- 2:23:25, 2000- 2:26:27. pbs: 10000m 32:55.32 '93, Rd 10km 32:39 '95, HMar 69:43 '97.
Six wins in 14 Marathons: set national records in three wins in 1996: 2:30:50 Marrakech, 2:29:05 Rome, 2:26:05 Olympics and again when won Boston in 1998. Also won Boston 1997 and 1999.

Derartu TULU b. 21 Mar 1972 Bejoki, Arusi province 1.55m 45kg. Employed by the prison police in Addis Ababa.
At 10000m (3000m): OG: '92- 1, '96- 4, '00- 1; WCh: '91- 8, '95- 2, '97- h; WJ: '90- 1; AfG: '91- 1; AfCh: '90- 1 (1), '92- 1 (1); WCp: '92- 1 (1). World CC: '89- 23, '90-1-5-6-7-00: 15/2/1/4/1/1; HMar: '99- 15.
Three African 10000m records 1992-2000. World junior 10000m record 1991 (32:08.74), Ethiopian records 1500m, 5000m (4), 10000m (5) 1991-2000, HMar 1995 & 2000.
Progression at 5000m, 10000m: 1990- 16:56.7, 32:56.26; 1991- 15:21.29, 31:45.95; 1992- 15:36.5, 31:06.02; 1994- 15:40.29, 31:48.93; 1995- 14:57.65, 31:08.10; 1996- 14:50.88, 31:10.46; 1997- 33:25.99; 2000- 14:44.57, 30:17.49. pbs: 1500m 4:12.08 '92, 3000m 8:46.32 '00, HMar 68:04 '00, Mar 2:26:09 '00.
Undefeated on the track in 1992, but missed most of 1993 season through injury. Daughter born 1998. Returned to road racing in 1999 and to a third world CC title and second Olympic title in 2000. 5th Boston on marathon debut 1997; 6th London and 3rd Tokyo in 2000.

Gete WAMI b. 11 Dec 1974 Debre Birhan 1.54m 45kg. Married Geteneh Tessema November 1999.
At 10000m (5000m): OG: '96- 2 (3); WCh: '95- 18, '97- dnf, '99- 1; WJ: '92- 2; AfG: '95/9- 3/1; AfCh: '92- 4. Won GP 3000m 1998, 2nd 5000m 1996.

World CC: '91-2: 5J/9J, '95-6-7-8-9-00-01: 5/1/3/3/1/2/2 & 1 4k; Rd Rly team: '96/8- 1/1. African records 5000m 2000, 10000m 1999. Ethiopian records: 3000m 1998, 5000m (4) 1996-8.
Progression at 5000m, 10000m: 1992- 32:34.68, 1994- 36:15.0A, 1995- 15:28.65, 32:17.41; 1996- 14:46.45, 31:06.65; 1997- 14:54.05, 32:05.73; 1998- 14:36.08, 34:23.4A; 1999- 15:25.5, 30:24.56; 2000- 14:30.88, 30:22.48. pbs: 1500m 4:01.47 '98, 3000m 8:29.24 '98.

Ayelech WORKU b. 12 Jun 1979 1.62m 47kg.
At 5000m: OG: '96- 12, '00- 4; WCh: '97- 12, '99- 3; WJ: '96- 1 (3000m 4); AfG: '95- 2, '99- 1. World CC: '95-6-7: 11J/11J/3J, '98-9-00: 9/4/9. Rd Rly team: '98- 1. Won ETH 5000m 1995.
Progression at 5000m: 1995- 15:48.3A, 1996- 15:16.74, 1997- 15:18.19, 1998- 15:12.43, 1999- 14:44.22; 2000- 14:41.23. pbs: 1500m: 4:15.93 '98, 3000m 8:39.51 '99, 10000m 37:09.1A '94.

FINLAND

Governing body: Suomen Urheiluliitto, Radiokatu 20, SF-00240 Helsinki. Founded 1906.
National Championships first held in 1907 (men), 1913 (women). **2000 Champions**: **Men**: 100m: Tuomas Näsi 10.55, 200m: Tommi Hartonen 20.76, 400m/800m/1500m: Wilson Kirwa 47.31/1:50.39/3:48.07, 5000m: Marko Kotila 14:06.23, 10000m: Janne Holmen 28:38.42; HMar: Jussi Utrainen 65:47, Mar: Yrjö Pesonen 2:22:36, 3000mSt: Kim Bergdahl 8:35.30, 110mh: Jarno Jokihaara 13.79, 400mh: Janne Mäkela 51.19, HJ: Mika Polku 2.28, PV: Vesa Rantanen 5.50, LJ: Kenneth Kastrén 7.70, TJ: Johan Meriluoto 15.97, SP: Arsi Harju 20.84, DT: Timo Tompuri 60.95, HT: Olli-Pekka Karjalainen 78.32, JT: Aki Parviainen 84.29, Dec: Eduard Hämäläinen 8224, 20000mW: Valentin Kononen 1:22:34.76, 50kmW: Asko Turkki 4:54:48. **Women**: 100m: Heidi Hannula 11.54, 200m: Johanna Manninen 23.28, 400m: Petra Söderström 53.79, 800m/1500m: Tytti Reho 2:03.59/4:14.87, 5000m: Annemari Sandell 16:32.00, 10000m/HMar: Maria Söderström 34:53.55/79:26, Mar: Erja Nurkkala 2:54:33, 3000mSt: Johanna Risku 10:34.92, 100mh: Manuela Bosco 13.30, 400mh: Anja Rantanen 59.96, HJ: Hanna Mikkonen 1.85, PV: Annu Mäkelä 3.95, LJ/Hep: Susanna Rajamäki 6.45/6014, TJ: Heli Koivula 13.68, SP: Anna Rauhala 15.49, DT: Tiina Kankaanpää 57.44, HT: Mia Strömmer 63.32, JT: Mikaela Ingberg 63.44, 10000mW; Tiina Muinonen 47:54.68, 20kmW: Outi Sillanpää 1:43:36

Timo AALTONEN b. 11 Apr 1969 Vehmaa 1.89m 129kg. Turun Urhelluliitto.
At SP: OG: '00- 12; EC: '98- 12; WI: '01- 4; EI: 00- 1.
Progression at SP: 1992- 14.97, 1993- 16.39, 1994- 16.79, 1995- 17.86, 1996- 18.50, 1997- 19.05, 1998- 20.12, 1999- 20.48, 2000- 20.70.
Took European Indoor gold after Bagach's disqualification. Won national U16 title and then gave up shot putting until 1992, becoming a construction worker.

Harri HAATAINEN b. 5 Jan 1978 Lapua 1.85m 86kg. Lapuan Virkiä.
At JT: OG:'00- dnq 19; WCh: '99- 11; WJ: '96- 2; EU23: '99- 1; EJ: '95- 2.
World junior javelin record 1996.
Progression at JT: 1993- 62.74, 1994- 72.02, 1995- 77.50, 1996- 82.52, 1997- 80.16, 1998- 79.07, 1999- 83.02, 2000- 86.10.

Harri HAKKARAINEN b. 16 Oct 1969 Kaavi 1.94m 110kg. Kuopion Sisu-Veikot.
At JT: OG: '96- dnq 14, '00- dnq; WCh: '95- 12; EC: '94- dnq 13; ECp: '96- 3.
Progression at JT: 1986- 60.38, 1987- 63.88, 1988- 65.78, 1989- 70.06, 1990- 71.52, 1991- 83.16, 1992- 83.46, 1993- 84.36, 1994- 85.46, 1995- 87.82, 1996- 87.44, 1997- 86.48, 1998- 85.34, 1999- 85.00, 2000- 85.65.

Mika HALVARI b. 13 Feb 1970 Kemi 1.91m 135kg. Kemin Kunto.
At SP: OG: '96- dnq 14; WCh: '95- 2, '97- 5, '99- dnq 15; WI: '95- 1, '97- 6; EC: '94- 4, '98- 6; EI: '98- 2; WJ: '88- 7; EJ: '89- 5; ECp: '98- 1. Finnish champion 1994-5, 1997.
Progression at SP: 1986- 14.64, 1987- 16.06, 1988- 17.62, 1989- 17.96, 1990- 18.65, 1991- 18.71, 1992- 18.60i/18.45, 1993- 20.08, 1994- 19.93i/19.87, 1995- 21.50, 1996- 20.81i/20.42, 1997- 21.11, 1998- 20.79, 1999- 21.00, 2000- 22.09i/21.04. pbs: DT 47.72 '88, HT 42.16 '89.
A 'spinner', he ruptured his Achilles tendon in February 1996, which meant that he was below par in Atlanta. He produced a startling 22.09 indoors in February 2000, but suffered another Achilles rupture in August 2000.

Eduard HÄMÄLÄINEN (ex-BLR) b. 21 Jan 1969 Karaganda, Kazakhstan 1.94m 93kg. Kuortaneen Kunto.
At Dec: OG: '92- dnf, '96- 5, '00- 24; WCh: '91- 7, '93- 2, '95- 2, '97- 2; EC: '94- dnf, '98- 2; WJ: '88- 3. CIS champion 1992, Finnish 2000. At Hep: WI inv: '93- 3.
BLR decathlon records 1993-4, two Finnish 1997.
Progression at Dec: 1987- 7369, 1988- 7596, 1989- 7891, 1990- 7845, 1991- 8233, 1992- 8483w, 1993- 8724, 1994- 8735, 1995- 8489, 1996- 8613, 1997- 8730, 1998- 8587, 2000- 8224. pbs: 100m 10.69/10.50w '94, 400m 46.71 '97, 1500m 4:22.5 '87, 60mh 7.93i '93, 110mh 13.57 '93, HJ 2.15i '95, 2.11 '94, PV 5.30 '93, LJ 7.56 '97, 7.67w '93; SP 16.74 '96, DT 52.20 '94, JT 61.88 '93, Hep 6096i '92.
Won Götzis decathlon 1993 and 1994, Talence 1995. In 1993 he set world decathlon records for 100mh at 13.65 and 13.57 in the World Champs. However, he fell in the 110mh when leading the 1994 Europeans. His grandfather was deported from Finland to the USSR in 1917, and home-

town was Grodno, Belarus, but has lived in Kuortane, Finland since 1996 and became eligible to compete for Finland in 1997. Missed 1999 season after an Achilles tendon operation.

Arsi HARJU b. 18 Mar 1974 Kurikka 1.83m 110kg. Perhon Kiri.
At SP: OG: '96- dnq, '00- 1; WCh: '95- dnq 17, '97- dnq 15, '99- nt; EC: '98- 9; WI: '97- 8, '99- 5; EI: '98- 3; WJ: '92- 11; EJ: '93- 3. Finnish champion 1998, 2000.
Progression at SP: 1989- 11.82, 1990- 15.65, 1991- 16.27, 1992- 17.60, 1993- 18.40, 1994- 18.74, 1995- 19.58, 1996- 19.84, 1997- 20.66, 1998- 21.04, 1999- 20.60, 2000- 21.39.
A 'spinner' since 1996, he improved his pb by 35cm in the 2000 Olympic qualifying.

Olli-Pekka KARJALAINEN b. 7 Mar 1980 Töysä 1.94m 118kg. Töysän Veto.
At HT: OG:'00- dnq 34; WCh: '99- 11; WJ: '98- 1; EJ: '97- 3, '99- 1. Finnish champion 1998-2000. World junior hammer record 2000.
Progression at HT: 1995- 48.26, 1996- 58.80, 1997- 69.84, 1998- 75.08, 1999- 78.33, 2000- 80.55.

Juha LAUKKANEN b. 6 Jan 1969 Pielavesi 1.86m 90kg. Laukkalan Luja. Marketing student.
At JT: OG: '92- 6; EC: '94- dnq 18, '98- 5; WJ: '88- 10; EJ: '87- 6. Finnish champion 1992, 1994.
World junior javelin record 1987.
Progression at JT: 1986- 74.40, 1987- 79.46, 1988- 77.08, 1989- 78.68, 1990- 83.36, 1991- 87.06, 1992- 88.22, 1993- 84.58, 1994- 85.54, 1995- 82.54, 1996- 87.12, 1997- 87.10, 1998- 86.96, 1999- 85.53, 2000- 82.35. pb DT 42.50.

Matti NÄRHI b. 17 Aug 1975 Viitasaari 1.88m 100kg. Viitasaaren Viesti.
At JT: WCh: '99- 12; EC: '98- 8; E23: '97- 2; WJ: '94- 2; EJ: '93- 2.
World indoor javelin best 85.78 in 1996.
Progression at JT: 1992- 70.24, 1993- 73.18, 1994- 76.14, 1995- 83.14, 1996- 85.78i/84.42, 1997- 88.24, 1998- 84.38, 1999- 87.88, 2000- 82.74. pb PV 3.90 '93.
Suffered a ruptured Achilles tendon at the 1999 World Championships.

Aki PARVIAINEN b. 26 Oct 1974 Helsinki 1.91m 96kg. Joensuun Kataja.
At JT: OG: '00- 5; WCh: '95- 9, '97- 8, '99- 1; EC: '98- 9; WJ: '92- 1; EJ: '91- 3; ECp: '98- 3. Finnish champion 1999-2000.
Progression at JT: 1990- 63.50, 1991- 79.96, 1992- 80.94, 1993- 78.18i/69.94, 1994- 78.76, 1995- 85.60, 1996- 84.96, 1997- 87.48, 1998- 90.88, 1999- 93.09, 2000- 90.97. pbs: SP 12.26 '96, DT 36.78 '96.
Set world age records at 14-16-17-18. The first Finn to win world titles at junior and senior level. Missed most of 1993 and 1994 seasons through an arm injury. Older brother Mika threw 80.26 in 1992.

Ville TIISANOJA b. 24 Dec 1975 Vantaa 1.92m 119kg. Kenttäurheilijat-58 (Vantaa).
At SP: OG: '00- dnq 15; WCh: '99- 8; EU23: '97- 4; WJ: '94- 3 (10 DT); EJ: '93- 7. Finnish champion 1999.
Progression at SP: 1992- 16.41, 1993- 17.35, 1994- 17.90, 1995- 19.10, 1996- 18.29, 1997- 19.40, 1998- 19.13, 1999- 20.49, 2000- 20.76. pbs: DT 54.10 '94, HT 51.36 '94.

Women

Tiia HAUTALA b. 3 Apr 1972 Pori 1.72m 64kg. Porin Yleisurheilu.
At Hep: OG: '96- 21, '00- 8; WCh: '95- 13, '97- 14, '99- 5; EC: '94- 20, '98- 11; EU23: '97- 4; WJ: '94- 3; ECp: '99- 5. At Pen: EI: '96- 5, '98- 4, '00- 4. Won FIN Hep 1994-7, 100mh 1999.
Progression at Hep: 1988- 4726, 1989- 4788, 1990- 4893, 1991- 5149, 1992- 5606, 1993- 5513, 1994- 6042, 1995- 6135, 1996- 6039, 1997- 6026, 1998- 6102, 1999- 6369, 2000- 6219. pbs: 200m 24.74 '00, 800m 2:13.98 '97, 60mh 8.36i '00, 100mh 13.43 '00, HJ 1.84 '99, LJ 6.52 '98, SP 14.43i '96, 13.98 '98, JT 47.61 '99, Pen 4580i '00.

Mikaela INGBERG b. 29 Jul 1974 Vaasa 1.74m 72kg. Vasa Idrottssällskap.
At JT: OG: '96- 7, '00- 9; WCh: '95- 3, '97- 4, '99- 9; EC: '94- dnq 16, '98- 3; EJ: '91- 15, '93- 1; WCp: '98- 3. Finnish champion 1994, 1999-2000.
Finnish record new javelin 2000
Progression at JT: 1987- 33.70, 1988- 41.78, 1989- 43.92, 1990- 51.96, 1991- 52.30, 1992- 54.00, 1993- 58.26, 1994- 58.70, 1995- 65.16, 1996- 65.66, 1997- 67.32, 1998- 66.43; new 1999- 61.50, 2000- 64.03. pbs: HJ 1.57 '88, SP 12.67 '99, DT 39.56 '95.

Heli RANTANEN b. 26 Feb 1970 Lammi 1.74m 70kg. Esbo Idrottsförening.
At JT: OG: '92- 6, '96- 1; WCh: '91- 9, '93- 11, '95- 4, '97- 10; EC: '90- 13, '98- 5; EJ: '89- 5. Won ECp B 1991. Finnish champion 1991-2, 1995-7.
Progression at JT: 1983- 35.24, 1984- 39.46, 1985- 48.68, 1986- 51.34, 1987- 50.04, 1988- 47.94, 1989- 54.74, 1990- 60.88, 1991- 64.66, 1992- 63.98, 1993- 61.38, 1994- 61.68, 1995- 65.04, 1996- 67.94, 1997- 66.52, 1998- 63.60; new: 1999- 61.61, 2000- 60.98. pbs: SP 12.85 '90, Hep 3982 '87.
Improved pb from 66.18 to 66.54 in qualifying and then to 67.94 in the 1st round to win 1996 Olympic gold medal, the first ever by a Finnish woman athlete. Shoulder operation in 1999.

Taina UPPA b. 24 Oct 1976 Pori 1.73m 74kg. Porin Tarmo.
At JT: OG: '96- dnq 19, '00- dnq 20; WCh: '95- dnq 24, '97- dnq 20, '99- 10; EC: '94- 10, '98=- dnq 14; EU23: '97- 1; WJ: '94- 1; EJ: '95- 1.
Finnish record new javelin 2000.
Progression at JT: 1990- 39.58, 1991- 49.78, 1992- 54.78, 1993- 52.08, 1994- 61.78, 1995- 66.00, 1996- 63.78, 1997- 61.00, 1998- 62.31; new 1999- 63.63, 2000- 64.06.

FRANCE

Governing body: Fédération Française d'Athlétisme, 33 avenue Pierre de Coubertin, 75640 Paris cedex 13. Founded 1920.

National Championships first held in 1888 (men), 1918 (women). **2000 Champions**: **Men**: 100m: David Patros 10.48, 200m: Christophe Cheval 20.66, 400m: Ibrahima Wade 45.28, 800m: David Divad 1:48.29, 1500m: Driss Maazouzi 3:42.16, 5000m/Driss El Himer 13:28.13/28:19.33, HMar: Mohamed Serbouti 63:21, Mar: Benoît Zwierzchiewski 2:10:47, 3000mSt: Mohamed Belabbes 8:26.08, 110mh: Frédéric Denis 13.85, 400mh: David Kafka 50.01, HJ: Dieudonne Opota 2.19, PV: Romain Mesnil 5.75, LJ: Cheikh Touré 8.43w, TJ: Jimmy Gabriel 16.68, SP: Yves Niaré 19.00, DT: Jean-Claude Retel 62.01, HT: David Chaussinand 77.38, JT: Laurent Dorique 78.86, Dec: Laurent Hernu 8178, 20kmW: Denis Langlois 1:23:20, 50kmW: Sylvain Caudron 3:52:27. **Women**: 100m: Christine Arron 11.32, 200m: Muriel Hurtis 22.99w, 400m: Marie-Louise Bévis 52.40, 800m: Laetitia Valdonado 2:01.24, 1500m: Yamna Belkacem 4:12.26, 5000m: Fatima Yvelain 16:04.88, 10000m: Rakiya Quetier-Maraoui 31:56.1, HMar/Mar: Chantal Dällenbach 73:08/2:33:34, 100mh: Nicole Ramalalanirina 13.06, 400mh: Olivia Abderrhamanne 58.11, HJ: Gaëlle Niaré 1.82, PV: Caroline Ammel Ammel 4.30, LJ: Aurélie Félix 6.62, TJ: Sandrine Domain 13.77, SP: Laurence Manfrédi 17.56, DT: Mélina Robert-Michon 61.23, HT: Manuela Montebrun 67.90, JT: Bina Ramesh 57.03, Hep: Nathalie Teppe 6214, 10kmW: Fatiha Ouali 45:48, 20kmW: Nora Leksir 1:36:26.

Mehdi BAALA b. 17 Aug 1978 Strasbourg 1.83m 66kg. ASPTT Strasbourg.
At 1500m (800m): OG: '00- 4; WJ: '96- h; EU23: '99- 3; EJ: '97- 7; EI: '00- 3; ECp: '00- 1 (1).
Progression at 1500m: 1994- 4:08.1, 1995- 3:48.74, 1996- 3:43.50, 1997- 3:45.34, 1998- 3:41.86, 1999- 3:34.83, 2000- 3:32.05. pbs: 800m 1:46.24 '00, 1000m 2:15.45 '00.

Stéphane DIAGANA b. 23 Jul 1969 Saint-Affrique, Aveyron 1.86m 75kg. EA Franconville. Biology student.
At 400mh/4x400mR: OG: '92- 4; WCh: '93- 4, '95- 3, '97- 1, '99- 2; EC: '90- 5, '94- 3/2R, '98- sf; WCp: '92- 3, '94- 3R; ECp: '93- 1/3R, '94- 3/3R, '99- 6. Won GP 1998 (3rd 1994). Won French 400m 1992-5, 1997; 400mh 1990.
European 400mh record 1995, eight French 1990-5.
Progression at 400mh: 1987- 54.1, 1989- 51.60, 1990- 48.92, 1992- 48.13, 1993- 47.64, 1994- 48.22, 1995- 47.37, 1997- 47.70, 1998- 48.04, 1999- 48.12, 2000- 48.70. pbs: 200m 20.81i '92, 20.95 '93; 300m 33.25 '99, 400m 45.18 '92, 60mh 8.10i '88, 110mh 14.56 '87, 200mh 22.94 '94, 22.9 '99.
Big advance in 1990, when he ran 50.11 to win the French title, then 49.26 and 48.92 at the European Championships in Split. In 1992 he ran 48.55 and then French records in each round at Olympics. In 1995 he took the European record, which had stood at 47.48 to Harald Schmid since 1982. Missed most of 1996 season through injury (stress fracture in foot) and was restricted by injury to just one hurdles race in 2000. Was elected president of the French athletes' association in October 1996. In 1999 he completed a set of World Champs 1-2-3-4.

Christophe ÉPALLE b. 23 Jan 1969 St Etienne 1.94m 109kg. Neuilly-Plaisance Sports.
At HT: OG: '92- 10, '96- dnq 17, '00- dnq 23; WCh: '93- 8, '95- dnq 15, '97- dnq; EC: '94- 7, '98- 12; WJ: '88- 8; WUG: '91- 5, '93- 3; ECp: '93-4-5-7-00: 2/3/4/4/1. French champion 1995, 1998. Won Med G 1997, NCAA HT & 35lbWt indoors 1991. French hammer record 1993.
Progression at HT: 1985- 49.76, 1986- 56.76, 1987- 60.54, 1988- 63.52, 1989- 67.00, 1990- 68.90, 1991- 73.52, 1992- 76.86, 1993- 79.98, 1994- 79.20, 1995- 79.94, 1996- 77.38, 1997- 78.44, 1998- 79.04, 1999- 77.65, 2000- 81.79. pbs: SP 17.48 '91, DT 54.98 '92, JT 61.92 '90, 35lbWt 22.73i '91.
His brother Thierry had a DT pb of 58.42 '98.

Mustapha ESSAÏD b. 20 Jan 1970 El Ksiba, Morocco 1.80m 61kg. APPTT Grenoble.
At 5000m: OG: '00- h; WCh: '93/7/9- h; EC: '98- 4; ECp: '97-8-00: 5/2/1. World CC: '93-4-5-6: 24/18/16/20; Eur CC: '94-5-6-7: 10/5/3/4. Won FRA 10000m 1993, 1996; CC 1994, 1996.
French records 3000m (2), 5000m 1998.
Progression at 5000m: 1991- 13:48.7, 1992- 13:42.25, 1993- 13:23.94, 1994- 13:22.34, 1995- 13:44.90, 1996- 13:27.95, 1997- 13:18.41, 1998- 13:02.15, 1999- 13:06.87, 2000- 13:09.93. pbs: 1500m 3:39.96 '99, 2000m 5:00.49 '98, 3000m 7:30.78 '98, 10000m 28:01.70 '96.

Jean GALFIONE b. 9 Jun 1971 Paris 1.84m 82kg. Stade Français (Paris).
At PV: OG: '92- dnq 13, '96- 1, '00- dnq 16=; WCh: '91- 10, '93- 8, '95- 3, '97/9- nh; EC: '94- 3, '98- 3; WJ: '90- 1; EJ: 89- 9; WI: '93- 3, '99- 1; EI: '92- 4, '94- 2; WUG: '93- 3; WCp: '94- 2; ECp: '93-4-6-7-8: 4/1/5=/2/5=; 2nd GP 1998. French champion 1993-8, Med G 1993.
Five French pole vault records 1993-9.
Progression at PV: 1987- 4.15, 1988- 5.16, 1989- 5.50, 1990- 5.60i/5.45, 1991- 5.80, 1992- 5.90, 1993- 5.93, 1994- 5.94, 1995- 5.86, 1996- 5.92, 1997- 5.80/6.00exh, 1998- 5.97, 1999- 6.00i/5.98, 2000- 5.81i/5.80. pbs: 100m 10.7 '92, 10.90 '94; 400m 48.96 '96, 1500m 4:51.48 '95, 110mh 14.75, HJ 2.01 '92, LJ 7.21 '95, TJ 14.00 '87, SP 11.90, DT 35.84 '95, JT 49.88 '95, Dec 7415 '95.
Set (then) world decathlon PV best of 5.75 in 7206 decathlon at Talence 1996. Had an operation on a collapsed lung in May 2000. Nephew of 1968 Olympic fencing gold medallist (team foil) Jean-Claude Magnan.

Sébastien LEVICQ b. 25 Jun 1971 Le Havre 1.86m 81kg. Stade Sotteville 76.
At Dec: OG: '96- 17, '00- dnf; WCh: '93- 14, '95- 9, '97- dnf, '99- 4; EC: '98- dnf; WJ: '90- 12; WUG: '93- 1; ECp: '94-5-6-9: 8/4/5/3. French champion 1994. At Hep: WI: '95- 8, '97- 7.
Progression at Dec: 1989- 6732, 1990- 7511, 1991- 7434, 1992- 7867, 1993- 7874, 1994- 8105, 1995- 8273, 1996- 8393, 1997- 8120, 1998- 8214, 1999- 8524, 2000- dnf. pbs: 100m 11.05 '99, 11.0 '92; 400m 50.13 '99, 1500m 4:23.74 '93, 60mh 8.09i '96, 110mh 14.23 '96, HJ 2.04 '95, PV 5.60 '97, LJ 7.52 '99, SP 14.98 '99, DT 47.96 '94, JT 72.22 '94, Hep 5886i '96. Made a storming finish in final three events (from 5.50 PV) to miss taking bronze at 1999 World Champs by just 3.6 secs at 1500m.

Driss MAAZOUZI b. 15 Oct 1969 Meknès, Morocco 1.80m 65kg. Athlé. 42 Saint-Etienne.
At 1500m: OG: '96- 10, '00- 11; WCh: '97- sf, '99- 8. At 3000m: ECp: '99-00: 3/1. Won FRA 1500m 1997-2000, 4k CC 1998-9; Med G 1500m 1997. French records 1000 (2), 1500m (2) 1998-9.
Progression at 1500m: 1990- 3:45.8, 1991- 3:42.12, 1993- 3:43.3, 1994- 3:37.04, 1995- 3:35.45, 1996- 3:34.08, 1997- 3:35.26, 1998- 3:31.59, 1999- 3:31.51, 2000- 3:32.01. pbs: 800m 1:46.3 '96, 1000m 2:15.26 '99, 1M 3:51.79 '00, 2000m 4:59.80 '95, 3000m 7:36.21 '98, 5000m 13:50.12 '94, HMar 64:44 '95, 3000mSt 9:08.6 '91.
Competed for Morocco to 1997, then switched allegiance (naturalised for France 23/7/96), but unable to compete for France until clearance granted by Morocco for 1999.

Romain MESNIL b. 13 Jul 1977 Plessis Bouchard 1.88m 79kg. ECLA Albi. Engineering student.
At PV: OG: '00- dnq 31; WCh: '99- nh; EU23: '99-1; WJ: '96- dnq 13=; WI: '99- 6=, '01- 3; ECp: '00- 5. French champion 2000.
Progression at PV: 1993- 4.30, 1994- 4.65, 1995- 5.15, 1996- 5.30, 1997- 5.40, 1998- 5.80, 1999- 5.93, 2000- 5.75, 2001- 5.86i. Former gymnast.

Jérôme ROMAIN (ex DOMINICA) b. 12 Jun 1971 Saint-Martin 1.83m 76kg. Student at University of Arkansas.
At TJ (LJ): OG: '96- nj; WCh: '91- dnq (h 100m), '93- 11 (dnq); '95- 3, '97- 6, '99- 7; CG: '94- 4 (7); PAm: '95- 2 (8); ECp: '99- 5. Won CAC TJ 1995 (2 LJ), 1997; French TJ 1999.
Progression at TJ: 1991- 16.39, 1992- 16.67, 1993- 16.98, 1994- 16.82i/16.79/17.05w, 1995- 17.48/ 17.59w, 1996- 17.14, 1997- 17.17/17.53w, 1998- 17.03i/17.01/17.18w, 1999- 17.31, 2000- 16.95i/ 16.93. pbs: 100m 10.70 '92, LJ 7.90 '93.
Took up French citizenship from 16 March 1999.

Smaïl SGHIR b. 16 Mar 1972 Taroudante 1.68m 50kg. Stade Bordelaise. Bordeaux University.
At 5000m: OG: '96- 11; WCh: '95- 4, '97- 4. At 10000m: WCh: '99- 15. At 3000m: WI: '97- 3. World CC: '96- 8, '97- 8. Won Med G 10000m 1997. French 5000m record 2000.
Progression at 5000m, 10000m: 1993- 14:15.03, 28:42.76; 1994- 13:13.47, 1995- 13:04.19, 1996- 12:58.99, 1997- 13:00.62, 28:05.74; 1999- 13:03.69, 27:12.39; 2000- 12:58.83, 27:33.20. pbs: 1500m 3:36.20 '95, 1M 3:54.2 '95, 2000m 4:52.88 '95, 3000m 7:30.09 '95, 2M 8:11.73 '96, 10000m 28:05.74 '97, HMar 63:55 '95, 3000mSt 8:57.28 '95.
Switched nationality from Morocco in 2000, but not cleared to compete for France until 24 Sep 2002.

Women

Christine ARRON b. 13 Sep 1973 Abymes, Guadeloupe 1.79m 64kg. Ile de France.
At 100m/4x100m (200m): OG: '00- sf/4R; WCh: '97- 4/3R, '99- 6/2R; EC: '98- 1/1R, '00- 2/1R; ECp: '97- (1), '98- 2, '99- 1/1R; WJ: '92- sf. Won French 100m 2000, 200m 1997. Med G 200m 1997. European and four French 100m records 1998.
Progression at 100m, 200m: 1988- 12.04, 1989- 11.64/11.6, 25.43; 1990- 12.41/12.3/12.0w, 1991- 11.97, 24.4; 1992- 11.51, 23.75; 1993- 11.93/11.92w, 1994- 24.18, 1995- 23.92, 1996- 23.26, 1997- 11.03, 22.62/22.57w, 1998- 10.73, 22.95i; 1999- 10.97, 22.26; 2000- 10.99/10.89w. pbs: 50m 6.05+ '99, 60m 7.00+ '99, 400m 53.76 '95.
The superstar of the 1998 European Championships followed a majestic 100m victory in a European record 10.73 with an awesome final sprint relay leg to take France to gold. She first set French age records at 11 in 1988 (for 80m and 150m). Made great breakthrough in 1997, setting a French indoor 200m record (23.13), stepping in for Marie-José Pérec to win European Cup 200m and placing 4th in World 100m.

Eunice BARBER b. 17 Nov 1974 Freetown, Sierra Leone 1.75m 68kg. EFS Reims.
At Hep: OG: '92- 26 (h 100mh), '96- 5 (dnq LJ), '00- dnf; WCh: '93- dnf, '95 4, '97- dnf, '99- 1; WJ: '92- 14. At Pen: WI: '97- 6. At LJ: AfG: '95- 1; ECp: '99- 1.
French long jump and heptathlon records 1999. African heptathlon record 1996. SLE records 100mh, HJ, LJ, SP, JT, Hep 1992-8.
Progression at LJ, Hep: 1990- 5.47, 1991- 5.66, 1992- 6.02, 5048; 1993- 5.94, 5308; 1994- 5.93, 5378; 1995- 6.57/6.70Aw, 6340; 1996- 6.59/6.66w, 6416; 1997- 6.70, 1998- 6.86i/6.75/6.90w, 1999- 7.01, 6861; 2000- 6.85, 6842. pbs: 60m 7.36i '00, 100m 11.90 '99, 200m 23.53 '99, 800m 2:10.75 '99, 60mh 8.11i '00, 100mh 12.89 '99, 200mh 27.47 '99, HJ 1.93 '99, SP 13.05i '97, 13.03 '99; JT 52.44 '95, new: 51.91 '00; Pen 4558i '97.
Became a French citizen in February 1999, having previously represented Sierra Leone, but living in Reims from 1992. After concentrating on the long jump for a couple of years and taking the French record to 7.01, she returned in 1999 to the heptathlon where she had wins at 6461 (Arles) and 6501 (European Cup) before adding 356 points to her pb with a superlative display in Seville to take the world title.Another win at

Talence (6514) secured her the IAAF Combined Events Challenge award. Won at Götzis with world's best score of 2000, but then held back by injuries; returned for Olympics but unable to continue beyond long jump in heptathlon.

Yamna BELKACEM b. 20 Feb 1974 Hagou, Morocco 1.64m 52kg. née Oubouhou. CS Meaux.
At 5000m: OG: '00- h; WCh: '99- 8; ECp: '00- 3. At 3000m: WI: '99- 4. World 4k CC: '99-00-01: 2/11/7; Eur CC: '96-7-8: 7/7/6. Won French 1500m 1999-2000.
French records: 3000m 1999, 5000m (5) -2000.
Progression at 3000m, 5000m: 1991- 9:50.0, 1993- 9:53.29, 1995- 9:46.94, 1996- 9:22.85, 16:03.90; 1997- 9:22.15, 15:50.92; 1999- 8:38.13, 15:02.34; 2000- 8:41.54, 14:47.79. pbs: 800m 2:10.8 '94, 1000m 2:52.9 '94, 1500m 4:08.60 '99, 2000m 5:39.44 '99, Rd 10km 34:33 '98.
Married to Henri Belkacem (b. 16 Mar 1964) 3000mSt pb 8:23.47 '99, French champion 1999.

Linda FERGA b. 24 Dec 1976 Paris 1.69m 51kg. Ile de France.
At 110mh (/LJ): OG: '00- 7/4R; WCh: '97- (dnq); EC: '98- 8/7; EJ: '95- 3/1; EU23: '99- 2/1R; EI: '98- (3); ECp: '98- (3), '00- 1/1R. At 60mh: WI: '99- 5, '01- 6; EI: '00- 1. Won FRA LJ 1997.
Progression at 100mh: 1994- 14.12, 1995- 13.61, 1996- 13.32/13.2, 1997- 13.34/13.02w, 1998- 12.95, 1999- 12.98/12.84w, 2000- 12.81/12.77w. pbs: 60m 7.23i '97, 100m 11.35 '98, 50mh 6.82i '00, 60mh 7.88i '00, LJ 6.80 '97, 6.82w '98.

Patricia GIRARD b. 8 Apr 1968 Pointe-à-Pitre, Guadeloupe 1.62m 48kg. Neuilly Plaisance Sports.
At 100mh/4x100m (100m): OG: '88- 7R, '92- 4R (sf), '96- 3/6R, '00- qf; WCh: '93- sf/4R, '95- sf/5R, '97- sf/3R, '99- 8/2R; EC: '94- (sf), '98- 5; ECp: '93- 2R, '95- 3R, '97- 2/2R, '98- 2, '99- 1/1R; Won FRA 1993, 1995, 1997, 1999; Med G 1997. At 60mh: WI: '93- 3; EI: '90- 4, '96- 1, '98- 1, '00- 2. At 60m: WI: '93- 8, '95- dnf, '97- 3=; EI: '94- 3.
Progression at 100mh: 1985- 14.4, 1986- 14.54/13.82w, 1987- 13.45, 1988- 13.42, 1989- 13.53, 1992- 12.91, 1993- 12.91, 1994- 12.93, 1995- 12.87, 1996- 12.59, 1997- 12.67, 1998- 12.80, 1999- 12.73, 2000- 12.88. pbs: 50m 6.27i '95, 60m 7.16i '94, 100m 11.11 '94, 10.9w '96; 200m 23.40 '95, 50mh 6.76i '00, 60mh 7.84i '95, 200mh 25.82 '99 (world best on auto timing), LJ 5.72 '93.
Two year drugs ban from 17 Mar 1990. Formerly married (1995) to European kick-boxing champion Eddy Léno.

Muriel HURTIS b. 25 Mar 1979 Bondy 1.80m 68kg. Ile de France.
At 200m/4x100m: OG: '00- sf/4R; WCh: '99- sf/2R; WJ: '98- 1/2R; EJ: '97- 2; EU23: '99- 2/1R; WI: '01- 5; EI: '00- 1; ECp: '00- 1/1R. Won FRA 200m 2000.
Progression at 200m: 1995- 23.91, 1996- 23.92, 1997- 23.79, 1998- 22.76/22.72w, 1999- 22.31, 2000- 22.70. pbs: 60m 7.43i '00, 100m 11.33/11.3 '99, 11.28w '00; 400m 54.44 '98, LJ 6.04i '97, 5.86 '95.

Manuela MONTEBRUN b. 13 Nov 1979 Laval 1.75m 90kg. Stade Laval. Student.
At HT: OG: '00- dnq 24; WCh: '99- 12; WJ: '98- 5; EU23: '99- 4; WUG: '99- 3; ECp: '00- 4. French champion 2000.
Five French hammer records 1999-2000.
Progression at HT: 1996- 47.34, 1997- 52.58, 1998- 62.79, 1999- 68.11, 2000- 71.18. pb SP 13.99 '98.

Marie-José PÉREC b. 9 May 1968 Basse Terre, Guadeloupe 1.80m 60kg. Stade Français.
At 400m/4x100m (4x400m): OG: '92- 1, '96- 1 (1 200m); WCh: '91- 1/5R, '95- 1; EC: '90- 3, '94- 1 (1R); WCp: '89- dq, '94- (4R); ECp: '91-1 (won B 1989). At 200m: OG: '88- qf; WCh: '93- 4/4R, '97- sf; EI: '89- 1; WI: '89- 6; WCp: '92- 1/2R; ECp: '93- 2/2R (2 100m), '96- 1/3R. At 400mh: ECp: '95- 1. Won GP 400m 1994, French 100m 1991, 200m 1992, 1995; 400m 1988, 400mh 1989.
French records: 100m 1991, three 200m 1991-3, eight 400m 1988-96, four 400mh 1995.
Progression at 200m, 400m: 1984- 25.44/25.0; 1985- 24.14; 1986- 24.33/24.00w; 1987- 24.52; 1988- 22.72, 51.35; 1989- 22.36, 51.05; 1990- 22.92, 50.84; 1991- 22.26, 49.13; 1992- 22.20, 48.83; 1993- 21.99; 1994- 22.61, 49.77; 1995- 22.79, 49.28; 1996- 22.07, 48.25; 1997- 22.67, 1999- 23.25, 2000- 22.71, 50.32. At 400mh: 1989- 55.76, 1995- 53.21. pbs: 60m 7.29i '92, 100m 10.96 '91, 300m 36.81 '88.
Preceded Michael Johnson to win 1996 Olympic double at 200m and 400m. Disqualified for breaking lane after winning the 1989 World Cup 400m in 50.30. Ran French records of 50.53 and 49.32 in her first two races at 400m in 1991, then 49.76 to win in Nice and then improved to 49.13 to win the world title. Did not compete in 1998 due to the effects of a virus illness but returned in 1999, although not regaining enough form to go to Seville. Had one race at 200m and one at 400m (3rd in Nice, her first at 400m for three years) and went to Sydney but fled from there when confronted with the pressure of the much-hyped intended clash with Cathy Freeman at 400m.

Nicole RAMALALANIRINA b. 5 Mar 1972 Soavinandriana, Madagascar 1.64m 57kg. Married name Válerie. 1.67m 58kg. Neuilly Plaisance Sports.
At 100mh: OG: '92- h, '96- sf, '00- 6; WCh: '93/95- sf, '97- ht, '99- sf; EC: '98- 4; AfG: '91- 3/3R, '95- 4; AfC: '90- 6, '92- 4/3R, '93- 1/2R; WCp: '94- 4, '98- dnf; WSG: '93- 3, '95- 1. At 60mh: WI: '01- 3. Won FRA 100mh 1998, 2000.
African record 60mh indoors 1996.
Progression at 100mh: 1990- 13.91, 1991- 13.69, 1992- 13.40, 1993- 13.11/12.92w, 1994- 13.11, 1995- 12.92, 1996- 12.90, 1997- 13.02, 1998- 12.85/12.76w, 1999- 12.84, 2000- 12.76. pbs: 60m 7.51i '95, 100m 11.56 '96, 11.53w '95; 200m 24.3A '91, 24.34w '00; 400m 56.42 '91, 50mh 6.94i '95, 60mh

7.89i '96, 400mh 59.88 '94. LJ 5.54 '94.
Changed citizenship from Madagascar (for whom she was also a basketball international) to France in 1998.

GERMANY

Governing body: Deutscher Leichtathletik Verband (DLV), Alsfelder Str. 27, 64289 Darmstadt. Founded 1898.
National Championships first held in 1891. **2000 Champions**: **Men**: 100m/200m: Holger Blume 10.19/20.82, 400m: Lars Figura 46.54, 800m: Nils Schumann 1:47.82, 1500m: Dirk Heinze 3:38.75, 5000m: Jitka Arndt 13:45.66, 10000m: Thorsten Naumann 28:44.88, Mar: Matthias Körner 2:20:05, HMar: Carsten Eich 62:47, 3000mSt: Damian Kallabis 8:31.64, 110mh: Florian Schwarthoff 13.42, 400mh: Thomas Goller 50.38, HJ: Wolfgang Kreissig 2.30, PV: Tim Lobinger 5.85, LJ: Kofi Amoah Prah 8.11, TJ: Charles Friedek 17.00, SP: Oliver-Sven Buder 20.41, DT: Lars Riedel 65.67, HT: Karsten Kobs 80.21, JT: Boris Henry 84.40, Dec: Florian Schönbeck 8127, 10000mW/20kmW: Andreas Erm 39:54.23/1:20:30, 50kmW: Denis Trautmann 3:52:06. **Women**: 100m: Esther Möller 11.44, 200m: Andrea Philipp 22.99, 400m: Grit Breuer 51.22, 800m: Claudia Gesell 2:00.53, 1500m: Kathleen Friedrich 4:17.99, 5000m: Irina Mikitenko 15:50.55, 10000m: Petra Wassiluk 32:20.49; HMar: Katrin Dörre-Heinig 71:44, Mar: Ines Cronjäger 2:41:00, 100mh: Kirsten Bolm 13.04, 400mh: Ulrike Urbansky 55.51, HJ: Amewu Mensah 1.90, PV: Yvonne Buschbaum 4.45, LJ: Heike Drechsler 6.72, TJ: Tanja König 13.64, SP: Nadine Kleinert 18.79, DT: Franka Dietzsch 65.25, HT: Simone Mathes 65.29, JT: Tanja Damaske 66.73, Hep: Kathleen Gutjahr 6079, 5000mW: Beate Gummelt 21:15.49, 20kmW: Kathrin Boyde 1:30:42.

Falk BALZER b. 14 Dec 1973 Leipzig 1.89m 80kg. TuS Jena.
At 110mh. OG. '00- sf; WCh: '97- sf, '99- 5; EC: '98- 2; EU23: '94- 1; WCp: '98- 1; ECp: '98-9-00 2/1/1. At 60mh: WI: '99- 3; EI: '96- 4, '00- 5. Won GER 110mh 1998.
Progression at 110mh: 1990 15.6, 1991- 14.64, 1992- 14.17, 1993- 13.96, 1994- 13.76, 1995- 13.59/13.47dt, 1996- 13.34, 1997- 13.31, 1998- 13.10rA/13.12, 1999- 13.21, 2000- 13.19. pbs: 100m 10.74 '98, 200m 21.79 '99, 60mh 7.41i '99, LJ 7.01 '95.
Won the 1998 World Cup 110mh, but was shown to have had a unacceptable reaction time of .031. Coached by his mother Karin Balzer (née Richert), the first GDR Olympic champion, at 80mh (10.54) in 1964 adding a bronze at 100mh in 1972. After a silver in 1962, she won three European gold medals (80mh 1966, 100mh 1969 and 1971). She set five world records at 100mh (13.3 in 1969 to 12.6 in 1971) and 29 world indoor bests at sprint hurdles, including three at the European Indoors, which she won for five successive years 1967-71. His father Karl-Heinz Balzer was GDR PV champion 1949-54.

Peter BLANK b. 10 Apr 1962 Frankfurt-am-Main 1.95m 103kg. Eintracht Frankfurt.
At JT: OG: '96- 9; WCh: '91- 11, '93- dnq 29, '99- dnq 13; EC: '90- dnq, '94- dnq 20, '98- 7; ECp: '91- 3. FRG champion 1988, 1990.
Progression at JT: 1978- 58.42, 1979- 64.92, 1980- 65.76, 1981- 72.84, 1982- 76.04, 1983- 78.22, 1984- 81.98, 1985- 82.34, new: 1986- 71.02, 1987- 77.94, 1988- 80.84, 1989- 79.60, 1990- 82.82R, 1991- 82.62, 1992- 81.12, 1993- 80.76, 1994- 82.56, 1995- 83.18, 1996- 88.12, 1997- 86.84, 1998- 86.99, 1999- 87.11, 2000- 85.45. pbs: HJ 2.23 '83, LJ 7.41 '88, Dec 7651 '90.
Set a world decathlon javelin best 79.80 in 1992.

Oliver-**Sven BUDER** b. 23 Jun 1966 Erlabrunn 2.00m 130kg. MTV Ingolstadt. Clerk.
At SP: OG: '96- 5, '00- 8; WCh: '91- 4, '93- 7, '95- 6, '97- 2, '99- 2; EC: '90- 2, '94- dnq 16, '98- 2; EJ: '85- 1; WCp: '94- 4, '98- 3; ECp: '93-4-5-6-7-8-9: 4/4/2/2/1/2/1; WI: '91- 7, '93- 8, '97- 4; EI: '90- 3, '96- 3, '98- 1. Won GER 1991, 1993-2000.
Progression at SP: 1984- 16.58, 1985- 19.34, 1986- 19.29, 1987- 20.14, 1988- 19.05, 1989- 20.22, 1990- 21.06, 1991- 20.20, 1992- 19.76i/19.70, 1993- 20.15, 1994- 20.44, 1995- 20.84, 1996- 20.67, 1997- 21.24, 1998- 21.47i/20.98, 1999- 21.42, 2000- 20.71i/20.41. pb DT 54.14 '91.
Improved 7 year-old personal best to take 1997 world silver medal.

Frank BUSEMANN b. 26 Feb 1975 Recklinghausen 1.92m 87kg. Bayer Leverkusen. Student.
At Dec: OG: '96- 2, '00- 7; WCh: '97- 3, '99- dnf; ECp: '96- 1. At 110mh: WJ: '94- 1; EJ: '93- 3; EU23: '97- 1. World junior 60mh best 7.67i '94.
Progression at 110mh, Dec: 1992- 14.33, 1993- 14.06, 1994- 13.56/13.47w, 7938; 1995- 13.68/13.58dt, 7879; 1996- 13.45, 8706; 1997- 13.49, 8652; 1998- 13.70, 8231; 1999- 13.85, 8411; 2000 13.98, 8531. pbs: 100m 10.59 '93, 200m 21.61 '96, 400m 48.32 '97, 1500m 4:23.04 '98, 60mh 7.52i '97, HJ 2.09 '97, PV 5.10 '99, LJ 8.07 '96, SP 15.24 '99, DT 46.70 '97, JT 66.96 '97.
Five personal bests and a decathlon world best 13.47 for 110mh at the 1996 Olympics. His mother won a German U21 shot title and his brother Lars Achim Busemann (b. 31 Jan 1978) has a pole vault pb of 5.26 '98.

Martin BUSS b. 7 Apr 1976 Berlin 1.95m 82kg. LG Bayer Leverkusen.
At HJ: WCh: '97- 9, '99- 3; EC: '98- 4; EJ: '95- 2; EU23: '97- 2; WI: '99- 4, '01- 5=; EI: '00- 2; WCp: '98- 4; ECp: '97-8-9: 3/4=/1. Won GER 1997-9.
Progression at HJ: 1993- 1.85, 1994- 2.04, 1995- 2.19, 1996- 2.27, 1997- 2.31, 1998- 2.33, 1999- 2.35, 2000- 2.34i. pb LJ 7.75 '99.

Danny ECKER b. 21 Jul 1977 Leverkusen 1.92m 76kg. TSV Bayer Leverkusen.
At PV: OG: '00- 8; WCh: '99- 4=; EC: '98- 4; WI: '99- 3; EI: '98- 3; WJ: '96- 3; ECp: '98- 4.
Progression at PV: 1990- 2.90, 1991- 3.30, 1992- 3.80, 1993- 4.40, 1994- 4.70, 1995- 5.12, 1996- 5.61, 1997- 5.72i/5.71, 1998- 5.93, 1999- 5.90, 2000- 5.90, 2001- 6.00i. pbs: HJ 2.00 '99. LJ 6.83 99.
Son of Heide Rosendahl, 1972 Olympic LJ champion (and 2nd Pen) (WR 6.84 '70), and US basketball player John Ecker.

Andreas ERM b. 12 Mar 1976 Berlin 1.84m 70kg. TV Friesen Naumburg. Soldier.
At 20kmW: OG: '96- 24, '00- 5; WCh: '97- dq, '99- dnf; EC: '98- 4; EU23: '97- 5; ECp: '98- 4, '00- 2. At 10000mW: WJ: '94- 9; EJ: '95- 1. Won GER 20kmW 1998-2000, 10000m W 2000.
German 20km walk record 2000, world best indoor 3000m walk 2001.
Progression at 20kmW: 1994- 1:26:41, 1995- 1:23:20, 1996- 1:22:16, 1997- 1:21:05, 1998- 1:20:57, 1999- 1:19:24, 2000- 1:18:42. pbs: 3000mW 10:31.42i '01, 5000mW 18:22.25i '01, 10000mW 39:54.23 '00.

Charles-Michael **FRIEDEK** b. 26 Aug 1971 Giessen 1.84m 80kg. TSV Beyer Leverkusen. Law student.
At TJ: OG: '00- nj (12); WCh: '97- 11, '99- 1; EC: '98- 6; WJ: '90- 12; EJ: '89- dnq; WI: '97- 4, '99- 1, '01- 4; EI: '98- 2, '00- 1; WUG: '97- 5, '99- 2; WCp: '98- 1; ECp: '96-7-8: 4/3/3. Won GP 1998, GER 1996-2000.
Progression at TJ: 1987- 13.67, 1988- 15.13, 1989- 15.85, 1990- 16.34, 1991- 15.77, 1992- 16.10, 1993- 16.32i/16.26/16.51w, 1994- 16.31, 1995- 16.34/16.60w, 1996- 17.10, 1997- 17.59, 1998- 17.42A/17.38, 1999- 17.59, 2000- 17.41. pbs: 100m 11.01 '92, 200m 22.23 '89, LJ 7.66 '97.

Raymond HECHT b. 11 Nov 1968 Gardelegen 1.91m 95kg. SG Magdeburg. Mechanical engineer.
At JT: OG: '96- 4, '00- 4; WCh: '91- 12, '93- dnq 23, '95- 4, '97- dnq 13, '99- 5; EC: '90- 10, '94- 5, '98- 3; WCp: '94- 2, '98- 3; ECp: '93-4-5-6-9: 4/2/1/1/1; EJ: '87- 3. GER champion 1993-4, 1996, 1999. 2nd GP 1993, 1995.
Five German javelin records 1991-5.
Progression at JT: 1984- 66.20, 1985- 69.32; new: 1986- 71.08 (71.14 old), 1987- 75.90, 1990- 83.24, 1991- 90.84R, 1992- 79.58, 1993- 88.90, 1994- 90.06, 1995- 92.60, 1996- 92.28, 1997- 87.32, 1998- 88.08, 1999- 88.67, 2000- 87.76.
As a junior was ranked fourth in the world in 1987. Injured 1988-9.

Boris HENRY b. 14 Dec 1973 Völklingen 1.93m 108kg. SV Saar 05 Saarbrücken. Army staff sergeant.
At JT: OG: '96- 5, '00- 7; WCh: '93- dnq, '95- 3, '97- 6, '99- 6; EC: '94- 11; WJ: '92- 2; EJ: '91- 4; ECp: '97-8-00: 3/1/3. 2nd GP 1997. GER champion 1995, 1997-8, 2000.
Progression at JT: 1989- 58.20, 1990- 65.86, 1991- 74.78, 1992- 76.92, 1993- 84.12, 1994- 82.02, 1995- 88.46, 1996- 88.00, 1997- 90.44, 1998- 89.21. 1999- 88.62, 2000- 86.65. pbs: SP 14.37 '94, DT 46.24 '94, Pen 3503 '93.
For several years wore a red baseball cap given to him as an 18th birthday present, now sports a white one.

Damian KALLABIS b. 10 Jun 1973 Gleiwitz (Gliwice), Poland 1.77m 64kg. SCC Berlin. Was at the University of Texas, El Paso, USA.
At 3000mSt: OG: '00- 15; WCh: '99- 4; EC: '98- 1; WCp: '98- 1; ECp: '99-00: 2/2. German champion 1998, 2000.
German 3000m steeplechase record 1999.
Progression at 3000mSt: 1991- 9:24.6, 1992- 8:49.99, 1993- 8:43.92, 1994- 8:40.40, 1995- 8:38.39, 1996- 8:42.13, 1997- 8:37.35, 1998- 8:13.10, 1999- 8:09.48, 2000- 8:14.53. pbs: 1500m 3:43.77 '98, 3000m 7:49.38 '99, 5000m 14:29.87 '97.
Made a superb breakthrough in 1998, running away with the European title and later upsetting Bernard Barmasai to win at the World Cup. Coached by Stéphane Franke. At 14 he was regional champion at 80mh and HJ (1.73m).

Karsten KOBS b. 16 Sep 1971 Dortmund 1.96m 118kg. TSV Bayer Leverkusen.
At HT: OG: '96- dnq 18, '00- dnq 31; WCh: '93- dnq 16, '95- dnq 16, '97- 9, '99- 1; EC: '94- 10, '98- 3; WJ: '90- 4; EJ: '89- 10; ECp: '93-5-6-9-00: 7/3/1/3/3. German champion 1996, 1999-2000. 3rd GP 2000.
Progression at HT: 1988- 59.80, 1989- 65.02, 1990- 70.02, 1991- 71.82, 1992- 74.36, 1993- 75.94, 1994- 76.30, 1995- 76.80, 1996- 78.92, 1997- 79.08, 1998- 81.21, 1999- 82.78, 2000- 80.21. pb SP 15.53 '98.
Has improved every year of his career to reach the world number one ranking in 1999. His father, Reiner, had HT pb of 58.90 (1974).

Wolfgang KREISSIG b. 29 Aug 1970 Gehrden 1.97m 82kg. MTG Mannheim.
At HJ: OG: '96- 9, '00- 8; WCh: '95- dnq 20=, '99- dnq 14=; EC: '94- 13; EJ: '89- 3; WI: '97- 5; WCp: '94- 5; ECp: '96- 4, '00- 2; WUG: '95- 2. Won GER HJ 1996, 2000.
Progression at HJ: 1987- 2.01, 1988- 2.16, 1989- 2.24, 1990- 2.22, 1991- 2.12, 1992- 2.19, 1993- 2.25, 1994- 2.28, 1995- 2.29, 1996- 2.33, 1997- 2.30i/2.25, 1998- 2.30, 1999- 2.34, 2000- 2.30. pb LJ 7.12w? '99.

Tim LOBINGER b. 3 Sep 1972 Rheinbach 1.93m 83kg. Quelle Fürth/München.
At PV: OG: '96- 7, '00- 13; WCh: '93- dnq, '95- 11, '97- 4, '99- 6; EC: '94- dnq 21=, '98- 2; WI: '97- 5; EI: '98- 1; WJ: '90- dnq; EJ: '91- 3; WCp: '98- 2; ECp: '93-4-5-6-7-00: 5/3/nh/2/3/2. Won GP 2000, 3rd 1997, won EU23Cp 1992; German champion 1993-4, 1997-2000.
Three German pole vault records 1997-9.
Progression at PV: 1986- 3.46, 1987- 3.90, 1988-

4.60, 1989- 4.85, 1990- 5.32, 1991- 5.35, 1992- 5.50, 1993- 5.55, 1994- 5.60, 1995- 5.70, 1996- 5.91, 1997- 6.00, 1998- 5.92, 1999- 6.00, 2000- 5.95i/5.85. pbs: 110mh 14.78 '99, HJ 1.97 '99, DT 42.76 '99, Dec 7346 '99.
Set (then) world decathlon PV best of 5.75 in 7346 decathlon at Leverkusen 1999. His wife **Petra** (b. 24 Jan 1967 Siegen-Weidenau, née Laux) set four German indoor TJ records from 14.15 '96 to 14.36 '97 (5 WI), outdoor pb 14.31/ 14.35w '97; German champion 1992, 1996-7, 10 WCh '97; they have one child.

Michael MÖLLENBECK b. 12 Dec 1969 Wesel 2.00m 120kg. TV Wattenscheid. Businessman.
At DT: OG: '96- dnq, '00- 10; WCh: '95- dnq 16, '99- 6; WJ: '88- 9; EJ: '87- 6.
Progression at DT: 1988- 53.00, 1989- 59.26, 1990- 60.16, 1991- 58.86, 1992- 62.12, 1993- 62.82, 1994- 58.26, 1995- 65.78, 1996- 67.44, 1997- 66.66, 1998- 67.18, 1999- 67.00, 2000- 65.49. pb SP 16.78 '95.
Married **Anja** Gündler (b. 18 Mar 1972, DT pb 64.63 '98, 3 WJ 1990, 1 EJ 1991, 5 WCh 1993) in 1996.

Kofi Amoah PRAH b. 20 Dec 1974 Accra, Ghana 1.75m 75kg. LG Nike Berlin. Office clerk.
At LJ: OG: '00- 5; WCh: '99- dnq 17; EC: '98- 11; WCp: '98- 7; ECp: '99-00: 2/2. Won GER 2000.
Progression at LJ: 1991- 6.96, 1992- 7.16, 1993- 7.43, 1994- 7.58, 1995- 7.25, 1996- 7.66, 1997- 8.02, 1998- 7.95, 1999- 8.15/8.19w, 2000- 8.20. pb 100m 10.61 '99.
Naturalised German since 1998.

Lars RIEDEL b. 28 Jun 1967 Zwickau 1.99m 110kg. LAC Erdgas Chemnitz. Computer salesman.
At DT: OG: '92- dnq 14, '96- 1, '00- 2; WCh: '91- 1, '93- 1, '95- 1, '97- 1, '99- 3; EC: '90- dnq 15, '94- dns, '98- 1; WJ: '86- 4; WUG: '93- 1; WCp: '98- 2; ECp: '93-5-7-00: 1/1/1/1. GER champion 1992-8, 2000. Won GP 1993, 1995, 1997 (2nd overall), 1999; 2nd 1991.
Progression at DT: 1985- 52.02, 1986- 58.66, 1988- 62.26, 1989- 60.84, 1990- 64.86, 1991- 67.78, 1992- 68.66, 1993- 68.42, 1994- 66.08, 1995- 69.08, 1996- 71.06, 1997- 71.50, 1998- 68.21, 1999- 69.18, 2000- 69.72. pbs: SP 15.93 '91, JT 61.14 '93, Dec 6087 '93.
The top discus thrower of the 1990s with four world titles and the 1996 Olympic gold. In 1992 improved to 67.90, but failed at the Olympics before making a fine comeback with four throws over 68m at the ISTAF meeting. In 1994 a bad back caused his withdrawal from European final. He exceeded 70m for the first time in Zürich in 1995.

Stefan SCHMID b. 6 May 1970 Würzburg 1.87m 85kg. LG Karlstadt.
At Dec: OG: '00- 9; WCh: '97- 7; EC: '94- 5, '98- 14; ECp: '93- 6; WUG: '91- 4. Won GER 1992.
Progression at Dec: 1990- 7532, 1991- 7866, 1992- 8012, 1993- 8061, 1994- 8309, 1996- 8478dq, 1997- 8360, 1998- 8011, 1999- 7981, 2000- 8485. pbs: 100m 10.69 '00, 10.67w '90; 200m 21.68 '91, 400m 48.14 '97, 1500m 4:26.51 '94, 60mh 7.98i '97, 110mh 13.93dq '96, 14.20 '90; HJ 2.01 '00, 2.06dq '96; PV 5.06 '00, LJ 7.83 '94, SP 14.73 '98, DT 45.16 '98, JT 71.68 '94, Hep 6058i '97.
After a season in which he broke into the world's top ten he had a cartilege operation at the end of 1994. Returned for his best decathlon in two years to win German title late in 1996 with four pbs; but a drugs test on this occasion found him to have taken a banned stimulant, although one that had been prescribed by a doctor for shoulder pains earlier in the year.

Jürgen SCHULT b. 11 May 1960 Neuhaus/Kreis Hagenow 1.93m 110kg. Schweriner SC.
At DT: OG: '88- 1, '92- 2, '96- 6, '00- 8; WCh: '83- 5, '87- 1, '91- 6, '93- 3, '95- 5, '97- 3, '99- 2; EC: '86- 7, '90- 1, '94- 3, '98- 2; EJ: '79- 1; WCp: '85- 2, '89- 1, '94- 5; ECp: '83-5-7-9-91-4-6-8-9: 1/4/2/1/2/2/ 3/2/1. GDR champion 1983-90, GER 1999. 3rd GP 1993.
World discus record 1986.
Progression at DT: 1978- 51.82, 1979- 57.22, 1980- 61.26, 1981- 61.56, 1982- 63.18, 1983- 66.78, 1984- 68.82, 1985- 69.74, 1986- 74.08, 1987- 69.52, 1988- 70.46, 1989- 68.12, 1990- 67.08, 1991- 67.20, 1992- 69.04, 1993- 66.12, 1994- 66.08, 1995- 65.04, 1996- 66.94, 1997- 66.24, 1998- 66.69, 1999- 68.18, 2000- 65.81. pb SP 17.45 '82.
Although never again approaching his world record distance of 1986 he has been most consistent, winning World, Olympic and European titles, and being undefeated in 1988 and 1989. The only man to have competed at all seven World Championships 1983-99, he has also placed in the top six each time. Apppinted German national coach for discus at end of 2000.

Nils SCHUMANN b. 20 May 1978 Bad Frankenhausen 1.92m 77kg. LC Nike Berlin.
At 800m: OG: '00- 1; WCh: '99- 8; EC: '98- 1; WJ: '96- 5; EJ: '97- 1; EU23: '99- 1; EI: '98- 1, '00- 2; WCp: '98- 1; ECp: '00- 2. German champion 1999-2000.
Progression at 800m: 1988- 2:26.5, 1989- 2:21.0, 1990- 2:18.3, 1991- 2:14.0, 1994- 2:03.6, 1995- 1:53.0, 1996- 1:48.35, 1997- 1:46.61, 1998- 1:44.89, 1999- 1:44.47, 2000- 1:44.22. pbs: 400m 46.62 '99, 1000m 2:17.44 '99, 1500m 3:40.36 '00.
Has burst to the fore with an astonishing sequence of championship victories.

Florian SCHWARTHOFF b. 7 May 1968 Dortmund 2.01m 83kg. OSC Berlin. Studied architecture.
At 110mh: OG: '88- qf, '92- 5. '96- 3, '00- 6; WCh: '87- sf, '91- 7, '93- 5, '95- sf (fell), '97- 4, '99- 7; EC: '90- sf, '94- 2, '98- 4; WCp: '94- 4; ECp: '89- 3, '91- 2 (5 200m), '93-4-5-6-7: 2/1/1/1/1; EJ: '87- 2; WUG: '89- 3. 3rd GP 1995, 2nd 1997. FRG/GER champion 1987-8, 1990-2, 1994-7, 1999-2000. At

60mh: WI: '93- 4; EI: '90- 3.
Four FRG 110mh records 1988-92 and three at 60mh indoors in 1990; GER 110mh record 1995.
Progression at 110mh: 1986- 14.13, 1987- 13.69, 1988- 13.50, 1989- 13.37, 1990- 13.37, 1991- 13.38, 1992- 13.13, 1993- 13.27. 1994- 13.16, 1995- 13.05, 1996- 13.11, 1997- 13.11, 1998- 13.19, 1999- 13.19, 2000- 13.23. pbs: 100m 10.57 '96, 10.46w '90; 200m 20.86 '91, 60mh 7.52i '90, LJ 7.69 '86.
Perhaps the tallest ever top-class high hurdler. His European silver in 1994, one place ahead of Tony Jarrett, was his first since the 1987 European Juniors when he was second to Jarrett.

Andreas SEELIG b. 6 Jul 1970 Berlin 2.00m 103kg. USC Mainz.
At DT: WCh: '97- 6, '99- dnq 14; EC: '94- 10, '98- 7; WJ: '88- 1; EJ: '89- 1.
Progression at DT: 1986- 45.06, 1987- 54.24, 1988- 61.84, 1989- 59.72, 1990- 59.36, 1991- 58.88, 1992- 60.82, 1993- 61.90, 1994- 62.22, 1995- 62.90, 1996- 63.62, 1997- 66.00, 1998- 65.47, 1999- 65.83, 2000- 64.51.

Michael STOLLE b. 17 Dec 1974 Buxtehude 1.92m 85kg. TSV Bayer Leverkusen.
At PV: OG: '96- 9=, '00- 4; WCh: '99- 7=; WI: '97- 8=, '01- 9=; EI: '98- 2; WJ: '90- dnq; EJ: '91- dnq; ECp: '99- 1. German champion 1996.
Progression at PV: 1989- 3.70, 1990- 4.20, 1991- 4.75, 1992- 5.05, 1993- 5.10i/5.05, 1994- 5.41, 1995- 5.50, 1996- 5.71i/5.70, 1997- 5.70i/5.60, 1998- 5.83, 1999- 5.91, 2000- 5.95. pb Dec 5817 '99.

Heinz WEIS b. 14 Jul 1963 Trier 1.93m 120kg. TSV Bayer Leverkusen. Businessman.
At HT: OG: '88- 5, '92- 6, '96- 5, '00- dnq 26; WCh: '87- 6, '91- 3, '97- 1, '99- dnq 18; EC: '90- 8, '94- 3, '98- 4; WUG: '85- 1, '87- 2, '89- 2, '91- 3; WCp: '89- 1, '94- 3, '98- 2; ECp: '89-91-4-7-8: 1/4/4/1/1. FRG/GER champion 1988-92, 1994, 1997-8. 3rd GP 1990, 1996.
Three FRG hammer records 1988-9.
Progression at HT: 1980- 53.34, 1981- 60.86, 1982- 61.56, 1983- 65.30, 1984- 68.98, 1985- 78.18, 1986- 76.08, 1987- 80.18, 1988- 82.52, 1989- 82.84, 1990- 81.36, 1991- 80.44, 1992- 80.46, 1993- 75.56, 1994- 81.20, 1995- 78.42, 1996- 80.90, 1997- 83.04, 1998- 81.27, 1999- 79.48, 2000- 80.13. pb SP 14.30 '87.
Has compiled a fine competitive record, world number one 1989. To gain the world title in 1997 he improved with each throw taking the lead from an opponent each time.

Women

Bianca ACHILLES b. 17 Apr 1981 Hagen 1.80m 98kg. Bayer Leverkusen.
At HT: EJ: '97- 4, '99- 1; WJ: '98- 1.
Three world junior hammer records 1999, German record 1999.
Progression at HT: 1996- 59.14, 1997- 61.70, 1998- 62.50, 1999- 68.40, 2000- 66.58. pbs: SP 12.98 '99, DT 42.72 '99.

Sabine BRAUN b. 19 Jun 1965 Essen 1.74m 62kg. TV Wattenscheid. Studied sport and biology.
At Hep: OG: '84- 6, '88- 14, '92- 3, '96- 7, '00- 5; WCh: '87- 18, '91- 1, '93- 2, '95- dnf, '97- 1 (dnq LJ), '99- 4; EC: '90- 1, '94- 1, '98- 6; EJ: '83- 2; WUG: '89- 2; ECp: '85- 4, '89- 5. At Pen: WI: '97- 1, '01- 5. At LJ: EJ: '83- 8; WCp: '85- 5, '94- 5; ECp: '85- 3, '89- 6. Won FRG LJ 1985, Hep 1989, GER 100mh 1992, Hep 1996.
Three FRG heptathlon records 1989-90, GER record 1992.
Progression at Hep: 1982- 5477, 1983- 6254, 1984- 6436, 1985- 6323, 1986- 6418, 1987- 5621, 1988- 6432, 1989- 6575, 1990- 6688, 1991- 6672, 1992- 6985, 1993- 6797, 1994- 6665, 1995- 6617, 1996- 6636, 1997- 6787, 1998- 6381, 1999- 6497, 2000- 6464. pbs: 100m 11.58 '97, 200m 23.65 '92, 23.60w '85; 400m 55.03 '83, 800m 2:09.41 '84, 50mh 7.04i '98, 60mh 8.09i '96, 100mh 13.05 '92, HJ 1.94 '92, LJ 6.76/6.83w '97; SP 15.08 '97, JT 54.10 '86, new: 51.71 '99; Pen 4780i '97.
Missed major events in 1986-7 through injury. Won at Götzis 1990-2, 1994. World best 6214 for 45-minute heptathlon 1993. Won IAAF Combined Events Challenge 2000.

Grit BREUER b. 16 Feb 1972 Röbel 1.66m 63kg. SC Magdeburg.
At 400m/4x400mR: OG: '88- resR, '96- 8/3R; WCh: '91- 2/3R (3 4x100mR), '97- 4/1R, '99- 7/3R; EC: '90- 1/1R, '98- 1/1R; WJ: '88- 1 (1R & 1 4x100mR); WI: '91- 1R (3 200m), '97- 6/3R, '99- 1; EI: '96- 1, '98- 1; WCp: '89- 2/2R, '98- 2/1R; ECp: '89-91-6-7: 1/2/1/1 (1R/2R/1R/-). Won GDR 400m 1989-90, GER 200m 1997, 400m 1996-7, 1999-2000.
World junior records 400m 1990 and 1991, 4x100m and 4x400m 1988, indoor 200m 1991. WIR 4x400m 1991.
Progression at 200m, 400m: 1985- 56.21, 1986- 55.7/55.5i, 1987- 24.03, 52.59; 1988- 23.04, 51.14; 1989- 22.82, 50.48; 1990- 22.49, 49.50; 1991- 22.45, 49.42; 1992- 22.71i, 1995- 23.63, 51.68; 1996- 50.22, 1997- 22.73, 49.98; 1998- 22.95i, 49.51; 1999- 23.02, 50.16; 2000- 23.46, 51.06. pbs: 100m 11.13 '90, 300m 36.51+ '99.
Set world age records for 400m at 16-17-18-19. Olympic bronze at age 16 as she ran in heats of 4x400m relay. Although a junior until 1991, she did not contest the 1989 or 1991 European or 1990 World Juniors, but concentrated with great success on senior competition. Drugs ban in 1992, first for allegedly tampering with sample. That ban was lifted by the DLV, but then caught again for use of Clenbuterol. She returned to competition when her three-year ban ended in August 1995. Ran a brilliant final leg of 48.69 to come from behind and take the gold medal for Germany in the 1997 World 4x400m. Withdrew from 2000 Olympic team due to back trouble and underwent surgery on 11 September.

(Above) Donna Fraser (right) congratulates a shell-shocked Kathy Freeman after the Australian won the Olympic 400m title in front of her own Sydney crowd.
(right) Merlene Ottey, now 40 but still going strong.

Konstadínos Kedéris cannot believe he has won the Olympic 200 metres title while Darren Campbell dips for silver.

Virgilijus Alekna belied his reputation of choking in major championships by winning Olympic gold.

Hadi Al-Somaily, the surprise of the season, won silver in the Sydney Olympics 400 metres hurdles.

The race of the year. Haile Gebrselassie (left) squeezes past Paul Tergat in the last few metres of the Sydney Olympic 10,000m to win by a smaller margin than Maurice Greene in the 100m.

Stacy Dragila set three indoor world records and three outdoors in 2000 before winning the inaugural Olympic title.

They do not give Olympic medals for courage but if they did surely Paula Radcliffe (1842) would have been awarded one for her front running in the Olympic 10,000m. But she was passed by three women in the latter stages. (right) Angelo Taylor won the 400m hurdles title from lane one.

Maurice Greene celebrates while Obadele Thompson checks to make sure he was third in the Sydney Olympic 100m.

Adam Nelson was the no.1 shot putter last year even though he suffered a surprise defeat in the Olympic final.

Yvonne BUSCHBAUM b. 14 Jul 1980 Ulm 1.70m 55kg. LG Stuttgart.
At PV: OG: '00- 6; WCh: '99- 14=; EC: '98- 3; WI: '01- 6; WJ: '98- 4; ECp: '99-00: 1/2. German champion 1999-2000.
Four world junior pole vault records 1999, German record 1999.
Progression at PV: 1994- 2.81, 1995- 3.30, 1996- 3.55, 1997- 4.00, 1998- 4.31, 1999- 4.42/4.45ex, 2000- 4.45. pbs: 100mh 14.54 '98, HJ 1.75 '98, LJ 5.81 '98.

Tanja DAMASKE b. 16 Nov 1971 Berlin 1.77m 69kg. OSC Berlin. Psychology student.
At JT: WCh: '95- 6, '97- 3; EC: '94- 6, '98- 1; WJ: '90- 1; WUG: '93- 2; WCp: '98- 5; ECp: '96-7-8-9: 3/3/1/1. Won GP 1996, 1998. GER champion 1995, 1997-2000.
Two world bests new javelin 1999.
Progression at JT: 1986- 44.38, 1987- 48.04, 1988- 52.50, 1989- 51.20, 1990- 61.06, 1991- 59.84, 1992- 55.86, 1993- 60.96, 1994- 64.24, 1995- 65.94, 1996- 66.62, 1997- 69.36, 1998- 70.10; new: 1999- 66.91, 2000- 66.73. pb SP 15.49i '97.
Set pb in last round for World bronze medal 1997 and had a splendid season in 1998 including the first 70m plus throw for three years when she threw 70.10 to win the German title in her hometown of Berlin. Warmed up but unable to compete at 1999 Worlds through injury, and also missed the 2000 Olympics.

Franka DIETZSCH b. 22 Jan 1968 Wolgast 1.83m 92kg. SC Neubrandenburg. Bank employee.
At DT: OG: '92- 12, '96- 4, '00- 6; WCh: '91- dnq 13, '93- 8, '95- 7, '97- dnq, '99- 1; EC: '94- 9, '98- 1; WJ: '86- 2; WUG: '89- 4; WCp: '98- 1; ECp: '97- 2, '99- 3; Won GP 2000, 2nd 1998. GER champion 1997-2000.
Progression at DT: 1981- 27.70, 1982- 43.80, 1983- 50.04, 1984- 51.16, 1985- 56.94, 1986- 64.34, 1987- 66.34, 1988- 65.56, 1989- 68.26, 1990- 67.42, 1991- 61.22, 1992- 61.61, 1993- 62.06, 1994- 62.76, 1995- 62.26, 1996- 66.66, 1997- 67.66, 1998- 68.91, 1999- 69.51, 2000- 68.06. pb SP 15.02 '85.

Heike DRECHSLER b. 16 Dec 1964 Gera 1.81m 68kg. née Daute. Karlsruher SC.
At LJ/R- 4x100mR: OG: '88- 2 (3 100m & 200m), '92- 1, '00- 1; WCh: '83 1, '87 3 (2 100m), '91- 2/3R, '93- 1, '95- 9 (dnf Hep), '97-4; EC: '82- 4, '86- 1 (1 200m), '90- 1 (2 200m), '94- 1, '98- 1; WI: '87- 1 (1 200m), '91- 2, '97- 7, '01- 5; EI: '83- 3, '85- 3, '86- 1, '87- 1, '88- 1, '94- 1, '00- 2; EJ: '81- 1; WCp: '85- 1, '92- 1, '98- 1; ECp: '83- 1, '85- 2, '87- 1/1R (2 4x400mR), '91- 1/2R, '93-4-5: 1/1/1. Won GDR LJ 1981, 1983-8, 1990; 200m 1986, 1988; GER LJ 1991-2, 1994-5, 1998-2000; 100m 1992; GWG LJ 1994. Won GP LJ 1990, 1992, 2000 (2nd 1996, 3rd 1994); won overall 1992 (2nd 1990).
World records: three LJ 1985-6, two 200m 1986. WIB: LJ (6): 6.88 '83, 6.99 '84 & '85, 7.25 & 7.29 '86, 7.37 '88; 100y: 10.24 '86, 10.24 & 10.15 '87; 200m: 22.27 '87. World junior LJ records 1981 and 1982, heptathlon 1981. 8 GDR LJ records 1983-8, GER record 1992.
Progression at 100m, 200m, LJ, Hep: 1977- 13.1, 4.40; 1978- 5.69, 1979- 12.3, 6.07; 1980- 6.64/6.70w, 5780; 1981- 11.75, 24.16, 6.91/7.01w, 5812; 1982- 6.98, 1983- 7.14/7.27w, 1984- 7.40, 1985- 23.19, 7.44; 1986- 10.91/10.80w, 21.71, 7.45; 1987- 10.95, 22.18, 7.40; 1988- 10.91/10.85w, 21.84, 7.48; 1990- 11.14, 22.19, 7.30; 1991- 11.09, 22.58/22.4, 7.37/7.39w; 1992- 11.24, 7.48/7.63Aw; 1993- 11.36, 23.16, 7.21; 1994- 11.38, 22.84, 7.29/7.39Aw, 6741; 1995- 23.02i/23.04, 7.09i/7.07, 6375; 1996- 23.17i, 6.96i/ 6.75/6.87w; 1997- 11.70, 6.95i/6.89/7.02w; 1998- 11.82w, 7.16; 1999- 6.91, 2000- 6.99/7.07w. pbs: 800m 2:11.53 '94, 100mh 13.34 '94, HJ 1.88i '92, TJ 13.94i '97, 13.35 '93; SP 13.88 '95, JT 40.64 '94.
World age records for long jump each age 15-19. The youngest gold medallist of the 1983 world championships, at LJ she had 27 successive wins until injured at the 1987 World Champs and from 1982 to 2000 won 235 of 312 competitions. She has had more than 409 jumps and 159 competitions over 7m (her 100th came at the 1992 Olympics). Her 7.63w at the high altitude of Sestriere in 1992 was the first 25 ft long jump by a woman; the wind just over the legal limit at +2.1. Missed 1996 Olympics and 1999 Worlds through injury, but came back in triumph in 2000 to regain her Olympic title. In all she has won 29 GDR/GER LJ titles – 14 indoors (1981, 1983-4, 1986-8, 1991-5, 1997, 1999-2000) 15 out. She made a sensational breakthrough in 1986 into a great sprinter, winning the GDR indoor 100y title in 10.24, and equalling Marita Koch's world 200m record and she showed further versatility with a 50.0 400m relay leg in the 1987 European Cup. In her first heptathlon since her world junior record in 1981, she scored a marvellous 6741 points to win at Talence in 1994.
Son, Toni Drechsler, born 1 Nov 1989. Her partner and coach is French decathlete Alain Blondel.

Karin ERTL b. 23 Jun 1974 Immenstadt 1.76m 60kg. née Specht. LAC Quelle Fürth/München.
At Hep: OG: '00- 7; WCh: '99- 6; EC: '98- 7; EJ: '93- 2; ECp: '97- 6. German champion 1999. At Pen: WI: '01- 3; EI: '98- 3, '00- 1.
Progression at Hep: 1993- 5591, 1994- 5779, 1995- 5871, 1996- 6047, 1997- 6128, 1998- 6366, 1999- 6332, 2000- 6396. pbs: 100m 12.10 '97, 200m 23.92 '98, 800m 2:16.08 '99, 60mh 8.26i 98, 100mh 13.24 '98, HJ 1.87 '96, LJ 6.47 '98, SP 14.79i '01, 14.17 '00; JT 45.07 '99, Pen 4678i '01.

Claudia GESELL b. 18 Dec 1977 Tirschenreuth 1.70m 58kg. TSV Bayer Leverkusen.
At 800m: OG: '00- sf; WCh: '99- sf; WJ: '96- 1 (1R); EU23: '97- 4, '99- 1. Won GER 1998-2000.
Progression at 800m: 1993- 2:12.16, 1994- 2:18.61, 1995- 2:07.20, 1996- 2:02.67, 1997- 2:02.52, 1998- 2:01.28, 1999- 1:59.87, 2000-

1:58.34. pbs: 400m 54.37 '96, 1000m 2:37.86 '99. Won a German Universities title at triathlon.

Nicole HUMBERT b. 5 Feb 1972 Landau/Pfalz 1.68m 53kg. née Rieger. ASV Landau.
At PV: OG: '00- 5; WCh: '99- 5; EC: '98- 2; WI: '99- 3=; EI: '98- 5; ECp: '98- 3, '99- 1.
Pole vault records: Seven European 1989-94, world 1994, 21 German 1989-2000. World indoor 1999, eleven European 1991-9.
Progression at PV: 1988- 2.90, 1989- 3.50, 1990- 3.45, 1991- 3.90, 1992- 3.92, 1993- 3.80, 1994- 4.08i/4.00, 1995- 4.01, 1996- 4.16, 1997- 4.17i/4.10, 1998- 4.35/4.36ex, 1999- 4.56i/4.41, 2000- 4.50. pbs: HJ 1.57 '91, LJ 5.43 '89.
An early pioneer of pole vaulting in Europe, she set nine European indoor records to 4.08 in 1994, and regained the record with 4.51 and then a WIR 4.56 in February 1999.

Nadine KLEINERT-SCHMITT b. 20 Oct 1975 Magdeburg 1.90m 90kg. Née Kleinert. SC Magdeburg.
At SP: OG: '00- 8; WCh: '97- 7, '99- 2; EC: '98- 6; WJ: '92- 12, '94- 6; EU23: '97- 1; EJ: '93- 2; WI: '99- 5, '01- 4; EI: '00- 2; ECp: '99- 2. Won GP 1999. German champion 1998, 2000.
Progression at SP: 1990- 13.85, 1991- 15.08, 1992- 16.32, 1993- 17.07, 1994- 17.44, 1995- 17.13, 1996- 18.37, 1997- 18.91, 1998- 19.22, 1999- 19.61, 2000- 19.81. pb DT 50.20 '00.

Astrid KUMBERNUSS b. 5 Feb 1970 Grevesmühlen 1.86m 89kg. SC Neubrandenburg.
At SP (DT): OG: '96- 1, '00- 3; WCh: '93- 6, '95- 1, '97- 1, '99- 1; EC: '90- 1, '94- 2; WI: '97- 2; EI: '92- 3, '94- 1, '96- 1, '00- 3; WJ: '88- (2); EJ: '87- (2), '89- 1 (1); WCp: '94- 3; ECp: '91-4-5-6-7-00: 2/1/1/1/1/1. Won GP 1995, 1997 (and Overall), 2nd 1993, 1999; 3rd 1991. Won GER SP 1995, 1999.
World junior shot record 1989.
Progression at SP, DT: 1983- 11.16, 33.48; 1984- 13.44/14.01i, 44.00; 1985- 14.23, 46.96; 1986- 15.39, 53.92; 1987- 18.20, 63.88; 1988- 18.73, 66.60; 1989- 20.54, 64.74; 1990- 20.77, 65.42; 1991- 19.67, 60.88; 1992- 20.03i/19.69, 1993- 19.92, 59.64; 1994- 20.06, 1995- 21.22, 59.90; 1996- 20.97, 1997- 21.22, 1999- 19.85, 2000- 20.23.
Unbeaten in 51 competitions 1995-6. In 1995 she had eight GP wins prior to the final, and won the world title by 1.18m, the largest ever margin of victory at World/Olympic level. She had knee surgery in November 1997 and missed the 1998 season; her son Philipp was born on 7 July 1998. Returned to take third world title in 1999.

Simone MATHES b. 13 Mar 1975 Stadtsteinach 1.71m 77kg. TSV Beyer Leverkusen.
At HT: WCh: '99- 7; EC: '98- 4; EU23: '97- 2; ECp: '97- 7. German champion 1993-4, 1997-9.
Nine German hammer records 1994-9.
Progression at HT: 1992- 55.42, 1993- 55.42, 1994- 59.02, 1995- 64.58, 1996- 61.86, 1997- 64.54, 1998- 66.17, 1999- 67.13, 2000- 65.90. pbs: SP 13.10 '91, DT 46.40 '92.

Irina MIKITENKO b. 23 Aug 1972 Bakankas, Kazahstan 1.58m 49kg. LG Eintracht Frankfurt.
At 5000m: OG: '96- h, '00- 5; WCh: '99- 4; ECp: '99-00: 2/2. At 10000m: EC: '98- 8; WCp: '98- 5. 3rd GP 3000m 1999. World 4k CC: '00- 19. Won Central Asian 1500m 1995; German 10000m 1998, 5000m 1999-2000.
German records 3000m 2000, 5000m (3) 1999.
Progression at 5000m, 10000m: 1995- 15:47.85, 1996- 15:49.59, 1997- 15:48.29, 1998- 15:18.86, 32:10.61; 1999- 14:42.03, 31:38.68; 2000- 14:43.59. pbs: 800m 2:09.97 '98, 1500m 4:06.68 '99, 3000m 8:30.39 '00
German parents; changed nationality from Kazakhstan to Germany in March 1998.

Kirsten MÜNCHOW b. 21 Jan 1977 Auetal-Rehren 1.72m 75kg. LG Eintracht Frankfurt. Designer.
At HT: OG: '00- 3; WCh: '99- 8; EC: '98- 3; EU23: '97- 5, '99- 2; ECp: '98-9-00: 2/5/3. German champion 2000.
Four German hammer records 1998-2000.
Progression at HT: 1992- 42.48, 1994- 50.96, 1995- 57.62, 1996- 59.40, 1997- 63.06, 1998- 66.82, 1999- 66.08, 2000- 69.28. pbs: SP 12.65 '98, DT 37.88 '96.

Steffi NERIUS b. 1 Jul 1972 Bergen/Rügen 1.78m 72kg. TSV Bayer Leverkusen. PE teacher.
At JT: OG: '96- 9, '00- 4; WCh: '93- 9, '95- 11, '99- dnq 16; EC: '98- 6; EJ: '91- 3; WUG: '97- 5; WCp: '92- 6; ECp: '95- 1. 2nd GP 1996.
Progression at JT: 1985- 30.12, 1987- 45.16, 1988- 48.00, 1989- 56.88, 1990- 56.14, 1991- 60.02, 1992- 59.46, 1993- 63.88, 1995- 68.42, 1996- 69.42, 1997- 64.58, 1998- 67.33; new: 1999- 61.56. 2000- 65.76.

Andrea **PHILIPP** b. 29 Jul 1971 Bützow 1.65m 54kg. LG Olympia Dortmund.
At 100m/(200m)/4x100mR: OG: '92- qf, '96- qf; WCh: '91- qf; '93- 5R, '97- sf/4R, '99- sf/3=; EC: '98- 2R; WJ: '90- 1; EJ: '89- 3R; WCp: '98- 6/3R; ECp: '91/3- 2R/3R, '97- 2/2/3R, '98- 3/2R, '99- 7/3R, '00- 4/3/3R. Won German 100m 1997-9, 200m 1999-2000.
Indoor world record 4x200m 1999.
Progression at 100m, 200m: 1985- 12.0, 1986- 11.8, 24.9; 1987- 11.93, 25.5; 1988- 11.78, 1989- 11.71, 1990- 11.36, 23.95; 1991- 11.45, 1992- 11.41/11.34w, 1993- 11.51, 23.49; 1994- 11.50/11.26w, 23.56; 1995- 11.34, 23.42; 1996- 11.25, 23.22w; 1997- 11.05, 22.75; 1998- 11.17, 23.12/22.77w; 1999- 11.06, 22.25; 2000- 11.21/11.15w, 22.69. pbs: 50m 6.30i '92, 60m 7.19i '99.
Missed 2000 Olympics through injury.

Anja **RÜCKER** b. 20 Dec 1972 Lobenstein 1.74m 56kg. TuS Jena.
At 400m/4x400mR: OG: '92- qf, '96- 3R; WCh: '93- sf; '97- 1R, '99- 2/3R; EC: '94- 5/3R; WI: '97- 3R; WJ: '90- 8/4R; EJ: '89- 1R, '91- 2/1R; EU23:

'94- 1/1R; WCp: '92- 6, '94- 8/2R; ECp: '93- 5/3R, '94- dnf, '99- 3. German champion 1992.
Progression at 400m: 1986- 56.25, 1987- 55.39, 1988- 54.51, 1989- 54.47, 1990- 53.01, 1991- 52.73, 1992- 51.33, 1993- 51.91, 1994- 51.42, 1996- 51.11, 1997- 51.36, 1999- 49.74, 2000- 51.99i/52.05. pbs: 100m 11.8 '89, 12.00 '96; 200m 23.34i '00, 23.40 '96; 300m 36.21+ '99.
Withdrew from 2000 Olympic team due to Achilles tendon injury.

Anastasija **'Nastja' RYSHICH** b. 19 Sep 1977 Omsk, Russia 1.70m 59kg. LAZ Zweibrücken.
At PV: WCh: '99- nh; EC: '98- 4=; WI: '99- 1; EU23: '99- 2.
Pole vault records: four World junior and five European junior 1996, two German 1999.
Progression at PV: 1992- 2.90, 1993- 3.50, 1994- 3.71, 1995- 3.80, 1996- 4.15, 1997- 4.10, 1998- 4.32/4.42ex, 1999- 4.50i/4.44, 2000- 4.31.
Her family left Omsk in Siberia in 1992 to live in Ulm. Her mother Yekaterina Ryzhikh (b. 20 Jan 1959) had a high jump best of 1.91i in 1985 and her father, Vladimir, is a pole vault coach.

Susen TIEDTKE b. 23 Jan 1969 Berlin 1.74m 56kg. LAC Erdgas Chemnitz. Married US long jumper Joe Greene 4 Dec 1993, divorced in 1998.
At LJ: OG: '92- 8, '00- 6; WCh: '91- 5, '93- 9, '97- 6, '99- 7; EC: '98- 8; WI: '93- 2, '95- 3; EJ: '87- 3; ECp: '97-8-00: 3/4/4. GER champion 1993, 1997.
Progression at LJ: 1986- 6.22, 1987- 6.44, 1988- 6.08, 1989- 6.53, 1990- 6.58, 1991- 7.00, 1992- 6.74/7.02w, 1993- 6.85/7.19Aw, 1994- 6.54/6.65i/ 6.81w, 1995- 6.90i, 1997- 6.86, 1998- 6.91, 1999- 6.78, 2000- 6.78.
Drugs ban (2 years) following positive test 13 Mar 1995. Was GDR youth champion gymnast at 13, and a candidate for the 1984 Olympics, which the GDR boycotted. Coached by her father Jürgen Tiedtke (PV 4.50 in 1964). In 1966 her mother Ingrid was 5th in the European 200m and ran a pb of 23.5. Her uncle Manfred Tiedtke was 10th in 1968 OG decathlon.

Ulrike URBANSKY b. 6 Apr 1977 Jena 1.70m 48kg. Bayer Leverkusen
At 400mh/4x400m: OG: '00- sf; WCh: '99- sf; EC: '98- 6; WJ: '94- 3R, '96- 1/1R; EU23: '99- 2; EJ: '95- 2; WUG: '99- 3; WCp: '98- 1R; ECp: '00: 2. German champion 2000.
Progression at 400mh: 1994- 58.27, 1995- 57.05, 1996- 56.09, 1997- 56.52, 1998- 55.38, 1999- 54.67, 2000- 54.57. pbs: 200m 24.16 '98, 400m 52.51i '99, 52.58 '98; 800m 2:02.96 '96, 1500m 4:41.64 '92, 3000m 10:01.92 '93.

Ilke WYLUDDA b. 28 Mar 1969 Leipzig 1.84m 95kg. LAC Erdgas Chemnitz.
At DT: OG: '92- 9, '96- 1, '00- 7; WCh: '87- 4, '91- 2, '93- 11, '95- 2; EC: '90- 1, '94- 1, '98- 6; WJ: '86- 1, '88- 1; EJ: '85- 1 (2 SP), '87- 1 (1 SP); WCp: '89- 1, '92- 2, '94- 1; ECp: '89-91-4-5-6: 1/1/1/2/1. Won GDR DT 1989-90, GER 1991-2, 1994-6. Won GWG 1990, GP 1990, 1992, 1994, 1996.
Eleven world junior records at discus 1986-8 and two at shot 1987-8.
Progression at SP, DT: 1982- 13.72, 46.54; 1983- 15.18, 51.12; 1984- 16.42, 57.74; 1985- 18.27, 62.36; 1986- 19.08, 65.86; 1987- 20.11, 71.64; 1988- 20.23, 74.40; 1989- 19.18, 74.56; 1990- 18.42, 71.10; 1991- 18.96, 69.12; 1992- 70.96, 1993- 64.06, 1994- 68.72, 1995- 69.20, 1996- 69.66, 1998- 63.46, 1999- 62.66, 2000- 65.76.
Holds GDR age records for DT age 13-15, SP 14-15 as well as discus world bests each age 15-19. Unbeaten in her senior career, 1989 to World championships 1991, where she was beaten by Tsvetanka Khristova after 41 successive discus victories. Operation on right knee March 1993 and left knee September 1993; two Achilles operations meant that she missed 1997 season.

GHANA

Governing body: Ghana Amateur Athletic Association, National Sports Council, PO Box 1272, Accra. Founded 1944.

Leonard MYLES-MILLS b. 9 May 1973 Accra 1.72m 68kg. Was at Brigham Young University, USA.
At 100m: OG: '00- sf; WCh: '99- sf; AfG: '99- 1; AfCh: '98- 3. Won NCAA 1998-9.
Ghana 100m record 1999. Two African records 60m indoors 1999.
Progression at 100m: 1995- 10.42, 1996- 10.43, 1997- 10.39A, 1998- 10.10, 1999- 9.98, 2000- 10.15. pbs: 50m 5.64i '00, 55m 6.02iA '97, 60m 6.45iA '99, 6.52i '00, 200m 20.54 '98, 20.11wA '99.
Younger brother of John Myles-Mills, 2nd 1989 WI 60m, pb 100m 10.21 '88.

Abdul **Aziz ZAKARI** b. 8 Jun 1976 1.71m 68kg.
At 100m (/200m): OG: '00- dnf; WCh: '97- sf; CG: '98- sf/sf; AfCh: '98/4, '00-1/1/1R.
Progression at 100m, 200m: 1995- 10.4, 21.36/21.0; 1996- 10.30, 20.90; 1997- 10.26, 20.88; 1998- 10.29, 20.62; 1999 10.35/10.08w, 20.84; 2000- 10.06, 20.23.

GREECE

Governing body: Hellenic Amateur Athletic Association (SEGAS), 137 Siggroú Avenue, 171 21 Nea Smirni, Athens. Founded 1897.
National Championships first held in 1896 (men), 1930 (women). **2000 Champions**: **Men**: 100m: Ággelos Pavlakákis 10.13, 200m/400m: Anastásios Goúsis 20.69/45.63, 800m: Panayiótis Stroubákos 1:46.62, 1500m: Stávros Karrés 3:48.30, 5000m/10000m: Panayiótis Haramís 13:52.44/29:17.43, Mar: Nikólaos Poliás 2:20:50, 3000mSt: Nikólaos Maxoúris 8.58.11, 110mh: Dimítrios Siatoúnis 13.94, 400mh: Periklís Iakovákis 50.26, HJ: Lábros Papakóstas 2.34, PV: Mários Evaggélou 5.30, LJ: Konstadínos

Koukodímos 7.85, TJ: Stamátios Lénis 16.77, SP: Váios Tíggas 18.61, DT: Stéfanos Kónstas 57.95, HT: Aléxandros Papadimitríou 80.45, JT: Konstadínos Gatsioúdis 87.89, Dec: Georgios Andreou CYP 7801, 20kmW: Theódoros Stamatópoulos 1:25:37, 50kmW: Spirídon Kastánis 3:56:47. **Women**: 100m: Ekateríni Thánou 10.93, 200m: Ekateríni Kóffa 23.33, 400m: Marína Vasarmídou 53.90, 800m: Ekateríni Koutalá 2:05.52, 1500m: María Tsírba 4:17.87, 5000m: María Polízou 16:16.04, 10000m: Yeoryía Abatzídou 34:40.50, Mar: Vasilikí Sikopéti 3:04:04, 100mh: Hristiána Tabáki 13.35, 400mh: Hrísa Goudenoúdi 58.09, HJ: María Hotokourídou 1.85, PV: Yeoryía Tsiliggíri 4.15, LJ: Hristína Athanasíou 6.34, TJ: Ioánna Kafetzí 13.65, SP: Kalliópi Ouzoúni 18.59, DT: Anastasía Kelesídou 64.00, HT: Evdokía Tsámoglou 63.20, JT: Aggelikí Tsiolakoúdi 59.83, Hep: Asimína Vanakára 5927, 20kmW: Hristína Déskou 1:31:38.

Konstadínos '**Kostas**' **GATSIOUDIS** b. 17 Dec 1973 Didimótiho 1.89m 94kg. Panellínios GS (Athens). Officer of the Fire Brigade.
At JT: OG: '96- 10, '00- 6; WCh: '93- dnq 17, '97- 3, '99- 2; EC: '94- dnq 14; WJ: '90- 6, '92- 3; EJ: '91- 9; ECp: '97-9-00: 2/3/2. Won GP 1999 (2nd overall), EU23Cp 1994, Greek champion 1992-4, 1999-2000; Balkan 1992, Med G 1997.
Eleven Greek javelin records 1992-2000. World junior record 1992.
Progression at JT: 1990- 70.20, 1991- 72.58, 1992- 80.30, 1993- 78.44, 1994- 83.82, 1995- 82.70, 1996- 87.12, 1997- 89.22, 1998- 88.13, 1999- 89.84, 2000- 91.69.
Threw Greek record 87.12 in qualifying at 1996 Olympics, but only 81.46 in the final. Over 84m in all 35 competitions in 1999 and 2000.

Konstadínos KEDÉRIS b. 11 Jun 1973 Mitilíni 1.80m 78kg. Olympiakós SF Piraeus. Air Force officer. PE Graduate of Thessaloníki University.
At 200m: OG: '00- 1; WCh: '99- fq; WJ: '92- 6; EI: '00- 5; ECp: '00- 3. At 400m: EC: '98- sf; EJ: '91- 4; ECp: '99- 3. Won MedG 400m 1993, Greek champion 200m 1999, 400m 1991-3, 1998.
Greek records 200m (3) 2000, 400m 1993, 1998.
Progression at 200m: 1991- 21.63, 1992- 21.05, 1993- 20.76, 1994- 20.93i, 1995- 20.89, 1996- 21.17, 1997- 20.83/20.64w, 1999- 20.50, 2000- 20.09. pbs: 100m 10.16 '00, 300m 32,99i '99, 400m 45.60 '98.
Kedéris started 2000 by running a Greek record of 20.25 for 200m and ended it by becoming the most surprising gold medallist of the Olympic Games in Sydney, where he improved his Greek record twice more – to 20.14 and 20.09. From early on he was considered a rare talent with big potential in both 200m/400m. However a series of injuries from the 1994 indoor season prevented his evolution for many years. In March 2000 he eventually decided to leave Thessaloníki due to its poor training facilities, relocate to Athens and concentrate on 200m.

Aléxandros PAPADIMITRÍOU b. 18 Jun 1973 Lárisa 1.83m 123kg, G.S. Iraklís Thessaloníki. MSc in kinesiology at UTEP, Texas, USA.
At HT: OG: '96- dnq 16; '00- 12; WCh: '97- dnq 19, '99- dnq 27; WJ: '92- 6; EC: '98- dnq 27; EU23: '94- 2; EJ: '91- 7; ECp: '97-00: 3/2. Greek champion 1994-7, 2000; Balkan 1997, 2000.
Three Greek hammer records 1996-2000.
Progression at HT: 1990- 61.72, 1991- 65.82, 1992- 69.48, 1993- 70.74, 1994- 73.74, 1995- 74.80, 1996- 77.84, 1997- 76.72, 1998- 77.60, 1999- 78.88, 2000- 80.45.

Hrístos POLÍHRONÍOU b. 31 Mar 1972 Athína 1.86m 107kg. Olympiakós SF Piraeus. Studied PE at Athens University.
At HT: OG: '96- dnq, '00- dnq 24; WCh: '95/97- dnq, '99- 6; EC: '98- 6; WJ: '90- 9; EJ: '91- 5; WUG: '99- 2; ECp: '99- 1. Greek champion 1998-9.
Five Greek hammer records 1995-9.
Progression at HT: 1989- 60.00, 1990- 63.52, 1991- 67.74, 1992- 67.50, 1993- 73.16, 1994- 73.04, 1995- 76.68, 1996- 77.36, 1997- 75.58, 1998- 78.92, 1999- 79.83, 2000- 79.57.

Women

Anastasía KELESÍDOU b. 28 Nov 1972 Hamburg, Germany 1.92m 91kg. GS Iraklís Thessaloníki. Navy Officer. PE graduate of Thessaloniki University.
At DT: OG: '96- dnq 18, '00- 2; WCh: '95- 11, '97- dnq 15, '99- 2; EC: '94- dnq 22, '98- 7; EU23: '94- 2; EJ: '91- 11; ECp: '00- 3. Won Med G 1997, Greek 1991, 1993-7, 1999-2000.
Eight Greek discus records 1994-9.
Progression at DT: 1987- 41.82, 1988- 45.00, 1989- 48.36/49.74u, 1990- 47.90, 1991- 50.90, 1992- 54.34, 1993- 57.44, 1994- 60.50, 1995- 60.92, 1996- 62.76, 1997- 66.18, 1998- 66.18, 1999- 67.70, 2000- 67.12. pb SP 12.68 '92.

Kalliópi OUZOÚNI b. 8 Feb 1973 Thessaloniki 1.83m 83kg. Panellínios GS (Athens). Army officer. PE graduate of Thessaloníki University.
At SP: OG: '00- 7; WCh: '97- dnq, '99- dnq 16; EU23: '94- 3; ECp: '00- 2. Greek champion 1993-4, 1996, 1998-2000.
Two Greek shot records 2000.
Progression at SP: 1991- 14.38, 1992- 15.03i/15.00, 1993- 15.86, 1994- 16.69, 1995- 17.47, 1996- 17.07i/16.73, 1997- 18.12i/18.06, 1998- 18.13, 1999- 18.39, 2000- 19.03i/18.63. pb DT 46.24 '92.
Engaged to javelin thrower Dimítrios Polimérou (pb 81.20 '99, 1 EJ 1993).

Ekateríni '**Kateŕina**' **THÁNOU** b. 1 Feb 1975 Athína 1.65m 61kg. Olympiakós SF Piraeus. Air Force Officer. Was at University of Athens.
At 100m: OG: '96- qf, '00- 2; WCh: '95- sf, '97- sf, '99- 3; EC: '94- qf, '98- 3; WJ: '94- 4; WUG: '95- 2, '97- 1. At 60m: WI: '99- 1; EI: '96- 1, '98- 4, '00- 1. Won GRE 100m 1995, 2000; Med G 100m 1997.
Seven Greek 100m records 1995-9.

Progression at 100m: 1993- 12.09/12.07w, 1994- 11.43, 1995- 11.09, 1996- 11.28, 1997- 11.13, 1998- 10.87/10.8w, 1999- 10.83/10.77w, 2000- 10.91/ 10.84w. pbs: 50m 6.01+ '99, 60m 6.96i/6.96+ '99, 200m 24.46/23.93w '94.
Brilliant run to win 1999 World Indoor 60m; Greek records in semi and final 1998 Europeans and in quarter and semi at 1999 Worlds.

Paraskeví TSIAMÍTA b. 10 Mar 1972 Vólos 1.74m 60kg. Panellínios GS (Athens). Air Force officer. PE graduate of Athens University.
At TJ: WCh: '99- 1; EC: '98- 9; WI: '99- 5; EU23: '94- 3. 2nd GP 1999. At LJ: EJ: '87- dnq. Won Greek LJ 1998, TJ 1999.
Three Greek triple jump records 1999.
Progression at TJ: 1994- 13.17, 1995- 13.27, 1998- 14.23, 1999- 15.07. pb LJ 6.93 '99.
Jumped 5.34 LJ at age 12 in 1984 and 6.00/6.07w in 1987 at 15 at the European Juniors. Out of action 1992-3 and 1996-7 due to injuries, studies and lack of motivation, but remained fit by working as aerobics teacher. Triple jumped 13.07i in her comeback competition in 1998, adding 2m with her world-leading mark of 1999. Suffered from a stress fracture in 2000.

Stilianí '**Stella**' **TSIKOÚNA** b. 19 Oct 1972 Halkída 1.71m 88kg. ASE Doúka (Athens). Navy officer. Was at University of Texas, El Paso, USA. PE student at Athens University.
At DT: OG: '96- dnq 31, '00- 5; WCh: '95- dnq 29, '97- 7, '99- 8; EC: '98- 12. Greek champion 1992, Balkan 2000.
Two Greek records 1992.
Progression at DT: 1987- 41.84, 1988- 44.18, 1989- 43.90, 1990- 45.38, 1991- 52.10, 1992- 56.48, 1993- 55.48, 1994- 56.98, 1995- 61.02, 1996- 61.30A, 1997- 63.30, 1998- 65.00, 1999- 64.16, 2000- 65.13. pb SP 14.78i '95.

Miréla TZELÍLI b. 21 Dec 1976 Dirráhio (Durrás), Albania 1.65m 65kg, née Manjani. Olympiakós SF Piraeus. Navy Officer.
At JT: OG: '96- dnq 24, '00- 2; WCh: '95- 12, '97- 11, '99- 1; EC: '94- dnq 22, 98- 9; WJ: '94- 8; EJ: '95- 2; ECp: '00- 3. Greek champion 1999, Balkan 1994, 1997.
Two World records (64.99 and 67.09) new javelin 1999. Six Greek records 1999-2000.
Progression at JT: 1993- 54.86, 1994- 57.20, 1995- 62.40, 1996- 62.46, 1997- 63.50, 1998- 65.14, 1999- 67.09, 2000- 67.51.
Switched from Albania to become Greek citizen in 1997. Married to weightlifter Yeóryios Tzelílis, 4th 1996 Olympics 64kg, 2nd 1999 Worlds 69kg.

Ólga-Anastasia VASDÉKI b. 26 Sep 1973 Vólos 1.74m 59kg. Panellínios GS (Athens). Harbour guard officer. PE graduate of Athens University
At TJ: OG: '96- 5, '00- 7; WCh: '97- 4, '99- 3; EC: '98- 1; EI: '96- 3, '98- 4; WCp: '98- 1. Won GRE 1993, 1995-6, 1998; Med G 1997.
Eleven Greek triple jump records 1993-8.
Progression at TJ: 1992- 12.77, 1993- 13.37, 1994- 13.25i, 1995- 13.45/13.73w, 1996- 14.48/14.51w, 1997- 14.62, 1998- 14.64A/14.59, 1999- 14.67, 2000- 14.26. pb LJ 6.60 '98, 6.66w '99.
Huge improvement in 1996. Her brother Spirídon Vasdékis (b. 23 Jan 1970) had LJ best of 8.19 '95 and 8.29Aw '96, 3 EI '96, 8 WI '97, 16 OG '92, 14 OG '96.

Ekateríni '**Katerina**' **VÓGGOLI** b. 30 Oct 1970 Lárisa 1.75m 87kg. Olympiakós SF Piraeus. PE graduate of Thessaloniki University.
At DT: OG: '96- dnq 22, '00- 9; WCh: '99- 11; EC: '98- 5; WJ: '88- 10. Greek champion 1989-90, 1998, Balkan 1994.
Four Greek discus records 1992-4.
Progression at DT: 1985- 39.84, 1986- 46.10, 1987- 46.74, 1988- 51.18, 1989- 51.96, 1990- 51.94, 1991- 53.24, 1992- 57.86, 1993- 59.70, 1994- 62.32, 1996- 60.34, 1997- 61.24, 1998- 64.78, 1999- 64.82, 2000- 64.35. pb SP 13.53 '00.

Níki XÁNTHOU b. 11 Oct 1973 Rhodos 1.74m 56kg. Olympiakós SF Piraeus. Harbour guard officer.
At LJ: OG: '96- 4, '00- dnq 18; WCh: '95- dnq 15, '97- 2, '99- dnq 26; EC: '94- 10; WJ: '92- 8, WI: '95- 9, '97- 5, '99- 4; EI: '98- 5, '00- 8; EU23: '94- 1. Greek champion 1992, 1995, 1997, 1999; Med G 1997.
Nine Greek long jump records 1994-7.
Progression at LJ: 1987- 5.32, 1988- 5.42, 1989- 5.60/5.73w, 1990- 5.96, 1991- 5.90/5.99w, 1992- 6.60, 1993- 6.09, 1994- 6.74, 1995- 6.94/7.12Aw, 1996- 7.01, 1997- 7.03, 1998- 6.83/6.84w, 1999- 6.98/7.01w, 2000- 6.81.
Married to her coach Dimítrios Hatzópoulos (pb LJ 8.07 '94, 8.08w '89).

GUATEMALA

Governing body: Federación National de Atletismo, Palacio de los Deportes, 26 Calle 9-31, Zona 5, Guatemala Ciudad. Founded 1896

Julio MARTÍNEZ b. 27 Sep 1973 1.65m 44kg.
At 20kmW: OG: '96- dq, '00- 43; WCh: '97/99- dq; WCp: '97- 5; PAm: '95- 3, CAG: '93- 3, '98- 3. Won CAC 1997.
World road best 20km walk 1999, four Guatemalan 20km walk records 1995-9.
Progression at 20kmW: 1992- 1:28:55, 1993- 1:29:43, 1994- 1:26:51, 1995- 1:23:50, 1996- 1:22:22, 1997- 1:18:51, 1998- 1:19:42, 1999- 1:17:46, 2000- 1:23:13.
Set world road best for 20km walk at Eisenhüttenstadt in 1999 just a week after being disqualified while with the leaders in the World Cup.

HAITI

Governing body: Fédération Haitienne d'Athlétisme Amateur, BP 2405, Port-au-Prince. F'd 1969.

Dudley DORIVAL b. 1 Sep 1975 Elizabeth, New Jersey, USA 1.85m 77kg. Sales consultant, studied sociology at University of Connecticut, At 110mh: OG: '00- 7; WCh: '99- sf; WJ: '94- 2; WUG: '97- 3. At 60mh: WI: '01- 7.
Four Haitian 110mh records from 3 at 13.42 in 1999 to 2000.
Progression at 110mh: 1994- 13.79/13.65w, 1995- 13.53A, 1996- 13.60/13.59w, 1997- 13.48, 1998- 13.30, 1999- 13.38/13.29w, 2000- 13.33. pbs: 200m 20.64w '98, 50mh 6.50i '01, 55mh 7.16i '96, 60mh 7.55i '01.
Switched from USA to take up Haitian nationality (his parents are from Haiti) from July 1999.

HUNGARY

Governing body: Magyar Atlétikai Szövetség, 1143 Budapest, Dózsa György utca 1-3. Founded 1897.
National Championships first held in 1896 (men), 1932 (women). **2000 Champions**. **Men**: 100m: Viktor Kovács 10.41, 200m: Géza Pauer 20.93 (drugs dq Gábor Dobos 10.21/20.63), 400m: Attila Kilvinger 45.92, 800m: Balázs Korányi 1:50.24, 1500m: Balázs Tölgyesi 3:48.46, 5000m/HMar: Imre Berkovics 14:25.71/63:53, 10000m: Ferenc Sági 29:36.26, Mar: János Szemán 2:24:45, 3000mSt: Levente Tímár 9:02.95, 110mh: Levente Csillag 13.58, 400mh: Tibor Bédi 50.68, HJ: Román Fehér 2.16, PV: Deszö Szabó 5.00, LJ: Balázs Dömötör 7.77, TJ: Zsolt Czingler 17.06, SP: Zsolt Bíber 19.46, DT: Róbert Fazekas 65.07, HT: Balázs Kiss 79.22, JT: Gergely Horváth 77.30, Dec: Zsolt Kürtösi 8036, 20kmW: Sándor Urbanik 1:22:12, 50kmW: Zoltán Czukor 3:55:48. **Women**: 100m/200m: Enikö Szabó 11.73/23.35w, 400m: Barbara Petráhn 52.05, 800m: Judit Varga 2:03.75, 1500m/HMar/Mar: Erika Csomor 4:23.31/72:06/2:41:57, 5000m: Anikó Kálovics 16:06.31, 10000m: Beáta Rakonczai 33:37.86, 100mh: Zita Bálint 13.69, 400mh: Orsolya Dóczi 57.94 (drugs dq Judit Szekeres 57.63), HJ: Dóra Györffy 1.85, PV: Zsuzsanna Szabó 4.00, LJ/TJ: Zita Ajkler 6.63/13.74, SP/DT/HT: Katalin Divós 15.91/56.44/66.09, JT: Nikolett Szabó 59.92, Hep: Enikö Kiss 5811, 10kmW: Mónika Pesti 50:37, 20kmW: Anikó Szebenszky 1:30:31.

Adrián ANNUS b. 28 Jun 1973 Szeged 1.94m 102kg. Dobó SE.
At HT: OG: '96- dnq 28, '00- dnq 17; EC: '98- 8; WJ: '92- 11. Hungarian champion 1996.
Progression at HT: 1990- 50.80, 1991- 57.42, 1992- 68.50, 1993- 69.26, 1994- 72.56, 1995- 74.68, 1996- 76.48, 1997- 76.62, 1998- 81.22, 1999- 81.73, 2000- 78.15. pbs: SP 16.87 '99, DT 50.16 '95.

Zsolt CZINGLER b. 28 Apr 1971 Budapest 1.87m 72kg. Újpesti TE.
At TJ: OG: '96- dnq 24, '00- dnq 18; WCh: '93- dnq 30, '95- dnq, 97- dnq 34, '99- dnq; EC: '94- 11, '98- 7; WJ: '90- 10; EJ: '89- 6; WI: '99- 3; EI: '00- 4. Won HUN 1992, 1995-2000.
Hungarian triple jump record 1998.
Progression at TJ: 1986- 13.88, 1987- 14.72, 1988- 15.59, 1989- 15.93, 1990- 16.01, 1991- 16.20, 1992- 16.49, 1993- 16.87/17.25w, 1994- 16.51/16.68w, 1995- 16.73, 1996- 16.98, 1997- 16.90, 1998- 17.24, 1999- 17.15i/16.99, 2000- 17.06. pbs: HJ 2.17 '90, LJ 7.60 '96.

Róbert FAZEKAS b. 18 Aug 1975 Szombathely 1.93m 105kg. Dobó SE.
At DT: OG: '00- dnq 16; WCh: '99- 11; EC: '98- 4; EU23: '97- 6; WJ: '94- 6 (dnq 18 HT). HUN champion 1998, 2000.
Progression at DT: 1992- 40.08, 1993- 53.48, 1994- 58.00, 1995- 60.34, 1996- 55.08, 1997- 59.32, 1998- 66.61, 1999- 64.92, 2000- 66.11. pb HT 75.33 '98.

Tibor GÉCSEK b. 22 Sep 1964 Szentgotthárd 1.85m 107kg. Dobó SE. Entrepreneur, formerly diesel engine mechanic.
At HT: OG: '88- 6, '92- 4, '00- 7; WCh: '87- 7, '91- 4, '93- 3, '95- 3, '99- 4; EC: '90- 2, '94- 5, '98- 1; EJ: '83- 6; WCp: 92- 1, '98- 1; ECp: '91- 2. Won HUN 1986-94, 1999. Won GP 1988, 1998 (2nd 1990).
Six Hungarian hammer records 1987-98.
Progression at HT: 1980- 34.26, 1981- 50.62, 1982- 60.60, 1983- 67.90, 1984- 73.66, 1985- 77.62, 1986- 77.66, 1987- 79.14, 1988- 81.68, 1989- 77.30, 1990- 80.92, 1991- 80.72, 1992- 81.02, 1993- 81.00, 1994- 80.22, 1995- 80.98, 1996- 74.18dq, 1997- 77.00, 1998- 83.68, 1999- 82.57, 2000- 81.92. pbs: SP 14.65 '85, DT 48.72 '85.
Positive drugs test at Berlin on 30 Aug 1995 was originally overturned by the Hungarian federation, but confirmed as four-year ban in 1996. He returned, however, to competition in September 1997 with the reduction by the IAAF of such suspensions to two years. In 1998 he smashed his 10-year-old pb to win the European title, went on to win the Grand Prix Final and World Cup and add two national records to the four he had set in 1987-8.

Balázs KISS b. 21 Mar 1972 Veszprém 1.92m 115kg. VEDAC. Was at University of Southern California, USA.
At HT: OG: '96- 1; WCh: '95- 4, '97- 4, '99- dnq 20; EC: '94- 12, '98- 2; WUG: '93- 2, '95- 1, '97- 1; EJ: '91- 3. 2nd GP 1998, HUN champion 1995, 1998, 2000; won NCAA 1993-6 (5th 4-time winner).
Five Hungarian hammer records 1995-8.
Progression at HT: 1988- 56.24, 1989- 61.24, 1990- 62.82, 1991- 70.66, 1993- 77.18, 1994- 77.74, 1995- 82.56, 1996- 81.76, 1997- 82.90, 1998- 83.00, 1999- 80.87, 2000- 79.22. pb DT 39.72 '91.

Zoltán KÖVAGÓ b. 10 Apr 1979 Szolnok 2.04m 127kg. Szolnoki MÁV.
At DT: OG: '00- dnq; WJ: '96- 4, '98- 1; EJ: '97- 3.
Progression at DT: 1995- 49.78, 1996- 59.70, 1997- 62.16, 1998- 60.27, 1999- 63.23, 2000- 66.76. pb SP 15.72 '99.

Zsolt NÉMETH b.9 Nov 1971 Szombathely 1.90m 110kg. Dobó SE.
At HT: OG: '96- dnq 22, '00- dnq 25; WCh: '97- dnq 26, '99- 2; WJ: '90- 6; WUG: '99- 1. HUN champion 1997.
Progression at HT: 1986- 41.00, 1987- 51.02, 1988- 56.60, 1989- 61.60, 1990- 67.66, 1991- 68.32, 1992- 71.14, 1993- 68.88, 1994- 73.14, 1995- 75.22, 1996- 77.48, 1997- 76.04, 1998- 80.19, 1999- 81.56, 2000- 80.02. pbs: SP 18.51 '00, DT 54.33 '98.

Attila ZSIVÓCZKY b. 29 Apr 1977 Budapest 1.93m 82kg. Újpesti TE. Was at Kansas State University, USA.
At Dec: OG: '00- 8; WCh: '99- 10; EC: '98- 16; WJ: '96- 1; EU23: '97- 4, '99- 1; ECp: '98- 5, '99- 5. At Hep: EI: '00- 4.
Progression at Dec: 1995- 7242, 1996- 7582, 1997- 7804, 1998- 8103, 1999- 8379, 2000- 8554. pbs: 100m 11.10/10.64w '00, 400m 47.93 '00, 1500m 4:20.94 '99, 110mh 14.87 '00, HJ 2.23i '98, 2.22 '94; PV 4.90i '00, 4.80 '99; LJ 7.31 '99, SP 15.72 '00, DT 47.43 '00, JT 65.87 '00, Hep 6033i '00.

Women

Katalin DIVÓS b. 11 May 1974 Szombathely 1.80m 84kg. Dobó SE and AC Pardubice, CZE
At HT: OG: '00- dnq 13; WCh: '99- 4; EC: '98- 5; Won HUN HT 1995-2000, SP & DT 1998-2000.
23 Hungarian hammer records 1995-2000.
Progression at HT: 1991- 45.94, 1992- 50.30, 1993- 50.76, 1994- 53.72, 1995- 55.42, 1996- 54.48, 1997- 59.88, 1998- 63.95, 1999- 67.64, 2000- 68.98. pbs: SP 16.04 '99, DT 56.44 '00.

Nikolett SZABÓ b. 3 Mar 1980 Budapest 1.68m 65kg. FTC.
At JT: OG: '00- dnq 14; WCh: '97- dnq 19; EC: '98- 8; WJ; '96- 2, '98- 4; EJ: '95- 7, '97- 1, '99- 1. HUN champion 1997-2000.
Hungarian record new javelin 1999.
Progression at JT: 1993- 45.28, 1994- 49.78, 1995- 55.32, 1996- 58.88, 1997- 61.76, 1998- 65.10; new: 1999- 61.79, 2000- 61.23. pbs: SP 12.92 '95, DT 36.43 '98.

Katalin SZENTGYÖRGYI b. 1 Jan 1979 Szeged 1.66m 48kg Szeged Nyíregyházi VSC
At 5000m (3000m): WCh: '99- 14; WJ: '96- 13 (dnq); EJ: '95- (8), '97- 1; EU23: '99- 1. Eur CC: '98- 1J, '00- 1. Won Hungarian 5000m 1999.
Hungarian 5000m record 1999.
Progression at 5000m: 1996- 16:35.32, 1997- 16:10.15, 1999- 15:18.80. pbs: 800m 2:10.26 '94, 1500m 4:11.18 '99, 3000m 8:53.92 '99, 10000m 35:56.92 '96.
Missed 2000 outdoor season due to stress fracture of the right foot.

Tünde VASZI b. 18 Apr 1972 Piskolt, Romania 1.70m 60kg. Honvéd-Steffl.
At LJ: OG: '96- 8, '00- 8; WCh: '95/97/99- dnq; EC: '98- 4; WI: '97- 9, '99- 5; EI: '00- 5; WCp: '98- 5. Won HUN 100m 1999, LJ 1996-9, TJ 1995.
Progression at LJ: 1990- 5.80, 1991- 6.05, 1992- 6.22, 1993- 5.81/6.04w, 1994- 6.43/6.46w, 1995- 6.58, 1996- 6.73/6.82Aw, 1997- 6.76/6.78w, 1998- 6.77/6.82w, 1999- 6.82i/6.66, 2000- 6.70. pbs: 100m 11.50 '96, 200m 24.11 '96, 100mh 13.84 95, HJ 1.63 '96, PV 4.22i/4.15 '99, TJ 13.39i '97, 13.38 '95.

ICELAND

Governing body: Frjálsíthróttasamband Islands, Sport Centre Laugardalur, 104 Reykjavik. Founded 1947. **National Championships** first held in 1927. **2000 Champions: Men**: 100m/200m/110mh/LJ: Jón Arnar Magnússon 10.9/21.6/?/8.01w, 400m: Davíd Hardarson 49.4, 800m: Björgvin Vikingsson 1:57.0, 1500m: Sigbjörn Arngímsson 4:20.3, 5000m: Björn Margeirsson 15:58.1, 3000mSt: Daníel Smári Gudmundsson 10:00.5, 400mh: Unnstein Grétarsson 55.3, HJ: Björgvin Reynir Helgason 1.85, PV: Kristján Gissurarson 4.20, TJ: Sigtryggur Adalbjörnsson 14.84, SP: Eggert Bogason 15.00, DT: Magnus Hallgrimsson 58.60, HT: Jón Sigurjónsson 51.43, JT: Jón Ásgrímsson 64.00. **Women**: 100m/200m/100mh/400mh: Gudrún Arnardottir 12.0/24.3/13.4/57.6, 400m: Silja Úlfarsdóttir 56.8, 800m: Eva Rós Stefánsdóttir 2:16.4, 1500m: Frída Rún Þórdardóttir 4:40.0, 5000m: Gudrún Bára Skúladóttir 19:09.3, HJ: Íris Svavarsdóttir 1.60, PV: Vala Flosadóttir 4.00, LJ: Gudny Eypórsdóttir 5.78w, TJ: Ágústa Tryggvadóttir 11.02, SP: Audur Adalbjarnardóttir 11.79, DT: Halla Heimisdóttir 40.50, HT: Gudleif Hardardóttir 41.94, JT: Vigdís Gudjónsdóttir 50.63.

Jón Arnar MAGNUSSON b. 28 Jul 1969 Selfoss 1.83m 87kg. UMSS. Teacher.
At Dec: OG: '96- 12, '00- dnf; WCh: '95, '97 & '99 dnf; EC: '98- 4; WJ: '87 dnf. At Hep: WI: '97- 3, '99- 5, '01 2; EI: '96- 3, '98- 5. Won ISL 100m 1994-5, 2000; 200m 1998-2000, 110mh 1994, 1998-2000; PV 1998-9, LJ 1995, 1999-2000; Dec 1992.
Icelandic records: 100m 1997, 110mh 1994-7, LJ 1994, decathlon 1994-8.
Progression at Dec: 1987- 6232, 1988- 6975, 1989- 7351, 1992- 7570, 1994- 7896, 1995- 8248, 1996- 8274, 1997- 8470, 1998- 8583w/8573, 1999- 6813, 2000- 8206. pbs: 60m 6.85i/6.6i '97, 100m 10.56 '97, 10.2w '95; 200m 21.17 '96, 300m 33.86 '94, 400m 46.49 '98, 1500m 4:32.23 '98, 50mh 6.76i '00, 60mh 7.98i '00, 7.8 '97; 110mh 13.91 '97, HJ 2.07 '98, PV 5.20 '98, LJ 8.00 '94, 8.01w '00; SP 16.61 '98, DT 51.30 '96, HT 40.02 '97, JT 64.16 '98, Hep 6293i '99.

Women

Gudrun ARNARDOTTIR b. 24 Sep 1971 1.68m 57kg. Was at University of Georgia, USA.
At 400mh: OG: '96- sf, '00- 7; WCh: '95- sf, '97- sf, '99- h; EC: '98- 4. At 100mh: WCh: '93- h. At 100/200: WJ: '86- h/h.
Icelandic records: 200m 1994-7, 400m 1997, 100mh 1993-6, 400mh (6) 1996-2000.

Progression at 400mh: 1993- 59.44, 1994- 61.50, 1995- 56.78, 1996- 54.81, 1997- 54.79, 1998- 54.59, 1999- 55.31, 2000- 54.37. pbs: 100m 11.97 '97, 11.84w '93; 200m 23.81/23.66w '97, 400m 52.83 '97, 800m 2:13.12 '97, 50mh 6.89i '99, 100mh 13.18/13.10w '96, LJ 5.59w '94, TJ 12.11 '93.

Vala FLOSADOTTIR b. 16 Feb 1978 Reykjavik 1.80m 67kg. Reykjavik and Malmö, Sweden.
At PV: OG: '00- 3; WCh: '99- 12; EC: '98- 9; WI: '97- 8, '99- 2; EI: '96- 1, '98- 3, '00- 4; EJ: '97- 2.
Two world and three European indoor pole vault records 1998, five world junior indoor records 1995-7, European junior record 1996.
Progression at PV: 1994- 3.40, 1995- 3.81, 1996- 4.17, 1997- 4.20i/4.10, 1998- 4.44i/4.36, 1999- 4.45i/4.30, 2000- 4.50. pbs: HJ 1.82 '96, Hep 4911 '96.
Has lived in Malmö, Sweden since 1992 while her parents are studying there.

INDIA

Governing body: Amateur Athletic Federation of India, Room No.1148, Gate No 28, East Block, Jawaharlal Nehru Stadium, Lodi Complex, New Delhi 110003. Founded 1946.
National Championships first held as Indian Games in 1924. **2000 National (Inter-State) Champions: Men**: 100m/200m: Anil Kumar 10.36/20.80, 400m: Paramjeet Singh 45.56, 800m: K M Binu 1:48.54, 1500m: Bahadur Prasad 3:43.71, 5000m/10000m Gulab Chand 14:07.9/30:41.27, 3000mSt: T D Verghese 9:15.43, 110mh: Gurpreet Singh 14.49, 400mh: K P Vishakamani 52.53 HJ: S Arumugam Pillay 2.12, PV: Jitendra Kumar Singh 4.60, LJ: Amit Kumar Saha 7.39, TJ: Pritpal Singh 15.48, SP: Shakti Singh 20.42, DT: Anil Kumar 59.70, HT: Pramod Kumar Tiwari 66.79, JT: Jagdish Bishnoi 79.69, Dec: Dharam Pal Singh 6570, 20kmW: Gurudev Singh 1:25:21.7. **Women:** 100m/200m: Rachita Mistry 11.45/23.10, 400m: Manjuma Kuriakose 53.22, 800m/1500m: Geeta Manral 2:03.67/4:21.84, 5000m: Pushpa Devi 16:18.5, 10000m: L Aruna Devi 34:30.2, 100mh: Anuradha Biswal 13.44, 400mh: Sapinder Kaur 58.68, HJ: Bobby Aloysius 1.84, PV: Karamjit Kaur 2.50, LJ: G Pramila Ganapathy 6.52, TJ: Manisha Dey 13.18, SP: Harwant Kaur 14.76, DT: Neelam J Singh 62.49, HT: Jebeshori Devi 58.36, JT: Gurpreet Kaur 48.73, Hep: Soma Biswas 6186.

IRELAND

Governing Body: The Athletic Association of Ireland (AAI), 11 Prospect Road, Glasnevin, Dublin 9. Founded in 1967. Original Irish AAA founded in 1885.
National Championships first held in 1873. **2000 champions**: **Men**: 100m: Garry Ryan 10.55, 200m: Paul Brizzel 20.73, 400m: Tomas Comyn 46.56; 800m: James Nolan 1:46.83, 1500m: Ken Nason 3:52.27, 5000m: Mark Carroll 13:55.76, 10000m: Seamus Power 28:54.61, HMar: Pauric McKinney 67:52, Mar: Gerry Healy 2:21:28, 3000mSt: Cormac Smith 8:51.22, 110mh: Peter Coghlan 14.08, 400mh: Tom McGuirk 50.69, HJ: Brendan Reilly 2.20, PV: Ken Morris 4.90, LJ: Gareth Devlin 7.22, TJ: Victor Congear 14.32, SP: John Dermody 17.86, DT: Nick Sweeney 57.48, HT: Patrick McGrath 69.00, JT: Terry McHugh (17th consecutive) 80.26, Dec: Jonathan McCabe 4292, 10000mW: Jamie Costin 42:49.84, 20kmW: Robert Heffernan 1:23:49. **Women**: 100m/200m: Sarah Reilly 11.64/23.55, 400m: Karen Shinkins 52.54, 800m/1500m: Sonia O'Sullivan 2:04.71/4:09.37, 5000m: Brid Dennehy-Willis 15:25.32, Mar: Mary Jennings 2:59:44, 100mh/400mh: Susan Smith-Walsh 13.49/56.23, HJ: Deirdre Ryan 1.70, PV: Juliet Claffey 3.00, LJ: Shauna Colhoun 5.65 , TJ: Siobhan Hoey 12.03, SP: Eva Massey 14.90, DT: Ailish O'Brien 45.99, HT: Olivia Kelleher 53.72, JT: Jennifer O'Sullivan 41.94, Hep: Fiona Kavanagh 4529, 5000mW: Niobe Menendez GBR 24:22.84, 20kmW: Gillian O'Sullivan 1:35:09.

Mark CARROLL b. 15 Jan 1972 Cork 1.77m 66kg. Was at Providence University, USA.
At 5000m: OG: '00- h; WCh: '95- 12, '97- h, '99- 14; EC: '98- 3; EJ: '91- 1. At 3000m: WI: '01- 7; EI: '00- 1. World CC: '90 19J. Won Irish 1500m 1995, 1999; 5000m 1999-2000.
Irish records 3000m (2) 1998-9, 5000m 1998, 10000m 2000.
Progression at 1500m, 5000m: 1990- 14:32.1, 1991- 3:43.36, 14:09.52; 1992- 4:00.81Mi, 1993- 3:39.67, 1994- 3:56.44Mi, 1995- 3:36.52, 13:13.94; 1996- 3:38.31, 1997- 3:37.50, 13:14.08; 1998- 3:38.12, 13:03.93; 1999- 3:35.00, 13:31.31; 2000- 3:34.91, 13:09.64. pbs: 800m 1:48.21i '00, 1:50.8 '98; 1000m 2:20.63i '94, 1M 3:50.62 '00, 3000m 7:30.36 '99, 10000m 27:46.82 '00.

Women

Sonia O'SULLIVAN b. 28 Nov 1969 Cobh 1.73m 53kg. Ballymore Cobh/Reebok RC. Studied accountancy at Villanova University, USA.
At 5000m (1500m): OG: '96- dnf (h), '00- 2 (6 10000m); WCh: '95- 1, '97- h (8); EC: '98- 1 (1 10000m); WCp: '98- 1. At 3000m (/1500m): OG: '92- 4/sf; WCh: '93- 4/2; WI: '97- 2, '01- 7/9; EC: '90- 11, '94- 1; WJ: '88- h; WUG: '91- 2/1; WCp: '94- (5). World CC: '92- 7, '97- 9, '98- 1 (1 4k), '00- 7 (15). Won 3000m GP 1993 (1st overall), 1995, 2000; 5000m 1992, 1994 (3rd overall); NCAA 3000m 1990-1, CC 1990; Irish CC 1987, 800m 1992, 1500m 1987, 1990, 1995-6, 2000; 5000m 1990, 1998.
Records: WIR 5000m 15:17.28 '91, World 2000m & European 3000m 1994, World best 2 miles 1998. Irish 1990-2000: 800m, 1000m, 1500m (6), 1M (2), 2000m (3), 3000m (6), 5000m (4), 10000m.
Progression at 1500m, 3000m, 5000m, 10000m: 1986- 10:02.7, 1987- 9:01.52, 1988- 9:13.6, 1989-

9:10.62, 1990- 4:08.49, 8:52.65, 15:26.9; 1991- 4:05.81, 8:54.16, 15:17.28i; 1992- 4:01.23, 8:39.67, 14:59.11; 1993- 3:59.60, 8:28.74, 14:45.92; 1994- 3:59.10, 8:21.64, 15:06.18; 1995- 3:58.85, 8:27.57, 14:41.40; 1996- 3:59.91, 8:35.32, 14:48.36; 1997- 4:05.31, 8:46.19i/8:53.53, 15:10.98; 1998- 4:01.05, 8:28.82, 14:51.61, 31:29.33; 2000- 4:01.70, 8:27.58, 14:41.02, 30:53.37. pbs: 800m 2:00.69 '94, 1000m 2:34.66 '93, 1M 4:17.25 '94, 2000m 5:25.36 '94, 2M 9:19.56 '98, HMar 70:05 '99, Mar 2:35:40 '00.
In 1994 she won the first ever European title for an Irish woman, but failed to finish the 5000m final due to illness at the 1996 Olympics. In 1998 she took both World CC titles and then won a 5000m/10,000m double at the Europeans, the latter in her track debut at 10k. She also won the Great North Run in her first half marathon. She gave birth to daughter Ciara on 10 July 1999, and was soon back in action, setting a world road best for 5 miles with 24:27 on 16 October. In 2000 she set her first Irish records for five years – both 5000m and 10000m (taking 36 secs off her previous best) at the Olympics. Later she won the Dublin Marathon at her debut at the distance.

ISRAEL

Governing body: Israeli Athletic Association, PO Box 24190, Tel Aviv 61241. Founded as Federation for Amateur Sport in Palestine 1931.
National Championships first held in 1935. **2000 Champions**: 100m: Tommy Kafri 10.27, 200m: Gidon Jablonka 20.89, 400m/800m: Ilan Moradi 49.30/1:53.68, 1500m: Tzahi Cohen 3:54.27, 5000m/10000m: Haile Satain 14:31.20/ 29:57.80, HMar: Hailemelkot Teshome 1:06:40, Mar: Asaf Bimro 2:19:45, 3000mSt: Itai Maggidi 9:11.79, 110mh: Ophir Shmueli 14.72, 400mh: David Nakhimovski 54.80, HJ: Konstantin Matusevich 2.32, PV: Aleksandr Averbukh 5.85, LJ: Mark Malisov 7.37, TJ: Rogel Nachum 16.83, SP: Shai Shalev 16.18, DT: Lior Peretz 53.12, HT: Shlomi Ben-Shoshan 57.71, JT: Vadim Bavikin 77.68. **Women**: 100m/100mh/Hep: Svetlana Gnezdilov 12.13/13.26/5632, 200m/400m/400mh: Olga Dor 24.92w/55.54/57.79, 800m/1500m: Noha Beitler 2:07.41/4:33.20, 5000m/10000m/ HMar/Mar: Nili Avramski 16:28.73/34:07.60/ 76:45/2.42.06, HJ/SP: Olga Kurkulin 1.71/12.85, PV: Vicki Argoss 3.74, LJ: Keren Serri 6.11, TJ: Rima Turevskiy 12.84, DT: Yael Dror 39.78, HT: Tzila Ben-Atar 44.32, JT: Dorit Naor 43.67.

Aleksandr AVERBUKH b. 1 Oct 1974 1.78m 76kg. Maccabi Tel-Aviv.
At PV: OG: '00- 10=; WCh: '99- 3; WI: '01- 4; EI: '00- 1; EJ: '93- dnq. EI Hep: '98- 6. Won ISR PV 2000, RUS Dec 1997.
Israeli pole vault records 1999 (5.80) and 2000.
Progression at PV, Dec: 1993- 5.30, 1994- 5.20, 1995- 5.50, 7598w; 1996- 5.40, 7716; 1997- 5.60, 8084; 1998- 5.70, 7658; 1999- 5.81, 2000- 5.85. pbs: 60m 6.89i '98, 6.6i '97; 100m 10.64 '00, 400m 48.74 '98, 1500m 4:33.79 '97, 60mh 8.36i '98, 8.2i '97; 110mh 14.14 '97, HJ 2.06 '95, LJ 7.53i/7.50 '97, SP 15.12 '98, DT 41.51 '00, JT 53.26 '97, Hep 6144i '98.
Emigrated from Russia to Israel, and became a citizen on 3 August 1999, just in time to compete at World Championships.

Konstantin MATUSEVICH b. 25 Jan 1971 Kiev, Ukraine 2.02m 85kg. Gvahim.
At HJ: OG: '96- dnq 17, '00- 5; WCh: '95- dnq 23, '97- 7, '99- dnq 20=; EC: '98- dnq; EI: '96- 4. ISR champion 1994, 1996, 1999-2000.
Eight Israeli high jump records 1995-2000.
Progression at HJ: 1988- 2.19, 1989- 2.13, 1991- 2.23, 1992- 2.28, 1993- 2.23, 1994- 2.22, 1995- 2.28, 1996- 2.34, 1997- 2.35, 1998- 2.26, 1999- 2.28, 2000- 2.36.
Ex Ukraine; became an ISR citizen in early 1995.

ITALY

Governing Body: Federazione Italiana di Atletica Leggera (FIDAL), Via Flaminia Nuova 830, 00191 Roma. Constituted 1926. First governing body formed 1896.
National Championships first held in 1906 (men), 1927 (women). **2000 champions**: **Men**: 100m: Francesco Scuderi 10.19, 200m: Alessandro Cavallaro 20.73, 400m: Ashraf Saber 46.68, 800m: Andrea Longo 1:48.03, 1500m: Christian Obrist 3:52.47, 5000m: Gennaro Di Napoli 13:39.82, 10000m: Daniele Caimmi 28:12.09, HMar: Rachid Berradi 61:52, Mar: Roberto Barbi 2:11:28, 3000mSt: Luciano Di Pardo 8:29.91, 110mh: Emiliano Pizzoli 13.62, 400mh: Giorgio Frinolli 49.81, HJ: Alessandro Talotti 2.25, PV: Maurilio Mariani 5.30, LJ: Bruno Frinolli 7.93, TJ: Fabrizio Donato 16.86w, SP: Paolo Dal Soglio 20.53, DT: Diego Fortuna 62.48, HT: Nicola Vizzoni 79.34, JT: Armin Kerer 75.86, Dec: Beniamino Poserina 7475, 10000mW/20kmW: Marco Giungi 39:35.87/ 1:24:39, 50kmW: Francesco Galdenzi 4:01:35. **Women**: 100m: Francesca Cola 11.54, 200m: Danielle Perpoli 23.66, 400m: Daniela Graglia 52.79, 800m: Claudia Salvarani 2:01.40, 1500m: Silvia Basso 4:20.66, 5000m: Roberta Brunet 15:37.13, 10,000: Silvia Sommaggio 32:35.10, HMar: Maura Viceconte 70:48, Mar: Patrizia Ritondo 2:48:56, 100mh: Margaret Macchiut 13.37, 400mh: Monika Niederstätter 56.72, HJ: Antonietta Di Martino 1.84, PV: Arianna Farfaletti 4.20, LJ: Laura Gatto 6.40, TJ: Silvia Biondini 13.71, SP: Assunta Legnante 17.84, DT: Agnese Maffeis 55.51, HT: Ester Balassini 65.45, JT: Claudia Coslovich 61.09, Hep: Karin Periginelli 5568, 5000W: Cristiana Pellino 21:24.07, 20kmW: Annarita Sidoti 1:34:53.

Stefano BALDINI b. 25 May 1971 Castelnovo di Sotto, Reggio Emilia 1.76m 58kg. Works for Corradini Excelsior Rubiera.

At 10,000m (5000m): OG: '96- 18 (sf); WCh: '95- 18, '97- 9; EC: '94- 20, '98- 1; WJ: '90- (6); EJ: '89- (9); ECp: '95- 1. At Mar: OG: '00- dnf. World HMar: '96-1, '97- 9. Eur CC: '99- 10. Won ITA 10,000m 1993-6, HMar 1995, 1998.
Italian records: half marathon 1997 & 2000, marathon 1997.
Progression at 10,000m, Mar: 1990- 29:48.5, 1992- 28:50.16, 1993- 28:25.98, 1994- 27:57.86, 1995- 27:50.17, 2:11:01sh; 1996- 27:43.98; 1997- 28:07.81, 2:07:57; 1998- 27:55.92, 2:09:33; 2000- 2:09:45. pbs: 1500m 3:45.7 '91, 3000m 7:43.14 '96, 5000m 13:23.43 '96, HMar 60:50 '00.
Won Rome and EC marathons 1998; 2nd London and 3rd New York 1997. On 9 Oct 1999 married **Virna De Angeli** (b. 27 Feb 1976) (2 WJ 400mh 1994, Italian record 400m 51.31 '97). Older brother Marco (b. 14 May 1968) has marathon best of 2:16:32 sh '95.

Ivano BRUGNETTI b. 1 Sep 1976 Milano 1.75m 62kg. Fiamme Gialle Ostia.
At 50kmW: OG: '00- dnf; WCh: '99- 2; WCp: '99- 26. At 10000mW: EJ: '95- 14. Won ITA 10000mW 1999.
Progression at 50kmW: 1997- 4:06:43, 1998- 4:02:15, 1999- 3:47:54. pbs: 5000mW 19:09.78i '00, 10000mW 39:53.34 '99, 20kmW 1:21:21 '00, 30kmW: 2:10:20 '99, 35kmW 2:33:43 '99.

Paolo CAMOSSI b. 6 Jan 1974 Gorizia 1.78m 65kg. Fiamme Azzure Roma.
At TJ (LJ): OG: '00- 8; WCh: '97- dnq, '99- 5; EC: '98- dnq 19 (5); EJ: '91- 11, '93- 1; WI: '01- 1; EI: '00- 3. Won Med G 1997, ITA 1996-9.
Progression at TJ: 1990- 14.36, 1991- 15.68, 1992- 15.43i/15.39, 1993- 16.41, 1994- 15.70i/15.46, 1995- 16.25, 1996- 16.49/16.68w, 1997- 16.82/16.96w, 1998- 17.20, 1999- 17.29, 2000- 17.45, 2001- 17.32i. pb LJ: 8.16 '98, 8.21ex '99.
Improved from 15.73 to 16.41 NJR to win the 1993 European Junior TJ, and in 1999 bettered the oldest Italian record (Gentile ex-WR 17.22 at the 1968 OG). In 1998 he married Giada Gallina (ex ITA 100m record 11.23 '97, 2nd EJ 200m 1991).

Paolo DAL SOGLIO b. 29 Jul 1970 Schio, Vicenza 1.89m 110kg. Carabinieri Bologna.
At SP: OG: 96- 4, '00- dnq 19; WCh: '93- dnq, '95- 9, '97- 9, '99- dnq 16; EC: '94- 8, '98- 5; WJ: '88- dnq; EJ: '89- 6; WUG: '93- 2, '97- 2; WI: '935/7/9/01- 5/7/6/5; EI: '96- 1; ECp: '93-4-5-6-9-00: 2/1/2/1/2/1. 3rd GP 1996. Won ITA 1994-6, 1998-2000; Med G 1993.
Progression at SP: 1988- 17.69, 1989- 18.23, 1990- 18.48, 1991- 18.60, 1992- 19.76, 1993- 20.40/20.65i, 1994- 20.68, 1995- 20.57, 1996- 21.23, 1997- 21.03i/20.69, 1998- 20.65, 1999- 20.46i/20.39, 2000- 20.75. pb DT 53.80 '89.

Giovanni DE BENEDICTIS b. 8 Jan 1968 Pescara 1.80m 63kg. Carabinieri Bologna.
At 20kmW (50kmW): OG: '88- 9, '92- 3, '96- 27 (dnf), '00- 16; WCh: '91- 4, '93- 2, '95- dq (dq), '97- 8; EC: '90- 8, '94- 4, '98- 10; WCp: '89- 14, '91- 5, '93- 7, '95- (12), 97- 23; ECp: '96- 10. At 10000mW: WJ: '86- 4; EJ: '85- 3, '87- 1. Won Italian 10000mW 1988-91, 1993, 1995, 1997; 20kmW 1989-91, 1993, 1996-7, 1999; 50kmW 1994, 1996. At 5000mW: WI: '89- 5, '91- 2; EI: '89- 3, '90- 2, '92- 1.
World walks bests: 2M 11:47.02 '89, 3000m '90.
Progression at 20kmW, 50kmW: 1986- 1:30:41, 1987- 1:26:47, 1988- 1:21:18, 1989- 1:22:01, 1990- 1:22:14, 1991- 1:20:29, 1992- 1:22:17.0t, 1993- 1:21:16, 1994- 1:20:39, 3:50:16; 1995- 1:20:41, 3:49:30; 1996- 1:22:31, 3:49:17; 1997- 1:20:49, 1998- 1:24:50t, 1999- 1:22:34, 2000- 1:21:20. pbs: 3000mW 10:47.11 '90, 5000mW 18:19.97i '92, 18:42.50 '91; 10000mW 38:40.18 '95, 1HrW 14680m '90.
Inside world record for 5000m walk but pipped by Shchennikov for world indoor title in 1991. Disqualified after 3rd at 20km in 1995 Worlds.

Michele DIDONI b. 7 Mar 1974 Milano 1.78m 71kg. Carabinieri Bologna.
At 20kmW: OG: '96- 34, '00- 11; WCh: '95- 1, '97- 7, '99- 10; EC: '94- 10, '98- 11; WCp: '95- 5. At 10000mW: WJ: '92- 6; EJ: '91- 3, '93- 1. At 5000mW: EI: '94- 4. Won Italian 10kmW 1994, 1996, 1998; 20km W 1995, 50kmW 1998.
Progression at 20kmW: 1992- 1:26:42.4t, 1993- 1:24:19, 1994- 1:21:44, 1995- 1:19:59, 1996- 1:21:47, 1997- 1:21:56, 1998- 1:22:09, 1999- 1:26:00, 2000- 1:21:43. pbs: 3000mW 11:24.53 '97, 5000mW 18:47.94i '00, 19:48.02 '96; 10000mW 38:48.01 '95, 15000mW 1:00:19.9 '00, 50kmW 3:51:53 '98.

Arturo DI MEZZA b. 16 Jul 1969 Napoli 1.73m 62kg. Fiamme Gialle Ostia.
At 50kmW (20kmW): OG: '96- 4, '00- dnf; WCh: 93- (13), '95- 7, '97- 7, '99- 7; EC: '94- 14, 98- 7; WCp: 97- 27; WUG: '91- (3), '97- (3); ECp: '96- 2. At 10000mW: WJ: '88- 9.
Progression at 50kmW: 1992- 4:00:47, 1994- 3:56:00, 1995- 3:49:46, 1996- 3:44:52, 1997- 3:51:33, 1998- 3:48:49, 1999- 3:53:50. pbs: 3000mW 11:48.19 '95, 5000mW 19:21.55 '93, 10000mW 39:11.7 '98, 20kmW 1:21:36 '98, 30km 2:07:44 '96.

Fabrizio DONATO b. 14 Aug 1976 Latina 1.90m 83kg. Fiamme Galle.
At TJ: OG: '00- dnq 25; WI: '01- 6; EJ: '95- 5; ECp: '00- 2. Italian champion 2000.
Italian triple jump record 2000.
Progression at TJ: 1993- 14.36, 1994- 15.27, 1995- 15.81, 1996- 16.35, 1997- 16.40A, 1998- 16.73, 1999- 16.66i/16.53w, 2000- 17.60.

Alessandro GANDELLINI b. 30 Apr 1973 Monza 1.79m 68kg. Fiamme Oro Padova. Policeman.
At 20kmW: OG: '00- 9; WCh: '97- 12, '99- 5; EC: '98- 12; WCp: '97- 17, '99- 8.
Progression at 20kmW: 1993- 1:28:55, 1994- 1:28:35, 1995- 1:25:22, 1996- 1:25:35, 1997- 1:20:31, 1998- 1:22:01, 1999- 1:21:01, 2000- 1:20:28. pbs: 3000mW 11:46.14i '98, 5000mW 18:27.15i '00, 10000mW 39:27.5 '98, 15000mW 1:00:01.2 '00.

Giacomo LEONE b. 10 Apr 1971 Francavilla Fontana, Brindisi 1.71m 56kg. Fiamme Oro Padova. Policeman.
At Mar: OG: '00- 5; WCh: '97- 7; EC: '98- dnf. World HMar: '95- 15, '96- 9. At 20kmRd: WJ: '90- 5; EJ: '89- 3.
Progression at Mar: 1991- 2:27:31, 1992- 2:14:49, 1995- 2:09:34sh, 1996- 2:09:54, 1997- 2:09:07, 1998- 2:09:46, 1999- 2:09:36, 2000- 2:08:41, 2001- 2:07:52. pbs: 3000m 8:04.87 '95, 5000m 13:47.90 '95, 10000m 28:47.93 '99, HMar 61:10 '97.
Was 15th at WUG in his first marathon in 1991, 2nd Venice 1995. New York 1996 is his one win in twelve marathons; 6th London and 4th New York 1999. 2nd Rome's Milennium Marathon 1 Jan 2000 and at Lake Biwa 2000.

Andrea LONGO b. 26 Jun 1975 Piove di Sacco, Padova 1.91m 83kg. Fiamme Oro Padova. Policeman.
At 800m: OG: '00- dq; WCh: '97- qf, '99- 6; EC: '98- 7; WJ: '94- sf; EU23: '97- 1; ECp: '98- 1, '00- 4. Italian champion 1998-2000.
Italian 800m record & European best 600m 2000.
Progression at 800m: 1992- 1:58.8, 1993- 1:51.92, 1994- 1:48.87, 1995- 1:48.82, 1996- 1:45.23, 1997- 1:44.40, 1998- 1:43.86, 1999- 1:43.93, 2000- 1:43.74. pbs: 400m: 46.65 '00, 600m 1:14.41 '00, 1000m 2:15.83 '97.

Vincenzo MODICA b. 2 Mar 1971 Mistretta, Messina 1.68m 53kg. Fiamme Oro Padova. Policeman.
At Mar: OG: '00- dnf; WCh: '97- dnf, '99- 2; EC: '98- 3. At 10000m: EC: '94- 11; WJ: '90- 7; EJ: '89- 3; WUG: '93- 3.
Italian half marathon record 1993.
Progression at Mar: 1996- 2:11:39, 1998- 2:12:53, 1999- 2:12:58, 2000- dnf. pbs: 1500m 3:45.0 '94, 3000m 7:52.74 '94, 5000m 13:30.31 '94, 10000m 28:01.65 '94, HMar 61:03 '93.
Made marathon debut with dnf at Carpi 1993, then 3rd in Venice 1996.

Fabrizio MORI b. 28 Jun 1969 Livorno 1.75m 68kg. Fiamme Gialle Ostia.
At 400mh: OG: '92- h, '96- 6, '00- 7; WCh: '91- sf, '93- sf, '95- sf, '97- 4, '99- 1; EC: '94- sf, '98- 3; ECp: '89-91-4-6-7-8-9-00: 8/3/4/1/1/2/1/3 (2R 95 & 98). Won Italian 400mh 1989, 1991, 1996.
Six Italian 400mh records 1996-9.
Progression at 400mh: 1987- 52.55, 1988- 51.46, 1989- 49.86, 1990- 52.00, 1991- 48.92, 1992- 49.16, 1993- 49.23, 1994- 49.24, 1995- 49.27, 1996- 48.33, 1997- 47.79, 1998- 48.36, 1999- 47.72, 2000- 48.40. pbs: 100m 10.6, 200m 21.8, 400m 46.19 '96, 300mh 35.7 '96.
Survived an initial disqualification in the semis, to win the World title in Seville.

Nicola VIZZONI b. 4 Nov 1973 Pietrasanta, Lucca 1.93m 122kg. Fiamme Gialle Ostia.
At HT: OG: '00- 2; WCh: '97- dnq 22, '99- 7; EC: '98- dnq 17; WJ: '92- 5; EJ: '91- 8; WUG: '97- 5, '99- 5; ECp: '99- 4. Won ITA 1998, 2000.
Progression at HT: 1991- 66.62, 1992- 69.32, 1993- 70.76, 1994- 71.78, 1995- 74.48, 1996- 75.30, 1997- 77.10, 1998- 77.89, 1999- 79.59, 2000- 79.64. Left-handed thrower.

Women

Erika ALFRIDI b. 22 Feb 1968 Tregnago, Verona 1.68m 51kg. Sai Assicura Roma.
At 20kmW: OG: '00- 4; WCh: '99- 6; ECp: '00- 4. At 10kmW: WCh: '97- 5; WCp: '97- 4; EC: '98- 2; ECp: '96- 7, '98- 9. Won ITA 5000mW 1998, 10kmW 1988, 1997; 20kmW 1996-7, 1999.
European 20km walk record 1997.
Progression at 10kmW, 20kmW: 1985- 55:30, 1987- 53:36, 1988- 46:57.5t, 1989- 44:34, 1993- 46:11.7t, 1995- 43:54, 1996- 43:27, 1:32:53; 1997- 42:15, 1:28:13; 1998- 42:54, 1999- 43:19.8, 1:31:52; 2000- 43:09, 1:28:06. pbs: 3000mW 11:58.06 '00, 5000mW 20:54.04 '98, 10000mW 43:19.8 '99.

Franca FIACCONI b. 4 Oct 1965 Roma 1.73m 56kg. Cus Universo Bologna.
At Mar: WCh: '97- 13; EC: '98- 4; WUG: '93- 2; WCp: '93- 30. Italian champion 1996, 1998.
Progression at Mar: 1989- 2:44:02, 1990- 2:41:27, 1991- 2:41:04, 1992- 2:39:26, 1993- 2:38:43, 1994- 2:37:43, 1995- 2:30:10, 1996- 2:28:22, 1997- 2:28:51, 1998- 2:25:17, 1999- 2:28:33, 2000- 2:26:03, 2001- 2:26:49. pbs: 5000m 17:22.1, 10000m 33:17.85 '99, HMar 72:37 '98.
Has won 12 of her 34 marathons: Cinzia Taroni 1989, Bologna 1990, Livorno 1993, Enschede and Merano 1994, Cesano Boscone 1995, Turin and Carpi 1996, Rome, Turin and New York 1998, Prague 1999, Padua 2000. 2nd New York 1996 & 2000, 3rd 1997; 2nd Osaka 2001. Ran three sub-2:30s in 1996 and in 1998 (with a fourth at 2:30:21). Unable to run in 1999 World Champs due to a broken arm, but returned for 4th in New York. Married to Luciano Milani.

Rossella GIORDANO b. 1 Dec 1972 Asti 1.72m 50kg. Fiamme Azzurre Roma.
At 20kmW: WCh: '99- 27. At 10kmW: OG: '96- 5, WCh: '95- 6; WCp: '95- 7, '97- 5; ECp: '96- 2; WUG: '93- 4, '95- 2, '97- 2, '99- 2. At 5000mW: WJ: '90- 18; EJ: '89- 7, '91- 6. Won ITA 10kmW 1996, 1998.
World record 20,000m track walk (1:30:48.3) 2000.
Progression at 10kmW, 20kmW: 1988- 50:42, 1989- 50:02, 1990- 48:22, 1991- 48:07, 1992- 46:35.2, 1993- 45:28.1, 1994- 44:20, 1995- 42:26, 1996- 42:20, 1997- 41:38, 1:29:12; 1998- 43:21, 1999- 43:14, 1:31:02; 2000- 43:36, 1:29:47. pbs: 3000mW 12:18.16 '96, 5000mW 20:48.11 '97, 10000mW 42:56.9 '96.

Maria GUIDA b. 23 Jan 1966 Vico Equense, Napoli 1.60m 49kg. Forestale.
At 10000m: OG: '96- dns; WCh: '95- 4; EC: '94- 6; ECp: '95- 1; WUG: '91- 6. World HMar: '98- 15. Won ITA 10000m 1991, 1993-6; HMar 1994, 1999; CC 1994.

Italian records 5000m (2), 10000m 1995-6.
Progression at 5000m, 10000m, Mar: 1987- 35:17.4, 1988- 16:06.07, 33:44.7; 1989- 15:58.38, 33:15.19; 1990- 34:10.65, 1991- 16:01.42, 32:45.36; 1992- 15:41.69, 32:10.29, 2:38:13; 1993- 15:36.98, 32:12.70; 1994- 15:40.96, 31:42.14; 1995- 15:04.13, 31:27.82; 1996- 14:58.84, 31:53.55; 1998- 15:38.68, 32:38.5, 2:35:47; 1999- 15:40.26, 31:50.40. 2:25:57; 2000- 2:26:12. pbs: 800m 2:12.4 '89, 1500m 4:17.01 '95, 3000m 8:54.59 '94, HMar 68:30 '96.
Having run two previous marathons, she had three wins in 1999, winning at Busseto 2:40:21, Turin 2:28:28 and Carpi 2:25:57.

Fiona MAY b. 12 Dec 1969 Slough, GBR 1.81m 60kg. Snam Gas Metano. Economics graduate of Leeds University. Married to Gianni Iapichino (PV 5.70 ITA rec '94).
At LJ: OG: '88- 6, '92- dnq, '96- 2, '00- 2; WCh: '91- dnq 19, '93- dnq 14, '95- 1, '97- 3, '99- 2; EC: '90- 7, '94- 3, '98- 2; CG: '90- 3; WJ: '86- 8, '88- 1; EJ: '87- 1; WI: '97- 1, '01- 4; EI: '98- 1; WUG: '91- 2; ECp: '89-91-3-5-7-8-9-00: 3/3/3/2/1/1/1/3 (TJ '98-9: 1/3). 3rd GP 1996, 1998. Won UK 1989, 1991, 1993; AAA 1989-92, Italian 1994, 1996.
Italian records: eight LJ 1994-8, three TJ 1998.
Progression at LJ, TJ: 1982- 5.34, 1983- 5.91, 1984- 6.30, 1985- 6.22/6.23w, 1986- 6.27/6.47w, 1987- 6.53/6.64w, 1988- 6.82/6.88w, 1989- 6.98w/6.80, 1990- 6.88, 1991- 6.77/6.91w, 1992- 6.73/6.76w, 1993- 6.86, 1994- 6.95A/6.90/7.00wA, 1995- 6.96/7.23Aw, 1996- 7.02/7.12w, 1997- 6.97/6.98w, 1998- 7.11, 14.65; 1999- 7.04, 14.39; 2000- 7.09. pbs: 60m 7.7i '92, 100m 11.94 '97, 11.88w '89; 200m 25.4 '89, HJ 1.72 '83.
Competed for Britain to 1993, Italy from 1994; now lives in Firenze. In her first ever triple jump competition in January 1998, she smashed the Italian indoor record with 14.56, ninth on the world all-time list indoors.

Elisabetta PERRONE b. 9 Jul 1968 Camburzano, Vercelli 1.68m 60kg. Forestale.
At 20kmW: OG: '00- dq; WCh: '99- 21; ECp: '00- 2. At 10kmW: OG: '92- 19, '96- 2; WCh: '93- 4, '95- 2, '97- 10; EC: '94- 7, '98- 11; WCp: '93- 10, '95- 6, 97- 25; ECp: '96- 5. At 20kmW: WCp: '99- 20. Won ITA 5000mW 1994, 1996-7; 10kmW 1994-5.
Italian record 20km walk 2000.
Progression at 10kmW, 20kmW: 1988- 53:08, 1989- 51:18, 1990- 48:23, 1991- 46:19, 1992- 44:19, 1993- 43:26/41:56sh/44:01.6t, 1:33:37; 1994- 42:15/43:27.6t, 1995- 42:16, 1996- 42:09, 1997- 42:39, 1998- 44:04, 1:34:32; 1999- 42:45, 1:32:21; 2000- 43:15, 1:27:42. pbs: 3000mW 11:56.40 '93, 2MW 13:03.87 '96, 5000mW 20:33.42 '95.

Annarita SIDOTI b. 25 Jul 1969 Gioiosa Marea, Messina 1.50m 42kg. Europa Capaci. Sports twon councilor in Gioiosa Marea.
At 20kmW: OG: '00- dnf; WCh: '99- dnq; ECp: '00- 5; At 10kmW OG: '92- 7, '96- 11; WCh: '91- 9, '93- 9, '95- 13, '97- 1; EC: '90- 1, '94- 2, '98- 1; WCp: '89- 8, '91- 9, '93- 7, '95- 8, 97- 6; ECp: '96- 1; WUG: '91- 3, '95- 1, '97- 3. At 5000mW: WJ: '88- 4; EJ: '87- 7. At 3000mW: WI: '93- 6; EI: '90- 3, '92- 4, '94- 1. Won Italian 5000mW 1995, 10kmW 1991, 20kmW 1992, 1995, 2000.
European 5000m walk record 1995.
Progression at 10kmW, 20kmW: 1986- 53:23, 1987- 49:37, 1988- 47:57.9t, 1989- 44:59, 1990- 44:00, 1991- 43:37, 1992- 43:03, 1:36:54; 1993- 42:41, 1994- 41:46, 1995- 42:04, 1996- 43:04, 1997- 42:20, 1:30:57; 1998- 42:49, 1999- 43:38.2, 1:34:00; 2000- 43:35, 1:28:38. Track pbs: 1MW 6:46.53 '90, 3000mW 11:54.32i '94, 12:09.3 '95; 5000mW 20:21.69 '95, 10000mW 42:55.49 '97.
Perhaps the smallest ever major champion when she won the 1990 European title. Took 1997 world title after coming in as a last-minute replacement for Rossella Giordano.

Maura VICECONTE b. 3 Oct 1967 Susa, Torino 1.55m 47kg. Maratona Torino Asics.
At Mar: OG: '96- dnf, '00- 12; EC: '98- 3; WCp: '95- 15. At 5000m: ECp: '00- 4. Won ITA HMar 2000, Mar 1995.
Italin records 10000m and marathon 2000.
Progression at Mar: 1994- 2:35:15, 1995- 2:29:11sh/2:38:22, 1997- 2:28:16, 1998- 2:28:31, 1999- 2:29:36, 2000- 2:23:47. pbs: 5000m 15:18.80 '00, 10000m 31:05.57 '00, HMar 70:48 '00.
Six wins in 12 marathons: Cesano Boscone 1994, Venice 1995, Monaco 1997, Carpi 1998, Rome 1999, Vienna 2000.

JAMAICA

Governing body: Jamaica Amateur Athletic Association, PO Box 272, Kingston 5. Founded 1932. **2000 Champions**: **Men**: 100m: Lindel Frater 10.10, 200m: Christopher Williams 20.32, 400m: Greg Haughton 44.98, 800m: Marvin Watts 1:47.20, 1500m: Omar Fagan 4:15.92, 5000m: Kevin Campbell 16:42.96, 10000m: Kevin Webb 35:53.36, 110mh: Robert Foster 13.59, 400mh: Kemel Thompson 49.33, HJ: Germaine Mason 2.18, PV: Fenton McDuffus 3.70, LJ: James Beckford 8.29, TJ: Nicholas Neufville 15.23, SP: Rory Marsh 15.14, DT: Kevin Brown 56.18, JT: Maurice Smith 56.87. **Women**: 100m: Peta-Gaye Dowdie 11.19, 200m: Beverley McDonald 22.70, 400m: Lorraine Graham 50.72, 800m: Charmaine Howell 2:02.54, 100mh: Delloreen Ennis-London 12.52, 400mh: Deon Hemmings 54.40, HJ: Sheree Francis 1.85, LJ: Elva Goulbourne 6.69, TJ: Keisha Spencer 13.93, SP/DT: Melissa Gibbons 13.97/51.90, JT: Olivia McKoy 57.39.

James BECKFORD b. 9 Jan 1975 St Mary 1.83m 73kg. Was a PE student at Blinn JC, USA.
At LJ (TJ): OG: '96- 2, '00- dnq 14; WCh: '95- 2 (6/4R), '97- 4; WI: '97- 5, '99- 5; CAG: '98- 1. 2nd GP LJ 1997, 1999 (3rd 1995). Won JAM LJ 1995-8, 2000; TJ 1995.
Commonwealth records: LJ 1995 & 1997, TJ

1995, Jamaican records: LJ (5), TJ (4) 1994-7.
Progression at LJ, TJ: 1993- 7.53, 15.70; 1994- 8.13/8.29w, 17.29; 1995- 8.45/8.68w, 17.92; 1996- 8.52, 16.43i; 1997- 8.62, 1998- 8.60/8.61w, 16.09; 1999- 8.50, 2000- 8.42.
After positive test for ephedrine on 25 June 1997 was re-admitted to competition with the IAAF new warning procedure and thus competed at the World Champs. Did not compete at 1999 Worlds as he had not attended the Jamaican Champs.

Gregory HAUGHTON b. 10 Nov 1973 St Mary 1.85m 79kg. Was at George Mason University, USA.
At 400m/4x400mR: OG: '96- 3R, '00- 3/3R; WCh: '93- 6, '95- 3/2R, '97- 3R, '99- 7/3R; CG: '98- 6/1R; PAm: '99- 1/1R; CAG: '98- 2R; WI: '97- 2R; WJ: '92- sf/2R. Won CAC 400m 1993, 1999; JAM 1994-5, 1999-2000; NCAA 1995.
Progression at 400m: 1991- 47.30, 1992- 46.88, 1993- 44.78, 1994- 44.93, 1995- 44.56, 1996- 45.07, 1997- 45.18, 1998- 45.24, 1999- 44.59, 2000- 44.70. pbs: 200m 20.64 '96, 300m 32.25+ '99.

Danny McFARLANE b. 14 Jun 1972 1.85m 81kg. Was at University of Oklahoma, USA.
At 400m/4x400mR: OG: '00- 8/3R; WCh: '95- sf/2R, '97- 3R, '99- sf/3R; WI: '01- 3; PAm: '99- 1R. Won CAC 1997.
Progression at 400m: 1993- 45.82, 1994- 45.74, 1995- 44.90, 1996- 46.18i/46.23, 1997- 45.47, 1998- 45.61, 1999- 45.37, 2000- 45.26. pb 200m 21.17 '95.

Dinsdale MORGAN b. 19 Nov 1972 St Elizabeth 1.88m 77kg. Was at Pittsburgh State University, USA.
At 400mh: OG: '96- h, '00- sf; WCh: '97- 7, '99- 7; CG: '98- 1; WI: '97- 2R; CAG: '98- 1; WCp: '98- 3. Won JAM 1996-8, NCAA 1996, CAC 1997.
Progression at 400mh: 1991- 54.97, 1992- 51.67, 1993- 52.5, 1994- 51.59, 1995- 50.26, 1996- 49.11, 1997- 48.41, 1998- 48.13, 1999- 48.59, 2000- 48.80. pb 400m 46.31 '96.

Women

Juliet CAMPBELL b. 17 Mar 1970 St Thomas 1.75m 62kg. Was at Auburn University, USA (business education).
At 400m/4x400mR: OG: '92- qf, '96- sf/4R; WCh: '93- 7/4R (3 4x100m). At 200m: OG: '00 qf; WCh: '97- sf, '99- 8; CG: '98- 2 (2 4x100m), CAG: '98- 2; WI: '99- 5, '01- 1/2R. Won NCAA 400m 1993, JAM 400m 1993, 1996.
Jamaican 400m record 1993.
Progression at 200m, 400m: 1987- 23.71w, 1988- 24.25, 1989- 24.20/23.7, 53.1; 1990- 23.52, 53.01; 1991- 53.59, 1992- 23.06, 51.11; 1993- 22.80/22.66w, 50.11; 1994- 23.69, 51.65; 1995- 22.77, 51.4/52.00; 1996- 22.71/22.55w, 50.11; 1997- 22.61, 52.30; 1998- 22.69/22.63w, 51.09; 1999- 22.50, 52.77; 2000- 22.70i/22.86, 2001- 22.64i. pbs: 60y 6.72i '90, 60m 7.23i '01, 100m 11.15w '93, 11.32/11.0 '95; 300m 36.59 '92. Lives in Auburn, USA.

Veronica CAMPBELL b. 15 May 1982 Trelawny 1.63m 61kg.
At 100m/4x100mR (200m): OG: '00- 2R; WJ: '98- qf, '00- 1/2R (1); WY: '99- 1/1R. Won CAC-J 100m 2000.
Progression at 100m, 200m: 1999- 11.49, 23.73; 2000- 11.12/11.1, 22.87.
In 2000 became the first woman to become World Junior champion at both 100m and 200m.

Delloreen ENNIS-LONDON b. 5 Mar 1975 St Catherine 1.78m 70kg. née Ennis. Business management graduate of Abilene Christian University, USA.
At 100mh: OG: '00- 4; WCh: '99- 7; WJ: '92- sf. 3rd GP 2000. Jamaican champion 1999-2000.
CAC 100mh record 2000.
Progression at 100mh: 1992- 13.81, 1996- 13.53/13.30w, 1997- 13.60/13.51w, 1998- 13.27/13.1w, 1999- 12.71/12.60w, 2000- 12.52. pbs: 100m 11.50 '99, 11.43w '00; 55mh 7.56i '99.

Bridgette FOSTER b. 7 Nov 1974 St Elizabeth 1.70m 61kg. Was at South West Texas State University, USA.
At 100mh: OG: '00- 8; CG: '98- 5/2R; WJ: '92- sf.
Jamaican champion 1999-2000.
CAC 100mh record 2000.
Progression at 100mh: 1993- 14.22, 1996- 13.34, 1998- 13.19/13.13w/12.9w, 1999- 13.35, 2000- 12.70. pbs:100m 11.54 '00, 11.38w '98; 200m 23.51/23.35w '98, 60mh 8.09i '01, 400mh 64.62 '93.

Merlene FRAZER b. 27 Dec1973 Trelawny 1.72m 57kg. Was at University of Texas, USA.
At 200m/4x100mR (100): OG: '00- res 2R; WCh: '91- res 1R, 97- sf/2R, '99- 3=/3R; CG: '94- 7; WI: '97- 4; WJ: '90- 1R (5), '92- 3/1R (3); PAm: '91- 3/1R. Won PAm-J 1991 (1R, 100m 2), NCAA 1994, JAM 1994. At 400m: OG: '96- sf (4 4x400m); WCh: '95- h.
Progression at 200m: 1990- 23.89, 1991- 23.48, 1992- 23.19, 1993- 22.91, 1994- 22.65/22.49w, 1995- 22.77, 1996- 23.10/22.63w, 1997- 22.66, 1998- 22.63, 1999- 22.18, 2000- 23.05. pbs: 60m 7.20i '97, 100m 11.20 '95, 300m 37.47 '96, 400m 51.18 '96.

Michelle FREEMAN b. 5 May 1969 St Catherine 1.70m 63kg. Was at University of Florida, now assistant coach at University of Texas.
At 100mh/4x100mR: OG: '92- qf, '96- 6/R, '00- qf; WCh: '91- sf, '93- 7/3R, '95- sf/res R (2), '97- 3; CG: '94- 1; WJ: '88- h (sf 100m); PAm: '91- 5. At 100m: CG: '90- h. At 60mh: WI: '93/5/7/01- dnf/7/1/2. Won JAM 100mh 1991-4, 1997; NCAA 1992. Won GP 100mh 1998 (3rd 1992), 3rd overall 1996.
WIR 55mh 1992. Eight Jamaican 100mh records 1990-8, inc. five Commonwealth 1992-8 and four CAC 1996-8.
Progression at 100mh: 1988- 13.70, 1989- 13.61/13.4, 1990- 13.18/13.09w, 1991- 12.98, 1992- 12.75, 1993- 12.77, 1994- 12.93/12.74w, 1995-

12.98, 1996- 12.57, 1997- 12.52/12.40w, 1998- 12.52, 2000- 12.57. pbs: 55m 6.66i '93, 60m 7.12i '98, 100m 11.16 '93, 11.13w '92; 200m 22.87 '92, 50mh 6.75i '96, 55mh 7.34i '92, 60mh 7.74i '98.
Had to withdraw from 1988 Olympic team through injury. Missed 1999 season due to multiple stress fractures in her left shin.

Lorraine GRAHAM b. 8 Sep 1973 Mandeville 1.73m 59kg. Graduated in criminal justice from Lincoln University, USA.
At 400m/4x400mR: OG: '00- 2/2R; WCh: '97- sf/3R, '99- 3. Won JAM 400m 1997, 1999-2000. Won GP 2000.
Progression at 400m: 1994- 53.31, 1995- 53.63, 1996- 51.85, 1997- 50.69, 1998- 50.23, 1999- 49.92, 2000- 49.58. pbs: 100m 11.73 '99, 200m 23.03 '97, 300m 36.00+ '00.

Deon HEMMINGS b. 9 Oct 1968 St Ann 1.76m 63kg. Studied business administration at Central State University, Ohio, USA.
At 400mh/4x400mR: OG: '92- 7, '96- 1, '00- 2/2R; WCh: '91- h, '93- 6, '95- 3, '97- 2/3R, '99- 3; CG: '94- 2/2R; PAm: '91- 2; CAG: '98- 1; WCp: '98- 2/2R; 3rd GP 1995, 2nd 1997 (2nd overall). At 400m: WI '93- 1R, '95- 4, '99- 6. Won CAC 400mh 1991; JAM 400m 1995, 400mh 1992-2000.
Five CAC & Jamaican 400mh records 1993-6.
Progression at 400mh: 1990- 61.72, 1991- 56.5, 1992- 54.70, 1993- 54.12, 1994- 54.48, 1995- 53.48, 1996- 52.82, 1997- 52.98, 1998- 53.03A/53.27, 1999- 53.16, 2000- 53.45. pbs: 100m 11.58/11.29w '97, 200m 22.64 '98, 22.6w '95, 300m 37.71 '93, 400m 50.63 '95.
Jamaica's first female Olympic champion.

Tayna LAWRENCE b. 17 Sep 1975 1.63m 61kg. Was at Fl;orida International University, USA.
At 100m/4x100mR: OG: '00- 3/2R; CAG: '98- 3.
Progression at 100m: 1997- 11.61, 1998- 11.30/11.23w, 1999- 11.37/11.36w, 2000- 11.07. pbs: 60m 7.21i '99, 200m 22.84/22.78w '00.

Beverley McDONALD b. 15 Feb 1970 St Mary 1.65m 59kg. Was at Texas Christian Univ., USA.
At 100m/4x100mR (200m): OG: '00- sf/2R (4); WCh: '91- sf/1R, '93- sf, '95-sf/2R (sf), '97- qf/2R, '99- (2)/3R; PAm: '91- 3/1R; CAG: '98- 2 (2); WJ: '88- 7; WCp: '98- 2R (4). At 60m: WI: '95- 5. 3rd GP 200m 1999. Won JAM 100m 1998, 200m 1998-2000.
Progression at 100m, 200m: 1987- 11.2, 23.40/ 23.3; 1988- 11.61, 24.15/23.7; 1990- 11.52/11.27w, 23.20w; 1991- 11.37/11.29w/11.2w, 23.48/23.31w; 1992- 11.43/11.19w, 23.31; 1993- 11.22/11.05w, 22.67; 1994- 11.47, 23.02w; 1995- 11.20/11.17w, 22.56; 1996- 11.16, 23.04; 1997- 11.13A/11.11w, 22.62; 1998- 10.99, 22.24; 1999- 11.10, 22.22; 2000- 11.11, 22.35. pb 60m 7.16i '95.
Her brother Michael (qv) is a top 400m runner.

Merlene OTTEY b. 10 May 1960 Cold Spring 1.73m 59kg. Graduate of Nebraska University. Formerly married to Nat Page (USA).
At 100m/200m/4x100mR: OG: '80- -/3R, '84- 3/3, '88- sf/4, '92- 5/3, '96- 2/2/3R. '00- 4/-/3R; WCh: '83- 4/2/3R, '87- 3/3, '91- 3/3/1R, '93- 2/1/3R, '95- 2/1/2R, '97- 7/3; WI 200m (60m): '87- 2 (4), '89- 1 (3), '91- 1 (2), '95 (1); CG: '82: 2/1/3R, '90- 1/1; PAm: '79- -/3/2R; WCp: '94- -/2. Won NCAA 100m 1982-3, 200m 1983; TAC 100m 1984-5, 200m 1982 and 1984-5; CAC 100m & 200m 1985. Won overall GP 1987 & 1990 (2nd 1991-2, 1996); 100m 1987, 1989, 1991, 1994, 1996; 200m 1990, 1992 (2nd 1997).
Commonwealth records: 200m (7), 100m (7) 1980-96, CAC 100m (7), 200m (9). WIR: 50m 6.00 '94, 60m 6.96 '92, 200m (3) 22.24 twice '91, 21.87 '93; 300y (8) 1980-2 best 32.63 '82, 300m (3), best 35.83 '81.
Progression at 100m, 200m: 1975- 25.9; 1976- 12.0, 24.7; 1977- 12.2, 25.1; 1978- 12.6, 24.5; 1979- 11.59/11.4, 23.10/22.79w; 1980- 11.36/11.0, 22.20; 1981- 11.07/10.97w, 22.35; 1982- 11.03/10.97Aw, 22.17; 1983- 11.07/10.98w, 22.19/22.11w/21.9w; 1984- 11.01, 22.09; 1985- 10.92, 21.93; 1986- 11.06/ 10.7w, 22.43; 1987- 10.87/10.8, 22.06; 1988- 11.00/ 10.7, 21.99; 1989- 10.95, 22.21; 1990- 10.78, 21.66; 1991- 10.79/10.78w, 21.64; 1992- 10.80, 21.94; 1993- 10.82, 21.77; 1994- 10.78, 22.07; 1995- 10.85, 21.93; 1996- 10.74, 22.08; 1997- 10.83, 22.06/ 21.92w; 1998- 11.01, 22.53; 1999- 10.97, 22.43; 2000- 10.99/10.91w. pbs: 150m 16.46 (world best) '89, 400m 51.12 '83.
Her 34 medals in major championships include a record 14 World Championships medals outdoors. In 1993 she at last won the World title outdoors at 200m, having lost the 100m by just 0.001 – on both occasions she received an overwhelming reception from the crowd on the victory rostrum. Before that she had won four Olympic and five World bronze medals and the 1983 World 200m silver, but anchored the Jamaican team to World gold in the sprint relay in 1991. She added three more Olympic medals in 1996. Ranked in the world's top ten each year 1980-98. Won 73 successive finals (and 15 heats) 21 May 1989 to 8 Mar 1991, when beaten by Irina Privalova in the World Indoor 60m. Her unbeaten runs at 100m: 57 finals from 3rd in 1987 World Champs, and 36 finals at 200m from 6 May 1989, were ended in Tokyo 1991. In 1990 she won all 36 finals, with a one-day 10.93 and 21.66 double at Zürich, both into the wind, and a one year record of seven sub-22.00 200m times. Has a record 66 legal times sub 11.00 for 100m and 106 legal times sub 22.50 for 200m to end 1999. The athletics world was shocked by reports of her positive test for nandrolene on 5 July 1999 in Lucerne, but a year later the IAAF Arbitration Panel decided that there were… " not the grounds to maintain (her) suspension from competition and accordingly the suspension ended with immediate effect". At the 2000 Olympics she became the oldest ever women's athletics medallist at 40y 143d when

she took bronze at 4x100m after missing one at 100m by 0.01.
Appointed a roving ambassador for Jamaica in 1993. Jamaican Sportswoman of the Year 15 times between 1979 and 1997. Now based in Ljubljana, Slovenia.

Debbie Ann **PARRIS** b. 24 Mar 1973 Trelawny 1.62m 52kg. Student at Louisiana State University, USA.
At 400mh: OG: '96- 4; WCh: '93- sf, '95- h, '97- 5, '99- 8; CG: '94- 3; CAG: '98- 3; WJ: '92- 8 (2 4x400m); WUG: '93- 2. NCAA champion 1993-4, CAC 1993.
Progression at 400mh: 1992- 57.34, 1993- 55.80, 1994- 55.17, 1995- 54.29, 1996- 53.97, 1997- 54.19, 1998- 54.49, 1999- 54.55, 2000- 55.90. pbs: 200m 23.50 '98, 400m 51.61 '95, 800m 2:13.35 '99, 100mh 13.51 '93.

Sandie RICHARDS b. 6 Nov 1968 Clarendon 1.77m 68kg. Was at University of Texas, USA (sociology).
At 400m/4x400mR: OG: '88- qf/5R, '92- 7/5R, '96- 7/4R, '00- sf/2R; WCh: '87- sf/6R, '93- 3/4R, '95- 8, '97- 2/3R; CG: '94- 3/2R, '98- 1; WI: '93- 1/2R, '95- 2, '97- 2, '99- 5, '01- 1/2R; WJ: '86- 3; WUG: '87- 3; PAm: '87- 8/3R, '91- 6/3R; CAG: '98- 1; WCp: '94- 3R, '98- 3/2R. Won JAM 400m 1991-2, 1994, 1998; PAm Jnr 1986, GP 1992.
Jamaican 400m record 1987.
Progression at 400m: 1986- 52.18, 1987- 50.92, 1988- 51.62, 1989- 51.46, 1990- 51.94, 1991- 51.06, 1992- 50.19, 1993- 50.44, 1994- 50.69, 1995- 50.53, 1996- 50.45, 1997- 49.79, 1998- 50.03, 1999- 51.54i/51.66, 2000- 50.42. pbs: 200m 23.38A '98, 23.66 '86, 23.15w '87; 300m 36.15 '93, 800m 2:04.60 '96.

Dionne ROSE b. 7 Nov 1969 Kingston 1.68m 52kg. Was at Universities of Florida and Middle Tennessee State, USA.
At 100mh (LJ): OG: '92- sf (dnq 25), '96- 5; WCh: '93- sf (dnq 25), '95- 7 (dnq 31), '97- 5, '99- 6; CG: '94- 4 (7); PAm: '90- dnf (7); CAG: '98- 1; WCp: '98- 4. At 60mh: WI: '99- 7. Won JAM LJ 1993, 1995; 100mh 1996, 1998.
Jamaican 100mh record 1995.
Progression at 100mh: 1988- 15.18/14.9, 1989- 14.42/14.1w, 1990- 14.44/13.49w, 1991- 13.39/13.29w, 1992- 13.03, 1993- 13.03, 1994- 13.13/13.06w, 1995- 12.86/12.85w, 1996- 12.64, 1997- 12.75, 1998- 12.64, 1999- 12.79, 2000- 13.15/12.93Aw. pbs: 100m 11.54 '98, 11.38w '95, 11.4 '97; 50mh 6.84i '99, 60mh 7.96i '97, LJ 6.72 '95, TJ 12.73w '90. Ran three personal bests in qualifying at 1996 Olympic Games.

JAPAN

Governing body: Nippon Rikujo-Kyogi Renmei, 1-1-1 Jinnan, Shibuya-Ku, Tokyo 150-8050. Founded 1911.
National Championships first held in 1914 (men), 1925 (women). **2000 Champions**: **Men**: 100m: Nobuharu Asahara 10.35, 200m: Hideki Ishizuka 20.79, 400m: Takahiko Yamamura 46.45, 800m: Hiroshi Sasano 1:51.06, 1500m: Junji Konomi 3:48.55, 5000m/10000m: Zakayo Ngatho KEN 13:35.95/27:44.01, Mar: Atsushi Fujita 2:06:51, 3000mSt: Yasunori Uchitomi 8:31.43, 110mh: Kimihiro Asami 13.72, 400mh: Hideaki Kawamura 48.85, HJ: Takahisa Yoshida 2.21, PV: Daichi Sawano 5.40, LJ: Masaki Morinaga 7.87, TJ: Takashi Komatsu 16.34, SP: Yasutada Noguchi 17.61, DT: Shigeo Hatakeyama 54.39, HT: Koji Murofushi 76.39, JT: Yukifumi Murakami 74.97, Dec: Hitoshi Maruono 7414, 20kmW: Satoshi Yanagisawa 1:19:29, 50kmW: Fumio Imamura 3:53:20. **Women**: 100m/200m: Motoka Arai 11.74/24.01, 400m: Kazue Kakinuma 54.07, 800m: Reina Sasaki 2:08.32, 1500m: Ikuko Tamura 4:19.49, 5000m: Yoshiko Fujinaga 15:27.82, 10000m: Yukiko Okamoto 32:06.42, Mar: Harumi Hiroyama 2:22:56, 100mh: Yvonne Kanazawa 13.46, 400mh: Makiko Yoshida 58.37, HJ: Yoko Ota 1.88, PV: Akane Eguchi 3.95, LJ/TJ: Maho Hanaoka 6.46w/13.50, SP: Yoko Toyonaga 16.46, DT: Yuka Murofushi 52.71, HT: Aya Suzuki 60.46, JT: Takako Miyake 56.26, Hep: Sayoko Sato 5637, 20kmW: Yuka Mitsumori 1:36:18.

Atsushi FUJITA b. 6 Nov 1976 Fukushima pref. 1.66m 52kg. Komazawa University.
At Mar: WCh: '99- 6. Japanese chanpion 2000. At HMar: WCh: '98- 30.
Asian marathon record 2000.
Progression at Mar: 1999- 2:10:07, 2000- 2:06:51. pbs: 5000m 14:02.58 '00, 10000m 28:19.94 '00, HMar 62:19 '00.
Second in debut marathon at Lake Biwa in March 1999. Won at Fukuoka in third marathon December 2000.

Takayuki INUBUSHI b. 11 Aug 1972 Tokushima prefecture 1.70m 58kg. Otsuka Pharmaceuticals.
At Mar: OG: '00- dnf.
Asian marathon record 1999.
Progression at Mar: 1995- 2:25:16, 1998- 2:13:15, 1999- 2:06:57, 2000- 2:08:16. pbs: 800m 1:53.9 '92, 1500m 3:48.86 '92, 3000m 8:12.8 '96, 5000m 13:46.74 '95, 10000m 28:26.98 '00; road: 10M 46:42 '93, HMar 62:47 '98, 30km 1:30:29 '94.
Shot to prominence with his second place in the 1999 Berlin marathon, when he took 5:27 off his previous pb, 2:12:20 for 7th at Tokyo on 14 Feb 1999. After his marathon debut in 1995 (59th at Lake Biwa), he did not finish at Fukuoka in 1995 and 1997 and was then 10th in Boston 1998. 4th Tokyo 2000.

Koji ITO b. 29 Jan 1970 Kobe 1.82m 72kg. Was at Tokai University. Fujitsu.
At 200m (100m)/4x100mR: OG: '96- sf, '00- sf/sf; WCh: '93- qf, '95- qf/5R, '97- h (h), '99- sf (qf); WI: '99- 5; AsiG: '94- 2/1R, '98- 1/1R (1); AsiC: '91- 3R, '98- 1/2R. At 400m/4x400mR:

OG: '96- 5R; WCh: '91- hR; WCp: '92- 6R; AsiC: '91- 3/1R, '93- 3/1R; Won Japanese 100m 1998, 200m 1995-6.
Asian records: 100m (3) 1998, 200m 1995-6 and 1998. Also Japanese 200m 1994.
Progression at 100m, 200m: 1983- 11.3, 23.3; 1984- 10.7, 21.8; 1985- 10.8, 21.9; 1986- 11.2, 21.8; 1987- 10.80/10.6, 21.2; 1988- 10.7, 21.92; 1989- 21.7, 1990- 21.35, 1991- 10.7, 21.02; 1992- 20.96, 1993- 10.52, 20.87; 1994- 10.34, 20.44; 1995- 10.21, 20.61; 1996- 10.36, 20.29; 1997- 10.34/10.1/10.22w, 20.46; 1998- 10.00, 20.16; 1999- 10.06/9.9, 20.41/ 20.34w; 2000- 10.25, 20.56. pbs: 60m 6.61i '97, 400m 46.11 '96.
Set a national senior high school record of 46.52 for 400m in 1987.

Koji MUROFUSHI b. 8 Oct 1974 Shizuoka 1.87m 89kg. Was at Chukyo Univ. Mizuno.
At HT: OG: '00- 9; WCh: '95- dnq, '97- 10, '99- dnq 14; WJ: '92- 8; AsiG: '94- 2, '98- 1; AsiC: '93- 2, '95- 2, '98- 2. 2nd GP 2000. Won E.Asian 1997. Japanese champion 1995-2000.
Eleven Japanese hammer records 1998-2000.
Progression at HT: 1991- 61.76, 1992- 66.30, 1993- 68.00, 1994- 69.54, 1995- 72.32, 1996- 73.82, 1997- 75.72, 1998- 78.57, 1999- 79.17, 2000- 81.08.
His father Shigenobu Murofushi won a record five Asian Games gold medals 1970-86 and held the Japanese hammer record with the 75.96 that he set in Los Angeles in 1984 until Koji broke it for the first time on 26 April 1998. His sister Yuka (b. 11 Feb 77) was Japanese discus champion and record setter (56.84) 1999 and 6th World Juniors 1996.

Women

Tomoe ABE b. 13 Aug 1971 Oita pref. 1.50m 38kg. Asahi Kasei Chemical.
At Mar: WCh: '93- 3, '97- 29. Japanese champion 1994. At 10,000m: WJ: '90- 11.
Japanese marathon record 1994.
Progression at Mar: 1993- 2:26:27, 1994- 2:26:09, 1996- 2:28:00, 1997- 2:45:19, 1998- 2:31:12, 1999- 2:27:05, 2000- 2:28:01. pbs: 3000m 9:22.15 '89, 5000m 15:53.46 '93, 10000m 32:55.78 '93, 20km Rd 67:39 '93, HMar 72:00 '99, 100km 6:33:11 '00.
Second in 2:26:27 on marathon début at Osaka 1993, and won there in a national record in 1994, returning for 5th in 1996 and 6th in 1999 and 2000. Won Sapporo 1996. Ran a sensational women's world best for 100km at Lake Saroma in 2000, improving the previous best by 27 minutes 37 seconds!

Harumi HIROYAMA b. 2 Sep 1968 Tokushima pref. 1.60m 47kg. née Suzuki. Graduate of Kokushikan University. Shiseido.
At 10000m: OG: '00- 20; WCh: '99- 4. At 5000m: OG: '96- h; WCh: '97- 8. At 3000m: WCh: '93- h (h 1500m); AsiG: '94- 2. Won E.Asian 5000m 1997, JPN 1500m & 3000m 1992, 10000m 1997, 1999, Mar 2000.
Japanese records: 1500m 1992 and 1994, 3000m (2) 1994, 5000m 1997 and 1998.
Progression at 5000m, 10000m, Mar: 1990- 17:18.21, 1991- 16:55.0, 1993- 15:30.78, 1994- 15:33.53, 1995- 15:28.17, 32:03.35; 1996- 15:09.69, 31:43.99; 1997- 15:07.75, 31:22.72; 1998- 15:03.67, 2:28:12; 1999- 15:21.04, 31:26.84; 2000- 15:20.36, 31:59.60, 2:22:56. pbs: 800m 2:06.19 '94, 1500m 4:11.10 '94, 3000m 8:50.40 '94, HMar 70:49 '00.
Third at Nagoya on marathon debut 1998, and 2nd at Osaka in 2000. Married to marathon runner Tsutomu Hiroyama (b. 22 Oct 1966, pb 2:11:37 '90).

Yuko KAWAKAMI b. 1 Aug 1975 Kobe 1.52m 45kg. Miyazaki Oki electric company.
At 10000m: OG: '96- 7, '00- 10; WCh: '99- 12; AsiG: '98- 1. At 5000m: WCh: '97- 15. Won JPN 10000m 1998.
Japanese 10000m record 2000.
Progression at 5000m, 10000m: 1991- 16:39.9, 1993- 16:13.4, 1994- 15:49.42, 1995- 15:45.83, 1996- 15:27.77, 31:20.19; 1997- 15:17.34, 31:26.67; 1998- 15:24.16, 31:39.35; 1999- 15:25.01, 31:43.01; 2000- 15:23.59, 31:09.46. pbs: 3000m 8:55.8 '98, 2M 9:35.04 '98, HMar 70:33 '99, Mar 2:34:09 '99.

Mizuki NOGUCHI b. 3 Jul 1978 Mie pref. Globaly. At HMar: WCh: '99- 2, '00- 4. Won Asian CC 1999. pbs: 5000m 15:34.36 '99, 10000m 32:05.23 '00, HMar 68:30 '99.

Yoko SHIBUI b. 14 Mar 1979 Kuroiso, Tochigi pref.1.65m 48kg.
Progression at 10000m, Mar: 1997- 33:53.20, 1999- 32:43.02, 2000- 31:48.89, 2001- 2:23:11. pbs: 5000m 15:35.79 '00, HMar 69:31 '00.
Ran the fastest ever debut marathon by a woman with 2:23:11 to win at Osaka in January 2001. Her breakthrough came with a 31:59 ekiden road relay leg in January 2000 and she had shown brilliant form with 10km legs of 31:09 and 31:11 in November 2000.

Chiemi TAKAHASHI b. 16 Feb 1976 Miyagi pref. 1.59m 43kg. Nihon Chemical.
At 10000m: OG: '00- 15; WCh: '97- 10, '99- 5; AsiG: '98- 3; AsiC: '98- 2. At 5000m: WCh: '95- h. At 3000m: WJ: '94- 6, Asi-J '92- 3. World CC: '95-97-01: 12J/17/10.
Progression at 10000m: 1995- 32:08.97, 1996- 32:03.61, 1997- 31:38.42, 1998- 31:27.57, 1999- 31:27.62, 2000- 31:52.59. pbs: 1500m 3:39.41 '97, 3000m 9:11.70 '94, 5000m 15:22.64 '99, HMar 71:35 '96.

Naoko TAKAHASHI b. 6 May 1972 Gifu 1.63m 47kg. Sekisui Chemical. Graduate of Osaka Gakuin University.
At Mar: OG: '00- 1; AsiG: '98- 1. At 5000m: WCh: '98- 13. Won JPN marathon 1998.
Asian and two Japanese marathon records 1998.
Progression at 10000m, Mar: 1994- 34:02.02, 1996- 31:48.23, 1997- 32:34.50, 2:31:32; 1998- 31:55.95, 2:21:47; 2000- 2:22:19. pbs: 1500m

4:22.89 '94, 3000m 9:13.00 '94, 5000m 15:21.15 '98, HMar 68:55 '00.
In 1998 she set national marathon records, 2:25:48 at Nagoya in March, and then a superb 2:21:47, on her own all the way and despite slowing in intense heat and humidity, to win the Asian Games gold medal in December. She had made her marathon debut with 7th at Osaka in 1997. After graduating from University she joined the Recruit team coached by Yoshio Koide and later followed him to the Sekisui team. Withdrew, injured, from 1999 World Champs on the eve of the race, but returned with a superb 2:22:19 (69:39 second half) to win at Nagoya in March 2000 and later took the Olympic gold in great style.

Eri YAMAGUCHI b. 14 Jan 1973 Takino, Hyogo pref. 1.63m 47kg. Tenmaya, Okayama.
At Mar: OG: '00- 7. Japanese champion 1999.
Progression at Mar: 1995- 2:32:47, 1996- 2:31:43, 1997- 2:39:46, 1998- 2:27:36, 1999- 2:22:12, 2000- 2:27:03. pbs: 3000m 9:26.86 '98, 5000m 15:42.3 '98, 10000m 32:07.25 '00. HMar 70:04 (69:31+) '99.
Made amazing breakthrough to win 1999 Tokyo women's marathon in 2:22:12, the fastest ever time in a women's only marathon on an out-and-back course. This was her second win in eight marathons; she had also won at Sapporo in 1998.

KAZAKHSTAN

Governing body: Athletic Federation of the Republic of Kazakhstan, Abai Street 48, 480072 Almaty. Founded 1959.

2000 National Champions: Men: 100m: Vitaliy Savin 10.74, 200m: Andrey Taranenko 21.74, 400m: Denis Rypakov 48.33, 800m: Yevgeniy Shelestov 1:50.14, 1500m: Boris Zhavoronkin 4:01.40, 5000m: Mikhail Kolganov 15:27.30, 10000m: Vladimir Gusev 31:23.18, 3000mSt: Nail Shakirov 10:14.61, 110mh: 110H: Andrey Korniyenko KGZ 15.07, 400mh: Yevgeniy Meleshenko 50.54, HJ: Yuriy Pakhlayev 2.26, PV: *none*, LJ: Andrey Pakhomov 7.41, TJ: Oleg Sakirkin 16.64, SP: Sergey Semenov UZB 15.91, DT: Chary Mamedov TKM 62.06; JT: Dmitriy Polyunin UZB 77.74, Dec: Ivan Yarkin 7612, 20kmW: Valeriy Borisov 1:26:48, 50kmW: Rustem Kuvatov 4:09:43. **Women**: 100m: Viktoriya Kovyreva 11.74, 200m: Alena Petrova TKM 25.10, 400m: Oksana Luneva KGZ 54.31, 800m: Gulmira Tasiybekova 2:04.96, 1500m: Svetlana Lukashova 4:30.50, 5000m: Garifa Kuku 17:29.8, 100mh: Yelena Nikitenko 14.62, 400mh: Natalya Torshina 55.61, HJ: Tatyana Efimenko KGZ 1.89, PV: Natalya Medvedeva 3.40, LJ: Yelena Bobrivskaya KGZ 6.39, TJ: Yelena Parfenova 13.60, SP: Iolanta Ulyeva 16.59, DT: Yekaterina Mitina 46.21, HT: Tatyana Kolesnikova 23.40, JT: Tatyana Morisova 34.42, Hep: Svetlana Kazanina 6117, 10kmW/20kmW: Svetlana Tolstaya 44:00/1:30:44.

Sergey KOREPANOV b. 9 May 1964 Almaty 1.70m 61kg. State Unversity, Izhevsk. Sports teacher.
At 50kmW: OG: '96- 8, '00- 15; WCh: '93- 10, '95- 9, '97- 12, '99- dnf; WCp: '95- 9, '99- 1; AsiG: '94- 1, '98- 2. At 20kmW: AsiC: '93- 3.
Asian 50km record 1999. KZK 50km walk records 1993-9.
Progression at 50kmW: 1989- 3:58:13, 1990- 3:56:33, 1991- 3:55:47, 1992- 4:08:02sh, 1993- 3:52:50, 1994- 3:54:37, 1995- 3:48:06, 1996- 3:48:42, 1997- 3:42:16, 1998- 3:45:15, 1999- 3:39:22, 2000- 3:53:05. pbs: 5000mW 19:14.00i '95, 20kmW 1:20:34 '95.
His World Cup win at 50km walk in 1999 was the first world medal for Kazakhstan.

Women

Olga SHISHIGINA b. 23 Dec 1968 1.62m 57kg.
At 100mh: OG: '00- 1; WCh: '95- 2, '99- 4; AsiG '94- 1, '98- 1; AsiC: '98- 1; WCp: '98- dnf; won Central Asian 1995, 1999 (and 100m). At 60mh: WI: '95/9/01- 2/1/4
Asian 100mh record 1995, Asian records indoors: 60mh (6) 1995-9 (two in 1996 lost due to positive drugs test), 50mh (3) 1995-9. KZK 100m record 2000.
Progression at 100mh: 1990- 14.04, 1991- 13.47, 1993- 13.29, 1994- 12.78, 1995- 12.44/12.41w, 1998- 12.63, 1999- 12.47, 2000- 12.65. pbs: 100m 11.13 '00, 200m 23.6 '94, 50mh 6.70i '99, 60mh 7.82i '99, 7.78i drugs dq '96.
Son Vitaliy born 1988. Lost just to Gail Devers (twice) at 100mh in 1995. Served two years drugs ban for positive test on 7 Feb 1996 at Gent. Became Kazakhstan's first individual Olympic champion in athletics in 2000.

Svetlana ZALEVSKAYA b. 14 Jun 1973 1.88m 65kg.
At HJ: OG: '96- 13, '00- 6; WCh: '93- 11=, '95- dnq 15, '99- 8; WJ: '92- 2=; EJ: '91- 5; WUG: '95- 2; WCp: '94- 5; AsiG: '94- 2; AsiC: '93- 1, '95- 1. Won C.Asian 1999.
Asian high jump record 1996.
Progression at HJ: 1990- 1.83, 1991- 1.89, 1992 1.89, 1993- 1.94, 1994- 1.89, 1995- 1.96, 1996- 1.98i/1.97, 1997- 1.96dq/1.95i/1.93, 1999- 1.93, 2000- 1.97.
Drugs disqualification 1997.

KENYA

Governing body: Kenya Amateur Athletic Association, Nyayo National Stadium, PO Box 46722, Nairobi. Founded 1951.
2000 National Champions: **Men**: 100m/200m: Ezra Sambu 10.51/20.71, 400m: David Kirui 45.71, 800m: Patrick Konchellah 1:45.8, 1500m: Noah Ngeny 3:38.3, 5000m: Julius Gitahi 13:24.4, 10000m: John Cheruiyot Korir 27:48.42, 3000mSt: Reuben Kosgei 8:17.6, 110mh: James Kotut 14.59, 400mh: James Karanja 50.27, HJ: Justus Musema 2.10, PV: Ken Kirui 4.60, LJ/TJ: Remmy Limo 7.54/16.52, SP: Gideon Mengich

14.75, DT: Joshua Pondo 49.60, JT: Paul Langat 72.9720kmW: Julius Sawe 1:21:21. **Women**: 100m/200m: Hellen Chemutai 12.13/24.6, 400m: Josephine Nyarunda 53.55, 800m: Jebet Langat 2:02.03, 1500m: Jeruto Kiptum 4:08.6, 5000m: Lydia Cheromei 15:45.7, 10000m: Tegla Loroupe 32:13.5, 2000mSt: Panistine Chepkorir 6:34.47, 100mh: Jemima Munyua 15.35, 400mh: Praxidis Chemaringo 60.69, HJ: Catherine Kagwiria 1.65, PV: Ann Too 2.25, LJ/TJ: Caroline Kola 5.65/12.36, SP/DT/HT: Elizabeth Tom 12.95/40.54/34.82, JT: Cecilia Kiplangat 51.47, 20kmW: Grace Wanjiru 1:45:38.

Bernard BARMASAI b. 6 May 1974 Keiyo 1.73m 55kg. Keiyo.
At 3000mSt: OG: '00- 4; WCh: '97- 3, '99- 5; CG: '98- 1; AfG: '95- 1; AfCh: '98- 1; WCp: '98- 2. Won GWG 1998, GP (and overall) 1999 (3rd 1997). Kenyan champion 1998-9. World CC: '97- 6.
World 3000m steeplechase record 1997.
Progression at 3000mSt: 1994- 8:14.18, 1995- 8:08.56, 1996- 8:10.84, 1997- 7:55.72, 1998- 8:00.67, 1999- 7:58.98, 2000- 8:02.76. pbs: 1500m 3:37.24 '00, 3000m 7:36.40 '97, 2000mSt 5:28.31 '95.
After setting a world record in 1997, Barmasai was ranked world number one at the steeplechase in 1998 and 1999. Won six of seven Golden League steeplechases in 1999, just losing to Ali Ezzine in the last, at Berlin. However, he had lost his chance of sharing the Jackpot when the IAAF determined that he had brought the sport into disrepute by apparently telling Christopher Kosgei not to beat him in Zürich.

Paul BITOK b. 26 Jun 1970 Kilibwoni 1.73m 58kg. Nandi. Airman (SPTE).
At 5000m: OG: '92- 2, '96- 2; WCh: '93- 8, '97- 13; WJ: '88- 9; AfG: '93- 4. At 3000m: WI: '97- 2, '99- 2. Won GP 5000m 1992, 2nd 3000m 1999. World Rd Rly team: '92- 1.
Progression at 5000m: 1988- 14:08.8, 1992- 13:08.89, 1993- 13:08.68, 1994- 13:07.30, 1995- 13:16.39, 1996- 13:04.48, 1997- 13:04.74, 1998- 13:14.26, 1999- 13:15.22i/13:31.01; 2000- 13:04.15. pbs: 1500m 3:35.82 '98, 1M 3:56.39i '00, 3:59.6 '96; 2000m 4:54.36 '99, 3000m 7:28.41 '96, 2M 8:13.28i '01, 8:16.44 '99; 10000m 28:51.6 '95, Rd 10km 28:31 '93.
Won the Paavo Nurmi Challenge 1997 with 1500m in 3:36.87 followed by 5000m in 13:26.25. No relation to the other notable Bitoks.

Wilson BOIT KIPKETER b. 6 Oct 1973 1.67m 52kg. Keiyo.
At 3000mSt: OG: '00- 2, WCh: '97- 1, '99- 2, AfG: '99- 2. 2nd GP 1999. World CC: '98- 5.
World 3000m steeplechase record 1997.
Progression at 3000mSt: 1993- 8:39.0A, 1994- 8:27.90A, 1995- 8:33.6A, 1996- 8:11.29, 1997- 7:59.08, 1998- 8:01.05, 1999- 8:07.10, 2000- 8:07.33. pbs: 2000m 5:02.1e '97, 3000m 7:33.96 '97, 10000m 28:43.89A '97.

David CHELULE b. 7 Jul 1977 1.70m 60kg.
At 10000 m (5000m): OG: '00- (5); WCh: '99- 9; WJ: '94- (h), '96- 2 (2); AfG: '99- 2. World CC: '95- 3J, '96- 1J. Won Kenyan 10000m 1999.
Progression at 5000m, 10000m: 1994- 13:56.8, 1995- 13:32.53, 1996- 13:24.48, 27:32.18; 1997- 13:02.52, 28:49.2A; 1999- 12:57.79, 27:51.90; 2000- 13:13.72, 27:57.10A. pbs: 2000m 5:01.7e '97, 3000m 7:37.36 '99, 3000mSt 8:55.2 '94, road 10km 27:19 '00.

Julius CHELULE b. 25 Dec 1978 Kapchumba 1.71m 55kg. Nandi
At 3000mSt: WJ: '94- 2, '96- 1.
Progression at 3000mSt: 1994- 8:33.64, 1995- 8:29.99, 1996- 8:33.09, 1997- 8:18.71, 1998- 8:12.91, 1999- 8:10.41, 2000- 8:21.21.
At 16, he became the yougest man to break 8:30 for 3000mSt. No relation to David Chelule.

William CHIRCHIR b. 6 Feb 1979 Bomet 1.77m 55kg. Kipsigis.
At 800m: WJ: '98- 1. At 1500m: OG: '00- h.
Ratified world junior 1500m record 1998.
Progression at 800m, 1500m: 1997- 1:47.08, 3:35.44; 1998- 1:44.69, 3:33.24; 1999- 1:43.33, 3:36.22; 2000- 1:43.84, 3:31.02. pbs: 1000m 2:14.99 '99, 1M 3:47.94 '00, 3000m 7:55.78 '97, HJ 1.90 '97.
Won Kenyan Schools decathlon in 1997. His younger brother **Cornelius** (b. 7 Oct 1983) won the 1500m at the 1999 World Youth Championships and at the 2000 World Juniors; he set a world age-16 best of 3:35.16 in 2000.

Julius GITAHI b. 29 Apr 1978 Nyeri 1.68m 52kg. Based in Japan.
At 5000m: OG: '00- 9; AfG: '99- 1; Kenyan champion 2000. At 10000m: Won GWG 1998, JPN Ch 1997. 3rd GP 3000m 1998.
Progression at 5000m, 10000m: 1994- 13:51.11, 28:43.96; 1995- 13:22.58, 28:00.12; 1996- 13:24.98, 27:28.60; 1997- 13:05.64, 27:44.49; 1998- 13:01.89, 27:11.17; 1999- 13:05.45, 27:17.66; 2000- 13:23.12. pbs: 3000m 7:31.13 '98. HMar 61:33 '98.
Started running when he went to Japan to study in 1994.

Patrick Mutuku **IVUTI** b. 30 Jun 1978 1.65m 52kg.
At 10000m: OG: '00- 4. World CC: '96-7-9-00-01: 9J/6J/2/4/7.
Progression at 5000m, 10000m: 1999- 28:48.0A, 2000- 13:02.68, 27:09.79. pb HMar 59:31 '00.

William KALYA b. 4 Aug 1974 1.71m 62kg.
At 10000m: CG: '98- 2. At 5000m: AfCh: '98- 3.
Progression at 5000m, 10000m: 1990- 14:00.3, 1995- 13:03.08, 1997- 13:12.76, 1998- 13:20.85, 28:06.3A; 1999- 28:31.30, 2000- 13:32.25, 27:23.65. pbs: 1500m 3:37.95 '91, 2000m 5:01.6+ '95, 3000m 7:31.14 '97.

Charles KAMATHI b. 18 May 1978 1.65m 51kg. Police constable.
World CC: '00- 7, '01- 3.

Progression at 5000m, 10000m: 1999- 13:05.29, 26:51.49; 2000- 13:23.24. pbs: 1500m 3:41.6? '99, 3000m 7:43.50 '00.
Made a sensational debut in European competition when he won at 10000m in 26:51.49 in Brussels in September 1999. He had won in India in July at 3000m 7:56.56 and 5000m 13:45.91 in his only previous races outside Kenya, where he had been 2nd at 5000m and 10,000m in the Kenyan Police Championships (c. 14:01 and 28:57) and had a 5000m best of c.13:43.

John Kemboi **KIBOWEN** 21 Apr 1969 Changach 1.75m 64kg. Nandi.
At 1500m: WCh: '97- h; CG: '98- 4. World CC 4k: '98-00-01: 1/1/7; Rd Rly team: '98- 1. Won KEN 1500m 1998.
Commonwealth 2000m record 1998.
Progression at 1500m: 1996- 3:38.6, 1997- 3:30.44, 1998- 3:30.18, 2000- 3:33.04. pbs: 1M 3:47.88 '97, 2000m 4:48.74 '98, 3000m 7:29.09 '98, 5000m 13:48.5 '96.
Trained as an aircraft technician 1992-5. before concentrating on running. Missed 1999 season through injury.

Joseph KIMANI Karanja b. 1 Sep 1972 Nakuru 1.70m 60kg.
At 10000m: WCh: '95- 6. World CC: '96- 6; HMar: '98- 21, '00- 4; Rd Rly team: '96- 1.
Progression at 5000m, 10000m: 1994- 13:26.44, 1995- 13:12.05, 27:28.07; 1997- 28:33.4, 2000- 28:30.32. pb 1M 4:03.11 '95, 3000m 7:44.77 '95, 2M 8:30.78 '95, Rd 15km 42:40 '96, HMar 60:04 '98, Mar 2:25:32 '98.
Has had outstanding success on the US road running circuit, including world bests for 10km on a loop course 27:41 '95 and 27:20 '96 and on a slightly downhill course 27:04 '96. His brother James Kuria ran a 63:59 half marathon in 1998.

Japheth KIMUTAI Butia b. 20 Dec 78 Lelmokwo, Nandi 1.73m 55kg.
At 800m: OG: '00- sf; WCh: '99- 5; CG: '98- 1; AfG: '99- 1; AfCh: '98- 1; WJ: '94- 2, '96- 4; WCp: '98- 4; AfJ: '95- 1 (1 1500m). 3rd GP 1999. Kenyan champion 1999.
World junior 800m record 1997.
Progression at 800m: 1994- 1:47.6, 1995- 1:47.0, 1996- 1:45.4, 1997- 1:43.64, 1998- 1:42.76, 1999- 1:42.69, 2000- 1:43.87. pbs: 1000m 2:14.28 '00, 1500m 3:34.14 '00.
A product of St Patrick's High School and the renowned coach Brother Colm O'Connell. After the disappointment of losing World Juniors in 1996, came back the following year to break Joaquim Cruz's 16 year-old 800m WJR. While still a teenager in 1998, ranked as world no.1 and in Zürich broke the three year unbeaten run of Wilson Kipketer. Trains in Iten, but based during the European summer in Tubingen, Germany.

Kenneth KIMWETICH (NGETICH) b. 1 Jan 1973 Eldoret 1.83m 73kg.
At 800m: WCh: '99- 7; CG: '98- 8; AfG: '99- 5. Kenyan champion 1998.
Progression at 800m: 1998- 1:43.03, 1999- 1:43.98, 2000- 1:44.20. pb 1000m 2:13.56 '99.
Did not race prior to 1998.

Sammy KIPKETER b. 29 Sep 1981 Keiyo 1.66m 52kg.
World CC: '99- 6J, 4k: '00-01: 2/4. 3rd GP 3000m 2000. Official world junior record 3000m 1999.
Progression at 5000m: 1999- 12:58.10, 2000- 12:54.07. pbs: 2000m 5:00.0e '99, 3000m 7:34.58 '99.
World age-17 bests at 3000m and 5000m 1999.

Luke KIPKOSGEI b. 27 Nov 1975 Iten 1.75m 55kg.
Won GWG 5000m 1998, GP 3000m 2000.
Progression at 5000m, 10000m: 1996- 13:15.00, 27:26.12; 1997- 13:22.68, 27:29.44; 1998- 12:57.32, 27:22.54; 1999- 13:00.83, 2000- 12:56.50, 27:57.11. pbs: 1500m 3:35.48 '98, 1M 3:56.4+ '98, 2000m 4:52.82 '98. 3000m 7:27.59 '98, 2M 8:17.53 '98.
Ran 27:26.12 on track debut at 10000m in Melbourne, December 1996.

Benjamin KIPKURUI b. 28 Dec 1980 Molo 1.74m 57kg. Kipsigis.
At 1500m (/800m): WJ: '98- 2; AfG: '99- (4); AfJ: '97- 1/1.
World junior records 1000m and 1500m 1999.
Progression at 800m, 1500m: 1997- 1:49.3, 3:44.17; 1998- 1:44.71, 3:35.35, 1999- 1:44.56, 3:33.16; 2000- 1:46.30, 3:30.73. pbs: 1000m 2:15.00 '99, 1M 3:49.34 '00.
World age-17 bests at 800m and 1500m in 1998.

Josephat KIPRONO b. 12 Dec 1973 Eldoret 1.72m 52kg. FILA, Italy.
At HMar: WCh: '96- 2.
Kenyan marathon record to win at Berlin 1999.
Progression at Mar: 1998- 2:07:27, 1999- 2:06:44, 2000- 2:07:29. pbs: 5000m 13:50.37 '95, 10000m 28:57.1 '93, Road: 10km 28:39 '96, 15km 43:46 '96, HMar 60:27 '98, 59:46sh '96; 3000mSt 8:42.2 '95.
Second in 1996 Stramilano half marathon, when course was short by 49m. Marathon debut with 4th at Rotterdam (2:09:11), then 2nd Berlin 1998. In 1999 he was 5th in London before winning at Berlin. He won the Milennium Marathon in Rome on 1 Jan 2000 and was second in Chicago 2000.

Fred KIPROP b. 3 Jun 1974. FILA.
Progression at Mar: 1997- 2:08:19, 1998- 2:11:15, 1999- 2:06:47, 2000- 2:08:23. pbs: road 10km 27:52 '99.
2nd in Chicago 1997, has three wins in his eight marathons: Gold Coast 1998 and 1999 before his fourth fastest of all-time at Amsterdam 1999.

Moses KIPTANUI b. 1 Oct 1970 Marakwet. 1.75m 57kg. Marakwet.
At 3000mSt: OG: '96- 2; WCh: '91- 1, '93- 1, '95- 1, '97- 2; AfG: '91- 1; WCp: '94- 1; won GP 1991, 1995 (1st overall); 2nd 1993, 1997. At 1500m: WJ:

'90- 1; AfCh: '90- 1. At 3000m: WI: '97- 5. 3rd GP 5000m 1994. Won Kenyan 3000mSt 1991, 1997; 1500m 1992; GWG 5000m 1994.
World records at 3000m (7:28.96) 1992, 5000m 1995, 3000m steeplechase 1992 and 1995, Kenyan records 2000m and 5000m 1992, 3000m 1995; WIRs 3000m (7:37.31 '92, 7:35.13 '95).
Progression at 1500m, 3000mSt, 5000m: 1989- 8:46.6, 1990- 3:36.73; 1991- 3:35.40, 8:06.46; 1992- 3:34.0, 8:02.08, 13:00.93; 1993- 3:35.44, 8:06.36, 13:14.62; 1994- 3:34.44, 8:08.80, 13:10.7; 1995- 3:34.82, 7:59.18, 12:55.30; 1996- 3:36.88i/3:38.2, 8:08.33, 12:54.85; 1997- 3:37.62, 13:03.00, 7:56.16; 1998- 13:14.82, 8:04.96; 1999- 8:09.23, 2000- 8:16.68. pbs: 1M 3:54.01 '91, 2000m 4:52.53 '92, 3000m 7:27.18 '95, 2M 8:09.01 '94.
In 1990, with no known form the previous year he won the World Junior and African senior titles at 1500m. He was then listed with a date of birth in 1971, but he has long insisted that he was a year older than this. In 1991 he turned to the steeplechase, running 8:31.0 to win the Kenyan services title in June, and then a month later threatened the world record with 8:07.89 in Stockholm. He went on to win the world title easily and to run 8:06.46. In 1992 he did not make the Kenyan Olympic team, but he showed great form in August when he set world records for 3000m in Köln and three days later for the steeplechase in Zürich, followed by close attempts at world records for 2000m and on his début at 5000m. Was a corporal in the army until 1994. In 1995 he ran the first sub 8-minute 3000m steeple at Zürich and followed with another at Brussels; at the end of 1996 he had run the six sub-8:05 times ever. He ran a further five sub-8:05 times in 1997, but his compatriots Boit and Barmasai both broke his world record. Now coaching leading runners, including Daniel Komen, at Nyahururu.

David Singoei **KIPTOO** b. 26 Jun 1965 (25 Jun 1967?) Kapsabat 1.75m 68kg. Economics graduate.
At 800m: OG: '96- 6. 3rd GP 1997 & 1999.
Progression at 800m: 1990- 1:49.60, 1991- 1:46.89, 1992- 1:48.10, 1993- 1:45.64, 1994- 1:44.07, 1995- 1:44.08, 1996- 1:43.38, 1997- 1:44.09, 1998- 1:43.60, 1999- 1:43.85, 2000- 1:44.6. pb 400m 46.34, 400mh 50.86/50.7 '91

Ismael KIRUI b. 20 Feb 1975 Marakwet 1.60m 55kg. Marakwet.
At 5000m: WCh: '93- 1, '95- 1, '97- h; WJ: '92- 2. Won GP 1993. At 10000m: WJ: '90- 2. World CC: '90-1-2-3-4-6-8: 4J/7J/1J/3/2/3/7. Won Kenyan 10000m 1993.
World junior records 3000m, 5000m (3) 1993.
Progression at 5000m, 10000m: 1990- 13:59.6, 28:40.77; 1992- 13:15.67, 29:35.0A; 1993- 13:02.75, 28:07.1; 1994- 13:14.46; 1995- 13:02.75, 27:06.59; 1996- 13:06.86, 28:49.13; 1997- 13:14.71, 27:44.27; 1999- 13:48.7A, 27:20.89; 2000- 13:11.18, 27:50.16. pbs: 2000m 5:04.4 '93, 3000m 7:39.82 '93. Road world bests: 10M: 45:38 '95, 12km 33:42 '94.
Won IAAF Cross Challenge 1992/3 and 1994/5. Younger brother of Richard Chelimo (b. 21 Apr 1972, but possibly c.1965) to whom he was runner-up at the 1990 World Juniors. At 10000m, Chelimo set a world record of 27:07.91 in 1993, and was 2nd in the 1991 Worlds and 1992 Olympics and 3rd 1993 Worlds. Their sister Catherine Kirui (b. 1 Mar 1976) was 6th in the World Junior CC in 1991 and 1993 and 11th in the seniors 1995. Married **Rose Cheruiyot** (pbs 3000m 8:39.34, 5000m 14:46.41 in 1994; 11 OG 5000m 2000) on 16 Nov 1996.

Daniel Kipngetich **KOMEN** b. 17 May 1976 Mwen 1.70m 60kg. Keiyo.
At 5000m (10000m): WCh: '97- 1, '99- 5; CG: '94- (9), '98- 1; AfCh: '98- 1; WJ: '94- 1 (1); WCp: '98- 1. Won overall & 5000m GP 1996. World CC: '94- 2J, '98- 2 4k. Won Kenyan 5000m 1997.
World record: 3000m 1996, 5000m 1997, world best 2 miles (8:03.54) 1996 and 1997. WIR 3000m 7:24.90 '98 and 5000m 12:51.48 '98. World junior records 1500m, 5000m 1995. Commonwealth & Kenyan records 2000m 1998, 3000m 1996, 5000m (4) 1996-7, Kenyan 1500m & 1M 1997.
Progression at 1500m, 5000m, 10000m: 1993- 13:58.30, 1994- 13:31.10, 28:29.74; 1995- 3:34.63, 12:56.15, 28:12.79; 1996- 3:34.17, 12:45.09; 1997- 3:29.46, 12:39.74; 1998- 3:30.49, 12:51.48i/12:54.82; 1999- 3:35.42, 12:55.16; 2000- 13:01.78. pbs: 1M 3:46.38 '97, 2000m 4:51.30 '98, 3000m 7:20.67 '96, 2M 7:58.61 '97, 3000mSt 8:54.5 '94, Road 10km 27:46 '94.
Ran 57.42 first lap in 1994 Commonwealth Games 5000m. In August 1996 he missed world records by narrow margins: 3000m by 0.05 at Monaco 10th, 5000m by 0.70 at Zürich on 14th, 3000m by 0.76 in Brussels on 23rd; then, on 1 September, came his superb 3000m at Rieti, in which he took 4.44 sec off Noureddine Morceli's old record, running under 60 secs for each 400m. In 1997 he ran first sub-8 minute 2 miles at Hechtel and lopped 2.12 secs off Gebrselassie's 9-day old 5000m world record at Brussels. Former high jumper and soccer goalkeeper.

Patrick KONCHELLAH b. 20 Apr 1968 1.81m 68kg. Masai.
At 800m: WCh: '97- 4; CG: '94- 1. Kenyan champion 1994, 1997, 2000.
Progression at 800m: 1989- 1:49.8, 1990- 1:47.3, 1991- 1:48.0, 1992- 1:46.6, 1993- 1:45.71, 1994- 1:44.24, 1997- 1:42.98, 1998- 1:46.32, 1999- 1:44.77, 2000- 1:44.58, pb 1000m 2:14.73 '00, 1500m 3:41.54 '94, 1M 4:03.50 '94.
Younger brother of Billy Konchellah (b. 20 Oct 1962), world 800m champion 1987 and 1991 (3rd 1993), 4th OG 1984, pb 1:43.06 '87.

John Cheruiyot **KORIR** b. 13 Dec 1981 1.67m 55kg.
At 10000m: OG: '00- 5. Kenyan champion 2000.

Progression at 5000m,10000m: 1999- 13:24.22, 27:38.86; 2000- 13:09.58, 27:24.75. pbs: 3000m 7:43.35 '00, 5000m 13:18.00 '98.
Ran fastest ever 10,000m at high altitude, 27:48,42, to win 2000 Kenyan title.

Christopher KOSGEI b. 14 Aug 1974 1.70m 62kg. Name in passport is Christopher Cherono Kipkosgei.
At 3000mSt: WCh: '95- 2, '99- 1; AfG: '99- 3; AfCh: '93- 2. World CC: '93- 2J.
Progression at 3000mSt: 1991- 9:05.5A, 1993- 8:24.58, 1994- 8:33.2, 1995- 8:06.86, 1996- 8:08.84, 1997- 8:10.19, 1998- 8:42.28, 1999- 8:05.43, 2000- 8:20.49. pbs: 3000m 7:57.12 '96, 5000m 13:40.17 '96, 10000m 29:45.62 '96.
When he first appeared he often ran barefoot, and, possessing a strong finishing kick, has long adopted outrageous tactics, sitting at the back of the field and then shooting through. Nicknamed "jogoo", meaning cockerel. His brother **Abraham Cherono** (b. 27 Jul 1980) was 2nd in the 1998 World Junior 3kmSt after 11th in the 1997 World Junior CC, pb 8:13.22 '00.

Japhet KOSGEI b. 20 Dec 1968. 1.65m 52kg. FILA, MIlan.
Progression at Mar: 1998- 2:09:59, 1999- 2:07:09, 2000- 2:07:15. pb HMar 60:01 '99.
Won first four marathons: Turin and Venice 1998, Rotterdam 1999, Tokyo 2000; then dnf London and 2nd New York 2000. Also won 1999 Lisbon half marathon in 60:01.

John KOSGEI b. 13 Jul 1973 Elgayo Marakwet 1.84m 71kg.
At 3000mSt: CG: '98- 1; AfCh: '92- 7. World CC 4k: '98- 5, '99- 8; Rd Rly team: '98- 1. Won KEN 4k CC 1998.
Progression at 1500m, 3000mSt: 1990- 9:12.0A, 1991- 8:54.0A, 1992- 3:43.98, 8:32.03; 1994- 8:48.5A, 1995- 3:40.25, 1996- 3:34.50, 8:05.68; 1997- 3:34.09, 8:03.89; 1998- 3:41.55, 8:09.08; 1999- 3:43.2, 8:42.52; 2000- 3:37.74, 8:19.47. pbs: 1M 3:54.7 '96, 2000m 4:53.7 '96, 3000m 7:37.39 '96, 5000m 13:28.62 '96, road 10km 28:56.
As pacemaker, took Daniel Komen to 2000m in his epic 3000m world record in Rieti in 1996. Six days later he made an extraordinary breakthrough at 3000m steeplechase at Milan, beating a top-class field in 8:05.68.

Paul KOSGEI Malakwen b. 22 Apr 1978 Marakwet 1.75m 57kg.
At 3000mSt: WCh: '99- 7. World CC: '97- 3J, 4k: '98-9-00: 3/2/3; 12k: '01- 5; Rd Rly team: '98- 1. World junior record 3000m steeplechase 1997.
Progression at 5000m, 10000m, 3000mSt: 1997- 8:07.69, 1998- 8:07.86, 1999- 8:07.13, 2000- 13:05.44, 27:38.22, 8:29.57. pbs: 2000m 5:03.1+ '00, 3000m 7:39.15 '00, 2000mSt 5:19.78 '98.
Won his heat at 1999 World Champs in 8:10.34, the fastest ever time in a preliminary round. Ran world road best 10km 27:03 in 2000.

Reuben KOSGEI b. 2 Aug 1979 Kapsabet 1.73m 54kg.
At 3000mSt: OG: '00- 1; WJ: '98- 1; Afr-J: '97- 1. Kenyan champion 2000.
Progression at 3000mSt: 1998- 8:23.76, 1999- 8:12.33, 2000- 8:03.92. pbs: 1500m 3:37.24 '00, 3000m 7:41.86i '00.

Bernard LAGAT b. 12 Dec 1974 Kapsabet 1.75m 61kg. Business management student at Washington State University, USA. Nandi.
At 1500m: OG: '00- 3; WUG: '99- 1; 2nd GP 1999-2000. At 3000m: WI: '01- 6. Won NCAA 5000m 1999 (and indoor 1M/3000m).
Progression at 1500m: 1996- 3:37.7A, 1997- 3:41.19, 1998- 3:34.48, 1999- 3:30.56, 2000- 3:28.51. pbs: 800m 1:46.02 '98, 1000m 2:18.70 '00, 1M 3:49.84 '00, 2000m 4:55.49 '99, 3000m 7:33.51 '00, 5000m 13:23.46 '00.
After impressive results in GP races he gave up his final year of scholastic eligibilty (as under NCAA rules no payments can be received) at his university in order to compete (for money) in the 1999 Grand Prix Final, in which he was 2nd.

Elijah LAGAT b. 19 Jun 1966 Saniak, Kapsabet district 58kg. Nandi.
At Mar: OG: '00- dnf.
Progression at Mar: 1993- 2:17:14, 1994- 2:18:07, 1995- 2:12:40, 1996- 2:11:54, 1997- 2:07:41, 1998- 2:08:52, 1999- 2:08:50, 2000- 2:09:47. pbs: 10000m 28:09.1A '98; HMar 60:24 '99.
Four wins in 13 marathons: Jerez 1994, Berlin 1997, Prague 1998, Boston 2000; 2nd Mombasa 1993, Frankfurt 1995, Turin 1997. Based in Italy with the FILA group of Dr Gabriele Rosa.

David LELEI b. 10 May 1971 Uasin Gishu 1.76m 60kg.
At 1500m: WCh: '99- 7; AfG: '99- 2. At 800m: WI: '01- 4.
Progression at 800m, 1500m: 1996- 1:47.51A, 1997- 1:45.44, 3:33.83; 1998- 1:46.96, 3:31.53; 1999- 1:45.35, 3:32.84; 2000- 1:43.97, 3:36.38. pbs: 1000m 2:22.71 '97, 1M 3:53.14 '99, 2000m 5:01.1 '98. Also known as David Kimeli.

Benjamin LIMO b. 23 Aug 1974 Kaptagat 1.78m 65kg. Army engineer.
At 5000m: WCh: '99- 2. Won GP 3000m 1999. World 4k CC: '98-9-01- 4/1/3; Rd Rly team: '98- 1.
Progression at 5000m: 1998- 13:07.38, 1999- 12:55.86, 2000- 12:55.82. pbs: 1500m 3:37.59 '99, 2000m 4:59.2e '99, 3000m 7:28.67 '99.
Only began running seriously in November 1997. Has great finishing speed.

Felix LIMO b. 22 Aug 1980.
Progression at 5000m, 10000m: 1999- 13:23.43, 28:23.30; 2000- 13:33.90, 27:04.54. pbs: 3000m 7:43.50 '00.

Richard Kipkemei **LIMO** b. 18 Nov 1980 Cheptigit 1.67m 53kg. Kalenjin.
At 5000m: OG: '00- 10; CG: '98- 3; AfG: '99- 6. At

3000mSt: AfCh: '98- 2. World CC: '98- 2J, '99- 2J. World junior records 3000m 1998, 2M 1999.
Progression at 5000m: 1998- 13:21.59, 1999- 12:58.15, 2000- 12:58.70. pbs: 2000m 5:00.6 '99, 3000m 7:34.32 '99, 2M 8:13.47 '99, 3000mSt 8:20.67 '98; Road: 10km 27:12 '00.

Simon MAINA Munyi b. 18 Mar 1978 Nyeri 1.77m 52kg. Kikuyu. Lives in Japan.
At 10000m: CG: '98- 1; AfG: '99- 4. Won JPN 5000m 1997-8, KEN 10000m 1998.
Progression at 5000m, 10000m: 1997- 13:33.1, 27:36.5; 1998- 13:10.71, 27:21.14; 1999- 13:15.88, 27:18.74; 2000- 13:19.60, 27:18.95. pb HMar 60:48 '00.

Benjamin MAIYO b. 6 Oct 1978 Trans Nzoia 1.75m 58kg.
At 10000m: WCh: '99- 7; AfG: '99- 5.
Progression at 5000m, 10000m: 1998- 13:18.98, 27:34.38; 1999- 13:02.38, 28:01.8A; 2000- 13:02.28, 28:28.7A. pbs: 1500m 3:42.30 '99, 2000m 5:01.9+ '00; 3000m 7:32.36 '00.

Kipkirui MISOI b. 23 Dec 1978 Bomet 1.77m 59kg.
At 3000mSt: CG: '98- 3; WJ: '96- 2; AfG: '99- 1. World CC: '98- 8 4k.
World junior record 3000m steeplechase 1998.
Progression at 3000mSt: 1995- 8:56.0A, 1996- 8:33.31, 1997- 8:16.76, 1998- 8:09.46, 1999- 8:08.62, 2000- 8:07.21. pbs: 1500m 3:39.17 '98, 3000m 7:40.93 '00, 5000m 13:26.83 '98.

Phillip MOSIMA b. 2 Jan 1977 (or 1976?) 1.68m 55kg.
At 5000m: WCh: '99- h; CG: '94- 5. At 1500m: WJ: '94- 3. World CC: '93- 1J, '94- 1J, '95- 5J, '00- 7 (4k). Won Afr J 1500m 1994; KEN 5000m 1999.
World junior records: 3000m (3) 1996, 5000m 1996.
Progression at 5000m: 1991- 14:02.0, 1993- 13:43.77, 1994- 13:24.07, 1995- 13:08.95, 1996- 12:53.72, 1997- 13:13.27, 1998- 13:29.06, 1999- 13:12.67, 2000- 13:09.69. pbs: 1500m 3:35.65 '97, 2000m 4:59.8+ '99, 3000m 7:35.52 '96, 2M 8:14.45 '97, 10km rd 28:30 '96.
Seriously injured in a car crash in July 1996.

Noah Kiprono **NGENY** b. 2 Nov 1978 Kabenas 1.82m 68kg.
At 1500m: OG: '00- 1; WCh: '99- 2; WI: '01- 3; WJ: '96- 8 (tripped on final lap). Won GP 1999-2000, KEN 1500m 1999-2000.
Records: World and two records 1000m 1999, Commonwealth: 1500m (3), 1M 1999-2000.
Progression at 1500m: 1996- 3:42.44, 1997- 3:32.91, 1998- 3:30.34, 1999- 3:28.73/3:28.6+u, 2000- 3:28.12. pbs: 800m 1:44.49 '00, 1000m 2:11.96 '99, 1M 3:43.40 '99, 2000m 4:50.08 '99, 3000m 7:35.46 '00.
Tripped on the first lap in the final of the 1996 World Juniors, sprinted to the front and led for three laps before being tripped again with 200m to go and losing his rhythm. Came through in 1997 to run world junior records. Although beaten three times by Hicham El Guerrouj, he had a wonderful season in 1999, following his World silver medal at 1500m, with the world record for 1000m (beating Seb Coe's 1981 mark) and a win in the Grand Prix Final 1500m. Then he ended El Guerrouj's winning run with Olympic gold in 2000. Brother of **Philip Kibitok** (b. 23 Mar 1971) pb 800m 1:43.55 '96.

Thomas NYARIKI 27 Sep 1971 Nyamira 1.70m 62kg.
At 5000m: OG: '96- 5; WCh: '97- 3; CG: '98- 2; AfG: '99- 3. 2nd GP 1997. Kenyan champion 1996, 1998. At 3000m: AfCh: '98- 1; WCp: '98- 3. World CC: '97- 3, '98- 4; Rd Rly team: '98- 1.
Progression at 5000m: 1996- 12:59.19, 1997- 12:55.94, 1998- 13:00.04, 1999- 13:04.07. pbs: 1500m 3:42.8 '95, 1M 3:59.6 '96, 2000m 4:55.79 '97, 3000m 7:27.75 '96, road 10km 27:30 '01.
Ex sprinter. Married to Jackline Maranga (qv).

Ondoro OSORO b. 3 Dec 1967 Masimba 1.68m 63kg. Civil servant working for Kenyan Armed Forces (private). Kisii.
At 5000m: WCh: '91- h; AfG: '91- 3. World CC: '91- 5, '93- 13.
Commonwealth marathon record 1998.
Progression at 5000m, 10000m, Mar: 1985- 14:05.4, 29:10.3; 1986- 30:03.2, 1987- 29:56.2, 1989- 13:36.2, 28:44.4; 1990- 14:02.1, 29:08.6; 1991- 13:11.77, 1992- 13:49.3, 1993- 13:15.21, 27:24.24; 1994- 13:16.39, 27:28.36; 1995- 27:32.82, 1996- 29:04.54, 1998- 29:05.1A, 2:06:54; 1999- 2:08:00, 2000- 2:10:29. pbs: 3000m 7:43.20 '93, 2M 8:29.67 '91; Road: 10M 45:36 '97, HMar 61:50 '00.
Won IAAF World Cross Challenge 1991 (2nd 1992). Seriously injured in a head-on car crash in 1995. On his return he concentrated on road running. In 1997 he set a world best for 10 miles on a loop course and in 1998 made a stunning marathon debut, with the fastest ever debut and third fastest of all-time to win in Chicago. 3rd Chicago 1999. A day after being selected to run in the 2000 Olympic marathon he was shot in the neck by car thieves and taken to hospital.

Laban ROTICH 20 Jan 1969 Mosoriot 1.63m 45kg. Fireman in Kenyan Air Force. Nandi.
At 1500m: OG: '96- 4; WCh: '97- 11, '99- 6; CG: '98- 1; AfCh: '98- 1; WI: '99- 2, '01- 4; WCp: '98- 1. 3rd GP 1996 & 1999. Won Kenyan 1500m 1997.
Kenyan records 1500m (3) 1996-7, 1000m & 1M 1997.
Progression at 800m, 1500m: 1995- 3:39.85, 1996- 1:45.8A, 3:31.06; 1997- 1:44.47, 3:30.13; 1998- 1:43.65, 3:29.91; 1999- 3:31.60, 2000- 3:32.93. pbs: 1000m 2:14.43 '97, 1M 3:47.65 '97, 2000m 4:56.09i '99, 4:57.63 '96.
World high altitude best 1500m 3:33.1 '98.

Evans RUTTO b. 8 Apr 1978 Marakwet.
World CC: 1999- 5.
Progression at 5000m, 10000m: 1999- 13:24.84,

28:06.60; 2000- 13:02.71, 27:21.32. pbs: 2000m 5:02.3+ '99; 3000m 7:36.38 '00.

Moses TANUI b. 20 Aug 1965 Nandi district 1.65m 65kg. FILA Club, Italy.
At 10000m (5000m): OG: '88- 8, '92- 8; WCh: '91- 1, '93- 2; CG: '90- 2 (5); AfCh: '89- 2 (3). Won Kenyan 10000m 1988-91. World CC: '87-8-9-90-1-3: 18/6/9/2/2/4. World HMar '94- 9, '95- 1, '97- 2. Commonwealth marathon record 1999.
Progression at 5000m, 10000m, Mar: 1986- 14:45.0, 1987- 13:54.0, 28:53.1; 1988- 13:36.74, 27:40.59; 1989- 13:24.85, 28:14.67; 1990- 13:28.31, 27:43.62; 1991- 13:21.75, 27:35.89; 1992- 13:17.80, 28:12.71; 1993- 13:22.82, 27:18.32, 2:15:36; 1994- 13:29.30, 28:06.76, 2:09:40; 1995- 13:35.97, 27:45.86, 2:10:22; 1996- 29:11.76, 2:09:15; 1997- 2:09:01, 1998- 2:07:34, 1999- 2:06:16, 2000- 2:07:47. pbs: 1500m 3:41.8 '89, 2000m 5:03.7 '95, 3000m 7:39.63 '95, 2M 8:33.47 '88.
Won the Stramilano Half Marathon each year 1990-3, setting a world best 59:47 in 1993, and Great North Run 1993 and 1995. Tenth in New York on his marathon début 1993. At Boston he went sub-2:10 for 10th in 1994, followed by 2nd 1995, 1st 1996, 5th 1997, 1st 1998, 3rd 2000. Won Chunchon Marathon 1997. Second in the 1999 Chicago Marathon in 2:06:16, the third fastest of all-time, and third in 2000.

Paul TERGAT b. 17 Jun 1969 Kabarnet, Barango 1.82m 62kg. Air Force sergeant (SPTE). Tugen.
At 10000m: OG: '96- 2, '00- 2; WCh: '95- 3, '97- 2, '99- 2. World HMar: '92-4-9-00: 5/11/1/1. World CC: '93-4-5-6-7-8-9-00: 10/4/1/1/1/1/1/3. Won Kenyan CC 1992, 1995-6.
World 10,000m record 1997. World road best 15km 1994 (42:13). World best half marathon 59:17 '98 and 59:06 '00 (40m dh at Lisbon) 58:51 at Milano 1996 was on course 49m short.
Progression at 5000m, 10000m: 1991- 29:46.8A, 1992- 13:48.64, 1993- 13:20.16, 27:18.43; 1994- 13:15.07, 27:23.89; 1995- 13:07.49, 27:14.08; 1996- 12:54.72, 26:54.41; 1997- 12:49.87, 26:27.85; 1998- 12:58.74, 26:44.44; 1999- 12:55.37, 27:10.08; 2000- 12:55.18, 27:03.87. pbs: 1500m 3:42.3 '96, 1M 3:58.4 '96, 2000m 4:57.4 '96, 3000m 7:28.70 '96, HMar 59:06 '00, 58:51sh '96.
A former basketball player, he made a sensational impact when he emerged to win the Kenyan CC title in 1992; he had however to miss his first run outside Now has a record five successive World Cross-country titles. Won the Stramilano half marathon each year 1994-9 and unbeaten at that distance 1995-2000. On the track he has won four silver medals and a bronze behind the great Haile Gebrselassie in global 10,000m races.

Eric WAINAINA b. 19 Dec 1973 Nyahururu 1.75m 58kg. Lives in Japan.
At Mar: OG: '96- 3, '00- 2; WCh: '95- 18.
Progression at Mar: 1994- 2:15:03, 1995- 2:10:31, 1996- 2:10:37, 1997- 2:13:35, 2000- 2:10:17. pbs: 10000m 28:52.6 '96, HMar 62:49 '95.
Marathon wins at Sapporo 1994, Tokyo 1995, Hokkaido 1997, Nagano 2000.

Raymond YATOR b. 7 Apr 1981 1.72m 55kg.
At 3000mSt: WJ: '00- 1; Af-J: '99-1.
World junior record 3000m steeplechase 2000.
Progression at 3000mSt: 1999- 8:15.31, 2000- 8:03.74. pbs: 1500m 3:41.20 '00, 5000m 13:30.02 '01, 10km Rd: 28:36 '00.

William YIAMPOY b. 15 May 1974 1.83m 70kg.
At 800m: OG: '00- sf.
Progression at 800m: 1999- 1:44.38, 2000- 1:44.23. pbs: 1000m 2:14.41 '99, 1500m 3:37.62 '00.

Women

Selina (Sally) BARSOSIO b. 21 Mar 1978 Keiyo 1.65m 46kg. Schoolgirl. Elgeyo Marakwet.
At 10000m (5000m): OG: '96- 10, '00- 17; WCh: '93- 3, '95- (11), '97- 1; WJ: '92- 3; AfG: '95- 1; AfCh: '92- 5 (5), '98- (2). Won GP 5000m 1997 (3rd 3000m 2000), Kenyan 5000m 1998, 10000m 1993, 1997; CC 1996-7, African Junior 1500m & 3000m 1994. World CC: '93-4-5-6-7-8-00-01: 3J/1J/3/11/5/10/8 (4k)/18; Rd Rly team: '98- 2.
World Junior records: 10000m 1993 (not ratified as no drugs test) and 1997, 3000m 1997; Kenyan records 10000m 1993, 5000m 1996, 3000m 1997.
Progression at 5000m, 10000m: 1992- 32:41.76, 1993- 31:15.38, 1994- 15:42.45; 1995- 15:05.75, 32:22.26, 1996- 14:47.81, 31:36.00; 1997- 14:46.71, 31:32.92; 1998- 15:27.22, 32:50.16; 1999- 15:42.79, 32:26.28; 2000- 14:53.61, 31:57.41. pbs: 1500m 4:21.6 '96, 2000m 5:39.4 '97, 3000m 8:35.89 '97.
A prodigious talent at 15 (18 according to some sources, including her mother !), but remarkably fortunate to be reinstated after disqualification in the 1993 World 10,000m to become the youngest ever World Championship medallist. She had caused havoc during the race by continually baulking Elana Meyer and running across several other runners. Four years later she became Kenya's first senior woman track world champion. Missed 1999 season through injury. Her elder sister Jepkemboi (Florence) Barsosio (b. 11 Aug 1976) was Kenyan champion and 13th in the World 5000m 1995, World CC '96- 16, '97- 13. Niece of Paul Koech.

Joyce CHEPCHUMBA Koech b. 6 Nov 1970 Kericho 1.60m 52kg. Kenyan postal service.
At Mar: OG: '96- dnf, '00- 3. World HMar: '97- 4, '98- 6, '99- 5; CC: '94- 18.
Kenyan marathon record 1997.
Progression at Mar: 1995- 2:33:51, 1996- 2:29:38, 1997- 2:26:51, 1998- 2:23:57, 1999- 2:23:22, 2000- 2:24:02. pbs: 800m 2:11.2 '94, 1500m 4:36.3A '91, 3000m 9:23.26 '95, 5000m 15:26.19 '00, 10000m 32:07.50 '99, road 5km 15:52 '94, 10km 32:19 '96, 15km 49:21 '97, 10M 54:27 '95, HMar 68:18 '00.
Five major wins in 13 marathons: London 1997

and 1999 (when she won the biggest ever prize of $230,000), Chicago 1998 and 1999, Tokyo 2000. 4th New York on marathon debut 1995, 2nd London and 3rd New York 1996, 2nd Tokyo 1997, 3rd London 1998 & 2000. Won Great North Run 1999. Has a training base in Dettmond, Germany. Son born in 1991.

Susan CHEPKEMEI b. 25 Jun 1975 1.64m 48kg.
World HMar: '00- 2; CC: '98-9-00-01: 12/5/3/3; Rd Rly team: '98- 2.
Progression at Mar: 1998- 2:28:19, 1999- 2:26:38. pbs: 3000m 8:59.45 '98, 5000m 15:06.14 '99, 10000m 33:01.2A '99; Road: 10km 31:54 '98, 10M 52:26 '98, HMar 69:10 '00.
Second in her two marathons to date: Berlin 1998, Rotterdam 1999.

Lydia CHEROMEI b. 11 May 1977 1.62m 47kg. Married Hosea Kogo (5000m 13:24.22 '97) in December 1996.
At 5000m: OG: '96- h, '00- 6; WCh: '97- 5; AfG: '95- 3; 2nd GP 1997 At 10000m: OG: '92- h; WJ: '90- 3, '92- 4; AfG: '91- 2; AfCh: '92- 2, '93- 2 (8 3000m). World CC: '91-2: 1J/3J, '97-00-01: 11/4/3. Won Kenyan 10000m 1991-2, 5000m 1997, 2000. Records: World junior 5000m 1995, African junior 3000m 1992, Kenyan 5000m 1995, 3000m 1997 and 2000.
Progression at 5000m, 10000m: 1990- 16:56.7, 33:20.83; 1991- 33:07.7, 1992- 15:17.31, 31:41.09; 1993- 32:54.55, 1994- 36:29.0, 1995- 14:53.44, 1996- 15:18.34, 1997- 14:46.72, 2000- 14:47.35. pbs: 1500m 4:09.32 '97, 2000m 5:38.9 '97, 3000m 8:29.14 '00.
At 13 in 1991, she is the youngest ever world junior cross-country champion. Set world age bests for 3000m, 5000m and 10000m at 13, 5000m at 15.

Lornah KIPLAGAT b. 20 Mar 1974.
Progression at Mar: 1997- 2:33:50, 1998- 2:34:03, 1999- 2:25:29, 2000- 2:22:36. pbs: 3000m 8:52.82 '00, 5000m 15:06.40 '99, Road: 5M 25:09 '97 (former world best), 10km 30:52 '00, 15km 49:08 '99, 10M 53:30 '99, HMar 66:56 '00.
Marathon wins: Los Angeles 1997 and 1998, Rotterdam 1999. Capped a brilliant series of road runs with second in Chicago marathon 2000.

Tegla LOROUPE Chepkite b. 9 May 1973 Kapsoit, West Pokot 1.53m 40kg. Pokot. Kenyan Post & Telecommunication Corporation.
At 10000m (Mar): OG: '92- 17, '96- 6, '00- 5 (13); WCh: '93- 4, '95- 3, '97- 6, '99- 3. World HMar: '93-7-8-9: 3/1/1/1; CC: '89- 28J, '90- 16J. Won GWG 10000m 1994, 1998; KEN 10000m 1995, 2000. World records: 1998 and 1999, 1 hour 1998, three African marathon records 1997-9, Kenyan records: 3000m 1999, 5000m 2000, 10000m 1993 & 1999, Marathon (3) 1994-8.
Progression at 5000m, 10000m, Mar: 1989- 34:36.1A, 1990- 35:06.0A, 1991- 35:02.8A, 1992- 31:34.30mx/32:34.07, 1993- 15:08.03, 31:21.20; 1994- 15:22.54, 31:52.39, 2:27:37; 1995- 15:08.86, 31:17.66, 2:28:06; 1996- 15:08.79, 31:23.22, 2:28:37; 1997- 15:19.78, 31:20.53, 2:22:07; 1998- 14:47.77, 32:15.44, 2:20:47; 1999- 14:49.12, 30:32.03, 2:20:43; 2000- 14:45.95, 30:37.26, 2:24:33. pbs: 1500m 4:29.39 '90, 3000m 8:30.95 '00, 1Hr 18340m '98, 20000m 1:05:26.6 '00; road 15km 48:52 '95, HMar 67:12 '96.
Eight wins in 17 marathons to 6th New York 2000. She made a brilliant début to win in New York in 1994 and won again there in 1995; 2nd Boston 1996 and won at Rotterdam in 1997 in the second fastest ever by a woman. Faded to 7th in New York marathon 1996 and 1997, but recovered speedily from what was at first thought a severe injury to place 7th in Osaka in January and then win in Rotterdam in a new world best time in April 1998. There was controversy, however, concerning this race as she was paced throughout by men. She was also illegally paced by a lapped runner in a 1 hour race at Borgholzhausen in August 1998 but this was ratified by the IAAF as a world record. 2nd Osaka and 1st in Rotterdam 1999. On the track in 1999 she won a World bronze at 10,000m and showed her speed by improving her pre-season 3000m pb of 9:01.62 to 8:33.36. Then she had an amazing 22 days in September-October, in which she ran on successive weekends: won HMar 69:20, world marathon record 2:20:43 in Berlin, won World HMar 68:48, 2nd Great North Run 69:35. Won London Marathon 2000, but ill for Olympic marathon.

Leah MALOT b. 7 Jun 1972 1.68m 46kg.
At 10000m: WCh: '87- h, 99- dnf; AfG: '87- 1, '99- 3. World CC: '98-9-00-01: 8/9/6/6; HMar: '98- 10; Rd Rly team: '98- 2. 2nd GP 3000m 2000. Kenyan s 3000m 1999, 5000m 2000.
Progression at 5000m, 10000m: 1987- 33:58.15, 1988- 38:09.8A, 1989- 36:40.4A, 1994- 35:53.2A, 1996- 16:20.91A, 1997- 15:10.12, 32:09.37, 1998- 15:09.75, 32:04.64; 1999- 15:03.75, 31:31.73; 2000- 14:39.83, 30:57.70. pbs: 800m 2:04.07 '00, 1000m 2:42.77 '99, 1500m 4:10.91 '97, 3000m 8:35.74 '99; Rd: 15km 49:06 '99, 10M 53:11 '98, HMar 69:46 '00.
Won African 10,000m title at age 15 in 1987. Ran for Kenyan World CC team in 1987 and 1994 before emerging in world class in 1997.

Naomi Wanjiku **MUGO** b. 2 Jan 1977 Nyahururu 1.63m 50kg.
At 1500m: OG: '96- dns, '00- h; CG: '98- 4; AfCh: '96- 1 (1 800m). Won Kenyan 1500m 1996-7. World CC: '94-6-7-8: 6J/3/8/11, 4k: '01- 11; Rd Rly team: '98- 2.
Kenyan 1500m record 1996 (also African Junior).
Progression at 1500m: 1993- 9:29.6, 1995- 4:19.0A, 1996- 4:04.29, 1997- 4:10.07, 1998- 3:58.12, 1999- 4:10.59, 2000- 4:01.64. pbs: 800m 2:02.13 '96, 1M 4:24.43 '98, 3000m 8:43.55 '00, 5000m 15:25.13 '00.

Catherine NDEREBA b. 21 Jul 1972.
At HMar: WCh: '99- 3.
Progression at Mar: 1999- 2:27:34, 2000- 2:21:33.

pbs: 1500m 4:27.6A '94, 3000m 9:25.10 '99, 5000m 15:27.84 '00, 10000m 32:17.58 '00; Road 5km 15:07 '98, 10km 31:41 '00, 15km 48:52 '99, 10M 52:25 '98. HMar 67:54 '01.
Has had great success on the US road running circuit, where she was top ranked in 1996 and 1998, having had a baby, Jane, in 1997. Made marathon debut with 6th in Boston, followed by second in New York 1999 and wins in Boston and Chicago 2000.

Esther WANJIRU b. 27 Mar 1977 1.62m 42kg. Based in Japan.
At 10000m: CG: '98- 1. At Mar: OG: '00- 4; WCh: '99- 11. Won Kenyan 10000m 1998.
World road 20km best (64:01) 2000, Kenyan Half Marathon record 1999.
Progression at 10000m, Mar: 1992- 34:38.05, 1994- 32:23.25, 1995- 32:04.27, 1996- 31:58.86, 1997- 31:52.44, 1998- 31:52.98, 1999- 32:07.05, 2:25:40; 2000- 2:23:31. pbs: 800m 2:09.43 '93, 1500m 4:19.97 '93, 3000m 9:11.71 '93, 5000m 15:16.42 '99, HMar 66:49 '99.
Brilliant marathon debut for 3rd in Osaka January 1999 and 3rd again in 2000.

KOREA

Governing body: Korea Amateur Athletic Federation, 10 Chamshil Dong, Songpa-Gu, Seoul. Founded 1945. **National Champions 2000**: **Men:** 100m: Kim Sang-do 10.52, 200m/400m: Kim Jae-da 21.51/46.67, 800m: Lee Jae-hoon 1:49.58, 1500m: Lee Du-haeng 3:44.73, 5000m: Cho Keun-hyung 14:19.88, 10000m: Ji Young-joon 30:23.69, 3000mSt: Ji Choon-keun 9:04.48, 110mh: Park Tae-kyong 14.30, 400mh: Lee Doo-yeon 50.00, HJ: Lee Jin-taek 2.20, PV: Kim Do-kyun 5.00, LJ: Sung Hee-joon 7.74, TJ: Lee Jae-ku 15.76, SP: Kim Jae-il 17.85, DT: Choi Jong-bum 52.27, HT: Lee Sung-dae 56.14, JT: Park Jae-myong 75.87, Dec: Kim Kun-woo 7040, 20kmW: Lee Dae-ro 1:26:09. **Women**: 100m: Baek Myong-ju 12.03, 200m: Kim Dong-hyun 24.92, 400m: Choi Hae-nam 54.80, 800m: Noh Jung-ae 2:13.04, 1500m: Ryu Su-hee 4:38.79, 5000m: Lee Cho-ae 16:28.91, 10000m: Bae Hae-jin 34:37.89, 400mh: Choi Hae-nam 58.40, HJ: Kim Ho-soon 1.70, PV: An You-rim 3.30, LJ: Kim Su-yeon 6.13, TJ: Lee Kyong-sun 13.18, SP: Yoo Young-kyung 15.20, DT: Won Soon-mi 49.95, HT: Chang Bok-shim 45.85, JT: Lee Young-sun 55.22, Hep: Park Sun-hee 4665, 20kmW: Kim Mi-jung 1:38:57.
Winners at 81st National Games 2000: Men: 100m: Kim Sang-do 10.60w, 200m: Kim Dong-hwan 21.74, 400m Shin Dae-chul 48.18, 800m: Kim Soon-hyung 1:55.84, 1500m: Lee Jae-hoon 3:54.41, 5000m: Shon Mun-kyu 14:40.10, 10000m: Oh Sung-keun 29:20.92, 3000mSt: Yeun Sun-ho 9:12.22, 110mh: Park Tae-kyong 14.41, 400mh: Lee Doo-yeon 50.93, HJ: Lee Jin-taek 2.21, PV: Kim Se-in 5.00, LJ: Sung Hee-jun 7.53, TJ: Kim Young-mo 16.22, SP: Kim Jae-il 17.59, DT: Kim Young-chul 51.70, HT: Mun Jun-heum 60.04, JT: Chu Ki-young 77.01, Dec: Kim Kun-woo 7117, 20kmW: Shin Il-yong 1:30:08. **Women**: 100m: Baek Myong-ju 12.42, 200m: Huh Soon-bok 24.82, 400m: Choi Hae-nam 55.66, 800m/1500m: Han Jung-yeon 2:10.64/4:49.10, 5000m: Choi Kyung-hee 16:49.17, 10000m/20kmRd: Oh Mi-ja 33:47.68/72:46, 100mh: Shim Mi-ra 13.98, 400mh: Choi Hae-nam 59.05, HJ: Kim Mi-ok 1.76, LJ: Yu Soon-chun 6.05, TJ: Lee Kyong-Sun 13.31, SP: Lee Myung-sun 16.23, DT: Won Soon-mi 50.38, JT: Lee Young-sun 53.68, Hep: Han Sang-won 4958, 10kmW: Kim Mi-jung 47:36.

LEE Bong-ju b. 11 Oct 1970 1.68m 56kg. Samsung Ekectronics.
At Mar: OG: '96- 2, '00- 24; WCh: '95- 22; AsiG: '98- 1. Korean champion 1992-3.
Korean marathon records 1998 and 2000.
Progression at Mar: 1992- 2:13:32, 1993- 2:13:16, 1994- 2:09:57, 1995- 2:10:58, 1996- 2:08:26, 1997- 2:10:33, 1998- 2:07:44, 1999- 2:12:11, 2000- 2:07:20.
Won Kwangju and Honolulu marathons 1993, Gyeongju 1995, Fukuoka 1996. 2nd Rotterdam 1998, Tokyo 2000.

LATVIA

Governing body: Latvian Athletic Association, 1 Augsiela Str, Riga LV-1009. Founded 1921. Athletes competed for USSR prior to 1992.
National Championships first held in 1920 (men), 1922 (women). **2000 Champions**: **Men**: 100m/200m: Sergejs Insakovs 10.53/21.04, 400m: Inguns Sviklins 47.55, 800m/400mh: Egils Tebelis 1:50.54/51.95, 1500m: Vitalijs Bulatnijs 3:53.04, 5000m: Andrejs Tokarevs 14:47.09, 10000m: Dmitrijs Slesarjonoks 30:54.16, HMar/Mar: Ziedonis Zalkalns 69.16/2:30:59, 3000mSt: Martins Alksnis 8:47.2, 110mh: Janis Votols 15.38, HJ: Alvis Erglis 2.10, PV: Egons Lacis 4.20, LJ: Andrejs Tolstiks 7.41, TJ: Juris Iljins 15.56, SP: Maris Petrasko 16.93, DT: Maris Urtans 52.16, HT: Janis Podnieks 56.26, JT: Eriks Rags 83.10, Dec: Aigars Bruveris 6572, 20kmW: Modris Liepins 1:25:02, 50kmW: Ugis Bruvelis 4:01:10. **Women**: 100m: Zanda Grava 12.35, 200m/400m/400mh: Irena Zauna 24.78/53.95/56.77, 800m: Irina Latva 2:02.14, 1500m/3000m: Inna Poluskina 4:24.99/9:42.02, 5000m: Jelena Prokopcuka 15:44.52, HMar: Inara Luse 73:36, Mar: Laila Ceika 3:16:08, 2000mSt: Inga Dauskane 7:38.2, 100mh: Anita Trumpe 13.64, HJ: Liga Klavina 1.83, PV: Elina Ringa 3.70, LJ: Ineta Radevica 6.16, TJ: Iveta Pence 13.06, SP/Hep: Kristine Sukharevska 12.69/5239, DT: Dace Ruskule 47.17, HT: Inguna Gailite 39.11, JT: Ieva Skrastina 54.19, 10000mW: Yolanta Dukure 47:07, 20kmW: Anita Liepina 1:35:14.

Aigars FADEJEVS b. 27 Dec 1975 Valmiera 1.75m 69kg. Liepaja District SC.
At 20kmW (50kmW): OG: '96- 6, '00- 14 (2);

WCh: '97- dnf, 99- dnf (dq); EC: '94- 17, '98- 2; EU23: '97- 1; WCp: '97- 15, '99- (9); ECp: '98- 3, '00- 6. At 10kmW: EJ: '93- 11; WJ: '94- dq. Won LAT 50kmW 1998.
Latvian records 20kmW 1996, 50kmW 1998.
Progression at 20kmW, 50kmW: 1993- 1:36:19, 1994- 1:23:41, 4:02:18; 1995- 1:22:56, 1996- 1:20:40, 1997- 1:19:36, 1998- 1:19:44, 3:43:18; 1999- 1:20:31, 3:46:36; 2000- 1:20:18, 3:43:40. pbs: 5000mW 18:48.30 '98, 10000mW 39:17.8 '98.

Stanislav OLIJARS b. 22 Mar 1979 Chelyabinsk, Russia 1.90m 80kg.
At 110mh: OG: '00- sf; WCh: '97- qf, '99- sf; EC: '98- sf; WJ: '96- h (dnq LJ), '98- 1; EJ: '97- 2; EU23: '99- 2. At 60mh: WI: '01- 8; EI: '00- 2.
Latvian 110mh record 2000.
Progression at 110mh: 1996- 14.52, 1997- 13.62, 1998- 13.49, 1999- 13.28, 2000- 13.25. pbs: 100m 10.45 '98, 200m 20.97 '00, 400m 46.66 '00, 50mh 7.56i '01, 60mh 7.50i '00. LJ 7.94i '00, 7.57A '97.
His mother (and coach) Ludmila Olijar (b. 5 Feb 1958) was the Latvian record holder for 100mh 12.90 (1989).

Women

Jelena PROKOPCUKA b. 21 Sep 1976 Riga 1.68m 51kg. née Chelnova.
At 5000m (/10000m): OG: '96- h, '00- 9/19; WCh: '97- h; EC: '98- 16; EU23: '97- 5/6. At 3000m (/10000m): WJ: '94: h/13; EJ: '95- 5/4; EI: '98- 4, '00- 4. Won LAT 1500m 1994, 1997-8, 3000m 1992-3, 1998-9, 5000m 1995-7, HMar 1995, 1999.
Latvian records 5000m (4) 1997-2000, 10000m 2000.
Progression at 5000m, 10000m: 1994- 35:22.44, 1995-16:20.7, 34:21.84; 1996- 15:59.00, 33:59.9; 1997- 15:40.68, 33:41.51, 1998- 15:30.76, 33:29.04; 1999- 16:09.22, 2000- 14:47.71, 31:27.86. pbs: 400m 60.46 '98, 800m 2:05.82 '00, 1500m 4:12.36 '00, 3000m 8:44.66i/8:46.97 '00, HMar 71:05 '99.
Took over two minutes off her 10000m pb when winning European Challenge B race in 2000. Married to Aleksandrs Prokopchuks (Latvian marathon record 2:15:56 '95).

LITHUANIA

Governing body: Athletic Federation of Lithuania, Zemaites 6, Vilnius LT 2009. Founded 1921. Athletes competed for USSR prior to 1991.
2000 National Champions: **Men**: 100m: Ilja Andriusenko 10.90, 200m/400m: Jonas Motiejunas 21.3/45.4, 800m: Mindaugas Narbutas 1:49.9, 1500m: Evaldas Martinka 4:00.70, 5000m/10000m: Mindaugas Pukstas 14:47.9/30:20.66, 3000mSt: Dainius Saucikovas 9:18.28, 110mh: Ridas Karaska 15.1, 400mh: Arturas Marcenko 53.1, HJ: Deividas Rinkevicius 2.09, PV: Raimundas Stackunas 3.60, LJ: Andrius Daunoravicius 7.66, TJ: Audrius Raizgys 15.95, SP: Saulius Kleiza 19.16, DT: Virgilijus Alekna 73.88, HT: Dalius Cizauskas 55.93, JT: Arunas Jurksas 77.58, Dec: Jonas Spudis 6696, 20kmW: Daugvinas Zujus 1:28:52, 30kmW: Gintaras Andriuskevicius 2:12:29. **Women**: 100m: Audra Dagelyté 11.64, 200m: Zana Minina 24.1, 400m/400mh: Inesa Kliukoityté 56.98/63.1, 800m:Vida Bytautiené 2:10.3, 1500m: Irina Krakoviak 4:19.83, 5000m: Vilija Birbalaité 16:23.2, 10000m: Zivile Balciunaité 33:04.46, 2000mSt: Sandra Staneviciuté 6:58.7, 100mh: Austra Skujyté 14.0, HJ: Nelé Zilinskiené 1.88, PV: Rita Snarskaité 3.10, LJ/TJ: Adrija Grociené 5.83/13.21, SP: Ruta Rakstyté 15.27, DT: Renata Gustaityté 53.42, HT: Laimuté Venclovaité 40.03, JT: Rita Ramanauskaité 61.46, Hep: Viktorija Zemaityté 4641, 10kmW/20kmW: Kristina Saltanovic 44:50/1:35:23.67t.

Virgilijus ALEKNA b. 13 Feb 1972 Terpeikiai, Kupiskis 2.00m 130kg. PE student and (from 1995) guard of the Lithuanian president.
At DT: OG: '96- 5, '00- 1; WCh: '95- dnq 19, '97- 2, '99- 4; EC: '98- 3; WCp: '98- 1. 2nd GP 1999. LIT champion 2000.
Four Lithuanian discus records 2000.
Progression at DT: 1990- 52.84, 1991- 57.16, 1992- 60.86, 1993- 62.84, 1994- 64.20, 1995- 62.78, 1996- 67.82, 1997- 67.70, 1998- 69.66A, 1999- 68.25, 2000- 73.88. pb SP: 19.99 '97.
His 69.66 discus throw at the 1999 World Cup is the longest ever in a major event, and his 69.30 to win the 2000 Olympic title got close. His throws of 72.35 and 73.88 at the 2000 Lithuanian Championships were the second and third longest ever. On 4 Mar 2000 he married Kristina Sablovskyte (pb LJ 6.14 '96, TJ 12.90 '97, sister of Remigija Nazaroviene).

LUXEMBOURG

Governing body: Fédération Luxembourgeoise d'Athlétisme, Boite Postale 503, 2015 Luxembourg. Founded 1928.
2000 National Champions: **Men**: 100m/400m: Christian Kemp 11.29/51.08, 200m: Sebastien Scheer 22.82, 800m/1500m: David Wagner 1:54.66/3:57.55, 5000m/10000m: Jeff Hommel 15:25.09/31:51.09, Mar: Francis Hoeser 2:35:10, 3000mSt: Pascal Groben 9:41.95, 110mh/400mh: Claude Godart 14.69/51.98, HJ: Sam Besch 1.96, PV: Fabien Mores 4.60, LJ: Richard Czerwonka 7.07, TJ: Frank Krier 14.30, SP: Fernand Heintz 14.66, DT: Stéphane Bignoli 38.89, HT: Charles De Ridder 61.56, JT: Edmond Libens 54.78. **Women**: 100m/200m: Sandra Frisch 12.40/25.44, 400m/400mh: Esther Gasperini 61.26/67.47, 800m: Chantal Hayen 2.22.40, 1500m: Marie Anne Reding 4:51.28, 3000m/10000m: Pascale Schmoetten 10:03.55/38:04.32, Mar: Mariella Baum 3:20:08, 100mh: Martine Brachtenbach 14.63, HJ: Laurence Baum 1.68, PV: Joëlle Scheer 3.10, LJ: Claudia Czerwonka 5.82, TJ: Laurence Kipgen 11.02, SP/DT: Christiane Liefgen 11.62/ 34.15, HT: Tessy Biver 39.27, JT: Nathalie Thill 38.12.

MEXICO

Governing body: Federación Mexicana de Atletismo, Anillo Periférico y Av. del Conscripto, 11200 México D.F. Founded 1933.

2000 National Champions: Men: 100m: Ebener Dueñas 10.69, 200m: Alejandro Cárdenas 20.71, 400m: Juan Pedro Toledo 46.08, 800m/1500m: Héctor Torres 1:50.69/3:45.27, 5000m: Fidencio Torres 13:57.37, 10000m: Jesús Capula 29:54.2, 3000mSt: Salvador Miranda 8:45.11, 110mh: Roberto Castrejón 14.70, 400mh: Salvador Chamor 52.22, HJ: Gerardo Martínez 2.00, PV: Robinson Pratt 5.31, LJ: Sergio Sauceda 7.24, TJ: Gerardo Carrasco 15.05, SP: Daniel Chapa 16.08 (light), DT: Mauricio Serna 52.24, HT: Guillermo Guzmán 65.66, JT: Juan de la Garza 74.15, Dec: José Herrera 6809, 20kmW: Edgar Hernández 1:24:20. **Women**: 100m: Liliana Allen 11.33, 200m: Yessica Torres 24.06, 400m/800m: Ana Guevara 51.68/2:02.88, 1500m: Dulce Rodríguez 4:25.70, 5000m: Nora Rocha 16:20.30, 10000m: Estela Chávez 35:36.0, 100mh: Jaqueline Taváres 14.69, 400mh: Mayra González 59.73, HJ/LJ: Romary Rifka 1.74/5.90, PV: Lorena Espinosa 3.60, TJ: Mónica Martínez 12.43, SP: Dulce Flores 12.71, DT: Flor Acosta 42.96, HT: Violeta Guzmán 56.01, JT: Nereida Ríos 46.72, Hep: Erándi Arteaga 4276, 20kmW: Rosario Sánchez 1:34:56.7.

Manuel **Alejandro CÁRDENAS** Robles b. 4 Sep 74. Hermosillo, Sonora 1.86m 73kg.
At 400m/4x400mR: OG: '96/00- qf; WCh: '97-qf, '99- 3; WI: '99- 3; PAm: '99- 3; CAG: '98- 3; CAC: '95- 2R; IbAm: '94- 2, '98- 1R (1 4x100m). At 100m: WJ: '92- h. At Dec/4x100m: PAm: '95-3/3R; IbAm: '96- 2/1R.
MEX records 200m 1998, 400m 1996-9, Dec 1995-6.
Progression at 400m: 1994- 48.52, 1995- 46.68A, 1996- 45.05A/45.33, 1997- 46.26, 1998- 44.92, 1999- 44.31, 2000- 44.92. pbs: 100m 10.2A '96/10.56W '94, 200m 20.63A '98, 20.71 '00; 300m 32.11+ '99, LJ: 7.72A '96, Dec 7614A '96.
Having set a Mexican record of 44.92 for the Pan-American bronze, he improved substantially to 44.37 in the semi-final and 44.31 in the World final in 1999.

Daniel GARCÍA Córdova b. 28 Oct 1971 Ciudad de México 1.68m 56kg. Instituto Mexicano del Seguro Social.
At 20kmW (50kmW): OG: '92- 7, '96- 19 (9), '00-12; WCh: '93- dq, '95- dq, '97- 1, '99- 3; WCp: '93- 1, '95- 11, '97- 2, '99- 5; PAm: '95- 2, '99- 2; WUG: '93- 2, '95- 1; CAG: '93- 1, '98- 1. Won IbAm 1994. PAmCp 1996.
Progression at 20kmW, 50kmW: 1991- 4:04:51, 1992- 1:22:16.1t, 3:57:38; 1993- 1:19:42, 3:53:23; 1994- 1:20:33, 4:00:17; 1995- 1:21:05, 3:54:45.6t; 1996- 1:18:50, 3:50:05; 1997- 1:18:27, 1998- 1:19:41, 1999- 1:19:05, 3:51:26; 2000- 1:22:05. pb 5000mW 19:14.2 '97.
Was disqualified while in a medal position in the closing stages of the World Championships of 1993 and 1995, but won in 1997.

Noé HERNÁNDEZ b. 15 Mar 1978 Chimalhuacán, Estado de México 1.75m 64kg.
At 20kmW: OG: '00- 2. Won CAC 1999, IbAm 2000, 2nd PAm Cup 2000.
Progression at 20kmW: 1998- 1:26:17, 1999-1:20:12, 2000- 1:19:03.

Miguel Ángel **RODRÍGUEZ** Gallegos b. 15 Jan 1967 Chihuahua 1.74m 62kg. Chihuahua. Trained as an engineer.
At 50kmW: OG: '92- 8 (dq 20k), '00- 7; WCh: '93-dq, '95- 4, '97- 3; WCp: '89-91-3-5-7-9: 17/7/4/5/6/19; PAm: '91- 2, '95- 2, '99- 2; CAmG: '93- 4. Won PAm Cup 2000, Aztec Cup 1997, 2nd America's Cup 1992 & 1994.
Progression at 50kmW: 1989- 3:58:41, 1990-4:08:30, 1991- 3:54:36, 1992- 3:50:55, 1993- 3:54:22, 1994- 3:52:06, 1995- 3:44:07, 1996- 4:00:11, 1997-3:42:45, 1998- 3:43:15, 1999- 3:49:53, 2000- 3:43:52. pb 20kmW 1:20:59 '93.

Joel SÁNCHEZ b. 15 Sep 1966 Ciudad de México 1.66m 60kg.
At 50kmW (20kmW): OG: 00- 3; WCh: '97- dq (16), '99- dnf; PAm: '99- 1; WCp: '97 (13). 2nd PAm Cup 20kmW 1990.
Progression at 20kmW, 50kmW: 1988- 1:22:00, 1989- 1:24:53, 1990- 1:22:09. 1991- 1:21:17, 1992-1:21:07.8t, 1993- 1:22:55, 4:01:06; 1996- 1:23:54.4t, 4:22:17; 1997- 1:20:05, 1998- 1:19:45, 4:01:16; 1999- 1:19:00, 3:49:51A; 2000- 1:20:53, 3:44:36.

Bernardo SEGURA Rivera b. 11 Feb 1970 San Mateo Atenco 1.75m 62kg. Estado de México.
At 20kmW: OG: '96- 3, '00- dq; WCh: '93- dq, '95- dnf, '99- dnf; WCp: '95- 3, '99- 1; PAm: '95- dq, '99- 1; CAG: '98- 2; WUG: '93- 3. Won America's Cup 1992, PAmCp 1994, 2000; GWG 1994.
World record 20,000m track walk 1994.
Progression at 20kmW: 1991- 1:22:01, 1992-1:24:09, 1993- 1:19:39, 1994- 1:17:25.6t, 1995- 1:19:09, 1996- 1:19:05, 1997- 1:23:19, 1998- 1:19:46, 1999-1:20:17, 2000- 1:22:47. pbs: 10,000mW 38:24 '94, 1HrW: 15,577.3m '94, 50kmW 4:03:51 '94.
Disqualified after 'winning' the Olympic 20km walk in 2000 and taking his lap of honour, President of the Sports Commission of the Mexican Congress. He has named his son Jefferson Daniel Segura after the last two 20kmW Olympic gold medallists. His brother **Jorge** (b. 23 Apr 1975) won the world junior 10,000m walk title in 1994 and at 20km was CAC champion 1995, pb 1:22:50 '95.

Women

Adriana FERNÁNDEZ b. 4 Apr 1971 Ciudad de México 1.64m 52kg.
At Mar: OG: '96- 51, '00- 16. At 5000m (10000m): WCh: '95- h, '97: h (h), '99- h; PAm: '95- 1, '99- 1; CAG: '98- (1). At 1500m/3000m: CAC: '93- 2/2, '95- 2/1.

Records: CAC 10000m 1996 & 2000, marathon 1998 and 1999. MEX 5000m 1995-7, 3000m 2000. Progression at 5000m, 10000m, Mar: 1995- 15:46.32, 33:06.66; 1996- 31:53.36, 2:31:59; 1997- 15:23.8, 33:09.22; 1998- 34:06.16, 2:26:33; 1999- 15:14.33, 32:39.05, 2:24:06; 2000- 15:16.45, 31:10.12, 2:25:42. pbs: 1500m: 4:18.02 '00, 3000m 8:53.53 '00. Completed five years of study for a law degree before taking up running seriously. Three major marathon 2nd places: Houston 1996 (debut), New York 1998, London 1999, followed by win in New York 1999. Coached by Rodolfo Gómez (2:09:12 marathon in 1983).

Ana Gabriela **GUEVARA** b. 4 Mar 77 Nogales, Sonora. 1.73m 61kg.
At 400m/4x400m (800m): OG: '00- 5; WCh: '99- sf; WI: '99- 4. WJ: '96- sf; PAm: '99- 1; CAG: '98- 2 (2); WUG: '97- (6). Won IbAm 400m 1998.
MEX records 400m (4) 1998-2000, 800m (2) 1998.
Progression at 400m, 800m: 1996- 54.75A, 2:09.80; 1997- 52.46A, 2:02.90; 1998- 50.65, 2:01.12; 1999- 50.70, 2:03.69, 2000- 49.70A/49.96, 2:02.88; 2001- 50.25A. pb 200m: 23.78A '98.

Guadalupe SÁNCHEZ b. 3 Jan 1971 Ciudad de México 1.69m 53kg.
At 20kmW: OG: '00- 5; WCh: '99- 25; WCp: '99- 34. Won PAm Cup 2000.
Progression at 10kmW, 20kmW: 1994- 50:12.2, 1997- 47:24, 1998- 46:21, 1:34:50; 1999- 43:27, 1:35:33; 2000- 44:34, 1:30:49.

MOROCCO

Governing Body: Fédération Royale Marocaine d'Athlétisme, Complex Sportif Prince Moulay Abdellah, PO Box 1778 R/P, Rabat. Founded 1957.

Saïd BÉRIOUI b. 3 Jun 1975? 1.78m 65kg.
At 10000m: OG: '00- 6; WCh: '97- 17, '99- 16; WJ: '98- dnf (birthdate then given as 3.4.79). At 5000m: AfCh: '00- 2.
Progession at 5000m, 10000m: 1996- 13:39.2, 1997- 13:20.93, 27:35.34; 1998- 13:21.92, 27:31.00; 1999- 13:15.10, 2000- 13:23.38, 27:37.83. pbs: 3000m 7:42.39 '98.

Brahim BOULAMI b. 20 Apr 1972 1.80m 64kg.
At 3000mSt: OG: '96- 7, 00- 7; WCh: '97- 10; AfCh: '98- 3; won MedG 1997. World CC: '97- 22, 4k: '98-01: 6/7. Won Moroccan CC 1997.
Two Moroccan 3000m steeplechase records 2000.
At 3000mSt: 1995- 8:20.64, 1996- 8:18.49, 1997- 8:10.84, 1998- 8:11.30, 2000- 8:02.90. pbs: 3000m 7:42.99 '98, 5000m 13:28.06 '98.
Younger brother of **Khalid Boulami** (b. 7 Aug 1969, 5000m: 3 OG 1996, 2 WCh 1995 & 1998, pb 12:53.41 ''97). Succeeded Ali Ezzine as fastest ever non-Kenyan steeplechaser in 2000.

Hicham EL GUERROUJ b. 14 Sep 1974 Berkane 1.76m 58kg.
At 1500m: OG: '96- 12, '00- 2; WCh: '95- 2, '97- 1, '99- 1; WI: '95- 1, '97- 1. At 3000m: WI: '01- 1; At 5000m: WJ: '92- 3. World Rd Rly team: '94- 1. World CC: '92- 14J. Won GP 1500m 1996 and 1998 (2nd 1M 1997).
World records: 1500m 1998, 1M and 2000m 1999. World indoor records 1500m (3:31.18) and 1M (3:48.45) 1997. Moroccan records: 1500m & 1M 1997 and 1998, 2000m 1998.
Progression at 1500m, 1M: 1994- 3:33.61, 3:53.71; 1995- 3:31.16, 3:48.69; 1996- 3:29.05, 1997- 3:28.91, 3:44.90; 1998- 3:26.00, 3:44.60; 1999- 3:27.65, 3:43.13; 2000- 3:27.21, 3:45.96. pbs: 1000m 2:16.85 '95, 2000m 4:44.79 '99, 3000m 7:23.09 '99, 2M 8:09.89i '01, 5000m 13:46.79 '92.
He won 51 of 54 races at 1500m or 1M 1996-2000. His only losses being when he fell just before the bell in the 1996 Olympic 1500m final, a loss in his last race of 1997 to Robert Andersen at 1M in the Grand Prix Final, and second to Noah Ngeny in the 2000 Olympics. In 1998 he took 1.37 secs off Morceli's 1500m WR with a majestic run at Rome on 14 July, and a year later added world records at 1M and 2000m and a superb World Championships win at 1500m. His unbeaten record in 1999 also included the 2nd best ever 3000m time of 7:23.09 at Brussels in 1999, from a previous best of 7:49.84 (1994) and a time-trial 7:39.74 in February 1996.
Made a great breakthrough in 1994 to run 3:33.61 for 1500m at Nice with no known form at this event before, although he had taken the 5000m bronze medal at the 1992 World Juniors. At Stuttgart on 2 Feb 1997 he took 2.98 secs off Morceli's world indoor 1500m record.

Abdelkader EL MOUAZIZ b. 1969. 1.72m 58kg.
At Mar: OG: '96- 44, '00- 7; WCh: '97- dnf.
Progression at Mar: 1994- 2:15:45, 1995- 2:14:45, 1996- 2:09:50, 1997- 2:09:50, 1998- 2:08:07, 1999- 2:07:57, 2000- 2:07:33. pb HMar 61:49 '96.
Seven wins in 17 marathons. He had won at Marrakech in 1996 and 1997 in the same time of 2:09:50 and again in 1999 in 2:08:15. Won London 1999, 2nd 1998 and 2000; won New York 2000. Spent four years 1990-4 in Granada, Spain.

Ali EZZINE b. 3 Sep 1978 1.80m 61kg.
At 3000mSt: OG: '00- 3; WCh: '99- 3; WJ: '96- 3. World CC: '97- 11J; 4k: '98- 12, '00- 13.
Three Moroccan 3000mSt records 1999-2000.
Progression at 3000mSt: 1996- 8:34.2, 1997- 8:23.18, 1998- 8:15.85, 1999- 8:06.70, 2000- 8:03.57. pbs: 1500m 3:43.8 '98, 2000m 5:00.84 '98, 3000m 7:51.6/7:48.62i '98, 5000m 13:32.56 '97.
Became the fastest ever non-Kenyan steeplechaser in 1999 with 8:07.31 in Paris and 8:06.70 when he ended Bernard Barmasai's hopes of winning at all seven Golden League meetings; improving to 8:03.57 in 2000.

Salah HISSOU b. 16 Jan 1972 Kasba Tadla 1.76m 62kg.

At 5000m: WCh: '99- 1; WJ: '90: dnf h. At 10000m: OG: '96- 3; WCh: '95- 4, '97- 3. 2nd GP 5000m 1996. Won Pan-Arab 10000m & CC, 2nd 5000m 1992, Moroccan 5000m 1991. World CC: '90- 12J, '91- 14J, '94- 11, '95- 3, '96- 2, '97- 2; HMar: '94- 18; Rd Rly team: '94- 1.
World 10000m record 1996, Moroccan records: 5000m 1996, 10000m 1995-6, 3000m 1999.
Progession at 5000m, 10000m: 1989- 14:15.0, 1990- 14:05.9, 1991- 13:37.40, 1992- 13:41.55, 28:31.62; 1993- 13:49.5, 1994- 13:04.93, 27:21.75; 1995- 13:02.25, 27:09.30; 1996- 12:50.80, 26:38.08; 1997- 12:52.39, 27:09.07; 1998- 12:57.73; 1999- 12:52.53, 2000- 13:00.06. pbs: 1500m 3:33.95 '96, 1M 3:52.54 '99, 2000m 4:58.4 '99, 3000m 7:28.93 '99; Road: 20km 58:20 '94 (world best), HMar 62:20 '94.
Great breakthrough in 1994. 3rd World Cross Challenge 1994/5.

Elarbi KHATTABI b. 16 May 1967 Casablanca 1.74m 61kg.
At 3000mSt: OG: '92- 10, '00- h; WCh: '93- 7, '95- sf, '97- 11, '99- h. Won Moroccan 1997. World CC: '94- 14, '95- 11, '97- 16, '98- 11; Rd Rly team: '94- 1.
Progression at 3000mSt: 1986- 9:28.1, 1987- 9:00.2, 1988- 8:52.55, 1989- 8:30.87, 1990- 8:40.0, 1991- 8:42.39, 1992- 8:23.82, 1993- 8:16.60, 1994- 8:16.18, 1995- 8:12.02, 1996- 8:17.29, 1997- 8:11.50, 1998- 8:10.67, 1999- 8:09.03, 2000- 8:10.15. pbs: 1500m 3:44.0 '94, 3000m 7:43.06 '98, 5000m 13:18.92 '95, HMar 62:43 '93.

Brahim LAHLAFI b. 15 Apr 1968 1.72m 62kg. Stade Sotteville CC, France.
At 5000m: OG: '96- 8, '00- 3; WCh: '95- 5, '99- 4; WCp: '94- 1. At 3000m: AfCh: '98- 2. World CC: '93- 11, '95- 5, '98- 17.
Moroccan 5000m record 2000.
Progession at 5000m: 1988- 14:02.2, 1989- 14:13.0, 1990- 13:21.11, 1991- 13:23.79, 1993- 13:15.85, 1994- 13:03.36, 1995- 13:18.46, 1996- 13:08.05, 1998- 13:00.56, 1999- 12:59.09, 2000- 12:49.28. pbs: 1500m 3:43.2 '97, 2000m 4:58.6 '00, 3000m 7:28.94 '99, 2M 8:16.11 '94, 10000m 27:43.05 '95, HMar 61:39 '94.

Younès MOUDRIK b. 1 Oct 1977 1.84m 72kg.
At LJ: OG: '00- dnq 17; WCh: '97- dnq 24, '99- 8; WJ: '94- dnq 24, '96- 8; AfCh: '00- 1; Af-J: '94- 3 (1 HJ). Arab & MAR champion 1997.
Moroccan long jump records 1997 & 1999.
Progression at LJ: 1994: 7.55, 1995- 7.76, 1996- 7.80/ 8.04w, 1997- 8.11, 1998- 8.10/8.12w, 1999- 8.20, 2000- 8.34. pbs: 100m 10.4 '95, HJ 2.12 '94.

Khalid SKAH b. 29 Jan 1967 Midelt 1.70m 58kg. Based in the summer in Norway. IL i BUL, Oslo.
At 10000m (5000m): OG: '92- 1, '96- 7; WCh: '91- 3 (6), '93- (5), '95- 2, '99- 10; WCp: '94- 1; AfCh: '89- (5). Won GP 5000m 1990, 1994. World CC: '90- 1, '91- 1, '92- 4, '93- 6, '94- 5, '96- 7. World HMar: '94- 1, '98- 3; Rd Rly team: '94- 1. Won NOR 5000m 1997-8, 2000.
World 2 miles best 1993. Moroccan 10000m record 1993.
Progression at 5000m, 10000m: 1986- 14:28.4, 1987- 14:26.11, 1988- 13:56.1, 1989- 13:17.30, 1990- 13:09.55, 27:29.27; 1991- 13:17.72, 27:23.29; 1992- 13:09.10, 27:46.70; 1993- 13:06.82, 27:17.74; 1994- 13:00.54, 27:38.74; 1995- 13:04.20, 27:14.53; 1996- 13:15.32, 27:46.98; 1997- 13:23.71, 27:44.33; 1998- 13:32.41, 27:31.87; 1999- 13:19.94, 28:25.10; 2000- 27:37.44. pbs: 1000m 2:26.0 '90, 1500m 3:38.10 '92, 2000m 5:03.9 '90, 3000m 7:36.76 '94, 2M 8:12.17 '93, 3000mSt 8:19.30 '94, HMar 60:24 '98.
2nd Arab junior CC and 68th World Junior CC in 1986. After winning the World CC he ran 27:29.27 in his 10000m track début in Brussels 1990. At first disqualified after Olympic 10000m in 1992 due to the alleged help rendered by lapped compatriot Hammou Boutayeb, he was reinstated and awarded gold medal. His wife is Norwegian and he was granted NOR citizenship on 18 Sep 1995, but has continued to compete for Morocco.

Women

Hasna BENHASSI b. 1 Jun 1978 1.66m 47kg.
At 800m: OG: '00- 8; WCh: '97- sf; AfCh: '98- 2, '00- 1; WJ: '96- sf; WI: '99- 5; won MedG 1997, Moroccan 1996. At 1500m: WI: '01- 1.
Moroccan records 800m (3), 1000m, 1500m (2) 1998-9.
Progression at 800m, 1500m: 1995- 2:11.0, 1996- 2:04.6, 4:31.4; 1997- 2:00.48, 4:27.1; 1998- 1:58.47, 4:05.15; 1999- 1:57.45, 4:05.29; 2000- 1:58.47, 4:14.28; 2001- 4:04.48i. pbs: 400m 54.04 '00, 1000m 2:33.15 '99, 1M 4:32.99 '98.

Nezha BIDOUANE b. 18 Sep 1969 1.74m 65kg.
At 400mh: OG: '92- sf, '00- 3; WCh: '91- sf, '93- h, '95- h, '97- 1, '99- 2; AfCh: '90- 1 (2 100mh), '98- 1; WCp: '92- 6, '94- 5, '98- 1; won Med G 1991, 1993, 1997. Arab champion 100m, 200m, 100mh & 400mh 1992 & 1995, 400m 1992; Moroccan 100m 1991, 200m 1988-90, 1992-3; 400m 1994, 100mh 1989-91, 1995; 400mh 1988-91, 1995.
Five African and Moroccan 400mh records 1997-9. Moroccan records: 200m 1998 400m (3) 1996-8.
Progression at 400mh: 1987- 65.2, 1988- 59.88, 1989- 59.45, 1990- 56.69/56.3, 1991- 55.13, 1992- 55.08, 1993- 56.09, 1994- 55.19, 1995- 55.85, 1996- 55.31, 1997- 52.97, 1998- 52.96A/53.23, 1999- 52.90, 2000- 53.53. pbs: 100m 11.73 '95, 11.5 '94; 200m 23.29 '98, 23.0 '00; 400m 51.67 '98, 800m 2:09.8 '96, 100mh 13.55 '90.
After not finishing in her heat in 1993 and being disqualified in heat in 1995, she became Morocco's first female world champion in 1997. Married to Abdelaziz Sahere (b. 18 Sep 1967), African champion at 3000mSt 1990, six MAR 3000mSt record to 8:09.02 '95.

Zahra OUAZIZ b. 20 Dec 1969 Oulmes 1.66m 50kg. Based in France.
At 5000m: OG: '96- h; WCh: '95- 3, '97- h, '99- 2.

At 3000m: AfCh: '98- 1; WI: '95- 7, '99- 2; WCp: '98- 2; 2nd GP 1998-9. World CC: '95- 12, 4k: '98/00: 2/2. Won French CC 1994, Arab 5000m 1997, Moroccan 3000m 1992, 5000m 1994.
African records: 3000m (5) and 5000m 1998-9. Moroccan records 1995-8: 1500m, 3000m (6), 5000m (6).
Progression at 3000m, 5000m: 1989- 9:40.0, 1990- 9:28.3, 1991- 9:59.9, 1992- 9:32.07, 16:19.03; 1993- 9:00.55; 1994- 8:54.40, 15:50.1; 1995- 8:43.19, 14:53.77; 1996- 8:54.86, 15:18.15; 1997- 8:46.56, 15:11.10; 1998- 8:27.26, 14:32.08; 1999- 8:26.48, 14:41.34; 2000- 8:47.18. pbs: 800m 2:06.6+ '98, 1500m 4:00.60 '98, 2000m 5:37.55 '99, 10000m 34:04.64 '94.
Injury caused her to cut short her 2000 season. Sisters: Nadia had 3000m pb 9:08.58 '88, and **Seloua** (b. 27 Jul 1974) was 24th in 1998 World 4k CC and at 1500m in 2000 ran a pb 4:08.18 and reached the Olympic semis.

MOZAMBIQUE

Governing body: Federaçao Moçambicana de Atletismo,Parque dos Continuardores, CP 1094, Maputo. Founded 1978.

Maria de Lourdes **MUTOLA** b. 27 Oct 1972 Maputo 1.62m 61kg.
At 800m (1500m): OG: '88- h, '92- 5 (9), '96- 3, '00- 1; WCh: '91- 4, '93- 1, '95 dq sf, '97- 3, '99- 2; WI: '93/5/7/9/01- 1/1/1/2/1; CG: '98- 1; AfCh: '88- 2, '90- 1 (1), '93- 1, '98- 1; AfG: '91- 1, '95- 1, '99- 1; WCp: '92- 1/3R, '94- 1, '98- 1. Won GWG 1994, GP 1993, 1995 (won overall), 1999 (2nd overall), 2nd 1997.
Records: World 1000m 1995, two WIR 1000m (2:32.08 '96 and 2:30.94 '99). African: 800m (8) 1991-4, 1000m (4) 1993-5; Commonwealth 800m 1997. African junior 800m (3) and 1500m 1991. MOZ 200m to 3000m.
Progression at 800m, 1500m: 1988- 2:04.36, 1989- 2:05.7, 4:31.5; 1990- 2:13.54, 4:25.27; 1991- 1:57.63, 4:12.72; 1992- 1:57.49, 4:02.60; 1993- 1:55.43, 4:04.97; 1994- 1:55.19, 4:13.93; 1995- 1:55.72, 4:01.6mx; 1996- 1:57.07, 4:01.63; 1997- 1:55.29, 4:09.1mx; 1998- 1:56.11, 1999- 1:56.04, 2000- 1:56.15, 4:02.39. pbs: 200m 23.86 '94, 300m 37.16mx '94, 400m 51.37 '94, 600m 1:25.8i '99, 1000m 2:29.34 '95, 1M 4:36.09 '91, 2000m 6:03.84 '92, 3000m 9:27.37 '91, 5000m 18:15.1 '90; Rd 1M 4:32.4 '95.
Star soccer player at school in Maputo; enabled to attend school in Eugene, Oregon, USA by a grant from the Olympic Solidarity Committee. 50 successive wins in 800m finals 1992-6, excluding her disqualification for stepping out of her lane after finishing first in her World Championship semi-final, ending with her Olympic bronze in 1996. Her 1:56.36 for 800m in 1998 was disallowed as a world indoor record as she ran inside the lane. She became Mozambique's first ever CG champion in 1998, following her country's admittance to the Commonwealth.

NAMIBIA

Governing body: Namibia AAU, PO Box 332, Windhoek. Founded 1990.

Frank FREDERICKS b. 2 Oct 1967 Windhoek 1.80m 73kg. Graduate of Brigham Young University, USA.
At 100m/200m: OG: '92- 2/2, '96- 2/2; WCh: '91- 5/2, '93- 6/1, '95- 4/2, '97- 4/2, '99- sf, dns; CG: '94- 3/1, '98- 2/-; AfG: '91- 1/1, '99- 3/; AfCh: '98- 2/1. At 200m: WI: '99- 1; WCp: '94- 1, '98- 1/3R. At 60m: WI: '93- 2. Won NCAA 100m & 200m 1991, South African 200m 1987. Won GP 100m 1998, 200m 1993, 1997 (2nd 1991, 1995).
WIR 100m (10.05), 200m (19.92) 1996. African records: 100m 1991 & 1996 (2), 200m (9) 1989-96.
Progression at 100m, 200m: 1985- 10.73, 21.68; 1986- 10.1, 20.6A; 1987- 10.36A, 20.58/20.41Aw; 1988- 10.32A, 20.57; 1989- 10.02A, 20.31A/ 20.09Aw; 1990- 10.16A/10.14Aw, 20.32/20.20Aw; 1991- 9.95/9.89w; 20.08/20.0/19.90w; 1992- 10.02/9.91w, 19.97; 1993- 10.03, 19.85; 1994- 10.04/10.00w, 19.97; 1995- 10.03A, 19.93A; 1996- 9.86, 19.68; 1997- 9.90, 19.81; 1998- 9.93, 19.97A/ 19.99; 1999- 9.94, 19.87; 2000- 20.79. pbs: 50m 5.59+ '97, 55m 6.13i '93, 60m 6.45+ '97, 400m 46.28 '89, LJ 7.57i '91, 7.46A '90.
The first to win an Olympic medal (he has now won all four Namibian Olympic medals) and the first to win a world title for his country. A former soccer player, he was sent to the USA by the Rossing Uranium Mine, for whom he now works, to study computer science. He became the first non-US sprinter to win the NCAA double. Able to compete internationally once Namibia gained independence in 1990 and IAAF affiliation 1991. At Oslo in 1996 he ended Michael Johnson's 2-year undefeated run at 200m. He ran nine sub-20 sec 200m times in 1996, easily a season's record and at 100m had a record nine legal sub-10.00 times in 1997 with a career record 26 in all to end 1999. Withdrew injured from semi of 100m and then from final of 200m at 1999 World Championships. Restricted by injury to just one race in 2000.

NETHERLANDS

Governing body: Koninklijke Nederlandse Atletiek-Unie (KNAU), PO Box 230, 3400 AE IJsselstein. Founded 1901.
National Championships first held in 1910 (men), 1921 (women). **2000 Champions**: **Men**: 100m: Martin Ungerer 10.45, 200m: Patrick van Balkom 20.95, 400m: Julien Hagen 46.47, 800m: Bram Som 1:49.80; 1500m: Stefan Beumer 3:55.98, 5000m: Kamiel Maase 13:47.84, 10000m: Ramses Bekkenk 29:27.92, HMar: Greg van Hest 62:52, Mar: Aiduna Aitnafa 2:11:46, 3000mSt: Simon Vroemen 8:35.57, 110mh: Robin Korving 13.44, 400mh: Jeroen Prent 51.87, HJ: Wilbert Pennings 2.14, PV: Christian Tamminga 5.50, LJ: Jurgen

Cools 7.69, TJ: Jermaine Sedoc 15.51, SP: Rutger Smith 18.46, DT: Pieter van der Kruk 61.32, HT: Frank van der Dool 66.41, JT: Oscar Schermer 72.00, Dec: Chiel Warners 7805, 20kmW: Marcel van Gemert 1:40:12. **Women**: 100m: Jacqueline Poelman 11.63, 200m: Mireille Donders SUI 23.54, 400m: Lotte Visschers 54.76, 800m: Anjolie Wisse 2:11.15, 1500m: Silvia Kruijer 4:22.18, 5000m: Erika van de Bilt 15:50.71; 10000m: Wilma van Onna 34:06:31, HMar: Nadezhda Wijenberg 71:39, Mar: Anne van Schuppen 2:35:35, 100mh: Ilja Voltman 13.75, 400mh: Marjolein de Jong 59.72, HJ: Denise Lewis GBR 1.70, PV: Monique van der Wilt 4.15, LJ: Sharon Jaklofsky 6.57w, TJ: Janneke Hulshof 12.03, SP: Lieja Koeman 17.39, DT: Jacqueline Goormachtigh 58.94, HT: Renate Beunder 59.79, JT: Kitty van Haperen 51.71, Hep: Saskia Meijer 5764.

Robin KORVING b. 29 Jul 1974 Heerhugowaard 1.88m 87kg. AAC Amsterdam. Construction engineering student.
At 110mh: WCh: '97/99- sf; EC: '98- 3; WJ: '92- 4; EJ: '93- 1; WCp: '99- 4; WUG: '97- 4. Dutch champion 1993-2000.
Eleven Dutch 110mh records 1993-9.
Progression at 110mh: 1992- 14.04, 1993- 13.85, 1994- 13.83, 1995- 13.83/13.65w, 1996- 13.58, 1997- 13.34, 1998- 13.20, 1999- 13.15, 2000- 13.25. pbs: 100m 10.90 '93, 200m 21.78 '95, 400m 47.79 '97, 60mh 7.60i '99, 200mh 23.67 '97.

NEW ZEALAND

Governing body: Athletics New Zealand, PO Box 741, Wellington.
National Championships first held in 1887 (men), 1926 (women). **2000 Champions: Men**: 100m/200m: Chris Donaldson 10.39/20.88, 400m: Bjørn Jansen 46.81, 800m: Mark Rodgers 1:47.61, 1500m: Adrian Blincoe 3:45.09, 3000m: Simon Maunder 8:01.14, 5000m/10000m: Richard Potts 14:01.84/29:19.12, HMar: Alan Bunce 64:15, Mar: Mark Hutchinson 2:24:58, 3000mSt: Phil Costley 8:57.65, 110mh: Tony Pownall 14.47, 400mh: Zion Armstrong 49.95, HJ: Glenn Howard 2.30, PV: Paul Gibbons 5.00, LJ: Aaron Langdon 7.69, TJ: Scott Clements 15.00, SP/DT: Ian Winchester 17.42/58.96, HT: Phil Jensen 69.19, JT: Stuart Farquhar 72.22, Dec: Sean Gourley 6639, 3000mW/20kmW: Craig Barrett 11:47.09/1:25:52, 50kmW: Tony Sargisson 4:28:27. **Women**: 100m/200m: Caro Hunt 11.86/24.02, 400m: Jane Arnott 52.44, 800m/1500m: Toni Hodgkinson 2:00.95/4:15.18, 3000m: Karen Murphy 9:45.45, 5000m/HMar: Sarah Christie 16:28.75/75:24, 10000m: Shireen Crumpton 34:26.67, Mar: Melissa Moon 2:45:42, 2000mSt: Karen Murphy 6:42.39, 100mh: Rowena Morton 13.56, 400mh: Nicola Kidd 60.37, HJ: Angela McKee 1.80, PV: Melina Hamilton 3.85, LJ: Nadia Smith 6.01, TJ: Shelley Avery 13.26, SP: Tania Senior 15.72, DT: Beatrice Faumuina 62.06, HT: Tasha Williams 62.31, JT: Andrea McBride 45.53, Hep: Joanne Henry 5198, 3000mW: Lynley Young 14:06.21, 10kmW: Diana Pittwood 60:04, 20kmW: Diane Barrett 1:49:36.

Women

Beatrice FAUMUINÁ b. 23 Oct 1974 Auckland 1.85m 124kg. Student.
At DT (SP): OG: '96- dnq 23, '00- 12; WCh: '95- dnq 28, '97- 1, '99- 5; CG: '94- 2 (9), '98- 1 (4); WJ: '92- 5; WCp: '98- 4. 3rd GP 2000. Won NZ DT 1993-2000, SP 1994, 1997-9; AUS SP 1998, DT 1997-8.
Eleven NZ discus records 1993-7.
Progression at DT: 1990- 45.06, 1991- 46.04, 1992- 53.02, 1993- 55.20, 1994- 57.94, 1995- 60.28, 1996- 64.04, 1997- 68.52, 1998- 67.58, 1999- 64.62, 2000- 65.41A. pbs: SP 16.96 '98, HT 44.24 '95.
Had 37 successive wins at discus Jan 1997 - June 1998. Parents came from Western Samoa. Her first important success was winning the discus at the Pacific Schools Games in 1992.

Toni HODGKINSON b. 12 Dec 1971 Takaka 1.80m 62kg. Physiotherapist.
At 800m (1500m): OG: '96- 8, '00- sf (h); WCh: '97- 6, '99- h; CG: '90- 9, '98- sf (8); WI: '97- 5; WJ: '90- sf. Won NZ 400m 1995, 800m 1994-6, 1999-2000; 1500m 1996, 2000.
Five NZ 800m records 1996.
Progression at 800m: 1985- 2:15.0, 1986- 2:11.3, 1987- 2:11.5, 1988- 2:09.73, 1989- 2:04.31, 1990- 2:05.86, 1991- 2:07.96, 1992- 2:07.36, 1993- 2:07.92, 1994- 2:05.82, 1995- 2:05.31, 1996- 1:58.25, 1997- 1:59.39, 1998- 2:00.86, 1999- 2:00.15, 2000- 1:59.31. pbs: 400m 53.40 '96, 1000m 2:36.96i '00, 2:38.68 '96; 1500m 4:06.23 '00, 1M 4:31.19 '98.
Having set many age records as a teenager from 13, it was not until 1996, coached by John Davies, that she improved the 800m time that she ran at 17, but then made a dramatic burst into top world class.

NIGERIA

Governing body: The Athletic Federation of Nigeria, P.O.Box 211, Marina, Lagos. F'd 1944.
2000 National Champions: **Men**: 100m: Francis Obikwelu 10.14, 200m: Ambrose Ezenwa 20.85, 400m: Jude Monye 45.41, LJ: Idika Uduma 7.87, SP: Chima Ugwu 20.26. **Women**: 100m/200m: Mary Onyali 11.22/22.76, 400m: Charity Opara 50.23, 100mh: Glory Alozie 12.85. *Others?*

Deji ALIU b. 22 Nov 1975 1.87m 75kg.
At 100m/4x100m (200m): OG: '96- qf, '00- sf; WCh: '95- qf, '97- (sf), '99- qf; CG: '94- qf; WJ: '92- 3R, '94- 1 (2); AfG: '99- 4/1R; WUG: '95- 4; Af-J: '94- 1 (1). At 60m: WI: '99- 5, '01- dq.
Two African indoor 60m records 1999.
Progression at 100m: 1993- 10.64, 1994- 10.17/10.0, 1995- 10.02, 1996- 10.12/10.11w/9.9, 1997- 10.15/10.09w, 1998- 10.20/10.08w, 1999- 10.11A/10.15/10.07w, 2000- 10.15/10.10w. pbs: 50m 5.61i '99,

60m 6.48i '99, 200m 20.43A '98, 20.43 '99.

Francis Obiorah **OBIKWELU** b. 22 Nov 1978 1.95m 74kg. Sporting Clube de Portugal.
At 200m (/100m): OG: '96- sf, '00- sf; WCh: '97- 2R (sf), '99- 3; WI: '97- 3, '99- 4; WJ: '96- 1/1; AfG: '99- 1/2/1R. 3rd GP 200m 1999. At 400m: WJ: '94- sf;Af-J: '94- 2. Won NGR 100m 1999-200m, 200m 1997, 1999.
Two Nigerian 200m records 1999
Progression at 100m, 200m: 1994- 21.16, 1995- 10.31, 21.22; 1996- 10.12, 20.24; 1997- 10.10, 20.53/20.27Aw; 1998- 10.01, 20.17; 1999- 10.01A/ 10.13/10.11w, 19.84; 2000- 9.97, 20.01. pb 400m 46.79 '94.
An Ibo, and thus in an ethnic minority group in Nigeria, his family emigrated to Portugal in 1994.

Women

Olabisi AFOLABI b. 31 Oct 1975 1.71m 59kg.
At 400m/4x400mR: OG: '96- sf/2R, '00- qf/4R; WCh: '95- h, '97/99- sf; WJ: '94- 1; CG: '94- 7; AfG: '95- 3, '99- 2/1R; WUG: '95- 1; Af-J: '94- 1. Nigerian champion 1995-6.
Two African 4x400m records 1996.
Progression at 400m: 1993- 53.42, 1994- 51.97, 1995- 50.50, 1996- 50.49/50.4, 1997- 50.41A/50.58, 1998- 50.85, 1999- 50.34A/50.40, 2000- 50.30. pbs: 100m 11.68 '96, 200m 23.37 '96, 600m 1:27.99 '95, 800m 2:06.92 '96.

Glory ALOZIE b. 30 Dec 1977 1.55m 51kg. Valencia, Spain.
At 100mh: OG: '00- 2; WCh: '99- 2; WJ: '96- 2; AfG: '99- 1/1R; AfCh: '96- 1, '98- 1, '00- 1; Af-J: '95- 2; WCp: '98- 1. 2nd GP 2000, 3rd 1998. At 60mh: WI: '99- 2. Won NGR 100mh 1999-2000.
African records: 100m 1999, 100mh (5) 1998-9; two Commonwealth 100mh records 1999.
Progression at 100mh: 1993- 14.99, 1994- 14.25, 1995- 13.86, 1996- 13.30, 1997- 12.96, 1998- 12.44/ 12.4w, 1999- 12.44, 2000- 12.54. pbs: 60m 7.20i '99, 100m 10.90 '99; 200m 22.91w '98, 50mh 6.86i '01, 60mh 7.82i '99.
Based in Spain since January 1997 and reportedly looking for Spanish citizenship. Won 17 of 19 finals in 1998 at 100mh. Her fiancée Hyginus Anugo was killed in a road accident in Sydney just prior to the 2000 Games.

Mercy NKU b. 17 Jul 1976 1.70m 67kg.
At 100m/(200m): OG: '96- sf, '00- sf/sf; WCh: '99- 8/qf; AfG: '99- 1/1R; AfCh: '96- h/sf; Af-J: '94- 3/4/1R, '95- 1/1. At 60m: WI: '01- 5.
Progression at 100m. 200m: 1992- 12.36, 1993- 12.20, 1994- 11.35, 24.11; 1995- 11.38/11.3, 23.63; 1996- 11.38/11.3, 24.15; 1997- 11.19/11.1, 23.35; 1998- 11.52/11.4, 23.9; 1999- 11.03A/11.08/10.98w, 22.53; 2000- 11.20, 22.95. pbs: 50m 6.13i '01, 60m 7.11i '01.
World's fastest junior at 100m in 1994.

Falilat OGUNKOYA b. 12 May 1968 1.72m 66kg. LIAZ Jablonec. Was at Mississippi State University, USA. Married to former 800m runner Tony Osheku.
At 400m/4x400mR: OG: '96- 3/2R, '00- 7/4R; WCh: '95- 6, '97- 5, '99- 4; WI: '99- 2; WCp: '89- 3, '98- 2; AfG: '95- 2/1R, '99- 1/1R; AfCh: '89- 1/1R, '98- 1; won GWG 1998, GP 1998 (2nd 1996, 2000). At 200m/4x100m: OG: '88- qf; WCh: '87- sf; WJ: '86- 1/3R; WUG: '87- 3R; WCp: '98- 1; AfG: '87- 2/1R (2 100m, 1 4x400mR); AfCh: '88- 1 (2 100m), '89- 2, '98- 1.
African records: 400m 1996, 4x100m 1987, 4x400m (3) 1987-96; Nigerian 800m 1997.
Progression at 200m, 400m: 1984- 24.3, 1985- 23.5, 1986- 23.11, 1987- 22.95A/22.87w, 52.2A; 1988- 22.88, 1989- 22.82A, 51.22; 1990- 23.53, 52.26; 1994- 24.05, 53.54; 1995- 22.99, 50.31A/ 50.72; 1996- 22.97/22.58w, 49.10; 1997- 22.94, 49.48; 1998- 22.22, 49.52A/49.60; 1999- 22.77, 49.62; 2000- 23.18, 22.93Aw, 50.04. pbs: 100m 11.19 '88, 300m 35.95+ '99, 800m 2:04.57 '97.
The former world junior champion, who has one child, made a great return to top-class action in 1995 after five years out. Son, Tony, born in 1993.

Charity OPARA b. 20 May 1972 Owerri 1.70m 60kg.
At 400m/4x400mR: OG: '96- 2R, '00- qf/4R; WCh: '91- dq/5R, '99- sf; WI: '97- 5; CG: '90- 3 (3 4x100mR); WJ: '90- 2; AfG: '91- 2/1R, '99- 5/1R; AfCh: '89- 1R, '90- 2/1R; 2nd GP 1998, 3rd 2000. Won NGR 400m 1989, 2000.
African records: 400m (2) 1990, 4x400m (3) 1991-6.
Progression at 400m: 1988- 55.80, 1989- 52.36, 1990- 51.12, 1991- 50.86, 1992- 49.86, 1996- 51.79, 1997- 49.79A/50.27/50.2, 1998- 49.29, 1999- 50.52, 2000- 50.23. pbs: 100m 11.46 '97, 200m 22.60 '92.
Unfortunate to be disqualified for running out of her lane after winning her second round heat very easily in 50.57 in the 1991 World Champs. Four-year drugs ban 1992-6. Lives in Trento, Italy.

NORWAY

Governing body: Norges Fri-Idrettsforbund, Serviceboks 1, Ullevaal Stadium, 0840 Oslo. Founded 1896.
National Championships first held in 1897 (men), 1947 (women). **2000 Champions**: **Men**: 100m/200m: John Ertzgaard 10.43/20.71, 400m: Quincy Douglas 46.63, 800m: Vebjørn Rodal 1:46.52, 1500m: Kjetil Hodnekvam 3:46.27, 5000m: Khalid Skah 13:36.35, 10000m: Knut Erik Rame 29:25.07, HMar: Karl Johan Rasmussen 64:22, Mar: Terje Næss 2:21:59, 3000mSt: Jim Svenøy 8:36.42, 110mh: Tom Erik Olsen 14.23, 400mh: Atle McAdam 51.96, HJ: Arjan Bos 2.11, PV: Tom Erik Olsen 5.50, LJ: Lars Jakob Woie 7.50, TJ: Sigurd Njerve 16.14, SP: Gjøran Sørli 19.03, DT: Einar Kristian Tveitå 59.63, HT: Anders Halvorsen 61.52, JT: Ronny Nilsen 75.39, Dec: Lukas Udelhoven GER 6683, 5000mW/10000mW:

Erik Tysse 20:00.51/41:44.6, 20000mW: Trond Nymark 1:29:50.9, 50kmW: 2 men dnf. Women: 100m/200m/400m: Ann Helen Rinden 11.77/23.95/54.64, 800m: Kristin Roset 2:07.43, 1500m/5000m/10000m: Gunhild Halle Haugen 4:20.63/16:02.26/32:24.06 , HMar: Bente Landøy 75:01, Mar: Jorunn Rekkedal 2:43:58, 3000mSt: Susanne Wigene 10:01.54, 100mh: Rannveig Kvalvik 14.26, 400mh: Mari Bjone 59.94, HJ: Hanne Haugland 1.90, PV: Monika Grimsrud 3.50, LJ/TJ: Lene Espegren 6.09/13.56, SP: Katarina Sederholm 16.30, DT: Mette Bergmann 59.08 (17th successive), HT: Unn Merete Lie 55.23, JT: Trine Hattestad 63.52, Hep: Tania Longe 5397, 5000mW/10000mW: Kjersti Plätzer 20:46.3/43:21.1, 20km: Anne Haaland Simonsen 1:38:15.

Pål Arne FAGERNES b. 8 Jun 1974 Asker 1.85m 103kg. IK Tjalve
At JT: OG: '96- dnq 13, '00- 9, WCh: '97- dnq 20, '99- 4; EC: '98- dnq 16;. Norwegian champion 1996, 1998-9; won NCAA 1996.
Eight Norwegian javelin records 1996-2000.
Progression at JT: 1990- 55.70, 1991- 59.86, 1992- 65.56, 1993- 67.82, 1994- 74.10, 1995- 77.46, 1996- 85.06, 1997- 82.80, 1998- 84.46, 1999- 86.24, 2000- 86.74.
Accomplished all-round sportsman, especially at skiing (at which he has won 72 national competitions) and cycling as well as javelin.

Jim SVENØY b. 22 Apr 1972 Molde 1.85m 69kg. Fræna FIK. Was at UTEP, USA.
At 3000mSt: OG: '96- 8, '00- 9; WCh: '93- h, '95- sf, '97- 7, '99- h; EC: '94- 7, '98- 3; WJ: '90- h; EJ: '91- 3. Won NOR 1500m 1992, 5000 1996, 3000mSt 1993-2000, NCAA 1994-5.
Five Norwegian 3000mSt records 1995-7.
Progression at 3000mSt: 1990- 8:57.83, 1991- 8:50.02, 1992- 8:42.67, 1993- 8:28.51, 1994- 8:28.12, 1995- 8:18.26, 1996- 8:19.79, 1997- 8:12.05, 1998- 8:15.24, 1999- 8:16.50, 2000- 8:23.61. pbs: 800m 1:52.82 '92, 1500m 3:40.49 '99, 1M 3:58.74 '94, 3000m 7:45.37 '98, 5000m 13:37.18 '96, 10000m 28:42.29 '99, 2000mSt 5:26.18 '99.

Women

Kjersti TYSSE PLÄTZER b. 18 Jan 1972 Os, Bergen 1.74m 54kg. née Tysse. Søfteland TIL.
At 20kmW: OG: '00- 2; WCh: '99- 9; EC: '94- 16, '98- 9; ECp: '00- 3. At 5000mW: WJ: '86- 5. Won NOR 5000mW 1985-7, 1992, 1994-6, 1998-2000, 10kmW 1994-5, 1998, 2000; 20kmW 1998-9.
Norwegian walks records: 3000m (2), 5000m (3), 10km (5), 10000m, 20km (4) 1996-2000.
Progression at 10kmW, 20kmW: 1986- 48:01, 1987- 45:45, 1994- 46:10, 1995- 45:12, 1996- 44:40, 1:39:36; 1998- 42:44, 1:32:55; 1999- 41:54, 1:28:35; 2000- 43:21.10t, 1:27:53. pbs: 3000mW 12:08.63i '01, 12:18.02 '00; 5000mW 20:46.2 '00.
Married to Stephan Plätzer GER (b. 12 Sep 66), pbs 800m 1:46.53 '89, 1500m 3:40.26 '89.

POLAND

Governing body: Polski Zwiazek Lekkiej Atletyki (PZLA), 01-809 Warszawa, ul. Ceglowska 68/70. Founded 1919.
National Championships first held in 1920 (men), 1922 (women). **2000 Champions**: **Men**: 100m: Marcin Nowak 10.22, 200m: Marcin Urbas 20.49, 400m: Robert Mackowiak 45.13, 800m: Grzegorz Krzosek 1:46.33, 1500m: Leszek Zblewski 3:41.03, 5000m: Piotr Drwal 13:56.49, 10000m/HMar: Jan Bialk 28:49.84/63:38, Mar: Miroslaw Plawgo 2:15:57, 3000mSt: Rafal Wójcik 8:22.82, 110mh: Marcin Kuszewski 13.52, 400mh: Pawel Januszewski 48.89, HJ: Artur Partyka 2.22, PV: Krzysztof Kusiak 5.40, LJ: Grzegorz Marciniszyn 7.82, TJ: Jacek Kazimierowski 16.13, SP: Przemyslaw Zabawski 18.65, DT: Olgierd Stanski 63.30, HT: Szymon Ziólkowski 80.39, JT: Grzegorz Krasinski 81.94, Dec: Michal Modelski 7685, 20kmW: Robert Korzeniowski 1:20:52, 50kmW: Jan Holender 4:15:23. **Women**: 100m/200m: Zuzanna Radecka 11.37/22.96, 400m: Grazyna Prokopek 52.15, 800m: Anna Zagórska 2:04.25, 1500m: Lidia Chojecka 4:07.16, 5000m/10000m: Justyna Bak 15:44.56/32:58.97, 3000mSt: Malgorzata Jamróz 10:33.84, HMar: Doruta Gruca-Giezek 73:03, Mar: Janina Malska 2:44:07, 100mh: Aneta Sosnowska 13.17, 400mh: Anna Olichwierczuk 55.75, HJ: Donata Jancewicz 1.86, PV: Monika Pyrek 4.00, LJ: Agata Karczmarek 6.54, TJ: Liliana Zagacka 13.87, SP: Krystyna Zabawska 18.35, DT: Joanna Wisniewska 61.12, HT: Kamila Skolimowska 66.20, JT: Genowefa Patla 56.51, Hep: Elzbieta Raczka 5801, 10mW: Katarzyna Radtke 44:28, 20kmW: Silwia Korzeniowska 1:34:24.

Pawel JANUSZEWSKI b. 2 Jan 1972 Pyrzyce 1.80m 75kg. Skra Waszawa.
At 400mh (4x400mR): OG: 96- h, '00- 6; WCh: '95- h, '97- sf, '99- 5; EC: '94- sf, '98- 1; EJ: '91- 2R; WUG: '99- 1; WCp: '98- 4; ECp: '95- 7, '99- 3. Polish champion 1995, 1997, 1999-2000.
Three Polish 400mh records 1997-8.
Progression at 400mh: 1991- 52.96, 1992- 51.71, 1993- 51.88, 1994- 49.95, 1995- 49.43, 1996- 49.63, 1997- 48.94, 1998- 48.17, 1999- 48.19, 2000- 48.42. pbs: 200m 21.64 '96, 400m 46.79 '96.
Survived a serious car crash in September 1997 (at first reported dead).

Robert KORZENIOWSKI b. 30 Jul 68 Lubaczów 1.70m 63kg. US Tourcoing, France & Wawel Kraków TC. PE teacher.
At 20kmW (50kmW): OG: '92- dnf (dq), '96- 8 (1), '00- 1 (1); WCh: '91- 10 (dnf), '93- (dq), '95- (3), '97- (1), '99- (dq); EC: '90- 4, '94- dq (5), '98- (1); WCp: '89- 40, '91- 7, '93- 4, '95- 9, '99- 4; ECp: '96- 1, '98- 2, '00- 1; WUG: '91- 1, '93- 1. At 10kmW: EJ: '87- dq. At 5000mW: WI: '93- 2. Won Polish 20kmW 1990-2000, 50kmW 1993.
World bests: 5km road walk (18:21 '90), track

1997. Polish records 1990-2000: 5000mW (5), 10kmW (3), 20kmW (5), 50km W (3).
Progression at 20kmW, 50kmW: 1986- 1:32:33, 1987- 1:29:48, 1988- 1:26:04, 1989- 1:23:19, 1990- 1:19.32, 1991- 1:21:19, 1992- 1:19:14, 3:46:42; 1993- 1:20:55, 3:44:24; 1994- 1:20:55, 3:45:57; 1995- 1:20:52, 3:45:57; 1996- 1:20:51, 3:42:40; 1997- 1:19:43, 3:44:46; 1998- 1:19:36, 3:43:51; 1999- 1:18:40, 2000- 1:18:22, 3:41:50. pbs: 3000mW 11:05.20 '97, 5000mW 18:17.22 '92, 10000mW 39:00.11 '94, 1 Hr 14,794m '92; road 35kmW 2:28:30 (world best) '93.
Disqualified in 2nd place in the stadium just before finish of the 1992 Olympic 50km walk, but won this event in 19996. In 2000 won a unique Olympics walks double and became the first man ever to retain the 50km title. His sister Silwia was Polish 20km walk champion in 2000.

Tomasz LIPIEC b. 10 May 1971 Warszawa 1.87m 75kg. Polonia Warszawa.
At 50kmW (20kmW): OG: '00- dnfWCh: '97- 5, '99- dq; EC: '98- 5; WCp: '93- 13, '97- 5, '99- 2; ECp: '98- 1, '00- (7). At 10kmW: EJ: 89- 10. Won POL 50kmW 1992, 1996, 1999.
Polish 50km walk records 1997 and 1999.
Progression at 50kmW: 1992- 4:01:13, 1993- 4:03:09, 1996- 3:49:30, 1997- 3:41:58, 1998- 3:42:57, 1999- 3:40:08. pbs: 5000mW 19:27.64 '00, 10000mW 39:56.00 '00, 20kmW 1:20:48 '00.

Robert MACKOWIAK b. 13 May 1970 Rawicz 1.81m 76kg. Slask Wroclaw. Soldier.
At 400m/4x400mR: OG: '00- 5; WCh: '97- sf/4R, '99- qf/2R; EC: '94- 6R, 98- 2/2R; WI: '97- 4, '99- 2R, '01- 1R; EI: '98- 3; ECp: '99- 4/2R. At 200m/ 4x100mR: OG: '96- qf; WCh: '91- hR, 95- h; EJ: '89- 1R. Won POL 200m 1995-7, 400m 1998, 2000.
Three Polish 400m records 1997-8.
Progression at 400m: 1991- 47.43, 1994- 46.50, 1995- 46.05, 1996- 45.91, 1997- 45.26, 1998- 45.04, 1999- 45.17, 2000- 45.01. pbs: 100m 10.45 '90, 10.44w '93; 200m 20.61 '96.

Tomasz SCIGACZEWSKI b. 18 Nov 1978 Zgierz 1.88m 88kg. Warszawianka Warszawa.
At 110mh: OG: '00- sf; WCh: '97/99- qf; WJ: '96- 2; EU23: '99- 1; EJ: '95- 3, '97- 1; ECp: '99- 3. Won POL 1998-9. At 60mh: WI: '99- 5; EI: '98- 2, '00- 3.
European U23 110mh record 1999.
Progression at 110mh: 1994- 15.30, 1995- 14.05, 1996- 13.64/13.55w, 1997- 13.51, 1998- 13.40/ 13.0/13.25w, 1999- 13.29, 2000- 13.42. pbs: 50mh 6.48i '99, 60mh 7.51i '99.
His mother Halina Kaminska long jumped 6.25 at the age of 18 in 1973.

Marcin URBAS b. 17 Sep 1976 Kraków 1.80m 77kg. AZS-AWF Kraków. Typography technician.
At 200m/4x100mR: OG: '00- qf; WCh: '99- 5; EC: '98- h; ECp: '99- 1. Won POL 1998-2000.
Polish 200m record 1999.
Progression at 200m: 1992- 23.07, 1993- 22.43, 1994- 22.01, 1995- 21.60, 1996- 21.45, 1997- 20.83, 1998- 20.64, 1999- 19.98, 2000- 20.43. pbs: 60m 6.73i '00, 100m 10.30 '99.
Improved from 20.64 in 1998 to 20.62, 20.34 (to win European Cup), 20.32 and, becoming the third European under 20-seconds, 19.98 (World Championships) in 1999. Sings with the group 'Sceptic'.

Szymon ZIÓLKOWSKI b. 1 Jul 1976 Poznan 1.90m 110kg. AZS Poznan.
At HT: OG: '96- 10, '00- 1; WCh: '95- dnq 22, '99- dnq 23; EC: '98- 5; WJ: '94- 1; EJ: '93= 7, '95- 1; EU23: '97- 2; ECp: '95- 6, '99- 2. Polish champion 1996-7, 1999-2000.
Three Polish hammer records 2000-01.
Progression at HT: 1991- 55.96, 1992- 63.84, 1993- 67.34, 1994- 72.48, 1995- 75.42, 1996- 79.52, 1997- 79.14, 1998- 79.58, 1999- 79.01, 2000- 81.42, 2001- 82.13.
His sister Michalina (b. 1983) was second in the 2000 Polish U18 Championships, pb 52.94 '00.

Women

Lidia CHOJECKA b. 25 Jan 1977 Siedlce 1.63m 47kg. WLKS Siedlce.
At 1500m (3000m): OG: '00- 5; WCh: '99- 9; EC: '98- 6; WJ: '94- 7, '96- 5; EJ: '95- 1; EU23: '97- 2, '99- 1; WUG: '97- 3; WI: '97- 4, '99- 3; EI: '98- 2, '00- (2); ECp: '99 (3). Won POL 800m 1996, 1500m 1999-2000.
Polish records: 1500m 2000, 3000m (3) 1999-2000.
Progression at 1500m: 1993- 4:40.84, 1994- 4:18.70, 1995- 4:15.27, 1996- 4:11.36, 1997- 4:05.74, 1998- 4:03.32, 1999- 4:01.36, 2000- 3:59.22. pbs: 800m 1:59.97 '99, 1000m 2:40.49 '98, 1M 4:24.44i '00, 4:25.18 '98; 3000m 8:33.35 '00, 5000m 16:29.87 '99.

Anna JAKUBCZAK b. 2 Feb 1973 Zamosc 1.66m 53kg. Skra Warszawa.
At 1500m: OG: '00- 6; WCh: '99- 7; EC: '98- 4; ECp: '99- 2. Won POL 800m 1994, 1997, 1999; 1500m 1998.
Progression at 1500m: 1990- 4:38.54, 1991- 4:36.73, 1992- 4:32.62, 1993- 4:17.84, 1994- 4:14.72, 1995- 4:21.54, 1996- 4:13.84, 1997- 4:13.71, 1998- 4:03.63, 1999- 4:01.43, 2000- 4:06.49. pbs: 800m 2:00.78 '99, 1000m 2:35.96 '00, 3000m 9:17.75 '98.

Monika PYREK b. 11 Aug 1980 Gdynia 1.66m 64kg. KS Lechia Gdansk.
At PV: OG: '00- 7; EC: '98- 7; WJ: '98- 2=; EJ: '97- 10, '99- 4.. Polish champion 1999-2000.
16 (+) Polish pole vault records 1997-2000.
Progression at PV: 1995- 2.30, 1996- 3.60, 1997- 3.83, 1998- 4.15, 1999- 4.21i/4.16, 2000- 4.40. pb HJ 1.70.

Kamila SKOLIMOWSKA b. 4 Nov 1982 Warszawa 1.80m 88kg. Warszawianka. Schoolgirl.
At HT: OG: '00- 1; WCh: '99- 21; WJ: '98 & '00- dnq; WY: '99- 1; EC: '98- 7; EJ: '97- 1, ECp: '99- 4. Polish champion 1996-7, 1999.
Four World junior hammer records 1999-2000, eight Polish hammer records 1997-2000.

Progression at HT: 1996- 47.66, 1997- 63.48, 1998- 62.72, 1999- 66.62, 2000- 71.16.
Youngest ever Polish champion and record holder (at 13y 229d), won European Junior title at 14y 264 and became the youngest Olympic champion in Sydney 2000 at 17 years 331 days. Father, Robert, was junior world champion at weightlifting in 1976 and 7th at super-heavyweight at the 1980 Olympics (his weight 155kg).

Urszula WLODARCZYK b. 22 Dec 1965 Walbrzych 1.80m 67kg. AZS-AWF Wroclaw and LIAZ Jablonec, CZE. PE teacher.
At Hep (TJ): OG: '92- 8, '96- 4, '00- 4; WCh: '91- 6, '93- 5 (8), '95- 9, '97- 4, '99- 7; EC: '94- 3, '98- 2; WUG: 91- 2 (4), '93- 1; ECp: '91-3-4-7-8-9-00: 4/3/5/2/3/4/4. At Pen: WI: '93/7/9/01-2inv/4/3/8; EI: '92- 3, '94- 3, '96- 2, '98- 1, '00- 3. At 100mh: ECp: '91- 6, '95- 8. Won POL 100mh 1991, TJ 1990-4; Hep 1988, 1990-3, 1996-7.
Two Polish triple jump records 1991.
Progression at Hep: 1982- 4779*, 1983- 4914, 1984- 5173, 1985- 5504, 1986- 5721, 1987- 5831, 1988- 5825, 1989- 5898, 1990- 6021, 1991- 6425, 1992- 6407, 1993- 6394, 1994- 6322, 1995- 6248, 1996- 6484, 1997- 6542, 1998- 6460, 1999- 6287, 2000- 6470. pbs: 100m 11.94 '91, 200m 24.02 '95, 23.89w '92; 800m 2:09.59 '97, 60mh 8.25i '98, 100mh 13.19 '94, HJ 1.86 '95, LJ 6.63 '97, 6.67w '93; TJ 13.98 '93, SP 15.48 '00, JT 47.60 '97, Pen 4808i '98.
Won IAAF Combined Events Challenge 1998. Completed 91 heptathlons 1982-2000 with 54 scores over 6000.

Krystyna DANILCZYK-ZABAWSKA b. 14 Jan 1968 Dabrowa Bialostocka 1.83m 82kg. née Danilczyk. Podlasie Bialystok. Storekeeper.
At SP: OG: '92- 10, '00- 5; WCh: '91- 12, '93 dnq 17, '97- 8, '99- 8; EC: '94- 9, 98- '11; WI: '99- 2, '01- 8; EI: '98- 4, '00- 5; ECp: '91-3-9: 5/5/1. Polish champion 1991-4, 1997-2000.
Progression at SP: 1985- 10.98, 1986- 12.20, 1987- 14.48, 1988- 15.70, 1990- 18.21, 1991- 19.03, 1992- 19.42, 1993- 18.31, 1994- 19.23, 1995- 16.38, 1996- 18.62, 1997- 19.06, 1998- 19.24, 1999- 19.26i/19.23, 2000- 19.18.
Married to Przemyslaw Zabawski, Polish shot champion 1997 & 2000, pb 18.76 '00.

PORTUGAL

Governing body: Federação Portuguesa de Atletismo, Largo da Lagoa, 15-B, 2795 Linda-a-Velha. Founded 1921.
National Championships first held in 1910 (men), 1937 (women). **2000 Champions**: **Men**: 100m/200m: Ricardo Alves 10.44/21.00, 400m: Vítor Moreno 47.72, 800m: Alberto Bispo 1:50.04, 1500m: Luís Feiteira 3:39.36, 5000m: Domingos Castro 13:29.58, 10000m: José Ramos 28:03.52, Mar: António Sousa 2:16:15, 3000mSt: Manuel Silva 8:37.16, 110mh: Rui Palma 13.91w, 400mh: Edivaldo Monteiro 50.76, HJ: Jonas Mattes 2.11, PV: João André 5.60, LJ: Gaspar Araújo 7.35w, TJ: Eduardo Martingo 15.37w, SP: Fernando Alves 17.91, DT: Paulo Bernardo 53.70, HT: Sérgio Coelho 59.61, JT: João Reis 65.33, Dec: Mário Aníbal 6747, 20000mW: João Vieira 1:26:41.81, 50kmW: Pedro Martins 3:55:55. **Women**: 100m/200m: Severina Cravid 11.69/24.14, 400m: Carmo Tavares 54.00, 800m/1500m: Nédia Semedo 2:04.28/4:28.36, 5000m: Fernanda Ribeiro 15:01.49, 10000m Helena Sampaio 32:08.67, Mar: Fatima Siulva 2:34:40, 100mh: Isabel Abrantes 13.14, 400mh: Patrícia Lopes 60.31, HJ: Sónia Machado 1.78, PV: Marisa Vieira 3.88, LJ/TJ: Marta Godinho 6.33w/12.45, SP/DT: Teresa Machado 15.82/59.79, HT: Vânia Silva 61.27, JT: Sílvia Cruz 48.60, Hep: Sónia Machado 4911, 10000mW: Susana Feitor 44:36.79, 20kmW: Isilda Gonçalves 1:39:00.

Paulo GUERRA b. 21 Aug 1970 Barrancos 1.74m 64kg. Maratona CP.
At 10000m: OG: '96- h; WCh: '95- 8; EC: '94- 5, '98- 14. At 3000mSt: EJ: '89- 8. World CC: '93-4-5-6-7-8-9-2000-01: 21/13/6/dnf/12/3/25/4. Eur CC '94-5-6-8-9-00: 1/1/2/11/1/1. Won POR 10000m 1994-5, CC 1995-7, 1999, 2001.
Progression at 5000m, 10000m: 1990- 14:00.90, 1991- 14:12.02, 1992- 14:07.11, 1993- 13:42.35, 28:11.14; 1994- 13:25.13, 27:52.44; 1995- 13:18.59, 27:52.55; 1996- 13:18.60, 28:09.56; 1998- 13:59.87, 27:50.17; 1999- 27:55.43. pbs: 1500m 3:45.21 '95, 1M 4:09.7 '91, 3000m 7:49.94 '96, 3000mSt 8:43.86 '91, HMar 61:53 '96, Mar 2:11:02 '98.
In a breakthrough 1994 season he was the top European placer in the World cross-country, won the Iberian 10,000m and was 5th in the Europeans, and then ran away with the inaugural European cross-country, a title he has now won four times. 2nd World Cross Challenge 1994/5. He is the only European senior man to earn a World Cross medal in the 1990s.

António PINTO b. 22 Mar 1966 Amarante 1.71m 61kg. Maratona CP
At 10000m: OG: '88- 13, WCh: '95- 19, '99- 5; EC: '90- 14, '98- 1. At Mar: OG: '92- dnf, '96- 14, '00- 11; WCh: '97- dnf; EC: '94- 9. Eur CC: '94- 8. Won POR CC 1992, 5000m 1994, 1999.
World best half marathon 1998, European records: 10000m 1999, Marathon 2000; Portuguese 5000m 1998.
Progression at 10000m, Mar: 1986- 31:13.3, 1987- 28:28.73, 1988- 28:01.00, 1989- 28:30.11, 1990- 28:14.32; 1991- 28:30.3, 2:12:39; 1992- 28:59.02, 2:10:02; 1994- 27:48.1, 2:08:31; 1995- 28:06.18, 2:08:48; 1996- 2:08:38, 1997- 2:07:55, 1998- 27:15.76, 2:08:13; 1999- 27:12.47, 2:09:00; 2000- 2:06:36. pbs: 1500m 3:39.25 '98, 3000m 7:41.33 '99, 5000m 13:02.86 '98, HMar 59:43 '98.
Previously a cyclist, started running in 1986. Has run 16 marathons, 7th at Carpi 1991 on his début and wins at London 1992, 1997 and 2000, and Berlin 1994; 2nd Paris 1994, Tokyo 1996,

London 1999; 3rd London and Berlin 1995, London 1998. Had four in succession under 2:09 in 1994-6 and after the Olympics ran his best yet, 2:07:55, to win his second London marathon. Had a poor record in championships until his European 10,000m title during a sensational season in 1998, when his times ranged from 3:39.25 for 1500m to 2:08:13 for marathon.

Rui SILVA b. 3 Aug 1977 1.74m 62kg. Sporting Club de Portugal.
At 1500m:OG: '00- h; WCh: '99- sf (fell); EC: '98- 2; WJ: '96- 6; EJ: '95- 8; EU23: '99- 1; WI: '99- 5. '01- 1; EI: '98- 1; WCp: '98- 2. At 3000m: EI: '00- 2. Won POR 1500m 1999, CC sh 2001.
Portuguese records: 1500m (4) 1998-9, 1000m, 1M, 2000m 1999.
Progression at 1500m: 1994- 3:50.9, 1995- 3:44.8, 1996- 3:40.09, 1997- 3:44.6, 1998- 3:34.00, 1999- 3:30.88, 2000- 3:32.60. pbs: 800m 1:45.29 '00, 1000m 2:16.30 '99, 1M 3:50.91 '99, 2000m 4:54.66 '99, 3000m 7:39.44i '00, 7:53.87 '99.

Women

Susana FEITOR b. 28 Jan 1975 Alcobertas 1.60m 54kg. C Natação Rio Maior.
At 20kmW: OG: '00- 14; WCh: '99- 4; WCp: '99- 9. At 10kmW: OG: '92- dq, '96- 13; WCh: '93- 11, '95- 17, '97- h; EC: '94- 8, '98- 3; EU23: '97- 3; WUG: '95- 4, '97- 4; WCp: '93- 8, '95- 15; ECp: '96- 3. At 5000mW: WJ: '90- 1, '92- dq, 94- 2; EJ: '89- 6, '91- 2, '93- 1. Won POR 10kmW 1992, 1994-2000, 20kmW 1998-9, 2001.
POR walks records 1989-2000: 3000m (9), 5000m (8), 10km (8), 20km (2). World junior 5000m best (21:01.8) 1993.
Progression at 10kmW, 20kmW: 1991- 45:37, 1992- 45:24, 1993- 43:44, 1994- 43:30, 1995- 44:05, 1996- 43:37, 1997- 44:26, 1998- 42:55, 1:31:03, 1999- 44:36, 1:30:13; 2000: 43:55, 1:28:19. Track pbs: 3000mW 12:21.7i '94, 5000mW 20:55.90 '96, 10000mW 44:36.79 '00.
Had a hugely successful junior career to her world silver medal in front of her home crowd in 1994, four years after she had won this title.

M Manuela MACHADO b. 9 Aug 1963 Viana do Castelo 1.61m 52kg. Sporting Club de Braga.
At Mar: OG: '92- 7, '96- 7, '00- 21; WCh: '91- 7, '93- 2, '95- 1, '97- 2, '99- 7; EC: '90- 10, '94- 1, '98- 1. Won POR Mar 1993.
Progression at Mar: 1988- 2:45:37, 1989- 2:38:45, 1990- 2:33:46, 1991- 2:32:33, 1992- 2:27:42, 1993- 2:30:54, 1994- 2:29.54, 1995- 2:27:53/2:25:39sh, 1996- 2:29:32, 1997- 2:28:12, 1998- 2:27:10, 1999- 2:25:09, 2000- 2:26:41. pbs: 800m 2:14.01 '87, 1500m 4:24.0 '91, 3000m 9:09.28 '92, 5000m 15:55.09 '95, 10000m 32:09.1 '94, HMar 70:18 '98.
Her World silver in 1993 was her best ever placing in her 12th marathon, but in December 1993 she won at Lisbon and after 7th in Nagoya went on to win the 1994 European title. Record now is four wins (including three major titles) and five 2nds in 29 marathons. 2nd in London and New York 1995 and Tokyo 1996; 3rd London 1999 in W35 world best.

Fernanda RIBEIRO b. 23 Jun 1969 Penafiel 1.61m 48kg. FC Porto,
At 10000m (5000m): OG: '96- 1, '00- 3; WCh: '93- 10, '95- 1 (2), '97- 2 (3), '99- dnf; EC: '94- 1, '98- 2; WCp: '94- 2; won E.Chall '98. At 3000m: OG: '88- h, '92- h; WCh: '87- h, '91- h; WI: '97- 3; EC: '86- h, '90- h; EI: '94- 1, '96- 1, '98- 2; WJ: '86- 4, '88- 2; EJ: '83- 11, '85- 4, '87- 1. World CC: '94- 10, '96- 6, '00- 10 (4k); Rd Rly team: '92- 1. Eur CC: '94- 6, '98- 4. Won IbAm 5000m 2000, POR 1500m 1989-90, 1995, 1998-9; 3000m 1985, 1993; 5000m 2000, 10000m 1992, 1996; CC 1996-9.
World 5000m record 1995. Portuguese records: 3000m (3), 5000m (3), 10000m (4) 1994-2000.
Progression at 3000m, 5000m, 10000m: 1982- 9:53.7, 1983- 9:21.71, 1984- 9:11.62, 1985- 9:14.19, 1986- 9:09.39, 1987- 8:56.33, 1988- 9:00.38, 1989- 9:04.33, 32:38.07; 1990- 9:03.35, 32:39.34; 1991- 8:57.64, 33:45.45; 1992- 8:56.10, 32:22.70; 1993- 8:51.91, 31:50.51; 1994- 8:42.13, 15:06.91, 31:04.25; 1995- 8:41.99, 14:36.45, 31:04.99; 1996- 8:39.49i/ 8:45.56, 14:41.07, 31:01.63; 1997- 8:37.14, 14:53.25, 31:39.15; 1998- 8:42.95, 15:22.8, 30:48.06; 1999- 8:30.66, 14:52.59; 2000- 8:34.99, 15:01.49, 30:22.88. pbs: 800m 2:05.83 '94, 1500m 4:05.97 '97, 1M 4:32.66 '99, HMar 68:23 '00.
At 11 was second in a half marathon in 1:24:02, just 4 secs behind Rosa Mota. Made international debut at 13 and set national age records each age 13-22 at 3000m and 14-18 and 20 at 1500m. She fulfilled her long-time promise in 1994 with brilliant performances to win European titles indoors and out, and has added World and Olympic titles in the following years.

Carla SACRAMENTO b. 10 Dec 1971 Lisboa 1.73m 58kg. Maratona Clube da Maia.
At 1500m (800m): OG: '92- sf (sf), '96- 6, '00- 10; WCh: '93- 11 (h), '95- 3, '97- 1, '99- 5; EC: '94- 6 (6), '98- 2; WI: '93/5/7/01- 7/2/5/4; EI: '92- (4), '94- (3), '96- 1; EJ: '89- (4); WUG: '97- 2; WCp: '98- 3. World 4k CC: '98-00-01: 19/7/7; Eur CC: '94- 11. Won GP 1M 1997 (3rd 1500m 1998), IbAm 1500m 1998, Portuguese 800m 1986-7, 1993-5; 1500m 1991, CC 2000-1.
Portuguese records 1989-99: 800m (7), 1500m (9), 1M (4), 1000m (2), 2000m and 3000m (1)
Progression at 800m, 1500m: 1985- 2:15.15/ 2:13.56dq, 1986- 2:10.48, 1987- 2:09.3, 4:35.96; 1988- 2:04.27, 4:29.41; 1989- 2:03.89, 4:21.92; 1990- 2:04.83, 4:15.06; 1991- 2:04.94, 4:20.43; 1992- 2:00.57, 4:04.10, 1993- 1:59.12, 4:06.33; 1994- 1:59.39, 4:06.05; 1995- 1:59.78, 4:03.79; 1996- 2:00.24, 4:02.64; 1997- 1:58.94, 4:01.86; 1998- 2:02.3, 3:57.71; 1999- 1:59.54, 4:01.29; 2000- 2:00.22, 4:00.35. pbs: 200m 25.49 '92, 400m 55.21 '89, 500m 1:10.83 '96, 1000m 2:34.85 '95, 1M 4:23.41 '98, 2000m 5:40.25 '96, 3000m 8:30.22 '99, 5000m 15:52.54 '00.

ROMANIA

Governing body: Federatia Romana de Atletism, Str. Aleea Strandului nr.2, Bucuresti 71331. Founded 1912.

National Championships first held in 1914 (men), 1925 (women). **2000 Champions**: **Men**: 100m: Bogdan Tarus 10.66, 200m: Adrian Guianu 21.45, 400m: Alexandru Mardan 47.28, 800m/1500m: Daniel Oniciuc 1.48.13/3:45.85, 5000m: Ovidiu Olteanu 13:52.27, 10000m: Niculae Negru 29:21.25, HMar: Laurentiu Staicu 66:06, Mar: Arthur Miklos 2:25:34, 3000mSt: Florin Ionescu 8:47.74, 110mh: Mihai Marghescu 14.50, 400mh: Mugur Mateescu 51.45, HJ: Stefan Vasilache 2.18, PV: Tiberiu Agoston 5.20, LJ: Bogdan Tudor 7.79, TJ: Ionut Punga 16.78, SP: Gheorghe Guset 20.18, DT: Ionel Oprea 60.67, HT: Cosmin Sorescu 69.69, JT: Levente Bartha 71.47, Dec: Romeo Hurduc 6911, 20kmW/50kmW: Silviu Casandra 1:21:35/4:03:30. **Women**: 100m/200m: Evelina Lisenco 11.52/23.73, 400m: Otilia Ruicu 51.85, 800m/1500m: Elena Iagar 2:01.29/4:04.94, 5000m: Elena Fidatov 15:20.59, 10000m: Alina Gherasim 32:14.18, HMar: Mihaela Botezan 70:07, Mar: Valentina Delion 2:47:30, 3000mSt: Cristina Iloc-Casandra 9:43.64, 100mh/LJ: Viorica Tigau 13.35/6.87w, 400mh: Otilia Lungu 59.45, HJ: Monica Dinescu 1.95, PV: Gabriela Mihalcea 3.80, TJ: Adelina Gavrila 14.44, SP: Livia Mehes 17.68, DT: Nicoleta Grasu 64.90, HT: Mihaela Melinte 73.95, JT: Ana-Mirela Termure 59.74, Hep: Elena Dumitrascu 5647, 10kmW/20kmW: Norica Cîmpean 43:51/1:29:39.

Women

Norica CÎMPEAN b. 22 Mar 1972 Teius 1.64m 58kg. CSM Unirea Alba Iulia. Civil servant.
At 20kmW: OG: '00- 6; WCh: '99- dnf; WCp: '99- 3; ECp: '00- 6. At 10kmW: OG: '96- 29; WCh: '95- 20; EC: '98- dq; WCp: '97- 17; ECp: '98- 12. Won ROM 10kmW 1993-7, 1999-2000; 20kmW 1995-8, 2000; Balkan 1994, 1999.
ROM walks records: 10km (4), 20km (2) 1995-9.
Progression at 10kmW, 20kmW: 1990- 53:45, 1991- 51:51, 1992- 46:05, 1993- 45:42, 1994- 45:10.4, 1995- 43:48, 1:37:14; 1996- 42:55, 1997- 43:21, 1:35:20; 1998- 42:57, 1:35:44, 1999- 42:16, 1:27:46; 2000- 43:51, 1:28:59. pb 5000mW 21:34.20/21:05R '98.

Monica DINESCU b. 1 Apr 1973 Sighetul Marmatiei 1.86m 68kg. née Iagar. Steaua Bucuresti. Sports teacher.
At HJ: OG: '00- 9=; WCh: '95- dnq 17=, '97- 13, '99- 10=; EC: '94- dnq, '98- 1; WI: '97/9/01- 9=/4/8; EI: '96- 5, '98- 1; WUG: '97- 2, '99- 1; WCp: '98- 1; ECp: '94-7-9-00: 2/5/2/1; 3rd GP 1997, ROM champion 1995-8, 2000; Balkan 1997.
Four Romanian high jump records 1997-2000.
Progression at HJ: 1987- 1.70, 1988- 1.78, 1989- 1.64, 1990- 1.78, 1992- 1.78, 1993- 1.87i/1.84, 1994- 1.91, 1995- 1.97i/1.92, 1996- 1.96i/1.95dq/1.93, 1997- 2.00, 1998- 2.02, 1999- 2.03i/2.01, 2000- 2.02. World number one high jumper of 1998. Six months drugs suspension 1996.

Nicoleta GRASU b. 11 Sep 1971 Secuieni 1.76m 88kg. née Gradinaru. Administration officer. Dinamo Bucuresti.
At DT: OG: '92- dnq 13, '96- 7, '00- dnq 19; WCh: '93- 7, '95- dnq 18, '97- 10, '99- 3; EC: '94- 4, '98- 3; WJ: '90- 6; WUG: '97- 3, '99- 1; WCp: '98- 2; ECp: '97-9-00: 4/2/1. Won Balkan 1992, 1997, 1999; ROM 1992-3, 1995-7, 1999-2000. 3rd GP 1996.
Progression at DT: 1985- 36.02, 1986- 43.56, 1987- 50.82, 1988- 51.06, 1989- 52.54, 1990- 56.02, 1991- 59.90, 1992- 65.66, 1993- 65.16, 1994- 64.40, 1995- 64.62, 1996- 65.26, 1997- 64.68, 1998- 67.80, 1999- 68.80, 2000- 68.70. pb SP 15.00i '92, 14.56 '91. Married to Costel Grasu (b. 5 Jul 1967) DT pb 67.08 '92; 4 OG 1992.

Mihaela MELINTE b. 27 Mar 1975 Bacau 1.73m 92kg. SC VILA Bacau. Student.
At HT: WCh: '99- 1; EC: '98- 1; WUG: '97- 1, '99- 1; EU23: '97- 1; ECp: '97-9-00: 2/1/1; ROM champion 1992-2000.
Eight world hammer records 1995-9, 21 ROM records 1992-9, three world junior records 1992-4.
Progression at HT: 1991- 37.76, 1992- 58.70, 1993- 62.52, 1994- 65.48, 1995- 66.86, 1996- 69.42, 1997- 71.24, 1998- 73.14, 1999- 76.07, 2000- 72.90/74.80dq. pbs: SP 13.98 '94, DT 43.12 '97.
Won 42 successive hammer competitions between losses to Olga Kuzenkova on 27 Jun 1997 and 25 Jun 2000. Positive drugs test (on 7 June 2000) announced just as she was about to compete at the 2000 Olympic Games; case referred by IAAF to arbitration in March 2001.

Cristina NICOLAU b. 9 Aug 1977 Bucuresti 1.84m 66kg. Steaua Bucuresti. Civil Servant.
At TJ (LJ): OG: '00- 6; WCh: '97- dnq 34, '99- 8; WJ: '94- (9), '96- 2 (2); EJ: '95- (2); EU23: '97- 1 (2), '99- 1 (4); WI: '01- 6; EI: '00- 2; WUG: '97- 5 (3); ECp: '99- 1. At LJ: WJ: '96- 2; EJ: '93- 3, '95- 2. Won ROM LJ 1996, 1999; TJ 1999.
Progression at TJ: 1996- 13.89, 1997- 14.22/14.23i, 1998- 14.20, 1999- 14.70, 2000- 14.94i/14.19/14.22w. pbs: HJ 1.82 '95, LJ 6.61i '00, 6.58 '96, 6.69w '99.
Set European age-14 LJ best (6.19 '91). Her father Mihai Nicolau won the ROM decathlon in 1975 and 1977, pb 7465 '75.

Oana PANTELIMON b. 27 Sep 1972 Tecuci 1.78m 61kg. née Musunoi.
At HJ: OG: '00- 3=; WJ: '90- dnq. Romanian champion 1999.
Progression at HJ: 1987- 1.78, 1988- 1.86, 1989- 1.90, 1990- 1.85, 1991- 1.87i/1.86, 1992- 1.94, 1993- 1.91i/1.87, 1994- 1.88, 1995- 1.92, 1996- 1.92, 1997- 1.93, 1999- 1.80+, 2000- 1.99.
Her bronze medal at the 2000 Olympics was a startling accomplishment, as this was her first major championship and after matching her pb of 1.94 to qualify she raised it with 1.96 and 1.99 in the final.

Lidia SIMON b. 4 Sep 1973 Târgu Carbunesti 1.57m 44kg. née Slavuteanu. CORA Craiova.
At Mar: OG: '96- 6, '00- 2; WCh: '95- 10, '97- 3, '99- 3; EC: '94- 10; WCp: '95- 2; won Balkan 1994. At 10000m: EC: '98- 3. World HMar: '96-7-8-00: 2/3/3/3.
Romanian marathon records 1997 and 1999, half marathon 2000.
Progression at 10000m, Mar: 1990- 2:58:18, 1991- 34:23.52, 2:52:20; 1993- 2:56:10, 1994- 2:32:38, 1995- 2:31:46, 1996- 2:30:13, 1997- 2:27:04, 1998- 31:32.64, 2:28:31; 1999- 2:23:24, 2000- 2:22:54. pbs: 1500m 4:22.57 '91, 3000m 9:25.84 '91, HMar 68:34 '00.
Won marathons at Kastoria and Lyon 1994. Took over 3 minutes off her pb for 3rd in Osaka (2:27:04), almost matched that when 3rd in London (2:27:11) and had third 3rd of 1997 at the Worlds. Won Osaka 1998, 1999 in a brilliant ROM record 2:23:24, the then fastest ever in a women's only race on an out and back course, and in 2000, when she moved to eighth on world all-time list with 2:22:54. 2nd London 2000.

Gabriela SZABO b. 14 Nov 1975 Bistrita 1.58m 42kg. Student. Rapid Bucuresti.
At 5000m (1500m): OG: '96- h (2), '00- 1 (3); WCh: '95- 4, '97- 1, '99- 1; EC: '98- 2; WUG: '95- 1 (1), '97- (1); ECp: '95- 1B, '97- 1 (2), '99 (1 1500 & 3000). At 3000m: EC: '94- 3; WJ: '92- 2, '94- 1; EJ: '91- 1, '93-1; WI: '95- 1, '97- 1, '99- 1 (1), '01- 2; EI: '98- 1, '00- 1; WCp: '94- 3, '98- 1. Won GP 3000m (and overall) 1999. World CC: '94- 4J, '95- 10, '96- 9. Won ROM 3000m 1993.
Records: World indoor 2000m 1998, 5000m (14:47.35)1999, 3000m (8:32.88) 2001; European 5000m 1998, European junior 3000m 1994. Romanian 3000m 1998, 5000m (4) 1995-8.
Progression at 1500m, 3000m, 5000m: 1991- 4:17.07, 9:19.28; 1992- 4:12.57, 8:48.28; 1993- 4:10.32, 8:50.97; 1994- 4:14.43, 8:40.08; 1995- 4:11.73, 8:30.03, 14:53.91; 1996- 4:01.54, 8:36.07, 14:41.12; 1997- 4:06.14i/4:06.25, 8:27.78, 14:42.43; 1998- 3:56.97, 8:24.31, 14:31.48; 1999- 4:03.23i/ 4:13.61, 8:25.03, 14:40.59; 2000- 4:00.73, 8:26.35, 14:40.61. pbs: 1M 4:19.30 '98, 2000m 5:30.53i '98, 5:36.88+ '97.
Had a marvellous season in 1997 when she won World titles indoors and out and lost just once, to Kelly Holmes at 1500m. In 1998 she was the world's fastest at 1500m, 1M, 2000m, 3000m and 5000m, the only woman to beat Svetlana Masterkova at 1500m, and after the disappointment of a European silver, ran a European record at 5000m in Berlin. In 1999 she won a brilliant double at 1500m and 3000m at the World Indoors and went on outdoors to annex the World title at 5000m, a half-share of the $1 million jackpot for her seven wins at 3000m/5000m in Golden League meetings and to become the overall IAAF Grand Prix champion. She also won a 1500m/3000m double for Romania in the European Cup and had 15 successive wins from 2nd to Kutre Dulecha in an indoor 1500m on 7 Feb 1999. Quieter but successful year in 2000. She has not raced in Romania since 1994. Married her coach Zsolt Gyöngyössy on 2 October 1999.

Violeta SZEKELY b. 26 Mar 1965 Dolhestii Mari 1.69m 52kg. née Beclea. Technician. Rapid Bucuresti.
At 1500m (800m): OG: '92- sf, '00- 2; WCh: '91- 10, '93- 9, '99- 4; EC: '94- h, '98- 5 (4); WI: '89- (4), '91- (2), '93- 2, '95 dq, '99- 2 (5 3000m), '01- 2; EI: '90- (3), '98- 3, '00- 1; ECp: '93- 2, '94- 3 (5). Won ROM 800m 1993-4, 1500m 1990-1, 1993-4. Won GP 1500m 1999-2000 (3rd 1M 1993).
Progression at 800m, 1500m: 1982- 2:05.07, 4:23.85, 1983- 2:03.63, 1985- 2:00.75, 4:11.01; 1986- 1:58.7, 4:04.56; 1987- 1:59.53, 4:07.56; 1988- 1:59.35, 4:07.94; 1989- 1:58.94, 4:07.24; 1990- 2:01.05, 4:03.14; 1991- 2:00.19, 4:02.21; 1992- 4:03.29; 1993- 1:59.13, 3:59.35; 1994- 1:59.30i/2:00.47, 4:03.76; 1998- 1:58.57, 3:59.67; 1999- 3:59.31, 2000- 2:00.81i, 3:58.29. pbs: 1000m 2:34.89i '95, 2:36.74 '89; 1M 4:21.69 '93, 2000m 5:39.36i '00, 3000m 8:46.39i '01, 8:47.3 '98.
Three year drugs ban from 15 Feb 1995, which cost her the World Indoor 1500m 4th place.

Felicea TILEA b. 29 Sep 1967 Magura Ilvei 1.69m 70kg. Married name **Moldovan**. Teacher. Rapid Bucuresti. Sports teacher.
At JT: OG: '96- 10, '00- dnq 15; WCh: '93- 8, '95- 2, '97- 5, '99- 11; EC: '90- dq (9), '94- 3, '98- 10; WUG: '95- 1; ECp: '93-4-6-7: 1/3/1B/2. ROM champion 1990, 1994, 1996-8.
Romanian javelin record 1996, new spec (2) 2000.
Progression at JT: 1981- 36.62, 1982- 44.00, 1983- 48.40, 1984- 46.80, 1985- 47.74, 1986- 51.42, 1987- 51.44, 1988- 47.42, 1989- 59.54, 1990- 64.02, 1993- 65.62, 1994- 66.40, 1995- 65.22, 1996- 69.26, 1997- 65.76, 1998- 65.10, 1999- 65.27; new: 60.97, 2000- 63.12.
Two-year drugs ban after positive test for steroids when 9th at 1990 European Champs.

Ionela TÎRLEA b. 9 Feb 1976 Horezu 1.69m 54kg. Student. Oltchim Rîmnicu Vîlcea and Fenerbace, TUR. Sports teacher.
At 400mh/4x400mR (200m): OG: '96- 7, '00- 6; WCh: '95- 7; EC: '94- 7, '98- 1/4R; WJ: '94- 1/3R; EJ: '93- 1, '95- 1; WUG: '95- 2; WCp: '98- 4; ECp: '93- (7), '94- 7 (8), '97- 8, '99- 3R (4, 1-400, 4-100). At 400m: WUG: '99- 1; WJ: '92- 3/1R; WI: '97- 4; EI: '94- 4, '96- 4, '98- 2. At 200m: WI: '99- 1. Won ROM 100m 1998, 200m 1998-9, 400m 1996, 1999; 400mh 1994-6.
Romanian records: 100m (2) 1998-9, 200m (3) 1998-9, 400m (2) 1998-9, 400mh (6) 1996-9.
Progression at 200m, 400m, 400mh: 1991- 24.51, 1992- 23.84, 52.13; 1993- 23.49, 56.30H; 1994- 23.60, 56.25H; 1995- 23.54, 55.26H; 1996- 54.40, 1997- 23.07, 52.06i, 55.04; 1998- 22.65/22.5A, 50.32, 53.37; 1999- 22.35, 49.88, 53.25; 2000-

51.84, 54.35. pb 100m 11.30 '99.
Was enjoying a brilliant season in 1999 until curtailed by injury in July.

RUSSIA

Governing body: All-Russia Athletic Federation, Luzhnetskaya Naberezhnaya 8, Moscow 119871. Founded 1911.

National Championships first held 1908, USSR women's from 1922. **2000 Champions**: **Men**: 100m: Sergey Bychkov 10.27, 200m: Anton Galkin 21.07, 400m: Dmitriy Golovastov 45.83, 800m: Dmitriy Bogdanov 1:45.76, 1500m: Aleksandr Skvortsov 3:41.59, 5000m: Sergey Drygin 13:53.50, 10000m: Dmitriy Maksimov 28:39.87, Mar: Aleksey Korobov 2:14:50, 3000mSt: Vladimir Pronin 8:27.15, 110mh: Yevgeniy Pechonkin 13.45, 400mh: Vladislav Shiryayev 49.02, HJ: Sergey Klyugin 2.33, PV: Pavel Gerasimov 5.85, LJ: Danila Burkenya 8.12, TJ: Denis Kapustin 17.24, SP: Pavel Chumechenko 20.04, DT: Dmitriy Shevchenko 64.61, HT: Vasiliy Sidorenko 81.75, JT: Sergey Makarov 86.11, Dec: Roman Razbeyko 7997, 20kmW: Roman Rasskazov 1:17:46, 50kmW: Valeriy Spitsyn 3:37:26. **Women**: 100m: Natalya Ignatova 11.12, 200m: Svetlana Pospelova 22.85, 400m: Natalya Nazarova 50.10, 800m: Natalya Tsyganova 1:56.60, 1500m: Lyudmila Rogachova 4:01.73, 5000m: Tatyana Tomashova 15:05.18, 10000m: Galina Bogomolova 31:29.66, Mar: Irina Safarova 2:34:44, 3000mSt: Yekaterina Volkova 10:09.18, 100mh: Natalya Shekhodanova 12.88, 400mh: Irina Privalova 54.21, HJ: Marina Kuptsova 1.96, PV: Yelena Belyakova 4.40, LJ: Tatyana Kotova 6.77, TJ: Tatyana Lebedeva 14.82, SP: Svetlana Krivelyova 20.59, DT: Natalya Sadova 67.33, HT: Olga Kuzenkova 68.51, JT: Tatyana Shikolenko 65.57, Hep: Yelena Prokhorova 6765, 20kmW: Tatyana Gudkina 1:25:18.
Note: Clubs abbreviations: Dyn – Dynamo, MS – Moskva City sports club, TU – Trade Union sports society, VS – Army, YR – Yunest Rossii.

Vladimir ANDREYEV b. 7 Sep 1966 Yamanchurino, Chuvashiya 1.80m 68kg. Cheboksary VS. Electrician.
At 20kmW: OG: '92- 13, '00- 3; WCh: '93- 19, '97- dnf, '99- dq; WCp: '93- 11, '97- 10, '99- 3. USSR champion 1989, CIS 1992, Russian 1993-4.
Progression at 20kmW: 1989- 1:20:08, 1990- 1:19:21, 1991- 1:19:17, 1992- 1:19:53, 1993- 1:19:43, 1994- 1:21:53, 1995- 1:18:32, 1996- 1:19:11, 1997- 1:18:39, 1998- 1:18:40, 1999- 1:19:57, 2000- 1:18:16. pbs: 5000mW 18:31.63i '92, 10000mW 39:27.0i '95, 1HrW 14,735m '92, 35kmW 2:29:31 '01.
Won the Russian winter 20km title 1995-8.

Aleksandr BORICHEVSKIY b. 25 Jun 1970 Zhukovskiy 1.95m 120kg. St.Petersburg VS.
At DT: OG: '96- dnq 31, '00- dnq 15; WCh: '97- dnq 28; '99- 8; EC: '98- dq; WCp: '97- 2; ECp: '99- 2. Russian champion 1997-8.
Progression at DT: 1990- 52.64, 1991- 59.12, 1992- 58.48, 1993- 60.78, 1994- 62.46, 1995- 63.00, 1996- 64.32, 1997- 62.32, 1998- 64.05, 1999- 65.08, 2000- 64.38A.

Yuriy BORZAKOVSKIY b. 12 Apr 1981 Kratovo, Moskva reg. 1.81m 70kg. Zhukovskiy Dyn. Student.
At 800m: OG: '00- 6; EJ: '99- 1; WI: '01- 1; EI: '00- 1; ECp: '99- 1.
Records: Two world junior indoor 800m 2000, European Junior 800m (2) & 1000m 2000.
Progression at 800m: 1997- 1:52.8i/1:53.69, 1998- 1:47.71, 1999- 1:46.13, 2000- 1:44.33, 2001- 1:44.15i pbs: 200m 22.56 '99, 400m 45.84 '00, 1000m 2:17.40 '00, 1500m 3:47.1 '98.
He won at the World Youth Games in 1998, and at the age of 18 startled Nico Motchebon and others when he sprinted to victory in the European Cup 800m. In January 2000 he set Russian senior and world junior indoors records of 1:45.91 to win in Sindelfingen, then a startling and hugely impressive 1:44.38 in Dortmund. He impressed outdoors also, but leaves himself a tremendous amount to do on the second lap of his 800m races.

Rodion GATAULLIN b. 23 Nov 1965 Tashkent UZB 1.89m 79kg. St Petersburg VS. Doctor.
At PV: OG: '88- 2; WCh: '87- 3, '91- 4, '95- 5; WI: '89- 1, '93- 1; EC: '86- nh, '90- 1, '94- 1; EI: '88- 1, '90- 1; EJ: '83- 1; WUG: '85- 1, '87- 2; ECp: '89-93-4-9: 1/1/nh/2. USSR champion 1985, 1989, 1991. Won GWG 1990, GP 1989.
World junior pole vault record 1984. WIB 6.00 and 6.02 '89, three Russian records 1992-4.
Progression at PV: 1977- 2.80, 1978- 3.10, 1979- 3.80, 1980- 4.20, 1981- 4.80, 1982- 5.20, 1983- 5.55, 1984- 5.65, 1985- 5.75, 1986- 5.85, 1987- 5.90, 1988- 5.95, 1989- 6.02i/6.00, 1990- 5.92, 1991- 5.90, 1992- 5.95, 1993- 6.00, 1994- 6.00, 1995- 5.90, 1996- 5.90i/5.80, 1997- 5.70i/5.20, 1998- 5.66, 1999- 5.70i/5.63, 2000- 5.70, 2001- 5.70i. pbs: 110mh 14.4, LJ 7.27 '90.
The world's second six-metre vaulter, a height he matched in retaining his European title in 1994, equalling the world best in a championship. Moved from Tashkent to St Petersburg in order to compete for Russia. Married to Tatyana Reshetnikova (100mh: 4 WCh 95, pb 12.53 '94).

Pavel GERASIMOV b. 29 May 1979 Aleksin, Tula reg. 1.93m 84kg. Moskva TU.
At PV: OG: '00- dnq 26=; WJ: '98- 1; EJ: '97- 2; WI: '01- 5.
Progression at PV: 1995- 4.40, 1996- 5.10i/5.00, 1997- 5.30, 1998- 5.55, 1999- 5.65/5.70ex, 2000- 5.90.

Oleg ISHUTKIN b. 22 Jul 1975 Atyashevo, Mordoviya 1.81m 70kg. Saransk TU
At 50kmW: WCh: '97- 4; EC: '98- dq; WCp: '97- 2. Russian champion 1999. At 10kmW: WJ: '94- 7.
Progression at 20kmW, 50kmW: 1995- 1:24:27,

1997- 3:40:12, 1999- 3:44:18, 2000- 3:45:47. pbs: 10000mW 41:46.30t '94, 20kmW 1:23:06 '98, 30kmW 2:06:30 '97, 35kmW 2:26:46 '97.

Denis KAPUSTIN b. 5 Oct 1970 Kazan 1.90m 86kg. KazanVS. Teacher.
At TJ: OG: '00- 3; WCh: '93- 6, '95- dnq 23, '97- 4, '99- 9; EC: '94- 1, '98- 2; EI: '94- 2; EJ: '89- 1; WUG: '91- 4; WCp: '98- 2; ECp: '94-7-9: 1/2/1. 2nd GP 1998. Russian champion 2000.
Progression at TJ: 1989- 16.37/16.63w, 1990- 16.68, 1991- 17.34, 1992- 17.48, 1993- 17.54, 1994- 17.62/17.86w, 1995- 17.42, 1996- 17.06, 1997- 17.59, 1998- 17.65, 1999- 17.40/17.65w, 2000- 17.46. pb LJ: 7.68i '91.

Vadim KHERSONTSEV b. 8 Jul 1974 Kursk region 1.92m 106kg. St Petersburg TU.
At HT: OG: '96- dnq 15; WCh: '97- 7, '99- 8; EJ: '93- 3; WUG: '97- 4; ECp: '97- 2. Russian champion 1996.
Progression at HT: 1992- 68.58, 1993- 72.72, 1994- 76.78, 1995- 76.94, 1996- 80.68, 1997- 78.58, 1998- 79.10, 1999- 78.82, 2000- 78.16.

Sergey KIRMASOV b. 25 Mar 1970 Mcensk Oryol region 1.80m 115kg. Mcensk VS. Soldier.
At HT: EC: '98- dnq 18; EJ: '89-1; ECp: '99- 7, '00- 5. Russian champion 1992, 1998.
Progression at HT: 1988- 71.20, 1989- 75.52, 1990- 77.66, 1991- 81.14, 1992- 79.92, 1993- 82.54, 1994- 79.20dq, 1998- 82.62, 1999- 79.55, 2000- 78.44. Four year drugs ban 1994.

Sergey KLYUGIN b. 24 Mar 1974 Kineshma, Ivanova region 1.92m 82kg. Moskva TU. Teacher.
At HJ: OG: '00- 1; WCh: '97- 11, '99- dnq 24; EC: '98- 3; WJ: '92- 5=, EJ: '91- 2; EU23Cp: '94- 2; ECp: '97-8-00: 2/1/3=. Russian champion 2000.
Progression at HJ: 1986- 1.55, 1987- 1.65, 1988- 1.80, 1989- 1.98, 1990- 2.16, 1991- 2.27, 1992- 2.28i/2.24, 1993- 2.26i/2.24, 1994- 2.28i/2.26, 1995- 2.26, 1996- 2.28, 1997- 2.31i/2.30, 1998- 2.36, 1999- 2.33, 2000- 2.35.

Ilya KONOVALOV b. 4 Mar 1971 Kursk region 1.92m 109kg. Kursk Dyn. Soldier.
At HT: OG: '96- 6, '00- 5; WCh: '95- 7, '97- 6, '99- 10; EC: '98- 9; WUG: '97- 3; ECp: '95- 1, '98- 2. Russian champion 1995, 1999.
Progression at HT: 1988- 63.10, 1989- 71.30, 1990- 74.66, 1991- 76.26, 1992- 77.04, 1993- 77.44, 1994- 78.30, 1995- 79.66, 1996- 79.46, 1997- 78.92, 1998- 79.82, 1999- 80.51, 2000- 81.93.

Lev LOBODIN b. 1 Apr 1969 Voronezh 1.88m 93kg. Luch Moskva. Teacher.
At Dec: OG: '96- dnf, '00- 13; WCh: '95- 7, '97- dnf, '99- 5; EC: '94- 3, '98- 3; ECp: '94- 2, '95- 6. UKR champion 1991. At Hep: WI: '93- 4, '99- 6, '01- 3; EI: '92- 6, '98- 3.
Progression at Dec: 1988- 7091h, 1991- 8018, 1992- 7998, 1993- 8156, 1994- 8201, 1995- 8286, 1996- 8315, 1997- 8184, 1998- 8571, 1999- 8494, 2000- 8071. pbs: 60m 6.83i '98, 100m 10.75 '98, 10.65w '94; 400m 48.39 '96, 1500m 4:29.95 '91, 60mh 7.79i '98, 110mh 13.94 '99, HJ 2.10 '91, PV 5.25i '99, 5.20 '98; LJ 7.56/7.68i?/7.74w '99, SP 16.39i '01, 16.19 '00; DT 50.72 '99, JT 59.00 '95, Hep 6226i '98.
Changed nationality UKR to RUS at end of 1996.

Sergey MAKAROV b. 19 Mar 1973 Lyubertsy 1.92m 100kg. Moskva Dyn.
At JT: OG: '96- 6, '00- 3; WCh: '97- 5, '99- 9; EC: '98- 4; WCp: '98- 2; ECp: '96-7-8-9-00: 2/4/2/2/2; EU23Cp: '94-2. Won GWG 1998, RUS 1996-7, 2000. Three Russian records 1996-9.
Progression at JT: 1991- 73.48, 1992- 76.08, 1993- 75.78, 1994- 82.54, 1995- 84.42, 1996- 88.86, 1997- 88.54, 1998- 86.96, 1999- 89.93, 2000- 89.92.
His father Aleksandr Makarov (b. 11 Feb 1951) was 2nd in the 1980 Olympic JT with a pb 89.64 (old javelin). Married to Oksana Ovchinnikova, Russian women's javelin record holder (qv).

Ilya MARKOV b. 19 Jun 1972 Asbest, Sverdlovsk reg. 1.76m 64kg. Asbest VS. Soldier.
At 20kmW: OG: '96- 2, '00- 15; WCh: '95- 4, '97- dq, '99- 1; EC: '94- 18, '98- 1; WUG: '97- 1; WCp: '95- 30, '97- 3, '99- 7; Won RUS 1995, GWG 1998. At 10kmW: WJ: '90- 1; EJ: '91- 1.
Progression at 20kmW: 1991- 1:33:46, 1992- 1:23:27, 1993- 1:20:19, 1994- 1:24:07, 1995- 1:18:53, 1996- 1:18:48, 1997- 1:18:30, 1998- 1:19:46, 1999- 1:18:50, 2000- 1:20:53. pbs: 3000mW 11:08.2i '92, 5000mW 18:36.71i/18:47.15 '99, 10000mW 39:15.6 '98.

Ruslan MASHCHENKO b. 11 Nov 1971 Voronezh 1.93m 89kg. Moskva Dyn.
At 400mh/4x400mR: OG: '96- h, '00- sf; WCh: '95- 4, '97- 6; EC: '94- sf, '98- 2; WUG: '97- 2; ECp: '94-5-6-7-8-9-00: 7/2/5/3/1/4/2 (2R '94). At 400m: WI: '01- 3R; EI: '98- 1. Won RUS 400mh 1995-6, 400m 1997.
Russian 400mh record 1995.
Progression at 400mh: 1986- 59.7, 1987- 57.9, 1988- 55.7, 1989- 53.5, 1990- 52.12, 1991- 51.87, 1993- 51.11, 1994- 49.13, 1995- 48.47, 1996- 49.16, 1997- 48.51, 1998- 48.06, 1999- 49.39, 2000- 48.76. pb 400m 45.89 '97.
Sister Lyudmila (b. 19 Apr 1974) was 3rd in 1993 European Junior heptathlon.

Nikolay MATYUKHIN b. 13 Dec 1968 Zhukovskiy, Moskva region 1.79m 68kg. Moskva Dyn. Teacher.
At 50kmW: OG: '96- 25, '00- 5; WCh: '95- 10, '97- 15, '99- 3; EC: '98- 16; WCp: '95- 17, '97- 4, '99- 3. Russian champion 1995.
Progression at 20kmW, 50kmW: 1990- 1:23:52, 4:10.04; 1991- 1:22:36, 1992- 1:21:16, 1993- 1:19:42, 1994- 3:45:34, 1995- 3:51:13, 1996- 1:22:18, 3:42:30; 1997- 1:24:51, 3:41:36; 1998- 1:20:12, 3:45:29; 1999- 3:40:13, 2000- 3:42:02. pbs: 10000mW 41:46.30t '94, 30kmW 2:06:36 '97, 35kmW 2:27:29 '97.

Andrey PLOTNIKOV b. 12 Aug 1967 Vladimir 1.86m 77kg. Vladimir VS. Soldier.

At 50kmW: OG: '96- dnf; EC: '90- dq, '94- 8, '98- 3; WCp: '97- 10. Russian champion 1996, 1998.
Progression at 50kmW: 1986- 4;08:40, 1987- 3:58:21, 1988- 3:53:42, 1989- 3:46:14, 1990- 3:40:07, 1991- 3:48:43, 1992- 3:37:05sh, 1993- 4:14:45, 1994- 3:47:53, 1995- 4:02:09, 1996- 3:40:58, 1997- 3:44:00, 1998- 3:41:14, 2000- 3:44:30. pbs: 20kmW 1:21:36 '91, 30kmW 2:05:53 '93, 35kmW 2:28:22 '97.

Vladimir POTEMIN b. 15 Jan 1980 Insar, Morodoviya 1.70m 67kg. Saransk VS.
At 20kmW: OG: '00- 26. 10000mW: EJ: '99- 2.
World U23 best 50km walk 2000.
Progression at 50kmW: 2000- 3:39:21. pbs: 10000mW 40:28.26 '99, 30kmW 2:08:05 '01, 35kmW 2:29:03 '01.

Roman RASSKAZOV b. 28 Apr 1979 Mordoviya 1.80m 64kg. Saransk VS. Student.
At 20kmW: OG: '00- 6; Russian champion 1999-2000. At 10000mW: WJ: '98- 1.
World best and two RUS records 20km walk 2000.
Progression at 20kmW: 1997- 1:31:24, 1999- 1:19:36, 2000- 1:17:46. pbs: 5000mW 19:02.1i '00, 10kmW 37:11 (world best) '00.

Vyacheslav SHABUNIN b. 27 Sep 1969 Kamyshlov, Sverdlovsk region 1.75m 56kg. Luch Moskva. Teacher.
At 1500m: OG: '96/00- h; WCh: '95- sf, '97/99- h; EC: '94- 5, '98- 9; WI: '95- 5; EI: '00- 5; ECp: '94-5-7-8-00: 6/2/3/7 (5 5000)/3. At 5000m: WCp: '92- 8. At 3000m: ECp: '99- 2. Won RUS 1500m 1992, 1994-6.
Russian records 1500m (3) 1997-2000, 1M (3) 1994-2000, 2000m, 3000m 1994-5.
Progression at 1500m/1M: 1988- 4:12.7, 1990- 3;54.6, 1991- 3:44.68, 1992- 3:40.49, 1993- 3:36.59, 1994- 3:38.61/3:53.54M, 1995- 3:34.79/3:51.02M, 1996- 3:34.50, 1997- 3:33.47, 1998- 3:33.30/3:53.30M, 1999- 3:34.01/3:52.23M, 2000- 3:32.28/3:50.54M. pbs: 800m 1:47.00 '96, 2000m 4:57.18 '97, 3000m 7:39.24 '95, 5000m 13:43.39 '94, HMar 61:29 '96.

Dmitriy SHEVCHENKO b. 13 May 1968 Taganrog, Rostov-na-Donu 2.00m 140kg. Krasnodar Dyn. Teacher.
At DT: OG: '92- 8, '00- 11; WCh: '91- 7, '93- 2, '95- 8, '99- dnq 19; EC: '94- 2, '98- dnq; ECp '93-4-8: 2/1/1; won GP 1995. USSR champion 1991, CIS 1992, Russian 1992-3, 1999-2000; GWG 1994.
Progression at DT: 1986- 57.30, 1987- 60.34, 1988- 59.68, 1989- 59.38/61.62?, 1990- 64.10, 1991- 63.70, 1992- 67.30, 1993- 66.90, 1994- 64.74, 1995- 68.04dq/66.74, 1998- 65.14, 1999- 65.68, 2000- 66.66. pb SP 17.94 '99.
Four year drugs ban for positive test at Cologne 18 Aug 1995, so he was disqualified from his Grand Prix Final win three weeks later; reinstated 1998.

Vitaliy SHKURLATOV b. 25 May 1979 Volgograd 1.82m 76kg. Volgograd VS.
At LJ: WJ: '98- 8; EU23: '99- 2; EJ: '97- 4; WI: '01- 8; EI: '00- 3; ECp: '00- 1.
Progression at LJ: 1995- 6.84, 1996- 7.64, 1997- 7.92, 1998- 7.79i, 1999- 8.06, 2000- 8.38i/8.22.

Yevgeniy SHMALYUK b. 14 Jan 1976 1.82m 74kg.
At 50kmW: WCh: '99- dnf; WCp: '99- 6; ECp: '00- 2. At 20kmW: EC: '98- 8; EU23: '97- 4.
Progression at 20kmW, 50kmW: 1995- 1:21:16, 1996- 1:21:01, 1997- 1:21:24, 1998- 1:20:13, 1999- 3:41:56, 2000- 3:44:33. pbs: 3000mW 11:29.0i '00, 5000mW 18:42.98i '01, 10000mW 39:45.0i '00, 30kmW 2:09:35 '99, 35kmW 2:27:02 '00.

Vasiliy SIDORENKO b. 1 May 1961 Volgograd 1.87m 110kg. Volgograd Dyn. Welder.
At HT: OG: '96- 12, '00- dnq 21; WCh: '93- 5, '95- dnq, '97- 3, '99- dnq 17; EC: '94- 1, '98- dnq 13; WCp: '94- 4; ECp: '94- 1. 3rd GP 1994. Russian champion 1992, 1997, 2000.
Progression at HT: 1979- 59.98, 1980- 68.78, 1981- 69.30, 1983- 74.10, 1984- 76.80, 1985- 80.40, 1986- 80.70, 1987- 80.02, 1988- 80.52, 1989- 82.30, 1990- 80.98, 1991- 79.76, 1992- 82.54, 1993- 80.04, 1994- 82.02, 1995- 81.46, 1996- 78.82, 1997- 80.76, 1998- 80.89, 1999- 79.95, 2000- 81.75.

Vitaliy SIDOROV 23 Mar 1970 V.Khichuri, Georgia 1.93m 125kg. Odessa Dyn.
At DT: OG: '96- 7, '00- dnq 26; WCh: '95- dnq, '97- 10; EC: '98- dnq 14; WUG: '95- 1; ECp: '96- 4, '00- 3. UKR champion 1995-8.
Progression at DT: 1989- 58.64, 1990- 55.50, 1991- 58.40, 1992- 59.60, 1993- 60.46, 1994- 64.40, 1995- 65.08, 1996- 65.60, 1997- 63.38, 1998- 67.90, 1999- 63.14, 2000- 65.69. pb SP 18.90 '97.
Changed nationality form UKR to RUS 2000.

German SKURYGIN b. 15 Sep 1963 Vutno Udmurtiya 1.64m 61kg. Izhevsk TU. Teacher.
At 50kW: WCh: '93- 23, '99- 1; EC: '94- 6; WCp: '95- 18, '99 5. RUS champion 1994.
Progression at 50kmW: 1989- 3:50:25, 1990- 3:51:04, 1991- 3:53:33, 1992- 3:59:42, 1993- 3:56:19, 1994- 3:46:30, 1995- 3:51:44, 1996- 3:44:33, 1997- 3:52:57, 1998- 3:47:44, 1999- 3:40:54. pbs: 20kmW 1:22:12 '88, 30kmW 2:05:37 '98, 35kmW 2:25:58 '98.

Yevgeniy SMIRYAGIN b. 17 May 1976 Leningrad 1.84m 79kg. St-Peterburg TU.
At PV: OG: '00- 10=, WCh: '97- 8; WJ: '94- 11; EJ: '95- 1; EU23: '97- 1; ECp: '98- 1, '00- 1.
Progression at PV: 1992- 4.80, 1993- 5.20, 1994- 5.40, 1995- 5.55, 1996- 5.65i/5.60, 1997- 5.85, 1998- 5.85, 1999- 5.65, 2000- 5.85.

Kirill SOSUNOV b. 1 Nov 1975 Ryazan 1.95m 86kg. Ryazan TU. Student.
At LJ: OG: '00- dnq 16; WCh: '97- 3; EC: '98- 1; WI: '97- 2; WUG: '95- 1; WJ: '94- dnq; EU23: '97- 2; WCp: '98- 4; ECp: '96-7-8-9: 4/1/1/7.
Progression at LJ: 1990- 6.70, 1991- 6.85, 1992- 7.11, 1993- 7.66, 1994- 7.96, 1995- 8.28/8.48w, 1996- 8.27i/8.17, 1997- 8.41i/8.30, 1998- 8.38, 1999- 7.98, 2000- 8.34. pb 60m 6.5i '98.
Married to **Olga Kaliturina** (b. 9 Mar 1976), HJ

1.96 '98, 1 WJ '94, 2= WCh '97.

Valeriy SPITSYN b. 5 Dec 1965 Magnitogorsk 1.78m 67kg. Magnitogorsk Sp. Teacher.
At 50kmW: OG: '92- 4, '00- dnf; WCh: '93- 3, '95- dq; EC: '94- 1; WCp: '91- 8, '95- 4. CIS champion 1992, RUS 1988, 2000.
World best 50kmW 2000.
Progression at 50kmW: 1988- 4:06:02, 1989- 3:48:38, 1990- 3:54:26, 1991- 3:50:18, 1992- 3:54:39/ 3:33:32 short, 1993- 3:42:50, 1994- 3:41:07, 1995- 3:43:36, 1996- 3:43:00, 1999- 3:47:16, 2000- 3:37:26. pbs: 20kmW 1:22:15 '91, 30kmW 2:04:24 '92, 35kmW 2:28:26 '98.

Vadim STROGALYOV b. 9 Feb 1975 Moskva 1.84m 77kg. Moskva MS.
At PV: WCh: 97- 7, '99- dnq 19=. Russian champion 1997.
Progression at PV: 1992- 4.80, 1993- 5.00, 1994- 5.20, 1995- 5.75i/5.70, 1996- 5.80, 1997- 5.80, 1998- 5.85, 1999- 5.80, 2000- 5.75.

Maksim TARASOV b. 2 Dec 1970 Yaroslavl 1.94m 80kg. Yaroslavl TU. Student.
At PV: OG: '92- 1, '00- 3; WCh: '91- 3, '93- 3=, '95- 2, '97- 2, '99- 1; EC: '98- 1; WJ: '88- 2; EJ: '89- 1; WI: '95- 7=, '97- 3; WCp: '98- 1. Won GP 1996, 1998, 1999 (2nd 1997, 3rd 1993, 1995), CIS PV 1992.
Three world junior records 1989.
Progression at PV: 1982- 2.90, 1983- 3.30, 1984- 3.80, 1985- 4.50, 1986- 5.00, 1987- 5.40, 1988- 5.60, 1989- 5.80, 1990- 5.85, 1991- 5.85/5.90ex, 1992- 5.90, 1993- 5.90, 1994- 5.90, 1995- 5.91, 1996- 5.90, 1997- 6.00, 1998- 5.95, 1999- 6.05, 2000- 5.90. pbs: 100m 10.8 '89, HJ 1.95, LJ 7.40.
All world age bests from 16 to 19, 1987-90. Very consistent vaulter, world number one of 1998 and 1999. Has lived in Budapest since 1992.

Vyacheslav VORONIN b. 5 Apr 1974 Vladikavkaz 1.90m 78m. Vladikavkaz Dyn.
At HJ: OG: '00- 10; WCh: '99- 1; EJ: '93- 2; WI: '99- 2, '01- 9; EI: '98- 2, '00- 1; ECp: '99- 2. Won GP 2000, Russian champion 1999.
Russian high jump record 2000.
Progression at HJ: 1992- 2.15, 1993- 2.18, 1995- 2.18, 1996- 2.29, 1997- 2.26/2.30sq, 1998- 2.32i/ 2.28, 1999- 2.37, 2000- 2.40.

Women

Yelena AFANASYEVA b. 1 Mar 1967 Kulebyaki Gorkiy reg. 1.64m 56kg. née Vlasova. Moskva reg. Dyn. Teacher.
At 800m: OG: '96- 5; WCh: '93- h, '95- sf, '97- 2; EC: '98- 1; WI: '93- 4, '95- 2; EI: '92- 3; WCp: '92- 3, '98- 2; ECp: '94-5-7: 7/1/1. Won RUS 800m 1995, 1998. WIR 4 x 800m relay 1994.
Progression at 1500m: 1985- 2:07.83, 1986- 2:00.90, 1988- 1:57.77, 1991- 1:59.85, 1992- 1:59.12, 1993- 1:58.88, 1994- 2:00.52, 1995- 1:59.20, 1996- 1:57.77, 1997- 1:56.61, 1998- 1:56.63, 1999- 2:00.37. pbs: 400m 52.78 '97, 1000m 2:34.60 '98, 1500m 4:07.8 '88.

Yelena BELYAKOVA b. 7 Apr 1976 Moskva 1.78m 55m. Luch Moskva. Teacher.
At PV: OG: '00- dnq; WCh: '99- 8; EC: '98- nh; EI: '00- 2; ECp: '98- nh, '99- 4; Won GWG 1998, RUS 1998-9.
Three Russian pole vault records 1998-2000.
Progression at PV: 1995- 3.40, 1996- 3.90, 1997- 4.15, 1998- 4.38, 1999- 4.46, 2000- 4.50, 2001- 4.55i.

Madina BIKTAGIROVA b. 20 Sep 1964 Osh, Kirgizstan 1.58m 50kg. Moskva Dyn.
At Mar: OG: '92- dq (4), '96- dnf, '00- 5; WCh: '93- 5; EC: '98- 2. USSR champion 1991.
BLR marathon record 1992.
Progression at Mar: 1987- 2:38:18sh, 1988- 2:38:00, 1989- 2:38:56, 1990- 2:36:02, 1991- 2:32:02, 1992- 2:26:23, 1993- 2:31:32, 1994- 2:30:00, 1995- 2:29:00, 1996- 2:31:38, 1997- 2:24:46, 1998- 2:27:19, 2000- 2:26:33. pb HMar 71:30 '95.
Won Los Angeles marathon 1992, Nagoya 1997; 2nd New York 1994, Berlin 1997, Nagoya 1998; 3rd Boston 1995. Lost Olympic 4th place in 1992 due to a positive test for stimulants, for which she received a three-month ban. Transferred nationality to Russia in 1997. Baby born 1999.

Olga CHERNYAVSKAYA b. 17 Sep 1963 Irbit Sverdlovsk region 1.80m 80kg. née Davydova, then Burova. Stavropol VS. Teacher.
At DT: OG: '92- 5, '96- 6; WCh: '93- 1, '95- 3; EC: '90- 2, '94- 5; WUG: '91- 4; WCp: '89- 5; ECp: '89- 4, '96- 2, '00- 4. USSR champion 1989-90, RUS 1994.
Progression at DT: 1981- 54.72, 1982- 47.90, 1983- 58.30, 1984- 56.88, 1985- 59.20, 1986- 58.28, 1987- 60.20, 1988- 65.34, 1989- 68.10, 1990- 68.32, 1991- 63.68, 1992- 68.38, 1993- 67.40, 1994- 65.60, 1995- 66.86, 1996- 65.38, 1998- 59.20, 1999- 64.68, 2000- 64.55.

Alla DAVYDOVA b. 21 May 1966 Frunze, Kirgizstan 1.67m 86kg. née Fyodorova. Luch Moskva. Teacher
At HT: OG: '00- dnq 18; EC: '98- 8. RUS champion 1996. Two world hammer records 1991.
Progression at HT: 1989- 58.30, 1990- 59.66, 1991- 64.44, 1992- 60.80, 1994- 61.84, 1995- 63.20, 1996- 67.48, 1998- 64.61, 1999- 66.06, 2000- 68.47.

Natalya FEDOSKINA b. 25 Jun 1980 Saransk 1.69m 52m. Saransk.
At 20kmW: WCh: '99- dq; WCp: '99- 2
Two world junior 20km walk records 1999.
Progression at 10kmW, 20kmW: 1998- 44:59, 1999- 43:58, 1:27:35; 2000- 43:56, 1:28:52; 2001- 1:27:30. pb 3000mW 12:18.29 '00.

Svetlana FEOFANOVA b. 16 Jul 1980 Moskva 1.63m 52kg. Luch Moskva.
At PV: OG: '00- dnq; WI: '01- 2; EI: '00- 5, ECp: '00- 1.
Two Russian pole vault records 2000, three European indoor records 2001.
Progression at PV: 1998- 3.90, 1999- 4.10, 2000- 4.50, 2001- 4.64i.

Lyudmila GALKINA b. 20 Jan 1972 Saratov 1.72m 57kg. Saratov TU.
At LJ (TJ): OG: '96- dnq, '00- 9; WCh: '93- 5, '95- dnq 17, '97- 1, '99- 4; EC: '94- dnq 16, '98- 3; WJ: '90- (7); EJ: '89- 3, '91- 2 (1); WI: '95- 1, '01- 6; WUG: '95- 3; WCp: '98- 4; ECp: '98-99- 2/3. Won RUS LJ 1997.
Progression at LJ: 1985- 5.52, 1986- 5.85, 1987- 6.14, 1988- 6.34, 1989- 6.52/6.62w, 1990- 6.63, 1991- 6.62, 1992- 6.60, 1993- 6.75, 1994- 6.78, 1995- 6.95i/6.71/6.85w, 1996- 6.88, 1997- 7.05, 1998- 6.99/7.06w, 1999- 6.95/7.08w, 2000- 6.89, 2001- 7.00i. pb TJ 13.67 '91.
Set personal best to win 1995 World Indoor title and 1997 World outdoor win was her first time over 7m.

Svetlana GONCHARENKO b. 28 May 1971 Rostov na Donu 1.76m 61kg. née Doronina. Stavropol VS.
At 400m/4x400mR: OG: '96- sf, '00- 3R; WCh: '95- 2R, '99- sf/1R; EC: '94- 2/2R; EI: '94- 1, WUG: '97- 1R; WCp: '98- 3R; ECp: '94- 1/3R. At 200m: EC: '98- sf/2R; EJ: '87- 5 (2 4x100mR); WI: '95- 1R; '97- 3/1R, '99- 2/1R; EI: '98- 1; ECp: '99- 1/2R. Won RUS 200m 1998, 400m 1996.
World indoor 4x400m world record 1999.
Progression at 200m, 400m: 1987- 23,93, 1988- 23.5, 54.22; 1989- 23.61, 1990- 24.11, 1991- 24.02, 1992- 23.62, 53.69; 1993- 23.40, 54.00; 1994- 22.6/23.58, 51.00; 1995- 22.89, 51.47; 1996- 23.01, 50.84; 1997- 22.84i, 53.06i; 1998- 22.46/21.9/22.43i; 1999- 22.59/22.4/22.52w, 50.75; 2000- 23.24i/23.42, 50.23. pbs: 60m 7.21i '99, 100m 11.13/10.7 '98, 300m 35.48i '98.

Natalya GORELOVA b. 18 Apr 1973 Moskva 1.73m 56m. née Zaytseva. Luch Moskva. Teacher.
At 800m: WCh: '99- 6. At 1500m: OG: '00- h; WI: '01- 3. Won Russian 800m 1999.
Progression at 800m, 1500m: 1997- 2:02.44, 1998- 2:02.21, 4:13.43; 1999- 1:57.90, 4:05:12; 2000- 2:00.24, 4:01.50; 2001- 1:59.15i, 4:03.51i.

Tatyana GUDKOVA b. 23 Jan 1978 Magnitogorsk 1.72m 54kg. Magnitogorsk TU. Teacher
At 20kmW: OG: '00- 8. Russian champion 2000.
World best 20km walk 2000.
Progression at 10kmW, 20kmW: 1998- 44:42, 1999- 42:51, 1:33:05; 2000- 42:42, 1:25:18.

Yelena GULYAYEVA b. 14 Aug 1967 Moskva 1.82m 61kg. née Rodina. Luch Moskva. Teacher.
At HJ: OG: '96- 4; WCh: '93- 4=, '99- 12; EC: '94- 2, '98- 6; ECp: '91-4-8-9: dq (1)/3/3/1; WI: '91- 6=, '95- 5; EI: '98- 4; WCp: '98- 4; 3rd GP 1995. USSR champion 1988, 1991.
Progression at HJ: 1981- 1.70, 1982- 1.70, 1983- 1.80, 1984- 1.84, 1985- 1.80, 1987- 1.80, 1988- 1.94, 1989- 1.89i/1.88, 1990- 1.92i/1.91, 1991- 1.99, 1993- 1.98, 1994- 2.00i/1.98, 1995- 1.99, 1996- 2.00, 1998- 2.01, 1999- 1.99, 2000- 1.95.
Two years suspension for positive drugs test at the 1991 European Cup ('won' HJ).

Yelena ISINBAYEVA b. 3 Jun 1982 Volgograd 1.74m 65kg. Volgograd SA.
At PV: OG: '00- dnq; WI: '01- 7; WJ: '98- 9, '00- 1, WY: '99 - 1.
World junior indoor PV records 2000 and 2001.
Progression at PV: 1997- 3.30, 1998- 4.00, 1999- 4.20, 2000- 4.45i/4.40, 2001- 4.47i.

Olimpiada IVANOVA b. 5 May 1970 Munsyuty Chuvashiya 1.67m 49kg. Cheboksary Dyn.
At 20kmW: ECp: '00- 1. At 10kmW: WCh: '97- drugs dq (2); WCp: '93- 12, '97- 2; won GWG 1994. At 5000mW: EJ: '85- 9.
World best 20km walk 2001.
Progression at 10kmW, 20kmW: 1987- 45:15, 1992- 45:18, 1993- 42:24, 1994- 42:30.31t, 1995- 41:30, 1996- 41:46, 1:30:58; 1997- 41:24, 1999- 43:31, 1:28:21; 2000- 42:43, 1:26:08; 2001- 1:24:50. pbs: 3000mW 12:02.2 '95, 5000mW 20:50.6i '97, 20:56.10 '94, 20:51R '97.
Lost her 1997 World silver medal when she tested positive for Stanozolol, receiving a two-year ban. World best 20km walk time when she won Russian winter championship in March 2001.

Tatyana KONSTANTINOVA b. 18 Nov 1970 Smolensk 1.79m 95lg. Smolensk Dyn
At HT: OG: '00- dnq 15; WCh: '99- 11; EC: '98- dnq 16.
Progression at HT: 1990- 57.42, 1991- 56.72, 1992- 55.58, 1993- 56.00, 1994- 59.50, 1995- 62.16, 1996- 60.64, 1997- 58.68, 1998- 65.77, 1999- 72.09, 2000- 69.73.

Larisa KOROTKEVICH b. 3 Jan 1967 Krivye Vitebsk region 1.80m 90kg. Krasnodar Dyn. Teacher.
At DT: OG: '92- 4, '00- dnq 20; WCh: '87- 10, '93- dnq 14, '97- 4, '99- dnq 15; EJ: '85- 3; WCp: '92- 4; ECp: '93- 1, '94- 4. Russian champion 1993, 1997.
Progression at DT: 1983- 52.74, 1984- 56.70, 1985- 59.02, 1986- 64.42, 1987- 64.94, 1988- 66.08, 1989- 60.74, 1990- 67.50, 1991- 63.44, 1992- 71.30, 1993- 68.14, 1994- 62.08, 1996- 59.00, 1997- 64.92, 1998- 61.66, 1999- 67.65, 2000- 64.37

Olga KOTLYAROVA b. 12 Apr 1976 Sverdlovsk 1.80m 65kg. Student. Yekaterinburg TU.
At 400m/4x400mR: OG: '96- qf/5R, '00- 8/3R; WCh: '97- sf, '99- 8/1R; EC: '98 3/2R; WJ: '94- 4R; EJ: '95- 1/2R; EU23: '97- 2R; WI: '97- 1R, '99- 1R, '01- 2/1R; EI: '96- 2; WUG: '97- 2/1R; WCp: '98- 3R; ECp: '96- 4/3R, '97- 3/1R, '99- 2/1R. Russian champion 1998.
World indoor 4x400m record 1997 & 1999.
Progression at 400m: 1994- 53.67, 1995- 52.03/51.8, 1996- 51.17, 1997- 50.63, 1998- 50.38, 1999- 50.32, 2000- 49.95. pbs: 200m 23.35A '98, 300m 36.91+ '99, 800m 2:05.17 '00.

Tatyana KOTOVA b. 11 Dec 1976 Kokand, Uzbekistan 1.82m 59kg. Moskva TU.
At LJ: OG: '00- 4; WCh: '99- dnq 13; WI: '99- 1, '01- 2; EU23: '97- 1. Russian champion 1999-2000.

Progression at LJ: 1994- 6.32, 1995- 6.32, 1996- 6.65, 1997- 6.76, 1998- 6.82/6.97w, 1999- 6.99/ 7.01w, 2000- 7.04 (7.05iu). pb TJ 13.69i/13.64 '98.
Born in Uzbekistan, she moved to Taboshari (Tadjikistan) and now lives in Central Siberia. Her father came from Cherkassy in the Ukraine.

Tamara KOVALENKO b. 5 Jun 1964 Sverdlovsk reg. 1.61m 48kg. Yaroslavl VS.
At 10kmW: EC: '90- 4; WCp: '89- 6, '95- 9, '97- 8; ECp: '98- 4. At 20kmW: WCp: '99- 10.
Progression at 10kmW, 20kmW: 1984- 47:17, 1985- 44:55, 1986- 46:23, 1987- 45:06, 1988- 43:43, 1989- 43:13.5t, 1990- 42:46, 1991- 43:43, 1992- 44:37, 1993- 44:49, 1994- 42:50, 1995- 42:01, 1996- 42:36, 1997- 42:02, 1998- 42:46, 1999- 43:38, 1:28:33; 2000- 42:42, 1:25:59. pbs: 3000mW 12:19.3i '97, 5000mW 21:00.0i '00, 21:25.62 '94, 20:51R '98.

Svetlana KRIVELYOVA b. 13 Jun 1969 Bryansk 1.83m 95kg. Moskva Dyn. Teacher.
At SP: OG: '92- 1, '96- dnq 15, '00- 4; WCh: '91- 3, '93- 2, '97- 10, '99- 3; EC: '98- 4; WJ: '88- 4; WI: '91/3/9/01- 8/1/1/3; EI: '00- 4; WUG: '91- 1; ECp: '96- 3, '99- 3. USSR champion 1991, Russian 1992, 1998-2000. Won GP 1993.
Progression at SP: 1985- 15.18, 1986- 16.76, 1987- 17.51, 1988- 18.35, 1989- 18.36, 1990- 19.70, 1991- 20.36, 1992- 21.06, 1993- 20.84, 1996- 18.97, 1997- 19.32i/19.18, 1998- 20.53, 1999- 20.69i/20.26, 2000- 20.72.
Took World Student Games gold medal in 1991 after Sui Xinmei disqualified, and World Indoor gold in 1999 after both Pavlysh and Korzhanenko disqualified.

Olga KUZENKOVA b. 4 Oct 1970 Smolensk 1.76m 76kg. Smolensk Dyn. Army Officer, has a diploma in physical education.
At HT: OG: '00- 2; WCh: '99- 2; EC: '98- 2; WUG: '97- 2; ECp: '97-8-9-00: 1/1/2/1. Russian champion 1992-4, 1997-2000; CIS 1992.
Ten world hammer records 1993-7, inc. unratified 69.46 '96 and 73.80 '98 due to no drugs testing procedures; 66.84 in 1994 was the first record for the event accepted by the IAAF. 14 Russian records 1993-2000.
Progression at HT: 1990- 59.50, 1991- 61.52, 1992- 65.40, 1993- 64.64, 1994- 66.84, 1995- 68.16, 1996- 69.46, 1997- 73.10, 1998- 73.80, 1999- 74.30, 2000- 75.68, 2001- 73.62.
Became the first 70-m hammer thrower in 1997.

Svetlana LAPINA b. 12 Apr 1978 Makhachkala 1.80m 59kg. Makhachkala VS. Student.
At HJ: OG: '00 dnq 15; WCh: '99 3; WJ: '96 3; EJ: '97- 3; EU23: '99- 1; WUG: '99- 2
Progression at HJ: 1990- 1.55, 1991- 1.76, 1992- 1.78, 1993- 1.82, 1994- 1.83, 1995- 1.89, 1996- 1.92, 1997- 1.90, 1998- 1.92i/1.90, 1999- 1.99, 2000- 1.94.

Yelena LEBEDENKO b. 16 Jan 1971 Moskva 1.77m 63kg. Moskva VS. Teacher.
At Hep: OG: '96- 17; WCh: '95- 18. At Pen: EI: '96- 1. At TJ: EC: '98- 10; WI: '99- 6; EI: '98- 3; ECp: '99- 4.
Progression at Hep: 1989- 5308, 1990- 5703, 1994- 5963, 1995- 6342, 1996- 6143. At TJ: 1998- 14.57i/14.41, 1999- 14.74i/14.37, 2000- 14.66i, 2001- 14.83i. pbs: 200m 24.67 '96, 800m 2:18.50 '95, 60mh 8.23i '96, 100mh 13.37 '96, HJ 1.85i '96, 1.83 '95; LJ 6.75 '96, SP 14.71 '95, JT 45.02 '96, Pen 4735i 96.
Former football and rugby player. Made triple jump debut with 14.33 indoors in January 1998, improving to 14.57 to win Russian indoor title.

Tatyana LEBEDEVA b. 21 Jul 1976 Sterlitamak, Bashkortostan 1.71m 60kg. Volgograd VS.
At TJ (LJ): OG: '00- 2; WCh: '99- 4; EC: '98- 5; WJ: '94- 3 (10); EJ: '95- 2 (6); WI: '01- 2; EI: '00- 1; WCp: '98- 2; ECp: '00- 1. 3rd GP 1999. Russian champion 1998-2000.
Two Russian triple jump records 2000.
Progression at TJ: 1991- 12.91, 1992- 13.03, 1993- 13.13i/12.94, 1994- 13.69, 1995- 13.88, 1996- 13.62, 1997- 13.89i/13.56, 1998- 14.45/14.58w, 1999- 14.89, 2000- 15.32, 2001- 15.00i. pb LJ 6.71i '01, 6.65 '94.

Yuliya LYAKHOVA b. 8 Jul 1977 Moskva 1.85m 60kg. Luch Moskva.
At HJ: OG: '96- dnq 19=; WCh: '97- 4; EC: '98- 12; WJ: '96- 1; EJ: '95- 3; EU23: '97- 1; WI: '99- 6; ECp: '00- 2. 2nd GP 1997.
Progression at HJ: 1993- 1.75, 1994- 1.90, 1995- 1.92i/1.90, 1996- 1.94, 1997- 1.99, 1998- 1.96i/1.95, 1999- 2.00i, 2000- 1.96, 2001- 1.96i.
Sister of **Sergey Lyakhov** (b. 1 Mar 1968) pbs: SP 20.03 '00, DT 66.78 '95.

Oksana MAKAROVA b. 21 Jul 1971 Volgograd 1.80m 70kg. née Chernyenko, then Ovchinnikova. Moskva reg. Dyn. Married to Sergey Makarov.
At JT: OG: '96- dnq 20; WCh: '95- dnq, '97- 9, '99- 8; WJ: '90- 2; ECp: '96-7-8-9: 1/1/3/2. Russian champion 1996. 3rd GP 1996.
Russian javelin record 1996.
Progression at JT: 1987- 51.40, 1988- 54.82, 1989- 55.76, 1990- 59.00, 1993- 52.98, 1994- 60.04, 1995- 62.74, 1996- 68.72, 1997- 68.38, 1998- 65.68, new: 1999- 64.61, 2000- 59.92.

Svetlana MASTERKOVA b. 17 Jan 1968 Achinsk. Krasnoyarsk reg. 1.72m 59kg. Luch Moskva.
At 800m (/1500m): OG: '96- 1/1, '00- (h); WCh: '91- 8, '97- (sf), '99- 3/1; EC: '98- (1); WI: '93- 2; EI: '96- 3; EJ: '85- 6; WCp: '98- (1); ECp: '91- 3, '96- 1. Won USSR 800m 1991, RUS 800m 1996, 1500m 1996-7. Won GWG 1M 1998, GP 1500m 1996, 3rd 800m 1993 & 1999.
World records 1000m and 1 mile 1996.
Progression at 800m, 1500m: 1982- 2:11.7, 1983- 2:04.3, 1984- 2:04.59, 4:24+?; 1985- 2:02.69, 1986- 2:03.34, 1989- 2:02.70, 1990- 1:59.83, 1991- 1:57.23, 1992- 1:57.63, 1993- 1:57.48, 1996- 1:56.04, 3:56.77; 1997- 1:58.89, 4:03.51; 1998- 2:01.78, 3:57.11; 1999- 1:55.87, 3:59.53; 2000- 4:01.15. pbs: 400m

53.12 '92, 1000m 2:28.98 '96, 1M 4:12.56 '96.
Emulated Tatyana Kazankina (1976) by winning Olympic 800/1500 double. Married professional cyclist, Asyat Saitov in 1993. Daughter Anastasiya born March 1995. Lives in Alicante, Spain.

Larisa MIKHAYLOVA b.3 Jan 1969 Yoshkar Ola region 1.64m 50kg. Moskva City.
At 800m: EC: '98- dnf; ECp: '98- 1.
Progression at 800m: 1994- 2:02.54, 1995- 2:02.64, 1996- 2:00.4, 1997- 2:00.49, 1998- 1:58.01, 1999- 1:57.70, 2000- 2:00.61. pbs: 1000m 2:37.31i '99, 1500m 4:06.08 '98, 1M 4:25.58 '98.

Irina MISTYUKEVICH b. 17 Jun 1977 Kurgan region 1.82m 69kg. Kurgan VS. Teacher.
At 800m: OG: '00- sf; EU23: '99- 7; EJ: '95- 2R; ECp: 00- 1.
Progression at 800m: 1995- 2:06.40, 1996- 2:03.8, 1997- 2:03.85, 1998- 2:01.93, 1999- 1:58.33, 2000- 1:57.49. pb 400m 51.87 '00.

Natalya NAZAROVA b. 26 May 1979 Moskva 1.65m 55kg. Luch Moskva. Student
At 400m/4x400mR: OG: '00- sf/3resR; WCh: '99- 6/1R; WJ: '98- 1/2R; WI: '99- 1R; EI: '00- 2; EJ: '97- 7; ECp: '99- 1R. RUS champion 1999-2000. World indoor 4x400m world record 1999.
Progression at 400m: 1995- 55.79, 1996- 54.59, 1997- 52.94, 1998- 51.50, 1999- 50.48, 2000- 50.10. pbs: 100m 11.57 '99, 200m 23.01/22.9 '99, 300m 36.91+ '99, 600m 1:26.35i '00.
Ran a mature last leg, holding off Jearl Miles-Clark and Grit Breuer, to ensure gold for the Russian 4x400m relay team at the 1999 Worlds.

Yelena NIKOLAYEVA b. 1 Feb 1966 Akshiki Chuvashia 1.68m 58kg. née Kuznetsova. Cheboksary Dyn.
At 10kmW: OG: '92- 2, '96- 1; WCh: '87- 5, '93- 7, '95- 3, '97- 9; EC: '94- 3; WCp: '87- 5, '93- 3, '95- 2. Won GWG 1998, USSR champion 1987-8, CIS 1992, RUS 1996. At 20kmW: WCh: '99- 12; WCp: '99- 4. At 3000mW: WI: '91- 5, '93- 1; EI: '94- 4.
Three world 10km track walk records 1986-8, road best 1996, European records 3000m 1992, 5000m: 21:32.4 '87, 21:08.65 '88.
Progression at 10kmW, 20kmW: 1984- 48:29.1, 1985- 46:37, 1986- 44:32.50t, 1987- 43:57, 1988- 43:36.41t, 1991- 43:25, 1992- 42:40, 1993- 43:11, 1994- 42:43, 1995- 42:20, 1996- 41:04, 1997- 41:41, 1998- 43:51.97t, 1999- 42:04, 1:28:01; 2000- 45:55. pbs: 3000mW 11:49.73i '93, 12:01.53 '98; 5000mW 21:00.80 '91, 20:48R '94.

Larisa PELESHENKO b. 29 Feb 1964 Slantsy, Leningrad region 1.87m 95kg. née Agapova. St Petersburg VS. Teacher.
At SP: OG: '00- 2; WCh: '93- 9; EC: '94- 5; WI: '95- 1, '01- 1; EI: '88- 2, '94- 2, '00- 1; WUG: '87- 3, '89- 4; ECp: '89- 3, '94- 3.
Progression at SP: 1981- 14.60, 1982- 15.95, 1983- 18.23, 1984- 19.30, 1985- 18.78i, 1986- 19.26, 1987- 20.99, 1988- 20.89, 1989- 19.68, 1990- 19.56, 1992- 19.65, 1993- 19.90i/19.23, 1994- 20.00i/19.81, 1995- 19.89i/19.93i dq, 1999- 19.18, 2000- 21.46.
4 year drugs ban 20 Feb 95. Has a son, Grigoriy.

Olga POLYAKOVA b. 23 Sep 1980 Penza reg. 1.71m 49kg. Saransk VS, Student.
At 20kmW: OG: '00- dnf.
World road best 5km walk 2000.
Progression at 20kmW: 1999- 1:29:09, 2000- 1:25:20. pbs: 5kmW 20:05 '00, 10kmW 42:43 '00.

Irina PRIVALOVA b. 22 Nov 1968 Malakhovka, Moskva region 1.75m 66kg. Married name was Sergeyeva. Moskva TU. Degree in journalism from Moscow State University.
At 100m (/200m, 4x100mR): OG: '92- 3/4/2R; '96- sf/sf/4R; WCh: '91- 4/4/2R, '93- 4/3/1R (2 4x400mR), '95- 3/2, '97- qf; EC: '90- 6, '94- 1/1/2R, '98- 2/1/3R; WJ: '86- sf/5R; EJ: '85- h; WCp: '94- 1/2 (1 400m), '98- 5/5; ECp: '89- 3/5; '91- 1/1/1R, '93- 1/1/1R, '98- 1/1R. At 60m/200m: WI: '91- 1/2, '93- 2/1, '97- 6/-. At 400m: WI: '95- 1. At 400mh/4x400m: OG: '00- 1/3R. Won USSR 100m 1989-90, CIS 100m/200m 1992, RUS 100m 1999, 200m 1993, 1996; 400mh 2000. GP 100m: 2nd 1993, 3rd 1994.
Records: European 100m 1994. Two USSR/CIS 100m 1991-2, three 200m 1992, Russian 200m (2) 1993-5, 100m 1994; WIR: 50m 6.05 and 6.00 (not ratified due to inaccurate camera alignment) '93, 6.03 '94, 5.96 '95; 60m 6.92 '93 & '95, 300m 1993. European IR 60m 6.97 '92, 200m 22.26 '92, 22.10 '95.
Progression at 100m, 200m, 400m: 1982- 11.9, 1983- 11.7, 1984- 11.79; 1985- 11.59, 24.54; 1986- 11.3i/11.52/11.37w, 24.10; 1987- 11.44/11.2, 23.3; 1989- 11.26, 23.00; 1990- 11.21, 23.01; 1991- 10.98, 22.21; 1992- 10.82/10.81w, 21.93; 1993- 10.94, 21.88, 49.89; 1994- 10.77, 22.02/21.82w, 50.62; 1995- 10.90, 21.87, 50.23i; 1996- 11.03/11.00w, 22.27; 1997- 22.52i; 1998- 10.83, 22.61A/22.62; 1999- 11.05, 23.09i; 2000- 11.37, 51.63. At 400mh: 2000- 53.02. pbs 300m 35.45i '93, 60mh 8.16i '00, 100mh 13.4 '87, HJ 1.72 '82, LJ 6.48i '85, 6.45 '84, TJ 13.72i '89.
Son Aleksey born 1988. Formerly a speed skater. Long jumped 6.45 at 15 in 1984. Won CIS 100m in 1992 with 10.81 to equal European record, but time later adjusted to 10.82. On successive days at the 1994 World Cup she won the 100m, was 2nd at 200m and then won the 400m in just her second ever race at the distance (ran 49.89 on debut July 1993). Missed outdoor season after injury at World Indoors 1997 and withdrew from 1999 World Champs (qf 100m) through injury. In 2000 she ran at 60mh indoors and outdoors made her 400mh debut with 54.49 – improving to 54.21 and 54.06 then 54.02 and 53.02 at the Olympics, taking the gold medal in just her eighth race at the event.

Yelena PROKHOROVA b. 16 Apr 1978 Kemerovo 1.71m 59kg. Kemerovo TU. Student.

At Hep: OG: '00- 2; EU23: '99- 2; ECp: '99- 6. At Pen: WI: '01- 2; EI: '00- 5. Won RUS Hep 2000.
Progression at Hep: 1994- 4919, 1995- 4621, 1996- 5152, 1997- 5600, 1998- 5776, 1999- 6132, 2000- 6765. pbs: 200m 23.37 '00, 800m 2:04.27 '00, 60mh 8.46i '01, 100mh 13.54 '00, HJ 1.82 '00, LJ 6.72 '00, SP 14.30 '00, JT 45.05 '00, Hep 4711i '01.

Olga RASPOPOVA b. 27 Dec 1978 Barabinsk, Novosibirsk reg 1.76m 62kg. Novosibirsk Dyn. Student.
At 800m: OG: '00- h.
Progression at 800m: 1997- 2:12.0, 1999- 2:03.88, 2000- 1:56.85.

Lyudmila ROGACHOVA b. 30 Oct 1966 Lad Balka Stavropol region 1.66m 57kg. Stavropol VS. Teacher.
At 1500m: OG: '92- 2, '96- sf, '00- sf; WCh: '91- 3, '93- 13, '95- 9, '99- h; EC: '90- 4, '94- 1 (3 800m); WI: '91- 1; EI: '94- 2; WUG: '89- 3. Won USSR 1500m 1990, CIS 800m 1992, RUS 1500m 1993-4, 1999-2000; GP 1500m 1992.
Progression at 800m, 1500m: 1980- 2:14.4, 4:44.6; 1981- 2:10.2, 4:32.4; 1982- 2:09.2, 4:30.6; 1983- 2:06.46, 4:26.6; 1984- 2:03.7, 4:15.8; 1985- 2:05.84, 4:19.2; 1986- 2:05.6, 4:17.6; 1987- 2:00.54, 4:08.10; 1988- 1:56.82, 4:04.29; 1989- 1:59.08, 4:07.5; 1990- 1:57.1, 4:02.3i/4:03.07; 1991- 1:58.67, 4:02.72; 1992- 1:57.93, 3:56.91; 1993- 1:58.13, 4:05.77; 1994- 1:58.43, 4:02.40; 1995- 1:58.70, 4:05.18; 1996- 2:00.17, 4:02.38; 1999- 2:02.43i, 4:04.19; 2000- 2:00.52, 4:01.73. pbs: 1000m 2:33.96 '93, 1M 4:21.30 '92.
Front ran Olympic 1500m 1992, and held on to smash through 4 minutes for the first time, but run down by Hassiba Boulmerka.

Oksana ROGOVA b. 7 Oct 1978 Tambov 1.80m 60kg. Tambov Sp. Student, Tambov University.
At TJ: OG: '00- 8; WCh: '99- 9; WJ: '96- 4; EU23: '99- 2; WI: '01- 5; EI: '00- 5.
Progression at TJ: 1993- 11.52, 1994- 12.48, 1995- 13.14, 1996- 13.49, 1997- 13.31, 1998- 14.14, 1999- 14.59/14.65w, 2000- 14.28i/14.27, 2001- 14.37i.

Natalya ROSHCHUPKINA b. 13 Jan1978 Lipetsk 1.82m 70kg. Lipetsk Dyn. Teacher.
At Hep: OG: '00- 6; WCh: '99- 10; EC: '98- 9; WJ: '96- 5; EU23: '99- 1; ECp: '98- 2, '00- 1. At Pen: WI: '99- 7, '01- 4.
Progression at Hep: 1993- 4772, 1994- 5191, 1995- 5383, 1996- 5767, 1997- 5920, 1998- 6370h, 1999- 6219, 2000- 6633. pbs: 200m 23.47 '00, 23.3 '98; 800m 2:07.93 '00, 60mh 8.60i '01, 100mh 13.49 '00, HJ 1.91 '00, LJ 6.45 '00, SP 14.63i '01, 11.28 '00, JT 45.16 '98, Pen 4664i '01.

Olga RUBLYOVA b. 28 Oct 1974 Volgograd 1.76m 65kg. Volgograd VS.
At LJ: OG: '96- dnq 19, '00- 5; WCh: '95- 4, '99- 11; EC: '94- 11; WJ: '92- 17; EJ: '93- 2; EI: '00- 4; ECp: '94- 2 (8 TJ), '95- 4, '00- 1. Russian champion 1995-6, 1998.
Progression at LJ: 1988- 5.77, 1989- 6.10, 1990- 6.29, 1991- 6.17, 1992- 6.46, 1993- 6.74, 1994- 6.76, 1995- 6.90/7.01w, 1996- 6.87, 1998- 6.88, 1999- 6.82, 2000- 6.90i/6.89. pb TJ 14.45i/14.21 '00.
Married to **Viktor Sotnikov** (b. 12 Sep 1974) TJ 17.11 '96, 9th OG 1996.

Nadezhda RYASHKINA b. 22 Jan 1967 Sokol 1.60m 47kg. Chelyabinsk Sp.
At 10kmW: EC: '90- dq, '98- 7; WCp: '91- 8; ECp: '98- 1. Won GWG 1990; USSR champion 1990, Russian 1997. 3000mW: WI: '89- 4.
World 10km track walk records 1989 and 1990, equalled world best for 20km road walk 1999.
Progression at 10kmW, 20kmW: 1988- 44:07.97t, 1:32:33; 1989- 43:08.4t, 1990- 41:56.23t, 1991- 44:29, 1:33:13; 1992- 44:30, 1994- 44:15.76t, 1997- 44:29, 1998- 42:25, 1999- 42:45, 1:27:30; 2000- 42:42, 1:28:06. pbs: 3000mW 12:12.98i '89, 5000mW 20:49.4 '90.
Previously a runner, took up walking in 1987.

Natalya SADOVA b. 15 Jun 1972 Gorkiy 1.80m 100kg. née Koptyukh. Nizhniy Novgorod VS. Teacher.
At DT: OG: '96- 2, '00- 4; WCh: '95- 5, '97- 3, '99- 4; EC: '94- 11, '98- 2; WJ: '90- 1; EJ: '89- 5; WUG: '95- 1, '97- 1; WCp: '98- 3; ECp: '95-7-8-9: 1/1/1/1; EU23Cp: '94- 1. Won GP 1998, Russian champion 1995-6, 1999-2000.
Progression at DT: 1988- 53.02, 1989- 55.34, 1990- 61.44, 1991- 59.10, 1992- 57.82, 1993- 58.14, 1994- 62.12, 1995- 66.86, 1996- 67.22, 1997- 67.72, 1998- 68.50, 1999- 70.02, 2000- 67.33. pb SP 14.21 '99. Has a daughter Viktoriya.

Tatyana SHIKOLENKO b. 10 May 1968 Gelenjik, 1.75m 79kg. Gelenjik Krasnodar TU.
At JT: OG: '00- 7; WCh: '93- 4, '97- 8, '99- 2; EC: '98- 2; WJ: '86- 4; EJ: '85- 5; WUG: '91- 1; WCp: '98- 4; ECp: '00- 2; 2nd GP 1998, Russian champion 1997-2000.
Russian javelin record 2000
Progression at JT: 1984- 59.40, 1985- 59.90, 1986- 55.70, 1987- 59.74, 1988- 64.70, 1989- 60.74, 1990- 64.98, 1991- 63.56, 1992- 62.20, 1993- 65.18, 1994- 64.94, 1996- 60.94, 1997- 67.34, 1998- 67.84; new: 1999- 66.37, 2000- 67.20.
Belarus prior to 1996. Younger sister of Natalya (1 WCh '95, 2 OG '92, pb 71.40 '94).

Irina STANKINA b. 25 Mar 1977 Saransk 1.67m 50kg. Saransk VS. Student.
At 20kmW: OG: '00- dnf; WCh: '99- 17. At 10kmW: OG: '96- dq; WCh: '95- 1, '97- dq; WCp: '97- 1. At 5000mW: WJ: '94- 1, '96- 1; EJ: '93- 3, '95- 1. Won RUS 20kmW 1999.
World junior road best 10km walk 1995, world junior record 5000m walk 1996.
Progression at 10kmW, 20kmW: 1995- 41:55, 1996- 42:01. 1997- 41:17, 1999- 1:29:00, 2000- 42:44, 1:25:29. pb 5000mW 20:31.4 '96.
At 18 years 135 days she became the youngest ever world champion in 1995. Twin sister Inna

and older brother **Vladimir** (b. 2 Jan 1974, pb 1:19:14 '01) are also race walkers. She has a daughter, Yekaterina.

Natalya TSYGANOVA b. 7 Feb 1971 Frunze, Kirgizstan 1.62m 52kg. Moskva Dyn. ex Ukraine. Teacher.
At 800m: OG: '00- h; WCh: '99- 5; EC: '98- sf; WI: '99- 3; EI: '00- 2; ECp: '99- 1. Won RUS 800m 2000.
Progression at 800m: 1992- 2:04.97, 1993- 2:02.7, 1994- 2:04.26, 1995- 2:02.30, 1998- 1:58.92, 1999- 1:57.15, 2000- 1:56.60. pbs: 400m 52.02 '98, 600m 1:25.9+i '99, 1000m 2:32.77 '99, 1500m 4:08.07 '99.

Irina VOSTRIKOVA b. 30 Aug 1970 Nizhnekamsk, Tatarstan 1.78m 68kg. Nizhekamsk TU. Economist.
At Hep: WCh: '97- 8, '99- 13; WUG: '95- 6, '97- 2; ECp: '94-5-6-7-9: 8/4/10/1/3. At Pen: EI: '96- 3, '00- 2. Won RUS Hep 1997.
Progression at Hep: 1989- 5444, 1990- 5428, 1991- 5835, 1992- 5892 (5987?), 1993- 6066, 1994- 6379, 1995- 6284, 1996- 5961, 1997- 6390, 1998- 6220, 1999- 6278, 2000- 6271. pbs: 200m 25.40/ 25.3 '94, 800m 2:15.77 '94, 60mh 8.49i '96, 100mh 13.67 '94, HJ 1.88 '94, LJ 6.52 '94, SP 16.06i '00, 15.92 '97; JT 49.90 '97, Hep 4615i '00.

Olga YEGOROVA b. 28 Mar 1972 Novocheboksarsk, Chuvashiya 1.60m 48kg. Cheboksary SA. Economist.
At 5000m: OG: '00- 8; WCh: '99- h; EC: '98- 11. At 3000m: WI: '97/6/01- 6/6/1; EI: '00- 6; ECp: '98- 1, '99- 3. At 1500m: WJ: '90- 9; EJ: '91- 3. Won RUS 5000m 1999.
Russian 5000m record 2000.
Progression at 5000m: 1996- 16:00.07, 1997- 15:42.47, 1998- 15:32.74, 1999- 15:22.80, 2000- 14:42.91. pbs: 1500m 4:04.75 '00, 1M 4:25.54i '00, 3000m 8:33.02 '99, 8:37.48i '01.

Yelena YELESINA b. 4 Apr 1970 Chelyabinsk 1.83m 64kg. Moskva VS.
At HJ: OG: '00- 1; WCh: '91- 2, '99- 2; EC: '90- 3; WJ: '88- 2; EJ: '87- 3=, '89- 1; WUG: '91- 4; EI: '92- 3, '98- 3. Won GWG & USSR 1990, Russian 1999.
Progression at HJ: 1983- 1.55, 1984- 1.65, 1985- 1.70, 1986- 1.83, 1987- 1.89, 1988- 1.98, 1989- 1.95, 1990- 2.02, 1991- 1.98, 1992- 1.94i/1.93, 1993- 1.91, 1994- 1.95, 1997- 1.95, 1998- 1.98i/1.94, 1999- 2.01, 2000- 2.01.
She has a son, Boris. Lives in Melbourne with her husband, Agvan Grigoryan ARM who plans to represent Australia at wrestling from 2002.

SAUDI ARABIA

Governing body: Saudi Arabian Amateur Athletic Federation, PO Box 5802, Riyadh 11432. Founded 1963.

Hamdan Obah **AL-BISHI** b. 5 May 1981 1.80m 70kg.
At 400mh: OG: '00- 2; WJ: '98- sf, '00- 1; AsiC: '00- 2; AsiJ: '97/99- 2.
Four Asian junior 400m records 2000. Six KSA 400m records 1998-2000.
Progression at 400m: 1996- 47.74, 1997- 46.51A, 1998- 46.2, 1999- 45.98, 2000- 44.66. pbs: 200m 21.1 '00, 300m 33.42 '00.

Hadi Sou'an AL-SOMAILY b. 30 Dec 1976 Taïf 1.90m 75kg. Teacher.
At 400mh: OG: '96- h, '00- 2; WCh: '95/99- h; AsiG: '94- 6; AsiC: '00- 1. Pan-Arab champion 1995, 1999. 2nd GP 2000.
Two Asian 400mh records 2000. Six KSA records 1994-2000.
Progression at 400mh: 1993- 52.28, 1994- 50.58, 1995- 49.30, 1996- 49.48, 1998- 51.1, 1999- 49.14/ 49.1A, 2000- 47.53. pb 400m 47.10 '95.
Lives in the mountainous area of Saudi Arabia. Coached by John Smith in Los Angeles.

SLOVAKIA

Governing body: Slovak Athletic Federation, Junácka 6, 832 80 Bratislava. Founded 1939.
National Championships first held in 1939.
2000 Champions: Men: 100m/200m: Martin Brinarsky 10.50/20.84, 400m: Stefan Balosák 45.72, 800m/1500m: Dusan Hlubocky 1:52.18/ 3:51.22, 5000m: Michal Kavacky 15:02.82, 10000m: Jan Krizak 30:14.77, HMar: Róbert Stefko 63:51, Mar: Václav Zupa 2:26:19, 3000mSt: Pavol Michalcik 9:37.28, 110mh: Igor Kovác 13.71, 400mh: Radoslav Holúbek 50.54, HJ: Lubos Benko 2.17, PV: Peter Krska 4.90, LJ: Martin Bercel 7.47, TJ: Martin Malovec 15.75, SP: Mikulás Konopka 19.84, DT: Milan Haborák 50.86, HT: Miloslav Konopka 70.91, JT: Marián Bokor 80.19, Dec: Marek Anestik 7035, 20kmW: Milos Bátovsky 1:27:56, 50kmW: Peter Korcok 3:54:56. **Women**: 100m: Anna Záhumenská 12.07, 200m/400mh: Miriam Hrdlicková 24.25/58.35, 400m: Janka Dubovská 54.07, 800m: Barbora Bronisová 2:16.28, 1500m: Adriana Vitková 4:27.59, 5000m: Alena Mocariová 17:01.65, 10000m: Helena Sluková 36:43.81, HMar: Dana Janecková 78:30, Mar: Anna Balosáková 2:52:55, 100mh: Miriam Bobková 13.63, HJ: Renata Medgyesová 1.84, PV: Slavomíra Slúková 3.50, LJ: Jana Veldáková 5.91, TJ: Irina Beskrovnaja 13.20, SP: Lucia Korceková 14.69, DT: Ivona Tomanová 49.81, HT: Martina Danisová 61.62, JT. Silvia Strasíková 43.89, Hep: Miriam Hrdlicková 4929, 20kmW: Zuzana Blazeková 1:41:14.

SLOVENIA

Governing body: Atletska Zveza Slovenije, Aljazeva ul.32, 1000 Ljubljana. Current organisation founded 1945. Athletes competed for Yugoslavia to 1991.
2000 National Champions: **Men**: 100m: Matic Osovnikar 10.34, 200m: Bostjan Horvat 21.26, 400m: Matija Sestak 46.31, 800m: Borut Veber 1:54.01, 1500m/5000m/10000m: Joze Petkovsek 3:48.51/14:31.59/30:38.32, HMar: Roman Kejzar

66:55, Mar: Mirko Vindis 2:28:00, 3000mSt: Bostjan Buc 9:18.61, 110mh: Damjan Zlatnar 14.01, 400mh: Sergej Salamon 52.03, HJ: Rozle Prezelj 2.17, PV: Jurij Rovan 5.21, LJ: Gregor Cankar 7.74, TJ: Marko Lenko 16.04, SP: Miran Vodovnik 17.64, DT: Miro Medic 52.50, HT: Primoz Kozmus 70.18, JT: Robi Tersek 68.50, Dec: Bostjan Bradesko 7233. **Women**: 100m: Alenka Bikar 11.43, 200m: Sasa Prokofjev 23.71, 400m: Brigita Langerholc 52.59, 800m: Jolanda Ceplak 2:02.00, 1500m/10000m: Helena Javornik 4:18.21/35:39.08, 3000m: Marjana Zajfrid 9:55.29, 5000m: Veronika Zupanc 18:06.37, HMar: Ida Surbek 79:52, Mar: Lidija Perse 3:08:58, 100mh: Katka Jankovic 14.09, 400mh: Maja Gorjup 61.62, HJ: Lea Cimperman 1.71, PV: Nina Zega 3.80, LJ/TJ: Anja Valant 6.16/13.65, SP/DT: Natasa Erjavec 15.15/44.81, HT: Lidija Novak 42.90, JT: Evfemija Storga 53.52, Hep: Desanka Calasan 5596.

Gregor CANKAR b. 25 Jan 1975 Celje 1.80m 68kg. Kladivar Cetis, Celje. Sports student.
At LJ: OG: '96- 6, '00- dnq 15; WCh: '95/97- dnq, '99- 3; EC: '94- dnq 23, '98- 6; WJ: '94- 1; WUG: '95- 3, '97- 3; WI: '97- 7, '99- 4; EI: '96- 4, '00- 5. Won SLO LJ 1995-7, 1998, 2000; TJ 1995, Med G LJ 1997.
Two Slovenian long jump records 1996-7.
Progression at LJ: 1989- 6.00, 1990- 6.70, 1991- 7.35, 1992- 7.51, 1993- 7.60/7.65w, 1994- 7.92/8.04w, 1995- 8.04/8.28sq/8.18w, 1996- 8.30, 1997- 8.40, 1998- 8.07, 1999- 8.36, 2000- 8.15/8.23w. pbs: 100m 10.61 '95, HJ 2.13 '94, TJ 16.51 '99.
First Slovenian to win a World Junior title.

Women

Brigita LANGERHOLC b. 23 Jul 1976 Kranj 1.70m 56kg. Was at University of South Califormia, USA. Marketing and finance manager.
At 800m: OG: '00- 4; WCh: '99- dnq sf; WUG: '99- 2. At 400m: EJ: '95- 5, '97- 5.
SLO records: 400m 2000m, 800m (3) 1999-2000.
Progression at 800m: 1996- 2:06.57, 1998- 2:04.16, 1999- 1:59.87, 2000- 1:58.51. pb 400m 52.02 '00.

Anja VALANT b. 8 Sep 1977 1.83m 64kg.
At TJ: OG: '00- 9; WCh: '97- dnq 30; '99- dnq 24; WJ: '96- 5; EU23: '97- 2, '99- 4; EJ: '95- 5. Won SLO LJ 2000, TJ 1997-2000.
Five Slovenian triple jump records 1996-2000.
Progression at TJ: 1994- 12.84/12.95w, 1995- 13.54, 1996- 13.79, 1997- 13.98, 1998- 13.85, 1999- 14.29, 2000- 14.69. pb 400m 6.51 '98.

SOUTH AFRICA

Governing body: Athletics South Africa, P.O. Box 15616, Doornfontein 2028. Original body founded 1894.
National Championships first held in 1894 (men), 1929 (women). **2000 Champions**: **Men**: 100m/200m: Matthew Quinn 10.33/20.90, 400m: Hendrik Mokganyetsi 45.52, 800m: Shawn Abrahams 1:45.03, 1500m: Clyde Colenso 3:43.8, 5000m: Whaddon Niewoudt 14:04.71, 10000m: Hendrick Ramaala 28:48.28, HMar: Shadrack Hoff 61:11, Mar: Johannes Maremane 2:11:15, 3000mSt: Simon Mayisela 8:35.67, 110mh: Shaun Bownes 13.94, 400mh: Llewellyn Herbert 49.06, HJ: Jacques Freitag 2.29, PV: Okkert Brits 5.50, LJ: Felix Coetzee 7.64, TJ: Willie Coetzee 15.35, SP: Burger Lambrechts 20.56, DT: Frantz Kruger 63.87, HT: Chris Harmse 70.94, JT: Marius Corbett 80.29, Dec: Jannie Botha 6864, 20kmW: Tapelo Mangole 1:35.14, 50kmW: Andre Enslin 4:59:24. **Women**: 100m: Wendy Hartman 11.32, 200m/400m: Heide Seyerling 23.06/51.26, 800m: Chantal Breet 2:04.88, 1500m: Zanelle Grobler 4:15.16, 5000m: Rene Kalmer 16:20.29, 10000m: Elana Meyer 31:47.32, HMar: Carlien Cornelissen 74:38, Mar: Gwen van Lingen 2:39:08, 3000mSt: Poppy Mlambo 10:54.03, 100mh/400mh: Surita Febbraio 13.42/56.43, HJ: Hestrie Cloete 1.90, PV: Elmarie Gerryts 4.20, LJ: Delia Visser 6.18, TJ: Petrusa Marais 12.51, SP: Veronica Abrahamse 16.67, DT: Elizna Naude 55.64, HT: Elmarie Knoetzen 57.98, JT: Rhona Dwinger 54.98, Hep: Maralize Fouche 5787, 20kmW: Susan Vermeulen 1:45:46.

Johan BOTHA b. 10 Jan 1974 Pretoria 1.81m 68kg. Mr Price AC. Former prison guard.
At 800m: OG: '96/00- sf; WCh: '99- sf; CG: '98- 3; WI: '99- 1, '01- 2; AfG: '99- 6.
Progression at 800m: 1991- 1:50.01, 1992- 1:49.4, 1993- 1:46.79, 1994- 1:46.37, 1995- 1:45.89, 1996- 1:45.17, 1997- 1:47.45, 1998- 1:44.57, 1999- 1:43.91, 2000- 1:44.85. pbs: 400m 47.3A '95, 47.39 '96; 1000m 2:16.71i/2:17.19 '99, 1500m 3:36.30 '00, 1M 3:57.00 '96, 3000m 8:23.59A '99.

Shaun BOWNES b. 24 Oct 1970 Johannesburg 1,94m 90kg. Computer operator. Mr Price AC.
At 110mh: OG: '00- sf; WCh: '99- qf; CG: '98- 3; AfG: '99- 5; AfCh: '98- 1; Won SA 1994, 1998, 2000. At 60mh: WI: '01- 3.
Records: African 110mh (6) 1998-2001, 60mh indoors (3) 2000-01. Seven SA 110mh 1998-2000.
Progression at 110mh: 1989- 14.5A, 1990- 15.00A, 1991- 14.43A, 1992- 13.97A, 1993- 14.19A, 1994- 13.98A, 1995- 14.21A/14.19Aw, 1997- 13.97A/13.5A, 1998- 13.53/13.2A, 1999- 13.39, 2000- 13.41/13.38w, 2001- 13.34A. pbs: 50mh 6.48i '01, 60mh 7.52 '01. Four-year drugs ban for steroid use in 1995, commuted to two years.

Okkert BRITS b. 22 Aug 1973 Uitenhage 1.98m 84kg. Stellenbosch AC.
At PV: OG: '96 dnq, '00 7; WCh: '93 dnq 16=, 95- 4, '97- dnq, '99- 10; CG: '94- nh; WJ: '92- 3; WI: '95- 3=, '97- 6, '01- 7; AfCh: '92- 1, '93- 1; AfG: '95- 1, '99- 1; AfCh: '98- 1; WCp: '92- 3, '94- 1. Won GP 1995, 3rd 2000. SA champion 1993-5, 1998, 2000.
23 SA (1992-5), 19 African (1993-5) and 9 Commonwealth (1994-5) pole vault records.

Progression at PV: 1989- 4.50, 1990- 4.80, 1991- 5.25, 1992- 5.46, 1993- 5.71, 1994- 5.90, 1995- 6.03, 1996- 6.01, 1997- 5.92, 1998- 5.90, 1999- 5.75A, 2000- 5.85/5.90ex. pb 100m 10.96 '96.
Younger brother Pieter (b. 14 Oct 1975) has PV best of 5.50 '97.

Marius CORBETT b. 26 Sep 1975 Potchefstroom 1.95m 115kg. Sports student at Potchefstroom University.
At JT: WCh: '97- 1, '99- dnq 22; CG: '98- 1; AfCh: '98- 1; WJ: '94- 1; WUG: '97- 1; WCp: '98- 4; AfG: '99- 1; Af-J: '94- 1. SA champion 1997-2001.
African javelin records 1997 and 1998, African Junior 1994.
Progression at JT: 1992- 64.02, 1993- 73.00, 1994- 77.98, 1996- 74.94, 1997- 88.40, 1998- 88.75, 1999- 87.17A, 2000- 83.43A.
Serious elbow and shoulder injuries followed his World Junior title in 1994, and he contemplated returning to play rugby, but he came back to the javelin in 1997, when he improved to 83.90 in April and than added 4.50m to this pb to win the World title. Showing his big meeting ability, he improved this record to 88.75 to win the 1998 Commonwealth Games gold; surprising Steve Backley as this was far better than the form he had showed in preceding months. An injury also kept him out of 2000 Olympics.

Llewellyn HERBERT b. 21 Jul 1977 Bethal 1.85m 80kg. Tuks AC, Pretoria.
At 400mh: OG: '96- h, '00- 3; WCh: '97- 2; WJ: '96- 2; WUG: '97- 1. Won SA 110mh 1996-7, 400mh 1996-2000.
Seven SA 400mh records 1997-2001.
Progression at 400mh: 1995- 51.25, 1996- 48.76A, 1997- 47.86, 1998- 48.43A/48.76, 1999- 47.83A/ 48.28, 2000- 47.81. pbs: 100m 10.30A/10.20Aw '99; 200m 20.50wA/21.06 '99, 400m 46.16A '98, 110mh 13.91A '98, 13.7A '97.
Customarily faces away from direction of running before taking his marks. Season cut short by injury in 1998 and again in 1999.

Frantz KRUGER b. 22 May 1975 Kempton Park 2.03m 118kg. Medical student at Free State University, Bloemfontein
At DT: OG: '00- 3; WCh: '99- dnq 17; CG: '98- 2; WJ: '94- 1; AfG: '99- 1; AfCh: '98- 1, WUG: '97- 6, '99- 1; WCp: '98- 3. Won SA DT 1996, 1999-2001; Af-J SP & DT 1994.
African and Commonwealth discus record 2000.
Progression at DT: 1993- 58.28, 1994- 58.52, 1995- 60.06, 1996- 60.66, 1997- 61.64, 1998- 65.73, 1999- 67.38, 2000- 69.75A.

Burger LAMBRECHTS b. 3 Apr 1973 Pretoria 2.00m 145kg. Rentmeester AC.
At SP: OG: '00- dnq 14; WCh: '97- 10, '99- 9; CG: '94- 6, '98- 1; WJ: '92- dnq 15; AfG: '99- 1; AfCh: '93- 4, '98- 1; WCp: '98- 4. SA champion 1993-4, 1997, 1999-2000.
Progression at SP: 1991- 15.94, 1992- 17.01, 1993- 18.43, 1994- 19.06, 1995- 19.26i/19.11, 1996- 19.07, 1997- 19.91, 1998- 20.29, 1999- 19.93, 2000- 20.56, 2001- 20.90dq?. pbs: DT 53.50A '97, HT 53.68 '96.
Set an African shot record of 20.90 on 23 Feb 2001, but then tested positive for Stanozolol at this meeting and was suspended pending further investigation.

Hendrik MOKGANYETSI b. 7 Sep 1975 1.90m 86kg. Rentmeester AC.
At 400m: OG: '96- qf, '00- 6; CG: '98- qf; At 800m: WCh: '97- qf. Won SA 400m 2000-01.
SA 400m record 2000.
Progression at 400m, 800m: 1995- 47.25, 1996- 45.39A, 1:46.93; 1997- 45.52A, 1:44.62; 1998- 45.30A, 1:45.62A; 1999- 45.92A, 1:46.60; 2000- 44.59, 1:47.60. pbs: 200m 21.79A '96, 600m 1:15.57 '97.

Hendrick RAMAALA b. 2 Feb 1972 GaMalepo, Pietersburg 1.72m 58kg. Law graduate of Wits University. Mr Price AC.
At 10000m: OG: '96- h; WCh: '95- 17, '97- 14, '99- 11; AfG: '99- 7. At Mar: OG: '00- 12. World HMar: '97- 4, '98- 2, '99- 2. Won SA 5000m 1995, 1999; 10000m 1995, 1999-2001; HMar 1997.
SA records 10000m (3) 1997-9, HMar 1997 and 2000.
Progression at 10000m: 1995- 27:54.59, 1996- 27:57.8, 1997- 27:36.30, 1998- 27:30.57, 1999- 27:29.94, 2000- 27:46.38, 2001- 27:38.36. pbs: 3000m 8:10.38 '95, 5000m 13:24.43 '98, HMar 59:20 '00, Mar 2:09:43 '00.
Won Great North Run half marathon 1997. Did not finish on his marathon debut at Chicago 1999.

Janus ROBBERTS b. 10 Mar 1979 Louis Trichardt 1.97m 117kg. Rentmeester AC. Southern Methodist University, USA.
At SP (DT): OG: '00- 7; WCh: '99- dnq 20; CG: '98- 5; WJ: '98- 2 (7); AfG: '99- 2. Won NCAA SP 1999, Afr-J SP/DT 1997.
Official world junior shot record 1998, African indoor record (twice) 2001.
Progression at SP: 1997- 18.61, 1998- 20.39, 1999- 20.10, 2000- 20.34, 2001- 21.36i. pb DT 61.18 '99.

Hezekiél SEPENG b. 30 Jun 1974 Potchefstroom 1.82m 70kg. Was at Rand Afrikaans University. Mr Price AC, Johannesburg.
At 800m: OG: '96- 2, '00- 4; WCh: '93- 5, '95- sf, '97- sf, '99- 2; CG: '94- 2, '98- 2; WJ: '92- 5; AfG: '95- 6, '99- 3; AfCh: '93- 4; WUG: '95- 1, '97- 2. 2nd GP 1999. Won SA 800m 1993-4, 1997-8; 1500m 2001. Three SA 800m records 1996-9.
Progression at 800m: 1992- 1:47.51, 1993- 1:45.46, 1994- 1:45.32, 1995- 1:45.36, 1996- 1:42.74, 1997- 1:43.19, 1998- 1:44.44, 1999- 1:42.69, 2000- 1:43.98. pbs: 400m 46.75 '93, 1000m 2:16.47 '00, 1500m 3:38.24 '96, 1M 3:57.33 '96, 3000m 8:21.58A '01.
Lost to Wilson Kipketer by just 0.02 in 1999 World Champs.

Gert THYS b. 12 Nov 1971 Prieska 1.67m 55kg. Security officer, Johannesburg City Council.
At Mar: OG: '96- 33; WCh: '93- dnf, '99- 15. World HMar: '97- 6, '98- 5.
African & Commonwealth marathon record 1999.
Progression at Mar: 19909- 2:19:05, 1992- 2:17:16, 1993- 2:09:31, 1995- 2:13:28, 1996- 2:08:30, 1997- 2:11:55, 1998- 2:07:45, 1999- 2:06:33, 2000- 2:11:32. pbs: 5000m 13:55.30 '91, 10000m 28:26.71 '01; Road: 10km 27:58 '96, 15km 43:04 '92, HMar 60:23 '97.
Won three of 16 marathons: on his debut in 1990 and then Beppu 1996 and Tokyo in February 1999, when he ran the second fastest ever time and became the first man to have run three sub-2:08 times, having been the first ever to run two sub-2:08s in one year with 3rd at Boston and Chicago 1998. 2nd Fukuoka 1993.

Women

Hestrie CLOETE b. 26 Aug 1978 Germiston 1.85m 68kg. née Storbeck. Mr Price AC.
At HJ: OG: '00- 2; WCh: '97- 10=, '99- dnq 14=; WJ: '96- 6=; AfG: '95- 1, '99- 1; AfCh: '98- 1; WCp: '98- 2. Won GP 1999, RSA 1996-2001, African Jnr 1997.
12 African high jump records 1998-9, four Commonwealth and two South African 1999, African Junior 1996.
Progression at HJ: 1993- 1.75, 1994- 1.79, 1995- 1.91, 1996- 1.92, 1997- 1.94, 1998- 1.96, 1999- 2.04, 2000- 2.01. pbs: 400m 56.0A '94, 800m 2:11.9 '95, LJ 5.75A '95.
Top world ranked in 1999, but had a lapse of concentration in failing to qualify for world final. Top junior in the world in 1997.

Elmarie GERRYTS b. 25 Aug 1972 Cape Town 1.70m 62kg. Mr Price Maties AC. Was at Stellenbosch University. Physiotherapist.
At PV: OG: '00- nh (12=); WCh: '99- 10; CG: '98- 2; AfG: '99- 2; WCp: '98- 2. AfCh: '92- 4 Hep, '93- 5 HJ. Won SA PV 1995-2001.
18 African pole vault records from 2.85, 3.30 and 3.70 in 1995 to 4.42 in 2000.
Progression at PV: 1995- 3.70, 1996- 3.85, 1997- 4.00, 1998- 4.30, 1999- 4.35, 2000- 4.42. pbs: 100mh 14.07 '90, HJ 1.85 '90, LJ 6.27 '90, TJ 12.03A '95, Hep 5250 '92.
A talented all-rounder who has excelled since taking up the pole vault. She set four African indoor records in 1999 and a further three in 2000. She was RSA U19 champion at pentathlon 1989-90 and HJ 1990.

Elana MEYER b. 10 Oct 1966 Albertinia 1.58m 55kg. née van Zyl. Mr Price Maties AC. Graduate of Stellenbosch University.
At 10000m: OG: '92- 2, '00- 8; WCh: '93- dnf, '95- 5, '97- 17; CG: '94- 2; WCp: '94- 1. At 5000m: AfG: '99- 2. At 1500m: AfCh: '92- 1, '93- 1. At Mar: OG: '96- dnf. World CC: '93-4: 6/6; HMar '94- 1, '98- 2, '99- 8. Won SA 1500m 1992; 3000m 1987-9, 1992-3; 10000m 1991, 1999-2001; HMar 1990-1, 1999.
World road bests Half Marathon 1991, 1998 & 1999; 15km 1991. African marathon & 10000m records 1994, 5000m 1993 and 1995. Commonwealth records 10000m 1994, 5000m 1995, Half Marathon 1999.
SA records 2000m 1987, 3000m 1991, 5000m (3) 1991-5, 10000m (5) 1989-94, Mar 1994.
Progression at 3000m, 5000m, 10000m, Mar: 1981- 10:00.2, 1982- 9:24.9, 1983- 9:09.32, 1984- 9:12.20, 1985- 8:58.73; 1986- 9:17.16, 1987- 8:52.39, 1988- 8:54.84, 1989- 8:55.78, 15:35.07, 32:28.9; 1990- 8:54.83, 1991- 8:32.00, 14:49.35, 31:33.46; 1992- 8:38.45, 14:44.15, 31:11.75; 1993- 8:32.81, 14:46.41, 32:28.02; 1994- 9:02.43, 15:25.59, 30:52.51, 2:25:15; 1995- 8:44.70, 14:44.05, 31:23.96, 2:26:51; 1996- 15:19.56, 32:23.53; 1997- 33:05.82, 2:27:09; 1998- 2:27:20, 1999- 15:42.76, 32:15.25, 2:27:17; 2000- 14:57.48, 31:14.70, 2:31:59. pbs: 800m 2:06.23 '85, 1000m 2:43.63 '87, 1500m 4:02.15 '92, 1M 4:30.21 '89, 2000m 5:40.7 '92. Road (all RSA records): 10km 31:19 '97, 15km 46:57 '91, HMar 66:44 '99.
Gave up in World 10000m final in 1993 after being repeatedly baulked by Sally Barsosio. Has run ten marathons, with six sub-2:28 times, but no wins. Boston: 3rd 1994 (début), 2nd 1995 & 1997; 3rd Chicago 1998 & 1999, 4th 2000; 5th London 1999. Her husband Michael ran 1500m in 3:47.47 at age of 19 in 1986.

Heidi SEYERLING b. 19 Aug 1976 Port Elizabeth 1.68m 55kg. Rentmeester AC, Durban.
At 400m: OG: '00- 6; AfG: '99- 7. At 200m: WCh: '95- h, '99- h; CG: '98- 5; WJ: '94- 1; AfCh: '98- 3, Af-J: '94- 1 (100m 2). Won SA 100m 1998-9, 200m 1995, 1998-2001, 400m 2000-01.
SA 400m record 2000.
Progression at 200m, 400m: 1991- 24.4, 1992- 23.8, 1993- 24.08A/23.94Aw, 1994- 23.22A/22.80w, 1995- 23.36, 1996- 23.28, 1997- 24.19A, 1998- 22.89, 53.8; 1999- 22.88A, 51.33A; 2000- 22.87A/22.59Aw, 50.05; 2001- 22.70A, 50.64A. pbs: 100m 11.35 '99, 11.33Aw '01, 11.1w '97; 300m 37.02 '00.

SPAIN

Governing body: Real Federación Española de Atletismo, Avda. Valladolid, 81 - 1°, 28008 Madrid, Spain. Founded 1918.
National Championships first held in 1917 (men), 1931 (women). **2000 Champions**: **Men**: 100m: Venancio José 10.18, 200m: Jordi Mayoral 21.20, 400m: David Canal 45.56, 800m: Roberto Parra 1:48.18, 1500m: Juan Carlos Higuero 3:38.54, 5000m: Yusef El Nasri 13:32.61, 10000m: José Rios 27:22.20, HMar: Antonio Peña 63:14, Mar: Benito Ojeda 2:18:37, 3000mSt: Luis Miguel Martín 8:18.97, 110mh: Francisco López 14.08, 400mh: Iván Rodríguez 50.03, HJ: David Antona 2.18, PV: Montxu Miranda 5.81, LJ: Yago Lamela 7.86, TJ: Raúl Chapado 16.26, SP: Manuel

Martínez 19.40, DT: David Martínez 60.83, HT: Moises Campeny 69.71, JT: Gustavo Dacal 72.61, Dec: Marcos Moreno 7790, 20kmW: Francisco Fernández 1:22:33, 50kmW: Jesús A García 3:45:14, **Women**: 100m: Carme Blay 11.87, 200m: Arantxa Reinares 24.41, 400m: Norfalia Carabali 52.47, 800m: Mayte Martínez 2:06.55, 1500m: Natalia Rodríguez 4:17.06, 5000m: Marta Domínguez 15:26.00, 10000m: Teresa Recio 31:44.3, HMar: Griselda González 71:40, Mar: María Luisa Muñoz 2:32:34, 100mh: Nerea Azkarate 13.50, 400mh: Miriam Alonso 57.69, HJ: Marta Mendía 1.90, PV: Mar Sánchez 4.05, LJ: Niurka Montalvo 6.73, TJ: Carlota Castrejana 13.94, SP: Martina de la Puente 17.13, DT: Alice Matejková 59.25, HT: Dolores Pedrares 58.74, JT: Marta Míguez 59.02, Hep: Imma Clopés 5843, 10,000W: Encarna Granados 43:30.22, 20kmW: Eva Pérez 1:32:03.

Abel ANTÓN b. 24 Oct 1962 Ojoel, Soria 1.79m 61kg. Reebok.
At Mar: OG: '00- 53; WCh: '97- 1, '99- 1. At 5000m (10000m): OG: '88- sf, '92- 8, '96- (13); WCh: '87- 14, '91- 11, '93- 11, '95- (dnf); EC: '86- h, '90- 11, '94- 3 (1); EJ: '81- 5; WCp: '92- 4, '94- 7; ECp: '87- (1), '93- 3. At 3000m: EI: '89- 2. Won Spanish 5000m 1991-3, 10000m 1994.
Progression at 5000m, 10000m, Mar: 1980- 14:43.5, 1981- 14:18.29, 1982- 14:13.94, 1983- 14:06.04, 1984- 13:27.95, 1985- 13:25.81, 1986- 13:32.61, 1987- 13:21.44, 28:46.65; 1988- 13:20.67, 1990- 13:29.81, 1991- 13:26.52, 28:38.27; 1992- 13:21.86, 1993- 13:17.48, 28:09.04; 1994- 13:15.17, 28:06.03; 1995- 13:34.21, 27:51.37; 1996- 13:20.93, 27:54.05, 2:09:15; 1997- 28:29.89, 2:10:27; 1998- 2:07:57, 1999- 2:09:41, 2000- 2:12:49. pbs: 1000m 2:20.44 '86, 1500m 3:37.5 '85, 2000m 5:01.35 '87, 3000m 7:46.08 '87, HMar 63:03 '98.
Won European Cup in his first year at 10,000m and has won five of his ten marathons: Berlin 1996, Kyongju and Worlds 1997, before 4th at Fukuoka 1997, then a pb in London 1998, but did not finish at New York. 3rd London 1999. Retained world marathon title in 1999; at 36 years 300 days the oldest world champion at any event from 1983.

Fermín CACHO b. 16 Feb 1969 Agreda, Soria 1.75m 65kg. Reebok.
At 1500m: OG: '92- 1, '96- 2; WCh: '91- 5, '93- 2, '95- 8, '97- 2, '99- 4; EC: '90- 11, '94- 1, '98- 3; WJ: '88- 3; EJ: '87- 12; WCp: '89- 6, '92- 4; ECp: '93-5-6-7: 2/3/1/1; WI: '91- 2, '95- 6; EI: '90- 2. Won Spanish 1500m 1989-93, 1995-6.
European records: 1500m 1997, indoor 3000m 1996, Spanish records 1000m 1993, 1500m 1997.
Progression at 1500m: 1986- 3:58.17, 1987- 3:45.9, 1988- 3:42.56, 1989- 3:36.23, 1990- 3:37.04, 1991- 3:32.03, 1992- 3:32.69, 1993- 3:32.01, 1994- 3:35.27, 1995- 3:34.25, 1996- 3:32.58, 1997- 3:28.95, 1998- 3:32.62, 1999- 3:31.34, 2000- 3:42.56. pbs: 800m 1:45.37 '91, 1000m 2:16.13 '93, 1M 3:49.56 '96, 2000m 5:02.68 '97, 3000m 7:36.61i '96, 7:37.02 '99.
Good footballer at school, concentrated on athletics from age 17. Having compiled a great championships record, at last ran a very fast time, with 3:28.95 to take Steve Cram's European record at 1500m in Zürich 1997. Completed five successive World Champs top eight placings at 1500m in 1999.

Andrés Manuel **DÍAZ** b. 12 Jul 1969 La Coruña 1.87m 71kg. Nike International
At 1500m: OG: '00- 7; WCh: '99- 5; EC: '98- 11; WI: '97- 5, '99- 3; EI: '98- 4. At 800m: OG: '96- h; WCh: '95- h; EC: '94- h; WUG: '95- 2, EI: '96- 4. At 3000m: EI: '00- 5. Won Spanish 1500m 1999.
European indoor 1500m record 1999.
Progression at 1500m: 1988- 3:47.7, 1989- 3:42.27, 1990- 3:41.85, 1991- 3:41.32, 1992- 3:47.1, 1993- 3:43.04, 1994- 3:48.32i, 1996- 3:42.32, 1997- 3:34.52, 1998- 3:32.17, 1999- 3:31.83, 2000- 3:31.48. pbs: 800m 1:45.89 '96, 1000m 2:19.2 '92, 1M 3:51.15 '99, 2000m 4:56.87i '99, 5:05.66 '00; 3000m 7:46.15i '99, 8:01.65 '00.

Réyes ESTÉVEZ b. 2 Aug 1976 Cornella de Llobregat, Barcelona 1.87m 70kg. Adidas.
At 1500m: OG: '96- sf; WCh: '97- 3, '99- 3; EC: '98- 1; WJ: '94- 4; EJ: '93- 1, '95- 1; EU23: '97- 1; WI: '01- 2; ECp: '98- 2. World CC: '94- 8J. Won Spanish 1500m 1997-8.
European Junior 1500m record 1995.
Progression at 1500m: 1992- 3:54.7, 1993- 3:42.36, 1994- 3:39.28, 1995- 3:35.51, 1996- 3:34.86, 1997- 3:33.40, 1998- 3:30.87, 1999- 3:30.57, 2000- 3:40.64. pbs: 800m 1:46.90 '96, 1000m 2:17.45 '00, 1M 3:52.61 '97, 2000m 5:10.64 '00, 3000m 7:44.87 '99, 5000m 14:08.8 '96.
Has won four European titles U20 to senior.

Francisco Javier **FERNÁNDEZ** b. 5 Mar 1977 Guadix, Granada 1.73m 57kg. Puma Sevilla Abierta.
At 20kmW: OG: '00- 7; WCh: '99- 15; WCp: '97- 47, '99- 12; EC: '98- 3; EU23: '97- 2; ECp: '98- 1, '00- 3. Spanish champion 1998-2000. At 10kmW: WJ: '96- 1; EJ: '95- 2.
Spanish walks records 10000m 1999, 20km 2000.
Progression at 20kmW: 1997- 1:21:59, 1998- 1:20:31, 1999- 1:21:55, 2000- 1:18:56. pb 5000mW 18:54.4 '99, 10000mW 38:42.38 '99.

Martín FIZ b. 3 Mar 1963 Vitoria 1.69m 53kg. Reebok.
At Mar: OG: '96- 4, '00- 6; WCh: '95- 1, '97- 2, '99- 8; EC: '94- 1. At 5000m: OG: '92- h; WC: '91- h; EC: '90- h. World CC: '90- 15, '91- 20, '93- 14, '95- 10; HMar: '98- 15; Eur CC: '98- 13. Won Spanish CC 1990, 1992.
Spanish records: Marathon (4) 1994-7, HMar 1996 (2).
Progression at 10000m, Mar: 1981- 31:40.6, 1987- 29:17.2, 1990- 28:40.81, 1991- 28:00.19, 1992- 28:12.07, 1993- 28:00.97, 2:12:47; 1994- 28:37.71, 2:10:21; 1995- 2:08:57, 1996- 2:08:25, 1997- 2:08:05,

1998- 27:49.61, 2:09:33; 1999- 2:08:50, 2000- 2:08:14. pbs: 1500m 3:44.0 '88, 3000m 7:50.17 '90, 5000m 13:20.01 '91, 3000mSt 8:28.9 '88, HMar 61:08 '96.
In 1982 he was 16th in the World Junior cross-country and Spanish junior champion at 5000m. Has 8 wins in 17 marathons from Helsinki on début in 1993. Won the European title in great style in 1994, with further wins in Rotterdam and World marathons 1995, Seoul 1996, Lake Biwa 1997 and 2000, Otsu 1999.

Jesús Ángel GARCÍA b. 17 Oct 1969 Madrid 1.71m 62kg. Canal de Isabel II.
At 50kmW: OG: '92- 10, '96- dnf, '00- 12; WCh: '93- 1, '95- 5, '97- 2, '99- dnf; EC: '94- 4, '98- dq; WCp: '93- 2, '95- 2, '97- 1, '99- 4; ECp: '96-8-00: 1/2/1. At 20kmW: WUG: '91- 5. Won SPA 50kmW 1997, 2000.
Progression at 50kmW: 1991- 4:05:10, 1992- 3:48:24, 1993- 3:41:41, 1994- 3:41:28, 1995- 3:41:54, 1996- 3:46:59, 1997- 3:39.54, 1998- 3:43:17, 1999- 3:40:40, 2000- 3:42:51. pbs: 10000mW 42:27.52 '90, road: 10kmW 40:38 '91, 20kmW 1:24:07 '95.
In 1997 he married Carmen Acedo, who won a rhythmic gymnastics world title in 1993.

Yago LAMELA b. 24 Jul 1977 Avilé, Asturias 1.78m 68kg. Computer engineering student at University of Oviedo. A.A.Avilesina.
At LJ (TJ): OG: '00- dnq 19; WCh: '99- 2; EC: '98- 8; WJ: '94- (dnq 14), '96- 4; EU23: '99- 1; EJ: '95 (12); WI: '99- 2; ECp: '98- 7. Won IbAm LJ 1998, Spanish LJ 1998-2000.
Five Spanish long jump records 1999.
Progression at LJ: 1991- 5.91, 1992- 6.62, 1993- 6.89, 1994- 7.27, 1995- 7.66, 1996- 7.80/8.04w, 1997- 7.87/7.97w, 1998- 8.14/8.20w, 1999- 8.56, 2000- 8.22. pb TJ 16.72 '98.
In 1999, after setting Spanish indoor records at 8.20 and 8.22 in Jan-Feb, had a superb World Indoors, with successive records of 8.29, 8.42 and 8.56, when second to Iván Pedroso, as he was also at the outdoor Worlds.

Eliseo MARTÍN b. 5 Nov 1973 Monzón, Huesca 1.73m 62kg. Transbaso Monzón Polidux.
At 3000mSt: OG: '00- 6; WCh: '99- 6; EC: '98- 7. At 10000m: WJ: '92- 7. Won ESP 3000mSt 1999.
Progression at 3000mSt: 1992- 9:02.55, 1993- 8:45.77, 1994- 8:32.89, 1995- 8:31.27, 1996- 8:31.99, 1997- 8:30.50, 1998- 8:25.92, 1999- 8:13.59, 2000- 8:13.63. pbs: 1500m 3:40.96 '00, 3000m 7:58.60 '00, 5000m 14:02.37 '94, 10000m 28:39.11 '99, 2000mSt 5:30.39 '00.

Luis Miguel MARTÍN b. 11 Jan 1972 Madrid 1.80m 69kg. Nike.
At 3000mSt: OG: '00- 5; WCh: '99- h; EC: '98- 4; won IbAm 1998, Spanish 2000. At 1500m: WJ: '90- h; EJ: '91- h.
Spanish record 3000mSt 1999 and 2000.
Progression at 3000mSt: 1998- 8:20.54, 1999- 8:11.18, 2000- 8:09.77. pbs: 1500m 3:39.07 '96, 3000m 7:50.27 '00.

Manuel MARTÍNEZ b. 7 Dec 1974 León 1.85m 117kg. Universidad de León.
At SP: OG: '96- dnq 15, '00- 6; WCh: '93- 11, '95- dnq 21, '97- dnq 13; EC: '94- dnq 14, '98- 7; EU23: '94- 1; WI: '95/7/9/01- 4/5/4/3; EI: '94- 4, '00- 2; WJ: '92- 2; EJ: '93- 1; ECp: '93/5/6/7/8- 7/4/4/3/3. Won Spanish 1993-8, 2000; IbAm 1998, 2000.
Fourteen Spanish shot records 1993-2000.
Progression at SP: 1991- 15.57, 1992- 18.14, 1993- 19.53, 1994- 20.16, 1995- 19.97i/19.69, 1996- 20.12, 1997- 20.37i/20.27, 1998- 20.50i/20.08; 1999- 20.79i/20.04, 2000- 20.55, 2001- 20.91i.

Valentí MASSANA b. 5 Jul 1970 Viladecans, Barcelona 1.68m 51kg. Integra 2.
At 20kmW (50kmW): OG: '92- dq, '96- 20 (3), '00- (4); WCh: '91- 5, '93- 1, '95- 2, '99- (5); EC: '90- 5, '94- 3, '98- 9; WCp: '91- 10, '93- 2, '97- 19, '99- (8); ECp: '96- 6, '98- 10. At 10kmW: WJ: '88- 2; EJ: '87- 2, '89- 1. At 5000mW: WI: '91- 5. Won Spanish 20kmW 1991-5, 1997; 50kmW 1993-6.
Spanish walks records 20km 1992, 50km 1994, 10,000m track 1997.
Progression at 20kmW, 50kmW: 1987- 1:31:50, 1990- 1:22:33, 1991- 1:20:29, 1992- 1:19:25, 1993- 1:20:50, 3:46:11; 1994- 1:20:33, 3:38:43; 1995- 1:20:23, 3:42:13; 1996- 1:22:23, 3:44:19; 1997- 1:20:39, 1998- 1:21:21, 1999- 1:26:33, 3:45:29; 2000- 1:26:19, 3:46:01. pbs: 5000mW 18:59.60i '91, 19:36.5 '89; 10000mW 39:31.81 '97, 1HrW 14,367m '90; road 10kmW 39:27 '92, 30kmW 2:07:58 '93.

Enrique MOLINA b. 25 Feb 1968 La Zubia, Granada 1.75m 62kg. Adidas.
At 10000m: OG: '00- dnf; WCh: '99- 14; EC: '98- 6. At 5000m: OG: '92- 7; WCh: '95- h, '97- 8. At 3000m: WI: '93- 3. World CC: '00- 17. Won Spanish 5000m 1995, CC 2000; EChall 10k 2000.
Spanish records: 3000m 1996, 5000m (2) 1996-7.
Progression at 5000m, 10000m: 1991- 13:46.84, 1993- 13:31.18, 1994- 13:37.60, 1995- 13:13.55, 1996- 13:11.05, 1997- 13:07.34, 1998- 13:21.95, 27:49.71; 1999- 13:25.44, 27:52.54; 2000- 13:15.75, 27:59.80. pbs: 800m 1:51.0 '87, 1500m 3:38.43 '91, 2000m 5:02.1 '97, 3000m 7:32.32 '97.

Antonio PEÑA b. 26 Aug 1970 Felanitx, Mallorca 1.75m 60kg. Hermes Logist.
At Mar: WCh: '99- dnf; EC: '94- 32, '98- 6. Spanish champion 1997. World HMar: '92- 13.
Progression at Mar: 1992- 2:11:35, 1993- 2:13:06, 1994- 2:17:19, 1995- 2:13:39, 1997- 2:10:49dh, 1998- 2:13:53, 2000- 2:07:47, 2001- 2:07:34. pbs: 5000m 13:52.72 '92, 10000m 28:02.1 '00, HMar 61:48 '92.
Won at Lake Biwa 2001 for his third win in 12 marathons; 5th Rotterdam and 2nd Berlin 2000.

Fabián RONCERO b. 19 Oct 1970 Madrid 1.71m 58kg. Nike.
At Mar: WCh: '97- 6, '99- dnf. World CC: '98- 10. Won Spanish HMar 199, CC 2001.
Spanish records 10000m 1998, Mar 1998 & 1999.

Progression at 10000m, Mar: 1991- 30:35.40, 1992- 29:59.55, 1993- 29:26.10, 1995- 28:38.2, 2:14:36; 1996- 28:47.87, 2:09:43; 1997- 28:21.38, 2:16:53; 1998- 27:14.44, 2:07:26; 1999- 27:58.02, 2:07:23. pbs: 3000m 7:41.48 '00, 5000m 13:28.10 '99, HMar 61:12 '00.
Two wins in six marathons: Carpi 1996 and Rotterdam 1998, the latter in a Spanish record just two weeks after taking over a minute off his best with a Spanish record to win the European Challenge 10,000m. He improved his marathon record by 3 secs when 2nd in Rotterdam 1999.

Women

Marta DOMÍNGUEZ b. 3 Nov 1975 Palencia 1.63m 52kg. Nike International.
At 5000m: OG: '00- h; WCh: '99- 9; EC: '98- 3; EU23: '97- 3 (1500m 5). At 3000m: WI: '95- 6, '97- 5; WI: '01- 4; EI: '96- 3, '98- 3, '00- 3; ECp: '96- 3. At 1500m: OG: '96- h; WCh: '95- sf; WJ: '94- 2; EJ: '93- 1. World 4k CC: '00- 14. Won Spanish 1500m 1996, 5000m 1998-2000.
Spanish record 3000m 2000.
Progression at 3000m, 5000m: 1990- 10:15.0, 1991- 9:47.03, 1993- 9:35.16, 1994- 9:24.10, 1995- 9:01.79i, 1996- 8:53.34i/9:06.27, 1997- 8:52.74i/ 9:01.96, 15:41.91; 1998- 8:44.10, 14:59.49; 1999- 8:46.14, 15:16.93; 2000- 8:28.80, 15:26.00; 2001- 8:40.98i. pbs: 800m 2:06.1 '95, 1000m 2:50.1 '91, 1500m 4:06.08 '00, 2000m 5:49.55i '98.

Niurka MONTALVO b. 4 Jun 1968 La Habana, Cuba 1.72m 57kg. CA Linense.
At TJ (LJ): OG: '96- (dnq 18); WCh: '93- 4, '95- dnq (2), '99- (1); WI: '91- (5), '95- 6, '01- 3; PAm: '91- (10), '95- 2 (1); WUG: '93- 1; WCp: '94- 5 (2); CAG: '93- 1 (1). 3rd GP LJ 2000. Won CAC LJ 1987, 1990, 1993; TJ 1993, Cuban LJ 1988, 1990, 1993-5, TJ 1993-4; Spanish LJ 1999-2000, TJ 1999.
Cuban records: LJ (3) 1990-3 (and two unrecognised 1998), TJ (6, also CAC) 1992-4; Spanish LJ (4) 1999.
Progression at LJ, TJ: 1984- 5.83, 1985- 6.18, 1986- 6.29, 1987- 6.32/6.52w, 1988- 6.62, 1989- 6.53, 1990- 6.87, 1991- 6.69, 12.51; 1992- 6.88, 13.92; 1993- 6.64/6.75w, 14.51; 1994- 6.71/6.78w, 14.60; 1995- 6.89, 14.31; 1996- 6.62, 13.68; 1997- 6.72/6.73w, 13.96; 1998- 6.93, 1999- 7.06, 13.93/ 14.17w; 2000- 6.87/6.95w, 13.20/13.86w. pb 100mh 13.57 '90.
Married a Spaniard on 26 Jan 1998, and became a Spanish citizen on 5 May 1999. Just over three months later she won the first gold medal for Spain at the 1999 World Champs in Seville, moving from 2nd at 6.88 to a Spanish record 7.06 to win in the final round. The Cuban Federation did not recognise would-be Cuban records 6.92 and 6.93 in 1998, due to her defection, and did not allow her to compete for Spain at the 2000 OG.

María VASCO b. 26 Dec 1975 Barcelona 1.56m 47kg. Integra 2.
At 20kmW: OG: '00- 3; WCh: '99- 10; WCp: '99- 23. At 10kmW: OG: '96- 28; WCh: '95- 26; EC: '98- 5; EU23: '97- 2; WCp '95- 26, '97- 22. At 5000mW: WJ: '90- 15, '92- 6, '94- 4; EJ: '93- 4. Won Spanish 10kmW 1996, 10000mW (t) 1997-9, 20kmW 1998 and 2000.
Spanish records 5000m 1997, 10,000m track 1997 and 1998, 10km 1998, 20km (3) 1998-2001.
Progression at 10kmW, 20kmW: 1993- 47:11, 1994- 47:05, 1995- 44:53, 1996- 44:51.60t, 1997- 43:54, 1998- 43:02, 1:34:11; 1999- 43:35, 1:32:38; 2000- 43:33.92t, 1:30:20; 2001- 1:30:09. pb 5000mW 21:36.22 '97, 21:26R '98.

SRI LANKA

Governing body: Amateur Athletic Association of Sri Lanka, 7 Upper Grand Stand, Reid Avenue, Colombo 7. Founded 1922. **National Champions 2000**: **Men:** 100m: Chintake De Zoysa 10.54, 200m: Manura Perera Kuranage 21.59, 400m: Rohan Pradeep Kumara 45.25, 800m: Vajira Kularatne 1:50.17, 1500m: Sunil Jayaweera 3:48.15, 5000m/10000m: A Indrijath Cooray 14:24.80,/30:37.53, 110mh: Inndika Kumara 14.74, 400mh: Harijan Ratnayake 50.11, HJ: Arosha Rangana Pigeira 2.10, LJ: Sujith Rohitha 7.65, TJ: Nelan Siriwardana 15.35, JT: Pradeep Nishantha 64.69. **Women**: 100m/100mh: Sriyani Kulawansa-Fonseka 11.92/13.27, 200m: Nimmi De Zoysa 24.73, 400m: Damayanthi Dharsha 52.12, 800m: Mangala Priyadharshani 2:08.57, 1500m: Keshani Samarakoon 4:38.25, 5000m/ 10000m: Nilmini Jayasena 17:42.21/36:27.84, 400mh: S V A Kusumawathi 61.96, LJ/TJ: Anusha Ekanaliyagoda Kariyawasam 6.17/12.86, JT: Anne Maheshi De Silva 51.69.

Sugath TILLAKARATNE b. 30 Jul 1973 1.70m 57kg.
At 400m: OG: '96/00- qf; WCh: '97/99- qf; CG: '98- 3; AsiG: '98- 1 (200m 3); AsiC: '95- 3, '98- 1; WCp: '98- 6.
SRI records: 400m (6) 1995-8, 200m (3) 1998.
Progression at 400m: 1993- 46.58, 1994- 46.45, 1995- 46.12, 1996- 45.78, 1997- 45.58, 1998- 44.61, 1999- 44.84, 2000- 45.31. pb 200m 20.69 '98.

Women

Susanthika JAYASINGHE b. 17 Dec 1975 1.70m 62kg. Married Dhammika Nandakumara 1994.
At 200m (/100m): OG: '96- (qf); , '00- sf/3; WCh: '95- h/qf, '97- 2, '99- (qf); WI: '01- 4; AsiG: '94- 2; AsiC: '95- 1/2; Won Asi-J 200m 1994.
Two Asian 200m records 1997, SRI records: 100m (4) 1995-2000, 200m (6) 1993-2000. Asian indoor 60m record 1999.
Progression at 100m, 200m: 1992- 12.36, 25.67; 1993- 12.17, 24.56; 1994- 11.49, 23.16; 1995- 11.30, 22.95; 1996- 11.18, 23.18; 1997- 11.25+/11.38, 22.33; 1998- 11.27, 23.28; 1999- 11.17, 22.74; 2000- 11.04, 22.29. pb 60m 7.09i '99.
Suspended after random doping test in April 1998, but cleared by Sri Lankan AAA; she claimed she was the victim of a conspiracy.

SURINAM

Governing body: Surinaamse Athletiek Bond, PO Box 1758, Paramaribo. Founded 1955.

Letitia Alma **VRIESDE** b. 5 Oct 1964 Paramaribo 1.59m 55kg. AVR, Netherlands.
At 800m (/1500m): OG: '88- sf/h, '92- sf/sf, '96- sf, '00- h; WCh: '91- 5/9, '95- 2, '97- 4, '99- sf; WI: '95- 3, '97- 4; PAm: '91- 4/2, '95- 3/4, '99- 1; CAG '90- 2/1, '93- 1/1, '98- 1; WCp: '98- 3. 3rd GP 1997. South American records 1990-5: 800m (6), 1000m (3) 1500m (2); indoors 1992-5: 800m (3), 1000m, 1500m, 3000m. SUR records 400m 1990-7, 3000m 1990-1.
Progression at 800m, 1500m: 1981- 5:25.41, 1982- 2:41.6, 5:24.0; 1983- 2:25.4, 5:11.3; 1984- 2:22.2, 5:19.1; 1986- 2:14.6, 4:34.01; 1987- 2:08.37, 4:36.86; 1988- 2:01.83, 4:16.29; 1989- 2:03.44, 4:24.64; 1990- 1:59.79, 4:11.88; 1991- 1:58.25, 4:05.67; 1992- 1:57.96, 4:08.82; 1993- 2:00.30, 1994- 2:01.53i/ 2:02.94, 1995- 1:56.68, 1996- 1:57.09, 1997- 1:57.86, 1998- 1:58.16, 1999- 1:58.99, 4:18.84; 2000- 1:58.62. pbs: 200m 24.41w '95, 400m 52.01 '97, 1000m 2:32.25 '91, 1M 4:30.45 '92, 3000m 9:07.08i '93, 9:15.64 '91.
The military administration in Surinam rejected her nomination for the 1984 Olympic Games, and did not grant funds to enable her to participate. She felt humiliated by that and went to the Netherlands, returning to athletics two years later. In 1995 she became the first South American female athlete to win medals in the indoor and outdoor World Championships.

SWEDEN

Governing body: Svenska Friidrottsförbundet, Box 11, 171 18 Solna. Founded 1895.
National Championships first held in 1896 (men), 1927 (women). **2000 Champions**: **Men**: 100m: Torbjörn Mårtensson 10.65, 200m: Johan Engberg 20.83w, 400m: Jimisola Laursen 45.68, 800m: Rizak Dirshe 1:48.23, 1500m: Patrik Johansson 3:44.75, 5000m: Erik Sjöqvist 14:34.03, 10000m: Claes Nyberg 29:41.09, HMar/Mar: Alfred Shemweta 64:48/2:18:49, 3000mSt: Henrik Skoog 8:48.47, 110mh: Robert Kronberg 13.62, 400mh: Mikael Jakobsson 50.85, HJ: Stefan Holm 2.29, PV: Martin Eriksson 5.62, LJ: Peter Häggström 8.01, TJ: Christian Olsson 16.97, SP: Jimmy Nordin 20.07, DT: Mattias Borrman 57.53, HT: Bengt Johansson 73.11, JT: Mikael Snällfot 75.10, Dec: Christer Holger 7836, 10000mW: Bo Gustafsson 42:38.6, 20000mW: Bengt Bengtsson 1:27:21.8, 50kmW: Fredrik Svensson 4:05:48. **Women**: 100m/200m: Annika Amundin 11.73/23.62, 400m: Andrea Geurtsen 54.84, 800m: Monica Lundgren 2:06.48, 1500m: Kristin Ahlepil 4:26.55, 5000m/10000m/HMar/Mar: Marie Söderström-Lundberg 16:25.95/33:36.80/74:39/2:37:57, 100mh: Susanna Kallur 13.43, 400mh: Frida Svensson 57.68, HJ: Kajsa Bergqvist 2.01, PV: Malin Ericsson 3.85, LJ: Jessica Larsson 6.25, TJ: Camilla Johansson 14.14, SP: Linda-Marie Mårtensson 16.79, DT: Anna Söderberg 60.22, HT: Cecilia Nilsson 61.87, JT: Elisabet Wahlander 53.02, Hep: Maria Richtnér 5620, 5000mW: Siw Vera-Ibanez 23:52.6, 10000mW/20kmW: Monika Svensson 49:51.5/1:40:30.

Patrik BODÉN b. 30 Jun 1967 Fryksände 1.87m 107kg. IF Göta. Studied engineering at University of Texas.
At JT: OG: '92- dnq 16, '00- dnq 23; WCh: '91- 8, '93- 8, '95- dnq 15, '97- 12, '99- dnq 24; EC: '90- 3, '94- 4, '98- 12; WJ: '86- 8; WCp: '94- 4; ECp: '94-6-00: 4/4/4. 3rd GP 1997. Swedish champion 1992-5, 1997-9; won NCAA 1989-91.
World javelin record 1990.
Progression at JT: 1983- 58.14, 1984- 63.58, 1985- 74.26; new: 1986- 74.66, 1987- 78.10, 1988- 76.52, 1989- 82.28, 1990- 89.10, 1991- 85.58R/79.82, 1992- 84.20, 1993- 88.26, 1994- 86.76, 1995- 83.10, 1996- 83.52, 1997- 86.98, 1998- 85.15, 1999- 84.52, 2000- 85.16. pbs: SP 15.76 '93, DT 49.28 '89, HT 53.44 '92.
Was 4th at LJ in National age 12 championships in 1979. Beset by injuries, with numerous operations on knees, elbow, feet and shoulder.

Stefan HOLM b. 25 May 1976 Forshaga 1.81m 69kg. Kils AIK.
At HJ: OG: '00- 4; WCh: '99- 10=; EC: '98- 7; WJ: '94- 7=; EJ: '93- 11, '95- 6; WI: '97- 8=, 99- 6=, '01- 1; EI: '00- 4; WUG: '99- 4; ECp: '00- 1. Swedish champion 1998-2000.
Progression at HJ: 1987- 1.40, 1988- 1.51, 1989- 1.61, 1990- 1.83, 1991- 1.94, 1992- 2.09i/2.06, 1993- 2.14, 1994- 2.18, 1995- 2.21, 1996- 2.26, 1997- 2.30i/2.22, 1998- 2.33, 1999- 2.32, 2000- 2.34, 2001- 2.34i. pbs: 100m 11.42 '99, 110mh 16.23 '99, LJ 7.18 '99; TJ 12.35i '91.
One of the smallest top high jumpers.

Robert KRONBERG b. 15 Aug 1976 Göteborg 1.82m 80kg. IF Kville.
At 110mh: OG: '00- 8; WCh: '97/99- qf; WJ: '94- sf; EJ: '95- 2; ECp: '00- 3. At 60mh: WI: '01- 4; EI: '00- 6. Won Swedish 110mh 1997-2000.
Two Swedish 110mh records 2000.
Progression at 110mh: 1993- 15.09, 1994- 14.21, 1995- 14.06, 1996- 13.97, 1997- 13.63, 1998- 13.61, 1999- 13.58, 2000- 13.36. pbs: 100m 10.73 '98, 200m 22.31 '98, 50mh 6.46i '01, 60mh 7.54i '01, HJ 1.90 '95, LJ 7.52 '97, TJ 14.23 '94.

Staffan STRAND b. 18 Apr 1976 Upplands-Väsby 1.88m 74kg. Hässelby SK. Was at University of Minnesota, USA.
At HJ: OG: '00- 6=; WCh: '97- dnq, '99- 5; EC: '98- 8; EU23: '97- 1; EJ: '95- 5; WI: '99- 5, '01- 3. Won Swedish 1995-7.
Progression at HJ: 1987- 1.45i, 1988- 1.60i, 1989- 1.65i, 1990- 1.70, 1991- 1.71, 1992- 1.80, 1993- 1.91i/1.88, 1994- 2.11, 1995- 2.22, 1996- 2.27, 1997- 2.28, 1998- 2.31, 1999- 2.30, 2000- 2.32,

2001- 2.34i. pbs: PV 3.40 '95, LJ 6.90 '96, TJ 15.16 '96, 15.23w '00; Dec 5022 '95.

Women

Kajsa BERGQVIST b. 12 Oct 1976 Sollentuna 1.75m 59kg. Turebergs FK. Was at Southern Methodist University, USA.
At HJ: OG: '96- dnq 14, '00- 3=; WCh: '95- dnq 17=, 97- 5=, '99- 4=; EC: '98- dnq 14; WJ: '94- 2; EU23: '97- 2; EJ: '93- 8, '95- 2; WI: '97- 8, '01- 1; EI: '00- 1. Swedish champion 1997-2000, NCAA 1997, 1999.
Six Swedish high jump records 1997-2000.
Progression at HJ: 1988- 1.38, 1989- 1.56, 1990- 1.61i/1.56, 1991- 1.61, 1992- 1.77, 1993- 1.84, 1994- 1.90, 1995- 1.92i/1.90, 1996- 1.93, 1997- 1.95, 1998- 1.93, 1999- 1.98A, 2000- 2.01, 2001- 2.00i. pbs: 100mh 14.98/14.8w '94, LJ 5.73 '95, TJ 11.74 '98, SP 11.95 '96, JT 36.60 '99, Hep 4952 '94.

Erica JOHANSSON b. 5 Feb 1974 Mölndal 1.78m 69kg. Mölndals AIK.
At LJ: OG: '00- dnq 17; WCh: '97- 8, '99- 10; EC: '94- dnq 22, '98- 5; WJ: '90-2; '92- 1; EJ: '89- 2, '91- 4, '93- 1; WI: '93- 6, '99- 9; EI: '00- 1. Won SWE LJ 1990-3, 1996-9; 100mh 1999.
Ten Swedish records 1989-99.
Progression at LJ: 1988- 5.71, 1989- 6.50, 1990- 6.56i/6.53, 1991- 6.55i/6.52, 1992- 6.72, 1993- 6.78i/6.56, 1994- 6.17/6.39w, 1995- 6.21/6.50w, 1996- 6.71, 1997- 6.64/6.66w, 1998- 6.85, 1999- 6.92/6.95w, 2000- 6.99/7.07Aw. pbs: 60m 7.63i '99, 100m 11.82 '99, 200m 23.75 '97, 800m 2:21.95 '89, 60mh 8.93i '97, 100mh 13.63 '98, HJ 1.78 '89, TJ 13.95/14.32w '99.
Foot injury caused her to miss much of the 1993 season, yet she still won the European Junior title after eight weeks out of competition. At the 1989 European Juniors, aged 15, she improved from 6.25 to 6.50 to take the silver medal and equal the Swedish senior record. On her competitive debut at triple jump – in the match against Finland in 1999 – she won at 14.32w, and also set a national record 13.95.

Anna SÖDERBERG b. 11 Jun 1973 Örebro 1.77m 82kg. Ullevi FK, Was at Northern Arizona University, USA.
At DT: OG: '00- dnq 24; WCh: '97- 11, '99- dnq 18; EC: '98- dnq; WJ: '92- dnq. Won SWE DT 1993-2000, HT 1996-7.
10 SWE discus records 1994-9, 10 hammer 1995-7.
Progression at DT: 1986- 28.62, 1987- 35.50, 1988- 41.52, 1989- 46.44, 1990- 45.06, 1991- 48.80, 1992- 52.88, 1993- 52.24, 1994- 58.74, 1995- 56.84, 1996- 59.96, 1997- 61.30, 1998- 64.00, 1999- 64.54, 2000- 62.91. pbs: HJ 1.67 '94, SP: 16.30 '99, HT 59.45 '99.

SWITZERLAND

Governing body: Schweizerischer Leichtathletikverband (SLV), Postfach 8222, CH 3001, Bern. Formed 1905 as Athletischer Ausschuss des Schweizerischen Fussball-Verbandes.
National Championships first held in 1906 (men), 1934 (women). **2000 Champions**: **Men**: 100m: Daniel Dubois 10.26w, 200m: Patric Clerc 21.12, 400m: Laurent Clerc 46.14, 800m: Ramon Wächter 1:51.34, 1500m: Philippe Bandi 3:49.12, 5000m: Mehdi Khelifi TUN 14:18.99, 10000m: Oliver Amann 29:50.28, HMar: Van Orlandi 66:42, Mar: Bruno Heuberger 2:21:15, 3000mSt: Markus Hagmann 9:13.60, 110mh: Raphaël Monachon 13.61, 400mh: Marcel Schelbert 50.78, HJ: Martin Stauffer 2.20, PV: Michel Gigandet 5.30, LJ: Daniel Hagspiel 7.50, TJ: Ruben Kiefer 15.21, SP: Marc Sandmeier 18.00, DT: Stanislav Kovar CZE 54.17, HT: Patric Suter 69.99, JT: Terry McHugh IRL 81.22, Dec: Adrian Krebs 7694, 10000mW: Yann Banderet 47:18.96, 20kmW: Pascal Charrière 1:30:32; 50kmW: Raymond Buffet 4:19:48. **Women**: 100m: Martina Feusi 11.67w, 200m: Mireille Donders 23.06, 400m: Anita Brägger 54.41, 800m: Christa Salt GBR 2:06.84, 1500m: Sabine Fischer 4:08.72, 5000m: Tanja Fischer 16:37.94, 10000m: Chantal Dällenbach 34:52.37, HMar: Sonja Knoepfli 75:02, Mar: Elisabeth Krieg 2:45:26, 100mh: Monica Pelegrinelli 13.28, 400mh: Nathalie Zamboni 56.89, HJ: Sylvie Dufour 1.74, PV: Nadine Rohr 3.70, LJ: Emmanuelle Devaud 5.80, TJ: Dejana Cachot 13.18, SP: Denise Keller 13.46, DT: Valérie Glayre 45.83. HT: Laurence Locatelli 51.98, JT: Alma von Planta 45.04, Hep: Manuela Kobelt 5541, 20mW Marie Polli 1:44:36.

André BUCHER b. 19 Oct 1976 Neudorf 1.85m 75kg. LR Beromünster. History graduate of Bern University. Teacher.
At 800m: OG: '96- sf, '00- 5; WCh: '97- sf, '99- sf; EC: '98- 2; EU23: '97- 2; EJ: '95- 2; WI: '01- 3; WUG: '99- 2. At 1500m: WJ: '94- 2. Won Swiss 800m 1995, 1997-9, 1500m 1994, 1996.
Swiss records 800m (3) 1998-9, 1000m 1999.
Progression at 800m: 1993- 1:56.40, 1994- 1:48.32, 1995- 1:45.71, 1996- 1:46.41, 1997- 1:45.33, 1998- 1:44.96, 1999- 1:42.92, 2000- 1:43.12. pbs: 400m 46.32 '00, 600m 1:14.72 (European best) '99, 1000m 2:15.66 '99, 1500m 3:38.44 '96, 3000m 8:16.9 '98, 5000m 14:06.77 '98, 10000m 30:40.5 '95, 3000mSt 9:09.73 '95.

Marcel SCHELBERT b. 26 Feb 1976 1.91m 83kg. LC Zürich. Economics student.
At 400mh: OG: '96- h; WCh: '97- hR, '99- 3; WJ: '94- sf; EJ: '95- 2; EU23: '97- 2; WUG: '99- 3. Won Swiss 400mh 1996-7, 1999-2000.
Six Swiss 400mh records 1997-9.
Progression at 400mh: 1992- 56.96, 1993- 53.36, 1994- 51.45, 1995- 50.44, 1996- 50.11, 1997- 49.33, 1998- 50.16, 1999- 48.13, 2000- 49.49. pbs: 200m 21.73 '95, 3000m 33.57 '97, 400m 46.05 '97, 60mh 8.15i '97, 110mh 14.14 '97.

Women

Anita WEYERMANN b. 8 Dec 1977 1.62m 50kg. GG Bern. Student.
At 5000m: OG: '96- 14. At 1500m: OG: '00- sf; WCh: '97- 3, '99- 12; EC: '98- 3; WJ: '94- 1, '96- 7. At 3000m: WJ: '96- 1; EJ: '95- 2. World CC 4k: '98- 4; Eur CC: '99- 1. 2nd GP 1500m 1999. Won Swiss 1500m 1996, CC 1995-8, 2000; 4k CC 1999-2000.
European junior records 1500m and 5000m 1996. Swiss records: 1500m & 1M 1998, 3000m 1997 & 1999, 5000m 1996.
Progression at 1500m, 3000m, 5000m: 1993- 4:28.37, 10:08.62; 1994- 4:13.97, 9:19.25; 1995- 4:15.53, 9:10.89, 16:01.72; 1996- 4:03.45, 8:50.73, 14:59.28; 1997- 4:04.70, 8:37.69, 15:06.97; 1998- 3:58.20, 8:54.97, 15:26.41; 1999- 3:59.82, 8:35.83, 15:41.91; 2000- 4:05.38. pbs: 400m 58.50 '93, 800m 2:02.73 '98, 1000m 2:39.44 '00, 1M 4:23.92 '98.
Skis downhill and slalom for regional team.

TANZANIA

Governing body: Tanzania Amateur Athletic Association, PO Box 2172, Dar es Salaam. Founded 1954.

Faustin BAHA Sulle b. 30 May 1982.
At World HMar: '99- 15, '00- 2; CC: '00- 6J.
World Junior and Tanzanian half marathon record 2000.
pbs: road: 10km 27:43 '00, HMar 59:38 '00.

TRINIDAD & TOBAGO

Governing body: National Amateur Athletic Association of Trinidad & Tobago, PO Box 605, Port of Spain, Trinidad. Founded 1945, reformed 1971.
2000 National Champions: **Men**: 100m: Niconnor Alexander 10.0, 200m/400m: Julien Raeburn 20.63/45.67, 800m: Sheridan Kirk 1:52.09, 1500m: Nigel Sinaswee 4:12.13, 5000m/10000m: Pamenos Ballantyne STV 14:40.62/31:13.0, 110mh: Kerl Chaihong 14.15, 400mh: Charles Gittens 50.38, HJ: Brent Romeo 2.00, PV: Kenneth Goodridge, LJ: Cleavon Dillon 7.38, TJ: Quincy Howe 15.54, SP: Dave Stoute 18.19, JT: Kurt Thompson 65.91. **Women**: 100m: Heather Samuel ANT 11.23, 200m: Ayanna Hutchinson 23.44, 400m/400mh: Romona Modeste 54.96/63.19, 800m/1500m: Janil Williams ANT 2:10.08/4:39.27, 100mh: Marsha Mark 14.23, HJ: Chanua Johnson 1.65, LJ: Onika James 16.05, TJ: Sheron Mark, SP/DT: Candice Scott 14.09/37.06, DT: Keron Modeste, JT: Geraldine George 47.27.

Ato BOLDON b. 30 Dec 1973 Port of Spain 1.76m 75kg. Studied engineering at San José City College and at UCLA, USA.
At 100m/200m: OG: '92- h/h, '96- 3/3, '00- 2/3; WCh: '93- qf/-, '95- 3/qf, '97- 5/1; WI: '97- dnf 200m; CG: '94- 4/sf, '98- 1/-; WJ: '92- 1/1. Won GWG 200m 1998, NCAA 200m 1995, 100m 1996; TRI 100m 1993-4, 200m 1992.
CAC records: 100m (9), 200m (3) 1996-9; TRI records: 100m (13) 1995-9, 200m (3) 1996-7.
Progression at 100m, 200m: 1990- 10.8, 21.3; 1991- 10.54/10.44w, 21.07; 1992- 10.22, 20.63/20.6; 1993- 10.23/10.0, 20.59; 1994- 10.07, 20.53; 1995- 10.03/10.01w, 20.08; 1996- 9.90, 19.80; 1997- 9.87, 19.77; 1998- 9.86, 19.88; 1999- 9.86, 19.86; 2000- 9.95, 19.97. pbs: 50m 5.58+ '97, 55m 6.04Ai '97, 60m 6.45+ '97.
Moved to Queens, New York at age 14 with his mother – and starred at soccer. In 1990 he went to live with an uncle in San José. Best ever one-day sprint double, 9.90 and 19.77 in Stuttgart 1997. Missed 1999 World Championships through injury, having had early season wins over Maurice Greene at both 100m and 200m, but made a big hit with his knowledgeable interviewing. Lives in Los Angeles.

TUNISIA

Governing body: Fédération Tunisienne d'Athlétisme, 6 rue Abdelmoumen Ben Ali, B.P. 264, Cité Mahrajane 1082, Tunis. Founded 1957.

Ali HAKIMI b. 24 Apr 1976 1.76m 55kg.
At 1500m: OG: '96- 8; WCh: '95- sf, '97- 5, '99- sf; WJ: '92- h, '94- 11; AfG: '95- 4, '99- 5; WI: '97- 6, '99- 6; Af-J: '94- 2. Won Pan Arab 800m 1995, 1999; 1500m 1999.
World junior 1000m record 1995. Tunisian records 1000m 1994, 1500m (5) 1996-7, 1M (2) 1996-7, 2000m 1996.
Progression at 1500m: 1992- 3:44.93, 1993- 3:44.5, 1994- 3:40.22, 1995- 3:35.97, 1996- 3:34.95, 1997- 3:31.70, 1998- 3:38.05, 1999- 3:33.00, 2000- 3:34.96. pbs: 800m 1:46.51 '96, 1000m 2:16.71 '99, 1M 3:50.57 '97, 2000m 4:54.54 '96, 3000m 7:59.12 '99.

TURKEY

Governing body: Türkiye Amator Atletizm Federasyonu, Ulus Ishani A Blok Kat 3, Ankara. Founded 1922. **National Champions 2000**: **Men**: 100m: Erol Mutlusoy 10.3, 200m: Gökhan Filiz 21.71, 400m: Volkan Karacali 47.53, 800m: Cevat Kücük 1:52.81, 1500m: Alibey Sükürov 3:51.47, 5000m/10000m: Abdülkadir Türk 14:25.52/ 29:52.44, 3000mSt: Bilal Yerlikaya 9:12.56, 110mh: Gürsel Özyurt 14.89w, 400mh: Yasar Yilmaz 53.7, HJ: Umut Toyer 1.99, PV: Bülent Erkaya 4.75, LJ: Mesut Yavas 7.73, TJ: Berk Tuna 15.66, SP: Ufuk Üstuna 14.96, DT: Ercüment Olgundeniz 57.51, HT: Fatih Eryildirim 65.81, JT: Gürbüz Cam 64.56, 10000mW: Abdülkadir Öz 44:51.55. **Women**: 100m: Aksel Gürcan 11.77, 200m: Züleyha Tokay 25.32, 400m: Fatma Ünal 58.16, 800m: Aybüke Kizilaslan 2:17.95, 1500m: Sebile Özyurt-Bekele 4:24.14, 3000m: Tezeta Sürekli-Desalegn 9:26.55, 5000m: Serap Aktas 16:42.23, 100mh: *not held*, 400mh: Fatma Ünal 62.35, HJ: Candeger Kilincer

1.72, LJ/TJ: Aysegül Baklaci 5.72w/13.28w, SP: Filiz Kadogan 14.35, DT: Ahu Sulak 49.36, HT: Zübeyde Yildiz 54.63, JT: Nazan Pehlivan 53.50, 5000mW: Yeliz Ay 23:45.00.

UKRAINE

Governing body: Ukrainian Athletic Federation, Esplanadnaya Str. 42, Kiev 23. Founded 1991.

National Champions 2000: **Men**: 100m: Konstantin Rurak 10.25, 200m: Sergey Polinkov 21.20, 400m: Aleksandr Kaydash 45.94, 800m: Anatoliy Yakimovich, 1500m: Ivan Geshko 3:38.48, 5000m: Sergey Lebed 13:27.53, 10000m: Yuriy Gychun 29:26.80, 3000mSt: Sergey Redko 8:29.63, 110mh: Denis Kozhemyakin 14.21, 400mh: Gennadiy Gorbenko 49.78, HJ: Andrey Sokolovskiy 2.28, PV: Denis Yurchenko 5.72, LJ: Aleksey Lukashevich 8.11, TJ: Sergey Izmailov 17.01, SP: Roman Virastyuk 20.55, DT: Kirill Chuprinin 61.89, HT: Vladislav Piskunov 80.88, JT: Oleg Statsenko 70.52, Dec: Fyodor Laukhin 8073, 20kmW: Aleksey Shelest 1:25:41. **Women**: 100m: Anzhela Kravchenko 11.35, 200m: Yelena Pastushenko 23.08, 400m: Yelena Rurak 51.73, 800m: Yelena Buzhenko 2:00.45, 1500m: Tatyana Krivobok 4:09.01, 5000m/10000m: Natalya Berkut 15:52.90/32:52.19, 3000mSt: Anzhelika Averkova 9:54.10, 100mh: Yelena Krasovskaya 12.82, 400mh: Tatyana Debelaya 55.79, HJ: Irina Mikhalchenko 1.98, PV: Anzhela Balakhonova 4.52, LJ: Yelena Shekhovtsova 6.86, TJ: Yelena Govorova 14.35, SP: Yelena Dementiy 16.95, DT: Yelena Antonova 66.38, HT: Irina Sekachova 61.73, JT: Nadezhda Kobrin 59.79, Hep: Lyudmila Blonskaya 6009, 20kmW: Vera Zozulya 1:31:26.

Yuriy BELONOG b. 9 Mar 1974 2.00m 125kg. Odessa Dyn.
At SP: OG: '00- 5; WCh: '97- 4, '99- 5; EC: '98- 3; WI: '95/7/9/01- 5/1/3/8; WJ: '92- 1; WUG: '95- 1, '97- 1; ECp: '96- 3. 2nd GP 1998, 2nd overall 2000. UKR shot record 2000.
Progression at SP: 1990- 15.60, 1991- 17.91, 1992- 19.02, 1993- 18.39, 1994- 18.72, 1995- 20.05, 1996- 21.20i/20.05, 1997- 21.02i/20.75, 1998- 20.92, 1999- 20.89i/20.65, 2000- 21.64. pb DT 65.32 '99. Mother-in-law Valentina Korsak: DT 63.92 '84.

Gennadiy GORBENKO b. 22 Sep 1975 1.87m 82kg.
At 400mh: OG: '00- 8; WCh: '95- h; WJ: '94- 1; WUG: '95- 4. UKR champion 1994-5, 2000.
Progression at 400mh: 1993- 53.48, 1994- 50.56, 1995- 48.92, 1996- 51.23, 1997- 51.28, 2000- 48.40. pb 400m 46.55 ' 95.

Sergey LEBED b. 15 Jul 1975 1.79m 63kg.
At 5000m: OG: '00- 7; WCh: '99- h; EC: '98- 13; WUG: '99- 1; EU23: '97- 7 (10000m 2). At 3000m: EI: '98- 5. World CC: '00- 8 (10 4k), '01- 2; Eur CC: '95-7-8-9-00: 11/3/1/7/2. Won UKR 1500m 1998, 5000m 1995-6, 1999-2000.
Progression at 5000m: 1993- 14:23.54, 1994- 14:11.27, 1995- 13:52.39, 1996- 13:39.31, 1997- 13:50.51, 1998- 13:30.23, 1999- 13:18.18, 2000- 13:27.53. pbs: 1500m 3:39.95 '98, 3000m 7:37.76 '99, 10000m 28:39.71 '97., 10km Rd 28:23 '99.

Aleksey LUKASHEVICH b. 11 Jan 1977 Dnepropetrovsk 1.75m 70kg.
At LJ: OG: '00- 4; WCh: '97- dnq 16, '99- dnq 22; EC: '98- dnq 20; WJ: '96- 1; EU23: '97- 3; EI: '98- 1, '00- 4; WUG: '99- 1. UKR champion 2000.
Progression at LJ: 1994- 7.68, 1995- 7.57, 1996- 7.91/8.10w, 1997- 7.95/8.09w, 1998- 8.06i/8.03, 1999- 8.16/8.17w, 2000- 8.27.

Vladislav PISKUNOV b. 7 Jun 1978 Novaya Kavhokva 1.83m 106kg.
At HT: OG: '00- dnq 14; WCh: '99- 3; EC: '98- 10; WJ: '94- dq; EU23: '99- 1; WUG: '99- 3. UKR champion 1998-2000.
Progression at HT: 1993- 68.96, 1994- 73.66, 1998- 78.66, 1999- 80.00, 2000- 81.56.
Used five turns when gaining 1999 World bronze medal. Threw the hammer 73.64 in June 1994 at 16 years 4 days, but a month later for disqualified for drugs use after winning (71.66) at the World Junior Championships. Returned to competition in 1998 after four-year ban.

Roman SHCHURENKO b. 14 Sep 1976 Nikipol 1.88m 82kg. University of PE, Kiev
At LJ: OG: '00- 3; WCh: '99- dnq 15; EJ: 95- 1; WUG: '99- 4. UKR champion 1998-9.
UKR Long jump record 2000.
Progression at LJ: 1993- 7.47, 1995- 7.85, 1996- 7.85, 1997- 7.98, 1998- 8.02, 1999- 8.30, 2000- 8.35.

Andrey SKVARUK b. 9 Mar 1967 Brodivski 1.86m 106kg. Rovno ZS.
At HT: OG: '96- 4, '00- 10; WCh: '93- nt, '97- 2, '99- 5; EC: '94- 1, '98- dnq 14; ECp: '93-4-00: 3/2/10. Won GP 2000. UKR champion 1992, 1994-6.
Progression at HT: 1985- 65.42, 1986- 72.54, 1989- 73.60, 1990- 77.24, 1991- 71.60, 1992- 80.22, 1993- 80.80, 1994- 81.72, 1995- 78.00, 1996- 80.52, 1997- 81.46, 1998- 78.96, 1999- 80.75, 2000- 81.43.

Andrey SOKOLOVSKIY b. 16 Jul 1978 Moskva, Russia 1.96m 76kg. Sports instructor.
At HJ: OG: '00- dnq 16=; WCh: '99- dnq 27=; WI: '99- 6=, '01- 2; U23: '99- 2. UKR champion 2000.
Progression at HJ: 1997- 2.10, 1998- 2.22, 1999- 2.32, 2000- 2.28, 2001- 2.35i.

Roman VIRASTYUK b. 20 Apr 1968 Ivano Frankovsk 1.89m 135kg. Ivano Frankovsk ZS.
At SP: OG: '96- , '00- dnq 20; WCh: '95- 7, '97- 6, '99- dnq 13; ECh: '94- 3; EI: '98- 5, '00- 5; ECp: '94- 2. UKR champion 2000.
Progression at SP: 1986- 16.69, 1987- 18.53, 1988- 18.47i/18.25, 1989- 19.62, 1990- 20.03, 1991- 20.04i, 1993- 19.48, 1994- 20.00, 1995- 20.71, 1996- 21.23, 1997- 20.66, 1998- 20.63i/20.37, 1999- 20.59, 2000- 21.34. Two-year drugs ban 1991.
Younger brother **Vasiliy** (b. 22 Apr 1974) has shot pb of 19.75 '00 (EC: '98- dnq 13).

Aleksandr YURKOV b. 21 Jul 1975 Prosyanaya 1.83m 84kg. Dnepropetrovsk Dyn. Sports instructor.
At Dec: OG: '00- 16; WJ: '94- dnf; EU23: '97-2, ECp: '00- 1. At Hep: WI: '01- 6.
Progression at Dec: 1994- 7161, 1995- 7617, 1996- 7676, 1997- 7888, 1998- 8034, 1999- 8215, 2000- 8574. pbs: 60m 6.94i '01, 100m 10.69 '00, 400m 48.66 '00, 1500m 4:32.49 '00, 60mh 8.13i '00, 110mh 14.56 '00, HJ 2.06 '99, PV 5.25i '01, 5.15 '00; LJ 7.93 '00, SP 15.35i '01, 15.26 '00; DT 50.44 '99, JT 59.52 '99, Hep 6160i '02.

Women

Olena (Yelena) ANTONOVA b. 16 Jun 1972 Nikipol 1.82m 95kg. Elektrometallurg Nikipol.
At DT: OG: '96- dnq 29, '00- dnq 13; WCh: '97- dnq 13, '99- 7; EC: '98- 11; EJ: '91- 3; WUG: '97- 4; ECp: '97-8-00: 3/3/6. UKR champion 1995-7, 1999-2000.
Progression at HJ: 1989- 55.84, 1990- 57.30, 1991- 57.12, 1992- 61.94, 1993- 58.34, 1994- 59.80, 1995- 61.54, 1996- 63.60, 1997- 61.62, 1998- 65.44, 1999- 64.32, 2000- 66.67. pb HT 54.82 '95.

Inha (Inga) **BABAKOVA** b. 27 Jun 1967 Ashkabad, Turkmenistan 1.80m 60kg. née Butkus.
At HJ: OG: '96- 3, '00- 5; WCh: '91/5/7/9/01- 3/3/2/1/2; EC: '94- 4; WI: '93- 3, '97- 2; ECp: '93- 4=. Won GP 1995, 1997; 2= 1999, 3rd 1991. UKR champion 1991-2.
Three UKR high jump records 1995.
Progression at HJ: 1987- 1.89, 1988- 1.92, 1989- 1.89i, 1991- 2.02, 1992- 2.00, 1993- 2.00i/1.96, 1994- 2.00, 1995- 2.05, 1996- 2.03, 1997- 2.02, 1999- 2.01, 2000- 2.00.
Born in Turkmenistan, Lithuanian by nationality and lives in Ukraine. Improved 10cm in 1991, with no previous international experience. After four World/Olympic silver and bronze medals, won gold at the 1999 Worlds. Coached by her husband Sergey Babakov, son Georgiy born June 1990. 13 competitions at 2.00 or higher in 1995 and 10 in 1996.

Anzhela BALAKHONOVA b. 18 Dec 1972 1.62m 55kg. Kiev Dyn.
At PV: OG: '00- nh (12=); WCh: '99- 2; EC: '98- 1; WI: '97- 9; EI: '98- 1; WUG: '97- 4=. UKR champion 1996-7, 1999.
PV Records: WIR and two European indoor 1998, 8 European 1997-2000, 17 UKR 1996-9.
Progression at PV: 1996- 3.98/4.05sq, 1997- 4.36/4.45ex, 1998- 4.45i/4.40, 1999- 4.55, 2000- 4.56. pbs: 100m 11.60/11.2 '95, 200m 23.63 '94, 23.4 '95; LJ 6.40 '96.
Started as a sprinter and rhythmic gymnast.

Olena (Yelena) GOVOROVA b. 18 Sep 1973 Izmail 1.75m 63kg. Odessa ZS.
At TJ: OG: '96- 9, '00- 3; WCh: '95- 10, '97- 3, '99- 7; EC: '98- 6; WJ: '92- 3; WI: '95- 7, '97- 7; EI: '00- 4; WUG: '97- 1, '99- 1; ECp: '96-8-00: 2/3/2. UKR champion 1997-2000.
Progression at TJ: 1990- 12.70, 1991- 13.19i/13.10, 1992- 13.43, 1993- 13.14i, 1994- 14.22, 1995- 14.08i/14.07, 1996- 14.60/14.75w, 1997- 14.67, 1998- 14.51/14.70w, 1999- 14.66/14.99w, 2000- 14.96. pb LJ 6.36 '98.

Viktoriya PALAMAR b. 12 Oct 1977 1.87m 64kg.
At HJ: OG: '00- 7; WJ: '96- 6=; WI: ' 01- 5=; EI: '00- 5.
Progression at HJ: 1992-, 1993- 1.83, 1994- 1.91, 1995- 1.88, 1996- 1.89, 1997- 1.88, 1998- 1.89, 1999- 1.93, 2000- 1.98.

Viktoriya PAVLYSH b. 15 Jan 1969 Kharkov 1.74m 85kg. Kharkov Dyn.
At SP: OG: '92- 8, '96- 4; WCh: '93- dnq, '95- 11, '97- 2; WI: '97- 1, '99- dq; EC: '94- 1, '98- 1; EI: '98- 2; EJ: '87- 6; WCp: '94- 4, '98- 1. 2nd GP 1997, 3rd 1993. UKR champion 1993, 1995-6.
Ukrainian shot record 1998.
Progression at SP: 1986- 15.73, 1987- 16.48, 1988- 16.28, 1989- 17.28, 1990- 17.86, 1991- 18.76, 1992- 19.66, 1993- 19.22, 1994- 19.61, 1995- 19.30, 1996- 19.79, 1997- 20.73, 1998- 21.69, 1999- 21.43idq.
Married Aristotle Mavridis on 22 Jul 1995. Her 21.69 to win the 1998 European title was the longest SP in the world for ten years, although she said afterwards that she had thrown 21.73 in a practice session in Kharkov. Disqualified and two-year drugs ban after 'winning' at 1999 World Indoors with 21.43. Returned to win European Throws Challenge SP in March 2001.

Zhanna PINTUSEVICH-BLOCK b. 6 Jul 1972 Nezhin, nr Chernigov 1.64m 62kg. née Tarnopolskaya. Kiev Dyn.
At 100m (/200m): OG: '96- 8/qf, '00- 5/8; WCh: '93- sf, '95- 5/h, '97- 2/1, '99- 4/qf; EC: '94- 2/2/4R, '98- 4/2; EJ: '91- 1/1/4R; WCp: '98- 4/3; ECp: '93- 3/4, '94- 1/1R. At 60m: WI: '93- 3; EI: '92- 1. Won UKR 100m 1994-5.
WIR 50m at 6.09 for a few minutes in 1993.
Ukrainian records: 100m (4) 1994-7, 200m 1997.
Progression at 100m, 200m: 1987- 11.8, 1988- 11.75/11.5, 23.75; 1989- 11.64/11.5, 24.03; 1990- 11.99, 1991- 11.29/11.0, 23.56; 1992- 11.17, 1993- 11.08, 22.79; 1994- 10.99, 22.66; 1995- 11.01, 22.71/22.64w; 1996- 11.07, 23.15; 1997- 10.85/10.6, 22.17A/22.32; 1998- 10.92/10.9A, 22.35A/22.46; 1999- 10.94, 22.42; 2000- 10.93, 22.66. pbs: 50m 6.03+ '97, 60m 6.97+ '97.
Married athletics agent Mark Block in 1999. Formerly married to Igor Pintsuvich (3rd WJ 110mh 1992).

Olena (Yelena) SHEKHOVTSOVA b. 31 May 1972 1.78m 58kg. Sports instructor. Kiev Dyn.
At LJ: OG '96- 5, '00- 12; WCh: '97- dnq 14, '99- dnq 24; EC: '98- dnq 16; WUG: '97- 1, '99- 1; ECp: '00- 2. Ukrainian champion 1996-7.
Progression at LJ: 1989- 6.43, 1991- 6.52, 1994- 6.36, 1995- 6.38i, 1996- 6.97, 1997- 6.88, 1998- 6.71i/6.64/6.73w, 1999- 6.92, 2000- 6.86. pb TJ 13.77 '97.

Tetyana TERESHCHUK b. 11 Oct 1969 1.85m 63kg. Lugansk Dyn.
At 400mh: OG: '96- sf, '00- 5; WCh: '95- 5, '97- 4, '99- 7; EC: '94- 6, '98- 2; WUG: '97- 1; ECp: '94-5-6-8-00: 2/3/4/1/1. 3rd GP 1997. UKR champion 1994, 1996, 1999.
Four UKR 400mh records 1997.
Progression at 400mh: 1989- 57.58, 1990- 57.98, 1991- 57.19, 1993- 58.20/57.9, 1994- 54.96, 1995- 54.88, 1996- 54.68, 1997- 53.64, 1998- 53.40, 1999- 53.46, 2000- 53.98., 2001- 53.89A. pbs: 200m 24.03 '97, 100mh 12.8 '95, 13.12A '98, 13.14 '97.
Set UKR 400mh records in four successive races in 12 days in 1997: World semi and final, then Zürich and Monaco.

UNITED KINGDOM

Governing body: UK Athletics, Athletics House, 10 Harborne Road, Edgbaston, Birmingham B15 3AA. Founded 1999 (replacing British Athletics, founded 1991, which succeeded BAAB, founded 1932). The Amateur Athletic Association was founded in 1880 and the Women's Amateur Athletic Association in 1922.
National Championships (first were English Championships 1863-79). **AAA Championships** first held 1880 (women 1922). **2000 Champions: Men**: 100m: Dwain Chambers 10.11, 200m Darren Campbell 20.49, 400m: Mark Richardson 45.55, 800m: James McIlroy 1:50.08, 1500m: John Mayock 3:45.29, 5000m/10000m: Andres Jones 13:45.86/28:00.50, HMar: Nick Wetheridge 64:09, Mar: Mark Hudspith 2:15:17, 3000mSt: Christian Stephenson 8:28.21, 110mh: Colin Jackson 13.54, 400mh: Chris Rawlinson 48.95, HJ: Ben Challenger 2.22, PV: Kevin Hughes 5.50, LJ: George Audu 7.89, TJ: Phillips Idowu 16.87, SP: Stephan Hayward 18.24, DT: Robert Weir 62.13, HT: Michael Jones 71.51, JT: Steve Backley 86.70, Dec: Alex Kruger 6975, 10000mW: Matthew Hales 43:12.85. **Women**: 100m: Marcia Richardson 11.41, 200m: Sarah Wilhelmy 23.39, 400m: Donna Fraser 50.94, 800m: Kelly Holmes 2:02.08, 1500m: Hayley Tullett 4:06.44, 5000m: Paula Radcliffe 15:05.48, 10000m: Birhan Dagne 32:30.4, HMar: Susan Reinsford 74:21, Mar: Jo Lodge 2:40:52, 100mh: Diane Allahgreen 13.24, 400mh: Keri Maddox 55.22, HJ: Jo Jennings-Steele 1.89, PV: Janine Whitlock 4.10, LJ: Joanne Wise 6.44, TJ: Michelle Griffith 13.67, SP: Judy Oakes 17.91, DT: Shelley Drew 59.03, HT: Lorraine Shaw 66.85, JT: Kelly Morgan 58.45, Hep: Julie Hollman 5560, 10000mW: Lisa Kehler 45:09.57.
Road Walk Champions: **Men**: 20kmW/50kmW: Darrell Stone 1:27:08/4:21:23 **Women**: 10km: Sharon Tonks 52:00, 20km: Lisa Kehler 1:39:28.

Onochie '**Larry**' **ACHIKE** b. 31 Jan 1975 Islington, London 1.88m 75kg. Shaftesbury Barnet.
At TJ: OG: '00- 5; WCh: '99- 11; EC: '98- dnq 21; CG: '98- 1; WJ: '92- 11, '94- 1; EJ: '93- 3; ECp: '00- 1. 3rd GP 2000.
Progression at TJ: 1989- 13.71, 1990- 14.18, 1991- 15.28, 1992- 15.97, 1993- 16.49, 1994- 16.53/16.67w, 1995- 15.91/15.94w, 1996- 16.36, 1997- 15.77, 1998- 17.10, 1999- 16.96, 2000- 17.30/17.31w. pbs: 100m 10.95 '94, 200m 21.68 '97, 21.6 '96; LJ 7.46 '93.
Over 17m for the first time in June 1998 with 17.07, improving to 17.10 for Commonwealth title. Lifetime best 17.31w to win the European Cup in 2000, and maintained that form with 17.30 (q) and 17.29 for fifth at the Olympics.

Stephen BACKLEY b. 12 Feb 1969 Sidcup 1.96m 100kg. Cambridge H.
At JT: OG: '92- 3, '96- 2, '00- 2; WCh: '91- dnq 15, '93- 4, '95- 2, '97- 2, '99- 8; EC: '90- 1, '94- 1, '98- 1; CG: '90- 1, '94- 1, '98- 2; WJ: '88- 2; EJ: '87- 1; WCp: '89- 1, '94- 1, '98- 1; ECp: '89-95-97: 1/3/1; WUG: '89- 1, '91- 1. Won GP 1989 (3rd overall), 3rd 1995, UK 1988-90, 1997; AAA 1989, 1992, 1998-2000.
Javelin records: Three world 1990-2, world junior 1988. Eight UK and Commonwealth 1989-92.
Progression at JT (old): 1985- 64.34, new: 1986- 64.98 (69.74), 1987- 78.16, 1988- 79.50, 1989- 85.90, 1990- 90.98, 1991- 91.36, 1992- 91.46, 1993- 85.10, 1994- 85.20, 1995- 88.54, 1996- 87.44, 1997- 89.02, 1998- 89.89, 1999- 87.59, 2000- 89.85.
The first British male thrower to set a world record: 89.58 in Stockholm with a Sandvik javelin, and 90.98 at Crystal Palace on his second throw with a Németh model, both 1990. When these were banned at the end of 1991 his 89.58 was reinstated as the world record and in New Zealand in 1992 he achieved the first 90m throw with the revised javelin specification. Won third successive European title in 1998, and just missed the same feat at the Commonwealth Games. In 2000 he became the first Briton in any athletics event to win an Olympic medal in three Games.

Jon BROWN b. 27 Feb 1971 Bridgend 1.75m 57kg. Sheffield. Studied journalism at Iowa State University, USA.
At Mar: OG: '00- 4. At 10000m: OG: '96- 10; WCh: '99- dnf; EC: '98- 4. At 5000m: WCh: '93- h; CG: '94- 4; WJ: '90- 13; WSG: '91- 4; EU23Cp: '92- 3. World CC: '96- 12, '97- 14; Eur CC: '95- 6, '96- 1, '99- 3. Won UK and AAA 5000m 1993.
Progression at 5000m, 10000m, Mar: 1988- 14:24.82, 1989- 14:23.38, 1990- 14:03.09, 29:21.9; 1991- 13:35.62, 28:38.36; 1992- 13:24.84, 28:19.6; 1993- 13:19.78, 1994- 13:23.96, 1995- 13:37.83, 28:08.31; 1996- 13:20.10, 27:59.72; 1997- 13:44.9, 27:27.47, 2:10:13; 1998- 13:19.03, 27:18.14, 2:11:10; 1999- 13:23.35, 2:09:44; 2000- 2:11:17. pbs: 800m 1:54.9 '93, 1500m 3:40.53 '92, 1M 4:06.2 '89, 3000m 7:45.41 '98. Rd 15km 42:39 '94, HMar 61:47 '97.
Lived in Germany for 15 months before moving to Vancouver, Canada in 1996, in which year he won the Gasparilla 15km in a UK best, then was first non-African in the World CC, and at the end of the year won the European CC. He was

the first non-African in the 2000 Olympic marathon.

Daniel CAINES b. 15 May 1979 Solihull 1.80m 72kg. Birchfield H. Law graduate of Swansea University.
At 400m/4x400mR: OG: '00- sf/6R; WJ: '98- 5R; WI: '01; EI: '00-6.
Progression at 400m: 1998- 47.13, 1999- 47.29i, 2000- 45.37, 2001- 45.75i. pbs: 60m 6.99i '98, 200m 21.11i '01, 21.26 '00; 300m 32.8i '01.
His mother, Blondelle Thompson, set a British record at 13.0 for 100mh in 1974 and his father Joe Caines was a British junior international in 1970-1 with a 400m best of 48.2 at age 19 in 1971.

Darren CAMPBELL b. 12 Sep 1973 Manchester 1.85m 86kg. Belgrave H.
At 100m/4x100mR (200m): OG: '96- ht R, '00- 6 (2); WCh: '97- sf/3R, '99- sf/2R; EC: '98- 1/1R; CG: '98- 5/1R; WJ: '92- 2/1R (2); EJ: '91- 1/2R (1); ECp: '96-8-9-00: 3R/1R/1R/1&1R; Won AAA 100m 1998, 200m 2000; GP 100m 2000.
Progression at 100m, 200m: 1988- 11.39, 23.2; 1989- 10.78w/11.0, 21.8/21.72w; 1990- 10.81, 21.51; 1991- 10.37/10.28w, 20.89/20.61w; 1992- 10.37, 20.87/20.68w; 1993- 10.39/10.29w, 20.86/20.69w; 1994- 10.54, 21.23i; 1995- 10.34, 1996- 10.17, 20.98; 1997- 10.13, 20.84; 1998- 10.04, 20.48; 1999- 10.12/10.11w, 21.05/20.51w; 2000- 10.06, 20.13. pbs: 50m 5.77i '99, 60m 6.60i '99, LJ 6.63w? '89.
After junior successes played football for two years 1993-5.

Dwain CHAMBERS b. 5 Apr 1978 London 1.80m 83kg. Belgrave H.
At 100m/4x100mR: OG: '00- 4; WCh: '97- resR, '99- 3/2R; EC: '98- 2/resR; CG: '98- sf/1R; WJ: '96- 5; EJ: '95- 1/1R, '97- 1/1R; WCp: '98- 3/1R; ECp: '99- 1. Won AAA 2000.
World junior 100m record 1997.
Progression at 100m: 1994- 10.75/10.56w, 1995- 10.41, 1996- 10.42, 1997- 10.06, 1998- 10.03rA/10.10, 1999- 9.97, 2000- 10.08. pbs: 50m 5.57+ '99, 60m 6.41+ '99, 200m 20.68 '99.
Older sister Christine Chambers (b. 4 Mar 1969) was 8th at 100m at 1987 European Juniors. pbs: 60m 7.46i '92, 100m 11.84 '87, 11.68w '92.

Jonathan EDWARDS b. 10 May 1966 London 1.82m 73kg. Gateshead. Physics graduate from Durham University.
At TJ: OG: '88- dnq 23, '92- dnq 35, '96- 2, '00- 1; WCh: '93- 3, '95- 1, '97- 2, '99- 3; EC: '94- 6, '98- 1; CG: '90- 2, '94- 2; WI: '93- 6, '01- 2; EI: '98- 1; WCp: '89- 3, '92- 1; ECp: '93-4-5-6-7-8-9: 2/4/1/1/1/1/2. Won GP 1996 (2nd overall), 2000; UK 1989, 1992; AAA 1989, 1994, 1998.
3 world and 7 British triple jump records 1995.
Progression at TJ: 1983- 13.84, 1984- 14.87/15.01w, 1985- 15.09, 1986- 16.05, 1987- 16.35, 1988- 16.74, 1989- 17.28, 1990- 16.51/16.93w, 1991- 17.43, 1992- 17.34, 1993- 17.44/17.70w, 1994- 17.39, 1995- 18.29/18.43w, 1996- 17.88, 1997- 17.74, 1998- 18.01, 1999- 17.52/17.71w, 2000- 17.71. pbs: 60m 6.73i '98, 100m 10.48 '96, 200m 22.2 '89, LJ 7.41/7.45w '92.
A committed Christian who previously refused to compete on Sundays, thus passing the 1991 World Championships, until 1993. He hit wondrous form in 1995, taking triple jumping into a new era, sailing well beyond 18m at the European Cup, with a wind just over the limit. His best of 18.43w was comprised: 6.50 hop, 5.60 step, 6.33 jump. After taking the world record with 17.98 at Salamanca, he achieved the unprecedented feat of world records on his first two jumps in the World final in Göteborg – 18.16 and 18.29, thus the first 18m and 60ft jumps with legal wind. His run of 22 successive victories was ended by Kenny Harrison at the 1996 Olympic Games. Had keyhole surgery on his left ankle at the end of the 1998 season, causing him to miss the Commonwealth Games. Although ranked number one in the world , he had to settle for silver and bronze at World Championships in 1997 and 1999, but returned to top the podium at the 2000 Olympics.

Jason GARDENER b. 18 Sep 1975 Bath 1.75m 70kg. Bath & Wessex.
At 100m/4x100mR: OG: '00- qf; WCh: '95- sf R, '99- 7/2R; CG: '98- res (1)R; WJ: '94- 2/1R; ECp: '95-7-9: 1R/3R/1R. At 60m: WI: '99- 3; EI: '98- 2, '00- 1. Won AAA 100m 1997, 1999.
Progression at 100m: 1992- 11.0, 1993- 10.62/10.46w, 1994- 10.25, 1995- 10.33, 1996- 10.5/10.41w, 1997- 10.31/10.17w, 1998- 10.30/10.17w/10.0w, 1999- 9.98, 2000- 10.09/10.04w. pbs: 50m 5.61i '00 (= European record), 60m 6.46i '99, 200m 20.65 '99.
Broke Linford Christie's European record for 60m with 6.46 for 3rd in World Indoors 1999, and outdoors became the third European to break 10 seconds for 100m.

Michael **'Mick' HILL** b. 22 Oct 1964 Leeds 1.90m 95kg. Leeds City. Athletics development officer for Leeds.
At JT: OG: '88- dnq 20, '92- 11, '96- 12, 00- 11; WCh: '87- 7, '91- 5, '93- 3, '95- 6, '97- 4, '99- dnq 14; EC: '86- 8, '90- 4, '94- 6, '98- 2; CG: '86- 2, '90- 2, '94- 2, '98- 3; EJ: '83- 11; WCp: '92- 5; ECp: '87-91-3-4-8-9: 4/5/2/3/4/4. Won UK 1985-7, 1992-3; AAA 1987, 1990-1, 1994-5. 2nd GP 1987, 3rd 1993.
UK and Commonwealth javelin record 1987.
Progression at JT: 1980- 56.32, 1981- 59.14, 1982- 64.72, 1983- 74.36, 1984- 71.08, 1985- 82.30, 1986- 82.04; new: 1986- 78.56, 1987- 85.24, 1988- 81.30, 1989- 82.56, 1990- 85.88, 1991- 86.32, 1992- 85.32, 1993- 86.94, 1994- 86.36, 1995- 84.14, 1996- 81.42, 1997- 86.54, 1998- 86.92, 1999- 84.94, 2000- 83.71.
Earned World bronze 1993 after disqualification of Dmitriy Polyunin. Operations on left knee in 1989 and March 1990. Missed only two finals in 18 major championships 1986-2000. A seven handicap golfer.

Phillips IDOWU b. 30 Dec 1978 Hackney, London 1.92m 87kg. Belgrave H.
At TJ: OG: '00- 6; EU23: '99-5; EJ: '97- 4. Won AAA 2000.
Progression at TJ: 1995- 13.90, 1996- 15.12/15.53w, 1997- 15.86/16.34w, 1998- 16.35, 1999- 16.41, 2000- 17.12. pb LJ 7.83 '00.

Colin JACKSON b. 18 Feb 1967 Cardiff 1.82m 73kg. Brecon.
At 110mh: OG: '88- 2, '92- 7, '96- 4, '00- 5; WCh: '87- 3, '91- sf, '93- 1/2 4x100mR, '97- 2, '99- 1; EC: '90- 1, '94- 1, '98- 1; CG: '86- 2, '90- 1, '94- 1; WJ: '86- 1; EJ: '85- 2; WCp: '89- 2, '92- 1; ECp: '87-9-91-3-6-7-8: 2/1/1/1/2/2/1 (3 100m). Won UK 1986, 1989-90, 1992; AAA 1986, 1988-90, 1992-3, 1996, 1998-2000; GWG 1994. Won GP 1993, 3rd 1989. At 60mh: WI: '87- 4, '89- 2, '93- 2, '97- 2, '99- 1; EI: '87- 2, '89- 1, '94- 1 (1 60m).
Records: World 110mh 1993, 60mh indoors 1994; 7 European 8 Commonwealth and 9 UK 110mh 1988-93; 9 UK, 4 Commonwealth & European 60mh to WIRs 7.36 & 7.30 '94. European indoor 50mh 1999. European junior 110mh 1986. World best 200mh 1991.
Progression at 110mh: 1984- 13.92, 1985- 13.69, 1986- 13.44/13.42w, 1987- 13.37, 1988- 13.11, 1989- 13.11/12.95w, 1990- 13.08/12.8w, 1991- 13.09, 1992- 13.04, 1993- 12.91, 1994- 12.98/ 12.94Aw, 1995- 13.17, 1996- 13.13, 1997- 13.05, 1998- 13.02, 1999- 13.04, 2000- 13.10. pbs: 60m 6.49i '94, 100m 10.29 '90, 200m 21.19/21.0 '88, 21.18w '89; 50mh 6.40i '99, 200mh 22.63 '91, HJ 1.81 '82, LJ 7.96w '86, 7.56 '85; JT 52.86 '84.
Ranked in the world top ten at 110mh each year 1986-2000, and top ranked each year 1992-4. He had a record 15 sub-13.20 times in 1992 although an injury held him back to 7th in the Olympics, and he had 13 sub-13.20 in 1993, when he set the world record to win his first World title, and in 1994, when he was undefeated. 44 successive hurdles victories 29 Aug 1993 to 9 Feb 1995 when Allen Johnson beat him at Madrid at 60mh, both running 7.42. Injury cost him the chance of medal at the 1986 Europeans, and he had operations on right knee 1990 and on left in 1991, after he had to withdraw from World semis following a warm-up accident. Unique double with European Indoor 60m/60mh 1994. After three silvers at last won World Indoor 60mh in 1999 and completed a double by regaining the world title at 110mh.

Mark LEWIS-FRANCIS b. 4 Sep 1982 1.83m 88kg. Birchfield H.
At 100m/4x100mR: WJ: '00- 1/1R; WY: '99- 1; EJ: '99- 2. At 60m: WI: '01- 3.
World junior record 60m indoors 2001.
Progression at 100m: 1996- 11.37/11.31w, 1997- 10.93, 1998- 10.49/10.36w, 1999- 10.31/10.26w, 2000- 10.10. pbs: 60m 6.51i '01, 200m 21.82 '99, 21.8 '98.
Improved his pb of 6.65 to successive British junior records of 6.61, 6.56 and 6.51 in 2001 World Indoor 60m.

Dean MACEY b. 12 Dec 1977 Rochford, Essex 1.96m 92kg. Harrow.
At Dec: OG: '00- 4; WCh: '99- 2; WJ: '96- 2; EU23: '97/99- dnf.
Progression at Dec: 1994- 5648, 1995- 6662, 1996- 7480, 1999- 8556, 2000- 8567. pbs: 100m 10.69/ 10.65w '99, 400m 46.41 '00, 1500m 4:23.45 '00, 110mh 14.35 '99, HJ 2.13 '95, PV 4.80 '00, LJ 7.77 '00, TJ 14.26/14.53w '94, SP 15.50 '99, DT 47.77 '99, JT 64.03 '99.
Dean's brilliant silver medal at the World championships, when he improved his best to 8556 points and set six individual event personal bests, came on his senior international debut for Britain! Earlier he had won at Arles with 8347, a huge improvement on his pb from his last completed decathlon, 7480 for 2nd at the 1996 World Juniors. He was heading for a similar score and a gold or silver medal when he fell in the 110mh at the European Under-23 championships after a first-day score of 4358 and 'legal' pbs at 100m and long jump. Despite only one competition (at which he did three events) pre-Sydney in 2000, he excelled to take fourth at the Olympics, setting pbs at LJ, 400m, PV and 1500m but held back in the throws by elbow problems.

Christian MALCOLM b. 3 Jun 1979 Cardiff 1.72m 66kg. Cardiff AAC.
At 200m/4x100mR (100m): OG: '00- 5; CG: '98- 2 (4 4x100m); WJ: '96- sf, '98- 1 (1); EJ: '97- 1/1R (2); EU23: '99- 2/1R (2=); WI: '01- 2; EI: '00- 1.
European Junior 200m record 1998.
Progression at 100m, 200m: 1993- 11.74, 1994- 10.88, 22.36/22.2; 1995- 10.85, 21.58/21.41w; 1996- 10.60/10.5, 21.27; 1997- 10.24, 20.83/20.48w; 1998- 10.12, 20.29; 1999- 10.22/10.20w, 20.47; 2000- 10.29, 20.19. pb 60m 6.64i '01, 6.65 '00.

John MAYOCK b. 26 Oct 1970 Barnsley 1.77m 66kg. Barnsley. Sports development officer.
At 1500m: OG: '96- 11, '00- 9; WCh: '95- sf, '97- 9, '99- sf; EC: '98- 5; CG: '94- 3, '98- 2; ECp: '97-8-9: 4/3/4. At 3000m: WI: '93- 6, '95- 5, '97- 6, '01- 4; EI: '92- 2, '98- 1, '00- 3. At 5000m: EJ: '89- 2; WUG: '91- 1; WCp: '92- 7; ECp: '94- 4. World CC: '89- 29J; Rd Rly team: '92- 3. Won AAA 1500m 1995-6, 1998-2000; UK 1997.
Progression at 1500m: 1987- 4:00.02, 1988- 3:48.46, 1989- 3:45.9, 1990- 3:48.05, 1991- 3:41.68, 1992- 3:37.76, 1993- 3:36.45, 1994- 3:37.20, 1995- 3:34.05, 1996- 3:33.38, 1997- 3:31.86, 1998- 3:32.82, 1999- 3:33.97, 2000- 3:34.69. pbs: 800m 1:47.8 '98, 1000m 2:18.48 '96, 1M 3:50.32 '96, 2000m 4:56.75 '99, 3000m 7:43.31i '97, 7:47.28 '95; 2M 8:32.54 '91, 5000m 13:26.97 '92.
Competed at 5000m at the 1991 World Student Games as a late replacement; took 5.39 off his pb in the heat and a further 22.16 secs off to win the gold medal. Showed similar ability to improve

his 3000m pb from 8:01.54 to 7:53.11 in his heat and 7:48.47 in the final to take the silver medal at the 1992 European Indoors.

Chris RAWLINSON b. 19 May 1972 Rotherham 1.85m 82kg. Belgrave H, Loughborough Univ.
At 400mh/4x400mR: OG: '00- sf; Worlds: '97- h; EC: '98- h; WUG: '97- (res 3R), '99- 5/2R; ECp: '97-0-00: 5/5/1&2R. Won AAA 1999-2000, UK 1997.
Progression at 400mh: 1992- 54.6, 1993- 52.9/53.62, 1994- 52.0/52.32, 1995- 50.90, 1996- 50.36, 1997- 49.69, 1998- 49.81, 1999- 48.14, 2000- 48.22. pbs: 200m 21.77 '97, 400m 47.18 '99, 60mh 8.17i '97, 110mh 14.2/14.25w '97, 300mh 34.59 '00, PV 4.40 '92, Dec 6291 '95 (6562u).
Fractured right ankle in 1999 and missed World Championships.

Mark RICHARDSON b. 26 Jul 1972 Slough 1.80m 74kg. Windsor, Slough & Eton AC. Sports science degree from Loughborough University.
At 400m/4x400mR: OG: '92- resR, '96- 2R; WCh: '91- resR, '95- 5/4R, '97- 4/2R, '99- 6; EC: '98- 3/1R; CG: '98- 2/2R; WJ: '88-4, '90- 3/2R; EJ: '89- h, '91- 2/1R (2 4x100mR); WCp: '92- 2/3R; ECp: '95-6-7-8-9: 1 & 1R/1R/1R/1 & 1R/1 & 1R. Won GP 1998, 2000; AAA 1995, 2000.
Progression at 400m: 1987- 50.8, 1988- 46.43, 1989- 47.13, 1990- 46.33, 1991- 45.53, 1992- 45.09, 1993- 45.94i/46.46, 1994- 46.11i, 1995- 44.81, 1996- 44.74, 1997- 44.47, 1998- 44.37, 1999- 44.47, 2000- 44.72. pbs: 100m 10.35 '98, 200m 20.62 '97, 20.6w '96; 300m 31.87 '98, 800m 1:55.9 '97.
Set a UK age-15 best for 400m of 47.57 in 1988, improving to 47.32 on his junior international debut, and then age-16 bests of 46.63 and 46.43 in the heats and semis of the World Juniors. Injuries cost him most of 1989, 1993-4 seasons. After gold and silver at the European Juniors he won relay medals as a reserve, running heats not finals: World gold 1991 and Olympic bronze 1992. At the 1996 Olympics his 43.62 for the 3rd leg in the final was the fastest split at the Games and the fastest ever run by a British runner. Tested marginally positive for nandrolene in February 2000; he vehemently denies knowingly taking any banned substance, and was cleared to compete but case pending with IAAF.

Iwan THOMAS b. 5 Jan 1974 Huntington, Cambridge 1.88m 80kg. Newham & Essex Beagles. Sports management student at West London Institute.
At 400m/4x400mR: OG: '96- 5/2R, '00- 6R; WCh: '97- 6/2R; EC: '98- 1/1R; CG: '94- sf/7R (qf 200m), '98- 1/3R; WJ: '92- 5R; WCp: '98- 1/2R; ECp: '95-7-8: 1R/1R/1R; EU23Cp: '94- 3R. 3rd GP 1998. Won AAA 1998.
Two British 400m records 1997.
Progression at 400m: 1992- 47.37, 1993- 47.94i/48.04, 1994- 45.98, 1995- 45.58, 1996- 44.66A/44.69, 1997- 44.36, 1998- 44.38, 2000- 45.82. pbs: 200m 20.87 '97, 300m 32.08+ '97.
Started athletics in 1992 after being ranked fourth in Europe at BMX cycle racing. Powered to three major titles in 1998. Missed 1999 season and struggled to return to form in 2000.

Women

Donna FRASER b. 7 Nov 1972 Shirley, Surrey 1.81m 70kg. Croydon H.
At 400m/4x400mR (200m): OG: '96- qf, '00- 4/6R; WCh: '97- 6R, '99- qf; EC: '98: 6/3R; CG: '98- 3/2R (3 4x100R); WJ: '90- 2 4x100R; EJ: '91- 1/5R (2 4x100R); EU23: '94- 5/5R; EI: '98- (5); ECp: '96-7-8-9-00: 7/2&3R/3R/7/2&3R (6). Won UK 1997, AAA 2000.
Progression at 400m: 1988- 55.03; 1989- 55.3, 1991- 52.54, 1992- 56.54, 1994- 53.44, 1995- 52.04, 1996- 51.58, 1997- 50.87, 1998- 50.85, 1999- 51.80, 2000- 49.79. pbs: 60m 7.46i '98, 100m 11.57 '00. 11.32w '97, 11.2wA '98; 200m 22.96i/22.90w '97, 23.08 '00; 300m 35.71 '00.
Confirmed a leap forward into top world class at the Sydney Olympics, where she reduced her pb from 50.85 to 50.77 in the quarter-final, 50.21 in the semi and 49.79 in the final of the 400m.

Ashia HANSEN b. 5 Dec 1971 Evansville, Indiana, USA 1.70m 63kg. Shaftesbury Barnet.
At TJ: OG: '96- 4, '00- 11; WCh: '95- dnq 21, '97- 5, '99- 12; EC: '94- dnq 15; CG: '98- 1; WI: '97- 2, '99- 1; EI: '98- 1; ECp: '95-6-7-9: 1/1/3/2. Won GP 1997, 1999; AAA 1996, UK 1997.
Records: 10 UK & Commonwealth triple jump 1994-7 and 1 unratified (no wind gauge) 1994. WIR 1998, 9 UK & Commonwealth indoor 1994-8.
Progression at TJ: 1990- 10.84, 1991- 12.68, 1992- 13.31, 1993- 13.48i/13.25/13.55w, 1994- 14.22, 1995- 14.66, 1996- 14.78, 1997- 15.15, 1998- 15.16i/14.32, 1999- 15.02i/14.96, 2000- 14.29. pbs: 60m 7.51i '98, 100m 11.7 '95, 11.95 '96, 11.81w '94; 200m 24.57i '95, 25.1 '92; LJ 6.47A '96.
Born in the USA, original name Ashia Nana Koramdina, she was adopted at three months by an English woman and her Ghanaian husband, They lived in Ghana for six years before settling in London. Injured heel at 1998 European Indoor Championships at which she set WIR – returned just in time to win Commonwealth Games gold, and was back in top form indoors in 1999.

Kelly HOLMES b. 19 Apr 1970 Pembury, Kent 1.64m 55kg. Middlesex Ladies.
At 1500m (800m): OG: '96- 11 (4), '00- 7 (3); WCh: '93- (sf), '95- 2 (3), '97- h, '99- (sf); EC: '94- 2; CG: '94- 1, '98- 2; WCp: '94- 3; ECp: '94- 2, '95- 1, '96- (2), '97- 1. 2nd GP 800m 1995. Won UK 800m 1993, 1995, 1997; AAA 800m 1993, 1995-6, 1999-2000; 1500m 1994, 1996.
Commonwealth 1500m record 1997. UK records 800m (2) 1995, 1000m 1995 & 1997.
Progression at 800m, 1500m: 1984- 2:15.1, 4:35.3; 1985- 2:13.1, 4:41.4; 1986- 2:11.0, 4:26.9; 1987-

2:09.45, 4:26.10; 1989- 2:12.1, 1991- 2:11.8, 1992- 2:03.94, 4:27.7; 1993- 1:58.64, 4:17.3; 1994- 1:59.43, 4:01.41; 1995- 1:56.21, 4:03.04; 1996- 1:57.84, 4:01.13; 1997- 1:57.14, 3:58.07; 1998- 4:06.10; 1999- 1:58.24, 4:04.58; 2000- 1:56.80, 4:05.35. pbs: 200m 25.29 '95, 400m 53.8 '96, 1000m 2:32.55 '97, 1M 4:28.04 '98, 3000m 9:08.7 '95, 10km Rd 34:54 '96.

The winner of the English Schools Junior 1500m in 1983, she hardly competed for four years after being a Junior International in 1987, and joining the Army at 18. Made a breakthrough to world class in 1993. Ran with a stress fracture of her left leg at the 1996 Olympics and was injured again at the 1997 Worlds when she had to drop out of her 1500m heat. Returned to gain 1998 Commonwealth silver and again in 2000 where she ran wondrously well at the Olympics after a very limited racing programme of just four competitions at 800m during the year. In 1997 she left the Army, for whom she had played at volleyball and been judo champion.

Denise LEWIS b. 27 Aug 1972 West Bromwich 1.73m 64kg. Birchfield H.

At Hep (LJ): OG: '96- 3 (dnq 24), '00- 1; WCh: '95- 7, '97- 2, '99- 2; EC: '94- (dnq 19), '98- 1; CG: '94- 1 (8), '98- 1; EJ: '91- 5; ECp: '94- 12 (5), '95- 1 (8), '96- (4), '97- (4). Won AAA LJ 1996, 1998.

Three UK and two Commonwealth heptathlon records 1996-2000.

Progression at Hep: 1989- 5277, 1990- 5193, 1991- 5484, 1992- 5812, 1993- 5774, 1994- 6325, 1995- 6299, 1996- 6645, 1997- 6736, 1998- 6559, 1999- 6724, 2000- 6831. pbs: 200m 24.10 '97, 24.01w '00; 800m 2:12.20 '00, 60mh 8.30i/8.2i '96, 100mh 13.13 '00, HJ 1.87 '99, LJ 6.69 '00, 6.77w '97; SP 16.12 '99, JT 56.50 '96, new 51.13 '00.

A 5.1m improvement to her javelin pb followed by 2 seconds off her best for 800m gave her a narrow heptathlon victory at the 1994 Commonwealth Games. Despite missing crucial weeks through injury, won double gold in 1998, and, again with an injury-shortened season, took World silver in 1999 with pbs at HJ and SP, ending just 12 points short of her record score. Despite the recurrence of an Achilles injury, she held on to take the Olympic gold in Sydney, having earlier set five pbs when she added 95 points to her Commonwealth heptathlon record at Talence.

Katharine MERRY b. 21 Sep 1974 Dunchurch 1.70m 61kg Birchfield H.

At 400m: OG: '00- 3; WCh: '99- 5. At 200m/4x100mR (100m): OG: '96- qf/8R; WCh: '93- qf; EC: '94- sf/5R; WJ: '90- (8)/2R; '92- 5/4R (6); EJ: '89- 5 (7 100m), '91- 3/2R, '93- 1/1R (2); ECp: '93- 6/6R, '94- 2/2R (2), '96- 3, '99- 8. Won UK 200m 1993 & 1997, AAA 100m & 200m 1994, 200m 1998, 400m 1999.

Progression at 200m, 400m: 1987- 25.4, 1988- 24.9, 1989- 23.94/23.54w/23.9, 1990- 23.65, 1991- 23.50/ 23.41w, 1992- 23.38, 1993- 23.20, 1994- 22.85, 54.0; 1995- 1996- 22.88, 1997- 22.77, 1998- 22.93, 51.01; 1999- 22.83i/22.90, 50.21; 2000- 22.76, 49.72. pbs: 60m 7.34i '94, 100m: 11.34/11.27w '94, 300m 36.00 '00, HJ 1.74 '88, LJ 5.55 '87, 6.05w '88.

She has overcome injury problems of recent years to make a big impression at 400m. Ran numerous UK age records and still holds the British best at under-13 for 70 and 75m hurdles, high jump and pentathlon and at under-15 for 100m, 200m and pentathlon. In 1989 she won the AAA girls (U15) indoor 60m with a stunning 7.35. Six years as a British junior international, with 11 national age-group titles. Engaged to Olivier-Jean Théodore FRA, who has a 400mh best of 49.93 (2000).

Joanne PAVEY b. 20 Sep 1973 Honiton 1.62m 51kg. née Davis. Bristol.

At 5000m: OG: '00- 12. At 1500m: WCh: '97- sf. Won UK 1500m 1997.

Progression at 3000m, 5000m: 1993- 9:56.1, 1996- 9:37.6, 1997- 9:05.87, 1998- 8:58.2, 2000- 8:36.70, 14:58.27. pbs: 800m 2:09.68 '90, 1500m 4:07.28 '97, 1M 4:30.77 '97, 2000m 5:44.0e '00.

Set a British under-15 record at 1500m with 4:27.9 in 1988 and won four national titles at U15/U17 level, but did not compete much in the early 1990s. Missed two years through injury 1998-2000. Married to middle-distance runner Gavin Pavey.

Paula RADCLIFFE b. 17 Dec 1973 Northwich 1.73m 54kg. Bedford & County. Degree in European languages from Loughborough University.

At 10000m: OG: '00- 4; WCh: '99- 2; EC: '98- 5; At 5000m: OG: '96- 5; WCh: '95- 5, '97- 4; ECp: '98- 1 (2 1500m), '99- 1; 3rd GP 1997. At 3000m: WCh: '93- 7; WJ: '92- 4; EJ: '91- 4; ECp: '97- 3. World HMar: '00- 1; CC: '91- 15J, '92- 1J, '93-5-6-7-8-9: 18/18/19/2/2/3; '00- 5 (4 4k), '01- 1 (2) Eur CC: '98- 1. Won AAA 5000m 1996, 2000; UK 1997.

Records: Commonwealth & UK: 10000m (4) 1998-2000, 3000m & 5000m 1999; British 5000m (3) 1996-9. European half marathon 2000.

Progression at 1500m, 3000m, 5000m, 10000m: 1988- 4:41.0, 1989- 4:34.9, 1990- 4:31.3, 9:41.4; 1991- 4:23.68, 9:23.29; 1992- 4:16.82, 8:51.78, 16:16.77i; 1993- 4:11.6, 8:40.40; 1994- 4:23.84, 1995- 4:06.84, 8:40.82, 14:49.27; 1996- 4:08.42, 8:37.07, 14:46.76; 1997 4:06.93, 8:35.28, 14:45.51; 1998- 4:05.81, 8:38.84, 14:51.27, 30:48.58; 1999- 4:06.71, 8:27.40, 14:43.54, 30:27.13; 2000- 4:11.45, 8:28.85, 14:44.36, 30:26.97. pbs: 400m 58.9 '92, 800m 2:05.22 '95, 1000m 2:47.17 '93, 1M 4:24.94 '96, 2000m 5:39.20 '93, 2M 9:27.5e (1998), 9:32.07 (1999); HMar 67:07 '00.

Fastest ever track debut for 10,000m when 2nd in 1998 European Challenge, 30:48.58. She improved this Commonwealth record to 30:40.70 to win this race in 1999 and in Seville to 30:27.13. There, forcing the pace throughout, despite searing heat; she was passed on the last lap by Gete Wami, but won a glorious silver medal. She set an even faster pace at the 2000 Olympics, but was outkicked and finished fourth. Followed that with brilliant form on the roads, including European half marathon record to win Great North Run and then the World Half marathon title by a margin of 33 seconds. Won 5th Avenue Mile 1996 & 1997. Her great aunt Charlotte Radcliffe won an Olympic swimming silver medal at 4x100m freestyle relay in 1920. Married 3:34.76 1500 man Gary Lough on 15 April 2000 but continues to race under her maiden name.

Lorraine SHAW b. 2 Apr 1968 1.70m 86kg. Sale H.
At HT: OG: '00- 9; EC: '98- 11; CG: '98- 2; ECp: '98-9-00: 5/6/5. Won UK 1993, AAA 1994, 1998, 2000. At DT: CG: '94- 10. Won Irish DT 1990-2, HT 1992.
15 British hammer records 1994-2001, Commonwealth records 1995 and 2000.
Progression at HT: 1991- 35.52, 1992- 44.40/45.24lt, 1993- 56.56, 1994- 59.94, 1995- 64.90, 1996- 61.34, 1998- 63.30, 1999- 67.10, 2000- 67.44, 2001- 68.15. pbs: SP 14.21 '94, DT 55.04 '94.
Having competed for Ireland at discus in 1992, opted for British nationality in 1993. Had a disc removed from her back and missed nearly two years of competition before return in April 1998.

Hayley TULLETT b. 17 Feb 1973 Swansea 1.66m 58kg. née Parry. Swansea H.
At 1500m (800m): OG: '00- 11; WCh: '99- h; WUG: '97- 4 (5); ECp: '97- (7), '99- 4. At 3000m: WI: '01- 8; ECp: '00- 3. Won AAA 1500m 1999-2000.
Progression at 1500m: 1988- 4:52.9, 1990- 5:01.4, 1994- 4:43.9, 1995- 4:25.51, 1996- 4:16.9, 1997- 4:08.98, 1999- 4:05.72, 2000- 4:01.23, 2001- 4:06.75i. pbs: 400m 55.6 '97, 800m 2:01.25 '00, 1M 4:26.50i '00, 4:48.88 '95; 3000m 8:45.36i '01, 8:45.39 '00; 2M 9:49.73 '99.
Married pole vaulter Ian Tullett (b. 15 Aug 1969, pb 5.35 '98, 2 CG 90) in 1999.

USA

Governing body: USA Track and Field, P.O. Box 120, Indianapolis, Indiana 46206-0120. Founded 1979, when it replaced the AAU (founded 1888) as the governing body.
National Championships first held in 1876 (men), 1923 (women). **2000 Champions (inc. Olympic Trials)**: **Men**: 100m: Maurice Greene 10.01, 200m: John Capel 19.85, 400m: Michael Johnson 43.68, 800m: Mark Everett 1:45.67, 1500m: Gabe Jennings 3:35.90, 5000m: Adam Goucher 13:27.06, 10000m: Meb Keflezighi 28:03.32, HMar/Mar: Rod DeHaven 63:06/2:15:30, 3000mSt: Pascal Dobert 8:15.77, 110mh: Allen Johnson 12.97, 400mh: Angelo Taylor 47.62, HJ: Charles Austin 2.32, PV: Lawrence Johnson 5.82, LJ: Melvin Lister 8.32, TJ: Robert Howard 16.99, SP: Adam Nelson 22.12, DT: Adam Setliff 63.95, HT: Lance Deal 78.87, JT: Breaux Greer 81.08, Dec: Tom Pappas 8467, 20000mW: Tim Seaman 1:25:41, 50kmW: Curt Clausen 3:56:16. **Women**: 100m/200m/LJ: Marion Jones 10.88/21.94/7.02, 400m: LaTasha Colander-Richardson 49.87, 800m: Hazel Clark 1:58.97, 1500m/5000m: Regina Jacobs 4:01.01/14:45.35, 10000m: Deena Drossin 31:51.05, HMar: Libbie Hickman 71:01, Mar: Christine Clark 2:33:31, 3000mSt: Elizabeth Jackson 9:57.20, 100mh: Gail Devers 12.33, 400mh: Sandra Glover 53.33, HJ: Karol Damon 1.93, PV: Stacy Dragila 4.63, TJ: Nicole Gamble 13.96, SP: Connie Price-Smith 18.63, DT: Seilala Sua 65.90, HT: Dawn Ellerbe 69.20, JT: Linda Bluetrich 58.28, Hep: DeDee Nathan 6343, 20kmW: Michelle Rohl 1:32:39.

NCAA Championships first held in 1921 (men), 1982 (women). **2000 champions**: **Men**: 100m: Bernard Williams 10.03, 200m: Shawn Crawford 20.09, 400m: Avard Moncur BAH 44.72, 800m: Patrick Nduwimana BUR 1:45.08, 1500m: Gabe Jennings 3:33.76, 5000m/10000m: Brad Hauser 13:48.80/30:38.57, 3000mSt: Tim Broe 8:39.03, 110mh: Terrence Trammell 13.43, 400mh: Felix Sanchez DOM 48.41, HJ: Mark Boswell CAN 2.31, PV: Russ Buller 5.60, LJ: Savante Stringfellow 8.17, TJ: Melvin Lister 16.96, SP: Joachim Olsen 20.26, DT: Gábor Maté HUN 65.74, HT: Libor Charfreitag SVK 77.22, JT: Esko Mikola FIN 72.62, Dec: Bevan Hart 8002. **Women**: 100m: Angela Williams 11.12, 200m: Peta-Gaye Dowdie 22.51, 400m: Miki Barber 51.14, 800m: Tytti Reho FIN 2:01.43, 1500m: Susan Taylor 4:13.03, 3000m/5000m: Kara Wheeler 9:02.15/15:54.30, 10000m: Tara Rohatinsky 33:49.24, 100mh: Joyce Bates 12.85, 400mh: Natasha Danvers GBR 55.26, HJ: Erin Aldrich 1.90, PV: Tracy O'Hara 4.40, LJ: Jenny Adams 6.54, TJ: Keisha Spencer JAM 13.97, SP/DT: Seilala Sua 17.36/61.20, HT: Florence Ezeh FRA 64.58, JT: Aggelíki Tsiolakoúdi GRE 60.24, Hep: Christi Smith 5797.

Dominique ARNOLD b. 14 Sep 1973 Long Beach, California 1.85m 76kg. Was at Washington State University.
At 110mh: PAm: '99- 4. NCAA champion 1996.
Progression at 110mh: 1992- 14.55, 1993- 14.17, 1995- 14.00, 1996- 13.46/13.32w, 1998- 13.54/13.5/13.48w, 1999- 13.21/13.2, 2000- 13.11. pbs: 55mh 7.15i '98, 60mh 7.51i '00.

Charles AUSTIN b. 19 Dec 1967 Bay City, Texas 1.84m 77kg. Was at Southwest Texas State University.
At HJ: OG: '92- 8=, '96- 1, '00- dnq 20; WCh: '91- 1, '95- dnq 13=, '97- dnq 13, '99- 8=; WI: '91- 6=, '97- 1, '99- 3; WCp: '98- 1. Won NCAA 1990, US 1995-2000.
US high jump record 1991.
Progression at HJ: 1986- 2.11, 1987- 2.16, 1988- 2.19, 1989- 2.27, 1990- 2.35, 1991- 2.40, 1992- 2.33i/2.32, 1993- 2.35i, 1994- 2.32, 1995- 2.34i/2.33, 1996- 2.39, 1997- 2.35i/2.32, 1998- 2.33, 1999- 2.33i/2.32, 2000- 2.32. pb TJ 14.91i '90.
Decline after 1991 world title due to right knee

injury, which was operated on in July 1993. Made slow recovery, climaxed by Olympic victory in Atlanta with his best jump for five years. His older brother Russell ran on 4x100m team that set a world Masters record in 1992.

Andy BLOOM b. 11 Aug 1973 Stamford, Ct. 1.85m 125kg. Nike. Was at Wake Forest University.
At SP (/DT): OG: '00- 4; WCh: '97- (dnq 16), '99- 4/nt; WJ: '92- 9/6; WI: '99- 9; WUG: '97- (2), '99- 1/2. Won GP SP 2000, NCAA SP & DT 1996.
Progression at SP, DT: 1991- 16.44, 48.66; 1992- 17.52, 53.50; 1993- 18.21, 55.34; 1994- 18.31, 54.28; 1995- 18.56, 63.48; 1996- 19.82, 64.86; 1997- 20.19i/ 19.96, 65.30; 1998- 20.45, 66.42; 1999- 21.27, 67.46; 2000- 21.82, 68.46.
Ssecond best ever SP/DT combination thrower (after John Godina).

Milton CAMPBELL b. 15 May 1976 Atlanta 1.78m 75kg. Was at University of North Carolina.
At 400m: WI: '99- 2/1R, '01- 2/2R; WJ: '94- 3R.
Progression at 400m: 1993- 47.17, 1994- 46.09, 1995- 45.84, 1996- 45.29, 1997- 44.67, 1998- 45.04, 1999- 45.02, 2000- 45.37. pb 200m 20.56i/20.66 '98.

John CAPEL b. 27 Oct 1978 Brooksville, Florida 1.80m 82kg. Was at University of Florida.
At 200m: OG: 00- 8. At 100m/4x100mR: WUG: '99- 2/1R. Won US 200m 2000, NCAA 200m 1999 (2nd 100m).
Progression at 100m, 200m: 1997- 10.46/10.2, 21.01; 1998- 10.40, 1999- 10.03, 19.87; 2000- 10.12, 19.85. pbs: 55m 6.15i '00, 60m 6.62i '99.
Promising footballer (wide receiver) at University of Florida, but withdrew in April 2000 to concentrate on trying for Olympic success. After running the fastest time in the semis (20.10), moved too early, then settled back onto his blocks and was virtually left at start of Olympic 200m final.

James CARTER b. 7 May 1978 Baltimore 1.80m 83kg. Maryland Elite. Hampton College.
At 400mh: OG: 00- 4.
Progression at 400mh: 1997- 10.46/10.2, 21.01; 1998- 50.17, 1999- 49.45, 2000- 48.04. pb LJ 7.25 '99.

LaMark CARTER b. 23 Aug 1970 Shreveport, Louisiana 1.80m 75kg. Nike. Graduate (now assistant track coach) of Northwestern Louisiana University.
At TJ: OG: '00- dnq 19; WCh: '95- dnq 18, '99- 6; PAm: '95- 4, '99- 2; WI: '95- 6, '99- 2; WUG: '95- 3; WCp: '98- 5. US champion 1998-9.
Progression at TJ: 1987- 13.91, 1988- 15.06, 1989- 15.58, 1991- 15.98/16.07w, 1992- 16.68, 1993- 16.78/16.83w, 1994- 16.94, 1995- 16.92i/16.77, 1996- 17.12i/17.06, 1997- 17.06i/16.76/17.15w, 1998- 17.44, 1999- 17.10/17.15w, 2000- 16.96/ 16.97w. pb LJ 7.98 '96.

Shawn CRAWFORD b. 14 Jan 1978 Van Wyck, SC 1.81m 75kg. Clemson University.
At 200m: WI: '01- 1; NCAA champion 2000.
Progression at 200m: 1997- 20.83; 1998- 20.44A/ 20.12w, 1999- 20.39, 2000- 20.09. pbs: 60m 6.56i '00, 100m 10.16 '00, 10.15w '98.
US indoor record 20.26 to win NCAA indoor 200m 2000.

Mark CREAR b. 2 Oct 1968 San Francisco 1.86m 79kg. Sociology degree from University of Southern California.
At 110mh: OG: '96- 2, '00- 3; WCh: '93- sf, '97- 7. Won GP 110mh 1995, 1997, 1999; 3rd overall 1995, 1997; NCAA champion 1992, US 1994, 1999; GWG 1998.
Progression at 110mh: 1990- 13.65/13.51w, 1992- 13.33, 1993- 13.26/13.22w/12.9w, 1994- 13.07, 1995- 13.02, 1996- 13.05, 1997- 13.03, 1998- 13.00, 1999- 12.98, 2000- 13.11/13.10w. pbs: 50mh 6.41Ai '95, 55mh 7.18i '94, 60mh 7.38i '98.
World's top high hurdler of 1995, but he went out in the semi-finals of the US Champs. Disqualified for two false starts in his quarter-final at the Worlds, but ranked no.1 in the world on his overall record in 1999. Formerly married to Keisha Marvin (2nd 1994 NCAA 400mh in pb 56.62).

Calvin DAVIS b. 2 Apr 1972 Eutaw, Alabama 1.83m 79kg. Adidas. Was at University of Arkansas.
At 400mh: OG: '96- 3. At 400m/4x400m: WI: '95- 6/1R. Won NCAA indoor 400m 1994.
Progression at 400m: 1989- 47.51, 1992- 45.85, 1993- 45.04, 1994- 45.20, 1995- 45.94, 1996- 45.06, 1997- 46.14i, 1998- 46.31i/46.68. At 400mh: 1996- 47.91, 1997- 48.75, 1998- 48.57, 1999- 48.33, 2000- 48.92.
Made his debut at 400mh in 1996 and was 3rd in the US Trials in his 7th race at the event – progressing to Olympic bronze.

Jerome DAVIS b. 20 Aug 1977 Ridgecrest, California 1.88m 81kg. University of Southern California.
At 400m/4x400m: WCh: '99- sf/1R; WJ: '96- 2/1R (1 4x100R); WUG: '97- 2/1R, '99- 1/1R. Won NCAA 1998.
Progression at 400m: 1994- 47.45, 1996- 46.62, 1997- 45.30, 1998- 45.04, 1999- 44.51, 2000- 45.09. pbs: 200m 20.51 '98.
Ran pb 44.51 in fifth in first semi at 1999 Worlds, with second semi then being won in 44.55. Top basketball player in high school.

Lance DEAL b. 21 Aug 1961 Riverton, Wyoming 1.88m 116kg. New York AC. Was at Montana State University. Wood and metal worker.
At HT: OG: '88- dnq 17, '92- 7, '96- 2, '00- dnq 16; WCh: '91- dnq 13, '93- 9, '95- 5, '99- dnq 13; PAm: '95- 1, '99- 1; WCp: '89- 2, '92- 3, '94- 2. Won GP 1996. US champion 1989, 1993-6, 1998-2000; GWG 1994. Won PAm-J discus 1980.
World bests 35lb weight: outdoors 24.05 '90, 25.41 '93; and nine indoors: from 24.17 '91 to 25.86 '95. Three US hammer records 1994-6.
Progression at HT: 1984- 62.52, 1985- 68.48,

1986- 74.66, 1987- 75.94, 1988- 75.64, 1989- 78.34, 1990- 77.66, 1991- 78.44, 1992- 81.08, 1993- 80.80, 1994- 82.50, 1995- 78.66, 1996- 82.52, 1998- 80.88, 1999- 80.35, 2000- 80.99. pbs: SP 18.35i '81, 18.22 '84; DT 61.62 '84.
An all-American linebacker at American football in high school, he switched from discus (left-handed) to hammer in 1984. Having been only 8th equal and thinking he was 9th and out after three rounds, came through to gain 1996 Olympic silver, and ended the year by matching his US record 82.50 at the ISTAF (actually measured at 82.51) and then added 2cm at the GP Final with 82.52. Missed the 1997 season with a back injury. Has 12 US indoor titles (record for any event) at 35lb Wt (1987, 1989-96, 1998-2000).

Tony DEES 6 Aug 1963 Pascagoula, Mississippi 1.93m 95kg. Vector Sports. Degree in education from University of Mississippi.
At 110mh: OG: '92- 2; WCh: '93- 8, '99- 4. Won GP 1991. At 60mh: WI: '93- 3, '97- 3.
Progression at 110mh: 1982- 13.98, 1983- 13.68/13.6, 1984- 13.65, 1985- 13.86, 1986- 13.65, 1987- 13.86, 1988- 13.54/13.51w, 1989- 13.61, 1990- 13.24/13.09w, 1991- 13.05, 1992- 13.08, 1993- 13.12, 1994- 13.40, 1995- 13.32/13.17Aw, 1996- 13.37/13.32w, 1997- 13.34, 1998- 13.28, 1999- 13.22/13.19w, 2000- 13.40/13.29w. pbs: 55m 6.12i '90, 100m 10.15/10.03w '91, 200m 20.54 '84, 20.37w/20.2w '83; 50mh 6.37i '00, 55mh 6.98i '90, 60mh 7.37i '00.
Has maintained world-class form into late 30s.

Kevin DILWORTH b. 14 Feb 1974 Jacksonville, Texas 1.80m 76kg. Adidas, Was at Abilene Christian University.
At LJ: WCh: '97- 8, '99- 8; WI: '01- 6. US champion 1999.
Progression at LJ: 1992- 7.52/7.73w, 1993- 7.66/7.87w, 1994- 7.73; 1995- 7.83/7.90w; 1996- 8.47, 1997- 8.29, 1998- 8.30, 1999- 8.09/8.12w, 2000- 8.28. pb 200m 20.98 '96, 20.87w '95, 20.6w '94.

Jon DRUMMOND b. 9 Sep 1968 Philadelphia 1.75m 75kg. Nike. Was at Texas Christian Univ.
At 200m/4x100mR (100m): OG: '96- 2R (sf), '00- 1R (5); WCh: '93- 1R, '95- hR, '97- 7, '99- 1R; WUG: '91- 1/1R. Won US 200m 1997. 3rd GP 100m 1994, 200m 1997. At 60m: WI: '93- 4.
World record 4x100m relay 1993.
Progression at 100m, 200m: 1986- 10.5; 1987- 10.28/10.23w, 20.64; 1988- 10.25/10.0w, 20.79i; 1989- 10.21, 20.82; 1990- 10.10, 1991- 10.19/10.03w, 20.58; 1992- 10.12, 20.37; 1993- 10.03/9.92w, 21.05i, 1994 9.99, 1995- 10.10/10.00w, 20.49/20.10w; 1996- 9.98, 20.05; 1997- 9.92, 20.03; 1998- 9.94, 20.15; 1999- 10.04, 20.29/20.24w; 2000- 9.96, 20.17. pbs: 50m 5.63i '99, 55m 6.14i '90, 60m 6.46i '98, 100y 9.33 '94, 400m 45.55 '00.
Self-styled 'Crown Prince of Track'. Sings with the gospel group 'Kirk Franklin & The Family'; their first album reached No.1 on the *Billboard* gospel chart in 1993. Returned from viral meningitis to run 5th at 100m and 6th at 200m at US Champs in 1999, qualifying for World team where he ran first leg on gold medal-winning sprint relay team.

John GODINA b. 31 May 1972 Fort Sill, Oklahoma 1.93m 129kg. Reebok Bruin. Studied biology at UCLA.
At SP/DT: OG: '96- 2/dnq 14, '00- 3/dnq 17; WCh: '95- 1/10, '97- 1/5, '99- 7/dnq 16; WI: '97- 3, '99- 2, '01- 1; WCp: '98- 1/5. Won GP SP 1996 (3rd 2000), 3rd DT 1997. Won US SP 1998-9, DT 1997-8, NCAA SP 1995, DT 1994-5, PAm-J SP & DT 1991; GWG SP 1998.
Progression at SP, DT: 1990- 53.58, 1991- 17.75, 58.60; 1992- 19.68, 61.52; 1993- 20.03, 60.48; 1994- 20.03, 62.24; 1995- 22.00, 64.92; 1996- 21.25, 64.58; 1997- 21.75, 67.40; 1998- 21.78, 69.91; 1999- 22.02, 69.05; 2000- 21.51, 68.32.
Undefeated in 24 shot competitions July 1997 to February 1999. Only 4th in the US trials shot in 1997, but gained World Championships place with a 'wild card entry for a defending champion; came second but took gold after the disqualification of Aleksandr Bagach. He achieved the best ever one day SP-DT doubles with 21.78 and 66.47 at Mt SAC and 21.58 and 69.91 at Salinas in 1998. He stepped into the US Olympic shot team after the withdrawal of CJ Hunter in 2000 and took bronze.

Maurice GREENE b. 23 Jul 1974 Kansas City, Kansas 1.76m 75kg. Nike.
At 100m(/200m)/4x100mR: OG: '00- 1/1R; WCh: '95- qf, '97- 1, '99- 1/1/1R; Won US 100m 1997, 1999-2000; 200m 1999; GWG 100m 1998. 2nd GP 200m 1999. At 60m: WI: '95- 4, '99- 1.
World 100m record 1999; three world indoor 60m records 1998-2001.
Progression at 100m, 200m: 1993- 10.43, 21.00; 1995- 10.19/9.88w, 1996- 10.08, 1997- 9.86, 19.86; 1998- 9.90/9.79w, 20.03/19.88w; 1999- 9.79, 19.90; 2000- 9.86, 20.02/19.93w. pbs: 50m 5.55+ '97, 55m 6.15i '96, 60m 6.39i/6.39+ '98.
Moved from Kansas to train with John Smith in Los Angeles in September 1996. In 1997 ran 100m in 9.90 to win US Champs and twice in Athens before 9.86 to win World 100m title. Took 0.05 off world record for 100m at Athens in June 1999, and went on the confirm his place as world's fastest man with World Champs treble (the first man to win 100m and 200m at World Champs). His elder brother Ernest was a former US junior college champion at 200m (20.60 '92).

Tim HARDEN b. 27 Jan 1974 Kansas City, Missouri 1.78m 77kg. Nike. Was at University of Kentucky.
At 100m/4x100mR: OG: '96- 1R; WCh: '99- 5; PAm: '99- 4; WCp: '98- 4/2R. 2nd PAm-J 1993. Won US 100m 1998, NCAA 1995 (2nd 1994, 1996). At 60m: WI: '99- 2, '01- 1.

Progression at 100m: 1992- 10.3/10.2w, 1993- 10.32, 1994- 10.14/10.03w, 1995- 10.05, 1996- 10.02/9.94w, 1997- 10.26, 1998- 10.03A/10.09/ 9.88w, 1999- 9.92, 2000- 10.20. pbs: 50m 5.60+ '99, 55m 6.06i '95, 60m 6.43i '99, 200m 20.54/20.38w '94.
Won US indoor 60m 1998 but then stripped of title and given public warning for doping violation (ephedrine). He won this title in 1999 in a pb 6.44 ahead of Maurice Greene and improved to third fastest of all-time at 60m when 2nd to Greene in Maebashi.

Alvin HARRISON b. 20 Jan 1974 Orlando, Florida 1.88m 80kg. Nike.
At 400m/4x400mR: OG: '96- 4/1R, '00- 2/1R; PAm: '99- 3R; PAm-J: '93- 3/1R.
Progression at 400m: 1993- 46.25, 1996- 44.09, 1997- 45.37, 1998- 44.19, 1999- 45.17, 2000- 44.18. pbs: 100m 10.52 '99, 200m 20.41 '96, 300m 32.00 '96.
The twins Alvin and Calvin, who both ran at the Pam Juniors in 1993, were homeless in 1995 and sleeping in an old Ford Mustang. Returning to the sport in 1996 Alvin made a huge breakthrough when he ran sub-45 seconds for the first time at the 1996 US Trials – running successively 44.93, 44.66, 44.43 and 44.09 in the four rounds.

Calvin HARRISON b. 20 Jan 1974 Orlando, Florida 1.86m 75kg. Nike.
At 400m/4x400mR: OG: '00- 1R; PAm-J: '93- 1/1R.
Progression at 400m: 1993- 45.25/45.07dq, 1994- 46.26, 1996- 44.70, 1997- 45.59, 1998- 44.68A/45.13, 2000- 44.64. pb 200m 20.57 '93.
Tested positive for pseudoephedrine at 1993 US Junior Championships in 45.07. Dropped out of school, Hartnell Junior College, Salinas, in 1994 and returned to Florida. Came back to California and to the sport in 1996.

Jeff HARTWIG b. 25 Sep 1967 St Louis 1.90m 82kg. Goldwin. Was at Arkansas State University.
At PV: OG: '96- 11=; WCh: '99- dnq 14=; WI: '99- 2; WCp: '98- 3. Won GWG 1998, US 1998-9. 2nd GP 1999. Four US pole vault records 1998-2000.
Progression at PV: 1983- 3.35, 1984- 3.81, 1985- 4.42, 1986- 4.57, 1987- 4.90, 1988- 5.10, 1989- 5.34, 1990- 5.40i/5.35, 1991- 5.35, 1992- 5.60i/5.50, 1993- 5.35, 1994- 5.63, 1995- 5.72, 1996- 5.80, 1997- 5.85, 1998- 6.01, 1999- 6.02, 2000- 6.03.
The first 6m-vaulter from the USA, Hartwig is also a snake rancher, with a herd of pythons and boa constrictors. Clearly headed world rankings in 2000, but failed to clear his opening height in the qualifying round of the US Trials, when he had problems with his eyes.

Tye HARVEY b. 25 Sep 1974 1.86m 73kg. Bell Athletics. Was at University of Minnesota.
At PV: WI: '01- 2
Progression at PV: 1992- 4.87, 1993- 5.21, 1994- 5.10, 1995- 5.35, 1996- 5.20, 1997- 5.55i/5.52, 1998- 5.47, 1999- 5.67, 2000- 5.80, 2001- 5.93i.

Matt HEMINGWAY b. 24 Oct 1972 San Pedro, California 2.01m 81kg. US West. Was at University of Arkansas. Sales manager.
At HJ: WI: '99- 6. Won NCAA 1996.
Progression at HJ: 1990- 2.08, 1991- 2.23, 1992- 2.10, 1993- 2.25, 1994- 2.17, 1995- 2.25i/2.21, 1996- 2.30, 1997- 2.21i/2.20, 2000- 2.38i/2.30.
Having been out for the sport for two and a half years 'tired of everything about track', but keeping fit playing basketball, he returned in sensational style in the 2000 indoor season, jumping a pb 2.32 in January, 2.36 in February and winning the US indoor title with 2.38 in March. He had been 2nd in the NCAA and 4th in the US Trials in 1996. He is a distant relative of author Ernest Hemingway.

Ja'Warren HOOKER b. 24 Sep 1978 1.83m 77kg. Student at University of Washington.
Won 100m & 4x100m PAm-J 1997.
Progression at 200m, 400m: 1996- 47.77, 1997- 21.02, 46.23; 1998- 20.54, 46.42; 1999- 20.48A, 2000- 20.23A/20.33, 44.78. pbs: 55m 6.09A '98, 60m 6.51A/6.57i '01, 100m 10.18 '98.

Robert HOWARD b. 26 Nov 1975 Brooklyn, New York 1.78m 75kg. Was at Univ. of Arkansas.
At TJ: OG: '96- 8, '00- 7; WCh: '97- dnq 17; WUG: '97- 3. Won NCAA LJ 1997-8, TJ 1996-8; US TJ 2000.
Progression at LJ, TJ: 1992- 14.80/14.93w, 1993- 15.21i/15.03/15.29w, 1994- 7.53, 15.69; 1995- 7.31, 16.12i; 1996- 8.26, 17.19; 1997- 8.40, 17.08; 1998- 8.03i/7.87/8.37w, 17.11/17.12w; 2000- 8.07, 17.05.
Achilles surgery in 1999. Eleven NCAA titles indoors and out. Is delaying a career in medicine.

Chris HUFFINS b. 15 Apr 1970 Brooklyn, New York 1.90m 82kg. Mizuno TC. Was at Purdue and California Universities.
At Dec: OG: '96- 10, '00- 3; WCh: '95- 8, '97- dnf, '99- 3; PAm: '99- 1. US champion 1998-9, NCAA 1993. At Hep: WI: '97- 4.
Progression at Dec: 1992- 7854, 1993- 8007, 1995- 8351, 1996- 8546, 1997- 8458, 1998- 8694, 1999- 8547, 2000- 8595. pbs. 60m 6.61i '97, 100m 10.22 '96, 200m 21.11 '91, 20.79w '90; 400m 48.05 '96, 1500m 4:38.71 '00, 60mh 7.82i '97, 110mh 13.82 '97, HJ 2.18 '98, PV 4.90 '97, LJ 8.01 '93, 8.07w '96; TJ 16.14 '92, SP 16.44 '96, DT 54.14 '97, JT 64.35 '99, Hep 6128i '97.
Ran decathlon 100m record (10.22) in US Trials 1996. Having led after the first day and still in 3rd place after 8 events, he had three no throws in the javelin at 1997 World Championships. Won Talence decathlon 1997. Needing to run hard to get the bronze medal, he took 12.49 secs off his 1500m best at the Sydney Olympics. Is now assistant coach at Georgia Tech University.

Nick HYSONG b. 9 Dec 1971 Winslow, Arizona 1.83m 77kg. Nike. Marketing degree from Arizona State University.
At PV: OG: '00- 1; WCh: '99- 4=; WJ: '90- 6; WI:

'95- 5=, '99- 8. Won NCAA 1994. 2nd GP 2000.
Progression at PV: 1989- 4.87, 1990- 5.30, 1991- 5.45, 1992- 5.52, 1993- 5.57i/5.50, 1994- 5.70, 1995- 5.85i/5.70, 1996- 5.71A, 1997- 5.67A, 1998- 5.70, 1999- 5.85i/5.80, 2000- 5.90.

Allen JOHNSON b. 1 Mar 1971 Washington DC 1.78m 70kg. Was at Univ. of North Carolina.
At 110mh: OG: '96- 1, '00- 4; WCh: '95- 1, '97- 1, '99- sf; WCp: '94- 2, '98- 2R; 2nd GP 1995. US champion 1996-7, 2000. At 60mh: WI: '95- 1.
US 110mh record 1996.
Progression at 110mh: 1991- 14.11, 1992- 13.63, 1993- 13.47/13.34w, 1994- 13.25/13.23Aw, 1995- 12.98, 1996- 12.92, 1997- 12.93, 1998- 12.98, 1999- 13.01, 2000- 12.97. pbs: 60m 6.62i '98, 100m 10.41/10.10w '99, 200m 20.26 '97, 400m 48.27 '96, 50mh 6.47i '95, 55mh 7.03i '94, 60mh 7.38i '95, 400mh 52.00 '91, HJ 2.11 '89, LJ 8.14i/7.91w '93, 7.85 '91; TJ 14.83 '89.
Having leapt into world class in 1994, on 8 Feb 1995 in Madrid he ended Colin Jackson string of 44 sprint hurdles victories. He went on to win world titles indoors and out, adding Olympic gold in 1996, when he missed the world record by just 0.01 at the US Trials, and another world gold in 1997. Had to withdraw from the 1999 World semis through injury.

Lawrence JOHNSON b. 7 May 1974 Norfolk, Virginia 1.83m 85kg. Adidas. Was at University of Tennessee. Pianist and composer.
At PV: OG: '96- 8, '00- 2; WCh: '97- dnq; WI: '97- 2, '01- 1; WUG: '95- 2. US champion 1996-7, NCAA 1995-6. PAm-J 1993.
US pole vault record 1996 (and indoors 2001).
Progression at PV: 1991- 4.87, 1992- 5.33, 1993- 5.71, 1994- 5.83i/5.80, 1995- 5.70, 1996- 5.98, 1997- 5.90, 1998- 5.80, 1999- 5.85, 2000- 5.90, 2000- 5.96i. pbs: 400m 49.55 '93, 110mh 14.60 '93, HJ 1.99 '93, Dec 7576 '93.
Broke an ankle in a motorcycle accident in 1999.

Michael JOHNSON b. 13 Sep 1967 Dallas 1.85m 78kg. Nike. Degree in marketing from Baylor University.
At 400m/4x400mR (200m): OG: '92- (sf)/1R, '96- 1 (1), '00- 1/1R; WCh: ' 91- (1), '93- 1/1R, '95- 1/1R (1), '97- 1, '99- 1/1R; WUG: '89- 2R. Won NCAA 200m 1990, GWG 200m 1990, 1994; 400 1998; US 200m 1990-2, 1995-6; 400m 1993, 1995-6, 2000. Won GP 200m 1991 (third overall), 1995; 400m 1996; 3rd 200m 1993.
World records: 200m 1996, 400m 1999, 4x400m relay 1992, 1993, 1998. World best 300m 2000. WIR 44.97 '94 and 44.63 '95.
Progression at 200m, 400m: 1986- 21.30, 1987- 20.41, 46.29; 1988- 20.07, 45.23; 1989- 20.47/ 20.06w, 46.49; 1990- 19.85, 44.21; 1991- 19.88, 44.17; 1992- 19.79, 43.98; 1993- 20.06, 43.65; 1994- 19.94, 43.90; 1995- 19.79, 43.39; 1996- 19.32, 43.44; 1997- 20.05, 43.75; 1998- 20.31/20.28w, 43.68; 1999- 19.93, 43.18; 2000- 19.71A/19.89, 43.68. pbs: 100m 10.09 '94, 300m 30.85A '00, 31.56 '94.
Won his fourth successive world title at 400m in 1999, when at last he found, in Seville, full fitness and ideal conditions to take the world record for 400m, sealing his place as the world's greatest ever 400m runner. His upright style, with little knee lift and rapid, short strides made a considerable impact when he burst onto the international scene and was the best in the world at both 200m and 400m in 1990. He ran a 43.5 400m relay split in April 1988 before a broken leg curtailed his season. His run of 32 successive wins at 200m from May 1990 was ended by Frank Fredericks in Rome on 9 Jun 1992 and he was ill at the 1992 Olympics, but at 400m he won 58 successive finals from 1990 to his 5th place in Paris on 25 Jun 1997. His 42.93 anchor on the 1993 US gold medal team is the fastest 400m relay leg ever run. In 1995 he recorded the first US 200m/400m championships double since 1899 and then won these events for a unique World Championship double, just missing the world record on each occasion. He repeated the US double and achieved a unique 200m/400 Olympic double in 1996, taking a stunning 0.34 off the world record for 200m that he had run at the US Champs. Having become the first man to retain a 400m title, he now has five Olympic gold medals. Has a record 22 sub-20 sec. times at 200m and 20 sub-44.00 times at 400m. Sullivan Award winner 1996.

Bob KENNEDY b. 18 Aug 1970 Bloomington, Indiana 1.83m 66kg. Nike. Was at Indiana Univ..
At 5000m: OG: '92- 12, '96- 6; WCh: '91- 12, '93- h, '95- 7, '97- 6, '99- 9. At 3000m: WI: '93- 4. World CC: '95-98-01: 14/16/12. . Won US 5000m 1995-7, CC 1992, PAm-J 1500m 1989, NCAA CC 1988, 1992; 1500m 1990.
US records 3000m (4) 1994-8, 2M 1997, 5000m (2) 1996.
Progression at 5000m: 1989- 14:21.40, 1990- 13:42.80, 1991- 13:22.17, 1992- 13:28.18, 1993- 13:14.91, 1994- 13:02.93, 1995- 13:03.37, 1996- 12:58.21, 1997- 13:06.62, 1998- 13:03.57, 1999- 13:05.54, 2000- 13:42.15. pbs: 800m 1:53.44 '89, 1500m 3:38.32 '91, 1M 3:56.21 '94, 2000m 4:59.9 '96, 3000m 7:30.84 '98, 2M 8:11.59 '97, 10000m 27:38.37 '99. Injured in a car accident May 2000.

Khalid KHANNOUCHI b. 22 Dec 1971 Meknès, Morocco.
At 5000m: WUG: '93- 1.
World best for the marathon 1999. World best road 20km 1998 (57:37). Moroccan records HMar and Mar 1997, US marathon record 2000.
Progression at Mar: 1997- 2:07:10, 1998- 2:07:19, 1999- 2:05:42, 2000- 2:07:01. pbs: 3000m 8:01.89i '96, 5000m 13:41.6 '95, 10000m 29:00.8 sh '89; Rd: 5km 13:24 '97, 10km 27:47 '98, 15km 42:57 '98, HMar 60:27 '97.
Won the WUG 5000m in Buffalo, New York, USA. Having felt that he was not appreciated in

his home country, he returned to Buffalo a few months later and eventually settled in Brooklyn, becoming a US citizen in 2000. He is coached and managed by his wife Sandra Natal, who originally came from the Dominican Republic. He showed great form at shorter distances on the roads in 1997 before running the fastest ever debut marathon to win at Chicago in 1997, just 20 seconds off the world record. A year later he was second in Chicago and in 1999 returned there to earn $165,000 for his win in a new world best time of 2:05:42. After 3rd in London, won again in Chicago 2000.

Nathan LEEPER b. 13 Jun 1977 Greensburg, Kansas 1.88m 82kg. Nike. Was at Kansas State University.
At HJ: OG: '00- 11; WI: '01- 4. Won NCAA 1998. 2nd GP 2000.
Progression at HJ: 1995- 2.16, 1996- 2.14, 1997- 2.23i/2.21, 1998- 2.30, 2000- 2.35.

Brian LEWIS b. 5 Dec 1974 Sacramento 1.72m 72kg. Reebok. Was at Norfolk State University.
At 100m/4x100mR: OG: '00- 1R; WCh: '97- hR, 99- sf/1R. US champion 1999.
Progression at 100m, 200m: 1992- 10.59, 21.36; 1993- 10.37w, 21.38/21.13w; 1994- 10.27, 20.70; 1995- 10.24/10.03w, 20.75/20.61w; 1996- 10.03, 20.54, 1997- 10.00, 1998- 10.03/9.98w, 20.40A/ 20.52; 1999- 10.02/10.00w, 20.34; 2000- 10.02/ 9.96w, 20.06r/20.26. pbs: 50m 5.70i '98, 60m 6.54i '98.
Led off, but failed to transfer baton to Tim Montgomery in 1997 World Champs relay heat.

Melvin LISTER b. 29 Aug 1977 New York 1.83m 77kg. HSI. University of Arkansas.
At LJ: OG: '00- dnq 25; WI: '01- 5; WJ: '96- 11. Won NCAA LJ 1999, TJ 2000.
Progression at LJ, TJ: 1996- 7.70, 15.65; 1997- 7.86, 1998- 8.05i/7.98w, 16.37i/15.48; 1999- 8.18, 17.02; 2000- 8.49, 16.96. pbs: 200m 20.51 '00, 400m 45.67 '98.

Kevin LITTLE b. 3 Apr 1968 Des Moines 1.83m 73kg. US West. Degree in marketing from Drake University.
At 200m: WCh: '95- qf, '97- sf, '99- 6; WI: '89- 3, '93- 3, '97- 1, '99- 3, '01- dns; PAm: '91- 2; WUG: '89- 6
Progression at 200m: 1984- 22.62, 1985- 22.30, 1986- 21.5, 1987- 21.04/20.80w, 1988- 20.55, 1989- 20.37A/20.39, 1990- 20.37, 1991- 20.63/ 20.48w; 1992- 20.33, 1993- 20.56, 1995- 20.60/ 19.94w, 1996- 20.29/20.09w, 1997- 20.24, 1998- 20.49, 1999- 20.10/20.08w, 2000- 20.30. pbs: 55m 6.14Ai '98, 100m 10.13/10.12w '98, 10.11Aw '92, 400m 44.77 '96.
Severed left Achilles tendon in 1993.

Anthuan MAYBANK b. 30 Dec 1969 Georgetown, South Carolina 1.88m 81kg. Reebok. Was at University of Iowa.
At 200m/4x400mR: OG: '96- 1R; WUG: '95- 1/1R. 2nd GP 400m 1996.
Progression at 200m, 400m, LJ: 1988- 46.82, 1989- 21.2, 46.39, 7.83; 1990- 21.36, 47.25, 1991- 21.04, 45.76, 7.81i; 1992- 20.70, 45.04, 8.06i/7.81; 1993- 20.79, 44.99, 8.25/8.40w; 1994- 20.59/ 20.55w, 45.76, 7.84w; 1995- 20.46/20.22w, 45.73, 8.25i/7.62; 1996- 20.41/20.19w, 44.15; 1997- 45.42, 1998- 20.74, 44.88; 1999- 20.61/20.44w, 44.76; 2000- 20.71, 44.80. pb 300m 31.61 '96.
Disqualified for running inside lane when 5th at US Trials 1996. Ran 43.87 last leg for gold at 1996 Olympics. Uniquely long jumped over 27ft (8.23m) and ran 400m in under 45 sec at same meeting in 1993 Drake Relays. Partner of Marie-José Pérec, and looking for French citizenship.

Coby MILLER b. 19 Oct 1976 Ackermann, Miss. 1.68m 68kg. Studying criminal justice at Auburn University.
At 200m/4x100m: OG: '00- 7; WUG: '99- 1/1R.
Progression at 100m, 200m: 1997- 10.24/10.19w, 20.73; 1998- 10.32/10.23w, 20.64; 1999- 10.03, 20.04; 2000- 9.98/9.88w, 19.96. pbs: 50m 5.70i '01, 55m 6.11i '99, 60m 6.50A/6.52i '99.
Was All-American at both football and track in high school and played football for a year in junior college before concentrating on sprinting.

Tim MONTGOMERY b. 28 Jan 1975 Gaffney, SC 1.78m 69kg. Asics. Was at Norfolk State University.
At 100m/4x100m: OG: '96- res (2)R, '00- res (1)R; WCh: '97- 3, '99- 6/1R; 2nd GP 2000. At 60m: WI: '01- 2.
Progression at 100m: 1992- 10.45w, 1993- 10.61/ 10.3, 1994- 10.11/9.96 irreg, 1995- 10.27/9.95w, 1996- 10.08, 1997- 9.92, 1998- 10.00/9.99w, 1999- 10.01/10.00w, 2000- 10.01/9.96w. pbs: 50m 5.57+ '97, 60m 6.43+ '97, 200m 20.52 '99, 20.44w '97.
Ran 100m in 9.96 to win the Junior Colleges title in 1994; but the wind gauge (+1.7) illegally placed on the outside of the track prevented ratification as world junior record; there were also doubts about whether the track measured 99.96m or 100m. Ran in heat and semi on US 4x100m team at 1996 Olympics and in heat in 2000.

Adam NELSON b. 7 Jul 1975 Atlanta 1.81m 115kg. Nike. Was at Dartmouth University. Training as a financial consultant.
At SP: OG: '00- 2; WI: '01- 2; WJ: '94- 1; WUG: '99- 2. 2nd GP 2000 (3rd overall). Won PAm-J 1993, NCAA 1997, US 2000.
Progression at SP: 1993- 16.56, 1994- 18.34, 1995- 18.27, 1996- 19.14, 1997- 19.62, 1998- 20.61, 1999- 20.64, 2000- 22.12. pb DT 54.38 '97.
Had a great season in 2000, when he improved his best from 20.64 to 21.70 and then the wortd's longest throw for four years, 22.12 (to take the US title) in July. Small for a shot putter, but very fast and dynamic in the circle. Played American Football at high school and college.

Tom PAPPAS b. 6 Sep 1976 Azalea, Oregon 1.93m 93kg. University of Tennessee.
At Dec: OG: '00- 5; WCh: '99- dnf. Won Pam-J 1995, NCAA 1999, US 2000.
Progression at Dec: 1995- 7198, 1996- 7499, 1997- 7677, 1999- 8463, 2000- 8467. pbs: 100m 10.70 '00, 400m 48.34 '99, 1500m 4:45.10 '00, 110mh 14.00 '99, HJ 2.21 '00, PV 5.10 '00, LJ 7.52 '99, SP 15.71i/15.38 '99, DT 48.66 '99, JT 66.12 '00.
Grandfather was a professional wrestler, father (Nick) set a world motor speed record.

Antonio PETTIGREW b. 3 Nov 1967 Macon, Georgia 1.83m 76kg. Reebok TC. Was at St Augustine's College.
At 400m/4x400m relay: OG: '00- 7/1R; WCh: '91- 1/2R, '93- res (1)R, '97- 7/1R, '99- 5/1R; WCp: '89- 5/2R, '92- 4R, '94- 1, '98- 1R. 2nd GP 1994, 3rd 2000. US champion 1989, 1991, 1994, 1997.
World record 4x400m 1998.
Progression at 400m: 1986- 47.19, 1987- 46.31, 1988- 45.36, 1989- 44.27, 1990- 45.26, 1991- 44.36, 1992- 44.71, 1993- 44.45, 1994- 44.43, 1995- 45.74, 1996- 45.19, 1997- 44.23, 1998- 44.40, 1999- 44.21, 2000- 44.57. pbs: 100m 10.42 '94, 200m 20.38 '94, 300m 32.15+ '99.
Ran a 43.1 relay (2nd) leg at 1997 Worlds.

Dwight PHILLIPS b. 1 Oct 1977 Decatur, Georgia 1.81m 82kg. Nike. Arizona State Univ..
At LJ: OG: '00- 8; PAm: '99- 7. 2nd US and NCAA 2000.
Progression at LJ: 1999- 8.18, 2000- 8.21/8.30w. pbs: 60m 6.68A '01, 100m 10.28/10.11w '00, TJ 16.41 '99.

Tom PUKSTYS b. 28 May 1968 Glen Ellyn, Illinois 1.88m 98kg. Adidas. Degree in public relations from University of Florida.
At JT: OG: '92- 10, '96- 8; WCh: '91- dnq 26, '93- 9, '95- dnq 19, '97- dnq 14; WCp: '92- 4. US champion 1992-3, 1995, 1997-9.
Six US javelin records 1993-7.
Progression at JT: 1987- 71.34, 1988- 75.72, 1989- 74.82, 1990- 83.30, 1991- 81.68, 1992- 83.20, 1993- 85.70, 1994- 82.32, 1995- 84.50, 1996- 86.82, 1997- 87.12, 1998- 85.06, 1999- 84.11, 2000- 84.25.

Duane ROSS b. 5 Dec 1972 Shelby, North Carolina 1.83m 78kg. Nike. Graduate of Clemson University.
At 110mh: WCh: '99- 3; Won NCAA 1995. At 60mh: WI: '97- 4, '99- 4.
Progression at 110mh: 1992- 13.97/13.61w, 1993- 13.74, 1994- 13.48, 1995- 13.32, 1996- 13.45, 1997- 13.50, 1998- 13.24, 1999- 13.12, 2000- 13.53. pbs: 200m 21.35w '95, 50mh 6.36i '99, 55mh 7.12i '93, 60mh 7.43i '99.
Only 4th at US Trials, but top US 110 hurdler at 1999 Worlds.

Gred SADDLER b. 29 Jun 1974 Sacramento 1.72m 72kg. Reebok. Was at Univ. of Mississippi.
At 100m: 3rd GP 2000.
Progression at 100m: 1992- 10.51, 1993- 10.38/10.25w, 1994- 10.20/10.11w, 1997- 10.26, 1998- 10.20/10.10w, 1999- 10.11, 2000- 10.08. pbs: 50m 5.66i '00, 55m 6.11i '94, 60m 6.51i '00, 200m 20.56 '99, 20.46w '98.

Adam SETLIFF b. 15 Dec 1969 El Dorado, Arizona 1.93m 125kg. Nike. Was at University of Washington.
At DT: OG: '96- 12, '00- 5; WCh: '97- 7. 2nd GP 1997.
Progression at DT: 1990- 55.46, 1991- 59.40, 1992- 61.54, 1993- 64.08, 1994- 62.08, 1995- 64.96, 1996- 66.86, 1997- 66.14, 1998- 68.45, 2000- 68.51.
Portrayed Mac Wilkins in Steve Prefontaine movie 1998. Missed 1999 season due to a hernia.

Savanté STRINGFELLOW b. 6 Nov 1978 Jackson, Miss. 1.90m 84kg. New York AC. University of Mississippi.
At LJ: OG: '00- dnq 22; WCh: '99-dnq 39; PAm: '99- 8. Won NCAA 2000.
Progression at LJ: 1999- 8.12, 2000- 8.30. pbs: 100m 10.43w '01, 200m 20.84w '00, HJ 2.14 '01, 2.18i '98?.

Angelo TAYLOR b. 29 Dec 1978 Albany, Georgia 1.88m 77kg. Nike. Was at Georgia Tech Univ., plane to enroll at Morris Brown College.
At 400mh/4x400mR: OG: '00- 1/res (1)R; WCh: '99- h/1R; WJ: '96- 3; won GP 2000 (and overall), PAm-J 1997, NCAA 1998, US 1999-2000.
Progression at 400mh: 1995- 52.76, 1996- 50.18, 1997- 48.72, 1998- 47.90, 1999- 48.15, 2000- 47.50. pbs: 200m 20.67 '97, 400m 44.89 '00.
Had a brilliant year in 1998, when he ran the fastest ever time by a 19 year-old and lost just twice, on both occasions to Bryan Bronson, at 400mh. Went out in his heat (misjudging the finish) when favourite for the 400mh title at the 1999 Worlds, but made amends with relay gold. Won US indoor 400m 1999.

Eric THOMAS b. 1 Dec 1973 Carthage, Texas 1.90m 88kg. Nike. Was at Abilene Christian University.
At 400mh: OG: '00- sf; PAm: '99- 2.
Progression at 400mh: 1993- 49.83, 1994- 49.29, 1995- 49.14, 1996- 48.20, 1997- 48.57, 1998- 48.45, 1999- 48.40, 2000- 47.94. pb 400m 46.33 '97.

Reggie TORIAN b. 22 Apr 1975 Harvey, Illinois 1.91m 89kg. Asics. Student at University of Wisconsin.
At 110mh: WCp: '98- 8; US champion 1998, NCAA 1997. At 60mh: WI: '99- 2.
Progression at 110mh: 1994- 14.17, 1995- 13.92, 1996- 13.57/13.45w, 1997- 13.26/13.24w, 1998- 13.03, 1999- 13.17, 2000- 13.42. pbs: 100m 10.55/10.18w '97, 50mh 6.43i '99, 55mh 7.07i '97. 60mh 7.38i '99, LJ 7.97 '94.
Was a star wide receiver at American football in college until 1997, but then concentrated on track. Won US indoor 60mh title 1997 and 1999.

Kevin TOTH b. 29 Dec 1967 Cleveland 1.93m 134kg. Nike. Was at McNeese State University. General manager of engineering company.
At SP: WCh: '93- 9, '97- 7, '99- nt.
Progression at SP: 1990- 18.06, 1991- 18.78, 1992- 20.99, 1993- 21.29, 1994- 21.25i/21.07, 1995- 21.17i/20.71, 1996- 21.15, 1997- 21.78, 1998- 21.10i/20.95, 1999- 21.59, 2000- 21.46.

Terrrence TRAMMELL b. 23 Nov 1978 Atlanta 1.88m 84kg. Student at University of South Carolina.
At 110mh/4x100m: OG: '00- 2; WUG: '99- 1/1R; Won NCAA 1999-2000. At 60mh: WI: '01- 1.
Progression at 110mh: 1997- 13.87, 1998- 13.32, 1999- 13.28, 2000- 13.16. pbs: 55m 6.12i '99, 60m 6.45Ai/6.51i '00, 100m 10.04 '00, 200m 20.74 '98, 20.45w '99; 55mh 6.94i '99, 60mh 7.47i '01.

Larry WADE b. 22 Nov 1974 Giddings, Texas 1.86m 79kg. Nike. Was at Texas A&M Univ.
At 110mh: Won NCAA 1998, 3rd GP 1999.
Progression at 110mh: 1994- 14.06/13.74w, 1995- 13.41, 1997- 13.38, 1998- 13.37, 1999- 13.01, 2000- 13.26. pbs: 50mh 6.51i '99, 55mh 7.08A '98, 60mh 7.59i '99, 400mh 50.82 '95.
Fine year in 1999, but only 7th (cramp) at US Trials. Moved from Elgin, Texas to Los Angeles in October 1998 to train with John Smith's group.

Erick WALDER b. 5 Nov 1971 Mobile, Alabama 1.86m 80kg. Adidas. Was at Univ. of Arkansas.
At LJ: WCh: '93- 4, '97- 2, '99- dnq 20; WI: '95- 3, '97- 4, '99- 3. At TJ: WJ: '90- 15. 3rd GP LJ 1997, 1999. Won NCAA LJ 1992-4, TJ 1994, indoor LJ & TJ 1992-4.
Progression at LJ, TJ: 1989- 7.36, 15.56; 1990- 16.25/16.31w, 1991- 7.79/7.84w, 16.05i; 1992- 8.47/8.58w, 16.88i/16.58/16.66w; 1993- 8.53, 16.86i/16.67/16.87w; 1994- 8.74A, 17.24i/17.12; 1995- 8.32, 1996- 8.58, 17.03; 1997- 8.49, 1998- 8.48/8.54w, 1999- 8.35i/8.22/8.50w, 2000- 8.14. pbs: 55m 6.0i '97, 200m 21.34 '92, HJ 2.11 '90.
His ten NCAA titles is a record for field events. Broke Carl Lewis's collegiate LJ record in 1994.

Anthony WASHINGTON b. 16 Jan 1966 Glasgow, Montana 1.86m 109kg. US West. Graphic artist. Graduate of Syracuse University.
At DT: OG: '92- 12, '96- 4, '00- 12; WCh: '91- dnq 28, '93- 11, '99- 1; PAm: '91- 1, '99- 1; WUG: '91- 2; WCp: '92- 1. US champion 1991, 1993, 1996, 1999. 2nd GP 1993 (3rd 1999).
Progression at DT: 1985- 52.88, 1986- 56.46, 1987- 60.16, 1988- 61.86, 1989- 64.18, 1990- 61.34, 1991- 65.04, 1992- 67.88, 1993- 66.86, 1994- 64.18, 1995- 66.70, 1996- 71.14, 1997- 63.12, 1998- 69.79, 1999- 69.08, 2000- 66.93. pb HT 59.58 '89.
Set pbs when 4th at 1989 TAC and when winning TAC and Pan-Am Games in 1991.

Tyree WASHINGTON b. 28 Aug 1976 1.85m 84kg. Reebok, San Bernardino Valley TC, California.
At 400m/4x400mR: WCh: '97- 3/1R.
World record 4x400m 1998.
Progression at 200m, 400m: 1995- 46.34, 1996- 20.88w, 46.00; 1997- 20.10, 44.38; 1998- 20.29, 44.29; 1999- 20.09, 45.50; 2000- 44.72. pb 500y 55.6i '98.
Made substantial breakthrough in 1997. Started as sprinter and long jumper; won 1994 California prep LJ title.

Bernard WILLIAMS b. 19 Jan 1978 Baltimore 1.83m 81kg. Was at University of Florida, moving to UCLA.
At 100m/4x100mR: OG: '00- 1R; PAm: '99- 1/4R. NCAA champion 2000.
Progression at 100m, 200m: 1997- 10.45, 21.13; 1998- 10.03, 20.46w; 1999- 10.08, 20.69Ai/20.71; 2000- 9.99, 20.03. pbs: 55m 6.08A '98, 60m 6.56iA '99, 6.59i '01.

Joey WOODY b. 22 May 1973 Iowa City 1.88m 78kg. Reebok. Degree in public relations from Northern Iowa University.
At 400mh/4x400mR: WCh: '97- sf, '99- 6/ res (1)R; WUG: '97- 5; WCp: '98- 5/1R. NCAA champion 1997. WIR 4x800m 2000.
Progression at 400mh: 1993- 50.76, 1994- 50.42, 1995- 49.97, 1996- 48.62, 1997- 48.18, 1998- 47.97, 1999- 48.22, 2000- 48.72. pbs: 400m 46.04 '99, 800m 1:47.75i '96, 1:48.41 '94; 110mh 13.98/13.63w '97.

Jerome YOUNG b. 14 Aug 1976 Jamaica 1.81m 79kg. Adidas. Was at Wallace State CC.
At 400m/4x400mR: OG: '00- res (1)R; WCh: '97- 5/1R, '99- 4; WI: '01- 2R; WCp: '98- 2/1R; PAm-J: '95- 2/1R (2 4x100R). US champion 1998-9. World record 4x400m 1998.
Progression at 400m: 1993- 47.25, 1994- 46.31, 1995- 45.01, 1996- 44.96, 1997- 44.50, 1998- 44.09, 1999- 44.24, 2000- 44.70. pbs: 200m 20.41 '98, 20.31w '00; 300m 31.95+ '99.
Ex-Jamaican, raised in Hartford, Connecticut, became US citizen in May 1995.

Torrance ZELLNER b. 6 Jan 1970 Baltimore 1.87m 75kg. Adidas. Was at University of Florida. Web page designer.
At 400mh: WCh: '99- 8; PAm: '91- 3, '99- 3/3R. 2nd GP 1996.
Progression at 400mh: 1987- c.55.4, 1988- 51.36, 1989- 53.90+, 1990- 50.56, 1991- 49.30, 1992- 49.10, 1993- 48.97, 1994- 49.07, 1996- 48.18, 1997- 48.71, 1998- 49.40, 1999- 48.45, 2000- 49.12. pb 110mh 13.98 '91.

Women

Amy ACUFF b. 14 Jul 1975 Port Arthur, Texas 1.88m 66kg. New Balance. Biology graduate of UCLA. Part-time model.
At HJ: OG: '96- dnq 24=, '00- dnq 31; WCh: '95- 8=, '97- dnq 14, '99- 9; WI: '01- 4; WJ: '92- 9, '94-3=; WUG: '97- 1. Won PAm-J 1993, NCAA 1995-6, US 1995, 1997.
Progression at HJ: 1988- 1.73, 1990- 1.83, 1991- 1.89, 1992- 1.90, 1993- 1.93, 1994- 1.89, 1995- 1.98,

1996- 1.94, 1997- 2.00, 1998- 1.94, 1999- 1.95, 2000- 1.91, 2001- 1.96i.

Kim BATTEN b. 29 Mar 1969 McRae, Georgia 1.70m 57kg. Reebok RC. Was at Florida State University.
At 400mh: OG: '96- 2, '00- sf; WCh: '91- 5, '93- 4, '95- 1, '97- 3/2R; PAm: '95- 1; WCp: '98- 3; won GP 1995, 1997 (3rd overall), 3rd 1993. At 400m: WI: '93 -6. Won US 400mh 1991, 1994-8.
World record 400mh 1995.
Progression at 400mh: 1986- 61.1, 1987- 60.94, 1988- 58.31, 1989- 58.60, 1990- 55.45, 1991- 53.98, 1992- 54.35, 1993- 53.84, 1994- 53.72, 1995- 52.61, 1996- 53.08, 1997- 52.97, 1998- 52.74, 1999- 53.99, 2000- 54.70. pbs: 55m 6.85i '96, 200m 23.52 '90, 400m 50.61 '98, 800m 2:10.35 '97, 50mh 7.01i '92, 55mh 7.55i '92, 100mh 13.14/13.06w '91, 13.0 '90; LJ 6.21i '91, 6.15/6.34w '90, TJ 12.95i '91, 12.92 '90.
Set collegiate 400m hurdles record in 1991, and improved her best by 1.11 secs to take the world record and world title at Göteborg 1995.

Dawn BURRELL b. 1 Nov 1973 1.75m 58kg. US Army. Was at University of Houston.
At LJ: OG: '00- 11; WCh: '99- 6; WI: '01- 1; PAm: '95- 5; WI: '99- 8; 2nd GP 2000. US champion 1999, indoors 1997-8. At 100mh: WJ: '92- 7.
Progession at LJ: 1989- 5.62, 1990- 6.09, 1991- 6.16i/6.08, 1992- 5.87, 1993- 6.01/6.02w, 1994- 6.46/6.55w, 1995- 6.22/6.38w, 1996- 6.46, 1997- 6.57/6.78w, 1998- 6.92i/6.90, 1999- 6.96, 2000- 6.98/6.99w, 2001- 7.03i. pbs: 100m 11.56/11.37w '99, 100mh 13.21 '99, TJ 12.34 '93.
Her brother Leroy (b. 21 Feb 1967) ran world records for 100m 9.88 '91 and 9.85 '94 (OG 92 5/1R, WCh 91- 2/1R, 93- 1R).

Shelia BURRELL b. 15 Jan 1972 Albuquerque 1.73m 64kg. Was at UCLA.
At Hep: OG: '00-26 (nh HJ); WCh: '99- 11; PAm: '99- 2. US champion 1999.
Progression at Hep: 1995- 5735, 1996- 5601, 1998- 6294w/6270, 1999- 6261, 2000- 6422. pbs: 100m 11.63 '95, 200m 23.32 '99, 400m 56.1 '90, 800m 2:10.29 '00, 100mh 13.19/13.14w '00, HJ 1.76 '99, LJ 6.46 '00, SP 13.76 '00, JT 50.31 '00.

Hazel CLARK b. 3 Oct 1977 Livingston, NJ 1.78m 55kg. Nike. Was at University of Florida.
At 800m: OG: '00- 7. Won NCAA 1998.
Progression at 800m: 1994- 2:10.24, 1995- 2:05.50, 1996- 2:05.08i/2:06.66, 1997- 2:01.42, 1998- 2:00.23, 1999- 2:01.77i/2:02.01, 2000- 1:58.75. pbs: 400m 53.69 '98, 1500m 4:16.04 '00, 1M 4:40.82 '00.
Sister of **Joetta** (b. 1 Aug 1962) who competed at four Olympics 1988-2000 (7th 1992) and five World Champs (7th 1997) and has ranked in US top ten at 800m for 22 successive years 1979-2000; pb 1:57.84 (1998). Their brother (and coach) J J Clark married Jearl Miles-Clark and their father is the celebrated school principal, Joe Clark, portrayed in the movie *Lean On Me*.

LaTasha COLANDER-RICHARDSON b. 23 Aug 1976 Portsmouth, Va 1.66m 52kg. Nike. Was at University of North Carolina.
At 400m/4x400mR: OG: '00- qf/1R. At 100mh: WJ: '94- 2. Won US 400m 2000.
Progression at 200m, 400m: 1993- 23.99, 1994- 23.56/23.3w, 1995- 23.80/23.60w, 1996- 23.26w, 1997- 23.21, 1998- 23.50i, 2000- 22.49, 49.87. pbs: 100m 11.64/11.60w '95, 300m 36.00 '00, 100mh 13.07 '96, 12.99w '97; 400mh 56.88 '99.
Having first made her name as a 100m hurdler, she won the US title in her first season at 400m in 2000.

Michelle COLLINS b. 12 Feb 1971 Canal Zone, Panama 1.77m 62kg. Graduate of University of Houston.
At 400m/4x400mR: OG: '00- h; WCh: '93- sf/res (1)R, '97- res (2)R, '99- sf/2R; WI: '99- 3R; PAm: '99- 2/2R; WCp: '94- 5R; WUG: '91- (200m 3), '93- 1/1R.
Progression at 400m: 1993- 51.59, 1994- 51.19, 1995- 50.84A, 1996- 51.84, 1997- 50.77, 1998- 51.17, 1999- 50.67, 2000- 50.11. pbs: 100m 11.19 '00, 200m 22.57 '00.
Limited by a right hip stress fracture at the 2000 Olympics.

Sharon COUCH-JEWELL b. 13 Sep 1967 Richmond, Virginia 1.72m 63kg. Reebok. Was at University of North Carolina. Business development manager. Married to Maurice Jewell.
At LJ: OG: '92- 6; WCh: '93/5/7- dnq 24/28/25=; WJ: '88- 11; WCp: '92- 4. At 100mh: OG: '00- sf.
Progression at 100mh, LJ: 1987- 13.82A/13.96w, 5.86A; 1988- 13.74, 6.32; 1989- 13.74w, 6.29; 1990- 13.65/13.40w, 6.23i/6.44w; 1991- 13.38, 6.54; 1992- 6.68; 1993- 6.51/6.62w, 1994- 13.24, 6.54/6.57w; 1995- 13.38/13.34w, 6.90; 1996- 6.70, 1997- 13.06, 6.77/7.07wA; 1998- 6.57/6.72w, 1999- 12.73/12.65w, 2000- 12.68. pbs: 100m 11.66/11.64w '93, 200m 24.23 '93, 55mh 7.63i 91, 60mh 7.94i '00, TJ 12.62i '90.

Gail DEVERS b. 19 Nov 1966 Seattle 1.60m 55kg. Nike International. Studied sociology at UCLA. Married to Ron Roberts 1988-92; now partner of Kenny Harrison.
At 100mh/4x100mR (100m): OG: '88- sf; '92- 5 (1), '96-4/1R (1), '00- sf; WCh: '91- 2, '3- 1/2R (1), '95- 1, '97- 1R, '99- 1 (5); PAm: '87- (1)/1R. At 60m: WI: '93- 1, '99- 2. Won NCAA 100m 1988, US 100m 1993-4, 100mh 1991-2, 1995-6, 1999. Won GP 100mh 2000 (2nd 1992), 2nd 100m 1996. 3rd overall 2000.
US records 100mh (6) 1988-2000, indoor 60m 1993.
Progression at 100m, 100mh: 1983- 11.69; 1984- 11.51/11.34w, 14.32; 1985- 11.19, 13.16/13.15w; 1986- 11.12/10.96w, 13.08; 1987- 10.98/10.85w, 13.28/13.1w; 1988- 10.97/10.86w, 12.61; 1991- 11.29, 12.48; 1992- 10.82, 12.55; 1993- 10.82, 12.46; 1994- 11.12/10.77w; 1995- 11.04/10.8w, 12.61; 1996- 10.83, 12.62; 1997- 10.88; 1999- 10.94,

12.37; 2000- 10.99, 12.33. pbs: 50m 6.00+ '99, 60m 6.95i '93, 200m 22.71/22.55w '87, 400m 52.66 '87, 800m 2:11.07 '82, 55mh 7.58i '92, 60mh 7.85i '94, 400mh 59.26 '85, LJ 6.77 '88, TJ 12.97/13.31w '86.
The fastest ever woman sprinter-hurdler. A serious thyroid disorder (Graves's Disease) caused her to miss competition in 1989-90, but after being close to having to have a foot amputated she made an astonishingly speedy return to the top to win the TAC 100mh in 1991, and on to world silver and the US record in Berlin. In 1992 she was a surprise winner of the Olympic 100m but tripped over the last hurdle when well clear of the field in the 100mh. Won 16 successive 100mh finals from 18 Jun 93 to Olympic 4th 1996, after she had become only the second woman to retain Olympic 100m title. Missed 1998 outdoor season, but was back in prime form indoors in 1999 and won the World outdoor title at 100mh, with her first US record for six years. Having been a class apart during the season, she was a clear favourite to take the 2000 Olympic gold at 100mh (at last), but, feeling a hamstring problem, pulled up after four hurdles in her semi final. She was also unable to run in the sprint relay in Sydney, but, needing to compete to ensure her share of the Golden League jackpot, she ran in the GP Final 100mh a week later, and, although heavily strapped, did more than just start but won to ensure a huge payday, including third in the overall Grand Prix.

Stacy DRAGILA b. 25 Mar 1971 Auburn, California 1.72m 63kg. née Mikaelson. Reebok. Graduate of Idaho State University.
At PV: OG: '00- 1; WCh: '99- 1; WI: '97- 1, '99- 8, '01- 4. US champion 1996-7, 1999-2000.
Three world pole vault records 1999-2000, 8 WIR 1997-2001. 16 US records 1996-2000 (and 18 indoors 1996-2001).
Progression at PV: 1995- 3.70, 1996- 4.20, 1997- 4.45, 1998- 4.48i/4.42A, 1999- 4.60, 2000- 4.70b/ 4.63. 2001- 4.70iA pbs: 100mh 13.88A '98, HJ 1.70 '97, LJ 5.81A '98, 5.97w '01; JT 44.28A '98, Hep 5488A '98.
Won first women's world pole vault titles both indoors (1997) and outdoors (1999), and both in world records.

Dawn ELLERBE b. 3 Apr 1974 Brooklyn, New York 1.88m 109kg. New York AC. Graduate of University of South Carolina, now assistant coach at University of Wyoming.
At HT: OG: '00- 7; WCh: '99- 10; PAm: '99- 1; WUG: '97- 6. US champion 1995-7, 1999-2000, NCAA 1996-7.
Eight US hammer records 1996-2000. Eight WIB 20lb weight from 21.86 to 23.60 '00.
Progression at HT: 1994- 51.72, 1995- 58.00, 1996- 63.76, 1997- 64.22, 1998- 63.56, 1999- 70.16, 2000- 70.46. pbs: SP 16.83i '98, 16.70 '97; DT 59.56 '00.

Suzy FAVOR HAMILTON b. 8 Aug 1968 Stevens Point, Wisconsin 1.62m 50kg. née Favor. Reebok RC. Graphic design graduate of University of Wisconsin.
At 1500m (800m): OG: '92- h, '96- (h), '00- 12; WCh: '91- h, '95- sf, '97- sf; WUG: '89- 2; WJ: '86- 9; WCp: '98- 4. Won PAm-J 1984 & 1986. US champion 1990-1, 1998, and record nine NCAA titles: 800m 1990, 1500m 1987-90, indoor 1M 1987, 1989-90; 3000m 1990.
US 1000m record 1995.
Progression at 1500m: 1983- 4:55.23 1M, 1984- 4:19.46, 1985- 4:19.43, 1986- 4:18.62, 1987- 4:09.20, 1988- 4:13.91, 1989- 4:09.7, 1990- 4:08.00, 1991- 4:06.13, 1992- 4:04.53, 1993- 4:10.69, 1994- 4:04.57, 1995- 4:05.14, 1996- 4:08.18, 1997- 4:03.50, 1998- 3:58.43, 1999- 4:13.96i, 2000- 3:57.40. pbs: 800m 1:58.10 '00, 1000m 2:33.93 '95, 1M 4:22.93 '98, 2000m 5:42.86 '94, 3000m 8:46.16 '00, 5000m 15:06.48 '00.
Won 21 individual and two relay Big 10 conference titles. Married Mark Hamilton, former baseball player, in 1991. Broke 4 minutes for 1500m for the first time on her 30th birthday.

Chrsyte GAINES b. 14 Sep 1970 Lawton, Oklahoma 1.70m 59kg. Adidas. Graduate of Stanford University.
At 100m/4x100mR: OG: '96- 1R, '00- sf/3R; WCh: '95- 1R, '97- 8/1R; PAm: '91-1 2/3R, '95- 1/1R; WUG: '91- 1/1R, '93- 5/1R; PAm-J: '89- 2/1R; 2nd GP 2000. At 200m: WCp: '94- 8, '98- 1R. At 60m: WI: '95- 7, '01- 3. Won NCAA 100m 1992.
Progression at 100m, 200m: 1985- 24.11/23.7, 1986- 11.76/11.4w, 23.68y; 1987- 11.50, 23.56/ 23.3; 1988- 11.50, 23.30y; 1989- 11.44, 24.24; 1990- 11.31, 23.71; 1991- 11.27/11.09w, 23.21/22.96w; 1992- 11.16/10.90w, 23.00; 1993- 11.25, 22.81; 1994- 11.32/11.2/10.99w, 23.32; 1995- 11.02, 22.92; 1996- 10.96, 22.82; 1997- 11.06, 22.91/22.53w; 1998- 10.89/10.8A, 23.08; 1999- 11.56A, 2000- 10.97, 23.04/22.83w. pbs: 50m 6.16i '99, 55m 6.68i '92, 60m 7.12i '01, LJ 5.84w '86.
1992 Olympic relay reserve, but did not compete.

Sandra GLOVER b. 30 Dec 1968 Palestine, Texas 1.72m 59kg. née Cummings. Teacher, graduate of University of Houston.
At 400mh: OG: '00- sf; WCh: 99- 5; US champion 1999-2000. 3rd GP 1999.
Progression at 400mh: 1988- 61.08, 1989- 59.99, 1990- 57.68, 1991- 56.97, 1992- 55.77, 1993- 56.76, 1994- 56.66, 1995- 57.39, 1996- 56.31mx/56.92, 1997- 55.63, 1998- 55.11, 1999- 53.65, 2000- 53.33. pbs: 200m 23.73 '00, 100mh 13.79/13.62w '91.
Made huge improvement in 1999 at the age of 30. Coached by her husband, Don Glover.

Monique HENNAGAN b. 26 May 1976 Columbia, SC 1.73m 55kg. Adidas. Degree in psychology from University of North Carolina.
At 400m/4x400mR: OG: '00- qf/1R; WI: '99- 3R, '01- 5/4R; WJ: '92- sf/4R, '94- 2/1R; PAm-J: '93-

2/2R. Won NCAA 800m 1996.
Progression at 400m: 1992- 53.58, 1993- 52.30, 1994- 52.19, 1995- 52.32, 1996- 51.44, 1997- 52.00, 1998- 51.11, 1999- 51.05, 2000- 50.82. pbs: 100m 11.86 '92, 11.3 '93, 11.69w '94; 200m 23.50 '97, 300m 36.68 '00, 800m 2:02.5 '96.

Regina JACOBS b. 28 Aug 1963 Los Angeles 1.68m 51kg. Nike. Graduate of Stanford Univ. Married her coach Tom Craig in December 1995.
At 1500m: OG: '88- h, '92- sf, '96- 10; WCh: '87- h, '97- 2, '99- 2; WI: '95- 1; WCp: '89- 9. At 3000m (5000m): WI: '99- 3; WCp: '98- 3 (2). Won US 1500m 1987, 1989, 1992, 1994-7, 1999-2000; 5000m 1998-2000.
US records 5000m 1998 and 2000, 1000m 1999. World best 2 miles (with illegal pacing) 1999.
Progression at 1500m, 5000m: 1980- 4:32.6, 1981- 4:25.0, 1983- 4:13.09, 1984- 4:11.33, 1985- 4:15.41, 1986- 4:02.6, 1987- 4:03.70, 1988- 4:00.46, 1989- 4:10.91, 1992- 4:03.72, 1993- 4:15.71, 1994- 4:02.15, 1995- 4:05.18, 1996- 4:01.77, 1997- 4:03.42, 14:58.79; 1998- 4:02.29, 14:52.49; 1999- 4:00.35, 15:24.80; 2000- 4:01.01, 14:45.35. pbs: 400m 56.79 '99 (54.49 '86?), 800m 1:58.08 '00, 1000m 2:31.80 '99, 1M 4:20.93 '98, 2000m 5:38.42 '94, 3000m 8:39.14i '99, 8:39.56 '98, 2M 9:11.97mx '99.
Had a fine year in 1999, when she reduced her pb at 800m after 12 years and at 1500m after 11 years, and won a fine double at the 2000 US Trials, taking seven seconds off her US record for 5000m. Withdrew from 1995 Worlds and 2000 Olympics through injury and viral infection respectively. Cousin of Wayne Collett (1972 Olympic silver at 400m).

LaTasha JENKINS b. 19 Dec 1977 Calumet Park, Illinois 1.70m 56kg. Was at Ball State University.
At 200m: WI: '01- 2; Won NCAA 1999.
Progression at 200m: 1996- 24.00/23.63w, 1997- 23.13/23.09w, 1998- 22.93, 1999- 22.29/22.22w, 2000- 22.86/22.54w. pb 100m 11.08 '99.
Withdrew through injury form 1999 Worlds after 2nd in US 200m.

Marion JONES b. 12 Oct 1975 Los Angeles 1.78m 68kg. Nike. Studied journalism at North Carolina State University.
At 100m/4x100m (200m): OG: 1/3R (1, 3 LJ, 1 4x400); WCh: '97- 1/1R (10 LJ), '99- 1 (sf, 3 LJ); WJ: '92- 5/2R (7); WCp: '98- 1 (1, 2 LJ). Won GP 100m 1998, 2000; 200m 1997; won overall 1998. 2nd 2000. Won US 100m 1997-8, 200m 1998-9, LJ 1997-8; GWG 100m/200m 1998.
Progression at 100m, 200m, 400m, LJ: 1988- 13.0, c.59.0, 1989- 12.01, 24.46/24.06w/23.8w, 56.73, 1990- 11.62, 23.70, 54.21; 1991- 11.17, 22.76, 52.91; 1992- 11.14, 22.58, 54.44; 1993- 11.28/11.2, 23.01/22.79w, 6.71/6.75w; 1994- 11.40, 23.32, 6.75; 1995- 11.68, 23.96w, 6.64; 1997- 10.76, 21.76, 6.93; 1998- 10.65A/10.71, 21.62A/21.80, 50.36, 7.31; 1999- 10.70, 21.81, 50.79, 7.01; 2000- 10.75/10.68w, 21.84, 49.59, 7.02. pbs: 50m 5.93+ '97, 60m 6.85+ '99.
The woman athlete of 1998, when she won 34 individual events until her 2nd to Heike Drechsler in World Cup LJ, her last competition of the year. Had another brilliant season in 1999, with 5 wins at 100m to World gold and 10 at 200m until pulled up with back spasms in her semi at the Worlds. In 2000 she won a record five medals at the Olympic Games, including three golds. Had dual nationality as mother was born in Belize, but opted for the USA. US junior champion at 100m & 200m 1991-2. 5th at 100m and 4th at 200m in 1992 US Olympic Trials, but declined Olympic relay reserve place. World 100m age bests for age 14-15-16 and 200m 15-16. She played point guard on the North Carolina basketball team that won the NCAA Divison 1 title 1994, but broke her left foot in August and December 1995. Her return to a track career in 1997 was stunning. Married shot putter **C J Hunter** (1999 World champ) on 3 Oct 1998.

Anjanette KIRKLAND b. 24 Feb 1974 Pineville, Louisiana 1.72m 66kg. Was at Texas A & M University.
At 100mh: WCh: '97- sf. At 60mh: WI: '01- 1.
US hammer record 1998.
Progression at 100mh: 1992- 13.99, 1993- 13.49/13.47w, 1994- 13.22, 1995- 13.09/12.89w, 1996- 13.24, 1997- 12.74/12.70w, 1998- 12.83, 1999- 12.91/12.68w, 2000- 12.63. pbs: 50mh 6.83i '01, 55mh 7.61i '96, 60mh 7.85i '01, 400mh 57.75 '97.

Kelly LaBOUNTY b. 24 Nov 1970 Prosser, Washington 1.81m 61kg. née Blair, married Matt LaBounty, a defensive end for the Seattle Seahawks on 31 Jan 1998. Nike. Was at University of Oregon.
At Hep: OG: '96- 8; WCh: '95- 10, '97- 10; WUG: '93- 3; NCAA champion 1993, US 1996-8. 2nd PAm-J 1989.
Progression at Hep: 1987- 4436, 1988- 5231, 1989- 5152, 1990- 5042, 1991- 5404, 1992- 5485w, 1993- 6038, 1994- 5907, 1995- 6354, 1996- 6406, 1997- 6465, 1998- 6465, 2000- 6217w/6180. pbs: 200m 24.13 '97, 800m 2:12.23 '96, 100mh 13.40 '95, 13.30w '98; 400mh 58.75 '93, HJ 1.81 '98, LJ 6.50 '98, 6.57w '95; SP 13.38 '98, JT 52.16 '98, new 46.48 '00.
Played for Oregon at basketball. Missed the 1999 season with a spinal disc injury, and also had to withdraw from the 2000 Olympics.

Jearl MILES-CLARK b. 4 Sep 1966 Gainesville 1.70m 60kg. Reebok. Was at Alabama A&M University.
At 400m (800m): OG: '92- sf/2R, '96- 5/1R, '00 1R (sf); WCh: '91- 5/2R, '93- 1/1R, '95- 3/1R, '97- 3/2R, '99 (4)/2R; WI: '93- 3, '95- 5, '97- 1/2R, '99- 3; PAm: '91- 3; WUG: '89- 2/1R; WCp: '92- 1, '94- 3, '98- (4). Won US 400m 1993, 1995, 1997; 800m 1998-9; GWG 400m 1994.
Three US 800m records 1997-9. WIR 500y 60.61 '00.

Progression at 400m, 800m: 1986- 52.41, 1987- 52.36, 1988- 51.28, 1989- 51.52, 1990- 51.76, 1991- 50.19, 1992- 50.30, 2:04.78; 1993- 49.82, 1994- 50.11, 1995- 50.00, 2:00.86; 1996- 49.55, 1:58.91; 1997- 49.40, 1:56.78; 1998- 50.11, 1:56.43; 1999- 49.98, 1:56.40; 2000- 50.04, 1:59.12. pbs: 100m 11.78/11.50w '93, 200m 23.03 '97, 300m 36.0 '95, 36.07 '00; LJ 6.45 '86, 6.47w '88.
Married long-time coach J J Clark, who had a 1500m pb of 3:41.5 (1988) and is brother of Joettta and Hazel Clark, on 30 Nov 1996.

Inger MILLER b. 12 Jun 1972 Los Angeles 1.63m 55kg. Nike. Degree in biological sciences from University of Southern California.
At 200m/4x100m (100m): OG: '96- 4/1R; WCh: '97- 5/1R (5), '99- 1 (2); WUG: '95- 1R; WCp: '98- 1R. Won US 100m 1999, 200m 1997. At 60m: WI: '99- 3.
Progression at 100m, 200m: 1988- 11.64/11.43w, 23.69; 1989- 11.53/11.38w, 23.62; 1990- 11.48, 23.57; 1991- 11.64/11.52w, 1992- 11.16/10.9w, 23.19/22.8/22.43w; 1993- 11.11, 22.33; 1994- 11.32/10.99w, 22.73/22.47w; 1995- 11.47; 1996- 10.96, 22.25; 1997- 11.04, 22.37/22.27w; 1998- 11.01/10.84w, 22.20; 1999- 10.79, 21.77; 2000- 10.91, 22.09. pbs: 50m 6.00+ '99, 60m 6.94+ '99, 400m 52.76 '94.
Her father Lennox Miller (Jam) won Olympic silver in 1968 and bronze in 1972 at 100m; they are the first ever father-daughter Olympic medallists at individual events in athletics – following the 4x100m silvers of Friedrich Hendrix (1932) and Brunhilde Hendrix (1960) for Germany. At the 1999 World Champs Miller improved her pb at 100m of 10.96 to 10.86, 10.81 and 10.79 (2nd) and at 200m from 22.10 to 21.77 when winning in great style. Withdrew from 2000 Olympic team through injury.

Melissa MORRISON b. 9 Jul 1971 Mooresville, NC 1.64m 56kg. Reebok. Was at Appalachian State University .
At 100mh: OG: '00- 3; WCh: '97- h; US champion 1997. At 60mh: WI: '97- 5, '99- 6.
Progression at 100mh: 1988- 14.37, 1989- 14.09, 1991- 13.63w, 1992- 13.24, 1993- 13.24, 1994- 13.24, 1995- 13.05A, 1996- 12.92/12.81w, 1997- 12.61, 1998- 12.53, 1999- 12.67/12.55w, 2000- 12.57. pbs. 100m 11.45A '93, 200m 24.07 '93, 50mh 6.81i '99, 60mh 7.85i '99, LJ 6.23 '93, TJ 12.55 '93.

Melissa MUELLER b. 16 Nov 1972 Waukesha WI 1.78m 68kg. Nike. Was at Wisconsin State University/Oshkosh. Married to Michael Clark.
At PV: OG: '00- dnq 14; WI: '99- 5.
Progression at PV: 1996- 3.53, 1997- 3.95, 1998- 4.22, 1999- 4.50i/4.38, 2000- 4.50b/4.45. pbs: 100mh 14.22, HJ 1.77 '93.
Started out as a hurdler and later a high jumper, before starting vaulting in 1995. She made a great breakthrough in the 1999 indoor season, improving from 4.22 to US records 4.49 and 4.50.

LeShundra '**DeDee**' **NATHAN** b. 20 Apr 1968 Fort Wayne 1.80m 75kg. Indiana Invaders. Was at Indiana University.
At Hep: OG: '00- 9; WCh: '93- 17, '95- 8, '97- 7; PAm: '91- 1, '95- 3. At Pen: WI: '97- 7, '99- 1.
Progression at Hep: 1990- 5855, 1991- 5998, 1992- 6162, 1993- 6038, 1994- 6189, 1995- 6283, 1996- 6327, 1997- 6317, 1998- 6479, 1999- 6577, 2000- 6343. pbs: 200m 24.11 '98, 800m 2:13.82 '96, 60mh 8.26i '99, 100mh 13.10 '96, 400mh 57.39A '89, 57.78 '88; HJ 1.86i '99, 1.83 '96; LJ 6.59/6.65w '98, SP 15.16 '97, JT 50.08 '99, Pen 4743i '99.
Added 230 points to pb when taking the 1999 World Indoor heptathlon gold. Won at Götzis but then missed Worlds after no height in the high jump in US heptathlon.

Amy PALMER b. 20 Apr 1975 Tooele, Utah 1.80m 100kg. née Christiansen. New York AC. Was at Brigham Young University.
At HT: OG: '00- 8; WCh: '99- 17. At SP: WJ: '94- 11. US hammer record 1998.
Progression at HT: 1995- 49.86, 1996- 56.48, 1997- 61.96, 1998- 67.08, 1999- 67.24, 2000- 68.28. pbs: SP 18.04i/17.71 '98, DT 51.90 '98, JT 44.42 '93. Married Rick Palmer on 30 Jan 1998.

Nanceen PERRY b. 19 Aug 1977 Fairfield, Texas 1.75m 69kg. Was at University of Texas.
At 200m/4x100mR: OG: '00- sf/3R; WCh: '99- qf/4R; WJ: '96- 6/1R; WUG: '99- 3/1R.
Progression at 200m: 1993- 23.57, 1994- 23.98/ 23.66w, 1995- 23.49, 1996- 23.17/22.88w, 1997- 22.73, 1998- 23.05/22.98w, 1999- 22.55/22.49w, 2000- 22.38/22.16w. pbs: 60m 7.13i '00, 100m 11.15 '99, 11.10w '00; LJ 5.93/6.03w '94, TJ 12.36 '94.

Connie PRICE-SMITH b. 3 Jun 1962 St. Charles, Missouri 1.92m 93kg. née Price, married John Smith (pb SP 19.59i '86, 19.58 '86) 1991. Reebok. Was at Southern Illinois University on a basketball scholarship.
At SP (DT): OG: '88-dnq 18 (dnq 16), '92- (dnq), '96- 5, '00- dnq 16; WCh: '87- (nt), '91- (11), '93- dnq 14 (dnq 19), '95- 9, '97- 5, '99- 11; PAm: '87- (3), '91- 2, '95- 1, '99- 1; WI: '91- 7, '95- 3, '97- 6, '99- 4; WCp: '89- (7), '94- (6), '98- 3. 3rd GP 1999. Won US SP 1988, 1990, 1992-2000; DT 1987, 1989-90, 1992-4; US Olympic Trials DT 1988.
Progression at SP, DT: 1985- 15.24i, 50.32; 1986- 17.28, 53.52; 1987- 18.29, 64.82; 1988- 19.15, 62.54; 1989- 18.55i, 62.86; 1990- 18.92, 59.00; 1991- 19.34, 59.24; 1992- 19.06, 64.00; 1993- 19.25, 63.52; 1994- 19.60, 62.32; 1995- 19.58, 58.72; 1996- 19.56, 59.84; 1997- 19.19, 1998- 19.46, 1999- 19.46, 2000- 19.18. Has won 24 US titles indoors and out.

Seilala SUA b. 25 Feb 1978 1.87m 109kg. Student at UCLA.
At DT/(SP): OG: '00- 10; WCh:'99- 6; WJ: '96- 2/8; PAm-J: '95- 2/1, '97- 1/1. Won US DT 1998-2000, NCAA SP 1999-2000, DT 1997-2000.
Progression at DT: 1994- 44.22, 1995- 53.84,

1996- 56.78, 1997- 63.44, 1998- 64.67, 1999- 64.89, 2000- 65.90. pbs: SP 17.65 '99, HT 60.60 '00, JT 49.12 '99, 20lb Wt 20.52i '99.
With the discus 1997-2000, Sua is only the second woman ever to win four successive NCAA titles at the same event (after Suzy Hamilton 1500m 1987-90). Her 107 points at shot, discus and weight indoors (38) and out (69) is a new NCAA record for any athlete.

Kellie SUTTLE b. 9 May 1973 St Peters, Missouri 1.70m 59kg. Nike. Was at Arkansas State University.
At PV: OG: '00- 11; WCh: '99- 9; WI: '01- 2=; PAm: '99- 2. Won US 1998.
Progression at PV: 1995- 3.71i/3.67, 1996- 3.85i/3.66, 1997- 3.90, 1998- 4.27, 1999- 4.46i/4.35, 2000- 4.53, 2001- 4.56i. pb LJ 5.86 '93.
Started pole vaulting while working as a gymnastics instructor.

Tisha WALLER b. 1 Dec 1970 South Boston, Virginia 1.83m 61kg. Was at University of North Carolina. Kindergarten teacher.
At HJ: OG: '96- 9=; WCh: '91- dnq 20, '93- dnq 17=, '99- 4=; WUG: '91- 3; WI: '99- 3; WCp: '98- 3. Won GWG 1998, US 1996, 1998-9.
Progression at HJ: 1986- 1.65, 1987- 1.65, 1988- 1.78, 1989- 1.78, 1990- 1.83, 1991- 1.93i/1.92, 1992- 1.92, 1993- 1.94, 1994- 1.96, 1995- 1.98, 1996- 1.99i/1.98, 1997- 1.84, 1998- 2.01i/1.98, 1999- 2.00, 2000- 1.96i/1.94. pb LJ 5.61 '88, TJ 12.74 '92.
Set a US indoor record when winning the US indoor title in 1998.

Angela WILLIAMS b. 30 Jan 1980 Bellflower, California 1.56m 52kg. Student at University of Southern California.
At 100m/4x100mR: WJ: '98- 2/1R; PAm: '99- 2/2R; WUG: '99- 1/1R; PAm-J: '95- 2, '97- 1/1R; Won NCAA 1999. At 60m: WI: '01- 2.
Progression at 100m: 1990- 12.85, 1992- 12.10, 1993- 11.79, 1994- 11.78, 1995- 11.24, 1996- 11.73/11.4w, 1997- 11.14/10.98w, 1998- 11.11/11.10w, 1999- 11.04/10.96w, 2000- 11.12/11.1/11.01w. pbs: 50m 6.17i '01, 60m 7.09i '01, 200m 23.02 '98, 22.78w '00; 400m 53.40 '95, 800m 2:16.78 '92, LJ: 5.83/6.00w '97.

Shana WILLIAMS b. 7 Apr 1972 Bridgeton, New Jersey 1.78m 66kg. Graduate of Seton Hall University.
At LJ: OG: '96- dnq, '00- dnq 21; WCh: '99- 12; WI: '99- 2. US indoor champion 1996. At Hep: WUG: '93- 7.
Progression at LJ: 1989- 5.74, 1990- 6.17i/6.05, 1991- 6.06, 1992- 6.28, 1993- 6.63, 1994- 6.31/6.53w, 1995- 6.57/6.63w, 1996- 7.01, 1997- 6.64/6.70w, 1998- 6.97, 1999- 6.82i/6.76, 2000- 6.80/6.87w. pbs: 100mh 13.74/13.66w '93, HJ 1.80i '93, 1.79 '92; Hep 5641w/5640 '93.
Moved to Eugene, Oregon after graduating in New Jersey.

UZBEKISTAN

Governing body: Light Athletic Federation of the Republic of Uzbekistan, Fourkat str. 1, office 208, Tashkent 700027. Founded 1950.

Andrey ABDUVALIYEV b. 30 Jun 1966 Leningrad, Russia 1.86m 112kg. Dushanbe Dyn.
At HT: OG: '92- 1, '00- dnq 15; WCh: '91- 5, '93- 1, '95- 1, '97/99- dnq 15; EJ: '85- 1; AsiG: '98- 2; AsiC: '98- 1; WCp: '94- 1, '98- 3. Won GP 1994, USSR HT 1991, Central Asian 1995, 1999.
Three Asian hammer records 1993-4.
Progression at HT: 1981- 52.40, 1982- 59.70, 1983- 65.20, 1984- 71.54, 1985- 73.20, 1986- 74.76, 1987- 74.06, 1988- 80.38, 1989- 81.00, 1990- 83.46, 1991- 82.80, 1992- 82.54, 1993- 82.78, 1994- 83.36, 1995- 83.10, 1997- 82.66, 1998- 80.70, 1999- 80.68, 2000- 80.51.
In 1990 he withdrew from the Europeans at the warm-up, and in 1991 disappointed by failing to complete the USSR clean sweep in the hammer in the Worlds. He won the Olympic gold, although that was one of only two wins in ten competitions during 1992. After Tajikistan became a member of the Asian AA in May 1993, he won the World title with his second Asian record of the year. Retained that title in 1995, but did not compete in 1996. Transferred nationality to Uzbekistan for 1997.

VENEZUELA

Governing body: Federación Venezolana de Atletismo, Apartado Postal 29059, Montalbán II, Calle 30, con 32-A Qunita Capinde, Caracas 1020. Founded 1948.
National Champions 2000: **Men**: 100m: Freddy Ávila 10.91, 200m: Jonathan Palma 21.61, 400m: William Hernández 47.28, 800m: Simoncito Silvera 1:51.09, 1500m/5000m: Néstor Nieves 3:51.82/14:21.91, 10000m: Lervis Arias 30:51.0, 3000mSt: Giovanny Valero 9:21.79, 110mh: Marleán Reina 14.40, 400mh: José Turbay 52.45, HJ: León Beltrán 2.03, PV: Edgar Reverón 4.10, LJ: Esteban Copland 7.97, TJ: Johnny Rodríguez 15.65, SP/DT: Yoger Medina 18.06/48.20, HT: Aldo Bello 63.80, JT: Edwin Cuesta 67.00, Dec: Marcos Reyes 6315, 20kmW: Carlos Ramones 1:36:13. **Women**: 100m/200m: Wilmary Álvarez 11.95/24.84, 400m: Eleana Pacheco 55.10, 800m: Yenny Mejías 2:13.58, 1500m: Adriana Moreno 4:53.71, 5000m: Norelis Lugo 18:17.36, 2000mSt: Yanileth Viloria 7:58.41, 100mh: Tamara Chourio 14.89, 400mh: Osmaira Sequea 63.31, HJ: María Thoris Luque 1.73, LJ: Nathaniel Gómez 5.90, TJ: Jennifer Arveláez 13.10, SP/DT: Neolanis Suárez 14.37/45.68, HT: Adriana Benaventa 44.56, JT: Carolina Castillo 45.04, Hep: Thaimara Rivas 4602, 20kmW: Karina Dueñas 1:51:48.

YUGOSLAVIA

Governing body: Atletski Savez Jugoslavije,

Strahinjica Bana 73a, 11000 Beograd. Founded in 1921.

National Championships first held in 1920 (men) and 1923 (women). **2000 champions**: **Men**: 100m: Milos Sakic 10.77, 200m: Marko Jankovic 21.52, 400m/400mh: Sinisa Pesa 46.54/50.48, 800m/1500m: Darko Radomirovic 1:49.79/3:40.02, 5000m: Ivan Cvetanovic 14:37.80, 10000m/HMar: Ramiz Taipi 31:44.29/63:06 (short), Mar: Sreten Ninkovic 2:28:08, 3000mSt: Dejan Bogicevic 9:10.44, 110mh: Nenad Loncar 14.63, HJ: Dragutin Topic 2.33, PV: Fedja Kamasi 4.70, LJ: Danial Jahic 7.99, TJ: Zoran Djurdjevic 16.43, SP: Dragan Peric 19.88, DT: Caba Guljas 59.59, HT: Nemenja Strbac 55.19, JT: Bojan Ilic 69.20, Dec: Dejan Mandaric 6973, 10,000mW/20kmW: Predrag Filipovic 41:34.2/1:30:35. **Women**: 100m: Elvira Pancic 11.78, 200m/100mh/Hep: Mila Savic 24.24/14.35/5336, 400m: Jelena Stanisavljevic 54.23, 800m: Nevena Lizdek 2:13.08, 1500m: Sonja Stolic 4:17.37, 5000m: Mirjana Kalajdzic 18:37.0 (lap too many), 10000m: Mira Preradovic (b.1987) 36:02.85, HMar: Enisa Salijevic 80:42 (short), Mar: Vesna Stevanovic 3:11:16, 400mh: Ivana Jovanovic 62.19, HJ: Jelena Scekic 1.75, PV: Ljiljana Novkovic 3.20, LJ: Marija Martinovic 6.10, TJ: Radojka Kurcubic 12.32, SP: Snezana Milinkovic 14.61, DT: Danijela Curovic 57.52, HT: Danijela Jankovic 50.36, JT: Maja Janjic 47.60, 5000mW/10kmW: Ankica Barzut 25:15.39/56:42.

Dragan PERIC b. 8 May 1964 Zivinice 1.86m 115kg. Crvena Zvezda, Beograd.
At SP: OG: '92- 7, '96- 8, '00- dnq 16; WCh: '91- 7, '93- 5, '97- dnq 19, '99- 6; EC: '90- 13, '94- 6, '98- 4; WI: '95- 3; EI: '94- 2, '98- 4. Yugoslav champion SP 1990-4, 1996-2000; DT 1992-4, 1997; Balkan SP 1996, 1998.
Yugoslav records: shot (3) 1993-8, discus 1991.
Progression at SP: 1980- 11.35, 1981- 12.23, 1982- 14.88, 1983- 17.24, 1985- 16.89, 1986- 17.70, 1987- 18.86, 1988- 19.92, 1989- 20.42, 1990- 20.06, 1991- 20.47, 1992- 20.91, 1993- 21.26, 1994- 20.64i/20.57, 1995- 20.36i/20.14, 1996- 20.90, 1997 20.78, 1998- 21.77, 1999- 20.74, 2000- 19.88. pb DT 61.94 '91.

Dragutin TOPIC b. 12 Mar 1971 Belgrade 1.97m 74kg. AK Partizan, Beograd. Was at Belgrade University of PE.
At HJ: OG: '92- 8=, '96- 4, '00- dnq 21=; WCh: '91- 9, '93- dnq, '95- 8=, '97- dnq, '99- 4; EC: '90- 1, '94- 5=, '98- 9=; WJ: '90- 1; EJ: '89- 4; WI: '97- 3; EI: '92- 3=, '96- 1, '00- 3; WUG: '95- 1. 3rd GP 1994, 2000. Yugoslav champion 1993, 1996, 1999-2000; Balkan 1998.
World junior high jump record 1990, five Yugoslav records 1990-3.
Progression at HJ: 1985- 1.85, 1986- 1.95, 1987- 1.95, 1988- 2.06, 1989- 2.23, 1990- 2.37, 1991- 2.32/2.34i, 1992- 2.35, 1993- 2.38, 1994- 2.32, 1995- 2.29, 1996- 2.35, 1997- 2.32i/2.31, 1998- 2.33, 1999- 2.32, 2000- 2.34i/2.33. pbs: LJ 7.48i '93, TJ 15.66 '92, Dec 6155h '93.
Won World Junior and European senior HJ titles in 1990. Was at high school in Illinois, USA for a year in 1987/8, but played basketball while there and did not compete as a high jumper. Reported to have failed a drugs test on 2 Feb 2001.

Women

Olivera JEVTIC b. 24 Jul 1977 Titovo Uzice 1.74m 52kg. Mladost-Niskogradnja, Uzice.
At 10000m (5000m): OG: '00- 11 (dnf); WCh: '97- h (h), '99- 10; EC: '98- 4 (4); EU23: '97- 1, '99- 1 (3); WJ: '94- (3000m 10), 96- (2, 3000m 5); EJ: '95- 2 (3000m 3). World HMar: '98- 4, '99- 22; CC: '95- 17J, '00-01 15/9; Eur CC: '96-7-8-9-00: 13/3/3/3/3. Won Yugoslav 1500m 1996, 5000m 1996, HMar 1998-9, CC 1994-7, 1999; Balkan 5000m 1998.
Yugoslav records: 5000m (7) 1995-2000, 10000m (2) 1998-2000, HMar (2) 1998.
Progression at 5000m, 10000m: 1995- 16:03.34, 33:48.61; 1996- 15:40.59, 32:38.0; 1997- 15:34.65, 32:43.42; 1998- 15:16.61, 31:34.26; 1999- 15:19.08, 31:57.67; 2000- 15:11.25, 31:29.65. pbs: 8000m 2:12.41 '93, 1500m 4:16.16 '98, 3000m 8:59.21 '98, HMar 70:02 '98 (69:58 short '97).

ZAMBIA

Governing body: Zambia Amateur Athletic Association, PO Box 30521 Lusaka.

Samuel MATETEb. 27 Jul 1968 Chingola 1.83m 81kg. Student at Auburn University, formerly at Blinn CC, USA 1988-90.
At 400mh: OG: '88- h, '92- dq sf, '96- 2, '00- sf; WCh: '91- 1. '93- 2, '95- 2, '97- 5, '99- sf; CG: '90- 5, '94- 1; AfG: '87- sf; AfCh: '88- 5 (4.400m), '98- 1; WJ: '88- 5; WCp: '92- 1/1R, '94- 1/2R, '98- 1. Won GP 1994 (2nd overall), 2nd 1990, 1992; 3rd 1996, 2000. Won NCAA 1991.
African 400mh record 1991. Zambian records 1989-91: 11 at 400mh, 2 at 400m.
Progression at 400mh: 1987- 51.48, 1988- 50.5, 1989- 48.67, 1990- 47.91, 1991- 47.10, 1992- 47.91, 1993- 47.60, 1994- 47.90, 1995- 47.52, 1996- 47.78, 1997- 47.84, 1998- 48.08A/48.32, 1999- 47.91, 2000- 48.01. pbs: 100m 10.77 '89, 200m 21.04 '89, 400m 44.88 '91.
Five national records in a month in 1989 from 49.94 to 48.67. He moved up to world number two in 1990. In 1991 he was unbeaten in 23 races at 400mh, improving to 47.80 and then to 47.10 (the second fastest ever run) in Zürich prior to becoming the first Zambian world champion. In 1992 he was disqualified after finishing third in his Olympic semi for trailing leg knocking down hurdle in another lane. In 1994 he won Zambia's first Commonwealth athletics gold medal. Apparently over age when he competed in the 1988 World Juniors.

INTRODUCTION TO WORLD LISTS AND INDEX

Records

World, World Junior, Olympic, Continental and Area records are listed for standard events. In running events up to and including 400 metres, only fully automatic times are shown. Marks listed are those which are considered statistically acceptable by the ATFS, and thus may differ from official records where, for instance the performance was set indoors.

World All-time and Year Lists

These lists are presented in the following format: Mark, Wind reading (where appropriate), Name, Nationality (abbreviated), Date of birth, Position in competition, Meeting name (if significant), Venue, Date of performance.
In standard events the best 30 or so performances are listed followed by the best marks for other athletes. Position, meet and venue details have been omitted for reasons of space beyond 100th in year lists.
In the all-time lists performances which have been world records (or world bests, thus including some unratified marks) are shown with WR against them – outdoor records only.

Indexes

These lists contain the names of all athletes ranked with full details in the world year lists for standard events (and others such as half marathon). The format of the index is as follows:
Family name, First name, Nationality, Birthdate, Height (cm) and Weight (kg), 2000 best mark, Lifetime best (with year) as at the end of 1999.
* before the name indicates an athlete who is profiled in the Biographies section, and a ^ symbol one who has been profiled in previous editions.

General Notes

Altitude aid

Marks set at an altitude of 1000m or higher have been suffixed by the letter "A".
Although there are not as yet separate world records for altitude assisted events, it is understood by experts that in all events up to 400m in length (with the possible exclusion of the 110m hurdles), and in the horizontal jumps, altitude gives a material benefit to performances. For events beyond 800m, however, the thinner air of high altitude has a detrimental effect.
Supplementary lists are included in relevant events for athletes with seasonal bests at altitude who have low altitude marks qualifying for the main list.

Some leading venues over 1000m

Addis Ababa ETH	2365m
Air Force Academy USA	2194
Albuquerque USA	1555
Antananarivo MAD	1350
Arusha TAN	c.1400
Bloemfontein RSA	1392
Bogotá COL	2644
Boulder USA	1655
Calgary CAN	1045
Cali COL	1046
Ciudad de México MEX	2247
Colorado Springs USA	1823
Denver USA	1609
Echo Summit USA	2250
El Paso USA	1187
Flagstaff USA	2105
Font-Romeu FRA	1850
Fort Collins USA	1521
Germiston RSA	1661
Guadalajara MEX	1567
Harare ZIM	1473
Johannesburg RSA	1748
Krugersdorp RSA	1740
Gyumri (Leninaken) ARM	1556
Medellín COL	1541
Nairobi KEN	1675
Pietersberg RSA	1230
Pocatello USA	1361
Potchefstroom RSA	1351
Pretoria RSA	1400
Provo USA	1380
Reno USA	1369
Roodepoort RSA	1720
Rustenburg RSA	1157
Secunda RSA	1628
Sestriere ITA	2050
Soría ESP	1056
South Lake Tahoe USA	1909
Toluca MEX	2700
Tsakhkadzor ARM	1980
Windhoek NAM	1725

Some others over 500m

Almaty KZK	847
Ankara TUR	902
Bern SUI	555
Boise USA	818
Canberra AUS	581
La Chaux de Fonds SUI	997
Caracas VEN	922
Edmonton CAN	652
Las Vegas USA	619
Lubbock USA	988
Madrid ESP	640
Malles ITA	980
Moscow, Idaho USA	787
München GER	520
Salamanca ESP	806
Santiago de Chile CHI	520
São Paulo BRA	725

Sofia BUL	564
Spokane USA	576
Tucson USA	728
300m-500m	
Annecy FRA	448
Atlanta USA	302
Banská Bystrica SVK	362
Genève SUI	385
Götzis AUS	448
Johnson City USA	499
Lausanne SUI	375
Rieti ITA	402
Sindelfingen GER	440
Tashkent UZB	477
Zürich SUI	410

Automatic timing

In the main lists for sprints and hurdles, only times recorded by fully automatic timing devices are included.

Hand timing

In the sprints and hurdles supplementary lists are included for races which are hand timed. Any athlete with a hand timed best 0.01 seconds or more better than his or her automatically timed best has been included, but hand timed lists have been terminated close to the differential levels considered by the IAAF to be equivalent to automatic times, i.e. 0.24 sec. for 100m, 200m, 100mh, 110mh, and 0.14 sec. for 400m and 400mh. It should be noted that this effectively recognises bad hand timekeeping, for there should be no material difference between hand and auto times, but what often happens is that badly trained timekeepers anticipate the finish, as opposed to reacting to the flash at the start.

In events beyond 400m, automatically timed marks are integrated with hand timed marks, the latter identifiable by times being shown to tenths. All-time lists also include some auto times in tenths of a second, where the 1/100th time is not known, but these are identified with the symbol ′.

Indoor marks

Indoor marks are included in the main lists for field events and straightway track events, but not for other track events. This is because track sizes vary in circumference (200m is the international standard) and banking, while outdoor tracks are standardised at 400m. Outdoor marks for athletes whose seasonal bests were set indoors are shown in a supplemental list.

Mixed races

For record purposes athletes may not, except in road races, compete in mixed sex races. Statistically there would not appear to be any particular logic in this, and women's marks set in such races are shown in our lists - annotated with mx. In such cases the athlete's best mark in single sex competition is appended.

Field event series

I have tried to include field event series for marks in the top 30 performances list for 2000. Sadly such information is missing from some meetings, and I hope that correspondents will help provide such more details in future.

Tracks

As with climatic conditions, the type and composition of tracks and runways will affect standards of performance.

Wind assistance

In the lists for sprints, long jump and triple jump, anemometer readings have been shown where available. The readings are given in metres per second to one decimal place. Where the figure was given originally to two decimal places, it has been rounded to the next tenth upwards, e.g. a wind reading of +2.01 m/s, beyond the IAAF legal limit of 2.0, is rounded to +2.1; or -1.22 m/s is rounded up to -1.2.

For multi-events a wind-assisted mark in one in which any of these events is aided by a wind over 4.0 m/s; such assisted marks are shown with a capital W.

Drugs bans

The IAAF have determined that the IAAF Executive Council may decertify an athlete's records, titles and results if he or she later admits to having used a banned substance before those performances. We have not removed any such athletes from all-time lists, but for information have shown ¶ after the name of any athlete who has at any stage in his or her career undergone a drugs suspension of a year or more (thus not including athletes receiving 3 month bans (now warnings) for stimulants etc., which for that year only are indicated with a #). This should not be taken as implying that the athlete was using drugs at that time. Nor have those athletes who have subsequently unofficially admitted to using banned substances been indicated; the ¶ is used only for those who have been caught.

Venues

From time to time place names are changed. Our policy is to use names in force at the time that the performance was set. Thus Leningrad prior to 1991, St Petersburg from its re-naming.

Amendments

Keen observers may spot errors in the lists. They are invited to send corrections to the editor, who will also welcome news and results for 2001.

Peter Matthews, 10 Madgeways Close, Great Amwell, Ware, Herts SG12 9RU, England
Fax 44 1920 877392
Email peter@matthews.in2home.co.uk

Amendments to ATHLETICS 2000

p.15 Feb 21, Liévin: Szabo 8:34.09 for 3000m
Feb 26-27, US Champs: Griffin 20.32 for 200m
p.22 Aug 11, Zürich: C Kosgei 8:05.43
p.51 17 Oct Graz Marathon: Roba 2:12:25
p.70 Drugs Disqualifications 1999. Men – Robert Koss AUT 4 Nov 2 years; Women – Deng Xiaochen CHN 8 Jul Pending – this could affect her 12.87 for 100mh on 17 Oct
p.84 World Champs 100m: at 60m: Montgomery 6.52.
p.97 Pan-Am Junior Dec: 1. Bryan Clay USA 7207, 2. Marcell Allmond USA 7111, 3. Maurice Smith JAM 6996
p.335 Junior Women's All-time 100mh: delete 12.76 Liu Jing in 1997 – she was at the time thought to have been born on 9.1.78, but later confirmed as 8.8.77.
p.591 European Indoor Champs: Men Shot: Bagach disqualified from 1st, so move up the rest and add 6. Tepa Reinikainen FIN 19.93.

World Lists 1999 – Men

High altitude: Karl Graf has found the track at Malles, Italy to be just below our 1000m high altitude level (perhaps c.980m). So that means that the A should be removed from the following 1999 marks: Men: 100m: 10.32 Amici, 800m: 1:46.47 Daum, 110mh: 13.55 Giaconi (remove 13.61 best la), 13.63 Rossi; LJ: 8.07 Trentin (7.93), 7.81 Campus; Women: 400m: 51.58 Ekpo-Umoh, 52.96 Carbone

Men

100m: 10.27A 1.8 Sherwin Vries NAM-J 22.3.80 1 Windhoek 19 Jun (& Jnrs), 10.27w Braziel 27.11.80 (& his twin Jerrod at 20.80w); hand: add 10.1 Fidelis Gadzama NGR 20.10.79 18 Jun, 10.1 Taiwo Ajibade NGR-J .82 Kaduna 19 Jun (add to juniors), 9.8w Al-Saker

200m: 20.67A 1.2 Sherwin Vries NAM-J 22.3.80 1 Windhoek 19 Jun (& Jnrs), 20.68 Alpha Babacar Sall SEN 15 May, 20.73A Christie van Wyk NAM 12.10.77 19 Jun, 20.74 Asahara; Hand: 20.7 Themba Ncube ZIM .77 4 Jul; Jnrs 20.82 2.0 Yang

400m: 46.01 Takahiko Yamamura, 46.04 Dozier 1.6.79 (& 200m 20.85w), 46.12 Alexandre Marchand, 46.12A Masvanshise 25 Jul (from 46.30A)

800m: 1:45.13 Luka Kipkoech, 1:47.3 Saïd Allali MAR 23 Jun, 1:47.6A James Maritim KEN 5 Jun, 1:47.9 Kennedy Osei GHA 21.10.66 30 Jul; Juniors: 1:48.1 Abdelkébir Louraïbi MAR 9.2.81 Meknés 5 Jun, 1:48.7 Noureddine Azzouzi MAR .80 Rabat 16 May

1500m: 3:31.51 Maaziouzi 15.10.69 (and in 1000, 2000), 3:35.63 Mekonnen 4.4.80 (& 3k, 5k), 3:40.12 Luke Kipkosgei 27.11.75 (& 7:35.30, 13:00.83); 3:41.0A Basweti (not 3:40.8)

1 Mile indoors: 3:58.2e+ Sammy Rono KEN 74 14 Feb

3000m: 7:42.98 Girma Tolla 13.10.75 (& 10k), 7:49.53 Felix Limo KEN-J 22.8.80 (& 13:23.43, 28:23.30, 28:22R); Jnrs: 7:58.90 Abraham Cherono KEN 21.7.80 3 Barletta 9 Sep, 8:04.6 Ridouane Haroufi MAR 30.7.81 Rabat 16 May

5000m: 13:39.5 Ali Saïdi-Sief ALG 15.3.78 22 May, 13:44.2 Saïd Bara MAR 9 May, 13:44,4 John Muriuthi

10000m: 27:38.86 John Cheruiyot Korir KEN 13.12.81 (not .75 John Korir) = 8th Junior AT, 28:03.67 Lagat; Juniors: 28:48.4A Thomas Nyakundi KEN .80 2 Nairobi 18 Jun, 29:02.5 Kipsigei .80, 29:04.37 James Wainaina KEN 16.6.81 Hachioji 1 Dec, 29:21.0A Willy Kirui KEN .82 Nairobi 2 Jul

HMar: 60:58 Zéroual FRA, 62:52 Michael Kite, 62:52 Willy Cheruiyot KEN 19 Sep

Mar: 2:06:57 T Tola 19.10.74 (& 10k, 10M, HMar), 2:10:37 L David Kemboi KEN 1 Palermo 8 Dec 2:11:36 Obed Gisemba 4 Jul (not 2:12:36), 2:13:17 Daniel Shungea

3000mSt: 8:18.46 Dobert 8.8.74, 8:33.55 Turki (and delete at 8:35.55). 8:37.74 Uchitomi 29.10.72; Jnrs: 8:45.08 Chemlal at Casablanca 13 Jul

110mh: 13.82 Ebine 27.7.77, delete 13.86 Korniyenko; Juniors: 14.19 0.0 Liu Xiang CHN 23.7.83 4 Shanghai 17 Apr (to 14.20)

400mh: 50.61 Ratnayake 8.12.74, 50.80 Osita Okeafu NGR 78 and 50.84 Glory Okfako NGR both 3 Jul

HJ: 2.22 Jara ARG; Jnrs: 2.18 Vincent 6.3.81

LJ: (8.31) Mersal also 8.30 nwi 1 El Maadi 1 Oct, 8.17A 1.2 Stephan Louw NAM 26.2.75 1 Windhoek 19 Jun, 7.86 Rohitha 27.10.69, 7.83 0.8 Chou Chien-Cheng TPE 10.9.77 & 7.81 0.0 Chao Chih-Kuo TPE 9.12.72 29 Dec, 7.80 -2.0 Hsu Chih-Hsiung TPE .77 27 Mar; Jnrs: 7.70 Idika Uduma NGR 82 NC Lagos 31 Jul

TJ: 16.70 Al-Ahmadi KSA, 16.36 drugs dq Wu Ji ¶ Jnrs: 16.00/16.02w Sands 16.8.81

SP: 20.74 Peric 8 Aug, 19.94 Stevimir Ercegovac, drugs dq 18.86 Nikolayev ¶; 18.59 (not 18.89) Neighbour 9 Jan; Juniors: 17.45 Kulwinder Singh IND 5.5.80 5 New Delhi 12 Oct, 17.40 Kuldeep Singh Maan IND 16.10.82 7 New Delhi 12 Oct

DT: 62.40 Conjungo, 53.41 Wu Tao 1987 d.o.b. unlikely!

HT: 80.51 Konovalov 4.3.71, 70.36 Tikhon 24.7.76

JT: 78.20A Paul Lagat KEN 69 1 Nairobi 21 Jun, 75.30 Ue 29 Aug, 74.38 Dejan Angelovski MKD .76. 100th best 75.78

Dec: 8107 Mewes 7.10.76, 7763 Sander 1500m 4:38.0; 7702 probably Nikolay not Sergey Afanasyev? 7550 Williams 16.8.74, 7538 Brophy 6.1.69, 7424 Yarkin; best auto: Sander 7430 on 28 May

4x100m: 39.82A NAM 17 Jun

4x400m: 2:56.45 USA (1st leg Jerome Davis), 3:05.28A and 3:05.71A

20kmW: 1:22:33A Kimutai 1 Narobi 4 Jun (from 1:22:37), Jnrs: 1:27:42 Bian Aiguo CHN 10.6.80 7 Shangqiu 9 May

50kmW: 3:51:26, 3:54:18, 3:54:47 at Naucalpan 21 Mar, delete 4:05:35 Seaman

Women

100m: 11.09A 1.9 Allen, 11.37 Perepelova 26.2.79; hand: 11.3 Calista Onyejiaka NGR 18 Jun

200m: 22.99 Aminita Diouf 1 Dakar 30 May (from 23.24), world 100th 23.22; 23.26 –1.0 Mame Tacko Diouf SEN 17.10.76 5 Apr; 23.52 Bu Fanfang; wa: 23.47 2.7 Angela Atede NGR 8.2.72; low alt: 22.96 Dharsha (b. 13.2.75, change at 11.19A, 22.68A, 52.11A); hand: 23.2 Calista Onyejiaka NGR and 23.3 Chinedu Odozor NGR .77 at Lagos 3 Jul

400m: 51.21A Komgang 21.2.74, 51.98 George 7.8.76, Juniors: 53.21 Zhou 3s1

800m: 2:03.4A (not .32) Sidelil J 1 May, 2:03.5 Saadia Saadi MAR 17 Jul

1500m: 4:14.12 Fatima Lanouar TUN 14.3.78 4 Jul, 4:14.18 Abir Nakhli TUN .81 Bucuresti 4 Jul (add to Jnrs). 4:14.2 Samira Raït MAR .74 16 Jul; Juniors: 4:15.47 Méryem Kirouani Boucetta MAR .81 Casablanca 13 Jul

3000m: 9:07.71 Hashim at Casablanca 13 Jul (from 9:08.43 & Jnrs), 9:08.13 Souad Benallal MAR .71 13 Jul; Jnrs: 9:09.60 Asahssah 24.9.82, 9:11.2A Kibiwott .83 (& 5000m 15:55.5)

5000m: 15:29.25 Lan 4.2.79 (& 1500m 4:11.62), 15:30.89 Yuko Manabe, 15:37.5 Ikuko Tamura, 15:44.01 Tsutsumi 23 Jun

10,000m: 33:48.8 Chebiego .84
Mar: 2:29:20 Ai Dongmei dob 15.10.79 (not 15.10.81 as previously reported), see also 10k 32:40.6 and junior all-time list)
3000mSt: Elizabeth Jackson 27.10.77
100mh: 12.53 Alozie and 3 others at Monaco 4 Aug; 12.87 Deng relegate to after drugs dq; 12.98 0.4 Ferga, 13.25 Zhu Shuiying, 13.36 Vu Bich Huong, 13.53 1.6 Huang Mei-Hua TPE 18.3.72 1h Kaohsiung 29 May
400mh: 55.99 Li Yulian 17.2.79, 56.66 Jia Wanhong, 57.60 Yao Yuehua, 57.94 Laraba Nasiru, 58.22 Fan Min-Hua TPE 24.11.75 28 Dec
HJ: 1.85 Netnapa Thaiking. 1.84i Zaytseva 14.8.81
PV: 4.50 Melissa Mueller, 3.90 Yang Fei 18.5.80
LJ: 6.96 1.9 Burrell, 6.75 0.0 Johansson, 6.67 Chinedu Odozor 1 Lagos 3 Jul (from 6.45A), 6.60 Peng Fengmei 9.7.79 (& TJ 13.49), 6.43 G. Pramila Ganapathy 8.5.77 (& Hep), 6.36 0.0 Lin Chao-Hsiu TPE 4.1.75 28 Dec
TJ: 13.82i Rhodes – relegate to footnote drugs suspension (public warning) and replace by 13.52i 1 Houston 23 Jan; 100th best 13.64; 13.63 1.3 Wang Kuo-Huei TPE 12.9.78 26 Dec, 13.46 Li Xiaoling, 13.45 Li Jing 1.9.79, 13.27 Markose 9 Aug
SP: 18.91 Cheng Xiaoyan 30.11.75, 16.12 Yu Xin CHN 23.2.77 8 May; Jnrs: 15.91 Bai Fengling 8 Shenyang 19 Jun; drugs dq: 21.43i Pavlysh
DT: 67.60 Zvereva at Staiki, 57.27 Chang 24.3.74, 54.62 Saroj Sihad Kumari IND-J 1 Gandhinagar 7 Dec (from 54.14)
HT: 68.21 Sudak 20.3.71 at Staiki 16 Jul, 58.97 Marwa Ahmed Hussein .78, delete 55.61 Zhang (JT mark)
JT: Menéndez 65.85 on 25 Jul; 55.39 Du 5 Jinan 2 May, 53.32 Tang Xiaoling CHN 8 May; old: 55.58 Aïda Sellam TUN .77 Tunis 18 Jan
Hep: 6004 Parfyonova 13 Jul, 5657h Ganapathy (13.9, 1.71, 11.52, 24.4, 6.31, 36.39, 2:26.5), 5558 Shen
4x100m: 43.28A NGR – Alozie, Ojokolo, Ekah, Nku; 45.68 TPE 27 Dec; Juniors: 43.69 JAM – Goulbourne, A Bailey, V Campbell, Sharpe
4x400m: 3:29.22 NGR – Madojemu, Afolabi, Opara, Ogunkoya; 3:42.5A KEN (Armed Forces) 26 Jun; Juniors: delete 3:32.35 CHN – as one athlete (Lu) born 1979
5000mW: 19:33.20 Gillet outdoors not in
10kmW: 42:51 Gudkova 23.1.78, 46:21+ Yuka Mitsumori JPN 8.1.72 2 May
20kmW: 1:32:19 Sazonova 28.5.65, 1:33:05 Gudkova 23.1.78; distance? 1:33:31 Kuznetsova 4.8.77

World Indoor Lists 2000

Men: 800m: 1:47.72 Knight 4.4.78; **50mh**: 6.52+ Denis 19 Feb (from 6.56); **60mh**: 7.56 Lichtenegger 4 El Gent 26 Feb; **HJ**: 2.26 Mike Ponikvar CAN 26.12.79 19 Feb; **LJ**: 8.04 OK Tudor, 7.95 Walter Davis USA 2.7.79 29 Jan; **SP**: 20.57 Proctor 17 Feb
Women: 60m: 7.14 OK Ottey; 200m: 23.22 Dunn 26.3.78; **1500m**: in 1M at Stuttgart 6 Feb: Chojecka 4:08.9, Szabo 4:09.1, Yegorova 4:09.9e; **1M**: 4:25.73 Dulecha, 4:34.75 Harrelson 17.6.78; **50mh**: 6.76 Girard 13 Feb; **HJ**: 1.91 Inna Gliznutsa MDA 18.4.73 16 Feb, 1.89 Babashkina (née Motkova) 23.11.68; **PV**: 4.30 Schulte 4 Mar (not 13 Feb), 4.22 Gao Shuying CHN 28.10.79 22 Mar, 4.17 Warlick 11.10.77; **LJ**: 6.72 Shekhovtsova 23 Jan (from 6.66); **TJ**: 14.41 Olga Yershova RUS 13.8.76 1 Barnaul 26 Feb; **SP**: 17.55 Lucica Ciobanu ROM 10.5.79 19 Feb, delete 18.11 Fields; **Hep**: 4261 Klüft 2.2.83

Previous World Lists

1984: Men SP: 21.42 Sergey Donskikh RUS 1 Leningrad 25 Aug
1989: Men HJ: 2.21 Kim Deok-hyung KOR 27 Sep; PV: Sergey Dzhamiyev UKR 5.60 4 Donyetsk 18 Sep (not 5.50); JT: 75.18 Lee Wook-jong KOR 66 23 Apr, 74.94 Kim Ki-hoon KOR 68 10 Jun
1992: Men 200m: 20.40 –0.2 Sidnei de Souza
1994: World Cross-country – Women: 18th J. Koech was Joyce Chepchumba.
1998: Men: Discus: Alekna add 66.85 1 NC Kaunas 18 Jul (x, 64.25, x, x, 63.55, 66.85)
Women 200m: Low altitude best: 22.62 Privalova 21 Aug; 4x200m: 1:29.64 Nike International

---

Additions to Records Set in 2000

Women's Marathon: WJR W Mar: 2:26:34 WEI Yanan CHN Beijing 15 Oct 00
Women's Javelin: Asl 63.04 WEI Jianhua CHN Shijiazhuang 28 Apr 2000

Obituary – ATFS Members

Dr Alphonse Juilland USA died in early 2001.
Louis Weisscher NED (b. 11 May 1928) died on 20 Mar 2001.

Long Careers as Juniors

Two of the medallists at the 2000 World Junior Championships had placed prominently at the two previous championships!
Chebet Langat (Kenya, b. 22 Aug 1981) was 3rd at 800m (2:03.21) in 1996, 2nd (2:05.43) in 1998 and 1st (2:01.51) in 2000 – a unique progression!
Rose Kosgei (Kenya, b. 22 Aug 1981 – the same birthdate!) was 4th at 1500m in 1996 (4:10.64), 4th in 1998 (4:13.14) and 2nd in 2000 (4:20.16).
Also competing at these three Championships was: Troy Sundstrom (Australia, b. 30 Apr 1981) who was 14th in the 10,000m walk in 1996 (43:46.02), 11th in 1998 (44:45.92) and 10th this time in 43:32.79.

World Indoor Championships 2001

Competition was intense at the 8th IAAF World Indoor Championships, but the standards were down on those of the previous Championships, held at Maebashi, Japan in 1999, and for the first time in the history of this event no indoor world records were set. There were just two championship bests – by Pavla Hamácková in the pole vault and Natalya Sazanovich in the pentathlon. Three 2000 Olympic champions won their events – Iván Pedroso LJ, Maria Mutola 800m and Tereza Marinova TJ, but ten had to settle for lesser placings. The most impressive performances came from Tim Harden at 60m, Yuriy Borzakovskiy 800m, Hicham El Guerrouj 3000m, Pedroso (a fifth world indoor title, a record for any event), Roman Sebrle Hep, Olga Yegorova 3000m and Sazanovich, with the Mutola v Stephanie Graf 800m clash the most thrilling race. Mark Lewis-Francis set a world junior record in taking the bronze medal at 60m. The USA (7 gold, 8 silver, 2 bronze) and Russia (4 gold, 5 silver, 6 bronze) were easily the two most dominant teams with Jamaica faring next best with five medals and also placing third, just ahead of Britain, on point scores determined by top eight placings. A total of 15 countries won titles and 28 a medal of some description, slightly down on the 1999 figures of 16 and 32.
See pages 591-2 for Results

CHANGES IN WORLD ATHLETICS

WHEN working on world lists and looking back over previous year, one is struck by just how much the world of athletics has changed. To demonstrate this I have taken a sample of four men's events and analysed the constituent nations of the top 50s for five Olympic years – every 12 years over the past half century.

This, of course, only gives a sample of changing trends – and perhaps an ATFS member might like to do a deeper and more exhaustive study of this theme.

But a few of the changes can be seen, such as:

1. The USA remains by far the strongest power in world athletics, but as worldwide participation has increased, its dominance has reduced.
2. The Eastern bloc rose in strength through the 1960, 1970s and 1980s, but has fallen back in the new economic and political societies of the past decade.
3. Almost every nation now has athletes that make the world lists.
4. African athletes have emerged, with especial force in the distance running events.
5. There has been a huge decline in distance running standards in most of the developed world over the past 15-20 years.
6. The Caribbean and Central American nations achieve success far beyond their proportion of population.
7. Australia has perhaps throughout the period been, by head of population, a hugely successful sporting nation.

Constituents of World Top 50s

400m	1952	'64	'76	'88	'00
Africa					
South Africa	3	2	-	-	4
East Africa	-	1	1	-	-
North Africa	-	-	-	-	-
West Africa	-	-	1	2	-
Americas					
USA	24	27	25.5	25.5	19
CAC	5	4	3	6	10
Canada	2	-	1		-
S.America	-	1	-	1	1
Asia					
Japan	-	-	-	1	2
Other Asia	-	1	-	1	4
Europe					
USSR *	1	-	-		1
East Europe	1	2	5	1	2
Scandinavia	2.5	1	1.5		-
Germany	2	5	8	4.5	-
GBR	2.5	2	2	4	3
France	4	1	-	-	2
Italy	-	-	-	-	1
ESP & POR	-	-	-	1	-
Other Europe	1	1	1	-	-
Oceania					
AUS & NZ	2	2	1	3	1

10,000m	1952	'64	'76	'88	'00
Africa					
South Africa	-	-	-	1	2
East Africa	-	1	3	8	25
North Africa	-	1	2	1	2
West Africa	-	-	-	-	-
Americas					
USA	3	4	4	3	3
CAC (MEX)	-		-	4	1
Canada	-		-	2	1
S. America	-		2	1	
Asia			-		
Japan	-	3	1	3	3
Other Asia	-		-		
Europe			-		
USSR *	8	15	11	1	
East Europe	12	4	1	1	
Scandinavia	15	2	5	2	
Germany	2	7	2	3	
GBR	3	4	4	5	1
France	3	2	1	2	1
Italy	-		1	4	2
ESP & POR	-	1	2	8	4
Other Europe	3	2	7	1	3
Oceania					
AUS & NZ	1	4	4	-	2

Long Jump	1952	'64	'76	'88	'00
Africa					
South Africa	3	-	-	1	-
East Africa	-	-	-	-	-
North Africa	-	-	-	-	2
West Africa	1	1	3	1	-
Americas					
USA	24	17	14	15	9
CAC	1	1	3	5	5
Canada	-		1	-	1
S.America	2	-	1	-	1
Asia					
China	-	1	-	2	3
Japan	1	1	-	1	-
Other Asia	-	-	-	-	1
Europe					
USSR *	4	6	3	12	8
East Europe	3	5	4	1	4
Scandinavia	1	4	-	-	2
Germany	5	5	11	3	2
GBR	-	3	2	-	-
France	1	2	4	1	4
Italy	-	-	1	1	-
ESP & POR	-	1	1	1	2
Other Europe	1	1	1	4	3
Oceania	-				-
AUS & NZ	3	2	1	2	3

Discus	1952	'64	'76	'88	'00
Africa					
South Africa	-	-	1	-	2
East Africa	-	-	-	-	-
North Africa	-	-	-	-	-
West Africa	-	-	-	1	-
Americas					
USA	20	14	10	6	11
CAC	-	-	1	3	2
Canada	-	-	1	-	2
S.America	1	-	-	-	-
Asia		-			
China	-	-	-	-	-
Japan	-	-	-	-	-
Other Asia	-	-	-	-	-
Europe					
USSR *	9	8	9	12	10
East Europe	5	10	10	8	8
Scandinavia	8	4	7	6	2
Germany	3	8	8	10	5
GBR	-	2	1	-	2
France	-	-	-	-	-
Italy	2	-	2	1	2
ESP & POR	-	-	-	-	1
Other Europe	1	2	-	2	2
Oceania				-	
AUS & NZ	1	2	-	1	1

* now including all ex-USSR republics

WORLD & CONTINENTAL RECORDS

As at end of 2000. **Key:** W = World, Afr = Africa, Asi = Asia, CAC = Central America & Caribbean, Eur = Europe, NAm = North America, Oce = Oceania, SAm = South America, Com = Commonwealth, WJ = World Junior.
Successive columns show: World or Continent as above, performance, name, nationality, venue, date.
A altitude over 1000m, + timing by photo-electric-cell, * awaiting ratification, § not officially ratified

100 METRES

W, NAm	9.79	Maurice GREENE	USA	Athína	16 Jun 1999
Com	9.84	Donovan BAILEY	CAN	Atlanta	27 Jul 1996
	9.84	Bruny SURIN	CAN	Sevilla	22 Aug 1999
Afr	9.86	Frank FREDERICKS	NAM	Atlanta	27 Jul 1996
CAC	9.86	Ato BOLDON	TRI	Walnut	19 Apr 1998
	9.86	BOLDON also at Athína 17 Jun 1998, Athína 16 Jun 1999 and Lausanne			2 Jul 1999
Eur	9.87	Linford CHRISTIE	GBR	Stuttgart	15 Aug 1993
SAm	10.00A	Róbson da SILVA	BRA	Ciudad de México	22 Jul 1988
Asi	10.00	Koji ITO	JPN	Bangkok	13 Dec 1998
Oce	10.03	Matt SHIRVINGTON	AUS	Kuala Lumpur	17 Sep 1998
WJ	10.05 §	Davidson EZINWA	NGR	Bauchi	3 Jan 1990
	10.06	Dwain CHAMBERS	GBR	Ljubljana	25 Jul 1997

200 METRES

W, NAm	19.32	Michael JOHNSON	USA	Atlanta	1 Aug 1996
Afr	19.68	Frank FREDERICKS	NAM	Atlanta	1 Aug 1996
Eur	19.72A	Pietro MENNEA	ITA	Ciudad de México	12 Sep 1979
CAC	19.77	Ato BOLDON	TRI	Stuttgart	13 Jul 1997
Com	19.68	Frank FREDERICKS	NAM	Atlanta	1 Aug 1996
SAm	19.89	Claudinei da SILVA	BRA	München	11 Sep 1999
Oce	20.06A	Peter NORMAN	AUS	Ciudad de México	16 Oct 1968
Asi	20.16	Koji ITO	JPN	Kumamoto	2 Oct 1998
WJ	20.07 §	Lorenzo DANIEL	USA	Starkville	18 May 1985
	20.13	Roy MARTIN	USA	Indianapolis	16 Jun 1985

400 METRES

W, NAm	43.18	Michael JOHNSON	USA	Sevilla	26 Aug 1999
CAC	44.14	Roberto HERNÁNDEZ	CUB	Sevilla	30 May 1990
Afr, Com	44.17	Innocent EGBUNIKE	NGR	Zürich	19 Aug 1987
SAm	44.29	Sanderlei PARRELA	BRA	Sevilla	26 Aug 1999
Eur	44.33	Thomas SCHÖNLEBE	GER	Roma	3 Sep 1987
Oce	44.38	Darren CLARK	AUS	Seoul	26 Sep 1988
Asi	44.56	Mohamed AL-MALKY	OMN	Budapest	12 Aug 1988
WJ	43.87	Steve LEWIS	USA	Seoul	28 Sep 1988

800 METRES

W, Eur	1:41.11	Wilson KIPKETER	DEN	Köln	24 Aug 1997
Com	1:41.73	Sebastian COE	GBR	Firenze	10 Jun 1981
SAm	1:41.77	Joaquim CRUZ	BRA	Koln	26 Aug 1984
Afr	1:42.28	Sammy KOSKEI	KEN	Koln	26 Aug 1984
NAm	1:42.60	Johnny GRAY	USA	Koblenz	28 Aug 1985
CAC	1:42.85	Norberto TELLEZ	CUB	Atlanta	31 Jul 1996
Asi	1:44.14	LEE Jin-il	KOR	Seoul	17 Jun 1994
Oce	1:44.3 m	Peter SNELL	NZL	Christchurch	3 Feb 1962
WJ	1:43.64	Japheth KIMUTAI	KEN	Zürich	13 Aug 1997

1000 METRES

W, Afr, Com	2:11.96	Noah NGENY	KEN	Rieti	5 Sep 1999
Eur	2:12.18	Sebastian COE	GBR	Oslo	11 Jul 1981
NAm	2:13.9	Rick WOHLHUTER	USA	Oslo	30 Jul 1974
SAm	2:14.09	Joaquim CRUZ	BRA	Nice	20 Aug 1984
Oce	2:16.57	John WALKER	NZL	Oslo	1 Jul 1980
CAC	2:17.0	Byron DYCE	JAM	København	15 Aug 1973
Asi	2:18.91	Mohamed SULEIMAN	QAT	Lindau	28 Jul 1995
WJ	2:15.00	Benjamim KIPKURUI	KEN	Nice	17 Jul 1999

1500 METRES

W, Afr	3:26.00	Hicham EL GUERROUJ	MAR	Roma	14 Jul 1998
Com	3:28.12	Noah NGENY	KEN	Zürich	11 Aug 2000
Eur	3:28.95	Fermin CACHO	ESP	Zürich	13 Aug 1997
NAm	3:29.77	Sydney MAREE	USA	Köln	25 Aug 1985

Oce	3:31.96	Simon DOYLE	AUS	Stockholm	3 Jul 1991
Asi	3:32.10	Mohammed SULEIMAN	QAT	Zürich	13 Aug 1997
SAm	3:34.63	Joaquim CRUZ	BRA	Hengelo	14 Aug 1988
CAC	3:36.60	Stephen AGAR (now CAN)	DMN	Abbotsford	2 Jun 1996
WJ	3:32.91 §	Noah NGENY (no doping control)	KEN	Monaco	16 Aug 1997
	3:33.16	Benjamin KIPKIRUI	KEN	Zürich	11 Aug 1999

1 MILE

W, Afr	3:43.13	Hicham El GUERROUJ	MAR	Roma	7 Jul 1999
Com	3:43.40	Noah NGENY	KEN	Roma	7 Jul 1999
Eur	3:46.32	Steve CRAM	GBR	Oslo	27 Jul 1985
NAm	3:47.69	Steve SCOTT	USA	Oslo	7 Jul 1982
Oce	3:49.08	John WALKER	NZL	Oslo	7 Jul 1982
Asi	3:51.12	Mohammed SULEIMAN	QAT	Zürich	16 Aug 1995
SAm	3:53.00	Joaquim CRUZ	BRA	Los Angeles	13 May 1984
CAC	3:57.34	Byron DYCE	JAM	Stockholm	1 Jul 1974
WJ	3:50.41 *	Noah NGENY	KEN	Nice	16 Jul 1997

2000 METRES

W, Afr	4:44.79	Hicham EL GUERROUJ	MAR	Berlin	7 Sep 1999
Com	4:48.74	John KIBOWEN	KEN	Hechtel	1 Aug 1998
Eur	4:51.39	Steve CRAM	GBR	Budapest	4 Aug 1985
Oce	4:51.52	John WALKER	NZL	Oslo	30 Jun 1976
NAm	4:52.44	Jim SPIVEY	USA	Lausanne	15 Sep 1987
Asi	4:55.57	Mohammed SULEIMAN	QAT	Roma	8 Jun 1995
WJ	4:59.14	Ali SAÏDI-SIEF	ALG	Villeneuve d'Ascq	29 Jun 1997
CAC	5:03.4	Arturo BARRIOS	MEX	Nice	10 Jul 1989
SAm	5:03.58	Hudson Santos de SOUZA	BRA	Hechtel	1 Aug 1998

3000 METRES

W, Afr, Com	7:20.67	Daniel KOMEN	KEN	Rieti	1 Sep 1996
Eur	7:26.62	Mohammed MOURHIT	BEL	Monaco	18 Aug 2000
NAm	7:30.84	Bob KENNEDY	USA	Monte Carlo	8 Aug 1998
CAC	7:35.71	Arturo BARRIOS	MEX	Nice	10 Jul 1989
Oce	7:37.49	John WALKER	NZL	London	17 Jul 1982
Asi	7:38.20	Mohammed SULEIMAN	QAT	Berlin	27 Aug 1993
SAm	7:45.34	Clodoaldo do CARMO	BRA	Koblenz	26 Aug 1992
WJ	7:33.00	Hailu MEKONNEN	ETH	Stuttgart	6 Jun 1999

5000 METRES

W, Afr	12:39.36	Haile GEBRSELASSIE	ETH	Helsinki	13 Jun 1998
Com	12:39.74	Daniel KOMEN	KEN	Bruxelles	22 Aug 1997
Eur	12:49.71	Mohammed MOURHIT	BEL	Bruxelles	25 Aug 2000
NAm	12:58.21	Bob KENNEDY	USA	Zürich	14 Aug 1996
CAC	13:07.79	Arturo BARRIOS	MEX	London	14 Jul 1989
Oce	13:12.87	Dick QUAX	NZL	Stockholm	5 Jul 1977
Asi	13:13.40	Toshinari TAKAOKA	JPN	Hechtel	1 Aug 1998
SAm	13:19.64	Antonio SILIO	ARG	Roma	17 Jul 1991
WJ	12:53.72	Philip MOSIMA	KEN	Roma	5 Jun 1996

10,000 METRES

W, Afr	26:22.75	Haile GEBRSELASSIE	ETH	Hengelo	1 Jun 1998
Com	26:27.85	Paul TERGAT	KEN	Bruxelles	22 Aug 1997
Eur	26:52.30	Mohammed MOURHIT	BEL	Bruxelles	3 Sep 1999
CAC	27:08.23	Arturo BARRIOS	MEX	Berlin	18 Aug 1989
NAm	27:20.56	Mark NENOW	USA	Bruxelles	5 Sep 1986
Oce	27:31.92	Shaun CREIGHTON	AUS	Melbourne	25 Nov 1996
Asi	27:35.33	Takeyuki NAKAYAMA	JPN	Helsinki	2 Jul 1987
SAm	27:38.72	Antonio SILIO	ARG	Bruxelles	3 Sep 1993
WJ	27:11.18	Richard CHELIMO	KEN	Hengelo	25 Jun 1991

MARATHON

W, Afr	2:05:42	Khalid KHANNOUCHI	MAR	Chicago	24 Oct 1999
SAm	2:06:05	Ronaldo da COSTA	BRA	Berlin	20 Sep 1998
Com	2:06:16	Moses TANUI	KEN	Chicago	24 Oct 1999
Eur	2:06:36	António PINTO	POR	London	16 Apr 2000
Asi	2:06:51	Atsushi FUJITA	JPN	Fukuoka	3 Dec 2000
NAm	2:07:01	Khalid KHANNOUCHI (ex MAR)	USA	Chicago	22 Oct 2000
CAC	2:07:19	Andrés ESPINOSA	MEX	Boston	18 Apr 1994
Oce	2:07:51	Rob DE CASTELLA	AUS	Boston	21 Apr 1986

WJ	2:12:49	Negash DUBE	ETH	Beijing	18 Oct 1987
	2:12:49	Tesfaye DADI	ETH	Berlin	9 Oct 1988

Boston course has an overall net drop of 139m (0.33%), and in 1994 there was a strong following wind.

3000 METRES STEEPLECHASE

W, Afr, Com	7:55.72	Bernard BARMASAI	KEN	Köln	24 Aug 1997
Eur	8:07.62	Joseph MAHMOUD	FRA	Bruxelles	24 Aug 1984
Asi	8:08.26	Saad AL-ASMARI	SAU	Stockholm	7 Jul 1997
NAm	8:09.17	Henry MARSH	USA	Koblenz	28 Aug 1985
Oce	8:14.05	Peter RENNER	NZL	Koblenz	29 Aug 1984
SAm	8:14.41	Wander MOURA	BRA	Mar del Plata	22 Mar 1995
CAC	8:25.69	Salvador MIRANDA	MEX	Barakaldo	9 Jul 2000
WJ	8:03.74	Raymond YATOR	KEN	Monaco	18 Aug 2000

110 METRES HURDLES

W, Eur, Com	12.91	Colin JACKSON	GBR	Stuttgart	20 Aug 1993
NAm	12.92	Roger KINGDOM	USA	Zürich	16 Aug 1989
	12.92	Allen JOHNSON	USA	Atlanta	23 Jun 1996
	12.92	Allen JOHNSON	USA	Bruxelles	23 Aug 1996
CAC	13.00	Anier GARCIA	CUB	Sydney	25 Sep 2000
Asi	13.25	LI Tong	CHN	Linz	4 Jul 1994
Oce	13.29	Kyle VANDER-KUYP	AUS	Göteborg	11 Aug 1995
SAm	13.38	Márcio de SOUZA	BRA	Rio de Janeiro	3 Jun 1999
Afr	13.39	Shaun BOWNES	RSA	Luzern	5 Jul 1999
WJ	13.23	Renaldo NEHEMIAH	USA	Zürich	16 Aug 1978

400 METRES HURDLES

W, NAm	46.78	Kevin YOUNG	USA	Barcelona	6 Aug 1992
Afr, Com	47.10	Samuel MATETE	ZAM	Zürich	7 Aug 1991
Eur	47.37	Stéphane DIAGANA	FRA	Lausanne	5 Jul 1995
Asi	47.53	Hadi Sou'an AL-SOMAILY	KSA	Sydney	27 Sep 2000
CAC	47.60	Winthrop GRAHAM	JAM	Zürich	4 Aug 1993
SAm	48.04	Eronilde de ARAUJO	BRA	Nice	12 Jul 1995
Oce	48.28	Rohan ROBINSON	AUS	Atlanta	31 Jul 1996
WJ	48.02	Danny HARRIS	USA	Los Angeles	17 Jun 1984

HIGH JUMP

W, CAC	2.45	Javier SOTOMAYOR	CUB	Salamanca	27 Jul 1993
Eur	2.42	Patrik SJÖBERG	SWE	Stockholm	30 Jun 1987
	2.42 i§	Carlos THRÄNHARDT	GER	Berlin	26 Feb 1988
NAm	2.40 i§	Hollis CONWAY	USA	Sevilla	10 Mar 1991
		Charles AUSTIN	USA	Zürich	7 Aug 1991
Asi	2.39	ZHU Jianhua	CHN	Eberstadt	10 Jun 1984
Com	2.38i	Steve SMITH	GBR	Wuppertal	4 Feb 1994
	2.38	Troy KEMP	BAH	Nice	12 Jul 1995
Oce	2.36	Tim FORSYTH	AUS	Melbourne	2 Mar 1997
Afr	2.34	Abderrahmane HAMMAD	ALG	Alger	14 Jul 2000
SAm	2.33	Gilmar MAYO	COL	Pereira	17 Oct 1994
WJ	2.37	Dragutin TOPIC	YUG	Plovdiv	12 Aug 1990
		Steve SMITH	GBR	Seoul	20 Sep 1992

POLE VAULT

W, Eur	6.15 i§	Sergey BUBKA	UKR	Donetsk	21 Feb 1993
	6.14 A	Sergey BUBKA	UKR	Sestriere	31 Jul 1994
Afr, Com	6.03	Okkert BRITS	RSA	Köln	18 Aug 1995
NAm	6.03	Jeff HARTWIG	USA	Jonesboro	14 Jun 2000
Oce	5.95	Dmitriy MARKOV	AUS	Athína	16 Jun 1999
	5.95	Dmitriy MARKOV	AUS	Monaco	4 Aug 1999
Asi	5.92i	Igor POTAPOVICH	KAZ	Stockholm	19 Feb 1998
	5.90	Grigoriy YEGOROV	KAZ	Stuttgart	19 Aug 1993
	5.90	Grigoriy YEGOROV	KAZ	London	10 Sep 1993
	5.90	Igor POTAPOVICH	KAZ	Nice	10 Jul 1996
SAm	5.76	Tom HINTNAUS	BRA	Zürich	21 Aug 1985
CAC	5.70A	Dominic JOHNSON	LCA	El Paso	26 Aug 2000
	5.72 §	Paul BENAVIDES	MEX	El Paso	18 Jun 1994
WJ	5.80	Maksim TARASOV	RUS	Bryansk	14 Jul 1989

LONG JUMP

W, NAm	8.95	Mike POWELL	USA	Tokyo	30 Aug 1991
Eur	8.86 A	Robert EMMIYAN	ARM	Tsakhkadzor	22 May 1987

CAC	8.71	Iván PEDROSO	CUB	Salamanca	18 Jul 1995
Com	8.62	James BECKFORD	JAM	Orlando	5 Apr 1997
Oce	8.49	Jai TAURIMA	AUS	Sydney	28 Sep 2000
Afr	8.46	Cheikh TOURÉ	SEN	Bad Langensalza	15 Jun 1997
SAm	8.40	Douglas de SOUZA	BRA	São Paulo	15 Feb 1995
Asi	8.40	LAO Jianfeng	CHN	Zhaoqing	28 May 1997
WJ	8.34	Randy WILLIAMS	USA	München	8 Sep 1972

TRIPLE JUMP

W, Eur, Com	18.29	Jonathan EDWARDS	GBR	Göteborg	7 Aug 1995
NAm	18.09	Kenny HARRISON	USA	Atlanta	27 Jul 1996
CAC	17.92	James BECKFORD	JAM	Odessa, Texas	20 May 1995
SAm	17.89 A	João Carlos de OLIVEIRA	BRA	Ciudad de México	15 Oct 1975
Oce	17.46	Ken LORRAWAY	AUS	London	7 Aug 1982
Asi	17.35	Oleg SAKIRKIN	KAZ	Moskva	5 Jun 1994
Afr	17.34	Ndabezinhle MDHLONGWA	ZIM	Lafayette	28 Mar 1998
WJ	17.50	Volker MAI	GER	Erfurt	23 Jun 1985

SHOT

W, NAm	23.12	Randy BARNES	USA	Westwood	20 May 1990
Eur	23.06	Ulf TIMMERMANN	GER	Hania	22 May 1988
Com	21.68	Geoff CAPES	GBR	Cwmbrân	18 May 1980
SAm	20.90	Gert WEIL	CHL	Wirges	17 Aug 1986
CAC	20.78	Alexis PAUMIER	CUB	La Habana	29 Jul 2000
Afr	20.76	Ahmed Kamel SHATTA	EGY	Al Qâhira	24 Mar 1988
Asi	20.60	Shakti SINGH	IND	Bangalore	5 Jul 2000
Oce	20.35	Justin ANLEZARK	AUS	Gold Coast (RB)	10 Sep 2000
WJ	21.05 i§	Terry ALBRITTON	USA	New York	22 Feb 1974
	20.65 §	Mike CARTER	USA	Boston	4 Jul 1979
	20.39	Jannus ROBERTS	RSA	Germiston	7 Mar 1998

DISCUS

W, Eur	74.08	Jürgen SCHULT	GER	Neubrandenburg	6 Jun 1986
NAm	72.34 ¶	Ben PLUCKNETT	USA	Stockholm	7 Jul 1981
	71.32 §	Ben PLUCKNETT	USA	Eugene	4 Jun 1983
CAC	71.06	Luis DELIS	CUB	La Habana	21 May 1983
Afr, Com	69.75A	Frantz KRUGER	RSA	Bloemfontein	15 Sep 2000
Oce	65.62 §	Werner REITERER	AUS	Melbourne	15 Dec 1987
	65.06	Wayne MARTIN	AUS	Newcastle	3 Jan 1979
Asi	65.16	LI Shaojie	CHN	Nanjing	7 May 1996
SAm	64.30	Ramón JIMÉNEZ-GAONA	PAR	Eugene	23 May 1992
WJ	65.62 §	Werner REITERER	AUS	Melbourne	15 Dec 1987
	63.64	Werner HARTMANN	GER	Strasbourg	25 Jun 1978

¶ Disallowed by the IAAF following retrospective disqualification for drug abuse, but ratified by the AAU/TAC

HAMMER

W, Eur	86.74	Yuriy SEDYKH	UKR/RUS	Stuttgart	30 Aug 1986
Asi	83.36	Andrey ABDUVALIYEV	TJK	Budapest	3 Jun 1994
NAm	82.52	Lance DEAL	USA	Milano	7 Sep 1996
Afr, Com	78.71	Chris HARMSE	RSA	Pretoria	23 Sep 2000
CAC	77.78	Alberto SANCHEZ	CUB	La Habana	15 May 1998
Oce	77.68	Stuart RENDELL	AUS	Pietersburg	18 Mar 2000
SAm	74.66	Andrés CHARADIA	ARG	Córdoba	9 Oct 1994
WJ	78.14	Roland STEUK	GER	Leipzig	30 Jun 1978

JAVELIN

W, Eur	98.48	Jan ZELEZNY	CZE	Jena	25 May 1996
Com	91.46	Steve BACKLEY	GBR	Auckland (NS)	25 Jan 1992
NAm	89.16 §	Tom PETRANOFF	USA	Potchefstroom	1 Mar 1991
	87.12	Tom PUKSTYS	USA	Jena	25 May 1997
Afr	88.75	Marius CORBETT	RSA	Kuala Lumpur	21 Sep 1998
Oce	88.20	Gavin LOVEGROVE	NZL	Oslo	5 Jul 1996
Asi	87.60	Kazuhiro MIZOGUCHI	JPN	San José	27 May 1989
CAC	87.12	Emeterio GONZALEZ	CUB	Jena	3 Jun 2000
SAm	84.70	Edgar BAUMANN	PAR	San Marcos	17 Oct 1999
WJ	82.52	Harri HAATAINEN	FIN	Leppävirta	25 May 1996

DECATHLON

W,Eur	8994	Tomás DVORÁK	CZE	Praha	4 Jul 1999
NAm	8891	Dan O'BRIEN	USA	Talence	5 Sep 1992

Com	8847	Daley THOMPSON	GBR	Los Angeles	9 Aug 1984
Oce	8490	Jagan HAMES	AUS	Kuala Lumpur	18 Sep 1998
Asi	8445	Ramil GANIYEV	UZB	Athína	6 Aug 1997
CAC	8252	Ra'l DUANY	CUB	La Habana	24 Jul 2000
SAm	8291 m	Tito STEINER	ARG	Provo	23 Jun 1983
	8266	Pedro da SILVA	BRA	Walnut	24 Apr 1987
Afr	7934 h	Ahmed MAHOUR BACHA	ALG	El Djezair (Alger)	9 Jul 1985
	7642	Anis RIAHI	TUN	Talence	31 Jul 2000
WJ	8397	Torsten VOSS	GER	Erfurt	7 Jul 1982

20 KILOMETRES WALK

CAC	1:17:25.6 t	Bernardo SEGURA	MEX	Fana	7 May 1994
W, Eur	1:17:46	Roman RASSKAZOV	RUS	Moskva	19 May 2000
Asi	1:18:04	BO Lingtang	CHN	Beijing	7 Apr 1994
SAm	1:18:24	Jefferson PEREZ	ECU	Podebrady	19 Apr 1997
Afr	1:19:02	Hatem GHOULA	TUN	Eisenhüttenstadt	10 May 1997
Oce, Com	1:19:22	Dave SMITH	AUS	Hobart	19 Jul 1987
NAm	1:21:03	Arturo HUERTA	CAN	Etobicoke	7 Jul 2000
WJ	1:19:38	YU Guohui	CHN	Zhuhai	10 Mar 1996

20,000 METRES TRACK WALK

W, CAC	1:17:25.6	Bernardo SEGURA	MEX	Fana	7 May 1994
Eur	1:18:35.2	Stefan JOHANSSON	SWE	Fana	15 May 1992
Oce, Com	1:20:12.3	Nick A'HERN	AUS	Fana	8 May 1993
Asi	1:20:24.4	LI Mingcai	CHN	Jinan	15 Mar 1992
SAm	1:20:55.4	Jefferson PEREZ	ECU	Fana	4 May 1996
NAm	1:22:27.0	Tim BERRETT	CAN	Edmonds, WA	9 Jun 1996
Afr	1:22:51.84	Hatem GHOULA	TUN	Leutkirch	8 Sep 1994
WJ	1:22:16.0	LI Mingcai	CHN	Hefei	3 Mar 1990

50 KILOMETRES WALK

W, Eur	3:37:26	Valeriy SPITSYN	RUS	Moskva	21 May 2000
Asi	3:39:22	Sergey KOREPANOV	KAZ	Mézidon-Canon	2 May 1999
CAC	3:41:20	Raúl GONZALEZ	MEX	Praha-Podebrady	11 Jun 1978
Oce, Com	3:43:13	Simon BAKER	AUS	L'Hospitalet	28 May 1989
NAm	3:47:48	Marcel JOBIN	CAN	Québec	20 Jun 1981
SAm	3:52:16	Héctor MORENO	COL	Naumberg	25 May 1997
Afr	4:07:30	Johan MOERDYK	RSA	Durban	14 Sep 1996
WJ	3:43:41	ZHANG Huiqiang	CHN	Zhuhai	12 Mar 1996

50,000 METRES TRACK WALK

W, Eur	3:40:57.9	Thierry TOUTAIN	FRA	Héricourt	29 Sep 1996
CAC	3:41:38.4	Raúl GONZALEZ	MEX	Fana	25 May 1979
Oce, Com	3:43:50.0	Simon BAKER	AUS	Melbourne	9 Sep 1990
Asi	3:48:13.7	ZHAO Yongshen	CHN	Fana	7 May 1994
NAm	3:56:13.0	Tim BERRETT	CAN	Saskatoon	21 Jul 1991
SAm	4:14:28.5	Jorge LOREFICE	ARG	Buenos Aires	9 May 1993
	4:14:28.5	Benjamin LOREFICE	ARG	Buenos Aires	9 May 1993
Afr	4:21:44.5	Abdelwahab FERGUÈNE	ALG	Toulouse	25 Mar 1984

4 X 100 METRES RELAY

W, NAm	37.40	USA (Marsh, Burrell, Mitchell, C.Lewis)	Barcelona	8 Aug 1992
	37.40	USA (Drummond, Cason, Mitchell, Burrell)	Stuttgart	21 Aug 1993
Com	37.69	CAN (Esmie, Gilbert, Surin, Bailey)	Atlanta	3 Aug 1996
Eur	37.73	GBR (Gardener, Campbell, Devonish, Chambers)	Sevilla	29 Aug 1999
SAm	37.90	BRA (V Lima, Ribeiro, A da Silva, Cl da Silva)	Sydney	30 Sep 2000
Afr	37.91	NGR (Asonze, Obikwelu, Effiong, Aliu)	Sevilla	29 Aug 1999
CAC	38.00	CUB (Simón, Lamela, Isasi, Aguilera)	Barcelona	8 Aug 1992
Oce	38.17	AUS (Henderson, Jackson, Brimacombe, Marsh)	Göteborg	12 Aug 1995
Asi	38.31	JPN (Inoue, K Ito, Tsuchie, Asahara)	Athína	9 Aug 1997
	38.31	JPN (Kawabata, K ito, Suetsugu, Asahara)	Sydney	29 Sep 2000
WJ	39.00A	USA (Jessie, Franklin, Blalock, Mitchell)	USAF Academy	18 Jul 1983

4 X 400 METRES RELAY

W, NAm	2:54.20	USA (Young, Pettigrew, Washington, Johnson)	Uniondale, NY	22 Jul 1998
Eur	2:56.60	GBR (Thomas, Baulch, Richardson, Black)	Atlanta	3 Aug 1996
CAC, Com	2:56.75	JAM (McDonald, Haughton, McFarlane, Clarke)	Athína	10 Aug 1997
SAm	2:58.56	BRA (C da Silva, A J dosSantos, de Araújo, Parrela)	Winnipeg	30 Jul 1999
Afr	2:58.68	NGR (Chukwu, Monye, Nada, Udo-Obong)	Sydney	30 Sep 2000

Oce	2:59.70	AUS (Frayne, Clark, Minihan, Mitchell)	Los Angeles	11 Aug 1984
Asi	3:00.76	JPN (Karube, K Ito, Osakada, Omori)	Atlanta	3 Aug 1996
WJ	3:01.90	USA (Campbell, Rish, Waddle, Reed)	Athína	20 Jul 1986

World Records at other men's events recognised by the IAAF

20km	56:55.6	Arturo BARRIOS (now USA)	MEX	La Flèche	30 Mar 1991
1 Hour	21,101 m	Arturo BARRIOS (now USA)	MEX	La Flèche	30 Mar 1991
25km	1:13:55.8	Toshihiko SEKO	JPN	Christchurch	22 Mar 1981
30km	1:29:18.8	Toshihiko SEKO	JPN	Christchurch	22 Mar 1981
4 x 200m	1:18.68	Santa Monica Track Club	USA	Walnut	17 Apr 1994
		(Michael Marsh, Leroy Burrell, Floyd Heard, Carl Lewis)			
4 x 800m	7:03.89	United Kingdom Team	GBR	London	30 Aug 1982
		(Peter Elliott, Garry Cook, Steve Cram, Sebastian Coe)			
4 x l500m	14:38.8 m	F.R.Germany Team	GER	Köln	17 Aug 1977
		(Thomas Wessinghage, Harald Hudak, Michael Lederer, Karl Fleschen)			
Track Walking					
2 Hours	29,572m	Maurizio DAMILANO	ITA	Cuneo	4 Oct 1992
30km	2:01:44.1	Maurizio DAMILANO	ITA	Cuneo	4 Oct 1992

WOMEN

100 METRES

W, NAm	10.49	Florence GRIFFITH JOYNER	USA	Indianapolis	16 Jul 1988
Eur	10.73	Christine ARRON	FRA	Budapest	19 Aug 1998
CAC, Com	10.74	Merlene OTTEY	JAM	Milano	7 Sep 1996
Asi	10.79	LI Xuemei	CHN	Shanghai	18 Oct 1997
Afr	10.90	Glory ALOZIE	NGR	La Laguna	5 Jun 1999
	10.84 §	Chioma AJUNWA	NGR	Lagos	11 Apr 1992
Oce	11.12A	Melinda GAINSFORD/TAYLOR	AUS	Sestriere	31 Jul 1994
SAm	11.17A	Lucimar de MOURA	BRA	Bogotá (sf)	25 Jun 1999
	11.17A	Lucimar de MOURA	BRA	Bogotá	25 Jun 1999
WJ	10.88 *	Marlies OELSNER/GÖHR	GER	Dresden	1 Jul 1977
	10.89	Kathrin KRABBE	GER	Berlin	20 Jul 1988

200 METRES

W, NAm	21.34	Florence GRIFFITH JOYNER	USA	Seoul	29 Sep 1988
CAC, Com	21.64	Merlene OTTEY	JAM	Bruxelles	13 Sep 1991
Eur	21.71	Marita KOCH	GER	Chemnitz	10 Jun 1979
	21.71 §	Marita KOCH	GER	Potsdam	21 Jul 1984
	21.71	Heike DRECHSLER	GER	Jena	29 Jun 1986
	21.71 §	Heike DRECHSLER	GER	Stuttgart	29 Aug 1986
Asi	22.01	LI Xuemei	CHN	Shanghai	22 Oct 1997
Afr	22.06 A§	Evette DE KLERK	RSA	Pietersburg	8 Apr 1989
	22.07	Mary ONYALI	NGR	Zürich	14 Aug 1996
Oce	22.23	Melinda GAINSFORD-TAYLOR	AUS	Stuttgart	13 Jul 1997
SAm	22.60A	Lucimar de MOURA	BRA	Bogotá	26 Jun 1999
WJ	22.19	Natalya BOCHINA	RUS	Moskva	30 Jul 1980

400 METRES

W, Eur	47.60	Marita KOCH	GER	Canberra	6 Oct 1985
Oce, Com	48.63	Cathy FREEMAN	AUS	Atlanta	29 Jul 1996
NAm	48.83	Valerie BRISCO	USA	Los Angeles	6 Aug 1984
Afr	49.10	Falilat OGUNKOYA	NGR	Atlanta	29 Jul 1996
CAC	49.28	Pauline DAVIS	BAH	Atlanta	29 Jul 1996
	49.2 mA	Ana Fidelia QUIROT	CUB	Bogotá	13 Aug 1989
SAm	49.64	Ximena RESTREPO	COL	Barcelona	5 Aug 1992
Asi	49.81	MA Yuqin	CHN	Beijing	11 Sep 1993
WJ	49.42	Grit BREUER	GER	Tokyo	27 Aug 1991

800 METRES

W, Eur	1:53.28	Jarmila KRATOCHVÍLOVÁ	CZE	München	26 Jul 1983
CAC	1:54.44	Ana Fidelia QUIROT	CUB	Barcelona	9 Sep 1989
Afr	1:55.19	Maria Lurdes MUTOLA	MOZ	Zürich	17 Aug 1994
Com	1:55.29	Maria Lurdes MUTOLA	MOZ	Köln	24 Aug 1997
Asi	1:55.54	LIU Dong	CHN	Beijing	9 Sep 1993
NAm	1:56.40	Jearl MILES-CLARK	USA	Zürich	11 Aug 1999
SAm	1:56.68	Letitia VRIESDE	SUR	Göteborg	13 Aug 1995
Oce	1:58.25	Toni HODGKINSON	NZL	Atlanta	27 Jul 1996
WJ	1:57.18	WANG Yuan	CHN	Beijing	8 Sep 1993

1000 METRES

W, Eur	2:28.98	Svetlana MASTERKOVA	RUS	Bruxelles	23 Aug 1996
Afr	2:29.34	Maria Lurdes MUTOLA	MOZ	Bruxelles	25 Aug 1995
Com	2:29.66	Maria Lurdes MUTOLA	MOZ	Bruxelles	23 Aug 1996
NAm	2:31.80	Regina JACOBS	USA	Brunswick	3 Jul 1999
SAm	2:32.25	Letitia VRIESDE	SUR	Berlin	10 Sep 1991
CAC	2:33.21	Ana Fidelia QUIROT	CUB	Jerez de la Frontera	13 Sep 1989
Asi	2:33.6 §	Svetlana ULMASOVA	UZB	Podolsk	5 Aug 1979
Oce	2:38.54	JAlison WRIGHT	NZL	Berlin	17 Aug 1979
WJ	2:35.4	Irina NIKITINA	RUS	Podolsk	5 Aug 1979
	2:35.4	Katrin WÜHN	GDR	Potsdam	12 Jul 1984

1500 METRES

W, Asi	3:50.46	QU Yunxia	CHN	Beijing	11 Sep 1993
Eur	3:52.47	Tatyana KAZANKINA	RUS	Zürich	13 Aug 1980
Afr	3:55.30	Hassiba BOULMERKA	ALG	Barcelona	8 Aug 1992
NAm	3:57.12	Mary DECKER/SLANEY	USA	Stockholm	26 Jul 1983
Com	3:57.41	Jackline MARANGA	KEN	Monaco	8 Aug 1998
Oce	4:01.34	Margaret CROWLEY	AUS	Oslo	5 Jul 1996
CAC	4:01.84	Yvonne GRAHAM	JAM	Monaco	25 Jul 1995
SAm	4:05.67	Letitia VRIESDE	SUR	Tokyo	31 Aug 1991
WJ	3:51.34	LANG Yinglai	CHN	Shanghai	18 Oct 1997

1 MILE

W, Eur	4:12.56	Svetlana MASTERKOVA	RUS	Zürich	14 Aug 1996
NAm	4:16.71	Mary SLANEY	USA	Zürich	21 Aug 1985
Com	4:17.57	Zola BUDD	GBR	Zürich	21 Aug 1985
Afr	4:20.79	Hassiba BOULMERKA	ALG	Oslo	6 Jul 1991
CAC	4:24.64	Yvonne GRAHAM	JAM	Zürich	17 Aug 1994
Oce	4:25.84	Margaret CROWLEY	AUS	Monaco	10 Aug 1996
SAm	4:30.05	Soraya TELLES	BRA	Praha	9 Jun 1988
Asi	4:35.34	WANG Qingfen	CHN	Linz	5 Jul 1998
WJ	4:17.57*	Zola BUDD	GBR	Zürich	21 Aug 1985

2000 METRES

W, Eur	5:25.36	Sonia O'SULLIVAN	IRL	Edinburgh	8 Jul 1994
Com	5:26.93	Yvonne MURRAY	GBR	Edinburgh	8 Jul 1994
Asi	5:29.43 §	WANG Junxia	CHN	Beijing	12 Sep 1993
NAm	5:32.7	Mary SLANEY	USA	Eugene	3 Aug 1984
Afr	5:37.6 §	Zahra OUAZIZ	MAR	Bruxelles	3 Sep 1999
Oce	5:44.67	Anne HARE	NZL	London (CP)	11 Jul 1986
WJ	5:33.15	Zola BUDD	GBR	London (CP)	13 Jul 1984

3000 METRES

W, Asi	8:06.11	WANG Junxia	CHN	Beijing	13 Sep 1993
Eur	8:21.64	Sonia O'SULLIVAN	IRL	London	15 Jul 1994
NAm	8:25.83	Mary SLANEY	USA	Roma	7 Sep 1985
Afr	8:26.48	Zahra OUAZIZ	MAR	Zürich	11 Aug 1999
Com	8:27.40	Paula RADCLIFFE	GBR	Zürich	11 Aug 1999
CAC	8:37.07	Yvonne GRAHAM	JAM	Zürich	16 Aug 1995
Oce	8:44.1 m	Donna GOULD (in mixed race)	AUS	Eugene	13 Jul 1984
	8:45.53	Anne AUDAIN	NZL	Brisbane	4 Oct 1982
SAm	9:02.37	Delirde BERNARDI	BRA	Linz	4 Jul 1994
WJ	8:28.83 *	Zola BUDD	GBR	Roma	7 Sep 1985

5000 METRES

W, Asi	14:28.09	JIANG Bo	CHN	Shanghai	23 Oct 1997
Afr	14:30.88	Getenesh WAMI	ETH	Heusden	5 Aug 2000
Eur	14:31.48	Gabriela SZABO	ROM	Berlin	1 Sep 1998
Com	14:39.83	Leah MALOT	KEN	Berlin	1 Sep 2000
NAm	14:45.35	Regina JACOBS	USA	Sacramento	21 Jul 2000
CAC	15:06.54	Nora ROCHA	MEX	Berlin	1 Sep 1998
Oce	15:08.69	Kerryn McCANN	AUS	Brisbane	3 Sep 2000
SAm	15:22.01	Carmen de OLIVEIRA	BRA	Hechtel	31 Jul 1993
WJ	14:39.96 §	YIN Lili (no doping control)	CHN	Shanghai	22 Oct 1997
	14:45.90	JIANG Bo	CHN	Nanjing	24 Oct 1995

10,000 METRES

W, Asi	29:31.78	WANG Junxia	CHN	Beijing	8 Sep 1993

Eur	30:13.74	Ingrid KRISTIANSEN	NOR	Oslo	5 Jul 1986
Afr	30:17.49	Derertu TULU	ETH	Sydney	30 Sep 2000
Com	30:26.97	Paula RADCLIFFE	GBR	Sydney	30 Sep 2000
CAC	31:10.12	Adriana FERNANDEZ	MEX	Brunswick	1 Jul 2000
Oce	31:11.72	Lisa ONDIEKI	AUS	Helsinki	30 Jun 1992
NAm	31:19.89	Lynn JENNINGS	USA	Barcelona	7 Aug 1992
SAm	31:47.76	Carmen de OLIVEIRA	BRA	Stuttgart	21 Aug 1993
WJ	30:39.41	LAN Lixin	CHN	Shanghai	19 Oct 1997

MARATHON

W, Afr, Com	2:20:43	Tegla LOROUPE	KEN	Rotterdam	26 Sep 1999

Note that Loroupe received assistance from male pacemakers throughout this race

Eur	2:21:06	Ingrid KRISTIANSEN	NOR	London	21 Apr 1985
NAm	2:21:21	Joan BENOIT/SAMUELSON	USA	Chicago	20 Oct 1985
Asi	2:21:47	Naoko TAKAHASHI	JPN	Bangkok	6 Dec 1998
Oce	2:23:51	Lisa MARTIN/ONDIEKI	AUS	Osaka	31 Jan 1988
CAC	2:24:06	Adriana FERNANDEZ	MEX	London	18 Apr 1999
SAm	2:27:41	Carmen de OLIVEIRA	BRA	Boston	18 Apr 1994

Boston course has an overall net drop of 139m (0.33%), and in 1994 there was a strong following wind.

WJ	2:26:34	WEI Yanan	CHN	Beijing	15 Oct 2000

3000 METRES STEEPLECHASE

W, Eur	9:40.20	Cristina ILOC-CASANDRA	ROM	Reims	30 Aug 2000
NAm	9:57.20	Elizabeth JACKSON	USA	Sacramento	17 Jul 2000
Com	10:08.11	Tara KRZYWICKI	GBR	Stretford	5 Sep 2000
Oce, WJ	10:10.73	Melissa ROLLISON	AUS	Sydney	25 Feb 2000
Afr	10:23.55	Sonia AGOUN	TUN	Bucuresti	7 Aug 2000
SAm	10:26.00	Michelle Barreto DA COSTA	BRA	Rio de Janeiro	5 Aug 2000

100 METRES HURDLES

W, Eur	12.21	Yordanka DONKOVA	BUL	Stara Zagora	20 Aug 1988
NAm	12.33	Gail DEVERS	USA	Sacramento	23 Jul 2000
Asi	12.44	Olga SHISHIGINA	KAZ	Luzern	27 Jun 1995
Afr, Com	12.44	Glory ALOZIE	NGR	Monaco	8 Aug 1998
	12.44	Glory ALOZIE	NGR	Bruxelles	28 Aug 1998
	12.44	Glory ALOZIE	NGR	Sevilla	28 Aug 1999
CAC	12.52	Michelle FREEMAN	JAM	Athína	10 Aug 1997
	12.52	Michelle FREEMAN	JAM	Zürich	12 Aug 1998
	12.52	Delloreen ENNIS-LONDON	JAM	Kingston	22 Jul 2000
SAm	12.86	Maurren MAGGI	BRA	Winnipeg	30 Jul 1999
Oce	12.93	Pam RYAN	AUS	München	4 Sep 1972
WJ	12.84	Aliuska LÓPEZ	CUB	Zagreb	16 Jul 1987

400 METRES HURDLES

W, NAm	52.61	Kim BATTEN	USA	Göteborg	11 Aug 1995
Eur, Com	52.74	Sally GUNNELL	GBR	Stuttgart	19 Aug 1993
CAC	52.82	Deon HEMMINGS	JAM	Atlanta	31 Jul 1996
Afr	52.90	Nezha BIDOUANE	MAR	Sevilla	25 Aug 1999
Oce	53.17	Debbie FLINTOFF-KING	AUS	Seoul	28 Sep 1988
Asi	53.96	HAN Qing	CHN	Beijing	9 Sep 1993
SAm	56.05	Ximena RESTREPO	ECU	Valencia, VEN	26 Nov 1994
WJ	55.20	Leslie MAXIE	USA	San Jose	9 Jun 1984
	55.20A	Jana PITTMAN	AUS	Pietersburg	18 Mar 2000
	54.93 §	LI Rui (no doping control)	CHN	Shanghai	22 Oct 1997

HIGH JUMP

W, Eur	2.09	Stefka KOSTADINOVA	BUL	Roma	30 Aug 1987
CAC	2.04	Silvia COSTA	CUB	Barcelona	9 Sep 1989
Afr, Com	2.04	Hestrie CLOETE	RSA	Monaco	4 Aug 1999
NAm	2.03	Louise RITTER	USA	Austin	8 Jul 1988
		Louise RITTER	USA	Seoul	30 Sep 1988
Oce	1.98	Vanessa WARD	AUS	Perth	12 Feb 1989
	1.98	Alison INVERARITY	AUS	Ingolstadt	17 Jul 1994
Asi	1.97	JIN Ling	CHN	Hamamatsu	7 May 1989
	1.97*	Svetlana ZALEVSKAYA	KAZ	Pierre-Benité	14 Jun 1996
	1.97	Svetlana ZALEVSKAYA	KAZ	Lausanne	5 Jul 2000
SAm	1.96	Solange WITTEVEEN	ARG	Oristano	8 Sep 1997
WJ	2.01 §	Olga TURCHAK	KAZ	Moskva	7 Jul 1986
	2.01	Heike BALCK	GER	Chemnitz	18 Jun 1989

POLE VAULT

W, NAm	4.63	Stacy DRAGILA	USA	Sacramento	23 Jul 2000
Oce, Com	4.60	Emma GEORGE	AUS	Sydney	20 Feb 1999
Eur	4.56	Anzhela BALAKHONOVA	UKR	Linz	8 Aug 2000
SAm	4.42	Alejandra GARCIA	ARG	Sydney	20 Feb 2000
Afr	4.42	Elmarie GERRYTS	RSA	Wesel	12 Jun 2000
Asi	4.33	CAI Weiyan	CHN	Shenzhen	5 Oct 1996
CAC	3.95	Katiuska PEREZ	CUB	La Habana	29 Jul 2000
WJ	4.42 ?	Yvonne BUSCHBAUM	GER	Freistett	27 Jun 1999
	4.40 §	Yelena ISINBAYEVA	RUS	Tula	24 Jul 2000

LONG JUMP

W, Eur	7.52	Galina CHISTYAKOVA	RUS	Sankt-Peterburg	11 Jun 1988
		now CISTJAKOVÁ	SVK		
NAm	7.49	Jackie JOYNER-KERSEE	USA	New York	22 May 1994
	7.49A*	Jackie JOYNER-KERSEE	USA	Sestriere	31 Jul 1994
SAm	7.26A	Maurren MAGGI	BRA	Bogotá	26 Jun 1999
Afr	7.12	Chioma AJUNWA	NGR	Atlanta	1 Aug 1996
Asi	7.01	YAO Weili	CHN	Jinan	5 Jun 1993
CAC	6.99	Lissette CUZA	CUB	Jena	3 Jun 2000
Com	6.90	Beverly KINCH	GBR	Helsinki	14 Aug 1983
Oce	6.87	Nicole BOEGMAN	AUS	Gateshead	14 Aug 1988
WJ	7.14 *	Heike DAUTE/DRECHSLER	GER	Bratislava	4 Jun 1983
	6.98	Heike DAUTE/DRECHSLER	GER	Potsdam	18 Aug 1982

TRIPLE JUMP

W, Eur	15.50	Inessa KRAVETS	UKR	Göteborg	10 Aug 1995
Com	15.16i	Ashia HANSEN	GBR	Valencia	26 Feb 1998
	15.16	Ashia HANSEN	GBR	Fukuoka	13 Sep 1997
CAC	14.77	Yamilé ALDAMA	CUB	Winnipeg	28 Jul 1999
Afr	14.70A	Françoise MBANGO	CMR	Johannesburg	18 Sep 1999
Asi	14.66	REN Ruiping	CHN	Hiroshima	29 Apr 1997
NAm	14.41	Sheila HUDSON	USA	Stockholm	8 Jul 1996
SAm	14.01	Luciana dos SANTOS	BRA	São Paulo	18 Jun 2000
Oce	13.82	Nicole MLADENIS	AUS	Perth	9 Dec 2000
WJ	14.62	Tereza MARINOVA	BUL	Sydney	25 Aug 1996

SHOT

W, Eur	22.63	Natalya LISOVSKAYA	RUS	Moskva	7 Jun 1987
Asi	21.76	LI Meisu	CHN	Shijiazhuang	23 Apr 1988
CAC	20.96	Belsy LAZA	CUB	Ciudad de México	2 May 1992
NAm	20.18	Ramona PAGEL	USA	San Diego	25 Jun 1988
Oce, Com	19.74	Gael MARTIN	AUS	Berkeley	14 Jul 1984
SAm	19.02	Elisângela ADRIANO	BRA	Bogotá	26 Jun 1999
Afr	17.93	Vivian PETERS	NGR	Dortmund	8 Jul 2000
WJ	20.54	Astrid KUMBERNUSS	GER	Orimattila	1 Jul 1989

DISCUS

W, Eur	76.80	Gabriele REINSCH	GER	Neubrandenburg	9 Jul 1988
Asi	71.68	XIAO Yanling	CHN	Beijing	14 Mar 1992
CAC	70.88	Hilda RAMOS	CUB	La Habana	8 May 1992
Oce, Com	68.72	Daniela COSTIAN	AUS	Auckland	22 Jan 1994
NAm	66.10	Carol CADY	USA	San José	31 May 1986
SAm	62.23	Elisângela ADRIANO	BRA	Palma de Mallorca	12 Jul 1999
Afr	61.74	Monia KARI	TUN	Tunis	1 May 1996
WJ	74.40	Ilke WYLUDDA	GER	Berlin	13 Sep 1988

HAMMER

W, Eur	76.07	Mihaela MELINTE	ROM	Rüdingen	29 Aug 1999
NAm	70.46	Dawn ELLERBE	USA	Philadelphia	29 Apr 2000
CAC	69.36	Yipsi MORENO	CUB	Rhede	23 Jun 2000
Oce, Com	67.95	Debbie SOSIMENKO	AUS	Sydney	29 Sep 2000
Asi	65.70	ZHAO Wei	CHN	Deyang	14 May 2000
Afr	62.06	Caroline FOURNIER	MRI	Montgeron	29 Jun 1996
SAm	61.85	Carina MOYA	ARG	Santa Fé	13 Jun 1998
WJ	71.16	Kamila SKOLIMOWSKA	POL	Sydney	29 Sep 2000

JAVELIN (NEW)

W, Eur	69.48	Trine HATTESTAD	NOR	Oslo	28 Jul 2000

CAC	67.83	Osleidys MENENDEZ	CUB	Berlin	1 Sep 2000
Oce, Com	66.80	Louise CURREY	AUS	Gold Coast	5 Aug 2000
Asi	63.92	WEI Jianhua	CHN	Beijing	18 Aug 2000
SAm	61.98A	Sueli dos SANTOS	BRA	Bogotá	6 May 2000
NAm	58.61	Lynda BLUTREICH	USA	New Haven	1 Jul 2000
Afr	55.90	Aïda SALLEM	TUN	Tunis	3 Jun 2000
WJ	61.99	WANG Yaning	CHN	Huizhou	14 Oct 1999

JAVELIN (OLD)

See ATHLETICS 2000 for final list

HEPTATHLON

W, NAm	7291	Jackie JOYNER-KERSEE	USA	Seoul	24 Sep 1988
Eur	7007	Larisa NIKITINA	RUS	Bryansk	11 Jun 1989
Asi	6942	Ghada SHOUAA	SYR	Götzis	26 May 1996
Com	6831	Denise LEWIS	GBR	Talence	30 Jul 2000
Oce	6695	Jane FLEMMING	AUS	Auckland	28 Jan 1990
CAC	6527	Diane GUTHRIE-GRESHAM	JAM	Knoxville	3 Jun 1995
Afr	6416	Eunice BARBER	SLE	Talence	15 Sep 1996
SAm	6017	Conceição GEREMIAS	BRA	Caracas	25 Aug 1983
WJ	6465	Sibylle THIELE	GER	Schwechat	28 Aug 1983

5000 METRES TRACK WALK

W, Oce, Com	20:03.0 §	Kerry SAXBY-JUNNA	AUS	Sydney	11 Feb 1996
	20:13.26	Kerry SAXBY-JUNNA	AUS	Hobart	25 Feb 1996
W, Eur	20:07.52 §	Beate ANDERS	GER	Rostock	23 Jun 1990
	20:21.69	Annarita SIDOTI	ITA	Cesenatico	1 Jul 1995
Asi	20:37.7 m	JIN Bingjie	CHN	Hefei	3 Mar 1990
NAm	20:56.88	Michelle ROHL	USA	Philadelphia	27 Apr 1996
SAm	22:30.45	Bertha VERA	ECU	Seoul	20 Sep 1992
CAC	22:38.25	Maria COLIN	MEX	Monterrey	9 Apr 1986
Afr	23:10.88	Amsale YAKOBE	ETH	Seoul	20 Sep 1992
WJ	20:31.4 m	Irina STANKINA	RUS	Adler	10 Feb 1996

10 KILOMETRES WALK

W, Eur	41:04	Yelena NIKOLAYEVA	RUS	Sochi	20 Apr 1996
Asi	41:16	WANG Yan	CHN	Eisenhüttenstadt	8 May 1999
Oce, Com	41:30	Kerry SAXBY-JUNNA	AUS	Canberra	27 Aug 1988
CAC	42:42	Graciella MENDOZA	MEX	Naumburg	25 May 1997
NAm	44:17	Michelle ROHL	USA	Göteborg	7 Aug 1995
SAm	45:03	Geovana IRUSTA	BOL	Podebrady	19 Apr 1997
Afr	45:06A	Susan VERMEULEN	RSA	Bloemfontein	17 Apr 1999
WJ	41:55	Irina STANKINA	RUS	Adler	11 Feb 1995

10,000 METRES TRACK WALK

W, Eur	41:56.23	Nadyezhda RYASHKINA	RUS	Seattle	24 Jul 1990
Oce	41:57.22	Kerry SAXBY-JUNNA	AUS	Seattle	24 Jul 1990
Asi	42:30.13	GAO Hongmiao	CHN	Nanjing	24 Oct 1995
NAm	44:30.1 m	Alison BAKER	CAN	Fana	15 May 1992
	44:06 no kerb	Michelle ROHL	USA	Kenosha	2 Jun 1996
CAC	44:51.81	Graciela MENDOZA	MEX	Athína	4 Aug 1997
SAm	45:59.95	Geovana IRUSTA	BOL	Rio de Janeiro	20 May 2000
Afr	51:11.2 m	Sabeha MANSOURI	ALG	Cairo	26 Aug 1995
WJ	42:49.7 m	GAO Hongmiao	CHN	Jinan	15 Mar 1992

20 KILOMETRES WALK

W, Eur	1:25:18	Tatyana GUDKOVA	RUS	Moskva	19 May 2000
Asi	1:27:30	LIU Hongyu	CHN	Beijing	1 May 1995
Oce, Com	1:28:56	Jane SAVILLE	AUS	Vallansbæk	6 May 2000
CAC	1:30:03	Graciela MENDOZA	MEX	Mézidon-Canon	2 May 1999
NAm	1:31:51	Michelle ROHL	USA	Kenosha	13 May 2000
SAm	1:34:37	Geovana IRUSTA	BOL	Naumburg	30 Apr 2000
Afr	1:36:18	Susan VERMEULEN	RSA	Mézidon-Canon	2 May 1999
WJ	1:27:35	Natalya FEDOSKINA	RUS	Mézidon-Canon	2 May 1999

4 X 100 METRES RELAY

W, Eur	41.37	GDR (Gladisch, Rieger, Auerswald, Göhr)	Canberra	6 Oct 1985
NAm	41.47	USA (Gaines, Jones, Miller, Devers)	Athína	9 Aug 1997
CAC, Com	41.92	BAH (Fynes, Sturrup, Davis-Thompson, Ferguson)	Sevilla	29 Aug 1999

Asi	42.23	Sichuan CHN (Xiao Lin, Li Yali, Liu Xiaomei, Li Xuemei)	Shanghai	23 Oct 1997
Afr	42.39	NGR (Utondu, Idehen, Opara-Thompson, Onyali)	Barcelona	7 Aug 1992
Oce	42.99A	AUS (Massey, Broadrick, Lambert, Gainsford-Taylor)	Pietersburg	18 Mar 2000
SAm	43.42	COL (Mera, Palacios, Rodríguez, Brock)	Göteborg	12 Aug 1995
WJ	43.33 §	GDR (Breuer, Krabbe, Dietz, Henke)	Berlin	20 Jul 1988
	43.38	USA (A Joyce, Aleah Williams, Robinson, Buchanan)	Tampa	11 Jul 1999

4 X 400 METRES RELAY

W, Eur	3:15.17	URS (Ledovskaya, Nazarova, Pinigina, Bryzgina)	Seoul	1 Oct 1988
NAm	3:15.51	USA (D.Howard, Dixon, Brisco, Griffith Joyner)	Seoul	1 Oct 1988
Afr	3:21.04	NGR (Bisi Afolabi, Yusuf, Opara, Ogunkoya)	Atlanta	3 Aug 1996
Com	3:21.21	CAN (Crooks, Richardson, Killingbeck, Payne)	Los Angeles	11 Aug 1984
CAC	3:21.30	JAM (Turner, L Graham, Hemmings, Richards)	Athína	10 Aug 1997
Oce	3:23.81	AUS (Peris-Kneebone, Lewis, Gainsford-Taylor, Freeman)	Sydney	30 Sep 2000
Asi	3:24.28	CHN / Hebei (An, Bai, Cao, Ma)	Beijing	13 Sep 1993
SAm	3:29.22A	BRA (Montalvão, R de Oliveira, Telles, Figueiredo)	Ciudad de México	24 Jul 1988
WJ	3:28.39	GDR (Derr, Fabert, Wöhlk, Breuer)	Sudbury	31 Jul 1988

World Records at other events recognised by the IAAF

1 Hour	18,340 m	Tegla LOROUPE	KEN	Borgholzhausen	7 Aug 1998
20km	1:05:26.6	Tegla LOROUPE	KEN	Borgholzhausen	3 Sep 2000
25km	1:29:29.2	Karolina SZABÓ	HUN	Budapest	22 Apr 1988
30km	1:47:05.6	Karolina SZABÓ	HUN	Budapest	22 Apr 1988
4x200m	1:28.15	GDR (Göhr, R Müller, Wöckel, Koch)		Jena	9 Aug 1980
4x800m	7:50.17	USSR (Olizarenko, Gurina, Borisova, Podyalovskaya)		Moskva	5 Aug 1984

WORLD BESTS AT NON-STANDARD BESTS

Men

50m	5.53	Bruny Surin	CAN	Sevilla (in 100m)	22 Aug 1999
	6.53	Ben Johnson ¶	CAN	Rome (in 100m)	30 Aug 1987
	drugs dq 6.52	Ben Johnson		Seoul (in 100m)	24 Sep 1988
60m	6.38	Bruny Surin	CAN	Sevilla (in 100m)	22 Aug 1999
	6.38	Ben Johnson ¶	CAN	Roma (in 100m)	30 Aug 1987
drugs dq	6.37	Ben Johnson	CAN	Seoul (in 100m)	24 Sep 1988
150m	14.8	Pietro Mennea	ITA	Cassino	22 May 1983
	14.93	John Regis	GBR	Stuttgart (in 200m)	20 Aug 1993
300m	30.85A	Michael Johnson	USA	Pretoria	24 Mar 2000
	31.48	Danny Everett	USA	Jerez de la Frontera	3 Sep 1990
	31.48	Roberto Hernández	CUB	Jerez de la Frontera	3 Sep 1990
500m	1:00.08	Donato Sabia	ITA	Busto Arsizio	26 May 1984
600m	1:12.81	Johnny Gray	USA	Santa Monica	24 May 1986
2 miles	7:58.61	Daniel Komen	KEN	Hechtel	19 Jul 1997
2000m Steeple	5:14.43	Julius Kariuki	KEN	Rovereto	21 Aug 1990
200mh	22.55	Laurent Ottoz	ITA	Milano	31 May 1995
(hand time)	22.5	Martin Lauer	FRG	Zürich	7 Jul 1959
220yh straight	21.9	Don Styron	USA	Baton Rouge	2 Apr 1960
300mh	34.59	Chris Rawlinson	GBR	Loughboroigh	30 Jul 2000
35lb weight	25.41	Lance Deal	USA	Azusa	20 Feb 1993
Pentathlon	4282 points	Bill Toomey	USA	London (CP)	16 Aug 1969
(1985 tables)		(7.58, 66.18, 21.3, 44.52, 4:20.3)			
Double decathlon	14274 pts	Indrek Kaseorg	EST	Punkalaidun	12/13 Sep 1992

11.75, 7.00, 200mh 25.01, 12.13, 5k 17:36.07, 2:04.84, 1.99, 400m 50.72, HT 32.26, 3kSt 10:50.14
15.11, DT 37.04, 200m 23.30, 4.30, 10:18.50, 400mh 54.00, 57.78, 4:47.36, TJ 14.05, 10k 45:35.95

Women

60m	5.93	Marion Jones	USA	Sevilla (in 100m)	22 Aug 1999
60m	6.85	Marion Jones	USA	Sevilla (in 100m)	22 Aug 1999
150m	16.10	Florence Griffith-Joyner	USA	Seoul (in 200m)	29 Sep 1988
300m	34.1	Marita Koch	GDR	Canberra (in 400m)	6 Oct 1985
500m	1:05.9	Tatána Kocembová	CZE	Ostrava	2 Aug 1984
600m	1:22.63	Ana Fidelia Quirot	CUB	Guadalajara	25 Jul 1997
2 miles	9:19.56	Sonia O'Sullivan	IRL	Cork	27 Jun 1998
2000m Steeple	6:11.84	Marina Pluzhnikova	RUS	Sankt Peterburg	25 Jul 1994
200mh	25.7	Pamela Ryan	AUS	Melbourne	25 Nov 1971
Double heptathlon	10824 pts	Irina Stasenko	RUS	Punkalaidun	12/13 Sep 1992
	100mh 14.95, HJ 1.57, 1500m 4:44.41, 400mh 61.82, SP 12.71, 200m 25.58, 100m 12.86				
	LJ 5.56, 400m 59.09, JT 37.52, 800m 2:17.88, 200mh 28.98, DT 30.32, 3000m 10:46.93				
Decathlon	7731	Marie Collonvillé	FRA	Lage	9/10 Sep 2000
	12.61, 6.03, 11.55, 1.75, 56.48, 14.28, 31.91, 3.40, 43.94, 5:13.70				

LONG DISTANCE WORLD BESTS – MEN TRACK

	hr:min:sec	*Name*	*Nat*	*Venue*	*Date*
15 km	0:42:34.0	Arturo Barrios	MEX	La Flèche	30 Mar 1991
10 miles	0:45:57.6	Jos Hermens	NED	Papendal	14 Sep 1975
15 miles	1:11:43.1	Bill Rodgers	USA	Saratoga, Cal.	21 Feb 1979
20 miles	1:39:14.4	Jack Foster	NZL	Hamilton, NZ	15 Aug 1971
30 miles	2:42:00	Jeff Norman	GBR	Timperley, Cheshire	7 Jun 1980
50 km	2:48:06	Jeff Norman	GBR	Timperley, Cheshire	7 Jun 1980
40 miles	3:48:35	Don Ritchie	GBR	London (Hendon)	16 Oct 1982
50 miles	4:51:49	Don Ritchie	GBR	London (Hendon)	12 Mar 1983
100 km	6:10:20	Don Ritchie	GBR	London (CP)	28 Oct 1978
150 km	10:36:42	Don Ritchie	GBR	London (CP)	15 Oct 1977
100 miles	11:30:51	Don Ritchie	GBR	London (CP)	15 Oct 1977
200 km	15:10:27	Yiannis Kouros	GRE	Adelaide	4-5 Oct 1997
200 miles	27:48:35	Yiannis Kouros	GRE	Montauban	15-16 Mar 1985
500 km	60:23.00	Yiannis Kouros	GRE	Colac, Aus	26-29 Nov 1984
500 miles	105:42:09	Yiannis Kouros	GRE	Colac, Aus	26-30 Nov 1984
1000 km	136:17:00	Yiannis Kouros	GRE	Colac, Aus	26-31 Nov 1984
1500 km	10d 17:28:26	Petrus Silkinas	LTU	Nanango, Qld	11-21 Mar 1998
1000 mile	11d 13:54:58	Petrus Silkinas	LTU	Nanango, Qld	11-22 Mar 1998
2 hrs	37.994 km	Jim Alder	GBR	Walton-on-Thames	17 Oct 1964
12 hrs	162.400 km	Yiannis Kouros	GRE	Montauban	15 Mar 1985
24 hrs	303.506 km *	Yiannis Kouros	GRE	Adelaide	4-5 Oct 1997
48 hrs	473.797 km	Yiannis Kouros	GRE	Surgères	3-5 May 1996
6 days	1030.000 indoor	Jean-Gilles Bousiquet	FRA	La Rochelle	16-23 Nov 1992
Outdoors	1023.200 km *	Yiannis Kouros	GRE	Colac, Aus	26 Nov-1 Dec 1984
	1022.068 km	Yiannis Kouros	GRE	New York	2-8 Jul 1984

 # Running watch time, no stopped times known.

LONG DISTANCE ROAD BESTS – MEN

Where superior to track bests and run on properly measured road courses.

	hr:min:sec	*Name*	*Nat*	*Venue*	*Date*
15 km	0:42:04+	Paul Tergat	KEN	Milano	4 Apr 1998
10 miles	0:44:45	Paul Koech	KEN	Amsterdam-Zaandam	21 Sep 1997
20 km	0:56:18+	Paul Tergat	KEN	Milano	4 Apr 1998
Half mar	0:59:17	Paul Tergat	KEN	Milano	4 Apr 1998
	0:59:06	Paul Tergat	KEN	Lisboa (downhill 40m)	26 Mar 2000
30 km	1:28:40+	Steve Jones	GBR	Chicago	10 Oct 1985
20 miles	1:35:22+	Steve Jones	GBR	Chicago	10 Oct 1985
30 miles	2:37:31+	Thompson Magawana	RSA	Claremont-Kirstenbosch	12 Apr 1988
50km	2:43:38	Thompson Magawana	RSA	Claremont-Kirstenbosch	12 Apr 1988
40 miles	3:45:39	Andy Jones	CAN	Houston	23 Feb 1991
50 miles	4:50:21	Bruce Fordyce	RSA	London-Brighton	25 Sep 1983
1000 miles	10d:10:30:35	Yiannis Kouros	GRE	New York	21-30 May 1988
Ekiden (6)	1:57:56		MAR	Litóhoro, GRE	17 Apr 1994
12 hrs	162.543 km	Yiannis Kouros	GRE	Queen's, New York	7 Nov 1984
6 days	1028.370 km	Yiannis Kouros	GRE	New York	21-26 May 1988

LONG DISTANCE WORLD BESTS – WOMEN TRACK

	hr:min:sec	*Name*	*Nat*	*Venue*	*Date*
15 km	0:49:44.0	Silvana Cruciata	ITA	Roma	4 May 1981
10 miles	0:54:21.8	Lorraine Moller	NZL	Auckland	9 Jan 1993
20 miles	1:59:09 !	Chantal Langlacé	FRA	Amiens	3 Sep 1983
30 miles	3:12:25	Carolyn Hunter-Rowe	GBR	Barry, Wales	3 Mar 1996
50 km	3:18:52	Carolyn Hunter-Rowe	GBR	Barry, Wales	3 Mar 1996
40 miles	4:26:43	Carolyn Hunter-Rowe	GBR	Barry, Wales	7 Mar 1993
50 miles	5:55:41	Valentina Lyakhova	RUS	Nantes	28 Sep 1996
100 km	7:23:28	Valentina Lyakhova	RUS	Nantes	28 Sep 1996
150 km	13:45:54	Hilary Walker	GBR	Blackpool	5-6 Nov 1988
100 miles	14:29:44	Ann Trason	USA	Santa Rosa, Cal.	18-19 Mar 1989
200 km	19:28:48 *	Eleanor Adams	GBR	Melbourne	19-20 Aug 1989
	19:49:36	Irina Reutovich	RUS	Verona	25-26 Sep 1999
200 miles	39:09:03	Hilary Walker	GBR	Blackpool	5-7 Nov 1988
500 km	77:53:46	Eleanor Adams	GBR	Colac, Aus.	13-16 Nov 1989
500 miles	130:59:58	Sandra Barwick	NZL	Campbelltown, AUS	18-23 Nov 1990
1000 km	8d 00:27:06	Eleanor Robinson	GBR	Nanango, Qld	11-19 Mar 1998
1500 km	12d 06:52:12	Eleanor Robinson	GBR	Nanango, Qld	11-23 Mar 1998
1000 miles	13d 02:16:49	Eleanor Robinson	GBR	Nanango, Qld	11-24 Mar 1998
2 hrs	32.652 km	Chantal Langlacé	FRA	Amiens	3 Sep 1983

12 hrs	147.600 km	Ann Trason	USA	Hayward, Cal	3-4 Aug 1991
24 hrs	242.624 km *	Irina Reutovich	RUS	Moskva	9-10 May 1998
	240.169 km	Eleanor Adams/Robinson	GBR	Melbourne	19-20 Aug 1989
48 hrs	377.892 km	Sue Ellen Trapp	USA	Surgères	2-4 May 1997
6 days	883.631 km	Sandra Barwick	NZL	Campbelltown, AUS	18-24 Nov 1990
Indoors where superior to track best					
200 km	19:00:31	Eleanor Adams	GBR	Milton Keynes	3/4 Feb 1990
24 hrs	248.901 km	Yelena Siderenkova	RUS	Podolsk	10-11 Feb 1996

! Timed on one running watch only, * lap recorded by computer

LONG DISTANCE ROAD BESTS - WOMEN

	hr:min:sec	*Name*	*Nat*	*Venue*	*Date*
10 km	0:30:39	Liz McColgan	GBR	Orlando	11 Mar 1989
15 km	0:46:57	Elana Meyer	RSA	Cape Town	2 Nov 1991
10 miles	0:51:16	Colleen de Reuck	RSA	Washington, DC	5 Apr 1998
	0:50:31 u	Ingrid Kristiansen	NOR	Amsterdam	11 Oct 1989
20 km	1:04:01	Esther Wanjiru	KEN	Kobe	17 Dec 2000
Half mar	1:06:40 ?	Ingrid Kristiansen	NOR	Sandnes	5 Apr 1987
	1:06:43	Masako Chiba	JPN	Tokyo - 33m drop	19 Jan 1997
25 km	1:21:21+	Ingrid Kristiansen	NOR	London	10 May 1987
30 km	1:38:27+	Ingrid Kristiansen	NOR	London	10 May 1987
20 miles	1:46:04+	Ingrid Kristiansen	NOR	London	10 May 1987
30 miles	3:01:16+	Frith van der Merwe	RSA	Claremont-Kirstenbosch	25 Mar 1989
50 km	3:08:39	Frith van der Merwe	RSA	Claremont-Kirstenbosch	25 Mar 1989
40 miles	4:26:13+	Ann Trason	USA	Houston	23 Feb 1991
50 miles	5:40:18	Ann Trason	USA	Houston	23 Feb 1991
100 km	7:00:48	Ann Trason	USA	Winschoten	16 Sep 1995
100 miles	13:47:41	Ann Trason	USA	Queen's, New York	4 May 1991
200 km	19:00:31	Eleanor Adams	GBR	Milton Keynes (indoor)	3-4 Feb 1990
1000 km	7d 01:11:00	Sandra Barwick	NZL	New York	16-23 Sep 1991
1000 miles	12d 14:38:40	Sandra Barwick	NZL	New York	16-29 Sep 1991
Ekiden (6)	2:11:41		CHN	Beijing	28 Feb 1998
12 hours	144.840 km	Ann Trason	USA	Queen's, New York	4 May 1991
24 hours	243.657 km	Sigrid Lomsky	GER	Basel	1-2 May 1993

100 KILOMETRES CONTINENTAL RECORDS

MEN					
W, Asi	6:13:33	Takahiro SUNADA	JPN	Yubetsu	21 Jun 1998
Eur	6:16:41	Jean-Paul PRAET	BEL	Torhout	24 Jun 1989
SAm	6:18:09	Valmir NUNES	BRA	Winschoten	16 Sep 1995
Afr	6:25:07	Bruce FORDYCE	RSA	Stellenbosch	4 Feb 1989
Oce	6:29:23	Tim SLOAN	AUS	Ross-Richmond	23 Apr 1995
NAm	6:30:11	Tom JOHNSON	USA	Winschoten	16 Sep 1995
WOMEN					
W, Asi	6:33:11	Tomoe ABE	JPN	Yufutsu	25 Jun 2000
NAm	7:00:48	Ann TRASON	USA	Winschoten	16 Sep 1995
Eur	7:18:57	Birgit LENNARTZ	GER	Hanau	28 Apr 1990
SAm	7:20:22	Maria VENANCIO	BRA	Cubatão	8 Aug 1998
Afr	7:31:47	Helena JOUBERT	RSA	Winschoten	16 Sep 1995
Oce	7:40:58	Linda MEADOWS	AUS	North Otago	18 Nov 1995

WORLD INDOOR RECORDS

Men					to March 2001
50 metres	5.56A	Donovan Bailey	CAN	Reno	9 Feb 1996
	5.50r	Maurice Greene	USA	Los Angeles	13 Feb 1999
	5.55 §	Ben Johnson ¶	CAN	Ottawa	31 Jan 1987
60 metres	6.39	Maurice Greene	USA	Madrid	3 Feb 1998
	6.39	Maurice Greene		Atlanta	3 Mar 2001
200 metres	19.92	Frank Fredericks	NAM	Liévin	18 Feb 1996
400 metres	44.63	Michael Johnson	USA	Atlanta	4 Mar 1995
800 metres	1:42.67	Wilson Kipketer	KEN	Paris (Bercy)	9 Mar 1997
1000 metres	2:14.96	Wilson Kipketer	KEN	Birmingham	20 Feb 2000
1500 metres	3:31.18	Hicham El Guerrouj	MAR	Stuttgart	2 Feb 1997
1 mile	3:48.45	Hicham El Guerrouj	MAR	Gent	12 Feb 1997
2000 metres #	4:52.86	Haile Gebrselassie	ETH	Birmingham	16 Feb 1998
3000 metres	7:24.90	Daniel Komen	KEN	Budapest	6 Feb 1998
2 miles #	8:09.66	Hailu Mekonnen	ETH	Birmingham	20 Feb 2000
5000 metres	12:50.38	Haile Gebrselassie	ETH	Birmingham	14 Feb 1999
50 m hurdles	6.25	Mark McKoy	CAN	Kobe	5 Mar 1986

60 m hurdles	7.30	Colin Jackson	GBR	Sindelfingen	6 Mar 1994
High jump	2.43	Javier Sotomayor	CUB	Budapest	4 Mar 1989
Pole vault	6.15	Sergey Bubka	UKR	Donetsk	21 Feb 1993
Long jump	8.79	Carl Lewis	USA	New York	27 Jan 1984
Triple jump	17.83	Aliecer Urrutia	CUB	Sindelfingen	1 Mar 1997
Shot	22.66	Randy Barnes	USA	Los Angeles	20 Jan 1989
Javelin #	85.78	Matti Närhi	FIN	Kajaani	3 Mar 1997
35 lb weight #	25.86	Lance Deal	USA	Atlanta	4 Mar 1995
5000m walk	18:07.78	Mikhail Shchennikov	RUS	Moskva	14 Feb 1995
4 x 200m	1:22.11	United Kingdom		Glasgow	3 Mar 1991
		(Linford Christie, Darren Braithwaite, Ade Mafe, John Regis)			
4 x 400m	3:02.83	USA		Maebashi	7 Mar 1999
		(Andre Morris, Desmond Johnson, Deon Minor, Milton Campbell))			
4 x 800m	7:13.94	USA/Global Athletics & Marketing		Roxbury	6 Feb 2000
		(Joey Woody, Karl Paranya, Rich Kenah, David Krummenacker)			
Heptathlon	6476 points	Dan O'Brien	USA	Toronto	13/14 Mar 1993
	(6.67 60m, 7.84 LJ, 16.02 SP, 2.13 HJ, 7.85 60mh, 5.20 PV, 2:57.96 1000m)				

Women

50 metres	5.96	Irina Privalova	RUS	Madrid	9 Feb 1995
60 metres	6.92	Irina Privalova	RUS	Madrid	11 Feb 1993
	6.92	Irina Privalova	RUS	Madrid	9 Feb 1995
200 metres	21.87	Merlene Ottey	JAM	Liévin	13 Feb 1993
400 metres	49.59	Jarmila Kratochvílová	CZE	Milano	7 Mar 1982
800 metres	1:56.40	Christine Wachtel	GDR	Wien	13 Feb 1988
1000 metres	2:30.94	Maria Lurdes Mutola	MOZ	Stockholm	25 Feb 1999
1500 metres	4:00.27 +	Doina Melinte	ROM	East Rutherford	9 Feb 1990
1 mile	4:17.14	Doina Melinte	ROM	East Rutherford	9 Feb 1990
2000 metres #	5:30.53	Gabriela Szabo	ROM	Sindelfingen	8 Mar 1998
3000 metres	8:32.88	Gabriela Szabo	ROM	Birmingham	18 Feb 2001
2 miles	9:28.15	Lynn Jennings	USA	New York	28 Feb 1986
5000 metres	14:47.35	Gabriela Szabo	ROM	Dortmund	13 Feb 1999
50 m hurdles	6.58	Cornelia Oschkenat	GDR	Berlin	20 Feb 1988
60 m hurdles	7.69	Lyudmila Narozhilenko	RUS	Chelyabinsk	4 Feb 1990
		now Ludmila Engquist	SWE		
High jump	2.07	Heike Henkel	GER	Karlsruhe	9 Feb 1992
Pole vault	4.70A	Stacy Dragila	USA	Pocatello	17 Feb 2001
Long jump	7.37	Heike Drechsler	GDR	Wien	13 Feb 1988
Triple jump	15.16	Ashia Hansen	GBR	Valencia	28 Feb 1998
Shot	22.50	Helena Fibingerová	CZE	Jablonec	19 Feb 1977
Javelin #	64.68	Mikaela Ingberg	FIN	Kajaani	5 Mar 1995
20 lb weight #	23.11	Dawn Ellerbe	USA	New York	4 Feb 2000
3000m walk	11:40.33	Claudia Iovan	ROM	Bucuresti	30 Jan 1999
5000m walk #	20:42.33	Yelena Gruzinova	RUS	Samara	1 Mar 1997
4 x 200m	1:32.55	SC Eintracht Hamm	FRG	Dortmund	20 Feb 1988
		(Helga Arendt, Silke-Beate Knoll, Mechthild Kluth, Gisela Kinzel)			
	1:32.55	LG Olympia Dortmund	GER	Karlsruhe	21 Feb 1999
		(Esther Möller, Gabi Rockmeier, Birgit Rockmeier, Andrea Philipp)			
4 x 400m	3:24.25	Russia		Maebashi	7 Mar 1999
		(Tatyana Chebykina, Svetlana Goncharenko, Olga Kotlyarova, Natalya Nazarova)			
4 x 800m	8:18.71	Russia		Moskva	4 Feb 1994
		(Olga Kuznetsova, Yelena Afanasyeva, Yelena Zaytseva, Yekaterina Podkopayeva)			
Pentathlon	4991 points	Irina Belova	RUS	Berlin	14/15 Feb 1992
		(8.22 60mh, 1.93 HJ, 13.25 SP, 6.67 LJ, 2:10.26 800m)			

 # events not official recognised by the IAAF

¶ The IAAF stripped Johnson of his records in January 1990, after he had admitted long-term steroid use.

WORLD VETERANS' RECORDS

MEN - Aged 40 or over at time of performances

100 metres	10.87	Eddie Hart (24.4.49)	USA	Eugene	30 Jul 1989
	10.6	Eddie Hart		Berkeley	16 Sep 1989
200 metres	21.80	Bill Collins (20.11.50)	USA	Spokane	15 Aug 1992
400 metres	47.87	Manuel Ulacio	VEN	Santiago de Chile	14 Nov 1981
	47.5u	Lee Evans (25.2.47)	USA		Apr 1989
800 metres	1:50.69	Colin Rothery (.60)	IRL	Stretford	5 Sep 2000
	1:48.81i	Johnny Gray (19.6.60)	USA	Atlanta	2 Mar 2001
1000 metres	2:27.8	Anselm LeBourne (20.4.59)	USA	Uniondale, NY	19 Aug 1999
1500 metres	3:44.89	Luiz José Gonçalves (4.12.58)	BRA	Rio de Janeiro	4 Jun 1999
1 mile	4:02.53	David Moorcroft (10.4.53)	GBR	Belfast	19 Jun 1993
	3:58.15i	Eamonn Coghlan (21.11.52)	IRL	Boston	20 Feb 1994

3000 metres	8:05.08	Martti Vainio (30.12.50)	FIN	Mikkeli	12 Jun 1991
5000 metres	13:43.15	Mohamed Ezzher (26.4.60)	FRA	Sotteville	3 Jul 2000
10000 metres	28:30.88	Martti Vainio (30.12.50)	FIN	Hengelo	25 Jun 1991
Marathon	2:11:04	John Campbell (6.2.49)	NZL	Boston	16 Apr 1990
3000m steeple	8:41.5	Gaston Roelants (5.2.37)	BEL	Oslo	6 Jul 1977
110m hurdles	14.16	Carlos Sala (20.3.60)	ESP	Castellón	16 Aug 2000
400m hurdles	52.62	Antônio Eusébio Dias Ferreira (2.3.60)	BRA	Rio de Janeiro	23 Jul 2000
High jump	2.15	Glen Conley (9.1.57)	USA	Troy, New York	2 Aug 1997
Pole vault	5.50A	Larry Jessee (31.3.52)	USA	El Paso	24 Aug 1996
Long jump	7.57	Hans Schicker (3.10.47)	FRG	Kitzingen	16 Jul 1989
Triple jump	16.58	Ray Kimble (19.4.53)	USA	Edinburgh	2 Jul 1993
Shot	21.41	Brian Oldfield (1.6.45)	USA	Innsbruck	22 Aug 1985
Discus	69.46	Al Oerter (19.9.36)	USA	Wichita	31 May 1980
Hammer	75.66	Yuriy Sedykh (11.6.55)	RUS	Dreux	29 Jun 1995
Javelin	78.84	Jorma Markus (28.11.52)	FIN	Kempele	21 Jun 1994
Pentathlon	3510 pts	Werner Schallau (8.9.38)	FRG	Gelsenkirchen	24 Sep 1978
		6.74, 59.20, 23.0, 43.76, 5:05.7			
Decathlon	6642 pts	Greg Richards (25.4.56)	GBR	Enfield	4 Aug 1996
		12.02, 6.81, 13.71, 1.86, 54.51, 15.63, 44.86, 4.00, 50.84, 5:18.14			
20 km walk	1:21:36	Willi Sawall (7.11.41)	AUS	Melbourne	4 Jul 1982
50 km walk	3:49:06	José Marín (21.1.50)	ESP	Badalona	22 Mar 1992
4x100m	42.79	Austin, Collins, Mitchell, Hartfield	USA		5 Feb 1992
4x400m	3:21.54	Thiel, Brinker, Tucker, King	USA	Eugene	8 Jun 1989

WOMEN – aged 35 or more

100 metres	10.74	Merlene Ottey (10.5.60)	JAM	Milano	7 Sep 1996
200 metres	21.93	Merlene Ottey (10.5.60)	JAM	Bruxelles	25 Aug 1995
400 metres	50.56	Aurelia Penton (18.2.43)	CUB	Medellin	16 Jul 1978
800 metres	1:56.53	Lyubov Gurina (6.8.57)	RUS	Hechtel	30 Jul 1994
1000 metres	2:31.5	Maricica Puica (29.7.50)	ROM	Poiana Brasov	1 Jun 1986
1500 metres	3:57.73	Maricica Puica (29.7.50)	ROM	Bruxelles	30 Aug 1985
1 mile	4:17.33	Maricica Puica (29.7.50)	ROM	Zürich	21 Aug 1985
2000 metres	5:28.69	Maricica Puica (29.7.50)	ROM	London	11 Jul 1986
3000 metres	8:27.83	Maricica Puica (29.7.50)	ROM	Roma	7 Sep 1985
5000 metres	14:45.35	Regina Jacobs (28.8.63)	USA	Sacramento	21 Jul 2000
10000 metres	31:20.28	Ingrid Kristiansen (21.3.56)	NOR	Hechtel	10 Aug 1991
2000m steeple	6:30.83	Leslie Lehane (12.3.63)	USA	Orono	31 Jul 1998
3000m steeple	10:06.8	Marina Pluzhnikova (25.2.63)	RUS	Moskva	5 Jun 1999
Marathon	2:24:35	Katrin Dörre-Heinig (6.10.61)	GER	Hamburg	25 Apr 1999
100m hurdles	12.47	Ludmila Engqvist (21.4.64)	SWE	Sevilla	28 Aug 1999
400m hurdles	52.94	Marina Styepanova (1.5.50)	RUS	Tashkent	17 Sep 1986
High jump	1.94i	Yelena Panikarovskikh (4.12.59)	RUS	Banská Bystrica	8 Feb 1995
	1.92	Yelena Panikarovskikh		St Peterburg	4 Jul 1996
Pole vault	4.22	Gabriela Mihalcea (27.1.64)	ROM	Dreux	11 Jun 1999
	4.25i	Gabriela Mihalcea (27.1.64)	ROM	Pireas	13 Feb 1999
Long jump	6.99	Heike Drechsler (16.12.64)	GER	Sydney	29 Sep 2000
Triple jump	14.02	Galina Chistyakova (26.7.62)	SVK	Athína	2 Aug 1997
Shot	21.46	Larisa Peleshenko (29.2.64)	RUS	Moskva	26 Aug 2000
	21.47i	Helena Fibingerová (13.7.49)	CZE	Jablonec	9 Feb 1985
Discus	69.60	Faina Melnik (9.7.45)	RUS	Donetsk	9 Sep 1980
Hammer	61.68	Lyubov Karpova (14.8.57)	RUS	Moskva	4 Sep 1994
Javelin (old)	67.00	Tuula Laaksalo (21.4.53)	FIN	Lappeenranta	10 Sep 1988
Heptathlon	6533 pts	Jane Frederick (7.4.52)	USA	Talence	27 Sep 1987
		13.60, 1.82, 15.50, 24.73; 6.29, 49.70, 2:14.88			
5000m walk	21:23.07	Anne Manning (13.11.59)	AUS	Sydney	17 Feb 1996
10km walk	42:42+	Tamara Kovalenko (5.6.64)	RUS	Moskva	19 May 2000
20km walk	1:25:59	Tamara Kovalenko (5.6.64)	RUS	Moskva	19 May 2000
4x100m	48.63	Desmier, Sulter, Andreas, Apavou	FRA	Eugene	8 Jun 1989
4x400m	3:50.80	Mitchell, Mathews, Beadnall, Gabriel	GBR	Gateshead	8 Aug 1999

WOMEN – aged 40 or more

100 metres	10.99	Merlene Ottey (10.5.60)	JAM	Thessaloniki	30 Aug 2000
200 metres	24.66A	Sara Montecinos (8.3.54)	CHI	Cali	18 Mar 1994
	24.84	Phil Raschker (21.2.47)	USA	Eugene	3 Aug 1989
400 metres	53.68A	Sara Montecinos (8.3.54)	CHI	Cali	19 Mar 1994
	53.73	Sara Montecinos (8.3.54)	CHI	Santiago de Chile	12 Nov 1994
800 metres	1:59.25	Yekaterina Podkopayeva (11.6.52)	RUS	Luxembourg	30 Jun 1994
1000 metres	2:36.16	Yekaterina Podkopayeva (11.6.52)	RUS	Nancy	14 Sep 1994
	2:36.08i	Yekaterina Podkopayeva (11.6.52	RUS	Liévin	13 Feb 1993
1500 metres	3:59.78	Yekaterina Podkopayeva (11.6.52)	RUS	Nice	18 Jul 1994
1 mile	4:23.78	Yekaterina Podkopayeva (11.6.52)	RUS	Roma	9 Jun 1993
3000 metres	9:11.2	Joyce Smith (26.10.37)	GBR	London	30 Apr1978

5000 metres	15:51.7	Nicole Lévêque (27.1.51)	FRA	Bonneuil/Marne	18 Jun 1994
10000 metres	32:12.07	Nicole Lévêque (27.1.51)	FRA	Helsinki	13 Aug 1994
Marathon	2:26:51	Priscilla Welch (22.11.44)	GBR	London	10 May 1987
3000m steeple	10:38.98	Soraya Telles (15.9.58)	BRA	Rio de Janeiro	5 Jun 1999
100 m hurdles	14.4	Jocelyn Harwood (21.11.57)	GBR	Basildon	6 Jun 1999
	14.61	Jocelyn Harwood		Bedford	30 May 1999
200 m hurdles	29.0	Maeve Kyle (6.10.28)	IRL	Dublin	29 Jul 1969
400 m hurdles	58.88	Maria José dos Santos (12.9.59)	BRA	Americana	3 Jun 2000
High jump	1.76	Debbie Brill (10.3.53) #	CAN	Gateshead	6 Aug 1999
Pole vault	3.38	Phil Raschker (21.2.47) #	USA	Atlanta	17 May 1994
Long jump	6.21	Franciska Janssen (23.8.44)	NED	Zwolle	7 Jul 1985
Triple jump	12.31	Conceição Geremias (23.7.56)	BRA	São Paulo	24 May 1997
Shot	19.05	Antonina Ivanova (25.12.32)	RUS	Oryol	28 Aug 1973
	19.16i	Antonina Ivanova	RUS	Moskva	24 Feb 1974
Discus	64.09 #	Zdenka Silhavá (15.6.54)	CZE	Pardubice	11 Aug 1999
Hammer	51.12	Margrith Duss-Müller (5.12.58)	SUI	Olten	15 Jul 2000
Javelin (old)	64.06	Tessa Sanderson (14.3.56)	GBR	London (CP)	12 Jul 1996
Heptathlon	4359 pts	Conceição Geremias (23.7.56)	BRA	São Caetano do Sul	7 Sep 1997
		15.61, 1.57, 12.14, 28.26, 5.49, 32.08, 2:56.10			
5000m walk	22:49.06	Suzanne Griesbach (22.4.45)	FRA	Annecy	9 Aug 1987
10km walk	47:16.8	Suzanne Griesbach (22.4.45)	FRA	Epinay-sur-Seine	12 Apr 1987
	47:03	Susanne Griesbach (22.4.45)	FRA	Montreal	21 Apr 1990
20km walk	1:42:22	Heather McDonald (13.8.49)	AUS	Melbourne	12 Sep 1993
4x100m	50.07	Horwedel, Fritsche, Grissmer, Stopka	GER	Gateshead	8 Aug 1999
4x400m	3:58.70	Foreman, Thompson, Board, Libal	GBR	Eugene	24 Aug 1996

 # W45 record

WORLD AND CONTINENTAL RECORDS SET IN 2000

OUTDOORS - MEN

1500m	Com	3:28.12	Noah NGENY	KEN	Zürich	11 Aug 2000
3000m	Eur	7:26.62	Mohammed MOURHIT	BEL	Monaco	18 Aug 2000
5000m	Eur	12:49.71	Mohammed MOURHIT	BEL	Bruxelles	25 Aug 2000
Marathon	Eur	2:06:36	António PINTO	POR	London	16 Apr 2000
	NAm	2:07:01	Khalid KHANNOUCHI (ex MAR)	USA	Chicago	22 Oct 2000
	Asi	2:06:51	Atsushi FUJITA	JPN	Fukuoka	3 Dec 2000
3000mSt	CAC	8:25.69	Salvador MIRANDA	MEX	Barakaldo	9 Jul 2000
	WJ	8:03.74	Raymond YATOR	KEN	Monaco	18 Aug 2000
110mH	CAC	13.07=	Anier GARCIA	CUB	Lausanne	5 Jul 2000
	CAC	13.00	Anier GARCIA	CUB	Sydney	25 Sep 2000
400mH	Asi	48.14	Hadi Sou'an AL-SOMAILY	KSA	Sydney	25 Sep 2000
	Asi	47.53	Hadi Sou'an AL-SOMAILY	KSA	Sydney	27 Sep 2000
High Jump	Afr	2.34	Abderrahmane HAMMAD	ALG	Alger	14 Jul 2000
Pole Vault	NAm	6.03	Jeff HARTWIG	USA	Jonesboro	14 Jun 2000
	CAC	5.70A	Dominic JOHNSON	LCA	El Paso	26 Aug 2000
Long Jump	Oce	8.40	Jai TAURIMA	AUS	Sydney	28 Sep 2000
	Oce	8.49	Jai TAURIMA	AUS	Sydney	28 Sep 2000
Shot	Oce	19.87A	Justin ANLEZARK	AUS	Roodepoort	13 Mar 2000
	Asi	20.60	Shakti SINGH	IND	Bangalore	5 Jul 2000
	CAC	20.78	Alexis PAUMIER	CUB	La Habana	29 Jul 2000
	Oce	19.88	Justin ANLEZARK	AUS	Brisbane	8 Sep 2000
	Oce	19.88=	Justin ANLEZARK	AUS	Gold Coast	10 Sep 2000
	Oce	20.35	Justin ANLEZARK	AUS	Gold Coast	10 Sep 2000
Discus	Afr	67.81	Frantz KRUGER	RSA	Zürich	11 Aug 2000
	Afr, Com	68.13	Frantz KRUGER	RSA	Cottbus	23 Aug 2000
	Afr, Com	69.75A	Frantz KRUGER	RSA	Bloemfontein	15 Sep 2000
Hammer	Afr	76.28	Chris HARMSE	RSA	Stellenbosch	18 Feb 2000
	Afr	76.71	Chris HARMSE	RSA	Port Elizabeth	25 Feb 2000
	Oce, Com	77.68A	Stuart RENDELL	AUS	Pietersburg	18 Mar 2000
	Afr, Com	77.92	Chris HARMSE	RSA	Cape Town	31 Mar 2000
	Afr, Com	78.71A	Chris HARMSE	RSA	Pretoria	23 Sep 2000
Javelin	CAC	84.83	Emeterio GONZALEZ	CUB	Dessau	31 May 2000
	CAC	87.12	Emeterio GONZALEZ	CUB	Jena	3 Jun 2000
Decathlon	CAC	8244	Raúl DUANY	CUB	Arles	4 Jun 2000
	CAC	8252	Raúl DUANY	CUB	La Habana	24 Jul 2000
	Afr	7642	Anis RIAHI	TUN	Talence	31 Jul 2000
10000m Walk	WJ	38:46.4 §	Viktor BURAYEV	RUS	Moskva	19 May 2000
20km Walk	Eur	1:18:07	Roman RASSKAZOV	RUS	Adler	20 Feb 2000
	W, Eur	1:17:46	Roman RASSKAZOV	RUS	Moskva	19 May 2000
	NAm	1:21:03	Arturo HUERTA	CAN	Etobicoke	7 Jul 2000
50km Walk	W, Eur	3:37:26	Valeriy SPITSYN	RUS	Moskva	21 May 2000

4x100m	SAm	37.90	BRA (V Lima, Ribeiro, A da Silva, Cl da Silva)		Sydney	30 Sep 2000
	Asi	38.31=	JPN (Kawabata, K Ito, Suetsugu, Asahara)		Sydney	29 Sep 2000
4x400m	Afr	2:58.68	NGR (Chukwu, Monye, Bada, Udo-Obong)		Sydney	30 Sep 2000

OUTDOORS - WOMEN

5000m	NAm	14:45.35	Regina JACOBS	USA	Sacramento	21 Jul 2000
	Afr	14:30.88	Getenesh WAMI	ETH	Heusden	5 Aug 2000
	Com	14:39.83	Leah MALOT	KEN	Berlin	1 Sep 2000
	Oce	15:08.69	Kerryn McCANN	AUS	Brisbane	3 Sep 2000
10000m	CAC	31:10.12	Adriana FERNANDEZ	MEX	Brunswick	1 Jul 2000
	Afr	30:17.49	Derartu TULU	ETH	Sydney	30 Sep 2000
	Com	30:26.97	Paula RADCLIFFE	Eng	Sydney	30 Sep 2000
20km	W	1:05:26.6	Tegla LOROUPE	KEN	Borgholzhausen	3 Sep 2000
3000mSt	Oce, Com, WJ	10:10.73	Melissa ROLLISON	AUS	Sydney	25 Feb 2000
	SAm	10:32.9	Michelle Barreto DA COSTA	BRA	Rio de Janeiro	16 Jul 2000
	NAm	9:57.20	Elizabeth JACKSON	USA	Sacramento	17 Jul 2000
	Afr	10:25.94	Sonia AGOUN	TUN	Sfântu Gheorghe	23 Jul 2000
	SAm	10:26.00	Michelle Barreto DA COSTA	BRA	Rio de Janeiro	5 Aug 2000
	W, Eur	9:43.64	Cristina ILOC-CASANDRA	ROM	Bucuresti	7 Aug 2000
	Afr	10:23.55	Sonia AGOUN	TUN	Bucuresti	7 Aug 2000
	W, Eur	9:40.20	Cristina ILOC-CASANDRA	ROM	Reims	30 Aug 2000
	Com	10:08.11	Tara KRZYWICKI	Eng	Stretford	5 Sep 2000
100mH	CAC	12.52=	Delloreen ENNIS-LONDON	JAM	Kingston	22 Jul 2000
	NAm	12.33	Gail DEVERS	USA	Sacramento	23 Jul 2000
400mH	WJ	55.20A=	Jana PITTMAN	AUS	Pietersburg	18 Mar 2000
High Jump	Asi	1.97=	Svetlana ZALEVSKAYA	KAZ	Lausanne	5 Jul 2000
Pole Vault	CAC	3.85	Katiuska PEREZ	CUB	La Habana	19 Feb 2000
	SAm	4.42	Alejandra GARCIA	ARG	Sydney	20 Feb 2000
	Afr	4.40	Elmarie GERRYTS	RSA	Port Elizabeth	25 Feb 2000
	Asi	4.35	GAO Shuying	CHN	Chengdu	10 May 2000
	W, NAm	4.60= §	Stacy DRAGILA	USA	Modesto	13 May 2000
	W, NAm	4.62 §	Stacy DRAGILA	USA	Phoenix	26 May 2000
	W, NAm	4.70 u	Stacy DRAGILA (board runway)	USA	Santa Barbara	11 Jun 2000
	Afr	4.42	Elmarie GERRYTS	RSA	Wesel	12 Jun 2000
	CAC	3.90	Katiuska PEREZ	CUB	La Habana	24 Jun 2000
	W, NAm	4.63	Stacy DRAGILA	USA	Sacramento	23 Jul 2000
	WJ	4.40 §	Yelena ISINBAYEVA	RUS	Tula	24 Jul 2000
	CAC	3.95	Katiuska PEREZ	CUB	La Habana	29 Jul 2000
	Eur	4.56	Anzhela BALAKHONOVA	UKR	Linz	8 Aug 2000
Long Jump	CAC	6.99	Lissette CUZA	CUB	Jena	3 Jun 2000
Triple Jump	SAm	14.01	Luciana dos SANTOS	BRA	São Paulo	18 Jun 2000
	Oce	13.82	Nicole MLADENIS	AUS	Perth	9 Dec 2000
Shot	Afr	17.74	Vivian PETERS	NGR	Stendal	10 Jun 2000
	Afr	17.93	Vivian PETERS	NGR	Dortmund	8 Jul 2000
Hammer	CAC	66.80	Yipsi MORENO	CUB	La Habana	17 Feb 2000
	CAC	67.25	Yipsi MORENO	CUB	La Habana	24 Feb 2000
	CAC	67.26	Yipsi MORENO	CUB	La Habana	24 Feb 2000
	Oce	67.36	Lisa MISIPEKA	ASA	Gainesville	24 Mar 2000
	Oce	67.42	Lisa MISIPEKA	ASA	Durham	7 Apr 2000
	Asi	63.80	LI Xiaoxue	CHN	Shanghai	19 Apr 2000
	NAm	70.46	Dawn ELLERBE	USA	Philadelphia	29 Apr 2000
	Asi	63.87	LI Xiaoxue	CHN	Tianjin	4 May 2000
	Asi	65.44	ZHAO Wei	CHN	Chengdu	10 May 2000
	Asi	65.70	ZHAO Wei	CHN	Deyang	14 May 2000
	CAC	69.09	Yipsi MORENO	CUB	Halle	27 May 2000
	WJ	69.13	Kamila SKOLIMOWSKA	POL	Warszawa	10 Jun 2000
	CAC	69.36	Yipsi MORENO	CUB	Rhede	23 Jun 2000
	Com	67.44	Lorraine SHAW	Eng	Gateshead	15 Jul 2000
	WJ	70.62	Kamila SKOLIMOWSKA	POL	Rüdlingen	13 Aug 2000
	Oce	67.55	Lisa MISIPEKA	ASA	Rüdlingen	13 Aug 2000
	Oce, Com	67.95	Debbie SOSIMENKO	AUS	Sydney	29 Sep 2000
	WJ	71.16	Kamila SKOLIMOWSKA	POL	Sydney	29 Sep 2000
Javelin (New)	Afr	55.78A	Rhona DWINGER	RSA	Potchefstroom	14 Feb 2000
	SAm	60.47	Sueli dos SANTOS	BRA	Montevideo	9 Apr 2000
	Asi	63.04	WEI Jianhua	CHN	Shijiazhuang	28 Apr 2000
	SAm	61.98A	Sueli dos SANTOS	BRA	Bogotá	6 May 2000
	Afr	55.90	Aïda SALLEM	TUN	Tunis	3 Jun 2000
	Asi	63.69	LI Lei	CHN	Jinxhou	8 Jun 2000
	W, Eur	68.22	Trine HATTESTAD	NOR	Roma	30 Jun 2000
	NAm	58.61	Lynda BLUTREICH	USA	New Haven	1 Jul 2000
	W, Eur	69.48	Trine HATTESTAD	NOR	Oslo	28 Jul 2000

	Oce, Com	66.80	Louise CURREY	AUS	Gold Coast	5 Aug 2000
	CAC	67.83	Osleidys MENENDEZ	CUB	Berlin	1 Sep 2000
Heptathlon	Com	6831	Denise LEWIS	Eng	Talence	30 Jul 2000
10000m Walk	WJ	43:35.2 §	Lyudmila YEFIMKINA	RUS	Moscow	20 May 2000
	SAm	45:59.95	Geovana IRUSTA	BOL	Rio de Janeiro	20 May 2000
	WJ	44:07.74 §	Lyudmila YEFIMKINA	RUS	Santiago de Chile	20 Oct 2000
20000m Walk	W	1:35:23.7	Kristina SALTANOVIC	LTU	Kaunas	3 Aug 2000
	W	1:30:48.3 §	Rossella GIORDANO	ITA	Almada	4 Aug 2000
20km Walk	Oce, Com	1:29:36	Kerry SAXBY-JUNNA	AUS	Naumburg	30 Apr 2000
	SAm	1:34:37	Geovana IRUSTA	BOL	Naumburg	30 Apr 2000
	Oce, Com	1:28:56	Jane SAVILLE	AUS	Vallansbæk	6 May 2000
	NAm	1:31:51	Michelle ROHL	USA	Kenosha	13 May 2000
	W, Eur	1:25:18	Tatyana GUDKOVA	RUS	Moskva	19 May 2000
4x100m	Oce	42.99A	AUS (Massey, Broadrick, Lambert, Gainsford-Taylor)		Pietersburg	18 Mar 2000
4x200m	W	1:27:46 §	USA (Jenkins, Colander-Richardson, Perry, Jones)		Philadelphia	29 Apr 2000
4x400m	Oce	3:24.05	AUS (Lewis, Andrews, Pittman, Peris-Kneebone)		Sydney	29 Sep 2000
	Oce	3:23.81	AUS (Peris-Kneebone, Lewis, Gainsford-Taylor, Freeman)		Sydney	30 Sep 2000

INDOORS - MEN

50m	Eur	5.61= §	Jason GARDENER	GBR	Madrid	16 Feb 2000
	CAC	5.61=	Freddy MAYOLA	CUB	Madrid	16 Feb 2000
	WJ	5.67	Kareem KELLY	USA	Los Angeles	19 Feb 2000
60m	CAC	6.49=	Freddy MAYOLA	CUB	Madrid	16 Feb 2000
200m	Nam	20.26	Shawn CRAWFORD	USA	Fayetteville	11 Mar 2000
		20.26	John CAPEL	USA	Fayetteville	11 Mar 2000
800m	WJ	1:45.91	Yuriy BORZAKOVSKIY	RUS	Sindelfingen	22 Jan 2000
	Asi	1:47.56	Boris KAVESHNIKOV	KGZ	Karlsruhe	29 Jan 2000
	WJ	1:44.35	Yuriy BORZAKOVSKIY	RUS	Dortmund	30 Jan 2000
1000m	W, Eur	2:15.25	Wilson KIPKETER	DEN	Stuttgart	6 Feb 2000
	Com	2:15.50	Kennedy KIMWETICH	KEN	Stuttgart	6 Feb 2000
	CAC	2:19.96	Mario VERNON-WATSON	JAM	Allston	12 Feb 2000
	W, Eur	2:14.96	Wilson KIPKETER	DEN	Birmingham	20 Feb 2000
5000m	Oce	13:49.83	Michael AISH	NZL	Indianapolis	12 Feb 2000
	Oce	13:48.28	Michael AISH	NZL	Roxbury	11 Mar 2000
50mH	CAC	6.42	Anier GARCIA	CUB	Liévin	13 Feb 2000
	SAm	6.65	Marcio Simão DE SOUZA	BRA	Liévin	13 Feb 2000
	CAC	6.36	Anier GARCIA	CUB	Liévin	13 Feb 2000
60mH	Afr	7.59	Shaun BOWNES	RSA	Karlsruhe	29 Jan 2000
	CAC	7.47	Anier GARCIA	CUB	Dortmund	30 Jan 2000
	CAC	7.45	Yoel HERNANDEZ	CUB	Erfurt	2 Feb 2000
	CAC	7.37	Anier GARCIA	CUB	Pireás	9 Feb 2000
	SAm	7.79=	Marcio Simão DE SOUZA	BRA	Liévin	13 Feb 2000
	SAm	7.75	Marcio Simão DE SOUZA	BRA	Madrid	16 Feb 2000
High Jump	Afr	2.28	Anthony IDIATA	NGR	Pireás	9 Feb 2000
	Afr	2.32	Anthony IDIATA	NGR	Patra	15 Feb 2000
Pole Vault	Oce	5.60	Viktor CHISTYAKOV	AUS	Zweibrücken	21 Jan 2000
Heptathlon	Eur	6424	Tomás DVORAK	CZE	Gent	26 Feb 2000
4x800m	W, NAm	7:13.94	Global Athletics & Marketing	USA	Roxbury	6 Feb 2000
			(Joey Woody, Karl Paranya, Rich Kenah, David Krummenacker)			

INDOORS - WOMEN

1000m	NAm	2:35.29	Regina JACOBS	USA	Roxbury	6 Feb 2000
	Oce	2:36.96	Toni HODGKINSON	NZL	Roxbury	6 Feb 2000
1 mile	Afr	4:25.73	Kutre DULECHA	ETH	Stuttgart	6 Feb 2000
	CAC	4:37.31	Mardrea HYMAN	JAM	Los Angeles	19 Feb 2000
2000m	Afr	5:46.67	Nourah MERAH-BENIDA	ALG	Liévin	13 Feb 2000
3000m	Asi	8:46.32	YIN Lili	CHN	Beijing	22 Feb 2000
50mH	CAC, Com	6.69	Michelle FREEMAN	JAM	Liévin	13 Feb 2000
	CAC, Com	6.67	Michelle FREEMAN	JAM	Liévin	13 Feb 2000
60mH	SAm	8.13	Maurren MAGGI	BRA	Pireás	9 Feb 2000
	SAm	8.12	Maurren MAGGI	BRA	Gent	11 Feb 2000
High Jump	SAm	1.94	Solange WITTEVEEN	ARG	Brno	9 Feb 2000
Pole Vault	NAm	4.51A	Stacy DRAGILA	USA	Pocatello	28 Jan 2000
	WJ	4.45	Yelena ISINBAYEVA	RUS	Volgograd	4 Feb 2000
	Afr	4.30=	Elmarie GERRYTS	RSA	Gent	11 Feb 2000
	Afr	4.40	Elmarie GERRYTS	RSA	Chemnitz	18 Feb 2000
	W, NAm	4.57A §	Stacy DRAGILA	USA	Pocatello	19 Feb 2000
	W, NAm	4.61A §	Stacy DRAGILA	USA	Pocatello	19 Feb 2000
	Afr	4.41	Elmarie GERRYTS	RSA	Birmingham	20 Feb 2000
	W,Nam	4.62	Stacy DRAGILA	USA	Atlanta	3 Mar 2000
Long Jump	SAm	6.66	Maurren MAGGI	BRA	Pireás	9 Feb 2000
	SAm	6.67	Maurren MAGGI	BRA	Birmingham	20 Feb 2000

WORLD MEN'S ALL-TIME LISTS

100 METRES

Mark	Wind		Name	Nat	Born	Pos	Meet	Venue	Date
9.79 WR	0.1	Maurice	Greene	USA	23.7.74	1rA	GP II	Athína	16 Jun 99
9.80	0.2		Greene			1	WCh	Sevilla	22 Aug 99
9.84 WR	0.7	Donovan	Bailey	CAN	16.12.67	1	OG	Atlanta	27 Jul 96
9.84	0.2	Bruny	Surin	CAN	12.7.67	2	WCh	Sevilla	22 Aug 99
9.85 WR	1.2	Leroy	Burrell	USA	21.2.67	1rA	Athl	Lausanne	6 Jul 94
9.85	0.8		Greene			1	GGala	Roma	7 Jul 99
9.86 WR	1.2	Carl	Lewis	USA	1.7.61	1	WCh	Tokyo	25 Aug 91
9.86	-0.4	Frank	Fredericks	NAM	2.10.67	1rA	Athl	Lausanne	3 Jul 96
9.86	0.2		Greene			1	WCh	Athína	3 Aug 97
9.86	1.8	Ato	Boldon	TRI	30.12.73	1rA	MSR	Walnut	19 Apr 98
9.86	-0.4		Boldon			1		Athína	17 Jun 98
9.86	0.1		Boldon			2rA	GP II	Athína	16 Jun 99
9.86	0.4		Boldon			1rA	Athl	Lausanne	2 Jul 99
9.86	-0.2		Greene			1	ISTAF	Berlin	1 Sep 00
9.87	0.3	Linford	Christie	GBR	2.4.60	1	WCh	Stuttgart	15 Aug 93
9.87	1.9		Fredericks			1	WG	Helsinki	25 Jun 96
9.87	1.3		Boldon			1q1	WCh	Athína	2 Aug 97
9.87A	-0.2	Obadele	Thompson	BAR	30.3.76	1	WCp	Johannesburg	11 Sep 98
9.87	0.6		Greene			1	DNG	Stockholm	30 Jul 99
9.87	-0.3		Greene			1	OG	Sydney	23 Sep 00
9.88	1.2		Burrell			2	WCh	Tokyo	25 Aug 91
9.88	-0.1		Boldon			1	CG	Kuala Lumpur	17 Sep 98
9.89	0.7		Fredericks			2	OG	Atlanta	27 Jul 96
9.89	0.8		Boldon			1r2	ModR	Modesto	10 May 97
9.89	1.5		Surin			1	NC	Montreal	1 Aug 98
9.90 WR	1.9		Burrell			1	TAC	New York	14 Jun 91
9.90	0.7		Boldon			3	OG	Atlanta	27 Jul 96
9.90	0.2		M Greene			1	NC	Indianapolis	13 Jun 97
9.90	1.0		M Greene			1rA	Athl	Lausanne	2 Jul 97
9.90	0.0		Boldon			1rA		Stuttgart	13 Jul 97
9.90	1.3		M Greene			2q1	WCh	Athína	2 Aug 97
9.90	0.5		M Greene			1s2	WCh	Athína	3 Aug 97
9.90	0.2		Fredericks			1	VD	Bruxelles	22 Aug 97
9.90	0.3		Greene			1	DNG	Stockholm	5 Aug 98
		(34 performances by 9 athletes)							
9.91	1.2	Dennis	Mitchell ¶	USA	20.2.66	3	WCh	Tokyo	25 Aug 91
9.92	0.3	Andre	Cason	USA	20.1.69	2	WCh	Stuttgart	15 Aug 93
9.92	0.8	Jon	Drummond	USA	9.9.68	1h3	NC	Indianapolis	12 Jun 97
9.92	0.2	Tim	Montgomery	USA	28.1.75	2	NC	Indianapolis	13 Jun 97
9.92A	-0.2	Seun	Ogunkoya	NGR	28.12.77	2	WCp	Johannesburg	11 Sep 98
9.92	1.0	Tim	Harden	USA	27.1.74	1		Luzern	5 Jul 99
9.93A WR	1.4	Calvin	Smith	USA	8.1.61	1	USOF	USAF Academy	3 Jul 83
9.93	-0.6	Michael	Marsh	USA	4.8.67	1	MSR	Walnut	18 Apr 92
9.94	0.2	Davidson	Ezinwa	NGR	22.11.71	1	Gugl	Linz	4 Jul 94
9.95A WR	0.3	Jim	Hines	USA	10.9.46	1	OG	Ciudad de México	14 Oct 68
9.95A	1.9	Olapade	Adeniken	NGR	19.8.69	1A		El Paso	16 Apr 94
		(20)							
9.95	0.8	Vincent	Henderson	USA	20.10.72	1		Leverkusen	9 Aug 98
9.96	0.1	Mel	Lattany	USA	10.8.59	1r1		Athens, Ga.	5 May 84
9.96	1.2	Ray	Stewart	JAM	18.3.65	6	WCh	Tokyo	25 Aug 91
9.96	0.8	Kareem	Streete-Thompson	CAY/USA	30.3.73	2h3	NC	Indianapolis	12 Jun 97
9.97	0.2	Dwain	Chambers	GBR	5.4.78	3	WCh	Sevilla	22 Aug 99
9.97	1.0	Francis	Obikwelu	NGR	22.11.78	2	Athl	Lausanne	5 Jul 00
9.98A	0.6	Silvio	Leonard	CUB	20.9.55	1	WPT	Guadalajara	11 Aug 77
9.98	0.3	Daniel	Effiong ¶	NGR	17.6.72	2s1	WCh	Stuttgart	15 Aug 93
9.98	1.4	Percy	Spencer	JAM	24.2.75	1	NC	Kingston	20 Jun 97
9.98	1.6	Leonard	Myles-Mills	GHA	9.5.73	1	NCAA	Boise	5 Jun 99
		(30)							
9.98	0.4	Jason	Gardener	GBR	18.9.75	3rA	Athl	Lausanne	2 Jul 99
9.98	0.4	Coby	Miller	USA	19.10.76	1s1	NCAA	Durham	2 Jun 00
9.99	0.4	Bernard	Williams	USA	19.1.78	2s1	NCAA	Durham	2 Jun 00
10.00	2.0	Marian	Woronin	POL	13.8.56	1	Kuso	Warszawa	9 Jun 84
10.00	1.0	Chidi	Imo ¶	NGR	27.8.63	1	ISTAF	Berlin	15 Aug 86
10.00#A	1.6	Robson	da Silva	BRA	4.9.64	1	IbAm	Ciudad de México	22 Jul 88

May not have been with auto-timing. Next best: 10.02 1.8 1 IbAm La Habana 27 Sep 86

MEN All-time

Mark	Wind	Name		Nat	Born	Pos	Meet	Venue	Date
10.00	0.9	Brian	Lewis	USA	5.12.74	1h2	NC	Indianapolis	12 Jun 97
10.00	1.9	Koji	Ito	JPN	29.1.70	1s2	AsiG	Bangkok	13 Dec 98
10.00	1.1	Eric	Nkansah	GHA	12.12.74	3		Nürnberg	13 Jun 99
10.01A	0.9	Pietro	Mennea	ITA	28.6.52	1		Ciudad de México	4 Sep 79
		(40)							
10.01A	1.9	Bode	Osagiobare	NGR	1.12.70	2A		El Paso	16 Apr 94
10.01	0.6	Jeff	Laynes	USA	3.10.70	1		Tempe	6 Apr 96
10.02A	WR2.0	Charles	Greene	USA	21.3.45	1q4	OG	Ciudad de México	13 Oct 68
10.02	1.0	James	Sanford	USA	27.12.57	1	Pepsi	Westwood	11 May 80
10.02	0.7	Daniel	Sangouma	FRA	7.2.65	2	BNP	Villeneuve d'Ascq	29 Jun 90

Some observers felt that this was run with the benefit of a flying start, but it was ratified as a French record

Mark	Wind	Name		Nat	Born	Pos	Meet	Venue	Date
10.02	-0.1	Deji	Aliu	NGR	22.11.75	1		Bauchi	18 Mar 95
10.02@	0.9	Vladislav	Dologodin	UKR	23.2.72	1		Kiyev	17 May 96
10.02	0.3	Jeff	Williams	USA	31.12.65	1h2	NC	Atlanta	14 Jun 96
10.02	1.7	Michael	Green	JAM	7.11.70	1		Knoxville	11 Apr 97
10.03A	1.9	Stanley	Floyd	USA	23.6.61	1r1	NCAA	Provo	5 Jun 82
		(50) with five more men at 10.03		100th man 10.08, 200th man 10.15					

Doubtful wind readings

Mark	Wind	Name		Nat	Born	Pos	Meet	Venue	Date
9.91	-2.3	Davidson	Ezinwa	NGR	22.11.71	1		Azusa	11 Apr 92
10.02	1.2	Ronald	Desruelles ¶	BEL	14.2.55	1		Naimette	11 May 85

Low altitude marks for athletes with lifetime bests at high altitude

9.94 0.1 Ogunkoya 1 AfCh Dakar 19 Aug 98 — 9.97 1.6 Smith 1 WK Zürich 24 Aug 83

9.96 0.6 O Thompson 2 DNG Stockholm 30 Jul 99

Wind-assisted marks to 9.96

Mark	Wind	Name		Nat	Born	Pos	Meet	Venue	Date
9.69A	5+	Obadele	Thompson	BAR	30.3.76	1		El Paso	13 Apr 96
9.78	5.2	Carl	Lewis	USA	1.7.61	1	OT	Indianapolis	16 Jul 88
9.79	5.3	Andre	Cason	USA	20.1.69	1h4	NC	Eugene	16 Jun 93
9.79	4.5		Cason			1s1	NC	Eugene	16 Jun 93
9.79	2.9	Maurice	Greene	USA	23.7.74	1	Pre	Eugene	31 May 98
9.80	4.3		Lewis			1q2	WCh	Tokyo	24 Aug 91
9.83	7.1	Leonard	Scott	USA	19.1.80	1r1	Sea Ray	Knoxville	9 Apr 99
9.84	3.3		Greene			1h2	NC	New Orleans	19 Jun 98
9.84	3.5		Greene			1	Pre	Eugene	30 May 99
9.84	3.5		Greene			1	Pre	Eugene	30 May 99
9.85	5.3		Burrell			2h4	NC	Eugene	16 Jun 93
9.85	4.8		Cason			1	NC	Eugene	17 Jun 93
9.85	4.8	Dennis	Mitchell ¶	USA	20.2.66	2	NC	Eugene	17 Jun 93
9.86	5.2		Mitchell			2	OT	Indianapolis	16 Jul 88
9.86	2.5		Burrell			1rA	TexR	Austin	9 Apr 94
9.87	11.2	William	Snoddy	USA	6.12.57	1		Dallas	1 Apr 78
9.87	4.9	Calvin	Smith	USA	8.1.61	1s2	OT	Indianapolis	16 Jul 88
9.87	5.2		C.Smith			3	OT	Indianapolis	16 Jul 88
9.87	2.4	Michael	Marsh	USA	4.8.67	1rA	MSR	Walnut	20 Apr 97
		19 wind assisted marks to 9.87							
9.88	2.3	James	Sanford	USA	27.12.57	1		Westwood	3 May 80
9.88	5.2	Albert	Robinson	USA	28.11.64	4	OT	Indianapolis	16 Jul 88
9.88	4.9	Tim	Harden	USA	27.1.74	1	NC	New Orleans	20 Jun 98
9.88	4.5	Coby	Miller	USA	19.10.76	1		Auburn	1 Apr 00
9.89	4.2	Ray	Stewart	JAM	18.3.65	1s1	PAm	Indianapolis	9 Aug 87
9.90	5.2	Joe	DeLoach	USA	5.6.67	5	OT	Indianapolis	16 Jul 88
9.90	7.1	Kenny	Brokenburr	USA	29.10.68	2r1	Sea Ray	Knoxville	9 Apr 99
9.91	5.3	Bob	Hayes	USA	20.12.42	1s1	OG	Tokyo	15 Oct 64
9.91	4.2	Mark	Witherspoon	USA	3.9.63	2s1	PAm	Indianapolis	9 Aug 87
9.92A	4.4	Chidi	Imo ¶	NGR	27.8.63	1s1	AfG	Nairobi	8 Aug 87
9.92A	2.8	Olapade	Adeniken	NGR	19.8.69	1rA		Sestriere	29 Jul 95
9.93	7.5	Pablo	Montes	CUB	23.11.47	1s	CAC	Panama City	1 Mar 70
9.94	2.7	Vitaliy	Savin	KZK	23.1.66	1	CIS Ch	Moskva	22 Jun 92
9.94	2.5	Daniel	Effiong ¶	NGR	17.6.72	2	TexR	Austin	9 Apr 94
9.94	7.0	Ousmane	Diarra	MLI	30.9.66	1		La Laguna	13 Jul 96
9.94	5.2	Osmond	Ezinwa	NGR	22.11.71	1		Pula	4 Sep 96
9.94	3.9	Vincent	Henderson	USA	20.10.72	1s1	WUG	Catania	29 Aug 97
9.94	2.8	Bryan	Howard	USA	7.10.76	2r7	MSR	Walnut	16 Apr 00
9.95	8.9	Willie	Gault	USA	5.9.60	1		Knoxville	2 Apr 83
9.95	2.4	Mel	Lattany	USA	10.8.59	1		Athens, Ga	7 May 83
9.95	7.1	Anthony	Jones	USA	12.12.71	3r1	Sea Ray	Knoxville	9 Apr 99
9.96	8.5	Anthony	Barnes	USA	23.12.65	1		Fresno	1 Apr 95
9.96	3.2	Percy	Spencer	JAM	24.2.75	1		Arlington	2 May 98
9.96	3.4	Brian	Lewis	USA	5.12.74	1h1	Conseil	Fort-de-France	29 Apr 00

Mark	Wind	Name		Nat	Born	Pos	Meet	Venue	Date
Disqualified for drug abuse									
9.79	1.1	Ben	Johnson ¶	CAN	30.12.61	-	OG	Seoul	24 Sep 88
9.83	1.0		Johnson			(1)	WCh	Roma	30 Aug 87
10.02	1.9	Horace	Dove-Edwin ¶	SLE	10.2.67	(2)	CG	Victoria	23 Aug 94
Hand timing									
9.7	1.9	Donovan	Powell ¶	JAM	31.10.71	1rA		Houston	19 May 95
9.7	1.9	Carl	Lewis	USA	1.7.61	2rA		Houston	19 May 95
9.7	1.9	Olapade	Adeniken	NGR	19.8.69	3rA		Houston	19 May 95
9.7w	3.8	Osvaldo	Lara	CUB	13.7.55	1		Santiago de Cuba	24 Feb 82
9.7w	3.5	Ben	Johnson ¶	CAN	30.12.61	1		Perth	24 Jan 87
9.7w	6.6	Rod	Mapstone	AUS	19.11.69	1r1		Perth	21 Dec 96
9.7w	8.1	Sayon	Cooper	LBR	26.4.74	1		Abilene	28 Mar 98

200 METRES

Mark	Wind	Name		Nat	Born	Pos	Meet	Venue	Date
19.32	WR 0.4	Michael	Johnson	USA	13.9.67	1	OG	Atlanta	1 Aug 96
19.66	WR 1.7		Johnson			1	NC	Atlanta	23 Jun 96
19.68	0.4	Frank	Fredericks	NAM	2.10.67	2	OG	Atlanta	1 Aug 96
19.71A	1.8		Johnson			1rA		Pietersburg	18 Mar 00
19.72A	WR 1.8	Pietro	Mennea	ITA	28.6.52	1	WUG	Ciudad de México	12 Sep 79
19.73	-0.2	Michael	Marsh	USA	4.8.67	1s1	OG	Barcelona	5 Aug 92
19.75	1.5	Carl	Lewis	USA	1.7.61	1	TAC	Indianapolis	19 Jun 83
19.75	1.7	Joe	DeLoach	USA	5.6.67	1	OG	Seoul	28 Sep 88
19.77	0.6		Johnson			1	DNG	Stockholm	8 Jul 96
19.77	0.7	Ato	Boldon	TRI	30.12.73	1rA		Stuttgart	13 Jul 97
19.79	1.7		Lewis			2	OG	Seoul	28 Sep 88
19.79	1.0		Johnson			1	OT	New Orleans	28 Jun 92
19.79	0.5		Johnson			1	WCh	Göteborg	11 Aug 95
19.80	-0.9		Lewis			1	OG	Los Angeles	8 Aug 84
19.80	0.4		Boldon			3	OG	Atlanta	1 Aug 96
19.81	0.3		Fredericks			1	GPF	Fukuoka	13 Sep 97
19.82A	2.0		Lewis			1		Sestriere	11 Aug 88
19.82	1.1		Fredericks			1	Bisl	Oslo	5 Jul 96
19.82	1.6		Boldon			1rA	DNG	Stockholm	7 Jul 97
19.83A	WR 0.9	Tommie	Smith	USA	12.6.44	1	OG	Ciudad de México	16 Oct 68
19.83	1.7		Johnson			1	GP I	Atlanta	18 May 96
19.84	0.2		Lewis			1q3	OT	Los Angeles	19 Jun 84
19.84	1.7	Francis	Obikwelu	NGR	22.11.78	1s2	WCh	Sevilla	25 Aug 99
19.85	0.4		Johnson			1	IAC	Edinburgh	6 Jul 90
19.85	0.3		Fredericks			1	WCh	Stuttgart	20 Aug 93
19.85	-0.9		Boldon			1	Athl	Lausanne	3 Jul 96
19.85	1.1		Johnson			2	Bisl	Oslo	5 Jul 96
19.85	-0.3	John	Capel (10)	USA	27.10.78	1	NC	Sacramento	23 Jul 00
19.86A	1.0	Don	Quarrie	JAM	25.2.51	1	PAm	Cali	3 Aug 71
19.86	-0.2		Lewis			1	OT	Los Angeles	21 Jun 84
19.86	1.0		Marsh			2	OT	New Orleans	28 Jun 92
19.86	1.6	Maurice	Greene	USA	23.7.74	2rA	DNG	Stockholm	7 Jul 97
19.86	0.4		Boldon			1rA	GP II	Athína	16 Jun 99
		(33/12)							
19.87	0.8	Lorenzo	Daniel	USA	23.3.66	1	NCAA	Eugene	3 Jun 88
19.87A	1.8	John	Regis	GBR	13.10.66	1		Sestriere	31 Jul 94
19.87	1.2	Jeff	Williams	USA	31.12.65	1		Fresno	13 Apr 96
19.88	-0.3	Floyd	Heard	USA	24.3.66	2	NC	Sacramento	23 Jul 00
19.89	-0.8	Claudinei	da Silva	BRA	19.11.70	1	GPF	München	11 Sep 99
19.92A	WR 1.9	John	Carlos	USA	5.6.45	1	FOT	Echo Summit	12 Sep 68
19.96	-0.9	Kirk	Baptiste	USA	20.6.63	2	OG	Los Angeles	8 Aug 84
19.96	0.4	Robson	da Silva	BRA	4.9.64	1	VD	Bruxelles	25 Aug 89
		(20)							
19.96	-0.3	Coby	Miller	USA	19.10.76	3	NC	Sacramento	23 Jul 00
19.97	-0.9	Obadele	Thompson	BAR	30.3.76	1	Super	Yokohama	9 Sep 00
19.98	1.7	Marcin	Urbas	POL	17.9.76	2s2	WCh	Sevilla	25 Aug 99
19.99	0.6	Calvin	Smith	USA	8.1.61	1	WK	Zürich	24 Aug 83
20.00	0.0	Valeriy	Borzov	UKR	20.10.49	1	OG	München	4 Sep 72
20.01	-1.0	Michael	Bates	USA	19.12.69	3rA	WK	Zürich	19 Aug 92
20.02	1.7	Christopher	Williams	JAM	15.3.72	1r5	MSR	Walnut	16 Apr 00
20.03	1.6	Clancy	Edwards	USA	9.8.55	1		Westwood	29 Apr 78
20.03	1.5	Larry	Myricks	USA	10.3.56	2	TAC	Indianapolis	19 Jun 83
20.03	1.2	Jon	Drummond	USA	9.9.68	1	VD	Bruxelles	22 Aug 97
		(30)							
20.03	-0.3	Bernard	Williams	USA	19.1.78	4	NC	Sacramento	23 Jul 00

Mark	Wind	Name		Nat	Born	Pos	Meet	Venue	Date
20.04	1.7	Kenny	Brokenburr	USA	29.10.68	2r5	MSR	Walnut	16 Apr 00
20.05	1.0	Roy	Martin	USA	25.12.66	3	OT	Indianapolis	20 Jul 88
20.05	1.0	Albert	Robinson	USA	28.11.64	4	OT	Indianapolis	20 Jul 88
20.06A	0.9	Peter	Norman	AUS	15.6.42	2	OG	Ciudad de México	16 Oct 68
20.06	1.7	Silvio	Leonard	CUB	20.9.55	1	Kuso	Warszawa	19 Jun 78
20.06	0.3	Ramon	Clay	USA	29.6.75	1	GP II	Doha	7 May 98
20.07		James	Mallard	USA	29.11.57	1		Tuscaloosa	20 Apr 79
20.08	0.9	LaMonte	King	USA	18.12.59	1	TAC	Walnut	15 Jun 80
20.08A	1.6	Dwayne	Evans	USA	13.10.58	1		Albuquerque	13 Jun 87
		(40)							
20.08	0.3	Danny	Everett	USA	1.11.66	2	TAC	Norwalk	16 Jun 90
20.08	1.7	Aaron	Armstrong	USA	14.10.77	1		Norman	10 Apr 99
20.09	1.7	Linford	Christie	GBR	2.4.60	4	OG	Seoul	28 Sep 88
20.09A	1.9	Dennis	Mitchell ¶	USA	20.2.66	1	NCAA	Provo	2 Jun 89
20.09	2.0	Tyree	Washington	USA	28.8.76	1	GP	Edwardsville	22 May 99
20.09	1.0	Shawn	Crawford	USA	14.1.78	1	NCAA	Durham	3 Jun 00
20.09	-0.6	Konstadínos	Kedéris	GRE	11.6.73	1	OG	Sydney	28 Sep 00
20.10	1.7	Millard	Hampton	USA	8.7.56	1	OT	Eugene	22 Jun 76
20.10	-0.2	Daniel	Effiong ¶	NGR	17.6.72	1	Jen	San José	28 May 94
20.10	1.7	Kevin	Little	USA	3.4.68	3s2	WCh	Sevilla	25 Aug 99
		(50)	100th man 20.22, 200th man 20.38						

Wind-assisted marks to 20.06

Mark	Wind	Name		Nat	Born	Pos	Meet	Venue	Date
19.61	>4.0	Leroy	Burrell	USA	21.2.67	1	SWC	College Station	19 May 90
19.70	2.7		Johnson			1s1	NC	Atlanta	22 Jun 96
19.79A	4.0		Marsh			1		Sestriere	21 Jul 92
19.83	3.5		Johnson			1	NC	Sacramento	18 Jun 95
19.83	9.2	Bobby	Cruse	USA	20.3.78	1r2	Sea Ray	Knoxville	9 Apr 99
19.86	4.6	Roy	Martin	USA	25.12.66	1	SWC	Houston	18 May 86
19.91		James	Jett	USA	28.12.70	1		Morgantown	18 Apr 92
19.93	2.4	Sebastián	Keitel	CHI	14.2.73	1		São Leopoldo	26 Apr 98
19.94	4.0	James	Sanford	USA	27.12.57	1s1	NCAA	Austin	7 Jun 80
19.94	3.7	Chris	Nelloms	USA	14.8.71	1	Big 10	Minneapolis	23 May 92
19.94	2.3	Kevin	Little	USA	3.4.68	1s3	NC	Sacramento	17 Jun 95
19.95	3.4	Mike	Roberson	USA	25.3.56	1h3	NCAA	Austin	5 Jun 80
19.96	2.2	Rohsaan	Griffin	USA	21.2.74	1s1	NC	Eugene	26 Jun 99
19.99	2.7	Ramon	Clay	USA	29.6.75	2s1	NC	Atlanta	22 Jun 96
20.00A	3.4	Olapade	Adeniken	NGR	19.8.69	1		USAF Academy	23 May 92
20.01	2.5	Derald	Harris	USA	5.4.58	1		San José	9 Apr 77
20.03	6.5	Alvis	Whitted	USA	4.9.74	1		College Park	20 Apr 96
20.05A	3.8	Cyprean	Enweani	CAN	19.3.64	1		Calgary	3 Jul 88
20.06		Renward	Wells	BAH	23.2.70	1		Stillwater	2 Apr 94

Low altitude marks for athletes with lifetime bests at high altitude

19.94	0.3	Regis	2	WCh	Stuttgart	20 Aug 93	20.06	0.4	Quarrie	1	WK	Zürich	16 Aug 74
19.96	0.0	Mennea	1		Barletta	17 Aug 80							

Hand timing

Mark	Wind	Name		Nat	Born	Pos	Meet	Venue	Date
19.7A		James	Sanford	USA	27.12.57	1		El Paso	19 Apr 80
19.7A	0.2	Robson C.	da Silva	BRA	4.9.64	1	AmCp	Bogotá	13 Aug 89
19.8"	WR1.3	Don	Quarrie	JAM	25.2.51	1	Pre	Eugene	7 Jun 75
19.8*	WR1.3	Steve	Williams	USA	13.11.53	2	Pre	Eugene	7 Jun 75
19.8	1.6	James	Mallard	USA	29.11.57	1	SEC	Tuscaloosa	13 May 79
19.8*w		Carl	Lawson	JAM	27.10.47	1		Moscow	19 May 73
19.8*w	3.4	James	Gilkes	GUY	21.9.52	1	NCAA	Austin	8 Jun 74
19.8w	4.4	Desmond	Ross	USA	30.12.61	1	Big8	Manhattan	11 May 85

*" during 220 yards race, * 220 yards less 0.1 seconds*

300 METRES

In 300m races only, not including intermediate times in 400m races

Mark	Name		Nat	Born	Pos	Meet	Venue	Date
30.85A	Michael	Johnson	USA	13.9.67	1		Pretoria	24 Mar 00
31.48	Danny	Everett	USA	1.11.66	1		Jerez de la Frontera	3 Sep 90
31.48	Roberto	Hernández	CUB	6.3.67	2		Jerez de la Frontera	3 Sep 90
31.56		Johnson			1		Salamanca	22 Jul 94
31.56	Doug	Walker	GBR	28.7.73	1		Gateshead	10 Jul 00
31.61	Anthuan	Maybank	USA	30.12.69	1		Durham	13 Jul 96
31.67	John	Regis	GBR	13.10.66	1	Vaux	Gateshead	17 Jul 92
31.70	Kirk	Baptiste	USA	20.6.63	1	Nike	London (CP)	18 Aug 84
31.73	Thomas	Jefferson	USA	8.6.62	1	DCG	London (CP)	22 Aug 87
31.74	Gabriel	Tiacoh	CIV	10.9.63	1		La Coruña	6 Aug 86
31.82	Steve	Lewis (10)	USA	16.5.69	2	Vaux	Gateshead	17 Jul 92
31.87	Mark	Richardson	GBR	26.7.72	2		Gateshead	19 Jul 98
31.88	Darren	Clark	AUS	6.9.65	1	UlstG	Belfast	30 Jun 86

Mark Wind	Name		Nat	Born	Pos	Meet	Venue	Date
31.96	Marc	Foucan	FRA	14.10.71	1r1		Strasbourg	29 Jun 99
31.97	Innocent	Egbunike	NGR	30.11.61	1	IAC	London (CP)	8 Aug 86
32.00	Alvin	Harrison	USA	20.1.74	2		Durham	13 Jul 96
32.04	Andrew	Valmon	USA	1.1.65	3		Jerez de la Frontera	3 Sep 90
32.05	Butch	Reynolds ¶	USA	8.6.64	1	Giro	Belfast	20 Jul 87
32.05	Robson	da Silva	BRA	4.9.64	1		Jerez de la Frontera	17 Sep 91
32.06	Jamie	Baulch	GBR	3.5.73	1	WelshG	Cardiff	31 May 97
32.07	Quincy	Watts	USA	19.6.70	2	Vaux	Gateshead	30 Jul 93
	(20)							

400 METRES

Mark Wind	Name		Nat	Born	Pos	Meet	Venue	Date
43.18 WR	Michael	Johnson	USA	13.9.67	1	WCh	Sevilla	26 Aug 99
43.29 WR	Butch	Reynolds ¶	USA	8.6.64	1	WK	Zürich	17 Aug 88
43.39		Johnson			1	WCh	Göteborg	9 Aug 95
43.44		Johnson			1	NC	Atlanta	19 Jun 96
43.49		Johnson			1	OG	Atlanta	29 Jul 96
43.50	Quincy	Watts	USA	19.6.70	1	OG	Barcelona	5 Aug 92
43.65		Johnson			1	WCh	Stuttgart	17 Aug 93
43.66		Johnson			1	NC	Sacramento	16 Jun 95
43.66		Johnson			1rA	Athl	Lausanne	3 Jul 96
43.68		Johnson			1	WK	Zürich	12 Aug 98
43.68		Johnson			1	NC	Sacramento	16 Jul 00
43.71		Watts			1s2	OG	Barcelona	3 Aug 92
43.74		Johnson			1	NC	Eugene	19 Jun 93
43.75		Johnson			1		Waco	19 Apr 97
43.76		Johnson			1	GWG	Uniondale, NY	22 Jul 98
43.81	Danny	Everett	USA	1.11.66	1	OT	New Orleans	26 Jun 92
43.83		Watts			1	WK	Zürich	19 Aug 92
43.84		Johnson			1	OG	Sydney	25 Sep 00
43.86A WR	Lee	Evans	USA	25.2.47	1	OG	Ciudad de México	18 Oct 68
43.86		Johnson			1	Bisl	Oslo	21 Jul 95
43.87	Steve	Lewis	USA	16.5.69	1	OG	Seoul	28 Sep 88
43.88		Johnson			1	WK	Zürich	16 Aug 95
43.90		Johnson			1		Madrid	6 Sep 94
43.91		Reynolds			2	NC	Atlanta	19 Jun 96
43.92		Johnson			1	Athl	Lausanne	2 Jul 99
43.92		Johnson			1	Pre	Eugene	24 Jun 00
43.93		Reynolds			1	OT	Indianapolis	20 Jul 88
43.93		Reynolds			2	OG	Seoul	28 Sep 88
43.94		Johnson			1	ISTAF	Berlin	27 Aug 93
43.95		Johnson			1s1	WCh	Sevilla	24 Aug 99
	(30/6)							
43.97A	Larry	James	USA	6.11.47	2	OG	Ciudad de México	18 Oct 68
44.09	Alvin	Harrison	USA	20.1.74	3	NC	Atlanta	19 Jun 96
44.09	Jerome	Young	USA	14.8.76	1	NC	New Orleans	21 Jun 98
44.13	Derek	Mills	USA	9.7.72	1	Pre	Eugene	4 Jun 95
	(10)							
44.14	Roberto	Hernández	CUB	6.3.67	2		Sevilla	30 May 90
44.15	Anthuan	Maybank	USA	30.12.69	1rB	Athl	Lausanne	3 Jul 96
44.17	Innocent	Egbunike	NGR	30.11.61	1rA	WK	Zürich	19 Aug 87
44.18	Samson	Kitur	KEN	25.2.66	2s2	OG	Barcelona	3 Aug 92
44.20A	Charles	Gitonga	KEN	5.10.71	1	NC	Nairobi	29 Jun 96
44.21	Ian	Morris	TRI	30.11.61	3s2	OG	Barcelona	3 Aug 92
44.21	Antonio	Pettigrew	USA	3.11.67	1		Nassau	26 May 99
44.26	Alberto	Juantorena	CUB	3.12.50	1	OG	Montreal	29 Jul 76
44.27	Alonzo	Babers	USA	31.10.61	1	OG	Los Angeles	8 Aug 84
44.28	Andrew	Valmon	USA	1.1.65	4	NC	Eugene	19 Jun 93
	(20)							
44.29	Tyree	Washington	USA	28.8.76	2	Herc	Monaco	8 Aug 98
44.29	Derrick	Brew	USA	28.12.77	1	SEC	Athens, Ga	16 May 99
44.29	Sanderlei	Parrela	BRA	7.10.74	2	WCh	Sevilla	26 Aug 99
44.30	Gabriel	Tiacoh	CIV	10.9.63	1	NCAA	Indianapolis	7 Jun 86
44.30	Lamont	Smith	USA	11.12.72	4	NC	Atlanta	19 Jun 96
44.31	Alejandro	Cárdenas	MEX	4.9.74	3	WCh	Sevilla	26 Aug 99
44.33	Thomas	Schönlebe	GDR	6.8.65	1	WCh	Roma	3 Sep 87
44.34	Darnell	Hall	USA	26.9.71	1	Athl	Lausanne	5 Jul 95
44.36	Iwan	Thomas	GBR	5.1.74	1	NC	Birmingham	13 Jul 97
44.37	Roger	Black	GBR	31.3.66	2rA	Athl	Lausanne	3 Jul 96
	(30)							

Mark Wind	Name		Nat	Born	Pos	Meet	Venue	Date
44.37	Davis	Kamoga	UGA	17.7.68	2	WCh	Athína	5 Aug 97
44.37	Mark	Richardson	GBR	26.7.72	1	Bisl	Oslo	9 Jul 98
44.38	Darren	Clark	AUS	6.9.65	3s1	OG	Seoul	26 Sep 88
44.40	Fred	Newhouse	USA	8.11.48	2	OG	Montreal	29 Jul 76
44.41A	Ron	Freeman	USA	12.6.47	3	OG	Ciudad de México	18 Oct 68
44.45A	Ronnie	Ray	USA	2.1.54	1	PAm	Ciudad de México	18 Oct 75
44.45	Darrell	Robinson	USA	23.12.63	2	Pepsi	Westwood	17 May 86
44.47	Michael	Franks	USA	23.9.63	1	WCp	Canberra	5 Oct 85
44.47	David	Grindley	GBR	29.10.72	4s2	OG	Barcelona	3 Aug 92
44.48	Roddie	Haley	USA	6.12.65	1	SWC	Houston	18 May 86
	(40)							
44.49	Roxbert	Martin	JAM	5.11.69	1	NC	Kingston	21 Jun 97
44.50	Erwin	Skamrahl	FRG	8.3.58	1r1		München	26 Jul 83
44.50	Derek	Redmond	GBR	3.9.65	1s2	WCh	Roma	1 Sep 87
44.50	Bert	Cameron	JAM	16.11.59	4s1	OG	Seoul	26 Sep 88
44.51	Jerome	Davis	USA	20.8.77	5s1	WCh	Sevilla	24 Aug 99
44.56	Mohamed	Al Malky	OMN	1.12.62	1	BGP	Budapest	12 Aug 88
44.56	Greg	Haughton	JAM	10.11.73	3	WCh	Göteborg	9 Aug 95
44.57	Jamie	Baulch	GBR	3.5.73	3rB	Athl	Lausanne	3 Jul 96
44.58	Patrick	Delice	TRI	12.11.67	1	NCAA II	Abilene	29 May 93
44.59A	Raymond	Pierre (50)	USA	19.9.67	1	NCAA	Provo	3 Jun 89
	44.60				1	PAm	Indianapolis	13 Aug 87
44.59	Mark	Everett	USA	2.9.68	1	WG	Helsinki	27 Jun 91
44.59A	Arnaud	Malherbe	RSA	20.11.72	2	GP II	Roodepoort	19 Mar 99
44.59	Hendrik	Mokganyetsi	RSA	7.9.75	2	Super	Yokohama	9 Sep 00
	(53)	100th man 44.79, 200th man 45.15						
Hand timing								
44.1	Wayne	Collett	USA	20.10.49	1	OT	Eugene	9 Jul 72
44.2*	John	Smith	USA	5.8.50	1	AAU	Eugene	26 Jun 71
44.2	Fred	Newhouse	USA	8.11.48	1s1	OT	Eugene	7 Jul 72
44.4A WR	Vince	Matthews	USA	16.12.47	1		Echo Summit	31 Aug 68

600 METRES

1:12.81	Johnny	Gray	USA	19.6.60	1		Santa Monica	24 May 86
1:13.2 + ?	John	Kipkurgat	KEN	16.3.44	1		Pointe-à-Pierre	23 Mar 74
1:13.80	Earl	Jones	USA	17.7.64	2		Santa Monica	24 May 86
1:14.15	David	Mack	USA	30.5.61	3		Santa Monica	24 May 86
1:14.3 A	Lee	Evans	USA	25.2.47	1		Echo Summit	31 Aug 68
1:14.41	Andrea	Longo	ITA	26.6.75	1		Rovereto	30 Aug 00
1:14.48	Trinity	Gray	USA	19.4.78	2		Rovereto	30 Aug 00
1:14.6 A	Larry	James	USA	6.11.47	2		Echo Summit	31 Aug 68

800 METRES

1:41.11 WR	Wilson	Kipketer	DEN	12.12.70	1	ASV	Köln	24 Aug 97
1:41.24 WR		Kipketer			1rA	WK	Zürich	13 Aug 97
1:41.73! WR	Sebastian	Coe	GBR	29.9.56	1		Firenze	10 Jun 81
1:41.73		Kipketer			1rA	DNG	Stockholm	7 Jul 97
1:41.77	Joaquim	Cruz	BRA	12.3.63	1	ASV	Köln	26 Aug 84
1:41.83		Kipketer			1	GP II	Rieti	1 Sep 96
1:42.17		Kipketer			1	TOTO	Tokyo	16 Sep 96
1:42.20		Kipketer			1	VD	Bruxelles	22 Aug 97
1:42.27		Kipketer			1	VD	Bruxelles	3 Sep 99
1:42.28	Sammy	Koskei	KEN	14.5.61	2	ASV	Köln	26 Aug 84
1:42.33 WR		Coe			1	Bisl	Oslo	5 Jul 79
1:42.34		Cruz			1r1	WK	Zürich	22 Aug 84
1:42.41		Cruz			1	VD	Bruxelles	24 Aug 84
1:42.49		Cruz			1		Koblenz	28 Aug 85
1:42.51		Kipketer			1	Nik	Nice	10 Jul 96
1:42.54		Cruz			1	ASV	Köln	25 Aug 85
1:42.57		Kipketer			1	Herc	Monaco	4 Aug 99
1:42.58	Vebjørn	Rodal	NOR	16.9.72	1	OG	Atlanta	31 Jul 96
1:42.59		Kipketer			1	Herc	Monaco	10 Aug 96
1:42.60	Johnny	Gray	USA	19.6.60	2r1		Koblenz	28 Aug 85
1:42.61		Kipketer			1rA	WK	Zürich	14 Aug 96
1:42.61		Kipketer			1rA	Athl	Lausanne	2 Jul 97
1:42.62	Patrick	Ndururi	KEN	12.1.69	2rA	WK	Zürich	13 Aug 97
1:42.65		Gray			1	WK	Zürich	17 Aug 88
1:42.69	Hezekiél	Sepeng	RSA	30.6.74	2	VD	Bruxelles	3 Sep 99
1:42.69	Japheth	Kimutai	KEN	20.12.78	3	VD	Bruxelles	3 Sep 99

Mark Wind	Name		Nat	Born	Pos	Meet	Venue	Date
1:42.74		Sepeng			2	OG	Atlanta	31 Jul 96
1:42.76		Kipketer			1	Bisl	Oslo	5 Jul 96
1:42.76		Kimutai			1		Stuttgart	19 Jul 98
1:42.77		Kipketer			1	VD	Bruxelles	23 Aug 96
1:42.77		Kipketer			1	Herc	Monaco	16 Aug 97
1:42.79	Fred	Onyancha !	KEN	25.12.69	3	OG	Atlanta	31 Jul 96
1:42.79		Kipketer			1	GGala	Roma	7 Jul 99
	(33/10)							
1:42.85	Norberto	Téllez	CUB	22.1.72	4	OG	Atlanta	31 Jul 96
1:42.88	Steve	Cram	GBR	14.10.60	1rA	WK	Zürich	21 Aug 85
1:42.92	André	Bucher	SUI	19.10.76	4	VD	Bruxelles	3 Sep 99
1:42.97	Peter	Elliott	GBR	9.10.62	1		Sevilla	30 May 90
1:42.98	Patrick	Konchellah	KEN	20.4.68	2	ASV	Köln	24 Aug 97
1:43.03	Kennedy	Kimwetich	KEN	1.1.73	2		Stuttgart	19 Jul 98
1:43.06	Billy	Konchellah	KEN	20.10.62	1	WCh	Roma	1 Sep 87
1:43.08	José Luiz	Barbosa	BRA	27.5.61	1		Rieti	6 Sep 91
1:43.09	Djabir	Saïd Guerni	ALG	29.3.77	5	VD	Bruxelles	3 Sep 99
1:43.16	Paul	Ereng	KEN	22.8.67	1	WK	Zürich	16 Aug 89
	(20)							
1:43.17	Benson	Koech	KEN	10.11.74	1		Rieti	28 Aug 94
1:43.20	Mark	Everett	USA	2.9.68	1rA	Gugl	Linz	9 Jul 97
1:43.26	Sammy	Langat (Kibet)	KEN	24.1.70	1rB	WK	Zürich	14 Aug 96
1:43.30	William	Tanui	KEN	22.2.64	2		Rieti	6 Sep 91
1:43.31	Nixon	Kiprotich	KEN	4.12.62	1		Rieti	6 Sep 92
1:43.33	Robert	Chirchir	KEN	26.11.72	3		Stuttgart	19 Jul 98
1:43.33	William	Chirchir	KEN	6.2.79	6	VD	Bruxelles	3 Sep 99
1:43.35	David	Mack	USA	30.5.61	3r1		Koblenz	28 Aug 85
1:43.38	David (Singoei)	Kiptoo	KEN	26.6.65	2	Herc	Monaco	10 Aug 96
1:43.38	Rich	Kenah	USA	4.8.70	3rA	WK	Zürich	13 Aug 97
	(30)							
1:43.44 WR	Alberto	Juantorena	CUB	3.12.50	1	WUG	Sofiya	21 Aug 77
1:43.46	Arthémon	Hatungimana	BUR	21.1.74	2rB	WK	Zürich	14 Aug 96
1:43.50	Mahjoub	Haïda	MAR	1.7.70	2	GGala	Roma	14 Jul 98
1:43.5* WR	Rick	Wohlhuter	USA	23.12.48	1		Eugene	8 Jun 74
1:43.54	William	Wuycke	VEN	21.5.58	2		Rieti	7 Sep 86
1:43.55	Philip	Kibitok	KEN	23.3.71	3	GP II	Rieti	1 Sep 96
1:43.56	Rob	Druppers	NED	29.4.62	4	ASV	Köln	25 Aug 85
1:43.57	Mike	Boit	KEN	6.1.49	1	ISTAF	Berlin	20 Aug 76
1:43.57	Joseph	Tengelei	KEN	8.12.72	3rB	WK	Zürich	16 Aug 95
1:43.60	Abdi	Bile	SOM	28.12.62	3	WK	Zürich	16 Aug 89
	(40)							
1:43.62	Earl	Jones	USA	17.7.64	2r1	WK	Zürich	13 Aug 86
1:43.63	Agberto	Guimarães	BRA	18.8.57	3		Koblenz	29 Aug 84
1:43.65	Willi	Wülbeck	FRG	18.12.54	1	WCh	Helsinki	9 Aug 83
1:43.65	Laban	Rotich	KEN	20.1.69	4		Stuttgart	19 Jul 98
1:43.66	Robert	Kibet	KEN	15.12.65	4	GP II	Rieti	1 Sep 96
1:43.69	Atle	Douglas	NOR	9.6.68	1		Rieti	5 Sep 95
1:43.7 WR	Marcello	Fiasconaro	ITA	19.7.49	1	vTCH	Milano	27 Jun 73
1:43.74	Andrea	Longo	ITA	26.6.75	1	GP II	Rieti	3 Sep 00
1:43.76	Benyounès	Lahlou	MAR	3.11.64	2	Nik	Nice	10 Jul 96
1:43.84	Olaf	Beyer	GDR	4.8.57	1	EC	Praha	31 Aug 78
	(50)	100th man 1:44.40, 200th man 1:45.17						
1:43.84	Martin	Steele	GBR	20.9.62	1rA	Bisl	Oslo	10 Jul 93
Indoors			*! photo-electric cell time*					
1:42.67i		Kipketer			1	WI	Paris (B)	9 Mar 97

1000 METRES

Mark Wind	Name		Nat	Born	Pos	Meet	Venue	Date
2:11.96 WR	Noah	Ngeny	KEN	2.11.78	1	GP II	Rieti	5 Sep 99
2:12.18 WR	Sebastian	Coe	GBR	29.9.56	1	OsloG	Oslo	11 Jul 81
2:12.66		Ngeny			1	Nik	Nice	17 Jul 99
2:12.88	Steve	Cram	GBR	14.10.60	1		Gateshead	9 Aug 85
2:13.40 WR		Coe			1	Bisl	Oslo	1 Jul 80
2:13.56	Kenneth	Kimwetich	KEN	1.1.73	2	Nik	Nice	17 Jul 99
2:13.73	Noureddine	Morceli	ALG	28.2.70	1	BNP	Villeneuve d'Ascq	2 Jul 93
2:13.9 WR	Rick	Wohlhuter	USA	23.12.48	1	King	Oslo	30 Jul 74
2:14.09	Joaquim	Cruz	BRA	12.3.63	1	Nik	Nice	20 Aug 84
2:14.28	Japheth	Kimutai	KEN	20.12.78	1	DNG	Stockholm	1 Aug 00
2:14.41	William	Yampoy	KEN	19.5.74	2	GP II	Rieti	5 Sep 99
2:14.43	Laban	Rotich (10)	KEN	20.1.69	1	Nik	Nice	16 Jul 97
2:14.50	Abdi	Bile	SOM	28.12.62	1		Jerez de la Frontera	13 Sep 89

Mark	Wind	Name		Nat	Born	Pos	Meet	Venue	Date
2:14.52		Djabir Saïd	Guerni	ALG	29.3.77	3	GP II	Rieti	5 Sep 99
2:14.53		Willi	Wülbeck	FRG	18.12.54	2	Bisl	Oslo	1 Jul 80
2:14.69		Mahjoub	Haïda	MAR	1.7.70	1	Nik	Nice	12 Jul 95
2:14.73		Joseph	Tengelei	KEN	8.12.72	2	Nik	Nice	12 Jul 95
2:14.73		Patrick	Konchellah	KEN	20.4.68	2	DNG	Stockholm	1 Aug 00

1500 METRES

Mark	Wind	Name		Nat	Born	Pos	Meet	Venue	Date
3:26.00	WR	Hicham	El Guerrouj	MAR	14.9.74	1	GGala	Roma	14 Jul 98
3:26.45			El Guerrouj			1 rA	WK	Zürich	12 Aug 98
3:27.21			El Guerrouj			1	WK	Zürich	11 Aug 00
3:27.37	WR	Noureddine	Morceli	ALG	28.2.70	1	Nik	Nice	12 Jul 95
3.27.52			Morceli			1	Herc	Monaco	25 Jul 95
3:27.65			El Guerrouj			1	WCh	Sevilla	24 Aug 99
3:28.12		Noah	Ngeny	KEN	2.11.78	2	WK	Zürich	11 Aug 00
3:28.21+			El Guerrouj			1	in 1M	Roma	7 Jul 99
3.28.37			Morceli			1	GPF	Monaco	9 Sep 95
3:28.37			El Guerrouj			1	Herc	Monaco	8 Aug 98
3:28.51		Bernard	Lagat	KEN	12.12.74	3	WK	Zürich	11 Aug 00
3:28.57			El Guerrouj			1rA	WK	Zürich	11 Aug 99
3:28.6+			Ngeny			2	in 1M	Roma	7 Jul 99
3:28.73			Ngeny			2	WCh	Sevilla	24 Aug 99
3:28.84			Ngeny			1	GP	Paris (C)	21 Jul 99
3:28.86	WR		Morceli			1		Rieti	6 Sep 92
3:28.91			El Guerrouj			1rA	WK	Zürich	13 Aug 97
3:28.92			El Guerrouj			1	VD	Bruxelles	22 Aug 97
3:28.93			Ngeny			1	GPF	München	11 Sep 99
3:28.95		Fermín	Cacho	ESP	16.2.69	2rA	WK	Zürich	13 Aug 97
3:29.05			El Guerrouj			1	VD	Bruxelles	23 Aug 96
3:29.12			El Guerrouj			1	Bisl	Oslo	9 Jul 98
3:29.18		Vénuste	Niyongabo	BUR	9.12.73	2	VD	Bruxelles	22 Aug 97
3:29.19			Ngeny			1	VD	Bruxelles	3 Sep 99
3:29.20			Morceli			1	MedG	Narbonne	20 Jun 93
3:29.30			El Guerrouj			1rA	DNG	Stockholm	7 Jul 97
3:29.43			Niyongabo			3rA	WK	Zürich	13 Aug 97
3:29.46	WR	Saïd	Aouita	MAR	2.11.59	1	ISTAF	Berlin	23 Aug 85
3:29.46		Daniel	Komen	KEN	17.5.76	1	Herc	Monaco	16 Aug 97
3:29.50			Morceli			1	Gaz	Paris (C)	28 Jun 96
		(30/8)							
3:29.67	WR	Steve	Cram	GBR	14.10.60	1	Nik	Nice	16 Jul 85
3:29.77		Sydney	Maree	USA	9.9.56	1	ASV	Köln	25 Aug 85
		(10)							
3:29.77		Sebastian	Coe	GBR	29.9.56	1		Rieti	7 Sep 86
3:29.91		Laban	Rotich	KEN	20.1.69	2rA	WK	Zürich	12 Aug 98
3:30.18		John	Kibowen	KEN	21.4.69	3rA	WK	Zürich	12 Aug 98
3:30.55		Abdi	Bile	SOM	28.12.62	1		Rieti	3 Sep 89
3:30.57		Reyes	Estévez	ESP	2.8.76	3	WCh	Sevilla	24 Aug 99
3:30.58		William	Tanui	KEN	22.2.64	3	Herc	Monaco	16 Aug 97
3:30.73		Benjamin	Kipkurui	KEN	28.12.80	2	GP II	Rieti	3 Sep 00
3:30.77	WR	Steve	Ovett	GBR	9.10.55	1		Rieti	4 Sep 83
3:30.82		Ali	Saïdi-Sief	ALG	15.3.78	1	GP II	Gateshead	28 Aug 00
3:30.88		Rui	Silva	POR	3.8.77	4rA	WK	Zürich	11 Aug 99
		(20)							
3:30.92		José Luis	González	ESP	8.12.57	3	Nik	Nice	16 Jul 85
3:30.94		Isaac	Viciosa	ESP	26.12.69	5	Herc	Monaco	8 Aug 98
3:31.01		Jim	Spivey	USA	7.3.60	1	R-W	Koblenz	28 Aug 88
3:31.02		William	Chirchir	KEN	6.2.79	1	Herc	Monaco	18 Aug 00
3:31.13		José Manuel	Abascal	ESP	17.3.58	1		Barcelona	16 Aug 86
3:31.17		Robert K.	Andersen	DEN	12.12.72	5rA	WK	Zürich	13 Aug 97
3:31.40		William	Kemoi	KEN	22.2.69	2	Nik	Nice	12 Jul 95
3:31.48		Azzedine	Sediki	MAR	21.5.70	3rA	ASV	Köln	18 Aug 95
3:31.48		José Antonio	Redolat	ESP	17.2.76	3	GGala	Roma	30 Jun 00
3:31.48		Andrés	Díaz	ESP	12.7.69	2	Herc	Monaco	18 Aug 00
		(30)							
3:31.51		Driss	Maazouzi	FRA	15.10.69	3	GP	Paris (C)	21 Jul 99
3:31.52		Steve	Holman	USA	2.3.70	6	VD	Bruxelles	22 Aug 97
3:31.53		David	Lelei	KEN	10.5.71	3		Stuttgart	19 Jul 98
3:31.58		Thomas	Wessinghage	FRG	22.2.52	2		Koblenz	27 Aug 80
3:31.70		Ali	Hakimi	TUN	24.4.76	7	VD	Bruxelles	22 Aug 97
3:31.71		Kevin	Sullivan	CAN	20.3.74	4	GGala	Roma	30 Jun 00

Mark	Wind	Name		Nat	Born	Pos	Meet	Venue	Date
3:31.75		Pierre	Délèze	SUI	25.9.58	1	WK	Zürich	21 Aug 85
3:31.76		Steve	Scott	USA	5.5.56	4	Nik	Nice	16 Jul 85
3:31.86		John	Mayock	GBR	26.10.70	8	VD	Bruxelles	22 Aug 97
3:31.87		Stephen	Kipkorir	KEN	24.10.70	2	Athl	Lausanne	3 Jul 96
		(40)							
3:31.89		Sammy	Rono	KEN	74	4		Stuttgart	19 Jul 98
3:31.96		Harald	Hudak	FRG	28.1.57	3		Koblenz	27 Aug 80
3:31.96		Simon	Doyle	AUS	9.11.66	2	DNG	Stockholm	3 Jul 91
3:32.05		Mehdi	Baala	FRA	17.8.78	6	WK	Zürich	11 Aug 00
3:32.06		Nadir	Bosch	FRA	16.5.73	4	GP	Paris (C)	21 Jul 99
3:32.07		Elijah Kipruto	Maru	KEN	12.6.76	4	GP II	Rieti	1 Sep 96
3:32.09		Benson	Koech	KEN	10.11.74	2	VD	Bruxelles	3 Sep 99
3:32.10		Mohammed	Suleiman	QAT	23.11.69	8rA	WK	Zürich	13 Aug 97
3:32.13		David	Kibet	KEN	24.11.63	2		Rieti	6 Sep 92
3:32.16	WR	Filbert	Bayi	TAN	23.6.53	1	CG	Christchurch	2 Feb 74
		(50)	100th man 3:33.95, 200th man 3:35.67						
Indoors									
3:31.76		Haile	Gebrselassie	ETH	18.4.73	1		Stuttgart	1 Feb 98

1 MILE

Mark	Wind	Name		Nat	Born	Pos	Meet	Venue	Date
3:43.13	WR	Hicham	El Guerrouj	MAR	14.9.74	1	GGala	Roma	7 Jul 99
3:43.40		Noah	Ngeny	KEN	2.11.78	2	GGala	Roma	7 Jul 99
3:44.39	WR	Noureddine	Morceli	ALG	28.2.70	1		Rieti	5 Sep 93
3:44.60			El Guerrouj			1	Nik	Nice	16 Jul 98
3:44.90			El Guerrouj			1	Bisl	Oslo	4 Jul 97
3:45.19			Morceli			1	WK	Zürich	16 Aug 95
3:45.64			El Guerrouj			1	ISTAF	Berlin	26 Aug 97
3:45.96			El Guerrouj			1	BrGP	London (CP)	5 Aug 00
3:46.24			El Guerrouj			1	Bisl	Oslo	28 Jul 00
3:46.32	WR	Steve	Cram	GBR	14.10.60	1	Bisl	Oslo	27 Jul 85
3:46.38		Daniel	Komen	KEN	17.5.76	2	ISTAF	Berlin	26 Aug 97
3:46.70		Vénuste	Niyongabo	BUR	9.12.73	3	ISTAF	Berlin	26 Aug 97
3:46.76		Saïd	Aouita	MAR	2.11.59	1	WG	Helsinki	2 Jul 87
3:46.78			Morceli			1	ISTAF	Berlin	27 Aug 93
3:46.92			Aouita			1	WK	Zürich	21 Aug 85
3:47.10			El Guerrouj			1	BrGP	London (CP)	7 Aug 99
3:47.30			Morceli			1	VD	Bruxelles	3 Sep 93
3:47.33	WR	Sebastian	Coe	GBR	29.9.56	1	VD	Bruxelles	28 Aug 81
3:47.65		Laban	Rotich	KEN	20.1.69	2	Bisl	Oslo	4 Jul 97
3:47.67			Ngeny			2	BrGP	London (CP)	5 Aug 00
3:47.69		Steve	Scott	USA	5.5.56	1	OsloG	Oslo	7 Jul 82
		(21/10)							
3:47.79		José Luis	González	ESP	8.12.57	2	Bisl	Oslo	27 Jul 85
3:47.88		John	Kibowen	KEN	21.4.69	3	Bisl	Oslo	4 Jul 97
3:47.94		William	Chirchir	KEN	6.2.79	2	Bisl	Oslo	28 Jul 00
3:48.40	WR	Steve	Ovett	GBR	9.10.55	1	R-W	Koblenz	26 Aug 81
3:48.80		William	Kemei	KEN	22.2.69	1	ISTAF	Berlin	21 Aug 92
3:48.83		Sydney	Maree	USA	9.9.56	1		Rieti	9 Sep 81
3:49.08		John	Walker	NZL	12.1.52	2	OsloG	Oslo	7 Jul 82
3:49.20		Peter	Elliott	GBR	9.10.62	2	Bisl	Oslo	2 Jul 88
3:49.22		Jens-Peter	Herold	GDR	2.6.65	3	Bisl	Oslo	2 Jul 88
3:49.31		Joe	Falcon	USA	23.6.66	1	Bisl	Oslo	14 Jul 90
		(20)							
3:49.34		David	Moorcroft	GBR	10.4.53	3	Bisl	Oslo	26 Jun 82
3:49.34		Benjamin	Kipkurui	KEN	28.12.80	3	VD	Bruxelles	25 Aug 00
3:49.40		Abdi	Bile	SOM	28.12.62	4	Bisl	Oslo	2 Jul 88
3:49.45		Mike	Boit	KEN	6.1.49	2	VD	Bruxelles	28 Aug 81
3:49.56		Fermín	Cacho	ESP	16.2.69	2	Bisl	Oslo	5 Jul 96
3:49.77		Ray	Flynn	IRL	22.1.57	3	OsloG	Oslo	7 Jul 82
3:49.77		Wilfred	Kirochi	KEN	12.12.69	2	Bisl	Oslo	6 Jul 91
3:49.80		Jim	Spivey	USA	7.3.60	3	Bisl	Oslo	5 Jul 86
3:49.84		Bernard	Lagat	KEN	12.12.74	4	VD	Bruxelles	25 Aug 00
3:49.91		Simon	Doyle	AUS	9.11.66	4	Bisl	Oslo	6 Jul 91
		(30)							
3:49.98		Thomas	Wessinghage	FRG	22.2.52	3	ISTAF	Berlin	17 Aug 83
3:50.26		Kevin	Sullivan	CAN	20.3.74	4	Bisl	Oslo	28 Jul 00
3:50.32		John	Mayock	GBR	26.10.70	3	Bisl	Oslo	5 Jul 96
3:50.33		Eric	Dubus	FRA	28.2.66	3	WK	Zürich	16 Aug 95

Mark	Wind	Name		Nat	Born	Pos	Meet	Venue	Date
3:50.34		Todd	Harbour	USA	24.3.59	5	OsloG	Oslo	11 Jul 81
3:50.38		Pierre	Délèze	SUI	25.9.58	4	R-W	Koblenz	25 Aug 82
3:50.40		Steve	Holman	USA	2.3.70	5	Bisl	Oslo	4 Jul 97
3:50.52		Hauke	Fuhlbrügge	GER	21.3.66	6	Bisl	Oslo	6 Jul 91
3:50.54		José Manuel	Abascal	ESP	17.3.58	2	GP-GG	Roma	10 Sep 86
3:50.54		Vyacheslav	Shabunin	RUS	27.9.69	5	VD	Bruxelles	25 Aug 00
		(40)							
3:50.57		William	Tanui	KEN	22.2.64	5	ISTAF	Berlin	26 Aug 97
3:50.57		Ali	Hakimi	TUN	24.4.76	6	ISTAF	Berlin	26 Aug 97
3:50.62		Mark	Carroll	IRL	15.1.72	7	Bisl	Oslo	28 Jul 00
3:50.64		Graham	Williamson	GBR	15.6.60	4		Cork	13 Jul 82
3:50.73		Wilson	Waigwa	KEN	15.2.49	2	R-W	Koblenz	31 Aug 83
3:50.79		Robert K.	Andersen	DEN	12.12.72	7	ISTAF	Berlin	26 Aug 97
3:50.82		Johan	Fourie	RSA	2.12.59	1		Port Elizabeth	11 Mar 87
3:50.84		Tom	Byers	USA	12.5.55	6	R-W	Koblenz	25 Aug 82
3:50.91		Rui	Silva	POR	3.8.77	3	GGala	Roma	7 Jul 99
3:50.98		José	Marajo	FRA	10.8.54	4	OsloG	Oslo	9 Jul 83
		(50)	100th man 3:52.72, 200th man 3:55.18						
Indoor marks									
3:49.78		Eamonn	Coghlan	IRL	24.11.52	1		East Rutherford	27 Feb 83
3:50.94		Marcus	O'Sullivan	IRL	22.12.61	1		East Rutherford	13 Feb 88

2000 METRES

Mark	Wind	Name		Nat	Born	Pos	Meet	Venue	Date
4:44.79	WR	Hicham	El Guerrouj	MAR	14.9.74	1	ISTAF	Berlin	7 Sep 99
4:47.88	WR	Noureddine	Morceli	ALG	28.2.70	1		Paris	3 Jul 95
4:48.36			El Guerrouj			1		Gateshead	19 Jul 98
4:48.69		Vénuste	Niyongabo	BUR	9.12.73	1	Nik	Nice	12 Jul 95
4:48.74		John	Kibowen	KEN	21.4.69	1		Hechtel	1 Aug 98
4:49.00			Niyongabo			1		Rieti	3 Sep 97
4:49.55			Morceli			1	Nik	Nice	10 Jul 96
4:50.08		Noah	Ngeny	KEN	2.11.78	1	DNG	Stockholm	30 Jul 99
4:50.81	WR	Saïd	Aouita	MAR	2.11.59	1	BNP	Paris	16 Jul 87
4:51.30		Daniel	Komen	KEN	17.5.76	1		Milano	5 Jun 98
4:51.39	WR	Steve	Cram	GBR	14.10.60	1	BGP	Budapest	4 Aug 85
4:51.52	WR	John	Walker	NZL	12.1.52	1	Bisl	Oslo	30 Jun 76
4:51.98			Aouita			1	VD	Bruxelles	5 Sep 86
4:52.20		Thomas	Wessinghage	FRG	22.2.52	1		Ingelheim	31 Aug 82
		(14/10)							
4:52.40		José Manuel	Abascal	ESP	17.3.58	1		Santander	7 Sep 86
4:52.44		Jim	Spivey	USA	7.3.60	1	Athl	Lausanne	15 Sep 87
4:52.53		Moses	Kiptanui	KEN	1.10.70	1	ISTAF	Berlin	21 Aug 92
4:52.82		Peter	Elliott	GBR	9.10.62	2	Athl	Lausanne	15 Sep 87
4:52.82		Luke	Kipkosgei	KEN	27.11.75	2	Slovn	Bratislava	9 Jun 98
4:52.88		Smaïl	Sghir	MAR	16.3.72	2	Nik	Nice	12 Jul 95
4:53.06		Jack	Buckner	GBR	22.9.61	3	Athl	Lausanne	15 Sep 87
4:53.69		Gary	Staines	GBR	3.7.63	4	Athl	Lausanne	15 Sep 87
4:53.7+		John	Kosgei	KEN	13.7.73	2	in 3k	Rieti	1 Sep 96
4:53.84		Martin	Keino (20)	KEN	20.6.72	2	Nik	Nice	10 Jul 96
Indoors									
4:52.86		Haile	Gebrselassie	ETH	18.4.73	1	BUPA	Birmingham	15 Feb 98

3000 METRES

Mark	Wind	Name		Nat	Born	Pos	Meet	Venue	Date
7:20.67	WR	Daniel	Komen	KEN	17.5.76	1		Rieti	1 Sep 96
7:23.09		Hicham	El Guerrouj	MAR	14.9.74	1	VD	Bruxelles	3 Sep 99
7:25.02		Ali	Saïdi-Sief	ALG	15.3.78	1	Herc	Monaco	18 Aug 00
7:25.09		Haile	Gebrselassie	ETH	18.4.73	1	VD	Bruxelles	28 Aug 98
7:25.11	WR	Noureddine	Morceli	ALG	28.2.70	1	Herc	Monaco	2 Aug 94
7:25.16			Komen			1	Herc	Monaco	10 Aug 96
7:25.54			Gebrselassie			1	Herc	Monaco	8 Aug 98
7:25.87			Komen			1	VD	Bruxelles	23 Aug 96
7:26.02			Gebrselassie			1	VD	Bruxelles	22 Aug 97
7:26.03			Gebrselassie			1	GP II	Helsinki	10 Jun 99
7:26.5 e			Komen			1	in 2M	Sydney	28 Feb 98
7:26.62		Mohammed	Mourhit	BEL	10.10.70	2	Herc	Monaco	18 Aug 00
7:27.18		Moses	Kiptanui	KEN	1.10.70	1	Herc	Monaco	25 Jul 95
7:27.3+			Komen			1	in 2M	Hechtel	19 Jul 97
7:27.42			Gebrselassie			1	Bisl	Oslo	9 Jul 98
7:27.50			Morceli			1	VD	Bruxelles	25 Aug 95

Mark Wind	Name		Nat	Born	Pos	Meet	Venue	Date
7:27.59	Luke	Kipkosgei	KEN	27.11.75	2	Herc	Monaco	8 Aug 98
7:27.67		Saïdi-Sief			1	Gaz	Saint-Denis	23 Jun 00
7:27.75	Tom	Nyariki	KEN	27.9.71	2	Herc	Monaco	10 Aug 96
7.28.04		Kiptanui			1	ASV	Köln	18 Aug 95
7:28.28		Kipkosgei			2	Bisl	Oslo	9 Jul 98
7:28.41	Paul	Bitok (10)	KEN	26.6.70	3	Herc	Monaco	10 Aug 96
7:28.45	Assefa	Mezegebu	ETH	19.6.78	3	Herc	Monaco	8 Aug 98
7:28.67	Benjamin	Limo	KEN	23.8.74	1	Herc	Monaco	4 Aug 99
7:28.70	Paul	Tergat	KEN	17.6.69	4	Herc	Monaco	10 Aug 96
7:28.92		Komen			3	Herc	Monaco	18 Aug 00
7:28.93	Salah	Hissou	MAR	16.1.72	2	Herc	Monaco	4 Aug 99
7:28.94	Brahim	Lahlafi	MAR	15.4.68	3	Herc	Monaco	4 Aug 99
7:28.96 WR		Kiptanui			1	ASV	Köln	16 Aug 92
7:29.09	John	Kibowen	KEN	21.4.69	3	Bisl	Oslo	9 Jul 98
	(30/16)							
7:29.34	Isaac	Viciosa	ESP	26.12.69	4	Bisl	Oslo	9 Jul 98
7:29.45 WR	Saïd	Aouita	MAR	2.11.59	1	ASV	Köln	20 Aug 89
7:30.09	Smaïl	Sghir	MAR	16.3.72	2	Herc	Monaco	25 Jul 95
7:30.36	Mark	Carroll	IRL	15.1.72	5	Herc	Monaco	4 Aug 99
	(20)							
7:30.50	Dieter	Baumann	GER	9.2.65	6	Herc	Monaco	8 Aug 98
7:30.53	El Hassan	Lahssini	MAR	1.1.74	6	Herc	Monaco	10 Aug 96
7:30.78	Mustapha	Essaïd	FRA	20.1.70	7	Herc	Monaco	8 Aug 98
7:30.84	Bob	Kennedy	USA	18.8.70	8	Herc	Monaco	8 Aug 98
7:30.99	Khalid	Boulami	MAR	7.8.69	1	Nik	Nice	16 Jul 97
7:31.13	Julius	Gitahi	KEN	29.4.78	6	Bisl	Oslo	9 Jul 98
7:31.14	William	Kalya	KEN	4.8.74	3	Herc	Monaco	16 Aug 97
7:31.59	Manuel	Pancorbo	ESP	7.7.66	7	Bisl	Oslo	9 Jul 98
7:32.1 WR	Henry	Rono	KEN	12.2.52	1	Bisl	Oslo	27 Jun 78
7:32.32	Enrique	Molina	ESP	25.2.68	5	Bisl	Oslo	4 Jul 97
	(30)							
7:32.36	Million	Wolde	ETH	17.3.79	3	Gaz	Saint-Denis	23 Jun 00
7:32.36	Benjamin	Maiyo	KEN	6.10.78	2	GPII	Athína	28 Jun 00
7:32.79	David	Moorcroft	GBR	10.4.53	1		London (CP)	17 Jul 82
7:33.00	Hailu	Mekonnen	ETH	4.4.80	2		Stuttgart	6 Jun 99
7:33.13	Shem	Kororia	KEN	25.9.72	7	Herc	Monaco	10 Aug 96
7:33.37	Sydney	Maree	USA	9.9.56	2		London (CP)	17 Jul 82
7:33.51	Bernard	Lagat	KEN	12.12.74	5	Herc	Monaco	18 Aug 00
7:33.79	Paul	Koech	KEN	25.6.69	5	Herc	Monaco	16 Aug 97
7:33.96	Wilson	Kipketer (Boit)	KEN	6.10.73	7	Nik	Nice	16 Jul 97
7:34.03	Vénuste	Niyongabo	BUR	9.12.73	3	ASV	Köln	16 Aug 96
	(40)							
7:34.18	Yobes	Ondieki	KEN	21.2.61	3	ASV	Köln	16 Aug 92
7:34.32	Richard	Limo	KEN	18.11.80	4	VD	Bruxelles	3 Sep 99
7:34.46	Driss	El Himer	FRA	4.4.74	5	GP	Paris	29 Jul 98
7:34.58	Sammy	Kipketer	KEN	29.9.81	5	VD	Bruxelles	3 Sep 99
7:34.67	Mohamed Saïd	El Wardi	MAR	19.4.72	4	Gaz	Saint-Denis	23 Jun 00
7:35.08	Aloÿs	Nizigama	BUR	18.6.66	2	Nik	Nice	18 Jul 94
7:35.1 WR	Brendan	Foster	GBR	12.1.48	1		Gateshead	3 Aug 74
7:35.32	Fita	Bayissa	ETH	15.12.72	5	ASV	Köln	16 Aug 96
7:35.41	Hicham	Bouaouiche	MAR	16.6.74	2		Villeneuve d'Ascq	11 Jul 98
7:35.46	Noah	Ngeny	KEN	2.11.78	1	GPII	Sevilla	9 Jun 00
	(50)	100th man 7:39.52, 200th man 7:43.86						
Indoors								
7:24.90		Komen			1		Budapest	6 Feb 98
7:26.15		Gebrselassie			1		Karlsruhe	25 Jan 98
7:26.80		Gebrselassie			1		Karlsruhe	24 Jan 99

2 MILES

7:58.61 WR	Daniel	Komen	KEN	17.5.76	1		Hechtel	19 Jul 97
7:58.91		Komen			1		Sydney	28 Feb 98
8:01.08 WR	Haile	Gebrselassie	ETH	18.4.73	1	APM	Hengelo	31 May 97
8:01.72		Gebrselassie			1	BrGP	London (CP)	7 Aug 99
8:01.86		Gebrselassie			1	APM	Hengelo	30 May 99
8:03.54 WR		Komen			1		Lappeenranta	14 Jul 96
8:07.46 WR		Gebrselassie			1		Kerkrade	28 May 95
8:09.01 WR	Moses	Kiptanui	KEN	10.10.70	1		Hechtel	30 Jul 94
8:10.98	Khalid	Boulami	MAR	7.8.69	1		Hechtel	6 Jul 96

Mark Wind	Name		Nat	Born	Pos	Meet	Venue	Date
8:11.59	Bob	Kennedy	USA	18.8.70	2		Hechtel	19 Jul 97
8:11.73	Smail	Sghir	MAR	16.3.72	2		Hechtel	6 Jul 96
8:09.66 i	Hailu	Mekonen	ETH	4.4.80	1		Birmingham	20 Feb 00

5000 METRES

Mark Wind	Name		Nat	Born	Pos	Meet	Venue	Date
12:39.36WR	Haile	Gebrselassie	ETH	18.4.73	1	GP II	Helsinki	13 Jun 98
12:39.74WR	Daniel	Komen	KEN	17.5.76	1	VD	Bruxelles	22 Aug 97
12:41.86WR		Gebrselassie			1	WK	Zürich	13 Aug 97
12:44.39WR		Gebrselassie			1	WK	Zürich	16 Aug 95
12:44.90		Komen			2	WK	Zürich	13 Aug 97
12:45.09		Komen			1	WK	Zürich	14 Aug 96
12:48.98		Komen			1	GGala	Roma	5 Jun 97
12:49.28	Brahim	Lahlafi	MAR	15.4.68	1	VD	Bruxelles	25 Aug 00
12:49.64		Gebrselassie			1	WK	Zürich	11 Aug 99
12:49.71	Mohammed	Mourhit	BEL	10.10.70	2	VD	Bruxelles	25 Aug 00
12:49.87	Paul	Tergat	KEN	17.6.69	3	WK	Zürich	13 Aug 97
12:50.80	Salah	Hissou	MAR	16.1.72	1	GGala	Roma	5 Jun 96
12:50.86	Ali	Saïdi Sief	ALG	15.3.78	1	GGala	Roma	30 Jun 00
12:51.60		Komen			1	DNG	Stockholm	8 Jul 96
12:52.38		Komen			1	GPF	Milano	7 Sep 96
12:52.39		Hissou			2	GGala	Roma	5 Jun 97
12:52.53		Hissou			1		Milano	9 Jun 99
12.52.70		Gebrselassie			2	WK	Zürich	14 Aug 96
12.53.19		Gebrselassie			1	ISTAF	Berlin	1 Sep 95
12:53.41	Khalid	Boulami	MAR	7.8.69	4	WK	Zürich	13 Aug 97
12:53.45		Hissou			2	WK	Zürich	11 Aug 99
12:53.72	Philip	Mosima	KEN	2.1.77	2	GGala	Roma	5 Jun 96
12:53.84	Assefa	Mezegebu (10)	ETH	19.6.78	1	VD	Bruxelles	28 Aug 98
12:53.92		Gebrselassie			1	Bisl	Oslo	30 Jun 99
12:54.07	Sammy	Kipketer	KEN-J	29.9.81	2	GGala	Roma	30 Jun 00
12:54.08		Gebrselassie			1	WK	Zürich	12 Aug 98
12:54.60		Gebrselassie			1		Nürnberg	13 Jun 97
12:54.70	Dieter	Baumann	GER	9.2.65	5	WK	Zürich	13 Aug 97
12:54.72		Tergat			3	WK	Zürich	14 Aug 96
12:54.82		Komen			2	VD	Bruxelles	28 Aug 98
	(30/12)							
12:54.85	Moses	Kiptanui	KEN	1.10.70	3	GGala	Roma	5 Jun 96
12:55.63	Mark	Bett	KEN	22.12.76	2	Bisl	Oslo	28 Jul 00
12:55.82	Benjamin	Limo	KEN	23.8.74	3	Bisl	Oslo	28 Jul 00
12:55.94	Tom	Nyariki	KEN	27.9.71	1	DNG	Stockholm	7 Jul 97
12:56.29	Paul	Koech	KEN	25.6.69	6	WK	Zürich	13 Aug 97
12:56.50	Luke	Kipkosgei	KEN	27.11.75	5	Bisl	Oslo	28 Jul 00
12:57.23	Worku	Bikila	ETH	6.5.68	3	GGala	Roma	8 Jun 95
12:57.79	David	Chelule	KEN	7.7.77	5	GGala	Roma	7 Jul 99
	(20)							
12:58.15	Richard	Limo	KEN	18.11.80	6	GGala	Roma	7 Jul 99
12:58.21	Bob	Kennedy	USA	18.8.70	5	WK	Zürich	14 Aug 96
12:58.39WR	Saïd	Aouita	MAR	2.11.59	1	GGala	Roma	22 Jul 87
12:58.99	Smaïl	Sghir	MAR	16.3.72	6	WK	Zürich	14 Aug 96
12:59.39	Million	Wolde	ETH	17.3.79	5	WK	Zürich	12 Aug 98
12:59.90	Albert	Chepkirui	KEN	4.4.81	8	Bisl	Oslo	28 Jul 00
13:00.41WR	David	Moorcroft	GBR	10.4.53	1	OsloG	Oslo	7 Jul 82
13:00.54	Khalid	Skah	MAR	29.1.67	1	BNP	Villeneuve d'Ascq	8 Jul 94
13:01.15	Sydney	Maree	USA	9.9.56	2	Bisl	Oslo	27 Jul 85
13:01.41	Brahim	Jabbour	MAR	2.10.70	1	GP II	Saint-Denis	3 Jul 99
	(30)							
13:01.82	Yobes	Ondieki	KEN	21.2.61	1	WK	Zürich	7 Aug 91
13:01.89	Julius	Gitahi	KEN	29.4.78	5	DNG	Stockholm	5 Aug 98
13:01.9	Abraham	Chebii	KEN	23.12.79	2		Milano	7 Jun 00
13:02.15	Mustapha	Essaïd	FRA	20.1.70	4	VD	Bruxelles	28 Aug 98
13:02.38	Benjamin	Maiyo	KEN	6.10.78	8	ISTAF	Berlin	7 Sep 99
13:02.68	Patrick	Ivuti	KEN	30.6.78	7	WK	Zürich	11 Aug 00
13:02.71	Evans	Rutto	KEN	8.4.78	2	Live	Nürnberg	25 Jun 00
13:02.75	Ismael	Kirui	KEN	20.2.75	1	WCh	Stuttgart	16 Aug 93
13:02.80	Shem	Kororia	KEN	25.9.72	1	DNG	Stockholm	10 Jul 95
13:02.86	António	Pinto	POR	22.3.66	9	WK	Zürich	12 Aug 98
	(40)							
13:03.08	William	Kalya	KEN	4.8.74	2	DNG	Stockholm	10 Jul 95

Mark	Wind	Name		Nat	Born	Pos	Meet	Venue	Date
13:03.29		Vénuste	Niyongabo	BUR	9.12.73	1		Saint-Denis	3 Jun 96
13:03.76		Stéphane	Franke	GER	12.2.64	5	WK	Zürich	16 Aug 95
13:03.85		Noureddine	Morceli	ALG	28.2.70	1	WK	Zürich	17 Aug 94
13:03.93		Mark	Carroll	IRL	15.1.72	7	ISTAF	Berlin	1 Sep 98
13:04.04		Josphat	Machuka	KEN	12.12.73	4	DNG	Stockholm	8 Jul 96
13:04.15		Paul	Bitok	KEN	26.6.70	10	Bisl	Oslo	28 Jul 00
13:04.3		James Kimutai	Koskei	KEN	23.11.68	4		Milano	7 Jun 00
13:04.32		El Hassane	Lahssini	MAR	1.1.74	7	GPF	Milano	7 Sep 96
13:04.46		Mohamed Saïd	El Wardi	MAR	19.4.72	3	Live	Nürnberg	25 Jun 00
		(50)	100th man 13:11.77, 200th man 13:18.32						
Indoors									
12:50.38			Gebrselassie			1	BUPA	Birmingham	14 Feb 99
12:51.48			Komen			1		Stockholm	19 Feb 98

MEN All-time

10,000 METRES

Mark	Wind	Name		Nat	Born	Pos	Meet	Venue	Date
26:22.75WR		Haile	Gebrselassie	ETH	18.4.73	1	APM	Hengelo	1 Jun 98
26:27.85WR		Paul	Tergat	KEN	17.6.69	1	VD	Bruxelles	22 Aug 97
26:31.32WR			Gebrselassie			1	Bisl	Oslo	4 Jul 97
26:36.26		Paul	Koech	KEN	25.6.69	2	VD	Bruxelles	22 Aug 97
26:38.08WR		Salah	Hissou	MAR	16.1.72	1	VD	Bruxelles	23 Aug 96
26:43.53WR			Gebrselassie			1	APM	Hengelo	5 Jun 95
26:46.44			Tergat			1	VD	Bruxelles	28 Aug 98
26:47.89			Koech			2	VD	Bruxelles	28 Aug 98
26:51.49		Charles	Kamathi	KEN	18.5.78	1	VD	Bruxelles	3 Sep 99
26:52.23WR		William	Sigei	KEN	11.10.69	1	Bisl	Oslo	22 Jul 94
26:52.30		Mohammed	Mourhit	BEL	10.10.70	2	VD	Bruxelles	3 Sep 99
26:54.41			Tergat			2	VD	Bruxelles	23 Aug 96
26:56.78			Koech			3	VD	Bruxelles	23 Aug 96
26:58.38WR		Yobes	Ondieki	KEN	21.2.61	1	Bisl	Oslo	10 Jul 93
27:03.87			Tergat			1	VD	Bruxelles	25 Aug 00
27:04.54		Felix	Limo (10)	KEN	22.8.80	2	VD	Bruxelles	25 Aug 00
27:06.44		Worku	Bikila	ETH	6.5.68	1	VD	Bruxelles	25 Aug 95
27:06.45		Habte	Jifar	ETH	29.1.76	1	APM	Hengelo	30 May 99
27:06.59		Ismael	Kirui	KEN	20.2.75	2	VD	Bruxelles	25 Aug 95
27:07.34			Gebrselassie			1	OG	Atlanta	29 Jul 96
27:07.91WR		Richard	Chelimo	KEN	21.4.72	1	DNG	Stockholm	5 Jul 93
27:09.79		Patrick	Ivuti	KEN	30.6.78	3	VD	Bruxelles	25 Aug 00
27:08.17			Tergat			2	OG	Atlanta	29 Jul 96
27:08.23WR		Arturo	Barrios	MEX	12.12.63	1	ISTAF	Berlin	18 Aug 89
27:09.07			Hissou			3	VD	Bruxelles	22 Aug 97
27:09.30			Hissou			3	VD	Bruxelles	25 Aug 95
27:10.08			Tergat			1	DNG	Stockholm	30 Jul 99
27:10.34		Josphat	Machuka	KEN	12.12.73	4	VD	Bruxelles	25 Aug 95
27:10.38			Koech			3	VD	Bruxelles	3 Sep 99
27:11.17		Julius	Gitahi	KEN	29.4.78	1		Kobe	26 Apr 98
27:11.18			Chelimo			1	APM	Hengelo	25 Jun 91
27:11.62		John	Ngugi ¶	KEN	10.5.62	1	VD	Bruxelles	13 Sep 91
27:12.39		Smaïl	Sghir	MAR	16.3.72	2	DNG	Stockholm	30 Jul 99
		(33/20)							
27:12.47		António	Pinto	POR	22.3.66	3	DNG	Stockholm	30 Jul 99
27:13.38		Girma	Tolla	ETH	13.10.75	2	APM	Hengelo	30 May 99
27:13.81WR		Fernando	Mamede	POR	1.11.51	1	DNG	Stockholm	2 Jul 84
27:14.26		Fita	Bayissa	ETH	15.12.72	1	Bisl	Oslo	4 Jul 92
27:14.44		Fabián	Roncero	ESP	19.10.70	1rA	EChall	Lisboa	4 Apr 98
27:14.53		Khalid	Skah	MAR	29.1.67	2	WCh	Göteborg	8 Aug 95
27:16.50		Salvatore	Antibo	ITA	7.2.62	1	WG	Helsinki	29 Jun 89
27:17.20		William	Kiptum	KEN	30.3.71	2	Bisl	Oslo	22 Jul 94
27:17.48		Carlos	Lopes	POR	18.2.47	2	DNG	Stockholm	2 Jul 84
27:17.82		Addis	Abebe	ETH	.70	2	WG	Helsinki	29 Jun 89
		(30)							
27:18.02		Shem	Kororia	KEN	25.9.72	6	VD	Bruxelles	25 Aug 95
27:18.14		Jon	Brown	GBR	27.2.71	4	VD	Bruxelles	28 Aug 98
27:18.28		Assefa	Mezegebu	ETH	19.6.78	4	APM	Hengelo	30 May 99
27:18.32		Moses	Tanui	KEN	20.8.65	2	VD	Bruxelles	3 Sep 93
27:18.59		Armando	Quintanilla	MEX	19.4.68	3	Bisl	Oslo	22 Jul 94
27:18.66		Mark	Bett	KEN	22.12.76	5	VD	Bruxelles	28 Aug 98
27:18.74		Simon	Maina Munyi	KEN	18.3.78	5	APM	Hengelo	30 May 99
27:20.38		Aloÿs	Nizigama	BUR	18.6.66	1		London (CP)	7 Jul 95

Mark	Wind	Name		Nat	Born	Pos	Meet	Venue	Date
27:20.56		Mark	Nenow	USA	16.11.57	1	VD	Bruxelles	5 Sep 86
27:21.29		Luka	Keitany	KEN	.79	7	APM	Hengelo	30 May 99
		(40)							
27:21.32		Evans	Rutto	KEN	8.4.78	3		Villeneuve d'Ascq	17 Jun 00
27:21.46		M Brahim	Boutayeb	MAR	15.8.67	1	OG	Seoul	26 Sep 88
27:21.53		Dieter	Baumann	GER	9.2.65	1	EChall	Barakaldo	5 Apr 97
27:22.20		José	Rios	ESP	15.3.74	1	NC	Gijón	12 Aug 00
27:22.47!WR		Henry	Rono	KEN	12.2.52	1		Wien	11 Jun 78
27:22.54		Luke	Kipkosgei	KEN	27.11.75	1	Zat	Melbourne	5 Dec 98
27:22.78		Antonio	Martins	FRA	23.8.63	3	Bisl	Oslo	4 Jul 92
27:23.06		Eamonn	Martin	GBR	9.10.58	1	Bisl	Oslo	2 Jul 88
27:23.18		Vincent	Rousseau	BEL	29.7.62	5	VD	Bruxelles	3 Sep 93
27:23.65		William	Kalya	KEN	4.8.74	4	VD	Bruxelles	25 Aug 00
		(50)	100th man 27:36.62, 200th man 27:47.16						

20,000m 1 HOUR

56:55.6	21 101m	Arturo	Barrios	MEX	12.12.63	1	La Flèche	30 Mar 91
57:24.19+	20 944	Jos	Hermens	NED	8.1.50	1	Papendal	1 May 76
57:18.4+	20 943	Dionísio	Castro	POR	22.11.63	1	La Flèche	31 Mar 90
57:28.7+	20 855	Carl	Thackery	GBR	14.10.62	2	La Flèche	31 Mar 90
57:44.4+	20 784	Gaston	Roelants	BEL	5.2.37	1	Bruxelles	20 Sep 72
57:48.7		Toshihiko	Seko	JPN	15.7.56	1	Odawara	11 May 85
58:01.8		Yutaka	Kanai	JPN	16.10.59	2	Odawara	11 May 85
58:05.3	20 639	Sammy	Nyangicha	KEN	10.11.62	2	La Flèche	30 Mar 91
58:10.8	20 620	Godfrey	Kiprotich	KEN	23.11.64	3	La Flèche	30 Mar 91
58:18.4+	20 601	Bertrand	Itsweire	FRA	30.8.65	3	La Flèche	31 Mar 90

HALF MARATHON

Included in these lists are the slightly downhill courses: Newcastle to South Shields 30.5m, Tokyo 33m. Lisboa 40m

59:06		Paul	Tergat	KEN	17.6.69	1		Lisboa	26 Mar 00
59:17			Tergat			1		Milano	4 Apr 98
59:20		Hendrick	Ramaala	RSA	2.2.72	2		Lisboa	26 Mar 00
59:22			Tergat			1	Stra	Milano	17 Apr 99
59:31		Patrick	Ivuti	KEN	30.6.78	3		Lisboa	26 Mar 00
59:38		Faustin	Baha	TAN	30.5.82	4		Lisboa	26 Mar 00
59:43		António	Pinto	POR	22.3.66	1		Lisboa	15 Mar 98
59:47		Moses	Tanui	KEN	20.8.65	1		Milano	3 Apr 93
59:51		William	Kiplagat	KEN	.72	5		Lisboa	26 Mar 00
59:51	w	Tesfaye	Tolla	ETH	19.10.74	1		Malmö	12 Jun 00
59:56			Tergat			1		Milano	1 Apr 95
59:56		Shem	Kororia	KEN	25.9.72	1	WCh	Kosice	4 Oct 97
59:58			Tanui			2	WCh	Kosice	4 Oct 97
60:00		Kenneth	Cheruiyot (10)	KEN	2.8.74	3	WCh	Kosice	4 Oct 97
60:00	w	Philip	Rugut	KEN	18.5.77	2		Malmö	12 Jun 00
60:01		Paul	Koech	KEN	25.6.69	1	WCh	Uster	27 Sep 98
60:01		Japhet	Kosgei	KEN	68	1		Lisboa	21 Mar 99
60:02		Benson	Masya	KEN	14.5.70	1	GNR	South Shields	18 Sep 94
60:02		Darren	Wilson	AUS	9.8.68	1		Tokyo	19 Jan 97
60:03			Tanui			2	GNR	South Shields	18 Sep 94
60:04		Joseph	Kimani	KEN	21.9.72	2		Lisboa	15 Mar 98
60:05			Rugut			1		Trieste	2 May 99
60:05	w		Baha			3		Malmö	12 Jun 00
60:06		Steve	Moneghetti	AUS	26.9.62	1		Tokyo	24 Jan 93
60:07			Ramaala			4	WCh	Kosice	4 Oct 97
60:09	Sh?	Paul	Evans	GBR	13.4.61	1		Marrakesh	15 Jan 95
60:11		Matthews	Temane	RSA	14.12.60	1	NC	East London	25 Jul 87
60:11		Zithulele	Sinqe	RSA	9.6.63	2	NC	East London	25 Jul 87
60:11		Todd	Williams	USA	7.3.69	2		Tokyo	24 Jan 93
60:12	Sh?	Laban	Chege	KEN	70	2		Marrakesh	15 Jan 95
		(30/20)							
60:14		Armando	Quintanilla	MEX	19.4.68	1		Tokyo	21 Jan 96
60:15		Sammy	Korir	KEN	12.12.71	1	RdVin	Grevenmacher	27 Sep 98
60:17		Dionicio	Cerón	MEX	9.10.65	3		Tokyo	24 Jan 93
60:18		Mohamed	Mourhit	BEL	10.10.70	5	WCh	Kosice	4 Oct 97
60:23		Vincent	Rousseau	BEL	29.7.62	1		Tokyo	23 Jan 94
60:23		Gert	Thys	RSA	12.11.71	6	WCh	Kosice	4 Oct 97
60:24		Philip	Tarus	KEN	11.9.74	2		Milano	4 Apr 98
60:24		Khalid	Skah	MAR	29.1.67	3	WCh	Uster	27 Sep 98

Mark	Wind	Name		Nat	Born	Pos	Meet	Venue	Date
60:24		Elijah	Lagat	KEN	72	1		Grevenmacher	26 Sep 99
60:26		Simon	Lopuyet	KEN	24.12.72	1		Lisboa	12 Mar 95
		(30)							
60:26		Tendai	Chimusasa	ZIM	28.1.71	1		Grevenmacher	24 Sep 95
60:26		Zebedayo	Bayo	TAN	20.5.76	3		Lisboa	15 Mar 98
60:27		Joseph	Kibor	KEN	22.12.72	2		Gualtieri	31 Mar 97
60:27		Khalid	Khannouchi	MAR/USA	22.12.71	1		Philadelphia	28 Sep 97
60:27		Josephat	Kiprono	KEN	12.12.73	4		Lisboa	15 Mar 98
60:28		Germán	Silva	MEX	9.1.68	2	WCh	Oslo	24 Sep 94
60:29	w	Róbert	Stefko	SVK	28.5.68	4		Malmö	12 Jun 00
60:30		Eduardo do	Nascimento	BRA	2.8.72	5		Lisboa	15 Mar 98
60:30		Ken-ichi	Takahashi	JPN	16.1.73	1		Tokyo	10 Jan 00
60:30		Gezahegne	Abera	ETH	23.4.78	5		Malmö	12 Jun 00
		(40)							
60:31		Julius	Korir	KEN	12.5.58	1		Grevenmacher	22 Sep 91
60:31		Ibrahim	Seïd	ETH	65	4	WCh	Uster	27 Sep 98
60:32		Peter	Ndirangu	KEN	24.5.71	6		Lisboa	15 Mar 98
60:33		Joseph	Keino	KEN	.63	2		Grevenmacher	22 Sep 91
60:34		Carsten	Eich	GER	9.1.70	1		Berlin	4 Apr 93
60:36		Thomas	Osano	KEN	4.6.70	2		Grevenmacher	24 Sep 95
60:39		Daniel	Njenga	KEN	7.5.76	2		Tokyo	21 Jan 96
60:39		Simon	Bor	KEN	13.2.69	2		Grevenmacher	26 Sep 99
60:40		Antonio	Silio	ARG	9.5.66	2	WC	South Shields	20 Sep 92
60:42		Arturo	Barrios	MEX	12.12.62	2		Tokyo	26 Jan 92
		(50)	100th man 61:03, 200th man 61:28						
60:42		Andrew	Masai	KEN	13.12.60	2		Milano	3 Apr 93
60:42		Sammy	Lelei	KEN	14.8.64	2		Berlin	4 Apr 93
60:42		Sakae	Osaki	JPN	18.8.64	4		Tokyo	21 Jan 96
60:42		Toshiyuki	Hayata	JPN	2.5.68	5		Tokyo	21 Jan 96
Short courses									
58:51		Paul	Tergat	KEN	17.6.69	1	Stra	Milano 49m sh	30 Mar 96
59:24		Sammy	Lelei	KEN	14.8.64	1		Lisboa 97m	13 Mar 93
59:46		Josephat	Kiprono	KEN	12.12.73	2	Stra	Milano 49m	30 Mar 96
Downhill: 59:53		Benoit	Zwierzchlewski	FRA	19.8.76	1		Las Vegas	9 Feb 97

MARATHON

Note Boston marathon is downhill overall (139m) and, as a point-to-point course, in some years, such as 1994, has been strongly wind-aided - next bests are shown if to standard as a supplement.
In second column: L = loop course or start and finish within 30%, P = point-to-point or start and finish more than 30% apart, D = point-to-point and downhil over 1/1000

Mark		Name		Nat	Born	Pos	Meet	Venue	Date
2:05:42	L WR	Khalid	Khannouchi	MAR/USA	22.12.71	1		Chicago	24 Oct 99
2:06:05	L WR	Ronaldo da	Costa	BRA	7.6.70	1		Berlin	20 Sep 98
2:06:16	L	Moses	Tanui	KEN	20.8.65	2		Chicago	24 Oct 99
2:06:33	L	Gert	Thys	RSA	12.11.71	1		Tokyo	14 Feb 99
2:06:36	L	António	Pinto	POR	22.3.66	1		London	16 Apr 00
2:06:44	L	Josephat	Kiprono	KEN	12.12.73	1		Berlin	26 Sep 99
2:06:47	L	Fred	Kiprop	KEN	3.6.74	1		Amsterdam	17 Oct 99
2:06:49	L	Tesfaye	Jifar	ETH	23.4.76	2		Amsterdam	17 Oct 99
2:06:50	L WR	Belayneh	Dinsamo	ETH	28.6.65	1		Rotterdam	17 Apr 88
2:06:50	L	William	Kiplagat	KEN	72	3		Amsterdam	17 Oct 99
		(10)							
2:06:51	L	Atsushi	Fujita	JPN	6.11.76	1		Fukuoka	3 Dec 00
2:06:54	L	Ondoro	Osoro	KEN	3.12.67	1		Chicago	11 Oct 98
2:06:57	L	Takayuki	Inubushi	JPN	11.8.72	2		Berlin	26 Sep 99
2:06:57	L	Tesfaye	Tolla	ETH	19.10.74	4		Amsterdam	17 Oct 99
2:07:01	L		Khannouchi			1		Chicago	22 Oct 00
2:07:02	L	Sammy	Lelei	KEN	14.8.64	1		Berlin	24 Sep 95
2:07:07	L	Ahmed	Salah	DJI	31.12.56	2		Rotterdam	17 Apr 88
2:07:09	L	Japheth	Kosgei	KEN	68	1		Rotterdam	18 Apr 99
2:07:10	L		Khannouchi			1		Chicago	19 Oct 97
2:07:12	L WR	Carlos	Lopes	POR	18.2.47	1		Rotterdam	20 Apr 85
2:07:13	L	Steve	Jones	GBR	4.8.55	1		Chicago	20 Oct 85
2:07:15	D	Cosmas	Ndeti (20)	KEN	24.11.71	1		Boston	18 Apr 94
2:07:15	L		Japheth Kosgei			1		Tokyo	13 Feb 00
2:07:19	D	Andrés	Espinosa	MEX	4.2.63	2		Boston	18 Apr 94
2:07:19	L		Khannouchi			2		Chicago	11 Oct 98
2:07:20	L	Vincent	Rousseau	BEL	29.7.62	2		Berlin	24 Sep 95
2:07:20	L		Lee Bong-ju	KOR	11.10.70	2		Tokyo	13 Feb 00

Mark	Wind	Name		Nat	Born	Pos	Meet	Venue	Date
2:07:20	L		Lee Bong-ju	KOR	11.10.70	2		Tokyo	13 Feb 00
2:07:23	L	Fabián	Roncero	ESP	19.10.70	2		Rotterdam	18 Apr 99
2:07:26	L		Roncero			1		Rotterdam	19 Apr 98
2:07:27	L		J Kiprono			2		Berlin	20 Sep 98
		(30/24)							
2:07:28	L	Josiah	Thugwane	RSA	15.4.71	1		Fukuoka	7 Dec 97
2:07:33	L	Abdelkader	El Mouaziz	MAR	1.1.69	2		London	16 Apr 00
2:07:35	L	Taisuke	Kodama	JPN	26.7.58	1		Beijing	19 Oct 86
2:07:35	L	Abebe	Mekonnen	ETH	9.1.64	1		Beijing	16 Oct 88
2:07:37	D	Joseph	Chebet	KEN	23.8.70	2		Boston	20 Apr 98
2:07:40	L	Hiromi	Taniguchi	JPN	5.4.60	2		Beijing	16 Oct 88
		(30)							
2:07:41	L	Elijah	Lagat	KEN	19.6.66	1		Berlin	28 Sep 97
2:07:41	L	Simon	Biwott	KEN	3.3.70	4		Rotterdam	18 Apr 99
2:07:43	L	Erick	Kimaiyo	KEN	8.7.69	2		Berlin	28 Sep 97
2:07:47	L	Antonio	Peña	ESP	26.8.70	2		Berlin	10 Sep 00
2:07:49	L		Kim Yi-yong	KOR	20.9.73	4		Rotterdam	18 Apr 99
2:07:51	D	Robert	de Castella	AUS	27.2.57	1		Boston	21 Apr 86
2:07:51	L	Domingos	Castro	POR	22.11.63	1		Rotterdam	20 Apr 97
2:07:54	L	Alejandro	Gómez	ESP	11.4.67	2		Rotterdam	20 Apr 97
2:07:54	L	Gezhange	Abera	ETH	78	1		Fukuoka	5 Dec 99
2:07:55	L	Mohamed	Ouaadi	FRA	1.1.69	2		Fukuoka	5 Dec 99
		(40)							
2:07:57	L	Kunimitsu	Ito	JPN	6.1.55	2		Beijing	19 Oct 86
2:07:57	L	Stefano	Baldini	ITA	25.5.71	2		London	13 Apr 97
2:07:57	L	Abel	Antón	ESP	24.10.62	1		London	26 Apr 98
2:07:59	L	Joseph	Kahugu	KEN	7.6.71	4		Chicago	11 Oct 98
2:08:01	P	Juma	Ikangaa	TAN	19.7.57	1		New York	5 Nov 89
2:08:01	L	Alberto	Juzdado	ESP	20.8.66	1		Tokyo	8 Feb 98
2:08:02	L	Sammy	Korir	KEN	12.12.71	3		Rotterdam	20 Apr 97
2:08:02	L	Peter	Githuka	KEN	14.2.69	4		Chicago	22 Oct 00
2:08:04	D	Zithulele	Sinqe	RSA	9.6.63	1	NC	Port Elizabeth	3 May 86
2:08:05	L	Martin	Fíz	ESP	3.3.63	1		Otsu	2 Mar 97
		(50)	100th man 2:08:49, 200th man 2:09:54						
2:08:05	L	Hiroshi	Miki	JPN	10.6.75	2		Tokyo	14 Feb 99
Drugs Disqualification									
2:07:37		Julio	Rey ¶	ESP	13.1.72	(3)		Rotterdam	18 Apr 99

2000 METRES STEEPLECHASE

Mark	Name		Nat	Born	Pos	Meet	Venue	Date
5:14.43	Julius	Kariuki	KEN	12.6.61	1		Rovereto	21 Aug 90
5:16.22	Phillip	Barkutwo	KEN	6.10.66	2		Rovereto	21 Aug 90
5:16.85	Eliud	Barngetuny	KEN	20.5.73	1		Parma	13 Jun 95
5:18.28	Richard	Kosgei	KEN	29.12.70	2		Parma	13 Jun 95
5:18.36	Alessandro	Lambruschini	ITA	7.1.65	1		Verona	12 Sep 89
5:18.38	Azzedine	Brahmi	ALG	13.9.66	1		Verona	17 Jun 92
5:19.21	Joseph	Keter	KEN	13.6.69	3		Rovereto	23 Aug 95
5:19.68	Samson	Obwocha	KEN	7.10.54	1		Birmingham	19 Jul 86
5:19.78	Paul	Kosgei	KEN	22.4.78	1		La Spezia	20 Jun 98
5:19.86	Mark	Rowland	GBR	7.3.63	1	McV	London (CP)	28 Aug 88

3000 METRES STEEPLECHASE

Mark		Name		Nat	Born	Pos	Meet	Venue	Date
7:55.72	WR	Bernard	Barmasai	KEN	6.5.74	1	ASV	Köln	24 Aug 97
7:56.16		Moses	Kiptanui	KEN	1.10.70	2	ASV	Köln	24 Aug 97
7:58.98			Barmasai			1	Herc	Monaco	4 Aug 99
7:59.08	WR	Wilson	Boit Kipketer	KEN	6.10.73	1	WK	Zürich	13 Aug 97
7:59.18	WR		Kiptanui			1	WK	Zürich	16 Aug 95
7.59.52			Kiptanui			1	VD	Bruxelles	25 Aug 95
8:00.35			Barmasai			2	WK	Zürich	13 Aug 97
8:00.54			Kiptanui			1		Rieti	3 Sep 97
8:00.67			Barmasai			1	Herc	Monaco	8 Aug 98
8:00.78			Kiptanui			3	WK	Zürich	13 Aug 97
8:01.05			Boit Kipketer			1		Stuttgart	19 Jul 98
8:01.53			Barmasai			1	Nik	Nice	16 Jul 98
8:01.80			Kiptanui			1	DNG	Stockholm	7 Jul 97
8:01.98			Barmasai			1	WK	Zürich	12 Aug 98
8:02.08	WR		Kiptanui			1	WK	Zürich	19 Aug 92
8:02.45			Kiptanui			1	GPF	Monaco	9 Sep 95
8:02.76			Barmasai			1	Herc	Monaco	18 Aug 00
8:02.77			Kipketer			2	DNG	Stockholm	7 Jul 97

Mark	Wind	Name		Nat	Born	Pos	Meet	Venue	Date
8:02.81			Barmasai			1		Paris	29 Jul 98
8:02.85			Kiptanui			1	Herc	Monaco	16 Aug 97
8:02.90		Brahim	Boulami	MAR	20.4.72	2	Herc	Monaco	18 Aug 00
8:02.94			Barmasai			2	Herc	Monaco	16 Aug 97
8:03.08			Barmasai			1	VD	Bruxelles	3 Sep 99
8:03.30			Barmasai			1	GGala	Roma	7 Jul 99
8:03.30			Boulami			1	Nik	Nice	8 Jul 00
8:03.36			Kiptanui			1	Bisl	Oslo	21 Jul 95
8:03.41		Patrick	Sang	KEN	11.4.64	3	ASV	Köln	24 Aug 97
8:03.51			Barmasai			3	DNG	Stockholm	7 Jul 97
8:03.57		Ali	Ezzine	MAR	3.9.78	1	Gaz	Saint-Denis	23 Jun 00
8:03.74		Raymond	Yator	KEN	7.4.81	3	Herc	Monaco	18 Aug 00
		(30/7)							
8:03.89		John	Kosgei	KEN	13.7.73	3	Herc	Monaco	16 Aug 97
8:03.92		Reuben	Kosgei	KEN	2.8.79	2	Gaz	Saint-Denis	23 Jun 00
8:05.01		Eliud	Barngetuny	KEN	20.5.73	1	Herc	Monaco	25 Jul 95
		(10)							
8:05.35	WR	Peter	Koech	KEN	18.2.58	1	DNG	Stockholm	3 Jul 89
8:05.37		Philip	Barkutwo	KEN	6.10.66	2		Rieti	6 Sep 92
8:05.4	WR	Henry	Rono	KEN	12.2.52	1		Seattle	13 May 78
8:05.43		Christopher	Kosgei	KEN	14.8.74	2	WK	Zürich	11 Aug 99
8:05.51		Julius	Kariuki	KEN	12.6.61	1	OG	Seoul	30 Sep 88
8:05.99		Joseph	Keter	KEN	13.6.69	1	Herc	Monaco	10 Aug 96
8:06.77		Gideon	Chirchir	KEN	24.2.66	2	WK	Zürich	16 Aug 95
8:06.88		Richard	Kosgei	KEN	29.12.70	2	GPF	Monaco	9 Sep 95
8:07.13		Paul	Kosgei	KEN	22.4.78	2	GP II	Saint-Denis	3 Jul 99
8:07.21		Kipkirui	Misoi	KEN	23.12.78	2	GGala	Roma	30 Jun 00
		(20)							
8:07.62		Joseph	Mahmoud	FRA	13.12.55	1	VD	Bruxelles	24 Aug 84
8:07.96		Mark	Rowland	GBR	7.3.63	3	OG	Seoul	30 Sep 88
8:08.02	WR	Anders	Gärderud	SWE	28.8.46	1	OG	Montreal	28 Jul 76
8:08.12		Matthew	Birir	KEN	5.7.72	3	GGala	Roma	8 Jun 95
8:08.26		Saad Shaddad	Al-Asmari	KSA	24.9.68	6	DNG	Stockholm	7 Jul 97
8:08.57		Francesco	Panetta	ITA	10.1.63	1	WCh	Roma	5 Sep 87
8:08.78		Alessandro	Lambruschini	ITA	7.1.65	3	WCh	Stuttgart	21 Aug 93
8:09.02		Abdelaziz	Sahere	MAR	18.9.67	5	GGala	Roma	8 Jun 95
8:09.03		Elarbi	Khattabi	MAR	16.5.67	3	GGala	Roma	7 Jul 99
8:09.11		Bronislaw	Malinowski	POL	4.6.51	2	OG	Montreal	28 Jul 76
		(30)							
8:09.17		Henry	Marsh	USA	15.3.54	1	R-W	Koblenz	28 Aug 85
8:09.18		Boguslaw	Maminski	POL	18.12.55	2	VD	Bruxelles	24 Aug 84
8:09.48		Damian	Kallabis	GER	10.6.73	4	WK	Zürich	11 Aug 99
8:09.54		Johnstone	Kipkoech	KEN	20.12.68	2	VD	Bruxelles	25 Aug 95
8:09.76		Mark	Croghan	USA	8.1.68	5	WCh	Stuttgart	21 Aug 93
8:09.77		Luis Miguel	Martín	ESP	11.1.72	5	Herc	Monaco	18 Aug 00
8:10.01		William	van Dijck	BEL	24.1.61	1	VD	Bruxelles	5 Sep 86
8:10.10		Hicham	Bouaouiche	MAR	16.6.74	3	Nik	Nice	16 Jul 98
8:10.23		Laïd	Bessou	ALG	5.2.76	8	Herc	Monaco	18 Aug 00
8:10.32		Hagen	Melzer	GDR	16.6.59	2	WCh	Roma	5 Sep 87
		(40)							
8:10.36		Frank	Baumgartl	GDR	29.5.55	3	OG	Montreal	28 Jul 76
8:10.41		Julius	Chelule	KEN	25.12.78	6	VD	Bruxelles	3 Sep 99
8:10.46			Sun Ripeng	CHN	25.1.74	1	NG	Shanghai	19 Oct 97
8:10.74		William	Mutwol	KEN	10.10.67	3	OG	Barcelona	7 Aug 92
8:10.83		Günther	Weidlinger	AUT	5.4.78	4h1	WCh	Sevilla	21 Aug 99
8:11.04		Krzysztof	Wesolowski	POL	9.12.56	1	VD	Bruxelles	30 Aug 85
8:11.14		Jonathan	Kandie	KEN	20.12.67	3	Herc	Monaco	4 Aug 99
8:11.27		Azzedine	Brahmi	ALG	13.9.66	1	Bisl	Oslo	4 Jul 92
8:11.80		Julius	Korir	KEN	21.4.60	1	OG	Los Angeles	10 Aug 84
8:11.85		Giuseppe	Maffei	ITA	28.1.74	2	ASV	Köln	8 Aug 99
		(50)	100th man 8:17.22, 200th man 8:22.82						

110 METRES HURDLES

Mark	Wind	Name		Nat	Born	Pos	Meet	Venue	Date
12.91	WR 0.5	Colin	Jackson	GBR	18.2.67	1	WCh	Stuttgart	20 Aug 93
12.92	WR -0.1	Roger	Kingdom	USA	26.8.62	1	WK	Zürich	16 Aug 89
12.92	0.9	Allen	Johnson	USA	1.3.71	1	NC	Atlanta	23 Jun 96
12.92	0.2		Johnson			1	VD	Bruxelles	23 Aug 96
12.93	WR -0.2	Renaldo	Nehemiah	USA	24.3.59	1	WK	Zürich	19 Aug 81
12.93	0.0		Johnson			1	WCh	Athína	7 Aug 97

Mark	Wind	Name		Nat	Born	Pos	Meet	Venue	Date
12.94	1.6	Jack	Pierce	USA	23.9.62	1s2	NC	Atlanta	22 Jun 96
12.95	0.6		Johnson			1	OG	Atlanta	29 Jul 96
12.97A	2.0		Kingdom			1		Sestriere	11 Aug 88
12.97A	-1.6		Jackson			1A		Sestriere	28 Jul 93
12.97	-0.5		Johnson			1		Stuttgart	13 Jul 97
12.97	1.5		Johnson			1	NC	Sacramento	23 Jul 00
12.98	1.5		Kingdom			1	OG	Seoul	26 Sep 88
12.98	0.2		Jackson			1	TOTO	Tokyo	15 Sep 94
12.98	0.2		Johnson			1	ASV	Köln	18 Aug 95
12.98	-0.3		Johnson			1rA	WK	Zürich	12 Aug 98
12.98	0.6	Mark	Crear	USA	2.10.68	1		Zagreb	5 Jul 99
12.99	1.2		Jackson			1	VD	Bruxelles	3 Sep 93
12.99	-0.3		Jackson			1		Madrid	6 Sep 94
13.00 WR	0.9		Nehemiah			1	Pepsi	Westwood	6 May 79
13.00	0.5	Anthony	Jarrett	GBR	13.8.68	2	WCh	Stuttgart	20 Aug 93
13.00	-0.1		Johnson			1	WCh	Göteborg	12 Aug 95
13.00	-0.3		Crear			2rA	WK	Zürich	12 Aug 98
13.00	0.6	Anier	García	CUB	9.3.76	1	OG	Sydney	25 Sep 00
13.01	0.3	Larry	Wade	USA	22.11.74	1rA	Athl	Lausanne	2 Jul 99
13.01	0.8		Johnson			1	GGala	Roma	7 Jul 99
13.02	0.6		Kingdom			1	ISTAF	Berlin	18 Aug 89
13.02	0.9		Jackson			1A	ISTAF	Berlin	30 Aug 94
13.02	1.5		Crear			1		Luzern	27 Jun 95
13.02	1.9		Jackson			1s1	EC	Budapest	22 Aug 98
13.02	1.5		Jackson			1	EC	Budapest	22 Aug 98
		(31/9)							
13.03	-0.2	Greg	Foster (10)	USA	4.8.58	2	WK	Zürich	19 Aug 81
13.03	1.0	Reggie	Torian	USA	22.4.75	1	NC	New Orleans	21 Jun 98
13.05	1.4	Tony	Dees	USA	6.8.63	1		Vigo	23 Jul 91
13.05	-0.8	Florian	Schwarthoff	GER	7.5.68	1	NC	Bremen	2 Jul 95
13.08	1.2	Mark	McKoy	CAN	10.12.61	1	BNP	Villeneuve d'Ascq	2 Jul 93
13.11	1.4	Dominique	Arnold	USA	14.9.73	2		Leverkusen	20 Aug 00
13.12	1.5	Falk	Balzer	GER	14.12.73	2	EC	Budapest	22 Aug 98
13.12	1.0	Duane	Ross	USA	5.12.72	3	WCh	Sevilla	25 Aug 99
13.13	1.6	Igor	Kovác	SVK	12.5.69	1	DNG	Stockholm	7 Jul 97
13.15	0.3	Robin	Korving	NED	29.7.74	5rA	Athl	Lausanne	2 Jul 99
13.16	0.6	Terrence	Trammell	USA	23.11.78	2	OG	Sydney	25 Sep 00
		(20)							
13.17	-0.4	Sam	Turner	USA	17.6.57	2	Pepsi	Westwood	15 May 83
13.17	0.0	Tonie	Campbell	USA	14.6.60	3	WK	Zürich	17 Aug 88
13.17	0.5	Courtney	Hawkins	USA	11.7.67	1		Ingolstadt	26 Jul 98
13.17	0.4	Mike	Fenner	GER	24.4.71	1		Leverkusen	9 Aug 98
13.18	0.5	Emilio	Valle	CUB	21.4.67	3s1	OG	Atlanta	29 Jul 96
13.19	1.9	Steve	Brown	USA/TRI	6.1.69	1h4	NC	Atlanta	21 Jun 96
13.20	2.0	Stéphane	Caristan	FRA	31.5.64	1	EC	Stuttgart	30 Aug 86
13.20	1.8	Aleksandr	Markin ¶	RUS	8.9.62	1	Znam	Leningrad	11 Jun 88
13.20	1.7	Larry	Harrington	USA	24.11.70	2s1	NC	Atlanta	22 Jun 96
13.21 WR	0.6	Alejandro	Casañas	CUB	29.1.54	1	WUG	Sofiya	21 Aug 77
		(30)							
13.21	1.8	Vladimir	Shishkin	RUS	12.1.64	2	Znam	Leningrad	11 Jun 88
13.21	0.9	Eugene	Swift	USA	14.9.64	3	NC	Atlanta	23 Jun 96
13.22	-0.2	Terry	Reese	USA	20.6.67	2	ASV	Köln	24 Aug 97
13.22	1.5	Dawane	Wallace	USA	30.12.76	4	NC	Sacramento	23 Jul 00
13.24 WR	0.3	Rod	Milburn	USA	18.5.50	1	OG	München	7 Sep 72
13.24	2.0	Arthur	Blake	USA	19.8.66	2	Athl	Lausanne	24 Jun 88
13.24	1.1	Yoel	Hernández	CUB	12.12.77	2	PAm	Winnipeg	30 Jul 99
13.25	0.1	Andre	Phillips	USA	5.9.59	1	USOF	Baton Rouge	28 Jul 85
13.25	-0.1		Li Tong	CHN	6.5.67	2rA	Gugl	Linz	4 Jul 94
13.25	1.9	Jonathan	N'senga	BEL	21.4.73	3s1	EC	Budapest	22 Aug 98
		(40)							
13.25	0.2	Stanislavs	Olijars	LAT	22.3.79	2	Herc	Monaco	18 Aug 00
13.26	1.6	Willie	Gault	USA	5.9.60	1	USOF	Indianapolis	25 Jul 82
13.26	0.0	Igor	Kazanov	LAT	24.9.63	2s1	WCh	Stuttgart	19 Aug 93
13.26	1.7	Erik	Batte	CUB	10.12.74	4s2	OG	Atlanta	29 Jul 96
13.26	0.0	Dan	Philibert	FRA	6.8.70	5	WCh	Athína	7 Aug 97
13.27	1.8	Sergey	Usov	BLR	16.1.64	3	Znam	Leningrad	11 Jun 88
13.27	1.2	Artur	Kohutek	POL	1.5.71	2q2	WCh	Athína	5 Aug 97
13.27	1.6	Chris	Phillips	USA	24.7.72	3		Palo Alto	1 Jul 00
13.28	1.1	Guy	Drut	FRA	6.12.50	1	NC	St. Etienne	29 Jun 75

Mark	Wind	Name		Nat	Born	Pos	Meet	Venue	Date
13.28	1.0	Andrey	Prokofyev	RUS	6.6.59	1r2	GWG	Moskva	6 Jul 86
13.28	-1.0	Philippe	Tourret	FRA	8.7.67	1	Herc	Monaco	12 Aug 90
		(51)	100th man 13.42, 200th man 13.55						
Rolling start but accepted by race officials									
13.10A	2.0	Falk	Balzer	GER	14.12.73	1	WCp	Johannesburg	13 Sep 98
Doubtful timing									
13.06	1.3	Mike	Fenner	GER	24.4.71	1		Scheessel	4 Jun 95
13.08	1.3	Eric	Kaiser	GER	7.3.71	2		Scheessel	4 Jun 95
Wind-assisted marks to 13.26									
12.87	2.6	Roger	Kingdom	USA	26.8.62	1	WCp	Barcelona	10 Sep 89
12.91	3.5	Renaldo	Nehemiah	USA	24.3.59	1	NCAA	Champaign	1 Jun 79
12.94A	2.8		Jackson			1rA		Sestriere	31 Jul 94
12.95	2.6		Jackson			2	WCp	Barcelona	10 Sep 89
12.99	2.7		Jackson			1	v3N	Birmingham	23 Jun 89
13.00	3.5		Nehemiah			1	USOF	Syracuse	26 Jul 81
13.00	2.7		Kingdom			1		Sacramento	21 Jul 84
13.00	3.8		Johnson			1s1	NC	Sacramento	17 Jun 95
13.06	2.1	Mark	McKoy	CAN	10.12.61	1	Gugl	Linz	13 Aug 92
13.14	2.9	Igor	Kazanov	LAT	24.9.63	1r1	Znam	Leningrad	8 Jun 86
13.15	2.1	Courtney	Hawkins	USA	11.7.67	1		Salamanca	10 Jul 98
13.18	4.7	Robert	Reading	USA	9.6.67	1		Azusa	23 Apr 94
13.20	2.4	Arthur	Blake	USA	19.8.66	2	IAC	Edinburgh	6 Jul 90
13.20	3.1	Yoel	Hernández	CUB	12.12.77	2		Camagüey	10 Mar 00
13.21A	2.5	Eric	Cannon	USA	2.3.67	2	NCAA	Provo	3 Jun 89
13.24	2.4	Glenn	Terry	USA	10.2.71	1s2	WUG	Buffalo	18 Jul 93
13.25	2.7	Tomasz	Scigaczewski	POL	18.11.78	1		Grudziadz	20 Jun 98
13.26A	2.6	Antti	Haapakoski	FIN	6.2.71	1rB		Sestriere	31 Jul 94
13.26	7.8		Chen Yanhao	CHN	7.2.72	1		Maebashi	27 Apr 96
Hand timing									
12.8	1.0	Renaldo	Nehemiah	USA	24.3.59	1		Kingston	11 May 79
13.0 WR	1.8	Guy	Drut	FRA	6.12.50	1	ISTAF	Berlin	22 Aug 75
13.0	1.0	Greg	Foster	USA	4.8.58	2		Kingston	11 May 79
13.0	0.8	Mark	McKoy	CAN	10.12.61	1	Nik	Nice	16 Jul 85
13.0		Stéphane	Caristan	FRA	25.1.64	1		Creteil	3 May 86
13.0		Vladimir	Shishkin	RUS	12.1.64	1		Stayki	7 May 88
13.0* WR	2.0	Rod	Milburn	USA	18.5.50	1s1	AAU	Eugene	25 Jun 71
13.0	0.4	Tomasz	Scigaczewski	POL	18.11.78	1	NC	Wroclaw	28 Jun 98
Wind-assisted									
12.8	2.4	Colin	Jackson	GBR	18.2.67	1		Sydney	10 Jan 90
12.9	4.1	Mark	Crear	USA	2.10.68	1rA	S&W	Modesto	8 May 93
13.0		Alejandro	Casañas	CUB	29.1.54	1	Barr	La Habana	22 May 77
13.0		Tonie	Campbell	USA	14.6.60	1		Los Angeles	16 Jul 86
13.0		Keith	Talley	USA	28.1.64	1		Tuscaloosa	26 Mar 88
13.0	4.1		Li Tong	CHN	6.5.67	2rA	S&W	Modesto	8 May 93

200 METRES HURDLES

Mark	Wind	Name		Nat	Born	Pos	Meet	Venue	Date
22.55		Laurent	Ottoz	ITA	10.4.70	1		Milano	31 May 95
22.59	0.2	Darryl	Wohlsen	AUS	6.3.73	1		Brisbane	14 Mar 96
22.63	-0.3	Colin	Jackson	GBR	18.2.67	1		Cardiff	1 Jun 91
22.68		Stefano	Cellario	ITA	16.3.72	1		Modena	17 Sep 97
22.69 WR	0.0	Glenn	Davis	USA	12.9.34	1		Bern	20 Aug 60

400 METRES HURDLES

Mark	Wind	Name		Nat	Born	Pos	Meet	Venue	Date
46.78 WR		Kevin	Young	USA	16.9.66	1	OG	Barcelona	6 Aug 92
47.02 WR		Edwin	Moses	USA	31.8.55	1		Koblenz	31 Aug 83
47.03		Bryan	Bronson	USA	9.9.72	1	NC	New Orleans	21 Jun 98
47.10		Samuel	Matete	ZAM	27.7.68	1rA	WK	Zürich	7 Aug 91
47.13 WR			Moses			1		Milano	3 Jul 80
47.14			Moses			1	Athl	Lausanne	14 Jul 81
47.15			Bronson			1	GWG	Uniondale, NY	19 Jul 98
47.17			Moses			1	ISTAF	Berlin	8 Aug 80
47.18			Young			1	WCh	Stuttgart	19 Aug 93
47.19		Andre	Phillips	USA	5.9.59	1	OG	Seoul	25 Sep 88
47.23		Amadou	Dia Bâ	SEN	22.9.58	2	OG	Seoul	25 Sep 88
47.27			Moses			1	ISTAF	Berlin	21 Aug 81
47.32			Moses			1		Koblenz	29 Aug 84
47.37			Moses			1	WCp	Roma	4 Sep 81
47.37			Moses			1	WK	Zürich	24 Aug 83
47.37			Moses			1	OT	Indianapolis	17 Jul 88

Mark Wind	Name		Nat	Born	Pos	Meet	Venue	Date
47.37		Young			1	Athl	Lausanne	7 Jul 93
47.37	Stéphane	Diagana	FRA	23.7.69	1	Athl	Lausanne	5 Jul 95
47.38		Moses			1	Athl	Lausanne	2 Sep 86
47.38	Danny	Harris	USA	7.9.65	1	Athl	Lausanne	10 Jul 91
47.40		Young			1	WK	Zürich	19 Aug 92
47.42		Young			1	ASV	Köln	16 Aug 92
47.43		Moses			1	ASV	Köln	28 Aug 83
47.45 WR		Moses			1	AAU	Westwood	11 Jun 77
47.46		Moses			1	WCh	Roma	1 Sep 87
47.48	Harald	Schmid	FRG	29.9.57	1	EC	Athína	8 Sep 82
47.48		Harris			2	WCh	Roma	1 Sep 87
47.48		Schmid			3	WCh	Roma	1 Sep 87
47.49		Harris			1	Athl	Lausanne	12 Jul 90
47.50		Moses			1	WCh	Helsinki	9 Aug 83
47.50	Angelo	Taylor	USA	29.12.78	1	OG	Sydney	27 Sep 00
	(31/10)							
47.53	Hadi Soua'an	Al-Somaily	KSA	30.12.76	2	OG	Sydney	27 Sep 00
47.54	Derrick	Adkins	USA	2.7.70	2	Athl	Lausanne	5 Jul 95
47.60	Winthrop	Graham	JAM	17.11.65	1	WK	Zürich	4 Aug 93
47.72	Fabrizio	Mori	ITA	28.6.69	1	WCh	Sevilla	27 Aug 99
47.75	David	Patrick	USA	12.6.60	4	OT	Indianapolis	17 Jul 88
47.81	Llewellyn	Herbert	RSA	21.7.77	3	OG	Sydney	27 Sep 00
47.82 WR	John	Akii-Bua	UGA	3.12.49	1	OG	München	2 Sep 72
47.82	Kriss	Akabusi	GBR	28.11.58	3	OG	Barcelona	6 Aug 92
47.91	Calvin	Davis	USA	2.4.72	1s2	OG	Atlanta	31 Jul 96
47.92	Aleksandr	Vasilyev	BLR	26.7.61	2	ECp	Moskva	17 Aug 85
	(20)							
47.94	Eric	Thomas	USA	1.12.73	1	GGala	Roma	30 Jun 00
47.97	Maurice	Mitchell	USA	14.5.71	2rA	WK	Zürich	14 Aug 96
47.97	Joey	Woody	USA	22.5.73	3	NC	New Orleans	21 Jun 98
47.98	Sven	Nylander	SWE	1.1.62	4	OG	Atlanta	1 Aug 96
48.04	Eronilde	de Araújo	BRA	31.12.70	2	Nik	Nice	12 Jul 95
48.04	James	Carter	USA	7.5.78	4	OG	Sydney	27 Sep 00
48.05	Ken	Harnden	ZIM	31.3.73	1	GP	Paris	29 Jul 98
48.06	Oleg	Tverdokhleb	UKR	3.11.69	1	EC	Helsinki	10 Aug 94
48.06	Ruslan	Mashchenko	RUS	11.11.71	1	GP II	Helsinki	13 Jun 98
48.12A WR	David	Hemery	GBR	18.7.44	1	OG	Ciudad de México	15 Oct 68
	(30)							
48.13	Dinsdale	Morgan	JAM	19.11.72	2	GGala	Roma	14 Jul 98
48.13	Marcel	Schelbert	SUI	26.2.76	3	WCh	Sevilla	27 Aug 99
48.14	Chris	Rawlinson	GBR	19.5.72	1rB	WK	Zürich	11 Aug 99
48.16	Tony	Rambo	USA	30.5.60	3s1	OT	Los Angeles	17 Jun 84
48.17	Pawel	Januszewski	POL	2.1.72	1	EC	Budapest	20 Aug 98
48.17A	Mubarak	Al-Nubi	QAT	30.12.77	2	WCp	Johannesburg	11 Sep 98
48.18	Torrance	Zellner	USA	6.1.70	4rA	WK	Zürich	14 Aug 96
48.24	Erick	Keter	KEN	22.7.66	2s2	WCh	Stuttgart	17 Aug 93
48.26	Kazuhiko	Yamazaki	JPN	10.5.71	3	GP	Osaka	8 May 99
48.27	Jirí	Muzík	CZE	1.9.76	3s3	WCh	Athína	3 Aug 97
	(40)							
48.28	Tranel	Hawkins	USA	17.9.62	3	OT	Los Angeles	18 Jun 84
48.28	Everson	Teixeira	BRA	23.11.74	2s2	OG	Atlanta	31 Jul 96
48.28	Rohan	Robinson	AUS	15.11.71	4s2	OG	Atlanta	31 Jul 96
48.30	Neil	Gardner	JAM	8.12.74	5s2	OG	Atlanta	31 Jul 96
48.30A	Ibou	Faye	SEN	13.12.69	1	AfG	Johannesburg	17 Sep 99
48.33	Felix	Sanchez	DOM	30.8.77	2	GP	Athína	28 Jun 00
48.34	Vasiliy	Arkhipenko	UKR	28.1.57	2	ECp	Torino	4 Aug 79
48.34	McClinton	Neal	USA	11.7.68	4rA	Athl	Lausanne	8 Jul 92
48.34	Shunji	Karube	JPN	8.5.69	1	NC	Tokyo	5 Oct 97
48.35	Niklas	Wallenlind	SWE	21.11.68	3s1	OG	Barcelona	5 Aug 92
	(50)	100th man 48.81, 200th man 49.37						
48.1 **Hand**	Jim	Bolding	USA	24.3.49	1		Milano	2 Jul 74

HIGH JUMP

Mark	Name		Nat	Born	Pos	Meet	Venue	Date
2.45 WR	Javier	Sotomayor	CUB	13.10.67	1		Salamanca	27 Jul 93
2.44 WR		Sotomayor			1	CAC	San Juan	29 Jul 89
2.43 WR		Sotomayor			1		Salamanca	8 Sep 88
2.43i		Sotomayor			1	WI	Budapest	4 Mar 89
2.42 WR	Patrik	Sjöberg	SWE	5.1.65	1	DNG	Stockholm	30 Jun 87
2.42i WR	Carlo	Thränhardt	FRG	5.7.57	1		Berlin	26 Feb 88

Mark Wind	Name		Nat	Born	Pos	Meet	Venue	Date
2.42		Sotomayor			1		Sevilla	5 Jun 94
2.41 WR	Igor	Paklin	KGZ	15.6.63	1	WUG	Kobe	4 Sep 85
2.41i		Sjöberg			1		Pireás	1 Feb 87
2.41i		Sotomayor			1	WI	Toronto	14 Mar 93
2.41		Sotomayor			1	NC	La Habana	25 Jun 94
2.41		Sotomayor			1	TSB	London (CP)	15 Jul 94
2.40 WR	Rudolf	Povarnitsyn	UKR	13.6.62	1		Donetsk	11 Aug 85
2.40i		Thränhardt			1		Simmerath	16 Jan 87
2.40i		Sjöberg			1		Berlin	27 Feb 87
2.40		Sotomayor			1	NC	La Habana	12 Mar 89
2.40		Sjöberg			1	ECp-B	Bruxelles	5 Aug 89
2.40		Sotomayor			1	AmCp	Bogota	13 Aug 89
2.40	Sorin	Matei	ROM	6.7.63	1	PTS	Bratislava	20 Jun 90
2.40i	Hollis	Conway	USA	8.1.67	1	WI	Sevilla	10 Mar 91
2.40		Sotomayor			1		Saint Denis	19 Jul 91
2.40	Charles	Austin	USA	19.12.67	1	WK	Zürich	7 Aug 91
2.40		Sotomayor			1	Barr	La Habana	22 May 93
2.40		Sotomayor			1	TSB	London (CP)	23 Jul 93
2.40		Sotomayor			1	WCh	Stuttgart	22 Aug 93
2.40i		Sotomayor			1		Wuppertal	4 Feb 94
2.40i		Sotomayor			1	TSB	Birmingham	26 Feb 94
2.40		Sotomayor			1		Eberstadt	10 Jul 94
2.40		Sotomayor			1	Nik	Nice	18 Jul 94
2.40		Sotomayor			1	GWG	Sankt-Peterburg	29 Jul 94
2.40		Sotomayor			1	WCp	London (CP)	11 Sep 94
2.40		Sotomayor			1	PAm	Mar del Plata	25 Mar 95
2.40	Vyacheslav	Voronin	RUS	5.4.74	1	BrGP	London (CP)	5 Aug 00
	(33/9)							
2.39 WR		Zhu Jianhua	CHN	29.5.63	1		Eberstadt	10 Jun 84
2.39i	Dietmar	Mögenburg	FRG	15.8.61	1		Köln	24 Feb 85
2.39i	Ralf	Sonn	GER	17.1.67	1		Berlin	1 Mar 91
2.38i	Gennadiy	Avdeyenko	UKR	4.11.63	2	WI	Indianapolis	7 Mar 87
2.38	Sergey	Malchenko	RUS	2.11.63	1		Banská Bystrica	4 Sep 88
2.38	Dragutin	Topic	YUG	12.3.71	1		Beograd	1 Aug 93
2.38i	Steve	Smith	GBR	29.3.73	2		Wuppertal	4 Feb 94
2.38i	Wolf-Hendrik	Beyer	GER	14.2.72	1		Weinheim	18 Mar 94
2.38	Troy	Kemp	BAH	18.6.66	1	Nik	Nice	12 Jul 95
2.38	Artur	Partyka	POL	25.7.69	1		Eberstadt	18 Aug 96
2.38i	Matt	Hemingway	USA	24.10.72	1	NC	Atlanta	4 Mar 00
	(20)							
2.37	Valeriy	Sereda	RUS	30.6.59	1		Rieti	2 Sep 84
2.37	Tom	McCants	USA	27.11.62	1	Owens	Columbus	8 May 88
2.37	Jerome	Carter	USA	25.3.63	2	Owens	Columbus	8 May 88
2.37	Sergey	Dymchenko	UKR	23.8.67	1		Kiyev	16 Sep 90
2.37i	Dalton	Grant	GBR	8.4.66	1	EI	Paris	13 Mar 94
2.37	Vyacheslav	Voronin	RUS	5.4.74	1	WCh	Sevilla	23 Aug 99
2.36 WR	Gerd	Wessig	GDR	16.7.59	1	OG	Moskva	1 Aug 80
2.36	Sergey	Zasimovich	KZK	6.9.62	1		Tashkent	5 May 84
2.36	Eddy	Annys	BEL	15.12.58	1		Ghent	26 May 85
2.36i	Jim	Howard	USA	11.9.59	1		Albuquerque	25 Jan 86
2.36i	Jan	Zvara	CZE	12.2.63	1	vGDR	Jablonec	14 Feb 87
	(30)							
2.36i	Gerd	Nagel	FRG	22.10.57	1		Sulingen	17 Mar 89
2.36	Nick	Saunders	BER	14.9.63	1	CG	Auckland	1 Feb 90
2.36	Doug	Nordquist	USA	20.12.58	2	TAC	Norwalk	15 Jun 90
2.36	Georgi	Dakov	BUL	21.10.67	2	VD	Bruxelles	10 Aug 90
2.36	Lábros	Papakóstas	GRE	20.10.69	1	NC	Athína	21 Jun 92
2.36i	Steinar	Hoen	NOR	8.2.71	1		Balingen	12 Feb 94
2.36	Tim	Forsyth	AUS	17.8.73	1	NC	Melbourne	2 Mar 97
2.36	Sergey	Klyugin	RUS	24.3.74	1	WK	Zürich	12 Aug 98
2.36	Konstantin	Matusevich	ISR	25.2.71	1		Perth	5 Feb 00
2.35i	Vladimir	Yashchenko	UKR	12.1.59	1	EI	Milano	12 Mar 78
	(40)							
2.35 WR	Jacek	Wszola	POL	30.12.56	1		Eberstadt	25 May 80
2.35i	Aleksandr	Kotovich	UKR	6.11.61	1		Vilnius	13 Jan 85
2.35i	Brent	Harken	USA	1.12.61	1		Moscow	15 Feb 91
2.35	Darrin	Plab	USA	26.9.70	2	NC	New Orleans	28 Jun 92
2.35i	Jean-Charles	Gicquel	FRA	24.2.67	2	EI	Paris	13 Feb 94

Mark Wind	Name		Nat	Born	Pos	Meet	Venue	Date
2.35	Konstantin	Matusevich	ISR	25.2.71	1		Byrkjelo	13 Jul 97
2.35	Martin	Buss	GER	7.4.76	1		Dortmund	26 Jun 99
2.35	Mark	Boswell	CAN	28.7.77	2	WCh	Sevilla	23 Aug 99
2.35	Nathan	Leeper	USA	13.6.77	1		Sacramento	21 May 00
		(48)	18 men at 2.34, 100th man 2.32, 200th man 2.29					

Best outdoor marks for athletes with indoor bests

Mark	Name	Pos	Meet	Venue	Date
2.39	Conway	1	USOF	Norman	30 Jul 89
2.38	Avdeyenko	2=	WCh	Roma	6 Sep 87
2.37	Thranhärdt	2		Rieti	2 Sep 84
2.37	Smith	1	WJ	Seoul	20 Sep 92
2.36	Mögenburg	3		Eberstadt	10 Jun 84
2.36	Howard	1		Rehlingen	8 Jun 87
2.36	Zvara	1		Praha	23 Aug 87
2.36	Grant	4	WCh	Tokyo	1 Sep 91
2.36	Hoen	1		Oslo	1 Jul 97
2.35	Nagel	1		Forbach	7 Aug 88

POLE VAULT

Mark Wind	Name		Nat	Born	Pos	Meet	Venue	Date
6.15i	Sergey	Bubka	UKR	4.12.63	1		Donetsk	21 Feb 93
6.14i		Bubka			1		Liévin	13 Feb 93
6.14A WR		Bubka			1		Sestriere	31 Jul 94
6.13i		Bubka			1		Berlin	21 Feb 92
6.13 WR		Bubka			1	TOTO	Tokyo	19 Sep 92
6.12i		Bubka			1	Mast	Grenoble	23 Mar 91
6.12 WR		Bubka			1		Padova	30 Aug 92
6.11i		S.Bubka			1		Donetsk	19 Mar 91
6.11 WR		Bubka			1		Dijon	13 Jun 92
6.10i		S.Bubka			1		San Sebastián	15 Mar 91
6.10 WR		Bubka			1	MAI	Malmö	5 Aug 91
6.09 WR		Bubka			1		Formia	8 Jul 91
6.08i		S.Bubka			1	NC	Volgograd	9 Feb 91
6.08 WR		Bubka			1	Znam	Moskva	9 Jun 91
6.07 WR		S.Bubka			1	Super	Shizuoka	6 May 91
6.06 WR		S.Bubka			1	Nik	Nice	10 Jul 88
6.05 WR		S.Bubka			1	PTS	Bratislava	9 Jun 88
6.05i		S.Bubka			1		Donetsk	17 Mar 90
6.05i		Bubka			1		Berlin	5 Mar 93
6.05		Bubka			1	GPF	London (CP)	10 Sep 93
6.05i		Bubka			1	Mast	Grenoble	6 Feb 94
6.05		Bubka			1	ISTAF	Berlin	30 Aug 94
6.05		Bubka			1	GPF	Fukuoka	13 Sep 97
6.05	Maksim	Tarasov	RUS	2.12.70	1	GP II	Athína	16 Jun 99
6.03 WR		S.Bubka			1	Ros	Praha	23 Jun 87
6.03i		S.Bubka			1		Osaka	11 Feb 89
6.03	Okkert	Brits	RSA	22.8.73	1	ASV	Köln	18 Aug 95
6.03	Jeff	Hartwig	USA	25.9.67	1		Jonesboro	14 Jun 00
6.02i	Rodion	Gataullin	RUS	23.11.65	1	NC	Gomel	4 Feb 89
6.02		Bubka			1	GP	Atlanta	18 May 96
6.02		Hartwig			1	NC	Eugene	27 Jun 99
6.02		Tarasov			1	WCh	Sevilla	26 Aug 99
	(32/5)							
6.01	Igor	Trandenkov	RUS	17.8.66	1	NC	Sankt Peterburg	4 Jul 96
6.00	Tim	Lobinger	GER	3.9.72	1	ASV	Köln	24 Aug 97
6.00	Dmitriy	Markov	BLR/AUS	14.3.75	1		Auckland (NS)	20 Feb 98
6.00i	Jean	Galfione	FRA	9.6.71	1	WI	Maebashi	6 Mar 99
5.98	Lawrence	Johnson	USA	7.5.74	1		Knoxville	25 May 96
	(10)							
5.97	Scott	Huffman	USA	30.11.64	1	NC	Knoxville	18 Jun 94
5.96	Joe	Dial	USA	26.10.62	1		Norman	18 Jun 87
5.95	Andrei	Tivontchik	GER	13.7.70	1	ASV	Köln	16 Aug 96
5.95	Michael	Stolle	GER	17.12.74	1	Herc	Monaco	18 Aug 00
5.94i	Philippe	Collet	FRA	13.12.63	1	Mast	Grenoble	10 Mar 90
5.93i	Billy	Olson	USA	19.7.58	1		East Rutherford	8 Feb 86
5.93	Danny	Ecker	GER	21.7.77	1		Ingolstadt	20 Jul 00
5.93	Romain	Mesnil	FRA	13.7.77	1	EU23	Göteborg	1 Aug 99
5.92	István	Bagyula	HUN	2.1.69	1	Gugl	Linz	5 Jul 91
5.92	Igor	Potapovich	KZK	6.9.67	2		Dijon	13 Jun 92
	(20)							
5.92	Dean	Starkey	USA	27.3.67	1	Banes	São Paulo	21 May 94
5.91 WR	Thierry	Vigneron	FRA	9.3.60	2	GGala	Roma	31 Aug 84
5.91i	Viktor	Ryzhenkov	UZB	25.8.66	2		San Sebastián	15 Mar 91
5.91A	Riaan	Botha	RSA	8.11.70	1		Pretoria	2 Apr 97

Mark	Wind	Name		Nat	Born	Pos	Meet	Venue	Date
5.90		Pierre	Quinon	FRA	20.2.62	2	Nik	Nice	16 Jul 85
5.90i		Ferenc	Salbert	FRA	5.8.60	1	Mast	Grenoble	14 Mar 87
5.90		Miroslaw	Chmara	POL	9.5.64	1	BNP	Villeneuve d'Ascq	27 Jun 88
5.90i		Grigoriy	Yegorov	KZK	12.1.67	1		Yokohama	11 Mar 90
5.90		Denis	Petushinskiy	RUS	29.1.67	1	Znam	Moskva	13 Jun 93
5.90i		Pyotr	Bochkaryov	RUS	3.11.67	1	EI	Paris	12 Mar 94
		(30)							
5.90		Jacob	Davis	USA	29.4.78	1	Tex R	Austin	4 Apr 98
5.90		Viktor	Chistyakov	RUS/AUS	9.2.75	1		Salamanca	15 Jul 99
5.90		Pavel	Gerasimov	RUS	29.5.79	1		Rüdlingen	12 Aug 00
5.90		Nick	Hysong	USA	9.12.71	1	OG	Sydney	29 Sep 00
5.89		Kory	Tarpenning	USA	27.2.62	1	OT	Indianopolis	21 Jul 88
5.87		Earl	Bell	USA	25.8.55	1		Jonesboro	14 May 88
5.86		Vasiliy	Bubka	UKR	26.11.60	1		Chelyabinsk	16 Jul 88
5.86		Bill	Payne	USA	21.12.67	1	SWC	Houston	19 May 91
5.86		Valeri	Bukrejev	EST	15.6.64	1		Somero	3 Jul 94
5.85		Konstantin	Volkov	RUS	28.2.60	1	Izv	Kiyev	22 Jun 84
		(40)							
5.85		Pat	Manson	USA	29.11.67	2	TOTO	Tokyo	15 Sep 94
5.85		Alain	Andji	FRA	20.11.74	1		Bonneuil-sur-Marne	18 May 97
5.85		Yevgeniy	Smiryagin	RUS	17.5.76	1	Nurmi	Turku	12 Jun 97
5.85		Vadim	Strogalyov	RUS	9.2.75	2		Hania	27 May 98
5.85		Aleksandr	Averbukh	ISR	1.10.74	1	NC	Tel Aviv	24 Jul 00
5.84		Mike	Tully	USA	21.10.56	1		Irvine	1 May 88
5.83i		Jani	Lehtonen	FIN	11.8.68	1	DNG	Stockholm	8 Mar 94
5.82		Aleksandr	Krupskiy	RUS	4.1.60	1	BGP	Budapest	20 Aug 84
5.82		Aleksandr	Parnov	UZB	10.5.59	1		Sumgait	21 Aug 85
5.82		Tim	Bright	USA	28.7.60	1	Nik	Nice	10 Jul 90
		(50)	100th man 5.75, 200th man 5.65						

Best outdoor marks for athletes with lifetime bests indoors

6.00	Gataullin	1		Tokyo	16 Sep 89	5.85	Collet	2	Paris	22 Jul 86
5.98	Galfione	1		Amiens	23 Jul 99	5.83	Stolle	3	Ingolstadt	26 Jul 98
5.90	Yegorov	2	WCh	Stuttgart	19 Aug 93	5.82	Lehtonen	1	Kuortane	26 Jun 93
5.86	Bochkaryov	5	OG	Atlanta	2 Aug 96					

Outdoors on built-up runway

5.90		Pyotr	Bochkaryov	RUS	3.11.67	1		Karlskrona	28 Jun 96
5.86		Denis	Petushinskiy	RUS	28.6.67	1		Karlskrona	23 Jul 94

Exhibition or Market Square competitions

6.00		Jean	Galfione	FRA	9.6.71	1		Besançon	23 May 97
5.95		Viktor	Chistyakov	AUS	9.2.75	1		Chiari	8 Sep 99
5.86		Gennadiy	Sukharev	BLR	3.2.65	1		Bisceglie	23 Jul 91
5.86i		Larry	Jessee	USA	31.3.52	1		Newcastle	16 Oct 85

LONG JUMP

8.95 WR	0.3	Mike	Powell	USA	10.11.63	1	WCh	Tokyo	30 Aug 91
8.90A WR	2.0	Bob	Beamon	USA	29.8.46	1	OG	Ciudad de México	18 Oct 68
8.87	-0.2	Carl	Lewis	USA	1.7.61	*	WCh	Tokyo	30 Aug 91
8.86A	1.9	Robert	Emmiyan	ARM	16.2.65	1		Tsakhkadzor	22 May 87
8.79	1.9		Lewis			1	TAC	Indianapolis	19 Jun 83
8.79i	-		Lewis			1		New York	27 Jan 84
8.76	1.0		Lewis			1	USOF	Indianapolis	24 Jul 82
8.76	0.8		Lewis			1	OT	Indianapolis	18 Jul 88
8.75	1.7		Lewis			1	PAm	Indianapolis	16 Aug 87
8.74	1.4	Larry	Myricks	USA	10.3.56	2	OT	Indianapolis	18 Jul 88
8.74A	2.0	Erick	Walder	USA	5.11.71	1		El Paso	2 Apr 94
8.72	-0.2		Lewis			1	OG	Seoul	26 Sep 88
8.71	-0.4		Lewis			1	Pepsi	Westwood	13 May 84
8.71	0.1		Lewis			1	OT	Los Angeles	19 Jun 84
8.71	1.9	Iván	Pedroso	CUB	17.12.72	1		Salamanca	18 Jul 95
8.70	0.8		Myricks			1	TAC	Houston	17 Jun 89
8.70	0.7		Powell			1		Salamanca	27 Jul 93
8.70	1.6		Pedroso			1	WCh	Göteborg	12 Aug 95
8.68	1.0		Lewis			Q	OG	Barcelona	5 Aug 92
8.68	1.6		Pedroso			1		Lisboa	17 Jun 96
8.67	0.4		Lewis			1	WCh	Roma	5 Sep 87
8.67	-0.7		Lewis			1	OG	Barcelona	6 Aug 92
8.66	0.8		Lewis			*	MSR	Walnut	26 Apr 87
8.66	1.0		Myricks			1		Tokyo	23 Sep 87

Mark	Wind	Name		Nat	Born	Pos	Meet	Venue	Date
8.66	0.9		Powell			1	BNP	Villeneuve d'Ascq	29 Jun 90
8.66A	1.4		Lewis			*		Sestriere	31 Jul 94
8.66	0.3		Pedroso			1		Linz	22 Aug 95
8.65	0.2		Lewis			1	VD	Bruxelles	24 Aug 84
8.65	0.7		Lewis			1	TAC	San José	26 Jun 87
8.65	1.5		Pedroso			1	OD	Jena	3 Jun 00
		(30/7)							
Most 'legal' competitions over 8.50m: 39 Lewis, 30 Pedroso, 17 Myricks, 16 Powell, 4 Beckford									
8.63	0.5	Kareem	Streete-Thompson	CAY/USA	30.3.73	1	GP II	Linz	4 Jul 94
8.62	0.7	James	Beckford	JAM	9.1.75	1		Orlando	5 Apr 97
8.56i	-	Yago	Lamela	ESP	24.7.77	2	WI	Maebashi	7 Mar 99
		(10)							
8.54	0.9	Lutz	Dombrowski	GDR	25.6.59	1	OG	Moskva	28 Jul 80
8.53	1.2	Jaime	Jefferson	CUB	17.1.62	1	Barr	La Habana	12 May 90
8.51	1.7	Roland	McGhee	USA	15.10.71	2		São Paulo	14 May 95
8.50	0.2	Llewellyn	Starks	USA	10.2.67	2		Rhede	7 Jul 91
8.49	2.0	Melvin	Lister	USA	29.8.77	1	SEC	Baton Rouge	13 May 00
8.49	0.6	Jai	Taurima	AUS	26.6.72	2	OG	Sydney	28 Sep 00
8.48	0.8	Joe	Greene	USA	17.2.67	3		São Paulo	14 May 95
8.47	1.9	Kevin	Dilworth	USA	14.2.74	1		Abilene	9 May 96
8.46	1.2	Leonid	Voloshin	RUS	30.3.66	1	NC	Tallinn	5 Jul 88
8.46	1.6	Mike	Conley	USA	5.10.62	2		Springfield	4 May 96
		(20)							
8.46	1.8	Cheikh Tidiane	Touré	SEN	25.1.70	1		Bad Langensalza	15 Jun 97
8.45	2.0	Nenad	Stekic	YUG	7.3.51	1	PO	Montreal	25 Jul 75
8.44	1.7	Eric	Metcalf	USA	23.1.68	1	TAC	Tampa	17 Jun 88
8.43	0.8	Jason	Grimes	USA	10.9.59	-	TAC	Indianapolis	16 Jun 85
8.43	1.8	Giovanni	Evangelisti	ITA	11.9.61	1		San Giovanni Valdarno	16 May 87
8.43i	-	Stanislav	Tarasenko	RUS	23.7.66	1		Moskva	26 Jan 94
8.43	0.1	Luis	Meliz	CUB	11.8.79	2	OD	Jena	3 Jun 00
8.41	1.5	Craig	Hepburn	BAH	10.12.69	1	NC	Nassau	17 Jun 93
8.41i	-	Kirill	Sosunov	RUS	1.11.75	2	WI	Paris (B)	8 Mar 97
8.40	1.4	Douglas de	Souza	BRA	6.8.72	1		São Paulo	15 Feb 95
		(30)							
8.40	0.4	Robert	Howard	USA	26.11.75	1	SEC	Auburn	17 May 97
8.40	2.0	Gregor	Cankar	SLO	25.1.75	1		Celje	18 May 97
8.40	0.0		Lao Jianfeng	CHN	24.5.75	1	NC	Zhaoqing	28 May 97
8.39	0.8	Dion	Bentley	USA	26.8.71	2	NCAA	New Orleans	3 Jun 93
8.38	0.4	Konstantin	Semykin	RUS	26.5.60	1	Drz	Moskva	17 Aug 84
8.38A	1.1		Huang Geng	CHN	10.7.70	1	NC	Taiyuan	18 May 95
8.38i	–	Vitaliy	Shkurlatov	RUS	25.5.79	1		Samara	30 Jan 00
8.37A	0.4	Leroy	Burrell	USA	21.2.67	2	NCAA	Provo	2 Jun 89
8.37	1.5	Bogdan	Tudor	ROM	1.2.70	2		Bad Cannstatt	9 Jul 95
8.36	1.0	João Carlos	de Oliveira	BRA	28.5.54	1		Rieti	21 Jul 79
		(40)							
8.36	1.6	Frank	Paschek	GDR	25.6.56	1	OD	Berlin	28 May 80
8.36	1.5		Chen Zunrong	CHN	20.10.62	*		Shizuoka	5 May 92
8.36	1.6	Konstadinos	Koukodímos	GRE	14.9.69	1		Hania	5 Jun 94
8.36A	0.8	Nelson	Ferreira Jr	BRA	1.1.73	*	IbAm	Medellín	10 May 96
8.36	1.2	Carlos	Calado	POR	5.10.75	1		Lisboa	20 Jun 97
8.35 WR	0.0	Ralph	Boston	USA	9.5.39	1	CalR	Modesto	29 May 65
8.35A WR	0.0	Igor	Ter-Ovanesyan	RUS	19.5.38	1	PreO	Ciudad de México	19 Oct 67
8.35	0.8	Josef	Schwarz	FRG	20.5.41	1	vUSA	Stuttgart	15 Jul 70
8.35	-0.6	Arnie	Robinson	USA	7.4.48	1	OG	Montreal	29 Jul 76
8.35	2.0	Henry	Lauterbach	GDR	22.10.57	1		Erfurt	2 Aug 81
8.35	2.0	Sergey	Layevskiy	UKR	3.3.59	1		Dnepropetrovsk	16 Jul 88
8.35	1.4	Dmitriy	Bagryanov	RUS	18.12.67	1		Granada	30 May 92
8.35	0.7	Roman	Shchurenko	UKR	14.9.76	1		Kiev	25 Jul 00
		(53)	100th man 8.26, 200th man 8.16						
Sand layer insufficient: 8.37i			Sean Robbins	USA	9.10.72	1		Bowling Green	10 Feb 96
Irregular conditions: 8.39 1.2			Ioan Lino Martínez	CUB	17.1.78	1		La Habana	5 Feb 99
Wind-assisted marks performances to 8.70, performers to 8.39									
8.99A	4.4	Mike	Powell	USA	10.11.63	1		Sestriere	21 Jul 92
8.96A	1.2+	Iván	Pedroso	CUB	17.12.72	1		Sestriere	29 Jul 95
8.95A	3.9		Powell			1		Sestriere	31 Jul 94
8.91	2.9	Carl	Lewis	USA	1.7.61	2	WCh	Tokyo	30 Aug 91
8.90	3.7		Powell			1	S&W	Modesto	16 May 92
8.79	3.0		Pedroso			1	Barr	La Habana	21 May 92
8.77	3.9		Lewis			1	Pepsi	Westwood	18 May 85
8.77	3.4		Lewis			1	MSR	Walnut	26 Apr 87

Mark	Wind	Name		Nat	Born	Pos	Meet	Venue	Date
8.73	4.6		Lewis			Q	TAC	Sacramento	19 Jun 81
8.73	3.2		Lewis			Q	TAC	Indianapolis	17 Jun 83
8.73A	2.6		Powell			1		Sestriere	31 Jul 91
8.73	4.8		Pedroso			1		Madrid	20 Jun 95
8.72	2.2		Lewis			1	NYG	New York	24 May 92
8.72A	3.9		Lewis			2		Sestriere	31 Jul 94
8.70	2.5		Pedroso			1		Padova	16 Jul 95
8.68	4.9	James	Beckford	JAM	9.1.75	1	JUCO	Odessa, Tx	19 May 95
8.66A	4.0	Joe	Greene	USA	17.2.67	2		Sestriere	21 Jul 92
8.64	3.5	Kareem	Streete-Thompson	CAY/USA	30.3.73	2	NC	Knoxville	18 Jun 94
8.63	3.9	Mike	Conley	USA	5.10.62	2	TAC	Eugene	20 Jun 86
8.57	5.2	Jason	Grimes	USA	10.9.59	1	vFRG,AFR	Durham	27 Jun 82
8.49	2.6	Ralph	Boston	USA	9.5.39	1	FOT	Los Angeles	12 Sep 64
8.49	4.5	Stanislav	Tarasenko	RUS	23.7.66	2		Madrid	20 Jun 95
8.48	2.8	Kirill	Sosunov	RUS	1.11.75	1		Oristano	18 Sep 95
8.48	3.4	Peter	Burge	AUS	3.7.74	1		Gold Coast (RB)	10 Sep 00
8.46	3.4	Randy	Williams	USA	23.8.53	1		Eugene	18 May 73
8.46		Vernon	George	USA	6.10.64	1		Houston	21 May 89
8.44		Keith	Talley	USA	28.1.64	Q		Odessa, Tx	16 May 85
8.42		Anthony	Bailous	USA	6.4.65	Q		Odessa, Tx	16 May 85
8.42A	4.5	Milan	Gombala	CZE	29.1.68	3		Sestriere	21 Jul 92
8.41	4.3	Shamil	Abbyasov	KGZ	16.4.57	2	vUSA	Indianapolis	3 Jul 82
8.41	3.3	Andre	Ester	USA	27.4.65	1	TexR	Austin	4 Apr 87
8.41A	3.2	Nelson	Ferreira Jr	BRA	1.1.73	1	IbAm	Medellín	10 May 96
8.40	4.3	Henry	Hines	USA	12.2.49	1	CalR	Modesto	27 May 72
8.40	2.1	Anthuan	Maybank	USA	30.12.69	1	DrakeR	Des Moines	24 Apr 93
8.40	3.4	Konstadínos	Koukodímos	GRE	14.9.69	1	ECp I	Valencia	11 Jun 94
8.39	6.2	Gary	Honey	AUS	26.7.59	2		Sacramento	21 Jul 84
8.39	3.5	Edrick	Floreal	CAN	5.10.66	1		Fayetteville	22 Apr 89
8.39	5.7	Yusuf	Alli	NGR	28.7.60	1	CG	Auckland	1 Feb 90
8.39	2.4		Chen Zunrong	CHN	20.10.62	1		Shizuoka	5 May 92
Exhibition: 8.46		Yuriy	Naumkin	RUS	4.11.68	1		Iglesias	6 Sep 96

Best outdoors

8.56 1.3 Lamela 1 Torino 24 Jun 99 8.38 1.1 Sosunov 1 ECp Sankt-Peterburg 27 Jun 98

TRIPLE JUMP

Mark	Wind	Name		Nat	Born	Pos	Meet	Venue	Date
18.29 WR	1.3	Jonathan	Edwards	GBR	10.5.66	1	WCh	Göteborg	7 Aug 95
18.09	-0.4	Kenny	Harrison	USA	13.2.65	1	OG	Atlanta	27 Jul 96
18.01	0.4		Edwards			1	Bisl	Oslo	9 Jul 98
18.00	1.3		Edwards			1	McD	London (CP)	27 Aug 95
17.99	0.5		Edwards			1	EC	Budapest	23 Aug 98
17.98 WR	1.8		Edwards			1		Salamanca	18 Jul 95
17.97 WR	1.5	Willie	Banks	USA	11.3.56	1	TAC	Indianapolis	16 Jun 85
17.93	1.6		Harrison			1	DNG	Stockholm	2 Jul 90
17.92	1.6	Khristo	Markov	BUL	27.1.65	1	WCh	Roma	31 Aug 87
17.92	1.9	James	Beckford	JAM	9.1.75	1	JUCO	Odessa, Tex	20 May 95
17.90	1.0	Vladimir	Inozemtsev	UKR	25.5.64	1	GPB	Bratislava	20 Jun 90
17.89A WR	0.0	João Carlos	de Oliveira	BRA	28.5.54	1	PAm	Ciudad de México	15 Oct 75
17.88	0.9		Edwards			2	OG	Atlanta	27 Jul 96
17.87	1.7	Mike	Conley	USA	5.10.62	1	TAC	San José	27 Jun 87
17.86	1.3	Charles	Simpkins	USA	19.10.63	1	WUG	Kobe	2 Sep 85
17.86	0.3		Conley			1	WCh	Stuttgart	16 Aug 93
17.85	0.9	Yoelbi	Quesada (10)	CUB	4.8.73	1	WCh	Athína	8 Aug 97
17.84	0.7		Conley			1		Bad Cannstatt	4 Jul 93
17.83i	-	Aliecer	Urrutia	CUB	22.9.74	1		Sindelfingen	1 Mar 97
17.82	1.6		Edwards			1	WG	Helsinki	25 Jun 96
17.81	2.0		Markov			1	Nar	Sofia	31 May 87
17.80	0.6		Markov			1	BGP	Budapest	11 Aug 86
17.79	-0.8		Harrison			1	OD	Berlin	4 Jul 90
17.79	-0.7		Edwards			1	WK	Zürich	14 Aug 96
17.78	1.0	Nikolay	Musiyenko	UKR	16.12.59	1	Znam	Leningrad	7 Jun 86
17.78	0.6	Lázaro	Betancourt ¶	CUB	18.3.63	1	Barr	La Habana	15 Jun 86
17.78	-0.8		Harrison			1	WCh	Tokyo	26 Aug 91
17.77	1.9		Markov			1	ECp-B	Budapest	11 Aug 85
17.77	1.0	Aleksandr	Kovalenko	RUS	8.5.63	1	NC	Bryansk	18 Jul 87
17.77	1.4		Markov			1	NC	Sofia	3 Sep 88
17.77i	-	Leonid	Voloshin	RUS	30.3.66	1		Grenoble	6 Feb 94
		(31/15)							

Mark	Wind	Name		Nat	Born	Pos	Meet	Venue	Date
17.75	0.3	Oleg	Protsenko	RUS	11.8.63	1	Znam	Moskva	10 Jun 90
17.72i		Brian	Wellman	BER	8.9.67	1	WI	Barcelona	12 Mar 95
17.69	1.5	Igor	Lapshin	BLR	8.8.63	1		Stayki	31 Jul 88
17.66	1.7	Ralf	Jaros	GER	13.12.65	1	ECp	Frankfurt-am-Main	30 Jun 91
17.65	1.0	Aleksandr	Yakovlev	UKR	8.9.57	1	Znam	Moskva	6 Jun 87
		(20)							
17.65	0.8	Denis	Kapustin	RUS	5.10.70	2	Bisl	Oslo	9 Jul 98
17.62i	-	Yoel	García	CUB	25.11.73	2		Sindelfingen	1 Mar 97
17.60	0.6	Vladimir	Plekhanov	RUS	11.4.58	2	NC	Leningrad	4 Aug 85
17.60	1.9	Fabrizio	Donato	ITA	14.8.76	1		Milano	7 Jun 00
17.59i	-	Pierre	Camara	FRA	10.9.65	1	WI	Toronto	13 Mar 93
17.59	0.3	Vasiliy	Sokov	RUS	7.4.68	1	NC	Moskva	19 Jun 93
17.59	0.8	Charles	Friedek	GER	26.8.71	1		Hamburg	23 Jul 97
17.58	1.5	Oleg	Sakirkin	KZK	23.1.66	2	NC	Gorkiy	23 Jul 89
17.57A	0.0	Keith	Connor	GBR	16.9.57	1	NCAA	Provo	5 Jun 82
17.56	1.9	Maris	Bruziks	LAT	25.8.62	1		Riga	3 Sep 88
		(30)							
17.55	0.3	Vasiliy	Grishchenkov	RUS	23.1.58	1	Spart	Moskva	19 Jun 83
17.55	0.9	Serge	Hélan	FRA	24.2.64	2	EC	Helsinki	13 Aug 94
17.53	1.0	Aleksandr	Beskrovniy	RUS	5.4.60	2	Spart	Moskva	19 Jun 83
17.53	1.6	Zdzislaw	Hoffmann	POL	27.8.59	1		Madrid	4 Jun 85
17.53	1.0	Gennadiy	Valyukevich	BLR	1.6.58	1		Erfurt	1 Jun 86
17.53	1.6	Al	Joyner	USA	19.1.60	Q	TAC	San José	26 Jun 87
17.53	0.9	Milán	Mikulás	CZE	1.4.63	1	NC	Praha	17 Jul 88
17.53	1.9	Oleg	Denishchik	BLR	10.11.69	2	NC	Kiyev	12 Jul 91
17.53	0.5	Aleksandr	Glavatskiy	BLR	2.5.70	2	WK	Zürich	12 Aug 98
17.50	0.4	Volker	Mai	GDR	3.5.66	1	vURS	Erfurt	23 Jun 85
		(40)							
17.49	1.4	Rostislav	Dimitrov	BUL	29.12.74	2	WCh	Sevilla	25 Aug 99
17.48	1.9	Jorge	Reyna	CUB	10.1.63	1		Santiago de Cuba	27 Feb 87
17.48	1.6	Jerome	Romain	DMN	12.6.71	Q	WCh	Göteborg	5 Aug 95
17.46	1.7	Ken	Lorraway	AUS	6.2.56	1		London (CP)	7 Aug 82
17.45	1.9	Aleksandr	Leonov ¶	BLR	7.2.62	1		Sochi	24 May 87
17.45	1.5	Paolo	Camossi	ITA	6.1.74	2		Milano	7 Jun 00
17.44	WR-0.?	Viktor	Saneyev	GEO	3.10.45	1		Sukhumi	17 Oct 72
17.44	2.0	Dirk	Gamlin	GDR	26.10.63	1		Dresden	7 Jul 85
17.44	0.4	Andrey	Kurennoy	RUS	12.5.72	1	NC	Tula	9 Jul 97
17.44	1.7	LaMark	Carter	USA	23.8.70	1	NC	New Orleans	20 Jun 98
		(50)	17.23, 200th man 17.02						

Wind-assisted marks – performances to 17.80

Mark	Wind	Name		Nat	Born	Pos	Meet	Venue	Date
18.43	2.4	Jonathan	Edwards	GBR	10.5.66	1	ECp	Villeneuve d'Ascq	25 Jun 95
18.20	5.2	Willie	Banks	USA	11.3.56	1	OT	Indianapolis	16 Jul 88
18.17	2.1	Mike	Conley	USA	5.10.62	1	OG	Barcelona	3 Aug 92
18.08	2.5		Edwards			1	BUPA	Sheffield	23 Jul 95
18.03	2.9		Edwards			1	GhG	Gateshead	2 Jul 95
18.01	3.7		Harrison			1	NC	Atlanta	15 Jun 96
17.97	7.5	Yoelbi	Quesada	CUB	4.8.73	1		Madrid	20 Jun 95
17.93	5.2	Charles	Simpkins	USA	19.10.63	2	OT	Indianapolis	16 Jul 88
17.91	3.2		Simpkins			1	TAC	Eugene	21 Jun 86
17.86	3.9		Simpkins			1	OT	New Orleans	21 Jun 92
17.86	5.7	Denis	Kapustin	RUS	5.10.70	1		Sevilla	5 Jun 94
17.84	2.3		Conley			2	TAC	Eugene	21 Jun 86
17.82	3.6		Banks			1	Jen	San José	31 May 86
17.81	4.6	Keith	Connor	GBR	16.9.57	1	CG	Brisbane	9 Oct 82
17.75		Gennadiy	Valyukevich	BLR	1.6.58	1		Uzhgorod	27 Apr 86
17.75	7.1	Brian	Wellman	BER	8.9.67	2		Madrid	20 Jun 95
17.73	4.1	Vasiliy	Sokov	RUS	7.4.68	1		Riga	3 Jun 89
17.63	4.3	Robert	Cannon	USA	9.7.58	3	OT	Indianapolis	16 Jul 88
17.59	2.1	Jerome	Romain	DMN	12.6.71	3	WCh	Göteborg	7 Aug 95
17.58	5.2	Al	Joyner	USA	19.1.60	5	OT	Indianapolis	16 Jul 88
17.56	3.7	Ron	Livers	USA	20.7.55	1	AAU	Walnut	17 Jun 79
17.55	3.6	Zdzislaw	Hoffmann	POL	27.8.59	1	Kuso	Warszawa	9 Jun 84
17.54	3.2	Ken	Lorraway	AUS	6.2.56	2	CG	Brisbane	9 Oct 82
17.53	4.8	Ray	Kimble	USA	19.4.53	7	OT	Indianapolis	16 Jul 88
17.51	3.0		Chen Yanping	CHN	17.1.66	1	AsiG	Beijing	3 Oct 90
17.49	4.5	Vladimir	Melikhov	RUS	30.3.69	2		Sevilla	5 Jun 94
17.48	2.9	Georges	Sainte-Rose	FRA	3.9.69	1		Montgeron	23 Jun 91
17.47	3.7	Joseph	Taiwo	NGR	24.8.59	1	GP	São Paulo	17 May 92

Mark	Wind	Name	Nat	Born	Pos	Meet	Venue	Date

Best outdoor marks for athletes with lifetime bests indoors

17.75	1.0	Voloshin	2	WCh	Tokyo	26 Aug 91
17.70	1.7	Urrutia	1	GP II	Sevilla	6 Jun 96
17.62A		Wellman	1		El Paso	15 Apr 95
17.47	1.8	García	1		Bad Cannstatt	9 Jul 95

SHOT

Mark		Name		Nat	Born	Pos	Meet	Venue	Date
23.12	WR	Randy	Barnes ¶	USA	16.6.66	1		Westwood	20 May 90
23.10			Barnes			1	Jen	San José	26 May 90
23.06	WR	Ulf	Timmermann	GDR	1.11.62	1		Hania	22 May 88
22.91	WR	Alessandro	Andrei	ITA	3.1.59	1		Viareggio	12 Aug 87
22.86		Brian	Oldfield	USA	1.6.45	1	ITA	El Paso	10 May 75
22.75		Werner	Günthör	SUI	1.6.61	1		Bern	23 Aug 88
22.66i			Barnes			1	Sunkist	Los Angeles	20 Jan 89
22.64	WR	Udo	Beyer	GDR	9.8.55	1		Berlin	20 Aug 86
22.62	WR		Timmermann			1		Berlin	22 Sep 85
22.61			Timmermann			1		Potsdam	8 Sep 88
22.60			Timmermann			1	vURS	Tallinn	21 Jun 86
22.56			Timmermann			1		Berlin	13 Sep 88
22.55i			Timmermann			1	NC	Senftenberg	11 Feb 89
22.52		John	Brenner	USA	4.1.61	1	MSR	Walnut	26 Apr 87
22.51			Timmermann			1		Erfurt	1 Jun 86
22.47			Timmermann			1		Dresden	17 Aug 86
22.47			Günthör			1	WG	Helsinki	2 Jul 87
22.47			Timmermann			1	OG	Seoul	23 Sep 88
22.45			Oldfield			1	ITA	El Paso	22 May 76
22.43			Günthör			1	v3-N	Lüdenscheid	18 Jun 87
22.42			Barnes			1	WK	Zürich	17 Aug 88
22.40			Barnes			1		Rüdlingen	13 Jul 96
22.39			Barnes			2	OG	Seoul	23 Sep 88
22.36	@		Timmermann			1		Athína	16 May 88
22.31			Beyer			1	NC	Potsdam	20 Aug 87
22.28			Oldfield			1	ITA	Edinburgh	18 Jun 75
22.28			Barnes			1	MSR	Walnut	22 Apr 90
22.26i			Günthör			1	NC	Magglingen	8 Feb 87
22.26			Brenner			1		Westwood	18 Apr 87
22.25			Günthör			1	WK	Zürich	19 Aug 87
22.24		Sergey	Smirnov	RUS	17.9.60	2	vGDR	Tallinn	21 Jun 86
22.24i			Timmermann			1	WCh	Indianapolis	7 Mar 87
		(32/8)							
22.12		Adam	Nelson	USA	7.7.75	1	NC	Sacramento	15 Jul 00
22.10		Sergey	Gavryushin	RUS	27.6.59	1		Tbilisi	31 Aug 86
		(10)							
22.09		Sergey	Kasnauskas	BLR	20.4.61	1		Stayki	23 Aug 84
22.09i		Mika	Halvari	FIN	13.2.70	1		Tampere	7 Feb 00
22.02i		George	Woods	USA	11.2.43	1	LAT	Inglewood	8 Feb 74
22.02		Dave	Laut	USA	21.12.56	1		Koblenz	25 Aug 82
22.02		John	Godina	USA	31.5.72	1	NC	Eugene	27 Jun 99
22.00	WR	Aleksandr	Baryshnikov	RUS	11.11.48	1	vFRA	Colombes	10 Jul 76
21.98		Gregg	Tafralis ¶	USA	9.4.58	1		Los Gatos	13 Jun 92
21.96		Mikhail	Kostin	RUS	10.5.59	1		Vitebsk	20 Jul 86
21.93		Remigius	Machura ¶	CZE	3.7.60	1		Praha	23 Aug 87
21.87		C.J.	Hunter ¶	USA	14.12.68	2	NC	Sacramento	15 Jul 00
		(20)							
21.85	WR	Terry	Albritton	USA	14.1.55	1		Honolulu	21 Feb 76
21.83i		Aleksandr	Bagach ¶	UKR	21.11.66	1		Brovary	21 Feb 99
21.82	WR	Al	Feuerbach	USA	14.1.48	1		San José	5 May 73
21.82		Andy	Bloom	USA	11.8.73	1	GPF	Doha	5 Oct 00
21.78	WR	Randy	Matson	USA	5.3.45	1		College Station	22 Apr 67
21.78		Kevin	Toth	USA	29.12.67	2	NC	Indianapolis	12 Jun 97
21.77i		Mike	Stulce ¶	USA	21.7.69	1	v GBR	Birmingham	13 Feb 93
21.77		Dragan	Peric	YUG	8.5.64	1		Bar	25 Apr 98
21.76		Mike	Carter	USA	29.10.60	2	NCAA	Eugene	2 Jun 84
21.74		Janis	Bojars	LAT	12.5.56	1		Riga	14 Jul 84
		(30)							
21.73		Augie	Wolf ¶	USA	3.9.61	1		Leverkusen	12 Apr 84
21.69		Reijo	Ståhlberg	FIN	21.9.52	1	WCR	Fresno	5 May 79
21.68		Geoff	Capes	GBR	23.8.49	1	4-N	Cwmbrân	18 May 80
21.68		Edward	Sarul	POL	16.11.58	1		Sopot	31 Jul 83
21.67		Hartmut	Briesenick	GDR	17.3.49	1		Potsdam	1 Sep 73

Mark Wind	Name		Nat	Born	Pos	Meet	Venue	Date
21.64	Yuriy	Belonog	UKR	9.3.74	1		Koncha-Zaspa	28 Apr 00
21.61	Kevin	Akins	USA	27.1.60	1	S&W	Modesto	14 May 83
21.60	Jim	Doehring ¶	USA	27.1.62	2		Los Gatos	13 Jun 92
21.58	Vladimir	Kiselyov	UKR	1.1.57	3	Drz	Moskva	17 Aug 84
21.53	Yevgeniy	Mironov ¶	RUS	1.11.49	1	NC	Kiyev	24 Jun 76
	(40)							
21.51	Ralf	Reichenbach	FRG	31.7.50	1	ISTAF	Berlin	8 Aug 80
21.47	Brent	Noon ¶	USA	29.8.71	1	SEC	Tuscaloosa	21 May 95
21.47i	Oliver-Sven	Buder	GER	23.6.66	1	EI	Valencia	28 Feb 98
21.44	Mikhail	Domorosov	BLR	5.3.55	2		Stayki	23 Aug 84
21.43	Mike	Lehmann	USA	11.3.60	2	Jen	San José	28 May 83
21.42i	Fred	DeBernardi	USA	2.3.49	1	ITA	Portland	20 Apr 74
21.42	Sergey	Donskikh	RUS	25.1.56	1		Leningrad	25 Aug 84
21.39	Arsi	Harju	FIN	18.3.74	1	OG	Sydney	22 Sep 00
21.35	Ron	Semkiw	USA	28.3.54	1		Mesa	5 Mar 74
21.35	Sergey	Nikolayev	RUS	12.11.66	1		Voronezh	5 Aug 89
	(50) 100th man 20.85, 200th 20.30		@ competitive meeting but unsanctioned by GDR federation					

Not recognised by GDR authorities

22.11	Rolf	Oesterreich	GDR	24.8.49	1		Zschopau	12 Sep 76

Drugs disqualification

22.84		Barnes			1		Malmö	7 Aug 90
21.82	Mike	Stulce ¶	USA	21.7.69	1		Brenham	9 May 90

Best outdoor marks for athletes with lifetime bests indoors

21.70	Stulce ¶	1	OG	Barcelona	31 Jul 92
21.63	Woods	2	CalR	Modesto	22 May 76
21.50	Halvari	1		Hämeenkyrö	9 Jul 95
21.47	Bagach ¶	1	Veniz	Haniá	31 May 97
21.42	Buder	2	WCh	Sevilla	21 Aug 99
21.41	DeBernardi	1	ITA	El Paso	27 Apr 74

DISCUS

Mark Wind	Name		Nat	Born	Pos	Meet	Venue	Date
74.08 WR	Jürgen	Schult	GDR	11.5.60	1		Neubrandenburg	6 Jun 86
73.88	Virgilijus	Alekna	LTU	13.2.72	1	NC	Kaunas	3 Aug 00
71.86 WR	Yuriy	Dumchev	RUS	5.8.58	1		Moskva	29 May 83
71.50	Lars	Riedel	GER	28.6.67	1		Wiesbaden	3 May 97
71.32	Ben	Plucknett ¶	USA	13.4.54	1	Pre	Eugene	4 Jun 83
71.26	John	Powell	USA	25.6.47	1	TAC	San José	9 Jun 84
71.26	Rickard	Bruch	SWE	2.7.46	1		Malmö	15 Nov 84
71.26	Imrich	Bugár	CZE	14.4.55	1	Jen	San José	25 May 85
71.18	Art	Burns	USA	19.7.54	1		San José	19 Jul 83
71.16 WR	Wolfgang	Schmidt	GDR	16.1.54	1		Berlin	9 Aug 78
71.14		Plucknett			1		Berkeley	12 Jun 83
71.14	Anthony	Washington (10)	USA	16.1.66	1eA		Salinas	22 May 96
71.12		Alekna			1	WK	Zürich	11 Aug 00
71.06	Luis M.	Delís ¶	CUB	6.12.57	1	Barr	La Habana	21 May 83
71.06		Riedel			1	WK	Zürich	14 Aug 96
71.00		Bruch			1		Malmö	14 Oct 84
70.98	Mac	Wilkins	USA	15.11.50	1	WG	Helsinki	9 Jul 80
70.98		Burns			1	Pre	Eugene	21 Jul 84
70.92		Schmidt	FRG		1		Norden	9 Sep 89
70.86 WR		Wilkins			1		San José	1 May 76
70.82		Plucknett			1		Salinas	1 Jun 83
70.72		Bugár			1	vHUN,AUT	Schwechat	18 Jun 83
70.66		Wilkins			1	AAU	Walnut	16 Jun 79
70.60		Riedel			1	ISTAF	Berlin	30 Aug 96
70.58		Delís			1		Salinas	19 May 82
70.48		Wilkins			1		San José	29 Apr 78
70.48		Wilkins			1	Pre	Eugene	31 May 78
70.48		Bruch			1		Malmö	12 Sep 84
70.46		Schult			1		Berlin	13 Sep 88
70.44		Wilkins			2	TAC	San José	9 Jun 84
	(30/13)	46 performances over 70m						
70.38 WRu	Jay	Silvester	USA	27.8.37	1		Lancaster	16 May 71
70.06	Romas	Ubartas ¶	LIT	26.5.60	1		Smolininkay	8 May 88
70.00	Juan	Martínez ¶	CUB	17.5.58	2	Barr	La Habana	21 May 83
69.91	John	Godina	USA	31.5.72	1		Salinas	19 May 98
69.75 A	Frantz	Kruger	RSA	22.5.75	1		Bloemfontein	15 Sep 00
69.70	Gejza	Valent	CZE	3.10.53	2		Nitra	26 Aug 84
69.62	Knut	Hjeltnes ¶	NOR	8.12.51	2	Jen	San José	25 May 85
	(20)							
69.46	Al	Oerter	USA	19.9.36	1	TFA	Wichita	31 May 80

Mark	Wind	Name		Nat	Born	Pos	Meet	Venue	Date
69.44		Georgiy	Kolnootchenko	BLR	7.5.59	1	vUSA	Indianapolis	3 Jul 82
69.40		Art	Swarts ¶	USA	14.2.45	1		Scotch Plains	8 Dec 79
69.36		Mike	Buncic	USA	25.7.62	1		Fresno	6 Apr 91
69.28		Vladimir	Dubrovshchik	BLR	7.1.72	1	NC-w	Stayki	3 Jun 00
69.26		Ken	Stadel	USA	19.2.52	2	AAU	Walnut	16 Jun 79
68.88		Vladimir	Zinchenko	UKR	25.7.59	1		Dnepropetrovsk	16 Jul 88
68.64		Dmitriy	Kovtsun ¶	UKR	29.9.55	1		Riga	6 Jul 84
68.58		Attila	Horváth	HUN	28.7.67	1		Budapest	24 Jun 94
68.52		Igor	Duginyets	UKR	20.5.56	1	NC	Kiyev	21 Aug 82
		(30)							
68.51		Adam	Setliff	USA	15.12.69	1cA		La Jolla	25 Mar 00
68.50		Armin	Lemme	GDR	28.10.55	1	vUSA	Karl-Marx-Stadt	10 Jul 82
68.48	WR	John	van Reenen	RSA	26.3.47	1		Stellenbosch	14 Mar 75
68.46		Andy	Bloom	USA	11.8.73	2cA		La Jolla	25 Mar 00
68.44		Vaclovas	Kidykas	LIT	17.10.61	1		Sochi	1 Jun 88
68.30		Stefan	Fernholm	SWE	2.7.59	1		Västerås	15 Jul 87
68.12		Markku	Tuokko ¶	FIN	24.6.51	1	WCR	Fresno	5 May 79
68.12		Iosif	Nagy	ROM	20.11.46	2		Zaragoza	22 May 83
68.12		Erik	de Bruin ¶	NED	25.5.63	1		Sneek	1 Apr 91
68.08		Hein-Direck	Neu ¶	FRG	13.2.44	1		Bremerhaven	27 May 77
		(40)							
68.00		Svein Inge	Valvik	NOR	20.9.56	1		Juarez	31 May 82
67.90		Vitaliy	Sidorov	UKR	23.3.70	1		Kiev	3 May 98
67.89		Nick	Sweeney	IRL	26.3.68	1		Helsingborg	4 Sep 98
67.88		Jason	Tunks	CAN	7.5.75	1		Abilene	14 May 98
67.82		Velko	Velev ¶	BUL	4.1.48	1		Riga	13 Aug 78
67.80		Alwin	Wagner	FRG	11.8.50	1		Melsungen	1 Jul 87
67.80		Adewale	Olukoju	NGR	27.7.68	1	S&W	Modesto	11 May 91
67.76		Vitaliy	Pishchalnikov	RUS	1.4.58	1		Stavropol	9 May 84
67.64		Vésteinn	Hafsteinsson ¶	ISL	12.12.60	1		Selfoss	31 May 89
67.62		Randy	Heisler	USA	7.8.61	1		Bloomington	29 Jun 87
67.62		Marco	Martino	ITA	21.2.60	1	v4N	Spoleto	28 May 89
		(51)	100th man 66.16, 200th man 64.36						
Subsequent to or at drugs disqualification			! recognised as US record						
72.34!		Ben	Plucknett ¶	USA	13.4.54	1	DNG	Stockholm	7 Jul 81
71.20			Plucknett			1	CalR	Modesto	16 May 81
70.84		Kamy	Keshmiri ¶	USA	23.1.69	1		Salinas	27 May 92
68.04		Dmitriy	Shevchenko ¶	RUS	13.5.68	(1)	ASV	Köln	18 Aug 95
Sloping ground									
72.08		John	Powell	USA	25.6.47	1		Klagshamn	11 Sep 87
69.80		Stefan	Fernholm	SWE	2.7.59	1		Klagshamn	13 Aug 87

HAMMER

Mark	Wind	Name		Nat	Born	Pos	Meet	Venue	Date
86.74	WR	Yuriy	Sedykh	RUS	11.6.55	1	EC	Stuttgart	30 Aug 86
86.66	WR		Sedykh			1	vGDR	Tallinn	22 Jun 86
86.34	WR		Sedykh			1		Cork	3 Jul 84
86.04		Sergey	Litvinov	RUS	23.1.58	1	OD	Dresden	3 Jul 86
85.74			Litvinov			2	EC	Stuttgart	30 Aug 86
85.68			Sedykh			1	BGP	Budapest	11 Aug 86
85.60			Sedykh			1	PTG	London (CP)	13 Jul 84
85.60			Sedykh			1	Drz	Moskva	17 Aug 84
85.20			Litvinov			2		Cork	3 Jul 84
85.14			Litvinov			1	PTG	London	11 Jul 86
85.14			Sedykh			1	Kuts	Moskva	4 Sep 88
85.02			Sedykh			1	BGP	Budapest	20 Aug 84
84.92			Sedykh			2	OD	Dresden	3 Jul 86
84.88			Litvinov			1	GP-GG	Roma	10 Sep 86
84.80			Litvinov			1	OG	Seoul	26 Sep 88
84.72			Sedykh			1	GWG	Moskva	9 Jul 86
84.64			Litvinov			2	GWG	Moskva	9 Jul 86
84.62		Igor	Astapkovich	BLR	4.1.63	1	Expo	Sevilla	6 Jun 92
84.60			Sedykh			1	8-N	Tokyo	14 Sep 84
84.58			Sedykh			1	Znam	Leningrad	8 Jun 86
84.48		Igor	Nikulin	RUS	14.8.60	1	Athl	Lausanne	12 Jul 90
84.46			Sedykh			1		Vladivostok	14 Sep 88
84.40		Jüri	Tamm	EST	5.2.57	1		Banská Bystrica	9 Sep 84
84.36			Litvinov			2	vGDR	Tallinn	22 Jun 86
84.26			Sedykh			1	Nik	Nice	15 Jul 86

Mark Wind	Name		Nat	Born	Pos	Meet	Venue	Date
84.26		Astapkovich			1		Reims	3 Jul 91
84.16		Tamm			1		Kharkov	19 Jun 88
84.14 WR		Litvinov			1	Spart	Moskva	21 Jun 83
84.14		Sedykh			1	WG	Helsinki	7 Jul 86
84.14		Astapkovich			1	EC	Split	31 Aug 90
	(30/5)							
83.68	Tibor	Gécsek ¶	HUN	22.9.64	1		Zalaegerszeg	19 Sep 98
83.46	Andrey	Abduvaliyev TJK/	UZB	30.6.66	1		Adler	26 May 90
83.40 @	Ralf	Haber	GDR	18.8.62	1		Athína	16 May 88
	82.54				1		Potsdam	9 Sep 88
83.04	Heinz	Weis	GER	14.7.63	1	NC	Frankfurt	29 Jun 97
83.00	Balázs	Kiss	HUN	21.3.72	1	GP II	Saint-Denis	4 Jun 98
	(10)	@ competitive meeting but unsanctioned by GDR federation						
82.78	Karsten	Kobs	GER	16.9.71	1		Dortmund	26 Jun 99
82.64	Günther	Rodehau	GDR	6.7.59	1		Dresden	3 Aug 85
82.62	Sergey	Kirmasov ¶	RUS	25.3.70	1		Bryansk	30 May 98
82.54	Vasiliy	Sidorenko	RUS	1.5.61	1		Krasnodar	13 May 92
82.52	Lance	Deal	USA	21.8.61	1	GPF	Milano	7 Sep 96
82.40	Plamen	Minev	BUL	28.4.65	1	NM	Plovdiv	1 Jun 91
82.38	Gilles	Dupray	FRA	2.1.70	1		Chelles	21 Jun 00
82.24	Benjaminas	Viluckis	LIT	20.3.61	1		Klaipeda	24 Aug 86
82.24	Vyacheslav	Korovin	RUS	8.9.62	1		Chelyabinsk	20 Jun 87
82.22	Holger	Klose	GER	5.12.72	1		Dortmund	2 May 98
	(20)							
82.16	Vitaliy	Alisevich	BLR	15.6.67	1		Parnu	13 Jul 88
82.08	Ivan	Tanev	BUL	1.5.57	1	NC	Sofia	3 Sep 88
82.00	Sergey	Alay	BLR	11.6.65	1		Stayki	12 May 92
81.88	Jud	Logan ¶	USA	19.7.59	1		University Park	22 Apr 88
81.79	Christophe	Épalle	FRA	23.1.69	1		Clermont-Ferrand	30 Jun 00
81.78	Christoph	Sahner	FRG	23.9.63	1		Wemmetsweiler	11 Sep 88
81.73	Adrián	Annus	HUN	28.6.73	1		Nitra	7 Aug 99
81.72	Andrey	Skvaryuk	UKR	9.3.67	1	NC	Kiyev	27 May 94
81.70	Aleksandr	Seleznyov	RUS	25.1.63	2		Sochi	22 May 93
81.64	Enrico	Sgrulletti	ITA	24.4.65	1		Ostia	9 Mar 97
	(30)							
81.56	Sergey	Gavrilov	RUS	22.5.70	1	Army	Rostov	16 Jun 96
81.56	Zsolt	Németh	HUN	9.11.71	1		Veszprém	14 Aug 99
81.56	Vladislav	Piskunov	UKR	7.6.78	1		Yalta	25 Mar 00
81.52	Juha	Tiainen	FIN	5.12.55	1		Tampere	11 Jun 84
81.44	Yuriy	Tarasyuk	BLR	11.4.57	1		Minsk	10 Aug 84
81.42	Szymon	Ziolkówski	POL	1.7.76	1		Warszawa	20 Aug 00
81.36	Vadim	Devyatovskiy ¶	BLR	20.3.77	1	NC	Brest	1 Aug 00
81.32	Klaus	Ploghaus	FRG	31.1.56	1		Paderborn	25 May 86
81.28	Vladimir	Maska	CZE	6.2.73	1		Pacov	25 Sep 99
81.20	Igor	Grigorash	RUS	18.8.59	1		Kiyev	23 Aug 84
	(40)							
81.18	Albert	Sinka	HUN	22.11.62	1		Székesfehérvár	7 Aug 88
81.10	Sergey	Ivanov	RUS	3.1.62	1		Chelyabinsk	27 Jun 87
81.08	Koji	Murofushi	JPN	8.10.74	1	Super	Yokohama	9 Sep 00
80.98	Loris	Paoluzzi	ITA	14.5.74	1	NC	Pescara	4 Jul 99
80.92	Matthias	Moder	GDR	17.6.63	1		Halle	11 Jun 85
80.90	Yaroslav	Chmyr	UKR	29.11.66	1		Chernigov	2 Jun 90
80.80	Karl-Hans	Riehm	FRG	31.5.51	1		Rhede	30 Jul 80
80.78	Donatas	Plunge	LIT	11.11.60	1		Volgograd	22 Sep 89
80.78	Aleksandr	Krasko	BLR	7.4.72	1		Minsk	22 Jul 94
80.68	Viktor	Litvinenko	UKR	22.12.57	2		Kiyev	23 Aug 84
80.68	Vadim	Khersontsev	RUS	8.7.74	1		Sankt Peterburg	11 May 96
	(51)	100th man 78.71, 200th man 76.14						
Extra trial: 81.04	Mariusz	Tomaszewski	POL	23.4.56	-		Zabrze	1 Jul 84
Over-long Chain: 81.12	Grigoriy	Shevtsov	RUS	16.8.58	1		Sochi	12 May 83

JAVELIN

98.48 WR	Jan	Zelezny	CZE	16.6.66	1		Jena	25 May 96
95.66 WR		Zelezny			1	McD	Sheffield	29 Aug 93
95.54A WR		Zelezny			1		Pietersburg	6 Apr 93
94.64		Zelezny			1	GS	Ostrava	31 May 96
94.02		Zelezny			1		Stellenbosch	26 Mar 97
93.09	Aki	Parviainen	FIN	26.10.74	1		Kuortane	26 Jun 99
92.60	Raymond	Hecht	GER	11.11.68	1	Bisl	Oslo	21 Jul 95
92.42		Zelezny			1	GS	Ostrava	28 May 97

Mark	Wind	Name		Nat	Born	Pos	Meet	Venue	Date
92.28			Zelezny			1	GPF	Monaco	9 Sep 95
92.28			Hecht			1	WK	Zürich	14 Aug 96
92.12			Zelezny			1	McD	London (CP)	27 Aug 95
92.12			Zelezny			1	TOTO	Tokyo	15 Sep 95
91.82			Zelezny			1	McD	Sheffield	4 Sep 94
91.69		Kostadínos	Gatsioúdis	GRE	17.12.73	1		Kuortane	24 Jun 00
91.68			Zelezny			1	GP	Gateshead	1 Jul 94
91.50			Zelezny			1	Kuso	Lublin	4 Jun 94
91.50A			Zelezny			1		Pretoria	8 Apr 96
91.50			Hecht			1		Gengenbach	1 Sep 96
91.46	WR	Steve	Backley	GBR	12.2.69	1		Auckland	25 Jan 92
91.40			Zelezny			1	BNP	Villeneuve d'Ascq	2 Jul 93
91.34			Zelezny			1		Cape Town	8 Apr 97
91.30			Zelezny			1	ISTAF	Berlin	1 Sep 95
91.28			Zelezny			1	BNP	Villeneuve d'Ascq	8 Jul 94
91.04			Zelezny			1		Kuortane	22 Jun 96
90.97			Parviainen			2		Kuortane	24 Jun 00
90.88			Parviainen			1		Tartu	11 Jun 98
90.80			Zelezny			1		Bratislava	30 May 95
90.80			Parviainen			1		Vantaa	20 Jun 00
90.68			Zelezny			1	Nik	Nice	21 Jul 93
90.60			Zelezny			1		Stellenbosch	13 Apr 93
90.60		Seppo	Räty	FIN	27.4.62	1		Nurmijärvi	20 Jul 92
90.60			Zelezny			1		Osaka	11 May 96
		(32/6)	47 performances over 90m, 9 more for Zelezny, 3 more for Hecht and 2 more for Parviainen						
90.44		Boris	Henry	GER	14.12.73	1	Gugl	Linz	9 Jul 97
89.93		Sergey	Makarov	RUS	19.3.73	1	GP II	Athína	16 Jun 99
89.16A		Tom	Petranoff	USA	8.4.58	1		Potchefstroom	1 Mar 91
89.10	WR	Patrik	Bodén	SWE	30.6.67	1		Austin	24 Mar 90
		(10)							
88.75		Marius	Corbett	RSA	26.9.75	1	CG	Kuala Lumpur	21 Sep 98
88.24		Matti	Närhi	FIN	17.8.75	1		Soini	27 Jul 97
88.22		Juha	Laukkanen	FIN	6.1.69	1		Kuortane	20 Jun 92
88.20		Gavin	Lovegrove	NZL	21.10.67	1	Bisl	Oslo	5 Jul 96
88.12		Peter	Blank	GER	10.4.62	2	NC	Köln	21 Jun 96
88.00		Vladimir	Ovchinnikov	RUS	2.8.70	1		Tolyatti	14 May 95
87.82		Harri	Hakkarainen	FIN	16.10.69	1		Kuortane	24 Jun 95
87.60		Kazuhiro	Mizoguchi	JPN	18.3.62	1	Jen	San José	27 May 89
87.40		Vladimir	Sasimovich	BLR	14.9.68	2		Kuortane	24 Jun 95
87.34		Andrey	Moruyev	RUS	6.5.70	1	ECp	Birmingham	25 Jun 94
		(20)							
87.20		Viktor	Zaytsev	UZB	6.6.66	1	OT	Moskva	23 Jun 92
87.17		Dariusz	Trafas	POL	16.5.72	1		Gold Coast (RB)	17 Sep 00
87.12		Tom	Pukstys	USA	28.5.68	2	OD	Jena	25 May 97
87.12		Emeterio	González	CUB	11.4.73	1	OD	Jena	3 Jun 00
86.98		Yuriy	Rybin	RUS	5.3.63	1		Nitra	26 Aug 95
86.94		Mick	Hill	GBR	22.10.64	1	NC	London (CP)	13 Jun 93
86.80		Einar	Vihljálmsson	ISL	1.6.60	1		Reykjavik	29 Aug 92
86.74		Pål Arne	Fagernes	NOR	8.6.74	q	OG	Sydney	22 Sep 00
86.64		Klaus	Tafelmeier	FRG	12.4.58	1	NC	Gelsenkirchen	12 Jul 87
86.50		Tapio	Korjus	FIN	10.2.61	1		Lahti	25 Aug 88
		(30)							
86.10		Harri	Haatainen	FIN	5.1.78	2		Lapinlahti	16 Jul 00
85.96		Kimmo	Kinnunen	FIN	31.3.68	3	NC	Seinäjoki	8 Aug 99
85.75		Andrew	Currey	AUS	7.2.71	1		Adelaide	26 Jan 98
85.74		Dmitriy	Polyunin ¶	UZB	6.4.69	2	OT	Moskva	23 Jun 92
85.70		Andrey	Shevchuk	RUS	8.3.70	2	Slovn	Bratislava	1 Jun 93
85.67		Mark	Roberson	GBR	13.3.67	2		Gateshead	19 Jul 98
85.60		Peter	Esenwein	GER	7.12.67	1		Riederich	25 May 97
85.42		Andreas	Linden	GER	20.2.65	2		Mülheim-Kärlich	17 Sep 95
85.28		Donald-Aik	Sild	EST	3.10.68	2		St Denis	10 Jun 94
85.18		Ari	Pakarinen	FIN	14.5.69	Q		Lapua	22 Jul 95
		(40)							
85.16		Viktor	Yevsyukov	KZK	6.10.56	1	vGDR	Karl-Marx-Stadt	21 Jun 87
85.09		Nick	Nieland	GBR	31.1.72	2	NC	Birmingham	13 Aug 00
85.02		Dag	Wennlund	SWE	9.10.63	1		Alvesta	28 May 95
84.84		Volker	Hadwich	GDR	23.9.64	1	vITA,TCH	Macerata	5 Sep 89
84.80		Pascal	Lefévre	FRA	25.1.65	2	Nik	Nice	10 Jul 90
84.80		Sergey	Voynov	UZB	26.2.77	1		Villeneuve d'Ascq	17 Jun 00

Mark	Wind	Name		Nat	Born	Pos	Meet	Venue	Date
84.76		Peter	Borglund	SWE	29.1.64	1	vFIN	Stockholm	19 Aug 89
84.70		Edgar	Baumann	PAR	16.4.70	1		San Marcos	17 Oct 99
84.60		Carlo	Sonego	ITA	20.2.72	3		Osaka	8 May 99
84.56		Klaus-Peter	Schneider	FRG	7.4.58	1	NC	Hamburg	13 Aug 89
		(50)	100th man 81.78, 200th man 79.46						

Javelins with roughened tails, now banned by the IAAF

Mark	Wind	Name		Nat	Born	Pos	Meet	Venue	Date
96.96	WR	Seppo	Räty	FIN	27.4.62	1		Punkalaidun	2 Jun 91
94.74	Irreg		Zelezny			1	Bisl	Oslo	4 Jul 92
91.98	WR		Räty			1	Super	Shizuoka	6 May 91
91.36			Backley			1	McV	Sheffield	15 Sep 91
90.98	WR		Backley			1	PG	London (CP)	20 Jul 90
90.84			Hecht			1		Gengenbach	8 Sep 91
90.82		Kimmo	Kinnunen	FIN	31.3.68	1	WCh	Tokyo	26 Aug 91
90.72			Zelezny			1	Athl	Lausanne	10 Jul 91
87.00		Peter	Borglund	SWE	29.1.64	1		Stockholm	13 Aug 91
85.52		Dag	Wennlund	SWE	9.10.63	1	NC	Helsingborg	27 Jul 91
85.08		Radoman	Scekic	YUG	1.10.67	1		Zagreb	12 Jun 91
84.94		Sigurdur	Einarsson	ISL	28.9.62	2	Super	Shizuoka	6 May 91
84.86		Ramón	González	CUB	24.8.66	1		Potsdam	3 Jul 90

DECATHLON

Mark										
8994 WR	Tomás	Dvorák	CZE	11.5.72	1	ECp	Praha			4 Jul 99
	10.54/-0.1	7.90/1.1	16.78	2.04	48.08	13.73/0.0	48.33	4.90	72.32	4:37.20
8900		Dvorák			1		Götzis			4 Jun 00
	10.54/1.3	8.03/0.0	16.68	2.09	48.36	13.89/-1.0	47.89	4.85	67.21	4:42.33
8891 WR	Dan	O'Brien	USA	18.7.66	1		Talence			5 Sep 92
	10.43w/2.1	8.08/1.8	16.69	2.07	48.51	13.98/-0.5	48.56	5.00	62.58	4:42.10
8847 WR	Daley	Thompson	GBR	30.7.58	1	OG	Los Angeles			9 Aug 84
	10.44/-1.0	8.01/0.4	15.72	2.03	46.97	14.33/-1.1	46.56	5.00	65.24	4:35.00
8844w		O'Brien			1	TAC	New York			13 Jun 91
	10.23	7.96	16.06	2.08	47.70	13.95W/4.2	48.08	5.10	57.40	4:45.54
8837	Tomás	Dvorák	CZE	11.5.72	1	WCh	Athína			6 Aug 97
	10.60/0.8	7.64/-0.7	16.32	2.00	47.56	13.61/0.8	45.16	5.00	70.34	4:35.40
8832 WR	Jürgen	Hingsen	FRG	25.1.58	1	OT	Mannheim			9 Jun 84
	10.70w/2.9	7.76/	16.42	2.07	48.05	14.07/0.2	49.36	4.90	59.86	4:19.75
8825 WR		Hingsen			1		Bernhausen			5 Jun 83
	10.92/0.0	7.74	15.94	2.15	47.89	14.10	46.80	4.70	67.26	4:19.74
8824		O'Brien			1	OG	Atlanta			1 Aug 96
	10.50/0.7	7.57/1.4	15.66	2.07	46.82	13.87/0.3	48.78	5.00	66.90	4:45.89
8817		O'Brien			1	WCh	Stuttgart			20 Aug 93
	10.57/0.9	7.99/0.4	15.41	2.03	47.46	14.08/0.0	47.92	5.20	62.56	4:40.08
8812		O'Brien			1	WCh	Tokyo			30 Aug 91
	10.41/-1.6	7.90/0.8	16.24	1.91	46.53	13.94/-1.2	47.20	5.20	60.66	4:37.50
8811		Thompson			1	EC	Stuttgart			28 Aug 86
	10.26/2.0	7.72/1.0	15.73	2.00	47.02	14.04/-0.3	43.38	5.10	62.78	4:26.16
8792	Uwe	Freimuth	GDR	10.9.61	1	OD	Potsdam			21 Jul 84
	11.06/	7.79/	16.30	2.03	48.43	14.66/	46.58	5.15	72.42	4:25.19
8774 WR		Thompson			1	EC	Athína			8 Sep 82
	10.51/0.3	7.80/0.8	15.44	2.03	47.11	14.39/0.9	45.48	5.00	63.56	4:23.71
8762	Siegfried	Wentz	FRG	7.3.60	2		Bernhausen			5 Jun 83
	10.89	7.49/	15.35	2.09	47.38	14.00	46.90	4.80	70.68	4:24.90
8757	Roman	Sebrle	CZE	26.11.74	2		Götzis			4 Jun 00
	10.64/1.3	7.88/1.6	15.19	2.15	49.05	13.99/-1.0	47.21	4.75	67.23	4:35.06
8755		O'Brien			1	GWG	Uniondale, NY			20 Jul 98
	10.71/-2.3	7.78w/2.2	15.67	2.11	48.04	13.67/0.4	48.87	5.20	66.31	5:08.77
8744		Dvorák			1	WCh	Sevilla			25 Aug 99
	10.60/0.1	7.98/0.1	16.49	2.00	48.42	13.75/0.7	46.26	4.60	70.11	4:39.87
8742	Erki	Nool	EST	25.6.70	3		Götzis			4 Jun 00
	10.69/1.3	7.78/1.8	14.14	1.97	47.18	14.37/-0.1	44.16	5.55	69.10	4:35.59
8741 WR		Hingsen			1	NO	Ulm			15 Aug 82
	10.74w	7.85	16.00	2.15	47.65	14.64	44.92	4.60	63.10	4:15.13
8738		Dvorák			1		Götzis			30 May 99
	10.71/-1.2	7.77/-0.9	16.43	2.00	48.21	13.85/-0.9	46.54	4.80	68.66	4:33.99
8735	Eduard	Hämäläinen	FIN/BLR	21.1.69	1		Götzis			29 May 94
	10.50w/2.1	7.26/1.0	16.05	2.11	47.63	13.82/-3.0	49.70	4.90	60.32	4:35.09
8733		Dvorák			1	Deca	Talence			30 Jul 00
	10.75/-1.2	7.58/2.0	16.14	1.95	48.07	13.93/0.8	49.22	4.90	69.37	4:30.83
8730 WR		Thompson			1		Götzis			23 May 82
	10.50w/2.3	7.95/1.8	15.31	2.08	46.86	14.31/-0.8	44.34	4.90	60.52	4:30.55

Mark Wind	Name				Nat	Born	Pos	Meet	Venue	Date
8730		Hingsen					2	EC	Stuttgart	28 Aug 86
	10.87w/2.5	7.89w/2.8	16.46	2.12	48.79	14.52/-0.3	48.42	4.60	64.38	4:21.61
8730		Hämäläinen					2	WCh	Athína	6 Aug 97
	10.81/0.8	7.56/0.9	15.71	1.97	46.71	13.74/0.8	50.50	5.20	59.82	4:37.10
8727w/8705	Dave	Johnson			USA	7.4.63	1		Azusa	24 Apr 92
	10.96/0.4	7.52W/4.5 (7.43)	14.61	2.04	48.19	14.17/0.3	49.88	5.28	66.96	4:29.38
8726		O'Brien					1	NC	Atlanta	22 Jun 96
	10.32/1.7	7.46/0.7	15.64	2.08	46.81	14.04/0.3	49.38	5.20	65.22	5:12.01
8724		Hämäläinen					2	WCh	Stuttgart	20 Aug 93
	10.72/-0.9	7.05/0.0	15.49	2.09	47.64	13.57/0.0	49.26	5.30	61.88	4:39.34
8715		O'Brien					1	GWG	Sankt-Peterburg	29 Jul 94
	10.49/-0.3	7.81/1.4	15.70	2.20	47.73	13.81/0.6	48.10	4.90	62.20	5:10.9
	(30/10)									
8709	Aleksandr	Apaychev			UKR	6.5.61	1	vGDR	Neubrandenburg	3 Jun 84
	10.96/	7.57/	16.00	1.97	48.72	13.93/	48.00	4.90	72.24	4:26.51
8698	Grigoriy	Degtyaryov			RUS	16.8.58	1	NC	Kiyev	22 Jun 84
	10.87/0.7	7.42/0.1	16.03	2.10	49.75	14.53/0.3	51.20	4.90	67.08	4:23.09
8694	Chris	Huffins			USA	15.4.70	1	NC	New Orleans	20 Jun 98
	10.31w/3.5	7.76w/2.5	15.43	2.18	49.02	14.02/1.0	53.22	4.60	61.59	4:59.43
8680	Torsten	Voss			GDR	24.3.63	1	WCh	Roma	4 Sep 87
	10.69/-0.3	7.88/1.2	14.98	2.10	47.96	14.13/0.1	43.96	5.10	58.02	4:25.93
8667 WR	Guido	Kratschmer			FRG	10.1.53	1		Bernhausen	14 Jun 80
	10.58w/2.4	7.80/	15.47	2.00	48.04	13.92/	45.52	4.60	66.50	4:24.15
8644	Steve	Fritz			USA	1.11.67	4	OG	Atlanta	1 Aug 96
	10.90/0.8	7.77/0.9	15.31	2.04	50.13	13.97/0.3	49.84	5.10	65.70	4:38.26
8634 WR	Bruce	Jenner			USA	28.10.49	1	OG	Montreal	30 Jul 76
	10.94/0.0	7.22/0.0	15.35	2.03	47.51	14.84/0.0	50.04	4.80	68.52	4:12.61
8627	Robert	Zmelík			CZE	18.4.69	1		Götzis	31 May 92
	10.62w/2.1	8.02/0.2	13.93	2.05	48.73	13.84/1.2	44.44	4.90	61.26	4:24.83
8626	Michael	Smith			CAN	16.9.67	1		Götzis	26 May 96
	11.23/-0.6	7.72/0.6	16.94	1.97	48.69	14.77/-2.4	52.90	4.90	71.22	4:41.95
	(20)									
8583w	Jón Arnar	Magnússon			ISL	28.7.69	1	ECp-2	Reykjavik	5 Jul 98
	10.68/2.0	7.63/2.0	15.57	2.07	47.78	14.33W/5.2	44.53	5.00	64.16	4:41.60
8574	Christian	Plaziat			FRA	28.10.63	1	EC	Split	29 Aug 90
	10.72/-0.6	7.77/1.1	14.19	2.10	47.10	13.98/0.7	44.36	5.00	54.72	4:27.83
8574	Aleksandr	Yurkov			UKR	21.7.75	4		Götzis	4 Jun 00
	10.69/0.9	7.93/1.8	15.26	2.03	49.74	14.56/-0.9	47.85	5.15	58.92	4:32.49
8571	Lev	Lobodin			RUS	1.4.69	3	EC	Budapest	20 Aug 98
	10.66w/2.2	7.42/0.2	15.67	2.03	48.65	13.97/0.9	46.55	5.20	56.55	4:30.27
8567	Dean	Macey			GBR	12.12.77	4	OG	Sydney	28 Sep 00
	10.81/-1.1	7.77/-0.5	14.62	2.09	46.41	14.53/-1.4	43.37	4.80	60.38	4:23.45
8566	Sebastian	Chmara			POL	21.11.71	1		Alhama de Murcia	17 May 98
	10.97w/2.9	7.56/1.2	16.03	2.10	48.27	14.32/1.8	44.39	5.20	57.25	4:29.66
8554	Attila	Zsivóczky			HUN	29.4.77	5		Götzis	4 Jun 00
	10.64w/2.1	7.24/-1.0	15.72	2.18	48.13	14.87/-0.9	45.64	4.65	63.57	4:23.13
8548	Paul	Meier			GER	27.7.71	3	WCh	Stuttgart	20 Aug 93
	10.57/0.9	7.57/1.1	15.45	2.15	47.73	14.63/0.0	45.72	4.60	61.22	4:32.05
8547	Igor	Sobolevskiy			UKR	4.5.62	2	NC	Kiyev	22 Jun 84
	10.64/0.7	7.71/0.2	15.93	2.01	48.24	14.82/0.3	50.54	4.40	67.40	4:32.84
8534	Siegfried	Stark			GDR	12.6.55	1		Halle	4 May 80
	11.10w	7.64	15.81	2.03	49.53	14.86w	47.20	5.00	68.70	4:27.7
	(30)									
8534w/8478	Antonio	Peñalver			ESP	1.12.68	1		Alhama	24 May 92
	10.76w/3.9	7.42W/6.2 (7.19w/4.0)	16.50	2.12	49.50	14.32/0.8	47.38	5.00	59.32	4:39.94
8526	Francisco Javier	Benet			ESP	25.3.68	2		Alhama de Murcia	17 May 98
	10.72w/2.9	7.45/-1.2	14.57	1.92	48.10	13.83/1.8	46.12	5.00	65.37	4:26.81
8524	Sébastien	Levicq			FRA	25.6.71	4	WCh	Sevilla	25 Aug 99
	11.05/0.2	7.52/-0.4	14.22	2.00	50.13	14.48/0.6	44.65	5.50	69.01	4:26.81
8519	Yuriy	Kutsenko			RUS	5.3.52	3	NC	Kiyev	22 Jun 84
	11.07/0.5	7.54/-0.1	15.11	2.13	49.07	14.94/0.3	50.38	4.60	61.70	4:12.68
8506	Valter	Külvet			EST	19.2.64	1		Stayki	3 Jul 88
	11.05/-1.4	7.35/0.4	15.78	2.00	48.08	14.55/-0.8	52.04	4.60	61.72	4:15.93
8500	Christian	Schenk			GER	9.2.65	4	WCh	Stuttgart	20 Aug 93
	11.22/-0.9	7.63/0.0	15.72	2.15	48.78	15.29/0.0	46.94	4.80	65.32	4:24.44
8491	Aleksandr	Nevskiy			UKR	21.2.58	2		Götzis	20 May 84
	10.97/-1.6	7.24/1.2	15.04	2.08	48.44	14.67/1.0	46.06	4.70	69.56	4:19.62
8490	Jagan	Hames			AUS	31.10.75	1	CG	Kuala Lumpur	18 Sep 98
	10.77/0.0	7.64/0.8	14.73	2.19	49.67	14.07/0.4	46.40	5.00	64.67	5:02.68

Mark	Wind	Name		Nat	Born	Pos	Meet	Venue	Date
8485		Konstantin	Akhapkin	RUS	19.1.56	1	NC	Moskva	2 Aug 82
		11.10/0.2 7.72/0.2 15.25 2.02 49.14 14.38/1.8 45.68 4.90 62.42 4:19.60							
8485		Stefan	Schmid	GER	6.5.70	1	OT	Ratingen	23 Jul 00
		10.82/0.0 7.59/-0.6 14.14 2.01 48.99 14.20/-1.6 44.24 5.06 67.63 4:31.76							
		(40)							
8467		Tom	Pappas	USA	6.9.76	1	NC	Sacramento	21 Jul 00
		10.70/1.1 7.41/-1.4 15.32 2.14 48.91 14.27/-0.4 45.81 5.10 63.45 4:59.74							
8466 WR		Nikolay	Avilov	UKR	6.8.48	1	OG	München	8 Sep 72
		11.00/ 7.68/ 14.36 2.12 48.45 14.31/ 46.98 4.55 61.66 4:22.82							
8462w		Kip	Janvrin	USA	8.7.65	1	vGER	Edwardsville	18 Jul 96
		10.61W/4.1 7.34w/3.1 14.64 1.96 48.20 14.48W/5.7 45.84 5.00 61.82 4:20.12							
8461		Mike	Maczey	GER	28.9.72	7		Götzis	4 Jun 00
		10.99/0.9 7.59/0.3 14.75 2.06 49.83 14.16/-1.0 44.56 5.15 62.27 4:29.93							
8453		Alain	Blondel	FRA	7.12.62	1	EC	Helsinki	13 Aug 94
		11.12/0.6 7.50w/3.2 13.78 1.99 48.91 14.18/0.9 45.08 5.40 60.64 4:20.48							
8447		Robert	de Wit	NED	7.8.62	1	NC	Eindhoven	22 May 88
		11.07/0.5 6.98/0.2 15.88 2.04 48.80 14.32/0.7 46.20 5.00 63.94 4:20.98							
8445		Ramil	Ganiyev	UZB	23.9.68	5	WCh	Athína	6 Aug 97
		10.94/0.2 7.58/0.7 14.76 2.06 48.34 14.34/-0.1 46.04 5.30 55.14 4:36.78							
8437		Richardas	Malakhovskis	LIT	28.4.65	2		Stayki	3 Jul 88
		10.93/0.6 7.04/0.6 14.94 2.09 47.77 14.34/-0.9 44.04 4.90 59.58 4:13.67							
8436		Dezsö	Szabó	HUN	4.9.67	2	EC	Split	29 Aug 90
		11.06/-0.2 7.49/1.1 13.65 1.98 47.17 14.67/0.0 40.78 5.30 61.94 4:11.07							
8417		Sergey	Zhelanov	RUS	14.6.57	4	NC	Kiyev	22 Jun 84
		11.04/0.5 7.50/-0.0 14.31 2.13 48.94 14.40/-0.1 43.44 5.00 65.90 4:37.24							
		(50)	100th man 8248, 200th man 8076						

Drugs suspension

Mark	Wind	Name		Nat	Born	Pos	Meet	Venue	Date
8478		Stefan	Schmid #	GER	6.5.70	1	NC	Vaterstetten	1 Sep 96
		10.70/0.8 7.82/0.5 13.69 2.06 48.79 13.93/1.6 44.96 4.90 68.04 4:52.28							

ONE-HOUR DECATHLON

Mark	Name		Nat	Born	Pos	Venue	Date
7897	Robert	Zmelík	CZE	18.4.69	1	Ostrava	24 Sep 92
	10.89 7.64 14.52 2.08 55.53 14.25 41.92 4.80 60.34 4:55.16						
7891	Dan	O'Brien	USA	18.7.66	1	Pullman	8 Sep 95
	10.68 7.28 15.50 2.10 58.68 14.60 49.36 5.10 62.22 5:23.18						

4 x 100 METRES RELAY

Mark	Team	Pos	Meet	Venue	Date
37.40 WR	USA Marsh, Burrell, Mitchell, C Lewis	1	OG	Barcelona	8 Aug 92
37.40 WR	USA Drummond, Cason, D.Mitchell, L.Burrell	1s1	WCh	Stuttgart	21 Aug 93
37.48	USA Drummond, Cason, D.Mitchell, L.Burrell	1	WCh	Stuttgart	22 Aug 93
37.50 WR	USA Cason, Burrell, Mitchell, C Lewis	1	WCh	Tokyo	1 Sep 91
37.59	USA Drummond, Montgomery, B Lewis, Greene	1	WCh	Sevilla	29 Aug 99
37.61	USA Drummond, Williams, B.Lewis, Greene	1	OG	Sydney	30 Sep 00
37.65	USA Drummond, Williams, C.Johnson, Greene	1	ISTAF	Berlin	1 Sep 00
37.67 WR	USA Marsh, Burrell, Mitchell, C Lewis	1	WK	Zürich	7 Aug 91
37.69	CAN Esmie 10.47, Gilbert 9.02, Surin 9.25, Bailey 8.95	1	OG	Atlanta	3 Aug 96
37.73	GBR Gardener, Campbell, Devonish, Chambers	2	WCh	Sevilla	29 Aug 99
37.75	USA Cason, Burrell, Mitchell, Marsh	1h2	WCh	Tokyo	31 Aug 91
37.77	GBR C.Jackson, Jarrett, Regis, L.Christie	2	WCh	Stuttgart	22 Aug 93
37.79 WR	FRA Morinière, Sangouma, Trouabal, Marie-Rose	1	EC	Split	1 Sep 90
37.79 WR	Santa Monica TC/USA Marsh, Burrell, Heard, C Lewis	1	Herc	Monaco	3 Aug 91
37.79	USA - Santa Monica TC Marsh, Burrell, Heard, C Lewis	1	MSR	Walnut	17 Apr 94
37.82	USA Drummond, Williams, B.Lewis, Greene	1s1	OG	Sydney	29 Sep 00
37.83 WR	USA Graddy, R.Brown, C.Smith, C Lewis	1	OG	Los Angeles	11 Aug 84
37.83	CAN Esmie, Gilbert, Surin, Mahorn	3	WCh	Stuttgart	22 Aug 93
37.86 WR	USA E.King, Gault, C.Smith, C Lewis	1	WCh	Helsinki	10 Aug 83
37.86	CAN Esmie, Gilbert, Surin, Bailey	1	WCh	Athína	10 Aug 97
37.87	FRA Morinière, Sangouma, Trouabal, Marie-Rose	2	WCh	Tokyo	1 Sep 91
37.89	Santa Monica TC (USA) Marsh, Burrell, Heard, C Lewis	1	TexR	Austin	9 Apr 94
37.90	USA McRae, L.McNeill, Glance, C Lewis	1	WCh	Roma	6 Sep 87
37.90	USA Drummond, Harden, Mitchell, Greene	1	GWG	Uniondale, NY.	22 Jul 98
37.90	BRA de Lima, Ribeiro, A da Silva, Cl da Silva	2	OG	Sydney	30 Sep 00
37.91	NGR Asonze, Obikwelu, Effiong, Aliu	3	WCh	Sevilla	29 Aug 99
37.93	Santa Monica TC/USA Witherspoon, Burrell, Heard, C Lewis	1		Barcelona	16 Jul 90
37.94	NGR O Ezinwa, Adeniken, Obikwelu, D Ezinwa	1s2	WCh	Athína	9 Aug 97
37.95	USA Drummond, Williams, A.Johnson, Greene	1	GP II	Gateshead	28 Aug 00
37.96	USA Drummond, Harden, Montgomery, Mitchell	1s2	OG	Atlanta	2 Aug 96
37.96	USA Saddler, Henderson, Griffin, Mitchell	1	Gugl	Linz	9 Jul 97
(31 by 6 nations)					

Mark	Wind	Name	Nat	Born	Pos	Meet	Venue	Date
38.00	CUB	Simón, Lamela, Isasi, Aguilera			3	OG	Barcelona	8 Aug 92
38.02	URS	Yevgenyev, Bryzgin, Muravyov, Krylov			2	WCh	Roma	6 Sep 87
38.12	GHA	Duah, Nkansah, Zakari, Tuffour			1s1	WCh	Athína	9 Aug 97
38.17	AUS	Henderson, Jackson, Brimacombe, Marsh			1s2	WCh	Göteborg	12 Aug 95
	(10)							
38.20	JAM	L Frater, D Thomas, C Williams, Bredwood			4	OG	Sydney	30 Sep 00
38.29	GDR	Schröder, Kübeck, Prenzler, Emmelmann			2	vUSA	Karl-Marx-Stadt	9 Jul 82
38.31	JPN	Inoue, K Ito, Tsuchie, Asahara			5s2	WCh	Athína	9 Aug 97
38.33	POL	Zwolinski, Licznerski, Dunecki, Woronin			2	OG	Moskva	1 Aug 80
38.37	ITA	Tilli, Simionato, Pavoni, Mennea			2	WCh	Helsinki	10 Aug 83
38.46	URS/RUS	Zharov, Krylov, Fatun, Goremykin			4	EC	Split	1 Sep 90
38.50A	RSA	Newton, Gorries, La Grange, Quinn			1		Pretoria	24 Mar 00
38.53	UKR	Rurak, Osovich, Kramarenko, Dologodin			1	ECp	Madrid	1 Jun 96
38.54	FRG	Heer, Haas, Klein, Schweisfurth			1	R-W	Koblenz	28 Aug 88
38.60	ESP	Feo, José, Mayoral, Berlanga			3s1	WCh	Athína	9 Aug 97
38.61	GRE	Séggos, Alexópoulos, Panayiotópoulos, Hoídis			2	ECp	Paris (C)	19 Jun 99
	(20, with RUS and UKR for USSR)							
38.63	SWE	Karlsson, Mårtensson, Hedner, Strenius			3s2	OG	Atlanta	2 Aug 96
38.67	HUN	Karaffa, Nagy, Tatár, Kovács			1	BGP	Budapest	11 Aug 86
38.73A	CIV	Ouré, Meité, Nogboum, Kablan			2	WUG	Ciudad de México	13 Sep 79
38.74	RSA	Nagel, la Grange, Newton, Quinn			7	WCh	Sevilla	29 Aug 99
38.80	THA	Natenee, Sophanich, Janthana, Suwonprateep			1	AsiC	Jakarta	31 Aug 00
38.81	CHN	Li Xiaoping, Lin Wei, Huang Danwei, Chen Wenzhong			2h3	WCh	Göteborg	12 Aug 95
38.81	ISR	Jaar, Jablonka, Kafri, Porkhomovskiy			3h2	WCh	Sevilla	28 Aug 99
38.82	TCH/CZE	Matousek, Demec, Kynos, Bohman			4	OG	München	10 Sep 72
38.91	SLE	Lisk, Ganda, Jos. Thomas, Turay			5s1	OG	Atlanta	2 Aug 96
38.92	TRI	Alexander, Raeburn, Burns, Boldon			6s2	OG	Sydney	29 Sep 00
38.96	NOR	Ramirez, Ertzgaard, Sivle, Moen			2	ECp	München	21 Jun 97
Multi-nation team								
37.82		World All-Stars			2	MSR	Walnut	17 Apr 94
		Drummond/USA, Jarrett/GBR, Regis/GBR, Mitchell/USA						
Best low altitude marks								
38.74	RSA	Nagel, la Grange, Newton, Quinn			7	WCh	Sevilla	29 Aug 99
38.76	CIV	N'Dri Pacone, Zirignon, Douhou, Meité			1	AfCh	Dakar	20 Aug 98

4 x 200 METRES RELAY

Mark	Team	Name	Pos	Meet	Venue	Date
1:18.68 WR	USA - Santa Monica TC	Marsh, Burrell, Heard, Lewis	1	MSR	Walnut	17 Apr 94
1:19.10	World All-Stars		2	MSR	Walnut	17 Apr 94
		Drummond/USA, Mitchell/USA, Bridgewater/USA, Regis/GBR				
1:19.11 WR	Santa Monica TC/USA	M.Marsh, L.Burrell, F.Heard, C.Lewis	1	Penn	Philadelphia	25 Apr 92
1:19.38 WR	Santa Monica TC/USA	Everett, Burrell, Heard, C.Lewis	1	R-W	Koblenz	23 Aug 89
1:19.45	Santa Monica TC/USA	DeLoach, Burrell, C.Lewis, Heard	1	Penn	Philadelphia	27 Apr 91
1:19.47	Nike Int./USA	Brokenburr, A Harrison, Greene, M Johnson	1	Penn	Philadelphia	24 Apr 99
Best non-US nations						
1:20.79	Central Arizona DC/Jamaica		1		Walnut	24 Apr 88
		Bucknor, Campbell, O'Conner, Davis)				
1:21.10	ITA	Tilli, Simionato, Bongiorno, Mennea	1		Cagliari	29 Sep 83
1:21.29	GBR	Adam, Mafe, Christie, Regis	1		Birmingham	23 Jun 89
1.21.32	UKR	Vanyaykin, Tverdokhleb, Streltsov, Dolgodin	1	EurR	Portsmouth	5 Jun 93

4 x 400 METRES RELAY

Mark	Team	Name	Pos	Meet	Venue	Date
2:54.20 WR	USA	Young 44.3, Pettigrew 43.2, Washington 43.5, M. Johnson 43.2	1	GWG	Uniondale, NY.	22 Jul 98
2:54.29 WR	USA	Valmon 44.43, Watts 43.59, Reynolds 43.23, Johnson 42.94	1	WCh	Stuttgart	22 Aug 93
2:55.74 WR	USA	Valmon 44.6, Watts 43.00, M.Johnson 44.73, S.Lewis 43.41	1	OG	Barcelona	8 Aug 92
2:55.99	USA	L Smith 44.62, A Harrison 43.84, Mills 43.66, Maybank 43.87	1	OG	Atlanta	3 Aug 96
2:56.16A WR	USA	Matthews 45.0, Freeman 43.2, James 43.9, Evans 44.1	1	OG	Ciu. México	20 Oct 68
2:56.16 WR	USA	Everett 44.0, S.Lewis 43.6, Robinzine 44.74, Reynolds 43.94	1	OG	Seoul	1 Oct 88
2:56.35	USA	A Harrison 44.36, Pettigrew 44.17, C Harrison 43.53, Johnson 44.29	1	OG	Sydney	30 Sep 00
2:56.45	USA	J Davis 45.2, Pettigrew 43.9, Taylor 43.92, M.Johnson 43.49	1	WCh	Sevilla	29 Aug 99
2:56.47	USA	Young 44.6, Pettigrew 43.1, Jones 44.80, Washington 44.80	1	WCh	Athína	10 Aug 97
2:56.60	GBR	I Thomas 44.92, Baulch 44.19, Richardson 43.62, Black 43.87	2	OG	Atlanta	3 Aug 96
2:56.60	USA Red	Taylor 45.0, Pettigrew 44.2, Washington 43.7, Johnson 43.7	1	PennR	Philadelphia	29 Apr 00
2:56.65	GBR	Thomas 44.8, Black 44.2, Baulch 44.08, Richardson 43.57	2	WCh	Athína	10 Aug 97
2:56.75	JAM	McDonald 44.5, Haughton 44.4, McFarlane 44.37, Clarke 43.51	3	WCh	Athína	10 Aug 97
2:57.29	USA	Everett 45.1, Haley 44.0, McKay 44.20, Reynolds 44.00	1	WCh	Roma	6 Sep 87
2:57.32	USA	Ramsey 44.9, Mills 44.6, Reynolds 43.74, Johnson 44.11	1	WCh	Göteborg	13 Aug 95
2:57.53	GBR	Black 44.7, Redmond 44.0, Regis 44.22, Akabusi 44.59	1	WCh	Tokyo	1 Sep 91
2:57.57	USA	Valmon 44.9, Watts 43.4, D.Everett 44.31, Pettigrew 44.93	2	WCh	Tokyo	1 Sep 91
2:57.87	USA	L Smith 44.59, Rouser 44.33, Mills 44.32, Maybank 44.63	1s2	OG	Atlanta	2 Aug 96

Mark	Wind	Name	Nat	Born	Pos	Meet	Venue	Date
2:57.91		Nix 45.59, Armstead 43.97, Babers 43.75, McKay 44.60	USA		1	OG	Los Angeles	11 Aug 84
2:57.97		McDonald , Haughton , McFarlane, D Clarke	JAM		1	PAm	Winnipeg	30 Jul 99
2:58.00		Rysiukiewicz 45.6, Czubak 44.2, Haczek 44.0, Mackowiak 44.2	POL		2	GWG	Uniondale, NY.	22 Jul 98
2:58.22		Sanders 45.85, Akabusi 44.48, Regis 43.93, Black 43.96	GBR		1	EC	Split	1 Sep 90
2:58.23		Ramsey 44.6, Mills 44.0, Lyles 44.41, Hall 45.22	USA		1h1	WCh	Göteborg	12 Aug 95
2:58.29		McDonald 45.1, D Clarke 43.8, Blake 44.80, McFarlane 44.60	JAM		2h1	WCh	Göteborg	12 Aug 95
2:58.33		Haughton, M McDonald, Blackwood, D Clarke	JAM		3	GWG	Uniondale, NY.	22 Jul 98
2:58.42		McDonald 44.54, Blake 44.75, Haughton 44.60, Martin 44.53	JAM		2s2	OG	Atlanta	2 Aug 96
2:58.56		Parrela, da Silva, dos Santos, de Araújo	BRA		2	PAm	Winnipeg	30 Jul 99
2:58.65		Frazier 45.3, B.Brown 44.62, Newhouse 43.8, Parks 45.00	USA		1	OG	Montreal	31 Jul 76
2:58.68		Hylton 45.42, Baulch 44.66, Thomas 44.21, Richardson 44.39	GBR		1	EC	Budapest	23 Aug 98
2:58.68		Chukwu 45.18, Monye 44.49, Bada 44.70, Udo-Obong 44.31	NGR		2	OG	Sydney	30 Sep 00
		(30/6)						
2:59.02		Moncur 44.73, McIntosh 45.74, Oliver 44.79, Brown 44.46	BAH		3s1	OG	Sydney	29 Sep 00
2:59.13		Martínez 45.6, Herrera 44.38, Tellez 44.81, Hernández 44.34	CUB		1h2	OG	Barcelona	7 Aug 92
2:59.63		D.Kitur 45.4, S.Kitur 45.13, Kipkemboi 44.76, Kemboi 44.34	KEN		3h2	OG	Barcelona	7 Aug 92
2:59.70		Frayne 45.38, Clark 43.86, Minihan 45.07, Mitchell 45.39	AUS		4	OG	Los Angeles	11 Aug 84
		(10)						
2:59.86		Möller 45.8, Schersing 44.8, Carlowitz 45.3, Schönlebe 44.1	GDR		1	vURS	Erfurt	23 Jun 85
2:59.95		Jovkovic, Djurovic, Macev, Brankovic 44.3	YUG		2h3	WCh	Tokyo	31 Aug 91
2:59.96		Dobeleit 45.7, Henrich 44.3, Itt 45.12, Schmid 44.93	FRG		4	WCh	Roma	6 Sep 87
3:00.09		Rapnouil 45.5, Hilaire 45.5, Farraudière 44.86, Diagana 44.19	FRA		4	WCh	Stuttgart	22 Aug 93
3:00.16		Lovachov, Lomtyev, Kurochkin, Markin 43.9	URS		1	Drz	Moskva	18 Aug 84
3:00.20		van Oudtshoorn 46.5, Mokganyetsi 44.5, A.Botha 45.43, Malherbe 43.78	RSA		4	WCh	Sevilla	29 Aug 99
3:00.44		Kliger 45.72, Kosov 45.09, Vdovin 44.73, Golovastov 44.90	RUS		5	WCh	Stuttgart	22 Aug 93
3:00.64		Diarra 46.53, Dia 44.94, Ndiaye 44.70, Faye 44.47	SEN		4	OG	Atlanta	3 Aug 96
3:00.76		Karube 45.88, Ito 44.86, Osakada 45.08, Omori 44.94	JPN		5	OG	Atlanta	3 Aug 96
3:00.79		Chiwira 46.2, Mukomana 44.6, Ngidhi 45.79, Harnden 44.20	ZIM		2h3	WCh	Athína	9 Aug 97
		(20 inc. both URS and RUS)						
3:01.05		Delice, A Daniel, De Silva, Morris	TRI		1h1	OG	Barcelona	7 Aug 92
3:01.12		Lönnqvist 46.7, Salin 45.1, Karttunen 44.8, Kukkoaho 44.5	FIN		6	OG	München	10 Sep 72
3:01.37		Bongiorni 46.2, Zuliani 45.0, Petrella 45.3, Ribaud 44.9	ITA		4	EC	Stuttgart	31 Aug 86
3:01.60		Louis 46.67, Peltier 44.97, Edwards 45.04, Forde 44.92	BAR		6	OG	Los Angeles	11 Aug 84
3:01.61		Georgiev 45.9, Stankulov 46.0, Raykov 45.07, Ivanov 44.66	BUL		2h1	WCh	Stuttgart	21 Aug 93
3:02.09		Govile 46.72, Kyeswa 44.60, Rwamu 46.40, Okot 44.37	UGA		7	OG	Los Angeles	11 Aug 84
3:02.11		Kasbane, Dahane, Belcaid, Lahlou 44.5	MAR		1h2	WCh	Tokyo	31 Aug 91
3:02.46		Clerc 46.55, Rusterholz 45.28, Rohr 45.72, Schelbert 44.91	SUI		5h3	WCh	Sevilla	28 Aug 99
3:02.47		Andres 46.60, Trull 45.41, Martínez 45.75, Canal 44.71	ESP		3	EC	Budapest	23 Aug 98
3:02.57		Carlgren 46.0, Faager 45.5, Öhman 45.3, Rönner 45.8	SWE		7	OG	München	10 Sep 72

4 x 800 METRES RELAY

Mark		Team	Pos	Meet	Venue	Date
7:03.89	WR	GBR Elliott 1:49.14, Cook 1:46.20, Cram 1:44.54, Coe 1:44.01	1		London (CP)	30 Aug 82
7:04.70		RSA G van Oudtshoorn 1:46.9, Sepeng 1:45.2, J Kotze 1:48.3, J, Botha 1:44.3	1		Stuttgart	6 Jun 99
7:04.89		KEN/ex-St Patrick's School D Kiptoo 1:46.4, Tengelei 1:48.2, W Chirchir 1:45.7, Kimutai 1:44.6	2		Stuttgart	6 Jun 99
7:06.5		Santa Monica TC/USA) J Robinson 1:49.8, Mack 1:46.7, E Jones 1:45.2, Gray 1:44.8	1	MSR	Walnut	26 Apr 86
7:07.40		URS Masunov, Kostetskiy, Matvetev, Kalinkin	1		Moskva	5 Aug 84

4 x 1500 METRES RELAY

Mark		Team	Pos	Meet	Venue	Date
14:38.8	WR	FRG Wessinghage 3:38.8, Hudak 3:40.2, Lederer 3:42.6, Fleschen 3:37.3	1		Köln	16 Aug 77
14:40.4	WR	NZL Polhill 3:42.9, Walker 3:40.4, Dixon 3:41.2, Quax 3:35.9	1		Oslo	22 Aug 73
14:45.63		URS Kalutskiy, Yakovlev, Legeda, Lotarev	1		Leningrad	4 Aug 85
14:46.16		Larios, ESP Jiménez 3:40.9, Pancorbo 3:41.2, A García 3:43.9, Viciosa 3:40.2	1		Madrid	5 Sep 97
14:46.3		USA Aldridge, Clifford, Harbour, Duits	1	Int	Bourges	23 Jun 79
14:48.2		FRA Begouin, Lequement, Philippe, Dien	2	Int	Bourges	23 Jun 79

4 x 1 MILE RELAY

Mark	Team	Pos	Venue	Date
15:49.08	IRL Coghlan 4:00.2, O'Sullivan 3:55.3, O'Mara 3:56.6, Flynn 3:56.98	1	Dublin	17 Aug 85

20 KILOMETRES WALK

Mark	Name		Nat	Born	Pos	Meet	Venue	Date
1:17:25.6t	Bernardo	Segura	MEX	11.2.70	1	SGP	Fana	7 May 94
1:17:46	Roman	Rasskazov	RUS	28.4.79	1	NC	Moskva	19 May 00
1:17:46	Julio	Martínez	GUA	27.9.73	1		Eisenhüttenstadt	8 May 99
1:17:56	Alejandro	López	MEX	9.2.75	2		Eisenhüttenstadt	8 May 99

Mark Wind	Name		Nat	Born	Pos	Meet	Venue	Date
1:18:04 WR		Bo Lingtang	CHN	12.8.70	1	NC	Beijing	7 Apr 94
1:18:07		Rasskazov			1	NC-w	Adler	20 Feb 00
1:18:13 WR	Pavol	Blazek	SVK	9.7.58	1		Hildesheim	16 Sep 90
1:18:14	Mikhail	Khmelnitskiy	BLR	24.7.69	1	NC	Soligorsk	13 May 00
1:18:16	Vladimir	Andreyev	RUS	7.9.66	2	NC	Moskva	19 May 00
1:18:18	Yevgeniy	Misyulya	BLR	9.3.64	1		Eisenhüttenstadt	11 May 96
1:18:20 WR	Andrey	Perlov (10)	RUS	12.12.61	1	NC	Moskva	26 May 90
1:18:22	Robert	Korzeniowski	POL	30.7.68	1		Hildesheim	9 Jul 00
1:18:23	Andrey	Makarov	BLR	2.1.71	2	NC	Soligorsk	13 May 00
1:18:24	Jefferson	Pérez	ECU	1.7.74	1	WCp	Podebrady	19 Apr 97
1:18:27	Daniel	García	MEX	28.10.71	2	WCp	Podebrady	19 Apr 97
1:18:29		Korzeniowski			1	ECp	Eisenhüttenstadt	17 Jun 00
1:18:30	Ilya	Markov	RUS	19.6.72	3	WCp	Podebrady	19 Apr 97
1:18:32		Andreyev			1	NC-w	Adler	11 Feb 95
1:18:32		Li Zewen	CHN	5.12.73	4	WCp	Podebrady	19 Apr 97
1:18:35.2t	Stefan	Johansson	SWE	11.4.67	1	SGP	Fana	15 May 92
1:18:36	Mikhail	Shchennikov	RUS	24.12.67	1	NC	Sochi	20 Apr 96
1:18:37	Aleksandr	Pershin	RUS	4.9.68	2	NC	Moskva	26 May 90
1:18:37	Ruslan	Shafikov (20)	RUS	27.6.75	1	NC-w23	Adler	11 Feb 95
1:18:37		Shchennikov			1		Eisenhüttenstadt	14 May 95
1:18:37		Shchennikov			2		Eisenhüttenstadt	11 May 96
1:18:40.0t WR	Ernesto	Canto	MEX	18.10.59	1	SGP	Fana	5 May 84
1:18:40		Andreyev			1		Cheboksary	30 Aug 98
1:18:40		Korzeniowski			1		Turku	22 May 99
1:18:41	Igor	Kollár	SVK	26.6.65	3		Eisenhüttenstadt	11 May 96
1:18:42	Andreas	Erm	GER	12.3.76	2	ECp	Eisenhüttenstadt	17 Jun 00
	(30/23)							
1:18:46		Tan Mingjun	CHN	17.7.70	2	NC	Beijing	7 Apr 94
1:18:48	Rishat	Shafikov	RUS	23.1.70	2		Cheboksary	30 Aug 98
1:18:49 WR?	Daniel	Bautista	MEX	4.8.52	1	LT	Eschborn	29 Sep 79
1:18:51	Frants	Kostyukevich	BLR	4.4.63	3	NC	Moskva	26 May 90
1:18:54	Maurizio	Damilano	ITA	6.4.57	1	7N	La Coruña	6 Jun 92
1:18:56	Grigoriy	Kornev	RUS	14.3.61	4	NC	Moskva	26 May 90
1:18:56	Francisco	Fernández	ESP	5.3.77	3	ECp	Eisenhüttenstadt	17 Jun 00
	(30)							
1:19:00	Joel	Sánchez	MEX	15.9.67	3		Eisenhüttenstadt	8 May 99
1:19:02	Hatem	Ghoula	TUN	7.6.73	2		Eisenhüttenstadt	10 May 97
1:19:03	Noe	Hernández	MEX	15.3.78	2	OG	Sydney	22 Sep 00
1:19:12	Axel	Noack	GDR	23.9.61	1	vURS	Karl-Marx-Stadt	21 Jun 87
1:19:15	Artur	Meleshkevich	BLR	11.4.75	3	NC	Soligorsk	13 May 00
1:19:16		Chen Shaoguo	CHN	20.1.71	3	NC	Beijing	7 Apr 94
1:19:18	Jirí	Malysa	CZE	14.8.66	4	ECp	Eisenhüttenstadt	17 Jun 00
1:19:18.3t	Ronald	Weigel	GDR	8.8.59	1	SGP	Fana	26 May 90
1:19:19	Mikhail	Orlov	RUS	25.6.67	4	NC-w	Adler	11 Feb 95
1:19:22	David	Smith	AUS	24.7.55	1		Hobart	19 Jul 87
	(40)							
1:19:22	Dmitriy	Yesipchuk	RUS	17.11.74	4	NC-w	Adler	9 Feb 97
1:19:22.5t	Aleksey	Pershin	RUS	23.9.62	1	SGP	Fana	7 May 88
1:19:24	Carlos	Mercenário	MEX	3.5.67	1	LT	New York	3 May 87
1:19:24.1t	Walter	Arena	ITA	30.5.64	2	SGP	Fana	26 May 90
1:19:25	Valentí	Massana	ESP	5.7.70	2	7N	La Coruña	6 Jun 92
1:19:28	Ruslan	Alukayev	RUS	8.9.78	3		Cheboksary	30 Aug 98
1:19:29	Valdas	Kazlauskas	LIT	25.2.58	2	NC-w	Sochi	19 Feb 89
1:19:29	Satoshi	Yanagisawa	JPN	19.1.71	1		Kobe	30 Jan 00
1:19:30	Jozef	Pribilinec	SVK	6.7.60	1	LT	Bergen	24 Sep 83
1:19:31	Aleksey	Voyevodin	RUS	9.8.70	4		Cheboksary	30 Aug 98
	(50)	100th man 1:20:34, 200th man 1:21:55						

50 KILOMETRES WALK

Mark	Name		Nat	Born	Pos	Meet	Venue	Date
3:37:26 WR	Valeriy	Spitsyn	RUS	5.12.65	1	NC	Moskva	21 May 00
3:37:41 WR	Andrey	Perlov	RUS	12.12.61	1	NC	Leningrad	5 Aug 89
3:38:17 WR	Ronald	Weigel	GDR	8.8.59	1	IM	Potsdam	25 May 86
3:38:29	Vyacheslav	Ivanenko	RUS	3.3.61	1	OG	Seoul	30 Sep 88
3:38:31 WR		Weigel			1		Berlin	20 Jul 84
3:38:43	Valentin	Massana	ESP	5.7.70	1	NC	Orense	20 Mar 94
3:38:56		Weigel			2	OG	Seoul	30 Sep 88
3:39:21	Vladimir	Potemin	RUS	15.1.80	2	NC	Moskva	21 May 00
3:39:22	Sergey	Korepanov	KAZ	9.5.64	1	WCp	Mézidon-Canon	2 May 99
3:39:34	Valentin	Kononen	FIN	7.3.69	1		Dudince	25 Mar 00

Mark	Wind	Name		Nat	Born	Pos	Meet	Venue	Date
3:39:45		Hartwig	Gauder	GDR	10.11.54	3	OG	Seoul	30 Sep 88
3:39:47			Perlov			1		Leningrad	3 Aug 85
3:39:54		Jesús Angel	García (10)	ESP	17.10.69	1	WCp	Podebrady	20 Apr 97
3:40:02		Aleksandr	Potashov	BLR	12.3.62	1	NC	Moskva	27 May 90
3:40:07			Perlov			1		Kharkov	5 Sep 87
3:40:07		Andrey	Plotnikov	RUS	12.8.67	2	NC	Moskva	27 May 90
3:40:08		Tomasz	Lipiec	POL	10.5.71	2	WCp	Mézidon-Canon	2 May 99
3:40:12		Oleg	Ishutkin	RUS	22.7.75	2	WCp	Podebrady	20 Apr 97
3:40:13		Nikolay	Matyukhin	RUS	13.12.68	3	WCp	Mézidon-Canon	2 May 99
3:40:40			J A García			4	WCp	Mézidon-Canon	2 May 99
3:40:46	WR	José	Marin	ESP	21.1.50	1		Valencia	13 Mar 83
3:40:53			Gauder			1	WCh	Roma	5 Sep 87
3:40:54		German	Skurygin	RUS	15.9.63	5	WCp	Mézidon-Canon	2 May 99
3:40:55			Gauder			1	EC	Stuttgart	31 Aug 86
3:40:57.9t		Thierry	Toutain	FRA	14.2.62	1		Héricourt	29 Sep 96
3:40:58			Plotnikov			1	NC	Sochi	21 Apr 96
3:41:00			Potashov			4	OG	Seoul	30 Sep 88
3:41:07			Spitsyn			1	EC	Helsinki	13 Aug 94
3:41:09			Kononen			3	WCp	Podebrady	20 Apr 97
3:41:20	WR	Raul	González	MEX	29.2.52	1		Podebrady	11 Jun 78
3:41:14			Plotnikov			1	NC	Izhevsk	16 May 98
3:41:20			Zhao Yongsheng	CHN	16.4.70	1	WCp	Beijing	30 Apr 95
		(32/20)							
3:41:28.2t		René	Piller	FRA	23.4.65	1	SGP	Fana	7 May 94
3:41:33		Aleksey	Voyevodin	RUS	9.8.70	1		Naumburg	25 May 97
3:41:50		Robert	Korzeniowski	POL	30.7.68	1	NC	Ponte de Sôr	5 Mar 00
3:41:51		Venyamin	Nikolayev	RUS	7.10.58	2		Leningrad	3 Aug 85
3:41:56		Yevgeniy	Shmalyuk	RUS	14.1.76	6	WCp	Mézidon-Canon	2 May 99
3:42:00		Stanislav	Vezhel	BLR	11.10.58	3	NC	Moskva	27 May 90
3:42:03		Carlos	Mercenario	MEX	3.5.67	1	WCp	San José	2 Jun 91
3:42:04		Yevgeniy	Yevsyukov	RUS	2.1.50	3		Leningrad	3 Aug 85
3:42:20		Pavel	Szikora	SVK	26.3.52	1		Dudince	4 Apr 87
3:42:20		Viktor	Ginko	BLR	7.12.65	2		Palma	5 Mar 95
		(30)							
3:42:36		Reima	Salonen	FIN	19.11.55	1	NC	Vantaa	24 May 86
3:42:37		Valeriy	Suntsov	RUS	10.7.55	4		Leningrad	3 Aug 85
3:42:45		Miguel Angel	Rodríguez	MEX	15.1.67	6	WCp	Podebrady	20 Apr 97
3:43:13		Simon	Baker	AUS	6.2.58	1	LT	L'Hospitalet	28 May 89
3:43:14		Dietmar	Meisch	GDR	10.2.59	3	LT	New York	2 May 87
3:43:16			Zhou Yongshen	CHN	15.10.72	1	NC	Beijing	10 Apr 94
3:43:18		Aigars	Fadejevs	LAT	27.12.75	1	NC	Ogre	6 Jun 98
3:43:36		Martín	Bermúdez	MEX	19.7.58	1	LT	Eschborn	30 Sep 79
3:43:41			Zhang Huiqiang	CHN	14.10.76	2	NC	Zhuhai	12 Mar 96
3:43:46		Mikhail	Shchennikov	RUS	24.12.67	2	OG	Atlanta	2 Aug 96
		(40)							
3:43:50		Axel	Noack	GER	23.9.61	4	WCh	Stuttgart	21 Aug 93
3:43:55		Giovanni	Perricelli	ITA	25.8.67	3	EC	Helsinki	13 Aug 94
3:43:57		Vitaliy	Matsko	RUS	8.6.60	2	NC	Leningrad	5 Aug 89
3:43:57		Vitaliy	Popovich	UKR	22.10.62	3	NC	Leningrad	5 Aug 89
3:43:59		Enrique	Vera-Ybánez	MEX	31.5.54	2	LT	Eschborn	30 Sep 79
3:44:08		Viktor	Dorovskikh	RUS	19.10.50	5		Leningrad	3 Aug 85
3:44.12		Anatoliy	Grigoryev	RUS	24.12.60	1		Yevpatoriya	1 Oct 89
3:44:24		Erling	Andersen	NOR	22.9.60	2	WCp-s	Borås	15 Jun 85
3:44:24		Daniel	Plaza	ESP	3.7.66	3	NC	Palma	5 Mar 95
3:44:33		Jorge	Llopart	ESP	5.5.52	1		Reus	26 Aug 79
		(50)	100th man 3:48:24						

100 KILOMETRES WALK

8:43:30	Viktor	Ginko	BLR	7.12.65	1		Scanzorosciate	29 Oct 00
8:54:35	Aleksey	Rodionov	RUS	5.3.57	1		Scanzorosciate	15 Nov 98
8:55:12	Pascal	Kieffer	FRA	6.5.61	1		Besançon	18 Oct 92
8:55:40	Vitaliy	Popovich	UKR	22.10.62	1		Scanzorosciate	31 Oct 99
8:58:12	Gérard	Lelievre	FRA	13.11.49	1		Laval	7 Oct 84
8:59:14	Modris	Liepins	LAT	3.8.66	2		Scanzorosciate	29 Oct 00
9:00:58	Zoltán	Czukor	HUN	18.12.62	2		Scanzorosciate	31 Oct 99
9:01:29	Sten	Reichel	GER	16.5.75	3		Scanzorosciate	29 Oct 00
9:04:27	Denis	Franke	GER	27.11.69	2		Scanzorosciate	15 Nov 98
9:06:34	Peter	Tichy	SVK	12.3.69	5		Scanzorosciate	29 Oct 00

JUNIOR MEN'S ALL-TIME LISTS

100 METRES

Mark	Wind	Name		Nat	Born	Pos	Meet	Venue	Date
10.05		Davidson	Ezinwa	NGR	22.11.71	1		Bauchi	4 Jan 90
10.06	2.0	Dwain	Chambers	GBR	5.4.78	1	EJ	Ljubljana	25 Jul 97
10.07	2.0	Stanley	Floyd	USA	23.6.61	1		Austin	24 May 80
10.08	0.0	Andre	Cason	USA	13.1.69	1	TAC-j	Tallahassee	24 Jun 88
10.08A	1.9	Obadele	Thompson	BAR	30.3.76	3		El Paso	16 Apr 94
10.09A	1.8	Mel	Lattany	USA	10.8.59	2r2	USOF	USAF Academy	30 Jul 78
10.10	1.9	Stanley	Kerr	USA	19.6.67	1	TAC-j	Towson	28 Jun 86
10.10	1.2	Francis	Obikwelu	NGR	22.11.78	1		Lisboa	20 Jun 97
10.10	1.9	Mark	Lewis-Francis	GBR	4.9.82	1B	BrGP	London (CP)	5 Aug 00
10.11	1.9	Harvey	Glance	USA	28.3.57	1	OT	Eugene	20 Jun 76
10.11	2.0	Tim	Montgomery	USA	28.1.75	3h3	NC	Knoxville	15 Jun 94
Wind assisted									
9.83	7.1	Leonard	Scott	USA	19.1.80	1		Knoxville	9 Apr 99
10.07	2.9	Lee	McRae	USA	23.1.66	2h5	NCAA	Austin	30 May 85
10.08	4.0	Johnny	Jones	USA	4.4.58	1		Austin	20 May 77
10.08	2.2	Billy	Fobbs	USA	29.2.76	1r3		Houston	19 May 95
10.09	4.1	Stanley	Blalock	USA	18.3.64	1		Athens, Ga	19 Mar 83
10.09	3.1	Innocent	Asunze	NGR	30.12.72	1r1		Lagos	10 Jun 90

200 METRES

Mark	Wind	Name		Nat	Born	Pos	Meet	Venue	Date
20.07	1.5	Lorenzo	Daniel	USA	23.3.66	1	SEC	Starkville	18 May 85
20.13	1.7	Roy	Martin	USA	25.12.66	1		Austin	11 May 85
20.16A	-0.2	Riaan	Dempers	RSA	4.3.77	1	NC-j	Germiston	7 Apr 95
20.22	1.7	Dwayne	Evans	USA	13.10.58	2	OT	Eugene	22 Jun 76
20.23	0.5	Michael	Timpson	USA	6.6.67	1		University Park	16 May 86
20.24	0.2	Joe	DeLoach	USA	5.6.67	3		Los Angeles	8 Jun 85
20.24	0.2	Francis	Obikwelu	NGR	22.11.78	2rB		Granada	29 May 96
20.29	1.5	Clinton	Davis	USA	17.8.65	1	TAC-j	University Park	26 Jun 83
20.29	-0.2	Christian	Malcolm	GBR	3.6.79	2	CG	Kuala Lumpur	19 Sep 98
20.30		Davidson	Ezinwa	NGR	22.11.71	1h1		Bauchi	3 Jan 90
Wind assisted									
20.01	2.5	Derald	Harris	USA	5.4.58	1		San José	9 Apr 77
20.08	9.2	Leonard	Scott	USA	19.1.80	2r2		Knoxville	9 Apr 99
20.10	4.6	Stanley	Kerr	USA	19.6.67	2r2	SWC	Houston	18 May 86
Hand timing									
19.9		Davidson	Ezinwa	NGR	22.11.71	1		Bauchi	18 Mar 89

400 METRES

Mark	Name		Nat	Born	Pos	Meet	Venue	Date
43.87	Steve	Lewis	USA	16.5.69	1	OG	Seoul	28 Sep 88
44.66	Hamdam	Al-Bishi	KSA	5.5.81	1	WJ	Santiago de Chile	20 Oct 00
44.69	Darrell	Robinson	USA	23.12.63	2	USOF	Indianapolis	24 Jul 82
44.73A	James	Rolle	USA	2.2.64	1	USOF	USAF Academy	2 Jul 83
44.75	Darren	Clark	AUS	6.9.65	4	OG	Los Angeles	8 Aug 84
44.75	Deon	Minor	USA	22.1.73	1s1	NCAA	Austin	5 Jun 92
45.01	Thomas	Schönlebe	GDR	6.8.65	1		Berlin	15 Jul 84
45.01	Jerome	Young	USA	14.8.76	1	NC-j	Walnut	24 Jun 95
45.04A	Wayne	Collett	USA	20.10.49	1q2	OT	Echo Summit	13 Sep 68
45.04	Brandon	Couts	USA	17.2.79	1	DrakeR	Des Moines	25 Apr 98
45.05	Roberto	Hernández	CUB	6.3.67	2		Santiago de Cuba	21 Feb00
44.9+A	Steve	Williams	USA	13.11.53	1	WAC	El Paso	13 May 72

800 METRES

Mark	Name		Nat	Born	Pos	Meet	Venue	Date
1:43.64	Japheth	Kimutai	KEN	20.12.78	3rB	WK	Zürich	13 Aug 97
1:44.3*	Jim	Ryun	USA	29.4.47	1	USTFF	Terre Haute	10 Jun 66
1:44.3	Joaquim	Cruz	BRA	12.3.63	1		Rio de Janeiro	27 Jun 81
1:44.33	Yuriy	Borzakovskiy	RUS	12.4.81	2s2	OG	Sydney	25 Sep 00
1:44.56	Benjamin	Kipkurui	KEN	28.12.80	2		Rehlingen	24 May 99
1:44.69	William	Chirchir	KEN	6.2.79	6	Herc	Monaco	8 Aug 98
1:44.77	Benson	Koech	KEN	10.11.74	1	WJ	Seoul	19 Sep 92
1:45.05	Nicholas	Wachira	KEN	19.11.82	5rB	WK	Zürich	11 Aug 00
1:45.14	Wilfred	Bungei	KEN	24.7.80	3		Pátra	1 Aug 99
1:45.3A	Emmanuel	Kemboi	KEN	.81	1		Kakamega	9 Apr 00
1:45.34	José	Parrilla	USA	31.3.72	1	SEC	Baton Rouge	19 May 91
1:45.45	Andreas	Busse	GDR	6.5.59	1	GS	Ostrava	7 Jun 78
1:45.46	Hezekiel	Sepeng	RSA	30.6.74	3s1	WCh	Stuttgart	15 Aug 93

Mark Wind	Name		Nat	Born	Pos	Meet	Venue	Date

1000 METRES

2:15.00	Benjamin	Kipkurui	KEN	28.12.80	5	Nik	Nice	17 Jul 99
2:16.84	Ali	Hakimi	TUN	24.4.76	1		Lindau	28 Jul 95
2:16.86	Japheth	Kimutai	KEN	20.12.78	1	VD	Bruxelles	22 Aug 97
2:17.10	Julius	Achon	UGA	12.12.76	1		Rhede	30 Jul 95
2:17.40	Yuriy	Borzakovskiy	RUS	12.4.81	5	Nik	Nice	8 Jul 00

1500 METRES

3:32.91	Noah	Ngeny	KEN	2.11.78	9	Herc	Monaco	16 Aug 97
3:33.16	Benjamin	Kipkurui	KEN	28.12.80	1rB	WK	Zürich	11 Aug 99
3:33.24	William	Chirchir	KEN	6.2.79	8rA	WK	Zürich	12 Aug 98
3:34.63	Daniel	Komen	KEN	17.5.76	2	Znam	Moskva	5 Jun 95
3:34.92	Kipkoech	Cheruiyot	KEN	2.12.64	1		München	26 Jul 83
3:35.16	Cornelius	Chirchir	KEN	7.10.83	6	GP II	Rieti	3 Sep 00
3:35.51	Reyes	Estévez	ESP	2.8.76	2	WK	Zürich	16 Aug 95
3:35.63	Hailu	Mekonnen	ETH	4.4.80	3		Arnhem	10 Jul 99
3:35.67	Birhane	Alemu	ETH	16.7.82	1	NA	Heusden	5 Aug 00
3:35.97	Ali	Hakimi	TUN	24.4.76	1rB	ASV	Köln	18 Aug 95
3:36.07	Wilfred Oanda	Kirochi	KEN	12.12.69	4		Rieti	31 Aug 88
3:36.1+	Jim	Ryun	USA	29.4.47	1		Berkeley	17 Jul 66

1 MILE

3:50.41	Noah	Ngeny	KEN	2.11.78	2	Nik	Nice	16 Jul 97
3:51.3	Jim	Ryun	USA	29.4.47	1		Berkeley	17 Jul 66
3:53.15	Graham	Williamson	GBR	15.6.60	3	OsloG	Oslo	17 Jul 79
3:53.92	Kipkoech	Cheruiyot	KEN	2.12.64	8	ISTAF	Berlin	17 Aug 83

2000 METRES

4:59.14	Ali	Saïdi-Sief	ALG	15.3.78	9	Gaz	Villeneuve d'Ascq	29 Jun 97
5:00.0+	Sammy	Kipketer	KEN	29.9.81	8	in3k	Monaco	4 Aug 99
5:00.6+	Richard	Limo	KEN	18.11.80	2	APM	Hengelo	30 May 99

3000 METRES

7:33.00	Hailu	Mekonnen	ETH	4.4.80	2		Stuttgart	6 Jun 99
7:34.32	Richard	Limo	KEN	18.11.80	4	VD	Bruxelles	3 Sep 99
7:34.58	Sammy	Kipketer	KEN	29.9.81	5	VD	Bruxelles	3 Sep 99
7:35.52	Philip	Mosima	KEN	2.1.77	1	GP	London (CP)	12 Jul 96
7:38.09	Daniel	Komen	KEN	17.5.76	7	GPF	Monaco	9 Sep 95
7:39.82	Ismael	Kirui	KEN	20.2.75	3	ISTAF	Berlin	27 Aug 93
7:42.93	Andrew	Sambu	TAN	5.10.72	1		Grossetto	11 Aug 91
7:43.01	Albert	Chepkirui	KEN	4.4.81	2		Caorle	10 Jul 99
7:43.1+	Million	Wolde	ETH	17.3.79	5	in 5k	Zürich	12 Aug 98
7:43.20	Ari	Paunonen	FIN	10.3.58	3		Köln	22 Jun 77

5000 METRES

12:53.72	Philip	Mosima	KEN	2.1.77	2	GGala	Roma	5 Jun 96
12:54.07	Sammy	Kipketer	KEN	29.9.81	2	GGala	Roma	30 Jun 00
12:56.15	Daniel	Komen	KEN	17.5.76	2	GG	Roma	8 Jun 95
12:58.15	Richard	Limo	KEN	18.11.80	6	GGala	Roma	7 Jul 99
12:59.39	Million	Wolde	ETH	17.3.79	5	WK	Zürich	12 Aug 98
12:59.90	Albert	Chepkirui	KEN	4.4.81	8	Bisl	Oslo	28 Jul 00
13:02.75	Ismael	Kirui	KEN	20.2.75	1	WCh	Stuttgart	16 Aug 93
13:05.48	Assefa	Mezegebu	ETH	19.6.78	4	GGala	Roma	5 Jun 97
13:05.64	Julius	Gitahi	KEN	29.4.78	2	GP	Osaka	10 May 97
13:09.58	John Cheruiyot	Korir	KEN	13.12.81	11	WK	Zürich	11 Aug 00
13:10.98	Hailu	Mekonnen	ETH	4.4.80	12	GGala	Roma	7 Jul 99

10,000 METRES

27:11.18	Richard	Chelimo	KEN	21.4.72	1	APM	Hengelo	25 Jun 91
27:17.82	Addis	Abebe	ETH	5.9.70	2	WG	Helsinki	29 Jun 89
27:24.75	John Cheruiyot	Korir	KEN	13.12.81	5	OG	Sydney	25 Sep 00
27:25.01	Assefa	Mezegebu	ETH	19.6.78	1	APM	Hengelo	31 May 97
27:27.87	Elijah H.	Korir	KEN	15.4.78	5	VD	Bruxelles	22 Aug 97
27:28.60	Julius	Gitahi	KEN	29.4.78	1		Konosu	5 Oct 96
27:32.18	David	Chelule	KEN	7.7.77	2	Slovn	Bratislava	29 May 96
27:36.5	Simon	Maina Munyi	KEN	18.3.78	1		Hachioji	30 Nov 97
27:42.75	Salim	Kipsang	KEN	22.12.79	10	VD	Bruxelles	28 Aug 98
27:43.14	Robert	Kipchumba	KEN-J	24.2.84	3		Rovereto	30 Aug 00

Mark	Wind	Name		Nat	Born	Pos	Meet	Venue	Date

3000 METRES STEEPLECHASE

8:03.74		Raymond	Yator	KEN	7.4.81	3	Herc	Monaco	18 Aug 00
8:07.69		Paul	Kosgei	KEN	22.4.78	5	DNG	Stockholm	7 Jul 97
8:16.76		Kipkirui	Misoi	KEN	23.10.78	2		Dortmund	8 Jun 97
8:18.71		Julius	Chelule	KEN	25.12.78	4	Slovn	Bratislava	10 Jun 97
8:19.12		Stephen	Cherono	KEN	15.10.82	11	WK	Zürich	11 Aug 99
8:19.21		Daniel	Njenga	KEN	7.5.76	1	JPN Ch	Tokyo	12 Jun 94
8:20.07		Christopher	Soget	KEN	15.5.80	2	Afr-J	Tunis	23 Jul 99
8:20.67		Richard	Limo	KEN	18.11.80	2	AfrC	Dakar	20 Aug 98
8:20.73		Paul	Chemase	KEN	24.8.76	10	Herc	Monaco	25 Jul 95
8:22.96		Abraham	Cherono	KEN	21.7.80	2		Linz	26 Jul 99
8:23.18		Ali	Ezzine	MAR	3.9.78	14	WK	Zürich	13 Aug 97

110 METRES HURDLES

13.23	0.0	Renaldo	Nehemiah	USA	24.3.59	1r2	WK	Zürich	16 Aug 78
13.44	-0.8	Colin	Jackson	GBR	18.2.67	1	WJ	Athína	19 Jul 86
13.46	1.8	Jon	Ridgeon	GBR	14.2.67	1	EJ	Cottbus	23 Aug 85
13.47	1.9	Holger	Pohland	GDR	5.4.63	2	vUSA	Karl-Marx-Stadt	10 Jul 82
13.49	0.6	Stanislavs	Olijars	LAT	22.3.79	1		Valmiera	11 Jul 98
13.51!	1.2	Tomasz	Scigaczewski	POL	18.11.78	1		Lodz	7 Sep 97
13.52	2.0	Alejandro	Casañas	CUB	29.1.54	1		Warszawa	28 Jun 72
13.52	0.6	Ubeja	Anderson	USA	30.3.74	1		Knoxville	16 May 93
13.53	-0.2	William	Erese	NGR	12.9.76	1s1	NC	Lagos	17 Jun 95
13.56	0.5	Frank	Busemann	GER	26.2.75	1h2		Mannheim	4 Jun 94
Wind assisted									
13.42	4.5	Colin	Jackson	GBR	18.2.67	2	CG	Edinburgh	27 Jul 86
13.47	2.1	Frank	Busemann	GER	26.2.75	1	WJ	Lisboa	22 Jul 94
13.54	4.1	Rod	Wilson	USA	24.9.61	1h2	NCAA	Austin	6 Jun 80
13.55	3.1	Arto	Bryggare	FIN	26.5.58	1	vGBR	Oulu	10 Jul 77

400 METRES HURDLES

48.02		Danny	Harris	USA	7.9.65	2s1	OT	Los Angeles	17 Jun 84
48.68		Bayano	Kamani	USA	17.4.80	1	NCAA	Boise	4 Jun 99
48.72		Angelo	Taylor	USA	29.12.78	2	NCAA	Bloomington	6 Jun 97
48.74		Vladimir	Budko	BLR	4.2.65	2	DRZ	Moskva	18 Aug 84
48.76A		Llewellyn	Herbert	RSA	21.7.77	1		Pretoria	7 Apr 96
		49.15				2	WJ	Sydney	23 Aug 96
49.07		Mubarak	Al-Nubi	QAT	30.12.77	1	WJ	Sydney	23 Aug 96
49.09		Dai	Tamesue	JPN	3.5.78	1		Hiroshima	14 Oct 96
49.10		Yoshihiko	Saito	JPN	12.2.72	1		Kanazawa	17 Oct 91
49.23		Marek	Plawgo	POL	25.2.81	1	WJ	Santiago de Chile	21 Oct 00
49.30		Hadi Soua'an	Al-Somaily	KSA	30.12.76	1	PArab	Cairo	27 Aug 95

HIGH JUMP

2.37		Dragutin	Topic	YUG	12.3.71	1	WJ	Plovdiv	12 Aug 90
2.37		Steve	Smith	GBR	29.3.73	1	WJ	Seoul	20 Sep 92
2.36		Javier	Sotomayor	CUB	13.10.67	1		Santiago de Cuba	23 Feb 86
2.35i		Vladimir	Yashchenko	UKR	12.1.59	1	EI	Milano	12 Mar 78
		2.34				1	Prv	Tbilisi	16 Jun 78
2.35		Dietmar	Mögenburg	FRG	15.8.61	1		Rehlingen	26 May 80
2.34		Tim	Forsyth	AUS	17.8.73	1	Bisl	Oslo	4 Jul 92
2.33			Zhu Jianhua	CHN	29.5.63	1	AsiG	New Delhi	1 Dec 82
2.33		Patrik	Sjöberg	SWE	5.1.65	1	OsloG	Oslo	9 Jul 83
2.31		Jörg	Freimuth	GDR	10.9.61	3	OG	Moskva	1 Aug 80
2.31		Lochsley	Thomson	AUS	20.8.73	3	NC	Adelaide	8 Mar 92

POLE VAULT

5.80		Maksim	Tarasov	RUS	2.12.70	1	vGDR-j	Bryansk	14 Jul 89
5.71		Lawrence	Johnson	USA	7.5.74	1		Knoxville	12 Jun 93
5.70		Viktor	Chistyakov	RUS	9.2.75	1		Leppävirta	7 Jun 94
5.65		Radion	Gataullin	UZB	23.11.65	2	NC	Donetsk	8 Sep 84
5.65		István	Bagyula	HUN	2.1.69	1	WJ	Sudbury	28 Jul 88
5.65i		Jacob	Davis	USA	29.4.78	1	Big 12	Lincoln	21 Feb 97
		5.62				2		Austin	5 Apr 97
5.62		Gérald	Baudouin	FRA	15.11.72	1	NC-j	Dreux	7 Jul 91
5.62		Lars	Börgeling	GER	16.4.79	1		Mannheim	13 Jun 98
5.61		Thierry	Vigneron	FRA	9.3.60	1		Longwy	30 Sep 79
5.61i		Grigoriy	Yegorov	KZK	12.1.67	1	vGDR-j	Moskva	16 Feb 86
5.61		Danny	Ecker	GER	21.7.77	1		Ljubljana	28 Sep 96

Mark	Wind	Name		Nat	Born	Pos	Meet	Venue	Date

LONG JUMP

Mark	Wind	Name		Nat	Born	Pos	Meet	Venue	Date
8.34	0.0	Randy	Williams	USA	23.8.53	Q	OG	München	8 Sep 72
8.28	0.8	Luis A	Bueno	CUB	22.5.69	1		La Habana	16 Jul 88
8.24	0.2	Eric	Metcalf	USA	23.1.68	1	NCAA	Indianapolis	6 Jun 86
8.24	1.8	Vladimir	Ochkan	UKR	13.1.68	1	vGDR-j	Leningrad	21 Jun 87
8.22		Larry	Doubley	USA	15.3.58	1	NCAA	Champaign	3 Jun 77
8.22		Ivan	Pedroso	CUB	17.12.72	1		Santiago de Cuba	3 May 91
8.21A	2.0	Vance	Johnson	USA	13.3.63	1	NCAA	Provo	4 Jun 82
8.20	1.5	James	Stallworth	USA	29.4.71	Q	WJ	Plovdiv	9 Aug 90
8.18		LaMonte	King	USA	18.12.59	2	CalR	Modesto	20 May 78
8.16	1.1	Dion	Bentley	USA	26.8.71	1	PAm-j	Santa Fé	23 Jun 89
8.16	1.8		Wang Cheng	CHN	4.11.80	1		Chengdu	19 Apr 98
Wind assisted									
8.40	3.2	Kareem	Streete-Thompson	CAY	30.3.73	1		Houston	5 May 91
8.35	2.2	Carl	Lewis	USA	1.7.61	1	NCAA	Austin	6 Jun 80
8.29	2.3	James	Beckford	JAM	9.1.75	1		Tempe	2 Apr 94
8.23	4.4	Peller	Phillips	USA	23.6.70	1		Sacramento	11 Jun 88
8.21	2.8	Masaki	Morinaga	JPN	27.3.72	1		Hamamatsu	7 Sep 91

TRIPLE JUMP

Mark	Wind	Name		Nat	Born	Pos	Meet	Venue	Date
17.50	0.4	Volker	Mai	GDR	3.5.66	1	vURS	Erfurt	23 Jun 85
17.42	1.3	Khristo	Markov	BUL	27.1.65	1	Nar	Sofiya	19 May 84
17.40A	0.4	Pedro	Pérez	CUB	23.2.52	1	PAm	Cali	5 Aug 71
17.29	1.3	James	Beckford	JAM	9.1.75	1		Tempe	2 Apr 94
17.27		Aliecer	Urrutia	CUB	22.9.74	1		Artemisa	23 Apr 93
17.23	0.2	Yoelbi	Quesada	CUB	4.8.73	1	NC	La Habana	13 May 92
17.03	0.6	Osiris	Mora	CUB	3.10.73	2	WJ	Seoul	19 Sep 92
17.00		Gustavo	Plá	CUB	29.7.54	1		La Habana	5 May 73
17.00		Yevgeniy	Timofeyev	RUS	22.2.74	1		Krasnodar	26 May 93
16.98	-0.2	Sergey	Bykov	UKR	11.5.71	1	WJ	Plovdiv	12 Aug 90
16.97	0.2	Igor	Parygin	RUS	3.2.67	1	WJ	Athína	20 Jul 86

SHOT

Mark	Wind	Name		Nat	Born	Pos	Meet	Venue	Date
21.05i		Terry	Albritton	USA	14.1.55	1	AAU	New York	22 Feb 74
		20.38				2	MSR	Walnut	27 Apr 74
20.65		Mike	Carter	USA	29.10.60	1	vSU-j	Boston	4 Jul 79
20.39		Janus	Robberts	RSA	10.3.79	1	NC	Germiston	7 Mar 98
20.20		Randy	Matson	USA	5.3.45	2	OG	Tokyo	17 Oct 64
20.20		Udo	Beyer	GDR	9.8.55	2	NC	Leipzig	6 Jul 74
20.08i		Jeff	Chakouian	USA	20.4.82	1		Lexington	8 Dec 00
19.99		Karl	Salb	USA	19.5.49	4	OT	Echo Summit	10 Sep 68
19.74		Andreas	Horn	GDR	31.1.62	2	vSU-j	Cottbus	24 Jun 81
19.71		Vladimir	Kiselyov -1	UKR	1.1.57	1		Yalta	15 May 76
19.69		Mikulás	Konopka	SVK	23.1.79	2	NC	Nitra	11 Jul 98
19.68		Ron	Semkiw	USA	28.3.54	1	vAFR	Dakar	4 Aug 73

DISCUS

Mark	Wind	Name		Nat	Born	Pos	Meet	Venue	Date
65.62		Werner	Reiterer	AUS	27.1.68	1		Melbourne	15 Dec 87
63.64		Werner	Hartmann	FRG	20.4.59	1	vFRA	Strasbourg	25 Jun 78
63.26		Sergey	Pachin	UKR	24.5.68	2		Moskva	25 Jul 87
63.22		Brian	Milne	USA	7.1.73	1		University Park	28 Mar 92
62.52		John	Nichols	USA	23.8.69	1		Baton Rouge	23 Apr 88
62.16		Zoltán	Kövágó	HUN	10.4.79	1		Budapest	9 May 97
62.04		Kenth	Gardenkrans	SWE	2.10.55	2		Helsingborg	11 Aug 74
61.84		Attila	Horváth	HUN	28.7.67	2		Budapest	18 May 85
61.84		Andreas	Seelig	GDR	6.7.70	1		Halle	15 May 88
61.54		Pedro	Acosta	CUB	15.1.70	1		La Habana	15 Jul 89

HAMMER

Mark	Wind	Name		Nat	Born	Pos	Meet	Venue	Date
78.33		Olli-Pekka	Karjalainen	FIN	7.3.80	1	NC	Seinäjoki	5 Aug 99
78.14		Roland	Steuk	GDR	5.3.59	1	NC	Leipzig	30 Jun 78
78.00		Sergey	Dorozhon	UKR	17.2.64	1		Moskva	7 Aug 83
76.54		Valeriy	Gubkin	BLR	3.9.67	2		Minsk	27 Jun 86
76.42		Ruslan	Dikiy	TJK	18.1.72	1		Togliatti	7 Sep 91
75.52		Sergey	Kirmasov	RUS	25.3.70	1		Kharkov	4 Jun 89
75.42		Szymon	Ziolkowski	POL	1.7.76	1	EJ	Nyíregyhazá	30 Jul 95
75.24		Christoph	Sahner	FRG	23.9.63	1	vPOL-j	Göttingen	26 Jun 82
75.22		Yaroslav	Chmyr	UKR	29.11.66	1		Kiyev	9 Sep 85
75.20		Igor	Nikulin	RUS	14.8.60	2		Leselidze	1 Jun 79

JAVELIN

Mark	Wind	Name		Nat	Born	Pos	Meet	Venue	Date
82.52		Harri	Haatainen	FIN	5.1.78	4		Leppävirta	25 May 96
81.80		Sergey	Voynov	UZB	26.2.77	1		Tashkent	6 Jun 96
80.94		Aki	Parviainen	FIN	26.10.74	4	NC	Jyväskylä	5 Jul 92
80.30		Konstadínos	Gatsioúdis	GRE	17.12.73	1	NC	Athína	20 Jun 92
80.26		Vladimir	Ovchinnikov	RUS	2.8.70	Q	OG	Seoul	24 Sep 88
79.58		Gavin	Lovegrove	NZL	21.10.67	2		Nouméa	26 Oct 86
79.50		Steve	Backley	GBR	12.12.69	1	NC	Derby	5 Jun 88
79.46		Juha	Laukkanen	FIN	6.1.69	1		Joutsa	19 Jul 87
79.30			Li Rongxiang	CHN	.2.72			Beijing	25 Apr 91
78.84		Vladimir	Sasimovich	BLR	14.9.68	1	WJ	Athína	18 Jul 86

DECATHLON

Mark	Name		Nat	Born	Pos	Meet	Venue	Date
8397	Torsten	Voss	GDR	24.3.63	1	NC	Erfurt	7 Jul 82
	10.76/ 7.66/ 14.41 2.09 48.37 14.37/ 41.76 4.80 62.90 4:34.04							
8114	Michael	Kohnle	FRG	3.5.70	1	EJ	Varazdin	26 Aug 89
	10.95/ 7.09/0.1 15.27 2.02 49.91 14.40/ 45.82 4.90 60.82 4:49.43							
8104	Valter	Külvet	EST	19.2.64	1		Viimsi	23 Aug 81
	10.7 / 7.26/ 13.86 2.09 48.5 14.8 / 47.92 4.50 60.34 4:37.8							
8082	Daley	Thompson	GBR	30.7.58	1	ECp/s	Sittard	31 Jul 77
	10.70/0.8 7.54/0.7 13.84 2.01 47.31 15.26/2.0 41.70 4.70 54.48 4:30.4							
8036	Christian	Schenk	GDR	9.2.65	5		Potsdam	21 Jul 84
	11.54/ 7.18/ 14.26 2.16 49.23 15.06/ 44.74 4.20 65.98 4:24.11							
7938	Frank	Busemann	GER	26.2.75	1		Zeven	2 Oct 94
	10.68/1.6 7.37/1.1 13.08 2.03 50.41 14.34/-1.139.84 4.40 63.00 4:37.31)							
7913	Raul	Duany	CUB	4.1.75	2		La Habana	26 May 94
	11.50/ 7.13/ 13.99 2.10 49.70 14.77/ 37.76 4.50 65.58 4:24.03							
7906	Mikhail	Romanyuk	UKR	6.2.62	1	EJ	Utrecht	21 Aug 81
	11.26/1.8 7.11w/3.7 13.50 1.98 49.98 14.72w/4.042.94 4.90 59.74 4:30.63							
7897	Dennis	Leyckes	GER	20.4.82	1	WJ	Santiago de Chile	19 Oct 00
	10.98/1.6 7.22/0.4 13.46 1.95 47.59 14.61/-0.139.52 4.80 54.76 4:33.10							
7881	Aki	Heikkinen	FIN	24.2.80	1	EJ	Riga	6 Aug 99
	11.10/0.5 7.23w/2.4 13.87 1.92 49.71 15.25/-1.140.96 4.80 66.75 4:36.62							

10,000 METRES WALK

Mark	Name		Nat	Born	Pos	Meet	Venue	Date
38:46.4	Viktor	Burayev	RUS	23.8.82	1	NC-j	Moskva	20 May 00
38:54.75	Ralf	Kowalsky	GDR	22.3.62	1		Cottbus	24 Jun 81
39:44.71	Giovanni	De Benedictis	ITA	8.1.68	1	EJ	Birmingham	7 Aug 87
39:49.22		Pei Chuang	CHN	5.12.81	2	NSG	Chengdu	8 Sep 00
39:50.73	Jefferson	Pérez	ECU	1.7.74	1	PAmJ	Winnipeg	15 Jul 93
39:55.52	Ilya	Markov	RUS	19.6.72	1	WJ	Plovdiv	10 Aug 90
39:56.49	Alberto	Cruz	MEX	6.6.72	2	WJ	Plovdiv	10 Aug 90
39:59.58	Sergey	Tyulenyev	RUS	14.3.71	1		Kharkov	4 Jun 90
40:05.62	Michele	Didoni	ITA	7.3.74	1	EJ	San Sebastián	30 Jul 93
40:13.11	Yevgeniy	Shmalyuk	RUS	14.1.76	1		Sankt-Peterburg	28 May 94

4 x 100 METRES RELAY

Mark	Nat	Team	Pos	Meet	Venue	Date
39.00A	USA	Jessle, Franklin, Blalock, Mitchell	1		Colorado Springs	18 Jul 83
39.13	USA	Nelloms, Bridges, Harris, Stallworth	1	WJ	Plovdiv	12 Aug 90
39.05	GBR	Edgar, Grant, Benjamin, Lewis-Francis	1	WJ	Santiago de Chile	22 Oct 00
39.25	FRG	Dobeleit, Klameth, Evers, Lübke	1	EJ	Schwechat	28 Aug 83
39.33	FRA	Pognon, Calligny, Doucoure, Djhone	2	WJ	Santiago de Chile	22 Oct 00
39.47	JPN	Mogi, Kitamura, Omaer, Miyazaki	3	WJ	Santiago de Chile	22 Oct 00
39.51	CIV	Y.Sonan, Ahmed Douhou, A.Byo, Ibrahim Meité	1	Afr-J	Bouaké	22 Jul 95
39.53	URS	Inshakov, Gromadskiy, Semyonov, Goremykin	1h3	WJ	Plovdiv	11 Aug 90
39.54	NGR	Tetengi, D Ezinwa, Nwankwo, Adeniken	1h2	WJ	Sudbury	30 Jul 88
39.61	ITA	Alaimo, Ibba, Paggi, Comparini	2	EJ	Nyíregyhazá	30 Jul 95
39.61	POL	Latkowski, Jedrusinski, Niczyporuk, Chyla	1h3	WJ	Santiago	22 Oct 00

4 x 400 METRES RELAY

Mark	Nat	Team	Pos	Meet	Venue	Date
3:01.90	USA	Campbell, Rish, Waddle, Reed	1	WJ	Athína	20 Jul 86
3:03.80	GBR	Grindley, Patrick, Winrow, Richardson	2	WJ	Plovdiv	12 Aug 90
3:04.12	JAM	R McDonald, D Clarke, Watts, M McDonald	2	WJ	Lisboa	24 Jul 94
3:04.22	CUB	Cadogan, Mordoche, González, Hernández	2	WJ	Athína	20 Jul 86
3:04.58	GDR	Preusche, Löper, Trylus, Carlowitz	1	EJ	Utrecht	23 Aug 81
3:04.74	AUS	McFarlane, Batman, Thom, Vincent	1	WJ	Annecy	2 Aug 98
3:05.60	URS	Angelov, Oleynikov, Belikov, Golovastov	4	WJ	Plovdiv	12 Aug 90
3:05.77	FRG	Grüber, Seybold, Mikisch, Just	2	EJ	Schwechat	28 Aug 83
3:06.01	JPN	Takahashi, Tamesue, Okusako, Morita	2	WJ	Sydney	25 Aug 96
3:06.17A	RSA	- Transvaal	1	NC	Secunda	7 May 94

Mark	Wind	Name		Nat	Born	Pos	Meet	Venue	Date

WOMEN'S ALL-TIME WORLD LISTS

100 METRES

Mark	Wind	Name		Nat	Born	Pos	Meet	Venue	Date
10.49 WR	0.0	Florence	Griffith-Joyner	USA	21.12.59	1q1	OT	Indianapolis	16 Jul 88
		@ Probably strongly wind-assisted, but recognised as a US and world record							
10.61	1.2		Griffith-Joyner			1	OT	Indianapolis	17 Jul 88
10.62	1.0		Griffith-Joyner			1q3	OG	Seoul	24 Sep 88
10.65A	1.1	Marion	Jones	USA	12.10.75	1	WCp	Johannesburg	12 Sep 98
10.70	1.6		Griffith-Joyner			1s1	OT	Indianapolis	17 Jul 88
10.70	-0.1		Jones			1	WCh	Sevilla	22 Aug 99
10.71	0.1		Jones			1		Chengdu	12 May 98
10.71	2.0		Jones			1s2	NC	New Orleans	19 Jun 98
10.72	2.0		Jones			1	NC	New Orleans	20 Jun 98
10.72	0.0		Jones			1	Herc	Monaco	8 Aug 98
10.72	0.0		Jones			1	Athl	Lausanne	25 Aug 98
10.73	2.0	Christine	Arron	FRA	13.9.73	1	EC	Budapest	19 Aug 98
10.74	1.3	Merlene	Ottey	JAM	10.5.60	1	GPF	Milano	7 Sep 96
10.75	0.6		Jones			1	GGala	Roma	14 Jul 98
10.75	-0.4		Jones			1	OG	Sydney	23 Sep 00
10.76 WR	1.7	Evelyn	Ashford	USA	15.4.57	1	WK	Zürich	22 Aug 84
10.76	0.9		Jones			1	VD	Bruxelles	22 Aug 97
10.76	0.3		Jones			1q4	WCh	Sevilla	21 Aug 99
10.77	0.9	Irina	Privalova	RUS	22.11.68	1rA	Athl	Lausanne	6 Jul 94
10.77	-0.9		Jones			1rA	WK	Zürich	12 Aug 98
10.78A	1.0	Dawn	Sowell	USA	27.3.66	1	NCAA	Provo	3 Jun 89
10.78	1.7		Ottey			1	Expo	Sevilla	30 May 90
10.78	0.4		Ottey			1	GPF	Paris	3 Sep 94
10.78	1.1		Jones			1	BrGP	London (CP)	5 Aug 00
10.78	0.1		Jones			1	ISTAF	Berlin	1 Sep 00
10.79A WR	0.6		Ashford			1	USOF	USAF Academy	3 Jul 83
10.79	1.7		Ottey			1		Vigo	23 Jul 91
10.79	0.0		Li Xuemei	CHN	5.1.77	1	NG	Shanghai	18 Oct 97
10.79	-0.6		Jones			1		Osaka	9 May 98
10.79	-0.1	Inger	Miller	USA	12.6.72	2	WCh	Sevilla	22 Aug 99
		(30 performances by 9 athletes)							
10.81 WR	1.7	Marlies	Göhr' (10)	GDR	21.3.58	1	OD	Berlin	8 Jun 83
10.82	-1.0	Gail	Devers	USA	19.11.66	1	OG	Barcelona	1 Aug 92
10.82	0.4	Gwen	Torrence	USA	12.6.65	2	GPF	Paris	3 Sep 94
10.83	1.7	Marita	Koch	GDR	18.2.57	2	OD	Berlin	8 Jun 83
10.83	0.0	Sheila	Echols	USA	2.10.64	1q2	OT	Indianapolis	16 Jul 88
10.83	-1.0	Juliet	Cuthbert	JAM	9.4.64	2	OG	Barcelona	1 Aug 92
10.83	0.1	Ekateríni	Thánou	GRE	1.2.75	2s1	WCh	Sevilla	22 Aug 99
10.84	1.3	Chioma	Ajunwa ¶	NGR	25.12.70	1		Lagos	11 Apr 92
10.85	2.0	Anelia	Nuneva	BUL	30.6.62	1h1	NC	Sofiya	2 Sep 88
10.85	0.4	Zhanna	Pintusevich	UKR	6.7.72	2	WCh	Athína	3 Aug 97
10.86	0.6	Silke	Gladisch/Möller	GDR	20.6.64	1	NC	Potsdam	20 Aug 87
		(20)							
10.86@	0.0	Diane	Williams	USA	14.12.60	2q1	OT	Indianapolis	16 Jul 88
		10.94A	0.6			2	USOF	USAF Academy	3 Jul 83
10.86	0.1	Chandra	Sturrup	BAH	12.9.71	1	NC	Nassau	21 Jul 00
10.89	1.8	Katrin	Krabbe ¶	GDR	22.11.69	1		Berlin	20 Jul 88
10.89	0.0		Liu Xiaomei	CHN	11.1.72	2	NG	Shanghai	18 Oct 97
10.89	2.0	Chryste	Gaines	USA	14.9.70	2	NC	New Orleans	20 Jun 98
10.90	1.4	Glory	Alozie	NGR	30.12.77	1		La Laguna	5 Jun 99
10.91	0.2	Heike	Drechsler'	GDR	16.12.64	2	GWG	Moskva	6 Jul 86
10.91	1.1	Sevatheda	Fynes	BAH	17.10.74	2	Athl	Lausanne	2 Jul 99
10.92	0.0	Alice	Brown	USA	20.9.60	2q2	OT	Indianapolis	16 Jul 88
10.92	1.1	D'Andre	Hill	USA	19.4.73	3	NC	Atlanta	15 Jun 96
		(30)							
10.93	1.8	Ewa	Kasprzyk	POL	7.9.57	1	NC	Grudziadz	27 Jun 86
10.94	1.0	Carlette	Guidry	USA	4.9.68	1	TAC	New York	14 Jun 91
10.95	1.0	Bärbel	Wöckel'	GDR	21.3.55	2	NC	Dresden	1 Jul 82
10.96	1.2	Marie-José	Pérec	FRA	9.5.68	1	NC	Dijon	27 Jul 91
10.96	2.0	Galina	Malchugina	RUS	17.12.62	2	CIS Ch	Moskva	22 Jun 92
10.96	1.0	Eldece	Clarke-Lewis	BAH	13.2.65	1	Conseil	Fort-de-France	29 Apr 00
10.96	0.1	Debbie	Ferguson	BAH	16.1.76	2	NC	Nassau	21 Jul 00
10.97	0.0	Angella	Issajenko' ¶	CAN	28.9.58	3	ASV	Köln	16 Aug 87

Mark	Wind	Name		Nat	Born	Pos	Meet	Venue	Date
10.97	0.2	Mary	Onyali	NGR	3.2.68	1q2	WCh	Stuttgart	15 Aug 93
10.97	0.1	Pauline	Davis-Thompson	BAH	9.7.66	3	NC	Nassau	21 Jul 00
		(40)							
10.98	0.1	Marina	Zhirova	RUS	6.6.63	2	ECp	Moskva	17 Aug 85
10.98	0.8	Angela	Bailey	CAN	28.2.62	2	BGP	Budapest	6 Jul 87
10.98	1.6	Natalya	Pomoshchnikova'	RUS	9.7.65	2q2	OG	Seoul	24 Sep 88
10.99	1.3	Valerie	Brisco-Hooks	USA	6.7.60	1	Pepsi	Westwood	17 May 86
10.99	0.7	Beverly	McDonald	JAM	15.2.70	1	GP II	Doha	7 May 98
11.01 WR	0.6	Annegret	Richter	FRG	13.10.50	1s1	OG	Montreal	25 Jul 76
11.01	0.8	Pam	Marshall	USA	16.8.60	2	Athl	Lausanne	15 Sep 87
11.01	1.3	Léonie Myriam	Mani	CMR	21.5.77	1	OD	Jena	3 Jun 00
11.02	2.0	Romy	Müller'	GDR	26.7.58	3	OT	Dresden	24 May 80
11.02	-0.2	Lyudmila	Kondratyeva	RUS	11.4.58	2	Drz	Praha	16 Aug 84
		(51)	100th women 11.11, 200th women 11.22						

Probably semi-automatic timing

Mark	Wind	Name		Nat	Born	Pos	Meet	Venue	Date
10.87	1.9	Lyudmila	Kondratyeva	RUS	11.4.58	1		Leningrad	3 Jun 80
10.99	1.9	Natalya	Bochina	RUS	4.1.62	2		Leningrad	3 Jun 80

Low altitude best: 10.91 1.6 Sowell 1 TAC Houston 16 Jun 89

Wind-assisted to 10.78 performances and 10.96 performers

Mark	Wind	Name		Nat	Born	Pos	Meet	Venue	Date
10.54	3.0		Griffith-Joyner			1	OG	Seoul	25 Sep 88
10.60	3.2		Griffith-Joyner			1h1	OT	Indianapolis	16 Jul 88
10.68	2.2		Jones			1	DNG	Stockholm	1 Aug 00
10.70	2.6		Griffith-Joyner			1s2	OG	Seoul	25 Sep 88
10.75	4.1		Jones			1h3	NC	New Orleans	19 Jun 98
10.77	2.3	Gail	Devers	USA	19.11.66	1	Jen	San José	28 May 94
10.77	2.1		Jones			1	Pre	Eugene	31 May 98
10.77	2.3	Ekateríni	Thánou	GRE	1.2.75	1		Rethymno	28 May 99
10.78	3.1		Ashford			1		Modesto	12 May 84
10.78	5.0	Gwen	Torrence	USA	12.6.65	1q3	OT	Indianapolis	16 Jul 88
10.78	2.3		Ottey			1s2	WCh	Tokyo	27 Aug 91
10.79	3.3	Marlies	Göhr'	GDR	21.3.58	1	NC	Cottbus	16 Jul 80
10.80	2.9	Pam	Marshall	USA	16.8.60	1	TAC	Eugene	20 Jun 86
10.80	2.8	Heike	Drechsler'	GDR	16.12.64	1	Bisl	Oslo	5 Jul 86
10.82	2.2	Silke	Gladisch/Möller	GDR	20.6.64	1s1	WCh	Roma	30 Aug 87
10.84	2.9	Alice	Brown	USA	20.9.60	2	TAC	Eugene	20 Jun 86
10.89	3.1	Kerstin	Behrendt	GDR	2.9.67	2		Berlin	13 Sep 88
10.91	4.6	Carlette	Guidry	USA	4.9.68	1s1	NCAA	Eugene	31 May 91
10.91	2.5	Debbie	Ferguson	BAH	16.1.76	1	NC	Nassau	18 Jun 99
10.92	3.3	Bärbel	Wöckel'	GDR	21.3.55	2	NC	Cottbus	16 Jul 80
10.92	3.4	Angella	Taylor' ¶	CAN	28.9.58	1s2	CG	Brisbane	4 Oct 82
10.92	3.4	Torri	Edwards	USA	31.1.77	1	MAI	Malmö	7 Aug 00
10.93	3.8	Sonia	Lannaman	GBR	24.3.56	1	ECp/sf	Dublin	17 Jul 77
10.93	3.3	Ingrid	Auerswald'	GDR	2.9.57	3	NC	Cottbus	16 Jul 80
10.93	4.2	Holli	Hyche	USA	6.9.71	2h2	NC	Eugene	16 Jun 93
10.94	3.9	Jackie	Washington	USA	17.7.62	1		Houston	18 May 86
10.94A	3.0	Evette	de Klerk'	RSA	21.8.65	1h	NC	Germiston	20 Apr 90
10.96	2.9	Brenda	Morehead	USA	5.10.57	1s2	AAU	Walnut	16 Jun 79
10.96	4.2	Olga	Naumkina'	RUS	20.5.64	1	Znam	Volgograd	11 Jun 89
10.96A	2.5	Michelle	Finn	USA	8.5.65	1		Sestriere	8 Aug 90
10.96	3.7	Angela	Williams	USA	30.1.80	1		Las Vegas	3 Apr 99
10.96	5.5	Kelli	White	USA	1.4.77	1r1	Sea Ray	Knoxville	9 Apr 99

Hand timing

Mark	Wind	Name		Nat	Born	Pos	Meet	Venue	Date
10.6	0.1	Zhanna	Pintusevich	UKR	6.7.72	1		Kiev	12 Jun 97
10.7		Merlene	Ottey	JAM	10.5.60	1h		Kingston	15 Jul 88
10.7	1.1	Juliet	Cuthbert	JAM	9.4.64	1	NC	Kingston	4 Jul 92
10.7		Mary	Onyali	NGR	3.2.68	1	NC	Lagos	22 Jun 96
10.7	-0.2	Svetlana	Goncharenko	RUS	28.5.71	1		Rostov	30 May 98
10.8		seven women from Renate Stecher GDR WR at Dresden on 20 Jul 73 and six at 10.8w							
10.7w	2.6	Sevatheda	Fynes	BAH	17.10.74	1		Nassau	22 Jun 95

200 METRES

Mark	Wind	Name		Nat	Born	Pos	Meet	Venue	Date
21.34 WR	1.3	Florence	Griffith-Joyner	USA	21.12.59	1	OG	Seoul	29 Sep 88
21.56 WR	1.7		Griffith-Joyner			1s1	OG	Seoul	29 Sep 88
21.62A	-0.6	Marion	Jones	USA	12.10.75	1	WCp	Johannesburg	11 Sep 98
21.64	0.8	Merlene	Ottey	JAM	10.5.60	1	VD	Bruxelles	13 Sep 91
21.66	-1.0		Ottey			1	WK	Zürich	15 Aug 90
21.71 WR	0.7	Marita	Koch	GDR	18.2.57	1	v Can	Karl-Marx-Stadt	10 Jun 79
21.71 WR	0.3		Koch			1	OD	Potsdam	21 Jul 84
21.71 WR	1.2	Heike	Drechsler'	GDR	16.12.64	1	NC	Jena	29 Jun 86
21.71 WR	-0.8		Drechsler			1	EC	Stuttgart	29 Aug 86

Mark	Wind	Name		Nat	Born	Pos	Meet	Venue	Date
21.72	1.3	Grace	Jackson	JAM	14.6.61	2	OG	Seoul	29 Sep 88
21.72	-0.1	Gwen	Torrence	USA	12.6.65	1s2	OG	Barcelona	5 Aug 92
21.74	0.4	Marlies	Göhr'	GDR	21.3.58	1	NC	Erfurt	3 Jun 84
21.74	1.2	Silke	Gladisch'	GDR	20.6.64	1	WCh	Roma	3 Sep 87
21.75	-0.1	Juliet	Cuthbert (10)	JAM	9.4.64	2s2	OG	Barcelona	5 Aug 92
21.76	0.3		Koch			1	NC	Dresden	3 Jul 82
21.76	0.7		Griffith-Joyner			1q1	OG	Seoul	28 Sep 88
21.76	-0.8		Jones			1	WK	Zürich	13 Aug 97
21.77	-0.1		Griffith-Joyner			1q2	OT	Indianapolis	22 Jul 88
21.77	1.0		Ottey			1	Herc	Monaco	7 Aug 93
21.77	-0.3		Torrence			1	ASV	Köln	18 Aug 95
21.77	0.6	Inger	Miller	USA	12.6.72	1	WCh	Sevilla	27 Aug 99
21.78	-1.3		Koch			1	NC	Leipzig	11 Aug 85
21.79	1.7		Gladisch			1	NC	Potsdam	22 Aug 87
21.80	-1.1		Ottey			1	Nik	Nice	10 Jul 90
21.80	0.4		Jones			1	GWG	Uniondale, NY	20 Jul 98
21.81	-0.1	Valerie	Brisco	USA	6.7.60	1	OG	Los Angeles	9 Aug 84
21.81	0.4		Ottey			1	ASV	Köln	19 Aug 90
21.81	-0.6		Torrence			1	OG	Barcelona	6 Aug 92
21.81	0.0		Torrence			1	Herc	Monaco	25 Jul 95
21.81	1.6		Jones			1	Pre	Eugene	30 May 99
		(30/12)							
21.83	-0.2	Evelyn	Ashford	USA	15.4.57	1	WCp	Montreal	24 Aug 79
21.85	0.3	Bärbel	Wöckel'	GDR	21.3.55	2	OD	Potsdam	21 Jul 84
21.87	0.0	Irina	Privalova	RUS	22.11.68	2	Herc	Monaco	25 Jul 95
21.93	1.3	Pam	Marshall	USA	16.8.60	2	OT	Indianapolis	23 Jul 88
21.95	0.3	Katrin	Krabbe ¶	GDR	22.11.69	1	EC	Split	30 Aug 90
21.97	1.9	Jarmila	Kratochvílová	CZE	26.1.51	1	PTS	Bratislava	6 Jun 81
21.99	0.9	Chandra	Cheeseborough	USA	10.1.59	2	TAC	Indianapolis	19 Jun 83
21.99	1.1	Marie-José	Pérec	FRA	9.5.68	1	BNP	Villeneuve d'Ascq	2 Jul 93
		(20)							
22.01	-0.5	Anelia	Nuneva'	BUL	30.6.62	1	NC	Sofiya	16 Aug 87
22.01	0.0		Li Xuemei	CHN	5.1.77	1	NG	Shanghai	22 Oct 97
22.04A	0.7	Dawn	Sowell	USA	27.3.66	1	NCAA	Provo	2 Jun 89
22.06A	0.7	Evette	de Klerk'	RSA	21.8.65	1		Pietersburg	8 Apr 89
22.07	-0.1	Mary	Onyali	NGR	3.2.68	1	WK	Zürich	14 Aug 96
22.10	-0.1	Kathy	Cook'	GBR	3.5.60	4	OG	Los Angeles	9 Aug 84
22.13	1.2	Ewa	Kasprzyk	POL	7.9.57	2	GWG	Moskva	8 Jul 86
22.14	-0.6	Carlette	Guidry	USA	4.9.68	1	NC	Atlanta	23 Jun 96
22.17A	-2.3	Zhanna	Pintusevich	UKR	6.7.72	1		Monachil	9 Jul 97
22.18	-0.6	Dannette	Young-Stone	USA	6.10.64	2	NC	Atlanta	23 Jun 96
		(30)							
22.18	0.9	Galina	Malchugina	RUS	17.12.62	1s2	NC	Sankt Peterburg	4 Jul 96
22.18	0.5	Merlene	Frazer	JAM	27.12.73	1s2	WCh	Sevilla	25 Aug 99
22.19	1.5	Natalya	Bochina	RUS	4.1.62	2	OG	Moskva	30 Jul 80
22.19	0.0	Debbie	Ferguson	BAH	16.1.76	1	GP II	Saint-Denis	3 Jul 99
22.22	0.6	Beverly	McDonald	JAM	15.2.70	2	WCh	Sevilla	27 Aug 99
22.21 WR	1.9	Irena	Szewinska'	POL	24.5.46	1		Potsdam	13 Jun 74
22.22	-0.9	Falilat	Ogunkoya	NGR	12.5.68	1	AfCh	Dakar	22 Aug 98
22.23	0.8	Melinda	Gainsford-Taylor	AUS	1.10.71	1		Stuttgart	13 Jul 97
22.24	0.3	Gesine	Walther	GDR	6.10.62	2	NC	Dresden	3 Jul 82
22.24	0.1	Maya	Azarashvili	GEO	6.4.64	1		Kiyev	16 Aug 88
		(40)							
22.25A	0.8	Angella	Taylor'	CAN	28.9.58	1		Colorado Springs	20 Jul 82
22.25	1.3	Cathy	Freeman	AUS	16.2.73	1	CG	Victoria	26 Aug 94
22.25	1.8	Andrea	Philipp	GER	29.7.71	2s1	WCh	Sevilla	25 Aug 99
22.26	0.0	Christine	Arron	FRA	13.9.73	2	GP II	Saint-Denis	3 Jul 99
22.27	1.2	Elvira	Barbashina'	UZB	25.2.63	3	GWG	Moskva	8 Jul 86
22.27	0.7	Pauline	Davis-Thompson	BAH	9.7.66	2	OG	Sydney	28 Sep 00
22.28	1.1	Fatima	Yusuf	NGR	2.5.71	2q2	WCh	Sevilla	24 Aug 00
22.28	0.7	Susanthika	Jayasinghe	SRI	17.12.75	3	OG	Sydney	28 Sep 00
22.29	0.7	Silke-Beate	Knoll	GER	21.2.67	1		Ingolstadt	19 Jul 92
22.29	0.6	LaTasha	Jenkins	USA	19.12.77	1	NCAA	Boise	5 Jun 99
		(50)	100th woman 22.52, 200th woman 22.80						

Wind-assisted

21.82	3.1	Irina	Privalova	RUS	22.11.68	1	Athl	Lausanne	6 Jul 94
22.16	3.1	Dannette	Young-Stone	USA	6.10.64	2	Athl	Lausanne	6 Jul 94
22.16	3.2	Nanceen	Perry	USA	19.4.77	1		Austin	6 May 00
22.18A	2.8	Melinda	Gainsford-Taylor	AUS	1.10.71	1		Pietersburg	18 Mar 00

Mark	Wind	Name		Nat	Born	Pos	Meet	Venue	Date
22.19A	3.1	Angella	Taylor'	CAN	28.9.58	1		Colorado Springs	21 Jul 82
22.22	2.7	LaTasha	Jenkins	USA	19.12.77	1s1	NCAA	Boise	4 Jun 99
22.25	3.8	Peta-Gaye	Dowdie	JAM	18.1.77	1		Baton Rouge	17 Apr 99
Hand timing									
21.9	-0.1	Svetlana	Goncharenko	RUS	28.5.71	1		Rostov-na-Donu	31 May 98
22.0	-0.6	Marina	Molokova	RUS	24.8.62	1	Ros	Praha	23 Jun 87
21.6w	2.5	Pam	Marshall	USA	16.8.60	1	TAC	San José	26 Jun 87

300 METRES

Times in 300m races

Mark	Wind	Name		Nat	Born	Pos	Meet	Venue	Date
35.46		Kathy	Cook'	GBR	3.5.60	1	Nike	London (CP)	18 Aug 84
35.46		Chandra	Cheeseborough	USA	10.1.59	2	Nike	London (CP)	18 Aug 84
35.70		Irena	Szewinska'	POL	24.5.46	1		London (CP)	4 Jul 75
35.71		Donna	Fraser	GBR	7.11.72	1		Gateshead	28 Aug 00
35.82		Cydonie	Mothersill	CAY	19.3.78	1r3		Sydney	14 Sep 00
35.99		Merlene	Ottey	JAM	10.5.60	3	Nike	London (CP)	18 Aug 84
Indoors									
35.45i		Irina	Privalova	RUS	22.11.68	1		Moskva	17 Jan 93
35.48	#	Svetlana	Goncharenko	RUS	28.5.71	1		Tampere	4 Feb 98
35.83		Merlene	Ottey	JAM	10.5.60	1	AIAW	Pocatello	14 Mar 81

400 METRES

Mark	Wind	Name		Nat	Born	Pos	Meet	Venue	Date
47.60 WR		Marita	Koch	GDR	18.2.57	1	WCp	Canberra	6 Oct 85
47.99 WR		Jarmila	Kratochvílová	CZE	26.1.51	1	WCh	Helsinki	10 Aug 83
48.16 WR			Koch			1	EC	Athína	8 Sep 82
48.16			Koch			1	Drz	Praha	16 Aug 84
48.22			Koch			1	EC	Stuttgart	28 Aug 86
48.25		Marie-José	Pérec	FRA	9.5.68	1	OG	Atlanta	29 Jul 96
48.26			Koch			1	GO	Dresden	27 Jul 84
48.27		Olga	Vladykina'	UKR	30.6.63	2	WCp	Canberra	6 Oct 85
48.45			Kratochvílová			1	NC	Praha	23 Jul 83
48.59		Tatána	Kocembová'	CZE	2.5.62	2	WCh	Helsinki	10 Aug 83
48.60 WR			Koch			1	ECp	Torino	4 Aug 79
48.60			Vladykina			1	ECp	Moskva	17 Aug 85
48.61			Kratochvílová			1	WCp	Roma	6 Sep 81
48.63		Cathy	Freeman	AUS	16.2.73	2	OG	Atlanta	29 Jul 96
48.65			Bryzgina'			1	OG	Seoul	26 Sep 88
48.73			Kocembová			2	Drz	Praha	16 Aug 84
48.77			Koch			1	v USA	Karl-Marx-Stadt	9 Jul 82
48.82			Kratochvílová			1	Ros	Praha	23 Jun 83
48.83		Valerie	Brisco	USA	6.7.60	1	OG	Los Angeles	6 Aug 84
48.83			Pérec			1	OG	Barcelona	5 Aug 92
48.85			Kratochvílová			2	EC	Athína	8 Sep 82
48.86			Kratochvílová			1	WK	Zürich	18 Aug 82
48.86			Koch			1	NC	Erfurt	2 Jun 84
48.87			Koch			1	VD	Bruxelles	27 Aug 82
48.88			Koch			1	OG	Moskva	28 Jul 80
48.89 WR			Koch			1		Potsdam	29 Jul 79
48.89			Koch			1		Berlin	15 Jul 84
48.94 WR			Koch			1	EC	Praha	31 Aug 78
48.96			Vladykina			1	NC	Leningrad	3 Aug 85
48.97			Koch			1	WCp	Montreal	26 Aug 79
48.97			Koch			1		Berlin	22 Sep 85
		(31/7)							
49.05		Chandra	Cheeseborough	USA	10.1.59	2	OG	Los Angeles	6 Aug 84
49.10		Falilat	Ogunkoya	NGR	12.5.68	3	OG	Atlanta	29 Jul 96
49.11		Olga	Nazarova ¶	RUS	1.6.65	1s1	OG	Seoul	25 Sep 88
			(10)						
49.19		Mariya	Pinigina'	UKR	9.2.58	3	WCh	Helsinki	10 Aug 83
49.24		Sabine	Busch	GDR	21.11.62	2	NC	Erfurt	2 Jun 84
49.28 WR		Irena	Szewinska'	POL	24.5.46	1	OG	Montreal	29 Jul 76
49.28		Pauline	Davis	BAH	9.7.66	4	OG	Atlanta	29 Jul 96
49.29		Charity	Opara ¶	NGR	20.5.72	1	GGala	Roma	14 Jul 98
49.30		Petra	Müller'	GDR	18.7.65	1		Jena	3 Jun 88
49.40		Jearl	Miles-Clark	USA	4.9.66	1	NC	Indianapolis	14 Jun 97
49.42		Grit	Breuer ¶	GER	16.2.72	2	WCh	Tokyo	27 Aug 91
49.43		Kathy	Cook'	GBR	3.5.60	3	OG	Los Angeles	6 Aug 84
49.43A		Fatima	Yusuf	NGR	2.5.71	1		Harare	15 Sep 95
		(20)							
49.47		Aelita	Yurchenko	UKR	1.1.65	2	Kuts	Moskva	4 Sep 88

Mark Wind	Name		Nat	Born	Pos	Meet	Venue	Date
49.56	Bärbel	Wöckel'	GDR	21.3.55	1		Erfurt	30 May 82
49.57	Grace	Jackson	JAM	14.6.61	1	Nik	Nice	10 Jul 88
49.58	Dagmar	Rübsam'	GDR	3.6.62	3	NC	Erfurt	2 Jun 84
49.58	Lorraine	Graham	JAM	8.9.73	2	OG	Sydney	25 Sep 00
49.59	Marion	Jones	USA	12.10.75	1r6	MSR	Walnut	16 Apr 00
49.61	Ana Fidelia	Quirot	CUB	23.3.63	1	PAm	Habana	5 Aug 91
49.64	Gwen	Torrence	USA	12.6.65	2	Nik	Nice	15 Jul 92
49.64	Ximena	Restrepo	COL	10.3.69	3	OG	Barcelona	5 Aug 92
49.66	Christina	Lathan'	GDR	28.2.58	3	OG	Moskva	28 Jul 80
	(30)							
49.66	Lillie	Leatherwood	USA	6.7.64	1	TAC	New York	15 Jun 91
49.67	Sandra	Myers	ESP	9.1.61	1	Bisl	Oslo	6 Jul 91
49.70A	Ana	Guevara	MEX	4.3.77	1	IMSS	Ciudad de México	1 Jul 00
49.72	Katharine	Merry	GBR	21.9.74	3	OG	Sydney	25 Sep 00
49.74	Anja	Rücker	GER	20.12.72	2	WCh	Sevilla	26 Aug 99
49.75	Gaby	Bussmann	FRG	8.10.59	4	WCh	Helsinki	10 Aug 83
49.79	Sandie	Richards	JAM	6.11.68	2	WCh	Athína	4 Aug 97
49.79	Donna	Fraser	GBR	7.11.72	4	OG	Sydney	25 Sep 00
49.81		Ma Yuqin	CHN	11.9.72	1	NG	Beijing	11 Sep 93
49.84	Diane	Dixon	USA	23.9.64	3s1	OG	Seoul	25 Sep 88
	(40)							
49.87	Denean	Howard/Hill	USA	5.10.64	4s1	OG	Seoul	25 Sep 88
49.87	LaTasha	Colander-Richardson	USA	23.8.76	1	NC	Sacramento	16 Jul 00
49.88	Ionela	Tîrlea	ROM	9.2.76	1	WUG	Palma de Mallorca	12 Jul 99
49.89	Irina	Privalova	RUS	22.11.68	1	Kuts	Moskva	30 Jul 93
49.91	Marita	Payne'	CAN	7.10.60	4	OG	Los Angeles	6 Aug 84
49.91	Jillian	Richardson	CAN	10.3.65	5s1	OG	Seoul	25 Sep 88
49.95	Olga	Kotlyarova	RUS	12.4.76	1	Super	Yokohama	9 Sep 00
49.98	Tatyana	Alekseyeva	RUS	7.10.63	1	NC	Tula	8 Jul 97
49.99	Pam	Marshall	USA	16.8.60	1	Pepsi	Westwood	17 May 86
50.01		Li Jing	CHN	14.2.80	1	NG	Shanghai	18 Oct 97
	(50)	100th woman 50.62, 200th woman 51.19						
Low altitude best: 49.77		Yusuf			6	OG	Atlanta	29 Jul 96
Hand timing								
48.9	Olga	Nazarova ¶	RUS	1.6.65	1	NP	Vladivostok	13 Sep 88
49.2A	Ana Fidelia	Quirot	CUB	23.3.63	1	AmCp	Bogotá	13 Aug 89

600 METRES

Mark	Name		Nat	Born	Pos	Meet	Venue	Date
1:22.63	Ana Fidelia	Quirot	CUB	23.3.63	1		Guadalajara	25 Jul 97
1:23.5	Doina	Melinte	ROM	27.12.56	1		Poiana Brasov	27 Jul 86
1:24.4	Patrizia	Spuri	ITA	18.2.73	1		Rieti	29 Sep 99
1:24.48+	Sigrun	Wodars	GDR	7.11.65	1	WCp	Barcelona	7 Sep 89
1:24.56	Martina	Steuk'	GDR	11.11.59	1		Erfurt	1 Aug 81

800 METRES

Mark	Name		Nat	Born	Pos	Meet	Venue	Date
1:53.28 WR	Jarmila	Kratochvílová	CZE	26.1.51	1		München	26 Jul 83
1:53.43 WR	Nadezhda	Olizarenko'	UKR	28.11.53	1	OG	Moskva	27 Jul 80
1:54.44	Ana Fidelia	Quirot	CUB	23.3.63	1	WCp	Barcelona	9 Sep 89
1:54.68		Kratochvílová			1	WCh	Helsinki	9 Aug 83
1:54.81	Olga	Mineyeva	RUS	1.9.52	2	OG	Moskva	27 Jul 80
1:54.82		Quirot			1	ASV	Köln	24 Aug 97
1:54.85 WR		Olizarenko			1	Prav	Moskva	12 Jun 80
1:54.94 WR	Tatyana	Kazankina ¶	RUS	17.12.51	1	OG	Montreal	26 Jul 76
1:55.04		Kratochvílová			1	OsloG	Oslo	23 Aug 83
1:55.05	Doina	Melinte	ROM	27.12.56	1	NC	Bucuresti	1 Aug 82
1:55.1 '		Mineyeva			1	Znam	Moskva	6 Jul 80
1:55.19	Maria Lurdes	Mutola	MOZ	27.10.72	1	WK	Zürich	17 Aug 94
1:55.26	Sigrun	Wodars/Grau	GDR	7.11.65	1	WCh	Roma	31 Aug 87
1:55.29		Mutola			2	ASV	Köln	24 Aug 97
1:55.32	Christine	Wachtel	GDR	6.1.65	2	WCh	Roma	31 Aug 87
1:55.41		Mineyeva			1	EC	Athína	8 Sep 82
1:55.42	Nikolina	Shtereva (10)	BUL	25.1.55	2	OG	Montreal	26 Jul 76
1:55.43		Mutola			1	WCh	Stuttgart	17 Aug 93
1:55.46	Tatyana	Providokhina	RUS	26.3.53	3	OG	Moskva	27 Jul 80
1:55.5		Mineyeva			1	Kuts	Podolsk	21 Aug 82
1:55.54	Ellen	van Langen	NED	9.2.66	1	OG	Barcelona	3 Aug 92
1:55.54		Liu Dong	CHN	24.12.73	1	NG	Beijing	9 Sep 93
1:55.56	Lyubov	Gurina	RUS	6.8.57	3	WCh	Roma	31 Aug 87

Mark Wind		Name	Nat	Born	Pos	Meet	Venue	Date
1:55.60	Elfi	Zinn	GDR	24.8.53	3	OG	Montreal	26 Jul 76
1:55.62		Mutola			1A	WK	Zürich	4 Aug 93
1:55.68	Ella	Kovacs	ROM	11.12.64	1	RomIC	Bucuresti	2 Jun 85
1:55.69	Irina	Podyalovskaya	RUS	19.10.59	1	Izv	Kiyev	22 Jun 84
1:55.70		Wodars			2	WCp	Barcelona	9 Sep 89
1:55.72		Mutola			1	GPF	Monaco	9 Sep 95
1:55.74	Anita	Weiss'	GDR	16.7.55	4	OG	Montreal	26 Jul 76
	(30/18)							
1:55.87	Svetlana	Masterkova	RUS	17.1.68	1	Kuts	Moskva	18 Jun 99
1:55.96	Lyudmila	Veselkova	RUS	25.10.50	2	EC	Athína	8 Sep 82
	(20)							
1:55.96	Yekaterina	Podkopayeva'	RUS	11.6.52	1		Leningrad	27 Jul 83
1:55.99	Lilia	Nurutdinova ¶	RUS	15.12.63	2	OG	Barcelona	3 Aug 92
1:56.0 WR	Valentina	Gerasimova	KZK	15.5.48	1	NC	Kiyev	12 Jun 76
1:56.0	Inna	Yevseyeva	UKR	14.8.64	1		Kiyev	25 Jun 88
1:56.1	Ravilya	Agletdinova'	BLR	10.2.60	2	Kuts	Podolsk	21 Aug 82
1:56.2 '	Totka	Petrova ¶	BUL	17.12.56	1		Paris	6 Jul 79
1:56.2	Tatyana	Mishkel	UKR	10.6.52	3	Kuts	Podolsk	21 Aug 82
1:56.21	Martina	Kämpfert'	GDR	11.11.59	4	OG	Moskva	27 Jul 80
1:56.21	Zamira	Zaytseva	UZB	16.2.53	2		Leningrad	27 Jul 83
1:56.21	Kelly	Holmes	GBR	19.4.70	2	GPF	Monaco	9 Sep 95
	(30)							
1:56.24		Qu Yunxia	CHN	25.12.72	2	NG	Beijing	9 Sep 93
1:56.40	Jearl	Miles-Clark	USA	4.9.66	3	WK	Zürich	11 Aug 99
1:56.42	Paula	Ivan	ROM	20.7.63	1	Balk	Ankara	16 Jul 88
1:56.44	Svetlana	Styrkina	RUS	1.1.49	5	OG	Montreal	26 Jul 76
1:56.51	Slobodanka	Colovic	YUG	10.1.65	1		Beograd	17 Jun 87
1:56.53	Patricia	Djaté	FRA	3.1.71	3	GPF	Mpnaco	9 Sep 95
1:56.56	Ludmila	Formanová	CZE	2.1.74	4	WK	Zürich	11 Aug 99
1:56.57	Zoya	Rigel	RUS	15.10.52	3	EC	Praha	31 Aug 78
1:56.60	Natalya	Tsyganova	RUS	7.2.71	1	NC	Tula	25 Jul 00
1:56.6	Tamara	Sorokina'	RUS	15.8.50	5	Kuts	Podolsk	21 Aug 82
	(40)							
1:56.61	Yelena	Afanasyeva	RUS	1.3.67	3	WK	Zürich	13 Aug 97
1:56.62	Tina	Paulino	MOZ	7.7.73	2	NYG	New York	22 May 93
1:56.64	Nadezhda	Loboyko	KAZ	30.6.61	1	NC	Kiyev	7 Jul 90
1:56.64	Stephanie	Graf	AUT	26.4.73	2	OG	Sydney	25 Sep 00
1:56.67	Fita	Lovin'	ROM	14.1.51	2	Prav	Moskva	12 Jun 80
1:56.68	Letitia	Vriesde	SUR	5.10.64	2	WCh	Göteborg	13 Aug 95
1:56.7	Dalia	Matuseviciene	LIT	12.11.62	2		Kiyev	25 Jun 88
1:56.78	Lyudmila	Borisova	RUS	30.7.59	3	Izv	Kiyev	22 Jun 84
1:56.82	Lyudmila	Rogachova	RUS	10.10.66	1		Parnu	13 Jul 88
1:56.84	Nina	Ruchayeva	RUS	17.4.56	2r1	NP/s	Moskva	19 Jul 84
	(50)	100th woman 1:58.0, 200th woman 1:59.23						

1000 METRES

Mark Wind		Name	Nat	Born	Pos	Meet	Venue	Date
2:28.98 WR	Svetlana	Masterkova	RUS	17.1.68	1	VD	Bruxelles	23 Aug 96
2:29.34 WR	Maria Lurdes	Mutola	MOZ	27.10.72	1	VD	Bruxelles	25 Aug 95
2:29.66		Mutola			2	VD	Bruxelles	23 Aug 96
2:30.6 WR	Tatyana	Providokhina	RUS	26.3.53	1		Podolsk	20 Aug 78
2:30.67 WR	Christine	Wachtel	GDR	6.1.65	1	ISTAF	Berlin	17 Aug 90
2:30.85	Martina	Kämpfert'	GDR	11.11.59	1		Berlin	9 Jul 80
2:31.50	Natalya	Artyomova ¶	RUS	5.1.63	1	ISTAF	Berlin	10 Sep 91
2:31.5	Maricica	Puica	ROM	29.7.50	1		Poiana Brasov	1 Jun 86
2:31.51	Sandra	Gasser ¶	SUI	27.7.62	1		Jerez de la Frontera	13 Sep 89
2:31.6 '	Beate	Liebich	GDR	21.2.58	2		Berlin	9 Jul 80
2:31.65	Olga	Dvirna	RUS	11.2.53	1		Athína	1 Sep 82
	(10)							

1500 METRES

Mark Wind		Name	Nat	Born	Pos	Meet	Venue	Date
3:50.46 WR		Qu Yunxia	CHN	25.12.72	1	NG	Beijing	11 Sep 93
3:50.98		Jiang Bo	CHN	13.3.77	1	NG	Shanghai	18 Oct 97
3:51.34		Lang Yinglai	CHN	22.8.79	2	NG	Shanghai	18 Oct 97
3:51.92		Wang Junxia	CHN	9.1.73	2	NG	Beijing	11 Sep 93
3:52.47 WR	Tatyana	Kazankina ¶	RUS	17.12.51	1	WK	Zürich	13 Aug 80
3:53.91		Yin Lili	CHN	11.11.79	3	NG	Shanghai	18 Oct 97
3:53.96	Paula	Ivan'	ROM	20.7.63	1	OG	Seoul	1 Oct 88
3:53.97		Lan Lixin	CHN	14.2.79	4	NG	Shanghai	18 Oct 97
3:54.23	Olga	Dvirna	RUS	11.2.53	1	NC	Kiyev	27 Jul 82
3:54.52		Zhang Ling (10)	CHN	13.4.80	5	NG	Shanghai	18 Oct 97

Mark Wind	Name		Nat	Born	Pos	Meet	Venue	Date
3:55.0 ' WR		Kazankina ¶			1	Znam	Moskva	6 Jul 80
3:55.01		Lan Lixin			1h2	NG	Shanghai	17 Oct 97
3:55.07		Dong Yanmei	CHN	16.2.77	6	NG	Shanghai	18 Oct 97
3:55.30	Hassiba	Boulmerka	ALG	10.7.68	1	OG	Barcelona	8 Aug 92
3:55.38		Qu Yunxia			2h2	NG	Shanghai	17 Oct 97
3:55.47		Zhang Ling			3h2	NG	Shanghai	17 Oct 97
3:55.82		Dong Yanmei			4h2	NG	Shanghai	17 Oct 97
3:56.0 WR		Kazankina ¶			1		Podolsk	28 Jun 76
3:56.14	Zamira	Zaytseva	UZB	16.2.53	2	NC	Kiyev	27 Jul 82
3:56.22		Ivan			1	WK	Zürich	17 Aug 88
3:56.31		Liu Dong	CHN	24.12.73	5h2	NG	Shanghai	17 Oct 97
3:56.50	Tatyana	Pozdnyakova	RUS	4.3.56	3	NC	Kiyev	27 Jul 82
3:56.56		Kazankina ¶			1	OG	Moskva	1 Aug 80
3:56.63	Nadezhda	Ralldugina	UKR	15.11.57	1	Drz	Praha	18 Aug 84
3:56.65	Yekaterina	Podkopayeva'	RUS	11.6.52	1		Rieti	2 Sep 84
3:56.7 '	Lyubov	Smolka	UKR	29.11.52	2	Znam	Moskva	6 Jul 80
3:56.7	Doina	Melinte	ROM	27.12.56	1		Bucuresti	12 Jul 86
3:56.77+	Svetlana	Masterkova (20)	RUS	17.1.68	1	WK	Zürich	14 Aug 96
3:56.8 '	Nadezhda	Olizarenko'	UKR	28.11.53	3	Znam	Moskva	6 Jul 80
3:56.9 '		Zaytseva			4	Znam	Moskva	6 Jul 80
	(30/21)							
3:56.91	Lyudmila	Rogachova	RUS	10.10.66	2	OG	Barcelona	8 Aug 92
3:56.97	Gabriela	Szabo	ROM	14.11.75	1	Herc	Monaco	8 Aug 98
3:57.03		Liu Jing	CHN	.2.71	6h2	NG	Shanghai	17 Oct 97
3:57.05	Svetlana	Guskova	MDA	19.8.59	4	NC	Kiyev	27 Jul 82
3:57.12	Mary	Decker/Slaney	USA	4.8.58	1	vNord	Stockholm	26 Jul 83
3:57.22	Maricica	Puica	ROM	29.7.50	1		Bucuresti	1 Jul 84
3:57.40	Suzy	Favor Hamilton	USA	8.8.68	1	Bisl	Oslo	28 Jul 00
3:57.4 '	Totka	Petrova ¶	BUL	17.12.56	1	Balk	Athína	11 Aug 79
3:57.41	Jackline	Maranga	KEN	16.12.77	3	Herc	Monaco	8 Aug 98
	(30)							
3:57.46		Zhang Linli	CHN	6.3.73	3	NG	Beijing	11 Sep 93
3:57.71	Christiane	Wartenberg'	GDR	27.10.56	2	OG	Moskva	1 Aug 80
3:57.71	Carla	Sacramento	POR	10.12.71	4	Herc	Monaco	8 Aug 98
3:57.72	Galina	Zakharova	RUS	7.9.56	1	NP	Baku	14 Sep 84
3:57.92	Tatyana	Dorovskikh ¶	UKR	12.8.61	4	OG	Barcelona	8 Aug 92
3:58.07	Kelly	Holmes	GBR	19.4.70	1		Sheffield	29 Jun 97
3:58.12	Naomi	Mugo	KEN	2.1.77	5	Herc	Monaco	8 Aug 98
3:58.20	Anita	Weyermann	SUI	8.12.77	6	Herc	Monaco	8 Aug 98
3:58.2 '	Natalia	Marasescu' ¶	ROM	3.10.52	1	NC	Bucuresti	13 Jul 79
3:58.29	Violeta	Szekely' ¶	ROM	26.3.65	1	Herc	Monaco	18 Aug 00
	(40)							
3:58.37	Tatyana	Providokhina	RUS	26.3.53	1	Kuts	Podolsk	22 Aug 82
3:58.38	Kutre	Dulecha	ETH	22.8.78	7	Herc	Monaco	8 Aug 98
3:58.40	Ravilya	Agletdinova'	BLR	10.2.60	1	ECp	Moskva	18 Aug 85
3:58.5 '	Ileana	Silai ¶	ROM	14.10.41	2	NC	Bucuresti	13 Jul 79
3:58.64		Wang Renmei	CHN	5.7.70	4	NG	Beijing	11 Sep 93
3:58.65	Gabriella	Dorio	ITA	26.6.57	2		Tirrenia	25 Aug 82
3:58.67	Hildegard	Körner'	GDR	20.12.59	2	WCh	Roma	5 Sep 87
3:58.71	Lyubov	Kremlyova ¶	RUS	21.12.61	1	WK	Zürich	19 Aug 92
3:58.74		Yan Wei	CHN	12.10.71	4h1	NG	Shanghai	17 Oct 97
3:58.76	Svetlana	Ulmasova	UZB	4.2.53	2	Kuts	Podolsk	22 Aug 82
	(50)	100th woman 4:01.4, 200th woman 4:04.81						

1 MILE

Mark Wind	Name		Nat	Born	Pos	Meet	Venue	Date
4:12.56 WR	Svetlana	Masterkova	RUS	17.1.68	1	WK	Zürich	14 Aug 96
4:15.61 WR	Paula	Ivan'	ROM	20.7.63	1	Nik	Nice	10 Jul 89
4:15.8	Natalya	Artyomova ¶	RUS	5.1.63	1		Leningrad	5 Aug 84
4:16.71 WR	Mary	Slaney (Decker)	USA	4.8.58	1	WK	Zürich	21 Aug 85
4:17.25	Sonia	O'Sullivan	IRL	28.11.69	1	Bisl	Oslo	22 Jul 94
4:17.33	Maricica	Puica	ROM	29.7.50	2	WK	Zürich	21 Aug 85
4:17.57	Zola	Budd'	GBR	26.5.66	3	WK	Zürich	21 Aug 85
4:18.13	Doina	Melinte	ROM	27.12.56	1	Bisl	Oslo	14 Jul 90
4:19.30	Gabriela	Szabo	ROM	14.11.75	1		Bellinzona	1 Jul 98
4:19.41	Kirsty	McDermott/Wade	GBR	6.8.62	2	Bisl	Oslo	27 Jul 85
	(10)							

Indoors

4:17.14	Doina	Melinte	ROM	27.12.56	1		East Rutherford	9 Feb 90

Mark Wind	Name		Nat	Born	Pos	Meet	Venue	Date

2000 METRES

Mark Wind	Name		Nat	Born	Pos	Meet	Venue	Date
5:25.36 WR	Sonia	O'Sullivan	IRL	28.11.69	1	TSB	Edinburgh	8 Jul 94
5:26.93	Yvonne	Murray	GBR	4.10.64	2	TSB	Edinburgh	8 Jul 94
5:28.69 WR	Maricica	Puica	ROM	29.7.50	1	PTG	London (CP)	11 Jul 86
5:28.72 WR	Tatyana	Kazankina ¶	RUS	17.12.51	1		Moskva	4 Aug 84
5:29.43+		Wang Junxia	CHN	9.1.73	1h2	NG	Beijing	12 Sep 93
5:29.64	Tatyana	Pozdnyakova	UKR	4.3.56	2		Moskva	4 Aug 84
5:30.19	Zola	Budd'	GBR	26.5.66	3	PTG	London (CP)	11 Jul 86
5:30.92	Galina	Zakharova	RUS	7.9.56	3		Moskva	4 Aug 84
5:32.7 ' WR	Mary	Decker/Slaney	USA	4.8.58	1		Eugene	3 Aug 84
5:32.83	Roberta	Brunet (10)	ITA	20.5.65	1		Torino	14 Sep 96
Indoors								
5:30.53	Gabriela	Szabo	ROM	14.11.75	1		Sindelfingen	8 Mar 98

3000 METRES

Mark Wind	Name		Nat	Born	Pos	Meet	Venue	Date
8:06.11 WR		Wang Junxia	CHN	9.1.73	1	NG	Beijing	13 Sep 93
8:12.18		Qu Yunxia	CHN	25.12.72	2	NG	Beijing	13 Sep 93
8:12.19 WR		Wang Junxia			1h2	NG	Beijing	12 Sep 93
8:12.27		Qu Yunxia			2h2	NG	Beijing	12 Sep 93
8:16.50		Zhang Linli	CHN	6.3.73	3	NG	Beijing	13 Sep 93
8:19.78		Ma Liyan	CHN	6.9.68	3h2	NG	Beijing	12 Sep 93
8:21.26		Ma Liyan			4	NG	Beijing	13 Sep 93
8:21.64	Sonia	O'Sullivan	IRL	28.11.69	1	TSB	London (CP)	15 Jul 94
8:21.84		Zhang Lirong	CHN	3.3.73	5	NG	Beijing	13 Sep 93
8:22.06 WR		Zhang Linli			1h1	NG	Beijing	12 Sep 93
8:22.44		Zhang Lirong			2h1	NG	Beijing	12 Sep 93
8:22.62 WR	Tatyana	Kazankina ¶	RUS	17.12.51	1		Leningrad	26 Aug 84
8:24.31	Gabriela	Szabo	ROM	14.11.75	1	GP	Paris	29 Jul 98
8:25.03		Szabo			1	WK	Zürich	11 Aug 99
8:25.59		Szabo			1	GP	Paris (C)	21 Jul 99
8:25.82		Szabo			1	VD	Bruxelles	3 Sep 99
8:25.83	Mary	Slaney	USA	4.8.58	1	GGALA	Roma	7 Sep 85
8:26.35		Szabo			1	WK	Zürich	11 Aug 00
8:26.48	Zahra	Ouaziz (10)	MAR	20.12.69	2	WK	Zürich	11 Aug 99
8:26.53	Tatyana	Samolenko' ¶	UKR	12.8.61	1	OG	Seoul	25 Sep 88
8:26.64		Ouaziz			2	GP	Paris (C)	21 Jul 99
8:26.78 WR	Svetlana	Ulmasova	UZB	4.2.53	1	NC	Kiyev	25 Jul 82
8:27.01		Ouaziz			2	VD	Bruxelles	3 Sep 99
8:27.12 WR	Lyudmila	Bragina	RUS	24.7.43	1	v USA	College Park	7 Aug 76
8:27.15	Paula	Ivan'	ROM	20.7.63	2	OG	Seoul	25 Sep 88
8:27.21		Szabo			1	Bisl	Oslo	30 Jun 99
8:27.26		Ouaziz			2	GP	Paris	29 Jul 98
8:27.40	Paula	Radcliffe	GBR	17.12.73	3	WK	Zürich	11 Aug 99
8:27.57		O'Sullivan			1	WK	Zürich	16 Aug 95
8:27.58		O'Sullivan			2	WK	Zürich	11 Aug 00
	(30/15)							
8:27.83	Maricica	Puica	ROM	29.7.50	2	GGALA	Roma	7 Sep 85
8:28.80	Marta	Domínguez	ESP	3.11.75	3	WK	Zürich	11 Aug 00
8:28.83	Zola	Budd'	GBR	26.5.66	3	GGALA	Roma	7 Sep 85
8:29.02	Yvonne	Murray	GBR	4.10.64	3	OG	Seoul	25 Sep 88
8:29.14	Lydia	Cheromei	KEN	11.5.77	5	WK	Zürich	11 Aug 00
	(20)							
8:29.24	Gete	Wami	ETH	11.12.74	3	GP	Paris	29 Jul 98
8:29.36	Svetlana	Guskova	MDA	19.8.59	2	NC	Kiyev	25 Jul 82
8:30.18	Mariya	Pantyukhova	RUS	14.8.74	4	WK	Zürich	11 Aug 99
8:30.22	Carla	Sacramento	POR	10.12.71	2	Herc	Monaco	4 Aug 99
8:30.39	Irina	Mikitenko	GER	23.8.72	6	WK	Zürich	11 Aug 00
8:30.45	Yelena	Romanova	RUS	20.3.63	4	OG	Seoul	25 Sep 88
8:30.66	Fernanda	Ribeiro	POR	23.6.69	3	Herc	Monaco	4 Aug 99
8:30.95	Tegla	Loroupe	KEN	9.5.73	2	Herc	Monaco	18 Aug 00
8:31.67	Natalya	Artyomova ¶	RUS	5.1.63	5	OG	Seoul	25 Sep 88
8:31.75	Grete	Waitz'	NOR	1.10.53	1	OsloG	Oslo	17 Jul 79
	(30)							
8:32.00	Elana	Meyer'	RSA	10.10.66	1		Durban	29 Apr 91
8:32.0	Tatyana	Pozdnyakova	UKR	4.3.56	1		Ryazan	11 Aug 84
8:32.17	Angela	Chalmers	CAN	6.9.63	1	CG	Victoria	23 Aug 94
8:33.02	Olga	Yegorova	RUS	28.3.72	4	Bisl	Oslo	30 Jun 99
8:33.07		Dong Yanmei	CHN	16.2.77	1	GP	Athína	28 Jun 00

Mark Wind		Name	Nat	Born	Pos	Meet	Venue	Date
8:33.35	Lidia	Chojecka	POL	25.1.77	1	Gaz	Saint-Denis	23 Jun 00
8:33.40	Galina	Zakharova	RUS	7.9.56	3	NC	Kiyev	25 Jul 82
8:33.53	Natalia	Marasescu' ¶	ROM	3.10.52	2	EC	Praha	29 Aug 78
8:33.53	Yelena	Sipatova	RUS	7.6.55	1		Moskva	12 Jul 80
8:33.85	Asmae	Laghzaoui	MAR	30.8.76	3	Herc	Monaco	18 Aug 00
	(40)							
8:33.9 '	Tatyana	Sychova	RUS	29.11.57	2		Moskva	12 Jul 80
8:33.97	Elly	van Hulst	NED	9.6.59	1	WK	Zürich	17 Aug 88
8:33.99	Olga	Bondarenko'	RUS	2.6.60	1	EC	Stuttgart	28 Aug 86
8:34.0 '	Faina	Krasnova'	RUS	7.12.57	3		Moskva	12 Jul 80
8:34.02	Alla	Yushina	RUS	20.8.58	2		Leningrad	27 Jul 83
8:34.10	Ingrid	Kristiansen'	NOR	21.3.56	1	WK	Zürich	13 Aug 86
8:34.53	Tatyana	Tomashova	RUS	1.7.75	3	GP	Athína	28 Jun 00
8:35.02	Libbie	Hickman	USA	17.2.65	2	GP II	Gateshead	28 Aug 00
8:35.11	Brigitte	Kraus	FRG	12.8.56	2	WCh	Helsinki	10 Aug 83
8:35.65	Roberta	Brunet	ITA	20.5.65	1	Herc	Monaco	16 Aug 97
	(50)	100th woman 8:41.23, 200th 8:48.37						
Indoors								
8:33.82	Elly	van Hulst	NED	9.6.59	1	WI	Budapest	4 Mar 89
8:34.80	Liz	McColgan'	GBR	24.5.64	2	WI	Budapest	4 Mar 89

2 MILES

9:11.97mx	Regina	Jacobs	USA	28.8.63	1		Los Gatos	12 Aug 99
9:19.56	Sonia	O'Sullivan	IRL	28.11.69	1		Cork	27 Jun 98

5000 METRES

14:28.09WR		Jiang Bo	CHN	13.3.77	1	NG	Shanghai	23 Oct 97
14:29.82		Dong Yanmei	CHN	16.2.77	2	NG	Shanghai	23 Oct 97
14:30.88	Gete	Wami	ETH	11.12.74	1	NA	Heusden	5 Aug 00
14:31.27WR		Dong Yanmei			1h1	NG	Shanghai	21 Oct 97
14:31.30		Jiang Bo			2h1	NG	Shanghai	21 Oct 97
14:31.48	Gabriela	Szabo	ROM	14.11.75	1	ISTAF	Berlin	1 Sep 98
14:32.08	Zahra	Ouaziz	MAR	20.12.69	2	ISTAF	Berlin	1 Sep 98
14:32.33		Liu Shixiang	CHN	13.1.71	3h1	NG	Shanghai	21 Oct 97
14:36.08		Wami		4	3	ISTAF	Berlin	1 Sep 98
14:36.45WR	Fernanda	Ribeiro	POR	23.6.69	1		Hechtel	22 Jul 95
14:37.33WR	Ingrid	Kristiansen'	NOR	21.3.56	1		Stockholm	5 Aug 86
14:38.14		Liu Shixiang			3	NG	Shanghai	23 Oct 97
14:39.83	Leah	Malot	KEN	7.6.72	1	ISTAF	Berlin	1 Sep 00
14:39.96		Yin Lili (10)	CHN	11.11.79	4	NG	Shanghai	23 Oct 97
14:40.19		Ouaziz			1	DNG	Stockholm	5 Aug 98
14:40.59		Szabo			1	ISTAF	Berlin	7 Sep 99
14:40.61		Szabo			2	ISTAF	Berlin	1 Sep 00
14:40.79		Szabo			1	OG	Sydney	25 Sep 00
14:41.02	Sonia	O'Sullivan	IRL	28.11.69	2	OG	Sydney	25 Sep 00
14:41.07		Ribeiro			1	Bisl	Oslo	5 Jul 96
14:41.12		Szabo			2	Bisl	Oslo	5 Jul 96
14:41.23	Ayelech	Worku	ETH	12.6.79	1	BrGP	London (CP)	5 Aug 00
14:41.34		Ouaziz			2	ISTAF	Berlin	7 Sep 99
14:41.40		O'Sullivan			1	ISTAF	Berlin	1 Sep 95
14:41.47		Yin Lili			1h2	NG	Shanghai	21 Oct 97
14:41.82		Szabo			1	WCh	Sevilla	27 Aug 99
14:42.03		Ouaziz			1	BrGP	London (CP)	7 Aug 99
14:42.03	Irina	Mikitenko	GER	23.8.72	3	ISTAF	Berlin	7 Sep 99
14:42.11		Ouaziz			1	GP II	Saint-Denis	4 Jun 98
14:42.23		Wami			3	OG	Sydney	25 Sep 00
	(30/13)							
14:42.91	Olga	Yegorova	RUS	28.3.72	1	DNG	Stockholm	1 Aug 00
14:43.54	Paula	Radcliffe	GBR	17.12.73	2	BrGP	London (CP)	7 Aug 99
14:44.05	Elana	Meyer	RSA	10.10.66	2		Hechtel	22 Jul 95
14:44.50	Roberta	Brunet	ITA	20.5.65	2	ASV	Köln	16 Aug 96
14:44.57	Derartu	Tulu	ETH	21.3.72	3	DNG	Stockholm	1 Aug 00
14:44.95	Julia	Vaquero	ESP	18.9.70	3	Bisl	Oslo	5 Jul 96
14:45.33		Lan Lixin	CHN	14.2.79	2h2	NG	Shanghai	21 Oct 97
	(20)							
14:45.35	Regina	Jacobs	USA	28.8.63	1	NC	Sacramento	21 Jul 00
14:45.71		Song Liqing	CHN	.1.80	3h2	NG	Shanghai	21 Oct 97
14:45.95	Tegla	Loroupe	KEN	9.5.73	3	BrGP	London (CP)	5 Aug 00
14:46.41	Rose	Cheruiyot	KEN	21.7.76	3	ASV	Köln	16 Aug 96

Mark Wind		Name	Nat	Born	Pos	Meet	Venue	Date
14:46.71	Sally	Barsosio	KEN	21.3.78	3	VD	Bruxelles	22 Aug 97
14:46.72	Lydia	Cheromei	KEN	11.5.77	2	ISTAF	Berlin	26 Aug 97
14:47.20		Dong Zhaoxia	CHN	13.11.74	5	NG	Shanghai	23 Oct 97
14:47.40	Worknesh	Kidane	ETH	21.11.81	7	OG	Sydney	25 Sep 00
14:47.51	Pauline	Konga	KEN	10.4.70	6	ASV	Köln	16 Aug 96
14:47.71	Jelena	Prokopcuka	LAT	21.9.76	5	DNG	Stockholm	1 Aug 00
	(30)							
14:47.79	Yamna	Belkacem	FRA	20.2.74	6	DNG	Stockholm	1 Aug 00
14:48.07WR	Zola	Budd'	GBR	26.5.66	1	McV	London (CP)	26 Aug 85
14:48.31	Asmae	Laghzaoui	MAR	30.8.76	4	ISTAF	Berlin	1 Sep 00
14:48.45		Wang Dongmei	CHN	3.12.72	6	NG	Shanghai	23 Oct 97
14:49.40	Catherina	McKiernan	IRL	30.11.69	7	ASV	Köln	16 Aug 96
14:50.88	Derartu	Tulu	ETH	21.3.71	1		Saint-Denis	3 Jun 96
14:51.62	Deena	Drossin	USA	14.2.73	9	DNG	Stockholm	1 Aug 00
14:51.69	Ebru	Kavaklioglou	TUR	14.3.70	5	WCh	Sevilla	27 Aug 99
	(ex Yelena	Kopytova	RUS)					
14:51.87		Wang Junxia	CHN	9.1.73	1	NC	Nanjing	5 May 96
14:52.61	Berhane	Adere	ETH	21.7.73	10	DNG	Stockholm	1 Aug 00
14:53.00	Tatyana	Tomashova	RUS	1.7.75	1	ECp-S	Gateshead	16 Jul 00
	(40)							
14:54.08	Natalya	Artyomova ¶	RUS	5.1.63	1		Podolsk	9 Sep 85
14:55.76	Olga	Bondarenko'	RUS	2.6.60	2		Podolsk	9 Sep 85
14:55.82	Viktoriya	Nenasheva	RUS	26.6.70	1	DNG	Stockholm	8 Jul 96
14:56.04	Amy	Rudolph	USA	18.9.73	2	DNG	Stockholm	8 Jul 96
14:56.07	Annette	Peters	USA	31.5.65	2	ISTAF	Berlin	27 Aug 93
14:56.22	Annemari	Sandell	FIN	2.1.77	4	DNG	Stockholm	8 Jul 96
14:56.94	Yvonne	Murray	GBR	4.10.64	4	BrGP	London (CP)	7 Jul 95
14:56.95	Daniela	Yordanova	BUL	8.3.76	10	OG	Sydney	25 Sep 00
14:58.18	Fatima	Yvelain	FRA	31.12.69	6	ISTAF	Berlin	7 Sep 99
14:58.27	Jo	Pavey	GBR	20.9.73	12	OG	Sydney	25 Sep 00
	(50)	100th woman 15:09.05, 200th woman 15:21.98						

10,000 METRES

Mark Wind		Name	Nat	Born	Pos	Meet	Venue	Date
29:31.78WR		Wang Junxia	CHN	9.1.73	1	NG	Beijing	8 Sep 93
30:13.37		Zhong Huandi	CHN	28.6.67	2	NG	Beijing	8 Sep 93
30:13.74WR	Ingrid	Kristiansen'	NOR	21.3.56	1	Bisl	Oslo	5 Jul 86
30:17.49	Derartu	Tulu	ETH	21.3.72	1	OG	Sydney	30 Sep 00
30:22.48	Gete	Wami	ETH	11.12.74	2	OG	Sydney	30 Sep 00
30:22.88	Fernanda	Ribeiro	POR	23.6.69	3	OG	Sydney	30 Sep 00
30:23.25		Kristiansen			1	EC	Stuttgart	30 Aug 86
30:24.56		Wami			1	WCh	Sevilla	26 Aug 99
30:26.97	Paula	Radcliffe	GBR	17.12.73	4	OG	Sydney	30 Sep 00
30:27.13		Radcliffe			2	WCh	Sevilla	26 Aug 99
30:32.03	Tegla	Loroupe	KEN	9.5.73	3	WCh	Sevilla	26 Aug 99
30:37.26		Loroupe			5	OG	Sydney	30 Sep 00
30:38.09		Dong Yanmei	CHN	16.2.77	1	NG	Shanghai	19 Oct 97
30:39.41		Lan Lixin (10)	CHN	14.2.79	2	NG	Shanghai	19 Oct 97
30:39.98		Yin Lili	CHN	11.11.79	3	NG	Shanghai	19 Oct 97
30:40.70		Radcliffe			1rA	EChall	Barakaldo	10 Apr 99
30:47.22		Dong Zhaoxia	CHN	13.11.74	4	NG	Shanghai	19 Oct 97
30:47.72		Wang Dongmei	CHN	3.12.72	5	NG	Shanghai	19 Oct 97
30:48.06		Ribeiro			1	EChall	Lisboa	4 Apr 98
30:48.51		Kristiansen			1	Bisl	Oslo	1 Jul 89
30:48.58		Radcliffe			2	EChall	Lisboa	4 Apr 98
30:49.30		Wang Junxia			1	WCh	Stuttgart	21 Aug 93
30:50.34		Wang Junxia			1	AsiG	Hiroshima	15 Oct 94
30:51.30	Berhane	Adere	ETH	21.7.73	1	NA	Heusden	5 Aug 00
30:52.51	Elana	Meyer	RSA	10.10.66	1	WCp	London (CP)	10 Sep 94
30:53.37	Sonia	O'Sullivan	IRL	28.11.69	6	OG	Sydney	30 Sep 00
30:55.83		Liu Shixiang	CHN	13.1.71	6	NG	Shanghai	19 Oct 97
30:56.4		Tulu			1		Gijón	12 Aug 00
30:57.07	Liz	McColgan	GBR	24.5.64	1	APM	Hengelo	25 Jun 91
30:57.21	Olga	Bondarenko'	RUS	2.6.60	2	EC	Stuttgart	30 Aug 86
30:57.70	Leah	Malot	KEN	7.6.72	2	NA	Heusden	5 Aug 00
30:59.42WR		Kristiansen			1	Bisl	Oslo	27 Jul 85
30:59.92	Merima	Hashim	ETH	.81	3	NA	Heusden	5 Aug 00
	(33/21)							
31:03.60	Marleen	Renders	BEL	24.12.68	4	NA	Heusden	5 Aug 00
31:03.62	Kathrin	Ullrich'	GER	14.8.67	1	ECp	Frankfurt-am-Main	30 Jun 91

Mark	Wind	Name		Nat	Born	Pos	Meet	Venue	Date
31:05.57		Maura	Viceconte	ITA	3.10.67	5	NA	Heusden	5 Aug 00
31:06.94			Li Ji	CHN	19.9.79	7	OG	Sydney	30 Sep 00
31:07.88		Jill	Hunter	GBR	14.10.66	2	ECp	Frankfurt-am-Main	30 Jun 91
31:08.41		Catherina	McKiernan	IRL	30.11.69	1		Villeneuve d'Ascq	17 Jun 95
31:09.25			Zhang Lirong	CHN	3.3.73	3	NG	Beijing	8 Sep 93
31:09.40		Yelena	Zhupiyova'	UKR	18.4.60	2	WCh	Roma	4 Sep 87
31:09.46		Yuko	Kawakami	JPN	1.8.75	2		Brunswick	1 Jul 00
		(30)							
31:10.12		Adriana	Fernández	MEX	4.4.71	3		Brunswick	1 Jul 00
31:10.46			Ma Liyan	CHN	6.9.68	4	NG	Beijing	8 Sep 93
31:11.26			Song Liqing	CHN	.1.80	7	NG	Shanghai	19 Oct 97
31:11.72		Lisa	Ondieki'	AUS	12.5.60	1	WG	Helsinki	30 Jun 92
31:12.58			Wang Mingxia	CHN	6.6.71	8	NG	Shanghai	19 Oct 97
31:13.21			Ren Xiujuan	CHN	14.9.74	2	NT	Nanjing	8 May 96
31:14.51		Julia	Vaquero	ESP	18.9.70	1	EChall	Barakaldo	5 Apr 97
31:15.00		Galina	Zakharova	RUS	7.9.56	2	Izv	Kiyev	24 Jun 84
31:15.38		Sally	Barsosio	KEN	21.3.78	3	WCh	Stuttgart	21 Aug 93
31:16.28			Zhang Linli	CHN	6.3.73	5	NG	Beijing	8 Sep 93
		(40)							
31:16.39			Yang Siju	CHN	19.4.73	9	NG	Shanghai	19 Oct 97
31:16.42		M Conceição	Ferreira	POR	13.3.62	2	WG	Helsinki	30 Jun 92
31:18.18		Viorica	Ghican	ROM	9.6.65	1	WG	Helsinki	27 Jun 90
31:19.40		Hiromi	Suzuki	JPN	6.12.68	1	NC	Osaka	9 Jun 96
31:19.76		Ulrike	Bruns'	GDR	17.11.53	3	EC	Stuttgart	30 Aug 86
31:19.89		Lynn	Jennings	USA	10.7.60	3	OG	Barcelona	7 Aug 92
31:20.46		Masako	Chiba	JPN	18.7.76	3	NC	Osaka	9 Jun 96
31:21.27		Lidiya	Grigoryeva	RUS	21.1.74	9	OG	Sydney	30 Sep 00
31:21.36		Uta	Pippig	GER	7.9.65	2	OD	Jena	28 May 92
31:22.72		Harumi	Hiroyama	JPN	2.9.68	1	NC	Tokyo	5 Oct 97
		(50)	100th woman 31:51.68, 200th woman 32:14.08						

1 HOUR

Mark	Wind	Name		Nat	Born	Pos	Meet	Venue	Date
18,340 WR		Tegla	Loroupe	KEN	9.5.73	1		Borgholzhausen	7 Aug 98
18,084 WR		Silvana	Cruciata	ITA	15.2.53	1		Roma	2 May 81
18,027		Rosa	Mota	POR	29.6.58	1		Lisbon	14 May 83

20,000 METRES

Mark	Wind	Name		Nat	Born	Pos	Meet	Venue	Date
1:05:26.6WR		Tegla	Loroupe	KEN	9.5.73	1		Borgholzhausen	3 Sep 00
1:06:48.8WR		Izumi	Maki	JPN	10.12.68	1		Amagasaki	19 Sep 93
1:06:55.5WR		Rosa	Mota	POR	29.6.58	1		Lisboa	14 May 83

HALF MARATHON

Included are the slightly downhill courses: Newcastle to South Shields 30.5m, Tokyo 33m (to 1998), Lisboa 40m

Mark	Wind	Name		Nat	Born	Pos	Meet	Venue	Date
66:40*		Ingrid	Kristiansen	NOR	21.3.56	1	NC	Sandnes	5 Apr 87
66:43		Masako	Chiba	JPN	18.7.76	1		Tokyo	19 Jan 97
66:44		Elana	Meyer	RSA	10.10.66	1		Tokyo	15 Jan 99
66:49		Esther	Wanjiru	ETH	27.3.77	2		Tokyo	15 Jan 99
66:56		Lornah	Kiplagat	KEN	20.3.74	1	City-Pier	Den Haag	25 Mar 00
67:07		Paula	Radcliffe	GBR	17.12.73	1	GNR	South Shields	22 Oct 00
67:11		Liz	McColgan	GBR	24.5.64	1		Tokyo	26 Jan 92
67:12		Tegla	Loroupe	KEN	9.5.73	1		Lisboa	10 Mar 96
67:22			Meyer			1		Tokyo	24 Jan 93
67:24			Loroupe			1		Lisboa	26 Mar 00
67:29			Meyer			1		Kyoto	8 Mar 98
67:32			Loroupe			1		Den Haag	28 Mar 98
67:33			Meyer			1		Tokyo	10 Jan 00
67:36			Meyer			1		Kyoto	9 Mar 97
67:37			Kiplagat			1		Zaandam	17 Sep 00
67:41			Wanjiru			2		Tokyo	10 Jan 00
67:43			Loroupe			2		Tokyo	19 Jan 97
67:48		Kerryn	McCann	AUS	2.5.67	3		Tokyo	10 Jan 00
67:50		Catherina	McKiernan (10)	IRL	30.11.69	1		Lisboa	15 Mar 98
67:52			Loroupe			1		Lisboa	21 Mar 99
67:57			Meyer			1		Kyoto	14 Mar 99
67:58		Uta	Pippig	GER	7.9.65	1		Kyoto	19 Mar 95
67:59			Meyer			1	NC	East London	18 May 91
67:59			Pippig			1		Kyoto	20 Mar 94
67:59			Wanjiru			1		Sendai	14 Mar 99
67:59	w	Restituta	Joseph	TAN	30.7.71	1		Malmö	12 Jun 00

Mark	Wind	Name		Nat	Born	Pos	Meet	Venue	Date
68:04		Derartu	Tulu	ETH	21.3.72	2		Lisboa	26 Mar 00
68:09			Loroupe			1		Tokyo	21 Jan 96
68:09		Cristina	Pomacu	ROM	15.9.73	2		Lisboa	15 Mar 98
68:12			Loroupe			1	RdVin	Grevenmacher	24 Sep 95
		(30/14)							
68:18		Izumi	Maki	JPN	10.12.68	2		Tokyo	21 Jan 96
68:18		Yoshiko	Ichikawa	JPN	18.4.76	3		Tokyo	19 Jan 97
68:18	w	Joyce	Chepchumba	KEN	6.11.70	2		Malmö	12 Jun 00
68:21		Albertina	Dias	POR	26.4.65	3		Lisboa	10 Mar 96
68:23		Fernanda	Ribeiro	POR	23.6.69	3		Lisboa	26 Mar 00
68:30		Maria	Guida	ITA	23.1.66	4		Lisboa	10 Mar 96
		(20)							
68:30		Mizuki	Noguchi	JPN	3.7.78	1		Nagoya	23 Nov 99
68:33		Lisa	Ondieki	AUS	12.5.60	2		Tokyo	26 Jan 92
68:34		Joan	Benoit	USA	16.5.57	1		Philadelphia	16 Sep 84
68:34		Olga	Appell	MEX	2.8.63	2		Tokyo	24 Jan 93
68:34		Asmae	Laghzaoui	MAR	30.8.76	1		Marrakech	31 Jan 99
68:34		Lidia	Simon	ROM	4.9.73	4		Tokyo	10 Jan 00
68:38		Colleen	de Reuck	RSA	13.4.64	1	NC	Durban	23 Jul 89
68:41		Junko	Kataoka	JPN	13.6.70	1		Tokyo	23 Jan 94
68:45	w	Lyubov	Morgunova	RUS	14.1.71	3		Malmö	12 Jun 00
68:48	w	Abeba	Tolla	ETH	3.6.77	4		Malmö	12 Jun 00
		(30)							
68:49		Grete	Waitz	NOR	1.10.53	1	GNR	South Shields	24 Jul 88
68:55		Naoko	Takahashi	JPN	6.5.72	1		Chiba	23 Jan 00
68:56		Carla	Beurskens	NED	10.2.52	1		Grevenmacher	21 Sep 86
68:58		Nadezhda	Ilyina	RUS	2.4.64	1		Chelyabinsk	18 Jun 94
69:02		Catherine	Ndereba	KEN	21.7.72	1		Como	26 Mar 00
69:03		Margaret	Okayo	KEN	30.5.76	1		Udine	1 Oct 00
69:05		Delillah	Asiago	KEN	24.2.72	1	GWR	Exeter	5 May 91
69:08		Firaya	Sultanova	RUS	29.4.61	2		Chelyabinsk	18 Jun 94
69:10		Alina	Tecuta-Gherasim	ROM	10.11.71	3		Marrakech	31 Jan 99
69:10		Susan	Chepkemei	KEN	25.6.75	2		Lisboa	22 Oct 00
		(40)							
69:12		Yukiko	Okamoto	JPN	29.11.74	1		Yamaguchi	12 Mar 00
69:13		Hellen	Kimaiyo	KEN	8.9.68	4		Grevenmacher	24 Sep 95
69:13		Sachie	Ozaki	JPN	12.3.77	4		Tokyo	19 Jan 97
69:15		Iulia	Negura ¶	ROM	26.1.67	2	WCh	Oslo	24 Sep 94
69:15		Nadia	Prasad'	FRA	6.10.67	1		Paris	17 Mar 96
69:15		Katrin	Dörre -Heinig	GER	6.10.61	2	RdVin	Grevenmacher	27 Sep 98
69:16		Anuta	Catuna	ROM	1.10.68	2		Lisboa	12 Mar 95
69:21		Megumi	Fujiwara	JPN	19.6.69	2	WCh	South Shields	20 Sep 92
69:21		Ann	Wamuchi	KEN	29.9.78	5		Tokyo	19 Jan 97
69:22		Takako	Tobise	JPN	20.6.74	6		Tokyo	19 Jan 97
		(50)	100th woman 69:59, 200th 71:02						
Downhill			* uncertain course measurement						
68:12		Claudia	Metzner	GER	5.5.66	1		Las Vegas (260m)	4 Feb 95
68:13		Petra	Wassiluk	GER	27.10.69	1		Las Vegas	9 Feb 97
69:05		Nadia	Bernard-Prasad	FRA	6.10.67	1		Las Vegas	5 Feb 94
Uncertain distance									
68:37		Rosa	Mota	POR	29.6.58	1		Québec	11 Jun 89
69:03		Carole	Rouillard	CAN	15.3.60	1		Québec	10 Jun 90
Drugs disqualification: 68:50			Yasuko Kimura #	JPN	6.1.76	(3)		Tokyo	21 Jan 96

MARATHON

Note Boston times included in main list, but course is downhill overall (139m) and sometimes, as in 1994, strongly wind-aided - next bests are shown if to standard

In second column: first character: L = loop course or start and finish within 30%, P = point-to-point or start and finish more than 30% apart, D + point-to-point and downhil over 1/1000

Second character: M mixed marathon (men and women), W women only race or separated start by time

Mark		Name		Nat	Born	Pos	Meet	Venue	Date
2:20:43	LM	Tegla	Loroupe	KEN	9.5.73	1		Berlin	26 Sep 99
2:20:47	LM		Loroupe			1		Rotterdam	19 Apr 98
2:21:06	LM	Ingrid	Kristiansen	NOR	21.3.56	1		London	21 Apr 85
2:21:21	LM	Joan	Benoit'	USA	16.5.57	1		Chicago	20 Oct 85
2:21:33	LM	Catherine	Ndereba	KEN	21.7.72	1		Chicago	22 Oct 00
2:21:45	DM	Uta	Pippig	GER	7.9.65	1		Boston	18 Apr 94
2:21:47	PW	Naoko	Takahashi	JPN	6.5.72	1	AsiG	Bangkok	6 Dec 98
2:22:07	LM		Loroupe			1		Rotterdam	20 Apr 97
2:22:12	LW	Eri	Yamaguchi	JPN	14.1.73	1		Tokyo	22 Nov 99
2:22:19	LW		N Takahashi			1		Nagoya	13 Mar 00

WOMEN All-time

Mark	Wind	Name		Nat	Born	Pos	Meet	Venue	Date
2:22:19	LW		N Takahashi			1		Nagoya	12 Mar 00
2:22:23	LM	Catherina	McKiernan	IRL	30.11.69	1		Amsterdam	1 Nov 98
2:22:36	LM	Lornah	Kiplagat	KEN	20.3.74	2		Chicago	22 Oct 00
2:22:43	DM		Benoit			1		Boston	18 Apr 83
2:22:48	LM		Kristiansen			1		London	10 May 87
2:22:48	LM		Loroupe			1		Rotterdam	18 Apr 99
2:22:54	LW	Lidia	Simon (10)	ROM	4.9.73	1		Osaka	30 Jan 00
2:22:56	LW	Harumi	Hiroyama	JPN	2.9.68	2		Osaka	30 Jan 00
2:23:05	LM		Kristiansen			2		Chicago	20 Oct 85
2:23:14	PW		N Takahashi			1	OG	Sydney	24 Sep 00
2:23:21	DM	Fatuma	Roba	ETH	18.12.73	1		Boston	20 Apr 98
2:23:22	LW	Joyce	Chepchumba	KEN	6.11.70	1		London	18 Apr 99
2:23:22	PW		Simon			2	OG	Sydney	24 Sep 00
2:23:24	LW		Simon			1		Osaka	31 Jan 99
2:23:25	DM		Roba			1		Boston	19 Apr 99
2:23:29	LM	Rosa	Mota	POR	29.6.58	3		Chicago	20 Oct 85
2:23:31	LW	Esther	Wanjiru	KEN	27.3.77	3		Osaka	30 Jan 00
2:23:33	DM	Valentina	Yegorova	RUS	16.2.64	2		Boston	18 Apr 94
2:23:43	DM	Olga	Markova	RUS	6.8.68	1		Boston	20 Apr 92
2:23:43	LM	Marleen	Renders	BEL	24.12.68	1		Paris	9 Apr 00
		(30/18)							
2:23:47	LM	Maura	Viceconte	ITA	3.10.67	1		Wien	21 May 00
2:23:51	LW	Lisa	Martin/Ondieki	AUS	12.5.60	1		Osaka	31 Jan 88
2:24:06	LW	Adriana	Fernández	MEX	4.4.71	2		London	18 Apr 99
2:24:07	LW		Wang Junxia	CHN	9.1.73	1		Tianjin	4 Apr 93
2:24:18	DM	Wanda	Panfil	POL	26.1.59	1		Boston	15 Apr 91
2:24:32	LW		Qu Yunxia	CHN	25.12.72	2		Tianjin	4 Apr 93
2:24:35	PM	Katrin	Dörre-Heinig	GER	6.10.61	1		Hamburg	25 Apr 99
2:24:36	LW	Reiko	Tosa	JPN	11.6.76	2		Nagoya	12 Mar 00
2:24:42	LW		Zhang Linli	CHN	6.3.73	3		Tianjin	4 Apr 93
2:24:46	LM	Madina	Biktagirova ¶	RUS	20.9.64	2		Berlin	28 Sep 97
2:24:47	LW	Elfenesh	Alemu	ETH	10.6.75	4		Osaka	30 Jan 00
2:24:52	LW		Zhang Lirong	CHN	3.3.73	4		Tianjin	4 Apr 93
		(30)							
2:24:54	LM	Grete	Waitz	NOR	1.10.53	1		London	20 Apr 86
2:25:09	LW	Manuela	Machado	POR	9.8.63	3		London	18 Apr 99
2:25:14	LW	Kayoko	Obata	JPN	18.9.71	5		Osaka	30 Jan 00
2:25:15	DM	Elana	Meyer	RSA	10.10.66	3		Boston	18 Apr 94
2:25:17	PM	Franca	Fiacconi	ITA	4.10.65	1		New York	1 Nov 98
2:25:19	LM	Alena	Peterková ¶	CZE	13.11.60	4		Boston	18 Apr 94
2:25:32			Ren Xiujuan	CHN	14.9.74	1	NC	Jinan	2 Apr 00
2:25:36	LW		Zhong Huandi	CHN	28.6.67	5		Tianjin	4 Apr 93
2:25:45	LW		Sun Yingjie	CHN	3.10.77	1	NC	Tianjin	11 Apr 98
2:25:45	PM	Lyudmila	Petrova	RUS	7.10.68	1		New York	5 Nov 00
		(40)							
2:25:46	LW		Ma Liyan	CHN	3.11.68	6		Tianjin	4 Apr 93
2:25:51	DM	Franziska	Rochat-Moser	SUI	17.8.66	2		Boston	19 Apr 99
2:25:52	LM	Miyoko	Asahina	JPN	24.9.69	1		Rotterdam	17 Apr 94
2:25:52	LW	Nicole	Carroll	AUS	14.1.72	4		London	18 Apr 99
2:25:56	LM	Véronique	Marot	GBR	16.9.55	1		London	23 Apr 89
2:25:57	PM	Maria	Guida	ITA	23.1.66	1		Carpi	10 Oct 99
2:25:59	LW	Kerryn	McCann	AUS	2.5.67	5		London	16 Apr 00
2:26:00	LM	Margaret	Okayo	KEN	30.5.76	2		Chicago	24 Oct 99
2:26:03	LM	Makiko	Ito	JPN	18.1.73	3		Rotterdam	20 Apr 97
2:26:09	LW	Tomoe	Abe	JPN	13.8.71	1		Osaka	30 Jan 94
2:26:09	LW	Nobuko	Fujimura	JPN	18.12.65	2		Osaka	30 Jan 94
2:26:10	LW	Junko	Asari	JPN	22.9.69	3		Osaka	30 Jan 94
		(52)	100th woman 2:27:25, 200th woman 2:29:29						

Short course performances

Mark	Wind	Name		Nat	Born	Pos	Meet	Venue	Date
2:25:25		Lyubov	Klochko	UKR	26.9.62	1		Belaya Cerkov	6 Sep 87
2:25:29		Allison	Roe	NZL	30.5.56	1		New York	25 Oct 81

2000 METRES STEEPLECHASE

Mark	Name		Nat	Born	Pos	Meet	Venue	Date
6:11.84	Marina	Pluzhnikova	RUS	25.2.63	1	GWG	Sankt-Peterburg	25 Jul 94
6:14.52	Svetlana	Rogova	RUS	4.8.67	1	Znam	Moskva	11 Jun 92
6:16.49	Yelena	Motalova	RUS	28.1.71	1	NC	Moskva	2 Aug 98
6:17.80	Irina	Mozharova	RUS	19.7.58	1	NC	Gorkiy	23 Jul 89
6:18.2	Svetlana	Vinogradova	RUS	71	1	Army	Rostov	16 Jun 96

Mark	Wind	Name		Nat	Born	Pos	Meet	Venue	Date

3000 METRES STEEPLECHASE

Mark	Wind	Name		Nat	Born	Pos	Meet	Venue	Date
9:40.20 WR		Cristina	Iloc-Casandra	ROM	21.10.77	1		Reims	30 Aug 00
9:43.64 WR			Iloc-Casandra			1	NC	Bucuresti	7 Aug 00
9:48.88 WR		Yelena	Motalova	RUS	28.1.71	1	NC	Tula	31 Jul 99
9:51.76			Iloc-Casandra			1		Stántu Gheorghe	23 Jul 00
9:52.40		Yekaterina	Volkova	RUS	.78	1	Znam	Sankt-Peterburg	17 Jun 00
9:54.10		Anzhelika	Averkova	UKR	13.3.69	1	NC	Kiev	5 Aug 00
9:54.86		Daniela	Petrescu	ROM	13.4.68	2	NC	Bucuresti	7 Aug 00
9:55.28			Petrescu			1	ROM IC	Bucuresti	21 Jun 98
9:55.69		Laurence	Duquénoy	FRA	29.9.69	1		Castres	8 Aug 99
9:56.6			Motalova			1	Znam	Moskva	5 Jun 99
9:56.99		Luminita	Gogîrlea	ROM	5.11.71	3	NC	Bucuresti	7 Aug 00
9:57.03		Justyna	Bak	POL	1.8.74	1	Kuso	Warszawa	24 Jun 00
9:57.20		Elizabeth	Jackson	USA	27.10.77	1	NC	Sacramento	17 Jul 00
9:57.62		Svetlana	Rogova	RUS	4.8.67	1	GWG	Uniondale, NY	19 Jul 98
		(10)							
10:00.63		Lisa	Nye	USA	17.11.68	2	NC	Sacramento	17 Jul 00
10:01.54		Susanne	Wigene	NOR	12.2.78	1	NC	Steinkjer	11 Aug 00
10:02.60		Olimpia	Pop	ROM	25.2.76	4	NC	Bucuresti	7 Aug 00
10:03.09		Kara	Ormond	USA	17.6.77	3	NC	Sacramento	17 Jul 00
10:03.68		Alina	Cucerzan	ROM	28.7.74	1	NC	Bucuresti	5 Jul 99
10:04.41		Courtney	Meldrum	USA	31.1.77	4	NC	Sacramento	17 Jul 00
10:04.45		Tara	Haynes	USA	6.8.78	5	NC	Sacramento	17 Jul 00
10:04.85		Céline	Rajot	FRA	22.3.75	1	NC	Nice	5 Aug 00

100 METRES HURDLES

Mark	Wind	Name		Nat	Born	Pos	Meet	Venue	Date
12.21 WR	0.7	Yordanka	Donkova	BUL	28.9.61	1		Stara Zagora	20 Aug 88
12.24	0.9		Donkova			1h		Stara Zagora	28 Aug 88
12.25 WR	1.4	Ginka	Zagorcheva	BUL	12.4.58	1	v TCH,GRE	Drama	8 Aug 87
12.26 WR	1.5		Donkova			1	Balk	Ljubljana	7 Sep 86
12.26	1.7	Lyudmila	Narozhilenko ¶	RUS	21.4.64	1rB		Sevilla	6 Jun 92
		(now Ludmila Engquist SWE)							
12.27	-1.2		Donkova			1		Stara Zagora	28 Aug 88
12.28	1.8		Narozhilenko			1	NC	Kiyev	11 Jul 91
12.28	0.9		Narozhilenko			1rA		Sevilla	6 Jun 92
12.29 WR	-0.4		Donkova			1	ASV	Köln	17 Aug 86
12.32	1.6		Narozhilenko			1		Saint-Denis	4 Jun 92
12.33	1.4		Donkova			1		Fürth	14 Jun 87
12.33	-0.3	Gail	Devers	USA	19.11.66	1	NC	Sacramento	23 Jul 00
12.34	-0.5		Zagorcheva			1	WCh	Roma	4 Sep 87
12.35 WR	0.1		Donkova			1h2	ASV	Köln	17 Aug 86
12.36 WR	1.9	Grazyna	Rabsztyn	POL	20.9.52	1	Kuso	Warszawa	13 Jun 80
12.36 WR	-0.6		Donkova			1	NC	Sofiya	13 Aug 86
12.36	1.1		Donkova			1		Schwechat	15 Jun 88
12.37	1.4		Donkova			1	ISTAF	Berlin	15 Aug 86
12.37	0.7		Devers			1	WCh	Sevilla	28 Aug 99
12.38	0.0		Donkova			1	BGP	Budapest	11 Aug 86
12.38	-0.7		Donkova			1	EC	Stuttgart	29 Aug 86
12.38	0.2		Donkova			1	OG	Seoul	30 Sep 88
12.39	1.5	Vera	Komisova'	RUS	11.6.53	1	GGala	Roma	5 Aug 80
12.39	1.5		Zagorcheva			2	Balk	Ljubljana	7 Sep 86
12.39	1.8	Natalya	Grigoryeva ¶	UKR	3.12.62	2	NC	Kiyev	11 Jul 91
12.39	-0.7		Devers			1	WK	Zürich	11 Aug 00
12.40	0.4		Donkova			1	GWG	Moskva	8 Jul 86
12.42	1.8	Bettine	Jahn	GDR	3.8.58	1	OD	Berlin	8 Jun 83
12.42	1.0		Zagorcheva			1		Sofiya	14 Aug 85
12.42	-0.2		Donkova			1	VD	Bruxelles	5 Sep 86
12.42	0.2		Narozhilenko			1	GGala	Roma	9 Jun 92
		(31/8)							
12.43	-0.9	Lucyna	Kalek (Langer)	POL	9.1.56	1		Hannover	19 Aug 84
12.44	-0.5	Gloria	Uibel (-Siebert) (10)	GDR	13.1.64	2	WCh	Roma	4 Sep 87
12.44	-0.8	Olga	Shishigina	KZK	23.12.68	1		Luzern	27 Jun 95
12.44	0.4	Glory	Alozie	NGR	30.12.77	1	Herc	Monaco	8 Aug 98
12.45	1.3	Cornelia	Oschkenat'	GDR	29.10.61	1		Neubrandenburg	11 Jun 87
12.47	1.1	Marina	Azyabina	RUS	15.6.63	1s2	NC	Moskva	19 Jun 93
12.50	0.0	Vera	Akimova'	RUS	5.6.59	1		Sochi	19 May 84
12.52	-0.4	Michelle	Freeman	JAM	5.5.69	1s1	WCh	Athína	10 Aug 97
12.52	1.9	Delloreen	Ennis-London	JAM	5.3.75	1	NC	Kingston	22 Jul 00

Mark	Wind	Name		Nat	Born	Pos	Meet	Venue	Date
12.53	0.2	Tatyana	Reshetnikova	RUS	14.10.66	1rA	GP II	Linz	4 Jul 94
12.53	-0.4	Svetla	Dimitrova ¶	BUL	27.1.70	1	Herc	Stara Zagora	16 Jul 94
12.53	1.0	Melissa	Morrison	USA	9.7.71	1	DNG	Stockholm	5 Aug 98
		(20)							
12.54	0.4	Kerstin	Knabe	GDR	7.7.59	3	EC	Athína	9 Sep 82
12.54	0.9	Sabine	Paetz/John'	GDR	16.10.57	1		Berlin	15 Jul 84
12.56	1.2	Johanna	Klier'	GDR	13.9.52	1	NC	Cottbus	17 Jul 80
12.56	1.2	Monique	Ewanje-Epée	FRA	11.7.67	1	BNP	Villeneuve d'Ascq	29 Jun 90
12.59 WR	-0.6	Anneliese	Ehrhardt	GDR	18.6.50	1	OG	München	8 Sep 72
12.59	0.0	Natalya	Shekhodanova ¶	RUS	29.12.71	1	NC	Sankt Peterburg	3 Jul 96
12.59	1.0	Patricia	Girard	FRA	8.4.68	2s2	OG	Atlanta	31 Jul 96
12.59	0.2	Brigita	Bukovec	SLO	21.5.70	2	OG	Atlanta	31 Jul 96
12.61	0.3	Svetlana	Gusarova	KZK	29.5.59	2	NC	Leningrad	3 Aug 85
12.61	0.2	Jackie	Joyner-Kersee	USA	3.3.62	1	Jenn	San José	28 May 88
		(30)							
12.61	1.4	Katie	Anderson	CAN	9.1.68	1		Villeneuve d'Ascq	13 Jun 99
12.62	1.2	Mihaela	Pogacian'	ROM	27.1.58	2	BNP	Villeneuve d'Ascq	29 Jun 90
12.62	1.1	Yuliya	Graudyn	RUS	13.11.70	1A	ISTAF	Berlin	30 Aug 94
12.63	1.8	Zofia	Bielczyk	POL	22.9.58	1h1	Kuso	Warszawa	18 Jun 79
12.63	1.4	Heike	Terpe/Theele	GDR	4.10.64	2	NC	Jena	27 Jun 86
12.63	0.0	Angie	Vaughn	USA	4.11.76	1	GP	Edwardsville	25 Jul 98
12.63	1.6	Anjanette	Kirkland	USA	24.2.74	1r5	MSR	Walnut	16 Apr 00
12.64	0.4	Paraskeví	Patoulídou	GRE	29.3.65	1	OG	Barcelona	6 Aug 92
12.64	0.1		Zhang Yu	CHN	8.4.71	1	NG	Beijing	9 Sep 93
12.64	1.0	Dionne	Rose	JAM	7.11.69	4s2	OG	Atlanta	31 Jul 96
		(40)							
12.65A	0.0	Danuta	Perka	POL	22.6.56	1h3	WUG	Ciudad de México	9 Sep 79
12.65	0.0	Nadezhda	Korshunova'	UKR	18.5.61	2		Sochi	19 May 84
12.66	0.0	Yelena	Biserova	RUS	24.3.62	3		Sochi	19 May 84
12.66	0.7	Lidiya	Yurkova '	BLR	15.1.67	1s2	NC	Kiyev	5 Jul 90
12.66	2.0	Gillian	Russell	JAM	28.9.73	2	CAG	Maracaibo	16 Aug 98
12.67	0.6	Tatyana	Anisimova	RUS	19.10.49	2	EC	Praha	2 Sep 78
12.67	0.2	Lynda	Tolbert/Goode	USA	3.10.67	3	WCh	Stuttgart	20 Aug 93
12.67	1.4	Aliuska	López	CUB	29.8.69	2q2	OG	Atlanta	29 Jul 96
12.67	1.3	Joanna	Hayes	USA	23.12.76	2s1	NC	Sacramento	23 Jul 00
12.68	1.1	Yelizaveta	Chernyshova	RUS	26.1.58	1h1	Znam	Volgograd	10 Jun 89
12.68	1.3	Sharon	Couch	USA	13.9.69	3s1	NC	Sacramento	23 Jul 00
		(51)	100th woman 12.82, 200th woman 13.02						

Wind assisted performers to 12.66

Mark	Wind	Name		Nat	Born	Pos	Meet	Venue	Date
12.28	2.7	Cornelia	Oschkenat'	GDR	29.10.61	1		Berlin	25 Aug 87
12.29	3.5		Donkova			1	Athl	Lausanne	24 Jun 88
12.35	2.4	Bettine	Jahn	GDR	3.8.58	1	WCh	Helsinki	13 Aug 83
12.37	2.7	Gloria	Uibel/Siebert'	GDR	13.1.64	2		Berlin	25 Aug 87
12.39	2.8		Rabsztyn			1	4-N	Bremen	24 Jun 79
12.40	2.1	Michelle	Freeman	JAM	5.5.69	1	GPF	Fukuoka	13 Sep 97
12.41	2.2	Olga	Shishigina	KZK	23.12.68	1rA	Athl	Lausanne	5 Jul 95
12.42	2.4	Kerstin	Knabe	GDR	7.7.59	2	WCh	Helsinki	13 Aug 83
12.50	2.7	Svetla	Dimitrova ¶	BUL	27.1.70	1		Saint-Denis	10 Jun 94
12.51	3.2	Johanna	Klier'	GDR	13.9.52	1	NC	Cottbus	17 Jul 80
12.51	3.6	Sabine	Paetz/John'	GDR	16.10.57	1		Dresden	27 Jul 84
12.51A	3.3	Yuliya	Graudyn	RUS	13.11.70	1		Sestriere	31 Jul 94
12.53	2.2	Mihaela	Pogacian	ROM	27.1.58	1	IAC	Edinburgh	6 Jul 90
12.60	4.2	Delloreen	Ennis-London	JPN	5.3.75	1r2	PennR	Philadelphia	24 Apr 99
12.63	2.8	Eva	Sokolova	RUS	25.3.62	1s1	NC	Moskva	19 Jun 93
12.64	5.0	Anne	Piquereau	FRA	15.6.64	3		Dijon	12 Jun 94
12.65	3.2	Dawn	Bowles	USA	12.11.68	1q1	NC	Atlanta	22 Jun 96
12.65	2.6	Sharon	Couch-Jewell	USA	13.9.69	1		Hechtel	7 Aug 99
12.66	2.6	Yelena	Politika	UKR	24.8.64	3	NC	Tallinn	5 Jul 88
12.66	4.7	Lynda	Tolbert/Goode	USA	3.10.67	1	BNP	Villeneuve d'Ascq	6 Jul 92
12.66	2.7	Nadezhda	Bodrova	UKR	13.7.61	1	NC	Kiyev	8 Jun 96

Probably hand timed

Mark	Wind	Name		Nat	Born	Pos	Meet	Venue	Date
12.4	0.7	Svetla	Dimitrova	BUL	27.1.70	1		Stara Zagora	9 Jul 97
Officially 12.36, but subsequent investigations showed this unlikely to have been auto-timed									
12.63		Angela	Atede	NGR	8.2.72	1	NC	Lagos	28 Jun 97

Hand timed

Mark	Wind	Name		Nat	Born	Pos	Meet	Venue	Date
12.3 WR	1.5	Anneliese	Ehrhardt	GDR	18.6.50	1	NC	Dresden	22 Jul 73
12.3		Marina	Azyabina	RUS	15.6.63	1		Yekaterinburg	30 May 93
12.0w	2.1	Yordanka	Donkova	BUL	28.9.61	1		Sofiya	3 Aug 86
12.1w	2.1	Ginka	Zagorcheva	BUL	12.4.58	2		Sofiya	3Aug 86

400 METRES HURDLES

Mark Wind	Name		Nat	Born	Pos	Meet	Venue	Date
52.61 WR	Kim	Batten	USA	29.3.69	1	WCh	Göteborg	11 Aug 95
52.62	Tonja	Buford-Bailey	USA	13.12.70	2	WCh	Göteborg	11 Aug 95
52.74 WR	Sally	Gunnell	GBR	29.7.66	1	WCh	Stuttgart	19 Aug 93
52.74		Batten			1	Herc	Monaco	8 Aug 98
52.79	Sandra	Farmer-Patrick	USA	18.8.62	2	WCh	Stuttgart	19 Aug 93
52.82	Deon	Hemmings	JAM	9.10.68	1	OG	Atlanta	31 Jul 96
52.84		Batten			1	WK	Zürich	12 Aug 98
52.89	Daimí	Pernía	CUB	27.12.76	1	WCh	Sevilla	25 Aug 99
52.90		Buford			1	WK	Zürich	16 Aug 95
52.90	Nezha	Bidouane	MAR	18.9.69	2	WCh	Sevilla	25 Aug 99
52.94 WR	Marina	Styepanova'	RUS	1.5.50	1s	Spart	Tashkent	17 Sep 86
52.96A		Bidouane			1	WCp	Johannesburg	11 Sep 98
52.97		Batten			1	NC	Indianapolis	14 Jun 97
52.97		Bidouane			1	WCh	Athína	8 Aug 97
52.98		Hemmings			1rA	WK	Zürich	13 Aug 97
52.99		Hemmings			1s1	OG	Atlanta	29 Jul 96
53.02	Irina	Privalova	RUS	22.11.68	1	OG	Sydney	27 Sep 00
53.03A		Hemmings			2	WCp	Johannesburg	11 Sep 98
53.05		Bidouane			1	GGala	Roma	7 Jul 99
53.06		Batten			1	Herc	Monaco	16 Aug 97
53.06		Batten			1	Gaz	Paris	29 Jul 98
53.08		Batten			2	OG	Atlanta	31 Jul 96
53.08		Bidouane			1	Athl	Lausanne	2 Jul 99
53.09		Hemmings			2	WCh	Ath'na	8 Aug 97
53.11	Tatyana	Ledovskaya	BLR	21.5.66	1	WCh	Tokyo	29 Aug 91
53.16		Gunnell			2	WCh	Tokyo	29 Aug 91
53.16		Hemmings			3	WCh	Sevilla	25 Aug 99
53.17	Debbie	Flintoff-King	AUS	20.4.60	1	OG	Seoul	28 Sep 88
53.17		Batten			1	Nik	Nice	16 Jul 98
53.17A		Batten			1	WCp	Johannesburg	11 Sep 98
	(30/11)							
53.21	Marie-José	Pérec	FRA	9.5.68	2	WK	Zürich	16 Aug 95
53.24	Sabine	Busch	GDR	21.11.62	1	NC	Potsdam	21 Aug 87
53.25	Ionela	Tîrlea	ROM	9.2.76	2	GGala	Roma	7 Jul 99
53.33	Sandra	Glover	USA	30.12.68	1	NC	Sacramento	17 Jul 00
53.36	Andrea	Blackett	BAR	24.1.76	4	WCh	Sevilla	25 Aug 99
53.40	Tatyana	Tereshchuk	UKR	11.10.69	2		Villeneuve d'Ascq	11 Jul 98
53.47	Janeene	Vickers	USA	3.10.68	3	WCh	Tokyo	29 Aug 91
53.48	Margarita	Ponomaryova'	RUS	19.6.63	3	WCh	Stuttgart	19 Aug 93
53.58	Cornelia	Ullrich'	GDR	26.4.63	2	NC	Potsdam	21 Aug 87
	(20)							
53.63	Ellen	Fiedler'	GDR	26.11.58	3	OG	Seoul	28 Sep 88
53.65A	Myrtle	Bothma'	RSA	18.2.64	mx		Pretoria	12 Mar 90
	53.74A				1		Johannesburg	18 Apr 86
53.96		Han Qing ¶	CHN	4.3.70	1	NG	Beijing	9 Sep 93
53.97	Debbie-Ann	Parris	JAM	24.3.73	4	OG	Atlanta	31 Jul 96
53.98	Yuliya	Nosova	RUS	21.4.78	1	Znam	Moskva	5 Jun 99
54.02 WR	Anna	Ambraziené'	LIT	14.4.55	1	Znam	Moskva	11 Jun 83
54.02A	Judit	Szekeres	HUN	18.11.66	1		Roodepoort	23 Jan 98
54.03	Heike	Meissner	GER	29.1.70	5	OG	Atlanta	31 Jul 96
54.04	Gudrun	Abt	FRG	3.8.62	6	OG	Seoul	28 Sep 88
54.11	Anna	Knoroz	RUS	30.7.70	3	Nik	Nice	18 Jul 94
	(30)							
54.14	Yekaterina	Fesenko/Grun	RUS	10.8.58	1	WCh	Helsinki	10 Aug 83
54.15	Ann-Louise	Skoglund	SWE	28.6.62	4	EC	Stuttgart	30 Aug 86
54.15	Michelle	Johnson	USA	12.4.74	5	WK	Zürich	11 Aug 99
54.17	Tonya	Williams	USA	5.10.74	3	Athl	Lausanne	3 Jul 96
54.21	Ryan	Tolbert	USA	16.6.76	3	NC	Indianapolis	14 Jun 97
54.22A	Silvia	Rieger	GER	14.11.70	5	WCp	Johannesburg	11 Sep 98
54.23	Judi	Brown King	USA	14.7.61	1	PAm	Indianapolis	12 Aug 87
54.24	Susanne	Losch	GDR	12.2.66	1	v FRG	Düsseldorf	19 Jun 88
54.25	Anita	Protti	SUI	4.8.64	6	WCh	Tokyo	29 Aug 91
54.27	Genowefa	Blaszak'	POL	22.8.57	1	DNG	Stockholm	2 Jul 85
	(40)							
54.28 WR	Karin	Rossley	GDR	5.4.57	1		Jena	17 May 80
54.31	Susan	Smith	IRL	14.9.71	7	WK	Zürich	12 Aug 98
54.34	Tatyana	Pavlova'	UZB	12.12.58	1h1	NC	Leningrad	2 Aug 85
54.35	Petra	Krug	GDR	9.11.63	1	vSU	Bryansk	14 Jul 89

Mark Wind		Name	Nat	Born	Pos	Meet	Venue	Date
54.36	LaTanya	Sheffield	USA	11.10.63	3s1	OG	Seoul	26 Sep 88
54.37	Vera	Ordina	RUS	4.6.68	2s1	OG	Barcelona	3 Aug 92
54.37	Gudrun	Arnardóttir	ISL	24.9.71	2	BrGP	London (CP)	5 Aug 00
54.39	Tatyana	Kurochkina'	BLR	15.9.67	7	OG	Seoul	28 Sep 88
54.39	Rosey	Edeh	CAN	13.8.66	6	OG	Atlanta	31 Jul 96
54.50	Natalya	Torshina	KAZ	4.10.68	1	ECCp	V R San António	27 May 00
	(50)	100th woman 55.23, 200th woman 56.04						

Low altitude bests

54.27 Rieger 2s2 OG Atlanta 29 Jul 96 54.44 Bothma 1 NC Durban 22 Apr 89

Drugs disqualification

53.38		Jiang Limei ¶	CHN	.3.70	(1)	NG	Shanghai	22 Oct 97
54.47		Guo Yue ¶	CHN	23.1.69	(2)	NG	Beijing	9 Sep 93

HIGH JUMP

2.09 WR	Stefka	Kostadinova	BUL	25.3.65	1	WCh	Roma	30 Aug 87
2.08 WR		Kostadinova			1	NM	Sofiya	31 May 86
2.07 WR	Lyudmila	Andonova ¶	BUL	6.5.60	1	OD	Berlin	20 Jul 84
2.07 WR		Kostadinova			1		Sofiya	25 May 86
2.07		Kostadinova			1		Cagliari	16 Sep 87
2.07		Kostadinova			1	NC	Sofiya	3 Sep 88
2.07i	Heike	Henkel'	GER	5.5.64	1	NC	Karlsruhe	8 Feb 92
2.06		Kostadinova			1	ECp	Moskva	18 Aug 85
2.06		Kostadinova			1		Fürth	15 Jun 86
2.06		Kostadinova			1		Cagliari	14 Sep 86
2.06		Kostadinova			1		Wörrstadt	6 Jun 87
2.06		Kostadinova			1		Rieti	8 Sep 87
2.06i		Kostadinova			1		Pireás	20 Feb 88
2.05 WR	Tamara	Bykova	RUS	21.12.58	1	Izv	Kiyev	22 Jun 84
2.05		Kostadinova			1		Wörrstadt	14 Jun 86
2.05		Kostadinova			1		Rieti	7 Sep 86
2.05i		Kostadinova			1	WI	Indianapolis	8 Mar 87
2.05		Kostadinova			1	Bisl	Oslo	4 Jul 87
2.05		Kostadinova			1		Padova	13 Sep 87
2.05		Kostadinova			1	BGP	Budapest	12 Aug 88
2.05		Henkel			1	WCh	Tokyo	31 Aug 91
2.05i		Kostadinova			1	NC	Sofiya	1 Feb 92
2.05		Kostadinova			1		San Marino	4 Jul 92
2.05		Kostadinova			1	Toto	Fukuoka	18 Sep 93
2.05	Inga	Babakova	UKR	27.6.67	1		Tokyo	15 Sep 95
2.05		Kostadinova			1	OG	Atlanta	3 Aug 96
	(26/5) 2.04 performances: 12 Kostadinova, 5 Henkel, 2 Bykova, 1 Costa, Astafei, Babakova, Cloete							
2.04	Silvia	Costa	CUB	4.5.64	1	WCp	Barcelona	9 Sep 89
2.04i	Alina	Astafei	GER	7.6.69	1		Berlin	3 Mar 95
2.04	Hestrie	Cloete	RSA	26.8.78	1	Herc	Monaco	4 Aug 99
2.03 WR	Ulrike	Meyfarth	FRG	4.5.56	1	ECp	London (CP)	21 Aug 83
2.03	Louise	Ritter	USA	18.2.58	1		Austin	8 Jul 88
	(10)							
2.03	Tatyana	Motkova	RUS	23.11.68	2		Bratislava	30 May 95
2.03	Níki	Bakoyiánni	GRE	9.6.68	2	OG	Atlanta	3 Aug 96
2.03	Venelina	Veneva	BUL	13.6.74	1		Kalamata	23 May 98
2.03i	Monica	Iagar/Dinescu	ROM	1.4.73	1		Bucuresti	23 Jan 99
2.02i	Susanne	Beyer'	GDR	24.6.61	2	WI	Indianapolis	8 Mar 87
2.02	Yelena	Yelesina	RUS	5.4.70	1	GWG	Seattle	23 Jul 90
2.01 WR	Sara	Simeoni	ITA	19.4.53	1	v Pol	Brescia	4 Aug 78
2.01	Olga	Turchak	UKR	5.3.67	2	GWG	Moskva	7 Jul 86
2.01	Desiré	du Plessis	RSA	20.5.65	1		Johannesburg	16 Sep 86
2.01i	Gabriele	Günz	GDR	8.9.61	2		Stuttgart	31 Jan 88
	(20)							
2.01	Heike	Balck	GDR	19.8.70	1	vSU-j	Karl-Marx-Stadt	18 Jun 89
2.01i	Ioamnet	Quintero	CUB	8.9.72	1		Berlin	5 Mar 00
2.01	Hanne	Haugland	NOR	14.12.67	1	WK	Zürich	13 Aug 97
2.01i	Tisha	Waller	USA	1.12.70	1	NC	Atlanta	28 Feb 98
2.01	Yelena	Gulyayeva	RUS	14.8.67	2		Kalamata	23 May 98
2.01	Kajsa	Bergqvist	SWE	12.10.76	1	NC	Uppsala	19 Aug 00
2.00 WR	Rosemarie	Ackermann'	GDR	4.4.52	1	ISTAF	Berlin	26 Aug 77
2.00i	Coleen	Sommer'	USA	6.6.60	1		Ottawa	14 Feb 82
2.00	Charmaine	Gale/Weavers	RSA	27.2.64	1		Pretoria	25 Mar 85
2.00i	Emilia	Dragieva'	BUL	11.1.65	3	WI	Indianapolis	8 Mar 87
	(30)							

Mark Wind		Name	Nat	Born	Pos	Meet	Venue	Date
2.00	Lyudmila	Avdyeyenko'	UKR	14.12.63	1	NC	Bryansk	17 Jul 87
2.00	Svetlana	Isaeva/Leseva	BUL	18.3.67	2	v TCH,GRE	Drama	8 Aug 87
2.00i	Larisa	Kositsyna	RUS	14.12.63	2	NC	Volgograd	11 Feb 88
2.00	Jan	Wohlschlag'	USA	14.7.58	1	Bisl	Oslo	1 Jul 89
2.00	Yolanda	Henry	USA	2.12.64	1	Expo	Sevilla	30 May 90
2.00	Biljana	Petrovic ¶	YUG	28.2.61	1		St. Denis	22 Jun 90
2.00	Tatyana	Shevchik ¶	BLR	11.6.69	1		Gomel	14 May 93
2.00i	Britta	Bilac'	SLO	4.12.68	1		Frankfurt	9 Feb 94
2.00	Amy	Acuff	USA	14.7.75	2	VD	Bruxelles	22 Aug 97
2.00i	Yuliya	Lyakhova	RUS	8.7.77	1		Wuppertal	5 Feb 99
	(40)							
2.00	Zuzana	Hlavonová	CZE	16.4.73	1	Odlozil	Praha	5 Jun 00
1.99i	Debbie	Brill	CAN	10.3.53	1		Edmonton	23 Jan 82
1.99i	Andrea	Bienias'	GDR	11.11.59	2	EI	Milano	7 Mar 82
1.99i	Katalin	Sterk	HUN	30.9.61	3	EI	Milano	7 Mar 82
1.99	Kerstin	Brandt'	GDR	9.12.61	3	ECp	London (CP)	21 Aug 83
1.99	Yelena	Topchina ¶	RUS	28.9.66	1		Rieti	5 Sep 93
1.99	Khristina	Kalcheva	BUL	29.5.77	1		Sofia	16 May 98
1.99	Svetlana	Lapina	RUS	12.4.78	3	WCh	Sevilla	29 Aug 99
1.99	Oana	Pantelimon	ROM	27.9.72	3=	OG	Sydney	30 Sep 00
	(49)	17 women at 1.98, 100th woman 1.96, 200th woman 1.93						

Best outdoor marks

Mark	Name	Pos	Meet	Venue	Date
2.02	Iagar/Dinescu	1		Budapest	6 Jun 98
2.01	Astafei	2		Wörrstadt	27 May 95
2.00	Quintero	1	Herc	Monaco	7 Aug 93
2.00	Kositsyna	1		Chelyabinsk	16 Jul 88
2.00	Bilac	1	EC	Helsinki	14 Aug 94
2.00	Waller	1	MSR	Walnut	18 Apr 99
1.99	Beyer'	3	WCh	Roma	30 Aug 87
1.99	Lyakhova	2	GPF	Fukuoka	13 Sep 97

Drugs disqualification: 1.99 Antonella Bevilacqua # ITA 15.10.71 (4) OG Atlanta 3 Aug 96

POLE VAULT

Mark Wind		Name	Nat	Born	Pos	Meet	Venue	Date
4.70 b	Stacy	Dragila	USA	25.3.71	1		Santa Barbara	11 Jun 00
	Above mark was statistically valid, but made on a platform runway, unacceptable for world records							
4.63 WR		Dragila			1	NC	Sacramento	23 Jul 00
4.62i		Dragila			1	NC	Atlanta	3 Mar 00
4.62 WR		Dragila			1		Phoenix	26 May 00
4.61Ai		Dragila			1		Pocatello	19 Feb 00
4.60 WR	Emma	George	AUS	1.11.74	1		Sydney	20 Feb 99
4.60 WR		Dragila			1	WCh	Sevilla	21 Aug 99
4.60 WR		Dragila			1	ModR	Modesto	12 May 00
4.60		Dragila			1	OG	Sydney	25 Sep 00
4.59 WR		George			1		Brisbane	21 Mar 98
4.59b		Dragila			1		Santa Barbara	19 Jun 99
4.58 WR		George			1	NC	Melbourne	14 Mar 98
4.57 WR		George			1	Tait	Auckland (NS)	20 Feb 98
4.57		Dragila			1		Sacramento	21 May 00
4.56i	Nicole	Rieger/Humbert	GER	5.2.72	1		Stockholm	25 Feb 99
4.56	Anzhela	Balakhonova	UKR	18.12.72	1	Gugl	Linz	8 Aug 00
4.55 WR		George			1	Nike	Melbourne	20 Feb 97
4.55i		George			1		Adelaide	26 Mar 98
4.55	Anzhela	Balakhonova	UKR	18.12.72	1	GP II	Saint-Denis	3 Jul 99
4.55		Balakhonova			2	WCh	Sevilla	21 Aug 99
4.55		Dragila			1		Brisbane	11 Feb 00
4.55	Tatiana	Grigorieva	AUS	8.10.75	2	OG	Sydney	25 Sep 00
4.54		Dragila			1		Uniondale, NY	6 Jun 99
4.54		Balakhonova			2		Uniondale, NY	6 Jun 99
4.53		Dragila			1		Palo Alto	1 Jul 00
4.53	Kellie	Suttle	USA	9.3.73	2		Palo Alto	1 Jul 00
4.52		Balakhonova			1	NC	Kiev	4 Aug 00
4.51	Daniela	Bártová	CZE	6.5.74	1	Slovn	Bratislava	9 Jun 98
4.51i	Zsuzsanna	Szabó	HUN	6.5.73	1		Budapest	4 Feb 99
4.51		Dragila			1		Ingolstadt	11 Jul 99
4.51Ai		Dragila			1		Pocatello	28 Jan 00
	(31/8)							
4.50i	Melissa	Mueller	USA	16.11.72	1		Roxbury	7 Feb 99
4.50i	Nastja	Ryshich (10)	GER	19.9.77	1	WI	Maebashi	5 Mar 99
4.50	Svetlana	Feofanova	RUS	16.7.80	1	GPII	Helsinki	15 Jun 00
4.50	Yelena	Belyakova	RUS	7.4.76	3	GP	Athína	28 Jun 00
4.50	Vala	Flosadóttir	ISL	16.2.78	3	OG	Sydney	25 Sep 00
4.47	Mary	Sauer	USA	31.10.75	2		Sacramento	21 May 00
4.45i	Yelena	Isinbayeva	RUS	3.6.82	1	NC	Volgograd	4 Feb 00

Mark	Wind	Name		Nat	Born	Pos	Meet	Venue	Date
4.45		Tracy	O'Hara	USA	20.7.80	1	USTCA	Austin	22 Apr 00
4.45		Pavla	Hamácková	CZE	20.5.78	2		Turnov	11 Jun 00
4.45		Yvonne	Buschbaum	GER	14.7.80	1		Ingolstadt	18 Jun 00
4.42		Alejandra	García	ARG	13.6.73	1		Sydney	20 Feb 00
4.42		Tanya	Koleva	BUL	8.3.72	1		Sofia	11 Jun 00
		(20)							
4.42		Elmarie	Gerryts	RSA	25.8.72	1		Wesel	12 Jun 00
4.40i		Christine	Adams	GER	28.2.74	2		Chemnitz	18 Feb 00
4.40		Doris	Auer	AUT	10.5.71	2		Gold Coast (RB)	17 Sep 00
4.40		Monika	Pyrek	POL	11.8.80	7	OG	Sydney	25 Sep 00
4.37i		Thórey	Elísdóttir	ISL	30.6.77	1		Reykjavik	16 Mar 99
4.37		Lesa	Kubishta	USA	19.4.78	1		Irvine	7 May 00
4.36		Melissa	Price	USA	20.9.77	1		Houston	23 May 98
4.35i			Cai Weiyan	CHN	25.10.73	3	WI	Paris (B)	9 Mar 97
4.35		Marie	Poissonnier	FRA	4.5.79	1		Bron	7 May 00
4.35			Gao Shuying	CHN	28.10.79	1		Chengdu	10 May 00
		(30)							
4.35		Alicia	Warlick	USA	11.10.77	3	ModR	Modesto	13 May 00
4.35		Janine	Whitlock	GBR	11.8.73	2=		Praha	5 Jun 00
4.35		Marie B	Rasmussen	DEN	1.11.72	8	OG	Sydney	25 Sep 00
4.33i		Eszter	Szemerédi	HUN	12.2.76	2		Karlsruhe	25 Jan 98
4.32		Vanessa	Boslak	FRA	11.6.82	1		La Roche-sur-Yon	23 Sep 00
4.31		Monika	Götz	GER	15.6.81	1		Troisdorf	9 May 98
4.31i		Tatyana	Gubareva	RUS	4.12.73	1		Moskva	14 Feb 99
4.31		Amandine	Homo	FRA	24.12.80	3	GP II	Saint-Denis	3 Jul 99
4.30		Andrea	Müller	GER	29.6.74	1		Worms	31 May 97
4.30		Annika	Becker	GER	12.11.81	2		Mannheim	18 Jun 99
		(40)							
4.30i		Krisztina	Molnár	HUN	8.4.76	1	NC	Budapest	13 Feb 00
4.30		Sabine	Schulte	GER	29.1.76	2		Dessau	31 May 00
4.30		Monique	de Wilt	NED	21.3.76	3		Dessau	31 May 00
4.30		Katerina	Badurová	CZE	18.12.82	3		Turnov	11 Jun 00
4.30b		Aimee	Crabtree	USA	22.1.78	4		Santa Barbara	11 Jun 00
4.30		Katalin	Donáth	HUN	12.11.79	1		Budapest	22 Jul 00
4.30		Caroline	Ammel	FRA	22.11.73	1		Bron	23 Jul 00
4.30		Maria Mar	Sánchez	ESP	25.12.79	1		Castellón	26 Aug 00
4.28i			Sun Caiyun	CHN	21.7.73	1		Tianjin	27 Feb 96
4.28		Arianna	Farfaletti	ITA	22.6.76	1		Rovellasca	23 Sep 00
		(50)	100th woman 4.10						

Outdoor best

4.50	Humbert	1		Salamanca	20 Jul 00	4.40	Isinbayeva	2	NC	Tula	24 Jul 00
4.45	Mueller	1		Portland	25 Jun 00	4.33	Cai Weiyan	1		Shenzhen	5 Oct 96
4.44	Ryshich	3	Nik	Nice	17 Jul 99	4.30	Adams	1		Dessau	31 May 00
4.40	Szabó	4	WCh	Sevilla	21 Aug 99	4.30	Elisdóttir	1		Vellinge	3 Jun 00

Exhibition or 'town square' meetings under questionable conditions

4.55		Grigoryeva			1		Iglesias	4 Sep 99
4.40	Andrea	Müller	GER	29.6.74	1		Zweibrücken	8 Oct 95
4.35sq	Monique	de Wilt	NED	21.3.76	1		Jockgrimm	19 Jul 00
4.31	Janet	Zach	GER	19.6.75	1		Recklinghausen	30 May 97

LONG JUMP

Mark	Wind	Name		Nat	Born	Pos	Meet	Venue	Date
7.52 WR	1.4	Galina	Chistyakova	RUS	26.7.62	1	Znam	Leningrad	11 Jun 88
7.49	1.3	Jackie	Joyner-Kersee	USA	3.3.62	1	NYG	New York	22 May 94
7.49A	1.7		Joyner-Kersee			1		Sestriere	31 Jul 94
7.48	1.2	Heike	Drechsler	GER	16.12.64	1	v ITA	Neubrandenburg	9 Jul 88
7.48	0.4		Drechsler			1	Athl	Lausanne	8 Jul 92
7.45 WR	0.9		Drechsler'			1	v URS	Tallinn	21 Jun 86
7.45 WR	1.1		Drechsler			1	OD	Dresden	3 Jul 86
7.45 WR	0.6		Joyner-Kersee			1	PAm	Indianapolis	13 Aug 87
7.45	1.6		Chistyakova			1	BGP	Budapest	12 Aug 88
7.44 WR	2.0		Drechsler			1		Berlin	22 Sep 85
7.43 WR	1.4	Anisoara	Cusmir/Stanciu	ROM	28.6.62	1	RomIC	Bucuresti	4 Jun 83
7.40	1.8		Daute' (Drechsler)			1		Dresden	26 Jul 84
7.40	0.7		Drechsler			1	NC	Potsdam	21 Aug 87
7.40	0.9		Joyner-Kersee			1	OG	Seoul	29 Sep 88
7.39	0.3		Drechsler			1	WK	Zürich	21 Aug 85
7.39	0.5	Yelena	Byelevskaya'	BLR	11.10.63	1	NC	Bryansk	18 Jul 87
7.39			Joyner-Kersee			1		San Diego	25 Jun 88
7.37i	-		Drechsler			1	v2N	Wien	13 Feb 88

Mark	Wind	Name		Nat	Born	Pos	Meet	Venue	Date
7.37A	1.8		Drechsler			1		Sestriere	31 Jul 91
7.37		Inessa	Kravets	UKR	5.10.66	1		Kiyev	13 Jun 92
7.36	0.4		Joyner			1	WCh	Roma	4 Sep 87
7.36	1.8		Byelevskaya			2	Znam	Leningrad	11 Jun 88
7.36	1.8		Drechsler			1		Jena	28 May 92
7.35	1.9		Chistyakova			1	GPB	Bratislava	20 Jun 90
7.34	1.6		Daute'			1		Dresden	19 May 84
7.34	1.4		Chistyakova			2	v GDR	Tallinn	21 Jun 86
7.34			Byelevskaya			1		Sukhumi	17 May 87
7.34	0.7		Drechsler			1	v URS	Karl-Marx-Stadt	20 Jun 87
7.33	0.4		Drechsler			1	v URS	Erfurt	22 Jun 85
7.33	2.0		Drechsler			1		Dresden	2 Aug 85
7.33	-0.3		Drechsler			1	Herc	Monaco	11 Aug 92
		(31/6)							
7.31	1.5	Yelena	Kokonova'	UKR	4.8.63	1	NP	Alma-Ata	12 Sep 85
7.31	1.9	Marion	Jones	USA	12.10.75	1	Pre	Eugene	31 May 98
7.26A	1.8	Maurren	Maggi	BRA	25.6.76	1	SACh	Bogotá	26 Jun 99
7.24	1.0	Larisa	Berezhnaya	UKR	28.2.61	1	Blanc	Granada	25 May 91
		(10)							
7.21	1.6	Helga	Radtke	GDR	16.5.62	2		Dresden	26 Jul 84
7.20 WR	-0.5	Valy	Ionescu	ROM	31.8.60	1	NC	Bucuresti	1 Aug 82
7.20	2.0	Irena	Ozhenko'	LIT	13.11.62	1		Budapest	12 Sep 86
7.20	0.8	Yelena	Sinchukova'	RUS	23.1.61	1	BGP	Budapest	20 Jun 91
7.20	0.7	Irina	Mushayilova	RUS	6.1.67	1	NC	Sankt-Peterburg	14 Jul 94
7.17	1.8	Irina	Valyukevich	BLR	19.11.59	2	NC	Bryansk	18 Jul 87
7.16		Iolanda	Chen	RUS	26.7.61	1		Moskva	30 Jul 88
7.14	1.8	Niole	Medvedyeva ¶	LIT	20.10.60	1		Riga	4 Jun 88
7.14	1.2	Mirela	Dulgheru	ROM	5.10.66	1	Balk G	Sofiya	5 Jul 92
7.12	1.6	Sabine	Paetz/John'	GDR	16.10.57	2		Dresden	19 May 84
		(20)							
7.12	0.9	Chioma	Ajunwa ¶	NGR	25.12.70	1	OG	Atlanta	2 Aug 96
7.11	0.8	Fiona	May	ITA	12.12.69	2	EC	Budapest	22 Aug 98
7.09 WR	0.0	Vilma	Bardauskiene	LIT	15.6.53	Q	EC	Praha	29 Aug 78
7.09	1.5	Ljudmila	Ninova	AUT	25.6.60	1	GP II	Sevilla	5 Jun 94
7.08	0.5	Marieta	Ilcu	ROM	16.10.62	1	RumIC	Pitesti	25 Jun 89
7.07	0.0	Svetlana	Zorina	RUS	2.2.60	1		Krasnodar	15 Aug 87
7.06	0.4	Tatyana	Kolpakova	KGZ	18.10.59	1	OG	Moskva	31 Jul 80
7.06	-0.1	Niurka	Montalvo	CUB/ESP	4.6.68	1	WCh	Sevilla	23 Aug 99
7.05	0.6	Lyudmila	Galkina	RUS	20.1.72	1	WCh	Athína	9 Aug 97
7.04	0.5	Brigitte	Künzel/Wujak	GDR	6.3.55	2	OG	Moskva	31 Jul 80
		(30)							
7.04	0.9	Tatyana	Proskuryakova'	RUS	13.1.56	1		Kiyev	25 Aug 83
7.04	2.0	Yelena	Yatsuk	UKR	16.3.61	1	Znam	Moskva	8 Jun 85
7.04	0.3	Carol	Lewis	USA	8.8.63	5	WK	Zürich	21 Aug 85
7.04	0.3	Tatyana	Kotova	RUS	11.12.76	1	Gaz	Saint-Denis	23 Jun 00
7.03	0.6	Níki	Xánthou	GRE	11.10.73	1		Bellinzona	18 Aug 97
7.01	-0.4	Tatyana	Skachko	UKR	18.8.54	3	OG	Moskva	31 Jul 80
7.01	0.3	Eva	Murková	SVK	29.5.62	1	PTS	Bratislava	26 May 84
7.01	-1.0	Marina	Kibakina'	RUS	2.8.60	1		Krasnoyarsk	10 Aug 85
7.01	1.4		Yao Weili	CHN	6.5.68	1	NC	Jinan	5 Jun 93
7.01	1.1	Shana	Williams	USA	7.4.72	Q	NC	Atlanta	21 Jun 96
		(40)							
7.01	-0.4	Eunice	Barber	FRA	17.11.74	1	GP	Paris (C)	21 Jul 99
7.00	2.0	Jodi	Anderson	USA	10.11.57	1	OT	Eugene	28 Jun 80
7.00		Margarita	Butkiene	LIT	19.8.49	1		Vilnius	25 May 83
7.00	-0.2	Birgit	Grosshennig	GDR	21.2.65	2		Berlin	9 Jun 84
7.00	0.6	Silvia	Khristova'	BUL	22.8.65	1		Sofiya	3 Aug 86
7.00		Susen	Tiedtke ¶	GER	23.1.69	2		Seoul	18 Aug 91
6.99 WR	2.0	Sigrun	Thon/Siegl	GDR	29.10.54	1	OD	Dresden	19 May 76
6.99	0.4	Lissette	Cuza	CUB	26.2.75	1	OD	Jena	3 Jun 00
6.99	1.9	Erica	Johansson	SWE	5.2.74	*	Athl	Lausanne	5 Jul 00
6.98	1.1	Dawn	Burrell	USA	1.11.73	1	DNG	Stockholm	1 Aug 00
		(50)	100th woman 6.85, 100th woman 6.75						
Exhibition: 6.98 sq		Viktoriya	Vershinina	UKR	11.6.71	1		Iglesias	10 Sep 95
Drugs dq: 7.03	0.1		Xiong Qiying	CHN	14.10.67	Q	NG	Shanghai	21 Oct 97
Wind assisted									
7.63A	2.1	Heike	Drechsler	GER	16.12.64	1		Sestriere	21 Jul 92
7.45	2.6		Joyner-Kersee			1	OT	Indianapolis	23 Jul 88
7.39	2.6		Drechsler			1		Padova	15 Sep 91

Mark	Wind		Name	Nat	Born	Pos	Meet	Venue	Date
7.39	2.9		Drechsler			1	Expo	Sevilla	6 Jun 92
7.39A	3.3		Drechsler			2		Sestriere	31 Jul 94
7.36	2.2		Chistyakova			1	Znam	Volgograd	11 Jun 89
7.35	3.4		Drechsler			1	NC	Jena	29 Jun 86
7.23A	4.3	Fiona	May	ITA	12.12.69	1		Sestriere	29 Jul 95
7.19A	3.7	Susen	Tiedtke ¶	GER	23.1.69	1		Sestriere	28 Jul 93
7.17	3.6	Eva	Murková	SVK	29.5.62	1		Nitra	26 Aug 84
7.14A	4.5	Marieke	Veltman	USA	18.9.71	2		Sestriere	29 Jul 95
7.12A	5.8	Níki	Xánthou	GRE	11.10.73	3		Sestriere	29 Jul 95
7.12A	4.3	Nicole	Boegman	AUS	5.3.67	4		Sestriere	29 Jul 95
7.09	2.9	Renata	Nielsen	DEN	18.5.66	2		Sevilla	5 Jun 94
7.08	2.2	Lyudmila	Galkina	RUS	20.1.72	1		Thessaloniki	23 Jun 99
7.07A	5.6	Valentina	Uccheddu	ITA	26.10.66	5		Sestriere	29 Jul 95
7.07A	2.7	Sharon	Couch	USA	13.9.67	1		El Paso	12 Apr 97
7.07A	w	Erica	Johansson	SWE	5.2.74	1		Vygieskraal	15 Jan 00
7.06	3.4		Ma Miaolan	CHN	18.1.70	1	NG	Beijing	10 Sep 93
7.01	2.2	Olga	Rublyova	RUS	28.10.74	1	NC	Moskva	16 Jun 95
7.00	3.8	Ramona	Neubert'	GDR	26.7.58	1	v GBR	Dresden	14 Jun 81
7.00	4.2	Sue	Hearnshaw'	GBR	26.5.61	1	NC	Cwmbran	27 May 84

Best at low altitude

7.12w 3.4 May 1 NC Bologna 25 May 96 7.02Aw4.8 Tiedtke-Greene 2 Sestriere 21 Jul 92

TRIPLE JUMP

Mark	Wind		Name	Nat	Born	Pos	Meet	Venue	Date
15.50 WR	0.9	Inessa	Kravets	UKR	5.10.66	1	WCh	Göteborg	10 Aug 95
15.33	-0.1		Kravets			1	OG	Atlanta	31 Jul 96
15.32	0.5	Tatyana	Lebedeva	RUS	21.7.76	1	Super	Yokohama	9 Sep 00
15.20	0.0	Sarka	Kaspárková	CZE	20.5.71	1	WCh	Athína	4 Aug 9
15.20	-0.3	Tereza	Marinova	BUL	5.9.77	1	OG	Sydney	24 Sep 00
15.18	0.3	Iva	Prandzheva ¶	BUL	15.2.72	2	WCh	Göteborg	10 Aug 95
15.16	0.1	Rodica	Mateescu	ROM	13.3.71	2	WCh	Athína	4 Aug 97
15.16i	-	Ashia	Hansen	GBR	5.12.71	1	EI	Valencia	28 Feb 98
15.15	1.7		Hansen			1	GPF	Fukuoka	13 Sep 97
15.14	-0.1		Mateescu			1	RomIC	Bucuresti	14 Jun 97
15.12	2.0		Prandzheva			1	TOTO	Tokyo	19 Sep 98
15.09 WR	0.5	Anna	Biryukova	RUS	27.9.67	1	WCh	Stuttgart	21 Aug 93
15.09	-0.5	Inna	Lasovskaya	RUS	17.12.69	1	ECCp-A	Valencia	31 May 97
15.08	1.4		Biryukova			3	WCh	Göteborg	10 Aug 95
15.08	0.7		Lasovskaya			1		Madrid	12 Jun 96
15.07	-0.6	Paraskeví	Tsiamíta (10)	GRE	10.3.72	Q	WCh	Sevilla	22 Aug 99
15.04	0.9		Prandzheva			1	NC	Sofia	17 Jun 00
15.03i		Iolanda	Chen	RUS	26.7.61	1	WI	Barcelona	11 Mar 95
15.03	0.0		Biryukova			1	WK	Zürich	16 Aug 95
15.02i	-		Hansen			1	WI	Maebashi	7 Mar 99
15.01i	-		Lasovskaya			1	WI	Paris (B)	8 Mar 97
15.01	1.9		Mateescu			1		Villeneuve d'Ascq	11 Jul 98
15.01	1.1		Lebedeva			1	Veniz	Haniá	14 Jun 00
15.00	1.3		Lebedeva			2	OG	Sydney	24 Sep 00
14.99	-0.2		Biryukova			1	GPF	Monaco	9 Sep 95
14.98	1.8	Sofiya	Bozhanova ¶	BUL	4.10.67	1		Stara Zagora	16 Jul 94
14.98	1.1		Lasovskaya			2	OG	Atlanta	31 Jul 96
14.98	-0.6		Kaspárková			3	OG	Atlanta	31 Jul 96
14.98	0.5		Kaspárková			1		Rovereto	26 Aug 98
14.98	0.9		Lebedeva			1	ECp-S	Gateshead	16 Jul 00
		(30/12)							
14.96	0.7	Yelena	Govorova	UKR	18.9.73	4	OG	Sydney	24 Sep 00
14.94i	–	Cristina	Nicolau	ROM	9.8.77	1	NC	Bucuresti	5 Feb 00
14.79	1.7	Irina	Mushayilova	RUS	6.1.67	1	DNG	Stockholm	5 Jul 93
14.77	1.2	Yamilé	Aldama	CUB	14.8.72	1	PAm	Winnipeg	28 Jul 99
14.76	0.9	Galina	Chistyakova	RUS	26.7.62	1		Luzern	27 Jun 95
		now Cistjaková SVK							
14.76	1.1	Gundega	Sproge	LAT	12.12.72	3		Sheffield	29 Jun 97
14.74i	-	Yelena	Lebedenko	RUS	16.1.71	1		Moskva	15 Jan 99
14.71	0.5	Adelina	Gavrila	ROM	26.11.78	1		Bucuresti	12 Jun 99
		(20)							
14.70A	0.5	Françoise	Mbango	CMR	14.4.76	1	AfG	Johannesburg	18 Sep 99
14.69	1.2	Anja	Valant	SLO	8.9.77	3		Kalamáta	4 Jun 00
14.67	1.2	Ólga	Vasdéki	GRE	26.9.73	1		Haniá	28 Jul 99
14.66	1.9		Ren Ruiping	CHN	1.2.76	1	Oda	Hiroshima	29 Apr 97

Mark	Wind	Name		Nat	Born	Pos	Meet	Venue	Date
14.65	0.3	Fiona	May	ITA	12.12.69	1	ECp	Sankt-Peterburg	27 Jun 98
14.65	2.0	Natalya	Safronova	BLR	11.4.74	1	NCp	Stayki	3 Jun 00
14.64A	0.2	Baya	Rahouli	ALG	27.7.79	2	AfG	Johannesburg	18 Sep 99
14.60	0.7	Niurka	Montalvo	CUB/ESP	4.6.68	1	NC	La Habana	24 Jun 94
14.59	1.1	Oksana	Rogova	RUS	7.10.78	*	EU23	Göteborg	1 Aug 99
14.58	0.3	Yelena	Donkina	RUS	15.3.73	2	NC	Tula	10 Jul 97
		(30)							
14.57	0.2		Huang Qiuyan	CHN	25.1.80	1	NG	Shanghai	19 Oct 97
14.55	0.9		Li Huirong	CHN	14.4.65	1	Nambu	Sapporo	19 Jul 92
14.55	-0.3	Jelena	Blazevica	LAT	11.5.70	1	NC	Riga	8 Jun 96
14.54i	-	Mariya	Sokova	RUS	2.9.70	1	NC	Volgograd	24 Feb 95
14.52	0.6	Anastasiya	Ilyina	RUS	16.1.82	q	WJ	Santiago de Chile	20 Oct 00
14.51		Natalya	Kayukova	RUS	10.12.66	1		Vladivostok	29 May 99
14.50	-0.1	Betty	Lise	FRA	5.9.72	Q	WCh	Athína	2 Aug 97
14.47	1.8	Olga	Yershova	RUS	13.8.76	4	Veniz	Haniá	14 Jun 00
14.46	1.0	Helga	Radtke	GER	16.5.62	1	NC	Erfurt	3 Jul 94
14.46			Peng Fengmei	CHN	2.7.79	1		Chengdu	19 Apr 98
		(40)							
14.45		Yelena	Stakhova	BLR	4.1.69	1		Bialystok	17 Jun 96
14.45i	–	Olga	Rublyova	RUS	28.10.74	2		Moskva	27 Jan 00
14.43	1.1	Laiza	Carrillo	CUB	27.11.68	1		La Habana	23 Feb 95
14.43	0.7	Olga	Cepero	CUB	4.5.75	1		La Habana	6 Feb 98
14.41	1.1	Sheila	Hudson	USA	30.6.67	2	DNG	Stockholm	8 Jul 96
14.40	0.7	Magdelín	Martínez	CUB	10.2.76	1		La Habana	23 Jun 00
14.39	-0.5		Wu Lingmei	CHN	16.2.73	2		Beijing	6 Jun 98
14.38	0.1	Yelena	Khlusovich	UKR	2.11.66	Q	OG	Atlanta	29 Jul 96
14.36i	-	Petra	Lobinger	GER	24.1.67	5	WI	Paris (B)	8 Mar 97
14.35	0.5	Yelena	Semiraz	UKR	21.11.65	2	NC	Kiyev	13 Jul 91
14.35	0.3	Zhanna	Gureyeva	BLR	10.6.70	Q	WCh	Athína	2 Aug 97
		(51)	100th woman 14.05, 200th woman 13.74						
Wind assisted									
15.07w	2.5		Marinova			1		Réthimno	10 Jun 00
15.05	2.7		Lasovskaya			1		Sevilla	3 Jun 95
15.00w	2.5		Lebedeva			2		Réthimno	10 Jun 00
14.99	6.8	Yelena	Govorova	UKR	18.9.73	1	WUG	Palma de Mallorca	11 Jul 99
14.84	4.1	Galina	Chistyakova	RUS	26.7.62	1		Innsbruck	28 Jun 95
14.83A	8.3		Ren Ruiping	CHN	1.2.76	1	NC	Taiyuan	21 May 95
14.75	4.2	Jelena	Blazevica	LAT	11.5.70	1	v2N	Kaunas	23 Aug 97
14.66	3.2	Sheila	Hudson	USA	30.6.67	1	NC	Sacramento	17 Jun 95
14.65	2.6	Oksana	Rogova	RUS	7.10.78	2	EU23	Göteborg	1 Aug 99
14.55	5.5		Wu Lingmei	CHN	16.2.73	2	WUG	Palma de Mallorca	11 Jul 99
14.43	2.7	Yelena	Lysak ¶	RUS	15.3.75	1	EJ	Lisboa	21 Jul 94
14.41	2.5	Zhanna	Gureyeva	BLR	10.6.70	Q	WCh	Göteborg	8 Aug 95

Best outdoor mark for athlete with all-time best indoors

14.70 1.3 Nicolau 1 EU23 Göteborg 1 Aug 99 | 14.41 -0.2 Lebedenko 1 ECCp-A Vilamoura 30 May 98

14.50 Sokova 2 Znam Moskva 5 Jun 99

Best low altitude:

14.65 1.8 Mbango 1 La-Roche-sur-Yon 11 Jul 99 | 14.42w 2.6 Rahouli 1 Adelaide 8 Mar 00

SHOT

Mark	Name		Nat	Born	Pos	Meet	Venue	Date
22.63 WR	Natalya	Lisovskaya	RUS	16.7.62	1	Znam	Moskva	7 Jun 87
22.55		Lisovskaya			1	NC	Tallinn	5 Jul 88
22.53 WR		Lisovskaya			1		Sochi	27 May 84
22.53		Lisovskaya			1		Kiyev	14 Aug 88
22.50i	Helena	Fibingerová	CZE	13.7.49	1		Jablonec	19 Feb 77
22.45 WR	Ilona	Slupianek' ¶	GDR	24.9.56	1		Potsdam	11 May 80
22.41		Slupianek			1	OG	Moskva	24 Jul 80
22.40		Slupianek			1		Berlin	3 Jun 83
22.38		Slupianek			1		Karl-Marx-Stadt	25 May 80
22.36 WR		Slupianek			1		Celje	2 May 80
22.34		Slupianek			1		Berlin	7 May 80
22.34		Slupianek			1	NC	Cottbus	18 Jul 80
22.32 WR		Fibingerová			1		Nitra	20 Aug 77
22.24		Lisovskaya			1	OG	Seoul	1 Oct 88
22.22		Slupianek			1		Potsdam	13 Jul 80
22.19	Claudia	Losch	FRG	10.1.60	1		Hainfeld	23 Aug 87
22.14i		Lisovskaya			1	NC	Penza	7 Feb 87
22.13		Slupianek			1		Split	29 Apr 80
22.06		Slupianek			1		Berlin	15 Aug 78

WOMEN All-time

Mark	Wind	Name		Nat	Born	Pos	Meet	Venue	Date
22.06			Lisovskaya			1		Moskva	6 Aug 88
22.05			Slupianek			1	OD	Berlin	28 May 80
22.05			Slupianek			1		Potsdam	31 May 80
22.04			Slupianek			1		Potsdam	4 Jul 79
22.04			Slupianek			1		Potsdam	29 Jul 79
21.99	WR		Fibingerová			1		Opava	26 Sep 76
21.98			Slupianek			1		Berlin	17 Jul 79
21.96			Fibingerová			1	GS	Ostrava	8 Jun 77
21.96			Lisovskaya			1	Drz	Praha	16 Aug 84
21.96			Lisovskaya			1		Vilnius	28 Aug 88
21.95			Lisovskaya			1	IAC	Edinburgh	29 Jul 88
		(30/4)							
21.89	WR	Ivanka	Khristova	BUL	19.11.41	1		Belmeken	4 Jul 76
21.86		Marianne	Adam	GDR	19.9.51	1	v URS	Leipzig	23 Jun 79
21.76			Li Meisu	CHN	17.4.59	1		Shijiazhuang	23 Apr 88
21.73		Natalya	Akhrimenko	RUS	12.5.55	1		Leselidze	21 May 88
21.69		Viktoriya	Pavlysh ¶	UKR	15.1.69	1	EC	Budapest	20 Aug 98
21.66			Sui Xinmei ¶	CHN	29.1.65	1		Beijing	9 Jun 90
		(10)							
21.61		Verzhinia	Veselinova	BUL	18.11.57	1		Sofiya	21 Aug 82
21.60i		Valentina	Fedyushina	UKR	18.2.65	1		Simferopol	28 Dec 91
21.58		Margitta	Droese/Pufe	GDR	10.9.52	1		Erfurt	28 May 78
21.57 @		Ines	Müller'	GDR	2.1.59	1		Athína	16 May 88
		21.45				1		Schwerin	4 Jun 86
21.53		Nunu	Abashidze ¶	UKR	27.3.55	2	Izv	Kiyev	20 Jun 84
21.52			Huang Zhihong	CHN	7.5.65	1	NC	Beijing	27 Jun 90
21.46		Larisa	Peleshenko ¶	RUS	29.2.64	1	Kuts	Moskva	26 Aug 00
21.45	WR	Nadezhda	Chizhova	RUS	29.9.45	1		Varna	29 Sep 73
21.43		Eva	Wilms	FRG	28.7.52	2	HB	München	17 Jun 77
21.42		Svetlana	Krachevskaya'	RUS	23.11.44	2	OG	Moskva	24 Jul 80
		(20)	*@ competitive meeting, but unsanctioned by GDR federation*						
21.31 @		Heike	Hartwig'	GDR	30.12.62	2		Athína	16 May 88
		21.27				1		Haniá	22 May 88
21.27		Liane	Schmuhl	GDR	29.6.61	1		Cottbus	26 Jun 82
21.22		Astrid	Kumbernuss	GER	5.2.70	1	WCh	Göteborg	5 Aug 95
21.21		Kathrin	Neimke	GDR	18.7.66	2	WCh	Roma	5 Sep 87
21.19		Helma	Knorscheidt	GDR	31.12.56	1		Berlin	24 May 84
21.15i		Irina	Korzhanenko ¶	RUS	16.5.74	1	NC	Moskva	18 Feb 99
21.10		Heidi	Krieger	GDR	20.7.65	1	EC	Stuttgart	26 Aug 86
21.06		Svetlana	Krivelyova	RUS	13.6.69	1	OG	Barcelona	7 Aug 92
21.05		Zdenka	Silhavá' ¶	CZE	15.6.54	2	NC	Praha	23 Jul 83
21.01		Ivanka	Petrova-Stoycheva	BUL	3.2.51	1	NC	Sofiya	28 Jul 79
		(30)							
21.00		Mihaela	Loghin	ROM	1.6.52	1		Formia	30 Jun 84
21.00		Cordula	Schulze	GDR	11.9.59	4	OD	Potsdam	21 Jul 84
20.96		Belsy	Laza	CUB	5.6.67	1		Ciudad de México	2 May 92
20.95		Elena	Stoyanova ¶	BUL	23.1.52	2	Balk	Sofiya	14 Jun 80
20.91		Svetla	Mitkova	BUL	17.6.64	1		Sofiya	24 May 87
20.80		Sona	Vasícková	CZE	14.3.62	1		Praha	2 Jun 88
20.72		Grit	Haupt/Hammer	GDR	4.6.66	3		Neubrandenburg	11 Jun 87
20.61		María Elena	Sarría	CUB	14.9.54	1		Habana	22 Jul 82
20.60		Marina	Antonyuk	RUS	12.5.62	1		Chelyabinsk	10 Aug 86
20.56		Yanina	Korolchik	BLR	26.12.76	1	OG	Sydney	28 Sep 00
		(40)							
20.54			Zhang Liuhong	CHN	16.1.69	1	NC	Beijing	5 Jun 94
20.53		Iris	Plotzitzka	FRG	7.1.66	1	ASV	Köln	21 Aug 88
20.50i		Christa	Wiese	GDR	25.12.67	2	NC	Senftenberg	12 Feb 89
20.47		Nina	Isayeva	RUS	6.7.50	1		Bryansk	28 Aug 82
20.47			Cong Yuzhen	CHN	22.1.63	2	IntC	Tianjin	3 Sep 88
20.44		Tatyana	Orlova	BLR	19.7.55	1		Staiki	28 May 83
20.40			Zhou Tianhua ¶	CHN	10.4.66	1		Beijing	5 Sep 91
20.34		Stephanie	Storp	FRG	28.11.68	1		Wolfsburg	1 Jul 90
20.32		Irina	Khudorozhkina	RUS	13.10.68	1		Sochi	25 May 96
20.27		Danguole	Bimbaite'	LIT	10.12.62	2		Leselidze	13 May 87
20.27		Lyudmila	Voyevudskaya	UKR	22.6.59	1		Nikolayev	7 Aug 87
		(51)	100th woman 19.42, 200th woman c.18.44						

Best outdoor marks

21.08	Fedyushina	1	Leselidze	15 May 88
20.82	Korzhanenko ¶	1	Rostov na Donu	30 May 98

DISCUS

Mark	Wind		Name	Nat	Born	Pos	Meet	Venue	Date
76.80	WR	Gabriele	Reinsch	GDR	23.9.63	1	v Ita	Neubrandenburg	9 Jul 88
74.56	WR	Zdenka	Silhavá' ¶	CZE	15.6.54	1		Nitra	26 Aug 84
74.56		Ilke	Wyludda	GDR	28.3.69	1	NC	Neubrandenburg	23 Jul 89
74.44			Reinsch			1		Berlin	13 Sep 88
74.40			Wyludda			2		Berlin	13 Sep 88
74.08		Diana	Gansky'	GDR	14.12.63	1	v URS	Karl-Marx-Stadt	20 Jun 87
73.90			Gansky			1	ECp	Praha	27 Jun 87
73.84		Daniela	Costian ¶	ROM	30.4.65	1		Bucuresti	30 Apr 88
73.78			Costian			1		Bucuresti	24 Apr 88
73.42			Reinsch			1		Karl-Marx-Stadt	12 Jun 88
73.36	WR	Irina	Meszynski	GDR	24.3.62	1	Drz	Praha	17 Aug 84
73.32			Gansky			1		Neubrandenburg	11 Jun 87
73.28		Galina	Savinkova'	RUS	15.7.53	1	NC	Donetsk	8 Sep 84
73.26	WR		Savinkova			1		Leselidze	21 May 83
73.26			Sachse/Gansky			1		Neubrandenburg	6 Jun 86
73.24			Gansky			1		Leipzig	29 May 87
73.22		Tsvetanka	Khristova ¶	BUL	14.3.62	1		Kazanlak	19 Apr 87
73.10		Gisela	Beyer	GDR	16.7.60	1	OD	Berlin	20 Jul 84
73.04			Gansky			1		Potsdam	6 Jun 87
73.04			Wyludda			1	ECp	Gateshead	5 Aug 89
72.96			Savinkova			1	v GDR	Erfurt	23 Jun 85
72.94			Gansky			2	v Ita	Neubrandenburg	9 Jul 88
72.92		Martina	Opitz/Hellmann	GDR	12.12.60	1	NC	Potsdam	20 Aug 87
72.90			Costian			1		Bucuresti	14 May 88
72.78			Hellmann			2		Neubrandenburg	11 Jun 87
72.78			Reinsch			1	OD	Berlin	29 Jun 88
72.72			Wyludda			1		Neubrandenburg	23 Jun 89
72.70			Wyludda			1	NC-j	Karl-Marx-Stadt	15 Jul 88
72.54			Gansky			1	NC	Rostock	25 Jun 88
72.52			Hellmann			1		Frohburg	15 Jun 86
72.52			Khristova			1	BGP	Budapest	11 Aug 86
		(31/10)							
72.14		Galina	Murashova	LIT	22.12.55	2	Drz	Praha	17 Aug 84
71.80	WR	Maria	Vergova/Petkova	BUL	3.11.50	1	NC	Sofiya	13 Jul 80
71.68			Xiao Yanling ¶	CHN	27.3.68	1		Beijing	14 Mar 92
71.58		Ellina	Zvereva' ¶	BLR	16.11.60	1	Znam	Leningrad	12 Jun 88
71.50	WR	Evelin	Schlaak/Jahl	GDR	28.3.56	1		Potsdam	10 May 80
71.30		Larisa	Korotkevich	RUS	3.1.67	1	RusCp	Sochi	29 May 92
71.22		Ria	Stalman	NED	11.12.51	1		Walnut	15 Jul 84
70.88		Hilda	Ramos	CUB	1.9.64	1		Habana	8 May 92
70.80		Larisa	Mikhalchenko	UKR	16.5.63	1		Kharkov	18 Jun 88
70.68		Maritza	Martén	CUB	16.8.63	1	Ib Am	Sevilla	18 Jul 92
		(20)							
70.50	WR	Faina	Melnik	RUS	9.6.45	1	Znam	Sochi	24 Apr 76
70.34	@	Silvia	Madetzky	GDR	24.6.62	3		Athína	16 May 88
		69.34				1		Halle	26 Jun 87
70.02		Natalya	Sadova	RUS	15.6.72	1		Thessaloniki	23 Jun 99
69.86		Valentina	Kharchenko	RUS	.49	1		Feodosiya	16 May 81
69.72		Svetla	Mitkova	BUL	17.6.64	2	NC	Sofiya	15 Aug 87
69.68		Mette	Bergmann	NOR	9.11.62	1		Florø	27 May 95
69.51		Franka	Dietzsch	GER	22.1.68	1		Wiesbaden	8 May 99
69.50		Florenta	Craciunescu'	ROM	7.5.55	1	Balk	Stara Zagora	2 Aug 85
69.08		Carmen	Romero	CUB	6.10.50	1	NC	Habana	17 Apr 76
69.08		Mariana	Ionescu/Lengyel	ROM	14.4.53	1		Constanta	19 Apr 86
		(30)							
68.94		Irina	Yatchenko	BLR	31.10.65	1	Nik	Nice	15 Jul 92
68.92		Sabine	Engel	GDR	21.4.54	1	v URS,POL	Karl-Marx-Stadt	25 Jun 77
68.80		Nicoleta	Grasu	ROM	11.9.71	1		Poiana Brasov	7 Aug 99
68.64		Margitta	Pufe'	GDR	10.9.52	1	ISTAF	Berlin	17 Aug 79
68.62			Yu Hourun	CHN	9.7.64	1		Beijing	6 May 88
68.62			Hou Xuemei	CHN	27.2.62	1	IntC	Tianjin	4 Sep 88
68.60		Nadezhda	Kugayevskikh	RUS	19.4.60	1		Oryol	30 Aug 83
68.58		Lyubov	Zverkova	RUS	14.6.55	1	Izv	Kiyev	22 Jun 84
68.52		Beatrice	Faumuiná	NZL	23.10.74	1	Bisl	Oslo	4 Jul 97
68.38		Olga	Burova'	RUS	17.9.63	2	RusCp	Sochi	29 May 92
		(40)							

Mark	Wind	Name		Nat	Born	Pos	Meet	Venue	Date
68.18		Tatyana	Lesovaya	KZK	24.4.56	1		Alma-Ata	23 Sep 82
68.18		Irina	Khval	RUS	17.5.62	1		Moskva	8 Jul 88
68.18		Barbara	Hechevarría	CUB	6.8.66	2		Habana	17 Feb 89
67.96		Argentina	Menis	ROM	19.7.48	1	RomIC	Bucuresti	15 May 76
67.90		Petra	Sziegaud	GDR	17.10.58	1		Berlin	19 May 82
67.82		Tatyana	Belova	RUS	12.2.62	1		Irkutsk	10 Aug 87
67.80		Stefenia	Simova ¶	BUL	5.6.63	1		Stara Zagora	27 Jun 92
67.70		Anastasía	Kelesídou	GRE	28.11.72	2		Réthimno	29 May 99
67.54		Svetlana	Petrova	BLR	19.12.51	1		Brest-Litovsk	20 Sep 78
67.50			Li Qiumei	CHN	20.4.74	1		Beijing	10 May 94
		(50)	100th woman 65.20, 200th woman c.62.80						
Unofficial meeting									
78.14		Martina	Hellmann	GDR	12.12.60	1		Berlin	6 Sep 88
75.36		Ilke	Wyludda	GDR	28.3.69	2		Berlin	6 Sep 88

HAMMER

Mark	Wind	Name		Nat	Born	Pos	Meet	Venue	Date
76.07 WR		Mihaela	Melinte ¶	ROM	27.3.75	1		Rüdlingen	29 Aug 99
75.97 WR			Melinte			1		Clermont-Ferrand	13 May 99
75.68		Olga	Kuzenkova	RUS	4.10.70	1	NCp	Tula	4 Jun 00
75.21			Melinte			1c1		Rüdlingen	28 Aug 99
75.20			Melinte			1	WCh	Sevilla	24 Aug 99
74.90			Melinte			1		Bucuresti	4 Jul 99
74.77			Melinte			1		Nürnberg	13 Jun 99
74.48			Melinte			1	ECp	Paris (C)	20 Jun 99
74.30			Kuzenkova			1	Znam	Moskva	4 Jun 99
74.24			Melinte			1	WUG	Palma de Mallorca	9 Jul 99
74.22			Melinte			1		Bucuresti	29 May 99
74.20			Melinte			1		Poiana Brasov	7 Aug 99
74.00			Kuzenkova			1	Kuts	Moskva	26 Aug 00
73.85			Kuzenkova			1		Togliatti	14 May 00
73.80 uWR			Kuzenkova			1		Tolyatti	15 May 98
73.60			Melinte			1		Bugeat	28 Jun 99
73.14 WR			Melinte			1		Poiana Brasov	16 Jul 98
73.10 WR			Kuzenkova			1	ECp	München	22 Jun 97
72.81			Kuzenkova			1	Live	Nürnberg	25 Jun 00
72.74			Kuzenkova			1		Clermont-Ferrand	30 Jun 00
72.64			Melinte			1	GWG	Uniondale, NY	21 Jul 98
72.56			Kuzenkova			2	WCh	Sevilla	24 Aug 99
72.19			Melinte			1		Mersin	29 Mar 00
72.17			Kuzenkova			2c1		Rüdlingen	28 Aug 99
72.12			Melinte			1		Halle	15 May 99
72.10			Melinte			1		Onesti	20 May 00
72.09		Tatyana	Konstantinova	RUS	18.11.70	2	Znam	Moskva	4 Jun 99
71.92			Kuzenkova			1	NC	Tula	1 Aug 99
71.85			Melinte			1	ECCp	Vilamoura	30 May 98
71.81			Kuzenkova			1	Znam	Sankt-Peterburg	18 Jun 00
		(30/3)							
71.18		Manuela	Montebrun	FRA	13.11.79	1		Vittel	2 Sep 00
71.16		Kamila	Skolimowska	POL	4.11.82	1	OG	Sydney	29 Sep 00
70.46		Dawn	Ellerbe	USA	3.4.74	1	PennR	Philadelphia	29 Apr 00
69.92		Lyudmila	Gubkina	BLR	28.5.73	1		Staiki	19 Aug 00
69.81		Olga	Tsander	BLR	18.5.76	1		Sochi	26 Feb 00
69.53		Irina	Sekacheva	UKR	21.7.76	1		Kiev	16 Jun 00
69.36		Yipsi	Moreno	CUB	19.11.80	1		Rhede	23 Jun 00
		(10)							
69.28		Kirsten	Münchow	GER	21.1.77	3	OG	Sydney	29 Sep 00
68.98		Katalin	Divós	HUN	11.5.74	1		Szombathely	24 Jun 00
68.47		Alla	Davydova	RUS	21.5.66	1	Mos Ch	Moskva	11 Jul 00
68.40		Bianca	Achilles	GER	17.4.81	1		Dortmund	25 Sep 99
68.28		Amy	Palmer	USA	20.4.75	2	PennR	Philadelphia	29 Apr 00
68.21		Svetlana	Sudak	BLR	20.3.71	1		Minsk	17 Jul 99
68.18		Ivana	Brkljacic	CRO	25.1.83	1		Pula	28 Apr 00
67.95		Debbie	Sosimenko	AUS	5.4.74	5	OG	Sydney	29 Sep 00
67.55		Lisa	Misipeka	ASA	3.1.75	4		Rüdlingen	12 Aug 00
67.44		Lorraine	Shaw	GBR	2.4.68	5	ECp-S	Gateshead	15 Jul 00
		(20)							
67.13		Simone	Mathes	GER	13.5.75	3		Halle	15 May 99
66.55		Bronwyn	Eagles	AUS	23.8.80	1		Sydney (B)	3 Dec 00

Mark	Wind	Name		Nat	Born	Pos	Meet	Venue	Date
66.52		Jesseca	Cross	USA	10.5.75	3		Logan	1 Jul 00
66.37		Mia	Strömmer	FIN	26.2.74	2		Lapinlahti	16 Jul 00
66.30		Manuela	Priemer	GER	29.11.78	1		Mannheim	18 Jun 99
66.17		Ester	Balassini	ITA	20.10.77	1		Pescara	22 Jul 00
66.13		Florence	Ezeh	FRA	29.12.77	1		Denton, TX.	7 May 99
65.88		Yunaika	Crawford	CUB	2.11.82	1		Las Tunas	3 Mar 00
65.88		Anna	Norgren	USA	19.12.74	1		West Point	13 May 00
65.70			Zhao Wei	CHN	27.1.79	1		Deyang	14 May 00
		(30)							
65.50		Sini	Pöyry	FIN	3.2.80	3		Lapinlahti	16 Jul 00
65.39		Cécile	Lignot	FRA	19.11.71	2		Castres	8 Aug 99
65.38		Karyne	Perkins-Dimarco	AUS	14.3.78	2		Brisbane (N)	6 Sep 00
65.35		Anelia	Yordanova	BUL	27.4.72	1		Sofia	10 Jun 00
65.26		Agnieszka	Pogroszewska	POL	20.2.77	3		Nitra	26 Aug 00
65.20		Norbi	Balantén	CUB	24.6.72	3		La Habana	24 Feb 00
65.11		Marina	Grin	BLR	23.1.76	3		Minsk	27 Jun 00
65.06			Liu Yinghui	CHN	29.6.79	1	NC	Luohe	20 Oct 00
64.94		Melissa	Price	USA	5.9.79	1		Seward, NE	12 May 99
64.86		Natalya	Kunitskaya	UKR	17.8.72	1		Kiev	15 Jul 00
		(40)							
64.80		Tina	Schäfer	GER	27.12.77	1		Rastatt	12 Jun 00
64.72			Gu Yuan	CHN	9.5.82	2	NGP	Deyang	14 May 00
64.60		Tasha	Williams	NZL	31.7.73	1		Flagstaff	6 Jul 00
64.50		Susanne	Keil	GER	18.5.78	4		Rüdlingen	23 Aug 98
64.50			Li Xiaoxue	CHN	1.11.80	3	NGP	Deyang	14 May 00
64.46		Michelle	Fournier	CAN	9.5.77	1		Flagstaff	4 Jul 00
64.44		Robin	Lyons ¶	CAN	15.4.77	1		Albuquerque	6 May 00
64.29		Windy	Dean	USA	7.9.76	2	MSR	Walnut	18 Apr 99
64.26		Tamika	Powell	USA	25.9.75	2	NC	Eugene	24 Jun 99
64.24		Natalya	Samusenkova	RUS	12.2.79	1	NC-23	Cheboksary	1 Jul 00
		(50)	100th woman 61.40						

WOMEN All-time

JAVELIN

Mark	Wind	Name		Nat	Born	Pos	Meet	Venue	Date
69.48 WR		Trine	Hattestad	NOR	18.4.66	1	Bisl	Oslo	28 Jul 00
68.91			Hattestad			1	OG	Sydney	30 Sep 00
68.32			Hattestad			1	ISTAF	Berlin	1 Sep 00
68.22 WR			Hattestad			1	GGala	Roma	30 Jun 00
68.19 WRu			Hattestad			1		Fana	28 Jul 99
67.92			Hattestad			1	DNG	Stockholm	1 Aug 00
67.83		Osleidys	Menéndez	CUB	14.11.79	2	ISTAF	Berlin	1 Sep 00
67.76			Hattestad			1	VD	Bruxelles	25 Aug 00
67.51 WR		Miréla	Tzelíli	GRE	21.12.76	2	OG	Sydney	30 Sep 00
67.34			Menéndez			Q	OG	Sydney	29 Sep 00
67.20		Tatyana	Shikolenko	RUS	10.5.68	1	Herc	Monaco	18 Aug 00
67.09			Tzelíli			1	WCh	Sevilla	28 Aug 99
66.96			Hattestad			1	ECp1A	Nadderud	8 Jul 00
66.91		Tanja	Damaske	GER	16.11.71	1	NC	Erfurt	4 Jul 99
66.80		Louise	Currey	AUS	24.1.69	1		Gold Coast (RB)	5 Aug 00
66.73			Damaske			1	NC	Braunschweig	29 Jul 00
66.73			Hattestad			2	Herc	Monaco	18 Aug 00
66.55			Tzelíli			1	NC	Athína	7 Aug 99
66.54			Hattestad			1		Fana	27 Jun 00
66.50			Hattestad			1	WK	Zürich	11 Aug 00
66.49			Menéndez			1		Leverkusen	5 Sep 99
66.45			Menéndez			1	Athl	Lausanne	2 Jul 99
66.44			Hattestad			1		Lapinlahti	16 Jul 00
66.37			T Shikolenko			2	WCh	Sevilla	28 Aug 99
66.38			Menéndez			2	VD	Bruxelles	25 Aug 00
66.35			Menéndez			1	GP	Athína	28 Jun 00
66.18			Menéndez			3	OG	Sydney	30 Sep 00
66.06			Hattestad			3	WCh	Sevilla	28 Aug 99
66.03			Currey			1	GP II	Linz	26 Jul 99
65.87		Sonia	Bisset	CUB	1.4.71	1	GPF	Doha	5 Oct 00
		(30/7)							
65.76		Steffi	Nerius	GER	1.7.72	Q	OG	Sydney	29 Sep 00
65.30		Claudia	Coslovich	ITA	26.4.72	1		Ljubljana	10 Jun 00
65.17		Karen	Forkel	GER	24.3.70	2	NC	Erfurt	4 Jul 99
		(10)							

Mark Wind	Name		Nat	Born	Pos	Meet	Venue	Date
64.89	Yekaterina	Ivakina	RUS	4.12.64	4	Bisl	Oslo	28 Jul 00
64.62	Joanna	Stone	AUS	4.10.72	2		Gold Coast (RB)	5 Aug 00
64.61	Oksana	Makarova	RUS	21.7.71	2	ECp	Paris (C)	19 Jun 99
64.19	Nikola	Tomecková	CZE	25.6.74	3	WK	Zürich	11 Aug 00
64.06	Taina	Uppa	FIN	24.10.76	1		Pihtipudas	23 Jul 00
64.03	Mihaela	Ingberg	FIN	29.7.74	6	ISTAF	Berlin	1 Sep 00
63.92		Wei Jianhua	CHN	23.3.79	1		Beijing	18 Aug 00
63.73	Laverne	Eve	BAH	16.6.65	1		Nashville	22 Apr 00
63.69		Li Lei	CHN	4.5.74	1	OT	Jinzhou	8 Jun 00
63.32	Khristina (20)	Georgieva	BUL	3.1.72	3	GP	Athína	28 Jun 00

Specification changed from 1 May 1999. See ATHLETICS 2000 for Old specification all-time list - Top 10:

Mark Wind	Name		Nat	Born	Pos	Meet	Venue	Date
80.00 WR	Petra	Felke	GDR	30.7.59	1		Potsdam	9 Sep 88
77.44 WR	Fatima	Whitbread	GBR	3.3.61	Q	EC	Stuttgart	28 Aug 86
74.76 WR	Tiina	Lillak	FIN	15.4.61	1		Tampere	13 Jun 83
74.20 WR	Sofía	Sakorafa	GRE	29.4.57	1	NC	Haniá	26 Sep 82
73.58	Tessa	Sanderson	GBR	14.3.56	1		Edinburgh	26 Jun 83
72.70	Anna	Veroúli ¶	GRE	13.11.56	1		Haniá	20 May 84
72.16	Antje	Kempe-Zöllkau	GDR	23.6.63	2		Celje	5 May 84
72.12	Trine	Hattestad'	NOR	18.4.66	1	Bisl	Oslo	10 Jul 93
71.88 WR	Antoaneta	Todorova'	BUL	8.6.63	1	ECp	Zagreb	15 Aug 81
71.82	Ivonne	Leal	CUB	27.2.66	1	WUG	Kobe	30 Aug 85

HEPTATHLON

Mark	Name			Nat	Born	Pos	Meet	Venue		Date
7291 WR	Jackie	Joyner-Kersee		USA	3.3.62	1	OG	Seoul		24 Sep 88
	12.69/0.5	1.86	15.80		22.56/1.6	7.27/0.7		45.66	2:08.51	
7215 WR		Joyner-Kersee				1	OT	Indianapolis		16 Jul 88
	12.71/-0.9	1.93	15.65		22.30/ 0.0	7.00/-1.3		50.08	2:20.70	
7158 WR		Joyner-Kersee				1	USOF	Houston		2 Aug 86
	13.18/-0.5	1.88	15.20		22.85/1.2	7.03/2.9		50.12	2:09.69	
7148 WR		Joyner-Kersee				1	GWG	Moskva		7 Jul 86
	12.85/0.2	1.88	14.76		23.00/0.3	7.01/-0.5		49.86	2:10.02	
7128		Joyner-Kersee				1	WCh	Roma		1 Sep 87
	12.91/0.2	1.90	16.00		22.95/1.2	7.14/0.9		45.68	2:16.29	
7044		Joyner-Kersee				1	OG	Barcelona		2 Aug 92
	12.85/-0.9	1.91	14.13		23.12/0.7	7.10/1.3		44.98	2:11.78	
7007	Larisa	Nikitina ¶		RUS	29.4.65	1	NC	Bryansk		11 Jun 89
	13.40/1.4	1.89	16.45		23.97/1.1	6.73/4.0		53.94	2:15.31	
6985	Sabine	Braun		GER	19.6.65	1		Götzis		31 May 92
	13.11/-0.4	1.93	14.84		23.65/2.0	6.63/2.9		51.62	2:12.67	
6979		Joyner-Kersee				1	TAC	San José		24 Jun 87
	12.90/2.0	1.85	15.17		23.02/0.4	7.25/2.3		40.24	2:13.07	
6946 WR	Sabine	Paetz'		GDR	16.10.57	1	NC	Potsdam		6 May 84
	12.64/0.3	1.80	15.37		23.37/0.7	6.86/-0.2		44.62	2:08.93	
6942	Ghada	Shouaa		SYR	10.9.72	1		Götzis		26 May 96
	13.78/0.3	1.87	15.64		23.78/0.6	6.77/0.6		54.74	2:13.61	
6935 WR	Ramona	Neubert		GDR	26.7.58	1	v URS	Moskva		19 Jun 83
	13.42/1.7	1.82	15.25		23.49/0.5	6.79/0.7		49.94	2:07.51	
6910		Joyner				1	MSR	Walnut		25 Apr 86
	12.9/0.0	1.86	14.75		23.24/2.8	6.85/2.1		48.30	2:14.11	
6897		John'				2	OG	Seoul		24 Sep 88
	12.85/0.5	1.80	16.23		23.65/1.6	6.71/ 0.0		42.56	2:06.14	
6878		Joyner-Kersee				1	TAC	New York		13 Jun 91
	12.77	1.89	15.62		23.42	6.97/0.4		43.28	2:22.12	
6875		Nikitina				1	ECp-A	Helmond		16 Jul 89
	13.55/-2.1	1.84	15.99		24.29/-2.1	6.75/-2.5		56.78	2:18.67	
6861	Eunice	Barber		FRA	17.11.74	1	WCh	Sevilla		22 Aug 99
	12.89/-0.5	1.93	12.37		23.57/0.5	6.86/-0.3		49.88	2:15.65	
6859	Natalya	Shubenkova		RUS	25.9.57	1	NC	Kiyev		21 Jun 84
	12.93/1.0	1.83	13.00		23.57/0.0	6.70/0.4		40.00	2:01.60	
6858	Anke	Vater/Behmer		GDR	5.6.61	3	OG	Seoul		24 Sep 88
	13.20/0.5	1.83	14.20		23.10/1.6	6.68/0.1		44.54	2:04.20	
6847		Nikitina				1	WUG	Duisburg		29 Aug 89
	13.47	1.81	16.12		24.12	6.66		59.28	2:22.07	
6845 WR		Neubert				1	v URS	Halle		20 Jun 82
	13.58/1.8	1.83	15.10		23.14/1.4	6.84w/2.3		42.54	2:06.16	
6845	Irina	Belova ¶ (10)		RUS	27.3.68	2	OG	Barcelona		2 Aug 92
	13.25/-0.1	1.88	13.77		23.34/0.2	6.82/0.0		41.90	2:05.08	

Mark	Wind	Name	Nat	Born	Pos	Meet	Venue	Date
6842		Barber			1		Götzis	4 Jun 00
	12.97/0.2	1.88	12.23	23.84/0.5	6.85/-0.1	51.91	2:11.55	
6841		Joyner			1	Int	Götzis	25 May 86
	13.09/-1.3	1.87	14.34	23.63/-0.8	6.76/-0.3	48.88	2:14.58	
6837		Joyner-Kersee			1	WCh	Stuttgart	17 Aug 93
	12.89/0.1	1.81	14.38	23.19/0.0	7.04/1.4	43.76	2:14.49	
6831		Denise Lewis	GBR	27.8.72	1	Deca	Talence	30 Jul 00
	13.13/1.0	1.84	15.07	24.01w/3.6	6.69/-0.4	49.42	2:12.20	
6813		Paetz			1	OD	Potsdam	21 Jul 84
	12.71/0.4	1.74	16.16	23.23w	6.58	41.94	2:07.03	
6805		Behmer			1	Int	Götzis	19 Jun 88
	13.28/1.6	1.84	14.38	22.73/4.0	6.62/1.1	40.48	2:04.64	
6803		Jane Frederick	USA	7.4.52	1	Int	Talence	16 Sep 84
	13.27/1.2	1.87	15.49	24.15/1.6	6.43/0.2	51.74	2:13.55	
6797		Braun			2	WCh	Stuttgart	17 Aug 93
	13.25/0.1	1.90	14.62	24.12/0.0	6.54/1.0	53.44	2:17.82	
	(30/12)							
6765		Yelena Prokhorova	RUS	16.4.78	1	NC	Tula	23 Jul 00
	13.54/-2.8	1.82	14.30	23.37/-0.2	6.72/1.0	43.40	2:04.27	
6750		Ma Miaolan	CHN	18.1.70	1	NG	Beijing	12 Sep 93
	13.28/1.5	1.89	14.98	23.86/	6.64/	45.82	2:15.33	
6741		Heike Drechsler	GER	16.12.64	1		Talence	11 Sep 94
	13.34/-0.3	1.84	13.58	22.84/-1.1	6.95/1.0	40.64	2:11.53	
6703		Tatyana Blokhina	RUS	12.3.70	1	Decast	Talence	11 Sep 93
	13.69/-0.6	1.91	14.94	23.95/-0.4	5.99/-0.3	52.16	2:09.65	
6702		Chantal Beaugeant ¶	FRA	16.2.61	2	Int	Götzis	19 Jun 88
	13.10/1.6	1.78	13.74	23.96/3.5	6.45/0.2	50.96	2:07.09	
6695		Jane Flemming	AUS	14.4.65	1	CG	Auckland	28 Jan 90
	13.21/1.4	1.82	13.76	23.62/2.4	6.57/1.6	49.28	2:12.53	
6660		Ines Schulz	GDR	10.7.65	3	Int	Götzis	19 Jun 88
	13.56/0.4	1.84	13.95	23.93/2.8	6.70/0.7	42.82	2:06.31	
6658		Svetla Dimitrova ¶	BUL	27.1.70	2		Götzis	31 May 92
	13.41/-0.7	1.75	14.72	23.06/2.4	6.64/1.9	43.84	2:09.60	
	(20)							
6646		Natalya Grachova	UKR	21.2.52	1	NC	Moskva	2 Aug 82
	13.80	1.80	16.18	23.86	6.65/3.5	39.42	2:06.59	
6635		Sibylle Thiele	GDR	6.3.65	2	GWG	Moskva	7 Jul 86
	13.14/0.6	1.76	16.00	24.18	6.62/1.0	45.74	2:15.30	
6635		Svetlana Buraga	BLR	4.9.65	3	WCh	Stuttgart	17 Aug 93
	12.95/0.1	1.84	14.55	23.69/	6.58/-0.2	41.04	2:13.65	
6633		Natalya Roshchupkina	RUS	13.1.78	2	NC	Tula	23 Jul 00
	14.05/-2.8	1.88	14.28	23.47/-0.2	6.45/0.4	44.34	2:07.93	
6623		Judy Simpson'	GBR	14.11.60	3	EC	Stuttgart	30 Aug 86
	13.05/0.8	1.92	14.73	25.09/0.0	6.56/2.5	40.92	2:11.70	
6619		Liliana Nastase	ROM	1.8.62	4	OG	Barcelona	2 Aug 92
	12.86/-0.9	1.82	14.34	23.70/0.2	6.49/-0.3	41.30	2:11.22	
6616		Malgorzata Nowak'	POL	9.2.59	1	WUG	Kobe	31 Aug 85
	13.27/4.0	1.95	15.35	24.20/0.0	6.37/3.9	43.36	2:20.39	
6604		Remigia Nazaroviene'	LIT	2.6.67	2	URSCh	Bryansk	11 Jun 89
	13.26/1.4	1.86	14.27	24.12/0.7	6.58/0.9	40.94	2:09.98	
6604		Irina Tyukhay	RUS	14.1.67	3		Götzis	28 May 95
	13.20/-0.7	1.84	14.97	24.33/1.7	6.71/0.5	43.84	2:17.64	
6598		Svetlana Moskalets	RUS	1.11.69	1	NC	Vladimir	17 Jun 94
	13.20/0.8	1.82	13.78	23.56/0.1	6.74/0.8	42.48	2:14.54	
	(30)							
6577		DeDee Nathan	USA	20.4.68	1		Götzis	30 May 99
	13.28/-0.1	1.76	14.74	24.23/0.2	6.59/1.6	50.08	2:16.92	
6573		Rita Ináncsi	HUN	6.1.71	3		Götzis	29 May 94
	13.66/2.0	1.84	13.94	24.20/2.5	6.78/1.4	46.28	2:16.02	
6572		Heike Tischler	GDR	4.2.64	2	EC	Split	31 Aug 90
	14.08/-0.9	1.82	13.73	24.29/0.9	6.22/-0.7	53.24	2:05.50	
6563		Natalya Sazanovich	BLR	15.8.73	2	OG	Atlanta	28 Jul 96
	13.56/-1.6	1.80	14.52	23.72/-0.3	6.70/1.1	46.00	2:17.92	
6552		Nadezhda Vinogradova'	RUS	1.5.58	2	NC	Kiyev	21 Jun 84
	13.92/1.0	1.80	15.19	23.84/0.2	6.67/0.1	38.60	2:06.80	
6551		Yelena Martsenyuk	RUS	21.2.61	2		Staiki	2 Jul 88
	13.54/-0.4	1.82	15.32	24.25/0.3	6.25/0.7	47.56	2:12.72	
6546		Mona Steigauf	GER	17.1.70	1	WUG	Catania	27 Aug 97
	13.13/1.6	1.85	12.83	24.14/1.7	6.56/1.3	43.86	2:11.15	

Mark Wind	Name		Nat	Born	Pos	Meet	Venue		Date
6542	Urszula	Wlodarczyk	POL	22.12.65	4	WCh	Athína		4 Aug 97
	13.55/0.3	1.81	14.16	24.48/0.1	6.63/0.6		44.18	2:09.59	
6541	Mila	Kolyadina	RUS	31.12.60	4	v GDR	Moskva		19 Jun 83
	14.05	1.82	16.28	24.81	6.48/0.8		48.26	2:15.26	
6539	Tatyana	Shpak	UKR	17.11.60	3		Staiki		2 Jul 88
	13.57/-0.4	1.76	15.30	23.61/0.5	6.52/-0.6		39.28	2:07.25	
	(40)								
6536	Yekaterina	Smirnova	RUS	22.10.56	3	v GDR	Moskva		19 Jun 83
	13.41	1.82	14.82	24.84	6.56/1.1		45.66	2:13.38	
6531	Peggy	Beer	GDR	15.9.69	3	EC	Split		31 Aug 90
	13.27/-0.2	1.82	13.46	23.99/0.4	6.38/0.9		42.10	2:05.79	
6527	Diane	Guthrie-Gresham	JAM	24.10.71	1	NCAA	Knoxville		3 Jun 95
	13.86w/2.5	1.86	13.80	24.91/-1.3	6.92w/2.5		49.04	2:20.82	
6523	Sabine	Everts	FRG	4.3.61	1	v URS	Mannheim		10 Jun 82
	13.45	1.89	12.39	23.73	6.75		36.02	2:07.73	
6500	Birgit	Clarius	GER	18.3.65	1	NC	Vaterstetten		20 Jun 93
	13.61/1.3	1.81	15.22	24.69w/2.1	6.08/-0.6		50.20	2:11.29	
6493	Svetlana	Filatyeva '	RUS	3.4.64	1		Kiyev		14 Aug 88
	13.77	1.89	13.89	24.94	6.30		48.44	2:11.89	
6487	Birgit	Dressel	FRG	4.5.60	4	EC	Stuttgart		30 Aug 86
	13.56/-1.6	1.92	14.12	24.68/0.0	6.28/1.1		45.70	2:15.78	
6474	Marianna	Maslennikova	RUS	17.5.61	2	NC	Kiyev		2 Aug 88
	13.37/0.4	1.83	13.68	24.07/-0.0	6.28/0.2		40.42	2:05.60	
6465	Kelly	Blair-LaBounty	USA	24.11.70	1	NC	Indianapolis		12 Jun 97
	13.47w/2.5	1.74	13.28	24.13/1.0	6.52w/2.2		51.60	2:15.31	
6461	Valentina	Kurochkina	RUS	13.12.59	1		Tallinn		11 Aug 83
	13.89	1.85	14.40	24.51	6.63/1.2		43.98	2:15.94	
	(50)	100th woman 6300, 200th woman 6078							

45-MINUTE HEPTATHLON

6214	Sabine	Braun	GER	19.6.65	1		Ingelheim		28 Aug 93
	13.43	1.83	14.44	24.82	6.43		44.96	2:32.35	
6154	Petra	Vaideanu'	ROM	24.8.65	2		Ingelheim		28 Aug 93
	13.62	1.77	14.56	25.71	5.92		47.90	2:15.73	
6043	Kym	Carter	USA	12.3.64	3		Ingelheim		28 Aug 93
	13.53	1.74	14.78	24.18	5.91		36.84	2:17.61	

DECATHLON

7731	Marie	Collonvillé	FRA	23.11.73	1	Lage				10 Sep 00
	12.61	6.03	11.55	1.75	56.48	14.28	31.91	3.40	43.94	5:13.70
7615	Mona	Steigauf	GER	17.1.70	1	Ahlen				21 Sep 97
	12.15/1.2	5.93	12.49	1.73	55.34	13.75/0.2	34.68	3.10	42.24	5:07.95
7577	Tiffany	Lott-Hogan	USA	1.8.75	2	Lage				10 Sep 00
	12.31	5.77	13.86	1.69	58.01	13.57	38.39	3.00	46.93	6:01.24

4 x 100 METRES RELAY

41.37 WR	GDR	Gladisch, Rieger, Auerswald, Göhr	1	WCp	Canberra	6 Oct 85
41.47	USA	Gaines, Jones, Miller, Devers	1	WCh	Athína	9 Aug 97
41.49	RUS	Bogoslovskaya, Malchugina, Voronova, Privalova	1	WCh	Stuttgart	22 Aug 93
41.49	USA	Finn, Torrence, Vereen, Devers	2	WCh	Stuttgart	22 Aug 93
41.52	USA	Gaines, Jones, Miller, Devers	1h1	WCh	Athína	8 Aug 97
41.53 WR	GDR	Gladisch, Koch, Auerswald, Göhr	1		Berlin	31 Jul 83
41.55	USA	Brown, Williams, Griffith, Marshall	1	ISTAF	Berlin	21 Aug 87
41.58	USA	Brown, Williams, Griffith, Marshall	1	WCh	Roma	6 Sep 87
41.60 WR	GDR	Müller, Wöckel, Auerswald, Göhr	1	OG	Moskva	1 Aug 80
41.61A	USA	Brown, Williams, Cheeseborough, Ashford	1	USOF	USAF Academy	3 Jul 83
41.63	USA	Brown, Williams, Cheeseborough, Ashford	1	v GDR	Los Angeles	25 Jun 83
41.65	USA	Brown, Bolden, Cheeseborough, Ashford	1	OG	Los Angeles	11 Aug 84
41.65	GDR	Gladisch, Koch, Auerswald, Göhr	1	ECp	Moskva	17 Aug 85
41.68	GDR	Möller, Krabbe, Behrendt, Günther	1	EC	Split	1 Sep 90
41.69	GDR	Gladisch, Koch, Auerswald, Göhr	1	OD	Potsdam	21 Jul 84
41.73	GDR	Möller, Behrendt, Lange, Göhr	1		Berlin	13 Sep 88
41.76	GDR	Gladisch, Koch, Auerswald, Göhr	1	WCh	Helsinki	10 Aug 83
41.79	GDR	Gladisch, Drechsler, Auerswald, Göhr	1	v URS	Karl-Marx-Stadt	20 Jun 87
41.84	GDR	Gladisch, Gunther, Auerswald, Göhr	1	EC	Stuttgart	31 Aug 86
41.85 WR	GDR	Müller, Wöckel, Auerswald, Göhr	1	OT	Potsdam	13 Jul 80
		(20 performances by 3 nations) from here just best by nation				
41.92	BAH	Fynes, Sturrup, Davis-Thompson, Ferguson	1	WCh	Sevilla	29 Aug 99

Mark	Wind / Nat	Name	Pos	Meet	Venue	Date
41.94	JAM	Duhaney, Cuthbert, McDonald, Ottey	1	WCh	Tokyo	1 Sep 91
42.06	FRA	Girard, Hurtis, Benth, Arron	2	WCh	Sevilla	29 Aug 99
42.08mx	BUL	Pavlova, Nuneva, Georgieva, Ivanova	mx		Sofiya	8 Aug 84
	42.29	Pencheva, Nuneva, Georgieva, Donkova	1		Sofiya	26 Jun 88
42.23	Sichuan, CHN	Xiao Lin, Li Yali, Liu Xiaomei, Li Xuemei	1	NG	Shanghai	23 Oct 97
42.39	NGR	Utondu, Idehen, Opara-Thompson, Onyali	2h2	OG	Barcelona	7 Aug 92
42.43	GBR	Hunte, Smallwood, Goddard, Lannaman	3	OG	Moskva	1 Aug 80
	(10)					
42.59	FRG	Possekel, Helten, Richter, Kroniger	2	OG	Montreal	31 Jul 76
42.71	POL	Tomczak, Pakula, Pisiewicz, Kasprzyk	3	ECp	Moskva	17 Aug 85
42.77	CAN	Bailey, Payne, Taylor, Gareau	2	OG	Los Angeles	11 Aug 84
42.89	CUB	Ferrer, López, Duporty, Allen	6	WCh	Stuttgart	22 Aug 93
42.97	UKR	Khristosenko, Kot, I Slyusar, German	1	SPART	Taskent	16 Sep 86
42.98	CZE/TCH	Sokolová, Soborová, Kocembová, Kratochvilová	1	WK	Zürich	18 Aug 82
42.99A	AUS	Massey, Broadrick, Lambert, Gainsford-Taylor	1		Pietersburg	18 Mar 00
43.07	GRE	Tsóni, Kóffa, Vasarmídou, Thánou	2	MedG	Bari	18 Jun 97
43.19	GHA	Akoto, Twum, Anim, Nsiah	5s1	OG	Sydney	29 Sep 00
43.25A	RSA	Hartman, Moropane, Holtshausen, Seyerling	2		Pietersburg	18 Mar 00
	(20)					
43.35	KZK	Aleksandrova, Kvast, Miljauskiene, Sevalnikova	2	SPART	Taskent	16 Sep 86
43.37	FIN	Pirtimaa, Hanhijoki, Hernesniemi, Salmela	7	WCh	Stuttgart	22 Aug 93
43.42	COL	Mera, Palacios, Rodriguez, Brock	4h2	WCh	Göteborg	12 Aug 95
43.44A WR	NED	van den Berg, Sterk, Hennipman, Bakker	4	OG	Ciudad de México	20 Oct 68
43.44	ITA	Pistone, Graglia, Grillo, Levorato	1		Barletta	26 Jul 00
43.61	MAD	Rahanitraniriana, Ratsimbazafy, Rakotozafy, Rakotondrabé	4h4	OG	Sydney	29 Sep 00
43.62	BLR	Molchan, Safronnikova, Sologub, Grigorovska	5	ECp	Madrid	1 Jun 96
43.82	UZB	Shmonina, Olenchenko, Barabashina, Vilisova	3	SPART	Moskva	20 Jun 83
43.89	BRA	Gomes, K Santos, Amaral, Moura	7h1	WCh	Athína	8 Aug 97
44.08	ESP	Morales, Castro, Garcia, Myers	5h2	WCh	Tokyo	31 Aug 91

Best at low altitude

Mark	Nat	Name	Pos	Meet	Venue	Date
43.18	AUS	Wilson, Wells, Robertson, Boyle	5	OG	Montreal	31 Jul 76
43.48	NED	Cooman, Tromp, Olyslager, Vader	5s1	OG	Seoul	1 Oct 88

4 x 200 METRES RELAY

Mark	Team	Name	Pos	Meet	Venue	Date
1:27.46 WR	USA Blue	Jenkins, Colander-Richardson, Perry, Jones	1	PennR	Philadelphia	29 Apr 00
1:28.15 WR	GDR	Göhr, R.Müller, Wöckel, Koch	1		Jena	9 Aug 80
1:29.24	Nike International USA	Roberts, Miller, Green, M Jones	1	Penn	Philadelphia	25 Apr 98
1:30.20	Nike International USA	Mondie-Milner, Green, Gaines, Miller	1	Penn	Philadelphia	26 Apr 97

4 x 400 METRES RELAY

Mark	Nat	Name	Pos	Meet	Venue	Date
3:15.17 WR	URS		1	OG	Seoul	1 Oct 88
		Ledovskaya 50.12, O.Nazarova 47.82, Pinigina 49.43, Bryzgina 47.80				
3.15.51	USA		2	OG	Seoul	1 Oct 88
		D.Howard 49.82, Dixon 49.17, Brisco 48.44, Griffith-Joyner 48.08				
3:15.92 WR	GDR	G.Walther 49.8, Busch 48.9, Rübsam 49.4, Koch 47.8	1	NC	Erfurt	3 Jun 84
3:16.71	USA		1	WCh	Stuttgart	22 Aug 93
		Torrence 49.0, Malone 49.4, Kaiser-Brown 49.48, Miles 48.78				
3:16.87	GDR	Emmelmann 50.9, Busch 48.8, Müller 48.9, Koch 48.3	1	EC	Stuttgart	31 Aug 86
3:18.29	USA		1	OG	Los Angeles	11 Aug 84
		Leatherwood 50.50, S.Howard 48.83, Brisco-Hooks 49.23, Cheeseborough 49.73				
3:18.29	GDR	Neubauer 50.58, Emmelmann 49.89, Busch 48.81, Müller 48.99	3	OG	Seoul	1 Oct 88
3:18.38	RUS		2	WCh	Stuttgart	22 Aug 93
		Ruzina 50.8, Alekseyeva 49.3, Ponomaryova 49.78, Privalova 48.47				
3:18.43	URS		1	WCh	Tokyo	1 Sep 91
		Ledovskaya 51.7, Dzhigalova 49.2, Nazarova 48.87, Bryzgina 48.67				
3:18.58	URS	I.Nazarova, Olizarenko, Pinigina, Vladykina	1	ECp	Moskva	18 Aug 85
3:18.63	GDR	Neubauer 51.4, Emmelmann 49.1, Müller 48.64, Busch 49.48	1	WCh	Roma	6 Sep 87
3:19.04 WR	GDR	Siemon' 51.0, Busch 50.0, Rübsam 50.2, Koch 47.9	1	EC	Athína	11 Sep 82
3:19.12	URS	Baskakova, I.Nazarova, Pinigina, Vladykina	1	Drz	Praha	18 Aug 84
3:19.23 WR	GDR	Maletzki, Rohde, Streidt, Brehmer	1	OG	Montreal	31 Jul 76
3:19.49	GDR	Emmelmann, Busch, Neubauer, Koch	1	WCp	Canberra	4 Oct 85
3:19.50	URS	Yurchenko, O.Nazarova, Pinigina, Bryzgina	2	WCh	Roma	6 Sep 87
3:19.60	USA	Leatherwood, S.Howard, Brisco-Hooks, Cheeseborough	1		Walnut	25 Jul 84
3:19.62	GDR	Kotte, Brehmer, Köhn, Koch	1	ECp	Torino	5 Aug 79
3:19.66	GDR	Busch, Emmelmann, Neubauer, Müller	1	v FRG	Düsseldorf	20 Jun 88
3:19.73	GDR	K.Walther, Busch, Koch, Rübsam	1	WCh	Helsinki	14 Aug 83
		(20/4 with USSR and Russia counted separately)				
3:20.32	CZE/TCH	Kocembová, Matejkovicová, Moravcíková, Kratochvílová	2	WCh	Helsinki	14 Aug 83
3:21.04	NGR	Afolabi 51.13, Yusuf 49.72, Opara 51.29, Ogunkoya 48.90	2	OG	Atlanta	3 Aug 96

Mark	Wind/Nat	Name	Pos	Meet	Venue	Date
3:21.21	CAN	Crooks, Richardson, Killingbeck, Payne	2	OG	Los Angeles	11 Aug 84
3:21.30	JAM	Turner 52.4, L Graham 49.9, Hemmings 49.58, Richards 49.45	3	WCh	Athína	10 Aug 97
3:21.94	UKR	Dzhigalova, Olizarenko, Pinigina, Vladykina	1	URSCh	Kiyev	17 Jul 86
3:22.01	GBR	Hanson, Smith, Gunnell, Keough	4	WCh	Tokyo	1 Sep 91
	(10)					
3:22.34	FRA	Landre 51.3, Dorsile 51.1, Elien 50.54, Pérec 49.36	1	EC	Helsinki	14 Aug 94
3:22.49	FRG	Thimm, Arendt, Thomas, Abt	4	OG	Seoul	1 Oct 88
3:23.81	AUS	Peris-Kneebone, Lewis, Gainsford-Taylor, Freeman	5	OG	Sydney	30 Sep 00
3:24.23	CUB	Bonne, Duporty, Morales, Quirot	2h2	OG	Atlanta	2 Aug 96
3:24.28	Hebei (CHN)	An X, Bai X, Cao C, Ma Y	1	NG	Beijing	13 Sep 93
3:24.65	POL	Kasprzyk, Wojdecka, Kapusta, Blaszak	3	EC	Stuttgart	31 Aug 86
3:25.68	ROM	Ruicu, Rîpanu, Barbu, Tîrlea	2	ECp	Paris (C)	20 Jun 99
3:25.7a	FIN	Eklund, Pursiainen, Wilmi, Salin	2	EC	Roma	8 Sep 74
3:25.81	BUL	Ilieva, Stamenova, Penkova, Damyanova	1	v Hun,Pol	Sofiya	24 Jul 83
3:26.31	BLR	Sologub, Budnik, Khlyustova, Kozak	3h1	OG	Sydney	29 Sep 00
	(20)					
3:26.69	ITA	Perpoli, Spuri, Carbone, De Angeli	5	ECp	Paris (C)	20 Jun 99
3:27.54	LIT	Navickaite, Valiuliene, Mendzoryte, Ambraziene	3	SPART	Moskva	22 Jun 83
3:27.57	ESP	Merino, Lacambra, Myers, Ferrer	7	WCh	Tokyo	1 Sep 91
3:27.86	HUN	Orosz, Forgács, Tóth, Pál	5	OG	Moskva	1 Aug 80
3:28.02	SEN	Diop, M T Diouf, A Diouf, Thiam	4h3	OG	Sydney	29 Sep 00
3:28.11	IND	Kuriakose, Philip, P Kaur, Beenamol	1	NC	Chennai	31 Jul 00
3:28.52	SUI	Burkart, Zürcher/Scalabrin, Brillante, Lüthi	8	WCh	Stuttgart	22 Aug 93
3:28.94A	KEN	Shitandayi, Wanjiru, Kavaya, Chepkurui	2	AfG	Nairobi	12 Aug 87
3:29.22A	BRA	Montalvão, Oliveira, Telles, Figueiredo	1	IbAm	Cd de México	24 Jul 88
3:29.38	POR	Moreira, Coelho, Amaral, Jardim	4h2	OG	Barcelona	7 Aug 92

3000 METRES WALK (TRACK)

Mark	Name		Nat	Born	Pos	Meet	Venue	Date
11:48.24WR	Ileana	Salvador	ITA	16.1.62	1		Padova	29 Aug 93
11:51.26WR	Kerry	Saxby-Junna	AUS	2.6.61	1		Melbourne	7 Feb 91
11:52.01	Beate	Anders/Gummelt	GER	4.2.68	1		Lapinlahti	27 Jun 93
11:56.40	Elisabetta	Perrone	ITA	9.7.68	2		Padova	29 Aug 93
11:57.68	Yelena	Nikolayeva	RUS	1.2.66	1		Formia	18 May 96
11:58.06	Erica	Alfridi	ITA	22.2.68	1		Milano	7 Jun 00
11:58.9	Yelena	Sayko	RUS	24.12.67	1		Novosibirsk	4 Sep 95
11:59.60	Sari	Essayah	FIN	21.2.67	2		Lapinlahti	27 Jun 93
12:00.58	Claudia	Iovan	ROM	25.2.78	2		Milano	9 Jun 99
12:02.2	Olimpiada	Ivanova ¶	RUS	5.5.70	2		Novosibirsk	4 Sep 95
Indoors								
11:40.33	Claudia	Iovan	ROM	25.2.78	1		Bucuresti	30 Jan 99
11:41.85	Norica	Cîmpean	ROM	22.3.72	1		Bucuresti	6 Feb 99
11:44.00	Alina	Ivanova	RUS	16.3.69	1		Moskva	7 Feb 92
11:49.73	Yelena	Nikolayeva	RUS	1.2.66	1	WI	Toronto	13 Mar 93
11:50.90	Beate	Anders/Gummelt	GER	4.2.68	1	WI	Sevilla	9 Mar 91
11:54.32	Annarita	Sidoti	ITA	25.7.69	1	EI	Paris	12 Mar 94
11:57.48	Yelena	Arshintseva	RUS	5.4.71	3	EI	Paris	12 Mar 94
12:00.13	Erika	Alfridi	ITA	22.2.68	1	NC	Genova	22 Feb 97
12:04.46	Leonarda	Yukhnevich	BLR	1.5.63	5	EI	Paris	12 Mar 94

5000 METRES WALK (TRACK)

Mark	Name		Nat	Born	Pos	Meet	Venue	Date
20:03.0WR	Kerry	Saxby-Junna	AUS	2.6.61	1		Sydney	11 Feb 96
20:07.52WR	Beate	Anders/Gummelt	GDR	4.2.68	1	vURS	Rostock	23 Jun 90
20:21.69	Annarita	Sidoti	ITA	25.7.69	1	NC	Cesenatico	1 Jul 95
20:27.59WR	Ileana	Salvador	ITA	16.1.62	1		Trento	3 Jun 89
20:28.62	Sari	Essayah	FIN	21.2.67	1	NC	Tuusula	9 Jul 94
20:29.63	Claudia	Iovan	ROM	25.2.78	1		Istanbul	19 Jun 99
20:31.4	Irina	Stankina	RUS	25.3.77	1	NC-wj	Adler	10 Feb 96
20:33.42	Elisabetta	Perrone	ITA	9.7.68	2	NC	Cesenatico	1 Jul 95
20:37.7		Jin Bingjie	CHN	1.4.71	1	NC	Hefei	3 Mar 90
20:38.0		Chen Yueling	CHN	1.4.68	2	NC	Hefei	3 Mar 90
	(10)							
20:40.6	Olga	Kardopoltseva	BLR	11.9.66	1		Alushta	5 May 90
20:46.23	Kjersti	Plätzer	NOR	18.1.72	1	NC	Kristiansand	20 Aug 00
20:48.11	Rossella	Giordano	ITA	1.12.72	1		Roma	10 May 97
20:49.4+	Nadezhda	Ryashkina	RUS	22.1.67	1=	GWG	Seattle	24 Jul 90
20:50.3		Fan Xiaoling	CHN	14.5.71	2	NC	Zhengzhou	3 Mar 91
20:50.60	Alina	Ivanova	RUS	16.3.69	1	vGDR	Bryansk	15 Jul 89
20:51.96	Katarzyna	Radtke	POL	31.8.69	1		Sopot	20 Jun 93
20:52.24	Tamara	Surovtseva	BLR	12.6.60	2	vGDR	Rostock	23 Jun 90

Mark	Wind	Name		Nat	Born	Pos	Meet	Venue	Date
20:53.34		Vera	Zozulya	UKR	31.8.70	1		Uzhgorod	8 May 98
20:54.04		Erica	Alfridi	ITA	22.2.68	1	NC	Roma	10 Jul 98
		(20)							
Indoors									
20:42.33		Yelena	Gruzinova	RUS	24.12.67	1		Samara	1 Mar 97
20:50.6		Olimpiada	Ivanova ¶	RUS	5.5.70	1	Army	Moskva	21 Jan 97

5 KILOMETRES WALK (ROAD)

Mark	Wind	Name		Nat	Born	Pos	Meet	Venue	Date
20:05	WB	Olga	Polyakova	RUS	23.9.80	1		Saransk	28 May 00
20:19+	WB	Yelena	Nikolayeva	RUS	1.2.66	1	in 10k	Sochi	20 Apr 96
20:19		Yuliya	Voyevodina	RUS	5.5.70	2		Saransk	28 May 00
20:24		Lyudmila	Yefimkina	RUS	22.8.81	3		Saransk	28 May 00
20:26		Ileana	Salvador	ITA	16.1.62	1		Barcelona	5 Apr 92
20:27		Tatyana	Kozlova	RUS	2.9.83	4		Saransk	28 May 00
20:30		Olimpiada	Ivanova ¶	RUS	5.5.70	5		Saransk	28 May 00
Where better than track									
20:36		Alina	Ivanova	RUS	16.3.69	1		L'Hospitalet	21 Apr 91
20:37		Olga	Kardopoltseva	BLR	11.9.66	2		L'Hospitalet	21 Apr 91
20:38		Vera	Makolova	RUS	17.2.66	1	NC	Leningrad	5 Aug 89
20:38		Nadezhda	Ryashkina	RUS	22.1.67	1		Saransk	6 Jun 98
20:40+		Valentina	Tsybulskaya	BLR	19.2.68	1	in 10k	Eisenhüttenstadt	10 May 97
20:40		Elisabetta	Perrone	ITA	9.7.68	1		Ivrea	8 Oct 00
20:41+			Liu Hongyu	CHN	11.1.75	1	in 10k	Eisenhüttenstadt	8 May 99
20:42+			Wang Yan	CHN	2.5.71	2	in 10k	Eisenhüttenstadt	8 May 99
20:45+		M del Rosario	Sánchez	MEX	16.10.73	3	in 10k	Eisenhüttenstadt	8 May 99
20:46+		Irina	Stankina	RUS	25.3.77	1	in 10k	Adler	9 Feb 97
20:47+		Natalya	Misyulya	BLR	16.4.66	5	in 10k	Eisenhüttenstadt	8 May 99
20:50+		Yelena	Gruzinova	RUS	24.12.67	2=	in 10k	Eisenhüttenstadt	10 May 97
20:50+		Larisa	Khmelnitskaya	BLR	23.9.71	2=	in 10k	Eisenhüttenstadt	10 May 97
20:51		Tamara	Kovalenko	RUS	5.6.64	1		Moskva	3 May 98
20:52+		Olga	Panfyorova	RUS	21.8.77	1=	in 10k	Izhevsk	16 May 98
20:53		Sada	Eidikite'	LIT	22.6.67	2		Hildesheim	10 Jun 89

10 KILOMETRES WALK

Mark	Wind	Name		Nat	Born	Pos	Meet	Venue	Date
41:04	WR	Yelena	Nikolayeva	RUS	1.2.66	1	NC	Sochi	20 Apr 96
41:16			Wang Yan	CHN	3.5.71	1		Eisenhüttenstadt	8 May 99
41:17		Irina	Stankina	RUS	25.3.77	1	NC-w	Adler	9 Feb 97
41:24		Olimpiada	Ivanova ¶	RUS	5.5.70	2	NC-w	Adler	9 Feb 97
41:29	WR	Larisa	Ramazanova	RUS	23.9.71	1	NC	Izhevsk	4 Jun 95
41:30	WR	Kerry	Saxby-Junna	AUS	2.6.61	1	NC	Canberra	27 Aug 88
41:30			O Ivanova			2	NC	Izhevsk	4 Jun 95
41:31		Yelena	Gruzinova	RUS	24.12.67	2	NC	Sochi	20 Apr 96
41:38			Gao Hongmiao	CHN	17.3.74	1	NC	Beijing	7 Apr 94
41:38		Rossella	Giordano	ITA	1.12.72	1		Naumburg	25 May 97
41:41			Nikolayeva			2		Naumburg	25 May 97
41:45			Liu Hongyu (10)	CHN	11.1.75	2		Eisenhüttenstadt	8 May 99
41:46		Annarita	Sidoti	ITA	25.7.69	1		Livorno	12 Jun 94
41:46			O Ivanova			1	NC/w	Adler	11 Feb 96
41:47			Saxby-Junna			1		Eisenhüttenstadt	11 May 96
41:48			Li Chunxiu	CHN	13.8.69	1	NG	Beijing	8 Sep 93
41:49			Ramazanova			3	NC	Sochi	20 Apr 96
41:49			Nikolayeva			1	OG	Atlanta	29 Jul 96
41:50		Yelena	Arshintseva	RUS	5.4.71	1	NC-w	Adler	11 Feb 95
41:51		Beate	Anders/Gummelt	GER	4.2.68	2		Eisenhüttenstadt	11 May 96
41:52			Stankina			1	WCp	Podebrady	19 Apr 97
41:54		Kjersti	Plätzer	NOR	18.1.72	3		Eisenhüttenstadt	8 May 99
41:55			Stankina			1	NC-wj	Adler	11 Feb 95
41:56		Yelena	Sayko	RUS	24.12.67	2	NC/w	Adler	11 Feb 96
41:56			Khmelnitskaya	(Ramazanova)		1		Eisenhüttenstadt	10 May 97
41:56.23t		Nadezhda	Ryashkina	RUS	22.1.67	1	GWG	Seattle	24 Jul 90
41:57			Gao Hongmiao			2	NG	Beijing	8 Sep 93
41:57.22t			Saxby-Junna			2	GWG	Seattle	24 Jul 90
41:58			Gruzinova			2	NC-w	Adler	11 Feb 95
41:59			O Ivanova			2	WCp	Podebrady	19 Apr 97
		(30/17)							
42:01		Tamara	Kovalenko	RUS	5.6.64	3	NC-w	Adler	11 Feb 95
42:01			Stankina			3		Eisenhüttenstadt	11 May 96
42:01		Olga	Panfyorova	RUS	21.8.77	1	NC-23	Izhevsk	16 May 98

Mark Wind	Name		Nat	Born	Pos	Meet	Venue	Date
42:06	Valentina	Tsybulskaya	BLR	19.2.68	4		Eisenhüttenstadt	8 May 99
	(20)							
42:07	Ileana	Salvador	ITA	16.1.62	1		Sesto San Giovanni	1 May 92
42:09	Elisabetta	Perrone	ITA	9.7.68	4		Eisenhüttenstadt	11 May 96
42:11	Nina	Alyushenko	RUS	29.5.68	3	NC	Izhevsk	4 Jun 95
42:13	Natalya	Misyulya	BLR	16.4.66	5		Eisenhüttenstadt	8 May 99
42:13.7t	Madelein	Svensson	SWE	20.7.69	2	SGP	Fana	15 May 92
42:15		Gu Yan	CHN	17.3.74	3	WCp	Podebrady	19 Apr 97
42:15	Erica	Alfridi	ITA	22.2.68	5		Naumburg	25 May 97
42:15	Jane	Saville	AUS	5.11.74	6		Eisenhüttenstadt	8 May 99
42:16	Alina	Ivanova	RUS	16.3.69	1		Novopolotsk	27 May 89
42:16	Norica	Cîmpean	ROM	22.3.72	1		Calella	9 May 99
	(30)							
42:17	Katarzyna	Radtke	POL	31.8.69	5		Eisenhüttenstadt	11 May 96
42:20	Sari	Essayah	FIN	21.2.67	4	WCh	Göteborg	7 Aug 95
42:29	Olga	Kardopoltseva	BLR	11.9.66	4		Eisenhüttenstadt	10 May 97
42:31	Vera	Nacharkina'	RUS	17.2.66	1	NC	Izhevsk	16 May 98
42:32	Maya	Sazonova	KZK	28.5.68	4	Rus Ch	Sochi	20 Apr 96
42:34	Mária	Rosza/Urbaník	HUN	12.2.67	7	WCh	Göteborg	7 Aug 95
42:37	Claudia	Iovan	ROM	25.2.78	2		Calella	9 May 99
42:37	Olga	Lukyanchuk	UKR	7.12.76	1		Mukachevo	21 Oct 00
42:40	Yuliya	Odzilyayeva	RUS	17.10.71	5		Livorno	12 Jun 94
42:40.37t		Feng Haixia	CHN	23.2.75	3		Nanjing	24 Oct 95
	(40)							
42:42	Graciela	Mendoza	MEX	22.3.63	11		Naumburg	25 May 97
42:42+	Tatyana	Gudkova	RUS	23.1.78	1=	in 20k	Moskva	19 May 00
42:43+	Olga	Polyakova	RUS	23.9.80	4=	in 20k	Moskva	19 May 00
42:44	Irina	Strakhova	RUS	4.3.59	3		Sochi	17 Feb 91
42:44		Long Yuwen	CHN	1.8.75	3		Shenzhen	18 Feb 93
42:45		Li Yuxin	CHN	4.12.74	4		Shenzhen	18 Feb 93
42:46.7t		Cui Yingzi	CHN	26.1.71	1	NC	Jinan	15 Mar 92
42:46.7t		Chen Yueling	CHN	1.4.68	2	NC	Jinan	15 Mar 92
42:48	M del Rosario	Sánchez	MEX	26.10.73	8		Eisenhüttenstadt	8 May 99
42:50.0t		Guan Ping	CHN	1.2.66	5	NC	Jinan	15 Mar 92
	(50)	100th woman 43:47, 200th woman 44:52						
Probable short course								
41:30	Ileana	Salvador	ITA	16.1.62	1	4-N	Livorno	10 Jul 93
41:56	Elisabeta	Perrone	ITA	9.7.68	2	4-N	Livorno	10 Jul 93
Best track times								
41:57.22	Kerry	Saxby-Junna	AUS	2.6.61	2	GWG	Seattle	24 Jul 90
42:11.5	Beate	Anders/Gummelt	GER	4.2.68	1	SGP	Fana	15 May 92
42:23.7	Ileana	Salvador		16.1.62	2	SGP	Fana	8 May 93
42:30.13		Gao Hongmiao	CHN	17.3.74	1		Nanjing	24 Oct 95
42:30.31	Olimpiada	Ivanova ¶	RUS	5.5.70	1	GWG	Sankt-Peterburg	26 Jul 94
42:37.0	Sari	Essayah	FIN	21.2.67	3	SGP	Fana	8 May 93
42:38.24		Liu Hongyu	CHN	11.1.75	2		Nanjing	24 Oct 95
42:43.23	Yelena	Sayko	RUS	16.2.68	2	GWG	Sankt-Peterburg	26 Jul 94
42:45.0	Elisabetta	Perrone	ITA	9.7.68	1		Catania	30 May 99
42:47.4	Katarzyna	Radtke	POL	31.8.69	4	SGP	Fana	8 May 93

20 KILOMETRES WALK

1:25:18 WR	Tatyana	Gudkova	RUS	23.1.78	1	NC	Moskva	19 May 00
1:25:20	Olga	Polyakova	RUS	23.9.80	2	NC	Moskva	19 May 00
1:25:29	Irina	Stankina	RUS	25.3.77	3	NC	Moskva	19 May 00
1:25:59	Tamara	Kovalenko	RUS	5.6.64	4	NC	Moskva	19 May 00
1:26:08	Olimpiada	Ivanova	RUS	5.5.70	5	NC	Moskva	19 May 00
1:26:48		Ivanova			1	ECp	Eisenhüttenstadt	17 Jun 00
1:27:30 WR		Liu Hongyu	CHN	11.1.75	1		Beijing	1 May 95
1:27:30 WR	Nadezhda	Ryashkina	RUS	22.1.67	1	NC-w	Adler	7 Feb 99
1:27:32		Liu Hongyu			1	WCp	Mézidon-Canon	2 May 99
1:27:35	Natalya	Fedoskina	RUS	25.6.80	2	WCp	Mézidon-Canon	2 May 99
1:27:42	Elisabetta	Perrone	ITA	9.7.68	2	ECp	Eisenhüttenstadt	17 Jun 00
1:27:46	Norica	Cîmpean (10)	ROM	22.3.72	1		Békéscsaba	28 Mar 99
1:27:48		Cîmpean			3	WCp	Mézidon-Canon	2 May 99
1:27:53	Kjersti	Tysse Plätzer	NOR	18.1.72	3	ECp	Eisenhüttenstadt	17 Jun 00
1:27:54		Song Lijuan	CHN	9.2.75	2		Beijing	1 May 95
1:27:55		Liu Hongyu			1		Rio Maior	15 Apr 00
1:28:01	Yelena	Nikolayeva	RUS	1.2.66	2	NC-w	Adler	7 Feb 99
1:28:06		Ryashkina			6	NC	Moskva	19 May 00

Mark Wind		Name	Nat	Born	Pos	Meet	Venue	Date
1:28:06	Erica	Alfridi	ITA	22.2.68	4	ECp	Eisenhüttenstadt	17 Jun 00
1:28:08		Stankina			1	NC-w	Adler	20 Feb 00
1:28:13		Alfridi			1	NC	Cassino	9 Mar 97
1:28:16		Ryashkina			2	NC-w	Adler	20 Feb 00
1:28:18		Kong Yan	CHN	6.7.73	3		Beijing	1 May 95
1:28:19	Susana	Feitor	POR	28.1.75	1		Hildesheim	9 Jul 00
1:28:21		O Ivanova			1		Cheboksary	4 Sep 99
1:28:23		Nikolayeva			4	WCp	Mézidon-Canon	2 May 99
1:28:24	Natalya	Misyulya	BLR	16.4.66	1	NC	Soligorsk	13 May 00
1:28:27		Wang Yan	CHN	3.5.71	2		Rio Maior	15 Apr 00
1:28:33		Kovalenko			3	NC-w	Adler	7 Feb 99
1:28:33		Wang Liping	CHN	8.7.76	1	NC2	Lushun	3 Jun 00
	(30/19)							
1:28:38	Annarita	Sidoti (20)	ITA	25.7.69	5	ECp	Eisenhüttenstadt	17 Jun 00
1:28:39		Gu Yan	CHN	17.3.74	4		Beijing	1 May 95
1:28:51	Olga	Kardopoltseva	BLR	11.9.66	2		Brest	4 Jun 99
1:28:56	Jane	Saville	AUS	5.11.74	1		København	6 May 00
1:28:56	Larisa	Khmelnitskaya	BLR	23.9.71	2	NC	Soligorsk	13 May 00
1:29:06	Valentina	Savchuk	UKR	19.1.75	4	RUS-w	Adler	20 Feb 00
1:29:12	Rossella	Giordano	ITA	1.12.72	2	NC	Cassino	9 Mar 97
1:29:15		Feng Haixia	CHN	23.2.75	1	NC	Zhuhai	12 Mar 96
1:29:20	Valentina	Tsybulskaya	BLR	19.2.68	4		Brest	4 Jun 99
1:29:23	Lyudmila	Dolgopolova	BLR	11.8.69	3	NC	Soligorsk	13 May 00
1:29:36	Kerry	Saxby-Junna	AUS	2.6.61	2		Naumburg	30 Apr 00
	(30)							
1:29:39	Claudia	Iovan ¶	ROM	25.2.78	6	WCp	Mézidon-Canon	2 May 99
1:29:39	Yuliya	Voyevodina	RUS	17.10.71	7	NC	Moskva	19 May 00
1:29:45		Sun Chunfang	CHN	1.3.77	2	NC2	Lushun	3 Jun 00
1:29:53	Tatyana	Sibileva	RUS	17.5.80	1	NC	Cheboksary	29 Aug 98
1:29:59	Ana Maria	Groza	ROM	1.6.76	2		Békéscsaba	9 Apr 00
1:30:03		Li Jingxue	CHN	10.2.70	7		Beijing	1 May 95
1:30:03		Gao Hongmiao	CHN	17.3.74	7	WCp	Mézidon-Canon	2 May 99
1:30:03	Graciela	Mendoza	MEX	23.3.63	8	WCp	Mézidon-Canon	2 May 99
1:30:12	Lyudmila	Yefimkina	RUS	22.8.81	4	NC	Saransk	12 Jun 99
1:30:17	Tatyana	Korotkova	RUS	24.4.80	6	NC-w	Adler	20 Feb 00
	(40)							
1:30:18	Maya	Sazonova	KAZ	28.5.65	8	RUS Ch	Moskva	19 May 00
1:30:20	Maria	Vasco	ESP	26.12.75	4	v4N	Leamington	23 Apr 00
1:30:31	Vera	Nacharkina	RUS	17.2.68	1	RusCup	Cheboksary	23 Aug 97
1:30:31	Anikó	Szebenszky	HUN	12.8.65	3	NC	Békéscsaba	9 Apr 00
1:30:34	Olga	Panfyorova	RUS	21.8.77	8	NC-w	Adler	7 Feb 99
1:30:35		Li Hong	CHN	1.6.79	11	WCp	Mézidon-Canon	2 May 99
1:30:36		Tang Yinghua	CHN	18.5.73	3	NC2	Lushun	3 Jun 00
1:30:37		Sun Chunfang	CHN	1.3.77	8		Beijing	1 May 95
1:30:40	Rimma	Makarova	RUS	25.2.63	7	NC-w	Adler	20 Feb 00
1:30:41	Larisa	Safronova	RUS	6.1.80	1		Cheboksary	6 Oct 00
	(50)	100th best woman 1:34:30						
Uncertain distance								
1:29:23	Svetlana	Tolstaya	KZK	9.8.71	1	NC	Almaty	27 Mar99

50 KILOMETRES WALK

4:41:57	Kora	Boufflért	FRA	23.4.66	1		Ay-Champagne	17 Sep 95
4:49:25	Jacqueline	Delasseaux	FRA	14.12.46	1		Chaumontel	17 Sep 78
4:50:05+	Lyudmila	Lyubomirova	RUS	13.11.62	1	in 100k	Perpignan	15 Oct 95

SOME WOMEN'S NAME CHANGES

Anders	Gummelt	Makolova	Nacharkina
Beclea	Szekely	Martin L	Ondieki
Burova	Chernyavskaya	Narozhilenko	Engquist
Celnova	Prokopcuka	Negura	Olteanu
Daute	Drechsler	Perkins	DiMarco
Davis P	Davis-Thompson	Pomoshchnikova	Voronova
Decker	Slaney	Rieger	Humbert
Ilyina	Wijenberg	Storbeck	Cloete
Johnson	Hickman	Tysse	Plätzer
Kováciková	Hamácková	Taylor A	Issajenko
McPaul	Currey	Ullrich K	Wessel

JUNIOR WOMEN'S ALL-TIME LISTS

Based on the age regulations introduced for 1988, that is under 20 in year of competition.

100 METRES

Mark	Wind	Name		Nat	Born	Pos	Meet	Venue	Date
10.88	2.0	Marlies	Oelsner	GDR	21.3.58	1	NC	Dresden	1 Jul 77
10.89	1.8	Katrin	Krabbe	GDR	22.11.69	1rB		Berlin	20 Jul 88
11.03	1.7	Silke	Gladisch	GDR	20.6.64	3	OD	Berlin	8 Jun 83
11.04	1.4	Angela	Williams	USA	30.1.80	1	NCAA	Boise	5 Jun 99
11.08	2.0	Brenda	Morehead	USA	5.10.57	1	OT	Eugene	21 Jun 76
11.11	0.2	Shakedia	Jones	USA	15.3.79	1		Los Angeles (Ww)	2 May 98
11.11	1.1	Joan Uduak	Ekah	NGR	16.12.80	5	Athl	Lausanne	2 Jul 99
11.12	2.0	Veronica	Campbell	JAM	15.5.82	1	WJ	Santiago de Chile	18 Oct 00
11.13	2.0	Chandra	Cheeseborough	USA	10.1.59	2	OT	Eugene	21 Jun 76
11.13	-1.0	Grit	Breuer	GDR	16.2.72	1		Jena	6 Jun 90

Uncertain timing: 10.99 1.9 Natalya Bochina RUS 4.1.62 2 Leningrad 3 Jun 80

Wind assisted

Mark	Wind	Name		Nat	Born	Pos	Meet	Venue	Date
10.96	3.7	Angela	Williams	USA	30.1.80	1		Las Vegas	3 Apr 99
10.97	3.3	Gesine	Walther	GDR	6.10.62	4	NC	Cottbus	16 Jul 80
11.02	2.1	Nikole	Mitchell	JAM	5.6.74	1	Mutual	Kingston	1 May 93
11.06	2.2	Brenda	Morehead	USA	5.10.57	1s	OT	Eugene	21 Jun 76
11.09		Angela	Williams	TRI	15.5.65	1		Nashville	14 Apr 84
11.12	4.1	Marion	Jones	USA	12.10.75	1h		Cerritos	31 May 91

200 METRES

Mark	Wind	Name		Nat	Born	Pos	Meet	Venue	Date
22.19	1.5	Natalya	Bochina	RUS	4.1.62	2	OG	Moskva	30 Jul 80
22.37	1.3	Sabine	Rieger	GDR	6.11.63	2	vURS	Cottbus	26 Jun 82
22.42	0.4	Gesine	Walther	GDR	6.10.62	1		Potsdam	29 Aug 81
22.45	0.5	Grit	Breuer	GER	16.2.72	2	ASV	Köln	8 Sep 91
22.51	2.0	Katrin	Krabbe	GDR	22.11.69	3		Berlin	13 Sep 88
22.52	1.2	Mary	Onyali	NGR	3.2.68	6	WCh	Roma	3 Sep 87
22.58	0.8	Marion	Jones	USA	12.10.75	4	TAC	New Orleans	28 Jun 92
22.70		Marita	Koch	GDR	18.2.57	1		Halle	16 May 76
22.70A	1.9	Kathy	Smallwood	GBR	3.5.60	2	WUG	Ciudad de México	12 Sep 79
22.72	1.3	Silke	Gladisch	GDR	20.6.64	3	NC	Karl-Marx-Stadt	18 Jun 83
22.72	0.4	Nora	Ivanova	BUL	1.6.77	1		Zagreb	21 Jun 96

Wind assisted

Mark	Wind	Name		Nat	Born	Pos	Meet	Venue	Date
22.34	2.3	Kathrin	Krabbe	GDR	22.11.69	1	WJ	Sudbury	30 Jul 88
22.49	2.3	Brenda	Morehead	USA	5.10.57	1	OT	Eugene	24 Jun 76
22.53	2.5	Valerie	Brisco	USA	6.7.60	2	AAU	Walnut	17 Jun 79
22.64	2.3	Chandra	Cheeseborough	USA	16.1.59	2	OT	Eugene	24 Jun 76
22.65	3.5	Shakedia	Jones	USA	15.3.79	1	NC-j	Edwardsville IL	27 Jun 98
22.66	5.0	Lauren	Hewitt	AUS	25.11.78	3	NC	Melbourne	2 Mar 97
22.70	2.5	Kinshasa	Davis	USA	10.7.79	1		Long Beach	30 May 97

400 METRES

Mark	Wind	Name		Nat	Born	Pos	Meet	Venue	Date
49.42		Grit	Breuer	GER	16.2.72	2	WCh	Tokyo	27 Aug 91
49.77		Christina	Brehmer	GDR	28.2.58	1		Dresden	9 May 76
50.01			Li Jing	CHN	14.2.80	1	NG	Shanghai	18 Oct 97
50.19		Marita	Koch	GDR	18.2.57	3	OD	Berlin	10 Jul 76
50.59		Fatima	Yusuf	NGR	2.5.71	1	HGP	Budapest	5 Aug 90
		50.5 hand				1	NC	Lagos	25 Aug 90
50.74		Monique	Henderson	USA	18.2.83	1		Norwalk	3 Jun 00
50.86		Charity	Opara	NGR	20.5.72	2		Bologna	7 Sep 91
50.87		Denean	Howard	USA	5.10.64	1	TAC	Knoxville	20 Jun 82
50.87		Magdalena	Nedelcu	ROM	12.5.74	1	NC-j	Bucuresti	31 Jul 92
50.90		Sheila	Ingram	USA	23.3.57	3s1	OG	Montreal	28 Jul 76

800 METRES

Mark	Wind	Name		Nat	Born	Pos	Meet	Venue	Date
1:57.18			Wang Yuan	CHN	8.4.76	2h2	NG	Beijing	8 Sep 93
1:57.45		Hildegard	Ullrich	GDR	20.12.59	5	EC	Praha	31 Aug 78
1:57.62			Lang Yinglai	CHN	.8.79	1	NG	Shanghai	22 Oct 97
1:57.63		Maria	Mutola	MOZ	27.10.72	4	WCh	Tokyo	26 Aug 91
1:57.77			Lu Yi	CHN	10.4.74	4	NG	Beijing	9 Sep 93
1:57.86		Katrin	Wühn	GDR	19.11.65	1		Celje	5 May 84
1:58.16			Lin Nuo	CHN	.1.80	3	NG	Shanghai	22 Oct 97
1:58.18		Marion	Hübner	GDR	29.9.62	2		Erfurt	2 Aug 81
1:58.24		Christine	Wachtel	GDR	6.1.65	3		Potsdam	25 May 84
1:58.37		Gabriela	Sedláková	SVK	2.3.68	4	ISTAF	Berlin	21 Aug 87

Mark	Wind	Name		Nat	Born	Pos	Meet	Venue	Date

1000 METRES

Mark		Name		Nat	Born	Pos	Meet	Venue	Date
2:35.4		Irina	Nikitina	RUS	16.1.61	5	Kuts	Podolsk	5 Aug 79
2:35.4		Katrin	Wühn	GDR	19.11.65	3		Potsdam	12 Jul 84

1500 METRES

Mark		Name		Nat	Born	Pos	Meet	Venue	Date
3:51.34			Lang Yinglai	CHN	.8.79	2	NG	Shanghai	18 Oct 97
3:53.91			Yin Lili	CHN	11.11.79	3	NG	Shanghai	18 Oct 97
3:53.97			Lan Lixin	CHN	14.2.79	4	NG	Shanghai	18 Oct 97
3:54.52			Zhang Ling	CHN	13.4.80	5	NG	Shanghai	18 Oct 97
3:59.81			Wang Yuan	CHN	8.4.76	7	NG	Beijing	11 Sep 93
3:59.96		Zola	Budd	GBR	26.5.66	3	VD	Bruxelles	30 Aug 85
4:00.05			Lu Yi	CHN	10.4.74	8	NG	Beijing	11 Sep 93
4:01.71			Li Ying	CHN	24.6.75	4h2	NG	Beijing	10 Sep 93
4:03.45		Anita	Weyermann	SUI	8.12.77	1	Athl	Lausanne	3 Jul 96
4:03.5		Svetlana	Guskova	MOL	19.8.59	3	Kuts	Podolsk	13 Aug 78

1 MILE: 4:17.57 Zola Budd GBR 26.5.66 3 WK Zürich 21 Aug 85

2000 METRES: 5:33.15 Zola Budd GBR 26.5.66 1 London 13 Jul 84

3000 METRES

Mark		Name		Nat	Born	Pos	Meet	Venue	Date
8:28.83		Zola	Budd	GBR	26.5.66	3	GG	Roma	7 Sep 85
8:35.89		Sally	Barsosio	KEN	21.3.78	2	Herc	Monaco	16 Aug 97
8:36.45			Ma Ningning	CHN	1.6.76	4	NC	Jinan	6 Jun 93
8:40.08		Gabriela	Szabo	ROM	14.11.75	3	EC	Helsinki	12 Aug 94
8:42.39			Li Ying	CHN	24.6.75	8	NG	Beijing	13 Sep 93
8:44.1mx		Donna	Gould	AUS	10.6.66	-		Eugene	13 Jul 84
8:44.14		Worknesh	Kidane	ETH	21.11.81	6		Milano	7 Jun 00
8:44.57		Ayelech	Worku	ETH	12.6.79	3	APM	Hengelo	1 Jun 98
8:46.86			Zhang Linli	CHN	6.3.73	1	WJ	Seoul	20 Sep 92
8:47.35		Rose	Cheruiyot	KEN	21.7.76	3	McD	London	27 Aug 95

5000 METRES

Mark		Name		Nat	Born	Pos	Meet	Venue	Date
14:39.96			Yin Lili	CHN	11.11.79	4	NG	Shanghai	23 Oct 97
14:45.33			Lan Lixin	CHN	14.2.79	2h2	NG	Shanghai	21 Oct 97
14:45.71			Song Liqing	CHN	20.1.80	3h2	NG	Shanghai	21 Oct 97
14:45.90			Jiang Bo	CHN	13.3.77	1		Nanjing	24 Oct 95
14:46.71		Sally	Barsosio	KEN	21.3.78	3	VD	Bruxelles	22 Aug 97
14:47.40		Worknesh	Kidane	ETH	21.11.81	7	OG	Sydney	25 Sep 00
14:48.07		Zola	Budd	GBR	26.5.66	1	McV	London (CP)	26 Aug 85
14:53.44		Lydia	Cheromei	KEN	11.5.77	3	ISTAF	Berlin	1 Sep 95
14:56.22		Annemari	Sandell	FIN	2.1.77	4	DNG	Stockholm	8 Jul 96
14:57.79		Rose	Cheruiyot	KEN	21.7.76	3	ASV	Köln	18 Aug 95

10,000 METRES

Mark		Name		Nat	Born	Pos	Meet	Venue	Date
30:39.41			Lan Lixin	CHN	14.2.79	2	NG	Shanghai	19 Oct 97
30:39.98			Yin Lili	CHN	11.11.79	3	NG	Shanghai	19 Oct 97
30:59.92		Merima	Hashim	ETH	.81	3	NA	Heusden	5 Aug 00
31:11.26			Song Liqing	CHN	20.1.80	7	NG	Shanghai	19 Oct 97
31:15.38		Sally	Barsosio	KEN	21.3.78	3	WCh	Stuttgart	21 Aug 93
31:32.15			Feng Wenhui	CHN	21.1.74	9	NG	Beijing	8 Sep 93
31:40.42		Annemari	Sandell	FIN	2.1.77	6h2	OG	Atlanta	27 Jul 96
31:40.56		Delillah	Asiago	KEN	24.2.72	1	JPN Ch	Tokyo	15 Jun 91
31:41.09		Lydia	Cheromei	KEN	11.5.77	2	AfrCh	Belle Vue Mauricia	27 Jun 92
31:43.7		Masako	Chiba	JPN	18.7.76	1		Nobeoka	11 Nov 95

HALF MARATHON

Mark		Name		Nat	Born	Pos	Meet	Venue	Date
69:05		Delillah	Asiago	KEN	24.2.72	1	GWR	Exeter	5 May 91
69:21		Ann	Wamuchi	KEN	29.9.78	5		Tokyo	19 Jan 97
69:48		Yuka	Hata	JPN	3.2.79	4		Lisboa	15 Mar 98
71:00		Maiko	Kawasaki	JPN	27.2.74	2		Sapporo	18 Jul 93

MARATHON

Mark		Name		Nat	Born	Pos	Meet	Venue	Date
2:26:34			Wei Yanan	CHN	6.12.81	1		Beijing	15 Oct 00
2:27:30			Ai Dongmei	CHN	15.10.79	3	NG	Beijing	4 Oct 97
2:29:12		Chika	Horie	JPN	15.2.81	4		Nagano	9 Apr 00
2:30:15			Gu Dongmei	CHN	5.11.74	9		Tianjin	4 Apr 93
2:30:30		Akemi	Masuda	JPN	1.1.64	1		Eugene	11 Sep 83
2:31:03			Feng Wenhui	CHN	21.1.74	10		Tianjin	4 Apr 93
2:31:29			Ri Myong-sil	PRK	24.4.81	4		Beijing	9 Oct 99

Mark	Wind	Name		Nat	Born	Pos	Meet	Venue	Date

3000 METRES STEEPLECHASE

10:10.73		Melissa	Rollison	AUS	13.4.83	1	NC	Sydney	25 Feb 00

100 METRES HURDLES

12.84	1.5	Aliuska	López	CUB	29.8.69	2	WUG	Zagreb	16 Jul 87
12.88	1.5	Yelena	Ovcharova	UKR	17.6.76	2	ECp	Villeneuve d'Ascq	25 Jun 95
12.92	0.0		Sun Hongwei	CHN	24.11.79	6	NG	Shanghai	18 Oct 97
12.95	1.5	Candy	Young	USA	21.5.62	2	AAU	Walnut	16 Jun 79
12.95A	1.5	Cinnamon	Sheffield	USA	8.3.70	2	NCAA	Provo	3 Jun 89
13.00	0.7	Gloria	Kovarik	GDR	13.1.64	3h2	NC	Karl-Marx-Stadt	16 Jun 83
13.00	2.0	Lyudmila	Khristosenko	UKR	14.10.66	1	NC-j	Krasnodar	16 Jul 85
13.02	-1.7	Susanna	Kallur	SWE	16.2.81	1	WJ	Santiago de Chile	19 Oct 00
13.05	1.8	Heike	Terpe	GDR	4.10.64	4	OD	Berlin	8 Jun 83
13.07	0.2	Monique	Ewanje-Epée	FRA	11.7.67	2		Paris	22 Jul 86
13.07	1.1	Gillian	Russell	JAM	28.9.73	3	NC	Kingston	3 Jul 92
Wind assisted to 13.05									
13.02	4.1	LaVonna	Martin	USA	18.11.66	5	NCAA	Austin	1 Jun 85
13.03	2.5	Dominiqué	Calloway	USA	19.7.78	2h3	NC	Atlanta	21 Jun 96

400 METRES HURDLES

54.93		Li Rui	CHN	22.11.79	1	NG	Shanghai	22 Oct 97
55.20	Lesley	Maxie	USA	4.1.67	2	TAC	San Jose	9 Jun 84
55.20A	Jana	Pittman	AUS	9.11.82	1		Pietersburg	18 Mar 00
	55.63				1		Sydney	13 Feb 00
55.26	Ionela	Tîrlea	ROM	9.2.76	1	Nik	Nice	12 Jul 95
55.43		Li Shuju	CHN	20.7.81	1h2	NG	Shanghai	21 Oct 97
55.53	Radostina	Dimitrova	BUL	1.6.66	3	OD	Potsdam	21 Jul 84
55.65	Schowonda	Williams	USA	3.12.66	3	NCAA	Austin	31 May 85
55.72		Zheng Liyuan	CHN	1.4.74	5	NG	Beijing	9 Sep 93
55.72		Li Yulian	CHN	20.1.79	3h2	NG	Shanghai	21 Oct 97
55.74A	Myrtle	Simpson	RSA	18.2.64	2	NC	Bloemfontein	16 Apr 83
Drugs disqualification: 54.54		Peng Yinghua ¶	CHN	21.2.79	(2)	NG	Shanghai	22 Oct 97

HIGH JUMP

2.01	Olga	Turchak	KZK	5.3.67	2	GWG	Moskva	7 Jul 86
2.01	Heike	Balck	GDR	19.8.70	1	vURS-j	Karl-Marx-Stadt	18 Jun 89
2.00	Stefka	Kostadinova	BUL	25.3.65	1		Sofiya	25 Aug 84
2.00	Alina	Astafei	ROM	7.6.69	1	WJ	Sudbury	29 Jul 88
1.98	Silvia	Costa	CUB	4.5.64	2	WUG	Edmonton	11 Jul 83
1.98	Yelena	Yelesina	RUS	5.4.70	1	Druzh	Nyiregyháza	13 Aug 88
1.97	Svetlana	Isaeva	BUL	18.3.67	2		Sofiya	25 May 86
1.96A	Charmaine	Gale	RSA	27.2.64	1	NC-j	Bloemfontein	4 Apr 81
1.96i	Desislava	Aleksandrova	BUL	27.10.75	2	EI	Paris	12 Mar 94
1.96	Marina	Kuptsova	RUS	22.12.81	1	NC	Tula	26 Jul 00

POLE VAULT

4.45i	Yelena	Isinbayeva	RUS	3.6.82	1	NC	Volgograd	4 Feb 00
	4.40				2	NC	Tula	24 Jul 00
4.42	Yvonne	Buschbaum	GER	14.7.80	1		Rheinau-Freistett	27 Jun 99
4.32	Vanessa	Boslak	FRA	11.6.82	1		La Roche-sur-Yon	23 Sep 00
4.31	Monika	Götz	GER	15.6.81	1		Troisdorf	9 May 98
4.31	Amandine	Homo	FRA	24.12.80	3	GP-II	Saint-Denis	3 Jul 99
4.30	Annika	Becker	GER	12.11.81	2		Mannheim	18 Jun 99
4.30	Katerina	Badurová	CZE	18.12.82	3		Turnov	11 Jun 00
4.25	Bridgid	Isworth	AUS	15.10.81	4		Brisbane	11 Feb 00
4.21i	Monika	Pyrek	POL	11.8.80	1		Spala	13 Feb 99
4.20i	Vala	Flosadóttir	ISL	16.2.78	2		Reykjavik	25 Jan 97
4.20	Michaela	Boulová	CZE	2.8.81	2	OD	Jena	3 Jun 00
4.20	Martina	Strutz	GER	4.11.81	2		Mannheim	11 Aug 00

LONG JUMP

7.14	1.1	Heike	Daute	GDR	16.12.64	1	PTS	Bratislava	4 Jun 83
7.00	-0.2	Birgit	Grosshennig	GDR	21.2.65	2		Berlin	9 Jun 84
6.94	-0.5	Magdalena	Khristova	BUL	25.2.77	2		Kalamata	22 Jun 96
6.91	0.0	Anisoara	Cusmir	ROM	29.6.62	1		Bucuresti	23 May 81
6.90	1.4	Beverly	Kinch	GBR	14.1.64	*	WCh	Helsinki	14 Aug 83
6.88	0.6	Natalya	Shevchenko	RUS	28.12.66	2		Sochi	26 May 84
6.84		Larisa	Baluta	UKR	13.8.65	2		Krasnodar	6 Aug 83
6.82	1.8	Fiona	May	GBR	12.12.69	*	WJ	Sudbury	30 Jul 88

Mark	Wind	Name		Nat	Born	Pos	Meet	Venue	Date
6.81	1.6	Carol	Lewis	USA	8.8.63	1	TAC	Knoxville	20 Jun 82
6.81	1.4	Yelena	Davydova	KZK	16.11.67	1	NC-j	Krasnodar	17 Jul 85
Wind assisted									
7.27	2.2	Heike	Daute	GDR	16.12.64	1	WCh	Helsinki	14 Aug 83
6.93	4.6	Beverly	Kinch	GBR	14.1.64	5	WCh	Helsinki	14 Aug 83
6.88	2.1	Fiona	May	GBR	12.12.69	1	WJ	Sudbury	30 Jul 88
6.84	2.8	Anu	Kaljurand	EST	16.4.69	2		Riga	4 Jun 88

TRIPLE JUMP

Mark	Wind	Name		Nat	Born	Pos	Meet	Venue	Date
14.62	1.0	Teresa	Marinova	BUL	5.9.77	1	WC	Sydney	25 Aug 96
14.57	0.2		Huang Qiuyan	CHN	25.1.80	1	NG	Shanghai	19 Oct 97
14.52	0.6	Anastasiya	Ilyina	RUS	16.1.82	q	WJ	Santiago de Chile	20 Oct 00
14.46	1.0		Peng Fengmei	CHN	2.7.79	1		Chengdu	18 Apr 98
14.37i	-		Ren Ruiping	CHN	1.2.76	3	WI	Barcelona	11 Mar 95
		14.36	0.0			1	NC	Beijing	1 Jun 94
14.32	-0.1	Yelena	Lysak ¶	RUS	19.10.75	1		Voronezh	18 Jun 94
14.23			Li Jiahui	CHN	8.8.79	1	Asi-J	Bangkok	6 Nov 97
14.19	2.0	Anna	Pyatkh	RUS	4.4.81	1		Lapinlahti	16 Jul 00
14.18i	-	Yevgeniya	Stavchanskaya	UKR	25.9.81	2		Lvov	7 Feb 99
14.10	1.4		Wang Zhuri	CHN	.9.80	Q	NG	Shanghai	17 Oct 97
1**Wind assisted**									
14.83A	8.3		Ren Ruiping	CHN	1.2.76	1	NC	Taiyuan	21 May 95
14.43	2.7	Yelena	Lysak ¶	RUS	19.10.75	1	WJ	Lisboa	21 Jul 94

SHOT

Mark	Name		Nat	Born	Pos	Meet	Venue	Date
20.54	Astrid	Kumbernuss	GDR	5.2.70	1	vFIN-j	Orimattila	1 Jul 89
20.51i	Heidi	Krieger	GDR	20.7.65	2		Budapest	8 Feb 84
	20.24				5		Spilt	30 Apr 84
20.23	Ilke	Wyludda	GDR	28.3.69	1	NC-j	Karl-Marx-Stadt	16 Jul 88
20.12	Ilona	Schoknecht	GDR	24.9.56	2	NC	Erfurt	23 Aug 75
20.02		Cheng Xiaoyan	CHN	30.11.75	3	NC	Beijing	5 Jun 94
19.90	Stephanie	Storp	FRG	28.11.68	1		Hamburg	16 Aug 87
19.63		Wang Yawen	CHN	23.8.73	1		Shijiazhuang	25 Apr 92
19.57	Grit	Haupt	GDR	4.6.66	1		Gera	7 Jul 84
19.48	Ines	Wittich	GDR	14.11.69	5		Leipzig	29 Jul 87
19.42	Simone	Michel	GDR	18.12.60	3	vSU	Leipzig	23 Jun 79

DISCUS

Mark	Name		Nat	Born	Pos	Meet	Venue	Date
74.40	Ilke	Wyludda	GDR	28.3.69	2		Berlin	13 Sep 88
67.38	Irina	Meszynski	GDR	24.3.62	1		Berlin	14 Aug 81
67.00	Jana	Günther	GDR	7.1.68	6	NC	Potsdam	20 Aug 87
66.80	Svetla	Mitkova	BUL	17.6.64	1		Sofiya	2 Aug 83
66.60	Astrid	Kumbernuss	GDR	5.2.70	1		Berlin	20 Jul 88
66.34	Franka	Dietzsch	GDR	22.1.68	2		St Denis	11 Jun 87
66.30	Jana	Lauren	GDR	28.6.70	1	vURS-j	Karl-Marx-Stadt	18 Jun 89
66.08		Cao Qi	CHN	1.1.74	1	NG	Beijing	12 Sep 93
65.96	Grit	Haupt	GDR	4.6.66	3		Leipzig	13 Jul 84
65.22	Daniela	Costian	ROM	30.4.65	3		Nitra	26 Aug 84

HAMMER

Mark	Name		Nat	Born	Pos	Meet	Venue	Date
71.16	Kamila	Skolimowska	POL	4.11.82	1	OG	Sydney	29 Sep 00
68.40	Bianca	Achilles	GER	17.4.81	1		Dortmund	25 Sep 99
68.18	Ivana	Brkljacic	CRO	25.1.83	1		Pula	28 Apr 00
66.34	Yipsi	Moreno	CUB	19.11.80	1		Ciudad de México	29 May 99
65.88	Yunaika	Crawford	CUB	2.11.82	1		Las Tunas	3 Mar 00
65.48	Mihaela	Melinte	ROM	27.3.75	1		Bucuresti	25 Feb 94
64.72		Gu Yuan	CHN	9.5.82	2	NGP	Deyang	14 May 00
63.60	Sini	Pöyry	FIN	3.2.80	2	EJ	Riga	7 Aug 99
62.79	Manuela	Montebrun	FRA	13.11.79	1	NC-j	Dreux	11 Jul 98
62.02	Bronwyn	Eagles	AUS	23.8.80	1		Sydney	9 Dec 99

JAVELIN

Mark	Name		Nat	Born	Pos	Meet	Venue	Date
61.99		Wang Yaning	CHN	4.1.80	1	NC	Huizhou	14 Oct 99
61.79	Nikolett	Szabó	HUN	3.3.80	1		Schwechat	23 May 99
60.90		Liang Lili	CHN	16.11.83	2		Shenyang	18 Jun 99
Pre 1999 specification								
71.88	Antoaneta	Todorova	BUL	8.6.63	1	ECp	Zagreb	15 Aug 81
71.82	Ivonne	Leal	CUB	27.2.66	1	WUG	Kobe	30 Aug 85
70.12	Karen	Forkel	GDR	24.9.70	1	EJ	Varazdin	26 Aug 89
68.94	Trine	Solberg	NOR	18.4.66	1	vURS	Oslo	16 Jul 85

Mark	Wind	Name		Nat	Born	Pos	Meet	Venue	Date
68.38		Antje	Kempe	GDR	23.6.63	Q	EC	Athína	8 Sep 82
68.17		Osleidys	Menéndez	CUB	14.11.79	1	WJ	Annecy	29 Jul 98

HEPTATHLON

Mark	Wind	Name		Nat	Born	Pos	Meet	Venue	Date
6465		Sibylle	Thiele	GDR	6.3.65	1	EJ	Schwechat	28 Aug 83
		13.49	1.90	14.63	24.07		6.65	36.22	2:18.36
6436		Sabine	Braun	FRG	19.6.65	1	vBUL	Mannheim	9 Jun 84
		13.68	1.78	13.09	23.88		6.03	52.14	2:09.41
6428		Svetla	Dimitrova ¶	BUL	27.1.70	1	NC	Sofiya	18 Jun 89
		13.49/-0/7	1.77	13.98	23.59/-0.2		6.49/0.7	40.10	2:11.10
6403		Emilia	Dimitrova	BUL	13.11.67	6	GWG	Moskva	7 Jul 86
		13.73	1.76	13.46	23.17		6.29	43.30	2:09.85
6276		Larisa	Nikitina	RUS	29.4.65	8	URS Ch	Kiyev	21 Jun 84
		13.87/1.6	1.86	14.04	25.26/-0.7		6.31/0.1	48.62	2:22.76
6218		Jana	Sobotka	GDR	3.10.65	6	OD	Potsdam	21 Jul 84
		14.40	1.74	13.28	24.19		6.27	43.64	2:06.83
6198		Anke	Schmidt	GDR	5.2.68	7		Götzis	24 May 87
		13.80/0.9	1.72	13.32	23.82/0.3		6.63/2.0	35.78	2:12.44
6194		Camelia	Cornateanu	ROM	23.1.67	2	NC	Pitesti	8 Aug 86
		14.35	1.86	14.70	24.97		6.15	38.94	2:11.93
6187		Ionica	Domniteanu	ROM	8.1.69	1	Bal-j	Pitesti	26 Jul 87
		13.51	1.77	14.56	24.66		6.00	43.86	2:17.60
6185			Shen Shengfei	CHN	1.11.80	2	NG	Shanghai	18 Oct 97
		14.23/1.6	1.83	14.37	24.13/0.0		5.93/-1.1	44.50	2:17.81

Disqualified for positive drugs test

Mark	Wind	Name		Nat	Born	Pos	Meet	Venue	Date
6534		Svetla	Dimitrova	BUL	27.1.70	H	ECp	Helmond	16 Jul 89
		13.30/1.0	1.84	14.35	23.33/-2.2		6.47/-1.4	39.20	2:13.56

5000 METRES WALK

Mark	Wind	Name		Nat	Born	Pos	Meet	Venue	Date
20:31.4		Irina	Stankina	RUS	25.3.77	1	NC-wj	Adler	10 Feb 96
20:32.44		Claudia	Iovan	ROM	25.2.78	1	NC-j	Bucuresti	8 Aug 97
20:37.7			Jin Bingjie	CHN	1.4.71	1	NC	Hefei	3 Mar 90
21:01.8		Susana	Feitor	POR	28.1.75	1	SGP	Fana	8 May 93
21:02.6			Li Jingxue	CHN	10.2.70	2		Anshan	2 Sep 89

10 KILOMETRES WALK

Mark	Wind	Name		Nat	Born	Pos	Meet	Venue	Date
41:55		Irina	Stankina	RUS	25.3.77	1	NCw-j	Adler	11 Feb 95
41:57			Gao Hongmiao	CHN	17.3.74	2	NG	Beijing	8 Sep 93
42:44			Long Yuwen	CHN	1.8.75	3	NC	Shenzen	18 Feb 93
42:45			Li Yuxin	CHN	4.12.74	4		Shenzhen	18 Feb 93
42:47			Liu Hongyu	CHN	1.12.75	5	NC	Shenzen	18 Feb 93
42:50			Gu Yan	CHN	17.3.74	4	NG	Beijing	8 Sep 93
42:53.9t			Tan Lihong	CHN	13.2.73	6	NC	Jinan	15 Mar 92
43:07			Song Lijuan	CHN	1.2.76	6	NG	Beijing	8 Sep 93
43:10.4			Zhang Qinghua	CHN	6.3.73	8	NC	Jinan	15 Mar 92
43:15			Li Hong	CHN	1.6.79	7	NC	Zhuhai	10 Mar 96

4 X 100 METRES RELAY

Mark	Nat	Team	Pos	Meet	Venue	Date
43.38	USA	Joyce, A.Williams, Robinson, Buchanan	1	PAm-J	Tampa	11 Jul 99
43.44A	NGR	Utondu, Iheagwam, Onyali, Ogunkoya	1	AfrG	Nairobi	9 Aug 87
43.48	GDR	Breuer, Krabbe, Dietz, Henke	1	WJ	Sudbury	31 Jul 88
	Unsanctioned race 43.33	Breuer, Krabbe, Dietz, Henke	1		Berlin	20 Jul 88
43.69	JAM	Goulbourne, A Bailey, V Campbell, Sharpe	2	PAm-J	Tampa	11 Jul 99
43.87	URS	Lapshina, Doronina, Bulatova, Kovalyova	1	vGDR-j	Leningrad	20 Jun 87
44.04	CUB	Riquelme, Allen, López, Valdivia	2	WJ	Sudbury	31 Jul 88
44.07	FRA	Thélamon, Hurtis, Imalouan, Rapp	2	WJ	Annecy	2 Aug 98
44.16	GBR	Soper, DSmith, Fraser, Merry	2	WJ	Plovdiv	12 Aug 90
43.9 h	FRA	Ropars, Simioneck, Declerk, Sidibé	1		Thaon	12 Aug 89

4 X 400 METRES RELAY

Mark	Nat	Team	Pos	Meet	Venue	Date
3:28.39	GDR	Derr, Fabert, Wohlk, Breuer	1	WJ	Sudbury	31 Jul 88
3:30.38	AUS	Scamps, R Poetschka, Hanigan, Andrews	1	WJ	Plovdiv	12 Aug 90
3:30.45	USA	Harris, Pritchett, Downing, Vickers	1	WJ	Athína	20 Jul 86
3:30.72	BUL	Kireva, Angelova, Rashova, Dimitrova	3	v2N	Sofiya	24 Jul 83
3:31.09	JAM	Williams, Cole, Turner, Scott	2	WJ	Plovdiv	12 Aug 90
3:31.41	URS	Zakharova, Kiryukhina, Ponomaryova, Zhdanova	2	EJ	Utrecht	23 Aug 81
3:31.57	ROM	Petrea, Florea, Tîrlea, Nedelcu	1	WJ	Seoul	20 Sep 92
3:31.81	CUB	Casanova, Duporty, Limonta, McLeon	3	WJ	Plovdiv	12 Aug 90
3:32.35	RUS	Lukashevich, Khripankova, Chebykina, Pesnopevtseva	3	WJ	Athiná	20 Jul 86

MEN'S WORLD LISTS 2000

100 METRES

Mark	Wind	Name		Nat	Born	Pos	Meet	Venue	Date
9.86	-0.2	Maurice	Greene	USA	23.7.74	1	ISTAF	Berlin	1 Sep
9.87	-0.3		Greene			1	OG	Sydney	23 Sep
9.91	-0.4		Greene			1	GP	Osaka	13 May
9.93	0.3		Greene			1h4	NC	Sacramento	14 Jul
9.94	-1.0		Greene			1	WK	Zürich	11 Aug
9.95	1.0	Ato	Boldon	TRI	30.12.73	1	Athl	Lausanne	5 Jul
9.96	-0.2	Jon	Drummond	USA	9.9.68	2	ISTAF	Berlin	1 Sep
9.97	0.7		Greene			1	GGala	Roma	30 Jun
9.97	1.0	Francis	Obikwelu	NGR	22.11.78	2	Athl	Lausanne	5 Jul
9.97	-1.0	Obadele	Thompson	BAR	30.3.76	2	WK	Zürich	11 Aug
9.98	0.4	Coby	Miller	USA	19.10.76	1s1	NCAA	Durham	2 Jun
9.98	2.0		Obikwelu			1		Braga	21 Jun
9.99	0.4	Bernard	Williams	USA	19.1.78	2s1	NCAA	Durham	2 Jun
9.99	-0.3		Boldon			2	OG	Sydney	23 Sep
10.00	1.9		Miller			1	Pre	Eugene	24 Jun
10.00	0.7		Obikwelu			2	GGala	Roma	30 Jun
10.00	0.7		Boldon			3	GGala	Roma	30 Jun
10.00	0.2		Boldon			1rA	Bisl	Oslo	28 Jul
10.00	-1.0		Boldon			3	WK	Zürich	11 Aug
10.01	0.2	Mike	Marsh	USA	4.8.67	1	GP	Raleigh	17 Jun
10.01	0.5		Obikwelu			1r2	GP	Athína	28 Jun
10.01	-1.7		Greene			1	NC	Sacramento	15 Jul
10.01	0.4		Boldon			1	DNG	Stockholm	1 Aug
10.01	0.4		Thompson			2	DNG	Stockholm	1 Aug
10.01	-0.1		Greene			1	Herc	Monaco	18 Aug
10.01	-0.2	Tim	Montgomery	USA	28.1.75	3	ISTAF	Berlin	1 Sep
10.02	0.7	Brian	Lewis	USA	5.12.74	4	GGala	Roma	30 Jun
10.02	-1.0		Lewis			4	WK	Zürich	11 Aug
10.03	1.6		Montgomery			1		Atlanta	20 May
10.03	1.2		Williams			1	NCAA	Durham	3 Jun
10.03	0.4		Lewis			1h5	NC	Sacramento	14 Jul
		(31/10)							
10.04	1.8	Kenny	Brokenburr	USA	29.10.68	1		Durham	8 Apr
10.04	0.5	Terrence	Trammell	USA	23.11.78	1s2	NCAA	Durham	2 Jun
10.05A	1.0	Kaaron	Conwright	USA	8.8.76	1r2		Flagstaff	8 Jul
10.05	1.0	Christopher	Williams	JAM	15.3.72	1s1	NC	Kingston	21 Jul
10.06	1.8	Tony	McCall	USA	16.6.74	2		Durham	8 Apr
10.06	1.5	Donovan	Bailey	CAN	16.12.67	1h2		Luzern	27 Jun
10.06	0.4	Darren	Campbell	GBR	12.9.73	3	DNG	Stockholm	1 Aug
10.06	0.7	Abdul Aziz	Zakari	GHA	2.9.76	2	Gugl	Linz	8 Aug
10.07	0.4	Lindel	Frater	JAM	13.11.77	3s1	NCAA	Durham	2 Jun
10.07	-1.7	Curtis	Johnson	USA	24.12.73	2	NC	Sacramento	15 Jul
		(20)							
10.08	0.7	Bruny	Surin	CAN	12.7.67	1		Villeneuve d'Ascq	17 Jun
10.08	-0.8	Greg	Saddler	USA	29.6.74	1	GP	Athína	28 Jun
10.08	-0.3	Dwain	Chambers	GBR	5.4.78	4	OG	Sydney	23 Sep
10.09	1.4	Dennis	Mitchell	USA	20.2.66	2r1	Veniz	Haniá	14 Jun
10.09	1.0	Jason	Gardener	GBR	18.9.75	3	Athl	Lausanne	5 Jul
10.09	1.0	Llewellyn	Bredwood	JAM	30.4.76	2s1	NC	Kingston	21 Jul
10.10	1.6	Patrick	Johnson	AUS	26.9.72	1rA	GP II	Melbourne	2 Mar
10.10	1.0	Roland	Németh	HUN	19.9.74	4	Athl	Lausanne	5 Jul
10.10	1.9	Mark	Lewis-Francis	GBR-J	4.9.82	1B	BrGP	London (CP)	5 Aug
10.11	1.4	Marquis	Davis	USA	14.8.80	1		Knoxville	18 May
		(30)							
10.11	-0.3	Matt	Shirvington	AUS	25.10.78	1	OT	Sydney	18 Aug
10.11	0.3	Shingo	Kawabata	JPN	15.5.78	1	Coll Ch	Tokyo	2 Sep
10.12	1.9	Bryan	Howard	USA	7.10.76	3	Pre	Eugene	24 Jun
10.12	0.4	John	Capel	USA	27.10.78	2h5	NC	Sacramento	14 Jul
10.12	1.0	Dwight	Thomas	JAM	23.9.80	3s1	NC	Kingston	21 Jul
10.13A	0.6	Kim	Collins	SKN	5.4.76	1	WAC	El Paso	20 May
10.13A	0.2	André D	da Silva	BRA	26.11.72	1	IMSS	Ciudad de México	1 Jul
10.13	0.2	Ággelos	Pavlakákis	GRE	7.11.76	1	NC	Athína	8 Jul
10.13	1.1	David	Patros	FRA	11.9.77	1		Castres	27 Jul
10.13	1.3	Antoine	Boussombo	GAB	18.5.68	1h3	FRA Ch	Nice	4 Aug
		(40)							

Mark	Wind	Name		Nat	Born	Pos	Meet	Venue	Date
10.14	0.0	Elston	Cawley	JAM	24.6.76	1		Natchitoches	16 May
10.14	0.5	Patrick	Jarrett	JAM	2.10.77	3	NC	Kingston	21 Jul
10.14	0.1	Freddy	Mayola	CUB	1.11.77	1	NC	La Habana	24 Jul
10.15	1.1	Deji	Aliu	NGR	22.11.75	2		Lisboa (U)	5 Aug
10.15	1.9	Leonard	Myles-Mills	GHA	9.5.73	3h8	OG	Sydney	22 Sep
10.16	1.0	Chris	Chandler	USA	27.10.78	1	Quad	Los Angeles	1 Apr
10.16	1.6	Shawn	Crawford	USA	14.1.78	1r2	GaTech	Atlanta	20 May
10.16	0.5	Lawrence	Armstrong	USA	19.3.78	2h1	NCAA	Durham	1 Jun
10.16	0.4	Claudinei	da Silva	BRA	19.11.70	3	GPII	Helsinki	15 Jun
10.16	0.2	Jeff	Laynes	USA	3.10.70	5	GP	Raleigh	17 Jun
		(50)							
10.16	0.2	Konstadínos	Kedéris	GRE	11.6.73	2	NC	Athína	8 Jul
10.16	1.7	Stéphane	Buckland	MRI	12.1.77	1		Funchal	29 Jul
10.17A	1.6	Roland	Promesse	LCA	31.8.74	1		El Paso	6 May
10.17	0.4	Sultan	McCullough	USA	2.2.80	4s1	NCAA	Durham	2 Jun
10.17	0.5	Daymon	Carroll	USA	27.4.77	3s2	NCAA	Durham	2 Jun
10.17	1.6	Konstantin	Rurak	UKR	9.4.74	1h2	NC	Kiev	3 Aug
10.17	1.3	Venancio	José	ESP	19.4.76	1		Castellón	9 Aug
10.18	2.0	Jerome	Avery	USA	22.12.78	2	FresnoR	Fresno	1 Apr
10.18	0.7	Michael	Bennett	USA	13.8.78	1h1	Big 10	Iowa City	20 May
10.18	1.0	Floyd	Heard	USA	24.3.66	2		Chapel Hill	18 Jun
		(60)							
10.18	2.0	Rae	Edwards	USA-J	7.5.81	1	NC-j	Denton	23 Jun
10.18A	0.7	Andrew	Tynes	BAH	13.2.72	1		El Paso	24 Jun
10.18	0.3	Jonathan	Carter	USA	5.5.72	3h4	NC	Sacramento	14 Jul
10.18A	0.0	Vicente	de Lima	BRA	4.6.77	1		Medellín	29 Jul
10.19	0.9	Matthew	Quinn	RSA	17.4.76	1	Engen	Cape Town	31 Mar
10.19	1.8	Niconnor	Alexander	TRI	4.2.77	1r6	MSR	Walnut	16 Apr
10.19	1.6	Christian	Nsiah	GHA	25.12.75	1rA		Lapinlahti	16 Jul
10.19	-0.7	Marc	Blume	GER	28.12.73	1	NC	Braunschweig	29 Jul
10.19	1.8	Nicolas	Macrozonaris	CAN	22.8.80	1h2	NC	Victoria	12 Aug
10.19	0.3	Shingo	Suetsugu	JPN	2.6.80	2	Univ Ch	Tokyo	2 Sep
		(70)							
10.19	1.2	Francesco	Scuderi	ITA	4.10.77	1	NC	Milano	6 Sep
10.20	1.8	Ja'Warren	Hooker	USA	24.9.78	1h4	DrakeR	Des Moines	28 Apr
10.20A	0.9	Raphael R	de Oliveira	BRA	5.2.79	1		Bogotá	7 May
10.20A	0.7	Wayne	Johnson	JAM	17.1.75	2		El Paso	24 Jun
10.20	1.5	Shigeyuki	Kojima	JPN	25.9.79	1r2		Kobe	2 Jul
10.20	-0.6	Mickey	Grimes	USA	10.10.76	4h3	NC	Sacramento	14 Jul
10.20	0.4	Tim	Harden	USA	27.1.74	4h5	NC	Sacramento	14 Jul
10.20	1.0	Donovan	Powell	JAM	31.10.71	4s1	NC	Kingston	21 Jul
10.21	1.0	Kenneth	Andam	GHA	8.1.76	3h3	NCAA	Durham	1 Jun
10.21	1.0	Justin	Anderson	USA	9.10.79	1		Norwalk	4 Jun
		(80)							
10.21	0.5	Jarmiene	Holloway	USA	6.3.77	2		Nassau	9 Jun
10.21	2.0	Akihiro	Yasui	JPN	2.10.77	1		Otsu	24 Jun
10.21	2.0	Anil	Kumar	IND	28.8.73	1		Bangalore	5 Jul
10.21	0.4	Marcin	Nowak	POL	2.8.77	1h1	NC	Kraków	4 Aug
10.22	1.7	Tre	Gardner	USA	25.10.79	1		Waco	25 Mar
10.22A	0.6	Darvis	Patton	USA	4.12.77	2	WAC	El Paso	20 May
10.22	-0.9	Travis	Grant	USA	31.8.72	1		Indianapolis	24 Jun
10.22	0.6	Vincent	Henderson	USA	20.10.72	1r2	Athl	Lausanne	5 Jul
10.22		Sunday	Emmanuel	NGR	8.10.78	2	NC	Lagos	22 Jul
10.23	0.2	Chris	Donaldson	NZL	26.5.75	1q3	NC	Sydney	24 Feb
		(90)							
10.23	1.2	Randall	Evans	USA	26.10.70	1h2		Atlanta	3 Jun
10.23	1.4	Andrea	Colombo	ITA	14.2.74	1		Milano	3 Jun
10.23	2.0	Andra	Fifer	USA-J	22.5.81	2	NC-j	Denton	23 Jun
10.23A	1.0	Shomari	Wilson	USA	6.6.76	2r1		Flagstaff	8 Jul
10.23	0.8	Ricardo	Williams	JAM	29.9.76	2h6	NC	Kingston	20 Jul
10.24A	0.0	Patrick	van Balkom	NED	14.9.74	1rA	Engen	Pretoria	24 Mar
10.24	0.3	Cláudio	Souza	BRA	14.10.73	2		Manaus	25 Mar
10.24	1.8	Pierre	Browne	CAN	14.1.80	4	SEC	Baton Rouge	14 May
10.24	1.7	Aimé-Issa	Nthépé	FRA	26.6.73	2r1		Arles	3 Jun
10.24	1.1	Ian	Mackie	GBR	27.2.75	1		Bedford	4 Jun
		(100)							
10.24	-0.9	Joshua	Johnson	USA	10.5.76	2		Indianapolis	24 Jun
10.24A	0.2	Oumar	Loum	SEN	31.12.73	2	IMSS	Ciudad de México	1 Jul
10.24	0.2	Geir	Moen	NOR	26.6.69	1		Uddevalla	22 Jul
10.24	1.3	Stéphane	Cali	FRA	26.4.72	2h3	NC	Nice	4 Aug

Mark	Wind	Name		Nat	Born	Pos	Meet	Venue	Date
10.24	1.9	Ibrahim	Meité	CIV	18.11.76	4h8	OG	Sydney	22 Sep

10.25	0.8		Zhou Wei ¶	CHN	6.3.76	3 May
10.25	1.9	Masahiko	Fukunaga	JPN	25.7.79	27 May
10.25	1.9	Sayon	Cooper	LBR	26.4.74	1 Jul
10.25A	0.0	Milton	Mallard	USA	24.11.73	6 Jul
10.25	0.7	Anatoliy	Dovgal	UKR	29.1.76	15 Jul
10.25	1.9	Hiroyasu	Tsuchie	JPN	14.6.74	16 Jul
10.25	0.1	Luis	Pérez-Rionda	CUB	16.8.69	24 Jul
10.25	1.0	Stefano	Tilli	ITA	22.8.62	20 Aug
10.25	0.8	Koji	Ito	JPN	29.1.70	22 Sep
10.26	0.5	Leonard	Scott	USA	19.1.80	14 Apr
10.26	1.9	Daniel	Effiong	NGR	17.6.72	29 Apr
10.26	0.4	Sebastián	Keitel	CHI	14.2.73	29 Apr
10.26	1.9	Géza	Pauer	HUN	7.1.76	16 Jun
10.26A	0.2	Édson	Ribeiro	BRA	8.12.72	1 Jul
10.26A	1.0	Lorenzo	Hathorne	USA	27.9.72	8 Jul
10.26	1.1	Frédéric	Krantz	FRA	13.9.78	27 Jul
10.26	1.3	Patrick	Stevens	BEL	31.1.68	3 Aug
10.26	0.2	Paul	Di Bella	AUS	12.2.77	18 Aug
10.26	-0.1	Martin	Lachkovics	AUT	25.1.75	19 Aug
10.26	1.9	Renward	Wells	BAH	23.2.70	10 Sep
10.27A	-1.0	Lee-Roy	Newton	RSA	19.12.78	14 Apr
10.27	1.1	Marlon	Devonish	GBR	1.6.76	27 Apr
10.27		Vitaliy	Seniv	UKR	11.3.75	9 May
10.27	1.6	Leon	Gordon	JAM	1.7.74	22 Jun
10.27A	1.0	Ibukun	Akinremi	NGR	26.3.76	8 Jul
10.27	2.0	Tommi	Hartonen	FIN	12.5.77	16 Jul
10.27	0.5	Omar	Brown	JAM-J	21.6.82	21 Jul
10.27	0.5	Tommy	Kafri	ISR	3.10.76	23 Jul
10.27	1.9	Sergey	Bychkov	RUS	1.9.75	23 Jul
10.27	-0.6	Salem Mubarak	Al-Yami	KSA-J	9.2.82	17 Oct
10.28	1.8	Jeremy	Taylor	USA	2.3.77	18 Mar
10.28	0.0	Dwight	Phillips	USA	1.10.77	15 Apr
10.28	1.1	Nobuharu	Asahara	JPN	21.6.72	29 Apr
10.28	0.7	Joey	Harris	USA	18.12.80	17 Jun
10.28	0.3	Jonathan	Barbour	GBR	3.11.80	17 Jun
10.28	1.7	Ryszard	Pilarczyk	POL	5.11.75	15 Aug
10.29A	1.6	Nnamdi	Anusim	NGR	11.7.72	28 Jan
10.29	1.0	Kieran	Noonan	AUS	7.9.76	5 Feb
10.29	1.1		Yin Hanzhao	CHN	18.2.76	29 Apr
10.29	2.0	Nicholas	Johnson	USA-J	12.11.83	23 Jun
10.29	0.5	Yeóryios	Theorídis	GRE	12.12.72	28 Jun
10.29	0.6	Ramon	Clay	USA	29.6.75	5 Jul
10.29	0.5	Gideon	Jablonka	ISR	30.10.77	23 Jul
10.29	1.0	Bradley	McCuaig	CAN	12.12.70	12 Aug
10.29	0.0	Alexander	Kosenkow	GER	14.3.77	13 Aug
10.29	0.6	Christian	Malcolm	GBR	3.6.79	17 Sep
10.30	0.4	David	Baxter	AUS	27.3.77	15 Jan
10.30A	1.1	Vitaliy	Medvedev	KAZ	6.1.77	1 Apr
10.30	0.8	Chad	Bullett	USA	20.12.78	6 May
10.30	0.8	LeShaunte	Edwards	USA	26.7.79	6 May
10.30	1.3	Brandon	Evans	USA	30.10.79	20 May
10.30	1.6	LaCra	Jenkins	USA	22.10.77	20 May
10.30	1.0	Gerald	Williams	USA	24.2.78	4 Jun
10.30	0.7	Okechukwu	Ejiogu	NGR	.76	9 Jun
10.30	0.0	Ronny	Ostwald	GER	7.4.74	11 Jun
10.30	0.0	Tadashi	Imori	JPN	11.4.77	1 Jul
10.30A	1.4	Doug	Bignall	GBR	20.10.74	6 Jul
10.30	1.0	Wayne	Fenton	JAM	9.10.74	21 Jul
10.30	1.9	Dmitriy	Vasilyev	RUS	24.1.78	23 Jul
10.30	1.2	Jérôme	Éyana	FRA	5.7.77	4 Aug
10.30	-0.8	Glenroy	Gilbert	CAN	31.8.68	12 Aug
10.30	1.2	Andrea	Rabino	ITA	23.4.78	6 Sep
10.30	-0.2		Chen Haijian	CHN	5.4.80	20 Oct
10.31	1.6	Damien	Marsh	AUS	28.3.71	2 Mar
10.31A		Benedictus	Botha	NAM	21.6.78	15 Apr
10.31	1.7	Owusu	Dako	GBR	23.5.73	16 Apr
10.31	0.3	Marcus	Brunson	USA	24.4.78	6 May
10.31	1.4	Virgil	Maddox	USA	31.8.78	20 May
10.31	1.7	Marco	Torrieri	ITA	14.5.78	24 Jun
10.31	2.0	Christie	van Wyk	NAM	12.10.77	16 Jul
10.31	1.0	Garth	Robinson	JAM	11.10.70	21 Jul
10.31	0.5	Raymond	Stewart	JAM	18.3.65	21 Jul
10.31	1.3	Piotr	Balcerzak	POL	25.6.75	23 Jul
10.31	1.5	Yosuke	Kitagawa	JPN	4.7.75	29 Jul
10.32	1.7	John	Stone	USA	7.7.79	15 Apr
10.32		Charlton	Raphaela	AHO	23.7.77	16 Jun
10.32A		Leon	Settle	USA	19.10.75	17 Jun
10.32	1.6	Aleksandr	Smirnov	RUS	25.2.74	25 Jun
10.32	0.7	Maurizio	Checcucci	ITA	26.2.74	30 Jun
10.32	1.6	John	Ertzgaard	NOR	18.6.77	16 Jul
10.32	1.0	Aston	Morgan	JAM	18.2.69	21 Jul
10.32	0.6	Kevin	Braunskill	USA	31.3.69	23 Jul
10.32	-1.2	Kareem	Streete-Thompson	CAY	30.3.73	11 Aug
10.32	0.2	Jamal	Al-Saffar	KSA	24.10.71	30 Aug
10.32	1.9	Anninos	Marcoullides	CYP	8.2.71	22 Sep
10.33A	1.1	Johann	Venter	RSA	30.12.71	4 Feb
10.33	0.9	Adam	Basil	AUS	14.4.75	24 Feb
10.33	-2.3	Kareem	Kelly	USA-J	1.4.81	4 Mar
10.33	2.0	Franklin	Nwankpa	NGR	26.5.73	22 Apr
10.33	1.0	Albert	Agyemang	GHA	4.10.77	6 May
10.33	1.6	Curtis	Coleman	USA		20 May
10.33	1.1	Byron	Logan	JAM	19.7.74	22 Jun
10.33	1.3	Patrick	Schneider	GER	21.12.72	8 Jul
10.33	1.8	Bongelomba	Bongelo	COD	2.12.73	16 Jul
10.33	1.8	Lueyi	Dovy	GAB	10.11.75	29 Jul
10.33	2.0	László	Babály	HUN	13.11.77	2 Sep

(201) 10 men at 10.34w

Wind assisted to 10.23/10.33

9.88	4.5	Coby	Miller	USA	19.10.76	1		Auburn	1 Apr
9.88	2.1		Greene			1	VD	Bruxelles	25 Aug
9.90	2.8	Mike	Marsh	USA	4.8.67	1r7	MSR	Walnut	16 Apr
9.94	2.8	Bryan	Howard	USA	7.10.76	2r7	MSR	Walnut	16 Apr
9.96	2.8	Tim	Montgomery	USA	28.1.75	3r7	MSR	Walnut	16 Apr
9.96	3.4	Brian	Lewis	USA	5.12.74	1h1	Conseil	Fort-de-France	29 Apr
9.96	2.5		Lewis			1	Conseil	Fort-de-France	29 Apr
9.99	6.7	Raymond	Stewart	JAM	18.3.65	1		Abilene	11 May
10.00	4.8	Michael	Bennett	USA	13.8.78	1r1		Austin	6 May
10.00	2.6	Donovan	Bailey	CAN	16.12.67	1		Baton Rouge	19 May
10.01	2.1		Williams			2	VD	Bruxelles	25 Aug
10.02	3.6	Kim	Collins	SKN	5.4.76	1		Arlington	6 May
10.02	2.1	Antoine	Boussombo	GAB	18.5.68	1		La Chaux de Fonds	13 Aug
10.02	2.1		Boldon			3	VD	Bruxelles	25 Aug
10.04	2.1	Christopher	Williams	JAM	15.3.72	1r1		Azusa	8 Apr
10.04	2.6	Dennis	Mitchell	USA	20.2.66	1		Atlanta	3 Jun
10.04	3.1	Jason	Gardener	GBR	18.9.75	1		Gold Coast (RB)	10 Sep
10.05A	4.4	Wayne	Fenton	JAM	9.10.74	1r1		Flagstaff	6 Jul
10.05	2.2	Bruny	Surin	CAN	12.7.67	1	NC	Victoria	12 Aug
10.05	3.1	Ian	Mackie	GBR	27.2.75	2		Gold Coast (RB)	10 Sep
10.06A	4.0	Oumar	Loum	SEN	31.12.73	1rA		Pietersburg	18 Mar
10.06A	4.0	Patrick	van Balkom	NED	14.9.74	2rA		Pietersburg	18 Mar
10.07	3.4	Lawrence	Armstrong	USA	19.3.78	1	USTCA	Austin	22 Apr
10.07	2.6	Llewellyn	Bredwood	JAM	30.4.76	2		Atlanta	3 Jun

Mark	Wind	Name		Nat	Born	Pos	Meet	Venue	Date
10.09A	2.5	Nnamdi	Anusim	NGR	11.7.72	1rB		Pietersburg	18 Mar
10.09	5.0	Darvis	Patton	USA	4.12.77	2r1	TexR	Austin	8 Apr
10.10	2.5	Deji	Aliu	NGR	22.11.75	3	Conseil	Fort-de-France	29 Apr
10.10A	3.5	Lee-Roy	Newton	RSA	19.12.78	1s1	NC-23	Pietersburg	14 Apr
10.10	3.4	Freddy	Mayola	CUB	1.11.77	1		Maia	15 Jul
10.10	4.2	Jeff	Laynes	USA	3.10.70	2	MAI	Malmö	7 Aug
10.11	4.6	Dwight	Phillips	USA	1.10.77	1h7	TexR	Austin	7 Apr
10.11	2.6	Randall	Evans	USA	26.10.70	3		Atlanta	3 Jun
10.12	2.6	Vincent	Henderson	USA	20.10.72	2		Baton Rouge	19 May
10.12	3.0	Donovan	Powell	JAM	31.10.71	1		Houston	6 Jul
10.12	2.1	Patrick	Stevens	BEL	31.1.68	2		La Chaux de Fonds	13 Aug
10.13A	3.4	Kenneth	Andam	GHA	8.1.76	1		Salt Lake City	10 May
10.13	2.2	Okechukwu	Ejiogu	NGR	.76	1rC		Gavá	28 May
10.13	4.0	Luis	Pérez Rionda	CUB	16.8.69	1		La Laguna	15 Jul
10.14	4.9	Travis	Grant	USA	31.8.72	1r3	KanR	Lawrence	22 Apr
10.14	3.3	Floyd	Heard	USA	24.3.66	1r3		College Station	11 May
10.14	3.1	Geir	Moen	NOR	26.6.69	1		Fana	27 Jun
10.14	2.9	Konstantin	Rurak	UKR	9.4.74	1		Ljubljana	25 Jul
10.15	2.5	Jarmiene	Holloway	USA	6.3.77	4	Conseil	Fort-de-France	29 Apr
10.15	2.8	Paul	Di Bella	AUS	12.2.77	1r4		Gold Coast (RB)	5 Aug
10.16	3.1	Brandon	Evans	USA	30.10.79	1r1		College Station	15 Apr
10.17A	4.0	Matthew	Quinn	RSA	17.4.76	3rA		Pietersburg	18 Mar
10.17	4.8	Glenroy	Gilbert	CAN	31.8.68	4r1		Austin	6 May
10.17	3.3	Rohsaan	Griffin	USA	21.2.74	1r2		Austin	6 May
10.17	2.4	Mickey	Grimes	USA	10.10.76	1		San Diego	24 Jul
10.17	2.1	Needy	Guims	FRA	8.9.74	3rA		La Chaux-de-Fonds	13 Aug
10.18	2.8	Ja'Warren	Hooker	USA	24.9.78	1		Palo Alto	26 Mar
10.18	4.5	Leonard	Scott	USA	19.1.80	3		Auburn	1 Apr
10.18A	9.9	Nicolas	Macrozonaris	CAN	22.8.80	1r4		Flagstaff	3 Jul
10.18A	3.9	Milton	Mallard	USA	24.11.73	1r6		Flagstaff	3 Jul
10.18	2.2	Bradley	McCuaig	CAN	12.12.70	2	NC	Victoria	12 Aug
10.19	3.6	Andra	Fifer	USA-J	22.5.81	3r1		Arlington	6 May
10.19	2.2	Joshua	Johnson	USA	10.5.76	1r2		Arlington	6 May
10.19	6.7	Oscar	Meneses	GUA	12.5.77	2		Abilene	11 May
10.19	2.9		To Wai Lok	HKG	7.8.79	1		Hong Kong	4 Jun
10.19A	3.0	Aaron	Armstrong	USA	14.10.77	1r1		Flagstaff	3 Jul
10.19A	7.0	Xavier	James	BER		1r2		Flagstaff	4 Jul
10.19A	4.4	Shomari	Wilson	USA	6.6.76	2r1		Flagstaff	6 Jul
10.20	4.3	Akihiro	Yasui	JPN	2.10.77	1h1		Shizuoka	3 May
10.20	2.3	Omar	Brown	JAM-J	21.6.82	1=h1	NC	Kingston	20 Jul
10.20	4.5	Kieran	Noonan	AUS	7.9.76	2r1		Gold Coast (RB)	5 Aug
10.21A	4.0	Damien	Marsh	AUS	28.3.71	4rA		Pietersburg	18 Mar
10.21A	4.0	Kevin	Braunskill	USA	31.3.69	5rA		Pietersburg	18 Mar
10.21	5.0	Pierre	Browne	CAN	14.1.80	5r1	TexR	Austin	8 Apr
10.21A	5.0	Vitaliy	Medvedev	KAZ	6.1.77	2r1		El Paso	15 Apr
10.21	2.9	LaCra	Jenkins	USA	22.10.77	1h2	GaTech	Atlanta	20 May
10.21	w	Nicholas	Johnson	USA-J	12.11.83	1		Converse	8 Jul
10.22A	2.5	Adam	Basil	AUS	14.4.75	2rB		Pietersburg	18 Mar
10.22	3.7	Mario	Ponds	USA	18.3.79	1h3	TexR	Austin	7 Apr
10.22	4.6	Tomas	Alexander	USA	16.5.80	2h7	TexR	Austin	7 Apr
10.22A	5.0	Kareem	Streete-Thompson	CAY	30.3.73	3r1		El Paso	15 Apr
10.22	2.6	Tetsuya	Nakamura	JPN	7.1.73	2	Oda	Hiroshima	29 Apr
10.22	3.7	Ike	Okenwa	USA	18.4.80	1r1		Ann Arbor	13 May
10.22	5.3	Gary	Ryan	IRL	12.6.72	1		Castleisland	11 Jun
10.22A	3.9	Trevino	Betty	CAN	10.10.71	2r6		Flagstaff	3 Jul
10.22	2.9	Anatoliy	Dovgal	UKR	29.1.76	2		Ljubljana	25 Jul
10.22	3.0	Aimé-Issa	Nthépé	FRA	26.6.73	1h2	NC	Nice	4 Aug
10.23	2.8	Obadiah	Cooper	USA	8.3.70	4r7	MSR	Walnut	16 Apr
10.23	4.9	Marlon	Barnaby	JAM	26.10.79	2r3	KansR	Lawrence KS	22 Apr
10.23	w	Andre	Totton	USA	17.7.80	1		Great Bend	29 Apr
10.23A	4.8	Ibukun	Akinremi	NGR	.76	2r2		Flagstaff	3 Jul
10.23	2.7	Stefano	Tilli	ITA	22.8.62	1		Nuoro	12 Jul
10.23	2.7	Gentry	Bradley	USA	19.1.74	1		Hamburg	3 Sep

10.24	3.6	Virgil	Maddox	USA	31.8.78	6 May
10.24	3.9	Nikela	Ndebele	ZIM	.80	20 May
10.24	2.6	Frédéric	Krantz	FRA	13.9.78	4 Jun
10.25	3.3	David	Baxter	AUS	27.3.77	15 Jan
10.25	3.7	Mike	Price	USA	24.2.77	15 Apr
10.25	3.6	Kendrick	Campbell	USA	16.12.77	6 May
10.25A	8.1	Lorenzo	Hathorne	USA	27.9.72	4 Jul
10.25	3.1	Renward	Wells	BAH	23.2.70	10 Sep
10.26	4.5	Serge	Bengono II	CMR	3.8.77	7 Apr
10.26	w	Jamal	Williams	USA	4.6.77	15 Apr
10.26	2.4	Terry	Bowen	USA	15.9.71	13 May
10.26	2.9	Aston	Morgan	JAM	18.2.69	20 May
10.26	2.7	Daniel	Dubois	SUI	24.12.71	29 Jul
10.27	4.9	Carlos	Francis	USA-J	3.1.81	21 Apr

Mark	Wind	Name		Nat	Born	Date
10.27	2.6		Yin Hanzhao	CHN	18.2.76	29 Apr
10.27A	5.3	Eric	Frempong	CAN	1.10.75	3 Jul
10.27A	8.1	Michael	James	BER	.77	4 Jul
10.27A	7.0	Doug	Bignall	GBR	20.10.74	4 Jul
10.27	2.8	Maurizio	Checcucci	ITA	26.2.74	27 Aug
10.28	w	Saidric	Williams	USA-J	16.12.81	29 Apr
		10.24w	unconfirmed			13 Apr
10.28	4.3	Tatsuo	Sugimoto	JPN	25.11.70	3 May
10.28	3.2	Len	Herring	USA	4.12.78	6 May
10.28	6.7	Suleman	Tunde	NGR	11.9.77	11 May
10.28	3.1	Paul	Brizzel	IRL	3.10.76	27 Jun
10.28	3.5	Thierry	Lubin	FRA	10.11.70	2 Jul
10.28	5.6	Didier	Héry	FRA	18.1.78	14 Jul
10.28	2.7	Alexander	Kosenkow	GER	14.3.77	3 Sep
10.28	4.5	John	McAdorey	IRL	16.9.74	9 Sep
10.29	3.4	Percival	Spencer	JAM	24.2.75	22 Apr
10.29	2.7	Kofi	Owusu-Ansah	GHA		7 May
10.29	6.7	Blaine	Wiley	USA		11 May
10.29	2.4	E.J.	Jackson	USA	3.2.78	13 May
10.29	3.0	Aléxios	Alexópoulos	GRE	21.5.71	13 May
10.29	5.0	Albert	Hollis	USA-J	15.4.82	26 May
10.29	4.2	Marco	Torrieri	ITA	14.5.78	3 Jun
10.29A	4.4	Jason	Young	USA	30.8.72	6 Jul
10.29	3.3	Dmitriy	Vasilyev	RUS	24.1.78	23 Jul
10.29	2.9	Seun	Ogunkoya	NGR	28.12.77	27 Aug
10.29	4.9	Masahide	Ueno	JPN-J	10.9.83	21 Oct
10.30	4.5	Reggie	Austin	USA	21.1.77	17 Mar
10.30A	3.2	Caimin	Douglas	AHO	11.5.77	15 Apr
10.30	w	Roy	Williams	USA-J	.81	29 Apr
10.30A	3.5	Sean	Ingram	USA	15.11.79	29 Apr
10.30	2.2	Julian	Raeburn	TRI	18.9.78	6 May
10.30	6.7	Trafton	Rodgers	USA	3.2.72	11 May
10.31	2.7	Carlos	Garcia	USA	20.9.76	25 Mar
10.31	2.2	Anthony	Authorlee	USA	10.7.77	6 May
10.31	3.5	Nicola	Asuni	ITA	4.1.73	17 May
10.31	2.6	Michael	Green	JAM	7.11.70	3 Jun
10.31	2.3	Aleksandr	Ryabov	RUS	22.12.75	15 Jul
10.31	2.7	Takashi	Mogi	JPN-J	28.12.82	3 Aug
10.31	4.5	Darryl	Wohlsen	AUS	6.3.73	5 Aug
10.31	3.9	Yusuke	Omae	JPN-J	6.4.82	19 Aug
10.32	2.7	Clint	Crenshaw	USA	11.9.79	7 May
10.32A	2.3	Bobby	Cruse	USA	20.3.78	20 May
10.32	3.8	Rajeev	Balakrishnan	IND	31.3.71	10 Jun
10.32	3.4	Lueyi	Dovy	GAB	10.11.75	29 Jul
10.32	2.3	Hideki	Ishizuka	JPN	14.10.74	20 Aug
10.32	5.6	Matías	Roberto Fayos	ARG	28.1.80	18 Nov

10.33/10.34w 18 men

Best at low altitude

10.10 0.5 Conwright 1h1 NCAA Durham 1 Jun | 10.15 1.3 Collins 1 Brisbane (N) 3 Sep

10.25 0.3 A D da Silva 25 Mar | 10.28 0.0 de Lima 20 May | 10.34 -0.4 Ribeiro 21 Jun

10.27 1.8 Mallard 3 Jun | 10.30 0.4 R de Oliveira 29 Apr | 10.28w 2.1 16 Jun

10.31w 3.3 Frempong 6 May

Rolling start

Mark	Wind	Name		Nat	Born	Pos	Venue	Date
9.98	-0.7	Donovan	Bailey	CAN	16.12.67	1	Luzern	27 Jun
10.00w	2.2	Freddy	Mayola	CUB	1.11.77	1	Camagüey	10 Mar
10.22w	2.2	José A.	César	CUB	4.1.78	2	Camagüey	10 Mar
10.32w	2.2	Jorge	Chacón	CUB	15.1.80	3	Camagüey	10 Mar

Doubtful timing: 23 Jun, Sidoarjo (NG): (1.4) 1. Janis Raubaba INA 24.4.71 10.13, 2. Erwin Heru Susanto INA 24.6.74 10.16, 3. John Muray INA 6.6.78 10.13; 21 Apr, Troy: 1h2 Jon Underhill USA 10.34

Hand timing

Mark	Wind	Name		Nat	Born	Pos	Venue	Date
9.9	0.0	Joseph	Batangdon	CMR	29.7.78	1	Yaoundé	27 May
10.0		Anatoliy	Dovgal	UKR	29.1.76	1=	Kharkov	3 Jun
10.0		Vladislav	Dologodin	UKR	23.2.72	1=	Kharkov	3 Jun
10.0		Niconnor	Alexander	TRI	4.2.77	1	Port of Spain	16 Jun
10.1		Seun	Ogunkoya	NGR	28.12.77			31 Mar
10.1		Chinedu	Oriala	NGR-J	17.12.81			31 Mar
10.1		Chad	Miller	USA				28 Apr
10.1	1.9	Slobodan	Spasic	YUG	16.5.77			13 May
10.1A	0.0	Moumi	Sébergue	CHA	1.7.77			27 May
10.1	1.5	Yordan	Yovchev	BUL	9.8.79			3 Jun
10.1	-0.1	Andrés	Martínez	ESP	10.6.78			21 Jul
10.1A		Josef	van der Linde	RSA	8.4.79			4 Oct

Wind assisted

Mark	Wind	Name		Nat	Born	Pos	Venue	Date
10.0		Omar	Brown	JAM-J	21.6.82	1	Kirkvine	28 Jun
10.1	5.3	Morne	James	RSA	26.3.76			26 Feb
10.1	3.7	Mahasse	Cornelius	USA				1 Apr
10.1	w	Devon	Ward	USA	10.11.80			29 Apr
10.1	w	Kenny	Mannie	USA-J	.82			20 May
10.1	5.4	Lueyi	Dovy	GAB	10.11.75			18 Jun
10.1	5.4	Stéphane	Peccatus	FRA	12.3.77			18 Jun
10.1		Marvin	Anderson	JAM-J	12.5.82			28 Jun
10.1A		Jean-Jacky	Randriamamitiana	MAD	.73			6 Aug

Following drugs disqualification

Mark	Wind	Name		Nat	Born	Pos	Venue	Date
10.13	1.1	Gábor	Dobos ¶	HUN	21.2.76	1	Lisboa (U)	5 Aug

JUNIORS

Mark	Wind	Name		Nat	Born	Pos	Meet	Venue	Date
10.10	1.9	Mark	Lewis-Francis	GBR	4.9.82	1B	BrGP	London (CP)	5 Aug
		10.12 0.1 1 WJ Santiago 18 Oct	10.24 -0.3 1s1 WJ Santiago 18 Oct						
		10.13 -0.6 1q2 WJ Santiago 17 Oct	10.25 1.9 1 Loughborough 21 May						
		10.24 0.8 3 NC Birmingham 12 Aug	10.25w 2.2 1h1 WJ Santiago 17 Oct						
10.18	2.0	Rae	Edwards	USA	7.5.81		NC	Denton	23 Jun
		10.26 1.8 1 Starkville 15 Apr	11 performances by 5 juniors to 10.27						
10.23	2.0	Andra	Fifer	USA	22.5.81		NC	Denton	23 Jun
10.27	0.5	Omar	Brown	JAM	21.6.82	7	NC	Kingston	21 Jul
10.27	-0.6	Salem Mubarak	Al-Yami	KSA	9.2.82	1h3	WJ	Santiago de Chile	17 Oct
10.29	2.0	Nicholas	Johnson	USA	12.11.83	3	NC	Denton	23 Jun
10.33	-2.3	Kareem	Kelly	USA	1.4.81	1r2	Trojan	Los Angeles	4 Mar
10.34	-0.6	Darrell	Brown	TRI	11.10.84	2q2	WJ	Santiago de Chile	17 Oct
10.35	2.0	Jamar	Ervin	USA	15.6.83	1		South Brunswick	7 Jun
10.35	0.2	Ville	Vakkuri	FIN	29.9.81	1		Pudasjärvi	22 Jun
10.35	2.0	Robert	Foster	USA	15.5.81	4	NC	Denton	23 Jun
10.35!	1.8	Lukasz	Chyla	POL	31.3.81	1h2		Sopot	22 Aug
10.36	1.9	Leo	Bookman	USA	3.1.82	1r2		Austin	12 May
10.36	0.7	Justin	Gatlin	USA	10.2.82	3	NSch	Raleigh	17 Jun
10.39		Paul	Thompson	JAM	9.9.81	1s	CarC	St. Georges	22 Apr
10.39	-0.2	Ricardo	Alves	POR	10.1.81	1		Braga	29 Jul

Mark	Wind	Name		Nat	Born	Pos	Meet	Venue	Date
10.39	1.2	Tyrone	Edgar	GBR	29.3.82	1	v3N	Grosseto	7 Oct
10.40	1.9	Nick	Nichols	USA	16.12.81	1r1		Austin	13 May
10.40	0.1	Marc	Burns	TRI	7.1.83	3	WJ	Santiago de Chile	18 Oct
10.41	1.8	Bennie	Robinson	USA	6.7.82	1		Glendora	8 Apr
10.41		Ahmad	Carroll	USA	.83	1		Knoxville	9 Jul
Wind assisted to 10.35									
10.19	3.6	Andra	Fifer	USA	22.5.81	3r1		Arlington	6 May
10.20	2.3	Omar	Brown	JAM	21.6.82	1=h1	NC	Kingston	20 Jul
10.21	w	Nicholas	Johnson	USA	12.11.83	1		Converse	8 Jul
10.27	4.9	Carlos	Francis	USA	3.1.81	1		Lubbock	21 Apr
10.28	w	Saidric	Williams	USA	16.12.81	1		San Angelo	29 Apr
10.29	5.0	Albert	Hollis	USA	15.4.82	1		Modesto	26 May
10.29	4.9	Masahide	Ueno	JPN	10.9.83	1		Fukui	21 Oct
10.30	w	Roy	Williams	USA	.81	1		Lubbock	29 Apr
10.31	2.7	Takashi	Mogi	JPN	28.12.82	1s3		Gifu	3 Aug
10.31	3.9	Yusuke	Omae	JPN	6.4.82	1		Tokyo	19 Aug
10.33	w	Adam	Wooten	USA	18.3.82	2		Lubbock	29 Apr
10.34	3.4	Ricardo	Alves	POR	10.1.81	3		Maia	15 Jul
10.34	3.4	Kazuya	Kitamura	JPN	1.5.82	1r2		Kitakyushu	3 Nov
10.35	4.6	Lewis	Hyman	USA	11.10.83	1r2	TexR	Austin	8 Apr
10.35	6.5	David	Socrier	FRA	2.3.81	1s1	NC	Bondoufle	14 Jul
Hand timed									
10.1		Chinedu	Oriala	NGR	17.12.81	2		Enugu	31 Mar
10.0w		Omar	Brown	JAM	21.6.82	1		Kirkvine	28 Jun
10.1w		Kenny	Mannie	USA	.82	1		Dolton IL	20 May
10.1w		Marvin	Anderson	JAM	12.5.82	2		Kirkvine	28 Jun

200 METRES

Mark	Wind	Name		Nat	Born	Pos	Meet	Venue	Date
19.71A	1.8	Michael	Johnson	USA	13.9.67	1rA		Pietersburg	18 Mar
19.85	-0.3	John	Capel	USA	27.10.78	1	NC	Sacramento	23 Jul
19.88	-0.3	Floyd	Heard	USA	24.3.66	2	NC	Sacramento	23 Jul
19.89	0.3		Johnson			1h4	NC	Sacramento	22 Jul
19.91	0.0		Johnson			1		Sevilla	9 Jun
19.96	-0.3	Coby	Miller	USA	19.10.76	3	NC	Sacramento	23 Jul
19.97	0.3	Ato	Boldon	TRI	30.12.73	1	Athl	Lausanne	5 Jul
19.97	-0.9	Obadele	Thompson	BAR	30.3.76	1	Super	Yokohama	9 Sep
20.01	0.3	Francis	Obikwelu	NGR	22.11.78	2	Athl	Lausanne	5 Jul
20.02	1.7	Christopher	Williams	JAM	15.3.72	1r5	MSR	Walnut	16 Apr
20.02	0.9	Maurice	Greene	USA	23.7.74	1	GGala	Roma	30 Jun
20.03	-0.7		Capel			1s1	NC	Sacramento	23 Jul
20.03	-0.3	Bernard	Williams	USA	19.1.78	4	NC	Sacramento	23 Jul
20.04	1.7	Kenny	Brokenburr	USA	29.10.68	2r5	MSR	Walnut	16 Apr
20.04	1.1		B Williams			1s2	NC	Sacramento	23 Jul
20.08	-0.6		Obikwelu			1	GP	Athína	28 Jun
20.09	1.0	Shawn	Crawford	USA	14.1.78	1	NCAA	Durham	3 Jun
20.09	-0.6	Konstadínos	Kedéris	GRE	11.6.73	1	OG	Sydney	28 Sep
20.10	0.3		Thompson			3	Athl	Lausanne	5 Jul
20.10	-1.1		Capel			1s1	OG	Sydney	28 Sep
20.11	0.5		Thompson			1	Gugl	Linz	8 Aug
20.12	1.0		Miller			2	NCAA	Durham	3 Jun
20.13	0.3	Darren	Campbell	GBR	12.9.73	1q1	OG	Sydney	27 Sep
20.13	-0.2		Capel			1q3	OG	Sydney	27 Sep
20.14	0.3		Heard			1h2	NC	Sacramento	22 Jul
20.14	0.9		Capel			2h4	NC	Sacramento	22 Jul
20.14	-0.7		Johnson			2s1	NC	Sacramento	23 Jul
20.14	0.3		Kéderis			2q1	OG	Sydney	27 Sep
20.14	-0.6		Campbell			2	OG	Sydney	28 Sep
20.15	1.1		Heard			2s2	NC	Sacramento	23 Jul
		(30/13)							
20.17	1.7	Jon	Drummond	USA	9.9.68	3r5	MSR	Walnut	16 Apr
20.17A	0.6	André D	da Silva	BRA	26.11.72	1	IMSS	Ciudad de México	1 Jul
20.19	-0.2	Christian	Malcolm	GBR	3.6.79	2q3	OG	Sydney	27 Sep
20.20A	0.6	Wayne	Johnson	JAM	17.1.75	2	IMSS	Ciudad de México	1 Jul
20.21A	0.6	Oumar	Loum	SEN	31.12.73	3	IMSS	Ciudad de México	1 Jul
20.23A	0.9	Ja'Warren	Hooker	USA	24.9.78	1		Provo	6 May
20.23	0.6	Claudinei	da Silva	BRA	19.11.70	1	IbAm	Rio de Janeiro	21 May
		(20)							
20.23	0.2	Abdul Aziz	Zakari	GHA	2.9.76	1	AfCh	Alger	14 Jul

Mark	Wind	Name		Nat	Born	Pos	Meet	Venue	Date
20.26	1.2	Mike	Marsh	USA	4.8.67	2h1	NC	Sacramento	22 Jul
20.26	1.1	Brian	Lewis	USA	5.12.74	3s2	NC	Sacramento	23 Jul
20.26	-0.9	Shingo	Suetsugu	JPN	2.6.80	2	Super	Yokohama	9 Sep
20.27	1.0	Marquis	Davis	USA	14.8.80	1		Knoxville	18 May
20.29	0.6	Darvis	Patton	USA	4.12.77	2s2	NCAA	Durham	2 Jun
20.30	2.0	Brandon	Evans	USA	30.10.79	1r4		College Station	15 Apr
20.30	1.1	Ramon	Clay	USA	29.6.75	5=s2	NC	Sacramento	23 Jul
20.30	1.1	Kevin	Little	USA	3.4.68	5=s2	NC	Sacramento	23 Jul
20.31A	1.3	Kim	Collins	SKN	5.4.76	1h1	WAC	El Paso	19 May
		(30)							
20.31	0.2	Joseph	Batangdon	CMR	29.7.78	2	AfCh	Alger	14 Jul
20.31	-0.5	Stéphane	Buckland	MRI	12.1.77	1		Funchal	29 Jul
20.33	-0.9	Ricardo	Williams	JAM	29.9.76	3	Super	Yokohama	9 Sep
20.35	-0.6	Marcus	la Grange	RSA	12.12.77	1		Bellville	12 Feb
20.36A	1.8	Patrick	van Balkom	NED	14.9.74	3rA		Pietersburg	18 Mar
20.39	0.5	Dennis	Mitchell	USA	20.2.66	2	Gugl	Linz	8 Aug
20.40	-0.2	Patrick	Stevens	BEL	31.1.68	3	VD	Bruxelles	25 Aug
20.42	0.9	Rohsaan	Griffin	USA	21.2.74	2		Portland	25 Jun
20.43A	2.0	Darryl	Wohlsen	AUS	6.3.73	1rB		Pietersburg	18 Mar
20.43	1.3	Jerome	Young	USA	14.8.76	1		Durham	8 Apr
		(40)							
20.43	0.3	Marcin	Urbas	POL	17.9.76	5q1	OG	Sydney	27 Sep
20.44A	0.6	Randall	Evans	USA	26.10.70	1r2		Flagstaff	8 Jul
20.45	0.5	LeShaunte	Edwards	USA	26.7.79	2s1	NCAA	Durham	2 Jun
20.47	1.8	Derrick	Brew	USA	28.12.77	2	SEC	Baton Rouge	14 May
20.47	-0.2	Tommi	Hartonen	FIN	12.5.77	4q3	OG	Sydney	27 Sep
20.48	1.9	Brandon	Couts	USA	17.2.79	1	Big12	Columbia	21 May
20.48	0.4	Alessandro	Cavallaro	ITA	22.2.80	1		Torino	10 Jun
20.49	1.8	Pierre	Browne	CAN	14.1.80	3	SEC	Baton Rouge	14 May
20.49A	0.6	Antoine	Boussombo	GAB	18.5.68	5	IMSS	Ciudad de México	1 Jul
20.50	0.5	Sayon	Cooper	LBR	26.4.74	2rA		Kourou	21 May
		(50)							
20.50A		Leon	Settle	USA	19.10.75			Juarez	17 Jun
20.50	-0.3	Christophe	Cheval	FRA	25.2.71	1r1		Paris (C)	23 Jul
20.50	0.8	Christie	van Wyk	NAM	12.10.77	1	Karelia	Lappeenranta	13 Aug
20.50A	-0.4	Andrew	Tynes	BAH	13.2.72	1		El Paso	26 Aug
20.51	0.8	Melvin	Lister	USA	29.8.77	1r1		Fayetteville	22 Apr
20.51		Gentry	Bradley	USA	19.1.74	1		Ponce	10 Jun
20.51	-0.3	David	Patros	FRA	11.9.77	2r1		Paris (C)	23 Jul
20.51	0.1	Marcin	Nowak	POL	2.8.77	2	NC	Kraków	6 Aug
20.53	0.7	Dominic	Demeritte	BAH	22.2.78	1	NC	Nassau	22 Jul
20.54A	2.0	Paul	Brizzel	IRL	3.10.76	2rB		Pietersburg	18 Mar
		(60)							
20.56	0.0	Koji	Ito	JPN	29.1.70	4q2	OG	Sydney	27 Sep
20.57A	2.0	David	Baxter	AUS	27.3.77	3rB		Pietersburg	18 Mar
20.57A	2.0	Kevin	Braunskill	USA	31.3.69	4rB		Pietersburg	18 Mar
20.57	0.8	Rae	Edwards	USA-J	7.5.81	1	NC-j	Denton	24 Jun
20.57	-0.9	Masahiko	Fukunaga	JPN	25.7.79	5	Super	Yokohama	9 Sep
20.58	1.1	Chris	Donaldson	NZL	26.5.75	2	GP II	Melbourne	2 Mar
20.58A	-0.1	Vicente	de Lima	BRA	4.6.77	1		Medellín	29 Jul
20.58	0.0	Dwight	Thomas	JAM	23.9.80	5q2	OG	Sydney	27 Sep
20.59A	-0.6	Paul	Gorries	RSA-J	28.2.81	1r1	vAUS	Roodepoort	13 Mar
20.59	1.2	Leonard	Scott	USA	19.1.80	3r2		Auburn	1 Apr
		(70)							
20.59	0.2	Michael	Mitchell	USA-J	.81	1		Bakersfield	20 May
20.59	1.9	Chris	Chandler	USA	27.10.78	2	Big 12	Columbia MO	21 May
20.59	0.9	Marlon	Devonish	GBR	1.6.76	5	GGala	Roma	30 Jun
20.59	-0.7	Iván	García	CUB	29.2.72	1		Madrid	18 Jul
20.60	1.9	Georkis	Vera	CUB	22.5.75	1		La Habana	11 Feb
20.60	1.9	JJ (Joshua)	Johnson	USA	10.5.76	1rC		Arlington	6 May
20.60A	0.5	Sanderlei	Parrela	BRA	7.10.74	1		Bogotá	7 May
20.60	0.7	Renward	Wells	BAH	23.2.70	3	NC	Nassau	22 Jul
20.61A	0.6	Jake	Jensen	USA	29.5.74	2r1		Flagstaff	8 Jul
20.61	-0.4	Martin	Lachkovics	AUT	25.1.75	1	NC	Wien	20 Aug
		(80)							
20.62A	-0.6	Matt	Shirvington	AUS	25.10.78	2r1		Roodepoort	13 Mar
20.62	0.3		Xu Zizhou	CHN-J	8.1.81	1	NGP	Shanghai	19 Apr
20.62	0.4	Bobby	Cruse	USA	20.3.78	1r2		Akron	13 May
20.62	-0.2	Greg	Saddler	USA	29.6.74	2r1	Veniz	Haniá	14 Jun
20.63A	1.8	Damien	Marsh	AUS	28.3.71	5rA		Pietersburg	18 Mar

Mark	Wind	Name		Nat	Born	Pos	Meet	Venue	Date
20.63	1.8	Aaron	Armstrong	USA	14.10.77	5	SEC	Baton Rouge	14 May
20.63	1.8	Daymon	Carroll	USA	27.4.77	6	SEC	Baton Rouge	14 May
20.63	0.0	Elston	Cawley	JAM	24.6.76	1h5		Natchitoches	15 May
20.63		Julian	Raeburn	TRI	18.9.78	1	NC	Port of Spain	17 Jun
20.63	2.0	Dave	Dopek	USA	8.2.73	1		Indianapolis	1 Jul
		(90)							
20.63	-0.3	Frédéric	Krantz	FRA	13.9.78	3r1		Paris (C)	23 Jul
20.63	1.2	Geir	Moen	NOR	26.6.69	1		Uddevalla	23 Jul
20.64	0.2	Jarmiene	Holloway	USA	6.3.77	1		Nassau	9 Jun
20.64	-1.2	Julian	Golding	GBR	17.2.75	2	GDN	Villeneuve d'Ascq	17 Jun
20.64	-0.3	Aimé-Issa	Nthépé	FRA	26.6.73	4r1		Paris (C)	23 Jul
20.65	1.7	Marcus	Adam	GBR	28.2.68	1r1		Ljubljana	25 Jul
20.66	1.1	Michael	Bennett	USA	13.8.78	1r1	USTCA	Tempe	18 Mar
20.66	0.8	Lawrence	Armstrong	USA	19.3.78	1h3	UCTA	Austin	21 Apr
20.66A	1.3	Kendrick	Campbell	USA	16.12.77	2h1	WAC	El Paso	19 May
20.67	0.5	Leo	Bookman	USA-J	3.1.82	1r4		Austin	12 May
		(100)							
20.67	1.9	Petko	Yankov	BUL	6.10.77	1r1	Papaf	Kalamáta	4 Jun
20.67	0.4	Alessandro	Attene	ITA	10.9.77	1		Rieti	25 Jun
20.67A	0.2	Lorenzo	Hathorne	USA	27.9.72	1r2		Flagstaff	8 Jul

20.68	0.0	Patrick	Johnson	AUS	26.9.72	30 Jan
20.68	1.9	Robert	Williams	USA	30.8.80	8 Apr
20.68	1.7	Jeremy	Taylor	USA	2.3.77	16 Apr
20.68A	0.9	Kenneth	Andam	GHA	8.1.76	20 May
20.68A	1.0	Lindel	Frater	JAM	13.11.77	20 May
20.68	-0.2	Tim	Montgomery	USA	28.1.75	14 Jun
20.68	-0.6	Sergey	Osovich	UKR	16.12.73	28 Jun
20.68	1.8	Olivier	Borderan	FRA	20.2.76	13 Aug
20.69A	-0.1	Matthew	Quinn	RSA	17.4.76	4 Feb
20.69A	2.0	Andre	Morris	USA	26.10.72	18 Mar
20.69	-1.3	Roland	Németh	HUN	19.9.74	22 Jun
20.69	0.5	Anastásios	Goúsis	GRE	7.7.79	9 Jul
20.69	0.6	Uchenna	Emedolu	NGR	17.9.76	13 Aug
20.69	-0.5	Marcin	Jedrusinski	POL-J	28.8.81	20 Oct
20.70	1.0	Tony	McCall	USA	16.6.74	1 Apr
20.70	1.5	Travis	Grant	USA	31.8.72	13 May
20.70		Curtis	Perry	USA	26.10.74	14 May
20.70	1.0	Russell	Frye	USA	25.3.79	18 May
20.71	1.6	Rico	Tilley	USA	10.2.77	14 May
20.71	0.3	Anthuan	Maybank	USA	30.12.69	5 Jul
20.71	1.4	Alejandro	Cárdenas	MEX	4.9.74	15 Jul
20.71A		Ezra	Sambu	KEN	4.9.78	22 Jul
20.71	-0.3	Aléxandros	Alexópoulos	GRE	21.5.71	30 Jul
20.71	0.7	John	Ertzgaard	NOR	18.6.77	13 Aug
20.71	0.4	Anninos	Marcoullides	CYP	8.2.71	27 Sep
20.72	-1.2	Pat	Dwyer	AUS	3.11.77	22 Jan
20.72	-0.3	Jimmy	Melfort	FRA	28.12.78	27 Jun
20.72	0.6	Mathias	Mertens	GER	24.11.80	2 Jul
20.72	0.1	Piotr	Balcerzak	POL	25.6.75	6 Aug
20.72A	-0.4	Vitaliy	Medvedev	KAZ	6.1.77	26 Aug
20.72	-1.1	Nobuharu	Asahara	JPN	21.6.72	27 Aug
20.73	-1.7	Anil	Kumar	IND	28.8.73	17 Jul
20.73	0.8	Christian	Nsiah	GHA	25.12.75	13 Aug
20.74A	0.9	Thobias	Akwenye	NAM	27.3.78	20 May
20.74	0.2	Chris	Hughes	USA		20 May
20.74	-0.7	Venancio	José	ESP	19.4.76	18 Jul
20.74	1.8	Didier	Héry	FRA	18.1.78	13 Aug
20.74	-0.8	Hirofumi	Nakagawa	JPN	3.1.80	9 Sep
20.75A	1.4	Lee-Roy	Newton	RSA	19.12.78	15 Apr
20.75	1.7	Martin	Brinarsky	SVK	23.1.76	25 Jul
20.75	2.0	Johan	Engberg	SWE-J	11.10.81	7 Aug
20.76	0.4	Sebastián	Keitel	CHI	14.2.73	14 May
20.76	-0.2	Marián	Vanderka	SVK	18.4.72	22 Jun
20.76A	0.6	Edson	Ribeiro	BRA	8.12.72	1 Jul
20.76	0.2	Andrea	Colombo	ITA	14.3.74	23 Jul
20.76	0.0	Tim	Benjamin	GBR-J	2.5.82	5 Aug
20.77	1.7	Brian	Bridgewater	USA	7.9.70	16 Apr
20.77	0.7	Kazuhiro	Takahashi	JPN	27.7.76	10 Jun
20.77	-1.3	Sunday	Emmanuel	NGR	8.10.78	22 Jun
20.78A		Sherwin	Vries	NAM	22.3.80	15 Apr
20.78	1.7	Andra	Fifer	USA-J	22.5.81	6 May
20.78	0.5	Brendan	Christian	USA-J	.84?	12 May
20.78	1.6	Corey	Nelson	USA	9.10.77	13 May
20.78	-0.1	Shingo	Kawabata	JPN	15.5.78	21 May
20.78	-1.1	Deji	Aliu	NGR	22.11.75	24 May
20.78	0.0	Vitor	Jorge	POR	28.11.74	28 Jun
20.78	1.2	Daniel	Batman	AUS-J	20.3.81	14 Jul
20.78	-1.5	Dwain	Chambers	GBR	5.4.78	12 Aug
20.79	0.6	Chad	Bullett	USA	20.12.78	2 Jun
20.79	2.0	Thomas	Müller	GER	9.3..78	20 Aug
20.79	0.4	Sittichai	Suwonprateep	THA	17.11.80	31 Aug
20.79	0.9	Troy	Douglas	NED	30.11.62	3 Sep
20.79	0.3	Frank	Fredericks	NAM	2.10.67	3 Sep
20.79	-0.8	Jonathan	Barbour	GBR	3.11.80	9 Sep
20.79	0.4	Hideki	Ishizuka	JPN	14.10.74	7 Oct
20.80A	0.5	Augusto de	Oliveira Santos	BRA	13.10.72	7 May
20.80		Niconnor	Alexander	TRI	4.2.77	17 Jun
20.80	0.5	Anastásios	Poulióglou	GRE	24.5.77	9 Jul
20.80	1.7	Allyn	Condon	GBR	24.8.74	25 Jul
20.80	1.1	Enefiok	Udo-Obong	NGR-J	22.5.82	26 Aug
20.81		Clement	Chukwu	NGR	7.7.73	5 May
20.81	1.0	Andre	Ammons	USA	12.11.78	20 May
20.81	1.0	Jermaine	Joseph	CAN	25.7.80	20 May
20.81A	0.6	Rod	Tolbert	USA	11.6.67	8 Jul
20.81	0.4	Mohamed	Al-Houti	OMN	8.9.72	31 Aug
20.81	1.2	Yusuke	Omae	JPN-J	6.4.82	20 Oct
20.82	2.0	Robert	Staten	USA	19.5.77	11 May
20.82	-0.6	Marc	Blume	GER	28.12.73	30 Jul
20.82	0.4	Heber	Viera	URU	29.4.79	27 Sep
20.83A	2.0	Corné	du Plessis	RSA	20.3.78	18 Mar
20.83	0.9	Milton	Mallard	USA	24.11.73	25 Jun
20.83	1.2	Shintaro	Sato	JPN	20.8.80	26 Aug
20.83	-0.8	John	Stewart	GBR	30.12.79	9 Sep
20.84	1.2	Marvin	Anderson	JAM-J	12.5.82	20 Oct
20.85	1.3	Jamel	Ashley	USA		25 Mar
20.85	1.2	Albert	Agyemang	GHA	4.10.77	13 May
20.85	1.4	Robert	Foster	USA-J	15.5.81	13 May
20.85	-0.6	Jeff	Laynes	USA	3.10.70	22 Jul
20.85		Ambrose	Ezenwa	NGR	10.4.77	22 Jul
20.85	2.0	Jerome	Davis	USA	20.8.77	7 Aug
20.85	0.2	Jimmy	Pino	COL	10.0.70	10 Aug
20.85	0.0	Robert	Mackowiak	POL	13.5.70	6 Sep
		(195)				

Indoors

20.55i	Leonard	Scott	USA	19.1.80	4	NCAA	Fayetteville	10 Mar
20.66i	Petko	Yankov	BUL	6.10.77	1rA	Gaz	Liévin	13 Feb

Wind assisted

19.93	2.1	Maurice	Greene	USA	23.7.74	1	Pre	Eugene	24 Jun
20.10		Mike	Marsh	USA	4.8.67	1		Houston	6 May
20.12	2.1		Brokenburr			1	Pre	Eugene	24 Jun
20.17A	5.0	Leon	Settle	USA	19.10.75	2r1		El Paso	15 Apr

Mark	Wind	Name		Nat	Born	Pos	Meet	Venue	Date
20.18	3.5	Kim	Collins	SKN	5.4.76	1		Arlington	6 May
20.19	2.3	Oumar	Loum	SEN	31.12.73	1		La Chaux de Fonds	13 Aug
20.25	2.3	Patrick	Stevens	BEL	31.1.68	2		La Chaux de Fonds	13 Aug
20.31	2.4	Jerome	Young	USA	14.8.76	1h1		Durham	8 Apr
20.34	3.7	LeShaunte	Edwards	USA	26.7.79	1		Akron	6 May
20.35	2.4	Tony	McCall	USA	16.6.74	2h1		Durham	8 Apr
20.35	2.3	Antoine	Boussombo	GAB	18.5.68	3		La Chaux de Fonds	13 Aug
20.37	2.4	Elston	Cawley	JAM	24.6.76	1		Natchitoches	16 May
20.37A	2.1	Milton	Mallard	USA	24.11.73	1r1		Flagstaff	6 Jul
20.38	3.7	Chad	Bullett	USA	20.12.78	2		Akron	6 May
20.41	3.1	Rohsaan	Griffin	USA	21.2.74	1		Austin	6 May
20.41A	2.1	Jake	Jensen	USA	29.5.74	2r1		Flagstaff	6 Jul
20.42A	2.3	Aaron	Armstrong	USA	14.10.77	2r3		Flagstaff	3 Jul
20.42	3.2	Dominic	Demeritte	BAH	22.2.78	1r3		Montauban	15 Aug
20.44	4.3	Lawrence	Armstrong	USA	19.3.78	1	USTCA	Austin	22 Apr
20.52	2.1	Curtis	Perry	USA	26.10.74	5	Pre	Eugene	24 Jun
20.52A	2.2	Geno	White	USA	10.3.78	1r2		Flagstaff	3 Jul
20.55A	2.4	Matthew	Quinn	RSA	17.4.76	1rA		Rustenburg	22 Jan
20.55	4.0	Niconnor	Alexander	TRI	4.2.77	1		San Angelo	22 Apr
20.56	4.3	Chris	Chandler	USA	27.10.78	2	UCTA	Austin	22 Apr
20.56	2.1	Tim	Montgomery	USA	28.1.75	2r1	GaTech	Atlanta	20 May
20.56	4.4	Kaaron	Conwright	USA	8.8.76	1		Moscow ID	20 May
20.58	2.3	Martin	Lachkovics	AUT	25.1.75	5rA		La Chaux-de-Fonds	13 Aug
20.60	2.3	Alex	Ménal	FRA	9.8.72	6rA		La Chaux-de-Fonds	13 Aug
20.61	4.1	Julian	Raeburn	TRI	18.9.78	1		Newcastle	9 Sep
20.62	4.5	Shane	Niemi	CAN	2.6.78	2	NC	Victoria	13 Aug
20.62	3.2	Venancio	José	ESP	19.4.76	2r3		Montauban	15 Aug
20.63A	4.0	Rod	Tolbert	USA	11.6.67	1r2		Flagstaff	6 Jul
20.64	3.8	Starr	Roberts	USA	24.7.79	1		Fargo ND	8 Apr
20.64	3.7	Rah'Sheen	Clay	USA	18.10.76	3	USTCA	Akron	6 May
20.64A	4.0	Andrew	Pierce	USA	8.6.79	2r2		Flagstaff	6 Jul
20.65A	4.8	Paul	Lewis	USA	30.10.77	2r1		Flagstaff	3 Jul
20.66	w	Anthony	Authorlee	USA	10.7.77	2r1		Houston	6 May
20.66	5.4	Clement	Chukwu	NGR	7.7.73	2r1	Owens	Columbus	7 May
20.66	2.5	Gabriel	Burnett	BAR	20.9.75	1r1		Durham	10 May

20.68	5.4	Kofi	Owusu-Ansah	GHA		7 May
20.68	2.9	Ian	Mackie	GBR	27.2.75	29 May
20.68	4.1	Martin	Brinarsky	SVK	23.1.76	31 Jul
20.68	2.5	Hideki	Ishizuka	JPN	14.10.74	19 Aug
20.69	3.8	Hirofumi	Nakagawa	JPN	3.1.80	3 May
20.69	4.4	Tawanda	Chiwira	ZIM	27.8.74	20 May
20.70	3.1	Bruny	Surin	CAN	12.7.67	6 May
20.71	2.3	Jorge	Chacón	CUB-J	15.1.80	26 Feb
20.71	2.4	Chris	Stewart	USA		16 May
20.73	2.1	Tony	Wheeler	USA	19.1.75	18 Mar
20.73	2.4	Andra	Fifer	USA-J	22.5.81	16 May
20.73	3.9	Ronny	Ostwald	GER	7.4.74	27 May
20.74	w	Andre	Totton	USA	17.7.80	29 Apr
20.75	2.1	Bryan	Harrison	USA	12.10.78	21 May
20.76	2.5	Fabian	Moore	BAR	.79	10 May
20.76		Darrell	Brown	TRI-J	11.10.84	21 May
20.77	2.8	Alvin	Harrison	USA	20.1.74	26 Mar
20.78	3.7	Martin	Jackson	USA		6 May
20.79	3.2	DaBryan	Blanton	USA-J	.82	13 May
20.80A	6.3	Ronald	Promesse	LCA	31.8.74	15 Apr
20.81	3.1	Glenroy	Gilbert	CAN	31.8.68	6 May
20.81	2.9	Julien	Arame	FRA	12.4.80	16 Jul
20.82	2.9	Marco	Torrieri	ITA	14.5.78	4 Jun
20.82	3.2	Thierry	Lubin	FRA	10.11.70	15 Aug
20.83	2.1	Angelo	Taylor	USA	29.12.78	20 May
20.83A	2.3	Eric	Frempong	CAN	1.10.75	3 Jul
20.84	3.4	Savante	Stringfellow	USA	6.11.78	12 May
20.84	2.3	Prodromos	Katsantonis	CYP	20.10.75	2 Jul
20.84	5.1	Carlos	Gats	ARG	11.12.69	15 Jul

Best at low altitude

20.33	1.5	Hooker	2		Tempe	15 Apr
20.35	0.1	A D da Silva	1		Velenje	23 Jun
20.43	1.9	Loum	1	NC	Dakar	11 Jun
20.55	0.7	Tynes	2	NC	Nassau	22 Jul
20.08	-0.0	de Lima				8 Aug
20.73	0.2	Settle				9 Jun
20.83	0.0	D Marsh				30 Jan
20.57	1.1	Wohlsen	1	GPII	Melbourne	2 Mar
20.62	-0.5	Gorries	1s2	WJ	Santiago	20 Oct
20.65	0.5	Brizzel	1rB		Ljubljana	25 Jul
20.66	2.0	Braunskill	2		Indianapolis	1 Jul
	20.61w 3.6		1		Nitra	26 Aug
20.49w	2.1	R Evans	1r4		Atlanta	3 Jun

Rolling start: 20.06 0.5 Brian Lewis USA 5.12.74 1 Kourou 14 May

Doubtful timing: 20.14 1.2 Paul Lewis USA 30.10.77 1 Fairfax 6 May

Hand timing

20.3	0.0	Jarmiene	Holloway	USA	6.3.77	1	Pointe-à-Pitre	1 May
20.3	0.0	Joseph	Batangdon	CMR	29.7.78	1	Yaoundé	27 May

20.5		Enefiok	Udo-Obong	NGR-J	22.5.82	31 Mar
20.5	1.3	Paul	Gorries	RSA-J	28.2.81	31 Mar
20.5	1.3	Andre	Morris	USA	26.10.72	31 Mar
20.6		Anton	Galkin	RUS	.79	18 May

Wind assisted

20.4	2.4	Mohamed	Al-Houti	OMN	8.9.72	8 Jul
20.6	w	Charles	Rogers	USA-J	23.5.81	30 May

Subsequent to drugs disqualification

20.63	-2.4	Gábor	Dobos ¶	HUN	21.2.76	1	NC	Budapest	30 Jul
		20.4w	2.4			2		Budapest	8 Jul
20.69	0.9	Daniel	Effiong	NGR	17.6.72	2r1		Rehlingen	12 Jun
		20.58	3.5			4r2	Conseil	Fort-de-France	29 Apr

Mark	Wind	Name		Nat	Born	Pos	Meet	Venue	Date

JUNIORS

See main list for top 5 juniors. 10 performances by 5 men to 20.67. Additional marks and further juniors

Gorries 20.59A 0.0 2 Pretoria 24 Mar | 20.62A -0.1 1 Bloemfontein 4 Feb
20.62 -0.5 1s2 WJ Santiago 20 Oct | 20.64 1.3 1 WJ Santiago 21 Oct
Xu Zizhou 20.65 0.5 1 NC Luohe 22 Oct

Mark	Wind	Name		Nat	Born	Pos	Meet	Venue	Date
20.69	-0.5	Marcin	Jedrusinski	POL	28.8.81	2s2	WJ	Santiago de Chile	20 Oct
20.75	2.0	Johan	Engberg	SWE	11.10.81	1rB	MAI	Malmö	7 Aug
20.76	0.0	Tim	Benjamin	GBR	2.5.82	2		Bern	5 Aug
20.78	1.7	Andra	Fifer	USA	22.5.81	2r1		Arlington	6 May
20.78	0.5	Brendan	Christian	USA	.84?	2r4		Austin	12 May
20.78	1.2	Daniel	Batman	AUS	20.3.81	1		Darwin	14 Jul
20.81	1.2	Yusuke	Omae	JPN	6.4.82	1s1	WJ	Santiago de Chile	20 Oct
20.84	1.2	Marvin	Anderson	JAM	12.5.82	2s1	WJ	Santiago de Chile	20 Oct
20.85	1.4	Robert	Foster	USA	15.5.81	1		New Orleans	13 May
20.86	0.0		Yang Yaozu	CHN	9.1.81	1	NC	Deyang	17 Jun
20.88	1.2	Dwayne	Grant	GBR	17.7.82	4s1	WJ	Santiago de Chile	20 Oct
20.89	0.5	Omar	Brown	JAM	21.6.82	4rA		Kourou	21 May
20.91	0.5	Saidric	Williams	USA	16.12.81	3r4		Austin	12 May
20.93	-0.1	Ville	Vakkuri	FIN	29.9.81	1		Pudasjärvi	22 Jun
20.94	1.9	Salem Mubarak	Al-Yami	KSA	9.2.82	4s1	AsiC	Jakarta	29 Aug
Wind assisted									
20.73	2.4	Andra	Fifer	USA	22.5.81	3		Natchitoches	16 May
20.76		Darrell	Brown	TRI	11.10.84	1		Port of Spain	21 May
20.79	3.2	DaBryan	Blanton	USA	.82	1r3		Austin	13 May
20.88	2.3	José Carlos	Peña	CUB	18.7.82	2		La Habana	26 Feb
20.90	4.8	Yuji	Okumo	JPN	31.7.82	1		Ise	8 Jul
20.91		Adam	Wooten	USA	18.3.82	1		Lubbock	29 Apr
20.93	2.1	Ladji	Doucouré	FRA	28.3.83			Hagetmau	26 Jul
Hand timed									
20.5		Enefiok	Udo-Obong	NGR	22.5.82	1		Enugu	31 Mar
20.5	1.3	Paul	Gorries	RSA	28.2.81	2		Cape Town	31 Mar
20.7		Anthony	Buchanan	USA	10.9.81	1		Yakima	8 Apr
20.6w		Charles	Rogers	USA	23.5.81	1		Saginaw	30 May

300 METRES

Mark	Name		Nat	Born	Pos	Venue	Date
30.85A	Michael	Johnson	USA	13.9.67	1	Pretoria	24 Mar
32.44	Joseph	Batangdon	CMR	29.7.78	1r3	Sydney	11 Sep
32.56	Sofiene	Labidi	TUN	29.9.79	1r3	Sydney	14 Sep
32.65	Enefiok	Udo-Obong	NGR-J	22.5.82	1r1	Sydney	11 Sep

Mark	Name		Nat	Born	Date	Mark	Name		Nat	Born	Date
32.67	Ibrahima	Wade	FRA	6.9.68	20 Jun	32.81	Sanjay	Ayre	JAM	19.6.80	14 Sep
32.70	Sunday	Bada	NGR	22.6.69	11 Sep	32.84A	Louis	Malherbe	RSA	23.6.75	24 Mar
32.72	Clement	Chukwu	NGR	7.7.73	14 Sep	32.87	Juan Pedro	Toledo	MEX	17.6.78	14 Sep
32.73A	Zétény	Dombi	HUN	10.1.75	24 Mar	32.94	Marc	Raquil	FRA	2.4.77	20 Jun
32.79	Éric	Milazar	MRI	1.6.75	14 Sep	32.98	Timothy	Munnings	BAH	22.6.66	14 Sep

Hand timing

Mark	Name		Nat	Born	Pos	Venue	Date
32.3	Paul	Gorries	RSA-J	28.2.81	1	Parow	29 Dec

Mark	Name		Nat	Born	Date	Mark	Name		Nat	Born	Date
32.7	David	Canal	ESP	7.12.78	14 May	32.8	Marcus	la Grange	RSA	12.12.77	29 Dec

400 METRES

Mark	Name		Nat	Born	Pos	Meet	Venue	Date
43.68	Michael	Johnson	USA	13.9.67	1	NC	Sacramento	16 Jul
43.84		Johnson			1	OG	Sydney	25 Sep
43.92		Johnson			1	Pre	Eugene	24 Jun
44.07		Johnson			1	VD	Bruxelles	25 Aug
44.18	Alvin	Harrison	USA	20.1.74	1		Brisbane	8 Sep
44.25		A Harrison			1q3	OG	Sydney	23 Sep
44.40		A Harrison			2	OG	Sydney	25 Sep
44.46		Johnson			1		Rieti	3 Sep
44.53		A Harrison			1s1	OG	Sydney	24 Sep
44.57	Antonio	Pettigrew	USA	3.11.67	1	Super	Yokohama	9 Sep
44.59	Hendrik	Mokganyetsi	RSA	7.9.75	2	Super	Yokohama	9 Sep
44.63		Johnson			1s1	NC	Sacramento	15 Jul
44.63		A Harrison			2	NC	Sacramento	16 Jul
44.64	Calvin	Harrison	USA	20.1.74	2		Brisbane	8 Sep
44.65		Pettigrew			1	GP	Raleigh	17 Jun
44.65	Sanderlei	Parrela	BRA	7.10.74	1		Portland	25 Jun
44.65		Johnson			2s1	OG	Sydney	24 Sep
44.66		Pettigrew			3	NC	Sacramento	16 Jul
44.66	Ibrahim	Ismail	QAT	10.5.72	1	AsiC	Jakarta	30 Aug
44.66	Hamdan Obah	Al-Bishi	KSA-J	5.5.81	1	WJ	Santiago de Chile	20 Oct

Mark	Name		Nat	Born	Pos	Meet	Venue	Date
44.69	Michael	Blackwood	JAM	29.8.76	1	Big12	Columbia	21 May
44.70	Derrick	Brew	USA	28.12.77	1	SEC	Baton Rouge	14 May
44.70	Jerome	Young	USA	14.8.76	4	NC	Sacramento	16 Jul
44.70	Greg	Haughton	JAM	10.11.73	3	OG	Sydney	25 Sep
44.72	Brandon	Couts	USA	17.2.79	2	Big12	Columbia	21 May
44.72	Avard	Moncur	BAH	2.11.78	1	NCAA	Durham	3 Jun
44.72	Tyree	Washington	USA	28.8.76	2	Pre	Eugene	24 Jun
44.72	Mark	Richardson	GBR	26.7.72	2	VD	Bruxelles	25 Aug
44.73A	Pat	Dwyer	AUS	3.11.77	1		Pretoria	24 Mar
44.73		Parrela			1	GP	Athína	28 Jun
	(30/17)							
44.74	Arnaud	Malherbe	RSA	20.11.72	3	Super	Yokohama	9 Sep
44.78	Ja'Warren	Hooker	USA	24.9.78	1s2	NC	Sacramento	15 Jul
44.80	Anthuan	Maybank	USA	30.12.69	1	Nik	Nice	8 Jul
	(20)							
44.87	Andrew	Pierce	USA	8.6.79	1	Big10	Iowa City	21 May
44.87	Éric	Milazar	MRI	1.6.75	1		La Chaux de Fonds	13 Aug
44.89	Angelo	Taylor	USA	29.12.78	2	GP	Raleigh	17 Jun
44.92	Alejandro	Cárdenas	MEX	4.9.74	1	GP II	Bratislava	22 Jun
44.99A	Marcus	la Grange	RSA	12.12.77	3		Pretoria	24 Mar
45.00	Leonard	Byrd	USA	17.3.75	3s2	NC	Sacramento	15 Jul
45.00	Danny	McCray	USA	11.3.74	6	NC	Sacramento	16 Jul
45.01	Robert	Mackowiak	POL	13.5.70	1q4	OG	Sydney	23 Sep
45.02	Geno	White	USA	10.3.78	2	NCAA	Durham	3 Jun
45.03	Takahiko	Yamamura	JPN	13.8.79	4	Super	Yokohama	9 Sep
	(30)							
45.05	Jun	Osakada	JPN	2.4.74	5	Super	Yokohama	9 Sep
45.06	Jamie	Baulch	GBR	3.5.73	1s1	NC	Birmingham	12 Aug
45.06	Davian	Clarke	JAM	30.4.76	1q2	OG	Sydney	23 Sep
45.08	Christopher	Brown	BAH	15.10.78	3	NCAA	Durham	3 Jun
45.09	Jerome	Davis	USA	20.8.77	5	Pre	Eugene	24 Jun
45.20	Sean	Baldock	GBR	3.12.76	2s1	NC	Birmingham	12 Aug
45.24	Michael	McDonald	JAM	17.3.75	2		Portland	25 Jun
45.24A	Juan Pedro	Toledo	MEX	17.6.78	1	IMSS	Ciudad de México	1 Jul
45.24	Ibrahima	Wade	FRA	6.9.68	2B	WK	Zürich	11 Aug
45.25	Rohan Pradeep	Kumara	SRI	10.3.75	1	NC	Colombo	15 Jul
	(40)							
45.26	James	Davis	USA	19.3.76	1		Sacramento	22 Apr
45.26A	Johnny	Collins	USA	28.7.78	1	WAC	El Paso	20 May
45.26	Danny	McFarlane	JAM	14.2.72	2	NC	Kingston	22 Jul
45.26	Dmitriy	Golovastov	RUS	14.7.71	6	Super	Yokohama	9 Sep
45.28	Troy	McIntosh	BAH	29.3.73	2		Nassau	9 Jun
45.31A	Kempa	Busby	USA	9.10.73	2		Flagstaff	6 Jul
45.31	Sugath	Thilakaratne	SRI	30.7.73	2	NC	Colombo	15 Jul
45.31	Marc	Raquil	FRA	2.4.77	2	NC	Nice	6 Aug
45.32	Iliya	Dzhivondov	BUL	6.3.78	1		Sofia	3 Jun
45.35	Alessandro	Attene	ITA	10.9.77	3q3	OG	Sydney	23 Sep
	(50)							
45.36	Bryan	Swarn	USA	19.11.79	2	GaTech	Atlanta	20 May
45.36	Casey	Vincent	AUS	17.3.79	4		Brisbane	8 Sep
45.37	Milton	Campbell	USA	15.5.76	3		Nassau	9 Jun
45.37	Deon	Minor	USA	22.1.73	3		Portland	25 Jun
45.37	Daniel	Caines	GBR	15.5.79	3q4	OG	Sydney	23 Sep
45.41	Judo	Monyo	NGR	16.11.73	1	NC	Lagos	22 Jul
45.43	Piotr	Haczek	POL	26.1.77	2q1	OG	Sydney	23 Sep
45.46	Tawanda	Chiwira	ZIM	27.8.74	1r5	MSR	Walnut	16 Apr
45.48	Matija	Sestak	SLO	30.12.72	1		Ljubljana	14 Aug
45.52	Derek	Mills	USA	9.7.72	6	GP	Raleigh	17 Jun
	(60)							
45.53	David	Canal	ESP	7.12.78	2h7	OG	Sydney	22 Sep
45.55	Jon	Drummond	USA	9.9.68	1r2		Los Angeles (Ww)	1 Apr
45.55	Malik	Louahla	ALG	19.12.77	1		Bugeat	23 Jul
45.55	Anastásios	Goúsis	GRE	7.7.79	1	NC-23	Kastoriá	5 Aug
45.55		Xu Zizhou	CHN-J	8.1.81	3	AsiC	Jakarta	30 Aug
45.56	Paramjeet	Singh	IND	22.8.71	1	Inter-St	Chennai	29 Jul
45.58	Sanjay	Ayre	JAM	19.6.80	4h1	NCAA	Durham	1 Jun
45.58A	Shane	Niemi	CAN	2.6.78	2r2		Flagstaff	8 Jul
45.59	Godfrey	Herring	USA	18.5.78	1r1		Knoxville	14 Apr
45.59	Anderson Jorge	dos Santos	BRA	23.4.72	2	IbAm	Rio de Janeiro	20 May
	(70)							

Mark	Name		Nat	Born	Pos	Meet	Venue	Date
45.59	Mike	Decker	USA	13.6.78	5h1	NCAA	Durham	1 Jun
45.59	Paul	Lewis	USA	30.10.77	2r2		Chapel Hill	18 Jun
45.60	Daniel	Batman	AUS-J	20.3.81	1h2	OT	Sydney	17 Aug
45.61	Jopie	Van Oudtshoorn	RSA	5.2.76	2	NC	Stellenbosch	3 Mar
45.63	Purukottam	Ramachandran	IND	20.5.71	2	Inter-St	Chennai	29 Jul
45.64	Jimmie	Hackley	USA	11.9.75	1	UCTA	Austin	22 Apr
45.67	Jonas	Motiejunas	LTU	7.12.74	6r1	GaTech	Atlanta	20 May
45.67	Julian	Raeburn	TRI	18.9.78	1	NC	Port of Spain	16 Jun
45.67A	Simon	Kemboi ¶	KEN	1.3.67	1h1	NC	Nairobi	21 Jul
45.67	Piotr	Rysiukiewicz	POL	14.7.74	3	NC	Kraków	5 Aug
	(80)							
45.68	Torrance	Chaplin	USA	12.6.77	1		Princeton	6 May
45.68	Dennis	Blake	JAM	6.9.70	3r2		Chapel Hill	18 Jun
45.68	Jimisola	Laursen	SWE	13.7.77	1	NC	Uppsala	19 Aug
45.69	Nduka	Awazie	NGR-J	4.4.81	2		Lagos	22 Jul
45.69	Jared	Deacon	GBR	15.10.75	2r1	DIG	Dublin	29 Jul
45.69	David	Kirui	KEN	15.12.74	2h4	OG	Sydney	22 Sep
45.71	Gavin	Herring	USA	2.6.75	1		Indianapolis	24 Jun
45.72	Ronnie	Williams	USA	14.10.74	3r2		Tempe	15 Apr
45.72	Stefan	Balosák	SVK	23.11.72	1	NC	Banská Bystrica	2 Jul
45.72	Norberto	Téllez	CUB	22.1.72	1		Madrid	18 Jul
	(90)							
45.72	Marc	Foucan	FRA	14.10.71	3	NC	Nice	6 Aug
45.73	Kenji	Tabata	JPN	24.9.74	7	Super	Yokohama	9 Sep
45.73	Brandon	Simpson	JAM-J	6.9.81	2	WJ	Santiago de Chile	20 Oct
45.74	Sunday	Bada	NGR	22.6.69	3	NC	Lagos	22 Jul
45.74	Davis	Kamoga	UGA	17.7.68	6q2	OG	Sydney	23 Sep
45.75	Enefiok	Udo-Obong	NGR-J	22.5.82	1		Abidjan	12 May
45.77	Kennedy	Ochieng	KEN	30.12.71	3	OD	Jena	3 Jun
45.77	Alain	Rohr	SUI	25.12.71	2		La Chaux-de-Fonds	13 Aug
45.77	Shinji	Ishikawa	JPN-J	18.3.81	3	WJ	Santiago de Chile	20 Oct
45.78	Mike	Kenyon	USA	26.8.79	1		Tucson	6 May
	(100)							

45.79	Ingo	Schultz	GER	26.7.75	18 Jun
45.80	Emmanuel	Front	FRA	27.1.73	6 Aug
45.81	Sofiane	Labidi	TUN	29.9.79	12 Jul
45.82	Kevin	Jefferson	USA	16.7.75	13 May
45.82	Karel	Bláha	CZE	1.6.75	16 Jul
45.82	Iwan	Thomas	GBR	5.1.74	15 Aug
45.83	Ken	Harnden	ZIM	31.3.73	7 May
45.83	Salaheddine	Bakar Safi	QAT	.80	15 Jul
45.83	Geoff	Dearman	GBR	4.8.77	29 Jul
45.84	Yuriy	Borzakovskiy	RUS-J	12.4.81	24 Jul
45.84	Tomas	Coman	IRL	10.11.79	29 Jul
45.84	Pierre-Marie	Hilaire	FRA	19.11.65	6 Aug
45.84	Clement	Chukwu	NGR	7.7.73	27 Aug
45.85	Darrick	Ingram	USA	24.7.78	6 May
45.85	Andrey	Semyonov	RUS	16.8.77	24 Jul
45.85	Shunji	Karube	JPN	8.5.69	9 Sep
45.86	Tom	Gerding	USA	17.12.78	29 Apr
45.86A	Philip	Mukomana	ZIM	21.4.74	1 Jul
45.86	Damion	Barry	TRI-J	3.3.82	20 Oct
45.87A	Andre	Morris	USA	26.10.72	18 Mar
45.87	Valdinei A	da Silva	BRA	29.3.72	14 May
45.87	Robert	Wilson	USA	19.6.77	3 Jun
45.87	Fabian	Rollins	BAR	4.1.76	10 Jun
45.89A	Roy	Williams	JAM	9.12.78	19 May
45.89	Luis	Eloi	BRA	22.7.70	3 Jun
45.90	Brad	Jamieson	AUS	16.3.78	15 Jan
45.91	Travis	Hannah	USA	31.1.70	16 Apr
45.91	Lancford	Davis	JAM	.78	12 May
45.91A	Cori	Loving	USA	17.1.77	8 Jul
45.91	Kjell	Provost	BEL	21.6.77	25 Aug
45.91	Ato	Modibo	TRI	19.6.79	22 Sep
45.92	Paul	McKee	IRL	15.11.77	1 May
45.92	Attila	Kilvinger	HUN	27.3.77	29 Jul
45.94	Aleksandr	Kaydash	UKR	30.5.76	4 Aug
45.94	Fred	Mango	FRA	26.6.73	13 Aug
45.94	Blair	Young	AUS	5.4.71	8 Sep
45.94	William	Hernández	VEN-J	18.2.81	20 Oct
45.95	Leon	Settle	USA	19.10.75	25 Mar
45.95	Dahesh Fawzi	Al Shammari	KUW	13.2.79	18 Apr
45.95	Jirí	Muzík	CZE	1.9.76	16 Jul
45.96A	Sam	Singleton	USA	27.3.78	6 May
45.97	Wagner	Souza	BRA	27.2.76	3 Jun
45.97	Richard	Sharp	RSA-J	1.8.81	20 Oct
45.98	Tony	Berrian	USA	12.2.79	25 Mar
45.98	Michael	Campbell	JAM	11.9.78	6 May
45.98	Bruno	Wavelet	FRA	20.11.74	23 Jul
45.99	Arnold	Payne	ZIM	17.10.72	15 Apr
45.99	Jacek	Bocian	POL	15.9.76	5 Aug
46.00	Chris	Jones	USA	8.10.73	6 May
46.00	Laurent	Clerc	SUI	12.4.72	11 Aug
46.01A	Brian	Fell	USA	25.2.77	6 Jul
46.02	Julien	Hagen	NED	4.5.75	10 Sep
46.03	Dedrick	Evans	USA	4.2.73	19 May
46.04A	Robbie	Stevens	RSA-J	18.2.81	20 May
46.04	Marcel	Lopuchovsky	SVK	2.5.77	1 Jun
46.04	Ruslan	Mashchenko	RUS	11.11.71	9 Sep
46.05	Mark	Everett	USA	2.9.68	14 Jun
46.05	Felix	Gadzama	NGR	20.10.79	22 Jul
46.06A	Lewis	Young	USA	6.9.76	6 May
46.06	Eronilde	de Araújo	BRA	31.12.70	4 Aug
46.07	Anthony	Authorlee	USA	10.7.77	20 May
46.07	Petko	Yankov	BUL	6.10.77	15 Jul
46.08A	Adriaan	Botha	RSA	8.3.77	24 Mar
46.08	Zsolt	Szeglet	HUN	4.5.77	21 May
46.08	Sylvester	Omodiale	NGR	5.9.77	3 Sep
46.09	Leroy	Jordan	USA	1.9.78	13 May
46.09	Anton	Galkin	RUS	.79	18 Jun
46.10A	Zétény	Dombi	HUN	10.1.75	18 Mar
46.11A	Dennis	Darling	BAH	6.5.75	8 Jul
46.12	Timothy	Munnings	BAH	22.6.66	21 Jul
46.13	Brian	Vernon	USA-J	2.1.81	20 May
46.13	Oleg	Kovalyov	RUS	26.5.77	24 Jul
46.14	Richard	Knowles	GBR	12.11.75	22 Jun
46.14	Solomon	Wariso	GBR	11.11.66	12 Aug
46.14	Claudinei	da Silva	BRA	19.11.70	22 Aug
46.14	Quincy	Douglas	NOR	7.9.75	22 Aug
46.15	Djabir	Saïd-Guerni	ALG	29.3.77	12 Mar
46.15	Yevgeniy	Zyukov	UKR	31.5.78	3 Aug
46.16	Andre	Ammons	USA	12.11.78	13 May
46.17	Dave	Dopek	USA	8.2.73	24 Jun
46.18	Michael	Granville	USA	14.2.78	13 May
46.18	Courtney	Hale	USA-J	5.8.81	16 May

Mark	Name		Nat	Born	Date	Mark	Name		Nat	Born	Date
46.19A	Tshepo	Thobelangope	RSA-J	10.8.81	18 Mar	46.24	Flávio	Godoy	BRA	13.12.69	4 Aug
46.19	Terrence	Williams	USA	14.8.78	13 May	46.25	Jarrod	Macklin	USA		6 May
46.19	Adrian	Patrick	GBR	15.6.73	18 Jun	46.25	Kevin	Baker	USA	26.5.80	20 May
46.19A	Felix	Lebo	KEN		21 Jul	46.26	Johan	Lannefors	SWE	24.10.76	20 May
46.20	Darryl	Wohlsen	AUS	6.3.73	23 Jan	46.26	Naoya	Hayashi	JPN	13.7.77	24 May
46.21	Rickey	Harris	USA-J	29.9.81	10 Jun	46.26	Rafal	Wieruszewski	POL-J	24.2.81	10 Jun
46.21	Magnus	Aare	SWE	9.9.74	2 Sep	46.26	Edel	Hevia	CUB	22.2.77	23 Jun
46.22	Dimitri	Demonière	FRA	28.3.79	23 Jul		(201)	16 men 46.27 to 46.34			
46.23A	Georkis	Vera	CUB	22.5.75	13 May	**Indoors**					
46.23	Takahiro	Ueno	JPN	11.4.78	24 May	46.08	Stefan	Holz	GER	25.2.79	6 Feb
46.24	Greg	McKinley	USA	25.3.76	20 May	46.15	Tyrone	Dozier	USA	22.11.79	19 Feb
46.24	Mark	Hylton	GBR	24.9.76	29 Jul	46.16	Leroy	Colquhoun	JAM	1.3.80	11 Mar

Best at low altitude

45.19	Dwyer	1	Canberra	15 Jan	45.79	Collins	1 Jun	45.93	Morris	6 May
45.76	Busby	3h1NC	Sacramento	14 Jul	45.79	Niemi	12 Aug	46.01	Toledo	27 Aug

Hand timing

43.9		Johnson			1		Cape Town	31 Mar
45.4	Daniel	Batman	AUS-J	20.3.81	1		Darwin	2 Jul
45.4	Jonas	Motiejunas	LTU	7.12.74	1	NC	Kaunas	3 Aug
45.5	Tyrone	Dozier	USA	22.11.79	1r2	GaTech	Atlanta	20 May
45.6	Corey	Nelson	USA	9.10.77	1		Bosie	6 May
45.6	Luis	Eloi	BRA	22.7.70	1		São Paulo	17 Jun
45.6A	David	Kirui	KEN	15.12.74	1		Nairobi	23 Jun

45.7	Michael	Johnson II	USA	13.5.78	20 May	46.0A	Felix	Lebo	KEN		27 May
45.8A	Ousmane	Niang	SEN	10.4.80	12 Apr	46.0	Abdrahim	El Haouzy	MAR	.75	29 Jul
45.9	Ato	Modibo	TRI	19.6.79	20 May	46.0A	Japheth	Ogamba	KEN-J	2.4.82	22 Sep
45.9A	Julius	Chepkwony	KEN	6.6.69	23 Jun	46.2	Johnson	Kubisa	BOT	23.4.72	28 May

JUNIORS

See main list for top 7 juniors. Additional marks and further juniors

Al-Bishi	45.22	1h8 OG	Sydney	22 Sep	45.41	2		Barcelona	25 Jul
	45.32	2 AsiC	Jakarta	30 Aug	45.46	1s2	AsiC	Jakarta	29 Aug
	45.35	3q2 OG	Sydney	23 Sep	10 performances by 3 men to 45.68				
Batman	45.66	2	Canberra	15 Jan	45.68A	4	vRSA	Roodepoort	13 Mar

45.84	Yuriy	Borzakovskiy	RUS	12.4.81	2	NC	Tula	24 Jul
45.86	Damion	Barry	TRI	3.3.82	4	WJ	Santiago de Chile	20 Oct
45.94	William	Hernández (10)	VEN	18.2.81	5	WJ	Santiago de Chile	20 Oct
45.97	Richard	Sharp	RSA	1.8.81	6	WJ	Santiago de Chile	20 Oct
46.04A	Robbie	Stevens	RSA	18.2.81	3	WAC	El Paso	20 May
46.13	Brian	Vernon	USA	2.1.81	1		Bakersfield	20 May
46.18	Courtney	Hale	USA	5.8.81	1		Natchitoches	16 May
46.19A	Tshepo	Thobelangope	RSA	10.8.81	1rB		Pietersburg	18 Mar
46.21	Rickey	Harris	USA	29.9.81	1		Richmond VA	10 Jun
46.26	Rafal	Wieruszewski	POL	24.2.81	1		Warszawa	10 Jun
46.36	Jonathan	Palma	VEN	8.12.81	7	WJ	Santiago de Chile	20 Oct
46.39	LeVar	Norris	USA	28.8.81	1		Humble TX	29 Apr
46.45	Marnus	Kritzinger (20)	RSA	10.2.82	1		Durban	18 Mar
46.45	Katsuya	Terada	JPN	13.7.82	1r6		Ichihara	20 Jul

Hand timed

45.4	Daniel	Batman	AUS	20.3.81	1		Darwin	2 Jul
46.0A	Japheth	Ogamba	KEN	2.4.82	1	NC	Nairobi	22 Sep
46.3A	Victor	Kibet	KEN		2	NC	Nairobi	22 Sep

600 METRES

1:14.41	Andrea	Longo	ITA	26.6.75	1		Rovereto	30 Aug
1:14.48	Trinity	Gray	USA	3.4.78	2		Rovereto	30 Aug
1:14.96	André	Bucher	SUI	19.10.76	1		Gold Coast (RB)	17 Sep
1:15.00	Glody	Dube	BOT	2.7.78	1		Sydney	14 Sep
1:15.13	Hezekiél	Sepeng	RSA	30.6.74	1		Gold Coast (RB)	10 Sep
1:15.26	Bram	Som	NED	20.2.80	2		Gold Coast (RB)	17 Sep
1:15.30	Milton	Browne	BAR	1.6.76	2		Gold Coast (RB)	10 Sep
1:15.74	Werner	Botha	RSA	31.1.78	3		Gold Coast (RB)	10 Sep

1:16.04	Khalid	Tighazouine	MAR	18.6.77	17 Sep	1:16.40	Charles	Makau	KEN	13.3.71	30 Aug
1:16.07	Kris	McCarthy	AUS	15.10.79	10 Sep	1:16.44	Zach	Whitmarsh	CAN	5.4.77	14 Sep
1:16.14	Vebjørn	Rodal	NOR	16.9.72	22 Aug	1:16.45	Japheth	Kimutai	KEN	20.12.78	21 May

800 METRES

1:43.12	André	Bucher	SUI	19.10.76	1rA	Athl	Lausanne	5 Jul
1:43.25	Djabir	Saïd-Guerni	ALG	29.3.77	1rA	VD	Bruxelles	25 Aug
1:43.31		Bucher			2rA	VD	Bruxelles	25 Aug
1:43.32		Saïd-Guerni			2rA	Athl	Lausanne	5 Jul
1:43.35	Wilson	Kipketer	DEN	12.12.70	3rA	VD	Bruxelles	25 Aug

Mark	Name		Nat	Born	Pos	Meet	Venue	Date
1:43.72		Bucher			1rA	WK	Zürich	11 Aug
1:43.74	Andrea	Longo	ITA	26.6.75	1	GP II	Rieti	3 Sep
1:43.79		Saïd-Guerni			1	Herc	Monaco	18 Aug
1:43.84	William	Chirchir	KEN	6.2.79	3rA	Athl	Lausanne	5 Jul
1:43.87	Japheth	Kimutai	KEN	20.12.78	2rA	WK	Zürich	11 Aug
1:43.92		Saïd-Guerni			3rA	WK	Zürich	11 Aug
1:43.93		Kimutai			2	Herc	Monaco	18 Aug
1:43.97	David	Lelei	KEN	10.5.71	1rA	GP II	Melbourne	2 Mar
1:43.98	Hezekiél	Sepeng	RSA	30.6.74	4rA	WK	Zürich	11 Aug
1:44.00		Sepeng			4rA	VD	Bruxelles	25 Aug
1:44.01	Bram	Som	NED	20.2.80	5rA	WK	Zürich	11 Aug
1:44.06	Jean-Patrick	Nduwimana	BDI	9.5.78	5rA	VD	Bruxelles	25 Aug
1:44.16		Nduwimana			6rA	WK	Zürich	11 Aug
1:44.19		Saïd-Guerni			1s2	OG	Sydney	25 Sep
1:44.20	Kenneth	Kimwetich	KEN	1.1.73	1rB	WK	Zürich	11 Aug
1:44.21		Nduwimana			1	NA	Heusden	5 Aug
1:44.21	Paul	Korir	KEN	.77	1		La Chaux de Fonds	13 Aug
1:44.22	Nils	Schumann	GER	20.5.78	1s1	OG	Sydney	25 Sep
1:44.22		Kipketer			1s3	OG	Sydney	25 Sep
1:44.23	William	Yiampoy	KEN	15.5.74	7rA	WK	Zürich	11 Aug
1:44.23	Wilfred	Bungei	KEN	24.7.80	2rB	WK	Zürich	11 Aug
1:44.25		Yiampoy			2	GP II	Rieti	3 Sep
1:44.27		Kipketer			1		Helsinki	15 Jun
1:44.28		Saïd-Guerni			1	AUS Ch	Sydney	26 Feb
1:44.32		Saïd-Guerni			1	GGala	Roma	30 Jun
	(30/15)							
1:44.33	Yuriy	Borzakovskiy	RUS-J	12.4.81	2s2	OG	Sydney	25 Sep
1:44.41	Werner	Botha	RSA	31.1.78	2	NA	Heusden	5 Aug
1:44.49	Noah	Ngeny	KEN	2.11.78	1	Bisl	Oslo	28 Jul
1:44.58	Patrick	Konchellah	KEN	20.4.68	2		Ingolstadt	18 Jun
1:44.6	David	Kiptoo	KEN	26.6.65	2		Milano	7 Jun
	(20)							
1:44.67	Adem	Hecini	ALG	13.12.75	3	GP II	Rieti	3 Sep
1:44.69	Wilson	Kirwa	FIN	28.12.74	1		Lappeenranta	13 Aug
1:44.70	Glody	Dube	BOT	2.7.78	3s1	OG	Sydney	25 Sep
1:44.84	Vebjørn	Rodal	NOR	16.9.72	3	Bisl	Oslo	28 Jul
1:44.85	Johan	Botha	RSA	10.1.74	4rB	WK	Zürich	11 Aug
1:44.87	Osmar	dos Santos	BRA	20.10.68	1		Rio de Janeiro	22 Jul
1:44.91	Trinity	Gray	USA	3.4.78	4	GP II	Rieti	3 Sep
1:44.98	Nathan	Kahan	BEL	12.2.71	4	NA	Heusden	5 Aug
1:45.03	Shawn	Abrahams	RSA	4.7.70	1	NC	Stellenbosch	4 Mar
1:45.05	Nicholas	Wachira	KEN-J	19.11.82	5rB	WK	Zürich	11 Aug
	(30)							
1:45.11	Joel	Marwa	KEN	30.8.74	6rB	WK	Zürich	11 Aug
1:45.12	Arthémon	Hatungimana	BDI	21.1.74	6	GP II	Rieti	3 Sep
1:45.18	Derrick	Peterson	USA	28.11.77	2	NCAA	Durham	2 Jun
1:45.29	Rui	Silva	POR	3.8.77	3		Lisboa (U)	5 Aug
1:45.3A	Emmanuel	Kemboi	KEN-J	.81	1		Kakamega	9 Apr
1:45.31	José Manuel	Cerezo	ESP	23.6.73	7rB	WK	Zürich	11 Aug
1:45.33	Rich	Kenah	USA	4.8.70	8rB	WK	Zürich	11 Aug
1:45.38	Gideon	van Oudtshoorn	RSA	23.9.76	5	NA	Heusden	5 Aug
1:45.38	Khalid	Tighazouine	MAR	18.6.77	3s2	OG	Sydney	25 Sep
1:45.39	José Antonio	Redolat	ESP	17.2.76	1		Barcelona	25 Jul
	(40)							
1:45.39	Norberto	Téllez	CUB	22.1.72	7	GP II	Rieti	3 Sep
1:45.40	Khadevis	Robinson	USA	19.7.76	1		Portland	25 Jun
1:45.44	Frederick	Onyancha	KEN	25.12.69	9rB	WK	Zürich	11 Aug
1:45.49A	Joseph Mwengi	Mutua	KEN	10.12.78	2s2	NC	Nairobi	21 Jul
1:45.51	Bryan	Woodward	USA	3.3.74	4		Thessaloníki	30 Aug
1:45.55	Mbulaeni	Mulaudzi	RSA	8.9.80	1r2		Budapest	22 Jul
1:45.57	Kris	McCarthy	AUS	15.10.79	3rA	GP II	Melbourne	2 Mar
1:45.57	Charles	Makau	KEN	13.3.71	8	GP II	Rieti	3 Sep
1:45.59	João	Pires	POR	10.6.79	10rB	WK	Zürich	11 Aug
1:45.60	Mahjoub	Haïda	MAR	1.7.70	2		Leverkusen	20 Aug
	(50)							
1:45.67	Mark	Everett	USA	2.9.68	1	NC	Sacramento	23 Jul
1:45.68	Trinity	Townsend	USA	7.2.74	2		Portland	25 Jun
1:45.69	Hudson	de Souza	BRA	25.2.77	3		Portland	25 Jun

Mark	Name		Nat	Born	Pos	Meet	Venue	Date
1:45.71	Boris	Kaveshnikov	RUS	30.9.74	4rB	Athl	Lausanne	5 Jul
1:45.76	Dmitriy	Bogdanov	RUS	11.4.79	1	NC	Tula	25 Jul
1:45.8	Pavel	Pelepyagin	BLR	29.6.78	1	NC	Brest	1 Aug
1:45.81	Anthony	Whiteman	GBR	13.11.71	1	BrGP	London (CP)	5 Aug
1:45.86	Grant	Cremer	AUS	9.6.78	3h6	OG	Sydney	23 Sep
1:45.96	James	McIlroy	GBR	30.12.76	3	BrGP	London (CP)	5 Aug
1:45.99	Lucky	Hadebe	RSA	2.1.80	1r1	MAL	Budapest	22 Jul
	(60)							
1:46.02	David	Divad	FRA	8.3.73	1		Paris (C)	23 Jul
1:46.03	Jess	Strutzel	USA	4.1.78	1r1		Eagle Rock	13 May
1:46.04	Nico	Motchebon	GER	13.11.69	7	GGala	Roma	30 Jun
1:46.04	Artyom	Mastrov	RUS	12.11.76	2	NC	Tula	25 Jul
1:46.07	Zach	Whitmarsh	CAN	5.4.77	2	DIG	Dublin	29 Jul
1:46.07	Pawel	Czapiewski	POL	30.3.78	1h2	NC	Kraków	4 Aug
1:46.12	Jurgens	Kotzé	RSA	11.4.73	2r2	MAL	Budapest	22 Jul
1:46.12	Joeri	Jansen	BEL	28.5.79	6	NA	Heusden	5 Aug
1:46.20	Michael	Stember	USA	30.1.78	4	NCAA	Durham	2 Jun
1:46.2	Mouhsin	Chehibi	MAR	28.1.78	5		Milano	7 Jun
	(70)							
1:46.21	Jeff	Kuzma	USA	21.2.72	2r2		Palo Alto	1 Jul
1:46.21	Balázs	Korányi	HUN	30.5.74	4h6	OG	Sydney	23 Sep
1:46.24	Mehdi	Baala	FRA	17.8.78	1		Nancy	3 Sep
1:46.25	Marko	Koers	NED	3.11.72	1		Palo Alto	5 May
1:46.26	Saïd	Lakhal	MAR	16.4.70	1		Zug	26 Aug
1:46.27	Sergey	Kozhevnikov	RUS	24.3.70	4	NC	Tula	25 Jul
1:46.30	Benjamin	Kipkurui	KEN	28.12.80	5		Ingolstadt	18 Jun
1:46.33	Grzegorz	Krzosek	POL	10.1.76	1	NC	Kraków	5 Aug
1:46.4	Assane	Diallo	SEN	10.2.75	1		Abidjan	12 May
1:46.42	Juan Carlos	Higuero	ESP	3.8.78	3rB	VD	Bruxelles	25 Aug
	(80)							
1:46.42	Panayiótis	Stroubákos	GRE	8.9.72	7		Thessaloníki	30 Aug
1:46.43	Andrea	Abelli	ITA	9.2.71	2		Torino	10 Jun
1:46.45	Martin	Byron	AUS	6.6.69	2		Canberra	15 Jan
1:46.46	James	Karanu	KEN	5.1.76	6	NCAA	Durham	2 Jun
1:46.50	Ned	Brooks	USA	22.7.76	7	NCAA	Durham	2 Jun
1:46.52	Sammy	Langat	KEN	24.1.70	4r2		Palo Alto	1 Jul
1:46.52	Andy	Hart	GBR	13.9.69	4r2	MAL	Budapest	22 Jul
1:46.57	Marvin	Watts	JAM	21.5.75	1r1		Chapel Hill	18 Jun
1:46.57A	Francis	Marwa	KEN	.76	7s1	NC	Nairobi	21 Jul
1:46.59	Tarik	Bourrouag	GER	9.7.76	1		Köln	1 Jun
	(90)							
1:46.62	Elliott	Gaskins	USA	3.1.74	2h2	NC	Sacramento	20 Jul
1:46.62	Jason	Pyrah	USA	6.4.69	1h4	NC	Sacramento	20 Jul
1:46.62	David	Krummenacker	USA	24.5.75	4		La Chaux-de-Fonds	13 Aug
1:46.64	Marius	van Heerden	RSA	8.9.74	6	NC	Stellenbosch	4 Mar
1:46.64	Luke	Kipkoech	KEN	9.12.70	1		Cardiff	5 Jul
1:46.65	Daniel	Caulfield	IRL	16.10.72	8		Gateshead	28 Aug
1:46.67	Oliver	Daum	GER	25.6.71	4		Chemnitz	22 Jul
1:46.70	Willy	Rotich	KEN	23.3.78	1		Hämeenlinna	9 Jun
1:46.71	Bernard	Kisilu	KEN	6.12.74	2		Cardiff	5 Jul
1:46.71	Philip	Kibitok	KEN	23.3.71	3	Karelia	Lappeenranta	13 Aug
	(100)							

1:46.72	Kamel	Boulahfane	ALG	1.7.76	17 Jun
1:46.72	Lubert	Lewis	USA	6.8.78	24 Jun
1:46.73	Shaun	Farrell	NZL	5.3.75	2 Mar
1:46.77	Pávlos	Faroúggias	GRE	6.6.77	8 Jul
1:46.77A	David	Cheruiyot	KEN	1.9.72	21 Jul
1:46.8A ?	Mike	Gichuki	KEN		23 Jun
1:46.81	Roman	Oravec	CZE	5.4.78	29 Aug
1:46.83	James	Nolan	IRL	27.1.77	20 Aug
1:46.85	Bernard	Lagat	KEN	12.12.74	15 Jun
1:46.86	Jimmy	Jean-Joseph	FRA	15.10.72	17 Jun
1:46.87	Wojciech	Kaldowski	POL	16.4.76	7 Jun
1:46.87	Lukás	Vydra	CZE	23.8.73	5 Aug
1:46.88	Darren	Dinneen	IRL	8.12.77	29 Jul
1:46.92	Joseph	Ischia	AUS	23.2.74	9 Aug
1:46.92	Mechal	Gebreab	ETH	1.1.72	13 Aug
1:46.92	Giacomo	Mazzoni	ITA	30.1.72	30 Aug
1:46.93	Meyer	Kotzé	RSA	7.9.76	3 Mar
1:46.94	Viktors	Lacis	LAT	28.11.77	23 Sep
1:46.96	Paul	Mwangi	KEN	19.11.73	19 Aug
1:46.99	Charlie	Gruber	USA	6.8.78	24 Jun
1:47.0A	Maswi	Ntambe	KEN		11 Jul
1:47.01	Ivan	Komar	BLR	18.3.70	3 Jun
1:47.01	Brian	Berryhill	USA	15.12.77	20 Jul
1:47.01	Kjetil	Hodnekvam	NOR	25.6.77	28 Jul
1:47.04	Bobby	True	LBR	5.11.77	29 Apr
1:47.04	Tom	Omey	BEL	24.4.75	13 Aug
1:47.05	Sebastian	Miller	POL	24.7.76	5 Jun
1:47.07	Rizak	Dirshe	SWE	5.1.72	13 Aug
1:47.08	Paskar	Owor	UGA	22.12.80	12 Jun
1:47.08	Gabe	Jennings	USA	25.1.79	28 Aug
1:47.1A	Dedan	Maina	KEN		24 Jun
1:47.1A	Roberto	Parra	ESP	6.4.76	16 Aug
1:47.15	Evans	Ndungu	KEN	22.2.79	24 Jun
1:47.17	Wolfram	Müller	GER-J	8.7.81	22 Jul
1:47.17	Abdou Ibrahim Youssef		QAT	.80	23 Jul
1:47.18	Todd	MacDonald	AUS	8.7.76	29 Jul
1:47.18	Vitaliy	Cherkes	MDA	.73	19 Aug
1:47.20	Heath	Fitzpatrick	AUS	17.8.75	11 Feb
1:47.2	Andrea	Giocondi	ITA	17.1.69	7 Jun
1:47.22	Márcio	de Oliveira	BRA	1.2.73	22 Jul

Mark	Name		Nat	Born	Date
1:47.23	Stefan	Beumer	NED-J	28.4.81	10 Jun
1:47.24	Henry	Rotich	KEN-J	5.12.81	27 Aug
1:47.27	Guillaume	Douceret	FRA	7.2.75	23 Jun
1:47.29	Karel	Znojil	CZE	3.1.75	18 Jun
1:47.29	Ibrahim	Aden	SOM	11.11.72	18 Jun
1:47.3A	Isaac	Sang	KEN		12 Apr
1:47.31	Abdelkebir	Louraibi	MAR-J	9.2.81	27 May
1:47.31	Saïd	El Allali	MAR		10 Jun
1:47.31	Mohamed Habib	Belhaj	TUN	27.11.72	22 Jul
1:47.32	Nuno	Lopes	POR	5.3.75	18 Jun
1:47.32	Alasdair	Donaldson	GBR	21.6.77	5 Aug
1:47.33	António	Reina	ESP-J	13.6.81	25 Jul
1:47.35	Brendan	Hanigan	AUS	19.3.73	8 Mar
1:47.36	Peter	Biwott	KEN	22.8.76	10 Jun
1:47.36	Torbjörn	Johansson	SWE	23.1.70	11 Jun
1:47.37	Rachid	Khouia	MAR	9.11.79	27 Jul
1:47.38	Juha	Kukkamo	FIN	1.4.76	2 Sep
1:47.41	Florent	Lacasse	FRA-J	21.1.81	7 Oct
1:47.45	Mike	Schroer	USA	29.4.74	1 Jul
1:47.45	Mohamed	Yagoub	SUD	2.9.77	3 Sep
1:47.46	Scott	Petersen	AUS	14.11.73	9 Aug
1:47.48	Marco	Chiavarini	ITA	25.2.72	5 Aug
1:47.48	Sammy	Rono	KEN	.74	30 Aug
1:47.49	Romain	De Bock	FRA	21.8.79	1 Jul
1:47.5A	Elkana	Angwenyi	KEN		9 Apr
1:47.5A	Vincent	Kemboi	KEN-J	29.5.82	22 Sep
1:47.52	Mark	Rodgers	NZL	24.7.76	15 Jan
1:47.53	Matt	Kalwinsky	USA	4.7.76	24 Jun
1:47.54	Mario	Vernon-Watson	JAM	26.4.71	22 Jul
1:47.55	Ricardo	Etheridge	USA	12.5.78	24 Jun
1:47.55	Solomon	Birir	KEN	.77	24 Jun
1:47.59	Ashraf	Tadili	CAN	8.7.80	27 Jun
1:47.60A	Hendrik	Mokganyetsi	RSA	7.9.75	18 Mar
1:47.60	Vanco	Stojanov	MKD	9.11.77	22 Jul
1:47.6	Leonard	Kivati	KEN		20 Jul
1:47.61	Jean-Gilles	Talin	FRA	2.11.76	1 Jul
1:47.62	Kennedy	Osei	GHA	21.10.66	12 Jul
1:47.62	Sergio	Gallardo	ESP	22.3.79	25 Jul
1:47.63	Milton	Browne	BAR	1.6.76	23 Sep
1:47.66	Patrick	Grammens	BEL	10.4.71	25 Aug
1:47.66	Crispen	Mutakanyi	ZIM	15.3.70	23 Sep
1:47.70A	Graham	Davidson	RSA	14.10.78	14 Feb
1:47.70	Fouad	Chouki	FRA	1.10.78	19 Jul
1:47.71	Abdelmoug	Raji	MAR	.74	27 Jun
1:47.73	Ryan	Locklin	USA		13 May
1:47.75	Chris	Moss	GBR	17.6.79	19 Aug
1:47.76	Fraser	Dowling	AUS	4.12.79	11 Feb
1:47.76	Vyacheslav	Shabunin	RUS	27.9.69	18 Jun
1:47.76	Akinori	Mori	JPN	4.4.74	22 Jul
1:47.77	Jeff	DeLong	USA	7.11.77	5 May
1:47.78	Robert	Chirchir	KEN	26.11.72	7 Jun
1:47.80	Farid	Essaki	MAR		27 May
1:47.80	Pavel	Soukup	CZE	2.1.71	18 Jun
1:47.81	Martin	Jares	CZE	3.5.76	5 Jun
1:47.81	Jason	Lobo	GBR	18.9.69	20 Aug
1:47.82	Nicolas	Aïssat	FRA	24.7.80	13 Aug
1:47.83	Miroslaw	Formela	POL	31.10.78	1 Jul
1:47.84	Aaron	Richberg	USA	25.11.76	1 Apr
1:47.86	Mickaël	Hotyat	FRA	3.5.77	1 Jul
1:47.86	Jai	Thomas	AUS	6.1.76	5 Jul
1:47.87	David	Matthews	IRL	9.4.74	20 Aug
	(200)	and 12 men 1:47.88 to 1:47.99			

Indoors

Mark	Name		Nat	Born	Pos	Meet	Venue	Date
1:46.54	Roman	Oravec	CZE	5.4.78	3	Spark	Dortmund	30 Jan
1:47.01	Roberto	Parra	ESP	6.4.76				19 Feb
1:47.71	Marcel	Burke	USA	2.9.78				11 Mar
1:47.72	Bryce	Knight	USA	27.7.78				11 Mar
1:47.78	Robert	Chirchir	KEN	26.11.72				30 Jan

JUNIORS

Mark	Name		Nat	Born	Pos	Meet	Venue	Date
1:44.33	Yuriy	Borzakovskiy	RUS	12.4.81	2s2	OG	Sydney	25 Sep
	1:44.35i	1					Dortmund	30 Jan
	1:45.61	5				GGala	Roma	30 Jun
	1:44.63	4				Athl	Lausanne	5 Jul
	1:45.83	6				OG	Sydney	27 Sep
	1:45.39	1h6				OG	Sydney	23 Sep
	1:45.91i	1					Sindelfingen	22 Jan
1:45.05	Nicholas	Wachira	KEN	19.11.82	5rB	WK	Zürich	11 Aug
	1:45.25	1B				Athl	Lausanne	5 Jul
	1:45.94	1					Selargius	23 Aug
1:45.3A	Emmanuel	Kemboi	KEN	.81	1		Kakamega	9 Apr
1:47.17	Wolfram	Müller	GER	8.7.81	5		Chemnitz	22 Jull
1:47.23	Stefan	Beumer	NED	28.4.81	2		Leiden	10 Jun
1:47.24	Henry	Rotich	KEN	5.12.81	1		Kuopio	27 Aug
1:47.31	Abdelkebir	Louraibi	MAR	9.2.81	2		Meknès	27 May
1:47.33	António	Reina	ESP	13.6.81	7		Barcelona	25 Jul
1:47.41	Florent	Lacasse	FRA	21.1.81	1	v3N	Grosseto	7 Oct
1:47.5A	Vincent	Kemboi (10)	KEN	29.5.82	2	NC	Nairobi	22 Sep
1:47.95	Othman	Mohamed Othman	KSA	3.4.82	5	Karelia	Lappeenranta	13 Aug
1:48.08	Arnoud	Okken	NED	20.4.82	3		Leiden	10 Jun
1:48.1	Ebrima	Ceesay	GAM	5.11.83	2		Abidjan	12 May
1:48.20	Salem Amer	Al-Badri	QAT	12.12.85	2		Gent	19 Jul
1:48.23	Samuel	Burley	USA	13.2.81	2	Heps	Philadelphia	14 May
1:48.34	Fernando	Almeida	POR	22.6.81	7		Lisboa (U)	5 Aug
1:48.4A	Silas	Kimutai	KEN		3	NC	Nairobi	22 Sep
1:48.53	Tom	Vanchaze	BEL	22.12.82	11rB	VD	Bruxelles	25 Aug
1:48.73	Jason	Stewart	NZL	21.11.81	5	MarleyG	Papakura	26 Jan
1:49.10A	Thabo	Thobelangope	RSA	10.8.81	1rB		Pretoria	24 Mar
1:49.10	Ali Abubaker	Kamal	QAT	.83	2		Nivelles	20 Aug
1:49.1	Ryan	Hayden (22)	CAN	27.1.82	1		Burnaby	1 Aug

1000 METRES

Mark	Name		Nat	Born	Pos	Meet	Venue	Date
2:14.28	Japheth	Kimutai	KEN	20.12.78	1	DNG	Stockholm	1 Aug
2:14.73	Patrick	Konchellah	KEN	20.4.68	2	DNG	Stockholm	1 Aug
2:14.78	Noah	Ngeny	KEN	2.11.78	1	Nik	Nice	8 Jul
2:14.79	William	Yiampoy	KEN	15.5.74	3	DNG	Stockholm	1 Aug
2:15.45	Mehdi	Baala	FRA	17.8.78	2	Nik	Nice	8 Jul
2:15.53		Ngeny			1	GP	Athína	28 Jun
2:15.73	André	Bucher	SUI	19.10.76	1		Langenthal	10 Jun
2:15.87		Baala			1		Marly	19 Jun
2:15.91		Konchellah			2	GP	Athína	28 Jun

Mark	Name		Nat	Born	Pos	Meet	Venue	Date
2:15.91	William	Chirchir	KEN	6.2.79	4	DNG	Stockholm	1 Aug
	(10/7)							
2:16.28	Kennedy	Kimwetich	KEN	1.1.73	5	DNG	Stockholm	1 Aug
2:16.45	Laban	Rotich	KEN	20.1.69	3	Nik	Nice	8 Jul
2:16.47	Hezekiél	Sepeng	RSA	30.6.74	6	DNG	Stockholm	1 Aug
2:16.61	Grant	Cremer	AUS	9.6.78	7	DNG	Stockholm	1 Aug
2:16.86	Ali	Hakimi	TUN	24.4.76	4	Nik	Nice	8 Jul
2:16.98	Jean-Patrick	Nduwimana	BDI	9.5.78	8	DNG	Stockholm	1 Aug
2:17.40	Yuriy	Borzakovskiy	RUS-J	12.4.81	5	Nik	Nice	8 Jul
2:17.45	Reyes	Estévez	ESP	2.8.76	1		Andújar	5 Sep
2:17.59	Kevin	Sullivan	CAN	20.3.74	3	GP	Athína	28 Jun
2:17.97	Andrea	Longo	ITA	26.6.75	6	Nik	Nice	8 Jul
2:17.99	Rich	Kenah	USA	4.8.70	4	GP	Athína	28 Jun

Mark	Name		Nat	Born	Date	Mark	Name		Nat	Born	Date
2:18.06	Boris	Kaveshnikov	RUS	30.9.74	8 Jul	2:18.94	Pávlos	Faroúggias	GRE	6.6.77	28 Jun
2:18.08	David	Krummenacker	USA	24.5.75	28 Jun	2:18.97	Branko	Zorko	CRO	1.7.67	17 Jun
2:18.11	James	Nolan	IRL	27.1.77	28 Jun	2:19.09	Aléxis	Abraham	FRA	14.2.76	19 Jun
2:18.20	Arthémon	Hatungimana	BDI	21.1.74	14 Sep	2:19.13	Nils	Schumann	GER	20.5.78	3 Sep
2:18.67	Johan	Botha	RSA	10.1.74	1 Aug	2:19.28	Moses	Kigen	KEN	22.4.73	3 Sep
2:18.69	Hudson	de Souza	BRA	25.2.77	28 Jun	2:19.37	Benson	Koech	KEN	10.11.74	8 Jul
2:18.70	Bernard	Lagat	KEN	12.12.74	14 Sep	2:19.38	Philip	Kibitok	KEN	23.3.71	28 Jun
2:18.89	Kamel	Boulahfane	ALG	1.7.76	19 Jun	2:19.41	Willy	Rotich	KEN	23.3.76	3 Aug

Indoors

Mark	Name		Nat	Born	Pos	Meet	Venue	Date
2:14.96	Wilson	Kipketer	DEN	12.12.70	1		Birmingham	20 Feb
2:15.25		Kipketer			1	Spark	Stuttgart	6 Feb
2:15.50	Kenneth	Kimwetich	KEN	1.1.73	2	Spark	Stuttgart	6 Feb

Mark	Name		Nat	Born	Date	Mark	Name		Nat	Born	Date
2:19.02	Nils	Schumann	GER	20.5.78	2 Feb	2:19.30A	Jason	Pyrah	USA	6.4.69	19 Feb
2:19.20	William	Tanui	KEN	22.2.64	20 Feb	2:19.35	Wojciech	Kaldowski	POL	16.4.76	2 Feb
2:19.20	John	Mayock	GBR	26.10.70	20 Feb						

Juniors

Mark	Name		Nat	Born	Pos	Meet	Venue	Date
2:17.40	Yuriy	Borzakovskiy	RUS	12.4.81	5	Nik	Nice	8 Jul
2:19.64	Florent	Lacasse	FRA	21.1.81	4		Marly	19 Jun
2:20.38	Stefan	Beumer	NED	28.4.81	1	VD	Bruxelles	25 Aug
2:21.35	Matthieu	Van Diest	BEL	10.2.81	2	VD	Bruxelles	25 Aug

1500 METRES

Mark	Name		Nat	Born	Pos	Meet	Venue	Date
3:27.21	Hicham	El Guerrouj	MAR	14.9.74	1	WK	Zürich	11 Aug
3:28.12	Noah	Ngeny	KEN	2.11.78	2	WK	Zürich	11 Aug
3:28.51	Bernard	Lagat	KEN	12.12.74	3	WK	Zürich	11 Aug
3:29.99		Ngeny			1	GGala	Roma	30 Jun
3:30.2+		El Guerrouj			1	in 1M	London (CP)	5 Aug
3:30.42		Ngeny			1	GP II	Rieti	3 Sep
3:30.73	Benjamin	Kipkurui	KEN	28.12.80	2	GP II	Rieti	3 Sep
3:30.75		El Guerrouj			1	GP	Saint-Denis	23 Jun
3:30.78		Lagat			2	GGala	Roma	30 Jun
3:30.82	Ali	Saïdi-Sief	ALG	15.3.78	1	GP II	Gateshead	28 Aug
3:30.90		El Guerrouj			1	ISTAF	Berlin	1 Sep
3:31.02	William	Chirchir	KEN	6.2.79	1	Herc	Monaco	18 Aug
3:31.10+		El Guerrouj			1	in 1M	Oslo	28 Jul
3:31.48	José Antonio	Redolat	ESP	17.2.76	3	GGala	Roma	30 Jun
3:31.48	Andrés	Díaz	ESP	12.7.69	2	Herc	Monaco	18 Aug
3:31.6+		Ngeny			2	in 1M	London (CP)	5 Aug
3:31.61		Ngeny			1	Athl	Lausanne	5 Jul
3:31.71	Kevin	Sullivan	CAN	20.3.74	4	GGala	Roma	30 Jun
3:31.72		Chirchir			2	ISTAF	Berlin	1 Sep
3:31.79		Díaz			4	WK	Zürich	11 Aug
3:32.01	Driss	Maazouzi	FRA	15.10.69	5	WK	Zürich	11 Aug
3:32.05	Mehdi	Baala	FRA	17.8.78	6	WK	Zürich	11 Aug
3:32.06		Maazouzi			3	Herc	Monaco	18 Aug
3:32.07		Ngeny			1	OG	Sydney	29 Sep
3:32.13+		Chirchir			2	in 1M	Oslo	28 Jul
3:32.28	Vyacheslav	Shabunin	RUS	27.9.69	5	GGala	Roma	30 Jun
3:32.32		El Guerrouj			2	OG	Sydney	29 Sep
3:32.41		Maazouzi			2	Athl	Lausanne	5 Jul
3:32.44		Lagat			3	OG	Sydney	29 Sep
3:32.55		Chirchir			1	GP II	Melbourne	2 Mar
3:32.58		Kipkurui			4	Herc	Monaco	18 Aug
	(31/12)							
3:32.60	Rui	Silva	POR	3.8.77	6	GGala	Roma	30 Jun
3:32.76	Benson	Koech	KEN	10.11.74	1		Lisboa (U)	5 Aug

Mark	Name		Nat	Born	Pos	Meet	Venue	Date
3:32.93	Laban	Rotich	KEN	20.1.69	7	WK	Zürich	11 Aug
3:33.04	John	Kibowen	KEN	21.4.69	5	Athl	Lausanne	5 Jul
3:33.07	Kamel	Boulahfane	ALG	1.7.76	3	GP II	Rieti	3 Sep
3:33.14	Hailu	Mekonnen	ETH	4.4.80	7	GGala	Roma	30 Jun
3:33.40	Mohamed	Khaldi	ALG	3.5.75	4	GP II	Rieti	3 Sep
3:33.59	Steve	Holman	USA	2.3.70	9	WK	Zürich	11 Aug
	(20)							
3:33.89	Nadir	Bosch	FRA	16.5.73	6	Herc	Monaco	18 Aug
3:33.92	Youssef	Baba	MAR	7.8.79	8	GGala	Roma	30 Jun
3:34.14	Japheth	Kimutai	KEN	20.12.78	1	GP	Osaka	13 May
3:34.29	Paul	Mwangi	KEN	19.11.73	1	Gugl	Linz	8 Aug
3:34.41	Adil	Kaouch	MAR	1.1.79	9	GGala	Roma	30 Jun
3:34.44	Marko	Koers	NED	3.11.72	10	GGala	Roma	30 Jun
3:34.69	Günther	Weidlinger	AUT	5.4.78	2		Kassel	7 Jun
3:34.69	John	Mayock	GBR	26.10.70	8	Herc	Monaco	18 Aug
3:34.85	Mohamed Saïd	El Wardi	MAR	19.4.72	11	GGala	Roma	30 Jun
3:34.91	Mark	Carroll	IRL	15.1.72	1	GP	Raleigh	17 Jun
	(30)							
3:34.93	Anthony	Whiteman	GBR	13.11.71	7	DNG	Stockholm	1 Aug
3:34.96	Ali	Hakimi	TUN	24.4.76	10	WK	Zürich	11 Aug
3:34.97	Hudson	de Souza	BRA	25.2.77	2	GP	Raleigh	17 Jun
3:35.11	Michael	Stember	USA	30.1.78	9	Herc	Monaco	18 Aug
3:35.16	Cornelius	Chirchir	KEN-J	7.10.83	6	GP II	Rieti	3 Sep
3:35.21	Gabe	Jennings	USA	25.1.79	7	GP II	Rieti	3 Sep
3:35.25	Peter	Biwott	KEN	22.8.76	2B	WK	Zürich	11 Aug
3:35.57	Shadrack	Langat	KEN	22.7.78	2	GP II	Zagreb	3 Jul
3:35.6A	Isaac	Sang	KEN		1		Nairobi	25 Mar
3:35.66	James Kimutai	Koskei	KEN	23.11.68	3B	WK	Zürich	11 Aug
	(40)							
3:35.67	Birhane	Alemu	ETH-J	16.7.82	1	NA	Heusden	5 Aug
3:35.67	Martin	Keino	KEN	20.6.72	8	GP II	Rieti	3 Sep
3:35.68	William	Tanui	KEN	22.2.64	9	GP II	Rieti	3 Sep
3:35.78	Mohammed	Amine	MAR	.76	3		Strasbourg	27 Jun
3:35.86	Julius	Achon	UGA	12.12.76	2		Leverkusen	20 Aug
3:36.00	Richard	Geemi	KEN	23.8.73	2		Lisboa (U)	5 Aug
3:36.08	Musa	Kimeli	KEN	23.6.68	5	GP II	Zagreb	3 Jul
3:36.14	Mohammed	Mourhit	BEL	10.10.70	2	NA	Heusden	5 Aug
3:36.15	David	Krummenacker	USA	24.5.75	3	GP	Raleigh	17 Jun
3:36.17	Paul	Bitok	KEN	26.6.70	2	GP II	Gateshead	28 Aug
	(50)							
3:36.18	Andrew	Graffin	GBR	20.12.77	3		Leverkusen	20 Aug
3:36.28	Aléxis	Abraham	FRA	14.2.76	4		Strasbourg	27 Jun
3:36.30	Johan	Botha	RSA	10.1.74	2		Nijmegen	23 May
3:36.30	James	Nolan	IRL	27.1.77	3	GP II	Gateshead	28 Aug
3:36.33	Daniel	Zegeye	ETH	13.3.79	6	Gugl	Linz	8 Aug
3:36.38	David	Lelei	KEN	10.5.71	7	Nik	Nice	8 Jul
3:36.55	Saïd	Chébili	FRA	6.5.73	12	Herc	Monaco	18 Aug
3:36.60	Abdelkader	Chékhémani	FRA	18.7.71	13	Herc	Monaco	18 Aug
3:36.62	Sammy	Rono	KEN	.74	4		Leverkusen	20 Aug
3:36.63	Juan Carlos	Higuero	ESP	3.8.78	4		Barcelona	25 Jul
	(60)							
3:36.70	Jason	Pyrah	USA	6.4.69	4	NC	Sacramento	16 Jul
3:36.71	Dirk	Heinze	GER	2.7.76	6	GP II	Zagreb	3 Jul
3:36.72	Peter	Philipp	SUI	18.2.72	6	NA	Heusden	5 Aug
3:36.74	Jason	Lunn	USA	19.9.74	7B	WK	Zürich	11 Aug
3:36.80	Ismaïl	Sghir	FRA	16.3.72	10	GP II	Rieti	3 Sep
3:36.83	Fouad	Chouki	FRA	1.10.78	8rB	WK	Zürich	11 Aug
3:37.08	Branko	Zorko	CRO	1.7.67	4	Veniz	Haniá	14 Jun
3:37.09	Salah	El Ghazi	MAR	2.11.75	10	Gaz	Saint-Denis	23 Jun
3:37.12	Edwin	Maranga	KEN	15.8.71	1	Karelia	Lappeenranta	13 Aug
3:37.24	Bernard	Barmasai	KEN	6.5.74	9	NA	Heusden	5 Aug
	(70)							
3:37.24	Reuben	Kosgei	KEN	2.8.79	10	NA	Heusden	5 Aug
3:37.25	Manuel	Damião	POR	9.7.78	3		Lisboa (U)	5 Aug
3:37.34	Kevin	McKay	GBR	9.2.69	9	Gugl	Linz	8 Aug
3:37.46	Luke	Kipkosgei	KEN	27.11.75	4	GP	Raleigh	17 Jun
3:37.47	Andrea	Abelli	ITA	9.2.71	14	GGala	Roma	30 Jun
3:37.48	Seneca	Lassiter	USA	12.3.77	5	GP	Raleigh	17 Jun
3:37.52	Darko	Radomirovic	YUG	5.8.77	1		Beograd	29 Aug
3:37.62	Mickaël	Damian	FRA	9.11.69	3		Amiens	25 Jul

Mark	Name		Nat	Born	Pos	Meet	Venue	Date
3:37.62	William	Yiampoy	KEN	15.5.74	1		Padova	27 Aug
3:37.72	Harrison	Makau	KEN	.74	2	Karelia	Lappeenranta	13 Aug
	(80)							
3:37.74	John	Kosgei	KEN	13.7.73	1		Brisbane	11 Feb
3:37.75	Samir	Benfarès	FRA	6.6.68	5		Strasbourg	27 Jun
3:37.75	Jonathan	McCallum	GBR	19.11.75	11	DNG	Stockholm	1 Aug
3:38.00	Ibrahim	Aden	SOM	11.11.72	8	GP II	Zagreb	3 Jul
3:38.03	Luís	Feiteira	POR	21.4.73	4		Lisboa (U)	5 Aug
3:38.16	Alexis	Sharangabo	RWA	9.11.78	2		Palo Alto	29 Jul
3:38.27	Craig	Mottram	AUS	18.6.80	9	GP II	Zagreb	3 Jul
3:38.30	Mohamed	Suleiman	QAT	23.11.69	8	-	Leverkusen	20 Aug
3:38.36	Andy	Downin	USA	12.5.73	6	NC	Sacramento	16 Jul
3:38.37	Matt	Holthaus	USA	2.11.71	3		Palo Alto	29 Jul
	(90)							
3:38.41	Noureddine	Morceli	ALG	28.2.70	2h3	OG	Sydney	25 Sep
3:38.44	Abdelhak	Abdellah	MAR	13.8.68	11	GP II	Rieti	3 Sep
3:38.48	Ivan	Geshko	UKR	19.8.79	1	NC	Kiev	4 Aug
3:38.51	Sammy	Mutai	KEN	20.12.74	2		Brisbane	11 Feb
3:38.52	António	Travassos	POR	24.9.71	5		Lisboa (U)	5 Aug
3:38.58	Mohamed	Yagoub	SUD	2.9.77	8	ISTAF	Berlin	1 Sep
3:38.61	Roberto	García	ESP	20.8.75	1		Zaragoza	9 Jul
3:38.61	Mustapha	Riyad	MAR	5.8.75	4		Amiens	25 Jul
3:38.63	Jürgen	Vandewiele	BEL	10.5.74	11rA	NA	Heusden	5 Aug
3:38.68	David	Kisang	KEN	.74	1		Loughborough	21 May
	(100)							

3:38.70	Scott	Anderson	USA	30.1.74	29 Jul
3:38.79	Laïd	Bessou	ALG	5.2.76	3 Sep
3:38.82	Gennaro	Di Napoli	ITA	5.3.68	3 Jun
3:38.86	Karl	Paranya	USA	27.6.75	14 Jul
3:38.90	Jonathon	Riley	USA	29.12.78	1 Jul
3:38.96	Alastair	Stevenson	AUS	28.5.79	11 Feb
3:39.03	Neil	Caddy	GBR	18.3.75	22 Jul
3:39.07	Leszek	Zblewski	POL	25.12.73	22 Jul
3:39.08	Gareth	Turnbull	IRL	14.5.79	21 May
3:39.09	Wolfram	Müller	GER-J	8.7.81	30 Jul
3:39.13	Richie	Boulet	USA	14.6.73	1 Jul
3:39.23	Boris	Kaveshnikov	RUS	30.9.74	3 Jul
3:39.25+	Bert	Leenaerts	BEL	1.7.80	25 Aug
3:39.28	Abdelkader	Hachlaf	MAR	.79	27 Jul
3:39.33	Kipkurui	Misoi	KEN	23.12.78	5 Aug
3:39.40	Christian	Obrist	ITA	20.11.80	3 Jun
3:39.49	Nick	Howarth	AUS	24.6.76	18 Jan
3:39.51	Fred	Cheruiyot	KEN	20.9.70	27 Jul
3:39.56	Balázs	Tölgyesi	HUN	10.1.73	14 Jun
3:39.60	Kiyoharu	Sato	JPN-J	28.5.81	13 May
3:39.63	Matthieu	Van Diest	BEL-J	10.2.81	5 Aug
3:39.66	Vénuste	Niyongabo	BDI	9.12.73	3 Jul
3:39.71	Dan	Wilson	USA	19.2.79	3 Jun
3:39.72	Hamid	El Mouaziz	MAR		27 Jul
3:39.76	Abraham	Chebii	KEN	23.12.79	21 May
3:39.77	Youcef	Abdi	AUS	7.12.77	11 Feb
3:39.80	Matthew	Dixon	GBR	26.12.78	21 May
3:39.94	David	Galván	MEX	6.4.76	4 Jun
3:40.02	Abraham Maiyo	Kipkemboi	KEN		3 Jun
3:40.03	Vasil	Tsikalo	UKR	2.3.80	4 Aug
3:40.05	Bouaza	El Mastati	MAR	.72	25 Jul
3:40.08	Jeremy	Huffman	USA	13.2.76	1 Jul
3:40.10	Moses	Kigen	KEN	22.4.73	27 Aug
3:40.13	Michael	East	GBR	20.1.78	21 May
3:40.14	Felix	Limo	KEN	22.8.80	1 Jul
3:40.14	Allen	Graffin	GBR	20.12.77	28 Aug
3:40.2	Mohamed	Abdelli	ALG	.74	8 Jun
3:40.22	Richard	Limo	KEN	18.11.80	23 May
3:40.23	Terrance	Herrington	USA	31.7.66	17 Jun
3:40.24	Jake	Maas	USA	17.2.77	25 Jun
3:40.28	Víctor	Morente	ESP	28.4.71	9 Jun
3:40.29	Wilson	Boit Kipketer	KEN	6.10.73	3 Jun
3:40.30	Brian	Berryhill	USA	15.12.77	25 Jun
3:40.36	Nils	Schumann	GER	20.5.78	7 Jun
3:40.40	Keita	Takahashi	JPN	7.4.75	13 May
3:40.41	Rubén	Villarroya	ESP	30.10.76	25 Jul
3:40.42	Colm	McLean	IRL	7.6.80	25 Jul
3:40.47	Michael	Ryan II	USA	16.7.76	14 Jul
3:40.5A	Enock	Koech	KEN-J	4.4.81	21 Jul
3:40.51	Javier	Moro	ESP	16.4.75	25 Jul
3:40.52	Esau	Faro	RSA	24.9.74	31 Mar
3:40.56	Erik	Nedeau	USA	30.8.71	1 Jul
3:40.58	David	Kimani	KEN	20.2.77	3 Jun
3:40.62	Roberto	Parra	ESP	6.4.76	9 Jun
3:40.64	Siakha	Bamba	FRA	24.5.75	30 Jun
3:40.64	Reyes	Estévez	ESP	2.8.76	18 Aug
3:40.65	Andy	Powell	USA	23.5.80	1 Jul
3:40.68	Darin	Shearer	USA	3.4.74	8 Aug
3:40.73	Panayiótis	Stroubákos	GRE	8.9.72	14 Jun
3:40.74	Philippe	Bandi	SUI	31.12.70	12 Jun
3:40.75	Sam	Gabremariam	USA	16.6.75	18 Jun
3:40.77	Djordje	Milic	YUG	12.10.72	22 Jul
3:40.77	Philemon	Kibet	KEN-J	20.11.82	22 Oct
3:40.82	Patrick	Grammens	BEL	10.4.71	5 Aug
3:40.83	Nabil	Maataoui	MAR		27 Jul
3:40.86	Massimo	Pegoretti	ITA	16.7.74	3 Jun
3:40.86	Héctor	Torres	MEX	8.9.73	7 Jul
3:40.87	Philip	Price	USA	21.8.74	22 Apr
3:40.87	Txomin	Martín	ESP	10.9.70	15 Jul
3:40.93	Mouhcine	Khoudaoui	MAR		27 Jul
3:40.94	Michael	Power	AUS	9.5.76	13 Feb
3:40.94	Alberto	Bispo	POR	14.1.75	15 Jul
3:40.95	Carlos	Suárez	ESP	25.9.75	15 Jul
3:40.96	Rédouane	Harroufi	MAR-J	30.7.81	27 Jul
3:40.96	Eliseo	Martín	ESP	5.11.73	21 Aug
3:40.97	Julius	Kiptoo	KEN	4.9.77	3 Jul
3:41.00	Youcef	Allem	ALG	16.11.69	27 Jun
3:41.02	Luc	Michard	FRA	4.10.73	27 Jun
3:41.05	Daniel	Kinyua	KEN	29.11.74	22 Apr
3:41.08	Tarek	Boukensa	ALG-J	19.11.81	24 Aug
3:41.09	Alemu	Dagne	ETH	15.10.80	3 Jun
3:41.10	Sharif	Karie	SOM	1.1.78	3 Jun
3:41.15	Jesús	España	ESP	21.8.78	21 Aug
3:41.15	Stefan	Beumer	NED-J	28.4.81	3 Sep
3:41.19	Angus	MacLean	GBR	20.9.80	3 Sep
3:41.20	Charlie	Gruber	USA	6.8.78	1 Jul
3:41.20	Raymond	Yator	KEN-J	7.4.81	5 Aug
3:41.2	Khamis Seif	Abdullah	QAT	1.12.76	8 Jun
3:41.21	Johan	Cronje	RSA-J	13.4.82	31 Mar
3:41.26	Tom	Nohilly	USA	27.4.66	1 Jul
3:41.28	Graham	Hood	CAN	2.4.72	13 Feb
3:41.3A	Paul	Korir	KEN	.77	29 Apr
3:41.32	Miguel Angel	Penas	ESP	9.11.77	15 Jul
3:41.36	Daniel	Oniciuc	ROM	23.1.77	24 Jun
3:41.36	Richard	Ashe	GBR	5.10.74	22 Jul
3:41.39	Andy	McKessock	CAN	27.2.79	5 May
3:41.39	Sebastien	Cosson	FRA	15.3.80	30 Jun
3:41.39	Rachid	Chékhémani	FRA	1.10.73	8 Jul
3:41.40	James	Karanu	KEN	5.1.76	14 May
3:41.40	Marco	Cepeda	ESP	1.7.74	21 Aug
	(200)				

Indoors

Mark	Name		Nat	Born	Date
3:39.75+i	Paul	McMullen	USA	19.2.72	8 Jan
3:40.25i	Rüdiger	Stenzel	GER	16.4.68	18 Feb
3:40.93i	Piotr	Rostkowski	POL	8.1.72	6 Feb

Subsequent to drugs disqualification

Mark	Name		Nat	Born	Pos	Meet	Venue	Date
3:37.18	Dieter	Baumann	GER	9.2.65	8rA	NA	Heusden	5 Aug

JUNIORS

Mark	Name		Nat	Born	Pos	Meet	Venue	Date
3:35.16	Cornelius	Chirchir	KEN	7.10.83	6	GP II	Rieti	3 Sep
	3:38.223	Lappeenranta	13 Aug	3:38.80	1	WJ	Santiago	22 Oct
3:35.67	Birhane	Alemu	ETH	16.7.82	1	NA	Heusden	5 Aug
	3:36.684 Nijmegen	23 May	3:38.79		5h3	OG	Sydney	25 Spe
	3:36.818 Gugl	Linz	8 Aug					
3:39.09	Wolfram	Müller	GER	8.7.81	2	NC	Braunschweig	30 Jul
	3:39.372 WJ	Santiago	22 Oct	10 performances by 4 men to 3:39.60				
3:39.60	Kiyoharu	Sato	JPN	28.5.81	5	GP	Osaka	13 May
3:39.63	Matthieu	Van Diest	BEL	10.2.81	14rA	NA	Heusden	5 Aug
3:40.5A	Enock	Koech	KEN	4.4.81	3s1	NC	Nairobi	21 Jul
3:40.77	Philemon	Kibet	KEN	20.11.82	3	WJ	Santiago de Chile	22 Oct
3:40.96	Rédouane	Harroufi	MAR	30.7.81	9		Casablanca	27 Jul
3:41.08	Tarek	Boukensa	ALG	19.11.81	2		Nantes	24 Aug
3:41.15	Stefan	Beumer	NED	28.4.81	1		Glasgow	3 Sep
3:41.20	Raymond	Yator	KEN	14.7.82	2rB	NA	Heusden	5 Aug
3:41.21	Johan	Cronje	RSA	13.4.82	4		Cape Town	31 Mar
3:41.70	Lorenzo	Perrone	ITA	26.9.81	1		Cles	11 Aug
3:41.97	Jamal Noor	Youssef	QAT	13.8.82	1		Gent	19 Jul
3:42.61	Ali Abubaker	Kamel	QAT	.83	3		Wespelaar	23 Jul
3:42.8	Ryan	Hayden	CAN	27.1.82	2		Burnaby	5 Aug
3:42.98	Abdul Rahman	Sulaiman	QAT	.84	3		Gent	19 Jul
3:43.36	Alvaro	Fernández	ESP	7.4.81	6h2	NC	Barcelona	2 Sep
3:43.66	Florent	Lacasse	FRA	21.1.81	2		Montgeron	18 Jun
3:43.81+	Donald	Sage	USA-J	5.10.81	9	Pre	Eugene	24 Jun

1 MILE

Mark	Name		Nat	Born	Pos	Meet	Venue	Date
3:45.96	Hicham	El Guerrouj	MAR	14.9.74	1	BrGP	London (CP)	5 Aug
3:46.24		El Guerrouj			1	Bisl	Oslo	28 Jul
3:47.67	Noah	Ngeny	KEN	2.11.78	2	BrGP	London (CP)	5 Aug
3:47.91		El Guerrouj			1	VD	Bruxelles	25 Aug
3:47.94	William	Chirchir	KEN	6.2.79	2	Bisl	Oslo	28 Jul
3:48.23		Chirchir			2	VD	Bruxelles	25 Aug
3:49.34	Benjamin	Kipkurui	KEN	28.12.80	3	VD	Bruxelles	25 Aug
3:49.84	Bernard	Lagat	KEN	12.12.74	4	VD	Bruxelles	25 Aug
3:49.87	John	Kibowen	KEN	21.4.69	3	Bisl	Oslo	28 Jul
3:50.26	Kevin	Sullivan	CAN	20.3.74	4	Bisl	Oslo	28 Jul
3:50.31	Laban	Rotich	KEN	20.1.69	5	Bisl	Oslo	28 Jul
3:50.54	Vyacheslav	Shabunin	RUS	27.9.69	5	VD	Bruxelles	25 Aug
3:50.61	John	Mayock	GBR	26.10.70	6	Bisl	Oslo	28 Jul
3:50.62	Mark	Carroll	IRL	15.1.72	7	Bisl	Oslo	28 Jul
3:51.79	Driss	Maazouzi	FRA	15.10.69	6	VD	Bruxelles	25 Aug
3:51.84		Chirchir			1	Pre	Eugene	24 Jun
3:52.04	Nadir	Bosch	FRA	16.5.73	7	VD	Bruxelles	25 Aug
	(17/13)							
3:52.22	Adil	Kaouch	MAR	1.1.79	8	Bisl	Oslo	28 Jul
3:52.85	Youssef	Baba	MAR	7.8.79	9	Bisl	Oslo	28 Jul
3:53.40	Hailu	Mekonnen	ETH	4.4.80	10	Bisl	Oslo	28 Jul
3:53.74	Hudson	de Souza	BRA	25.2.77	3	Pre	Eugene	24 Jun
3:54.66	Mohamed	Khaldi	ALG	3.5.75	11	VD	Bruxelles	25 Aug
3:54.85	Seneca	Lassiter	USA	12.3.77	5	Pre	Eugene	24 Jun
3:54.90	Bert	Leenaerts	BEL	1.7.80	13	VD	Bruxelles	25 Aug
3:55.07	Kevin	McKay	GBR	9.2.69	7	BrGP	London (CP)	5 Aug
3:55.24	David	Kisang	KEN	.74	1		London (BP)	4 Jun
3:55.31	Abraham	Chebii	KEN	23.12.79	2		London (BP)	4 Jun
	(20)							
3:55.74	Jason	Pyrah	USA	6.4.69	6	Pre	Eugene	24 Jun
3:56.01	Steve	Holman	USA	2.3.70	14	VD	Bruxelles	25 Aug
3:56.13	Andrew	Graffin	GBR	20.12.77	9	BrGP	London (CP)	5 Aug
3:56.43	Leonard	Mucheru	KEN	13.6.78	1		San Francisco	29 Oct
3:56.48	Reyes	Estévez	ESP	2.8.76	15	VD	Bruxelles	25 Aug

Mark	Name		Nat	Born	Date
3:56.68	Rui	Silva	POR	3.8.77	25 Aug
3:57.00	Martin	Keino	KEN	20.6.72	5 Aug
3:57.07	David	Kimani	KEN	20.2.77	29 Apr
3:57.32	Mohamed	Amine	MAR	.76	5 Aug
3:57.5	Charles	Makau	KEN	13.3.71	27 Aug
3:57.5	Edwin	Maranga	KEN	15.8.71	27 Aug
3:57.82	Alexis	Sharangabo	RWA	9.11.78	19 Aug
3:57.89	Gareth	Turnbull	IRL	14.5.79	29 Apr

Mark	Name		Nat	Born	Date
3:58.13	Phil	Clode	NZL	11.3.65	22 Jan
3:58.31	Neil	Caddy	GBR	18.3.75	5 Aug
3:58.38	Alastair	Stevenson	AUS	28.5.79	22 Jan
3:58.49	Clyde	Colenso	RSA	11.5.77	13 May
3:58.74	Karl	Paranya	USA	27.6.75	29 Apr
3:58.96	Andrew	Walker	IRL	6.5.77	29 Oct
3:59.04	Steve	Willis	NZL	24.4.75	22 Jan
3:59.17	Sam	Gabremariam	USA	16.6.75	29 Apr
3:59.23	Emmanuel	Kemboi	KEN-J	.81	28 Jul
3:59.28	Simon	Maunder	NZL	20.8.72	22 Jan
3:59.29	Dwight	Davis	USA	25.12.77	16 Apr
3:59.29	John	Kosgei	KEN	13.7.73	24 Jun
3:59.3	Cornelius	Chirchir	KEN-J	7.10.83	27 Aug
3:59.34	Brian	Berryhill	USA	15.12.77	22 Jan
3:59.35	Steve	Fein	USA	4.6.77	13 May
3:59.71	Dan	Browne	USA	24.6.75	13 May
3:59.71	Rich	Tremain	CAN	30.6.71	19 Aug
3:59.86	Mike	Miller	USA	19.1.74	13 May
3:59.86	Allen	Graffin	GBR	20.12.77	5 Aug
3:59.91	Gabe	Jennings	USA	25.1.79	24 Jun
3:59.97	Paul	McMullen	USA	19.2.72	29 Apr

Indoors

Mark	Name		Nat	Born	Pos	Meet	Venue	Date
3:56.39	Paul	Bitok	KEN	26.6.70	3	Gaz	Liévin	13 Feb

Mark	Name		Nat	Born	Date
3:56.76	William	Tanui	KEN	22.2.64	13 Feb
3:57.00	Richie	Boulet	USA	14.6.73	8 Jan
3:57.88	Paul	McMullen	USA	19.2.72	8 Jan
3:58.21	Jason	Lunn	USA	19.7.74	12 Feb
3:58.34	Saïd	Chébili	FRA	6.5.73	13 Feb
3:58.40	Michael	Stember	USA	30.1.78	31 Jan
3:58.87	Shadrack	Langat	KEN	22.7.78	13 Feb
3:59.17	James	Karanu	KEN	5.1.76	12 Feb
3:59.43	Rich	Kenah	USA	4.8.70	12 Feb
3:59.46	Gabe	Jennings	USA	25.1.79	11 Mar
3:59.67	Tim	Broe	USA	20.6.77	27 Feb
3:59.80	Ibrahim	Aden	SOM	11.11.72	29 Jan
3:59.90#	Jay	Cantin	CAN	23.4.77	5 Feb
3:59.93	Darin	Shearer	USA	3.4.74	4 Mar

JUNIORS

Mark	Name		Nat	Born	Pos	Meet	Venue	Date
3:59.23	Emmanuel	Kemboi	KEN	.81	11	Bisl	Oslo	28 Jul
3:59.3	Cornelius	Chirchir	KEN	5.6.83	3		Aberdeen	27 Aug
4:00.29	Donald	Sage	USA	5.10.81	9	Pre	Eugene	24 Jun

2000 METRES

Mark	Name		Nat	Born	Pos	Meet	Venue	Date
4:58.6+	Brahim	Lahlafi	MAR	15.4.68	1	in 3k	Monaco	18 Aug
4:58.7+	Ali	Saïdi-Sief	ALG	15.3.78	2	in 3k	Monaco	18 Aug
4:58.8+	Mohammed	Mourhit	BEL	10.10.70	3	in 3k	Monaco	18 Aug
4:59.0+	Daniel	Komen	KEN	17.5.76	4	in 3k	Monaco	18 Aug
5:00.21	Bouabdallah	Tahri	FRA	20.12.78	1		Marly	19 Jun
5:00.66	David	Kisang	KEN	.74	1		London (BP)	25 Jun
5:01.28	Andrew	Graffin	GBR	20.12.77	2		London (BP)	25 Jun
5:01.6+	Million	Wolde	ETH	17.3.79	4	Gaz	Saint-Denis	23 Jun
5:01.85+	William	Tanui	KEN	22.2.64	1	in 3k	Sevilla	9 Jun
5:01.9+	Benjamin	Maiyo	KEN	6.10.78	2	GP	Athína	28 Jun

Mark	Name		Nat	Born	Date
5:02.1+	Mohamed Said	El Wardi	MAR	19.4.72	23 Jun
5:02.3+	Evans	Rutto	KEN	8.4.78	28 Jun
5:02.6+	Driss	Maazouzi	FRA	15.10.69	23 Jun
5:02.90	Allen	Graffin	GBR	20.12.77	25 Jun
5:03.08	Salah	El Ghazi	MAR	2.11.75	5 Jun
5:03.1+	Paul	Kosgei	KEN	22.4.78	28 Jun
5:03.91	Ivan	Geshko	UKR	19.8.79	24 Jun
5:03.92	Ibrahim	Aden	SOM	11.11.72	5 Jun

Indoors

Mark	Name		Nat	Born	Date
5:02.53	John	Mayock	GBR	26.10.70	11 Feb
5:03.75	Girma	Tolla	ETH	13.10.75	11 Feb

3000 METRES

Mark	Name		Nat	Born	Pos	Meet	Venue	Date
7:25.02	Ali	Saïdi-Sief	ALG	15.3.78	1	Herc	Monaco	18 Aug
7:26.62	Mohammed	Mourhit	BEL	10.10.70	2	Herc	Monaco	18 Aug
7:27.67		Saïdi-Sief			1	Gaz	Saint-Denis	23 Jun
7:28.92	Daniel	Komen	KEN	17.5.76	3	Herc	Monaco	18 Aug
7:29.25	Brahim	Lahlafi	MAR	15.4.68	4	Herc	Monaco	18 Aug
7:30.76		Saïdi-Sief			1	ISTAF	Berlin	1 Sep
7:31.47		Komen			2	Gaz	Saint-Denis	23 Jun
7:31.96		Komen			1	GPII	Athína	28 Jun
7:31.98		Lahlafi			2	ISTAF	Berlin	1 Sep
7:32.36	Million	Wolde	ETH	17.3.79	3	Gaz	Saint-Denis	23 Jun
7:32.36	Benjamin	Maiyo	KEN	6.10.78	2	GPII	Athína	28 Jun
7:33.51	Bernard	Lagat	KEN	12.12.74	5	Herc	Monaco	18 Aug
7:34.67	Mohamed Saïd	El Wardi	MAR	19.4.72	4	Gaz	Saint-Denis	23 Jun
7:34.86	Luke	Kipkosgei	KEN	27.11.75	6	Herc	Monaco	18 Aug
7:35.18		Lahlafi			5	Gaz	Saint-Denis	23 Jun
7:35.20	Paul	Bitok	KEN	26.6.70	7	Herc	Monaco	18 Aug
7:35.46	Noah	Ngeny	KEN	2.11.78	1	GPII	Sevilla	9 Jun
7:35.72	Sammy	Kipketer	KEN-J	29.9.81	8	Herc	Monaco	18 Aug
7:35.80		Komen			3	ISTAF	Berlin	1 Sep
7:36.10		Lahlafi			2	GPII	Sevilla	9 Jun
	(20/12)							
7:36.33	James Kimutai	Koskei	KEN	23.11.68	6	Gaz	Saint-Denis	23 Jun
7:36.38	Evans	Rutto	KEN	8.4.78	3	GPII	Athína	28 Jun
7:36.79	Bernard	Barmasai	KEN	6.5.74	4	GPII	Athína	28 Jun
7:37.12	Richard	Limo	KEN	18.11.80	9	Herc	Monaco	18 Aug
7:37.16	Salah	Hissou	MAR	16.1.72	5	ISTAF	Berlin	1 Sep
7:37.73	Benjamin	Limo	KEN	23.8.74	1	Nik	Nice	8 Jul

Mark	Name		Nat	Born	Pos	Meet	Venue	Date
7:37.91	Ismail	Sghir	FRA	16.3.72	2	Nik	Nice	8 Jul
7:38.03	Mustapha	Essaïd	FRA	20.1.70	3	Nik	Nice	8 Jul
	(20)							
7:38.30	David	Chelule	KEN	7.7.77	10	Herc	Monaco	18 Aug
7:39.15	Paul	Kosgei	KEN	22.4.78	5	GPII	Athína	28 Jun
7:39.29	Daniel	Gachara	KEN	19.12.72	6	GPII	Athína	28 Jun
7:39.93	Driss	Maazouzi	FRA	15.10.69	9	Gaz	Saint-Denis	23 Jun
7:40.56	Martin	Keino	KEN	20.6.72	5	Nik	Nice	8 Jul
7:40.82	Alberto	García	ESP	22.2.71	1		Barcelona	25 Jul
7:40.93	Kipkirui	Misoi	KEN	23.12.78	2		Ingolstadt	18 Jun
7:41.03	Mark	Carroll	IRL	15.1.72	8	ISTAF	Berlin	1 Sep
7:41.48	Fabián	Roncero	ESP	19.10.70	2		Barcelona	25 Jul
7:41.56	Leonard	Mucheru Maina	KEN	13.6.78	9	ISTAF	Berlin	1 Sep
	(30)							
7:41.85	Réda	Benzine	ALG	19.4.71	12	Herc	Monaco	18 Aug
7:42.05	Marius	Bakken	NOR	27.3.78	1		Florø	8 Jun
7:42.19	David	Galván	MEX	6.4.76	10	ISTAF	Berlin	1 Sep
7:42.51	José	Rios	ESP	15.3.74	3		Barcelona	25 Jul
7:42.58	Abiyote	Abate	ETH	20.11.80	1	GPII	Helsinki	15 Jun
7:43.00	Ahmed	Ibrahim Warsama	QAT	4.2.66	4		Barcelona	25 Jul
7:43.05	David	Tuwei	KEN	22.2.79	2	GPII	Helsinki	15 Jun
7:43.35	John Cheruiyot	Korir	KEN-J	13.12.81	2		Torino	10 Jun
7:43.41	Enrique	Molina	ESP	25.2.68	5		Barcelona	25 Jul
7:43.48	Moses	Kiptanui	KEN	1.10.70	7	GPII	Athína	28 Jun
	(40)							
7:43.49	Albert	Chepkirui	KEN-J	4.4.81	11	ISTAF	Berlin	1 Sep
7:43.50	Charles	Kamathi	KEN	18.5.78	3	GPII	Helsinki	15 Jun
7:43.50	Felix	Limo	KEN	22.8.80	3		Ingolstadt	18 Jun
7:43.73	Roberto	García	ESP	20.8.75	6		Barcelona	25 Jul
7:44.06	Aloÿs	Nizigama	BDI	18.6.66	6	Nik	Nice	8 Jul
7:44.39+	Haile	Gebrselassie	ETH	18.4.73	1	in 5k	Zürich	11 Aug
7:44.50	Boniface	Usisivu	KEN	5.9.74	3		Torino	10 Jun
7:45.63	Abraham	Chebii	KEN	23.12.79	11	Gaz	Saint-Denis	23 Jun
7:45.72	Josphat	Boit	KEN		2		Florø	8 Jun
7:46.07	Laïd	Bessou	ALG	5.2.76	4		Torino	10 Jun
	(50)							
7:46.22	Michael	Power	AUS	9.5.76	1		Brisbane	8 Sep
7:46.40	Mark	Bett	KEN	22.12.76	1		Caorle	8 Jul
7:46.88	Shaun	Creighton	AUS	14.5.67	1		Portland	25 Jun
7:46.95	Kenenisa	Bekele	ETH-J	.81	1		Cottbus	23 Aug
7:47.39	Philemon	Kemei	KEN-J	12.2.82	1		Viareggio	22 Aug
7:47.52	Alemu	Dagne	ETH	15.10.80	9	GP	Athína	28 Jun
7:48.09	Sergey	Lebed	UKR	15.7.75	7		Barcelona	25 Jul
7:48.19	Julius	Maritim	KEN	.80	2		Cottbus	23 Aug
7:48.71	Salim	Kipsang	KEN	22.12.79	5	GP II	Helsinki	15 Jun
7:49.12	Teodoro	Cuñado	ESP	13.2.70	8		Barcelona	25 Jul
	(60)							
7:49.67	Anacleto	Jiménez	ESP	24.2.67	9		Barcelona	25 Jul
7:50.02	Helder	Ornelas	POR	6.5.74	13	ISTAF	Berlin	1 Sep

7:50.22	Yousef	El Nasri	ESP	28.7.79	18 Aug
7:50.27	Luis M	Martín	ESP	11.1.72	25 Jul
7:50.30	Antonio D	Jiménez	ESP	18.2.77	5 Sep
7:50.4+	Paul	Tergat	KEN	17.6.69	5 Jul
7:50.83	Bruno	Toledo	ESP	23.11.73	25 Jul
7:50.96	Driss	El Himer	FRA	4.4.74	8 Jul
7:51.17	Abraham	Cherono	KEN	21.7.80	10 Jun
7:51.20	Pablo	Olmedo	MEX	8.5.75	1 Sep
7:51.25	Nadir	Bosch	FRA	16.5.73	15 Jun
7:51.32	Craig	Mottram	AUS	18.6.80	14 Jun
7:51.35	Biruk	Deberework	ETH-J	25.8.82	31 May
7:51.37	James	Getanda	KEN-J	.7.82	8 Jul
7:51.54	Julius	Kiptoo	KEN	1.9.77	11 Jun
7:51.90	José Manuel	Martínez	ESP	22.10.71	25 Jul
7:51.95	Jirka	Arndt	GER	1.8.73	18 Jun
7:51.99	Philip	Kemei	KEN	6.6.77	10 Jun
7:52.17	Cyrus	Kataron	KEN-J	16.5.82	31 May
7:52.19	David	Kisang	KEN	.74	5 Jul
7:52.27	Kris	Bowditch	GBR	14.1.75	14 Jun
7:52.32	Salvatore	Vincenti	ITA	5.3.72	8 Jul
7:52.37	Iván	Hierro	ESP	14.2.78	25 Jul
7:52.46	Wolfram	Müller	GER-J	8.7.81	31 May
7:52.82	Jeff	Schiebler	CAN	1.6.73	31 May
7:52.84	Brahim	Jabbour	MAR	2.10.70	25 Jul
7:53.04	Paul	Mwangi	KEN	19.11.73	8 Jul
7:53.11	Bouabdallah	Tahri	FRA	20.12.78	6 May
7:53.11	Julian	Moorhouse	GBR	13.11.71	14 Jun
7:53.19	Eduardo	Vargas	ESP	13.11.76	5 Sep
7:53.22	Brian	Baker	USA	8.6.70	1 Jul
7:53.23	Christian	Stephenson	GBR	22.7.74	5 Jul
7:53.41	Matt	Lane	USA	5.9.77	1 Jul
7:53.46	Alan	Culpepper	USA	15.9.72	25 Jun
7:53.54	John	Nuttall	GBR	11.1.67	5 Jul
7:53.65	Sebastian	Hallmann	GER	7.1.77	31 May
7:53.67	José Antonio	Redolat	ESP	17.2.76	9 Jun
7:53.68	Adrian	Passey	GBR	2.9.64	14 Jun
7:53.98	Andrea	Arlati	ITA	7.5.70	10 Jun
7:54.12	Andres	Jones	GBR	3.2.77	5 Jul
7:54.23	Abdelhak	Abdellah	MAR	13.8.68	22 Aug
7:54.34	Alejandro	Suárez	MEX	.80	31 May
7:54.49	Michal	Bartoszak	POL	21.6.70	23 Aug
7:54.62	Pete	Sherry	USA	22.8.68	1 Jul
7:54.88	Fidencio	Torres	MEX	16.8.73	31 May
7:54.97	Tijani	Errahmouni	FRA	30.12.70	25 Jul

Mark	Name		Nat	Born	Pos	Meet	Venue	Date
Subsequent to drugs disqualification								
7:47.22	Dieter	Baumann	GER	9.2.65	1		Cuxhaven	19 Jul
Indoors								
7:35.34		Wolde			1	Spark	Stuttgart	6 Feb
7:36.25		Saïdi-Sief			2	Spark	Stuttgart	6 Feb
7:38.33	Moses	Kiptanui	KEN	1.10.70	3	Spark	Stuttgart	6 Feb
7:38.39+	Hailu	Mekonnen	ETH	4.4.80	1		Birmingham	20 Feb
7:38.68	Girma	Tolla	ETH	13.10.75	2		Karlsruhe	29 Jan
7:39.44	Rui	Silva	POR	3.8.77	4	Spark	Stuttgart	6 Feb
7:41.86	Reuben	Kosgei	KEN	2.8.79	6	Spark	Stuttgart	6 Feb
7:47.09	El Hassan	Lahssini	FRA	1.1.74	7	Spark	Stuttgart	6 Feb
7:47.19	Yousef	El Nasri	ESP	28.7.79	3	IHM	Karlsruhe	29 Jan
7:47.20	Gennaro	Di Napoli	ITA	5.3.68	3		Stockholm	17 Feb
7:47.65	Saïd	Chébili	FRA	6.5.73	4	IHM	Karlsruhe	29 Jan
7:47.79	Günther	Weidlinger	AUT	5.4.78	1	NC	Wien	13 Feb
7:48.90	Kent	Claesson	SWE	29.7.71	4		Stockholm	17 Feb
7:48.91	Vyacheslav	Shabunin	RUS	27.9.69	1		Erfurt	2 Feb
7:49.03	Adam	Goucher	USA	18.2.75	2	Mill	New York	4 Feb
7:49.37	Michael	Buchleitner	AUT	14.10.69	2	NC	Wien	13 Feb
7:49.97	John	Mayock	GBR	26.10.70	3	EI	Gent	27 Feb

7:50.26 ?	Moses	Kigen	KEN	22.4.73	9 Feb	7:53.63	Rob	Whalley	GBR	11.2.68	6 Feb
7:52.12	Eric	Dubus	FRA	28.2.66	9 Feb	7:53.85	Jan	Fitschen	GER	2.5.77	2 Feb
7:52.35	Ovidiu	Olteanu	ROM	6.8.70	9 Feb	7:53.97	Andrés	Díaz	ESP	12.7.69	27 Feb
7:52.64	David	Kimani	KEN	20.2.77	11 Mar	7:54.0	Abdelhak	Abdellah	MAR	13.8.68	13 Feb
7:53.37+	Kevin	Sullivan	CAN	20.3.74	6 Feb	7:54.59	Miroslav	Vanko	SVK	14.2.73	17 Feb
						7:54.6	Massimo	Pegoretti	ITA	16.7.74	13 Feb

JUNIORS

See main list for top 5 juniors. 11 performances by 5 men under 7:48.5. Additional marks and further juniors:

Kipketer	7:38.06	8	Gaz	Saint-Denis	23 Jun	7:47.31	3	GPF	Doha	5 Oct
	7:46.2+	4	in 5k	Oslo	28 Jul	7:48.47+	1	in 5k	Milano	7 Jun
Chepkirui	7:46.0+	3	in 5k	Oslo	28 Jul	7:47.53	3		Caorle	8 Jul

7:51.35	Biruk	Deberework	ETH	25.8.82	1		Dessau	31 May
7:51.37	James	Getanda	KEN	.7.82	4		Caorle	8 Jul
7:52.17	Cyrus	Kataron	KEN	16.5.82	2		Dessau	31 May
7:52.46	Wolfram	Müller	GER	8.7.81	3		Dessau	31 May
8:01.95	Alene	Emere (10)	ETH	5.3.82	19	ISTAF	Berlin	1 Sep
8:04.42	Khoudir	Aggoune	ALG	5.1.81	3		Nantes	24 Aug
8:04.63	Lorenzo	Perrone	ITA	26.9.81	1		Modena	1 Oct
8:04.93	Chris	Thompson	GBR	17.4.81	2		Manchester	14 Jun
8:05.64	Ionut	Bura	ROM	21.9.81	3		Constanta	27 May
8:05.83	Mohammed	Chouqrati	ITA	24.8.81	2		Modena	1 Oct
8:07.0+	James	Wainaina	KEN	16.6.81	1		Tottori	11 Jun
8:07.17	Gustav	Svedbrandt	SWE	10.7.81	5		Karlstad	23 Aug

2 MILES

Indoors

8:09.66	Hailu	Mekonnen	ETH	4.4.80	1		Birmingham	20 Feb
8:16.15	Paul	Bitok	KEN	26.6.70	1		Boston	6 Feb
8:17.68	Million	Wolde	ETH	17.3.79	2		Birmingham	20 Feb
8:19.88	Moses	Kiptanui	KEN	1.10.70	4		Birmingham	20 Feb
8:21.14	Youssef	Baba	MAR	7.8.79	5		Birmingham	20 Feb
8:23.35	Mohamed Saïd	El Wardi	MAR	19.4.72	6		Birmingham	20 Feb

8:26.49	Kevin	Sullivan	CAN	20.3.74	6 Feb	8:30.22	Berhanu	Adane	ETH		6 Feb
8:28.21	Sean	Kaley	CAN	26.2.75	6 Feb	8:30.62	Dan	Browne	USA	24.6.75	6 Feb

5000 METRES

12:49.28	Brahim	Lahlafi	MAR	15.4.68	1	VD	Bruxelles	25 Aug
12:49.71	Mohammed	Mourhit	BEL	10.10.70	2	VD	Bruxelles	25 Aug
12:50.86	Ali	Saïdi Sief	ALG	15.3.78	1	GGala	Roma	30 Jun
12:54.07	Sammy	Kipketer	KEN-J	29.9.81	2	GGala	Roma	30 Jun
12:55.03		Kipketer			1	Bisl	Oslo	28 Jul
12:55.18	Paul	Tergat	KEN	17.6.69	3	GGala	Roma	30 Jun
12:55.63	Mark	Bett	KEN	22.12.76	2	Bisl	Oslo	28 Jul
12:55.82	Benjamin	Limo	KEN	23.8.74	3	Bisl	Oslo	28 Jul
12:56.18		Lahlafi			4	Bisl	Oslo	28 Jul
12:56.50	Luke	Kipkosgei	KEN	27.11.75	5	Bisl	Oslo	28 Jul
12:56.60		Mourhit			6	Bisl	Oslo	28 Jul
12:57.95	Haile	Gebrselassie	ETH	18.4.73	1	WK	Zürich	11 Aug
12:58.21		Tergat			2	WK	Zürich	11 Aug
12:58.63		Kipketer			3	WK	Zürich	11 Aug

Mark	Name		Nat	Born	Pos	Meet	Venue	Date
12:58.70	Richard	Limo	KEN	18.11.80	4	GGala	Roma	30 Jun
12:58.83	Ismail	Sghir	FRA	16.3.72	7	Bisl	Oslo	28 Jul
12:59.90	Albert	Chepkirui	KEN-J	4.4.81	8	Bisl	Oslo	28 Jul
13:00.06	Salah	Hissou	MAR	16.1.72	9	Bisl	Oslo	28 Jul
13:00.50		Mourhit			4	WK	Zürich	11 Aug
13:00.75		Hissou			5	WK	Zürich	11 Aug
13:01.07		Gebrselassie			1	Live	Nürnberg	25 Jun
13:01.6		Gebrselassie			1		Milano	7 Jun
13:01.78	Daniel	Komen	KEN	17.5.76	3	VD	Bruxelles	25 Aug
13:01.9	Abraham	Chebii	KEN	23.12.79	2		Milano	7 Jun
13:01.93		Kipketer			1	Athl	Lausanne	5 Jul
13:02.19		B Limo			5	GGala	Roma	30 Jun
13:02.28	Benjamin	Maiyo	KEN	6.10.78	2	Athl	Lausanne	5 Jul
13:02.43		R Limo			6	WK	Zürich	11 Aug
13:02.49		Tergat			3	Athl	Lausanne	5 Jul
13:02.5		Kipketer			3		Milano	7 Jun
13:02.68	Patrick	Ivuti	KEN	30.6.78	7	WK	Zürich	11 Aug
13:02.71	Evans	Rutto	KEN	8.4.78	2	Live	Nürnberg	25 Jun
13:02.96	Million	Wolde	ETH	17.3.79	4	Athl	Lausanne	5 Jul
	(33/19)							
13:04.15	Paul	Bitok	KEN	26.6.70	10	Bisl	Oslo	28 Jul
13:04.3	James Kimutai	Koskei	KEN	23.11.68	4		Milano	7 Jun
13:04.46	Mohamed Saïd	El Wardi	MAR	19.4.72	3	Live	Nürnberg	25 Jun
13:05.44	Paul	Kosgei	KEN	22.4.78	12	Bisl	Oslo	28 Jul
13:06.13	Assefa	Mezegebu	ETH	19.6.78	9	WK	Zürich	11 Aug
13:07.59	José	Rios	ESP	15.3.74	5	DNG	Stockholm	1 Aug
13:07.73	Alemu	Dagne	ETH	15.10.80	6	Live	Nürnberg	25 Jun
13:08.15	Fita	Bayissa	ETH	15.12.72	7	GGala	Roma	30 Jun
13:09.50	Alberto	García	ESP	22.2.71	7	DNG	Stockholm	1 Aug
13:09.58	John Cheruiyot	Korir	KEN-J	13.12.81	11	WK	Zürich	11 Aug
13:09.64	Mark	Carroll	IRL	15.1.72	8	DNG	Stockholm	1 Aug
	(30)							
13:09.69	Philip	Mosima	KEN	2.1.77	9	DNG	Stockholm	1 Aug
13:09.93	Mustapha	Essaïd	FRA	20.1.70	10	DNG	Stockholm	1 Aug
13:10.7	Abiyot	Abate	ETH	20.11.80	7		Milano	7 Jun
13:10.99	Driss	El Himer	FRA	4.4.74	7	VD	Bruxelles	25 Aug
13:11.18	Ismael	Kirui	KEN	20.2.75	1	NA	Heusden	5 Aug
13:11.30	Marius	Bakken	NOR	27.3.78	10	GGala	Roma	30 Jun
13:11.77	Mebrahtom	Keflezighi	USA	5.5.75	2	NA	Heusden	5 Aug
13:13.15	Wilberforce	Talel	KEN	10.1.80	14	DNG	Stockholm	1 Aug
13:13.52	Ahmed	Ibrahim Warsama	QAT	4.2.66	3	NA	Heusden	5 Aug
13:13.72	David	Chelule	KEN	7.7.77	8	VD	Bruxelles	25 Aug
	(40)							
13:14.13	Kamiel	Maase	NED	20.10.71	4	NA	Heusden	5 Aug
13:14.68	Daniel	Gachara	KEN	19.12.72	8	Athl	Lausanne	5 Jul
13:15.34	Toshinari	Takaoka	JPN	24.9.70	5	NA	Heusden	5 Aug
13:15.7	Abraham	Cherono	KEN	21.7.80	8		Milano	7 Jun
13:15.75	Enrique	Molina	ESP	25.2.68	16	DNG	Stockholm	1 Aug
13:16.76	Joshua	Chelanga	KEN	7.4.73	12	GGala	Roma	30 Jun
13:17.39	Yusef	El Nasri	ESP	28.7.79	7	NA	Heusden	5 Aug
13:18.50	Nick	Rogers	USA	2.5.75	8	NA	Heusden	5 Aug
13:18.56	Hélder	Ornelas	POR	6.5.74	13	GGala	Roma	30 Jun
13:18.67	Lemma	Alemayehu	ETH	.77	9	NA	Heusden	5 Aug
	(50)							
13:19.55	Enoch	Mitei	KEN	26.11.80	2		Lisboa (U)	5 Aug
13:19.60	Simon	Maina Munyi	KEN	18.3.78	1	GP	Osaka	13 May
13:20.57	Kenenisa	Bekele	ETH-J	.81	3	GP II	Rieti	3 Sep
13:20.83	David	Tuwei	KEN	22.2.79	1		Luminy	28 Jun
13:21.04	Girma	Tolla	ETH	13.10.75	14	Bisl	Oslo	28 Jul
13:21.14	Leonard	Mucheru Maina	KEN	13.6.78	13	VD	Bruxelles	25 Aug
13:21.17	Alene	Emere	ETH-J	5.3.82	4	GP II	Rieti	3 Sep
13:21.33	Zakayo	Ngatho	KEN	18.3.78	1rA		Shizuoka	3 May
13:21.45	Shaun	Creighton	AUS	14.5.67	2		Dedham	3 Jun
13:21.47	Jirka	Arndt	GER	1.8.73	14	GGala	Roma	30 Jun
	(60)							
13:21.62	Aloÿs	Nizigama	BDI	18.6.66	2rA		Shizuoka	3 May
13:22.00	Salvatore	Vincenti	ITA	5.3.72	15	GGala	Roma	30 Jun
13:23.10	Réda	Benzine	ALG	19.4.71	4h1	OG	Sydney	27 Sep

Mark	Name		Nat	Born	Pos	Meet	Venue	Date
13:23.12	Julius	Gitahi	KEN	29.4.78	5h1	OG	Sydney	27 Sep
13:23.24	Charles	Kamathi	KEN	18.5.78	2	GP II	Bratislava	22 Jun
13:23.38	Saïd	Bérioui	MAR	3.6.75	11	BrGP	London (CP)	5 Aug
13:23.46	Bernard	Lagat	KEN	12.12.74	1r2	MSR	Walnut	14 Apr
13:23.83	Gennaro	Di Napoli	ITA	5.3.68	16	GGala	Roma	30 Jun
13:23.96	Gabriel	Muchiri	KEN		3	GP II	Bratislava	22 Jun
13:24.04	Philemon	Kemei	KEN-J	12.2.82	3		Formia	3 Jun
	(70)							
13:24.22	Mohamed	Suleiman	QAT	23.11.69	10	NA	Heusden	5 Aug
13:24.34	Adam	Goucher	USA	18.2.75	7h1	OG	Sydney	27 Sep
13:24.37	Roberto	García	ESP	20.8.75	18	DNG	Stockholm	1 Aug
13:24.56	Mizan	Mehari	AUS	28.12.80	8h1	OG	Sydney	27 Sep
13:24.84	Pablo	Olmedo	MEX	8.5.75	4	GP II	Bratislava	22 Jun
13:25.04	Jeff	Schiebler	CAN	1.6.73	4rA		Shizuoka	3 May
13:25.16	Sean	Kaley	CAN	26.2.75	1	NC	Victoria	11 Aug
13:25.37	David	Kimani	KEN	20.2.77	1		Tuscaloosa	25 Mar
13:25.39	Dennis	Jensen	DEN	11.9.69	11	NA	Heusden	5 Aug
13:25.46	Simone	Zanon	ITA	30.5.75	4		Formia	3 Jun
	(80)							
13:25.72	Hiroyuki	Ikegaya	JPN	29.4.75	12	NA	Heusden	5 Aug
13:25.95	Matt	Giusto	USA	25.10.66	1r1		Palo Alto	5 May
13:26.20	Craig	Mottram	AUS	18.6.80	1		London (BP)	25 Jun
13:26.43	Sebastian	Hallmann	GER	7.1.77	8	Live	Nürnberg	25 Jun
13:26.81	Carsten	Schütz	GER	28.8.75	9	Live	Nürnberg	25 Jun
13:26.88	Shadrack	Hoff	RSA	19.5.73	1		Stellenbosch	18 Feb
13:27.05	Marc	Davis	USA	17.12.69	2r2	MSR	Walnut	14 Apr
13:27.07	Michael	Power	AUS	9.5.76	2		Brisbane	11 Feb
13:27.24	Matt	Lane	USA	5.9.77	2r1		Palo Alto	5 May
13:27.31	Brad	Hauser	USA	28.3.77	2	NC	Sacramento	21 Jul
	(90)							
13:27.39	Hendrick	Ramaala	RSA	2.2.72	2		Stellenbosch	18 Feb
13:27.4	Eduardo	Vargas	ESP	13.11.76	1		Jerez de la Frontera	12 Aug
13:27.53	Sergey	Lebed	UKR	15.7.75	1	NC	Kiev	6 Aug
13:27.65	Paul	Biwott	KEN	.78	5	GP II	Bratislava	22 Jun
13:28.00	Halez	Taguelmint	FRA	29.3.73	5		Formia	3 Jun
13:28.12	Andrea	Arlati	ITA	7.5.70	6		Formia	3 Jun
13:28.22	Kris	Bowditch	GBR	14.1.75	2		London (BP)	25 Jun
13:28.29	Andre	Williams	USA	11.10.71	3r1		Palo Alto	5 May
13:28.60	José Manuel	Martínez	ESP	22.10.71	18	GGala	Roma	30 Jun
13:28.62	Brian	Baker	USA	8.6.70	4		Dedham	3 Jun
	(100)							

13:28.65	Rachid	Chékhémani	FRA	1.10.73	4 Aug
13:28.99	Ray	Appenheimer	USA	18.10.72	5 May
13:29.08	Kebede	Tadesse	ETH-J	.81	3 Jun
13:29.19	George	Okworo	KEN	12.5.79	25 Jun
13:29.41	Alan	Culpepper	USA	15.9.72	5 May
13:29.58	Domingos	Castro	POR	22.11.63	12 Aug
13:29.65	James	Wainaina	KEN-J	16.6.81	3 May
13:29.95	Salim	Kipsang	KEN	22.12.79	25 Jun
13:30.12	Martin	Keino	KEN	20.6.72	11 Feb
13:30.12	Koichiro	Nagata	JPN	19.12.78	3 May
13:30.22	David	Kisang	KEN	.74	25 Jun
13:30.45	Manuel	Pancorbo	ESP	7.7.66	1 Aug
13:30.63	Jason	Stewart	USA	22.4.72	5 May
13:30.67	Adrian	Passey	GBR	2.9.64	5 Aug
13:30.92	Danielle	Caimmi	ITA	17.12.72	30 Jun
13:30.96	Darren	Lynch	AUS	30.8.66	5 Feb
13:31.02	James	Getanda	KEN-J	.7.82	3 Sep
13:31.20	Vénuste	Niyongabo	BDI	9.12.73	25 Aug
13:31.32	Seamus	Power	IRL	28.11.70	25 Jun
13:31.34	Tom	Compernolle	BEL	13.11.75	5 Aug
13:31.51	Nobuya	Matsunaga	JPN	8.11.74	5 Aug
13:31.57	Dmitriy	Maksimov	RUS	6.5.77	18 Jun
13:31.96	Víctor	Morente	ESP	28.4.71	30 Jun
13:32.09	Toshihiro	Iwasa	JPN	18.5.76	11 Jun
13:32.15	Richie	Boulet	USA	14.6.73	5 May
13:32.18	Cyrus	Kataron	KEN-J	16.5.82	3 Jun
13:32.20	Michitane	Noda	JPN	25.3.75	11 Jun
13:32.25	William	Kalya	KEN	4.8.74	2 Sep
13:32.48	Bolota	Asmerom	ERI	12.10.78	14 Apr
13:32.51	Whaddon	Niewoudt	RSA	6.1.70	18 Feb
13:32.55	Laban	Kagika	KEN	17.7.78	11 Jun
13:32.69	Tom	Van Hooste	BEL	23.9.72	5 Aug
13:33.14	Luka	Keitany	KEN		25 Jun
13:33.23	Sisay	Bezabeh	AUS	9.9.77	26 Feb
13:33.29	El Hassan	Lahssini	MAR/FRA	1.1.74	4 Aug
13:33.41	Aleksandr	Vasilyev	RUS	6.12.70	18 Jun
13:33.90	Felix	Limo	KEN	22.8.80	11 Jun
13:34.00	Rachid	Berradi	ITA	29.8.75	2 Sep
13:34.04	Elarbi	Khattabi	MAR	16.5.67	5 Aug
13:34.42	Samir	Moussaoui	ALG	17.5.75	3 Sep
13:34.63	Jan	Fitschen	GER	2.5.77	7 Jun
13:34.91	Thomas	Omwenga	KEN		12 Jun
13:34.94	Solomon	Wachira	KEN	5.11.76	3 May
13:34.96	Simon	Khambule	RSA	11.6.76	31 Mar
13:34.99	Ali Zayed	Mabrouk	LBA	13.1.74	5 Aug
13:35.65	Jean Philippe	Vindex	FRA	6.11.60	4 Aug
13:35.74	Philip	Price	USA	21.8.74	5 May
13:35.78	Mauricio	Díaz	CHI	7.8.68	15 Jul
13:36.0A	Gordon	Mugi	KEN-J	27.11.81	22 Sep
13:36.21	Biruk	Deberework	ETH-J	25.8.82	23 May
13:36.29	Julius	Kiptoo	KEN	4.9.77	22 Jun
13:36.30	Mark	Thompson	AUS	5.3.79	11 Feb
13:36.35	Khalid	Skah	MAR/NOR	29.1.67	11 Aug
13:36.42	Tomohiro	Seto	JPN	19.10.76	8 Oct
13:36.58	Birhanu	Dejene	ETH	.80	7 Jun
13:36.78	Fabián	Roncero	ESP	19.10.70	30 Jun
13:36.79	Naoki	Mishiro	JPN	16.3.77	8 Oct
13:36.82	Claes	Nyberg	SWE	3.3.71	5 Aug
13:36.84	Hisayuki	Okawa	JPN	27.8.71	2 Aug
13:37.01	Abdi	Abdirahman	USA	1.1.77	14 Apr
13:37.08	Michael	Aish	NZL	24.7.76	14 Apr
13:37.12	André	Green	GER	21.4.73	7 Jun
13:37.12	David	Galván	MEX	6.4.76	24 Jun
13:37.29	Janne	Holmén	FIN	26.9.77	2 Aug

Mark	Name		Nat	Born	Date
13:37.3A	Ibrahim	Songok	KEN-J		22 Sep
13:37.37	Yoji	Yamaguchi	JPN	12.6.75	29 Apr
13:37.45	Tijani	Errahmouni	FRA	30.12.70	5 Aug
13:37.50	Dan	Middleman	USA	19.10.69	31 Mar
13:37.97	Michael	Openshaw	GBR	8.4.72	25 Jun
13:38.10	Silah	Misoi	KEN	26.2.74	2 Aug
13:38.12	Mustapha	Bamouh	MAR	21.12.72	3 Jun
13:38.15	David	Kariuki	KEN	23.5.80	21 May
13:38.17	Pete	Sherry	USA	22.8.68	5 May
13:38.18	Hailu	Mesfin	ETH-J	.81	15 Aug
13:38.31	Jeremy	Deere	CAN	5.10.75	11 Aug
13:38.37	Glen	Stewart	GBR	7.12.70	11 Jul
13:38.42	Dan	Browne	USA	24.6.75	5 May
13:38.57	Richard	Mavuso	RSA	30.3.78	18 Feb
13:38.73	Luc	Krotwaar	NED	25.1.68	5 Jul
13:38.74	José	Ramos	POR	27.7.68	15 Jul
13:38.87	Jay	Schoenfelder	USA	17.4.77	31 Mar
13:39.02	John	Nuttall	GBR	11.1.67	11 Jul
13:39.1 A	Kipchumba	Mitei	KEN	15.1.80	22 Jul
13:39.43	Andres	Jones	GBR	3.2.77	5 Aug
13:39.45	Enos	Matalane	RSA	11.8.79	31 Mar
13:39.8 A	Hosea	Kogo	KEN	11.8.72	21 Jul
13:40.23	Umberto	Pusterla	ITA	21.10.67	30 Jun
13:40.40	Dmitriy	Baranovskiy	UKR	28.7.79	1 Jul
13:40.46	Francis	Komu	KEN	5.5.74	28 Jun
13:40.49	Susumu	Ichinose	JPN	11.7.75	5 Jul
13:40.57	Satoshi	Irifune	JPN	14.12.75	13 May
13:40.67	Ahmed	Boulahia	ALG	3.4.73	5 Aug
13:40.89	Mohamed	Amine	MAR	.76	25 Aug
13:40.93	Shigeru	Aburaya	JPN	8.2.77	5 Jul
13:41.31	Katsuhiko	Hanada	JPN	12.6.71	27 Sep
13:41.42	Allen	Graffin	GBR	20.12.77	19 Aug
13:41.5A	Nicholas	Kemboi	KEN-J		22 Sep
13:41.58	Mike	Klass	USA	11.3.77	5 May
13:41.59	Chris	Graff	USA	5.10.75	3 Jun
13:41.72	Sam	Mwape	ZAM	19.5.76	27 Sep
	(200) and further 41 men under 13:45.0				
Indoors					
13:37.60	Berhanu	Adane	ETH		31 Jan

Drugs disqualification

Mark	Name		Nat	Born	Pos	Meet	Venue	Date
13:13.84	Dieter	Baumann	GER	9.2.65	15	WK	Zürich	11 Aug

JUNIORS

See main list for top 6 juniors. 14 performances by 3 men under 13:20. Additional marks and further juniors:

Kipketer 5+	13:06.99	2	BrGP	London (CP)	5 Aug	13:15.99	9	VD	Bruxelles	25 Aug
Chepkirui	13:04.78	5	Athl	Lausanne	5 Jul	13:17.82	16	WK	Zürich	11 Aug
J C Korir	13:11.04	1		Bratislava	22 Jun	13:16.65	10	VD	Bruxelles	25 Aug
	13:13.74	15	DNG	Stockholm	1 Aug					

Mark	Name		Nat	Born	Pos	Meet	Venue	Date
13:29.08	Kebede	Tekeste	ETH	.81	4		Dedham	3 Jun
13:29.65	James	Wainaina	KEN	16.6.81	5rA		Shizuoka	3 May
13:31.02	James	Getanda	KEN	.7.82	7	GP II	Rieti	3 Sep
13:32.18	Cyrus	Kataron (10)	KEN	16.5.82	4		Kerkrade	3 Jun
13:36.0A	Gordon	Mugi	KEN	27.11.81	2	NC-j	Nairobi	22 Sep
13:36.21	Biruk	Deberework	ETH	25.8.82	1		Nijmegen	23 May
13:37.3A	Ibrahim	Songok	KEN		3	NC-j	Nairobi	22 Sep
13:38.18	Hailu	Mesfin	ETH	.81	1		Brasschaat	15 Aug
13:41.5A	Nicholas	Kemboi	KEN		4	NC-j	Nairobi	22 Sep
13:41.9A	Shadrack	Koskei	KEN		5	NC-j	Nairobi	22 Sep
13:46.03	Robert	Kipchumba	KEN	24.2.84	24	VD	Bruxelles	25 Aug
13:46.33	Obed	Mutanya	ZAM	15.3.83	4	WJ	Santiago de Chile	21 Oct
13:50.30	Samuel	Kabiru	KEN	6.6.83	1r24		Yokohama	3 Dec
13:51.49	Wolfram	Müller (20)	GER	8.7.81	1		Koblenz	17 May

10,000 METRES

Mark	Name		Nat	Born	Pos	Meet	Venue	Date
27:03.87	Paul	Tergat	KEN	17.6.69	1	VD	Bruxelles	25 Aug
27:04.54	Felix	Limo	KEN	22.8.80	2	VD	Bruxelles	25 Aug
27:09.79	Patrick	Ivuti	KEN	30.6.78	3	VD	Bruxelles	25 Aug
27:18.20	Haile	Gebrselassie	ETH	18.4.73	1	OG	Sydney	25 Sep
27:18.29		Tergat			2	OG	Sydney	25 Sep
27:18.95	Simon	Maina Munyi	KEN	18.3.78	1rA	Hyogo	Kobe	23 Apr
27:19.75	Assefa	Mezegebu	ETH	19.6.78	3	OG	Sydney	25 Sep
27:19.79		Mezegebu			1		Villeneuve d'Ascq	17 Jun
27:20.03	Girma	Tolla	ETH	13.10.75	2		Villeneuve d'Ascq	17 Jun
27:20.44		Ivuti			2	OG	Sydney	25 Sep
27:21.32	Evans	Rutto	KEN	8.4.78	3		Villeneuve d'Ascq	17 Jun
27:22.20	José	Rios	ESP	15.3.74	1	NC	Gijón	12 Aug
27:23.65	William	Kalya	KEN	4.8.74	4	VD	Bruxelles	25 Aug
27:23.93		Maina Munyi			4		Villeneuve d'Ascq	17 Jun
27:24.75	John Cheruiyot	Korir	KEN-J	13.12.81	5	OG	Sydney	25 Sep
27:28.0		Ivuti			1		Baracaldo	8 Jul
27:30.23		Korir			1	Odlozil	Praha	5 Jun
27:30.[illegible]		Maina Munyi			5	VD	Bruxelles	25 Aug
27:32.8		Rios			2		Baracaldo	8 Jul
27:32.97	Salim	Kipsang	KEN	22.12.79	6	VD	Bruxelles	25 Aug
27:33.20	Ismail	Sghir	FRA	16.3.72	7	VD	Bruxelles	25 Aug
27:33.59		Rutto			8	VD	Bruxelles	25 Aug
27:36.48	Wilberforce	Talel	KEN	10.1.80	2	Odlozil	Praha	5 Jun
27:36.90	Teodoro	Cuñado	ESP	13.2.70	2	NC	Gijón	12 Aug
27:37.44	Khalid	Skah	MAR/NOR	29.1.67	5		Villeneuve d'Ascq	17 Jun
27:37.69	David	Galván	MEX	6.4.76	1r2	MSR	Walnut	14 Apr
27:37.83	Saïd	Bérioui	MAR	3.6.75	6	OG	Sydney	25 Sep

Mark	Name		Nat	Born	Pos	Meet	Venue	Date
27:38.22	Paul	Kosgei	KEN	22.4.78	9	VD	Bruxelles	25 Aug
27:39.31	David	Maritim	KEN	.79	1		Rovereto	30 Aug
27:39.70		Bérioui			6		Villeneuve d'Ascq	17 Jun
	(30/20)							
27:40.08	Philimon	Kemei	KEN	12.2.82	2		Rovereto	30 Aug
27:40.44	Toshinari	Takaoka	JPN	24.9.70	7	OG	Sydney	25 Sep
27:43.14	Robert	Kipchumba	KEN-J	24.2.84	3		Rovereto	30 Aug
27:44.01	Zakayo	Ngatho	KEN	18.3.78	1	JPN Ch	Rifu	7 Oct
27:44.09	Karl	Keska	GBR	7.5.72	8	OG	Sydney	25 Sep
27:44.56	Aloÿs	Nizigama	BDI	18.6.66	9	OG	Sydney	25 Sep
27:45.13	Katsuhiko	Hanada	JPN	12.6.71	3h2	OG	Sydney	22 Sep
27:45.75	Mohammed	Mourhit	BEL	10.10.70	4h2	OG	Sydney	22 Sep
27:46.08	Shadrack	Hoff	RSA	19.5.73	1		Port Elizabeth	25 Feb
27:46.17	Abdi	Abdirahman	USA	1.1.77	10	OG	Sydney	25 Sep
	(30)							
27:46.38	Hendrick	Ramaala	RSA	2.2.72	2		Port Elizabeth	25 Feb
27:46.82	Mark	Carroll	IRL	15.1.72	1r1		Palo Alto	5 May
27:47.44	John	Kanyi	KEN	6.9.80	2	JPN Ch	Rifu	7 Oct
27:47.97	Gabriel	Muchiri	KEN	.78	7		Villeneuve d'Ascq	17 Jun
27:48.34	Alene	Emere	ETH-J	5.3.82	3	Odlozil	Praha	5 Jun
27:48.64	Daniele	Caimmi	ITA	17.12.72	4		Rovereto	30 Aug
27:49.20	Shaun	Creighton	AUS	14.5.67	2r1		Palo Alto	5 May
27:49.9	Joshua	Chelanga	KEN	7.4.73	3		Baracaldo	8 Jul
27:50.16	Ismael	Kirui	KEN	20.2.75	11	VD	Bruxelles	25 Aug
27:53.19	Koichiro	Nagata	JPN	19.12.78	1		Isahaya	2 Dec
	(40)							
27:53.63	Mebrahtom	Keflezighi	USA	5.5.75	12	OG	Sydney	25 Sep
27:53.85	Jeff	Schiebler	CAN	1.6.73	2rA	Hyogo	Kobe	23 Apr
27:53.9	José Manuel	Martínez	ESP	22.10.71	4		Baracaldo	8 Jul
27:54.23	Rachid	Berradi	ITA	29.8.75	1		Nembro	25 Jul
27:55.17	Nick	Rogers	USA	2.5.75	4r1		Palo Alto	5 May
27:55.85	Tadesse	Feyissa	ETH-J	.81	13	VD	Bruxelles	25 Aug
27:55.89	Luka	Keitany	KEN		8		Villeneuve d'Ascq	17 Jun
27:56.30	José	Ramos	POR	27.7.68	10h2	OG	Sydney	22 Sep
27:56.64	Sisay	Bezabeh	AUS	9.9.77	5r1		Palo Alto	5 May
27:56.94	Kamiel	Maase	NED	20.10.71	1		Watford	22 Jul
	(50)							
27:57.10A	David	Chelule	KEN	7.7.77	2	NC	Nairobi	22 Jul
27:57.11	Luke	Kipkosgei	KEN	27.11.75	1	Zat	Melbourne	4 Dec
27:57.19	Solomon	Wachira	KEN	5.11.76	3	JPN Ch	Rifu	7 Oct
27:57.81	Laban	Kagika	KEN	17.7.78	4	JPN Ch	Rifu	7 Oct
27:58.57	Satoshi	Irifune	JPN	14.12.75	2rA		Hachioji	29 Nov
27:59.39	Naoko	Mishiro	JPN	16.3.77	5	NC	Rifu	7 Oct
27:59.64	Kamel	Kohil	ALG	26.12.71	15	VD	Bruxelles	25 Aug
27:59.80	Enrique	Molina	ESP	25.2.68	1rA	EChall	Lisboa (I)	1 Apr
28:00.1	Stephen	Sego	KEN	.78	6		Baracaldo	8 Jul
28:00.50	Andres	Jones	GBR	3.2.77	2	1 AAA	Watford	22 Jul
	(60)							
28:01.06	Sean	Kaley	CAN	26.2.75	6r1		Palo Alto	5 May
28:01.11	Alberto	García	ESP	22.2.71	3rA	EChall	Lisboa (I)	1 Apr
28:01.21	James	Wainaina	KEN-J	16.6.81	1		Shizuoka	14 Oct
28:01.55	Michele	Gamba	ITA	2.10.72	5		Rovereto	30 Aug
28:02.06	James	Ndungu	KEN	30.4.79	2		Shizuoka	14 Oct
28:02.1	Antonio	Peña	ESP	26.8.70	7		Baracaldo	8 Jul
28:02.80	Takayuki	Matsumiya	JPN	21.2.80	3rA		Hachioji	29 Nov
28:03.00	Toshiaki	Tezuka	JPN	7.12.76	1rA		Tottori	10 Jun
28:03.31	Rob	Denmark	GBR	23.11.68	3	2 AAA	Watford	22 Jul
28:03.35	Alan	Culpepper	USA	15.9.72	2	NC	Sacramento	14 Jul
	(70)							
28:03.43	Yuko	Matsumiya	JPN	21.2.80	4rA		Hachioji	29 Nov
28:03.6	Armando	Quintanilla	MEX	19.4.68	8		Baracaldo	8 Jul
28:04.48	Mark	Steinle	GBR	22.11.74	4	3 AAA	Watford	22 Jul
28:04.71	Marco	Mazza	ITA	25.6.77	6		Rovereto	30 Aug
28:05.61	Mauricio	Díaz	CHI	7.8.68	13h2	OG	Sydney	22 Sep
28:05.86	Manuel	Pancorbo	ESP	7.7.66	5rA	EChall	Lisboa (I)	1 Apr
28:06.15	Alberto	Chaíça	POR	17.9.73	6rA	EChall	Lisboa (I)	1 Apr
28:06.27	Michael	Njenga	KEN	5.5.72	7r1		Palo Alto	5 May
28:06.71	Eduardo	Henriques	POR	24.3.68	7rA	EChall	Lisboa (I)	1 Apr
28:06.89	Toshihiro	Iwasa	JPN	18.5.76	1		Montréal (McG)	7 Jul
	(80)							

Mark	Name		Nat	Born	Pos	Meet	Venue	Date
28:07.09	Hiroyuki	Ikegaya	JPN	29.4.75	7	NC	Rifu	7 Oct
28:07.15	Yonas	Kifle	ERI	24.3.77	1		Hamburg	26 Aug
28:07.20	Samir	Moussaoui	ALG	15.5.75	9	GDN	Villeneuve d'Ascq	17 Jun
28:07.37 A	William	Kiptum Muigei	KEN	30.3.71	6	NC	Nairobi	21 Jul
28:08.23	Takeshi	Hamano	JPN	30.7.74	8	NC	Rifu	7 Oct
28:08.45	Tadakatsu	Mukae	JPN	17.10.76	5rA		Hachioji	29 Nov
28:08.46	Michael	Aish	NZL	24.7.76	5		Watford	22 Jul
28:11.26	Driss	El Himer	FRA	4.4.74	8rA	EChall	Lisboa (I)	1 Apr
28:11.42	Koen	Allaert	BEL	29.9.72	9rA	EChall	Lisboa (I)	1 Apr
28:11.43	Susumu	Ichinose	JPN	11.7.75	2rA		Tottori	10 Jun
	(90)							
28:12.0A	Duncan Kipkorir Lebo		KEN-J	30.12.82	1		Nairobi	23 Sep
28:13.01	Pablo	Olmedo	MEX	8.5.75	2r2	MSR	Walnut	14 Apr
28:13.22	Ken-ichi	Takahashi	JPN	16.1.73	6rA	Hyogo	Kobe	23 Apr
28:13.69	Eleniíson	da Silva	BRA	24.1.72	2		Montréal (McG)	7 Jul
28:13.76	Shigeru	Aburaya	JPN	8.2.77	3rA		Tottori	10 Jun
28:14.61	Yoji	Yamaguchi	JPN	12.6.75	7rA	Hyogo	Kobe	23 Apr
28:15.06	Kazuyoshi	Tokumoto	JPN	22.6.79	1		Yokohama	2 Dec
28:15.63	Tomohiro	Seto	JPN	19.10.76	2		Yokohama	2 Dec
28:15.85	Dmitriy	Maksimov	RUS	6.5.77	1rB	EChall	Lisboa (I)	1 Apr
28:15.98	Mark	Bett	KEN	15.7.76	4	Odlozil	Praha	5 Jun
	(100)							

28:16.00	Toshiyuki	Hayata	JPN	2.5.68	29 Nov
28:16.31	David	Muturi Kariuki	KEN	23.5.80	3 Jun
28:16.31	Kenji	Takemoto	JPN	14.8.75	7 Oct
28:16.75	Toshinari	Fujimoto	JPN	2.10.75	29 Nov
28:17.25	Rod	DeHaven	USA	21.9.66	25 Mar
28:17.31	Darren	Wilson	AUS	9.8.68	7 Jul
28:17.38	Masakazu	Fujiwara	JPN-J	6.3.81	2 Dec
28:17.46	Alejandro	Salvador	MEX	14.4.66	7 Jul
28:18.10	Kazuo	Ietani	JPN	.77	7 Oct
28:18.55	Francesco	Bennici	ITA	3.10.71	1 Apr
28:18.58	Michael	Buchleitner	AUT	14.10.69	22 Jul
28:19.94	Atsushi	Fujita	JPN	6.11.76	27 May
28:22.03	Oscar	Martín	ESP	28.7.74	12 Aug
28:22.06	Keith	Cullen	GBR	13.6.72	1 Apr
28:22.17	Jirka	Arndt	GER	1.8.73	14 Apr
28:22.48	Toshiyuki	Sakai	JPN	23.5.76	29 Nov
28:22.53	Viktor	Röthlin	SUI	14.10.74	1 Apr
28:23.00	Dean	Cavuoto	AUS	4.6.75	17 Aug
28:23.01A	Benson	Barus	KEN	4.7.80	21 Jul
28:23.11	Seamus	Power	IRL	28.11.70	22 Jul
28:23.37	Brent	Hauser	USA	28.3.77	25 Mar
28:23.78	Chris	Weber	CAN	22.9.66	5 May
28:23.95	Abraham	Chebii	KEN	23.12.79	4 Dec
28:24.13	Kenta	Oshima	JPN	29.6.79	2 Dec
28:24.22	Mike	Donnelly	USA	2.1.75	5 May
28:24.38	Nobuyuki	Sato	JPN	8.8.72	23 Apr
28:24.63	Manabu	Itayama	JPN	26.6.78	2 Dec
28:25.25	Yuki	Mori	JPN	8.3.79	7 Oct
28:25.47	Simone	Zanon	ITA	30.5.75	17 Jun
28:25.78	Yoichiro	Akiyama	JPN	25.12.79	3 Dec
28:25.84	Atsushi	Sato	JPN	8.5.78	27 May
28:26.26	Hisayuki	Okawa	JPN	27.8.71	29 Nov
28:26.36	Marius	Bakken	NOR	27.3.78	1 Apr
28:26.63	Vincenzo	Modica	ITA	2.3.71	1 Apr
28:26.91	Ryan	Shay	USA	4.5.79	14 Apr
28:26.98	Takayuki	Inubushi	JPN	11.8.72	29 Nov
28:27.0 A	John	Kipngeno	KEN		20 Jul
28:27.16	Cheren	Simatwa	KEN		28 May
28:27.32	Peter	Matthews	IRL	17.11.69	22 Jul
28:27.34	Tetsuo	Nishikawa	JPN	14.7.77	29 Nov
28:27.4 A	Elijah	Korir II	KEN	15.4.78	25 Jun
28:27.4 A	David	Busenei	KEN	22.12.74	20 Jul
28:27.4A	Mark	Rotich	KEN-J	.81	22 Sep
28:27.58	Weldon	Johnson	USA	24.7.73	14 Apr
28:27.98	Tomonori	Onitsuka	JPN	21.3.80	29 Nov
28:28.27	Yoshiteru	Morishita	JPN	26.5.71	13 May
28:28.35	Halez	Taguelmint	FRA	29.3.73	1 Apr
28:28.45	Danilo	Goffi	ITA	3.12.72	17 Jun
28:28.7 A	Benjamin	Maiyo	KEN	6.10.78	20 Jul
28:28.72	Samuel	Mucheke	KEN	3.10.74	23 Apr
28:28.82	Dan	Middleman	USA	19.10.69	14 Apr
28:28.94	Nobuya	Matsunaga	JPN	8.11.74	29 Nov
28:29.25	Toyokazu	Tsuchida	JPN	14.5.76	29 Nov
28:29.50	Tomoo	Tsubota	JPN	16.6.77	29 Nov
28:29.52	Francisco Javier Cortés		ESP	25.10.71	1 Apr
28:29.77	Masatoshi	Ibata	JPN	20.8.72	29 Nov
28:29.94	Ryuji	Matsushita	JPN	7.11.80	3 Dec
28:30.32	Joseph	Kimani	KEN	1.9.72	2 Mar
28:30.36	Tomoaki	Kunichika	JPN	22.4.73	30 Sep
28:30.4 A	Peter	Githuka	KEN	14.2.69	23 Jun
28:30.46	Aaron	Gabonewe	RSA	28.9.77	25 Feb
28:30.48	Toshiya	Kono	JPN	28.3.71	29 Nov
28:30.5	Ignacio	Cáceres	ESP	18.6.76	8 Jul
28:31.19	Andrés	Espinosa	MEX	4.2.63	3 Jun
28:31.28	Kenichiro	Setoguchi	JPN	12.12.80	10 Jun
28:31.40	Tsunaki	Kalamore	RSA	6.7.73	29 Nov
28:31.41	Tadashi	Fukushima	JPN	29.9.64	3 Dec
28:31.63	Maurizio	Leone	ITA	17.8.73	17 Jun
28:31.66	Shawn	Found	USA	11.10.70	14 Apr
28:31.75	Dennis	Jensen	DEN	11.9.69	1 Apr
28:32.53	Masayuki	Kobayashi	JPN	4.4.74	13 May
28:32.75	Makhosonke	Fika	RSA	20.1.73	25 Feb
28:32.76	Hideyuki	Obinata	JPN	2.12.76	3 Dec
28:33.0	Kiyara	Kamzee	KEN	2.3.80	20 May
28:33.2	Jun	Hiratsuka	JPN	8.1.69	12 Mar
28:34.23	Michitane	Noda	JPN	25.3.75	23 Apr
28:34.31	David	Galindo	MEX	27.2.77	7 Jul
28:34.41	Adam	Dailey	USA	5.9.76	25 Mar
28:34.58	Satoshi	Sanpei	JPN	30.6.74	13 May
28:34.94	Kim	Gillard	AUS	18.8.70	3 Jun
28:35.06	Scott	Westcott	AUS	25.9.75	3 Jun
28:35.28	Takashi	Matsuyama	JPN	15.1.74	3 Dec
28:35.34	Clint	Wells	USA	2.5.75	5 May
28:35.74	Takamasa	Uchida	JPN-J	17.10.81	3 Dec
28:36.09	Chad	Johnson	USA	20.4.76	5 May
28:36.22	Mustapha	El Ahmadi	FRA	8.7.68	17 Jun
28:36.39	Stephen	Mayaka	KEN	27.11.72	7 Oct
28:36.46	Janne	Holmén	FIN	26.9.77	19 Jul
28:36.53	Brad	Hauser	USA	28.3.77	14 Jul
28:36.82	Daisuke	Isomatsu	JPN	17.12.73	29 Nov
28:37.06	Andrew	Letherby	AUS	19.9.73	17 Aug
28:37.29	Tatsumi	Morimasa	JPN	3.4.76	10 Jun
28:37.30	Hiroshi	Miki	JPN	10.6.75	10 Jun
28:37.3A	Gilbert	Koech	KEN-J	.81	22 Sep
28:37.72	Simon	Mpholo	RSA	17.8.75	25 Feb
28:38.43	Tadayuki	Ojima	JPN	22.11.76	29 Nov
28:38.55	Tsuyoshi	Nakano	JPN	12.3.73	29 Nov
28:38.9	Saïd	Bara	MAR		11 Jun
28:39.20	Jim	Jurcevich	USA	25.5.76	14 Jul
28:39.45	Seiji	Kushibe	JPN	11.11.71	2 Dec
	(200)	239 under 28:45.0			
28:39.7 A	Daniel	Kirui	KEN	29.12.77	27 May
28:39.87	Marílson	dos Santos	BRA	6.8.77	8 Apr

Road race?: Arusha (A) 13 May: 28:21.6 Zebedayo Bayo TAN 20.5.76, 28:23.5 Safari Ingi TAN, 28:25.1 Anthony Mwingereza TAN

JUNIORS

See main list for top 7 juniors. 10 performances by 6 men to 28:12.0. Additional marks and further juniors:

J C Korir 2+ 27:48.42A 1 NC Nairobi 22 Jul 27:50.19 3h1 OG Sydney 22 Sep

Kemei 28:06.09 1 Carpi 17 Jun

Mark	Name		Nat	Born	Pos	Meet	Venue	Date
28:17.38	Masakazu	Fujiwara	JPN	6.3.81	3		Yokohama	3 Dec
28:27.4A	Mark	Rotich	KEN	.81	3	NC-j	Nairobi	22 Sep
28:35.74	Takamasa	Uchida	JPN	17.10.81	13		Yokohama	3 Dec
28:36.4A	Cheruiyot (same as Philimon Kemei?)	Kemei	KEN		4	NC-j	Nairobi	22 Sep
28:37.3A	Gilbert	Koech	KEN	.81	5	NC-j	Nairobi	22 Sep
28:40.06	Hailu	Mesfin	ETH	.81	7		Rovereto	30 Aug
28:40.51	Abreta	Hadush	ETH	.81	1	AfrC	Alger	11 Jul
28:48.46	Kazuhiro	Maeda	JPN	19.4.81	2r2		Ishaya	2 Dec
28:51.5A	Peter	Kiplangat	KEN		6	NC-j	Nairobi	22 Sep
28:54.30	Louis	Luchini	USA	24.5.81	5r2		Palo Alto	5 May
28:58.04	Shuichi	Fujii	JPN	14.2.82	8r3		Shizuoka	14 Oct
28:58.81		Zhang Yunshan	CHN	16.3.84	1	NGPF	Jinzhou	8 Jun
28:59.4	Naosato	Yoshimura	JPN	5.12.81	3		Yokohama	1 Oct

5 KILOMETRES ROAD

Mar 26, Carlsbad: 1. Sammy Kipketer KEN 13:00, 2. James Koskei KEN 13:22, 3. Reuben Cheruiyot KEN 13:30, 4. Philip Kirui KEN 13:30, 5. Felix Limo KEN 13:31

10 KILOMETRES ROAD

Mark	Name		Nat	Born	Pos	Meet	Venue	Date
27:36	James	Koskei	KEN	23.11.68	1		Vancouver	16 Apr
27:38	Paul	Kosgei	KEN	22.4.78	1		Brunssum	9 Apr
27:38		J Koskei			1		New Orleans	22 Apr
27:39	Reuben	Cheruiyot	KEN	13.3.74	2		New Orleans	22 Apr
27:40		J Koskei			1		Charleston	1 Apr
27:42	Lazarus (6/4)	Nyakeraka	KEN	22.11.75	3		New Orleans	22 Apr
27:49	Dominic	Kirui	KEN	12.4.67	1		Mobile	25 Mar
27:54	Joseph	Kimani	KEN	1.9.72	4		New Orleans	22 Apr
27:56	Ambesse	Tolossa	ETH	28.8.77	1		Groesbeek	10 Jun
27:56	Philip	Singoei	KEN		2		Groesbeek	10 Jun
27:58	Felix	Limo	KEN	22.8.80	4		Charleston	1 Apr
Others where superior to track bests								
28:02	Francis	Komu	KEN	5.5.74	1		Clermont-Ferrand	16 Jun
28:03	Philip	Kirui	KEN		5		Charleston	1 Apr
28:04	Greg	van Hest	NED	3.6.73	3		Groesbeek	10 Jun
28:06	William	Kiplagat	KEN	.72	2		Punta del Este	5 Jan
28:06	Simon	Bor	KEN	13.2.69	1		Cuneo	12 Nov
28:07	Daniel	Lopes Ferreira	BRA	2.2.67	1		São Paulo	13 Mar
28:07	David	Ngeny Cheruiyot	KEN	.80	2		Cuneo	12 Nov
28:08	Simson	Limareng	KEN	2.6.77	4	Peach	Atlanta	4 Jul
28:10	Vanderlei	de Lima	BRA	11.8.69	2		São Paulo	13 Mar
28:11	Vincenzo	Modica	ITA	2.3.71	1		Ravanusa	3 Sep
28:13	Gert	Thys	RSA	12.11.71	2	NC	Port Elizabeth	14 Oct
28:13	Gabriele	De Nard	ITA	3.11.74	3		Cuneo	12 Nov
28:16	Motsehi	Moeketsana	RSA	2.1.70	3	NC	Port Elizabeth	14 Oct

Mark	Name		Nat	Born	Date
28:17	Laban	Kipkemboi	KEN		24 Sep
28:19	Francesco	Bennici	ITA	3.10.71	3 Sep
28:19	Josiah	Bembe	RSA	28.11.74	14 Oct
28:21	Titus	Munji	KEN		8 Jul
28:22	Wilson	Omwoyo	KEN	25.11.65	10 Jun
28:22	Aiduna	Aitnafa	NED	28.10.74	10 Jun
28:22	Julius	Kimutai	KEN		24 Sep
28:22	Johannes	Kekana	RSA	25.4.72	14 Oct
28:23	Whaddon	Niewoudt	RSA	6.1.70	14 Oct
28:24	Fita	Bayissa	ETH	15.12.72	30 Apr
28:24	George	Mofokeng	RSA	19.2.79	14 Oct
28:25	David	Makori	KEN	6.11.73	1 Apr
28:26	Ronald	Munyao	KEN	2.2.74	10 Jun
28:27	Berhanu	Adane	ETH	.74	1 Apr
28:28	David	Chepkwony	KEN		2 Apr
28:28	Sergey	Lebed	UKR	15.7.75	31 Dec
28:29	Benoît	Zwierzchlewski	FRA	19.8.76	5 Nov
28:29	Wilson	Onsare	KEN	.76	5 Nov
28:30	Tesfaye	Tolla	ETH	19.10.74	5 Jan
28:30	Evance	Rotich	KEN		8 Jul
28:30A	Gilbert	Koech	KEN-J	.81	15 Oct
28:30	Mohamed	Belasri	MAR	.73	5 Nov
28:31	Vincent	Kutoane	RSA	20.9.79	14 Oct
28:32	Brahim	Lahlafi	MAR	15.4.68	2 Jan
28:32	Dereje	Denboba	ETH	.79	1 Apr
28:33	Philip	Kemei	KEN	6.6.77	10 Jun
28:33	Marcel	Versteeg	NED	20.8.65	10 Jun
28:33	Rene	Godlieb	NED	1.12.66	10 Jun
28:33	Thomas	Omwenga	KEN	.81	8 Oct
28:33	Joseph	Waweru	KEN	.77	15 Oct
28:34	Simon	Rono	KEN	9.4.72	15 Oct
28:35	Khalid	Khannouchi	MAR/USA	22.12.71	27 Feb
28:35	Günther	Weidlinger	AUT	5.4.78	10 Sep
28:35	Neo	Molema	RSA	29.9.80	14 Oct
28:35A	Benedict	Kimondiu	KEN	30.11.77	15 Oct
28:35	Philip	Tanui	KEN	20.12.75	26 Nov
28:36	Joshua	Killy	KEN		2 Jan
28:36	Raymond	Yator	KEN-J	14.7.82	12 Nov
28:36	Joseph	Sitienei	KEN	.75	26 Nov
28:37A	Wilson	Kigen	KEN	.75	5 Nov
28:38	Tendai	Chimusasa	ZIM	28.1.71	9 Apr
28:38	Sylvester	Moleko	RSA	10.6.70	14 Oct

Mark	Name		Nat	Born	Date	Mark	Name		Nat	Born	Date
28:38	Oscar	Fernández	ESP	23.1.74	22 Oct	28:39	Kenneth	Cheruiyot	KEN	8.2.74	4 Jul
28:39	John Thuo	Ithai	KEN	26.12.73	16 Apr	28:39	Wilson	Kibet	KEN	.69	9 Sep
28:39	Benjamin	Itok	KEN	.72	22 Apr	28:39	Makhosonke	Fika	RSA	20.1.72	14 Oct

Uncertified: Montevideo 7 Jan: 3. Jafred Lorono USA 28:12. 4, Néstro García URU 6.7.75 28:14.

Downhill: Sep 24, Pittsburgh: 1. Aleme Emere ETH 27:49, 2. Leonard Mucheru KEN 28:03, 4. David Njuguna KEN 28:14,5. Abraham Assefa ETH 28:17, 8. Mohammed Amine 28:25, 6. Mohammed Amine 28:25, 7. Stephenson Nyamu KEN 28:34, 8. Julius Kiptoo KEN 28:36, 9. Amos Gitagama KEN 28:37

15 KILOMETRES ROAD

Mark	Name		Nat	Born	Pos	Meet	Venue	Date
42:53	Felix	Limo	KEN	22.8.80	1		Nijmegen	19 Nov
42:56	Salim	Kipsang	KEN	22.12.79	2		Nijmegen	19 Nov
43:07	Reuben	Cheruiyot	KEN	13.3.74	1		Utica	9 Jul
43:09	Kenenisa	Bekele	ETH-J	.81	1		Heerenberg	3 Dec
43:10	Joseph	Kimani	KEN	1.9.72	2		Utica	9 Jul
43:14	Gert	Thys	RSA	12.11.71	3		Nijmegen	19 Nov
43:23	Lazarus	Nyakeraka	KEN	22.11.75	3		Utica	9 Jul
43:26	Reuben Kiyara	Kamzee	KEN	2.3.80	2		Heerenberg	3 Dec
43:28	Assefa	Mezegebu	ETH	19.6.78	4		Nijmegen	19 Nov
43:30	Jackson	Koech	KEN		5		Nijmegen	19 Nov
43:34	David	Makori	KEN	6.11.73	4		Utica	9 Jul

Mark	Name		Nat	Born	Date	Mark	Name		Nat	Born	Date
43:42	Simon	Rono	KEN	9.4.72	28 Oct	43:53	Hezron	Otwori	KEN	25.12.76	28 Oct
43:43	Thomas	Omwenga	KEN	.79	28 Oct	43:54	Wilberforce	Talel	KEN	10.1.80	30 Apr
43:44	John	Korir	KEN	15.12.75	9 Jul	43:54	Daniel	Kirwa Too	KEN	21.11.76	9 Jul
43:47	Alene	Emere	ETH-J	5.3.82	9 Jul	43:55	Hilaire	Ntirampéba	BDI	.70	10 Jun
43:48	Enock	Mitei	KEN	26.11.80	16 Apr	43:57	Paul	Tergat	KEN	17.6.69	31 Dec
43:49	Andrew	Sambu	TAN	5.10.72	30 Apr	43:58	Gebremehden	Gebremairan	ETH	.80	9 Jul
43:49	Mark	Yatich	KEN	.76	9 Jul	43:58	Philip	Mosima	KEN	2.1.77	19 Nov
43:50	Kenneth	Cheruiyot	KEN	8.2.74	9 Jul	43:58	Tesfaye	Tolla	ETH	19.10.74	31 Dec
43:50	Dominic	Kirui	KEN	12.4.67	28 Oct	43:59	Tesfaye	Jifar	ETH	23.4.76	31 Dec
43:53	Roland	Mogaka	KEN	17.4.78	9 Jul	44:00	Luke	Metto	KEN	.76	30 Apr

10 MILES ROAD

Mark	Name		Nat	Born	Pos	Meet	Venue	Date
45:48	Ken-ichi	Takahashi	JPN	16.1.73	1		Karatsu	13 Feb
46:07	Reuben	Cheruiyot	KEN	13.3.74	1		Washington	9 Apr
46:10	Joseph	Kimani	KEN	1.9.72	2		Washington	9 Apr
46:19	John	Korir	KEN	15.12.75	3		Washington	9 Apr
46:21	Dominic	Kirui	KEN	12.4.67	4		Washington	9 Apr
46:25	Joshua	Chelanga	KEN	7.4.73	5		Washington	9 Apr
46:28	Timothy	Cherigat	KEN	29.12.76	1		Erewash	20 Aug
46:41	Benjamin	Itok	KEN	.72	1		Antwerpen	16 Apr
46:44	Solomon	Wachira	KEN	5.11.76	1		Kosa	17 Dec
46:45	Greg	van Hest	NED	3.6.73	1		Lelystad	24 Jun
46:45	Julius	Maritim	KEN	.80	1		Schortens	19 Aug
46:48	Christopher	Kandie	KEN	.69	2		Schortens	19 Aug
46:49	Kazuo	Ietani	JPN		2		Kosa	17 Dec

Mark	Name		Nat	Born	Date	Mark	Name		Nat	Born	Date
46:52	Wilson	Kibet	KEN	.77	3 Sep	46:54	Hisayuki	Okawa	JPN	27.8.71	11 Feb
46:53	Eliud	Kurgat	KEN	20.8.73	4 Jun	46:56	Tadayuki	Ojima	JPN	22.11.76	17 Dec
46:53	Jacob	Losian	KEN	6.6.71	19 Aug	46:57	David	Makori	KEN	6.11.73	9 Apr

20 KILOMETRES ROAD

Mark	Name		Nat	Born	Pos	Meet	Venue	Date
57:58	Hendrick	Ramaala	RSA	2.2.72	1		Alphen aan den Rijn	12 Mar
58:16	Christopher	Kandie	KEN	.69	2		Alphen aan den Rijn	12 Mar
58:45	José	Ramos	POR	28.7.68	1		Almeirim	16 Jan
58:45	Worku	Bikila	ETH	6.5.68	3		Alphen aan den Rijn	12 Mar
58:50	Larbi	Zéroual	FRA	10.1.71	4		Alphen aan den Rijn	12 Mar

Mark	Name		Nat	Born	Date	Mark	Name		Nat	Born	Date
58:59	Peter	Musyoki	KEN		29 Apr	59:10	Greg	van Hest	NED	4.6.73	12 Mar

HALF MARATHON

Note – Lisboa course slightly downhill (69m?)

Mark		Name		Nat	Born	Pos	Meet	Venue	Date
59:06		Paul	Tergat	KEN	17.6.69	1		Lisboa	26 Mar
59:20		Hendrick	Ramaala	RSA	2.2.72	2		Lisboa	26 Mar
59:31		Patrick	Ivuti	KEN	30.6.78	3		Lisboa	26 Mar
59:38		Faustin	Baha	TAN-J	30.5.82	4		Lisboa	26 Mar
59:51		William	Kiplagat	KEN	.72	5		Lisboa	26 Mar
59:51	w	Tesfaye	Tolla	ETH	19.10.74	1		Malmö	12 Jun
60:00	w	Philip	Rugut	KEN	18.5.77	2		Malmö	12 Jun
60:05	w		Baha			3		Malmö	12 Jun
60:22		Japhet	Kosgei	KEN	.68	1		Udine	1 Oct
60:28		Khalid	Khannouchi	MAR/USA	22.12.71	6		Lisboa	26 Mar
60:29	w	Róbert	Stefko	SVK	28.5.68	4		Malmö	12 Jun

Mark		Name		Nat	Born	Pos	Meet	Venue	Date
60:30		Ken-ichi	Takahashi	JPN	16.1.73	1		Tokyo	10 Jan
60:30		Gezahegne	Abera	ETH	23.4.78	5		Malmö	12 Jun
60:35		António	Pinto	POR	22.3.66	7		Lisboa	26 Mar
60:40	w	Tendai	Chimusasa	ZIM	28.1.71	6		Malmö	12 Jun
60:44		David	Rutto	KEN		1		Gargnano	24 Sep
60:48		Simon	Maina Munyi	KEN	18.3.78	1		Nagoya	23 Nov
60:49			Ivuti			1	Stram	Milano	15 Apr
60:49		Christopher	Cheboiboch	KEN	3.3.77	1		Zaandam	17 Sep
60:50		Zebedayo	Bayo	TAN	20.5.76	1		Paris	12 Mar
60:50		Mohammed	Mourhit	BEL	10.10.70	2	Stram	Milano	15 Apr
60:50	w	Stefano	Baldini	ITA	25.5.71	7		Malmö	12 Jun
60:50		James	Ndungu	KEN	30.4.79	2		Nagoya	23 Nov
60:53		Eliud	Lagat	KEN	.77	2		Udine	1 Oct
61:04		Lahoussine	Mrikik	MAR		2		Paris	12 Mar
61:04		Masayuki	Kobayashi	JPN	4.4.74	3		Nagoya	23 Nov
61:06		Anthony	Korir	KEN	25.10.80	2		Gargnano	24 Sep
61:07		Philip	Kirui	KEN	11.9.73	1		Granollers	23 Jan
61:07			Bayo			1		Den Haag	25 Mar
61:08		David	Ndegwa	KEN	17.12.72	3		Gargnano	24 Sep
61:09		Stephen	Kiogora	KEN	29.11.76	3		Paris	12 Mar
61:09			Mrikik			1	RSA Ch	Durban	6 Aug
		(32/28)							
61:10		Alberto	Juzdado	ESP	20.8.66	2		Granollers	23 Jan
61:11		Shadrack	Hoff	RSA	19.5.73	2	1 NC	Durban	6 Aug
		(30)							
61:12		Joseph	Waweru	KEN	.77	3	Stram	Milano	15 Apr
61:12		Fabián	Roncero	ESP	19.10.70	1		Liverpool	13 Aug
61:14		Simon	Kasimili	KEN	12.12.80	4		Paris	12 Mar
61:15		Joseph	Kibor	KEN	22.12.72	5		Paris	12 Mar
61:16		Gert	Thys	RSA	12.11.71	4	3 NC	Durban	6 Aug
61:19		Francesco	Ingargiola	ITA	15.2.73	1		Ostia	19 Mar
61:19		John	Nada Saya	TAN	8.8.78	1		Vitry-sur-Seine	26 Mar
61:21		Albert	Okemwa	KEN	.66	2		Den Haag	25 Mar
61:21		Luke	Metto	KEN	.76	9		Lisboa	26 Mar
61:21		João	N'Tyamba	ANG	20.3.68	11		Lisboa	26 Mar
		(40)							
61:21		Saïd	Bouhmandi	MAR	18.7.74	2		Vitry-sur-Seine	26 Mar
61:22		Motsehi	Moeketsana	RSA	2.1.70	5	4 NC	Durban	6 Aug
61:23		Elijah	Nyabuti	KEN	10.2.79	2		Ostia	19 Mar
61:23		Timothy	Cherigat	KEN	29.12.76	3		Vitry-sur-Seine	26 Mar
61:24		Daniel	Lopes Ferreira	BRA	2.2.67	12		Lisboa	26 Mar
61:25		William	Kiptum	KEN	30.3.71	2		Philadelphia	17 Sep
61:26		James	Wainaina	KEN-J	16.6.81	4		Nagoya	23 Nov
61:27		Mbarak	Hussein	KEN	4.4.65	3		Philadelphia	17 Sep
61:28		Robert	Cheruiyot	KEN		6		Paris	12 Mar
61:29		Giacomo	Leone	ITA	10.4.71	3		Ostia	19 Mar
		(50)							
61:29		Larbi	Zéroual	FRA	10.1.71	3		Den Haag	25 Mar
61:30		Susumu	Ichinose	JPN	11.7.75	1		Yamaguchi	12 Mar
61:30		Abdellah	Béhar	FRA	5.7.63	1		Lille	2 Sep
61:33		Benjamin	Itok	KEN	.72	7		Paris	12 Mar
61:33		Francis	Komu	KEN	5.5.74	8		Paris	12 Mar
61:33		John	Gwako	KEN	4.9.78	2		Zaandam	17 Sep
61:33		Barnabas	Rutto	KEN		4		Udine	1 Oct
61:35		Joseph	Sitienei	KEN	.75	9		Paris	12 Mar
61:35		Piotr	Gladki	POL	8.2.72	4		Den Haag	25 Mar
61:35		Laban	Nkete	RSA	13.11.70	6	NC	Durban	6 Aug
		(60)							
61:36		Satoshi	Irifune	JPN	14.12.75	2		Yamaguchi	12 Mar
61:36		Rachid	Aitbensalem	MAR	10.11.72	9		Malmö	12 Jun
61:37		Tomonori	Onitsuka	JPN	21.3.80	3		Yamaguchi	12 Mar
61:38		Yoshifumi	Miyamoto	JPN	9.2.73	4		Yamaguchi	12 Mar
61:39		Thomas	Lotik	KEN	7.7.70	5		Den Haag	25 Mar
61:39		Haron	Toroitich	KEN	.78	3		Lille	2 Sep
61:39		Godfrey	Nyombi	UGA	10.10.78	4		Gargnano	24 Sep
61:40		Simon	Mphulanyane	RSA	10.9.70	13		Lisboa	26 Mar
61:40		David	Makori	KEN	6.11.73	1		Lisboa	22 Oct
61:41		Mathias	Ntawulikura	RWA	14.7.64	4		Vitry-sur-Seine	26 Mar
		(70)							

Mark		Name		Nat	Born	Pos	Meet	Venue	Date
61:41		Boniface	Usisivu	KEN	5.9.74	1		Prato	24 Apr
61:42		Michael	Kite	KEN	.73	1		Merano	30 Apr
61:42		George	Mofokeng	RSA	19.2.79	7	NC	Durban	6 Aug
61:43		Domingos	Castro	POR	22.11.63	4		Lille	2 Sep
61:44		William	Cheruiyot	KEN	.67	1		Torino	27 Feb
61:45		Egoberto Robert	Naali	TAN	.72	2		Merano	30 Apr
61:49		Tatsumi	Morimasa	JPN	3.4.76	5		Yamaguchi	12 Mar
61:49		Roberto	Barbi	ITA	25.3.65	5		Gargano	24 Sep
61:50		Ondoro	Osoro	KEN	3.12.67	1		Kyoto	12 Mar
61:50		Laban	Chege Kipkemboi	KEN	10.9.69	1		Stroud	22 Oct
		(80)							
61:52		Daisuke	Isomatsu	JPN	17.12.73	6		Yamaguchi	12 Mar
61:52		Joseph	Mereng	KEN	3.1.71	1		Berlin	2 Apr
61:52		Rachid	Berradi	ITA	29.8.75	4	Stram	Milano	15 Apr
61:53A		Martin	Hhaway Sulle	TAN-J	28.12.82	2		Arusha	1 Jan
61:53		Yuko	Matsumiya	JPN	21.2.80	7		Yamaguchi	12 Mar
61:53		Christopher	Kandie	KEN	.69	6		Den Haag	25 Mar
61:53		Salaho	Ngadi	TAN	12.3.79	1		Gravellona Toce	24 Sep
61:53	?	Benedict	Ako	TAN	5.8.68	1		Kisongo	8 Oct
61:54		Nicolae	Negru	ROM	2.8.72	7		Den Haag	25 Mar
61:55		Toshihide	Kato	JPN	4.7.73	8		Yamaguchi	12 Mar
		(90)							
61:56	?	John	Yuda	KEN	9.9.79	2		Kisongo	8 Oct
61:57		Toshiyuki	Hayata	JPN	2.5.68	3		Tokyo	10 Jan
61:57		Bethuel	Netshifhefhe	RSA	16.3.72	8	NC	Durban	6 Aug
61:57		Julius	Maritim	KEN	.80	5		Lille	2 Sep
61:57		Philip	Singoei	KEN		5		Amsterdam	17 Sep
61:59		Naotaka	Takahashi	JPN	28.6.76	9		Yamaguchi	12 Mar
61:59		Giuliano	Battocletti	ITA	1.8.75	4		Parma	10 Sep
61:59		Peter	Kipkassi	KEN		2		Ovar	5 Oct
62:00		Jiro	Itoyama	JPN	16.10.75	10		Yamaguchi	12 Mar
62:00		John	Kipchumba	KEN	.77	8		Den Haag	25 Mar
		(100)							
62:00		Aaron	Gabonewe	RSA	28.9.77	9	NC	Durban	6 Aug

62:01	Philip	Manyim	KEN		15 Apr
62:02	William	Cheseret	KEN	.71	2 Sep
62:03	Wilson	Omwoyo	KEN	25.11.65	25 Mar
62:03	Abel	Ondeyo	KEN	.78	17 Sep
62:05	Dmitriy	Kapitonov	RUS	10.4.68	25 Mar
62:05	Philip	Kipketer	KEN-J	7.12.82	26 Mar
62:05	David	Ngeny Cheruiyot	KEN	.80	24 Apr
62:06	José Ramon	Rey	ESP	3.11.67	23 Jan
62:06	Stephen	Ariga	KEN	31.12.73	20 Aug
62:07	Peter	Musyoki	KEN	.80	26 Mar
62:07	Benson	Lokorwa	KEN	5.5.71	1 Apr
62:07	Kamel	Kohil	ALG	26.12.71	16 Apr
62:07	Armando	Quintanilla	MEX	19.4.68	20 Aug
62:07	Jackson	Koech	KEN		24 Sep
62:08	David	Chelule	KEN	7.7.77	15 Apr
62:08	Abdelkader	El Mouaziz	MAR	1.1.69	12 Jun
62:08	Kamiel	Maase	NED	20.10.71	20 Aug
62:09	Joshua	Chelanga	KEN	7.4.73	26 Mar
62:10	Toshiaki	Tezuka	JPN	7.12.76	12 Mar
62:10	Isaac	Kiprono	KEN	5.9.73	12 Mar
62:11	Shinji	Matsumura	JPN	21.5.72	10 Jan
62:11	Makoto	Otsu	JPN	3.7.80	12 Mar
62:11	Keith	Cullen	GBR	13.6.72	20 Aug
62:12	Marco	Mazza	ITA	25.6.77	15 Apr
62:12	Marílson	dos Santos	BRA	6.8.77	20 Aug
62:14	Pavel	Kokin	RUS	21.7.74	26 Mar
62:14	Fabio	Rinaldi	ITA	15.7.73	1 Oct
62:14	Enock	Kiptoo Keter	KEN-J	.83	16 Dec
62:15	Eliud	Kurgat	KEN	20.8.73	26 Mar
62:16	Philip	Tarus	KEN	11.3.74	26 Mar
62:16	Laban	Kagika	KEN	17.7.78	2 Jul
62:16	Greg	van Hest	NED	3.6.73	17 Sep
62:18	Charles	Kwambai	KEN	4.5.78	24 Sep
62:19	Mustapha	Errebbah	MAR	1.8.71	12 Jun
62:19	Atsushi	Fujita	JPN	6.11.76	2 Jul
62:20	Takashi	Matsuyama	JPN	15.1.74	12 Mar
62:20	Gideon	Chirchir	KEN	24.2.66	26 Mar
62:20	Alberto	Chaíça	POR	17.9.73	15 Apr
62:20	Christopher	Kipkoech	KEN		24 Apr
62:20	Eduardo	Henriques	POR	24.3.68	24 Sep
62:21	Takashi	Ota	JPN	27.4.76	10 Jan
62:21	Yoshitaka	Iwamizu	JPN	20.6.79	12 Mar
62:21	Philip	Tanui	KEN	20.12.75	15 Apr
62:21	Ibrahim	Mitei	KEN	15.8.78	24 Sep
62:21	Augustine	Togom	KEN		5 Oct
62:23	Makhosonke	Fika	RSA	20.1.73	6 Aug
62:23	Wilberforce	Talel	KEN	10.1.80	2 Sep
62:23	Denis	Curzi	ITA	14.5.75	24 Sep
62:23	Katsuhiko	Hanada	JPN	12.6.71	23 Dec
62:24	Peter	Githuka	KEN	14.2.69	13 Aug
62:26A	Ben	Kimondiu	KEN	30.11.77	30 Jan
62:26	Ottavio	Andriani	ITA	4.1.74	26 Mar
62:26	Titus	Munji	KEN		15 Oct
62:27	Kenta	Oshima	JPN	29.6.79	12 Mar
62:27	Toshiyuki	Sakai	JPN	23.5.76	12 Mar
62:27	Eric	Biyase	RSA	31.1.76	6 Aug
62:28	W	Kipkering	KEN		27 Feb
62:28	John	Kiyai	KEN	8.12.70	12 Mar
62:28	Kanji	Moriso	JPN	27.6.74	12 Mar
62:28	Francesco	Bennici	ITA	3.10.71	15 Apr
62:28	Richard	Mutai	KEN		15 Oct
62:28	Andy	Coleman	GBR	29.9.74	22 Oct
62:29	Saïd	Barra	MAR	.70	2 Sep
62:30	Hideki	Kodama	JPN	26.11.71	12 Mar
62:30	Giovanni	Ruggiero	ITA	19.1.74	12 Jun
62:31	Evans	Ogaro	KEN		12 Mar
62:31	Tsuyoshi	Ogata	JPN	11.5.73	12 Mar
62:31	Isaac	Chemobwo	KEN	25.10.73	30 Apr
62:32	Manabu	Hayama	JPN	26.6.78	23 Nov
62:33	Paulo	Guerra	POR	21.8.70	26 Mar
62:34	Tadayuki	Tsutsumi	JPN	12.8.77	12 Mar
62:34	John	Mutai	KEN	26.5.66	22 Oct
62:34	Lazarus	Nyakeraka	KEN	22.11.75	26 Nov
62:35	Jeff	Schiebler	CAN	1.6.73	10 Jan
62:35	Domenico	D'Ambrosio	ITA	18.7.75	1 Oct
62:35	Migidio	Bourifa	ITA	31.1.69	1 Oct
62:35	Barnabas	Koskei	KEN	.71	15 Oct
62:35	Vincenzo	Modica	ITA	2.3.71	22 Oct

Mark	Name		Nat	Born	Date
62:36	Erick	Wainaina	KEN	19.12.73	2 Jul
62:36	Toyokazu	Tsuchida	JPN	14.5.76	23 Nov
62:37	Marco	Gielen	NED	30.5.70	22 Oct
62:38	Janko	Bensa	YUG	28.6.77	16 Jan
62:41	Wilson	Kigen	KEN	.75	9 Jan
62:41	David	Kipruto	KEN	20.11.75	15 Apr
62:43	Nobusuke	Takanashi	JPN	26.3.72	12 Mar
62:43	William	Kalya	KEN	4.8.74	22 Oct
62:44	James	Kibiwott Tanui	KEN	.74	12 Jun
62:45	David	Kirui	KEN	29.12.77	20 Feb
62:45	Kazunobu	Fuse	JPN	8.10.80	12 Mar
62:45	Amos	Gitagama	KEN	29.8.78	10 Sep
62:45	Paulo	Catarino	POR	30.9.63	5 Oct
62:46	Gabriel	Mutai Kiprono	KEN	5.6.76	25 Mar
62:47	Philemon	Kipkering	KEN	10.8.74	19 Mar
62:47	Carsten	Eich	GER	9.1.70	25 Mar
62:48	Seiji	Hamada	JPN	31.8.73	12 Mar
62:48	Antonio	Armuzzi	ITA	14.8.69	26 Mar
62:49	Roman	Kejzar	SLO	11.2.66	20 Feb
62:49	Francis	Mbiu	KEN	12.6.74	25 Mar
62:49	Fred	Getanga	KEN	.75	13 May
62:49	Geoffrey	Letting	KEN		17 Sep
62:49	Ryuji	Matsushita	JPN	7.11.80	23 Nov
62:50	David	Chepkwony	KEN		25 Mar
62:50	Aziz	Larachi	MAR	.72	16 Apr
	(204)	223 men under 63:00			

Downhill

62:28	Juan	Martínez	MEX	.65	6 Feb
62:33	Jonathan	Ndambuki	KEN	3.8.76	6 Feb
62:36	Gregorio	Domínguez	MEX	.67	6 Feb

Uncertain course

62:42	Miroslaw	Plawgo	POL	4.1.70	9 Apr

JUNIORS

See main list for top 3 juniors. More:

62:05	Philip	Kipketer	KEN	7.12.82	1	Como	26 Mar
62:14	Enock	Kiptoo Keter	KEN	.83	1	Dronten	16 Dec
63:06	Kiplimo	Muneria	KEN	28.8.83	9	Amsterdam	17 Sep
63:30	Takuya	Yamawaki	JPN	1.4.81	1	Ageo	11 Nov
63:33	Naoto	Yoneda	JPN	6.1.81	2	Ageo	19 Nov
63:38	Jun-ichi	Shibata	JPN	22.6.81	4	Ageo	19 Nov
63:53	Keisuke	Nakatani	JPN	6.4.81	5	Fuchu	23 Nov
63:56	Takamasa	Uchida	JPN	17.10.81	6	Fuchu	23 Nov
63:57	Takayuki	Kawano	JPN	7.3.82	9	Ageo	19 Nov
64:14	Robert	Kipchumba	KEN	24.2.84	6	Prato	24 Apr
64:15		Wang Yonghua II	CHN	23.5.81	2	Seoul	19 Nov
64:45	Koichi	Mitsuyuki	JPN	12.12.81	13	Ageo	19 Nov

MARATHON

D in second column = aided course due to possible net tailwind or downslope from point-to-point arrangement (>30% start/finish separation). L = loop or out-and-back course, P - Point-to-point

2:06:36	L	António	Pinto	POR	22.3.66	1		London	16 Apr
2:06:51	L	Atsushi	Fujita	JPN	6.11.76	1		Fukuoka	3 Dec
2:07:01	L	Khalid	Khannouchi	MAR/USA	22.12.71	1		Chicago	22 Oct
2:07:15	L	Japhet	Kosgei	KEN	20.12.68	1		Tokyo	13 Feb
2:07:20	L		Lee Bong-ju	KOR	11.10.70	2		Tokyo	13 Feb
2:07:29	L	Josephat	Kiprono	KEN	12.12.73	2		Chicago	22 Oct
2:07:33	L	Abdelkader	El Mouaziz	MAR	1.1.69	2		London	16 Apr
2:07:42	L	Simon	Biwott	KEN	3.3.70	1		Berlin	10 Sep
2:07:47	L	Antonio	Peña	ESP	26.8.70	2		Berlin	10 Sep
2:07:47	L	Moses	Tanui	KEN	20.8.65	3		Chicago	22 Oct
2:08:02	L	Peter	Githuka	KEN	14.2.69	4		Chicago	22 Oct
2:08:08	L	Alberto	Juzdado	ESP	20.8.66	3		Tokyo	13 Feb
2:08:14	L	Martín	Fiz	ESP	3.3.63	1	L.Biwa	Otsu	5 Mar
2:08:16	L	Takayuki	Inubushi	JPN	11.8.72	4		Tokyo	13 Feb
2:08:22	L	Kenneth	Cheruiyot	KEN	8.2.74	1		Rotterdam	16 Apr
2:08:23	L	Fred	Kiprop	KEN	3.6.74	5		Chicago	22 Oct
2:08:27	L		Kiprono			1	Mill	Roma	1 Jan
2:08:30	L	Francisco Javier	Cortés	ESP	25.10.71	2		Rotterdam	16 Apr
2:08:33	L	Simretu	Alemayehu	ETH	18.10.70	1		Torino	26 Mar
2:08:34	L	Vanderlei	de Lima	BRA	11.8.69	3		Rotterdam	16 Apr
2:08:36	L		Khannouchi			3		London	16 Apr
2:08:41	L	Giacomo	Leone	ITA	10.4.71	2	Mill	Roma	1 Jan
2:08:48	L	William	Cheruiyot	KEN	.67	1		Wien	21 May
2:08:49	L	Francesco	Ingargiola	ITA	15.2.73	3	Mill	Roma	1 Jan
2:08:49	L		Baek Seung-do	KOR	16.6.68	5		Tokyo	13 Feb
2:08:49	L	Mohamed	Ouaadi	FRA	1.1.69	1		Paris	9 Apr
2:08:49	L	Joseph	Ngolepus	KEN	.75	4		Rotterdam	16 Apr
2:08:50	L	Simon	Bor	KEN	13.2.69	2		Wien	21 May
2:08:57	L		Cortés			1		Amsterdam	15 Oct
2:08:59	L	Elijah	Korir	KEN	13.3.66	2		Torino	26 Mar
2:08:59	L		Peña			5		Rotterdam	16 Apr
		(31/27)							
2:09:00	L	Mark	Sainah	KEN	10.11.70	3		Torino	26 Mar
2:09:04	L	Shinji	Kawashima	JPN	4.6.66	2	L.Biwa	Otsu	5 Mar
2:09:06	L	William	Kiplagat	KEN	.72	4		London	16 Apr
		(30)							

MEN 2000

Mark		Name		Nat	Born	Pos	Meet	Venue	Date
2:09:09	L	Abdellah	Béhar	FRA	5.7.63	3		Fukuoka	3 Dec
2:09:10	L	Samuel	Otieno	KEN	10.4.73	2		Paris	9 Apr
2:09:17	L	Abraham	Limo	KEN	10.12.63	2		Amsterdam	15 Oct
2:09:18	L	Zebedayo	Bayo	TAN	20.5.76	4		Paris	9 Apr
2:09:23	L	Ryuji	Takei	JPN	18.5.71	3	L.Biwa	Otsu	5 Mar
2:09:26	L	Noriaki	Igarashi	JPN	28.10.72	4		Fukuoka	3 Dec
2:09:30	L	Hiroshi	Miki	JPN	10.6.75	6		Tokyo	13 Feb
2:09:35	L	Joseph	Mereng	KEN	3.1.71	6		Rotterdam	16 Apr
2:09:43	L	Hendrick	Ramaala	RSA	2.2.72	5		London	16 Apr
2:09:45	L	Stefano	Baldini	ITA	25.5.71	6		London	16 Apr
		(40)							
2:09:45	L	Gezahegne	Abera	ETH	23.4.78	5		Fukuoka	3 Dec
2:09:46	L	Michael	Kite	KEN	.73	1		München	15 Oct
2:09:47	D	Elijah	Lagat	KEN	19.6.66	1		Boston	17 Apr
2:09:47	L	Joel	Sankale	KEN	4.10.69	2		München	15 Oct
2:09:49	L	Moges	Taye	ETH	12.12.73	4	Mill	Roma	1 Jan
2:09:50	L	Atsushi	Sato	JPN	8.5.78	4	L.Biwa	Otsu	5 Mar
2:09:50	P	John	Bungei	KEN	9.11.76	1		Venezia	22 Oct
2:09:52	L	Jackson	Kabiga	KEN	1.12.76	3		Berlin	10 Sep
2:09:55	L	Mathias	Ntawalikura	RWA	14.7.64	7		London	16 Apr
2:10:00	L	Steve	Moneghetti	AUS	26.9.62	7		Tokyo	13 Feb
		(50)							
2:10:08	L	Takahiro	Sunada	JPN	19.1.73	4		Berlin	10 Sep
2:10:09	P	Isaac	Kiprono	KEN	5.9.73	2		Venezia	22 Oct
2:10:12	P	Roberto	Barbi	ITA	25.3.65	3		Venezia	22 Oct
2:10:14	L	Wesley	Chelule	KEN	4.9.74	5	Mill	Roma	1 Jan
2:10:15	P	Migidio	Bourifa	ITA	31.1.69	4		Venezia	22 Oct
2:10:17	D	Erick	Wainaina	KEN	19.12.73	1		Nagano	9 Apr
2:10:24	L	Kazuhiro	Matsuda	JPN	24.6.74	5	L.Biwa	Otsu	5 Mar
2:10:29	L	Josiah	Thugwane	RSA	15.4.71	8		London	16 Apr
2:10:29	D	Ondoro	Osoro	KEN	3.12.67	4		Boston	17 Apr
2:10:29	L	Pavel	Kokin	RUS	21.7.74	1		Cleveland	30 Apr
		(60)							
2:10:35	L	Mukhamet	Nazipov	RUS	10.9.61	9		London	16 Apr
2:10:35	L	Simon	Chemoiywo	KEN	20.4.68	1	NC	Praha	21 May
2:10:36	L	Willy Kalombo Mwenzé		COD	7.6.70	5		Paris	9 Apr
2:10:36	L	Larbi	Zéroual	FRA	10.1.71	7		Rotterdam	16 Apr
2:10:38	L	David	Kiptum Businei	KEN	22.12.74	3		Amsterdam	15 Oct
2:10:40	L	Henry	Cherono	KEN	17.7.78	1		Frankfurt	29 Oct
2:10:41	L	Koji	Shimizu	JPN	17.10.69	8		Tokyo	13 Feb
2:10:43	L	Paul	Kiptanui	KEN	.69	5		Berlin	10 Sep
2:10:44	L	Kazutaka	Enoki	JPN	7.6.74	1		Oita	6 Feb
2:10:44	L	Yasuaki	Yamamoto	JPN	5.8.72	6	L.Biwa	Otsu	5 Mar
		(70)							
2:10:45	L	Paul	Kipsambu	KEN	18.2.62	6		Paris	9 Apr
2:10:47	L	Benoît	Zwierzchlewski	FRA	19.8.76	1	NC	Reims	22 Oct
2:10:48	L	Shigeru	Aburaya	JPN	8.2.77	7	L.Biwa	Otsu	5 Mar
2:10:50	L	Samson	Kandie	KEN	20.4.71	4		Amsterdam	15 Oct
2:10:50	P	Christopher	Cheboiboch	KEN	3.3.77	5		Venezia	22 Oct
2:10:51	L	Josephat Kipchoge Rop		KEN	.69	4		Torino	26 Mar
2:10:52	L	Raymond	Chemwelo	KEN	.75	5		Torino	26 Mar
2:10:52	L	Kamel	Ziani	ESP	20.2.72	5		Amsterdam	15 Oct
2:10:54	L	Danilo	Goffi	ITA	3.12.72	10		London	16 Apr
2:10:57	L	Ambesa	Tolossa	ETH	28.8.77	8		Rotterdam	16 Apr
		(80)							
2:11:01	L	Abel	Gisemba	KEN	7.7.71	2		Frankfurt	29 Oct
2:11:02	L	Mohamed	Ezzher	FRA	26.4.60	7		Paris	9 Apr
2:11:04	L	John	Moiben	KEN	12.4.68	6		Amsterdam	15 Oct
2:11:05	L	Nelson	Ndereva	KEN	14.7.67	1		Pyongyang	9 Apr
2:11:06	L	Piotr	Gladki	POL	8.2.72	1		Hamburg	16 Apr
2:11:06	L	Elias	Chebet	KEN	.74	6		Berlin	10 Sep
2:11:07	L	Leonid	Shvetsov	RUS	28.3.69	8	L.Biwa	Otsu	5 Mar
2:11:07	L	Tumo	Turbo	ETH	23.2.70	6		Torino	26 Mar
2:11:10	L	Andrew	Eyapan	KEN	12.12.65	1		Napoli	2 Apr
2:11:10	P	Tesfaye	Tolla	ETH	19.10.74	3	OG	Sydney	1 Oct
		(90)							
2:11:15	L	Johannes	Maremane	RSA	27.9.65	1	NC	Pinelands	5 Mar
2:11:16	L	Luke	Kibet	KEN	19.6.73	7	Mill	Roma	1 Jan
2:11:16	L	Sergey	Fedotov	RUS	14.2.72	9		Rotterdam	16 Apr

Mark		Name		Nat	Born	Pos	Meet	Venue	Date
2:11:17	P	Jon	Brown	GBR	27.2.71	4	OG	Sydney	1 Oct
2:11:18	L	Ezael	Tlhobo	RSA	4.5.64	10		Rotterdam	16 Apr
2:11:18	L	Mark	Steinle	GBR	22.11.74	11		London	16 Apr
2:11:19	L	Joshua	Peterson	RSA	8.3.75	2	NC	Pinelands	5 Mar
2:11:19	L	Koen	Allaert	BEL	29.9.72	11		Rotterdam	16 Apr
2:11:20	L		Kim Jung-won	PRK	20.9.73	2		Pyongyang	9 Apr
2:11:24	L	Benjamin	Paredes	MEX	7.8.61	1		Torreón	5 Mar
		(100)							
2:11:24	L	Andrés	Espinosa	MEX	4.2.63	2		Torreón	5 Mar

2:11:25	L	Carlos	Tarazona	VEN	14.8.65	30 Apr
2:11:28	L	Stephen	Ndungu	KEN	1.6.67	16 Jan
2:11:28	L	Michael	Fietz	GER	13.11.67	16 Apr
2:11:29	L		Jung Nam-kyun	KOR	23.10.78	19 Mar
2:11:29	L	Luis	Novo	POR	29.5.70	16 Apr
2:11:32	L	Gert	Thys	RSA	12.11.71	16 Apr
2:11:33	L	Leonardo V	Guedes	BRA	23.1.73	16 Apr
2:11:39	L	Julius	Bitok	KEN	4.7.76	26 Mar
2:11:39	L		Hyung Jae-young	KOR	24.2.71	9 Apr
2:11:40	L	Waldermar	Glinka	POL	9.1.68	17 Dec
2:11:43	L	Tsuyoshi	Ogata	JPN	11.5.73	16 Apr
2:11:43		David	Kiptoo Kirui	KEN	29.12.77	1 Oct
2:11:44	L	Bethuel	Netshifhefhe	RSA	16.3.72	5 Mar
2:11:46	L	Aiduna	Aitnafa	NED	28.10.74	16 Apr
2:11:46	L	Yuriy	Chizhov	RUS	20.2.72	8 Oct
2:11:48	L	Diego	García	ESP	12.10.61	19 Mar
2:11:50	L	Roman	Kejzar	SLO	11.2.66	26 Mar
2:11:55		Benson	Mutisya	KEN	22.3.78	5 Mar
2:11:56	L	Benjamin	Rotich	KEN		29 Oct
2:11:58	L	Artur	Osman	POL	1.3.70	29 Oct
2:12:00	L	David	Morris	USA	17.5.70	22 Oct
2:12:01	L		Kim Jong-chol	PRK	30.3.72	9 Apr
2:12:02	P	David	Ngetich	KEN	12.5.72	22 Oct
2:12:08	L	Elias	Bastos	BRA	27.9.74	3 Dec
2:12:11	L	Luketz	Swartbooi	NAM	7.2.66	4 Mar
2:12:14	L	Dmitriy	Kapitonov	RUS	10.4.68	1 Jan
2:12:14	L	Toshiyuki	Hayata	JPN	2.5.68	5 Mar
2:12:15	L		Jang Chon-il	PRK		9 Apr
2:12:16	D	Maxwell	Musembi	KEN		9 Apr
2:12:18	L	William	Musyoki	KEN	25.11.66	19 Mar
2:12:19	L	Benjamin	Mutua	KEN	12.3.71	19 Mar
2:12:21		Wilson	Kibet	KEN	.77	14 Jan
2:12:21	L	Oleg	Strizhakov	RUS	18.7.63	16 Apr
2:12:22	L	Nelson	Chirchir	KEN	16.6.56	9 Apr
2:12:22	L	Tendai	Chimusasa	ZIM	28.1.71	16 Apr
2:12:24	L	Gideon	Chirchir	KEN	24.2.66	16 Apr
2:12:26	D	John	Kagwe	KEN	9.1.69	17 Apr
2:12:27	L	Abdelfatah	Aitzouri	MAR	6.6.70	22 Oct
2:12:28	L	Shem	Kororia	KEN	25.9.72	16 Apr
2:12:29	L		Kil Jae-son	PRK	5.5.75	9 Apr
2:12:30	D	Laban	Nkete	RSA	13.11.70	17 Apr
2:12:31	L	James	Moiben	KEN	20.4.77	10 Sep
2:12:33	L	Paul	Tangus	KEN		2 Apr
2:12:37	L	Michal	Bartoszak	POL	21.6.70	29 Oct
2:12:39	D	Joseph	Chebet	KEN	23.8.70	17 Apr
2:12:40	L	Eliud	Kurgat	KEN	20.8.73	16 Apr
2:12:41	L		Sim In-chol	PRK		9 Apr
2:12:41	P	Samuel	Kororia	KEN	.72	22 Oct
2:12:42	L	Eric	Mack	USA	31.8.74	22 Oct
2:12:45	L	Belaye	Wolashe	ETH	3.5.69	4 Jun
2:12:46	L	Motsehi	Moeketsana	RSA	2.1.70	10 Sep
2:12:46	L	Joshua	Kipkemboi	KEN	22.2.59	8 Oct
2:12:46	L	Philip	Tanui	KEN	20.12.75	3 Dec
2:12:47		Aleksandr	Kuzin	UKR	21.10.74	22 Oct
2:12:48	L	Pavel	Andreyev	RUS	20.4.70	8 Oct
2:12:49	L	Abel	Antón	ESP	24.10.62	19 Mar
2:12:49	L	Elias	Chelanga	KEN	.69	8 Oct
2:12:49	L	Fekadu	Degefu	ETH	.74	15 Oct
2:12:49	L	Hakim	Bagy	FRA	31.3.68	22 Oct
2:12:51	L	Carsten	Eich	GER	9.1.70	16 Apr
2:12:52	D	Cosmas	Ndeti	KEN	24.11.71	9 Apr
2:12:53	L	Patrick	Kaotsane	RSA	22.11.66	9 Apr
2:12:53	L	Viktor	Röthlin	SUI	14.10.74	16 Apr
2:12:53	L	Elly	Rono	KEN	5.5.70	8 Oct
2:12:54	L	Andrey	Gordeyev	BLR	7.8.73	26 Mar
2:12:58		Alejandro	Semprún	VEN	12.3.73	6 Feb
2:13:01	L	Jacob	Mazibuko	RSA	28.6.69	5 Mar
2:13:02	L		Kim Yi-yong	KOR	20.9.73	22 Oct
2:13:08	P	Ezekiel	Kibiwott Sanga	KEN	18.8.63	12 Mar
2:13:13	L	Bedaso	Turube	ETH	19.3.69	30 Apr
2:13:13	L	Yosuke	Osawa	JPN	1.9.67	8 Oct
2:13:14	L	Julius	Rutto	KEN	26.12.71	3 Dec
2:13:15	P	Giorgio	Calcaterra	ITA	11.2.72	12 Mar
2:13:16	L	Carlos	Bautista	MEX	17.2.68	5 Mar
2:13:16	P	Abraham	Assefa	ETH	9.12.72	5 Nov
2:13:19	L	John	Monyatso	RSA	5.10.73	16 Apr
2:13:20		John	Mutai	KEN	26.5.66	14 Jan
2:13:22	L	Chala	Kelele	ETH	7.10.66	9 Apr
2:13:23	L	Fabio	Rinaldi	ITA	15.7.73	3 Dec
2:13:24	L	Nobuhiko	Chiba	JPN	3.7.71	5 Mar
2:13:25	L	Tsutomu	Sassa	JPN	26.7.74	5 Mar
2:13:28	L	Patrick	Ndayisenga	BDI	28.10.71	16 Apr
2:13:28		Graziano	Calvaresi	ITA	18.10.66	7 May
2:13:29	L	Tadesse	Hailemariam	ETH		21 May
2:13:29	L	Andrey	Naumov	UKR	21.12.73	21 May
2:13:29	L	Sammy	Koskei	KEN	.74	8 Oct
2:13:30	L	Evans	Ogaro	KEN		22 Oct
2:13:32	L	Panayiótis	Haramís	GRE	28.1.71	16 Apr
2:13:33	P	Alberico	Di Cecco	ITA	19.4.74	15 Oct
2:13:34	L	John	Kipsang	KEN	.68	15 Oct
2:13:35		Patrick	Chumba	KEN	24.7.74	22 Oct
2:13:36	L	Daisuke	Tokunaga	JPN	28.11.65	5 Mar
2:13:37	L	Keith	Cullen	GBR	13.6.72	16 Apr
2:13:37	L	Kefah	Keraro	KEN		30 Apr
2:13:38		Samwel	Maritim	KEN	10.2.65	29 Apr
2:13:42		Oscar	Cortínez	ARG	4.8.73	23 Apr
2:13:42	L	Patrick	Kiptum	KEN	7.4.72	4 Jun
2:13:42	L	Stephen	Langat	KEN	.62	29 Oct
2:13:43	L	Juan	Camacho	MEX	5.9.72	30 Apr
		(200)	224 men under 2:14:00			

JUNIORS

2:15:07	Li Zhuhong	CHN-J	22.10.83	10	Beijing	15 Oct

100 KILOMETRES

6:17:17	Takahiro	Sunada	JPN	19.1.73	1	EC	Belvès	30 Apr
6:23:14	Grigoriy	Murzin	RUS	23.1.70	1		S.C.de Bezana	7 Oct
6:23:15	Pascal	Fétizon	FRA	30.8.62	1	WC	Winschoten	9 Sep
6:27:13	Yasufumi	Mikami	JPN	14.1.66	1		Yubetsu	25 Jun
6:29:13	Dmitriy	Radyuchenko	RUS	27.11.70	2	WC	Winschoten	9 Sep
6:29:29	Oleg	Kharitonov	RUS	13.4.68	3	WC	Winschoten	9 Sep
6:33:12	Dan	Held	USA	15.10.65	4	WC	Winschoten	9 Sep
6:33:19	Farid	Ganiyev	RUS	13.12.64	1		Torhout	16 Jun
6:33:36		Ganiyev			2	EC	Belvès	30 Apr
6:37:15	Shuji	Uchishiba	JPN		2		Yufutsu	25 Jun

Mark	Name		Nat	Born	Pos	Meet	Venue	Date
6:38:48	Rainer	Müller	GER	24.5.66	1	NC	Rodenbach	22 Apr
6:38:57		Ganiyev			5	WC	Winschoten	9 Sep
6:39:47	Jaroslav	Janicki	POL	6.7.66	1		Kalisz	1 Oct
6:41:35	Thierry	Guichard	FRA	29.5.60	6	WC	Winschoten	9 Sep
6:41:35	Gilles	Diehl	FRA	8.4.60	7	WC	Winschoten	9 Sep
6:42:31	János	Bogár	HUN	23.6.64	1	NC	Encs	15 Apr
6:43:40	Igor	Tupin	RUS	8.4.71	8	WC	Winschoten	9 Sep
6:44:28	Piotr	Sekowski	POL	5.9.67	3	EC	Belves	30 Apr
6:45:12		Kharitonov			2		Torhout	16 Jun
6:45:17		Sekowski			2		Kalisz	1 Oct
6:45:53	Tomasz	Chawawko	POL	9.7.74	3		Kalisz	1 Oct
	(21/17)							
6:46:10	Donovan	Wright	RSA	12.4.67	9	WC	Winschoten	9 Sep
6:46:22	Naruhisa	Kojima	JPN	16.8.64	3		Yufutsu	25 Jun
6:46:24	Aleksandr	Masarigin	RUS	18.10.60	3		Torhout	16 Jun
	(20)							
6:46:39	Dave	Dunham	USA	27.3.64	1		Boston	8 Oct
6:48:24	Jan	Vandendriessche	BEL	6.6.61	3		Torhout	16 Jun

6:50:00	Attila	Vozár	HUN	27.11.74	9 Sep	6:51:33	Csaba	Németh ¶	HUN	.68	15 Apr
6:50:53	Stefano	Sartori	ITA	28.5.65	9 Sep	6:53:48	Nicolas	Boisselier	FRA	7.6.66	9 Sep
6:50:54	Marcio	Oliveira	BRA		16 Jun	6:54:28	Aleksandr	Motorin	RUS	22.5.55	30 Apr
6:51:10	Aleksandr	Osypov	UKR	.67	22 Apr	6:54:59	Pascal	Piveteau	FRA	7.10.61	9 Sep

24 HOURS

Mark		Name		Nat	Born	Pos	Meet	Venue	Date
265,683	t	Yiannis	Kouros	GRE	13.2.56	1		Verona	23/24 Sep
261.437		Anatoliy	Kruglikov	RUS	9.10.57	1		Sankt-Peterburg	2/3 Sep
260.973		Alain	Prual	FRA	24.9.59	1	NC	Gravigny	1/2 Jul
259.273		Lubomir	Hrmo	SVK	25.2.61	1	EChall	Uden	22/23 Oct
257.760		Andrey	Kazantsev	RUS	.62	2	EChall	Uden	22/23 Oct
257.024		Vladimir	Kurbatov	RUS	.58	2		Sankt-Peterburg	2/3 Sep
256.869	t		Kazantsev			1	NC	Moskva	8/9 May
255.446	t		Kouros			1		Surgères	1/2 Jun
255.510			Prual			3	EChall	Uden	22/23 Oct
254.821		Jean-Pierre	Guyomarc'h	FRA	5.4.54	2	NC	Gravigny	1/2 Jul
254.512			Guyomarc'h			4	EChall	Uden	22/23 Oct
254.200		John	Geesler	USA	2.9.59	1	NC	Sylvania	16/17 Sep
252.748		Kenji	Okiyama	JPN	3.6.65	1		Tokyo	25/25 Mar
252.449		Alain	Mallereau	FRA	28.9.50	3	NC	Gravigny	1/2 Jul
		(14/10)							
249.694		Wim	Epskamp	NED	8.1.54	5	EChall	Uden	22/23 Oct
247.050		Nikolai	Machitov	RUS	.55	3		Sankt-Peterburg	2/3 Sep
246.704		William	Sichel	GBR	1.10.53	1		Basel	13/14 May
245.173	t	Antonio	Mazzeo	ITA	19.5.52	2		Verona	23/24 Sep
244.000		Emmanuel	Conraux	FRA	.68	1		Laurent-du-Pont	16/17 Sep
242.000	t	Kename	Sakurai	JPN	4.1.64	1		Tokyo	28/29 Mar
241.394	t	Ivan	Lubutin	RUS	20.3.59	2		Moskva	8/9 May

2000 METRES STEEPLECHASE

Mark	Name		Nat	Born	Pos	Meet	Venue	Date
5:20.42	Laïd	Bessou	ALG	5.2.76	1		Padova	27 Aug
5:21.13	Lotfi	Turki	TUN	6.3.75	2		Padova	27 Aug
5:25.25	Abraham	Cherono	KEN	21.7.80	3		Padova	27 Aug
5:25.69	Gaël	Pencréach	FRA	5.8.77	1		Châlon-sur-Saone	15 Jun
5:26.10	Simon	Vroemen	NED	11.5.69	1		Gold Coast (RB)	17 Sep
5:26.69	Kipkurui	Misoi	KEN	23.12.78	2		Nancy	3 Sep

5:27.86	Damian	Kallabis	GER	10.6.73	17 Sep	5:30.18	Amos Kipruto	Tanui	KEN	.75	3 Aug
5:28.97	Angelo	Carosi	ITA	20.1.64	27 Aug	5:30.39	Eliseo	Martín	ESP	5.11.73	3 Jun
5:29.88	Tony	Cosey	USA	5.10.74	3 Aug	5:30.52	Robert	Gary	USA	5.4.73	3 Aug

JUNIORS

Mark	Name		Nat	Born	Pos	Meet	Venue	Date
5:34.85	Grzegorz	Walaszek	POL	28.4.81	1	NC-j	Wroclaw	28 Aug
5:39.64	Jan	Förster	GER	.82	1	NC-j	Dresden	15 Jul
5:43.13	Mariusz	Gizynski	POL	26.6.81	2	NC-j	Wroclaw	20 Aug

3000 METRES STEEPLECHASE

Mark	Name		Nat	Born	Pos	Meet	Venue	Date
8:02.76	Bernard	Barmasai	KEN	6.5.74	1	Herc	Monaco	18 Aug
8:02.90	Brahim	Boulami	MAR	20.4.72	2	Herc	Monaco	18 Aug
8:03.30		Boulami			1	Nik	Nice	8 Jul
8:03.57	Ali	Ezzine	MAR	3.9.78	1	Gaz	Saint-Denis	23 Jun
8:03.74	Raymond	Yator	KEN-J	7.4.81	3	Herc	Monaco	18 Aug
8:03.82		Boulami			1	GGala	Roma	30 Jun

Mark	Name		Nat	Born	Pos	Meet	Venue	Date
8:03.92	Reuben	Kosgei	KEN	2.8.79	2	Gaz	Saint-Denis	23 Jun
8:04.06		Ezzine			2	Nik	Nice	8 Jul
8:04.27		Barmasai			3	Gaz	Saint-Denis	23 Jun
8:06.58		R Kosgei			1	DNG	Stockholm	1 Aug
8:06.62		Barmasai			2	DNG	Stockholm	1 Aug
8:07.21	Kipkirui	Misoi	KEN	23.12.78	2	GGala	Roma	30 Jun
8:07.33	Wilson	Boit Kipketer	KEN	6.10.73	3	DNG	Stockholm	1 Aug
8:07.64		Boit Kipketer			1	Veniz	Haniá	14 Jun
8:08.00		Misoi			4	Gaz	Saint-Denis	23 Jun
8:08.35		Misoi			4	Herc	Monaco	18 Aug
8:08.67		Boulami			4	DNG	Stockholm	1 Aug
8:09.32		Misoi			5	DNG	Stockholm	1 Aug
8:09.77	Luis Miguel	Martín	ESP	11.1.72	5	Herc	Monaco	18 Aug
8:09.78		Yator			5	Gaz	Saint-Denis	23 Jun
8:10.15		Boit Kipketer			6	Herc	Monaco	18 Aug
8:10.15	Elarbi	Khattabi	MAR	16.5.67	7	Herc	Monaco	18 Aug
8:10.23	Laïd	Bessou	ALG	5.2.76	8	Herc	Monaco	18 Aug
8:10.82		Boulami			2	Veniz	Haniá	14 Jun
8:11.19		Boit Kipketer			1	WK	Zürich	11 Aug
8:11.28		Boit Kipketer			1		Villeneuve d'Ascq	17 Jun
8:11.29	Mark	Croghan	USA	8.1.68	9	Herc	Monaco	18 Aug
8:11.51	Günther	Weidlinger	AUT	5.4.78	1	GS	Ostrava	1 Jun
8:11.65		R Kosgei			2	WK	Zürich	11 Aug
8:11.77		Barmasai			3	WK	Zürich	11 Aug
8:11.94		Yator			6	DNG	Stockholm	1 Aug
	(31/12)							
8:12.30	Jonathan	Kandie	KEN	20.12.67	3	Veniz	Haniá	14 Jun
8:13.22	Abraham	Cherono	KEN	21.7.80	2		Barcelona	25 Jul
8:13.45	Simon	Vroemen	NED	11.5.69	3	GGala	Roma	30 Jun
8:13.63	Eliseo	Martín	ESP	5.11.73	5	WK	Zürich	11 Aug
8:14.53	Damian	Kallabis	GER	10.6.73	4	GGala	Roma	30 Jun
8:14.74	Marco	Cepeda	ESP	1.7.74	3		Barcelona	25 Jul
8:14.94	Gaël	Pencréach	FRA	5.8.77	6	GGala	Roma	30 Jun
8:15.77	Pascal	Dobert	USA	27.10.73	1	NC	Sacramento	20 Jul
	(20)							
8:16.14	Bouabdallah	Tahri	FRA	20.12.78	8	WK	Zürich	11 Aug
8:16.68	Moses	Kiptanui	KEN	1.10.70	8	Gaz	Saint-Denis	23 Jun
8:17.09	Rafal	Wójcik	POL	18.9.72	4		Barcelona	25 Jul
8:17.56	Khamis Seif	Abdullah	QAT	1.12.76	2	GS	Ostrava	1 Jun
8:19.43	Vladimir	Pronin	RUS	27.5.69	9	GGala	Roma	30 Jun
8:19.47	John	Kosgei	KEN	13.7.73	1	GP II	Melbourne	2 Mar
8:20.34	Antonio	Jiménez	ESP	18.2.77	3	NC	Barcelona	2 Sep
8:20.44	Elisardo	de la Torre	ESP	10.10.71	1		Baracaldo	8 Jul
8:20.44	José Luis	Blanco	ESP	3.6.75	6		Barcelona	25 Jul
8:20.49	Christopher	Kosgei	KEN	14.8.74	9	DNG	Stockholm	1 Aug
	(30)							
8:21.14	Luciano	Di Pardo	ITA	3.2.75	10	DNG	Stockholm	1 Aug
8:21.21	Julius	Chelule	KEN	25.12.78	11	Gaz	Saint-Denis	23 Jun
8:21.25	Ramiro	Morán	ESP	17.5.69	4	NC	Barcelona	2 Sep
8:21.41	Tony	Cosey	USA	5.10.74	3	NC	Sacramento	20 Jul
8:21.50	Tim	Broe	USA	20.6.77	4	NC	Sacramento	20 Jul
8:21.62	Florin	Ionescu	ROM	3.2.71	13	Gaz	Saint-Denis	23 Jun
8:22.51	Sa'ad Shaddad	Al-Asmari	KSA	24.9.68	1		Rabat	17 Jun
8:22.98	Lotfi	Turki	TUN	6.3.75	2		Rabat	17 Jun
8:23.26	Clint	Wells	USA	2.5.75	5	NC	Sacramento	20 Jul
8:23.36	David	Chepkisa	KEN	.74	3	GP II	Zagreb	3 Jul
	(40)							
8:23.55	Frédéric	Denis	FRA	3.3.75	6	Nik	Nice	8 Jul
8:23.61	Jim	Svenøy	NOR	22.4.72	2h2	OG	Sydney	27 Sep
8:24.11	Ralf	Assmus	GER	28.1.77	2		Dortmund	8 Jul
8:24.2A	Matthew	Birir	KEN	5.7.72	5	NC	Nairobi	22 Jul
8:24.36	Henri	Belkacem	FRA	16.3.64	7	Nik	Nice	8 Jul
8:24.36	Yarba	Lakhal	MAR	12.2.75	7		Barcelona	25 Jul
8:24.56	Jan	Zakrzewski	POL	21.12.70	2	NC	Kraków	4 Aug
8:24.60	Manuel	Silva	POR	8.10.78	3		Baracaldo	8 Jul
8:25.09	Tom	Nohilly	USA	27.4.66	6	NC	Sacramento	20 Jul
8:25.32	Mourad	Benslimani	ALG	19.2.74	5	ESP Ch	Barcelona	2 Sep
	(50)							

Mark		Name		Nat	Born	Pos	Meet	Venue	Date
8:25.37		Anthony	Famiglietti	USA	8.11.78	7	NC	Sacramento	20 Jul
8:25.37		Christian	Stephenson	GBR	22.7.74	1		Solihull	19 Aug
8:25.68		Giuseppe	Maffei	ITA	28.1.74	1		Pescara	23 Jul
8:25.69		Salvador	Miranda	MEX	22.8.71	5		Baracaldo	8 Jul
8:25.87		Robert	Gary	USA	5.4.73	8	NC	Sacramento	20 Jul
8:25.92		Christian	Belz	SUI	11.9.74	8		Villeneuve d'Ascq	17 Jun
8:25.94		Joël	Bourgeois	CAN	25.4.71	12	DNG	Stockholm	1 Aug
8:25.97		Mohammed	Belabbès	FRA	11.3.66	1		Vanves	30 Jun
8:26.02		Billy	Herman	USA	3.7.77	2h2	NC	Sacramento	17 Jul
8:26.07		Justin	Chaston	GBR	4.11.68	2		Solihull	19 Aug
		(60)							
8:26.10		Badre Din	Zioini	FRA	25.3.76	9	GDN	Villeneuve d'Ascq	17 Jun
8:26.56		Christopher	Soget	KEN	15.8.80	3	GS	Ostrava	1 Jun
8:26.66		Chuck	Sloan	USA	9.1.77	9	NC	Sacramento	20 Jul
8:26.96		Roman	Usov	RUS	4.6.78	5	Gugl	Linz	8 Aug
8:27.04		Lyès	Ramoul	ALG	17.6.76	2	NC	Nice	5 Aug
8:27.08		André	Green	GER	21.4.73	4	GP II	Zagreb	3 Jul
8:27.10		José Maria	González	ESP	3.3.73	10		Barcelona	25 Jul
8:27.17		Angelo	Carosi	ITA	20.1.64	3		Pescara	23 Jul
8:27.19		Merzak Ould	Bouchiba	ALG	.75	5	GP II	Zagreb	3 Jul
8:27.36		Néstor	Nieves	VEN	29.12.74	6	NC	Barcelona	2 Sep
		(70)							
8:27.49		Carlos	Suárez	ESP	25.9.75	11		Barcelona	25 Jul
8:27.60		Michael	Nejedly	CZE	1.10.69	4	GS	Ostrava	1 Jun
8:27.67		Tom	Chorny	USA	23.11.76	3h3	NC	Sacramento	17 Jul
8:27.80		Chris	Unthank	AUS	31.8.72	1		Hobart	30 Jan
8:28.78		Hamid	Jaouane	FRA	3.4.72	11	GDN	Villeneuve d'Ascq	17 Jun
8:28.98		Darin	Shearer	USA	3.4.74	4h1	NC	Sacramento	17 Jul
8:29.36		Dmitriy	Drozdov	RUS	13.4.72	3	NC	Tula	25 Jul
8:29.57		Paul	Kosgei	KEN	22.4.78	16	Gaz	Saint-Denis	23 Jun
8:29.63		Sergey	Redko	UKR	24.1.73	1	NC	Kiev	6 Aug
8:29.73		Lemma	Alemayehu	ETH	.77	6	GP II	Zagreb	3 Jul
		(80)							
8:30.00		Vítor	Almeida	POR	6.3.70	1		Maia	15 Jul
8:30.22		Martin	Dent	AUS	8.2.79	2		Hobart	30 Jan
8:30.5	A	Wilfred	Kigen	KEN		1h1	NC	Nairobi	20 Jul
8:31.11		Momoun	Elouardani	MAR		3		Rabat	17 Jun
8:31.22		Stefano	Ciallella	ITA	22.4.74	4		Pescara	23 Jul
8:31.28		Abderrahmane	Daas	ALG	8.12.73	2		Tunis	3 Jun
8:31.43		Yasunori	Uchitomi	JPN	29.10.72	1	NC	Rifu	7 Oct
8:31.79		João	Junqueira	POR	24.6.65	3		Maia	15 Jul
8:31.95		David	Chemweno	KEN-J	18.12.81	2	WJ	Santiago de Chile	21 Oct
8:32.12		Gianni	Crepaldi	ITA	19.10.68	5		Pescara	23 Jul
		(90)							
8:32.46		Greg	Jimmerson	USA	1.2.75	5h2	NC	Sacramento	17 Jul
8:32.57		Luleseged	Wale	ETH-J	.82	9	Gugl	Linz	8 Aug
8:32.83		Frank	Bruder	GER	31.10.71	4		Cottbus	23 Aug
8:32.99		Yoshitaka	Iwamizu	JPN	20.6.79	1	Nambu	Sapporo	16 Jul
8:33.02		Aziz	Driouche	MAR	15.11.77	1	Oda	Hiroshima	29 Apr
8:33.06		Stephen	Thurston	AUS	26.3.77	2		Manchester	14 Jun
8:33.13		Gebremadhin	Gebremariam	ETH	.80	7		Portland	25 Jun
8:33.29		Ray	Hughes	USA	9.5.75	1r3		Palo Alto	5 May
8:33.34		Dave	Cullum	USA	26.10.73	5h3	NC	Sacramento	17 Jul
8:33.37		Stéphane	Desaulty	FRA	8.1.72	1		Villeneuve d'Ascq	8 May
		(100)							

8:33.5	Taoufik	Faouzi	MAR	73	11 Jun
8:33.5	Jaroslav	Muschinschi	MDA	8.8.76	10 Jun
8:33.5	Abdellatif	Chemlal	MAR-J	1.1.82	23 Jul
8:33.61	Stuart	Stokes	GBR	15.12.76	14 Jun
8:33.71	Alberto	Genovés	ESP	22.11.71	8 Jul
8:34.22	[illegible]	[illegible]	[illegible]	[illegible]	31 Mar
8:34.5	Ivan	Luchianov	MDA-J	31.1.81	10 Jun
8:34.56	Amos Kipruto	Tanui	KEN	.75	29 Aug
8:34.59	Jeremy	Tolman	USA	5.6.77	5 May
8:34.60	Christian	Knoblich	GER	1.10.76	29 Jul
8:34.6A	David	Chepngeno	KEN-J	.81	22 Jul
8:34.80	Yeóryios	Yiannélis	GRE	24.7.71	16 Jul
8:34.84	Hicham	Garmoud	MAR	.79	17 Jun
8:34.85	Chris	Dugan	USA	19.6.79	25 Jun
8:34.86	Jakub	Czaja	POL	12.9.80	4 Aug
8:34.90	Donovan	Bergstrom	USA	3.3.70	14 Apr
8:34.98	Marc	Ostendarp	GER	24.1.73	8 Jul
8:35.02	Sandy	Rebeniuc	USA	.69	17 Jul
8:35.09	Ian	Connor	USA	30.8.79	17 Jul
8:35.15	Steve	Slattery	USA	14.8.80	27 Apr
8:35.23	Martins	Alksnis	LAT	5.9.75	29 Aug
8:35.30	Kim	Bergdahl	FIN	5.3.78	18 Aug
8:35.34	Daba	Maru	ETH	12.12.80	27 Sep
8:35.49	Dave	Wittman	USA	4.7.69	14 Apr
8:35.67	Simon	Mayisela	RSA	9.5.72	3 Mar
8:35.87	Wataru	Izumi	JPN	22.9.72	15 Oct
8:35.90	Ryan	Pirtle	USA	3.6.77	21 May
8:36.57	Casper	Vroemen	NED	11.5.69	18 Aug
8:37.23	Cormac	Smith	IRL	8.10.73	30 Aug
8:37.34	Moses	Kigen	KEN	22.4.73	29 Aug
8:37.37	Joaquín	Torres	ESP	14.8.77	2 Sep
8:37.54	Eric	Segura	ESP	9.6.79	25 Jul

Mark	Name		Nat	Born	Date
8:37.60	Henrik	Skoog	SWE	17.4.79	29 Aug
8:37.63	Charlie	Low	GBR	9.10.74	19 Aug
8:37.84	Tuomo	Lehtinen	FIN	2.2.79	2 Aug
8:37.95	Alberto	Alvarez	ESP	22.12.75	2 Sep
8:38.06	Mickaël	Damian	FRA	9.11.69	12 Jun
8:38.08	Angelo	Iannelli	ITA	27.7.76	7 Sep
8:38.10	Adelar	Schuler	BRA	6.5.72	21 May
8:38.16	Richard	Lee	USA	29.1.71	14 Apr
8:38.40	Philip	Tarus	KEN	11.9.74	15 Jul
8:38.49	Takeshi	Yamamoto	JPN	1.8.73	7 May
8:38.73	Jamal	El Arbi	QAT	10.10.72	17 Jun
8:38.89	César	Pérez	ESP	7.4.75	14 Apr
8:38.89	Stéphane	Machon	FRA	1.4.74	7 Jun
8:38.89	Sergio	Martín	ESP	25.3.78	8 Jul
8:38.93	Vadim	Slobodenyuk	UKR-J	17.3.81	1 Jun
8:39.03	Jacques	Sallberg	USA	24.9.74	17 Jul
8:39.07	Celso	Ficagna	BRA	5.8.75	21 May
8:39.26	Casey	O'Shea	USA	6.2.74	14 Apr
8:39.29	Josephat	Kapkory	KEN	2.1.67	15 Jul
8:39.34	Joseph	Keter	KEN	13.6.69	30 Jan
8:39.35	Jan-Erik	Salo	FIN	26.6.75	27 Apr
8:39.38	Jay	Brock	USA		1 Jul
8:39.50	Brady	Bonsall	USA	4.11.72	14 Apr
8:39.72	Craig	Wheeler	GBR	14.6.76	13 Aug
8:39.74	Richard	Mestler	USA	8.8.69	17 Jul
8:39.79	William	Preira	FRA	8.1.75	5 Aug
8:39.90	Konstantin	Tomskiy	RUS	16.3.75	17 Jun
8:39.97	Boaz	Kisang	KEN		21 May
8:39.99	Francis	O'Neill	USA	25.2.70	17 Jul
8:39.99	Hilaire	Ntirampéba	BDI	.70	18 Aug

One hurdle missing: 25 Jun, Nürnberg: 1. Simon Vroemen 8:13.36, 3. Henri Belkacem 8:19.04, 5. André Green 8:20.29, 6. Christian Belz 8:25.55, 7. Rafal Wójcik POL 8:25.87

JUNIORS

See main list for top 3 juniors. Additional marks and further juniors:

Yator 3+	8:12.24	2		Villeneuve d'Ascq	17 Jun	
	8:12.29	4	WK	Zurich	11 Aug	
	8:16.34	1	WJ	Santiago	21 Oct	
	8:19.38	2		Luzern	27 Jun	
	8:19.94	1		Kerkrade	3 Jun	
	8:24.17	1		Rehlingen	12 Jun	
	8:24.5A	6	NC	Nairobi	22 Jul	
	10 performances by 1 men under 8:25.0.					

Mark	Name		Nat	Born	Pos	Meet	Venue	Date
8:33.5	Abdellatif	Chemlal	MAR	1.1.82	1		Casablanca	23 Jul
8:34.5	Ivan	Luchianov	MDA	31.1.81	2		Chisinau	10 Jun
8:34.6A	David	Chepngeno	KEN	.81	8	NC	Nairobi	22 Jul
8:38.93	Vadim	Slobodenyuk	UKR	17.3.81	8	GS	Ostrava	1 Jun
8:41.0A	David	Kirwa	KEN	.82	2		Nairobi	27 May
8:42.80	Mickaël	André	FRA	3.6.81	4		Bonneuil-sur-Marne	9 Jun
8:43.5A	Kenneth	Maiyo	KEN		3	NC-j	Nairobi	22 Sep
8:45.34	Adelino	Monteiro	POR	1.4.81	4	WJ	Santiago de Chile	21 Oct
8:45.60	Grzegorz	Walaszek	POL	28.4.81	7	NC	Kraków	4 Aug
8:46.80	Martin	Pröll	AUT	21.3.81	5	WJ	Santiago de Chile	21 Oct
8:47.68		Wang Jun	CHN	3.10.83	3	NC	Luohe	22 Oct
8:48.0A	Ezekieli	Kemboi	KEN		4	NC-j	Nairobi	22 Sep
8:48.65	Ali	Tachour	ALG	13.12.81	5		La Roche-sur-Yon	23 Aug
8:49.0A	Moses	Kigen	KEN		5	NC-j	Nairobi	22 Sep
8:50.19		Liu Dong	CHN	8.1.82	4	NC	Luohe	21 Oct
8:50.20	Mariusz	Gizynski	POL	26.6.81	7		Gruzdiadz	3 Sep
8:51.26	Itai	Maggidi	ISR	9.1.81	6	WJ	Santiago de Chile	21 Oct

110 METRES HURDLES

Mark	Wind	Name		Nat	Born	Pos	Meet	Venue	Date
12.97	1.5	Allen	Johnson	USA	1.3.71	1	NC	Sacramento	23 Jul
13.00	0.6	Anier	García	CUB	9.3.76	1	OG	Sydney	25 Sep
13.06	0.6		Johnson			1rA	Athl	Lausanne	5 Jul
13.07	0.6		García			2rA	Athl	Lausanne	5 Jul
13.10	0.0		Johnson			1		Zagreb	3 Jul
13.10	1.4	Colin	Jackson	GBR	18.2.67	1		Leverkusen	20 Aug
13.11	1.5	Mark	Crear	USA	2.10.68	2	NC	Sacramento	23 Jul
13.11	1.4	Dominique	Arnold	USA	14.9.73	2		Leverkusen	20 Aug
13.12	-0.8		García			1	Super	Yokohama	9 Sep
13.14	1.1		Arnold			1s1	NC	Sacramento	23 Jul
13.14	0.7		Johnson			1	Gugl	Linz	8 Aug
13.15	1.1		Johnson			2s1	NC	Sacramento	23 Jul
13.15	1.5		Johnson			1	DNG	Stockholm	1 Aug
13.15	0.5		Arnold			1	VD	Bruxelles	25 Aug
13.16	0.4		García			1s1	OG	Sydney	25 Sep
13.16	0.6	Terrence	Trammell	USA	23.11.78	2	OG	Sydney	25 Sep
13.17	-0.6		Johnson			1	WK	Zürich	11 Aug
13.18	0.2		García			1	NC	La Habana	24 Jul
13.18	0.2		García			1	Herc	Monaco	18 Aug
13.19	0.9		García			1		Helsinki	15 Jun
13.19	0.7		Johnson			1	GGala	Roma	30 Jun
13.19	1.5		Trammell			3	NC	Sacramento	23 Jul
13.19	1.4	Falk	Balzer	GER	14.12.73	3		Leverkusen	20 Aug
13.20	1.6		Crear			1		Palo Alto	1 Jul
13.20	-0.1		Jackson			1		Chemnitz	22 Jul
13.22	1.5		Johnson			1	Veniz	Haniá	14 Jun
13.22	1.5	Dawane	Wallace	USA	30.12.76	4	NC	Sacramento	23 Jul

Mark	Wind	Name		Nat	Born	Pos	Meet	Venue	Date
13.22	0.7		Trammell			2	Gugl	Linz	8 Aug
13.22	0.6		Crear			3	OG	Sydney	25 Sep
13.23	-0.6		García			2	WK	Zürich	11 Aug
13.23	1.4	Florian	Schwarthoff	GER	7.5.68	4		Leverkusen	20 Aug
13.23	2.0		Arnold			1	GP II	Gateshead	28 Aug
13.23	0.4		Crear			2s1	OG	Sydney	25 Sep
13.23	0.6		Johnson			4	OG	Sydney	25 Sep
		(34/9)							
13.24	0.5	Yoel	Hernández	CUB	12.12.77	2	VD	Bruxelles	25 Aug
13.25	1.5	Robin	Korving	NED	29.7.74	2	DNG	Stockholm	1 Aug
13.25	0.2	Stanislavs	Olijars	LAT	22.3.79	2	Herc	Monaco	18 Aug
13.26	1.5	Larry	Wade	USA	22.11.74	5	NC	Sacramento	23 Jul
13.27	1.6	Chris	Phillips	USA	24.7.72	3		Palo Alto	1 Jul
13.33	1.5	Zhivko	Videnov	BUL	23.5.77	2	Veniz	Haniá	14 Jun
13.33	0.4	Dudley	Dorival	HAI	1.9.75	1h2	OG	Sydney	24 Sep
13.34	0.3	Elmar	Lichtenegger	AUT	25.5.74	1h1	Gugl	Linz	8 Aug
13.36	1.5	Robert	Kronberg	SWE	15.8.76	1r2		Gold Coast (RB)	17 Sep
13.39	1.5	Yevgeniy	Pechonkin	RUS	9.10.73	3	DNG	Stockholm	1 Aug
13.40	1.5	Anthony	Dees	USA	6.8.63	3	Veniz	Haniá	14 Jun
		(20)							
13.40	1.9	Jean-Marc	Grava	FRA	2.12.71	1h2		Beaupréau	1 Jul
13.41	1.1	Mike	Fenner	GER	24.4.71	1r2		Dessau	31 May
13.41	0.4	Shaun	Bownes	RSA	24.10.70	5s1	OG	Sydney	25 Sep
13.42	1.3	Terry	Reese	USA	20.6.67	1	ModR	Modesto	13 May
13.42	0.1	Ralf	Leberer	GER	26.10.73	1r2		Osnabrück	24 Jun
13.42	-0.3	Reggie	Torian	USA	22.4.75	2s2	NC	Sacramento	23 Jul
13.42	-0.2	Tomasz	Scigaczewski	POL	18.11.78	1		Wroclaw	15 Aug
13.42	-0.2	Krzysztof	Mehlich	POL	2.8.74	2		Wroclaw	15 Aug
13.43	-0.5	Márcio	de Souza	BRA	24.1.75	1		Americana	3 Jun
13.44A	1.9	Deworski	Odom	USA	11.4.77	1r1		Flagstaff	6 Jul
		(30)							
13.45	-0.2	Marcin	Kuszewski	POL	19.5.77	3		Wroclaw	15 Aug
13.46	0.7	Andrea	Giaconi	ITA	11.4.74	1		La Chaux de Fonds	13 Aug
13.47	1.1	Ron	Bramlett	USA	22.10.79	3	GaTech	Atlanta	20 May
13.48	1.3	Raphaël	Monachon	SUI	8.2.73	1		Fribourg	19 Aug
13.49	-0.3	Aubrey	Herring	USA	19.9.78	2	NCAA	Durham	3 Jun
13.49	-0.6	Andrey	Kislykh	RUS	24.11.76	2	Sule	Tartu	11 Jun
13.49	1.2	Levente	Csillag	HUN	22.3.73	1r2		Budapest	16 Jun
13.49	1.1	Jeff	York	USA	3.9.71	5s1	NC	Sacramento	23 Jul
13.50	0.2	Eugene	Swift	USA	14.9.64	2r2	MSR	Walnut	16 Apr
13.51	0.2	Arend	Watkins	USA	23.5.79	3r2	MSR	Walnut	16 Apr
		(40)							
13.51	0.7	Jonathan	Nsenga	BEL	21.4.73	2		La Chaux de Fonds	13 Aug
13.52	2.0	Adrian	Woodley	CAN	25.11.75	1		Kitchener	22 Jul
13.53	0.2	Duane	Ross	USA	5.12.72	1		Chapel Hill	18 Jun
13.53	2.0	Anthony	Jarrett	GBR	13.8.68	6	GP II	Gateshead	28 Aug
13.54	1.7	Robert	Foster	JAM	12.7.70	1		Fullerton	27 Apr
13.54	0.7	Emiliano	Pizzoli	ITA	29.6.74	6	GGala	Roma	30 Jun
13.55	0.2		Chen Yanhao	CHN	2.1.72	2	GP	Osaka	13 May
13.55	1.5	Steve	Brown	TRI	6.1.69	4h1	GaTech	Atlanta	20 May
13.55	1.7	Paolo	Della Santa	SUI	12.9.73	1h1		Zofingen	12 Jun
13.55	0.9	Vincent	Clarico	FRA	8.1.66	2		Beaupréau	1 Jul
		(50)							
13.57	0.7	Luiz André	Balcers	BRA	18.10.73	1h1		Americana	3 Jun
13.57	-0.3	Todd	Matthews	USA	28.6.79	3	NCAA	Durham	3 Jun
13.57	-0.6	Jerome	Crews	GER	20.2.77	4	NC	Braunschweig	30 Jul
13.58	2.0	Kyle	Vander-Kuyp	AUS	30.5.71	1		Perth	5 Feb
13.58	1.5	Matt	Rush	USA	19.10.78	3		Knoxville	18 May
13.58	0.2	Erik	Batte	CUB	10.12.74	3	NC	La Habana	24 Jul
13.59	1.7	Redelén	dos Santos	BRA	24.4.76	2		São Paulo	6 May
13.59	1.3	Claude	Edorh	GER	27.2.72	1h5		Scheessel	11 Jun
13.60	0.9	Igor	Kovác	SVK	12.5.69	2		Cape Town	31 Mar
13.60	?	Derek	Knight	USA	11.10.67	1h		Sondershausen	25 Aug
		13.61	0.2			2h1		Königs Wusterhausen	29 Aug
		(60)							
13.60	-0.1	Yuniel	Hernández	CUB-J	28.3.81	1	WJ	Santiago de Chile	20 Oct
13.62		Gabriel	Burnett	BAR	20.9.75	1	NC	Bridgetown	24 Jun
13.62	1.6	Antti	Haapakoski	FIN	6.2.71	1		Jämsänkoski	6 Jul
13.62	1.3	Damien	Greaves	GBR	19.9.77	1		Loughborough	30 Jul

Mark	Wind	Name		Nat	Born	Pos	Meet	Venue	Date
13.63A	1.9	Robby	Hughes	USA	10.10.78	1r1		Flagstaff	6 Jul
13.63	0.2	Sébastien	Denis	FRA	4.5.71	7	Herc	Monaco	18 Aug
13.63	-0.4	Philip	Nossmy	SWE-J	6.12.82	2	vFIN	Helsinki	2 Sep
13.66	1.5	Uwezu	McReynolds	USA	20.9.70	6h1	GaTech	Atlanta	20 May
13.66	1.7	Satoru	Tanigawa	JPN	5.7.72	1h2		Toyama	18 Oct
13.67	1.5	Balázs	Kovács	HUN	14.6.77	2	NC	Budapest	29 Jul
		(70)							
13.67	0.6	Leonard	Hudec	AUT	13.6.73	6h2	Gugl	Linz	8 Aug
13.68	-0.1	Andrea	Putignani	ITA	31.12.70	2	NC	Milano	6 Sep
13.70	0.5	Rich	Benoy	USA	14.7.68	2		Norwalk	4 Jun
13.70A	0.0	J-Berlioz	Randriahihaja	MAD	30.11.75	3	IMSS	Ciudad de México	1 Jul
13.71	2.0	Maurice	Wignall	JAM	17.4.76	2		Harrisonburg	13 May
13.71	-0.2	Hajime	Hanazawa	JPN	30.1.73	1		Odawara	25 Jun
13.72	-0.4	Jean-Luc	Poussin	FRA	16.3.70	1		Saint-Brieuc	1 Jun
13.72	0.9	D'Marcus	Brown	USA	17.6.78	4s1	NCAA	Durham	2 Jun
13.72	1.2	Ronald	Mehlich	POL	26.9.69	1h2		Biala Podlaska	3 Jun
13.72	0.8	Hipólito	Montesinos	ESP	24.5.76	1		Vitoria	30 Jul
		(80)							
13.72	1.8	Jarno	Jokihaara	FIN	2.9.73	3	Nurmi	Turku	2 Aug
13.72	0.0	Kimihiro	Asami	JPN	8.11.72	1	NC	Rifu	7 Oct
13.74	0.6	Kenneth	Fambro	USA	13.9.77	3s2	NCAA	Durham	2 Jun
13.74	2.0	Kevin	Ellis	USA	29.6.73	1		Houston	22 Jun
13.74	1.5	Tomas	Dvorák	CZE	11.5.72	3	ECp-1A	Nadderud	9 Jul
13.74	0.6	Kehinde	Alad'efa	NGR	19.12.74	1rB		Namur	18 Aug
13.75	1.8	Greg	Scott	USA	8.2.80	3	SEC	Baton Rouge	14 May
13.75	1.2	Sherman	Armstrong	USA	22.9.78	2h1	NCAA	Durham	1 Jun
13.75	0.5	Philippe	Lamine	FRA	4.10.76	2		Bron	23 Jul
13.75	-0.3		Liu Xiang	CHN-J	23.7.83	1s2	WJ	Santiago de Chile	19 Oct
		(90)							
13.75	-0.3	Ladji	Doucouré	FRA-J	28.3.83	2s2	WJ	Santiago de Chile	19 Oct
13.76	1.5	Kris	Allen	USA	14.4.79	1		Houston	1 Apr
13.76	1.4	Tony	Galaviz	USA	23.9.78	1		Sacramento	20 May
13.76	0.9	Wenston	Riley	USA	24.4.77	5s1	NCAA	Durham	2 Jun
13.76	1.7	Ivan	Bitzi	SUI	4.8.75	2r1		Zofingen	12 Jun
13.76	2.0	Bashir	Ramzy	USA	4.5.79	2		Houston	22 Jun
13.76	2.0	Charles	Allen	GUY	29.3.77	2		Kitchener	22 Jul
13.76	-0.5	Egbert	Felix	CAN	22.11.73	1		Kitchener	29 Jul
13.76	1.3	Thomas	Keller	SUI	25.5.73	2		Fribourg	19 Aug
13.76	0.0	Ken-ichi	Sakurai	JPN	26.12.76	3	NC	Rifu	7 Oct
		(100)							

13.77	-1.9	Rusty	Fry	USA	8.3.78	31 Mar
13.77	0.5	Dominique	DeGrammont	USA	13.3.79	4 Jun
13.77	1.1	Tasuku	Tanonaka	JPN	23.9.78	3 Sep
13.78	0.4	Dmitriy	Kolesnichenko	UKR	28.2.72	28 May
13.78	0.9	Eddie	Jackson	USA	19.12.80	2 Jun
13.78	0.2	Emilio	Valle	CUB	21.4.67	24 Jul
13.78	-0.6	Thomas	Blaschek	GER-J	5.4.81	30 Jul
13.78	0.8	Alexis	Sánchez	CUB	13.4.71	30 Jul
13.79	1.4	Ron	Andrews	USA	12.10.79	20 May
13.79	1.1	Shinri	Yamada	JPN	17.6.79	3 Sep
13.80		Ricardo	Moody	USA	24.9.80	6 May
13.81A	0.0	Tim	Ewen	AUS	21.2.77	24 Mar
13.81	1.2		Zhang Feng	CHN	9.5.72	13 May
13.81A	1.9	Andrew	Lissade	CAN	7.1.76	6 Jul
13.81	1.8	Mubarak	Ata Mubarak	KSA-J	17.12.81	2 Aug
13.81	0.0	Rafal	Lis	POL	25.2.70	10 Sep
13.82	1.8	Masanori	Inoue	JPN	1.5.72	11 Jun
13.82	1.3	Mensah	Elliott	GBR	29.8.76	30 Jul
13.83	-0.5	Andrey	Sklyarenko	KAZ	10.1.76	3 Jun
13.83	1.8	Carlos	Patterson	CUB	20.2.78	30 Jun
13.83A	0.0	Derek	Spears	USA	22.3.73	1 Jul
13.84		Nicholas	Wade	USA		20 May
13.84	1.2	Jeff	Jackson	ISV	14.3.74	18 Jun
13.84	1.7	Andreas	Dengler	GER	22.12.80	12 Aug
13.84	1.4	Chris	Baillie	GBR-J	21.4.81	27 Aug
13.85	-0.4	T.J.	Nelson	USA	7.12.77	29 Apr
13.85	1.5	Gabe	Spezia	USA		18 May
13.85	0.0	Rui	Palma	POR	4.1.78	2 Jun
13.85	0.0	Masato	Naito	JPN	31.7.80	18 Oct
13.86	1.4	Stephen	Jones	BAR	25.7.78	14 Apr
13.86	1.7	Emerson	Perin	BRA	17.3.75	6 May
13.86	0.9	Dimítrios	Piétris	GRE	24.10.79	21 Jun
13.86	-0.2	Hubert	Grossard	BEL	28.3.68	2 Jul
13.86	0.4	Pavel	Oreshkin	RUS	25.4.78	11 Jul
13.86	0.8	Francisco J	López	ESP	28.9.73	30 Jul
13.86	0.3	Peter	Coghlan	IRL	27.3.75	24 Sep
13.87	0.7	Caldrequis	Lesley	USA	11.12.76	1 Apr
13.87	0.3	Luca	Giovannelli	ITA	29.9.75	16 Jun
13.87	1.6	Denis	Kozhemyakin	UKR	5.7.78	17 Jun
13.87	1.6	Gergely	Palágyi	HUN	19.4.79	8 Jul
13.87	-0.5	Jan	Schindzielorz	GER	8.8.78	20 Aug
13.87	-0.1	Denis	Favaro	ITA	14.7.72	6 Sep
13.87	-1.4	Roman	Sebrle	CZE	26.11.74	28 Sep
13.88		Rod	Jett	USA	28.10.66	25 Mar
13.88		Victor	Houston	BAR	24.2.74	1 May
13.88	0.6	Shogo	Kanzaki	JPN	1.7.78	21 May
13.88	0.6	Yasunori	Yoshioka	JPN	19.5.75	16 Jul
13.88	1.1	Eric	Ciolfi	FRA	14.5.77	23 Jul
13.88	1.2	Sven	Pieters	BEL	5.6.76	14 Aug
13.89	0.4	Austin	Wighaman	USA		16 May
13.89	0.5	William	Erese	NGR	12.9.76	4 Jun
13.89	0.8	Miguel	de los Santos	ESP	9.8.73	30 Jul
13.90	-1.1	Corey	Taylor	USA-J	2.5.81	25 Mar
13.90	1.6	Greg	Richardson	USA	27.12.76	6 May
13.90	2.0	Sean	Lightfoot	USA	8.6.79	13 May
13.90	-0.5	Jeramie	Thomas	USA	2.2.76	26 May
13.90	1.2	Eddie	Neufville	LBR	16.11.76	3 Jun
13.90	1.8	Mitsuhiko	Nagano	JPN	11.12.77	11 Jun
13.90	1.3	Damjan	Zlatnar	SLO	16.12.77	17 Jun
13.90	1.7	Garland	Martin	USA-J	1.3.81	23 Jun
13.91	1.2		Li Qiang	CHN	13.2.74	13 May
13.91	1.5	Artur	Kohutek	POL	1.5.71	28 Jun
13.91	1.6	Cédric	Lavanne	FRA	13.11.80	15 Jul
13.91	0.3	Dmitriy	Reykh	RUS	.71	24 Jul
13.91	-1.4	Chris	Huffins	USA	15.4.70	28 Sep
13.92	1.6	Jalilu	Mayo	USA	2.1.78	6 May

Mark	Wind	Name		Nat	Born	Date
13.92	-0.1	Dario	Volturara	ITA	1.4.70	6 Sep
13.93	0.0	Scott	Keys	USA	11.12.76	15 May
13.93	1.6	Marcell	Allmond	USA-J	28.5.81	23 Jun
13.93	1.5	Dimítrios	Siatoúnis	GRE	20.8.69	28 Jun
13.93	0.9	Paul	Gray	GBR	25.5.69	29 Jul
13.93	1.5	Neil	Owen	GBR	18.10.73	6 Aug
13.93!	0.7	Hubert	Tomczak	POL	25.3.76	12 Aug
13.93	1.2	Jens	Buchholz	GER	17.6.76	27 Aug
13.94A	1.2	Wes	Davis	USA	9.12.75	21 Apr
13.94	0.0	Darren	Youngstrom	USA	7.7.77	26 May
13.94	-0.3	Jörn	Lichtenhagen	GER	30.4.76	11 Jun
13.95	1.1	Jermaine	Cooper	USA	31.8.80	1 Jun
13.95	1.5	Felipe	Vivancos	ESP	16.6.80	10 Jun
13.95	0.0	Matthew	Love	JAM	1.8.70	18 Jun
13.95	0.7	Avery	Anderson	USA	16.3.73	1 Jul
13.95	0.9	Marcel	van der Westen	NED	1.8.76	2 Jul
13.95	2.0	Tom	Pappas	USA	6.9.76	13 Aug
13.95	1.4	Robert	Newton	GBR-J	10.5.81	27 Aug
13.95	0.7	Antonio	De Sanctis	ITA	18.10.72	30 Aug
13.96		Chris	Stokes	USA	1.2.79	6 May
13.96	-0.5	Sultan	Tucker	USA	24.10.78	14 May
13.96	1.5	Mihai	Marghescu	ROM	26.9.76	24 Jun
13.96	1.8	Carlos	Navarro	CUB-J	.83	29 Jun
13.96	-0.2	Piet	Deveughele	BEL	3.6.77	2 Jul
13.96	1.6	Thomas	Martin	FRA	19.2.80	15 Jul
13.96	0.3	Yusuke	Sugiyama	JPN	17.5.78	3 Sep
13.97	-0.4		Cao Jing	CHN	31.1.78	15 Apr
13.97	2.0	Jasper	Demps	USA	22.10.79	5 May
13.97	-0.1	Kevin	Walker	USA	26.2.78	7 May
13.97	1.3		Qi Zhen	CHN	4.8.76	8 Jun
13.97	-0.6	Emmanouíl	Sbókos	GRE	10.4.72	21 Jun
13.97	0.5	Nicola	Comencini	ITA	7.5.78	24 Jun
13.97	0.3	Viktor	Bolkun	RUS	2.7.70	24 Jul
13.98	1.5	Karl	Jennings	USA	14.5.79	18 May
13.98	-0.9	Frank	Busemann	GER	26.2.75	24 May
13.98A	0.1	Paulo	Villar	COL	28.7.78	30 Jul
13.98	0.1	Artur	Budzillo	POL	21.7.79	6 Aug
13.99	1.8	Stefan	Heinås	SWE	15.1.75	19 Jul

Disqualified – trailing leg

Mark	Wind	Name		Nat	Born	Date
13.79	1.6	Dan	O'Brien	USA	18.7.66	1 Jul

Wind assisted

Mark	Wind	Name		Nat	Born	Pos	Meet	Venue	Date
13.06	2.5		García			1	GP	Athína	28 Jun
13.10	3.1	Mark	Crear	USA	2.10.68	1	OD	Jena	3 Jun
13.17	3.1		García			1		Camagüey	10 Mar
13.17	2.2		Crear			1h1	OD	Jena	3 Jun
13.19	2.2		García			2h1	OD	Jena	3 Jun
13.19	3.1		García			2	OD	Jena	3 Jun
13.20	3.1	Yoel	Hernández	CUB	12.12.77	2		Camagüey	10 Mar
13.29	3.1	Anthony	Dees	USA	6.8.63	3	OD	Jena	3 Jun
13.37	2.3	Yevgeniy	Pechonkin	RUS	9.10.73	1		Caorle	8 Jul
13.38	3.1	Shaun	Bownes	RSA	24.10.70	4	OD	Jena	3 Jun
13.38A	2.3	Deworski	Odom	USA	11.4.77	1r2		Flagstaff	6 Jul
13.40	3.1	Ralf	Leberer	GER	26.10.73	5	OD	Jena	3 Jun
13.45	2.8	Paolo	Della Santa	SUI	12.9.73	1h1	NC	Lugano	29 Jul
13.50	2.3	Adrian	Woodley	CAN	25.11.75	1	Big East	Piscataway	7 May
13.52	2.8	Hipólito	Montesinos	ESP	24.5.76	1		Ibiza	12 Aug
13.54	3.1	Jerome	Crews	GER	20.2.77	1h2		Hamburg	3 Sep
13.55A	3.3	Igor	Kovác	SVK	12.5.69	3		Pietersburg	18 Mar
13.58	2.1	Satoru	Tanigawa	JPN	5.7.72	1	Oda	Hiroshima	29 Apr
13.59	3.5	Robby	Hughes	USA	10.10.78	1r2	GaTech	Atlanta	20 May
13.61	5.2	Kris	Allen	USA	14.4.79	1r2		College Station	11 May
13.61	3.7	Sébastien	Denis	FRA	4.5.71	1		Argentan	25 Jun
13.62	3.6	Jean-Luc	Poussin	FRA	16.3.70	2h1		Bron	23 Jul
13.65	3.2	Derek	Spears	USA	22.3.73	1r1	Johnson	Waco	22 Apr
13.66	4.5	Stephen	Jones	BAR	25.7.78	2	UCTA	Austin	22 Apr
13.66	3.6	Philippe	Lamine	FRA	4.10.76	3h1		Bron	23 Jul
13.67	3.1	Rich	Benoy	USA	14.7.68	2r1		Azusa	8 Apr
13.67	2.1	Bashir	Ramzy	USA	4.5.79	1	Big 12	Columbia MO	21 May
13.69	5.2	Kevin	Ellis	USA	29.6.73	2r2		College Station	11 May
13.69A	7.1	Kehinde	Alad'efa	NGR	19.12.74	1r3		Flagstaff	3 Jul
13.69	3.8	Mensah	Elliott	GBR	29.8.76	2	NCp	Bedford	19 Aug
13.72	2.6	Shorman	Armstrong	USA	22.9.78	1	Big 10	Iowa City	21 May
13.73	3.2	Jeremichael	Williams	USA	30.12.76	2r1	Johnson	Waco	22 Apr
13.74	3.8	Rusty	Fry	USA	8.3.78	2r2	Owens	Columbus	7 May
13.74	3.3	Sean	Lightfoot	USA	8.6.79	1h2	GaTech	Atlanta	20 May
13.74A	4.3	Francisco J	López	ESP	28.9.73	1		Soria	29 Jul
13.75	5.6	Austin	Wighaman	USA		1		Abilene	11 May
13.75	3.3	Eddio	Jackson	USA	19.12.80	2h2	GaTech	Atlanta	20 May
13.75	3.1	Ivan	Bitzi	SUI	4.8.75	6r1		Génève	24 Jun
13.75A	2.9	Miguel	de los Santos	ESP	9.8.73	2		Soria	29 Jul

Mark	Wind	Name		Nat	Born	Date
13.77	4.2	Rod	Jett	USA	28.10.66	1 Apr
13.78A	3.3	Tim	Ewen	AUS	21.2.77	18 Mar
13.78	2.1	Victor	Houston	BAR	24.2.74	29 Apr
13.79	4.5	Ryan	Wilson	USA	19.12.80	22 Apr
13.80	5.7	John	McAfee	USA	15.3.78	8 Apr
13.80	2.1	Jeff	Jackson	ISV	14.3.74	29 Apr
13.81A	4.3	Javier	Vega	ESP	10.12.75	29 Jul
13.81	2.4	Felipe	Vivancos	ESP	16.6.80	12 Aug
13.82	3.1	Carlos	Patterson	CUB	20.2.78	10 Mar
13.82	3.8	Michael	Thomas	USA-J	21.12.81	23 Jun
13.82		Jan	Schindzielorz	GER	8.8.78	24 Jun
13.83A	3.7	Wes	Davis	USA	9.12.75	10 May
13.83	2.1	Jermaine	Cooper	USA	31.8.80	21 May
13.84	4.2	William	Erese	NGR	12.9.76	8 Apr
13.84	2.6	Ryan	Grear	USA	11.4.79	21 May
13.86	2.1	Yasunori	Yoshioka	JPN	19.5.75	29 Apr
13.86	2.4	Sultan	Tucker	USA	24.10.78	21 Apr
13.86	2.7	Jens	Buchholz	GER	17.6.76	3 Sep
13.87	3.4	Chris	Stokes	USA	1.2.79	8 Apr
13.87		Mike	Henderson	USA		21 Apr
13.87	4.5	Lee	Mays	USA	18.9.78	22 Apr
13.87	2.2	Derrick	James	USA		19 May
13.87	3.4	Neil	Owen	GBR	18.10.73	18 Jun
13.87	2.1	Jalilu	Mayo	USA	2.1.78	1 Jul
13.88	w	Chris	Pinnock	USA-J	.82	29 Apr
13.88	2.3	Antoine	Johnson	USA	22.12.80	7 May

Mark	Wind	Name		Nat	Born	Pos	Meet	Venue	Date
13.88	2.3	Gus	Martin	USA	4.4.78				7 May
13.89	2.1	Calvin	Williams	USA	23.1.79				21 Apr
13.89	3.2	Marcell	Allmond	USA-J	28.5.81				21 May
13.90	2.4	Iain	Harnden	ZIM	23.9.76				21 Apr
13.91	3.3	Désiré	Delric	FRA	18.4.79				4 Aug
13.92	3.1	Djeke	Mambo	BEL	4.3.77				8 Apr
13.92	2.4	Zoran	Miljus	CRO	26.5.76				20 May
13.92	2.3	Darren	Youngstrom	USA	7.7.77				25 May
13.92A	2.4	Ben	Meyer	USA	12.9.77				3 Jul
13.92	3.8	Martin	Barrow	AUS	3.1.73				5 Aug
13.93	3.3	Derek	Zachary	USA					12 May
13.93	3.2	Marcel	van der Westen	NED	1.8.76				10 Jun
13.94	5.6	Brandon	May	USA	7.4.77				11 May
13.95	5.6	Shaka	Huggins	USA					11 May
13.96	4.2	David	Ashford	USA	24.1.64				8 Apr
13.96	5.2	Micah	Harris	USA					13 May
13.97A	3.3	Martin	Barrow	AUS	3.1.73				18 Mar
13.99		Casey	Swain	USA					8 Apr
13.99	2.8	Stéphane	Caristan	FRA	31.5.64				28 May
Best at low altitude									
13.59	-0.3		Odom			6s2	NC	Sacramento	23 Jul
13.66	1.8		Hughes			1rB	MSR	Walnut	16 Apr
13.74	1.9		Randriamihaja			1		Réduit	9 Apr
13.87	1.5		Ewen			1	NC	Sydney	26 Jan
Hand timing									
13.3	1.1	Levente	Csillag	HUN	22.3.73	1		Veszprém	9 Sep
13.4	-0.9	Emilio	Valle	CUB	21.4.67	1		La Habana	16 Jun
13.5	-0.9	Yuniel	Hernández	CUB-J	28.3.81	2		La Habana	16 Jun
13.5	-0.9	Carlos	Patterson	CUB	20.2.78	3		La Habana	16 Jun
13.5	0.8	Eric	Ciolfi	FRA	14.5.77	1	vENG	Vittel	2 Sep
13.6	0.0	Richard	Benoy	USA	14.6.68				1 Apr
13.6	1.0	Ken-ichi	Sakurai	JPN	26.12.76				22 Jul
13.6	0.8	Shinri	Yamada	JPN	17.6.79				12 Aug
13.7		Denis	Kozhemyakin	UKR	5.7.78				3 Jun
13.7	0.8	Tasuku	Tanonaka	JPN	23.9.78				12 Aug
13.7	0.8	Mensah	Elliott	GBR	29.8.76				2 Sep
13.7w	2.8	Stefan	Heinås	SWE	15.1.75				26 Jul

JUNIORS

Mark	Wind	Name		Nat	Born	Pos	Meet	Venue	Date
13.60	-0.1	Yuniel	Hernández	CUB-J	28.3.81	1	WJ	Santiago de Chile	20 Oct
		13.78 -1.8 1s1 WJ Santiago 19 Oct							
13.63	-0.4	Philip	Nossmy	SWE-J	6.12.82	2	vFIN	Helsinki	2 Sep
13.75	-0.3		Liu Xiang	CHN-J	23.7.83	1s2	WJ	Santiago de Chile	19 Oct
13.75	-0.3	Ladji	Doucouré	FRA-J	28.3.83	2s2	WJ	Santiago de Chile	19 Oct
		13.78 1.9 2 Réduit 9 Apr				11 performances by 6 men to 13.81			
13.78	-0.6	Thomas	Blaschek	GER-J	5.4.81	7	NC	Braunschweig	30 Jul
		13.80 -0.1 2 WJ Santiago 20 Oct				13.81 -0.3 3s2 WJ Santiago 19 Oct			
13.81	1.8	Mubarak	Ata Mubarak	KSA-J	17.12.81	4	Nurmi	Turku	2 Aug
13.84	1.4	Chris	Baillie	GBR-J	21.4.81	1	NC-j	Bedford	27 Aug
13.90	-1.1	Corey	Taylor	USA-J	2.5.81	1		Columbia SC	25 Mar
13.90	1.6	Garland	Martin	USA-J	1.3.81	1h3	NC-j	Denton	23 Jun
13.93	1.6	Marcell	Allmond	USA-J	28.5.81	2h3	NC-j	Denton	23 Jun
13.95	1.4	Robert	Newton	GBR-J	10.5.81	2		Bedford	27 Aug
13.96	1.8	Carlos	Navarro	CUB-J	.83	3r2		La Habana	29 Jun
14.06	-1.8	Dwayne	Robinson	JAM-J	31.3.83	1h2	NC	Kingston	22 Jul
14.07	-0.1	Nenad	Loncar	YUG-J	6.3.81	1h5	WJ	Santiago de Chile	18 Oct
14.08	0.0	Nassim	Meziane Brahimi	QAT-J	.84	1h4	WJ	Santiago de Chile	18 Oct
14.12	1.6	Chris	Pinnock	USA-J	.82	1	KansR	Lawrence KS	22 Apr
14.13	2.0	Ricardo	Melbourne	JAM-J	26.2.82	4	NC	Kingston	22 Jul
14.13	0.7		Shen Zhensheng	CHN-J	6.3.81	2	AsiC	Jakarta	30 Aug
14.19	-1.1	Bruce	Bickell	RSA-J	7.10.81	1		Pietersburg	15 Apr
14.19	0.9	Justin	Dyett	GER-J	15.5.81	3		Mannheim	12 Aug
14.19	-0.7	Nikolay	Koykov	BUL-J	12.10.81	1		Constanta	16 Sep
		(21)							
Wind assisted									
13.82	3.8	Michael	Thomas	USA-J	21.12.81	1h4	NC-j	Denton	23 Jun
13.88	w	Chris	Pinnock	USA-J	.82	1		Great Bend	29 Apr
13.89	3.2	Marcell	Allmond	USA-J	28.5.81	2	Pac 10	Eugene	21 May
14.05	2.3	Charles	Ryan	USA-J	10.2.81	1h1	NC-j	Denton	23 Jun
14.10A	3.3	Bruce	Bickell	RSA-J	7.10.81	6		Pietersburg	18 Mar
14.11	3.2	Gregory	Sedoc	NED-J	16.10.81	3		Leiden	10 Jun
14.17	2.2	Jacob	Garlick	USA-J	12.2.82	1h2	NC-j	Denton	23 Jun
Hand timed									
13.5	-0.9	Yuniel	Hernández	CUB-J	28.3.81	2		La Habana	16 Jun
13.8A	w?	Jacques	Greyling	RSA-J	31.8.81	1		Potchefstroom	11 Oct
13.9	-0.9	Carlos	Navarro	CUB-J	.83	4		La Habana	16 Jun

200 METRES HURDLES

23.03	1.0	Paolo	Della Santa	SUI	12.9.73	1		Langenthal	20 May

300 METRES HURDLES

34.59	Chris	Rawlinson	GBR	19.5.72	1	Loughborough	30 Jul
35.1	Thomas	Göller	GER	28.10.77	1h	Pliezhausen	21 May
35.25	Matt	Douglas	GBR	26.11.76	2	Loughborough	30 Jul
35.69	Rohan	Robinson	AUS	15.11.71	3	Loughborough	30 Jul

400 METRES HURDLES

Mark	Name		Nat	Born	Pos	Meet	Venue	Date
47.50	Angelo	Taylor	USA	29.12.78	1	OG	Sydney	27 Sep
47.53	Hadi Soua'an	Al-Somaily	KSA	30.12.76	2	OG	Sydney	27 Sep
47.62		Taylor			1	NC	Sacramento	22 Jul
47.81	Llewellyn	Herbert	RSA	21.7.77	3	OG	Sydney	27 Sep
47.90		Taylor			1rA	WK	Zürich	11 Aug
47.93		Herbert			2rA	WK	Zürich	11 Aug
47.94	Eric	Thomas	USA	1.12.73	1	GGala	Roma	30 Jun
47.98		Herbert			1rA	Athl	Lausanne	5 Jul
48.01	Samuel	Matete	ZAM	27.7.68	1	Super	Yokohama	9 Sep
48.03		Taylor			2	GGala	Roma	30 Jun
48.04	James	Carter	USA	7.5.78	4	OG	Sydney	27 Sep
48.09		Herbert			2	Super	Yokohama	9 Sep
48.14		Al-Somailly			1s1	OG	Sydney	25 Sep
48.14		Taylor			1	GPF	Doha	5 Oct
48.18		Herbert			1	Herc	Monaco	18 Aug
48.18		Al-Somailly			2	GPF	Doha	5 Oct
48.20		Thomas			1	Nik	Nice	8 Jul
48.22	Chris	Rawlinson	GBR	19.5.72	1		Milano	7 Jun
48.22		Rawlinson			2rA	Athl	Lausanne	5 Jul
48.22		Thomas			2	NC	Sacramento	22 Jul
48.25	Eronilde	de Araújo	BRA	31.12.70	1	GP	Athína	28 Jun
48.26		Taylor			1	ISTAF	Berlin	1 Sep
48.30		Herbert			1	VD	Bruxelles	25 Aug
48.32		Herbert			1		Luzern	27 Jun
48.32		Thomas			3rA	WK	Zürich	11 Aug
48.33	Felix	Sanchez	DOM	30.8.77	2	GP	Athína	28 Jun
48.33		Al-Somailly			1rB	Athl	Lausanne	5 Jul
48.33		Taylor			2	VD	Bruxelles	25 Aug
48.34		de Araújo			5	OG	Sydney	27 Sep
48.35		Rawlinson			2	Herc	Monaco	18 Aug
	(30/9)							
48.40	Fabrizio	Mori	ITA	28.6.69	2s1	OG	Sydney	25 Sep
48.40	Gennadiy	Gorbenko	UKR	22.9.75	3s1	OG	Sydney	25 Sep
48.42	Pawel	Januszewski	POL	2.1.72	4s1	OG	Sydney	25 Sep
48.43	Bayano	Kamani	USA	17.4.80	2	NCAA	Durham	2 Jun
48.47	Dai	Tamesue	JPN	3.5.78	3	Super	Yokohama	9 Sep
48.56	Kemel	Thompson	JAM	25.9.74	1	GaTech	Atlanta	20 May
48.61	Sherman	Armstrong	USA	22.9.78	3	NCAA	Durham	2 Jun
48.70	Stéphane	Diagana	FRA	23.7.69	3	Gaz	Saint-Denis	23 Jun
48.71	Jirí	Muzík	CZE	1.9.76	1rB	WK	Zürich	11 Aug
48.72	Joey	Woody	USA	22.5.73	1s2	NC	Sacramento	21 Jul
48.76	Ruslan	Mashchenko	RUS	11.11.71	2rB	Athl	Lausanne	5 Jul
	(20)							
48.80	Ibou	Faye	SEN	13.12.69	1		Chaux de Fonds	13 Aug
48.80	Dinsdale	Morgan	JAM	19.11.72	4	Super	Yokohama	9 Sep
48.82	Thomas	Goller	GER	28.10.77	3rB	WK	Zürich	11 Aug
48.84	Hideaki	Kawamura	JPN	15.9.74	5	Super	Yokohama	9 Sep
48.88	William	Porter	USA	15.4.73	5	NC	Sacramento	22 Jul
48.92	Calvin	Davis	USA	2.4.72	2	GaTech	Atlanta	20 May
49.02A	Hennie	Botha	RSA	20.2.75	1rA		Potchefstroom	14 Feb
49.02	Ken	Harnden	ZIM	31.3.73	2	Veniz	Haniá	14 Jun
49.02	Vladislav	Shiryayev	RUS	30.10.73	1	NC	Tula	25 Jul
49.07A	Alwyn	Myburgh	RSA	13.10.80	2rA		Pretoria	24 Mar
	(30)							
49.08A	Blair	Young	AUS	5.4.71	2		Pietersburg	18 Mar
49.08	Sam	Glover	USA	22.1.80	4	NCAA	Durham	2 Jun
49.08	Mario	Watts	JAM	21.5.75	1		Indianapolis	1 Jul
49.09	Boris	Gorban	RUS	26.9.78	2	NC	Tula	25 Jul
49.11	Ken	Yoshizawa	JPN	7.7.78	2		Yokohama	21 May
49.12	Ian	Weakley	JAM	24.2.74	2		Chapel Hill	18 Jun
49.12	Torrance	Zellner	USA	6.1.70	5s2	NC	Sacramento	21 Jul
49.17	Giorgio	Frinolli	ITA	12.7.70	1		Selargius	23 Aug
49.23	Maurice	Mitchell	USA	14.5.71	6s2	NC	Sacramento	21 Jul
49.23	Marek	Plawgo	POL-J	25.2.81	1	WJ	Santiago de Chile	21 Oct
	(40)							
49.25	John	McAfee	USA	15.3.78	2		Indianapolis	1 Jul
49.26	Matthew	Douglas	GBR	26.11.76	2		Rovereto	30 Aug

Mark	Name		Nat	Born	Pos	Meet	Venue	Date
49.27	Shunji	Karube	JPN	8.5.69	2		Shizuoka	3 May
49.33A	Tibor	Bédi	HUN	22.3.74	1rB		Pretoria	24 Mar
49.35	Yoshihiro	Chiba	JPN	29.4.79	3		Yokohama	21 May
49.35	Periklis	Iakovakis	GRE	24.3.79	2		Thessaloníki	30 Aug
49.36	Louis	Sales	USA	29.11.71	5	GaTech	Atlanta	20 May
49.41	Rohan	Robinson	AUS	15.11.71	1	GP II	Melbourne	2 Mar
49.44	Ziad Abou	Hamed	SYR/AUS	22.4.70	1		Canberra	15 Jan
49.44	Sylvester	Omodiale	NGR	5.9.77	1		L'Hospitalet	27 Aug
	(50)							
49.44	Harijan	Ratnayake	SRI	8.12.74	2	AsiC	Jakarta	31 Aug
49.47A	Willie	Smith	NAM	20.9.77	4r1		Roodepoort	13 Mar
49.47	Regan	Nichols	USA	26.7.73	1		Houston	6 Jul
49.48	Jean-Dominique	Dième	SEN	18.9.69	1	NC	Dakar	11 Jun
49.48	Pedro	Rodrigues	POR	8.7.71	7s1	OG	Sydney	25 Sep
49.49	Marcel	Schelbert	SUI	26.2.76	8rA	WK	Zürich	11 Aug
49.50	Neil	Gardner	JAM	8.12.74	2		Nassau	9 Jun
49.51	Cleverson	da Silva	BRA	5.9.73	2	Kuso	Warszawa	24 Jun
49.54	Wayne	Whyte	JAM	4.5.74	1		Königs Wusterhausen	29 Aug
49.55	Ferdana	Johnson	USA	6.10.72	1		Houston	23 Jun
	(60)							
49.60	Michael	Smith	USA	26.4.79	2	Big 12	Columbia MO	21 May
49.62	David	Aaron	USA	2.12.78	2		Houston	6 Jul
49.66	Mustapha	Sdad	MAR	11.4.70	1		Madrid	28 Jul
49.67	Zahirudin Abd.	Al-Najem	SYR	11.1.77	3	AsiC	Jakarta	31 Aug
49.68	Iain	Harnden	ZIM	23.9.76	2		Tallahassee	13 May
49.68	Adrian	Mann	USA	23.5.78	1r2		Atlanta	20 May
49.68	Anthony	Borsumato	GBR	13.12.73	5	vUSA	Glasgow	2 Jul
49.70	David	Kafka	FRA	2.7.72	3rA		La Chaux-de-Fonds	13 Aug
49.71	Kazuhiko	Yamazaki	JPN	10.5.71	4r2	Athl	Lausanne	5 Jul
49.74	Yvon	Rakotoarimaindry	MAD	5.1.76	1		Castres	27 Jul
	(70)							
49.74	Yuki	Omoto	JPN	29.10.78	3	Univ Ch	Tokyo	2 Sep
49.77		Tan Chunhua	CHN	13.3.77	1	NGPF	Jinzhou	8 Jun
49.77A	Nick	Stewart	CAN	6.4.79	1r1		Flagstaff	8 Jul
49.79A	Brett	Guymon	USA	9.1.77	1	USTCA	Provo	6 May
49.81	Bartosz	Gruman	POL	11.5.75	2	NC	Kraków	5 Aug
49.82A	Kyle	Grossarth	USA	4.1.77	2	USTCA	Provo	6 May
49.83	Octavius	Terry	USA	7.11.72	4h2	NC	Sacramento	20 Jul
49.84	Derrick	Adkins	USA	2.7.70	2h4	NC	Sacramento	20 Jul
49.86	Iñigo	Monreal	ESP	26.9.74	2	ECp1A	Nadderud	8 Jul
49.88	Jun	Iwasaki	JPN	3.6.78	1h3		Yokohama	20 May
	(80)							
49.88	Iliya	Dzhivondov	BUL	6.3.78	1		Sofia	11 Jun
49.90	Anderson	dos Santos	BRA	15.6.75	1		São Caetano do Sul	15 Apr
49.90	Olivier	Jean-Théodore	FRA	13.11.74	1		Loughborough	30 Jul
49.92	Gianni	Carabelli	ITA	30.5.79	1		Lecco	16 Jul
49.93	Josef	Rous	CZE	26.7.79	1		Praha	15 Jun
49.93		Chen Tien-Wen	TPE	1.6.78	5h2	OG	Sydney	24 Sep
49.95	Zion	Armstrong	NZL	21.1.75	1	NC	Christchurch	12 Mar
49.95	Paul	Tucker	GUY	30.1.76	1rB		La Chaux-de-Fonds	13 Aug
49.95	Kehinde	Alad'efa	NGR	19.12.74	2		Selargius	23 Aug
49.96	Omar A.	Brown	JAM	26.12.75	4		Torino	10 Jun
	(90)							
49.97A	Monté	Raymond	CAN	18.11.73	1r1		Flagstaff	6 Jul
49.98	Eduardo Iván	Rodríguez	ESP	7.4.78	1	NC-23	Puertollano	6 Aug
49.99	Calvin	Bostic	USA	26.3.71	2		Indianapolis	24 Jun
49.99	Andrey	Vinnitskiy	UKR	23.12.76	2h2	NC	Kiev	4 Aug
50.00	Jeff	Ellis	CAN	18.10.78	1r2	GaTech	Atlanta	20 May
50.00		Lee Doo-yeon	KOR	9.4.75	1	NC	Daejun	10 Jun
50.01	Victor	Houston	BAR	24.2.74	7r1	GaTech	Atlanta	20 May
50.04	Makio	Haywood	USA	19.10.78	1r1		Eagle Rock	13 May
50.05	Greg	Christie	JAM	1.10.78	1		New Orleans	13 May
50.06	Erick	Keter	KEN	22.7.66	6h2	OG	Sydney	24 Sep
	(100)							

50.07	Yoshihiko	Saito	JPN	12.2.72	3 May
50.07	Rickey	Harris	USA-J	29.9.81	23 Jun
50.08	Jaime	Juan	ESP	28.8.77	18 Jul
50.09	Aaron	Haynes	USA	1.11.75	14 May
50.09	Du'aine	Thorne-Ladejo	GBR	14.2.71	6 Aug
50.11	Carlos	Zbinden	CHI	2.12.76	29 Apr
50.11	Erkin	Isakov	UZB/RUS	25.11.74	17 May
50.11	Gary	Jennings	GBR	21.2.72	27 Jun
50.11	Jan	Schneider	GER	24.1.76	20 Aug
50.12	Matt	Beckenham	AUS	18.3.76	2 Jul
50.12	Jimmy	Coco	FRA	28.11.72	7 Jul
50.16	Alain	Rohr	SUI	25.12.71	5 Jul

Mark	Name		Nat	Born	Date
50.17	Tom	McGuirk	IRL	2.3.71	16 Apr
50.18	Travis	McAshan	USA	2.5.78	21 May
50.18	Radoslav	Holúbek	SVK	28.11.75	22 Jul
50.18	Roman	Voronko	UKR	1.4.78	5 Aug
50.19	Leonid	Vershinin	BLR	23.6.77	27 Jun
50.21A	Martin	Willemse	RSA	23.4.75	14 Feb
50.21	Darko	Juricic	CRO	28.8.69	9 Sep
50.21	Ter	de Villiers	RSA-J	13.7.82	19 Oct
50.24A	Curt	Young	PAN	18.1.74	1 Jul
50.25	LaBronze	Garrett	USA	9.11.76	6 May
50.26	Edivaldo	Monteiro	POR	28.4.76	15 Jul
50.27A	James	Karanja	KEN		22 Jul
50.28	Tomasz	Rudnik	POL	6.3.79	5 Aug
50.29	Jean-Laurent	Heusse	FRA	8.4.74	13 Aug
50.30	Quinton	Milner	USA	20.12.74	6 May
50.33	Steffen	Kolb	GER	7.9.73	12 Jun
50.36A	Laurier	Primeau	CAN	1.3.70	6 Jul
50.37	Eldridge	Darling	JAM	18.12.75	19 May
50.37	Tommaso	Galvanini	ITA	27.5.78	10 Sep
50.38	Steve	Gittens	TRI	25.4.68	17 Jun
50.39	Kirill	Sedykh	RUS	20.7.79	1 Jul
50.40	Naman	Keita	FRA	9.4.78	24 Aug
50.40	Masashi	Wakae	JPN	28.4.80	1 Sep
50.41	Minoru	Kobayashi	JPN	24.5.78	1 Sep
50.42		Liu Jiangfeng	CHN	10.2.77	19 Apr
50.42	Attila	Kilvinger	HUN	27.3.77	10 Jun
50.43	Fred	Sharpe	USA	21.8.78	31 May
50.44	Jamaal	Jackson	USA		27 May
50.44	John	Hall	USA	6.3.78	31 May
50.44	Greg	Hines	JAM	16.9.75	6 Jul
50.47A	Kevin	Henderson	USA	4.2.65	4 Jul
50.48A	Jorge	Chaverra	COL-J	13.3.81	13 May
50.48	Sinisa	Pesa	YUG	6.3.73	20 Aug
50.49	João Carlos	dos Santos	BRA	28.4.75	3 Jun
50.50	Carlos	Silva	POR	8.6.74	28 Jun
50.51A	Daniël	van Heerden	RSA	4.11.76	13 Mar
50.51	D'Marcus	Brown	USA	17.6.78	22 Apr
50.52A	Rerei	Sang	KEN	.72	22 Jul
50.52	Pascal	Maran	FRA	21.3.67	4 Aug
50.52	Paul	Hibbert	GBR	31.3.65	2 Sep
50.53	Jean-Paul	Bruwier	BEL	18.2.71	21 Jun
50.53A	Okkert	Cilliers	RSA-J	21.4.81	17 Sep
50.53		Meng Yan	CHN	30.9.80	22 Oct
50.54	Michael	Brown	USA	9.1.79	29 Apr
50.54	Yevgeniy	Meleshenko	KAZ-J	19.1.81	15 Jul
50.54A	John	Langat	KEN	.74	22 Jul
50.55	Martin	Leiser	SUI	17.6.78	11 Aug
50.56	Lynn	Stewart	USA	22.7.77	6 May
50.57	Aleksey	Zaykin	BLR	13.2.74	27 Jun
50.58	Mark	LeDoux	USA	11.8.78	16 May
50.59A	Francois	Coertze	RSA	23.2.79	28 Jan
50.59		Zhuang Zhenping	CHN	6.1.76	4 May
50.59	Nobuyuki	Suzuki	JPN	1.7.75	13 May
50.59	Daniel	Gómez	AND	11.5.79	3 Sep
50.60	Alessandro	Battinelli	ITA	2.3.79	7 Sep
50.60	Christian	Duma	GER-J	5.2.82	21 Oct
50.61	Laboris	Bean	USA	24.10.78	6 May
50.61	Naohiro	Kawakita	JPN	10.7.80	21 May
50.63	Marnus	Kritzinger	RSA-J	10.2.82	6 May
50.63A	Llimy	Rivas	COL	8.6.68	13 May
50.63	Stefan	Bönisch	GER	10.8.77	22 Jul
50.64A	Barend	Kotzé	RSA	14.3.77	14 Apr
50.66	Ryan	Clarke	JAM	3.11.80	20 Jul
50.66	Kimmo	Haapasalo	FIN	23.7.77	2 Aug
50.66	Francesco	Filisetti	ITA	13.6.77	30 Aug
50.68	Kurt	Duncan	JAM	3.6.78	21 May
50.69	Masatsugu	Takamura	JPN	3.4.80	20 May
50.70	Keith	Varga	USA	7.4.76	21 Apr
50.70	Kevin	Carter	USA	8.1.79	20 May
50.70	Kostas	Pochanis	CYP	29.7.73	28 Jun
50.72	Yevgeniy	Mikheyko	BLR-J	24.4.81	27 Jun
50.72	Karol	Radke	POL	13.1.76	5 Aug
50.74	Filipp	Salov	RUS	11.8.74	4 Jun
50.74	Sergej	Salamon	SLO	7.3.75	10 Jun
50.75	Derek	Spears	USA	22.3.73	6 May
50.75	So	Takebayashi	JPN	10.8.79	21 May
50.75	Jeroen	Prent	NED	26.3.65	30 Jul
50.76	Orentheus	Hutcherson	USA		15 Apr
50.76	Zane	Cole	USA	6.2.74	11 Jun
50.77	Francesco	Sartore	ITA	30.5.77	4 Jun
50.77	Tahar	Ghozali	ALG	27.1.79	2 Aug
50.78	Clayton	Brookins	USA	19.5.76	7 Jul
50.80	Nabil	Selmi	ALG	5.2.72	2 Aug
50.81	Omar	Clinton	USA	18.6.78	18 Jun
50.82	Derwin	Jones	TRI	8.5.75	14 Apr
50.85	Lukás	Soucek	CZE	10.7.75	22 Jun
50.85	Youssoupha	Sarr	SEN	16.10.78	12 Jul
50.85	Jorge	Moreno	CUB	.77	25 Jul
50.85	Mikael	Jakobsson	SWE-J	9.1.81	20 Aug
	(201)				

Best at low altitude

49.11	Myburgh	1		Dublin	29 Jul
49.20	Young	4s2	OG	Sydney	25 Sep
49.60	Botha	2	NC	Stellenbosch	4 Mar
49.77	Bédi	3		Cape Town	31 Mar
50.09	Redmond	1h1	NC	Victoria	12 Aug
50.50	C Young	3		Waco	22 Apr

Hand timing

49.6	Leonid	Vershinin	BLR	23.6.77	1	Brest	2 Aug
49.9	Matt	Beckenham	AUS	18.3.76	1	Darwin	24 Jun
50.2	Guilhem	Barthes	FRA	25.6.78	1	Bron	23 Jul

JUNIORS

49.23	Marek	Plawgo	POL	25.2.81	1	WJ	Santiago de Chile	21 Oct
	49.68	1		Wroclaw	29 Aug			
	50.30	5	Kuso	Warszawa	24 Jun			
	50.02	3	NC	Kraków	5 Aug			
	50.40	1s1	WJ	Santiago	19 Oct			
50.07	Rickey	Harris	USA	29.9.81	1h3	NC-j	Denton	23 Jun
	50.17	1	NC-j	Denton	24 Jun			
50.21	Ter	de Villiers	RSA	13.7.82	1s2	WJ	Santiago de Chile	19 Oct
	50.52	2	WJ	Santiago	21 Oct			
	10 performances by 4 men to 50.52							
50.48A	Jorge	Chaverra	COL	13.3.81	1		Medellín	13 May
50.53A	Okkert	Cilliers	RSA	21.4.81	1		Pretoria	17 Sep
50.54	Yevgeniy	Meleshenko	KAZ	19.1.81	1		Almaty	15 Jul
50.60	Christian	Duma	GER	5.2.82	4	WJ	Santiago de Chile	21 Oct
50.63	Marnus	Kritzinger	RSA	10.2.82	1		Sydney	6 May
50.72	Yevgeniy	Mikheyko	BLR	24.4.81			Staiki	27 Jun
50.85	Mikael	Jakobsson (10)	SWE	9.1.81	1	NC	Uppsala	20 Aug
51.04	Bennie	Brazell	USA	.82	1	JunOly	Amherst	30 Jul
51.06	Chris	Hickman	USA	24.2.81	2	NC-j	Denton	24 Jun
51.08	Sean	Avery	AUS	28.2.82	2h2	OT	Sydney	17 Aug
51.18	Sergio	Hierrezuelo	CUB	15.3.82	1		La Habana	19 Feb
51.18		Zhang Shibao	CHN	12.3.84	3	NGP	Tianjin	4 May
51.24	Hisatoshi	Hotta	JPN	30.10.81	3h2	Univ Ch	Tokyo	2 Sep

Mark	Name		Nat	Born	Pos	Meet	Venue	Date
51.24	Yuta	Otsuki	JPN	12.2.82	4h2	NC	Rifu	6 Oct
51.26	Masakatsu	Tanaka	JPN	11.9.82	1		Gifu	3 Aug
51.31	Frederico	Rubeca	ITA	10.6.81	5s2	WJ	Santiago de Chile	19 Oct
51.36	Danyne	Brown	USA	14.4.81	1r2		Gainesville	24 Mar

HIGH JUMP

Mark	Name		Nat	Born	Pos	Meet	Venue	Date
2.40	Vyacheslav	Voronin	RUS	5.4.74	1	BrGP	London (CP)	5 Aug
				2.31/2 2.34/1 2.40/3 2.46/xp				
2.37i				2.20/1 2.25/1 2.31/3 2/37/3 2.40/xp	1	v4N	Glasgow	5 Mar
2.36				2.20/1 2.27/1 2.33/1 2.36/3 2.41/xxx	1		Eberstadt	23 Jul
2.35i				2.20/1 2.24/2 2.31/2 2.35/3 2.38/xxx	1		Balingen	30 Jan
2.35				2.20/1 2.26/1 2.31/1 2.33/1 2.35/1 2.37/xxx	1	GGala	Roma	30 Jun
2.34i				2.20/1 2.24/1 2.30/1 2.34/2 2.36/xxx	1		Arnstadt	28 Jan
2.34i				2.24/1 2.30/1 2.34/1 2.36/xxx	1	EI	Gent	27 Feb
2.33i				2.21/1 2.25/2 2.30/1 2.33/2 2.37/xxx	1		Moskva	18 Jan
2.33				2.20/1 2.25/1 2.31/2 2.33/3 2.37/xxx	1	Super	Yokohama	9 Sep
2.38i	Matt	Hemingway	USA	24.10.72	1	NC	Atlanta	4 Mar
				2.17/2 2.22/1 2.27/1 2.32/1 2.35/1 2.38/1 2.41/xxx				
2.36iA				2.15/1 2.21/1 2.26/1 2.31/1 2.36/3 2.39/xxx	1		USAF Acadamy	19 Feb
2.37i	Artur	Partyka	POL	25.7.69	1		Spala	18 Feb
				2.15/1 2.24/1 2.30/1 2.37/3 2.40/xx				
2.36	Konstantin	Matusevich	ISR	25.2.71	1		Perth	5 Feb
2.33				2.15/1 2.20/1 2.26/1 2.29/1 2.31/3 2.33/3 2.35/xxx	3	GGala	Roma	30 Jun
2.35	Nathan	Leeper	USA	13.6.77	1		Sacramento	21 May
2.33				2.18/2 2.23/3 2.29/3 2.31/2 2.33/1 2.35/xxx	1		Modesto	13 May
2.35	Mark	Boswell	CAN	28.7.77	2	GGala	Roma	30 Jun
				2.20/1 2.26/3 2.31/1 2.33/1 2.35/3 2.37/xxx				
2.33i				2.20/1 2.26/1 2.31/1 2.33/1 2.39/xp	1	NCAA	Fayetteville	10 Mar
2.33				2.19/1 2.25/1 2.31/1 2.33/1	1	TexR	Austin	8 Apr
2.35	Sergey	Klyugin	RUS	24.3.74	1	OG	Sydney	24 Sep
				2.20/1 2.29/1 2.32/2 2.35/1 p				
2.33				2.16/1 2.20/1 2.24/1 2.28/1 2.33/1 2.35/xxx	1	NC	Tula	25 Jul
2.34i	Martin	Buss	GER	7.4.76	2	EI	Gent	27 Feb
				2.20/1 2.27/1 2.30/1 2.32/1 2.34/2 2.36/xxx				
2.34i	Dragutin	Topic	YUG	12.3.71	3	EI	Gent	27 Feb
				2.20/1 2.27/1 2.30/x 2.32/1 2.34/2 2.36/xxx				
2.33				2.15/1 2.21/2 2.25/x 2.27/1 2.31/x 2.33/2 2.36/xxx	1	NC	Beograd	20 Aug
2.34	Kwaku	Boateng (10)	CAN	30.6.74	1	GP II	Zagreb	3 Jul
				2.20/1 2.25/1 2.28/1 2.31/2 2.34/3 p				
2.34	Lábros	Papakóstas	GRE	20.10.69	1	NC	Athína	9 Jul
				2.21/1 2.26/1 2.30/1 2.34/2 2.37/xxx				
2.34	Abderahmane	Hammad	ALG	27.5.77	1	AfCh	Alger	14 Jul
				2.15/1 2.20/1 2.24/1 2.28/1 2.34/1 2.37/xxp				
2.34	Stefan	Holm	SWE	25.5.76	1	vFIN	Helsinki	3 Sep
				2.18/1 2.24/1 2.28/1 2.34/2 2.37/xxx				
	(28/13) and 26 performances at 2.32							
2.32i	Anthony	Idiata	NGR	5.1.75	1		Pátra	15 Feb
2.32i	Staffan	Strand	SWE	18.4.76	2		Stockholm	17 Feb
2.32i	Shane	Lavy	USA	15.2.76	1	LA Inv	Los Angeles	19 Feb
2.32	Charles	Austin	USA	19.12.67	2	Nik	Nice	8 Jul
2.32	Javier	Sotomayor	CUB	13.10.67	2	OG	Sydney	24 Sep
2.31i	Kenny	Evans	USA	6.4.79	2	NCAA	Fayetteville	10 Mar
2.31A	Charles	Clinger	USA	28.12.76	1		Ogden	8 Apr
	(20)							
2.31	Christian	Rhoden	GER	27.3.74	2	GP II	Zagreb	3 Jul
2.31	Mika	Polku	FIN	19.7.75	1		Viitasaari	22 Jul
2.30i	David	Furman	USA	5.11.78	1		Gainesville	16 Jan
2.30i	Jan	Jankú	CZE	10.8.71	2		Wuppertal	4 Feb
2.30i	Oskari	Frösén	FIN	24.1.76	1		Tampere	7 Feb
2.30i	Wolfgang	Kreissig	GER	29.8.70	3=		Pátra	15 Feb
2.30	Glenn	Howard	NZL	1.4.76	1	NC	Christchurch	12 Mar
2.30	Aleksey	Lyolin	BLR	27.11.78	1		Riga	22 Jun
2.30A	Jacques	Freitag	RSA-J	11.6.82	1		Pretoria	25 Aug
2.30	Sergey	Dymchenko	UKR	23.8.67	1		Pátra	2 Sep
	(30)							
2.29i	Henry	Patterson	USA	27.5.75	1		Ypsilanti	19 Feb
2.29	Jeremy	Fischer	USA	17.2.76	2c2	MSR	Walnut	16 Apr
2.28i	Pyotr	Brayko	RUS	27.3.77	3=		Balingen	30 Jan
2.28i	Brendan	Reilly	IRL	23.12.72	1		Reykjavik	5 Mar

MEN 2000

Mark	Name		Nat	Born	Pos	Meet	Venue	Date
2.28	Stevan	Zoric	YUG	25.5.71	1	Veniz	Haniá	14 Jun
2.28	Andrey	Chubsa	BLR-J	29.11.82	1		Gomel	2 Jul
2.28	Tim	Forsyth	AUS	17.8.73	6	GP II	Zagreb	3 Jul
2.28	Toni	Huikuri	FIN	17.9.79	1		Espoo	5 Jul
2.28	Takahisa	Yoshida	JPN	17.2.70	1	Nambu	Sapporo	16 Jul
2.28	Yaroslav	Rybakov	RUS	22.11.80	3	NC	Tula	25 Jul
	(40)							
2.28	Andrey	Sokolovskiy	UKR	16.7.78	1	NC	Kiev	5 Aug
2.28	Ruslan	Glivinskiy	UKR	7.2.75	2	NC	Kiev	5 Aug
2.27i	Martin	Stauffer	SUI	7.7.75	1	NC	Magglingen	13 Feb
2.26i	Mike	Ponikvar	CAN	26.12.79	1		Boston	19 Feb
2.26i	Marko	Aleksejev	EST	14.2.79	2	v2N	Tampere	20 Feb
2.26	Malcolm	Hendriks	RSA	27.4.77	2	NC	Stellenbosch	4 Mar
2.26	Jason	Boness	USA	11.2.80	1	Pac10	Eugene	21 May
2.26	Mustapha	Raïfak	FRA	9.9.75	1		Montgeron	18 Jun
2.26	Yuriy	Pakhlayev	KAZ	20.12.74	1	NC	Almaty	15 Jul
2.26	Giulio	Ciotti	ITA	5.10.76	1		Pescara	23 Jul
	(50)							
2.25i	Robert	Jordan	USA	22.6.80	1		Ames	22 Jan
2.25	Nick	Moroney	AUS	3.8.72	2		Hobart	30 Jan
2.25i	Igor	Sukharev	RUS	1.1.72	2		Samara	30 Jan
2.25i	Aleksey	Krysin	RUS	25.11.76	3		Samara	30 Jan
2.25i	Wilbert	Pennings	NED	23.2.75	3		Pireás	9 Feb
2.25i	Elvir	Krehmic	BIH	27.4.73	1	BalkC	Pireás	12 Feb
2.25i	Ben	Challenger	GBR	7.3.78	4		Birmingham	20 Feb
2.25i	Dalton	Grant	GBR	8.4.66	2	vRUS	Glasgow	5 Mar
2.25	Tim	Bell	USA	7.9.79	1		Gainesville	25 Mar
2.25	Ron	Nelson	USA	15.1.78	3cA	TexR	Austin	8 Apr
	(60)							
2.25	Fabricio	Romero	BRA	13.5.78	3c2	MSR	Walnut	16 Apr
2.25	Ray	Doakes	USA	12.8.73	2		Fayetteville	22 Apr
2.25	Takahiro	Kimino	JPN	19.2.73	1		Shizuoka	3 May
2.25A	Gilmar	Mayo	COL	30.9.69	1		Bogotá	6 May
2.25	Tora	Harris	USA	21.9.78	1		College Station	11 May
2.25		Lee Jin-taek	KOR	13.4.72	2	GP	Osaka	13 May
2.25	Rod	Newton	USA	3.11.76	1	SEC	Baton Rouge	14 May
2.25A	Marc	Chenn	USA	6.3.76	1		Provo	20 May
2.25	Pawel	Gulcz	POL	28.1.79	1		Biala Podlaska	4 Jun
2.25	Grzegorz	Sposób	POL	12.2.76	1		Lublin	11 Jun
	(70)							
2.25	Tomás	Jankú	CZE	27.12.74	1		Prague	15 Jun
2.25	Paul	Klemic	USA-J	12.8.81	1	NSch	Raleigh	17 Jun
2.25	Svatoslav	Ton	CZE	20.10.78	1		Praha	10 Jul
2.25	Jarrad	Pozzi	AUS	29.7.75	1		Brisbane (N)	29 Jul
2.25A	Hugo	Muñoz	PER	10.1.73	1		Arequipa	12 Aug
2.25	Gennadiy	Moroz	BLR	27.5.78	3		Berdichev	3 Sep
2.25	Alessandro	Talotti	ITA	7.10.80	1	NC	Milano	7 Sep
2.25i	Alfred	Neale	USA-J	1.7.81	1		Norman OK	2 Dec
2.24i	Steinar	Hoen	NOR	8.2.71	5=		Arnstadt	28 Jan
2.24i	Javier	Bermejo	ESP	8.3.78	1		Sevilla	8 Feb
	(80)							
2.24i	Vyacheslav	Tyrtyshnik	UKR	16.1.71	4		Brno	9 Feb
2.24i	Ivan	Bernasconi	ITA	19.10.74	1	NC	Genova	13 Feb
2.24		Tao Rui	CHN	26.1.72	1	NGP	Deyang	13 May
2.24	Djordje	Niketic	YUG	11.3.76	1		Kragujevac	14 May
2.24	Collat	Johnson	USA	.78	1	NCAA-II	Raleigh	27 May
2.24	Dimítrios	Sirrákos	GRE	26.1.74	3	Papaf	Kalamáta	4 Jun
2.24	Metin	Durmusoglu	TUR	11.1.74	1		Izmir	10 Jun
2.24	Grégory	Gabella	FRA	22.6.80	2		Montgeron	18 Jun
2.24	Aleksandr	Kravtsov	RUS	18.3.74	1		Rostov-na-Donu	26 Jun
2.24	Arturo	Ortiz	ESP	18.9.66	1	ECp IA	Nadderud	0 Jul
	(90)							
2.24	Igor	Savenkov	RUS	.73	1	MosCh	Moskva	12 Jul
2.24	Aleksey	Belov	RUS	.76	2	MosCh	Moskva	12 Jul
2.24	Germaine	Mason	JAM-J	1.4.83	2	WJ	Santiago de Chile	19 Oct
2.23i	Rozle	Prezelj	SLO	26.9.79	1		Ljubljana	15 Jan
2.23i	Shaun	Guice	USA	11.8.80	1		Indianapolis	22 Jan
2.23i	Dimítrios	Tomarás	GRE	7.6.72	2	BalkC	Pireás	12 Feb
2.23i	Frédéric	Schinz	SUI	25.6.77	2	NC	Magglingen	13 Feb
2.23i	Yoshiteru	Kaihoko	JPN	19.11.71	1	vCHN	Yokohama	26 Feb

Mark	Name		Nat	Born	Pos	Meet	Venue	Date
2.23i	Lavar	Miller	USA	16.2.77	2	SEC	Fayetteville	27 Feb
2.23	Mark	Bradley	USA-J	.81	1		Texarkana	31 Mar
	(100)							
2.23	Jeff	Mueller	USA	1.10.78	1	MSR	Walnut	15 Apr
2.23		Zhou Zhongge	CHN	15.2.67	1	NGP	Tianjin	4 May
2.23	Troy	Kemp	BAH	18.6.66	1		Boise	6 May
2.23	James	Nieto	USA	2.11.76	2c2	ModR	Modesto	13 May
2.23	Robert	Michniewski	POL	16.2.74	1		Turnov	11 Jun
2.23	Hiroyuki	Hokahori	JPN	31.5.76	1		Tsukuba	18 Jun
2.23	Ricardo	Perez	PUR	9.11.78	1		Houston	21 Jul
2.23	Raul	Touset	CUB	.78	1	Barr	La Habana	30 Jul
2.23	Branko	Djuricic	YUG-J	5.1.81	2	NC	Beograd	20 Aug
2.23		Wang Zhouzhou	CHN	20.4.77	2	AsiC	Jakarta	31 Aug
2.23i	Aleksey	Gordiyenko	UKR	9.5.79	2		Lvov	28 Dec
2.23i	Dan	Olson	USA-J	27.9.82	1		Providence	29 Dec

2.22i	Hannes	Zumsande	GER	28.7.79	21 Jan
2.22i	Stefan	Vasilache	ROM	9.5.79	22 Jan
2.22i	Bobby	Myers	USA	11.10.76	29 Jan
2.22	Chris	Anderson	AUS	6.4.68	5 Feb
2.22	Ron	Garlett	AUS	18.12.79	5 Feb
2.22	Jean-Claude	Rabbath	LIB	12.7.77	13 Feb
2.22i	Luca	Toso	ITA	15.2.64	13 Feb
2.22i	Igor	Prokopov	BLR	8.3.77	16 Feb
2.22i	Christian	Olsson	SWE	25.1.80	17 Feb
2.22i	Didier	Detchenique	FRA	4.10.72	20 Feb
2.22	Joey	Brunkhorst	USA	23.2.79	6 May
2.22	Shaun	Kologinczak	USA	13.10.79	7 May
2.22	Danny	Graham	GBR	3.8.79	20 May
2.22	Adam	Shunk	USA	29.8.79	20 May
2.22	David	Antona	ESP	18.11.78	20 May
2.22	Michal	Titinger	POL	23.9.77	10 Jun
2.22	Khemraj	Naïko	MRI	23.8.72	2 Jul
2.22	Ville	Vepsäläinen	FIN	16.8.76	22 Jul
2.22	Rafal	Kazimierczak	POL	27.10.74	6 Aug
2.21i	Alex	Rosen	ISR	2.6.73	22 Jan
2.21i	Ivan	Vadillo	ESP	13.6.78	22 Jan
2.21i	Terrance	Woods	USA	18.4.79	5 Feb
2.21Ai	Greg	Walker	USA	15.4.75	12 Feb
2.21i	Tomás	Ort	CZE	9.9.76	22 Feb
2.21Ai	Clinte	Motley	USA	16.10.79	25 Feb
2.21i	Tom	Pappas	USA	6.9.76	3 Mar
2.21i	Einar Karl	Hjartarson	ISL	28.10.80	3 Mar
2.21	Cameron	Wright	USA	7.11.72	18 Mar
2.21	Adrian	Shears	USA	.78	15 Apr
2.21	Pawel	Mankiewicz	POL	28.4.79	29 Apr
2.21	Tomohiro	Nomura	JPN	11.10.75	29 Apr
2.21		Huang Lin	CHN	31.3.79	9 May
2.21		Zheng Decheng	CHN	1.2.77	9 May
2.21		Li Baibing	CHN	22.2.79	13 May
2.21		Cui Kai	CHN-J	26.3.82	16 Jun
2.21	Shigeki	Toyoshima	JPN	5.3.71	20 Aug
2.21	Tomasz	Smialek	POL-J	16.1.81	19 Oct
2.20i	Tony	Barton	USA	17.10.09	8 Jan
2.20	Alfredo	Deza	PER	24.8.79	15 Jan
2.20i	Robert	Mitchell	GBR	14.9.80	16 Jan
2.20i	Nick	Decker	USA	18.4.78	22 Jan
2.20i	Aleksandr	Veryutin	BLR	18.11.79	23 Jan
2.20i	Dejan	Milosevic	SLO	2.9.73	29 Jan
2.20i	Pavel	Fomenko	RUS	.76	5 Feb
2.20i	Fabrizio	Borellini	ITA	5.7.68	13 Feb
2.20Ai	Lance	Thurston	USA	17.11.74	25 Feb
2.20i	J.J.	Barton	USA	16.1.77	3 Mar
2.20A	Vusumzi	Mtshatsheni	RSA	20.12.79	18 Mar
2.20i	Jean-Patrick	Thirion	FRA	4.6.72	25 Mar
2.20	Will	Montgomery	USA	23.6.80	25 Mar
2.20	Dave	Hoffman	USA		8 Apr
2.20	Nick	Decker	USA	18.4.78	16 Apr
2.20		Xu Shiwei	CHN-J	24.6.81	19 Apr
2.20		Niu Jian	CHN	26.12.72	23 Apr
2.20	Ryan	Fitzpatric	USA	1.3.80	7 May
2.20	Michiya	Onoue	JPN	28.10.71	13 May
2.20	Patrick	De Paepe	BEL	10.3.76	14 May
2.20	Masaaki	Uno	JPN	13.12.72	14 May
2.20	Raheim	Greenridge	USA		27 May
2.20	Marcin	Kaczocha	POL	22.9.77	3 Jun
2.20	Angel	Kararadev	BUL	18.11.79	3 Jun
2.20	Aleksandr	Veryutin	BLR	18.11.79	3 Jun
2.20	Shuhei	Manabe	JPN-J	31.8.82	4 Jun
2.20	Konstadínos	Liápis	GRE	1.5.73	25 Jun
2.20	Yoshihisa	Fukumoto	JPN	2.9.73	30 Jun
2.20	Steve	Smith	USA	11.1.71	1 Jul
2.20	James	Ballard	USA	11.12.75	1 Jul
2.20	Koji	Ishii	JPN	4.5.78	2 Jul
2.20	Aleksey	Lesnichy	BLR	3.2.78	2 Jul
2.20A	Mike	Caza	CAN	21.4.74	6 Jul
2.20A	James	Rolle	BAH	.72	8 Jul
2.20	Eugène	Ernesta	SEY	.76	14 Jul
2.20	Mauro	Tavella	ITA	20.10.71	23 Jul
2.20	Mikhail	Semyonok	RUS	12.9.76	25 Jul
2.20	Mikhail	Tsvetkov	RUS	.80	25 Jul
2.20	Mickaël	Hanany	FRA-J	25.3.83	26 Jul
2.20	Jirí	Krehula	CZE-J	17.7.82	5 Aug
2.20	Jesse	Lipscombe	CAN	4.4.80	5 Aug
2.20	Jeffrey	Caton	CAN	3.11.75	12 Aug
2.20	Aleksey	Zaytsev	BLR-J	31.10.81	3 Sep
2.20	Erasmo	Jara	ARG	25.3.76	5 Nov
	(193)				

Best outdoor mark for athlete with best indoors

2.32	Strand	1	Nik	Nice	8 Jul
2.30	K Evans	1		Fayetteville	22 Apr
2.30	Hemingway	2		Sacramento	21 May
2.30	Kreissig	1		Ettlingen	2 Jul
2.28	Brayko	2	NC	Tula	25 Jul
2.27	Frösén	1	Sule	Tartu	11 Jun
2.27	Patterson	6	Gaz	Saint-Denis	23 Jun
2.26	J Jankú	2=		Somoskó	17 Jun
2.26	Partyka	1		Bydgoszcz	15 Jul
2.25	Idiata	2		Cape Town	31 Mar
2.25	Furman	1	NCAA	Durham	3 Jun
2.25	Pennings	4	ISTAF	Berlin	1 Sep
2.24	Reilly	7	BrGP	London (CP)	5 Aug
2.24	Krehmic	14=q	OG	Sydney	22 Sep
2.23	Stauffer	4		Somoskö	17 Jun
2.23	Grant	1		Luton	9 Sep

2.22	Neale	8 Apr
2.22	Miller	3 Jun
2.22	Aleksejev	11 Jun
2.22	Challenger	13 Aug
2.22	Bernasconi	7 Sep
2.21	Guice	20 May
2.21	T Woods	27 May
2.21	Tomarás	14 Jun
2.21	Hoen	8 Jul
2.21	Pappas	27 Sep
2.20	Rosen	20 Feb
2.20	Kaihoko	9 Apr
2.20	Walker	21 May
2.20	Prezelj	24 May
2.20	Tyrtyshnik	1 Jun
2.20	Bermejo	3 Jun
2.20	Milosevic	4 Jun
2.20	Ort	28 Jun
2.20	Olsson	1 Jul
2.20	Fomenko	25 Jul
2.20	Hjartason	29 Jul
2.20	Prokopov	2 Aug
2.20	Gordiyenko	5 Aug
2.20	Mitchell	19 Aug

Low altitude best

2.30	Clinger	1		Palo Alto	26 Mar
2.29	Freitag	1	NC	Stellenbosch	4 Mar
2.24	Mayo	1	IbAm	Rio de Janeiro	21 May

MEN 2000

Mark	Name		Nat	Born	Pos	Meet	Venue	Date

JUNIORS

See main list for top 8 juniors. 10 performances by 4 men to 2.25. Additional marks and further juniors:

Freitag	2.29	1	NC	Stellenbosch	4 Mar	2.25	1	Cape Town	31 Mar
	2.25	1		Stellenbosch	18 Feb	2.25	1	Budapest	22 Jul
	2.25	1		Port Elizabeth	25 Feb	2.25	1	Belfast	31 Jul
	2.25A	1		Pretoria	24 Mar				
2.25i	Neale	best outdoors:				2.22	1	Owasso	8 Apr

Mark	Name		Nat	Born	Pos	Meet	Venue	Date
2.21		Cui Kai	CHN	26.3.82	1	NC-j	Deyang	16 Jun
2.21	Tomasz	Smialek (10)	POL	16.1.81	3	WJ	Santiago de Chile	19 Oct
2.20		Xu Shiwei	CHN	24.6.81	1	NGP	Shanghai	19 Apr
2.20	Shuhei	Manabe	JPN	31.8.82	1		Marugame	4 Jun
2.20	Mickaël	Hanany	FRA	25.3.83	1		Hagetmau	26 Jul
2.20	Jirí	Krehula	CZE	17.7.82	1		Olomouc	5 Aug
2.20	Aleksey	Zaytsev	BLR	31.10.81	4		Berdichev	3 Sep
2.19i	Samson	Oni	NGR	25.6.81	2=	AAA	Birmingham	30 Jan
2.18		Xu Hao	CHN	19.5.83	3	NGP	Wenzhou	23 Apr
2.18	Jimmy	Baxter	USA	17.11.81	1		St Petersburg ?	28 Apr
2.18	Joe	Squittieri	USA		2		Gainesville	12 May
2.18	Román	Fehér (20)	HUN	11.2.81	1		Olomouc	1 Jul
2.18	Pavel	Netsvetayev	BLR	.82			Brest	24 Aug
2.18	Jessé	de Lima	BRA	16.2.81	4	WJ	Santiago de Chile	19 Oct
2.18	Matt	Vincent	USA-J	6.3.81	5	WJ	Santiago de Chile	19 Oct

POLE VAULT

Mark	Name		Nat	Born	Pos	Meet	Venue	Date
6.03	Jeff	Hartwig	USA	25.9.67	1		Jonesboro	14 Jun
				5.60/2 5.80/2 5.91/2 6.03/2 6.10/xxx				
	5.95 1	Jonesboro	19 May	5.65/1 5.80/3 5.95/1 6.03/xxx				
	5.92 1	Modesto	13 May	5.50/1 5.70/1 5.81/1 5.92/3 6.03/xxx				
	5.90Ai 1	Reno	21 Jan	5.45/1 5.60/1 5.70/1 5.80/2 5.90/1 5.96/xxx				
	5.90 1	Norderney	1 Aug					
	5.90 2 Herc	Monaco	18 Aug	5.55/1 5.70/1 5.80/1 5.90/1 6.00/xxx				
	5.85i 1	Fayetteville	13 Feb	5.55/1 5.65/1 5.80/2 5.85/2 5.90/xxx				
	6.00ex 1	Köln	5 Aug					
5.95i	Tim	Lobinger	GER	3.9.72	1		Chemnitz	18 Feb
				5.70/2 5.80/1 5.85/1 5.90/2 5.95/3 6.00/xxx				
	5.85 1 NC	Braunschweig	29 Jul	5.40/1 5.60/1 5.85/1 5.91/xxx				
	5.83 1 Veniz	Haniá	14 Jun	5.53/1 5.63/1 5.73/1 5.83/2 5.91/xxx				
5.95	Michael	Stolle	GER	17.12.74	1	Herc	Monaco	18 Aug
				5.55/1 5.70/1 5.80/1 5.85/1 5.90/xx 5.95/1				
	5.90i 2	Chemnitz	18 Feb	5.50/1 5.70/1 5.80/3 5.90/3 6.00/x				
	5.90 4 OG	Sydney	29 Sep	5.50/3 5.70/1 5.80/2 5.90/3 5.96/xxx				
5.90A	Lawrence	Johnson	USA	7.5.74	1		Pretoria	24 Mar
				5.50/3 5.70/1 5.80/1 5.90/3 6.03/xxx				
	5.90 2 OG	Sydney	29 Sep	5.70/1 5.80/1 5.90/2 5.96/xxx				
	5.83 1 NC	Sacramento	16 Jul	5.63/1 5.73/2 5.83/3 5.90/xxx				
5.90	Pavel	Gerasimov	RUS	29.5.79	1		Rüdlingen	12 Aug
				5.50/1 5.70/1 5.80/1 5.90/3				
	5.85 1 NC	Tula	25 Jul	5.40/2 5.55/1 5.65/1 5.75/1 5.80/x 5.85/2 5.90/xxx				
5.90	Danny	Ecker	GER	21.7.77	1	VD	Bruxelles	25 Aug
				5.50/1 5.65/1 5.75/2 5.90/3 6.01/xxx				
	5.85 1 WK	Zürich	11 Aug	5.50/2 5.70/3 5.85/1 6.00/xxx				
5.90	Nick	Hysong	USA	9.12.71	1	OG	Sydney	29 Sep
				5.50/1 5.70/2 5.80/1 5.90/1 5.96/xxx				
	5.85 2	Norderney	1 Aug					
	5.83 1	Fresno	1 Apr					
5.90	Maksim	Tarasov	RUS	2.12.70	3	OG	Sydney	29 Sep
				5.50/1 5.80/2 5.90/3 5.96/xxx				
	5.82 1 Nik	Nice	8 Jul	5.60/1 5.82/3 5.92/xxx				
5.85	Okkert	Brits	RSA	22.8.73	1		Ingolstadt	18 Jun
	5.82 1	Recklinghausen	26 May					
	5.90u 1	Hof	3 Jun					
5.85	Dmitriy	Markov	AUS	14.3.75	1	Athl	Lausanne	5 Jul
				5.60/2 5.75/3 5.85/3 6.05/xx				
5.85	Yevgeniy	Smiryagin	RUS	17.5.76	1	ECp-S	Gateshead	16 Jul
				5.25/2 5.40/1 5.50/1 5.60/1 5.70/2 5.80/1 5.85/2				
5.85	Aleksandr	Averbukh	ISR	1.10.74	1	NC	Tel Aviv	24 Jul
				5.50/1 5.70/1 5.85/1 6.00/xp				
	(30/12)							
5.81i	Jean	Galfione	FRA	9.6.71	1		Rennes	5 Feb

Mark	Name		Nat	Born	Pos	Meet	Venue	Date
5.81	Tim	Mack	USA	15.9.72	1		Chapel Hill	18 Jun
5.81	Montxu	Miranda	ESP	27.12.76	1	NC	Barcelona	2 Sep
5.80Ai	Chad	Harting	USA	20.2.72	2		Reno	21 Jan
5.80A	Martin	Eriksson	SWE	15.6.71	2		Pietersburg	18 Mar
5.80A	Jim	Davis	USA	15.6.78	1	WAC	El Paso	20 May
5.80	Tye	Harvey	USA	25.9.74	1		Jonesboro	9 Jul
5.80	Viktor	Chistiakov	AUS	9.2.75	5=	OG	Sydney	29 Sep
	(20)							
5.75	Scott	Hennig	USA	17.4.69	1		Austin	6 May
5.75	Rens	Blom	NED	1.3.77	2		Ingolstadt	18 Jun
5.75	Vadim	Strogalyov	RUS	9.2.75	2	Mos Ch	Moskva	11 Jul
5.75	Romain	Mesnil	FRA	13.7.77	1		Bugeat	23 Jul
5.75	Lars	Börgeling	GER	16.4.79	4		Norderney	1 Aug
	above not recognised by some, next		5.70		2		Cuxhaven	19 Jul
5.73A	Toby	Stevenson	USA	19.11.76	2		Flagstaff	8 Jul
5.72	Stepan	Janácek	CZE	12.6.77	2		Lisboa (U)	5 Aug
5.72	Denis	Yurchenko	UKR	27.1.78	1		Kiev	6 Aug
5.71	Russ	Buller	USA	10.9.78	1cA	TexR	Austin	8 Apr
5.70i	Maurilio	Mariani	ITA	22.4.73	2		Pireás	9 Feb
	(30)							
5.70i	Rodion	Gataullin	RUS	23.11.65	3		Liévin	13 Feb
5.70	Manabu	Yokoyama	JPN	20.7.74	1	Oda	Hiroshima	29 Apr
5.70	Ruhan	Isim	TUR	5.6.70	2		Jonesboro	6 Jun
5.70	Thibaut	Duval	BEL	1.2.79	1		Oordegem	11 Jun
5.70	Daren	McDonough	USA	29.5.74	1		Terre Haute	11 Jun
5.70b	Dennis	Kholev	ISR	21.10.75	3=		Santa Barbara	11 Jun
	b - board runway, legitimate competition. Next			5.60A	1		El Paso	24 Jun
5.70	Patrik	Kristiansson	SWE	3.6.77	1		Helsingborg	8 Jul
5.70	Ilian	Efremov	BUL	2.8.70	1	ECp1B	Bydgoszcz	9 Jul
5.70	Giuseppe	Gibilisco	ITA	5.1.79	4	ECp-S	Gateshead	16 Jul
5.70	Pyotr	Bochkaryov	RUS	3.11.67	2		Rüdlingen	12 Aug
	(40)							
5.70A	Dominic	Johnson	LCA	31.10.75	1		El Paso	26 Aug
5.65i	Petr	Spacek	CZE	23.7.75	1		Praha	18 Jan
5.65i	Jacob	Davis	USA	29.4.78	1		Indianapolis	12 Feb
5.65i	Pavel	Burlachenko	RUS	7.4.76	2		Stockholm	17 Feb
5.65	Dean	Starkey	USA	27.3.67	1		Palo Alto	5 May
5.65	Scott	Slover	USA	9.7.75	2		Austin	6 May
5.65	Jake	Pauli	USA	15.6.79	1		Cedar Falls	6 May
5.65	Derek	Miles	USA	28.9.72	2		Jonesboro	19 May
5.65	Christian	Tamminga	NED	30.4.74	1		Arras	8 Jul
5.65	Khalid	Lachheb	FRA	16.1.75	2		Dijon	19 Jul
	(50)							
5.65	Taoufik	Lachheb	FRA	16.1.75	3		Dijon	19 Jul
5.65	Yevgeniy	Mikhaylichenko	RUS	13.2.79	4	NC	Tula	25 Jul
5.65	Björn	Otto	GER	16.10.77	5		Norderney	1 Aug
	or next best	5.60			2		Arnhem	5 Jul
5.63		Zhang Hongwei	CHN	26.4.75	1		Deyang	13 May
5.63	Pat	Manson	USA	29.11.67	3=	NC	Sacramento	16 Jul
5.62	Grigoriy	Yegorov	KAZ	12.1.67	1		Alicante	6 May
5.61i	Richard	Spiegelburg	GER	12.8.77	1		Bad Segeberg	15 Jan
5.61	Stávros	Tsítouras	GRE	15.6.69	1		Minsk	9 Jun
5.61	Adam	Ptácek	CZE	8.10.80	1		Jablonec	18 Jul
5.61	Javier	García	ESP	22.7.66	2		Vic	17 Aug
	(60)							
5.60i	Vasiliy	Gorshkov	RUS	5.2.77	1		Moskva	18 Jan
5.60i	Andrei	Tivontschik	GER	13.7.70	1		Halle	26 Jan
5.60i	Sergey	Bubka	UKR	4.12.63	1		Valencia	2 Feb
5.60A	Laurens	Loojie	NED	12.1.73	1		Potchefstroom	14 Feb
5.60A	Riaan	Botha	RSA	8.11.70	1		Pretoria	16 Feb
5.60	Paul	Burgess	AUS	14.8.79	1	GP II	Melbourne	2 Mar
5.60	Bill	Payne	USA	21.12.67	3		Austin	6 May
5.60	Kurt	Hanna	USA	23.4.75	4		Austin	6 May
5.60	Mike	McNamara	USA	27.3.79	1		Abilene	11 May
5.60	Brent	Burns	USA	2.5.69	1=		Sacramento	21 May
	(70)							
5.60	Piotr	Buciarski	DEN	22.11.75	2	Odlozil	Praha	5 Jun
5.60	Massimo	Allevi	ITA	23.11.69	1		Rieti	24 Jun
5.60	Konstantin	Semyonov	ISR	20.11.69	1		Staiki	27 Jun
5.60	Vesa	Rantanen	FIN	2.12.75	1		Raahe	5 Jul

Mark	Name		Nat	Born	Pos	Meet	Venue	Date
5.60	Brian	Hunter	USA	28.3.79	1		Houston	6 Jul
5.60	Gérald	Baudouin	FRA	15.11.72	2		Arras	8 Jul
5.60	José Manuel	Arcos	ESP	19.1.73	1		Getafe	12 Jul
5.60	João	André	POR	28.5.76	1		Lisboa (I)	15 Jul
5.60	Trond	Barthel	NOR	11.9.70	1		Halmstad	16 Jul
5.60	Martin	Voss	DEN	5.9.67	2		Halmstad	16 Jul
	(80)							
5.60	Nuno	Fernandes	POR	1.4.69	2		Salamanca	20 Jul
5.60A	Robison	Pratt	MEX	25.2.80	1		El Paso	24 Jul
5.56i	Jure	Rovan	SLO	23.1.75	1		Pireás	22 Jan
5.56	Photis	Stephani	CYP	4.10.71	2		Minsk	9 Jun
5.56i	Aleksey	Khanafin	RUS-J	12.4.81	1		Moskva	26 Dec
5.55i	Gildas	Verbist	FRA	9.6.79	6		Rennes	5 Feb
5.55i	Russell	Johnson	USA	12.10.76	1		Blacksburg	5 Feb
5.55i	Oscar	Janson	SWE	22.7.75	2	v2N	Tampere	20 Feb
5.55Ai	Dason	Phelps	USA	5.5.76	2		Flagstaff	20 Feb
5.55i		Xu Gang	CHN	4.2.79	2	vJPN	Yokohama	26 Feb
	(90)							
5.55	Borya	Celentano	USA	25.10.76	1		Azusa	8 Apr
5.55	Jon	Nance	USA	28.8.77	2	UCTA	Austin	22 Apr
5.55	Paul	Williamson	GBR	16.6.74	1=jo	ModR	Modesto	13 May
5.55	Eric	Eshbach	USA-J	4.2.81	1	Big 12	Columbia MO	21 May
5.55	Erki	Nool	EST	25.6.70	D	Hypo	Götzis	4 Jun
5.55	William	Inocencio	FRA	20.2.76	1		Clermont-Ferrand	13 Jul
5.55	Fabrice	Fortin	FRA	2.2.80	1	NC-23	Bondoufle	16 Jul
5.55	Alain	Andji	FRA	20.11.74	4		Dijon	19 Jul
5.55	Igor	Pavlov	RUS	.79	7	NC	Tula	25 Jul
5.55	Sergey	Porokhin	RUS	4.4.77	8	NC	Tula	25 Jul
	(100)							
5.55	Kevin	Hughes	GBR	30.4.73	16=q	OG	Sydney	27 Sep
5.55	Danny	Krasnov	ISR	27.5.70	20=q	OG	Sydney	27 Sep

5.52	Geoff	Fairbanks	USA	1.6.79	16 May
5.51A	Alan	Gulledge	USA	21.1.75	15 Apr
5.51	Mathieu	Boisrond	FRA	8.1.77	30 Jul
5.50i	Ryan	Barkdull	USA	29.12.73	22 Jan
5.50i	Konstadínos	Tsatalós	GRE	14.2.70	29 Jan
5.50i	Ralf	Schmidt	GER	1.9.75	12 Feb
5.50i	Jim	Autenreith	USA	20.9.79	19 Feb
5.50i	Brian	McLaughlin	USA	25.7.77	11 Mar
5.50i	Jeff	Dutoit	USA	3.3.78	11 Mar
5.50	Bill	Deering	USA	20.7.71	28 Apr
5.50	Satoru	Yasuda	JPN	27.7.75	14 May
5.50	Aleksandr	Korchagin	KAZ	25.1.72	27 May
5.50	Clark	Humphreys	USA	27.11.75	1 Jun
5.50	Krzysztof	Kusiak	POL	13.5.74	25 Jun
5.50	Kevin	Brown	USA	15.8.71	1 Jul
5.50	Kiyonobu	Kigoshi	JPN	7.5.76	1 Jul
5.50	Adam	Kolasa	POL	2.8.75	8 Jul
5.50	Michel	Gigandet	SUI	12.4.76	5 Aug
5.50	Aleksandr	Korchmyd	UKR-J	22.1.82	6 Aug
5.50	Tom Erik	Olsen	NOR	20.10.74	12 Aug
5.50	Stefan	Drews	GER	12.2.79	3 Sep
5.47i	Nicolas	Jolivet	FRA	24.3.77	22 Jan
5.47	Mike	Westlund	USA	24.3.80	21 May
5.46	Pierre-Charles	Peuf	FRA	27.4.79	23 Jul
5.45Ai	Mike	Drummey	USA	11.7.72	21 Jan
5.45i	Tiberiu	Agoston	ROM	25.12.76	6 Feb
5.45i	Spas	Bukhalov	BUL	14.11.80	19 Feb
5.45i	Ketil	Rønneberg	NOR	9.12.76	25 Feb
5.45	Matt	Phillips	USA	28.12.77	13 May
5.45	Daichi	Sawano	JPN	16.9.80	28 May
5.45	Viktor	von Bothmer	SWE	21.3.78	30 Jul
5.45	Wesley	Rombaut	BEL	12.11.77	30 Jul
5.45	Jussi	Autio	FIN	5.4.75	19 Aug
5.43i	Marc	Vandevoir	FRA	17.6.71	5 Mar
5.42	Adam	Keul	USA	27.1.80	16 May
5.42	Rocky	Danners	USA-J	21.6.81	18 May
5.42	Brad	Tyler	USA	14.7.80	20 May
5.42	Bevan	Hart	USA	1.8.77	20 May
5.42	Christoph	Völker	GER	26.11.79	17 Jun
5.41Ai	Jeff	Hansen	USA	13.10.76	29 Jan
5.41i	Hendrik	Hübner	GER	11.6.76	4 Feb
5.41	Brad	Parris	USA		11 May
5.41	Georgi	Wassilew	GER	16.2.80	2 Jul

5.40i	Christof	Gross	GER	11.3.76	15 Jan
5.40i	Matej	Urban	CZE	23.1.75	22 Jan
5.40i	Ruslan	Gataullin	RUS	1.12.79	22 Jan
5.40i	Javier	Gazol	ESP	27.10.80	23 Jan
5.40i	Fabio	Pizzolato	ITA	16.3.75	23 Jan
5.40i	Alberto	Giacchetto	ITA	21.2.73	23 Jan
5.40i	Aleksey	Gladkikh	RUS	17.4.71	5 Feb
5.40i	Andrey	Podkorytov	RUS	.73	5 Feb
5.40i	Igor	Kravtsov	BLR	2.4.77	5 Feb
5.40i	Giacomo	Befani	ITA	8.1.70	12 Feb
5.40i	Sergey	Blonskiy	UKR	7.1.73	19 Feb
5.40i	Andrey	Afonin	UKR	22.7.78	19 Feb
5.40i	Jeff	Beam	USA	8.6.76	20 Feb
5.40i	Fumiaki	Kobayashi	JPN	10.12.74	26 Feb
5.40i	Vasiliy	Petrov	RUS-J	5.2.83	29 Feb
5.40	Alex	Miroshnichenko	RUS	28.9.78	8 Mar
5.40	Hideji	Suzuki	JPN	10.3.74	29 Apr
5.40	Sébastien	Levicq	FRA	25.6.71	21 May
5.40	Brad	Pickett	USA	27.9.77	21 May
5.40	Igor	Potapovich	KAZ	6.9.67	10 Jun
5.40	Tim	Thomas	GBR	18.11.73	11 Jun
5.40	Martin	Kysela	CZE	25.3.74	11 Jun
5.40	Mários	Evaggélou	GRE-J	8.5.81	1 Jul
5.40	Mikko	Latvala	FIN	8.7.80	5 Jul
5.40	Ruslan	Yeremenko	UKR	31.7.78	8 Jul
5.40	Alhaji	Jeng	SWE-J	13.12.81	16 Jul
5.40	Pawel	Szczyrba	POL-J	1.9.81	16 Jul
5.40	Igor	Trandenkov	RUS	17.8.66	23 Jul
5.40	Yuriy	Yeliseyev	RUS	27.5.75	23 Jul
5.40	Nick	Buckfield	GBR	5.6.73	2 Aug
5.40	Pat	Jesser	AUS-J	11.6.81	17 Aug
5.40	Ariel	Mäki-Soini	FIN	23.7.75	19 Aug
5.40	Takuya	Kanno	JPN	17.1.79	1 Sep
5.39A	Eric	Boxley	USA	7.3.75	8 Jul
5.38i	Cédric	Nobilet	FRA	30.9.77	22 Jan
5.38	Sam	Boswell	USA	19.12.80	18 Mar
5.38	Nick	Paramo	USA	26.4.78	18 Mar
5.36i	François	Thénault	FRA	4.5.72	1 Feb
5.36i	Patrick	Tvarkunas	USA	23.9.78	12 Feb
5.36i	Mike	Brookins	USA	18.5.76	2 Mar
5.36	Sage	Thames	USA-J	23.5.82	10 Jun
5.36	Jukka	Nurmela	FIN	15.2.79	27 Jul
5.35i	Ben	Flint	GBR	16.9.78	29 Jan

Mark	Name		Nat	Born	Date
5.35i	William	Jones	USA	27.11.76	4 Feb
5.35i	Sean	Brown	USA	23.3.74	19 Feb
5.35	Scott	Wenholz	USA	23.8.77	1 Apr
5.35	Ricardo	Diez	VEN	29.3.75	6 May
5.35	Lon	Badeaux	USA	9.3.73	19 May
5.35	Gustavo	Rehder	BRA	10.12.79	28 May
5.35	Luke	Walker	USA	24.3.72	24 Jul
5.35	Nicolas	Guigon	FRA	10.10.80	30 Jul
5.35	Rob	Pike	CAN	8.1.70	1 Aug
5.35	Fílippos-Dimítrios	Sgoúros	GRE-J	26.9.81	6 Aug
5.35	Fanie	Jacobs	RSA	21.4.76	5 Dec
	(199)				

Best outdoor mark for athlete with best indoors

5.80	Galfione	1	Bisl	Oslo	28 Jul
5.80b	Harting	1		Santa Barbara	11 Jun
	5.65	3	Pre	Eugene	24 Jun
5.70	Gataullin	1		Villeneuve d'Ascq	17 Jun
5.60	Spiegelburg	5		Ingolstadt	18 Jun
5.60	Spacek	1=		Jablonec	22 Jul
5.55	Gorshkov	2	NCp	Tula	2 Jun
5.55	Bubka	9=	Herc	Monaco	18 Aug
5.55	Janson	3	vFIN	Helsinki	2 Sep

5.50	Dutoit	1 Jun
5.50	Khanafin	1 Jul
5.50	Schmidt	29 May
5.49	Phelps	18 Mar
5.42	Johnson	18 May
5.41	McLaughlin	26 Mar
5.40	Verbist	29 Apr
5.40	Tivontschik	31 May
5.40	Burlachenko	9 Jun
5.40	Gazol	10 Jun
5.40b	Beam	11 Jun
5.40	Drummey	17 Jun
5.40	Mariani	24 Jun
	5.50 exh	24 Aug
5.40	Gladkikh	26 Jun
5.40	Rønneberg	30 Jul
5.40	Kobayashi	27 Aug
5.40	Xu Gang	20 Oct
5.37	Davis	21 May
5.35	Agoston	24 Jun

Low altitude best

5.72i	Eriksson	1		Glasgow	5 Mar
5.72	Stevenson	1	Pac10	Eugene	21 May
5.61	D Johnson	1		Ljubljana	10 Jun
5.35i	Pratt	6		Los Angeles	19 Feb

Town square and exhibition marks

5.71	Björn	Otto	GER	16.10.77	5	Köln	4 Aug
5.70	Petr	Spacek	CZE	23.7.75	1	Jockgrimm	19 Jul
5.70 sq	Igor	Pavlov	RUS	.79	1	Lódz	11 Aug
5.70 sq	Martin	Kysela	CZE	25.3.74	2	Lódz	11 Aug
5.70	Vasiliy	Gorshkov	RUS	5.2.77	2	Carbonia	24 Aug
5.65 sq	Adam	Kolasa	POL	2.8.75	1	Miedzyzdrzóje	17 Aug
5.62	Martin	Voss	DEN	5.9.67	2	Recklinghausen	26 May
5.60	Krzysztof	Kusiak	POL	13.5.74	1	Sopot	12 Jul
5.60 sq	Aleksandr	Korchmyd	UKR-J	22.1.82	3=	Lódz	11 Aug
5.60 sq	Ruslan	Yeremenko	UKR	31.7.78	6	Lódz	11 Aug

JUNIORS

5.56i	Aleksey	Khanafin	RUS	12.4.81	1		Moskva	26 Dec
	5.50	1 NC-j Cheboksary		1 Jul				
5.55	Eric	Eshbach	USA	4.2.81	1	Big 12	Columbia MO	21 May
	5.50i	1 Lincoln		29 Jan	5.45i	2	Lincoln NE	12 Feb
	5.50i	5= NCAA Fayetteville		11 Mar				
5.50	Aleksandr	Korchmyd	UKR	22.1.82	2	NC	Kiev	6 Aug
5.42	Rocky	Danners	USA	21.6.81	1c2		Knoxville	18 May
	5.41	3=c1 Knoxville		18 May	9 performances by 4 men to 5.41			
5.40i	Vasiliy	Petrov	RUS	5.2.83	1		Moskva	29 Feb
5.40	Mários	Evaggélou	GRE	8.5.81	2	BalkG	Kavála	1 Jul
5.40	Alhaji	Jeng	SWE	13.12.81	3		Halmstad	16 Jul
5.40	Pawel	Szczyrba	POL	1.9.81	4		Halmstad	16 Jul
5.40	Pat	Jesser	AUS	11.6.81	2	OT	Sydney	17 Aug
5.36	Sage	Thames (10)	USA	23.5.82	1	GWest	Sacramento	10 Jun
5.35	Fílippos-Dimítrios	Sgoúros	GRE	26.9.81	1		Kastoriá	6 Aug
5.30i	Vyacheslav	Ostapenko	RUS	28.4.82	2		Sankt-Peterburg	4 Jan
5.30	Toshio	Imura	JPN	14.6.82	1		Kobe	24 Jun
5.30	Kevin	Rans	BEL	19.8.82	1	FlemCh	Brugge	2 Jul
5.30	Dmitriy	Kuptsov	RUS	.82	2		Cheboksary	8 Jul
5.30	Marvin	Osei-Tutu	GER	22.4.81	1	NC-j	Dresden	15 Jul
5.30	Andrey	Sergeyev	UKR	23.1.81	1		Minsk	24 Aug
5.30	Alberto	Martínez	ESP	4.4.82	1	vGBR23	Getafe	9 Sep
5.26i	Jonathan	Henley	USA	16.7.81	2	NIAC	Lincoln NE	19 Feb
5.25i	Sébastien	Homo (20)	FRA	27.4.82	1	v2N-j	Neubrandenburg	4 Mar
5.25	Rico	Tepper	GER	16.4.82	1		Zeulenroda	22 Jun
5.25	Robert	Villa	ESP	13.1.81	3		Barcelona	16 Jul

LONG JUMP

8.65	1.5	Iván	Pedroso	CUB	17.12.72	1	OD	Jena	3 Jun		
					x	x	8.14	8.65	p	p	
8.55	0.41	OG	Sydney	28 Sep	x	8.34/0.0	x	8.41/0.2	x	8.55	
8.44	0.61		Camagüey	5 Mar	x	x	7.76	x	8.44	x	
8.40i	- 1		Pireás	9 Feb	x	8.10	8.40	x	p	p	
8.39	1.01		Torino	10 Jun	x	x	x	x	7.61	8.39	
8.33i	- 1		Madrid	16 Feb	8.33	x	x	8.28	x	x	
8.33	0.91	Athl	Lausanne	5 Jul	8.11	7.75	8.23	8.11	x	8.33	
8.32	1.21	Super	Yokohama	9 Sep	x	7.92	8.14	8.32	p	p	
8.32	0.1Q	OG	Sydney	25 Sep	7.70	7.99	8.32				

Mark	Wind	Name		Nat	Born	Pos	Meet	Venue		Date
8.49	2.0	Melvin	Lister	USA	29.8.77	1	SEC	Baton Rouge		13 May
	8.32	0.5 1 MSR	Walnut	16 Apr	7.67	8.32	x	x	x	x
	8.32	1.6 1 NC	Sacramento	17 Jul	7.69	8.32	x	7.87	x	x
8.49	0.6	Jai	Taurima	AUS	26.6.72	2	OG	Sydney		28 Sep
					x	8.18	8.34/-0.2	8.40/0.6	8.49	8.28
8.43	0.1	Luis	Meliz	CUB	11.8.79	2	OD	Jena		3 Jun
					8.28	8.43	7.96	p	x	p
8.42		James	Beckford	JAM	9.1.75	1		Bad Langensalza		1 Jul
					7.98	8.15	8.42	x	8.31	8.24
	8.41	1.3 1	Villeneuve d'Ascq	17 Jun	7.99	x	8.25	x	8.41	x
	8.34	-1.3 *	Malles	15 Jul	7.85	8.19w	7.96	8.39w/2.5	x	8.34
	8.34	-1.1 1	Salamanca	20 Jul	x	7.92	8.34	x	x	8.02
	8.29	0.0 1	Rivas	21 Jun	7.81	7.94	x	8.19	8.14	8.29
	8.29	-0.6 1	Cuxhaven	19 Jul	8.10	8.09	8.01	8.19	x	8.29
	8.29	1.5 1 NC	Kingston	22 Jul	8.29	x	8.27/-1.4	p	p	p
8.38i	–	Vitaliy	Shkurlatov	RUS	25.5.79	1		Samara		30 Jan
					8.18	8.38	x	x	x	8.02
	8.30i	– 1	Moskva	27 Jan	8.16	8.27	8.13	p	p	8.20
8.35	0.7	Roman	Shchurenko	UKR	14.9.76	1		Kiev		25 Jul
	8.31	0.3 3 OG	Sydney	28 Sep	7.76	x	8.14	x	x	8.31
8.34	1.4	Younès	Moudrik	MAR	1.10.77	1	AfCh	Alger		13 Jul
					7.83	7.89	8.34	x	p	p
8.34	0.9	Kirill	Sosunov	RUS	1.11.75	1		Lisboa (U)		5 Aug
					8.34	7.94	x	x	p	8.02
8.33	0.8	Hussein	Al-Sabee (10)	KSA	14.11.79	1	AsiC	Jakarta		31 Aug
					x	8.33	8.02	5.77	7.97	8.30/0.5
	8.33Aw	5.2 1	Guadix	18 Jun						
8.31		Kareem	Streete-Thompson	CAY	30.3.73	2		Bad Langensalza		1 Jul
					7.87	x	8.11	7.83	x	8.31
8.30i	–	Bogdan	Tarus	ROM	1.8.75	1		Bucuresti		30 Jan
8.30	1.1	Peter	Burge	AUS	3.7.74	1	GP II	Melbourne		2 Mar
					x	8.21	8.21	8.30	8.23	8.18
8.30	2.0	Savanté	Stringfellow	USA	6.11.78	2	MSR	Walnut		16 Apr
					8.30	7.85	7.67	8.00	x	
8.30	1.1	Petar	Dachev	BUL	15.6.79	1		Nicosia		23 Jun
					7.96w	8.12	8.15w	x	7.94	8.30
		(33/15)								
8.28	1.3	Kevin	Dilworth	USA	14.2.74	1	Conseil	Fort-de-France		29 Apr
8.27	1.4	Aleksey	Lukashevich	UKR	11.1.77	1	Sule	Tartu		11 Jun
8.26	1.2	Miguel	Pate	USA	13.6.79	1	AlabR	Tuscaloosa		25 Mar
8.25	0.3	Vladimir	Malyavin	RUS	4.3.73	3	Znam	Sankt-Peterburg		18 Jun
8.24	0.8	Ronald	Servius	FRA	21.2.76	2	NC	Nice		6 Aug
		(20)								
8.23	1.6	Cheikh	Touré	FRA	25.1.70	*	NC	Nice		6 Aug
8.22	1.9	Kader	Klouchi	FRA	10.6.69	1		Arles		3 Jun
8.22	0.1	Yago	Lamela	ESP	24.7.77	1		Thessaloníki		30 Aug
8.21	0.2	Shane	Hair	AUS	24.10.75	1		Perth		5 Feb
8.21	1.3	Dwight	Phillips	USA	1.10.77	Q	NC	Sacramento		15 Jul
8.20	0.8	Kofi Amoah	Prah	GER	20.12.74	1		Wesel		12 Jun
8.20	1.1	Nikolay	Atanasov	BUL	11.12.74	1		Dimitrovgrad		19 Jul
8.19	1.9	Richard	Duncan	CAN	25.12.73	1		Houston		25 Mar
8.18	1.1	Nelson	Ferreira	BRA	1.1.73	1	NC	Rio de Janeiro		3 Aug
8.16	2.0		Wang Cheng	CHN	4.11.80	1		Hong Kong		8 Jul
		(30)								
8.16	0.9	Walter	Davis	USA	2.7.79	Q	NC	Sacramento		15 Jul
8.15	0.2	Gregor	Cankar	SLO	25.1.75	3		Bad Langensalza		1 Jul
8.14	0.9	Erick	Walder	USA	5.11.71	2		Portland		25 Jun
8.13	1.5	Carlos	Calado	POR	5.10.75	3		Thessaloníki		30 Aug
8.12	0.4	Hatem	Mersal	EGY	20.1.75	5		Torino		10 Jun
8.12	1.9	Danila	Burkenya	RUS	20.7.78	1	NC	Tula		25 Jul
8.11	1.5	Pedro	García	CUB	11.6.76	2		La Habana		19 Feb
8.10	1.9	Tomas	Bardauskas	LTU	22.3.75	1	v2N	Kaunas		19 Aug
8.09i	–	Mesut	Yavas	TUR	14.4.78	1		Ames		3 Mar
8.09	0.4		Liu Honglin	CHN	13.10.76	1	NGP	Shijiazhuang		28 Apr
		(40)								
8.09	0.7	Emmanuel	Bangué	FRA	21.7.71	2		Bron		23 Jul
8.09	1.2	Konstadínos	Koukodímos	GRE	14.9.69	5		Thessaloníki		30 Aug
8.08i	–	Dimítrios	Serélis	GRE	5.5.80	1	NC	Pireás		20 Feb
8.08	0.2		Lao Jianfeng	CHN	24.5.75	1	NGP	Tianjin		4 May

Mark	Wind	Name		Nat	Born	Pos	Meet	Venue	Date
8.08A	1.2	Shirak	Pogosian	ARM	24.9.69	1		Tsakhkadzor	26 May
8.08	1.3	Matthias	Sunneborn	SWE	27.9.70	1		Göteborg	3 Aug
8.07i	–	Konstantin	Krause	GER	8.10.67	2		Erfurt	2 Feb
8.07	1.7	Delvit	Rogers	USA	23.3.80	1		Baton Rouge	15 Apr
8.07	0.9	Robert	Howard	USA	26.11.75	4	NC	Sacramento	17 Jul
8.07	1.2	Peter	Häggström	SWE	27.1.76	1		Budapest	22 Jul
		(50)							
8.05	-0.2	Arnaud	Casquette	MRI	16.4.78	1		Réduit	8 Apr
8.05	1.5	Kenta	Bell	USA	16.3.77	1		Natchitoches	28 Apr
8.05	0.6	Masaki	Morinaga	JPN	27.3.72	1		Tottori	10 Jun
8.05A	1.8	Jonathan	Daniels	USA	.75	1		Flagstaff	8 Jul
8.04i		Bogdan	Tudor	ROM	1.2.70	1		Bucuresti	19 Feb
8.04	2.0	Darvis	Patton	USA	4.12.77	1	USTCA	Baton Rouge	25 Mar
8.04	1.7	Schahriar	Bigdeli	GER	26.3.80	*		Bad Camberg	10 Jun
8.03	0.0	Tomas	Dvorák	CZE	11.5.72	D		Götzis	3 Jun
8.03	0.0	Eric	Bowers	USA	20.7.74	1		Nassau	9 Jun
8.03	1.2	Krzysztof	Luczak	POL	13.1.75	1		Biala Podlaska	17 Jun
		(60)							
8.03A	0.0	Jayson	Duff	USA	15.8.72	1		Flagstaff	6 Jul
8.03	0.4	Sanjay Kumar	Rai	IND	1.5.79	2	AsiC	Jakarta	31 Aug
8.02i		Marcus	Thomas	USA	22.3.79	1	SEC	Fayetteville	26 Feb
8.02	0.7	Milan	Kovár	CZE	24.2.72	1		Turnov	11 Jun
8.01	0.0	Sinisa	Ergotic	CRO	14.9.68	1		Ljubljana	10 Jun
8.01A	2.0	Jerrod	Sanders	USA	.78	1		El Paso	24 Jun
8.01	1.3	Yann	Domenech	FRA	17.3.79	4		Pierre-Benité	24 Jun
8.01	-0.4	Abdulrahman	Al-Nubi	QAT	17.10.79	3	AsiC	Jakarta	31 Aug
8.00i		Maurice	Lewis	USA	14.1.78	1		Gainesville	6 Feb
8.00i		Grzegorz	Marciniszyn	POL	22.5.77	1	NC	Spala	12 Feb
		(70)							
8.00	1.4	Deandre	Free	USA-J	15.1.81	1		Kansas City MO	29 Apr
8.00	1.3	Nathan	Morgan	GBR	30.6.78	1	vESP23	Getafe	9 Sep
8.00	0.7	Astérios	Noúsios	GRE	.79	1	v3N23	Praha	9 Sep
7.99i		Maurice	Wignall	JAM	17.4.76	1		Blacksburg	25 Feb
7.99	1.5	Mickaël	Loria	FRA	9.6.73	1		Forbach	10 Jun
7.99	0.2	Danial	Jahic	YUG	1.7.79	1	NC	Beograd	19 Aug
7.98	1.4	Nicola	Trentin	ITA	20.6.74	1		Cagliari	5 Jul
7.98A	0.0	Ian	Lowe	CAN	23.2.73	2		Flagstaff	6 Jul
7.97i		Roman	Sebrle	CZE	26.11.74	H	Nool	Tallinn	29 Jan
7.97	1.3	Roland	McGhee	USA	15.10.71	7	NC	Sacramento	17 Jul
		(80)							
7.97	0.0	Esteban	Copland	VEN	12.10.79	1	NC	Barquisimeto	9 Sep
7.96i		Dimitrios	Filíndras	GRE	9.2.73	2	NC	Pireás	20 Feb
7.96	1.6	Niklas	Rorarius	FIN	7.6.78	2	GP II	Helsinki	15 Jun
7.96	1.3	Sean	Robbins	USA	9.10.72	3		Portland	25 Jun
7.96	1.3	Frédéric	Erin	FRA	23.4.80	1	NC-23	Bondoufle	15 Jul
7.95i		Krasimir	Argirov	BUL	13.4.80	1		Sofia	20 Feb
7.95	1.3	Yoelmis	Pacheco	CUB-J	9.6.82	2		La Habana	24 Feb
7.95	0.8	Salim	Sdiri	FRA	26.10.78	1		Noisy-le-Grand	20 Jun
7.95A	0.0	Brian	Thomas	CAN	27.1.70	3		Flagstaff	6 Jul
7.95	-0.2	Rustam	Khusnutdinov	UZB	14.11.75	1	NC	Tashkent	18 Aug
		(90)							
7.95	1.2	Antonio	Adsuar	ESP	4.7.78	2	vGBR23	Getafe	9 Sep
7.94i		Stanislavs	Olijars	LAT	22.3.79	1		Riga	5 Jan
7.94	1.2	Joan Lino	Martínez	CUB	17.1.78	*		La Habana	19 Feb
7.94	1.3	José J	Reyes	VEN	20.3.77	1		San Felipe	5 May
7.93i		Yevgeniy	Tretyak	RUS	18.7.71	1		Shakhty	16 Jan
7.93i		Shawn	Watson	USA	9.5.75	1		Mount Union	25 Feb
7.93	1.4	Diego	Boschiero	ITA	12.5.76	2	ECCp	Vila Real S.António	27 May
7.93	1.8	Aleksandr	Yurkov	UKR	21.7.75	D	Hypo	Götzis	3 Jun
7.93	0.7		Cai Peng	CHN-J	28.3.83	2	NGPF	Jinzhou	8 Jun
7.93	1.9	James	Stallworth	USA	29.4.71	1		Long Beach	10 Jun
		(100)							
7.93A	1.8	Michael	Laberge	CAN	10.2.74	2		Flagstaff	8 Jul
7.93	0.6	Bruno	Frinolli	ITA	27.2.68	1	NC	Milano	6 Sep

7.92i		Andrey	Bragin	RUS	.78	30 Jan
7.92i		Tamás	Margl	HUN	18.6.76	12 Feb
7.92A	0.9	Armen	Martirosyan	ARM	6.8.69	26 May
7.92A	1.6	Merudian	Sarkisian	ARM	20.11.76	26 May
7.92	1.8	Frank	Busemann	GER	26.2.75	3 Jun
7.92	0.9	Jamorya	Funderburk	USA	23.12.79	15 Jul
7.92	0.8	Cláudio	Novaes	BRA	18.6.72	3 Aug
7.91	1.9	Vasil	Gergov	BUL	1.7.77	2 Jul
7.91	1.0	Marco	Tremigliozzi	ITA	2.9.74	21 Jul
7.91	-0.7		Li Dalong	CHN	21.10.80	22 Oct
7.91A	0.6	Francois	Coetzee	RSA	30.7.75	25 Nov
7.90i		Andrey	Ignatov	RUS	3.2.68	2 Feb

Mark	Wind	Name		Nat	Born	Date
7.90	0.9	Denis	Savelyev	RUS	.74	3 Jun
7.90	0.6	Matthias	Eifert	GER	10.9.77	12 Jun
7.90	1.0	Mark Anthony	Awere	GHA	16.7.71	5 Aug
7.90		Darren	Ritchie	GBR	14.2.75	19 Aug
7.90	1.8	Erki	Nool	EST	25.6.70	3 Sep
7.89		Daniel	Hagspiel	AUT	3.9.73	23 Jun
7.89	0.0		Sung Hee-jun	KOR	8.6.74	10 Aug
7.89	1.2	George	Audu	GBR	18.1.77	12 Aug
7.89	0.0	Yusuke	Maeda	JPN	16.3.78	2 Sep
7.88i		Wendell	Williams	TRI	19.10.68	23 Jan
7.88	0.0		Zhou Can	CHN	20.5.79	22 Apr
7.88	0.6	Galin	Georgiev	BUL	23.3.70	4 Jun
7.88	0.0	Chris	Wright	BAH	8.8.71	9 Jun
7.88	1.2	Maksim	Smetanin	KGZ	17.2.74	2 Jul
7.88A	1.7	Devon	Bean	BER	13.9.75	8 Jul
7.88	-0.1	Méhdi	Ghazouani	MAR	1.1.76	13 Jul
7.87	1.6	Ibrahim	Camejo	CUB-J	28.6.82	11 Feb
7.87i		Romuald	Ducros	FRA	6.2.73	20 Feb
7.87	0.7	Jeremy	Taylor	USA	2.3.77	13 May
7.87	1.2	Daisuke	Watanabe	JPN	29.5.75	10 Jun
7.87	-0.6	Chris	Huffins	USA	15.4.70	20 Jul
7.87		Idika	Uduma	NGR-J	12.12.82	22 Jul
7.87	1.0	Georges Téko	Folligan	TOG	6.4.76	27 Jul
7.86i		Clayton	Porter	USA	7.6.78	25 Feb
7.86	1.8	Darius	Pemberton	USA	10.5.75	6 May
7.86		Stephan	Louw	NAM	26.2.75	13 May
7.86		Lenton	Herring	USA	4.12.78	20 May
7.86	1.8	Francesco	Agresti	ITA	20.10.77	15 Jul
7.86	0.5	Jirí	Kuntos	CZE	2.10.73	16 Jul
7.85		Jonathan	Chimier	MRI-J	6.8.82	11 Mar
7.85	0.9		Hsu Chih-Hsiung	TPE	17.7.77	24 Apr
7.85	0.1		Xu Bin	CHN	4.8.70	4 May
7.85	1.6	Leonard	Cobb	USA	20.1.75	11 May
7.85	0.7	Andrejs	Tolstiks	LAT	19.1.77	11 Jun
7.85	-0.4	Aaron	Langdon	NZL	19.7.71	2 Jul
7.85	-0.1	Giacomo	D'Apolito	ITA	23.10.71	23 Aug
7.85	-1.3		Huang Le	CHN	25.9.77	22 Oct
7.84	0.0		Chen Jing	CHN	10.3.76	25 Mar
7.84A	0.6	Martin	McClintock	RSA	30.6.75	7 Apr
7.84	1.2	Shin-ichi	Terano	JPN	10.7.79	16 Jul
7.84	1.0	Philip	Ibe	GER	5.5.75	22 Jul
7.84	-0.6	Vladimir	Zyuskov	UKR-J	29.8.81	22 Oct
7.83	0.1		Dong Baohua	CHN	14.2.80	15 Apr
7.83	1.2	Sergej	Rozman	SLO	20.5.71	17 Jun
7.83	-1.7	Stanislav	Tarasenko	RUS	23.7.66	26 Jun
7.83	0.8	Leevan	Sands	BAH-J	16.1.81	14 Jul
7.83	1.1	Phillips	Idowu	GBR	30.12.78	25 Jul
7.82i		Sergey	Novozhilov	RUS	21.4.69	6 Feb
7.82i		Jón Arnar	Magnússon	ISL	28.7.69	5 Mar
7.82	0.8	Tim	Bryant	USA	11.1.74	11 May
7.82	1.6	Ramon	Washington	USA-J	23.6.81	23 Jun
7.82	1.5	Balázs	Dömötör	HUN	24.6.75	22 Jul
7.81	0.3	Franck	Monnel	FRA	20.1.69	9 Jul
7.81		Sujith	Rohitha	SRI	27.10.69	18 Aug
7.80i		Eddie	Jackson	USA	19.12.80	5 Feb
7.80	1.9	Michael	Hessek	GER	15.3.75	12 Jun
7.80	-0.1	Erik	Nijs	BEL	27.7.73	25 Aug
7.80	0.0	Kentaro	Suzuki	JPN	29.9.78	2 Sep

(172)

Wind assisted

Mark	Wind	Name		Nat	Born	Pos	Meet	Venue	Date
8.48	3.4	Peter	Burge	AUS	3.7.74	1		Gold Coast (RB)	10 Sep
					8.48w	8.31w/5.0	8.30w/3.1	8.25w	
8.43	3.1	Cheikh	Touré	FRA	25.1.70	1	NC	Nice	6 Aug
					8.01	x	8.43w	p	x 8.23
8.34	3.0	Masaki	Morinaga	JPN	27.3.72	1		Shizuoka	3 May
					8.10w	8.03w	8.16w	8.34w	p p
8.30	2.5	Dwight	Phillips	USA	1.10.77	1		Portland	25 Jun
					7.89	8.04	8.09	x	8.30w x
8.23	4.7	Shane	Hair	AUS	24.10.75	1		Sydney	13 Feb
8.23	6.3	Gregor	Cankar	SLO	25.1.75	4		Gold Coast (RB)	10 Sep
8.22	2.1	Schahriar	Bigdeli	GER	26.3.80	1		Bad Camberg	10 Jun
8.20	6.1	Aaron	Langdon	NZL	19.7.71	3		Gold Coast (RB)	5 Aug
8.18	2.5	Joan Lino	Martínez	CUB	17.1.78	1		La Habana	19 Feb
8.18	2.9	Daisuke	Watanabe	JPN	29.5.75	2		Shizuoka	3 May
8.18	6.0	Sean	Robbins	USA	9.10.72	1	Owens	Columbus	7 May
8.17	3.3	Yann	Doménech	FRA	17.3.79	1		Pierrelatte	17 Jun
8.15	2.8	Carlos	Calado	POR	5.10.75	1		Maia	15 Jul
8.11	2.8	Paolo	Camossi	ITA	6.1.74	1		Roma	3 Jun
8.09	7.5	Darius	Pemberton	USA	10.5.75	2		Houston	6 May
8.09	3.9	Roland	McGhee	USA	15.10.71	1		Knoxville	18 May
8.09	2.9	Cleavon	Dillon	TRI-J	8.6.82	1	CAC-J	San Juan	14 Jul
8.08	5.4	Shin-ichi	Terano	JPN	10.7.79	3		Shizuoka	3 May
8.08	3.3	Peter	Häggström	SWE	27.1.76	3	ECp-S	Gateshead	15 Jul
8.07	5.3	Darvis	Patton	USA	4.12.77	1		Fort Worth	22 Apr
8.06	4.9	Sujith	Rohitha	SRI	27.10.69	1		Colombo	3 Jun
8.06	3.4	Antonio	Adsuar	ESP	4.7.78	1		Vic	17 Aug
8.05	4.3	Shigeru	Tagawa	JPN	22.11.75	4		Shizuoka	3 May
8.05	2.3	Rephel	Martin	USA	23.4.76	1		New Orleans	12 May
8.05	3.5	Nathan	Morgan	GBR	30.6.78	1		Ljubljana	25 Jul
8.04	4.1	Brian	Johnson	USA	25.3.80	1		Houston	22 Jun
8.01	6.0	Jón Arnar	Magnússon	ISL	28.7.69	1		Reykjavik	22 Jul
8.00	2.2	Mickaël	Loria	FRA	9.6.73	4	NC	Nice	6 Aug
7.98	2.2	Santana	Moss	USA	1.6.79	1	Big East	Piscataway	6 May
7.98	2.3	Milko	Campus	ITA	2.4.[illegible]	2		Roma	3 Jun
7.96	4.6	Tetsuya	Shida	JPN	27.6.71	6		Shizuoka	3 May
7.95	2.2	Will	Montgomery	USA	23.6.80	2		New Orleans	12 May
7.95	w	Tim	Bryant	USA	11.1.74	1		Houston	6 Jul
7.94	2.8		Xu Bin	CHN	4.8.70	2	NGP	Shijiazhuang	28 Apr
7.94A	2.3	Gaël	Ovois	FRA	10.5.72	1		Font-Romeu	9 Jul
7.93	3.1	Garfield	Swaby	JAM	21.2.77	1		Natchitoches	15 May
7.93	3.3	Andrea	Baldi	ITA	2.1.70	3		Roma	3 Jun

A = made at altitude of over 1000m

Mark	Wind	Name		Nat	Born	Pos	Meet	Venue	Date
7.92		Leonard	Cobb	USA	20.1.75				24 Mar
7.92	2.2	Chris	Wright	BAH	8.8.71				21 Jul
7.92	4.4	Darren	Ritchie	GBR	14.2.75				28 Aug
7.90	2.8		Wen Yutao	CHN	2.2.74				28 Apr
7.90	2.6	France	Davis	USA	23.8.77				6 May
7.89	3.9	Nabil	Adamou	ALG	8.4.75				6 Feb
7.89	2.4	Joe	Allen	USA	.77				1 Apr
7.88	2.7	Robert	Etheridge	USA-J	3.4.81				23 Jun
7.88	2.8	Fabrizio	Donato	ITA	14.8.76				24 Jun
7.87	3.7	Francisco	Caro	ESP	23.10.78				8 Sep
7.86	2.6	Steve	Phillips	GBR	17.3.72				29 May
7.85	2.2	Robert	Kennedy	USA-J	14.6.81				20 May
7.84	7.3	Tomasz	Mateusiak	POL	5.12.80				10 Jun
7.84	7.1	David	Vincent	FRA	1.4.75				17 Jun
7.83	2.1	Sérgio	dos Santos	BRA	13.5.76				3 Aug
7.82	2.7	Kazushige	Inatomi	JPN	14.5.78				3 May
7.82	2.9	Marshaun	West	USA	4.2.78				6 May
7.82	5.6	Anthony	Harris	USA					12 May
7.82	3.4	Leslie	Djhone	FRA-J	18.3.81				28 Jun
7.82	2.7	Kevin	Wiley	USA	30.10.72				1 Jul
7.82	3.0	Julien	Ruiz	FRA-J	25.8.82				2 Jul
7.81	2.1	Garfield	Swaby	JAM	21.2.77				6 May
7.81	2.2		Yang Chao	CHN	12.2.74				9 May
7.81		Marco	Kummie	GER	16.7.73				24 Jun
7.80	4.2	Panayiótis	Papázoglou	GRE	10.4.80				22 Apr
7.80		Jerome	Robinson	USA					11 Jun
7.80	2.2	Tommi	Evilä	FIN	6.4.80				15 Jun
7.80	3.0	Luka	Aracic	CRO-J	13.3.81				25 Jul

Best outdoor mark for athlete with best indoors

Mark	Wind	Name	Pos	Meet	Venue	Date
8.22	1.8	Shkurlatov	1	ECpS	Gateshead	15 Jul
8.12	-0.1	Tarus	1		Bucuresti	24 Jun
8.08	0.8	Yavas	1		Istanbul	24 Jun
8.01	1.8	M Thomas	q	NC	Sacramento	15 Jul
8.00	0.8	Serélis	6		Thessaloníki	30 Aug
7.96	0.2	Marciniszyn	1		Sopot	1 Jul
7.96	-0.6	Tudor	1		Poiana Brasov	22 Jul
7.95	1.7	Krause	2	NC	Braunschweig	29 Jul
7.93	1.8	Lewis	5	SEC	Baton Rouge	13 May
8.04w	2.1	Ser´´lis	2		Nicosia	23 Jun

Mark	Wind	Name	Date
7.88	1.6	Sebrle	3 Jun
7.85	1.0	Ignatov	25 Jul
7.84	0.0	Porter	19 May
7.80		Williams	7 Jun
7.80	1.6	Filíndras	10 May
		7.88w 6.0	22 Apr
7.88w	2.1	Margl	20 May
7.85w	2.9	Ducros	17 Jun

Best at low altitude

Mark	Wind	Name	Date
7.90w	2.4	Lowe	29 Apr
7.86	w	Daniels	25 Mar

JUNIORS

Mark	Wind	Name		Nat	Born	Pos	Meet	Venue	Date
8.00	1.4	Deandre	Free	USA	15.1.81	1		Kansas City MO	29 Apr
7.95	1.3	Yoelmis	Pacheco	CUB	9.6.82	2		La Habana	24 Feb
		7.92 0.2 2	La Habana	11 Feb	7.89	-0.3 2		Camag¨ëy	5 Mar
7.93	0.7		Cai Peng	CHN	28.3.83	2	NGPF	Jinzhou	8 Jun
		7.88 -0.5 1	WJ Santiago	22 Oct	7.87	0.3 2		Shanghai	18 Apr
7.87	1.6	Ibrahim	Camejo	CUB	28.6.82	3		La Habana	11 Feb
7.87		Idika	Uduma	NGR	12.12.82	1		Lagos	22 Jul
7.85		Jonathan	Chimier	MRI	6.8.82	1		Belle Vue Mauricia	11 Mar
		10 performances by six men to 7.85							
7.84	-0.6	Vladimir	Zyuskov	UKR	29.8.81	2	WJ	Santiago de Chile	22 Oct
7.83	0.8	Leevan	Sands	BAH	16.1.81	2	CAC-j	San Juan	14 Jul
7.82	1.6	Ramon	Washington	USA	23.6.81	3	NC-j	Denton	23 Jun
7.77	1.2	Kevone	Fair (10)	USA	24.4.81	1		Miami	13 May
7.77	0.0	Luka	Aracic	CRO	13.3.81	1		Zagreb	29 Jul
7.77	1.2	Leslie	Djhone	FRA	18.3.81	8	NC	Nice	6 Aug
7.77	1.0	Daisuke	Arakawa	JPN	19.9.81	1		Kyoto	26 Aug
7.76	0.6	Cleavon	Dillon	TRI	8.6.82	*	CAC-j	San Juan	14 Jul
7.75		Stéphane	Moreau	FRA	1.9.81	1		Fort-de-France	25 Mar
7.74	1.8	Robert	Kennedy	USA	14.6.81	*	NC-j	Denton	23 Jun
7.74	1.5	Anton	Andersson	SWE	12.3.81	1	NC-j	Västerås	12 Aug
7.73	0.3	Daniel	Kaczmarczyk	POL	28.6.81	*		Biala Podlaska	17 Jun
7.72	1.3	Dimitriy	Sapinskiy	RUS	.83	1	NC-y	Yekaterinburg	20 Jun
7.71		Tommy	Oleksy (20)	USA	26.3.81	2	DrakeR	Des Moines	28 Apr
7.71	1.5		Liang Xin	CHN	20.1.81	1	NC-j	Deyang	16 Jun
7.71	0.5	Víctor	Castillo	VEN	8.6.81	*	CAC-j	San Juan	14 Jul

Wind assisted

Mark	Wind	Name		Nat	Born	Pos	Meet	Venue	Date
8.09	2.9	Cleavon	Dillon	TRI	8.6.82	1	CAC	San Juan	14 Jul
7.88	2.7	Robert	Etheridge	USA	3.4.81	1	NC-j	Denton	23 Jun
7.85	2.2	Robert	Kennedy	USA	14.6.81	2	Pac 10	Eugene	20 May
7.82	3.4	Leslie	Djhone	FRA	18.3.81	2		Luminy	28 Jun
7.82	3.0	Julien	Ruiz	FRA	25.8.82	1		Miramas	2 Jul
7.80	3.0	Luka	Aracic	CRO	13.3.81	3		Ljubljana	25 Jul
7.79	2.1	Thiago	Dias	BRA	2.3.84	4	NC	Rio de Janeiro	3 Aug
7.78	2.8	Daniel	Kaczmarczyk	POL	28.6.81	2		Biala Podlaska	17 Jun
7.77	4.0	Roy	Williams	USA	.81?	1		Austin	13 May
7.77	2.8	Víctor	Castillo	VEN	8.6.81	3	CAC-j	San Juan	14 Jul
7.74	2.6	Blair	Woodward	USA	16.5.81	4	NC-j	Denton	23 Jun
7.73	2.4	Tommy	Oleksy	USA	26.3.81	2cB	TexR	Austin	7 Apr

TRIPLE JUMP

Mark	Wind	Name		Nat	Born	Pos	Meet	Venue	Date
17.71	0.2	Jonathan	Edwards	GBR	10.5.66	1	OG	Sydney	25 Sep

						17.12	17.37/1.2	17.71	17.06	p	x
17.62	1.4	1		Leverkusen	20 Aug	x	17.62	p	p	p	p
17.48	0.6	1	GP II	Gateshead	28 Aug	16.52	x	16.37	x	17.48	p
17.36	0.2	1	WK	Zürich	11 Aug	x	17.27	17.36	16.81	p	p
17.34	0.2	1	BrGP	London (CP)	5 Aug	17.34	17.23	p	p	p	p

Mark	Wind	Name		Nat	Born	Pos	Meet	Venue		Date
Edwards	17.32	1.2 1 Super	Yokohama	9 Sep	17.27	17.32	p	p	p	p
	17.23	1.5 1	Fana	27 Jun	17.23	14.73	x	17.05w	x	16.70
	17.20	1.8 1	Tallahassee	13 May						
17.60	1.9	Fabrizio	Donato	ITA	14.8.76	1		Milano		7 Jun
					13.87	16.79	17.23w	17.09	17.60	x
17.47	0.1	Yoel	García	CUB	25.11.73	2	OG	Sydney		25 Sep
					17.15	17.19	17.19	x	16.70	17.47
	17.24w	1	La Habana	26 Feb	x	17.09w	x	17.24w	p	p
17.46	0.3	Denis	Kapustin	RUS	5.10.70	3	OG	Sydney		25 Sep
					x	17.46	16.73	17.17	x	17.06
	17.24	0.4 1 NC	Tula	24 Jul	15.88w	17.00	17.24	p	x	p
17.45	1.5	Paolo	Camossi	ITA	6.1.74	2		Milano		7 Jun
					16.65	16.59	17.11	x	16.89	17.45
17.41	0.6	Charles	Friedek	GER	26.8.71	1		Wesel		12 Jun
					x	17.41	x	x	17.40/1.1	x
	17.31	-0.2 2 WK	Zürich	11 Aug	x	16.87	16.86	x	x	17.31
	17.29	1.5 3	Milano	7 Jun	x	17.29	x	p	p	x
	17.28i	- 1 EI	Gent	27 Feb	16.25	16.93	17.28	x	x	x
	17.21	0.4 1 Live	Nürnberg	25 Jun	16.85	17.03	p	p	x	17.21
	17.20	-0.1 1 ISTAF	Berlin	1 Sep	16.84	17.20	x	x	x	x
17.37	0.3	Yoelbi	Quesada	CUB	4.8.73	4	OG	Sydney		25 Sep
					17.19	x	x	x	x	17.37
17.30	0.4	Rostislav	Dimitrov	BUL	29.12.74	1	DNG	Stockholm		1 Aug
					16.91	17.30	x	p	x	17.08
	17.25	-0.3 1 GGala	Roma	30 Jun	17.25	x	16.62	16.58	p	p
	17.22i	- 2 EI	Gent	27 Feb	x	17.22	16.66	x	x	17.14
17.30	1.0	Larry	Achike	GBR	31.1.75	q	OG	Sydney		23 Sep
					16.71	17.30		two only		
	17.29	0.5 5 OG	Sydney	25 Sep	17.29	x	x	x	17.00	x
	17.16	0.3 1	Zagreb	3 Jul	16.52	17.11	x	16.77	16.93	17.16
17.26	-0.3	Michael	Calvo	CUB	26.12.77	1		La Habana		17 Jun
					16.58	16.78	17.26	17.04	17.05	x
	17.14	0.5 1 NC	La Habana	25 Jul	16.51	17.03	17.11	16.79	17.14	16.83
17.22	2.0	Kenta	Bell	USA	16.3.77	1		Natchitoches		28 Apr
17.18	1.8	Konstadínos	Zalaggítis	GRE	13.12.80	*	NC-23	Kastoriá		5 Aug
					16.66	17.05w	17.18	17.21w	x	x
		(30/12)								
17.12	-1.6	René	Hernández	CUB	18.5.77	1		La Habana		18 Feb
17.12	-0.6	Phillips	Idowu	GBR	30.12.78	q	OG	Sydney		23 Sep
17.12	1.2	Andrew	Murphy	AUS	18.12.69	q	OG	Sydney		23 Sep
17.09i	–	Gennadiy	Markov	RUS	15.6.67	1		Samara		30 Jan
17.08	-1.9	Aliecer	Urrutia	CUB	22.9.74	2		La Habana		18 Feb
17.07	0.3	Walter	Davis	USA	2.7.79	1		Baton Rouge		19 May
17.06	1.8	Zsolt	Czingler	HUN	28.4.71	1	NC	Budapest		30 Jul
17.05Ai	–	Brian	Wellman	BER	8.9.67	1		USAF Academy		19 Feb
		(20)								
17.05	0.5	Robert	Howard	USA	26.11.75	7	OG	Sydney		25 Sep
17.03	1.8	Oleg	Sakirkin	KAZ	23.1.66	1		Bangkok		18 May
17.02	2.0	Takanori	Sugibayashi	JPN	14.3.76	1	Nambu	Sapporo		16 Jul
17.01	1.5	Stamátios	Lénis	GRE	11.10.77	3	ECp-S	Gateshead		15 Jul
17.01	0.8	Sergey	Izmaylov	UKR	1.5.75	1	NC	Kiev		6 Aug
17.00i	–	LeVar	Anderson	USA	26.3.77	1		BatonRouge		15 Jan
17.00	0.7	Colomba	Fofana	FRA	11.4.77	1		Castres		27 Jul
16.98	1.0	Rogel	Nachum	ISR	21.5.67	1	Veniz	Haniá		14 Jun
16.97	1.9	Christian	Olsson	SWE	25.1.80	1	NC	Uppsala		20 Aug
16.96	0.4	Melvin	Lister	USA	29.8.77	1	NCAA	Durham		2 Jun
		(30)								
16.96	-0.6	LaMark	Carter	USA	23.8.70	2	NC	Sacramento		23 Jul
16.95i	–	Jérôme	Romain	FRA	12.6.71	3		Fayetteville		12 Feb
16.95	0.0	Julian	Golley	GBR	12.9.71	2	GP II	Zagreb		3 Jul
16.95	1.4	Johan	Meriluoto	FIN	22.3.74	1	Nurmi	Turku		2 Aug
16.93	1.2	Sergey	Kochkin	RUS	1.7.70	3	GP II	Zagreb		3 Jul
16.91	1.8	Ivailo	Rusenov	BUL	9.9.79	1		Sofia		3 Jun
16.91	1.0		Lao Jianfeng	CHN	24.5.75	1	OT	Jinzhou		7 Jun
16.90	0.1	Sergey	Arzamasov	KAZ	9.4.71	1		Almaty		27 May
16.89			Gu Junjie	CHN-J	5.5.85	1		Dalian		25 Aug
16.87	1.5	Kenny	Boudine	FRA	25.1.73	1		Forbach		10 Jun
		(40)								
16.86i	–	Igor	Spasovkhodskiy	RUS	1.8.79	1	NC	Volgograd		5 Feb

Mark	Wind	Name		Nat	Born	Pos	Meet	Venue	Date
16.85i		Igor	Gavrilenko	RUS	26.7.76	1		Volgograd	17 Dec
16.82i	–	Vyacheslav	Taranov	RUS	20.3.75	3		Samara	30 Jan
16.82	1.7	Yoandri	Betanzos	CUB-J	15.2.82	2		La Habana	17 Jun
16.80	1.4	Vladimir	Kravchenko	UKR	22.12.69	1		Kiev	16 Jun
16.80	0.8	Alexander	Martínez	CUB	23.8.77	1		La Habana	24 Jun
16.80	0.8	Leonard	Cobb	USA	20.1.75	4	NC	Sacramento	23 Jul
16.79	1.9	Yevgeniy	Timofeyev	RUS	22.2.74	2	NCp	Tula	4 Jun
16.79	0.2	Ketill	Hanstveit	NOR	2.11.73	4	WK	Zürich	11 Aug
16.78	0.0	Rodrigo	Mendes	BRA	21.6.68	1		São Paulo	6 May
		(50)							
16.78	0.8	Ionut	Punga	ROM	14.10.79	1	NC	Bucuresti	6 Aug
16.77	1.9	Galin	Georgiev	BUL	23.3.70	1		Sofia	24 Jun
16.76	0.4	Nikolay	Raev	BUL	29.1.71	1		Sofia	10 Jun
16.75	0.7	Andrey	Kurennoy	RUS	12.5.72	2	Mos Ch	Moskva	12 Jul
16.74i	–	Ambrus	Szabó	HUN	8.4.77	1	NC	Budapest	13 Feb
16.74	-1.0	Samuel	Douglas	CUB	18.6.77	3		La Habana	18 Feb
16.74	0.7	Andrew	Owusu	GHA	8.7.72	1		Göteborg	3 Aug
16.73	0.5	Andrey	Trots	UKR	17.1.78	2	NC	Kiev	6 Aug
16.72	-0.2	Vitaliy	Moskalenko	RUS	30.6.74	5	NC	Tula	24 Jul
16.71	0.7	Maksim	Smetanin	KGZ	17.2.74	1	NC	Bishkek	1 Jul
		(60)							
16.70A	1.3	Raúl	Chapado	ESP	4.5.70	1		Avila	12 Aug
16.69	0.7	Samuel	Okantey	GHA	3.11.74	2	AfrC	Alger	10 Jul
16.69	1.9	Sébastien	Pincemail	FRA	21.2.79	3		Montauban	15 Aug
16.68	1.9	Sérgio	dos Santos	BRA	13.5.76	1	NC	Rio de Janeiro	5 Aug
16.68	0.5	Jimmy	Gabriel	FRA	19.10.73	1	NC	Nice	5 Aug
16.68	1.4	Hrístos	Melétoglou	GRE	2.1.72	1		Pátra	2 Sep
16.68	0.0	Aleksandr	Glavatskiy	BLR	2.5.70	3	GP II	Rieti	3 Sep
16.67i		Igor	Sautkin	RUS	23.2.72	6		Samara	30 Jan
16.67	2.0	Yevgeniy	Petin	UZB	29.1.75	4	MosCh	Moskva	12 Jul
16.65i		Vasil	Gergov	BUL	1.7.77	7		Samara	30 Jan
		(70)							
16.64	-4.5	Etién	Hernández	CUB	19.8.79	4		La Habana	18 Feb
16.64	0.4	Zoran	Djurdjevic	YUG	3.4.68	1		Beograd	4 Jun
16.63	1.3	Chris	Hercules	USA	14.5.79	1		Coral Gables	18 Mar
16.63	1.5	Marcus	Thomas	USA	22.3.79	1	SEC	Baton Rouge	14 May
16.62i		Djeke	Mambo	BEL	4.3.77	1	NC	Gent	6 Feb
16.62	2.0	Richard	Duncan	CAN	25.12.73	1cB	TexR	Austin	7 Apr
16.62	-0.3	Clifton	Etheridge	USA	4.1.69	5	NC	Sacramento	23 Jul
16.62	1.1	Karl	Taillepierre	FRA	13.8.76	5		Castres	27 Jul
16.61i		Jason	Ward	USA-J	6.4.81	2	NCAA	Fayetteville	11 Mar
16.61	-0.3	Karsten	Richter	GER	25.7.72	1		Garbsen	3 Jun
		(80)							
16.58i		Tibor	Ordina	HUN	17.3.71	1		Budapest	22 Jan
16.57	0.7	Audrius	Raizgys	LTU	4.4.69	1	ECp2A	Kaunas	9 Jul
16.56i		Viktor	Gushchinskiy	RUS	12.8.78	3	NC	Volgograd	5 Feb
16.55	0.2		Lee Kang-min	KOR	26.5.80	1	NG	Pusan	13 Oct
16.54	0.7	Jacek	Kazimierowski	POL	2.7.74	1		Siedlce	25 Jun
16.54	1.6	Yevgeniy	Plotnir	RUS	.77	6	MosCh	Moskva	12 Jul
16.53		Dmitriy	Vasilyev	BLR	27.10.76	1	NC	Brest	1 Aug
16.53	0.4	Nattaporn	Nomkanha	THA	15.9.71	1	AsiC	Jakarta	29 Aug
16.52		Tim	Rusan	USA	25.6.77	1c2	PennR	Philadelphia	29 Apr
16.52A		Remmy	Limo	KEN	25.8.71	1	NC	Nairobi	20 Jul
		(90)							
16.52	0.6	Hrvoje	Verzi	GER	12.11.70	2	NC	Braunschweig	30 Jul
16.51	-0.9	Allen	Mortimer	BAH	1.9.77	1	NC	Nassau	22 Jul
16.50	-2.0	Salem Mouled	Al-Ahmadi	KSA	12.9.69	1	GulfCh	Al-Kuwait	20 Apr
16.50	-0.5	Olivier	Sanou	BKF	2.1.75	1		Dakar	22 Apr
16.50A		Paul	Koech	KEN	.69	2	NC	Nairobi	20 Jul
16.49	0.4	Marian	Oprea	ROM-J	6.6.82	1		Bucuresti	25 Jun
16.49	-0.1	Jirí	Kuntos	CZE	2.10.73	1	NC	Plzen	15 Jul
16.49	1.4	Von	Ware	USA	30.6.75	Q	NC	Sacramento	21 Jul
16.48i		Ronald	Servius	FRA	21.2.76	3	NC	Liévin	19 Feb
16.48	?	Jadel	Gregório	BRA	16.9.80	1	Silva	São Paulo	11 Jun
		(100)							

16.47		Mohammed Hamdi	Awadh	QAT-J	.81	20 Apr
16.47	1.2	Ndabazihle	Mdhlongwa	ZIM	30.5.73	21 Apr
16.47	0.3		Zou Sixin	CHN	5.8.67	10 May
16.47	0.9	Ike	Olekaibe	USA	2.2.78	2 Jun
16.47	0.2	Vasiliy	Sokov	RUS	7.4.68	22 Jul
16.46	0.8	Rustam	Khusnutdinov	UZB	14.11.75	1 Jul
16.44i		Greg	Yeldell	USA	14.10.80	11 Mar
16.44	1.9	Maksim	Ivanov	RUS	.77	12 Jul
16.41i		Andrey	Zirko	BLR	1.7.72	11 Feb
16.41	0.3	Takashi	Komatsu	JPN	30.12.67	7 May

MEN 2000

Mark	Wind	Name		Nat	Born	Date
16.40i		Jim	McCann	USA	2.11.72	3 Mar
16.40i		Robert	Johnson	USA	20.9.73	3 Mar
16.40	-0.3		Duan Qifeng	CHN	20.1.73	26 Mar
16.40	1.2	Luciano	Rigo	ITA	12.7.73	4 Jun
16.40	1.4	Francis	Agyepong	GBR	16.6.65	13 Aug
16.39i		Gregor	Cankar	SLO	25.1.75	22 Jan
16.39i		Maksim	Babenko	RUS	20.2.80	25 Jan
16.39i		Sheldon	Hutchinson	JAM	11.2.80	26 Feb
16.39	0.7	Dmitriy	Valyukevich	BLR-J	31.5.81	19 Oct
16.38i		Rich	Thompson	USA	16.6.69	3 Mar
16.38	-0.6	Pavel	Laza	CUB-J	.81	17 Jun
16.37	0.9	Denis	Saurambayev	KAZ	30.6.77	1 Jul
16.37	1.1	Daniel	Donovici	ROM	5.3.80	6 Aug
16.36	1.0	Del	Smutherman	USA	21.4.72	26 Mar
16.36	0.3		Zhang Jun	CHN	10.5.73	10 May
16.33	1.7	Arnis	Filet	FRA	17.12.77	27 Jul
16.32i		Yeóryios	Stáikos	GRE	14.6.75	15 Jan
16.32	1.0	Armen	Martirosyan	ARM	6.8.69	9 Jul
16.31	0.3	Sergey	Bochkov	AZE	20.8.79	4 Jun
16.31	-0.1	Aleksandr	Aseledchenko	RUS	18.10.73	9 Jul
16.31	1.4	Nicholas	Thomas	GBR	4.4.79	22 Jul
16.31	0.0	Nikolay	Savolaynen	UKR	25.3.80	6 Aug
16.30i		Bostjan	Simunic	SLO	28.12.74	5 Feb
16.30	0.2	Natale	Monopoli	ITA	21.3.67	7 Jun
		(134)				

Wind assisted

Mark	Wind	Name		Nat	Born	Pos	Meet	Venue	Date
17.31	4.4	Larry	Achike	GBR	31.1.75	1	ECp-S	Gateshead	15 Jul
					16.55	16.91	17.31w	16.72	fouonly
17.21	2.2	Konstadínos	Zalaggítis	GRE	15.12.80	1	NC-23	Kastoriá	5 Aug
17.20	2.3	Stamatis	Lénis	GRE	11.7.78	1		Istanbul	24 Jun
					16.69	17.20w	x	16.79w 16.30	16.84w
17.09A	2.9	Brian	Wellman	BER	8.9.67	1		El Paso	15 Apr
17.08	5.2	Walter	Davis	USA	2.7.79	1cA	TexR	Austin	8 Apr
16.97	2.7	LaMark	Carter	USA	23.8.70	1		Baton Rouge	15 Apr
16.88	2.1	Ketill	Hanstveit	NOR	2.11.73	2	MAI	Malmö	7 Aug
16.81	2.7	Greg	Yeldell	USA	14.10.80	1	Big10	Iowa City	21 May
16.80	3.2	Jimmy	Gabriel	FRA	19.10.73	2		Montauban	15 Aug
16.78	2.2	Andrew	Owusu	GHA	8.7.72	3	MAI	Malmö	7 Aug
16.75	3.7	Hrvoje	Verzi	GER	12.11.70	4	ECp-S	Gateshead	15 Jul
16.74A	3.5	Raúl	Chapado	ESP	4.5.70	1		Soria	29 Jul
16.68	4.3	Bostjan	Simunic	SLO	28.12.74	1		Nova Gorica	14 May
16.66	3.9	Etién	Hernández	CUB	19.8.79	3		La Habana	26 Feb
16.60	3.8	Ike	Olekaibe	NGR	2.2.78	2	Big 10	Iowa City	21 May
16.59	2.3	Jirí	Kuntos	CZE	2.10.73	2	ECp1A	Nadderud	9 Jul
16.57		Von	Ware	USA	30.6.75	1		Fullerton	27 Apr
16.56	2.7	Lenton	Herring	USA	4.12.78	3	Big 10	Iowa City	21 May
16.52	2.6	Bashir	Ramzy	USA	4.5.79	1	USTCA	Baton Rouge	25 Mar
16.52	2.9	Greg	Hughes	BAR		1		Wichita	20 May
16.50	2.5	Arnis	Filet	FRA	17.12.77	2	Conseil	Fort-de-France	29 Apr
16.50	2.2	Richard	Mestre	CUB-J	6.1.81	3		La Habana	17 Jun
16.48	3.1	Abdul	Rasheed	USA	14.11.79	2	KansR	Lawrence KS	22 Apr

Mark	Wind	Name		Nat	Born	Date
16.41	2.5	Tyson	Dillard	USA	11.5.79	28 Apr
16.40	4.5	Femi	Akinsanya	GBR	29.11.69	6 Aug
16.38	3.0	Julien	Kapek	FRA	12.1.79	15 Aug
16.37	3.2	Tosin	Oke	GBR	1.10.80	22 Jul
16.36	3.9	Tomás	Cholensky	CZE	25.4.78	6 Jun
16.35	2.9	Terrance	Woods	USA	18.4.79	24 Mar
16.35	3.4	Tyson	Dillard	USA	11.5.79	16 May
16.32	2.8	Delvit	Rogers	USA	23.3.80	13 May
16.32	4.2	Messias	Baptista	BRA	24.5.68	9 Jul
16.30	5.7	Josh	Rollins	USA		13 May
16.30	3.8	Sergey	Khurbatov	BLR	22.5.79	10 Jun

Best outdoor mark for athlete with best indoors

Mark	Wind	Name	Pos	Meet	Venue	Date
16.98	1.2	Anderson	2		Natchitoches	28 Apr
16.93	2.0	Romain	2		Montauban	15 Aug
16.89	0.2	Markov	2	NC	Tula	24 Jul
16.86	1.2	Spasovkhodskiy	1	Mos Ch	Moskva	12 Jul
16.41	1.4	Mambo	4		Mar	
16.38A	0.0	Thompson				8 Jul
16.82	-1.5	Gavrilenko	4	NC	Tula	22 Jul
16.50	-0.6	Wellman	3		Sydney	14 Sep
16.48	-0.3	Taranov	7	NC	Tula	24 Jul
16.72w	2.2		3	Mos Ch	Moskva	12 Jul
16.54w	2.6	Ward	1	NC-j	Denton	24 Jun

Best at low altitude

16.69i - Chapado 1 NC San Sebastián 12Feb and 16.61 0.6 1 Castellón 23 Aug

JUNIORS

See main list for top 4 juniors. 12 performances by 5 men to 16.41. Additional marks and further juniors:

Name	Mark	Wind	Pos	Meet	Venue	Date	Mark	Wind	Pos	Meet	Venue	Date
Betanzos	16.67	0.3	Q	WJ	Santiago	19 Oct	16.49	0.4	5		La Habana	26 Feb
Gu Junjie	16.81		1		Jinzhou	22 May	16.53	0.9	*	NGPF	Jinzhou	7 Jun
	16.47	0.8	3	Super	Yokohama	9 Sep	16.85W	2.3	2	NGPF	Jinzhou	7 Jun
Oprea	16.48	0.5	2		Bucuresti	6 Aug	16.41	1.9	1	WJ	Santiago	20 Oct

Mark	Wind	Name		Nat	Born	Pos	Meet	Venue	Date
16.47		Mohammed	Hamdi Awadh	QAT	.81	2	GulfCh	Al-Kuwait	20 Apr
16.39	0.7	Dmitriy	Valyukevich	BLR	31.5.81	2q	WJ	Santiago de Chile	19 Oct
16.38	-0.6	Pavel	Laza	CUB	.81	4		Beograd	20 Aug
16.29	1.5	Rudolf	Helpling	GER	23.2.81	2		Schwechat	10 Jun
16.22	0.5	Leevan	Sands	BAH	16.1.81	Q	WJ	Santiago de Chile	19 Oct
16.21	0.2	Ibrahim Moh.	Aboubaker (10)	QAT	10.12.82	6	AsiC	Jakarta	29 Aug
16.19	0.5	Richard	Mestre	CUB	6.1.81	8		La Habana	26 Feb
16.19	0.0	Viktor	Yastrebov	UKR	13.1.82	6	NC	Kiev	6 Aug
16.18	0.3	Dimítrios	Tsiámis	GRE	12.1.82	1	NC-j	Kavála	22 Jul
16.13	0.4	Arvidas	Nazarovas	LTU	17.4.81	6	WJ	Santiago de Chile	20 Oct
16.11	0.2	Allen	Simms	USA	26.7.82	1		Sacramento	10 Jun
16.11	1.4	Marcelo	da Costa	BRA	1.5.81	Q	WJ	Santiago de Chile	19 Oct
16.07	-0.2	Vladimir	Letnicov	MDA	7.10.81	1		Kaunas	9 Jul

Mark	Wind	Name		Nat	Born	Pos	Meet	Venue		Date
16.02	0.1	Jonathan	Moore	GBR	31.5.84	1		Edinburgh		13 Aug
16.00	0.6	Konstantin	Pozatsidi	RUS	.83	1		Vladivostok		20 May
16.00A		Erik	Nurijanian	ARM	19.5.81			Vanadzor		1 Jul
Wind assisted										
16.54	2.6	Jason	Ward	USA	6.4.81	1	NC-j	Denton		24 Jun
16.50	2.2	Richard	Mestre	CUB	6.1.81	3		La Habana		17 Jun
16.27	3.9	Anton	Andersson	SWE	12.3.81	1	v3Nj	Borgarnes		27 Aug
16.22	3.6	Marcelo	da Costa	BRA	1.5.81	1		São Leopoldo		8 Oct
16.21	3.0	Dimítrios	Tsiámis	GRE	12.1.82	2	NC-23	Kastoriá		5 Aug

SHOT

22.12		Adam	Nelson	USA	7.7.75	1	NC	Sacramento		15 Jul
					21.32	20.36	21.06	x	20.87	22.12
	21.94	1	Rüdlingen	13 Aug	20.60	21.94	x	20.54	x	x
	21.70	1	Palo Alto	1 Jul	20.95	x	20.83	21.15	20.89	21.70
	21.66	2 GPF	Doha	5 Oct	21.08	20.57	21.00	21.16	x	21.66
	21.64	1 WK	Zürich	11 Aug	21.64	20.99	21.17	x	21.12	21.46
	21.58	1 VD	Bruxelles	25 Aug	21.58	21.00	x	20.52	20.60	20.82
	21.53	1 MAI	Malmö	7 Aug	20.56	x	20.53	x	21.53	x
	21.43	1 Bisl	Oslo	28 Jul	19.89	20.71	21.02	20.26	21.43	x
	21.40	2 GP	Raleigh	17 Jun	20.50	21.02	21.40	x	21.18	x
	21.21	2 OG	Sydney	22 Sep	20.53	21.20	21.21	x	20.97	x
22.09i		Mika	Halvari	FIN	13.2.70	1		Tampere		7 Feb
					22.09	x	x	p	p	p
	21.29i	1 NC	Kuopio	13 Feb	20.33	21.29	20.39	20.63	x	x
	21.23i	1 v2N	Tampere	20 Feb	21.00	21.23	x	x	x	x
21.87		C.J.	Hunter ¶	USA	14.12.68	2	NC	Sacramento		15 Jul
					21.01	21.10	21.81	21.24	21.22	21.87
	21.86	1 GP	Raleigh	17 Jun	20.88	21.24	21.56	x	21.86	21.06
	21.74	1 MSR	Walnut	16 Apr	21.14	21.00	21.74	21.05	20.97	21.09
	21.49	1	Atlanta	19 May						
	21.38	1 Pre	Eugene	24 Jun	x	21.38	21.25	x	x	x
	21.34	1	Athens, Ga	6 May	21.34	x	x	21.00	x	x
	21.34	1 GGala	Roma	30 Jun	20.83	20.99	x	21.34	x	x
	21.33	1 GP	Osaka	13 May	20.61	20.71	21.02	21.33	20.87	x
	21.26dq	2 Bisl	Oslo	28 Jul	19.60	21.26	21.00	x	20.74	x
21.82		Andy	Bloom	USA	11.8.73	1	GPF	Doha		5 Oct
					19.77	20.86	20.81	20.40	x	21.82
	21.61	3 NC	Sacramento	15 Jul	x	20.01	x	x	19.57	21.61
	21.60i	1 NC	Atlanta	4 Mar	20.50	21.60	x	20.21	x	20.47
	21.43	2	Knoxville	15 Apr	20.15	x	21.15	21.07	x	21.43
21.64		Yuriy	Belonog	UKR	9.3.74	1		Koncha-Zaspa		28 Apr
					21.28	21.64	x	21.26	x	21.13
21.51		John	Godina	USA	31.5.72	3	GPF	Doha		5 Oct
					21.05	21.51	20.97	x	20.76	x
	21.25	1 Gaz	Saint-Denis	23 Jun	21.25	x	20.58	20.68	20.44	x
	21.20	3 OG	Sydney	22 Sep	x	20.40	20.25	20.71	21.20	x
21.46		Kevin	Toth	USA	29.12.67	1	Sea Ray	Knoxville		15 Apr
					19.87	20.91	21.22	21.42	21.46	21.11
21.39		Arsi	Harju	FIN	18.3.74	1	OG	Sydney		22 Sep
					21.20	21.29	20.77	x	20.37	x
	21.29	q OG	Sydney	22 Sep	19.40	21.39		two only		
21.34		Roman	Virastyuk	UKR	20.4.68	1		Ivano-Frankivsk		7 May
					x	20.86	21.04	21.34	x	20.98
21.27i		Aleksandr	Bagach ¶	UKR	21.11.66	1	NC	Brovary		9 Feb
					20.44	20.84	x	21.07	20.92	21.27
		(34/10) plus 1 by C J Hunter after positive drugs test								
20.98		Dennis	Black	USA	4.7.73	1		Missoula		5 May
		20.99 unconfirmed				1		Bozeman		13 May
20.88		Joachim	Olsen	DEN	31.5.77	1	NC	Aalborg		12 Aug
20.78		Alexis	Páumier	CUB	21.1.75	1	Barr	La Habana		29 Jul
20.76i		Gheorghe	Guset	ROM	28.5.68	1		Pireás		9 Feb
20.76		Ville	Tiisanoja	FIN	24.12.75	1		Espoo		12 Aug
20.75		Paolo	Dal Soglio	ITA	29.7.70	1	GP II	Rieti		3 Sep
20.71i		Oliver-Sven	Buder	GER	23.6.66	1		Erfurt		2 Feb
20.70		Timo	Aaltonen	FIN	11.4.69	1		Eurajoki		1 Jul
20.64		Miroslav	Menc	CZE	16.3.71	1		Ostrava		3 Sep
20.60		Shakti	Singh	IND	14.5.62	1		Bangalore		5 Jul
		(20)								

Mark		Name		Nat	Born	Pos	Meet	Venue	Date
20.57i		Mark	Proctor	GBR	15.1.63	1		Birmingham	17 Feb
20.56		Burger	Lambrechts	RSA	3.4.73	1	NC	Stellenbosch	4 Mar
20.55		Manuel	Martínez	ESP	7.12.74	6	OG	Sydney	22 Sep
20.48i		Andrey	Mikhnevich	BLR	12.7.76	1		Minsk	28 Jan
20.35		Milan	Haborák	SVK	11.1.73	1		Funchal	29 Jul
20.35		Justin	Anlezark	AUS	14.8.77	1		Gold Coast (RB)	10 Sep
20.34		Janus	Robberts	RSA	10.3.79	1		Fort Worth	22 Apr
20.31		Jarkko	Haukijärvi	FIN	10.6.77	2		Suodenniemi	26 Aug
20.29		Karel	Potgieter	RSA	21.9.75	1		Varazdin	15 Jul
20.28		Stevimir	Ercegovac	CRO	20.1.74	1		Rijeka	2 Sep
		(30)							
20.26i		Ivan	Yemelyanov	MDA	19.2.77	1		Chisinau	26 Feb
20.26		Chima	Ugwu	NGR	19.7.73	1	NC	Lagos	22 Jul
20.24		Brad	Snyder	CAN	8.1.76	2		Gold Coast (RB)	10 Sep
20.22		Chris	Merced	PUR	26.1.76	1		Irvine	28 May
20.19		John	Davis	USA	19.2.77	q	NC	Sacramento	14 Jul
20.16		Detlef	Bock	GER	15.8.74	1		Halle	27 May
20.12		Jani	Illikainen	FIN	26.1.76	1		Tornio	10 Jun
20.11		Tepa	Reininkainen	FIN	16.3.73	4		Eurajoki	1 Jul
20.10		Saulius	Kleiza	LTU	2.4.64	1		Kaunas	27 Jun
20.09i		Andy	Dittmar	GER	5.7.74	2		Erfurt	2 Feb
		(40)							
20.09		Jim	Roberts	USA	30.12.76	3	NCAA	Durham	1 Jun
20.09		Pavel	Chumachenko	RUS	5.4.71	1	Kuts	Moskva	26 Aug
20.08		Gunnar	Pfingsten	GER	24.3.75	1		Reinheim	30 Apr
20.08i		Jeff	Chakouian	USA-J	20.4.82	1		Lexington	8 Dec
20.07		Jimmy	Nordin	SWE	19.10.79	1	NC	Uppsala	18 Aug
20.03		Carlos	Fandiño	CUB	10.6.69	2	Barr	La Habana	29 Jul
20.03		Sergey	Lyakhov	RUS	1.5.68	2	Kuts	Moskva	26 Aug
20.01		Szilárd	Kiss	HUN	9.12.75	1		Szombathely	23 Jul
20.01		Bahadur	Singh	IND	7.5.73	2	NC	Chennai	29 Jul
20.01		Yoger	Medina	VEN	5.9.73	1		Maracaibo	26 Aug
		(50)							
19.98		Michael	Mertens	GER	27.12.65	1		Braunschweig	2 Jul
19.94		Mikulás	Konopka	SVK	23.1.79	3		Halle	27 May
19.93		Brian	Miller	USA	20.3.72	1		Carbondale	1 Apr
19.92		Sergey	Rubtsov	KAZ	4.9.65	1		Tashkent	15 Jun
19.88		Dragan	Peric	YUG	8.5.64	1	NC	Beograd	19 Aug
19.82		Yosvany	Obregón	CUB	3.11.72	3	Barr	La Habana	29 Jul
19.81i		Brad	Mears	USA	24.12.70	1		USAF Academy	29 Jan
19.79		Reese	Hoffa	USA	8.10.77	3	NCAA	Durham	1 Jun
19.76i		Josh	Hagedorn	USA	30.4.73	1		Ames	12 Feb
19.75		Vasiliy	Virastyuk	UKR	22.4.74	2		Ivano-Frankivsk	7 May
		(60)							
19.72		Mark	Edwards	GBR	2.12.74	1		Brighton	16 Aug
19.68i		Jason	Gervais	CAN	18.1.76	1		USAF Academy	26 Feb
19.68		Richard	Harrison	USA	13.5.70	1		Albuquerque	9 Jul
19.67		Christian	Cantwell	USA	30.9.80	1	Big12	Columbia	20 May
19.62		Leszek	Sliwa	POL	20.9.79	1		Bydgoszcz	8 Jul
19.58		Marcus	Clavelle	USA	23.6.78	1		Fayetteville	22 Apr
19.56		Petr	Stehlik	CZE	15.4.77	2	NC	Praha	15 Jul
19.55		Andrey	Nemchaninov	RUS	27.11.66	4		Koncha-Zaspa	28 Apr
19.50		Ben	Lindsey	USA	5.10.77	1	Pac 10	Eugene	20 May
19.50		Jarred	Rome	USA	21.12.76	2	NAm25	Monterrey	3 Aug
		(70)							
19.48		Rutger	Smith	NED-J	9.7.81	1	WJ	Santiago de Chile	19 Oct
19.46		Conny	Karlsson	FIN	30.12.75	4cA		Hämeenkyrö	22 Jul
19.46		Zsolt	Bíber	HUN	31.5.76	1	NC	Budapest	29 Jul
19.46		Michael	Lischka	GER	23.12.73			Fränkisch-Crumbach	3 Sep
19.41	?	David	Rodely	USA	7.6.68	1		Jonesboro	14 Jun
		18.69				3		Atlanta	19 May
19.40		Bilal Saad	Mubarak	QAT	18.12.72	1		Schapbach	22 Jul
19.35		Anders	Holmström	SWE	23.8.78	1	Big 10	Iowa City	21 May
19.34		Ralf	Bartels	GER	21.2.78	2		Wipperfürth	13 Aug
19.32		Jason	Hammond	USA	20.5.78	2		Laramie	25 Apr
19.32		Andreas	Vlasny	AUT	12.9.69	1		Linz	12 Aug
		(80)							
19.31		Pavol	Pankúch	SVK	20.2.75	1		Nitra	31 Jul
19.31		Váios	Tíggas	GRE	16.10.78	1		Thessaloníki	30 Aug
19.30		Aleksandr	Salnikov	RUS	.71	1		Cheboksary	20 May

Mark	Name		Nat	Born	Pos	Meet	Venue	Date
19.28i	Ian	Waltz	USA	15.4.77	1		Moscow, ID	4 Mar
19.27	Ivan	Yushkov	RUS-J	15.1.81	1		Krasnodar	16 Sep
19.24	Gjøran	Sørli	NOR	3.6.78	1		Oslo	23 Jun
19.22	Josef	Rosúlek	CZE	6.2.71	1		Praha	13 May
19.22	Yves	Niaré	FRA	20.7.77	1		Vanves	30 Jun
19.19	René	Sack	GER	14.7.76	3	OD	Jena	3 Jun
19.18i	Corrado	Fantini	ITA	7.2.67	1		Torino	29 Jan
	(90)							
19.16i	Sören	Tallhem	SWE	16.2.64	1		Sätra	12 Feb
19.15	Tonyo	Sylvester	USA	17.12.67	1		New Haven	30 Apr
19.12	Fernando	Alves	POR	24.6.67	1		Lisboa (U)	7 May
19.12	Pavel	Lyzhin	BLR-J	24.3.81			Brest	24 Aug
19.10	Steve	Albert	USA	1.4.64			Warrensburg	2 Jun
19.10	Dirk	Urban	GER	14.1.69	1		Lübeck	17 Jun
19.07	Alessandro	Andrei	ITA	3.1.59	2		Pescara	23 Jul
19.06	Margus	Tammaru	EST	24.8.71	2		Kaunas	20 Aug
19.05i	Doug	Reynolds	USA	11.8.75	1		Pocatello	15 Jan
19.05	Van	Mounts	USA	5.1.80	2	Pac 10	Eugene	20 May
	(100)							
19.05	Michalis	Louca	CYP	23.2.70	1		Nicosia	23 Jun

19.04i	Marco	Dodoni	ITA	5.9.72	26 Jan
19.04	Stefan	Blomqvist	SWE	7.2.65	21 Oct
19.01	Andrey	Borodkin	UKR	18.4.78	15 Jul
19.01	Sergio	Mottin	ITA	15.6.76	10 Sep
19.00	Andreas	Deuschle	GER	11.2.68	10 Jun
19.00	Dmitriy	Goncharuk	BLR	17.7.70	1 Aug
19.00	Tomasz	Chrzanowski	POL-J	12.7.81	19 Oct
18.99	Stéphane	Vial	FRA	9.2.73	27 Jul
18.99	Arpad	Sinko	YUG	30.10.77	28 Jun
18.98	Drazen	Kuljic	YUG	10.5.72	3 Jun
18.97i		Wen Jili	CHN	11.7.73	24 Feb
18.96	Mark	Hoxmeier	USA	16.7.79	19 May
18.96	Sergiu	Ursu	MDA	26.4.80	10 Jun
18.94		Wen Jili	CHN	11.7.73	7 Jun
18.93	Giovanni	Tubini	ITA	9.4.64	16 Jun
18.92i	Jamie	Beyer	USA	29.12.76	26 Feb
18.92		Zhong Fengzhu	CHN	24.7.79	29 Apr
18.92	Thorsten	Herbrand	GER	9.4.70	27 Jun
18.91	Dave	Stoute	TRI	27.3.78	3 Aug
18.90	Scott	Denbo	USA	2.6.78	20 May
18.89	Matt	Godbehere	USA	24.9.71	19 Feb
18.88	Aaron	Neighbour	AUS	2.12.77	24 Jun
18.86		Liu Hao	CHN	28.11.68	9 May
18.84i	Attila	Pintér	HUN	31.1.77	12 Feb
18.83i	Billy	Bush	USA	21.7.77	25 Feb
18.83	Yuriy	Belov	BLR-J	20.3.81	19 Oct
18.82	Iker	Sukía	ESP	24.1.78	15 Jul
18.82	Kristian	Pettersson	SWE	5.10.71	26 Aug
18.80	Ole	Hertel	GER	12.7.73	27 Jun
18.79	Stephan	Hayward	GBR	30.7.74	6 Sep
18.78	Giorgio	Venturi	ITA	23.6.66	28 Jun
18.78	Raphaël	Cécé	FRA	7.7.60	30 Jun
18.78	Teijo	Kööpikkä	FIN	7.10.80	26 Jul
18.78	Jaiveer	Singh	IND		12 Aug
18.78	Andreas	Anastasópoulos	GRE	2.4.76	30 Aug
18.77i	Ray	Wilks	USA	15.8.77	8 Jan
18.77	David	Estes	USA		18 Mar
18.76	Edhem	Kacevic	BIH	20.11.70	1 May
18.76	Przemyslaw	Zabawski	POL	8.4.75	17 Jun
	18.80 exhibition				17 Aug
18.75i	Mario	Pestano	ESP	8.4.78	15 Jan
18.75i	Aléxios	Leonídis	GRE	8.12.68	29 Jan
18.70i	Jeremy	Allen	USA	5.9.79	26 Feb
18.69	Andreas	Gustafsson	SWE	2.7.75	21 Jul
18.64	Vitaliy	Sidorov	RUS	23.3.70	26 Jul
18.60	Allen	Babayan	USA	14.11.71	1 Jul
18.59	Ahmed Hassab	Gholoum	KUW	31.5.80	20 Apr
18.59	Rocky	Vaïtanacki	FRA	7.4.73	1 Jun
18.57		Wang Zhiyong	CHN	3.1.79	29 Apr
18.57	Paolo	Capponi	ITA	25.3.76	4 Aug
18.56i	Ryan	Speers	USA	6.12.79	18 Feb
18.56i	Chris	Spurrier	USA	26.5.77	18 Feb
18.56	Alexander	Forst	GER	11.6.75	19 May
18.56	Wim	Blondeel	BEL	25.12.73	17 Jun
18.56	Sebastian	Wenta	POL	4.5.75	7 Oct
18.54i	Manuel	Brändeborn	SWE	7.4.73	23 Jan
18.53	Janne	Alakumpula	FIN	6.6.74	11 Jul
18.51	Jean-Louis	Lebon	FRA	13.6.67	22 Jul
18.51	Mikko	Rönkkö	FIN	29.3.78	5 Aug
18.51	Zsolt	Németh	HUN	9.11.71	19 Aug
18.50	Clay	Cross	AUS	26.11.77	13 Feb
18.50	Marc	Sandmeier	SUI	6.6.73	1 Jul
18.47i		Qu Yongzhao	CHN	27.4.77	24 Feb
18.46	Borivoje	Stanic	YUG	2.10.74	29 Aug
18.45	Edson	Miguel	BRA	11.4.65	29 Apr
18.45i	Chris	Adams	USA	.78	9 Dec
18.44	Matt	Eicholtz	USA	14.12.75	3 Jun
18.43i	Aaron	Banks	USA	11.11.73	29 Jan
18.42	Frits	Potgieter	RSA	13.3.74	4 Mar
18.42	Pavel	Sofyin	RUS-J	4.9.81	16 Sep
18.41	Ian	Douglas	USA	23.3.79	13 May
18.40	Dan	Ames	USA-J	16.1.81	20 May
18.39i	Håkan	Andersson	SWE	19.9.76	25 Feb
18.39	Okechukwu	Eziuka	NGR	.78	13 May
18.39	Jan	Sagedal	NOR	19.6.60	13 Aug
18.38i	Jaan	Talts	EST	18.6.75	16 Feb
18.36	Dmitriy	Kruchenok	BLR	7.4.79	3 Jun
18.36	Jhonny	Rodríguez	COL	12.11.79	11 Aug
18.35i	Yevgeniy	Palchikov	RUS	27.4.68	22 Jan
18.34	Jon	Mayhew	USA	7.4.77	22 Apr
18.34	Daniel	Jonsson	SWE	11.4.74	27 May
18.34	Steffen	Beck	GER	22.10.70	20 Jul
18.32i	Vladimir	Lukovkin	RUS	8.3.74	22 Jan
18.30	Oliver	Dück	GER	10.2.67	24 Jun
18.29	Robert	Garza	USA		15 Apr
18.29	Yasutada	Noguchi	JPN	11.8.76	13 May
18.29	Mikhail	Zabruskov	RUS	26.1.74	26 Jul
18.29i	Peter	Sack	GER	27.7.79	2 Dec
18.28	John	Dermody	IRL	30.8.73	21 May
18.28	Igor	Cagigas	ESP	1.2.77	8 Aug
18.28	Jakob	Vujcic	AUS	8.8.73	12 Aug
18.27A	Roelof	Potgieter	RSA	20.3.80	14 Apr
18.27		Li Wenkui	CHN	31.12.71	9 May
18.27	Alberto	Viejo	ESP	19.5.76	12 Aug
18.26	Yevgeniy	Kozlov	RUS	.78	20 Jun
18.26	Jaroslaw	Cichocki	POL-J	28.7.82	19 Oct
18.25	Ghufran	Hussain	PAK	1.7.69	21 May
18.23i	Piotr	Perzylo	POL	15.11.61	13 Feb
18.23	Rhys	Jones	AUS-J	19.3.81	3 Sep
18.22	Mukesh Singh	Kumar	IND		30 Oct
18.20	Khalid Salman	Al-Khalidi	KSA	14.2.65	20 Apr
	(201)				

Best outdoor marks for athlete with best indoors

21.04	Halvari	1	GPII	Helsinki	15 Jun
20.66	Guset	1		Poiana Brasov	22 Jul
20.41	Buder	1	NC	Braunschweig	30 Jul
20.12	Mikhnevich	1	NC	Brest	1 Aug
20.11	Proctor	1		Vila Real S.António	25 Mar
19.49	Gervais	1		Albuquerque	5 May

Mark		Name	Nat	Born	Pos	Meet	Venue	Date

19.26 Dittmar 3 NC Braunschweig 30 Jul | 19.13 Waltz 1 Tucson 17 Mar

19.14 Hagedorn 1 Lincoln NE 8 Apr | 19.05 Yemelyanov 2 Bucuresti 6 Aug

19.03	Dodoni	27 Jun	18.89	Chakouian	19 Oct	18.55	Allen	6 May	18.41	Bush	1 Apr
18.99	Mears	29 Apr	18.75	Pintér	16 Jun	18.50	Beyer	20 May	18.35	Qu Yongzhao	18 Apr
18.94	Wen Jili	7 Jun	18.66	Tallhem	20 May	18.49	Spurrier	14 Apr	18.26	Banks	14 Jul

Unsanctioned meeting

19.66	Aaron	Neighbour	AUS	2.12.77	1		Melbourne	16 Aug

Following drugs suspension

20.92	Aleksandr	Bagach ¶	UKR	21.11.66	2		Koncha-Zaspa	28 Apr
19.71i	Carl	Myerscough ¶	GBR	21.10.79	1		Lincoln NE	12 Feb

JUNIORS

20.08i	Jeff	Chakouian	USA	20.4.82	1		Lexington	8 Dec
	18.89				5	WJ	Santiago de Chile	19 Oct
19.48	Rutger	Smith	NED	9.7.81	1	WJ	Santiago de Chile	19 Oct
	19.31 1 Hioversum 10 Sep				19.18 1 NA		Heusden	5 Aug
	19.22 1 v2N Magglingen 1 Jul							
19.27	Ivan	Yushkov	RUS	15.1.81	1		Krasnodar	16 Sep
	19.06 2 WJ Santiago de Chile 19 Oct							
19.12	Pavel	Lyzhin	BLR	24.3.81			Brest	24 Aug
	19.00 4 WJ Santiago de Chile 19 Oct				10 performances by five men to 19.00			
19.00	Tomasz	Chrzanowski	POL	12.7.81	3	WJ	Santiago de Chile	19 Oct
18.83	Yuriy	Belov	BLR	20.3.81	6	WJ	Santiago de Chile	19 Oct
18.42	Pavel	Sofyin	RUS	4.9.81	2		Krasnodar	16 Sep
18.40	Dan	Ames	USA	16.1.81			Los Angeles	20 Ma
18.26	Jaroslaw	Cichocki	POL	28.7.82	8	WJ	Santiago de Chile	19 Oct
18.23	Rhys	Jones (10)	AUS	19.3.81	2		Brisbane	3 Sep
18.19	Nedzad	Mulabegovic	CRO	4.2.81	1		Rijeka	7 Sep
18.12	Mihaíl	Stamatóyiannis	GRE	20.5.82	9	WJ	Santiago de Chile	19 Oct
18.03	Kuldeep	Singh Mann	IND	16.10.82	4	Inter-St	Chennai	29 Jul
17.77	Tomasz	Majewski	POL	30.8.81	2		Bialystok	1 Sep
17.76	Josh	Sides	USA	14.4.81	6		Moscow ID	20 Ma
17.67	Ivan	Lesetskiy	BLR	.81	6		Brest	24 Aug
17.60	Scott	Martin	AUS	12.10.82	11	WJ	Santiago de Chile	19 Oct
17.59		Cong Wei	CHN	20.4.83	7	NGP	Tianjin	3 May
17.47	John	Sullivan	RSA	12.2.81	1		Pretoria	17 Sep
17.38		Dong Enxin (20)	CHN	22.2.81	2	NC	Singapore	9 Sep

DISCUS

73.88	Virgilijus		Alekna	LTU	13.2.72	1	NC	Kaunas			3 Aug
					70.22	72.35	69.26	73.88	x	x	
71.12	1	WK	Zürich	11 Aug	70.26	68.55	68.68	70.42	70.60	71.12	
70.39	1	Sule	Tartu	11 Jun	68.34	70.06	68.99	70.39	68.30	x	
69.74	1		Chemnitz	22 Jul	67.82	67.55	64.08	69.74	67.92	68.07	
69.70	2	ISTAF	Berlin	1 Sep	65.16	64.35	69.70	69.42	68.64	68.94	
69.41	1	Live	Nürnberg	25 Jun	x	64.44	67.35	67.74	69.41	68.39	
69.30	1	OG	Sydney	25 Sep	58.55	67.54	68.73	66.64	69.30	64.78	
68.60	1		Turnov	21 May	64.27	64.09	68.60	66.57	65.27	?	
68.48	1		Dortmund	8 Jul	67.75	65.80	67.03	64.53	68.48	65.54	
68.29	1	ECp2A	Kaunas	9 Jul	65.75	65.20	65.09	68.29	four only		
68.21	1		Barcelona	25 Jul	66.34	66.22	67.28	67.41	x	68.21	
68.06	1	VD	Bruxelles	25 Aug	x	63.76	68.06	65.20	67.96	x	
67.80	1	MSR	Walnut	16 Apr	67.12	65.70	x	65.46	67.80	64.60	
67.27	1	OD	Jena	3 Jun	62.97	x	67.27	x	63.62	64.92	
67.13	1		Milano	7 Jun	66.81	67.13	65.91	x	66.84	x	
67.10	q	OG	Sydney	24 Sep	67.10	only					
67.02A	1		Potchefstroom	14 Feb	64.16	64.91	x	65.63	67.02	x	
69.75 A	Frantz		Kruger	RSA	22.5.75	1		Bloemfontein			15 Sep
					x	69.75	x	x	p	p	
68.19	3	OG	Sydney	25 Sep	67.89	x	68.19	68.06	x	62.72	
68.13	1		Cottbus	20 Aug	61.06	66.87	65.64	68.13	x	65.65	
67.81	2	WK	Zürich	11 Aug	66.01	67.11	67.81	64.54	66.90	67.09	
67.54	q	OG	Sydney	24 Sep	67.54	only					
67.32	3	ISTAF	Berlin	1 Sep	66.44	67.32	66.32	65.28	65.81	63.91	
69.72	Lars		Riedel	GER	28.6.67	1	ISTAF	Berlin			1 Sep
					65.54	65.90	67.84	67.72	67.11	66.94	
68.50	2	OG	Sydney	25 Sep	65.18	x	68.50	68.08	67.33	63.87	
68.15	q	OG	Sydney	24 Sep	68.15	only					
67.83	2		Chemnitz	22 Jul	66.56	66.10	67.83	67.05	x	67.14	
67.13	2		Dortmund	8 Jul	x	65.52	66.52	66.72	67.13	x	

Mark	Name		Nat	Born	Pos	Meet	Venue		Date
69.28	Vladimir	Dubrovshchik	BLR	7.1.72	1	NC-w	Stayki		3 Jun
				64.49	64.86	60.66	65.90	66.40	69.28
68.51	Adam	Setliff	USA	15.12.69	1cA		La Jolla		25 Mar
				66.55	x	64.50	66.23	68.51	63.38
68.46	Andy	Bloom	USA	11.8.73	2cA		La Jolla		25 Mar
				68.46	65.21	66.98	68.10	67.08	68.03
67.25	2	Salinas	23 May	63.07	x	67.25	x	66.37	x
68.32	John	Godina	USA	31.5.72	1		Salinas		23 May
				66.94	67.91	65.86	65.66	66.60	68.32
67.59	Vasiliy	Kaptyukh	BLR	27.6.67	4	OG	Sydney		25 Sep
				58.93	64.50	67.59	64.42	65.07	66.70
67.41	Aleksander	Tammert	EST	2.2.73	1		Austin		6 May
				67.02	66.02	x	65.28	65.04	67.41
66.93	Anthony	Washington	USA	16.1.66	Q	NC	Sacramento		22 Jul
	(36/10)								
66.91	Gábor	Máté	HUN	28.3.79	1cB		La Jolla		25 Mar
66.76	Zoltán	Kövágó	HUN	10.4.79	1		Budapest		22 Jul
66.72	Jim	Seifert	USA	26.11.62	1		Piscataway		25 Mar
66.66	Dmitriy	Shevchenko	RUS	13.5.68	1	Kuts	Moskva		27 Aug
66.47	Doug	Reynolds	USA	11.8.75	1		Salinas		23 May
66.28	Jason	Tunks	CAN	7.5.75	2		Austin		6 May
66.11	Róbert	Fazekas	HUN	18.8.75	1		Budapest		8 Jul
65.81	Jürgen	Schult	GER	11.5.60	2		Halle		27 May
65.69	Vitaliy	Sidorov	RUS	23.3.70	2	Kuts	Moskva		27 Aug
65.56	Leonid	Cherevko	BLR	21.4.74			Brest		3 Mar
	(20)								
65.49	Michael	Möllenbeck	GER	12.12.69	2	Live	Nürnberg		25 Jun
65.39	Roland	Varga	HUN	22.10.77	2		Tatabánya		27 May
65.13	Timo	Tompuri	FIN	9.6.69	1		Espoo		13 May
65.10	Kristian	Pettersson	SWE	5.10.71	1		Mesa		14 Apr
65.08	Robert	Weir	GBR	4.2.61	1	NCp	Bedford		19 Aug
64.74	Nick	Petrucci	USA	10.11.75	1		San Diego		24 Jul
64.69	Diego	Fortuna	ITA	14.2.68	1		Ravenna		24 Jun
64.65	Perriss	Wilkins	GBR	12.12.69	1		Redditch		22 Jul
64.61	Romas	Ubartas	LTU	26.5.60	2	NC	Kaunas		3 Aug
64.60	David	Martínez	ESP	31.1.67	1		Las Palmas		30 Aug
	(30)								
64.51	Andreas	Seelig	GER	6.7.70	4		Halle		27 May
64.47A	Casey	Malone	USA	6.4.77	1		Fort Collins		29 Apr
64.44	Michel	Hemmings	CUB	10.9.75	1		La Habana		15 Jun
64.40	Dragan	Mustapic	CRO	23.3.63	1		Ljubljana		25 Jul
64.38A	Aleksandr	Borichevskiy	RUS	25.6.70	1		Bloemfontein		4 Feb
64.26A	Jason	Gervais	CAN	18.1.76	1		USAF Academy		12 May
64.26	Ian	Winchester	NZL	27.5.73	2A	ModR	Modesto		13 May
64.20	Olgierd	Stanski	POL	4.4.73	1	ECp1B	Bydgoszcz		9 Jul
64.13	Alexis	Elizalde	CUB	19.9.67	1		La Habana		7 Jul
64.00	Jarred	Rome	USA	21.12.76	4		Salinas		23 May
	(40)								
63.94	Tolga	Köseoglu	GER	16.11.76	1		College Station		15 Apr
63.90A	Frits	Potgieter	RSA	13.3.74	2		Potchefstroom		14 Feb
63.73	Libor	Malina	CZE	14.6.73	1		Ostrava		3 Sep
63.70	John	Menton	IRL	7.5.70	1		Oakhurst		5 Jul
63.67	Mark	White	USA	10.6.67	3cA		La Jolla		25 Mar
63.56	Andrzej	Krawczyk	POL	11.4.76	1		Kraków		30 Jul
63.55	Cristiano	Andrei	ITA	14.5.73	1		Tuscania		10 Sep
63.54	Kirill	Chuprinin	UKR	22.7.75	1		Koncha-Zaspa		9 May
63.54	James	Dennis	USA	25.2.76	1		Kent		13 May
63.49	Jo	Van Daele	BEL	6.4.72	4		Wiesbaden		20 May
	(50)								
63.35	Carl	Brown	USA	11.2.70	2		San Diego		24 Jul
63.32	Frank	Casañas	CUB	18.10.78	1		La Habana		23 Jun
63.17	Michael	Lischka	GER	23.12.73	1		Eppstein		18 Jul
63.11	David	Dumble	USA	11.11.74	2cB		La Jolla		25 Mar
63.09	Magnús	Hallgrimsson	ISL	23.3.76	1		Helsingborg		17 Jun
63.08	Glen	Smith	GBR	21.5.72	1		Watford		9 Aug
62.90	Ercüment	Olgundeniz	TUR	7.7.76	1		Izmir		16 Apr
62.90	Torsten	Schmidt	GER	9.12.74	1		Medelby		8 Jul
62.84	Chima	Ugwu	NGR	19.7.73	1		Tempe		21 Apr
62.80	Vésteinn	Hafsteinsson	ISL	12.12.60	1		Hafnarfjördur		26 Jun
	(60)								

MEN 2000

Mark	Name		Nat	Born	Pos	Meet	Venue	Date
62.79	Ionel	Oprea	ROM	12.10.70	1	NC-w	Bucuresti	4 Mar
62.59	Petri	Hakala	FIN	21.2.79	1		Hämeenlinna	24 Aug
62.54	Igor	Primc	SLO	8.1.66	2	ECp1B	Bydgoszcz	9 Jul
62.52	Aleksandr	Malasevich	BLR	7.4.77	4		Nitra	26 Aug
62.50	Marcelo	Pugliese	ARG	2.9.68	1		Buenos Aires	15 Jul
62.46	Roman	Poltoratskiy	UZB	22.7.72	1		Tashkent	15 Jun
62.38	Marco	Jakobs	GER	30.5.74	6		Wiesbaden	20 May
62.34	Reedus	Thurmond	USA	15.12.79	3cB		La Jolla	25 Mar
62.29		Li Shaojie	CHN	26.11.75	13q	OG	Sydney	24 Sep
62.27	Yuriy	Seskin	RUS	7.7.66	1	NC-w	Adler	19 Feb
	(70)							
62.26	Jean-Claude	Retel	FRA	11.2.68	1	vENG	Vittel	2 Sep
62.22	Pertti	Hynni	FIN	14.2.60	2		Porvoo	26 Aug
62.20	Pieter	van der Kruk	NED	10.2.72	1		Den Haag	13 Aug
62.10	Kevin	Brown	GBR/JAM	10.9.64	1		Ipswich	3 Aug
62.07	Emeka	Udechuku	GBR	10.7.79	2	NCp	Bedford	19 Aug
62.06	Chary	Mamedov	TKM	12.10.63	1	NC	Almaty	15 Jul
61.78	Vaclovas	Kidykas	LTU	17.10.61	7	Sule	Tartu	11 Jun
61.76	Nick	Sweeney	IRL	26.3.68	1		Newcastle	9 Sep
61.63	Mario	Pestano	ESP	8.4.78	5		Barcelona	25 Jul
61.62	Timo	Sinervo	FIN	5.8.75	2		Ikaalinen	23 Jun
	(80)							
61.57	Svein Inge	Valvik	NOR	20.9.56	2c1		Helsingborg	17 Jun
61.55	Thomas	Rosvold	NOR	21.7.67	1		Oslo (S)	28 May
61.43	Einar Kristian	Tveitå	NOR	22.2.73	1		Ski	3 Sep
61.40	Werner	Reiterer	AUS	27.1.68	1		Melbourne	16 Mar
61.35	Yuriy	Belonog	UKR	9.3.74	2	NC	Kiev	6 Aug
61.31	Ben	Lindsey	USA	5.10.77	1c2		Salinas	23 May
61.30	Anil	Kumar	IND	1.9.74	1		Trivandrum	12 Aug
61.16	Jeff	Kremer	USA	22.2.75	1		Joplin	7 Apr
61.08A	Mattias	Borrman	SWE	20.6.72	1		Fort Collins	1 Apr
61.06	Stéfanos	Kónstas	GRE	16.5.77	1		Iráklio	25 Jun
	(90)							
60.72	Sergey	Lyakhov	RUS	1.5.68	1	MosCh	Moskva	11 Jul
60.60	Frank	Vicet	CUB	13.11.71	2		Arles	3 Jun
60.52	Ian	Waltz	USA	15.4.77	1	Pac 10	Eugene	21 May
60.45	Mika	Loikkanen	FIN	20.2.74	2	Nurmi	Turku	2 Aug
60.45	Peter	Elvy	AUS	3.6.80	1		Sydney	12 Aug
60.41	Kevin	Fitzpatrick	USA	26.9.69	4		San Diego	24 Jul
60.34	Mark	Simmons	USA	14.9.78	4		Austin	6 May
60.32	Mark	Hoxmeier	USA	16.7.79	8	NCAA	Durham	31 May
60.18	Olav	Jenssen	NOR	11.5.62	2		Oslo (S)	28 May
60.16	Luke	Sullivan	USA	4.6.76	4cB		La Jolla	25 Mar
	(100)							
60.16	Rasheed	Al-Dosari	QAT-J	8.5.81	1		Al-Kuwait	18 Apr

60.12	Attila	Horváth	HUN	28.7.67	8 Oct
60.00	Tom	Barrett	USA	12.6.78	28 Apr
60.00	Olaf	Többen	GER	19.12.62	9 Sep
59.99	Jouni	Helppikangas	FIN	10.2.71	29 Jul
59.91	Jon	O'Neil	USA	23.3.79	13 Apr
59.84	Zech	Schiebout	USA	19.9.77	6 May
59.83	Caba	Guljas	YUG	5.2.78	16 Jul
59.78	Scott	Moser	USA	15.7.79	25 Mar
59.63	Sávvas	Panávoglou	GRE	14.8.74	28 May
59.59	Jason	Stuke	USA	22.8.75	25 Mar
59.58	Mickaël	Conjungo	CAF	6.5.68	12 Jul
59.55	Jean	Pons	FRA	29.5.69	4 Jun
59.51A	Janus	Robberts	RSA	10.3.79	20 May
59.51	Hannes	Hopley	RSA-J	26.1.81	21 Oct
59.44	Janne	Hummastenniemi	FIN	4.10.79	24 Aug
59.36		Yu Wenge	CHN	18.2.66	3 May
59.29	Patrick	Stang	GER	17.5.78	27 May
59.28A	Mike	Mielke	USA	29.4.62	6 Jul
59.22	Nathan	Fanger	USA	15.9.76	13 May
59.21	Curry	Dawson	USA	4.8.79	22 Apr
59.20	Gjøran	Sørli	NOR	3.6.78	10 Sep
59.19	Niklas	Arrhenius	SWE-J	10.9.82	21 Oct
59.14	Mike	Walsh	USA	25.7.71	25 Mar
59.10A	Roberto	Moya	CUB	11.2.65	18 Mar
59.10	Ben	Vet	NED	2.2.68	16 Jul
59.09	Abbas	Samimi	IRI	9.6.77	1 Jul
59.08A	James	Parker	USA	3.12.75	4 May
59.06	Hridayanand	Singh	IND	.75	17 Jul
59.00	Mikko	Kyyrö	FIN	12.7.80	16 Sep
58.90	Joe	Erdkamp	USA	10.1.76	28 Apr
58.83	Travis	Pendleton	USA-J	.81	13 Apr
58.82A	Brian	Trainor	USA	14.3.80	29 Apr
58.80A	Jason	Young	USA-J	27.5.81	15 Apr
58.77	Jean-Baptiste	Tiercelin	FRA	1.2.77	28 May
58.75	Pavel	Pirozhkov	UKR	10.4.74	6 Aug
58.74	Rutger	Smith	NED-J	9.7.81	16 Jul
58.69	Cameron	Bolles	USA	.76	23 May
58.68	Sean	McKeown	USA	9.5.74	13 Apr
58.64	Valeriy	Borisov	BLR	24.2.75	2 Aug
58.62	Michal	Hodun	POL-J	17.2.83	21 Oct
58.61	Stéphane	Nativel	FRA	4.4.75	5 Jul
58.53A	Chris	Harmse	RSA	31.5.73	7 Apr
58.53	Dan	Ames	USA-J	16.1.81	13 May
58.51	Joachim	Olsen	DEN	31.5.77	13 Aug
58.51		Zhang Cunbiao	CHN	11.2.69	21 Oct
58.47	Aleksey	Ryzhenko	RUS	19.7.71	19 Feb
58.46	Mattihas	Thriene	GER	28.12.71	9 Sep
58.36	Julio César	Piñero	ARG	4.6.75	25 Mar
58.29	Luciano	Zerbini	ITA	16.2.60	6 Sep
58.27	Veljko	Cegar	YUG	30.7.74	30 Aug
58.22	Alexander	Forst	GER	11.6.75	15 Apr
58.21	Simone	Sbrogiò	ITA	4.10.74	26 Feb
58.16	Kevin	Mannon	USA	12.8.76	1 Apr
58.15	Paulo	Bernardo	POR	21.11.74	28 Jun

Mark	Name		Nat	Born	Date
58.10	Cristian	Ponton	ITA	23.3.72	15 Jul
58.06A	Deon	Geldenhuys	RSA	12.6.71	14 Feb
57.90	Khalid Salman	Al-Khalidi	KSA	14.2.65	6 Apr
57.90	Loy	Martínez	CUB-J	3.6.81	23 Jun
57.90	Eivind	Smørgrav	NOR	7.6.74	26 Jul
57.88	Dmitriy	Kipryushin	UZB	29.1.70	15 Jun
57.86	Russ	Bell	USA-J	27.2.81	25 Mar
57.82A	Carlos	Scott	USA	7.7.60	15 Apr
57.82	Stefano	Lomater	ITA	23.4.74	3 Jun
57.82	Heinrich	Seitz	GER	6.4.80	22 Aug
57.80	Shakti	Singh	IND	14.5.62	12 Aug
	(166)				

Unconfirmed

Mark	Name		Nat	Born	Pos	Meet	Venue	Date
63.55	Sean	McKeown	USA	9.5.74	1		Fresno	3 Apr

JUNIORS

Mark	Name		Nat	Born	Pos	Meet	Venue	Date
60.16	Rasheed	Al-Dosari	QAT	8.5.81	1		Al-Kuwait	18 Apr
59.51	Hannes	Hopley	RSA	26.1.81	1	WJ	Santiago de Chile	21 Oct
59.19	Niklas	Arrhenius	SWE	10.9.82	2	WJ	Santiago de Chile	21 Oct
	58.58A 3	Logan	1 Jul					
58.83	Travis	Pendleton	USA	.81	1cC		Lancaster	13 Apr
58.80A	Jason	Young	USA	27.5.81	2		El Paso	15 Apr
58.74	Rutger	Smith	NED	9.7.81	3	NC	Amsterdam	16 Jul
	58.70 3	WJ Santiago	21 Oct	10 performaces by eight men over 58.50				
58.62	Michal	Hodun	POL	17.2.83	4	WJ	Santiago de Chile	21 Oct
58.53	Dan	Ames	USA	16.1.81	1c3	ModR	Modesto	13 May
57.90	Loy	Martínez	CUB	3.6.81	3		La Habana	23 Jun
57.86	Russ	Bell (10)	USA	27.2.81	1		Gainesville	25 Mar
57.38	Omer	Inan	USA	20.10.81	2	NC-j	Denton	23 Jun
56.82	Pavel	Lyzhin	BLR	24.3.81			Brest	24 Aug
56.42	Kibwe	Johnson	USA	17.7.81	1		Athens GA	22 Apr
55.88		Wu Tao	CHN	3.10.83	3	NGP	Shanghai	19 Apr
55.57	Lucais	MacKay	USA	13.4.81	2c2	ModR	Modesto	13 May
55.35	Omar	El Ghazaly	EGY	9.2.84	1		Cairo	7 Sep
55.31		Nuermei Meiti	CHN	8.3.84	2		Chengdu	10 May
54.60	Dylan	Armstrong	CAN	15.1.81	2	vUSA-j	Montreal	18 Jul
54.54	Krishnakumar	Sharma	IND	5.5.81	1	NC	Calcutta	10 Oct
54.21		Xu Yongyi (20)	CHN	28.7.84	7	NC	Luohe	21 Oct

HAMMER

Mark	Name		Nat	Born	Pos	Meet	Venue		Date
82.58	Igor	Astapkovich	BLR	4.1.63	1		Stayki		18 Aug
				80.73	82.58	p	p	80.36	82.02
81.25	1	Stayki	27 Jun	80.33	x	81.25	p	x	p
81.00	1	Minsk	11 Feb						
80.90	1	Hengelo	28 May	80.90	79.08	78.18	x	x	x
82.38	Gilles	Dupray	FRA	2.1.70	1		Chelles		21 Jun
				78.42	82.38	80.36	p	p	p
81.93	Ilya	Konovalov	RUS	14.3.71	1		Rostov-na-Donu		28 Jun
81.92	Tibor	Gécsek	HUN	22.9.64	1		Szombathely		4 Jun
80.85	1	Szombathely	10 Sep		only best throw measured both meets				
80.53	1	Szombathely	23 Jul	77.00	79.63	78.94	x	x	80.53
80.50	2	Clermont-Ferrand	30 Jun	78.87	80.50	78.95	78.48	77.38	x
81.79	Christophe	Épalle	FRA	23.1.69	1		Clermont-Ferrand		30 Jun
				80.63	81.31	81.04	81.79	81.18	80.94
81.45	1	Reims	30 Aug	76.87	79.35	81.45	x	80.35	80.78
81.75	Vasiliy	Sidorenko	RUS	1.5.61	1	NC	Tula		24 Jul
				80.06	x	81.75	80.44	80.59	80.72
81.57	1	Rüdlingen	13 Aug	76.76	80.41	81.57	81.12	78.58	78.94
81.56	Vladislav	Piskunov	UKR	7.6.78	1		Yalta		25 Mar
80.88	1 NC	Kiev	5 Aug	79.47	79.98	80.58	x	80.27	80.88
81.43	Andrey	Skvaruk	UKR	9.3.67	1	GPF	Doha		5 Oct
				81.43	78.20	77.86	x	p	x
80.70	2 NC	Kiev	5 Aug	79.44	79.38	78.57	79.89	80.50	80.70
81.42	Szymon	Ziolkówski	POL	1.7.76	1		Warszawa		20 Aug
				78.30	78.90	79.77	79.35	80.06	81.42
80.39	1 NC	Kraków	6 Aug	76.23	78.55	80.39	76.55	77.54	75.92
80.26	1	Gold Coast (RB)	17 Sep	77.25	79.17	80.26	78.42	79.93	78.72
81.36	Vadim	Devyatovskiy ¶ (10)	BLR	20.3.77	1	NC	Brest		1 Aug
				78.13	79.64	79.18	81.36	78.90	79.98
80.96	2	Stayki	18 Aug	80.22	78.56	80.18	77.80	78.32	80.96
80.25	2	Stayki	27 Jun	79.29	79.15	80.25	79.60	79.22	78.90
81.08	Koji	Murofushi	JPN	8.10.74	1	Super	Yokohama		9 Sep
				77.41	81.08	80.26	80.72	79.74	80.29
80.56	1	Sapporo	16 Jul	x	77.69	80.47	78.38	80.56	79.81
80.38	1	Budapest	22 Jul	76.94	79.65	x	x	78.43	80.38
80.32	2 GPF	Doha	5 Oct	79.04	79.67	78.97	78.63	79.69	80.32

Mark	Name		Nat	Born	Pos	Meet	Venue	Date
80.99	Lance	Deal	USA	21.8.61	1	Nik	Nice	8 Jul
				78.59 78.67 80.99 78.98 78.33 79.12				
80.98	Vladimir	Maska	CZE	6.2.73	1	NC	Plzen	16 Jul
				80.43 80.98 79.60 x x x				
80.55	Olli-Pekka	Karjalainen	FIN	7.3.80	1		Tampere	19 Jul
				80.55 78.18 79.00 x x x				
80.51	Andrey	Abduvaliyev	UZB	30.6.66	1	NC	Tashkent	17 Aug
80.45	Aléxandros	Papadimitríou	GRE	18.6.73	1	NC	Athína	9 Jul
				77.91 78.94 79.07 79.71 80.45 79.17				
80.25	Maciej	Palyszko	POL	4.1.78	2		Gold Coast (RB)	17 Sep
	(34/17)			79.03 79.32 79.93 80.25 78.96 x				
80.21	Karsten	Kobs	GER	16.9.71	1	NC	Braunschweig	29 Jul
80.13	Heinz	Weis	GER	14.7.63	3		Rüdlingen	12 Aug
80.02	Zsolt	Németh	HUN	9.11.71	2		Budapest	22 Jul
	(20)							
79.85	Ivan	Tikhon	BLR	24.7.76	3		Stayki	27 Jun
79.68	Aleksey	Zagornyy	RUS	31.5.78	1	NC-23	Cheboksary	1 Jul
79.64	Nicola	Vizzoni	ITA	4.11.73	2	OG	Sydney	24 Sep
79.57	Hrístos	Polihroníou	GRE	31.3.72	1		Iráklio	25 Jun
79.52	Aleksandr	Krykun	UKR	1.3.68	3	NC	Kiev	5 Aug
79.47	Loris	Paoluzzi	ITA	14.5.74	1		Lucca	20 May
79.29	David	Chaussinand	FRA	19.4.73	1		Castres	27 Jul
79.29	Pavel	Sedlácek	CZE	5.4.68	1		Ostrava	3 Sep
79.22	Balázs	Kiss	HUN	21.3.72	1	NC	Budapest	30 Jul
79.01	Nicolas	Figère	FRA	19.5.79	4		Clermont-Ferrand	30 Jun
	(30)							
78.71	Chris	Harmse	RSA	31.5.73	1		Pretoria	23 Sep
78.55	Kevin	McMahon	USA	26.5.72	2	Jerome	Burnaby	4 Jun
78.44	Sergey	Kirmasov	RUS	25.3.70	1	NCp	Tula	3 Jun
78.16	Vadim	Khersontsev	RUS	8.7.74	4	NC	Tula	24 Jul
78.15	Adrián	Annus	HUN	28.6.73	6	Nik	Nice	8 Jul
78.02	Nikólaos	Yedékos	GRE	9.7.66	1		Limassol	28 Jul
77.75	András	Haklits	CRO	23.9.77	2		Szombathely	19 Aug
77.68	Stuart	Rendell	AUS	30.6.72	1		Pietersburg	18 Mar
77.42	Péter	Botfa	HUN	30.6.79	1		Szombathely	19 Jul
77.22	Libor	Charfreitag	SVK	11.9.77	1	NCAA	Durham	1 Jun
	(40)							
77.21	Konstantin	Astapkovich	BLR	23.10.70	4		Staiki	27 Jun
77.04	Holger	Klose	GER	5.12.72	1		Wiesbaden	25 Jun
76.95	Vadim	Kolesnik	UKR	29.4.69	4	NC	Kiev	5 Aug
76.84	Primoz	Kozmus	SLO	30.9.79	1		Tapolca	5 Aug
76.66	Markus	Esser	GER	3.2.80	3	NC	Braunschweig	29 Jul
76.60	Marko	Wahlman	FIN	6.4.69	2		El Paso	15 Apr
76.59	Wojciech	Kondratowicz	POL	18.4.80	1		Warszawa	25 Jun
76.41	Zoltán	Fábián	HUN	22.4.69	2		Szombathely	19 Jul
76.34	Vitor	Costa	POR	28.5.74	1		Paris (I)	12 Jul
76.30	Vadim	Grabovoy	UKR	5.4.73	3		Kiev	16 Jun
	(50)							
76.20	Kazimierz	Boulge	POL	13.2.76	1		Skórcz	1 Jun
76.12	Miloslav	Konopka	SVK	23.1.79	1		Banská Bystrica	4 Jun
76.05	Jan	Bielecki	DEN	20.2.71	1		Minden	1 Jul
76.03	Yuriy	Voronkin	RUS	18.5.79	2		Rostov-na-Donu	28 Jun
76.02	Andrey	Vorontsov	BLR	24.7.75	2	NC	Brest	1 Aug
75.94	Michael	Jones	GBR	23.7.63	1		Crawley	6 Sep
75.78	Per	Karlsson	SWE	21.4.67	1		Västerås	4 Aug
75.77	Viktor	Ustinov	UZB	20.7.74	1		Tashkent	14 Jun
75.74	Igor	Tugay	UKR	22.3.75	1	Univ Ch	Kiev	15 Jul
75.62	Vitaliy	Khozhatelyov	UZB	12.8.67	2		Tashkent	14 Jun
	(60)							
75.62	Bengt	Johansson	SWE	7.7.73	1		Helsingborg	7 Jul
75.62	Jud	Logan	USA	19.7.59	1cB		Rüdlingen	12 Aug
75.61	Raphaël	Piolanti	FRA	14.11.67	2		Castres	27 Jul
75.59	Dmitriy	Shako	BLR	25.3.79	3		Stayki	18 Aug
75.10	Vitaliy	Alisevich	BLR	12.7.67	2	NC	Stayki	3 Jun
75.07	Vladimir	Bykov	RUS	29.4.70	3		Togliatti	14 May
75.04	Andrey	Vikhrov	RUS	.73	3		Rostov-na-Donu	28 Jun
74.85	Mikko	Dannbäck	FIN	16.3.77	1		Kuortane	8 Jul
74.82	Roman	Konevtsov	RUS	4.4.77	5	NCp	Tula	3 Jun
74.68	Róbert	Fazekas	HUN	18.8.75	5	NC	Budapest	30 Jul
	(70)							

Mark	Name		Nat	Born	Pos	Meet	Venue	Date
74.32	Juan Ignacio	Cerra	ARG	16.10.76	1	IbAm	Rio de Janeiro	20 May
74.03	Mark	McGehearty	USA	3.7.75	1		New Haven	1 Jul
73.67		Ye Kuigang	CHN	4.1.75	1	NC	Luohe	19 Oct
73.62	Samu-Petri	Simo	FIN	22.6.78	1		Kaustinen	6 Jul
73.52	Marco	Lingua	ITA	4.6.78	3	NC	Milano	7 Sep
73.29	Stanislav	Zakharov	RUS	10.4.77	2		Sankt-Peterburg	26 Jun
73.09	Andrey	Yevgenyev	RUS	9.7.73	3	MosCh	Moskva	11 Jul
72.85	Jerry	Ingalls	USA	24.9.74	1		New York	8 Jul
72.84	Dan	Bourque	USA	4.7.76	1		West Point	14 Jun
72.81	José Manuel	Pérez	ESP	6.5.73	1		Madrid (Rivas)	13 May
	(80)							
72.47	Wataru	Ebihara	JPN	12.12.73	1		Odawara	25 Jun
72.40	Walter	Ciofani	FRA	17.2.62	1cB		Clermont-Ferrand	30 Jun
72.31	Mika	Laaksonen	FIN	21.3.68	3	Karelia	Lappeenranta	13 Aug
72.30	James	Parker	USA	3.12.75	1		Logan	1 Jul
72.20	Roman	Rozna	MDA	25.3.76	1		Chisinau	10 Jun
72.13	Patric	Suter	SUI	17.5.77	1		Basel	1 May
72.13	Ioannis	Barlís	GRE	26.11.79	3	NC	Athína	9 Jul
72.01	Norbert	Horváth	HUN	13.6.75	6		Szombathely	23 Jul
71.99	Yosmel	Monte	CUB	26.6.77	1	Barr	La Habana	29 Jul
71.97	Krzysztof	Kaliszewski	POL	9.9.72	1		Warszawa	3 Jun
	(90)							
71.90	Janne	Vartia	FIN	18.3.77	3	NCAA	Durham	1 Jun
71.89	Claus	Dethloff	GER	24.9.68	2		Krefeld	1 Jul
71.76	William	Beauchamp	GBR	9.9.70	1		North Wembley	23 Apr
71.69	Aleksandr	Baburkin	RUS	.74	4		Rostov-na-Donu	28 Jun
71.52	Marco	Quintarelli	ITA	20.6.73	1		Padova	14 Jun
71.50	Kevin	Mannon	USA	12.8.76	1		Greeley	22 Apr
71.35	Alexander	Sporrer	GER	20.1.71	2		Karlsruhe	6 May
71.30	Xavier	Tison	FRA	20.9.77	7	NC	Nice	5 Aug
71.30	Giovanni	Sanguin	ITA	14.5.69	4	NC	Milano	7 Sep
71.28	Moisés	Campeny	ESP	27.5.79	1	NC-23	Puertollano	5 Aug
	(100)							

71.24	Paddy	McGrath	IRL	1.7.71	13 May
71.18	Sergey	Gavrilov	RUS	22.5.70	3 Jun
71.10	Aleksandr	Yeroshin	RUS	.69	8 Jul
71.09		Bi Zhong	CHN	5.9.68	10 May
70.90	Jay	Harvard	USA	14.3.76	25 Mar
70.90	Paul	Head	GBR	1.7.65	29 May
70.76	Jarkko	Paljakka	FIN	7.2.79	30 Jul
70.73	Michal	Kozlowski	POL	13.3.78	6 Aug
70.66	Dylan	Armstrong	CAN-J	15.1.81	6 Jul
70.58	Éric	Albert	FRA	30.7.79	10 Jun
70.51	Yosvany	Suárez	CUB	20.12.72	24 Jul
70.50	Dorian	Collaku	ALB	2.6.77	9 Aug
70.48	Samir	Haouam	ALG	20.6.68	17 Jun
70.48	Alberto	Sánchez	CUB	3.2.73	14 Jul
70.40	Harálabos	Arsoniádis	GRE	19.1.78	27 May
70.36	Peter	Kubera	GER	22.6.74	6 May
70.36	Nikolay	Davydov	KGZ	11.4.70	4 Jun
70.34	Athanásios	Koukouzíkis	GRE	24.9.76	18 Jun
70.33	John	Pearson	GBR	30.4.66	30 Jul
70.32	Hrístos	Tsíntzos	GRE	3.9.80	29 Jul
70.25	Cosmin	Sorescu	ROM	11.7.75	22 Jul
70.15	Jean-Charles	De Ridder	LUX	7.6.71	30 Apr
70.13	Ishtiyaque	Ahmed	IND	6.4.78	17 Jul
70.12	Adrián	Marzo	ARG	24.1.68	9 Apr
69.97	Esref	Apak	TUR-J	3.1.82	18 Oct
69.95	Ronald	Gram	NED	31.3.74	28 May
69.84	John	McEwen	USA	5.3.74	13 May
69.63		Liu Fuxiang	CHN	24.3.75	14 May
69.61	Kay	Maybach	GER	10.1.72	17 Jun
69.55	Sándor	Vegh	HUN	10.3.77	13 Oct
69.49	Nikólaos	Koronákos	GRE	18.11.77	9 Jul
69.46		Cong Changqing	CHN	19.4.75	10 May
69.44	Enrico	Sgrulletti	ITA	24.4.65	27 Feb
69.40	Bernard	Reibel	FRA	13.8.67	12 Jun
69.40	Roman	Linscheid	IRL	29.12.70	4 Jul
69.38	Oleg	Sergeyev	RUS	6.8.77	3 Jun
69.38	Mike	Floyd	GBR	26.9.76	18 Jun
69.32	Denis	Kulagin	RUS	23.5.80	19 Feb
69.27	Xavier	Dallet	FRA	24.12.79	21 Jun
69.24	Grigoriy	Khatantsev	RUS	.78	26 Aug
69.21	Stefan	Paukner	GER	16.8.76	1 Jul
69.19	Phil	Jensen	NZL	8.11.67	12 Mar
69.19	Travis	Nutter	USA	9.2.75	24 Jun
69.08	Lukás	Melich	CZE	16.9.80	25 Jun
69.02	Mohd. Karim	Horchani	TUN	13.3.76	29 Aug
69.00	Kristóf	Páli	HUN	29.12.80	19 May
68.92	Gianni	Nadalini	ITA	17.5.66	12 Jul
68.91	Ilmari	Verho	FIN	10.8.75	20 Aug
68.81	Szabolcs	Maróti	HUN	30.9.76	24 Mar
68.75	Scott	Boothby	USA	9.4.73	1 Apr
68.70	Kirill	Chuprinin	UKR	22.7.75	25 Mar
68.67	Aaron	Fish	AUS-J	27.2.81	6 Sep
68.53	David	Söderberg	FIN	11.8.79	7 Jun
68.49	Nasser Abd.	Al Jarallah	KUW	20.11.73	20 Apr
68.48	Aleksey	Mukhortov	RUS	13.7.79	26 Feb
68.34	Frank	van den Dool	NED	10.7.67	10 Sep
68.32	Aleksey	Yeliseyev	RUS-J	12.3.82	20 Aug
68.24	Marco	Felice	ITA	20.10.79	21 Sep
68.16	Roland	Ciofani	FRA	29.9.71	21 May
68.09	Steffen	Reumann	GER	6.3.68	28 May
68.02	David	Smith II	GBR	2.11.74	16 Apr
	(161)				

JUNIORS

70.66	Dylan	Armstrong	CAN	15.1.81	1		Flagstaff	6 Jul
	70.44 1 Flagstaff 8 Jul				69.15 4	MSR	Walnut	15 Apr
69.97	Esref	Apak	TUR	3.1.82	1	WJ	Santiago de Chile	18 Oct
	68.76 1 Istanbul 20 Aug				67.69 1		Ankara	16 Jul
	68.44 1 Balk-j Constanta 17 Sep							
68.67	Aaron	Fish	AUS	27.2.81	2		Brisbane	6 Sep
68.32	Aleksey	Yeliseyev	RUS	12.3.82	2		Moskva	20 Aug
	67.88 1 NC-w Adler 19 Feb				10 performaces by 4 men to 67.69			

Mark	Name		Nat	Born	Pos	Meet	Venue	Date
67.45	Vladimir	Stepanenko	UKR	26.4.81	1		Kiev	20 May
67.28	Aleksandr	Vaschilo	BLR	.81			Staiki	3 Jun
66.88	Aleksey	Korolyov	RUS	5.4.82	5		Sochi	26 Feb
66.80	Krisztián	Pars	HUN	18.2.82	2c2		Szombathely	23 Jul
66.15	Alessandro	Beschi	ITA	5.8.81	1		Milano	4 Jun
65.77		Liu Yi (10)	CHN	5.6.81	4	NC	Luohe	19 Oct
65.38	Andrey	Mezhevov	RUS	.82	2		Cheboksary	8 Jul
64.45	Noleysi	Vicet	CUB	.81	3		La Habana	14 Jul
64.32	Jari	Polvi	FIN	26.8.81	1		Ylivieska	30 Sep
64.28		Shen Yi	CHN	15.12.84	8	NC	Luohe	19 Oct
64.24	Johannes	Kaczmarek	FIN	15.6.83	1		Helsinki	17 Sep
64.00	Yuriy	Kravchuk	BLR	.81	7	NC	Brest	1 Aug
63.20	Aleksandr	Lutsenko	UKR	3.3.82	8	NC	Kiev	5 Aug
63.16	Sergey	Karpovich	UKR	23.4.81	2		Kiev	20 May
63.09	Riaan	Smit	RSA	1.12.82	2		Parow	29 Dec
62.54	József	Horváth (20)	HUN	3.4.84	4B		Budapest	30 Jul

JAVELIN

91.69	Kostadínos		Gatsioúdis	GRE	17.12.73	1		Kuortane		24 Jun
					87.62	88.15	x	x	91.69	x
89.48	1		Pireás	23 Apr	89.48	x	x	x	x	x
88.76	1		Kalamáta	4 Jun	81.30	85.49	88.76	x	x	85.20
88.74	1	GP	Helsinki	15 Jun	88.75	85.11	85.41	86.80	x	86.77
88.46	1	GP	Athína	28 Jun	88.46	x	x	x	86.57	x
88.41	q	OG	Sydney	22 Sep	88.41	only				
87.93	2		Vantaa	20 Jun	86.57	87.93	x	86.42	x	x
87.89	1	NC	Athína	8 Jul	87.89	86.76	x	x	p	p
87.37	2	Athl	Lausanne	5 Jul	87.37	84.24	83.75	x	x	83.19
87.29	1	ECCp	V R St António	27 May	84.40	87.29	x	x	four only	
90.97	Aki		Parviainen	FIN	26.10.74	2		Kuortane		24 Jun
					x	x	83.28	90.97	84.78	85.65
90.80	1		Vantaa	20 Jun	x	87.15	90.80	86.23	x	82.57
90.34	1		Lapinlahti	16 Jul	x	90.34	x	89.31	x	85.81
89.88	1	ECp!A	Nadderud	9 Jul	89.88	p	p	p	p	p
89.62	1		Joensuu	14 Jul						
88.33	2	GP	Athína	28 Jun	x	80.52	84.88	88.33	84.90	x
88.10	1	Nurmi	Turku	2 Aug	87.96	84.63	88.10	82.04	p	x
87.81	1	BrGP	London (CP)	5 Aug	x	85.56	83.79	87.81	x	x
87.59	2	GP	Helsinki	15 Jun	80.74	85.71	82.44	85.83	87.59	x
90.59A	Jan		Zelezny	CZE	16.6.66	1		Pretoria		24 Mar
					81.84	79.79	83.52	87.39	90.59	x
90.56	1		Praha	5 Jun	82.60	90.56	x	88.81	x	x
90.56	1	Bisl	Oslo	28 Jul	83.66	x	p	x	p	90.56
90.17	1	OG	Sydney	23 Sep	89.41	x	90.17	x	x	88.97
89.39	q	OG	Sydney	22 Sep	89.39	only				
88.84	1		Réthimno	10 Jun	83.97	80.27	82.11	88.84	p	x
87.80	3		Kuortane	24 Jun	87.57	87.80	x	x	x	x
87.66	1	Athl	Lausanne	5 Jul	83.38	87.66	p	p	p	p
89.92	Sergey		Makarov	RUS	19.3.73	1	ECp-S	Gateshead		16 Jul
					84.88	x	82.62	89.92	four only	
88.67	3	OG	Sydney	23 Sep	88.67	85.90	x	x	86.67	85.30
88.53	2	Bisl	Oslo	28 Jul	86.64	88.53	x	85.80	86.16	85.60
89.85	Steve		Backley	GBR	12.2.69	2	OG	Sydney		23 Sep
					86.25	89.85	x	80.99	x	x
87.76	Raymond		Hecht	GER	11.11.68	4	OG	Sydney		23 Sep
					87.76	x	x	x	76.11	p
87.17	Dariusz		Trafas	POL	16.5.72	1		Gold Coast (RB)		17 Sep
					87.17	79.64	81.01	84.73	x	x
87.12	Emeterio		González	CUB	11.4.73	1	OD	Jena		3 Jun
	(34/8)				81.83	x	81.64	82.67	81.77	87.12
86.74	Pål Arne		Fagernes	NOR	8.6.74	q	OG	Sydney		22 Sep
86.65	Boris (10)		Henry	GER	14.12.73	1		Saarbrücken		1 Jul
86.10	Harri		Haatainen	FIN	5.1.78	2		Lapinlahti		16 Jul
85.65	Harri		Hakkarainen	FIN	16.10.69	1		Eurajoki		1 Jul
85.45	Peter		Blank	GER	10.4.62	1		Stendal		10 Jun
85.28	Andrew		Currey	AUS	7.2.71	1		Sydney		13 Feb
85.16	Patrik		Bodén	SWE	30.6.67	1		Karlstad		18 Jun
85.09	Nick		Nieland	GBR	31.1.72	2	NC	Birmingham		13 Aug
84.80	Sergey		Voynov	UZB	26.2.77	1		Villeneuve d'Ascq		17 Jun

Mark	Name		Nat	Born	Pos	Meet	Venue	Date
84.79	Peter	Esenwein	GER	7.12.67	2		Mainz	7 Jul
84.42	Vladimir	Sasimovich	BLR	14.9.68	1	NC	Brest	2 Aug
84.29		Li Rongxiang	CHN	8.1.72	1		Chengdu	10 May
	(20)							
84.25	Tom	Pukstys	USA	28.5.68	1		Karlstad	23 Aug
84.20	Andrew	Martin	AUS	12.5.80	1		Gold Coast (RB)	5 Aug
83.71	Mick	Hill	GBR	22.10.64	1		Cape Town	31 Mar
83.61	Eriks	Rags	LAT	1.6.75	1		Ventspils	17 Jun
83.46A	Adrian	Hatcher	AUS	6.5.70	1		Pietersburg	18 Mar
83.43A	Marius	Corbett	RSA	26.9.75	2		Pietersburg	18 Mar
83.38	Marián	Bokor	SVK	17.4.77	1		Nitra	31 Jul
83.30	Isbel	Luaces	CUB	20.7.75	2	OD	Jena	3 Jun
83.08	Voldemars	Lusis	LAT	7.12.74	2		Ventspils	17 Jun
83.04	Manuel	Nau	GER	2.7.77	1		Halle	27 May
	(30)							
82.75	Terry	McHugh	IRL	22.8.63	4	BrGP	London (CP)	5 Aug
82.74	Matti	Närhi	FIN	17.8.75	q	NC	Lahti	18 Aug
82.63	Breaux	Greer	USA	19.10.76	q	OG	Sydney	22 Sep
82.60	Vladimir	Ovchinnikov	RUS	2.8.70	2	NC	Tula	23 Jul
82.37	Grzegorz	Krasinski	POL	11.1.75	1		Lappeenranta	13 Aug
82.35	Juha	Laukkanen	FIN	6.1.69	3		Eurajoki	1 Jul
82.28	Rajmund	Kólko	POL	1.3.71	1		Zielona Góra	6 May
82.24	Arunas	Jurksas	LTU	3.5.72	4		Pihtipudas	23 Jul
82.16	Andrus	Värnik	EST	27.9.77	1		Haapsalu	29 Jul
82.03A	Gregor	Högler	AUT	27.6.72	3		Pretoria	24 Mar
	(40)							
81.49	Björn	Lange	GER	15.6.79	1	NC-23	Jena	19 Aug
81.43	Maximo	Rigondeaux	CUB	17.10.76	3		Dessau	31 May
81.41	Kimmo	Kinnunen	FIN	31.3.68	3	Nurmi	Turku	2 Aug
80.83	Sami	Saksio	FIN	28.4.69	5		Eurajoki	1 Jul
80.54A	Johan	Vosloo	RSA	26.3.77	1		Potchefstroom	14 Feb
80.48	Vadim	Bavikin	ISR	4.10.70	1		Tel Aviv	3 Jun
80.42	Daniel	Daub	GER	3.2.76	2	NC	Braunschweig	30 Jul
80.26	Pekka	Alaräisänen	FIN	27.12.75	2		Äanekoski	9 Aug
80.19	Christian	Nicolay	GER	4.3.76	3	NC	Braunschweig	30 Jul
80.18	Maher	Ridane	TUN	11.11.77	1		Tunis	3 Jun
	(50)							
80.16	Ty	Sevin	USA	17.6.71	1		College Station	15 Apr
79.93	Laurent	Dorique	FRA	10.7.76	1		Tergnier	1 Jun
79.90	Andreas	Linden	GER	20.2.65	5		Dessau	31 May
79.85	David	Brisseault	FRA	7.3.69	1		Boulouris	4 Mar
79.76A	Johannes	van Eck	RSA	28.1.74	1		Pietersburg	8 Apr
79.67	Jagdish	Singh Bishnoi	IND	20.5.72	1	Inter-St	Chennai	31 Jul
79.57	Gergely	Horváth	HUN	5.6.75	1		Lisboa	18 Jun
79.50	Luiz F	da Silva	BRA	2.7.71	1		Asunción	29 Jul
79.40	Mark	Roberson	GBR	13.3.67	1	NCp	Bedford	19 Aug
79.21	Marko	Hyytiäinen	FIN	27.11.66	7		Kuortane	24 Jun
	(60)							
79.13	Miroslav	Guzdek	CZE	3.8.75	1		Praha	30 Jul
79.04	Todd	Riech	USA	24.10.70	5	vGBR	Glasgow	2 Jul
78.94	Scott	Russell	CAN	16.1.79	1		Waco	25 Mar
78.85		Zhang Lianbiao	CHN	25.1.69	2	NGP	Shijiazhuang	28 Apr
78.71	Ari	Pakarinen	FIN	14.5.69	1		Joensuu	25 Jul
78.57	Yukifumi	Murakami	JPN	23.12.79	1		Itoman	19 Mar
78.55		Song Dong-hyun	KOR-J	17.11.81	1		Kimchun	19 Jun
78.26	Dimitríos	Martátos	GRE	21.5.74	2		Pireás	23 Apr
78.24	David	Parker	GBR	28.2.80	1cB		Halle	27 May
78.13	Dominique	Pausé	FRA	11.1.76	2		Miramas	5 Jul
	(70)							
78.11	Hardus	Pienaar	RSA-J	10.8.81	1	WJ	Santiago de Chile	22 Oct
77.95	Adrian	Markowski	POL	14.10.78	3		Biala Podlaska	17 Jun
77.95	Jarkko	Koski-Vähälä	FIN	21.11.78	q	NC	Lahti	18 Aug
77.88		Chen Qi	CHN-J	10.3.82	2	NGP	Tianjin	3 May
77.77	Dmitriy	Shnayder	KGZ	30.5.76	1	NC	Bishkek	1 Jul
77.74	Nery	Kennedy	PAR	28.5.73	1		Austin	6 May
77.74	Dmitriy	Polyunin	UZB	6.4.69	1	NC	Almaty	15 Jul
77.68	Ronny	Nilsen	NOR	7.5.71	1		Fana	10 Sep
77.65		Chu Ki-young	KOR	4.3.77	2		Kimchun	19 Jun
77.58	Yuriy	Rybin	RUS	5.3.63	5	Kuso	Warszawa	24 Jun
	(80)							

Mark	Name		Nat	Born	Pos	Meet	Venue	Date
77.56	Philippe	Gandrey	FRA	14.3.73	1		Dijon	7 Jul
77.54		Sun Shipeng	CHN	10.3.76	2	NGPF	Jinzhou	7 Jun
77.48	Andreas	Thorkildsen	NOR-J	1.4.82	1		Düdingen	30 Sep
77.47	Brahman Shankar	Dubey	IND		1		Bangalore	17 Jul
77.20	Gustavo	Dacal	ESP	30.3.77	1		Pontevedra	8 Jul
77.16A	Brian	Erasmus	RSA	28.2.80	1		Pietersburg	18 Nov
77.11	Aleksandr	Ivanov	RUS-J	25.5.82	1	NC-23	Cheboksary	2 Jul
77.07	Armin	Kerer	ITA	27.6.72	1	NC	Pordenone	1 Sep
77.00	Teemu	Pasanen	FIN	24.5.77	6		Eurajoki	1 Jul
76.96	Roald	Bradstock	USA	24.4.62	1	Towns	Athens GA	1 Apr
	(90)							
76.96	Om Prakash	Dudi	IND	.77	1	NC	Calcutta	11 Oct
76.79	Dimítrios	Polimérou	GRE	17.5.74	1cB		Pireás	23 Apr
76.78		Zhang Houxi	CHN-J	15.1.81	3	NGP	Tianjin	3 May
76.74	Satbir	Singh	IND	25.8.72	1		Nagercoil	1 Jul
76.64	Kurt	Thompson	TRI	13.12.67	1		Indianapolis	22 Apr
76.60	Tomasz	Damszel	POL	25.3.72	4	NC	Kraków	5 Aug
76.48	Pietari	Skyttä	FIN	24.5.76	1		Kangasala	27 Jul
76.43	Pavel	Stasyuk	BLR	14.6.77	2	Klim	Stayki	27 Jun
76.25	Jarkko	Kinnunen	FIN	21.4.70	5		Äänekoski	9 Aug
76.06	Janis	Liepa	LAT-J	14.3.81	1		Ventspils	17 Jun
	(100)							

Mark	First	Last	Nat	Born	Date
76.01	Christian	Fusenig	GER	9.5.78	25 Aug
76.00	Raimundo	Fernández	ESP	5.6.70	19 Aug
75.89		Cao Jun	CHN-J	12.11.83	13 May
75.89	Gaëtan	Siakinou-Schmidt	FRA	6.4.74	4 Aug
75.87		Park Jae-myong	KOR-J	15.12.81	9 Jun
75.78	Ireneusz	Karasinski	POL	1.11.71	17 Jun
75.76	José Manuel	Hermoso	ESP	10.8.75	30 Apr
75.56	Walid	Mohamed	EGY		3 Jun
75.55A	Johan	Kloeck	BEL	4.12.75	18 Mar
75.55	Patrick	Landmesser	CZE	7.1.69	30 Jul
75.51	Alejandro	García	ESP	15.3.76	28 Jun
75.48	Andis	Anskins	LAT	25.1.79	29 Jul
75.47	Jari	Hartikainen	FIN	28.4.67	27 Jul
75.37	Stuart	Faben	GBR	28.2.75	22 Apr
75.36	Felix	Loretz	SUI	13.11.75	20 Aug
75.29	Daniel	Kratzmann	AUS-J	19.2.81	5 Feb
75.26	Tim	Werner	GER	25.9.80	31 May
75.25	Alberto	Desiderio	ITA	26.3.73	3 Aug
75.20	Richard	Knudsen	DEN	28.7.72	26 Aug
75.18	Marc	Van Mensel	BEL	18.5.71	30 Sep
75.10	Mikael	Snällfot	SWE	23.5.80	19 Aug
75.07	Matthias	Rau	GER	21.12.74	18 Jun
75.06	Artur	Wszelaki	POL	.79	22 Sep
75.04	József	Belák	HUN	13.8.58	2 Jul
74.81	Ramandeep	Singh	IND	.78	1 Jul
74.80	Vadim	Yevtukhovich	BLR-J	.81	4 Mar
74.70	Jan	Navara	CZE	12.6.79	11 Jun
74.66	Paolo	Valt	ITA	15.7.72	14 May
74.63		Gao Wenxu	CHN	1.3.73	26 Mar
74.63A	Noraldo	Palacios	COL	8.7.80	7 Dec
74.59		An Hyuk-yun	KOR	23.3.79	3 May
74.59	Richard	Alneroth	SWE	10.2.80	7 Jun
74.58	Oleg	Statsenko	UKR	22.10.80	24 Mar
74.58	Marko	Kantanen	FIN	17.4.78	20 Jul
74.51A	Mats	Nilsson	SWE	16.7.75	19 May
74.38	Ari	Weckström	FIN	23.10.67	14 Jun
74.37	Joachim	Kiteau	FRA-J	23.6.82	29 Jul
74.30A	Willie	Human	RSA-J	8.3.82	17 Sep
74.28	Oscar	Duncan	USA	5.3.75	29 Apr
74.21	Igor	Lisovskiy	BLR	4.2.77	2 Aug
74.15	Francesco	Pignata	ITA	14.2.78	27 Feb
74.15A	Juan	de la Garza	MEX	20.9.61	16 Jul
74.12	Oliver	Zschunke	GER	29.4.70	4 Aug
74.10	Robi	Tersek	SLO	1.7.70	7 May
74.10	Daniel	Ragnvaldsson	SWE	3.1.76	7 Jun
74.06	Esko	Mikkola	FIN	14.2.75	11 Jun
74.03A	Luis Carlos	Lucumí	COL	25.12.58	6 May
74.00	Mariusz	Roszkowski	POL	16.11.75	20 Aug
	(148)				

Best at low altitude

Mark	Name		Nat	Born	Pos	Meet	Venue	Date
83.42	Adrian	Hatcher	AUS	6.5.70	1		Perth	5 Feb
80.89	Gregor	Högler	AUT	27.6.72	17q	OG	Sydney	23 Sep
80.29	Marius	Corbett	RSA	26.9.75	1	NC	Stellenbosch	4 Mar
80.05	Johan	Vosloo	RSA	26.3.77	2		Ljubljana	25 Jul

JUNIORS

See main list for top 7 men. 10 performances to 76.78 by 6 men. Additional marks and further juniors:

Pienaar	78.07A	1		Pretoria	10 Sep	77.46A	1	Krugersdorp	8 Sep
Ivanov	77.10	3	Znam	St-Peterburg	17 Jun				
Song	77.02	1		Jaechun	3 May				

Mark	Name		Nat	Born	Pos	Meet	Venue	Date
75.89		Cao Jun	CHN	12.11.83	2	NGP	Deyang	13 May
75.87		Park Jae-myong	KOR	15.12.81	1	NC	Daejun	9 Jun
75.29	Daniel	Kratzmann (10)	AUS	19.2.81	3		Perth	5 Feb
74.80	Vadim	Yevtukhovich	BLR	.81			Brest	4 Mar
74.37	Joachim	Kiteau	FRA	23.6.82	q		Angers	29 Jul
74.30A	Willie	Human	RSA	8.3.82	2		Pretoria	17 Sep
73.75	Tero	Pitkämäki	FIN	19.12.82	1		Pihtipudas	20 Jul
73.45	Harri	Hietala	FIN	8.10.81	2		Alavus	11 Jun
73.29	Pasi	Kuusinen	FIN	8.5.81	1	NC-j	Tampere	5 Aug
73.16A	Fanie	du Toit	RSA	25.3.81	1	NC-j	Pietersburg	14 Apr
73.13	Sergey	Tsydikh	BLR	.81			Brest	4 Mar
73.07	Vadims	Vasilevskis	LAT	5.1.82	2		Riga	4 Aug
73.06	Stefan	Wenk (20)	GER	13.3.81	1		Girona	16 Sep

Mark	Name		Nat	Born	Pos	Meet	Venue	Date

PENTATHLON

3866	6.99	59.24	22.49	43.88	4:28.98	Jirí	Ryba	CZE	15.6.76	1	Olomouc	7 May
3835	7.49	65.52	22.42	39.25	4:54.44	Klaus	Ambrosch	AUT	23.5.73	1	Lienz	21 May
3624	6.83	55.20	22.56	41.65	4:43.64	Thorsten	Didio	GER	1.9.76	1	Ulm	29 Jul
3584	6.68	62.96	22.59	41.38	5:02.64	Michael	Schnallinger	AUT	29.4.80	2	Lienz	21 May
3549	7.62	45.62	22.85	39.75	4:52.91	Roland	Schwarzl	AUT	10.12.80	3	Lienz	21 May
3492	6.99	54.57	23.12	34.25	4:36.60	Stefan	Wimmer	GER	4.4.77		T'rkheim	12 Aug
3471	7.08	56.95	22.85	32.07	4:46.38	Sebastian	Nehring	GER	12.6.78		Gelsenkirchen	30 Sep
3463	6.65	59.95	23.97	39.99	4:47.48	Vit	Rus	CZE	19.12.75	2	Olomouc	7 May
3458	6.62	55.37	23.36	44.17	4:59.50	Ales	Pastrnak	CZE	9.4.76	1	Kolín	27 Aug

DECATHLON

8900	Tomás	Dvorák	CZE	11.5.72	1		Götzis	4 Jun		
	10.54/1.3	8.03/0.0	16.68	2.09	48.36	13.89/-1.0	47.89	4.85	67.21	4:42.33
8757	Roman	Sebrle	CZE	26.11.74	2		Götzis	4 Jun		
	10.64/1.3	7.88/1.6	15.19	2.15	49.05	13.99/-1.0	47.21	4.75	67.23	4:35.06
8742	Erki	Nool	EST	25.6.70	3		Götzis	4 Jun		
	10.69/1.3	7.78/1.8	14.14	1.97	47.18	14.37/-0.1	44.16	5.55	69.10	4:35.59
8733		Dvorák			1	Deca	Talence	30 Jul		
	10.75/-1.2	7.58/2.0	16.14	1.95	48.07	13.93/0.8	49.22	4.90	69.37	4:30.83
8706		Nool			2	Deca	Talence	30 Jul		
	10.69/-1.2	7.81/1.2	14.20	1.95	46.95	14.43/0.8	41.84	5.50	68.89	4:30.40
8641		Nool			1	OG	Sydney	28 Sep		
	10.68/-1.1	7.76/-0.7	15.11	2.00	46.71	14.48/-1.4	43.66	5.00	65.82	4:29.48
8606		Sebrle			2	OG	Sydney	28 Sep		
	10.92/-1.1	7.62/0.0	15.22	2.12	48.20	13.87/-1.4	44.39	4.80	64.04	4:28.79
8595	Chris	Huffins	USA	15.4.70	3	OG	Sydney	28 Sep		
	10.48/0.4	7.71/-0.3	15.27	2.09	48.31	13.91/-1.4	49.55	4.70	56.62	4:38.71
8574	Aleksandr	Yurkov	UKR	21.7.75	4		Götzis	4 Jun		
	10.69/0.9	7.93/1.8	15.26	2.03	49.74	14.56/-0.9	47.85	5.15	58.92	4:32.49
8567	Dean	Macey	GBR	12.12.77	4	OG	Sydney	28 Sep		
	10.81/-1.1	7.77/-0.5	14.62	2.09	46.41	14.53/-1.4	43.37	4.80	60.38	4:23.45
8554	Attila	Zsivóczky	HUN	29.4.77	5		Götzis	4 Jun		
	10.64w/2.1	7.24/-1.0	15.72	2.18	48.13	14.87/-0.9	45.64	4.65	63.57	4:23.13
8531	Frank	Busemann	GER	26.2.75	6		Götzis	4 Jun		
	10.76/-0.1	7.92/1.8	14.50	2.03	48.87	14.72/-1.0	43.66	5.05	62.78	4:23.23
8485	Stefan	Schmid	GER	6.5.70	1	OT	Ratingen	23 Jul		
	10.82/0.0	7.59/-0.6	14.14	2.01	48.99	14.20/-1.6	44.24	5.06	67.63	4:31.76
8467	Tom	Pappas (10)	USA	6.9.76	1	NC	Sacramento	21 Jul		
	10.70/1.1	7.41/-1.4	15.32	2.14	48.91	14.27/-0.4	45.81	5.10	63.45	4:59.74
8461	Mike	Maczey	GER	28.9.72	7		Götzis	4 Jun		
	10.99/0.9	7.59/0.3	14.75	2.06	49.83	14.16/-1.0	44.56	5.15	62.27	4:29.93
8445		Schmid			8		Götzis	4 Jun		
	10.82/0.9	7.65/-0.2	14.39	2.00	49.03	14.45/-2.2	42.14	5.05	69.16	4:32.46
8425		Pappas			5	OG	Sydney	28 Sep		
	10.82/0.4	7.41/-0.4	14.87	2.21	48.64	14.15/-1.4	41.42	4.90	62.26	4:45.10
8385		Dvorák			6	OG	Sydney	28 Sep		
	10.91/-1.1	7.50/-0.1	15.91	1.97	49.11	14.34/-1.4	47.15	4.40	69.94	4:32.23
8351		Busemann			7	OG	Sydney	28 Sep		
	10.91/-1.1	7.64/-0.9	14.52	2.09	48.97	14.16/-1.4	33.71	5.00	64.91	4:25.32
8339	Jirí	Ryba	CZE	15.6.76	1		Desenzano del Garda	14 May		
	11.10/0.2	6.83/0.2	14.33	2.03	48.30	14.55/0.6	45.26	5.20	61.55	4:12.14
8314	Jan	Podebradsky	CZE	1.3.74	1		Arles	4 Jun		
	10.73/1.9	7.20/1.6	15.30	1.90	46.78	14.32/0.0	43.51	4.85	55.92	4:17.69
8293		Zsivóczky			3	Deca	Talence	30 Jul		
	11.00/2.1	7.06/3.0	14.69	2.16	48.68	15.23/0.8	46.75	4.60	65.26	4:25.81
8285		Huffins			2	NC	Sacramento	21 Jul		
	10.45/0.5	7.87/-0.6	14.60	2.11	48.64	14.31/-0.9	50.27	4.50	54.35	5:11.01
8277		Zsivóczky			8	OG	Sydney	28 Sep		
	11.10/-1.1	7.00/0.2	14.96	2.06	48.61	15.27/0.0	47.43	4.80	65.87	4:23.37
8253	Wilfrid	Boulineau	FRA	13.5.70	2		Arles	4 Jun		
	10.82w/3.2	7.39w/3.0	14.16	2.05	48.81	14.95/0.0	41.21	5.05	62.59	4:31.07
8252	Raúl	Duany	CUB	4.1.75	1	NC	La Habana	24 Jul		
	10.66/-0.8	7.48/0.2	13.96	2.01	49.52	13.9h/-1.8	41.38	4.60	64.20	4:26.56
8244		Duany			3		Arles	4 Jun		
	10.82/3.2	7.19/1.2	13.95	2.11	49.31	14.24/0.0	40.85	4.65	64.71	4:26.54
8228		Sebrle			4	Deca	Talence	30 Jul		
	10.96/-1.2	7.33/0.0	14.76	2.07	48.78	14.23/0.8	46.37	4.40	62.71	4:36.87

Mark	Name		Nat	Born	Pos	Meet	Venue			Date
8224	Eduard	Hämäläinen	FIN	21.1.69	1	NC	Lahti			20 Aug
	11.01/-0.1	7.32/2.0	15.30	1.96	48.43	14.25/0.1	43.48	5.10	56.12	4:34.83
8209h	Roman	Razbeyko	RUS	9.3.73	1		Novosibirk			20 Aug
	10.9	7.52	15.49	2.06	51.5	14.3	46.50	5.00	60.43	4:43.1
	(30/17)									
8206	Jón Arnar	Magnússon	ISL	28.7.69	9		Götzis			4 Jun
	10.81/-0.1	7.68/0.7	15.64	2.00	48.15	16.17/-2.1	46.68	5.05	58.85	4:48.64
8188	Aki	Heikkinen	FIN	24.2.80	2	NC	Lahti			20 Aug
	10.93/-0.1	7.57w/2.3	14.11	1.90	49.23	14.88/0.1	40.81	5.00	68.50	4:30.82
8178	Laurent	Hernu	FRA	22.8.76	5	1 NC	Talence			30 Jul
	11.15w/2.1	7.26/-0.4	14.12	2.10	49.98	14.25/0.0	44.81	5.10	56.16	4:36.68
	(20)									
8178	Henrik	Dagård	SWE	7.8.69	10	OG	Sydney			28 Sep
	10.84/0.2	7.08/0.1	14.97	1.94	48.75	14.30/0.0	42.95	5.10	65.05	4:49.51
8153	Philipp	Huber	SUI	18.2.74	10		Götzis			4 Jun
	11.00/0.9	7.32/0.4	14.19	1.88	48.80	14.78/-2.2	44.60	5.05	59.44	4:21.06
8149	Zsolt	Kürtösi	HUN	21.3.71	11	OG	Sydney			28 Sep
	11.00/0.4	7.19/-0.1	15.13	2.00	48.81	14.15/0.0	46.62	4.80	57.16	4:43.39
8136	Mário	Aníbal	POR	25.3.72	12	OG	Sydney			28 Sep
	10.97/0.4	6.90/-0.3	15.39	2.03	48.71	14.71/0.0	45.01	4.90	57.51	4:32.68
8127	Florian	Schönbeck	GER	13.1.74	1	NC	Wesel			3 Sep
	11.34/0.1	7.28/0.0	14.13	1.91	49.07	14.54/0.1	42.22	5.20	64.70	4:29.74
8113	Klaus	Ambrosch	AUT	23.5.73	11		Götzis			4 Jun
	10.84w/2.1	7.37/1.4	15.09	1.91	49.54	14.62/-2.2	40.92	4.55	68.16	4:30.12
8108	David	Mewes	GER	7.10.76	12		Götzis			4 Jun
	11.32w/2.1	7.46/1.2	15.64	2.00	50.39	14.82/-2.1	47.51	4.65	61.19	4:34.83
8097	Phil	McMullen	USA	3.2.75	1		Knoxville			13 Apr
	11.20/1.3	7.02/1.8	14.36	2.00	49.17	14.63/1.0	46.96	4.97	56.10	4:25.54
8094	Lionel	Marceny	FRA	17.7.74	4		Arles			4 Jun
	10.84/1.9	7.72w/2.6	12.90	1.99	48.61	14.29/0.6	40.43	5.15	50.82	4:36.26
8073	Fyodor	Laukhin	UKR	13.2.74	1	NC	Kiev			28 Jul
	11.09/0.5	7.35/0.6	12.70	2.06	49.86	14.56/1.5	39.66	5.00	58.80	4:19.62
	(30)									
8071	Lev	Lobodin	RUS	1.4.69	13	OG	Sydney			28 Sep
	10.75/0.4	7.18/0.6	15.75	1.94	48.87	14.02/-1.4	44.55	5.00	50.16	4:50.73
8069	Pródromos	Korkízoglou	GRE	27.2.75	1	ECp-1	Schwyz/Ibach			2 Jul
	10.60/1.3	7.24/1.1	14.39	2.01	49.86	14.25/0.4	41.82	5.00	56.93	4:50.77
8058	Eugenio	Balanqué	CUB	20.12.68	5		Arles			4 Jun
	10.71w/3.2	7.07w/2.6	14.90	1.93	48.20	14.25/0.6	42.14	4.85	61.21	4:51.75
8057	Kip	Janvrin	USA	8.7.65	3	NC	Sacramento			21 Jul
	11.03/0.5	6.92/-1.5	13.94	1.90	48.39	14.88/-1.8	42.30	5.00	59.30	4:12.01
8052	Vladimir	Mikhaylenko	UKR	27.8.73	1	NCp	Kiev			4 Jun
	11.07/0.7	7.53/1.1	14.20	2.00	48.56	14.56/1.0	41.00	4.90	50.70	4:25.91
8030	Trond	Høiby	NOR	24.1.73	1	SWE Ch	Huddinge			6 Aug
	11.30w/2.3	6.82w/2.3	14.32	1.92	49.65	14.97/1.1	46.83	4.71	70.18	4:24.39
8024	Indrek	Kaseorg	EST	16.12.67	3	ECp-1	Schwyz/Ibach			2 Jul
	11.38/1.3	7.26/-0.6	13.89	1.98	49.52	14.48/0.4	41.53	4.60	68.37	4:27.32
8002	Bevan	Hart	USA	1.8.77	1	NCAA	Durham			3 Jun
	11.07/0.8	6.75w/2.4	13.93	2.02	48.41	14.92/-0.4	39.86	5.40	53.76	4:26.65
8002	Klaus	Isekenmeier	GER	14.4.75	3	OT	Ratingen			23 Jul
	11.36/0.0	7.28/0.7	15.20	1.98	50.22	14.73/-1.6	47.11	4.66	59.34	4:33.64
7984	Rolf	Schläfli	SUI	15.3.71	4	ECp-1	Schwyz/Ibach			2 Jul
	11.08/1.3	7.30w/2.2	14.43	1.95	48.62	14.80/0.0	46.94	4.20	63.42	4:33.84
	(40)									
7974	Philip	Ibe	GER	5.5.75	4	OT	Ratingen			23 Jul
	10.86/0.0	7.84/1.0	15.17	1.95	52.87	14.69/ 1.6	45.72	4.66	61.88	4:57.36
7954	Brian	Brophy	USA	6.1.69	1		Manhattan KS			8 Jul
	11.29w/2.6	7.12w/4.0	16.50	2.00	50.57	15.44w/3.5	51.51	4.90	56.23	4:56.3h
7952	Avery	Anderson	USA	16.3.73	1		Northridge			1 Jul
	10.78/0.9	7.41/0.7	12.43	2.10	49.24	13.95/0.7	44.60	4.50	49.46	4:41.81
7951h	Brendon	Falconer	USA	15.4.75	1		Indianapolis			9 Jul
	10.9	7.42	14.25	1.97	48.6	14.0	38.82	4.50	57.58	4:26.8
7929	Dmitriy	Ivanov	RUS	23.3.77	2	NC	Tula			25 Jul
	10.92/-1.5	7.10/1.4	14.40	1.94	48.02	14.57/-0.7	41.67	4.80	54.53	4:37.42
7919	Ross	Bomben	USA	6.4.75	1		Chula Vista			23 Jun
	10.78	7.36	12.96	1.92	49.93	14.11	41.74	5.10	52.94	4:43.00
7914A	Mike	Nolan	CAN	22.9.73	1		Logan			27 May
	11.38/-0.5	7.33/0.6	14.23	2.02	50.98	15.05w/2.7	48.06	4.90	64.37	5:01.28
7909	Gaëtan	Blouin	FRA	4.1.74	7		Arles			4 Jun
	10.88/1.9	7.36w/2.4	12.31	2.02	49.36	14.64/0.0	40.68	4.75	58.68	4:35.99

Mark	Name			Nat	Born	Pos	Meet	Venue		Date
7903w	Ricky	Barker		USA	14.11.69	1	TexR	Austin		6 Apr
	10.73w/3.6	7.29w/3.8	14.12	2.03	50.20	14.64W/4.5	42.18	4.90	58.52	5:05.82
7897	Dennis	Leyckes		GER-J	20.4.82	1	WJ	Santiago de Chile		19 Oct
	10.98/1.6	7.22/0.4	13.46	1.95	47.59	14.61/-0.1	39.52	4.80	54.76	4:33.10
	(50)									
7890	Dan	Steele		USA	20.3.69	5	NC	Sacramento		21 Jul
	10.85/1.1	6.90/0.9	13.84	1.84	47.80	14.70/-0.4	47.26	4.40	64.03	4:40.44
7847	Chiel	Warners		NED	2.4.78	6	ECp-1	Schwyz/Ibach		2 Jul
	10.79/1.3	7.62/1.9	14.45	1.86	48.17	14.39/0.4	36.35	4.80	58.23	4:59.59
7840	Kamil	Damasek		CZE	22.9.73	8		Arles		4 Jun
	11.17w/3.4	7.09/1.3	14.47	1.99	49.24	15.03/0.7	41.98	4.85	54.20	4:34.73
7836	Christer	Holger		SWE	16.1.74	2	NC	Huddinge		6 Aug
	10.90w/2.3	7.29w/4.0	13.79	1.92	50.37	14.96/1.1	40.85	4.81	55.26	4:26.05
7830w	Jeff	Sander		USA	13.2.76	2		Manhattan KS		8 Jul
	11.18/1.4	7.40W/4.4	13.19	2.06	50.81	14.14w/3.5	40.33	4.70	51.90	4:33.9h
7830	Stephan	Zeyen		GER	11.9.78	1	v2N23	Val-de-Reuil		13 Aug
	11.02/-0.5	7.21w/2.1	13.27	1.97	49.24	14.38/0.5	38.63	4.75	64.35	4:53.08
7827	Chad	Smith		USA	9.1.74	18		Götzis		4 Jun
	11.07/-0.1	7.24/1.2	14.19	1.85	49.16	14.73/-2.1	45.39	4.85	60.46	4:56.52
7812	Sebastian	Knabe		GER	13.10.78	1		Bernhausen		28 May
	10.97/0.2	7.29/-1.5	14.26	1.95	49.21	14.49/-0.3	44.90	4.50	48.95	4:37.08
7812	Stefan	Drews		GER	12.2.79	4	vUSA	Uniondale		13 Aug
	11.02/-0.2	7.17/1.3	11.01	2.00	47.85	14.23/1.3	36.89	5.21	51.90	4:37.29
7806	Claston	Bernard		JAM	22.3.79	2	NCAA	Durham		3 Jun
	10.98/0.8	6.71/0.7	15.26	2.11	48.22	14.87/0.8	46.26	3.90	56.40	4:44.46
	(60)									
7803	Stephen	Moore		USA	13.8.75	5	vGER	Uniondale		13 Aug
	10.91/-0.2	7.53w/3.5	12.33	2.12	48.60	14.76/1.3	41.27	4.41	50.73	4:43.69
7802	Georgios	Andréou		CYP	26.7.74	1	GRE Ch	Volos		12 Aug
	10.83	7.16	15.16	1.96	51.21	15.37/0.7	45.13	4.90	59.31	5:03.03
7801	Ales	Pastrnák		CZE	9.4.76	1		Praha		23 Jul
	11.48/0.2	7.13/0.2	14.16	2.01	51.59	14.86/-1.3	44.54	4.80	60.94	4:39.99
7793	Peter	Sóldos		SVK	27.4.73	3		Desenzano del Garda		14 May
	11.07/0.9	6.90/0.4	15.38	1.94	49.68	14.69/0.6	42.82	4.70	62.64	4:59.73
7790	Marcos	Moreno		ESP	14.3.73	1	NC	Logroño		20 Aug
	11.08/-0.1	7.30/0.6	13.68	2.05	51.01	15.13/0.7	46.39	4.40	53.62	4:32.31
7788	Boris	Kawohl		GER	1.4.77	3	NCAA	Durham		3 Jun
	11.48/0.7	6.89/0.7	13.24	1.96	49.02	14.97/-0.5	44.26	4.80	56.46	4:22.46
7784	Nikolay	Afanasyev		RUS	11.8.65	2	NCp	Tula		3 Jun
	11.18	6.86	15.27	2.02	52.32	14.64	43.92	4.70	59.53	4:44.17
7783	Marc	Magrans		ESP	26.9.76	2		Alhama de Murcia		4 Jun
	10.83/1.2	7.26/1.5	13.18	1.92	48.89	14.98/0.8	38.46	4.80	52.28	4:25.08
7780	Jari	Olli		FIN	3.4.77	3	NC	Lahti		20 Aug
	10.95/-0.1	7.58/0.8	13.64	1.93	50.41	14.85/0.1	40.29	4.80	60.87	4:57.26
7772	Jörg	Goedicke		GER	25.6.74	6	vUSA	Uniondale		13 Aug
	11.22/-0.2	7.52w/2.7	14.42	2.00	50.40	14.48w/2.6	40.63	4.81	52.20	4:52.43
	(70)									
7772	David	Gómez		ESP-J	13.2.81	2	WJ	Santiago de Chile		19 Oct
	11.03/-0.4	7.12/-0.3	13.06	1.92	47.81	14.52/-0.1	39.17	4.30	58.64	4:24.55
7763w	Paul	Elson		USA	.66	3		Manhattan KS		8 Jul
	11.09w/2.6	6.93W/4.6	13.10	2.00	49.44	14.94w/3.5	41.49	4.70	55.72	4:27.2h
7758	Adrian	Krebs		SUI	8.6.77	1		Zofingen		10 Sep
	10.74/1.7	7.25/-0.4	13.55	1.90	48.81	14.50/0.4	40.61	4.50	56.34	4:45.02
7756	Tomás	Komenda		CZE	24.7.78	1		Maribor		28 May
	11.12w/2.4	7.66/1.6	13.95	2.02	50.77	14.92/0.7	39.30	4.80	51.52	4:44.57
7753	Thomas	Pöge		GER	6.9.79	2		Bernhausen		28 May
	11.20/0.2	7.15/-0.2	14.99	2.01	50.97	14.97/-0.3	39.16	4.60	58.78	4:36.38
7751	Stéphane	Bamboux		FRA	28.2.74	9		Arles		4 Jun
	10.76/1.9	7.14/1.7	13.21	1.84	49.52	14.49/0.0	42.11	5.05	54.67	4:51.94
7746	Rojs	Piziks		LAT	12.2.71	1	ECp-2	Esbjerg		2 Jul
	11.58w/2.1	6.99/1.0	14.50	2.13	52.55	15.42/0.0	46.21	4.70	59.03	4:39.84
7732		Du Xiaopeng		CHN	8.1.77	1	NC	Luohe		22 Oct
	10.88	7.17	13.93	1.96	50.81	15.01	46.76	4.50	55.10	4:45.52
7720	Jagan	Hames		AUS	31.10.75	2	NC	Sydney		25 Feb
	11.20/-1.3	7.29/0.5	14.03	2.09	50.93	14.76/0.0	45.68	4.60	56.44	5:11.17
7714	Xavier	Brunet		ESP	5.2.71	3		Alhama de Murcia		4 Jun
	11.17/0.9	7.02/0.5	13.66	2.13	50.00	14.73/0.8	40.03	4.80	48.02	4:41.63
	(80)									
7712	André	Niklaus		GER-J	30.8.81	3	WJ	Santiago de Chile		19 Oct
	11.09/0.6	6.94/0.7	13.25	1.92	48.55	14.61/-0.1	39.32	4.90	49.51	4:26.58

Mark	Name			Nat	Born	Pos	Meet	Venue		Date
7706	Oscar	González		ESP	8.8.76	4		Alhama de Murcia		4 Jun
	10.83/1.2	7.58/1.5	12.18	2.04	48.60	14.51/0.8	38.24	4.20	46.25	4:26.09
7705	Darrin	Steele		USA	20.3.69	1cA		Sacramento		31 Mar
	10.67/2.0	6.68w/2.5	13.35	1.74	47.89	14.31w/2.3	46.38	4.50	62.02	4:54.26
7702	Viktor	Kovalenko		MDA		1		Chisinau		11 Jun
7701	Harri	Laiho		FIN	1.3.77	4	NC	Lahti		20 Aug
	11.04/-0.1	7.25/0.7	13.88	1.99	49.99	14.99/0.1	37.81	4.80	57.75	4:49.59
7701	Matthias	Spahn		GER	3.1.79	1	NC-23	Wesel		3 Sep
	11.05w/2.1	6.81/0.2	15.05	1.97	50.30	15.13/0.5	43.95	4.40	64.42	4:53.67
7700	Scott	Ferrier		AUS	12.6.74	1	OT	Sydney		18 Aug
	11.09/-0.6	7.18/0.7	14.36	1.95	49.88	14.86/-0.2	43.69	4.90	55.47	5:07.59
7690	André	Röttger		GER	26.3.79	1		Neustadt		11 Jun
	11.22/0.4	7.05	13.92	1.92	49.96	15.38/-0.2	42.58	4.30	67.49	4:35.66
7689	Francisco José	Caro		ESP	23.10.78	1		Valladolid		23 Jul
	10.96/-1.2	7.59/0.9	14.21	1.96	49.80	15.35/-0.8	40.28	4.60	56.40	4:56.82
7685	Michal	Modelski		POL	16.4.75	1	NC	Kraków		5 Aug
	11.07/0.0	7.27/1.4	14.10	1.98	49.25	14.70/1.6	39.26	4.70	48.98	4:42.46
	(90)									
7684	Efthímios	Andréoglou		GRE	12.8.70	7	ECp-1	Schwyz/Ibach		2 Jul
	11.26/1.2	7.36/1.7	13.74	2.07	51.72	14.70/0.0	41.60	4.50	57.44	4:49.55
7679	Vladimir	Shatkovskiy		UKR	8.10.75	5		Desenzano del Garda		14 May
	11.20/0.9	6.87/0.6	14.22	1.91	50.32	14.99/1.0	44.90	4.80	58.42	4:47.28
7667	Jamie	Quarry		GBR	15.11.72	10		Arles		4 Jun
	10.83/1.9	7.42w/2.9	13.15	1.87	49.30	14.38/0.6	39.32	4.45	48.92	4:29.67
7651	Stephen	Harris		USA	5.12.80	4	NCAA	Durham		3 Jun
	10.92/0.7	7.13/0.7	12.27	2.11	48.17	14.70/-0.8	37.16	3.90	54.00	4:26.57
7650	Bruno	Lambèse		FRA	11.4.69	11		Arles		4 Jun
	10.78w/3.2	7.37/1.9	14.28	1.96	49.69	15.04/0.6	39.61	4.75	43.68	4:42.66
7649	Santiago	Lorenzo		ARG	4.4.78	2	Pac 10	Eugene		14 May
	11.36/-1.3	7.07/-1.1	13.33	1.88	48.76	15.18w/2.3	41.96	4.60	58.94	4:31.14
7647	William	Gallardo		CUB	17.1.73	2	NC	La Habana		24 Jul
	11.00/-0.6	7.33/1.8	14.30	1.95	51.37	14.1h/-1.1	39.13	4.00	59.94	4:36.46
7642	Anis	Riahi		TUN	30.5.71	7	3 FRA	Talence		30 Jul
	11.01/-1.2	7.22/-0.6	11.20	1.89	47.72	15.31/0.0	38.97	4.40	57.46	4:15.12
7639	Mark	Schumacher		GER	27.6.76	2	NC	Wesel		3 Sep
	11.07/-0.6	6.78/0.5	13.49	1.94	48.10	14.61/1.4	44.68	4.30	52.43	4:37.19
7634	Michael	Schnallinger		AUT	29.4.80	20		Götzis		4 Jun
	11.21/0.4	7.12/-1.1	13.25	2.00	49.79	14.86/-0.1	41.12	4.55	61.97	4:57.92
	(100)									

7633A	Darwin	VandeHoef	USA	16.4.70	27 May
7631	Matt	McEwen	AUS	16.10.71	25 Feb
7630	Yuriy	Zhuravskiy	UKR	10.4.74	14 May
7626	Elliott	Young	USA	23.3.75	10 Jun
7624w	Joe	Cebulski	USA	25.10.76	31 Mar
7624	Cédric	Lopez	FRA	13.2.73	30 Jul
7620	Dmitriy	Karpov	KAZ-J	23.7.81	28 May
7612w	Viktor	Kovács	HUN	5.4.76	28 May
7612	Ivan	Yarkin	KAZ	21.11.74	15 Jul
7611h	Kamau	Sullivan	USA	2.3.70	27 Apr
7609	Romain	Barras	FRA	1.8.80	30 Jul
7600	Tom Erik	Olsen	NOR	20.10.74	4 Jun
7594	Jim	Dunkleberger	USA	27.3.73	1 Jul
7592	Todd	Doughty	USA	11.7.74	21 Jun
7586	Paolo	Casarsa	ITA	2.7.75	14 May
7567	Henri	Kokkonen	FIN	11.8.78	20 Aug
7559	Marzio	Viti	ITA	10.8.73	2 Jul
7554	Brondan	Tennant	AUS	22.4.72	8 Jul
7546	Douglas	Pirini	NZL	6.9.69	9 Jan
7539	Edson Luques	Bindilatti	BRA	13.3.79	21 May
7538	Hitoshi	Maruono	JPN	27.10.71	4 Jun
7536	Robert	Pendergist	USA	12.7.70	1 Jul
7533	Sven	Böhm	GER	5.12.78	2 Jul
7533	Nikolay	Tishchenko	RUS	.77	25 Jul
7532	David	Lemen	USA	13.11.79	2 Ma
7531	Curtis	Pugsley	USA	.78	3 Jun
7527	Igor	Peresypkin	UKR	7.4.75	28 Jul
7521	Jason	Wilson	USA	.78	12 May
7520	Yves	Bourgey	FRA	4.4.71	4 Jun
7517w	James	Johnson	USA	22.11.77	8 Apr
7508	Krzysztof	Andrzejak	POL	10.1.75	14 May
7501	Sergey	Blonskiy	UKR	7.1.73	28 Jul
7497A	Karl	Lerum	USA	23.7.74	27 May
7495	Mirko	Spada	SUI	26.1.69	4 Jun
7495	Ireneusz	Zurawicz	POL	24.1.78	5 Aug
7480	Aivo	Normak	EST	19.8.78	2 Jul
7475	Beniamino	Poserina	ITA	6.11.70	6 Sep
7456	Jurren	Valkenburg	NED	16.4.77	21 May
7452	Pávlos	Kouromihalákis	GRE	16.2.76	28 May
7451w	Mike	Kuoppamaki	USA	22.3.75	31 Mar
7451	Indrek	Turi	EST-J	30.7.81	16 Jul
7451	Erik	Svensson	SWE	10.8.79	10 Sep
7449	Toru	Yasui	JPN	21.4.76	23 Apr
7449	Gerd	Brinkmann	GER	7.2.77	3 Sep
7438	André	Gautschi	SUI	4.7.77	4 Jun
7426	Patrick	Pfingsten	GER	1.2.78	28 May
7426	Jacob	Predmore	USA	17.4.77	3 Jun
7426	Aleksandr	Shtepa	RUS	15.5.79	25 Jul
7418w	Márk	Váczi	HUN	25.4.74	28 May
7416	Luigi	Llanos	PUR	22.8.78	2 Aug
7414	Takeshi	Yoneshima	JPN	1.9.77	23 Apr
7414	Cristian	Gasparro	ITA	15.12.74	6 Sep
7413	Sven	Simuste	EST	25.8.75	2 Jul
7430		Qi Haifeng	CHN-J	7.8.83	4 May
7407	Edemar	dos Santos	BRA	5.9.73	21 May
7407	Barry	Thomas	GBR	28.4.72	20 Aug
	(156)				

Best without wind assistance

7577	Jeff	Sander			1 Apr

Best with automatic timing

7997	Roman	Razbeyko		RUS	9.3.73	1	NC	Tula		25 Jul
	11.30/-1.5	7.30/-0.5	15.31	2.12	51.62	14.69/-0.7	42.69	4.80	63.64	4:52.68

Mark | Name | Nat | Born | Pos | Meet | Venue | Date

JUNIORS

See main list for top 3 marks. Additional marks and jhuniors:

Leyckes 7802 1 v2N-j Val-de-Reuil 13 Aug

Gómez 7649 1 NC-j Santander 1 Oct

Niklaus 7627 1 Bad Oeynhausen 25 Jun

7620 Dmitriy Karpov KAZ 23.7.81 1 Almaty 28 May

11.29/-0.3 7.37/-1.8 13.47 1.96 48.53 14.58/0.2 43.96 4.40 47.40 4:45.59

7451 Indrek Turi EST 30.7.81 1 Tartu 16 Jul

11.44/-1.5 6.67/0.7 12.59 1.90 50.14 14.84/-0.4 35.24 4.80 59.51 4:26.13

7430 Qi Haifeng CHN 7.8.84 1 Tianjin 4 May

11.25 6.86 13.34 1.89 49.84 15.29 45.09 4.00 56.62 4:30.74

7412 1B NSG Chengdu 10 Sep 10 performances by 7 men to 7366

7373 Cao Wen CHN 15.3.81 1 Chengdu 10 May

11.31 7.20 12.76 2.00 50.31 15.61 40.36 4.40 57.00 4:55.00

7275 Sébastien Maillard FRA 2.5.81 2 v2N-j Val-de-Reuil 13 Aug

11.12/1.2 6.99/0.3 12.58 1.94 49.80 14.86/1.5 35.03 4.35 45.59 4:30.15

7257 Marcus Pallentin GER 21.4.81 3 v2N Val-de-Reuil 13 Aug

11.46/1.0 7.22/0.0 13.46 1.94 50.89 14.55/1.5 37.96 3.65 53.10 4:32.72

7248 Liu Jun (10) CHN .81 2 Tianjin 4 May

11.53 6.94 12.65 2.04 50.28 15.40 38.95 4.10 51.10 4:33.77

7222 Ahmed Hassan Moussa QAT .81 1 GulfCh Al-Kuwait 20 Apr

11.32 6.92 12.56 1.81 50.35 15.45 41.69 3.90 63.93 4:40.17

7179 Daniel Baganz GER 15.3.81 3 Bad Oeynhausen 25 Jun

12.10/-0.4 7.15/0.4 14.44 2.00 55.10 15.82/-1.2 38.96 4.50 61.76 4:48.98

7174 Mikk Joorits EST 12.2.81 2 Tartu 16 Jul

11.26/-1.5 7.08/0.1 11.89 1.87 49.43 15.49/-0.4 37.19 4.10 50.62 4:26.59

7164 Virgil Spier NED 8.1.81 5 NC Apeldoorn 27 Aug

10.62/1.0 6.83/-0.7 12.16 1.98 49.22 14.66 37.56 3.80 41.01 4:42.21

7156 Lars Albert GER 9.2.82 4 Bad Oeynhausen 25 Jun

11.70/-0.4 6.94/0.5 14.24 1.91 53.14 15.50/0.5 39.67 4.60 53.49 4:48.74

7152 Marcell Allmond USA 28.5.81 1 Eagle Rock 12 Mar

11.12 6.86 12.66 2.00 50.19 14.58 36.25 4.10 45.11 4:48.31

7131 Pavel Havlícek CZE 3.11.81 6 WJ Santiago de Chile 19 Oct

11.60/1.6 6.86/0.4 12.71 1.98 51.50 15.79/0.2 39.57 4.70 56.15 5:06.21

7087 Yosbel Gómez CUB 19.4.82 1 Santiago de Cuba 5 Mar

11.17/0.5 6.43/-1.2 12.82 1.84 50.12 15.71/0.2 40.94 3.60 61.73 4:31.73

7025 Calen Powell USA 1 Kirkland WA 3 Jun

junior implements?

7000 Leonid Andreyev (20) UZB 6.11.83 2 NC Tashkent 18 Aug

11.46/0.2 7.14/0.4 11.36 1.9651.80 - 15.98/-0.1 31.20 4.70 58.80 4:59.80

4 X 100 METRES RELAY

Mark	Team	Members	Pos	Meet	Venue	Date
37.61	USA	Drummond, Williams, B.Lewis, Greene	1	OG	Sydney	30 Sep
37.65	USA	Drummond, Williams, C.Johnson, Greene	1	ISTAF	Berlin	1 Sep
37.82	USA	Drummond, Williams, B.Lewis, Greene	1s1	OG	Sydney	29 Sep
37.90	BRA	de Lima, Ribeiro, A da Silva, Cl da Silva	2	OG	Sydney	30 Sep
37.95	USA	Drummond, Williams, C Johnson, Greene	1	GP II	Gateshead	28 Aug
38.04	CUB	Cesar, Pérez-Rionda, I García, Mayola	3	OG	Sydney	30 Sep
38.15	USA	Brokenburr, Montgomery, Lewis, Greene	1h5	OG	Sydney	29 Sep
38.16	CUB	Cesar, Pérez-Rionda, I García, Mayola	1s2	OG	Sydney	29 Sep
38.18	USA B	Brokenburr, Montgomery, B.Lewis, Capel	2	ISTAF	Berlin	1 Sep
38.20	JAM	L Frater, D Thomas, C Williams, Bredwood	4	OG	Sydney	30 Sep
38.22	USA Red	Drummond, Harden, Montgomery, Greene	1	PennR	Philadelphia	29 Apr
38.24	BRA	de Lima, Ribeiro, A da Silva, Cl da Silva	1	IbAm	Rio de Janeiro	20 May
38.27	JAM	L Frater, D Thomas, C Williams, Bredwood	2s1	OG	Sydney	29 Sep
38.27	BRA	de Lima, Ribeiro, A da Silva, Cl da Silva	2s2	OG	Sydney	29 Sep
38.31	JPN	Kawabata, K Ito, Suetsugu, Asahara	3s2	OG	Sydney	29 Sep
38.32	BRA	de Lima, Ribeiro, A da Silva, C Sousa	1h2	OG	Sydney	29 Sep
38.35	Univ of Florida (USA)	Carroll, B.Williams, A.Armstrong, G.Whit	1	NCAA	Durham	2 Jun
38.35	GBR	Chambers, Campbell, Devonish, Gardener	2	GP II	Gateshead	28 Aug
38.36	USA Blue	C.Johnson, Brokenburr, Howard, Griffin	2	PennR	Philadelphia	29 Apr
38.36	CUB		1r3		Montauban	15 Aug
38.41	GBR	Malcolm, Campbell, Devonish, Chambers	1	ECp-S	Gateshead	15 Jul
38.45	Univ of S Carolina (USA)	Crenshaw, Trammell, Hackley, J.Howard	2	NCAA	Durham	2 Jun
38.45	BRA	de Lima, Ribeiro, A da Silva, Cl da Silva	1r3		Sydney	14 Sep
38.49	FRA	Krantz, Patros, Cheval, Guims	5	OG	Sydney	30 Sep
38.50A	RSA	Newton, Gorries, La Grange, Quinn	1		Pretoria	24 Mar

25 performances by teams from 8 nations

MEN 2000

Mark	Nat	Name	Pos	Meet	Venue	Date
38.60	POL	Nowak, Urbas, Balcerzak, Pilarczyk	4s2	OG	Sydney	29 Sep
38.67	GRE	Theodorídis, Kedéris, Alexópoulos, Pavlakákis	2	ECp-S	Gateshead	15 Jul
	(10)					
38.67	ITA	Scuderi, Cavallaro, Checcucci, Colombo	4s1	OG	Sydney	29 Sep
38.76A	AUS	Noonan, Di Bella, Baxter, Shirvington	1		Pietersburg	18 Mar
	38.76	Shirvington, Di Bella, Wohlsen, Johnson	2h4	OG	Sydney	29 Sep
38.80	THA	Natenee, Sophanich, Janthana, Suwonprateep	1	AsiC	Jakarta	31 Aug
38.82	CIV	N'Dri, Douhou, Sonan, Meité	5s1	OG	Sydney	29 Sep
38.85	NGR	Emedolu, Anusim, Emmanuel, Aliu	3h2	OG	Sydney	29 Sep
38.88	GER	Kosenkow, Schacht, Schneider, M.Blume	1		Chemnitz	22 Jul
38.92	CAN	McCuaig, Gilbert, Browne, Woodley	6s1	OG	Sydney	29 Sep
38.92	TRI	Alexander, Raeburn, Burns, Boldon	6s2	OG	Sydney	29 Sep
38.98	BAH	Wells, Demeritte, Lewis, Tynes	3r3		Montauban	15 Aug
39.10	HUN	Babály, Pauer, R Németh, Gyulai	1		Budapest	22 Jul
	(20)					
39.19	MRI	Chimier, Milazar, Buckland, Augustin	2r3		Sydney	14 Sep
39.23	ISR	Golan, Jablonka, T Kafri, Porkhomovskiy	1r1	ECp2B	Banská Bystrica	8 Jul
39.25	GUA	Blanco, O Meneses, J Meneses, Tinoco	1		La Habana	30 Jul
39.25	SLO	Sustersic, Osovnikar, Fridrih, Acman	5h2	OG	Sydney	29 Sep
39.26	IRL	McAdorey, Ryan, Comyns, Brizzel	4h3	OG	Sydney	29 Sep
39.29	RUS	Vasilyev, Ryabov, Smirnov, Bychkov	4h5	OG	Sydney	29 Sep
39.36	ESP	Feo, José, Navarro, Nolet	1		Majadahonda	28 Jun
39.42	FIN	Tuikka, Louramo, Hartonen, Näsi	1	Nurmi	Turku	2 Aug
39.45	VEN	Morillo, Peña, Carabalí, Ollarves	5h5	OG	Sydney	29 Sep
39.49	CHI	Faúndez, Ri.Roach, Keitel, Ro.Roach	1		São Paulo	10 Jun
	(30)					
39.49	CYP	Kokkinos, Marcoullides, Katsantonis, Zisimides	1		Nicosia	23 Jun

39.52	SWE	2 Sep	39.77	NED	8 Jul	39.96	YUG	8 Jul	40.31	MAS	25 Feb	40.46	KAZ	28 May
39.57	NOR	8 Jul	39.77	UKR	8 Jul	39.97	HKG	9 May	40.31	KOR	31 Aug	40.46?	PNG	29 Jun
39.60	KSA	31 Aug	39.77	LBR	29 Sep	40.04	SUI	8 Jul	40.35	CZE	15 Jul	40.48	TUR	8 Jul
39.62	CMR	29 Sep	39.81	SVK	1 Jul	40.07	AUT	8 Jul	40.38	BAR	29 Sep	40.49	BUL	8 Jul
39.65	PUR	10 Jun	39.82	OMN	29 Sep	40.11	INA	19 May	40.42	POR	25 Jun	**Best at Low altitude**		
39.68	CHN	10 May	39.90	UZB	15 Jun	40.14	SLE	10 Sep	40.42	NZL-J	22 Oct	39.68	RSA	22 Jul
39.70	IND	31 Aug	39.90	GHA	12 Jul	40.23	BLR	8 Jul	40.43	HAI	20 Aug			
39.76	CRO	29 Jul	39.90	QAT	31 Aug	40.26	ARG	20 May	40.44	BEL	8 Jul			

Mixed nation teams (majority from nation shown in brackets)

Mark	Nat	Name	Pos	Meet	Venue	Date
38.15	HSI (USA)	Drummond, Bolden TRI, B.Howard, C.Johnson	1	MSR	Walnut	16 Apr
38.17	HSI (USA)	Drummond, Bolden TRI, B.Howard, C.Johnson	1		Los Angeles	1 Apr
38.45	HIS (USA)	Johnson, BoldenTRI, Howard, Greene	1		Lawrence	22 Apr
39.70	NED	Beck, van Balkom, Kempen, Douglas AHO	3		Tel Aviv	24 Jul

JUNIORS

Mark	Nat	Name	Pos	Meet	Venue	Date
39.05	GBR	Edgar, Grant, Benjamin, Lewis-Francis	1	WJ	Santiago	22 Oct
39.14	GBR	Edgar, Grant, Benjamin, Lewis-Francis	1h1	WJ	Santiago	22 Oct
39.33	FRA	Pognon, Calligny, Doucouré, Djhone	2	WJ	Santiago	22 Oct
39.47	JPN	Mogi, Kitamura, Omaer, Miyazaki	3	WJ	Santiago	22 Oct
39.61	POL	Latkowski, Jedrusinski, Niczyporuk, Chyla	1h3	WJ	Santiago	22 Oct
39.94	JAM	M Frater, W Smith, Shakespeare, Anderson	2h3	WJ	Santiago	22 Oct
40.03	TRI	Rudder, Burns, Dillon, D Brown	4	WJ	Santiago	22 Oct
40.23	USA	(Duncanville HS)	1		Austin	13 May
40.31	HUN	L Szabó, G Nagy, G Németh, Lörincz	3h1	WJ	Santiago	22 Oct
40.34	GER	Pfennig, Mörsch, Gatzka, Pinnock	3h3	WJ	Santiago	22 Oct
40.42	NZL	Madgwick, Townsend, Jones, McLellan	4h3	WJ	Santiago	22 Oct
40.49	ITA	Oliverio, Gaschi, Rigato, Marsadri	5		Ljubljana	10 Jun
40.57	SUI	Trolliet, Oggier, Mühlbauer, Schneeberger	5h3	WJ	Santiago	22 Oct
40.58	POR	Pacheco, Alves, P Silva, Tavares	1		Maia	6 Aug
40.61	KSA		1	Arab-J	Damascus	5 Nov
40.77A	BRA	L A da Silva, A C Oliveira, Ambrosio, Pacheco	1		Bogotá	4 Nov
40.89	FIN	Javanainen, Johansson, Sillanpää, Vakkuri	2	Nurmi	Turku	2 Aug
	40.7 hand	Javanainen, Johansson, Sillanpää, Vakkuri	2		Tampere	19 Jul

4 X 200 METRES RELAY

Mark	Team	Pos	Meet	Venue	Date
1:19.67	Texas Christian University	1	PennR	Philadelphia	29 Apr
	L Frater JAM, R Williams JAM, Patton USA, Collins SKN				
1:19.92	Nike/USA Brokenburr, Howard, Griffin, Greene	1	PennR	Philadelphia	29 Apr
1:20.39	Texas Christian University	1h3	PennR	Philadelphia	28 Apr
1:20.81	Sprint Capital USA	1		Raleigh	1 Apr
1:21.53	Univ of S.Carolina/USA Hockley, Trammell, Crenshaw, Taylor	1		Knoxville	15 Apr
1:21.57	Florida Univ Mann, Wiliiams, Armstrong, White	2		Knoxville	15 Apr
1:22.66	THA Seehawong, Sophanich, Janthana, Suwonprateep	3	PennR	Philadelphia	29 Apr

4 X 400 METRES RELAY

Mark	Nat	Name	Pos	Meet	Venue	Date
2:56.35	USA	A Harrison 44.36, Pettigrew 44.17, C Harrison 43.53, MJohnson 44.29	1	OG	Sydney	30 Sep
2:56.60	USA Red	Taylor 45.0, Pettigrew 44.2, Washington 43.7, M Johnson 43.7	1	PennR	Philadelphia	29 Apr
2:58.68	NGR	Chukwu 45.18, Monye 44.49, Bada 44.70, Udo-Obong 44.31	2	OG	Sydney	30 Sep
2:58.71	USA Blue	Campbell 45.3, C Harrison 44.8, Byrd 44.6, Je.Davis 44.0	2	PennR	Philadelphia	29 Apr
2:58.78	USA	Young 45.23, Taylor 44.17, C.Harrison 43.56, A.Harrison 45.82	1s1	OG	Sydney	29 Sep
2:58.78	JAM	Blackwood 45.14, Haughton 44.29, C Williams 44.73, McFarlane 44.62	3	OG	Sydney	30 Sep
2:58.84	JAM	Ayre 45.86, Haughton 44.37, McFarlane 44.16, Blackwood 44.45	2s1	OG	Sydney	29 Sep
2:58.92	JAM	Clarke 45.0, McFarlane 45.2, C Williams 44.2, Haughton 44.5	3	PennR	Philadelphia	29 Apr
2:59.02	BAH	Moncur 44.73, McIntosh 45.74, Oliver 44.79, Brown 44.46	3s1	OG	Sydney	29 Sep
2:59.23	BAH	Moncur 44,65, McIntosh 44.23, Oliver 44.83, Brown 45.52	4	OG	Sydney	29 Sep
3:00.59	USA	Lister 47.5, Hooker 45.3, C Harrison 43.8, A Harrison 44.0	1		Gold Coast	10 Sep
3:00.64	FRA	Front, Foucan, Wade, Raquil	4s1	OG	Sydney	29 Sep
3:00.65		Sprint Capital (USA)	1		Atlanta	20 May
3:00.66	POL		5s1	OG	Sydney	29 Sep
		Rysiukiewicz 45.48, Haczek 45.38, Dlugosielski 45.20, Mackowiak 44.60				
3:01.02	FRA	Front 46.22, Foucan 44.92, Wade 44.46, Raquil 45.42	5	OG	Sydney	30 Sep
3:01.06	NGR	Chukwu 45.49, Monye 45.03, Udo-Obong 45.81, Bada 44.73	1s2	OG	Sydney	29 Sep
3:01.20	NGR	Awazie 46.67, Chukwu 44.92, Gadzama 45.35, Udo-Obong 44.26	1h5	OG	Sydney	29 Sep
3:01.22	GBR	Deacon 45.63, Caines 44.65, Thomas 45.26, Baulch 45.68	6	OG	Sydney	30 Sep
3:01.25	RSA	Myburgh 46.04, Sepeng 45.28, Herbert 45.73, Malherbe 44.20	6s1	OG	Sydney	29 Sep
3:01.30	POL	Walotka 47.02, Dlugosielski 44.96, Bocian 45.23, Mackowiak 44.09	2h5	OG	Sydney	29 Sep
3:01.35	GBR	Deacon 45.97, Caines 44.84, Thomas 45.83, Baulch 44.71	2s2	OG	Sydney	29 Sep
	21 performances by teams from 8 nations					
3:01.91	AUS	Vincent 46.30, Young 45.20, Dwyer 45.37, Hazel 45.04	3s2	OG	Sydney	29 Sep
3:02.28	RUS	Semyonov, Bogdanov, Mashchenko, Golovastov 44.70	4s2	OG	Sydney	29 Sep
	(10)					
3:02.67	SEN	Loum 46.91, Niang 45.35, Sarr 45.64, Faye 44.77	4h5	OG	Sydney	29 Sep
3:02.68	UKR	Kaydash 46.50, Voronkov 46.27, Zyukov 44.83, Gorbenko 45.08	5s2	OG	Sydney	29 Sep
3:02.71	SRI	Perera, Ratnakumara, Wimalawansa, Kumara	1	AsiC	Jakarta	31 Aug
3:02.78	IND	Thottan, Ramachandran, Shankar, P Singh	2	AsiC	Jakarta	31 Aug
3:03.33	BRA	Eloy, V da Silva, A dos Santos, Parrela	1	IbAm	Rio de Janeiro	21 May
3:03.71		Nippon University JPN Kobayashi, Mukai, Nakagawa, Yamamura	1		Yokohama	21 May
3:04.19	BOT	Molefe, Basinyi, Kubisa, Matshameko	5h5	OG	Sydney	29 Sep
3:05.00	KSA	Hamdan Al-Bishi, Moh.Al-Bishi, Hamed Al-Bishi, Al-Somaily	3	AsiC	Jakarta	31 Aug
3:05.34	TRI		2		Ljubljana	25 Jul
3:05.42	CRO	Persic, Habun, Bakaric, Juricic	3		Ljubljana	25 Jul
	(20)					
3:05.45	NED	Mabelis, van Rhee, Som, Hagen	2	ECp1B	Bydgoszcz	9 Jul
3:05.45	ALG	M Louahla, S Louahla, Hecini, Saïd-Guerni	1	AfrC	Alger	14 Jul
3:05.47A		Armed Forces (KEN)	1		Nairobi	22 Jul
3:05.60	ZIM	Mutakanyi, Chiwira, Mukomana, K Harnden	3h4	OG	Sydney	29 Sep
3:05.62	YUG	Gajovic, Vranes, Jankovic, Pesa	1	ECp2B	Banská Bystrica	9 Jul
3:05.66	KUW	Al-Johar, Al-Harbi, Al-Azimi, Al-Shammari	4	AsiC	Jakarta	31 Aug
3:05.88	HUN	Dombi, Szeglet, Kilvinger, Bédi	3	ECp-S	Gateshead	16 Jul
3:05.89	GRE	Ikonomídis, Iakovákis, Dimótsios, Goúsis	4	ECp-S	Gateshead	16 Jul
3:05.89	THA	Linglom, Kongtong, Noohlong, Nilploy	5	AsiC	Jakarta	31 Aug
3:05.90	CZE	Muzík, Stejta, Hanz, Blaha	1	ECp1A	Nadderud	9 Jul
	(30)					
3:05.93	SUI	Baeriswyl, L Clerc, Hänggi, Rohr	2	ECp1A	Nadderud	9 Jul

3:06.02 SVK 9 Jul	3:06.46 POR 9 Jul	3:06.87 ESP 29 Sep	3:09.13 BAR 8 Sep	**Indoors**
3:06.02 ITA 16 Jul	3:06.48 QAT 20 Apr	3:07.24 BLR 9 Jul	3:09.16 MAR 14 Jul	3:06.61 GER 27 Feb
3:06.07 IRL 9 Jul	3:06.56 GHA 31 Aug	3:07.37A CAN 8 Jul	3:09.26 CHN 22 Oct	
3:06.24 BUL 9 Jul	3:06.63 SLO 9 Jul	3:07.68 NOR 9 Jul	3:09.71 PUR 10 Jun	
3:06.35 SWE 16 Jul	3:06.79 GER-J 22 Oct	3:08.69 BEL 9 Jul	3:09.71 VEN-J 22 Oct	

JUNIORS

Mark	Nat	Name	Pos	Meet	Venue	Date
3:06.06	JAM	S Clarke, Sappleton, Coley, Simpson	1	WJ	Santiago	22 Oct
3:06.79	GER	Gatzka, Duma, Hönig, Swillims	2	WJ	Santiago	22 Oct
3:07.05	POL	Wieruszewski, Terejlis, Garaszewski, Plawgo	3	WJ	Santiago	22 Oct
3:07.66	RSA	Sharp, Nkose, P de Villiers, Thobelangope	4	WJ	Santiago	22 Oct
3:08.50	ESP	Melo, Ruiz, Melo, Reina	2h2	WJ	Santiago	21 Oct
3:08.82	KSA		1	Arab-J	Damascus	5 Nov
3:09.71	VEN	Hernández, Palma, Silvera, Nuñez	6	WJ	Santiago	22 Oct
3:09.88		New Wave TC, USA	1		Buffalo	30 Jul
3:10.41	AUS	McLeod, C Brown, Cappellano, Ormrod	2h1	WJ	Santiago	21 Oct
3:10.92	CHI	S Martínez, Cavagnaro, Cantuarias, Mayer	5h2	WJ	Santiago	21 Oct
3:10.99	TRI	Kirk, Rodriguez, Rudder, Barry	4h1	WJ	Santiago	21 Oct
3:11.17	KEN	D Kibet, Wachira, V Kemboi, Ogamba	5h1	WJ	Santiago	21 Oct

Mark	Name		Pos	Meet	Venue	Date
3:11.22	JPN	Ishikawa, Tanaka, Itabashi, Hotta	6h2	WJ	Santiago	21 Oct
3:12.22	FRA	Lefebvre, Maillard, Panel, Lacroix	1	v3N-j	Grosseto	7 Oct
3:12.55	RSA	de Villiers, van Soest, Roelf, Ramokoka	1	CommY	Edinburgh	13 Aug
3:12.69	GBR	Bryan, Nicholls, Christie, Bradbury	2	v3N-j	Grosseto	7 Oct
3:12.96	BRA	(Rio de Janeiro)	1		Manaus	3 Sep

4 X 800 METRES RELAY

Mark	Team	Pos	Meet	Venue	Date
7:13.94i	USA Global	1		Boston (R)	6 Feb
	Woody 1:49.34, Paranya 1:48.31, Kenah 1:48.48, Krummenacker 1:47.81				
7:14.78i	Reebok Enclave	2		Boston (R)	6 Feb
	Gaskins 1:50.66, Murphy 1:49.19, Schroer 1:48.23, Woodward 1:46.70				
7:16.33	Univ of Missouri/USA Hansard, Councilor, Dunne, Peterson	1	DrakeR	Des Moines	28 Apr
	Frater JAM, R Williams JAM, Patton USA, Collins SKN				

4 X 1500 METRES RELAY

Mark	Team	Pos	Meet	Venue	Date
14:52.13	Arkanas TC	1	PennR	Philadelphia	29 Apr
	Kerr CAN 3:46.6, Bruton IRL 3:43.3, Price USA 3:39.0, Lassiter USA 3:43.2				
14:52.37	Reebok Enclave/USA	2	PennR	Philadelphia	29 Apr
	Anderson 3:45.5, Honnerkamp 3:44.1, Ryan 3:42.0, Holthaus 3:40.8				

4 X 1 MILE RELAY

Mark	Team	Pos	Meet	Venue	Date
16:08.81	Univ of Arkanas	1	PennR	Philadelphia	29 Apr
	Link CAN 4:05.7, Karie SOM 4:01.2, Travis 4:00.1, Karanu KEN 4:01.8				

4 X 110 METRES HURDLES

Mark	Team		Pos	Meet	Venue	Date
55.37	Univ of Arkanas, USA	Lightfoot, Jackson, Glover, Brown	1	PennR	Philadelphia	28 Apr
55.47	Clemson Univ, USA	Tucker, Allen, Potter, Matthews	2	PennR	Philadelphia	28 Apr

3000 METRES WALK

Mark	Name		Nat	Born	Pos	Meet	Venue	Date
11:27.06	Robert	Heffernan	IRL	20.2.78	1		Tullamore	13 Aug
11:30.94	Troy	Sundstrom	AUS	30.5.81	1		Sydney	23 Jan
11:39.89+	Andreas	Erm	GER	12.3.76	1	in 10k	Braunschweig	29 Jul
11:42.5 A	Denis	Trautmann	GER	15.8.72	1		Pretoria	28 Jan
11:46.2 A	Mike	Trautmann	GER	13.3.74	2		Pretoria	28 Jan
Indoors								
11:29.0	Yebgeniy	Shmalyuk	RUS	14.1.76	1		Sankt-Peterburg	1 Dec
11:31.47+	Andreas	Erm	GER	12.3.76	1	in 5k	Sindelfingen	13 Feb
11:37.0	Kazimir	Verkin	SVK	27.3.72	1		Hlohovec	24 Nov
11:39.0	Yevgeniy	Zybizov	RUS	27.1.83	1		Insar	27 Feb

5000 METRES WALK

Mark	Name		Nat	Born	Pos	Meet	Venue	Date
18:33.16	João	Vieira	POR	20.2.76	1		Rio Maior	10 May
18:41.44	Ilya	Markov	RUS	19.6.72	1		Spala	10 Jun
18:48.92	Robert	Korzeniowski	POL	30.7.68	2		Spala	10 Jun
18:58.29		Korzeniowski			1		Belfort	21 May
19:02.88		Korzeniowski			1		Warszawa	24 Jun
	(5/3							
19:17.65	Denis	Langlois	FRA	10.10.68	1		Arras	8 Jul
19:20.87	Brent	Vallance	AUS	30.4.72	1		Sydney	20 Feb
19:27.64	Tomasz	Lipiec	POL	10.5.71	2		Warszawa	24 Jun
19:28.9	Mikel	Odriozola	ESP	25.5.73	1		L'Hospitalet	13 May
19:30.4	David	Márquez	ESP	13.10.77	2		L'Hospitalet	13 May

Mark	Name		Nat	Born	Date
19:31.97	Pascal	Servanty	FRA	26.5.66	2 Sep
19:32.4	Alejandro	Cambil	ESP	26.1.75	13 May
19:34.15	Roman	Magdziarczyk	POL	5.7.77	24 Jun
19:34.68	Luke	Adams	AUS	22.10.76	20 Feb
19:38.22	Troy	Sundstrom	AUS	30.5.81	20 Feb
19:38.4	Juan Manuel	Molina	ESP	15.3.79	30 Jan
19:39.3	Maris	Putenis	LAT-J	20.6.82	4 Jul
19:39.92	Grzegorz	Sudol	POL	28.8.78	10 Jun

Indoors

Mark	Name		Nat	Born	Pos	Meet	Venue	Date
18:27.15	Alessandro	Gandellini	ITA	30.4.73	1	NC	Genova	12 Feb
18:34.59	Giovanni	De Benedictis	ITA	8.1.68	2	NC	Genova	12 Feb
18:47.94	Michele	Didoni	ITA	7.3.74	3	NC	Genova	12 Feb
18:51.2+	Vladimir	Andreyev	RUS	7.9.66	1	in5152m	Yekaterinburg	7 Jan
18:53.71	Robert	Korzeniowski	POL	30.7.68	1	NC	Liévin	19 Feb
18:56.8		Andreyev			1		Samara	30 Jan
18:59.24	Costica	Balan	ROM	25.8.64	1		Bucuresti	19 Feb
19:00.53		Korzeniowski			1	NC	Spala	13 Feb
19:00.7	Dmitriy	Yesipchuk	RUS	17.11.74	2		Samara	30 Jan
19:02.1+	Roman	Rasskazov	RUS	28.4.79	2	in5152m	Yekaterinburg	7 Jan
19:05.2+	Sergey	Khripunov	RUS	15.9.76	3	in5152m	Yekaterinburg	7 Jan
19:06.28	Giovanni	Perricelli	ITA	25.8.67	4	NC	Genova	12 Feb

Mark	Name		Nat	Born	Pos	Meet	Venue	Date
19:08.2	Vitaliy	Shvetsov	RUS	20.2.73	3		Samara	30 Jan
19:08.53		Balan			1		Bucuresti	5 Feb
19:09.78	Ivano	Brugnetti	ITA	1.9.76	5	NC	Genova	12 Feb
	(15/12)							
19:17.19	Andreas	Erm	GER	12.3.76	1	NC	Sindelfingen	13 Feb
19:27.21	Silviu	Casandra	ROM	27.10.75	2	NC	Bucuresti	5 Feb
19:27.3	Matej	Spisiak	SVK	5.4.78	1		Banská Bystrica	27 Dec
19:29.9	Aleksey	Kronin	RUS	23.10.70	4		Samara	30 Jan
19:30.55	Tomasz	Lipiec	POL	10.5.71	2	NC	Spala	13 Feb

19:32.11	Tim	Seaman	USA	14.5.72	4 Mar
19:32.2	Sergey	Melentyev	RUS	5.12.76	4 Mar
19:33.5	Andrey	Stadnichuk	RUS	14.12.73	4 Mar
19:38.19	Lorenzo	Civallero	ITA	8.8.75	12 Feb
19:40.80#	Milos	Holusa	CZE	2.5.65	8 Jan
19:41.3	Andrey	Savin	RUS	26.2.77	4 Mar
19:41.84	Enrico	Lang	ITA	31.3.72	12 Feb
19:43.36	Denis	Trautmann	GER	15.8.72	13 Feb

10000 METRES WALK

Mark	Name		Nat	Born	Pos	Meet	Venue	Date
38:39.82	Hatem	Ghoula	TUN	7.6.73	1		Tunis	3 Jun
38:46.4	Viktor	Burayev	RUS-J	23.8.82	1	NC-j	Moskva	20 May
39:14.0	Sergey	Khripunov	RUS	15.9.76	1		Magnitogorsk	23 Sep
39:18.0	Vitaliy	Shvetsov	RUS	20.2.73	2		Magnitogorsk	23 Sep
39:30.30	Alessandro	Gandellini	ITA	30.4.73	1		Pescara	22 Jul
39:33.18		Li Zewen	CHN	5.12.73	1	NSG	Chengdu	8 Sep
39:35.87	Marco	Giungi	ITA	30.10.74	1	NC	Milano	6 Sep
39:37.4		Shvetsov			1		Cheboksary	8 Oct
39:42.50	Giovanni	De Benedictis	ITA	8.1.68	2		Pescara	22 Jul
39:46.14	Moussa	Aouanouk	ALG	2.8.72	2		Tunis	3 Jun
39:49.22		Pei Chuang	CHN-J	5.12.81	2	NSG	Chengdu	8 Sep
39:53.9	Sergey	Lovkin	RUS	14.7.77	2		Cheboksary	8 Oct
39:54.23	Andreas	Erm	GER	12.3.76	1	NC	Braunschweig	29 Jul
	(12/11)							
39:55.07	Daisuke	Ikeshima	JPN	30.1.75	1		Tottori	10 Jun
39:55.2	Dmitriy	Yesipchuk	RUS	17.11.74	3		Magnitogorsk	23 Sep
39:56.00	Tomasz	Lipiec	POL	10.5.71	1		Spala	7 May
40:11.05	Vittorino	Mucci	ITA	29.11.74	2	NC	Milano	6 Sep
40:15.0	Yevgeniy	Yakovlyev	RUS	17.6.79	4		Magnitogorsk	23 Sep
40:15.18	Enrico	Lang	ITA	31.3.72	3	NC	Milano	6 Sep
40:16.68	Robert	Heffernan	IRL	20.2.78	1		Tullamore	23 Jul

40:27.35	Yoshimi	Hara	JPN	2.3.68	10 Jun
40:29.88	Michele	Didoni	ITA	7.3.74	3 Jun
40:30.9	Yevgeniy	Demkov	RUS-J	3.12.82	20 May
40:31.41	Akihiko	Koike	JPN	10.4.73	10 Jun
40:36.50	Lorenzo	Civallero	ITA	8.8.75	6 Sep
40:36.6	Vincenzo	Magliulo	ITA	16.11.76	15 Jul
40:42.24	Ivano	Brugnetti	ITA	1.9.76	6 Sep
40:42.8	Aivars	Kadaks	LAT-J	11.2.81	20 May
40:44.9+	Noe	Hernández	MEX	15.3.79	20 May
40:44.91		Wang Yu	CHN	20.1.79	8 Sep

Indoors

39:45.0	Yevgeniy	Shmalyuk	RUS	14.1.76	1		Sankt-Peterburg	3 Dec
39:48.0	Sergey	Melentyev	RUS	5.12.76	1		Novokuznetsk	31 Dec
39:53.0	Georgiy	Sergeyev	RUS	27.4.76	2		Novokuznetsk	31 Dec

JUNIORS

38:46.4	Viktor	Burayev	RUS	23.8.82	1	NC-j	Moskva	20 May
	40:51.9 1 Adler 19 Feb	40:56.57 3 WJ Santiago de Chile 19 Oct						
39:49.22		Pei Chuang	CHN	5.12.81	2	NSG	Chengdu	8 Sep
40:30.9	Yevgeniy	Demkov	RUS	3.12.82	2	NC-j	Moskva	20 May
	40:56.53 2 WJ Santiago de Chile 19 Oct							
40:42.8	Aivars	Kadaks	LAT	11.2.81	1		Stockholm	20 May
40:46.1	Maris	Putenis	LAT	20.6.82	1		Haapsalu	13 May
40:40.74	David	Berdeja	MEX	21.6.81	1		Guadalajara	14 May
	40:56.47 1 WJ Santiago de Chile 19 Oct							
41:19.8	Sergey	Lystsov	RUS	14.11.82	2		Adler	19 Feb
41:26.8	Denis	Shalgin	RUS	29.6.81	3	NC-j	Moskva	20 May
41:44.3	Aleksandr	Strokov	RUS	21.8.82	4	NC-j	Moskva	20 May
41:47.5	Konstantin	Maksimov (10)	RUS	17.6.82	1		Novosibirsk	1 Apr
41:49.0	Aleksandr	Yargunkin	RUS	6.1.81	2		Cheboksary	8 Oct
41:50.08	Beniamin	Kucinski	POL	1.6.82	1		Wroclaw	28 Aug
41:53.7	Anatoliy	Kupriyanov	RUS	2.1.81	5	NC-j	Moskva	20 May
41:54.43	Patrick	Ennemoser	ITA	12.1.81	1		Piovene Rocchette	28 Jul
41:58.0	Yevgeniy	Petrov	RUS	23.11.82	6	NC-j	Moskva	20 May
41:58.54	Troy	Sundstrom	AUS	30.5.81	1		Sydney	18 Aug
41.59,15	Gabriel	Ortíz	MEX	8.12.81	1		Nakazawa	26 Aug
42.01,1	Omar	Segura	MEX	24.4.81	2	1	León	19 Feb
42:05.31	Jan	Albrecht	GER	23.7.81	3	NC	Braunschweig	29 Jul
42:14.20	Takeaki	Akatsuma (20)	JPN	27.11.81	1		Matto	4 Jun
Indoors: 41:59.0	Roman	Shavalyev	RUS	6.9.82	1		Novokuznetsk	31 Dec

20 KILOMETRES WALK

Mark	Name		Nat	Born	Pos	Meet	Venue	Date
1:17:46	Roman	Rasskazov	RUS	28.4.79	1	NC	Moskva	19 May
1:18:07		Rasskazov			1	NC-w	Adler	20 Feb
1:18:14	Mikhail	Khmelnitskiy	BLR	24.7.69	1	NC	Soligorsk	13 May
1:18:16	Vladimir	Andreyev	RUS	7.9.66	2	NC	Moskva	19 May
1:18:22	Robert	Korzeniowski	POL	30.7.68	1		Hildesheim	9 Jul
1:18:23	Andrey	Makarov	BLR	2.1.71	2	NC	Soligorsk	13 May
1:18:29		Korzeniowski			1	ECp	Eisenhüttenstadt	17 Jun
1:18:42	Andreas	Erm	GER	12.3.76	2	ECp	Eisenhüttenstadt	17 Jun
1:18:56	Francisco	Fernández	ESP	5.3.77	3	ECp	Eisenhüttenstadt	17 Jun
1:18:59		Korzeniowski			1	OG	Sydney	22 Sep
1:19:03	Noe	Hernández	MEX	15.3.78	2	OG	Sydney	22 Sep
1:19:15	Artur	Meleshkevich	BLR	11.4.75	3	NC	Soligorsk	13 May
1:19:18	Jirí	Malysa (10)	CZE	14.8.66	4	ECp	Eisenhüttenstadt	17 Jun
1:19:27		Andreyev			3	OG	Sydney	22 Sep
1:19:29	Satoshi	Yanagisawa	JPN	19.1.71	1		Kobe	30 Jan
1:19:33	Yevgeniy	Misyulya	BLR	9.3.64	2		Hildesheim	9 Jul
1:19:42	Daisuke	Ikeshima	JPN	30.1.75	2		Kobe	30 Jan
1:19:56	Dmitriy	Yesipchuk	RUS	17.11.74	5	ECp	Eisenhüttenstadt	17 Jun
1:20:01		Liu Yunfeng ¶	CHN	3.8.79	1		Rio Maior	15 Apr
1:20:09	Alejandro	López	MEX	9.2.75	1		København	6 May
1:20:12	Semyon	Lovkin	RUS	14.7.77	2	NC-w	Adler	20 Feb
1:20:16	Akihiko	Koike	JPN	10.4.73	3		Kobe	30 Jan
1:20:17		Misyulya			4	NC	Soligorsk	13 May
1:20:18		Fernández			1		Leamington	23 Apr
1:20:18	Aigars	Fadejevs	LAT	27.12.75	5	ECp	Eisenhüttenstadt	17 Jun
1:20:18	Jefferson	Pérez (20)	ECU	1.7.74	4	OG	Sydney	22 Sep
1:20:19		Liu Yunfeng			2		Leamington	23 Apr
1:20:19	Marco	Giungi	ITA	30.10.74	3		Hildesheim	9 Jul
1:20:25		Erm			5	OG	Sydney	22 Sep
1:20:28	Alessandro (30/22)	Gandellini	ITA	30.4.73	3		Leamington	23 Apr
1:20:31	Vladimir	Stankin	RUS	2.1.74	3	NC-w	Adler	20 Feb
1:20:42	Valentin	Kononen	FIN	7.3.69	1		Heinola	7 May
1:20:48	Tomasz	Lipiec	POL	10.5.71	7	ECp	Eisenhüttenstadt	17 Jun
1:20:50	Modris	Liepins	LAT	3.8.66	1		Aizpute	21 Jul
1:20:53	Joel	Sánchez	MEX	15.9.66	4	v4N	Leamington	23 Apr
1:20:53	Nick	A'Hern	AUS	6.1.69	3		Naumburg	30 Apr
1:20:53	Ilya	Markov	RUS	19.6.72	3		Turku	21 May
1:21:01	Vitaliy (30)	Shvetsov	RUS	20.2.73	1		Cheboksary	6 Oct
1:21:03	Arturo	Huerta	CAN	30.3.64	1		Toronto (Et)	7 Jul
1:21:03	Nathan	Deakes	AUS	17.8.77	8	OG	Sydney	22 Sep
1:21:04	Gyula	Dudás	HUN	20.8.66	1	NC	Békéscsaba	9 Apr
1:21:12		Li Zewen	CHN	5.12.73	5	v4N	Leamington	23 Apr
1:21:14	Róbert	Valícek	SVK	10.3.69	1		Hronov	2 Apr
1:21:14	Maris	Putenis	LAT-J	20.6.82	2		Aizpute	21 Jul
1:21:20	Giovanni	De Benedictis	ITA	8.1.68	2		Pomigliano	1 Apr
1:21:21	Ivano	Brugnetti	ITA	1.9.76	3		Pomigliano	1 Apr
1:21:21A	Julius	Sawe	KEN	21.11.71	1	NC	Nairobi	20 Jul
1:21:23A	David (40)	Kimutai	KEN	19.8.69	2	NC	Nairobi	20 Jul
1:21:26	Denis	Langlois	FRA	10.10.68	6	v4N	Leamington	23 Apr
1:21:26	Anthony	Gillet	FRA	7.2.76	7	v4N	Leamington	23 Apr
1:21:30	Vitaliy	Gordey	BLR	11.7.73	2	NC	Békéscsaba	9 Apr
1:21:30	Edgar	Hernández	MEX	6.8.77	4		Turku	21 May
1:21:35	Silviu	Casandra	ROM	27.10.75	1	NC	Bucuresti	6 Aug
1:21:36	Sergey	Khripunov	RUS	15.9.76	4	NC-w	Adler	20 Feb
1:21:37	Hironori	Kawai	JPN	3.2.76	4		Kobe	30 Jan
1:21:39	Costica	Balan	ROM	25.8.64	11	ECp	Eisenhüttenstadt	17 Jun
1:21:43	Michele	Didoni	ITA	7.3.74	11	OG	Sydney	22 Sep
1:21:44	David (50)	Márquez	ESP	13.10.77	13	ECp	Eisenhüttenstadt	17 Jun
1:21:45	Valeriy	Borisov	KAZ	18.9.66	5	RUS-w	Adler	20 Feb
1:21:46	Tim	Berrett	CAN	23.1.65	2	NC	Victoria	13 Aug
1:21:47	Denis	Nizhegorodov	RUS	.80	4	NC	Moskva	19 May
1:21:58	Yevgeniy	Yakovlev	RUS	17.6.79	6	NC-w	Adler	20 Feb
1:22:00	Masato	Yoshihara	JPN	14.3.77	5		Kobe	30 Jan

Mark	Name		Nat	Born	Pos	Meet	Venue	Date
1:22:05	Andre	Höhne	GER	10.3.78	1		Dublin	15 Jul
1:22:05	Daniel	García	MEX	28.10.71	12	OG	Sydney	22 Sep
1:22:12	Sándor	Urbanik	HUN	15.12.64	1	NC	Ózd	21 May
1:22:13	Konstantin	Golubtsov	RUS	1.6.73	8	NC-w	Adler	20 Feb
1:22:14	Stepan	Yudin	RUS	3.4.80	9	NC-w	Adler	20 Feb
	(60)							
1:22:16	Aleksey	Lopatin	RUS	30.4.77	10	NC-w	Adler	20 Feb
1:22:25	Igor	Kollár	SVK	26.6.65	15	ECp	Eisenhüttenstadt	17 Jun
1:22:29	Mikel	Odriozola	ESP	25.5.73	8	v4N	Leamington	23 Apr
1:22:30	Sergey	Melentyev	RUS	5.12.76	11	NC-w	Adler	20 Feb
1:22:32		Yu Guohui	CHN	30.4.77	13	OG	Sydney	22 Sep
1:22:34	José David	Domínguez	ESP	29.7.80	16	ECp	Eisenhüttenstadt	17 Jun
1:22:42		He Xiaodong	CHN	14.1.78	2		Xinzheng	5 May
1:22:43	Juan M	Molina	ESP	15.3.79	9	v4N	Leamington	23 Apr
1:22:43	Robert	Heffernan	IRL	28.2.78	18	ECp	Eisenhüttenstadt	17 Jun
1:22:46	Arturo	Di Mezza	ITA	16.7.69	19	ECp	Eisenhüttenstadt	17 Jun
	(70)							
1:22:47	Bernardo	Segura	MEX	11.2.70	1	PAmCp	Poza Rica	8 Apr
1:22:52	Nikolay	Matyukhin	RUS	13.12.68	12	NC-w	Adler	20 Feb
1:22:53	João	Vieira	POR	20.2.76	2		Rio Maior	15 Apr
1:22:54	Lorenzo	Civallero	ITA	8.8.75	11	v4N	Leamington	23 Apr
1:23:00	Robert	Ihly	GER	5.5.63	20	ECp	Eisenhüttenstadt	17 Jun
1:23:12	Francesco	Galdenzi	ITA	16.12.76	4		Pomigliano d'Arco	1 Apr
1:23:13	Aleksandr	Arkhipov	RUS	7.8.73	13	NC-w	Adler	20 Feb
1:23:13	Julio	Martínez	GUA	27.9.73	2		La Coruña	20 May
1:23:14	Nichan	Daimer	GER	19.7.67	21	ECp	Eisenhüttenstadt	17 Jun
1:23:17	Daniel	Plaza	ESP	3.7.66	2		L'Hospitalet	30 Apr
	(80)							
1:23:20	Eiichi	Yoshizawa	JPN	5.9.80	2		Takahata	29 Oct
1:23:24	Milos	Holusa	CZE	2.5.65	22	ECp	Eisenhüttenstadt	17 Jun
1:23:34		Zhu Hongjun	CHN-J	18.8.83	3		Xinzheng	5 May
1:23:34	Andrey	Stadnichuk	RUS	14.12.73	6	NC	Moskva	19 May
1:23:34		Bai Liansheng	CHN	28.7.78	2	NC-2	Lushun	1 Jun
1:23:34	Moussa	Aouanouk	ALG	2.8.72	1		Alger	11 Jun
1:23:35		Yu Chaohong	CHN	3.11.75	3		Rio Maior	15 Apr
1:23:40.0t	Tim	Seaman	USA	14.5.72	2		San Diego	19 Aug
1:23:46	David	Berdeja	MEX-J	21.6.81	3	PAmCp	Poza Rica	8 Apr
1:23:47		Cui Xucai	CHN	24.8.76	2	NC1	Shangqiu	3 May
	(90)							
1:23:48	Jorge I	Silva	ESP	19.4.79	1		Cieza	19 Mar
1:23:50	Aivars	Kadaks	LAT-J	11.2.81	3		Aizpute	21 Jul
1:23:55.8t	Curt	Clausen	USA	9.10.67	3		San Diego	19 Aug
1:24:08	Aleksey	Kronin	RUS	23.10.70	8	NC	Moskva	19 May
1:24:09	Dion	Russell	AUS	8.5.75	4	NC	Sydney	26 Feb
1:24:13	Kazimir	Verkin	SVK	27.3.72	2		Dublin	15 Jul
1:24:14	Jorge	Pino	CUB	6.7.69	1		Sancti Spiritus	17 Mar
1:24:18	Luke	Adams	AUS	22.10.76	1		Canberra	16 Jan
1:24:21	Aleksey	Trifonov	RUS	8.5.80	9	NC	Moskva	19 May
1.24.22		Han Qiang	CHN	28.6.77	5	NC2	Lushun	3 Jun
	(100)							

1:24:23.9t	Pascal	Servanty	FRA	26.5.66	11 Jun
1:24:25	Giovanni	Perricelli	ITA	25.8.67	9 Jul
1:24:28	Vasiliy	Ivanov	RUS	26.12.76	20 Feb
1:24:33	Stanislaw	Stosik	POL	26.3.72	5 Aug
1:24:34	Ivan	Azaranok	BLR	17.7.79	13 May
1:24:35	Nikolay	Ivanov	RUS	14.7.75	6 Oct
1:24:41+	Yevgeniy	Shmalyuk	RUS	14.1.76	20 Feb
1:24:45		Xi Shaohui	CHN	7.9.74	5 May
1:24:45	Jirí	Masita	CZE	5.5.73	14 May
1:24:47	Alejandro	Cambil	ESP	26.1.75	7 May
1:24:48	Birger	Fält	SWE	12.8.68	17 Jun
1.24.49	Andrey	Kovenko	UKR	25.11.73	17 Jun
1:24:51+	Valeriy	Spitsyn	RUS	5.12.65	20 Feb
1:24:53	José M	Rodríguez	ESP	7.11.72	20 May
1:24:57	Theódoros	Stamatópoulos	GRE	24.4.70	17 Jun
1:25:00	Jesús Angel	García	ESP	17.10.69	30 Apr

Other best track times

1:20:55.8	Jefferson	Pérez	ECU	1.7.74	1		San Diego	19 Aug
1:23:37.5	Julio	Martínez	GUA	27.9.73	2		Fana	6 May
1:24:50.5	Noe	Hernández	MEX	15.3.79	1	IbAm	Rio de Janeiro	20 May
1:24:59.9	Vitaliy	Gordey	BLR	11.7.73	1		Brest	1 Aug

JUNIORS

1:21:14	Maris	Putenis	LAT	20.6.82	2		Aizpute	21 Jul
1:23:34		Zhu Hongjun	CHN	18.8.83	3		Xinzheng	5 May
	1:24:37 4 NC1	Shangqiu	3 May	1:24:58	6	NC2	Lushun	3 Jun
1:23:46	David	Berdeja	MEX	21.6.81	3	PAmCp	Poza Rica	8 Apr
1:23:50	Aivars	Kadaks	LAT	2.11.81	3		Aizpute	21 Jul
1:25:43		Chang Chunhu	CHN	1.5.82	7	NC2	Lushun	3 Jun

Mark	Name		Nat	Born	Pos	Meet	Venue	Date
1:26:37	Troy	Sundstrom	AUS	30.5.81	7	NC	Sydney	26 Feb
1:26:58		Zhang Tianping	CHN	11.1.82	10		Xincheng	5 May
1:27:03	Vitaliy	Talankov	BLR	.82			Brest	1 Aug
1:27:04		Pei Chuang	CHN	5.12.81	2rA	NSG	Chengdu	11 Sep
1:27:12	Konstantin	Maksimov (10)	RUS	17.6.82	12	NC	Moskva	19 May
1:27:16	Denis	Shalgin	RUS	29.6.81	21	NC-w	Adler	20 Feb
1:27:16	Sergey	Ostapchuk	BLR	.81			Brest	1 Aug
1:27:17		Wang Pu	CHN	.73	11		Xinzheng	5 May
1:27:24		Wang Shigang	CHN	22.2.81	11	NC2	Lushun	3 Jun
1:27:25	Aleksandr	Kuzmin	BLR	24.3.81	10	NC	Békéscsaba	9 Apr
1:27:39	Vitaliy	Averkin	RUS	.82	24	NC-w	Adler	20 Feb
1:27:42	Andrey	Sobolev	RUS	6.3.82	25	NC-w	Adler	20 Feb
1:28:36	Aleksandr	Yargunkin	RUS	6.1.81	29	NC-w	Adler	20 Feb
1:28:40	Dmitriy	Yutkin	RUS	10.11.82	30	NC-w	Adler	20 Feb
1:28:40	Rafal	Dys (20)	POL	14.1.82	1	NC-j	Zamosc	24 Sep

30 KILOMETRES WALK

Mark	Name		Nat	Born	Pos	Meet	Venue	Date
2:05:20+	Yevgeniy	Shmalyuk	RUS	14.1.76	1	NC-w	Adler	20 Feb
2:06:20	Marco	Giungi	ITA	30.10.74	1		Pescara	12 Mar
2:06:35+	Valeriy	Spitsyn	RUS	5.12.65	2	NC-w	Adler	20 Feb
2:06:54+	Andrey	Stadnichuk	RUS	14.12.73	3	NC-w	Adler	20 Feb
2:07:52+	Dmitriy	Dolnikov	RUS	19.11.72	4	NC-w	Adler	20 Feb
2:08:01	Francesco	Galdenzi	ITA	16.12.76	2		Pescara	12 Mar
2:08:20+	Aleksandr	Nadezhdin	RUS	22.3.76	5	NC-w	Adler	20 Feb
2:08:24	Alessandro	Mistretta	ITA	6.3.71	3		Pescara	12 Mar
2:08:27+	Vitaliy	Gordey	BLR	11.7.73	6	NC-w	Adler	20 Feb
2:08:57+	Robert	Heffernan	IRL	20.2.78	1		Dublin	15 Jul
2:09:13	Mikel	Odriozola	ESP	25.5.73	1		EL Prat de Llobergat	13 Feb
2:09:29+	Vladimir	Potemin	RUS	15.1.80	1=	in 50k	Moskva	21 May
2:09:29+		Spitsyn			1=	in 50k	Moskva	21 May
2:09:47	Daniel	Plaza	ESP	3.7.66	2		El Prat de Llobergat	13 Feb
2:09:56+		Shmalyuk			3	in 50k	Moskva	21 May
2:10:02	Dion	Russell	AUS	8.5.75	1	NC	Melbourne	6 Aug
2:10:10+	Andrey	Plotnikov	RUS	12.8.67	7	NC-w	Adler	20 Feb
2:10:11+	Yuriy	Andronov	RUS	6.11.71	8	NC-w	Adler	20 Feb
2:10:37	José Manuel	Rodríguez	ESP	7.11.72	3		El Prat de Llobergat	13 Feb
2:10:50+	Oleg	Ishutkin	RUS	22.7.75	4	in 50k	Moskva	21 May
2:11:00.4t	Curt	Clausen	USA	9.10.67	1		Chula Vista	23 Jan
2:11:05	Juan	Molina	ESP	15.3.79	4		El Prat de Llobergat	13 Feb
2:11:13+	Nikolay	Matyukhin	RUS	13.12.68	5	in 50k	Moskva	21 May
2:11:27	Lorenzo	Civallero	ITA	8.8.75	4		Pescara	12 Mar
2:11:44	Ivano	Brugnetti	ITA	1.9.76	5		Pescara	12 Mar
2:11:50	Juan Antonio	Porras	ESP	19.2.72	5		El Prat de Llobergat	13 Feb
2:12:15	Daugvinas	Zujus	LTU	16.10.75	1	NC	Birstonas	6 May
2:12:20	Jesús Angel	García	ESP	17.10.69	6		El Prat de Llobergat	13 Feb
2:12:21	Massimo	Passoni	ITA	25.3.71	6		Pescara	12 Mar
2:12:25+	Valentin	Kononen	FIN	7.3.69	1	in 50k	Dudince	25 Mar
2:12:29	Gintaras	Andriukevicius	LTU	6.7.75	2	NC	Birstonas	6 May
2:12:31.2t	Andrew	Hermann	USA	22.2.71	2		Chula Vista	23 Jan
2:12:36	Alfio	Corsaro	ITA	31.10.79	7		Pescara	12 Mar
2:12:38+	Grigoriy	Sergeyev	RUS	27.4.76	11	NC-w	Adler	20 Feb
2:12:56	Trond	Nymark	NOR	28.12.76	1		Søfteland	2 Apr

2:13:06	Mario	Avellaneda	ESP	12.11.74	13 Feb
2:13:30+	Robert	Korzeniowski	POL	30.7.68	29 Sep
2:13:30+	Aigars	Fadejevs	LAT	27.12.75	29 Sep
2:13:31+	Nathan	Deakes	AUS	17.8.77	29 Sep
2:13:31+	Miguel Angel	Rodríguez	MEX	15.1.67	29 Sep
2:13:31+	Germán	Sánchez	MEX	31.7.67	29 Sep
2:13:32+	Joel	Sánchez	MEX	15.9.66	29 Sep
2:13:55	João	Vieira	POR	20.2.76	30 Jan

35 KILOMETRES WALK

Mark	Name		Nat	Born	Pos	Meet	Venue	Date
2:27:02	Yevgeniy	Shmalyuk	RUS	14.1.76	1	NC-w	Adler	20 Feb
2:27:54	Valeriy	Spitsyn	RUS	5.12.65	2	NC-w	Adler	20 Feb
2:29:14	Andrey	Stadnichuk	RUS	14.12.73	3	NC-w	Adler	20 Feb
2:29:49	Dmitriy	Dolnikov	RUS	19.11.72	4	NC-w	Adler	20 Feb
2:30:30	Aleksandr	Nadezhdin	RUS	22.3.76	5	NC-w	Adler	20 Feb
2:30:57+		Spitsyn			1	in 50k	Moskva	21 May
2:30:58+	Vladimir	Potemin	RUS	15.1.80	2	in 50k	Moskva	21 May
2:31:12	Yuriy	Andronov	RUS	6.11.71	6	NC-w	Adler	20 Feb
2:31:19+	Robert	Heffernan	IRL	20.2.78	1		Dublin	15 Jul
2:31:43	Vitaliy	Gordey	BLR	11.7.73	7	NC-w	Adler	20 Feb
2:32:38+	Oleg	Ishutkin	RUS	22.7.75	3	in 50k	Moskva	21 May
2:33:06	Andrey	Plotnikov	RUS	12.8.67	8	NC-w	Adler	20 Feb

Mark	Name		Nat	Born	Pos	Meet	Venue	Date
2:33:45+	Nikolay	Matyukhin	RUS	13.12.68	4	in 50k	Moskva	21 May
2:35:03+	Robert	Korzeniowski	POL	30.7.68	1	in 50k	Sydney	29 Sep
2:35:04+	Joel	Sánchez	MEX	15.9.66	2=	in 50k	Sydney	29 Sep
2:35:04+	Germán	Sánchez	MEX	31.7.67	2=	in 50k	Sydney	29 Sep
2:35:05+	Nathan	Deakes	AUS	17.8.77	4	in 50k	Sydney	29 Sep
2:35:21+	Miguel Angel	Rodríguez	MEX	15.1.67	5	in 50k	Sydney	29 Sep
2:35:22+	Valentin	Kononen	FIN	7.3.69				29 Sep
2:35:25+	Aigars	Fadejevs	LAT	27.12.75				29 Sep
2:35:52+	Jesús Angel	García	ESP	17.10.69				18 Jun
2:36:22	Anton	Trotskiy	BLR	2.11.72				13 May
2:36:26	Aleksey	Nazhibulin	BLR	12.12.75				13 May
2:36:55	Aleksandr	Andrushevskiy	BLR	4.3.78				13 May
2:36:59+	Marco	Giungi	ITA	30.10.74				24 Apr
2:37:38+	Valentí	Massana	ESP	5.7.70				29 Sep

50 KILOMETRES WALK

Mark	Name		Nat	Born	Pos	Meet	Venue	Date
3:37:26	Valeriy	Spitsyn	RUS	5.12.65	1	NC	Moskva	21 May
3:39:21	Vladimir	Potemin	RUS	15.1.80	2	NC	Moskva	21 May
3:39:34	Valentin	Kononen	FIN	7.3.69	1		Dudince	25 Mar
3:41:50	Robert	Korzeniowski	POL	30.7.68	1	NC	Ponte de Sôr	5 Mar
3:42:02	Nikolay	Matyukhin	RUS	13.12.68	3	NC	Moskva	21 May
3:42:22		Korzeniowski			1	OG	Sydney	29 Sep
3:42:51	Jesús Angel	García	ESP	17.10.69	1	ECp	Eisenhüttenstadt	18 Jun
3:43:40	Aigars	Fadejevs	LAT	27.12.75	2	OG	Sydney	29 Sep
3:43:52	Miguel Angel	Rodríguez	MEX	15.1.67	1	PAmCp	Poza Rica	9 Apr
3:44:30	Andrey	Plotnikov	RUS	12.8.67	4	NC	Moskva	21 May
3:44:33	Yevgeniy	Shmalyuk (10)	RUS	14.1.76	2	ECp	Eisenhüttenstadt	18 Jun
3:44:36	Joel	Sánchez	MEX	15.9.66	3	OG	Sydney	29 Sep
3:45:14		García			1	NC	Cieza	19 Mar
3:45:47	Oleg	Ishutkin	RUS	22.7.75	5	NC	Moskva	21 May
3:45:57	Mikel	Odriozola	ESP	25.5.73	2	NC	Cieza	19 Mar
3:46:01	Valentí	Massana	ESP	5.7.70	4	OG	Sydney	29 Sep
3:46:37		Matyukhin			5	OG	Sydney	29 Sep
3:47:29	Nathan	Deakes	AUS	17.8.77	6	OG	Sydney	29 Sep
3:47:38	Denis	Langlois	FRA	10.10.68	3	ECp	Eisenhüttenstadt	18 Jun
3:47:49	René	Piller	FRA	23.4.65	4	ECp	Eisenhüttenstadt	18 Jun
3:47:53	Viktor	Ginko	BLR	7.12.65	1		Naumburg	30 Apr
3:47:55		J Sánchez			2	PAmCp	Poza Rica	9 Apr
3:48:06	Germán	Sánchez	MEX	31.7.67	3	PAmCp	Poza Rica	9 Apr
3:48:09	Sylvain	Caudron (20)	FRA	10.9.69	5	ECp	Eisenhüttenstadt	18 Jun
3:48:12		Rodríguez			7	OG	Sydney	29 Sep
3:48:17	Roman	Magdziarczyk	POL	5.7.77	8	OG	Sydney	29 Sep
3:48:36	Modris	Liepins	LAT	3.8.66	9	OG	Sydney	29 Sep
3:48:42		Yang Yongjian	CHN	28.4.73	10	OG	Sydney	29 Sep
3:49:16	Aleksandar	Rakovic	YUG	13.1.68	11	OG	Sydney	29 Sep
3:49:31		García			12	OG	Sydney	29 Sep
3:49:50	Mario (31/25)	Avellaneda	ESP	12.11.74	6	ECp	Eisenhüttenstadt	18 Jun
3:50:19		Wang Yinhang	CHN	15.2.77	13	OG	Sydney	29 Sep
3:50:21	Giovanni	Perricelli	ITA	25.8.67	1	v4N	Leamington	23 Apr
3:50:27	Aleksey	Voyevodin	RUS	9.8.70	6	NC	Moskva	21 May
3:50:28	Carlos	Mercenario	MEX	23.5.67	4	PAmCp	Poza Rica	9 Apr
3:50:28	Denis (30)	Trautmann	GER	15.8.72	7	ECp	Eisenhüttenstadt	18 Jun
3:51:24	Santiago	Pérez	ESP	15.1.72	8	ECp	Eisenhüttenstadt	18 Jun
3:52:21t	Tim	Berrett	CAN	23.1.65	1		Victoria	29 Oct
3:52:20	Yoshimi	Hara	JPN	2.3.68	1		Takahata	29 Oct
3:52:38	Robert	Ihly	GER	5.5.63	3		Naumburg	30 Apr
3:52:41	Mike	Trautmann	GER	13.3.74	4		Naumburg	30 Apr
3:53:01	Francesco	Galdenzi	ITA	16.12.76	9	ECp	Eisenhüttenstadt	18 Jun
3:53:05	Sergey	Korepanov	KAZ	9.5.64	5		Naumburg	30 Apr
3:53:10	Trond	Nymark	NOR	28.12.76	1		Dublin	15 Jul
3:53:20	Fumio	Imamura	JPN	5.11.66	1		Wajima	16 Apr
3:53:48	Milos (40)	Holusa	CZE	2.5.65	16	OG	Sydney	29 Sep
3:54:18	José Manuel	Rodríguez	ESP	7.11.72	5	NC	Cieza	19 Mar
3:54:20	Thomas	Wallstab	GER	29.1.68	12	ECp	Eisenhüttenstadt	18 Jun
3:54:38	Alessandro	Mistretta	ITA	6.3.71	13	ECp	Eisenhüttenstadt	18 Jun
3:54:40		Zhang Huiqiang	CHN	14.10.77	1	NC1	Shangqiu	3 May
3:54:47	Peter	Tichy	SVK	12.3.69	17	OG	Sydney	29 Sep
3:54:56	Peter	Korcok	SVK	12.8.74	2		Dudince	25 Mar
3:54:56		Li Guoqing	CHN	1.10.79	1		Xincheng	7 May
3:55:18	Stanislaw	Stosik	POL	26.3.72	2	NC	Podebrady	16 Apr

Mark	Name		Nat	Born	Pos	Meet	Venue	Date
3:55:20		Yu Guohui	CHN	30.4.77	3	NC2	Lushun	3 Jun
3:55:48	Zóltan	Czukor	HUN	18.12.62	3		Dudince	25 Mar
	(50)							
3:55:53	Craig	Barrett	NZL	16.11.71	18	OG	Sydney	29 Sep
3:55:55	Pedro	Martins	POR	12.1.68	2	NC	Ponte de Sôr	5 Mar
3:56:01	Arturo	Huerta	CAN	30.3.64	5	PAmCp	Poza Rica	9 Apr
3:56:16	Curt	Clausen	USA	9.10.67	1	OT	Sacramento	13 Feb
3:56:20		Pei Chuang	CHN-J	5.12.81	4		Xincheng	7 May
3:56:36	Edgar	Hernández	MEX	6.8.77	6	PAmCp	Poza Rica	9 Apr
3:56:42	David	Boulanger	FRA	11.12.74	2		Velaines	26 Mar
3:56:44	Stefan	Malík	SVK	11.2.66	20	OG	Sydney	29 Sep
3:56:47	Spirídon	Kastánis	GRE	23.9.64	1	NC	Marathónas	18 Mar
3:57:10	Chris	Maddocks	GBR	28.3.57	1		Sint-Oedenrode	12 Mar
	(60)							
3:57:19	Valeriy	Borisov	KAZ	18.9.66	7		Naumburg	30 Apr
3:57:27		Ma Hongye	CHN	16.4.74	5		Xincheng	7 May
3:57:44	Theódoros	Stamatópoulos	GRE	24.4.70	2	NC	Marathónas	18 Mar
3:57:51	Dominic	McGrath	AUS	4.6.72	2		Leamington	23 Apr
3:57:51		Liu Jun	CHN	28.2.75	6		Xincheng	7 May
3:57:54	Andrew	Hermann	USA	25.2.71	2	OT	Sacramento	13 Feb
3:57:59		Qu Fanhua	CHN	21.2.77	7		Xincheng	7 May
3:58:09	Jacob	Sørensen	DEN	27.12.74	16	ECp	Eisenhüttenstadt	18 Jun
3:58:26	Denis	Franke	GER	27.11.69	3	NC	Ponte de Sôr	5 Mar
3:58:27	Vitaliy	Popovich	UKR	22.10.62	5		Dudince	25 Mar
	(70)							
3:58:39	Daugvinas	Zujus	LTU	16.10.75	6		Dudince	25 Mar
3:58:44		Yu Chaohong	CHN	3.11.75	8		Xincheng	7 May
3:58:49	Marek	Janek	SVK	29.1.77	7		Dudince	25 Mar
3:58:52	Axel	Noack	GER	23.9.61	9		Naumburg	30 Apr
3:59:02	Jamie	Costin	IRL	1.6.77	17	ECp	Eisenhüttenstadt	18 Jun
3:59:08	Grzegorz	Müller	POL	3.11.73	3	NC	Podebrady	16 Apr
3:59:08		Bai Liansheng	CHN	28.7.78	6	NC2	Lushun	3 Jun
3:59:13	Martin	Pupis	SVK	19.10.78	3		Dublin	15 Jul
3:59:16	Kazimir	Verkin	SVK	27.3.72	8		Dudince	25 Mar
3:59:27	Aleksey	Shelest	UKR	27.3.73	18	ECp	Eisenhüttenstadt	18 Jun
	(80)							
3:59:41		Li Mingcai	CHN	22.1.71	7	NC2	Lushun	3 Jun
3:59:44		Wang Libo	CHN	28.10.79	3	NC1	Shangqiu	3 May
4:00:16	Francisco	Martín	ESP	27.5.75	3		Leamington	23 Apr
4:00:40		Zou Menghui	CHN	21.9.75	4	NC1	Shangqiu	3 May
4:01:10	Ugis	Bruvelis	LAT	28.6.71	1	NC	Ogre	6 May
4:01:15	Erick	Cordero	CUB	8.7.75	1		Ranchuelo	5 Feb
4:01:27	Virgiíio	Soares	POR	13.11.59	20	ECp	Eisenhüttenstadt	18 Jun
4:01:46	Benjamin	Leroy	BEL	9.1.73	21	ECp	Eisenhüttenstadt	18 Jun
4:02:02	Bengt	Bengtsson	SWE	4.9.61	4	NC	Podebrady	16 Apr
4:02:09	Jorge	Pino	CUB	6.7.69	2		Ranchuelo	5 Feb
	(90)							
4:02:17	Massimo	Passoni	ITA	25.3.71	4		Leamington	23 Apr
4:02:50	Dion	Russell	AUS	8.5.75	27	OG	Sydney	29 Sep
4:03:05	Philip	Dunn	USA	12.6.71	28	OG	Sydney	29 Sep
4:03:08	Alfio	Corsaro	ITA	31.10.79	5		Leamington	23 Apr
4:03:08	Takehito	Hirakawa	JPN	28.7.72	2		Takahata	29 Oct
4:03:30	Silviu	Casandra	ROM	27.10.75	1	NC	Craiova	23 Sep
4:03:42	Fredrik	Svensson	SWE	10.9.73	24	ECp	Eisenhüttenstadt	18 Jun
4:03:51	Ihosvany	Díaz	CUB	25.11.70	3		Ranchuelo	5 Feb
4:04:19	David	Sánchez	ESP	23.8.73	7	NC	Cieza	19 Mar
4:04:34	Peter	Ferrari	SWE	24.2.65	25	ECp	Eisenhüttenstadt	18 Jun
	(100)							

4:04:57	Hirofumi	Tadamasa	JPN	29.8.76	29 Oct	4:07:33	Mark	Easton	GBR	24.5.63	12 Mar
4:04:58	Anton	Trotskiy	BLR	2.11.72	18 Jun	4:07:59	Pascal	Charrière	SUI	14.11.64	18 Jun
4:05:21	Jeffrey	Cassin	IRL	15.12.71	15 Jul	4:08:18	Gyula	Dudás	HUN	[illegible]	[illegible] Mar
4:05:33	Milan	Bátovsky	SVK	26.5.79	25 Mar	4:08:29		Chang Wei	CHN	5.7.83	7 May
4:06:02	Francisco	Pinardo	ESP	15.3.75	19 Mar	4:08:35	Aleksandr	Andruschevsky	BLR	4.3.78	18 Jun
4:06:22		Xi Shaohui	CHN	7.9.74	3 Jun	4:08:47		Wang Yu	CHN	20.1.79	3 Jun
4:06:27	Kenji	Katsurayama	JPN	9.9.70	16 Apr	4:08:56	José	Magalhães	POR	30.10.54	5 Mar
4:06:30	Diego	Cafagna	ITA	9.7.75	23 Apr	4:09:34	Klaus David	Jensen	DEN	15.7.71	25 Mar
4:06:54	Sergio	Galdino	BRA	7.5.69	30 Apr	4:09:36	Matej	Spisiak	SVK	5.4.78	25 Mar
4:07:08		Bian Aiguo	CHN	10.6.80	3 May	4:09:40		Wang Shengtang	CHN	8.3.77	18 Sep
4:07:18	Steve	Hollier	GBR	27.2.76	18 Jun	4:09:43	Rustam	Kuvatov	KAZ	9.11.77	31 Mar
4:07:22		Liu Xiaochun	CHN	12.8.72	7 May						

Short course 48125m at Yverdon 1. Bengtsson SWE 3:49:24, 2. Bruvelis LAT 3:52:38, 3. D Franke GER 3:55:04

Mark	Name		Nat	Born	Pos	Meet	Venue	Date

100 KILOMETRES WALK

8:43:30	Viktor	Ginko	BLR	7.12.65	1		Scanzorosciate	29 Oct
8:59:14	Modris	Liepins	LAT	3.8.66	2		Scanzorosciate	29 Oct
9:01:29	Sten	Reichel	GER	16.5.75	3		Scanzorosciate	29 Oct
9:04.15	Aleksey	Rodionov	RUS	5.3.57	4		Scanzorosciate	29 Oct
9:06:34	Peter	Tichy	SVK	12.3.69	5		Scanzorosciate	29 Oct
9:13:59	Aleksey	Shelest	UKR	27.3.73	6		Scanzorosciate	29 Oct
9:22:31	Denis	Franke	GER	27.11.69	7		Scanzorosciate	29 Oct
9:37:01	Yuriy	Burban	UKR	18.4.80	8		Scanzorosciate	29 Oct
9:39.23	Roberto	Defendenti	ITA	30.5.68	9		Scanzorosciate	29 Oct
9:48:40	Zóltan	Czukor	HUN	18.12.62	10		Scanzorosciate	29 Oct
9:53:46	David	Regi	FRA	1.5.69	1	NC	Ligny-en-Barrois	15 Oct
9:54:15	Sergey	Lazar	UKR	24.3.80	11		Scanzorosciate	29 Oct

WORLD LIST TRENDS

Men 10th Bests

	1980	1984	1988	1992	1995	1996	1997	1998	1999	2000
100m	10.18	10.14	10.06	10.07	10.07	10.01	**9.98**	10.00	10.00	10.03
200m	20.36	20.34	20.18	20.15	20.20	20.17	20.21	20.27	20.08	**20.03**
400m	45.33	44.83	44.61	44.52	44.81	**44.51**	44.65	44.65	44.59	44.70
800m	1:45.6	1:43.93	1:44.10	1:44.33	1:44.05	**1:43.66**	1:44.01	1:44.17	1:43.98	1:44.06
1500m	3:34.11	3:34.20	3:34.61	3:33.80	3:33.69	3:33.00	**3:31.52**	3:31.89	3:31.60	3:32.01
5000m	13:19.8	13:16.41	3:17.48	13:10.47	13:03.21	12:59.19	13:02.52	13:00.59	12:59.09	**12:58.70**
10000m	27:46.71	27:47.00	7:40.36	27:45.46	27:25.82	27:30.37	27:29.44	27:22.54	**27:18.28**	27:23.65
Marathon	2:10:23	2:10:05	2:08:49	2:09:30	2:09:33	2:09:15	2:08:02	2:07:57	**2:07:09**	2:07:47
3000mSt	8:18.78	8:17.27	8:16.04	8:13.65	**8:09.54**	8:12.54	8:10.20	8:10.67	8:10.56	8:10.23
110mh	13.53	13.45	13.36	13.33	13.27	13.24	13.26	**13.20**	13.21	13.24
400mh	49.24	48.74	48.65	48.60	48.53	48.28	48.39	48.30	**48.22**	48.40
HJ	2.29	2.33	**2.36**	2.34	2.34	2.34	2.32	2.32	2.32	2.34
PV	5.65	5.75	5.80	5.85	5.80	**5.90**	5.85	**5.90**	5.85	5.85
LJ	8.13	8.27	8.31	8.28	8.34	8.34	**8.36**	8.28	8.26	8.33
TJ	17.03	17.34	17.43	17.30	17.30	17.20	17.33	17.24	17.27	17.26
SP	21.10	**21.63**	21.16	20.93	20.57	20.78	20.88	20.79	20.84	21.27
DT	67.68	67.76	67.38	66.64	65.72	66.70	65.76	66.69	66.95	66.93
HT	77.96	80.50	**81.88**	80.46	79.66	79.52	79.14	80.88	80.51	81.36
JT (Old)	(89.48)	(90.94)	82.70	85.74	85.60	**87.12**	**87.12**	86.92	87.11	86.65
Decathlon	(8196)	8491	8387	8237	8286	8462	8380	**8526**	8379	8467
20kmW	1:20:57	1:21:49	1:20:10	1:20:32	1:19:36	1:19:31	**1:19:05**	1:19:43	1:19:55	1:19:18
50kmW	3.48.59	3:48:50	3:46:30	3:50:01	3:45:56	**3:44:19**	3:44:45	3:45:29	3:46:36	3:44:33

Other peaks: TJ 17.48 (1985), DT: 68.20 (1982).

Men 100th Bests

	1980	1984	1988	1992	1995	1996	1997	1998	1999	2000
100m	10.44	10.36	10.34	10.32	10.31	10.27	10.27	10.27	10.26	**10.24**
200m	20.94	20.78	20.79	20.78	20.73	**20.66**	20.69	20.67	20.66	20.67
400m	46.35	46.03	45.99	45.98	45.96	45.91	45.96	45.91	45.88	**45.78**
800m	1:47.85	1:46.97	1:46.91	1:46.95	1:47.0	1:46.82	1:46.96	1:46.87	**1:46.54**	1:46.71
1500m	3:40.41	3:38.89	3:39.46	3:39.11	3:39.94	3:38.66	**3:38.42**	3:39.10	3:39.05	3:38.68
5000m	13:40.1	13:35.10	13:37.20	13:31.44	13:36.12	13:34.29	13:36.06	13:34.34	13:32.94	**13:28.62**
10000m	28:36.6	28:26.10	28:27.28	28:30.42	28:27.6	28:20.9	28:26.71	28:26.4	28:19.07	**28:15.98**
Marathon	2:14:25	2:13:20	2:13:08	2:13:22	2:12:32	2:12:25	2:12:03	2:11:50	2:11:26	**2:11:24**
3000mSt	8:36.3	8:35.35	8:35.24	8:34.43	8:36.0	8:34.91	8:36.07	8:36.24	8:34.04	**8:33.37**
110mh	14.07	13.91	13.83	13.78	13.81	**13.72**	13.79	13.80	13.80	13.76
400mh	50.99	50.53	50.52	50.50	50.32	50.17	50.26	50.20	50.10	**50.06**
HJ	2.20	**2.24**	**2.24**	**2.24**	2.23	**2.24**	2.24	2.23	2.22	2.23
PV	5.28	5.41	5.50	5.50	5.50	5.50	5.50	5.50	5.50	**5.55**
LJ	7.78	7.90	7.93	7.93	7.89	**7.94**	7.91	7.90	7.92	7.93
TJ	16.22	16.41	**16.60**	16.59	16.53	16.56	16.46	16.42	16.37	16.48
SP	19.15	**19.48**	19.17	18.79	18.56	18.81	18.73	18.89	18.81	19.05
DT	60.32	**60.96**	60.84	59.80	58.82	59.82	59.60	59.98	59.87	60.16
HT	69.98	**73.08**	72.34	70.70	70.92	70.88	70.76	71.10	70.93	71.28
JT	(80.68)	(81.52)	76.48	76.40	76.26	76.20	76.18	76.20	75.78	76.06
Decathlon	(7685)	7630	**7702**	7567	7633	7701	7649	7607	7592	7634
20kmW	1:25:55	1:25:57	1:24:54	1:24:09	**1:23:39**	1:23:55	1:23:58	1:24:30	1:24:31	1:24:22
50kmW		4:09:40	4:06:34	4:07:33	4:06:01	4:06:31	4:05:42	4:08:00	**4:03:49**	4:04:34

Other peaks: HJ 2.24 (also 1989), JT 77.14 (1991).

MEN 2000

WORLD LIST TRENDS

Women 10th Bests

100m	11.20	11.10	**10.92**	11.07	11.09	11.03	11.05	10.99	10.98	10.99
200m	22.47	22.36	**22.24**	22.44	22.50	22.27	22.45	22.53	22.31	22.49
400m	51.00	**49.74**	49.90	50.30	50.50	50.32	50.41	50.33	50.34	50.04
800m	1:57.0	1:57.20	**1:56.91**	1:57.93	1:58.74	1:58.22	1:58.48	1:58.39	1:58.24	1:58.34
1500m	3:59.82	4:00.18	4:01.02	4:01.23	4:04.31	4:02.38	**3:58.07**	4:00.60	4:03.14	4:01.23
3000m	8:44.7	8:37.36	8:37.70	8:42.09	8:43.19	8:43.72	8:45.70	8:44.10	8:34.19	**8:33.85**
5000m	16:03.9	15:30.63	15:17.89	15:19.20	14:56.94	14:48.36	14:46.72	15:03.67	14:56.00	**14:45.35**
10000m	33:48.49	32:30.91	31:42.02	31:28.06	31:43.41	31:24.08	31:16.39	31:52.98	31:32.63	**31:03.60**
Marathon	2:35:06	2:29:10	2:28:40	2:27:42	2:28:00	2:27:41	2:26:51	2:26:11	2:25:29	**2:24:33**
100mh	12.80	12.74	12.73	12.76	12.86	12.69	12.74	**12.67**	12.73	12.70
400mh	56.16	54.93	54.49	54.70	55.01	54.40	54.63	54.49	**54.15**	54.41
HJ	1.94	1.97	1.98	1.96	1.98	1.98	1.97	1.96	**1.99**	1.98
PV			-	3.70	4.01	4.15	4.20	4.34	4.46	**4.50**
LJ	6.81	7.01	**7.07**	6.92	6.90	6.92	6.86	6.91	6.93	6.93
TJ			13.07	14.07	14.46	14.55	14.58	14.53	**14.70**	14.52
SP	20.54	20.55	20.81	19.78	19.56	19.46	19.19	19.12	19.21	19.32
DT	66.02	68.56	**70.34**	67.08	63.90	64.90	65.86	65.05	64.68	65.41
HT			-	56.40	60.90	61.84	63.48	64.61	67.24	**69.36**
JT	66.40	66.56	**68.42**	65.02	65.22	66.14	66.52	66.43	63.52*	64.89*
Heptathlon	6424		**6540**	6460	6374	6406	6350	6381	6287	6396
10kmW	50:17	47:08	44:20	42:50	42:18	42:16	**42:15**	42:49	42:37	43:11
20kmW									1:28:51	**1:28:06**

Other peaks: SP 20.85 (1987). Note 5000m standard event from 1995, 20km walk from 1999.

Women 100th Bests

100m	11.65	11.51	11.43	11.45	11.47	11.44	11.40	11.39	11.41	**11.36**
200m	23.64	23.39	23.32	23.36	23.36	23.32	23.25	23.24	23.22	**23.21**
400m	53.00	52.63	52.50	52.60	52.59	52.29	52.66	52.40	52.46	**52.26**
800m	2:02.5	**2:01.50**	2:01.66	2:02.80	2:03.23	2:02.96	2:02.56	2:02.6	2:02.53	2:02..50
1500m	4:13.2	**4:10.22**	4:11.70	4:11.80	4:13.97	4:11.87	4:11.97	4:12.68	4:11.79	4:11.18
3000m	9:16.21	9:01.50	9:01.60	9:01.83	9:07.95*	- -				
5000m					15:39.12	15:35.62	15:39.95	15:40.74	15:37.76	**15:29.36**
10000m		34:26.36	33:11.31	33:05.80	33:00.33	32:56.63	32:59.33	33:11.36	32:59.05	**32:32.47**
Marathon	2:49:08	2:37:29	2:35:29	2:36:14	2:34:25	2:33:24	2:33:38	2:33:45	2:33:05	**2:32:25**
100mh	13.77	13.48	13.39	13.35	13.37	13.31	13.35	13.33	13.32	**13.22**
400mh	59.69	58.07	57.50	57.60	57.91	57.63	57.64	57.74	57.59	**57.48**
HJ	1.85	1.87	**1.88**	**1.88**	1.87	1.87	1.86	1.86	1.86	1.87
PV					-	3.60	3.77	3.90	4.00	**4.10**
LJ	6.34	6.48	**6.53**	6.45	6.46	6.50	6.48	6.48	6.48	6.49
TJ				13.16	13.36	13.45	13.53	13.51	13.64	**13.68**
SP	16.33	17.18	17.02	16.40	16.33	16.34	16.70	16.58	16.53	16.44
DT	56.46	**58.50**	57.40	56.20	55.84	56.86	56.04	56.28	56.02	56.22
HT					-	53.84	55.72	57.66	59.08	**60.66**
JT	55.48	57.74	**58.14**	56.36	56.04	56.16	55.48	54.80	54.54*	55.55*
Heptathlon	c5590		**5741**	5661	5609	5649	5620	5604	5596	5647
10kmW		50:17	?	45:59	46:06	**45:48**	46:01	46:05		
20kmW									1:36:59	**1:34:44**

All-time record levels indicated in bold. * Note new javelin from 1999.

Other peaks: 3000m 9:00.65 (1993), HJ 1.88 (also 1986, 1987, 1993), SP 17.19 (1987)

WOMEN'S WORLD LISTS 2000

100 METRES

Mark	Wind	Name		Nat	Born	Pos	Meet	Venue	Date
10.75	-0.4	Marion	Jones	USA	12.10.75	1	OG	Sydney	23 Sep
10.78	1.1		Jones			1	BrGP	London (CP)	5 Aug
10.78	0.1		Jones			1	ISTAF	Berlin	1 Sep
10.83	-1.3		Jones			1	VD	Bruxelles	25 Aug
10.83	1.0		Jones			1q2	OG	Sydney	22 Sep
10.84	-0.7		Jones			1	GP	Osaka	13 May
10.86	0.1	Chandra	Sturrup	BAH	12.9.71	1	NC	Nassau	21 Jul
10.88	-1.0		Jones			1	NC	Sacramento	15 Jul
10.91	1.0		Jones			1	GGala	Roma	30 Jun
10.91	0.9	Ekateríni	Thánou	GRE	1.2.75	1	Athl	Lausanne	5 Jul
10.91	-0.3	Inger	Miller	USA	12.6.72	1	Herc	Monaco	18 Aug
10.92	-0.2		Jones			1h1	NC	Sacramento	14 Jul
10.93	1.3		Thánou			1	Veniz	Haniá	14 Jun
10.93	-0.1		Thánou			1	NC	Athína	8 Jul
10.93	-0.4		Jones			1s1	NC	Sacramento	15 Jul
10.93	0.3	Zhanna	Pintusevich-Block	UKR	6.7.72	1	Bisl	Oslo	28 Jul
10.94	0.9		Pintusevich			2	Athl	Lausanne	5 Jul
10.95	-1.2		Jones			1	WK	Zürich	11 Aug
10.96	1.0	Eldece	Clarke-Lewis	BAH	13.2.65	1	Conseil	Fort-de-France	29 Apr
10.96	0.1	Debbie	Ferguson	BAH	16.1.76	2	NC	Nassau	21 Jul
10.96	-1.2		Miller			2	WK	Zürich	11 Aug
10.97	1.7	Chryste	Gaines	USA	14.9.70	1r1	GP	Athína	28 Jun
10.97	0.1	Pauline	Davis-Thompson	BAH	9.7.66	3	NC	Nassau	21 Jul
10.97	1.1		Miller			2	BrGP	London (CP)	5 Aug
10.99	1.0	Christine	Arron	FRA	13.9.73	2	GGala	Roma	30 Jun
10.99	1.3	Gail	Devers	USA	19.11.66	1h3	NC	Sacramento	14 Jul
10.99	1.2	Mary	Onyali	NGR	3.2.68	1		Chaux de Fonds	13 Aug
10.99	-1.2	Merlene	Ottey	JAM	10.5.60	1		Thessaloníki	30 Aug
10.99	1.0		Thánou			2q2	OG	Sydney	22 Sep
11.00	0.9		Thánou			1r2	GP	Athína	28 Jun
11.00	1.3		Ottey			1		Ljubljana	14 Aug
11.00	1.6		Jones			1	GPF	Doha	5 Oct
		(32/13)							
11.01	1.3	Léonie Myriam	Mani	CMR	21.5.77	1	OD	Jena	3 Jun
11.03	1.3	Carlette	Guidry	USA	4.9.68	2h3	NC	Sacramento	14 Jul
11.03	-1.2	Savatheda	Fynes	BAH	17.10.74	2		Thessaloníki	30 Aug
11.04	2.0	Lyubov	Perepelova	UZB	26.2.79	1h		Bishkek	3 Jun
11.04	-0.5	Susanthika	Jayasinghe	SRI	17.12.75	1	Super	Yokohama	9 Sep
11.06	0.9	Torri	Edwards	USA	31.1.77	4r2	GP	Athína	28 Jun
11.07	0.1	Tayna	Lawrence	JAM	17.9.75	3	ISTAF	Berlin	1 Sep
		(20)							
11.11	0.0	Beverly	McDonald	JAM	15.2.70	1s1	NC	Kingston	21 Jul
11.11	1.6	Natalya	Voronova	RUS	9.7.65	1s2	NC	Tula	23 Jul
11.12	-0.4	Angela	Williams	USA	30.1.80	1	NCAA	Durham	3 Jun
11.12	1.3	Irina	Pukha	UKR	10.1.73	4	Veniz	Haniá	14 Jun
11.12	0.9	Natalya	Ignatova	RUS	28.12.73	1	NC	Tula	23 Jul
11.12	2.0	Veronica	Campbell	JAM-J	16.5.82	1	WJ	Santiago de Chile	18 Oct
11.13	1.6	Olga	Shishigina	KAZ	23.12.68	1		Almaty	27 May
11.13	1.5	Peta-Gaye	Dowdie	JAM	18.1.77	1s2	NC	Kingston	21 Jul
11.14	1.2	LaTasha	Jenkins	USA	19.12.77	2		Chaux de Fonds	13 Aug
11.17	1.3	Nanceen	Perry	USA	19.4.77	2		Portland	25 Jun
		(30)							
11.17	0.9	Marina	Trandenkova	RUS	7.1.67	2	NC	Tula	23 Jul
11.17	1.5	Sandra	Citté	FRA	28.3.76	1h3	NC	Nice	4 Aug
11.18	0.3	Vida	Nsiah	GHA	13.4.76	3h10	OG	Sydney	22 Sep
11.19	2.0	Kelli	White	USA	1.4.77	1r1	Sea Ray	Knoxville	14 Apr
11.19	1.6	Michelle	Collins	USA	12.2.71	1		Atlanta	3 Jun
11.19A	0.1	Liliana	Allen	MEX	24.5.70	1	IMSS	Ciudad de México	1 Jul
11.20	0.5	Kisha	Jett	USA	11.2.75	1h2		Chapel Hill	18 Jun
11.20	1.1	Mercy	Nku	NGR	17.7.76	1		Rieti	3 Sep
11.21	1.7	Virgen	Benavídes	CUB	31.12.74	1		Camagüey	10 Mar
11.21	1.0	Manuela	Levorato	ITA	16.3.77	7	GGala	Roma	30 Jun
		(40)							
11.21	1.2	Andrea	Philipp	GER	29.7.71	1r1		Gold Coast (RB)	17 Sep

Mark	Wind	Name		Nat	Born	Pos	Meet	Venue	Date
11.22	-0.5	Marina	Kislova	RUS	12.12.78	1		Sanky-Peterburg	10 Jun
11.23	1.7		Cui Danfeng	CHN	10.1.77	1	NGP	Shijiazhuang	28 Apr
11.23	-0.4	Heather	Samuel	ANT	6.7.70	1		Ponce	10 Jun
11.23	1.1	Petya	Pendareva	BUL	20.1.71	2		Rieti	3 Sep
11.24		Natasha	Mayers	VIN	10.3.79	2		Port of Spain	16 Jun
11.24	0.5	Teneeshia	Jones	USA	28.1.79	2h2		Chapel Hill	18 Jun
11.24	1.0	Melinda	Gainsford-Taylor	AUS	1.10.71	4q2	OG	Sydney	22 Sep
11.25	1.3	Shakedia	Jones	USA	15.3.79	4h3	NC	Sacramento	14 Jul
11.25	-0.4		Li Xuemei	CHN	5.1.77	2h8	OG	Sydney	22 Sep
		(50)							
11.26		Ayanna	Hutchinson	TRI	18.2.78	3	NC	Port of Spain	16 Jun
11.26	0.5	Rachita	Mistry	IND	4.3.74	1		Bangalore	5 Jul
11.27	0.9	Shaunta	Pelham	USA	12.2.78	1s2	NCAA	Durham	2 Jun
11.27	1.3	Ameerah	Bello	ISV	3.10.75	1		Chapel Hill	18 Jun
11.27	1.4	Oksana	Ekk	RUS	26.11.74	1h3	NC	Tula	22 Jul
11.28	0.1	Yelena	Pastushenko	UKR	14.7.79	1		Kiev	26 May
11.28	0.5	Juan	Ball	USA	8.3.72	3h2		Chapel Hill	18 Jun
11.28	0.2	Anzhela	Kravchenko	UKR	25.1.71	1s2	NC	Kiev	4 Aug
11.28	1.2	Aminata	Diouf	SEN	18.2.77	3rA		La Chaux-de-Fonds	13 Aug
11.29	1.4	Martha	Adusei	CAN	8.6.76	2		Helsinki	15 Jun
		(60)							
11.29	1.1	Karin	Mayr	AUT	4.6.71	1	Live	Nürnberg	25 Jun
11.29	-0.2	Passion	Richardson	USA	25.1.75	2h1	NC	Sacramento	14 Jul
11.29	1.2	Zuzanna	Radecka	POL	2.4.75	1h3	NC	Kraków	4 Aug
11.29	0.0	Lauren	Hewitt	AUS	25.11.78	1	OT	Sydney	18 Aug
11.30	0.6	Tonya	Carter	USA	22.3.78	2h2	NCAA	Durham	1 Jun
11.30	0.6		Qin Wangping	CHN-J	16.6.82	1h1	OT	Jinzhou	7 Jun
11.30	0.5	Celena	Mondie-Milner	USA	6.8.68	4h2		Chapel Hill	18 Jun
11.30	0.3	Elva	Goulbourne	JAM	21.1.80	3h3	NC	Kingston	20 Jul
11.30	0.2	Oksana	Guskova	UKR	16.6.74	2s2	NC	Kiev	4 Aug
11.30	1.0	Esi	Benyarku	CAN	28.11.76	1	NC	Victoria	12 Aug
		(70)							
11.31	-0.2	Angela	Manuel	USA	10.5.75	3h1	NC	Sacramento	14 Jul
11.31	1.9	Viktoriya	Koviryeva	KAZ	17.12.75	1		Almaty	11 Aug
11.32	0.0	Wendy	Hartman	RSA	28.2.76	1	NC	Stellenbosch	3 Mar
11.32		Erica	Whipple	USA-J	4.12.82	1h1		Plant City	4 May
11.32	1.0	Michelle	Burrell	USA	8.5.65	2r1		Houston	6 May
11.32	-2.5	Glory	Alozie	NGR	30.12.77	2	ECCp	Vila Real S.António	27 May
11.32	1.4	Paraskeví	Patoulídou	GRE	29.3.65	1h4	NC	Athína	8 Jul
11.32	0.9	Irina	Khabarova	RUS	18.3.66	5	NC	Tula	23 Jul
11.33	0.9	Brianna	Glenn	USA	18.4.80	3s2	NCAA	Durham	2 Jun
11.33	0.0	Astia	Walker	JAM	4.4.75	3s1	NC	Kingston	21 Jul
		(80)							
11.33	1.2	Esther	Möller	GER	13.9.77	2r1		Gold Coast (RB)	17 Sep
11.34	1.7	Kim	Gevaert	BEL	5.8.78	1		Jambes	1 May
11.34	1.6	Tatyana	Barashko	BLR	7.10.76	1	NC	Brest	1 Aug
11.34	-0.2	Anzhelika	Shevchuk	UKR	23.2.69	1	Univ Ch	Kiev	15 Jul
11.34	1.7	Shani	Anderson	GBR	7.8.75	1		Nitra	26 Aug
11.35	1.3	Agné	Visockaite	LTU	4.8.78	1		Lebanon IL	15 Apr
11.35	-0.7	Philomena	Mensah	CAN	11.5.75	5	GP	Osaka	13 May
11.35	1.6	Louise	Ayétotché	CIV	3.6.75	1		Sacramento	21 May
11.35	0.4	SaDonna	Thornton	USA	16.8.78	3s1	NCAA	Durham	2 Jun
11.35	2.0	Marcia	Richardson	GBR	10.2.72	2		Bedford	4 Jun
		(90)							
11.35	0.2	Nora	Ivanova-Güner	TUR	1.6.77	1	ECp-2B	Banská Bystrica	8 Jul
11.35	0.4	Monica	Twum	GHA	14.3.78	2s2	AfrC	Alger	10 Jul
11.35	0.0	Alenka	Bikar	SLO	7.1.74	1		Ravne na Koroskem	21 Jul
11.35	1.4	Frédérique	Bangue	FRA	31.12.76	1r1		Castres	27 Jul
11.36	1.8	Aleah	Williams	USA-J	7.1.81	1h7	TexR	Austin	7 Apr
11.36	0.7	Cathy	Freeman	AUS	16.2.73	5r3	ModR	Modesto	13 May
11.36	0.4	Lakeesha	White	USA	29.7.80	4s1	NCAA	Durham	2 Jun
11.36	1.2	Nadine	Palmer	JAM-J	9.2.83	2	CAC	San Juan	14 Jul
11.36	1.3	Muna	Lee	USA-J	30.10.81	5h3	NC	Sacramento	14 Jul
11.36	1.6	Yekaterina	Stankevich	BLR	5.6.77	h	NC	Brest	31 Jul
		(100)							
11.36	2.0	Katia	Benth	FRA	16.11.75	2h1	NC	Nice	4 Aug
11.36	0.0	Muriel	Hurtis	FRA	25.3.79	4rB	Herc	Monaco	18 Aug

Symbols/Abbreviations

+ intermediate time in longer race, A made at an altitude of 1000m or higher, H made in a heptathlon, h made in a heat, qf quarter-final, sf semi-final, i indoors, Q qualifying round, r race number, -J juniors (born 1981 or later)

Mark	Wind		Name	Nat	Born	Date
11.37	0.2		Liu Xiaomei	CHN	11.1.72	13 May
11.37	0.2	Nadine	Faustin	HAI	14.4.76	21 May
11.37	1.1	Angela	Daigle	USA	28.5.76	4 Jun
11.37	0.3	Irina	Privalova	RUS	22.11.68	22 Jul
11.37	-0.5	Lucimar	de Moura	BRA	22.3.74	3 Aug
11.37	0.7	Natalya	Safronnikova	BLR	28.2.73	18 Aug
11.37		Bolanie	Aikema	NGR-J		Nov
11.38	1.8	Cydonie	Mothersill	CAY	19.3.78	20 May
11.38	0.5	Donna	Howard	USA	28.8.74	18 Jun
11.38	0.2	Joan	Ekah Uduak	NGR	16.12.80	21 Jun
11.38	1.0	Tarama	Perry	CAN	20.11.74	12 Aug
11.38	1.2	Delphine	Combe	FRA	6.12.74	13 Aug
11.39A	0.0	Dikeledi	Morapane	RSA	12.3.76	14 Feb
11.39	0.4		Zeng Xiujun	CHN	10.2.79	9 May
11.39	1.9	Mary	Grant	USA	.78	14 May
11.39	2.0	Tania	Van Heer-Murphy	AUS	30.12.70	4 Jun
11.39	1.2	Khalilah	Carpenter	USA-J	27.1.83	23 Jun
11.39	1.9	Véronique	Mang	CMR-J	15.12.84	26 Jul
11.39	1.2	Mireille	Donders	SUI	7.7.74	13 Aug
11.39	2.0	Katchi	Habel	GER-J	22.10.82	18 Oct
11.40		Fana	Ashby	TRI-J	15.6.81	18 Mar
11.40	2.0	Miesha	McKelvy	USA	26.7.76	10 Jun
11.40A	0.1	Richelle	Webb	USA	8.10.71	1 Jul
11.40	0.5	Yuliya	Tabakova	RUS	.80	22 Jul
11.40	1.0	Atia	Weekes	CAN	29.5.80	12 Aug
11.40	1.2	Sanna	Kyllönen	FIN	9.3.71	19 Aug
11.40	1.0	Saraswati	Dey	IND	23.11.79	30 Aug
11.41A	1.0	Nova	Peris-Kneebone	AUS	25.2.71	13 Mar
11.41	2.0	Heather	Sumpter	USA	12.11.77	14 Apr
11.41	1.1	Marion	Wagner	GER	1.2.78	25 Jun
11.41	2.0	Yessica	Torres	MEX	.80	14 Jul
11.41	1.9	Odiah	Sidibé	FRA	13.1.70	4 Aug
11.42A	1.0	Aïda	Diop	SEN	27.4.70	13 Mar
11.42	1.7	Merlene	Frazer	JAM	27.12.73	14 May
11.42	1.6	Natalya	Vorobyeva	KAZ	15.11.71	27 May
11.42	1.0	Kátia	Santos	BRA	31.12.67	3 Jun
11.42	-1.3	Svetlana	Pospelova ¶	RUS	24.12.79	10 Jun
11.42	0.7	Kaori	Sakagami	JPN	12.5.74	9 Jul
11.42	1.3	Cheryl	Taplin	USA	2.9.72	14 Jul
11.42	0.4	Joice	Maduaka	GBR	30.9.73	8 Aug
11.42	0.7		Wang Xiaoqian	CHN	5.1.79	20 Oct
11.43A	-0.1	Heide	Seyerling	RSA	19.8.76	4 Feb
11.43	1.0	Valma	Bass	SKN	12.3.74	15 Apr
11.43A	0.8	Mirtha	Brock	COL	9.4.70	13 May
11.43	-0.5	Evelina	Lisenco	ROM	4.2.75	10 Jun
11.43	1.0	Donita	Benjamin	GBR	7.3.72	11 Aug
11.44	-5.0	Jasmine	Reynolds	USA		18 Jun
11.44	0.8	Samantha	Davies	GBR	20.9.79	11 Aug
11.45	-0.4	Yohandra	Neyra	CUB	18.4.76	11 Feb
11.45	1.5	Rodena	Barr	USA	5.3.78	8 Apr
11.45	1.1	Chinedu	Odozor	NGR	24.12.77	29 Apr
11.46A	0.8	Digna Luz	Murillo	COL-J	22.5.81	13 May
11.46	0.2	LaQuinta	Manahan	USA	27.1.79	16 May
11.46	1.3	Shanta	Ghosh	GER	3.1.75	1 Jul
11.46	1.5	Patricia	Girard	FRA	8.4.68	4 Aug
11.46	0.0	Sina	Schielke	GER-J	19.5.81	12 Aug
11.47	1.1	Jodi	Lambert	AUS	1.9.70	5 Feb
11.47	1.5	Nolle	Graham	JAM-J	12.9.81	8 Apr
11.47	2.0	Staciann	Brown	JAM	17.12.77	14 Apr
11.47	0.0	Vonette	Dixon	JAM	26.11.75	15 Apr
11.47	1.9	Oluwaseum	Adetiba	USA	27.5.79	22 Apr
11.47	1.7		Yan Jiankui	CHN	19.3.76	28 Apr
11.47	-1.5	Zhanna	Zhabchenko	RUS	.73	10 Jun
11.47	1.9	Jacqueline	Poelman	NED	5.10.73	2 Jul
11.47	-0.4	LaKeisha	Backus	USA	15.12.76	14 Jul
11.47	0.0	Aleen	Bailey	JAM	25.11.80	21 Jul
11.47	1.9	Céline	Thélamon	FRA	1.3.79	4 Aug
11.48	0.6	Rosemar	Coelho Neto	BRA	2.1.77	3 Jun
11.48	-0.7	Yelena	Anisimova	RUS	12.6.71	18 Jun
11.48	0.3	Yuliya	Skotnikova	RUS	.76	26 Jun
11.48	1.1	Michelle	Bookman	USA	8.10.71	7 Jul
11.48	1.2	Sharon	Cripps	AUS	29.6.77	14 Jul
11.48	0.3	Yekaterina	Leshchova	RUS	21.4.74	22 Jul
11.48	1.6	Larisa	Kruglova	RUS	27.10.72	23 Jul
11.49A	0.0	Surita	Febbraio	RSA	27.12.73	22 Jan
11.49	-1.0	Candace	Young	USA	8.1.79	18 Mar
11.49	1.1	LaTrese	Taylor	USA	18.7.78	6 May
11.49		Donica	Merriman	USA	24.1.79	20 May
11.49	0.9	Rachelle	Boone	USA-J	30.6.81	2 Jun
11.49	1.2	Sarah	Reilly	IRL	3.7.73	17 Jun
11.49A	1.6	Trinity	Davis	USA		4 Jul
11.49	0.2	Effrosíni	Patsoú	GRE	5.6.74	8 Jul
11.49	0.3	Irina	Titova	RUS	.78	11 Jul
11.49	1.7	Rosa	Rakotozafy	MAD	12.11.77	27 Jul
11.49	0.1	Johanna	Manninen	FIN	4.4.80	2 Aug
11.49	1.7	Heidi	Hannula	FIN	26.2.80	19 Aug
11.49	0.7	Sarah	Wilhelmy	GBR	2.2.80	17 Sep
11.50	1.1	Mechelle	Lewis	USA	20.9.80	12 Apr
11.50	1.7	Kerine	Black	JAM		12 May
11.50	-1.3	Roxana	Díaz	CUB-J	17.5.81	16 Jun
11.50	1.7	Enikő	Szabó	HUN	10.11.79	16 Jun
11.50	0.4	Tatyana	Bonenko	UKR	7.6.76	18 Jun
11.50	1.2	Tatyana	Tkalich	UKR	30.5.75	3 Aug
11.50	0.0	Elly	Hutton	AUS	2.6.76	18 Aug
11.50	-0.8	Hanitriniana	Rakotondrabe	MAD	1.1.67	22 Sep
11.51	-0.9	Yelena	Tishkova	RUS	11.5.75	11 Jul
11.51	0.9	Cynthia	Octavia	FRA	16.6.78	14 Jul
		(199)	18 more women 11.52 to 11.54			

Mark	Wind		Name	Nat	Born	Pos	Meet	Venue	Date
Rolling start: 11.16	1.6	Manuela	Levorato	ITA	16.3.77	1		Padova	27 Aug
Indoors: 11.35		Natalya	Safronnikova	BLR	28.2.73	2		Tampere	7 Feb
Wind assisted									
10.68	2.2	Marion	Jones	USA	12.10.75	1	DNG	Stockholm	1 Aug
10.84	2.9	Ekateríni	Thánou	GRE	1.2.75	1	ECp-S	Gateshead	15 Jul
10.89	3.4	Christine	Arron	FRA	13.9.73	1r4		Montauban	15 Aug
10.91	2.4	Merlene	Ottey	JAM	10.5.60	1		Gold Coast (RB)	10 Sep
10.92	3.4	Torri	Edwards	USA	31.1.77	1	MAI	Malmö	7 Aug
10.93	2.6		Jones			1	Pre	Eugene	24 Jun
10.95	3.1		Sturrup			1	MSR	Walnut	16 Apr
10.98	4.0	Peta-Gaye	Dowdie	JAM	18.1.77	1		Houston	6 Jul
10.98	2.2		Pintusevich			2	DNG	Stockholm	1 Aug
11.01	2.2	Angela	Williams	USA	30.1.80	1	Pac10	Eugene	21 May
11.02A	3.0	Melinda	Gainsford-Taylor	AUS	1.10.71	1		Pietersburg	18 Mar
11.08	2.6	Natalya	Ignatova	RUS	28.12.73	1s1	NC	Tula	23 Jul
11.10	2.1	Nanceen	Perry	USA	19.4.77	1		Austin	6 May
11.13	2.9	Manuela	Levorato	ITA	16.3.77	3	ECp-S	Gateshead	15 Jul
11.14	3.4	Marina	Trandenkova	RUS	7.1.67	4	MAI	Malmö	7 Aug
11.15	5.5	Tonya	Carter	USA	22.3.78	1	Owens	Columbus	7 May
11.15	2.9	Andrea	Philipp	GER	29.7.71	4	ECp-S	Gateshead	15 Jul
11.16	5.5	Donica	Merriman	USA	24.1.79	2	Owens	Columbus	7 May
11.18	3.3	Lauren	Hewitt	AUS	25.11.78	1		Canberra	15 Jan
11.18A	3.0	Nova	Peris-Kneebone	AUS	25.2.71	2		Pietersburg	18 Mar
11.18	4.0	Kisha	Jett	USA	11.2.75	1	GaTech	Atlanta	20 May
11.19	3.7	Virgen	Benavídes	CUB	31.12.74	1		La Habana	11 Feb

Mark	Wind	Name		Nat	Born	Pos	Meet	Venue	Date
11.19	2.1	Passion	Richardson	USA	25.1.75	4		Palo Alto	1 Jul
11.19	2.6	Irina	Khabarova	RUS	18.3.66	2s1	NC	Tula	23 Jul
11.20A	3.0	Wendy	Hartman	RSA	28.2.76	3		Pietersburg	18 Mar
11.21	2.1	LaKeisha	Backus	USA	15.12.76	3		Austin	6 May
11.21	4.0	Cydonie	Mothersill	CAY	19.3.78	2	GaTech	Atlanta	20 May
11.22	2.5		Cui Danfeng	CHN	10.1.77	1	NGP	Nanjing	14 Apr
11.22	4.7	Lakeesha	White	USA	29.7.80	1	USTCA	Austin	22 Apr
11.23A	3.0	Aïda	Diop	SEN	27.4.70	4		Pietersburg	18 Mar
11.24	2.8	Brianna	Glenn	USA	18.4.80	1r1	TexR	Austin	8 Apr
11.25	4.7	Aleah	Williams	USA-J	7.1.81	2	USTCA	Austin	22 Apr
11.26	2.6	Karin	Mayr	AUT	4.6.71	1		Schwechat	17 Jun
11.28	3.9	Muriel	Hurtis	FRA	25.3.79	1		Arles	3 Jun
11.28	2.1	Benedicta	Ajudua	NGR	10.7.80	1r2		Sydney	11 Sep
11.29	4.7	Marcia	Richardson	GBR	10.2.72	1s1	CAU	Bedford	29 May
11.29	3.4	Kaori	Sakagami	JPN	12.5.74	1r2		Fukui	9 Jul
11.29	3.9	Delphine	Combe	FRA	6.12.74	1r3		Montauban	15 Aug
11.30	4.7	SaDonna	Thornton	USA	16.8.78	3	UCTA	Austin	22 Apr
11.30	3.7	LaQuinta	Manahan	USA	10.4.78	1r2		Arlington	6 May
11.30	2.4	Wyllesheia	Myrick	USA	21.11.79	1	Big East	Piscataway	7 May
11.31	3.7	Heidi	Hannula	FIN	26.2.80	1		Lapinlahti	16 Jul
11.32A	3.0	Dikeledi	Morapane	RSA	12.3.76	5		Pietersburg	18 Mar
11.32	3.7	Sanna	Kyllönen	FIN	9.3.71	2		Lapinlahti	16 Jul
11.32	3.4	Frédérique	Bangue	FRA	31.12.76	3r4		Montauban	15 Aug
11.33	w	Angela	Daigle	USA	28.5.76	3h1		Sacramento	21 May
11.34A	2.5	Falilat	Ogunkoya	NGR	12.5.68	1		El Paso	15 Apr
11.34	3.2	Tami	Zachery	USA	27.11.78	1		Lubbock	21 Apr
11.34	3.4	Katia	Benth	FRA	16.11.75	4r4		Montauban	15 Aug
11.35	3.1	Tarama	Perry	CAN	20.11.74	4r7	MSR	Walnut	16 Apr

11.36A	3.0	Suzanne	Broadrick	AUS	24.10.68	18 Mar
11.36	3.1	Angie	Vaughn	USA	4.11.76	8 Apr
11.36	3.0	Monique	Wright-Cruse	USA	28.10.80	11 May
11.36	2.4	Erica	Burrell	USA	24.5.78	19 May
11.36	2.8	Rosemar	Coelho Neto	BRA	2.1.77	15 Jul
11.37	2.9	Irina	Titova	RUS	.78	1 Jul
11.38	5.5	Mechelle	Lewis	USA	20.9.80	7 May
11.38	4.0	Aleen	Bailey	JAM	25.11.80	13 May
11.38		Michelle	Brown	USA	12.3.75	11 Jun
11.38A	7.3	Trinity	Davis	USA		3 Jul
11.38	2.6	Yuliya	Tabakova	RUS	.80	23 Jul
11.38	3.9	Céline	Thélamon	FRA	1.3.79	15 Aug
11.39	2.4	Rosa	Rakotozafy	MAD	12.11.77	8 Apr
11.39	3.3	Rachelle	Boone	USA-J	30.6.81	21 May
11.40	2.4	Jodi	Lambert	AUS	1.9.70	5 Feb
11.40	3.7	Vonette	Dixon	JAM	26.11.75	13 May
11.40	3.5	Sharon	Cripps	AUS	29.6.77	5 Aug
11.41	2.1	Tania	Woods	USA	23.9.80	16 Apr
11.41	2.7	Anna	Voskanyan	RUS	11.10.77	28 May
11.41	2.4	Elly	Hutton	AUS	2.6.76	10 Sep
11.42A	3.0	Rachael	Massey	AUS	23.3.76	18 Mar
11.42	4.7	Valma	Bass	SKN	12.3.74	22 Apr
11.42	2.2	Kinshasa	Davis	USA	10.7.79	21 May
11.43	2.4	Delloreen	Ennis-London	JAM	5.3.75	6 May
11.43	4.0	Michelle	Bookman	USA	8.10.71	6 Jul
11.45	3.2	Donna	Fraser	GBR	7.11.72	8 Apr
11.45	4.7	Me'Lisa	Barber	USA	4.10.80	22 Apr
11.45	3.2	Sarah	Reilly	IRL	3.7.73	16 Jul
11.45	2.6	Yekaterina	Leshchova	RUS	21.4.74	23 Jul
11.45	2.3	Patricia	Girard	FRA	8.4.68	27 Jul
11.46	2.1	Motoka	Arai	JPN	4.7.74	16 Apr
11.46	3.4	Adrianna	Lamalle	FRA-J	27.9.82	27 May
11.47	w	Camille	Pouncy	USA	20.1.80	28 Apr
11.47	5.5	D'Andre	Hill	USA	19.4.73	7 May
11.47	5.2	Cynthia	Octavia	FRA	16.6.78	14 Jul
11.48	2.1	Candace	Young	USA	8.1.79	16 Apr
11.48	4.0	Maicel	Malone-Wallace	USA	12.6.69	28 Apr
11.48	3.9	Linda	Ferga	FRA	24.12.76	3 Jun
11.49	3.7	Mercedes	Carnesolta	CUB	13.5.75	11 Feb
11.49	3.0	Donnette	Brown	JAM	19.9.71	11 May
11.49	4.9	Sonia	Williams	ANT	28.5.79	12 May
11.49	4.3	Enikő	Szabó	HUN	10.11.79	20 May
11.49	4.7	Ellena	Ruddock	GBR	23.2.76	29 May
11.49A	7.3	Karen	Clarke	CAN	7.10.71	3 Jul
11.49	2.6	Christine	Bloomfield	GBR	12.2.68	19 Aug
11.50	4.7	Sharika	Higgins	USA	10.4.78	22 Apr
11.50	4.3	Enikő	Szakács	HUN	26.4.77	20 May
11.50	2.3	Doris	Deruel	FRA	13.11.77	27 Jul
11.51	4.1	Stacy	Minott	USA	9.12.77	8 Apr
11.51		Hellena	Wrappah	GHA	9.12.73	21 Apr
11.51	4.2	Mila	Savic	YUG	24.4.74	17 Jun
11.51	3.4	Annika	Amundin	SWE	9.2.77	7 Aug

18 women 11.52w-11.54w

Doubtful timing

11.37		Monique	Tubbs	USA-J	23.1.81	21 Apr
11.51	4.1	Stacey	Minott	USA	9.12.77	8 Apr

Best at low altitude

11.24	-1.6	Allen	1		Funchal	29 Jul
11.23w	2.2		2		Lisboa (U)	5 Aug
11.32	0.0	Hartman	1	NC	Stellenbosch	3 Mar
11.44	0.0	Morapane				3 Mar
11.45w	2.1	Peris-Kneebone				3 Sep

Hand timing

11.0		Yelena	Pastushenko	UKR	14.7.79	1h	Kharkov	3 Jun
11.0		Evelina	Lisenco	ROM	4.2.75	1	Meknès	27 May
11.1		Veronica	Campbell	JAM-J	15.5.82	1	Kingston	15 Jan
11.1	0.0	Angela	Williams	USA	30.1.80	1	Los Angeles (ww)	6 May
11.1		Viktoriya	Fomenko	UKR	2.10.70	h	Kharkov	3 Jun
11.1		Tatyana	Tkalich	UKR	30.5.75	h	Kharkov	3 Jun

11.2	-0.9	Candace	Young	USA	8.1.79	4 Mar
11.2		Chinedu	Odozor	NGR	24.12.77	31 Mar
11.2A	-0.2	Rosa	Rakotozafy	MAD	12.11.77	12 Apr
11.2		Aminata	Diouf	SEN	18.2.77	12 May
11.2		Anna	Voskanyan	RUS	11.10.77	17 May
11.2	0.4	Nora	Güner	TUR	1.6.77	20 May
11.2	-0.4	Oksana	Guskova	UKR	16.6.74	16 Jun
11.2	1.6	Tatyana	Bonenko	UKR	7.6.76	16 Jun
11.2A		Hanitriniana	Rakotondrabe	MAD	1.1.67	25 Aug
11.3		Nadine	Palmer	JAM-J	9.2.83	11 Mar
11.3		Tracee	Thomas	USA-J	17.4.84	16 Mar
11.3		Lerma	Bulauitan	PHI	17.10.74	5 May
11.3	1.6	Anzhelika	Shevchuk	UKR	23.2.69	16 Jun
11.3	1.0	Monika	Gachevska	BUL	30.10.74	17 Jun

Mark	Wind	Name		Nat	Born	Pos	Meet	Venue	Date
Wind assisted									
11.0	2.1	Tatyana	Bonenko	UKR	7.6.76	1h2		Kiev	16 Jun
11.2	2.1	Yuliya	Shcherbak	UKR	23.9.75				16 Jun
11.2		Aleen	Bailey	JAM	25.11.80				28 Jun
11.3	3.0	Shani	Anderson	GBR	7.8.75				19 Aug

JUNIORS

See main list for top 6 juniors. 10 performances by 6 women to 11.36. Additional marks and further juniors:

Campbell 11.16 1.5 2s2 NC Kingston 21 Jul; 11.30 -0.5 1h2 NC Kingston 20 Jul
11.18 1.2 1 CAC-j San Juan 14 Jul; 11.31 0.5 1 NC Kingston 21 Jul
11.28 0.0 1 Brisbane 8 Sep; 11.33 0.0 1 NC-j Kingston 30 Jun

Mark	Wind	Name		Nat	Born	Pos	Meet	Venue	Date
11.37		Bolanie	Aikema	NGR		1		Bauchi	Nov
11.39	1.2	Khalilah	Carpenter	USA	27.1.83	1	NC-j	Denton	23 Jun
11.39	1.9	Véronique	Mang	CMR	15.12.84	1s		Hagetmau	26 Jul
11.39	2.0	Katchi	Habel (10)	GER	22.10.82	2	WJ	Santiago de Chile	18 Oct
11.40		Fana	Ashby	TRI	15.6.81	2		Port of Spain	18 Mar
11.46A	0.8	Digna Luz	Murillo	COL	22.5.81	2		Medellín	13 May
11.46	0.0	Sina	Schielke	GER	19.5.81	1		Mannheim	12 Aug
11.47	1.5	Nolle	Graham	JAM	12.9.81	2		Durham	8 Apr
11.49	0.9	Rachelle	Boone	USA	30.6.81	7s2	NCAA	Durham	2 Jun
11.50	-1.3	Roxana	Díaz	CUB	17.5.81	1		La Habana	16 Jun
11.52	0.8	Monique	Tubbs	USA	23.1.81	1		Troy	22 Apr
		11.37w	doubtful timing			1h1		Troy	21 Apr
11.53	1.6	Gwladys	Bélliard	FRA	10.11.82	1		Hagetmau	26 Jul
11.53	1.9	Thatiana	Ignâcio	BRA	2.7.83	1		Manaus	2 Sep
11.57	1.2	Consuella	Moore	USA	29.8.81	3	NC-j	Denton	23 Jun

Wind assisted see main lists for three women – and:

Campbell 11.18w 2.1 2r1 Brisbane 3 Sep; 11.25w 2.9 1h2 CAC-j San Juan 14 Jul
Williams 11.29w 2.8 3 TexR Austin 8 Apr

Mark	Wind	Name		Nat	Born	Pos	Meet	Venue	Date
11.39	3.3	Rachelle	Boone	USA	30.6.81	1	Big 10	Iowa City	21 May
11.46	3.4	Adrianna	Lamalle	FRA	27.9.82	1		Fort-de-France	27 May
11.52	w	Porchea	Carroll	USA	23.10.83	1		Camarillo	18 Mar
11.52	2.2	Alexis	Joyce	USA	9.5.83	1h1	NC-j	Denton	23 Jun
11.53	2.1	Zenobia	Reed	USA	24.1.84	1r5		Austin	13 May
11.53	2.1	Angel	Perkins	USA	5.10.84	1h2	JunOly	Amherst	28 Jul
11.54	2.1	Calista	Onyejiaka	NGR	3.4.83	3r2		Sydney	11 Sep

200 METRES

Mark	Wind	Name		Nat	Born	Pos	Meet	Venue	Date
21.84	0.7	Marion	Jones	USA	12.10.75	1	OG	Sydney	28 Sep
21.94	0.5		Jones			1	NC	Sacramento	23 Jul
22.09	0.5	Inger	Miller	USA	12.6.72	2	NC	Sacramento	23 Jul
22.27	0.7	Pauline	Davis-Thompson	BAH	9.7.66	2	OG	Sydney	28 Sep
22.28	0.7	Susanthika	Jayasinghe	SRI	17.12.75	3	OG	Sydney	28 Sep
22.32	-0.5		Jayasinghe			1	Super	Yokohama	9 Sep
22.35	0.7	Beverly	McDonald	JAM	15.2.70	4	OG	Sydney	28 Sep
22.37	0.7	Debbie	Ferguson	BAH	16.1.76	5	OG	Sydney	28 Sep
22.38	0.5	Nanceen	Perry	USA	19.4.77	3	NC	Sacramento	23 Jul
22.38	0.7		Davis-Thompson			1s2	OG	Sydney	28 Sep
22.40	-1.4		Jones			1s1	OG	Sydney	28 Sep
22.41	0.2	Léonie Myriam	Mani	CMR	21.5.77	1		Kourou	21 May
22.42	0.7	Melinda	Gainsford-Taylor	AUS	1.10.71	6	OG	Sydney	28 Sep
22.43	1.2		Gainsford-Taylor			1		Hobart	30 Jan
22.43	1.0		Ferguson			1	Athl	Lausanne	5 Jul
22.44A	1.0		Davis-Thompson			1	IMSS	Ciudad de México	1 Jul
22.44	-0.5		McDonald			2	Super	Yokohama	9 Sep
22.44	-0.2		McDonald			1q1	OG	Sydney	27 Sep
22.45	0.7		Jayasinghe			2s2	OG	Sydney	28 Sep
22.46	-0.2		Ferguson			1	NC	Nassau	26 Jul
22.48	-0.2		Davis-Thompson			2	NC	Nassau	26 Jul
22.49	0.0	LaTasha	Colander-Richardson	USA	23.8.76	1		Nassau	9 Jun
22.49	1.0	Mary	Onyali	NGR	3.2.68	1		Chaux de Fonds	13 Aug
22.49	-0.3		Gainsford-Taylor			1q2	OG	Sydney	27 Sep
22.50	-0.6		McDonald			1h5	OG	Sydney	27 Sep
22.50	-0.3		Jones			2q2	OG	Sydney	27 Sep
22.51	0.7	Peta-Gaye	Dowdie	JAM	18.1.77	1	NCAA	Durham	3 Jun
22.51	0.7		Gainsford-Taylor			1		Brisbane	8 Sep
22.52	1.5	Lauren	Hewitt	AUS	25.11.78	1		Canberra	15 Jan
22.52	1.7		Perry			1s2	NC	Sacramento	23 Jul
		(30/13)							
22.53	0.7	Cathy	Freeman	AUS	16.2.73	7	OG	Sydney	28 Sep

Mark	Wind	Name		Nat	Born	Pos	Meet	Venue	Date
22.57	-0.2	Chandra	Sturrup	BAH	12.9.71	1	NC	Nassau	22 Jul
22.57	1.7	Michelle	Collins	USA	12.2.71	2s2	NC	Sacramento	23 Jul
22.64A	1.0	Aida	Diop	SEN	27.4.70	2	IMSS	Ciudad de México	1 Jul
22.65	1.7	Torri	Edwards	USA	31.1.77	3s2	NC	Sacramento	23 Jul
22.66	0.4	Cydonie	Mothersill	CAY	19.3.78	1		Clemson	14 May
22.66	0.7	Zhanna	Pintusevich-Block	UKR	6.7.72	8	OG	Sydney	28 Sep
		(20)							
22.69	2.0	Kinshasa	Davis	USA	10.7.79	1r4	MSR	Walnut	16 Apr
22.69	0.0	Andrea	Philipp	GER	29.7.71	1A	Live	Nürnberg	25 Jun
22.69	0.5	Oksana	Ekk	RUS	26.11.74	1		Moskva	20 Aug
22.70	-0.3	Muriel	Hurtis	FRA	25.3.79	1	ECp-S	Gateshead	16 Jul
22.71	1.0	Marie-José	Pérec	FRA	9.5.68	2	Athl	Lausanne	5 Jul
22.72	-0.4	Lyubov	Perepelova	UZB	26.2.79	1		Bishkek	4 Jun
22.75	0.9	Sabrina	Mulrain	GER	10.6.78	1	NC-23	Jena	20 Aug
22.76	1.2		Liu Xiaomei	CHN	11.1.72	1	OT	Jinzhou	8 Jun
22.76	-1.0	Katharine	Merry	GBR	21.9.74	2		Barcelona	25 Jul
22.76	0.5	Irina	Khabarova	RUS	18.3.66	2		Moskva	20 Aug
		(30)							
22.76	0.7	Louise	Ayétoché	CIV	3.6.75	5s2	OG	Sydney	28 Sep
22.78	1.9	Olesya	Zykina	RUS	7.10.80	1h3	NCp	Tula	3 Jun
22.79	0.7	Astia	Walker	JAM	4.4.75	2	Gugl	Linz	8 Aug
22.80	0.9	Shanta	Ghosh	GER	3.1.75	2B	Live	Nürnberg	25 Jun
22.80	-2.0	Svetlana	Pospelova ¶	RUS	24.12.79	1h6	NC	Tula	24 Jul
22.81	0.0	Esther	Möller	GER	13.9.77	2A	Live	Nürnberg	25 Jun
22.81	-0.3	Natalya	Voronova	RUS	9.7.65	2	ECp-S	Gateshead	16 Jul
22.84	0.6	Tayna	Lawrence	JAM	17.9.75	2		Basse-Terre	1 May
22.84	0.7	Damayanthi	Darsha	SRI	13.2.75	1	AsiC	Jakarta	31 Aug
22.85A	1.0	Celena	Mondie-Milner	USA	6.8.68	3	IMSS	Ciudad de México	1 Jul
		(40)							
22.85	0.2	Yelena	Pastushenko	UKR	14.7.79	1		Dortmund	8 Jul
22.86	-0.3	LaTasha	Jenkins	USA	19.12.77	4		Milano	7 Jun
22.86	0.9	Eldece	Clarke-Lewis	BAH	13.2.65	3B	Live	Nürnberg	25 Jun
22.86	-2.0	Juliet	Campbell	JAM	17.3.70	1	NC	Kingston	22 Jul
22.87A	0.7	Heide	Seyerling	RSA	19.8.76	1		Bloemfontein	4 Feb
22.87	-0.2	Savatheda	Fynes	BAH	17.10.74	4	NC	Nassau	22 Jul
22.87	0.7	Veronica	Campbell	JAM-J	15.5.82	1	WJ	Santiago de Chile	21 Oct
22.88	0.9	Shaunta	Pelham	USA	12.2.78	1		Tallahassee	13 May
22.89	-0.3	Manuela	Levorato	ITA	16.3.77	4	ECp-S	Gateshead	16 Jul
22.90	0.9	Alenka	Bikar	SLO	7.1.74	4B	Live	Nürnberg	25 Jun
		(50)							
22.90	1.0	Fatima	Yusuf	NGR	2.5.71	5	Athl	Lausanne	5 Jul
22.90	-0.4	Marina	Trandenkova	RUS	7.1.67	2	NC	Tula	25 Jul
22.93	0.6	Virgen	Benavídes	CUB	31.12.74	1		Camagüey	11 Mar
22.94	-0.3	Mercy	Nku	NGR	17.7.76	4q2	OG	Sydney	27 Sep
22.96	0.2	Viktoriya	Fomenko	UKR	2.10.70	1	Kiev Ch	Kiev	17 Jun
22.96	-0.2	Zuzanna	Radecka	POL	2.4.75	1	NC	Kraków	6 Aug
22.98	-0.5	Mikele	Barber	USA	4.10.80	1r1		Chapel Hill	18 Jun
22.99	-0.5	Marina	Kislova	RUS	12.12.78	4	Super	Yokohama	9 Sep
23.00	-0.5	Flirtisha	Harris	USA	21.2.72	2r1		Chapel Hill	18 Jun
23.03	1.7	Carlette	Guidry	USA	4.9.68	4s2	NC	Sacramento	23 Jul
		(60)							
23.04	1.0	Chryste	Gaines	USA	14.9.70	1h2		Sacramento	21 May
23.04	1.8	Vinitha	Tripathi	IND	15.10.80	1		Bangalore	5 Jul
23.05	-1.8		Li Xuemei	CHN	5.1.77	1	NGP	Chengdu	10 May
23.05	-2.0	Merlene	Frazer	JAM	27.12.73	4	NC	Kingston	22 Jul
23.06	0.2	Tatyana	Bonenko	UKR	7.6.76	2	Kiev Ch	Kiev	17 Jun
23.06	1.2	Mireille	Donders	SUI	7.7.74	1	NC	Lugano	30 Jul
23.06	0.4	Samantha	Davies	GBR	20.9.79	5		Gateshead	28 Aug
23.07A	-0.4	Dikeledi	Morapane	RSA	12.3.76	1		Pretoria	24 Mar
23.07	1.7	Valma	Bass	SKN	12.3.74	2r1		Baton Rouge	15 Apr
23.07	0.9	Sina	Schielke	GER-J	19.5.81	2	NC-23	Jena	20 Aug
		(70)							
23.08		Donica	Merriman	USA	24.1.79	1h1	Big 10	Iowa City	20 May
23.08	1.5	Kelli	White	USA	1.4.77	1r1		Atlanta	20 May
23.08	1.2		Qin Wangping	CHN-J	16.6.82	2	NGP	Jinzhou	8 Jun
23.08	-0.5	Donna	Fraser	GBR	7.11.72	1r2		Budapest	22 Jul
23.08	0.2	Felipa	Palacios	COL	1.12.75	3h1	OG	Sydney	27 Sep
23.09A	0.5	Wendy	Hartman	RSA	28.2.76	1		Potchefstroom	14 Feb
23.09	0.5	Kim	Gevaert	BEL	5.8.78	2		Oordegem	11 Jun
23.10	1.1	Natalya	Safronnikova	BLR	28.2.73	2r2		Kalamáta	4 Jun

Mark	Wind	Name		Nat	Born	Pos	Meet	Venue	Date
23.10	0.4	Rachita	Mistry	IND	4.3.74	1	Inter-St	Chennai	31 Jul
23.11	-0.5	Ameerah	Bello	ISV	3.10.75	3r1		Chapel Hill	18 Jun
		(80)							
23.12	2.0	Christiane	Amertil	BAH	18.8.79	1		Natchitoches	16 May
23.12	-0.5	Sarah	Reilly	IRL	3.7.73	2r2		Budapest	22 Jul
23.13	-0.5	Jearl	Miles-Clark	USA	4.9.66	4r1		Chapel Hill	18 Jun
23.13	-0.4	Nora	Ivanova-Güner	TUR	1.6.77	1	BalkG	Kavála	2 Jul
23.13	0.0	Sharon	Cripps	AUS	29.6.77	1		Brisbane (N)	22 Jul
23.14	1.7	Teneeshia	Jones	USA	28.1.79	1h2	SEC	Baton Rouge	12 May
23.14	0.7	Michele	Davis	USA	4.9.80	4	NCAA	Durham	3 Jun
23.14	1.7	Wyllesheia	Myrick	USA	21.11.79	6s2	NC	Sacramento	23 Jul
23.16	1.6	Khalilah	Carpenter	USA-J	27.1.83	1	NC-j	Denton	24 Jun
23.16	-0.4	Ekateríni	Koffa	GRE	10.4.69	1		Pátra	2 Sep
		(90)							
23.17	0.7	Joice	Maduaka	GBR	30.9.73	3	Gugl	Linz	8 Aug
23.18	-0.5	Kisha	Jett	USA	11.2.75	5r1		Chapel Hill	18 Jun
23.18	1.0	Aminata	Diouf	SEN	18.2.77	3rA		La Chaux-de-Fonds	13 Aug
23.18	0.6	Falilat	Ogunkoya	NGR	12.5.68	4	GP II	Rieti	3 Sep
23.19	-0.6	Monique	Henderson	USA-J	18.2.83	1		Norwalk	3 Jun
23.20A	0.0	Nova	Peris-Kneebone	AUS	25.2.71	4		Roodepoort	13 Mar
23.20	1.3	Jacqueline	Poelman	NED	5.10.73	1		Oordegem	26 Aug
23.20	1.9	Shani	Anderson	GBR	7.8.75	3		Gold Coast (RB)	10 Sep
23.21	0.7	Hellena	Wrappah	GHA	9.12.73	1		New Orleans	13 May
23.21	0.4	Monica	Twum	GHA	14.3.78	2		Clemson	14 May
		(100)							
23.21	0.1	Juan	Ball	USA	8.3.72	1r4		Chapel Hill	18 Jun

Mark	Wind	Name		Nat	Born	Date
23.22	1.0	Agné	Visockaite	LTU	4.8.78	25 Mar
23.22	0.7	Angela	Williams	USA	30.1.80	20 May
23.23	1.7	Me'Lisa	Barber	USA	4.10.80	12 May
23.24	-0.3	Aleah	Williams	USA-J	7.1.81	21 Apr
23.24	0.3	Tania	Van Heer-Murphy	AUS	30.12.70	4 Jun
23.24	0.9	Birgit	Rockmeier	GER	29.11.73	25 Jun
23.25	0.4	Shekera	Weston	USA	17.10.77	14 May
23.25	0.3	Lakeesha	White	USA	29.7.80	2 Jun
23.25	-0.6	Shakedia	Jones	USA	15.3.79	22 Jul
23.25	0.0	Anzhela	Kravchenko	UKR	25.1.71	6 Aug
23.26	0.6	Juliett	Brown	USA		15 Apr
23.26	-0.6	Sarah	Wilhelmy	GBR	2.2.80	29 Jul
23.26	1.9	Johanna	Manninen	FIN	4.4.80	20 Aug
23.27	0.5	Joan	Ekah Uduak	NGR	16.12.80	6 May
23.27	1.0	Fabé	Dia	FRA	14.2.77	13 Aug
23.28	1.9	Angel	Patterson	USA	6.8.79	20 May
23.29	1.3	Erica	Witter	CAN	10.12.76	18 May
23.29		Rosemar	Coelho Neto	BRA	2.1.77	11 Jun
23.31	1.9	Tanya	Oxley	BAR	13.5.79	27 May
23.31	-0.1	Jitka	Burianová	CZE	17.1.77	15 Jun
23.32A	0.4	Surita	Febbraio	RSA	27.12.73	22 Jan
23.32	0.4	Donna	Howard	USA	28.8.74	14 May
23.32	1.9	Tania	Woods	USA	23.9.80	21 May
23.32	-0.8	Natalya	Sologub	BLR	31.3.75	2 Aug
23.32	1.3	Vida	Anim	GHA-J	7.12.83	26 Aug
23.32	0.5		Yan Jiankui	CHN	19.3.76	29 Aug
23.34	-0.4	Svetla	Dimitrova	BUL	27.1.70	4 Jun
23.34	-0.6	Emily	Maher	IRL-J	2.5.81	29 Jul
23.34A	0.0	Lucimar	de Moura	BRA	22.3.74	29 Jul
23.34	1.4	Tatyana	Tkalich	UKR	30.5.75	5 Aug
23.35A	0.3	LaDonna	Antoine	CAN	20.11.74	8 Jul
23.35		Caliste	Ubah	NGR	15.11.73	22 Jul
23.36	0.9	Nadjina	Kaltouma	CHA	16.11.76	25 Jun
23.37	1.3	Rachelle	Boone	USA-J	30.6.81	13 May
23.37	-1.1	Evelina	Lisenco	ROM	4.2.75	10 Jun
23.37	-0.2	Yelena	Prokhorova	RUS	16.4.78	22 Jul
23.38	1.6	Aisha	Margain	USA-J	26.9.81	24 Jun
23.38	0.1	Irina	Rosikhina	RUS	11.5.75	27 Jun
23.38	0.7	Michelle	Bookman	USA	8.10.71	7 Jul
23.38	0.2		Zeng Xiujun	CHN	10.2.79	22 Oct
23.39	0.7	Karin	Mayr	AUT	4.6.71	8 Aug
23.40A	0.7	Susanna	Holtzhausen	RSA	7.10.76	4 Feb
23.40	-0.6	Angel	Perkins	USA-J	5.10.84	3 Jun
23.40	-0.6	Ciara	Sheehy	IRL	12.8.80	29 Jul
23.40	1.9	Delphine	Combe	FRA	6.12.74	6 Aug
23.41	0.1	Erica	Whipple	USA-J	4.12.82	13 May
23.41	-0.7	Gabi	Rockmeier	GER	29.11.73	30 Jul
23.42	1.0	Tarama	Perry	CAN	20.11.74	25 Mar
23.42	1.0	Svetlana	Goncharenko	RUS	28.5.71	5 Jul
23.42	-1.6	Yelena	Anisimova	RUS	12.6.71	12 Jul
23.43	2.0	Tracey	Ball	USA-J	10.2.81	16 Apr
23.43	1.7	Mame Tacko	Diouf	SEN	17.10.76	6 May
23.43	1.3	Demetria	Washington	USA	31.12.79	12 May
23.43	-1.2	Monika	Gachevska	BUL	30.10.74	11 Jun
23.43	0.5	Larisa	Kruglova	RUS	27.10.72	20 Aug
23.44	1.2	Nadine	Palmer	JAM-J	9.2.83	23 Apr
23.44	0.6	LaKeisha	Backus	USA	15.12.76	1 May
23.44	-2.8	Chinedu	Odozor	NGR	24.12.77	3 May
23.44	1.9	Andrea	Anderson	USA	17.9.77	13 May
23.44		Ayanna	Hutchinson	TRI	18.2.78	17 Jun
23.44	-0.2	Anita	Mormand	FRA	20.2.71	24 Aug
23.45	1.0	LaTrese	Taylor	USA	18.7.78	6 May
23.45	1.7	Kerine	Black	JAM		12 May
23.45	0.8	Myra	Combs	USA	17.4.79	19 May
23.45	0.8	Celena	Clarke	JAM	3.1.75	19 May
23.45	0.2	Alice	Reuss	GER	3.6.78	8 Jul
23.45	-2.0	Aleen	Bailey	JAM	25.11.80	22 Jul
23.46	-1.0	Grit	Breuer	GER	16.2.72	27 Jun
23.46	2.0	Enikõ	Szabó	HUN	10.11.79	2 Jul
23.46	1.5	Olga	Maksimova	RUS	9.8.76	12 Jul
23.46	1.0	Monica	Bumbescu	ROM	21.8.77	22 Jul
23.47	-1.1	Debbie	Dunn	JAM	26.3.78	15 Apr
23.47		Fana	Ashby	TRI-J	15.6.81	17 Jun
23.47	-0.2	Natalya	Roshchupkina	RUS	13.1.78	22 Jul
23.47	-1.8	Yekaterina	Leshchova	RUS	21.4.74	25 Jul
23.48	2.0	Motoka	Arai	JPN	4.7.74	16 Apr
23.48A	0.7	Digna Luz	Murillo	COL-J	22.5.81	13 May
23.48	2.0	LaQuinta	Manahan	USA	10.4.78	16 May
23.48	1.6	Ashlee	Williams	USA-J	27.3.84	24 Jun
23.48	0.2		Xu Lingling	CHN	26.2.79	22 Oct
23.49	1.0	Oluwaseum	Adetiba	USA	27.5.79	21 May
23.51A	0.5	Maralize	Fouché	RSA	2.3.74	3 Jun
23.51			Li Yali	CHN	26.1.75	9 Sep
23.52A	-0.4	Jodi	Lambert	AUS	1.9.70	24 Mar
23.53	0.4	Maicel	Malone-Wallace	USA	12.6.69	16 Apr
23.53	1.2	Marcia	Richardson	GBR	10.2.72	27 Apr
23.53	-0.2	Fabienne	Féraez	FRA	6.8.76	24 Aug
23.54	0.3	Shemeeka	Hopkins	USA	3.9.79	14 May
23.54	-0.4	Mila	Savic	YUG	24.4.74	2 Jul
23.54	0.5		Chen Yueqin	CHN		29 Aug
		(191)				

Indoors

Mark	Wind	Name		Nat	Born	Pos	Meet	Venue	Date
22.52	-		Perry			1r3		Liévin	13 Feb
22.70		Juliet	Campbell	JAM	17.3.70	1		Birmingham	20 Feb
22.90		Carlette	Guidry	USA	4.9.68	2	NC	Atlanta	4 Mar

Mark	Wind	Name		Nat	Born	Pos	Meet	Venue	Date
23.07		Birgit	Rockmeier	GER	29.11.73	1	NC	Sindelfingen	13 Feb
23.09		Yekaterina	Leshchova	RUS	21.4.74	1r1		Karlsruhe	29 Jan
23.12		Nora	Ivanova-Güner	TUR	1.6.77	1	BalkC	Pireás	12 Feb
23.15		Fabé	Dia	FRA	14.2.77	1	NC	Liévin	20 Feb

Mark	Name		Nat	Born	Date
23.22	Debbie	Dunn	JAM	26.3.78	10 Mar
23.24	Svetlana	Goncharenko	RUS	28.5.71	13 Feb
23.31	Christine	Bloomfield	GBR	12.2.68	30 Jan
23.34	Anja	Rücker	GER	20.12.72	18 Feb
23.46	Catherine	Murphy	GBR	21.9.75	5 Feb
23.46	Sylviane	Félix	FRA	31.10.77	20 Feb
23.49	Vernicha	James	GBR-J	6.6.84	30 Jan

Wind assisted

Mark	Wind	Name		Nat	Born	Pos	Meet	Venue	Date
22.08	2.3		Jones			1s1	NC	Sacramento	23 Jul
22.16	3.2	Nanceen	Perry	USA	19.4.77	1		Austin	6 May
22.18A	2.8	Melinda	Gainsford-Taylor	AUS	1.10.71	1		Pietersburg	18 Mar
22.40	2.3		Miller			2s1	NC	Sacramento	23 Jul
22.43	4.7	Peta-Gaye	Dowdie	JAM	18.1.77	1	USTCA	Austin	22 Apr
22.54	2.3	LaTasha	Jenkins	USA	19.12.77	3s1	NC	Sacramento	23 Jul
22.57	2.3	Shakedia	Jones	USA	15.3.79	5s1	NC	Sacramento	23 Jul
22.59A	2.8	Heide	Seyerling	RSA	19.8.76	2		Pietersburg	18 Mar
22.70A	2.8	Nova	Peris-Kneebone	AUS	25.2.71	3		Pietersburg	18 Mar
22.74	4.7	Lakeesha	White	USA	29.7.80	2	USTCA	Austin	22 Apr
22.75	5.1	Donica	Merriman	USA	24.1.79	1	Owens	Columbus	7 May
22.78	4.5	Tayna	Lawrence	JAM	17.9.75	1r3		College Station	11 May
22.78	2.4	Angela	Williams	USA	30.1.80	1	Pac10	Eugene	21 May
22.81	4.7	Aleah	Williams	USA-J	7.1.81	3	USTCA	Austin	22 Apr
22.82	5.6	LaDonna	Antoine	CAN	20.11.74	1	NC	Victoria	13 Aug
22.83	3.2	Chryste	Gaines	USA	14.9.70	2		Austin	6 May
22.84	2.5	Mikele	Barber	USA	4.10.80	1	SEC	Baton Rouge	14 May
22.86	2.7	Aleen	Bailey	JAM	25.11.80	1	KansR	Lawrence	22 Apr
22.91A	2.8	Jodi	Lambert	AUS	1.9.70	4		Pietersburg	18 Mar
22.93A	2.5	Falilat	Ogunkoya	NGR	12.5.68	1		El Paso	15 Apr
22.94	3.1	Kelli	White	USA	1.4.77	1	Conseil	Fort-de-France	29 Apr
22.96	2.2	Deon	Hemmings	JAM	9.10.68	1		Harrisonburg	13 May
22.97A	2.5	Brianna	Glenn	USA	18.4.80	2		El Paso	15 Apr
22.99	2.9	Rosemar	Coelho Neto	BRA	2.1.77	1h1		São Caetano do Sul	9 Jul
23.02	4.5	Joanne	Durant	BAR	25.5.75	2r3		College Station	11 May
23.05A	5.1	Omotayo	Akinremi	NGR	13.9.74	1r2		Flagstaff	3 Jul
23.09A	4.9	Erica	Witter	CAN	10.12.76	1r1		Flagstaff	3 Jul
23.10	4.0	Aisha	Margain	USA-J	26.9.81	1	MSR	Walnut	15 Apr
23.14	3.2	Donna	Howard	USA	28.8.74	4r1		Austin	6 May
23.15	2.3	Kisha	Jett	USA	11.2.75	6s1	NC	Sacramento	23 Jul
23.16	4.0	Monique	Henderson	USA-J	18.2.83	2	MSR	Walnut	15 Apr
23.21	2.7	Passion	Richardson	USA	25.1.75	2	KansR	Lawrence KS	22 Apr

Mark	Wind	Name		Nat	Born	Date
23.22mx	3.8	Tania	Van Heer-Murphy	AUS	30.12.70	28 Jan
23.23	4.6	Angel	Patterson	USA	6.8.79	6 May
23.23	2.4	Sinead	Dudgeon	GBR	9.7.76	29 Jul
23.24A	4.9	Trinity	Davis	USA		3 Jul
23.25	2.9	Tanya	Oxley	BAR	13.5.79	8 Apr
23.26	2.4	Fabé	Dia	FRA	14.2.77	6 Aug
23.26	5.6	Tarama	Perry	CAN	20.11.74	13 Aug
23.28	3.9	Sherri	Coleman	USA	2.10.76	11 May
23.29	4.7	Mila	Savic	YUG	24.4.74	18 Jun
23.31	2.5	Lisa	Sharpe	JAM-J	18.1.84	23 Apr
23.32	2.7	Shelia	Burrell	USA	15.1.72	22 Apr
23.32	3.0	Chinedu	Odozor	NGR	24.12.77	3 May
23.32A	5.1	Candice	Jones	CAN	3.2.73	3 Jul
23.33	3.9	Mercedes	Carnesolta	CUB	13.5.75	19 Feb
23.33	4.7	Mechelle	Lewis	USA	20.9.80	22 Apr
23.34A	4.9	Omolade	Akinremi	NGR	13.9.74	3 Jul
23.35	2.6	Enikõ	Szabó	HUN	10.11.79	30 Jul
23.35	3.6	Maralize	Fouché	RSA	2.3.74	30 Jul
23.38	2.5	Demetria	Washington	USA	31.12.79	14 May
23.38	2.4	Delphine	Combe	FRA	6.12.74	6 Aug
23.39	3.5	Ciara	Sheehy	IRL	12.8.80	9 Sep
23.40	2.6	Grit	Breuer	GER	16.2.72	2 Jul
23.43	4.7	Sharika	Higgins	USA	10.4.78	22 Apr
23.44	2.2	Chequetta	Bearfield	USA	16.4.80	1 Apr
23.45	2.7	Camille	Clarke	JAM	3.12.77	22 Apr
23.45	w	Michelle	Burrell	USA	8.5.65	6 May
23.47	2.2	Heather	Samuel	ANT	6.7.70	1 Apr
23.47	5.1	Jasmine	Reynolds	USA		7 May
23.47	2.6	Barbara	Petráhn	HUN	16.9.78	30 Jul
23.48	2.9	Catherine	Murphy	GBR	21.9.75	15 Apr
23.48	3.2	Moushami	Robinson	USA-J	13.4.81	6 May
23.48	3.6	Vonette	Dixon	JAM	26.11.75	12 May
23.48	2.3	Hrísa	Goudenoúdi	GRE	28.3.77	10 Jun
23.49	2.7	Rosa	Rakotozafy	MAD	12.11.77	9 Apr
23.49	3.9	Julia	Alba	ESP	30.5.72	15 Aug

Best at low altitude

Mark	Wind	Name	Pos	Meet	Venue	Date
22.76	1.0	Diop	2		La Chaux-de-Fonds	13 Aug
22.95	0.6	Seyerling	1rA		Budapest	22 Jul
23.21	1.1	Peris-Kneebone	1h3		Melbourne	17 Feb
23.35	0.0	de Moura	1	NC	Rio de Janeiro	6 Aug

Hand timing

Mark	Wind	Name		Nat	Born	Pos	Venue	Date
22.9		Viktoriya	Fomenko	UKR	2.10.70	1	Kharkov	3 Jun
22.9	-1.0	Nora	Ivanova-Güner	TUR	1.6.77	1	Ankara	16 Jul

Mark	Wind	Name		Nat	Born	Date
23.0		Caliste	Ubah	NGR	15.11.73	31 Mar
23.0		Tatyana	Tkalich	UKR	30.5.75	22 . Jul
23.0		Nezha	Bidouane	MAR	18.9.69	6 Aug
23.1	0.6	Chinedu	Odozor	NGR	24.12.77	31 May
23.2		Nadine	Palmer	JAM-J	9.2.83	11 Mar
23.2	0.0	Claudine	Komgang	CMR	21.2.74	27 May

JUNIORS

See main list for top 5 juniors. 10 performances by 6 women to 23.24. Additional marks and further juniors:

Name	Mark	Wind	Pos	Meet	Venue	Date	Mark	Wind	Pos	Meet	Venue	Date
Campbell	23.05	1.2	1	CAC-j	St Georges	23 Apr	23.19	1.6	1s2	WJ	Santiago	20 Oct
Schielke	23.14	0.0	1r2		Mannheim	12 Aug	23.20	0.7	2	WJ	Santiago	21 Oct

Mark	Wind	Name		Nat	Born	Pos	Meet	Venue	Date
23.24	-0.3	Aleah	Williams	USA	7.1.81	1h3	UCTA	Austin	21 Apr
23.32	1.3	Vida	Anim	GHA	7.12.83	2		Oordegem	26 Aug
23.34	-0.6	Emily	Maher	IRL	2.5.81	2		Dublin (S)	29 Jul
23.37	1.3	Rachelle	Boone	USA	30.6.81	1r2		Bloomington	13 May
23.38	1.6	Aisha	Margain (10)	USA	26.9.81	2	NC-j	Denton	24 Jun
23.40	-0.6	Angel	Perkins	USA	5.10.84	2		Norwalk	3 Jun
23.41	0.1	Erica	Whipple	USA	4.12.82	1h1		Gainesville	13 May
23.43	2.0	Tracey	Ball	USA	10.2.81	3r4	MSR	Walnut	16 Apr
23.44		Nadine	Palmer	JAM	9.2.83	2	CarC	St. Georges	23 Apr
23.47		Fana	Ashby	TRI	15.6.81	2	NC	Port of Spain	17 Jun
23.48A	0.7	Digna Luz	Murillo	COL	22.5.81	2		Medellín	13 May
23.48	1.6	Ashlee	Williams	USA	27.3.84	3	NC-j	Denton	24 Jun
23.49i		Vernicha	James	GBR	6.6.84	1-17		Birmingham	30 Jan
		23.59	1.6			2s2	WJ	Santiago de Chile	20 Oct
23.57	-1.5	Sanya	Richards	JAM	26.2.85	1		Gainesville	12 May
23.57	0.3	Roxana	Díaz (20)	CUB	17.5.81	1		La Habana	25 Jul

Wind assisted see main list for two three juniors, and:

Mark	Wind	Name		Nat	Born	Pos	Meet	Venue	Date
23.31	2.5	Lisa	Sharpe	JAM	18.1.84	1	Car-18	St. Georges	23 Apr
23.48	3.2	Moushami	Robinson	USA	13.4.81	5r1		Austin	6 May
23.54		Nolle	Graham	JAM	12.9.81	2		Harrisonburg	13 May

300 METRES

Mark	Name		Nat	Born	Pos	Venue	Date
35.71	Donna	Fraser	GBR	7.11.72	1	Gateshead	28 Aug
35.82	Cydonie	Mothersill	CAY	19.3.78	1r3	Sydney	14 Sep
36.00	Katharine	Merry	GBR	21.9.74	2	Gateshead	28 Aug
36.00	LaTasha	Colander-Richardson	USA	23.8.76	3	Gateshead	28 Aug
36.07	Jearl	Miles-Clark	USA	4.9.66	1r4	Sydney	14 Sep
36.30	Manuela	Levorato	ITA	16.3.77	1	Viareggio	22 Aug
36.37	Ami Mbacké	Thiam	SEN	10.11.76	1r1	Sydney	14 Sep
36.40	Mireille	Nguimgo	CMR	7.11.76	2r1	Sydney	14 Sep
36.48	Shanta	Ghosh	GER	3.1.75	1r2	Pliezhausen	21 May
36.51	Sandie	Richards	JAM	6.11.68	4	Gateshead	28 Aug
36.55	Claudine	Komgang	CMR	21.2.74	1r2	Sydney	14 Sep
36.64	LaDonna	Antoine	CAN	20.11.74	1	Gold Coast (S)	15 Sep
36.68	Monique	Hennagan	USA	26.5.76	5	Gateshead	28 Aug
36.75	Mireille	Donders	SUI	7.7.74	1	Langenthal	1 Jun
36.77	Nadjina	Kaltouma	CHA	16.11.76	2r3	Sydney	14 Sep
36.83	Nova	Peris-Kneebone	AUS	25.2.71	2r4	Sydney	14 Sep
36.98	Corinne	Simasotchi	SUI	11.6.71	2	Langenthal	1 Jun

Mark	Name		Nat	Born	Date	Mark	Name		Nat	Born	Date
37.02	Heide	Seyerling	RSA	19.8.76	11 Sep	37.42	Omotayo	Akinremi	NGR	13.9.74	11 Sep
37.06	Tanya	Oxley	BAR	13.5.79	14 Sep	37.48	Catherine	Murphy	GBR	21.9.75	28 Aug
37.07	Florence	Ekpo-Umoh	GER	27.12.77	21 May	37.52	Melissa	Straker-Taylor	BAR	23.1.76	14 Sep
37.16	Aïda	Diop	SEN	27.4.70	14 Sep	37.54	Aliann	Pompey	GUY	9.3.78	14 Sep
37.22	Olabisi	Afolabi	NGR	31.10.75	22 Aug	37.55	Helen	Frost	GBR	12.3.74	28 Aug
37.30	Michelle	Burgher	JAM	12.3.77	14 Sep	37.59	Jennifer	Stoute	GBR	16.4.65	30 Jul
37.33	Charity	Opara	NGR	20.5.72	28 Aug	**Indoors**					
37.33	Rosemary	Okafor	NGR-J	22.5.81	11 Sep	37.56#	Natalya	Sologub	BLR	31.3.75	7 Feb

During 300m: 25 Sep, Sydney: 1. Lorraine Graham 36.00, 2. Merry 36.08, 3. Cathy Freeman 36.14.

400 METRES

Mark	Name		Nat	Born	Pos	Meet	Venue	Date
49.11	Cathy	Freeman	AUS	16.2.73	1	OG	Sydney	25 Sep
49.48		Freeman			1	Herc	Monaco	18 Aug
49.56		Freeman			1	Athl	Lausanne	5 Jul
49.58	Lorraine	Graham	JAM	8.9.73	2	OG	Sydney	25 Sep
49.59	Marion	Jones	USA	12.10.75	1r6	MSR	Walnut	16 Apr
49.70A	Ana	Guevara	MEX	4.3.77	1	IMSS	Ciudad de México	1 Jul
49.72	Katharine	Merry	GBR	21.9.74	3	OG	Sydney	25 Sep
49.78		Freeman			1	VD	Bruxelles	25 Aug
49.79	Donna	Fraser	GBR	7.11.72	4	OG	Sydney	25 Sep
49.87	LaTasha	Colander-Richardson	USA	23.8.76	1	NC	Sacramento	16 Jul
49.95	Olga	Kotlyarova	RUS	12.4.76	1	Super	Yokohama	9 Sep
49.96		Guevara			5	OG	Sydney	25 Sep
50.00		Freeman			1	NC	Sydney	26 Feb
50.01		Freeman			1s2	OG	Sydney	24 Sep
50.04	Falilat	Ogunkoya	NGR	12.5.68	1	GP	Osaka	13 May
50.04		Freeman			1	GP	Athína	28 Jun
50.04	Jearl	Miles-Clark	USA	4.9.66	2	Herc	Monaco	18 Aug
50.05		Merry			1	Nik	Nice	8 Jul
50.05	Heide	Seyerling	RSA	19.8.76	6	OG	Sydney	25 Sep

WOMEN 2000

Mark	Name		Nat	Born	Pos	Meet	Venue	Date
50.07		Graham			2	Athl	Lausanne	5 Jul
50.08		Graham			3	Herc	Monaco	18 Aug
50.10		Graham			2	Nik	Nice	8 Jul
50.10	Natalya	Nazarova	RUS	26.5.79	1	NC	Tula	24 Jul
50.11	Michelle	Collins	USA	12.2.71	2	GP	Osaka	13 May
50.11		Guevara			2s2	OG	Sydney	24 Sep
50.12		Guevara			1	BrGP	London (CP)	5 Aug
50.12		Ogunkoya			7	OG	Sydney	25 Sep
50.15		Collins			2	BrGP	London (CP)	5 Aug
50.18		Ogunkoya			3s2	OG	Sydney	24 Sep
	(29/13)							
50.23	Charity	Opara	NGR	20.5.72	1	NC	Lagos	22 Jul
50.23	Svetlana	Goncharenko	RUS	28.5.71	2s1	NC	Tula	23 Jul
50.30	Olabisi	Afolabi	NGR	31.10.75	3	NC	Lagos	22 Jul
50.32	Marie-José	Pérec	FRA	9.5.68	3	Nik	Nice	8 Jul
50.36	Olesya	Zykina	RUS	7.10.80	1s1	NC	Tula	23 Jul
50.42	Sandie	Richards	JAM	6.11.68	5s2	OG	Sydney	24 Sep
50.47	Svetlana	Pospelova ¶	RUS	24.12.79	1		Luzern	27 Jun
	(20)							
50.67	Anna	Tkach	RUS	17.4.75	1h3	NC	Tula	22 Jul
50.69	Mireille	Nguimbo	CMR	7.11.76	1		Chaux de Fonds	13 Aug
50.71	Helena	Fuchsová	CZE	3.6.65	1	GS	Ostrava	1 Jun
50.73A	Claudine	Komgang	CMR	21.2.74	3	IMSS	Ciudad de México	1 Jul
50.73	Yuliya	Sotnikova	RUS	18.11.70	2s2	NC	Tula	23 Jul
50.74	Monique	Henderson	USA-J	18.2.83	1		Norwalk	3 Jun
50.76	Irina	Rosikhina	RUS	11.5.75	1r3	NCp	Tula	2 Jun
50.82	Monique	Hennagan	USA	26.5.76	4	NC	Sacramento	16 Jul
50.85	Jitka	Burianová	CZE	17.1.77	1q1	OG	Sydney	23 Sep
50.88	Ami Mbacké	Thiam	SEN	10.11.76	2		Chaux de Fonds	13 Aug
	(30)							
50.92	LaDonna	Antoine	CAN	20.11.74	2q1	OG	Sydney	23 Sep
50.98	Mikele	Barber	USA	4.10.80	1	SEC	Baton Rouge	14 May
51.05	Damayanthi	Darsha	SRI	13.2.75	1	AsiC	Jakarta	30 Aug
51.06	Grit	Breuer	GER	16.2.72	3	Live	Nürnberg	25 Jun
51.06	Maicel	Malone	USA	12.6.69	2s1	NC	Sacramento	15 Jul
51.09A	Celena	Mondie-Milner	USA	6.8.68	4	IMSS	Ciudad de México	1 Jul
51.13	Daimí	Pernía	CUB	27.12.76	2	GP II	Rieti	3 Sep
51.16	Yekaterina	Kulikova	RUS	7.11.68	4s1	NC	Tula	23 Jul
51.18	Andrea	Anderson	USA	17.9.77	3s1	NC	Sacramento	15 Jul
51.21	Shanelle	Porter	USA	20.1.72	1	Elite	Tempe	22 Apr
	(40)							
51.21	K.Mathews	Beenamol	IND	15.8.75	1		Kiev	18 Jun
51.27	Daniela	Georgieva	BUL	22.9.69	4	Live	Nürnberg	25 Jun
51.28	Nova	Peris-Kneebone	AUS	25.2.71	3q1	OG	Sydney	23 Sep
51.35	Youlanda	Warren	USA	13.3.72	5s1	NC	Sacramento	15 Jul
51.37	Lee	Naylor	AUS	26.1.71	3	NC	Sydney	26 Feb
51.41	Suziann	Reid	USA	14.1.77	6	GP	Raleigh	17 Jun
51.42	Kim	Graham	USA	26.3.71	1	GaTech	Atlanta	20 May
51.42	Uta	Rohländer-Fromm	GER	30.6.69	3		Dortmund	8 Jul
51.45	Birgit	Rockmeier	GER	29.11.73	4		Dortmund	8 Jul
51.49	Natalya	Khrushchelyova	RUS	20.3.73	5s1	NC	Tula	23 Jul
	(50)							
51.50	Allison	Curbishley	GBR	3.6.76	2	NC	Birmingham	13 Aug
51.51	Tamsyn	Lewis	AUS	20.7.78	1		Brisbane	11 Feb
51.56	Gelena	Bodunova	RUS	.76	2h1	NC	Tula	22 Jul
51.59	Tatyana	Chebykina	RUS	22.11.68	2	Mos Ch	Moskva	11 Jul
51.62A	Foy	Williams	CAN	27.9.73	1		Flagstaff	4 Jul
51.63	Irina	Privalova	RUS	22.11.68	1	Kuts	Moskva	26 Aug
51.64A	Susanna	Holtzhausen	RSA	7.10.76	2		Roodepoort	13 Mar
51.65	Catherine	Scott	JAM	27.8.73	3		Portland	25 Jun
51.67	Anna	Kozak	BLR	22.6.74	1		Minsk	20 May
51.67	Florence	Ekpo-Umoh	GER	27.12.77	1rA		Chemnitz	22 Jul
	(60)							
51.69	Karen	Shinkins	IRL	15.10.76	1r2		Budapest	22 Jul
51.69	Zulia	Calatayud	CUB	9.11.79	1	Barr	La Habana	29 Jul
51.70	Natalya	Sologub	BLR	31.3.75	1	NC	Brest	1 Aug
51.71	Demetria	Washington	USA	31.12.79	1	SEC	Baton Rouge	14 May
51.73	Melinda	Gainsford-Taylor	AUS	1.10.71	1		Brisbane	22 Jul
51.73	Yelena	Rurak	UKR	7.2.72	1	NC	Kiev	4 Aug
51.74	Shanta	Ghosh	GER	3.1.75	3	NC	Braunschweig	30 Jul

Mark	Name		Nat	Born	Pos	Meet	Venue	Date
51.76A	Jana	Pittman	AUS-J	9.11.82	3		Roodepoort	13 Mar
51.77	Norfalia	Carabalí	ESP	21.1.64	3		Barcelona	25 Jul
51.80	Deon	Hemmings	JAM	9.10.68	1		Harrisonburg	13 May
	(70)							
51.84	Ionela	Tîrlea	ROM	9.2.76	4	GP	Osaka	13 May
51.85	Otilia	Ruicu	ROM	20.8.78	1	NC	Bucuresti	6 Aug
51.87	Irina	Mistyukevich	RUS	17.6.77	1		Sankt-Peterburg	10 Jun
51.95	Antonina	Yefremova	UKR-J	19.7.81	1		Schwechat	10 Jun
51.95		Bu Fanfang	CHN	.2.78	1	NC	Luohe	20 Oct
51.96	Susan	Andrews	AUS	26.5.71	1		Perth	30 Jan
52.00	Alice	Kun	HUN	7.6.76	1		Senta	6 May
52.00	Christine	Amertil	BAH	18.8.79	1	NC	Nassau	21 Jul
52.02	Brigita	Langerholc	SLO	23.7.76	1		Ljubljana	14 Aug
52.03	Samantha	George	CAN	7.8.76	2r1		Atlanta	20 May
	(80)							
52.03	Hana	Benesová	CZE	19.4.75	2	NC	Plzen	16 Jul
52.04	Idalmis	Bonne	CUB	2.2.71	3	GP II	Rieti	3 Sep
52.04		Chen Yuxiang	CHN	28.2.78	2	NC	Luohe	20 Oct
52.05	Anja	Rücker	GER	20.12.72	7	Live	Nürnberg	25 Jun
52.05	Barbara	Petráhn	HUN	16.9.78	1	NC	Budapest	29 Jul
52.07	Natalya	Sharova	RUS	4.10.72	5r3	NCp	Tula	2 Jun
52.12	Carolyn	Jackson	USA	6.12.77	2h1	NCAA	Durham	1 Jun
52.15	Grazyna	Prokopek	POL	20.4.77	1	NC	Kraków	5 Aug
52.15	Marie-Louise	Bévis	FRA	12.10.72	3		La Chaux-de-Fonds	13 Aug
52.17	Svetlana	Bodritskaya	KAZ	7.11.71	1		Almaty	28 May
	(90)							
52.17	Anita	Mormand	FRA	20.2.71	4		La Chaux-de-Fonds	13 Aug
52.17	Julia	Duporty	CUB	9.2.71	4	GP II	Rieti	3 Sep
52.19	Nakiya	Johnson	USA-J	12.5.81	1		Austin	6 May
52.19	Julian	Reynolds	USA	2.11.77	7		Raleigh	17 Jun
52.21	Yelena	Budnik	BLR	9.5.76			Staiki	1 Sep
52.23	Jane	Arnott	NZL	3.1.76	6	NC	Sydney	26 Feb
52.24	Corinne	Simasotchi	SUI	11.6.71	2		Genève	24 Jun
52.25	Zana	Minina	LTU	11.6.77	3		Riga	22 Jun
52.26	Tanya	Oxley	BAR	13.5.79	1	NC	Bridgetown	25 Jun
52.26	Linetta	Wilson	USA	11.10.67	5h1	NC	Sacramento	14 Jul
	(100)							

52.27	Donna	Howard	USA	28.8.74	20 May
52.27	Nadjina	Kaltouma	CHA	16.11.76	12 Jul
52.27	Andrea	Thomas	JAM	18.3.68	21 Jul
52.28	Angel	Perkins	USA-J	5.10.84	20 May
52.31	Debbie	Dunn	JAM	26.3.78	6 May
52.32	Anke	Feller	GER	26.9.71	8 Jul
52.35	Tonique	Williams	BAH	17.1.76	16 Apr
52.37	Moushami	Robinson	USA-J	13.4.81	22 Apr
52.37	Celena	Clarke	JAM	3.1.75	6 Jul
52.39	Tatyana	Levina	RUS	28.2.77	11 Jul
52.40	Helen	Frost	GBR	12.3.74	17 Sep
52.44	Claudia	Marx	GER	16.9.78	20 Aug
52.45	Michelle	Burgher	JAM	12.3.77	22 Jul
52.46	Khadijah	Conda	USA	26.6.78	6 May
52.48	Francine	Landre	FRA	26.7.70	29 Apr
52.49	Jerrika	Chapple	USA-J	11.9.84	24 Jun
(valid mark, but disqualified as she had not run her 200m heat)					
52.50A	Surita	Febbraio	RSA	27.12.73	19 Feb
52.50	Flirtisha	Harris	USA	21.2.72	14 Jul
52.50	Tatyana	Vorovchenko	UKR	13.8.78	15 Jul
52.52	Aliann	Pompey	GUY	9.3.78	18 Mar
52.54	Sandra	Stals	BEL	5.6.75	8 Jul
52.55	Tania	Van Heer-Murphy	AUS	30.12.70	8 Jul
52.55	Tatyana	Movchan	UKR	19.9.70	4 Aug
52.58	Patrizia	Spuri	ITA	18.2.73	13 Aug
52.60	Irina	Khlyustova	BLR	14.6.78	1 Sep
52.61A	Candice	Jones	CAN	3.2.73	4 Jul
52.62	Irina	Anashkina	RUS	.72	19 Aug
52.64	Stephanie	Smith	USA-J	27.6.85	30 Jul
52.64	Olga	Mishchenko	UKR	24.11.71	4 Aug
52.65	Virna	De Angeli	ITA	27.2.76	16 Jun
52.66	Stella	Klassen	USA	14.8.78	7 May
52.67	Kudirat	Akhigbe	NGR		18 Jun
52.68	Michele	Davis	USA	4.9.80	3 Jun
52.68		Zhong Shaoting	CHN	30.1.80	20 Oct
52.70	Fabiola	Piroddi	ITA	23.5.69	17 Sep
52.71	Rebecca	Wardell	NZL	21.12.77	12 Mar
52.71	Sinead	Dudgeon	GBR	9.7.76	17 Sep
52.72	Justyna	Karolkiewicz	POL	29.10.80	5 Aug
52.72	Catherine	Murphy	GBR	21.9.75	17 Sep
52.73	Yudalis	Díaz	CUB	20.9.79	29 Jul
52.73A	Norma	González	COL-J	11.8.82	4 Dec
52.74	Anna	Pacholak	POL	15.1.80	5 Aug
52.75	Omolade	Akinremi	NGR	13.9.74	22 Apr
52.78	Lauren	Poetschka	AUS	22.10.74	5 Feb
52.78	Yelena	Piskunova	UZB	2.8.80	16 May
52.78	Marina	Grishakova	RUS	.78	23 Jul
52.78	Aneta	Lemiesz	POL-J	17.1.81	20 Oct
52.79	Daniela	Graglia	ITA	20.5.76	7 Sep
52.80		Xu Lingling	CHN	26.2.79	7 Jun
52.81	Zuzanna	Radecka	POL	2.4.75	3 Jun
52.82	Luiza	Lancuchowska	POL	1.6.76	5 Aug
52.82	Lucie	Rangassamy	FRA	6.8.74	13 Aug
52.87	Natalya	Pygyda	UKR-J	30.1.81	4 Aug
52.89		Zhou Wei	CHN-J	23.1.82	19 Oct
52.91	Adia	McKinnon	TRI-J	18.4.81	20 May
52.91	Petra	Söderström	FIN	12.3.74	1 Jul
52.92	Janice	Davis	USA-J	27.10.84	30 Jul
52.93	Mame Tacko	Diouf	SEN	17.10.76	12 May
52.95A	Felipa	Palacios	COL	1.12.75	4 Dec
52.96	Carron	Allen	USA	14.9.78	13 May
52.96	Oksana	Luneva	KGZ	2.8.79	14 Jun
52.97	Lashinda	Demus	USA-J	10.3.83	20 May
52.98	Ludmila	Formanová	CZE	2.1.74	11 Jun
52.98	Hrísa	Goudenoúdi	GRE	28.3.77	28 Jun
52.99	Kari	Karhoff	USA	15.5.79	20 May
53.00	Fatima	Yusuf-Olukoju	NGR	2.5.71	25 Jun
53.01	Marína	Vasarmídou	GRE	16.7.72	28 Jun
53.02	Lesley	Owusu	GBR	21.12.78	20 May
53.03	Luciana	Mendes	BRA	26.7.71	14 May
53.03	Galina	Misiruk	UKR	18.12.70	3 Aug
53.03	Jacqueline	Poelman	NED	5.10.73	10 Sep

Mark	Name		Nat	Born	Date	
53.04	Kinshasa	Davis	USA	10.7.79	21	Apr
53.05	Malika	Edmondson	USA	13.4.79	6	May
53.05	Awatef	Benhassine	TUN	5.4.80	24	Jun
53.07	Kristina	Perica	CRO	5.11.79	16	Jun
53.08A	Dywana	Crudup	USA	30.9.78	20	May
53.08	Paramjeet	Kaur	IND	2.4.76	30	Aug
53.08	Francesca	Carbone	ITA	17.7.68	17	Sep
53.10	Liz	Grow	USA	17.10.79	20	May
53.10	Anika	Ahrens	GER	19.7.78	20	May
53.10	Jennifer	Fontenot	USA	9.8.78	21	May
53.11	Nicole	Green	USA	28.10.71	22	Apr
53.13	Tatyana	Ledovskaya	BLR	21.5.66	27	Jun
53.15A	Rita	Onyebuchi	NGR	23.6.72	28	Jan
53.15	Yolanda	Brown-Moore	USA	25.3.78	25	Mar
53.18	Lorena	Franco de Oliveira	BRA	5.5.78	21	May
53.20	Viviane	Dorsile	FRA	1.6.67	29	Apr
53.20A	Tiffany	Williams	USA	1.10.78	20	May
53.20	Ina	Cordes	GER	25.10.68	1	Jul
53.21	Candyee	DeLoatch	USA	27.6.78	22	Apr
53.22	Marina	Makarova	UKR	3.1.75	2	Jun
53.22	Manjuma	Kuriakose	IND	29.10.76	29	Jul
53.22	Anja	Knippel	GER	19.8.74	30	Jul
53.22	Shellene	Williams	BAR	20.7.77	4	Aug
53.22	Ulrike	Urbansky	GER	6.4.77	3	Sep
53.22	Stephanie	Price	AUS	17.7.72	8	Sep
53.24	Anna	Potapchenko	RUS	.78	11	Jul
53.24	Dawn	Higgins	GBR	10.12.75	16	Jul
53.24	Danielle	Perpoli	ITA	7.3.68	27	Aug

(199) and further eight women 53.26-53.29

Indoors

Mark	Name		Nat	Born	Pos	Meet	Venue	Date
51.99	Anja	Rücker	GER	20.12.72	1rA	NC	Sindelfingen	13 Feb
52.21	Aliann	Pompey	GUY	9.3.78	1	NCAA	Fayetteville	11 Mar
52.25	Claudia	Marx	GER	16.9.78	2rA	NC	Sindelfingen	13 Feb

Mark	Name		Nat	Born	Date	
52.61	Stella	Klassen	USA	14.8.78	11	Mar
52.73	Yelena	Andreyeva	RUS	9.5.69	27	Jan
52.81	Yolanda	Brown-Moore	USA	25.3.78	27	Feb
53.01	Francesca	Carbone	ITA	17.7.68	12	Feb
53.02	Ulrike	Urbansky	GER	6.4.77	2	Feb
53.06	Natalya	Tsyganova	RUS	7.2.71	24	Jan
53.10	Linda	Kisabaka	GER	9.4.69	2	Feb
53.14	Gudrún	Arnardóttir	ISL	24.9.71	26	Feb
53.17	Saidat	Onanuga	NGR	18.6.74	10	Mar
53.29	Peta-Gaye	Gayle	JAM	19.1.79	10	Mar

Best at low altitude

Mark	Name	Pos	Meet	Venue	Date
51.35	Komgang	1	AfCh	Alger	12 Jul
51.85	Pittman	4	NC	Sydney	26 Feb
51.98	Mondie-Milner	6s1	NC	Sacramento	15 Jul
52.00	F Williams	2		Rehlingen	12 Jun
52.15	Holzhausen	2	NC	Stellenbosch	3 Mar
53.00	González	1	IbAm	Rio de Janeiro	21 May

Hand timing

Mark	Name		Nat	Born	Date	
52.4	Virna	De Angeli	ITA	27.2.76	22	Jul
52.6	Marina	Kalashinova	RUS		4	Jul
52.6	Danielle	Perpoli	ITA	7.3.68	22	Jul
52.7	Marina	Makarova	UKR	3.1.75	16	Jun
52.8	Francesca	Carbone	ITA	17.7.68	22	Jul
53.1	Yvonne	Harrison	USA	2.12.75	22	Apr
53.1	Justine	Bayiga	UGA	.78	20	May
53.1	Hortense	Béwouda Kaméni	CMR	19.10.78	27	May

JUNIORS

See main list for top 4 juniors. 10 performances by 6 women to 23.24. Additional marks and further juniors:

Name	Mark	Pos	Meet	Venue	Date
Henderson	51.24	4s1	NC	Sacramento	16 Jul
	51.31	1		Poway CA	27 May
	51.77	2h4	NC	Sacramento	15 Jul
	51.78	4	Pre	Eugene	24 Jun
	51.79	8	NC	Sacramento	16 Jul
Pittman	51.85	4	NC	Sydney	26 Feb
	51.90	2		Darwin	2 Jul
	51.93	2		Brisbane	8 Sep

11 performances by 3 women to 51.95

Mark	Name		Nat	Born	Pos	Meet	Venue	Date
52.28	Angel	Perkins	USA	5.10.84	1		Norwalk	20 May
52.37	Moushami	Robinson	USA	13.4.81	3	UCTA	Austin	22 Apr
52.49	Jerrika	Chapple	USA	11.9.84	(2)	NC-j	Denton	24 Jun
	(valid mark, but she was disqualified, because she had not run her 200m heat)							
52.64	Stephanie	Smith	USA	27.6.85	1	JunOly	Amherst	30 Jul
52.73A	Norma	González	COL	11.8.82	1	NG	Paipa	4 Dec
	53.00				1	IbAm	Rio de Janeiro	21 May
52.78	Aneta	Lemiesz (10)	POL	17.1.81	2	WJ	Santiago de Chile	20 Oct
52.87	Natalya	Pygyda	UKR	30.1.81	4	NC	Kiev	4 Aug
52.89		Zhou Wei	CHN	23.1.82	1s2	NC	Luohe	19 Oct
52.91	Adia	McKinnon	TRI	18.4.81	1		Champaign	20 May
52.92	Janice	Davis	USA	27.10.84	2	JunOly	Amherst	30 Jul
52.97	Lashinda	Demus	USA	10.3.83	2		Norwalk	20 May
53.27A	Tracey	Ball	USA	10.2.81	3	WAC	El Paso	20 May
53.29	Hazel-Ann	Regis	GRN	1.2.81	1	CarC	St. Georges	22 Apr
53.33	Sheryl	Morgan	JAM	6.11.83	6	NC	Kingston	22 Jul
53.35	Licretia	Sibley	USA	3.8.83	1		Orlando	5 Aug
53.38	Maria	Rus (20)	ROM	19.1.83	3s1	WJ	Santiago de Chile	18 Oct
Hand timed: 53.2	Irene	Zauna	LAT	16.3.81			Riga	5 Jul

600 METRES

Mark	Name		Nat	Born	Pos	Meet	Venue	Date
1:24.82	Helena	Fuchsová	CZE	3.6.65	1		Gold Coast (RB)	17 Sep
1:25.37	Charmaine	Howell	JAM	13.3.75	1		Sydney	11 Sep
1:27.02	Lwiza	John	TAN	18.5.80	1		Pliezhausen	21 May
1:27.18	Diane	Modahl	GBR	17.6.66	2		Gold Coast (RB)	17 Sep
1:27.37	Leontine	Tsiba	CGO	20.11.73				14 Sep
1:27.47	Mina	Aït Hamou	MAR	18.7.78				17 Sep
1:27.57	Florencia	Hunt	AHO	14.5.78				14 Sep

Indoors

Mark	Name		Nat	Born	Pos	Meet	Venue	Date
1:26.35	Natalya	Nazarova	RUS	22.5.79	1		Moskva	6 Jan
1:27.18	Svetlana	Cherkasova	RUS	20.5.78	2		Moskva	6 Jan
1:27.82	Irina	Mistyukevich	RUS	17.6.77	3		Moskva	6 Jan

800 METRES

Mark	Name		Nat	Born	Pos	Meet	Venue	Date
1:56.15	Maria Lurdes	Mutola	MOZ	27.10.72	1	OG	Sydney	25 Sep
1:56.60	Natalya	Tsyganova	RUS	7.2.71	1	NC	Tula	25 Jul
1:56.64	Stephanie	Graf	AUT	26.4.73	2	OG	Sydney	25 Sep
1:56.80	Kelly	Holmes	GBR	19.4.70	3	OG	Sydney	25 Sep
1:56.85	Olga	Raspopova	RUS	27.12.78	2	NC	Tula	25 Jul
1:56.90		Mutola			1	WK	Zürich	11 Aug
1:56.98		Mutola			1	DNG	Stockholm	1 Aug
1:57.32		Graf			2	DNG	Stockholm	1 Aug
1:57.34		Graf			2	WK	Zürich	11 Aug
1:57.49	Irina	Mistyukevich	RUS	17.6.77	1r2	Znam	Sankt-Peterburg	18 Jun
1:57.53	Ludmila	Formanová	CZE	2.1.74	3	WK	Zürich	11 Aug
1:57.56		Graf			1s2	OG	Sydney	23 Sep
1:57.65		Mutola			1	Pre	Eugene	24 Jun
1:57.68		Tsyganova			1	Mos Ch	Moskva	11 Jul
1:57.70		Raspopova			3	DNG	Stockholm	1 Aug
1:57.72		Formanová			4	DNG	Stockholm	1 Aug
1:57.83		Tsyganova			4	WK	Zürich	11 Aug
1:57.98		Raspopova			5	WK	Zürich	11 Aug
1:58.01		Mistyukevich			5	DNG	Stockholm	1 Aug
1:58.04		Tsyganova			6	DNG	Stockholm	1 Aug
1:58.06		Mutola			1	VD	Bruxelles	25 Aug
1:58.08	Regina	Jacobs	USA	28.8.63	2	Pre	Eugene	24 Jun
1:58.10	Suzy	Favor Hamilton	USA	8.8.68	7	DNG	Stockholm	1 Aug
1:58.30		Raspopova			2	Mos Ch	Moskva	11 Jul
1:58.34	Claudia	Gesell	GER	18.12.77	1		Leverkusen	20 Aug
1:58.39		Graf			1h5	OG	Sydney	22 Sep
1:58.45		Holmes			2s2	OG	Sydney	23 Sep
1:58.47	Hasna	Benhassi	MAR	1.6.78	1	Live	Nürnberg	25 Jun
1:58.51	Brigita	Langerholc	SLO	23.7.76	4	OG	Sydney	25 Sep
1:58.52		Mistyukevich			3	NC	Tula	25 Jul
	(30/12)							
1:58.56	Helena	Fuchsová	CZE	3.6.65	5	OG	Sydney	25 Sep
1:58.62	Letitia	Vriesde	SUR	5.10.64	2	VD	Bruxelles	25 Aug
1:58.66	Zulia	Calatayud	CUB	9.11.79	6	OG	Sydney	25 Sep
1:58.75	Hazel	Clark	USA	3.10.77	7	OG	Sydney	25 Sep
1:58.77	Marina	Anisimova	RUS	4.3.73	4	NC	Tula	25 Jul
1:59.09	Sandra	Stals	BEL	5.6.75	7	WK	Zürich	11 Aug
1:59.12	Jearl	Miles-Clark	USA	4.9.66	2	NC	Sacramento	23 Jul
1:59.20	Ivonne	Teichmann	GER	11.4.77	1	NA	Heusden	5 Aug
	(20)							
1:59.21	Tamsyn	Lewis	AUS	20.7.78	1		Canberra	15 Jan
1:59.23	Svetlana	Cherkasova	RUS	20.5.78	1r2	Mos Ch	Moskva	11 Jul
1:59.31	Toni	Hodgkinson	NZL	12.12.71	1		Brisbane	8 Sep
1:59.49	Joetta	Clark-Diggs	USA	1.8.62	3	NC	Sacramento	23 Jul
1:59.50	Meredith	Valmon	USA	15.10.68	4	NC	Sacramento	23 Jul
1:59.58	Lwiza	John	TAN	18.5.80	2	Super	Yokohama	9 Sep
1:59.60	Mayte	Martínez	ESP	17.5.76	1h3	OG	Sydney	22 Sep
1:59.68	Nouria	Mérah-Benida	ALG	19.10.70	1		Alger	2 Aug
1:59.8 mx	Susan	Andrews	AUS	26.5.71	1		Perth	15 Jul
	2:00.32				1		Brisbane	3 Sep
1:59.97	Linda	Kisabaka	GER	9.4.69	3		Leverkusen	20 Aug
	(30)							
1:59.97	Margaret	Crowley	AUS	24.5.67	3		Brisbane	8 Sep
2:00.07	Yelena	Buzhenko	UKR	16.11.72	3	GP	Athína	28 Jun
2:00.1	Larisa	Mikhaylova	RUS	3.1.69	1		Cherepovets	16 Jul
2:00.22	Carla	Sacramento	POR	10.12.71	2	ECp1A	Nadderud	8 Jul
2:00.24	Natalya	Gorelova	RUS	18.4.73	2r2	Mos Ch	Moskva	11 Jul
2:00.32	Lyudmila	Goncharova	BLR	17.10.76	1		Stayki	27 Jun
2:00.32	Gladys	Wamuyu	KEN	23.12.72	3	AfCh	Alger	14 Jul
2:00.47	Natalya	Dukhnova	BLR	16.7.66	4	GP	Athína	28 Jun
2:00.52	Lyudmila	Rogachova	RUS	30.10.66	4	Super	Yokohama	9 Sep
2:00.53	Diane	Modahl	GBR	17.6.66	3	OD	Jena	3 Jun
	(40)							
2:00.54	Galina	Misiruk	UKR	18.12.70	2	NC	Kiev	6 Aug
2:00.61	Luciana	Mendes	BRA	26.7.71	5	GP	Athína	28 Jun
2:00.63		Wang Yuanping	CHN	8.12.76	1	OT	Jinzhou	7 Jun

Mark	Name		Nat	Born	Pos	Meet	Venue	Date
2:00.63	Charmaine	Howell	JAM	13.3.75	7s1	OG	Sydney	23 Sep
2:00.64	Süreyya	Ayhan	TUR	6.9.78	1		Istanbul	20 Aug
2:00.67		Lin Na	CHN	18.1.80	2	OT	Jinzhou	7 Jun
2:00.67	Mardrea	Hyman	JAM	22.12.72	3	Veniz	Haniá	14 Jun
2:00.67	Patricia	Djaté	FRA	3.1.71	1		Castres	27 Jul
2:00.80	Jolanda	Ceplak	SLO	12.9.76	1		Ljubljana	10 Jun
2:00.92	Tina	Paulino	MOZ	7.7.73	1r7	MSR	Walnut	16 Apr
	(50)							
2:00.97	Grace	Birungi	UGA	10.10.73	4	AfCh	Alger	14 Jul
2:01.01	Amy	Ross-Schroer	USA	13.12.74	5	NC	Sacramento	23 Jul
2:01.06	Tanya	Blake	GBR	16.1.71	4		Leverkusen	20 Aug
2:01.09	Faith	Macharia	KEN	.76	5		Milano	7 Jun
2:01.11	Anita	Brägger	SUI	6.10.72	7	Live	Nürnberg	25 Jun
2:01.13	Kristina	da Fonseca-Wollheim	GER	10.2.72	8	Live	Nürnberg	25 Jun
2:01.15	Marina	Makarova	UKR	3.1.75	3r4	RUS Cp	Tula	4 Jun
2:01.24	Laetitia	Valdonado	FRA	4.8.77	1	NC	Nice	6 Aug
2:01.25	Hayley	Tullett	GBR	17.2.73	1r1		Budapest	22 Jul
2:01.26	Chebet	Langat	KEN-J	22.8.81	3	Gugl	Linz	8 Aug
	(60)							
2:01.28	Yuliya	Taranova	RUS	15.2.77	3r2	Znam	Sankt-Peterburg	18 Jun
2:01.29	Elena	Buhaianu-Iagar	ROM	16.1.75	1	NC	Bucuresti	7 Aug
2:01.30	Malin	Ewerlöf-Krepp	SWE	2.6.72	3	ECp-1A	Nadderud	8 Jul
2:01.30	Viviane	Dorsile	FRA	1.6.67	2	NC	Nice	6 Aug
2:01.38	Nuria	Fernández	ESP	16.8.76	4	NA	Heusden	5 Aug
2:01.39	Tytti	Reho	FIN	5.8.77	4	ECp-1A	Nadderud	8 Jul
2:01.40	Claudia	Salvarani	ITA	8.3.75	1	NC	Milano	7 Sep
2:01.44	Öznur	Dursun	TUR	24.10.71	1	Cezmi	Istanbul	24 Jun
2:01.51	Natalya	Yevkodimova	RUS	17.3.78	1r1	Znam	Sankt-Peterburg	18 Jun
2:01.59	Nicole	Teter	USA	8.11.73	3r2		Palo Alto	1 Jul
	(70)							
2:01.61	Tatyana	Lisnichenko	RUS	28.3.66	6		Milano	7 Jun
2:01.61	Irina	Krakoviak	LTU	27.11.77	1	ECp-2A	Kaunas	8 Jul
2:01.63	Yuliya	Kosenkova	RUS	28.3.73	5	Veniz	Hánia	14 Jun
2:01.64	Judit	Varga	HUN	16.4.76	5	ECp-1A	Nadderud	8 Jul
2:01.68	Yekaterina	Fedotova	RUS	4.11.75	1		New Delhi	25 Feb
2:01.70	Fabiane	dos Santos	BRA	30.5.76	5		Barcelona	25 Jul
2:01.73	Olga	Kuznetsova	RUS	23.10.67	1		Sankt Peterburg	10 Jun
2:01.73	Georgie	Clarke	AUS-J	17.6.84	6		Brisbane	8 Sep
2:01.8	Tatyana	Buloychik	BLR	7.1.75	1	NC	Brest	2 Aug
2:01.86	Yekaterina	Puzanova	RUS	1.1.79	6r2	Znam	Sankt-Peterburg	18 Jun
	(80)							
2:01.95	Diane	Cummins	CAN	19.1.74	4r2		Palo Alto	1 Jul
2:01.98	Irina	Prokofyeva	RUS	13.3.72	4r1	Znam	Sankt-Peterburg	18 Jun
2:01.99	Mina	Aït Hamou	MAR	18.7.78	1		Rabat	17 Jun
2:02.06	Oksana	Meltsayeva	UKR	16.8.75	1	Kiev Ch	Kiev	17 Jun
2:02.08	Simona	Ionescu	ROM	24.8.73	1		Torino	10 Jun
2:02.12	Dorota	Fiut	POL	10.12.76	3	Kuso	Warszawa	24 Jun
2:02.14	Irina	Latve	LAT-J	26.8.81	1	NC	Riga	29 Jul
2:02.15	Sunita	Rani	IND	4.12.79	2		New Delhi	25 Feb
2:02.18	Yuliya	Gurtovenko	UKR	8.12.80	3	NC	Kiev	6 Aug
2:02.20	Heidi	Jensen	DEN	14.8.66	3		Cottbus	23 Aug
	(90)							
2:02.21	Olga	Moroz	BLR	17.12.74			Staiki	3 Jun
2:02.22	Elizabeth	Diaz	USA	18.10.77	2h2	NC	Sacramento	20 Jul
2:02.28	Michelle	Ave	USA	15.5.67	2s1	NC	Sacramento	21 Jul
2:02.31	Elisabeth	Grousselle	FRA	6.2.73	1		Montauban	15 Aug
2:02.34	Olga	Mikayeva	RUS	22.10.79	2h1	NC	Tula	22 Jul
2:02.35	Mary Jayne	Harrelson	USA	17.6.78	6	NC	Sacramento	23 Jul
2:02.36	Larisa	Chzhao	RUS	4.2.71	5r1	Znam	Sankt-Peterburg	18 Jun
2:02.36	Hanane	Sabri	FRA	8.12.75	6	-	Leverkusen	20 Aug
2:02.40	Virginie	Fouquet	FRA	9.9.75	2		Castres	27 Jul
2:02.50	Patrizia	Spuri	ITA	18.2.73	6		Barcelona	25 Jul
	(100)							

2:02.51	Shayne	Culpepper	USA	3.12.73	1 Jul
2:02.52	Nédia	Semedo	POR	14.11.78	19 Jul
2:02.54	Chantee	Earl	USA	17.7.78	2 Jun
2:02.54	Carine	van Dorp	NED	11.9.71	26 Aug
2:02.57	Vicky	Lynch-Pounds	CAN	6.6.70	29 Jul
2:02.59	Brigitte	Mühlbacher	AUT	5.12.75	3 Jul
2:02.61		Yang Wei	CHN-J	24.7.83	7 Jun
2:02.73	Aleksandra	Deren	POL	1.2.78	10 Jun
2:02.74	Anjolie	Wisse	NED	17.9.76	5 Aug
2:02.75	Yekaterina	Dedkova	RUS	8.3.72	11 Jul
2:02.76	Lyubov	Kremlyova	RUS	21.12.61	11 Jul
2:02.8	Svetlana	Suvorova	RUS	.78	16 Jul
2:02.85	Madhuri A	Singh	IND		25 Feb
2:02.86	Sandra	Teixeira	POR	13.3.78	25 Jul

Mark	Name		Nat	Born	Date
2:02.87	Oksana	Kochetkova	UKR	25.5.74	24 Jun
2:02.87	Fatima	Lanouar	TUN	14.3.78	7 Aug
2:02.88	Ana	Guevara	MEX	4.3.77	16 Jul
2:02.94	Ashley	Wysong	USA	26.1.79	2 Jun
2:02.95	Hareg	Sidelil	ETH-J	20.4.81	7 Jun
2:02.96	Stephanie	Best	USA	16.10.69	20 Jul
2:03.04	Yuliya	Kumpan	UKR	19.10.77	6 Aug
2:03.05	Anna	Bagmut	RUS	8.7.76	22 Jul
2:03.07	Elisabetta	Artuso	ITA	25.4.74	7 Jun
2:03.09	Peggy	Babin	FRA	24.12.76	23 Jul
2:03.1	Natalya	Vasko	BLR	20.5.80	2 Aug
2:03.12	Svetlana	Tverdokhleb	UKR	12.10.72	15 Jul
2:03.17	Miesha	Marzell	USA	29.1.75	20 Jul
2:03.23	Shaquandra	Roberson	USA	3.2.77	2 Jun
2:03.27	Debbie	Grant	USA	5.8.65	18 Jun
2:03.29	Natalya	Keiko	BLR	2.12.79	21 May
2:03.36	Sasha	Spencer	USA	4.8.79	2 Jun
2:03.37		Li Jingnan	CHN-J	17.2.83	28 Jun
2:03.38	Marlén	Estévez	ESP	29.8.71	25 Jul
2:03.39	Monica	Lundgren	SWE	12.1.73	19 Jul
2:03.40	Melanie	Steere	USA		2 Jun
2:03.41	Berit	Bauer	GER	17.4.75	3 Jun
2:03.45		Shi Hua	CHN-J	21.6.81	7 Jun
2:03.48mx	Kelly	Caffell	GBR	10.2.79	30 Aug
	2:04.35				6 Sep
2:03.50	Kim	Cornelius	USA	.72	17 Jun
2:03.50	Melanie	Collins	AUS	28.10.67	4 Aug
2:03.51	René	Kalmer	RSA	3.11.80	23 May
2:03.52	Simone	Beutelspacher	GER	8.12.74	3 Jun
2:03.58	Jennifer	Toomey	USA	.72	4 Jul
2:03.59	Ieva	Zunda	LAT	20.7.78	27 Aug
2:03.60	Natalya	Mayorova	RUS	.77	4 Jun
2:03.64	Maren	Schott	GER	11.2.76	20 Aug
2:03.64	Alina	Rîpanu	ROM-J	29.10.81	17 Sep
2:03.65	Birhane	Hirpassa	ETH		15 Aug
2:03.67	Geeta	Manral	IND	11.12.80	30 Jul
2:03.72	Korine	Hinds	JAM	18.1.76	21 May
2:03.75	Olga	Moroz	UKR	16.8.70	18 Jun
2:03.75	Helen	Pattinson	GBR	2.1.74	28 Aug
2:03.76	Anna	Zagórska	POL	26.7.80	23 Aug
2:03.78mx	Alex	Carter	GBR	1.4.80	5 Sep
2:03.78	Florencia	Hunt	AHO	14.5.78	22 Sep
2:03.79	Svetlana	Kanatova	RUS	10.9.70	11 Jul
2:03.80	Nadiha	Touhami	ALG	.78	15 Aug
2:03.82	Amy	Wickus	USA	25.6.72	20 Jul
2:03.83	Yelena	Afanasyeva	RUS	1.3.67	5 Jul
2:03.84	Tsvetelina	Kirilova	BUL	14.7.77	28 Jun
2:03.90	Miriam	Bravo	ESP	29.9.74	25 Jul
2:03.92	Malgorzata	Jamróz	POL	16.10.73	24 Jun
2:03.92	Mary	McClung	GBR	19.12.71	22 Jul
2:03.96	Olga	Karchaleva	BLR		22 Jun
2:03.96	Anna	Anfinogentova	LAT	22.7.78	29 Jul
2:03.99	Agnes	Samaria	NAM	11.8.72	22 Jul
2:04.00	Miki	Nishimura	JPN-J	14.4.82	5 Aug
2:04.00	Lucia	Klocová	SVK-J	20.11.83	20 Oct
2:04.02	Jurga	Marcinkeviciute	LTU	17.10.74	3 Jun
2:04.04	Tatyana	Krivobok	UKR	17.1.72	25 Jul
2:04.06A	Julia	Sakara	ZIM	12.7.69	24 Mar
2:04.07	Leah	Malot	KEN	7.6.72	25 Aug
2:04.07	Emma	Davies	GBR	9.10.78	3 Aug
2:04.08	Leontine	Tsiba	CGO	20.11.73	22 Sep
2:04.09	Julian	Reynolds	USA	2.11.77	1 Apr
2:04.09	Anna	Jakubczak	POL	2.2.73	17 Jun
2:04.09	Kim	Voyticky	USA	17.10.75	18 Jun
2:04.10	Mónica	Alcázar	ESP	21.6.77	9 Jun
2:04.11	Natalya	Sidorenko	UKR	22.11.80	15 Jul
2:04.13	Abebech	Negussie	ETH-J	2.1.83	12 Jun
2:04.15	Sonja	Roman	SLO	11.3.79	10 Jun
2:04.15	Jeina	Mitchell	GBR	21.1.75	3 Sep
2:04.19	Akosua	Serwah	GHA-J	3.1.81	14 Jul
2:04.19	Joanne	Fenn	GBR	19.10.74	22 Jul
2:04.24	Fabiana	da Silva	BRA	3.9.78	21 Jun
2:04.25	Alisa	Harvey	USA	16.9.65	1 Jul
2:04.26	Yekaterina	Nikishina	RUS	5.8.78	2 Jul
2:04.27	Yelena	Prokhorova	RUS	16.4.78	23 Jul
2:04.27	Linda	Olsson	SWE	21.8.72	3 Sep
2:04.28	Marjo	Venäläinen	FIN	29.5.71	16 Jul
2:04.31	Olga	Komyagina	RUS	10.2.74	4 Jun
2:04.32	Hope	Sanders	USA	24.3.73	24 Jun
2:04.37	Nadezhda	Vorobyeva	RUS	.77	22 Jul
2:04.41	Mary	Cobb	USA	10.12.76	3 Jun
2:04.42		Bu Weili	CHN-J	25.8.81	7 Jun
2:04.47	Chiara	Grossutti	ITA	13.7.71	10 Jun
2:04.48	Tamieka	Grizzle	USA	14.7.77	1 Apr
2:04.50	Geraldine	Nolan	IRL	11.4.74	29 Jul
	(198)				

Indoors

Mark	Name		Nat	Born	Pos	Meet	Venue	Date
1:57.80		Graf			1		Birmingham	20 Feb
1:58.43		Graf			1		Stockholm	17 Feb
2:00.46	Lidia	Chojecka	POL	25.1.77	2		Karlsruhe	29 Jan
2:00.6	Stella	Jongmans	NED	17.5.71	2		Erfurt	2 Feb
2:00.81	Violeta	Szekely	ROM	26.3.65	1	NC	Bucuresti	6 Feb
2:01.40	Heike	Meissner	GER	29.1.70	1		Chemnitz	18 Feb
2:01.72	Simone	Beutelspacher	GER	8.12.74	4	IHS	Sindelfingen	22 Jan
2:02.19	Chantee	Earl	USA	17.7.78	1	NCAA	Fayetteville	11 Mar
2:03.13	Kutre	Dulecha	ETH	22.8.78				30 Jan
2:03.19	Svetlana	Badrankova	KAZ	25.3.77				11 Mar
2:03.4	Kathleen	Friedrich	GER	13.7.77				2 Feb
2:04.36	Anca	Safta	ROM	9.1.78				6 Feb

JUNIORS

Mark	Name		Nat	Born	Pos	Meet	Venue	Date
2:01.26	Chebet	Langat	KEN	22.8.81	3	Gugl	Linz	8 Aug
	2:01.51 1 WJ Santiago 20 Oct				2:02.03A 1 NC Nairobi 22 Jul			
	2:01.92 2 Rovereto 30 Aug							
2:01.73	Georgie	Clarke	AUS	17.6.84	6		Brisbane	8 Sep
	2:01.81 2 Canberra 15 Jan				2:02.59 4 Sydney 27 Feb			
	2:02.28 2 WJ Santiago 20 Oct				10 performances by 4 women to 2:02.61			
2:02.14	Irina	Latve	LAT	26.8.81	1	NC	Riga	29 Jul
2:02.61		Yang Wei	CHN	24.7.83	1h1	OT	Jinzhou	7 Jun
2:02.95	Hareg	Sidelil	ETH	20.4.81	7		Milano	7 Jun
2:03.37		Li Jingnan	CHN	17.2.83	9	GP	Athína	28 Jun
2:03.45		Shi Hua	CHN	21.6.81	4	OT	Jinzhou	7 Jun
2:03.64	Alina	Rîpanu	ROM	29.10.81	1	Balk-j	Constanta	17 Sep
2:04.00	Miki	Nishimura	JPN	14.4.82	1		Gifu	5 Aug
2:04.00	Lucia	Klocová (10)	SVK	20.11.83	3	WJ	Santiago de Chile	20 Oct
2:04.13	Abebech	Negussie	ETH	2.1.83	4		Rehlingen	12 Jun
2:04.19	Akosua	Serwah	GHA	3.1.81	6	AfrC	Alger	14 Jul
2:04.42		Bu Weili	CHN	7.6.81	2h2	OT	Jinzhou	7 Jun
2:04.74	Tatyana	Petlyuk	UKR	22.2.82	5		Kiev	18 Jun
2:04.77	Mari	Järvenpää	FIN	29.11.81	3	vSWE	Helsinki	3 Sep

Mark	Name		Nat	Born	Pos	Meet	Venue	Date
2:04.86	Saray	Valverde	CUB	10.4.84	1		La Habana	24 Jun
2:04.86	Kerstin	Werner	GER	18.9.82	1	v2N-23	Liverpool	22 Jul
2:04.88	Joanna	Buza	POL	15.4.81	2		Wroclaw	6 Sep
2:04.96	Gulmira	Tasiybekova	KZK	2.7.81	1	NC	Almaty	15 Jul
2:05.13	Anasatasiya	Fesenko (20)	RUS	.82	7r1		Sankt-Peterburg	18 Jun

1000 METRES

Mark	Name		Nat	Born	Pos	Meet	Venue	Date
2:35.96	Anna	Jakubczak	POL	2.2.73	1		Gold Coast (RB)	17 Sep
2:37.22	Violeta	Szekely	ROM	26.3.65	1	Nik	Nice	8 Jul
2:37.42	Letitia	Vriesde	SUR	5.10.64	2	Nik	Nice	8 Jul
2:37.89	Yelena	Buzhenko	UKR	16.11.72	3	Nik	Nice	8 Jul
2:38.39	Yelena	Afanasyeva	RUS	1.3.67				8 Jul
2:39.23	Fabiane	dos Santos	BRA	30.5.76				8 Jul
2:39.30	Natalya	Dukhnova	BLR	16.7.66				8 Jul
2:39.35	Luciana	Mendes	BRA	26.7.71				8 Jul
2:39.44	Anita	Weyermann	SUI	8.12.77				22 Sep
2:40.39	Sabine	Fischer	SUI	29.6.73				22 Sep
2:40.56	Renata	Hoppová	CZE	11.6.76				21 May
2:41.02	Simone	Beutelspacher	GER	8.12.74				21 May
Indoors								
2:35.29	Regina	Jacobs	USA	28.8.63	1		Boston (R)	6 Feb
2:35.68	Maria Lurdes	Mutola	MOZ	27.10.72	1	Gaz	Liévin	13 Feb
2:36.73	Natalya	Tsyganova	RUS	7.2.71	2	Gaz	Liévin	13 Feb
2:36.96	Toni	Hodgkinson	NZL	12.12.71	2		Boston (R)	6 Feb
2:39.47	Kutre	Dulecha	ETH	22.8.78	3	Gaz	Liévin	13 Feb
2:39.67	Amy	Ross-Schroer	USA	13.12.74				6 Feb
2:40.15	Carmen	Wüstenhagen	GER	15.8.73				6 Feb
2:41.08	Sandra	Stals	BEL	5.6.75				13 Feb
		JUNIORS						
2:43.72	Georgie	Clarke	AUS	17.6.84	3		Castleisland	11 Jun
2:45.98A	Zanelle	Grobler	RSA	27.1.83	1		Johannesburg	5 Aug

1500 METRES

Mark	Name		Nat	Born	Pos	Meet	Venue	Date
3:57.40	Suzy	Favor Hamilton	USA	8.8.68	1	Bisl	Oslo	28 Jul
3:58.29	Violeta	Szekely	ROM	26.3.65	1	Herc	Monaco	18 Aug
3:59.02	Kutre	Dulecha	ETH	22.8.78	2	Herc	Monaco	18 Aug
3:59.12	Nouria	Mérah-Benida	ALG	19.10.70	3	Herc	Monaco	18 Aug
3:59.22	Lidia	Chojecka	POL	25.1.77	2	Bisl	Oslo	28 Jul
3:59.34		Szekely			3	Bisl	Oslo	28 Jul
4:00.35	Carla	Sacramento	POR	10.12.71	1	VD	Bruxelles	25 Aug
4:00.37		Chojecka			1	WK	Zürich	11 Aug
4:00.60		Dulecha			4	Bisl	Oslo	28 Jul
4:00.73	Gabriela	Szabo	ROM	14.11.75	1	Pre	Eugene	24 Jun
4:00.79		Favor Hamilton			2	Pre	Eugene	24 Jun
4:00.92		Dulecha			2	WK	Zürich	11 Aug
4:00.99		Szekely			2	VD	Bruxelles	25 Aug
4:01.01	Regina	Jacobs	USA	28.8.63	1	NC	Sacramento	16 Jul
4:01.15	Svetlana	Masterkova	RUS	17.1.68	5	Bisl	Oslo	28 Jul
4:01.18		Sacramento			6	Bisl	Oslo	28 Jul
4:01.18		Szekely			3	WK	Zürich	11 Aug
4:01.23	Hayley	Tullett	GBR	17.2.73	7	Bisl	Oslo	28 Jul
4:01.23		Mérah-Benida			3	VD	Bruxelles	25 Aug
4:01.50	Natalya	Gorelova	RUS	18.4.73	8	Bisl	Oslo	28 Jul
4:01.64	Naomi	Mugo	KEN	2.1.77	4	WK	Zürich	11 Aug
4:01.70	Sonia	O'Sullivan	IRL	28.11.69	9	Bisl	Oslo	28 Jul
4:01.73	Lyudmila	Rogachova	RUS	30.10.66	1	NC	Tula	26 Jul
4:01.79		Sacramento			5	WK	Zürich	11 Aug
4:01.80		Mérah-Benida			6	WK	Zürich	11 Aug
4:01.81		Favor Hamilton			2	NC	Sacramento	16 Jul
4:02.21	Olga	Nelyubova	RUS	12.6.64	7	WK	Zürich	11 Aug
4:02.32	Olga	Komyagina	RUS	10.2.74	1		Leverkusen	20 Aug
4:02.39	Maria Lurdes	Mutola	MOZ	27.10.72	4	Herc	Monaco	18 Aug
4:02.60		Komyagina			4	VD	Bruxelles	25 Aug
	(00/17)							
4:03.02	Süreyya	Ayhan	TUR	6.9.78	5	VD	Bruxelles	25 Aug
4:03.10	Lyubov	Kremlyova	RUS	21.12.61	3	NC	Tula	26 Jul
4:03.18	Olga	Kuznetsova	RUS	23.10.67	10	Bisl	Oslo	28 Jul
	(20)							
4:03.32	Yelena	Zadorozhnaya	RUS	3.12.77	4	NC	Tula	26 Jul
4:03.83	Daniela	Yordanova	BUL	8.3.76	2	ECp1B	Bydgoszcz	9 Jul
4:03.95		Lan Lixin	CHN	14.2.79	1	OT	Jinzhou	8 Jun
4:04.24	Natalia	Rodríguez	ESP	2.6.79	2	NA	Heusden	5 Aug
4:04.28	Yuliya	Kosenkova	RUS	28.3.73	3	NA	Heusden	5 Aug

Mark	Name		Nat	Born	Pos	Meet	Venue	Date
4:04.66	Paula	Ivan	ROM	20.7.63	5	Herc	Monaco	18 Aug
4:04.75	Olga	Yegorova	RUS	28.3.72	2	Mos Ch	Moskva	12 Jul
4:04.80	Tatyana	Tomashova	RUS	1.7.75	5	Znam	Sankt-Peterburg	18 Jun
4:04.82	Helen	Pattinson	GBR	2.1.74	2		Barcelona	25 Jul
4:04.84		Li Jingnan	CHN-J	17.2.83	2	Gaz	Saint-Denis	23 Jun
	(30)							
4:04.94	Elena	Buhaianu-lagar	ROM	16.1.75	1	NC	Bucuresti	6 Aug
4:05.07	Kristiba	da Fonseca-Wollheim	GER	10.2.72	9	GGala	Roma	30 Jun
4:05.07	Lyudmila	Vasilyeva	RUS	20.10.69	7	NC	Tula	26 Jul
4:05.14	Sabine	Fischer	SUI	29.6.73	9	WK	Zürich	11 Aug
4:05.28	Sinead	Delahunty	IRL	12.2.71	3		Barcelona	25 Jul
4:05.35	Kelly	Holmes	GBR	19.4.70	4s1	OG	Sydney	28 Sep
4:05.38	Anita	Weyermann	SUI	8.12.77	10	WK	Zürich	11 Aug
4:05.76	Zoya	Kaznovskaya	UKR	22.9.66	1		Strasbourg	27 Jun
4:05.77	Veerle	Dejaeghere	BEL	1.8.73	4	NA	Heusden	5 Aug
4:05.94	Kathleen	Friedrich	GER	13.7.77	1		Neustadt	6 Aug
	(40)							
4:05.99	Alesya	Turova	BLR	6.12.79	7	Znam	Sankt-Peterburg	18 Jun
4:06.02	Amy	Rudolph	USA	18.9.73	5	NA	Heusden	5 Aug
4:06.08	Marta	Domínguez	ESP	3.11.75	4		Barcelona	25 Jul
4:06.09	Sarah	Jamieson	AUS	24.3.75	4	Nik	Nice	8 Jul
4:06.14	Marla	Runyan	USA	4.1.69	6s1	OG	Sydney	28 Sep
4:06.19	Svetlana	Kanatova	RUS	10.9.70	8	NC	Tula	26 Jul
4:06.20	Abebech	Negussie	ETH-J	2.1.83	12	Bisl	Oslo	28 Jul
4:06.20	Maria	Cioncan	ROM	19.6.77	3	NC	Bucuresti	6 Aug
4:06.23	Toni	Hodgkinson	NZL	12.12.71	1	GP II	Melbourne	2 Mar
4:06.37	Nuria	Fernández	ESP	16.8.76	5		Barcelona	25 Jul
	(50)							
4:06.49	Anna	Jakubczak	POL	2.2.73	6	OG	Sydney	30 Sep
4:06.77	Georgie	Clarke	AUS-J	17.6.84	1		Hobart	30 Jan
4:06.77	Helena	Javornik	SLO	26.3.66	3	ECp1B	Bydgoszcz	9 Jul
4:06.91	Fatima	Lanouar	TUN	14.3.78	5	ROM Ch	Bucuresti	6 Aug
4:07.00	Silvia	Kühnemund	GER	25.7.74	2		Dortmund	8 Jul
4:07.02	Hareg	Sidelil	ETH-J	20.4.81	12	WK	Zürich	11 Aug
4:07.05	Benita	Willis	AUS	6.5.79	3	GP II	Melbourne	2 Mar
4:07.13	Irina	Mikitenko	GER	23.8.72	3	Live	Nürnberg	25 Jun
4:07.23	Margaret	Crowley	AUS	24.5.67	1		Gold Coast (RB)	9 Aug
4:07.25		Yin Lili	CHN	11.11.79	3	OT	Jinzhou	8 Jun
	(60)							
4:07.82	Deena	Drossin	USA	14.2.73	6	NA	Heusden	5 Aug
4:07.88	Leah	Pells	CAN	9.11.64	3	Pre	Eugene	24 Jun
4:07.99	Irina	Krakoviak	LTU	27.11.77	1	GS	Ostrava	1 Jun
4:07.99	Shayne	Culpepper	USA	3.12.73	1	Jerome	Burnaby	4 Jun
4:08.03		Zhang Ling	CHN	13.4.80	4	NGPF	Jinzhou	8 Jun
4:08.06	Margarita	Marusova	RUS	25.11.67	13	GGala	Roma	30 Jun
4:08.18	Saloua	Ouaziz	MAR	27.7.74	14	GGala	Roma	30 Jun
4:08.25	Tatyana	Krivobok	UKR	17.1.72	1h1	NC	Kiev	3 Aug
4:08.32	Heidi	Jensen	DEN	14.8.66	3		Leverkusen	20 Aug
4:08.42	Fatima	Yvelain	FRA	31.12.69	2		Strasbourg	27 Jun
	(70)							
4:08.6A	Jeruto	Kiptum	KEN-J	12.12.81	1	NC	Nairobi	22 Jul
4:08.70	Patricia	Djaté	FRA	3.1.71	9	Gaz	Saint-Denis	23 Jun
4:08.76	Mary Jayne	Harrelson	USA	17.6.78	5	NC	Sacramento	16 Jul
4:08.83	Fernanda	Ribeiro	POR	23.6.69	1		Funchal	29 Jul
4:09.08	Luminita	Zaituc	GER	9.10.68	7	NA	Heusden	5 Aug
4:09.19	Natalya	Yevkodimova	RUS	17.3.78	10	NC	Tula	26 Jul
4:09.21	Grete	Koens	NED	26.5.67	5		Leverkusen	20 Aug
4:09.57	Faith	Macharia	KEN	.76	3		Brisbane	11 Feb
4:09.83	Mardrea	Hyman	JAM	22.12.72	8	Znam	Sankt-Peterburg	18 Jun
4:09.95	Tatyana	Belovol	UKR	7.10.69	2	NC	Kiev	4 Aug
	(80)							
4:10.03	Zhor	El Kamch	MAR	15.3.73	17	GGala	Roma	30 Jun
4:10.08	Malin	Ewerlöf-Krepp	SWE	2.6.72	9	Live	Nürnberg	25 Jun
4:10.1	Sunita	Rani	IND	4.12.79	1		Lucknow	15 Mar
4:10.14	Natalya	Sidorenko	UKR	22.11.80	3	NC	Kiev	4 Aug
4:10.22	Kelly	Caffell	GBR	10.2.79	6	-	Leverkusen	20 Aug
4:10.28	Andrea	Suldesová	CZE	11.2.75	3		Kassel	7 Jun
4:10.34	Anne	Cross	AUS	16.4.65	4		Brisbane	11 Feb
4:10.51	Yimenashu	Taye	ETH	1.1.79	5	GP II	Rieti	3 Sep

Mark	Name		Nat	Born	Pos	Meet	Venue	Date
4:10.68	Elva	Dryer	USA	26.9.71	3	Jerome	Burnaby	4 Jun
4:10.73	Birhane (90)	Hirpassa	ETH		3		Dessau	31 May
4:10.75	Gete	Urge	ETH	30.8.70	6		Luzern	27 Jun
4:10.80	Doreen	Walter	GER	1.2.76	2		Neustadt	6 Aug
4:10.81	Laurence	Duquénoy	FRA	29.9.69	3		Strasbourg	27 Jun
4:10.96	Yelena	Gorodnicheva	UKR	5.9.70	7		Luzern	27 Jun
4:11.00	Debbie	Grant	USA	5.8.65	3h1	NC	Sacramento	14 Jul
4:11.03	Leah	Malot	KEN	7.6.72	1		Cottbus	23 Aug
4:11.05	Rocío	Rodríguez	ESP	23.5.77	10		Barcelona	25 Jul
4:11.14	Carmen	Wüstenhagen	GER	15.8.73	11	Live	Nürnberg	25 Jun
4:11.18		Wang Chunmei	CHN	10.4.76	5	NGPF	Jinzhou	8 Jun
4:11.18	Oksana (100)	Meltsayeva	UKR	16.8.75	5	NC	Kiev	4 Aug

Mark	Name		Nat	Born	Date	
4:11.24	Collette	Liss	USA	29.4.73	1	Jul
4:11.24	Jacinta	Muraguri	KEN	28.5.70	5	Aug
4:11.28	Almitu	Colakoglu (Bekele)	TUR	17.9.77	2	Jul
4:11.45	Paula	Radcliffe	GBR	17.12.73	25	Jul
4:11.46	Karen	Candaele	USA	27.5.72	1	Jul
4:11.67	Cristina	Grosu	ROM	11.11.76	6	Aug
4:11.72	Galina	Bogomolova	RUS	15.10.77	2	Jul
4:11.81	Breeda	Dennehy-Willis	IRL	2.3.70	6	May
4:11.91	Sibel	Özyurt (Bekele)	TUR	21.4.80	20	Aug
4:11.94	Gladys	Wamuyu	KEN	23.12.72	11	Feb
4:12.12	Stephanie	Best	USA	16.10.69	14	Jul
4:12.15	Kara	Wheeler	USA	9.7.78	21	May
4:12.20	Simona	Ionescu	ROM	24.8.73	5	Aug
4:12.20	Cláudia	Pereira	POR	20.2.76	5	Aug
4:12.26	Yamna	Belkacem	FRA	20.2.74	6	Aug
4:12.36	Jelena	Prokopcuka	LAT	21.9.76	22	Jul
4:12.39	Svetlana	Cherkasova	RUS	20.5.78	12	Jul
4:12.40	Malgorzata	Jamróz	POL	16.10.73	23	Aug
4:12.53	Susan	Taylor	USA		14	Jul
4:12.53	Justyna	Bak	POL	1.8.74	23	Aug
4:12.56	Sally	Glynn	USA	3.11.78	1	Jul
4:12.67	Fabiana	da Silva	BRA	3.9.78	18	Jun
4:12.72	Gete	Wami	ETH	11.12.74	23	May
4:12.73	Melanie	Collins	AUS	28.10.67	11	Feb
4:12.77	Tatyana	Buloychik	BLR	7.1.75	27	Jun
4:13.00	Michiko	Shimizu	JPN	22.9.70	11	Feb
4:13.00	Janet	Trujillo	USA	7.8.75	25	Jun
4:13.01	Judit	Varga	HUN	16.4.76	2	Sep
4:13.05	Rose	Cheruiyot	KEN	21.7.76	23	May
4:13.06	Lydia	Cheromei	KEN	11.5.77	23	May
4:13.11	Sally	Barsosio	KEN	21.3.78	3	Sep
4:13.13	Brigitte	Mühlbacher	AUT	5.12.75	31	Mar
4:13.14		Wu Qingdong	CHN	11.11.79	22	Apr
4:13.22	Vera	Norkina	RUS	20.8.68	12	Jul
4:13.40	Mandy	Giblin	AUS	27.6.74	9	Aug
4:13.41	Jennifer	Peck	USA	.75	24	Jun
4:13.43	Sonja	Stolic	YUG	21.4.80	3	Jun
4:13.45	René	Kalmer	RSA	3.11.80	31	Mar
4:13.49	Jenelle	Deatherage	USA	25.9.77	14	Jul
4:13.52		Sun Qiuhong	CHN	1.2.79	8	Jun
4:13.52	Jamie	King	USA		14	Jul
4:13.56	Nédia	Semedo	POR	14.11.78	29	Jul
4:13.58	Tytti	Reho	FIN	5.8.77	2	Sep
4:13.72		Yan Wei	CHN	12.10.71	18	Apr
4:13.78	Yelena	Fadeyeva	UKR	23.6.66	4	Aug
4:13.91	Silvia	Kruijer	NED	6.9.74	23	May
4:13.96	Sonja	Friend-Uhl	USA		24	Jun
4:13.99	Tezeta	Sürekli	TUR	8.4.80	2	Sep
4:14.01	Priscilla	Hein	USA	15.7.76	1	Jul
4:14.02		Shi Hua	CHN-J	21.6.81	8	Jun
4:14.03	Hanane	Sabri	FRA	8.12.75	27	Jun
4:14.04	Nathalie	Côte	CAN	21.1.73	7	Jul
4:14.13	Yekaterina	Dedkova	RUS	8.3.72	26	Jul
4:14.15	Niamh	Beirne	IRL	20.7.74	1	Jul
4:14.26	Yekaterina	Fedotova	RUS	4.11.75	3	Mar
4:14.26	Kathy	Fleming	USA	25.12.67	24	Jun
4:14.26	Anjolie	Wisse	NED	17.9.76	23	Aug
4:14.28	Hasna	Benhassi	MAR	1.6.78	28	May
4:14.33	Rasa	Drazdauskaite	LTU-J	20.3.81	1	Jul
4:14.37	Renata	Hoppová	CZE	11.6.76	16	Jul
4:14.41	Diane	Modahl	GBR	17.6.66	31	May
4:14.42	Lwiza	John	TAN	18.5.80	31	Mar
4:14.43	Mary	Cobb	USA	10.12.76	27	May
4:14.47		Lin Na	CHN	18.1.80	22	Oct
4:14.58	Melissa	Teemant	USA	30.5.74	24	Jun
4:14.63	Etaferahu	Tarekegne	ETH	20.3.80	23	May
4:14.64	Agata	Balsamo	ITA	11.11.70	3	Jun
4:14.70	Susie	Power	AUS	26.3.75	2	Mar
4:14.85	Geraldine	Nolan	IRL	11.4.74	13	Aug
4:14.9	Oksana	Barak-Zhelznyak	TUR	9.9.75	15	Jul
4:14.97	Amy	Wickus	USA	25.6.72	14	Jul
4:15.11		Wang Hua	CHN	14.6.80	22	Oct
4:15.13	Yuliya	Vinokurova	RUS	.72	26	Jul
4:15.13	Susanne	Pumper	AUT	1.9.70	20	Aug
4:15.14	Ronel	Thomas	RSA	19.1.72	18	Feb
4:15.16	Zanelle	Grobler	RSA-J	27.1.83	3	Mar
4:15.19	Meseret	Defar	ETH-J	.83	15	Aug
4:15.23	Julia	Sakara	ZIM	12.7.69	18	Feb
4:15.24	Letitia	Vriesde	SUR	5.10.64	25	Jun
4:15.28	Angela	Newport	GBR	21.10.70	14	Jun
4:15.35	Marjo	Venäläinen	FIN	29.5.71	2	Sep
4:15.39	Nicole	Jefferson	USA	8.3.76	29	Jul
4:15.40	Mónica	Rosa	POR	5.5.78	5	Aug
4:15.40	María	Protópapa	GRE	5.5.73	2	Sep
4:15.44	Juli	Henner	USA	13.5.70	1	Jul
4:15.46	Vicky	Lynch-Pounds	CAN	6.6.70	25	Mar
4:15.46	Kathy (187)	Butler	GBR	22.10.73	24	Jun

Indoors

Mark	Name		Nat	Born	Pos	Venue	Date
4:10.65	Carmen	Wüstenhagen	GER	15.8.73	4	Chemnitz	18 Feb

Mark	Name		Nat	Born	Date	
4:12.40	Tatyana	Lisnichenko	RUS	.66	5	Feb
4:13.10	Cheri	Kenah	USA	26.12.70	6	Feb
4:15.14		Song Liqing	CHN	20.1.80	23	Feb
4:15.31	Anne	Bruns	GER	3.7.74	26	Jan

JUNIORS

See main list for top 6 juniors. 12 performances by 5 women to 4:08.63. Additional marks and further juniors:

Li Jingnan	4:05.332	NGPF	Jinzhou	[illegible] Jun					
Negussie	4:08.147	BrGP	London (CP)	5 Aug	4:08.63	2	GS	Ostrava	1 Jun
Clarke	4:06.973		Melbourne	2 Mar	4:07.30	13	Bisl	Oslo	28 Jul
Sidelil	4:07.785	BrGP	London (CP)	5 Aug	4:08.43	5	Athl	Lausanne	5 Jul

Mark	Name		Nat	Born	Pos	Meet	Venue	Date
4:14.02		Shi Hua	CHN	21.6.81	8	NGPF	Jinzhou	8 Jun
4:14.33	Rasa	Drazdauskaite	LTU	20.3.81	3		Sopot	1 Jul
4:15.16	Zanelle	Grobler	RSA	27.1.83	1	NC	Stellenbosch	3 Mar
4:15.19	Meseret	Defaru (10)	ETH	.83	2		Brasschaat	15 Aug
4:15.94		Yan Junli	CHN	9.1.81	6	NGP	Shanghai	18 Apr
4:16.78	Amy	Mortimer	USA	16.8.81	2	Big 12	Columbia MO	21 May

Mark	Name		Nat	Born	Pos	Meet	Venue	Date
4:17.33	Olga	Rosseyeva	RUS	1.8.81	8h2	NC	Tula	24 Jul
4:17.67	Carol	Henry	CAN	20.6.82	3		Montréal (McG)	7 Jul
4:17.76	Lauren	Fleshman	USA	26.9.81	5	NCAA	Durham	3 Jun
4:18.10		Chen Fang	CHN	28.10.81	1h2	WJ	Santiago de Chile	19 Oct
4:18.12	Kerstin	Werner	GER	18.9.82	1		Mannheim	12 Aug
4:18.21	Irina	Latve	LAT	26.8.81	1		Riga	12 Aug
4:18.7	Elvan	Can	TUR	9.11.82	2		Izmir	20 May
4:18.74	Liljana	Culibrk (20)	CRO	27.10.82	1		Rijeka	16 Sep

1 MILE

Mark	Name		Nat	Born	Pos	Meet	Venue	Date
4:31.62	Lyudmila	Vasilyeva	RUS	20.10.69	1		San Francisco	29 Oct
4:32.29	Courtney	Babcock	CAN	30.6.72	2		San Francisco	29 Oct

Mark	Name		Nat	Born	Date	Mark	Name		Nat	Born	Date
4:32.87	Cheri	Kenah	USA	26.12.70	29 Apr	4:34.40	Mary Jayne	Harrelson	USA	17.6.78	19 Aug
4:33.90	Mardrea	Hyman	JAM	22.12.72	29 Apr	4:34.49	Almitu	Colakoglu	TUR	17.9.77	24 Jun
4:34.14	Amy	Rudolph	USA	18.9.73	29 Apr	4:35.25	Simona	Ionescu	ROM	24.8.73	28 May
4:34.40	Ebru	Kavaklioglu	TUR	14.3.70	24 Jun	4:35.31	Stephanie	Best	USA	16.10.69	29 Apr

Indoors

Mark	Name		Nat	Born	Pos	Meet	Venue	Date
4:21.79	Regina	Jacobs	USA	28.8.63	1		New York	8 Jan
4:23.90	Gabriela	Szabo	ROM	14.11.75	1	Spark	Stuttgart	6 Feb
4:24.04		Jacobs			1	Mill	New York	4 Feb
4:24.44	Lidia	Chojecka	POL	25.1.77	2	Spark	Stuttgart	6 Feb
4:25.54	Olga	Yegorova	RUS	28.3.72	3	Spark	Stuttgart	6 Feb
4:25.73	Kutre	Dulecha	ETH	22.8.78	4	Spark	Stuttgart	6 Feb
4:26.50	Hayley	Tullett	GBR	17.2.73	5	Spark	Stuttgart	6 Feb
4:28.90	Nouriah	Mérah-Benida	ALG	19.10.70	6	Spark	Stuttgart	6 Feb
4:30.41	Sinead	Delahunty	IRL	12.2.71	2		New York	8 Jan
4:32.02	Olga	Komyagina	RUS	10.2.74	7	Spark	Stuttgart	6 Feb

Mark	Name		Nat	Born	Date	Mark	Name		Nat	Born	Date
4:33.28	Collette	Liss	USA	29.4.73	4 Mar	4:35.17	Hareg	Sidelil	ETH-J	20.4.81	31 Jan

2000 METRES

Mark	Name		Nat	Born	Pos	Meet	Venue	Date
5:38.09mx	Amy	Rudolph	USA	18.9.73	1		Sydney	14 Sep
5:39.39	Fatima	Yvelain	FRA	31.12.69	1		Nancy	3 Sep
5:40.4+	Gabriela	Szabo	ROM	14.11.75	1	in 3k	Zürich	11 Aug
5:41.4+		Dong Yanmei	CHN	16.2.77	1	in 3k	Saint-Denis	23 Jun
5:43.5+	Lydia	Cheromei	KEN	11.5.77	1	in 3k	Monaco	18 Aug
5:43.79	Yamna	Belkacem	FRA	20.2.74	2		Nancy	3 Sep
5:43.32+	Paula	Radcliffe	GBR	17.12.73	1	in 3k	Gateshead	28 Aug
5:43.6+	Tegla	Loroupe	KEN	9.5.71	2	in 3k	Monaco	18 Aug
5:43.6+	Sonia	O'Sullivan	IRL	28.11.69	2	in 3k	Gateshead	28 Aug
5:43.8+		Lan Lixin	CHN	14.2.79	3	in 3k	Athína	28 Jun
5:43.8+	Asmae	Laghzaoui	MAR	30.8.76	3	in 3k	Monaco	18 Aug
5:43.8e+	Sally	Barsosio	KEN	21.3.78	3	in 3k	Gateshead	28 Aug
5:44.0+	Fernanda	Ribeiro	POR	23.6.69	4	in 3k	Monaco	18 Aug
5:44.0e+	Libbie	Hickman	USA	17.2.65	4	in 3k	Gateshead	28 Aug
5:44.4e+	Jo	Pavey	GBR	20.9.73	5	in 3k	Gateshead	28 Aug
5:44.2+	Rose	Cheruiyot	KEN	21.7.76	5	in 3k	Monaco	18 Aug
5:44.5+		Yin Lili	CHN	11.11.79	5	in3k	Athína	28 Jun
5:44.7+	Tatyana	Tomashova	RUS	1.7.75	6	in 3k	Athína	28 Jun

Indoors

Mark	Name		Nat	Born	Pos	Meet	Venue	Date
5:38.76	Gabriela	Szabo	ROM	14.11.75	1		Liévin	13 Feb
5:39.30	Olga	Yegorova	RUS	28.3.72	2		Liévin	13 Feb
5:39.36	Violeta	Szekely	ROM	26.3.65	3		Liévin	13 Feb

Mark	Name		Nat	Born	Date	Mark	Name		Nat	Born	Date
5:46.67	Nouria	Mérah-Benida	ALG	19.10.70	13 Feb	5:48.67	Ebru	Kavakliogluo	TUR	14.3.70	13 Feb

3000 METRES

Mark	Name		Nat	Born	Pos	Meet	Venue	Date
8:26.35	Gabriela	Szabo	ROM	14.11.75	1	WK	Zürich	11 Aug
8:27.58	Sonia	O'Sullivan	IRL	28.11.69	2	WK	Zürich	11 Aug
8:28.80	Marta	Domínguez	ESP	3.11.75	3	WK	Zürich	11 Aug
8:28.85	Paula	Radcliffe	GBR	17.12.73	4	WK	Zürich	11 Aug
8:29.14	Lydia	Cheromei	KEN	11.5.77	5	WK	Zürich	11 Aug
8:30.39	Irina	Mikitenko	GER	23.8.72	6	WK	Zürich	11 Aug
8:30.80		Cheromei			1	Herc	Monaco	18 Aug
8:30.95	Tegla	Loroupe	KEN	9.5.73	2	Herc	Monaco	18 Aug
8:33.00		O'Sullivan			1	GP II	Gateshead	28 Aug
8:33.07		Dong Yanmei	CHN	16.2.77	1	GP	Athína	28 Jun
8:33.12		Loroupe			7	WK	Zürich	11 Aug
8:33.35	Lidia	Chojecka	POL	25.1.77	1	Gaz	Saint-Denis	23 Jun
8:33.53		Cheromei			2	GP	Athína	28 Jun
8:33.85	Asmae	Laghzaoui	MAR	30.8.76	3	Herc	Monaco	18 Aug

Mark	Name		Nat	Born	Pos	Meet	Venue	Date
8:34.53	Tatyana	Tomashova	RUS	1.7.75	3	GP	Athína	28 Jun
8:34.99	Fernanda	Ribeiro	POR	23.6.69	4	Herc	Monaco	18 Aug
8:35.02	Libbie	Hickman	USA	17.2.65	2	GP II	Gateshead	28 Aug
8:36.11		Radcliffe			3	GP II	Gateshead	28 Aug
8:36.25		Dong Yanmei			2	Gaz	Saint-Denis	23 Jun
8:36.37		Tomashova			1	Nik	Nice	8 Jul
8:36.70	Jo	Pavey	GBR	20.9.73	4	GP II	Gateshead	28 Aug
8:36.92	Gete	Wami	ETH	11.12.74	2	Nik	Nice	8 Jul
8:36.96		O'Sullivan			3	Gaz	Saint-Denis	23 Jun
8:37.55		Cheromei			4	Gaz	Saint-Denis	23 Jun
8:37.58		Wami			1		Milano	7 Jun
8:37.65		Loroupe			3	Nik	Nice	8 Jul
8:39.06	Yimenashu	Taye	ETH	1.1.79	8	WK	Zürich	11 Aug
8:39.22		Wami			1		Kerkrade	3 Jun
8:39.67		Lan Lixin	CHN	14.2.79	4	GP	Athína	28 Jun
8:39.86	Amy	Rudolph	USA	18.9.73	9	WK	Zürich	11 Aug
8:39.88	Rose	Cheruiyot	KEN	21.7.76	5	Herc	Monaco	18 Aug
	(31/19)							
8:40.15	Sally	Barsosio	KEN	21.3.78	10	WK	Zürich	11 Aug
8:41.05		Yin Lili	CHN	11.11.79	5	Gaz	Saint-Denis	23 Jun
8:41.23	Leah	Malot	KEN	7.6.72	6	Herc	Monaco	18 Aug
8:41.54	Yamna	Belkacem	FRA	20.2.74	7	Herc	Monaco	18 Aug
8:41.96	Zhor	El Kamch	MAR	15.3.73	3		Milano	7 Jun
8:42.55	Regina	Jacobs	USA	28.8.63	1		Portland	25 Jun
8:42.59	Deena	Drossin	USA	14.2.73	11	WK	Zürich	11 Aug
8:43.45	Galina	Bogomolova	RUS	15.10.77	2	ECp-S	Gateshead	15 Jul
8:43.53	Fatima	Yvelain	FRA	31.12.69	8	Herc	Monaco	18 Aug
8:43.55	Naomi	Mugo	KEN	2.1.77	4		Milano	7 Jun
8:43.74	Getenesh	Urge	ETH	30.8.70	5		Milano	7 Jun
	(30)							
8:44.14	Worknesh	Kidane	ETH-J	21.11.81	6		Milano	7 Jun
8:44.28	Ayelech	Worku	ETH	12.6.79	7		Milano	7 Jun
8:44.81	Alesya	Turova	BLR	6.12.79	8		Milano	7 Jun
8:45.26	Daniela	Yordanova	BUL	8.3.76	2	ECp1B	Bydgoszcz	8 Jul
8:45.39	Hayley	Tullett	GBR	17.2.73	3	ECp-S	Gateshead	15 Jul
8:46.16	Suzy	Favor Hamilton	USA	8.8.68	1		Madison	6 May
8:46.32	Derartu	Tulu	ETH	21.3.72	2		Portland	25 Jun
8:46.65	Berhane	Adere	ETH	21.7.73	2	Gugl	Linz	8 Aug
8:46.92	Jelena	Prokopcuka	LAT	21.9.76	3	Gugl	Linz	8 Aug
8:47.04	Susanne	Pumper	AUT	1.9.70	4	Gugl	Linz	8 Aug
	(40)							
8:47.18	Zahra	Ouaziz	MAR	20.12.69	7	Gaz	Saint-Denis	23 Jun
8:49.31	Veerle	Dejaeghere	BEL	1.8.73	5	GPII	Helsinki	15 Jun
8:50.71	Helena	Javornik	SLO	26.3.66	3	ECp1B	Bydgoszcz	8 Jul
8:50.72	Jennifer	Rhines	USA	1.7.74	6	Gugl	Linz	8 Aug
8:51.2	Yelena	Zadorozhnaya	RUS	3.12.77	1		Rovereto	30 Aug
8:51.97	Laurence	Duquénoy	FRA	29.9.69	10	Gaz	Saint-Denis	23 Jun
8:52.60	Roberta	Brunet	ITA	20.5.65	10	Herc	Monaco	18 Aug
8:52.82	Lornah	Kiplagat	KEN	20.3.74	1		Leiden	10 Jun
8:53.53	Adriana	Fernández	MEX	4.4.71	6		Portland	25 Jun
8:53.58mx	Natalie	Harvey	AUS	19.1.75	1		Cardiff	5 Jul
	9:05.06				10		Athína	28 Jun
	(50)							
8:53.76	Olga	Yegorova	RUS	28.3.72	10	Nik	Nice	8 Jul
8:54.03	Merima	Denboba	ETH	21.8.74	7	Gugl	Linz	8 Aug
8:54.82	Kara	Wheeler	USA	9.7.78	1		Palo Alto	5 May
8:56.42	Kerryn	McCann	AUS	2.5.67	1		Hobart	30 Jan
8:57.08	Susie	Power	AUS	26.3.75	2		Hobart	30 Jan
8:57.21	Anne	Cross	AUS	16.4.65	3		Hobart	30 Jan
8:57.75mx	Sarah	Young-Wilkinson	GBR	3.1.70	1		Stretford	27 Jun
8:57.84	Erika	van de Bilt	NED	7.4.71	2		Leiden	10 Jun
8:58.19	Olga	Komyagina	RUS	10.2.74	9		Milano	7 Jun
8:58.38+	Zoya	Kaznovskaya	UKR	22.9.66	1		Villeneuve d'Ascq	17 Jun
	(60)							
8:58.43mx	Kate	Richardson	AUS	5.11.73	1		Brisbane	21 Jul
8:58.49	Anja	Smolders	BEL	2.6.73	2	ECp-2A	Kaunas	9 Jul
8:58.99	Tatyana	Belovol	UKR	7.10.69	3	Odlozil	Praha	5 Jun
8:59.22	Jaqueline	Martín	ESP	14.4.74	12	Nik	Nice	8 Jul
8:59.28	Tezeta	Sürekli	TUR	8.4.80	2		Beograd	29 Aug

Mark	Name		Nat	Born	Pos	Meet	Venue	Date
8:59.4	Mari	Ozaki	JPN	16.7.75	1		Kyoto	3 Dec
8:59.90	Meseret	Defar	ETH-J	.83	5		Kerkrade	3 Jun
9:00.12	Klara	Kashapova	RUS	29.1.70				27 Aug
9:00.32	Gunhild	Haugen	NOR	1.6.72				8 Jul
9:00.73	Merima	Hashim	ETH-J	.81				8 Aug
9:00.86	Genet	Gebregiorgis	ETH	5.1.77				5 Jun
9:01.20	Nouriah	Mérah-Benida	ALG	19.10.70				3 Jun
9:01.22	Rose	Wanjiru	KEN-J	11.9.81				3 Aug
9:01.33	Naoko	Sakata	JPN-J	1.5.82				3 Aug
9:01.47	Ruth	Kutol	KEN	16.5.73				7 Jun
9:01.7mx	Georgie	Clarke	AUS-J	17.6.84				27 May
9:01.9	Marina	Dubrova	UKR	9.12.78				17 Jun
9:01.99	Sonja	Stolic	YUG	21.4.80				29 Aug
9:02.02	Andrea	Suldesová	CZE	11.2.75				8 Jul
9:02.03	Kylie	Risk	AUS	28.11.73				30 Jan
9:02.08	Clair	Fearnley	AUS	7.3.75				30 Jan
9:02.13	Olivera	Jevtic	YUG	24.7.77				9 Jul
9:02.19	Benita	Willis	AUS	6.5.79				8 Sep
9:02.30	Silvia	Sommaggio	ITA	20.11.69				7 Jun
9:02.35mx	Maria	McCambridge	IRL	10.7.75				5 Jul
9:02.62	Lidiya	Vasilevskaya	RUS	1.4.73				11 Jul
9:02.67	Beatriz	Santiago	ESP	28.10.68				8 Jul
9:02.67mx	Amanda	Parkinson	GBR	21.1.71				22 Aug
9:02.7	Agata	Balsamo	ITA	11.11.70				10 Jun
9:02.78mx	Sarah	Jamieson	AUS	24.3.75				30 Mar
9:02.88mx	Hayley	Yelling	GBR	3.1.74				5 Jul
9:03.19	Irene	Kwambai	KEN	25.10.78				7 Jun
9:03.20	Luminita	Zaituc	GER	9.10.68				15 Jul
9:03.59	Sabine	Fischer	SUI	29.06.73				5 Jun
9:04.03	Kristina	da Fonseca-Wollheim	GER	10.2.72				7 Jun
9:04.14	Mónica	Rosa	POR	5.5.78				8 Jul
9:04.16	Elena	Fidatov	ROM	24.7.60				7 Jun
9:05.50	Emi	Ikeda	JPN-J	29.8.83				3 Aug
9:05.70	Ikuko	Tamura	JPN	24.9.78				9 Apr
9:05.86mx	Angela	Newport	GBR	21.10.70				25 Jul
	9:08.46	(100)						28 Aug
9:06.08	Molly	Watcke	USA	10.4.71				1 Jul
9:06.23	Clare	Taylor	USA	7.12.69				8 Apr
9:06.27	Ana	Dias	POR	15.1.74				6 Aug
9:06.28	María	Protópappa	GRE	5.5.73				28 Jun
9:06.54	Blake	Russell	USA	24.7.75				20 May
9:07.06	Bouchra	Chaabi	MAR	19.5.79				17 Jun
9:07.09	Justyna	Bak	POL	1.8.74				2 Sep
9:07.15	René	Kalmer	RSA	3.11.80				3 Jun
9:07.25	Lyubov	Kremlyova	RUS	21.12.61				4 Jun
9:07.91	Viktoriya	Nenasheva	RUS	28.6.70				10 Jun

Indoors

Mark	Name		Nat	Born	Pos	Meet	Venue	Date
8:35.42		Szabo			1		Birmingham	20 Feb
8:44.66	Jelena	Prokopcuka	LAT	21.9.76	4	EI	Gent	27 Feb
8:49.18	Olga	Yegorova	RUS	28.3.72	6	EI	Gent	27 Feb
8:50.68		Wang Chunmei	CHN	10.4.76	1r2		Beijing	22 Feb
8:50.71		Li Ji	CHN	19.9.79	2r2		Beijing	22 Feb
8:51.40	Lyubov	Kremlyova	RUS	21.12.61	1	NC	Volgograd	6 Feb
8:52.74	Carla	Sacramento	POR	10.12.71	2		Birmingham	20 Feb
8:53.92		Song Liqing	CHN	20.1.80	1r4	NGP	Beijing	22 Feb
8:54.46	Zoya	Kaznovskaya	UKR	22.9.66	3		Birmingham	20 Feb
8:54.53	Olga	Churbanova	RUS	16.7.65	2	NC	Volgograd	6 Feb
8:56.13	Ebru	Kavaklioglu	TUR	14.3.70	4		Birmingham	20 Feb
8:56.27#	Marla	Runyan	USA	4.1.69	1		Moscow	18 Feb
8:58.47#	Collette	Liss	USA	29.4.73	1		South Bend	5 Feb
8:59.18	Silvia	Sommaggio	ITA	20.11.69	1	NC	Genova	13 Feb
9:01.66	Cheri	Kenah	USA	26.12.70				4 Mar
9:01.79	Aysen	Barak	TUR	9.9.75				20 Feb
9:03.75	Cristina	Petite	ESP	10.5.72				25 Feb
9:04.01	Ana	Dias	POR	15.1.74				23 Jan
9:04.50	Donna	Garcia	USA	26.3.68				4 Mar
9:05.92	Jana	Franke	GER	12.6.72				2 Feb
9:06.19		Dai Yanyan	CHN	8.1.80				22 Feb
9:06.23	Debbie	Grant	USA	5.8.65				4 Mar
9:06.47	Luminita	Gogîrlea	ROM	5.11.71				25 Feb
9:06.48		Wei Li	CHN	29.6.72				22 Feb
9:07.00		Chen Junwei	CHN-J	12.6.82				22 Feb
9:07.01	Inês	Monteiro	POR	18.5.80				13 Feb

JUNIORS

Mark	Name		Nat	Born	Pos	Meet	Venue	Date
8:44.14	Worknesh	Kidane	ETH	21.11.81	6		Milano	7 Jun
	8:46.48 12 WK Zürich 11 Aug				8:50.94	3	Kerkrade	3 Jun
8:59.90	Meseret	Defar	ETH	.83	5		Kerkrade	3 Jun
9:00.73	Merima	Hashim	ETH	.81	8	Gugl	Linz	8 Aug
9:01.22	Rose	Wanjiru	KEN	11.9.81	1		Gifu	3 Aug
9:01.33	Naoko	Sakata	JPN	1.5.82	2		Gifu	3 Aug
9:01.7 mx	Georgie	Clarke	AUS	17.6.84	1		Melbourne	27 May
9:05.50	Emi	Ikeda	JPN	29.8.83	3		Gifu	3 Aug
9:07.00i		Chen Junwei	CHN	12.6.82	4r2	NGP	Beijing	22 Feb
9:08.24i		Wang Xiaoming	CHN	3.2.85	3r5	NGP	Beijing	22 Feb
9:08.55i		Wei Yanan (10)	CHN	6.12.81	5r2	NGP	Beijing	22 Feb
9:08.7	Elvan	Can (Abeye)	TUR	11.9.82	1		Izmir	21 May
9:08.80	Beatrice	Chepchumba	KEN	25.11.83	1	WJ	Santiago de Chile	22 Oct
9:08.97i	Jessica	Augusto	POR	8.11.81	1		Braga	16 Dec
9:10.05	Jane	Chepkoech	KEN	8.8.82	2	WJ	Santiago de Chile	22 Oct
9:11.55	Etalemahu	Kidane	ETH	.83	3	WJ	Santiago de Chile	22 Oct
9:12.53		Chen Fang	CHN	28.10.81	4	WJ	Santiago de Chile	22 Oct
9:13.17	Eyerusalem	Kuma	ETH	14.11.81	10		Portland	25 Jun
9:13.56	Rina	Fujioka	JPN	18.10.82	2		Osaka	18 Jun
9:13.74	Amy	Mortimer	USA	16.8.81	2r2	MSR	Walnut	18 Apr
9:13.88	Tomomi	Tagao (20)	JPN	29.6.83	4		Gifu	3 Aug

Uncertain times:

KEN NC-j, Nairobi 22 Sep: 1. Jane Chepkoech 8:45.0A; 2. Beatrice Chepchumba 8:46.0
3. Salome Chepchumba 8:51.5, 4. Chelagat Kibiwott 8:53.0, 5. Elizabeth Rumokol 9:00.0
6. Emma Onchiri 9:03.0, 7. Caroline Kigen 9:13.4

5000 METRES

Mark	Name		Nat	Born	Pos	Meet	Venue	Date
14:30.88	Gete	Wami	ETH	11.12.74	1	NA	Heusden	5 Aug
14:39.83	Leah	Malot	KEN	7.6.72	1	ISTAF	Berlin	1 Sep
14:40.61	Gabriela	Szabo	ROM	14.11.75	2	ISTAF	Berlin	1 Sep
14:40.79		Szabo			1	OG	Sydney	25 Sep
14:41.02	Sonia	O'Sullivan	IRL	28.11.69	2	OG	Sydney	25 Sep
14:41.23	Ayelech	Worku	ETH	12.6.79	1	BrGP	London (CP)	5 Aug
14:42.23		Wami			3	OG	Sydney	25 Sep
14:42.67		Worku			4	OG	Sydney	25 Sep
14:42.91	Olga	Yegorova	RUS	28.3.72	1	DNG	Stockholm	1 Aug
14:43.59	Irina	Mikitenko	GER	23.8.72	5	OG	Sydney	25 Sep
14:44.34		Wami			2	DNG	Stockholm	1 Aug
14:44.36	Paula	Radcliffe	GBR	17.12.73	2	BrGP	London (CP)	5 Aug
14:44.57	Derartu	Tulu	ETH	21.3.72	3	DNG	Stockholm	1 Aug
14:45.35	Regina	Jacobs (10)	USA	28.8.63	1	NC	Sacramento	21 Jul
14:45.50		Worku			4	DNG	Stockholm	1 Aug
14:45.95	Tegla	Loroupe	KEN	9.5.73	3	BrGP	London (CP)	5 Aug
14:46.70		Loroupe			3	ISTAF	Berlin	1 Sep
14:47.35	Lydia	Cheromei	KEN	11.5.77	6	OG	Sydney	25 Sep
14:47.40	Worknesh	Kidane	ETH-J	21.11.81	7	OG	Sydney	25 Sep
14:47.71	Jelena	Prokopcuka	LAT	21.9.76	5	DNG	Stockholm	1 Aug
14:47.79	Yamna	Belkacem	FRA	20.2.74	6	DNG	Stockholm	1 Aug
14:48.04		Loroupe			7	DNG	Stockholm	1 Aug
14:48.09		Cheromei			8	DNG	Stockholm	1 Aug
14:48.31	Asmae	Laghzaoui	MAR	30.8.76	4	ISTAF	Berlin	1 Sep
14:50.31		Yegorova			8	OG	Sydney	25 Sep
14:50.75		Cheromei			4	BrGP	London (CP)	5 Aug
14:51.62	Deena	Drossin	USA	14.2.73	9	DNG	Stockholm	1 Aug
14:52.61	Berhane	Adere	ETH	21.7.73	10	DNG	Stockholm	1 Aug
14:53.00	Tatyana	Tomashova	RUS	1.7.75	1	ECp-S	Gateshead	16 Jul
14:53.61	Sally	Barsosio	KEN	21.3.78	5	ISTAF	Berlin	1 Sep
	(30/20)							
14:55.88	Rose	Cheruiyot	KEN	21.7.76	11	DNG	Stockholm	1 Aug
14:56.95	Daniela	Yordanova	BUL	8.3.76	10	OG	Sydney	25 Sep
14:57.48	Elana	Meyer	RSA	10.10.66	6	BrGP	London (CP)	5 Aug
14:58.27	Jo	Pavey	GBR	20.9.73	12	OG	Sydney	25 Sep
15:01.49	Fernanda	Ribeiro	POR	23.6.69	1	NC	Coimbra	13 Aug
15:03.99		Dong Yanmei	CHN	16.2.77	1	OT	Jinzhou	7 Jun
15:06.30		Yin Lili	CHN	11.11.79	2	OT	Jinzhou	7 Jun
15:06.48	Suzy	Favor Hamilton	USA	8.8.68	1		Long Beach	18 Mar
15:07.66	Marla	Runyan	USA	4.1.69	1		Eugene	13 May
15:08.36	Meseret	Defar	ETH-J	.83	2	NA	Heusden	5 Aug
	(30)							
15:08.61	Galina	Bogomolova	RUS	15.10.77	3	NC	Tula	22 Jul
15:08.69	Kerryn	McCann	AUS	2.5.67	1		Brisbane	8 Sep
15:08.82	Yemenashu	Taye	ETH	1.1.79	3	NA	Heusden	5 Aug
15:09.19	Elva	Dryer	USA	26.9.71	2		Eugene	13 May
15:10.50	Cheri	Kenah	USA	26.12.70	3		Eugene	13 May
15:11.11	Vivian	Cheruiyot	KEN-J	9.11.83	5h3	OG	Sydney	22 Sep
15:11.16	Amy	Rudolph	USA	18.9.73	15	DNG	Stockholm	1 Aug
15:11.25	Olivera	Jevtic	YUG	24.7.77	6h3	OG	Sydney	22 Sep
15:12.06	Teresa	Recio	ESP	7.7.63	4	NA	Heusden	5 Aug
15:12.23	Zhor	El Kamch	MAR	15.3.73	2	GPII	Sevilla	9 Jun
	(40)							
15:12.83	Breeda	Dennehy-Willis	IRL	2.3.70	5	NA	Heusden	5 Aug
15:13.07	Fatima	Yvelain	FRA	31.12.69	5		Villeneuve d'Ascq	17 Jun
15:14.26	Clair	Fearnley	AUS	7.3.75	2		Sydney	13 Feb
15:14.42	Merima	Hashim	ETH-J	.81	3	GPII	Sevilla	9 Jun
15:15.17	Merima	Denboba	ETH	21.8.74	4	GPII	Sevilla	9 Jun
15:15.35	Gunhild	Haugen	NOR	1.6.72	7	ISTAF	Berlin	1 Sep
15:15.64	Nora	Rocha	MEX	18.12.67	1r2	MSR	Walnut	14 Apr
15:15.94	Roberta	Brunet	ITA	20.5.65	1		Viareggio	22 Aug
15:16.32	Susanne	Pumper	AUT	1.9.70	15	DNG	Stockholm	1 Aug
15:16.45	Adriana	Fernández	MEX	4.4.71	1		Montreal	7 Jul
	(50)							
15:17.14	Beatriz	Santiago	ESP	28.10.68	6	NA	Heusden	5 Aug
15:17.57	Rosemary	Ryan	IRL	8.11.75	7	NA	Heusden	5 Aug
15:18.04mx	Anja	Smolders	BEL	2.6.73	1		Uden	1 Jul
	15:20.23				9	NA	Heusden	5 Aug

Mark	Name		Nat	Born	Pos	Meet	Venue	Date
15:18.09	Klara	Kashapova	RUS	29.1.70	4	NC	Tula	22 Jul
15:18.62		Song Liqing	CHN	20.1.80	3	OT	Jinzhou	7 Jun
15:18.78	Maria	McCambridge	IRL	10.7.75	8	NA	Heusden	5 Aug
15:18.80	Maura	Viceconte	ITA	3.10.67	4	ECp-S	Gateshead	16 Jul
15:18.82	Kate	Richardson	AUS	5.11.73	7		Villeneuve d'Ascq	17 Jun
15:19.65	Lidiya	Grigoryeva	RUS	21.1.74	2	Super	Yokohama	9 Sep
15:19.88	Jennifer	Rhines	USA	1.7.74	17	DNG	Stockholm	1 Aug
	(60)							
15:20.36	Harumi	Hiroyama	JPN	2.9.68	2	GP	Osaka	13 May
15:20.59	Elena	Fidatov	ROM	24.7.60	1	NC	Bucuresti	7 Aug
15:20.78	Anne	Cross	AUS	16.4.65	1		Melbourne	5 Feb
15:21.04	Michiko	Shimizu	JPN	22.9.70	3	GP	Osaka	13 May
15:21.37	Blake	Russell	USA	24.7.75	1r2	PennR	Philadelphia	28 Apr
15:21.37	Benita	Willis	AUS	6.5.79	6h1	OG	Sydney	22 Sep
15:21.55	Libbie	Hickman	USA	17.2.65	10	ISTAF	Berlin	1 Sep
15:22.44	Gete	Urge	ETH	30.8.70	8		Villeneuve d'Ascq	17 Jun
15:22.98	Lyudmila	Biktasheva	RUS	25.7.74	4	Super	Yokohama	9 Sep
15:23.27	Erika	van de Bilt	NED	7.4.71	10	NA	Heusden	5 Aug
	(70)							
15:23.41	Yoshiko	Ichikawa	JPN	18.4.76	7h3	OG	Sydney	22 Sep
15:23.59	Yuko	Kawakami	JPN	1.8.75	4	GP	Osaka	13 May
15:23.70	Yoshiko	Fujinaga	JPN-J	15.8.81	5	GP	Osaka	13 May
15:23.71	Anne Marie	Lauck	USA	7.3.69	5	NC	Sacramento	21 Jul
15:23.84	Alesya	Turova	BLR	6.12.79	2		Formia	3 Jun
15:23.9	Agata	Balsamo	ITA	11.11.70	1		Palermo	22 Apr
15:24.31	Laurence	Duquénoy	FRA	29.9.69	9		Villeneuve d'Ascq	17 Jun
15:24.9	Ikuko	Tamura	JPN	24.9.78	1		Kyoto	3 Dec
15:25.13	Naomi	Mugo	KEN	2.1.77	1		Adelaide	8 Mar
15:25.16	Hristosomiá	Iakóvou	GRE	9.4.71	4		Viareggio	22 Aug
	(80)							
15:26.00	Marta	Domínguez	ESP	3.11.75	1	NC	Barcelona	2 Sep
15:26.19	Joyce	Chepchumba	KEN	6.11.70	11	ISTAF	Berlin	1 Sep
15:26.36	Megumi	Tanaka	JPN	4.9.75	6	GP	Osaka	13 May
15:26.69	Una	English	IRL	14.8.70	2	NC	Dublin (S)	20 Aug
15:27.07	Susie	Power	AUS	26.3.75	2		Adelaide	8 Mar
15:27.46	Esther	Wanjiru	KEN	27.3.77	8	GP	Osaka	13 May
15:27.46	Dulce	Rodríguez	MEX	14.8.72	2		Montréal (McG)	7 Jul
15:27.58	Hiromi	Ominami	JPN	15.11.75	1		Dublin (S)	29 Jul
15:27.68	Helena	Javornik	SLO	26.3.66	11		Villeneuve d'Ascq	17 Jun
15:27.74	Ana	Dias	POR	15.1.74	2		Braga	21 Jun
	(90)							
15:27.82	Jacqueline	Martín	ESP	14.4.74	3		Barcelona	25 Jul
15:27.84	Catherine	Ndereba	KEN	21.7.72	9	GP	Osaka	13 May
15:27.88	Ruth	Kutol	KEN	16.5.73	5		Formia	3 Jun
15:28.41	Mari	Ozaki	JPN	16.7.75	2	NC	Rifu	7 Oct
15:28.66	Inga	Juodeskiene	LTU	21.10.71	11	NA	Heusden	5 Aug
15:28.78	Kara	Wheeler	USA	9.7.78	2r2	MSR	Walnut	14 Apr
15:28.91	Constantina	Dita	ROM	23.1.70	2	NC	Bucuresti	7 Aug
15:28.99	Naomi	Sakashita	JPN	25.5.75	2rA		Nobeoka	27 May
15:29.32	Chiemi	Takahashi	JPN	16.2.76	7	Super	Yokohama	9 Sep
15:29.36		Dai Yanyan	CHN	8.1.80	2	NGP	Nanjing	14 Apr
	(100)							
15:29.70	Kayoko	Fukushi	JPN-J	25.3.82	3	NC	Rifu	7 Oct

15:30.00	Tina	Connelly	CAN	16.8.70	7	Jul
15:30.40	Luminita	Talpos	ROM	9.10.72	15	Oct
15:30.43	Alina	Tecuta-Gherasim	ROM	10.11.71	7	Aug
15:30.44	Clare	Taylor	USA	7.12.69	21	Jul
15:30.55	Kylie	Risk	AUS	28.11.73	13	Feb
15:30.79	Natalie	Harvey	AUS	19.1.75	11	Jul
15:31.05		Lan Lixin	CHN	14.2.79	18	Apr
15:31.49	Shayne	Culpepper	USA	3.12.73	21	Jul
15:32.04	Ikumi	Nagayama	JPN	22.6.74	11	Jun
15:32.47	Kumiko	Takemoto	JPN	25.11.78	3	May
15:32.50	Nicole	Jefferson	USA	8.3.76	13	May
15:32.62	Andrea	Whitcombe	GBR	8.6.71	25	Jun
15:32.66	Cristina	Petite	ESP	10.5.72	5	Aug
15:32.91	Amaia	Piedra	ESP	2.6.72	5	Aug
15:32.94	Akiko	Kawashima	JPN	5.8.77	15	Oct
15:33.40	Noriko	Matsuoka	JPN	2.5.79	27	May
15:34.33	Sarah	Dillabaugh	CAN	4.12.73	7	Jul
15:34.47	Sonja	Stolic	YUG	21.4.80	20	May
15:34.84	Mónica	Rosa	POR	5.5.78	13	Aug
15:34.91	Courtney	Babcock	CAN	30.6.72	11	Aug
15:35.22	Wilma	van Onna	NED	13.6.65	5	Jul
15:35.25	Kazue	Ogoshi	JPN-J	2.3.81	7	Jul
15:35.28	Kristin	Ihle	USA	12.4.69	21	Jul
15:35.48	Silviya	Skvortsova	RUS	16.11.74	22	Jul
15:35.51	Analídia	Torre	POR	10.10.76	13	Aug
15:35.71		Song Dan	CHN		7	Jun
15:35.79	Yoko	Shibui	JPN	14.3.79	14	May
15:35.89	Debbie	Buhlers	CAN	1.1.73	7	Jul
15:36.27	Hayley	Yelling	GBR	3.1.74	16	Jul
15:36.35	Birhan	Dagne	GBR	8.4.78	5	Aug
15:36.57	Haruko	Okamoto	JPN	19.8.74	11	Jun
15:36.91	Luisa	Larraga	ESP	10.12.70	2	Sep
15:37.08	Reiko	Tosa	JPN	11.6.76	27	May
15:37.32	Tomoko	Isobe	JPN	3.9.74	11	Jun
15:37.32	Tatyana	Belovol	UKR	7.10.69	16	Jul
15:37.76	Olga	Romanova	RUS	23.5.80	22	Jul

Mark		Name	Nat	Born	Date
15:37.83	Yasuko	Hashimoto	JPN	12.8.75	11 Jun
15:37.92	Molly	Watcke	USA	10.4.71	3 Jun
15:37.99	Annette	Peters	USA	31.5.65	21 Jul
15:38.27	Yukiko	Okamoto	JPN	29.11.74	27 May
15:38.28		Zhou Chunxiu	CHN	8.3.79	7 Jun
15:38.31	Kaori	Kumasaka	JPN	23.6.80	11 Jun
15:38.35		Zhang Yang	CHN-J	20.7.83	7 Jun
15:38.66mx	Susan	Michelsson	AUS	29.2.72	17 Jun
15:38.93	Eyerusalem	Kuma	ETH-J	14.11.81	3 Jun
15:38.93	Leila	Aman	ETH	.76	23 Nov
15:39.19	Michelle	King	CAN	7.10.69	11 Aug
15:39.28		Li Helan	CHN	2.1.78	7 Jun
15:39.36	Michiyo	Ando	JPN	12.12.72	3 May
15:39.83		Zheng Guixia	CHN	24.6.73	20 Oct
15:39.97	Viktoriya	Nenasheva	RUS	26.6.70	17 Jun
15:40.07	Yuko	Manabe	JPN	8.2.79	21 May
15:40.12	Sarah	Dupré	CAN	29.3.76	11 Aug
15:40.13	María	Abel	ESP	23.10.74	2 Sep
15:40.24	Hayley	McGregor	AUS	27.5.79	19 Aug
15:40.24		Wang Hongxia	CHN	13.1.75	15 Oct
15:40.43	Samukeliso	Moyo	ZIM	1.1.74	8 Mar
15:40.54	Tatyana	Khmeleva	RUS	2.4.79	17 Jun
15:40.7A	Sharon	Cherop	KEN-J	16.3.84	22 Sep
15:40.75		Hu Xiuying	CHN	1.10.78	7 Jun
15:40.75	Kazumi	Matsuo	JPN	18.4.74	15 Oct
15:40.85	Sarah	Young-Wilkinson	GBR	2.1.70	11 Jul
15:41.18	Justyna	Bak	POL	1.8.74	18 Jun
15:41.43	Annemari	Sandell	FIN	2.1.77	9 Jul
15:41.48	Kristin	Beaney	USA	30.6.72	17 Jul
15:41.51	Silvia	Sommaggio	ITA	20.11.69	28 May
15:41.60	Mami	Kusunoki	JPN	8.9.75	3 May
15:41.79mx	Mandy	Giblin	AUS	27.6.74	21 Jul
15:42.06	Noriko	Takahashi	JPN	9.11.76	15 Oct
15:42.08	Mizuki	Noguchi	JPN	3.7.78	9 Apr
15:42.15	Yuliya	Vinokurova	RUS	.72	22 Jul
15:42.19	América	Mateos	MEX	20.12.71	20 May
15:42.2A	Fridah	Domongole (Ywalareng)	KEN-J	15.1.84	22 Sep
15:42.22	Kathy	Butler	GBR	22.10.73	14 Apr
15:42.36	Svetlana	Baygulova	RUS	13.7.75	22 Jul
15:42.36	Kyoko	Katafuchi	JPN	12.3.80	30 Sep
15:42.49	Yumiko	Suzuki	JPN	19.9.75	15 Oct
15:42.50	Makiko	Kawashima	JPN	5.8.77	9 Apr
15:42.64	Valerie	Vaughan	IRL	1.11.66	25 Jun
15:42.77	Anália	Rosa	POR	28.2.76	21 Jun
15:43.01		Wu Qingdong	CHN	11.11.79	14 Apr
15:43.18	Carlien	Cornelissen	RSA	28.4.72	18 Feb
15:43.76	Fumiko	Tsutsumi	JPN	13.5.72	3 May
15:43.89	Lidiya	Vasilevskaya	RUS	1.4.73	12 Jul
15:44.07	Margarita	Tapia	MEX	16.11.76	20 May
15:44.22		Zhang Yuhong	CHN-J	15.2.81	20 Oct
15:44.30		Cui Guomei	CHN	2.7.79	18 Apr
15:44.65	Yelena	Burykina	RUS	.72	22 Jul
15:44.7	Yukiko	Akaba	JPN	18.10.79	17 Dec
15:44.95	Blandine	Bitzner	FRA	1.12.65	5 Aug
15:44.96	Helena	Sampaio	POR	9.10.73	9 Jun
15:44.97	Robyn	Meagher	CAN	17.6.67	25 Mar
15:45.22	Rachel	Sauder	USA	16.3.74	5 May
15:45.74	Alessandra	Aguilar	ESP	1.7.78	2 Sep
15:45.79	Masayo	Kobayashi	JPN	4.2.80	15 Oct
15:46.39	Dorota	Gruca	POL	5.12.70	18 Jun
15:46.40	Rie	Matsuoka	JPN	9.3.77	18 Oct
15:46.44	Kate	Fonshell	USA	10.10.69	17 Jul
15:46.94		Tong Dejing	CHN	4.9.80	20 Oct
15:46.89	Amy (201)	Yoder	USA	11.1.78	10 Mar

JUNIORS

See main list for top 5 juniors. Additional marks and further juniors:

Kidane	14:59.31	3	Villeneuve d'Ascq	17 Jun	15:16.998	BrGp	London (CP)	5 Aug
	15:08.62	2h3	OG Sydney	22 Sep				
V Cheruiyot	15:16.10	5h3	Viareggio	23 Aug				
Fujinaga	15:24.64	6	Super Yokohama	9 Sep	10 performances by five women under 15:25.0			

15:29.70	Kayoko	Fukushi	JPN	25.3.82	3	NC	Rifu	7 Oct
15:35.25	Kazue	Ogoshi	JPN	2.3.81	5		Montréal (McG)	7 Jul
15:38.35		Zhang Yang	CHN	20.7.83	7	OT	Jinzhou	7 Jun
15:38.93	Eyerusalem	Kuma	ETH	14.11.81	2		Dedham	3 Jun
15:40.7A	Sharon	Cherop (10)	KEN	16.3.84	1		Nairobi	22 Sep
15:42.2A	Fridah	Domongole	KEN	15.1.84	2		Nairobi	22 Sep
15:44.22		Zhang Yuhong	CHN	15.2.81	3	NC	Luohe	20 Oct
15:48.71		Wang Xiaoming	CHN	3.2.85	8	NGP	Shanghai	18 Apr
15:49.7A	Sally	Chepyego	KEN	.82	3	NC-j	Nairobi	22 Sep
15:50.18	Lauren	Fleshman	USA	26.9.81	8r2	MSR	Walnut	14 Apr
15:51.52	Tereza	Yohannes	ETH	.82	6		Braga	21 Jun
15:53.01	Miyuki	Hikita	JPN	1.3.81	8r1		Tottori	11 Jun
15:53.6	Tomoko	Chakushi	JPN	12.8.81	2		Kyoto	3 Dec
15:54.59	Megumi	Hirayama	JPN	25.11.81	9		Toyama	18 Oct
15:54.8	Haruko	Yamamoto (20)	JPN	31.10.81	4r2		Tokyo	14 Sep

10,000 METRES

30:17.49	Derartu	Tulu	ETH	21.3.72	1	OG	Sydney	30 Sep
30:22.48	Gete	Wami	ETH	11.12.74	2	OG	Sydney	30 Sep
30:22.88	Fernanda	Ribeiro	POR	23.6.69	3	OG	Sydney	30 Sep
30:26.97	Paula	Radcliffe	GBR	17.12.73	4	OG	Sydney	30 Sep
30:37.26	Tegla	Loroupe	KEN	9.5.73	5	OG	Sydney	30 Sep
30:51.30	Berhane	Adere	ETH	21.7.73	1	NA	Heusden	5 Aug
30:53.37	Sonia	O'Sullivan	IRL	28.11.69	6	OG	Sydney	30 Sep
30:56.4		Tulu			1		Gijón	12 Aug
30:57.70	Leah	Malot	KEN	7.6.72	2	NA	Heusden	5 Aug
30:59.92	Merima	Hashim	ETH-J	.81	3	NA	Heusden	5 Aug
31:03.60	Marleen	Renders (10)	BEL	24.12.68	4	NA	Heusden	5 Aug
31:05.57	Maura	Viceconte	ITA	3.10.67	5	NA	Heusden	5 Aug
31:06.94		Li Ji	CHN	19.9.79	7	OG	Sydney	30 Sep
31:08.27		Tulu			1		Brunswick	1 Jul
31:09.46	Yuko	Kawakami	JPN	1.8.75	2		Brunswick	1 Jul
31:10.12	Adriana	Fernández	MEX	4.4.71	3		Brunswick	1 Jul
31:14.70	Elana	Meyer	RSA	10.10.66	8	OG	Sydney	30 Sep

Mark	Name		Nat	Born	Pos	Meet	Venue	Date
31:21.27	Lidiya	Grigoryeva	RUS	21.1.74	9	OG	Sydney	30 Sep
31:24.12	Silvia	Sommaggio	ITA	20.11.69	6	NA	Heusden	5 Aug
31:24.36		Ribeiro			1		Baracaldo	9 Jul
31:27.44		Kawakami			10	OG	Sydney	30 Sep
31:27.86	Jelena	Prokopcuka	LAT	21.9.76	1rB	EChall	Lisboa (I)	1 Apr
31:29.65	Olivera	Jevtic	YUG	24.7.77	11	OG	Sydney	30 Sep
31:29.66	Galina	Bogomolova (20)	RUS	15.10.77	1	NC	Tula	26 Jul
31:30.83		Grigoryeva			2	NC	Tula	26 Jul
31:33.58	Lyudmila	Biktasheva	RUS	25.7.74	3	NC	Tula	26 Jul
31:36.4		Loroupe			1		Strasbourg	27 Jun
31:40.14	Irina	Timofeyeva	RUS	5.4.70	4	NC	Tula	26 Jul
31:40.52		Adere			12	OG	Sydney	30 Sep
31:41.1		Meyer			1		Watford	22 Jul
	(30/22)							
31:43.28	Merima	Denboba	ETH	21.8.74	7	NA	Heusden	5 Aug
31:43.29	Fatima	Yvelain	FRA	31.12.69	1rA	EChall	Lisboa (I)	1 Apr
31:44.3	Teresa	Recio	ESP	7.7.63	2	1 NC	Gijón	12 Aug
31:46.4	Griselda	González	ESP	4.12.65	3	2 NC	Gijón	12 Aug
31:47.89	Gunhild	Haugen	NOR	1.6.72	2rA	EChall	Lisboa (I)	1 Apr
31:48.60	Eyerusalem	Kuma	ETH-J	14.11.81	4		Brunswick	1 Jul
31:48.89	Yoko	Shibui	JPN	14.3.79	2	Hyogo	Kobe	23 Apr
31:50.22	Alice	Timbilil	KEN-J	16.6.83	14	OG	Sydney	30 Sep
	(30)							
31:50.53	Noriko	Matsuoka	JPN	2.5.79	3	Hyogo	Kobe	23 Apr
31:50.89	Hiromi	Ominami	JPN	15.11.75	1rA		Kottori	10 Jun
31:51.05	Deena	Drossin	USA	14.2.73	1	NC	Sacramento	14 Jul
31:52.2	Petra	Wassiluk	GER	27.10.69	2		Strasbourg	27 Jun
31:52.50	Rie	Matsuoka	JPN	9.3.77	3rA		Kottori	10 Jun
31:52.59	Chiemi	Takahashi	JPN	16.2.76	15	OG	Sydney	30 Sep
31:52.75	Lyudmila	Petrova	RUS	7.10.68	5	NC	Tula	26 Jul
31:54.46	Kumiko	Takemoto	JPN	25.11.78	4	Hyogo	Kobe	23 Apr
31:55.65	Clair	Fearnley	AUS	7.3.75	2	NC	Sydney	24 Feb
31:56.1	Rakiya	Quétier	FRA	12.9.67	3	1 NC	Strasbourg	27 Jun
	(40)							
31:56.49	Agata	Balsamo	ITA	11.11.70	2		Trento	31 May
31:56.94	Libbie	Hickman	USA	17.2.65	16	OG	Sydney	30 Sep
31:57.41	Sally	Barsosio	KEN	21.3.78	17	OG	Sydney	30 Sep
31:58.34	Jennifer	Rhines	USA	1.7.74	2	NC	Sacramento	14 Jul
31:58.76	Klara	Kashapova	RUS	29.1.70	6	NC	Tula	26 Jul
31:58.93	Yoshiko	Fujinaga	JPN-J	15.8.81	5	Hyogo	Kobe	23 Apr
31:58.95	Kazue	Ogoshi	JPN-J	2.3.81	5		Brunswick	1 Jul
31:59.21	Asmae	Laghzaoui	MAR	30.8.76	18	OG	Sydney	30 Sep
31:59.60	Harumi	Hiroyama	JPN	2.9.68	1		Mito	7 May
32:00.4	Margarete	Atodonyang	KEN	.78	4		Strasbourg	27 Jun
	(50)							
32:01.04	Naomi	Sakashita	JPN	25.5.75	5rA		Kottori	10 Jun
32:01.86	Anne Marie	Lauck	USA	7.3.69	4	NC	Sacramento	14 Jul
32:02.2	María	Abel	ESP	23.10.74	5	3 NC	Gijón	12 Aug
32:02.86	Lydia	Vasilevskaya	RUS	1.4.73	7	NC	Tula	26 Jul
32:03.00	Mari	Ozaki	JPN	16.7.75	6rA		Kottori	10 Jun
32:03.06	Annette	Peters	USA	31.5.65	1r2	MSR	Walnut	14 Apr
32:04.81	Ana	Dias	POR	15.1.74	1	Nordic	Sandefjord	3 Jun
32:05.23	Mizuki	Noguchi	JPN	3.7.78	7rA		Kottori	10 Jun
32:06.42	Yukiko	Okamoto	JPN	29.11.74	1	NC	Rifu	8 Oct
32:07.25	Eri	Yamaguchi	JPN	14.1.73	8rA		Kottori	10 Jun
	(60)							
32:07.42	Iulia	Olteanu (Negura)	ROM	26.1.67	4rA	EChall	Lisboa (I)	1 Apr
32:07.44	Natalie	Harvey	AUS	19.1.75	2		Sandefjørd	3 Jun
32:07.58	Yuko	Manabe	JPN	8.2.79	9rA		Kottori	10 Jun
32:08.67	Helena	Sampaio	POR	9.10.73	5rA	EChall	Lisboa (I)	1 Apr
32:08.82	Nora	Rocha	MEX	18.12.67	1	Jerome	Burnaby	3 Jun
32:09.25	Ikumi	Nagayama	JPN	22.6.74	2	NC	Rifu	8 Oct
32:09.53	Marina	Bastos	POR	7.7.71	6rA	EChall	Lisboa (I)	1 Apr
32:11.30	Breeda	Dennehy-Willis	IRL	2.3.70	8rA	EChall	Lisboa (I)	1 Apr
32:11.79	Carol	Montgomery	CAN	24.8.66	2r2	MSR	Walnut	14 Apr
32:12.56	Yasuko	Hashimoto	JPN	12.8.75	8		Kobe	23 Apr
	(70)							
32:12.6	Beatriz	Santiago	ESP	28.10.68	6	NC	Gijón	12 Aug
32:13.03	Megumi	Tanaka	JPN	4.9.75	10rA		Tottori	10 Jun

Mark	Name		Nat	Born	Pos	Meet	Venue	Date
32:14.18	Alina	Tecuta-Gherasim	ROM	10.11.71	1	NC	Bucuresti	6 Aug
32:15.63	Reiko	Tosa	JPN	11.6.76	9		Kobe	23 Apr
32:16.33	Blake	Russell	USA	24.7.75	3r2	MSR	Walnut	14 Apr
32:16.4	Anikó	Kálovics	HUN	13.5.77	5		Strasbourg	27 Jun
32:16.95	Kim	Fitchen	USA	3.9.68	4r2	MSR	Walnut	14 Apr
32:17.58	Catherine	Ndereba	KEN	21.7.72	3		Mito	7 May
32:17.7	Bouchra	Chaabi	MAR		1		Rabat	11 Jun
32:17.71	Sylvia	Mosqueda	USA	8.4.66	5r2	MSR	Walnut	14 Apr
	(80)							
32:21.27	Tina	Connelly	CAN	16.8.70	6r2	MSR	Walnut	14 Apr
32:21.31	Melanie	Kraus	GER	24.10.74	2	NC	Troisdorf	27 May
32:22.72	Kristin	Beaney	USA	30.6.72	8	NC	Sacramento	14 Jul
32:23.21		Dong Yanmei	CHN	16.2.77	2	NGPF	Jinzhou	8 Jun
32:23.45		Dai Yanyan	CHN	8.1.80	2	NGP	Nanjing	15 Apr
32:23.57		Song Liqing	CHN	20.1.80	4	NGP	Nanjing	15 Apr
32:24.06	Cheri	Kenah	USA	26.12.70	1		Raleigh	31 Mar
32:24.45		Cui Guomei	CHN	2.7.79	5	NGP	Nanjing	15 Apr
32:24.52	Miyuki	Nishimura	JPN	16.4.80	11		Kobe	23 Apr
32:25.21	Kylie	Risk	AUS	28.11.73	3	NC	Sydney	24 Feb
	(90)							
32:25.44	Sara	Ferrari	ITA	30.9.77	8	NA	Heusden	5 Aug
32:27.68	Alena	Peterková	CZE	13.11.60	1	NC	Plzen	15 Jul
32:28.16	Stine	Larsen	NOR	5.11.75	10rA	EChall	Lisboa (I)	1 Apr
32:30.14	Haruko	Okamoto	JPN	19.8.74	6	NC	Rifu	8 Oct
32:30.4	Birhan	Dagne	GBR	8.4.78	2		Watford	22 Jul
32:31.5	Dorota	Gruca	POL	5.12.70	6		Strasbourg	27 Jun
32:31.9	Rosemary	Ryan	IRL	8.11.75	3		Watford	22 Jul
32:31.91	Michaela	Möller	GER	19.10.73	3	NC	Troisdorf	27 May
32:32.06		Dong Zhaoxia	CHN	13.11.74	7	NC	Rifu	8 Oct
32:32.47	Silviya	Skvortsova	RUS	16.11.74	8	NC	Tula	26 Jul
	(100)							

32:32.68		Zheng Guixia	CHN	24.6.73	15	Apr
32:32.77	Yuri	Kano	JPN	27.10.78	8	Oct
32:33.62	Katie	McGregor	USA	2.9.77	25	Mar
32:34.51	Donna	Garcia	USA	26.3.68	14	Apr
32:34.60	Takako	Kotorida	JPN	2.4.77	10	Jun
32:34.7	Sarah	Young-Wilkinson	GBR	2.1.70	22	Jul
32:35.00	Maya	Nishio	JPN	19.12.78	10	Jun
32:39.66	Kazumi	Matsuo	JPN	18.4.74	13	May
32:40.12	Rie	Honkawa	JPN	30.11.78	10	Jun
32:40.21	Chantal	Dällenbach	FRA/SUI	24.10.62	1	Apr
32:41.01	Elizabeth	Miller	AUS	8.11.63	17	Aug
32:41.66	Hristosomiá	Iakóvou	GRE	9.4.71	5	Aug
32:42.27	Makiko	Kawashima	JPN	5.8.77	10	Jun
32:42.46	Fumiko	Tsutsumi	JPN	13.5.72	13	May
32:42.82	Yumiko	Suzuki	JPN	19.9.75	8	Oct
32:43.22	Rachel	Sauder	USA	16.3.74	14	Apr
32:43.63	Luisa	Larraga	ESP	10.12.70	8	Jul
32:44.14	Fumi	Murata	JPN	13.3.75	23	Apr
32:44.40	Helena	Javornik	SLO	26.3.66	1	Apr
32:44.47	Firiya	Sultanova/Zhdanova	RUS	29.4.61	26	Jul
32:44.70	Jenny	Crain	USA	12.2.68	14	Jul
32:44.79	Lisa	Harvey	CAN	7.2.70	3	Jun
32:44.82	Gete	Urge	ETH	30.8.70	1	Apr
32:44.84		Wang Xiaoming	CHN-J	3.2.85	8	Jun
32:45.36	Natalie	Nalepa	USA	30.12.68	14	Jul
32:45.59		Zhang Yuhong	CHN-J	15.2.81	8	Jun
32:46.75		Wei Yanan	CHN-J	6.12.81	8	Jun
32:47.31	Blandine	Bitzner	FRA	1.12.65	27	May
32:47.43	Leigh	Daniel	USA	6.8.78	25	Mar
32:47.58	Yoshiko	Ichikawa	JPN	18.4.76	8	Oct
32:48.27	Ayano	Kozuka	JPN	27.10.77	10	Jun
32:48.79	Anne	Cross	AUS	16.4.65	24	Feb
32:48.89	Alessandra	Aguilar	ESP	1.7.70	8	Jul
32:49.07		Lu Jing	CHN	24.12.76	8	Jun
32:50.0A	Alice	Chelagat	KEN		23	Jun
32:50.29	Erica	Palmer	USA	22.11.79	14	Jul
32:50.73	Constantina	Dita	ROM	23.1.70	1	Apr
32:50.92		Liu Min	CHN-J	29.11.83	8	Jun
32:51.46	Milkah	Chepkieny	KEN	12.8.76	3	Sep
32:51.65	Cristina	Pomacu	ROM	15.9.73	1	Apr
32:52.19	Natalya	Berkut	UKR	30.5.75	3	Aug
32:52.5	Hayley	Yelling	GBR	3.1.74	22	Jul
32:52.60	Tomoko	Tamamushi	JPN	26.8.77	10	Jun
32:54.31	Iris	Biba-Pöschl	GER	27.5.64	3	Sep
32:55.10	Isabel	Juárez	MEX	10.9.66	14	Apr
32:55.12	Krishna	Stanton	AUS	10.5.66	17	Aug
32:55.42	Rosaria	Console	ITA	17.12.79	17	Jun
32:56.19	Silvia	Weissteiner	ITA	13.7.79	1	Apr
32:56.6	Fatima	Hajjami-Ouammou	FRA	29.7.66	27	Jun
32:57.20	Nami	Kurosawa	JPN	26.12.78	8	Oct
32:57.3	Bente	Landøy	NOR	16.12.72	22	Jul
32:58.41	Yelena	Burykina	RUS	72	26	Jul
32:58.68	Susanne	Wigene	NOR	12.2.78	1	Apr
32:58.91	Asami	Obi	JPN	22.3.76	13	May
32:58.97	Justyna	Bak	POL	1.8.74	6	Aug
32:59.31	Megumi	Kobayashi	JPN	4.8.76	23	Apr
33:00.03	Marta	Fernández	ESP	19.8.71	1	Apr
33:00.24	Akiko	Shinagawa	JPN	16.5.77	13	May
33:01.04	Miho	Kakehata	JPN	20.5.73	23	Apr
33:01.42	Sabrina	Varrone	ITA	24.4.72	17	Jun
33:02.74		Ju Limei	CHN	9.6.78	8	Jun
33:03.12	Noriko	Geji	JPN	31.5.73	10	Jun
33:03.13	Irina	Safarova	RUS	19.6.69	26	Jul
33:04.32	Tomoe	Yokoyama	JPN	.76	13	May
33:04.4A	Hellen	Kimaiyo	KEN	8.9.68	21	Jul
33:04.44	Nesira	Azaïdj	ALG	29.10.71	5	Aug
33:04.46	Zivile	Balciunaite	LTU	3.4.79	3	Aug
33:04.54	Maggie	Chan Man-Yee	HKG	28.10.75	12	May
33:04.73	Tereza	Yohanes	ETH-J	.82	8	Jul
33:04.98	América	Mateos	MEX	20.12.71	3	Jun
33:05.20		Jin Li	CHN-J	29.5.83	8	Jun
33:05.39		Wang Yanrong	CHN	16.10.76	15	Oct
33:05.5	Anne	Keenan-Buckley	IRL	7.1.62	22	Jul
33:05.60	Ari	Ichihashi	JPN	22.11.77	7	May
33:06.6	Asuka	Kato	JPN	7.3.80	26	Dec
[illegible]	Amy	Yoder	USA	11.1.78	25	Mar
33:07.69	Viktoriya	Klimina	RUS	.76	26	Jul
33:07.9	Liz	Yelling	GBR	5.12.74	22	Jul
33:07.96		Ren Xiujuan	CHN	14.9.74	25	Mar
33:08.22	Julia	Vaquero	ESP	18.9.70	1	Apr
33:08.41	Michelle	Borgert	USA	8.9.72	12	May
33:08.62	Kerryn	McCann	AUS	2.5.67	24	Feb
33:08.69	Susanne	Pumper	AUT	1.9.70	13	May
33:08.75	Zahia	Dahmani	FRA	2.6.72	1	Apr
33:09.47	Tatyana	Khmeleva	RUS	2.4.79	26	Jul
33:09.75	Shinobu	Yasuda	JPN	30.11.77	10	Jun

Mark	Name		Nat	Born	Pos	Date
33:09.87	Mayumi	Kumagai	JPN	22.3.68	14	May
33:09.96	Kazumi	Urata	JPN	1.2.80	10	Jun
33:10.32	Satomi	Matsuo	JPN	1.12.77	13	May
33:10.89	Tara	Krzywicki	GBR	9.3.74	1	Apr
33:11.5	Megumi	Hirayama	JPN-J	25.11.81	26	Dec
33:11.82	Sarah	Christie	NZL	11.1.73	24	Feb
33:12.18	Restituta	Joseph	TAN	30.7.71	27	Sep
33:12.3A	Irene	Kwambai	KEN	25.10.78	11	Jul
33:12.54	Naoko	Tanaka	JPN	23.3.77	10	Jun
33:12.56	Ai	Yamamoto	JPN	6.7.78	10	Jun
33:12.97	Sabrina	Mockenhaupt	GER	6.12.80	2	Sep
33:13.14	Mamiko	Kudo	JPN	2.10.75	13	May
33:13.2	Hafida	Gadi	FRA	14.7.74	27	Jun
33:13.25	Asuka	Maeda	JPN	4.10.78	30	Apr

(200) and further 24 women under 33:30 (3 more under 33:15)

JUNIORS

See main list for top 5 juniors. 10 performances by 5 women under 32:35.0. Additional marks and further juniors

Hashim 31:54.6 4 Gijón 12 Aug

Timbilil 32:18.0A 2 NC Nairobi 21 Jul 32:34.15 2h2 OG Sydney 30 Sep

Ogoshi 31:59.41 4r2 Tottori 10 Jun 32:00.03 1 Kakogawa 20 May

Mark		Name	Nat	Born	Pos	Meet	Venue	Date
32:44.84		Wang Xiaoming	CHN	3.2.85	5	NGPF	Jinzhou	8 Jun
32:45.59		Zhang Yuhong	CHN	15.2.81	6	NGPF	Jinzhou	8 Jun
32:46.75		Wei Yanan	CHN	6.12.81	7	NGPF	Jinzhou	8 Jun
32:50.92		Liu Min	CHN	29.11.83	9	NGPF	Jinzhou	8 Jun
33:04.73	Tereza	Yohanes (10)	ETH	.82	6		Baracaldo	8 Jul
33:05.20		Jin Li	CHN	29.5.83	11	NGPF	Jinzhou	8 Jun
33:11.5	Megumi	Hirayama	JPN	25.11.81	2		Yokohama	26 Dec
33:29.52		Zhang Yang	CHN	20.7.83	15	NGPF	Jinzhou	8 Jun
33:38.56	Tomoko	Motohira	JPN	13.2.81	1		Yokohama	19 May
33:45.83	Kumi	Tanabe	JPN	2.4.81	1		Osaka	25 Jun
33:56.1	Tomoni	Kinuta	JPN	4.11.81	6		Yokohama	26 Dec
34:00.68	Yuka	Matsumoto	JPN	2.3.81	10		Kakogawa	20 May
34:02.90	Yumiko	Hara	JPN	9.1.82	4		Kobe	15 Oct
34:08.59	Masa	Yoshida	JPN	20.1.81	4		Amagasaki	29 Oct
34:18.83		Kim Ok-bin (20)	KOR	23.7.81	3		Pusan	13 Oct

20,000 METRES

Mark	Name	Nat	Born	Pos	Venue	Date
1:05:26.6 and 18,287m 1Hr	Tegla Loroupe	KEN	9.5.73	1	Borgholzhausen	3 Sep

5 KILOMETRES ROAD

Mark		Name	Nat	Born	Pos	Venue	Date
15:08	Deena	Drossin	USA	14.2.73	1	Carlsbad	26 Mar
15:15	Lornah	Kiplagat	KEN	20.3.74	1	Trier	31 Dec
15:16	Irina	Mikitenko	GER	23.8.72	2	Trier	31 Dec
15:18	Lydia	Cheromei	KEN	11.5.77	1	Bern	18 Jun
15:18	Leah	Malot	KEN	7.6.72	3	Trier	31 Dec
15:20	Nora	Rocha	MEX	18.12.67	2	Carlsbad	26 Mar
15:20	Restituta	Joseph	TAN	30.7.71	2	Kassel	14 May
15:21	Luminita	Zaituc	GER	9.10.68	3	Kassel	14 May
15:23	Eyerusalem	Kuma	ETH-J	14.11.81	3	Carlsbad	26 Mar
15:24	Marla	Runyan	USA	4.1.69	4	Carlsbad	26 Mar
15:25	Sally	Barsosio	KEN	21.3.78	5	Carlsbad	26 Mar

10 KILOMETRES ROAD

Mark		Name	Nat	Born	Pos	Meet	Venue	Date
30:52	Lornah	Kiplagat	KEN	20.3.74	1	Peach	Atlanta	4 Jul
30:59	Sonia	O'Sullivan	IRL	28.11.69	1		Milano	21 May
31:14		L Kiplagat			1		Tilburg	4 Jun
31:20	Tegla	Loroupe	KEN	9.5.73	2		Milano	21 May
31:28	Elana	Meyer	RSA	10.10.66	2		Tilburg	4 Jun
31:28		O'Sullivan			1		Dublin	11 Jun
31:29		L Kiplagat			1		Tolkamer	2 Apr
31:30		Loroupe			1		San Juan	27 Feb
31:37		Loroupe			1		New York	10 Jun
31:38	Colleen	de Reuck	RSA	13.4.64	1		Durban	25 Jun
31:38	Derartu	Tulu	ETH	21.3.72	2	Peach	Atlanta	4 Jul
31:39	Hellen	Kimaiyo	KEN	8.9.68	3	Peach	Atlanta	4 Jul
31:40		Tulu			3		Milano	21 May
	(13/7)							
31:41	Catherine	Ndereba	KEN	21.7.72	4	Peach	Atlanta	4 Jul
31:54	Sally	Barsosio	KEN	21.3.78	2		Charleston	1 Apr
32:00	Jane	Ngotho	KEN	29.11.69	2		New Orleans	22 Apr
32:05	Restituta	Joseph	TAN	30.7.77	3		Tilburg	4 Jun
32:06	Eyerusalem	Kuma	ETH-J	14.11.81	5	Peach	Atlanta	4 Jul

Others where superior to 10,000m track bests

Mark		Name	Nat	Born	Pos	Venue	Date
32:15	Magdaline	Chemjor	KEN	12.11.78	2	Tolkamer	2 Apr
32:15	Stine	Larsen	NOR	5.11.75	1	Oslo	30 Apr
32:18	Isabellah	Ochichi	KEN		1	Tulle	9 Sep

Mark		First name	Last name	Nat	Born	Pos	Meet	Venue	Date
32:20		Firiya	Sultanova/Zhdanova	RUS	29.4.61	3		Cleveland	30 Apr
32:22		Patricia	Arribas	ESP	2.10.77	1		Madrid	31 Dec
32:25		Susan	Chepkemei	KEN	25.6.75	1		Brunssum	9 Apr
32:25		Fatuma	Roba	ETH	18.12.73	3		New York	10 Jun
32:28		Natalie	Nalepa	USA	30.12.68	3		Cape Elizabeth	5 Aug
32:29		Sonja	Oberem	GER	24.2.73	1		Leverkusen	12 Mar
32:29		Ruth	Kutol	KEN	16.5.73	3		Porto	18 Jun
32:29	u	Petra	Drajzatlová	CZE	19.1.73	1		Rijsbergen	17 Jun
32:30		Christine	Chepkonga	KEN		1		Oelde	9 Sep

Mark		First name	Last name	Nat	Born	Date
32:32		Jane	Omoro	KEN	12.9.74	30 Apr
32:33		Joyce	Chepchumba	KEN	6.11.70	14 May
32:33		M Luisa	Larraga	ESP	10.12.70	31 Dec
32:36		Elva	Dryer	USA	26.9.71	27 Feb
32:36		Luminita	Zaituc	GER	9.10.68	3 Sep
32:37		Grace	Momanyi	KEN		1 Apr
32:39		Claudia	Dreher	GER	2.5.71	5 Aug
32:40		Svetlana	Zakharova	RUS	15.9.70	5 Aug
32:42		Olga	Markova	RUS	6.8.68	25 Mar
32:42		Jane Jebiwott Rotich		KEN		10 Jun
32:44		Emiko	Kojima	JPN	4.7.79	13 Feb
32:46		Pauline	Konga	KEN	10.4.70	16 Apr
32:48		Gladys	Asiba	KEN	31.5.77	8 Oct
32:49	u	Wilma	van Onna	NED	13.6.65	18 Jun
32:51		Hawa	Hussein	TAN-J	5.12.82	31 Dec
32:55		Fabiana Cristine da Silva		BRA	3.9.78	13 Mar
32:57	u	Nadezhda	Wijenberg	NED	2.4.64	17 Jun
32:58		Ikuko	Nishida	JPN	16.11.78	13 Feb
32:58		Abeba	Tolla	ETH	3.6.77	24 Jun
32:58		Kathrin	Wessel	GER	14.8.67	5 Aug
32:59		Leah	Pells	CAN	9.11.64	16 Apr
33:00		Miyuki	Hikita	JPN-J	1.3.81	13 Feb
33:02		Asuka	Maeda	JPN	4.10.78	13 Feb
33:02		Hannah	Njeri	KEN	28.11.68	1 May

Downhill

Sep 24, Pittsburgh: 2. Gladys Asiba KEN 32:08, 3. Jane Omoro KEN 32:12, 5. Naomi Wangui KEN 32:29, 6. Kristy Johnston UA 32:34, Lucy Njeri KEN 32:41, 9, Ejagayoua Diaba ETH 32:42, 10. Martha Komu KEN 32:46

15 KILOMETRES ROAD

Mark	First name	Last name	Nat	Born	Pos	Meet	Venue	Date
48:06	Berhane	Adere	ETH	21.7.73	1		Nijmegen	19 Nov
48:15	Susan	Chepkemei	KEN	25.6.75	2		Nijmegen	19 Nov
48:32	Gete	Wami	ETH	11.12.74	3		Nijmegen	19 Nov
48:47	Catherine	Ndereba	KEN	21.7.72	1		Utica	9 Jul
49:03	Leah	Malot	KEN	7.6.72	1		Saint-Denis	30 Apr
49:09	Magdaline	Chemjor	KEN	12.11.78	4		Nijmegen	19 Nov
49:17	Maura	Viceconte	ITA	3.10.67	2		Saint-Denis	30 Apr
49:18	Restituta	Joseph	TAN	30.7.71	5		Nijmegen	19 Nov
49:34		Joseph			3		Saint-Denis	30 Apr
49:35	Manuela	Machado	POR	9.8.63	1	ECCp	Moskva	7 May
49:35	Hellen (11/10)	Kimaiyo	KEN	8.9.68	2		Utica	9 Jul
49:40	Deena	Drossin	USA	14.2.73	1	NC	Jacksonville	4 Mar
49:41	Lyudmila	Biktasheva	RUS	25.7.74	2	ECCp	Moskva	7 May
49:43	Ruth	Kutol	KEN	16.5.73	1		Lisboa	16 Apr
49:44	Margaret	Okayo	KEN	30.5.76	4		Saint-Denis	30 Apr
49:45	Lyubov	Morgunova	RUS	14.1.71	3	ECCp	Moskva	7 May
49:47	Helena	Sampaio	POR	9.10.73	2		Lisboa	16 Apr
49:54	Marleen	Renders	BEL	24.12.68	5		Saint-Denis	30 Apr
49:54	Irina	Timofeyeva	RUS	5.4.70	4	ECCp	Moskva	7 May
50:06	Jennifer	Rhines	USA	1.7.74	2	NC	Jacksonville	4 Mar
50:10	Isabellah	Ochichi	KEN		6		Saint-Denis	30 Apr
50:15	Simona	Staicu	HUN	5.5.71	6		Nijmegen	19 Nov
50:22	Irina	Suvorova	RUS	3.3.71	1		Tulsa	28 Oct
50:24	Mihaela	Botezan	ROM	21.2.76	7		Saint-Denis	30 Apr
50:24	Zinaida	Semyonova	RUS	19.3.62	5	ECCp	Moskva	7 May
50:33	Lydia	Cheromei	KEN	11.5.77	1		São Paulo	31 Dec
50:42	Annette	Peters	USA	31.5.65	3	NC	Jacksonville	4 Mar
50:44	Lidiya	Grigoryeva	RUS	21.1.74	2		Tulsa	28 Oct

10 MILES ROAD

Mark	First name	Last name	Nat	Born	Pos	Meet	Venue	Date
53:01	Catherine	Ndereba	KEN	21.7.72	1		Flint	26 Aug
53:07	Milkah	Chepkieny	KEN	12.8.76	1		Schortens	19 Aug
53:15	Petra	Wassiluk	GER	27.10.69	2		Schortens	19 Aug
53:18	Hellen	Kimaiyo	KEN	8.9.68	2		Flint	26 Aug
53:25	Marleen	Renders	BEL	24.12.68	3		Flint	26 Aug
53:50	Salome	Chepchumba	KEN	29.9.82	1		Bruges	5 Mar
53:52	Lyudmila	Petrova	RUS	7.10.68	4		Flint	26 Aug
54:06	Jane	Omoro	KEN	12.9.74	5		Flint	26 Aug
54:11	Nadezhda	Wijenberg	NED	2.4.64	1		Heerlen	3 Sep
54:15	Leah	Malot	KEN	7.6.72	1		Bern	13 May
54:27	Judith	Kiplimo	KEN	.68	3		Schortens	19 Aug
54:28	Svetlana	Zakharova	RUS	15.9.70	6		Flint	26 Aug

20 KILOMETRES ROAD

Mark		Name		Nat	Born	Pos	Meet	Venue	Date
64:01		Esther	Wanjiru	KEN	27.3.77	1		Kobe	17 Dec
65:16		Joyce	Chepchumba	KEN	6.11.70	1		Alphen aan den Rijn	12 Mar
65:28	u	Hellen	Kimutai	KEN	28.12.77	1		Paris	22 Oct
66:06		Stine	Larsen	NOR	5.11.75	2		Alphen aan den Rijn	12 Mar
66:12			Zheng Guixia	CHN	24.6.73	2		Kobe	17 Dec
66:15	u	Mihaela	Botezan	ROM	21.2.76	2		Paris	22 Oct
66:15		Miyuki	Nishimura	JPN	16.4.80	3		Kobe	17 Dec
66:25		Kazue	Ogoshi	JPN-J	2.3.81	4		Kobe	17 Dec
67:08	u	Margaret	Kerubo	KEN		3		Paris	22 Oct
67:12		Nadezhda	Wijenberg	NED	2.4.64	3		Alphen aan den Rijn	12 Mar
67:49		Simona	Staicu	ROM/HUN	5.5.71	4		Alphen aan den Rijn	12 Mar
68:08			Cui Guomei	CHN	2.7.79	5		Kobe	17 Dec
68:09		Isabellah	Ochichi	KEN		1		Le Mans	1 Jun

Mark	Name		Nat	Born	Date
68:37	Takako	Yamada	JPN	16.12.72	17 Dec
68:38	Lyudmila	Petrova	RUS	7.10.68	4 Sep
68:47	Rosa	Oliveira	POR	28.7.66	16 Jan
68:48	Eri	Kurotaki	JPN		17 Dec
68:54	Abeba	Tolla	ETH	3.6.77	12 Mar
69:02	Claudia	Dreher	GER	2.5.71	12 Mar
69:04	Jane	Ekimat	KEN	12.6.74	16 Jan
69:08	Colleen	de Reuck	RSA/USA	13.4.64	4 Sep
69:11	Mineko	Yamanouchi	JPN	10.12.72	15 Oct
69:15	Petra	Drajzajtlová	CZE	19.1.73	12 Mar

HALF MARATHON

Note - Lisboa course is slightly downhill

Mark		Name		Nat	Born	Pos	Meet	Venue	Date
66:56		Lornah	Kiplagat	KEN	20.3.74	1	City-Pier	Den Haag	25 Mar
67:07		Paula	Radcliffe	GBR	17.12.73	1	GNR	South Shields	22 Oct
67:24		Tegla	Loroupe	KEN	9.5.73	1		Lisboa	26 Mar
67:33		Elana	Meyer	RSA	10.10.66	1		Tokyo	10 Jan
67:37			Kiplagat			1		Zaandam	17 Sep
67:41		Esther	Wanjiru	KEN	27.3.77	2		Tokyo	10 Jan
67:48		Kerryn	McCann	AUS	2.5.67	3		Tokyo	10 Jan
67:59	w	Restituta	Joseph	TAN	30.7.71	1		Malmö	12 Jun
68:04		Derartu	Tulu	ETH	21.3.72	2		Lisboa	26 Mar
68:18	w	Joyce	Chepchumba	KEN	6.11.70	2		Malmö	12 Jun
68:22			Chepchumba			1		Berlin	2 Apr
68:23		Fernanda	Ribeiro (10)	POR	23.6.69	3		Lisboa	26 Mar
68:34		Lidia	Simon	ROM	4.9.73	4		Tokyo	10 Jan
68:45	w	Lyubov	Morgunova	RUS	14.1.71	3		Malmö	12 Jun
68:47			Joseph			1		Nice	16 Apr
68:48	w	Abeba	Tolla	ETH	3.6.77	4		Malmö	12 Jun
68:52			Chepchumba			1		Glasgow	22 Aug
68:55		Naoko	Takahashi	JPN	6.5.72	1		Chiba	23 Jan
69:00	w	Maria	Guida	ITA	23.1.66	5		Malmö	12 Jun
69:02		Catherine	Ndereba	KEN	21.7.72	1		Como	26 Mar
69:03		Margaret	Okayo	KEN	30.5.76	1		Udine	1 Oct
69:04		Yoshiko	Ichikawa	JPN	18.4.76	5		Tokyo	10 Jan
69:04			Meyer			1		Sendai	12 Mar
69:07			Radcliffe			1	WCh	Veracruz	12 Nov
69.09			Tulu			1		Lisboa	22 Oct
69:10			N Takahashi			1		Sapporo	2 Jul
69:10		Susan	Chepkemei	KEN	25.6.75	2		Lisboa	22 Oct
69:11			Wanjiru			2		Sendai	12 Mar
69:12		Yukiko	Okamoto	JPN	29.11.74	1		Yamaguchi	12 Mar
69.13			Chepchumba			1		Altötting	3 Sep
69:19			Chepchumba			3		Lisboa	22 Oct
		(31/20)							
69:24		Ruth	Kutol	KEN	16.5.73	2		Udine	1 Oct
69:25			Zheng Guixia	CHN	24.6.73	2		Yamaguchi	12 Mar
69:26		Fumi	Murata	JPN	13.3.75	3		Yamaguchi	12 Mar
69:26		Lyudmila	Petrova	RUS	7.10.68	4		Lisboa	22 Oct
69:28		Berhane	Adere	ETH	21.7.73	4		Lisboa	26 Mar
69:28		Stine	Larsen	NOR	5.11.75	1		Göteborg	13 May
69:31		Yoko	Shibui	JPN	14.3.79	1		Matsue	19 Mar
69:35		Marleen	Renders	BEL	24.12.68	6		Lisboa	26 Mar
69:39		Mami	Kusunoki	JPN	8.9.75	4		Yamaguchi	12 Mar
69:40		Hiromi	Ominami	JPN	15.11.75	1		Miyazaki	6 Jan
		(30)							
69:40		Ikumi	Nagayama	JPN	22.6.74	5		Yamaguchi	12 Mar
69:44		Mizuki	Noguchi	JPN	3.7.78	1		Okayama	3 Dec
69:46		Junko	Kumagai	JPN	31.12.74	6		Yamaguchi	12 Mar

Mark		Name		Nat	Born	Pos	Meet	Venue	Date
69:46	w	Elfenesh	Alemu	ETH	10.6.75	6		Malmö	12 Jun
69:46		Leah	Malot	KEN	7.6.72	2		Zaandam	17 Sep
69:48		Maya	Nishio	JPN	19.12.78	7		Yamaguchi	12 Mar
69:48		Hellen	Kimaiyo	KEN	8.9.68	3		Zaandam	17 Sep
69:50		Tomoko	Tamamushi	JPN	26.8.77	8		Yamaguchi	12 Mar
69:53		Naoko	Tanaka	JPN	23.3.77	9		Yamaguchi	12 Mar
69:55		Esther	Kiplagat	KEN	8.12.66	8		Lisboa	26 Mar
		(40)							
69:57		Rie	Ueno	JPN	11.6.76	1		Marugame	6 Feb
69:58		Annemari	Sandell	FIN	2.1.77	9		Lisboa	26 Mar
69:59		Hellen	Kimutai	KEN	28.12.77	1		Torino	17 Sep
70:01			Cui Guomei	CHN	2.7.79	10		Yamaguchi	12 Mar
70:04		Asami	Obi	JPN	22.3.76	11		Yamaguchi	12 Mar
70:05		Gladys	Asiba	KEN	31.5.77	2		Philadelphia	17 Sep
70:07		Mihaela	Botezan	ROM	21.2.76	1	NC	Buzau	30 Sep
70:11		Simona	Staicu	HUN	5.5.71	1		Den Haag	25 Mar
70:15		Isabellah	Ochichi	KEN		2		Nice	16 Apr
70:15		Helena	Sampaio	POR	9.10.73	1	ESP Ch	Zamora	27 Aug
		(50)							
70:16		Fatuma	Roba	ETH	18.12.73	1		Kyoto	12 Mar
70:16		Alice	Chelagat	KEN		3		Philadelphia	17 Sep
70:18		Jane	Ekimat	KEN	12.6.74	2		Como	26 Mar
70:21		Takami	Ominami	JPN	15.11.75	2		Miyazaki	6 Jan
70:23		Lidiya	Vasilevskaya	RUS	1.4.73	1		Zelenograd	30 Jul
70:25		Masako	Chiba	JPN	18.7.76	3		Miyazaki	6 Jan
70:29		Takako	Kotorida	JPN	2.4.77	12		Yamaguchi	12 Mar
70:33		Hisae	Yoshimatsu	JPN	13.5.79	6		Tokyo	10 Jan
70:36		Rie	Matsuoka	JPN	9.3.77	13		Yamaguchi	12 Mar
70:38		Yuko	Manabe	JPN	8.2.79	4		Miyazaki	6 Jan
		(60)							
70:39		Jackline	Jerotich	KEN	23.9.70	3		Udine	1 Oct
70:40		Hannah	Njeri	KEN	28.11.68	1		Paris	12 Mar
70:42		Yuko	Takakura	JPN	1.6.78	14		Yamaguchi	12 Mar
70:44		Cristina	Pomacu	ROM	15.9.73	1		San Diego	13 Aug
70:48		Maura	Viceconte	ITA	3.10.67	1	NC	Bologna	16 Apr
70:49		Harumi	Hiroyama	JPN	2.9.68	5		Miyazaki	6 Jan
70:55		Nuta	Olaru	ROM	28.8.70	2	NC	Buzau	30 Sep
70:56		Naomi	Sakashita	JPN	25.5.75	2		Matsue	19 Mar
71:01		Libbie	Hickman	USA	17.2.65	1		Parkersburg	19 Aug
71:03		Pamela	Chepchumba	KEN	28.2.78	2		Göteborg	13 May
		(70)							
71:03		Florence	Barsosio	KEN	11.8.76	5		Lisboa	22 Oct
71:05		Asuka	Maeda	JPN	4.10.78	15		Yamaguchi	12 Mar
71:06		Yukako	Goto	JPN	16.9.73	16		Yamaguchi	12 Mar
71:09		Irina	Timofeyeva	RUS	5.4.70	1		Nizhniy Novgorod	23 Apr
71:12	u	Wilma	van Onna	NED	13.6.65	1		Haarlem	24 Sep
71:16		Kazue	Ogoshi	JPN-J	2.3.81	2		Marugame	6 Feb
71:20		Sylvia	Mosqueda	USA	8.4.66	2		Parkersburg	19 Aug
71:22		Galina	Aleksandrova	RUS	15.10.76	2		Nizhniy Novgorod	23 Apr
71:22		Margaret	Kerubo	KEN	15.5.74	1		Le Canet	10 Jun
71:22		Ari	Ichihashi	JPN	22.11.77	2		Nagoya	23 Nov
		(80)							
71:25		Noriko	Geji	JPN	31.5.73	6		Sapporo	2 Jul
71:28		Alina	Tecuta-Gherasim	ROM	10.11.71	3		Paris	12 Mar
71:28		Margarete	Atodonyang	KEN	.78	1		Pietramurata	14 May
71:29		Aiko	Nitta	JPN	18.11.75	17		Yamaguchi	12 Mar
71:32		Luminita	Talpos	ROM	9.10.72	7		Tokyo	10 Jan
71:33		Akiko	Shinagawa	JPN	16.5.77	18		Yamaguchi	12 Mar
71:35		Irina	Safarova	RUS	19.6.69	3		Nizhniy Novgorod	23 Apr
71:35		Constantina	Dita-Tomescu	ROM	23.1.70	4	NC	Buzau	30 Sep
71:39		Nadezhda	Wijenberg	NED	2.4.64	3		Den Haag	25 Mar
71:40		Griselda	González	ESP	4.12.65	2	NC	Zamora	27 Aug
		(90)							
71:41		Irene	Kwambai	KEN	25.10.78	1		Vitry-sur-Seine	26 Mar
71:42		Lucilla	Andreucci	ITA	19.12.69	4		Udine	1 Oct
71:42		Kei	Satomura	JPN	31.1.79	3		Nagoya	23 Nov
71:44		Tomoko	Isobe	JPN	3.9.74	19		Yamaguchi	12 Mar
71:44		Katrin	Dörre-Heinig	GER	6.10.61	1	NC	Freiburg	25 Mar
71:44		Garifa	Kuku	KAZ	30.11.59	1		Almaty	12 Aug
71:44		Kaori	Tanabe	JPN	30.4.75	4		Nagoya	23 Nov

Mark	Name		Nat	Born	Pos	Meet	Venue	Date
71:45	Eri	Yamaguchi	JPN	14.1.73	3		Marugame	6 Feb
71:46	Colleen	de Reuck	RSA/USA	13.4.64	1		Hampton	5 Feb
71:46	Ornella (100)	Ferrara	ITA	17.4.68	1		Torino	27 Feb
71:46	Sakiko	Kato	JPN	8.5.79	20		Yamaguchi	12 Mar

Mark	Name		Nat	Born	Pos	Date
71:48	Gitte	Karlshøj	DEN	14.5.59	12	Jun
71:49	Magdeline	Chemjor	KEN	12.11.78	22	Oct
71:53	Isabela	Zatorska	POL	6.10.62	3	Dec
71:54	Erika	Olivera	CHI	14.1.76	10	Sep
71:56	Caroline	Kwambai	KEN	9.9.75	15	Oct
72:01	Hiromi	Katayama	JPN	15.12.74	6	Jan
72:01	Yasuko	Hashimoto	JPN	12.8.75	10	Jan
72:01	Judy	Kiplimo	KEN	.68	15	Oct
72:04		Wei Yanan	CHN-J	6.12.81	12	Mar
72:04	Gete	Urge	ETH	30.8.70	26	Mar
72:05	Rocío	Ríos	ESP	13.3.69	27	Aug
72:06	Yoko	Manabe	JPN	8.2.79	6	Feb
72:06	Erika	Csomor	HUN	8.11.73	16	Apr
72:07A	Martha	Tenorio	ECU	6.8.66	6	Aug
72:10	Fatima	Yvelain	FRA	31.12.69	16	Apr
72:11	Irina	Suvorova	RUS	3.3.71	17	Sep
72:14	Ayano	Kozuka	JPN	27.10.77	12	Mar
72:17	Kazumi	Matsuo	JPN	18.4.74	10	Jan
72:17	Judit	Földing-Nagy	HUN	9.12.65	3	Sep
72:18	Takami	Nishiyama	JPN	17.10.80	27	Feb
72:20	Yasuko	Nishida	JPN	16.11.78	6	Jan
72:21	Namie	Yamamoto	JPN	18.2.80	12	Mar
72:23	Masami	Deto	JPN	29.7.77	27	Feb
72:23	Lidiya	Grigoryeva	RUS	21.1.74	6	May
72:24	Klara	Kashapova	RUS	29.1.70	12	Mar
72:26	Milkah	Chepkieny	KEN	12.8.76	16	Sep
72:27	Kinuyo	Yoshida	JPN	21.2.75	12	Mar
72:27	Sonja	Oberem	GER	24.2.73	25	Mar
72:27	Marina	Bastos	POR	7.7.71	7	May
72:28	Shinobu	Yasuda	JPN	30.11.77	2	Jul
72:29	Franziska	Moser-Rochat	SUI	17.8.66	26	Mar
72:29	Manuela	Machado	POR	9.8.63	20	Aug
72:31	Maria Conceição	Ferreira	POR	13.3.62	23	Jan
72:31	Liz	Yelling	GBR	5.12.74	22	Oct
72:32	Rita	Jeptoo	KEN-J	15.2.81	19	Mar
72:33	Dorota	Gruca	POL	5.12.70	25	Mar
72:34	Rosaria	Console	ITA	17.12.79	16	Apr
72:34	Chantal	Dällenbach	SUI/FRA	24.10.62	2	Sep
72:34	Tomoko	Motohira	JPN-J	13.2.81	3	Dec
72:35	Marie	Söderström-Lundberg	SWE	21.10.60	13	May
72:36	Hafida	Gadi	FRA	14.7.74	22	Oct
72:37	Anne Mette	Jensen	DEN	11.4.72	2	Apr
72:37	Rie	Honkawa	JPN	30.11.78	25	Jun
72:38	Yukie	Murafuji	JPN		19	Mar
72:39	Nicole	Carroll	AUS	14.1.72	27	Aug
72:40	Tatyana	Pozdnyakova	UKR	4.3.56	30	Jan
72:40	Shoko	Kawashima	JPN	12.10.72	19	Mar
72:40	Gloria	Marconi	ITA	31.3.68	8	Oct
72:42	Galina	Zhulyeva	UKR	5.3.66	24	Sep
72:43	Kayoko	Obata	JPN	18.9.71	6	Jan
72:43	Noriko	Matsuoka	JPN	2.5.79	12	Mar
72:43	Ester	Barmasai	KEN	.72	15	Oct
72:44	Rie	Matsushima	JPN	19.2.75	12	Mar
72:44	Maria Luisa	Muñoz	ESP	6.5.59	27	Aug
72:45	Tiziana	Alagia	ITA	8.3.73	1	Oct
72:46	Kim	Pawelek	USA	20.1.74	30	Jan
72:47	Mineko	Yamanouchi	JPN	10.12.72	10	Jan
72:47	Marta	Fernández de Castro	ESP	19.8.71	27	Aug
72:48	Christine	Mallo	FRA	26.2.66	26	Mar
72:51	Nami	Kurosawa	JPN	26.12.78	6	Feb
72:51	Luminita	Gogîrlea	ROM	5.11.71	16	Apr
72:52	Yuko	Arimori	JPN	17.12.66	17	Sep
72:53	Mary	Ptikany	KEN	.78	5	Nov
72:54	Kyoko	Katafuchi	JPN	12.3.80	6	Jan
72:54	Megumi	Kobayashi	JPN	4.8.76	23	Nov
72:56	Silvana	Trampuz	AUS	15.9.66	19	Mar
72:58	Svetlana	Zakharova	RUS	15.9.70	13	Aug
72:59	Silviya (169)	Skvortsova	RUS	16.11.74	23	Apr

Short course

Mark	Name		Nat	Born	Pos	Date
72:36	Olivera	Jevtic	YUG	24.7.77	22	Apr

Downhill: Feb 6, Las Vegas (122m): 1. Melody Fairchild USA 10.9.73 71:38; María Portillo PER 10.4.72 72:52

Note – during Marathon

Mark	Name		Nat	Born	Pos	Meet	Venue	Date
70:46	Harumi	Hiroyama	JPN	2.9.68	1=		Osaka	30 Jan
70:46	Reiko	Tosa	JPN	11.6.76	1		Tokyo	19 Nov
70:47	Kayoko	Obata	JPN	18.9.71	3=		Osaka	30 Jan
70:48	Noriko	Geji	JPN	31.5.73	5=		Osaka	30 Jan

Mark	Name		Nat	Born	Pos	Date
71:48	Adriana	Fernández	MEX	4.4.71	24	Sep
71:56		Kim Chang-ok	PRK	16.4.75	24	Sep
72:01		Ren Xiujuan	CHN	14.9.74	24	Sep
72:18	Madina	Biktagirova	RUS	20.9.64	24	Sep
72:20	Manuela	Machado	POR	9.8.63	24	Sep
72:38	Irina	Bogachova	KGZ	30.5.61	24	Sep
72:39	Midori	Fumoto	JPN	18.12.71	12	Mar
72:40	Junko	Kataoka	JPN	13.6.70	19	Nov
72:54	Tomoe	Abe	JPN	13.8.71	30	Jan
72:58	Anuta	Catuna	ROM	1.10.68	24	Sep

JUNIORS

Mark	Name		Nat	Born	Pos	Meet	Venue	Date
71:16	Kazue	Ogoshi	JPN	2.3.81	2		Marugame	6 Feb
72:32	Rita	Jeptoo	KEN	15.2.81	3		Ostia	19 Mar
72:34	Tomoko	Motohira	JPN	13.2.81	6		Okayama	3 Dec
73:15	Yuko	Matsushita	JPN	28.2.81	28		Yamaguchi	12 Mar
73:17	Masa	Yoshida	JPN	20.1.81	4		Kyoto	12 Mar
73:50	Chika	Horie	JPN	15.2.81	3		Chiba	23 Jan
73:53	Naoko	Sato	JPN	22.1.81	16		Sapporo	2 Jul
73:58	Mai	Nobata	JPN	29.10.82	8		Matsue	19 Mar

MARATHON

In second column: first character: L = loop course or start and finish within 30%, P = point-to-point or start and finish more than 30% apart, D = point-to-point and downhil over 1/1000

Second character: M mixed marathon (men and women), W women only race or separated start by time

Mark		Name		Nat	Born	Pos	Meet	Venue	Date
2:21:33	LM	Catherine	Ndereba	KEN	21.7.72	1		Chicago	22 Oct
2:22:19	LW	Naoko	Takahashi	JPN	6.5.72	1		Nagoya	12 Mar
2:22:36	LM	Lornah	Kiplagat	KEN	20.3.74	2		Chicago	22 Oct
2:22:54	LW	Lidia	Simon	ROM	4.9.73	1		Osaka	30 Jan
2:22:56	LW	Harumi	Hiroyama	JPN	2.9.68	2		Osaka	30 Jan
2:23:14	PW		Takahashi			1	OG	Sydney	24 Sep
2:23:22	PW		Simon			2	OG	Sydney	24 Sep

Mark		Name		Nat	Born	Pos	Meet	Venue	Date
2:23:31	LW	Esther	Wanjiru	KEN	27.3.77	3		Osaka	30 Jan
2:23:43	LM	Marleen	Renders	BEL	24.12.68	1		Paris	9 Apr
2:23:47	LM	Maura	Viceconte	ITA	3.10.67	1		Wien	21 May
2:24:02	LW	Joyce	Chepchumba	KEN	6.11.70	1		Tokyo	19 Nov
2:24:33	LW	Tegla	Loroupe (10)	KEN	9.5.73	1		London	16 Apr
2:24:36	LW	Reiko	Tosa	JPN	11.6.76	2		Nagoya	12 Mar
2:24:45	PW		Chepchumba			3	OG	Sydney	24 Sep
2:24:46	LW		Simon			2		London	16 Apr
2:24:47	LW	Elfenesh	Alemu	ETH	10.6.75	4		Osaka	30 Jan
2:24:47	LW		Tosa			2		Tokyo	19 Nov
2:24:55	DM		Alemu			1		Nagano	9 Apr
2:24:57	LW		Chepchumba			3		London	16 Apr
2:25:14	LW	Kayoko	Obata	JPN	18.9.71	5		Osaka	30 Jan
2:25:32	LM		Ren Xiujuan	CHN	14.9.74	1	NC	Jinan	2 Apr
2:25:42	LW	Adriana	Fernández	MEX	4.4.71	4		London	16 Apr
2:25:45	PM	Lyudmila	Petrova	RUS	7.10.68	1		New York	5 Nov
2:25:59	LW	Kerryn	McCann	AUS	2.5.67	5		London	16 Apr
2:26:03	PM	Franca	Fiacconi	ITA	4.10.65	2		New York	5 Nov
2:26:09	LW	Derartu	Tulu	ETH	21.3.72	6		London	16 Apr
2:26:11	DM		Ndereba			1		Boston	17 Apr
2:26:12	LW	Maria	Guida (20)	ITA	23.1.66	7		London	16 Apr
2:26:15	LM	Kazumi	Matsuo	JPN	18.4.74	1		Berlin	10 Sep
2:26:17	PW		Wanjiru			4	OG	Sydney	24 Sep
2:26:26	DW	Valentina	Yegorova	RUS	16.2.64	2		Nagano	9 Apr
2:26:27	DM	Irina	Bogachova	KGZ	30.5.61	2		Boston	17 Apr
2:26:27	DM	Fatuma	Roba	ETH	18.12.73	3		Boston	17 Apr
2:26:33	LW	Lyubov	Morgunova	RUS	14.1.71	8		London	16 Apr
2:26:33	PW	Madina	Biktagirova	RUS	20.9.64	5	OG	Sydney	24 Sep
2:26:34	LM		Wei Yanan	CHN-J	6.12.81	1		Beijing	15 Oct
2:26:36	LM		Sun Yingjie	CHN	3.10.77	2		Beijing	15 Oct
2:26:36	PM	Margaret	Okayo	KEN	30.5.76	3		New York	5 Nov
2:26:38	LW		Tulu			3		Tokyo	19 Nov
2:26:41	LW	Manuela	Machado (30)	POR	9.8.63	9		London	16 Apr
2:26:42	LM		Fiacconi			2		Berlin	10 Sep
2:26:42	PM	Hellen (42/31)	Kimutai	KEN	28.12.77	4		New York	5 Nov
2:26:58	DW	Takami	Ominami	JPN	15.11.75	3		Nagoya	12 Mar
2:27:00	PM	Florence	Barsosio	KEN	11.8.76	5		New York	5 Nov
2:27:03	PW	Eri	Yamaguchi	JPN	14.1.73	7	OG	Sydney	24 Sep
2:27:07	PW		Ham Bong-sil	PRK	24.7.74	8	OG	Sydney	24 Sep
2:27:14	LM		Zhang Shujing	CHN	13.9.79	3		Berlin	10 Sep
2:27:25	LM	Sonja	Oberem	GER	24.2.73	3		Wien	21 May
2:27:41	LM	Noriko	Geji	JPN	31.5.73	4		Berlin	10 Sep
2:27:42	LM	Alina	Ivanova	RUS	16.3.69	1		Praha	21 May
2:27:52	LW	Malgorzata (40)	Sobanska	POL	25.4.69	4		Tokyo	19 Nov
2:27:55	LW	Midori	Fumoto (Shimizu)	JPN	18.12.71	4		Nagoya	12 Mar
2:27:58	LM	Melanie	Kraus	GER	24.10.74	5		Berlin	10 Sep
2:28:01	LW	Tomoe	Abe	JPN	13.8.71	6		Osaka	30 Jan
2:28:11	LW	Svetlana	Zakharova	RUS	15.9.70	10		London	16 Apr
2:28:16	PM	Ruth	Kutol	KEN	16.5.73	1		Venezia	22 Oct
2:28:17	LM	Alina	Gherasim	ROM	10.11.71	2		Paris	9 Apr
2:28:20	LW	Junko	Kataoka	JPN	13.6.70	5		Tokyo	19 Nov
2:28:27	DM	Alla	Zhilyayeva	RUS	5.2.69	3		Nagano	9 Apr
2:28:32	LW	Hiromi	Ominami	JPN	15.11.75	5		Nagoya	12 Mar
2:28:32	PM	Jackline (50)	Jerotich	KEN	23.9.70	1		Carpi	15 Oct
2:28:46	LW	Zinaida	Semyonova	RUS	19.3.62	11		London	16 Apr
2:28:51	LW	Mineko	Yamanouchi	JPN	10.12.72	7		Tokyo	19 Nov
2:28:59	PM	Ornella	Ferrara	ITA	17.4.68	2		Carpi	15 Oct
2:29:12	DM	Chika	Horie	JPN-J	15.2.81	4		Nagano	9 Apr
2:29:13	LM	Irina	Timofeyeva	RUS	5.4.70	3		Chicago	22 Oct
2:29:32	LW	Yukari	Komatsu	JPN	13.2.74	6		Nagoya	12 Mar
2:29:34	LM	Helena	Sampaio	POR	9.10.73	6		Berlin	10 Sep
2:29:39	LM	Hiromi	Igarashi	JPN	26.10.70	7		Berlin	10 Sep
2:29:43	LM	Irina	Suvorova	RUS	3.3.71	2		St.Paul	8 Oct
2:29:43	LM	Lucilla (60)	Andreucci	ITA	19.12.69	1		Milano	3 Dec

Mark		Name		Nat	Born	Pos	Meet	Venue	Date
2:29:44	LM		Oh Mi-ja	KOR	3.7.70	1		Kunsan	9 Apr
2:29:46	DM	Anuta	Catuna	ROM	1.10.68	4		Boston	17 Apr
2:29:54	LM	Abeba	Tolla	ETH	3.6.77	1		Amsterdam	15 Oct
2:30:02	LM	Aniela	Nikiel	POL	1.11.65	2		Torino	26 Mar
2:30:07	LM		Tian Mei	CHN	27.11.71	3		Beijing	15 Oct
2:30:18	DM		Ai Dongmei	CHN	15.10.79	6		Boston	17 Apr
2:30:21	LM	Ana Isabel	Alonso	ESP	16.8.63	1		Rotterdam	16 Apr
2:30:23	LW		Wang Yanrong	CHN	16.10.76	8		Tokyo	19 Nov
2:30:30	LW	Esther	Kiplagat	KEN	8.12.66	13		London	16 Apr
2:30:34	PW	Ari	Ichihashi	JPN	22.11.77	15	OG	Sydney	24 Sep
		(70)							
2:30:35	LM	Hellen	Kimaiyo	KEN	8.9.68	3		San Diego	4 Jun
2:30:43	LM		Lu Jingbo	CHN	18.4.73	3		Jinan	2 Apr
2:30:50	LW	Masako	Koide	JPN	3.1.74	9		Tokyo	19 Nov
2:30:54	PW	Judit	Földing-Nagy	HUN	9.12.65	17	OG	Sydney	24 Sep
2:31:04	LM	Esther	Barmasai	KEN	72	1		Frankfurt	29 Oct
2:31:08	LM	Alena	Peterková	CZE	13.11.60	2		Praha	21 May
2:31:12	LM	Griselda	Gonzalez	ESP	4.12.65	1		Barcelona	19 Mar
2:31:12	PM	Yuko	Arimori	JPN	17.12.66	10		New York	5 Nov
2:31:14	LW	Ramilya	Burangulova	RUS	11.7.61	14		London	16 Apr
2:31:20	LM	Tomoko	Kai	JPN	5.11.76	2		Frankfurt	29 Oct
		(80)							
2:31:25	LW	Aki	Fujikawa	JPN	14.11.78	8		Nagoya	12 Mar
2:31:25	LM	Milkah	Chepkieny	KEN	12.8.76	4		Paris	9 Apr
2:31:28	LM		Hong Myong-hui	PRK	29.7.78	1		Pyongyang	9 Apr
2:31:35	PW	Christine	Clark	USA	10.10.62	19	OG	Sydney	24 Sep
2:31:37	LM	Manuela	Zipse	GER	11.5.74	1		Hamburg	16 Apr
2:31:40	PW		Jong Yong-ok	PRK-J	24.1.81	20	OG	Sydney	24 Sep
2:31:44	LM	Tadelesh	Birra	ETH	24.4.75	3		Torino	26 Mar
2:31:48	LM	Sara	Ferrari	ITA	30.9.77	9		Berlin	10 Sep
2:31:49	LM		Kang Kum-sin	PRK	79	2		Pyongyang	9 Apr
2:31:49	DM	Martha	Tenorio	ECU	6.8.66	9		Boston	17 Apr
		(90)							
2:31:57	LM	Claudia	Dreher	GER	2.5.71	3		Frankfurt	29 Oct
2:31:59	LM	Elana	Meyer	RSA	10.10.66	4		Chicago	22 Oct
2:32:04	LM	Mary	Ptikany	KEN	78	2		Amsterdam	15 Oct
2:32:09	LM	Libbie	Hickman	USA	17.2.65	6		Chicago	22 Oct
2:32:11	LM	Gadissie	Edato	ETH	15.3.73	2		Roma	1 Jan
2:32:18	LM	Tiziana	Alagia	ITA	8.3.73	1		Firenze	26 Nov
2:32:20	LW	Hiroko	Kinuki	JPN	18.7.74	9		Nagoya	12 Mar
2:32:20	LW	Nadezhda	Wijenberg	NED	2.4.64	10		Tokyo	19 Nov
2:32:21	DM	Firiya	Zhdanova	RUS	29.4.61	11		Boston	17 Apr
2:32:25	LM	Tatyana	Pozdnyakova	UKR	4.3.56	1		Houston	16 Jan
		(100)							

2:32:30		Mayumi	Ichikawa	JPN	3.5.76	27 Aug
2:32:34		María Luisa	Muñoz	ESP	6.5.59	6 Feb
2:32:37	LW	Susan	Hobson	AUS	13.3.58	30 Jan
2:32:40		Lidiya	Grigoryeva	RUS	21.1.74	10 Dec
2:32:45	LM	Christine	Junkermann	USA	2.8.72	22 Oct
2:32:48	LM	Judy	Kiplimo	KEN	00	29 Oct
2:32:52		Cristina	Pomacu	ROM	15.9.73	19 Nov
2:32:58	LM		Oh Song-suk	PRK		9 Apr
2:33:00	LW	Azumi	Miyazaki	JPN	3.3.75	30 Jan
2:33:05	LW	Marie	Söderström-Lundberg	SWE	21.10.60	12 Mar
2:33:06			Park Ko-eun	KOR	11.4.76	19 Mar
2:33:10	LM	Katrin	Dörre-Heinig	GER	6.10.61	16 Apr
2:33:18	LW	Ryoko	Kitajima	JPN	12.6.76	19 Nov
2:33:20	LM	Kristy	Johnston	USA	3.6.65	22 Oct
2:33:27	LM	Valentina	Enaki	MDA	15.2.66	9 Apr
2:33:32	LM	Olga	Kovpotina	RUS	10.1.68	8 Oct
2:33:33	LM	Alla	Zadorozhnaya	BLR	4.4.72	29 Oct
2:33:34	LM	Jane	Salumäe	EST	17.1.68	5 Mar
2:33:34		Chantal	Dällenbach	SUI/FRA	24.10.62	22 Oct
2:33:35		Marlene	Fortunato	BRA	8.1.70	19 Mar
2:33:41	LM	Sue	Reinsford	GBR	24.3.69	16 Apr
2:33:45	DM	Renata	Paradowska	POL	14.6.70	17 Apr
2:33:47	LW	Masako	Kusakaya	JPN	26.2.72	12 Mar
2:33:52	LW	Ayumi	Noshita	JPN	7.9.77	30 Jan
2:33:53	PM	Svetlana	Shepeleva	MDA	10.5.69	17 Jun
2:33:57	LM		Pyo Un-suk	PRK		9 Apr
2:33:58	LM	Christine	Mallo	FRA	26.2.66	16 Apr
2:34:14	LM	Wioletta	Kryza	POL	10.8.68	16 Jan
2:34:18		Marcia	Narloch	BRA	28.3.69	7 May
2:34:33	PW	Marian	Sutton	GBR	7.10.63	24 Sep
2:34:33	LM		Ju Limei	CHN	9.6.78	15 Oct
2:34:35	LM	Galina	Zhulyeva	UKR	5.3.66	19 Mar
2:34:37	LW	Tomoe	Yokoyama	JPN	.76	12 Mar
2:34:38	LW	Kaori	Yamauchi	JPN	2.5.76	30 Jan
2:34:40	LM	Fatima	Silva	POR	6.5.70	26 Nov
2:34:44	PM	Francesca	Zanusso	ITA	25.10.75	15 Oct
2:34:45		Irina	Safarova	RUS	19.6.69	21 May
2:34:50	LM	Mónica	Pont	ESP	3.6.69	21 May
2:34:51	LM	Marta	Fernández de Castro	ESP	19.8.71	16 Apr
2:34:52	LM	Zahia	Dahmani	FRA	2.6.72	16 Apr
2:35:05	LW	Shiki	Terasaki	JPN	27.3.72	12 Mar
2:35:07	LM	Adriana	Barbu	ROM	17.1.61	30 Apr
2:35:07	PW	Erika	Oliveia	CHI	14.1.76	24 Sep
2:35:10		Rie	Matsuoka	JPN	9.3.77	27 Aug
2:35:11	LW	Cleuza María	Irineu	BRA	18.6.65	16 Apr
2:35:11	DM	Gitte	Karlshøj	DEN	14.5.59	17 Apr
2:35:12	DM	Annemari	Sandell	FIN	2.1.77	17 Apr
2:35:14	LM	Nuta	Olaru	ROM	28.8.70	5 Mar
2:35:16	LM		Jo Jong-hui	PRK	80	9 Apr
2:35:16	LM	Maryse	Le Gallo	FRA	27.4.60	9 Apr
2:35:18	LW	Tami	Yada	JPN	31.5.72	30 Jan
2:35:18	LW	Ritsuko	Sasaki	JPN	30.11.72	12 Mar
2:35:18		Luciene	de Deus	BRA	15.11.69	19 Mar
2:35:24	LM	María	Portillo	PER	10.4.72	5 Mar
2:35:30	LM	Alevtina	Naumova	RUS	16.1.61	30 Apr
2:35:31	DM	Naoko	Sato	JPN-J	22.1.81	9 Apr
2:35:32	LM		Han Sun-ran	PRK		9 Apr
2:35:32	PW		Kim Chang-ok	PRK	16.4.75	24 Sep

Mark		Name		Nat	Born	Date
2:35:33	LM	Annemette	Jensen	DEN	11.4.72	21 May
2:35:35	LM	Antje	van Schuppen	NED	11.10.60	16 Apr
2:35:42	LM	Dagmar	Rabensteiner	AUT	15.6.63	15 Oct
2:35:42	LM	Sonia	O'Sullivan	IRL	28.11.69	30 Oct
2:35:46	LW	Michiyo	Ando	JPN	12.12.72	30 Jan
2:35:47		Ai	Sugihara	JPN	12.10.75	27 Aug
2:35:48	LW	Akemi	Maeda	JPN	11.10.78	12 Mar
2:35:48	LW	Mina	Ogawa	JPN	9.1.75	19 Nov
2:35:54	LM	Marie-Luce	Romanens	SUI	19.1.73	9 Apr
2:35:54	LM	Pilar	Ramos	ESP	7.10.72	16 Apr
2:35:59	PM	Monica	Capelli	ITA	15.12.69	22 Oct
2:36:03	LW	Tomoko	Nishi	JPN	.76	12 Mar
2:36:05	LM		Won Chun-ae	PRK		9 Apr
2:36:06	LW	Anne Marie	Lauck	USA	7.3.69	26 Feb
2:36:06			Suh Ok-yeon	KOR	5.5.79	19 Mar
2:36:13	LM	Vilija	Birbalaite	LTU	11.8.66	16 Apr
2:36:13	LM	Zhanna	Malkova	RUS	27.10.67	1 Oct
2:36:19	LM	Natalya	Volguina	RUS	15.3.77	9 Apr
2:36:22	LW	Tomoko	Kitamura	JPN	26.10.73	12 Mar
2:36:25	LW	Shizuka	Oka	JPN	23.7.70	12 Mar
2:36:26	LM	Anfisa	Kosacheva	RUS	1.3.65	26 Nov
2:36:27	LM	Viviany	de Oliveira	BRA	17.7.69	16 Apr
2:36:28	LM	Marzanna	Helbik	POL	11.9.61	29 Oct
2:36:32	LW	Silvana	Trampuz	AUS	15.9.66	16 Apr
2:36:34		Svetlana	Nechayeva	RUS	24.7.61	1 Jan
2:36:35	LW	Kaoru	Yamada	JPN	24.11.75	12 Mar
2:36:40	PM	Yelena	Makolova	BLR	5.1.68	17 Jun
2:36:44		Karina	Szymanska	POL	16.1.75	2 Apr
2:36:46	LW	Susannah	Beck	USA	1.5.68	26 Feb
2:36:46	LM	Véronique	Vandersmissen	CAN	67	14 May
2:36:48	PW	Colleen	de Reuck	RSA	13.4.64	24 Sep
2:36:51	LM	Hilde	Hovdenak	NOR	15.2.71	16 Jan
2:36:54	LM	Faustina	María	ESP	28.4.71	21 May
2:36:54	LM		Li Juan	CHN	8.6.66	15 Oct
2:36:55	LW	Yuko	Maeda	JPN	3.3.78	12 Mar
2:36:56	LM	Lyudmila	Afonyushkina	RUS	10.10.67	16 Apr
2:37:02	LM	Lucia	Subano	KEN	15.12.67	29 Apr
2:37:02	LM		Yun Sun-sook	KOR	28.5.72	22 Oct
2:37:04u		Grace	Chebet	KEN	6.11.66	9 Jul
2:37:05	LW	Patricia	Jardón	MEX	17.3.67	16 Apr
2:37:17	LM		Kan Yongying	CHN	20.4.79	15 Oct
2:37:20	LM	Krystyna	Kuta	POL	21.9.67	16 Apr
		(200)				

Downhill

Mark		Name		Nat	Born	Date
2:34:03	DM	Tatyana	Titova	RUS	6.8.65	20 Feb
2:34:37	DM	Marzanna	Helbik	POL	11.9.61	20 Feb
2:36:01	DM	Joanna	Gront	POL	25.12.67	6 Feb

JUNIORS

Mark		Name		Nat	Born	Pos	Meet	Venue	Date
2:29:12	DM	Chika	Horie	JPN	15.2.81	4		Nagano	9 Apr
2:31:40	PW		Jong Yong-ok	PRK	24.1.81	20	OG	Sydney	24 Sep
2:35:31	DM	Naoko	Sato	JPN	22.1.81	5		Nagano	9 Apr
2:38:20		Meseret	Kotu	ETH	.81	2		München	15 Oct
2:42:32			Jiang Shuhui	CHN	19.1.82	6	NC	Jinan	2 Apr

100 KILOMETRES

Mark		Name		Nat	Born	Pos	Meet	Venue	Date
6:33:11		Tomoe	Abe	JPN	13.8.71	1		Yubetsu	25 Jun
7:25:21		Edit	Bérces	HUN	16.5.64	1	WC	Winschoten	9 Sep
7:30:26		Makiko	Hotta	JPN	5.10.66	2		Yubetsu	25 Jun
7:35:01		Elvira	Kolpakova	RUS	30.10.72	2	WC	Winschoten	9 Sep
7:39:35		Constanze	Wagner	GER	23.1.63	3	WC	Winschoten	9 Sep
7:46:05		Magali	Maggiolini	FRA	21.5.59	4	WC	Winschoten	9 Sep
7:48:57		Tania	Schäfer	GER	25.9.67	1	NC	Rodenbach	22 Apr
7:50:49	t	Birgit	Lennartz	GER	22.11.65	1		Otweiler	7 Oct
7:50:50			Bérces			1		Boston	8 Oct
7:52:16			Bérces			1		Torhout	16 Jun
7:52:50		Sylvie	Beaulieu	FRA	15.6.62	5	WC	Winschoten	9 Sep
7:53:12			Berces			1	EC	Belvès	30 Apr
7:54:32		Elke	Hiebl	GER	12.6.64	6	WC	Winschoten	9 Sep
7:54:35		Nadezhda	Karaseva	RUS	.60	7	WC	Winschoten	9 Sep
7:55:02		Hiroki	Noguchi	JPN	4.5.78	8	WC	Winschoten	9 Sep
7:57:34		Alzira	Lario	POR	8.4.57	1		S.C. de Bezana	7 Oct
7:58:17		Ute	Wollenberg	GER	1.10.66	2	NC	Rodenbach	22 Apr
7:58:49		Valentina	Shatyayeva	RUS	23.11.63	2		Boston	8 Oct
		(18/15)							
8:05:21		Ricarda	Botzon	GER	4.9.66	9	WC	Winschoten	9 Sep
8:06:46		Karine	Herry	FRA	2.1.68	2		Belvès	30 Apr
8:08:03		Deb	Bollig	USA		10	WC	Winschoten	9 Sep
8:12:51		Akiko	Sekiya	JPN	.65	4		Yubetsu	25 Jun
8:13:07		Anke	Drescher	GER	14.12.67	1		Neuwittenbek	30 Sep
8:17:24		Miyuki	Morishita	JPN	7.3.67	1		Shimanto	15 Oct
8:17:42		Oksana	Ladyzhina	RUS	21.7.67	2		S.C.de Bezana	7 Oct

Mark		Name		Nat	Born	Date
8:22:21		Dana	Parrot	USA		25 Mar
8:22:27	t	Ann	Trason	USA	30.8.60	29 Dec
8:22:37		Marietjie	Montgomery	RSA	17.10.59	9 Sep
8:22:58		Jennifer	Devine	USA	1.11.71	8 Oct
8:24:59		Luanne	Park	USA		9 Sep
8:25:39		Maria Luisa	Costetti	ITA	31.7.61	9 Sep
8:27:36		Murielle	Brionne	FRA	9.12.67	9 Sep
8:29:59		Danielle	Czerniak	USA	24.10.61	9 Sep

24 HOURS

Mark		Name		Nat	Born	Pos	Meet	Venue	Date
230.438t		Irina	Reutovich	RUS	21.1.50	1	NC	Moscow	8/9 May
226.299		Rimma	Paltseva	RUS	14.10.48	1		Sankt-Peterburg	2/3 Sep
225.418			Reutovich			1	EChall	Uden	22/23 Oct
221.867i			Reutovich			1		Brno	17/18 Mar
219.260		Joelle	Semur	FRA	22.12.60	2	EChall	Uden	22/23 Oct
218.037t			Paltseva			2	NC	Moscow	8/9 May
216.299			Paltseva		14.10.48	3	EChall	Uden	22/23 Oct

Mark		Name		Nat	Born	Pos	Meet	Venue	Date
215.755		Helga	Backhaus	GER	19.1.53	1		Basel	13/14 May
209.220		Colette	Musy	FRA	11.4.59	5	EChall	Uden	22/23 Oct
207.720		Julia	Alter	GER	24.2.72	6	EChall	Uden	22/23 Oct
205.775		Irina	Koval	RUS	19.11.58	7	EChall	Uden	22/23 Oct
203.929		Ursula	Alder	SUI	1.10.55	2		Basel	13/14 May
203.495		Calina	Gordeeva	RUS	18.4.55	8	EChall	Uden	22/23 Oct

2000 METRES STEEPLECHASE

Mark		Name		Nat	Born	Pos	Meet	Venue	Date
6:25.77		Melissa	Rollison	AUS-J	13.4.83	1		Sydney	1 May
6:27.69		Yekaterina	Volkova	RUS	.78	1		Rostov-na-Donu	27 Jun
6:27.76		Varvara	Shestok	UKR	17.12.74	1		Kiev	18 Jun
6:32.65		Lisa	Nye	USA	17.11.68	1		Eugene	1 Jul
6:34.52		Anzhelika	Averkova	UKR	13.3.69	2		Kiev	18 Jun
6:36.02		Jayne	Spark	GBR	16.9.70	1		Stretford	8 Aug
6:36.49		Tara	Krzywicki	GBR	9.3.74	1		Loughborough	21 May

3000 METRES STEEPLECHASE

Mark		Name		Nat	Born	Pos	Meet	Venue	Date
9:40.20		Cristina	Iloc-Casandra	ROM	21.10.77	1		Reims	30 Aug
9:43.64			Iloc-Casandra			1	NC	Bucuresti	7 Aug
9:51.76			Iloc-Casandra			1		Stántu Gheorghe	23 Jul
9:52.40		Yekaterina	Volkova	RUS	.78	1	Znam	Sankt-Peterburg	17 Jun
9:54.10		Anzhelika	Averkova	UKR	13.3.69	1	NC	Kiev	5 Aug
9:54.86		Daniela	Petrescu	ROM	13.4.68	2	NC	Bucuresti	7 Aug
9:56.99		Luminita	Gogîrlea	ROM	5.11.71	3	NC	Bucuresti	7 Aug
9:57.03		Justyna	Bak	POL	1.8.74	1	Kuso	Warszawa	24 Jun
9:57.20		Elizabeth	Jackson	USA	27.10.77	1	NC	Sacramento	17 Jul
10:00.63		Lisa	Nye	USA	17.11.68	2	NC	Sacramento	17 Jul
		(10/8)							
10:01.54		Susanne	Wigene	NOR	12.2.78	1	NC	Steinkjer	11 Aug
10:02.60		Olimpia	Pop	ROM	25.2.76	4	NC	Bucuresti	7 Aug
10:03.09		Kara	Ormond	USA	17.6.77	3	NC	Sacramento	17 Jul
10:04.41		Courtney	Meldrum	USA	31.1.77	4	NC	Sacramento	17 Jul
10:04.45		Tara	Haynes	USA	6.8.78	5	NC	Sacramento	17 Jul
10:04.85		Céline	Rajot	FRA	22.3.75	1	NC	Nice	5 Aug
10:05.12		Varvara	Shestok	UKR	17.12.74	2	NC	Kiev	5 Aug
10:07.63		Meriem	Méred	FRA	4.4.76	2	NC	Nice	5 Aug
10:08.11		Tara	Krzywicki	GBR	9.3.74	1		Stretford	5 Sep
10:08.18		Véronique	Bertel	FRA	12.4.69	3	NC	Nice	5 Aug
10:09.64		Elodie	Olivarès	FRA	22.5.76	1		Saint-Maur	7 Jun
10:10.73		Melissa	Rollison	AUS-J	13.4.83	1	NC	Sydney	25 Feb
		(20)							
10:11.86		Natalya	Cherepanova	RUS	.67	2	NC	Tula	24 Jul
10:12.07		Mariya	Vilisova	RUS	.69	3	NC	Tula	24 Jul
10:12.57		Analídia	Torre	POR	10.10.76	1		Viana do Castelo	14 Jun
10:12.97		Chantal	Dällenbach	SUI/FRA	24.10.62	1		Chartres	27 Jul
10:13.29		Alina	Cucerzan	ROM	28.7.74				25 Jun
10:13.83		Tonya	Dodge	USA	24.5.75				17 Jul
10:16.01		Leah	Rogers	AUS	17.2.76				25 Feb
10:18.85		Desiree	Owen	USA	22.2.75				17 Jul

JUNIORS

Mark		Name		Nat	Born	Pos	Meet	Venue	Date
10:22.92		Ida	Nilsson	SWE-J	8.2.81	1		Högby	2 Jun
10:25.85		Kerry	Hills	USA-J	21.3.81	3	MSR	Walnut	14 Apr
10:26.73		Marina	Ivanova	RUS-J	.82	1	NC-j	Krasnodar	17 Sep
10:34.29		Hana	Chaouach	TUN-J	18.9.81	6	NC	Bucuresti	7 Aug
10:34.45		Sigrid	Vandenbempt	BEL-J	10.2.81	4		Beveren	9 Sep
10:39.40		Valquíria	Santos	BRA-J	21.10.81	3	NC	Rio de Janeiro	5 Aug

100 METRES HURDLES

Mark	Wind	Name		Nat	Born	Pos	Meet	Venue	Date
12.33	-0.3	Gail	Devers	USA	19.11.66	1	NC	Sacramento	23 Jul
12.39	-0.7		Devers			1	WK	Zürich	11 Aug
12.47	0.5		Devers			1	GGala	Roma	30 Jun
12.50	0.8		Devers			1	Athl	Lausanne	5 Jul
12.52	1.9	Delloreen	Ennis-London	JAM	5.3.75	1	NC	Kingston	22 Jul
12.53	-0.8		Devers			1	VD	Bruxelles	25 Aug
12.54	-0.7	Glory	Alozie	NGR	30.12.77	2	WK	Zürich	11 Aug
12.54	-0.1		Devers			1	Herc	Monaco	18 Aug
12.56	0.8		Alozie			2	Athl	Lausanne	5 Jul
12.56	0.0		Devers			1	Bisl	Oslo	28 Jul
12.57	-1.1		Devers			1h3	NC	Sacramento	22 Jul
12.57	1.9	Michelle	Freeman	JAM	5.5.69	2	NC	Kingston	22 Jul

Mark	Wind	Name		Nat	Born	Pos	Meet	Venue	Date
12.57	1.3	Melissa	Morrison	USA	9.7.71	1s1	NC	Sacramento	23 Jul
12.62	0.7		Devers			1h5	OG	Sydney	25 Sep
12.63	1.6	Anjanette	Kirkland	USA	24.2.74	1r5	MSR	Walnut	16 Apr
12.63	-0.3		Morrison			2	NC	Sacramento	23 Jul
12.64	1.3		Devers			1	Pre	Eugene	24 Jun
12.65	0.8	Olga	Shishigina	KAZ	23.12.68	3	Athl	Lausanne	5 Jul
12.65	0.0		Shishigina			1	OG	Sydney	27 Sep
12.66	0.5		Kirkland			2	GGala	Roma	30 Jun
12.66	-0.1		Morrison			2	Herc	Monaco	18 Aug
12.66	-0.2		Alozie			1	ISTAF	Berlin	1 Sep
12.66	1.5		Shishigina			1q2	OG	Sydney	25 Sep
12.67	1.3	Joanna	Hayes	USA	23.12.76	2s1	NC	Sacramento	23 Jul
12.67	-0.2		Morrison			2	ISTAF	Berlin	1 Sep
12.68	2.0		Alozie			1		Barcelona	13 May
12.68	1.3		Kirkland			2	Pre	Eugene	24 Jun
12.68	0.5		Shishigina			3	GGala	Roma	30 Jun
12.68	1.3	Sharon	Couch	USA	13.9.69	3s1	NC	Sacramento	23 Jul
12.68	-0.1		Ennis-London			3	Herc	Monaco	18 Aug
12.68	-0.4		Alozie			1s2	OG	Sydney	27 Sep
12.68	0.0		Alozie			2	OG	Sydney	27 Sep
		(32/9)							
12.70	1.7	Donica	Merriman	USA	24.1.79	1r1	PennR	Philadelphia	29 Apr
12.70	-0.4	Bridgette	Foster	JAM	7.11.74	2s2	OG	Sydney	27 Sep
12.75	-0.7	Natalya	Shekhodanova	RUS	29.12.71	1	Super	Yokohama	9 Sep
12.76	0.6	Nicole	Ramalalanirina	FRA	5.3.72	1		Chaux de Fonds	13 Aug
12.77	1.3	Tonya	Lawson	USA	16.5.69	4s1	NC	Sacramento	23 Jul
12.78	1.9	Svetla	Dimitrova	BUL	27.1.70	1	Veniz	Haniá	14 Jun
12.78	1.3	Miesha	McKelvy	USA	26.7.76	5s1	NC	Sacramento	23 Jul
12.80	1.9	Nadine	Faustin	HAI	14.4.76	2	Veniz	Haniá	14 Jun
12.81	0.8	Linda	Ferga	FRA	24.12.76	6	Athl	Lausanne	5 Jul
12.81	-0.3	Ellakisha	Williamson	USA	19.3.75	4	NC	Sacramento	23 Jul
12.82	-0.8	Yelena	Krasovskaya	UKR	17.8.76	1	NC	Kiev	3 Aug
		(20)							
12.82	0.8	Astia	Walker	JAM	4.4.75	1		Leverkusen	20 Aug
12.82	-0.7	Aliuska	López	CUB	29.8.69	2	Super	Yokohama	9 Sep
12.82	0.2	Katie	Anderson	CAN	9.1.68	1h2	OG	Sydney	25 Sep
12.83	1.3	Angie	Vaughn	USA	4.11.76	6s1	NC	Sacramento	23 Jul
12.85	0.8	Joyce	Bates	USA	16.2.77	1	NCAA	Durham	3 Jun
12.85	1.1	Rosa	Rakotozafy	MAD	12.11.77	1h1		Chaux de Fonds	13 Aug
12.86	0.8	Jenny	Adams	USA	8.7.78	1s2	NCAA	Durham	2 Jun
12.87	0.1	Yuliya	Graudyn	RUS	13.11.70	1rB	Athl	Lausanne	5 Jul
12.88	1.9	Maya	Shemchishina	UKR	6.5.72	1		Kiev	18 Jun
12.88	0.8	Patricia	Girard	FRA	8.4.68	2		Bron	23 Jul
		(30)							
12.89	-0.8	Nadezhda	Bodrova	UKR	13.7.61	2	NC	Kiev	3 Aug
12.90	0.4	Vonette	Dixon	JAM	26.11.75	2h2	NCAA	Durham	1 Jun
12.90	0.8	Eunice	Barber	FRA	17.11.74	1		Montgeron	18 Jun
12.91	1.2	Perdita	Felicien	CAN	29.8.80	2h3	NCAA	Durham	1 Jun
12.92	0.4	Kirsten	Bolm	GER	4.3.75	1	GP II	Bratislava	22 Jun
12.92	1.3	Nicole	Harrison	USA	14.1.76	7s1	NC	Sacramento	23 Jul
12.92	1.0	Angela	Atede	NGR	8.2.72	1		Sydney	14 Sep
12.93	0.7	Dominqué	Calloway	USA	19.7.78	2		Tallahassee	15 Apr
12.93	1.9	Lacena	Golding	JAM	20.3.75	4	NC	Kingston	22 Jul
12.93	-0.7	Svetlana	Laukhova	RUS	7.5.73	3	Super	Yokohama	9 Sep
		(40)							
12.94	1.4	Mame Tacko	Diouf	SEN	17.10.76	1		Dakar	6 May
12.94	0.9	Yolanda	McCray	USA	11.9.76	2		Chapel Hill	18 Jun
12.94	1.9	Gillian	Russell	JAM	28.9.73	5	NC	Kingston	22 Jul
12.96	1.7	Reina-Flor	Okori	FRA	2.5.80	1r1		Arles	3 Jun
12.96	1.5	Trecia	Roberts	THA	4.2.71	5q2	OG	Sydney	25 Sep
12.97	1.2	Nicole	Hoxie	USA	22.7.79	3h3	NCAA	Durham	1 Jun
12.99	0.8		Su Yiping	CHN	4.8.79	1	AsiC	Jakarta	30 Aug
13.00	0.7	Yvonne	Kanazawa	JPN	19.11.74	1	Nambu	Sapporo	16 Jul
13.00	0.1	Juliane	Sprenger	GER	22.3.77	1		Sondershausen	25 Aug
13.02	-1.7	Susanna	Kallur	SWE-J	16.2.81	1	WJ	Santiago de Chile	19 Oct
		(50)							
13.03	0.5	Brandit	Copper	USA	25.8.78	3s1	NCAA	Durham	2 Jun
13.03	1.3	Monifa	Taylor	USA	3.3.71	8s1	NC	Sacramento	23 Jul
13.04	1.5	Patrina	Allen	JAM	17.4.75	1h2	GaTech	Atlanta	20 May

Mark	Wind	Name		Nat	Born	Pos	Meet	Venue	Date
13.04	-0.3	Bisa	Grant	USA	10.7.76	8	NC	Sacramento	23 Jul
13.05	0.9	Kyla	Shoemake	USA	6.6.77	3h1	NCAA	Durham	1 Jun
13.05	2.0	Irina	Lenskiy	ISR	12.6.71	1		Tel Aviv	10 Jun
13.05	0.0	Kim	Carson	USA	12.3.74	2		Ingolstadt	18 Jun
13.08	1.2	Jackie	Madison	USA	14.7.79	4h3	NCAA	Durham	1 Jun
13.08	0.8	Haydy	Aron	FRA	21.5.73	3		Bron	23 Jul
13.08	0.3	Adrianna	Lamalle	FRA-J	27.9.82	1h1		Mannheim	12 Aug
		(60)							
13.09	1.9	Svetlana	Gnezdilov	ISR	20.7.69	3		Kiev	18 Jun
13.10	2.0	Caren	Sonn	GER	18.1.68	2		Kassel	7 Jun
13.10	-1.3	Tiffany	Lott-Hogan	USA	1.8.75	H	NC	Sacramento	14 Jul
13.10	0.7	Sriyani	Kulawansa	SRI	1.3.70	3h5	OG	Sydney	25 Sep
13.11	-0.3		Liu Jing	CHN	8.8.77	1	NGP	Guangzhou	25 Mar
13.11	0.9	Andria	King	USA	22.6.76	1h1	OD	Jena	3 Jun
13.11A	1.5	Dawn	Riley	USA	17.11.73	3r1		Flagstaff	6 Jul
13.11	1.1	Diane	Allahgreen	GBR	21.2.75	5h4	OG	Sydney	25 Sep
13.12	-0.3		Feng Yun	CHN	23.2.76	2	NGP	Guangzhou	25 Mar
13.12	1.1	Jacquie	Munro	AUS-J	4.10.81	1		Darwin	14 Jul
		(70)							
13.13	1.9	Lutisha	Shittu	USA	7.5.79	1h1		Knoxville	18 May
13.13	1.6	Keri	Maddox	GBR	4.7.72	1		Loughborough	21 May
13.13	0.8	Charmaine	Walker	USA	5.5.78	6s2	NCAA	Durham	2 Jun
13.13	0.8	Christina	Ohaeri	USA	30.3.79	7s2	NCAA	Durham	2 Jun
13.13	1.9	Vera	Ordina	RUS	4.6.68	2h2	NC	Tula	25 Jul
13.13	1.0	Denise	Lewis	GBR	27.8.72	H	Deca	Talence	29 Jul
13.13	-0.2	Yahumara	Neyra	CUB	18.4.76	1	Barr	La Habana	30 Jul
13.13	0.2	Natacha	Casy	FRA	26.4.74	2h3	NC	Nice	4 Aug
13.14	1.8	Patricia	Buval	FRA	22.1.76	2h1	NC	Nice	4 Aug
13.14	2.0	Isabel	Abrantes	POR	20.2.73	1	NC	Coimbra	13 Aug
		(80)							
13.15	1.3	Michelle	Perry	USA	1.5.79	1h2	Pac 10	Eugene	20 May
13.15	1.9	Dionne	Rose	JAM	7.11.69	4	Veniz	Hánia	14 Jun
13.15	0.0	Valerie	Manning	USA	27.3.68	1		Namur	18 Aug
13.16	0.7	Viorica	Tigau	ROM	12.8.79	1H		Poiana Brasov	24 Jul
13.17	1.5	Selena	Lewis	USA	3.8.76	4r4	ModR	Modesto	13 May
13.17	1.7	Melanie	Wilkins	GBR	18.1.73	1		Brighton	18 Jun
13.17	1.9	Sonia	Paquette	CAN	7.2.73	1h1		Argentan	25 Jun
13.17	0.0	Aneta	Sosnowska	POL	10.5.74	1	NC	Kraków	6 Aug
13.18	1.3	Cheryl	Dickey	USA	12.12.66	4	Pre	Eugene	24 Jun
13.18	0.1	Jenny	Kallur	SWE-J	16.2.81	1h4	WJ	Santiago de Chile	17 Oct
		(90)							
13.19	0.8	Shelia	Burrell	USA	15.1.72	1H		Manhattan	6 May
13.19	0.9	Liliana	Nastase	ROM	1.8.62	H		Bucuresti	24 Jun
13.20	1.6	Tamika	Higgins-Francis	USA	19.4.71	6r5	MSR	Walnut	16 Apr
13.20	0.6	Natasha	Danvers	GBR	19.9.77	2		Los Angeles (Ww)	6 May
13.20	1.8	Nichole	Denby	USA-J	10.10.82	1		Norwalk	3 Jun
13.20	1.6	Debbi	Edwards	AUS	25.9.78	2		Gold Coast (RB)	10 Sep
13.21	1.7	Felicia	Stone	USA	10.8.77	1r1	ModR	Modesto	13 May
13.21	1.2	Zita	Bálint	HUN	25.10.71	1	ECCp-B	Dudelange	27 May
13.21	-1.7	Fanny	Gérance	FRA-J	4.1.81	2	WJ	Santiago de Chile	19 Oct
13.22	-0.2	Yasmina	Azzizi-Kettab	ALG	25.2.66	1r2		Noisy-le-Grand	20 Jun
		(100)							
13.22	2.0	Sandra	Turpin	POR	5.6.76	2	NC	Coimbra	13 Aug
13.22	0.6	Margaret	Macchiut	ITA	25.7.74	2		Lappeenranta	13 Aug

13.23	1.1	Gilvaneide	Oliveira	BRA	31.8.76	30 Apr
13.23	1.2	Dawn	Burrell	USA	1.11.73	5 Oct
13.24	0.8	Michelle	Johnson	USA	12.4.74	18 Mar
13.24	0.2	Birgit	Hamann	GER	11.9.69	16 Jul
13.25	0.9	Maíla Paula	Machado	BRA-J	22.1.81	21 May
13.26	1.1	Damu	Cherry	USA	.78	25 Mar
13.26	0.2	Hannah	Cooper	LBR	10.6.79	13 May
13.27	-0.8	Maurren	Maggi	BRA	25.6.76	3 Aug
13.28	1.0	Nikkie	Bouyer	USA	11.2.76	22 Apr
13.28	1.5	Vida	Nsiah	GHA	13.4.76	5 May
13.28	0.3	Monica	Pellegrinelli	SUI	14.5.65	29 Jul
13.28	0.1	Tessy	Prediger	GER	29.1.79	25 Aug
13.29	1.2	Manuela	Bosco	FIN-J	11.6.82	19 Jul
13.29	-1.7	Joni-Ann	Doyley	JAM-J	25.10.81	19 Oct
13.30	0.0	Tatyana	Ladovskaya	UKR	4.5.77	4 Jun
13.30	1.9	Natalya	Kosorukova	UKR	9.8.72	18 Jun
13.30	1.1	Nadine	Grouwels	BEL	1.11.73	13 Aug
13.31	0.4	April	Sams	USA	23.8.79	1 Jun
13.31	0.2	Karin	Ertl	GER	23.6.74	3 Jun
13.32	-0.1	Lesley	Tashlin	CAN	27.5.69	21 May
13.32	1.2	Peggy	Beer	GER	15.9.69	3 Jun
13.32		Ime	Akpan	NGR	27.4.72	22 Jul
13.33	1.4	Danielle	Carruthers	USA	22.12.79	20 May
13.33	1.0	Monique	Salter	USA	15.8.78	3 Jun
13.33	0.7	Nadine	Hentschke	GER-J	27.1.82	12 Aug
13.33	0.3	Urszula	Wlodarczyk	POL	22.12.65	23 Sep
13.34	-0.4	Nerea	Azkárate	ESP	4.1.74	28 Jun
13.34	0.8	DeDee	Nathan	USA	20.4.68	14 Jul
13.34	1.8	Veronica	Dyer	CAN	29.4.77	22 Jul
13.35	0.0	Hristiána	Tabáki	GRE	13.1.73	8 Jul
13.35	1.2	Yuliya	Cherepkova	RUS	.77	11 Jul
13.36	1.8	Gi-Gi	Miller	USA	12.1.79	22 Apr
13.36	0.2	Aurelia	Trywianska	POL	9.5.76	13 May
13.36	0.2	Gudrún	Arnardóttir	ISL	24.9.71	9 Jul

Mark	Wind	Name		Nat	Born	Date
13.36	-0.4	Mariya	Koroteyeva	RUS-J	10.11.81	16 Sep
13.37A	0.6	Surita	Febbraio	RSA	27.12.73	19 Feb
13.37A	1.6	Angela	Whyte	CAN	22.5.80	19 May
13.37	0.3		Xiong Yanling	CHN	5.5.80	7 Jun
13.38	0.6	Ingeborg	Leschnik	GER	15.2.72	3 Jun
13.38	0.2	Mona	Steigauf	GER	17.1.70	15 Jul
13.38	-0.2	Anay	Tejeda	CUB-J	3.4.83	30 Jul
13.38	1.3	Tomoko	Motegi	JPN	8.8.78	3 Nov
13.39	0.9	Patience	Itanyi	NGR	2.7.73	3 Jun
13.39	1.6	Nadia	Waeber	SUI	2.5.77	21 Jun
13.39	0.0	Brigita	Bukovec	SLO	21.5.70	14 Aug
13.39	-0.1	Lydie	Potin-Sinapayen	FRA	23.7.77	23 Aug
13.40	1.7	Julie	Pratt	GBR	20.3.79	18 Jun
13.40	0.4	Heike	Blassneck	GER	26.7.71	22 Jul
13.40	0.8	Yuliya	Kondakova	RUS-J	4.12.81	26 Aug
13.40	0.8	Anuradha	Biswal	IND	28.3.75	30 Aug
13.41	0.0	Staciann	Brown	JAM	17.12.77	14 Apr
13.41	-0.2	Nohadis	Ferrera	CUB	30.10.79	30 Jul
13.42	0.0	Eva	Miklos	ROM	30.7.78	10 Jun
13.42	1.9	Oksana	Kuchma	UKR	4.3.73	18 Jun
13.42	-0.3	Joanna	Bujak	FRA	30.8.79	22 Jul
13.43	0.2	Akiko	Morimoto	JPN	17.2.77	23 Apr
13.43	1.3	NeJuan	Bakewell	USA	9.12.78	14 May
13.43	0.8	Tiia	Hautala	FIN	3.4.72	3 Jun
13.44	1.0	Lyudmila	Meskhiya	RUS	.75	2 Jun
13.44	0.8	Natalya	Sazanovich	BLR	15.8.73	3 Jun
13.44	0.2	Elke	Wölfling	AUT	27.11.71	8 Aug
13.45	1.8	Hanna	Korell	FIN	16.3.79	5 Jun
13.46	1.8	Sally	Heagney-Bult	AUS	3.10.70	2 Mar
13.46	0.7	Ayumi	Fujita	JPN	2.11.77	16 Jul
13.46	0.5	Magalys	García	CUB	23.10.71	23 Sep
13.47			Zeng Xiaoling	CHN		8 Sep
13.48	0.9	Emily	Waibel	USA-J	10.2.81	7 May
13.48	-1.2		Du Xueru	CHN-J	20.4.84	7 Jun
13.48	0.9	Susan	Smith	IRL	14.9.71	18 Jun
13.48	1.0	Stephanie	Thomas	USA	6.7.64	24 Jul
13.49		Damaris	Agbugba	NGR		22 Jul
13.49	1.2	Oksana	Samoylenko	UZB/RUS	5.12.72	25 Jul
13.49	0.4	Polina	Denisova	RUS	.78	25 Jul
13.49	1.9	Liz	Fairs	GBR	1.12.77	30 Jul
13.49	1.5	Raquel	Fraguas	ESP	2.3.76	23 Aug
13.49	0.3	Sabine	Braun	GER	19.6.65	23 Sep
13.50	1.2	Astrid	Retzke	GER	13.7.73	3 Jun
13.50	0.8	Kathleen	Gutjahr	GER	27.7.75	3 Jun
13.50	0.8		Vu Bich Huong	VIE	30.11.69	30 Aug
13.51	1.9	Ranysah	LeBlanc	USA-J	1.1.83	12 May
13.51	1.6	Sónia	Machado	POR	19.10.76	15 Jul
13.51	-0.6	Rachel	King	GBR	11.5.76	12 Aug
13.52	1.8	Rachel	Joy	USA	29.4.78	16 Apr
13.52		Jennifer	Komoll	GER	17.4.80	28 May
13.52	1.2	Ursa	Beti	SLO	19.6.78	23 Jun
13.52	0.6	Marie	Collonvillé	FRA	23.11.73	29 Jul
13.52	1.9	Bianca	Liston	GBR	28.5.78	30 Jul
13.52	-0.4	Kumiko	Ikeda	JPN-J	10.1.81	18 Oct
13.53	0.3		Wang Junlin	CHN	13.4.79	7 Jun
13.53	0.6	Myriam	Tschomba	BEL	8.1.77	13 Aug
13.54	-2.8	Yelena	Prokhorova	RUS	16.4.78	22 Jul
13.55	0.1	Marisa	Robinson	USA	16.5.78	16 Apr
13.55	0.9	Sophie	Marrot	FRA	13.2.75	3 Jun
13.55	-0.1	Michaela	Hejnová	CZE	10.4.80	15 Jun
13.55	-2.8	Irina	Tyukhay	RUS	14.1.67	22 Jul
13.55	1.1	Clova	Court	GBR	10.2.60	19 Aug
		(198)	213 under 13.60			

Wind assisted

Mark	Wind	Name		Nat	Born	Pos	Meet	Venue	Date
12.45	2.3		Devers			1s2	NC	Sacramento	23 Jul
12.77	5.4	Linda	Ferga	FRA	24.12.76	1		Montauban	15 Aug
12.79	3.7	Joyce	Bates	USA	16.2.77	1	USTCA	Austin	22 Apr
12.83	3.9	Nicole	Hoxie	USA	22.7.79	2		Austin	6 May
12.86	4.8	Dominqué	Calloway	USA	19.7.78	2	Owens	Columbus	7 May
12.88	3.6		Feng Yun	CHN	23.2.76	1h1		Shizuoka	3 May
12.90A	2.5	Yvonne	Kanazawa	JPN	19.11.74	1r1		Flagstaff	8 Jul
12.91	w	Cheryl	Dickey	USA	12.12.66	1		Houston	6 May
12.91	2.1	Reina Flor	Okori	FRA	2.5.80	1h2		Bron	23 Jul
12.92	3.1	Haydy	Aron	FRA	21.5.73	3h1		Bron	23 Jul
12.93	4.8	Jackie	Madison	USA	14.7.79	2	Owens	Columbus	7 May
12.93A	3.0	Dionne	Rose	JAM	7.11.69	2r3		Flagstaff	6 Jul
12.95	2.3	Bisa	Grant	USA	10.7.76	4s2	NC	Sacramento	23 Jul
12.96A	2.1	Sonia	Paquette	CAN	7.2.73	3r2		Flagstaff	8 Jul
12.97	2.9		Su Yiping	CHN	4.8.79	1	NGP	Nanjing	14 Apr
13.01	2.5	Charmaine	Walker	USA	5.5.78	1	Big East	Piscataway	7 May
13.01	2.3	Valerie	Manning	USA	27.3.68	5s2	NC	Sacramento	23 Jul
13.02	2.2	Patrina	Allen	JAM	17.4.75	2	GaTech	Atlanta	20 May
13.03	3.5	Michelle	Perry	USA	1.5.79	1	Pac10	Eugene	21 May
13.03	3.5	Jacquie	Munro	AUS-J	4.10.81	1r2		Gold Coast (RB)	5 Aug
13.03	2.9	Caren	Sonn	GER	18.1.68	1		Arnstadt	12 Aug
13.04	3.9	Dawn	Riley	USA	17.11.73	5		Austin	6 May
13.04	2.3	Andria	King	USA	22.6.76	1	OD	Jena	3 Jun
13.06	3.7	Christina	Ohaeri	USA	30.3.79	1		College Station	15 Apr
13.08	4.0	Michelle	Johnson	USA	12.4.74	2r2	TexR	Austin	8 Apr
13.10	2.6	Danielle	Carruthers	USA	22.12.79	1		Bloomington	13 May
13.12	2.3	Lutisha	Shittu	USA	7.5.79	1		Knoxville	18 May
13.12	2.3	Birgit	Hamann	GER	11.9.69	5	OD	Jena	3 Jun
13.14	5.4	Shelia	Burrell	USA	15.1.72	1h4	KansR	Lawrence KS	22 Apr
13.14	5.5	Akiko	Morimoto	JPN	17.2.77	1h2		Shizuoka	3 May
13.14	3.0	Debbi	Edwards	AUS	25.9.78	1r1		Gold Coast (RB)	5 Aug
13.16	4.0	Tamika	Higgins-Francis	USA	10.4.71	0r2	TexR	Austin	8 Apr
13.17A	4.6	Nikkie	Bouyer	USA	11.2.76	1		El Paso	15 Apr
13.17	w	Andrea	Blackett	BAR	24.1.76	3		Houston	6 May
13.18	5.5	Naoko	Kobayashi	JPN	16.7.68	2h2		Shizuoka	3 May
13.19	3.7	Natasha	Danvers	GBR	19.9.77	7	UCTA	Austin	22 Apr

Mark	Wind	Name		Nat	Born	Date
13.22	3.7	Natasha	Neal	USA	22.7.80	22 Apr
13.24	3.7	April	Sams	USA	23.8.79	22 Apr
13.24	2.3	Damu	Cherry	USA	.78	13 May
13.26	5.4	Rachel	Joy	USA	29.4.78	22 Apr
13.27	3.6	Tomoko	Motegi	JPN	8.8.78	3 May
13.27	2.3	Ingeborg	Leschnik	GER	15.2.72	3 Jun
13.27	2.3	Nadine	Hentschke	GER-J	27.1.82	20 Aug
13.28	3.3	Julie	Pratt	GBR	20.3.79	11 Jun
13.28A	3.2	Nerea	Azkárate	ESP	4.1.74	29 Jul
13.30	3.5	Sally	Heagney-Bult	AUS	3.10.70	5 Aug

Mark	Wind	Name		Nat	Born	Pos	Meet	Venue	Date
13.32	3.0	Aurelia	Trywianska	POL	9.5.76				21 May
13.34	2.5	Elke	Wölfling	AUT	27.11.71				29 Jul
13.35	2.7	Ayumi	Fujita	JPN	2.11.77				11 Jun
13.36	4.2	Tiffany	Talbert	USA					11 May
13.37	2.3	Jennifer	Komoll	GER	17.4.80				3 Jun
13.37	2.9	Dalanda	Jackson	USA-J	21.1.82				24 Jun
13.39	3.3	NeJuan	Bakewell	USA	9.12.78				13 May
13.39	2.9	Ashlee	Williams	USA-J	27.3.84				24 Jun
13.40	3.3	Myriam	Tschomba	BEL	8.1.77				20 May
13.42	3.5	Katia	Brito	CUB	25.11.78				10 Mar
13.42A	4.5	Stephanie	Thomas	USA	6.7.64				6 Jul
13.43	3.4	Bertha	Peñalver	CUB-J	3.10.81				10 Mar
13.46	2.9	Izabela	Oblekowska	POL	18.2.72				3 Jun
13.48	2.1	Kia	Davis	USA	23.5.76				8 Apr
13.48	2.9	Beate	Gensel	GER	12.3.80				12 Aug
13.49	3.3	Trudy	Bihm	USA	22.12.78				19 May
13.50	3.6	Cecile	Michot	FRA	2.6.74				30 Jul
13.52	2.1	Susanne	Dickenson	JAM	12.2.78				24 Mar
13.52	4.2	Kelly	LaBounty	USA	24.11.70				5 Apr
13.52	4.0	Teneeshia	Jones	USA	28.1.79				8 Apr
13.52	5.5	Kuriya	Toyomori	JPN	26.6.73				3 May
13.53	3.4	Iselda	de la Torre	CUB-J	15.5.82				10 Mar
13.53	2.9		Xu Jia	CHN	23.9.79				14 Apr

Best at low altitude

13.22	1.5	Riley	13		May

Hand timing

Mark	Wind	Name		Nat	Born	Pos	Meet	Venue	Date
12.7		Dominqué	Calloway	USA	19.7.78	1		Berkeley	8 Apr
12.9	1.7	Tamika	Higgins-Francis	USA	19.4.71	1		Houston	7 Jul
13.1	0.9		Feng Yun	CHN	23.2.76				25 Mar
13.2			Vu Bich Huong	VIE	30.11.69				4 May
13.2		Oksana	Kuchma	UKR	4.3.73				11 May
13.2	0.6	Anita	Trumpe	LAT	6.8.68				18 Jun
13.2mx	2.0	Sally	Bult	AUS	3.10.70				23 Jul
13.3w		Nakeshia	Jackson	USA					22 Apr

JUNIORS

See main list for top 6 juniors. Additional marks and further juniors:

S Kallur	13.03	-0.9	1s1	WJ	Santiago	18 Oct	13.14	0.3	1		Turku	2 Aug
	13.07	0.0	1	vFIN	Helsinki	2 Sep	13.15	1.7	1		Söderhamn	7 Jun
	13.10	0.3	1	ECp1A	Nadderud	8 Jul	13.18	0.7	2		Karlstad	23 Aug
	13.13	0.6	1h6	WJ	Santiago	17 Oct	11 performances by 4 women to 13.18					

Mark	Wind	Name		Nat	Born	Pos	Meet	Venue	Date
13.25	0.9	Maíla Paula	Machado	BRA	22.1.81	2	IbAm	Rio de Janeiro	21 May
13.29	1.2	Manuela	Bosco	FIN	11.6.82	2		Tampere	19 Jul
13.29	-1.7	Joni-Ann	Doyley	JAM	25.10.81	4	WJ	Santiago de Chile	19 Oct
13.33	0.7	Nadine	Hentschke (10)	GER	27.1.82	2		Mannheim	12 Aug
13.36	-0.4	Mariya	Koroteyeva	RUS	10.11.81	1		Krasnodar	16 Sep
13.38	-0.2	Anay	Tejeda	CUB	3.4.83	2	Barr	La Habana	30 Jul
13.40	0.8	Yuliya	Kondakova	RUS	4.12.81	1	Kuts	Moskva	26 Aug
13.48	0.9	Emily	Waibel	USA	10.2.81	1r2	USTCA	Lincoln NE	7 May
13.48	-1.2		Du Xueru	CHN	20.4.84	H	OT	Jinzhou	7 Jun
13.51	1.9	Ranysah	LeBlanc	USA	1.1.83	1r4		Austin	12 May
13.52	-0.4	Kumiko	Ikeda	JPN	10.1.81	6s2	WJ	Santiago de Chile	18 Oct
13.56	1.7	Dalanda	Jackson	USA	21.1.82	1		Sherbrooke	21 Jul
13.56	0.0	Yana	Kasova	BUL	13.8.81	1		Beograd	29 Aug
13.60		Keitha	Moseley (20)	BAR	21.7.81	1		St. Georges	24 Apr

Wind assisted

Mark	Wind	Name		Nat	Born	Pos	Meet	Venue	Date
13.03w		Munro	in main list and		13.17 3.0		2r1	Gold Caost (RB)	5 Aug
13.27	2.3	Nadine	Hentschke	GER	27.1.82	1	NC-23	Jena	19 Aug
13.37	2.9	Dalanda	Jackson	USA	21.1.82	1	NC-j	Denton	24 Jun
13.39	2.9	Ashlee	Williams	USA	27.3.84	2	NC-j	Denton	24 Jun
13.43	3.4	Bertha	Peñalver	CUB	3.10.81	2		Camagüey	10 Mar
13.53	3.4	Iselda	de la Torre	CUB	15.5.82	3		Camagüey	10 Mar
13.59	2.9	LaTasha	Pharr	USA	6.5.83	3	NC-j	Denton	24 Jun

200 METRES HURDLES

Mark	Wind	Name		Nat	Born	Pos	Meet	Venue	Date
26.47	0.2	Monica	Niederstätter	ITA	2.3.74	1		Trento	31 May

400 METRES HURDLES

Mark	Name		Nat	Born	Pos	Meet	Venue	Date
53.02	Irina	Privalova	RUS	22.11.68	1	OG	Sydney	27 Sep
53.33	Sandra	Glover	USA	30.12.68	1	NC	Sacramento	17 Jul
53.45	Deon	Hemmings	JAM	9.10.68	2	OG	Sydney	27 Sep
53.53	Nezha	Bidouane	MAR	18.9.69	1	GGala	Roma	30 Jun
53.57		Bidouane			3	OG	Sydney	27 Sep
53.68	Daimí	Pernía	CUB	27.12.76	4	OG	Sydney	27 Sep
53.87		Glover			1s1	NC	Sacramento	16 Jul
53.92		Glover			1	BrGP	London (CP)	5 Aug
53.98	Tatyana	Tereshchuk	UKR	11.10.69	5	OG	Sydney	27 Sep
54.00		Hemmings			1s2	OG	Sydney	25 Sep
54.02		Privalova			1s1	OG	Sydney	25 Sep
54.06		Privalova			1	Herc	Monaco	18 Aug
54.08		Glover			1	Gugl	Linz	8 Aug
54.14		Pernía			1		Zagreb	3 Jul
54.18		Glover			1	GaTech	Atlanta	20 May
54.18		Hemmings			1	Athl	Lausanne	5 Jul
54.19		Bidouane			2s2	OG	Sydney	25 Sep
54.20		Tereshchuk			2		Zagreb	3 Jul

Mark	Name		Nat	Born	Pos	Meet	Venue	Date
54.21		Privalova			1	NC	Tula	25 Jul
54.25		Tereshchuk			3s2	OG	Sydney	25 Sep
54.27		Tereshchuk			2	Herc	Monaco	18 Aug
54.31	Yuliya	Nosova	RUS	21.4.78	1	NCp	Tula	4 Jun
54.31		Glover			2	GGala	Roma	30 Jun
54.35	Ionela	Tîrlea	ROM	9.2.76	6	OG	Sydney	27 Sep
54.37	Gudrun	Arnardóttir	ISL	24.9.71	2	BrGP	London (CP)	5 Aug
54.38		Hemmings			1		Villeneuve d'Ascq	17 Jul
54.39		Glover			1		Luzern	27 Jun
54.40		Hemmings			1	NC	Kingston	21 Jul
54.41		Hemmings			1	Veniz	Haniá	14 Jun
54.41	Andrea	Blackett	BAR	24.1.76	1		Chaux de Fonds	13 Aug
	(30/10)							
54.50	Natalya	Torshina	KAZ	4.10.68	1	ECCp	V R San António	27 May
54.57	Ulrike	Urbansky	GER	6.4.77	1		Barcelona	25 Jul
54.70	Kim	Batten	USA	29.3.69	2	NC	Sacramento	17 Jul
54.80	Tonja	Buford-Bailey	USA	13.12.70	3	NC	Sacramento	17 Jul
54.84	Heike	Meissner	GER	29.1.70	2		Barcelona	25 Jul
54.93	Catherine	Scott	JAM	24.8.73	2	NC	Kingston	21 Jul
54.95	Natasha	Danvers	GBR	19.9.77	3s1	OG	Sydney	25 Sep
54.97	Joanna	Hayes	USA	23.12.76	4	NC	Sacramento	17 Jul
55.09	Yvonne	Harrison	USA	2.12.75	2	GaTech	Atlanta	20 May
55.11	Mame Tacko	Diouf	SEN	17.10.76	3	Nik	Nice	8 Jul
	(20)							
55.20A	Jana	Pittman	AUS-J	9.11.82	1		Pietersburg	18 Mar
55.22A	Surita	Febbraio	RSA	27.12.73	1		Roodepoort	13 Mar
55.22	Keri	Maddox	GBR	4.7.72	1	NC	Birmingham	12 Aug
55.31	Michelle	Johnson	USA	12.4.74	1h3	NC	Sacramento	15 Jul
55.37	Lauren	Poetschka	AUS	22.10.74	1	GP II	Melbourne	2 Mar
55.42	Susan	Smith	IRL	14.9.71	1		Padova	27 Aug
55.45	Sinead	Dudgeon	GBR	9.7.76	1		Budapest	22 Jul
55.50	Angel	Patterson	USA	6.8.79	1	TexR	Austin	8 Apr
55.55	Tanya	Jarrett	JAM	18.9.77	4	Nik	Nice	8 Jul
55.56	Trevaia	Davis	USA	7.9.68	4s1	NC	Sacramento	16 Jul
	(30)							
55.57	Ryan	Tolbert	USA	16.6.76	5s1	NC	Sacramento	16 Jul
55.63	Patrina	Allen	JAM	17.4.75	3	GaTech	Atlanta	20 May
55.73	Natalya	Chulkova	RUS	5.12.77	3	NC	Tula	25 Jul
55.75	Anna	Olichwierczuk	POL	10.12.78	1	NC	Kraków	5 Aug
55.78	Monica	Niederstätter	ITA	2.3.74	4		Barcelona	25 Jul
55.79	Tatyana	Debelaya	UKR	28.1.70	1	NC	Kiev	5 Aug
55.83		Li Yulian	CHN	17.2.79	1	NC	Luohe	21 Oct
55.86	Nikkie	Bouyer	USA	11.2.76	2	GP	Raleigh	17 Jun
55.86	Malgorzata	Pskit	POL	25.5.76	1		Wroclaw	6 Sep
55.90	Debbie-Ann	Parris	JAM	24.3.73	1		Chapel Hill	18 Jun
	(40)							
55.91	Tatyana	Kurochkina	BLR	15.9.67	2		Riga	22 Jun
55.93	Peta-Gaye	Gayle	JAM	19.1.79	3	NCAA	Durham	2 Jun
55.98	Svetlana	Sagaydak	RUS	.70	2	NCp	Tula	4 Jun
56.00		Song Yinglan	CHN	14.9.75	1	OT	Jinzhou	8 Jun
56.02	Maren	Schott	GER	11.2.76	1		Wipperfürth	13 Aug
56.03	Stephanie	Price	AUS	17.7.62	3	GP II	Melbourne	2 Mar
56.07	Petra	Söderström	FIN	12.3.74	1		Lappeenranta	13 Aug
56.09	Irina	Lenskiy	ISR	12.6.71	2		Kiev	18 Jun
56.11A	Karlene	Haughton	CAN	18.10.72	2		Flagstaff	8 Jul
56.21	Silvia	Rieger	GER	14.11.70	2	OD	Jena	3 Jun
	(50)							
56.26	Marjorlein	de Jong	NED-J	12.6.81	2h1	WJ	Santiago de Chile	19 Oct
56.30A	Melinda	Sallins	USA	30.6.73	1		Flagstaff	6 Jul
56.30	Anika	Ahrens	GER	19.7.78	1	NC-23	Jena	20 Aug
56.32	Dominqué	Calloway	USA	19.7.78	1h1	NCAA	Durham	31 May
56.39	Natasha	Reynolds-Peeble	USA	7.6.72	3h1	NC	Sacramento	15 Jul
56.40	Irena	Zauna	LAT-J	16.3.81	1		Valmiera	14 Jul
56.42	Anna	Knoroz	RUS	30.7.70	1	Sule	Tartu	11 Jun
56.45	Saidat	Onanuga	NGR	18.6.74	2h1	NCAA	Durham	31 May
56.48	Tatyana	Ledovskaya	BLR	21.5.66	1		Staiki	27 Jun
56.50	Michelle	Perry	USA	1.5.79	4	NCAA	Durham	2 Jun
	(60)							
56.63		Li Rui	CHN	22.11.79	1	NGP	Tianjin	3 May

Mark	Name		Nat	Born	Pos	Meet	Venue	Date
56.64	Brenda	Taylor	USA	9.2.79	4h1	NC	Sacramento	15 Jul
56.65		Peng Yinghua	CHN	.2.79	2	NGP	Tianjin	3 May
56.67	Frances	Santin	USA	27.7.80	5h1	NC	Sacramento	15 Jul
56.73	Adrienne	McIvor	IRL	2.9.70	3		Riga	22 Jun
56.74	Anja	Höcke	GER	16.10.74	1		Stuttgart	18 Jun
56.77	Ann	Mercken	BEL	6.5.74	1		Brasschaat	15 Aug
56.82	Sheena	Johnson	USA-J	1.10.82	1	NC-j	Denton	24 Jun
56.83	Claudia	Jung	GER	17.6.76	2		Stuttgart	18 Jun
56.83	LaTanya	Sheffield	USA	11.10.63	2h4	NC	Sacramento	15 Jul
	(70)							
56.86	Olga	Dor	ISR	26.6.76	2h3	NC	Sydney	24 Feb
56.86	TaNisha	Mills	USA	2.11.74	3h2	NC	Sacramento	15 Jul
56.89	Nathalie	Zamboni	SUI	23.12.73	1	NC	Lugano	30 Jul
56.90	Hrísa	Goudenoúdi	GRE	28.3.77	7	Veniz	Hánia	14 Jun
56.94	Frida	Svensson	SWE	5.1.70	1	ECp-1A	Nadderud	8 Jul
56.96	Melanie	Walker	JAM-J	1.1.83	3	WJ	Santiago de Chile	21 Oct
57.02	Tawa	Babatunde	CAN	19.12.79	1r2		Atlanta	20 May
57.02	Omolade	Akinremi	NGR	13.9.74	1		Fullerton	17 Jun
57.05		Jia Wanhong	CHN-J	24.9.81	2	NGPF	Jinzhou	8 Jun
57.07	Randi	Smith	USA-J	14.5.81	2	NC-j	Denton	24 Jun
	(80)							
57.10	Julie	Bennion-Murdock	USA	12.3.75	6h1	NC	Sacramento	15 Jul
57.11A	Isabelle	Gervais	CAN	27.7.77	2		Flagstaff	6 Jul
57.13	Lara	Rocco	ITA	20.12.75	1		Trieste	26 Jul
57.15	Orsolya	Dóczi	HUN	28.9.75	6		Budapest	22 Jul
57.17	Eva	Paniagua	ESP	2.2.74	7		Barcelona	25 Jul
57.19	Ana Paula	Pereira	BRA	11.12.78	1		Rio de Janeiro	27 May
57.21	LaTasha	Colander-Richardson	USA	23.8.76	1		Raleigh	31 Mar
57.23	Ester	Goossens	NED	21.2.72	1		Vught	24 Sep
57.24	Martina	Stoop	SUI	1.1.73	1		Luzern	27 Jun
57.26	Miriam	Hrdlicková	SVK	4.1.76	7		Budapest	22 Jul
	(90)							
57.29	Natalya	Senkina	UZB	23.9.70	1	NC	Bangkok	17 May
57.29	Jupira	da Graça	BRA	20.2.70	2		Americana	3 Jun
57.29	Lantosoa	Razafinjanahary	MAD-J	13.5.81	1h2	WJ	Santiago de Chile	19 Oct
57.30	Le'Gretta	Hinds-Smith	USA	13.1.74	1		Indianapolis	1 Jul
57.31	Carla	Barbarino	ITA	16.5.67	1		Saronno	4 Jun
57.33	Omotayo	Akinremi	NGR	13.9.74	2		Tucson	17 Mar
57.36	Lana	Jekabsone	LAT	16.10.74	1	DrakeR	Des Moines	28 Apr
57.38	Olga	Salnikova	RUS	19.6.71	3r3	Mos Ch	Moskva	12 Jul
57.47	Sedell	Roberts	JAM		7r1		Atlanta	20 May
57.48	Gesine	Schmidt	GER	26.6.71	4		Rhede	23 Jun
	(100)							

57.49	Stephanie	Kampf	GER	25.4.78	22 Jul
57.50	Olivia	Abderrhamanne	FRA	2.8.79	2 Sep
57.51	Miriam	Alonso	ESP	6.6.70	24 Aug
57.52	Evette	Cordy	AUS	28.9.73	16 Jul
57.53	Luciana	França	BRA	19.5.77	6 Aug
57.54	Natasha	Neal	USA	22.7.80	8 Apr
57.55A	Kerryn	van Zyl	RSA	5.10.74	24 Mar
57.56A	Holly	Gibbons	USA	28.9.79	20 May
57.61	Inna	Tsud	UKR	17.1.67	16 Jul
57.64		Wang Yamei	CHN	30.9.78	19 Apr
57.67A	Lana	van Heerden	RSA	9.12.68	13 Mar
57.73A	Milena	Alver	EST	10.12.76	20 May
57.73	Perla	dos Santos	BRA-J	29.1.82	6 Aug
57.74	Corinne	Tafflet	FRA	8.11.75	15 Jul
57.75	Ellakisha	Williamson	USA	19.3.75	12 May
57.76	Meta	Macus	SLO	23.3.75	27 Aug
57.77	Eusheka	Bartley	USA	2.1.74	15 Apr
57.77	Nicole	Thomas	USA	3.8.79	6 May
57.79		Zeng Xiaoling	CHN		10 Sep
57.80	Sonia	Brito	AUS	10.6.79	27 Feb
57.80A	Deniece	Bell	CAN	11.1.78	8 Jul
57.82	Georgia	Harrison	JAM	6.9.70	1 Jul
57.82	Linise	Gordon	USA		1 Jul
57.83	Gnima	Touré	SEN	27.8.75	6 Aug
57.84	Sandra	Farmer-Patrick	USA	18.8.62	15 Jul
57.88	Corinne	Pierre-Joseph	FRA	27.10.66	13 Aug
57.89	Anja	Rantanen	FIN	18.7.79	3 Sep
57.90	Elke	Bogemans	BEL	22.6.77	2 Jul
57.90		Chen Lin	CHN-J	22.8.81	21 Oct
57.92	Tracey	Duncan	GBR	16.5.79	29 Jul
57.92	Makiko	Yoshida	JPN	16.7.76	2 Sep
57.97	Karolina	Tlustochowska	POL-J	19.9.81	19 Oct
57.97		Yang Hairong	CHN	8.6.78	21 Oct
57.98	Skye	Green	USA	3.5.74	16 Apr
58.01	Nicola	Kidd	NZL	4.7.75	27 Feb
58.01	Anastasiya	Rabchenyuk	UKR-J	14.9.83	18 Jun
58.04A	Jane	Durfey	USA	9.7.77	22 Apr
58.05	Yasnay	Lescay	CUB	25.7.78	11 Mar
58.07	Aleksandra	Pieluzek	POL	4.4.79	9 Sep
58.08		Xun Penghua	CHN	15.9.80	19 Apr
58.09	Åsa	Carlsson	SWE	19.12.72	18 Jun
58.10	Katia	Brito	CUB	25.11.78	8 Jul
58.11	Kylie	Wheeler	AUS	17.1.80	11 Feb
58.11	Yelena	Budnik	BLR	9.5.76	20 May
58.11	Sylvanie	Morandais	FRA	14.7.79	6 Aug
58.12A	Natalie	Gibson	USA	1.8.77	22 Apr
58.12	Cara	Evans	USA	23.7.78	3 Jun
58.12	Mari	Bjone	NOR	11.9.70	8 Jul
58.17	Yamelis	Ortiz	PUR	26.2.78	16 May
58.18	Brandy	Mack	USA	1.11.78	31 May
58.21	Ayanna	Reece	USA	18.4.76	31 May
58.23	Andrea	Bliss	JAM	5.10.80	13 Apr
58.27	Yasuko	Igari	JPN	25.4.77	3 May
58.27A	Princesa	Oliveros	COL	10.8.75	7 Dec
58.29A	Kelsey	Sheppard	USA	11.9.79	6 May
58.30	Natalya	Antyukh	RUS-J	26.6.81	9 Jul
58.33	Ayodele	Buraimoh	GER	24.4.78	20 Aug
58.33	Zofia	Malachowska	POL-J	14.5.82	19 Oct

Mark		Name	Nat	Born	Date
58.34	Kari	Karhoff	USA	15.5.79	20 May
58.34	Isabel	Silva	BRA	15.6.79	3 Jun
58.34	Tsvetelina	Kirilova	BUL	14.7.77	8 Jul
58.40		Choi Hae-nam	KOR	17.2.76	10 Jun
58.41	Mayte	Urcelay	ESP	8.9.72	27 May
58.43	Karla	Faulhaber	GER	13.5.74	29 Jul
58.43	Manuela	Gentili	ITA	7.2.78	27 Aug
58.44	Becky	Jackson	USA	5.4.77	13 May
58.44	Joanna	Helm	USA	31.3.78	14 May
58.45	Adneris	Griñán	CUB	12.5.73	11 Mar
58.47	Erica	Mårtensson	SWE	24.6.79	13 Aug
58.48	Nerelys	Rodriguez	CUB		4 Jun
58.50	Tiffany	Ross	USA-J	5.2.83	17 Jun
58.50	Tawana	Watkins	USA-J	27.3.84	17 Jun
	(172)				

Hand Timed

Mark		Name	Nat	Born	Pos	Meet	Venue	Date
57.2	Lantosoa	Razafinjanahary	MAD-J	13.5.81	1	NC	Antananarivo	27 Aug
57.3	Cendrino	Razaiarimalala	MAD	8.2.78	2	NC	Antananarivo	27 Aug
57.7	Gnima	Touré	SEN	27.8.75				23 Jul
58.1	Asik	Beevi	IND					2 Nov
58.3	Gowry	Hodge	GBR	21.6.60				2 Sep

Best at low altitude

Mark	Name	Pos	Venue	Date
55.63	Pittman	1	Sydney	13 Feb
55.77	Febbraio	2	Budapest	22 Jul
56.17	Haughton	3	Palo Alto	1 Jul
56.36	Sallins	3h3NC	Sacramento	15 Jul
57.68	van Heerden			4 Mar
58.15	van Zyl			4 Mar
58.37	Oliveros			31 Jul
58.43	Gibbons			31 May

Drugs disqualification

Mark		Name	Nat	Born	Pos	Venue	Date
55.96A	Judit	Szekeres ¶	HUN	18.11.66	2	Pretoria	28 Jan

JUNIORS

See main list for top 8 juniors. 10 Performances by 2 women to 56.27. Additional marks and further juniors:

	Mark	Pos	Meet	Venue	Date
Pittman	55.61	1		Brisbane	3 Sep
	55.63	1		Sydney	13 Feb
	55.82	1		Sydney	20 Feb
	55.88	1	OT	Sydney	19 Aug
	55.93	2		Melbourne	2 Feb
	56.12	1		Gold Coast (RB)	10 Sep
	56.161	s1	WJ	Santiago	19 Oct
	56.27	1	WJ	Santiago	19 Oct

Mark		Name	Nat	Born	Pos	Meet	Venue	Date
57.73	Perla	dos Santos	BRA	29.1.82	3	NC	Rio de Janeiro	6 Aug
57.90		Chen Lin (10)	CHN	22.8.81	4	NC	Luohe	21 Oct
57.97	Karolina	Tlustochowska	POL	19.9.81	2h2	WJ	Santiago de Chile	19 Oct
58.01	Anastasiya	Rabchenyuk	UKR	14.9.83	4		Kiev	18 Jun
58.30	Natalya	Antyukh	RUS	26.6.81	1		Cheboksary	9 Jul
58.33	Zofia	Malachowska	POL	14.5.82	2h3	WJ	Santiago de Chile	19 Oct
58.50	Tiffany	Ross	USA	5.2.83	2	NSch	Raleigh	17 Jun
58.50	Tawana	Watkins	USA	27.3.84	3	NSch	Raleigh	17 Jun
58.60	Sira	Córdoba	COL	17.5.81	4h3	WJ	Santiago de Chile	21 Oct
58.61	Patricia	Hall	JAM	16.10.82	2		Kingston	13 Apr
58.68	Sapinder	Kaur	IND	8.4.82	1	Inter-St	Chennai	31 Jul
58.70	Yekaterina	Kimovets (20)	BLR	10.10.82	7		Kiev	18 Jun

HIGH JUMP

2.02 Monica Iagar/Dinescu ROM 1.4.73 1 Villeneuve d'Ascq 17 Jun
1.80/1 1.85/1 1.90/1 1.94/1 1.97/3 2.00/3 2/02/3 2.04/xxp
1.98 1 Tunis 3 Jun
1.97 1 Milano 7 Jun 1.80/1 1.85/1 1.91/2 1.94/2 1.97/3 2.00/xxx
1.97 2 GGala Roma 30 Jun 1.80/1 1.85/1 1.91/1 1.94/1 1.97/2 2.00/xxx
2.01 Venelina Veneva BUL 13.6.74 1 Kalamáta 4 Jun
1.85/1 1.92/1 1.95/3 1.98/1 2.01/2 2.05/xxx
2.00 1 GP Athêna 30 May 1.85/1 1.91/1 1.97/3 2.00/1 -
1.97i 1 Brno 9 Feb 1.80/1 1.85/2 1.88/1 1.91/1 1.94/3 1.97/1 1.99/xxp
1.97 2 Zagreb 3 Jul 1.80/1 1.85/1 1.89/2 1.93/2 1.97/3 p
1.97 1 ECp1B Bydgoszcz 9 Jul 1.81/1 1.84/1 1.89/1 1.91/1 1.93/2 1.95/1 1.97/2
2.01 Kajsa Bergqvist SWE 12.10.76 1 NC Uppsala 19 Aug
1.83/1 1.91/1 1.96/1 2.01/3
2.00i 1 Pátra 16 Feb 1.85/1 1.91/2 1.94/2 1.96/1 2.00/2 p
2.00i 1 EI Gent 26 Feb 1.85/1 1.89/1 1.92/2 1.94/1 1.96/x 1.98/1 2.00/2
2.05/xx
2.00 1 Falköping 15 Aug 1.81/1 1.87/1 1.90/1 1.95/1 2.00/3 2.03/xxx
2.00 1 Gold Coast (RB) 17 Sep 1.90/1 1.95/1 2.00/1 2.03/xxx
1.99 3= OG Sydney 30 Sep 1.85/1 1.90/1 1.93/1 1.96/1 1.99/2 2.01/x 2.03/xx
1.97 1 Lapinlahti 16 Jul 1.82/1 1.89/1 1.94/2 1.97/1 2.00/xxx
2.01 Yelena Yelesina RUS 4.4.70 1 OG Sydney 30 Sep
1.85/1 1.90/1 1.93/1 1.96/1 1.99/1 2.01/2 2.03/xxx
1.99 1 Yokohama 9 Sep 1.80/1 1.85/1 1.90/2 1.93/1 1.96/3 1.99/3
1.97 3 GP Athêna 30 May 1.75/1 1.80/1 1.85/1 1.88/2 1.91/2 1.94/3 1.97/3
2.00/xxx
2.01 Hestrie Cloete RSA 26.8.78 2 OG Sydney 30 Sep
1.85/1 1.90/1 1.93/1 1.96/2 1.99/1 2.01/2 2.03/xxx
1.97 1 Athl Lausanne 5 Jul 1.80/1 1.85/1 1.90/1 1.94/1 1.97/3 2.00/xxx
1.97 1 MAI Malmö 7 Aug 1.80/1 1.85/2 1.88/1 1.91/2 1.94/1 1.97/1 2.00/xxx
2.00 Zuzana Hlavonová CZE 16.4.73 1 Odlozil Praha 5 Jun
1.80/1 1.84/1 1.88/1 1.91/2 1.94/1 1.96/xp 1.98/2 2.00/1
1.98i 2 EI Gent 26 Feb 1.80/2 1.85/1 1.89/2 1.92/2 1.94/2 1.98/2 2.00/xxx

Mark	Name		Nat	Born	Pos	Meet	Venue	Date
	1.97 1 GS Ostrava 1 Jun			1.80/1 1.85/1 1.88/1 1.91/2 1.94/1 1.97/1 2.00/xxx				
	1.97 1 GP II Bratislava 22 Jun			1.80/1 1.85/1 1.91/1 1.94/1 1.97/1 2.01/xx				
2.00	Inga	Babakova	UKR	27.6.67	2		Villeneuve d'Ascq	17 Jun
				1.80/1 1.85/1 1.90/1 1.94/1 1.97/1 2.00/3 2.02/xxx				
	2.00 2 Zagreb 3 Jul			1.80/1 1.85/1 1.89/1 1.93/1 1/97/1 2.00/2 2.03/xxp				
	1.97 1 Torino 10 Jun			1.80/1 1.85/1 1.90/1 1.93/1 1.97/1 1.99/xxx				
	1.97 1 GGala Roma 30 Jun			1.80/1 1.85/1 1.88/1 1.91/1 1.94/1 1.97/1 2.00/xxx				
1.99	Oana	Pantelimon	ROM	27.9.72	3=	OG	Sydney	30 Sep
				1.85/1 1.90/1 1.93/1 1.96/1 1.99/2 2.01/xxx				
1.98	Khristina	Kalcheva	BUL	29.5.77	2		Kalamáta	4 Jun
				1.80/1 1.85/1 1.89/1 1.92/2 1.95/2 1.98/3 2.01/xxx				
	1.97 2 GP Athêna 30 May			1.80/1 1.85/1 1.88/1 1.91/1 1.94/1 1.97/1 2.00/xxx				
1.98	Irina	Mikhalchenko	UKR	20.1.72	1	NC	Kiev	5 Aug
	(10)			1.80/1 1.85/1 1.89/1 1.92/1 1.94/1 1.96/2 1.98/2 2.00/xxx				
1.98	Viktoriya	Palamar	UKR	12.10.77	2	NC	Kiev	5 Aug
				1.85/1 1.89/1 1.92/2 1.94/1 1.96/3 1.98/2 2.00/xxx				
	1.97 1 Kiev 15 Jul							
1.97i	Dora	Györffy	HUN	23.2.78	1		Hanover, NH	27 Feb
	1.75/1			1.78/1 1.81/1 1.84/1 1.88/1 1.91/1 1.94/1 1.97/2 2.00/xxp				
1.97i	Viktoriya	Seryogina	RUS	22.5.73	1	v4N	Glasgow	5 Mar
				1.76/1 1.81/1 1.86/1 1.89/1 1.92/1 1.95/1 1.97/2 2.00/xxx				
1.97	Svetlana	Zalevskaya	KAZ	14.6.73	2	Athl	Lausanne	5 Jul
				1.80/1 1.85/1 1.90/3 1.94/1 1.97/3 2.00/xxx				
1.97	Tatyana	Shevchik	BLR	11.6.69	1		Berdichev	3 Sep
	(40/15)							
1.96i	Olga	Kaliturina	RUS	9.3.76	3	EI	Gent	26 Feb
1.96i	Tisha	Waller	USA	1.12.70	1	NC	Atlanta	4 Mar
1.96	Marina	Kuptsova	RUS-J	22.12.81	1	NC	Tula	26 Jul
1.96	Viktoriya	Styopina	UKR	21.2.76	3	NC	Kiev	5 Aug
1.96	Yuliya	Lyakhova	RUS	8.7.77	1		Leverkusen	20 Aug
	(20)							
1.95	Erin	Aldrich	USA	27.12.77	1	TexR	Austin	7 Apr
1.95	Eleonora	Milusheva	BUL	8.4.73	1		Mito	7 May
1.95	Yelena	Gulyayeva	RUS	14.8.67	3		Kalamáta	4 Jun
1.95	Hanne	Haugland	NOR	14.12.67	2	ECp1A	Nadderud	9 Jul
1.95	Sigrid	Kirchmann	AUT	29.3.66	2	ECp1B	Bydgoszcz	9 Jul
1.94i	Solange	Witteveen	ARG	6.2.76	4		Brno	9 Feb
1.94i	Viktoriya	Slivka	RUS	28.9.80	5		Brno	9 Feb
1.94	Liga	Klavina	LAT	27.1.80	1	Sule	Tartu	11 Jun
1.94	Amehu	Mensah	GER	21.3.77	1		Rehlingen	12 Jun
1.94	Tatyana	Babashkina	RUS	23.11.68	2	GP II	Bratislava	22 Jun
	(30)							
1.94	Svetlana	Lapina	RUS	12.4.78	3	NC	Tula	26 Jul
1.94	Yoko	Ota	JPN	14.1.75	Q	OG	Sydney	28 Sep
1.93i	Gwen	Wentland	USA	29.4.72	1		Fairfax	29 Jan
1.93	Miki	Imai	JPN	30.5.75	2	GP	Osaka	13 May
1.93	Inna	Gliznutsa	MDA	18.4.73	1		Chisinau	10 Jun
1.93	Tatyana	Nikolayeva	UKR	26.2.76	1		Kiev	16 Jun
1.93	Nele	Zilinskiené	LTU	29.12.69	5	GP II	Zagreb	3 Jul
1.93	Karol	Damon	USA	20.12.69	1	NC	Sacramento	16 Jul
1.93	Blanka	Vlasic	CRO-J	8.11.83	1		Zagreb	30 Jul
1.93	Linda	Horvath	AUT	10.2.78	1	NC	Wien	19 Aug
	(40)							
1.93	Marta	Mendía	ESP	18.5.75	1		Manresa	24 Aug
1.93	Susan	Jones	GBR	8.6.78	1	v FRA	Vittel	2 Sep
1.93	Michelle	Dunkley	GBR	26.1.78	2	v FRA	Vittel	2 Sep
1.92i	Antonella	Bevilacqua	ITA	15.10.71	2	v2N	Valencia	19 Feb
1.92i	Daniela	Galeotti	ITA	22.3.77	3	v2N	Valencia	19 Feb
1.92i	Nicole	Forrester	CAN	17.11.76	3	v4N	Glasgow	5 Mar
1.92	Ioamnet	Quintero	CUB	8.9.72	1		La Habana	25 Feb
1.92	Birgit	Kähler	GER	14.8.70	3		Rehlingen	12 Jun
1.91i	Heike	Henkel	GER	5.5.64	1	NC	Sindelfingen	12 Feb
1.91i	Nevena	Lendjel	CRO	18.7.79	Q	EI	Gent	25 Feb
	(50)							
1.91	Natalya	Roshchupkina	RUS	13.1.78	1H		Götzis	3 Jun
1.91	Stefania	Cadamuro	ITA	23.2.79	5		Milano	7 Jun
1.91	Amy	Acuff	USA	14.7.75	3jo	NC	Sacramento	16 Jul
1.91	Tatyana	Gordeyeva	RUS	3.6.73	1=H	NC	Tula	22 Jul
1.91	Yelena	Chernyavskaya	RUS	13.4.78	1=H	NC	Tula	22 Jul
1.90i	Miriam	Bielert	GER	17.6.75	1		Halle	29 Jan

Mark	Name		Nat	Born	Pos	Meet	Venue	Date
1.90i	Angie	Spangler	USA	4.9.68	2	NC	Atlanta	4 Mar
1.90	Marina	Korzhova	KAZ-J	13.9.82	2		Almaty	27 May
1.90	Olga	Shedova	BLR-J	6.4.81	1		Schwechat	10 Jun
1.90	Tatyana	Efimenko	KGZ-J	2.1.81	1	NC	Bishkek	2 Jul
	(60)							
1.90	Yekaterina	Aleksandrova	RUS	3.6.77	2	Mos Ch	Moskva	11 Jul
1.90	Mária	Melová	SVK	21.10.75	1		Dudelange	16 Jul
1.90	Sabrina	De Leeuw	BEL	19.8.74	1		Brasschaat	15 Aug
1.90	Anna	Chicherova	RUS-J	22.7.82	1=		Krasnodar	15 Sep
1.90	Natalya	Lebusova	RUS	.78	1=		Krasnodar	15 Sep
1.90A	Nicolize	Steyn	RSA-J	28.5.81	1		Pretoria	17 Sep
1.89	Karen	Beautle	JAM	13.6.71	1		Kingston	26 Feb
1.89	Wanita	May	CAN	30.1.75	2		Bedford	4 Jun
1.89	Tia	Hellebaut	BEL	16.2.78	1		Oordegem	11 Jun
1.89	Kärt	Siilats	EST	7.9.80	1		Haapsalu	20 Jun
	(70)							
1.89	Agni	Charalambous	CYP	2.9.75	1	NC	Nicosia	1 Jul
1.89	Natalya	Turayeva	RUS-J	.82	7=	NC	Tula	26 Jul
1.89	Jo	Jennings-Steele	GBR	20.9.69	1	NC	Birmingham	12 Aug
1.89	Katja	Schötz	GER-J	22.7.81	1	NC-23	Jena	19 Aug
1.88i	Inga	Janku	CZE	1.5.74	1		Siegen	21 Jan
1.88	Alison	Inverarity	AUS	12.8.70	1=		Perth	5 Feb
1.88i	Renata	Medgyesová	SVK-J	28.1.83	1	NC	Bratislava	5 Feb
1.88i	Tatyana	Gulevich	BLR	10.2.71	4		Banská Bystrica	16 Feb
1.88i	Ágota	Stáhl	HUN	17.12.78	1		Dunaújváros	26 Feb
1.88i	Sophie	Sagonas	GER-J	18.9.81	1	v2N	Neubrandenburg	4 Mar
	(80)							
1.88		Lu Jieming	CHN-J	25.1.83	1	NGP	Nanjing	15 Apr
1.88		Zhang Liwen	CHN	29.1.73	1	NGP	Wenzhou	22 Apr
1.88	Irina	Naumenko	KAZ	13.2.80	1H		Almaty	20 May
1.88	Heike	Balck	GER	19.8.70	5		Wörrstadt	27 May
1.88	Adriana	Maximiuc	ROM	1.10.73	6		Wörrstadt	27 May
1.88	Eunice	Barber	FRA	17.11.74	1H		Götzis	3 Jun
1.88	Irina	Zhukovskaya	RUS	.78	q	NC	Tula	24 Jul
1.88	Elena	Herzenberg	GER	24.6.79	1		Arnstadt	13 Aug
1.88	Lee	McConnell	GBR	9.10.78	2	NCp	Bedford	19 Aug
1.88	Níki	Bakoyiánni	GRE	9.6.68	4		Pátra	2 Sep
	(90)							
1.88	Yelena	Sivushenko	RUS-J	28.2.82	3		Krasnodar	15 Sep
1.88	Antonietta	Di Martino	ITA	1.6.78	1		Matera	20 Sep
1.88	Marizca	Gertenbach	RSA-J	20.10.82	3	WJ	Santiago de Chile	20 Oct
1.87i	Latifah	Long	USA	21.2.77	1		Minneapolis	29 Jan
1.87i	Barbora	Laláková	CZE-J	2.5.81	1	NC-j	Praha	19 Feb
1.87i	Orsolya	Appelt	HUN	27.5.78	1		Budapest	20 Feb
1.87i	Marianne	Mattas	FIN	20.8.79	1	NC-23	Jyväskylä	27 Feb
1.87i	Carri	Long	USA	23.4.77	2	NCAA	Fayetteville	11 Mar
1.87	Svetlana	Stavskaya	KAZ	9.5.77	3		Almaty	27 May
1.87	Alina	Astafei	GER	7.6.69	2	NC	Braunschweig	29 Jul
	(100)							
1.87	Anna	Ksok	POL-J	29.9.83	1	v3N-j	Bialystok	27 Aug

1.86i	Dalia	Mikneviciute	GBR	5.9.70	16 Jan
1.86i	Pia	Lindroth	FIN	19.10.79	23 Jan
1.86i	Ruth	Beitia	ESP	1.4.79	29 Jan
1.86i	Kathryn	Holinski	GER-J	19.7.82	4 Feb
1.86i	Anzhela	Laytinen	RUS	.71	6 Feb
1.86i	Karin	Ertl	GER	23.6.74	25 Feb
1.86	Tayibba	Haneef	USA	23.3.79	19 May
1.86	Tamika	Toppin	USA	5.6.79	17 Jun
1.86	Tatyana	Grigoryeva	RUS-J	13.5.81	20 Jun
1.86	Katja	Vainikainen	FIN	30.7.77	24 Jun
1.86	Sheree	Francis	JAM-J	20.10.83	30 Jun
1.86	Bobby	Aloysius	IND	.73	21 Jul
1.86	Donata	Jancewicz	POL	17.6.69	5 Aug
1.86	Melanie	Skotnik	GER-J	8.11.82	9 Sep
1.86	Ramona	Pop	ROM-J	5.4.82	7 Oct
1.85	Sherryl	Morrow	AUS	22.3.73	13 Jan
1.85i	Gaëlle	Niaré	FRA-J	12.3.82	15 Jan
1.85	Jane	Millington	AUS	16.7.76	16 Jan
1.85i	Julia	Bennett	GBR	26.3.70	23 Jan
1.85	Lisa	Bruty	AUS	2.5.77	30 Jan
1.85i	Stefania	Paesotto	ITA	20.1.79	5 Feb
1.85i	Lyudmila	Shevchuk	UKR	9.11.77	7 Feb
1.85i	Svetlana	Kazanina	KAZ	31.10.71	11 Feb
1.85i	Julie	Crane	GBR	26.9.76	13 Feb
1.85Ai	Jenna	Bingham	USA	22.6.78	19 Feb
1.85i	Lucie	Finez	FRA	25.11.76	19 Feb
1.85i	Olga	Bolshova	MDA	16.6.68	20 Feb
1.85i	Hanna	Mikkonen	FIN-J	15.1.81	27 Feb
1.85	Christina	Estrict	USA-J	25.7.82	28 Apr
1.85	Miyuki	Aoyama	JPN	4.1.77	29 Apr
1.85	Darnesha	Griffith	USA	11.6.80	6 May
1.85	Carrie	Braness	USA	24.3.78	7 May
1.85	Desislava	Aleksandrova	BUL	27.10.75	30 May
1.85	Dagmar	Kulma	GER-J	14.2.85	1 Jun
1.85	Sonja	Kesselschläger	GER	20.1.78	3 Jun
1.85	Carolina	Klüft	SWE-J	2.2.83	11 Jun
1.85	Debbie	Marti	GBR	14.5.68	17 Jun
1.85A	Arrate	Azkona	ESP-J	4.5.84	29 Jun
1.85	María	Hotkourídou	GRE	22.5.77	8 Jul
1.85	Stacy Ann	Grant	USA/JAM	18.8.77	16 Jul
1.85	Yelena	Tsolan	RUS	.78	24 Jul
1.85	Yelena	Shachina	RUS	.76	24 Jul
1.85	Elisa	Bozzola	ITA	18.1.76	2 Aug
1.85	Austra	Skujyte	LTU	12.8.79	3 Aug

Mark		Name	Nat	Born	Date
1.85	Yelena	Kholosha	UKR-J	26.1.82	5 Aug
1.85	Petrina	Price	AUS-J	26.4.84	10 Sep
1.85	Karen	Dickson	AUS	16.10.80	26 Nov
1.84i	Tatyana	Ivanova	RUS	22.1.76	22 Jan
1.84i	Iva	Straková	CZE	4.8.80	29 Jan
1.84Ai	Brooke	Cottle	USA		12 Feb
1.84i	Adriane	Sims	USA	8.12.79	25 Feb
1.84i	Nicole	McClain	USA		25 Feb
1.84i	Christelle	Préau	FRA-J	3.11.81	4 Mar
1.84i	Lynn	Houston	USA	7.10.75	4 Mar
1.84i	Yelena	Semyonova	RUS	.77	11 Mar
1.84i	Jessica	Thompson	USA	20.2.78	11 Mar
1.84	Lisa	Riech	USA	7.8.69	8 Apr
1.84		Jin Ling	CHN	25.1.67	15 Apr
1.84		Zhao Ning	CHN-J	26.7.81	15 Apr
1.84		Jing Xuezhu	CHN	20.4.75	18 Apr
1.84		Jiang Haiyan	CHN	19.12.79	18 Apr
1.84	Vanessa	Jones	USA	29.12.79	13 May
1.84	Katerina	Korcová	CZE	31.7.76	4 Jun
1.84	Agnieszka	Korogocka	POL	3.9.76	10 Jun
1.84	Sónia	Carvalho	POR	10.5.77	11 Jun
1.84	Ioulia	Farmaka	CYP	.78	1 Jul
1.84	Irina	Vostrikova	RUS	30.8.70	1 Jul
1.84	Jane	Jamieson	AUS	23.6.75	7 Jul
1.84	Tatyana	Kurinova	UKR	11.12.80	11 Jul
1.84	Netnapa	Thaiking	THA	11.6.80	21 Jul
1.84	Denise	Lewis	GBR	27.8.72	29 Jul
1.84	Marie	Norrman	SWE-J	10.11.81	12 Aug
1.84	Sofiya	Kabanova	UZB	29.5.70	17 Aug
1.84	Yelena	Fedoseyeva	RUS-J	.83	19 Aug
1.84	Natalya	Sazanovich	BLR	15.8.73	23 Sep
	(176)				

Best outdoor marks for athlete with best indoors

Mark	Name	Pos	Meet	Venue	Date
1.95	Györffy	1		Budapest	22 Jul
1.94	Waller	2		Rehlingen	12 Jun
1.94	Kaliturina	2		Leverkusen	20 Aug
1.93	Slivka	1		Pietersburg	18 Mar
1.93	Seryogina	1	Mos Ch	Moskva	11 Jul
1.93	Witteveen	1		Vic	17 Aug
1.91	Galeotti	1		Pescara	22 Jul
1.90	Henkel	2		Lorch	10 Jun
1.90	Bielert	4		Rehlingen	12 Jun
1.89	Forrester	4	GP	Osaka	13 May
1.89	Lendjel	3		Avezzano	20 Aug
1.88	Wentland	3	MSR	Walnut	16 Apr
1.88	Bevilacqua	4		Formia	3 Jun
1.88	Spangler	2	v4N	Glasgow	2 Jul
1.87	Medgyesová	2	ECp-2B	Banská Bystrica	9 Jul
1.87	Gulevich			Brest	23 Aug

Mark	Name	Date
1.86	Mikneviciute	4 Jun
1.86	Mattas	24 Jun
1.85	Ståhl	7 May
1.85	Bolshova	1 Jun
1.85	Sagonas	10 Jun
1.85	Beitia	24 Jun
1.85	Laytinen	22 Jul
1.85	Mikkonen	20 Aug
1.84	Préau	24 Jun
1.84	Sims	1 Jul
1.84	Laláková	19 Jul
1.84	Finez	23 Jul
1.84	Gulevich	1 Aug
1.84	Paesotto	6 Sep

JUNIORS

See main list for top 16 juniors. 8 Performances by 2 women to 1.91. Additional marks and further juniors:

Kuptsova	1.94	1		Rostov-na-Donu	9 Jul	1.91i	4		Spala 18 Feb
	1.91i	1		Pátra	15 Feb	1.91	3	Odlozil	Praha 5 Jun
Vlasic	1.92	17	OG	Sydney	28 Sep	1.91	1	WJ	Santiago 20 Oct

Mark		Name	Nat	Born	Pos	Meet	Venue	Date
1.86i	Kathryn	Holinski	GER-J	19.7.82	2		Wuppertal	4 Feb
1.86	Tatyana	Grigoryeva	RUS-J	13.5.81	1		Moskva	20 Jun
1.86	Sheree	Francis	JAM-J	20.10.83	1	NC-j	Kingston	30 Jun
1.86	Melanie	Skotnik	GER-J	8.11.82			Markheidenfeld	9 Sep
1.86	Ramona	Pop	ROM-J	5.4.82	1		Poiana Brasov	7 Oct

POLE VAULT

4.70 b Stacy Dragila USA 25.3.71 1 Santa Barbara 11 Jun
4.10/1 4.30/3 4.40/2 4.50/1 4.60/2 4.70/3 4.90/xxx

Above mark was statistically valid, but made on a platform runway, unacceptable for world records

4.63 1 NC Sacramento 23 Jul 4.18/1 4.33/1 4.43/1 4.53/2 4.63/1 4.70/xxx
4.62i 1 NC Atlanta 3 Mar 4.12/2 4.32/1 4.42/2 4.47/1 4.57/2 4.62/1 4.70/xxx
4.62 1 Phoenix 26 May 4.07/2 4.17/1 4.27/1 4.37/1 4.47/2 4.62/1 4.70/xxx
4.61Ai 1 Pocatello 19 Feb 4.15/2 4.30/1 4.45/1 4.57/2 4.61/2 4.90/xxx
4.60 1 ModR Modesto 12 May 4.10/3 4.25/1 4.35/1 4.45/1 4.60/2 4.70/xxx
4.60 1 OG Sydney 25 Sep 4.25/1 4.35/1 4.40/2 4.45/1 4.50/3 4.55/2 4.60/1 4.65/xxx
4.57 1 Sacramento 21 May 4.07/1 4.17/3 4.27/1 4.37/1 4.47/2 4.57/2 4.67/xxx
4.55 1 Brisbane 11 Feb 4.15/1 4.25/3 4.30/1 4.35/2 4.40/1 4.45/1 4.50/1 4.55/3 4.61/xxx
4.53 1 Palo Alto 1 Jul 4.08/2 4.23/1 4.38/3 4.53/2 4.63/xxx
4.51Ai 1 Pocatello 28 Jan 3.81/2 3.96/2 4.12/1 4.37/2 4.51/3 4.57/xxx
4.50A 1 Pocatello 4 May 4.04/1 4.19/1 4.34/3 4.50/2 4.65/xxx
4.50 1 Rüdlingen 12 Aug 4.20/2 4.30/1 4.40/1 4.45/1 4.50/3 4.64/xxx

4.56 Anzhela Balakhonova UKR 18.12.72 1 Gugl Linz 8 Aug
4.30/2 4.50/1 4.56/1 4.64/xxx

4.52 1 NC Kiev 4 Aug 4.25/1 4.40/1 4.52/1 4.57/xxx
4.50 1 DNG Stockholm 1 Aug 4.25/1 4.35/1 4.50/1 4.60/xxx
4.47i 1 Budapest 4 Feb 4.22/1 4.37/1 4.47/2 4.57/xxx

4.55 Tatiana Grigorieva AUS 8.10.75 2 OG Sydney 25 Sep
4.15/2 4.25/14.35/1 4.40/1 4.45/1 4.50/2 4.55/1 4.60/x 4.65/xx

4.53 Kellie Suttle USA 9.3.73 2 Palo Alto 1 Jul
4.08/1 4.23/2 4.38/2 4.53/3 4.63/xxx

4.47 1 Jonesboro 19 May 4.06/1 4.16/1 4.21/1 4.36/2 4.47/3 4.58/xxx

4.50 Emma George AUS 1.11.74 1 Perth 5 Feb
4.20/1 4.35/3 4.50/1 4.62/xxx

Mark	Name		Nat	Born	Pos	Meet	Venue	Date
4.50b	Melanie	Mueller	USA	16.11.72	2		Santa Barbara	11 Jun
				3.99/2 4.20/1 4.30/3 4.40/1 4.50/1 4.60/xxx				
	4.45				2		Portland	25 Jun
4.50	Svetlana	Feofanova	RUS	16.7.80	1	GPII	Helsinki	15 Jun
				4.10/1 4.20/1 4.30/1 4.40/1 4.50/3 4.56/xxx				
	4.50 1 GP Athína 28 Jun			4.20/1 4.30/1 4.40/2 4.50/2 4.56/xxx				
	4.46 1 Nik Nice 8 Jul			4.20/3 4.34/2 4.40/1 4.46/1 4.52/xxx				
4.50	Daniela	Bártová	CZE	6.5.74	2	GP	Athína	28 Jun
				4.10/3 4.30/2 4.50/2 4.56/xxx				
	4.50 4 OG Sydney 25 Sep			4.00/1 4.25/1 4.35/3 4.45/3 4.50/1 4.55/xxx				
	4.46 ex 1 Praha 21 Jun			4.00/1 4.26/1 4.46/1 4.56/xxx				
4.50	Yelena	Belyakova	RUS	7.4.76	3	GP	Athína	28 Jun
				4.20/1 4.30/1 4.40/2 4.50/3 4.56/xxx				
4.50	Nicole	Humbert (10)	GER	5.2.72	1		Salamanca	20 Jul
				4.20/2 4.35/2 4.45/1 4.50/2 4.56/xxx				
4.50	Vala	Flosadóttir	ISL	16.2.78	3	OG	Sydney	25 Sep
				4.00/1 4.15/1 4.25/1 4.35/1 4.40/1 4.45/1 4.50/1 4.55/xxx				
4.47	Mary	Sauer	USA	31.10.75	2		Sacramento	21 May
	(30/12) to 4.46 with 18 performances at 4.45							
4.45i	Yelena	Isinbayeva	RUS-J	3.6.82	1	NC	Volgograd	4 Feb
4.45	Tracy	O'Hara	USA	20.7.80	1	USTCA	Austin	22 Apr
4.45	Pavla	Hamácková	CZE	20.5.78	2		Turnov	11 Jun
4.45	Yvonne	Buschbaum	GER	14.7.80	1		Ingolstadt	18 Jun
4.42	Alejandra	García	ARG	13.6.73	1		Sydney	20 Feb
4.42	Tanya	Koleva	BUL	8.3.72	1		Sofia	11 Jun
4.42	Elmarie	Gerryts	RSA	25.8.72	1		Wesel	12 Jun
4.40i	Christine	Adams	GER	28.2.74	2		Chemnitz	18 Feb
	(20)							
4.40	Doris	Auer	AUT	10.5.71	2		Gold Coast (RB)	17 Sep
4.40	Monika	Pyrek	POL	11.8.80	7	OG	Sydney	25 Sep
4.37	Lesa	Kubishta	USA	19.4.78	1		Irvine	7 May
4.35	Marie	Poissonnier	FRA	4.5.79	1		Bron	7 May
4.35		Gao Shuying	CHN	28.10.79	1		Chengdu	10 May
4.35	Alicia	Warlick	USA	11.10.77	3	ModR	Modesto	13 May
4.35	Janine	Whitlock	GBR	11.8.73	2=		Praha	5 Jun
4.35	Marie B	Rasmussen	DEN	1.11.72	8	OG	Sydney	25 Sep
4.32	Vanessa	Boslak	FRA-J	11.6.82	1		La Roche-sur-Yon	23 Sep
4.31i	Amandine	Homo	FRA	24.12.80	1		Poissy	22 Jan
	(30)							
4.31	Nastja	Ryshich	GER	19.9.77	1		Düdingen	30 Sep
4.30i	Krisztina	Molnár	HUN	8.4.76	1	NC	Budapest	13 Feb
4.30	Sabine	Schulte	GER	29.1.76	2		Dessau	31 May
4.30	Monique	de Wilt	NED	21.3.76	3		Dessau	31 May
4.30	Thórey	Elisdóttir	ISL	30.6.77	1		Vellinge	3 Jun
4.30	Katerina	Badurová	CZE-J	18.12.82	3		Turnov	11 Jun
4.30b	Aimee	Crabtree	USA	22.1.78	4		Santa Barbara	11 Jun
	4.12				3		Azusa	8 Apr
4.30	Katalin	Donáth	HUN	12.11.79	1		Budapest	22 Jul
4.30	Caroline	Ammel	FRA	22.11.73	1		Bron	23 Jul
4.30	Maria Mar	Sánchez	ESP	25.12.79	1		Castellón	26 Aug
	(40)							
4.28	Arianna	Farfaletti	ITA	22.6.76	1		Rovellasca	23 Sep
4.27	Paula	Serrano	USA	28.12.76	1		Fullerton	27 Apr
4.27	Monika	Götz	GER-J	15.6.81	2		Beckum	25 Aug
4.27	Francesca	Dolcini	ITA	28.12.74	1		Rieti	21 Sep
4.25	Bridgid	Isworth	AUS-J	15.10.81	4		Brisbane	11 Feb
4.23A	Déborah	Gyurcsek	URU	7.12.78	1		Cochabamba	23 Jul
4.22i	Zsuzsanna	Szabó	HUN	6.5.73	2		Budapest	4 Feb
4.22i	Melissa	Price	USA	20.9.77	6	NC	Atlanta	4 Mar
4.22	Andrea	Branson	USA	9.11.78	1		Lawrence	22 Apr
4.22	Annika	Becker	GER-J	12.11.81	1		Holzminden	10 Jun
	(50)							
4.22	Thália	Iakovídou	GRE	10.9.72	1		Ródos	3 Sep
4.21i	Masumi	Ono	JPN	5.12.75	1	vCHN	Yokohama	26 Feb
4.20	Rachel	Dacy	AUS	10.11.76	1		Melbourne	11 Jan
4.20i	Tatyana	Köstem-Zaikova	TUR	20.4.79	1		Krasnodar	16 Jan
4.20i	Svetlana	Abramova	RUS	27.10.70	2		Moskva	27 Jan
4.20	Kym	Howe	AUS	12.6.80	4		Perth	5 Feb
4.20i	Andrea	Müller	GER	29.6.74	4	NC	Sindelfingen	13 Feb
4.20i	Maria Carla	Bresciani	ITA	16.7.73	1	v2N	Valencia	19 Feb

Mark	Name		Nat	Born	Pos	Meet	Venue	Date
4.20	Shae	Bair	USA	15.8.78	1		Pullman	8 Apr
4.20		Sun Caiyun	CHN	21.7.73	1		Shizuoka	3 May
	(60)							
4.20		Cai Weiyan	CHN	25.10.73	2	NGP	Chengdu	10 May
4.20	Erin	Anderson	USA	31.12.77	2	NCAA	Durham	2 Jun
4.20	Michaela	Boulová	CZE-J	2.8.81	2	OD	Jena	3 Jun
4.20	Yeoryía	Tsiliggíri	GRE	21.6.72	2	Balk	Kavála	2 Jul
4.20	Emilie	Bécot	FRA	20.10.80	2		Bron	23 Jul
4.20	Irie	Hill	GBR	16.1.69	1		Stoke-on-Trent	6 Aug
4.20	Martina	Strutz	GER-J	4.11.81	2		Mannheim	11 Aug
4.20	Sárka	Mládková	CZE	30.8.76	5		Rüdlingen	12 Aug
4.18	Alexa	Harz	USA	18.2.78	5	NC	Sacramento	23 Jul
4.16i	Aurore	Pignot	FRA	24.12.79	2		Montceau-les-Mines	11 Mar
	(70)							
4.16	Kim	Becker	USA	25.6.72	1		Jonesboro	19 May
4.15	Melina	Hamilton	NZL	15.6.76	1		Wellington	5 Feb
4.15	Rhian	Clarke	GBR	19.4.77	1	TexR	Austin	7 Apr
4.15	Julie	Vigourt	FRA	19.10.79	1		Tours	2 Jun
4.15	Paula	Fernández	ESP	8.6.78	1	NC-23	Puertollano	5 Aug
4.15	Floé	Kühnert	GER-J	6.3.84	4	NC-23	Jena	19 Aug
4.14	Erika	Hoernig	USA	19.10.78	1=	Pac 10	Eugene	21 May
4.12i	Kristen	Quackenbush	USA	9.1.76	1		Blacksburg	25 Feb
4.12	Annu	Mäkelä	FIN-J	20.9.82	1	NC-j	Tampere	6 Aug
4.11	Shannon	Gallagher	USA	10.3.75	3		Jonesboro	19 May
	(80)							
4.10i	Alla	Checheleva	RUS-J	1.7.81	1	Dyach	Moskva	14 Jan
4.10i	Lyudmila	Vaylenko-Prykhodko	UKR	18.3.74	1	NC	Brovary	9 Feb
4.10i	Petra	Pechstein	SUI	26.7.71	1	NC	Magglingen	13 Feb
4.10i	Natalya	Kushch	UKR-J	5.3.83	1		Donetsk	19 Feb
4.10i	Maria	Rendin	SWE-J	28.7.82	1	v2N	Tampere	20 Feb
4.10i	Niki	Reed	USA	1.4.80	4	NCAA	Fayetteville	10 Mar
4.10	Jenny	Dryburgh	NZL	30.8.78	1		Hamilton	15 Feb
4.10	Takayo	Kondo	JPN	17.11.75	2		Shizuoka	3 May
4.10	Shannon	Pierson	USA	30.9.74	1		Palo Alto	5 May
4.10	Andrea	Wildrick	USA	23.12.79	1		Lynchburg	11 May
	(90)							
4.10	Jillian	Schwartz	USA	19.9.79	3	NCAA	Durham	2 Jun
4.10	Anna	Tamburini	ITA	6.1.73	4		Milano	7 Jun
4.10b	Jaqueline	Honey	CAN	25.6.75	8		Santa Barbara	11 Jun
	4.00A				3		El Paso	6 May
4.10b	Ardin	Harrison	CAN	3.4.74	9		Santa Barbara	11 Jun
	4.00A				2		El Paso	6 May
4.10	Gabriela	Mihalcea	ROM	27.1.64	5	ECp	Gateshead	15 Jul
4.10	Fanny	Vieu	FRA	19.4.78	3	NC-23	Bondoufle	16 Jul
4.10	Eszter	Szemerédi	HUN	12.2.76	2		Budapest	22 Jul
4.10	Anastasiya	Ivanova	RUS	.79	4	NC	Tula	24 Jul
4.10	Naroa	Agirre	ESP	15.5.79	1		San Sebastián	9 Aug
4.10	Yuliya	Lukinskaya	RUS	.76	1		Moskva	19 Aug
	(100)							
4.10	Anna	Wielgus	POL-J	27.10.81	1	NC-j	Wroclaw	28 Aug
4.10	Fanni	Juhász	HUN-J	31.3.81	1		Budapest	7 Oct
4.10		Zhang Na	CHN	27.9.80	2	NC	Luohe	22 Oct

4.07i	Agnès	Livebardon	FRA	31.5.80	24 Mar
4.06	Stacie	Manuel	USA-J	6.12.83	25 May
4.05	Stefanie	Lax	GER-J	24.3.83	11 Aug
4.04	Heather	Sickler	USA	8.2.80	21 May
4.04	Lucy	Webber	GBR	5.2.72	15 Jul
4.03	Marisa	Vieira	POR	30.12.79	6 Aug
4.02i	Elise	Genévrier	FRA-J	27.6.83	24 Mar
4.02	Tracy	Carrington	USA	12.3.77	30 Apr
4.02A	Stephanie	McCann	CAN	22.4.77	8 Jul
4.02A	Dana	Ellis	CAN	7.12.79	8 Jul
4.02	Jill	Wittenwyler	USA	7.3.71	21 Jul
4.01	Caroline	Hingst	GER	18.9.80	27 May
4.01	Vanessa	Ríos	ESP	5.1.80	9 Sep
4.01	Yelena	Reznik	KAZ	20.8.78	15 Sep
4.00i	Teija	Saari	FIN	21.3.78	29 Jan
4.00i	Yevgeniya	Savina	UKR	21.4.76	9 Feb
4.00	Tracey	Shepherd	AUS	29.6.69	19 Feb
4.00i	Gaëlle	Delcourt	FRA	31.7.79	20 Feb
4.00i	Cécile	Lelong	FRA	23.6.77	20 Feb
4.00i		Peng Xiaoming	CHN	15.5.75	20 Feb
4.00	Andrea	Neary	USA	28.2.78	1 Apr
4.00	Dena	Dial	USA	31.8.77	7 Apr
4.00	Jennifer	Swanson	USA	4.1.78	15 Apr
4.00	Mami	Nakano	JPN	12.3.79	3 May
4.00		Tang Junmei	CHN	9.2.80	10 May
4.00	Meredith	Garner	USA	19.7.80	26 May
4.00	Maria	Lopez	USA	18.8.79	2 Jun
4.00	Jenni	Ashcroft	USA	2.7.80	2 Jun
4.00	Sirine	Balti	TUN-J	31.10.83	3 Jun
4.00	Sabine	Verbeek	NED	25.3.80	17 Jun
4.00	Vyara	Chavdarova	BUL	19.11.80	17 Jun
4.00	Stefanie	Pietsch	GER	14.6.76	18 Jun
4.00	Galina	Fyodorova	RUS	24.6.70	21 Jun
4.00	Elisabete	Tavares	POR	7.3.80	27 Jun
4.00	Solenne	Allain	FRA-J	5.3.82	8 Jul
4.00	Lucie	Palasová	CZE-J	26.3.81	8 Jul
4.00	Francesca	Zanini	ITA-J	4.4.82	22 Jul
4.00	Béatrice	Denis	FRA	18.6.72	23 Jul
4.00	Teja	Melink	SLO	23.3.80	6 Aug
4.00	Alison	Davies	GBR	6.4.61	12 Aug

Mark	Name		Nat	Born	Date
4.00		Du Na	CHN	7.1.79	22 Oct
3.97i	Jennifer	Hoffer	USA	24.7.76	28 Jan
3.97i	Amy	Spellmeyer	USA	4.9.79	19 Feb
3.97i	Samantha	Shepard	USA-J	11.11.83	3 Mar
3.97	Kathleen	Donoghue	USA-J	29.8.81	30 Apr
3.97A	Becky	Jackson	USA	5.4.77	19 May
3.97	Amy	Linnen	USA-J	15.7.82	16 Jun
3.97i	Molly	Lederman	USA-J	5.6.84	19 Dec
3.96i	Laura	Hawkins	USA	15.2.79	27 Feb
3.95	Sandy	Erickson	USA		29 Apr
3.95	Julia	Hütter	GER-J	26.7.83	6 May
3.95A	Brooke	Lankard	USA	3.5.80	19 May
3.95	Laura	Rosenberger	USA-J	25.9.81	23 Jun
3.95A	Melissa	Feinstein	CAN	18.3.79	4 Jul
3.95	Katiuska	Pérez	CUB	21.12.75	29 Jul
3.95	Akane	Eguchi	JPN	20.6.76	6 Oct
3.93	Ebby	Metzinger	USA	16.6.79	7 May
3.92	Hanna-Mai	Persson	SWE	11.2.78	7 Sep
3.91Ai	Shannon	Flett	USA	15.11.77	25 Feb
3.91	Suzanne	Krings	USA	3.10.80	20 May
3.90Ai	Ashley	Feinberg	USA	17.5.79	22 Jan
3.90i	Anna	Fitidou	CYP	22.4.77	22 Jan
3.90i	Anja	Wilhelm	GER	5.5.80	29 Jan
3.90i	Yelena	Chikachkova	UKR-J	18.4.82	9 Feb
3.90		Chang Kuo-Hsin	TPE	20.6.80	13 Feb
3.90i	Kristina	Zeyhle	GER	26.9.78	13 Feb
3.90i	Valerie	Jalajas	USA	14.6.78	18 Feb
3.90i	Irina	Saks	EST-J	21.5.82	20 Feb
3.90i	Eglantine	Colin	FRA	24.3.79	20 Feb
3.90Ai	Shannon	Agee	USA	7.3.79	4 Mar
3.90A	Chrisna	Oosthuizen	RSA	1.3.71	25 Mar
3.90		Yang Hongling	CHN	15.4.78	19 Apr
3.90		Zhong Guiqing	CHN	5.7.77	19 Apr
3.90		Kuan Mei-Lien	TPE	26.7.80	24 Apr
3.90	Ellie	Spain	GBR-J	23.8.82	6 May
3.90		Qin Xia	CHN	6.12.79	10 May
3.90	Pascale	Bourguignon	FRA	27.2.72	1 Jun
3.90	Tracy	Bloomfield	GBR	13.9.79	4 Jun
3.90	Karen	Borges da Silva	BRA	31.8.79	11 Jun
3.90	Sandrine	Toulouse	FRA	14.9.72	14 Jun
3.90	Fabiana	Murer	BRA-J	16.3.81	17 Jun
3.90	Séverine	Phélippon	FRA-J	19.1.81	17 Jun
3.90	Anastasiya	Kuznetsova	RUS	.80	21 Jun
3.90A	Yuliya	Kostina	KAZ	12.6.77	24 Jun
3.90	Annalisa	Meacci	ITA	8.3.76	25 Jun
3.90	Adigóni	Asteríou	GRE	2.11.76	28 Jun
3.90	Elke	Andries	BEL	4.8.76	2 Jul
3.90	Céline	Poissonnier	FRA	4.5.79	5 Jul
3.90	Merle	Kivimets	EST	21.7.74	8 Jul
3.90	Anastasiya	Kiryanova	RUS-J	.82	8 Jul
3.90	Dana	Cervantes	ESP	18.8.78	12 Jul
3.90	Natsue	Matsui	JPN	27.5.76	16 Jul
3.90	Andrea	Stürmer	GER	4.4.79	30 Jul
3.90	Ioánna	Volpánou	GRE	5.5.80	30 Jul
3.90	Liesbet	Van Roie	BEL-J	20.1.81	13 Aug
3.90i	Christina	Gadschiew	GER-J	3.7.84	17 Dec
3.88	Malin	Ericsson	SWE	12.1.80	10 Jun
	(200)	222 women at 3.85 or better			

Best outdoor marks for athlete with best indoors

4.40	Isinbayeva	2	NC	Tula	24 Jul
4.30	Adams	1		Dessau	31 May
4.22	Molnár	1		Budapest	8 Sep
4.20	Köstem-Zaikova	1		Krasnodar	13 May
4.20b	Price	5=		Santa Barbara	11 Jun
		8	NC	Sacramento	23 Jul
4.20	Müller	6=		Ingolstadt	18 Jun
4.20	Bresciani	1		Pergine Valsugana	26 Jul
4.20	Szabó	2		Budapest	5 Aug
4.15	Homo	1		Annecy	21 May
4.15	Pignot	1	NC-23	Bondoufle	16 Jul
4.10	Reed	2		Eugene	29 Apr
4.10	Checheleva	1		Moskva	17 May
4.10	Pechstein	3		Rheinau-Freistett	8 Jul

4.05	Abramova	11 Jul
4.02	Quackenbush	21 Jul
4.00	Peng Xiaoming	26 Mar
4.00	Ono	22 Apr
4.00	Kushch	22 May
4.00	V-Prykhodko	3 Jun
4.00	Delcourt	27 Jun
4.00	Genévrier	5 Jul
4.00	Lelong	27 Jul
3.95	Hoffer	22 Apr
3.91	Hawkins	8 Apr
3.90	Spellmeyer	1 Apr
3.90	Jalajas	7 May
3.90	Livebardon	28 May
3.90	Rendin	2 Jul
3.90	Saari	3 Sep

Town square and exhibition marks

4.35sq	Monique	de Wilt	NED	21.3.76	1	Jockgrimm	19 Jul
4.26sq	Sárka	Mládková	CZE	30.8.76	3	Praha	21 Jun

JUNIORS

See main list for top 15 juniors. 10 performances by 5 women to 4.25. Additional marks and further juniors:

Isinbayeva	4.40	2	NC	Tula	24 Jul	4.30i	Q	EI	Gent	25 Feb
	4.35	7	GP I	Athína	28 Jun					
Badurová	4.30	3=		Rüdlingen	12 Aug	4.25	1		Olomouc	1 Jul

4.06	Stacie	Manuel	USA	6.12.83	1	Albertville	25 May
4.05	Stefanie	Lax	GER	24.3.83	4	Mannheim	11 Aug
4.02i	Elise	Genévrier	FRA	27.6.83	1	Clermont Ferrand	24 Mar
4.00	Sirine	Balti	TUN	31.10.83	2	Tunis	3 Jun
4.00	Solenne	Allain	FRA	5.3.82	1	Antony	8 Jul
4.00	Lucie	Palasová	CZE	26.3.81	6	Rheinau-Freistett	8 Jul
4.00	Francesca	Zanini	ITA	4.4.82	1	Pescara	22 Jul

LONG JUMP

7.09	0.0	Fiona	May	ITA	12.12.69	1	GP	Rio de Janeiro			14 May
					6.89	7.02	x	6.83	6.84	7.09	
7.07	0.91		Milano	7 Jun	7.07	6.83	x	x	7.02/0/2	6.98/0.0	
6.95	-0.32	Bisl	Oslo	28 Jul	6.95	6.54	6.59	6.72	6.51	6.87	
6.94	0.11		Torino	10 Jun	x	x	x	6.76	6.77	6.94	
6.92	1.12	OG	Sydney	29 Sep	6.76	6.82	6.92	6.72	6.73	6.72	
7.04	0.3	Tatyana	Kotova	RUS	11.12.76	1	Gaz	Saint-Denis			23 Jun
					6.92/0.0	6.82	6.93/0.3	6.93/-0.6	5.30	7.04	
7.00	-0.21	Bisl	Oslo	28 Jul	6.50	x	6.61	6.85	6.72	7.00	
6.96	0.21	VD	Bruxelles	25 Aug	6.91/0.8	p	x	6.96	p	6.82	
6.96	0.91	ISTAF	Berlin	1 Sep	6.58	6.64	6.80	6.71	6.70	6.96	
6.95	0.21	GP	Athína	30 May	4.43	6.60	6.50	6.62	6.95	p	
6.90	1		Kalamáta	4 Jun	6.69	6.70	x	x	6.74	6.90	
6.89	-0.11	GGala	Roma	30 Jun	6.34	6.89	x	6.75	6.86	6.82	
7.05i	training competition		Barnaul	26 Feb							

Mark	Wind	Name		Nat	Born	Pos	Meet	Venue		Date
7.02	1.9	Marion	Jones	USA	12.10.75	1	NC	Sacramento		16 Jul
					x	x	6.75	6.88w	7.02	x
	6.97	1.9 1 Pre	Eugene	24 Jun	6.97	6.70	6.63w	6.69w	x	x
	6.93	0.7 1 WK	Zürich	11 Aug	6.62	6.67	6.74	6.72	6.93	6.86
	6.92	1.0 3 OG	Sydney	29 Sep	x	6.68	6.92	x	x	x
7.00	-1.0	Inessa	Kravets ¶	UKR	5.10.66	1		Kiev		15 Jul
6.99	0.4	Lissette	Cuza	CUB	26.2.75	1	OD	Jena		3 Jun
					x	6.82	6.99	p	6.87w	x
6.99	1.9	Erica	Johansson	SWE	5.2.74	*	Athl	Lausanne		5 Jul
					x	6.58	6.85	6.89	7.04w/2.2	6.99
	6.89i	- 1 EI	Gent	27 Feb	6.89	6.73	x	x	6.66	x
6.99	1.9	Heike	Drechsler	GER	16.12.64	1	OG	Sydney		29 Sep
					6.48	x	6.99	6.79	x	x
	6.95	0.4 2 ISTAF	Berlin	1 Sep	6.95	x	x	6.65	6.90	6.80
	6.91	0.1 3 WK	Zürich	11 Aug	6.80	6.86	x	x	x	6.91
6.98	1.1	Dawn	Burrell	USA	1.11.73	1	DNG	Stockholm		1 Aug
					6.63	x	x	6.79	6.78	6.98
	6.96	1.7 * NC	Sacramento	16 Jul	x	6.77	6.84	6.96	x	6.97w/2.6
6.95			Guan Yingnan	CHN	25.4.77	1		Tianjin		3 May
	6.92	1.3 1	Beijing	1 Sep						
6.93	0.0	Maurren	Maggi (10)	BRA	25.6.76	2	GP	Rio de Janeiro		14 May
					6.81	6.93	6.69	p	6.51	p
6.91	0.6	Valentina	Gotovska	LAT	3.9.65	1	Sule	Tartu		11 Jun
					6.72	x	6.84	x	6.91	x
6.90i	–	Olga	Rublyova	RUS	28.10.74	1		Samara		30 Jan
					6.76	6.84	6.90	x	x	x
	6.89	0.6 1 NCp	Tula	3 Jun						
6.89	2.0	Lyudmila	Galkina	RUS	20.1.72	2	Sule	Tartu		11 Jun
		(32/13)				6.84	x	6.83	6.78	6.89 6.81
6.87A	1.2	Meosha	Hubbard	USA		1		Flagstaff		6 Jul
6.87	0.6	Niurka	Montalvo	ESP	4.6.68	3	GPF	Doha		5 Oct
6.86	2.0	Yelena	Shekhovtsova	UKR	31.5.72	1	NC	Kiev		5 Aug
6.85	-0.1	Eunice	Barber	FRA	17.11.74	1H		Götzis		4 Jun
6.85	0.1	Viorica	Tigau	ROM	12.8.79	*	NC	Bucuresti		7 Aug
6.84	0.7	Viktoriya	Vershinina	UKR	11.6.71	2		Kiev		15 Jul
6.83	0.5	Iva	Prandzheva ¶	BUL	15.2.72	1	ECp1B	Bydgoszcz		9 Jul
		(20)								
6.82	0.9		Guo Chunfang	CHN	4.1.79	1	OT	Jinzhou		7 Jun
6.81	0.5	Niki	Xánthou	GRE	1.10.73	1		Athína (F)		31 May
6.80	1.4	Shana	Williams	USA	7.4.72	*	NC	Sacramento		16 Jul
6.79i	–	Tatyana	Ter-Mesrobyan	RUS	12.5.68	1		Moskva		25 Jan
6.78	2.0	Susen	Tiedtke	GER	23.1.69	1		Wesel		12 Jun
6.75	0.1	Déspina	Papavasiláki	GRE	24.3.73	2		Athína (F)		30 May
6.74	1.2	Elva	Goulbourne	JAM	21.1.80	1		Brisbane		3 Sep
6.72	1.3	Sofia	Schulte	GER	8.4.76	2		Siegen		27 May
6.72	0.2	Luciana	dos Santos	BRA	10.2.70	1		Americana		3 Jun
6.72	1.0	Yelena	Prokhorova	RUS	16.4.78	1H	NC	Tula		23 Jul
		(30)								
6.71i		Irina	Melnikova	RUS	14.5.75	1		Shakhty		16 Jan
6.71	0.4	Irina	Yermolayeva	RUS	.79	1		Rostov-na-Donu		20 May
6.70	0.9		Liang Shuyan	CHN	16.9.77	1	NGP	Guangzhou		26 Mar
6.70	-1.1	Chandra	Sturrup	BAH	12.9.71	1	GP	Raleigh		17 Jun
6.70	0.0	Zita	Ajkler	HUN	9.6.75	1		Budapest		19 Jul
6.70	1.3	Aurélie	Félix	FRA	20.3.79	*		Bron		23 Jul
6.70	0.1	Tünde	Vaszi	HUN	18.4.72	Q	OG	Sydney		27 Sep
6.69	1.9	Pam	Simpson	USA	28.4.77	5	NC	Sacramento		16 Jul
6.69	-0.4	Denise	Lewis	GBR	27.8.72	1H	Deca	Talence		30 Jul
6.68i		Mirela	Dulgheru/Renda	ROM	5.10.66	1		Ploesti		12 Feb
		(40)								
6.68	-1.1	Yelena	Kashcheyeva	KAZ	17.2.73	1		Tashkent		15 Jun
6.68A	0.3	Anna	Tarasova	KAZ	23.3.80	1		El Paso		24 Jun
6.68	0.8	Yelena	Pershina	KAZ	24.12.63	1		Dortmund		10 Aug
6.67	1.3	Jackie	Joyner-Kersee	USA	3.3.62	5	NC	Sacramento		16 Jul
6.67	1.1	Lacena	Golding	JAM	20.3.75	2	NC	Kingston		21 Jul
6.67	0.6		Ren Ruiping	CHN	1.2.76	2		Beijing		1 Sep
6.66		Marieke	Veltman/Miller	USA	18.9.71	1		Los Angeles		20 May
6.66A	0.4	Chantal	Brunner	NZL	5.11.70	2		Flagstaff		6 Jul
6.66	0.2	Yelena	Bobrovskaya	KGZ	11.4.75	1	AsiC	Jakarta		30 Aug
6.65A	0.4	Jackie	Edwards	BAH	14.4.71	3		Flagstaff		6 Jul
		(50)								

Mark	Wind	Name		Nat	Born	Pos	Meet	Venue	Date
6.65A	0.0	Brianna	Glenn	USA	18.4.80	1c1		Flagstaff	8 Jul
6.64	1.4	Jenny	Adams	USA	8.7.78	1	USTCA	Austin	22 Apr
6.64	1.0	Concepción	Montaner	ESP-J	14.1.81	1		Castellón	9 Aug
6.63	1.7	Tisha	Parker	USA	18.9.77	1	SEC	Baton Rouge	13 May
6.63	0.5	Natalya	Bastrygina	RUS	.71	2		Rostov-na-Donu	20 May
6.63A	0.5	Alice	Falaiye	CAN	24.12.78	4		Flagstaff	6 Jul
6.62	1.8	Trecia	Smith	JAM	5.11.75	1	Sea Ray	Knoxville	15 Apr
6.62	0.0	Natalya	Safronova	BLR	11.4.74	2	ECp1B	Bydgoszcz	9 Jul
6.62	1.5	Eva	Miklos	ROM	30.7.78	2	NC	Bucuresti	7 Aug
6.62			Zhong Mei	CHN	7.1.78	1		Chengdu	8 Sep
		(60)							
6.61i	–	Cristina	Nicolau	ROM	9.8.77	1	NC	Bucuresti	6 Feb
6.61	2.0	Maho	Hanaoka	JPN	3.8.76	1		Mito	7 May
6.61	1.7	Keisha	Spencer	JAM	16.2.78	2	SEC	Baton Rouge	13 May
6.61	1.9	Yelena	Kulikova	KAZ	27.8.76	1		Bishkek	3 Jun
6.61A	0.8	Nicole	Gilmore	CAN	24.8.73	2c2		Flagstaff	8 Jul
6.59	0.6	Anju K	Markose	IND	.77	1		Bhopal	23 Feb
6.59	1.7	Tasha	Mahone	USA	5.8.79	1		Athens	22 Apr
6.59	0.4	Johanna	Halkoaho	FIN	13.1.77	*	Sule	Tartu	11 Jun
6.59	1.4	Agata	Karczmarek	POL	29.11.63	1		Biala Podlaska	17 Jun
6.59	1.1	Adrien	Sawyer	USA	13.12.75	7	NC	Sacramento	16 Jul
		(70)							
6.59	0.1	Jo	Wise	GBR	15.3.71	13Q	OG	Sydney	27 Sep
6.58	1.4	Jade	Johnson	GBR	7.6.80	1		Arles	4 Jun
6.57	-1.8	Kylie	Reed	AUS	17.12.74	1	NC	Sydney	27 Feb
6.57	0.9	Yuan	Hunt	USA	18.12.74	1		Houston	22 Jun
6.57			Zhou Yangxia	CHN-J	10.2.83	2		Beijing	1 Sep
6.56	0.9	Bronwyn	Thompson	AUS	29.1.78	1	OT	Sydney	18 Aug
6.55	0.8	Bianca	Kappler	GER	8.8.77	3		Wesel	12 Jun
6.55	1.2	Sharon	Jaklofsky	NED	30.9.68	1	Kuso	Warszawa	24 Jun
6.54i		Marcela	Umnik	SLO	11.9.76	1	NC	Ljubljana	12 Feb
6.54	0.3	Patience	Itanyi	NGR	2.7.73	H		Arles	4 Jun
		(80)							
6.54	0.7	G Pramila	Ganapathy	IND	8.5.77	1		Bangalore	17 Jul
6.54	0.0	Liliana	Zagacka	POL	28.1.77	2	NC	Kraków	5 Aug
6.53		Olga Lidia	Cepero	CUB	4.2.75	2		La Habana	12 Feb
6.53	0.9	Nolle	Graham	JAM-J	12.9.81	2	NCAA	Durham	1 Jun
6.53	1.4	Stephanie	Hort	GER	13.2.75	1		Saarlouis	4 Jun
6.53A	0.5	Vanessa	Monar-Enweani	CAN	11.12.69	5		Flagstaff	6 Jul
6.52i		Anzhela	Kinet	TUR	14.11.70	P		Gomel	2 Feb
6.52i		Keyon	Soley	USA	8.9.79	1	NCAA	Fayetteville	10 Mar
6.52i		Monique	Freeman	USA	1.7.77	2	NCAA	Fayetteville	10 Mar
6.52	0.0	Flora	Hyacinth	ISV	10.3.66	1		Houston	14 Jul
		(90)							
6.52	0.1	Yolanta	Khropach	UKR	22.9.74	1		Kiev	25 Jul
6.52	1.6	Olesya	Belyayeva	KAZ	29.6.80	1		Almaty	11 Aug
6.51	0.5	Nadezhda	Bazhenova	RUS	.78	1		Vladimir	20 May
6.51	1.3	Julie	Hollman	GBR	16.2.77	1H		Waterford	3 Sep
6.51	0.4	Anastasiya	Ilyina	RUS-J	16.1.82	1		Krasnodar	15 Sep
6.50Ai		Tiffany	Greer	USA-J	5.12.81	1		Flagstaff	18 Feb
6.50i		Kirsten	Bolm	GER	4.3.75	3	NCAA	Fayetteville	10 Mar
6.50	1.9	Natalya	Sazanovich	BLR	15.8.73	H	ECp-1	Ibach	2 Jul
6.50	0.7	Stilianí	Pilátou	GRE	28.3.80	1		Praha	9 Sep
6.49	1.0		Zhao Fan	CHN	1.3.78	2	NGP	Shanghai	18 Apr
		(100)							
6.49	0.3	Olga	Salazhenkova	RUS	.76	1	Mos Ch	Moskva	11 Jul

6.48i		Svetlana	Parfyonova	RUS	.74	21 Jan
6.48		Yelena	Lebedenko	RUS	16.1.71	17 May
6.48	0.3	Hristína	Athanasíou	GRE	11.1.74	29 Jul
6.48	-0.2	Susanna	Rajamäki	FIN	19.9.79	3 Sep
6.47i		Tatyana	Kotova	UKR	2.1.70	9 Feb
6.47i		Ola	Sesay	USA	30.5.79	18 Feb
6.47A	1.9	Kène	Ndoye	SEN	20.11.78	18 Mar
6.47A	0.0	Grace	Upshaw	USA	22.9.75	8 Jul
6.46	1.8	Déborah	Grapotte	FRA	2.4.78	28 May
6.46		Shelia	Burrell	USA	15.1.72	23 Jun
6.46	0.6	Tereza	Marinova	BUL	5.9.77	2 Jul
6.46	-0.7	Nicole	Boegman	AUS	5.3.67	22 Jul
6.46	1.3	Anna	Pyatykh	RUS-J	4.4.81	19 Aug
6.45i		Yevgeniya	Stavchanskaya	UKR-J	25.9.81	9 Feb
6.45	1.1	Virginia	Martínez	CUB/ESP	3.9.68	6 May
6.45	0.8	Laura	Gatto	ITA	4.3.77	21 May
6.45	2.0	Marta	Godinho	POR	24.6.80	15 Jul
6.45	0.4	Natalya	Roshchupkina	RUS	13.1.78	23 Jul
6.45	2.0	Oluchi	Elechi	NGR	20.7.73	1 Sep
6.44i		Inna	Ivleva	RUS	.71	21 Jan
6.44i		Yelena	Khlopotnova	UKR	4.8.63	9 Feb
6.44	1.0	Ychlindria	Spears	USA-J	17.7.84	2 Aug
6.44	1.7	Sarah	Claxton	GBR	23.9.79	19 Aug
6.44	1.1	Svetlana	Zaytseva	RUS-J	14.8.81	19 Aug
6.43	1.5	Baya	Rahouli	ALG	27.7.79	13 Feb
6.43	1.9	Chinedu	Odozor	NGR	24.12.77	7 May
6.43	1.4		Peng Fengmei	CHN	9.7.79	10 May
6.43	-0.4	Sárka	Beránková	CZE	16.4.78	23 Jul
6.43	0.9	Viviane	Sildillia	FRA	23.2.74	23 Sep
6.43	0.8	Kumiko	Ikeda	JPN-J	10.1.81	18 Oct

Mark	Wind	Name		Nat	Born	Date
6.43i		Irina	Belova	RUS	27.3.68	24 Dec
6.42	0.8	Seun	Augustus	USA	9.5.78	21 Apr
6.42	0.7	Olga	Bolshova	MDA	16.6.68	29 Apr
6.42	0.9		Huang Jianfen	CHN	10.10.78	7 Jun
6.42	1.1	Yelena	Volf	RUS	2.3.69	23 Jul
6.42	1.8	Jessica	Larsson	SWE	9.4.75	26 Jul
6.41	0.5	Andrea	Ávila	ARG	4.4.70	20 May
6.41	1.3	Urszula	Wlodarczyk	POL	22.12.65	4 Jun
6.41	1.2	Vera	Olenchenko	RUS	21.3.59	26 Jun
6.41	0.7	DeDee	Nathan	USA	20.4.68	1 Jul
6.40i		Camilla	Johansson	SWE	3.11.76	6 Feb
6.40A	0.0	Ria	Fourie	RSA	2.11.75	28 Jan
6.40A	0.2	Elisa	Cossa	MOZ	3.6.80	24 Mar
6.40	1.7	Jernae	Wright	USA	22.11.78	13 May
6.40	0.0	Edyta	Sibiga	POL	16.2.77	4 Jun
6.40	1.4	Maria Chiara	Baccini	ITA-J	21.7.81	25 Jun
6.40	1.2	Kelly	LaBounty	USA	24.11.70	15 Jul
6.40	0.9	Sabine	Braun	GER	19.6.65	23 Jul
6.40	1.5	Korinna	Fink	GER-J	6.4.81	19 Aug
6.40	1.2	Ólga	Vasdeki	GRE	26.9.73	2 Sep
6.39i		Dahlia	Ingram	USA	17.7.78	25 Feb
6.39	1.2	Célia	Harmenil	FRA-J	7.9.81	7 May
6.38i		Antoinette	Wilks	USA	14.10.80	26 Feb
6.38i		Irina	Simagina	RUS-J	25.5.82	29 Feb
6.38	1.4	Nicole	Gamble	USA	21.6.77	13 May
6.38		Natalia	Kilpeläinen	FIN	19.7.70	18 Jun
6.38	1.4	Karin	Ertl	GER	23.6.74	23 Jul
6.38	1.6	Aleksandra	Stadnyuk	UKR	16.4.80	5 Aug
6.38	1.1	Nadia	Raymond	FRA-J	21.4.81	6 Aug
6.38			Lu Xin	CHN	1.12.80	7 Sep
6.37A	-2.2	Delia	Visser	RSA-J	9.4.83	8 Apr
6.37	0.9	Jada	Phelps	USA		13 May
6.36i		Lucie	Komrsková	CZE	24.10.77	13 Feb
6.36i		Valerie	Williams	USA	7.12.79	10 Mar
6.36A	0.4	Charlene	Lawrence (6.34?)	RSA	25.9.79	22 Jan
6.36		Marsha	Mark	TRI	20.1.74	14 May
6.36	1.9	Agneta	Rosenblad	SWE	8.8.77	20 May
6.36		Kateryna	Chernyavskaya	UKR-J	31.1.83	3 Jun
6.36	0.4	Anastasia	Mahob	FRA	28.7.72	30 Jun
6.36	0.5	Lerma	Bulauitan	PHI	17.10.74	30 Aug
6.35i		Diana	Koritskaya	RUS	22.2.75	18 Feb
6.35	1.1	Tameisha	King	USA-J	24.2.81	19 May
6.35	1.5	Irina	Naumenko	KAZ	13.2.80	3 Jun
6.35	0.9	Yelena	Ivanova	RUS	16.3.79	25 Jun
6.35	1.7	Starlie	Graves	USA	25.10.70	7 Jul
6.35	0.1	Anja	Valant	SLO	8.9.77	9 Jul
6.35	1.7	Astrid	Retzke	GER	13.7.73	23 Jul
6.35	0.5	Niina	Saarman-Bartholdi	FIN	28.2.77	3 Sep
6.35		Alina	Militaru	ROM-J	10.4.82	7 Oct
6.35	1.0	Eri	Yamamoto	JPN	25.9.79	17 Oct
6.35	0.7	Dana	Veldáková	SVK-J	3.6.81	18 Oct
		(182)	200 women at 6.33 or better			

Wind assisted

Mark	Wind	Name		Nat	Born	Pos	Meet	Venue	Date
7.07A	w	Erica	Johansson	SWE	5.2.74	1		Vygieskraal	15 Jan
					6.63w 6.91w 7.07w 6.88w 6.83w x				
7.01w						1	ECp1A	Nedderud	9 Jul
					6.76 6.68 6.81 7.01w four only				
7.07	2.4	Heike	Drechsler	GER	16.12.64	1	GPF	Doha	5 Oct
					6.97w/2.6 p x x x 7.07w				
6.99	2.5	Dawn	Burrell	USA	1.11.73	2	GPF	Doha	5 Oct
					x x 6,83 6.76 6.99w x				
6.95	5.1	Niurka	Montalvo	ESP	4.6.68	1		La Laguna	15 Jul
					6.59w 6.95w x x 6.92w/3.3 x				
6.93	4.3		Maggi			1		São Paulo	6 May
6.87	2.8	Shana	Williams	USA	7.4.72	3	NC	Sacramento	16 Jul
6.87	2.1	Viorica	Tigau	ROM	12.8.79	1	NC	Bucuresti	7 Aug
6.79	2.5	Concepción	Montaner	ESP-J	14.1.81	1		Valencia	12 Aug
6.79	3.3	Elva	Goulbourne	JAM	21.1.80	1		Gold Coast (RB)	10 Sep
6.77A	2.6	Chantal	Brunner	NZL	5.11.70	1		Flagstaff	3 Jul
6.73	2.1	Johanna	Halkoaho	FIN	13.1.77	3	Sule	Tartu	11 Jun
6.72	2.9	Aurélie	Félix	FRA	26.3.79	1		Bron	23 Jul
6.64	2.7	Bronwyn	Thompson	AUS	29.1.78	3		Gold Coast (RB)	10 Sep
6.63	3.2	Yuan	Hunt	USA	18.12.74	1		College Station	15 Apr
6.63	2.4	Adrien	Sawyer	USA	13.12.75	3	MAI	Malmö	7 Aug
6.57	3.8	Lynette	Wigington	USA	15.3.78	1cB	TexR	Austin	7 Apr
6.57	2.3	Marta	Godinho	POR	24.6.80	1		Maia	15 Jul
6.57	2.3	Sharon	Jaklofsky	NED	30.9.68	1	NC	Amsterdam	15 Jul
6.56	3.1	Keyon	Soley	USA	8.9.79	2	UCTA	Austin	22 Apr
6.56	4.6	Dahlia	Ingram	USA	17.7.78	3	UCTA	Austin	22 Apr
6.56	3.1	Brandi	Bentley	USA	7.3.78	1		Ann Arbor MI	13 May
6.55	3.8	Olga Lidia	Cepero	CUB	4.2.75	1		La Habana	19 Feb
6.55	3.1	Kirsten	Bolm	GER	4.3.75	1cA	TexR	Austin	7 Apr
6.54	2.2	Viviane	Sildillia	FRA	23.2.74	1		Marly	23 Sep
6.53	2.6	Ola	Sesay	USA	30.5.79	1		Atlanta	19 May

Mark	Wind	Name		Nat	Born	Date
6.48	4.2	Yolanda	Thompson	USA-J	29.5.81	23 Jun
6.48	2.4	Yelena	Ivanova	RUS	16.3.79	25 Jun
6.47	2.9	Chinedu	Odozor	NGR	24.12.77	13 Aug
6.46A	w	Charlene	Lawrence	RSA	25.9.79	15 Jan
6.46	3.7	Célia	Harmenil	FRA-J	7.9.81	26 Jul
6.46	2.7	Kumiko	Ikeda	JPN-J	10.1.81	16 Sep
6.45	2.2	Sarah	Claxton	GBR	23.9.79	11 Jun
6.45	5.1	Tameisha	King	USA-J	24.2.81	23 Jun
6.45	2.4	Donita	Benjamin	GBR	7.3.72	23 Jul
6.44	3.3	Antoinette	Wilks	USA	14.10.80	7 May
6.44	2.3	Beatrice	Albert	GER	9.5.70	12 Aug
6.43	3.3	Nadine	Caster	FRA	15.10.65	10 Jun
6.41	2.5	Emmanuelle	Desebe-Devaud	SUI	22.12.75	3 Jun
6.41	2.2	Narayane	Dossevi	FRA-J	3.2.83	26 Jul
6.40	2.9	Larisa	Necheporuk	UKR	24.12.70	28 May
6.39	2.3	Heli	Paloranta	FIN	24.1.80	26 Jul
6.38	5.4	Angel	Heath	USA	28.1.80	12 May
6.38	3.7	Annica	Sandström	SWE	25.2.68	10 Jun
6.38	4.2	Bozena	Trzcinska	POL	24.1.76	10 Jun
6.38	4.2	Marie	Guerdin	FRA	21.11.79	23 Jul
6.37		Zhanna	Gureyeva	BLR	10.6.70	21 May
6.37	2.1	LaShonda	Christopher	USA	23.10.76	18 Jun
6.37	3.4	Tracy	Joseph	GBR	29.11.69	23 Jul
6.36A	3.5	Lisa	Domico	USA	18.2.76	3 Jul
6.35	3.0	Chandi	Jones	USA-J	7.6.83	12 May
6.35	w	Libuse	Tománková	CZE	30.3.77	27 May

Best outdoor marks for athlete with best indoors

Mark	Wind	Name	Pos	Meet	Venue	Date
6.76	-1.2	Ter-Mesrobyan	q	NC	Tula	23 Jul
6.64	0.5	Melnikova	3	NC	Tula	25 Jul
6.50	0.7	Soley	1		Los Angeles (Ww)	6 May
6.47	0.2	Greer	1		Tucson	6 May

Mark	Wind	Name	Date	Mark	Wind	Name	Date	Mark	Wind	Name	Date
6.45A	1.4	Bolm	21 Apr	6.41	0.1	Dulgheru/Renda	7 Aug	6.36	1.9	Komrsková	23 Jul
6.45	1.8	Nicolau	3 Jun	6.38		Parfyonova	27 Jun	6.35	1.3	Sesay	18 May
6.43	0.5	Ivleva	19 Aug	6.38	-0.7	Simagina	8 Jul	6.49w	2.6	Freeman	25 Mar
6.42	1.7	Freeman	13 May	6.36	0.5	Ingram	1 Jun	6.42w	4.8	Umnik	14 May

Best at low altitude

6.61		Edwards	1	Barr	La Habana	30 Jul	6.47	1.1	Glenn	6 May
6.59	0.9	Hubbard	Q	NC	Sacramento	14 Jul	6.46	1.9	Falaiye	13 May
		6.84w 2.7	4	NC	Sacramento	16 Jul	6.34	w	Domico	24 Jul
6.54	0.8	Brunner	2		Sydney	18 Aug				

Mark	Wind	Name		Nat	Born	Pos	Meet	Venue		Date
Exhibition: 6.60		Hristína	Athanasíou	GRE	11.1.74	2		Carbonia		24 Aug
Pending – following positive drugs test										
6.92	0.3	Iva	Prandzheva ¶	BUL	15.2.72	2	WK	Zürich		11 Aug
					6.92	6.88	6.88	6.63	6.87	x
7.10w	2.1	Inessa	Kravets ¶	UKR	5.10.66	1		Barcelona		25 Jul
					6.82	6.78	7.10w	x	p	p
6.92	1.7	1 BrGP	London (CP)	5 Aug	6.88	6.92	p	p	p	p

JUNIORS

See main list for top 5 juniors. 10 performances by 4 women to 6.51. Additional marks and further juniors:

Montaner	6.64	0.8	1		Castellón	26 Aug	6.53	1.0	1		Castellón	3 Jun
	6.54	1.0	1		Alfaz del Pi	29 Apr	6.53	1.7	2		Selargius	23 Aug
	6.54	1.2	2	NC	Barcelona	3 Sep	6.51	1.5	1		Castellón	16 Aug

6.46	1.3	Anna	Pyatykh	RUS	4.4.81	1		Moskva	19 Aug
6.45i		Yevgeniya	Stavchanskaya	UKR	25.9.81	4	NC	Brovary	9 Feb
6.44	1.0	Ychlindria	Spears	USA	17.7.84	1		Orlando	2 Aug
6.44	1.1	Svetlana	Zaytseva	RUS	14.8.81	2		Moskva	19 Aug
6.43	0.8	Kumiko	Ikeda (10)	JPN	10.1.81	3	WJ	Santiago de Chile	18 Oct
6.40	1.4	Maria Chiara	Baccini	ITA	21.7.81	1		Sesto Fiorentino	25 Jun
6.40	1.5	Korinna	Fink	GER	6.4.81	1	NC-23	Jena	19 Aug
6.39	1.2	Célia	Harmenil	FRA	7.9.81	1		Bron	7 May
6.38i		Irina	Simagina	RUS	25.5.82	1		Moskva	29 Feb
6.38	1.1	Nadia	Raymond	FRA	21.4.81	2	NC	Nice	6 Aug
6.37A	-2.2	Delia	Visser	RSA	9.4.83	1	NC-y	Pretoria	8 Apr
6.36		Kateryna	Chernyavskaya	UKR	31.1.83	1		Kharkov	3 Jun
6.35	1.1	Tameisha	King	USA	24.2.81	3		Atlanta	19 May
6.35		Alina	Militaru	ROM	10.4.82	1		Poiana Brasov	7 Oct
6.35	0.7	Dana	Veldaková (20)	SVK	3.6.81	4	WJ	Santiago de Chile	18 Oct

Wind assisted

Montaner	6.64	3.9	1	Valencia	24 Jun	6.64w 2.2	2	Castellón	9 Aug
	6.57	2.5	1	Valencia	1 Jul	best was 6.79w			
6.48	4.2	Yolanda	Thompson	USA	29.5.81	1	NC-j	Denton	23 Jun
6.46	3.7	Célia	Harmenil	FRA	7.9.81	2		Hagetmau	26 Jul
6.46	2.7	Kumiko	Ikeda	JPN	10.1.81	1		Kokogawa	16 Sep
6.45	5.1	Tameisha	King	USA	24.2.81	2	NC-j	Denton	23 Jun
6.41	2.2	Narayane	Dossevi	FRA	3.2.83	2		Hagetmau	26 Jul
6.35	3.0	Chandi	Jones	USA	7.6.83	1c4		Austin	12 May

TRIPLE JUMP

15.32	0.5	Tatyana		Lebedeva	RUS	21.7.76	1	Super	Yokohama		9 Sep
						15.15	15.32	15.15	15.16	14.86	x
15.01	1.1	1	Veniz	Haniá	14 Jun	14.80/1.5	15.01	14.72	14.61	14.50w	14.88w/2
15.00	1.3	2	OG	Sydney	24 Sep	14.77	14.66	14.45	14.91/-0.8	15.00	14.90/0.6
14.98	0.9	1	ECp-S	Gateshead	16 Jul	14.55	14.34	14.56	14.98	four only	
14.91	0.3	q	OG	Sydney	22 Sep	11.71	14.91		two only		
14.89	0.4	1	GP II	Bratislava	22 Jun	14.70	13.55	14.65	14.61	x	14.89
14.82	-0.9	1	NC	Tula	24 Jul	14.60	14.69	14.82	x	13.87	14.76/-1.
14.78i	-	1		Pireás	9 Feb	14.51	x	13.58	14.78	x	14.71
14.78	0.0	1	GP	Athína	28 Jun	13.78	14.50w	14.68/0.8	14.31	12.65	14.78
14.75i	-	1	NC	Volgograd	6 Feb	14.52	14.75	14.69	14.54	14.62	x
14.68i	-	1	EI	Gent	26 Feb	14.50	14.68	14.66	x	p	p
14.66i		1		Karlsruhe	29 Jan	14.06	14.36	x	14.39	14.66	x
14.64i	-	1		Moskva	23 Jan	14.37	14.64	x	x	x	14.61
15.00w	2.5	2		Réthimno	10 Jun	14.66w	14.80w/3.0	14.95w/3.0	14.92w/4.0	14.78w	15.00w
15.20	-0.3	Tereza		Marinova	BUL	5.9.77	1	OG	Sydney		24 Sep
						15.20	x	x	x	x	x
14.90	0.6	1		Kalamáta	4 Jun	14.50	14.90	x	x	x	x
14.79	0.8	1		Thessaloníki	30 Aug	14.56	14.30w	14.79	14.51w		four only
14.74	0.8	1		Villeneuve d'Ascq	17 Jun	14.58	14.46	x	14.74	x	x
14.73	-0.5	q	OG	Sydney	22 Sep	14.73		two only			
14.65	-0.3	1		Athína	30 May	x	13.79	13.97	x	14.65	14.29

Mark	Wind	Name		Nat	Born	Pos	Meet	Venue	Date
	15.07w 2.5	1	Réthimno	10 Jun	14.66w	14.80w/3.0 x		14.75w/2.8 15.07w	x
	14.90w 2.1	2 Veniz	Haniá	14 Jun	14.90w	x	14.19	x x	x
15.04	0.9	Iva	Prandzheva ¶	BUL	15.2.72	1	NC	Sofia	17 Jun
					14.60	14.70	14.49	14.64 14.78/1.1	15.04
	14.76 0.5	2 GP	Athína	28 Jun	x	14.76	x	14.50/0.9p	14.68/-1.0
	14.68 0.2	1	Sofia	10 Jun	14.43	14.68	p	p p	p
	14.66i -	2	Pireás	9 Feb	14.66	14.54	x	14.18 13.91	x
	14.64 0.0	1 ECp1B	Bydgoszcz	8 Jul	14.64	14.25	14.34	p four only	
	14.63i -	3 EI	Gent	26 Feb	x	x	x	14.26 x	14.63
14.96	0.7	Yelena	Govorova	UKR	18.9.73	4	OG	Sydney	24 Sep
					14.96	x 14.74/-0.9	14.78/0.1	14.69 14.74/0.	
	14.80 1.0	3 Veniz	Haniá	14 Jun	14.63w	14.80	14.71	x x	14.67w
	14.76 0.2	q OG	Sydney	22 Sep	14.76	one only			
	14.72 0.7	2	Kalamáta	4 Jun	x	x	14.72	x 14.62	x
	14.70 2.0	3	Réthimno	10 Jun	x	x	x	14.50w 14.70	14.63
	14.60 1.6	3 GP	Athína	28 Jun	x	14.60	14.5	14.13 x	14.20
14.94i	–	Cristina	Nicolau	ROM	.8.77	1	NC	Bucuresti	5 Feb
					14.94	p	x	p p	p
	14.63i -	2 EI	Gent	26 Feb	14.63	14.49	x	14.44 p	x
14.69	1.2	Anja	Valant	SLO	8.9.77	3		Kalamáta	4 Jun
					x	14.69	14.29	x 14.55	14.14
	14.62 1.3	2	Thessaloníki	30 Aug	14.06	14.62	x	14.13	four only
14.66i	–	Yelena	Lebedenko	RUS	16.1.71	1		Samara	30 Jan
					13.81	14.16	13.94	14.66 14.26	14.44
14.65	2.0	Natalya	Safronova	BLR	11.4.74	1	NCp	Stayki	3 Jun
		(37/8)			14.65	14.15	14.21	14.14 x	14.30
14.57	0.0	Inessa	Kravets ¶	UKR	5.10.66	1		Ljubljana	10 Jun
14.52	0.6	Anastasiya	Ilyina (10)	RUS-J	16.1.82	q	WJ	Santiago de Chile	20 Oct
14.47	1.8	Olga	Yershova	RUS	13.8.76	4	Veniz	Haniá	14 Jun
14.47	2.0	Yamilé	Aldama	CUB	14.8.72	5	Veniz	Haniá	14 Jun
14.47	1.2		Ren Ruiping	CHN	1.2.76	1		Beijing	1 Sep
14.45i	–	Olga	Rublyova	RUS	28.10.74	2		Moskva	27 Jan
14.44	1.2	Anna	Biryukova	RUS	27.9.67	2	GP II	Bratislava	22 Jun
14.44	-0.5	Adelina	Gavrila	ROM	26.11.78	1	NC	Bucuresti	6 Aug
14.40	0.7	Magdelín	Martínez	CUB	10.2.76	1		La Habana	23 Jun
14.34	0.4	Sárka	Kaspárková	CZE	20.5.71	q	OG	Sydney	22 Sep
14.31i	–	Rodica	Mateescu	ROM	13.3.71	2	NC	Bucuresti	5 Feb
14.30	1.8	Baya	Rahouli	ALG	27.7.79	*		Adelaide	8 Mar
		(20)							
14.29	-0.4	Ashia	Hansen	GBR	5.12.71	q	OG	Sydney	22 Sep
14.28i	–	Oksana	Rogova	RUS	7.10.78	5	EI	Gent	26 Feb
14.27	0.9	Maria	Dimitrova	BUL	7.8.76	5		Kalamáta	4 Jun
14.27	-0.1	Yelena	Khlusovich	UKR	3.11.69	1		Kiev	16 Jul
14.26	0.3	Ólga	Vasdéki	GRE	26.9.73	q	OG	Sydney	22 Sep
14.25i	–	Irina	Lasovskaya	RUS	17.12.69	2		Samara	30 Jan
14.25	0.8	Yelena	Oleynikova	RUS	9.12.76	4	Znam	Sankt-Peterburg	18 Jun
14.21	-0.6		Miao Chunqing	CHN	27.2.79	1	OT	Jinzhou	8 Jun
14.20	1.6	Yelena	Parfyonova	KAZ	26.1.74	1		Almaty	28 May
14.19	2.0	Anna	Pyatkh	RUS-J	4.4.81	1		Lapinlahti	16 Jul
		(30)							
14.18	-0.9	Mariya	Sokova	RUS	2.9.70	2	Mos Ch	Moskva	12 Jul
14.18	0.8	Françoise	Mbango	CMR	14.4.76	1		Sydney	11 Sep
14.17A	2.0	Anna	Tarasova	KAZ	23.3.80	1		Juárez	21 Jul
14.14	1.2	Elena	Dumitrascu	ROM	14.5.74	2		Constanta	27 May
14.14		Irina	Vasilyeva	RUS	.79	1		Moskva	21 Jun
14.14	1.8	Camilla	Johansson	SWE	3.11.76	1	NC	Uppsala	19 Aug
14.13	1.8	Nadezhda	Bazhenova	RUS	.78	4	Mos Ch	Moskva	12 Jul
14.13	1.4	Concepción	Paredes	ESP	19.7.70	1		Castellón	23 Aug
14.10	0.9	Carlota	Castrejana	ESP	25.4.73	1		Pamplona	29 Jul
14.09i	–	Natalia	Kilpeläinen	FIN	19.7.70	5		Samara	30 Jan
		(40)							
14.09	2.0	Suzette	Lee	JAM	6.3.75	1		Baton Rouge	19 May
14.07	1.4	Lyudmila	Nikitina	RUS	2.3.70	1	NCp	Tula	3 Jun
14.07	0.2	Yelena	Lysak	RUS	19.10.75	q	NC	Tula	23 Jul
14.06i	–	Tiombé	Hurd	USA	17.8.73	1	NC	Atlanta	4 Mar
14.06i	–	Keisha	Spencer	JAM	16.2.78	1	NCAA	Fayetteville	11 Mar
14.06	0.7	Marija	Martinovic	YUG	17.4.79	1	ECp2B	Banská Bystrica	8 Jul
14.06	0.2	Barbara	Lah	ITA	24.3.72	1		Pescara	22 Jul
14.05	-0.8	Natalya	Kayukova	RUS	10.12.66	4		Lapinlahti	16 Jul

Mark	Wind	Name		Nat	Born	Pos	Meet	Venue	Date
14.05	1.3	Dímitra	Márkou	GRE	28.7.80	4		Thessaloníki	30 Aug
14.04	1.6	Olga	Cepero	CUB	4.2.75	2		La Habana	23 Jun
		(50)							
14.03	1.0	Kène	Ndoye	SEN	20.11.78	1		Funchal	29 Jul
14.02	-1.3	Mabel	Gay	CUB-J	5.5.83	2	Barr	La Habana	29 Jul
14.01i	–		Wu Lingmei	CHN	16.2.73	1		Tianjin	20 Feb
14.01	1.6	Stacey	Bowers	USA	22.8.77	1	Conseil	Fort-de-France	29 Apr
14.01	1.5	Luciana	dos Santos	BRA	10.2.70	1		São Paulo	18 Jun
14.00	0.7	Tatyana	Drozdova	RUS	7.2.75	2	NCp	Tula	3 Jun
13.96	0.8	Tanja	König	GER	11.4.70	1		Wesel	12 Jun
13.96	1.2	Viktoriya	Brigadnaya	TKM	4.8.80	1	Cezmi	Istanbul	24 Jun
13.96	1.7	Nicole	Gamble	USA	21.6.77	1	NC	Sacramento	22 Jul
13.96	1.2	Constanta	Stucan	ROM-J	12.7.81	1		Poiana Brasov	22 Jul
		(60)							
13.96	0.0	Liliana	Zagacka	POL	28.1.77	1		Zielona Góra	7 Sep
13.95		Sheila	Hudson	USA	30.6.67	*		Sacramento	19 Aug
13.93	0.3	Ilona	Pazola	POL	22.3.69	1		Bojanowo	3 May
13.92	1.4	Dana	Veldáková	SVK-J	3.6.81	3	WJ	Santiago de Chile	21 Oct
13.91i		Yevgeniya	Stavchanskaya	UKR-J	25.9.81	2	NC	Brovary	7 Feb
13.91	0.6	Yolanta	Khropach	UKR	22.9.74	3	NC	Kiev	6 Aug
13.91	1.4	Nicole	Herschmann	GER	27.10.75	1		Sondershausen	25 Aug
13.90		Tatyana	Kotova	UKR	2.1.70	1		Dnepropetrovsk	18 Jul
13.90	1.3	Aleksandra	Stadnyuk	UKR	16.4.80	4	NC	Kiev	6 Aug
13.88	-0.4		Li Jiahui	CHN	8.8.79	4	NGPF	Jinzhou	8 Jun
		(70)							
13.88	1.5	Olga	Bolshova	MDA	16.6.68	1		Mataró	22 Jul
13.87	0.5	Yelena	Donkina	RUS	15.3.73	5	Mos Ch	Moskva	12 Jul
13.86i		Marie-Véronique	Mazarin	FRA	18.10.76	1	NC	Liévin	19 Feb
13.83i		Zhanna	Gureyeva	BLR	10.6.70	1	Univ Ch	Minsk	11 Feb
13.83			Tang Zhimin	CHN	26.6.79	2	NGP	Wenzhou	23 Apr
13.83	1.2	Sandrine	Domain	FRA	6.9.71	1		Montgeron	18 Jun
13.83	-0.9	Natasha	Gibson	USA	12.7.69	5	NC	Sacramento	22 Jul
13.82	1.9	Nicole	Mladenis	AUS	22.9.75	1		Perth	9 Dec
13.80	0.4	Maho	Hanaoka	JPN	3.8.76	2		Mito	7 May
13.80	-1.0	Yusmay	Bicet	CUB-J	8.12.83	4		La Habana	23 Jun
		(80)							
13.78i			Huang Qiuyan	CHN	25.1.80	1	NGP	Beijing	22 Feb
13.78A	0.4	Althea	Williams	CAN	4.1.75	1		Flagstaff	4 Jul
13.76		Trecia	Smith	JAM	5.11.75	1		Clemson	14 May
13.75	0.8	Shelly-Ann	Gallimore	JAM-J	10.3.81	2	SEC	Baton Rouge	14 May
13.75	-0.1	Sylvie	Borda	FRA	4.9.66	2		Montgeron	18 Jun
13.75	0.0	Yelena	Ivanova	RUS	16.3.79	3	NC-23	Cheboksary	2 Jul
13.75		Nguyen	Thi Bich Van	VIE	21.2.75	1	NC	Ho Chi-Minh	15 Oct
13.74	1.5	Shakeema	Walker	USA	10.11.76	q	NC	Sacramento	20 Jul
13.74	1.8	Zita	Ajkler	HUN	9.6.75	1	NC	Budapest	30 Jul
13.73	0.8		Wang Zhuri	CHN	4.9.80	3	NGP	Shanghai	19 Apr
		(90)							
13.73	0.8	Lene	Espegren	NOR	8.5.71	3	ECp-1A	Nadderud	8 Jul
13.72	2.0	Oksana	Derkach	UKR	7.2.69	2	Kiev Ch	Kiev	17 Jun
13.72	1.2		Zhou Yangxia	CHN-J	10.2.83	5	WJ	Santiago de Chile	21 Oct
13.71	0.2		Ren Ni	CHN	14.5.79	3	NGP	Shijiazhuang	28 Apr
13.71	1.0	Michelle	Griffith	GBR	6.10.71	1		Solihull	5 Aug
13.71	2.0	Maria Costanza	Moroni	ITA	23.3.69	1		Avezzano	20 Aug
13.69i		Nathalie	Jacques-Gustave	FRA	12.5.76	2	NC	Liévin	19 Feb
13.69	1.2	Katja	Umlauft	GER	22.11.74	2		Sondershausen	25 Aug
13.68	0.1		Hu Yaoyao	CHN-J	16.4.83	1	NGP	Chengdu	9 May
13.68	0.5	Federica	Cresci	ITA	13.4.74	1		Piombino	16 Jul
		(100)							
13.68	-0.3	Colleen	Gillies	JAM	18.8.74	3	NC	Kingston	20 Jul
13.68	0.6	Heli	Koivula	FIN	27.6.75	1	NC	Lahti	20 Aug
13.68			Zhao Hanjun	CHN	.0.00	1qB	NSG	Chengdu	10 Sep

13.66i		Mariana	Solomon	ROM	8.9.80	5 Feb
13.66			Zhao Weiping	CHN		10 Sep
13.65	0.3	Ioánna	Kafetzí	GRE	30.5.76	8 Jul
13.65		Andrea	Ávila	ARG	4.4.70	28 Aug
13.64		Dahlia	Ingram	USA	17.7.78	23 Jun
13.64	-0.3	Caroline	Honoré	FRA	29.4.70	27 Jun
13.64			Peng Xiaoyan	CHN		10 Sep
13.63	1.9		Song Ying	CHN-J	18.1.82	14 Apr
13.63	0.0		Zhao Fan	CHN	1.3.78	28 Apr
13.62		Vanitta	Kinard	USA	26.7.75	23 Jun
13.62	0.1	Maria	Spirescu	ROM	2.4.80	24 Jun
13.61	1.4	Olga	Nechayeva	RUS	.74	23 Jul
13.60i		Yasmina	Soualhia	FRA	7.3.80	19 Feb
13.60	0.5		Lee Kyung-sun	KOR	11.9.77	2 May
13.57i		Anna	Yerokhina	UKR	24.9.76	7 Feb
13.56i		DeAnne	Davis	USA	9.11.77	19 Feb
13.56		Jackie	Edwards	BAH	14.4.71	26 Mar
13.56	0.0	Sofiya	Sukhina	RUS	.79	2 Jul

Mark	Wind	Name		Nat	Born	Date
13.56	1.8	Irina	Beskrovnajа	SVK-J	28.12.82	22 Jul
13.52	0.9	Connie	Henry	GBR	15.4.72	19 Feb
13.52	0.9	Oksana	Zelinskaya	KAZ	26.4.69	2 Jul
13.52	1.1	Sari	Kulmala	FIN	25.5.74	16 Jul
13.52	0.6	Galina	Sharova	RUS	30.1.79	23 Jul
13.52	0.5		Li Xiaoling	CHN	15.8.80	19 Oct
13.51i		Kerstin	Hodea	GER	9.8.77	19 Jan
13.51		Marina	Ogorodova	RUS	.76	20 May
13.49	0.4		Zhang Hao	CHN	26.2.78	28 Apr
13.49	1.4	Brandi	Prieto	USA	17.4.78	3 Jun
13.49	1.0	Kerine	Black	JAM		3 Jun
13.49	0.0	Martina	Darmovzalová	CZE	12.10.78	16 Jul
13.49	1.0	Alina	Dinu	ROM-J	2.9.82	22 Jul
13.48	1.5	Hrisopiyí	Devetzí	GRE	2.1.76	25 Jun
13.48A	1.5	Robyne	Johnson	USA	22.8.63	8 Jul
13.47i		Virge	Naeris	EST	12.12.69	20 Feb
13.47	0.0	Adrija	Grociene	LTU	25.7.74	8 Jul
13.45i		Silvia	Biondini	ITA	24.1.76	25 Jan
13.45	0.9	Aysegül	Baklaci	TUR	25.12.77	24 Jun
13.45	-0.8	Yelena	Portugal	RUS-J	.82	9 Jul
13.44	0.3	Michelle	Hastick	CAN	16.9.73	27 Jul
13.44	0.0	Viktoriya	Gurova	RUS-J	.82	2 Sep
13.43	0.6	Inmaculada	Beitia	ESP	8.9.75	2 Sep
13.42	0.6	Svetlana	Klimina	UZB	.67	28 May
13.42	0.5	Larisa	Kolchanova	RUS	.79	2 Jul
13.42	0.0	Olga	Voropinova	RUS-J	.81	17 Sep
13.41	1.6	Claudine	Szendrei	GER	22.7.76	29 Jul
13.40A		Chantal	Ouaba	BKF	.75	6 May
13.40	0.6	Mariana	Bogatie	ROM-J	12.6.81	27 May
13.38	0.2		Li Jing	CHN	10.7.79	25 Aug
13.37			Phan Thi Thu Lan	VIE	,79	4 Jul
13.37	0.5	Angela	Barylla	GER	6.1.71	29 Jul
13.36	0.5	Elena	Gilardoni	ITA	20.5.75	27 Jun
13.36	0.0	Dejana	Cachot	SUI	2.11.68	29 Aug
13.36	1.6	Jennifer	Arveláez	VEN-J	28.10.82	7 Oct
13.35			Wang Kuo-Huei	TPE	12.9.78	16 May
13.35	1.2	Shonda	Swift	USA	28.2.74	20 Jul
13.34	0.0		Yan Xueqin	CHN	1.11.73	25 Mar
13.34	0.0	Renata	Szykulska	POL	17.8.74	6 Aug
13.33		Kerstin	Hodea	GER	9.8.77	2 Jul
13.32	1.0	Olga	Lapina	KAZ	22.6.78	2 Jul
13.32	0.6	Eva	Dolezalová	CZE	24.5.79	16 Jul
13.32	-0.3	Deanna	Simmons	USA	22.10.78	20 Jul
13.32	-1.5	Giovanna	Franzon	ITA-J	26.5.81	7 Oct
13.31	1.9	Zita	Bálint	HUN	25.10.71	30 Jul
13.31	1.6	Fukuyo	Ihara	JPN	18.5.78	2 Sep
13.31	1.2		Yu Shaohua	CHN-J	4.1.85	19 Oct
13.30	1.4	Irina	Burmagina	RUS	14.1.80	2 Jul
13.29i		Sona	Klimácková	SVK	4.5.75	5 Feb
13.29	0.0	Eugenie	Gomis	FRA	1.7.80	9 Jun
13.29	2.0	Sandra	Swennen	BEL	12.2.73	17 Jun
13.28i		Stilianí	Pilátou	GRE	28.3.80	20 Feb
13.28i	-	Andreja	Ribac	SLO	14.1.76	3 Mar
13.27i			Kang Yan	CHN	22.6.80	19 Feb
13.27	0.0		Xu Junfang	CHN	10.2.79	23 Apr
13.27	0.4	Ksenija	Predikaka	SLO	11.3.70	25 Jun
13.26	0.1	Shelley	Avery	NZL	9.3.73	12 Mar
13.26	1.6	Marie	Åhlander	SWE	15.4.78	30 Jul
13.26	0.1	Olga	Saladukha	UKR-J	4.6.83	10 Sep
13.25	1.4	Penny	Blackwell	USA	24.12.69	10 Jun
13.25	-1.0	Stéphanie	Luzieux	FRA-J	7.7.82	7 Oct
		(182)				

Wind assisted

Mark	Wind	Name		Nat	Born	Pos	Meet	Venue	Date
14.42	2.6	Baya	Rahouli	ALG	27.7.79	1		Adelaide	8 Mar
14.15	4.6	Keisha	Spencer	JAM	16.2.78	1	USTCA	Austin	22 Apr
14.14	3.9	Michelle	Griffith	GBR	6.10.71	1		Ljubljana	25 Jul
14.00		Sheila	Hudson	USA	30.6.67	1		Sacramento	19 Aug
13.92	2.4	Trecia	Smith	JAM	5.11.75	1		Durham	7 Apr
13.86	2.9	Niurka	Montalvo	ESP	4.6.68	1		Palafrugell	27 May
13.86	2.3	Natasha	Gibson	USA	12.7.69	2		Durham	7 Apr
13.82	2.6	Vanitta	Kinard	USA	26.7.75	q	NC	Sacramento	20 Jul
13.80	2.2	Aysegül	Baklaci	TUR	25.12.77	9	Veniz	Hánia	14 Jun
13.74	2.1	Sari	Kulmala	FIN	25.5.74	1		Jämsä	8 Jul
13.72	2.8	Caroline	Honoré	FRA	29.4.70	3		Montgeron	18 Jun
13.72	4.4	Andreja	Ribac	SLO	14.1.76	2		Ljubljana	25 Jul
13.71	3.3	Silvia	Biondini	ITA	24.1.76	1	NC	Milano	7 Sep

Mark	Wind	Name		Nat	Born	Date
13.66	3.8	Connie	Henry	GBR	15.4.72	25 Jul
13.65	3.2	Keila da Silva Costa		BRA-J	6.2.83	7 Oct
13.53	3.4	Kareen	Clarke	JAM-J	10.4.81	1 Apr
13.52	3.7	Åsa	Lönn	SWE	18.3.78	20 May
13.47	w	Michelle	Hastick	CAN	16.9.73	28 Apr
13.47	2.2	Aurélie	Talbot	FRA-J	22.8.81	26 Jul
13.46	2.6	Rodena	Barr	USA	5.3.78	14 May
13.44	4.5	Renata	Szykulska	POL	17.8.74	17 Jun
13.41	2.5	Anja	Diezel	GER	17.5.79	20 Aug
13.37	2.5		Wang Kuo-Huei	TPE	12.9.78	20 Mar
13.37	3.1	Bianca	Rockett	USA	6.7.80	14 May
13.35		Christine	Guldbrandsen	NOR	4.5.77	21 May
13.35	2.1	Yelena	Bobrovskaya	KGZ	11.4.75	28 May
13.34	2.1	Tatyana	Obukhova	UKR	15.1.78	21 May
13.28	0.1	Katerina	Chernyavskaya	UKR-J	31.1.83	10 Jun

Best outdoor marks for athlete with boot indoors

Mark	Wind	Name	Pos	Meet	Venue	Date
14.27	-1.1	Rogova	2	NC	Tula	24 Jul
14.24	1.3	Lasovskaya	q	NC	Tula	23 Jul
14.21	1.6	Rublyova	1		Rostov-na-Donu	27 Jun
14.19	–	Nicolau	7	GP	Athína	28 Jun
		14.22w 3.1	4		Róthimno	10 Jun
13.99	-0.6	Wu Lingmei	3	OT	Jinzhou	8 Jun
13.97	1.6	Spencer	1cA	TexR	Austin	8 Apr
13.97	0.9	Hurd	1		Sacramento	16 Aug
13.76	0.6	Huang Qiuyan	1	NGP	Shijiazhuang	28 Apr

Mark	Wind	Name	Date
13.60	0.1	Solomon	6 Aug
13.51	1.2	Mazarin	29 Apr
13.45	-0.2	Kilpeläinen	24 Jun
13.44	1.4	Biondini	3 Jun
13.40		Gureyeva	21 May
13.36	0.6	Soualhia	9 Jun
13.34	0.7	Jacques-Gustave	8 Jul
13.27	1.4	Kang Yan	4 May
13.27	0.0	Davis	20 May
13.27	1.6	Ribac	3 Jun
13.27	0.7	Stavchanskaya	17 Jun
13.30w	2.1	Lebedenko	23 Jul

Low altitude best

Mark	Wind	Name	Pos	Meet	Venue	Date
13.73	1.0	A Williams	1	PennR	Philadelphia	28 Apr
13.59	-0.8	Tarasova	2		Almaty	12 Aug

Drugs disqualification

Mark	Wind	Name		Nat	Born	Pos	Venue	Date
14.18	0.1	Rodica	Mateescu	ROM	13.3.71	1	Bucuresti	25 Jun

JUNIORS

See main list for top 10 juniors. 11 performances by 6 women to 13.91. Additional marks and further juniors:

Name	Mark	Wind	Pos	Meet	Venue	Date	Mark	Wind	Pos	Meet	Venue	Date
Ilyina	14.24	-0.3	1	WJ	Santiago	21 Oct						
Pyatkh	14.18	1.2	2	WJ	Santiago	21 Oct	14.00	0.0	1	NC-j	Krasnodar	17 Sep
	14.15	0.3	Q	WJ	Santiago	20 Oct	13.95	-1.2	1		Cheboksary	9 Jul

Mark	Wind	Name		Nat	Born	Pos	Meet	Venue	Date
13.63			Song Ying	CHN	18.1.82	4	NGP	Nanjing	14 Apr
13.56	1.8	Irina	Beskrovnaja	SVK	28.12.82	3		Budapest	22 Jul

WOMEN 2000

Mark	Wind	Name		Nat	Born	Pos	Meet	Venue	Date
13.49	1.0	Alina	Dinu	ROM	2.9.82	2		Poiana Brasov	22 Jul
13.45	-0.8	Yelena	Portugal	RUS	.82	3		Cheboksary	9 Jul
13.44	0.0	Viktoriya	Gurova	RUS	.82	3		Krasnodar	2 Sep
13.42	0.0	Olga	Voropinova	RUS	.81	4		Krasnodar	17 Sep
13.40	0.6	Mariana	Bogatie	ROM	12.6.81	3		Constanta	27 May
13.36	1.6	Jennifer	Arveláez	VEN	28.10.82	2	SAm-J	São Leopoldo	7 Oct
13.32	-1.5	Giovanna	Franzon	ITA	26.5.81	1		Grosseto	7 Oct
13.31	1.2		Yu Shaohua (20)	CHN	4.1.85	q	NC	Luohe	19 Oct
Wind assisted									
Gay		13.96w 2.2	2 NC La Habana	24 Jul					
13.65	3.2	Keila da Silva	Costa	BRA	6.2.83	1	SAm-J	São Leopoldo	7 Oct
13.53	3.4	Kareen	Clarke	JAM	10.4.81	1		Coral Gables	1 Apr
13.47	2.2	Aurélie	Talbot	FRA	22.8.81	1		Hagetmau	26 Jul

SHOT

21.46		Larisa	Peleshenko	RUS	29.2.64	1	Kuts	Moskva		26 Aug
					21.01	21.03	x	21.07	21.46	20.98
	20.36i	1	Moskva	27 Jan	20.18	20.28	20.13	20.17	20.36	x
	20.29	2 NCp	Tula	2 Jun	19.66	19.76	19.48	20.29	x	20.07
	20.26	2 NC	Tula	26 Jul	20.17	x	x	20.26	20.10	20.11
	20.15i	1 EI	Gent	26 Feb	19.86	x	19.61	x	x	20.15
	20.05i	1	Moskva	21 Jan	20.05	x	19.67	x	19.89	19.87
	19.92	2 OG	Sydney	28 Sep	19.16	19.92	19.79	x	x	19.60
	19.69	2 Znam	Sankt-Peterburg	17 Jun	x	19.69	x	19.45	x	17.62
	19.51i	1 NC	Volgograd	5 Feb						
20.72		Svetlana	Krivelyova	RUS	13.6.69	1	NCp	Tula		2 Jun
					19.77	19.68	20.72	19.69	x	20.03
	20.59	1 NC	Tula	26 Jul	20.59	20.43	19.64	20.25	20.37	x
	20.15	1 Znam	Sankt-Peterburg	17 Jun	19.33	x	20.15	20.04	19.76	p
	20.11i	1	Moskva	24 Jan	x	19.71	20.11	x	19.57	x
	19.80	Q NC	Tula	25 Jul						
20.56		Yanina	Korolchik	BLR	26.12.76	1	OG	Sydney		28 Sep
					19.43	x	18.76	19.11	x	20.56
	20.31	1	Stayki	1 Sep	20.31	20.06	x	x	x	
	20.08	1	Minsk	21 May	19.35	x	x	19.42	19.80	20.08
20.23		Astrid	Kumbernuss	GER	5.2.70	1		Engers		25 Aug
	20.12	1	Bad Köstritz	3 Sep						
	20.03	1	Leverkusen	20 Aug	20.03	?				
	19.93	1	Halle	27 May	19.93	19.23	19.35	x	19.05	p
	19.77	1	Iffezheim	27 Jun	19.46	19.77	x	x	19.69	x
	19.70i	1	Neubrandenburg	4 Mar	18.94	19.68	19.70	19.38	19,54	19.26
	19.63	1	Chemnitz	22 Jul	19.63	19.22	x	19.38	x	p
	19.63	1	Cottbus	23 Aug	19.50	19.63	19.40	x	x	x
	19.62	3 OG	Sydney	28 Sep	19.38	19.24	18.73	18.76	18.89	19.62
19.81		Nadine	Kleinert-Schmitt	GER	20.10.75	2		Halle		27 May
					19.79	19.59	19.81	x	x	x
	19.67	1	Gotha	24 Jun	19.26	x	19.18	19.67	19.61	x
19.51		Lyudmila	Sechko	RUS	27.11.74	3	NCp	Tula		2 Jun
19.48		Yumileidi	Cumbá	CUB	11.2.75	1	Barr	La Habana		29 Jul
		(30/7)			18.92	x	18.41	19.34	18.70	19.48
19.36			Lee Myung-sun	KOR	12.2.76	1	NGP	Shanghai		19 Apr
19.32			Yu Xin	CHN	23.2.77	1	OT	Jinzhou		8 Jun
19.32		Olga	Ryabinkina	RUS	24.9.76	1		Sankt-Peterburg		25 Jun
		(10)								
19.31			Cheng Xiaoyan	CHN	30.12.75	1		Beijing		18 Aug
19.28		Katarzyna	Zakowicz	POL	12.5.75	1		Bydgoszcz		15 Jul
19.18		Connie	Price-Smith	USA	3.6.62	1		Portland		25 Jun
19.18		Krystyna	Zabawska	POL	14.1.68	5	OG	Sydney		28 Sep
19.17i		Jesseca	Cross	USA	10.5.75	1		Lawrence		8 Jan
19.13i		Nadezhda	Ostapchuk	BLR	12.10.80	1		Pireás		9 Feb
19.03i		Kalliópi	Ouzoúni	GRE	8.2.73	1		Pireás		22 Jan
18.94		Lucica	Ciobanu	ROM	10.5.79	1		Onesti		20 May
18.87i		Anna	Romanova	RUS	9.3.68	3		Moskva		27 Jan
18.85			Zhang Liuhong	CHN	16.1.69	2	OT	Jinzhou		8 Jun
		(20)								
18.81		Mara	Rosolen	ITA	27.7.65	1		Avezzano		20 Aug
18.79		Valentina	Fedyushina	AUT	18.2.65	1		Quinta del Anjo		18 Mar
18.73		Yuliya	Zaginay	RUS	3.8.63	5	NCp	Tula		2 Jun
18.69i		Laurence	Manfredi	FRA	20.5.74	Q	NC	Liévin		19 Feb
18.68			Song Feina	CHN	25.1.77	1	NC	Luohe		22 Oct

Mark		Name	Nat	Born	Pos	Meet	Venue	Date
18.62		Yu Juan	CHN	29.3.75	4	NGP	Shanghai	19 Apr
18.56	Irina	Khudoroshkina	RUS	13.10.68	4	Znam	Sankt-Peterburg	17 Jun
18.46i	Lieja	Koeman	NED	10.3.76	7	EI	Gent	26 Feb
18.42i	Tressa	Thompson ¶	USA	6.5.75	2		Fairfax	29 Jan
18.37i	Livia	Mehes	ROM	6.3.65	1		Bucuresti	30 Jan
	(30)							
18.35		Jiang Ping	CHN	10.1.79	2	NC	Luohe	22 Oct
18.32		Wang Yawen	CHN	23.8.73	1	NGP	Guangzhou	26 Mar
18.32	Teri	Tunks	USA	30.10.75	2		Sacramento	21 May
18.30i	Judy	Oakes	GBR	14.2.58	1	NC	Birmingham	30 Jan
18.25i	Svetla	Sinirtas	TUR	17.6.64	1	BUL Ch	Sofia	29 Jan
18.24		Sui Xinmei	CHN	29.1.65	1	NGP	Deyang	13 May
18.23		Tian Xiue	CHN	4.10.71	3	NGP	Tianjin	3 May
18.21		Li Meisu	CHN	17.4.59	3	NGP	Guangzhou	26 Mar
18.17	Martina	de la Puente	ESP	4.4.75	1		Cartagena	8 Aug
18.02i	Nadine	Beckel	GER	27.5.77	2		Halle	26 Jan
	(40)							
17.93	Vivian	Peters	NGR	4.5.77	6		Dortmund	8 Jul
17.87		Jia Lina	CHN	26.4.80	4	NC	Luohe	22 Oct
17.84	Assunta	Legnante	ITA	14.5.78	1	NC	Milano	6 Sep
17.83	Nada M	Kawar	JOR	23.11.75	1		Los Angeles (Ww)	6 May
17.82	Iolanta	Ulyeva	KAZ	27.7.76	1		Almaty	11 Aug
17.70		Zhang Peipei	CHN		1		Chengdu	7 Sep
17.67i	Stephanie	Storp	GER	28.11.68	3		Halle	29 Jan
17.64	Yelena	Ivanenko	BLR	5.5.78			Staiki	3 Jun
17.63	Ilona	Beyer	GER	8.1.76	3		Stendal	10 Jun
17.62	Elena	Hila	ROM	20.5.74	1		Poiana Brasov	22 Jul
	(50)							
17.62		Du Xianhui	CHN-J	4.1.81	1		Singapore	9 Sep
17.60	Dawn	Dumble	USA	25.2.72	1		Long Beach	10 Jun
17.59		Qian Chunhua	CHN	11.2.79	5	NC	Luohe	22 Oct
17.55	Misleydis	González	CUB	19.6.78	1		La Habana	29 Jun
17.54	Yelena	Dementiy	UKR	6.3.69	1		Koncha-Zaspa	8 May
17.53		Zhang Zhiying	CHN	19.7.73	9	NGP	Shijiazhuang	28 Apr
17.52	Jenny	Folz	USA	24.12.75	1		Indianapolis	1 Jul
17.48		Li Meiju	CHN-J	23.1.81	7	NGP	Nanjing	14 Apr
17.48	Natalya	Lisovskaya	FRA	16.7.62	2		Nantes	24 Aug
17.45		Zhang Guirong	CHN	.78	2	NC	Singapore	9 Sep
	(60)							
17.40i	Corrie	de Bruin	NED	26.10.76	2	NC	Gent	12 Feb
17.39i	Oksana	Chibisova	RUS	31.3.77	1		Shakhty	15 Jan
17.37	Kathleen	Kluge	GER-J	17.11.81	1	WJ	Santiago de Chile	17 Oct
17.36	Seilala	Sua	USA	25.2.78	1	NCAA	Durham	2 Jun
17.34	Christina	Tolson	USA	16.1.78	4	MSR	Walnut	16 Apr
17.33		Zhang Xiaoyu	CHN-J	16.3.83	2		Beijing	1 Sep
17.23		Gong Jian	CHN	16.1.77	10	NGP	Nanjing	14 Apr
17.22	Cheree	Hicks	USA	17.2.78	5	MSR	Walnut	16 Apr
17.21	Elisângela	Adriano	BRA	27.7.72	1	NC	Rio de Janeiro	6 Aug
17.18	Linda-Marie	Mårtensson	SWE	22.6.71	1		Karlstad	23 Aug
	(70)							
16.92		Mao Lingyan	CHN	12.2.78	12	NGP	Tianjin	3 May
16.89	Zdenka	Silhavá	CZE	15.6.54	2	ECp-1A	Nadderud	9 Jul
16.88	Iríni-Hrisovaládo	Terzóglou	GRE	2.2.79	1	v3N23	Praha	9 Sep
16.88i	Karin	Wurm	GER	6.2.78	2		Magdeburg	16 Dec
16.87	Maranelle	du Toit	RSA	31.12.78	1	NC-23	Pietersburg	14 Apr
16.86	Aleksandra	Kopaneva	RUS	.80	2		Rostov-na-Don	20 May
16.84	Martina	Greithanner	GER	21.10.74	4	NC	Braunschweig	29 Jul
16.82	Rhonda	Hackett	TRI	24.1.77	1		Tuscaloosa	25 Mar
16.82	Veronica	Abrahamse	RSA	18.3.80	2	NC-23	Pietersburg	14 Apr
16.81		Yu Jing	CHN-J	7.3.83	3		Beijing	1 Sep
	(80)							
16.80i	Alina	Frunza	ROM	17.4.79	3		Bucuresti	29 Jan
16.78i	Teresa	Machado	POR	22.7.69	1		Espinho	29 Jan
16.76i	Irache	Quintanal	ESP	18.9.78	6	v2N	Valencia	19 Feb
16.75		Li Xuemei	CHN	1.10.79	12	NGP	Nanjing	14 Apr
16.75	Helena	Engman	SWE	16.6.76	2	NC	Uppsala	19 Aug
16.72i	Vera	Yepimashko	BLR	.76			Gomel	3 Feb
16.60i	Dawn	Ellerbe	USA	3.4.74	2		Laramie	19 Feb
16.58	Natalya	Kharaneko	BLR-J	25.5.82			Brest	23 Aug
16.56i	Jessica	Marable	USA	3.5.77	1		USAF Academy	26 Feb

Mark	Name		Nat	Born	Pos	Meet	Venue	Date
16.56	Oksana	Zakharchuk	UKR	3.4.80	1	Univ Ch	Kiev	15 Jul
	(90)							
16.55	Anna	Rauhala	FIN	26.3.75	1		Kuortane	24 Jun
16.53		Hong Mei	CHN-J	16.1.82	15	NGP	Nanjing	14 Apr
16.53i	Beth	Obruba	USA	30.4.77	1		Lynchburg	9 Dec
16.51	Tania	Lutton-Senior	NZL	1.3.68	2		Brisbane	11 Feb
16.48	Chaniqua	Ross	USA	24.5.80	6	MSR	Walnut	16 Apr
16.46i	Lisa	Griebel	USA	8.3.79	1		Ames	12 Feb
16.46	Linda	Nestorsson	SWE	2.12.75	2		Göteborg	26 Jul
16.46	Lyudmila	Starovoytova	BLR	8.4.74	3	NC	Brest	2 Aug
16.46	Yoko	Toyonaga	JPN	15.4.77	1	NC	Rifu	7 Oct
16.44		Li Fengfeng	CHN	9.1.79	3		Beijing	18 Aug
	(100)							
16.44		Chang Xinhong	CHN	24.3.74	2cA	NSG	Chengdu	9 Sep

16.43	Chinatsu	Mori	JPN	20.5.80	23 Apr
16.43	Amel	Benkhaled	TUN	6.6.74	24 Aug
16.41	Veerle	Blondeel	BEL	14.1.75	23 Jun
16.40	Julie	Dunkley	GBR	11.9.79	12 Aug
16.36	Olympia	Menelaou	CYP	29.4.66	28 Mar
16.33i	Jennifer	Brown	USA	1.9.79	19 Feb
16.33	Jacqueline	Goormachtigh	NED	28.2.70	10 Jun
16.33i	Heather	Leverington	USA	20.2.79	8 Dec
16.30	Sumi	Ichioka	JPN	25.7.79	4 Jun
16.30	Katarina Hoff	(Sederholm)	NOR	19.6.68	11 Aug
16.26	Olga	Schukina	UZB	6.4.77	1 Jul
16.25	Katja	Kròl	GER	5.2.80	22 Jul
16.23i	Claudia	Venghaus	GER	2.4.77	5 Feb
16.23i	Eha	Rünne	EST	25.5.63	6 Feb
16.22	Hristína	Konstadínou	GRE	29.5.72	6 May
16.21	Luz Dary	Castro	COL	30.5.78	8 Dec
16.18i	Mandy	Kinney	USA-J	26.3.81	4 Mar
16.18		Wu Xiaoliang	CHN		7 Sep
16.17	Helen	Toussis	AUS	30.1.75	10 Mar
16.17i	Aubrey	Schmitt	USA	22.11.77	11 Mar
16.17		Jin Cuiping	CHN		7 Sep
16.16	Amber	Knighten	USA	28.6.80	8 Apr
16.16	Leann	Boerema	USA	25.8.80	7 May
16.13i	Safiya	Ingram	USA	18.6.77	27 Feb
16.13	Claudia	Villeneuve	FRA-J	22.8.83	26 Jul
16.12	Cynthia	Ademiluyi	USA	23.1.79	26 Feb
16.12	Anna	Tolokina	RUS-J	3.10.81	20 May
16.10i	Monique	Briche	FRA	12.10.71	20 Feb
16.10	Tina	McDonald	CAN	12.1.76	29 Jul
16.09	Joanne	Duncan	GBR	27.12.66	9 Jul
16.09	Alina	Lenghel	ROM	14.2.80	7 Aug
16.06i	Irina	Vostrikova	RUS	30.8.70	25 Feb
16.05	Anca	Vîlceanu	ROM	1.1.78	7 Aug
16.04	Georgette	Reed	CAN	26.1.67	9 Jul
16.03	Christina	Strovilidou	CYP	.74	21 May
16.03	Lucia	Korceková	SVK-J	23.7.82	24 Aug
16.02i	Magnolia	Iglesias	ESP	25.5.79	6 Feb
16.01	Hanaa Salah	El Melegi	EGY	29.3.75	10 Jul
16.01	Sandra	Harms	GER	22.1.77	29 Jul
16.00	Andrea	Pappas	USA	3.1.78	19 May
15.97	Oksana	Gromova	RUS	23.9.80	12 May
15.96	Svetlana	Shevchenko	UKR	11.2.80	4 Jun
15.94	Leslie	Vidmar	USA	10.10.75	1 Jul
15.94	Karolina	Konkolewska	POL	16.8.80	29 Jul
15.93i	Jodi	Borges	USA	28.1.80	3 Mar
15.91	Katalin	Divós	HUN	11.5.74	29 Jul
15.90i	Jessica	Winkler	GER	24.4.75	13 Feb
15.90i	Mary	LeJour	CAN	13.1.79	19 Feb
15.90	Yuliya	Savchenko	UKR	15.4.74	3 Aug
15.89	Adrienne	Judie	USA	4.8.79	6 May
15.89		Cho Jin-sook	KOR	21.2.77	10 Aug
15.87i	Marsha	French	USA	20.11.76	14 Jan
15.86	Lyudmila	Rublevskaya	RUS	7.6.77	20 May
15.85i	Naomi	Elliott	USA	4.4.80	19 Feb
15.85i	Liz	Toman	CAN	17.4.78	26 Feb
	(156)				

Best outdoor marks for athlete with best indoors

18.83	Ostapchuk			Staiki	1 Sep
18.68	Manfredi	1		Castres	17 Jul
18.63	Ouzoúni	7	OG	Sydney	28 Sep
18.29	Koeman	4		Leverkusen	20 Aug
18.22	Oakes	1		Feltham	2 Sep
18.01	Beckel	2	NC	Braunschweig	29 Jul
17.80	Cross	3		Sacramento	21 May
17.68	Mehes	1	NC	Bucuresti	7 Aug
17.54	Sinirtas	5	ECCp	V R S.António	28 May
17.21	Chibisova	7	NCp	Tula	2 Jun
17.17	Romanova	Q	NC	Tula	25 Jul
17.08	de Bruin	2	NC	Amsterdam	15 Jul
16.97	Thompson	1		Lincoln NE	8 Apr
16.78	Machado	2		Quinta do Anjo	19 Mar
16.69	Frunza	4	NC	Bucuresti	7 Aug

16.34 Wurm 29 Jul | 16.29 Griebel 21 Jul
16.29 Leverington 13 May | 16.25 Quintanal 1 Jul
16.05 Venghaus 7 May | 16.03 Brown 22 Apr

Drugs suspension: 17.31 best out Tressa Thompson ¶ 4 Portland 25 Jun

JUNIORS

See main list for top 7 juniors. 11 performances by 4 women to 17.00. Additional marks and further juniors:

Li Meiju	17.48	9		Tianjin	3 May			
	17.42	10		Shijiahuang	28 Apr			
	17.28	11		Shanghai	19 Apr			
	17.09	1	NC-j	Deyang	16 Jun			
	17.00i	3		Tianjin	19 Feb			
	17.00	1		Chengdu	9 Sep			
Kluge	17.20i	1	NC-j	Sindelfingen	19 Feb			

16.18i	Mandy	Kinney	USA	26.3.81	6	NC	Atlanta	4 Mar
16.13	Claudia	Villeneuve	FRA	22.8.83	1		Hagetmau	26 Jul
16.12	Anna	Tolokina (10)	RUS	3.10.81	3		Rostov-na-Donu	20 May
16.03	Lucia	Korceková	SVK	23.7.82	2		Bratislava	24 Aug
15.82	Laura	Gerraughty	USA	29.7.83	1	NSch	Raleigh	16 Jun
15.82i	Yelena	Voynova	RUS	.81	1		Shakhty	15 Jan
15.74	Mailin	Vargas	CUB	83	2		La Habana	15 Jun
15.73		Yang Yang	CHN	12.1.83	19		Shanghai	19 Apr
15.72	Valerie	Adamas	NZL	6.10.84	1		Papakura	26 Jan
15.54i	Gheorghita	Bosneaga	ROM	15.7.81			Bucuresti	27 Feb
15.50	Karen	Freberg	USA	30.9.82	1		San Luis Obispo	4 May
15.45		Yang Dehui	CHN	28.4.83	20		Shanghai	19 Apr
15.44	Chiara	Rosa (20)	ITA	28.1.83	4		Padova	27 Aug

DISCUS

Mark	Name		Nat	Born	Pos	Meet	Venue		Date
68.70	Nicoleta	Grasu	ROM	11.9.71	1	NC-w	Bucuresti		4 Mar
				65.05	68.70	67.16	66.37	68.30	x
66.17	1	Snagov	6 May	61.86	62.32	64.89	63.05	x	66.17
65.66	1	Sydney	13 Sep						
68.40	Ellina	Zvereva	BLR	16.11.60	1	OG	Sydney		27 Sep
				67.00	66.12	68.40	65.80	x	x
67.25	2 Veniz	Haniá	14 Jun	65.55	67.25	66.72	66.29	64.98	61.38
65.81	1	Stayki	1 Sep	65.81	64.54	64.14	61.57	62.40	p
65.51	1 GP	Osaka	13 May	59.94	63.97	63.92	x	62.63	65.51
68.06	Franka	Dietzsch	GER	22.1.68	1	Veniz	Haniá		14 Jun
				65.24	x	65.26	63.77	x	68.06
67.13	1	Halle	27 May	x	67.04	66.30	x	65.75	67.13
66.31	1	Stendal	10 Jun	x	66.31	62.61	63.51	x	61.30
66.11	1 Gugl	Linz	8 Aug	64.28	62.47	63.63	63.58	63.32	66.11
65.75	1	Obersuhl	11 Jun	65.75	64.75	x	65.14	63.28	x
65.41	1 GPF	Doha	5 Oct	64.91	63.41	x	65.41	x	62.69
67.33	Natalya	Sadova	RUS	15.6.72	1	NC	Tula		25 Jul
				61.33	64.25	67.33	x	65.75	62.94
66.52	1	Moskva	19 Aug						
66.50	1	Rüdlingen	12 Aug	64.57	66.00	66.50	64.95	64.22	66.31
65.98	1	Thessaloníki	30 Aug	64.21	65.98	63.49	62.71	four only	
65.84	1	Moskva	11 Jul	65.84	63.08	x	p	p	p
67.12	Anastasia	Kelesídou	GRE	28.11.72	3	Veniz	Haniá		14 Jun
				63.26	64.30	67.12	x	63.18	x
66.86	2	Halle	27 May	63.21	64.21	63.29	x	x	66.86
65.71	2 OG	Sydney	27 Sep	65.71	63.20	62.59	64.58	63.07	61.85
66.67	Yelena	Antonova	UKR	16.6.72	1	GP	Rio de Janeiro		14 May
				64.37	66.67	62.54	64.20	63.12	65.28
66.38	1 NC	Kiev	6 Aug	61.02	61.49	62.52	66.38	59.55	61.66
66.15	1	Koncha-Zaspa	28 Apr						
66.51	Irina	Yatchenko	BLR	31.10.65	1		Stayki		27 Jun
				60.64	66.08	x	66.51	x	64.16
65.42	1 Nik	Nice	8 Jun	x	65.43	62.32	64.83	63.30	62.72
65.90	Seilala	Sua	USA	25.2.78	1	NC	Sacramento		17 Jul
				65.90	63.19	x	x	62.67	x
65.76	Ilke	Wyludda	GER	28.3.69	1		Chemnitz		22 Jul
				65.53	64.81	64.28	65.76	63.82	x
65.41A	Beatrice	Faumuiná	NZL	23.10.74	1		Pietersburg		18 Mar
				61.68	61.87	65.41	63.80	61.61	x
65.35	Lisa-Marie	Vizaniari	AUS	14.12.71	1	Pre	Eugene		24 Jun
				65.35	62.82	63.14	64.87	x	62.45
65.34	Kris	Kuehl	USA	30.7.70	1		St Paul		8 Apr
	(31/12)			59.10	65.34	x	62.94	63.84	62.60
65.30	Suzy	Powell	USA	3.9.76	1	ModR	Modesto		13 May
65.18	Renata	Gustaitytė	LTU	7.4.74	1		Palanga		28 Jun
	perhaps doubtful, next 59.98				1		Kaunas		28 Jun
65.13	Stilianí	Tsikoúna	GRE	19.10.72	1		Tríkala		30 Jul
64.90		Yu Xin	CHN	23.2.77	1		Jinzhou		22 Jul
64.55	Olga	Chernyavskaya	RUS	17.9.63	6	Veniz	Haniá		14 Jun
64.37	Larisa	Korotkevich	RUS	3.1.67	2	NC	Tula		25 Jul
64.35	Ekateríni	Vóggoli	GRE	30.10.70	1		Athína		29 Jul
64.09	Teresa	Machado	POR	22.7.69	1		Aveiro		2 Sep
	(20)								
63.94	Joanna	Wisniewska	POL	24.5.72	1		Nitra		26 Aug
63.73	Alison	Lever	AUS	13.10.72	1	NC	Sydney		26 Feb
63.72	Vladimira	Racková	CZE	15.5.67	1		Pardubice		16 Aug
63.68	Oksana	Yesipchuk	RUS	13.12.76	2	NCp	Tula		2 Jun
63.68	Valentina	Ivanova	RUS	1.5.63	2	Mos Ch	Moskva		11 Jul
63.25		Li Qiumei	CHN	20.4.74	1		Beijing		1 Sep
63.19	Milina	Robert-Michon	FRA	18.7.79	1		Luminy		28 Jun
	63.65	downhill			1		Le Pontet		13 Feb
63.02	Neelam J	Singh	IND	8.1.71	1		Trivandrum		12 Aug
62.91	Aretha	Hill	USA	14.8.76	3		Salinas		23 May
62.91	Anna	Söderberg	SWE	11.6.73	2		Nitra		26 Aug
	(30)								
62.63	Anja	Möllenbeck	GER	18.3.72	3		Kassel		7 Jun
62.46	Mette	Bergmann	NOR	9.11.62	1		Aremark		18 Jun

Mark	Name		Nat	Born	Pos	Meet	Venue	Date
62.42	Lyudmila	Starovoytova	BLR	8.4.74	1		Brest	1 Aug
62.32	Oksana	Mert	TUR	26.3.73	2		Krasnodar	13 May
62.26		Cao Qi	CHN	15.1.74	1	NGP	Tianjin	4 May
62.26		Luan Zhili	CHN	6.1.73	1		Mito	7 May
62.12	Lacy	Barnes-Mileham	USA	23.12.64	1		Davis	15 Apr
61.76	Natalya	Ampleyeva	RUS	25.9.72	3	Mos Ch	Moskva	11 Jul
61.56	Lyudmila	Filimonova	BLR	22.3.71	2		Stayki	27 Jun
61.33	Daniela	Costian	AUS	30.4.65	1		Toowoomba	15 Jul
	(40)							
61.05	Jacqueline	Goormachtigh	NED	28.2.70	1		Leiden	10 Jun
61.02	Zdenka	Silhavá	CZE	15.6.54	1		Pacov	18 Jun
60.84		Li Yanfeng	CHN	15.5.79	2	OT	Jinzhou	7 Jun
60.81		Xiao Yanling	CHN	27.3.68	1	NC	Luohe	20 Oct
60.76		Liu Fengying	CHN	26.1.79	1		Shanghai	18 Apr
60.57	Agnese	Maffeis	ITA	9.3.65	1		Pescara	23 Jul
60.50	Tiina	Kankanpää	FIN	16.8.76	1		Ähtäri	1 Aug
60.40	Lacramioara	Ionescu	ROM	3.4.79	2	Nc-w	Bucuresti	4 Mar
60.39	Kathleen	Hering	GER	24.6.76	3		Wiesbaden	20 May
60.39		Song Aimin	CHN	15.3.78	6	OT	Jinzhou	7 Jun
	(50)							
60.35		Ma Shuli	CHN	20.1.78	1cA	NSG	Chengdu	6 Sep
60.22	Marzena	Wysocka	POL	17.2.69	1	Univ Ch	Biala Podlaska	3 Jun
60.10	Isabelle	Devaluez	FRA	17.3.66	2		Arles	3 Jun
59.73	Agnès	Teppe	FRA	4.5.68	1		Sorgues	15 Jul
59.72	Janet	Hill	USA	28.8.70	5	NC	Sacramento	17 Jul
59.71		Cheng Xianhong	CHN	24.10.68	4	NGP	Tianjin	4 May
59.60	Aretí	Abatzí	GRE	14.5.74	1		Trípoli	3 May
59.56	Dawn	Ellerbe	USA	3.4.74	1		Claremont	14 Apr
59.51		Huang Qun	CHN	12.4.79	5	NGP	Shanghai	18 Apr
59.25	Alice	Matejková	ESP	11.1.69	1	NC	Barcelona	3 Sep
	(60)							
59.03	Shelley	Drew	GBR	8.8.73	1	NC	Birmingham	13 Aug
58.90	Sabine	Sievers	GER	3.3.75	2		Wanganui	22 Jan
58.73		Hu Honglian	CHN	20.2.73	3	NGP	Deyang	13 May
58.63	Elisângela	Adriano	BRA	27.7.72	1	NC	Rio de Janeiro	5 Aug
58.60	Adina	Mocanu	ROM	4.3.80	2		Onesti	20 May
58.51	Elizna	Naude	RSA	14.9.78	1		Ljubljana	25 Jul
58.46	Monia	Kari	TUN	14.4.71	1	AfrC	Alger	11 Jul
58.37	Edie	Boyer	USA	15.2.66	6	NC	Sacramento	17 Jul
58.32	Roberta	Collins	USA	31.7.77	1	Owens	Columbus	7 May
58.28	Vera	Pospisilová	CZE	19.11.78	2		Praha	23 Jul
	(70)							
58.14		Tao Hongbo	CHN	20.9.79	3	NGP	Wenzhou	22 Apr
58.14	Wioletta	Potepa	POL	14.12.80	1		Biala Podlaska	17 Jun
57.92	Summer	Pierson	USA	3.9.78	3		Claremont	14 Apr
57.91	Danijela	Curovic	YUG	7.3.74	2	BalkG	Kavála	1 Jul
57.89	Lyudmila	Rublevskaya	RUS	7.6.77	5	NCp	Tula	2 Jun
57.78	Harwant	Kaur	IND	5.7.80	2		Trivandrum	12 Aug
57.67	Anaelys	Fernández	CUB	15.12.79	1		La Habana	10 Feb
57.63	Veerle	Blondeel	BEL	14.1.75	1		Eeklo	23 Jun
57.53A	Monique	Nacsa	AUS	26.10.76	3		Pietersburg	18 Mar
57.53		Qin Lei	CHN	15.10.76	7	NC	Luohe	20 Oct
	(80)							
57.40	Yania	Ferrales	CUB	28.7.77	1		La Habana	15 Jun
57.39	Annika	Larsson	SWE	10.7.70	1		Sollentuna	10 Jun
57.35	Nada M	Kawar	JOR	23.11.75	4		Salinas	23 May
57.20	Seema	Antil	IND-J	27.7.83	1	NC	Calcutta	11 Oct
57.06	Olga	Goncharenko	BLR-J	13.7.81	2	NC	Brest	2 Aug
57.04	Philippa	Roles	GBR	1.3.78	1		Rugby	23 Jul
57.02		Wang Pingping	CHN	27.2.79	3cA	NSG	Chengdu	6 Sep
57.00	Cheree	Hicks	USA	17.2.78	2	NCAA	Durham	1 Jun
56.80	Mara	Rosolen	ITA	27.7.65	1		Verona	25 Jun
56.72	Sugan	Yadav Kumar	IND	.77	2		Bangalore	17 Jul
	(90)							
56.71	Rita	Lora	ESP	23.3.73	1		L'Hospitalet	27 Aug
56.59	Katja	Tenhonen	FIN	18.11.77	1		Vampula	9 Sep
56.51	Miyoko	Nakanishi	JPN	17.1.75	1	NG	Toyama	18 Oct
56.49	Eha	Rünne	EST	25.5.63	2	ECp-2A	Kaunas	8 Jul
56.44	Katalin	Divós	HUN	11.5.74	1	NC	Budapest	29 Jul

Mark		Name		Nat	Born	Pos	Meet	Venue	Date
56.30	?	Maureen	Morrison	USA	2.5.78	1		Eugene	13 May
56.28			Dai Zuoying	CHN		1cB	NSG	Chengdu	9 Sep
56.25		Anita	Hietalahti	FIN	17.2.77	1		Järvenpää	11 Jun
56.24		Nadine	Beckel	GER	27.5.77	5	NC	Braunschweig	30 Jul
56.22		Vera	Begic	CRO-J	17.3.82	2		Ljubljana	25 Jul
		(100)							

56.00	Safiya	Ingram	USA	18.6.77	1 Jun
55.86	April	Malveo	USA	11.3.76	25 Mar
55.85		Chang Xinhong	CHN	24.3.74	22 Apr
55.80	Ina	Reiber	GER	19.3.80	20 May
55.78	Amalía	Láboura	GRE	16.3.68	27 May
55.60	Emma	Merry	GBR	2.7.74	30 Jul
55.58	Ileana	Brindusoiu	ROM	9.5.79	6 Aug
55.57	Christelle	Bornil	FRA	9.5.78	6 Aug
55.56	Katja	Schreiber	GER	30.6.78	13 May
55.53	Ilona	Rutjes	NED	28.5.80	20 May
55.50	Olga	Tarantayeva	RUS	12.1.79	19 Feb
55.50	Rhonda	Hackett	TRI	24.1.77	18 Mar
55.40		Wang Qiuju	CHN	12.10.75	6 Sep
55.35	Éva	Kürti	HUN	21.7.76	26 Aug
55.29		Gong Yaqin	CHN	20.7.79	25 Aug
55.21		Shao Jinling	CHN		9 Sep
55.02	Chaniqua	Ross	USA	24.5.80	23 May
54.97	Yuka	Murofushi	JPN	11.2.77	18 Oct
54.96	Manuela	Frauendorf	GER	21.11.78	20 May
54.94	Angie	Joy	USA	.76	6 May
54.90		Xu Shaoyang	CHN-J	10.5.82	4 May
54.88	Beth	Obruba	USA	30.4.77	6 May
54.87A	Felicia Nkiru	Ojiego	NGR		18 Mar
54.69	Christy	Thiel	AUS	30.4.74	11 Feb
54.68	Robin	Lyons ¶	CAN	15.4.77	29 Apr
54.58	Briona	Reynolds	USA-J	2.6.83	6 May
54.56	Giorgia	Baratella	ITA	8.1.75	16 Jul
54.55	Katja	Kròl	GER	5.2.80	20 May
54.54	Amélie	Perrin	FRA	30.3.80	16 Jul
54.51	Ivona	Tomanová	SVK	24.10.72	17 Jun
54.48	Mirjam	Burchard	GER	1.2.72	9 Sep
54.44	Niina	Kelo	FIN	26.3.80	11 Jun
54.43	Gheorghita	Bosneaga	ROM-J	15.7.81	24 Jun
54.28	Grete	Etholm	NOR	25.1.76	3 Aug
54.28		Liu Yanxia	CHN-J	3.4.81	1 Sep
54.16		Cao Liping	CHN	8.11.78	25 Aug
54.10		Tao Yinyan	CHN		9 Sep
54.08	Jill	Pedretti	USA	30.9.80	30 Apr
54.08	Ilona	Zakharchenko	UKR	16.6.67	16 Jul
54.04		Cao Shuang	CHN		4 May
54.00A	Lezelle	Duvenage	RSA	17.5.77	18 Mar
53.99	Tina	McDonald	CAN	12.1.76	20 May
53.97		Cui Limin	CHN	22.5.79	15 Apr
53.97	Jana	Tucholke	GER-J	27.5.81	19 Oct
53.96	Martina	Greithanner	GER	21.10.74	20 May
53.88	Yelena	Dementiy	UKR	6.3.69	17 Jun
53.88	Harjeet	Kaur	IND	21.9.71	1 Jul
53.83	Diane	Slinden	USA	7.4.80	13 May
53.76	Nicole	Chimko	CAN	31.7.78	25 Mar
53.66		Hong Mei	CHN-J	16.1.82	17 Jun
53.66	Krishna	Poonia	IND		5 Jul
53.62	Bianca	Overkamp	GER	17.3.75	10 Sep
	(152)				

JUNIORS

57.20	Seema	Antil	IND	27.7.83	1	NC	Calcutta	11 Oct
	55.27 1 WJ Santiago 19 Oct			54.83 q WJ Santiago 18 Oct				
	55.14 4 New Delhi 9 Sep							
57.06	Olga	Goncharenko	BLR	13.7.81	2	NC	Brest	2 Aug
56.22	Vera	Begic	CRO	17.3.82	2		Ljubljana	25 Jul
54.90		Xu Shaoyang	CHN	10.5.82	9	NGP	Tianjin	4 May
	54.49 8 Shijiazhuang 29 Apr			10 performances by 6 women over 54.40				
54.58	Briona	Reynolds	USA	2.6.83	1		Grand Forks	6 May
54.43	Gheorghita	Bosneaga	ROM	15.7.81	2		Bucuresti	24 Jun
54.28		Liu Yanxia	CHN	3.4.81	6		Beijing	1 Sep
53.97	Jana	Tucholke	GER	27.5.81	3	WJ	Santiago de Chile	19 Oct
53.66		Hong Mei	CHN	16.1.82	1	NC-j	Deyang	17 Jun
53.08	Julia	Bremser (10)	GER	27.4.82	1		Wiesbaden	24 Jun
52.96	Olga	Olshevskaya	RUS	82	1		Vladimir	21 May
52.71	Deborah	Lovely	AUS	20.6.83	2		Brisbane	3 Sep
52.55		Jing Junyan	CHN	4.1.83	11		Shijiazhuang	29 Apr
52.51	Carol	Stevenson	CAN	15.5.81	1		Abbotsford	22 Jul
52.48	Katrina	Steele	AUS	2.7.81	1		Sydney	20 Feb
52.29		Luo Xiaorong	CHN	4.11.83	8		Deyang	13 May
52.21	Emma	Carpenter	GBR	16.5.82	1		Exeter	17 Jun
52.20	Yelena	Lebusova	RUS	26.6.81	6	NCp	Tula	2 Jun
52.19	Claire	Smithson	GBR	3.8.83	1	v3N-j	Grosseto	7 Oct
52.14		Yang Hong (20)	CHN	3.3.81	20		Nanjing	15 Apr

WOMEN 2000

HAMMER

75.68	Olga	Kuzenkova	RUS	4.10.70	1	NCp	Tula			4 Jun
				72.84	75.16	x	72.97	73.54	75.68	
74.00	1	Kuts	Moskva	26 Aug	73.51	73.87	x	x	74.00	x
73.85	1		Togliatti	14 May	67.17	71.43	70.93	73.85	p	69.91
72.81	1	Live	Nürnberg	25 Jun	72.81	70.01	72.64	58.60	x	x
72.74	1		Clermont-Ferrand	30 Jun	72.25	72.74	x	x	72.58	x
71.81	1	Znam	Sankt-Peterburg	18 Jun	69.90	71.81	x	x		four only
70.60	q	OG	Sydney	27 Sep	70.60	only				
70.39	1	NC-w	Adler	19 Feb	68.84	70.39	70.23	x	70.07	p
70.20	2	ECp-S	Gateshead	15 Jul	66.13	x	70.20	x		four only
69.77	2	OG	Sydney	29 Sep	x	67.18	69.64	69.77	x	x
69.75	Q	NC	Tula	26 Jul						

A = made at altitude above 1000m, q = made in qualifying round, -J = Junior (born 1981 or later)

Mark	Name		Nat	Born	Pos Meet		Venue		Date
72.19	Mihaela	Melinte ¶	ROM	27.3.75	1		Mersin		29 Mar
				66.71	71.05	x	72.19	70.01	x
72.10	1	Onesti	20 May	67.80	69.60	x	69.26	72.10	71.20
71.37	1	Snagov	21 May	67.81	70.67	71.37	x	x	x
70.96	1	Mersin	25 Mar						
71.18	Manuela	Montebrun	FRA	13.11.79	1		Vittel		2 Sep
				67.29	69.71	71.18	67.89	69.40	68.95
71.16	Kamila	Skolimowska	POL-J	4.11.82	1	OG	Sydney		29 Sep
				x	66.33	71.16	66.06	69.91	p
70.62	2	Rüdlingen	12 Aug	66.41	70.62	69.45	x	68.37	68.99
70.06	1	Skórcz	31 Aug	65.63	x	65.97	x	x	70.06
69.13	1	Warszawa	10 Jun	66.00	x	69.13	67.60	p	p
70.46	Dawn	Ellerbe	USA	3.4.74	1	PennR	Philadelphia		29 Apr
				67.94	70.46	67.42	65.52	66.88	67.54
70.17	1	Logan	1 Jul						
69.20	1 NC	Sacramento	15 Jul	64.28	65.40	68.45	69.04	67.53	69.20
69.06	1	Winnipeg	9 Jul	68.52	68.37	69.06	68.38	x	x
69.92	Lyudmila	Gubkina	BLR	28.5.73	1		Staiki		19 Aug
69.81	Olga	Tsander	BLR	18.5.76	1		Sochi		26 Feb
				66.28	64.45	x	69.81	68.94	x
69.73	Tatyana	Konstantinova	RUS	18.11.70	2		Togliatti		14 May
				66.16	68.07	69.73	67.89	68.93	68.59
69.53	Irina	Sekacheva	UKR	21.7.76	1		Kiev		16 Jun
69.36	Yipsi	Moreno	CUB	19.11.80	1		Rhede		23 Jun
				x	69.36	61.83	66.05	67.72	x
69.09	1	Halle	27 May	x	x	66.63	69.09	68.84	68.60
69.28	Kirsten	Münchow	GER	21.1.77	3	OG	Sydney		29 Sep
	(31/11)			66.42	x	67.81	66.03	69.28	67.96
68.98	Katalin	Divós	HUN	11.5.74	1		Szombathely		24 Jun
68.47	Alla	Davydova	RUS	21.5.66	1	Mos Ch	Moskva		11 Jul
68.28	Amy	Palmer	USA	20.4.75	2	PennR	Philadelphia		29 Apr
68.18	Ivana	Brkljacic	CRO-J	25.1.83	1		Pula		28 Apr
67.95	Debbie	Sosimenko	AUS	5.4.74	5	OG	Sydney		29 Sep
67.55	Lisa	Misipeka	ASA	3.1.75	4		Rüdlingen		12 Aug
67.44	Lorraine	Shaw	GBR	2.4.68	5	ECp-S	Gateshead		15 Jul
67.15	Svetlana	Sudak	BLR	20.3.71	2		Stayki		27 Jun
66.58	Bianca	Achilles	GER-J	17.4.81	5		Clermont-Ferrand		30 Jun
	(20)								
66.55	Bronwyn	Eagles	AUS	23.8.80	1		Sydney (B)		3 Dec
66.52	Jesseca	Cross	USA	10.5.75	3		Logan		1 Jul
66.37	Mia	Strömmer	FIN	26.2.74	2		Lapinlahti		16 Jul
66.17	Ester	Balassini	ITA	20.10.77	1		Pescara		22 Jul
65.90	Simone	Mathes	GER	13.3.75	2		Stendal		10 Jun
65.88	Yunaika	Crawford	CUB-J	2.11.82	1		Las Tunas		3 Mar
65.88	Anna	Norgren	USA	19.12.74	1		West Point		13 May
65.70		Zhao Wei	CHN	27.1.79	1		Deyang		14 May
65.61	Manuela	Priemer	GER	29.11.78	5	Live	Nürnberg		25 Jun
65.50	Sini	Pöyry	FIN	3.2.80	3		Lapinlahti		16 Jul
	(30)								
65.38	Karyne	Perkins-Dimarco	AUS	14.3.78	2		Brisbane (N)		6 Sep
65.35	Anelia	Yordanova	BUL	27.4.72	1		Sofia		10 Jun
65.26	Agnieszka	Pogroszewska	POL	20.2.77	3		Nitra		26 Aug
65.20	Norbi	Balantén	CUB	24.6.72	3		La Habana		24 Feb
65.11	Marina	Grin	BLR	23.1.76	3		Minsk		27 Jun
65.06		Liu Yinghui	CHN	29.6.79	1	NC	Luohe		20 Oct
64.94	Melissa	Price	USA	5.9.79	1	USTCA	Austin		22 Apr
64.86	Natalya	Kunitskaya	UKR	17.8.72	1		Kiev		15 Jul
64.80	Tina	Schäfer	GER	27.12.77	1		Rastatt		12 Jun
64.74	Florence	Ezeh	FRA	29.12.77	1	TexR	Austin		6 Apr
	(40)								
64.72		Gu Yuan	CHN-J	9.5.82	2	NGP	Deyang		14 May
64.60	Tasha	Williams	NZL	31.7.73	1		Flagstaff		6 Jul
64.50		Li Xiaoxue	CHN	1.11.80	3	NGP	Deyang		14 May
64.46	Michelle	Fournier	CAN	9.5.77	1		Flagstaff		4 Jul
64.44	Robin	Lyons ¶	CAN	15.4.77	1		Albuquerque		6 May
64.25	Tamika	Powell	USA	25.9.75	1		Dedham		10 Jun
64.24	Natalya	Samusenkova	RUS	12.2.79	1	NC-23	Cheboksary		1 Jul
64.22	Jenny	Folz	USA	24.12.75	1		Bloomington		13 May
64.12	Windy	Dean	USA	7.9.76	6	PennR	Philadelphia		29 Apr

Mark	Name		Nat	Born	Pos	Meet	Venue	Date
64.04	Susanne	Keil	GER	18.5.78	2	v2N-23	Boulouris	5 Mar
	(50)							
64.00	Cécile	Lignot-Maubert	FRA	19.11.71	1		Clermont-Ferrand	19 Jul
63.96	Lyn	Sprules	GBR	11.9.75	1		Bedford	20 Aug
63.80	Leslie	Coons	USA	16.7.73	Q	NC	Sacramento	14 Jul
63.70	Aldenay	Vasallo	CUB	25.2.77	4		La Habana	24 Feb
63.68	Christina	Tolson	USA	16.1.78	2		Austin	22 Apr
63.66	Maureen	Griffin	USA	6.10.80	8	PennR	Philadelphia	29 Apr
63.61	Elizabeth	Pidegon	GBR	27.4.77	1B		Halle	27 May
63.20	Evdokiá	Tsámoglou	GRE	15.12.78	1	NC	Athína	8 Jul
63.09	Bethany	Hart	USA	10.4.77	1		Dedham	17 Jun
62.93		Chen Ying	CHN	4.11.75	3	NC	Luohe	20 Oct
	(60)							
62.86	Jennifer	Joyce	CAN	25.9.80	2	Pac10	Eugene	20 May
62.69	Amalía	Láboura	GRE	16.3.68	2	NC	Athína	8 Jul
62.62	Lucie	Vrbenská	CZE	12.5.77	1		Ostrava	3 Sep
62.60	Cristina	Fechita/Buzau	ROM	12.4.76	2		Mersin	29 Mar
62.54	Cecilia	Nilsson	SWE	22.6.79	1		Karlstad	23 Aug
62.28	Caroline	Wittrin	CAN	10.12.68	1		Abbotsford	22 Jul
62.26	Jennifer	Vail	USA	16.3.78	3	Pac 10	Eugene	20 May
62.16	Nancy	Guillén	ESA	14.10.76	2	TexR	Austin	6 Apr
62.14	Vânia	Silva	POR	8.6.80	1		Aveiro	11 May
62.00	Byrony	Glass	AUS	31.3.77	1		Perth	16 Jul
	(70)							
61.97	Brenda	MacNaughton	AUS	7.5.76	2		Sydney	13 Feb
61.89	Brooke	Krueger	AUS	9.7.80	4	NC	Sydney	27 Feb
61.82	Caroline	Fournier	MRI	7.5.75	1		Franconville	28 May
61.80	Markéta	Hajdu	CZE	9.9.74	1		Pardubice	31 May
61.80	Carrie	Myers	USA	12.9.77	2		Terre Haute	11 Jun
61.78		Cui Xiaohong	CHN	10.2.80	4	NC	Luohe	20 Oct
61.63	Carina	Moya	ARG	28.9.73	1		Santa F´é	9 Sep
61.62	Martina	Danisová	SVK-J	21.3.83	1	NC	Banská Bystrica	2 Jul
61.56	Ericka	Dice	USA	9.2.72	9	PennR	Philadelphia	29 Apr
61.50	Grettel	Miller	JAM	6.6.75	5	RM	Logan	1 Jul
	(80)							
61.50	Kaisa	Kiintonen	FIN	18.3.80	3		Tampere	19 Jul
61.44		Yang Meiping	CHN-J	23.10.85	3	NGP	Shanghai	19 Apr
61.42	Julianna	Tudja	HUN	13.10.79	4	DrakeR	Des Moines	29 Apr
61.40	Michelle	Clayton-Boswell	USA	29.10.76	1		Conway, SC	8 Jul
61.39	Dolores	Pedrares	ESP	17.1.73	1	IbAm	Rio de Janeiro	20 May
61.38	Kiyomi	Parish	USA	19.5.75	1		Norwalk	4 Jun
61.32	Aya	Suzuki	JPN	18.11.67	2cB		Halle	27 May
61.32	Denise	Passmore	AUS	11.6.74	2		Gold Coast (RB)	5 Aug
61.18	Irina	Martynenko	UKR	19.10.76	3		Koncha-Zaspa	8 May
61.12	Tatyana	Dyomina	BLR	29.9.73			Staiki	19 Aug
	(90)							
60.96	Meshell	Trotter	USA	2.9.78	4	UCTA	Austin	22 Apr
60.88	Svetlana	Sherina	RUS	29.4.71	3		Togliatti	14 May
60.86	Livia	Mehes	ROM	6.3.65	3		Onesti	20 May
60.84	Renate	Beunder	NED	31.8.70	1		Hoorn	20 May
60.84	Monica	Torazzi	ITA	26.2.71	2		Pescara	22 Jul
60.83	Clarissa	Claretti	ITA	7.10.80	1		Terni	23 Sep
60.78	Andrea	Bunjes	GER	5.2.76	1		Braunschweig	1 Jul
60.70	Katy	Craig	USA		1		Columbus	3 Sep
60.69		Wang Dan	CHN-J	.82	1	NC	Singapore	10 Sep
60.66	Patti	Pilsner-Steinke	CAN	9.7.73	1		Lethbridge	7 May
	(100)							

60.64	Asimína	Mórfi	GRE	4.5.73	3 May
60.62	Marina	Rezanova	UKR	28.8.74	15 Jul
60.60	Seilala	Sua	USA	25.2.78	1 Apr
60.60	Julie	Thomas	USA	11.7.79	25 Apr
60.55	Wendy	Koolhaas	NED	5.1.80	1 Jul
60.54	Veronika	Ushakova	RUS	8.11.77	15 Jul
60.50	Josiane	Soares	BRA	21.6.76	9 Jul
60.41	Yelena	Tauryanina	RUS	11.9.80	23 Sep
60.39	Olga	Markevich	BLR	13.10.79	19 Aug
60.30		Zhang Wenxiu	CHN-J	11.2.83	18 Aug
60.23	Barbara	Németh	HUN	7.11.80	3 Jun
60.23	Virginia	Balut	ROM-J	3.3.81	18 Oct
60.22	Carri	Soong	USA-J	11.7.81	31 May
60.19	Merja	Korpela	FIN-J	15.5.81	18 Aug
60.02	Natalya	Zledennaya	UKR	22.11.77	16 Jun
59.97	Marie	Brouzet	FRA	20.6.74	21 May
59.92	Sónia	Alves	POR	3.6.79	6 May
59.84	Olga	Klopova	UKR	19.2.80	16 Jun
59.75	Tatyana	Gramoda	BLR-J	.81	27 Jun
59.59	Jolanta	Borawska	POL	16.1.76	10 Jun
59.54	Anne Laure	Grémillet	FRA	27.9.78	20 May
59.51		Wang Xiaoyu	CHN-J	25.12.81	14 May
59.46	Erin	Wibbels	USA	3.7.78	22 Apr
59.38	Yuka	Murofushi	JPN	11.2.77	8 Jul
59.36	Anna	Whitham	USA	28.3.77	13 May
59.30	Melissa	Houston	USA	3.1.80	14 Jun
59.19	Natalya	Kravchenko	UKR-J	26.6.61	13 Feb
59.16	Beth	Howard	USA	8.10.77	15 Apr

WOMEN 2000

Mark	Name		Nat	Born	Date
59.06	Unn Merete	Lie	NOR	18.1.71	6 Jul
59.00	Sandrine	Gardes	FRA	13.10.75	30 Jun
58.99	Charlotte	Wåhlin	DEN	19.7.76	6 May
58.97	Anna	Söderberg	SWE	11.6.73	3 Sep
58.95	Hardeep	Kaur	IND		9 Oct
58.90	Silvia	Lazzari	ITA	12.7.75	6 May
58.90		Yang Jie	CHN-J	10.12.83	20 Oct
58.87	Maree	Ryabovitch	AUS	1.3.80	27 Feb
58.87	Masumi	Aya	JPN	1.1.80	8 Jul
58.86	Tina	Rankin	USA	5.1.73	6 May
58.84	Violeta	Guzmán	MEX	14.5.77	3 Aug
58.83	Suzanne	Roberts	GBR	19.12.78	9 Sep
58.76	Andrea	Thornton	USA	14.12.78	15 Apr
58.66	Dana	Dillon	USA	10.1.77	29 Apr
58.64	Yelena	Kiselyova	RUS	78	20 May
58.63	Alessandra	Coaccioli	ITA	11.9.75	8 Apr
58.60	Liz	Legault	USA	4.5.70	20 May
58.39	Anelis	Molina	CUB-J	25.8.81	24 Feb
58.36	K Jebeshori	Devi	IND	1.3.78	29 Jul
58.35	Elmarie	Knoetzen	RSA	18.7.78	31 Mar
58.33		Chen Juanying	CHN	13.7.74	19 Apr
58.28	Margarita	Grechikho	BLR-J	15.4.81	27 Jun
58.21	Sónia	Martins	POR	25.3.78	22 Jul
58.15	Evaggelía	Dervéni	GRE	2.5.80	15 Apr
58.12	Diandra	Bauer	USA	16.11.77	29 Apr
58.06	Jackie	Jeschelnig	USA	.78	13 May
58.04	Chantel	Goldsberry	USA	3.4.79	19 May
58.00	Yuliya	Denisova	RUS-J	7.4.82	17 Sep
57.90		Guo Peng	CHN-J	21.6.84	14 May
57.78	Serene	Ross	USA	15.10.77	19 May
57.74	Catherine	Madec	FRA	13.2.72	31 May
57.71	Wendy	Egbert	USA	29.6.73	15 Apr
57.70	Mariya	Smolyachkova	BLR-J	.85	3 Jun
57.67	Alexándra	Papayeoryíou	GRE	.80	11 Jun
57.64	Janet	Boettcher	USA		25 May
57.54	Zübeyde	Yildiz	TUR	7.9.80	6 Sep
57.52	Angela	Foster	USA	27.12.79	4 Jun
57.49	Alexandria	Earl-Givan	USA	25.4.70	1 Jul
57.42	Mette	Bergmann	NOR	9.11.62	29 Jul
57.40	Géraldine	Gravouil	FRA	25.5.74	5 Aug
57.36	Natalya	Vasilenko	UKR	30.10.74	5 Aug
57.33	Margit	Wahlbrink	BRA	20.5.75	3 Jun
57.30	Brenda	Start	USA	4.5.74	24 Mar
57.22	LaKeisha	Mose	USA	6.7.77	22 Apr
57.22		Cai Yan	CHN	26.3.80	14 May
57.20	Nesrin	Kaya	TUR	30.6.79	29 Mar
57.20	Gulfiya	Khanafeyeva	RUS-J	.82	15 Jul
57.18	Viktoriya	Polyanskaya	RUS	2.4.71	19 Feb
57.16	Mary	LeJour	CAN	13.1.79	25 Apr
57.15	Morwa Ahmed	Hussein	EGY	19.6.78	13 Jul
57.14	Kathrine	Johnston	USA-J	29.12.83	29 Apr
57.13	Inna	Sayenko	UKR-J	8.3.82	20 May
57.09	Rachael	Beverley	GBR	23.7.79	6 May
57.06	María Eugenia	Villamizar	COL	30.8.70	4 Dec
57.01	Amélie	Perrin	FRA	30.3.80	1 May
57.00	Vera	Petukhova	RUS	27.7.80	20 May
56.96	Jenny	Brown	USA	1.9.79	25 Mar
56.93	Gloria	Butler	USA		1 Apr
56.92	Nicola	Coffey	IRL	8.9.76	3 Jul
56.86	Maureen	Morrison	USA	2.5.78	22 Apr
56.86	Maria José	Conde	POR	26.8.80	12 Aug
56.86	Malgorzata	Zadura	POL-J	3.10.82	2 Sep
56.68A	Jennifer	Dahlgren	ARG-J	27.8.84	5 Nov
56.62	Elisa	Viganò	ITA	24.3.78	22 Jul
56.61	Larisa	Tarasyuk	RUS	14.6.70	26 Feb
56.53	Helena	Engman	SWE	16.6.76	29 Aug
56.50	Oksana	Menkova	BLR-J	.82	27 Jun
56.49	Rhonda	Snyder	USA		7 Apr
56.45	Silke	Grundmann	GER-J	7.8.82	27 May
56.44	Simona	Kozmus	SLO	18.3.78	3 Jun
56.42	Céline	Vandeville	FRA	5.11.79	16 Jul
56.40	Katherina	Gallahar	USA	20.3.76	19 May
56.40	Eva	Charfreitagová	SVK	9.9.79	16 Sep
	(201)	219 women over 56.00, 244 over 55.50			

Downhill

65.63	Michelle	Fournier	CAN	9.5.77	2		Lethbridge	22 Jul

Drugs suspension/pending hearing

74.80	Mihaela	Melinte ¶		ROM	27.3.75	1	Rüdlingen			12 Aug
					x	73.51	x	71.64	72.69	74.80
74.32	1		Nitra	26 Aug	74.32	72.59	73.78	71.31	x	x
73.75	1	NC	Bucuresti	6 Aug	x	71.04	72.15	73.75	71.23	72.22
73.74	1		Noisy-le-Grand	20 Jun	73.74	72.29	x	x	x	x
72.54	1		Milano	7 Jun	72.24	72.54	71.09	x	x	72.12
72.46	2		Clermont-Ferrand	30 Jun	70.41	72.06	70.61	x	70.11	72.46
71.91	1		Poiana Brasov	22 Jul						
71.44	2	Live	Nürnberg	25 Jun	71.44	70.37	x	x	x	66.92
70.20	1	ECp-S	Gateshead	15 Jul	66.13	70.20	x	68.16		
67.40dh	Robin	Lyons ¶		CAN	15.4.77	1	Lethbridge			22 Jul

JUNIORS

See main list for top 8 juniors. 13 performances by 3 women to 66.20. Additional marks and further juniors:

Skolimowska top 4 marks in main list plus:

68.73	1	Gold Coast (RB)	17 Sep	66.70	1		Warszawa	27 May
67.12	1	NC-j Wroclaw	29 Aug	66.35	1		Biala Podlaska	17 Jun
66.80	1	Kuso Warszawa	24 Jun	66.30	Q	OG	Sydney	27 Sep
				66.20	1	NC	Kraków	4 Aug

60.30		Zhang Wenxiu	CHN	11.2.83	2		Beijing	18 Aug
60.23	Virginia	Balut (10)	ROM	3.3.81	2	WJ	Santiago de Chile	18 Oct
60.22	Carri	Soong	USA	11.7.81	8	NCAA	Durham	31 May
60.19	Merja	Korpela	FIN	15.5.81	4	NC	Lahti	18 Aug
59.75	Tatyana	Gramoda	BLR	.81			Staiki	27 Jun
59.51		Wang Xiaoyu	CHN	25.12.81	6	NGP	Deyang	14 May
59.10	Natalya	Kravchenko	UKR	26.6.81	1		Brovary	13 Feb
58.90		Yang Jie	CHN	10.12.83	8	NC	Luohe	20 Oct
58.39	Anelis	Molina	CUB	25.8.81	5		La Habana	24 Feb
58.28	Margarita	Grechikho	BLR	15.4.81			Staiki	27 Jun
58.00	Yuliya	Denisova	RUS	7.4.82	1		Krasnodar	17 Sep
57.90		Guo Peng (20)	CHN	21.6.84	8	NGP	Deyang	14 May

The hammer has become a most popular event for women –indeed it is surely now more widely practised than the shot or discus. Progress in women's hammer standards is illustrated by the annual number of women exceeding 60m: 1989- 2, 1990- 4, 1991- 5, 1992- 3, 1993- 4, 1994- 9, 1995- 14, 1996- 18, 1997- 28, 1998- 57, 1999- 84, 2000- 115

JAVELIN

Mark	Name		Nat	Born	Pos	Meet	Venue	Date	Series
69.48	Trine	Hattestad	NOR	18.4.66	1	Bisl	Oslo	28 Jul	
									63.50 65.40 x 65.01 64.44 69.48
68.91					1	OG	Sydney	30 Sep	68.91 62.27 x 64.38 66.22 64.09
68.32					1	ISTAF	Berlin	1 Sep	64.48 63.94 68.32 66.64 x 64.91
68.22					1	GGala	Roma	30 Jun	63.22 65.17 x 68.22 p 62.32
67.92					1	DNG	Stockholm	1 Aug	67.92 64.62 65.21 63.72 63.13 ?
67.76					1	VD	Bruxelles	25 Aug	67.76 62.20 64.30 x x 63.27
66.96					1	ECp1A	Nadderud	8 Jul	63.48 66.96 64.32 62.55 four only
66.73					2	Herc	Monaco	18 Aug	66.73 62.86 64.84 65.75 x 66.12
66.54					1		Fana	27 Jun	63.22 66.54 x x 65.81 65.22
66.50					1	WK	Zürich	11 Aug	66.50 64.36 x x 59.85 64.27
66.44					1		Lapinlahti	16 Jul	66.44 63.70 x 63.52 ? ?
65.86					2	GPF	Doha	5 Oct	64.64 64.46 63.16 62.93 63.63 65.86
65.44					Q	OG	Sydney	29 Sep	65.44 only
67.83	Osleidys	Menéndez	CUB	14.11.79	2	ISTAF	Berlin	1 Sep	
									63.83 67.83 63.51 62.10 62.45 64.67
67.34					Q	OG	Sydney	29 Sep	67.34 only
66.38					2	VD	Bruxelles	25 Aug	58.80 q61.20 63.84 66.38 61.73 62.85
66.35					1	GP	Athína	28 Jun	60.85 66.35 x 61.32 58.43 58.99
66.18					3	OG	Sydney	30 Sep	66.03 64.99 65.17 63.95 62.47 66.18
65.79					3	GPF	Doha	5 Oct	65.67 61.38 x 64.95 65.79 64.81
65.50					2	DNG	Stockholm	1 Aug	65.50 59.15 inj p p p
65.33					2		Halle	27 May	62.60 62.35 x 59.01 61.47 65.33
67.51	Miréla	Tzelíli	GRE	21.12.76	2	OG	Sydney	30 Sep	
									x 65.56 67.51 61.96 65.34 67.51
67.20	Tatyana	Shikolenko	RUS	10.5.68	1	Herc	Monaco	18 Aug	
									67.20 60.83 x x p 62.24
65.57					2		Fana	27 Jun	60.36 61.75 65.57 x 59.85 64.98
65.57					1	NC	Tula	25 Jul	65.57 63.80 p 59.99 p p
66.80	Louise	Currey	AUS	24.1.69	1		Gold Coast (RB)	5 Aug	
66.73	Tanja	Damaske	GER	16.11.71	1	NC	Braunschweig	29 Jul	
									61.49 60.80 63.95 61.19 66.73 p
65.74					2	Bisl	Oslo	28 Jul	x 58.01 59.38 x 63.12 65.74
65.87	Sonia	Bisset	CUB	1.4.71	1	GPF	Doha	5 Oct	
									61.46 62.13 59.58 59.77 61.59 65.87
65.76	Steffi	Nerius	GER	1.7.72	Q	OG	Sydney	29 Sep	
									65.76 only
65.47					1		Halle	27 May	65.47 p 61.66 x p p
65.30	Claudia	Coslovich	ITA	26.4.72	1		Ljubljana	10 Jun	
	(32/9)								58.57 65.30 p p p p
64.09	Yekaterina	Ivakina	RUS	4.12.64	4	Bisl	Oslo	28 Jul	
64.62	Joanna	Stone	AUS	4.10.72	2		Gold Coast (RB)	5 Aug	
64.19	Nikola	Tomecková	CZE	25.6.74	3	WK	Zürich	11 Aug	
64.06	Taina	Uppa	FIN	24.10.76	1		Pihtipudas	23 Jul	
64.03	Mihaela	Ingberg	FIN	29.7.74	6	ISTAF	Berlin	1 Sep	
63.92		Wei Jianhua	CHN	23.3.79	1		Beijing	18 Aug	
63.73	Laverne	Eve	BAH	16.6.65	1		Nashville	22 Apr	
63.69		Li Lei	CHN	4.5.74	1	OT	Jinzhou	8 Jun	
63.32	Khristina	Georgieva	BUL	3.1.72	3	GP	Athína	28 Jun	
63.29	Ana Mirela	Termure	ROM	13.1.75	1		Snagov	5 May	
63.12	Felicia	Tilea-Moldovan	ROM	29.9.67	1		Poiana Brasov	22 Jul	
	(20)								
62.92	Xiomara	Rivero	CUB	22.11.68	6	OG	Sydney	30 Sep	
62.69	Rita	Ramanauskaité	LTU	22.2.70	6	Gaz	Saint-Denis	23 Jun	
62.35	Karen	Forkel	GER	24.3.70	1		Regensburg	7 Jul	
62.16	Nadine	Auzeil	FRA	19.8.64	1		Strasbourg	27 Jun	
62.06	Oksana	Velichko	BLR	26.3.75	1		Stayki	27 Jun	
61.98A	Sueli	dos Santos	BRA	8.1.65	1		Bogotá	6 May	
61.57	Maria de la C	Álvarez	CUB	30.8.75	1	Barr	La Habana	30 Jul	
61.50	Genowefa	Patla	POL	17.10.62	1		Siedlce	20 May	
61.24	Yanuris	La Montaña	CUB	29.8.75	1		La Habana	17 Feb	
61.23	Nikolett	Szabó	HUN	3.3.80	2		Pátra	2 Sep	
	(30)								
61.14	Evfemija	Storga	SLO	7.10.75	1		Koper	8 Apr	
61.01	Paula	Huhtaniemi	FIN	17.2.73	3		Kuortane	24 Jun	
60.98	Heli	Rantanen	FIN	26.2.70	2		Pihtipudas	23 Jul	
60.67	Nora	Bicet	CUB	29.10.77	2		La Habana	30 Jul	

Mark	Name		Nat	Born	Pos	Meet	Venue	Date
60.55	Isel	López	CUB	11.7.70	3	Janet	Santiago de Cuba	4 Mar
60.49	Valeriya	Zabruskova	RUS	29.7.75	2		Rostov-na-Donu	20 May
60.26A	Aggelikí	Tsiolakoúdi	GRE	10.5.76	1		El Paso	6 May
60.02		Zhang Li	CHN	19.10.78	1		Shanghai	18 Apr
59.93	Alina	Serdyuk	BLR	22.1.75			Staiki	3 Jun
59.92	Oksana	Makarova	RUS	21.7.71	3	NC-w	Adler	18 Feb
	(40)							
59.87	Dörthe	Friedrich	GER	21.6.73	3		Regensburg	7 Jul
59.79	Nadezhda	Kobrin	UKR	21.1.72	1	NC	Kiev	4 Aug
59.75	Kirsi	Ahonen	FIN	8.4.76	4		Kuortane	24 Jun
59.56		Chu Chunxia	CHN	28.1.78	1	NGP	Guangzhou	25 Mar
59.33		Liang Lili	CHN-J	16.11.83	1	NC	Luohe	22 Oct
59.33A	Zuleima	Araméndiz	COL	23.9.75	1	NG	Tunja	7 Dec
59.21	Carmen	Filip	ROM	2.5.76	q	NC-w	Bucuresti	2 Mar
59.06	Christina	Scherwin	DEN	11.7.76	1		Chapel Hill	4 Jun
59.02	Marta	Míguez	ESP	3.3.73	1	NC	Barcelona	2 Sep
58.64	Gurmeet	Kaur	IND	20.6.70	1		Bangalore	17 Jul
	(50)							
58.61	Lynda	Blutreich	USA	13.12.71	1		New Haven	1 Jul
58.54	Karen	Martin	GBR	24.11.74	1		Aldershot	5 Jul
58.45	Kelly	Morgan	GBR	17.6.80	1	NC	Birmingham	12 Aug
58.33		Ha Xiaoyan	CHN	30.1.72	1cA	NSG	Chengdu	10 Sep
58.29	Olivia	McKoy	JAM	1.12.73	2		Gold Coast (RB)	10 Sep
58.23	Sabina	Moya	COL	27.1.77	2	NG	Tunja	7 Dec
58.15		Lee Young-sun	KOR	21.2.74	1B		Suwon	22 May
57.91	Mercedes	Chilla	ESP	19.1.80	1		Oviedo	6 May
57.81		Wang Yaning	CHN	4.1.80	4	NGPF	Jinzhou	8 Jun
57.75	Olga	Ivankova	UKR	7.1.73	2		Kiev	18 Jun
	(60)							
57.64	Veera	Oksanen	FIN	23.5.78	6		Kuortane	24 Jun
57.61	Savva	Líka	GRE	.70	2		Pireás	22 Apr
57.58	Inga	Kozarenoka	LAT-J	16.3.82	2		Ventspils	17 Jun
57.50	Idoia	Mariezkurrena	ESP	11.7.70	1		Gavà	28 May
57.41	Tatyana	Lyakhovich	UKR	20.5.79	19q	OG	Sydney	29 Sep
57.34	Kim	Kreiner	USA	26.7.77	1		Schaan	20 Aug
57.29		Du Beibei	CHN-J	6.1.83	2	NC	Luohe	22 Oct
57.28	Tatyana	Sudarikova	KGZ	28.5.73	1	NC	Bishkek	1 Jul
57.22	Jana	Woytkowska	GER	7.8.77	5		Chemnitz	22 Jul
57.19	Lorna	Jackson	GBR	9.1.74	1		Peterborough	9 Jul
	(70)							
57.16	Claudia	Isaila	ROM	17.7.73	3		Onesti	20 May
57.03	Sarah	Walter	FRA	5.5.78	1		Tours	2 Jun
57.03	Bina	Ramesh	FRA	20.8.79	1	NC	Nice	4 Aug
56.98	Emily	Carlsten	USA	30.10.78	3	NC	Sacramento	17 Jul
56.90	Aysel	Tas	TUR	21.10.64	1		Izmir	20 May
56.88	Tiziana	Rocco	ITA	2.12.78	1		Piovene Rocchette	30 Jul
56.85	Lada	Chernova	RUS	1.1.70	q	NC	Tula	24 Jul
56.83	Nazan	Pehlivan	TUR	15.7.68	2		Izmir	20 May
56.70	Annika	Petersson	SWE	10.1.79	1	v2N	Magglingen	1 Jul
56.69	Constanta	Iancu	ROM	12.9.76	3		Bucuresti	2 Mar
	(80)							
56.59	Yayoi	Shibano	JPN	10.3.75	1		Odawara	25 Jun
56.52	Galina	Kakhova	BLR-J	26.3.82			Staiki	27 Jun
56.45	Barbara	Vontein	GER	7.6.78	4		Regensburg	7 Jul
56.44	Christine	Wiegelmann	GER	18.7.74	2		Arnstadt	12 Aug
56.44	Takako	Miyake	JPN	22.7.74	1		Toyama	20 Aug
56.42	Yelena	Burgiman	UZB	21.12.68	1		Tashkent	15 Jun
56.37	Magdalena	Czenska	POL-J	14.6.81	1		Riesa	23 Sep
56.36	Åsa	Lindberg	FIN	12.4.79	1		Pihtipudas	20 Jul
56.35	Oksana	Yarygina	RUS	24.12.72	2	NCp	Tula	3 Jun
56.28		Song Huiling	CHN	1.11.66	7	NGPF	Jinzhou	8 Jun
	(90)							
56.20	Ann	Crouse	USA	6.4.76	1	PennR	Philadelphia	28 Apr
56.05		Wu Jianfang	CHN	1.7.79	4	NGP	Shijiazhuang	29 Apr
56.04	Jarmila	Klimesová	CZE-J	9.2.81	2		Ostrava	3 Sep
55.96		Yi Chunmei	CHN-J	15.3.83	2	NGP	Deyang	14 May
55.90	Alda	Sellam	TUN	.77	1		Tunis	3 Jun
55.83	Tanja	Tesner	RSA	4.2.80	1		Ventspils	18 Jun
55.78A	Rhona	Dwinger	RSA	28.6.71	1		Potchefstroom	14 Feb

Mark	Name		Nat	Born	Pos	Meet	Venue	Date
55.73	Manuela	Kurrat	GER-J	25.12.81	1		Jena	3 Jun
55.66	Monica	Stoian	ROM-J	25.8.82	3		Bucuresti	4 Mar
55.55	Liliya (100)	Titarenko	UKR	17.2.78	2		Kharkov	22 Jul

55.43	Harumi	Yamamoto	JPN	8.5.74	11 Jun
55.36	Beth	Obruba	USA	30.4.77	1 Apr
55.29	Monika	Aava	EST	17.6.79	20 May
55.16	Cassie	Morelock	USA	21.1.78	21 Apr
55.12	Inga	Stasiulionyte	LTU-J	29.6.81	4 Jul
55.11	Tatyana	Noskova	RUS	.73	25 Jul
55.10	Ieva	Skrastina	LAT	8.11.69	14 Jul
55.10	Barbara	Madejczyk	POL	30.9.76	5 Aug
55.06	Susan	Mathies	GER	22.1.77	27 May
54.95	Izabela	Wojczakowska	POL	24.3.74	18 Jun
54.94	Elisabetta	Marin	ITA	5.11.77	4 Jun
54.90	Cindy	Stas	BEL	5.9.79	25 Aug
54.87		Liu Jingjing	CHN	18.3.74	14 May
54.86	Windy	Dean	USA	7.9.76	14 Apr
54.85	Andrea	Gránicz	HUN	5.7.79	26 Aug
54.70	Valeriya	Poryadina	UKR	14.1.69	29 Apr
54.68	Katy	Doyle	USA	1.8.80	17 Jul
54.65	Dana	Lehmann	GER	1.7.79	3 Jun
54.65	Yuko	Kojima	JPN	20.11.73	6 Oct
54.61	Inês de Souza	Fernandes	BRA	9.6.71	22 Jul
54.58	Goldie	Sayers	GBR-J	16.7.82	19 Oct
54.52	Khristina	Kleshchevskaya	UKR	17.12.74	4 Aug
54.50	Christina	Obergföll	GER-J	22.8.81	19 Aug
54.34	Anna	Makhmutova	RUS	.69	18 May
54.26	Nadia	Vigliano	FRA	24.6.77	2 Jun
54.26	Natalya	Shimchuk	BLR-J	1.10.81	27 Jun
54.26	Zahra	Bani	ITA	31.12.79	30 Jul
54.26	Zsuzsa	Füredi	HUN	26.9.71	30 Jul
54.17		Wang Yan	CHN	8.1.77	14 May
54.15	Barbora	Spotáková	CZE-J	30.6.81	21 Oct
54.10	Geraldine	George	TRI	25.2.72	8 Apr
54.05	Heidi	Marien	BEL-J	29.7.81	20 May
54.00	Stefanie	Hessler	GER-J	16.3.83	30 Jul
53.98	Yekaterina	Chernykh	RUS	.77	21 May
53.76	Oksana	Gromova	RUS	23.9.80	12 Feb
53.76	Nicole	Carroll	USA	18.4.68	16 Apr
53.75	Vigdís	Gudjónsdóttír	ISL	27.6.75	11 Aug
53.70	Jamie	Strieter	USA	14.11.75	4 May
53.70	Nathalie	Teppe	FRA	22.5.72	4 Jun
53.67	Kazuyo	Komasa	JPN	21.6.79	23 Apr
53.64	Valentina	Bukraba	BLR	6.3.70	3 Mar
53.53	Anna	Boyeva	UKR	4.9.77	4 Aug
53.52	Mariana	Melinte	ROM-J	1.3.81	25 Jun
53.49	Wilma	Jansen	GER	29.10.80	27 May
53.32		Liu Yunping	CHN		7 Sep
53.24	Candy	Mitchell	USA	17.3.77	17 Jul
53.22	Eva	Uroz	ESP	11.11.75	4 Mar
53.22	Sílvia	Cruz	POR	29.12.80	23 Jul
53.19	Olivia	Norris	GER-J	17.9.83	27 May
53.18	Kendra	Wecker	USA-J	16.12.82	5 Aug
53.15	Jana	Ladewig	GER-J	16.9.81	19 Aug
53.12	Andrea	Kvetová	CZE	27.2.84	23 Sep
53.10	Katy	Polansky	USA-J	15.7.82	17 Jul
53.06	Shelley	Holroyd	GBR	17.5.73	7 May
53.04	Linda	Lindqvist	FIN	3.4.79	20 May
53.02	Alessandra	Resende	BRA	5.3.75	15 Apr
53.02	Elisabet (157)	Wahlander	SWE	14.3.60	19 Aug

JUNIORS

See main list for top 9 juniors. 10 performances by 7 women to 55.96. Additional marks and further juniors:

Liang Lili	57.66	4	Shanghai	18 Apr	56.50	6	Jinzhou	8 Jun
Kozarenkova	56.03	1	Valmiera	14 Jul				

55.12	Inga	Stasiulionyte	LTU	29.6.81	1		Vilnius	4 Jul
54.58	Goldie	Sayers	GBR	16.7.82	Q	WJ	Santiago de Chile	19 Oct
54.50	Christina	Obergföll	GER	22.8.81	1	NC-23	Jena	19 Aug
54.26	Natalya	Shimchuk	BLR	1.10.81			Staiki	27 Jun
54.15	Barbora	Spotáková	CZE	30.6.81	1H	WJ	Santiago de Chile	21 Oct
54.05	Heidi	Marien	BEL	29.7.81	1		Aalst	20 May
54.00	Stefanie	Hessler	GER	16.3.83	1	v2N-j	St-Jean-de-Luz	30 Jul
53.52	Mariana	Melinte	ROM	1.3.81	3		Bucuresti	25 Jun
53.19	Olivia	Norris	GER	17.9.83	1		Halle	27 May
53.18	Kendra	Wecker	USA	16.12.82	1	NAm-25	Monterrey	5 Aug
53.15	Jana	Ladewig (20)	GER	16.9.81	3	NC-23	Jena	19 Aug

HEPTATHLON

6842	Eunice	Barber	FRA	17.11.74	1		Götzis	4 Jun
	12.97/0.2 1.88 12.23 23.84/0.5			6.85/-0.1		51.91	2:11.55	
6831	Denise	Lewis	GBR	27.8.72	1	Deca	Talence	30 Jul
	13.13/1.0 1.84 15.07 24.01w/3.6			6.69/-0.4		49.42	2:12.20	
6765	Yelena	Prokhorova	RUS	16.4.78	1	NC	Tula	23 Jul
	13.54/-2.8 1.82 14.30 23.37/-0.2			6.72/1.0		43.40	2:04.27	
6633	Natalya	Roshchupkina	RUS	13.1.78	2	NC	Tula	23 Jul
	14.05/-2.8 1.88 14.28 23.47/-0.2			6.45/0.4		44.34	2:07.93	
6584		Lewis			1	OG	Sydney	24 Sep
	13.23/0.3 1.75 15.55 24.34/-0.1			6.48/0.8		50.19	2:16.83	
6531		Prokhorova			2	OG	Sydney	24 Sep
	13.63/0.3 1.81 13.21 23.72/-0.1			6.59/-0.4		45.05	2:10.32	
6527	Natalya	Sazanovich	BLR	15.8.73	3	OG	Sydney	24 Sep
	13.45/-0.2 1.84 14.79 24.12/-0.6			6.50/-0.5		43.97	2:16.41	
6520		Prokhorova			1	NCp	Tula	3 Jun
	13.84 1.77 14.09 23.83			6.54		42.91	2:05.10	
6513		Roshchupkina			2		Götzis	4 Jun
	13.99/1.2 1.91 14.20 23.80/0.5			6.12/-0.1		44.11	2:09.36	
6470	Urszula	Wlodarczyk	POL	22.12.65	4	OG	Sydney	24 Sep
	13.33/0.3 1.78 14.45 24.29/-0.1			6.31/-0.8		46.16	2:12.15	

Mark	Name		Nat	Born	Pos	Meet	Venue	Date
6464	Sabine	Braun	GER	19.6.65	3		Götzis	4 Jun
	13.56/0.2 1.82 14.49 24.81/0.3			6.32/0.0		51.66	2:18.23	
6422	Sheila	Burrell	USA	15.1.72	4		Götzis	4 Jun
	13.45/0.2 1.70 12.97 23.65/0.1			6.30/0.5		50.31	2:10.29	
6401	Diana	Koritskaya	RUS	22.2.75	3	NC	Tula	23 Jul
	13.77/-2.8 1.79 13.41 23.79/-0.2			6.10/0.1		45.14	2:06.11	
6398		Wlodarczyk			1		Arles	4 Jun
	14.00/0.9 1.83 15.23 24.43w/2.7			6.41/1.3		44.02	2:16.99	
6396	Karin	Ertl (10)	GER	23.6.74	5		Götzis	4 Jun
	13.31/0.2 1.82 14.17 24.16/0.1			6.36/0.3		44.02	2:18.93	
6384	Yelena	Chernyavskaya	RUS	13.4.78	2	NCp	Tula	3 Jun
	13.71 1.80 13.36 24.12			6.19		42.87	2:05.20	
6379	Astrid	Retzke	GER	13.7.73	1	OT	Ratingen	23 Jul
	13.81/-1.1 1.77 14.48 24.55/0.7			6.35/1.7		49.17	2:16.28	
6377		Roshchupkina			1	ECp	Oulu	2 Jul
	13.91/0.7 1.84 13.49 23.61/0.8			6.07/1.1		44.34	2:10.53	
6355		Braun			5	OG	Sydney	24 Sep
	13.49/0.3 1.81 14.33 24.74/-0.1			6.22/-1.7		48.56	2:19.14	
6352	Irina	Tyukhay	RUS	14.1.67	4	NC	Tula	23 Jul
	13.55/-2.8 1.79 14.86 24.42/-0.2			6.28/-0.2		42.59	2:14.79	
6351		Wlodarczyk			2	Deca	Talence	30 Jul
	13.50/1.0 1.81 15.48 24.08w/3.6			6.02/1.6		42.76	2:16.74	
6343	DeDee	Nathan	USA	20.4.68	1	NC	Sacramento	15 Jul
	13.34/0.8 1.76 14.33 24.54/0.3			6.40/1.7		44.17	2:16.33	
6341	Kathleen	Gutjahr	GER	27.7.75	6		Götzis	4 Jun
	13.50/0.8 1.82 13.80 24.94/0.3			6.08/-0.4		47.23	2:12.10	
6339		Burrell			2	NC	Sacramento	15 Jul
	13.26/1.6 1.61 13.59 23.65/0.3			6.28/1.9		49.04	2:11.34	
6336	Tatyana	Gordeyeva	RUS	3.6.73	5	NC	Tula	23 Jul
	14.13/-2.6 1.91 14.35 25.00/-0.4			6.18/-0.6		39.99	2:08.87	
6332		Braun			2	OT	Ratingen	23 Jul
	13.71/-1.1 1.80 14.13 24.91/0.7			6.40/0.9		49.16	2:20.49	
6331	Larisa	Necheporuk	UKR	24.12.70	1		Maribor	28 May
	13.99w/2.9 1.79 13.85 24.74w/3.8			6.40w/2.9		50.50	2:18.43	
6326		Retzke			7		Götzis	4 Jun
	13.50/1.2 1.76 13.62 24.32/-0.8			6.13/-0.3		49.93	2:15.90	
6289	Viorica	Tigau	ROM	12.8.79	1		Bucuresti	25 Jun
	13.18/0.9 1.79 12.03 23.90/0.2			6.83/0.5		40.40	2:23.05	
6288		Sazanovich			1	ECp-1	Schwyz/Ibach	2 Jul
	13.46/0.4 1.78 14.74 23.94/-0.3			6.50/1.9		40.45	2:24.24	
	(30/18)							
6271	Irina	Vostrikova	RUS	30.8.70	8		Götzis	4 Jun
	13.78/0.1 1.82 15.64 25.49/-0.8			6.08/0.5		46.63	2:18.59	
6235	Nathalie	Teppe	FRA	22.5.72	2		Arles	4 Jun
	13.87/0.9 1.74 14.01 25.64/1.4			6.23/1.9		53.70	2:17.45	
	(20)							
6227	Jane	Jamieson	AUS	23.6.75	1		Darwin	8 Jul
	14.20/0.9 1.84 13.50 24.97/0.0			6.11/1.6		50.19	2:18.03	
6219	Tiia	Hautala	FIN	3.4.72	10		Götzis	4 Jun
	13.43/0.8 1.82 13.67 24.74/0.3			6.20/0.5		41.66	2:17.22	
6217w	Kelly	Blair-LaBounty	USA	24.11.70	1	TexR	Austin	6 Apr
	13.52W/4.2 1.74 13.64 24.34/-4.3			6.24W/5.2		45.04	2:17.25	
6187	Svetlana	Parfyonova	RUS	.74	5	NCp	Tula	3 Jun
	13.76 1.77 12.60 23.69			6.29		33.94	2:05.63	
6186	Soma	Biswas	IND	16.5.78	1	Inter-St	Chennai	31 Jul
	13.62 1.69 13.22 24.23			6.19		44.92	2:11.67	
6177	Rita	Ináncsi	HUN	6.1.71	2	ECp-1	Schwyz/Ibach	2 Jul
	14.10/-0.5 1.78 14.88 25.53/-0.3			6.26w/2.9		48.33	2:21.01	
6161	Svetlana	Kazanina	KAZ	31.10.71	11		Götzis	4 Jun
	14.28/0.1 1.82 12.96 24.60/0.5			5.94/-0.1		46.10	2:10.76	
6153	Peggy	Beer	GER	15.9.69	5	OT	Ratingen	23 Jul
	13.78/-1.1 1.77 13.29 25.04/0.7			6.15/1.4		46.95	2:16.27	
6146	Tatyana	Alisevich	BLR	22.1.69	3	ECp-1	Schwyz/Ibach	2 Jul
	13.83/0.0 1.66 14.70 24.52/-0.8			5.85/1.7		50.84	2:15.58	
6119	Marie	Collonvillé	FRA	23.11.73	4	2 NC	Talence	30 Jul
	13.52/0.6 1.78 12.03 24.90w/3.6			5.96/1.1		47.00	2:13.03	
	(30)							
6105	G Pramila	Ganapathy	IND	8.5.77	2	Inter-St	Chennai	31 Jul
	13.85 1.75 12.20 24.41			6.51		42.62	2:18.42	

Mark	Name		Nat	Born	Pos	Meet	Venue	Date
6104	Austra	Skujyté	LTU	12.8.79	1	ECp-2	Esbjerg	2 Jul
	14.44/1.2 1.81 14.70 25.66/1.3			6.30/0.4		44.98	2:20.1h	
6094	Tiffany	Lott-Hogan	USA	1.8.75	4	NC	Sacramento	15 Jul
	13.10/-1.3 1.70 13.41 24.61/0.3			5.87/1.6		49.60	2:22.51	
6079	Sárka	Beránková	CZE	16.4.78	1	NC	Praha	23 Jul
	14.06/-0.2 1.76 12.56 24.02w/2.4			6.43/-0.4		40.30	2:18.33	
6078	Irina	Naumenko	KAZ	13.2.80	1	KosM	Almaty	28 May
	14.30/-0.5 1.88 13.36 24.64/2.0			6.14/1.0		37.20	2:15.59	
6077	Lyudmila	Blonskaya	UKR	18.3.75	1	NCp	Kiev	4 Jun
	14.65/0.8 1.73 13.84 25.56/0.4			6.17/-0.6		46.12	2:08.16	
6077	Nicole	Haynes	CAN/USA	18.9.74	5	NC	Sacramento	15 Jul
	14.20/0.8 1.79 14.33 25.62/0.3			6.19/1.3		44.40	2:17.81	
6076	Anzhela	Kinet	TUR	14.11.70	13		Götzis	4 Jun
	13.56/0.8 1.76 13.25 24.07/0.3			6.14/0.8		39.11	2:18.35	
6056	Carolina	Klüft	SWE-J	2.2.83	1	WJ	Santiago de Chile	21 Oct
	13.92/0.6 1.80 13.27 24.61/-0.6			6.08/-0.2		42.00	2:18.77	
6054	Magalys	García	CUB	23.10.71	11	OG	Sydney	24 Sep
	13.46/0.5 1.66 13.29 24.58/-0.2			5.92/1.0		50.31	2:19.64	
	(40)							
6041	Beatrice	Mau-Repnak	GER	20.2.71	1		Bernhausen	28 May
	13.88/-1.3 1.70 13.78 25.33/-1.1			6.00/0.3		52.09	2:21.41	
6041	Wendi	Raatjes	USA	28.7.69	6	NC	Sacramento	15 Jul
	13.92/0.8 1.73 12.30 24.17/-0.7			6.23w/2.3		40.00	2:12.57	
6039	Sonja	Kesselschläger	GER	20.1.78	14		Götzis	4 Jun
	13.87/0.1 1.85 13.55 25.88/-0.8			6.14/0.7		42.46	2:20.18	
6021	Marina	Bryukhach	UKR	16.1.77	2	NCp	Kiev	4 Jun
	13.91/0.8 1.79 12.56 24.84/0.3			6.11/0.1		41.10	2:14.95	
6021	Muriel	Crozet	FRA	8.1.71	5	3 NC	Talence	30 Jul
	13.60/1.0 1.81 13.27 25.21/1.3			6.02/0.6		41.77	2:19.93	
6021	Susanna	Rajamäki	FIN	19.9.79	13	OG	Sydney	24 Sep
	13.60/0.5 1.66 13.87 24.03/-0.2			6.36/0.5		37.00	2:18.47	
6019	Maralize	Fouché	RSA	2.3.74	15		Götzis	4 Jun
	13.61/1.2 1.79 13.47 23.51/0.5			5.93/0.4		38.70	2:24.63	
6015	Michaela	Hejnová	CZE	10.4.80	2	NC	Praha	23 Jul
	13.65/-0.2 1.67 12.09 24.85w/2.4			6.09/2.0		47.89	2:14.14	
5995w	Tracye	Lawyer	USA	28.8.77	1	MSR	Azusa	14 Apr
	13.88w/2.9 1.82 14.26 24.35W/4.1			5.92/1.7		38.40	2:23.44	
5990	Gertrud	Bacher	ITA	28.2.71	4	ECp-1	Schwyz/Ibach	2 Jul
	13.85/0.4 1.75 12.79 24.52/-0.3			5.78/-0.7		40.05	2:09.05	
	(50)							
5984	Tatyana	Zhevnova	BLR	17.10.77			Staiki	3 Jun
	13.93 1.73 13.62 25.28			6.04		46.54	2:19.71 = 5991	
5979	Annika	Meyer	GER	9.6.80	8	OT	Ratingen	23 Jul
	13.93/-0.7 1.80 12.59 25.27/0.9			6.20/1.5		40.05	2:16.53	
5979	Lidiya	Bashlykova	RUS-J	10.1.81	1		Krasnodar	16 Sep
	14.33 1.82 14.60 24.55			6.05		39.00	2:24.23 =5978?	
5958	Clare	Thompson	AUS	28.12.77	2		Darwin	8 Jul
	13.65/0.9 1.75 11.67 24.56/0.0			6.06/0.8		42.14	2:16.55	
5943	Elzbieta	Raczka	POL	19.11.70	6		Arles	4 Jun
	14.08/1.8 1.77 12.71 25.08/1.8			6.14/0.6		42.72	2:19.15	
5932w	Christi	Smith	USA	5.11.77	2	TexR	Austin	6 Apr
	14.04W/6.2 1.68 13.04 24.18W/5.7			6.22w/2.2		39.30	2:17.04	
5931	Annu	Montell	FIN	7.5.76	2	NC	Lahti	18 Aug
	13.78/1.8 1.77 13.20 25.18/0.9			5.95/1.3		45.56	2:24.69	
5927	Asimína	Vanakára	GRE	14.7.79	1	NC	Vólos	12 Aug
	14.10/1.3 1.72 10.96 24.20			6.25/0.3		44.96	2:18.79	
5924	Liliana	Nastase	ROM	1.8.62	2		Bucuresti	25 Jun
	13.19/0.9 1.64 12.92 24.88/0.2			6.03/0.2		39.66	2:14.11	
5915	Izabella	Oblekowska	POL	18.2.72	8	ECp	Oulu	2 Jul
	13.63/-1.6 1.78 12.16 25.06/-0.8			5.82/0.0		40.27	2:13.72	
	(60)							
5915	Yuliya	Akulenko	UKR	3.6.77	2	NC	Kiev	28 Jul
	14.31/0.0 1.70 12.71 25.10/-1.0			6.23/0.6		48.00	2:22.00	
5896	Yasmina	Azzizi-Kettab	ALG	25.2.66	17	OG	Sydney	24 Sep
	13.64/0.5 1.60 14.17 24.59/-0.2			5.88/0.2		46.28	2:21.82	
5889		Du Xueru	CHN-J	6.4.83	1	NGPF	Jinzhou	8 Jun
	13.48/-1.2 1.63 13.97 24.83/0.3			6.08/-1.3		41.87	2:22.17	
5873	Barbora	Spotáková	CZE-J	30.6.81	3	NC	Praha	23 Jul
	14.26/-0.2 1.73 13.29 25.11w/2.4			5.60/1.1		48.97	2:18.29	

WOMEN 2000

Mark	Name		Nat	Born	Pos	Meet	Venue	Date
5850	Marina	Shcherbina	UKR	5.1.68	3	NCp	Kiev	4 Jun
	14.53/0.8 1.76	14.30 26.22/0.4		5.75/0.2		42.62	2:12.16	
5843	Imma	Clopés	ESP	19.1.68	1	NC	Logroño	20 Aug
	14.27/-0.3 1.74	13.56 25.75/-0.6		6.09/0.2		43.12	2:20.95	
5842	Sophie	Marrot	FRA	13.2.75	10		Arles	4 Jun
	13.55/0.9 1.71	11.68 25.10/1.8		6.00/1.1		46.15	2:23.36	
5839		Shen Shengfei	CHN-J	21.1.81	1cA	NSG	Chengdu	7 Sep
5835		Liu Xing	CHN	27.4.70	1	NC	Luohe	20 Oct
	13.96 1.62	12.99 24.21		6.11		41.71	2:20.19	
5826	Sabine	Krieger	GER	4.9.73	9	OT	Ratingen	23 Jul
	14.16/0.0 1.71	13.58 25.41/0.0		5.85w/2.2		43.77	2:18.60	
	(70)							
5817	Sherryl	Morrow	AUS	22.3.73	1	NC	Sydney	25 Feb
	13.65/1.8 1.85	11.54 25.63/-1.9		5.98/1.0		39.34	2:22.55	
5814	Taisiya	Dobrovitskaya	BLR	8.12.67	5	ECp-1	Schwyz/Ibach	2 Jul
	13.91/0.0 1.69	13.70 24.85/0.0		5.98/0.9		37.51	2:18.55	
5811	Enikõ	Kiss	HUN	23.9.75	1	NC	Budapest	6 Aug
	13.88/0.1 1.75	12.12 24.55/1.3		6.20/0.0		33.67	2:18.53	
5795	Silvia	Dalla Piana	ITA	3.2.75	6	ECp-1	Schwyz/Ibach	2 Jul
	14.29/0.0 1.81	11.30 25.83/-0.8		5.86w/3.4		45.40	2:17.26	
5777	Gigi	Miller	USA	12.1.79	2	NCAA	Durham	1 Jun
	13.58/0.4 1.69	12.00 24.15/-0.8		5.81/0.0		34.92	2:13.98	
5771	Piia	Peltosaari	FIN	27.2.73	6	Multi	Desenzano del Garda	14
	14.49/-2.2 1.70	12.81 25.23/-1.2		5.84/0.4		46.53	2:19.48	
5764	Saskia	Meijer	NED	8.2.79	1	NC	Apeldoorn	27 Aug
	14.49/-0.5 1.72	14.33 25.50/0.9		5.61/0.0		43.54	2:17.99	
5760	Sofiya	Kabanova	UZB	29.5.70	1	NC	Tashkent	17 Aug
	15.39/-0.1 1.84	13.12 28.13/0.2		6.01/0.3		49.20	2:15.44 =5761?	
5750	Marsha	Mark	TRI	20.1.74	2	CAN Ch	Windsor	6 Aug
	13.90/1.9 1.71	11.14 25.45w/3.1		6.13/0.7		45.07	2:22.84	
5748		Wang Hailan	CHN	6.4.76	2	NC	Luohe	20 Oct
	14.25 1.65	13.09 25.35		6.26		38.90	2:18.35	
	(80)							
5747	Mona	Steigauf	GER	17.1.70	10	OT	Ratingen	23 Jul
	13.77/-1.1 1.68	11.96 24.76/0.7		6.17/0.6		36.23	2:18.65	
5746		Hu Yaoyao	CHN-J	16.4.83	2	NSG	Chengdu	7 Sep
5743	Judith	Vis	NED	21.6.80	2	NC	Apeldoorn	27 Aug
	13.59/-0.5 1.75	12.20 24.26/0.2		6.00/0.2		29.91	2:19.19	
5739	Alena	Vindyuk	RUS	.74	9	NC	Tula	23 Jul
	14.38/-2.6 1.73	11.47 24.86/-0.4		6.04/-0.7		41.75	2:19.22	
5735	Kerry	Jury	GBR	19.11.68	2	ESP Ch	Logroño	20 Aug
	13.92/-0.3 1.77	11.58 24.26/-0.6		5.71/0.1		34.33	2:14.89	
5730	Patience	Itanyi	NGR	2.7.73	11		Arles	4 Jun
	13.39/0.9 1.71	10.01 24.60w/2.7		6.54/0.3		35.03	2:25.43	
5728	Niina	Kelo	FIN	26.3.80	18	ECp	Oulu	2 Jul
	14.45/0.7 1.72	14.60 26.85/-1.2		5.58/0.2		52.47	2:25.97	
5726w	Ifoma	Jones	USA	4.9.77	3	TexR	Austin	6 Apr
	14.21W/6.2 1.83	10.90 24.94W/5.7		5.89W/5.9		36.28	2:16.77	
5718	Sanna	Saarman	FIN-J	14.5.81	2	Nord-21	Geithus	16 Jul
	13.91/-0.7 1.69	12.67 25.99/-0.9		6.01/0.9		43.18	2:21.73	
5699	Salla	Käppi	FIN	22.5.80	3	Nord-21	Geithus	16 Jul
	14.13/-0.7 1.75	12.43 26.12/-0.9		5.69/0.5		47.18	2:22.94	
	(90)							
5688	Irina	Ilyina	RUS	.76	11	NC	Tula	23 Jul
	14.47/-2.2 1.61	13.26 25.25/-0.3		5.78/0.7		44.03	2:15.09	
5688	Jessica	Zelinka	CAN-J	3.9.81	5	WJ	Santiago de Chile	21 Oct
	14.02/-0.9 1.77	11.57 24.73/-0.2		5.85/0.1		37.40	2:21.34	
5685	Julie	Hollman	GBR	16.2.77	3	ESP Ch	Logroño	20 Aug
	14.55/-0.3 1.74	12.64 24.81/-0.6		6.06w/2.6		32.16	2:15.46	
5673	Anna	Snetkova	RUS	.80	12	NC	Tula	23 Jul
	14.66/-2.2 1.73	13.00 25.93/-0.3		6.12/1.0		38.54	2:18.85	
5671	Magdalena	Szczepanska	POL	25.1.80	11		Ratingen	23 Jul
	14.40/0.0 1.68	11.10 25.19/0.0		6.02/0.9		41.96	2:15.48	
5671	Enezenaide	Gomes	STP	10.11.79	4	ESP Ch	Logroño	20 Aug
	14.48/-0.3 1.80	13.12 25.87/-0.6		6.07/0.8		42.64	2:33.66	
5657	Anzhela	Laytinen	RUS	.71	13	NC	Tula	23 Jul
	14.83/-2.2 1.85	12.59 25.78/-0.3		6.06/1.5		34.36	2:21.18	

Mark	Name		Nat	Born	Pos	Meet	Venue	Date
5655	Joanne	Henry	NZL	2.10.71	1		Auckland	9 Jan
	14.57/-2.1 1.74	13.07	25.71/-1.0	5.97/0.7		40.98	2:23.81	
5647	Regla Maria	Cárdenas	CUB	21.1.75	1		Santiago de Cuba	4 Mar
	13.72w/2.5 1.71	14.56	25.78	5.75		38.07	2:28.64	
5647	Elena	Dumitrascu	ROM	14.5.74	1		Poiana Brasov	22 Jul
	14.86 1.78	13.29	26.23	6.29/1.6		37.94	2:31.69	
	(100)							

5646	Tia	Hellebaut	BEL	16.2.78	27 Aug
5644	Danielle	Freeman	GBR	11.2.80	4 Jun
5644	Vasilisa	Verlan	RUS	.78	23 Jul
5642	Yuki	Nakata	JPN	10.3.77	4 Jun
5637	Sayoko	Sato	JPN	23.10.77	7 Oct
5632	Svetlana	Gnezdilov	ISR	20.7.69	17 Apr
5621	Kim	Vanderhoek	CAN	30.11.70	21 May
5621	Oksana	Shutko	UKR	25.3.77	28 Jul
5620	Maria	Richtnér	SWE	5.2.73	6 Aug
5616	Karin	Periginelli	ITA	5.2.70	8 Oct
5614	Missy	Vanek	USA	.70	1 Jun
5602	Kim	Schiemenz	USA	13.4.77	26 May
5602	Nicola	Gautier	GBR	21.3.78	4 Jun
5596wA	Aja	Frary	USA	1.7.78	27 May
5596	Desanka	Calasan	SLO	7.6.70	28 May
5592	Lyudmila	Shevchuk	UKR	9.11.77	4 Jun
5590	Erin	Narzinski	USA	6.5.76	14 Apr
5590	Michelle	Moran	USA	23.3.79	20 May
5589w	Jennifer	Hoppe	USA	5.12.76	18 Jun
5584	Yevgeniya	Mazurenko	UKR	26.8.78	4 Jun
5584	Antonia	Schulze-Borges	GER-J	14.4.82	2 Sep
5584	Olga	Karas	RUS-J	9.7.82	21 Oct
5583	Kylie	Wheeler	AUS	17.1.80	8 Jul
5572	Jana	Klecková	CZE	19.3.75	23 Jul
5567	Alexandra	Barlet	FRA	17.2.77	4 Jun
5560	DeeDee	Brown	USA	5.5.78	12 May
5558	Euzinete	dos Reis	BRA	7.3.72	4 Aug
5555	Maren	Freisen	GER-J	15.2.82	13 Aug
5551	Aryiró	Stratáki	GRE	3.8.75	28 May
5548	María	Peinado	ESP	8.2.77	20 Aug
5547	Yuliya	Ignatkina	RUS-J	.82	2 Jul
5545	Zita	Bálint	HUN	25.10.71	21 May
5543	Margaret	Simpson	GHA-J	2.8.82	4 Jun
5541	Manuela	Kobelt	SUI	11.12.69	13 Aug
5539	Valentina	Boffelli	ITA	24.1.78	2 Jul
5538	Julia	Bennett	GBR	26.3.70	4 Jun
5533	Alma	von Planta	SUI	18.7.73	4 Jun
5530	Ottelien	Olsthoorn	NED	20.6.78	27 Aug
5523	Ursula	Neumair	GER-J	21.1.82	13 Aug
5518	Tania	Longe	NOR	4.4.74	4 Jun
5513	Elizete	da Silva	BRA	2.5.71	4 Aug
5507	Andrea	Geurtsen	SWE	13.6.79	20 May
5504	Lindsay	Taylor	USA	9.2.79	23 Mar
5502	Sylvie	Dufour	SUI	24.1.79	13 Aug
5500	Ionela	Haralambie	ROM	26.9.79	3 Jun
5500	Stefanie	Fuchs	GER	24.7.79	3 Sep
5499	Kristi	McGihon	USA	23.1.69	1 Jul
5488	Barbara	Szlendaková	CZE	6.8.78	20 May
5488	Katja	Keller	GER	9.8.80	25 Jun
5481	Monika	Marques	BRA	25.11.67	21 May
5474	Manuela	Kurrat	GER-J	25.12.81	25 Jun
5474	Kristina	Porsche	GER	25.2.80	2 Jul
5467		Dan Jiao	CHN-J	6.9.83	4 May
5466A	Janice	Josephs	RSA-J	31.3.82	15 Apr
5466	Rutti	Luksepp	EST	19.6.74	11 Jun
5464	Kerry	O'Bric	USA	22.9.78	1 Jun
5464	Gabriela	Kouassi	FRA	18.11.79	13 Aug
5463	Carmen	Wright	USA	27.4.79	6 May
5460	Jamie	Walker	USA-J	3.3.81	12 May
5458	Keiko	Kikugawa	JPN	10.10.79	4 Jun
5458	Alena	Shiman	RUS	2.12.69	23 Jul
5457	Catherine	Bond-Mills	CAN	20.9.67	6 Aug
5455	Ali	McKnight	USA	27.4.72	31 Mar
5455w	Kathrine	Nielsen	DEN	9.2.77	18 May
5451A	Marsha	Baird	USA		21 Apr
5449	Frenke	Bolt	NED	8.6.80	12 May
5446w	Rannveig	Kvalvik	NOR	2.10.76	14 Apr
5445	Annelies	De Meester	BEL	30.1.76	27 Aug
5441	Dagmar	Urbánková	CZE	8.4.62	18 Jun
5436	Antonietta	Di Martino	ITA	1.6.78	2 Jul
5435	Kym	Carter-Begel	USA	12.3.64	14 Apr
5435	Yvonne	Wisse	NED-J	6.6.82	27 Aug
5430	Déborah	Grapotte	FRA	2.4.78	9 Jul
5428	Kelly	Sotherton	GBR	13.11.76	4 Jun
5428	Svetlana	Grachova	UKR	23.1.79	28 Jul
5423w	Martha	Brennan	USA	13.12.72	6 Apr
5423	Beata	Lukaszewska	POL	19.2.80	4 Jun
5406wA	Peggy	Odita	USA	2.1.68	27 May
5406	Emilie	Boulleret	FRA	23.5.73	9 Jul
5402	Natalya	Germanyuk	BLR	30.3.75	24 Aug
	(180)				

Best without wind assistance

Mark	Name		Nat	Born	Pos	Meet	Venue	Date
6180	Kelly	LaBounty	USA	24.11.70	3	NC	Sacramento	15 Jul
	13.72/-1.3 1.70	13.30	24.92/-0.7	6.40/1.2		46.21	2:14.24	
5844	Tracye	Lawyer	USA	28.8.77	7	NC	Sacramento	15 Jul
	13.78/0.8 1.82	14.14	24.78/0.3	5.90/1.0		37.69	2:31.10	
5797	Christi	Smith	USA	5.11.77	1	NCAA	Durham	1 Jun
	14.35/1.3 1.69	13.26	24.55/-1.1	5.80/1.2		40.18	2:15.02	

5593 IJones 1 Jun 5438 Nielsen 1 Jun **Best at low altitude**: 5522 Frary 15 Jul

JUNIORS

See main list for top 7 juniors. 13 performances by 7 women over 5700. Additional marks and further juniors:

Klüft	5814	1		Växjö	28 Jun	5810 1	Lerum	21 May
	5764	1		Nordum	16 Jul			
Bashlykova	5898	2	WJ	Santiago de Chile	21 Oct			
Spotáková	5719	1		Hexham	21 May			
Du Xueru	5717	1		Tianjin	4 May			

Mark	Name		Nat	Born	Pos	Meet	Venue	Date
5584	Antonia	Schulze-Borges	GER	14.4.82	1	NC-j	Wesel	2 Sep
	14.35/1.5 1.78	11.80	25.91/-0.5	5.83/1.0		43.02	2:27.36	
5584	Olga	Karas	RUS	9.7.82	6	WJ	Santiago de Chile	21 Oct
	14.89/0.6 1.74	11.82	25.40/-0.6	6.05/1.1		40.10	2:22.32	
5555	Maren	Freisen (10)	GER	15.2.82	1	v2N	Val-de-Reuil	13 Aug
	14.20/1.1 1.67	11.40	25.90/0.3	5.72/1.4		46.69	2:21.78	
5547	Yuliya	Ignatkina	RUS	.82	1	NC-23	Cheboksary	2 Jul
	15.24 1.69	11.16	25.60	5.97		46.61	2:20.22	
5543	Margaret	Simpson	GHA	2.8.82	18	(1J)	Arles	4 Jun
	14.45/0.8 1.74	11.02	25.24/1.3	5.78/2.0		48.58	2:33.69	
5523	Ursula	Neumair	GER	21.1.82	2	v2N	Val-de-Reuil	13 Aug
	15.17/1.1 1.73	12.76	26.04/0.3	5.73w/2.1		43.75	2:21.69	

Mark	Name		Nat	Born	Pos	Meet	Venue	Date
5474	Manuela	Kurrat	GER	25.12.81	2J		Bad Oeynhausen	25 Jun
	14.88/-1.6 1.57 12.54 26.12			5.40/-0.4		48.06	2:11.90	
5467		Dan Jiao	CHN	.84	4		Tianjin	4 May
	14.14 1.57 13.03 24.97			5.65		40.26	2:23.85	
5466A	Janice	Josephs	RSA	31.3.82	1	NC-j	Pietersburg	15 Apr
	13.98/1.7 1.64 10.73 23.67			5.98		33.71	2:27.67	
5460	Jamie	Walker	USA	3.3.81	2	SEC	Baton Rouge	12 May
	14.12w/3.6 1.55 11.20 24.02w/2.2			5.92w		34.25	2:17.93	
5435	Yvonne	Wisse	NED	6.6.82	5	NC	Apeldoorn	27 Aug
	14.50/-0.5 1.81 10.88 24.94/0.2			5.77/-1.2		29.25	2:20.69	
5396	Fanny	Gérance	FRA	4.1.81	1	NC-j	St Etienne	9 Jul
	13.45/1.2 1.63 11.08 24.31/1.5			5.58/+1.9		28.84	2:18.96	
5388	Lucia	Tomaceková (20)	SVK	26.12.82	7	ECp-2	Esbjerg	2 Jul
	14.49/2.5 1.69 11.22 26.10w/2.1			5.69/-0.2		41.42	2:22.7	

DECATHLON

Mark	Name		Nat	Born	Pos	Meet	Venue	Date
7731	Marie	Collonvillé	FRA	23.11.73	1		Lage	10 Sep
	12.61	6.03	11.55	1.75	56.48	14.28	31.91	3.40
43.94	5:13.70							
7577	Tiffany	Lott-Hogan	USA	1.8.75	2		Lage	10 Sep
	12.31 5.77	13.86	1.69 58.01	13.57			38.39 3.00 46.93	6:01.24
7275	Mona	Steigauf	GER	17.1.70	3		Lage	10 Sep
	12.41 5.96	12.57	1.72 55.98	13.99			27.52 2.90 35.84	5:35.53

4 X 100 METRES RELAY

41.95	BAH	Fynes, Sturrup, Davis-Thompson, Ferguson	1	OG	Sydney	30 Sep
42.13	USA	Gaines, Devers, Miller, Edwards	1	Herc	Monaco	18 Aug
42.13	JAM	Lawrence, V Campbell, McDonald, Ottey	2	OG	Sydney	30 Sep
42.15	JAM	Lawrence, V Campbell, McDonald, Frazer	1s2	OG	Sydney	29 Sep
42.20	USA	Gaines, Edwards, Perry, Jones	3	OG	Sydney	30 Sep
42.33	USA Red	Gaines, Edwards, Miller, Jones	1	PennR	Philadelphia	29 Apr
42.35	BAH	Ferguson, Fynes, Clarke-Lewis, Davis-Thompson	2	Herc	Monaco	18 Aug
42.38	FRA	Citté, Hurtis, Dia, Arron	3	Herc	Monaco	18 Aug
42.42	BAH	Clarke-Lewis, Sturrup, Davis-Thompson, Fynes	1s1	OG	Sydney	29 Sep
42.42	FRA	Citté, Hurtis, Dia, Arron	2s2	OG	Sydney	29 Sep
42.42	FRA	Ferga, Hurtis, Dia, Arron	4	OG	Sydney	30 Sep
42.46	JAM	Lawrence, V Campbell, McDonald, Frazer	1h2	OG	Sydney	29 Sep
42.58	BAH	Clarke-Lewis, Sturrup, Davis-Thompson, Fynes	1h3	OG	Sydney	29 Sep
42.73	GER	Schielke, Möller, Philipp, Wagner	1		Chemnitz	22 Jul
42.74	USA Blue	Richardson, Perry, Anderson, Jenkins	2	PennR	Philadelphia	29 Apr
42.77	GER		1		Gold Coast (RB)	17 Sep
42.78	JAM	Golding, Frazer, A Walker, Campbell	3	PennR	Philadelphia	29 Apr
42.80	GER	G Rockmeier, Mulrain, Philipp, Wagner	1		KönigsWusterhausen	29 Aug
42.82	GER	G Rockmeier, Mulrain, Philipp, Wagner	2h2	OG	Sydney	29 Sep
42.82	USA	Gaines, Edwards, Perry, Richardson	2s1	OG	Sydney	29 Sep
42.82	NGR	Alozie, Ajudua, Nku, Onyali	3s1	OG	Sydney	29 Sep
42.84	BAH		1r1		Montauban	15 Aug
42.84	RUS	Ignatova, Trandenkova, Khabarova, Voronova	4s1	OG	Sydney	29 Sep
42.85	GER	G Rockmeier, Mulrain, Philipp, Wagner	3s2	OG	Sydney	29 Sep
42.92	USA	Gaines, Edwards, Perry, Richardson	1h4	OG	Sydney	29 Sep
42.95	FRA	Citté, Hurtis, Dia, Arron	1r2		Montauban	15 Aug
42.95	USA	Gaines, Burrell, Richardson, Jones	1	ISTAF	Berlin	1 Sep
42.97	FRA	Benth, Hurtis, Dia, Arron	1	ECp-S	Gateshead	15 Jul
42.99A	AUS	Massey, Broadrick, Lambert, Gainsford-Taylor	1		Pietersburg	18 Mar
	29 performances by teams from 8 nations					
43.04	CHN	Zeng Xiujun, Liu Xiaomei, Qin Wangping, Li Xuemei	4s2	OG	Sydney	29 Sep
43.18	UKR	Guskova, Kravchenko, Pastushenko, Pukha	1	NC	Kiev	5 Aug
43.19	GHA	Akoto, Twum, Anim, Nsiah	5s1	OG	Sydney	29 Sep
43.19	GBR	Maduaka, Richardson, Davies, Anderson	5s2	OG	Sydney	29 Sep
43.25A	RSA	Hartman, Moropane, Holtshausen, Seyerling	2		Pietersburg	18 Mar
43.44	ITA	Pistone, Graglia, Grillo, Levorato	1		Barletta	26 Jul
43.46	GRE	Patoulídou, Patsoú, Kóffa, Thánou	2h1	OG	Sydney	29 Sep
43.50	FIN	Bosco, Kyllönen, Manninen, Hannula	6s2	OG	Sydney	29 Sep
43.61	MAD	Rahanitraniriana, Ratsimbazafy, Rakotozafy, Rakotondrabé	4h4	OG	Sydney	29 Sep
43.89	CAN	Weekes, Benyarku, Perry, Adusei	2		Brisbane	8 Sep
43.95	POL	Pawlak, Nielacna, Rysiukiewicz, Radecka	3r2		Montauban	15 Aug
43.98	KAZ	Koviyreva, Gridasova, Vorobyeva, Shishigina	1		Almaty	20 May
	(20)					

Mark		Name	Pos	Meet	Venue	Date
44.08	COL	Murillo, Restrepo, Brock, Palacios	5h2	OG	Sydney	29 Sep
44.12	SWE	Amundin, J Kallur, S Kallur, Fernström	2	vFIN	Helsinki	2 Sep
44.19	BLR	Safronnikova, Stankevich, Barashkh, Sologub	1	ECp1B	Bydgoszcz	8 Jul
44.23	SRI	Samandeepika, Herath, De Zoysa, Dharsha	1	AsiC	Jakarta	31 Aug
44.34	CIV	Allou, Sanganoko, Gnahore, Ayétotché	5h3	OG	Sydney	29 Sep
44.36	SUI	Feusi, Donders, N'Koué, Riesen	1		La Chaux de Fonds	13 Aug
44.42	ROM	Bumbescu, Tigau, Lisenco, Miklòs	7	ECp-S	Gateshead	15 Jul
44.44	IND	Jayalakshmi, Tripathi, Biswal, Mistry	1		Chennai	29 Jul
44.44	Vasco da Gama (BRA)	dos Santos, Pina, A Gomes, de Moura	1		Rio de Janeiro	4 Aug
44.51	THA	Ruamsuk, Khawpeag, Klomdee, Roberts	4h1	OG	Sydney	29 Sep
	(30)					

44.62	SEN	12 Jul	44.99	TUR	8 Jul	45.11	IRL	20 Aug	45.46	NED	8 Jul	45.84	CHI	20 May
44.68	YUG	8 Jul	45.00	ESP	8 Jul	45.14	UZB	29 Sep	45.68	ISR	8 Jul	45.89	INA	31 Aug
44.86	BUL	8 Jul	45.02	SKN	2 Jul	45.26	JPN	31 Aug	45.71	NZL-J	22 Oct			
44.86	CZE	8 Jul	45.10	SLO	8 Jul	45.29	AUT	8 Jul	45.78	POR	8 Jul			
44.89	HUN	16 Jun	45.11	PUR	17 Jun	45.31	TRI-J	24 Apr	45.82	CMR	29 Sep			

Hand timned

43.4A	MAD	Rahanitraniriana, Ratsimbazafy, Rakotozafy, Rakotondrabé	1		Antananarivo	27 Aug
44.9	PUR	Ortiz, Caraballo, Diana, Rivera	1		Ponce	10 Jun

Best at low altitude

43.38	AUS	Hutton, Hewitt, Peris-Kneebone, Gainsford-Taylor	1		Brisbane	3 Sep
44.25	RSA		2		Budapest	22 Jul

JUNIORS

43.91	GER	Kaufmann, Schielke, Grötzinger, Habel	1	WJ	Santiago	22 Oct
44.05	JAM	V Campbell, Palmer, K Stewart, N Graham	2	WJ	Santiago	22 Oct
44.55	FRA	Huyghes, Lamalle, Gérance, Belliard	2h2	WJ	Santiago	22 Oct
44.78	SWE	Rienas, J Kallur, S Kallur, Fernström	3	WJ	Santiago	22 Oct
44.89	ITA	Marchetti, Amerighi, Avogadri, Cali	4	WJ	Santiago	22 Oct
44.96	USA	D Jackson, Carpenter, Moore, Heantz	1	vCAN-j	Montreal	19 Jul
45.04	AUS	Spencer, Munro, Kleeberg, Porter	5	WJ	Santiago	22 Oct
45.23	POL	Flejszar, Wardowska, Hennig, Radoszewska	6	WJ	Santiago	22 Oct
45.31	TRI		2	Carifta	St. Georges	24 Apr
45.43	GBR	Selley, Thomas, Maylor, V James	3	v3N-j	Grossetto	7 Oct
45.70/90?	CAN	Lepp, Bayley, Samuel, Lopes	2	vUSA	Montréal	19 Jul
45.71	NZL	Spragg, Miller, Cowley, Brough	5h1	WJ	Santiago	22 Oct
45.96	USA		1		Norwalk	3 Jun
45.99A	VEN	Y García, Mejías, Legenort, Álvarez	1	SAm-y	Bogotá	4 Nov

4 X 200 METRES RELAY

1:27.46	USA Blue	Jenkins, Colander-Richardson, Perry, Jones	1	PennR	Philadelphia	29 Apr
1:31.01	Univ of S.Carolina USA	Me.Barber, Washington, Me.Lewis, Mi.Barber	2	PennR	Philadelphia	29 Apr

4 X 400 METRES RELAY

3:22.62	USA	Miles-Clark 50.86, Hennagan 51.57, Jones 49.46, Colander-Richardson 50.73	1	OG	Sydney	30 Sep
3:22.99	NGR	Jacob 51.3, Afolabi 50.4, Okafor 50.36, Opara 51.00	1h3	OG	Sydney	29 Sep
3:23.25	JAM	Richards 51.14, Scott 51.18, Hemmings 51.30, Graham 49.63	2	OG	Sydney	30 Sep
3:23.46	RUS	Sotnikova 52.21, Goncharenko 51.18, Kotlyarova 50.20, Privalova 49.81	3	OG	Sydney	30 Sep
3:23.80	NGR	Afolabi 52.09, Opara 50.97, Okafor 51.13, Ogunkoya 49.61	4	OG	Sydney	30 Sep
3:23.81	AUS	Peris-K 51.71, Lewis 51.69, Gainsford-Taylor 51.06, Freeman 49.35	5	OG	Sydney	30 Sep
3:23.95	USA	Miles-Clark 50.43, Hennagan 51.15, Anderson 50.62, Colander-Richardson 51.75	1h1	OG	Sydney	29 Sep
3:24.05	AUS	Lewis 51.2, Andrews 51.2, Pittman 51.10, Peris-Kneebone 50.53	2h3	OG	Sydney	29 Sep
3:24.40	CZE	Burianová 51.07, Benesová 51.00, Ficková 52.24, Fuchsová 50.09	3h3	OG	Sydney	29 Sep
3:25.22	CUB	Calatayud 51.62, Duporty 51.12, Bonne 51.4, Pernía 51.0	2h1	OG	Sydney	29 Sep
3:25.28	GBR	Frost 52.5, Fraser 50.4, Curbishley 51.6, Merry 50.8	1h2	OG	Sydney	29 Sep
3:25.50	RUS	Zykina 51.3, Rosikhin 51.5, Kulikova 51.45, Sotnikova 51.28	1	ECpS	Gateshead	16 Jul
3:25.65	JAM	Howell 52.6, Scott 50.6, Burgher 51.4, Richards 51.1	2h2	OG	Sydney	29 Sep
3:25.67	GBR	Danvers 53.14, Fraser 50.30, Curbishley 52.46, Merry 49.77	6	OG	Sydney	30 Sep
3:25.96	USA Red	Reid, Collins, Graham 51.8, Miles-Clark 50.3	1	PennR	Philadelphia	29 Apr
3:26.05	RUS	Sotnikova 52.1, Zykina 52.0, Goncharenko 50.0, Nazarova 52.0	3h2	OG	Sydney	29 Sep
3:26.31	BLR	Sologub 52.06, Budnik 51.11, Khlyustova 52.05, Kozak 50.09	3h1	OG	Sydney	29 Sep
3:27.02	GER	Ghosh 52.65, Urbansky 51.29, B.Rockmeier 52.09, Ekpo-Umoh 50.99	4h1	OG	Sydney	29 Sep
3:27.23	ITA	Graglia 53.1, Carbone 51.4, Piroddi 50.9, De Angeli 51.8	4h2	OG	Sydney	29 Sep
3:27.36	CAN	Haughton 54.10, Antoine 50.77, Williams 51.29, George 51.20	5h1	OG	Sydney	29 Sep
3:27.51	CZE	Burianová, Formanová, Benesová, Fuchsová	1	ECp1A	Nadderud	9 Jul
3:27.60	USA Sprint Capital	Warren, Colander-Richardson, Reynolds, Collins	1		Raleigh	1 Apr
3:27.70	GER	Ghosh 51.9, Urbansky 52.7, G.Rockmeier 51.78, Rohländer 51.38	2	ECpS	Gateshead	16 Jul

23 performances by teams from 12 nations

Mark		Name	Pos	Meet	Venue	Date
3:28.02	SEN	Diop 51.27, M T Diouf 51.70, A Diouf 52.53, Thiam 51.52	4h3	OG	Sydney	29 Sep
3:28.11	IND	Kuriakose, Philip, P Kaur, Beenamol	1	NC	Chennai	31 Jul
3:30.83	BAR	Straker 54.96, Blackett 51.02, Williams 51.43, Oxley 53.42	5h3	OG	Sydney	29 Sep
3:31.16	POL	Pskit, Pacholak, Lancuchowska, Prokopek	1		Sopot	12 Aug
3:31.87	Kiev UKR	Vorovchenko, Debelaya, Movchan, Pygyda	1	NC	Kiev	6 Aug
3:32.24	IRL	Shinkins 52.0, McCarthy 53.1, Maher 53.94, Sheehy 53.28	6h3	OG	Sydney	29 Sep
3:32.36	ROM	Popovici, Rus, Burlacu, Ruicu	1	Balk	Kavala	2 Jul
3:32.45	ESP	Alba 53.67, Carabali 51.74, Bravo 53.95, Martínez 53.09	6h1	OG	Sydney	29 Sep
	(20)					
3:32.89	CMR	M Nguimgo, K Béwouda, Komgang, Mani	1	AfCh	Alger	14 Jul
3:33.07	UZB	Vorobyeva, Piskunova, Kremlyova, Senkina	1		Bangkok	18 May
3:33.11	HUN	E Szabò, Balazsic, Gróf, Petráhn	2	ECp1A	Nadderud	9 Jul
3:33.16	FRA	Bévis, Dorsile, Rangassamy, Mormand	5	ECp-S	Gateshead	16 Jul
3:33.16	Guangdong CHN	He Linlin, Zhou Wei, Li Xiashu, Zhong Shaoting	1	NC	Luohe	22 Oct
3:33.30	PUR	Castro Mortales, Moya, Cruz, Salas	6h2	OG	Sydney	29 Sep
3.34.51	COL	Brock, Palacios, Lucumi, González	1	IbAm	Rio de Janeiro	21 May
3.35.00	SLO	Macus, Langerholc, Steblovnik-Ceplak, Prokofijev	7h3	OG	Sydney	29 Sep
3.35.11	SWE	Geurtsen, F Svensson, L Olsson, Lundgren	4	ECp1A	Nadderud	9 Jul
3.35.26	Vasco da Gama BRA	Aquino, dos Reis Santos, França, Figueirêdo	1		Rio de Janeiro	6 Aug
	(30)					

3.35.36	YUG	2 Jul	3.37.86	SUI	9 Jul	3.40.57	TUR	9 Jul	3.42.76	CRO	9 Jul	3.44.13	NZL	12 Mar
3.36.37	POR	9 Jul	3.37.91	NED	9 Jul	3.41.03	LAT	20 Aug	3.42.91	MAR	14 Jul	3.44.84	EST	9 Jul
3.37.15	JPN	31 Aug	3.38.86	LTU	9 Jul	3.41.21	SVK	9 Jul	3.43.34	BEL	9 Jul	3.44.84	DEN	9 Jul
3.37.17	GRN	30 Jul	3.39.91	ISR	9 Jul	3.41.51	GRE	2 Jul	3.43.42	RSA	4 Mar			
3.37.42	FIN	3 Sep	3.40.25	BUL	9 Jul	3.41.91	SKN	10 Jun	3.43.46	TRI-J	24 Apr			

JUNIORS

3:33.82	GBR	Wall, Meadows, Thieme, Miller	1	WJ	Santiago	22 Oct
3:33.99	JAM	Morgan, Gayle, McLaughlin, M Walker	2	WJ	Santiago	22 Oct
3:34.49	ROM	Marchis, Barbulescu, Rus, Rîpanu	3	WJ	Santiago	22 Oct
3:36.11	POL	Bejnar, Dydo, Tlustochowska, Lemiesz	4	WJ	Santiago	22 Oct
3:36.70	GER	E Müller, Hoffman, Balkow, Kettenis	5	WJ	Santiago	22 Oct
3:37.83	UKR	Chervan, Petlyuk, Yefremova, Pygyda	6	WJ	Santiago	22 Oct
3:38.37	United Stars TC, USA		1		Buffalo	30 Jul
3:38.66	AUS	Jauncey, Dressler, Irwin, Pittman	7	WJ	Santiago	22 Oct
3:39.31	ITA	Ellecosta, Riva, Damiani, Reina	2	v3N-j	Grosseto	7 Oct
3:40.24	GRN	George, Bernard, Morain, Regis	2	CAC	San Juan	16 Jul
3:42.13	BAR		2	Carifta	St. Georges	24 Apr
3:42.92	RUS	Bufalova, Ryakhovskaya, Vecherkevich, Firova	1		Cheboksary	9 Jul
3:42.99	BRA	Araújo, Teodoro, de Acevedo, Dias	1	SAm-j	São Leopoldo	8 Oct
3:43.46	TRI		3	Carifta	St. Georges	24 Apr
3:45.48	VEN	Mesias, Garcia, Sequea, Sequea	2		São Leopoldo	8 Oct

4 X 1500 METRES RELAY

17:09.75	AUS	Harvey, Clarke, Richardson, Jamieson	1		London (BP)	25 Jun
17:19.09	IRL	Lynch, Fitzgerald, Thom, O'Sullivan	2		London (BP)	25 Jun

4 X 100 METRES HURDLES

54.57	Louisiana State University USA	Leaverton, Sams, Bethel, Bates	1	PennR	Philadelphia	29 Apr

3000 METRES WALK

11:58.06	Erica	Alfridi	ITA	22.2.68	1		Milano	7 Jun
12:02.44	Elisabetta	Perrone	ITA	9.7.68	2		Milano	7 Jun
12:07.82	Nadezhda	Ryashkina	RUS	22.1.67	3		Milano	7 Jun
12:17.81	Natalya	Fedoskina	RUS	25.6.80	1		Formia	3 Jun
12:18.02	Kjersti	Plätzer	NOR	18.1.72	1		Steinkjer	13 Aug
12:18.19	Gillian	O'Sullivan	IRL	21.8.76	1		Castleisland	11 Jun
12:26.21	Annarita	Sidoti	ITA	25.7.69	5		Milano	7 Jun
12:28.78	Susana	Feitor	POR	28.1.75	1		Braga	21 Jun
12:30.72	Beate	Gummelt	GER	4.2.68	1	NC	Braunschweig	30 Jul
12:38.00	Lisa	Barbieri	ITA	18.5.78	6		Milano	7 Jun
12:39.62	Sara	Stevenson	USA	.80	1		Burnaby	26 May

12:40.32	Nora	Leksir	FRA	13.5.74	3 Jun	12:47.5	Jolanta	Dukure	LAT	20.9.79	23 Jul
12:44.48	Olga	Panfyorova	RUS	21.8.77	3 Jun	12:48.36	Katarzyna	Radtke	POL	31.8.69	1 Jul

Indoors

12:05.66	Beate	Gummelt	GER	4.2.68	1	NC	Sindelfingen	13 Feb
12:10.18		Alfridi			1	NC	Genova	12 Feb
12:14.51	Annarita	Sidoti	ITA	25.7.69	2	NC	Genova	12 Feb

Mark	Name		Nat	Born	Pos	Meet	Venue	Date
12:16.92	Cristiana	Pellino	ITA	21.9.70	3	NC	Genova	12 Feb
12:25.76	Sabine	Zimmer	GER-J	6.2.81	2	NC	Sindelfingen	13 Feb
12:30.48	Ana Maria	Groza	ROM	1.6.76	1	NC	Bucuresti	5 Feb

12:39.82	Veronica	Budileanu	ROM	27.2.76	5 Feb	12:46.45	Fatiha	Ouali	FRA	28.10.74	19 Feb
12:41.98	Olive	Loughnane	IRL	14.1.76	12 Feb	12:48.79	Daniela	Cîrlan	ROM	18.9.80	5 Feb
12:45.28	Elke	Ennemoser	ITA	17.1.78	12 Feb	12:49.19	Anne Catherine	Berthonnaud	FRA	26.10.66	19 Feb

5000 METRES WALK

Mark	Name		Nat	Born	Pos	Meet	Venue	Date
20:46.3	Kjersti	Plätzer	NOR	18.1.72	1	NC	Kristiansand	20 Aug
21:01.66	Cristiana	Pellino	ITA	21.9.70	1		Roma	3 Jun
21:01.78	Annarita	Sidoti	ITA	25.7.69	2		Roma	3 Jun
21:02.0	Olga	Lukyanchuk	UKR	7.12.76	1		Kiev	17 Jun
21:02.99	Erica	Alfridi	ITA	22.2.68	1		Pescara	22 Jul
21:15.49	Beate	Gummelt	GER	4.2.68	1	NC	Braunschweig	30 Jul
21:18.96	Gillian	O'Sullivan	IRL	21.8.76	1		Castleisland	11 Jun
21:20.61	Maya	Sazonova	KAZ	28.5.65	1		Almaty	28 May
21:23.54		Gao Kelian	CHN-J	15.8.83	1		Chengdu	6 Sep
21:24.07		Pellino			1	NC	Milano	7 Sep
21:24.34	Jolanta	Dukure	LAT	20.9.79	1		Valmiera	14 Jul
21:29.39		Li Hong	CHN	1.6.79	2rA	NSG	Chengdu	6 Sep
	(12/11)							
21:35.08	Susana	Feitor	POR	28.1.75	1		Rio Maior	10 May
21:36.2	Lisa	Barbieri	ITA	18.5.78	1		Peschiera	27 Apr
21:39.46	Sabine	Zimmer	GER-J	6.2.81	2	NC	Braunschweig	30 Jul
21:42.10	Melanie	Seeger	GER	8.1.77	3	NC	Braunschweig	30 Jul
21:42.86	Kaori	Nikaido	JPN	25.7.79	1		Toyama	15 Oct
21:45.16	Lisa	Paolini	AUS	10.12.62	1		Sydney	20 Feb
21:49.0+	Tatyana	Kozlova	RUS-J	2.9.83	1	in 10km	Moskva	20 May
21:49.5	Nevena	Dimitrova	BUL	17.6.72	1	NC	Sofia	17 Jun

21:56.0+	Lyudmila	Yefimkina	RUS-J	22.8.81	20 May	22:00.88	Sara	Stevenson	USA	.80	29 Apr
21:56.07	Rossella	Giordano	ITA	1.12.72	7 Sep	22:00.97	Gisella	Orsini	ITA	9.12.71	7 Sep
21:59.2	Rocio	Florido	ESP	16.1.76	11 Aug	22:01.53	Olive	Loughnane	IRL	14.1.76	11 Jun
						22:02.01		Kim Mi-jung	KOR	10.6.79	10 Aug

Indoors

Mark	Name		Nat	Born	Pos	Meet	Venue	Date
21:00.0	Tamara	Kovalenko	RUS	5.6.64	1		Moskva	23 Jan
21:04.8	Olimpiada	Ivanova	RUS	5.5.70	2		Moskva	23 Jan
21:20.0	Tatyana	Gudkova	RUS	23.1.78	1		Chelyabinsk	31 Dec
21:26.06	Sonata	Milusauskaité	LTU	21.8.73	1		Panevezys	4 Feb
21:45.8	Margarita	Nazarova	RUS	1.10.76	3		Moskva	23 Jan
21:50.8	Tatyana	Matyushkina	RUS	22.1.79	4		Moskva	23 Jan

JUNIORS

Three above plus

Mark	Name		Nat	Born	Pos	Meet	Venue	Date
21:56.0+	Lyudmila	Yefimkina	RUS-J	22.8.81	2	in 10km	Moskva	20 May
22:13.84		Zuo Yan	CHN	.12.83	4		Chengdu	6 Sep
22:14.25		Jian Xingli	CHN	18.8.83	5		Chengdu	6 Sep
22:14.6	Sofiya	Kusevanova	RUS	12.6.84	1	NC-y	Moskva	20 May
22:24.37	Sachiko	Konishi	JPN	4.2.82	5		Toyama	15 Oct
22:27.8	Alena	Zenkova	RUS	1.1.82	1		Cheboksary	6 Oct
22:33.23	Beatriz	Pascual	ESP	9.5.82	1		Santander	30 Sep
22:38.4	Kseniya	Ishcheykina	RUS	.84	2	NC-y	Moskva	20 May
22:42.8	Yekaterina	Dergunova	RUS	13.8.82	2		Cheboksary	6 Oct
22:48,2	Irina	Petrova	RUS	27.5.85	3	NC-y	Moskva	20 May
22:49.8	Irina	Korotkova	RUS	31.5.82	3		Cheboksary	6 Oct

5 KILOMETRES ROAD WALK

Mark	Name		Nat	Born	Pos	Meet	Venue	Date
20:05	Olga	Polyakova	RUS	23.9.80	1		Saransk	28 May
20:19	Yuliya	Voyevodina	RUS	5.5.70	2		Saransk	28 May
20:24	Lyudmila	Yefimkina	RUS-J	22.8.81	3		Saransk	28 May
20:27	Tatyana	Kozlova	RUS-J	2.9.83	4		Saransk	28 May
20:30	Olimpiada	Ivanova	RUS	5.5.70	5		Saransk	28 May
20:40	Elisabetta	Perrone	ITA	9.7.68	1		Ivrea	8 Oct
20:58		Ivanova			2		Ovrea	8 Oct
21:02	Erica	Alfridi	ITA	22.2.68	1		San Pietro Clarenza	5 Aug
21:02	Cristiana	Pellino	ITA	21.9.70	2		San Pietro Clarenza	5 Aug
21.06	Valentina	Tsybulskaya	BLR	19.2.68	1		Druskininkai	3 Sep
21:12+	Tatyana	Gudkova	RUS	23.1.78	1=	in 20k	Moskva	19 May
21:12+	Nadezhda	Ryashkina	RUS	22.1.67	1=	in 20k	Moskva	19 May
21:13+		Polyakova			3=	in 20k	Moskva	19 May
21:13+	Irina	Stankina	RUS	25.3.77	3=	in 20k	Moskva	19 May
21:15+		Ivanova			5	in 20k	Moskva	19 May

Mark	Name		Nat	Born	Pos	Meet	Venue	Date
21:16+	Tamara	Kovalenko	RUS	5.6.64	6	in 20k	Moskva	19 May
21:19	Tatyana	Korotkova	RUS	24.4.80	6		Saransk	28 May
21:20	Katarzyna	Radtke	POL	31.8.69	1		Kraków	3 Jun
21:21+	Maya	Sazonova	KAZ	28.5.65	7	in 20k	Moskva	19 May
21:22+		Ivanova			1	in 20k	Eisenhüttenstadt	17 Jun
	(20/15)	Others where superior to track bests						
21:25	Vera	Nacharkina	RUS	17.2.66	7		Saransk	28 May
21:28	Larisa	Safronova	RUS	6.1.80	8	in 20k	Moskva	19 May
21:38	Natalya	Misyulya	BLR	14.4.66	2		Kraków	3 Jun
21:42+	Norica	Cîmpean	ROM	22.3.72	2	in 20k	Eisenhüttenstadt	17 Jun
21:45+	Rimma	Makarova	RUS	25.2.63	11	in 20k	Moskva	19 May
21:47	Eva	Pérez	ESP	18.7.75	1		Viladecans	6 Feb

10 KILOMETRES WALK

Mark	Name		Nat	Born	Pos	Meet	Venue	Date
42:37	Olga	Lukyanchuk	UKR	7.12.76	1		Mukachevo	21 Oct
42:42+	Tatyana	Gudkova	RUS	23.1.78	1=	in 20k	Moskva	19 May
42:42+	Tamara	Kovalenko	RUS	5.6.64	1=	in 20k	Moskva	19 May
42:42+	Nadezhda	Ryashkina	RUS	22.1.67	1=	in 20k	Moskva	19 May
42:43+	Olga	Polyakova	RUS	23.9.80	4=	in 20k	Moskva	19 May
42:43+	Olimpiada	Ivanova	RUS	5.5.70	4=	in 20k	Moskva	19 May
42:44+	Irina	Stankina	RUS	25.3.77	6	in 20k	Moskva	19 May
42:56		Ivanova			1	in 20k	Eisenhüttenstadt	17 Jun
42:59	Jolanta	Dukure	LAT	20.9.79	1		Aizpute	21 Jul
43:09	Erica	Alfridi	ITA	22.2.68	1		Vittorio Veneto	16 Jul
43:11		Wang Yan	CHN	2.5.71	1		L'Hospitalet	30 Apr
43:15	Elisabetta	Perrone	ITA	9.7.68	2		Vittorio Veneto	16 Jul
43:21.1t	Kjersti	Plätzer	NOR	18.1.72	1	NC	Kristiansand	18 Aug
43:29	Gillian	O'Sullivan	IRL	21.8.76	1		Dublin	15 Jul
43:30.22t	Encarna	Granados	ESP	30.1.72	1	NC	Barcelona	2 Sep
43:33	Svetlana	Tolstaya	KAZ	9.8.71	1		Birstonas	6 May
43:33.92t	Maria	Vasco	ESP	26.12.75	2	NC	Barcelona	2 Sep
	(17/16)							
43:35+	Annarita	Sidoti	ITA	25.7.69	2=	in 20k	Eisenhüttenstadt	17 Jun
43:35+	Valentina	Tsybulskaya	BLR	19.2.68	2=	in 20k	Eisenhüttenstadt	17 Jun
43:35.2 t	Lyudmila	Yefimkina	RUS-J	22.8.81	1	NC-j	Moskva	20 May
43:36+	Valentina	Savchuk	UKR	19.1.75	7=	in 20k	Eisenhüttenstadt	17 Jun
	(20)							
43:36+	Larisa	Khmelnitskaya	BLR	22.1.67	7=	in 20k	Eisenhüttenstadt	17 Jun
43:36	Rossella	Giordano	ITA	1.12.72	3		Vittorio Veneto	16 Jul
43:43+	Maya	Sazonova	KAZ	28.5.65	7	in 20k	Moskva	19 May
43:47	Anita	Liepina	LAT	17.11.67	2		Aizpute	21 Jul
43:49.5t	Cristiana	Pellino	ITA	21.9.70	1		Castelnovo Monti	26 Aug
43:51	Norica	Cîmpean	ROM	22.3.72	1	NC	Sf.Gheorghe	23 Jul
43:55+	Susana	Feitor	POR	28.1.75	1	in 20k	Hildesheim	9 Jul
43:56+	Natalya	Fedoskina	RUS	25.6.80	2	in 20k	Hildesheim	9 Jul
43:57+	Yuliya	Voyevodina	RUS	5.5.70	8=	in 20k	Moskva	19 May
43:57+	Larisa	Safronova	RUS	6.1.80	8=	in 20k	Moskva	19 May
	(30)							
43:57	Lyudmila	Yegorova	UKR	4.10.74	2		Mukachevo	21 Oct
43:58+	Tatyana	Korotkova	RUS	24.4.80	10	in 20k	Moskva	19 May
43:58		Li Hong	CHN	1.6.79	1	NC	Lushun	3 Jun
44:00		Xu Aihui	CHN	25.4.78	2	NC	Lushun	3 Jun
44:01	Ana-Maria	Groza	ROM	1.6.76	2	NC	Sf.Gheorghe	23 Jul
44:06+	Jane	Saville	AUS	5.11.74	1	in 20k	København	6 May
44:08+		Liu Hongyu	CHN	11.1.75	1	in 20k	Leamington	23 Apr
44:19+	Rimma	Makarova	RUS	25.2.63	4	in 20k	Adler	20 Feb
44:24	Eva	Pérez	ESP	18.7.75	1		El Prat de Llobergat	13 Feb
44:24.43 t	Tatyana	Kozlova	RUS-J	2.9.83	2	WJ	Santiago de Chile	20 Sep
	(40)							
44:26		Han Min	CHN-J	[illegible]	3	NC	Lushun	3 Jun
44:28+	Daniela	Cîrlan	ROM	18.9.80	10=	in 20k	Eisenhüttenstadt	17 Jun
44:28	Katarzyna	Radtke	POL	31.8.69	1	NC	Kraków	5 Aug
44:33+	Natalya	Misyulya	BLR	14.4.66	3	in 20k	Hildesheim	9 Jul
44:34+	Guadalupe	Sánchez	MEX	14.2.74	2	in 20k	Vallensbäk	6 May
44:36+	Margarita	Nazarova	RUS	1.10.76	5=	in 20k	Adler	20 Feb
44:36.0t		Gao Hongmiao	CHN	17.3.74	1	NC-t	Qufu	17 Sep
44:37+	Natalya	Shiviryeva	RUS	31.8.78	8	in 20k	Adler	20 Feb
44:39+		Xue Ailing	CHN	12.2.79	3	in 20k	Rio Maior	15 Apr
44:39		Gao Kelian	CHN-J	15.8.83	4	NC	Lushun	3 Jun
	(50)							

Mark	Name		Nat	Born	Pos	Meet	Venue	Date
44:39+	Tatyana	Ragozina	UKR	3.9.64	13	in 20k	Eisenhüttenstadt	17 Jun
44:39.9 t		Jiang Qiuyan	CHN-J	5.7.83	2	NC-t	Qufu	17 Sep
44:40+	Mária	Rosza-Urbanik	HUN	12.2.67	15	in 20k	Eisenhüttenstadt	17 Jun
44:42		Hu Guangkun	CHN	4.8.76	5	NC	Lushun	3 Jun
44:50+	Claudia	Iovan ¶	ROM	25.2.78	1	in 20k	Békéscsaba	9 Apr
44:50	Kristina	Saltanovic	LTU	20.2.75	2	NC	Birstonas	6 May
44:52	Lisa	Barbieri	ITA	18.5.78	6		Vittorio Veneto	16 Jul
44:52.2 t	Teresa	Linares	ESP	29.4.69	1		La Laguna	20 Feb
44:55+	Graciela	Mendoza	MEX	22.3.63	2=	in 20k	Sydney	28 Sep
44:55+		Wang Liping	CHN	8.7.76	2=	in 20k	Sydney	28 Sep
	(60)							
44:57+	Olga	Kardopoltseva	BLR	11.9.66	16	in 20k	Eisenhüttenstadt	17 Jun
44:59+	Kerry	Saxby-Junna	AUS	2.6.61	9	in 20k	Sydney	28 Sep
45:02	Melanie	Seeger	GER	8.1.77	1		Dubai	15 Jul
45:07	Oslaidis	Cruz	CUB	12.3.74	1		Sancti Spiritus	17 Mar
45:07+	Elena	Isar	ROM	7.12.71	4	in 20k	Békéscsaba	9 Apr
45:09.57 t	Lisa	Kehler	GBR	15.3.67	1	NC	Birmingham	13 Aug
45:10+	Tatyana	Sibileva	RUS	17.5.80	12	in 20k	Adler	20 Feb
45:10		Guo Dongmei	CHN-J	5.2.83	7	NC	Lushun	3 Jun
45:11		Chen Haiyan	CHN		8	NC	Lushun	3 Jun
45:11.3 t	Gisella	Orsini	ITA	9.12.71	5		Castelnovo Monti	26 Aug
	(70)							
45:12	Sonata	Milusauskaité	LTU	31.8.73	3	NC	Birstonas	6 May
45:13+	Mara	Ibañez	MEX	17.12.74	4	in 20k	Naumburg	30 Apr
45:13+	Abigail	Saenz	MEX	21.4.77	4	in 20k	Vallensbäk	6 May
45:13.6 t	Dina	Suleymanova	RUS	26.7.79				8 Oct
45:14+	Beate	Gummelt	GER	4.2.68	5	in 20k	Naumburg	30 Apr
45:15.21t	Lisa	Paolini	AUS	10.12.62	1		Sydney	18 Aug
45:16	Sabine	Zimmer	GER-J	6.2.81	1		Aschersleben	9 Apr
45:25+	Anikó	Szebenszky	HUN	12.8.65	5	in 20k	Békéscsaba	9 Apr
45:25.60 t	Rocío	Florido	ESP	16.1.76	4	NC	Barcelona	3 Sep
45:26	Lyudmila	Dolgopolova	BLR	11.8.69	3	NC	Podebrady	16 Apr
	(80)							
45:27	Yelena	Miroshnichenko	UKR	1.3.77	3		Mukachevo	21 Oct
45:30	Annett	Amberg	GER	9.2.73	2		Aschersleben	9 Apr
45:30+	Kathrin	Boyde	GER	4.12.70	22	in 20k	Eisenhüttenstadt	17 Jun
45:31+	Kaori	Nikaido	JPN	25.7.79	1	in 20k	Takahata	29 Oct
45:33+	María del R	Sánchez	MEX	26.10.73	12	in 20k	Naumburg	30 Apr
45:33+	Nora	Leksir	FRA	13.5.74	26	in 20k	Eisenhüttenstadt	17 Jun
45:33	Marina	Tikhonova	BLR-J	14.12.83	2	ECp-J	Eisenhüttenstadt	18 Jun
45:34+	Lyudmila	Dedekina	RUS	5.1.79	14	in 20k	Adler	20 Feb
45:34.5 t	Margarita	Turova	BLR	28.12.80	1	NC	Brest	1 Aug
45:35+	Vera	Zozulya	UKR	31.8.70	28	in 20k	Eisenhüttenstadt	17 Jun
	(90)							
45:35	Alena	Zenkova	RUS-J	1.1.82	3	ECp-J	Eisenhüttenstadt	18 Jun
45:37		Wang Qingqing	CHN-J	7.2.83	9	NC	Lushun	3 Jun
45:40	Olga	Panfyorova	RUS	21.8.77	3		Lanciano	12 Mar
45:42+	Michelle	Rohl	USA	12.11.65	1	in 20k	Kenosha	13 May
45:42.21 t	Anne Haaland	Simonsen	NOR	18.6.80	1		Fana	6 May
45:42.68 t		Sun Chunfang	CHN	1.3.77	2	AsiC	Jakarta	30 Aug
45:44		Zang Yan	CHN-J	13.12.83	10	NC	Lushun	3 Jun
45:48	Fatiha	Ouali	FRA	28.10.74	1	NC	Nice	6 Aug
45:50+	Athiná	Papayiánni	GRE	18.8.80	22=	in 20k	Sydney	28 Sep
45:50+		Yuan Yufang	MAS	1.2.76	22=	in 20k	Sydney	28 Sep
	(100)							

45:53	Andrea	Meloni	GER	1.10.67	29 Oct
45:55	Yelena	Nikolayeva	RUS	17.3.66	12 Mar
45:57		Yang Wenjing	CHN	26.9.79	3 Jun
45:59.95t	Giovana	Irusta	BOL	26.9.75	20 May
46:02+	Yelena	Arshintseva	RUS	5.4.71	20 Feb
46:05	Mónika	Pesti	HUN	27.6.75	16 Apr
46:05		Li Yurui	CHN-J	18.1.81	10 Sep
46:06.80t	Beatriz	Pascual	ESP-J	9.5.82	2 Sep
46:09+	Ryoko	Tadamasa	JPN	9.5.76	29 Oct
46:12+	Debbi	Lawrence	USA	15.10.61	13 May
46:14	Emanuela	Perilli	ITA	19.5.73	16 Jul
46:14.7 t	Tatyana	Dotsenko	RUS-J	24.4.81	20 May
46:18+	Natalya	Trofimova	RUS	17.1.75	20 Feb
46:20		Liu Qimei	CHN	16.5.77	3 Jun
46:27		Li Haiyan	CHN	27.5.79	3 Jun
46:32+	Tatyana	Matyushkina	RUS	22.1.79	19 May
46:32	Olive	Loughnane	IRL	14.1.76	15 Jul
46:32		Jian Xingli	CHN-J	18.8.83	10 Sep
46:34.5 t	Annarita	Fidanza	ITA	3.8.78	26 Aug
46:36+	Elisa	Rigaudo	ITA	17.6.80	23 Apr
46:40+	Sara	Stevenson	USA	.80	13 May
46:41+	Zuzana	Blazeková	SVK	1.7.80	17 Jun
46:42+	Ildikó	Ilyés	HUN	28.8.66	25 Mar
46:42+		Kim Mi-jung	KOR	10.6.79	28 Sep
46:43+	Cheryl	Webb	AUS	3.10.76	15 Apr
46:45		Shi Na	CHN-J	17.2.81	3 Jun
46:45	Elke	Ennemoser	ITA	17.1.78	16 Jul
46:46.12t	Natividad	Collado	GUA	20.11.71	6 May
46:47+	Svetlana	Kalitka	UKR	28.3.70	25 Mar
46:47+	Alexándra	Tzioúti ¶	GRE	1.1.71	17 Jun
46:49		Ha Mingming	CHN-J	15.4.82	3 Jun
46:52+	Ivis	Martínez	ESA	5.1.71	28 Sep

Mark		Name	Nat	Born	Pos	Meet	Venue	Date
46:55	Sylwia	Korzeniowska	POL	25.4.80				26 Aug
47:00+	Vanessa	Espinosa	ESP	4.2.79				20 May

Indoors

46:32.0 Tatyana Melnikova RUS 12.9.75 31 Dec

Other best track times

44:00.0 Kovalenko 1 Rostov-na-Donu 27 Jun

44:14.6 Perrone 2 Castelnovo Monti 26 Aug

44:16.2 Ivanova 1 Rostov-na-Donu 27 Jun

44:35.5 Sidoti 4 Castelnovo Monti 26 Aug

44:36.79 Feitor 1 NC Coimbra 13 Aug

44:59.90 Li Hong 1 AsiC Jakarta 30 Aug

45:02.96 Pérez 3 NC Barcelona 2 Sep

45:09.4+ Giordano 1 in 20k Almada 4 Aug

45:32.5 Safronova 27 Jun

45:38.90 R Sánchez 20 May

45:56.5 Dukure 20 May

46:06.1 Zenkova 20 May

46:12.66 Yuan Yufang 30 Aug

46:14.2 Perilli 26 Aug

46:19.8 Liepina 20 May

46:21.6 Guo Dongmei 17 Sep

46:33.1 Hu Guangkun 17 Sep

46:49.97 Zimmer 20 Oct

46:51.55 Saenz 20 May

46:57.40 Papayiánni 23 Apr

Drugs disqualification

Mark		Name	Nat	Born	Pos	Meet	Venue	Date
44:35	Claudia	Iovan ¶	ROM	25.2.78	(1)		La Coruña	20 May
45:47.6t	Alexándra	Tzioúti ¶	GRE	1.1.71	(1)		Athína	29 Jul

JUNIORS

See main list for top 11 juniors. 11 performances by 9 women to 45:30. Additional marks and further juniors:

Yefimkina 44:07.741 WJ Santiago 20 Oct

Kozlova 44:34.8 2 NC-j Moskva 20 May 45:28R 1 ECp-J Eisenhüttenstadt 18 Jun

Jiang Qiuyan 44:45 6 NC Lushun 3 Jun

Mark		Name	Nat	Born	Pos	Meet	Venue	Date
46:05		Li Yurui	CHN	18.1.81	2rA	NSG	Chengdu	10 Sep
46:06.80 t	Beatriz	Pascual	ESP	9.5.82	5		Barcelona	2 Sep
46:14.7 t	Tatyana	Dotsenko	RUS	24.4.81	4	NC-j	Moskva	20 May
46:32		Jian Xingli	CHN	18.8.83	3rA	NSG	Chengdu	10 Sep
46:45		Shi Na	CHN	17.2.81	14	NC	Lushun	3 Jun
46:49		Ha Mingming	CHN	15.4.82	15	NC	Lushun	3 Jun
47:01.91t	Edina	Füsti	HUN	24.6.82	1		Nyiregyháza	15 Jul
47:08	Alina	Olaru	ROM	13.10.82	7	ECp-J	Eisenhüttenstadt	18 Jun
47:10.96t	Athansia	Tsoumeléka (20)	GRE	2.1.82	4	WJ	Santiago de Chile	20 Oct

Best track

46:21.6 Guo Dongmei 4 NC-t Qufu 17 Sep

46:49.97 Zimmer 3 WJ Santiago de Chile 20 Oct

20 KILOMETRES WALK

Mark		Name	Nat	Born	Pos	Meet	Venue	Date
1:25:18	Tatyana	Gudkova	RUS	23.1.78	1	NC	Moskva	19 May
1:25:20	Olga	Polyakova	RUS	23.9.80	2	NC	Moskva	19 May
1:25:29	Irina	Stankina	RUS	25.3.77	3	NC	Moskva	19 May
1:25:59	Tamara	Kovalenko	RUS	5.6.64	4	NC	Moskva	19 May
1:26:08	Olimpiada	Ivanova	RUS	5.5.70	5	NC	Moskva	19 May
1:26:48		Ivanova			1	ECp	Eisenhüttenstadt	17 Jun
1:27:42	Elisabetta	Perrone	ITA	9.7.68	2	ECp	Eisenhüttenstadt	17 Jun
1:27:53	Kjersti	Plätzer	NOR	18.1.72	3	ECp	Eisenhüttenstadt	17 Jun
1:27:55		Liu Hongyu	CHN	11.1.75	1		Rio Maior	15 Apr
1:28:06	Nadezhda	Ryashkina	RUS	22.1.67	6	NC	Moskva	19 May
1:28:06	Erica	Alfridi (10)	ITA	22.2.68	4	ECp	Eisenhüttenstadt	17 Jun
1:28:08		Stankina			1	NC-w	Adler	20 Feb
1:28:16		Ryashkina			2	NC-w	Adler	20 Feb
1:28:19	Susana	Feitor	POR	28.1.75	1		Hildesheim	9 Jul
1:28:24	Natalya	Misyulya	BLR	16.4.66	1	NC	Soligorsk	13 May
1:28:27		Wang Yan	CHN	2.5.71	2		Rio Maior	15 Apr
1:28:33		Wang Liping	CHN	8.7.76	1	NC2	Lushun	3 Jun
1:28:38	Annarita	Sidoti	ITA	25.7.69	5	ECp	Eisenhüttenstadt	17 Jun
1:28:40		Liu Hongyu			1		Leamington	23 Apr
1:28:52		Ivanova			3	NC-w	Adler	20 Feb
1:28:52	Natalya	Fedoskina	RUS	25.6.80	2		Hildesheim	9 Jul
1:28:56	Jane	Saville	AUS	5.11.74	1		København	6 May
1:28:56	Larisa	Khmelnitskaya	BLR	23.9.71	2	NC	Soligorsk	13 May
1:28:59	Norica	Cîmpean	ROM	22.3.72	6	ECp	Eisenhüttenstadt	17 Jun
1:29:05		Wang Liping			1	OG	Sydney	28 Sep
1:29:06	Valentina	Savchuk	UKR	19.1.75	4	RUS-w	Adler	20 Feb
1:29:10		Alfridi			1		Taranto	19 Mar
1:29:10		Perrone			2		Taranto	10 Mar
1:29:16		Savchuk			7	ECp	Eisenhüttenstadt	17 Jun
1:29:20		Liu Hongyu			1		Naumburg	30 Apr
	(30/20)							
1:29:23	Lyudmila	Dolgopolova	BLR	11.8.69	3	NC	Soligorsk	13 May
1:29:36	Kerry	Saxby-Junna	AUS	2.6.61	2		Naumburg	30 Apr
1:29:39	Claudia	Iovan ¶	ROM	25.2.78	1	NC	Békéscsaba	9 Apr
1:29:39	Yuliya	Voyevodina	RUS	17.10.71	7	NC	Moskva	19 May
1:29:45		Sun Chunfang	CHN	1.3.77	2	NC2	Lushun	3 Jun

Mark	Name		Nat	Born	Pos	Meet	Venue	Date
1:29:47	Rossella	Giordano	ITA	1.12.72	3		Hildesheim	9 Jul
1:29:59	Ana-Maria	Groza	ROM	1.6.76	2	NC	Békéscsaba	9 Apr
1:30:17	Tatyana	Korotkova	RUS	24.4.80	6	NC-w	Adler	20 Feb
1:30:18	Maya	Sazonova	KAZ	28.5.65	8	RUS Ch	Moskva	19 May
1:30:19	Valentina	Tsybulskaya	BLR	19.2.68	8	ECp	Eisenhüttenstadt	17 Jun
	(30)							
1:30:20	Maria	Vasco	ESP	26.12.75	4	v4N	Leamington	23 Apr
1:30:31	Anikó	Szebenszky	HUN	12.8.65	3	NC	Békéscsaba	9 Apr
1:30:36		Tang Yinghua	CHN	18.5.73	3	NC2	Lushun	3 Jun
1:30:40	Rimma	Makarova	RUS	25.2.63	7	NC-w	Adler	20 Feb
1:30:41	Larisa	Safronova	RUS	6.1.80	1		Cheboksary	6 Oct
1:30:42	Kathrin	Boyde	GER	4.12.70	4		Naumburg	30 Apr
1:30:42	Cristiana	Pellino	ITA	21.9.70	9	ECp	Eisenhüttenstadt	17 Jun
1:30:44	Svetlana	Tolstaya	KAZ	9.8.71	1	NC	Almaty	31 Mar
1:30:49	Guadelupe	Sánchez	MEX	3.1.71	2		København	6 May
1:30:51	Tatyana	Sibilyova	RUS	17.5.80	8	NC-w	Adler	20 Feb
	(40)							
1:30:51		Pan Hailian	CHN	21.11.77	4	NC2	Lushun	3 Jun
1:30:58	Margarita	Nazarova	RUS	1.10.76	9	NC-w	Adler	20 Feb
1:31:13	Olga	Kardopoltseva	BLR	11.9.66	4	NC	Soligorsk	13 May
1:31:15	Nora	Leksir	FRA	13.5.74	11	ECp	Eisenhüttenstadt	17 Jun
1:31:21	Maria	Rosza-Urbanik	HUN	12.2.67	12	ECp	Eisenhüttenstadt	17 Jun
1:31:26	Vera	Zozulya	UKR	31.8.70	1	NC	Kiev	5 Aug
1:31:30	Daniela	Cîrlan	ROM	18.9.80	13	ECp	Eisenhüttenstadt	17 Jun
1:31:31		Li Hong	CHN	1.6.79	5	v4N	Leamington	23 Apr
1:31:31	Gillian	O'Sullivan	IRL	21.8.76	14	ECp	Eisenhüttenstadt	17 Jun
1:31:38	Hristína	Déskou	GRE	27.5.73	1	NC	Marathónas	18 Mar
	(50)							
1:31:45		Xue Ailing	CHN	12.2.79	3		Rio Maior	15 Apr
1:31:45	Beate	Gummelt	GER	4.2.68	6		Naumburg	30 Apr
1:31:51	Natalya	Shiviryeva	RUS	31.8.78	11	NC-w	Adler	20 Feb
1:31:51	Michelle	Rohl	USA	12.11.65	1		Kenosha	13 May
1:31:55	Teresa	Linares	ESP	29.4.69	5		Hildesheim	9 Jul
1:32:01	Olga	Lukyanchuk	UKR	7.12.76	12	RUS-w	Adler	20 Feb
1:32:02	Lyudmila	Yegorova	UKR	4.10.74	16	ECp	Eisenhüttenstadt	17 Jun
1:32:03	Eva	Pérez	ESP	18.7.75	1	NC	Cieza	19 Mar
1:32:07		Xu Aihui	CHN	25.4.78	2		Xinzheng	5 May
1:32:10	Melanie	Seeger	GER	8.1.77	1		Dublin	15 Jul
	(60)							
1:32:14	Fatiha	Ouali	FRA	28.10.74	7		Leamington	23 Apr
1:32:17	Tatyana	Ragozina	UKR	3.9.64	17	ECp	Eisenhüttenstadt	17 Jun
1:32:19	Elena	Isar	ROM	7.12.71	5		Békéscsaba	9 Apr
1:32:22	Graciela	Mendoza	MEX	22.3.63	8		Naumburg	30 Apr
1:32:23	Yelena	Kuznetsova	KAZ	4.8.77	2	NC	Almaty	31 Mar
1:32:34	Rosario	Sánchez	MEX	26.10.73	9		Naumburg	30 Apr
1:32:44	Kaori	Nikaido	JPN	25.7.79	1		Takahata	29 Oct
1:32:46	Abigail	Saenz	MEX	21.4.77	3		Vallensbæk	6 May
1:32:48	Kristina	Saltanovic	LTU	20.2.75	19	ECp	Eisenhüttenstadt	17 Jun
1:32:50	Elisa	Rigaudo	ITA	17.6.80	4		Taranto	19 Mar
	(70)							
1:32:54	Mara	Ibañez	MEX	17.12.74	11		Naumburg	30 Apr
1:32:57	Gisella	Orsini	ITA	9.12.71	5		Taranto	19 Mar
1:33:00	Lisa	Paolini	AUS	10.12.62	1		Sydney	8 Jul
1:33:01		Gao Hongmiao	CHN	17.3.74	3		Xinzheng	5 May
1:33:06	Encarna	Granados	ESP	30.1.72	9	v4N	Leamington	23 Apr
1:33:14	Athiná	Papayiánni	GRE	18.8.80	11	OG	Sydney	28 Sep
1:33:27	Lyudmila	Dedekina	RUS	5.1.79	14	NC-w	Adler	20 Feb
1:33:27		Han Min	CHN-J	8.7.83	4		Xinzheng	5 May
1:33:28		Jiang Qiuyan	CHN-J	5.7.83	6	NC	Lushun	3 Jun
1:33:38		Gao Kelian	CHN	15.8.83	5		Xinzheng	5 May
	(80)							
1:33:40	Tatyana	Matyushkina	RUS	22.1.79	12	NC	Moskva	19 May
1:33:40		Chen Yueling	USA	1.4.68	2	NC	Sacramento	16 Jul
1:33:48	Debbi	Lawrence	USA	15.10.61	3	NC	Sacramento	16 Jul
1:33:52	Katarzyna	Radtke	POL	31.8.69	1	NC	Ponte de Sôr	5 Mar
1:33:57	Lisa	Kehler	GBR	15.3.67	23	ECp	Eisenhüttenstadt	17 Jun
1:34:02		Li Yuxin	CHN	4.12.74	7		Xinzheng	5 May
1:34:08		Yang Wenjing	CHN	26.9.79	7	NC	Lushun	3 Jun
1:34:19		Yuan Yufang	MAS	1.2.76	15	OG	Sydney	28 Sep
1:34:20	Svetlana	Kalitka	UKR	28.3.70	4		Dudince	25 Mar

Mark	Name		Nat	Born	Pos	Meet	Venue	Date
1:34:22	Anne Haaland (90)	Simonsen	NOR	18.6.80	1		Fana	2 Apr
1:34:24	Sylwia	Korzeniowska	POL	25.4.80	1		Zamosc	23 Sep
1:34:25	Cheryl	Webb	AUS	3.10.76	6		Rio Maior	15 Apr
1:34:26		Gu Yan	CHN	17.3.74	8		Xincheng	5 May
1:34:26	Anita	Líepina	LAT	17.11.67	25	ECp	Eisenhüttenstadt	17 Jun
1:34:32	Natalya	Trofimova	RUS	17.1.75	15	NC-w	Adler	20 Feb
1:34:37	Geovanna	Irusta	BOL	26.9.75	17		Naumburg	30 Apr
1:34:42	Dina	Suleymanova	RUS	26.7.79	13	NC	Moskva	19 May
1:34:42		Li Haiyan	CHN	27.5.79	9	NC2	Lushun	3 Jun
1:34:44	Simone	Wolowiec	AUS	12.2.74	1		Canberra	16 Jan
1:34:44	Susan (100)	Armenta	USA	19.9.73	1		Kenosha	3 Jun

1:34:50	Jill	Zenner	USA	13.2.75	3 Jun
1:34:50	Janice	McCaffrey	CAN	20.10.59	13 Aug
1:34:59	Olive	Loughnane	IRL	14.1.76	17 Jun
1:34:59	Hristína	Kokótou	GRE	9.1.72	17 Jun
1:35:03	Alexándra	Tzioúti	GRE	1.1.71	17 Jun
1:35:07	Zuzana	Blazeková	SVK	1.7.80	17 Jun
1:35:13	Lisa	Barbieri	ITA	18.5.78	7 May
1:35:13	Sonata	Milusauskaité	LTU	21.8.73	17 Jun
1:35:22	Sara	Stevenson	USA	.80	13 May
1:35:26	Rocío	Florido	ESP	16.1.76	19 Mar
1:35:31		Guo Dongmei	CHN-J	5.2.83	5 May
1:35:46		Liu Shu	CHN-J	17.6.81	3 Jun
1:35:45	Theresa	Vaill	USA	20.11.62	2 Apr
1:35:46	Nevena	Mineva-Dimitrova	BUL	17.6.72	29 Jun
1:35:48	Ryoko	Tadamasa	JPN	9.5.76	29 Oct
1:35:49	Yelena	Arshintseva	RUS	5.4.71	20 Feb
1:35:50	Oslaidis	Cruz	CUB	12.3.74	5 Feb
1:35:50		Wang Qingqing	CHN-J	7.2.83	3 Jun
1:35:57	Mayumi	Kawasaki	JPN	10.5.80	16 Apr
1:36:09		Kim Mi-jung	KOR	10.6.79	28 Sep
1:36:17	Joanne	Dow	USA	19.3.64	16 Jul
1:36:18	Yuka	Mitsumori	JPN	8.1.72	30 Jan
1:36:22		Ha Mingming	CHN-J	15.4.82	3 Jun
1:36:26	Gretchen	Eastler-Fishman	USA	7.4.72	3 Jun
1:36:27	Natividad	Collado	GUA	20.11.71	30 Apr
1:36:34	Sara	Standley	USA	16.1.67	3 Jun
1:36:34.7t	Isilda	Gonçalves	POR	11.11.69	4 Aug
1:36:40	Sara-Jane	Cattermole	GBR	29.1.77	4 Mar
1:36:42		Song Hongmei	CHN	2.10.80	3 Jun
1:36:46	Danielle	Kirk	USA	14.2.74	30 Apr
1:36:48	Miki	Itakura	JPN	1.8.75	16 Apr
1:36:52	Yelena	Miroshnichenko	UKR	1.3.77	25 Mar
1:36:54	Jolanta	Dukure	LAT	20.9.79	28 Sep
1:37:05		Ha Guangkun	CHN	4.8.76	5 May
1:37:18	Tatyana	Melnikova	RUS	12.9.75	20 Feb
1:37:22		Shi Na	CHN-J	17.2.81	3 Jun
1:37:24	Aya	Kamikawa	JPN	22.1.77	30 Jan
1:37:26	Emanuela	Perilli	ITA	19.5.73	19 Mar
1:37:29.7t	Sofia	Avoila	POR	30.7.76	4 Aug
1:37:34	Takako	Terui	JPN	11.1.78	30 Jan
1:37:38	Tatiana	Denize-Boulanger	FRA	13.7.73	23 Apr
1:37:49	Sachiyo	Matsunobu	JPN	27.3.73	30 Jan
1:37:49		Hu Guangkun	CHN	4.8.76	3 May
1:37:51		Chen Haiyan	CHN-J	16.1.81	3 Jun
1:38:07	Ivis	Martínez	ESA	5.1.71	28 Sep
1:38:14	Andrea	Meloni	GER	1.10.67	22 Oct
1:38:21		Zang Yan	CHN-J	13.12.83	5 May
1:38:24	Mónika	Pesti	HUN	27.6.75	9 Apr
1:38:39	Valérie	Nadaud	FRA	16.3.68	17 Jun
1:38:42	Vanessa	Espinosa	ESP	4.2.79	19 Mar
1:38:43	Jurgita	Meskauskaité	LTU	27.8.76	25 Mar
1:38:49	Antonina	Petrova	RUS	1.5.77	19 May
1:38:52	Victoria	Palacios	MEX	29.3.77	16 Jul
1:39:01	Annett	Amberg	GER	9.2.73	15 Jul
1:39:04		Liu Shu	CHN-J	17.6.81	5 May
1:39:06	Annarita	Fidanza	ITA	3.8.78	19 Mar
1:39:07	Ivonne	Varas	MEX	31.10.70	8 Apr
1:39:10	Yoshimi	Morita	JPN	22.6.73	16 Apr
1:39:17	Anna	Zvarová	SVK	9.3.75	17 Jun
1:39:20.5t	Vera	Santos	POR-J	3.12.81	4 Aug
1:39:32	María	Ibars	ESP	26.3.78	19 Mar
1:39:33	Aleksandra	Sorokina	RUS	24.2.79	19 May
1:39:35		Liu Xiuping	CHN-J	1.10.83	3 Jun
1:39:36	Irina	Kovalchuk	UKR	26.11.77	21 May
1:39:40	Nicole	Best	GER	25.6.70	30 Apr
1:39:40		Qi Fei	CHN-J	18.5.82	3 Jun
1:39:48	Lucie	Nedomová	CZE	28.10.78	14 May
1:39:49	Yevkodia	Korotkova	RUS	28.2.79	7 Oct
1:39:53	Bahia	Boussad	ALG	31.1.79	27 Aug
1:39:58	Aida	Isayeva	AZE	12.9.73	19 May
1:39:59	Susan (171)	Vermeulen	RSA	10.2.73	15 Jul

Best track times

1:30:48.3	Rossella	Giordano	ITA	1.12.72	1		Almada	4 Aug

1:35:26.67	Kristina	Saltanovic	LTU	20.2.75	3 Aug
1:35:45.7		Chen Yueling	USA	1.4.68	23 Jan
1:36:11.6	Susana	Feitor	POR	28.1.75	4 Aug
1:36:55.88	Sonata	Milusauskaité	LTU	21.8.73	3 Aug
1:38:19.1	Danielle	Kirk	USA	14.2.74	12 Feb
1:39:54.0	Susan	Armenta	USA	19.9.73	12 Feb

JUNIORS

1:33:27		Han Min	CHN	8.7.83	4		Xinzheng	5 May
1:33:28		Jiang Qiuyan	CHN	5.7.83	6	NC	Lushun	3 Jun
1:35:31		Guo Dongmei	CHN	5.2.83	10		Xincheng	5 May
1:35:46		Liu Shu	CHN	17.6.81	10	NC2	Lushun	3 Jun
1:35:50		Wang Qingqing	CHN	7.2.83	11	NC	Lushun	3 Jun
1:36:22		Ha Mingming	CHN	15.4.82	12	NC	Lushun	3 Jun
1:37:22		Shi Na	CHN	17.2.81	16	NC	Lushun	3 Jun
1:37:51		Chen Haiyan	CHN	16.1.81	17	NC	Lushun	3 Jun
1:38:21		Zang Yan	CHN	13.12.83	13		Xinzheng	5 May
1:39:04		Liu Shu	CHN	17.6.81	15		Xinzheng	5 May
1:39:20.5 t	Vera	Santos	POR	3.12.81	5		Almada	4 Aug
1:39:35		Liu Xiuping	CHN	1.10.83	18	NC	Lushun	3 Jun
1:39:40		Qi Fei	CHN	18.5.82	19	NC	Lushun	3 Jun

50 KILOMETRES WALK

4:52:29	Natalia	Bruniko	ITA	23.2.73	1		Scanzorosciate	29 Oct
5:01:58	Silvia	Panseri	ITA	17.9.80	2		Scanzorosciate	29 Oct
5:03:11	Henrieta	Rusnáková	SVK	17.10.71	3		Scanzorosciate	29 Oct

MEN'S INDEX 2000

Athlete included are those ranked in ther top 100s at standard (World Champs) events (plus shorter lists for 1M and 3000m). Those with detailed biographical profiles are indicated in first column by: * in this year's Annual, ^ in a previous year's Annual

Name		Nat	Born	Ht/Wt	Event	2000 Mark	Pre-2000 Best
* Aaltonen	Timo	FIN	11.4.69	189/123	SP	20.70	20.48 -99
Aaron	David	USA	2.12.78	193/95	400H	49.62	50.58 -99
Abate	Abiyote	ETH	20.11.80	174/56	3000	7:42.58	7:45.45 –99
					5000	13:10.7	13:23.41 -99
Abdellah	Abdelhaq	MAR	13.8.68	174/57	1500	3:38.44	3:35.42 -96
Abdirahman	Abdi	USA	1.1.77	178/60	10000	27:46.17	28:06.65 -99
Abdullah	Khamis Seif	QAT	1.12.76	181/64	3kSt	8:17.56	8:18.58 -99
* Abduvaliyev	Andrey	UZB	30.6.66	186/112	HT	80.51	83.46 -90
Abelli	Andrea	ITA	9.2.71	175/68	800	1:46.43	1:45.4 -97
					1500	3:37.47	3:36.25 -97
* Abera	Gezahegne	ETH	13.4.78	168/57	HMar	60:30w	
					Mar	2:09:45	2:07:54 -99
Abraham	Aléxis	FRA	14.2.76	185/70	1500	3:36.28	3:42.21 -99
Abrahams	Shawn	RSA	23.10.73		800	1:45.03	1:46.70 -98
Aburaya	Shigeru	JPN	8.2.77	163/51	10000	28:13.76	28:21.02 -99
					Mar	2:10:48	-0-
* Achike	Larry	GBR	31.1.75	188/75	TJ	17.30, 17.31w	17.10 -98
Achon	Julius	UGA	12.12.76	168/55	1500	3:35.86	3:35.68 -97
^ Adam	Marcus	GBR	28.2.68	182/82	200	20.65	20.41 -92, 20.10w -90
Adams	Luke	AUS	22.10.76	182/64	20kW	1:24:18	1:23:52 -99
Aden	Ibrahim	SOM	11.11.72	177/57	1500	3:38.00	3:36.47 -97
^ Adkins	Derrick	USA	2.7.70	188/80	400H	49.84	47.54 -95
Adsuar	Antonio	ESP	4.7.78	178/79	LJ	7.95, 8.06w	7.93 -99
Afanasyev	Nikolay	RUS	11.8.64	187/80	Dec	7784	8090h -85
^ A'Hern	Nick	AUS	6.1.69	169/61	20kW	1:20:53	1:19:33 -90
Aish	Michael	NZL	24.7.76	175/60	10000	28:08.46	28:49.53 -99
Aitbensalim	Rachid	MAR	10.11.72		HMar	61:36w	
Akinremi	Ibukun	NGR	26.3.76		100	10.23Aw	10.54 –99
Ako	Benedict	TAN	5.8.68		HMar	61:53?	61:34u -97
Aladefa	Kehinde	NGR	19.12.74	193/89	110H	13.74, 13.69Aw	13.58 -95
					400H	49.95	49.60 -96
Al-Ahmadi	Salem Mouled	KSA	12.9.69	185/75	TJ	16.50	17.07 -97
Alaräisänen	Pekka	FIN	27.12.75	188/106	JT	80.26	77.03 -98
Al-Asmari	Sa'ad Shaddad	KSA	24.9.68	185/72	3kSt	8:22.51	8:08.26 -97
Albert	Steve	USA	1.4.64	180/114	SP	19.09	20.15 -98
* Al-Bishi	Hamdan Obah	KSA	5.5.81	175/68	400	44.66	45.98 -99
Al-Dosari	Rasheed	QAT	8.5.81	198/130	DT	60.16	59.51 -99
* Alekna	Virgilijus	LIT	13.2.72	200/130	DT	73.88	69.66A -98
Aleksejev	Marko	EST	14.2.79	196/78	HJ	2.26i	2.19i -99, 2.15 -97
Alemayehu	Lemma	ETH	77	175/55	5000	13:18.67	
					3kSt	8:29.73	8:28.28 -99
Alemayehu	Semiretu	ETH	18.10.70	182/68	Mar	2:08:33	2:12:46 -99
Alemu	Birhane	ETH	16.7.82	178/63	1500	3:35.67	
* Alemu	Dagne	ETH	15.10.80	174/57	3000	7:47.52	7:45.92 -99
					5000	13:07.73	13:18.39 -99
Alexander	Niconnor	TRI	4.2.77	178/68	100	10.19, 10.0	10.28, 10.13w -99
					200	20.55w	21.30 -98, 20.95w -99
Alexander	Tomas	USA	16.5.80	183/76	100	10.22w	10.40, 10.34w -99
Al-Houti	Mohamed	OMN	8.9.72	185/63	200	20.4w	20.80 -99
^ Alisevich	Vitaliy	BLR	15.6.67	186/112	HT	75.10	82.16 -88
* Aliu	Deji	NGR	22.11.75	187/75	100	10.15, 10.10w	10.02 -95, 9.9 -96
Allaert	Koen	BEL	29.9.72		10000	28:11.42	28:36.51 -99
					Mar	2:11:19	-0-
Allen	Charles	GUY	29.7.77	190/87	110H	13.77	
Allen	Kris	USA	14.4.79	178/68	110H	13.76, 13.61w	13.82, 13.76w -99
Allevi	Massimo	ITA	23.11.69	182/72	PV	5.60	5.60 -98
Almeida	Vitor	POR	6.3.70	170/58	3kSt	8:30.00	8:26.66 -95
Al-Najem	Zahirudin Abd.	SYR	11.1.77	184/75	400H	49.67	50.35 -99
Al-Nubi	Abdurahman	QAT	17.10.79	190/80	LJ	8.01	8.11 -98
Al-Sabee	Hussein	KSA	14.11.79	186/82	LJ	8.33	8.06 -99
* Al-Somaily	Hadi Sou'an	KSA	30.12.76	191/72	400H	47.53	49.14, 49.1A -99
Alves	Fernando	POR	24.6.67	190/110	SP	19.12	19.30 -99
Ambrosch	Klaus	AUT	23.5.73	188/88	Dec	8113	7615 -97, 7825w -98
Amine	Mohammed	MAR	76	168/53	1500	3:35.78	3:34.81 -99
Andam	Kenneth	GHA	8.1.76	186/70	100	10.21, 10,13Aw	10.22 -98. 10.20Aw -99

Name		Nat	Born	Ht/Wt	Event	2000 Mark	Pre-2000 Best
Anderson	Avery	USA	16.3.73	188/84	Dec	7952	
Anderson	Justin	USA	9.3.79		100	10.21	10.32 -99
Anderson	LeVar	USA	26.3.77	183/77	TJ	17.00i,16.98	16.78i,16.78A,16.73,17.12w -99
^ Andji	Alain	FRA	20.11.74	187/89	PV	5.55	5.85 -97
André	João	POR	28.5.76	181/82	PV	5.60	5.37 -99
^ Andrei	Alessandro	ITA	3.1.59	191/118	SP	19.07	22.91 -87
Andrei	Cristiano	ITA	14.5.73	198/115	DT	63.55	61.01 -99
Andréoglou	Efthímios	GRE	12.8.70	180/75	Dec	7684	7769 -97
Andréou	Georgios	CYP	26.7.74	188/80	Dec	7801	7714 -99
* Andreyev	Vladimir	RUS	7.9.66	180/68	20kW	1:18:16	1:18:32 -95
Aníbal	Mário	POR	25.3.72	187/90	Dec	8136	7937 -99
Anlerzak	Justin	AUS	14.8.77	187/118	SP	20.35	19.36 -98
* Annus	Adrián	HUN	28.6.73	194/102	HT	78.15	81.73 -99
Anusim	Nnamdi	NGR	11.7.72	175/71	100	10.09Aw	10.17 -94
Aounaouk	Moussa	ALG	2.8.72	173/62	20kW	1:23:34	1:23:35 -96
* de Araújo	Eronilde Nunes	BRA	31.12.70	182/78	400H	48.25	48.04 -95
Arcos	José Manuel	ESP	19.1.73	177/81	PV	5.60	5.76 -96, 5.80i -99
Argirov	Krasimir	BUL	13.4.80	180/70	LJ	7.95i	7.82 -98
Arkhipov	Aleksandr	RUS	7.8.73	178/69	20kW	1:23:13	1:22:07 -97
Arlati	Andrea	ITA	7.5.70	176/56	5000	13:28.12	13:38.55 -98
Armstrong	Aaron	USA	14.10.77	173/70	100	10.19Aw	10.59w, 10.3w -97, 9.8w -99
					200	20.63, 20.42Aw	20.08 -99
Armstrong	Lawrence	USA	19.3.78	178/77	100	10.16,10.07w	10.39 -97,10.23w -98, 9.9w -99
					200	20.66, 20.44w	21.24 -99, 21.00w -96
Armstrong	Sherman	USA	22.9.78	185/75	110H	13.75, 13.72w	14.01, 13.88w -99
					400H	48.61	50.13 -99
Armstrong	Zion	NZL	21.1.75	185/75	400H	49.95	50.23 -99
Arndt	Jirka	GER	1.8.73	179/63	5000	13:21.47	13:43.51 -99
* Arnold	Dominique	USA	14.9.73	185/76	110H	13.11	13.21, 13.2 -99
Arzamasov	Sergey	KZK	9.4.71	190/75	TJ	16.90	17.27 -95, 17.28w -93
Asami	Kimihiro	JPN	8.11.72	185/78	110H	13.72	13.90 -97, 13.87w -99
Assmus	Ralf	GER	28.1.77		3kSt	8:24.11	8:26.58 -99
* Astapkovich	Igor	BLR	4.1.63	191/118	HT	82.58	84.62 -92
Astapkovich	Konstantin	BLR	23.10.70	185/120	HT	77.21	79.08 -99
Atanasov	Nikolay	BUL	11.12.74	188/72	LJ	8.20	8.09i, 8.08, 8.12w -99
Attene	Alessandro	ITA	10.9.77	180/74	200	20.67	20.57 -97
					400	45.35	47.53 -96
* Austin	Charles	USA	19.12.67	184/77	HJ	2.32	2.40 -91
Authorlee	Anthony	USA	10.7.77	170/68	200	20.66w	20.79, 20.67w -97
Avellaneda	Mario	ESP	12.11.74	168/58	50kW	3:49:50	3:56:09 -98
* Averbukh	Aleksandr	ISR	1.10.74	178/76	PV	5.85	5.81 -99
Avery	Jerome	USA	18.4.78	170/68	100	10.18	10.23 -98
Awazie	Nduka	NGR	4.4.81	172/74	400	45.69	45.44 -98
Ayre	Sanjay	JAM	19.6.80	188/75	400	45.58	45.95 -99
* Baala	Mehdi	FRA	17.8.78	183/65	800	1:46.24	1:46.41 -99
					1500	3:32.05	3:34.83 -99
Baba	Youssef	MAR	7.8.79	173/55	1500	3:33.92	3:34.51 -99
					Mile	3:52.85	3:53.64 -99
Baburkin	Alreksandr	RUS	.74		HT	71.69	73.30 –99
* Backley	Steve	GBR	12.2.69	196/100	JT	89.85	91.46 -92
^ Bada	Sunday	NGR	22.6.69	188/79	400	45.74	44.63 -93
Baek	Seung-do	KOR	16.6.68	172/58	Mar	2:08:49	2:11:24 -99
^ Bagach	Aleksandr	UKR	21.11.66	194/135	SP	21.27i, 20.92dq	21.47 -97, 21.83i -99
* Baha Sulle	Faustin	TAN	30.5.82		HMar	59:38	60:38 -99
Bai	Liansheng	CHN	28.7.78		20kW	1:23:34	1:25:05.2t –97
					50kW	3:59:08	4:08:16 -99
* Bailey	Donovan	CAN	16.12.67	183/82	100	10.06, 9.98r, 10.00w	9.84 -96
Baker	Brian	USA	8.6.70	175/59	5000	13:28.62	13:26.81 -96
Bakken	Marius	NOR	27.3.78	183/63	3000	7:42.05	7:47.66 -99
					5000	13:11.30	13:22.58 -99
Balan	Constantin	ROM	25.8.64	172/62	20kW	1:21:00	1:21:00 -99
Balanqué	Eugenio	CUB	20.12.68	188/75	Dec	8058	8221 -95
Balcers	Luiz André	BRA	18.10.73	192/90	110H	13.57	13.46 -99
Baldi	Andrea	ITA	2.1.70	183/63	LJ	7.93w	7.77 -99, 7.87w -98
* Baldini	Stefano	ITA	25.5.71	176/58	HMar	60:50w	60:56 -97
					Mar	2:09:45	2:07:57 -97
Baldock	Sean	GBR	3.12.76	175/74	400	45.20	45.42 -97
Balosák	Stefan	SVK	23.11.72	180/72	400	45.72	45.32 -96
* Balzer	Falk	GER	14.12.73	189/80	110H	13.19	13.12, 13.10Ar -98
Bamboux	Stéphane	FRA	28.2.74	185/82	Dec	7751	7793 -99

	Name		Nat	Born	Ht/Wt	Event	2000 Mark	Pre-2000 Best
^	Bangué	Emmanuel	FRA	21.7.71	180/72	LJ	8.09	8.25 -96, 8.32w -99
	Barbi	Roberto	ITA	25.3.65		HMar	61:49	62:09 -99
						Mar	2:10:12	2:10:46 -99
	Bardauskas	Tomas	LIT	22.3.75	183/67	LJ	8.10	8.09 -97
	Barker	Ricky	USA	14.11.69	190/77	Dec	7903w	8404 -96
	Barlís	Ioannis	GRE	26.11.79	182/100	HT	72.13	71.54 -97
*	Barmasai	Bernard	KEN	6.5.74	173/55	1500	3:37.24	3:38.48 -99
						3000	7:36.79	7:36.40 -97
						3kSt	8:02.76	7:55.72 -97
	Barnaby	Marlon	JAM	26.10.79	179/71	100	10.23w	10.66 -97
	Barrett	Craig	NZL	16.11.71	183/70	50kW	3:55:53	3:48:14 -99
	Bartels	Ralf	GER	21.2.78	183/110	SP	19.34	18.95 -99
	Barthel	Trond	NOR	11.9.70	190/90	PV	5.60	5.72 -96
	Basil	Adam	AUS	14.4.75		100	10.22Aw	10.34, 10.24w -99
	Batangdon	Joseph	CMR	29.7.78	180/75	100	9.9	10.54 -98
						200	20.31	20.31A, 20.69, 20.3 -99
	Batman	Daniel	AUS	20.3.81	171/71	400	45.60, 45.4	46.57 -98
	Batte	Erik	CUB	10.12.74	185/79	110H	13.58	13.26 -96
	Battocletti	Giuliano	ITA	1.8.75	176/54	HMar	61:59	60:59 -98
^	Baudouin	Gérald	FRA	15.11.72	183/79	PV	5.60	5.80 -94
^	Baulch	Jamie	GBR	3.5.73	176/67	400	45.06	44.57 -96
^	Baumann	Dieter	GER	9.2.65	178/64	1500	3:37.18dq	3:33.51 -97
						3000	7:47.22dq	7:30.50 -98
						5000	13:13.84dq	12:54.70 -97
	Bavikin	Vadim	ISR	4.10.70	186/90	JT	80.48	78.48 -93, 81.56R -91
	Baxter	David	AUS	27.3.77	179/66	200	20.57A	20.74 -99
*	Bayissa	Fita	ETH	15.12.72	173/52	5000	13:08.15	13:05.40 -93
	Bayo	Zebedayio	TAN	20.5.76	178/64	HMar	60:50	60:26 -98
						Mar	2:09:18	2:08:51 -98
	Beauchamp	William	GBR	9.9.70	196/110	HT	71.76	72.63 -99
	Beckenham	Matt	AUS	18.3.76	182/73	400H	49.9	49.47 -99
*	Beckford	James	JAM	9.1.75	183/73	LJ	8.42	8.62 -97, 8.68w -95
	Bédi	Tibor	HUN	22.3.74	182/82	400H	49.33A, 49.77	49.00 -99
	Béhar	Abdellah	FRA	5.7.63	172/58	HMar	61:30	61:53 -99
						Mar	2:09:09	-0-
	Bekele	Kenenisa	ETH	81	160/54	3000	7:46.95	8:09.89 -99
						5000	13:20.57	
	Belabbès	Mohammed	ALG	11.3.66	177/62	3kSt	8:25.97	8:22.60 -95
	Belkacem	Henri	FRA	16.3.64	172/61	3kSt	8:24.36	8:23.47 -99
	Bell	Kenta	USA	16.3.77		LJ	8.05	7.92, 8.04w -99
						TJ	17.22	16.52, 16.67w -99
	Bell	Tim	USA	7.9.79	191/77	HJ	2.25	2.23 -98
*	Belonog	Yuriy	UKR	9.3.74	200/125	SP	21.64	21.20i -96, 20.92 -98
						DT	61.35	65.32 -99
	Belov	Aleksey	RUS	76		HJ	2.24	2.21 -99
	Belz	Christian	SUI	11.9.74	178/63	3kSt	8:25.92	8:24.10 -99
	Benfarès	Samir	FRA	6.6.68	186/66	1500	3:37.75	3:35.99 -94
	Bengtsson	Bengt	SWE	4.9.61	176/65	50kW	4:02:02, 3:49:24sh	3:59:27 -99
	Bennett	Michael	USA	13.0.70	178/92	100	10.18, 10.00w	10.33 -98
						200	20.66	20.68 -98
	Benoy	Rich	USA	14.7.68	193/90	110H	13.70, 13.67w	13.49 -95, 13.3 -99
	Benslimani	Mourad	ALG	19.2.74	178/64	3kSt	8:25.32	8:30.32 -99
	Benzine	Réda	ALG	19.4.71	180/63	3000	7:41.85	7:44.79 -98
						5000	13:23.10	13:20.85 -96
	Berdeja	David Cristian	MEX	21.6.81		20kW	1:23:46	1:32:02 -98
*	Bérioui	Saïd	MAR	3.6.75	171/57	5000	13:23.38	13:15.10 -99
						10000	27:37.83	27:31.00 -98
	Bermejo	Javier	ESP	8.3.78	191/77	HJ	2.24i	2.23 -98
	Bernard	Claston	JAM	22.3.79	193/90	Dec	7806	7444 -99
	Bernasconi	Ivan	ITA	19.10.74	193/74	HJ	2.24i	2.28 -99
	Berradi	Rachid	ITA	29.8.75	171/60	10000	27:54.23	28:10.48 -99
						HMar	61:52	63:03 -99
^	Berrett	Tim	CAN	23.1.65	179/66	20kW	1:21:46	1:22:27t -96
						50kW	3:52:21t	3:50:23 -93
	Bessou	Laïd	ALG	5.2.76	179/62	3000	7:46.07	7:47.70 -98
						3kSt	8:10.23	8:14.61 -99
	Betanzos	Yoandri	CUB	15.2.82	179/71	TJ	16.82	15.94, 16.07w -99
	Bett	Mark	KEN	22.12.76	180/64	3000	7:46.40	7:44.20 -98
						5000	12:55.63	13:14.27 -99
						10000	28:15.98	27:18.66 -98
	Betty	Trevino	CAN	10.10.71	180/76	100	10.22Aw	10.25 -98

Name		Nat	Born	Ht/Wt	Event	2000 Mark	Pre-2000 Best
Bezabeh	Sisay	AUS	9.9.77	168/52	10000	27:56.64	28:13.01 -99
Bíber	Zsolt	HUN	31.5.76	194/104	SP	19.46	19.42 -99
Bielicki	Jan	DEN	20.2.71	188/105	HT	76.05	76.11 -99
Bigdeli	Schahriar	GER	26.3.80	182/71	LJ	8.04, 8.22w	7.93 -99
^ Birir	Matthew	KEN	5.7.72	172/62	3kSt	8:24.2A	8:08.12 -95
* Bitok	Paul	KEN	26.6.70	173/58	1500	3:36.17	3:35.82 -98
					Mile	3:56.39i	3:59.6 -96
					3000	7:35.20	7:28.41 -96
					5000	13:04.15	13:04.48 -96
Bitzi	Ivan	SUI	4.8.75	185/73	110H	13.76, 13.75w	13.61 -99
Biwott	Paul	KEN	78		5000	13:27.65	
Biwott	Peter	KEN	22.8.76	182/67	1500	3:35.25	3:45.67 -99
Biwott	Simon	KEN	3.3.70		Mar	2:07:42	2:07:41 -99
Black	Dennis	USA	4.7.73	183/134	SP	20.98, 20.99u	19.44 -98
Blackwood	Michael	JAM	29.8.76	190/79	400	44.69	45.33 -99
Blake	Dennis	JAM	6.9.70	186/70	400	45.68	45.69 -95
Blanco	José Luis	ESP	3.6.75	175/61	3kSt	8:20.44	8:22.58 -99
* Blank	Peter	GER	10.4.62	195/103	JT	85.45	88.12 -96
Blom	Rens	NED	1.3.77	178/75	PV	5.75	5.62 -97, 5.70i -99
* Bloom	Andy	USA	11.8.73	185/120	SP	21.82	21.27 -99
					DT	68.46	67.46 -99
Blouin	Gaëtan	FRA	4.4.74	190/85	Dec	7909	7745 -99, 7998w -98
Blume	Marc	GER	28.12.73	180/68	100	10.19	10.13 -96
* Boateng	Kwaku	CAN	30.6.74	193/84	HJ	2.34	2.29 -99
^ Bochkaryov	Pyotr	RUS	3.11.67	186/82	PV	5.70	5.90i -94, 5.86 -96
Bock	Detlef	GER	15.8.74	194/114	SP	20.16	19.22 -98, 19.29i -99
* Bodén	Patrik	SWE	30.6.67	187/107	JT	85.16	89.10 -90
Bogdanov	Dmitriy	RUS	11.4.79	190/77	800	1:45.76	1:46.61 -99
Boit	Josphat	KEN			3000	7:45.72	
* Boit Kipketer	Wilson	KEN	6.10.73	167/52	3kSt	8:07.33	7:59.08 -97
Bokor	Marián	SVK	17.4.77	193/83	JT	83.38	76.65 -98
* Boldon	Ato	TRI	30.12.73	176/75	100	9.95	9.86 -98
					200	19.97	19.77 -97
Bomben	Ross	USA	6.4.75	185/84	Dec	7919	7808 -98
Boness	Jason	USA	11.2.80	191/75	HJ	2.26	2.25 -99
Bookman	Leo	USA	3.1.82	191/95	200	20.67	
Bor	Simon	KEN	13.2.69		Mar	2:08:50	2:08:47 -98
Börgeling	Lars	GER	16.4.79	187/84	PV	5.75x, 5.70	5.80 -99
* Borichevskiy	Aleksandr	RUS	25.6.70	195/120	DT	64.38A	65.08 -99
Borisov	Valeriy	KZK	18.9.66	180/62	20kW	1:21:45	1:19:55 -96
					50kW	3:57:19	
Borrman	Mattias	SWE	20.6.72	184/111	DT	61.08A	62.01 -99
Borsumato	Anthony	GBR	13.12.73	185/82	400H	49.68	49.78 -99
* Borzakovskiy	Yuriy	RUS	12.4.81	179/72	800	1:44.33	1:46.13 -99
Bosch	Nadir	FRA	16.5.73	191/68	1500	3:33.89	3:32.06 -99
					Mile	3:52.04	3:54.33 -98
Boschieri	Diego	ITA	12.5.76	180/62	LJ	7.93	7.85 -97
Bostic	Calvin	USA	26.3.71	183/70	400H	49.99	51.02 -94
* Boswell	Mark	CAN	28.7.77	189/77	HJ	2.35	2.35 -99
Botfa	Péter	HUN	30.6.79	187/123	HT	77.42	71.31 -99
Botha	Hennie	RSA	20.2.75	180/68	400H	49.02A, 49.60	49.91A -99
* Botha	Johan	RSA	10.1.74	181/68	800	1:44.85	1:43.91 -99
					1500	3:36.30	3:39.82 -99
^ Botha	Riaan	RSA	8.11.70	186/82	PV	5.60A	5.91A, 5.90 -97
Botha	Werner	RSA	31.1.78	186/73	800	1:44.41	1:48.95A -96
Bouchiba	Merzak Ould	ALG	75		3kSt	8:27.19	8:55.11 -99
Boudine	Kenny	FRA	25.1.73	189/83	TJ	16.87	17.05 –96
Bouhmandi	Saïd	MAR	18.7.74		HMar	61:21	61:53 –97
Boulahfane	Kamel	ALG	1.7.76	178/63	800	1:46.72	1:46.49 -99
					1500	3:33.07	3:34.72 -99
* Boulami	Brahim	MAR	20.4.72	180/64	3kSt	8:02.90	8:10.84 -97
Boulanger	David	FRA	11.12.74	176/64	50kW	3:56:42	3:59:35 -99
Boulge	Kazimierz	POL	13.2.76	195/99	HT	76.20	74.13 -99
Boulineau	Wilfrid	FRA	13.5.70	180/68	Dec	8253	8312 -99
Bourgeois	Joël	CAN	25.4.71	175/58	3kSt	8:25.94	8:20.08 -99
Bourifa	Migidio	ITA	31.1.69		Mar	2:10:14	2:11:37 -99
Bourque	Dan	USA	4.7.76		HT	72.84	70.86 -99
Bourrouag	Tarik	GER	9.7.76	185/74	800	1:46.59	1:45.98 -98
Boussombo	Antoine	GAB	18.5.68	178/69	100	10.13, 10.02w	10.18 -99, 10.0w -98
					200	20.49A, 20.35w	20.51 -99
Bowditch	Kris	GBR	14.1.75	183/63	5000	13:28.22	13:36.24 -98

	Name		Nat	Born	Ht/Wt	Event	2000 Mark	Pre-2000 Best
	Bowers	Eric	USA	20.7.74	183/82	LJ	8.03	7.99 -96, 8.08w -97
*	Bownes	Shawn	RSA	24.10.70	194/90	110H	13.41, 13.38w	13.39 -99, 13.2A -98
	Bradley	Gentry	USA	19.1.74	183/77	100	10.23w	10.26 -98
						200	20.51	20.34, 20.20w -96
	Bradley	Mark	USA	81		HJ	2.23	
^	Bradstock	Roald	USA	24.4.62	180/95	JT	76.96	83.84 -87
	Bramlett	Ron	USA	22.10.79	181/68	110H	13.47	13.72 -99
	Braunskill	Kevin	USA	31.3.69	170/70	100	10.21Aw	10.16 -98, 10.11w -93
						200	20.57A, 20.66, 20.61w	20.22A -94, 20.37 -98, 20.21w -91
	Brayko	Pyotr	RUS	27.3.77	202/75	HJ	2.28i, 2.28	2.30i -99, 2.26 -98
	Bredwood	Llewellyn	JAM	30.4.76	178/77	100	10.09, 10.07w	10.30, 10.20w -98
	Brew	Derrick	USA	28.12.77	185/82	200	20.47	20.42, 20.38Aw -99
						400	44.70	44.29 -99
	Brisseault	David	FRA	7.3.69	185/95	JT	79.85	79.59 -99
*	Brits	Okkert	RSA	22.8.73	198/84	PV	5.85, 5.90ex	6.03 -95
	Brizzel	Paul	IRL	3.10.76	186/70	200	20.54A, 20.65	20.74 -99
	Broe	Tim	USA	20.6.77		3kSt	8:21.50	8:42.69 -99
	Brokenburr	Kenny	USA	29.10.68	178/79	100	10.04	10.04 -97, 9.90w -99
						200	20.04	20.30, 20.24w -99
	Brooks	Ned	USA	22.7.76	185/73	800	1:46.50	1:47.94 -98
	Brophy	Brian	USA	6.1.69	188/95	Dec	7954	8276 -92
	Brown	Carl	USA	11.2.70	193/105	DT	63.35	62.52 -98
	Brown	Christopher	BAH	14.10.79	178/68	400	45.08	45.96 -99
	Brown	D'Marcus	USA	17.6.78	196/77	110H	13.72	13.90, 13.4w -98, 13.86w -99
*	Brown	Jon	GBR	27.2.71	175/57	Mar	2:11:17	2:09:44 -99
	Brown	Kevin	GBR/JAM	10.9.64	176/114	DT	62.10	61.10 -97
	Brown	Omar	JAM	21.6.82	177/70	100	10.20w, 10.0w	10.43 -99
	Brown	Omar A	JAM	26.12.75	180/68	400H	49.96	48.98 -98
^	Brown	Steve	TRI	6.1.69	188/87	110H	13.55	13.19 -96
	Browne	Pierre	CAN	14.1.80	178/75	100	10.24, 10.21w	10.55 -99, 10.54w -98
						200	20.49	
	Bruder	Frank	GER	31.10.71	188/78	3kSt	8:32.83	8:26.83 -99
*	Brugnetti	Ivano	ITA	1.9.76	175/62	20kW	1:21:21	1:25:12 -98
	Brunet	Xavier	ESP	5.2.71	180/78	Dec	7714	7783 -99
	Bruvelis	Ugis	LAT	28.6.71	173/67	50kW	4:01:10, 3:52:38sh	4:10:27 -98
	Bryant	Tim	USA	11.1.74	188/75	LJ	7.95w	8.07 -97, 8.31w -98
^	Bubka	Sergey	UKR	4.12.63	184/80	PV	5.60i, 5.55	6.15i -93, 6.14 -94
*	Bucher	André	SUI	19.10.76	185/75	800	1:43.12	1:42.92 -99
	Buchleitner	Michael	AUT	14.10.69	190/72	3000	7:49.37i	
	Buciarski	Piotr	DEN	22.11.75	183/79	PV	5.60	5.55i, 5.55 -98
	Buckland	Stéphane	MRI	12.1.78	187/73	100	10.16	10.22, 10.0A -99
						200	20.31	21.14 -96
*	Buder	Oliver-Sven	GER	23.6.66	200/130	SP	20.71i, 20.41	21.42 -99, 21.47i -98
	Buller	Russ	USA	10.9.78	178/72	PV	5.71	5.80i, 5.70A -99
	Bullett	Chad	USA	20.12.78	185/77	200	20.38w	20.54 -99
	Bungei	John	KEN	9.11.76		Mar	2:09:50	2:11:35 -99
	Bungei	Wilfred	KEN	24.7.80		800	1:44.23	1:45.14 -99
*	Burge	Peter	AUS	3.7.74	187/80	LJ	8.30, 8.48w	8.22 -98
	Burgess	Paul	AUS	14.8.79	183/78	PV	5.60	5.60 -98
	Burkenya	Danila	RUS	20.7.78	198/84	LJ	8.12	8.07i, 8.00 -99
	Burlachenko	Pavel	RUS	7.4.76	184/80	PV	5.65i	5.81 -98
	Burnett	Gabriel	BAR	20.9.75	170/73	200	20.66w	20.88 -99
						110H	13.62	13.77, 13.60w -99
	Burns	Brent	USA	2.5.69	193/88	PV	5.60	5.70 -92
	Busby	Kempa	USA	9.10.73	187/77	400	45.31A, 45.76	44.93 -98
*	Busemann	Frank	GER	26.2.75	191/80	Dec	8531	8706 -96
	Businei	David Kiptum	KEN	22.12.74		Mar	2:10:38	
*	Buss	Martin	GER	7.4.76	195/82	HJ	2.34i	2.35 -99
	Bykov	Vladimir	RUS	29.4.70		HT	75.07	76.60 -98
	Byrd	Leonard	USA	17.3.75	178/64	400	45.00	44.88 -96
	Byron	Martin	AUS	6.6.69		800	1:46.45	1:47.12 -96
	Cai	Peng	CHN	28.3.83		LJ	7.93	8.02 -99
	Caimmi	Daniele	ITA	17.12.72	180/64	10000	27:48.64	28:13.38 -99
*	Caines	Daniel	GBR	15.5.79	180/72	400	45.37	47.13 -98
	Calado	Carlos	POR	5.10.75	186/80	LJ	8.13, 8.15w	8.36 -97
	Cali	Stéphane	FRA	26.4.72	178/72	100	10.24	10.15 -97, 10.11w -98
	Calvo	Michael	CUB	26.12.77	182/65	TJ	17.26	17.30 -97
*	Camossi	Paolo	ITA	6.1.74	176/68	LJ	8.11w	8.16 -98, 8.21ex -99
						TJ	17.45	17.29 -99

	Name		Nat	Born	Ht/Wt	Event	2000 Mark	Pre-2000 Best
*	Campbell	Darren	GBR	12.9.73	180/72	100	10.06	10.04 -98
						200	20.13	20.48 -98
	Campbell	Kendrick	USA	16.12.77		200	20.66A	21.14, 20.7 -99
*	Campbell	Milton	USA	15.5.76	178/75	400	45.37	44.67 -97
	Campeny	Moisés	ESP	27.5.79	186/90	HT	71.28	73.65 -99
	Campus	Milko	ITA	2.4.69	173/65	LJ	7.98w	8.13, 8.15ex, 8.31Aw -94
	Canal	David	ESP	7.12.78	183/63	400	45.53	45.20 -98
*	Cankar	Gregor	SLO	25.1.75	180/68	LJ	8.15, 8.23w	8.40 -97
	Cantwell	Christian	USA	30.9.80	198/132	SP	19.67	15.85 -99
*	Capel	John	USA	27.10.78	180/82	100	10.12	10.03 -99
						200	19.85	19.87 -99
	Carabelli	Gianni	ITA	30.5.79	187/69	400H	49.92	51.09 -99
*	Cárdenas	Alejandro	MEX	4.9.74	186/73	400	44.92	44.31 -99
	Caro	Francisco José	ESP	23.10.78	190/80	Dec	7689	7401 -99
	Carosi	Angelo	ITA	20.1.64	182/66	3kSt	8:27.17	8:14.02 -94
	Carroll	Daymon	USA	27.4.77	178/82	100	10.17	10.19 -99
						200	20.63	20.56 -98
*	Carroll	Mark	IRL	15.1.72	177/66	1500	3:34.91	3:35.00 -99
						Mile	3:50.62	3:52.82 -97
						3000	7:41.03	7:30.36 -99
						5000	13:09.64	13:03.93 -98
						10000	27:46.82	-0-
*	Carter	James	USA	7.5.78	186/77	400H	48.04	49.45 -99
	Carter	Jonathan	USA	10.5.72	178/73	100	10.18	10.04, 10.00w -98
*	Carter	LaMark	USA	23.8.70	180/75	TJ	16.96, 16.97w	17.44 -98
	Casandra	Silviu	ROM	27.10.75	183/64	20kW	1:21:35	1:21:50 -99
						50kW	4:03:30	-0-
	Casañas	Frank	CUB	18.10.78	184/101	DT	63.32	63.90 -99
	Casquette	Arnaud	MRI	16.4.78	175/70	LJ	8.05	7.89A -99
^	Castro	Domingos	POR	22.11.63	167/56	HMar	61:43	61:22 -95
	Caudron	Sylvain	FRA	10.9.69	186/73	50kW	3:48:09	3:46:38 -97
	Caulfield	Daniel	IRL	16.10.72		800	1:46.65	1:47.75 -96
	Cavallaro	Alessandro	ITA	22.2.80	180/69	200	20.48	20.74, 20.46w -99
	Cawley	Elston	JAM	24.6.76	184/90	100	10.14	10.34 -97, 10.15w -98
						200	20.63, 20.37w	20.53 -97, 20.35w -98
	Celentano	Borya	USA	25.10.76		PV	5.55	5.65 -99
	Cepeda	Marco	ESP	1.7.74	188/68	3kSt	8:14.74	8:20.21 -99
	Cerezo	José Manuel	ESP	23.6.73	180/57	800	1:45.31	1:45.82 -95
	Cerra	Juan Ignacio	ARG	16.10.76	180/110	HT	74.32	72.20 -99
	César	José Angel	CUB	4.1.78	178/75	100	10.22w-rs	10.53 -98, 10.3 -97
	Chaíça	Alberto	POR	12.9.73		10000	28:06.15	28:17.99 -99
	Chakouian	Jeff	USA	20.4.83	183/118	SP	20.08i, 18.89	
	Challenger	Ben	GBR	7.3.78	186/75	HJ	2.25i	2.30 -99
*	Chambers	Dwain	GBR	5.4.78	180/83	100	10.08	9.97 -99
	Chandler	Chris	USA	27.10.78	185/75	100	10.16	10.32 -99
						200	20.59, 20.56w	20.94 -99, 20.52w -98
	Chapado	Raúl	ESP	4.5.70	194/85	TJ	16.70, 16.74Aw, 16.69i, 16.61	
								16.83 -97, 16.87i 98
	Chaplin	Torrence	USA	12.6.77		400	45.68	47.01 -99
	Charfreitag	Libor	SVK	11.9.77	191/110	HT	77.22	75.18 -99
	Chaston	Justin	GBR	4.11.68	178/64	3kSt	8:26.07	8:23.90 -94
	Chaussinand	David	FRA	19.4.73	193/105	HT	79.29	79.81 -99
	Chebe Kipkemboi	Laban	KEN		10.9.69	HMar	61:50	60:12 -95
	Chebet	Elias	KEN	74		Mar	2:11:06	2:10:52 -99
	Chebii	Abraham	KEN	23.12.79		Mile	3:55.31	
						3000	7:45.63	7:45.29 -99
						5000	13:01.9	13:30.41 -99
	Chébili	Saïd	FRA	6.5.73	180/66	1500	3:36.55	3:33.66 -99
						3000	7:47.65i	7:52.55i -97
	Cheboiboch	Christopher	KEN	3.3.77		HMar	60:49	61:11 -99
						Mar	2:10:50	2:10:00 -99
	Chehibi	Mouhsin	MAR	28.1.78	182/70	800	1:46.2	1:46.15 -99
	Chékhémani	Abdelkader	FRA	18.7.71	180/70	1500	3:36.60	3:33.10 -96
	Chelanga	Joshua	KEN	7.4.73		5000	13:16.76	13:27.19 -96
						10000	27:49.9	27:36.62 -98
*	Chelule	David	KEN	7.7.77	179/63	3000	7:38.30	7:37.36 -99
						5000	13:13.72	12:57.79 -99
						10000	27:57.10A	27:32.18 -96
*	Chelule	Julius	KEN	25.12.78	171/55	3kSt	8:21.21	8:10.41 -99
	Chelule	Wesley	KEN	4.9.74		Mar	2:10:14	2:12:04 -99
	Chemoiywo	Simon	KEN	20.4.68	170/60	Mar	2:10:35	

Name		Nat	Born	Ht/Wt	Event	2000 Mark	Pre-2000 Best
Chemwelo	Raymond	KEN	75		Mar	2:10:52	2:16:43 -99
Chemweno	David	KEN	18.12.81	175/58	3kSt	8:31.95	
Chen	Qi	CHN	10.3.82		JT	77.88	71.94 -99
Chen	Tien-Wen	TPE	1.6.78	180/70	400H	49.93	50.15 -98
Chen	Yanhao	CHN	2.1.72	183/72	110H	13.55	13.39 -94, 13.26w -96
Chenn	Marc	HKG	6.3.76	189/77	HJ	2.25A	2.23A -98
Chepkirui	Albert	KEN	4.4.81	172/57	3000	7:43.49	7:43.01 -99
					5000	12:59.90	13:25.18 -99
Chepkisa	David	KEN	.74		3kSt	8:23.36	8:31.24 -99
Cherevko	Leonid	BLR	21.4.74	198/126	DT	65.56	64.94 -97
Cherigat	Timothy	KEN	29.12.76		HMar	61:23	63:57 -99
Cherono	Abraham	KEN	21.7.80		5000	13:15.7	
					3kSt	8:13.22	8:22.96 -99
Cherono	Henry	KEN	17.7.78		Mar	2:10:40	2:10:37 -99
Cheruiyot	Kenneth	KEN	8.2.74	173/53	Mar	2:08.22	2:11:26 -99
Cheruiyot	Robert	KEN			HMar	61:28	
Cheruiyot	William	KEN	67		HMar	61:44	
					Mar	2:08:48	2:17:17 -98
Cheval	Christophe	FRA	25.2.71	177/72	200	20.50	20.41, 20.38w -98
Chiba	Yoshihiro	JPN	29.4.79	177/63	400H	49.35	49.55 -99
Chimusasa	Tendai	ZIM	28.1.71	180/60	HMar	60:40w	60:26 -95
Chirchir	Cornelius	KEN	7.10.83	172/58	1500	3:35.16	3:44.02 -99
* Chirchir	William	KEN	6.2.79	175/55	800	1:43.84	1:43.33 -99
					1500	3:31.02	3:33.24 -98
					Mile	3:47.94	-0-
* Chistiakov	Viktor	AUS	9.2.75	202/92	PV	5.80	5.90, 5.95ex -99
Chiwira	Tawanda	ZIM	27.8.74	178/68	400	45.46	45.26 -97
Chorny	Thomas	USA	23.11.76	183/70	3kSt	8:27.67	8:30.93 -99
Chouki	Fouad	FRA	1.10.78	183/69	1500	3:36.83	3:41.23 -99
Christie	Greg	JAM	1.10.78	188/64	400H	50.05	50.45 -99
Chu	Ki-young	KOR	4.3.77	180/80	JT	77.65	77.96 –98
Chubsa	Andrey	BLR	29.11.82		HJ	2.28	2.13 -99
^ Chukwu	Clement	NGR	7.7.73	190/82	200	20.66w	20.30 -98, 20.17w -99
Chumachenko	Pavel	RUS	5.4.71	187/128	SP	20.09	20.31i -99, 19.47 -98
Chung	Nam-kyun	KOR	23.10.78	178/60	Mar	2:11:29	2:22:02 -99
Chuprinin	Kirill	UKR	22.7.75	196/120	DT	63.54	58.86 -99
Ciallella	Stefano	ITA	22.4.74	175/64	3kSt	8:31.22	8:26.58 -98
^ Ciofani	Walter	FRA	17.2.62	185/110	HT	72.40	78.50 -85
Ciolfi	Eric	FRA	14.5.77	183/77	110H	13.5	13.88 -99
Ciotti	Giulio	ITA	5.10.76	187/75	HJ	2.26	2.23 -98, 2.24i -99
Civallero	Lorenzo	ITA	8.8.75	183/63	20kW	1:22:54	1:23:45 -97
Claesson	Kent	SWE	29.7.71	183/66	3000	7:48.90i	
Clarico	Vincent	FRA	8.1.66	184/79	110H	13.55	13.41 -97, 13.3 -98
Clarke	Davian	JAM	30.4.76	178/67	400	45.06	44.87 -96
^ Clausen	Curt	USA	9.10.67	188/71	20kW	1:23:55.8t	1:23:34 -99
					50kW	3:56:16	3:48:04 -99
Clavelle	Marcus	USA	23.6.78	203/152	SP	19.58	19.27 -99
Clay	Rah'Sheen	USA	18.10.76		200	20.64w	20.64 -98
^ Clay	Ramon	USA	29.6.75	188/77	200	20.30	20.00, 20.0A -98, 19.99w -98
Clinger	Charles	USA	28.12.76	206/100	HJ	2.31A, 2.30	2.27, 2.29A -99
Cobb	Leonard	USA	20.1.75	178/73	TJ	16.80	16.95 -95
Collins	Johnny	USA	28.7.78	175/75	400	45.26A, 45.79	45.90 -98
Collins	Kim	STK	4.5.76	180/77	100	10.13A, 10.15, 10.02w	10.18, 10.16w -98
					200	20.31A, 20.18w	20.43 -99
Colombo	Andrea	ITA	14.2.74	191/77	100	10.23	10.23 -99
Conwright	Kaaron	USA	8.8.76	175/73	100	10.05A, 10.10	10.22, 10.12w -99
Cooper	Obadiah	USA	8.3.70	173/74	100	10.23w	10.15 -98
Cooper	Sayon	LBR	24.4.74	175/74	200	20.50	20.78 -97
Copland	Esteban	VEN	15.10.79	179/62	LJ	7.97	7.82 -98
* Corbett	Marius	RSA	26.9.75	196/115	JT	83.43A, 80.29	88.75 -98
Cordero	Erich	CUB	8.7.75	177/70	50kW	4:01:15	
Corsaro	Alfio	ITA	31.10.79	175/63	50kW	4:03:08	-0-
Cortés	Francisco Javier	ESP	25.10.71	173/59	Mar	2:08:30	2:09:41 -99
Cosey	Tony	USA	5.10.74	180/66	3kSt	8:21.41	8:27.60 -98
Costa	Vitor	POR	28.5.74	183/105	HT	76.34	75.76 -98
Costin	Jamie	IRL	1.6.77	179/72	50kW	3:59:02	
Couts	Brandon	USA	17.2.79	175/71	200	20.48	20.65, 20.60w -98
					400	44.72	45.04 -98
* Crawford	Shawn	USA	14.1.78	181/75	100	10.16	10.34, 10.15w -98
					200	20.09	20.39 -99, 20.12w -98
* Crear	Mark	USA	2.10.68	186/79	110H	13.11, 13.10w	12.98 -99

Name		Nat	Born	Ht/Wt	Event	2000 Mark	Pre-2000 Best
^ Creighton	Shaun	AUS	14.5.67	180/65	3000	7:46.88	7:41.60 -95
					5000	13:21.45	13:17.76 -95
					10000	27:49.20	27:31.92 -96
Cremer	Grant	AUS	9.6.78	185/74	800	1:45.86	1:45.21 -99
Crepaldi	Gianni	ITA	19.10.68	182/65	3kSt	8:32.12	8:27.20 -95
Crews	Jerome	GER	20.2.77	188/77	110H	13.57, 13.54w	13.41 -98
^ Croghan	Mark	USA	8.1.68	175/60	3kSt	8:11.29	8:09.76 -93
Cruse	Bobby	USA	20.3.78	183/79	200	20.62	20.39, 19.83w -99
Csillag	Levente	HUN	22.3.73	190/81	110H	13.49, 13.3	13.44 -97, 13.4 -96
Cui Xucai		CHN	24.8.76		20kW	1:23:47	
Cullum	Dave	USA	26.10.73		3kSt	8:33.34	8:39.86 -99
Culpepper	Alan	USA	15.9.72	185/59	10000	28:03.35	27:39.27 -99
Cuñado	Teodoro	ESP	13.2.70	172/60	3000	7:49.12	7:59.53 -98
					10000	27:36.90	28:11.05 -96
Currey	Andrew	AUS	7.2.71	184/95	JT	85.28	85.75 -98
Cziapewski	Pawel	POL	30.3.78	178/57	800	1:46.07	1:46.57 -98
* Czingler	Zsolt	HUN	28.4.71	187/72	TJ	17.06	17.24 -98, 17.25w -93
Czukor	Zoltán	HUN	18.12.62	186/74	50kW	3:55:48	3:50:02 -95
Daas	Abderrahmane	ALG	8.12.73	170/55	3kSt	8:31.28	8:25.0 -97
Dacal	Gustavo	ESP	30.3.77	185/80	JT	77.20	73.14 -99
Dachev	Petar	BUL	15.6.79	181/77	LJ	8.30	8.14 -98
^ Dagård	Henrik	SWE	7.8.69	184/81	Dec	8178	8403 -94
Daimer	Nichan	GER	19.7.67	179/65	20kW	1:23:14	1:20:36 -96
* Dal Soglio	Paolo	ITA	29.7.70	189/115	SP	20.75	21.23 -96
Damasek	Kamil	CZE	22.9.73	195/91	Dec	7840	8256 -96
Damian	Mickaël	FRA	9.11.69	173/61	1500	3:37.62	3:34.52 -96
Damião	Manuel	POR	9.7.78		1500	3:37.25	3:42.09 -98
Damszel	Tomasz	POL	25.3.72	186/83	JT	76.60	77.60 -93
Daniels	Jonathan	USA	75		LJ	8.05A	7.43w -99
Dannbäck	Mikko	FIN	16.3.77	196/115	HT	74.85	73.02 -99
Daub	Daniel	GER	3.2.76	187/87	JT	80.42	81.72 -99
Daum	Oliver	GER	25.6.71	185/72	800	1:46.67	1:46.04 -97
* Davis	Calvin	USA	2.4.72	183/79	400H	48.92	47.91 -96
Davis	Jacob	USA	29.4.78	193/91	PV	5.65i	5.90 -98
Davis	James	USA	19.3.76	185/82	400	45.26	45.61 -99
* Davis	Jerome	USA	20.8.77	188/81	400	45.09	44.51 -99
Davis	Jim	USA	15.6.78	185/82	PV	5.80A, 5.60b	5.50 -99
Davis	John	USA	19.2.77	190/104	SP	20.19	19.68i -98, 19.32 -99
Davis	Marc	USA	17.12.69	186/66	5000	13:27.05	13:32.58 -89
Davis	Marquis	USA	14.8.80	185/84	100	10.11, 9.98w-dt	10.38, 10.19w -99
					200	20.27	20.77 -99
Davis	Walter	USA	2.7.79	188/78	LJ	8.16	7.70, 7.88i -99
					TJ	17.07, 17.08w	16.38, 16.47w -99
* De Benedictis	Giovanni	ITA	8.1.68	180/63	20kW	1:21:20	1:20:29 -91
de la Torre	Elisardo	ESP	10.10.71	175/65	3kSt	8:20.44	8:26.48 -96
de los Santos	Miguel	ESP	9.8.73	187/70	110H	13.75w	13.75 -96, 13.68A -99
Deacon	Jared	GBR	15.10.75	187/76	400	45.69	45.88 -99
^ Deakes	Nathan	AUS	17.8.77	183/66	20kW	1:21:03	1:20:15 -99
					50kW	3:47:29	3:52:53 -99
* Deal	Lance	USA	21.8.61	188/116	HT	80.99	82.52 -96
Decker	Mike	USA	13.6.78	185/84	400	45.59	45.67 -99
* Dees	Anthony	USA	6.8.63	193/90	110H	13.40, 13.29w	13.05 -91
Della Santa	Paolo	SUI	12.9.73	185/73	110H	13.55, 13.45w	13.81 -98
Demeritte	Dominic	BAH	22.2.78	180/67	200	20.53, 20.42w	20.67, 20.61w -99
Denis	Frédéric	FRA	3.3.75	172/57	3kSt	8:23.55	8:37.32 -99
Denis	Sébastien	FRA	4.5.71	185/71	110H	13.63, 13.61w	13.65 -98, 13.59w -97
^ Denmark	Rob	GBR	23.11.68	174/60	10000	28:03.31	28:03.34 -94
Dennis	James	USA	25.2.76		DT	63.54	60.22 -99
Dent	Martin	AUS	8.2.79	180/69	3kSt	8:30.22	8:31.55 -99
Desaulty	Stéphane	FRA	8.1.72	183/68	3kSt	8:33.37	8:22.74 -97
Dethloff	Claus	GER	24.9.68	187/97	HT	71.89	77.68 -94
Devonish	Marlon	GBR	1.6.76	180/72	200	20.59	20.25 -99
Devyatovskiy ¶	Vadim	BLR	20.3.77	194/120	HT	81.36	76.77 -99
Di Bella	Paul	AUS	12.2.77	178/69	100	10.15w	10.34, 10.30w -98
* Di Mezza	Arturo	ITA	16.7.69	173/62	20kW	1:22:46	1:21:36 -98
^ Di Napoli	Gennaro	ITA	5.3.68	185/61	3000	7:47.20i	7:39.54 -96
					5000	13:23.83	13:17.46 -95
Di Pardo	Luciano	ITA	3.2.75	182/66	3kSt	8:21.14	8:17.32 -99
* Diagana	Stéphane	FRA	23.7.69	184/75	400H	48.70	47.37 -95
Diallo	Assane	SEN	10.2.75		800	1:46.4	1:45.11 -99

Name		Nat	Born	Ht/Wt	Event	2000 Mark	Pre-2000 Best
* Díaz	Andrés	ESP	12.7.69	187/71	1500	3:31.48	3:31.83 -99
Díaz	Ihosvany	CUB	25.11.70	178/63	50kW	4:03:51	3:58:31 -99
Díaz	Mauricio	CHI	7.8.68	170/59	10000	28:05.61	28:19.48 -99
* Didoni	Michele	ITA	7.3.74	178/70	20kW	1:21:43	1:19:59 -95
Dième	Jean-Dominique	SEN	18.9.69	193/80	400H	49.48	49.96A -99
Dillon	Cleavon	TRI	5.10.82		LJ	8.09w	
* Dilworth	Kevin	USA	14.2.74	180/76	LJ	8.28	8.47 -96
* Dimitrov	Rostislav	BUL	29.12.74	182/80	TJ	17.30	17.49 -99
Dittmar	Andy	GER	5.7.74	196/115	SP	20.09i, 19.26	19.72 -97
Divad	David	FRA	8.3.73	175/62	800	1:46.02	1:45.94 -99
Djurdjevic	Zoran	YUG	3.4.68	183/74	TJ	16.64	16.94 -98, 17.17w -91
Djuricic	Branko	YUG	5.1.81	190/73	HJ	2.23	1.95 -99
Doakes	Ray	USA	12.8.73	203/82	HJ	2.25	2.30 -95, 2.32i -94
Dobert	Pascal	USA	27.10.73	185/68	3kSt	8:15.77	8:15.83 -98
Dobos ¶	Gábor	HUN	21.2.76	178/80	100	10.13dq	10.17 -99
					200	20.63dq, 20.4w-dq	20.67 -99, 20.52w -97
^ Dologodin	Vladislav	UKR	23.2.72	189/90	100	10.0	10.18, 9.9 -94, 10.02dt -96
Domenech	Yann	FRA	17.3.79	173/61	LJ	8.01, 8.17w	8.05 -98
Domínguez	José David	ESP	29.7.80	172/55	20kW	1:22:34	
Donaldson	Chris	NZL	26.5.75	188/80	100	10.23	10.17 -98
					200	20.58	20.42 -97
* Donato	Fabrizio	ITA	14.8.76	189/81	TJ	17.60	16.73 -98
Dopek	Dave	USA	8.2.73	196/89	200	20.63	20.31, 20.20w -95
Dorique	Laurent	FRA	10.7.76	191/92	JT	79.93	76.44 -99
* Dorival	Dudley	HAI	1.9.75	185/77	110H	13.33	13.30 -98, 13.29w -99
Doucouré	Ladji	FRA	28.3.83	183/65	110H	13.75	
Douglas	Matthew	GBR	26.11.76	190/82	400H	49.26	50.20 -98
Douglas	Samuel	CUB	18.6.77	175/68	TJ	16.74	16.69 -99
Dovgal	Anatoliy	UKR	29.1.76	174/73	100	10.0, 10.22w	10.30, 10.1 -99
Downin	Andy	USA	12.5.73	178/67	1500	3:38.36	3:39.21 -96
Dozier	Tyrone	USA	22.11.79		400	45.5	45.67 -98
Drews	Stefan	GER	12.2.79	189/77	Dec	7812	7427 -98
Driouche	Aziz	MAR	15.11.77	170/58	3kSt	8:33.02	8:32.08 -99
Drozdov	Dmitriy	RUS	13.4.72	185/72	3kSt	8:29.36	8:32.01 -96
* Drummond	Jon	USA	9.9.68	175/75	100	9.96	9.92 -97
					200	20.17	20.03 –97
					400	45.55	-0-
Du	Xiaopeng	CHN	8.1.77	187/83	Dec	7732	7335 -96, 7875dq -97
Duany	Raúl	CUB	4.1.75	179/79	Dec	8252	8189 -96
Dube	Glody	BOT	2.7.78	165/56	800	1:44.70	1:46.67 -99
* Dubrovshchik	Vladimir	BLR	7.1.72	191/115	DT	69.28	67.90 -96
Dudás	Gyula	HUN	20.8.66	175/68	20kW	1:21:04	1:21:16 -91
Dudi	Om Prakash	IND	77		JT	76.96	73.28 -96
Duff	Jason	USA	15.8.72	198/88	LJ	8.03A	7.86 -93, 7.95w -92
Dumble	David	USA	11.11.74	186/114	DT	63.11	61.34 -98
Duncan	Richard	CAN	25.12.73	190/80	LJ	8.19	8.14, 8.23w -97, 8.15A -99
					TJ	16.62	16.48 -95, 16.83w -96
Dunn	Philip	USA	12.6.71	175/60	50kW	4:03:05	3:59:53 -99
Dupray	Gilles	FRA	2.1.70	188/115	HT	82.38	80.71 -98
Durmusoglou	Metin	TUR	11.1.74		HJ	2.24	2.25, 2.26i -99
Duval	Thibaut	BEL	1.2.79	185/76	PV	5.70	5.62 -99
* Dvorák	Tomás	CZE	11.5.72	186/88	110H	13.72	13.61, 13.6 -97
					LJ	8.03	7.98 -99
					Dec	8900	8994 -99
Dwyer	Pat	AUS	3.11.77	186/80	400	44.73A, 45.19	45.67 -98
^ Dymchenko	Sergey	UKR	23.8.67	203/80	HJ	2.30	2.37 -90
Dzhivondov	Iliya	BUL	6.3.78	184/74	400	45.32	46.73 -99
					400H	49.88	51.15 -99
Ebihara	Wataru	JPN	12.12.73	182/92	HT	72.47	71.20 -99
* Ecker	Danny	GER	21.7.77	192/78	PV	5.90	5.93 -98
Edorh	Claude	GER	27.2.72	183/82	110H	13.59	13.41 -94
* Edwards	Jonathan	GBR	10.5.66	182/73	TJ	17.71	18.29, 18.43w -95
Edwards	LeShaunte	USA	26.7.79	167/57	200	20.45, 20.34w	20.58 -99
Edwards	Mark	GBR	2.12.74	180/115	SP	19.72	19.21 -99
Edwards	Monzavous Rae	USA	7.5.81	183/77	100	10.18	10.53, 10.4 -99
					200	20.57	
^ Effiong #	Daniel	NGR	17.6.72	187/80	200	20.58wdq	20.10 -94
Efremov	Ilian	BUL	2.8.70	191/84	PV	5.70	5.70i, 5.70 -98
Ejiogu	Okechukwu	NGR	76		100	10.13w	10.23w -99
El Ghazi	Salah	MAR	2.11.75	172/62	1500	3:37.09	3:33.21 -97

Name		Nat	Born	Ht/Wt	Event	2000 Mark	Pre-2000 Best
* El Guerrouj	Hicham	MAR	14.9.74	176/58	1500	3:27.21	3:26.00 -98
					Mile	3:45.96	3:43.13 -99
El Himer	Driss	FRA	4.4.74	178/58	5000	13:10.99	13:15.67 -98
					10000	28:11.26	-0-
* El Mouaziz	Abdelkader	MAR	1.1.69	172/58	Mar	2:07:33	2:07:57 -99
El Nasri	Yusef	ESP	28.7.79	178/65	3000	7:47.19i	7:39.80 -99
					5000	13:17.39	13:23.46 -99
El Wardi	Mohamed Saïd	MAR	19.4.72	178/65	1500	3:34.85	
					3000	7:34.67	7:38.82 -99
					5000	13:04.46	13:10.10 -99
* Elizalde	Alexis	CUB	19.9.67	192/118	DT	64.13	65.76 -97
Elliott	Mensah	GBR	29.8.76		110H	13.69w	14.26, 14.08w -99
Ellis	Jeff	CAN	18.10.78		400H	50.00	49.96 -99
Ellis	Kevin	USA	29.6.73	185/79	110H	13.74, 13.69w	13.68 -96
Eloi	Luís A	BRA	22.7.70	195/82	400	45.6	
Elouardani	Momoun	MAR			3kSt	8:31.11	
Elsen	Paul	USA			Dec	7763w	
Elvy	Peter	AUS	3.6.80	195/100	DT	60.45	55.45 -99
Emere	Alene	ETH	5.3.82	184/63	5000	13:21.17	
					10000	27:48.34	29:47.6A -98
Emmanuel	Sunday	NGR	8.10.78	174/73	100	10.22	10.14 -99, 10.06dt, 10.0 -97
Enoki	Kazutaka	JPN	7.6.74	175/55	Mar	2:10:44	2:13:18 -99
* Épalle	Christophe	FRA	23.1.69	194/116	HT	81.79	79.98 -93
Erasmus	Brian	RSA	28.2.80		JT	77.16A	66.10 -99
Ercegovac	Stevimir	CRO	20.1.74	185/130	SP	20.28	19.94 -99
Ergotic	Sinisa	CRO	14.9.68	179/63	LJ	8.01	8.06 -96
Eriksson	Martin	SWE	15.6.71	174/76	PV	5.80A, 5.72i	5.71i -98, 5.70 -97
Erin	Frédéric	FRA	23.4.80	189/83	LJ	7.96	7.78 -99
* Erm	Andreas	GER	12.3.76	184/70	20kW	1:18:42	1:19:24 -99
Esenwein	Peter	GER	7.12.67	188/85	JT	84.79	85.60 -97
Eshbach	Eric	USA	4.2.81	183/84	PV	5.55	5.54 -99
Espinosa	Andres	MEX	4.2.63	167/55	Mar	2:11:24	2:07:19 -94
* Essaïd	Mustapha	FRA	20.1.70	180/61	3000	7:38.03	7:30.78 -98
					5000	13:09.93	13:02.15 -98
Esser	Markus	GER	3.2.80	180/92	HT	76.66	73.10 -98
Estévez	Reyes	ESP	2.8.76	187/70	Mile	3:56.48	3:52.61 -97
Etheridge	Clifton	USA	4.1.69	172/68	TJ	16.62	16.62 -95
Evans	Brandon	USA	30.10.79	180/79	100	10.16w	10.42, 10.2 -98
					200	20.30	20.92 -98
Evans	Kenny	USA	6.4.79	188/74	HJ	2.31i, 2.30	2.27 -99, 2.29i -98
Evans	Randall	USA	26.10.70	180/79	100	10.23, 10.11w	10.12 -96, 10.05w -98, 9.9 -99
					200	20.44A, 20.49w	20.50 -93
^ Everett	Mark	USA	2.9.68	183/70	800	1:45.67	1:43.20 -97
Eyapan	Andrew	KEN	12.12.65		Mar	2:11:09	2:11:47 -98
Ezzher	Mohammed	FRA	26.4.60	176/58	Mar	2:11:02	2:19:41 -99
* Ezzine	Ali	MAR	3.9.78	180/61	3kSt	8:03.57	8:06.70 -99
Fábián	Zoltán	HUN	22.4.69	184/110	HT	76.41	78.20 -98
* Fadejevs	Aigars	LAT	27.12.75	175/59	20kW	1:20:18	1:19:36 -97
					50kW	3:43:40	3:43:18 -98
* Fagernes	Pål Arne	NOR	8.6.74	185/96	JT	86.74	86.24 -99
Falconer	Brendan	USA	15.4.75		Dec	7950	7865w -98
Fambro	Kenneth	USA	13.9.77		110H	13.74	14.08 -99
Famiglietti	Anthony	USA	8.11.78	173/57	3kSt	8:25.37	8:42.58 -99
Fandino	Carlos	CUB	10.6.69	186/110	SP	20.03	19.49 -93
^ Fantini	Corrado	ITA	7.2.67	191/120	SP	19.18i	20.78 -96
Faye	Ibou	SEN	13.12.69	190/75	400H	48.80	48.84 -96, 48.30A -99
* Fazekas	Róbert	HUN	18.8.75	193/105	DT	66.11	66.61 -98
					HT	74.68	75.33 -98
Fedotov	Sergey	RUS	12.2.72	175/68	Mar	2:11:16	2:13:54 -99
Feiteira	Luís	POR	21.4.73	178/58	1500	3:38.03	3:37.5 -96
Félix	Egbert	CAN	22.11.73		110H	13.76	14.00 -99
Fenner	Mike	GER	24.4.71	187/88	110H	13.41	13.17 -98, 13.06dt -95
Fenton	Wayne	JAM	9.10.74	165/64	100	10.05Aw	10.38, 10.31w -98
Fernandes	Nuno	POR	1.4.69	187/84	PV	5.60	5.66 -96
* Fernández	Francisco	ESP	5.3.77	172/65	20kW	1:18:56	1:20:31 -98
Ferrari	Peter	SWE	24.2.64	183/77	50kW	4:04:34	4:00:43 -97
^ Ferreira Junior	Nelson	BRA	1.1.73	188/87	LJ	8.18	8.36A, 8.32, 8.41Aw -96
Ferrier	Scott	AUS	12.6.74	190/85	Dec	7700	8307 -98
Feyisa	Tadesse	ETH	81		10000	27:55.85	-0-
Fifer	Andra	USA	22.5.81	168/68	100	10.23, 10.19w	

	Name		Nat	Born	Ht/Wt	Event	2000 Mark	Pre-2000 Best
	Figère	Nicolas	FRA	19.5.79	177/91	HT	79.01	75.13 -99
	Filet	Arnis	FRA	17.12.77	182/67	TJ	16.50w	17.01w -99
	Filíndras	Dimitrios	GRE	9.2.73	183/70	LJ	7.96i	8.03 -96
	Fischer	Jeremy	USA	16.2.76	175/66	HJ	2.29	2.25 -98
	Fitzpatrick	Kevin	USA	26.9.69	193/105	DT	60.41	65.28 -97
*	Fiz	Martín	ESP	3.3.63	169/55	Mar	2:08:14	2:08:05 -97
	Fofana	Colomba	FRA	11.4.77	186/76	TJ	17.00	16.83 -98, 16.86w -99
^	Forsyth	Tim	AUS	17.8.73	199/79	HJ	2.28	2.36 -97
	Fortin	Fabrice	FRA	2.2.80	175/68	PV	5.55	5.35 -98
	Fortuna	Diego	ITA	14.2.68	190/116	DT	64.69	64.68 -99
	Foster	Robert	JAM	12.7.70	190/88	110H	13.54	13.49 -95
	Foucan	Marc	FRA	14.10.71	177/80	400	45.72	45.31 -99
	Franke	Denis	GER	27.11.69	183/70	50kW	3:58:26, 3:55:04sh	3:51:27 -99
	Frater	Lindel	JAM	13.11.77	170/66	100	10.07	10.23, 10.12w, 9.9w -98
	Free	Deandre	USA	15.1.81	180/84	LJ	8.00	
	Freitag	Jacques	RSA	11.6.82	204/83	HJ	2.30A, 2.29	2.25A -99
*	Friedek	Charles-Michael	GER	26.8.71	184/76	TJ	17.41	17.59 -97
	Frinolli	Bruno	ITA	27.2.68	182/68	LJ	7.93	7.92 -96
	Frinolli	Giorgio	ITA	12.7.70	183/72	400H	49.17	49.22 -93
	Frösén	Oskari	FIN	24.1.76	194/85	HJ	2.30i, 2.27	2.27 -98
	Fry	Rusty	USA	8.3.78		110H	13.77, 13.74w	13.78 -98, 13.74w -99
*	Fujita	Atsushi	JPN	6.11.76	166/53	Mar	2:06:51	2:10:07 -99
	Fukunaga	Masahiko	JPN	25.7.79	172/68	200	20.57	20.83 -99
	Furman	David	USA	5.11.78	188/79	HJ	2.30i, 2.25	2.28 -97
	Gabella	Grégory	FRA	22.6.80	190/70	HJ	2.24	2.21 -99
	Gabonewe	Aaron	RSA	28.9.77		HMar	62:00	
	Gabriel	Jimmy	FRA	19.10.73	185/76	TJ	16.68, 16.80w	16.64 -99,16.70i -97,16.79w -96
	Gachara	Daniel	KEN	19.12.72	170/53	3000	7:39.29	7:38.19 -99
						5000	13:14.68	13:07.27 -98
	Galaviz	Tony	USA	23.9.78		110H	13.76	13.98 -99
	Galdenzi	Francesco	ITA	6.12.76	176/60	20kW	1:23:12	1:24:16 -99
						50kW	3:53:01	3:53:25 -99
*	Galfione	Jean	FRA	9.6.71	184/82	PV	5.81i, 5.80	5.98, 6.00i -99, 6.00ex -97
	Gallardo	William	CUB	17.1.73		Dec	7647	7770 -96
	Galván	David	MEX	6.4.76	172/60	3000	7:42.19	7:49.57 -99
						10000	27:37.69	28:12.53 -99
	Gamba	Michele	ITA	2.10.72	188/68	10000	28:01.55	28:49.56 -98
*	Gandellini	Alessandro	ITA	30.4.73	179/68	20kW	1:20:28	1:20:31 -97
	Gandrey	Philippe	FRA	14.3.73	175/77	JT	77.58	76.00 -99
	García	Alberto	ESP	22.2.71	163/45	3000	7:40.82	7:38.01 -98
						5000	13:09.50	13:04.64 -98
						10000	28:01.11	27:46.12 -99
*	García	Anier	CUB	9.3.76	183/79	110H	13.00	13.07 -99
*	García	Daniel	MEX	28.10.71	168/56	20kW	1:22:05	1:18:27 -97
^	García	Iván	CUB	29.2.72	182/70	200	20.59	20.17 -95
	García	Javier	ESP	22.7.66	177/71	PV	5.61	5.77i -92, 5.75 -90
*	García	Jesús Angel	ESP	17.10.69	171/62	50kW	3:42:51	3:39:54 -97
	García	Pedro	CUB	11.6.76	185/80	LJ	8.11	8.31 -97
	García	Roberto	ESP	20.8.75	168/55	1500	3:38.61	3:40.31 -98
						3000	7:43.73	7:54.20 -98
						5000	13:24.37	13:33.55 -99
*	García	Yoel	CUB	25.11.73	182/83	TJ	17.47	17.47 -95, 17.62i -97
*	Gardener	Jason	GBR	18.9.75	175/70	100	10.09, 10.04w	9.98 -99
	Gardner	Neil	JAM	8.12.74	178/72	400H	49.50	48.30 -98
	Gardner	Tre	USA	25.10.79	180/73	100	10.22	10.31, 10.29w -99
	Gary	Robert	USA	5.4.73	178/68	3kSt	8:25.87	8:19.26 -96
	Gaskins	Elliott	USA	3.1.74	172/62	800	1:46.62	1:46.05 -99
*	Gataullin	Rodion	RUS	23.11.65	189/78	PV	5.70i, 5.70	6.02i, 6.00 -89
*	Gatsioúdis	Kostadínos	GRE	17.12.73	189/94	JT	91.69	89.84 -99
	Gavrilenko	Igor	RUS	26.7.76	185/78	TJ	16.82	16.93 -98
	Gebremarian	Gebremadhin	ETH	80	164/50	3kSt	8:33.13	8:43.16 -98
*	Gebrselassie	Haile	ETH	18.4.73	164/53	3000	7:44.39+	7:25.09 -98
						5000	12:57.95	12:39.36 -98
						10000	27:18.20	26:22.75 -98
*	Gécsek	Tibor	HUN	22.9.64	184/100	HT	81.92	83.68 -98
	Geemi	Richard	KEN	23.8.73		1500	3:36.00	
^	Georgiev	Galin	BUL	23.3.70	184/78	TJ	16.77	17.14 -98, 17.18i -96
*	Gerasimov	Pavel	RUS	29.5.79	186/75	PV	5.90	5.65, 5.70ex -99
	Gergov	Vasil	BUL	1.7.77	188/76	TJ	16.65i	16.39, 16.53w -99
	Gervais	Jason	CAN	18.1.76	198/134	SP	19.68i, 19.49	18.29 -99
						DT	64.26A	63.67A -99

Name		Nat	Born	Ht/Wt	Event	2000 Mark	Pre-2000 Best
Geshko	Ivan	UKR	19.8.79	178/65	1500	3:38.48	3:42.33 -99
Giaconi	Andrea	ITA	11.4.74	181/72	110H	13.46	13.57 -98, 13.55A -99
Gibilisco	Giuseppe	ITA	5.1.79	182/71	PV	5.70	5.60 -99
Gilbert	Glenroy	CAN	31.8.68	183/79	100	10.17w	10.10 -94, 10.01w -93
Gillet	Anthony	FRA	7.2.76	175/63	20kW	1:21:26	1:23:10 -97
* Ginko	Viktor	BLR	7.12.65	186/77	50kW	3:47:53	3:42:20 -95
Gisemba	Abel	KEN	7.7.71		Mar	2:11:01	2:11:40 -98
* Gitahi	Julius	KEN	29.4.78	168/52	5000	13:23.12	13:01.89 -98
Githuka	Peter	KEN	14.2.69		Mar	2:08:02	2:11:20 -98
Giungi	Marco	ITA	30.10.74	175/58	20kW	1:20:19	1:21:47 -99
Giusto	Matt	USA	25.10.66	178/62	5000	13:25.95	13:23.60 -93
Gladki	Piotr	POL	8.2.72	180/61	HMar	61:35	
					Mar	2:11:06	-0-
* Glavatskiy	Aleksandr	BLR	2.5.70	185/72	TJ	16.68	17.53 -98
Glivinskiy	Ruslan	UKR	7.2.75	204/92	HJ	2.28	2.25 -98
Glover	Samuel	USA	22.1.80	180/66	400H	49.08	49.99 -99
* Godina	John	USA	31.5.72	193/129	SP	21.51	22.02 -99
					DT	68.32	69.91 -98
Goedicke	Jörg	GER	25.6.74	192/82	Dec	7772	7882 -99
Goffi	Danilo	ITA	3.12.72	173/52	Mar	2:10:55	2:08:33 -98
Golding	Julian	GBR	17.2.75	183/68	200	20.64	20.18 -98
Goller	Thomas	GER	28.10.77	190/80	400H	48.82	48.54 -99
^ Golley	Julian	GBR	12.9.71	186/80	TJ	16.95	17.06 -94
Golovastov	Dmitriy	RUS	14.7.71	190/79	400	45.26	45.59 -99
Golubtsov	Konstantin	RUS	1.6.73	172/60	20kW	1:22:13	1:22:10 -99
Gómez	David	ESP	13.2.81	185/85	Dec	7772	7323 -99
* González	Emeterio	CUB	11.4.73	184/105	JT	87.12	84.32 -99
González	José Maria	ESP	3.3.73	177/63	3kSt	8:27.10	8:22.72 -99
González	Oscar	ESP	8.8.76	193/83	Dec	7706	7260 -99
Gorban	Boris	RUS	26.9.78	192/74	400H	49.09	49.87 -98
* Gorbenko	Gennadiy	UKR	22.9.75	185/67	400H	48.40	48.92 -95
Gordey	Vitaliy	BLR	24.5.73	180/71	20kW	1:21:30	1:21:49 –98
Gordiyenko	Aleksey	UKR	9.5.79	186/73	HJ	2.23i	2.20 -98
Gorries	Paul	RSA	28.2.82	184/75	200	20.59A, 20.62	20.65 -99
Gorshkov	Vasiliy	RUS	5.2.77		PV	5.60i, 5.55, 5.70ex	5.70 -98
Goucher	Adam	USA	18.2.75	178/64	3000	7:49.03i	7:43.31 -99
					5000	13:24.34	13:11.25 -99
Goúsis	Anastásios	GRE	7.7.79	180/78	400	45.55	46.20 -99
Grabovoy	Vadim	UKR	5.4.73	190/102	HT	76.30	77.14 -94
Graffin	Andrew	GBR	20.12.77	179/63	1500	3:36.18	3:42.0 -99
					Mile	3:56.13	3:59.64 -99
^ Grant	Dalton	GBR	8.4.66	186/73	HJ	2.25i, 2.23	2.36 -91, 2.37i -94
Grant	Travis	USA	31.8.72	178/73	100	10.22, 10.14w	10.23 -98, 10.13w -96, 9.9w-99
Grava	Jean Marc	FRA	2.12.71	186/80	110H	13.40	13.43 -99
Gray	Trinity	USA	3.4.78	184/73	800	1:44.91	1:45.67 -98
Greaves	Damien	GBR	9.9.77	183/85	110H	13.62	13.82 -97
Green	André	GER	21.4.73	182/65	3kSt	8:27.08	8:20.24 -99
* Greene	Maurice	USA	23.7.74	175/75	100	9.86	9.79 -99
					200	20.02, 19.93w	19.86 -97
Greer	Breaux	USA	19.10.76	190/100	JT	82.63	79.98 -96
Gregório	Jadel	BRA	16.9.80		TJ	16.48	16.07 -99
^ Griffin	Rohsaan	USA	21.2.74	175/64	100	10.14w	10.36 -99, 10.32w -96
					200	20.42, 20.41w	20.13, 19.96w -99
Grimes	Mickey	USA	10.10.76	185/84	100	10.20,10.17w	10.32 -98,10.19A,10.18Aw -99
Grossarth	Kyle	USA	4.1.77	185/77	400H	49.82A	50.13A -99
Gruman	Bartosz	POL	11.5.75	191/82	400H	49.81	49.94 -99
Gu	Junjie	CHN	5.5.85		TJ	16.89	15.85 -99
Guice	Shaun	USA	11.8.80	180/70	HJ	2.23i	2.13 -99
Guims	Needy	FRA	8.9.74	187/81	100	10.17w	10.20, 10.19w -96
Gulcz	Pawel	POL	28.1.79	189/82	HJ	2.25	2.20 -99
Guset	Gheorghe	ROM	28.5.68	185/110	SP	20.76i, 20.66	20.84 -99
Gushchinskiy	Viktor	RUS	12.8.78	202/84	TJ	16.56i	16.78 -97
Guymon	Brett	USA	9.1.77		400H	49.79A	51.81A -99
Guzdek	Miroslaw	CZE	3.8.75		JT	79.13	77.36 -99
Gwako	John	KEN	4.9.78		HMar	61:33	61:00 -97
^ Haapakoski	Antti	FIN	6.2.71	191/87	110H	13.62	13.42 -95, 13.26Aw -94
* Haatainen	Harri	FIN	5.1.78	185/83	JT	86.10	83.02 -99
Haborák	Milan	SVK	11.1.73	191/106	SP	20.35	19.86 -99
Hackley	Jimmie	USA	11.9.75	175/69	400	45.64	45.17 -98
Haczek	Piotr	POL	26.1.77	188/72	400	45.43	45.46 -98

	Name		Nat	Born	Ht/Wt	Event	2000 Mark	Pre-2000 Best
	Hadebe	Lucky	RSA	2.1.80	172/59	800	1:45.99	1:45.73 -99
^	Hafsteinsson	Vésteinn	ISL	12.12.60	190/113	DT	62.80	67.64 -89
	Hagedorn	Josh	USA	30.4.73	190/130	SP	19.76i, 19.14	19.39 -97
	Häggström	Peter	SWE	27.1.76	173/70	LJ	8.07, 8.08w	7.90 -98, 7.94w -99
^	Haïda	Mahjoub	MAR	1.7.70	180/75	800	1:45.60	1:43.50 -98
	Hair	Shane	AUS	24.10.75	181/68	LJ	8.21, 8.23w	8.24, 8.35w -99
	Hakala	Petri	FIN	21.2.79	194/95	DT	62.59	59.68 -99
*	Hakimi	Ali	TUN	24.4.76	176/55	1500	3:34.96	3:31.70 -97
*	Hakkarainen	Harri	FIN	16.10.69	194/110	JT	85.65	87.82 -95
	Haklits	András	CRO	23.9.77	189/103	HT	77.75	76.47 -99
	Hallgrímsson	Magnus	ISL	23.3.76	192/110	DT	63.09	60.62 -98
	Hallmann	Sebastian	GER	7.1.77	181/62	5000	13:26.43	13:49.60 -99
*	Halvari	Mika	FIN	13.2.70	191/135	SP	22.09i, 21.04	21.50 -95
*	Hämäläinen	Eduard	FIN	21.1.69	192/88	Dec	8224	8735 -94
	Hamano	Takeshi	JPN	30.7.74	174/62	10000	28:08.23	28:45.1 -97
	Hamed	Ziad Abou	SYR/AUS	22.4.70	182/75	400H	49.44	48.87 -99
^	Hames	Jagan	AUS	31.10.75	190/83	Dec	7720	8490 -98
*	Hammad	Abderahmane	ALG	27.5.77	185/70	HJ	2.34	2.32 -99
	Hammond	Jason	USA	20.5.78		SP	19.32	18.02, 18.54i –99
	Han Qiang		CHN	28.6.77		20kW	1:24:22	
	Hanada	Katsuhiko	JPN	12.6.71	175/58	10000	27:45.13	27:50.46 -96
	Hanazawa	Hajime	JPN	30.1.73	181/75	110H	13.71	13.84 -99
	Hanna	Kurt	USA	23.4.75	178/73	PV	5.60	5.62 -97, 5.75i -98
	Hanstveit	Ketill	NOR	2.11.73	178/65	TJ	16.79, 16.88w	17.27 -99
	Hara	Yoshimi	JPN	2.3.68	170/60	50kW	3:52:26	3:55:17 -99
*	Harden	Tim	USA	27.1.74	178/79	100	10.20	9.92 -99, 9.88w -98
*	Harju	Arsi	FIN	18.3.74	183/125	SP	21.39	21.04 -98
	Harmse	Chris	RSA	31.5.73	184/118	HT	78.71	76.09 -99
	Harnden	Ian	ZIM	23.9.78	193/80	400H	49.68	51.17 -98
^	Harnden	Ken	ZIM	31.3.73	196/89	400H	49.02	48.05 -98
	Harris	Stephen	USA	5.12.80	191/82	Dec	7651	
	Harris	Tora	USA	21.9.78	190/83	HJ	2.25	2.24 -99
*	Harrison	Alvin	USA	20.1.74	188/80	400	44.18	44.09 -96
*	Harrison	Calvin	USA	20.1.74	186/75	400	44.64	44.70 -96, 44.68A -98
	Harrison	Richard	USA	13.5.70		SP	19.68	
	Hart	Andy	GBR	13.9.69	180/68	800	1:46.52	1:45.71 -98
	Hart	Bevan	USA	1.8.77	180/75	Dec	8002	7773 -99
	Harting	Chad	USA	20.2.72	183/75	PV	5.80Ai, 5.80b, 5.65	5.71i, 5.70 -99
	Hartonen	Tommi	FIN	12.5.77	188/85	200	20.47	21.31 -99
*	Hartwig	Jeff	USA	25.9.67	190/82	PV	6.03	6.02 -99
*	Harvey	Tye	USA	25.9.74	186/73	PV	5.80	5.67 -99
	Hatcher	Adrian	AUS	6.5.70	182/93	JT	83.46A, 83.42	84.36 -99
	Hathorne	Robbie	USA	27.9.72		200	20.67A	20.88A -99
^	Hatungimana	Arthémon	BDI	21.1.74	180/64	800	1:45.12	1:43.46 -96
*	Haughton	Greg	JAM	10.11.73	185/79	400	44.70	44.56 -95
	Haukijärvi	Jarkko	FIN	10.6.77	189/117	SP	20.31	19.23 -98, 19.53i -99
	Hauser	Brad	USA	28.3.77	190/68	5000	13:27.31	13:35.98 -98
	Hayata	Toshiyuki	JPN	2.5.68	176/61	HMar	61:57	60:42 -96
	Haywood	Maklo	USA	19.10.78		400H	50.04	50.68 -98
	He	Xiaodong	CHN	14.1.78		20kW	1:22:42	1:23:48 -98
^	Heard	Floyd	USA	24.3.66	178/71	100	10.18, 10.14w	10.10, 10.04w -91
						200	19.88	19.95 -87
*	Hecht	Raymond	GER	11.11.68	191/95	JT	87.76	92.60 -95
	Hecini	Adem	ALG	13.12.75	175/66	800	1:44.07	1:44.50 -97
	Heffernan	Robert	IRL	28.2.78	173/55	20kW	1:22:43	1:26:45 -99
	Heikkinen	Aki	FIN	24.2.80	187/77	Dec	8188	7881 -99
	Heinze	Dirk	GER	2.7.76	182/64	1500	3:36.71	3:36.55 -99
*	Hemingway	Matt	USA	24.10.72	198/81	HJ	2.38i, 2.30	2.30 -96
	Hemmings	Michel	CUB	10.9.75	189/100	DT	64.44	60.70 -99
^	Henderson	Vincent	USA	20.10.72	175/66	100	10.22, 10.12w	9.95 -98, 9.94w -97
	Hendriks	Malcolm	RSA	27.4.77	182/64	HJ	2.26	2.24A -99
	Hennig	Scott	USA	17.4.69	186/81	PV	5.75	5.80i -97, 5.80 -98
	Henriques	Eduardo	POR	24.3.68	185/58	10000	28:06.71	28:21.82 -98
*	Henry	Boris	GER	14.12.73	193/108	JT	86.65	90.44 -97
*	Herbert	Llewellyn	RSA	21.7.77	185/80	400H	47.81	47.83A -99, 47.86 -97
	Hercules	Chris	USA	14.5.79	188/86	TJ	16.63	16.35, 16.43w -99
	Herman	Billy	USA	3.7.77		3kSt	8:26.02	8:43.14 -99
	Hermann	Andrew	USA	25.2.71	191/75	50kW	3:57:54	3:58:54 -97
*	Hernández	Edgar	MEX	6.8.77		20kW	1:21:30	1:27:00 -99
						50kW	3:56:36	

Name		Nat	Born	Ht/Wt	Event	2000 Mark	Pre-2000 Best
Hernández	Etién	CUB	19.8.79	183/76	TJ	16.64, 16.66w	16.35, 16.76w -99
* Hernández	Noe	MEX	15.3.78	175/64	20kW	1:19:03	1:20:12 -99
Hernández	René	CUB	18.5.77	185/79	TJ	17.12	17.22 -97
* Hernández	Yoel	CUB	12.12.77	185/72	110H	13.24, 13.20w	13.24 -99
Hernández	Yunier	CUB	28.3.81	183/76	110H	13.60, 13.5	13.99, 13.81w -99
Hernu	Laurent	FRA	22.8.76	190/85	Dec	8178	7937 -99
Herring	Aubrey	USA	19.9.78	183/77	110H	13.49	13.74 -98, 1.67w -99
Herring	Gavin	USA	2.6.75		400	45.71	45.33 -97
Herring	Godfrey	USA	18.5.78	183/68	400	45.59	45.96 -99
Herring	Lenton	USA	4.12.78	180/73	TJ	16.56w	16.03, 16.18w -99
Hhaway Sulle	Martin	TAN	28.12.62		HMar	61:53A	
Higuero	Juan Carlos	ESP	3.8.78	178/72	800	1:46.42	1:48.37 -99
					1500	3:36.63	3:39.57 -99
* Hill	Mick	GBR	22.10.64	190/98	JT	83.71	86.94 -93
Hirakawa	Takehito	JPN	28.7.72	176/57	50kW	4:03:08	3:58:01 -99
* Hissou	Salah	MAR	16.1.72	176/62	3000	7:37.16	7:28.93 -99
					5000	13:00.06	12:50.80 -96
^ Hoen	Steinar	NOR	8.2.71	192/80	HJ	2.24i	2.36i, 2.35 -94
Hoff	Shadrack	RSA	19.5.73	169/51	5000	13:26.88	13:14.16 -95
					10000	27:46.08	27:43.89 -96
					HMar	61:11	62:04 -99
Hoffa	Reese	USA	8.10.77	183/115	SP	19.79	19.35 -99
Högler	Gregor	AUT	27.6.72	181/91	JT	82.03A, 80.89	84.03 -99
Höhne	Andre	GER	10.3.78	184/68	20kW	1:22:05	1:24:22 -99
Høiby	Trond	NOR	24.1.73	194/94	Dec	8030	8085 -99
Hokahori	Hiroyuki	JPN	31.5.76	188/73	HJ	2.23	2.22 -99
Holger	Christer	SWE	16.1.74	181/80	Dec	7836	7608 -96
Holloway	Jarmiene	USA	6.3.77	173/84	100	10.21, 10.15w	10.17, 10.14w -98
					200	20.64, 20.3	20.55, 20.52w -98
* Holm	Stefan	SWE	25.5.76	181/70	HJ	2.34	2.33 -98
^ Holman	Steve	USA	2.3.70	186/66	1500	3:33.59	3:31.52 -97
					Mile	3:56.01	3:50.40 -97
Holmström	Anders	SWE	23.8.78	213/150	SP	19.35	18.85 -99
Holthaus	Matt	USA	2.11.71	183/68	1500	3:38.37	3:38.65 -99
Holusa	Milos	CZE	2.5.65	174/62	20kW	1:23:24	1:21:58 -97
					50kW	3:53:48	3:49:08 -96
* Hooker	Ja'Warren	USA	24.9.78	183/77	100	10.20, 10.18w	10.18 -98
					200	20.23A, 20.33	20.54 -98, 20.48A -99
					400	44.78	46.23 -97
Horváth	Gergely	HUN	5.6.75	186/90	JT	79.57	80.53 -98
Horváth	Norbert	HUN	13.6.75	183/104	HT	72.01	73.75 -99
Houston	Victor	BAR	24.2.74	188/77	400H	50.01	49.21 -98
Howard	Bryan	USA	7.10.76	183/82	100	10.12, 9.94w	10.13, 10.11A -99
Howard	Glenn	NZL	1.4.76	193/81	HJ	2.30	2.25 -97
* Howard	Robert	USA	26.11.75	178/75	LJ	8.07	8.40 -97
					TJ	17.05	17.19 -96
Hoxmeier	Mark	USA	16.7.79	188/107	DT	60.32	55.74 -99
Huber	Philipp	SUI	18.2.74	184/82	Dec	8153	8107 -97
Hudec	Leonard	AUT	13.6.73	185/70	110H	13.67	13.75 -99
Huerta	Arturo	CAN	30.3.64	172/62	20kW	1:21:03	1:22:02 -99
					50kW	3:56:01	
* Huffins	Chris	USA	15.4.70	190/82	Dec	8595	8694 -98
Hughes	Greg	BAR			TJ	16.52w	
Hughes	Kevin	GBR	30.4.73	185/76	PV	5.55	5.61 -99
Hughes	Ray	USA	9.5.75		3kSt	8:33.29	8:34.25 -99
Hughes	Robby	USA	10.10.78		110H	13.63A, 13.66, 13.59w	14.14 -97
Huikuri	Toni	FIN	17.9.79	191/77	HJ	2.28	2.24 -96
Hunter	Brian	USA	28.3.79	185/88	PV	5.60	5.49 -99
^ Hunter ¶	C.J.	USA	14.12.68	186/149	SP	21.87	21.79 -99
Hussein	Mbarak	KEN	4.4.65		HMar	61:27	
Hynni	Pertti	FIN	14.2.60	193/110	DT	62.22	63.25 -98
* Hysong	Nick	USA	9.12.71	183/77	PV	5.90	5.85i -95, 5.80 -99
Hyytiäinen	Marko	FIN	27.11.66	191/88	JT	79.21	83.40 -90
Iakovakis	Periklis	GRE	24.3.79	184/73	400H	49.35	49.53 -99
Ibe	Philip	GER	5.5.75		Dec	7974	8000 -99
Ibrahim Warsama	Ahmed	QAT	4.2.66	182/62	3000	7:43.00	7:46.89 -99
					5000	13:13.52	13:31.78 -97
Ichinose	Susumu	JPN	11.7.75	175/57	10000	28:11.43	28:13.79 -99
					HMar	61:30	62:40 -99
Idiata	Anthony	NGR	5.1.75		HJ	2.32i, 2.25	2.27 -98
* Idowu	Phillips	GBR	30.12.78	192/87	TJ	17.12	16.41 -99

	Name		Nat	Born	Ht/Wt	Event	2000 Mark	Pre-2000 Best
	Igarashi	Noriaki	JPN	28.10.72	165/54	Mar	2:09:26	2:09:38 -98
^	Ihly	Robert	GER	5.5.63	174/64	20kW	1:23:00	1:19:59 -92
						50kW	3:52:38	3:49:22 -99
	Ikegaya	Hiroyuki	JPN	29.4.75	175/58	5000	13:25.72	13:46.77 -99
						10000	28:07.09	28:11.86 -99
	Ikeshima	Daisuke	JPN	30.1.75	183/68	20kW	1:19:42	1:19:50 -98
	Illikainen	Jani	FIN	26.1.76	196/110	SP	20.12	20.43i, 19.21 -99
	Imamura	Fumio	JPN	5.11.66	178/63	50kW	3:53:20	3:49:38 -98
	Ingalls	Jerry	USA	24.9.74	196/110	HT	72.85	72.52 -99
	Ingargiola	Francesco	ITA	15.2.73	172/60	HMar	61:19	63:12 -97
						Mar	2:08:49	2:12:01 -97
	Inocencio	William	FRA	20.2.76	180/64	PV	5.55	5.61 -98
*	Inubushi	Takayuki	JPN	11.8.72	170/58	Mar	2:08:16	2:06:57 -99
	Ionescu	Florin	ROM	3.2.71	179/66	3kSt	8:21.62	8:13.26 -99
	Irifune	Satoshi	JPN	14.12.75	176/60	10000	27:58.57	28:02.99 -99
						HMar	61:36	62:50 -99
	Isekenmeier	Klaus	GER	14.4.75	199/94	Dec	8002	8310 -97
	Ishikawa	Shinji	JPN	18.3.81	178/68	400	45.77	
*	Ishutkin	Oleg	RUS	22.7.75	181/70	50kW	3:45:47	3:40:12 -97
	Isim	Ruhan	TUR	5.6.70	190/82	PV	5.70	5.70Ai -98, 5.55 -99
	Ismail	Ibrahim	QAT	10.5.72	178/70	400	44.66	44.85 -93
	Isomatsu	Daisuke	JPN	17.12.73	162/53	HMar	61:52	
*	Ito	Koji	JPN	29.1.70	182/72	200	20.56	20.16 -98
	Itok	Benjamin	KEN	72		HMar	61:33	63:22 -99
	Itoyama	Jiro	JPN	16.10.75	173/54	HMar	62:00	63:48 -99
	Ivanov	Aleksandr	RUS	25.5.82	192/88	JT	77.11	71.76 -99
	Ivanov	Dmitriy	RUS	23.3.77	187/77	Dec	7899	7787 -99
*	Ivuti	Patrick	KEN	30.6.78	165/52	5000	13:02.68	
						10000	27:09.79	28:48.0A -98
						HMar	59:31	
	Iwamizu	Yoshitaka	JPN	20.6.79	173/53	3kSt	8:32.99	8:45.54 -99
	Iwasa	Toshihiro	JPN	18.5.76	172/58	10000	28:06.89	28:29.13 -98
	Iwasaki	Jun	JPN	3.6.78	178/68	400H	49.92	50.14 -99
	Izmaylov	Sergey	UKR	1.5.75	180/72	TJ	17.01	17.02 -96, 17.09dq -99
*	Jackson	Colin	GBR	18.2.67	182/75	110H	13.10	12.91 -93
	Jackson	Eddie	USA	19.12.80	187/84	110H	13.78, 13.75w	14.68w -99
	Jahic	Danial	YUG	1.7.79	191/77	LJ	7.99	8.18, 8.27w -99
	Jakobs	Marco	GER	30.5.74	200/100	DT	62.38	64.96 -97
	James	Xavier	BER			100	10.19Aw	10.63 -99
	Janácek	Stepan	CZE	12.6.77	189/79	PV	5.72	5.65, 5.66ex -99
	Janek	Marek	SVK	29.1.77		50kW	3:58:49	
	Jankú	Jan	CZE	10.8.71	197/84	HJ	2.30i, 2.26	2.30i -96, 2.29 -97
	Jankú	Tomás	CZE	27.12.74	192/78	HJ	2.25	2.32 -99
	Jansen	Joeri	BEL	28.5.79	180/62	800	1:46.12	1:47.63 -99
	Janson	Oscar	SWE	22.7.75	192/88	PV	5.55i, 5.55	5.50 -99
*	Januszewski	Pawel	POL	2.1.72	178/68	400H	48.42	48.17 –98
^	Janvrin	Kip	USA	8.7.65	183/84	Dec	8057	8462w, 8345 -96
	Jaouane	Hamid	FRA	3.4.72	180/63	3kSt	8:28.78	8:42.70 -99
^	Jarrett	Anthony	GBR	13.8.68	188/80	110H	13.63	13.00 -93
	Jarrett	Pat	JAM	2.10.77	186/82	100	10.14	10.22 -99
	Jean-Théodore	Olivier	FRA	13.11.74	183/75	400H	49.90	50.10 -97
	Jenkins	Lacra	USA	2.10.77		100	10.21w	10.64 -98
	Jennings	Gabe	USA	25.1.79	181/70	1500	3:35.21	3:39.85 -99
	Jensen	Dennis	DEN	11.9.69		5000	13:26.30	13:30.09 -99
	Jenson	Jake	USA	29.5.74		200	20.61A, 20.41Aw	21.03, 20.67w -98
	Jenssen	Olav	NOR	11.5.62	193/112	DT	60.18	66.28 -89
	Jiménez	Anacleto	ESP	24.2.67	180/67	3000	7:49.67	7:35.83 -98
	Jiménez	Antonio	ESP	18.2.77	178/61	3kSt	8:20.34	8:37.29 -99
	Jimmerson	Greg	USA	1.2.75		3kSt	8:32.46	8:41.84 -99
	Johansson	Bengt	SWE	7.7.73	190/102	HT	75.62	73.29 -98
*	Johnson	Allen	USA	1.3.71	178/70	110H	12.97	12.92 -96
	Johnson	Brian	USA	25.3.80		LJ	8.04w	7.47, 7.67w -99
	Johnson	Collat	USA	78	198/88	HJ	2.24	2.19 -98
	Johnson	Curtis	USA	24.12.73	180/80	100	10.07	10.09 -99
	Johnson	Dominic	STL	31.10.75	185/77	PV	5.70A, 5.61	5.65 -98
	Johnson	Ferdana	USA	6.10.72	183/69	400H	49.55	50.07 -99
	Johnson	Joshua 'J.J'	USA	10.5.76	191/91	100	10.24, 10.19w	
						200	20.60	
*	Johnson	Lawrence	USA	7.5.74	183/85	PV	5.90A, 5.90	5.98 -96
*	Johnson	Michael	USA	13.9.67	185/78	200	19.71A, 19.89	19.32 -96
						400	43.68	43.18 –99

Name		Nat	Born	Ht/Wt	Event	2000 Mark	Pre-2000 Best
Johnson	Nicholas	USA	12.11.83		100	10.21w	
Johnson	Patrick	AUS	26.9.72	177/73	100	10.10	10.17 -99
Johnson	Russell	USA	12.10.76	183/73	PV	5.55i	5.65 -98
Johnson	Wayne	JAM	17.1.75	172/70	100	10.20A	10.28A, 10.27Aw -98
					200	20.20A	20.64A -99
Jokihaara	Jarno	FIN	2.9.73	176/75	110H	13.72	13.88 -99
Jones	Andres	GBR	3.2.77	182/60	10000	28:00.50	29:17.69 -99
Jones	Michael	GBR	23.7.63	187/119	HT	75.94	75.20 -99
Jones	Stephen	BAR	25.7.78	184/66	110H	13.66w	13.76 -98
Jordan	Robert	USA	22.6.80	188/77	HJ	2.25i	2.24 -99
José	Venancio	ESP	19.4.76	180/70	100	10.17	10.18A -96, 10.22 -97
					200	20.62w	20.59 -97
Junqueira	João	POR	24.6.65	174/58	3kSt	8:31.79	8:25.81 -93
Jurksas	Arunas	LIT	3.5.72	198/108	JT	82.24	79.56 -99
^ Juzdado	Alberto	ESP	20.8.66	172/61	HMar	61:10	61:50 -98
					Mar	2:08:08	2:08:01 -98
Kabiga	Jackson	KEN	1.12.76	172/58	Mar	2:09:52	2:08:42 -98
Kadaks	Aivars	LAT	11.2.81	178/63	20kW	1:23:50	1:24:59 -99
Kafka	David	FRA	2.7.72	188/79	400H	49.70	49.74 -98
Kagika	Laban	KEN	17.7.78		10000	27:57.81	28:14.00 -99
Kahan	Nathan	BEL	12.2.71	187/68	800	1:44.98	1:44.87 -97
Kaihoko	Yoshiteru	JPN	19.11.71	182/70	HJ	2.23i	2.26 -98
Kaley	Sean	CAN	26.2.75	178/64	5000	13:25.16	13:41.15 -99
					10000	28:01.06	28:26.89 -99
Kaliszewski	Krzysztof	POL	9.8.72	185/110	HT	71.97	70.74 -99
* Kallabis	Damian	GER	10.6.73	177/67	3kSt	8:14.53	8:09.48 -99
Kalombo Mwenzé	Willie	ZAI	7.6.70	176/63	Mar	2:10:36	2:08:40 -99
* Kalya	William	KEN	4.8.74	171/62	10000	27:23.65	28:06.3A -98
Kamani	Bayano	USA	17.4.80	188/79	400H	48.43	48.68 -99
* Kamathi	Charles	KEN	18.5.78	165/51	3000	7:43.50	c.7:51+ -99
					5000	13:23.24	13:05.29 -99
^ Kamoga	Davis	UGA	17.7.68	180/73	400	45.74	44.37 -97
Kandie	Christopher	KEN	69		HMar	61:53	
Kandie	Jonathan	KEN	20.12.67	174/60	3kSt	8:12.30	8:11.14 -99
Kandie	Samson	KEN	20.4.71		Mar	2:10:50	2:08:31 -99
Kanyi	John	KEN	6.9.80		10000	27:47.44	28:11.00 -98
Kaouch	Adil	MAR	1.1.79	170/60	1500	3:34.41	3:34.28 -99
					Mile	3:52.22	3:51.62 -99
* Kaptyukh	Vasiliy	BLR	27.6.67	197/120	DT	67.59	66.92 -96
* Kapustin	Denis	RUS	5.10.70	189/86	TJ	17.46	17.65 -98, 17.86w -94
Karanu	James	KEN	5.1.76	175/62	800	1:46.46	1:46.60 -99
Kariuki	David	KEN	23.5.80		10000	28:16.31	28:18.33 -99
* Karjalainen	Olli-Pekka	FIN	7.3.80	194/108	HT	80.55	78.33 -99
Karlsson	Conny	FIN	30.12.75	193/118	SP	19.46	19.48 -97
Karlsson	Per	SWE	21.4.67	182/115	HT	75.78	75.29 -98
^ Karube	Shunji	JPN	8.5.69	184/69	400H	49.27	48.34 -97
Kaseorg	Indrek	EST	16.12.67	194/86	Dec	8024	8179 -98
Kasimili	Simon	KEN	12.12.80		HMar	61:14	
Kastánis	Spíridon	GRE	23.9.64	175/65	50kW	3:56:47	3:54:11 -90
Kato	Toshihide	JPN	4.7.73	174/55	HMar	61:55	
Kaveshnikov	Boris	RUS	30.9.74	180/64	800	1:45.71	1:46.04 -99
Kawabata	Shingo	JPN	15.5.78	175/70	100	10.11	10.37 -99
Kawai	Hironori	JPN	3.2.76		20kW	1:21:37	1:22:30 -98
Kawamura	Hideaki	JPN	15.9.74	175/67	400H	48.84	48.91 -98
Kawashima	Shinji	JPN	4.6.66	166/53	Mar	2:09:04	2:10:07 -98
Kawohl	Boris	GER	1.4.77	192/82	Dec	7788	7908 -99
Kazmierowski	Jacek	POL	2.7.74	185/76	TJ	16.54	16.59 -98
* Kedéris	Konstadínos	GRE	11.6.73	180/78	100	10.16	10.40 -97
					200	20.09	20.50 -99
Keflezighi	Mebrahtom	USA	5.5.75	169/58	5000	13:11.77	13:26.85 -98
					10000	27:53.63	28:10.70 -99
^ Keino	Martin	KEN	20.6.72	180/67	1500	3:35.67	3:33.00 -96
					3000	7:40.56	7:35.97 -97
Keitany	Luka	KEN		173/55	10000	27:55.89	27:21.29 -99
Keller	Thomas	SUI	25.5.73		110H	13.76	13.98 -99
Kemboi	Emmanuel	KEN	81		800	1:45.3A	1:48.4 -99
Kemboi	Simon	KEN	1.3.67	178/74	400	45.67A	44.94, 44.7A -93
Kemei	Philmon	KEN	12.2.82		3000	7:47.39	
					5000	13:24.04	13:38.4A -99
					10000	27:40.08	-0-
^ Kemp	Troy	BAH	18.6.66	187/69	HJ	2.23	2.38 -95

Name		Nat	Born	Ht/Wt	Event	2000 Mark	Pre-2000 Best
^ Kenah	Rich	USA	4.8.70	185/73	800	1:45.33	1:43.38 -97
Kennedy	Nery	PAR	28.5.73	186/95	JT	77.74	81.28 -98
Kenyon	Mike	USA	26.8.78	178/73	400	45.78	46.22 -99
Kerer	Armin	ITA	27.6.72	178/82	JT	77.07	80.25 -99
Keska	Karl	GBR	7.5.72	183/68	10000	27:44.09	29:10.40 -96
^ Keter	Erick	KEN	22.7.66	170/60	400H	50.06	48.24 -93
Khaldi	Mohamed	ALG	3.5.75	172/60	1500	3:33.40	3:36.28 -99
					Mile	3:54.66	
Khanafin	Aleksey	RUS	12.4.81	190/78	PV	5.56i, 5.50	5.40-99
* Khannouchi	Khalid	MAR/USA	22.12.71		HMar	60:28	60:27 -97
					Mar	2:07:01	2:05:42 -99
* Khattabi	Elarbi	MAR	16.5.67	174/61	3kSt	8:10.15	8:09.03 -99
* Khersontsev	Vadim	RUS	8.7.74	192/106	HT	78.16	80.68 -96
^ Khmelnitskiy	Mikhail	BLR	24.7.69	166/57	20kW	1:18:14	1:18:48 -98
Kholev	Dennis	ISR	21.10.75	182/76	PV	5.70b, 5.60A	5.50 -99
Khozhatelyov	Vitaliy	UZB	12.8.67	189/110	HT	75.62	72.22 -89
Khripunov	Sergey	RUS	15.9.76	181/70	20kW	1:21:36	1:22:29 -98
Khusnutdinov	Rustam	UZB	14.11.75	183/74	LJ	7.95	7.51 -99
Kibet	Lukas	KEN	19.6.73		Mar	2:11:16	2:12:55 -98
^ Kibitok	Philip	KEN	23.3.71	170/62	800	1:46.71	1:43.55 -96
Kibor	Joseph	KEN	22.12.72	178/60	HMar	61:15	60:27 -97
* Kibowen	John	KEN	21.4.69	175/64	1500	3:33.04	3:30.18 -98
					Mile	3:49.87	3:47.88 -97
^ Kidykas	Vaclovas	LIT	17.10.61	197/118	DT	61.78	68.44 -88
Kifle	Yonas	ERI	24.3.77	168/55	10000	28:07.15	
Kigen	Wilfred	KEN			3kSt	8:30.5A	
Kim	Jung-won	PRK	20.9.73	168/54	Mar	2:11:20	2:10:50 -96
* Kimani	David	KEN	28.2.78	183/66	5000	13:25.37	
Kimeli	Musa	KEN	23.6.68		1500	3:36.08	3:36.07 -99
Kimino	Takahiro	JPN	19.2.73	175/55	HJ	2.25	2.32 -93
Kimutai	David	KEN	19.8.69	165/57	20kW	1:21:23A	1:20:40A -96
* Kimutai	Japheth	KEN	20.12.78	173/55	800	1:43.87	1:42.69 -99
					1500	3:34.14	3:35.64 -98
* Kimwetich	Kenneth	KEN	1.1.73	183/73	800	1:44.20	1:43.03 -98
Kinnunen	Jarkko	FIN	21.4.70	176/75	JT	76.25	79.70 -90
^ Kinnunen	Kimmo	FIN	31.3.68	187/98	JT	81.41	90.82R -91, 85.96 -99
Kiogora	Stephen	KEN	10.11.74		HMar	61:09	61:37 -99
Kipchumba	John	KEN	74		HMar	62:00	62:30 -99
Kipchumba	Robert	KEN	24.2.84		10000	27:43.14	
Kipkassi	Peter	KEN			HMar	61:59	
* Kipketer	Sammy	KEN	29.9.81	166/52	3000	7:35.72	7:34.58 -99
					5000	12:54.07	12:58.10 -99
* Kipketer	Wilson	DEN	12.12.70	172/62	800	1:43.35	1:41.11 -97
Kipkoech	Luke Kiptoo	KEN	9.12.70	183/73	800	1:46.64	1:45.13 -99
* Kipkosgei	Luke	KEN	27.11.75	176/57	1500	3:37.46	3:35.48 -98
					3000	7:34.86	7:27.59 -98
					5000	12:56.50	12:57.32 –98
					10000	27:57.11	27:22.54 -98
* Kipkurui	Benjamin	KEN	28.12.80	174/57	800	1:46.30	1:44.50 -99
					1500	3:30.73	3:33.16 -99
					Mile	3:49.34	4:02.44 -98
Kiplagat	William	KEN	72		HMar	59:51	61:37 -99
					Mar	2:09:06	2:06:50 -99
Kiprono	Isaac	KEN	5.9.73		Mar	2:10:09	
* Kiprono	Josephat	KEN	12.12.73	172/52	Mar	2:07:29	2:06:44 -99
* Kiprop	Fred	KEN	3.6.74		Mar	2:08:23	2:06:47 -99
Kipsambu	Paul	KEN	18.2.62		Mar	2:10:45	2:08:25 -99
Kipsang	Salim	KEN	22.12.79	172/52	3000	7:48.71	7:57.21 -99
					10000	27:32.97	27:42.75 -98
* Kiptanui	Moses	KEN	1.10.70	175/60	3000	7:43.48, 7:38.33i	7:27.18 -95
					3kSt	8:16.68	7:56.16 -97
Kiptanui	Paul	KEN	69		Mar	2:10:43	2:09:09 -99
* Kiptoo Singoei	David	KEN	26.6.65	175/68	800	1:44.6	1:43.38 -96
^ Kiptum Muigei	William	KEN	30.3.71	168/55	10000	28:07.37A	27:17.20 -94
					HMar	61:25	60:54 -98
* Kirmasov	Sergey	RUS	25.3.70	181/115	HT	78.44	82.62 -98
Kirui	David	KEN	15.12.74	175/71	400	45.69, 45.6A	46.04 -99
* Kirui	Ismael	KEN	20.2.75	160/55	5000	13:11.18	13:02.75 -93
					10000	27:50.16	27:06.59 -95
Kirui	Philip	KEN	11.9.73		HMar	61:07	61:39 -99

	Name		Nat	Born	Ht/Wt	Event	2000 Mark	Pre-2000 Best
	Kirwa	Wilson	FIN	28.12.74	168/57	800	1:44.69	1:45.70 -99
	Kisang	David	KEN	74	168/58	1500	3:38.68	3:35.27 -96
						Mile	3:55.24	3:59.5 -98
	Kisilu	Bernard	KEN	6.12.74	173/64	800	1:46.71	1:44.76 -95
	Kislykh	Andrey	RUS	24.11.76	188/80	110H	13.49	13.43 -97
*	Kiss	Balázs	HUN	21.3.72	192/115	HT	79.22	83.00 -98
	Kiss	Szilárd	HUN	9.12.75	198/106	SP	20.01	19.06 -99
	Kite	Michael	KEN	73		HMar	61:42	
						Mar	2:09:46	
^	Kleiza	Saulius	LIT	2.4.64	196/125	SP	20.10	20.91 -87
	Klemic	Paul	USA	12.8.81		HJ	2.25	
	Klose	Holger	GER	5.12.72	191/104	HT	77.04	82.22 -98
	Klouchi	Kader	FRA	10.6.69	177/70	LJ	8.22	8.30, 8.33w -98
*	Klyugin	Sergey	RUS	24.3.74	192/82	HJ	2.35	2.36 -98
	Knabe	Sebastian	GER	13.10.78		Dec	7812	7754 -99
	Knight	Derek	USA	11.10.67	180/73	110H	13.60?, 13.61	13.37, 13.35w -95
	Kobayashi	Masayuki	JPN	4.4.74	175/62	HMar	61:04	62:21 -98
*	Kobs	Karsten	GER	16.9.71	196/118	HT	80.21	82.78 -99
	Kochkin	Sergey	RUS	1.7.70		TJ	16.93	17.30 -96
^	Koech	Benson	KEN	10.11.74	178/65	1500	3:32.76	3:32.09 -99
	Koech	Paul	KEN	69		TJ	16.50A	16.17A -98
^	Koers	Marko	NED	3.11.72	193/78	800	1:46.25	1:44.01 -97
						1500	3:34.44	3:33.05 -96
	Kohil	Kamel	ALG	26.12.71	155/52	10000	27:59.64	28:24.19 -97
	Koike	Akihiko	JPN	10.4.73	170/50	20kW	1:20:16	1:25:36 -97
	Kojima	Shigeyuki	JPN	25.9.79	173/64	100	10.20	10.26, 10.12w -99
	Kokin	Pavel	RUS	21.7.74	178/71	Mar	2:10:29	2:12:34 -99
	Kolasa	Adam	POL	2.8.75	191/75	PV	5.65sq	5.51 -99, 5.60sq -96
	Kolesnik	Vadim	UKR	29.4.69	185/115	HT	76.95	79.62 -94
	Kólko	Rajmund	POL	1.3.71	186/83	JT	82.28	82.50 -97
^	Kollár	Igor	SVK	26.6.65	175/62	20kW	1:22:25	1:18:41 -96
*	Komen	Daniel	KEN	17.5.76	170/60	3000	7:28.92	7:20.67 -96
						5000	13:01.78	12:39.74 -97
	Komenda	Tomás	CZE	24.7.78	187/78	Dec	7756	7622 -99
	Komu	Francis	KEN	74		HMar	61:33	
*	Konchellah	Patrick	KEN	20.4.68	181/68	800	1:44.58	1:42.98 -97
	Kondratowicz	Wojciech	POL	18.4.80	193/97	HT	76.59	74.12 -99
	Konevtsov	Roman	RUS	4.4.77	191/106	HT	74.82	78.70 -99
^	Kononen	Valentin	FIN	7.3.69	181/69	20kW	1:20:42	1:20:47 -99
						50kW	3:39:34	3:41:09 -97
	Konopka	Mikulás	SVK	23.1.79	192/102	SP	19.94	19.71 -99
	Konopka	Miloslav	SVK	23.1.79	189/102	HT	76.12	71.96 -99
*	Konovalov	Ilya	RUS	14.3.71	189/103	HT	81.93	80.51 -99
	Kónstas	Stáfanos	GRE	16.5.77	198/119	DT	61.06	59.17A -99
	Korányi	Balázs	HUN	30.5.74	177/75	800	1:46.21	1:45.39 -99
	Korchmyd	Aleksandr	UKR	22.1.82	187/75	PV	5.60sq	5.30 -99
	Korcok	Peter	SVK	12.8.74	178/64	50kW	3:54:56	3:59:01 -96
*	Korepanov	Sergey	KZK	9.5.64	170/61	50kW	3:53:05	3:39:22 -99
	Korir	Anthony	KEN	25.10.80		HMar	61:06	61:37 -99
^	Korir	Elijah	KEN	13.3.66		Mar	2:08:59	2:09:43 -99
*	Korir	John Cheruiyot	KEN	13.12.81	172/57	3000	7:43.35	
						5000	13:09.58	13:24.22 -99
						10000	27:24.75	27:38.86 -99
	Korir	Paul	KEN	77		800	1:44.21	1:47.6 -99
	Korkízoglou	Pródromos	GRE	27.2.75	190/84	Dec	8069	8025 -99
*	Korving	Robin	NED	29.7.74	188/87	110H	13.25	13.15 -99
*	Korzeniowski	Robert	POL	30.7.68	168/60	20kW	1:18:22	1:18:40 -99
						50kW	3:41:50	3:42:40 -96
	Köseoglu	Tolga	GER	16.11.76	194/90	DT	63.94	63.36 -96
*	Kosgei	Christopher	KEN	14.8.74	170/62	3kSt	8:20.49	8:05.43 -99
*	Kosgei	Japhet	KEN	20.12.[illegible]	[illegible]	HMar	[illegible]	60:01 -99
						Mar	2:07:15	2:07:09 -99
*	Kosgei	John	KEN	13.7.73	184/71	1500	3:37.74	3:34.09 -97
						3kSt	8:19.47	8:03.89 -97
*	Kosgei	Paul	KEN	22.4.78	175/57	3000	7:39.15	7:43.68 -98
						5000	13:05.44	-0-
						10000	27:38.22	
						3kSt	8:29.57	8:07.13 -99
*	Kosgei	Reuben	KEN	2.8.79	170/55	1500	3:37.24	
						3000	7:41.86i	
						3kSt	8:03.92	8:12.33- 99

Name		Nat	Born	Ht/Wt	Event	2000 Mark	Pre-2000 Best
Koskei	James Kimutai	KEN	23.11.68	172/62	1500	3:35.66	3:38.7A -99
					3000	7:36.33	7:36.55 -99
					5000	13:04.3	13:15.33 -99
Koski-Vähälä	Jarko	FIN	21.11.78	194/94	JT	77.95	74.90 -99
Kotzé	Jürgens	RSA	11.4.73	186/75	800	1:46.12	1:46.04 -95
^ Koukodímos	Konstadínos	GRE	14.9.69	186/80	LJ	8.09	8.36, 8.40w -94
^ Kovác	Igor	SVK	12.5.69	184/78	110H	13.60, 13.55Aw	13.13 -97
Kovács	Balázs	HUN	14.6.77	192/75	110H	13.67	13.81, 13.74i -99
* Kóvágó	Zoltán	HUN	10.4.79	204/127	DT	66.76	63.23 -99
Kovalenko	Viktor	MDA			Dec	7702	
Kovár	Milan	CZE	24.2.72	178/71	LJ	8.02	8.16 -98
Kozhevnikov	Sergey	RUS	12.5.70	180/64	800	1:46.27	1:46.34 -99
Kozmus	Primosz	SLO	30.9.79	188/102	HT	76.84	70.11 -99
Krantz	Frédéric	FRA	13.9.78	176/70	200	20.63	20.73, 20.40dq -99
Krasinski	Grzegorz	POL	11.1.75	188/90	JT	82.37	77.79 -98
^ Krasnov	Danny	ISR	27.5.70	184/82	PV	5.55	5.75 -94
Krause	Konstantin	GER	8.10.67	189/79	LJ	8.07i, 7.95	8.27 -97
Kravchenko	Vladimir	UKR	22.12.69	184/76	TJ	16.80	17.09 -97, 17.29w -96
Kravtsov	Aleksandr	RUS	18.3.74		HJ	2.24	2.22 -98
Krawczyk	Andrzej	POL	11.4.76	195/100	DT	63.56	63.60 -99
Krebs	Adrian	SUI	8.6.77	184/78	Dec	7758	7556 -99
Krehmic	Elvir	BIH	27.4.73	198/83	HJ	2.25i, 2.24	2.31 -98
* Kreissig	Wolfgang	GER	29.8.70	197/82	HJ	2.30i, 2.30	2.34 -99
Kremer	Jeff	USA	22.2.75	191/100	DT	61.16	60.20 -98
Kristiansson	Patrik	SWE	3.6.77	193/81	PV	5.70	5.77 -98
* Kronberg	Robert	SWE	15.8.76	181/77	110H	13.36	13.56 -99
Kronin	Aleksey	RUS	23.7.70	180/69	20kW	1:24:08	1:20:01 -99
* Kruger	Frantz	RSA	22.5.75	203/118	DT	69.75A	67.38 -99
Krummenacker	David	USA	24.5.75	190/79	800	1:46.62	1:44.57 -99
					1500	3:36.15	3:36.20 -99
^ Krykun	Aleksandr	UKR	1.3.68	194/110	HT	79.52	80.36 –93
Krysin	Aleksey	RUS	25.11.76	202/80	HJ	2.25i	2.30 -98
Krzosek	Grzegorz	POL	10.1.76	182/67	800	1:46.33	1:47.38 -97
Kumar	Anil	IND	28.8.73	178/74	100	10.21	10.33 -99
Kumar	Anil	IND	1.9.74		DT	61.30	60.48 -97
Kumara	Rohan Pradeep	SRI	10.3.75		400	45.25	45.77A -99
Kuntos	Jirí	CZE	2.10.73	188/78	TJ	16.49, 16.59w	17.29 -99
^ Kurennoy	Andrey	RUS	12.5.72	185/80	TJ	16.75	17.44 -97
Kürtösi	Zsolt	HUN	21.3.71	188/88	Dec	8149	8140 -98
Kusiak	Krzysztof	POL	13.5.74	198/89	PV	5.60sq	5.70 -98
Kuszewski	Marcin	POL	19.5.77	186/73	110H	13.45	13.60 -99
Kuzma	Jeff	USA	21.2.72	185/75	800	1:46.21	1:46.50 -99
Kysela	Martin	CZE	25.3.74	178/66	PV	5.70sq	5.60 -96, 5.65i -98
la Grange	Marcus	RSA	12.12.77	186/75	200	20.35	20.37A -99
					400	44.99A	-0-
Laaksonen	Mika	FIN	21.3.68	190/88	HT	72.31	76.22 -96
Laberge	Michael	CAN	10.2.74		LJ	7.93A	7.82A -97
Lachheb	Khalid	FRA	16.1.75	180/72	PV	5.65	5.80 -98
Lachheb	Taoufik	FRA	16.1.75	181/78	PV	5.65	5.72i, 5.63 -99
Lachkovics	Martin	AUT	25.1.75	178/80	200	20.61, 20.58w	20.48 -99
* Lagat	Bernard	KEN	12.12.74	175/61	1500	3:28.51	3:30.56 -99
					Mile	3:49.84	4:02.04, 3:55.65i -99
					3000	7:33.51	7:45.28 -98
					5000	13:23.46	13:36.12 -99
* Lagat	Elijah	KEN	19.6.66		Mar	2:09:47	2:07:41 -97
Lagat	Eliud	KEN	77		HMar	60:53	
* Lahlafi	Brahim	MAR	15.4.68	172/62	3000	7:29.25	7:28.94 -99
					5000	12:49.28	12:59.09 -99
^ Lahssini	El Hassan	MAR	1.1.74	177/64	3000	7:47.09i	7:30.53 -96
Laiho	Harri	FIN	1.3.77	188/85	Dec	7701	7394 -97
Lakhal	Saïd	MAR	16.4.70		800	1:46.26	1:46.20 -99
Lakhal	Yarba	MAR	12.2.75	168/61	3kSt	8:24.36	8:22.09 -95
Lambese	Bruno	FRA	11.4.69	190/96	Dec	7650	7643 -99
* Lambrechts	Burger	RSA	3.4.73	200/145	SP	20.56	20.29 -98
* Lamela	Yago	ESP	24.7.77	178/68	LJ	8.22	8.56i, 8.56 -99
Lamine	Philippe	FRA	4.10.76	183/80	110H	13.75, 13.66w	13.80 -98, 13.71w -99
Lane	Matt	USA	5.9.77	178/64	5000	13:27.24	13:46.90 -99
Langat	Sammy	KEN	24.1.70	168/57	800	1:46.52	1:43.26 -96
Langat	Shadrack	KEN	22.7.78	168/55	1500	3:35.57	3:34.93 -99
Langdon	Aaron	NZL	19.7.71		LJ	8.20w	7.99 -98

Name		Nat	Born	Ht/Wt	Event	2000 Mark	Pre-2000 Best
Lange	Björn	GER	15.6.79	193/90	JT	81.49	74.58 -99
Langlois	Denis	FRA	10.10.68	172/60	20kW	1:21:26	1:20:35 -97
					50kW	3:47:38	3:48:56 -99
Lao	Jianfeng	CHN	24.5.75	183/70	LJ	8.08	8.40 -97
					TJ	16.91	16.90 -97
Lassiter	Seneca	USA	12.3.77	175/60	1500	3:37.48	3:33.72 -99
					Mile	3:54.85	4:04.51 -97, 3:57.22i -99
Laukhin	Fyodor	UKR	13.2.74	184/75	Dec	8073	7829 -99
* Laukkanen	Juha	FIN	6.1.69	186/90	JT	82.35	88.22 -92
Laursen	Jimisola	SWE	13.7.77	184/86	400	45.68	46.04 -99
Lavy	Shane	USA	15.2.76	185/72	HJ	2.32i	2.30 -99
Laynes	Jeff	USA	3.10.70	178/84	100	10.16, 10.10w	10.01 -96, 9.9 -95
* Lebed	Sergey	UKR	15.7.75	179/63	3000	7:48.09	7:37.76 -99
					5000	13:27.53	13:18.18 -99
Leberer	Ralf	GER	26.10.73	184/78	110H	13.42, 13.40w	13.42 -99
Lebo	Duncan Kipkorir	KEN	30.12.82	167/52	10000	28:12.0A	28:14.5A -99
* Lee	Bong-ju	KOR	11.10.70	168/56	Mar	2:07:20	2:07:44 -98
Lee	Doo-yon	KOR	9.4.75	180/70	400H	50.00	50.79 -99
^ Lee	Jin-taek	KOR	13.4.72	190/72	HJ	2.25	2.34 -97
Lee	Kang-min	KOR	26.5.80		TJ	16.55	15.99 -99
Leenaerts	Bert	BEL	1.7.80		Mile	3:54.90	
* Leeper	Nathan	USA	13.6.77	188/82	HJ	2.35	2.30 -98
* Lelei	David	KEN	10.5.71	176/60	800	1:43.97	1:45.35 -99
					1500	3:36.38	3:31.53 -98
Lénis	Stamátios	GRE	11.10.77	185/75	TJ	17.01, 17.20w	16.62 -98
* Leone	Giacomo	ITA	10.4.71	171/59	HMar	61:29	61:10 -97
					Mar	2:08:41	2:09:07 -97
Leroy	Benjamin	BEL	9.1.73	173/66	50kW	4:01:46	4:03:49 -99
* Lewis	Brian	USA	5.12.74	170/72	100	10.02, 9.96w	10.00 -97, 9.98w -98
					200	20.26, 20.06rs	20.34 -99
Lewis	Maurice	USA	14.1.78	191/82	LJ	8.00i, 7.93	7.83 -99
Lewis	Paul	USA	30.10.77	178/73	200	20.14dt, 20.65Aw	20.78 -99
					400	45.59	45.82 -99
* Lewis-Francis	Mark	GBR	4.9.82	183/88	100	10.10	10.31, 10.26w -99
Leyckes	Dennis	GER	20.4.82	183/73	Dec	7897	
Li	Guoqing	CHN	1.10.79	165/57	50kW	3:54:56	3:57:24 –99
Li	Mingcai	CHN	22.1.71	168/55	50kW	3:59:41	3:49:17 -93
Li	Rongxian	CHN	8.1.72	180/80	JT	84.29	82.72 -99
Li	Shaojie	CHN	26.11.75	194/100	DT	62.29	65.16 -96
* Li	Zewen	CHN	5.12.73	172/55	20kW	1:21:12	1:18:32 -97
Lichtenneger	Elmar	AUT	25.5.74	187/83	110H	13.34	13.33 -99
Liepa	Janis	LAT	14.3.81	193/90	JT	76.06	76.12 -99
Liepins	Modris	LAT	3.8.66	178/68	20kW	1:20:50	1:20:09 -97
					50kW	3:48:36	3:47:48 -98
Lightfoot	Sean	USA	8.6.79	185/81	110H	13.74w	14.09, 13.87w -99
^ de Lima	Vanderlei	BRA	11.8.69	168/54	Mar	2:08:34	2:08:31 -98
de Lima	Vicente	BRA	4.6.77	165/63	100	10.18A	10.24 -99
					200	20.58A	20.56 -99
Limo	Abraham	KEN	10.12.63		Mar	2:09:17	2:11:37 -99
* Limo	Benjamin	KEN	23.8.74	178/65	3000	7:37.73	7:28.67 -99
					5000	12:55.82	12:55.86 -99
* Limo	Felix	KEN	22.8.80		3000	7:43.50	7:49.53 -99
					10000	27:04.54	28:23.30 -99
Limo	Remmy	KEN	25.8.71	182/79	TJ	16.52A	16.89 -98
* Limo	Richard	KEN	18.11.80	167/53	3000	7:37.12	7:34.32 -99
					5000	12:58.70	12:58.15 -99
Linden	Andreas	GER	20.2.65	185/90	JT	79.90	85.42 -95
Lindsey	Ben	USA	5.10.77	198/120	SP	19.50	19.91 -98
					DT	61.31	61.75 -98
Lingua	Marco	ITA	4.6.78	179/98	HT	73.52	76.72 -99
* Lipiec	Tomasz	POL	10.5.71	186/72	20kW	1:20:18	1:21:50 -93
Lischka	Michael	GER	23.12.73	197/135	SP	19.46	17.90 -99
					DT	63.17	63.42 -98
* Lister	Melvin	USA	29.8.77	188/75	200	20.51	20.95 -97
					LJ	8.49	8.18 -99
					TJ	16.96	17.02 -99
* Little	Kevin	USA	3.4.68	183/73	200	20.30	20.10 -99, 19.94w -95
Liu	Honglin	CHN	13.10.76	183/72	LJ	8.09	8.08 -97, 8.16w –99
Liu	Jun	CHN	28.2.75		50kW	3:57:51	3:57:10 -96
Liu	Xiang	CHN	23.7.83		110H	13.75	14.19 -99
Liu ¶	Yunfeng	CHN	3.8.79	173/62	20kW	1:20:01	1:21:12 -96

Name		Nat	Born	Ht/Wt	Event	2000 Mark	Pre-2000 Best
* Lobinger	Tim	GER	3.9.72	193/83	PV	5.95i, 5.85	6.00 -97
* Lobodin	Lev	RUS	1.4.69	188/88	Dec	8071	8571 -98
^ Logan	Jud	USA	19.7.59	193/123	HT	75.62	81.88 -88
Loikkanen	Mika	FIN	20.2.74	194/115	DT	60.45	62.24 -99
* Longo	Andrea	ITA	26.6.75	191/85	800	1:43.74	1:43.86 -98
Looije	Laurens	NED	12.1.73	185/75	PV	5.60A	5.71 -98
Lopatin	Aleksey	RUS	30.4.77	181/69	20kW	1:22:16	1:23:18 -98
Lopes Ferreira	Daniel	BRA	69		HMar	61:24	64:28 -99
López	Alejandro	MEX	9.2.75	173/61	20kW	1:20:09	1:17:56 -99
López	Francisco Javier	ESP	28.9.73	190/86	110H	13.74w	13.80A -99
Lorenzo	Santiago	ARG	4.4.78	191/88	Dec	7649	7344A -99
Loria	Mickaël	FRA	9.6.73	182/74	LJ	7.99, 8.00w	8.23A, 7.95 -98
Lotik	Thomas	KEN	7.7.70		HMar	61:39	
Louahala	Malik	ALG	19.12.77	174/72	400	45.55	
Louca	Mihalis	CYP	23.2.70	180/125	SP	19.05	19.70 -96
Loum	Omar	SEN	31.12.73	184/79	100	10.24A, 10.06Aw	10.19 -94
					200	20.21A, 20.43, 20.19w	20.42 -94
Lovkin	Semyon	RUS	14.7.77	180/67	20kW	1:20:12	1:22:29 -99
Lowe	Ian	CAN	23.2.73	183/75	LJ	7.98A	8.12A, 8.19Aw, 7.95 -99
Luaces	Isbel	CUB	20.7.75	187/97	JT	83.30	82.18 -99
Luczak	Krzysztof	POL	13.1.75	187/70	LJ	8.03	8.16 -97
* Lukashevich	Aleksey	UKR	11.1.77	174/68	LJ	8.27	8.16, 8.17w -99
Lunn	Jason	USA	19.7.74	187/71	1500	3:36.74	3:40.45 -99
Lusis	Voldemars	LAT	7.12.74	187/102	JT	83.08	81.48-99
^ Lyakhov	Sergey	RUS	1.5.68	195/107	SP	20.03	19.54 -99
					DT	60.72	66.78 -95
Lyolin	Aleksey	BLR	27.11.78	190/74	HJ	2.30	2.18 -99
Lyzhin	Pavel	BLR	24.3.81	189/110	SP	19.12	17.98 –99
Ma	Hongye	CHN	16.4.74		50kW	3:57:27	3:52:58 -97
Maase	Kamiel	NED	20.10.71	191/71	5000	13:14.13	13:25.17 -99
					10000	27:56.94	27:34.02 -99
* Maazouzi	Driss	FRA	20.10.69	180/65	1500	3:32.01	3:31.51 -99
					Mile	3:51.79	3:52.62 -98
					3000	7:39.93	7:36.21 -98
* Macey	Dean	GBR	12.12.77	196/92	Dec	8567	8556 -99
Mack	Tim	USA	15.9.72	188/78	PV	5.81	5.70 -98
Mackie	Ian	GBR	27.2.75	188/82	100	10.24, 10.05w	10.17 -96, 10.00w -98
* Mackowiak	Robert	POL	13.5.70	181/76	400	45.01	45.04 -98
Macrozonaris	Nicolas	CAN	22.8.80	178/82	100	10.19, 10.18Aw	10.33w -99
Maczey	Mike	GER	28.9.72	188/81	Dec	8461	8264 -99
Maddocks	Chris	GBR	28.3.57	176/67	50kW	3:57:10	3:51:37 -90
Maffei	Giuseppe	ITA	28.1.74	182/64	3kSt	8:25.68	8:11.85 -99
Magdziarczyk	Roman	POL	5.7.77	180/70	50kW	3:48:17	3:51:20 -99
* Magnússon	Jón Arnar	ISL	28.7.69	183/87	LJ	8.01w	8.00 -94
					Dec	8206	8573, 8583w -98
Magrans	Marc	ESP	26.9.76	185/80	Dec	7783	7673 -99
* Maina Munyi	Simon	KEN	18.3.78	177/52	5000	13:19.60	13:10.71 -98
					10000	27:18.95	27:18.74 -99
					HMar	60:48	0
* Maiyo	Benjamin	KEN	6.10.78	175/58	3000	7:32.36	7:42.88 -99
					5000	13:02.28	13:02.38 -99
* Makarov	Andrey	RUS	2.1.71	181/72	20kW	1:18:23	1:19:05 -97
Makarov	Sergey	RUS	19.3.73	192/95	JT	89.92	89.93 -99
Makau	Charles	KEN	13.3.71		800	1:45.57	1:45.70 -99
Makau	Harrison	KEN	74		1500	3:37.72	
Makori	David	KEN	6.11.73	178/63	HMar	61:40	61:45 -99
Maksimov	Dmitriy	RUS	6.5.77	174/57	10000	28:15.85	28:51.36 -98
Malasevich	Aleksandr	BLR	7.4.77	200/115	DT	62.52	63.78 -99
* Malcolm	Christian	GBR	3.6.79	174/67	200	20.19	20.29 -98
Malherbe	Arnaud	RSA	20.11.72	188/69	400	44.74	44.59A -99, 45.01 -98
Malík	Stefan	SVK	11.2.66	183/69	50kW	3:56:44	3:48:52 -97
Malina	Libor	CZE	14.6.73	192/120	DT	63.73	65.08 -98
Mallard	Milton	USA	24.11.73	183/75	100	10.18Aw	10.22 -99
					200	20.37Aw,20.57w	20.38 -99,20.3-97,20.18w -98
Malone	Casey	USA	6.4.77	203/106	DT	64.47A	61.49 -99
Malyavin	Vladimir	RUS	4.3.73	188/75	LJ	8.25	8.07 -97
Malysa	Jirí	CZE	14.8.66	180/71	20kW	1:19:18	1:20:16 -96
Mambo	Djeke	BEL	4.3.77	182/76	TJ	16.62i	16.21 -97
Mamedov	Chary	TKM	12.10.63	183/112	DT	62.06	56.50 -98
Mann	Adrian	USA	23.5.78	180/64	400H	49.68	50.32 -98
Mannon	Kevin	USA	12.8.76	193/118	HT	71.50	69.04 -99

Name		Nat	Born	Ht/Wt	Event	2000 Mark	Pre-2000 Best
^ Manson	Pat	USA	29.11.67	178/75	PV	5.63	5.85 -94
Maranga	Edwin	KEN	15.8.71	172/63	1500	3:37.12	3:35.62 -98
Marceny	Lionel	FRA	17.7.74	184/70	Dec	8094	7942 -99
Marciniszyn	Grzegorz	POL	22.5.77	187/82	LJ	8.00i, 7.96	8.04 -97, 8.12w -98
Maremane	Johannes	RSA	27.9.65	160/53	Mar	2:11:15	2:11:19 -96
Mariani	Maurillio	ITA	22.4.73	183/72	PV	5.70i	5.70 -99
Maritim	David	KEN	79		10000	27:39.31	28:36.4A -99
Maritim	Julius	KEN	80		3000	7:48.19	
					HMar	61:57	
* Markov	Dmitriy	AUS	14.3.75	182/85	PV	5.85	6.00 -98
^ Markov	Gennadiy	RUS	15.6.67	182/75	TJ	17.09i, 16.89	17.38 -94
* Markov	Ilya	RUS	19.6.72	178/65	20kW	1:20:53	1:18:30 -97
Markowski	Adrian	POL	14.10.78	184/75	JT	77.95	78.42 -97
Márquez	David	ESP	13.10.77	170/51	20kW	1:21:44	1:23:42 -99
^ Marsh	Damien	AUS	28.3.71	185/79	100	10.21Aw	10.13 -95
					200	20.63A	20.32 -95, 20.29w -93
^ Marsh	Mike	USA	4.8.67	178/75	100	10.01, 9.90w	9.93 -92, 9.87w -97
					200	20.26, 20.10w	19.73 -92
Martátos	Dimitríos	GRE	21.5.74	190/93	JT	78.26	78.79 -99
Martin	Andrew	AUS	12.5.80	191/94	JT	84.20	73.94 -99
* Martín	Eliseo	ESP	5.11.73	173/62	3kSt	8:13.63	8:13.59 -99
Martín	Francisco	ESP	27.5.75	173/74	50kW	4:00:16	4:12:28 -99
* Martín	Luis Miguel	ESP	11.1.72	180/69	3kSt	8:09.77	8:11.18 -99
Martin	Rephel	USA	23.4.76	170/70	LJ	8.05w	7.59 -99
Martínez	Alexander	CUB	23.8.77		TJ	16.80	16.67 -98
Martínez	David	ESP	31.1.67	195/105	DT	64.60	65.36 -92, 65.52dq -97
Martínez	Joan Lino	CUB	17.1.78	176/69	LJ	7.94, 8.18w	8.19 -98, 8.39ic -99
Martínez	José Manuel	ESP	22.10.71	176/65	5000	13:28.60	13:39.54 -99
					10000	27:53.9	27:51.82 -99
* Martínez	Julio	GUA	27.9.73	165/44	20kW	1:23:13	1:17:46 -99
* Martínez	Manuel	ESP	7.12.74	185/117	SP	20.55	20.79i -99, 20.27 -97
Martins	Pedro	POR	12.1.68	163/60	50kW	3:55:55	3:56:25 -99
Marwa	Francis	KEN	76		800	1:46.57A	1:45.78 -99
Marwa	Joel	KEN	30.8.74	179/63	800	1:45.11	1:44.5A -98
* Mashchenko	Ruslan	RUS	11.11.71	193/83	400H	48.76	48.06 -98
Maska	Vladimir	CZE	6.2.73	190/115	HT	80.98	81.28 -99
Mason	Germaine	JAM	1.4.83	187/68	HJ	2.24	2.03 -99
* Massana	Valentí	ESP	5.7.70	163/51	50kW	3:46:01	3:38:43 -94
Mastrov	Artyom	RUS	12.11.76	175/62	800	1:46.04	1:47.39 -99
Máté	Gábor	HUN	28.3.79	199/104	DT	66.91	61.74 -99
* Matete	Samuel	ZAM	27.7.68	183/81	400H	48.01	47.10 -91
Matsuda	Kazuhiro	JPN	24.6.74	177/62	Mar	2:10:24	2:12:25 -99
Matsumiya	Takayuki	JPN	21.2.80	162/47	10000	28:02.80	28:49.72 -99
Matsumiya	Yuko	JPN	21.2.80	163/48	10000	28:08.45	28:50.02 -99
					HMar	61:53	
Matthews	Todd	USA	28.6.79	193/86	110H	13.57	13.75 -99
* Matusevich	Konstantin	ISR	25.2.71	202/85	HJ	2.36	2.35 -97
* Matyukhin	Nikolay	RUS	13.12.68	178/68	20kW	1:22:52	1:19:43 -93
					50kW	3:42:02	3:40:13 -99
* Maybank	Anthuan	USA	30.12.69	188/81	400	44.80	44.15 -96
^ Mayo	Gilmar	COL	30.9.69	190/72	HJ	2.25A, 2.24	2.33 -94
* Mayock	John	GBR	26.10.70	177/66	1500	3:34.69	3:31.86 -97
					Mile	3:50.61	3:50.32 -96
					3000	7:49.97i	7:43.31i -97, 7:47.28 -95
* Mayola	Freddy	CUB	1.11.77	176/74	100	10.14, 10.10w, 10.00rw	10.10 -99
Mazza	Marco	ITA	25.6.77	168/53	10000	28:04.71	28:10.17 -99
McAfee	John	USA	15.3.78	186/64	400H	49.25	50.08 -99
McCall	Tony	USA	16.6.74	173/72	100	10.06	10.08 -97
					200	20.35w	20.27 -98
McCallun	Jonathan	GBR	19.11.75	181/62	1500	3:37.75	3:40.87 -99
McCarthy	Kris	AUS	15.10.79	180/75	800	1:46.57	1:47.59 -99
McCray	Danny	USA	11.3.74	181/84	400	45.00	44.81 -96
McCuaig	Bradley	CAN	12.12.70	176/77	100	10.18w	10.10A, 10.22 -98
McCullough	Sultan	USA	2.2.80	180/79	100	10.17	10.17 -99
^ McDonald	Michael	JAM	17.3.75	183/85	400	45.24	44.64A -96, 44.65 -97
McDonough	Daren	USA	30.5.74	183/78	PV	5.70	5.62 -94
* McFarlane	Danny	JAM	14.2.72	183/75	400	45.26	44.90 -95
McGehearty	Mark	USA	3.7.75	190/105	HT	74.03	71.65 -99
^ McGhee	Roland	USA	15.10.71	180/70	LJ	7.97, 8.09w	8.51 -95
McGrath	Dominic	AUS	4.6.72	180/70	50kW	3:57:51	3:59:15 -97
McGrath	Paddy	IRL	1.7.71	183/120	HT	71.24	77.49 -99

Name		Nat	Born	Ht/Wt	Event	2000 Mark	Pre-2000 Best
McHugh	Terry	IRL	22.8.63	191/106	JT	82.75	82.14 -94, 84.54R -91
McIlroy	James	GBR	30.12.76	180/68	800	1:45.96	1:45.32 -98
McIntosh	Troy	BAH	29.3.73	178/75	400	45.28	44.73A -96, 44.79 -99
McKay	Kevin	GBR	9.2.69	178/67	1500	3:37.34	3:34.59 -97
					Mile	3:55.07	3:53.64 -94
McKeown	Sean	USA	9.5.74		DT	63.55u	63.56 -99
McMahon	Kevin	USA	26.5.72	183/102	HT	78.55	79.26 -99
McMullen	Phil	USA	3.2.75	188/84	Dec	8097	8008w -98, 7731 -97
McNamara	Michael	USA	27.3.79	185/82	PV	5.60	5.18 -99
McReynolds	Uwezu	USA	20.9.70	183/77	110H	13.66	13.54 -99
Mears	Brad	USA	24.12.70	193/132	SP	19.81i	20.05 -99
Medina	Yoger	VEN	5.9.73	185/108	SP	20.01	19.56 -96
Medvedev	Vitaliy	KZK	6.1.77	172/64	100	10.21Aw	10.13 -99
Mehari	Mizan	AUS	28.12.80	165/51	5000	13:24.56	13:20.85 -98
Mehlich	Krzysztof	POL	2.8.74	190/80	110H	13.42	13.40 -96
Mehlich	Ronald	POL	26.9.69	190/86	110H	13.72	13.44 -97
Meité	Ibrahim	CIV	18.11.76	183/75	100	10.24	10.28 -95, 10.12w -96, 10.0A -99
* Mekonnen	Hailu	ETH	4.4.80	172/61	1500	3:33.14	3:35.63 -99
					Mile	3:53.40	-0-
					3000	7:38.39+i	7:33.00 -99
Melentyev	Sergey	RUS	5.12.76	178/68	20kW	1:22:30	1:24:39 -98
Meleshkevich	Artur	BLR	11.4.75	173/69	20kW	1:19:15	1:19:29 -97
Melétoglu	Hrístos	GRE	2.1.72	189/72	TJ	16.68	17.12 -97
* Meliz	Luis	CUB	11.8.79	177/76	LJ	8.43	8.14, 8.23ic -99
Ménal	Alex	FRA	9.8.72	180/72	200	20.60w	20.49 -96
* Menc	Miroslav	CZE	16.3.71	197/130	SP	20.64	20.15 -97, 20.58i -98, 21.19ex -99
Mendes	Rodrigo	BRA	21.6.68		TJ	16.78	16.27 -99
Meneses	Oscar	GUA	12.5.77	178/69	100	10.19w	10.32, 10.0w -98
Menton	John	IRL	7.5.70	201/120	DT	63.70	60.27 -99
Merced	Chris	PUR	26.1.76	180/128	SP	20.22	18.70 -99
^ Mercenario	Carlos	MEX	3.5.67	175/63	50kW	3:50:28	3:42:03 -91
Mereng	Joseph	KEN	3.1.71		HMar	61:52	61:36 -99
					Mar	2:09:35	2:09:36 -99
Meriluoto	Johan	FIN	22.3.74	187/73	TJ	16.95	16.85 -99
Mersal	Hatem	EGY	20.1.75	183/76	LJ	8.12	8.31 -99
Mertens	Michael	GER	27.12.65	191/105	SP	19.98	20.24 -98
* Mesnil	Romain	FRA	13.7.77	188/79	PV	5.75	5.93 -99
Mestre	Richard	CUB	6.1.81		TJ	16.50w	16.38 -99
Metto	Luke	KEN	.76		HMar	61:21	63:15 -99
Mewes	David	GER	7.10.76	196/95	Dec	8108	8107 -99
* Mezegebu	Assefa	ETH	19.6.78	175/55	5000	13:06.13	12:53.84 -98
					10000	27:19.75	27:18.28 -99
Michniewski	Robert	POL	16.2.74	188/76	HJ	2.23	2.15 -99
Mikhaylenko	Vladimir	UKR	27.8.73	196/84	Dec	8052	7992 -99
Mikhaylichenko	Yevgeniy	RUS	13.2.79	181/68	PV	5.65	5.40A, 5.40 -98, 5.50i -99
Mikhnevich	Andrey	BLR	12.7.76	202/115	SP	20.48i, 20.12	20.30, 20.52 i -99
Miki	Hiroshi	JPN	10.6.75	175/57	Mar	2:09:30	2:08:05 -99
Milazar	Éric	MRI	1.6.75	192/80	400	44.87	45.31 -98
Milos	Derek	USA	28.9.72	188/84	PV	5.65	5.50 -97
Miller	Brian	USA	20.3.72	193/135	SP	19.93	20.43 -97
* Miller	Coby	USA	19.10.76	168/68	100	9.98, 9.88w	10.03 -99
					200	19.96	20.04 -99
Miller	Lavar	USA	16.2.77	188/79	HJ	2.23i	2.25i, 2.22 -99
^ Mills	Derek	USA	9.7.72	175/68	400	45.52	44.13 -95
^ Minor	Deon	USA	22.1.73	193/82	400	45.37	44.75 -92
Miranda	Montxu	ESP	27.12.76	191/83	PV	5.81	5.78i -98, 5.71 -99
Miranda	Salvador	MEX	22.8.71	172/57	3kSt	8:25.69	8:36.24 -98
Mishiro	Yaoki	JPN	16.3.77	165/53	10000	27:59.39	28:09.59 -99
* Misoi	Kipkirui	KEN	23.12.78	177/59	3000	7:40.93	7:44.91 -98
					3kSt	8:07.21	8:08.62 -99
Mistretta	Alessandro	ITA	6.3.71	172/58	50kW	3:54:38	3:51:33 -99
^ Misyulya	Yevgeniy	BLR	9.3.64	178/68	20kW	1:19:33	1:18:18 -96
^ Mitchell	Dennis	USA	20.2.66	174/69	100	10.09, 10.04w	9.91 -91, 9.85w -93
					200	20.39	20.20 -92, 20.09A -89
^ Mitchell	Maurice	USA	14.5.71	196/86	400H	49.23	47.97 -96
Mitchell	Michael	USA	81		200	20.59	20.98, 20.92w -99
Mitei	Enoch	KEN	26.11.80		5000	13:19.55	
Miyamoto	Yoshifumi	JPN	9.2.73	175/61	HMar	61:38	64:17 -99
Modelski	Michal	POL	16.4.75	186/84	Dec	7685	7546 -99
Moeketsana	Motsehi	RSA	2.2.70		HMar	61:22	62:47 -99

Name		Nat	Born	Ht/Wt	Event	2000 Mark	Pre-2000 Best
^ Moen	Geir	NOR	26.6.69	190/85	100	10.24, 10.14w	10.08 -96
					200	20.63	20.17 -96
Mofokeng	George	RSA	19.2.79	155/44	HMar	61:42	
Moiben	John	KEN	12.4.68		Mar	2:11:04	2:10:07 -99
* Mokganyetsi	Hendrik	RSA	7.9.75	190/76	400	44.59	45.30A -98, 45.85 -97
* Molina	Enrique	ESP	25.2.68	175/62	3000	7:43.41	7:32.32 -97
					5000	13:15.75	13:07.34 -97
					10000	27:59.80	27:49.71 -98
Molina	Juan Manuel	ESP	15.3.79	170/52	20kW	1:22:43	1:23:39 -99
* Möllenbeck	Michael	GER	12.12.69	200/120	DT	65.49	67.44 -96
Monachon	Raphaël	SUI	8.2.73	186/80	110H	13.48	13.68 -98
Moncur	Avard	BAH	2.11.78	196/82	400	44.72	45.09 -99
^ Moneghetti	Steve	AUS	26.9.62	176/60	Mar	2:10:00	2:08:16 -90
Monreal	Iñigo	ESP	26.9.74	191/85	400H	49.86	49.88 -95
Monte	Yosmel	CUB	26.6.77	189/100	HT	71.99	67.80 -96
Montesinos	Hipólito	ESP	24.5.76	186/79	110H	13.72	13.59 -99
* Montgomery	Tim	USA	28.1.75	178/69	100	10.01, 9.96w	9.92 -97
					200	20.56w	20.52 -99, 20.44w -97
Montgomery	Will	USA	23.6.80	188/79	LJ	7.95w	7.59 -98
Monye	Jude	NGR	16.11.73	188/79	400	45.41	44.83 -96
Moore	Stephen	USA	13.8.75	180/75	Dec	7803	8037 -99
Morán	Ramiro	ESP	17.5.69	173/63	3kSt	8:21.25	8:17.49 -98
* Morceli	Noureddine	ALG	28.2.70	172/62	1500	3:38.41	3:27.37 -95
Moreno	Marcos	ESP	14.3.73	193/94	Dec	7790	7314 -99
* Morgan	Dinsdale	JAM	19.11.72	188/77	400H	48.80	48.13 -98
Morgan	Nathan	GBR	30.6.78	187/86	LJ	8.00, 8.05w	8.11 -98
* Mori	Fabrizio	ITA	28.6.69	175/68	400H	48.40	47.72 -99
Morimasa	Tatsumi	JPN	3.4.76	171/56	HMar	61:49	63:07 -97
^ Morinaga	Masaki	JPN	27.3.72	175/64	LJ	8.05, 8.34w	8.25 -92
Moroney	Nick	AUS	3.8.72		HJ	2.25	2.22 -94
Moroz	Gennadiy	BLR	27.5.78	200/77	HJ	2.25	2.25 -98, 2.28i -99
Mortimer	Allen	BAH	1.9.77	172/73	TJ	16.51	16.58 -96
* Mosima	Philip	KEN	2.1.77	168/55	5000	13:09.69	12:53.72 -96
Moskalenko	Vitaliy	RUS	30.6.74		TJ	16.72	17.00i, 16.84 -99
Moss	Santana	USA	1.6.79	178/79	LJ	7.98w	7.57 -99
^ Motchebon	Nico	GER	13.11.69	186/81	800	1:46.04	1:43.91 -96
Motiejunas	Jonas	USA	12.12.74	188/77	400	45.67, 45.4	45.64 -99
Mottram	Craig	AUS	18.6.80	188/72	1500	3:38.27	3:43.37 -99
					5000	13:26.20	13:40.48 -99
* Moudrik	Younès	MAR	1.10.77	176/72	LJ	8.34	8.20 -99
Mounts	Van	USA	5.1.80	183/120	SP	19.05	17.58 -98
* Mourhit	Mohammed	BEL	10.10.70	164/55	1500	3:36.14	3:37.73 -91
					3000	7:26.62	7:32.65 -99
					5000	12:49.71	12:58.45 -99
					10000	27:45.75	26:52.30 -99
					HMar	60:50	60:18 -97
Moussaoui	Samir	ALG	15.5.75	172/65	10000	28:07.20	28:01.34 -99
Mpulanyane	Simon	RSA	10.9.70	150/47	HMar	61:40	
Mrikik	Lahoussine	MAR			HMar	61:04	63:15 -99
Mubarak	Bilal Saad	QAT	18.12.72	189/110	SP	19.40	19.65 -97
Mucheru Maina	Leonard	KEN	13.6.78		3000	7:41.56	
					5000	13:21.14	
Muchiri	Gabriel	KEN	78		Mile	3:56.43	
					5000	13:23.96	
					10000	27:47.97	28:06.1A -99
Mueller	Jeff	USA	1.10.78	193/77	HJ	2.23	2.14 -96
Mukae	Tadakatsu	JPN	17.10.76	178/58	10000	28:08.45	28:27.90 -99
Mulaudzi	Mbulaeni	RSA	8.9.80	171/62	800	1:45.55	1:48.33A -99
Müller	Grzegorz	POL	3.11.73	168/59	50kW	3:59:08	-0-
Muñoz	Hugo	PER	10.1.73	188/73	HJ	2.25A	2.30 -95
Murakami	Yukifumi	JPN	23.12.79	183/80	JT	78.37	76.54 -97
* Murofushi	Koji	JPN	8.10.74	187/89	HT	81.08	79.17 -99
* Murphy	Andrew	AUS	18.12.69	185/82	TJ	17.12	17.32 -99
Murray	John	INA	6.6.78	163/58	100	10.23dt	10.54 -99
Mustapic	Dragan	CRO	23.3.63	196/106	DT	64.40	63.70 -97
Mutai	Sammy	KEN	20.12.74	180/68	1500	3:38.51	3:33.44 -99
Mutua	Joseph Mwengi	KEN	10.12.78	170/58	800	1:45.49A	1:46.3A -96
Muzík	Jirí	CZE	1.9.76	181/75	400H	48.71	48.27 -97
Mwangi	Paul	KEN	19.11.73	179/63	1500	3:34.29	3:36.51 -98
Myburgh	Alwyn	RSA	13.10.80	188/71	400H	49.07A, 49.11	50.15A -99
Myerscough	Carl	GBR	21.10.79	208/142	SP	19.71i-dq	19.46 -98

Name		Nat	Born	Ht/Wt	Event	2000 Mark	Pre-2000 Best
* Myles-Mills	Leonard	GHA	9.5.73	172/68	100	10.15	9.98 -99
Naali	Egoberto Robert	TAN	72		HMar	61:45	
^ Nachum	Rogel	ISR	21.5.67	181/73	TJ	16.98	17.20 -92, 17.31w -91
Nada Saya	John	TAN	8.8.78		HMar	61:19	61:27 -99
Nagata	Koichiro	JPN	19.12.78	175/59	10000	27:53.19	
Nakamura	Tetsuya	JPN	7.1.73	175/65	100	10.22w	10.26 -99, 10.25w -95
Nance	Jon	USA	28.8.77	183/73	PV	5.55	5.11 -97
* Närhi	Matti	FIN	17.8.75	188/100	JT	82.74	88.24 -97
Nau	Manuel	GER	2.7.77	190/90	JT	83.04	80.74 -99
Nazipov	Mukhamet	RUS	10.9.64	178/64	Mar	2:10:35	2:11:01 -98
Ndegwa	David	KEN	17.12.72		HMar	61:08	62:12 -99
Ndereva Njeru	Nelson	KEN	14.7.67		Mar	2:11:05	2:10:37 -96
Ndungu	James	KEN	30.4.79		10000	28:02.06	28:05.47 -99
					HMar	60:50	61:49 -99
Nduwimana	Jean-Patrick	BDI	9.5.78	178/61	800	1:44.06	1:46.03 -99
Neal	McClinton	USA	11.7.68	193/91	400H	49.76	48.34 –92
Neale	Alfred	USA	1.7.81		HJ	2.25i	
Negru	Nicolae	ROM	2.8.72	171/62	HMar	61:54	61:45 -97
Neighbour	Aaron	AUS	2.12.77	190/113	SP	19.66u	18.95 -98
Nejedly	Michael	CZE	1.10.69	/70	3kSt	8:27.60	8:33.00 -97
* Nelson	Adam	USA	7.7.75	183/114	SP	22.12	20.64 -99
Nelson	Corey	USA	9.10.77	183/77	400	45.6	45.36 -99
Nelson	Ron	USA	15.1.78		HJ	2.25	2.23i, 2.23 -99
Nemchaninov	Andrey	RUS	27.11.66	180/105	SP	19.55	20.95i -88, 20.60 -92
Németh	Roland	HUN	19.9.74	177/77	100	10.10	10.08 -99
* Németh	Zsolt	HUN	9.11.71	190/110	HT	80.02	81.56 -99
Netshifhefhe	Bethuel	RSA	16.3.72		HMar	61:57	63:02 -99
Newton	Rod	USA	3.11.76	190/79	HJ	2.25	2.17 -99
Ngadi	Salaho	TAN	12.3.79		HMar	61:53	
Ngatho	Zakayo	KEN	18.3.78	165/54	5000	13:21.33	
					10000	27:44.01	28:49.2A -99
* Ngeny	Noah	KEN	2.11.78	182/68	800	1:44.49	1:44.7+ -99
					1500	3:28.12	3:28.6+, 3:28.73 -99
					Mile	3:47.67	3:43.40 -99
					3000	7:35.46	-0-
Ngolebus	Joseph	KEN	75		Mar	2:08:49	2:11:44 -98
Niaré	Yves	FRA	20.7.77	195/100	SP	19.22	18.57i, 18.23 -99
Nichols	Regan	USA	26.7.73	183/79	400H	49.47	48.66 -98
Nicolay	Christian	GER	4.3.76	188/90	JT	80.19	79.96 -96
Nieland	Nick	GBR	31.1.72	193/95	JT	85.09	83.68 -99
Niemi	Shane	CAN	2.6.78	186/80	200	20.62w	20.69A -99
					400	45.58A, 45.79	45.52 -99
Nieto	James	USA	2.11.76	193/79	HJ	2.23	2.30 -99
Nieves	Néstor	VEN	29.12.74	169/65	3kSt	8:27.36	8:28.59 -99
Niketic	Djordje	YUG	11.3.76	200/75	HJ	2.24	2.26 -98
Niklaus	André	GER	30.8.81	190/78	Dec	7712	7339 -99
Nizhegorodov	Denis	RUS	80		20kW	1:21:47	
^ Nizigama	Aloÿs	BDI	18.6.66	172/53	3000	7:44.06	7:35.08 -94
					5000	13:21.62	13.12.14 -93
					10000	27:44.56	27:20.38 -95
Njenga	Michael	KEN	5.5.72		10000	28:06.27	27:43.37 -99
Nkete	Laban	RSA	13.11.70		HMar	61:35	62:40 -99
^ Noack	Axel	GER	23.9.61	181/68	50kW	3:58:52	3:43:50 -93
Nohilly	Tom	USA	27.4.66	183/65	3kSt	8:25.09	8.16.92 -92
Nolan	James	IRL	27.1.77	183/71	1500	3:36.30	3:40.2 -99
Nolan	Michael	CAN	22.9.73	188/93	Dec	7914A	7886 -96, 8009w -97
Nomkhuna	Nattaporn	THA	15.9.71		TJ	16.53	16.42 -98
* Nool	Erki	EST	25.6.70	184/84	PV	5.55	5.60 -98
					Dec	8742	8672 -98
Noonan	Kieran	AUS	7.9.76		100	10.20w	10.55, 10.33w -98
Nordin	Jimmy	SWE	19.10.79	179/115	SP	20.07	19.28 -99
Nossmy	Philip	SWE	6.12.82	187/83	110H	13.63	14.33 -99
Noúsios	Astérios	GRE	79		LJ	8.00	7.60, 7.94w -99
Nowak	Marcin	POL	2.8.77	174/71	100	10.21	10.23 -99
					200	20.51	20.74 -98
Nsenga	Jonathan	BEL	21.4.73	188/82	110H	13.51	13.25 -98
Nsiah	Christian	GHA	25.12.75	195/80	100	10.19	10.37, 10.28w -99
^ Ntawulikiura	Mathias	RWA	14.7.64	171/60	HMar	61:41	62:48 -98
					Mar	2:09:56	
Nthépé	Aimé-Issa	FRA	26.6.73	180/70	100	10.24, 10.22w	10.26, 10.16w -99
					200	20.64	21.33w -99

	Name		Nat	Born	Ht/Wt	Event	2000 Mark	Pre-2000 Best
	N'Tyamba	João	ANO	20.3.68	172/70	HMar	61:21	62:54 -98
	Nyabuti	Elijah	KEN	10.2.79		HMar	61:23	
	Nymark	Trond	NOR	28.12.76	180/62	50kW	3:53:10	3:54:36 -99
	Nyombi	Godfrey	UGA	10.10.78		HMar	61:39	62:07 -99
*	Obikwelu	Francis	NGR	22.11.78	195/74	100	9.97	10.01 -98
						200	20.01	19.84 -99
	Obregón	Yosvany	CUB	3.11.72	186/90	SP	19.82	19.00 -98
^	Ochieng	Kennedy	KEN	30.12.71	183/73	400	45.77	44.82, 44.5A -93, 44.77A -99
	Odom	Deworski	USA	11.4.77	188/84	110H	13.44A, 13.59, 13.38Aw	13.59, 13.56w -99
	Odriozola	Mikel	ESP	25.5.73	180/62	20kW	1:22:29	1:22:32 -99
						50kW	3:45:57	3:47:24 -98
	Ohlsson	Christian	SWE	25.1.80	192/70	TJ	16.97	16.30, 16.59w -99
	Okantey	Samuel	GHA	3.11.74	183/77	TJ	16.69	16.74 -99
	Okemwa	Albert	KEN	66		HMar	61:21	61:06 -99
	Okenwa	Ike	USA	18.4.80		100	10.22w	10.46 -99
	Olekaibe	Ike	USA	2.7.78		TJ	16.47, 16.60w	16.17 -99
	Olgundeniz	Ercüment	TUR	7.7.76		DT	62.90	62.25 -99
*	Olijars	Stanislavs	LAT	22.3.79	190/80	110H	13.25	13.28 -99
						LJ	7.94i	7.57A -97
	de Oliveira	Raphael R	BRA	5.2.79	172/68	100	10.20A	10.36 -99
	Olli	Jari	FIN	3.4.77	186/75	Dec	7783	7445 -98
	Olmedo	Pablo	MEX	8.5.75	175/60	5000	13:24.84	13:13.32 -98
						10000	28:13.01	28:23.07 -97
	Olsen	Joachim	DEN	31.5.77	184/120	SP	20.88	19.75 -99
	Olson	Dan	USA	27.9.82		HJ	2.23i	
	Omodiale	Sylvester	NGR	5.9.77	173/68	400H	49.44	50.02 -99
	Omoto	Yuki	JPN	29.10.78	172/60	400H	49.74	51.88 -99
	Onitsuka	Tomonori	JPN	21.3.80	160/48	HMar	61:37	
^	Onyancha	Frederick	KEN	25.12.69	170/64	800	1:45.44	1:42.79 -96
	Oprea	Ionel	ROM	12.10.70	190/120	DT	62.79	59.52 -90
	Oprea	Marian	ROM	6.6.82	190/80	TJ	16.49	15.98 -99
	Oravec	Roman	CZE	5.4.78	190/73	800	1:46.54i	1:45.06 -99
	Ordina	Tibor	HUN	17.3.71	191/80	TJ	16.58i	16.96i -98, 16.90 -96
	Ornellas	Hélder	POR	6.5.74	176/63	5000	13:18.56	13:32.65 -97
^	Ortíz	Arturo	ESP	18.9.66	190/73	HJ	2.24	2.34 -91
	Osakada	Jun	JPN	2.4.74	177/67	400	45.05	45.69 -99
*	Osoro	Ondoro	KEN	3.12.67	167/63	HMar	61:50	62:10 -93
						Mar	2:10:29	2:06:54 -98
	Otieno	Samuel	KEN	10.4.73		Mar	2:09:10	2:10:41 -99
	Otto	Björn	GER	16.10.77	188/84	PV	5.65x, 5.60, 5.71ex	5.55, 5.60ex -99
	Ouaadi	Mohamed	FRA	1.1.69	172/57	Mar	2:08:49	2:07:55 -99
^	Ovchinnikov	Vladimir	RUS	2.8.70	190/90	JT	82.60	88.00 -95
	Ovois	Gaël	FRA	10.5.72	181/72	LJ	7.94w	7.86 -98
	Owusu	Andrew	GHA	8.7.72	180/75	TJ	16.74, 16.78w	17.23 -98
	Pacheco	Yoelmis	CUB	9.6.82	180/74	LJ	7.95	7.62 -99
^	Pakarinen	Ari	FIN	14.5.69	182/98	JT	78.71	85.18 -95
	Pakhlayev	Yuriy	KZK	20.12.74	188/68	HJ	2.26	2.25, 2.27i -97
	Palyszko	Maciej	POL	4.1.78	186/110	HT	80.25	75.92 -99
^	Pancorbo	Manuel	ESP	7.7.66	178/63	3000	7:49.28	7:31.59 -98
						10000	28:05.86	-0-
	Pankúch	Pavol	SVK	20.2.75	193/115	SP	19.31	19.78 -99
	Paoluzzi	Loris	ITA	14.5.74	191/110	HT	79.47	80.98 -99
*	Papadimitríou	Aléxandros	GRE	18.6.73	183/123	HT	80.45	78.88 -99
^	Papakóstas	Lábros	GRE	20.10.69	193/73	HJ	2.34	2.36 -92
*	Pappas	Tom	USA	6.9.76	194/85	Dec	8467	8463 -99
	Paredes	Benjamin	MEX	30.4.62	162/50	Mar	2:11:24	2:10:40 -94
	Parker	David	GBR	28.2.80	189/93	JT	78.24	77.48 -99
	Parker	James	USA	3.12.75	180/107	HT	72.30	71.24 -99
*	Parrela	Sanderlei Claro	BRA	7.10.74	193/78	200	20.60A	20.83 -97
						400	44.65	44.29 -99
^	Partyka	Artur	POL	25.7.69	192/71	HJ	2.37i, 2.20	[illegible]
*	Parviainen	Aki	FIN	26.10.74	191/96	JT	90.97	93.09 -99
	Pasanen	Teemu	FIN	24.5.77	187/97	JT	77.00	78.37 -99
	Passoni	Massimo	ITA	25.3.71	170/64	50kW	4:02:17	4:02:45 -97
	Pastrnák	Ales	CZE	9.4.76	189/94	Dec	7801	7604 -98
	Pate	Miguel	USA	13.6.79		LJ	8.26	7.73 -98
	Patros	David	FRA	11.9.77	180/75	100	10.13	10.37, 10.36w -99
						200	20.51	21.19 -98
	Patterson	Carlos	CUB	20.2.78	186/79	110H	13.5	13.74w -99
	Patterson	Henry	USA	27.5.75	196/86	HJ	2.29i, 2.27	2.32 -99

Name		Nat	Born	Ht/Wt	Event	2000 Mark	Pre-2000 Best
Patton	Darvis	USA	4.12.77	183/75	100	10.22A, 10.09w	10.3 -98
					200	20.29	20.49w -98
					LJ	8.04, 8.07w	8.06w -98
Pauli	Jake	USA	15.6.79	191/86	PV	5.65	5.55 -99
Páumier	Alexis	CUB	21.1.75	191/100	SP	20.78	17.71 -99
Pausé	Dominique	FRA	11.1.76	176/72	JT	76.86	76.01 -98
Pavlakákis	Ággelos	GRE	7.11.76	173/68	100	10.13	10.11 -97
Pavlov	Igor	RUS	79		PV	5.70sq, 5.55	5.30i -99, 5.10 -98
^ Payne	Bill	USA	21.12.67	188/77	PV	5.60	5.86 -91
Pechonkin	Yevgeniy	RUS	9.10.73	192/82	110H	13.39, 13.37w	13.38 -96
* Pedroso	Iván	CUB	17.12.72	176/70	LJ	8.65	8.71, 8.96Adw -95, 8.79w-
Pei	Chuang	CHN	5.12.81		50kW	3:56:20	
Pelepyagin	Pavel	BLR	29.6.78	184/72	800	1:45.8	1:47.82 -99
Pemberton	Darius	USA	10.5.75	185/77	LJ	8.09w	8.07 -97, 8.12w -94
Pencréach	Gaël	FRA	5.8.77	180/68	3kSt	8:14.94	8:13.16 -99
Pennings	Wilbert	NED	12.2.75	194/81	HJ	2.25i, 2.25	2.30 -99
* Peña	Antonio	ESP	26.8.70	175/60	10000	28:02.1	28:50.67 -91
					Mar	2:07:47	2:11:35 -92, 2:10:49dh -97
* Pérez	Jefferson	ECU	1.7.74	174/59	20kW	1:20:18	1:18:24 -97
Pérez	José Manuel	ESP	6.5.73	185/115	HT	72.81	73.34 -95
Perez	Ricardo	PUR	9.11.78		HJ	2.23	
Pérez	Santiago	ESP	15.1.72	179/70	50kW	3:51:24	3:45:55 -98
Pérez Rionda	Luis	CUB	16.8.69	172/72	100	10.13w	10.18 -97
* Peric	Dragan	YUG	8.5.64	186/115	SP	19.88	21.77 -98
^ Perricelli	Giovanni	ITA	25.8.67	170/57	50kW	3:50:21	3:43:55 -94
Perry	Curtis	USA	26.10.74	191/91	200	20.52w	20.40 -98, 20.25A -97, 20.24w -99
Pestano	Mario	ESP	8.4.78	193/105	DT	61.63	61.73 -99
Peterson	Derrick	USA	28.11.77	182/73	800	1:45.18	1:45.88i, 1:46.75 -99
Peterson	Joshua	RSA	8.3.75		Mar	2:11:19	2:13:19 -99
Petin	Yevgeniy	UZB	29.1.75	182/71	TJ	16.67	16.55 -98, 16.67w -97
Petrucci	Nick	USA	10.11.75		DT	64.74	60.46A -99
Pettersson	Kristian	SWE	5.10.71	193/129	DT	65.10	62.66 -98
* Pettigrew	Antonio	USA	3.11.67	183/76	400	44.57	44.21 -99
Pfingsten	Gunnar	GER	24.3.75	196/120	SP	20.08	20.00 -99
Phelps	Dason	USA	5.5.76		PV	5.55i	5.25 -99
Philipp	Peter	SUI	18.2.72	184/68	1500	3:36.72	3:35.87 -99
Phillips	Chris	USA	24.7.72	183/77	110H	13.27	13.32A, 13.43 -99
* Phillips	Dwight	USA	1.10.77	183/77	100	10.11w	10.51 -99
					LJ	8.21, 8.30w	8.18 -99
Pienaar	Hardus	RSA	10.8.81	190/88	JT	78.11	75.71A -99
Pierce	Andrew	USA	8.6.79	196/77	200	20.64Aw	21.18, 21.13w -99
					400	44.87	45.86 -99
Piller	René	FRA	23.4.65	168/57	50kW	3:47:49	3:41:28.2t -94
Pincemail	Sébastien	FRA	21.2.79	186/84	TJ	16.69	16.14 -98, 16.34w -99
Pino	Jorge Luis	CUB	6.7.69	174/65	20kW	1:24:14	1:24:15 -96
					50kW	4:02:09	3:58:37 -96
* Pinto	António	POR	22.3.66	165/59	HMar	60:35	59:43 -98
					Mar	2:06:36	2:07:55 -97
Piolanti	Raphaël	FRA	14.11.67	192/103	HT	75.81	79.68 -92
Pires	João	POR	10.6.79	175/70	800	1:45.59	1:46.83 -99
* Piskunov	Vladislav	UKR	7.6.78	183/106	HT	81.56	80.00 -99
Piziks	Rojs	LAT	12.2.71	195/90	Dec	7746	8045 -96
Pizzoli	Emiliano	ITA	29.6.74	192/80	110H	13.54	13.60, 13.5 -99, 13.43r -98
Plawgo	Marek	POL	25.2.81	191/72	400H	49.23	51.97 -99
^ Plaza	Daniel	ESP	3.7.66	181/64	20kW	1:23:17	1:20:40 -97
* Plotnikov	Andrey	RUS	12.8.67	186/77	50kW	3:44:30	3:40:07 -90
Plotnir	Yevgeniy	RUS	77		TJ	16.54	16.30 -99
Podebradsky	Jan	CZE	1.3.74	186/80	Dec	8314	8147 -96
Pöge	Thomas	GER	6.9.79	190/80	Dec	7753	7666 -99
Pogosian	Shirak	ARM	24.9.69	178/71	LJ	8.08A	7.98 -89
Polku	Mika	FIN	19.7.75	184/64	HJ	2.31	2.27i, 2.25 -96
Poltoratskiy	Roman	UZB	22.7.72	195/120	DT	62.46	61.00 -95
* Polyhroníou	Hrístos	GRE	31.3.72	186/107	HT	79.57, 79.95ic	79.83 -99
Polymérou	Dimítrios	GRE	17.5.74	188/98	JT	76.79	81.20 -99
Polyunin	Dmitriy	UZB	6.4.69	186/85	JT	77.74	85.74 -92
Ponds	Mario	USA	18.3.79		100	10.22w	10.45, 10.28w -99
Ponikvar	Mike	CAN	26.12.79		HJ	2.26i	2.24 -97
^ Popovich	Vitaliy	UKR	22.10.62	172/66	50kW	3:58:27	3:43:57 -89
Porokhin	Sergey	RUS	4.4.77	190/80	PV	5.55	5.40 -99
Porter	William	USA	15.4.73	193/87	400H	48.88	48.65 -99

Name		Nat	Born	Ht/Wt	Event	2000 Mark	Pre-2000 Best
Potgieter	Frits	RSA	13.3.74	195/110	DT	63.90	64.16 -97
Potgieter	Karel	RSA	29.9.75	187/116	SP	20.29	19.74 -99
* Potomin	Vladimir	RUS	15.1.80	177/69	50kW	3:39:21	-0-
Poussin	Jean-Luc	FRA	16.3.70	186/78	110H	13.72, 13.62w	13.54, 13.44w -98
Powell	Donovan	JAM	31.10.71	183/79	100	10.20, 10.12w	10.07, 9.7 -95
Power	Michael	AUS	9.5.76	183/70	3000	7:46.22	7:50.05i -99
					5000	13:27.07	13:36.37 -99
Pozzi	Jarrad	AUS	29.7.75	194/82	HJ	2.25	2.20 -94
* Prah	Kofi Amoah	GER	20.12.74	178/73	LJ	8.20	8.15, 8.19w -99
Pratt	Robinson	MEX	25.2.80	197/80	PV	5.60A	5.35A -99
Prezelj	Rozle	SLO	26.9.79	193/73	HJ	2.23i	2.19 -99
Primc	Igor	SLO	8.1.66	183/108	DT	62.54	64.79 -99
Primus	Ashada	USA	2.6.75		100	10.20	10.37 -99
Proctor	Mark	GBR	15.1.63	193/131	SP	20.57i, 20.11	20.85i -98, 20.40 -99
Promesse	Ronald	STL	31.8.74	170/70	100	10.17A	10.27A, 10.21Aw -98
^ Pronin	Vladimir	RUS	27.5.69	180/72	3kSt	8:19.43	8:16.59 -95
Ptácek	Adam	CZE	8.10.80	178/65	PV	5.61sq, 5.60i, 5.60	5.60 -99
Pugliese	Marcelo	ARG	2.9.68	191/105	DT	62.50	64.20 -97
* Pukstys	Tom	USA	28.5.68	188/98	JT	84.25	87.12 -97
Punga	Ionut	ROM	14.10.79	180/66	TJ	16.78	17.04 -99
Pupis	Martin	SVK	19.10.78		50kW	3:59:13	
Putenis	Maris	LAT	20.6.82	180/69	20kW	1:21:14	1:26:04 -99
Putignani	Andrea	ITA	31.12.70		110H	13.68	13.81 -97, 13.69rs -98
Pyrah	Jason	USA	6.4.69	172/64	800	1:46.62	1:46.75 -96
					1500	3:36.70	3:35.21 -96
					Mile	3:55.74	3:55.14 –96
Qu	Fanhua	CHN	21.2.77		50kW	3:57:59	3:57:59 -95
Quarry	Jamie	GBR	15.11.72	185/88	Dec	7667	7739 -99
* Quesada	Yoelbi	CUB	4.8.73	181/71	TJ	17.37	17.85 -97, 17.97w -95
Quinn	Matthew	RSA	17.4.76	179/82	100	10.19, 10.17Aw	10.08A, 10.24 -99
					200	20.55Aw	20.64A -98, 20.27Aw -99
^ Quintanilla	Armando	MEX	19.4.68	175/56	10000	28:03.6	27:18.59 -94
Quintarelli	Marco	ITA	20.6.73		HT	71.52	69.50 -99
Radomirovic	Darko	YUG	5.8.77	183/60	1500	3:37.52	3:38.91 -98
Raeburn	Julian	TRI	18.9.78	188/82	200	20.63, 20.61w	20.93 -98
					400	45.67	47.25 -98
Raev	Nikolay	BUL	29.1.71	184/71	TJ	16.76	17.18 -98, 17.27idq -93
Rags	Eriks	LAT	1.6.75	183/93	JT	83.61	83.78 -99
Rai Kumar	Sanjay	IND	1.5.79	178/72	LJ	8.03	8.02 -99
Raïfak	Mustapha	FRA	9.9.75	184/67	HJ	2.26	2.28 -97
Raizgys	Andrius	LIT	4.4.69	185/80	TJ	16.57	17.29 -95
Rakotoarimiandry	Yvon	MAD	5.1.76	180/72	400H	49.74	49.91A -99
Rakovic	Aleksandar	YUG	13.4.68	183/70	50kW	3:49:16	3:48:01 -99
* Ramaala	Hendrick	RSA	2.2.72	172/58	5000	13:27.39	13:24.43 -98
					10000	27:46.38	27:29.94 -99
					HMar	59:20	60:07 -97
					Mar	2:09:43	-0-
Ramachandram	Purukottam	IND	20.5.71		400	45.63	46.10 -99
Ramos	José	POR	28.7.68	171/68	10000	27:56.30	27:57.66 -99
Ramoul	Lyès	ALG	17.6.76		3kSt	8:27.04	8:34.39 -97
Ramzy	Bashir	USA	4.5.79	185/86	110H	13.76, 13.67w	13.98, 13.83w -99
					TJ	16.52w	15.54 -99
Randriamihaja	Joseph-Berlioz	MAD	30.11.75	188/75	110H	13.70A, 13.74	13.85A -99
Rantanen	Vesa	FIN	2.12.75	181/65	PV	5.60	5.65 -97
Raquil	Marc	FRA	2.4.77	191/81	400	45.31	45.82 -99
Rasheed	Abdul	USA	11.2.79		TJ	16.48w	15.53 -98
* Rasskasov	Roman	RUS	28.4.79	186/64	20kW	1:17:46	1:19:36 -99
Ratnayake	Harijan	SRI	8.12.74		400H	49.44	50.61 -98
* Rawlinson	Chris	GBR	19.5.72	185/82	400H	48.22	48.14 -99
Raymond	Monté	CAN	18.11.73	188/86	400H	49.97A, 50.09	49.64A, 49.80 -99
Razbeyko	Roman	RUS	9.3.73	188/89	Dec	8209h, 7997	7866h -99
Redko	Sergey	UKR	24.1.73	184/67	3kSt	8:29.63	8:24.35 -99
Redolat	José Antonio	ESP	17.2.76	181/66	800	1:45.39	1:46.15 -98
					1500	3:31.48	3:35.65 -99
^ Reese	Terry	USA	20.6.67	183/79	110H	13.42	13.22 -97
Reilly	Brendan	IRL	23.12.72	195/80	HJ	2.28i, 2.24	2.32i -94, 2.31 -92
^ Reiterer	Werner	AUS	27.1.68	193/110	DT	61.40	65.62 -87
Rendell	Stuart	AUS	30.6.72	187/112	HT	77.68	76.86 -99
Renikainen	Tepa	FIN	16.3.76	198/130	SP	20.11	19.53 -99
Retel	Jean-Claude	FRA	11.2.68	193/100	DT	62.20	61.97 -99
Reyes	José J	VEN	20.3.77		LJ	7.94	7.78 -98

	Name		Nat	Born	Ht/Wt	Event	2000 Mark	Pre-2000 Best
	Reynolds	Doug	USA	11.8.75	196/124	SP	19.05i	18.89i -98
						DT	66.47	66.76 -99
	Rhoden	Christian	GER	27.3.74	192/75	HJ	2.31	2.32 -98
	Riahi	Anis	TUN	30.5.71	183/73	Dec	7642	7506 -97
*	Richardson	Mark	GBR	26.7.72	178/74	400	44.72	44.37 -98
	Richter	Karsten	GER	25.7.72	194/80	TJ	16.61	16.95 -93
	Ridane	Maher	TUN	11.11.71	177/90	JT	80.18	77.98 -95
	Riech	Todd	USA	24.10.70	188/95	JT	79.04	82.12 -96
*	Riedel	Lars	GER	28.6.67	199/110	DT	69.72	71.50 -97
	Rigondeaux	Maximo	CUB	17.10.76	182/85	JT	81.43	79.84 -99
	Riley	Wenston	USA	24.4.77		110H	13.76	13.88 -98
	Rios	José	ESP	15.3.74	170/50	3000	7:42.51	
						5000	13:07.59	13:41.03 -99
						10000	27:22.20	28:30.53 –99
	Riyad	Mustapha	MAR	5.8.75		1500	3:38.61	3:41.5 -98
	Robberts	Janus	RSA	10.3.79	197/117	SP	20.34	20.39 -98
	Robbins	Sean	USA	9.10.72	188/84	LJ	7.96, 8.18w	8.33 -98
	Roberson	Mark	GBR	13.3.67	193/104	JT	79.40	85.67 -98
	Roberts	Jim	USA	30.12.76	196/107	SP	20.09	19.71 -99
	Roberts	Starr	USA	24.7.79		200	20.64w	21.01 -99
	Robinson	Khadevis	USA	19.7.76	183/74	800	1:45.40	1:45.23 -99
^	Robinson	Rohan	AUS	15.11.71	188/77	400H	49.41	48.28 -96
^	Rodal	Vebjörn	NOR	16.9.72	188/78	800	1:44.84	1:42.58 -96
	Rodely	David	USA	7.6.68	193/118	SP	19.41?	18.94 -94
	Rodrigues	Pedro	POR	8.7.71	181/72	400H	49.48	48.77 -94
	Rodríguez	Eduardo Iván	ESP	7.4.78	179/64	400H	49.98	50.67 -99
	Rodríguez	José Manuel	ESP	7.11.72	170/62	50kW	3:54:18	3:58:55 -98
*	Rodríguez	Miguel Angel	MEX	15.1.67	174/62	50kW	3:43:52	3:42:45 -97
	Rogers	Delvit	USA	23.3.80	185/77	LJ	8.07	7.25 -99
	Rogers	Nick	USA	2.5.75	188/72	5000	13:18.50	13:43.05 -99
						10000	27:55.17	29:59.45 -97
	Rohitha	Sujith	SRI	27.10.69		LJ	8.06w	7.76 -99
	Rohr	Alain	SUI	25.12.71	182/74	400	45.77	46.22 -96
*	Romain	Jérôme	FRA	12.6.71	183/76	TJ	16.95i, 16.93	17.48, 17.59w -95
	Rome	Jarred	USA	21.12.76	196/145	SP	19.90	18.20i, 18.03 -97
						DT	64.00	59.78 -98
	Romero	Fabrício	BRA	13.5.78	190/72	HJ	2.25	2.26A, 2.24 -99
*	Roncero	Fabián	ESP	19.10.70	171/58	3000	7:41.48	7:59.36 -99
						HMar	61:12	61:38 -99
	Rono	Sammy	KEN	74	184/73	1500	3:36.62	3:31.89 -98
	Rop	Josephat Kipchoge	KEN	69		Mar	2:10:51	2:11:40 -99
	Rorarius	Niklas	FIN	7.6.78	186/77	LJ	7.96	7.85, 8.02w -99
*	Ross	Duane	USA	5.12.72	183/78	110H	13.53	13.12 -99
	Rosúlek	Josef	CZE	6.2.71	196/105	SP	19.22	19.18 -99
	Rosvold	Thomas	NOR	21.7.67	192/93	DT	61.55	59.96 -99
*	Rotich	Laban	KEN	20.1.69	163/45	1500	3:32.93	3:29.91 -98
						Mile	3:50.31	3:47.65 -97
	Rotich	Willy	KEN	23.3.76		800	1:46.70	1:47.47 -99
	Röttger	André	GER	26.3.79		Dec	7690	7747 -99
	Rous	Josef	CZE	26.7.79	195/78	400H	49.95	50.70 -99
	Rovan	Jure	SLO	23.1.75	187/81	PV	5.56i	5.55 -98
	Rozna	Roman	MDA	25.3.76	190/105	HT	72.20	70.12?, 67.75 -99
	Rubtsov	Sergey	KZK	4.9.65	190/140	SP	19.92	20.68 -88
	Rugut	Philip	KEN	18.5.77	165/50	HMar	60:00w	60:05 -99
	Rurak	Konstantin	UKR	9.4.74	178/74	100	10.17, 10.14w	10.30 -94, 10.03dt, 10.13w -96
	Rusan	Tim	USA	25.6.77		TJ	16.52	16.14 -96
	Rusenov	Ivailo	BUL	20.11.79	178/65	TJ	16.91	16.65 -98
	Rush	Matt	USA	19.10.78	188/79	110H	13.58	14.46 -99
	Russell	Dion	AUS	8.5.75	180/72	20kW	1:24:09	1:20:49 -99
						50kW	4:02:50	3:47:34 -98
	Russell	Scott	CAN	16.1.79	206/130	JT	78.94	76.80 -99
	Rutto	Barnabas	KEN			HMar	61:33	
	Rutto	David	KEN			HMar	60:44	
*	Rutto	Evans	KEN	8.4.78		3000	7:36.38	7:47.24 -99
						5000	13:02.71	13:24.84 -99
						10000	27:21.32	28:06.60 -99
	Ryan	Gary	IRL	12.6.72	175/70	100	10.22w	10.45, 10.18w -99
	Ryba	Jirí	CZE	15.6.76	192/89	Dec	8339	8088w, 8068 -97
	Rybakov	Yaroslav	RUS	22.11.80	194/76	HJ	2.28	2.20 -98
	Rybin	Yuriy	RUS	5.3.63	186/97	JT	77.58	86.98 -95

	Name		Nat	Born	Ht/Wt	Event	2000 Mark	Pre-2000 Best
	Ryland	Daniel	USA	6.8.79	185/82	200	19.89w-dt	
	Rysiukewicz	Piotr	POL	14.7.74	176/71	400	45.67	45.54 -99
	Sack	René	GER	14.7.76	190/120	SP	19.19	19.06 -99
*	Saddler	Greg	USA	29.6.74	175/73	100	10.08	10.11 -99, 10.10w -98
						200	20.62	20.56 -99, 20.46w -98
*	Saïd Guerni	Djabir	ALG	29.3.77	187/70	800	1:43.25	1:43.09 -99
*	Saïdi Sief	Ali	ALG	15.3.78	170/55	1500	3:30.82	3:30.91 -99
						3000	7:25.02	7:36.97 -99
						5000	12:50.86	13:39.5 -99
	Sainah	Mark	KEN	10.11.70		Mar	2:09:00	2:10:44 -99
^	Sakirkin	Oleg	KZK	23.1.66	182/72	TJ	17.03	17.58 -89
	Saksio	Sami	FIN	28.4.69	190/95	JT	80.83	84.26 -97
	Sakurai	Ken-ichi	JPN	26.12.76	179/65	110H	13.76	13.67 -99
	Sales	Louis	USA	29.11.71	185/81	400H	49.36	49.73 –99
	Salnikov	Aleksandr	RUS	.71		SP	19.30	19.52 -99
*	Sanchez	Felix	DOM	30.8.77	178/73	400H	48.33	48.60 -99
	Sánchez	David	ESP	23.8.73	176/63	50kW	4:04:19	3:56:00 -99
	Sánchez	German	MEX	31.7.67	173/63	50kW	3:48:06	3:49:29 -95
*	Sánchez	Joel	MEX	15.9.66	175/53	20kW	1:20:53	1:19:00 -99
						50kW	3:44:36	3:49:51A -99
	Sander	Jeff	USA	13.2.76		Dec	7830w	7763h -99
	Sanders	Jerrod	USA	78		LJ	8.01A	
	Sang	Isaac	KEN			1500	3:35.6A	
	Sanguin	Giovanni	ITA	14.5.69	180/95	HT	71.30	74.52 -97
	Sankale	Joel	KEN	4.10.69		Mar	2:09:47	
	Sanou	Olivier	BKF	2.1.75		TJ	16.50	16.04 -99
	dos Santos	Anderson C	BRA	15.6.75		400H	49.90	49.98 -99
	dos Santos	Anderson J	BRA	23.4.72	186/75	400	45.59	45.39A, 45.54 -99
	dos Santos	Osmar B	BRA	20.10.68	175/65	800	1:44.87	1:45.38 -97
	dos Santos	Redelén	BRA	24.4.76		110H	13.59	13.90 -98
	dos Santos	Sérgio	BRA	13.5.76		TJ	16.68	16.41 -97
^	Sasimovich	Vladimir	BLR	14.9.68	178/86	JT	84.42	87.40 -95
	Sato	Atsushi	JPN	8.5.78	170/55	Mar	2:09:50	-0-
	Sautkin	Igor	RUS	23.2.72	190/79	TJ	16.67i	17.15 -94
	Savenkov	Igor	RUS	73		HJ	2.24	2.22 -97
	Sawe	Julius	KEN	21.11.71	173/63	20kW	1:21:21A	1:21:22 -96
*	Schelbert	Marcel	SUI	26.2.76	191/83	400H	49.49	48.13 -99
	Schiebler	Jeff	CAN	1.6.73	171/55	5000	13:25.04	13:13.96 -98
						10000	27:53.85	27:45.75 -98
	Schinz	Frédéric	SUI	25.6.77	193/68	HJ	2.23i	2.20 -99
	Schläfi	Rolf	SUI	15.3.71	197/97	Dec	7984	7953 -95
*	Schmid	Stefan	GER	6.5.70	186/78	Dec	8485	8360 -97, 8478dq -96
	Schmidt	Torsten	GER	9.12.74	207/105	DT	62.90	61.04 -97
	Schnallinger	Michael	AUT	29.4.80	190/96	Dec	7634	7416 -99
	Schönbeck	Florian	GER	13.1.74	191/80	Dec	8127	7999 -99
*	Schult	Jürgen	GER	11.5.60	193/110	DT	65.81	74.08 -86
	Schultz	Ingo	GER	26.7.75	201/94	400	45.79	45.99 -99
	Schumacher	Mark	GER	27.6.76		Dec	7639	7661 -98
*	Schumann	Nils	GER	20.5.78	192/77	800	1:44.22	1:44.47 -99
	Schütz	Carsten	GER	30.8.75	188/69	5000	13:26.81	13:53.82 -99
*	Schwarthoff	Florian	GER	7.5.68	201/83	110H	13.23	13.05 -95
*	Scigaczewski	Tomasz	POL	18.11.78	188/88	110H	13.42	13.29 -99, 13.25w, 13.0 -98
	Scott	Greg	USA	8.2.80	180/83	110H	13.75	13.74 -99
	Scott	Leonard	USA	19.1.80	181/84	100	10.18w	10.29, 9.83w 99
						200	20.59, 20.55i	20.08w -99
	Scuderi	Francesco	ITA	4.10.77	171/70	100	10.19	10.34 -98
	Sdad	Mustapha	MAR	11.4.70	180/72	400H	49.66	49.05 -97
	Sdiri	Salim	FRA	26.10.78		LJ	7.95	7.37 -99
	Seaman	Tim	USA	14.5.72	175/64	20kW	1:23:40t	1:23:42 -99
*	Sebrle	Roman	CZE	26.11.74	185/86	LJ	7.97i	8.03 -98
						Dec	8757	8589 -98
	Sedlácek	Pavel	CZE	5.4.68	198/111	HT	79.29	79.56 -96
*	Seelig	Andreas	GER	6.7.70	200/120	DT	64.51	66.00 -97
	Sego	Stephen	KEN	78		10000	28:00.1	
*	Segura	Bernardo	MEX	11.2.70	175/62	20kW	1:22:47	1:17:25.6t -94
	Seifert	Jim	USA	26.11.62	188/114	DT	66.72	66.70 –96
	Semyonov	Konstantin	ISR	20.11.69	190/86	PV	5.60	5.76 -96
*	Sepeng	Hezekiél	RSA	30.6.74	182/70	800	1:43.98	1:42.69 -99
	Serélis	Dimítrios	GRE	5.5.80	186/83	LJ	8.08i, 8.00, 8.04w	7.86 -99
	Servius	Ronald	FRA	21.2.76	169/65	LJ	8.24	7.91 -98
						TJ	16.48i	16.72 -99

Name		Nat	Born	Ht/Wt	Event	2000 Mark	Pre-2000 Best
Seskin	Yuriy	RUS	7.7.66	196/110	DT	62.27	64.58 -88
Sestak	Matija	SLO	30.12.72	187/73	400	45.48	45.43 -99
* Setliff	Adam	USA	15.12.69	193/125	DT	68.51	68.45 -98
Settle	Leon	USA	19.10.75		200	20.17Aw	20.76 -97
Sevin	Ty	USA	17.6.71	186/94	JT	80.16	75.76 -96
* Sghir	Ismaïl	FRA	16.3.72	168/50	1500	3:36.80	3:36.20 -95
					3000	7:37.91	7:30.09 -95
					5000	12:58.83	12:58.99 -96
					10000	27:33.20	27:12.39 -99
* Shabunin	Vyacheslav	RUS	27.9.69	171/56	1500	3:32.28	3:33.30 -98
					Mile	3:50.54	3:51.02 -95
					3000	7:48.91i	7:39.24 -95
Shako	Dmitriy	BLR	27.5.79	192/92	HT	75.59	66.68 -98
Shankar Dubey	Brahma	IND			JT	77.47	76.75 -99
Sharangabo	Alexis	RWA	9.11.78		1500	3:38.16	3:43.40 -99
Shatkovskiy	Vladimir	UKR	8.10.75	189/84	Dec	7679	7966 -99
* Shchurenko	Roman	UKR	14.9.76	186/83	LJ	8.35	8.30 -99
Shearer	Darin	USA	3.4.74	178/72	3kSt	8:28.98	8:23.63 -99
Shelest	Aleksey	UKR	27.3.67	173/64	50kW	3:59:27	3:58:09 -99
* Shevchenko	Dmitriy	RUS	13.5.68	198/120	DT	66.66	67.30 -92, 68.04dq -95
Shida	Tetsuya	JPN	27.6.71	182/75	LJ	7.96w	7.95 -96, 8.04w -94
Shimizu	Koji	JPN	17.10.69	176/52	Mar	2:10:41	2:09:00 -99
* Shirvington	Matt	AUS	25.10.78	184/82	100	10.11	10.03 -98
					200	20.62A	20.45 -98
Shiryayev	Vladislav	RUS	30.10.73	176/72	400H	49.02	49.11 -98
* Shkurlatov	Vitaliy	RUS	25.5.79	185/70	LJ	8.38i, 8.22	8.06 -99
* Shmalyuk	Yevgeniy	RUS	14.1.76	182/74	50kW	3:44:33	3:41:56 -99
Shnayder	Dmitriy	KGZ	30.5.76	192/90	JT	77.77	74.10 -99
Shvetsov	Leonid	RUS	28.3.69	185/70	Mar	2:11:07	2:09:16 -97
Shvetsov	Vitaliy	RUS	20.2.73	181/67	20kW	1:21:01	1:21:14 -99
* Sidorenko	Vasiliy	RUS	1.5.61	187/106	HT	81.75	82.54 -92
* Sidorov	Vitaliy	RUS	23.3.70	193/125	DT	65.69	67.90 -98
da Silva	Andre Domingos	BRA	26.11.72	187/78	100	10.13A	10.16,10.05dt -97,10.10w -95,10.06A-99
					200	20.17A, 20.35	20.54 -99
* da Silva	Claudinei	BRA	19.11.70	186/86	100	10.16	10.12 -99, 10.0w -96, 10.08dt-97
					200	20.23	19.89 -99
da Silva	Cleverson O	BRA	5.9.73	185/75	400H	49.51	49.10 -99
da Silva	Elenílson	BRA	24.1.72	178/59	10000	28:13.69	28:40.34 -99
da Silva	Luiz Fernando	BRA	2.7.71	186/87	JT	79.50A	77.80 -96
Silva	Jorge	ESP	19.4.79	175/60	20kW	1:23:48	1:25:03 -99
Silva	Manuel	POR	8.10.78	179/65	3kSt	8:24.60	8:34.92 -99
* Silva	Rui	POR	3.8.77	174/62	800	1:45.29	1:46.40i, 1:46.71 - 99
					1500	3:32.60	3:30.88 -99
					3000	7:39.44i	7:53.87 -99
Simmons	Mark	USA	14.9.78	201/107	DT	60.34	59.68 -99
Simo	Samu-Petri	FIN	22.6.78	194/118	HT	73.62	72.62 -99
Simpson	Brandon	JAM	6.9.81	172/75	400	45.73	47.22 -99
Simunic	Bostjan	SLO	28.12.74	186/73	TJ	16.68w	16.13 -98
Sinervo	Timo	FIN	5.8.76	100/100	DT	61.62	61.61 -99
Singh	Bahadur	IND	7.5.73	187/95	SP	20.01	19.59 -98
Singh Bishnoi	Jagdish	IND	20.5.72	182/86	JT	79.67	78.01 -99
Singh	Paramjeet	IND	22.8.73		400	45.56	45.70 -98
Singh	Satvir	IND	25.8.72	180/90	JT	76.74	79.68 -98
Singh	Shakti	IND	14.5.62	185/100	SP	20.60	19.85 -99
Singoei	Philip	KEN			HMar	61:57	
Sirrákos	Dimítrios	GRE	26.1.74		HJ	2.24	2.15 -98
Sitienei	Joseph	KEN	75		HMar	61:35	
* Skah	Khalid	MAR/NOR29.1.67			170/58	10000	27:37.44
27:14.53 -95							
* Skvaruk	Andrey	UKR	9.3.67	186/104	HT	81.43	81.72 -94
Skyttä	Pietari	FIN	24.5.76	183/83	JT	76.48	83.28 -97
Sliwa	Leszek	POL	20.9.79	187/110	SP	19.62	18.39 -99
Sloan	Chuck	USA	9.1.77		3kSt	8:26.66	8:37.06 -99
Slover	Scott	USA	9.7.75	185/79	PV	5.65	5.70 -99
Smetanin	Maksim	KGZ	17.2.74	187/67	TJ	16.71	16.50 -96
* Smiryagin	Yevgeniy	RUS	17.5.76	185/77	PV	5.85	5.85 -97
Smith	Chad	USA	9.1.74	185/82	Dec	7827	8045 -99
Smith	Glen	GBR	21.5.72	190/110	DT	63.08	65.11 -99
Smith	Michael	USA	26.4.79	183/75	400H	49.60	50.12 -99
Smith	Rutger	NED	9.7.81	197/120	SP	19.48	18.27 -99
Smith	Willie	NAM	20.9.77	170/64	400H	49.47A	50.45 -97

	Name		Nat	Born	Ht/Wt	Event	2000 Mark	Pre-2000 Best
*	Snyder	Brad	CAN	8.1.76	196/122	SP	20.24	20.51 -99
	Soares	Virgílio	POR	13.11.59	184/75	50kW	4:01:27	4:03:54 -98
	Soget	Christopher	KEN	15.5.80		3kSt	8:26.56	8:20.07 -99
*	Sokolovskiy	Andrey	UKR	16.7.78	195/78	HJ	2.28	2.31i, 2.29, 2.32ex -99
	Sóldos	Peter	SVK	27.4.73	189/82	Dec	7793	7834 -96
	Som	Bram	NED	20.2.80	177/62	800	1:44.01	1:46.58 -99
	Song	Dong-hyun	KOR	17.11.81	178/90	JT	78.55	72.26 -99
	Sørensen	Jacob	DEN	27.12.74	186/76	50kW	3:58:09	3:59:18 -99
	Sørli	Gjøran	NOR	3.6.78	191/125	SP	19.24	18.28 -99
*	Sosunov	Kirill	RUS	1.11.75	195/86	LJ	8.34	8.41i -97, 8.38 -98, 8.48w -95
*	Sotomayor	Javier	CUB	13.10.67	193/80	HJ	2.32	2.45 -93
	Souza	Cláudio Roberto	BRA	14.10.73	168/68	100	10.24	10.33 -99
	de Souza	Hudson	BRA	25.2.77	180/65	800	1:45.69	1:46.33 -99
						1500	3:34.97	3:38.32 -99
						Mile	3:53.74	3:55.63 -98
	de Souza	Márcio	BRA	24.1.75	180/72	110H	13.43	13.38 -99
	Spacek	Petr	CZE	23.7.75	183/75	PV	5.65i, 5.61	5.60 -99
	Spahn	Matthias	GER	3.1.79		Dec	7701	7140 -97
	Spasovkhodskiy	Igor	RUS	1.8.79	192/86	TJ	16.86i, 16.86	16.32 -99
	Spears	Derek	USA	22.3.73	183/76	110H	13.65w	13.50, 13.48w -96
	Spiegelburg	Richard	GER	12.8.77	182/77	PV	5.61i, 5.60	5.65 -99
*	Spitsyn	Valeriy	RUS	5.12.65	178/67	50kW	3:37:26	3:41:07 -94
	Sporrer	Alexander	GER	20.1.71	184/88	HT	71.35	74.16 -96
	Sposób	Grzegorz	POL	12.2.76	200/87	HJ	2.25	2.14 -99
	Stadnichuk	Andrey	RUS	14.12.73	176/64	20kW	1:23:34	1:22:03 -98
^	Stallworth	James	USA	29.4.71	183/84	LJ	7.93	8.20 -90
	Stamatópoulos	Theódoros	GRE	24.4.70	182/70	50kW	3:57:44	3:58:37 -99
	Stankin	Vladimir	RUS	2.1.74	184/71	20kW	1:20:31	1:20:21 -99
	Stanski	Olgierd	POL	4.4.73	196/98	DT	64.20	62.53 -99
^	Starkey	Dean	USA	27.3.67	188/84	PV	5.65	5.92 -94
	Stasyuk	Pavel	BLR	14.6.77		JT	76.43	75.14 -99
	Stauffer	Martin	SUI	7.7.75	205/85	HJ	2.27i, 2.23	2.23 -99
	Steele	Dan	USA	20.3.69	188/84	Dec	7890	8130 -99
	Steele	Darrin	USA	20.3.69	188/87	Dec	7705	8129m -95
	Stefko	Róbert	SVK	28.5.68	178/61	HMar	60:29w	61:46 -96
	Stehlik	Petr	CZE	15.4.77	185/102	SP	19.56	19.42 -99
	Steinle	Mark	GBR	22.11.74	184/63	10000	28:04.48	29:07.33 -95
						Mar	2:11:18	-0-
	Stember	Michael	USA	30.1.78	179/66	800	1:46.20	1:47.11 -98
						1500	3:35.11	3:39.05 -99
	Stephani	Photis	CYP	4.10.71	187/78	PV	5.56	5.40 -94
	Stephenson	Christian	GBR	22.7.74	172/54	3kSt	8:25.37	8:29.09 -99
^	Stevens	Patrick	BEL	31.1.68	183/73	100	10.12w	10.14 -97, 10.00w -95
						200	20.40, 20.25w	20.19 -96
	Stevenson	Toby	USA	19.11.76		PV	5.73A, 5.72	5.55 -98
	Stewart	Nick	CAN	6.4.79		400H	49.77A	50.44A -99
^	Stewart	Raymond	JAM	18.3.65	178/73	100	9.99w	9.96 -91, 9.89w -87
*	Stolle	Michael	GER	17.12.74	192/85	PV	5.95	5.91 -99
	Stosik	Stanislaw	POL	26.3.72	175/64	50kW	3:55:18	3:53:55 -99
	Strand	Staffan	SWE	18.4.76	188/74	HJ	2.32i, 2.32	2.31 -98
*	Streete-Thompson	Kareem	CAY	30.3.73	183/84	100	10.22Aw	9.96 -97
						LJ	8.31	8.63, 8.64w -94
*	Stringfellow	Savanté	USA	6.11.78	191/84	LJ	8.30	8.12 -99
*	Strogalyov	Vadim	RUS	9.2.75	184/77	PV	5.75	5.85 -98
	Stroubákos	Panayiótis	GRE	8.9.72	187/73	800	1:46.42	1:45.00 -97
	Strutzel	Jess	USA	4.1.78	185/70	800	1:46.03	1:45.81 -99
	Suárez	Carlos	ESP	25.9.75	186/68	3kSt	8:27.49	8:33.39 -99
	Suetsugu	Shingo	JPN	2.6.80	178/62	100	10.19	10.37 -98
						200	20.26	21.08 -99
	Sugibayashi	Takanori	JPN	14.3.76	184/67	TJ	17.02	16.78 -99, 16.83w -98
	Sukharev	Igor	RUS	1.1.72		HJ	2.25i	2.33i -98
^	Suleiman	Mohammed	QAT	23.11.69	170/60	1500	3:38.30	3:32.10 -97
						5000	13:24.22	13:25.15 -92
*	Sullivan	Kevin	CAN	20.3.74	180/68	1500	3:31.71	3:34.61 -99
						Mile	3:50.26	3:52.25 -95
	Sullivan	Luke	USA	4.6.76	188/114	DT	60.16	61.06 -99
	Sun	Shipeng	CHN	10.3.76		JT	77.54	75.14 -99
	Sunada	Takahiro	JPN	19.1.73	167/54	Mar	2:10:07	2:11:03 -99
^	Sunneborn	Mattias	SWE	27.9.70	187/83	LJ	8.08	8.21 -96
*	Surin	Bruny	CAN	12.7.67	180/81	100	10.08, 10.05	9.84 -99
	Suter	Patrick	SUI	17.5.77	192/100	HT	72.13	72.96 -99

Name		Nat	Born	Ht/Wt	Event	2000 Mark	Pre-2000 Best
* Svenøy	Jim	NOR	22.4.72	186/70	3kSt	8:23.61	8:12.05 -97
Svensson	Fredrik	SWE	10.9.73	184/77	50kW	4:03:42	4:01:52 -98
Swarn	Bryan	USA	19.11.79	179/71	400	45.36	46.18 -99
Swaby	Garfield	JAM	21.2.77		LJ	7.93w	7.62 -99
^ Sweeney	Nick	IRL	26.3.68	195/121	DT	61.76	67.89 -98
Swift	Eugene	USA	14.9.64	183/79	110H	13.50	13.21 -96
Sylvester	Tonyo	USA	17.12.67	188/99	SP	19.15	18.32 -99
Szabó	Ambrus	HUN	8.4.77	185/81	TJ	16.74i	16.41 -99
Tabata	Kenji	JPN	24.9.74	174/64	400	45.73	45.69 -98
Tagawa	Shigeru	JPN	22.11.75	190/80	LJ	8.05w	8.15 -99
Taguelmint	Halez	FRA	29.3.73	174/57	5000	13:28.00	13:20.73 -99
Tahri	Bouabdallah	FRA	20.12.78	190/65	3kSt	8:16.14	8:12.24 -99
Taillepierre	Karl	FRA	13.8.76	176/64	TJ	16.62	16.28 -96
Takahashi	Ken-ichi	JPN	16.1.73	172/55	10000	28:13.22	28:11.18 -99
					HMar	60:30	63:53 -99
Takahashi	Naotaka	JPN	28.6.76	180/63	HMar	61:59	
Takaoka	Toshinari	JPN	24.9.70	178/52	5000	13:15.34	13:13.40 -98
					10000	27:40.44	27:49.89 -96
Takei	Ryuji	JPN	18.5.71	169/56	Mar	2:09:23	2:10:24 -99
Takemoto	Kenji	JPN	14.8.75	175/53	10000	28:16.31	28:20.55 -99
Talel	Wilberforce Kapkeny	KEN	10.1.80		5000	13:13.15	
					10000	27:36.48	29:33.4A -99
Tallhem	Sören	SWE	16.2.64	192/110	SP	19.16i	20.91, 21.24i -85
Talotti	Alessandro	ITA	7.10.80	193/73	HJ	2.25	2.20 -99
Tamesue	Dai	JPN	3.5.78	170/62	400H	48.47	49.09 -96
Tammaru	Margus	EST	24.8.71	192/110	SP	19.02	18.98 -99
* Tammert	Aleksander	EST	2.2.73	196/117	DT	67.41	66.95 -99
Tamminga	Christian	NED	30.4.74	172/67	PV	5.65	5.76 -98
Tan	Chunhua	CHN	13.3.77	183/76	400H	49.77	49.25 -98
Tanigawa	Satoru	JPN	5.7.72	183/74	110H	13.66, 13.58w	13.55 -99
* Tanui	Moses	KEN	20.8.65	165/55	Mar	2:07:47	2:06:16 -99
* Tanui	William	KEN	22.2.64	183/70	1500	3:35.68	3:30.58 -97
Tao	Rui	CHN	26.1.72	187/68	HJ	2.24	2.28 -94
Taranov	Vyacheslav	RUS	20.3.75	190/74	TJ	16.82i, 16.48	17.33 -97
* Tarasov	Maksim	RUS	2.12.70	194/80	PV	5.90	6.05 -99
Tarus	Bogdan	ROM	1.8.75	190/77	LJ	8.30i, 8.12	8.29 -96
* Taurima	Jai	AUS	26.6.72	187/74	LJ	8.49	8.35 -99
Taye	Moges	ETH	12.12.73	167/54	Mar	2:09:49	2:09:21 -98
* Taylor	Angelo	USA	29.12.78	188/77	400	44.89	45.14 -98
					400H	47.50	47.90 -98
* Téllez	Norberto	CUB	22.1.72	186/78	400	45.72	45.27 -94
					800	1:45.39	1:42.85 -96
Terano	Shin-ichi	JPN	10.7.79	175/65	LJ	8.08w	7.83 -99
* Tergat	Paul	KEN	17.6.69	182/62	5000	12:55.18	12:49.87 -97
					10000	27:03.87	26:27.85 -97
					HMar	59:06	59:17 -98, 58:51sc -96
^ Terry	Octavius	USA	7.11.72	189/74	400H	49.83	48.39 -97
Tezuka	Toshiaki	JPN	7.12.76	178/56	10000	28:03.00	28:15.17 -99
* Thilakeratne	Sugath	SRI	30.7.73	170/57	400	45.31	44.61 -98
Thomas	Brian	CAN	14.3.70	178/73	LJ	7.95A	8.04 -92
Thomas	Dwight	JAM	23.9.80	185/82	100	10.12	10.37 -99
					200	20.58	20.66 -99
* Thomas	Eric	USA	1.12.73	190/88	400H	47.94	48.20 -96
Thomas	Marcus	USA	22.3.70	183/82	LJ	8.02i, 8.01	7.64 -99
					TJ	16.63	16.30 -99
Thompson	Kemel	JAM	25.9.74	180/75	400H	48.56	48.82 -99
Thompson	Kurt	TRI	13.12.67	178/80	JT	76.64	78.06 -96
* Thompson	Obadele	BAR	30.3.76	175/67	100	9.97	9.87A-98, 9.96 -99, 9.69Aw -96
					200	19.97	20.03 -97
Thorkildsen	Andreas	NOR	1.4.82	188/90	JT	77.48	72.11 -99
^ Thugwane	Josiah	RSA	15.4.71	158/45	Mar	2:10:29	2:07:28 -97
Thurmond	Reedus	USA	15.12.79		DT	62.34	60.98 -99
Thurston	Stephen	AUS	26.3.77		3kSt	8:33.06	8:33.77 -99
* Thys	Gert	RSA	12.11.71	167/55	HMar	61:16	60:23 -97
Tichy	Peter	SVK	12.3.69	177/67	50kW	3:54:47	3:51:22 -96
Tiggas	Váios	GRE	16.10.78	186/96	SP	19.31	19.47 -99
Tighazomine	Khalid	MAR	18.6.77	175/68	800	1:45.38	1:48.8 -99
* Tiisanoja	Ville	FIN	24.12.75	192/119	SP	20.76	20.49 -99
Tikhon	Ivan	BLR	24.7.76	185/100	HT	79.85	78.03 -98
^ Tilli	Stefano	ITA	22.8.62	175/76	100	10.23w	10.16 -84, 10.06w -83
Timofeyev	Yevgeniy	RUS	22.2.74		TJ	16.79	17.00 -93

Name		Nat	Born	Ht/Wt	Event	2000 Mark	Pre-2000 Best
Tison	Xavier	FRA	20.9.77	193/110	HT	71.30	71.64 -97
^ Tivontschik	Andrei	GER	13.7.70	184/80	PV	5.60i	5.95 -96
Tlhobo	Ezael	RSA	4.5.64	175/60	Mar	2:11:18	2:09:54 -98
To	Wai Lok	HKG	7.8.79	170/60	100	10.19w	10.52 -99, 10.44w -97
Tokumoto	Kazuyoshi	JPN	22.6.79	173/59	10000	28:15.06	
Tolbert	Rod	USA	11.6.67	185/79	200	20.63Aw	20.38 -92
Toledo	Juan Pedro	MEX	17.6.78	185/82	400	45.24A	45.63 -98, 45.49A -99
* Tolla	Girma	ETH	13.10.75	174/57	3000	7:38.68i	7:42.98 -99
					5000	13:21.04	13:15.72 -98
					10000	27:20.03	27:13.48 -99
* Tolla	Tesfaye	ETH	19.10.74	167/60	HMar	59:51w	61:37 -97
					Mar	2:11:10	2:06:57 -99
Tolossa	Ambesse	ETH	28.8.77	171/53	Mar	2:10:57	2:10:13 -98
Tomarás	Dimítrios	GRE	6.6.72	192/67	HJ	2.23i	2.24 -96
Tompuri	Timo	FIN	9.6.69	189/117	DT	65.13	64.90 -99
Ton	Svatoslav	CZE	20.10.78	192/75	HJ	2.25	2.27i, 2.25 -97
* Topic	Dragutin	YUG	12.3.71	197/74	HJ	2.34i, 2.33	2.38 -93
* Torian	Reggie	USA	22.4.75	191/88	110H	13.42	13.03 -98
Torotoich	Haron	KEN	78		HMar	61:39	
* Toth	Kevin	USA	29.12.67	193/144	SP	21.46	21.78 -97
Totton	Andre	USA	17.7.80		100	10.23w	10.59 -98, 10.40w -99
^ Touré	Cheikh Tidiane	FRA	25.1.70	195/89	LJ	8.23, 8.43w	8.46 -97
Touset	Raul	CUB	78		HJ	2.23	2.15 -98
Townsend	Trinity	USA	7.2.74	175/66	800	1:45.68	1:45.75 -98
Trafas	Dariusz	POL	16.5.72	188/87	JT	87.17	83.23 -99
* Trammell	Terrance	USA	23.11.78	188/84	100	10.04	10.08 -99
					110H	13.16	13.28 -99
Trautmann	Denis	GER	15.8.72	182/71	50kW	3:50:28	3:48:05 -99
Trautmann	Mike	GER	13.3.74	180/72	50kW	3:52:41	4:01:48t -99
Travassos	António	POR	24.9.71	174/69	1500	3:38.52	3:37.2 -97
Trentin	Nicola	ITA	20.6.74	178/62	LJ	7.98	8.00sq, 8.32w -96, 8.07A, 7.93 –99
Tretyak	Yevgeniy	RUS	18.7.71	184/75	LJ	7.93i	8.29 -94
Trifonov	Aleksey	RUS	8.5.80	179/70	20kW	1:24:21	1:25:55 -97
Trots	Andrey	UKR	17.1.78	188/78	TJ	16.73	16.21 -99
Tsítouras	Stávros	GRE	15.6.69	190/75	PV	5.61	5.62 -97
Tucker	Paul	GUY	30.1.76	186/84	400H	49.95	50.83 -98
^ Tudor	Bogdan	ROM	1.2.70	187/70	LJ	8.04i, 7.96	8.37 -95
Tugay	Igor	UKR	22.3.75	185/95	HT	75.74	73.85 -98
* Tunks	Jason	CAN	7.5.75	197/120	DT	66.28	67.88 -98
Turbo	Tumo	ETH	23.2.70	170/63	Mar	2:11:07	2:09:00 -97
Turki	Lotfi	TUN	6.3.75	190/65	3kSt	8:22.98	8:33.33 -99
Tuwei	David	KEN	22.2.79	176/56	3000	7:43.05	
					5000	13:20.83	
Tveitå	Einar Kristian	NOR	22.2.73	185/120	DT	61.43	63.64 -99
^ Tynes	Andrew	BAH	13.2.72	193/82	100	10.18A	10.21 -94, 10.01Aw -96
					200	20.50A, 20.55	20.23 -95, 20.22A -93, 20.20w -94
Tyrtyshnik	Vyacheslav	UKR	16.1.71	186/75	HJ	2.24i	2.30 -96
^ Ubartas	Romas	LIT	26.5.60	202/128	DT	64.61	70.06 -88
Uchitomi	Yasunori	JPN	29.10.72	173/64	3kSt	8:31.43	8:26.48 -97
Udechuku	Emeka	GBR	10.7.79	176/102	DT	62.07	60.97 -98
Udo-Obong	Enefiok	NGR	22.5.82	185/82	400	45.75	46.72, 46.7 -99
Ugwu	Chima	NGR	19.7.73	196/140	SP	20.26	19.62 -96
					DT	62.84	61.71 -98
Unthank	Chris	AUS	31.8.72	181/63	3kSt	8:27.80	8:24.48 -97
Urban	Dirk	GER	14.1.69	188/101	SP	19.10	20.26 -96
^ Urbanik	Sándor	HUN	15.12.64	173/58	20kW	1:22:12	1:20:41 -97
* Urbas	Marcin	POL	17.9.76	179/75	200	20.43	19.98 -99
^ Urrutia	Aliecer	CUB	22.9.74	174/76	TJ	17.08	17.70 -96, 17.83i -97
Usiviyu	Boniface	KEN	5.9.74		3000	7:44.50	
					HMar	61:11	62:14 -99
Usov	Roman	RUS	4.6.78	176/56	3kSt	8:26.96	8:39.25 -99
Ustinov	Viktor	UZB	20.7.74	189/110	HT	75.77	69.21 -99
Valícek	Róbert	SVK	10.3.69	174/61	20kW	1:21:14	1:20:58 -97
^ Valle	Emilio	CUB	21.4.67	183/74	110H	13.4, 13.78	13.18 -96
Valvik	Svein-Inge	NOR	20.9.56	190/112	DT	61.57	68.00 -82
van Balkom	Patrick	NED	14.9.74	184/80	100	10.24A, 10.06Aw	10.23 -98, 10.20w -96
					200	20.36A	20.36 -99
Van Daele	Jo	BEL	6.4.72	191/110	DT	63.49	62.61 -99
van der Kruk	Pieter	NED	10.2.72	194/111	DT	61.32	66.03 -99

Name		Nat	Born	Ht/Wt	Event	2000 Mark	Pre-2000 Best
van Eck	Johannes	RSA	28.1.74	194/100	JT	79.76A	79.76 -96
van Heerden	Marius	RSA	8.9.74	178/69	800	1:46.64	1:44.57 -96
van Oudtshoorn	Gideon	RSA	23.9.76	184/75	800	1:45.38	1:46.10A -99
van Oudtshoorn	Jopie	RSA	5.2.76	189/80	400	45.61	44.75A, 45.21 -99
van Wyk	Christie	NAM	12.10.77	171/65	200	20.50	20.66A -99
^ Vander-Kuyp	Kyle	AUS	30.5.71	192/82	110H	13.58	13.29 -95, 13.27Aw, 13.2 -94
Vandewiele	Jürgen	BEL	10.5.74	182/68	1500	3:38.63	3:36.64 -99
Varga	Roland	HUN	22.10.77	197/102	DT	65.39	62.78 -99
Vargas	Eduardo	ESP	13.11.76	174/62	5000	13:27.4	13:32.96 -99
Värnik	Andrus	EST	27.9.77	182/93	JT	82.16	77.19 -99
Vartia	Janne	FIN	18.3.77	192/115	HT	71.90	66.66 -98
Vasilyev	Dmitriy	BLR	27.10.76	190/74	TJ	16.53	16.45 -96, 16.68i -98
Vera	Georkis	CUB	22.5.75	171/70	200	20.60	20.75A -99
Verbist	Gildas	FRA	9.6.79	180/70	PV	5.55i	5.50 -99
Verkin	Kazimir	SVK	27.3.72	178/68	20kW	1:24:13	1:24:34 -96
					50kW	3:59:16	4:04:14 -96
Verzl	Hrvoje	GER	12.11.70	183/78	TJ	16.52, 16.75w	16.74, 17.21w -98
Vicet	Frank	CUB	13.11.71	190/90	DT	60.60	61.02 -98
Videnov	Zhivko	BUL	23.5.77	193/80	110H	13.33	13.79 -97, 13.65w -99
Vieira	João	POR	20.2.76	174/58	20kW	1:22:53	1:20:59 –97
Vikhrov	Andrey	RUS	.73		HT	75.04	75.76 -99
Vincent	Casey	AUS	17.3.79	197/76	400	45.36	45.55 -98
Vincenti	Salvatore	ITA	5.3.72	176/53	5000	13:22.00	13:24.74 -99
Vinnitskiy	Andrey	UKR	23.12.76	184/71	400H	49.96	51.16 -99
* Virastyuk	Roman	UKR	20.4.68	189/135	SP	21.34	21.23 -96
Virastyuk	Vasiliy	UKR	22.4.74	191/120	SP	19.75	19.68 -98
* Vizzoni	Nicola	ITA	4.11.73	193/114	HT	79.64	79.59 -99
Vlasny	Andreas	AUT	12.9.69	182/96	SP	19.32	19.08 -99
* Voronin	Vyacheslav	RUS	5.4.74	190/78	HJ	2.40	2.37 -99
Voronkin	Yuriy	RUS	18.5.79	184/83	HT	76.03	70.22 -98
Vorontsov	Andrey	BLR	24.7.75		HT	76.02	75.06 -97
Vosloo	Johan	RSA	26.3.77	194/100	JT	80.54A, 80.05	79.96A -99
Voss	Martin	DEN	5.9.67	188/76	PV	5.60, 5.62ex	5.70 -96, 5.72i -95
Voyevodin	Aleksey	RUS	9.8.70	178/65	50kW	3:50:27	3:41:33 -97
Voynov	Sergey	UZB	26.2.77	188/89	JT	84.80	83.12 -99
Vroemen	Simon	NED	11.5.69	189/68	3kSt	8:13.45, 8:13.36inv	8:19.16 -97
Wachira	Nicholas	KEN	19.11.82		800	1:45.05	1:50.00 -99
Wachira	Solomon	KEN	5.11.76	170/55	10000	27:57.19	28:22.58 -98
Wade	Ibrahima	FRA	6.9.68	191/80	400	45.24	45.05 -98
* Wade	Larry	USA	22.11.74	187/83	110H	13.26	13.01 -99
Wahlman	Marko	FIN	6.4.69	194/104	HT	76.60	78.70 -95
* Wainana	Erick	KEN	19.12.73	175/58	Mar	2:10:17	2:10:31 -95
Wainana	James	KEN	16.6.81	163/55	HMar	61:20	
* Walder	Erick	USA	5.11.71	186/80	LJ	8.14	8.74A -94, 8.58 -96
Wale	Luleseged	ETH	82		3kSt	8:32.57	
Wallace	Dawane	USA	30.12.76	190/79	110H	13.22	13.57, 13.34w -99
Wallstab	Thomas	GER	29.1.68	178/64	50kW	3:54:20	3:51:19 -97
Waltz	Ian	USA	15.4.77	186/122	SP	19.28i, 19.13	19.45 -98
					DT	60.52	64.44 -98
Wang	Cheng	CHN	4.11.80	178/70	LJ	8.16	8.16 –98
Wang	Libo	CHN	28.10.79		50kW	3:59:44	4:08:57 -99
Wang	Yinhang	CHN	15.2.77	170/54	50kW	3:50:19	3:55:01 -99
Wang	Zhouzhou	CHN	20.4.77		HJ	2.23	2.27 -99
Ward	Jason	USA	6.4.81	188/79	TJ	16.61i, 16.54w	16.41 -99
Ware	Von	USA	30.6.75	175/79	TJ	16.49, 16.57w	16.97, 17.21w -98
Warners	Chiel	NED	2.4.78	194/85	Dec	7847	8363 -99
* Washington	Anthony	USA	16.1.66	186/109	DT	66.93	71.14 -96
* Washington	Tyree	USA	28.8.76	185/84	400	44.72	44.29 -98
Watanabe	Daisuke	JPN	29.5.75	185/72	LJ	8.18w	8.12 -99, 8.19w -97
Watkins	Arend	USA	23.5.79	190/86	110H	13.51	13.77, 13.63w -99
Watson	Shawn	USA	9.5.75	188/82	LJ	7.93i	7.96 -96
Watts	Mario	JAM	21.5.75	178/70	400H	49.08	49.45 -98
Watts	Marvin	JAM	1.5.75	188/71	800	1:46.57	1:47.74 -98
Waweru	Joseph	KEN	77		HMar	61:12	60:49 -99
Weakley	Ian	JAM	24.2.74	180/68	400H	49.12	48.83, 48.81dq -97
* Weidlinger	Günther	AUT	5.4.78	169/54	1500	3:34.69	3:42.40 -99
					3000	7:47.79i	
					3kSt	8:11.51	8:10.83 -99
Weir	Robert	GBR	4.2.61	191/119	DT	65.08	64.60 -97
* Weis	Heinz	GER	14.7.63	193/120	HT	80.13	83.04 -97

Name		Nat	Born	Ht/Wt	Event	2000 Mark	Pre-2000 Best
* Wellman	Brian	BER	8.9.67	175/72	TJ	17.05Ai, 16.50, 17.09Aw	
							17.62A, 17.72i, 17.75w -95
Wells	Clint	USA	2.5.75	185/68	3kSt	8:23.26	8:34.54 -99
Wells	Renward	BAH	23.2.70	173/72	200	20.60	20.53 -95, 20.06w -94
White	Geno	USA	10.3.78		200	20.52Aw	20.77, 20.5 -97
					400	45.02	45.66 -98
White	Mark	USA	10.6.67	190/101	DT	63.67	60.90 -99
^ Whiteman	Anthony	GBR	13.11.71	189/72	800	1:45.81	1:47.16 -97
					1500	3:34.93	3:32.34 -97
Whitmarsh	Zach	CAN	5.4.77	182/72	800	1:46.07	1:45.94 -99
Whyte	Wayne	JAM	4.5.74	187/77	400H	49.54	49.08 -98
Wighaman	Austin	USA			110H	13.75w	14.0w -98
Wignall	Maurice	JAM	17.4.76	186/75	110H	13.71	13.66 -99
					LJ	7.99i	8.09 -97
Wilkins	Perriss	GBR	12.12.69	188/112	DT	64.65	66.64 -98
Williams	Andre	USA	11.10.71	178/65	5000	13:28.29	13:34.74 -97
* Williams	Bernard	USA	19.1.78	183/81	100	9.99	10.03 -98
					200	20.03	20.71, 20.69Ai -99
Williams	Chris	JAM	15.3.72	177/68	100	10.05, 10.04w	10.30 -99
					200	20.02	20.48, 20.40w -99
Williams	Jeremichael	USA	30.12.76	183/80	110H	13.73w	13.53w -98
Williams	Ricardo	JAM	29.9.76	183/73	100	10.23	10.25, 10.19w -98
					200	20.33	20.58, 20.37w -98
Williams	Ronnie	USA	14.10.74	188/79	400	45.72	46.09 -98
Williamson	Paul	GBR	16.6.74	184/76	PV	5.55	5.50 -96
Wilson	Shomari	USA	6.6.76	183/73	100	10.23A, 10.19Aw	10.28A -99, 10.49 -98
Winchester	Ian	NZL	27.5.73	193/109	DT	64.26	63.74 -99
Wohlsen	Darryl	AUS	6.3.73	186/80	200	20.43A, 20.57	20.48 -98
Wójcik	Rafal	POL	18.9.72	180/66	3kSt	8:17.09	8:17.29 -99
* Wolde	Million	ETH	17.3.79	175/59	3000	7:32.36	7:35.61 -99
					5000	13:02.96	12:59.39 -98
Woodley	Adrian	CAN	25.11.75	180/73	110H	13.52, 13.50w	13.74 -99
Woodward	Bryan	USA	3.3.74	190/84	800	1:45.51	1:45.23 -99
* Woody	Joey	USA	22.5.73	188/78	400H	48.72	47.97 -98
Xu	Bin	CHN	4.8.70	178/62	LJ	7.94w	8.19 -92
Xu	Gang	CHN	9.2.79	187/70	PV	5.55i	5.50 -97, 5.52i -98
Xu	Zhizhou	CHN	8.1.81	179/64	200	20.62	20.87 -99
					400	45.55	45.88 -99
Yagoub	Mohamed	SUD	2.9.77	175/64	1500	3:38.58	3:33.73 -97
Yakovlev	Yevgeniy	RUS	17.6.79	176/65	20kW	1:21:58	1:24:31 -99
Yamaguchi	Yasi	JPN	12.6.75	183/64	10000	28:14.61	28:12.58 -99
Yamamoto	Yasuaki	JPN	5.8.72	168/57	Mar	2:10:44	2:11:13 -99
Yamamura	Takahiro	JPN	13.8.79	176/68	400	45.03	46.01 -99
^ Yamazaki	Kazuhiko	JPN	10.5.71	174/66	400H	49.71	48.26 -99
Yanagisawa	Satoshi	JPN	19.1.71	170/60	20kW	1:19:29	1:21:37 -95
Yang	Yongjian	CHN	28.4.73	177/65	50kW	3:48:42	3:55:23 -99
Yankov	Petko	BUL	6.10.77	185/73	200	20.67, 20.66i	20.27, 20.23w -99
Yasui	Akihiro	JPN	2.10.77	175/62	100	10.21, 10.20w	10.27, 10.21w -98
* Yator	Raymond	KEN	7.4.81	172/55	3kSt	8:03.74	8:15.31 -99
Yavas	Mesut	TUR	14.4.78	185/81	LJ	8.09i, 8.08	7.76, 7.89w -99
Ye	Kuigang	CHN	4.1.75		HT	73.67	72.62 -99
Yedékos	Nikólaos	GRE	9.7.66	186/100	HT	78.02	74.90 -96
^ Yegorov	Grigoriy	KZK	12.1.67	184/79	PV	5.62	5.90i, 5.90 -93
Yeldell	Greg	USA	14.10.80	180/84	TJ	16.44i. 16.81w	16.44 -98
Yemelyanov	Ivan	MOL	19.2.77	202/130	SP	20.26i, 19.05	17.81 -99
Yeremenko	Ruslan	UKR	31.7.78	185/75	PV	5.60sq	5.20 -99
Yesipchuk	Dmitriy	RUS	17.11.74	178/66	20kW	1:19:56	1:19:22 -97
Yevgenyev	Andrey	RUS	9.7.73	182/100	HT	73.09	77.92 -97
* Yiampoy	William	KEN	17.5.74	183/70	800	1:44.23	1:44.38 -99
					1500	3:37.62	
Yokoyama	Manabu	JPN	20.7.74	182/76	PV	5.70	5.63 -99
York	Jeff	USA	3.9.71	186/77	110H	13.49	13.59 -98, 13.56w -92
Yoshida	Takahisa	JPN	17.2.70	180/67	HJ	2.28	2.31 -93
Yoshihara	Masato	JPN	14.3.77	169/55	20kW	1:22:00	1:22:55 -99
Yoshizawa	Eiichi	JPN	5.9.80	170/54	20kW	1:23:20	1:27:05 -99
Yoshizawa	Ken	JPN	7.7.78	178/69	400H	49.11	49.44 -99
Young	Blair	AUS	5.4.71	194/83	400H	49.08A, 49.20	50.48 -99
* Young	Jerome	USA	14.8.76	181/79	200	20.43, 20.31w	20.41 -98
					400	44.70	44.09 -98
Yu	Chaohong	CHN	12.12.76	175/63	20kW	1:23:35	1:23:09 -99
					50kW	3:58:44	4:00:47 -97

	Name		Nat	Born	Ht/Wt	Event	2000 Mark	Pre-2000 Best
*	Yu	Guohui	CHN	30.4.77	182/70	20kW	1:22:32	1:19:38 -96
						50kW	3:55:20	4:02:17 -97
	Yuda	John	KEN	9.9.79		HMar	61:56?	
	Yudin	Stepan	RUS	3.4.80	175/61	20kW	1:22:14	1:26:00 -99
	Yurchenko	Denis	UKR	27.1.78	173/70	PV	5.72	5.59 -99
*	Yurkov	Aleksandr	UKR	21.7.75	183/80	LJ	7.93	7.58 -98
						Dec	8574	8215 -99
	Yushkov	Ivan	RUS	15.1.81	185/87	SP	19.27	16.02 -99
	Zagornyy	Aleksey	RUS	31.5.78	199/128	HT	79.68	77.20 -99
*	Zakari	Abdul Aziz	GHA	2.9.76	178/73	100	10.06	10.26 -97, 10.08w -99
						200	20.23	20.62 –98
	Zakharov	Stanislav	RUS	10.4.77		HT	73.29	70.10 -98
	Zakrzewski	Jan	POL	21.12.70	187/73	3kSt	8:24.56	8:26.13 -96
	Zalaggítis	Konstadinos	GRE	15.12.80	185/78	TJ	17.18,17.21w	16.14i -99,16.13 -97,16.59w-98
	Zanon	Simone	ITA	30.5.75	182/64	5000	13:25.46	13:22.48 -99
	Zegeye	Daniel	ETH	13.3.79	180/62	1500	3:36.33	3:40.94 -99
*	Zelezny	Ján	CZE	16.6.66	186/88	JT	90.59A, 90.56	98.48 -96
*	Zellner	Torrance	USA	6.1.70	187/75	400H	49.12	48.18 -96
	Zéroual	Larbi	MAR	10.1.71	178/65	HMar	61:29	60:58 -99
						Mar	2:10:36	2:12:20 -99
	Zeyen	Stephan	GER	11.9.78		Dec	7830	7706 -99
	Zhang	Hongwei	CHN	26.4.75		PV	5.63	5.40 -99
	Zhang	Houxi	CHN	15.1.81		JT	76.78	70.63 –99
	Zhang	Huiqiang	CHN	14.10.77	168/64	50kW	3:54:40	3:43:41 -96
	Zhang	Lianbiao	CHN	25.1.69	193/110	JT	78.85	83.38 -94
	Zhou	Zhongge	CHN	15.2.67	189/75	HJ	2.23	2.33 -90
	Zhu	Hongjun	CHN	18.8.83		20kW	1:23:34	1:24:28.3t -99
	Ziani	Kamal	ESP	20.2.72	178/68	Mar	2:10:52	2:15:21 -98
	Zioini	Badre Din	FRA	25.3.76	175/53	3kSt	8:26.10	8:45.93 -99
*	Ziolkówski	Szymon	POL	1.7.76	188/104	HT	81.42	79.58 -98
	Zoric	Steven	YUG	25.5.71	199/75	HJ	2.28	2.31i -91, 2.31 -96
^	Zorko	Branko	CRO	1.7.67	180/73	1500	3:37.08	3:33.30 –98
	Zou	Menghui	CHN	21.9.75		50kW	4:00:40	3:48:12 -97
*	Zsivóczky	Attila	HUN	29.4.77	193/82	Dec	8554	8379 -99
	Zujus	Daugvinas	LIT	16.10.75	182/65	50kW	3:58:39	3:55:10 -98
	Zwierzchiewski	Benoît	FRA	19.8.76	171/57	Mar	2:10:47	2:10:51 -98

Women's Name Changes

Kate	Anderson	Richardson
Oksana	Andrusina	Mert
Anzhela	Atroshchenko	Kinet
Tatyana	Babshkina	Motkova
Kelly	Blair	LaBounty
Angela	Bradburn	Spangler
Elena	Buhaianu	Iagar
Joetta	Clark	Diggs
Michelle	DiMuro	Ave
Mirela	Dulgheru	Renda
Wanita	Dykstra	May
Cristina	Fechita	Buzau
Colleen	Gillies	Scott
Gunhild	Halle	Haugen
Monica	Iagar	Dinescu
Nora	Ivanova	Güner
Jo	Jennings	Steele
Shae	Jones	Bair
Nadine	Kleinert	Schmitt
Cécile	Lignot	Maubert
Tania	Lutton	Senior
Svetla	Mitkova	Sinirtas
Oana	Musunolu	Pantelimon
Iulia	Negura	Olteanu
Mariya	Pantyukova	Konovalova
Karyne	Perkins	DiMarco
Irie	Pfeiler	Hill
Uta	Rohländer	Fromm
Maris	Rosza	Urbanik
Marina	Savitskaya	Grin
Midori	Shimnzu	Fumoto
Firiya	Sultanova	Zhdanova
Alina	Tecuta	Gherasim
Felicia	Tilea	Moldevan
Kjersti	Tysse	Plätzer
Lyudmila	Vaylenko	Prykhodko
Manuela	Veith	Zipse
Marieke	Veltman	Miller

WOMEN'S INDEX 2000

Athletes included are those ranked in the top 100s at standard events. Those with detailed biographical profiles are indicated in first column: * in this year's Annual, ^ in a previous year's Annual.* # old javelin

	Name		Nat	Born	Ht/Wt	Event	2000 Mark	Pre-2000 Best
	Abatzí	Aretí	GRE	14.5.74	183/78	DT	59.60	61.22 -97
*	Abe	Tomoe	JPN	13.8.71	149/38	Mar	2:28:01	2:26:09 -94
	Abel	María	ESP	23.10.74	162/45	10000	32:02.2	32:21.22 -99
	Abrahamse	Veronica	RSA	18.3.80	180/98	SP	16.82	16.53 -99
	Abramova	Svetlana	RUS	27.10.70	172/57	PV	4.20i, 4.05	4.20 -99
	Abrantes	Isabel	POR	20.2.73	170/55	100H	13.14	13.21 -95
*	Achilles	Bianca	GER	17.4.81	180/128	HT	66.58	68.40 -99
*	Acuff	Amy	USA	14.7.75	188/66	HJ	1.91	2.00 -97
^	Adams	Christine	GER	28.2.74	182/72	PV	4.40i, 4.30	4.21, 4.23ex -99
	Adams	Jenny	USA	8.7.78	165/55	100H	12.86	12.98, 12.86w -99
						LJ	6.64	6.45 -99, 6.53i, 6.59w -98
*	Adere	Berhane	ETH	21.7.73	170/48	3000	8:46.65	8:40.14 -97
						5000	14:52.61	14:54.88 -99
						10000	30:51.30	31:32.51 -99
						HMar	69:28	71:30 -97
	Adriano	Elisângela	BRA	27.7.72	180/95	SP	17.21	19.02 -99
						DT	58.63	62.23 -99
	Adusei	Martha	CAN	8.6.76	165/64	100	11.29, 11.0	11.33 -99, 11.29Aw -98
*	Afolabi	Olabisi	NGR	31.10.75	171/62	400	50.30	50.34A, 50.40 -99
	Agirre	Naroa	ESP	15.5.79	176/64	PV	4.10	4.01i, 4.00 -99
	Ahonen	Kirsi	FIN	8.4.76	170/78	JT	59.75	57.51 -99, 59.71# -98
	Ahrens	Anika	GER	19.7.78	168/54	400H	56.30	57.02 -99
	Ai	Dongmei	CHN	15.10.79	161/49	Mar	2:30:18	2:27:30 –97
	Aït Hamou	Mina	MAR	18.7.78		800	2:01.99	2:03.76 -99
	Ajkler	Zita	HUN	9.6.75	170/56	LJ	6.70	6.64 -98
						TJ	13.74	13.38 -98
	Ajudua	Benedicta	NGR	10.7.80	155/57	100	11.28w	
	Akinremi	Omolade	NGR	13.9.74	158/60	400H	57.02	55.44 -95
	Akinremi	Omotayo	NGR	13.9.74	158/60	200	23.05Aw	23.46 -96
						400H	57.33	56.66 -96, 56.4 -91
	Akulenko	Yulia	UKR	3.6.77	176/61	Hep	5915	6117 -97
	Alagia	Tiziana	ITA	8.3.73	171/54	Mar	2:32:18	2:52:12 -99
*	Aldama	Yamilé	CUB	14.8.72	172/65	TJ	14.47	14.77 -99
	Aldrich	Erin	USA	27.12.77	186/62	HJ	1.95	1.97i -98, 1.93 -97
	Aleksandrova	Galina	RUS	15.10.76		HMar	71:22	71:18 -99
	Aleksandrova	Yekaterina	RUS	3.6.77	181/57	HJ	1.90	1.96i -98, 1.94 -96
*	Alemu	Elfenesh	ETH	10.6.75	165/51	HMar	69:46	72:30 -97
						Mar	2:24:47	2:28:52 -99
*	Alfridi	Erica	ITA	22.2.68	168/53	20kW	1:28:06	1:28:13 -97
	Alisevich	Tatyana	BLR	22.1.69		Hep	6146	6073 -93
	Allahgreen	Diane	GBR	21.2.75	164/63	100H	13.11	12.99 -99
^	Allen	Liliana	MEX	24.5.70	170/62	100	11.19A,11.24, 11.23w	11.09A -99, 11.10 -92
	Allen	Patrina	JAM	17.4.75	175/68	100H	13.04, 13.02w	13.21 -98
						400H	55.63	57.43 -98
	Alonso	Ana Isabel	ESP	16.8.63	152/46	Mar	2:30:21	2:26:51 -95
*	Alozie	Glory	NGR	30.12.77	165/51	100	11.32	10.90 -99
						100H	12.54	12.44, 12.4w -98
	Álvarez	María Caridad	CUB	30.8.75	165/62	JT	61.57	58.34 –99, 63.02# -95
	Amertil	Christine	BAH	18.8.79	168/52	200	23.12	23.84 -99
						400	52.00	52.99 -99
	Ammel	Caroline	FRA	22.11.73	165/51	PV	4.30	4.25 -99
	Ampleyeva	Natalya	BLR	25.9.72		DT	61.76	58.62 -95
	Anderson	Andrea	USA	17.9.77	164/61	400	51.18	51.48 -98
	Anderson	Erin	USA	31.12.77		PV	4.20	3.85i, 3.83 -99
*	Anderson	Keturah 'Katie'	CAN	9.1.68	163/63	100H	12.82	12.61 -99
	Anderson	Shani	GBR	7.8.75	176/66	100	11.34	11.45, 11.36w -99
						200	23.20	23.22 -99
	Andreucci	Lucilla	ITA	19.12.69	168/52	HMar	71:42	71:32 -96
						Mar	2:29:43	2:30:34 -98
	Andrews	Susan	AUS	26.5.71	173/58	400	51.96	51.55 -98
						800	1:59.8mx, 2:00.32	2:04.54 -99
	Anisimova	Marina	RUS	4.3.73	172/65	800	1:58.77	2:01.11 -99
	Antil	Seema	IND	27.7.83	178/79	DT	57.20	
	Antoine	LaDonna	CAN	20.11.74	167/60	200	22.82w	23.23, 22.9 -97
						400	50.92	51.48 -97
*	Antonova	Yelena	UKR	16.6.72	182/90	DT	66.67	65.44 -98

Name		Nat	Born	Ht/Wt	Event	2000 Mark	Pre-2000 Best
Appelt	Orsolya	HUN	27.5.78	180/63	HJ	1.87i	1.86 -99
Araméndiz	Zuleima	COL	23.9.75	172/75	JT	59.33A	55.77A -99, 61.72# -96
^ Arimori	Yuko	JPN	17.12.66	166/47	Mar	2:31:12	2:26:39 -99
Armenta	Susan	USA	19.9.73	165/54	20kW	1:34:44	1:37:04 -99
* Arnardóttir	Gudrun	ISL	24.9.71	176/57	400H	54.37	54.59 -98
Arnott	Jane	NZL	3.1.76		400	52.23	52.80 -98
Aron	Haydy	FRA	21.5.73	169/57	100H	13.08, 12.92w	13.31 -96
* Arron	Christine	FRA	13.9.73	177/64	100	10.99, 10.89w	10.73 -98
Asiba	Gladys	KEN	31.5.77		HMar	70:05	72:46 -99
^ Astafei	Alina	GER	7.6.69	181/59	HJ	1.87	2.04i, 2.01 -95
^ Atede	Angela	NGR	8.2.72	170/66	100H	12.92	12.72 -98, 13.63dt -97
Athanasíou	Hristína	GRE	11.1.74	165/60	LJ	6.48, 6.60ex	6.60 -98
Atodonyang	Margarete	KEN	.78		10000	32:00.4	
					HMar	71:28	
* Auer	Doris	AUT	10.5.71	168/65	PV	4.40	4.33 -99
Auzeil	Nadine	FRA	19.8.64	176/64	JT	62.16	61.08 -99, 64.32# -94
Ave (DiMuro)	Michelle	USA	15.5.67	159/49	800	2:02.28	1:59.85 -96
Averkova	Anzhelika	UKR	13.3.69	165/48	3kSt	9:54.10	
Ayétotché	Louise	CIV	3.6.75	160/54	100	11.35	11.48A, 11.44w, 11.2A -99
					200	22.76	23.35A, 23.0A -99, 23.42 -96
Ayhan	Süreyya	TUR	6.9.78	163/52	800	2:00.64	2:06.72 -99
					1500	4:03.02	4:14.8 -99
^ Azzizi	Yasmina	ALG	25.2.66	174/70	100H	13.22	13.02 -92
(-Kettab)					Hep	5896	6392 -91
* Babakova	Inga	UKR	27.6.67	180/60	HJ	2.00	2.05 -95
^ Babashkina	Tatyana	RUS	23.11.68	175/68	HJ	1.94	2.03 -95
Babatunde	Tawa	CAN	19.12.79	175/60	400H	57.02	58.18 -99
Babcock	Courtney	CAN	30.6.72		1M	4:32.29	4:39.31i -94
Bacher	Gertrud	ITA	28.2.71	180/63	Hep	5990	6185 -99
Backus	LaKeisha	USA	15.12.76	158/52	100	11.21w	11.11 -98
Badurová	Katerina	CZE	18.12.82	167/50	PV	4.30	4.20 -99
Bailey	Aleen	JAM	25.11.80		200	22.86w	23.37 -99, 23.16w -98
Bair (Jones)	Shae	USA	15.8.78	163/57	PV	4.20	4.04 -99
Bak	Justyna	POL	1.8.74		3kSt	9:57.03	9:58.77 -99
Baklaci	Aysegül	TUR	25.12.77		TJ	13.80w	13.29 -99
^ Bakoyiánni	Níki	GRE	9.6.68	171/54	HJ	1.88	2.03 -96
* Balakhonova	Anzhela	UKR	18.12.72	162/55	PV	4.56	4.55 -99
Balantén	Norbi	CUB	24.6.72	176/83	HT	65.20	63.20 -98
Balassini	Ester	ITA	20.10.77	174/70	HT	66.17	64.44 -99
^ Balck	Heike	GER	19.8.70	180/60	HJ	1.88	2.01 -89
Bálint	Zita	HUN	25.10.71	169/55	100H	13.21	13.15 -99
Ball	Juan	USA	8.3.72	158/50	100	11.28	11.28A -99, 11.30, 11.23w -96
					200	23.21	23.34 -99, 22.86w -96
Balsamo	Agata	ITA	11.11.70	169/55	5000	15:23.9	15:14.70 -99
					10000	31:56.49	32:20.66 -99
Bangué	Frédérique	FRA	31.12.76	179/61	100	11.35, 11.32w	11.16 -98
Barashko	Tatyana	BLR	7.10.76		100	11.34	11.49 -98
Barbarino	Carla	ITA	16.5.67	168/53	400H	57.31	56.66 -97
* Barber	Eunice	FRA	17.11.74	175/68	100H	12.90	12.89 -99
					HJ	1.88	1.93 -99
					LJ	6.85	7.01 -99
					Hep	6842	6861 -99
Barber	Mikele	USA	4.10.80	159/50	200	22.98, 22.84w	23.05, 22.99w -99
					400	50.98	51.03 -99
Barmasai	Esther	KEN	.72		Mar	2:31:04	2:32:55 -99
Barnes-Mileham	Lacy	USA	23.12.64	165/70	DT	62.12	63.56 -96
Barsosio	Florence	KEN	11.8.76		HMar	71:03	
					Mar	2:27:00	
* Barsosio	Sally	KEN	21.3.78	165/46	3000	8:40.15	8:35.89 -97
					5000	14:53.61	14:46.71 -97
					10000	31:57.41	31:15.38 -99
* Bártová	Daniela	CZE	6.5.74	163/64	PV	4.50	4.51 -98
Bashlykova	Lidiya	RUS	10.1.81	169/56	Hep	5979	5618 -99
Bass	Valma	SKN	12.3.74	163/59	200	23.07	23.24 -98
Bastos	Marina	POR	7.7.71	165/50	10000	32:09.53	31:41.38 -99
Bastrygina	Natalya	RUS	.71		LJ	6.49	6.32 -99
Bates	Joyce	USA	16.2.77	163/59	100H	12.85, 12.79w	12.91, 12.85w -99
* Batten	Kim	USA	29.3.69	170/57	400H	54.70	52.61 -95
Bazhenova	Nadezhda	RUS	.78		LJ	6.51	6.04 -98
					TJ	14.13	15.25 -99

Name		Nat	Born	Ht/Wt	Event	2000 Mark	Pre-2000 Best
Beaney	Kristin	USA	30.6.72	158/48	10000	32:22.72	32:33.52 -97
Beautle	Karen	JAM	13.6.71	177/54	HJ	1.89	1.87 -98
Beckel	Nadine	GER	27.5.77	190/89	SP	18.02i, 18.01	17.69i, 17.55 -99
					DT	56.24	59.49 -99
Becker	Annika	GER	12.11.81	170/63	PV	4.22	4.30 -99
Becker	Kim	USA	25.6.72		PV	4.16	4.20i, 4.18 -99
Bécot	Emilie	FRA	20.10.80	165/58	PV	4.20	4.05 -99
Beenamol	K. Matthews	IND	15.8.75	163/52	400	51.21	52.69 -99
^ Beer	Peggy	GER	15.9.69	176/66	Hep	6153	6531 -90
Begic	Vera	CRO	17.3.82	169/69	DT	56.22	52.55 -99
* Belkacem	Yamna	FRA	20.2.74	164/52	3000	8:41.54	8:38.13 -99
					5000	14:47.79	15:02.34 -99
Bello	Ameerah	ISV	3.10.75	165/54	100	11.27	11.60 -97
					200	23.11	23.13 -98
Belovol	Tatyana	UKR	7.10.69	162/52	1500	4:09.95	4:08.06 -97
					3000	8:58.99	8:52.2 -95
* Belyakova	Yelena	RUS	7.4.76	178/55	PV	4.50	4.46 -99
Belyayeva	Olesya	KAZ	29.6.80		LJ	6.52	6.33 -99
Benavídes	Virgen	CUB	31.12.74	165/62	100	11.21, 11.19w	11.14, 11.10w -99
					200	22.93	23.31, 23.28w -98
Benesová	Hana	CZE	19.4.75	170/60	400	52.03	51.18 -97
* Benhassi	Hasna	MAR	1.6.78	166/55	800	1:58.47	1:57.45 -99
Bennion-Murdock	Julie	USA	12.3.75		400H	57.10	57.08A -99
Benth	Katia	FRA	16.11.75	172/56	100	11.36, 11.34w	11.20 -98
Bentley	Brandi	USA	7.3.78		LJ	6.56w	6.50 -99
Benyarku	Esi	CAN	28.11.76	168/55	100	11.30	11.57, 11.37w -99
Beránková	Sárká	CZE	16.4.78	176/69	Hep	6079	5670 -99
^ Bergmann	Mette	NOR	9.11.62	174/80	DT	62.46	69.68 -95
* Bergqvist	Kajsa	SWE	12.10.76	175/59	HJ	2.01	1.98A, 1.97 -99
Bertel	Véronique	FRA	12.4.69	162/52	3kSt	10:08.18	0
Beunder	Renate	NED	31.8.70		HT	60.84	59.71 -99
Beutelspacher	Simone	GER	8.12.74	170/60	800	2:01.72i	2:02.44 -99
^ Bevilacqua	Antonella	ITA	15.10.71	175/56	HJ	1.92i, 1.88	1.98, 1.99dq -96
Bévis	Marie-Louise	FRA	12.10.72	170/58	400	52.15	51.79 -96
Beyer	Ilona	GER	8.1.76	184/90	SP	17.63	17.19 -99
Bicet	Nora	CUB	29.10.77	178/78	JT	60.67	56.68# -95
Bicet	Yusmay	CUB	8.12.83		TJ	13.80	13.60 -99
* Bidouane	Nezha	MAR	18.9.69	174/60	400H	53.53	52.90 -99
Bielert	Miriam	GER	17.6.75		HJ	1.90i, 1.90	1.85 -97
Bikar	Alenka	SLO	7.1.74	161/53	100	11.35	11.30 -98
					200	22.90	22.79 -99
* Biktagirova	Madina	RUS	20.9.64	158/46	Mar	2:26:33	2:24:46 -97
Biktasheva	Lyudmila	RUS	25.7.74	160/48	5000	15:22.98	15:47.45 -96
					10000	31:33.58	32:29.27 -98
Biondini	Silvia	ITA	24.1.76	166/58	TJ	13.71w	13.70 -99
Birra	Tadelesh	ETH	24.4.75		Mar	2:31:44	2:36:40 -99
Birungi	Grace	UGA	10.10.73	164/48	800	2:00.97	2:01.76A -99
^ Biryukova	Anna	RUS	27.9.67	174/61	TJ	14.44	15.09 -93
* Bisset	Sonia	CUB	1.4.71	172/77	JT	65.87	63.52 -99, 68.24# -97
Biswas	Soma	IND	16.5.78	173/60	Hep	6186	5374 -99
* Blackett	Andrea	BAR	24.1.76	160/54	100H	13.17w	13.44 -97, 13.2 -98
					400H	54.41	53.36 -99
Blake	Tanya	GBR	16.1.71	167/58	800	2:01.06	2:00.10 -98
Blondeel	Veerle	BEL	14.1.75	179/86	DT	57.63	57.00 -96
Blonskaya	Lyudmila	UKR	18.3.75	173/62	Hep	6077	6230 -99
Blutreich	Lynda	USA	13.12.71	176/80	JT	58.61	57.14 –99, 60.82# -97
Bobrovskaya	Yelena	KGZ	11.4.75	175/56	LJ	6.66	6.58 -99
Bodritskaya	Svetlana	KAZ	7.11.71	171/54	400	52.17	52.53 -97
^ Bodrova	Nadezhda	UKR	13.7.61	170/58	100H	12.89	12.65 -84
Bodunova	Gelena	RUS	.76		400	51.56	52.63 -99
Bogachova	Irina	KGZ	30.5.61	167/52	Mar	2:26:27	2:27:46 -99
Bogomolova	Galina	RUS	15.10.77	158/41	3000	8:43.45	9:12.33 -99
					5000	15:08.61	15:52.72 -99
					10000	31:29.66	33:34.44 -97
Bolm	Kirsten	GER	4.3.75	179/65	100H	12.92	13.04, 12.86Aw -99
					LJ	6.50i, 6.55w	6.55 -94
Bolshova	Olga	MDA	16.6.68	174/60	TJ	13.88	
Bonenko	Tatyana	UKR	7.6.76	164/54	100	11.0w	11.46 -98
					200	23.06	23.23, 22.8 -98
Bonne	Idalmis	CUB	2.2.71	167/61	400	52.04	50.95A -95, 51.50 -96

Name		Nat	Born	Ht/Wt	Event	2000 Mark	Pre-2000 Best
Borda	Sylvie	FRA	4.9.66	172/66	TJ	13.75	14.07 -99
Boslak	Vanessa	FRA	11.6.82	169/57	PV	4.32	4.15i, 4.11 -99
Botezan	Mihaela	ROM	21.2.76	162/49	HMar	70:07	76:52 -99
Boulová	Michaela	CZE	2.8.81	165/52	PV	4.20	3.90 -99
Bouyer	Nikkie	USA	11.2.76	175/68	100H	13.17Aw	13.24A -99, 13.21w -98
					400H	55.86	56.34 -99
Bowers	Stacey	USA	22.8.77	168/59	TJ	14.01	14.05 -99
Boyde	Kathrin	GER	4.12.70	172/62	20kW	1:30:42	1:35:12 -98
Boyer	Edie	USA	15.2.66	183/86	DT	58.37	64.08 -96
Brägger	Anita	SUI	6.10.72	170/59	800	2:01.11	2:00.23 -99
Branson	Andrea	USA	9.11.78	175/59	PV	4.22	4.07 -99
* Braun	Sabine	GER	19.6.65	174/65	Hep	6464	6985 -92
Bresciani	Maria Carla	ITA	16.7.73	171/64	PV	4.20i, 4.20	4.06 -96
* Breuer	Grit	GER	16.2.72	166/63	400	51.06	49.42 -91
Brigadnaya	Viktoriya	TKM	4.8.80	176/60	TJ	13.96	13.97 -99
* Brkljacic	Ivana	CRO	25.1.83	170/65	HT	68.18	58.51 -99
^ Brunet	Roberta	ITA	20.5.65	170/58	3000	8:52.60	8:35.65 -97
					5000	15:15.94	14:44.50 -96
Brunner	Chantal	NZL	5.11.70	168/58	LJ	6.66A, 6.54, 6.77Aw	6.68 -97
Bryukhach	Marina	UKR	16.1.77	168/53	Hep	6022	5330 -97
Bu	Fanfang	CHN	02.78		400	51.95	51.85 -97
Budnik	Yelena	BLR	9.5.76	173/63	400	52.25	52.83 -99
^ Buford-Bailey	Tonja	USA	13.12.70	173/61	400H	54.80	52.62 -95
^ Buhaianu-Iagar	Elena	ROM	16.1.75	173/54	800	2:01.29	2:00.26 -99
		ROM			1500	4:04.94	4:04.27 -99
Buloychik	Tatyana	BLR	7.1.75		800	2:01.8	
Bunjes	Andrea	GER	5.2.76	175/80	HT	60.78	60.53 -98
^ Burangulova	Ramilya	RUS	11.7.61	154/50	Mar	2:31:14	2:27:58 -96
Burgiman	Yelena	UZB	21.12.68	179/66	JT	56.42	52.00 -99, 56.24# -96
Burianová	Jitka	CZE	17.1.77	174/57	400	50.85	51.72 -99
* Burrell	Dawn	USA	1.11.73	176/58	LJ	6.98, 6.99w	6.96 -99
* Burrell	Shelia	USA	15.1.72	173/64	100H	13.19,13.14w	13.20A -99,13.22,13.17w -98
					Hep	6422	6294w, 6270 -98
Burrell (Finn)	Michelle	USA	8.5.65	165/52	100	11.32	11.05, 10.96Aw -90
* Buschbaum	Yvonne	GER	14.7.80	173/56	PV	4.45	4.42, 4.45ex -99
Buval	Patricia	FRA	22.1.76	168/57	100H	13.14	13.35 -99
Buzhenko	Yelena	UKR	16.11.72	170/55	800	2:00.07	1:59.46 -99
Cadamuro	Stefania	ITA	23.2.79	178/58	HJ	1.91	1.88 -99
Caffel	Kelly	GBR	10.2.79	168/47	1500	4:10.22	4:16.64 -99
^ Cai	Weiyan	CHN	25.10.73	169/56	PV	4.20	4.35i, 4.33 -96
Calatayud	Zulia	CUB	9.11.79	169/59	400	51.69	52.03 -99
					800	1:58.66	2:00.67 -99
Calloway	Dominiqué	USA	19.7.78	175/60	100H	12.93, 12.7, 12.86w	12.85 -99
					400H	56.32	56.02 -99
* Campbell	Juliet	JAM	17.3.70	178/62	200	22.86, 22.70i	22.50 -99
* Campbell	Veronica	JAM	15.5.82	163/61	100	11.12, 11.1	11.49 -99
					200	22.87	23.73 -99
^ Cao	Qi	CHN	15.1.74	182/83	DT	62.26	66.08 -93
Carabalí	Norfalia	ESP	21.1.64	163/51	400	51.77	51.17 -93
Cárdenas	Regla María	CUB	21.1.75	186/77	Hep	5647	6306 -95
Carlsten	Emily	USA	30.10.78	180/77	JT	56.98	52.96 -99
Carpenter	Khalilah	USA	27.1.83	173/61	200	23.16	23.81 -99
Carruthers	Danielle	USA	22.12.79		100H	13.10w	13.88, 13.77w -99
^ Carson	Kim	USA	12.3.74	170/56	100H	13.06	12.72 -96, 12.69w -90
Carter	Tonya	USA	22.3.78		100	11.30, 11.15w	11.68, 11.32w -99
Castrejana	Carlota	ESP	25.4.73	188/67	TJ	14.10	14.05i, 14.05A, 13.83 -99
Casy	Natacha	FRA	26.4.74	174/64	100H	13.13	13.30, 13.15w -99
^ Catuna	Anuta	ROM	1.10.68	155/44	Mar	2:29:46	2:27:34 -98
Cepero	Olga Lidia	CUB	4.2.75	178/66	LJ	6.53, 6.55w	6.36 -97
					TJ	14.04	14.43 -98
Ceplak	Jolanda	SLO	12.9.76	168/55	800	2:00.80	2:00.94 -97
Chang	Xinhong	CHN	24.3.74		SP	16.44	16.34 -95
Charalambous	Agni	CYP	2.9.75	176/57	HJ	1.89	1.82 -96, 1.86dq -97
Chebykina	Tatyana	RUS	22.11.68	173/63	400	51.59	51.01 -95
Chechelyeva	Alla	RUS	1.7.81	166/54	PV	4.10i, 4.10	3.90 -98
Chelagat	Alice	KEN			HMar	70:16	
Chen	Ying	CHN	4.11.75	171/58	HT	62.93	
^ Chen	Yueling	USA	1.4.68	155/46	20kW	1:33:40	1:38:17 -99
Chen	Yuxiang	CHN	28.2.78	167/60	400	52.04	51.15 -97
Cheng	Xianhong	CHN	24.10.68		DT	59.71	66.00 -97

	Name		Nat	Born	Ht/Wt	Event	2000 Mark	Pre-2000 Best
	Cheng	Xiaoyan	CHN	30.12.75	176/90	SP	19.31	20.02 -94
*	Chepchumba	Joyce	KEN	6.11.70	160/52	5000	15:26.19	15:51.08 -99
						HMar	68:18	69:07 -97
						Mar	2:24:02	2:23:22 -99
	Chepchumba	Pamela	KEN	28.2.78		HMar	71:03sh	72:27 -99
*	Chepkemei	Susan	KEN	25.6.75	164/48	HMar	69:10	69:28 -99
	Chepkieny	Milkah	KEN	12.8.76		Mar	2:31:25	2:32:46 -99
	Cherepanova	Natalya	RUS	.67		3kSt	10:11.86	
	Cherkasova	Svetlana	RUS	20.5.78		800	1:59.23	2:00.91 -99
	Chernova	Lada	RUS	1.1.70		JT	56.85	56.65 -99, 61.34# -96
*	Chernyavskaya	Olga	RUS	17.9.63	180/80	DT	64.55	68.38 -92
	Chernyavskaya	Yelena	RUS	13.4.78		HJ	1.91	1.86 -99
						Hep	6384	5961 -99
*	Cheromei	Lydia	KEN	11.5.77	168/45	3000	8:29.14	8:36.11 -97
						5000	14:47.35	14:46.72 -97
^	Cheruiyot	Rose	KEN	21.7.76	163/48	3000	8:39.88	8:39.34 -96
						5000	14:55.88	14:46.41 -96
	Cheruiyot	Vivian	KEN	9.11.83		5000	15:11.11	15:42.79A -99
^	Chiba	Masako	JPN	18.7.76	156/39	HMar	70:25	66:43 -97
	Chibisova	Oksana	RUS	31.3.77	177/87	SP	17.39i, 17.21	16.83 -98
	Chicherova	Anna	RUS	22.7.82	178/53	HJ	1.90	1.89 -99
	Chilla	Mercedes	ESP	19.1.80	165/54	JT	57.91	54.41 -99, 55.32# -99
*	Chojecka	Lidia	POL	25.1.77	163/51	800	2:00.46i	1:59.97 -99
						1500	3:59.22	4:01.36 -99
						1M	4:24.44i	4:25.18 -98
						3000	8:33.35	8:34.19 -99
	Chu	Chunxia	CHN	28.1.78	182/60	JT	59.56	58.21 -99, 61.91# -98
	Chulkova	Natalya	RUS	5.12.77	170/56	400H	55.73	59.94 -99
	Churbanova	Olga	RUS	16.7.65	169/51	3000	8:54.53i	8:40.48 -94
*	Cîmpean	Norica	ROM	22.3.72	165/58	20kW	1:28:59	1:27:46 -99
	Ciobanu	Lucica	ROM	10.5.79	175/80	SP	18.94	17.30 -99
	Cioncan	Maria	ROM	19.6.77	172/51	1500	4:06.20	4:11.18 -99
	Cîrlan	Daniela	ROM	18.9.80	162/45	20kW	1:31:30	1:42:30 -99
	Citté	Sandra	FRA	28.3.76	162/57	100	11.17	11.35 -98, 11.25w -99, 11.1w -96
	Claretti	Clarissa	ITA	7.10.80	170/70	HT	60.83	55.83 -99
	Clark	Christine	USA	10.10.62	160/50	Mar	2:31:35	2:40:38 -99
*	Clark	Hazel	USA	3.10.77	175/55	800	1:58.75	2:00.23 -98
^	Clark-Diggs	Joetta	USA	1.8.62	168/56	800	1:59.49	1:57.84 -98
	Clarke	Georgie	AUS	17.6.84	167/46	800	2:01.73	2:02.49 -99
						1500	4:06.77	4:12.51 -99
	Clarke	Rhian	GBR	19.4.77	170/59	PV	4.15	3.90 -97
	Clarke-Lewis	Eldece	BAH	13.2.65	162/43	100	10.96	11.21 -96
						200	22.86	23.04 -95
	Clayton-Boswell	Michelle	USA	29.10.76		HT	61.40	59.22 -99
*	Cloete	Hestrie	RSA	26.8.78	185/68	HJ	2.01	2.04 -99
	Clopés	Inmaculada	ESP	19.1.68	170/60	Hep	5843	5810 -96
*	Colander-Richardson	LaTasha	USA	23.8.76	168/52	200	22.49	23.21 -97
						400	49.87	0
						400H	57.21	56.88 -99
*	Collins	Michelle	USA	12.2.71	176/62	100	11.19	11.36 -92, 11.22w -94
						200	22.57	22.74 -94
						400	50.11	50.67 -99
	Collins	Roberta	USA	31.7.77	170/112	DT	58.32	56.60 -98
	Collonvillé	Marie	FRA	23.11.73	163/54	Hep	6119	6350 -97
	Combe	Delphine	FRA	6.12.74	168/59	100	11.29w	11.30 -95
	Connelly	Tina	CAN	16.8.70	165/52	10000	32:21.27	32:54.96 -97
	Coons	Leslie	USA	16.7.73	175/74	HT	63.80	63.11 -99
	Copper	Brandit	USA	25.8.78		100H	13.03	13.38, 13.24w -99
	Coslovich	Claudia	ITA	26.4.72	170/70	JT	65.30	60.12 -99, 65.55# -98
^	Costian	Daniela	AUS	30.4.65	182/84	DT	61.33	73.84 -88
	Couch	Sharon	USA	[illegible]	170/[illegible]	100H	[illegible]	[illegible] -99
	Crabtree	Aimee	USA	22.1.78		PV	4.30b, 4.12	3.97 -99
	Craig	Katy	USA			HT	60.73	
	Crawford	Yunaika	CUB	2.11.82	165/75	HT	65.88	62.71 -99
	Cresci	Federica	ITA	13.4.74	179/65	TJ	13.68	13.69, 13.80w -99
	Cripps	Sharon	AUS	29.6.77	165/56	200	23.13	23.24 -98
	Cross	Anne	AUS	16.4.65	170/56	1500	4:10.34	4:11.15 -90
						3000	8:57.21	8:53.17 -95
						5000	15:20.78	15:25.8 -98

	Name		Nat	Born	Ht/Wt	Event	2000 Mark	Pre-2000 Best
	Cross	Jesseca	USA	10.5.75	178/88	SP	19.17i, 17.80	18.10 -99
						HT	66.52	63.25 -99
	Crouse	Ann	USA	6.4.76	183/84	JT	56.20	57.38 -99
^	Crowley	Margaret	AUS	24.5.67	167/55	800	1:59.97	1:59.73 -96
						1500	4:07.23	4:01.34 -96
	Crozet	Muriel	FRA	8.1.71	175/66	Hep	6021	5825 -99
	Cui	Danfeng	CHN	10.1.77		100	11.23, 11.22w	11.20 -97
	Cui	Guomei	CHN	2.7.79		10000	32:24.45	32:46.67 -97
						HMar	70:01	
	Cui	Xiaohong	CHN	10.2.80		HT	61.78	59.17 -99
	Culpepper	Shayne	USA			1500	4:07.99	4:08.69 -99
*	Cumbá	Yumileidi	CUB	11.2.75	183/100	SP	19.48	19.29 -99
	Cummins	Diane	CAN	19.1.74	165/50	800	2:01.95	2:02.14 -99
^	Curbishley	Allison	GBR	3.6.76	167/58	400	51.50	50.71 -98
	Curovic	Danijela	YUG	7.3.74	184/98	DT	57.91	59.92, 59.92u -95
*	Currey	Louise	AUS	24.1.69	174/65	JT	66.80	66.03 -99, 66.96# -98
	Cuza	Lissete	CUB	26.2.75	165/55	LJ	6.99	6.69 -96
	Czenska	Magdalena	POL	14.6.81	169/67	JT	56.37	54.38 -99
*	da Fonseca-Wollheim	Kristina	GER	10.2.72	180/56	800	2:01.13	2:00.76 -97
						1500	4:05.07	4:01.42 -98
	Dacy	Rachel	AUS	10.11.76	170/62	PV	4.20	4.15 -99
	Dagne	Birhan	GBR	8.4.78	166/47	10000	32:30.4	33:24.46 -99
	Dai	Yanyan	CHN	8.1.80	175/55	5000	15:29.36	16:21.76 -97
						10000	32:23.45	
	Dai	Zuoying	CHN			DT	56.28	
	Daigle	Angela	USA	28.5.76	157/57	100	11.37, 11.33w	11.34 -99
	Dalla Piana	Silvia	ITA	3.2.75	173/60	Hep	5795	5664 -98
	Dällenbach	Chantal	FRA	24.10.62	164/48	3kSt	10:12.94	0
*	Damaske	Tanja	GER	16.11.71	177/77	JT	66.73	66.91 -99, 70.10# -98
	Damon	Karol	USA	20.12.69	178/54	HJ	1.93	1.93 -99
	Danisová	Martina	SVK	21.3.83	176/75	HT	61.62	58.61 -99
	Danvers	Natasha	GBR	19.9.77	175/61	100H	13.20, 13.19w	13.20 -98, 12.8w -99
						400H	54.95	55.69 -98
	Darsha	Damayanthi	SRI	13.2.75	168/60	200	22.84	22.48 -98
						400	51.05	51.06 -98
	Davies	Samantha	GBR	20.9.79	157/52	200	23.06	24.22 -97, 24.02w -98
	Davis	Kinshasa	USA	10.7.79	178/	200	22.69	22.90 -97
	Davis	Michele	USA	4.9.80	170/60	200	23.14	23.65A, 23.03Aw -99
*	Davis-Thompson	Pauline	BAH	9.7.66	167/57	100	10.97	11.07 -98, 10.9A -89
						200	22.27	22.44 -92
	Davis	Trevaia	USA	7.9.68	183/68	400H	55.56	54.78 -99
*	Davydova	Alla	RUS	21.5.66	167/82	HT	68.47	67.48 -96
^	de Bruin	Corrie	NED	26.10.76	179/80	SP	17.40i, 17.08	18.97i, 18.87 -98
	de Jong	Marjolein	NED	12.6.81	184/62	400H	56.26	58.9 -99
	de la Puente	Martina	ESP	4.4.75	180/100	SP	18.17	18.17 -99
	De Leeuw	Sabrina	BEL	19.8.74	182/63	HJ	1.90	1.93 -93
^	de Reuck	Colleen	RSA	13.4.64	164/47	HMar	71:46	68:38 -89
	de Wilt	Monique	NED	21.3.76	170/60	PV	4.30, 4.35ex	4.21 -99
	Dean	Windy	USA	7.9.78	178/84	HT	64.12	64.29 -99
	Debelaya	Tatyana	UKR	28.1.70	170/56	400H	55.79	55.67 -99
	Dedekina	Lyudmila	RUS	5.1.79	165/55	20kW	1:33:27	1:30:52 -99
	Defar	Meseret	ETH	.83	155/42	3000	8:59.90	9:02.08 -99
						5000	15:08.36	
	Dejaeghere	Veerle	BEL	1.8.73	184/52	1500	4:05.77	4:10.40 -98
						3000	8:49.31	8:53.23 -99
	Delahunty	Sinead	IRL	12.2.71	172/60	1500	4:05.28	4:04.22 -98
						1M	4:30.41i	4:27.38 -97
	Dementiy	Yelena	UKR	6.3.69	180/80	SP	17.54	16.64 -98
*	Denboba	Merima	ETH	21.8.74	168/48	3000	8:54.03	8:44.21 -99
						5000	15:15.17	15:08.52 -99
						10000	31:43.28	31:32.63 -99
	Denby	Nichole	USA	10.10.82	163/52	100H	13.20	13.78, 13.36w -99
	Dennehy-Willis	Breeda	IRL	2.3.70	175/53	5000	15:12.83	15:42.49 -99
						10000	32:11.30	
	Derkach	Oksana	UKR	7.2.69	166/53	TJ	13.72	14.09 -99
	Déskou	Hristína	GRE	27.5.73	167/46	20kW	1:31:38	1:32:52 -99
	Devaluez	Isabelle	FRA	17.3.66	180/75	DT	60.10	62.02 -96
*	Devers	Gail	USA	19.11.66	160/55	100	10.99	10.82 -92, 10.8w -95
						100H	12.33	12.37 -99
	Di Martino	Antonietta	ITA	1.6.78	169/58	HJ	1.88	1.78 -97

Name		Nat	Born	Ht/Wt	Event	2000 Mark	Pre-2000 Best
Dia	Fabé	FRA	14.2.77	173/62	200	23.15i	23.02, 22.99w -99
Dias	Ana	POR	15.1.74	169/50	5000	15:27.74	15:29.32 -95
					10000	32:04.80	31:39.52 -99
Diaz	Elizabeth	USA	18.10.77		800	2:02.22	2:03.44 -99
Dice	Ericka	USA	9.2.72	168/68	HT	61.56	56.68 -98
^ Dickey	Cheryl	USA	12.12.66	165/62	100H	12.98, 12.91w	12.72 -98
* Dietzsch	Franka	GER	22.1.68	183/90	DT	68.06	69.51 -99
Dimitrova	Maria	BUL	7.8.76	170/52	TJ	14.27	14.28 -98
* Dimitrova	Svetla	BUL	27.1.70	170/65	100H	12.78	12.53, 12.50w -94, 12.4 -97
* Dinescu	Monica	ROM	1.4.73	186/68	HJ	2.02	2.03i -99, 2.02 -98
Diop	Aïda	SEN	27.4.70	164/59	100	11.23Aw	11.41A -99
					200	22.64A, 22.76	22.92 -99
Diouf	Aminata	SEN	18.2.77	172/60	100	11.28	11.24 -99, 10.9 -98
					200	23.18	22.90 -98
Diouf	Mame Tacko	SEN	17.10.76	169/57	100H	12.94	12.98 -98, 12.8 -99
					400H	55.11	54.75 -99
Dita-Tomescu	Constantina	ROM	23.1.70	165/48	5000	15:28.91	15:36.36 -99
					HMar	71:35	71:22 -99
* Divós	Katalin	HUN	11.5.74	180/84	DT	56.44	56.29 -99
					HT	68.98	67.64 -99
Dixon	Vonette	JAM	26.11.75		100H	12.90	13.26 -97
^ Djaté	Patricia	FRA	3.1.71	173/58	800	2:00.67	1:56.53 -95
					1500	4:08.70	4:02.26 -96
Dobrovitskaya	Taisia	BLR	8.12.67	179/62	Hep	5814	6337 -93
Dóczi	Orsolya	HUN	28.9.75	164/51	400H	57.15	57.57 -98
Dolcini	Francesca	ITA	28.12.74	162/55	PV	4.27	4.26 -99
Dolgopolova	Lyudmila	BLR	11.8.69	160/53	20kW	1:29:23	1:31:43 -99
Domain	Sandrine	FRA	6.9.71	176/63	TJ	13.83	14.15 -96
* Domínguez	Marta	ESP	3.11.75	163/52	1500	4:06.08	4:08.59 -96
					3000	8:28.80	8:44.10 -98
					5000	15:26.00	14:59.49 -98
Donáth	Katalin	HUN	12.11.79	161/50	PV	4.30	4.20 -99
Donders	Mireille	SUI	7.7.74	166/52	200	23.06	23.19 -96, 22.96i -98
* Dong	Yanmei	CHN	16.2.77	166/51	3000	8:33.07	
					5000	15:03.99	14:29.82 -97
					10000	32:23.21	30:38.09 -97
Dong	Zhaoxia	CHN	13.11.74	167/48	10000	32:32.06	30:47.22 -97
Donkina	Yelena	RUS	15.3.73	180/64	TJ	13.87	14.58 -97
Dor	Olga	ISR	26.6.76	166/58	400H	56.86	56.75 -99
^ Dörre-Heinig	Katrin	GER	6.10.61	170/57	HMar	71:44	69:15 -98
Dorsile	Viviane	FRA	1.6.67	167/51	800	2:01.30	1:59.29 -92
Dowdie	Peta-Gaye	JAM	18.1.77	172/61	100	11.13, 10.98w	11.03A, 11.06 -99
					200	22.51, 22.43w	22.56, 22.25w -99
* Dragila	Stacy	USA	25.3.71	173/64	PV	4.70b, 4.63	4.60 -99
* Drechsler	Heike	GER	16.12.64	180/67	LJ	6.99, 7.07w	7.48 -88, 7.63Aw -92
Dreher	Claudia	GER	2.5.71	170/53	Mar	2:31:57	2:27:55 -99
Drew	Shelley	GBR	8.8.73	182/81	DT	59.03	60.82 -98
Drossin	Deena	USA	14.2.73	163/48	1500	4:07.82	4:13.98 -99
					3000	8:42.59	8:45.13 -99
					5000	14:51.62	14:56.84 -99
					10000	31:51.05	32:00.72 -99
Drozdova	Tatyana	RUS	7.2.75	175/54	TJ	14.00	14.10 -99
Dryburgh	Jenny	NZL	30.8.78	173/65	PV	4.10	4.06 -99
Dryer	Elva	USA	26.9.71	165/51	1500	4:10.68	4:10.02 -98
					5000	15:09.19	15:17.37 -98
Du	Beibei	CHN	6.1.83		JT	57.29	55.39 -99
Du	Xianhui	CHN	4.1.81	188/90	SP	17.62	18.73i, 18.35 -99
Du	Xueru	CHN	6.4.83		Hep	5889	5520 -99
du Toit	Maranelle	RSA	31.12.78		SP	16.87	16.62 -99
Dudgeon	Sinead	GBR	9.7.76	169/57	400H	55.45	55.24 -99
^ Dukhnova	Natalya	BLR	16.7.66	174/60	800	2:00.47	1:57.24 -96
* Dulecha	Kutre	ETH	22.8.78	166/48	1500	3:59.02	3:58.38 -98
					1M	4:25.73i	4:39.04 -97
^ Dulgheru -Renda	Mirela	ROM/TUR	5.10.66	175/64	LJ	6.79, 6.68i	7.14 -92
Dumble	Dawn	USA	25.2.72	173/90	SP	17.60	18.08 -98
Dumitrascu	Elena	ROM	14.5.74	174/63	TJ	14.14	13.79 -94
					Hep	5647	5389 -94
Dunkley	Michelle	GBR	26.1.78	178/62	HJ	1.93	1.89i -97, 1.88 -98
^ Duporty	Julia	CUB	9.2.71	165/51	400	52.17	50.61 -94

Name		Nat	Born	Ht/Wt	Event	2000 Mark	Pre-2000 Best
Duquénoy	Laurence	FRA	29.9.69	160/46	1500	4:10.81	2:12.93 -99
					3000	8:51.97	9:01.36 -97, 8:59.60i -96
					5000	15:24.31	15:24.03 -97
Durant	Joanne	BAR	25.5.75	170/71	200	23.02w	23.93 -97, 23.6 -98
Dursun	Öznur	TUR	24.10.71		800	2:01.44	2:01.42 -97
Dwinger	Rhona	RSA	28.6.71		JT	55.78A	58.32# -96
Dyomina	Tatyana	BLR	29.9.73		HT	60.99	61.40 -99
Eagles	Bronwyn	AUS	23.8.80	176/80	HT	66.55	62.02 -99
Earl	Chantee	USA	17.7.78	152/45	800	2:02.19i, 2:02.54	2:04.20 -99
Edato	Gadissie	ETH	15.3.73	156/43	Mar	2:32:11	2:29:57 -99
Edwards	Debbie	AUS	25.9.78	170/61	100H	13.20, 13.14w	13.31, 13.19w -98
Edwards	Jackie	BAH	14.4.71	172/64	LJ	6.65A, 6.61	8.80 -96, 6.89Aw -95
Edwards	Torri	USA	31.1.77	163/52	100	11.06, 10.92w	11.10, 11.05w -99
					200	22.65	22.88 -98, 22.84w -99
Efimenko	Tatyana	KGZ	2.1.81	187/70	HJ	1.90	1.95 -99
Ekimat	Jane	KEN	12.6.74		HMar	70:18	72:38 -95
Ekk	Oksana	RUS	26.11.74	175/63	100	11.27	11.21 -98, 11.2 -94
					200	22.69	22.77 -98
Ekpo-Umoh	Florence	GER	27.12.77	178/64	400	51.67	51.32 -98
El Kamch	Zhor	MAR	15.3.73	167/52	1500	4:10.03	4:08.09 -99
					3000	8:41.96	8:42.32 -99
					5000	15:12.23	15:15.57 -98
Elisdóttir	Thórey	ISL	30.6.77	181/64	PV	4.30	4.37i, 4.22 -99
* Ellerbe	Dawn	USA	3.4.74	186/111	SP	16.60i	16.83i -98, 16.70 -97
					DT	59.56	59.04 -98
					HT	70.46	70.16 -99
English	Una	IRL	14.8.70	181/61	5000	15:26.69	15:28.57 -97
Engman	Helena	SWE	16.6.76		SP	16.75	16.46 -99
* Ennis-London	Delloreen	JAM	5.3.75	180/67	100H	12.52	12.71, 12.60w -99
* Ertl	Karin	GER	23.6.74	177/65	Hep	6396	6366 -98
Espegren	Lene	NOR	8.5.71	170/53	TJ	13.73	13.83, 13.97w -99
^ Eve	Laverne	BAH	16.6.65	179/77	JT	63.73	62.94 -99, 64.78# -89
Ewerlöf-Krepp	Malin	SWE	2.6.72	180/61	800	2:01.30	1:59.44 -98
					1500	4:10.08	4:05.49 -97
Ezeh	Florence	FRA	29.12.77	173/96	HT	64.74	66.12 -99
Fairchild	Melody	USA	10.9.73	157/43	HMar	71:38dh	76:57 -99
Falaiye	Alice	CAN	24.12.78		LJ	6.63A, 6.46	6.54A -99
Farfaletti	Arianna	ITA	22.6.76	158/51	PV	4.28	4.05 -99
* Faumuiná	Beatrice	NZL	23.10.74	180/125	DT	65.41A	68.52 -97
Faustin	Nadine	HAI	14.4.76	160/56	100H	12.80	13.04A, 13.14, 13.02w -99
* Favor Hamilton	Suzy	USA	8.8.68	160/44	800	1:58.10	1:58.66 -98
					1500	3:57.40	3:58.43 -98
					3000	8:46.16	9:12.33 -97, 9:02.30i -90
					5000	15:06.48	0
Fearnley	Clair	AUS	7.3.75	161/65	5000	15:14.26	15:36.06 -99
					10000	31:55.65	32:18.22 -99
Febbraio	Surita	RSA	27.12.73		400H	55.22A, 55.77	56.50A, 57.44 -99
Fechita-Buzau	Cristina	ROM	12.4.76	176/78	HT	62.60	62.60 -98
* Fedoskina	Natalya	RUS	25.6.80	167/52	20kW	1:28:52	1:27:35 -99
Fedotova	Yekaterina	RUS	4.11.75		800	2:01.68	2:02.70 -94
^ Fedyushina	Valentina	AUT	18.2.65	190/90	SP	18.79	21.08 -86
* Feitor	Susana	POR	28.1.75	160/52	20kW	1:28:19	1:30:13 -99
Felicien	Perdita	CAN	29.8.80	165/57	100H	12.91	13.69, 13.47w -98
Felix	Aurélie	FRA	26.3.79	180/60	LJ	6.70, 6.72w	6.85 -99
Feng	Yun	CHN	23.2.76	170/60	100H	13.12, 12.88w	12.85 -99
* Feofanova	Svetlana	RUS	16.7.80	162/52	PV	4.50	4.10 -99
* Ferga	Linda	FRA	24.12.76	169/51	100H	12.81, 12.77w	12.95 -98, 12.84w -99
* Ferguson	Debbie	BAH	16.1.76	170/57	100	10.96	10,97 -98, 10.91w -99
					200	22.37	22.19 -99
* Fernández	Adriana	MEX	4.4.71	163/59	3000	8:53.53	9:12.23 -93
					5000	15:16.45	15:14.33 -99
					10000	31:10.12	31:53.36 -96
					Mar	2:25:42	2:24:06 -99
Fernández	Anaelys	CUB	15.12.79	185/87	DT	57.67	58.48, 62.75db -99
Fernández	Nuria	ESP	16.8.76	168/58	800	2:01.38	2:01.76 -99
					1500	4:06.37	4:07.46 -99
Fernández	Paula	ESP	8.6.78	165/54	PV	4.15	4.10 -99
Ferrales	Yania	CUB	28.7.77	183/86	DT	57.40	56.94 -99
Ferrara	Ornella	ITA	17.4.68	153/40	HMar	71:46	71:30 -95
					Mar	2:28:59	2:28:01 -97

Name		Nat	Born	Ht/Wt	Event	2000 Mark	Pre-2000 Best
Ferrari	Sara	ITA	30.9.77	157/41	10000	32:25.44	33:16.50 -97
					Mar	2:31:48	2:25:22 -99
* Fiacconi	Franca	ITA	4.10.65	173/56	Mar	2:26:03	2:25:14 -98
^ Fidatov	Elena	ROM	24.7.60	168/52	5000	15:20.59	15:12.58 -95
Filimonova	Lyudmila	BLR	22.3.71	184/76	DT	61.56	64.44 -98
Filip	Carmen	ROM	2.5.76	174/64	JT	59.31	57.58 -99, 59.81# -98
Fischer	Sabine	SUI	29.6.73	175/58	1500	4:05.14	4:11.75 -99
Fitchen	Kim	USA	3.9.68		10000	32:16.95	33:17.88 -99
Fiut	Dorota	POL	10.12.76	170/54	800	2:02.12	2:00.99 -97
* Flosadóttir	Vala	ISL	16.2.78	181/70	PV	4.50	4.45i -99, 4.36 -98
Földing-Nagy	Judit	HUN	9.12.65	170/55	Mar	2:30:54	2:28:50 -96
Folz	Jennifer	USA	24.12.75		SP	17.52	15.78 -99
					HT	64.22	61.24 -99
Fomenko	Viktoriya	UKR	2.10.71	170/60	100	11.1	11.37 -93, 11.1 -99
					200	22.96, 22.9	22.59 -96, 22.1 -97
^ Forkel	Karen	GER	24.3.70	173/65	JT	62.35	65.17 -99, 70.20# -91
* Formanová	Ludmila	CZE	2.1.74	168/60	800	1:57.53	1:56.56 -99
Forrester	Nicole	CAN	17.11.76	191/73	HJ	1.92i, 1.89	1.93i -99, 1.91 -98
* Foster	Bridgette	JAM	7.11.74	170/61	100H	12.70	13.19, 13.13w, 12.9w -98
Fouché	Maralize	RSA	2.3.74	177/67	Hep	6019	5963 -99
Fouquet	Virginie	FRA	9.9.75	162/48	800	2:02.40	2:00.20mx -97, 2:01.08 -98
Fournier	Caroline	MRI	7.5.75	165/90	HT	61.82	62.06 -96
Fournier	Michelle	CAN	9.5.77	176/86	HT	64.46, 65.63dh	62.91 -99
* Fraser	Donna	GBR	7.11.72	181/70	200	23.08	23.13 -99, 22.96i, 22.90w -97
					400	49.79	50.85 -98
* Frazer	Merlene	JAM	27.12.73	174/62	200	23.05	22.18 -99
* Freeman	Cathy	AUS	16.2.73	164/52	100	11.36	11.24, 11.15w -94
					200	22.53	22.25 -94
					400	49.11	48.63 -96
Freeman	Danielle	GBR	11.2.80		Hep	5644	5258w -99, 5237 -98
* Freeman	Michelle	JAM	5.5.69	170/61	100H	12.57	12.52, 12.40w -97
Freeman	Monique	USA	1.7.77	173/59	LJ	6.52i, 6.49w	6.45i, 6.37 -99, 6.59w -98
Friedrich	Dörthe	GER	21.6.73	174/68	JT	59.87	60.30 -99, 65.25# -98
Friedrich	Kathleen	GER	13.7.77	174/57	1500	4:05.94	4:11.61 -99
Frunza	Alina	ROM	17.4.79	182/100	SP	16.80i, 16.69	17.31 -99
* Fuchsová	Helena	CZE	3.6.65	170/68	400	50.71	50.21 -98
					800	1:58.56	1:58.81 -99
Fujikawa	Aki	JPN	14.11.78	159/42	Mar	2:31:25	2:27:42 -99
Fujinaga	Yoshiko	JPN	15.8.81	168/50	5000	15:23.70	15:22.68 -99
					10000	31:58.93	0
Fumoto (Shimizu)	Midori	JPN	18.12.71	160/43	Mar	2:27:55	0
* Fynes	Sevatheda	BAH	17.10.74	165/58	100	11.03	10.91 -99, 10.7w -95
					200	22.87	22.32 -99
* Gaines	Chryste	USA	14.9.70	170/59	100	10.97	10.89, 10.8A -98
					200	23.04, 22.83w	22.81 -93, 22.53w -97
* Gainsford-Taylor	Melinda	AUS	1.10.71	173/66	100	11.24, 11.02Aw	
							11.12A -94, 11.15 -95, 11.03w -98
					200	22.42, 22.18w	22.23 -97
					400	51.73	52.29 -96
Galeotti	Daniela	ITA	22.3.77	183/68	HJ	1.92i, 1.91	1.92 -99
* Galkina	Lyudmila	RUS	20.1.72	172/58	LJ	6.89	7.05 -97, 7.08w -99
Gallagher	Shannon	USA	10.3.75		PV	4.11	4.00 -99
Gallimore	Shelly-Ann	JAM	10.3.81	174/61	TJ	13.75	13.41 -99
Gamble	Nicole	USA	21.6.77	163/55	TJ	13.96	14.05i, 14.08w -99, 13.48 -97
Ganapathy	G. Pramila	IND	8.5.77	167/57	LJ	6.54	6.43 -99
					Hep	6105	5705 -98
* Gao	Hongmiao	CHN	17.3.74	162/51	20kW	1:33:01	1:30:03 –99
Gao	Kelian	CHN	15.8.83		20kW	1:33:38	
Gao	Shuying	CHN	28.10.79	180/63	PV	4.35	4.10 -99
* García	Alejandra	ARG	13.6.73	172/58	PV	4.42	4.41 -99
García	Magalys	CUB	23.10.71	178/71	Hep	6054	6352 -96
Gavrila	Adelina	ROM	26.11.78	175/56	TJ	14.44	14.71 -99
Gay	Mabel	CUB	5.5.83	178/67	TJ	14.02	13.82 -99
Gayle	Peta-Gaye	JAM	19.1.79		400H	55.93	57.50 -97
Geji	Noriko	JPN	31.5.73	169/52	HMar	71:25, 70:48 (in Mar)	70:37 -97
					Mar	2:27:41	0
* George	Emma	AUS	1.11.74	172/64	PV	4.50	4.60 -99
George	Samantha	CAN	7.8.76	165/57	400	52.03	51.98 -99
^ Georgieva	Daniela	BUL	22.9.69	165/52	400	51.27	50.25 -95
Georgieva	Khristina	BUL	3.1.72	176/74	JT	63.32	59.48 -99

Name		Nat	Born	Ht/Wt	Event	2000 Mark	Pre-2000 Best
Gérance	Fanny	FRA	4.1.81	171/61	100H	13.21	13.27 -99
* Gerryts	Elmarie	RSA	25.8.72	170/62	PV	4.42	4.36 -99
Gertenbach	Marizca	RSA	20.10.82	177/65	HJ	1.88	1.81 -98
Gervais	Isabelle	CAN	27.7.77		400H	57.11A	58.30A -98
* Gesell	Claudia	GER	18.12.77	170/58	800	1:58.34	1:59.87 -99
Gevaert	Kim	BEL	5.8.78	170/60	100	11.34	11.17 -99
					200	23.09	23.03 -99
Ghosh	Shanta	GER	3.1.75	168/58	200	22.80	22.80 -97
					400	51.74	53.60i -99
Gibson	Natasha (ex TRI)	USA	12.7.69	170/54	TJ	13.83, 13.86w	13.78 -98
Gillies-Scott	Colleen	JAM	18.8.74	183/63	TJ	13.68	13.83 -98
Gilmore	Nicole	CAN	24.8.73	179/68	LJ	6.61A	6.66 -96
* Giordano	Rossella	ITA	1.12.72	172/50	20kW	1:29:47, 1:30:48,3t	1:29:12 -97
* Girard	Patricia	FRA	8.4.68	162/48	100H	12.88	12.59 -96
Glass	Byrony	AUS	31.3.77		HT	62.00	63.15 -99
Glenn	Brianna	USA	18.4.80		100	11.33, 11.24w	11.66, 11.54w -99
					200	22.97Aw	23.88 -99
					LJ	6.65A, 6.47	6.05, 6.09w -99
Gliznutsa	Inna	MDA	18.4.73	184/65	HJ	1.93	1.95 -99
* Glover	Sandra	USA	30.12.68	173/59	400H	53.33	53.65 -99
Gnezdilov	Svetlana	ISR	20.7.69	170/58	100H	13.09	13.31 -99
Godinho	Marta	POR	24.6.80		LJ	6.57w	5.98 -97
Gogîrlea	Luminita	ROM	5.11.71	160/46	3kSt	9:56.99	10:00.50 -98
Golding	Lacena	JAM	20.3.75	168/57	100H	12.93	13.00 -98
					LJ	6.67	6.87 -98
Gomes	Enezenaide	STP	10.11.79	175/62	Hep	5671	4974 -99
* Goncharenko	Olga	BLR	13.7.81		DT	57.06	53.70 -99
Goncharenko	Svetlana	RUS	28.5.71	176/61	400	50.23	50.75 -99
Goncharova	Lyudmila	BLR	17.10.76	168/55	800	2:00.32	2:00.01 -97
Gong	Jian	CHN	.80		SP	17.23	17.09 -99
González	Griselda	ESP	4.12.65	165/48	10000	31:46.4	33:17.9 -93
					HMar	71:40	73:11 -95
					Mar	2:31:12	2:30:32 -97
González	Misleydis	CUB	19.6.78		SP	17.55	16.19 -99
Goormachtigh	Jacqueline	NED	28.2.70	179/85	DT	61.05	63.86 -98
^ Goossens	Ester	NED	21.2.72	175/65	400H	57.23	54.62 -98
Gordeyeva	Tatyana	RUS	3.6.73	180/63	HJ	1.91	1.91 -97
					Hep	6336	6335 -97
* Gorelova	Natalya	RUS	18.4.73	173/56	800	2:00.24	1:57.90 -99
					1500	4:01.50	4:05.12 -99
Gorodnicheva	Yelena	UKR	5.9.70	168/54	1500	4:10.96	4:05.78 -99
Goto	Yukako	JPN	16.9.73	152/42	HMar	71:06	72:40 -96
^ Gotovska	Valentina	LAT	3.9.65	176/59	LJ	6.91	6.73 -99
^ Götz	Monika	GER	15.6.81	178/61	PV	4.27	4.31 -98
Goudenoúdi	Hrísa	GRE	28.3.77	175/54	400H	56.90	57.41 -99
Goulbourne	Elva	JAM	21.1.80	170/50	100	11.30	11.62 -98
					LJ	6.74, 6.79w	6.49 -99
* Govorova	Yelena	UKR	18.9.73	178/61	TJ	14.96	14.64 -97, 14.99w -99
da Graça	Jupira M	BRA	20.2.70	178/66	400H	57.29	57.61, 57.4 -93
* Graf	Stephanie	AUT	26.4.73	170/60	800	1:56.64	1:57.07 -99
^ Graham	Kim	USA	26.3.71	163/58	400	51.42	50.53 -96
* Graham	Lorraine	JAM	8.9.73	174/59	400	49.58	49.92 -99
Graham	Nolle	JAM	12.9.81	167/59	LJ	6.53	6.17 -99
^ Granados	Encarna	ESP	30.1.72	168/50	20kW	1:33:06	1:36:32 -98
Grant	Bisa	USA	10.7.76	166/60	100H	13.04, 12.95w	13.26 -97
Grant	Debbie	USA	5.8.65	169/55	1500	4:11.00	4:08.52 -99
* Grasu	Nicoleta	ROM	11.9.71	176/88	DT	68.70	68.80 -99
^ Graudyn	Yuliya	RUS	13.11.70	174/60	100H	12.87	12.62, 12.51Aw -94
Greer	Tiffany	USA	8.6.81	160/56	LJ	6.50Ai, 6.47	6.47 -99
Greithanner	Martina	GER	21.10.74	190/82	SP	16.84	16.63 -97
Griebel	Lisa	USA	8.3.79	173/	SP	16.46i	16.41 -99
Griffin	Maureen	USA	6.10.80	176/88	HT	63.66	61.44 -98
Griffith	Michelle	GBR	6.10.71	172/65	TJ	13.71, 14.14w	14.08 -94
* Grigorieva	Tatiana	AUS	8.10.75	180/68	PV	4.55	4.50, 4.55ex -99
Grigoryeva	Lidiya	RUS	21.1.74	163/48	5000	15:19.65	
					10000	31:21.27	32:49.64 -99
Grin	Marina	BLR	23.1.76	182/79	HT	65.11	63.78 -97
Grousselle	Elisabeth	FRA	6.2.73	163/49	800	2:02.31	2:02.62 -98
Groza	Ana Maria	ROM	1.6.76	167/53	20kW	1:29:59	1:32:28 -99
Gruca	Dorota	POL	5.12.70	159/46	10000	32:31.5	33:12.92 –98

	Name		Nat	Born	Ht/Wt	Event	2000 Mark	Pre-2000 Best
	Gu	Yan	CHN	17.3.74		20kW	1:34:26	
	Gu	Yuan	CHN	9.5.82		HT	64.72	63.38 -99
*	Guan	Yingnan	CHN	25.4.77	176/60	LJ	6.95	6.91 -98
*	Gubkina	Lyudmila	BLR	28.5.72	174/76	HT	69.92	68.27 -99
*	Gudkova	Tatyana	RUS	23.1.78	170/62	20kW	1:25:18	1:33:05 -99
*	Guevara	Ana	MEX	4.3.77	170/60	400	49.70A, 49.96	50.65 -98
*	Guida	Maria	ITA	23.1.66	160/49	HMar	69:00	68:30 -96
						Mar	2:26:12	2:25:57 -99
^	Guidry	Carlette	USA	4.9.68	168/50	100	11.03	10.94, 10.91w -91
						200	23.03, 22.90i	22.14 -96
	Guillén	Nancy	ESA	14.10.76	168/70	HT	62.16	61.35 -99
	Gulevich	Tatyana	BLR	10.2.71	187/66	HJ	1.88i, 1.87	1.92 -95
*	Gulyayeva	Yelena	RUS	14.8.67	182/64	HJ	1.95	2.01 -98
^	Gummelt	Beate	GER	4.2.68	169/53	20kW	1:31:45	1:33:10 -99
	Güner (Ivanova)	Nora	TUR	1.6.77	174/59	100	11.35	11.23 -98
						200	23.13, 22.9, 23.12i	22.72 -96
	Guo	Chunfang	CHN	4.1.79	174/65	LJ	6.82	6.53 -98
	Gureyeva	Zhanna	BLR	10.6.70	178/54	TJ	13.83i	14.35 -97, 147.41w -95
	Gurtovenko	Yuliya	UKR	8.12.80	170/52	800	2:02.18	2:03.81 -99
	Guskova	Oksana	UKR	16.6.74	169/58	100	11.30	11.34, 11.1 -99
	Gustaityté	Renata	LTU	7.4.74	180/87	DT	65.18?, 59.98	60.38 -98
	Gutjahr	Kathleen	GER	27.7.75	175/65	Hep	6341	6320 -98
	Györffy	Dora	HUN	23.2.78	175/55	HJ	1.97i, 1.95	1.94 -99
	Gyurcsek	Déborah	URU	7.12.78	163/59	PV	4.23A	4.15 -99
	Ha	Xiaoyan	CHN	30.1.72	176/73	JT	58.33	59.73 -99, 65.44# -93
	Hackett	Rhonda	TRI	24.1.77	180/90	SP	16.82	16.64 -99
	Hajdu	Markéta	CZE	9.9.74	178/90	HT	61.80	58.05 -99
	Halkoaho	Johanna	FIN	13.1.77	165/55	LJ	6.59, 6.73w	6.79 -98
	Ham	Bong-sil	PRK	24.7.74	155/44	Mar	2:27:07	2:30:28 -95
*	Hamácková	Pavla	CZE	20.5.78	170/66	PV	4.45	4.40 -99
	Hamann	Birgit	GER	11.9.69	175/58	100H	13.12w	12.96 -96
	Hamilton	Melina	NZL	15.6.76		PV	4.15	4.02 –99
	Han	Min	CHN	8.7.83		20kW	1:33:27	
	Hanaoka	Maho	JPN	3.8.76	170/56	LJ	6.61	6.36 -99
						TJ	13.80	14.04 -99
	Hannula	Heidi	FIN	26.2.80	165/53	100	11.31w	11.61, 11.58w -99
*	Hansen	Ashia	GBR	5.12.71	173/64	TJ	14.29	15.16i -98, 15.15 -97
	Harrelson	Mary Jayne	USA	17.6.78		800	2:02.35	2:03.85 -99
						1500	4:08.76	4:17.56 -99
	Harris	Flirtisha	USA	21.12.72	154/51	200	23.00	22.73 -98, 22.56w -93
	Harrison	Ardin	CAN	14.3.74	170/61	PV	4.10b, 4.00A	3.84 -99
	Harrison	Nicole	USA	14.1.76	163/57	100H	12.92	13.08 -97
	Harrison	Yvonne	USA	2.12.75	178/64	400H	55.09	55.87 -98
	Hart	Bethany	USA	10.4.77		HT	63.09	60.12 -99
	Hartman	Wendy	RSA	28.2.76	163/60	100	11.32, 11.20Aw	11.18A, 11.30 -99
						200	23.09A	22.74A, 23.16i, 23.27 -99
	Harvey	Natalie	AUS	19.1.75	164/50	3000	8:53.58mx	8:57.57 -99
						10000	32:07.44	32:20.58 -98
	Harz	Alexa	USA	18.2.78	169/52	PV	4.18	3.90 -99
*	Hashim	Merima	ETH	.81	162/42	5000	15:14.42	15:39.57 -98
						10000	30:59.92	31:32.06 -99
	Hashimoto	Yasuko	JPN	12.8.75	162/49	10000	32:12.56	33:01.6 -98
^	Hattestad	Trine	NOR	18.4.66	173/76	JT	69.48	68.19 -99, 72.12# -93
	Haugen	Gunhild	NOR	1.6.72	165/48	5000	15:15.35	15:09.00 -96
						10000	31:47.89	32:47.56 -99
	Haughton	Karlene	CAN	18.10.72	165/57	400H	56.11A, 56.17	55.11 -97
^	Haugland	Hanne	NOR	14.12.67	183/63	HJ	1.95	2.01 -97
*	Hautala	Tiia	FIN	3.4.72	171/65	Hep	6219	6369 -99
	Hayes	Joanna	USA	23.12.76	165/58	100H	12.67	12.89, 12.88w, 12.7w -99
						400H	54.97	54.57 -99
	Haynes	Nicole	CAN/USA	18.9.74	180/75	Hep	6077	6000 -99
	Haynes	Tara	USA	6.8.78	168/55	3kSt	10:04.45	10:32.04 -98
	Hejnová	Michaela	CZE	10.4.80	167/62	Hep	6015	5857 -99
	Hellebaut	Tia	BEL	16.2.78	182/66	HJ	1.89	1.87i, 1.82 -99
						Hep	5646	5629 -99
*	Hemmings	Deon	JAM	9.10.68	176/62	200	22.96w	22.64 -98
						400	51.80	50.63 -95
						400H	53.45	52.62 -96
	Henderson	Monique	USA	18.2.83	170/54	200	23.19, 23.16w	23.30 -99
						400	50.74	51.96 -99

Name		Nat	Born	Ht/Wt	Event	2000 Mark	Pre-2000 Best
^ Henkel	Heike	GER	5.5.64	181/62	HJ	1.91i, 1.90	2.07i -92, 2.05 -91
* Hennagan	Monique	USA	26.5.76	173/55	400	50.82	51.05 -99
Henry	Joanne	NZL	2.10.71	170/63	Hep	5655	6278 -92
Hering	Kathleen	GER	24.6.76	178/76	DT	60.39	61.85 -99
Herschmann	Nicole	GER	27.10.75	179/68	TJ	13.91	13.41 -99
Herzenberg	Elena	GER	24.6.79		HJ	1.88	1.88 -99
* Hewitt	Lauren	AUS	25.11.78	170/60	100	11.29, 11.18w	11.28 -99, 11.22w -98
					200	22.52	22.53 -99
Hickman	Libbie	USA	17.2.65	168/52	3000	8:35.02	8:43.32 -96
					5000	15:21.55	15:11.15 -97
					10000	31:56.94	31:41.33 -99
					HMar	71:01	71:40 -97
					Mar	2:32:09	2:28:34 -99
Hicks	Cheree	USA	17.2.78		SP	17.22	17.13 -99
					DT	57.00	60.86 -99
Hietalahti	Anita	FIN	17.2.77	177/69	DT	56.25	54.87 -99
Higgins-Francis	Tamika	USA	19.4.71	175/65	100H	13.20, 12.9, 13.16w	13.48 -99
Hila	Elena	ROM	20.5.74	180/98	SP	17.62	18.23 -99
Hill	Aretha	USA	14.8.76	181/98	DT	62.91	65.62 -98
Hill	Irie	GBR	16.1.69	176/60	PV	4.20	4.05 -99
Hill	Janet	USA	28.6.70	170/75	DT	59.72	59.48 -96
Hinds-Smith	Le'Gretta	USA	13.1.74	161/55	400H	57.30	57.36 -98
* Hiroyama	Harumi	JPN	2.9.68	160/47	5000	15:20.36	15:03.67 -98
					10000	31:59.60	31:22.72 -97
					HMar	70:49, 70.46 (in Mar)	70:58 -96
					Mar	2:22:56	2:28:12 -98
Hirpassa	Birhane	ETH			1500	4:10.73	
* Hlavonová	Zuzana	CZE	16.4.73	179/58	HJ	2.00	1.99 -99
Höcke	Anja	GER	16.10.74	169/52	400H	56.74	56.57 -96
* Hodgkinson	Toni	NZL	12.12.71	180/62	800	1:59.31	1:58.25 -96
					1500	4:06.23	4:10.07 -98
Hoernig	Erica	USA	19.10.78	178/61	PV	4.14	3.86 -99
Hollman	Julie	GBR	16.2.77	180/69	LJ	6.51	6.23 -99, 6.29w -97
					Hep	5685	5816w -98, 5595 -97
* Holmes	Kelly	GBR	19.4.70	164/55	800	1:56.80	1:56.21 -95
					1500	4:05.35	3:58.07 -97
Holtzhausen	Susanna	RSA	7.10.76	172/53	400	51.64A, 52.15	53.04A -99
Homo	Amandine	FRA	24.12.80	170/58	PV	4.31i, 4.15	4.31 -99
Honey	Jacqueline	CAN	25.6.75		PV	4.10b, 4.00A	3.75 -98
Hong	Mei	CHN	16.1.82		SP	16.53	16.53 -99
Hong	Myong-hui	PRK	29.7.78		Mar	2:31:28	
Honoré	Caroline	FRA	29.4.70	171/56	TJ	13.72w	13.78 -95
Horie	Chika	JPN	15.2.81	161/41	Mar	2:29:12	0
Hort	Stephanie	GER	13.2.75	180/58	LJ	6.53	6.48 -98
Horvath	Linda	AUT	10.2.78	190/70	HJ	1.93	1.93 -99
Howard	Donna	USA	28.8.74	163/56	200	23.14w	23.29 -98, 23.07w -96
Howe	Kym	AUS	12.6.80	176/63	PV	4.20	4.16 -99
Howell	Charmaine	JAM	13.3.75	170/60	800	2:00.63	2:02.35 -99
Hoxie	Nicole	USA	22.7.79		100H	12.97, 12.83w	13.27 -99
Hrdlicková	Miriam	SVK	4.1.76		400H	57.26	58.25 -99
Hu	Honglian	CHN	20.2.73		DT	58.73	62.22 -97
Hu	Yaoyao	CHN	16.4.83		TJ	13.68	
					Hep	5746	5144 -98
Huang	Qiuyan	CHN	25.1.80		TJ	13.78i, 13.76	14.57 -97
Huang	Qun	CHN	12.4.79		DT	59.51	57.30 -99
Hubbard	Meosha	USA			LJ	6.87A, 6.59, 6.84w	6.22 -97,6.48w -98
^ Hudson	Sheila	USA	30.6.67	165/50	TJ	13.95, 14.00w	14.41 -96, 14.66w -95
Huhtaniemi	Paula	FIN	17.2.73	167/65	JT	61.01	58.44 -99
* Humbert	Nicole	GER	5.2.72	168/53	PV	4.50	4.56i, 4.41 -99
Hunt	Yuan	USA	18.12.74		LJ	6.57, 6.63w	6.76 -98
Hurd	Tiombé	USA	17.8.73	178/64	TJ	14.06i, 13.97	14.00 -99
* Hurtis	Muriel	FRA	25.3.79	180/68	100	11.36, 11.28w	11.33, 11.3 -99
					200	22.70	22.31 -99
Hutchinson	Ayanna	TRI	18.2.78		100	11.26	11.51 -98
Hyacinth	Flora	UVI	10.3.66	170/61	LJ	6.52	6.72A -98, 6.71 -92
Hyman	Mardrea	JAM	22.12.72	168/52	800	2:00.67	1:59.71 -98
					1500	4:09.83	4:17.00 -97
Iakovídou	Thália	GRE	10.9.72	172/55	PV	4.22	4.15 -99
Iakóvou	Hrisostomía	GRE	9.4.71	170/52	5000	15:25.16	15:37.14 -97
Iancu	Constanta	ROM	12.9.76	179/82	JT	56.69	54.69 -99

Name		Nat	Born	Ht/Wt	Event	2000 Mark	Pre-2000 Best
Ibañez	Mara	MEX	17.12.74	173/60	20kW	1:32:54	1:48:58 -99
^ Ichihashi	Ari	JPN	22.11.77	157/42	HMar	71:22	69:23 -97
					Mar	2:30:34	2:27:02 -99
Ichikawa	Mayumi	JPN	3.5.76	154/41	Mar	2:32:30	2:27:57 -99
Ichikawa	Yoshiko	JPN	18.4.76	162/46	5000	15:23.41	15:20.53 -97
					HMar	69:04	68:18 -97
Igarashi	Hiromi	JPN	26.10.70	157/48	Mar	2:29:39	2:36:22 -98
Ignatova	Natalya	RUS	28.12.73	168/59	100	11.12, 11.08w	11.20 -99, 11.0 -98
Iloc-Casandra	Cristina	ROM	21.10.77	168/50	3kSt	9:40.20	0
Ilyina	Anastasia	RUS	16.1.82	172/57	LJ	6.51	6.36 -99
					TJ	14.52	13.59 -99
Ilyina	Irina	RUS	.76		Hep	5689	5893 -98
Imai	Miki	JPN	30.5.75	173/51	HJ	1.93	1.94 -98
^ Ináncsi	Rita	HUN	6.1.71	190/73	Hep	6177	6573 -94
* Ingberg	Mikaela	FIN	29.7.74	174/75	JT	64.03	61.50 -99, 67.32# -97
Ingram	Dahlia	USA	17.7.78	162/49	LJ	6.56w	6.44, 6.68w -99
^ Inverarity	Alison	AUS	12.8.70	181/61	HJ	1.88	1.98 -94
Ionescu	Lacramioara	ROM	3.4.79	180/85	DT	60.40	58.24 -99
Ionescu	Simona	ROM	24.8.73	170/60	800	2:02.08	2:03.08 -98
^ Iovan ¶	Claudia	ROM	25.2.78	167/53	20kW	1:29:39	1:29:39 -99
Irusta	Geovanna	BOL	26.9.75	157/48	20kW	1:34:37	1:35:56 -99
^ Isaila	Claudia	ROM	17.7.73	167/64	JT	57.16	53.28 -99, 66.56# -94
Isar	Elena	ROM	7.12.71	165/54	20kW	1:32:19	1:42:12 -99
* Isinbayeva	Yelena	RUS	3.6.82	172/56	PV	4.45i, 4.40	4.20 -99
Isobe	Tomoko	JPN	3.9.74	161/43	HMar	71:44	73:39 -99
Isworth	Bridgid	AUS	15.10.81	168/62	PV	4.25	4.15 -98
Itanyi	Patience	NGR	2.7.73	170/57	LJ	6.54	6.73 -95
					Hep	5730	5697 -99
^ Ivakina	Yekaterina	RUS	7.12.64	168/67	JT	64.89	62.94 -99, 65.36# -93
^ Ivan	Paula	ROM	20.7.63	170/57	1500	4:04.66	3:53.96 -88
Ivanenko	Yelena	BLR	5.5.78	180/90	SP	16.92	19.13 -99
Ivankova	Olga	UKR	7.1.73	173/62	JT	57.75	57.40 -99, 60.94# -96
^ Ivanova	Alina	RUS	16.3.69	163/52	Mar	2:27:42	2:31:44 -98
Ivanova	Anastasiya	RUS	.79		PV	4.10	3.90 -99
* Ivanova	Olimpiada	RUS	5.5.70	168/54	20kW	1:26.08	1:28:31 -99
Ivanova	Valentina	RUS	1.5.63	178/90	DT	63.68	63.25 -99
Ivanova	Yelena	RUS	16.3.79		TJ	13.75	13.48 -99
Jackson	Carolyn	USA	6.12.77	168/60	400	52.12	52.10 -99
Jackson	Elizabeth	USA	27.10.77	170/59	3kSt	9:57.20	10:07.23ir -99
Jackson	Lorna	GBR	9.1.74	180/80	JT	57.19	56.00 -99, 58.39# -98
* Jacobs	Regina	USA	28.8.63	168/51	800	1:58.08	1:58.55 -99
					1500	4:01.01	4:00.35 -99
					1M	4:21.79i	4:20.93 -98
					3000	8:42.55	9:39.56 -98, 8:39.14i -99
					5000	14:45.35	14:52.49 -98
Jacques-Gustave	Nathalie	FRA	12.5.76	183/72	TJ	13.69i	13.75 -99
Jaklofsky	Sharon	NED	30.9.68	170/60	LJ	6.55, 6.57w	6.75 -96
* Jakubczak	Anna	POL	2.2.73	166/53	1500	4:06.49	4:01.43 -99
Jamieson	Jane	AUS	23.6.75	170/59	Hep	6227	6354 -98
Jamieson	Sarah	AUS	24.3.75	172/57	1500	4:06.09	4:12.89 -99
Janku	Inga	CZE	1.5.74		HJ	1.88i	1.91 -98
Jarrett	Tanya	JAM	18.9.77	169/54	400H	55.55	55.78 -99
Javornik	Helena	SLO	26.3.66	163/50	1500	4:06.77	4:07.34 -99
					3000	8:50.71	8:58.14 -97, 8:53.40i -99
					5000	15:27.68	15:15.40 -99
* Jayasinghe	Susanthika	SRI	17.12.75	170/62	100	11.04	11.17 -99
					200	22.28	22.33 -97
Jekabsone	Lana	LAT	16.10.74	175/60	400H	57.36	55.46 -96
* Jenkins	LaTasha	USA	19.12.77	170/55	100	11.14	11.08 -99
					200	22.86, 22.54w	22.29, 22.22w -99
Jennings-Steele	Jo	GBR	20.9.69	174/60	HJ	1.89	1.94i -93, 1.91 -98
Jensen	Heidi	DEN	14.8.66	173/65	800	2:02.20	2:01.12 -99
					1500	4:08.32	4:12.73 -99
Jerotich	Jackline	KEN	23.9.70		HMar	70:39	71:51 -98
					Mar	2:28:32	2:34:28 -99
Jett	Kisha	USA	11.2.75	168/58	100	11.20,11.18w	11.29A,11.31 -95, 11.22w -99
					200	23.18, 23.15w	22.84 -96
* Jevtic	Olivera	YUG	24.7.77	176/52	5000	15:11.25	15:16.61 -98
					10000	31:29.65	31:34.26 -98
Jia	Lina	CHN	26.4.80		SP	17.87	16.45 -99

Name		Nat	Born	Ht/Wt	Event	2000 Mark	Pre-2000 Best
Jia	Wanghong	CHN	24.9.81		400H	57.05	56.66 -99
Jiang	Ping	CHN	10.1.79		SP	18.35	16.81 –98
Jiang	Qiuyan	CHN	4.8.76		20kW	1:33:28	
Johansson	Camilla	SWE	3.11.76	166/52	TJ	14.14	13.86 -99
* Johansson	Erica	SWE	5.2.74	178/69	LJ	6.99, 7.07Aw	6.92, 6.95w -99
John	Lwiza Msyani	TAN	18.5.80	156/48	800	1:59.58	2:00.10 -99
Johnson	Jade	GBR	7.6.80	187/72	LJ	6.58	6.52 -99
^ Johnson	Michelle	USA	12.4.74	170/61	100H	13.08w	12.88 -98
					400H	55.31	54.15 -99
Johnson	Nakiya	USA	12.5.81	173/59	400	52.19	52.09 -98
Johnson	Sheena	USA	1.10.82	163/53	400H	56.82	58.61 -98
Jones	Ifoma	USA	4.9.77	168/60	Hep	5726w	5649w -99 5173 -98
* Jones	Marion	USA	12.10.75	178/64	100	10.75, 10.68w	10.65A -98, 10.90 -99
					200	21.84	21.62A -98, 21.76 -97
					400	49.59	50.36 -98
					LJ	7.02	7.31 -98
Jones	Shakedia	USA	15.3.79	163/53	100	11.25	11.11 -98
					200	22.57w	22.84, 22.65w -99
Jones	Susan	GBR	8.6.78	179/62	HJ	1.93	1.92i -98, 1.91 -97
Jones	Teneeshia	USA	28.1.79	163/	100	11.24	11.43 -99
					200	23.14	23.65, 23.40w -99
Jong	Yong-ok	PRK	24.1.81	155/43	Mar	2:31:40	
^ Jongmans	Stella	NED	17.5.71	174/59	800	2:00.6i	1:58.61 -92
Joseph	Restituta	TAN	30.7.71	164/56	HMar	67:59w	70:13 -99
Joyce	Jennifer	CAN	25.9.80	178	HT	62.86	58.84 -99
^ Joyner-Kersee	Jackie	USA	3.3.62	178/70	LJ	6.67	7.49 -94
Juhász	Fanni	HUN	31.3.81	169/58	PV	4.10	4.11 -99
Jung	Claudia	GER	17.6.76	186/61	400H	56.83	57.24 -99
Juodeskiene	Inga	LTU	21.10.71	167/51	5000	15:10.71	15:50.17 -99
Jury	Kerry	GBR	19.11.68	178/67	Hep	5735	6005w -98, 5908 -99
Kabanova	Sofiya	UZB	29.5.70	182/67	Hep	5760	5501 -99
^ Kähler	Birgit	GER	14.8.70	182/60	HJ	1.92	1.94 -91
Kai	Tomoko	JPN	5.11.76	156/36	Mar	2:31:20	2:28:13 -98
Kakhova	Galina	BLR	26.3.82	167/62	JT	56.52	50.40 -99
* Kalcheva	Khristina	BUL	29.5.77	178/57	HJ	1.98	1.99 -98
Kalitka	Svetlana	UKR	28.3.70	173/60	20kW	1:34:20	1:34:24 -97
^ Kaliturina	Olga	RUS	9.3.76	180/57	HJ	1.96i, 1.94	1.96 -97
Kallur	Jenny	SWE	16.2.81	170/60	100H	13.18	13.70 -99
Kallur	Susanna	SWE	16.2.81	170/60	100H	13.02	13.41 -99
Kálovics	Anikó	HUN	13.5.77	174/60	10000	32:16.4	32:53.32 -98
Kanatova	Svetlana	RUS	10.9.70		1500	4:06.19	4:09.25 -98, 4:06.20i -99
Kanazawa	Yvonne	JPN	19.11.74	173/63	100H	13.00, 12.90Aw	13.08, 12.98w -96
Kang	Kum-sin	PRK	.79		Mar	2:31:49	
Kankaanpää	Tiina	FIN	16.8.76	180/80	DT	60.50	61.04 -99
Käppi	Salla	FIN	22.5.80	176/64	Hep	5699	4993 -97
Kappler	Bianca	GER	8.8.77	179/62	LJ	6.55	6.40 -99
^ Karczmarek	Agata	POL	29.11.63	172/60	LJ	6.59	6.97 -88
^ Kardopoltseva	Olga	BLR	11.9.66	170/56	20kW	1:31:13	1:28:51 -99
Kari	Monia	TUN	11.4.71	172/72	DT	58.46	61.74 06
Kashapova	Klara	RUS	29.1.70	158/47	5000	15:18.09	15:18.21 -96
					10000	31:58.76	31:55.99 -94
Kashcheyeva	Yelena	KAZ	17.2.73	175/58	LJ	6.68	6.76 -98
* Kaspárková	Sárka	CZE	20.5.71	186/69	TJ	14.34	15.20 -97
Kataoka	Junko	JPN	13.6.70	158/42	Mar	2:28:20	2:30:10 00
Kato	Sakiko	JPN	8.5.79		HMar	71:46	0
Kaur	Gurmeet	IND	20.6.70	174/75	JT	58.64	55.86 –99, 60.22#- 98
Kaur	Harwant	IND	5.7.80		DT	57.78	51.24 -99
^ Kavaklioglu	Ebru	TUR	14.3.70	167/58	3000	8:56.13i	8:38.98 -99
* Kawakami	Yuko	JPN	1.8.75	152/45	5000	15:23.59	15:17.34 -97
					10000	31:09.46	31:20.19 -96
Kawar	Nada	JOR	23.11.75	185/96	SP	17.83	17.79 -98
					DT	57.37	60.11 -98
Kayukova	Natalya	RUS	10.12.66	175/66	TJ	14.05	14.51 -99
Kazanina	Svetlana	KAZ	31.10.71	172/62	Hep	6161	6228 -99
Kaznovskaya	Zoya	UKR	22.9.66	172/62	1500	4:05.76	4:06.55 -99
					3000	8:58.38,8:54.46i	8:55.56 -94,8:50.78i -99
Kehler	Lisa	GBR	15.3.67	168/51	20kW	1:33:57	0
Keil	Susanne	GER	18.5.78	172/59	HT	64.04	64.50 -98
* Kelesídou	Anastasia	GRE	28.11.72	192/92	DT	67.12	67.70 -99
Kelo	Niina	FIN	26.3.80	179/67	Hep	5728	5359 -99

Name		Nat	Born	Ht/Wt	Event	2000 Mark	Pre-2000 Best
Kenah	Cheri	USA	26.12.70	176/57	5000	15:10.50	15:13.42 -99
					10000	32:24.06	32:55.43 -96
Kerubo	Margaret	KEN	15.5.74		HMar	71:22	
Kesselschläger	Sonja	GER	20.1.78	178/66	Hep	6039	5890 -99
Khabarova	Irina	RUS	18.3.66	170/62	100	11.32, 11.19w	11.38 -99
					200	22.76	22.96 -98, 22.92w -99
Kharaneko	Natalya	BLR	25.5.82	180/81	SP	16.58	16.12 -99
Khlusovich	Yelena	UKR	3.11.69	186/70	TJ	14.27	14.38 -96
^ Khmelnitskaya	Larisa	BLR	23.9.71	173/60	20kW	1:28:56	1:28:58 -99
Khropach	Yolanta	UKR	22.9.74	168/55	LJ	6.52	6.69 -97
					TJ	13.91	13.98 -99
Khrushchelyova	Natalya	RUS	20.3.73	172/55	400	51.49	51.73 -94, 51.5 -98
Khudoroshkina	Irina	RUS	13.10.68	182/98	SP	18.56	20.32 -96
* Kidane	Worknesh	ETH	21.11.81	158/42	3000	8:44.14	9:02.40 -98
					5000	14:47.70	15:24.56 -99
Kiintonen	Kaisa	FIN	18.3.80	167/67	HT	61.50	57.50 -99
Kilpeläinen	Natalia	FIN	19.7.70	168/57	TJ	14.09i	14.10 -94
^ Kimaiyo	Hellen	KEN	8.9.68	163/50	HMar	69:48	69:13 -95
					Mar	2:30:35	2:29:45 -97
Kimutai	Hellen	KEN	28.12.77		HMar	69:59	73:05 -99
					Mar	2:26:42	
Kinard	Vanitta	USA	26.7.75	178/58	TJ	13.82w	13.76 -97
Kinet	Anzhela	TUR	14.11.70	178/65	LJ	6.52i	6.72 -93
					Hep	6076	6339 -93
King	Andria	USA	22.6.76	178/65	100H	13.11, 13.04w	12.86, 12.73w -99
Kinuki	Hiroko	JPN	18.7.74	160/46	Mar	2:32:20	2:34:18 -97
^ Kiplagat	Esther	KEN	8.12.66	161/47	HMar	69:55	70:10 -97
					Mar	2:30:30	2:33:09 -99
* Kiplagat	Lornah	KEN	20.3.74		3000	8:52.82	
					HMar	66:56	69:11 -97
					Mar	2:22:36	2:25:29 -99
Kiptum	Jeruto	KEN	12.12.81		1500	4:08.6A	4:18.0 -99
^ Kirchmann	Sigrid	AUT	29.3.66	181/64	HJ	1.95	1.97 -93
* Kirkland	Anjanette	USA	24.2.74	172/66	100H	12.63	12.74 -97, 12.68w -99
^ Kisabaka	Linda	GER	9.4.69	166/52	800	1:59.97	1:58.24 -96
Kislova	Marina	RUS	12.12.78	166/57	100	11.26	11.54 -99
					200	22.99	23.50 -99
Kiss	Enikö	HUN	23.9.75	172/56	Hep	5811	5901 -99
Klavina	Liga	LAT	27.1.80	181/69	HJ	1.94	1.85 -99
* Kleinert-Schmitt	Nadine	GER	20.10.75	190/78	SP	19.81	19.61 -99
Klimesová	Jarmila	CZE	9.2.81	172/78	JT	56.04	53.90 -99, 54.03# -98
Klüft	Carolina	SWE	2.2.83	178/64	Hep	6056	5162 -99
Kluge	Kathleen	GER	17.11.81	170/92	SP	17.37	17.00 -99
^ Knoroz	Anna	RUS	30.7.70	162/50	400H	56.42	54.11 -94
Kobayashi	Naoko	JPN	16.7.68	167/57	100H	13.18w	13.17, 13.04w -96
Kobrin	Nadezhda	UKR	21.1.72	165/67	JT	59.79	55.34 -99. 62.04# -98
Koeman	Lieja	NED	10.3.76	183/95	SP	18.46i, 18.29	18.48 -99
Koens	Grete	NED	25.5.67	182/63	1500	4:09.21	4:13.86 -98
^ Koffa	Ekateríni	GRE	10.4.69	177/63	200	23.16	22.67 -96, 22.64w -97
Koide	Masako	JPN	3.1.74	160/49	Mar	2:30:50	2:36:51 -97
Koivula	Heli	FIN	27.6.75	174/60	TJ	13.68	14.34 -99
Koleva	Tanya	BUL	8.3.72	178/62	PV	4.42	4.25 -99
Komatsu	Yukari	JPN	13.2.74	163/44	Mar	2:29:32	2:28:48 -98
Komgang	Claudine	CMR	21.2.74	170/55	400	50.73A, 51.35	51.21A, 51.68 -99
Komyagina	Olga	RUS	10.2.74	162/48	1500	4:02.32	4:04.99 -98
					1M	4:32.02i	4:25.71 -99
					3000	8:58.19	8:42.58 -99
Kondo	Takayo	JPN	17.11.75	160/56	PV	4.10	4.10 -99
König	Tanja	GER	11.4.70	184/63	TJ	13.96	13.88 -93
* Konstantinova	Tatyana	RUS	18.1.70	178/95	HT	69.73	72.09 -99
Koritskaya	Diana	RUS	22.2.75	173/62	Hep	6401	6169 -97
* Korolchik	Yanina	BLR	26.12.76	187/87	SP	20.56	19.58 -99
* Korotkevich	Larisa	RUS	3.1.67	182/90	DT	64.37	71.30 -92
Korotkova	Tatyana	RUS	24.4.80	166/56	20kW	1:30:17	1:38:20 -99
Korzeniowska	Sylwia	POL	25.4.80	164/52	20kW	1:34:24	0
Korzhova	Marina	KAZ	13.9.82	180/60	HJ	1.90	1.86 -99
Kosenkova	Yuliya	RUS	28.3.73	170/58	800	2:01.63	2:00.71 -99
					1500	4:04.28	4:10.24 -99
Köstem-Zaikova	Tatyana	TUR	20.9.79	169/60	PV	4.20i, 4.20	4.10i, 3.90 -98
* Kotlyarova	Olga	RUS	12.4.76	180/65	400	49.95	50.32 -99

Name		Nat	Born	Ht/Wt	Event	2000 Mark	Pre-2000 Best
Kotorida	Takako	JPN	2.4.77	167/49	HMar	70:29	71:52 -98
* Kotova	Tatyana	RUS	11.12.76	182/59	LJ	7.04, 7.05iu	6.99, 7.01w -99
Kotova	Tatyana	UKR	2.1.70	175/61	TJ	13.90	14.19 -98
* Kovalenko	Tamara	RUS	5.6.64	161/48	20kW	1:25:59	1:28:33 -99
Koviryeva	Viktoria	KAZ	17.12.75	170/58	100	11.31	11.62 -98
Kozak	Anna	BLR	22.6.74	174/62	400	51.67	50.94 -96
Kozarenoka	Inga	LAT	16.3.82	174/70	JT	57.58	55.49 -99
Krakoviak	Irina	LTU	27.11.77	167/53	800	2:01.61	2:01.04 -98
					1500	4:07.99	4:28.00 -94
Krasovskaya	Yelena	UKR	17.8.76	176/62	100H	12.82	12.88 -95, 12.8 -97
Kraus	Melanie	GER	24.10.74	164/48	10000	32:21.31	32:12.40mx -99, 32:23.62 -98
					Mar	2:27:58	
Kravchenko	Anzhela	UKR	25.1.71	166/60	100	11.28	11.16 -98, 11.13w -99
^ Kravets	Inessa	UKR	5.10.66	178/60	LJ	7.00, 7.10wdq	7.37 -92
					TJ	14.57	15.50 -95
Kreiner	Kim	USA	26.7.77		JT	57.34	53.84 –99, 54.65# -98
^ Kremlyova	Lyubov	RUS	21.12.61	165/52	1500	4:03.10	3:58.71 -92
					3000	8:51.40i	8:46.94 -90
Krieger	Sabine	GER	4.9.73	180/64	Hep	5826	5766 -99
* Krivelyova	Svetlana	RUS	13.6.69	182/95	SP	20.72	21.06 -92
Krivobok	Tatyana	UKR	17.1.72	164/52	1500	4:08.25	4:07.57 -99
Krueger	Brooke	AUS	9.7.80	180/125	HT	61.89	56.89 -98
Krzywicki	Tara	GBR	9.3.74	160/52	3kSt	10:08.11	0
Ksok	Anna	POL	29.9.83	181/68	HJ	1.87	1.81 -99
Kubishta	Lesa	USA	19.4.78		PV	4.37	3.85 -99
Kuehl	Kris	USA	30.7.70	183/69	DT	65.34	63.26 -98
Kühnemund	Sylvia	GER	25.7.74	164/52	1500	4:07.00	4:05.96 -98
Kühnert	Floe	GER	6.3.84		PV	4.15	4.05 -99
Kuku	Garifa	KAZ	30.11.59	166/51	HMar	71:44	72:52 -94
Kulawansa	Sriyani	SRI	1.3.70	168/57	100H	13.10	12.91 -96
Kulikova	Yekaterina	RUS	7.11.68	172/59	400	51.16	51.42 -96
Kulikova	Yelena	KAZ	27.8.76	176/61	LJ	6.61	6.59 -99
Kulmala	Sari	FIN	25.5.74	166/52	TJ	13.74w	13.56 -99
Kuma	Eyerusalem	ETH	.81	157/45	10000	31:48.60	
Kumagai	Junko	JPN	31.12.74	167/49	HMar	69:46	73:09 -99
* Kumbernuss	Astrid	GER	5.2.70	181/86	SP	20.23	21.22 -95
Kun	Alice	HUN	7.6.76	169/54	400	52.00	53.29 -99
Kunitskaya	Natalya	UKR	17.8.72	170/70	HT	64.86	63.84 -99
Kuptsova	Marina	RUS	22.12.81	185/65	HJ	1.96	1.95i -98, 1.94 -99
^ Kurochkina	Tatyana	BLR	15.9.67	174/62	400H	55.91	54.39 -88
Kurrat	Manuela	GER	25.12.81	178/60	JT	55.73	53.48 -99
Kushch	Natalya	UKR	5.3.83	168/56	PV	4.10i, 4.00	3.70 -99
Kusunoki	Mami	JPN	8.9.75	160/48	HMar	69:39	74:07 -99
Kutol	Ruth	KEN	16.5.73		5000	15:27.88	
					HMar	69:24	71:56 -99
					Mar	2:28:16	
* Kuzenkova	Olga	RUS	4.10.70	176/76	HT	75.68	74.30 -99
Kuznetsova	Olga	RUS	23.10.67	168/53	800	2:01.73	1:58.77 -99
					1500	4:03.10	4.05.95 -99
Kuznetsova	Yelena	KAZ	4.8.77	164/53	20kW	1:32:23	1:33:21sh -99
Kwambai	Irene	KEN	25.10.78		HMar	71:41	73:11 -99
Kyllönen	Sanna	FIN	9.3.71	170/54	100	11.32w	11.30 -97, 11.28w -92
La Montaña	Yanuris	CUB	29.8.75	168/67	JT	61.24	59.36 -99, 62.57# -98
* LaBounty	Kelly	USA	24.11.70	170/65	Hep	6217w, 6180	6465 -97
Láboura	Amalía	GRE	16.3.68		HT	62.69	58.28 -99
Laghzaoui	Asmae	MAR	30.8.76	155/40	3000	8:33.85	8:37.81 -99
					5000	14:48.31	
					10000	31:59.21	32:18.1 -99
Lah	Barbara	ITA	24.3.72	180/61	TJ	14.06	14.17, 14.85w -95
Laláková	Barbora	CZE	2.5.81	178/58	HJ	1.87i	1.88 -99
Lamalle	Adrianna	FRA	27.9.82	170/58	100H	13.08	13.77, 13.43w -99
Lambert	Jodi	AUS	1.9.70	168/60	200	22.91Aw	23.13 -96, 22.87w -97
* Lan	Lixin	CHN	14.2.79	164/50	1500	4:03.95	3:53.97 -97
					3000	8:39.67	9:07.39 -98
Langat	Chebet	KEN	22.8.81	165/42	800	2:01.26	2:01.6 -97
* Langerholc	Brigita	SLO	23.7.76	170/56	400	52.02	53.26 -97
					800	1:58.51	1:59.87 -99
Lanouar	Fatima	TUN	14.3.78	165/52	1500	4:06.91	4:14.12 -99
* Lapina	Svetlana	RUS	12.4.78	180/58	HJ	1.94	1.99 -99
Larsen	Stine	NOR	5.11.75	157/48	10000	32:28.16	32:32.73 -99
					HMar	69:28	70:24 -99

Name		Nat	Born	Ht/Wt	Event	2000 Mark	Pre-2000 Best
Larsson	Annika	SWE	10.7.70	178/	DT	57.39	56.54 -96
^ Lasovskaya	Inna	RUS	17.12.69	177/67	TJ	14.25i, 14.24	15.09 -97
Latve	Irina	LAT	26.8.81	175/63	800	2:02.14	2:03.45 -99
^ Lauck	Anne Marie	USA	7.3.69	168/48	5000	15:23.71	15:43.37 -94
					10000	32:01.86	31:37.26 -93
Laukhova	Svetlana	RUS	7.5.73	170/60	100H	12.93	12.85 -99
Lawrence	Debbi	USA	15.10.61	175/58	20kW	1:33:48	1:40:51 -98
* Lawrence	Tayna	JAM	17.9.75	163/52	100	11.07	11.30, 11.23w -98
					200	22.84, 22.78w	22.89 -99
Lawson	Tonya	USA	16.5.69	162/54	100H	12.77	12.88 -98, 12.86w -99
Lawyer	Tracey	USA	28.8.77	178/67	Hep	5995w, 5844	5855w -99, 5809 -98
* Lebedenko	Yelena	RUS	16.1.71	177/63	TJ	14.66i	14.74i -99, 14.41 -98
* Lebedeva	Tatyana	RUS	21.7.76	171/60	TJ	15.32	14.89 -99
Lebusova	Natalya	RUS	.78		HJ	1.90	1.84i -99, 1.82 -97
^ Ledovskaya	Tatyana	BLR	21.5.66	171/60	400H	57.24	53.11 -91
Lee	Muna	USA	30.10.81		100	11.36	11.66 -99
Lee	Myung-sun	KOR	12.2.76	177/80	SP	19.36	18.79 -99
Lee	Suzette	JAM	6.3.75	185/67	TJ	14.09	14.25i -97, 14.09 -99
Lee	Young-sun	KOR	21.2.74	165/65	JT	58.15	56.80 -99, 63.32# -92
Legnante	Assunta	ITA	14.5.78	181/90	SP	17.84	16.61 -99
Leksir	Nora	FRA	13.5.74	158/49	20kW	1:31:15	1:34:35 -99
Lendjel	Nevena	CRO	18.7.79	181/62	HJ	1.91i, 1.89	1.91 -99
Lenskiy	Irina	ISR	12.6.71	176/54	100H	13.05	13.35 -99
					400H	56.09	55.59 -96
^ Leshchova	Yekaterina	RUS	21.4.74	176/68	200	23.09i	22.47 -97
Lever	Alison	AUS	13.10.72	182/85	DT	63.73	63.07 -99
Levorato	Manuela	ITA	16.3.77	179/65	100	11.21, 11.16rs, 11.13w	11.20 -99
					200	22.89	22.60 -99
* Lewis	Denise	GBR	27.8.72	173/65	100H	13.13	13.18 -96
					LJ	6.69	6.67 -95, 6.77w -97
					Hep	6831	6736 -99
Lewis	Selena	USA	3.8.76	163/61	100H	13.17	13.06 -99
Lewis	Tamsyn	AUS	20.7.78	168/57	400	51.51	52.58 -99
					800	1:59.21	2:00.95 –99
Li	Haiyan	CHN	27.5.79		20kW	1:34:42	1:35:46 -99
Li	Hong	CHN	1.6.79	158/58	20kW	1:31:31	1:30:35 -99
Li	Ji	CHN	19.9.79	155/45	3000	8:50.71i	
					10000	31:06.94	33:01.02 -99
Li	Jiahui	CHN	8.8.79		TJ	13.88	14.23 -97
Li	Jingnan	CHN	17.2.83	162/40	1500	4:04.84	4:16.47 -99
^ Li	Lei	CHN	4.5.74	175/74	JT	63.69	57.83 -99, 66.88# -98
Li	Meiju	CHN	23.1.81	173/85	SP	17.48	16.62 -99
^ Li	Meisu	CHN	17.4.59	176/92	SP	18.21	21.76 -88
Li	Qiumei	CHN	20.4.74	180/80	DT	60.54	67.50 -94
Li	Rui	CHN	22.11.79		400H	56.63	54.93 -97
Li	Xiaoxue	CHN	1.11.80		HT	64.50	57.72 -99
^ Li	Xuemei	CHN	5.11.77	166/60	100	11.25	10.79 -97
					200	23.05	22.01 -97
Li	Xuemei	CHN	1.10.79		SP	16.75	16.64i, 16.35 -99
Li	Yanfeng	CHN	15.5.79	179/76	DT	60.84	63.67 -99
Li	Yulian	CHN	17.2.79	166/52	400H	55.83	55.72 –97
Li	Yuxin	CHN	4.12.74	163/51	20kW	1:34:02	1:34:54- 99
Liang	Lili	CHN	16.11.83	170/75	JT	59.33	60.90 -99, 61.81# -98
Liang	Shuyan	CHN	16.9.77		LJ	6.70	6.62 -99
Liepina	Anita	LAT	17.11.67	164/55	20kW	1:34:26	1:33:01 -98
Lignot-Maubert	Cécile	FRA	19.11.71	168/70	HT	64.00	65.39 -99
Lika	Savva	GRE	.70		JT	57.61	52.15 -99
Lin	Na	CHN	18.1.80	180/63	800	2:00.67	1:58.16 -97
Linares	Teresa	ESP	29.4.69	157/49	20kW	1:31:55	1:34:30 -99
Lindberg	Åsa	FIN	12.4.79	173/75	JT	56.36	55.98# -97
Lishchenko	Tatyana	UKR	28.3.66	172/54	800	2:01.61	2:01.00 -90
^ Lisovskaya	Natalya	FRA	16.7.62	187/92	SP	17.48	22.63 -87
Liss	Collette	USA	29.4.73		3000	8:58.47i	9:26.29 -97
Liu	Fengying	CHN	26.1.79	178/80	DT	60.76	65.20 -97
* Liu	Hongyu	CHN	11.1.75	164/51	20kW	1:27:55	1:27:30 -95
Liu	Jing	CHN	8.8.77		100H	13.11	12.76 -87
Liu	Xiaomei	CHN	11.1.72	168/60	200	22.76	22.36 -97
Liu	Xing	CHN	27.4.70		Hep	5835	6184 -97
Liu	Yinghui	CHN	29.6.79		HT	65.06	63.75 -99
Long	Carri	USA	23.4.77	181/64	HJ	1.87i	1.86i -99

Name		Nat	Born	Ht/Wt	Event	2000 Mark	Pre-2000 Best
Long	Latifah	USA	21.2.77	181/	HJ	1.87i	1.83 -99
^ López	Aliuska	CUB	29.8.69	174/67	100H	12.82	12.67 -96
* López	Isel	CUB	11.7.70	174/76	JT	60.55	61.66 -99, 66.18# -90
Lora	Rita	ESP	23.3.73	175/80	DT	56.71	56.92 -98
* Loroupe	Tegla	KEN	9.5.73	156/48	3000	8:30.95	8:33.36 -99
					5000	14:45.95	14:49.12 -99
					10000	30:37.26	30:32.03 -99
					HMar	67:24	67:12 -96
					Mar	2:24:33	2:20:43 -99
Lott-Hogan	Tiffany	USA	1.8.75	170/61	100H	13.10	12.72A, 12.92, 12.8 -97
					Hep	6094	6211 -97
Lu	Jieming	CHN	25.1.83		HJ	1.88	1.82 -99
Lu	Jingbo	CHN	18.4.73	163/52	Mar	2:30:43	2:33:45 -99
Luan	Zhili	CHN	6.1.73	173/	DT	62.26	64.62 -93
Lukinskaya	Yuliya	RUS	.76		PV	4.10	3.70 -99
Lukyanchuk	Olga	UKR	7.12.76	168/56	20kW	1:32:01	1:39:39 -97
Lutton-Senior	Tania	NZL	1.3.68		SP	16.51	16.18 -98
* Lyakhova	Yulia	RUS	8.7.77	185/60	HJ	1.96	2.00i -99, 1.99 -97
Lyakhovich	Tatyana	UKR	20.5.79	171/68	JT	57.41	57.35 -99
Lyons ¶	Robin	CAN	15.4.77	173/79	HT	64.44, 67.40dh-dq	62.78 -99
^ Lysak	Yelena	RUS	19.10.75	175/55	TJ	14.07	14.32, 14.43w -94
Ma	Shuli	CHN	20.1.78	178/75	DT	60.35	61.23 -98
Macchiut	Margaret	ITA	25.7.74	171/48	100H	13.22	13.21 -99
* Machado	Manuela	POR	9.8.63	161/52	Mar	2:26:41	2:25:09 -99
^ Machado	Teresa	POR	22.7.69	170/80	SP	16.78i, 16.78	17.26i, 17.18 -96
					DT	64.09	65.40 -98
Macharia	Faith	KEN	.76		800	2:01.09	2:01.33 -99
					1500	4:09.57	4:08.04 -99
MacNaughton	Brenda	AUS	7.5.76		HT	61.97	62.49 -98
Maddox	Keri	GBR	4.7.72	172/63	100H	13.13	12.95 -99
					400H	55.22	55.33 -99
Madison	Jacqueline	USA	14.7.79	176/	100H	13.08, 12.93w	13.59 -99
Maduaka	Joice	GBR	30.9.73	173/62	200	23.17	22.83 -99
Maeda	Asuka	JPN	4.10.78	164/49	HMar	71:05	72:28 -98
Maffeis	Agnese	ITA	9.3.65	187/81	DT	60.57	63.66 -96
* Maggi	Maurren	BRA	25.6.76	173/62	LJ	6.93	7.26A, 6.79 -99
Mahone	Tasha	USA	5.8.79	165/	LJ	6.59	6.20A, 6.36Aw -99
Makarova	Marina	UKR	3.1.75	178/65	800	2:01.15	2:04.2 -94
Makarova	Oksana	RUS	21.7.71	180/90	JT	59.92	64.61 -99, 68.72# -96
* Makarova	Rimma	RUS	25.2.63	168/62	20kW	1:30:40	1:36:13 -97
Mäkelä	Annu	FIN	20.9.82	174/60	PV	4.12	4.00 -99
^ Malone	Maicel	USA	12.6.69	176/61	400	51.06	50.05 -94
* Malot	Leah	KEN	7.6.72	168/46	1500	4:11.03	4:10.17 -99
					3000	8:41.23	8:35.74 -99
					5000	14:39.83	15:03.75 -99
					10000	30:57.70	31:31.73 -99
					HMar	69:46	71:04 -98
Manabe	Yuko	JPN	8.2.79	158/41	10000	32:07.58	33:14.97 -99
					HMar	70.38	71.06 -99
Manahan	LaQuinta	USA	10.4.78		100	11.30w	11.70 -99
Manfredi	Laurence	FRA	20.5.74	175/92	SP	18.69i, 18.68	17.89 -99
* Mani	Léonie Myriam	CMR	21.5.77	169/57	100	11.01	11.24A, 11.22w -99, 11.1w -98
					200	22.41	22.66A -99, 23.01 -98
Manning	Valerie	USA	27.3.68	178/66	100H	13.15, 13.01w	13.00 -97
Manuel	Angela	USA	10.5.75		100	11.31	11.41w -98
Mao	Lingyan	CHN			SP	16.92	16.89 -99
Marable	Jessica	USA	3.5.77		SP	16.56i	15.92 -99
Margain	Aisha	USA	26.9.81	170/68	200	23.10w	24.03 -97
Mariezkurrena	Idoia	ESP	11.7.70	166/73	JT	57.50	55.51 –99, 57.18# -97
* Marinova	Tereza	BUL	5.9.77	173/56	TJ	15.20	14.76i -99, 14.64 -98
Mark	Marsha	TRI	20.1.74	168/54	Hep	5750	5706w –98, 5481 -97
Markose	Anju	IND	.77		LJ	6.59	6.37 -99
Márkou	Dímitra	GRE	28.7.80	178/58	TJ	14.05	13.47 -99
Marrot	Sophie	FRA	13.2.75	167/56	Hep	5842	6091 -98
Märtensson	Linda-Marie	SWE	22.6.71	185/81	SP	17.18	17.52 -99
Martín	Jacqueline	ESP	14.4.74	157/	3000	8:59.22	9:27.94, 9:18.55i -99
					5000	15:27.82	17:01.38 -98
Martin	Karen	GBR	24.11.74	174/73	JT	58.54	59.50 -99
Martínez	Magdelin	CUB	10.2.76	174/63	TJ	14.40	14.27 -98
Martínez	Maite	ESP	17.5.76	165/58	800	1:59.60	2:05.00 -95

Name		Nat	Born	Ht/Wt	Event	2000 Mark	Pre-2000 Best
Martinovic	Marija	YUG	17.4.79	173/58	TJ	14.06	13.62 -97
Martynenko	Irina	UKR	19.10.76	176/92	HT	61.18	61.60 -98
Marusova	Margarita	RUS	25.11.67	170/53	1500	4:08.06	4:02.86 -98
Marx	Claudia	GER	16.9.78	172/60	400	52.25i	52.26 -99
* Masterkova	Svetlana	RUS	17.1.68	168/58	1500	4:01.15	3:56.77 -96
^ Mateescu ¶	Rodica	ROM	13.3.71	180/63	TJ	14.31i, 14.18dq	15.16 -97
Matejková	Alice	ESP	11.1.69	170/69	DT	59.25	62.66 -97
* Mathes	Simone	GER	13.3.75	173/82	HT	65.90	67.13 -99
Matsuo	Kazumi	JPN	18.4.74	165/47	Mar	2:26:15	2:32:14 -99
Matsuoka	Noriko	JPN	2.5.79	142/35	10000	31:50.53	0
Matsuoka	Rie	JPN	9.3.77	142/35	10000	31:52.50	32:24.03 -97
					HMar	70:36	70:08 -98
Mattas	Marianne	FIN	20.8.79	176/63	HJ	1.87i, 1.86	1.87 -98
Matyushkina	Tatyana	RUS	22.1.79	176/63	20kW	1:33:40	1:40:55 -99
Mau-Repnak	Beatrice	GER	20.2.71	174/56	Hep	6041	6349 -99
Maximiuc	Adriana	ROM	1.10.73	176/60	HJ	1.88	1.92 -99
* May	Fiona	ITA	12.12.69	182/60	LJ	7.09	7.11 -98, 7.23Aw -95
May	Wanita	CAN	30.1.75	170/61	HJ	1.89	1.92 -93
Mayers	Natasha	VIN	10.3.79	168/69	100	11.24	11.88 -99
Mayr	Karin	AUT	4.6.71	179/69	100	11.29, 11.26w	11.57 -97
Mazarin	Marie-Véronique	FRA	18.10.76	167/60	TJ	13.86i	13.45i, 13.40 -98, 13.83w -99
Mbango	Françoise	CMR	14.4.76	172/63	TJ	14.18	14.70A, 14.65 -99
McCambridge	Maria	IRL	10.7.75		5000	15:18.78	
McCann	Kerryn	AUS	2.5.67	162/48	3000	8:56.42	8:50.4mx -99
					5000	15:08.69	15:19.87mx, 15:24.28 -99
					HMar	67:48	69:05 -99
					Mar	2:25:59	2:28:44 -99
McConnell	Lee	GBR	9.10.78		HJ	1.88	1.86 -99
McCray	Yolanda	USA	11.9.76	168/60	100H	12.94	12.78, 12.77w -99
* McDonald	Beverly	JAM	15.2.70	169/59	100	11.11	10.99 -98
					200	22.35	22.22 -99
McIvor	Adrienne	IRL	2.9.70	172/59	400H	56.73	56.85 -99
McKelvy	Miesha	USA	26.7.76	173/64	100H	12.78	12.82, 12.67w -99
McKoy	Olivia	JAM	1.12.73	165/73	JT	58.29	55.47 -99
Medgyesová	Renata	SVK	28.1.83	170/52	HJ	1.88i, 1.87	1.88 -98
Mehes	Livia	ROM	6.3.65	174/90	SP	18.37i, 17.68	19.61 -86
					HT	60.86	61.52 -99
Meijer	Saskia	NED	8.2.79		Hep	5764	4914 -98
^ Meissner	Heike	GER	29.1.70	172/57	800	2:01.40i	1:59.50 -98
					400H	54.84	54.03 -96
Meldrum	Courtney	USA	30.1.77	168/	3kSt	10:04.41	10:23.47 -96
* Melinte ¶	Mihaela	ROM	27.3.75	170/84	HT	72.19, 74.80dq	76.07 -99
Melnikova	Irina	RUS	14.5.75	169/57	LJ	6.71i, 6.64	6.68 -96
Melová	Mária	SVK	21.10.75	179/60	HJ	1.90	1.96i -97, 1.87 -96
Meltsayeva	Oksana	UKR	16.8.75	175/55	800	2:02.06	2:04.74 -99
					1500	4:11.18	4:10.12 -99
^ Mendes	Luciana	BRA	26.7.71	170/55	800	2:00.61	1:58.27 -94
Mendía	Marta	ESP	18.5.75	172/58	HJ	1.93	1.91 -99
Mendoza	Graciela	MEX	23.3.63	156/48	20kW	1:32:22	1:30:03 -99
Menéndez	Osleydis	CUB	14.11.79	174/78	JT	67.83	66.49 -99, 68.17# -98
Mensah	Amewu	GER	21.3.77	182/64	HJ	1.94	1.93 -99
^ Mensah	Philomena	CAN	11.5.75	166/57	100	11.35	11.03A -99, 11.08 -98, 11.0 -94
* Mérah-Benida	Nouria	ALG	19.10.70	162/52	800	1:59.68	1:59.49 -99
					1500	3:59.12	4:05.44 -99
					1M	4:28.90i	
Mercken	Ann	BEL	6.5.74	177/71	400H	56.77	54.95 -96
Méred	Meriem	FRA	4.4.76	166/48	3kSt	10:07.63	10:20.89 -99
Merriman	Donica	USA	24.1.79		100	11.16w	11.40 -99
					200	23.08, 22.75w	23.35, 23.03w -99
					100H	12.70	12.84 -99
* Merry	Katharine	GBR	21.9.74	173/63	200	22.76	22.77 -97
					400	49.72	50.21 -99
Mert	Oksana	TUR	26.3.73	187/82	DT	62.32	64.25 -99
Meyer	Annika	GER	9.6.80		Hep	5979	5538 -98
* Meyer	Elana	RSA	10.10.66	158/55	5000	14:57.48	14:44.05 -95
					10000	31:14.70	30:52.51 -94
					HMar	67:33	66:44 -99
					Mar	2:31:59	2:25:15 -94
Miao	Chunqing	CHN	27.2.79	178/66	TJ	14.21	14.31 -99
Míguez	Marta	ESP	3.3.73	171/62	JT	59.02	57.59 -99

Name		Nat	Born	Ht/Wt	Event	2000 Mark	Pre-2000 Best
Mihalcea	Gabriela	ROM	27.1.64	174/65	PV	4.10	4.25i, 4.22 -99
Mikayeva	Olga	RUS	22.10.79	163/49	800	2:02.34	2:03.09 -99
Mikhalchenko	Irina	UKR	20.1.72	174/58	HJ	1.98	1.96i -98, 1.96 -99
* Mikhaylova	Larisa	RUS	3.1.69	158/50	800	2:00.61	1:57.70 -99
* Mikitenko	Irina	GER	23.8.72	158/49	1500	4:07.13	4:06.68 -99
					3000	8:30.39	8:45.59 -99
					5000	14:43.59	14:42.03 -99
Miklos	Eva	ROM	30.7.78	174/56	LJ	6.62	6.58 -99
* Miles-Clark	Jearl	USA	4.9.66	170/60	200	23.13	23.03 -97
					400	50.04	49.40 -97
					800	1:59.12	1:56.40 -99
Miller	Virginia 'Gigi'	USA	12.1.79	165/55	Hep	5777	5242 -99
Miller	Gretel	JAM	6.6.75		HT	61.50	58.68 -98
* Miller	Inger	USA	12.6.72	163/55	100	10.91	10.79 -99
					200	22.09	21.77 -99
Mills	TaNisha	USA	2.11.74	172/62	400H	56.86	56.45 -99
Milusheva	Eleonora	BUL	8.4.73	176/59	HJ	1.95	1.92 -96
Minina	Zana	LTU	11.6.77	174/58	400	52.25	53.41 -99
* Misipeka	Lisa	ASA	3.1.75	170/84	HT	67.55	67.00 -99
Misiruk	Galina	UKR	18.12.70	168/54	800	2:00.54	2:01.87 -99
Mistry	Rachita	IND	4.3.74		100	11.26	11.46 -98
					200	23.10	23.75 -98
* Mistyukevich	Irina	RUS	17.6.77	177/63	400	51.87	54.2 -98
					800	1:57.49	1:58.33 -99
^ Misyulya	Natalya	BLR	16.4.66	162/48	20kW	1:28:24	1:28:40 -99
Miyake	Takako	JPN	22.7.74	161/58	JT	56.44	57.27 -99, 59.22# -66
Mladenis	Nicole	AUS	22.9.75	170/58	TJ	13.82	13.67 -99
Mládková	Sárka	CZE	30.8.76	173/58	PV	4.20, 4.26sq	4.20 -99
Mocanu	Adina	ROM	4.3.80	181/81	DT	58.60	55.90 -99
^ Modahl	Diane	GBR	17.6.66	170/56	800	2:00.53	1:58.65 -90
^ Möllenbeck	Anja	GER	18.3.72	184/86	DT	62.63	64.63 -98
Möller	Esther	GER	13.9.77	172/58	100	11.33	11.34 -97
					200	22.81	22.85 -99
Möller	Michaela	GER	19.10.73		10000	32:31.91	33:24.43 -99
Molnár	Krisztina	HUN	8.4.76	168/51	PV	4.30i, 4.22	4.11 -99
Monar-Enweani	Vanessa	CAN	11.12.69	180/64	LJ	6.53	6.62A -99
^ Mondie-Milner	Celena	USA	6.8.68	169/57	100	11.30	11.17 -96
					200	22.85A	22.55 -96
					400	51.09A, 51.98	51.14A, 51.45 -88
* Montalvo	Niurka	ESP	4.6.68	172/57	LJ	6.87, 6.95w	7.06 -99
					TJ	13.89w	14.60 -94
Montaner	Concepción	ESP	14.1.81	170/56	LJ	6.64, 6.79w	6.47 -99
* Montebrun	Manuela	FRA	13.11.79	175/92	HT	71.18	68.11 -99
Montell	Annu	FIN	7.5.76	173/64	Hep	5931	5767 -99
Montgomery	Carol	CAN	24.8.66	160/55	10000	32:11.79	32:26.42 -95
Morapane	Dikeledi	RSA	12.3.76		100	11.32w	11.83A -99
					200	23.07A	
* Moreno	Yipsi	CUB	19.11.80	178/80	HT	69.36	66.34 -99
Morgan	Kolly	GBR	17.6.80		JT	58.45	54.01 -99
Morgunova	Lyubov	RUS	14.1.71	167/48	HMar	68:45	71:09 -98
					Mar	2:26:33	2:27:43 -99
Morimoto	Akiko	JPN	17.2.77	163/49	100H	13.14w	13.29, 13.22w -99
Mormand	Anita	FRA	20.2.71	175/60	400	52.17	51.94 -98
Moroni	Maria Constanza	ITA	23.3.60	178/62	TJ	13.71	14.25 -90
Morrison	Maureen	USA	2.5.78	178/	DT	56.30	50.82 -98
* Morrison	Melissa	USA	9.7.71	163/50	100H	12.57	12.53 -98
Morrow	Sherryl	AUS	22.3.73		Hep	5817	5722 -99
Mosqueda	Sylvia	USA	8.4.66	160/48	10000	32:17.71	31:54.03 -96
					HMar	71:20	70:47 -87
Mothersill	Cydonie	CAY	19.3.78	170/54	100	11.21w	11.35 -96
					200	22.66	22.81 -99
Moya	Carina	ARG	28.9.73	171/76	HT	61.63	61.85 -95
Moya	Sabina	COL	27.1.77	162/70	JT	58.23	58.84 -99, 60.10# -98
* Mueller	Melissa	USA	16.11.72	178/66	PV	4.50b, 4.45	4.50i, 4.38 -99
* Mugo	Naomi	KEN	2.1.77	163/50	1500	4:01.64	3:58.12 -98
					3000	8:43.55	8:44.58 -98
					5000	15:25.13	0
^ Müller	Andrea	GER	29.6.74	164/57	PV	4.20i, 4.20	4.30 -97, 4.40sq -95
Mulrain	Sabrina	GER	10.6.78	174/63	200	22.75	22.73 -99
* Münchow	Kirsten	GER	21.1.77	174/75	HT	69.28	66.82 -98

	Name		Nat	Born	Ht/Wt	Event	2000 Mark	Pre-2000 Best
	Munro	Jacquie	AUS	4.10.81	166/57	100H	13.12, 13.03w	13.47 -99
	Murata	Fumi	JPN	13.3.75	151/40	HMar	69:26	72:41 -99
*	Mutola	Maria Lurdes	MOZ	27.10.72	162/61	800	1:56.15	1:55.19 -94
						1500	4:02.39	4:01.6mx -95, 4:01.63 -96
	Myers	Carrie	USA	12.9.77	176/	HT	61.80	60.00 -99
	Myrick	Wyllesheia	USA	21.11.79	163/	100	11.30w	11.59, 11.56w -98
						200	23.14	23.68 -98
	Nacsa	Monique	AUS	26.10.76	177/85	DT	57.53A	55.51 -99
	Nagayama	Ikumi	JPN	22.6.74	155/42	10000	32:09.25	31:55.08 -99
						HMar	69:40	70:36 -97
	Nakanishi	Miyoko	JPN	17.1.75	174/73	DT	56.51	54.64 -99
^	Nastase	Liliana	ROM	1.8.62	170/65	100H	13.19	12.81 -91
						Hep	5924	6619 -92
*	Nathan	DeDee	USA	20.4.68	180/75	Hep	6343	6577 -99
	Naude	Elizna	RSA	14.9.78		DT	58.51	55.92 -99
	Naumenko	Irina	KAZ	13.2.80	180/63	HJ	1.88	1.84 -99
						Hep	6078	5902 -99
	Naylor	Lee	AUS	26.1.71	165/58	400	51.37	51.35 -98
	Nazarova	Margarita	RUS	1.10.76	167/58	20kW	1:30:58	1:33:53 -99
*	Nazarova	Natalya	RUS	26.5.79	167/55	400	50.10	50.48 -99
*	Ndereba	Catherine	KEN	21.7.72		5000	15:27.84	15:53.6A -99
						10000	32:17.58	32:38.3A -99
						HMar	69:02	69:23 -99
						Mar	2:21:33	2:27:35 -99
	Ndoye	Kène	SEN	20.11.78	164/58	TJ	14.03	14.08A, 13.99 -99
	Necheporuk	Larisa	UKR	24.12.70	171/59	Hep	6331	6274 -94
	Negussie	Abebech	ETH	2.1.83	160/45	1500	4:06.20	
	Nelyubova	Olga	RUS	12.6.64	168/58	1500	4:02.21	4:01.42 -98
*	Nerius	Steffi	GER	1.7.72	176/72	JT	65.76	61.56 -99, 69.42# -96
	Nestorsson	Linda	SWE	2.12.75		SP	16.46	16.19 -99
	Neto	Rosemar Coelho	BRA	2.1.77		200	22.99w	23.8 -99
	Neyra	Yahumara	CUB	18.4.76	158/50	100H	13.13	13.17, 13.00w -99
	Nguimbo	Mireille	CMR	7.11.76	172/56	400	50.69	51.89 -99
	Nguyen Thi	Bich Van	VIE	21.2.75		TJ	13.75	13.30 -98
*	Nicolau	Cristina	ROM	9.8.77	186/66	LJ	6.61i	6.58 -96, 6.69w -99
						TJ	14.94, 14.19, 14.22w	14.70 -99
	Niederstatter	Monika	ITA	2.3.74	169/47	400H	55.78	55.10 -99
	Nikaido	Kaori	JPN	25.7.79	162/51	20kW	1:32:44	1:36:59 -99
	Nikiel	Aniela	POL	1.11.65	157/49	Mar	2:30:02	2:29:19 -95
	Nikitina	Lyudmila	RUS	2.3.70		TJ	14.07	14.33i, 14.14 -99
*	Nikolayeva	Tatyana	UKR	26.2.76	184/63	HJ	1.93	1.93 -99
	Nilsson	Cecilia	SWE	22.6.79	177/82	HT	62.54	61.37 -99
	Nishimura	Miyuki	JPN	16.4.80	157/47	10000	32:24.52	32:51.7 -99
	Nishio	Maya	JPN	19.12.78	161/44	HMar	69:48	69:56 -99
	Nitta	Aiko	JPN	18.11.75	163/48	HMar	71:29	76:50 -99
	Njeri	Hannah	KEN	28.11.68		HMar	70:40	71:49 -99
*	Nku	Mercy	NGR	17.7.76	170/67	100	11.20	11.03A, 11.09, 10.98w -99
						200	22.95	22.53 -99
*	Noguchi	Mizuki	JPN	3.7.78		10000	32:05.23	33:09.98 -98
						HMar	69:44	68:30 -99
	Norgren	Anna	USA	19.12.74	180/75	HT	65.88	64.72 -99
	Nosova	Yuliya	RUS	21.4.78	180/65	400H	54.31	53.98 -99
	Nsiah	Vida	GHA	13.4.76	172/65	100	11.18	11.25 -97
	Nye	Lisa	USA	17.11.68		3kSt	10:00.63	10:08.58 -99
^	Oakes	Judy	GBR	14.2.58	163/83	SP	18.30i, 18.22	19.36 -88
	Obata	Kayoko	JPN	18.9.71	156/46	Mar	2:25:14	2:26:18 -99
^	Oberem	Sonja	GER	24.2.73	170/50	Mar	2:27:25	2:28:02 -97
	Obi	Asami	JPN	22.3.76	157/43	HMar	70:04	73:01 -96
	Oblekowska	Izabella	POL	18.2.72	175/58	Hep	5915	5919 -99
	Obruba	Beth	USA	30.4.77		SP	16.53i	
	Uchichi	Isabellah	KEN			HMar	70:15	72:18 -99
	Ogoshi	Kazue	JPN	2.3.81	160/44	10000	31:58.95	32:25.0 -99
						HMar	71:16	0
*	Ogunkoya	Falilat	NGR	12.5.68	172/66	100	11.34Aw	11.19 -88
						200	23.18, 22.93Aw	22.22 -98
						400	50.04	49.10 -96
	Oh	Mi-ja	KOR	3.7.70	166/50	Mar	2:29:44	2:30:09 -96
	Ohaeri	Christine	USA	30.3.79	175/64	100H	13.13, 13.06w	13.44, 13.38w -99
	O'Hara	Tracy	USA	20.7.80	165/55	PV	4.45	4.07 -99
	Okamoto	Haruko	JPN	19.8.74	155/40	10000	32:30.14	33:29.70 -98

Name		Nat	Born	Ht/Wt	Event	2000 Mark	Pre-2000 Best
Okamoto	Yukiko	JPN	29.11.74	159/45	10000	32:06.42	32:09.76 -95
					HMar	69:12	70:28 -96
Okayo	Margaret	KEN	30.5.76		HMar	69:03	70:08 -99
					Mar	2:26:36	2:26:00 -99
Okori	Reina-Flor	FRA	2.5.80	165/56	100H	12.96, 12.91w	13.16 -99
Oksanen	Veera	FIN	23.5.78	174/70	JT	57.64	58.36 -99, 59.67# -98
Olaru	Nuta	ROM	28.8.70	161/40	HMar	70:55	69:52 -97
Oleynikova	Yelena	RUS	9.12.76		TJ	14.25	13.85 -99
Olichwierczuk	Anna	POL	10.12.78	168/56	400H	55.75	56.43 -99
Olivarès	Elodie	FRA	22.5.76	170/55	3kSt	10:09.64	0
^ Olteanu (Negura)	Iulia	ROM	26.1.67	166/57	10000	32:07.42	31:26.46 -96
Ominami	Hiromi	JPN	15.11.75	165/47	5000	15:27.58	15:27.14 -97
					10000	31:50.89	32:13.26 -98
					HMar	69:40	70:42 -99
					Mar	2:28:32	2:30:19 -99
Ominami	Takami	JPN	15.11.75	165/47	HMar	70:21	70:42 -99
					Mar	2:26:58	2:33:05 -99
Onanuga	Saidat	NGR	18.6.74	168/59	400H	56.45	56.10 -97
Ono	Masumi	JPN	5.12.75	161/52	PV	4.21i	4.20 -99
^ Onyali	Mary	NGR	3.2.68	168/54	100	10.99	10.97, 10.7 -96
					200	22.49	22.31 -90
* Opara	Charity	NGR	20.5.72	170/60	400	50.23	49.29 -98
^ Ordina	Vera	RUS	4.6.68	172/56	100H	13.13	13.26 -96, 13.0 -98
Ormond	Kara	USA	17.6.77	170/	3kSt	10:03.09	10:26.63 -99
Orsini	Gisella	ITA	9.12.71	161/49	20kW	1:32:57	1:34:36 -99
* Ostapchuk	Nadezhda	BLR	12.10.80	180/78	SP	19.13i, 18.82	18.73 -99
O'Sullivan	Gillian	IRL	21.8.76	163/61	20kW	1:31:31	1:36:44 -99
* O'Sullivan	Sonia	IRL	28.11.69	172/53	1500	4:01.70	3:58.85 -95
					3000	8:27.58	8:21.64 -94
					5000	14:41.02	14:41.40 -95
					10000	30:53.37	31:29.33 -98
Ota	Yoko	JPN	14.1.75	171/51	HJ	1.94	1.94 -99
* Ottey	Merlene	JAM	10.5.60	173/61	100	10.99, 10.91w	10.74 -96
Ouali	Fatiha	FRA	28.10.74	159/52	20kW	1:32:14	1:34:35 -99
Ouaziz	Saloua	MAR	27.7.74	161/45	1500	4:08.18	4:09.73 -99
* Ouaziz	Zahra	MAR	20.12.69	165/50	3000	8:47.18	8:26.45 -99
* Ouzoúni	Kallиópi	GRE	8.2.73	182/80	SP	19.03i, 18.63	18.39 -99
Oxley	Tanya	BAR	13.5.79	183/59	400	52.26	53.64 -99
Ozaki	Mari	JPN	16.7.75	163/46	3000	8:59.4	9:18.94 -98
					5000	15:28.41	15:25.99 -98
					10000	32:03.00	31:58.05 -99
Palacios	Felipa	COL	1.12.75	168/60	200	23.08	
							22.93A -96, 22.8A -98, 23.05 -99, 22.74Aw -97
* Palamar	Viktoriya	UKR	12.10.77	186/63	HJ	1.98	1.93 -99
* Palmer	Amy	USA	20.4.75	180/100	HT	68.28	67.27 -99
Palmer	Nadine	JAM	19.2.83	173/68	100	11.36	11.68, 11.2 -99
Pan	Hailian	CHN	21.11.77	163/55	20kW	1:30:51	1:31:17 -99
Paniagua	Eva	ESP	2.2.74	170/60	400H	57.17	56.11A, 56.74 -96
* Pantelimon	Oana	ROM	27.9.72	178/61	HJ	1.99	1.94 -92
Paolini	Lisa	AUS	10.12.62	147/45	20kW	1:33:00	1:36:20 -99
Papavasiláki	Déspina	GRE	24.3.73	174/56	LJ	6.75	6.48 -99
Papayiánni	Athiná	GRE	18.8.80	168/55	20kW	1:33:14	0
Paquette	Sonia	CAN	7.2.73	173/57	100H	13.17, 12.96Aw	13.11A -96, 13.16 -97
Paredes	Concepción	ESP	19.7.70	174/67	TJ	14.13	14.30A -94, 14.27 -95
Parfyonova	Svetlana	RUS	.74		Hep	6187	6004 -99
Parfyonova	Yelena	KAZ	26.1.74	176/58	TJ	14.20	13.80 -99
Parish	Kiyomi	USA	19.5.75	163/77	HT	61.38	61.54 -99
Parker	Tisha	USA	18.9.77	173/60	LJ	6.63	6.45, 6.51w -98
* Parris	Debbie-Ann	JAM	24.3.73	162/52	400H	55.90	53.97 -96
Passmore	Denise	AUS	11.6.74		HT	61.32	60.62 -98
Pastushenko	Yelena	UKR	14.7.79	175/61	100	11.28, 11.0	11.24 -99
					200	22.85	23.06 -99
Patla	Genowefa	POL	17.10.62	175/73	JT	61.50	61.05 -99, 65.96# -91
^ Patoulídou	Paraskeví	GRE	29.3.65	168/61	100	11.32	11.27 -90
Patterson	Angel	USA	6.8.79		400H	55.50	56.02 -99
Pattinson	Helen	GBR	2.1.74	170/57	1500	4:04.82	4:06.72 -99
^ Paulino	Argentina	MOZ	7.7.73	166/61	800	2:00.92	1:56.62 -93
* Pavey	Joanne	GBR	20.9.73	168/48	3000	8:36.70	8:58.2 -99
					5000	14:58.27	0

Name		Nat	Born	Ht/Wt	Event	2000 Mark	Pre-2000 Best
Pazola	Ilona	POL	22.3.69	170/55	TJ	13.93	13.78 -99
Pechstein	Petra	SUI	26.7.71	166/60	PV	4.10i, 4.10	4.00i -99, 3.90 -98
Pedrares	Dolores	ESP	17.1.73	168/69	HT	61.39	61.28 -99
Pehlivan	Nazan	TUR	15.7.68		JT	56.83	52.40 -99, 55.86# -91
* Peleshenko	Larisa	RUS	29.2.64	187/95	SP	21.46	20.99 -87
Pelham	Shaunta	USA	12.2.78		100	11.27	11.54 -99
					200	22.88	23.40 -99
Pellino	Cristiana	ITA	21.9.70	164/49	20kW	1:30:42	1:35:51 -98
^ Pells	Leah	CAN	9.11.64	173/55	1500	4:07.88	4:03.56 -96
Peltosaari	Piia	FIN	27.2.73	173/60	Hep	5771	5962 -99
* Pendareva	Petya	BUL	20.1.71	163/56	100	11.23	11.12 -98, 11.04w -99, 11.0 -95
Peng	Yinghua	CHN	21.2.79		400H	56.65	56.84, 54.54dq -97
* Pérec	Marie-José	FRA	9.5.68	180/60	200	22.71	21.99 -93
					400	50.32	48.25 -96
Pereira	Ana Paula	BRA	11.12.78		400H	57.19	57.29 -99
Perepelova	Lyubov	UZB	26.2.79	163/53	100	11.04	11.37 -99
					200	22.72	23.45 -99
Pérez	Eva	ESP	18.7.75	150/48	20kW	1:32:03	1:38:22 -99
Peris-Kneebone	Nova	AUS	25.2.71	170/58	100	11.18Aw	11.23 -98
					200	23.20A, 23.21, 22.70w	22.74 -99
					400	51.28	53.18 -99
Perkins-DiMarco	Karyne	AUS	14.3.78	168/77	HT	65.38	63.43 -99
* Pernía	Daimí	CUB	27.12.76	175/61	400	51.13	51.18 -99
					400H	53.68	52.89 -99
Perrone	Elisabetta	ITA	9.7.68	168/60	20kW	1:27:42	1:32:21 -99
Perry	Michelle	USA	1.5.79	175/60	100H	13.15, 13.03w	13.26, 13.08w, 12.9w -99
					400H	56.50	58.30 -99
* Perry	Nanceen	USA	19.4.77	176/68	100	11.17, 11.10w	11.15, 11.12w -99
					200	22.38, 22.16w	22.55, 22.49w -99
Perry	Tarama	CAN	2.10.74	168/63	100	11.35w	11.34A -98
Pershina	Yelena	KAZ	24.12.63	176/62	LJ	6.68	6.91 -92
Peterková	Alena	CZE	13.11.60	168/55	10000	32:27.68	33:46.46 -90
					Mar	2:31:08	2:25:19 -94
Peters	Annette	USA	31.5.65	165/50	10000	32:03.06	31:30.89 -97
Peters-Chukwuemeka	Vivian	NGR	4.5.75	178/90	SP	17.93	17.35 -99
Petersson	Annika	SWE	10.1.79	176/74	JT	56.70	54.19 -99
Petráhn	Barbara	HUN	16.9.78	170/56	400	52.05	52.82 -98
Petrescu	Daniela	ROM	13.4.68	170/52	3kSt	9:54.86	9:55.28 -98
Petrova	Lyudmila	RUS	7.10.68	160/44	10000	31:52.75	31:58.84 -96
					HMar	69:26	69:46 -98
					Mar	2:25:45	2:29:13 -99
* Philipp	Andrea	GER	29.7.71	165/60	100	11.21, 11.15w	11.05 -97
					200	22.69	22.25 -99
Pidgeon	Elizabeth	GBR	27.4.77	160/77	HT	63.61	60.37 -99
Pierson	Shannon	USA	30.9.74	175/	PV	4.10	3.95 -99
Pierson	Summer	USA	3.9.78		DT	57.92	55.24 -99
Pignot	Aurore	FRA	24.12.79	172/57	PV	4.16i, 4.15	4.13i, 4.12, 4.25ex -99
Pilátou	Stilianí	GRE	28.3.80		LJ	6.50	6.12 -99
Pilsner-Steinke	Patti	CAN	9.7.73	178/75	HT	60.66	60.85 -99
* Pintusevich-Block	Zhanna	UKR	6.7.72	164/62	100	10.93	10.85, 10.6 -97
					200	22.66	22.17A, 22.32 -97
* Pittman	Jana	AUS	9.11.82	177/62	400	51.76A	51.80 -99
					400H	55.20A, 55.63	56.23 -99
* Plätzer	Kjersti	NOR	18.1.72	176/57	20kW	1:27:53	1:28:35 -99
Poelman	Jacqueline	NED	5.10.73	171/63	200	23.20	23.17 -94
Poetschka	Lauren	AUS	22.10.74	172/57	400H	55.37	56.06 -94
Pogroszewska	Agnieszka	POL	20.2.77	170/75	HT	65.26	62.17 -98
Poissonnier	Marie	FRA	4.5.79	166/58	PV	4.35	4.30 -99
* Polyakova	Olga	RUS	23.9.80	168/50	20kW	1:25:20	1:29:09 -99
^ Pomacu	Cristina	ROM	15.9.73	164/46	HMar	70:44	68:08 -99
Pompey	Aliann	GUY	0.0.70	166/66	100	52.21i	52.66 -99
Pop	Olimpia	ROM	25.2.76	167/52	3kSt	10:02.60	10:09.83 -99
Porter	Shanelle	USA	20.1.72	178/66	400	51.21	50.67 -96
Pospelova ¶	Svetlana	RUS	24.12.79	170/60	200	22.80	23.82 -99
					400	50.47	52.58 -99
Pospisilová	Vera	CZE	19.11.78	178/78	DT	58.28	58.17 -99
Potepa	Wioleta	POL	14.12.80	186/83	DT	58.14	56.47 -99
Powell	Suzy	USA	3.9.76	178/73	DT	65.30	65.22 -97
Powell	Tamika	USA	25.9.75	178/73	HT	64.25	64.26 -99

	Name		Nat	Born	Ht/Wt	Event	2000 Mark	Pre-2000 Best
	Power	Susie	AUS	26.3.75	176/53	3000	8:57.08	8:56.93 -94
						5000	15:27.07	15:23.18 -99
	Pöyry	Sini	FIN	3.2.80	183/80	HT	65.50	63.60 -99
^	Pozdnyakova	Tatyana	UKR	4.3.56	164/59	Mar	2:32:25	2:29:25 -98
^	Prandzheva ¶	Iva	BUL	15.2.72	175/63	LJ	6.92dq, 6.83	6.90i, 6.97w -99, 6.88 -95
						TJ	15.04	15.18 -95
	Price	Melissa	USA	20.9.77	160/50	PV	4.22i, 4.20b, 4.18	4.36 -98
						HT	64.94	64.94 -99
	Price	Stephanie	AUS	17.7.72	168/56	400H	56.03	56.83 -99
*	Price-Smith	Connie	USA	3.6.62	192/95	SP	19.18	19.60 -94
	Priemer	Manuela	GER	29.11.78	178/75	HT	65.61	66.30 -99
*	Privalova	Irina	RUS	22.11.68	175/66	400	51.63	49.89 -93
						400H	53.02	0
*	Prokhorova	Yelena	RUS	16.4.78	175/62	LJ	6.72	6.48 -99
			S			Hep	6765	6132 -99
	Prokofyeva	Irina	RUS	13.3.72		800	2:01.98	2:00.77 -99
*	Prokopcuka	Jelena	LAT	21.9.76	162/43	3000	8:46.97	9:05.87 -98
						5000	14:47.71	15:30.76 -98
						10000	31:27.86	33:29.04 -98
	Prokopek	Grazyna	POL	20.4.77	170/51	400	52.15	52.28 -99
	Prykhodko	Lyudmila	UKR	18.3.74	168/52	PV	4.10i	3.90i -99, 3.87 -98
	Pskit	Malgorzata	POL	25.5.76	172/56	400H	55.86	57.29 -97
	Ptikany	Mary	KEN	.78		Mar	2:32:04	
	Pukha	Irina	UKR	10.1.73	168/60	100	11.12	11.17 -96
	Pumper	Susanne	AUT	1.9.70	170/50	3000	8:47.04	9:10.52 -99
						5000	15:16.32	15:24.38 -99
	Puzanova	Yekaterina	RUS	1.1.79		800	2:01.86	2:05.44 -99
	Pyatykh	Anna	RUS	4.4.81	175/64	TJ	14.19	13.59 -99
*	Pyrek	Monika	POL	11.8.80	166/64	PV	4.40	4.21i, 4.16 -99
	Qian	Chunhua	CHN	11.2.79		SP	17.59	17.58 -99
	Qin	Lei	CHN	4.4.76		DT	57.53	61.02 -98
	Qin	Wangping	CHN	16.6.82	164/53	100	11.30	11.53 -99
						200	23.08	23.29, 23.28w -99
	Quackenbush	Kristen	USA	9.1.75		PV	4.12i	4.08 -99
	Quétier	Rakiya	FRA	12.9.67	165/50	10000	31:56.1	0
	Quintanal	Irache	ESP	18.9.78	170/70	SP	16.76i	16.21 -99
^	Quintero	Ioamnet	CUB	8.9.72	178/61	HJ	1.92	2.01i, 2.00 -93
	Raatjes	Wendi	USA	28.7.69	168/57	Hep	6041	6078 -96
	Racková	Vladimira	CZE	15.5.67	180/85	DT	63.72	63.92 -93
	Raczka	Elzbieta	POL	19.11.70	178/63	Hep	5943	6051 -99
*	Radcliffe	Paula	GBR	17.12.73	173/54	3000	8:28.85	8:27.40 -99
						5000	14:44.36	14:43.54 -99
						10000	30:26.97	30.27.13 -99
						HMar	67:07	69:37 -99
	Radecka	Zuzanna	POL	2.4.75	172/58	100	11.29	11.40 -99
						200	22.96	22.96 -99
^	Radtke	Katarzyna	POL	31.8.69	162/49	20kW	1:33:52	1:31:26 -99
	Ragozina	Tatyana	UKR	3.9.64	162/51	20kW	1:32:17	1:33:25 -91
*	Rahouli	Baya	ALG	27.7.79	176/58	TJ	14.30, 14.42w	14.64A, 14.30 -99
	Rajamäki	Susanna	FIN	19.9.79	176/60	Hep	6021	5785 -98
	Rajot	Céline	FRA	22.3.75	162/50	3kSt	10:04.85	0
	Rakotozafy	Rosa	MAD	12.11.77	165/55	100H	12.85	12.84 -99
*	Ramalalanirina	Nicole	FRA	5.3.72	164/57	100H	12.76	12.84 -99, 12.76w -98
	Ramanauskaité	Rita	LTU	22.2.70	174/72	JT	62.69	62.21 -99, 65.46# -96
	Ramesh	Bina	FRA	20.8.79	176/62	JT	57.03	52.22 -99, 61.66# -97
	Rani	Sunita	IND	4.12.79	158/45	800	2:02.15	2:06.99 -99
						1500	4:10.1	4:08.1 -99
*	Rantanen	Heli	FIN	26.2.70	174/69	JT	60.98	61.61 -99, 67.94# -96
	Rasmussen	Marie Bagger	DEN	1.11.72	178/65	PV	4.35	4.03i, 4.00 -98
*	Raspopova	Olga	RUS	27.12.78	175/56	800	1:56.85	2:03.88 -99
	Rauhala	Anna	FIN	26.3.75	180/93	SP	16.55	17.14i -97, 17.04 -99
	Razafijanahary	Lantosoa	MAD	13.5.81	165/52	400H	57.29, 57.2	58.61 -99
	Razaiarimalala	Cendrino	MAD	8.2.78		400H	57.3	57.74, 57.5 -99
	Recio	Teresa	ESP	7.7.63	154/45	5000	15:12.06	15:12.13 -99
						10000	31:44.3	31:43.80 -99
	Reed	Kylie	AUS	17.12.74		LJ	6.57	6.47 -99
	Reed	Niki	USA	1.4.80		PV	4.10i, 4.10	3.90 -99
	Reho	Tytti	FIN	5.8.77	165/55	800	2:01.39	2:01.27 -99
	Reid	Suziann	USA	14.1.77	168/64	400	51.41	50.74 -99
	Reilly	Sarah	IRL	3.7.73	165/56	200	23.12	23.20 -97

Name		Nat	Born	Ht/Wt	Event	2000 Mark	Pre-2000 Best
Ren	Ni	CHN	14.5.79		TJ	13.71	12.92 -99
* Ren	Ruiping	CHN	1.2.76	176/64	LJ	6.67	6.51 -96
					TJ	14.47	14.66 -97, 14.83Aw -95
* Ren	Xiujuan	CHN	14.9.74	160/56	Mar	2:25:32	2:27:13 -96
* Renders	Marleen	BEL	24.12.68	166/47	10000	31:03.60	31:51.21 -99
					HMar	69:35	69:29 -94
					Mar	2:23:43	2:23:58 -99
Rendin	Maria	SWE	28.7.82	172/55	PV	4.10i	3.86 -99
Retzke	Astrid	GER	13.7.73	175/60	Hep	6379	6254 -98
Reynolds	Julian	JAM	2.11.77	163/48	400	52.19	54.63 -95
Reynolds-Peebles	Natasha	USA	7.6.72	155/48	400H	56.39	56.90 -99
Rhines	Jennifer	USA	1.7.74	160/50	3000	8:50.72	9:01.16 -99
					5000	15:19.88	15:25.52 -99
					10000	31:58.34	32:29.67 -99
Ribac	Andreja	SLO	14.1.76		TJ	13.72w	13.16, 13.40w -94
* Ribeiro	Fernanda	POR	23.6.69	161/48	1500	4:08.83	4:05.97 -97
					3000	8:34.99	8:30.66 -99
					5000	15:01.49	14:36.45 -95
					10000	30:22.88	30:48.06 -98
					HMar	68:23	68:44 -99
* Richards	Sandie	JAM	6.11.68	170/61	400	50.42	49.79 -97
Richardson	Marcia	GBR	10.2.72	173/63	100	11.35, 11.29w	11.40, 11.36w -98
Richardson	Passion	USA	25.1.75	155/47	100	11.29, 11.19w	11.28 -97, 11.27w -99
Richardson	Kate	AUS	5.11.73	168/51	3000	8:58.43mx	8:48.48 -97
(Anderson)					5000	15:18.82	15:10.78 -97
^ Rieger	Silvia	GER	14.11.70	176/60	400H	56.21	54.22A -98, 54.27 -96
Rigaudo	Elisa	ITA	17.6.80	169/56	20kW	1:32:50	1:42:40 -99
Riley	Dawn	USA	17.11.73	180/64	100H	13.11A, 13,22, 13.04w	13.00 -96
Risk	Kylie	AUS	28.11.73	160/49	10000	32:25.21	31:51.71 -96
* Rivero	Xiomara	CUB	22.12.68	176/78	JT	62.92	62.46 -99, 67.06# -95
* Roba	Fatuma	ETH	18.12.73	170/48	HMar	70:16	69:43 -97
					Mar	2:26:27	2:23:21 -98
Robert-Michon	Melina	FRA	18.7.79	178/87	DT	63.19, 63.65dh	60.17 -99
Roberts	Sedell	JAM			400H	57.47	59.49 -99
Roberts	Trecia	THA	4.2.71	163/59	100H	12.96	12.73A -98, 12.83 -99
Rocco	Lara	ITA	20.12.75	164/58	400H	57.13	56.43 -98
Rocco	Tiziana	ITA	2.12.78	166/62	JT	56.88	54.22 -99, 57.27# -99
Rocha	Nora	MEX	18.12.67	168/56	5000	15:15.64	15:06.54 -98
					10000	32:08.82	32:20.60 -97
Rockmeier	Birgit	GER	29.11.73	173/62	200	23.07i	23.11 -97, 22.89i -98
					400	51.45	52.86 -99
Rodríguez	Dulce	MEX	14.8.72	157/54	5000	15:27.46	16:51.50 -99
Rodríguez	Natalia	ESP	2.6.79	164/49	1500	4:04.24	4:10.65 -99
Rodríguez	Rocio	ESP	23.5.77	150/45	1500	4:11.05	4:15.67 -98, 4:10.17i -99
* Rogachova	Lyudmila	RUS	30.10.66	170/57	800	2:00.52	1:56.82 -88
					1500	4:01.73	3:56.91 -92
* Rogova	Oksana	RUS	7.10.78	183/60	TJ	14.28i, 14.27	14.59, 14.65w -99
Rohl	Michelle	USA	12.11.65	150/41	20kW	1:31:51	1:33:17 -99
^ Rohländer-Fromm	Uta	GER	30.6.69	173/60	400	51.42	50.33 -98
Roles	Philippa	GBR	1.3.78	180/100	DT	57.04	60.00 -99
Rollison	Melissa	AUS	13.4.83	165/51	3kSt	10:10.73	10:15.77 -99
^ Romanova	Anna	RUS	9.3.68	182/88	SP	18.87i, 17.17	20.24 -93
* Rose	Dionne	JAM	7.11.69	169/57	100H	13.15, 12.93Aw	12.64 -96
* Roshchupkina	Natalya	RUS	13.1.78	182/70	HJ	1.91	1.85 -98
					Hep	6633	6370h -98
Rosikhina	Irina	RUS	11.5.75	175/65	400	50.76	51.34, 50.5 -98
Rosolen	Mara	ITA	27.7.65	175/80	SP	18.81	18.89i, 18.61 -97
					DT	56.80	55.72 -96
Ross	Chaniqua	USA	24.5.80	173/80	SP	16.48	16.03 -99
Ross-Schoer	Amy	USA	13.12.74	175/61	800	2:01.01	2:03.32 -99
Rosseyeva	Olga	RUS	1.8.81		1500	4:10.67	4:10.97 -99
^ Rosza-Urbanik	Maria	HUN	12.2.67	169/52	20kW	1:31:21	1:31:43 -99
Rublevskaya	Lyudmila	RUS	7.6.77	186/87	DT	57.89	60.04 -99
* Rublyova	Olga	RUS	28.10.74	175/65	LJ	6.90i, 6.89	6.90, 7.01w -95
					TJ	14.45i, 14.21	14.13i -99, 13.84 -92
* Rücker	Anja	GER	20.12.72	174/58	400	52.05, 51.99i	49.74 -99
^ Rudolph	Amy	USA	18.9.73	176/55	1500	4:06.02	4:08.19 -99
					3000	8:39.86	8:42.40 -96
					5000	15:11.16	14:46.04 -96
Ruicu	Otilia	ROM	20.8.78	172/52	400	51.85	51.50 -99

Name		Nat	Born	Ht/Wt	Event	2000 Mark	Pre-2000 Best
Rünne	Eha	EST	25.5.63	183/88	DT	56.49	63.18 -88
Runyan	Marla	USA	4.1.69	170/60	1500	4:06.14	4:05.27 -99
					3000	8:56.27#i	0
					5000	15:07.66	0
Rurak	Yelena	UKR	7.2.72	166/55	400	51.73	50.93 -96
Russell	Blake	USA	24.7.75		5000	15:21.37	15:44.11 -99
					10000	32:16.33	0
^ Russell	Gillian	JAM	28.9.73	169/57	100H	12.94	12.66 -98
Ryabinkina	Olga	RUS	24.9.76	186/81	SP	19.20	17.99 -99
Ryan	Rosemary	IRL	8.11.75	168/50	5000	15:17.57	16:07.84 -98
					10000	32:31.9	0
* Ryashkina	Nadezhda	RUS	22.1.67	160/47	20kW	1:28:06	1:27:30 -99
* Ryshich	Nastja	GER	19.9.77	170/58	PV	4.31	4.50i, 4.44 -99
Saarman	Sanna	FIN	14.5.81	168/58	Hep	5718	5537 -99
Sabri	Hanane	FRA	8.12.75	178/58	800	2:02.36	2:04.27 -98
* Sacramento	Carla	POR	10.12.71	168/53	800	2:00.22	1:58.94 -97
					1500	4:00.35	3:57.71 -98
					3000	8:52.74i	8:30.22 -99
* Sadova	Natalya	RUS	15.6.72	180/100	DT	67.33	70.02 -99
Saenz	Abigail	MEX	21.4.77	160/52	20kW	1:32:46	1:45:16 -99
Safarova	Irina	RUS	19.6.69		HMar	71:35	70:03 -96
Safronnikova	Natalya	BLR	28.2.73	174/60	100	11.35i	11.17 -99, 10.9 -98
					200	23.10	22.74 -99, 22.3 -98
Safronova	Larisa	RUS	6.1.80	164/52	20kW	1:30:41	1:31:45 -99
Safronova	Natalya	BLR	11.4.74	176/60	LJ	6.62	6.34 -98
					TJ	14.65	14.26 -98
Sagaydak	Svetlana	RUS	.70		400H	55.98	56.30, 56.2 -98
Sagonas	Sophie	GER	18.9.81		HJ	1.88i	1.85 -99
Sakagami	Kaori	JPN	12.5.74	159/51	100	11.29w	11.55 -97, 11.46w -96
Sakashita	Naomi	JPN	25.5.75	158/42	5000	15:28.99	15:46.32 -99
					10000	32:01.04	31:53.40 -96
					HMar	70:56	70:17 -97
Salazhenkova	Olga	RUS	.76		LJ	6.49	6.41, 6.44w -98
Sallins	Melinda	USA	30.6.73	178/64	400H	56.30A, 56.36	56.06 -97
Salnikova	Olga	RUS	19.6.71		400H	57.38	56.72 -99
Saltanovic	Kristina	LTU	20.2.75	162/53	20kW	1:32:48	1:33:03 -99
Salvarani	Claudia	ITA	8.3.75	170/55	800	2:01.40	2:01.23 -99
Sampaio	Helena	POR	9.10.73	159/46	10000	32:08.67	31:43.22 -99
					HMar	70:15	71:29 -98
					Mar	2:29:34	
Samuel	Heather	ANT	6.7.70	160/60	100	11.23	11.20 -93, 11.0w -99
Samusenkova	Natalya	RUS	12.2.79	164/61	HT	64.24	61.80 -99
* Sánchez	Guadalupe	MEX	3.1.77	160/53	20kW	1:30:49	1:34:50 -98
Sánchez	Maria Mar	ESP	25.12.79	170/60	PV	4.30	4.20i, 4.16 -99
Sánchez	Rosario	MEX	26.10.73		20kW	1:32:34	1:30:52 -99
^ Sandell	Annemari	FIN	2.1.77	170/50	HMar	69:58	70:04 -98
Santiago	Beatriz	ESP	28.10.68	160/50	5000	15:17.14	15:26.07 -98
					10000	32:12.6	32:59.05 -98
Santin	Frances	USA	27.7.80	175/57	400H	56.67	60.37 -99
dos Santos	Fabiane	BRA	30.5.76		800	2:01.70	2:03.16 -99
dos Santos	Luciana Alves	BRA	10.2.70	160/56	LJ	6.72	6.81A -99, 6.58, 6.61w -97
					TJ	14.01	13.90A -99
^ dos Santos	Sueli Pereira	BRA	8.1.65	165/63	JT	61.98A	58.16 -99, 65.96# -94
Satomura	Kei	JPN	31.1.79	153/41	HMar	71:42	75:11 -97
Sauer	Mary	USA	31.10.75		PV	4.47	4.15 -99
Savchuk	Valentina	UKR	19.1.75	157/49	20kW	1:29:06	1:32:49 -98
* Saville	Jane	AUS	5.11.74	164/53	20kW	1:28:56	1:31:58 -99
Sawyer	Adrien	USA	13.12.75	170/57	LJ	6.59, 6.63w	6.87 -99
* Saxby-Junna	Kerry	AUS	2.6.61	166/59	20kW	1:29:36	1:29:40 -88
* Sazanovich	Natalya	BLR	15.8.73	179/65	LJ	6.50	6.86 -96
					Hep	6527	6563 -96
Sazonova	Maya	KAZ	28.5.65	166/53	20kW	1:30:18	1:32:19 -99
Schäfer	Tina	GER	27.12.77	170/68	HT	64.80	61.10 -99
Scherwin	Christina	DEN	11.7.76	177/63	JT	59.06	53.61 -99
Schielke	Sina	GER	19.5.81	167/56	200	23.07	23.03 -99
Schmidt	Gesine	GER	26.6.71	184/65	400H	57.48	55.76 -94
Schott	Maren	GER	11.2.76		400H	56.02	58.88 -99
Schötz	Katja	GER	22.7.81	183/57	HJ	1.89	1.81 -99
Schulte	Sabine	GER	29.1.76	169/58	PV	4.30i, 4.30	4.25 -98
Schulte	Sofia	GER	8.4.76	178/58	LJ	6.72	6.67 -99

Name		Nat	Born	Ht/Wt	Event	2000 Mark	Pre-2000 Best
Schwartz	Jillian	USA	19.9.79		PV	4.10	3.56 -99
Scott	Catherine	JAM	27.8.73	174/61	400	51.65	51.80 -99
					400H	54.93	55.00 -98
Sechko	Lyudmila	RUS	27.11.74	180/80	SP	19.51	18.67 -97
Seeger	Melanie	GER	8.1.77	166/49	20kW	1:32:10	1:34:17 -99
Sekachova	Irina	UKR	21.7.76	165/72	HT	69.53	65.93 -99
Sellam	Aida	TUN	.77		JT	55.90	54.34 -99
Semyonova	Zinaida	RUS	19.3.62	150/42	Mar	2:28:46	2:21:49 -98
Senkina	Natalya	UZB	23.9.70		400H	57.29	
Serdyuk	Alina	BLR	22.1.75	175/68	JT	58.48	58.38 -99, 58.68# -96
Serrano	Paula	USA	28.12.76	163/	PV	4.27	4.14 -99
Seryogina	Viktoriya	RUS	22.5.73	170/60	HJ	1.97i, 1.93	1.98i, 1.96 -99, 1.97sq -98
Sesay	Ola	USA	30.5.79		LJ	6.47i, 6.53w	6.40 -99
* Seyerling	Heide	RSA	19.8.76	168/55	200	22.87A, 22.95, 22.59w	22.88A -99, 22.89 -98, 22.80w -94
					400	50.05	51.33A, 52.43 -99
Sharova	Natalya	RUS	4.10.72	165/61	400	52.07	51.40 -99
* Shaw	Lorraine	GBR	2.4.68	171/87	HT	67.44	67.10 -99
Shcherbina	Marina	UKR	5.1.68	180/67	Hep	5851	6192 -89
Shedova	Oksana	BLR	6.4.81		HJ	1.90	1.85 -99
^ Sheffield	LaTanya	USA	11.10.63	165/57	400H	56.83	54.36 -88
Shekhodanova	Natalya	RUS	29.12.71	169/55	100H	12.75	12.59 -96
* Shekhovtsova	Yelena	UKR	31.5.72	178/58	LJ	6.86	6.97 -96
Shemchishina	Maya	UKR	6.5.72	174/52	100H	12.88	13.03 -97, 12.8 -98
Shen	Shengfei	CHN	21.1.81	178/70	Hep	5839	6185 -97
Sherina	Svetlana	RUS	29.4.71		HT	60.88	61.52 -97
Shestok	Varvara	UKR	17.12.74	166/51	3kSt	10:05.12	
^ Shevchik	Tatyana	BLR	11.6.69	178/60	HJ	1.97	2.00 -93
Shevchuk	Anzhelika	UKR	23.2.69		100	11.34	11.24 -92
Shibano	Yayoi	JPN	10.3.75	170/65	JT	56.59	57.07 -99
* Shibui	Yoko	JPN	14.3.79	165/50	10000	31:48.89	32:43.02 -99
					HMar	69:31	71:14 -98
* Shikolenko	Tatyana	RUS	10.5.68	174/65	JT	67.20	66.37 -99, 67.84# -98
^ Shimizu	Michiko	JPN	22.9.70	164/45	5000	15:21.04	15:09.05 -96
Shinagawa	Akiko	JPN	16.5.77	164/47	HMar	71:33	71:44 -99
Shinkins	Karen	IRL	15.10.76	165/53	400	51.69	51.07 -99
* Shishigina	Olga	KAZ	23.12.68	162/57	100	11.13	11.24 -99
					100H	12.65	12.44, 12.41w -95
Shittu	Lutisha	USA	9.5.79	170/56	100H	13.13, 13.12w	13.48, 13.32w -98
Shiviryeva	Natalya	RUS	31.8.78	164/54	20kW	1:31:51	1:34:13 -99
Shoemake	Kyla	USA	6.6.77	175/62	100H	13.05	13.21, 13.19w -98
Sibilyeva	Tatyana	RUS	17.5.80	164/51	20kW	1:30:51	1:29:53 -98
Sidelil	Hareg	ETH	20.4.81	162/51	1500	4:07.02	4:09.78 -99
Sidorenko	Natalya	UKR	22.11.80	160/49	1500	4:10.14	4:15.91 -99
* Sidoti	Annarita	ITA	25.7.69	150/42	20kW	1:28:38	1:30:57 -97
Sievers	Sabine	GER	3.3.75	181/84	DT	58.90	62.23 -99
Siilats	Kart	EST	7.9.80	184/62	HJ	1.89	1.89 -99
Sildillia	Viviane	FRA	23.2.74	172/60	LJ	6.54w	5.92, 6.37w -99
^ Silhavá	Zdenka	CZE	15.6.54	178/85	SP	16.89	21.05 -83
					DT	61.02	74.56 -84
Silva	Vánia	POR	8.6.80		HT	62.14	57.53 -99
Simasotchi	Corinne	SUI	11.6.71	170/57	400	52.24	51.86 -96
* Simon	Lidia	ROM	4.9.73	157/44	HMar	68:34	68:51 -99
					Mar	2:22:54	2:23:24 -99
Simonsen	Anne Haaland	NOR	18.6.80	169/56	20kW	1:34:22	1:36:10 -99
Simpson	Pamela	USA	28.4.77	160/	LJ	6.69	6.40, 6.46w -99
Singh	Neelam J	IND	8.1.71	166/80	DT	63.02	60.28 -99
Sinirtas	Svetla	TUR	17.6.64	178/96	SP	18.25i, 17.54	20.91 -87
Sivushenko	Yulia	RUS	28.2.82		HJ	1.88	1.82 -99
* Skolimowska	Kamila	POL	4.11.82	180/88	HT	71.16	66.62 -99
Skujyté	Austra	LTU	12.8.79	188/75	Hep	6104	5724 -99
Skvortsova	Silviya	RUS	16.11.74		10000	32:32.47	
Slivka	Viktoriya	RUS	28.9.80	178/54	HJ	1.94i, 1.93	1.94 -99
Smith	Christi	USA	5.11.77		Hep	5932w, 5797	5773w, 5528 -99
Smith	Randi	USA	14.5.81	175/61	400H	57.07	58.86 -99
Smith	Susan	IRL	14.9.71	168/60	400H	55.42	54.31 -98
Smith	Trecia	JAM	5.11.75	185/66	LJ	6.62	6.72, 6.84w -97
					TJ	13.76, 13.92w	14.22 -97
Smolders	Anja	BEL	2.6.73	168/52	3000	8:58.49	8:57.14 -99
					5000	15:20.23, 15:18.04mx	15:40.12 -98

Name		Nat	Born	Ht/Wt	Event	2000 Mark	Pre-2000 Best
Snetkova	Anna	RUS	.80		Hep	5673	
^ Sobanska	Malgorzata	POL	25.4.69	165/50	Mar	2:27:52	2:27:30 -99
* Söderberg	Anna	SWE	11.6.73	177/82	DT	62.91	64.54 -99
Söderström	Petra	FIN	12.3.74	170/55	400H	56.07	55.01 -99
^ Sokova	Mariya	RUS	2.9.70	170/58	TJ	14.18	14.54i -95, 14.50 -99
Soley	Keyon	USA	8.9.79	168/57	LJ	6.52i, 6.50, 6.56w	6.39 -99, 6.57w -97
Sologub	Natalya	BLR	31.3.75	176/64	400	51.70	51.97 -99
Sommaggio	Silvia	ITA	20.11.69	170/53	3000	8:59.18i	8:50.30 -94
					10000	31:24.12	31:38.94 -97
Song	Aimin	CHN	15.3.78		DT	60.39	60.50 -99
Song	Feina	CHN	25.1.77	183/95	SP	18.68	18.45 -97
Song	Liqing	CHN	20.1.80	166/51	3000	8:53.92i	
					5000	15:18.62	14:45.71 -97
					10000	32:23.57	31:11.26 -97
Song	Ruiling	CHN	1.11.66		JT	56.28	57.50 -99, 62.12# -93
Song	Yinlang	CHN	14.9.75		400H	56.00	55.58 -97
Sonn	Caren	GER	18.1.68	169/55	100H	13.10, 13.03w	12.88 -97, 12.87Aw -98
* Sosimenko	Debbie	AUS	5.4.74	170/90	HT	67.95	67.16 -98, 67.40dh -99
Sosnowska	Aneta	POL	10.5.74	168/58	100H	13.17	13.17 -97, 13.10w -96
Sotnikova	Yuliya	RUS	18.11.70	170/60	400	50.73	51.06 -95
Spangler	Angela	USA	4.9.68	178/61	HJ	1.90i, 1.88	1.95 -94
Spencer	Keisha	JAM	16.2.78	176/61	LJ	6.61	6.23 -99, 6.31w -98
					TJ	14.06i, 13.97, 14.15w	13.61, 13.72w -99
Spotáková	Barbora	CZE	30.6.81	182/75	Hep	5873	5096 -99
Sprenger	Juliane	GER	22.3.77	164/52	100H	13.00	13.14 -99
Sprules	Lyn	GBR	11.9.75	175/93	HT	63.96	63.05 -99
Spuri	Patrizia	ITA	18.2.73	173/57	800	2:02.50	1:59.96 -98
Stadnyuk	Aleksandra	UKR	16.4.80	170/55	TJ	13.90	13.61 -99
Stáhl	Ágota	HUN	17.12.78	180/60	HJ	1.88i	1.87 -99
Staicu	Simona	HUN	5.5.71	164/48	HMar	70:11	70:17 -97
Stals	Sandra	BEL	5.6.75	170/55	800	1:59.09	1:58.31 -98
Stankevich	Yekaterina	BLR	5.6.77		100	11.36	11.56 -99
* Stankina	Irina	RUS	25.3.77	165/50	20kW	1:25:29	1:29:00 -99
Starovoytova	Lyudmila	BLR	8.4.74		SP	16.46	15.12 -97
					DT	62.42	60.71 -99
Stavchanskaya	Yevgeniya	UKR	25.9.81	163/50	TJ	13.91i	14.18i, 13.77 -99
Stavskaya	Svetlana	KGZ	9.5.77	180/60	HJ	1.87	1.86 -99
^ Steigauf	Mona	GER	17.1.70	178/69	Hep	5747	6546 -97
Steyn	Nicolize	RSA	28.5.81	169/58	HJ	1.90	1.86 -99
Stoian	Monica	ROM	25.8.82		JT	55.65	51.25 -99
Stone	Felicia	USA	10.8.77		100H	13.21	13.55 -99
* Stone	Joanna	AUS	4.10.72	173/66	JT	64.62	69.85# -98
Stoop	Martina	SUI	1.1.73	168/55	400H	57.24	55.80 -96
Storga	Evfemija	SLO	7.10.75	168/68	JT	61.14	59.33 -99, 61.01# -98
^ Storp	Stephanie	GER	28.11.68	194/95	SP	17.67i	20.34 -90
Strömmer	Mia	FIN	26.2.74	170/70	HT	66.37	62.07 -99
Strutz	Martina	GER	4.11.81	160/53	PV	4.20	4.10 -99
Stucan	Constanta	ROM	12.7.81	174/60	TJ	13.96	13.41 -98
* Sturrup	Chandra	BAH	12.9.71	159/52	100	10.86	10.95 -98, 10.94w -99
					200	22.57	22.33 -96
					LJ	6.70	6.52 -99, 6.80w -95
^ Styopina	Viktoriya	UKR	21.2.76	175/58	HJ	1.96	1.96 -99
Su	Yiping	CHN	4.8.79		100H	12.99, 12.97w	12.91 -99
* Sua	Seilala	USA	25.2.78	188/109	SP	17.36	17.65 -99
					DT	65.90	64.89 -99
* Sudak	Svetlana	BLR	20.3.71	174/90	HT	67.15	68.21 -99
Sudarikova	Tatyana	KGZ	28.5.73	187/89	JT	57.28	51.62 -99
^ Sui	Xinmei	CHN	29.1.65	172/90	SP	18.24	21.66 -90
^ Suldesová	Andrea	CZE	11.2.75	164/51	1500	4:10.28	4:06.13 -98
Suleymanova	Dina	RUS	26.7.79	162/52	20kW	1:34:42	1:42:44 -99
^ Sun	Caiyun	CHN	21.7.73	173/57	PV	4.20	4.28i, 4.25 -96
Sun	Chunfang	CHN	1.3.77		20kW	1:29:45	1:30:37 -95
Sun	Yingjie	CHN	19.1.79	164/52	Mar	2:26:36	2:25:45 -98
Sürekli	Tezeta	TUR	8.4.80		3000	8:59.28	9:08.09 -99
* Suttle	Kellie	USA	9.3.73	170/59	PV	4.53	4.46i, 4.35 -99
Suvorova	Irina	RUS	3.3.71		Mar	2:29:43	2:34:30 -98
Suzuki	Aya	JPN	18.11.67	168/75	HT	61.32	61.33 -99
Svensson	Frida	SWE	5.1.70	167/56	400H	56.94	55.36 -91
* Szabo	Gabriela	ROM	14.11.75	158/43	1500	4:00.73	3:56.97 -98
					1M	4:23.90i	4:19.30 -98

Name		Nat	Born	Ht/Wt	Event	2000 Mark	Pre-2000 Best
Szabo *cont*					3000	8:26.35	8:24.31 -98
					5000	14:40.61	14:31.48 -98
* Szabó	Nikolett	HUN	3.3.80	168/65	JT	61.23	61.79 -99, 65.10# -98
Szabó	Zsuzsanna	HUN	6.5.73	176/63	PV	4.22i, 4.20	4.51i, 4.40 -99
Szczepanska	Magdalena	POL	25.1.80	176/58	Hep	5671	5619 -99
Szebenszky	Anikó	HUN	12.8.65	169/58	20kW	1:30:31	1:32:08 -99
* Szekely	Violeta	ROM	26.3.65	167/52	800	2:00.81i	1:58.57 -98
					1500	3:58.29	3:59.31 -99
Szekeres ¶	Judit	HUN	18.11.66	168/55	400H	55.96dq	54.02A -98
Szemerédi	Eszter	HUN	12.2.76	177/62	PV	4.10	4.33i, 4.22 -98
* Takahashi	Chiemi	JPN	16.2.76	160/43	5000	15:29.32	15:22.64 -99
					10000	31:52.59	31:27.57 -98
* Takahashi	Naoko	JPN	6.5.72	161/52	HMar	68:55	70:35 -97
					Mar	2:22:19	2:21:47 -98
Takakura	Yuko	JPN	1.6.78	159/43	HMar	70:42	72:04 -99
Takemoto	Kumiko	JPN	25.11.78	167/47	10000	31:54.56	32:10.68 -99
Talpos	Luminita	ROM	9.10.72	164/47	HMar	71:32	70:33 -99
Tamamushi	Tomoko	JPN	26.8.77	155/44	HMar	69:50	72:13 -99
Tamburini	Anna	ITA	6.1.73	165/67	PV	4.10	4.05 -98
Tamura	Ikuko	JPN	24.9.78	155/41	5000	15:24.9	15:37.5 -99
Tanabe	Kaori	JPN	30.4.75		HMar	71:44	73:57 -99
Tanaka	Megumi	JPN	4.9.75	162/46	5000	15:26.36	15:17.92 -99
					10000	32:13.03	31:53.35 -98
Tanaka	Naoko	JPN	23.3.77	160/42	HMar	69:53	71:27 -96
Tang	Yinghua	CHN	18.5.73		20kW	1:30:36	1:37:08 -94
Tang	Zhimin	CHN	26.6.79		TJ	13.83	13.81 -99
Tao	Hongbio	CHN	20.9.79		DT	58.14	60.83 -99
Taranova	Yuliya	RUS	15.2.77	172/59	800	2:01.28	1:59.63 -99
Tarasova	Anna	KAZ	23.3.80	176/62	LJ	6.68A	6.49 -99
					TJ	14.17A, 13.59	13.85 -98
Tas	Aysel	TUR	21.10.64		JT	56.90	52.21 -99, 61.13# -98
Taye	Yimenashu	ETH	.79	162/45	1500	4:10.51	4:11.97 -98
					3000	8:39.06	8:54.79 -98
					5000	15:08.82	15:46.70 -99
Taylor	Brenda	USA	9.2.79		400H	56.64	57.29 -99
Taylor	Monifa	USA	3.3.71	168/60	100H	13.03	12.80 -92
Tecuta	Alina	ROM	10.11.71	166/47	10000	32:14.18	31:48.28 -99
(-Gherasim)					HMar	71:28	69:10 -99
					Mar	2:28:17	2:28:37 -98
Teichmann	Ivonne	GER	11.4.77	167/45	800	1:59.20	2:02.58 -99
Tenorio	Martha	ECU	6.8.66	152/42	Mar	2:31:49	2:27:58 -99
Teppe	Agnès	FRA	4.5.68	182/78	DT	59.73	60.14 -92
^ Teppe	Nathalie	FRA	22.5.72	183/61	Hep	6235	6396 -94
Ter-Mesrobian	Tatyana	RUS	12.5.68	180/62	LJ	6.79i, 6.76	6.94 -98
* Tereshchuk	Tatyana	UKR	11.10.69	176/61	400H	53.98	53.40 -98
Termure	Ana Mirela	ROM	13.1.75	175/66	JT	63.29	61.35 -99, 62.87# -99
Terzóglou	Iríni- Hrisovaládo	GRE	2.2.79	176/86	SP	16.88	14.98i -99, 14.92 -98
Tesner	Tanja	RSA	4.2.80	179/74	JT	55.83	50.60 -99
Teter	Nicole	USA	8.11.73	172/57	800	2:01.59	2:02.55 -96
* Thánou	Ekateriní	GRE	1.2.75	165/56	100	10.91, 10.84w	10.83, 10.77w -99
Thiam	Amy Mbacké	SEN	10.11.76	183/70	400	50.88	50.77 -99
Thompson	Bronwyn	AUS	29.1.78	177/68	LJ	6.56, 6.64w	6.04, 6.14w -94
Thompson	Clare	AUS	28.12.77	176/58	Hep	5958	5766 -99
Thompson	Tressa	USA	6.5.75	178/93	SP	18.42i, 17.31dq	19.44i, 18.88 -99
Thornton	SaDonna	USA	16.8.78	157/48	100	11.35, 11.30w	11.37 -98
Tian	Mei	CHN	27.11.71	161/50	Mar	2:30:07	2:28:15 -97
Tian	Xiue	CHN	4.10.71		SP	18.23	18.51 -93
* Tiedtke	Susen	GER	23.1.69	171/54	LJ	6.78	7.00, 7.19Aw -93
Tigau	Viorica	ROM	12.8.79	171/60	100H	13.16	13.71 -99
					LJ	6.85, 6.87w	6.41i -99, 6.30 -98
					Hep	6289	5720 -98
* Tilea	Felicia	ROM	29.9.67	169/70	JT	63.12	60.97 -99, 69.26# -96
Timbilil	Alice	KEN	16.6.83	155/45	10000	31:50.22	32:02.2 -99
Timofeyeva	Irina	RUS	5.4.70	156/48	10000	31:40.14	32:24.70 -97
					HMar	71:09	71:02 -99
					Mar	2:29:13	2:27:46 -99
* Tîrlea	Ionela	ROM	9.2.76	169/54	400	51.84	49.88 -99
					400H	54.35	53.25 -99
Titarenko	Liliya	UKR	17.2.78		JT	55.55	
Tkach	Anna	RUS	17.4.75		400	50.67	52.18, 50.9 -99

Name		Nat	Born	Ht/Wt	Event	2000 Mark	Pre-2000 Best
Tkalich	Tatyana	UKR	30.5.75	160/50	100	11.1	11.54 -99, 11.1 -98
Tolbert	Ryan	USA	16.6.76	174/66	400H	55.57	54.21 -97
Tolla	Abeba	ETH	3.6.77		HMar	68:48	72:42 -97
					Mar	2:29:54	2:35:43 -98
Tolson	Christina	USA	16.1.78		SP	17.34	16.98 -99
					HT	63.68	61.21 -99
Tolstaya	Svetlana	KAZ	9.8.71	168/52	20kW	1:30:44	1:31:46 -99
Tomashova	Tatyana	RUS	1.7.75	168/47	1500	4:04.80	4:13.50 -98
					3000	8:34.53	8:52.42 -99
					5000	14:53.00	15:26.67 -99
* Tomecková	Nikola	CZE	25.6.74	180/77	JT	64.19	60.92A -99, 64.50# -96
Torazzi	Monica	ITA	26.2.71	174/88	HT	60.84	60.20 -99
Torre	Analidia	POR	10.10.76		3kSt	10:12.57	
^ Torshina	Natalya	KAZ	4.10.68	172/57	400H	54.50	54.53 -93
Tosa	Reiko	JPN	11.6.76	166/51	10000	32:15.63	0
					Mar	2:24:36	2:54:47 -98
Toyonaga	Yoko	JPN	15.4.77	164/87	SP	16.46	16.10 -99
^ Trandenkova	Marina	RUS	7.1.67	171/61	100	11.17, 11.14w	11.06 -96, 10.8 -99
					200	22.90	22.44A -97, 22.47 -96
Tripathi	Vinitha	IND	15.10.80		200	23.04	23.59A -99
Trofimova	Natalya	RUS	17.1.75	164/55	20kW	1:34:32	1:32:09 -99
Trotter	Meshell	USA	2.9.78	186/107	HT	60.96	56.00 -99
Tsámoglou	Evdokiá	GRE	15.12.78		HT	63.20	59.50 -99
Tsander	Olga	BLR	18.5.76	174/83	HT	69.81	64.56 -99
* Tsikoúna	Stilianí	GRE	19.10.72	171/84	DT	65.13	65.00 -98
Tsiliggíri	Yeoryía	GRE	21.6.72	158/46	PV	4.20	4.25i -99, 4.01 -98
Tsiolakoúdi	Aggelikí	GRE	10.5.76	171/66	JT	60.26A	56.91 -99, 63.32# -97
^ Tsybulskaya	Valentina	BLR	19.2.68	163/54	20kW	1:30:19	1:29:20 -99
* Tsyganova	Natalya	RUS	7.2.71	162/50	800	1:56.60	1:57.15 -99
Tudja	Julianna	HUN	13.10.79	175/77	HT	61.42	61.11 -99
* Tullett	Hayley	GBR	17.2.73	166/55	800	2:01.25	2:02.18 -97, 2:01.52i -98
					1500	4:01.23	4:05.72 -99
					1M	4:26.50i	4:48.88 -95
					3000	8:45.39	9:14.5 -99
* Tulu	Derartu	ETH	21.3.72	155/45	3000	8:46.32	8:52.9 -96
					5000	14:44.57	14:50.88 -96
					10000	30:17.49	31:06.02 -92
					HMar	68:04	68:26 -95
					Mar	2:26:09	2:30:28 -97
Tunks	Teri	USA	30.10.75	187/86	SP	18.32	19.04i, 18.80 -99
Turayeva	Natalya	RUS	.82		HJ	1.89	1.85 -99
Turova	Alesya	BLR	6.12.79	180/64	1500	4:05.99	4:12.08 -99
					3000	8.44.81	9:22.96i -99
					5000	15:23.84	
Turpin	Sandra	POR	5.6.76		100H	13.22	13.45, 13.34w -98
Twum	Monica	GHA	14.3.78	149/58	100	11.35	11.47, 11.29w -99
					200	23.21	22.98A -99
^ Tyukhay	Irina	RUS	14.1.67	171/64	Hep	6352	6604 -95
* Tzelíli	Miréla	GRE	21.12.76	165/64	JT	67.51	67.09 -99
Ueno	Rie	JPN	11.6.76	163/49	HMar	69:57	76:52 -98
Ulyeva	Iolanta	KAZ	27.7.76	172/85	SP	17.82	16.60 -97
Umlauft	Katja	GER	22.11.74	180/	TJ	13.69	13.72 -99
Umnik	Marcela	SLO	11.9.76	177/65	LJ	6.54i	6.53 -96, 6.54w, 6.75ex -99
* Uppa	Taina	FIN	24.10.76	173/74	JT	64.06	63.63 -99, 66.00# -95
* Urbansky	Ulrike	GER	6.4.77	170/52	400H	54.57	54.67 -99
Urge	Getenesh	ETH	30.8.70	157/52	1500	4:10.75	4:12.38 -91
					3000	8:43.74	8:51.85 -99
					5000	15:22.44	15:27.59 -99
Vail	Jennifer	USA	16.3.78	173/	HT	62.26	58.89 -99
* Valant	Anja	SLO	8.9.77	183/66	TJ	14.69	14.29 -99
Valdonado	Laetetia	FRA	4.8.77	160/48	800	2:01.24	2:01.51 -99
^ Valmon	Meredith	USA	15.10.68	168/55	800	1:59.50	1:57.04 -96
Van Onna	Wilma	NED	13.6.65	163/48	HMar	71:12	70:59 -92
Van de Bilt	Erika	NED	7.4.71		3000	8:57.84	9:14.2 -98
					5000	15:23.27	15:53.1mx -99
Vanakára	Asimína	GRE	14.7.79	173/56	Hep	5927	5258w -99
Varga	Judit	HUN	16.4.76	169/49	800	2:01.64	2:01.18 -98
Vasallo	Aldenay	CUB	25.2.77	170/73	HT	63.70	63.68 -99
* Vasco	Maria	ESP	26.12.75	156/47	20kW	1:30:20	1:32:38 -99

Name		Nat	Born	Ht/Wt	Event	2000 Mark	Pre-2000 Best
* Vasdéki	Ólga	GRE	26.9.73	174/59	TJ	14.26	14.67 -99
Vasilevskaya	Lidiya	RUS	1.4.73	163/48	10000	32:02.86	32:12.53 -97
					HMar	70:23	72:20 -98
Vasilyeva	Irina	RUS	.79		TJ	14.11	13.99 -99
Vasilyeva	Lyudmila	RUS	20.10.69	170/54	1500	4:05.07	4:11.01 -94
					1M	4:31.62	4:42.39i -93
* Vaszi	Tünde	HUN	18.4.72	172/58	LJ	6.70	6.82i -99, 6.77 -98, 6.82Aw -96
^ Vaughn	Angie	USA	4.11.76	170/64	100H	12.83	12.63 -98
Veldáková	Dana	SVK	3.6.81	178/59	TJ	13.92	13.13, 13.19w -99
Velichko	Oksana	UKR	26.3.75	172/69	JT	62.02	58.12 -99, 59.02# -99
Veltman/Miller	Marieke	USA	18.9.71	170/60	LJ	6.66	6.88 -96, 7.14Aw -95
* Veneva	Venelina	BUL	13.6.74	179/61	HJ	2.01	2.03 -98
Verlan	Vasilisa	RUS	.78		Hep	5644	5542h -98
^ Vershinina	Viktoriya	UKR	11.6.71	177/60	LJ	6.84	6.92 -96, 6.98ex -95
* Viceconte	Maura	ITA	3.10.67	155/47	5000	15:18.80	15:45.92 -98
					10000	31:05.57	32:05.44 -99
					HMar	70:48	70:54 -97
					Mar	2:23:47	2:28:16 -97
Vieu	Fanny	FRA	19.4.78	164/55	PV	4.10	3.95 -98
Vigourt	Julie	FRA	19.10.79	162/50	PV	4.15	4.02 -96
Vilisova	Maria	RUS	.69		3kSt	10:12.07	
Vindyuk	Alena	RUS	.74		Hep	5739	
Vis	Judith	NED	21.6.80	183/72	Hep	5743	5713 -99
Visockaite	Agné	LTU	4.8.78	172/63	100	11.35	11.42 -97
* Vizaniari	Lisa-Marie	AUS	14.2.71	174/100	DT	65.35	65.86 -97
Vlasic	Blanka	CRO	8.11.83	188/65	HJ	1.93	1.80 -99
* Vóggoli	Ekateríni	GRE	30.10.70	175/89	DT	64.35	64.82 -99
Volkova	Yekaterina	RUS	.78		3kSt	9:52.40	10:04.46 -99
Vontein	Barbara	GER	7.6.78	182/60	JT	56.45	54.64 -99
^ Voronova	Natalya	RUS	9.7.65	169/63	100	11.11	10.98 -98
					200	22.81	22.35 -93
* Vostrikova	Irina	RUS	30.8.70	178/68	Hep	6271	6390 -97
Voyevodina	Yuliya	RUS	17.10.71	169/56	20kW	1:29:39	1:30:07 -99
Vrbenská	Lucie	CZE	12.5.77	180/85	HT	62.62	57.89 -99
* Vriesde	Letitia	SUR	5.10.64	159/55	800	1:58.62	1:56.68 -95
Walker	Astia	JAM	4.4.75	180/60	100	11.33	11.44 -94, 11.4w -93
					200	22.79	22.69 -97
					100H	12.82	12.82 -97
Walker	Charmaine	USA	5.5.78	173/63	100H	13.13, 13.01w	13.15 -98
Walker	Melanie	JAM	1.1.83	165/53	400H	56.96	58.99 -99
Walker	Shakeema	USA	10.11.76		TJ	13.74	13.50 -99
* Waller	Tisha	USA	1.12.70	183/59	HJ	1.96i, 1.94	2.01i -98, 2.00 -99
Walter	Doreen	GER	1.2.76	176/58	1500	4:10.80	4:10.88 -99
Walter	Sarah	FRA	5.5.78	173/64	JT	57.03	59.02 -99
* Wami	Getenesh	ETH	11.12.74	153/44	3000	8:36.92	8:29.24 -98
					5000	14:30.88	14:36.08 -98
					10000	30:22.48	20:24.56 -99
Wamuyu	Gladys	KEN	23.12.72	167/63	800	2:00.32	2:00.0 -93
Wang	Chunmei	CHN	10.4.76	165/50	1500	4:11.18	3:59.48 -97
					3000	8:50.68i	8:53.44i -99
Wang	Dan	CHN	.82		HT	60.69	
Wang	Hailian	CHN	6.4.76		Hep	5748	5808 -99
* Wang	Liping	CHN	8.7.76	165/48	20kW	1:28:33	1:29:26 -95
Wang	Pingping	CHN	27.2.79		DT	57.02	53.25 -99
* Wang	Yan	CHN	2.5.71	170/52	20kW	1:28:27	1:28:54 -95
Wang	Yaning	CHN	4.1.80		JT	57.81	61.99 -99, 64.52#dq -97
Wang	Yanrong	CHN	16.10.76	155/43	Mar	2:30:23	2:28:41 -97
Wang	Yawen	CHN	23.8.73	187/90	SP	18.32	19.89 -93
Wang	Yuanping	CHN	8.12.76		800	2:00.63	2:00.76 -97
Wang	Zhuri	CHN	4.9.80		TJ	13.73	14.10 -97
* Wanjiru	Esther	KEN	27.3.77	162/48	5000	15:27.46	15:16.42 -99
					HMar	67:41	66:49 -99
					Mar	2:23:31	2:25:40 -99
Warlick	Alicia	USA	11.10.77		PV	4.35	3.85 -98
Warren	Youlanda	USA	13.3.72	160/50	400	51.35	50.90 -96
Washington	Demetria	USA	31.12.79	178/65	400	51.71	52.57 -99
Wassiluk	Petra	GER	27.10.69	167/50	10000	31:52.2	32:03.60 -97
Webb	Cheryl	AUS	3.10.76		20kW	1:34:25	1:39:46 -99
Wei	Jianhua	CHN	23.3.79	170/68	JT	63.92	62.97 -99, 66.64# -97

	Name		Nat	Born	Ht/Wt	Event	2000 Mark	Pre-2000 Best
	Wei	Yanan	CHN	6.12.81	162/49	Mar	2:26:34	0
	Wentland	Gwen	USA	29.4.72	178/64	HJ	1.93i, 1.88	1.96i, 1.94 -95
*	Weyermann	Anita	SUI	8.12.77	162/50	1500	4:05.38	3:58.20 -98
	Wheeler	Kara	USA	9.7.78		3000	8:54.82	9:16.53 -99
						5000	15:28.78	16:57.31 -99
	Whipple	Erica	USA	4.12.82		100	11.32	11.51 -98, 11.0 -99
	White	Kelli	USA	1.4.77	163/57	100	11.19	11.20, 10.96w -99
						200	23.08, 22.94w	22.58 -98, 22.49w -99
	White	LaKeesha	USA	29.7.80	168/57	100	11.36, 11.22	11.39, 11.34w -99
						200	22.74w	23.22 -99
	Whitlock	Janine	GBR	11.8.73	165/54	PV	4.35	4.31 -98
	Wiegelmann	Christine	GER	18.7.74		JT	56.44	50.07 -99
	Wielgus	Anna	POL	27.10.81	170/60	PV	4.10	4.00 -98
	Wigene	Susanne	NOR	12.2.78		3kSt	10:01.54	0
	Wigington	Lynette	USA	15.3.78		LJ	6.57w	6.37 -97
	Wijenberg	Nadezhda	NED	2.4.64	165/49	HMar	71:39	68:58 -94
						Mar	2:32:20	2:28:45 -99
	Wildrick	Andrea	USA	23.12.79		PV	4.10	3.35 -99
	Wilkins	Melanie	GBR	18.1.73	178/61	100H	13.17	13.34, 13.1 -95, 13.23w -96
	Wilkinson (Young)	Sarah	GBR	2.1.70	160/49	3000	8:57.75mx	9:04.27 -98
	Williams	Aleah	USA	7.1.81	172/64	100	11.36, 11.25w	11.70 -97, 11.49w -99
						200	22.81w	23.42 -99
	Williams	Althea	CAN	4.1.75		TJ	13.78A, 13.73	13.31A -99
*	Williams	Angela	USA	30.1.80	156/52	100	11.12, 11.1, 11.01w	11.04, 10.96w -99
						200	22.78w	23.02, 22.89w -98
	Williams	Foy	CAN	27.9.73	168/54	400	51.62A, 52.00	51.66A -99, 52.19 -98
*	Williams	Shana	USA	7.4.72	178/58	LJ	6.80, 6.87w	7.01 -96
	Williams	Tasha	NZL	31.7.73	174/72	HT	64.60	62.84 -99
	Williamson	Ellakisha	USA	19.3.75	160/59	100H	12.81	12.92 -99
	Willis	Benita	AUS	6.5.79	165/53	1500	4:07.05	4:13.69 -99
						5000	15:21.37	16:11.57 -97
	Wilson	Linetta	USA	11.10.67	165/65	400	52.26	51.02 -86
^	Wise	Joanne	GBR	15.3.71	165/56	LJ	6.59	6.76 -99
	Wisniewska	Joanna	POL	24.5.72	178/82	DT	63.94	63.97 -99
	Witter	Erica	CAN	10.12.76	180/65	200	23.09Aw	23.45, 23.43w -96
^	Witteveen	Solange	ARG	6.2.76	171/59	HJ	1.94i, 1.93	1.96 -97
	Wittrin	Caroline	CAN	10.12.68	175/84	HT	62.28	63.47 -99
*	Wlodarczyk	Urszula	POL	22.12.65	180/66	Hep	6470	6542 -97
	Wolowiec	Simone	AUS	12.2.74	182/70	20kW	1:34:44	1:35:14 -98
*	Worku	Ayelech	ETH	12.6.79	165/47	3000	8:44.28	8:39.51 -99
						5000	14:41.23	14:44.22 -99
	Woytkowska	Jana	GER	7.8.77		JT	57.22	58.35 -99
	Wrappah	Hellena	GHA	9.12.73	170/69	200	23.21	23.9 -99
	Wu	Jianfang	CHN	1.7.79		JT	56.05	55.33 -99
	Wu	Lingmei	CHN	16.2.73	168/60	TJ	14.01i, 13.99	14.39 -98, 14.55w -99
	Wurm	Karin	GER	6.2.78		SP	16.88i, 16.34	16.11 -97
	Wüstenhagen	Carmen	GER	15.8.73	175/58	1500	4:11.14, 4:10.65i	4:06.7 -99
*	Wyludda	Ilke	GER	28.3.69	183/91	DT	65.76	74.56 -89
	Wysocka	Marzena	POL	17.2.69	176/80	DT	60.22	63.20 -99
*	Xánthou	Niki	GRE	11.10.73	174/56	LJ	6.81	7.03 -97, 712Aw -95
	Xiao	Yanling	CHN	27.3.68	180/92	DT	60.81	71.68 -92
	Xu	Aihui	CHN	25.4.78	167/54	20kW	1:32:07	1:32:24 -95
	Xue	Ailing	CHN	12.2.79	173/52	20kW	1:31:45	1:33:10 -99
	Yadav Kumar	Sugan	IND	.77		DT	56.72	54.70 -98
*	Yamaguchi	Eri	JPN	14.1.73	163/47	10000	32:07.25	32:07.26 -99
						HMar	71:45	69:31 -99
						Mar	2:27:03	2:22:19 -99
	Yamanouchi	Mineko	JPN	10.12.72	161/45	Mar	2:28:51	2:28:52 -99
	Yang	Meiping	CHN	23.10.85		HT	61.44	59.26 –99
	Yang	Wenjing	CHN	26.9.79		20kW	1:34:08	
	Yarygina	Oksana	RUS	24.12.72	170/65	JT	56.35	58.80 -99, 64.62# -94
*	Yatchenko	Irina	BLR	31.10.65	187/96	DT	66.51	68.94 -92
	Yefremova	Antonina	UKR	19.7.81	176/58	400	51.95	54.85 -99
	Yegorova	Lyudmila	UKR	4.10.74	164/54	20kW	1:32:02	1:36:41 -97
*	Yegorova	Olga	RUS	28.3.72	160/48	1500	4:04.75	4:07.38 -99
						1M	4:25.54i	
						3000	8:53.76, 8:49.18i	8:33.02 -99
						5000	14:42.91	15:22.80 -99
^	Yegorova	Valentina	RUS	16.2.64	156/52	Mar	2:26:26	2:23:33 -94

	Name		Nat	Born	Ht/Wt	Event	2000 Mark	Pre-2000 Best
*	Yelesina	Yelena	RUS	4.4.70	182/62	HJ	2.01	2.02 -90
	Yermolayeva	Irina	RUS	.79		LJ	6.56	6.36 -99
	Yershova	Olga	RUS	13.8.76		TJ	14.47	14.25 -99
	Yesipchuk	Oksana	RUS	13.12.76	183/95	DT	63.68	61.59 -98
	Yevdokimova	Natalya	RUS	17.3.78	178/65	800	2:01.51	2:04.61 -95
						1500	4:09.19	4:20.28 -97
	Yi	Chunmei	CHN	15.3.83		JT	55.96	51.09 -99, 54.62# -98
^	Yin	Lili	CHN	11.11.79	168/60	1500	4:07.25	3:53.91 -97
						3000	8:41.05	8:57.09 -98
						5000	15:06.30	14:39.96 -97
	Yordanova	Anelia	BUL	27.4.72	174/74	HT	65.35	65.11 -99
	Yordanova	Daniela	BUL	8.3.76	165/50	1500	4:03.83	4:11.93 -99
						5000	14:56.95	16:07.28 -99
	Yoshimatsu	Hisae	JPN	13.5.79	163/46	HMar	70:33	0
	Yu	Jing	CHN	7.3.83		SP	16.75	16.72 -98
	Yu	Juan	CHN	29.3.75	175/85	SP	18.62	19.13 -95
	Yu	Xin	CHN	23.2.77	188/90	SP	19.32	19.16 -97
						DT	64.90	63.80 -96
	Yuan	Yufang	MAS	1.2.76	164/53	20kW	1:34:19	1:34:13 -99
^	Yusuf	Fatima	NGR	2.5.71	180/64	200	22.90	22.28 -99
	Yvelain	Fatima	FRA	31.12.69	165/52	1500	4:08.42	4:31.62 -98, 4:28.22i -99
						3000	8:43.53	8:55.32 -99
						5000	15:13.07	14:58.18 -99
						10000	31:43.29	33:48.69 -96
*	Zabawska	Krystyna	POL	14.1.68	183/92	SP	19.18	19.42 -96
	Zabruskova	Valeriya	RUS	29.7.75		JT	60.49	62.04 -99
	Zachery	Tami	USA	27.11.78	165/	100	11.34w	11.83, 11.62w -98
	Zadorozhnaya	Yelena	RUS	3.12.77	162/48	1500	4:03.32	4:09.03 -99
						3000	8:51.2	9:15.0 -98
	Zagacka	Liliana	POL	28.1.77	168/56	LJ	6.54	6.31 -97
						TJ	13.96	13.81 -99
	Zaginay	Yuliya	RUS	3.8.63		SP	18.73	19.06 -99
	Zaituc	Luminita	GER	9.10.68	163/47	1500	4:09.08	4:06.33 -98
	Zakharchuk	Oksana	UKR	3.4.80	178/78	SP	16.56	16.22 -97
	Zakharova	Svetlana	RUS	15.9.70		Mar	2:28:11	2:27:08 -99
	Zakowicz	Katarzyna	POL	12.5.75	184/94	SP	19.28	18.77 -98
*	Zalevskaya	Svetlana	KAZ	14.6.73	188/63	HJ	1.97	1.98i, 1.97 -96
	Zamboni	Nathalie	SUI	23.12.73		400H	56.89	57.79 -99
	Zauna	Irena	LAT	16.3.81	179/69	400H	56.40	61.5 -99
	Zelinka	Jessica	CAN	3.9.81		Hep	5688	
	Zhang	Guirong	CHN	.78		SP	17.45	
	Zhang	Li	CHN	19.10.78		JT	60.02	58.55 -99
	Zhang	Ling	CHN	13.4.80		1500	4:08.03	3:54.52 -97
	Zhang	Liuhong	CHN	16.1.69	181/86	SP	18.85	20.54 -94
	Zhang	Liwen	CHN	29.1.73	173/56	HJ	1.88	1.94 -86
	Zhang	Na	CHN	27.9.80		PV	4.10	3.80 -99
	Zhang	Peipei	CHN			SP	17.70	
	Zhang	Shujing	CHN	13.9.79	158/55	Mar	2:27:14	2:32:19 -99
	Zhang	Xiaoyu	CHN			SP	17.33	15.46 -99
	Zhang	Zhiying	CHN	19.7.73	174/80	SP	17.53	19.77 -93
	Zhao	Fan	CHN	1.3.78		LJ	6.49	6.18 -97
	Zhao	Hanjun	CHN	.8.80		TJ	13.68	13.19 -97
	Zhao	Larisa	RUS	4.2.71		800	2:02.36	2:01.33 -93
	Zhao	Wei	CHN	27.1.79	185/95	HT	65.70	63.20 -99
	Zhdanova (Sultanova)	Firiya	RUS	29.4.61	166/52	Mar	2:32:21	2:30:45 -99
	Zheng	Guixia	CHN	24.6.73	160/52	HMar	69:25	74:19 -97
	Zhevnova	Tatyana	BLR	17.10.77	173/60	Hep	5793	5871 -97
^	Zhilyayeva	Alla	RUS	5.2.69	163/47	Mar	2:28:27	2:27:38 -95
	Zhong	Mei	CHN	7.1.78		LJ	6.62	6.76 -97
	Zhou	Yangxia	CHN	10.2.83	167/58	LJ	6.57	6.29 -99
						TJ	10.70	13.26 00
	Zhukovskaya	Irina	RUS	.78		HJ	1.88	1.82i -95
^	Zilinskiené	Nele	LTU	29.12.69	176/58	HJ	1.93	1.96 -94
	Zipse (Veith)	Manuela	GER	11.5.74	167/51	Mar	2:31:37	2:30:58 -98
	Zozulya	Vera	UKR	31.8.70	166/56	20kW	1:31:26	1:35:26 -97
*	Zvereva	Ellina	BLR	16.11.60	186/96	DT	68.40	71.58 -88
	Zykina	Olesya	RUS	7.10.80	166/56	200	22.78	23.98 -98, 23.47i, 22.3 -99
						400	50.36	51.31, 50.8 -98

WORLD INDOOR LISTS 2001 - MEN

50 METRES

5.63+	Freddy	Mayola	CUB	1.11.77	1		Madrid	14 Mar
5.64	Jeff	Laynes	USA	3.10.70				20 Jan
5.65+	Deji	Aliu	NGR	22.11.75				25 Feb

55m: 6.10 Leonard Scott USA 19.1.80 16 Feb
6.12 Ja'Warren Hooker USA 24.9.78 20 Jan

60 METRES

6.39	Maurice	Greene	USA	23.7.74	1s1	NC	Atlanta	3 Mar
6.44	Tim	Harden	USA	27.1.74	1	WI	Lisboa	11 Mar
6.45A	Terrence	Trammell	USA	23.11.78	1		Pocatello	17 Feb
	6.51				1		Boston (R)	4 Feb
6.46	Tim	Montgomery	USA	28.1.75	2	WI	Lisboa	11 Mar
6.48	Leonard	Scott	USA	19.1.80	1h1	SEC	Lexington	24 Feb
6.51A	Ja'Warren	Hooker	USA	24.9.78	1		Flagstaff	24 Feb
6.51	Mark	Lewis-Francis	GBR	4.9.82	3	WI	Lisboa	11 Mar
6.54	Deji	Aliu	NGR	22.11.75	2	Euro	Gent	23 Feb
6.55	Coby	Miller	USA	19.10.76	1	Euro	Birmingham	18 Feb
6.55	Greg	Saddler	USA	29.6.74	3	Euro	Gent	23 Feb
6.55	Aggelos	Pavlakakis	GRE	7.11.76	1	NC	Pireás	24 Feb
6.55	Freddy	Mayola	CUB	1.11.77	4	WI	Lisboa	11 Mar
6.55	Matt	Shirvington	AUS	25.10.78	5	WI	Lisboa	11 Mar

6.57A	Robert	Spies	USA		27 Jan
6.57	Yeóryios	Theodorídis	GRE	12.12.72	21 Feb
6.57	Leonard	Myles-Mills	GHA	9.5.73	23 Feb
6.57	Brian	Lewis	USA	5.12.74	3 Mar
6.58	Venancio	José	ESP	19.4.76	24 Feb
6.58	Tim	Goebel	GER	4.3.82	25 Feb
6.58	Kim	Collins	SKN	5.4.76	9 Mar
6.59	Gennadiy	Chernoval	KAZ	6.6.76	1 Feb
6.59	Tuomas	Näsi	FIN	14.10.79	3 Mar
6.59	Bernard	Williams	USA	19.1.78	3 Mar
6.59	Jon	Drummond	USA	9.9.68	3 Mar

Drugs dq: 6.59 John Skeete GBR 8.9.78 27 Jan

200 METRES

20.31	Coby	Miller	USA	19.10.76	1	NC	Atlanta	3 Mar
20.44	Kevin	Little	USA	3.4.68	2	NC	Atlanta	3 Mar
20.45	Shawn	Crawford	USA	14.1.78	3	NC	Atlanta	3 Mar
20.46	Christian	Malcolm	GBR	3.6.79	1A	Euro	Liévin	25 Feb
20.55	Kim	Collins	SKN	5.4.76	1r2	NCAA	Fayetteville	9 Mar
20.56	Ja'Warren	Hooker	USA	24.9.78	2r2	NCAA	Fayetteville	9 Mar
20.60	Allyn	Condon	GBR	24.8.74	1		Birmingham	28 Jan
20.61	Leonard	Scott	USA	19.1.80	3r2	NCAA	Fayetteville	9 Mar
20.65	Justin	Gatlin	USA	10.2.82	4r2	NCAA	Fayetteville	9 Mar
20.68	Christopher	Williams	JAM	15.3.72	1r2		Pireás	21 Feb

20.69	Radek	Zachoval	CZE	6.7.78	12 Feb
20.73	Darvis	Patton	USA	4.12.77	9 Mar
20.74	Jimmie	Hackley	USA	11.9.75	2 Mar
20.77	Joseph	Batangdon	CMR	29.7.78	18 Feb
20.77	Patrick	van Balkom	NED	14.9.74	9 Mar
20.78	Timothy	Benjamin	GBR	2.5.82	24 Feb
20.79	Brandon	Evans	USA	30.10.79	24 Feb
20.81	Aaron	Armstrong	USA	14.10.77	9 Mar
20.84	Josephus	Howard	USA	14.4.78	9 Feb
20.84	Andrew	Pierce	USA	8.6.79	25 Feb
20.85	Bobby	Cruse	USA	20.3.78	9 Mar
20.86	Ramon	Clay	USA	29.6.75	2 Mar

Oversized track

20.47	Leonard	Scott	USA	19:1.80	1	SEC	Lexington	25 Feb
20.52	Justin	Gatlin	USA	10.2.82	1h4	SEC	Lexington	24 Feb

400 METRES

45.46	Andrew	Pierce	USA	8.6.79	1	Big10	University Park	25 Feb
45.61	Daniel	Caines	GBR	15.5.79	1A		Birmingham	18 Feb
45.78	Rickey	Harris	USA	29.9.81	1r2	NCAA	Fayetteville	10 Mar
45.79	James	Davis	USA	19.3.76	1h1	NC	Atlanta	2 Mar
46.03	Leonard	Byrd	USA	17.3.75	2h1	NC	Atlanta	2 Mar
46.03	Jerome	Young	USA	14.8.76	1h3	NC	Atlanta	2 Mar

46.09	Brandon	Couts	USA	17.2.79	24 Feb
46.19	Robert	Mackowiak	POL	13.5.70	9 Feb
46.20	Bayano	Kamani	USA	17.4.80	10 Mar
46.24	Mark	Hylton	GBR	24.9.76	28 Jan
46.25	Mitch	Potter	USA	16.9.80	9 Mar
46.27	Sunday	Bada	NGR	22.6.69	24 Feb
46.29	Davian	Clarke	JAM	30.4.76	4 Feb
46.31	Du'aine	Thorne-Ladejo	GBR	14.2.71	18 Feb
46.31	Alleyne	Francique	GRN	7.6.76	9 Mar
46.32	Milton	Campbell	USA	15.5.76	2 Mar
46.33	Boris	Gorban	RUS	26.9.78	17 Feb
46.33	Mike	Decker	USA	13.6.78	10 Mar

Oversized track

45.68	Arvad	Moncur	BAH	2.11.78	1	SEC	Lexington	25 Feb
45.73	Alleyne	Francique	GRN	7.6.76	2	SEC	Lexington	25 Feb

46.22A	Milton	Campbell	USA	15.5.76	16 Feb
46.34A	Tony	Berrian	USA	12.2.79	16 Feb

800 METRES

1:44.15	Yuriy	Borzakovskiy	RUS	12.4.81	1		Karlsruhe	27 Jan
1:45.32	André	Bucher	SUI	19.10.76	1	Euro	Stockholm	15 Feb

1:45.33	Patrick	Nduwimana	BDI	9.5.78	1	NCAA	Fayetteville	10 Mar
1:45.65	David	Lelei	KEN	10.5.71	2	Euro	Stockholm	15 Feb
1:45.80	Johan	Botha	RSA	10.1.74	3	Euro	Stockholm	15 Feb
1:45.95	Dirk	Heinze	GER	2.7.76	2	NCAA	Fayetteville	10 Mar
1:46.13	Otukile	Lekote	BOT	19.10.78	3	NCAA	Fayetteville	10 Mar
1:46.34	Benjamin	Kipkurui	KEN	28.12.80	1		Sindelfingen	4 Mar
1:46.42	Marko	Koers	NED	3.11.72	2		Sindelfingen	4 Mar
1:46.45 #	Dmitriy	Bogdanov	RUS	11.4.79	1		Tampere	12 Feb

1:46.48	Roberto	Parra	ESP	6.4.76	15 Feb
1:46.49	Japheth	Kimutai	KEN	20.12.78	15 Feb
1:46.82	Bram	Som	NED	20.2.80	11 Feb
1:46.90	Glory	Dube	BOT	2.7.78	11 Mar
1:47.01	Wolfram	Müller	GER	8.7.81	4 Feb
1:47.03	Florent	Lacasse	FRA	21.1.81	27 Jan
1:47.10	Boris	Kaveshnikov	RUS	30.9.74	27 Jan
1:47.10	Trinity	Gray	USA	3.4.78	3 Mar
1:47.12	Sergey	Kozhevnikov	RUS	12.5.70	21 Feb
1:47.21	Daniel	Caulfield	IRL	16.10.72	10 Feb
1:47.25	Elliot	Gaskins	USA	3.1.74	3 Mar
1:47.31	Khadevis	Robinson	USA	19.7.76	3 Mar
1:47.35	Pawel	Czapiewski	POL	30.3.78	10 Mar
1:47.41	Nico	Motchebon	GER	13.11.69	15 Feb
1:47.64	David	Kiptoo	KEN	26.6.65	10 Feb
1:47.67	João	Pires	POR	10.6.79	4 Feb
1:47.67	Tom	Omey	BEL	24.4.75	10 Mar
1:47.71	Roman	Oravec	CZE	5.4.78	10 Mar
1:47.72	Moise	Joseph	USA	.81	10 Mar
1:47.80	Lukas	Vydra	CZE	23.8.73	4 Feb

1000 Metres

2:17.26	Noah	Ngeny	KEN	2.11.78	1	Euro	Gent	23 Feb
2:17.36	Mehdi	Baala	FRA	17.8.78	2	Euro	Gent	23 Feb
2:17.36	Rui	Silva	POR	3.8.77	3	Euro	Gent	23 Feb
2:18.23	Bram	Som	NED	20.2.80	4	Euro	Gent	23 Feb
2:18.45	Marko	Koers	NED	3.11.72	5	Euro	Gent	23 Feb

2:18.61	Japheth	Kimutai	KEN	20.12.78	21 Feb
2:18.65	Joeri	Jansen	BEL	28.5.79	23 Feb
2:18.88	Johan	Botha	RSA	10.1.74	2 Feb
2:19.00	Pawel	Czapiewski	POL	30.3.78	2 Feb
2:19.22	Laban	Rotich	KEN	20.1.69	4 Feb
2:19.24	Benjamin	Kipkurui	KEN	28.12.80	16 Feb

1500 METRES

3:36.17	Noah	Ngeny	KEN	2.11.78	1	Euro	Birmingham	18 Feb
3:36.25	John	Mayock	GBR	26.10.70	2	Euro	Birmingham	18 Feb
3:36.78+	Rui	Silva	POR	3.8.77	1M	Euro	Stockholm	15 Feb
3:36.89	Youssef	Baba	MAR	7.8.79	3	Euro	Birmingham	18 Feb
3:36.90	Mehdi	Baala	FRA	17.8.78	1	Spark	Stuttgart	4 Feb
3:37.20	Hicham	El Guerrouj	MAR	14.9.74	1	Euro	Liévin	25 Feb
3:37.24	Japheth	Kimutai	KEN	20.12.78	2	Spark	Stuttgart	4 Feb
3:37.54	Vyacheslav	Shabunin	RUS	27.9.69	3	Spark	Stuttgart	4 Feb
3:37.76	Saïd	Chébili	FRA	6.5.76	4	Spark	Stuttgart	4 Feb
3:37.90	Adil	Kaouch	MAR	1.1.79	2h3	WI	Lisboa	9 Mar
3:37.93	Reyes	Estévez	ESP	2.8.76	1h1	WI	Lisboa	9 Mar

3:38.25	James	Nolan	IRL	27.1.77	18 Feb
3:38.25	Laban	Rotich	KEN	20.1.69	25 Feb
3:38.41	Hailu	Mekonnen	ETH	4.4.80	9 Mar
3:38.61	Kamel	Boulahfane	ALG	1.7.76	4 Feb
3:38.64	Abdelkader	Hachlaf	MAR	.79	18 Feb
3:38.74	Mohamed	Khaldi	ALG	3.5.75	4 Feb
3:38.75	Birhane	Alemu	ETH	16.7.82	18 Feb
3:38.82	Bernard	Lagat	KEN	12.12.74	25 Feb
3:38.86	Peter	Philipp	SUI	18.2.72	4 Feb
3:38.91	Marko	Koers	NED	3.11.72	18 Feb
3:39.04	Jurgen	Vandewiele	BEL	10.5.74	18 Feb
3:39.14	Julius	Achon	UGA	12.12.76	9 Mar
3:39.21	Juan Carlos	Higuero	ESP	3.8.78	9 Mar
3:39.35+	Benson	Koech	KEN	10.11.74	15 Feb
3:39.55	Branko	Zorko	CRO	1.7.67	9 Mar
3:39.79	José A	Redolat	ESP	17.2.76	3 Feb
3:39.81	Bouabdallah	Tahri	FRA	20.12.78	27 Jan
3:40.42	Mark	Carroll	IRL	15.1.72	4 Mar
3:40.42	Jason	Lunn	USA	19.9.74	9 Mar
3:40.68	Luis	Feiteira	POR	21.4.73	9 Mar

1 MILE

3:52.18	Rui	Silva	POR	3.8.77	1	Euro	Stockholm	15 Feb
3:53.31	Noah	Ngeny	KEN	2.11.78	2	Euro	Stockholm	15 Feb
3:53.49	Reyes	Estévez	ESP	2.8.76	3	Euro	Stockholm	15 Feb
3:53.64	Laban	Rotich	KEN	20.1.69	1	Tyson	Fayetteville	10 Feb
3:54.21	Seneca	Lassiter	USA	12.3.77	2	Tyson	Fayetteville	10 Feb
3:54.27	Clyde	Colenso	RSA	11.5.77	3	Tyson	Fayetteville	10 Feb
3:54.5	Mark	Carroll	IRL	15.1.72	1		Boston	18 Feb
3:55.07	John	Mayock	GBR	26.10.70	4	Euro	Stockholm	15 Feb
3:55.45	Benson	Koech	KEN	10.11.74	5	Euro	Stockholm	15 Feb

3:56.26	Hudson	de Souza	BRA	25.2.77	10 Feb
3:56.33	Jason	Pyrah	USA	6.4.69	10 Feb
3:56.50	James	Nolan	IRL	27.1.77	15 Feb
3:56.69	Kevin	Sullivan	CAN	20.3.74	4 Feb
3:56.84	Bryan	Berryhill	USA	15.12.77	10 Mar
3:57.37	Marko	Koers	NED	3.11.72	15 Feb
3:57.61	Bernard	Lagat	KEN	12.12.74	20 Jan
3:57.90	Leonard	Mucheru	KEN	13.6.78	20 Jan
3:58.02	Javier	Moro	ESP	16.4.75	15 Feb
3:58.42	Jason	Lunn	USA	19.9.74	4 Feb
3:58.51	Charlie	Gruber	USA	6.8.78	10 Mar
3:58.54	Gabe	Jennings	USA	25.1.79	10 Mar
3:58.90	Michael	Stember	USA	30.1.78	4 Feb

2000m: At Liévin 25 Feb: 4:56.40 Noah Negny KEN 2.11.78, 4:57.09 John Mayock GBR 26.10.70, 4:58.93 Youssef Baba MAR 7.8.79, 4:59.12 Vyacheslav Shabunin RUS 27.9.69, 5:01.99 Kamel Boulahfane ALG 1.7.76

3000 METRES

7:36.85+	Hicham	El Guerrouj	MAR	14.9.74	1M	Euro	Gent	23 Feb
7:37.99	Million	Wolde	ETH	17.3.79	1	Spark	Stuttgart	4 Feb
7:38.48	Girma	Tolla	ETH	13.10.75	2	Spark	Stuttgart	4 Feb
7:38.94	Mohammed	Mourhit	BEL	10.10.70	2	WI	Lisboa	11 Mar
7:38.95	Hailu	Mekonnen	ETH	4.4.80	3	Spark	Stuttgart	4 Feb
7:39.52	Rui	Silva	POR	3.8.77	4	Spark	Stuttgart	4 Feb
7:39.96	Alberto	García	ESP	22.2.71	3	WI	Lisboa	11 Mar
7:42.08	Assefa	Mezgebu	ETH	19.6.78	5	Spark	Stuttgart	4 Feb
7:42.32	Smail	Sghir	FRA	16.3.72	6	Spark	Stuttgart	4 Feb
7:42.68	Bouabdallah	Tahri	FRA	20.12.78	7	Spark	Stuttgart	4 Feb

7:43.1+	Daniel	Komen	KEN	17.5.76	18 Feb
7:43.3+	Paul	Bitok	KEN	26.6.70	18 Feb
7:43.38	Mohamed	Khaldi	ALG	3.5.75	12 Feb
7:43.59	Roberto	García	ESP	20.8.75	3 Feb
7:44.08	John	Mayock	GBR	26.10.70	11 Mar
7:45.52	Bernard	Lagat	KEN	12.12.74	11 Mar
7:46.79	Mark	Carroll	IRL	15.1.72	11 Mar
7:47.86	Günther	Weidlinger	AUT	5.4.78	12 Feb
7:47.96	Leonard	Mucheru	KEN	13.6.78	4 Feb
7:48.26	Yusef	El Nasri	ESP	28.7.79	11 Feb
7:48.34	Craig	Mottram	AUS	18.6.80	11 Mar
7:48.46	Daniel	Zegeye	ETH	13.3.79	4 Feb
7:48.66+	Saïd	Bérioui	MAR	3.6.75	23 Feb
7:48.69	Tim	Broe	USA	20.6.77	4 Feb
7:48.76	Jan	Fitschen	GER	2.5.77	2 Feb
7:48.79	Jonathon	Riley	USA	29.12.78	4 Feb
7:49.13	Rachid	Chékhémani	FRA	1.10.73	27 Jan
7:49.61+	Mohamed	Saïd El Wardi	MAR	19.4.72	23 Feb

Drugs suspension: 7:47.29 Dieter Baumann GER 9.2.65 1 NC Dortmund 25 Feb

2 MILES

8:09.89	Hicham	El Guerrouj	MAR	14.9.74	1	Euro	Gent	23 Feb
8:11.85	Hailu	Mekonnen	ETH	4.4.80	1	Euro	Birmingham	18 Feb
8:12.10	Million	Wolde	ETH	17.3.79	2	Euro	Birmingham	18 Feb
8:12.80	Girma	Tolla	ETH	13.10.75	3	Euro	Birmingham	18 Feb
8:13.28	Paul	Bitok	KEN	26.6.70	4	Euro	Birmingham	18 Feb
8:16.89	Daniel	Komen	KEN	17.5.76	5	Euro	Birmingham	18 Feb

8:21.16	Saïd	Bérioui	MAR	3.6.75	23 Feb
8:21.33	Smail	Sghir	FRA	16.3.72	18 Feb
8:21.57	Sergey	Lebed	UKR	15.7.75	18 Feb
8:23.67	Kevin	Sullivan	CAN	20.3.74	18 Feb
8:25.11	Mohamed	Saïd El Wardi	MAR	19.4.72	23 Feb

50 METRES HURDLES

6.44+	Tony	Dees	USA	6.8.63	1	Euro	Liévin	25 Feb
6.45	Anier	García	CUB	9.3.76	1r2	Spark	Stuttgart	4 Feb
6.46	Robert	Kronberg	SWE	15.8.76	1r1		Sindelfingen	4 Mar

6.48+	Stanislavs	Olijars	LAT	22.3.79	25 Feb
6.48+	Shaun	Bownes	RSA	24.10.70	25 Feb
6.48	Yevgeniy	Pechonkin	RUS	9.10.73	4 Mar
6.50+	Dudley	Dorival	HAI	1.9.75	25 Feb
6.51+	Yoel	Hernández	CUB	12.12.77	25 Feb
6.53	Falk	Balzer	GER	14.12.73	4 Feb
6.54	Eugene	Swift	USA	14.9.64	20 Jan
6.54	Elmar	Lichtenegger	AUT	25.5.74	4 Feb
6.56	Yuniel	Hernández	CUB	28.3.81	4 Feb
6.56	Peter	Coghlan	IRL	27.3.75	4 Mar

60 METRES HURDLES

7.47	Terrence	Trammell	USA	23.11.78	1	Mill	New York	2 Feb
7.52	Shaun	Bownes	RSA	24.10.70	1	Euro	Gent	23 Feb
7.52	Tony	Dees	USA	6.8.63	1	Euro	Liévin	25 Feb
7.53	Yevgeniy	Pechonkin	RUS	9.10.73	1		Glasgow	18 Mar
7.54	Falk	Balzer (drugs p)	GER	14.12.73	1		Karlsruhe	27 Jan
7.54	Robert	Kronberg	SWE	15.8.76	1s2	WI	Lisboa	9 Mar
7.54	Anier	García	CUB	9.3.76	2	WI	Lisboa	9 Mar
7.54	Elmar	Lichtenegger	AUT	25.5.74	3		Glasgow	18 Mar
7.55	Dudley	Dorival	HAI	1.9.75	1	Euro	Stockholm	15 Feb
7.55	Ron	Bramlett	USA	22.10.79	1	SEC	Lexington	25 Feb
7.55	Stanislavs	Olijars	LAT	22.3.79	1s1	WI	Lisboa	9 Mar

7.56	Yuniel	Hernández	CUB	28.3.81	4 Mar
7.57	Tomasz	Scigaczewski	POL	18.11.78	9 Feb
7.58	Yoel	Hernández	CUB	12.12.77	12 Feb
7.61	Aubrey	Herring	USA	19.9.78	9 Mar
7.63	Dawane	Wallace	USA	30.12.76	2 Feb
7.64	Maurice	Wignall	JAM	17.4.76	17 Feb
7.64	T J	Nelson	USA	7.12.77	25 Feb
7.64	Chris	Phillips	USA	24.7.72	3 Mar
7.65	Ralf	Leberer	GER	26.10.73	24 Feb
7.67	Zhivko	Videnov	BUL	23.5.77	27 Jan
7.67	Peter	Coghlan	IRL	27.3.75	9 Mar
7.68	Emiliano	Pizzoli	ITA	29.6.74	25 Feb
7.69	Andrey	Kislykh	RUS	24.11.76	4 Feb
7.69	Guy	Rose	USA	6.2.80	25 Feb
7.69	Jeffrey	York	USA	3.9.71	25 Feb
7.69	Sultan	Tucker	USA	24.10.78	9 Mar

HIGH JUMP

2.35	Andrey	Sokolovskiy	UKR	16.7.78	1		Arnstadt	17 Feb
2.34	Staffan	Strand	SWE	18.4.76	1	Euro	Stockholm	15 Feb
2.34	Stefan	Holm	SWE	25.5.76	2	Euro	Stockholm	15 Feb
2.33	Nathan	Leeper	USA	13.6.77	1		Manhattan, KS	19 Jan
2.33	Yaroslav	Rybakov	RUS	22.11.80	1		Moskva	25 Feb
2.31	Vyacheslav	Voronin	RUS	5.4.74	1		Vladikavkaz	29 Dec
	2.30				1	NC	Moskva	17 Feb

2.31	Andrey	Chubsa	BLR-J	29.11.82	1		Minsk	12 Jan
2.31	Dragutin	Topic (drugs p)	YUG	12.3.71	1		Wuppertal	2 Feb
2.31	Sergey	Dymchenko	UKR	23.8.67	1		Banská Bystrica	14 Feb
2.31	Charles	Austin	USA	19.12.67	1		Arnstadt	17 Feb
2.31	Javier	Sotomayor	CUB	13.10.67	1		Pireás	21 Feb
2.31 A	Charles	Clinger	USA	28.12.76	1		Bozeman	24 Feb

2.30	Martin	Buss	GER	7.4.76	9 Feb	2.27	Henry	Patterson	USA	27.5.75	2 Feb
2.28	Gennadiy	Moroz	BLR	27.5.78	20 Jan	2.27	Grzegorz	Sposób	POL	12.2.76	25 Feb
2.28	Sergey	Klyugin	RUS	24.3.74	15 Feb	2.26	Dalton	Grant	GBR	8.4.66	14 Feb
2.28	Oskari	Frösén	FIN	24.1.76	15 Feb	2.26	Djordje	Niketic	YUG	11.3.76	14 Feb
2.28	Einar Karl	Hjartarson	ISL	28.10.80	18 Feb	2.26	Shaun	Guice	USA	11.8.80	10 Mar
2.27	Jan	Janku	CZE	10.8.71	24 Jan	2.26	Kenny	Evans	USA	6.4.79	10 Mar

POLE VAULT

6.00	Danny	Ecker	GER	21.7.77	1		Dortmund	11 Feb
5.96	Lawrence	Johnson	USA	7.5.74	1	NC	Atlanta	3 Mar
5.93	Tye	Harvey	USA	25.9.74	2	NC	Atlanta	3 Mar
5.86	Aleksandr	Averbukh	ISR	1.10.74	1	Euro	Stockholm	15 Feb
5.86	Romain	Mesnil	FRA	13.7.77	1		Toulouse	4 Mar
5.85	Michael	Stolle	GER	17.12.74	2		Potsdam	18 Feb
5.81	Pavel	Gerasimov	RUS	29.5.79	2		Toulouse	4 Mar
5.80	Jeff	Hartwig	USA	25.9.67	1	Tyson	Fayetteville	10 Feb
5.80	Lars	Börgeling	GER	16.4.79	1		Sindelfingen	4 Mar
5.80	Timothy	Mack	USA	15.9.72	3	NC	Atlanta	3 Mar

5.75	Tim	Lobinger	GER	3.9.72	4 Mar	5.70	Grigoriy	Yegorov	KZK	12.1.67	4 Feb
5.75	Stepán	Janácek	CZE	12.6.77	4 Mar	5.70	Chad	Harting	USA	20.2.72	10 Feb
5.75	Russ	Buller	USA	10.9.78	3 Mar	5.70	Vasiliy	Gorshkov	RUS	5.2.77	17 Feb
5.72	Andrej	Tivontschik	GER	13.7.70	16 Mar	5.70	Rodion	Gataullin	RUS	23.11.65	23 Feb
5.71	Yevgeniy	Smiryagin	RUS	17.5.76	4 Mar	5.68	Jake	Pauli	USA	15.6.79	9 Mar
5.70 A	Derek	Miles	USA	28.9.72	19 Jan	5.68	Adam	Keul	USA	27.1.80	9 Mar
5.70	Montxu	Miranda	ESP	27.12.76	3 Feb	5.67	Ruslan	Yeremenko	UKR	31.7.78	21 Jan
5.70	Okkert	Brits	RSA	22.8.73	4 Feb	5.65	Pavel	Burlachenko	RUS	7.4.76	17 Feb
5.70	Denis	Yurchenko	UKR	27.1.78	4 Feb	5.60	11 men				

LONG JUMP

8.43	Iván	Pedroso	CUB	17.12.72	1	WI	Lisboa	11 Mar
8.23	Savante	Stringfellow	USA	6.11.78	1		Gainesville	3 Feb
8.16	Kareem	Streete-Thompson	CAY	30.3.73	2	WI	Lisboa	11 Mar
8.16	Carlos	Calado	POR	5.10.75	3	WI	Lisboa	11 Mar
8.14	Walter	Davis	USA	2.7.79	1	SEC	Lexington	24 Feb
8.13	Kofi Amoah	Prah	GER	20.12.74	1	TEAG	Erfurt	2 Feb
8.12	Dwight	Phillips	USA	1.10.77	1	NC	Atlanta	3 Mar
8.11	Gregor	Cankar	SLO	25.1.75	1		Eaubonne	7 Feb
8.11	Yevgeniy	Tretyak	RUS	18.7.71	1	NC	Moskva	18 Feb
8.11	Luis	Méliz	CUB	11.8.79	2		Pireás	21 Feb
8.11	Peter	Burge	AUS	3.7.74	1		Sindelfingen	4 Mar

8.10	Mickaël	Loria	FRA	9.6.73	18 Feb	8.00	Miguel	Pate	USA	13.6.79	3 Feb
8.10	Melvin	Lister	USA	29.8.77	11 Mar	8.00	Aleksey	Lukashevich	UKR	11.1.77	12 Feb
8.06	Vladimir	Malyavin	RUS	4.3.73	18 Feb	7.98	Allen	Simms	USA	26.7.82	6 Jan
8.05	Yago	Lamela	ESP	24.7.77	7 Feb	7.98	Dmitriy	Ruban	RUS		18 Feb
8.05	Vladimir	Zyuskov	UKR	29.8.81	10 Feb	7.98	Astérios	Noúsios	GRE	.79	21 Feb
8.05	Vitaliy	Shkurlatov	RUS	25.5.79	18 Feb	7.98	James	Beckford	JAM	9.1.75	21 Feb
8.05	Danila	Burkenya	RUS	20.7.78	18 Feb	7.98	Konstadínos	Koukodímos	GRE	14.9.69	25 Feb
8.05	Peter	Häggström	SWE	27.1.76	4 Mar	7.97	Roman	Shchurenko	UKR	14.9.76	21 Feb
8.03	Cheikh	Touré	FRA	25.1.70	18 Feb	7.97	Kevin	Dilworth	USA	14.2.74	11 Mar
8.02	Petar	Dachev	BUL	15.6.79	21 Jan	7.95	Bogdan	Tarus	ROM	1.8.75	21 Feb
8.02	Younès	Moudrik	MAR	1.10.77	2 Feb	7.95	Konstantin	Krause	GER	8.10.67	25 Feb

TRIPLE JUMP

17.60	Jonathan	Edwards	GBR	10.5.66	1		Samara	1 Feb
17.32	Paolo	Camossi	ITA	6.1.74	1	WI	Lisboa	9 Mar
17.20	Andrew	Murphy	AUS	18.12.69	3	WI	Lisboa	9 Mar
17.13	Charles	Friedek	GER	26.8.71	4	WI	Lisboa	9 Mar
17.06	Aleksandr	Glavatskiy	BLR	2.5.70	2		Samara	1 Feb
17.06	Walter	Davis	USA	2.7.79	1	Tyson	Fayetteville	9 Feb
17.05	Ionut	Punga	ROM	14.10.79	1		Bucuresti	27 Jan
17.00	Igor	Gavrilenko	RUS	26.7.76	1	NC	Moskva	17 Feb
17.00	Alexander	Martínez	CUB	23.8.77	1	SUICh	Magglingen	25 Feb
16.94	Fabrizio	Donato	ITA	14.8.76	1	NC	Torino	24 Feb
16.92	Robert	Howard	USA	26.11.75	9	Feb		

16.91	Rostislav	Dimitrov	BUL	29.12.74	9 Mar	16.90	LaMark	Carter	USA	23.8.70	3 Mar

16.86	Jimmy	Gabriel	FRA	19.10.73	18 Jan
16.82	Kenta	Bell	USA	16.3.77	27 Jan
16.82	Brian	Wellman	BER	8.9.67	27 Jan
16.80	Allen	Simms	USA	26.7.82	19 Jan
16.77	LeVar	Anderson	USA	26.3.77	27 Jan
16.76	Andrey	Kurennoy	RUS	12.5.72	1 Feb
16.75	Raul	Chapado	ESP	4.5.70	25 Feb
16.75	Johan	Meriluoto	FIN	22.3.74	24 Feb
16.75	Michael	Calvo	CUB	26.12.77	9 Mar
16.73	Denis	Kapustin	RUS	5.10.70	1 Feb
16.72	Marian	Oprea	ROM	6.6.82	24 Feb
16.70	Igor	Spasovkhodskiy	RUS	1.8.79	23 Feb
16.69A	Quincy	Howe	TRI		24 Feb
16.69	Chris	Hercules	USA	14.5.79	10 Mar
16.66	Lenton	Herring	USA	4.12.78	10 Mar
16.64	Igor	Sautkin	RUS	23.2.72	17 Feb
16.61	Yoel	García	CUB	25.11.73	11 Feb
16.61	Thomas	Moede	GER	26.7.77	24 Feb

Doubtful: 17.16 Vasiliy Sokov UZB 7.4.68 1 Tashkent 1 Mar

SHOT

21.40	Adam	Nelson	USA	7.7.75	1	NC	Atlanta	3 Mar
21.36	Janus	Robberts	RSA	10.3.79	1	WAC	Reno	24 Feb
20.91	Pavel	Chumachenko	RUS	5.4.71	1	NC	Moskva	16 Feb
20.91	Manuel	Martínez	ESP	7.12.74	1		Madrid	14 Mar
20.82	John	Godina	USA	31.5.72	1	WI	Lisboa	9 Mar
20.68	Gheorghe	Guset	ROM	18.5.68	1		Bucuresti	3 Feb
20.68	Miroslav	Menc	CZE	16.3.71	1	NC	Praha	18 Feb
20.46	Paolo	Dal Soglio	ITA	29.7.70	1	NC	Torino	25 Feb
20.45	Andy	Bloom	USA	11.8.73	3	NC	Atlanta	3 Mar
20.43	Joachim	Olsen	DEN	31.5.77	1		Moscow ID	16 Feb
20.43	Milan	Haborák	SVK	11.1.73	1		Bratislava	17 Feb

20.37	Jim	Roberts	USA	30.12.76	3 Feb
20.29	Brad	Snyder	CAN	8.1.76	24 Feb
20.27	Timo	Aaltonen	FIN	11.4.69	24 Feb
20.08	Jeffrey	Chakouian	USA	20.4.82	8 Dec
19.96	Jimmy	Nordin	SWE	19.10.79	20 Jan
19.93	Conny	Karlsson	FIN	30.12.75	18 Feb
19.86	Brian	Miller	USA	20..3.72	17 Feb
19.81	Stevimir	Ercegovac	CRO	20.1.74	13 Jan
19.72	Roman	Virastyuk	UKR	20.4.68	10 Feb
19.71	Yuriy	Belonog	UKR	9.3.74	9 Mar
19.70	Petr	Stehlik	CZE	15.4.77	3 Mar
19.69	Ralf	Bartels	GER	21.2.78	3 Mar
19.67	Oliver-Sven	Buder	GER	23.6.66	16 Feb
19.65	Marco	Dodoni	ITA	5.9.72	25 Feb
19.62	Sergio	Mottin	ITA	15.6.76	27 Jan
19.57	Zsolt	Bíber	HUN	31.5.76	3 Feb
19.56	Detlef	Bock	GER	15.8.74	16 Dec
19.55	Marcus	Clavelle	USA	23.6.78	17 Feb
19.52	Reese	Hoffa	USA	8.10.77	3 Feb
19.52	Jaroslaw	Cichocki	POL	28.7.82	18 Feb
19.51	Gjøran	Sørli	NOR	3.6.78	2 Mar

35 LBS WEIGHT

23.97	András	Haklits	CRO	23.9.77	*	NCAA	Fayetteville	9 Mar
	24.43 elongated implement				1	NCAA	Fayetteville	9 Mar
24.02	Libor	Charfreitag	SVK	11.9.77	2	NCAA	Fayetteville	9 Mar
23.36	Scott	Russell	CAN	16.1.79	3	NCAA	Fayetteville	9 Mar
22.67	John	McEwen	USA	5.3.74	1	NC	Atlanta	3 Mar
22.32	Kevin	Mannon	USA	12.8.76	2	NC	Atlanta	3 Mar
22.25	Jason	Gervais	CAN	18.1.76	1		USAF Academy	23 Feb
22.12	Dylan	Armstrong	CAN	15.1.81	4	NCAA	Fayetteville	9 Mar

21.99	James	Parker	USA	3.12.75	9 Mar
21.93	Chris	Brown	USA	8.1.78	25 Feb
21.87	Daniel	Bourquo	USA	4.7.76	17 Feb
21.43	Christian	Cantwell	USA	30.9.80	26 Jan

HEPTATHLON

6420	Roman	Sebrle	CZE	26.11.74	1	WI	Lisboa	11 Mar
	(7.00, 7.88, 15.75, 2.08, 7.86, 4.90, 2:37.86)							
6233	Jón Arnar	Magnússon	ISL	28.7.69	2	WI	Lisboa	11 Mar
	(7.07, 7.74, 16.34, 2.05, 8.09, 4.90, 2:44.99)							
6202	Lev	Lobodin	RUS	1.4.69	3	WI	Lisboa	11 Mar
	(6.99, 7.27, 16.39, 1.93, 7.86, 5.20, 2:43.59)							
6160	Aleksandr	Yurkov	UKR	21.7.75	3	Nool	Tallinn	4 Feb
	6.94, 7.53, 15.35, 1.98, 8.19, 5.25, 2:47.18)							
6132	Stephen	Moore	USA	13.8.75	4	WI	Lisboa	11 Mar
	(7.03, 7.46, 12.65, 2.14, 8.06, 5.10, 2:42.35)							
6074	Erki	Nool	EST	25.6.70	5	WI	Lisboa	11 Mar
	(7.01, 7.60, 14.89, 1.93, 8.02, 5.00, 2:44.38)							
6068	Vladimir	Mikhaylenko	UKR	27.8.73	4	Nool	Tallinn	4 Feb
	(7.03, 7.41, 13.40, 2.07, 8.09, 5.15, 2:46.07)							
6029	Stefan	Drews	GER	12.2.79	1		Frankfurt	11 Feb
	(6.94, 7.26, 11.78, 1.96, 7.90, 5.40, 2:42.41							

5867	Mário	Aníbal	POR	25.3.72	1 Mar
5863	Laurent	Hernu	FRA	22.8.76	1 Feb
5857	Andrey	Kurdeko	BLR	27.5.76	0 Jan
5847	Chiel	Warners	NED	2.4.78	4 Feb
5839	Kip	Janvrin	USA	8.7.65	3 Mar
5811	Phil	McMullen	USA	3.2.75	3 Mar
5810	Vesa	Rantanen	FIN	2.12.75	1 Feb

3000m Walk: 10:31.42 Andreas Erm GER 12.3.76 1 Halle 4 Feb

11:06.74+ Yevgeniy Shmalyuk RUS 14.1.76 1 Sankt-Peterburg 6 Jan

5000m Walk: dee page 590

WORLD INDOOR LISTS 2001 - WOMEN

50 METRES

6.12+	Sevatheda	Fynes	BAH	17.10.74	14 Mar
6.13+	Mercy	Nku	NGR	17.7.76	25 Feb
6.13+	Merlene	Ottey	JAM	10.5.60	14 Mar
6.15+	Petya	Pendareva	BUL	20.1.71	25 Feb
6.17	Angela	Williams	USA	30.1.80	20 Jan
6.18+	Marina	Kislova	RUS	12.12.78	25 Feb

60 METRES

7.04	Petya	Pendareva	BUL	20.1.71	1s1	WI	Lisboa	11 Mar
7.05	Chandra	Sturrup	BAH	12.9.71	1	WI	Lisboa	11 Mar
7.08	Natalya	Ignatova	RUS	28.12.73	1h4		Moskva	16 Jan
7.08	Marina	Kislova	RUS	12.12.78	1		Samara	1 Feb
7.09	Anzhela	Kravchenko	UKR	25.1.71	1	Spark	Stuttgart	4 Feb
7.09	Angela	Williams	USA	30.1.80	2	WI	Lisboa	11 Mar
7.11	Mercy	Nku	NGR	17.7.76	1	Euro	Liévin	25 Feb
7.12	Chryste	Gaines	USA	14.9.70	2s3	WI	Lisboa	11 Mar
7.12	Merlene	Ottey	JAM	10.5.60	1		Madrid	14 Mar
7.13	Endurance	Ojokolo	NGR	29.9.75	2s1	WI	Lisboa	11 Mar

7.15	Karin	Mayr	AUT	4.6.71	24 Feb
7.15	Sevatheda	Fynes	BAH	17.10.74	11 Mar
7.16	Irina	Pukha	UKR	10.1.73	27 Jan
7.17	Susanthika	Jayasinghe	SRI	17.12.75	4 Feb
7.18	Natalya	Mikhaylovskaya	RUS	.75	1 Feb
7.19	Larisa	Kruglova	RUS	27.10.72	1 Feb
7.19	Mary	Onyali	NGR	3.2.68	9 Feb
7.19		Li Xuemei	CHN	5.1.77	11 Mar
7.20	Sina	Schielke	GER	19.5.81	25 Feb
7.21	Nora	Ivanova-Güner	TUR	1.6.77	27 Jan
7.21	Kim	Gevaert	BEL	5.8.78	28 Jan
7.21	Natalya	Safronnikova	BLR	28.2.73	16 Feb
	7.04 doubtful time		1 NC	Minsk	21 Feb
7.21	Tayna	Lawrence	JAM	17.9.75	11 Mar
7.22	Marion	Wagner	GER	1.2.78	25 Feb
7.22	Torri	Edwards	USA	31.1.77	3 Mar
7.22	Alenka	Bikar	SLO	7.1.74	4 Mar
7.23	Juliet	Campbell	JAM	17.3.70	4 Feb
7.23	Glory	Alozie	NGR	30.12.77	21 Feb
7.24	Liliana	Allen	MEX	24.6.70	11 Mar

100m: at Tampare, 12 Feb: 11.21 Merlene Ottey JAM 10.5.60, 11.34 Natalya Safronnikova BLR 28.2.73

200 METRES

22.64	Juliet	Campbell	JAM	17.3.70	1	WI	Lisboa	10 Mar
22.84	Cydonie	Mothersill	CAY	19.3.78	1h1	NCAA	Fayetteville	9 Mar
22.96	LaTasha	Jenkins	USA	19.12.77	2	WI	Lisboa	10 Mar
22.97	Karin	Mayr	AUT	4.6.71	1	NC	Wien	25 Feb
22.99	Susanthika	Jayasinghe	SRI	17.12.75	1h1	WI	Lisboa	9 Mar
23.01	Gabriele	Rockmeier	GER	29.11.73	1		Sindelfingen	4 Mar
23.02	Natalya	Safronnikova	BLR	28.2.73	1s3	WI	Lisboa	9 Mar
23.06	Muriel	Hurtis	FRA	25.3.79	2s3	WI	Lisboa	9 Mar
23.08	Nora	Ivanova-Güner	TUR	1.6.77	2		Wien	12 Feb
23.11	Ionela	Tîrlea	ROM	9.2.76	3		Wien	12 Feb

23.17	Muna	Lee	USA	30.10.81	9 Feb
23.19	Birgit	Rockmeier	GER	29.11.73	25 Feb
23.24	Anastasiya	Kapachinskaya	RUS	79	17 Feb
23.27	Alenka	Bikar	SLO	7.1.74	9 Mar
23.29	Oksana	Ekk	RUS	26.11.74	17 Jan
23.31	Shanta	Ghosh	GER	3.1.75	27 Jan
23.31	Natalya	Mikhaylovskaya	RUS	.75	17 Feb
23.31	Fabé	Dia	FRA	14.2.77	18 Feb
23.33	Demetria	Washington	USA	31.12.79	9 Mar
23.33	Rachelle	Boone	USA	30.6.81	9 Mar
23.35	Catherine	Murphy	GBR	21.9.75	28 Jan
23.36	Teneeshia	Jones	USA	28.1.79	10 Feb

Oversized track: 23.04 Muna Lee USA 30.10.81 1h4 SEC Lexington 24 Feb

400 METRES

50.42	Olga	Kotlyarova	RUS	12.4.76	1r1		Moskva	27 Jan
50.53	Katharine	Merry	GBR	21.9.74	1	Euro	Birmingham	18 Feb
51.04	Sandie	Richards	JAM	6,11,68	1	WI	Lisboa	11 Mar
51.33	Olesya	Zykina	RUS	7.10.80	2	NC	Moskva	17 Feb
51.48	Shanta	Ghosh	GER	3.1.75	1	NC	Dortmund	25 Feb
51.84	Suziann	Reid	USA	14.1.77	2s2	WI	Lisboa	10 Mar
51.92	Nadjina	Kaltouma	CHA	16.11.76	3s2	WI	Lisboa	10 Mar
51.99	Helena	Fuchsová	CZE	3.6.65	1	NC	Praha	18 Feb
51.99	Catherine	Murphy	GBR	21.9.75	2	Euro	Birmingham	18 Feb
52.13	Yuliya	Sotnikova	RUS	18.11.70	3	NC	Moskva	17 Feb

52.15	Lesley	Owusu	GBR	21.12.78	9 Mar
52.16	Jearl	Miles Clark	USA	4.9.66	1 Feb
52.18	Monique	Hennagan	USA	26.5.76	3 Mar
52.23	Irina	Rosikhina	RUS	11.5.75	16 Jan
52.25	Yuliya	Nosova	RUS	21.4.78	17 Feb
52.31	Karen	Shinkins	IRL	15.10.76	24 Feb
52.37	Natalya	Antyukh	RUS	26.6.81	19 Jan
52.37	Demetria	Washington	USA	31.12.79	10 Mar
52.40	Yekaterina	Kulikova	RUS	7.11.68	27 Jan
52.46	Natalya	Khrushchelyova	RUS	30.5.73	19 Jan
52.47	Sinead	Dudgeon	GBR	9.7.76	27 Jan
52.53	Claudia	Marx	GER	16.9.78	25 Feb
52.55	Mikele	Barber	USA	4.10.80	9 Mar
52.62	Olga	Maksimova	RUS	9.8.76	17 Feb
52.64	Ionela	Tîrlea	ROM	9.2.76	4 Mar
52.68	Florence	Ekpo-Umoh	GER	27.12.77	2 Feb
52.69	Marina	Grishakova	RUS	76	27 Jan
52.69	Birgit	Rockmeier	GER	29.11.73	4 Feb
52.69	Bisi	Afolabi	NGR	31.10.75	24 Feb
52.71	Carmo	Tavares	POR	27.4.74	17 Feb
52.73	Irina	Anashkina	RUS		16 Jan
52.75	Deon	Hemmings	JAM	9.10.68	21 Feb

Oversized Track:52.06	Demetria	Washington	USA	31.12.79	1	SEC	Lexington	25 Feb
500y: 1:01.15A	Jearl	Miles-Clark	USA	4.9.66	1		Pocatello	17 Feb
500m: 1:10.0	Olga	Kotlyarova	RUS	12.4.76	1		Yekaterinburg	7 Jan
600y: 1:17.92	Lesley	Owusu	GBR	21.12.78	1		Lincoln, NE	3 Mar
600m: 1:26.72	Anna	Tkach	RUS	17.4.75	1r2		Moskva	6 Jan

800 METRES

1:57.53	Stephanie	Graf	AUT	26.4.73	1	Euro	Liévin	25 Feb
1:58.02	Maria	Mutola	MOZ	27.10.72	2	Euro	Liévin	25 Feb
1:58.37	Helena	Fuchsová	CZE	3.6.65	3	Euro	Liévin	25 Feb
1:58.73	Yelena	Afanasyeva	RUS	1.3.67	1	NC	Moskva	17 Feb
1:58.94	Olga	Kuznetsova	RUS	23.10.67	2	NC	Moskva	17 Feb
1:59.15	Natalya	Gorelova	RUS	18.4.73	3	NC	Moskva	17 Feb
1:59.81	Jolanda	Ceplak	SLO	12.9.76	1		Sindelfingen	4 Mar
1:59.86	Hasna	Benhassi	MAR	1.6.78	1	Euro	Birmingham	18 Feb
2:00.01	Ester	Goossens	NED	21.2.72	4	Euro	Stockholm	15 Feb
2:00.42	Svetlana	Cherkasova	RUS	20.5.78	4	NC	Moskva	17 Feb

2:00.52	Olga	Raspopova	RUS	27.12.78	4 Feb
2:00.75	Heike	Meissner	GER	29.1.70	27 Jan
2:00.96	Jearl	MIles-Clark	USA	4.9.66	3 Mar
2:00.98	Fabiane	dos Santos	BRA	30.5.76	15 Feb
2:00.98	Ivonne	Teichmann	GER	11.4.77	16 Feb
2:01.43	Hazel	Clark	USA	3.10.77	3 Mar
2:01.74	Lwiza	John	TAN	18.5.80	25 Feb
2:02.12	Anca	Safta	ROM	9.1.78	21 Feb
2:02.21	Yekaterina	Fedotova	RUS	4.11.75	17 Feb
2:02.47	Sandra	Teixeira	POR	13.3.78	17 Feb
2:02.50	Natalya	Dukhnova	BLR	16.7.66	21 Feb
2:02.82	Larisa	Mikhaylova	RUS	3.1.69	27 Jan
2:02.90	Joanne	Fenn	GBR	19.10.74	18 Feb
2:02.91	Tsvetelina	Kirilova	BUL	14.7.77	21 Jan
2:02.97	Maite	Martínez	ESP	17.5.76	17 Feb

1000m: 2:41.08A	Miesha	Marzell	USA	29.1.75	1		Pocatello	17 Feb

1500 METRES

4:03.42	Gabriela	Szabo	ROM	14.11.75	1	Euro	Liévin	25 Feb
4:03.51	Natalya	Gorelova	RUS	18.4.73	2	Euro	Liévin	25 Feb
4:03.61	Violeta	Szekely	ROM	26.3.65	1	Euro	Stockholm	15 Feb
4:04.11	Carla	Sacramento	POR	10.12.71	3	Euro	Liévin	25 Feb
4:04.26	Olga	Kuznetsova	RUS	23.10.67	4	Euro	Liévin	25 Feb
4:04.48	Hasna	Benhassi	MAR	1.6.78	2		Dortmund	11 Feb
4:05.74	Olga	Yegorova	RUS	28.3.72	1		Sindelfingen	4 Mar
4:05.75	Kutre	Dulecha	ETH	22.8.78	3		Dortmund	11 Feb
4:06.00	Daniela	Yordanova	BUL	8.3.76	1		Sofia	10 Feb
4:06.22	Helena	Javornik	SLO	26.3.66	4		Dortmund	11 Feb

4:06.75	Hayley	Tullett	GBR	17.2.73	18 Mar
4:07.25	Yelena	Zadorozhnaya	RUS	3.12.77	27 Jan
4:07.45	Irina	Mikitenko	GER	23.8.72	27 Jan
4:07.89	Maria	Cioncan	ROM	19.6.77	15 Feb
4:08.42	Kathleen	Friedrich	GER	13.7.77	20 Jan
4:08.55	Alesiya	Turova	RUS	6.12.79	4 Mar
4:08.98	Mariya	Pantyukhova	RUS	14.8.74	15 Feb
4:09.26	Elena	Iagar	ROM	16.1.75	4 Mar
4:09.43	Olga	Komyagina	RUS	10.2.74	4 Mar
4:10.45+	Amy	Rudolph	USA	18.9.73	20 Jan
4:10.95	Aysen	Barak	TUR	9.9.75	15 Feb
4:11.27	Sonia	O'Sullivan	IRL	28.11.69	10 Mar
4:11.41	Andrea	Suldesová	CZE	11.2.75	24 Feb
4:12.27	Gete	Wami	ETH	11.12.74	27 Jan
4:12.66	Nuria	Fernández	ESP	16.8.76	3 Feb
4:12.75	Svetlana	Kanatova	RUS	10.9.70	27 Jan
4:12.99	Judit	Varga	HUN	16.4.76	27 Jan

1 MILE

4:23.19	Gabriela	Szabo	ROM	14.11.75	1	Spark	Stuttgart	4 Feb
4:23.33	Kutre	Dulecha	ETH	22.8.78	2	Spark	Stuttgart	4 Feb
4:24.10	Yelena	Zadorozhnaya	RUS	3.12.77	3	Spark	Stuttgart	4 Feb
4:26.52	Hayley	Tullett	GBR	17.2.73	4	Spark	Stuttgart	4 Feb
4:28.47	Amy	Rudolph	USA	18.9.73	1		New York	20 Jan
2000m: 5:43.02+	Gabriela	Szabo	ROM	14.11.75	1k	Euro	Birmingham	18 Feb

3000 METRES

8:32.88	Gabriela	Szabo	ROM	14.11.75	1	Euro	Birmingham	18 Feb
8:37.48	Olga	Yegorova	RUS	28.3.72	1	WI	Lisboa	10 Mar
8:40.15	Yelena	Zadorozhnaya	RUS	3.12.77	3	WI	Lisboa	10 Mar
8:40.98	Marta	Domínguez	ESP	3.11.75	4	WI	Lisboa	10 Mar
8:41.34		Dong Yanmei	CHN	16.2.77	5	WI	Lisboa	10 Mar
8:42.75	Benita	Willis	AUS	6.5.79	6	WI	Lisboa	10 Mar
8:43.38	Gete	Wami	ETH	11.12.74	2	TEAG	Erfurt	2 Feb
8:43.38	Regina	Jacobs	USA	28.8.63	1		Boston (R)	4 Feb
8:44.33	Leah	Malot	KEN	7.6.72	3	TEAG	Erfurt	2 Feb
8:44.37	Sonia	O'Sullivan	IRL	28.11.69	7	WI	Lisboa	10 Mar

8:45.36	Hayley	Tullett	GBR	17.2.73	10 Mar
8:46.39	Violeta	Szekely	ROM	26.3.65	18 Feb
8:46.47	Lidia	Chojecka	POL	25.1.77	18 Feb
8:46.56	Werknesh	Kidane	ETH	21.11.81	10 Mar
8:47.60	Asmae	Leghzaoui	MAR	30.8.76	10 Mar
8:48.33	Amy	Rudolph	USA	18.9.73	4 Feb
8:48.57	Helena	Javornik	SLO	26.3.66	18 Feb
8:48.60	Aysen	Barak	TUR	9.9.75	18 Feb
8:49.55	Marina	Bastos	POR	7.7.71	4 Mar
8:50.36	Mariya	Pantyukhova	RUS	14.8.74	18 Feb

8:51.68	Sarah	Schwald	USA	2.1.73	4 Feb
8:52.41	Irina	Mikitenko	GER	23.8.72	24 Feb
8:53.41	Fernanda	Ribeiro	POR	23.6.69	4 Mar
8:54.96	Kathy	Butler	GBR	22.10.73	4 Feb
8:55.69	Cheri	Kenah	USA	26.12.70	3 Mar
8:57.53	Alla	Zhilyayeva	RUS	5.2.69	16 Feb
8:57.60	Elva	Dryer	USA	26.9.71	3 Mar
8:57.83	Maria	Cioncan	ROM	19.6.77	3 Feb
8:59.13	Daniela	Yordanova	BUL	8.3.76	3 Feb
8:59.73	Maria Cristina	Petite	ESP	10.5.72	24 Feb
8:59.99	Elena	Iagar	ROM	16.1.75	24 Feb
9:00.57	Collette	Liss	USA	29.4.73	10 Feb
9:00.88	Maria Cristina	Grosu	ROM	11.11.76	18 Feb
9:00.90	Margarita	Marusova	RUS	25.11.67	16 Feb

5000 METRES

14:49.36	Gete	Wami	ETH	11.12.74	1		Dortmund	11 Feb
14:55.99	Irina	Mikitenko	GER	23.8.72	2		Dortmund	11 Feb
15:07.33	Marla	Runyan	USA	4.1.69	1		New York (A)	18 Feb

15:27.99	Aysen	Barak	TUR	9.9.75	11 Feb
15:38.59	Leah	Malot	KEN	7.6.72	11 Feb

50 METRES HURDLES

6.72+	Michelle	Freeman	JAM	5.5.69	1	Euro	Liévin	25 Feb
6.76+	Glory	Alozie	NGR	30.12.77	2	Euro	Liévin	25 Feb

6.83+	Anjanette	Kirkland	USA	24.2.74	25 Feb
6.83	Yahumara	Neyra	CUB	18.4.76	4 Mar
6.84+	Olga	Shishigina	KAZ	23.12.68	25 Feb
6.87+	Vonette	Dixon	JAM	26.11.75	25 Feb
6.87+	Lacena	Golding	JAM	20.3.75	25 Feb
6.87	Dionne	Rose	JAM	7.11.69	4 Mar
6.88+	Svetlana	Laukhova	RUS	7.5.73	25 Feb

60 METRES HURDLES

7.83	Michelle	Freeman	JAM	5.5.69	1	Euro	Liévin	25 Feb
7.84	Glory	Alozie	NGR	30.12.77	2	Euro	Liévin	25 Feb
7.85	Anjanette	Kirkland	USA	24.2.74	1	WI	Lisboa	9 Mar
7.90	Olga	Shishigina	KAZ	23.12.68	1s2	WI	Lisboa	9 Mar
7.93	Nicole	Ramalalanirina	FRA	5.3.72	1h2	WI	Lisboa	9 Mar
7.95	Donica	Merriman	USA	24.1.79	1	NCAA	Fayetteville	9 Mar
7.96	Melissa	Morrison	USA	9.7.71	1		Boston (R)	4 Feb
7.98	Svetlana	Laukhova	RUS	7.5.73	1		Samara	1 Feb
7.98	Linda	Ferga	FRA	24.12.76	1	NC	Liévin	18 Feb
7.98	Yahumara	Neyra	CUB	18.4.76	1		Sindelfingen	4 Mar

7.99	Perdita	Felicien	CAN	29.8.80	9 Mar
8.00	Lacena	Golding	JAM	20.3.75	23 Feb
8.00	Vonette	Dixon	JAM	26.11.75	25 Feb
8.02	Dionne	Rose	JAM	7.11.69	4 Mar
8.02	Bisa	Grant	USA	16.7.76	3 Mar
8.06	Aliuska	López	CUB	29.8.69	27 Jan
8.06	Juliane	Sprenger	GER	22.3.77	24 Feb
8.07	Haydy	Aron	FRA	21.5.73	18 Feb
8.07	Natalya	Shekhodanova	RUS	29.12.71	4 Mar
8.07	Irina	Lenskiy	ISR	12.6.71	9 Mar
8.08	Isabel	Abrantes	POR	20.2.73	17 Feb
8.09	Bridgette	Foster	JAM	7.11.74	18 Feb
8.09	Yelena	Krasovskaya	UKR	17.8.76	4 Mar
8.11	Kim	Carson	USA	12.3.74	3 Mar
8.12	Danielle	Carruthers	USA	22.12.79	10 Feb
8.12	Dawn	Burrell	USA	1.11.73	11 Feb
8.12A	Joyce	Bates	USA	16.2.77	17 Feb
8.14	Maurren	Maggi	BRA	25.6.76	12 Feb
8.14	Nicole	Hoxie	USA	22.7.79	17 Feb
8.15	Melanie	Wilkins	GBR	18.1.73	18 Mar

HIGH JUMP

2.00	Kajsa	Bergqvist	SWE	12.10.76	1	WI	Lisboa	9 Mar
2.00	Inga	Babakova	UKR	27.6.67	2	WI	Lisboa	9 Mar
1.98	Venelina	Veneva	BUL	13.6.74	1		Budapest-OH	20 Jan
1.97	Hestrie	Cloete	RSA	26.8.78	1	Euro	Birmingham	18 Feb
1.97	Monica	Iagar-Dinescu	ROM	2.4.73	1	Euro	Liévin	25 Feb
1.96	Amy	Acuff	USA	14.7.75	1	Mill	New York	2 Feb
1.96	Viktoriya	Seryogina	RUS	22.5.73	1		Wien	12 Feb
1.96	Viktoriya	Palamar	UKR	12.10.77	1		Arnstadt	17 Feb
1.96	Yuliya	Lyakhova	RUS	8.7.77	1	NC	Moskva	18 Feb
1.96	Dóra	Györffy	HUN	23.2.78	1		Boston	18 Feb

1.94	Elena	Herzenberg	GER	24.6.79	9 Feb
1.94	Yelena	Gulyayeva	RUS	14.8.67	18 Feb
1.94	Marta	Mendía	ESP	18.5.75	25 Feb
1.94	Ruth	Beitia	ESP	1.4.79	25 Feb
1.93	Yelena	Sivushenko	RUS	28.2.82	24 Jan
1.93	Olga	Kaliturina	RUS	9.3.76	2 Feb
1.93	Alina	Astafei	GER	7.6.69	24 Feb
1.92	Anna	Chicherova	RUS	22.7.82	27 Jan
1.92	Karol	Damon	USA	20.12.69	10 Feb
1.91	Marina	Kuptsova	RUS	22.12.81	24 Jan
1.91	Miki	Imai	JPN	30.5.75	15 Feb
1.91	Solange	Witteveen	ARG	6.2.76	18 Feb
1.91	Svetlana	Zalevskaya	KAZ	14.6.73	25 Feb
1.90	Tatyana	Babashkina	RUS	23.11.68	20 Jan
1.90	Liga	Klavina	LAT	27.1.80	13 Jan
1.90	Anna	Ksok	POL	29.9.83	20 Jan
1.90	Antonietta	Di Martino	ITA	1.6.78	21 Jan
1.90	Anna	Visigalli	ITA	24.2.81	3 Feb
1.90	Blanka	Vlasic	CRO	8.11.83	17 Feb
1.89	Yekaterina	Aleksandrova	RUS	3.6.77	18 Feb
1.89	Inna	Gliznutsa	MDA	18.4.73	18 Feb
1.89	Tia	Hellebaut	BEL	16.2.78	23 Feb
1.89	Olga	Bolshova	MDA	16.6.68	25 Feb

POLE VAULT

4.70A	Stacy	Dragila	USA	25.3.71	1		Pocatello	17 Feb
4.65	Svetlana	Feofanova	RUS	16.7.80	1		Pireás	21 Feb
4.56	Kellie	Suttle	USA	9.3.73	2	NC	Atlanta	2 Mar
4.56	Pavla	Hamácková	CZE	20.5.78	1	WI	Lisboa	9 Mar

4.55	Yelena	Belyakova	RUS	7.4.76	2		Pireás	21 Feb
4.51	Thorey	Elisdóttir	ISL	30.6.77	1	NCAA	Fayetteville	10 Mar
4.47	Yelena	Isinbayeva	RUS	3.6.82	1		Budapest-OH	10 Feb
4.44	Doris	Auer	AUT	10.5.71	2		Glasgow	18 Mar
4.43	Anzhela	Balakhonova	UKR	18.12.72	2	Euro	Liévin	25 Feb
4.40	Tanya	Koleva	BUL	8.3.72	1		Sofia	3 Feb
4.40	Yvonne	Buschbaum	GER	14.7.80	2		Nördlingen	18 Feb

4.37	Krisztina	Molnár	HUN	8.4.76	12 Feb	4.25		Gao Shuying	CHN	28.10.79	24 Feb
4.36	Monika	Pyrek	POL	11.8.80	25 Feb	4.25	Francesca	Dolcini	ITA	28.12.74	25 Feb
4.36	Alicia	Warlick	USA	11.10.77	2 Mar	4.25	Janine	Whitlock	GBR	11.8.73	16 Mar
4.35	Georgia	Tsiliggiri	GRE	21.6.72	21 Feb	4.21	M.Mar	Sánchez	ESP	25.12.79	3 Feb
4.35	Nicole	Humbert	GER	5.2.72	25 Feb	4.20	Andrea	Müller	GER	29.6.74	26 Jan
4.35	Christine	Adams	GER	28.2.74	25 Feb	4.20	Floe	Kühnert	GER	6.3.84	9 Feb
4.34	Marie	Poissonnier	FRA	4.5.79	16 Mar	4.20	Natalya	Kushch	UKR	5.3.83	10 Feb
4.33	Vanessa	Boslak	FRA	11.6.82	25 Feb	4.20	Andrea	Dutoit	USA	28.8.78	10 Mar
4.31A	Tracy	O'Hara	USA	2.7.80	23 Feb	4.20	Rhian	Clarke	GBR	19.4.77	10 Mar
4.30	Nastja	Ryshich	GER	19.9.77	20 Jan	4.20	Amy	Linnen	USA	15.7.82	10 Mar
4.30	Annika	Becker	GER	12.11.81	2 Feb	4.15	Martina	Strutz	GER	4.11.81	11 Feb
4.27A	Mary	Sauer	USA	31.10.75	19 Jan	4.15	Marie B	Rasmussen	DEN	1.11.72	27 Jan
4.25	Anastasiya	Ivanova	RUS	.79	10 Feb	4.15 A	Jackie	Honey	CAN	25.6.75	3 Feb
4.25	Katerina	Badurová	CZE	18.12.82	17 Feb	4.15	Arianna	Farfaletti	ITA	22.6.76	25 Feb

LONG JUMP

7.03	Dawn	Burrell	USA	1.11.73	1	WI	Lisboa	10 Mar
7.00	Lyudmila	Galkina	RUS	20.1.72	1	NC	Moskva	16 Feb
6.98	Tatyana	Kotova	RUS	11.12.76	2	WI	Lisboa	10 Mar
6.88	Niurka	Montalvo	ESP	4.6.68	3	WI	Lisboa	10 Mar
6.87	Fiona	May	ITA	12.12.69	4	WI	Lisboa	10 Mar
6.75	Heike	Drechsler	GER	16.12.64	5	WI	Lisboa	10 Mar
6.73	Olga	Rublyova	RUS	28.10.74	1	Army	Moskva	19 Jan
6.71	Inna	Ivleva	RUS	.71	2	Army	Moskva	19 Jan
6.71	Tatyana	Lebedeva	RUS	21.7.76	3	Army	Moskva	19 Jan
6.69	Natalya	Sazanovich	BLR	15.8.73	1H	WI	Lisboa	9 Mar

6.68	Tatyana	Ter-Mesrobyan	RUS	12.5.68	16 Feb	6.59	Elisha	Williams	USA	9.1.79	9 Mar
6.68	Jenny	Adams	USA	8.7.78	9 Mar	6.58	Tünde	Vaszi	HUN	18.4.72	10 Feb
6.67		Guan Yingnan	CHN	25.4.77	17 Feb	6.56	Valentina	Gotovska	LAT	3.9.65	12 Jan
6.65	Yelena	Shekhovtsova	UKR	31.5.72	11 Feb	6.56	Jackie	Edwards	BAH	14.4.71	16 Feb
6.65	Stilianí	Pilátou	GRE	28.3.80	18 Feb	6.56		Wang Lina	CHN	28.2.83	17 Feb
6.64	Aurélie	Félix	FRA	26.3.79	18 Feb	6.56	Brianna	Glenn	USA	18.4.80	2 Mar
6.61	Irina	Yermolayeva	RUS	.79	16 Feb	6.54	Viviane	Sildillia	FRA	23.2.74	18 Feb
6.61	Yelena	Kashcheyeva	KAZ	17.2.73	18 Feb	6.52	Natalya	Budarina	RUS	.77	3 Feb
6.61	Concepción	Montaner	ESP	14.1.81	25 Feb	6.51	Alice	Falaiye	CAN	24.12.78	9 Mar
6.60	Antoinette	Wilks	USA	14.10.80	3 Feb	6.50	Irina	Melnikova	RUS	14.5.75	27 Jan
6.60	Niki	Xánthou	GRE	11.10.73	24 Feb	6.50		Hu Yaoyao	CHN	16.4.83	17 Feb

TRIPLE JUMP

15.00	Tatyana	Lebedeva	RUS	21.7.76	1	NC	Moskva	18 Feb
14.91	Tereza	Marinova	BUL	5.9.77	1	WI	Lisboa	11 Mar
14.83	Yelena	Lebedenko	RUS	16.1.71	1		Samara	1 Feb
14.53	Cristina	Nicolau	ROM	9.8.77	1	NC	Bucuresti	24 Feb
14.41	Natalya	Safronova	BLR	11.7.71	3		Samara	1 Feb
14.37	Oksana	Rogova	RUS	7.10.78	3		Pireás	21 Feb
14.31	Anja	Valant	SLO	8.9.77	2		Karlsruhe	27 Jan
14.26	Olga	Rublyova	RUS	28.10.74	1	Army	Moskva	21 Jan
14.24	Nadezhda	Bazhenova	RUS	78	3	NC	Moskva	18 Feb
14.19	Tiombé	Hurd	USA	17.8.73	3	WI	Lisboa	11 Mar

14.18	Maria	Dimitrova	BUL	7.8.76	21 Jan	13.96	Mariana	Solomon	ROM	8.9.80	3 Feb
14.17	Olga	Bolshova	MDA	16.6.68	11 Mar	13.95	Trecia	Smith	JAM	5.11.75	17 Feb
14.16	Yelena	Oleynikova	RUS	9.12.76	17 Jan	13.95	Yamilé	Aldama	CUB	14.8.72	25 Feb
14.13	Anastasiya	Ilyina	RUS	16.1.82	14 Feb	13.94	Carlota	Castrejana	ESP	25.4.73	14 Mar
14.04	Lyudmila	Nikitina	RUS	2.3.70	18 Feb	13.93		Ren Ruiping	CHN	6.2.76	20 Feb
14.03	Nicole	Herschmann	GER	27.10.75	25 Feb	13.91	Tatyana	Ter-Mesrobyan	RUS	12.5.68	6 Jan
14.02	Niurka	Montalvo	ESP	4.6.68	14 Mar	13.91	Adelina	Gavrila	ROM	26.11.78	24 Feb
14.01	Katja	Umlauft	GER	22.11.74	28 Jan	13.90	Anna	Pyatykh	RUS	4.4.81	17 Jan
14.01	Natalya	Kayukova	RUS	10.12.66	18 Feb	13.89	Yelena	Ivanova	RUS	16.3.79	6 Jan
14.00	Silvia	Biondini	ITA	24.1.76	13 Feb	13.87	Yelena	Govorova	UKR	18.9.73	27 Jan

SHOT

20.12	Larisa	Peleshenko	RUS	29.2.64	1	NC	Moskva	17 Feb
19.64	Svetlana	Krivelyova	RUS	13.6.69	2		Moskva	27 Jan
19.29	Lyudmila	Sechko	RUS	27.11.74	1		Sankt-Peterburg	5 Jan
19.24	Nadezhda	Ostapchuk	BLR	12.10.80	2	WI	Lisboa	10 Mar

19.10	Yumileidi	Cumbá	CUB	11.2.75	1	Balk	Pireás	18 Feb
19.05	Nadine	Kleinert-Schmitt	GER	20.10.75	1		Halle	16 Feb
18.59	Katarzyna	Zakowicz	POL	12.5.75	6	WI	Lisboa	10 Mar
18.44	Teri	Tunks	USA	30.10.75	1		Blacksburg	24 Feb
18.35	Connie	Price-Smith	USA	3.6.62	1	NC	Atlanta	3 Mar
18.22		Cheng Xioyan	CHN	30.11.75	7	WI	Lisboa	10 Mar

18.12	Krystyna	Zabawska	POL	14.1.68	10 Mar
18.11		Song Feina	CHN	25.1.77	24 Feb
17.88	Lieja	Koeman	NED	10.3.76	17 Feb
17.87		Zhang Zhaoyu	CHN		20 Feb
17.81	Yanina	Korolchik	BLR	26.12.76	3 Mar
17.79	Yuliya	Zaginay	RUS	3.8.63	19 Jan
17.78	Corrie	de Bruin	NED	26.10.76	17 Feb
17.75		Jia Lina	CHN	26.4.80	20 Feb
17.57		Jiang Ping	CHN	10.1.79	18 Feb
17.56	Alina	Frunza	ROM	17.4.79	24 Feb
17.55		Zhang Liuhong	CHN	16.1.69	20 Feb
17.50	Laurence	Manfredi	FRA	20.5.74	18 Feb

20 LBS WEIGHT

22.66	Dawn	Ellerbe	USA	3.4.74	1		Pocatello	9 Feb
22.24	Florence	Ezeh	FRA	29.12.77	1	WAC	Reno	23 Feb

21.02	Lisa	Misipeka	ASA	3.1.75	10 Feb
20.97	Christina	Tolson	USA	16.1.78	10 Mar
20.92	Anna	Norgren	USA	19.12.74	3 Mar
20.74	Jamine	Moton	USA	14.12.78	26 Jan
20.73	Maureen	Griffin	USA	6.10.80	27 Jan

PENTATHLON

4850	Natalya	Sazanovich	BLR	15.8.73	1	WI	Lisboa	9 Mar
	(8.25, 1.80, 16.31, 6.69, 2:23.20)							
4711	Yelena	Prokhorova	RUS	16.4.78	2	WI	Lisboa	9 Mar
	(8.46, 1.77, 14.03, 6.42, 2:09.85)							
4678	Karin	Ertl	GER	23.6.74	3	WI	Lisboa	9 Mar
	(8.51, 1.83, 14.79, 6.34, 2:18.48)							
4675	Irina	Belova	RUS	27.3.68	1		Kemerovo	24 Dec
	(8.0, 1.67, 14.38, 6.43, 2:09.1)							
4664	Natalya	Roshchupkina	RUS	13.1.78	4	WI	Lisboa	9 Mar
	(8.60, 1.83, 14.43, 6.08, 2:10.61)							
4646	Sabine	Braun	GER	19.6.65	5	WI	Lisboa	9 Mar
	(8.32, 1.80, 14.37, 6.27, 2:17.45)							
4577	Anzhela	Atroshchenko-Kinet	TUR	14.11.70	1		Gomel	25 Jan
	(8.26, 1.78, 13.31, 6.44, 2:20.39)							
4452	Liga	Klavina	LAT	27.1.80	1		Riga	11 Feb
	(8.61, 1.89, 13.72, 6.32, 2:34.10)							
4436	Tia	Hellebaut	BEL	16.2.78	1	NC	Gent	25 Feb
	(8.61, 1.88, 12,66, 5.96, 2:20.20)							
4392	Julie	Hollman	GBR	16.2.77	1	v4N	Praha	28 Jan
	(8.78, 1.81, 12.98, 6.13, 2:19.57)							

4351	Marina	Bryukhach	UKR	16.1.77	19 Feb
4303	Tiia	Hautala	FIN	3.4.72	11 Feb
4296	Sonja	Kesselschläger	GER	20.1.78	11 Feb
4294	Natalya	Dobrinskaya	UKR	29.5.82	16 Dec
4321?	Svetlana	Sokolova	RUS	9.1.81	24 Dec
4282	María	Peinado	ESP	8.2.77	25 Feb
4272	Svetlana	Parfyonova	RUS	74	20 Jan
4251	Vera	Yepimashko	UKR	10.7.76	19 Feb
4248	Jana	Kleckova	CZE	19.3.75	28 Jan
4241	Silvia	Dalla Piana	ITA	3.2.75	21 Jan
4228	Katja	Keller	GER	9.8.80	14 Jan
4223	Antonia	Schulze-Borges	GER	14.4.82	11 Feb

3000 METRES WALK

12:08.63	Kjersti	Plätzer	NOR	18.1.72	1	NC	Stange	25 Feb
12:20.62	Gillian	O'Sullivan	IRL	21.8.76	1	NC	Nenagh	4 Feb

12:25.97	Annarita	Sidoti	ITA	25.7.69	24 Feb
12:28.32	Michelle	Rohl	USA	12.11.65	3 Mar
12:29.08	Sabine	Zimmer	GER	6.2.81	25 Feb
12:29.17	Sysan	Feitor	POR	28.1.75	3 Mar
12:32.59	Erica	Alfridi	ITA	22.2.68	24 Feb
12:33.56	Norica	Cîmpean	ROM	22.3.72	24 Feb
12:35.71	Melanie	Seeger	GER	8.1.77	25 Feb
12:37.28	Lisa	Barbieri	ITA	18.5.78	24 Feb

5000mW: 21:20.0	Tatyana	Gudkova	RUS	23.12.77	1		Chelyabinsk	30 Dec
10,000mW: 44:38.8	Olimpiada	Ivanova	RUS	5.5.70	1	Army	Moskva	21 Jan

MEN – 5000 METRES WALK

18:22.25	Andreas	Erm	GER	12.3.76	1	NC	Dortmund	25 Feb
18:42.98	Yevgeniy	Shmalyuk	RUS	14.1.76	1		Sankt-Peterburg	6 Jan
18:55.5	Ilya	Markov	RUS	19.6.72	1		Yekaterinburg	7 Jan
18:58.97	Robert	Korzeniowski	POL	30.7.68	1	FRACh	Liévin	17 Feb
18:59.1	Vladimir	Andreyev	RUS	7.9.66	2		Yekaterinburg	7 Jan
19:00.12	Ivan	Brugnetti	ITA	1.9.76	1	NC	Torino	24 Feb
19:11.0	Dmitriy	Yesipchuk	RUS	17.11.74	1		Chelyabinsk	30 Dec

19:12.31	Robert	Heffernan	IRL	20.2.78	4 Feb
19:19.2	Sergey	Khripunov	RUS	15.9.76	7 Jan
19:21.0	Vitaliy	Shvetsov	RUS	20.2.73	30 Dec
19:25.61	Giovanni	Perricelli	ITA	25.8.67	24 Feb
19:27.14	Mike	Trautmann	GER	13.3.74	11 Feb
19:27.3	Matej	Spisiak	SVK	5.4.78	27 Dec
19:29.91	Lorenzo	Civallero	ITA	8.8.75	24 Feb
19:29.96	Tim	Seaman	USA	14.5.72	3 Mar

WORLD INDOOR CHAMPIONSHIPS 2001

At Lisboa, Portugal, 9-11 March

MEN – 60 Metres
1. Tim Harden USA 6.44
2. Tim Montgomery USA 6.46
3. Mark Lewis-Francis GBR 6.51
4. Freddy Mayola CUB 6.55
5. Matt Shirvington AUS 6.55
6. Tim Goebel GER 6.59
7. Yeóryios Theodorídis GRE 6.60

dq. Deji Aliu NGR 2 fs

200 Metres
1. Shawn Crawford USA 20.63
2. Christian Malcolm GBR 20.76
3. Patrick van Balkom NED 20.96
4. Christopher Williams JAM 21.12
5. Allyn Condon GBR 21.69

dns. Kevin Little USA –

400 Metres
1. Daniel Caines GBR 46.40
2. Milton Campbell USA 46.45
3. Danny McFarlane JAM 46.74
4. David Canal ESP 46.99
5. Mark Hylton GBR 47.03

dnf. James Davis USA –

800 Metres
1. Yuriy Borzakovskiy RUS 1:44.49
2. Johan Botha RSA 1:46.42
3. André Bucher SUI 1:46.46
4. David Lelei KEN 1:46.88
5. Glory Dube BOT 1:46.90
6. Pawel Czapiewski POL 1:50.51

1500 Metres
1. Rui Silva POR 3:51.06
2. Reyes Estévez ESP 3:51.25
3. Noah Ngeny KEN 3:51.63
4. Laban Rotich KEN 3:51.71
5. Adil Kaouch MAR 3:51.91
6. Seneca Lassiter USA 3:52.39
7. Hailu Mekonnen ETH 3:52.72
8. Julius Achon UGA 3:53.03
9. Juan Carlos Higuero ESP 3:56.71

3000 Metres
1. Hicham El Guerrouj MAR 7:37.74
2. Mohammed Mourhit BEL 7:38.94
3. Alberto García ESP 7:39.96
4. John Mayock GBR 7:44.08
5. Million Wolde ETH 7:44.54
6. Bernard Lagat KEN 7:45.52
7. Mark Carroll IRL 7:46.79
8. Craig Mottram AUS 7:48.34
9. Mohammed Khaldi ALG 7:52.76
10. Paul Bitok KEN 7:54.16

60 Metres Hurdles
1. Terrence Trammell USA 7.51
2. Anier García CUB 7.54
3. Shaun Bownes RSA 7.55
4. Robert Kronberg SWE 7.57
5. Yoel Hernández CUB 7.58
6. Elmar Lichtenegger AUT 7.65
7. Dudley Dorival HAI 7.73
8. Stanislav Olijars LAT 12.77

High Jump
1. Stefan Holm SWE 2.32
2. Andrey Sokolovskiy UKR 2.29
3. Steffen Strand SWE 2.29
4. Nathan Leeper USA 2.29

5= Martin Buss GER 2.25
5= Javier Sotomayor CUB 2.25

7. Yaroslav Rybakov RUS 2.25
8. Sergey Dymchenko UKR 2.25

Pole Vault
1. Lawrence Johnson USA 5.95
2. Tye Harvey USA 5.90
3. Romain Mesnil FRA 5.85
4. Aleksandr Averbukh ISR 5.70
5. Pavel Gerasimov RUS 5.70
6. Montxu Miranda ESP 5.70
7. Okkert Brits RSA 5.60
8. Stepán Janacek CZE 5.60

Long Jump
1. Iván Pedroso CUB 8.43
2. Kar. Streete-Thompson CAY 8.16
3. Carlos Calado POR 8.16
4. Peter Burge AUS 8.11
5. Melvin Lister USA 8.10
6. Kevin Dilworth USA 7.97
7. Vladmir Malyavin RUS 7.94
8. Vitaliy Shkurlatov RUS 7.80

Triple Jump
1. Paolo Camossi ITA 17.32
2. Jonathan Edwards GBR 17.26
3. Andrew Murphy AUS 17.20
4. Charles Friedek GER 17.13
5. Rostislav Dimitrov BUL 16.91
6. Fabrizio Donato ITA 16.77
7. Michael Calvo CUB 16.75
8. Aleksandr Glavatskiy BLR 16.49

Shot
1. John Godina USA 20.82
2. Adam Nelson USA 20.72
3. Manuel Martínez ESP 20.67
4. Timo Aaltonen FIN 20.24
5. Paolo Dal Soglio ITA 20.17
6. Miroslav Menc CZE 20.08
7. Milan Haborák SVK 20.05
8. Yuriy Belonog UKR 19.71

Heptathlon
1. Roman Sebrle CZE 6420
2. Jón-Arnar Magnússon ISL 6233
3. Lev Lobodin RUS 6202
4. Stephen Moore USA 6132
5. Erki Nool EST 6074
6. Aleksandr Yurkov UKR 6059
7. Mário Aníbal POR 5867

dnf. Chris Huffins USA

4 x 400 Metres Relay
1. POL P Ryskiewicz, P Haczek, J Bocian, R Mackowiak 3:04.47
2. USA M Campbell, L Byrd, T Gray, J Young 3:04.64
3. RUS Ladeyshchikov, Mashchenko, B Gorban, A Semyonov 3:04.82
4. JAM 3:05.45
5. GBR 3:09.21
6. NGR 3:16.53

WOMEN – 60 Metres
1. Chandra Sturrup BAH 7.05
2. Angela Williams USA 7.09
3. Chryste Gaines USA 7.12
4. Sevathedra Fynes BAH 7.15
5. Mercy Nku NGR 7.15
6. Petya Pendareva BUL 7.16
7. Li Xuemei CHN 7.20
8. Endurance Ojokolo NGR 7.23

200 Metres
1. Juliet Campbell JAM 22.64
2. LaTasha Jenkins USA 22.96
3. Natalya Safronnikova BLR 23.17
4. Susanthika Jayasinghe SRI 23.24
5. Muriel Hurtis FRA 23.63
6. Alenka Bikar SLO 23.74

400 Metres
1. Sandie Richards JAM 51.04
2. Olga Kotlyarova RUS 51.56
3. Olesya Zykina RUS 51.71
4. Nadjina Kaltouma CHA 52.49
5. Monique Hennagan USA 52.83
6. Suziann Reid USA 61.50

800 Metres
1. Maria Mutola MOZ 1:59.74
2. Stephanie Graf AUT 1:59.78
3. Helena Fuchsová CZE 2:01.18
4. Lwiza John TAN 2:01.76
5. Yelena Afanasyeva RUS 2:02.17
6. Jolanda Ceplak SLO 2:02.67

1500 Metres
1. Hasna Benhassi MAR 4:10.83
2. Violeta Szekely ROM 4:11.17
3. Natalya Gorelova RUS 4:11.74
4. Carla Sacramento POR 4:11.76
5. Daniela Yordanova BUL 4:12.79
6. Alesya Turova BLR 4:13.67
7. Nuria Fernández ESP 4:15.37
8. Helena Javornik SLO 4:15.76
9. Sonia O'Sullivan IRL 4:19.40

3000 Metres
1. Olga Yegorova RUS 8:37.48
2. Gabriela Szabo ROM 8:39.65
3. Yelena Zadorozhnaya RUS8:40.15
4. Marta Domínguez ESP 8:40.98
5. Dong Yanmei CHN 8:41.34
6. Benita Willis AUS 8:42.75
7. Sonia O'Sullivan IRL 8:44.37
8. Hayley Tullett GBR 8:45.36
9. Werknesh Kidane ETH 8:46.56
10. Asmae Leghzaoui MAR 8:47.60

60 Metres Hurdles
1. Anjanette Kirkland USA 7.85
2. Michelle Freeman JAM 7.92
3. Nicole Ramalalanirina FRA 7.96
4. Olga Shishigina KAZ 7.96
5. Svetlana Laukhova RUS 7.99
6. Linda Ferga FRA 8.06
7. Bisa Grant USA 8.09
8. Lacena Golding JAM 8.24

High Jump
1. Kajsa Bergqvist SWE 2.00
2. Inga Babakova UKR 2.00
3. Venelina Veneva BUL 1,96
4. Amy Acuff USA 1.96

5= Dóra Györffy HUN 1.93
5= Viktoriya Palamar UKR 1.93

7. Ruth Beitia ESP 1.93
8. Monica Dinescu ROM 1.93

Pole Vault
1. Pavla Hamácková CZE 4.56*

2= Svetlana Feofanova RUS 4.51
2= Kellie Suttle USA 4.51

4. Stacy Dragila USA 4.51
5. Tanya Koleva BUL 4.35
6. Yvonne Buschbaum GER 4.25

WORLD CROSS-COUNTRY CHAMPIONSHIPS 2001

At Oostende, Belgium 24 - 25 March

Men's Long Race

1	Mohammed Mourhit	BEL	39:53
2	Sergey Lebid	UKR	40:03
3	Charles Kamathi	KEN	40:05
4	Paulo Guerra	POR	40:06
5	Paul Kosgei	KEN	40:09
6	Driss El Himer	FRA	40:13
7	Patrick Ivuti	KEN	40:16
8	Hélder Ornelas	POR	40:33
9	Alejandro Gómez	ESP	40:37
10	Róbert Stefko	SVK	40:41
11	Mustapha El Hamadi	FRA	40:42
12	Bob Kennedy	USA	40:43
13	Mebrahtom Keflezighi	USA	40:46
14	Yibeltal Admasu	ETH	40:49
15	Abdi Abdirahman	USA	40:54
16	Alberto García	ESP	40:57
17	Giuliano Battocletti	ITA	40:59
18	Enock Mitei	KEN	41:01
19	Michele Gamba	ITA	41:01
20	Tom Van Hooste	BEL	41:02

159 finished. **Teams** (27 scored)

1 KEN 33	5 POR 100	9 ETH 170
2 FRA 72	6 ITA 103	10 ALG 200
3 USA 87	7 BEL 139	11 TAN 206
4 ESP 100	8 IRL 146	12 AUS 210

Men's Short Race

1	Enock Koech	KEN	12:40
2	Kenenisa Bekele	ETH	12:42
3	Benjamin Limo	KEN	12:43
4	Sammy Kipketer	KEN	12:44
5	Cyrus Kataron	KEN	12:45
6	Albert Chepkurui	KEN	12:46
7	John Kibowen	KEN	12:49
8	Craig Mottram	AUS	12:49
9	Brahim Boulami	MAR	13:00
10	Hailu Mekonnen	ETH	13:03
11	Adil Kaouch	MAR	13:06
12	Moh'd Saïd El Wardi	MAR	13:08
13	Dagne Alemu	ETH	13:08
14	John Yuda	TAN	13:09
15	Bradley Hauser	USA	13:09
16	Mohammed Amyn	MAR	13:09
17	Alejandro Suárez	MEX	13:10
18	Tim Broe	USA	13:10
19	Andrew Downin	USA	13:16
20	Luciano Di Pardo	ITA	13:18

156 finished. **Teams** (26 scored)

1 KEN 13	5 ESP 171	9 NZL 196
2 MAR 48	6 POR 183	10 GBR 196
3 ETH 51	7 CAN 187	11 RUS 198
4 USA 91	8 ITA 193	12 TAN 199

Junior Men

1	Kenenisa Bekele	ETH	25:04
2	Duncan Lebo	KEN	25:37
3	Dathan Ritzenhein	USA	25:46
4	Nicholas Kemboi	KEN	25:52
5	Mattew Tegenkamp	USA	25:55
6	Robert Kipchumba	KEN	26:00
7	Alemayehu Tedla	ETH	26:02
8	Maregu Zewdie	ETH	26:14
9	Beruk Debrework	ETH	26:15
10	Paul Wakou	UGA	26:17

149 finished. **Teams** (25 scored)

1 KEN 24	5 MAR 95	9 BEL 209
2 ETH 25	6 CAN 171	10 JPN 242
3 UGA 68	7 ERI 190	11 ITA 245
4 USA 71	8 ALG 206	12 ESP 258

Women's Long Race

1	Paula Radcliffe	GBR	27:49
2	Gete Wami	ETH	27:52
3	Lydia Cheromei	KEN	28:07
4	Susan Chepkemei	KEN	28:13
5	Pamela Chepchumba	KEN	28:20
6	Leah Malot	KEN	28:36
7	Yamna Belkacem	FRA	28:40
8	Merima Denboba	ETH	28:52
9	Olivera Jevtic	YUG	29:03
10	Anja Smolders	BEL	29:17
11	Rakiya Maraoui-Quétier	FRA	29:24
12	Deena Drossin	USA	29:28
13	Restituta Joseph	TAN	29:35
14	Hellen Chepchirchir	KEN	29:39
15	Analía Rosa	POR	29:41
16	Analídia Torre	POR	29:42
17	Liz Yelling	GBR	29:44
18	Sally Barsosio	KEN	29:50
19	Chiemi Takahashi	JPN	29:51
20	Rosita Rota Gelpi	ITA	29:53

107 finished. **Teams (18 scored)**

1 KEN 18	5 POR 95	9 TAN 163
2 ETH 70	6 ITA 117	10 JPN 178
3 FRA 77	7 ESP 119	11 BEL 191
4 GBR 83	8 USA 130	12 CAN 233

Women's Short Race

1	Gete Wami	ETH	14:46
2	Paula Radcliffe	GBR	14:47
3	Edith Masai	KEN	14:57
4	Merima Denboba	ETH	15:04
5	Werknesh Kidane	ETH	15:06
6	Benita Willis	AUS	15:06
7	Carla Sacramento	POR	15:07
8	Rose Cheruiyot	KEN	15:07
9	Asmae Leghzaoui	MAR	15:08
10	Margaret Ngotho	KEN	15:20
11	Naomi Mugo	KEN	15:24
12	Kathy Butler	GBR	15:25
13	Elena Fidatov	ROM	15:25
14	Anastasiya Zubova	RUS	15:31
15	Iulia Negura-Olteanu	ROM	15:32
16	Genet Gebregiorgis	ETH	15:33
17	Sabine Fischer	SUI	15:36
18	Ayelech Worku	ETH	15:36
19	Anna Ndege	TAN	15:37
20	Anne Keenan-Buckley	IRL	15:37

113 finished. **Teams** (19 scored)

1 ETH 26	5 MAR 109	9 RUS 172
2 KEN 32	6 IRL 152	10 USA 188
3 ROM 78	7 POR 157	11 CAN 194
4 GBR 81	8 TAN 158	12 ESP 199

Junior Women

1	Viola Kibiwot	KEN	22:05
2	Abebech Negussie	ETH	22:05
3	Aster Bacha	ETH	22:05
4	Vivian Cheruiyot	KEN	22:06
5	Tirunesh Dibaba	ETH	22:08
6	Tereza Yohannes	ETH	22:10
7	Fridah Domongole	KEN	22:12
8	Sally Kipyego	KEN	22:22
9	Peninah Chepchumba	KEN	22:24
10	Mestewat Tufa	ETH	22:24

123 finished. **Teams** (21 scored)

1 ETH 16	5 RSA 136	9 TUR 208
2 KEN 20	6 GBR 141	10 CAN 210
3 JPN 59	7 RUS 164	11 USA 215
4 AUS 107	8 ALG 201	12 ESP 230

Kenya won the men's long race title for the 16th successive year and the men's short race for the fourth time (of four). Their junior men's title was the 13th in 14 years.

World Indoor Championships (Continued)

7. Yelena Isinbayeva RUS	4.25
nh Anzhela Balakhonova UKR	–

Long Jump

1. Dawn Burrell USA	7.03
2. Tatyana Kotova RUS	6.98
3. Niurka Montalvo ESP	6.88
4. Fiona May ITA	6.87
5. Heike Drechsler GER	6.75
6. Lyudmila Galkina RUS	6.71
7. Guan Yingnan CHN	6.59
8. Valentina Gotovska LAT	6.46

Triple Jump

1. Tereza Marinova BUL	14.91
2. Tatyana Lebedeva RUS	14.85
3. Tiombé Hurd USA	14.19
4. Olga Bolshova MDA	14.17
5. Oksana Rogova RUS	14.17
6. Cristina Nicolau ROM	14.05
7. Anja Valant SLO	13.84
8. Adelina Gavrila ROM	13.77

Shot

1. Larisa Peleshenko RUS	19.84
2. Nadezhda Ostapchuk BLR	19.24
3. Svetlana Krivelyova RUS	19.18
4. Nadine Kleinert-Schmitt GER	18.87
5. Yumileidi Cumbá CUB	18.61
6. Katarzyna Zakowicz POL	18.59
7. Cheng Xiaoyan CHN	18.22
8. Krystyna Zabawska POL	18.12

Pentathlon

1. Natalya Sazanovich BLR	4850
2. Yelena Prokhorova RUS	4711
3. Karin Ertl GER	4678
4. Natalya Roshchupkina RUS	4664
5. Sabine Braun GER	4646
6. Anzhela Kinet TUR	4558
7. Liga Klavina LAT	4334
8. Urszula Wlodarczyk POL	3434

4 x 400 Metres Relay

1. RUS Y Nosova, O Zykina, Y Sotnikova, O Kotlyarova	3:30.00
2. JAM C Howell, J Campbell, C Scott, S Richards	3:30.79
3. GER C Marx, B Rockmeier, F Ekpo-Umoh, S Ghosh	3:31.00
4. USA	3:32.76